The BIOGRAPHICAL DICTIONARY of WOMEN in SCIENCE

The BIOGRAPHICAL DICTIONARY of WOMEN in SCIENCE

*Pioneering Lives
from Ancient Times to the
Mid-20th Century*

MARILYN OGILVIE
AND JOY HARVEY,

EDITORS

Volume 2
L–Z

ROUTLEDGE

New York and London

We dedicate these volumes to the memory of
Kerry Meek Whitney, who was an enthusiastic
supporter and contributor to this work.

Published in 2000 by
Routledge
29 West 35th Street
New York, NY 10001

Published in Great Britain by
Routledge
11 New Fetter Lane
London, EC4P 4EE

Copyright © 2000 by Marilyn Ogilvie
Interior Design by Publisher's Studio/Stratford Publishing Services
Printed in the United States on acid-free paper.

Library of Congress Cataloging-in-Publication Data

The biographical dictionary of women in science: pioneering lives
from ancient times to the mid-20th century. / Marilyn Ogilvie and Joy
Harvey, editors.
     p.   cm.
  Includes bibliographical references and index.
   ISBN 0-415-92038-8 (set : alk. paper). — ISBN 0-415-92039-6
(vol. 1 : alk. paper). — ISBN 0-415-92040-X (vol. 2 : alk. paper)
   1. Women scientists—Biography—Dictionaries.   I. Ogilvie,
Marilyn Bailey.   II. Harvey, Joy Dorothy.
Q141.B5285   2000
509' 2'2—dc21   99-17668
  [b]   CIP

CONTENTS

VOLUME 1

Foreword   *vii*

Acknowledgments   *ix*

Introduction   *xi*

Standard Sources   *xv*

Contributors   *xxi*

Alphabetical List of Entries   *xxiv*

Entries A–K   *1*

VOLUME 2

Standard Sources   *vii*

Alphabetical List of Entries   *xvii*

Entries L–Z   *731*

List of Scientists by Occupation   *1425*

List of Scientists by Time Period   *1444*

List of Scientists by Country   *1461*

Index   *1477*

STANDARD SOURCES

ADELMAN Adelman, Joseph. *Famous Women*. New York: Lonow, 1926.

AINLEY Ainley, Marianne Gosztonyi, ed. *Despite the Odds: Essays on Canadian Women and Science*. Montreal: Vehicule Press, 1990.

ALIC Alic, Margaret. *Hypatia's Heritage: A History of Women in Science from Antiquity through the Nineteenth Century*. Boston: Beacon Press, 1986.

AMERICAN WOMEN *American Women*. Ed. Durward Howes. Los Angeles: Richard Blank, 1935–1940.

AMERICAN WOMEN 1974 *American Women: The Standard Biographical Dictionary of Notable Women*. Ed. Durward Howes. Teaneck, N.J.: Zephyrus Press, 1974.

AMS *American Men of Science: A Biographical Dictionary*. New York: Bowker 1–11th, 1906–1968. Eds. 1–8 published by the Science Press, 9th ed. published by Bowker and Science Press, 10th and 11th ed. published by Jacques Cattell Press. 9th ed. issued in 3 vols.: vol. 1, *Physical Sciences;* vol. 2, *Biological Sciences;* and vol. 3, *Social Sciences.* 10th ed. issued in 5 vols.: vols. 1–4, *Physical and Biological Sciences,* A–Z; vol. 5, *Social and Behavioral Sciences.* 11th ed. issued in 8 vols.: vols. 1–6, *Physical and Biological Sciences;* vols. 7–8, *Social and Behavioral Sciences,* A–Z. Supplements issued between some editions. Continues as *American Men and Women of Science*. Titles of the 12th–19th eds. vary. The abbreviations for all citations, whether *American Men of Science* or *American Men and Women of Science,* will be *AMS*.

ANB *American National Biography*. New York: Oxford University Press, 1999.

ANNUAL OBITUARY *The Annual Obituary* (1980–1993). [editor varies with each volume.] 14 vols. New York: St. Martin's Press, 1981–1994.

AOU BIOGRAPHIES Palmer, T.S. *Biographies of Members of the American Ornithologists' Union*. Washington, D.C.: American Ornithologists' Union, 1954.

APA DIRECTORY *American Psychological Association Directory*. Washington, D.C.: American Psychological Association, annual.

APA MEMBERSHIP REGISTER *American Psychological Association Membership Register*. Washington, D.C.: American Psychological Association, annual.

APPIGNANESI Appignanesi, Lisa, and Forrester, John. *Freud's Women*. New York: Basic Books, 1992.

APPLETON'S CYCLOPAEDIA *Appletons' Cyclopaedia of American Biography*. Ed. James Grant Wilson and John Fiske. New York: D. Appleton and Co., 1888.

ARNOLD Arnold, Lois Barber. *Four Lives in Science: Women's Education in the Nineteenth Century*. New York: Schocken Books, 1984.

BAILEY Bailey, Martha J. *American Women in Science: A Biographical Dictionary*. Denver, Colo: ABC-CLIO, 1994.

BALLARD Ballard, George. *Memoirs of Several Ladies of Great Britain Who Have Been Celebrated for their Writings or Skill in the Learned Languages, Arts and Sciences*. London: Edwards, 1775.

BARNHART Barnhart, John Hendley. *Biographical Notes upon Botanists in the New York Botanical Garden Library*. Boston: G. K. Hall, 1965.

BARR Barr, Ernest Scott. *Index to Biographical Fragments in Unspecialized Scientific Journals*. University of Alabama Press, 1973.

BAUDOUIN Baudouin, Marce. *Femmes médecins d'autrefois*. Paris: Librairie Médicale et Scientifique Jules Rousset, 1906.

BDAS Elliott, Clark. *Biographical Dictionary of American Science: The Seventeenth Through the Nineteenth Centuries*. Westport, Conn: Greenwood Press, 1979.

BIBLIOGRAPHIE ASTRONOMIQUE Lalande, Jérôme de. *Bibliographie astronomique avec l'histoire de l'astronomie depuis 1781 jusqu'à 1802*. Paris: Imprimerie de la République, 1803.

BIOGRAFISCH WOORDENBOEK *Biografisch Woordenboek van Nederland*. Ed. by J. Charite. 4 vols. 's-Gravenhage: Nijhoff, 1979–1994.

BIOGRAPHICAL MEMOIRS Royal Society of London. *Biographical Memoirs of Fellows of the Royal Society*. London: Royal Society 1–44, 1955–1998.

BIOGRAPHIE UNIVERSELLE *Biographie universelle, ancienne et moderne*. 85 vols. Paris: L. G. Michaud, 1811–1826.

BOASE Boase, Frederic. *Modern English Biography*. 6 vols. London: Truro, Netherton and Worth, for the author, 1892–1921.

BONNER Bonner, Thomas Neville. "Rendezvous in Zürich: Seven Who Made a Revolution in Women's Medical Education, 1864–1874." *Journal of the History of Medicine* 44, no. 1: 7–27.

BONNER 1992 ———. *To the Ends of the Earth: Women's Search for Education in Medicine*. Cambridge, Mass: Harvard University Press, 1992.

BONTA Bonta, Marcia Myers. *Women in the Field: America's Pioneering Women Naturalists*. College Station: Texas A&M University Press, 1991.

BRINK Brink, J. R., ed. *Female Scholars: A Tradition of Learned Women before 1800*. Montreal: Eden Press, 1980.

BROOKE BAILEY Bailey, Brooke. *The Remarkable Lives of 100 Women Healers and Scientists*. Holbrook, Mass: Bob Adams, 1994.

CARR AND CARR Carr, D. J. and S. G. M. Carr. *People and Plants in Australia*. Sydney: Academic Press, 1981.

CATALOGUE ROYAL SOCIETY Royal Society of London. *Catalogue of Scientific Papers (1800– 1900)*. London: Royal Society, 1867–1925.

COLUMBIA ENCYCLOPEDIA *New Columbia Encyclopedia*. New York: Viking Press, 1953.

CONCISE UNIVERSAL BIOGRAPHY *Concise Universal Biography*. Ed. John Alexander Hammerton. London: Educational Book Company, 1934–1935.

CREATIVE COUPLES Pycior, Helena M., Nancy G. Slack, and Pnina G. Abir-Am, eds. *Creative Couples in the Sciences*. New Brunswick, N.J.: Rutgers University Press, 1996.

CREESE 1991 Creese, Mary R. S. "British Women and Research in the Chemical Sciences." *The British Journal for the History of Science*. 24 (September 1991): 275–305.

CREESE Creese, Mary R. S. *Ladies in the Laboratory? American and British Women in Science, 1800–1900*. Lanham, Md.: Scarecrow Press, 1998.

CREESE AND CREESE Creese, Mary R. S., and Creese, Thomas M. "British Women Who Contributed to Research in the Geological Sciences in the Nineteenth Century." *The British Journal for the History of Science* 27 (March 1994): 23–54.

CURRENT BIOGRAPHY *Current Biography*. New York: H. W. Wilson, *1940–*.

CYCLOPEDIA *A Cyclopedia of Female Biography*. Ed. H. G. Adams. Glasgow: Robert Forrester, Stockwell, 1866.

DAB *Dictionary of American Biography*. Ed. by Allen Johnson and Dumas Malone. 11 vols. New York: Scribner, 1964.

DANSK BIOGRAFISK *Dansk Biografisk Leksikon*. 16 vols. Engelstoft: Porl, 1876–.

DAS DEUTSCHE WW *Wer ist Wer?: Das Deutsche Who's Who*. Berlin: 1954–.

DBE *Deutsche Biographische Enzyclopadie*. Munich: K. G. Sour.

DBF *Dictionnaire de Biographie Française*. Paris: Letouzey, 1933–.

DEBUS *World Who's Who in Science: A Biographical Dictionary of Notable Scientists from Antiquity to the Present*. Ed. Allen G. Debus. Chicago: Marquis, 1968.

DESMOND Desmond, Ray. *Dictionary of British and Irish Botanists and Horticulturists*. London: Taylor and Francis, and the Natural History Museum (London), 1994.

DFC *Dictionnaire des femmes celebres, de tous les temps et de tous les pays*. Ed. Lucienne Mazenod and Ghislain Schoeller. Paris: R. Laffont, 1992.

DIB *Dictionary of International Biography*. Cambridge: International Biographical Centre, 1963–.

DICTIONARY OF SCIENTIFIC BIOGRAPHY *Dictionary of Scientific Biography*. Ed. Charles Coulston Gillispie. 16 vols. New York: Charles Scribner's Sons, 1970–1980. Supplement II, ed. Frederic L. Holmes. 2 vols. 1990.

DIZIONARIO ITALIANI *Dizionario biografico degli Italiani*. Ed. by Alberto Mario Ghisalberti. Rome: Instituto della Enciclopedia Italiani, 1964–.

DNB *The Dictionary of National Biography:* London: Oxford University Press, 1882–.

DNB, MISSING PERSONS *The Dictionary of National Biography: Missing Persons*. Oxford: Oxford University Press, 1994.

DOLAN Dolan, Josephine A. *Goodnow's History of Nursing*. 10th ed. Philadelphia: W. B. Saunders, 1958.

DORLAND Dorland, William Alexander Newman. *The Sum of Feminine Achievement: A Critical and Analytical Study of Woman's Contribution to the Intellectual Progress of the World*. Boston: Stratford, 1917.

DUBREIL-JACOTIN Dubreil-Jacotin, Marie Louise. "Women Mathematicians." In *Mathematics: Concepts and Development,* 168–180. Vol. 1 of *Great Currents of Mathematical Thought*. Ed. F. LeLionnais. New York: Dover, 1971.

ECHOLS AND WILLIAMS Echols, Anne and Marty Williams. *Annotated Index of Medieval Women*. New York: Markus Wiener Publishing, 1992.

ECKENSTEIN Eckenstein, Lina. *Woman Under Monasticism*. New York: Russell and Russell, 1963.

ENCYCLOPEDIA BRITTANICA *Encyclopedia Britannica: A Dictionary of Arts, Sciences, Literature and General Information.* 11th ed. 29 vols. Cambridge: Cambridge University Press, 1910.

ENCYCLOPEDIA OF PSYCHOLOGY *Encyclopedia of Psychology.* Ed. Raymond J. Corsini. 4 vols. New York: John Wiley and Sons, 1994.

EUROPA *The Europa Biographical Dictionary of British Women.* Ed. Anne Crawford, et al. London: Europa, and Detroit, Mich.: Gale Research, 1983.

FRS OBITUARY NOTICES Royal Society of London. *Obituary Notices of the Fellows of the Royal Society.* London: Royal Society, 1–9, 1932–1954.

GACS Gacs, Ute, et al., eds. *Women Anthropologists: A Biographical Dictionary.* New York: Greenwood Press, 1988.

GIRTON *Girton College Register* 1869–1946. Cambridge: privately printed for Girton College, 1948.

GREAT SOVIET ENCYCLOPEDIA *Great Soviet Encyclopedia* (Bol'shaia sovetskaia entsiklopediia). Ed. by A. M. Prokhorov, New York: Macmillan, 1973–1983. 31 vols.

GRINSTEIN 1993 Grinstein, Louise S., Rose K. Rose, and Miriam H. Rafailovich, eds. *Women in Chemistry and Physics: A Biobibliographic Sourcebook.* Westport, Conn.: Greenwood Press, 1993.

GRINSTEIN 1997 Grinstein, Louise S., Carol A. Biermann, and Rose K. Rose, eds. *Women in the Biological Sciences: A Biobibliographic Sourcebook.* Westport, Conn: Greenwood Press, 1997.

GRINSTEIN AND CAMPBELL Grinstein, Louise S. and Paul J. Campbell, eds. *Women of Mathematics: A Biobibliographic Sourcebook.* New York: Greenwood Press, 1987.

GUNN AND CODD Gunn, Mary, and L. E. W. Codd. *Botanical Exploration of Southern Africa: An Illustrated History of Early Botanical Literature on the Cape Flora: Biographical Accounts of the Leading Plant Collectors and Their Activities in Southern Africa from the Days of the East India Company until Modern Times.* Cape Town: Botanical Research Institute by A.A. Balkema, 1981.

HABER Haber, Louis. *Women Pioneers of Science.* New York: Harcourt Brace Jovanovich, 1979.

HACKER Hacker, Carlotta. *The Indomitable Lady Doctors.* Toronto: Clarke, Irwin & Co., 1974.

HARLESS Harless, Johann Christian Friedrich. *Die Verdienste der Frauen um Naturwissenschaft und Heilkunde.* Göttingen: Vandenhoeck-Ruprechtschen Verlage, 1830.

HELLSTEDT, AUTOBIOGRAPHIES Hellstedt, Leone. *Women Physicians of the World: Autobiographies of Medical Pioneers.* Washington, D.C.: Hemisphere Publ., 1978.

HERZENBERG Herzenberg, Caroline. *Women Scientists from Antiquity to the Present: an Index.* West Cornwall, Conn: Locust Hill Press, 1986.

HØYRUP Høyrup, Else. *Women of Science, Technology, and Medicine: A Bibliography.* Roskilde, Denmark: Roskilde University Library, 1987.

HUGHES Hughes, Muriel Joy. *Women Healers in Medieval Life and Literature.* Oxford: Oxford University Press, 1943.

HUNT INSTITUTE Hunt Institute for Botanical Documentation. *Biographical Dictionary of Botanists Represented in the Hunt Institute Portrait Collection.* Boston: G.K. Hall, 1972.

HURD-MEAD 1933 Hurd-Mead, Kate Campbell. *Medical Women of America.* New York: Froben, 1933.

HURD-MEAD 1938 Hurd-Mead, Kate Campbell. *A History of Women in Medicine: From the Earliest Times to the Beginning of the Nineteenth Century.* Haddam, Conn.: The Haddam Press, 1938.

IDA *International Dictionary of Anthropologists.* New York: Garland, 1991.

INTERNATIONAL WW *The International Who's Who of Women.* London: Europa Publications, 1992.

IRELAND Ireland, Norma Olin. *Index to Women of the World from Ancient to Modern Times: Biographies and Portraits.* Boston: Faxon, 1962.

JEWS IN MEDICINE Schreiber, Emanuel. *Jews in Medicine.* Chicago: n.p., 1902.

JONES AND BOYD Jones, Bessie Zaban, and Lyle Gifford Boyd. *The Harvard College Observatory: The First Four Directorships, 1839–1919.* Cambridge, Mass.: Harvard University Press, 1971.

KASS-SIMON AND FARNES Kass-Simon, G., and Patricia Farnes, eds. *Women of Science: Righting the Record.* Bloomington, IN: Indiana University Press, 1990.

KERSEY Kersey, Ethel M. *Women Philosophers: A Bio-Critical Source Book.* New York: Greenwood Press, 1989.

LA GRAN ENCICLOPEDIA DE PUERTO RICO *La Gran Enciclopedia de Puerto Rico.* Madrid: n.p., 1976.

LAROUSSE BIOGRAPHICAL DICTIONARY *Larousse Biographical Dictionary.* New York: Larousse, 1994.

LEXICON DER FRAU *Lexikon der Frau.* 2 vols. Zürich: Encyclios Verlag AG, 1953.

LIPINSKA 1900 Lipinska, Melanie. *Histoire des femmes médecins depuis l'antiquité jusqu'à nos jours.* Paris: Librairie G. Jacques, 1900.

LIPINSKA 1930 Lipinska, Melanie. *Les femmes et le progrès des sciences médicales.* Paris: Masson, 1930.

LKW Golemba, Beverly E. *Lesser Known Women: A Biographical Dictionary.* Boulder, Colo.: Lynne Rienner, 1992.

LOVEJOY Lovejoy, Esther Pohl. *Women Doctors of the World.* New York: Macmillan, 1957.

MALLIS Mallis, Arnold. *American Entomologists.* New Brunswick, N.J.: Rutgers University Press, 1971.

McGrayne McGrayne, Sharon Bertsch. *Nobel Prize Women in Science: Their Lives, Struggles, and Momentous Discoveries.* New York: Birch Lane Press, 1993.

Medical Women Jex-Blake, Sophia. *Medical Women: A Thesis and a History.* 2d ed. Edinburgh: Oliphant, Anderson and Ferrier, 1886.

Ménage Ménage, Gilles. *The History of Women Philosophers.* Trans. Beatrice H. Zedler. Lanham, Md.: University Press of America, 1984.

Meyer Meyer, Gerald Dennis. *The Scientific Lady in England, 1650–1760: An Account of Her Rise, with Emphasis on the Major Roles of the Telescope and Microscope.* Berkeley: University of California Press, 1955.

Meyer and von Schweidler Meyer, Stefan, and Egon von Schweidler. *Radioaktivität.* Leipzig: B. G. Teubner, 1927.

Modern Scientists and Engineers *McGraw-Hill Modern Scientists and Engineers.* New York: McGraw-Hill, 1980.

Mollan and Finucane Mollan, William Davis, and Brandan Finucane, eds. *Some People and Places in Irish Science and Technology.* Dublin: Royal Irish Academy, 1985.

Morantz-Sanchez Morantz-Sanchez, Regina Markell. *Sympathy and Science: Women Physicians in American Medicine.* New York: Oxford University Press, 1985.

Mothers and Daughters Stanley, Autumn. *Mothers and Daughters of Invention: Notes for a Revised History of Technology.* Metuchen, N.J.: Scarecrow Press, 1993.

Mozans Mozans, H. J. *Woman in Science.* Notre Dame: University of Notre Dame Press, 1991.

Munk's Roll *Lives of the Fellows of the Royal Society of Physicians: Continued to 1983 (Munk's Roll).* Oxford: IRL Press, 1984.

Nalivkin Nalivkin, D. V. *Nashi Pervye Zhenshchinye-geologi (Our First Women Geologists).* Leningrad: Nauka, 1979.

NBG *Nouvelle biographie générale: Depuis les temps les plus reculés jusqu'à nos jours.* 46 vols. Paris: Firmin Didot Frères, 1856.

NAW James, Edward T., ed. *Notable American Women, 1607–1950: a Biographical Dictionary.* 3 vols. Cambridge, Mass.: Belknap Press of Harvard University Press, 1973.

NAW(M) Sicherman, Barbara, and Carol Hurd Green, eds., *Notable American Women: The Modern Period: A Biographical Dictionary.* Cambridge, Mass.: Belknap Press of Harvard University Press, 1980.

NAW(UNUSED) *Notable American Women: The Modern Period Records, 1975–1980.* Schlesinger Library, Radcliffe Institute. MC 307, IV, series III.

NBAW Smith, Jessie Carney, ed. *Notable Black American Women.* 2 vols. Detroit: Gale, Research, 1992–1996.

NCAB *National Cyclopedia of American Biography.* Clifton, N.J.: J. T. White, 1891–.

NDB *Neue Deutsche Biographie.* Berlin: Duncker and Humblot, 1953–.

Newnham *Newnham College Register.* 3 vols. Cambridge: Newnham College, 1871–1971.

Newnham Roll *Newnham College Roll Letter.* Cambridge: printed for private circulation, 1957.

Notable Mathematicians *Notable Mathematicians from Ancient Times to the Present.* Ed. Robyn V. Young. Detroit: Gale, 1998.

Notable/Notable suppl. *Notable Twentieth-Century Scientists.* Ed. Emily McMurray. 4 vols. New York: Gale Research, 1995. Supplement, ed. K. M. Krapp, 1998.

O'Connell and Russo 1988 O'Connell, Agnes N., and Nancy Felipe Russo. *Models of Achievement.* New York: Columbia University Press, 1983–1988.

O'Connell and Russo 1990 O'Connell, Agnes N., and Nancy Felipe Russo. *Women in Psychology: A Bio-Bibliographic Sourcebook.* New York: Greenwood Press, 1990.

O'Connor O'Connor, W. J. *British Physiologists 1885–1914: A Biographical Dictionary.* Manchester: Manchester University Press, 1991.

Ogilvie 1986 Ogilvie, Marilyn Bailey. *Women in Science: Antiquity through the Nineteenth Century: A Biographical Dictionary with Annotated Bibliography.* Cambridge, Mass.: MIT Press, 1986.

Ogilvie 1996 ———. With Kerry Meek. *Women and Science: An Annotated Bibliography.* New York: Garland, 1996.

O'Hern O'Hern, Elizabeth Moot. *Profiles of Pioneer Woman Scientists.* New York: Acropolis Books: 1985.

O'Neill O'Neill, Lois Decker, ed. *The Women's Book of World Records and Achievements.* Garden City, N.Y.: 1979.

Opfell Opfell, Olga S. *The Lady Laureates: Women Who Have Won the Nobel Prize.* 2d ed. Metuchen, N.J.: Scarecrow Press, 1986.

Osborn Osborn, Herbert. *A Brief History of Entomology.* Columbus, Ohio: Spahr and Glenn Company, 1952.

Pauly-Wissowa Pauly, August Friedrich von. *Paulys Real-Encyclopädie der classichen Altertumswissenschaft.* Ed. G. Wissowa. Stuttgart: J. B. Metzler, 1891–.

Phillips Phillips, Patricia. *The Scientific Lady: A Social History of Women's Scientific Interests, 1520–1918.* New York: St. Martin's, 1990.

Poggendorff Poggendorff, J.C. *Biographisch-literarisches Handworterbuch der Exakten Naturwissenschaften.* 7 vols. Berlin: Akademie-Verlag, 1863–1992.

Praeger Praeger, R. Lloyd. *Some Irish Naturalists: A Biographical Notebook.* Dundalk, W. Tempest: Dundalgen Press, 1949.

Psychological Register *Psychological Register.* Ed. Carl Murchison. Worcester, Mass.: Clark University Press, 1929–.

Rayner-Canham 1997 Rayner-Canham, Marelene F., and Geoffrey W. Rayner-Canham. *A Devotion to Their Science: Pioneer Women of Radioactivity.* Philadelphia, Penn.: Chemical Heritage Foundation, 1997.

RAYNER-CANHAM 1998 Rayner-Canham, Marelene F., and Geoffrey W. Rayner-Canham. *Women in Chemistry*. American Chemical Society and Chemical Heritage Foundation, 1998.

REP *Routledge Encyclopedia of Philosophy*. Ed. Edward Craig. 10 vols. London: Routledge, 1998.

REBIÈRE Rebière, A. *Les femmes dans la Science*. Paris: Nony, 1897.

ROSSITER 1982 Rossiter, Margaret. *Women Scientists in America: Struggles and Strategies to 1948*. Baltimore: Johns Hopkins University Press, 1982.

ROSSITER 1995 Rossiter, Margaret. *Women Scientists in America: Before Affirmative Action, 1940–1972*. Baltimore: Johns Hopkins University Press, 1995.

SARJEANT Sarjeant, William Antony S. *Geologists and the History of Geology: An International Bibliography from the Origins to 1978*. New York: Arno Press, 1980; 1987; 1996.

SCHIEBINGER Schiebinger, Londa. *The Mind Has No Sex? Women in the Origins of Modern Science*. Cambridge, Mass.: Harvard University Press, 1989.

SHEARER AND SHEARER 1996 Shearer, Benjamin F. and Barbara S. Shearer, eds. *Notable Women in the Life Sciences: A Biographical Dictionary*. Westport, Conn.: Greenwood Press, 1996.

SHEARER AND SHEARER 1997 Shearer, Benjamin F., and Barbara S. Shearer, eds. *Notable Women in the Physical Sciences. A Biographical Dictionary*. Westport, Conn.: Greenwood Press, 1997.

SHTEIR Shteir, Ann B. *Cultivating Women Cultivating Science: Flora's Daughters and Botany in England 1760–1860*. Baltimore: Johns Hopkins Press, 1996.

SIEGEL AND FINLEY Siegel Patricia Joan and Kay Thomas Finley. *Women in the Scientific Search: An American Bio-bibliography, 1724–1979*. Metuchen, N.J.: Scarecrow Press, 1985.

SOUTH AFRICAN DNB Rosenthal, R. *Southern African Dictionary of National Biography*. N.p., 1966.

SOVIET UNION *The Soviet Union: A Biographical Dictionary*. New York: Macmillan, 1990.

SPENDER Spender, Dale, and Janet Todd, eds. *British Women Writers: An Anthology from the Fourteenth Century to the Present*. New York: P. Bedrick Books, 1989.

STAFLEU AND COWAN Stafleu, Frans A, and R.S. Cowan, eds. *Taxonomic Literature: A Selective Guide to Botanical Publications and Collections with Dates, Commentaries and Types*. Utrecht: Bohn, Scheltema & Holkema, 1976–1988. Supplement, Ed. F. A. Stafleu and E. A. Mennega. Königstein, Germany: Koeltz Scientific Books, 1992.

STEVENS AND GARDNER Stevens, Gwendolyn, and Sheldon Gardner. *Women of Psychology*. Cambridge, Mass.: Schenkman, 1982.

STROHMEIER Strohmeier, Renate. *Lexikon der Naturwissenschaftlerinnen und naturkundigen Frauen Europas von der Antike bis zum 20. Jahrhundert*. Thun and Frankfurt am Main: Harri Deutsch, 1998.

STUCKEY Stuckey, Ronald. *Women Botanists of Ohio Born Before 1900*. Columbus, Ohio: Ohio State University, 1992.

TURKEVICH AND TURKEVICH Turkevich, John, and Turkevich, Ludmilla, comp. *Prominent Scientists of Continental Europe*. New York: American Elsevier Publishing Co., 1968.

TUVE Tuve, Jeanette E. *The First Russian Women Physicians*. Newtonville, Mass.: Oriental Research Partners, 1984.

UGLOW 1982 Uglow, Jennifer S., ed. *International Dictionary of Women's Biography*. New York: Continuum, 1982; 1989.

UGLOW 1989 Uglow, Jennifer S., ed. *Macmillan Dictionary of Women's Biography*. 2d. ed. New York: Macmillan, 1989.

UNEASY CAREERS Abir-Am, Pnina, and Dorinda Outram, eds. *Uneasy Careers and Intimate Lives: Women in Science, 1787–1979*. New Brunswick: Rutgers University Press, 1987.

VARE AND PTACEK Vare, Ethlie Ann, and Ptacek, Greg. *Mothers of Invention*. New York: Morrow, 1988.

VOGT Vogt, Annette, "The Kaiser-Wilhelm-Gesellschaft and the Career Chances for Female Scientists Between 1911 and 1945." Paper for International Congress for the History of Science, Liége, Belgium, 1997.

WAITHE Waithe, Mary Ellen. *Ancient Women Philosophers, 600 B.C.–500 A.D.* Dordrecht: Kluwer, 1987.

WALSH Walsh, James Joseph. *Medieval Medicine*. London: A. and C. Black, 1920.

WHO'S WHO OF AMERICAN WOMEN *Who's Who of American Women*. Chicago: Marquis Who's Who.

WOMAN'S WHO'S WHO OF AMERICA *Woman's Who's Who of America: A Biographical Dictionary of Contemporary Women of the United States and Canada*. Ed. John William Leonard. New York: American Commonwealth, 1914.

WOMEN PHYSIOLOGISTS Bindman, Lynn, Alison Brading, and Tilli Tansey eds. *Women Physiologists: An Anniversary Celebration of their Contributions to British Physiology*. London: Portland Press, 1992.

WOMEN IN WHITE Marks, Geoffrey, and Beatty, William K. *Women in White*. New York: Scribner, [1972].

WORLD WW OF WOMEN *World Who's Who of Women*. Cambridge: Melrose Press, 1973–.

WW *Who's Who*. London: A. and C. Black, 1849–.

WW IN AMERICA *Who's Who in America*. Chicago: Marquis Who's Who, 1899–.

WW IN AMERICAN EDUCATION *Who's Who in American Education*. Nashville, Tenn.: Who's Who in American Education, 1928–.

WW IN EDUCATION *Who's Who in Education*. Ed. G. E. Bowman and Nellie C. Ryan. Greeley, Colo.: 1927–.

WW IN FRANCE *Who's Who in France.* Paris: J. LaFitte, 1953–.

WW IN ITALY *Who's Who in Italy.* London: Eurospan, 1994.

WW IN THE MIDWEST *Who's Who in the Midwest.* Chicago: Marquis Who's Who, 1949–.

WW IN NEW YORK *Who's Who in New York City and State.* New York: L.R. Hamersly Co., 1904–.

WW IN SCIENCE IN EUROPE *Who's Who in Science in Europe.* Vol. 3. London: Francis Hogson, 1967.

WW IN SOVIET SCIENCE *Who's Who in Soviet Science.* Ed. Ina Telberg. New York: Telberg Book Co., 1960.

WW IN SWITZERLAND *Who's Who in Switzerland.* Zurich: Central European Times Publishing Co., 1952–.

WWW *Who Was Who.* Vols. 1–9. London: A. and C. Black, 1920–1996.

WWW(A) *Who Was Who in America.* Chicago, Marquis Who's Who.

WWW(UUSR) *Who Was Who in the USSR: A Biographic Directory Containing Biographies of Prominent Soviet Historical Personalities.* Ed. Heinrich E. Schulz, Paul K. Urban, and Andrew I. Lebed. Metuchen, N.J., Scarecrow Press.

YOST Yost, Edna. *Women of Modern Science.* New York: Dodd, Mead & Co., 1959.

ZUSNE Zusne, L. *Names in the History of Psychology.* Washington, D.C.: Hemisphere, 1975.

ADDITIONAL REFERENCES

Allgemeine deutsche biographie. Ed. Rocus von Liliencron. 56 vols. Leipzig: Verlag von Duncker and Humblot, 1875–1912.

Allibone, S.A. *A Critical Dictionary of English Literature.* Philadelphia: Lippincott, 1872.

Burke's Peerage and Baronetage. 105th ed.; London: Burke's Peerage, 1980.

Crone, John S. *Concise Dictionary of Irish Biography.* Dublin: Talbot Press, 1928,

Cyclopedia of American Medical Biography. Philadelphia: W. B. Saunders, 1912.

Hall, Diana Long. "Academics, Blue Stockings and Biologists: Women at the University of Chicago, 1892–1932." *Annals of the New York Academy of Sciences* 323 (1979).

La Grande Encyclopédie, inventaire raisonné des sciences, des lettres et des arts, par une société de savants et de gens de lettres. Ed.
A. Berthelot. 31 vols. Paris: Lamirault et cie; vols. 23–31 published by the Societe anonyme de la grande encyclopédie, [1886–1902].

Leaders in American Science. Ed. Robert C. Cook. Who's Who in American Education, Inc., [1953–].

Larousse Biographical Dictionary of Scientists. Ed. Hazel Muir. New York: Larousse, 1994.

Lovejoy, Esther. *Women Physicians and Surgeons.* Livingston, N.Y.: Livingston Press, 1939.

Magill, Frank N., ed. *Physics,* 831–839. Vol. 2 of *The Nobel Prize Winners.* Pasadena, Calif. and Englewood Cliffs, N.J.: Salem Press, 1989.

National Academy of Sciences. *Biographical Memoirs (National Academy of Sciences).* New York: Columbia University Press, 1960.

National Union Catalog, Pre-1956 Imprints: A Cumulative Author List Representing Library of Congress Printed Cards and Titles Reported By Other American Libraries. Comp. and ed. with the cooperation of the Library of Congress and the National Union Catalog Subcommittee of the Resources and Technical Services Divisions, American Library Association. London: Mansell, 1968–1980.

Osborn, Herbert. *Fragments of Entomological History.: Including Some Personal Recollections of Men and Events.* Columbus, Ohio: privately printed, 1937.

Royal Society of London. 1902–1921. *International Catalogue of Scientific Literature, 1901–1914.* 14 vols. London: Royal Society, n.d. Reprint, 32 vols, New York: Johnson, 1968–1969.

Rudolph, E. D. "Women Who Studied Plants in the Pre-Twentieth Century United States and Canada." *Taxon,* 39, no. 2, 1990: 151–205.

Sammons, Vivian O. *Blacks in Science and Medicine.* New York: Hemisphere, 1990.

Sheehy, Noel, J. Chapman, and Wendy A. Conroy, eds. *Biographical Dictionary of Psychology.* London: Routledge, 1997.

Turkevich, John. *Soviet Men of Science: Academicians and Corresponding Members of the Academy of Sciences of the USSR.* Westport, Conn.: Greenwood, 1963.

Yost, Edna. *American Women of Science.* Philadelphia: Frederick A. Stokes Co., 1943.

ALPHABETICAL
LIST OF ENTRIES

Abbott, Maude Elizabeth Seymour
Abel, Mary Hinman
Abel, Theodora Mead
Abella
Aberle, Sophie Bledsoe
Abouchdid, Edna
Abramson, Jadwiga
Abrotelia
Achilles, Edith Mulhall
Acosta-Sison, Honoria
Acton, Frances (Knight)
Adametz, Lotte
Adams, Amy Elizabeth Kemper
Adams, Mildred
Adamson, Joy (Gessner)
Addams, Jane
Adelberger of Lombardy
Adelle of the Saracens
Adelmota of Carrara
Adkins, Dorothy Christina
Aelfleda
Aemilia
Aesara of Lucania
Agamede
Agassiz, Elizabeth Cary
Aglaonike
Agnes of Bohemia
Agnes of Jerusalem
Agnes of Silesia
Agnes, Countess of Aix
Agnesi, Maria Gaetana
Agnodike
Aitken, Janet Kerr
Akeley, Mary Lee (Jobe)
Albertson, Mary
Albrecht, Eleonore
Albrecht, Grete
Alcock, Nora Lilian Leopard
Aldrich-Blake, Louisa Brandreth
Alexander, Annie Montague
Alexander, Frances Elizabeth Somerville
    (Caldwell)
Alexander, Hattie Elizabeth
Ali, Safieh
Alimen, Henriette
Allan, Mary Eleanor (Mea)
Allen, Doris Twitchell

Allen, Eliza (Stevens)
Allen, Ruth Florence
Alper, Thelma Gorfinkle
Altmann, Margaret
Aluwihare, Florence Kaushalya (Ram)
Amalitskiya, Anna P.
Amalosunta
Ameline
Ames, Blanche (Ames)
Ames, Louise Bates
Ames, Mary E. Pulsifer
Amherst, Sarah (Archer), Countess.
Andersen, Dorothy Hansine
Anderson, Caroline Virginia (Still) Wiley
Anderson, Elda Emma
Anderson, Elizabeth Garrett
Anderson, Evelyn M.
Anderson, Louisa Garrett
Anderson, Rose Gustava
Anderson, Violet Louise
Anderton-Smith, Mrs. W.
Andreas-Salomé, Louise Lelia
Andrews, Eliza Frances
Andrews, Grace
Andromache
Andrus, Ruth
Angst-Horridge, Anita
Anicia or Amyte
Ann Medica of York
Anna of Bohemia
Anna Sophia of Denmark
Anna Sophia of Hesse
Anne, Electress of Denmark
Anning, Mary
Anslow, Gladys Amelia
Antipoff, Helene
Antoine, Lore
Antoinette de Bellegarde
Antonia, Maestra
Apgar, Virginia
Applin, Esther (Richards)
Apsley (Hutchinson), Lady Lucy
Arber, Agnes (Robertson)
Arbuthnot, Isobel Agnes
Arconville, Geneviève Charlotte d'
Arden, Lady Margaret Elizabeth (Spencer
    Wilson)

Ardinghelli, Maria Angela
Arete of Cyrene
Arignote of Samos
Arkhangel'skaia, Aleksandra Gavriilovna
Arlitt, Ada Hart
Armitage, Eleanora
Armitage, Ella Sophia A. (Bulley)
Armitt, Annie Maria
Armitt, Mary Louisa
Armitt, Sophia
Arnold, Magda Blondiau
Arnstein, Margaret Gene
Arsenjewa, A.
Artemisia of Caria II
Arthur, Mary Grace
Artner, Mathilde
Asclepigenia
Ashby, Winifred Mayer
Aspasia of Miletus
Aspasia the Physician
Astell, Mary
Atkins, Anna
Atkins, Louisa Catherine Fanny
Atkinson, Louisa (later Calvert)
Attersoll, Maria
Atwater, Helen Woodard
Atwood, Martha Maria
Atwood, Martha Maria
Auerbach, Charlotte
Auken, Kirsten
Austin, Mary Lellah
Austin, Rebecca
Axiothea of Phlius
Ayrton, Hertha Marks
Ayrton, Matilda (Chaplin)
Babcock, Harriet
Baber, Zonia
Bachman, Maria Martin
Bacon, Clara (Latimer)
Baetjer, Anna Medora
Bagley, Florence (Winger)
Bagshaw, Elizabeth Catherine
Bahr- Bergius, Eva Vilhelmina Julia von
Bailey, Ethel Zoe
Bailey, Florence Augusta (Merriam)
Baker, Anne Elizabeth
Baker, Sara Josephine

Baker, Sarah Martha
Bakwin, Ruth (Morris)
Balaam, Ellen
Balfour, Margaret Ida
Balk, Christina (Lochman)
Ball, Anne Elizabeth
Ball, Josephine
Ball, Mary
Ballard, Julia Perkins Pratt
Bancroft, Nellie
Bang, Duck-Heung
Banga, Ilona
Banham, Katherine May
Banks, Sarah Sophia
Barbapiccola, Giuseppa Eleonora
Barbarshova, Zoya
Barber, Helen Karen
Barber, Mary Elizabeth (Bowker)
Bari, Nina Karlovna
Barkly, Lady Anna Maria (Pratt)
Barkly, Lady Elizabeth Helen (Timins or
  Timmins)
Barlett, Helen Blair
Barlow, Lady Emma Nora Darwin
Barnard, Alicia Mildred
Barnard, Edith Ethel
Barnard, Lady Anne (Henslow)
Barnard, Lady Anne (Lindsay)
Barnes (Berners), Juliana
Barney, Ida
Barney, Nora Stanton (Blatch) De Forest
Barnothy, Madeleine (Forro)
Barnum, Charlotte Cynthia
Barrera, Oliva Sabuca de Nantes
Barringer, Emily Dunning
Barrows, Katherine Isabel Hayes Chapin
Barry, James (pseudonym)
Barton, Clara Harlowe
Barton, Lela Viola
Bascom, Florence
Bass, Mary Elizabeth
Bassi, Laura Maria Caterina
Batchelder, Esther Lord
Bate, Dorothea Minola Alice
Bates, Mary E.
Bateson, Anna
Bateson, Beatrice
Battle, Helen Irene
Bauer, Grace M.
Baum, Marie
Baumann, Frieda
Baumgarten-Tramer, Franziska
Baumgartner, Leona
Baxter, Mildred Frances
Bayern, Therese von
Bayley, Nancy
Baynard, Anne
Beanland, Sarah
Beatley, Janice Carson
Beatrice of Savoy, Countess of Provence
Beatrice, Medica of Candia
Beaufort, Countess Margaret
Beaufort, Harriet Henrietta
Beausoleil, Martine de Bertereau

Beauvallet, Marcelle Jeanne
Beck, Sarah Coker (Adams)
Becker, Lydia Ernestine
Becker-Rose, Herta
Beckman, A.
Beckwith, Angie Maria
Beckwith, Cora
Beckwith, Martha Warren
Beecher, Catharine Esther
Beers, Catherine Virginia
Beever, Mary
Beever, Susan
Behn, Aphra
Behre, Ellinor H.
Beilby, Winifred
Belaeva, Elizaveta Ivanovna
Belar, Maria
Bell, Julia
Belota [Johanna Belota]
Belyea, Helen Reynolds
Bender, Hedwig
Bender, Lauretta
Bender, W.
Benedek, Therese F.
Benedict, Ruth (Fulton)
Benett, Etheldred
Bengston, Ida Albertina
Bennett, Alice
Bennett, Dorothea
Benson, Margaret Jane
Bentham, Ethel
Bentham, Lady Mary Sophia (Fordyce)
Bentinck, Margaret Cavendish (Harley),
  Duchess of Portland
Berger, Emily V.
Berger, Katharina Bertha Charlotte
Berners, Juliana See Barnes, Juliana
Beronice
Berridge, Emily Mary
Bertereau, Martine de, Baroness de
  Beausoleil
Berthagyta, Abbess
Berthildis of Chelles
Bertile of Chelles
Bertillon, Caroline Schultze
Besant, Annie (Wood)
Beutler, Ruth
Bevier, Isabel
Bhatia, Sharju Pandit
Bibring, Grete Lehner
Bickerdyke, Mary Ann (Ball)
Bidder, Anna McClean
Bidder, Marion Greenwood
Biheron, Marie Catherine
Bilger, Leonora (Neuffer)
Billings, Katharine Stevens (Fowler-Lunn)
Bingham, Millicent (Todd)
Bird, Grace Electa
Bird, Isabella See Bishop, Isabella Bird
Birdsall, Lucy Ellen
Birstein, Vera
Biscot, Jeanne
Bishop, Ann
Bishop, Isabella Lucy Bird

Bishop, Katharine Scott
Bissell, Emily P.
Bitting, Katherine Eliza (Golden)
Black, Florence
Black, Hortensia
Blackburn, Kathleen Bever
Blackburne, Anna
Blacker, Margaret Constance Helen
Blackwell, Antoinette Louise (Brown)
Blackwell, Elizabeth
Blackwell, Elizabeth
Blackwell, Elizabeth Marianne
Blackwell, Emily
Blackwood, Beatrice Mary
Blagg, Mary Adela
Blake, Mary Safford
Blanchan, Neltje (pseud.)
Blanchard, Frieda Cobb
Blanchard, Phyllis
Blanquies, Lucie
Blatchford, Ellen C.
Blau, Marietta
Bledsoe, Lucybelle
Blinova, Ekaterina Nikitichna
Bliss, Dorothy Elizabeth
Bliss, Eleanor, Albert
Bliss, Mary Campbell
Block, Jeanne (Humphrey)
Blodgett, Katharine Burr
Bluhm, Agnes
Bluket, Nina Aleksandrovna
Blunt, Katharine
Bocchi (Bucca), Dorotea
Bochantseva, Zinaida Petrovna
Bodley, Rachel Littler
Bogdanovskaia, Vera Evstaf'evna
Böhm-Wendt, Cäcilia
Boivin, Marie Gillain
Bokova-Sechenova, Mariia Aleksandrovna
Boley, Gertrude Maud
Bolschanina, M. A.
Bolton, Edith
Bolus, Harriet Margaret Louisa (Kensit)
Bomhard, Miriam Lucile
Bonnay, Marchioness du
Bonnevie, Kristine
Boole, Mary (Everest)
Boos, Margaret Bradley (Fuller)
Booth, Mary Ann Allard
Boring, Alice Middleton
Borisova-Bekriasheva, Antoniia
  Georgievna
Boron, Elizabeth (Riddle) Graves
Borromeo, Clelia Grillo
Borsarelli, Fernanda
Boswell, Katherine Cumming
Bourdel, Léone
Bourgeoise, Louyse
Bouteiller, Marcelle
Bouthilet, Lorraine
Boveri, Marcella Imelda O'Grady
Bowen, Susan
Boyd, Elizabeth Margaret
Boyd, Louise Arner

Boyer, Esther Lydia
Bracher, Rose
Bradley, Amy Morris
Bradley, Frances Sage
Brahe, Sophia
Branch, Hazel Elisabeth
Brand, Martha
Brandegee, Mary Katharine Layne
Branham, Sara Elizabeth
Brant, Laura
Braun, (Emma) Lucy
Braun, Annette Frances
Brazier, Mary Agnes Burniston (Brown)
Breckinridge, Mary
Bredikhina, Evgeniia Aleksandrovna
Breed, Mary (Bidwell)
Brenchley, Winifred Elsie
Brenk, Irene
Brès Madeleine (Gébelin)
Breyer, Maria Gerdina (Brandwijk)
Brezina, Maria Aristides
Bridget, Saint, of Ireland
Bridget, Saint, of Scandinavia
Bridgman, Olga Louise
Brière, Nicole-Reine Etable de la.
Brière, Yvonne
Brightwen, Eliza (Elder)
Britten, Lilian Louisa
Britton, Elizabeth Knight
Broadhurst, Jean
Brock, Sylvia (DeAntonis)
Bromley, Helen Jean (Brown)
Bronner, Augusta Fox
Brooke, Winifred
Brooks, Harriet T.
Brooks, Matilda (Moldenhauer)
Brooks, Sarah Theresa
Broomall, Anna Elizabeth
Brousseau, Kate
Brown, Charlotte Amanda Blake
Brown, Dame Edith Mary
Brown, Elizabeth
Brown, Fay Cluff
Brown, Mabel Mary
Brown, Nellie Adalesa
Brown, Rachel Fuller
Browne, Ida Alison (Brown)
Browne, Lady Isabel Mary (Peyronnet)
Browne, Marjorie Lee
Bruce, Catherine Wolfe
Bruce, Eileen Adelaide
Brüch, Hilde
Brückner, Frau Dr.
Brunetta
Brunetti, R.
Brunfels, Frau Otto
Brunswick, Ruth Jane (Mack)
Bryan, Alice Isabel (Bever)
Bryan, Margaret
Bryan, Mary Katherine
Bryant, Louise Stevens
Bryant, Sophie (Willock)
Bucca, Dorotea.
Buchanan, Florence

Buchbinder, Laura G. Ordan
Buckel, Chloe A.
Buckland, Mary Morland
Buckley, Arabella
Buell, Mary Van Rensselaer
Buerk, Minerva (Smith)
Bühler, Charlotte Bertha (Malachowski)
Bülbring, Edith
Bull, Nina Wilcox
Bunch, Cordia
Bunting, Martha
Bunting-Smith, Mary (Ingraham)
Bunzel, Ruth Leah
Burges, Mary Anne
Burgess, May (Ayres)
Burkill, Ethel Maud (Morrison)
Burlingham, Dorothy (Tiffany)
Burlingham, Gertrude Simmons
Burns, Eleanor Irene
Burns, Louisa
Burr, Emily Thorp
Burrell, Anna Porter
Burton, Helen Marie Rousseay
    (Kannemeyer)
Burtt Davy, Alice (Bolton)
Bury, Elizabeth (Lawrence)
Bury, Priscilla Susan (Falkner)
Bush, Katharine Jeannette
Busk, Lady Marian (Balfour)
Bussecker, Erna
Buttelini, Marchesa
Bykhovskaia, Anna Markovna
Byrd, Mary Emma
Byrnes, Esther Fussell
Byron, Augusta Ada, Countess of Lovelace
Cadbury, Dorothy Adlington
Cadilla de Martínez, María
Cady, Bertha Louise Chapman
Caerellia (Caerelia)
Caetani-Bovatelli, Donna Ersilia
Calderone, Mary S.
Caldwell, Mary Letitia
Cale, F. M.
Calenda, Constanza or Laurea Constantia
Calkins, Mary Whiton
Callcott, Lady Maria Graham
Calvert, Catherine Louisa Waring
    (Atkinson)
Calvert, Emily Amelia (Adelia)
Cambrière, Clarisse
Campbell, Dame Janet Mary
Campbell, Helen Stuart
Campbell, May Sherwood
Campbell, Persia Crawford
Cannon, Annie Jump
Capen, Bessie
Carlson, Elizabeth
Carlson, Lucille
Carne, Elizabeth Catherine (Thomas)
Carothers, Estrella Eleanor
Carpenter, Esther
Carr, Emma Perry
Carroll, Chris tiane (Mendrez)
Carroll, Dorothy

Carson, Rachel Louise
Carter, Edna
Carter, Elizabeth
Cartwright, Dame Mary Lucy
Carus, Mary Hegeler
Carvajales y Camino, Laura M. de
Castle, Cora (Sutton)
Castra, Anna de
Catani, Giuseppina
Catherine of Bologna, Saint
Catherine of Genoa, Saint
Catherine of Siena, Saint
Catherine Ursula, Countess of Baden
Catherine, Medica of Cracow
Catlow, Maria Agnes
Cattell, Psyche
Cattoi, Noemí Violeta
Cauchois, Yvette
Caughlan, Georgeanne (Robertson)
Cauquil, Germaine Anne
Cavendish, Margaret, Duchess of
    Newcastle
Cellier, Elizabeth
Cesniece-Freudenfelde, Zelma
Chaix, Paulette Audemard
Chalubinska, Aniela
Chamié, Catherine
Chandler, Elizabeth
Chandler, Marjorie Elizabeth Jane
Chang, Moon Gyung
Chang, Vivian
Charles, Vera Katherine
Charlotte Sophia, Queen
Charsley, Fanny Anne
Chase, Mary Agnes Meara
Chasman, Renate Wiener
Châtelet, Gabrielle-Emilie Le Tonnelier de
    Breuteuil, Marquise du
Chauchard, B.
Chaudet, Maria Casanova de
Cheesman, Lucy Evelyn
Chenoweth, Alice Drew
Chesser, Elizabeth (Sloan)
Chick, Dame Harriette
Child, Lydia Maria (Francis)
Chinchon, Countess of
Chinn, May Edward
Chisholm, Catherine
Chisholm, Grace Emily
Chmielewska, Irene
Chodak-Gregory, Hazel Haward
    (Cuthbert)
Christen, Sydney Mary (Thompson)
Christina, Queen of Sweden
Church, Elda Rodman (MacIlvaine)
Chute, Hettie Morse
Cilento, Lady Phyllis
Cinquini, Maria dei Conti Cibrario
Cioranescu-Nenitzescu, Ecaterina
Clapp, Cornelia Maria
Clappe, Louisa Amelia (Smith)
Clara (Clare) of Assisi, Saint
Clarisse of Rotomago (or Clarice of
    Rouen)

Clark, Bertha
Clark, Frances N.
Clark, Janet Howell
Clark, Jessie Jane
Clark, Lois
Clark, Mamie Katherine (Phipps)
Clark, Nancy Talbot
Clarke, Cora Huidekoper
Clarke, Edith
Clarke, Lilian Jane
Clarke, Louisa (Lane)
Clay-Jolles, Tettje Clasina
Claypole, Agnes Mary
Claypole, Edith Jane
Clea
Cleachma
Clemens, Mary Knapp (Strong)
Clements, Edith Gertrude (Schwartz)
Clements, Margaret
Cleobulina of Rhodes
Cleopatra
Clerke, Agnes Mary
Clerke, Ellen Mary
Cleve-Euler, Astrid
Cleveland, Emeline Horton
Clifford, Lady Anne
Clinch, Phyllis E. M.
Clisby, Harriet Jemima Winifred
Clothilde of Burgundy
Coade, Eleanor
Coates, Sarah J.
Cobb, Margaret Vera
Cobb, Rosalie M. Karapetoff
Cobbe, Anne Phillipa
Cobbe, Frances Power
Cobbe, Margaret
Cochran, Doris Mabel
Cockburn, Catharine (Trotter)
Cockrell, Wilmatte (Porter)
Cohn, Essie White
Coignou, Caroline Pauline Marie
Colby, Martha Guernsey
Colcord, Mabel
Colden, Jane
Cole, Emma J.
Cole, Rebecca J.
Collet, Clara Elizabeth
Collett, Mary Elizabeth
Collins, Katharine Richards
Colvin, Brenda
Comnena (Comnenos), Anna
Comstock, Anna Botsford
Comyns-Lewer, Ethel
Cone, Claribel
Conklin, Marie (Eckhardt)
Conklin, Ruth Emelene
Converse, Jeanne
Conway, Anne
Conway, Elsie (Phillips)
Cook, A. Grace
Cook, Margaret C.
Cooke, Alice Sophia (Smart)
Cookson, Isabel Clifton
Cooley, Jacquelin Smith

Coombs, Helen Copeland
Cooper, Clara Chassell
Cooper, Elizabeth Morgan
Cooper, Susan Fenimore
Cooper, Sybil
Cooper-Ellis, Katharine Murdoch
Copeland, Lennie Phoebe
Cordier, Marguerite Jeanne
Cori, Gerty Theresa Radnitz
Cornaro (Cornero), Elena (Helena)
    Lucretia
Cornelius-Furlani, Marta
Coryndon, Shirley (Cameron)
Coste Blanche, Marie de
Cotelle, Sonia
Cotter, Brigid M.
Coudreau, Octavie
Cowan, Edwina Abbott
Cox, Gertrude Mary
Cox, Rachel (Dunaway)
Coyle, Elizabeth Eleanor
Cram, Eloise Blaine
Cramer, Catherine Gertrude du Tertre
    Schraders
Crandall, Ella Phillips
Crane, Agnes
Crane, Jocelyn
Cranwell, Lucy May
Cremer, Erika
Crespin, Irene
Crocker, Lucretia
Croll, Hilda M.
Crosbie, May
Crosby, Elizabeth Caroline
Crosfield, Margaret Chorley
Csepreghyné-Meznerics, Ilona
Cuffe, Lady Charlotte Wheeler (Williams)
Cullis, Winifred
Cumming, Lady Gordon (Eliza Maria
    Campbell)
Cummings, Clara Eaton
Cummings, Louise Duffield
Cunio, Isabella
Cunitz, Maria
Cunningham, Bess Virginia
Cunningham, Gladys Story
Cunningham, Susan
Curie, Marie (Maria Sklodowska)
Currie, Ethel Dobbie
Curtis, Doris Sarah (Malkin)
Curtis, Natalie
Cushier, Elizabeth
Cushing, Hazel Morton
Cushman, Florence
Cuthbert-Browne, Grace Johnston
Cutler, Catherine
Czaplicka, marie antoinette
Czeczottowa, Hanna (Peretiatkowicza)
Dalai, Maria Jolanda (Tosoni)
Dalby, Mary
Dale, Elizabeth
Dallas, A. E. M. M.
Dalle Donne, Maria
Damo

Dane, Elisabeth
Daniel, Anne Sturges
Daniels, Amy L.
Danti or Dante, Theodora
Darwin, Emma (Wedgwood)
Dashkova, Princess Ekaterina Romanovna
Daulton, Agnes Warner McClelland
Davenport, Gertrude (Crotty)
David, Florence N.
Davidson, Ada D.
Davis, Adelle
Davis, Alice (Rohde)
Davis, Frances (Elliott)
Davis, Grace Evangeline
Davis, Katharine Bement
Davis, Marguerite
Davis, Olive Griffith Stull
Davis, Rose May
Davy, Lady Joanna Charlotte (Flemmich)
Dawson, Maria
Day, Dorothy
Day, Gwendolen Helen
Day, Mary Anna
De Almania, Jacqueline Felicia
De Bréauté, Eléonore-Nell-Suzanne
De Chantal, Mme.
De Fraine, Ethel Louise
De Gorzano, Leonetta
De Graffenried, Mary Clare
De la Cruz, Juana Inés
De la Marche, Marguerite du Tertre
De Laguna, Fredericka Annis Lopez de
    Leo
De Lange, Cornelia Catharina
De Lebrix, Françoise
De Marillac, Louise, Mlle, Le Gras.
De Milt, Clara Marie
De Mole, Fanny Elizabeth
De Staël Holstein, Anne Louise Germaine
    Necker
De Valera, Mairin
De Valois, Madame
De Vesian, Dorothy Ellis
De Witt, Lydia Maria Adams
Decker, Jane Cynthia (McLaughlin)
Deflandre-Rigaud, Marthe
Deichmann, Elisabeth
Déjerine-Klumpke, Augusta
Delaney (or Delany), Mary (Granville),
Delap, Maude Jane
Delauney, Marguerite de Staël
Delf-Smith, Ellen Marion
Deloria, Ella Cara
Dembo, Tamara
Dempsey, Sister Mary Joseph
Demud
Dengel, Anna Maria
Denis, Willey Glover
Dennett, Mary Ware
Dennis, Olive Wetzel
Densmore, Frances Theresa
Derick, Carrie M.
Derscheid-Delcourt, Marie
Detmers, Frederica

Deutsch, Helene Rosenback
Dewey, Jane Mary (Clark)
Di Novella, Maria
Diana of Poitiers
Dick, Gladys Rowena Henry
Dickerson, Mary Cynthia
Dietrich, Amalie
Diggs, Ellen Irene
Dimock, Susan
Dimsdale, Helen Easdale (Brown)
Dinnerstein, Dorothy
Diotima of Mantinea
Dix, Dorothea Lynde
Dobrolubova, Tatiana A.
Dobroscky, Irene Dorothy
Dobrowolska, H.
Dobson, Mildred E.
Dock, Lavinia Lloyd
Dodd, Katharine
Dodds, Mary Letitia
Dodgson, Sarah Elizabeth
Dodson, Helen Walter
Doering, Kathleen Clara
Dohan, Edith Haywood Hall
Dokhman, Genrietta Isaakovna
Dolgopol de Saez, Mathilde
Dolley, Sarah Read Adamson
Dombrovskaia, Iuliia Fominichna
Donnay, Gabrielle (Hamburger)
Dooley, Lucile
Dorabialska, Alicja Domenica
Doreck, Hertha (Walburger Doris Sieverts)
Dorenfeldt, Margot
Dorety, Angela
Dormon, Caroline
Doubleday, Neltje Blanchan (De Graff)
Dougal, Margaret Douie
Douglas, Alice Vibert
Dover, Mary Violette
Downey, June Etta
Downey, K. Melvina
Downie, Dorothy G.
Downs, Cornelia Mitchell
Drake, Judith
Drant, Patricia (Hart)
Draper, Mary Anna Palmer
Drebeneva-Ukhova, Varvara Pavlovna
Drew, Kathleen Mary
Drinker, Katherine (Rotan)
Drummond, Margaret
Du Bois, Cora
Du Châtelet, Gabrielle-Emilie Le
    Tonnelier de Breteuil (Marquise)
Du Coudray, Angelique (Marguerite le
    Boursier)
Du Luys, Guillemette
Dubuisson-Brouha, Adele
Duffy, Elizabeth
Duges, Marie-Louise
Dumée, Jeanne
Dummer, Ethel (Sturges)
Dunbar, Helen Flanders
Duncan, Catherine (Gross)
Duncan, Helen

Duncan, Ursula Katherine
Dunham, Ethel Collins
Dunlop, Janette Gilchrist
Dunn, Mary Douglas
Dunn, Thelma Brumfield
Dunning, Wilhelmina Frances
Dupré, Marie
Durham, Mary Edith
Durocher, Marie (Josefina Mathilde)
Duryea, Nina
Dutcher, Adelaide
Dutton, Bertha Pauline
Dutton, Loraine Orr
Dye, Marie
Dyer, Helen Marie
Dylazanka, Maria
Earle, Marie Theresa (Villiers)
Eastwood, Alice
Eaves, Elsie
Ebers, Edith (Knote)
Eccello of Lucania
Echecratia the Philiasian
Echols, Dorothy Jung
Eckerson, Sophia Hennion
Eckstorm, Fannie Pearson (Hardy)
Eddy, Bernice Elaine
Edge, Rosalie Barrow
Edgell, Beatrice
Edgerton, Winifred Haring
Edgeworth, Maria
Edinger, Johanna Gabrielle Otellie (Tilly)
Edkins, Nora Tweedy
Edson, Fanny Carter
Edwards, Emma Ward
Edwards, Lena Frances
Edwards-Pilliet, Blanche
Efimenko, Aleksandra Iakovlevna
Eggleton, Marion Grace (Palmer)
Ehrenfest-Afanassjewa, Tatyana Alexeyevna
Eichelberger, Lillian
Eigenmann, Rosa Smith
Eimmart, Marie Claire
Einstein, Elizabeth Roboz
Einstein-Maric, Mileva
Eisele, Carolyn
Elam, Constance Fligg Tipper
Elderton, Ethel
Eleanora, Duchess of Mantua
Eleanora, Duchess of Troppau and
    Jagerndorf
Elephantis
Elgood, Cornelia Bonté Sheldon (Amos)
Elion, Gertrude Belle
Eliot, Martha May
Elizabeth of Bohemia
Elizabeth of Poland, Queen of Hungary
Elizabeth of Portugal, Saint
Elizabeth of Schönau
Elles, Gertrude Lilian
Elliott, Charlotte
Ellis, Florence Hawley
Ellisor, Alva Christine
Elsom, Katharine (O'Shea)
Emerson, Gladys Ludwina (Anderson)

Eng, Helga
Engelbrecht, Mildred Amanda
Erdmann, Rhoda
Erdmuthe, Sophie
Ermol'eva, Zinaida Vissarionovna
Erxleben, Dorothea Christiana (Leporin)
Esau, Katherine
Esdorn, Ilse
Etheldrida, Queen
Euphemia, Abbess of Wherwell
Evans, Alice Catherine
Evans, Alice Margaret
Everard, Barbara Mary Steyning
Everett, Alice
Evershed, Mary Orr
Eves, Florence
Ewing, Elizabeth Raymond (Burden)
Eyton, Charlotte
Fabiola
Fage, Winifred E.
Farenden, Emma
Farnsworth, Alice
Farnsworth, Vesta J.
Farquharson, Marian Sarah (Ridley)
Farr, Wanda Kirkbride
Farrar, Lillian K. P.
Fátima
Faustina
Favilla
Fawcett, Phillipa Garrett
Fearn, Anne Walter
Fedchenko, Ol'ga Aleksandrovna
Feichtinger, Nora
Felicie, Jacobina
Fell, Honor Bridget, Dame
Fenchel, Käte (Sperling)
Fenwick, Florence
Ferguson, Margaret Clay
Fernald, Grace Maxwell
Fernald, Maria Elizabeth (Smith)
Ferrand, Elizabeth M.
Ferrand, Jacqueline
Ferrero, Gina (Lombroso)
Fielde, Adele Marion
Fielding, Mary Maria (Simpson)
Fiennes, Celia
Fieser, Mary
Figner, Vera
Finch, Louisa (Thynne), Countess of
    Aylesford
Findlater, Doris
Finkler, Rita V. (Sapiro)
Fischer, Irene Kaminka
Fish, Margery
Fish, Marie Poland
Fishenden, Margaret White
Fisher, Edna Marie
Fisher, Elizabeth Florette
Fisher, Sara Carolyn
Fitton, Sarah Mary
FitzGerald, Mabel Purefoy
Flammel, Perrenelle
Fleming, Amalia Coutsouris, Lady
Fleming, Williamina Paton Stevens

Fletcher, Alice Cunningham
Flock, Eunice Verna
Flood, Margaret Greer
Florendo, Soledad Arcega
Flügge-Lotz, Irmgard
Foley, Mary Cecilia
Folmer, HerminE Jacoba
Fomina-Zhukovskaia, Evdokiia
    Aleksandrovna
Fonovits-Smereker, H.
Foot, Katharine
Forbes, Helena Madelain Lamond
Forster, Mary
Fossey, Dian
Fossler, Mary Louise
Foster, Josephine Curtis
Foster, Margaret D.
Fouquet, Marie de Maupeou, Vicomtesse
    de Vaux
Fowler, Lydia Folger
Fowler-Billings, Katharine Stevens
Fox, Ruth
Fraine, Ethel Louise de
Frampton, Mary
Frances of Brittany
Francini, Eleonora Corti
Françoise, Marie-Thérèse
Frank, Margaret
Franklin, Rosalind Elsie
Frantz, Virginia Kneeland
Freeman, Joan Maie
Freidlina, Rakhil' Khatskelevna
Frenkel-Brunswik, Else
Freud, Anna
Freund, Ida
Friant, M.
Friedlander, Kate
Friedmann, Friederike
Friend, Charlotte
Fritz, Madeleine Alberta
Fromm, Erika Oppenheimer
Frostig, Marianne Bellak
Fulford, Margaret Hannah
Fulhame, Elizabeth
Furness, Caroline Ellen
Fuss, Margarita
Gabler, Anna
Gage, Catherine
Gage, Susanna Phelps
Gaige, Helen (Thompson)
Galabert, Renée
Galindo, Beatrix
Galvani, Lucia (Galeazzi)
Gamble, Eleanor Acheson McCulloch
Gantt, Love Rosa
Gaposchkin, Cecilia Payne
Gardiner, Edith Gertrude (Willcock)
Gardiner, Margaret Isabella
Gardner, Elinor Wight
Gardner, Julia Anna
Gardner, Mary Sewall
Garfield, Viola Edmundson
Garlick, Constance
Garnett, Alice

Garnjobst, Laura Flora
Garretson, Mary (Welleck)
Garrett, Elizabeth
Garrod, Dorothy Anne Elizabeth
Gàta, Elena (Stefanescu)
Gates, Fanny Cook
Gatty, Margaret (Scott)
Gaw, Esther Allen
Gaw, Frances Isabel
Geiringer Hilda
Geldart, Alice Mary
Genet-Varcin, Emilienne
Genung, Elizabeth Faith
Gepp, Ethel Sarel (Barton)
Geppert, Maria Pia
Germain, Sophie
Gerould, Elizabeth Wood
Gerry, Eloise B.
Gey, Margaret Lewis
Ghilietta
Giammarino, Pia
Gibbons, E. Joan
Gibbons, Vernette Lois
Gibbs, Lilian Suzette
Gifford, Isabella
Gilbert, Ruth
Gilbreth, Lillian Evelyn Moller
Gilette of Narbonne
Giliani, Alessandra
Gilkey, Helen Margaret
Gill, Jocelyn Ruth
Gillett, Margaret (Clark)
Gilmore, Jane Georgina
Gilroy, Helen (Turnbull)
Giraud, Marthe
Gitelson, Frances H.
Gjellestad, Guro Else
Glagoleva-Arkad'yeva, Aleksandra
    Andreyevna
Glascott, Louisa S.
Glasgow, Maude
Glass, Jewell Jeanette
Gleason, Josephine Mixer
Gleason, Kate
Gleason, Rachel Brooks
Gleditsch, Ellen
Glueck, Eleanor (Touroff)
Gocholashvili, Mariia Mikievna
Godding, D. W.
Godfery, Hilda Margaret
Goeppert Mayer, Maria Gertrud Käte
Goldfeder, Anna
Goldfrank, Esther Schiff
Goldhaber, Sulamith
Goldman, Hetty
Goldring, Winifred
Goldschmidt, Frieda
Goldsmith, Grace Arabell
Goldsmith, Marie
Goldthwaite, Nellie Esther
Golinevich, Elena Mikhailovna
Goodenough, Florence Laura
Goodrich, Sarah Frances
Goodyear, Edith

Gordon, Kate
Gordon, Maria Matilda Ogilvie
Gorinevskaya, Valentina Valentinovna
Gorizdro-Kulczycka, Zinaida
Gorshkova, Tat'yana Ivanovna
Götz, Irén Julia (Dienes)
Gracheva, Yekaterina Konstantinovna
Graham, Helen (Treadway)
Graham, Maria Dundas (Lady Calcott)
Grainger, Jennie
Gravatt, Annie Evelyn (Rathbun)
Graves, Elizabeth (Riddle)
Gray, Etta
Gray, Maria Emma (Smith)
Gray, Susan Walton
Green, Arda Alden
Green, Mary Letitia
Green, Vera Mae
Greene, Catherine (Littlefield)
Greenwood, Marion
Gregory, Eliza Standerwick (Barnes)
Gregory, Emily Lovira
Gregory, Emily Ray
Gregory, Lady Isabella Augusta (Persse)
Gregory, Louisa Catherine (Allen)
Gregory, Louise Hoyt
Greig, Margaret Elizabeth
Greisheimer, Esther Maud
Griffin, Harriet Madeline
Griffiths, Amelia Elizabeth
Griffiths, Amelia Warren (Rogers)
Griggs, Mary Amerman
Grignan, Françoise Marguerite de Sévigné,
    Comtesse de
Grinnell, Hilda Wood
Griswold, Grace Hall
Gromova, Vera Isaacovna
Gruhn, Ruth
Grundy, Clara
Grundy, Ellen
Grundy, Maria Ann
Grzigorzewska, Marja
Gsell, Maria Dorothea Henrica (Graf)
Gualco, Sellina
Guarna, Rebecca
Guldberg, Estrid
Gullett, Lucy E.
Gundersen, Herdis
Gunn, Mary Davidson
Gunther, Erna
Guthrie, Mary Jane
Guyton de Morveau, Claudine Poullet
    Picardet
Gwynne-Vaughan, Dame Helen Charlotte
    Isabella (Fraser)
Haber-Immerwahr, Clara
Haccius, Barbara
Hagood, Margaret Loyd Jarman
Hahn, Dorothy Anna
Hainault, Countess of
Haldorsen, Inger Alida
Halicka, Antonina (Yaroszewicz)
Halket, Ann Cronin
Halket, Lady Anne (Murray)

Hall, Agnes C.
Hall, Dorothy
Hall, Edith Hayward
Hall, Julia Brainerd
Hall, Kate Marion
Hall, Rosetta Sherwood
Hall-Brown, Lucy
Halliday, Nellie
Hallowell, Susan Maria
Hamburger, Erna
Hamerstrom, Frances (Flint)
Hamilton, Alice
Hamilton, Peggy-Kay
Hammer, Marie Signe
Hanfmann, Eugenia
Hanks, Jane Richardson
Hansen, Hazel D.
Hansen, Julie Marie Vinter
Hanson, Emmeline Jean
Haoys (la meresse)
Hardcastle, Frances
Hardesty, Mary
Harding, Anita
Hardwick, Rose Standish
Hardy, Harriet
Hardy, Thora Marggraff Plitt
Harmon, Élise F.
Harrison, Jane Ellen
Harrison, Janet Mitchell Marr (Dingwall)
Harrower, Molly R.
Hart, Esther Hasting
Hart, Helen
Hart, J. B.
Hartt, Constance Endicott
Harvey, Elizabeth
Harvey, Ethel Nicholson Browne
Harwood, Margaret
Haslett, Dame Caroline
Hassall, Bessie Florence (Cory)
Hastings, Barbara, Marchioness of
Hathaway, Millicent Louise
Hatshepsut, Queen
Hausser, Isolde (Ganswindt)
Hawes, Harriet (Boyd)
Hawkes, Jacquetta (Hopkins)
Hawkins, Kate
Hawkins, Mary Esther (Sibthorp)
Hawn Mirabile, Margaret H.
Hayes, Ellen Amanda
Hayner, Lucy Julia
Hayward, Ida Margaret
Haywood, Charlotte
Hazen, Elizabeth Lee
Hazlett, Olive Clio
Hearst, Phoebe (Apperson)
Heath, Daisy Winifred
Hebb, Catherine Olding
Hebel, Medicienne
Heckter, Maria
Hedges, Florence
Hedwig of Silesia, Saint
Heermann, Margareta
Hefferan, Mary
Heidbreder, Edna Frances

Heim-Vögtlin, Marie
Heimann, Berta
Heimann, Paula
Heinlein, Julia Elizabeth Heil
Hélène, Duchess of Aosta
Hellman, Johanna
Hellstedt, Leone McGregor
Héloïse
Henderson, Nellie Frater
Hendricks, Eileen M.
Hennel, Cora Barbara
Henrey, Blanche Elizabeth Edith
Henry, Caroline (Orridge)
Henshaw, Julia Wilmotte
Heppenstall, Caroline A.
Herford, Ethilda B. Meakin
Herrad of Hohenburg
Herrick, Christine (Terhune)
Herrick, Julia Frances
Herrick, Sophia McIlvaine (Bledsoe)
Herschel, Caroline Lucretia
Hersende, Abbess of Fontevrault
Herskovits, Frances S. (Shapiro)
Hertwig, Paula
Hertz, Mathilde
Herwerden, Marianne van
Herwerden, Marianne van
Herxheimer, Franziska
Heslop, Mary Kingdon
Hesse, Fanny
Hetzer, Hildegard
Hevelius, Elisabetha Koopman
Hewer, Dorothy
Hewitt, Dorothy Carleton
Hibbard, Hope
Hickey, Amanda Sanford
Hicks, Beatrice Alice
Higgins, Vera (Cockburn)
Hightower, Ruby Usher
Hildegard of Bingen
Hildreth, Gertrude Howell
Hilgard, Josephine Rohrs
Hill, Dorothy
Hill, Justina Hamilton
Hill, Mary Elliott
Hines, Marion
Hinman, Alice Hamlin
Hinrichs, Marie Agnes
Hirschfeld-Tiburtius, Henriette (Pagelsen)
Hitchcock, Fanny Rysam Mulford
Hitchcock, Orra White
Hitchens, Ada Florence R.
Hitzenberger, Annaliese
Hoare, Sarah
Hobby, Gladys Lounsbury
Hoby, Lady
Hodgkin, Dorothy Mary Crowfoot
Hodgson, Eliza Amy
Hodgson, Elizabeth
Hoffleit, Ellen Dorrit
Hofmann, Elise
Hogg, Helen Sawyer
Hoggan, Ismé Aldyth
Hohl, Leonora Anita

Hoke, Calm ,(Morrison)
Hol, Jacoba Brigitta Louisa
Holley, Mary Austin
Hollingworth, Leta Anna Stetter
Holm, Esther (Aberdeen)
Holmes, Mary Emilee
Holton, Pamela Margaret (Watson-
    Williams)
Homer, Annie
Hoobler, Icie Gertrude Macy
Hooker, Frances Harriet Henslow
Hooker, Henrietta Edgecomb
Hooker, Marjorie
Hopkins, Esther (Burton)
Hopper, Grace (Brewster Murray)
Horenburg, Anna Elizabeth von
Horney, Karen Clementine (Danielsen)
Horowitz, Stephanie
Hough, Margaret Jean Ringier
Howard Beckman, Ruth Winifred
Howard Wylde, Hildegarde
Howard, Louise Ernestine (Matthaei),
    Lady
Howe Akeley, Delia Julia Denning
Howes, Ethel Dench Puffer
Howitt, Mary (Botham)
Hroswitha of Gandersheim
Hubbard, Marian Elizabeth
Hubbard, Ruth Marilla
Hubbs, Laura Cornelia (Clark)
Hudson, Hilda Phoebe
Hug-Hellmuth, Hermine von
Huggins, Margaret Lindsay (Murray)
Hughes, Ellen Kent
Hughes, Mary Caroline (Weston)
Hughes-Schrader, Sally Peris
Hugonnai-Wartha, Vilma
Hummel, Katharine Pattee
Hunscher, Helen Alvina
Hunt, Caroline Louisa
Hunt, Eva Verbitsky
Hunt, Harriot Kezia
Hurler, Gertrud (Zach)
Hurlock, Elizabeth Bergner
Hurston, Zora Neale
Hussey, Anna Maria (Reed)
Hussey, Priscilla Butler
Hutchins, Ellen
Hutchinson, Dorothy (Hewitt)
Hutton, Lady Isabel Emilie
Huxley, Henrietta Heathorn
Hyde, Ida Henrietta
Hyman, Libbie Henrietta
Hynes, Sarah
Hypatia of Alexandria
Ianovskaia, Sof'ia Aleksandrovna
Ibbetson, Agnes (Thomson)
Ide, Gladys Genevra
Ilg, Frances Lillian
Inglis, Elsie (Maude)
Irwin, Marian
Isaacs, Susan Sutherland (Fairhurst)
Iusupova, Saradzhan Mikhailovna
Ivanova, Elena Alekseevna

Ives, Margaret
Iwanowska, Wilhelmina
Jacobi, Mary Corinna Putnam
Jacobina Medica of Bologna
Jacobs, Aletta Henrietta
Jacobson, Clara
Jacopa of Passau
Jacson, Maria Elizabeth
Jahoda, Marie
James, Lucy Jones
Janaki Ammal, Edavaleth Kakkat
Janssen, Mme.
Janssen, Mme.
Jeanes, Allene Rosalind
Jekyll, Gertrude
Jensen, Estelle Louise
Jérémine, Elisabeth (Tschernaieff)
Jermoljeva, Zinaida Vissarionovna
Jesson, Enid Mary
Jex-Blake, Sophia
Ježowska-Trzebiatowska, Boguslawa
Jhirad, Jerusha
Johanna (Johanne, Joanna)
Johnson, Dorothy Durfee Montgomery
Johnson, Hildegarde (Binder)
Johnson, Mary
Johnson, Minnie May
Johnston, Mary Sophia
Joliot-Curie, Irène
Jonas, Anna I.
Jones, Amanda Theodosia
Jones, Eva Elizabeth
Jones, Katharine, Viscountess Ranelagh
Jones, Lorella Margaret
Jones, Mary Amanda Dixon
Jones, Mary Cover
Jordan, Louise
Jordan, Sara Claudia (Murray)
Jordan-Lloyd, Dorothy
Joslin, Lulu Broadbent
Josselyn, Irene (Milliken)
Joteyko, Joséphine
Joyce, Margaret Elizabeth
Juhn, Mary
Julian, Hester Forbes (Pengelly)
Justin, Margaret M.
Kaan, Helen Warton
Kaberry, Phyllis Mary
Kablick [Kablíková], Josephine (Ettel)
Kaczorowska, Zofia
Kahn, Ida
Kaltenbeiner, Victorine
Kane, Lady Katherine Sophia (Baily)
Kanouse, Bessie Bernice
Karamihailova, Elizabeth/Elizaveta [Kara-
    Michailova]
Kardymowiczowa, Irena
Karlik, Berta
Karp, Carol Ruth (Vander Velde)
Karpowicz, Ludmila
Karrer, Annie May Hurd
Kashevarova-Rudneva, Varvara
    Aleksandrovna
Katherine, la Surgiene (the Surgeon)

Katz, Rosa Heine
Kaye-Smith, A. Dulcie
Keeler, Harriet Louise
Keen, Angeline Myra
Keeney, Dorothea Lilian
Keil, Elizabeth Marbareta
Keil, Elsa Marie
Keith, Marcia Anna
Keldysh, Liudmila Vsevolodovna
Keller, Ida Augusta
Kellerman, Stella Victoria (Dennis)
Kelley, Louise
Kellogg, Louise
Kellor, Frances A.
Kelly, Agnes
Kelly, Isabel Truesdell
Kelly, Margaret G.
Kelly, Margaret W.
Kendall, Claribel
Kendrick, Pearl (Luella)
Kennard, Margaret Alice
Kennedy, Cornelia
Kenny, Elizabeth (Sister Kenny)
Kent, Elizabeth
Kent, Elizabeth Isis Pogson
Kent, Grace Helen
Kent, Kate Peck
Kenyon, Kathleen Mary
Kerling, Louise Catharina Petronella
Keur, Dorothy Louise (Strouse)
Kharuzina, Vera Nikolaevna
Kielan-Jaworowska, Zofia
Kil, Chung-Hee
King, Anastasia Kathleen (Murphy)
King, Georgina
King, Helen Dean
King, Jessie Luella
King, Louisa Boyd (Yeomans)
King, Martha
King, Susan (Raymond)
Kingsley, Louise
Kingsley, Mary Henrietta
Kirby, Elizabeth
Kirch, Christine
Kirch, Margaretha
Kirch, Maria Margaretha Winkelmann
Kirkbride, Mary Butler
Kirkham, Nellie
Kittrell, Flemmie Pansy
Kleegman, Sophia
Klein, Marthe
Klein, Melanie (Reizes)
Kletnova, E. N.
Klieneberger-Nobel, Emmy
Kline, Virginia Harriett
Klosterman, Mary Jo
Kluckhohn, Florence Rockwood
Klumpke, Dorothea
Knake, Else
Knight, Margaret
Knopf, Eleanora Frances (Bliss)
Knott-Ter Meer, Ilse
Knowles, Matilda Cullen
Knowles, Ruth Sheldon

Knull, Dorothy J.
Kobel, Maria
Koch, Helen Lois
Koch, Marie Louise
Kochanowská, Adéla
Kochina, Pelageia Iakovlevna
Kohler, Elsa
Kohn, Hedwig
Kohts, Nadie (Ladychin)
Kolaczkowska, Maria
Komarovsky, Mirra
Koprowska, Irena Grasberg
Korn, Doris Elfriede
Korobeinikova, Iuliia Ivanovna
Korringa, Marjorie K.
Korshunova, Olga Stepanovna
Koshland, Marian (Elliott)
Kovalevskaia, Sofia Vasilyevna
Kovrigina, Mariia Dmitrievna
Kozlova, Ol'ga Grigoriyevna
Krasnosel'skaia, Tat'iana Abramovna
Krasnow, Frances
Kraus Ragins, Ida
Kroeber, Theodora Kracaw
Krogh, Birthe Marie (Jorgensen)
Krupskaia, Nadezhda Konstantinovna
Krutikhovskaia, Zinaida Aleksandrovna
Kunde, Margarethe Meta H.
L'Esperance, Elise Depew Strang
La Chapelle, Marie Louise Dugès
La Mance, Lora Sarah (Nichols)
La Sablière, Marguerite Hessein, Madame
    de
La Vigne, Anne de
Ladd-Franklin, Christine
Ladygina-Kots, Nadezhda Nikolaevna
Laird, Carobeth (Tucker)
Laird, Elizabeth Rebecca
Laïs
Lalande, Marie Jeanne Amélie Harlay
    Lefrançais de
Lamarck, Cornelié
Lambin, Suzanne
Lamme, Bertha
LaMonte, Francesca Raimonde
Lampe, Lois
Lampl-de Groot, Jeanne
Lancefield, Rebecca Craighill
Landes, Ruth (Schlossberg)
Lane-Claypon, Janet Elizabeth
Langdon, Fanny E.
Langdon, LaDema M.
Lange, Linda Bartels
Lange, Mathilde Margarethe
Langecker, Hedwig
Langford, Grace
Langsdorff, Toni von
Lankester, Phoebe (Pope)
Lansdell, Kathleen Annie
Lapicque, Marcelle (de Heredia)
Larsson, Elisabeth
Larter, Clara Ethelinda
Laskey, Amelia (Rudolph)
Laski, Gerda

Lassar, Edna Ernestine (Kramer)
Lasthenia of Mantinea
Latham, Vida Annette
Latimer, Caroline Wormeley
Laubenstein, Linda
Laughlin, Emma Eliza
Laurie, Charlotte Louisa
Lavoisier, Marie Anne Pierrette Paulze
Law, Annie
Lawder, Margaret
Lawrence, Barbara
Lawrence, Penelope
Lawrenson, Alice Louisa
Lawton, Elva
Lazarus, Hilda Mary
Le Beau, Désirée
Le Breton, Elaine
Le Maître, Dorothée
Leach, Mary Frances
Leacock, Eleanor Burke
Leakey, Mary Douglas (Nicol)
Leavitt, Henrietta Swan
Lebedeva, Nataliia Ivanova
Lebedeva, Vera Pavlovna
Lebour, Marie Victoire
Leclercq, Suzanne (Céline)
Ledingham, Una Christina (Garvin)
Lee, Julia Southard
Lee, Rebecca
Lee, Rose Hum
Lee, Sarah Wallis Bowdich
Leebody, Mary Elizabeth
Lees, Florence Sarah
Lefroy, Helena (Trench)
Lehmann, Inge
Lehmus, Emilie
Lehr, Marguerite (Anna Marie)
Leighton, Dorothea (Cross)
Leland, Evelyn
Lemmon, Sarah Plummer
Leontium
Leoparda
Lepaute, Nicole-Reine Hortense (Etable
    de la Brière)
Lepeshinskaia, Ol'ga Borisovna
Lepin, Lidiia Karlovna
Lermontova, Ekaterina Vladimirovna
Lermontova, Iuliia Vsevolodovna
Leschi, Jeanne
Leslie (Burr), May Sybil
Leverton, Ruth Mandeville
Levi, Hilde
Levi-Montalcini, Rita
Levine, Lena
Levyns, Margaret Rutherford Bryan
    (Michell)
Lewis, Florence Parthenia
Lewis, Graceanna
Lewis, Helen Geneva
Lewis, Isabel (Martin)
Lewis, Lilian (Burwell)
Lewis, Madeline Dorothy (Kneberg)
Lewis, Margaret Adaline Reed
Lewis, Mary Butler

Leyel, Hilda Winifred Ivy (Wauton)
Libby, Leona Woods Marshall
Libert, Marie-Anne
Lieber, Clara Flora
Lieu, K. O. Victoria
Lin Qiaozhi (Lin Chiao-chi)
Lincoln, Almira Hart
Lind-Campbell, Hjördis
Lindsten- Thomasson, Marianne
Lines, Dorolyn (Boyd)
Linton, Laura Alberta
Lipinska, Mélanie
Lisitsian, Srbui Stepanova
Lisovskaia, Sofiya Nikolaievna
Lister, Gulielma
Litchfield Henrietta Emma (Darwin)
Litvinova, Elizaveta Fedorovna
Litzinger, Marie
Lloyd, Dorothy Jordan
Lloyd, Rachel
Lloyd-Green, Lorna
Lochman-Balk, Christina
Loewe, Lotte Luise Friedericke
Logan, Martha Daniell
Logan, Myra Adele
Logsdon, Mayme (Irwin)
Lomax, Elizabeth Anne (Smithson)
Longfield, Cynthia
Longshore, Hannah E. (Myers)
Longstaff, Mary Jane (Donald)
Lonsdale, Kathleen (Yardley)
Losa, Isabella
Löser, Margaret Sibylla von
Loudon, Jane (Webb)
Lovejoy, Esther Pohl
Lovelace, Augusta Ada Byron, Countess of
Loveless, Mary Hewitt
Lowater, Frances
Lowell, Frances Erma
Lozier, Clemence Sophia (Harned)
Lu Gwei Djen
Lubinska, Liliana
Lukanina, Adelaida N.
Lunn, Katharine Fowler
Luomala, Katharine
Lutwak-Mann, Cecelia
Lwoff, Marguerite (Bourdaleix)
Lyell, Katharine Murray (Horner)
Lyell, Mary Elizabeth (Horner)
Lynn, Mary Johnstone
Lyon, Mary
Lyubimova, Yelena Aleksandrovna
Maass, Clara Louise
Macaulay, Catharine (Sawbridge)
MacCallum, Bella Dytes (MacIntosh)
Macdonald, Eleanor Josephine
MacDougall, Mary Stuart
MacGill, Elsie Gregory
MacGillavry, Carolina Henriette
Macintyre, Sheila Scott
Mack, Pauline Beery
Mackay, Helen Marion MacPherson
Macklin, Madge (Thurlow)
Mackowsky, Marie-Therese

MacLaughlin, Florence Edith Carothers
MacLean, Ida (Smedley)
MacLeod, Annie Louise
MacLeod, Grace
Macrina
MacRobert, Rachel (Workman), Lady of
    Douneside and Cromar
Maddison, Ada Isabel
Mahler, Margaret Schönberger
Mahout, Countess of Artois
Mair, Lucy Philip
Makemson, Maude (Worcester)
Maling, Harriet Florence (Mylander)
Malleson, Elizabeth
Mallory, Edith (Brandt)
Maltby, Margaret Eliza
Man, Evelyn Brower
Mangold, Hilde (Proescholdt)
Mann, Harriet
Manning, Ann B. (Harned)
Manson, Grace Evelyn
Mantell, Mary Ann (Woodhouse)
Manton, Irene
Manton, Sidnie Milana
Manzolini, Anna Morandi
Maracineanu, Stefania
Marcella
Marcet, Jane Haldimand
Marche, Marguerite du Tertre de la
Margery
Margulova, Tereza Kristoforovna
Marianne Plehn
Maric, Mileva
Marillac, Louise de
Marinov, Evelina
Marks, Hertha
Marlatt, Abby Lillian
Marriott, Alice Lee
Marsh, Mary Elizabeth
Marshall, Clara
Marshall, Sheina Macalister
Martin, Ella May
Martin, Emilie Norton
Martin, Lillien Jane
Martineau, Harriet
Martinez-Alvarez, Josefina
Mary the Jewess
Mason, Carol Y.
Mason, Marianne Harriet
Massee, Ivy
Massevitch, Alla Genrikhovna
Massey, Patricia
Massy, Anne L.
Masters, Sybilla (Righton)
Mateer, Florence Edna
Mateyko, Gladys Mary
Mather, Sarah
Mathias, Mildred Esther
Mathisen, Karoline
Matikashvili, Nina
Matilde
Maunder, Annie Scott Dill Russell
Maury, Antonia Caetana de Paiva
Maury, Carlotta Joaquina

Maver, Mary Eugenie
Maxwell, Martha Dartt
May, Caroline Rebecca
Mayer, Maria Goeppert
Mayo, Clara Alexandra (Weiss)
McAvoy, Blanche
McBride, Katharine Elizabeth
McCarthy, Dorothea Agnes
McClintock, Barbara
McConney, Florence
McCracken, Eileen May
McCracken, Elizabeth (Unger)
McCracken, Mary Isabel
McCrea, Adelia
McDonald, Janet
McDowell, Louise Sherwood
McGee, Anita (Newcomb)
McGlamery, Josie Winifred
McGraw, Myrtle Byram
McGuire, Ruth Colvin Starrett
McHale, Kathryn
McKeag, Anna Jane
McKinney, Ruth Alden
McLaren, Agnes
McLean, Helen (Vincent)
McNab, Catherine Mary
McVeigh, Ilda
Mead, Kate Campbell (Hurd)
Mead, Margaret
Measham, Charlotte Elizabeth (Cowper)
Mechthild of Magdeburg
Medaglia, Diamante
Medes, Grace
Medvedeva, Nina Borisovna
Mee, Margaret Ursula (Brown)
Meek, Lois Hayden
Meigler, Marie J.
Meitner, Lise
Melissa
Mellanby, May (Tweedy)
Memmler, Ruth Lundeen
Mendenhall, Dorothy (Reed)
Mendrez-Carroll, Christiane
Menten, Maud L.
Mentuhetep, Queen
Mercuriade
Meredith, Louisa Anne (Twamley)
Mergler, Marie
Merian, Maria Sibylla
Meritt, Lucy Taxis (Shoe)
Merriam, Florence
Merrifield, Mary Philadelphia (Watkins)
Merrill, Helen Abbot
Merrill-James, Maud Amanda
Messina, Angelina Rose
Metchnikova, Olga (Belokopytova)
Metrodora
Metzger, Hélène (Bruhl)
Meurdrac, Marie
Mexia, Ynes
Meyer, Margaret Theodora
Meyer-Bjerrum, Kirstine
Meyling-Hylkema, Elisabeth
Meznevics, Ilona

Michael, Helen Cecilia DeSilver Abbott
Michelet, Athénaïs (Mialaret)
Mildmay, Grace Sherrington
Miles, Catherine Cox
Mill, Harriet Hardy Taylor
Miller, Bessie Irving
Miller, Elizabeth Cavert
Miller, Olive Thorne
Minoka-Hill, Lillie Rosa
Minor, Jessie Elizabeth
Minot, Ann Stone
Mirchink, Maria E.
Mises Geiringer, Hilda von
Missuna, Anna Boleslavovna
Mitchell, Anna Helena
Mitchell, Evelyn Groesbeeck
Mitchell, Helen Swift
Mitchell, Maria
Mitchell, Mildred Bessie
Miyaji, Kunie
Mockeridge, Florence Annie
Moffat, Agnes K.
Mohr, Erna W.
Molesworth, Caroline
Molza, Tarquinia
Monin-Molinier, Madeline
Monson, Lady Anne Vane
Montague, Lady Mary Wortley
Montel, Eliane
Montessori, Maria
Moody, Agnes Claypole
Moody, Mary Blair
Mooney-Slater, Rose Camille LeDieu
Moore, Anne
Moore, Charlotte Emma
Moore, Emmeline
Moore, Lillian Mary
Moore, Mary Mitchell
Moore, Ruth Ella
Morehouse, Kathleen M.
Morgan, Agnes Fay
Morgan, Ann Haven
Morgan, Elizabeth Frances
Morgan, Lilian Vaughan Sampson
Moriarity, Henrietta Maria
Morozova, Valentina Galaktionovna
Morris, Margaretta Hare
Morse, Elizabeth Eaton
Morse, Meroë Marston
Morton, Emily L.
Morton, Rosalie Slaughter
Moser, Fanny
Mosher, Clelia Duel
Mottl, Mária
Moufang, Ruth
Mueller, Kate Heuvner
Muir-Wood, Helen Marguerite
Muller, Marie Claire Eimmart
Murphy, Lois Barclay
Murray, Amelia Matilda
Murray, Lady Charlotte
Murray, Margaret Alice
Murray, Margaret Mary Alberta
Murray, Margaret Ransone

Murrell, Christine Mary
Murtfeldt, Mary
Muszhat, Aniela
Myers, Mabel Adelaide
Myia or Mya
Nance, Nellie Ward
Napper, Diana Margaret
Nasymuth, Dorothea Clara (Maude)
Naumova, Sofiya Nickolaevna
Naylor, Bertha
Neal, Marie Catherine
Necker, Susanne (Curchod)
Needham, Dorothy Mary (Moyle)
Neiburg, Maria Feodorovna
Nelson, Katherine Greacen
Nemcová-Hlobilová, Jindriska
Nemir, Rosa Lee
Netrasiri, Khunying Cherd-Chalong
Neuburg Maria Feodorovna
Neumann, Elsa
Neumann, Hanna (von Caemmerer)
Nevill, Lady Dorothy Frances (Walpole)
Newbigin, Marion Isabel
Newson, Mary Frances Winston
Newton, Margaret
Nice, Margaret Morse
Nicerata, Saint
Nichols, Mary Louise
Nichols, Mary Sargeant Neal Gove
Nicholson, Barbara Evelyn
Nickerson, Dorothy
Nickerson, Margaret (Lewis)
Nicosia, Maria Luisa
Nieh, Chung-en
Nightingale, Dorothy Virginia
Nightingale, Florence
Nihell, Elizabeth
Noddack, Ida Eva Tacke
Noel, Emilia Frances
Noether, Amalie Emmy
Nolde, Hélène Aldegonde de
Nolte, Margarethe
Norsworthy, Naomi
North, Marianne
Northrup, Ann Hero
Novoselova, Aleksandra Vasil'evna
Noyes, Mary Chilton
Nuttall, Gertrude (Clarke)
Nuttall, Zelia Maria Magdalena
Nutting, Mary Adelaide
O'Brien, Charlotte Grace
O'Brien, Ruth
O'Connell, Marjorie
O'Malley, Lady Emma Winifred
    (Hardcastle)
O'Reilly, Helen
O'Shea, Harriet Eastabrooks
Obrutsheva, A.
Occello of Lucania
Odlum, Doris
Ogilvie, Ida Helen
Ogilvie-Gordon, Dame Maria Matilda
Ogino, G.

Ohnesorge, Lena
Okey, Ruth Eliza
Olympias of Thebes
Onslow, Muriel (Wheldale)
Oppenheimer, Ella Hutzler
Oppenheimer, Jane Marion
Ordan, Laura G.
Orent-Keiles, Elsa
Origenia
Ormerod, Eleanor Anne
Orr, Mary
Osterhaut, Marian Irwin.
Oszast, Janina Celina
Owen, Luella Agnes
Owens, Margaret
Owens-Adair, Bethenia
Pabst, Marie B.
Pacaud, Suzanne
Page, Mary Maud
Page, Winifred Mary
Paget, Dame Mary Rosalind
Paget, Rose Elizabeth
Paine, Mary Esther (Trueblood)
Pajchlowa, Maria Leokadia
Pallis, Marietta
Palmer, Alice W.
Palmer, Dorothy Bryant (Kemper)
Palmer, Elizabeth Day
Palmer, Katherine Evangeline Hilton (Van
    Winkle)
Palmer, Margaretta
Palmer, Miriam Augusta
Palmer, Sophia French
Palmie, Anna Helene
Panajiotatou, Angeliki
Paphnutia the Virgin
Paris, Marie-Louise
Parke, Mary Winifred
Parker, Ivy May
Parkins, Phyllis Virginia
Parloa, Maria
Parmelee, Ruth A.
Parrish, Rebecca
Parry, Angenette
Parsons, Elizabeth Ingersoll
Parsons, Eloise
Parsons, Elsie Worthington (Clews)
Parsons, Emily Elizabeth
Parsons, Helen Tracy
Parsons, Mary, Countess of Rosse
Parthenay, Catherine de (Dame de Rohan)
Pasternak, Lydia
Pasteur, Marie (Laurent)
Pastori, Giuseppina
Pastori, Maria
Patch, Edith Marion
Patrick, Ruth
Patterson, Flora Wambaugh
Pattullo, June Grace
Paula
Paulsen, Alice Elizabeth
Paulucci, Marianna, Marchesa
Pavenstedt, Eleanor
Pavlova, Mariia Vasil'evna

Payne, Nellie Maria de Cottrell
Payne, Rose Marise
Payne, Sylvia May (Moore)
Payne-Gaposchkin, Cecilia Helena
Peak, Helen
Pearce, Louise
Pearl, Maud Dewitt
Pechey-Phipson, Mary Edith
Peckham, Elizabeth (Gifford)
Peebles, Florence
Pell, Anna Johnson
Pelletier, Madeleine
Pendleton, Ellen Fitz
Pennington, Mary Engle
Pensa-Joja, Josipa
Penston, Norah Lilian
Perceval, Anne Mary (Flower)
Pereiaslavtseva, Sof'ia Mikhailovna
Pereira de Queiroz, Carlota
Perette of Rouen
Peretti, Zaffira
Perey, Marguerite Catherine
Perictione
Perlmann, Gertrude Erika
Pernell
Péronelle
Perrette, Berthe
Pertz, Dorothea Frances Matilda
Péter, Rózsa
Petermann, Mary Locke
Peterson, Edith (Runne)
Peterson, Ruth Dixon
Petran, Elizabeth Irene
Petrova, Maria Kapitonovna
Pettersson, Dagmar
Pettit, Hannah Steele
Pettit, Mary Dewitt
Pettracini, Maria
Pfeiffer, Ida (Reyer)
Pfeiffer, Norma Etta
Pfiester, Lois Ann
Phelps, Almira Hart Lincoln
Phelps, Martha Austin
Philip, Anna-Ursula
Phillips, Melba Newell
Philpot, Elizabeth
Philpot, Margaret
Philpot, Mary
Phisalix, Marie (Picot)
Piazolla-Beloch, Margherita
Piccard, Sophie
Pickett, Lucy Weston
Pickford, Grace Evelyn
Pickford, Lilian Mary
Picotte, Susan (La Flesche)
Pierce, Madelene Evans
Pierce, Marion (Armbruster)
Pierry, Louise Elizabeth du
Pilliet, Blanche Edwards
Pinckney, Eliza (Lucas)
Pink, Olive Muriel
Piozzi, Hester Lynch
Pirami, Edmea
Pirie, Antoinette

Pirie, Mary
Pirret, Ruth
Pisan, Christine de
Piscopia, Helena Lucretia Cornaro
Pitt-Rivers, Rosalind Venetia (Henley)
Pittman, Margaret Jane
Platt, Julia Barlow
Plues, Margaret
Plues, Margaret
Plummer, Helen Jeanne (Skewes)
Pockels, Agnes
Pocock, Mary Agard
Pogson, Iris
Pokrovskaia, Irina Mitrofanovna
Pokrovskaia, Mariia Ivanovna
Polenova, Yelena Nikolayevna
Pollack, Flora
Polubarinova-Kochina, Pelageya
    Yakovelevna
Ponse, Kitty
Pool, Judith Graham
Pope, Clara Maria (Leigh)
Popenoe, Dorothy K. (Hughes)
Porada, Edith
Porter, Gene Stratton
Porter, Helen Kemp Archbold
Porter, Lilian E. (Baker)
Porter, Mary Winearls
Potter, Beatrix
Potter, Edith Louise
Potter, Ellen Culver
Potts, Eliza
Povitsky, Olga Raissa
Powdermaker, Hortense
Pozaryska, Krystyna (Maliszewski)
Prádacová, Marcella
Prankerd, Theodora Lisle
Pratt, Anne
Pressey, Luella (Cole)
Preston, Ann
Preston, Isabella
Prestwich, Grace Anne (Milne) M'Call
Price, Dorothy
Price, Dorothy (Stopford)
Prichard, Marjorie Mabel Lucy
Prince, Helen Walter (Dodson)
Pringle, Elizabeth Waties (Allston)
Pringle, Mia Lilly (Kellmer)
Prins, Ada
Proctor, Mary
Proskouriakoff, Tatiana
Pruette, Lorine Livingston
Prytz, Milda Dorothea
Puffer, Ethel Dench
Pulcheria, Empress
Putnam, Helen Cordelia
Putnam, Marian Cabot
Putnam, Mary Louise (Duncan)
Pye, Edith Mary
Pythias of Assos
Queiroz, Carlotta Pereira de
Quiggle, Dorothy
Quimby, Edith Smaw (Hinckley)
Quirk, Agnes

Quiroga, Margarita Delgado de Solis
Rabinoff, Sophie
Rabinovitch-Kempner, Lydia
Radegonde
Radnitz, Gerty.
Rafatdjah, Safieh
Ragins, Ida.
Raisin, Catherine Alice
Ramart-Lucas, Pauline
Ramirez, Rosita Rivera
Ramsay, Christina (Broun), Countess of
    Dalhousie
Ramsey, Elizabeth Mapelsden
Ramstedt, Eva Julia Augusta
Rancken, Saima Tawast
Rand, Marie Gertrude
Randoin, Lucie Gabrielle (Fandard)
Randolph, Harriet
Rasskazova, Yelena Stepanovna
Rathbone, Mary May
Rathbun, Mary Jane
Ratnayake, May
Ratner, Sarah
Rauzer-Chernousova, Dagmara M.
Ray, Dixy Lee
Raymond-Schroeder, Aimee J.
Rayner, Mabel Mary Cheveley
Rea, Margaret Williamson
Reames, Eleanor Louise
Reddick, Mary Logan
Reder, Ruth Elizabeth
Redfield, Helen
Reed, Eva M.
Rees, Florence Gwendolen
Rees, Mina Spiegel
Refshauge, Joan Janet
Reichard, Gladys Amanda
Reid, Eleanor Mary (Wynne Edwards)
Reid, Mary Elizabeth
Reimer, Marie
Reinhardt, Anna Barbara
Remond, Sarah Parker
Renooz, Céline
Reynolds, Doris Livesey
Rhine, Louise Ella (Weckesser)
Rhodes, Mary Louise
Rice, Elsie (Garrett)
Rice-Wray, Edris
Rich, Mary Florence
Richards, Audrey Isabel
Richards, Clarice Audrey
Richards, Ellen Henrietta Swallow
Richards, Mary Alice Eleanor (Stokes)
Richards, Mildred Hoge (Albro)
Richter, Emma (Hüther)
Richter, Grete
Riddle, Lumina Cotton
Ridenour, Nina
Rigas, Harriett B.
Ring, Barbara Taylor
Rioch, Margaret J.
Ripley, Martha (Rogers)
Rising, Mary Meda
Risseghem, Hortense van

Ritter, Mary Elizabeth (Bennett)
Riviere, Joan (Verrall)
Rob, Catherine Muriel
Robb, Jane (Sands)
Robb, Mary Anne (Boulton)
Roberts, Charlotte Fitch
Roberts, Dorothea Klumpke
Roberts, Edith Adelaide
Roberts, Lydia Jane
Roberts, Mary
Robertson, Florence
Robertson, Jeannie (Smillie)
Robertson, Muriel
Robeson, Eslanda Cordoza (Goode)
Robinson, Daisy Maude (Orleman)
Robinson, Gertrude Maud (Walsh)
Robinson, Harriet May Skidmore
Robinson, Julia (Bowman)
Robinson, Margaret (King)
Robinson, Pamela Lamplugh
Roboz-Einstein, Elizabeth
Robscheit-Robbins, Frieda Saur
Rockley, Lady Alicia Margaret (Amherst)
Rockwell, Alice Jones
Rockwell, Mabel Macferran
Rodde, Dorothea von (Schlözer)
Roe, Anne
Roe, Josephine Robinson
Roger, Muriel
Rogers, Agnes Lowe
Rogers, Julia Ellen
Rogers, Marguerite Moillet
Rogick, Mary Dora
Rohde, Eleanour Sinclair
Róna, Elisabeth
Ronzoni, Ethel (Bishop)
Roper, Ida Mary
Roper, Margaret
Rose Stoppel
Rose, Flora
Rose, Glenola Behling
Rose, Mary Davies Swartz
Rosenberg, Mary Elizabeth
Rosenfeld, Eva
Ross, Joan Margaret
Ross, Marion Amelia Spence
Ross, Mary G.
Rosse, Mary, Countess of
Rothschild, Miriam
Roupell, Arabella Elizabeth (Piggott)
Royer, Clémence
Rozanova, Mariia Aleksandrovna
Rozova, Evdokia Aleksandrovna
Rubin, Vera (Dourmashkin)
Rucker, Augusta
Rudnick, Dorothea
Rumbold, Caroline (Thomas)
Russell, Anna (Worsley)
Russell, Annie
Russell, Dorothy
Russell, Jane Anne
Ruth Tunnicliff
Ruys [Ruijs], Anna Charlotte
Ruysch, Rachel

Rydh, Hanna
Sabin, Florence Rena
Sablière, Marguerite (Hessein) de la
Sabuco Banera D'Alcaraz, Olivia
Sackville-West, Victoria Mary
Safford, Mary Jane
Sager, Ruth
Salbach, Hilde
Sale, Rhoda
Salmon, Eleanor Seely
Salpe
Sampson, Kathleen Samuel
Sanborn, Ethel
Sandford-Morgan, Elma (Linton)
Sandhouse, Grace Adelbert
Sandiford, Irene
Sanford, Vera
Sanger, Margaret Higgins
Sara of Saint-Gilles
Sara of Würzburg
Sargant, Ethel
Sargent, Winifred
Satur, Dorothy May
Saunders, Edith Rebecca
Savulescu, Olga
Sawin, Martha
Say, Lucy (Sistare)
Scarpellini, Caterina
Schaffner, Mabel (Brockett)
Schantz, Viola Shelly
Scharlieb, Dame Mary Ann Dacomb
    (Bird)
Scharrer, Berta (Vogel)
Schiemann, Elisabeth
Schliemann, Sophia (Kastromenos)
Schmid, Elisabeth
Schmideberg, Melitta (Klein)
Schmidt, Johanna Gertrud Alice
Schmidt-Fischer, Hildegard
Schoenfeld, Reba Willits
Schoental, Regina
Schofield, Brenda Muriel
Schraders, Catharina Geertruida
Schubert, Anna
Schulze, Caroline M. (Bertillon)
Schurman, Anna Marie van
Schwidetsky, Ilse
Scotland, Minnie (Brink)
Scott, Charlotte Angas
Scott, Flora Murray
Scott, Henderina Victoria (Klaassen)
Scudder, Ida Sophia
Seaman, Elizabeth Cochrane
Sears, Pauline Snedden
Seegal, Beatrice Carrier
Seibert, Florence Barbara
Seligman, Brenda Zara
Semikhatova, Sofia Viktorovna (Karpova)
Semple, Ellen Churchill
Serment, Louise-Anastasia
Sessions, Kate Olivia
Sewall, Lucy
Seward, Georgene Hoffman
Shabanova, Anna Nikolaevna

Shakespear, Dame Ethel Mary Reader (Wood)
Sharp, Emily Katharine (Dooris)
Sharp, Jane
Sharsmith, Helen Katherine
Shattuck, Lydia White
Shaw, Hester
Sheldon, Jennie Arms
Shepardson, Mary (Thygeson)
Sheps, Mindel (Cherniack)
Sherbourne, Margaret Dorothea (Willis)
Sherif, Carolyn (Wood)
Sherman, Althea Rosina
Sherman, Irene Case
Sherrill, Mary Lura
Shields, Margaret Calderwood
Shinn, Milicent Washburn
Shirley, Mary Margaret
Shishkina, Olga Vasil'yevna
Short, Jessie May
Shove, Rosamund Flora
Shtern, Lina Sol o monovna
Shubnikova, Ol'ga Mikhailovna
Shulga-Nesterenko, Maria I.
Sibelius, Helena
Sichel, Elsa Marie (Keil)
Sidgwick, Eleanor (Balfour)
Siebold, Charlotte Marianne Heidenreich von
Siebold, Josepha (Henning) von
Siegemund, Justine Dittrich
Sieverts, Hertha
Signeux, Jeanne
Silberberg, Ruth Katzenstein
Silliman, Hepsa Ely
Simons, Lao Genevra
Simpson, Anne Roe
Sinclair, Mary Emily
Sinskaia, Evgeniia Nikolaevna
Sitterly, Charlotte Emma (Moore)
Skeat, Ethel Gertrude
Skoczylas-Ciszewska, Kamila
Slater, Ida Lilian
Slater, Jesse Mabel Wilkins
Slavikova, Ludmila (Kaplanova)
Slosson, Annie Trumbull
Slye, Maud
Smart, Helen Edith (Fox)
Smedley, Ida
SmirnovaZamkova, Aleksandra Ivanovna
Smith, Adelia Calvert
Smith, Alice Emily
Smith, Anne Millspaugh (Cooke)
Smith, Annie Lorrain
Smith, Annie Morrill
Smith, Audrey U.
Smith, Clara Eliza
Smith, Elizabeth (Hight)
Smith, Emily Adelia (Pidgen)
Smith, Erma Anita
Smith, Erminnie Adele (Platt)
Smith, Isabel Fothergill
Smith, Isabel Seymour
Smith, Janice Minerva

Smith, Margaret Kiever
Smith, Marian Wesley
Smith, Matilda
Smith, Olive Watkins
Smith, Pleasance (Reeve)
Smith, Winifred
Snelling, Lilian
Snethlage, Emilie
Snow, Julia Warner
Snow, Mary (Pilkington)
Soddy, Winifred Moller (Beilby)
Sokol'skaya, Anna Nikolayevna
Solis Quiroga, Margarita Delgado de
Sollas, Igerna Brünhilda Johnson
Solomko-Sotiriadis, Evgeniia
Somerville, Mary (Fairfax) Greig
Sommer, Anna Louise
Sophia Charlotte, Queen of Prussia
Sophia, Electress of Hanover
Sorokin, Helen Petrovna (Beratynskaiia)
Soshkina, Elizabeth D.
Sotira
Souczek, Helene
South, Lillian Herrald
Sowton, Sarah C. M.
Spalding, Effie Southworth
Spence, Eliza Jane (Edmondson)
Spencer, Adelin Elam
Sperry, Pauline
Spiegel-Adolf, Mona
Sponer-Franck, Hertha Dorothea Elisabeth
Sprague, Mary Letitia (Green)
Spratt, Ethel Rose
Stackhouse, Emily
Stadnichenko, Tasia Maximovna
Stael-Holstein, Anne Louise Germaine Necker
Stanley, Louise
Stanton, Hazel Martha
Staudinger, Magda (Woit)
Stearns, Genevieve
Steed, Gitel Poznanski
Stefanescu, Sabba
Stein, Emmy
Steinhardt, Edna
Stelfox, Margarita Dawson (Mitchell)
Stenhouse, Caroline
Stephens, Jane
Stephens, Joanna
Stephenson, Marjory
Stern, Catherine (Brieger)
Stern, Frances
Stevens, Nettie Maria
Stevenson, Matilda Coxe (Evans)
Stevenson, Sara (Yorke)
Stevenson, Sarah Ann (Hackett)
Stewart, Grace Anne
Stewart, Isabel Maitland
Stewart, Maude
Stewart, Sarah Elizabeth
Stiebeling, Hazel Katherine
Stieglitz, Mary Rising
Stimson, Barbara Bartlett
Stinchfield, Sara Mae

Stokes, Margaret McNair
Stokey, Alma Gracey
Stone, Constance
Stone, Doris Zemurray
Stone, Isabelle
Stopes, Marie Charlotte Carmichael
Stose, Anna Isabel (Jonas)
Stott, Alicia (Boole)
Stovin, Margaret
Stowe, Emily Howard (Jennings)
Strachey, Alix (Sargant-Florence)
Strang, Ruth May
Strassmann-Heckter, Maria Caroline
Stratton Porter, Gene
Strobell, Ella Church
Strong, Harriet Williams (Russell)
Strong, Helen Mabel
Strong, Miriam Carpenter
Strozzi, Lorenza
Stuart, Miranda
Sullivan, Betty Julia
Sullivan, Elizabeth Teresa
Sullivan, Ellen Blythe
Summerskill, Edith Clara
Sundquist, Alma
Sunne, Dagny
Suslova, Nadezhda Prokof'evna
Sutter, Vera LaVerne
Svartz, Nanna Charlotta
Svihla, Ruth Dowell
Swain, Clara A.
Swallow, Ellen
Swanson, Pearl Pauline
Swift, Mary
Swindler, Mary Hamilton
Swope, Helen Gladys
Swope, Henrietta (Hill)
Sykes, Mary Gladys
Syniewska, Janina
Szeminska, Alina
Szeparowicz, Maria
Szmidt, Jadwiga
Szwajger, Adina Blady
Taeuber, Irene Barnes
Taft, Jessie
Takeuchi, Shigeyo
Talbot, Dorothy Amaury
Talbot, Marion
Talbot, Mary
Talbot, Mignon
Taliaferro, Lucy (Graves)
Tammes, Jantine
Tannery, Marie Alexandrine (Prisset)
Taussig, Helen Brooke
Taussky-Todd, Olga
Taylor, Charlotte De Bernier Scarborough
Taylor, Clara Mae
Taylor, Clara Millicent
Taylor, Eva Germaine Rimington
Taylor, Helen
Taylor, Janet
Taylor, Lucy Beaman (Hobbs)
Taylor, Monica
Taylor, Rose H.

Teagarden, Florence Mabel
Tebb, Mary Christine
Telfair, Annabella (Chamberlain)
Telkes, Maria
Tenenbaum, Estera
Terent'eva, Liudmila Nikolaevna
Terry, Ethel Mary
Terzaghi, Ruth Doggett
Tessier, Marguerite
Tetsuo, Tamayo
Theano
Thelander, Hulda Evelin
Thelberg, Elizabeth (Burr)
Thelka, Saint
Theodora, Empress
Theodosia, Saint
Theosebeia
Thiselton-Dyer, Lady Harriet Ann
    (Hooker)
Thoday, Mary Gladys Sykes
Thomas, Caroline (Bedell)
Thomas, Dorothy Swaine (Thomas)
Thomas, Ethel Nancy Miles
Thomas, Mary Frame (Myers)
Thome, Frances
Thompson, Caroline Burling
Thompson, Clara Mabel
Thompson, Helen
Thompson, Laura
Thompson, Mary Harris
Thompson, Rachel Ford
Thompson, Rose Elizabeth (Paget)
Thompson, Sydney Mary
Thoms, Adah B. (Samuels)
Thomson, Agnes C.
Thomson, Jane Smithson
Thring, Lydia Eliza Dyer (Meredith)
Thurstone, Thelma Gwinn
Tiburtius, Franziska
Tilden, Evelyn Butler
Tilden, Josephine Elizabeth
Timofe'eff-Ressovsky, Elena
    Aleksandrovna (Fiedler)
Tindall, Isabella Mary
Tinne, Alexandrina Petronella Francina
Tinsley, Beatrice Muriel (Hill)
Tipper, Constance Fligg (Elam)
Tisserand, M.
Todd, Emily Sophia
Todd, Mabel Loomis
Todd, Ruth
Todtmann, Emmy Mercedes
Tolman, Ruth (Sherman)
Tomaszewicz-Dobrska, Anna
Tompkins, Sally Louisa
Tonnelat, Marie-Antoinette (Baudot)
Toops, Laura Chassell (Merrill)
Towara, Hélène
Town, Clara Harrison
Tracy, Martha
Traill, Catharine Parr (Strickland)
Treat, Mary Lua Adelia (Davis)
Trimmer, Sarah (Kirby)
Tristram, Ruth Mary (Cardew)

Trizna, Valentina Borisovna
Trotter, Mildred
Trotula
Trower, Charlotte Georgiana
Tsvetaeva, Maria
Tum-Suden, Caroline
Tumanskaya, Olga G. (Shirokobruhova)
Tunakan, Seniha (Hüsnü)
Turnbull, Priscilla Freudenheim
Turner, Abby Howe
Turner, Mary (Palgrave)
Twining, Elizabeth Mary
Tyler, Leona Elizabeth
Tyler, Martha G.
Tyndall, A. C.
Tyng, Anita E.
Tyska, Maria
Ubisch, Gerta von
Underhill, Ruth Murray
Ushakova, Elizaveta Ivanovna
Uvarova, Countess Praskov'ia Sergeevna
Vachell, Eleanor
Valentine, Lila Hardaway (Meade)
Van Beverwijk, Agathe L.
Van Blarcom, Carolyn (Conant)
Van Deman, Esther Boise
Van Hoosen, Bertha
Van Rensselaer, Martha
Van Wagenen, Gertrude
Varsanof'eva, Vera Aleksandrovna
Vasilevich, Glafira Makar'evna 1895–1971
Vaughan, Dame Janet
Vavrinova, Milada
Veil, Suzanne Zélie Pauline
Veley, Lilian Jane (Nutcombe)
Venning, Eleanor (Hill)
Verder, Ada Elizabeth
Veretennikova, Anna Ivanovna
Vernon, Magdalen Dorothea
Vesian, Dorothy E. de
Vickers, Anna
Vilar, Lola
Vilmorin, Elisa (Bailly)
Vivian, Roxana Hayward
Vogt, Cécile (Mugnier)
Vogt, Marthe Louise
Vold, Marjorie Jean Young
Volkova, Anna Fedorovna
Von Schroeder, Edith
Vyssotsky, Emma T. R. (Williams)
Vytilingam, Kamala Israel
Waelsch, Salome Glueckschn
Wakefield, Elsie Maud
Wakefield, Priscilla (Bell)
Walcott, Helene B. (Stevens)
Walcott, Mary Morris (Vaux)
Wald, Lillian D.
Walker, Eliza
Walker, Elizabeth
Walker, Harriet Ann
Walker, Helen Mary
Walker, Mary Edward
Walker, Norma (Ford)
Wall, Florence

Wallace, Louise Baird
Wallis, Ruth Sawtell
Walworth, Ellen Hardin
Wang Chi Che
Wang Zhenyi
Ward, Mary (King)
Warga, Mary Elizabeth
Waring, Sister Mary Grace
Warren, Elizabeth Andrew
Warren, Madeleine (Field)
Washburn, Margaret Floy
Washburn, Ruth
Wassell, Helen Erma
Watkins, Della Elizabeth (Ingram)
Watson, Janet Vida
Watt, Helen Winifred Boyd (de Lisle)
Watt, Menie
Watts, Betty (Monaghan)
Way, Katharine
Webb, Jane
Weber, Anne Antoinette (van Bosse)
Webster, Mary McCallum
Wedderburn, Jemima
Wedgwood, Camilla Hildegarde
Wedgwood, Mary Louisa (Bell)
Weeks, Alice Mary (Dowse)
Weeks, Dorothy W.
Weeks, Mary Elvira
Weightman, Mary
Weinzierl, Laura (Lane)
Weishaupt, Clara Gertrude
Weiss, Marie Johanna
Weiss, Mary Catherine (Bishop)
Welch, Betty
Welch, Winona Hazel
Weld, Julia Tiffany
Wellman, Beth Lucy
Wells, Agnes Ermina
Wells, Charlotte Fowler
Wells, Louisa D.
Welser, Philippine
Welsh, Jane Kilby
Welsh, Lilian
Weltfish, Gene
Wertenstein, Mathilde
Wessel, Bessie (Bloom)
West, Ethel
Westall, Mary
Westcott, Cynthia
Westover, Cynthia May
Wharton, Martha Lucille
Whedon, Frances Lovisa
Wheeler, Anna Johnson Pell
Wheeler, Elizabeth Lockwood
Wheeler-Voeglin, Erminie Brooke
White, Edith Grace
White, Eliza Catherine (Quekett)
White, Elizabeth Juanita (Greer)
White, Florence Roy
White, Frances Emily
White, Margaret Pirie
White, Marian Emily
Whitehead, Lilian Elizabeth
Whiteley, Martha Annie

Whiting, Marian Muriel
Whiting, Sarah Frances
Whitney, Mary Watson
Wick, Frances Gertrude
Wickens, Aryness Joy
Widdowson, Elsie May
Wiebusch, Agnes (Townsend)
Wienholz, Eva
Wilder, Inez (Whipple)
Wiley, Grace Olive
Wilkinson, Helen Avina (Hunscher)
Willard, Emma (Hart)
Willard, Mary Louisa
Willcock, Edith Gertrude (Gardiner)
Willcox, Mary Alice
Williams, Anna Wessels
Williams, Cicely Delphine
Williams, Marguerite (Thomas)
Willmott, Ellen Ann
Wilson, Alice Evelyn
Wilson, Aphra Phyllis
Wilson, Edith
Wilson, Fiammetta Worthington
Wilson, Hilda E.
Wilson, Irene Mossom
Wilson, Louise (Palmer)
Wilson, Lucy
Wilson, Lucy Langdon (Williams)
Wilson, Mabel Florey
Wilson, May Georgiana
Wilson, Monica Hunter
Winlock, Anna

Winner, Dame Albertine
Winthrop, Hannah Fayerweather Tolman
Winton, Kate Grace (Barber)
Wipf, Frances Louise
Withers, Augusta Innes (Baker)
Woillard-Roucoux, Geneviève Marie-
  Aurélie
Woker, Gertrud Jan
Wolf, Katherine
Wollstein, Martha
Wong Ah Mae
Wood, Emily Elizabeth
Wood, Emily Margaret
Wood, Ethel
Wood, Ruth Goulding
Wood-Lorz, Thelma (Rittenhouse)
Woodard, Helen (Quincy)
Woodbridge, Mary Emily
Woods, Elizabeth Lindley
Woods, Ethel Gertrude (Skeat)
Woodward, Gladys Estelle
Wooldridge, Elizabeth (Taylor)
Woolley, Ann
Woolley, Helen Bradford (Thompson)
Woolley, Mildred Thompson
Wootton, Barbara Adam
Wormington, Hannah Marie
Worner, Ruby K.
Worthington, Euphemia R.
Wrangell, Margarethe von
Wreschner, Marie
Wright, Frances May

Wright, Frances Woodworth
Wright, Helena Rosa (Lowenfeld)
Wright, Jean Davies
Wright, Katharine
Wright, Lady Catherine
Wright, Mabel Osgood
Wrinch, Dorothy Maud
Wu Chien-Shiung
Wundt, Nora
Wyckoff, Delphine Grace (Rosa)
Wyckoff, Dorothy
Wylie, Margaret
Wynne, Frances Elizabeth
Wyttenbach, Jeanne Gallien
Young, Anne Sewell
Young, Grace Emily (Chisholm)
Young, Leona Esther
Young, Mabel Minerva
Young, Mary Sophie
Young, Roger Arliner
Zachry, Caroline Beaumont
Zaklinskaia, Elena Dmitrievna
Zakrzewska, Marie Elizabeth
Zalesskaya-Chirkova, Elena
Zaniewska-Chilpalska, Eugenia
Zeckwer, Isolde Therese
Zenari, Silvia
Zhuze, Anastasiya Panteleyemonovna
Ziegarnik, Bliuma
Zlatarovic, Rely

L

LA CHAPELLE, MARIE LOUISE DUGÈS (1769–1821)

French midwife. Born 1 January 1769 in Paris to Marie Jonet and Louis Dugès. Married M. La Chapelle (1792). One child. Educated by mother; studied under obstetrician Franz Carl Naegele in Heidelberg. Professional experience: maternity department, Hôtel Dieu, Paris, director and instructor (1797–1821). Died 4 October 1821.

Marie Louise Dugès was the daughter of an officer of health and a competent midwife. Her midwife mother was the child's constant companion, and taught her all she knew about midwifery.

Dugès assisted at births from an early age. She married a surgeon at the Hôtel St. Louis in 1792, but after his death three years later, she had to support herself and her daughter, so she worked again as a midwife. While her mother was still alive, she had reorganized the maternity ward, and La Chapelle assisted her as associate chief midwife. After her mother's death in 1797, La Chapelle became head of the maternity department of the Hôtel Dieu. In 1797, she was asked to organize a new maternity department to be part of the old Hôtel Dieu but located in a former religious institution at Port Royal de Paris. This new Hospice de la Maternité was organized as a teaching hospital. The surgeon-in-chief and head of obstetrics, Jean-Louis Baudelocque, realized the need for a systematically organized school for midwives. In order to be a part of the reforms, La Chapelle went to Heidelberg to study, and then returned to France to organize the maternity and children's hospital at Port Royal. Baudelocque had great respect for La Chapelle's skills and practical acumen. They worked well together and developed a course of study for training midwives. After a year-long course, the students took a rigorous examination, and, if they passed, received a diploma from the Ecole de Médicine.

La Chapelle published her ideas on midwifery. Her *Pratique des accouchements* went through many editions and rep-

resented an important teaching source. In her teaching, she stressed the importance of noninterference with the birth process unless it was absolutely essential. She opposed the use of forceps except in cases of absolute necessity.   JH/MBO

PRIMARY SOURCES

La Chapelle, Marie Louise Dugès. "Observations sur divers cas d'accouchements (rupture du vagin; présentation de la face; issue prématurée du cordon; accouchement précédé de convulsions)." *L'Annuaire des médecins et chirurgiens des hôpitaux* (1819):3.

———. *Pratique des accouchements, ou mémoires et observations choisies, sur les points les plus importants de l'art.* Paris: J. B. Ballière, 1821–1825.

SECONDARY SOURCES

Cutter, Irving S., and Henry R. Viets. *A Short History of Midwifery.* Philadelphia: W. B. Saunders, 1964.

Delacoux, Alexis. *Biographie des sage-femmes célèbres, anciennes, modernes et contemporaines.* Paris: Trinquart, 1834.

Jex-Blake, Sophia. *Medical Women: A Thesis and a History.* Edinburgh: Oliphant, Anderson, and Ferrier, 1886. Discusses La Chapelle on page 33.

STANDARD SOURCES

Alic; Hurd-Mead; Lipinska 1930 (includes a portrait); Ogilvie 1986; Shearer and Shearer 1996 (article by Irmgard Wolfe).

LADD-FRANKLIN, CHRISTINE (1847–1930)

U.S. logician and psychologist, known for her work on color vision. Born 1 December 1847 in Windsor, Conn., to Augusta (Niles) and Eliphalet Ladd. Married Fabian Franklin. One surviving daughter. Educated Wesleyan Academy, Wilbraham, Mass. (graduated, 1865); Vassar College (A.B., 1869); Johns Hopkins University (1878–

1882; Ph.D., 1926). Professional experience: Johns Hopkins University, lecturer in psychology and logic (1904–1909); Columbia University, lecturer in psychology and logic (1914–1927). Died 1847 in New York City.

Christine Ladd, the eldest of three children of a New York City merchant, was the product of old New England stock. She spent her early childhood in New York and Connecticut; after the death of her mother when she was twelve, she lived in Portsmouth, New Hampshire, with her paternal grandmother. In 1865 she was graduated from the Wesleyan Academy in Wilbraham, Massachusetts, as class valedictorian.

At Vassar College, where she spent two years (receiving a bachelor's degree in 1869), Ladd concentrated on mathematics. Her real interest, however, was in physics; but knowing that graduate laboratory facilities were unavailable to women, she chose instead a field she could pursue independently. For nine years after leaving Vassar, she taught science at the secondary-school level and published articles on mathematics in the British *Educational Times.*

Drawn to the research facilities at the newly founded Johns Hopkins University, Ladd applied for admission as a graduate student in 1878. Although the school was not open to women, a mathematics professor there, James Sylvester, recognized her name from her publications and prevailed upon the administration to allow her to attend his own lectures only. Upon demonstrating her abilities, she was permitted to attend the lectures of the mathematicians Charles Sanders Pierce and William Story. Ladd studied at Hopkins for four years and fulfilled the requirements for a doctorate, but was not awarded the degree until 1926. Nonetheless she held a lectureship in logic and psychology there from 1904 to 1909. In 1882, after completing her graduate studies, she married Fabian Franklin, a member of the mathematics department. One of the couple's two children, Margaret, survived to maturity.

Ladd-Franklin is remembered for her work in two disparate fields, symbolic logic and the theory of vision. She became interested in the former during her studies under C. S. Pierce, and contributed a paper, "The Algebra of Logic," to Pierce's 1883 volume *Studies in Logic by Members of the Johns Hopkins University.* Her major contributions, however, were in the field of psychology, specifically in the study of color vision.

Ladd-Franklin had been intrigued by visual problems since the mid-1880s. During her husband's sabbatical year in 1891–1892, she accompanied him to Europe and did research in the laboratories of G. E. Müller in Göttingen and Hermann von Helmholtz in Berlin. In Berlin she also attended the lectures of Arthur König. König and Helmholtz held a three-color theory of color vision, whereas Müller posited three opponent-color pairs; Ladd-Franklin developed her own hypothesis, in which the red and green senses

are held to have developed out of the more primitive yellow sense. Ladd-Franklin presented her theory at the International Congress of Psychology in London in 1892.

After Fabian Franklin took up journalism in 1895, he was made associate editor of the New York *Evening Post* in 1910. During the couple's years in New York, Christine Ladd-Franklin lectured on psychology and logic at Columbia University. Rossiter has detailed her anger at learning that the Society of Experimental Psychologists, which had rigorously excluded women, would meet at Columbia to discuss color theory in 1914. After unsuccessful attempts to attend, she finally resorted to the tactic of requesting James McKeen Cattell to take her as a guest. None of the men had the courage to throw her out of the "masculine session" on color theory upon which she was an international authority. Ladd-Franklin continued to be active throughout her life in the cause of women's suffrage and in support of women's educational opportunities. She died of pneumonia at age eighty-two.   JH/MBO

PRIMARY SOURCES

Ladd-Franklin, Christine. "The Algebra of Logic." In C. S. Pierce, *Studies in Logic.* Boston: Little, Brown, 1883.

———. *Colour and Colour Theories.* London: K. Paul, Trench, Trubner, 1929.

SECONDARY SOURCES

Hawkins, Hugh. *Pioneer: A History of the Johns Hopkins University, 1874–1889.* Ithaca, N.Y.: Cornell University Press, 1960. Discusses Ladd-Franklin's admission to the university.

STANDARD SOURCES

AMS 4; *DAB, NAW* (article by Dorothea Jameson Hurvich); *Notable;* Ogilvie 1986; Rossiter 1982.

LADYGINA-KOTS, NADEZHDA NIKOLAEVNA (1889–1963)

Russian zoopsychologist. Born 18 May 1889 in Penza. Educated Moscow Higher Women's Courses; Moscow University (doctor of biological sciences). Professional experience: Darwin Museum in Moscow, zoopsychology laboratory, director; Institute of Philosophy of the Soviet Academy of Sciences, senior research officer. Honors and memberships: Honored Scientist of the Russian Soviet Federated Social Republic (RSFSR). Died 3 September 1963 in Moscow.

Nadezhda Nikolaevna Ladygina-Kots's early career was connected with the Darwin Museum in Moscow, founded in 1907 by the biologist A. F. Kots as part of the Higher Women's Courses. (It became an independent institution in 1922.) In 1913, Ladygina-Kots set up a zoopsychology laboratory at the Darwin Museum, which she directed for many years. In 1916 she graduated from the Women's Higher Courses in Moscow and finished the course at Moscow University a year later. In 1945 she became a senior research assistant at the Institute of Philosophy of the Soviet Academy of Sciences.

Ladygina-Kots's chief object of research was comparative psychology of apes and humans. She studied the psychological activity of primates with particular emphasis on the behavior of chimpanzees. In her published studies, she compared the cognitive abilities, emotions, play behavior, intelligence, and habits of human children with those of young chimpanzees.

Ladygina's work demonstrated differences and similarities in the psychology of humans and animals and added to knowledge of zoopsychology, comparative psychology and anthropology. In 1960, she was named an Honored Scientist of the Russian Soviet Federated Socialist Republic (RSFSR). She was also awarded the Order of Lenin and other medals.

ACH

PRIMARY SOURCES

Ladygina-Kots, Nadezhda Nikolaevna. *Prisposobitel'nye motornye navyki makaka v usloviiakh eksperimenta.* Moscow: Izdanie Gosudarstvennnogo Darvinovskogo Muzeiia (Scientific Memoirs of the Darwin Museum, Moscow), 1928. Treats adaptive behavior of Macacus rhesus monkeys under experimental conditions.

———. *Ditia shimpanze i ditia cheloveka, v ikh instinktakh, emotsiakh, igrakh, privychkakh i vyrazitel'nykh kvizheniiakh s 145 tablitsami.* Moscow: Izvestiva Gosudarstvennogo Darvinskogo Muzei, 1935. On the instinctive and emotional behavior of chimpanzees.

———. *Predposylki chelovecheskogo myshleniia: podrazhatel'noe konstruirovanie obez'ianoi i det'mi.* Moscow: Nauka, 1965. On imitation in children.

SECONDARY SOURCES

Bol'shaia sovetskaia entsiklopediia. 3d. ed. Moscow: Izd-vo "Sovietskaia entsiklopediia," 1973.

LAIRD, CAROBETH (TUCKER) (1895–1983)

U.S. ethnographer and linguist. Born 20 July 1895 in Coleman, Tex. to Emma Cora (Chaddock) and James Tucker. Married (1) John Peabody Harrington (1916; divorced 1923?); (2) George Laird (died 1940). Seven children. Educated: San Diego Normal School, summer school (1915). Professional experience: Bureau of Ethnology field assistant (to Harrington) (1916–1923); Rancher (1924–1940); Christian Science practitioner (1940–1960). Honors and memberships: University of Arizona, Honorary Doctorate (1983). Member Southwestern Anthropological Society. Died 5 August 1983 in Poway, CA.

Carobeth Tucker had an unconventional background for an anthropologist. Raised in Texas as the only child of Methodist parents, she was an early reader with an uncanny ear for languages, encouraged by her father who was a printer. Accompaning her parents to Mexico on a summer trip at the age of fourteen, she met an older man in Mexico City with whom she had a brief romance resulting in the birth of a child. Her parents took over the raising of her daughter, and she moved with them to San Diego when she was seventeen. There, she was unable to finish high school, and instead took summer classes at the San Diego Normal School. There she met an eccentric linguist, John Peabody Harrington, who was delighted in her perfect ear for linguistic subtleties and trained her in his specialty. When the Bureau of Ethnology hired him the following year to record the dying Native American languages, the couple was married and Carobeth accompanied her husband as field assistant, chauffeur, secretary, and unpaid servant. Many years later she wrote extensively about her experiences in her book *Encounter with an Angry God.*

A child was born to the couple, but her husband insisted that this daughter also be left with her parents so that husband and wife could continue their gypsy life in the field. After three years, Harrington sent his wife on linguistic collecting trips by herself. In Parker, Arizona, she met George Laird, twenty years older than she, with whom she began to record materials on the disappearing Chemehuevi language and culture. After four years of working with George Laird as an informant, Carobeth decided to divorce Harrington and marry Laird. They moved to a small ranch in Poway, near San Diego, where they raised five children, and some crops, and George Laird also worked at a number of minor jobs.

Over the next twenty years, Carobeth Laird continued to record Chemehuevi myths in the Chemehuevi language, eventually producing an unusually complete collection. When her husband died suddenly in 1940, she sought work as a Christian Science practitioner, maintaining that position for the next twenty years while completing her manuscript on the Chemehuevis. Her attempts to publish it were frustrated by a dismissive anthropology professor at the University of California, Los Angeles, and for many years the manuscript disappeared from view until it was rediscovered in 1976.

In 1974, almost eighty and discouraged, Laird began to write and publish a few articles on Chemehuevi folklore. Encouraged to write about her life and marriage to Harrington, the book was published the following year. It touched many of those in the anthropologist community because of its frank depiction of field anthropology and there was a growing interest about the author. Laird was rediscovered living in a nursing home where she had been forced to retire because of ill health. Rescued from what she later (in her book *Limbo*) described as a dehumanizing situation, she found herself an accepted member of the anthropological community for the first time, at the age of eighty.

Laird began to see her work published; her major study on the Chemehuevi was rediscovered, and hailed; she attended and presented papers at anthropological meetings. As evidence of this reemergence, she was awarded an honorary doctorate of humane letters by the University of Arizona in 1983. Although she died that August at age eighty-seven, two other manuscripts were finished before her death: one a more complete look at George Laird's interpretation of Chemehuevi mythology, *Mirror and Pattern,* and the second, her final autobiography, *Pilgrim and Stranger.* Her field notes, tapes, and manuscripts are in the University of California, Riverside.

JH/MBO

PRIMARY SOURCES

Laird, Carobeth. "The Buffalo in Chemehuevi Folklore."
Journal of California Anthropology 1 (1974): 220–224.
———. *Encounter with an Angry God: Recollections of My Life with John Peabody Harrington.* Banning, Calif.: Malki Museum Press, 1975.
———. *Limbo: A Memoir about Life in a Nursing Home by a Survivor.* Novato, Calif.: Chandler & Sharp, 1979.
———. *Mirror and Pattern: George Laird's World of Chemehuevi Mythology.* Banning, Calif.: Malki Museum Press, 1984.
———. *Pilgrim and Stranger.* Novato, Calif.: Chandler & Sharp [1988?].

STANDARD SOURCES

Gacs (article by Ute Gacs).

LAIRD, ELIZABETH REBECCA (1874–1969)

Canadian/U.S. physicist. Born 6 December 1874 in Owen Sound, Ontario, to Rebecca (La Pierre) and John G. Laird, a Methodist minister. At least two siblings. Educated in London, Ontario; University of Toronto (A.B., 1896); University of Berlin (graduate studies, 1898–1899); Bryn Mawr College (Ph.D., 1901); Cambridge University (postdoctoral studies, 1905, 1909); University of Würzburg (1913–1914); University of Chicago (1919); Yale University (1925). Professional experience: Ontario Ladies' College, instructor (1896–1897); Bryn Mawr College, substitute demonstrator in physics (1900); Mount Holyoke College, assistant in physics (1901–1902), instructor (1902–1903), acting head physics department (1903–1904), professor (1904–1940), emerita professor (from 1940). Honors and memberships: Yale University, honorary research fellow (1925); National Research Council of Canada (1941–1945); University of Western Ontario, researcher (1941–1945), honorary professor (1945–1953); Mount Holyoke College, honorary D.Sc. (1927); American Physical Soci-
ety, Fellow; University of Western Ontario, honorary LL.D. (1954). Died 1969.

Rebecca Laird took the Honors Mathematics and Physics Course at Toronto, selecting the physics option during her fourth year. Up to that time she had preferred mathematics, but during that year new discoveries and teaching demonstrations made physics seem exciting. Because of her sex, Laird was ineligible for the 1851 scholarship, but she received a fellowship from Bryn Mawr the next year, which she used to go to Berlin. Before she left Canada, she spent a year teaching mathematics at the Ontario Ladies' College. By then both her parents were dead, leaving Laird dependent upon financial aid and her own earnings.

Laird's first scientific project, an application of Stokes's mathematical theory to wires vibrating in liquids, won her the Bryn Mawr President's European Fellowship. Laird spent 1898–1899 at the University of Berlin, where she worked on timelag in magnetization under Emil Warburg, and studied with Max Planck, Jacobus Henricus Van't Hoff, Immanuel Lazarus Fuchs, and Georg Ferdinand Frobenius. Warburg suggested that she present her work as a thesis, but since Laird felt obligated to Bryn Mawr, she returned to the United States. There she began new researches on chlorine's absorption spectrum with Bryn Mawr's state-of-the-art Rowland grating. Laird received her doctorate in physics and mathematics under A. S. MacKenzie in 1901. She then began teaching at Mount Holyoke, where she continued until her retirement in 1940, at which time she became an emerita professor.

Before she returned to Bryn Mawr, Laird had visited J. J. Thomson's former student John C. McLennan at Toronto, who stimulated her interest in ionization, X-rays, and, later, radioactivity. In 1903, Laird heard J. J. Thomson lecture at Yale, and in the summer of 1905 she was able to work in his laboratory in Cambridge. Here Laird was introduced to the mysterious discharge rays, penetrating rays associated with electric sparks, which became the major research subject of her career. Laird continued to study the discharge rays at Mount Holyoke, using thermoluminescence as well as ionization to detect them. She found that celluloid films would transmit the rays, which greatly facilitated experimental work. She also investigated ionization in various gases.

J. J. Thomson had predicted that spark discharges would give rise to soft X-rays. Upon her return to the Cavendish in 1909, Laird's experiments supported the idea that discharge rays were actually soft X-rays. During 1913–1914, she used a Sarah Berliner Fellowship to continue investigating discharge rays at Würzburg under Wien, whom she had met earlier that year in the United States. She found many similarities between discharge rays and X-rays. In 1919, Laird spent nine weeks at Chicago working under Robert

Millikan on transmission of short-wave radiation through celluloid films. Back at Mount Holyoke, she investigated reflection of discharge rays and searched for the minimum energy which would produce them. During a semester at Yale in 1925 (supported by an honorary research fellowship), Laird worked on developing a photographic method for investigating the discharge rays, by then identified as soft X-rays.

Laird supervised student work on the Raman effect and on thermal conductivity. During the war she applied her experience with radiation to radar development. Afterward she consulted for the Ontario Research Foundation on the medical uses of short-wave radiation. This led her to experiments in biophysics, in particular on the effect of keratin's structure on its electrical properties.

Laird was a Fellow of the American Association for the Advancement of Science and the American Physical Society, and a member of the Optical Society of America, the Association of Physics Teachers, the History of Science Society, the Canadian Association of Physicists, and the American Institute of Radio Engineers.   MM

PRIMARY SOURCES
Laird, Elizabeth R. "The Absorption Spectrum of Chlorine." *Astrophysical Journal* 14 (1901): 85–115.
———. "Ionization Produced by Entladungsstrahlung and Experiments Bearing on the Nature of the Radiation." *Physical Review* 30 (1910): 293–310.
———. "Entladungsstrahlung at Atmospheric Pressure and at Diminished Pressures." *Physical Review* 33 (1911): 512–527.
———. "Über die Erzeugung von Röntgenstrahlung durch langsame Kathodenstrahlungen." *Annalen der Physik* 46 (1915): 605–622.
———. With Vola P. Barton. *Physical Review* 14 (1919): 234–245.
———. "Note on Article by H. M. Dadourian on 'Soft X-Rays.'" *Physical Review* 15 (April 1920): 293–296.
———. With Vola P. Barton. "Soft X-Rays Produced by Cathode Rays of From 200 to 600 Volts Velocities." *Physical Review* 15 (April 1920): 297–311.
Autobiography in Niels Bohr Library, American Institute of Physics.

SECONDARY SOURCES
Baly, E. C. C. *Spectroscopy.* New York and Bombay: Longmans, Green, and Co., 1905.
Holweck, Fernand. *De la Lumière aux Rayons X.* Paris: Les Presses Universitaires de France, 1927.
Journal of the Optical Society of America 59 (December 1969): 1687. Obituary notice.
Kayser, Heinrich. *Handbuch der Spectroscopy.* Vol. 3. Leipzig: S. Hirzel, 1905.

Rayner-Canham, M. F., and G. W. Rayner-Canham. "Pioneer Women in Nuclear Science." *American Journal of Physics* 58 (1990): 1036–1043.

STANDARD SOURCES
AMS 1–8, P 9, P&B 10; Bailey; Rossiter 1982; Siegel and Finley; *Woman's Who's Who of America.*

LAÏS (1st or 2d century B.C.E.)
Greek midwife and physician.

In his *Natural History,* Pliny describes Laïs as a midwife who often opposed Elephantis regarding the use of drugs. Laïs, along with Salpe, he reports, devised a treatment for rabies and intermittent fevers: these maladies were "cured by the flux on wool from a black ram enclosed in a silver bracelet." Laïs and Elephantis, wrote Pliny, "do not agree in their statements about abortives, the burning root of cabbage, myrtle, or tamarisk extinguished by the menstrual blood, about asses not conceiving for as many years as they have eaten grains of barley contaminated with it, or in their other portentous or contradictory pronouncements, one saying that fertility, the other that barrenness is caused by the same measures. It is better not to believe them." If credulous Pliny was skeptical about the medical achievements of Laïs, it is likely that suspicion is warranted. Pliny is the only source available, and there is nothing in his report to indicate anything scientific about her medicine.   JH/MBO

SECONDARY SOURCES
Pliny, the Elder. *Natural History.* Vol. 8, Book 28. Ed. W.H.S. Jones. Loeb Classical Library. Cambridge, Mass.: Harvard University Press, 1938–1963. See pages 23, 80–82.

STANDARD SOURCES
Ogilvie 1986; Pauly-Wissowa, vol. 11.

LALANDE, MARIE JEANNE AMÉLIE HARLAY LEFRANÇAIS DE (1760–1832)
French astronomer. Born 1760 in Harlay. Married Michel Jean Jérôme Lefrançais de Lalande. Two children: Caroline and Isaac.

Little is known of Lalande's early life. Her husband, Michel (1776–1839), was the younger cousin and protégé of astronomer Joseph Jérôme Lefrançais de Lalande (1732–1807), who always referred to Michel and Amélie as his nephew and niece and who instructed them both in astronomy. The names of their children reflect the family saturation with astronomy. Since their daughter was born on 20 January 1790, the day on which a comet discovered by CAROLINE HERSCHEL was first visible in Paris, she was named Caroline; their son was named after Sir Isaac Newton.

Lalande assisted the two men, especially in the calculation of astronomical tables. She constructed the tables appended to Jérôme's *Albrégé de navigation* (1793), designed to help navigators calculate the time at sea by the altitude of the sun and stars; her calculations and reductions are included in an astronomical almanac, *Connaissance des temps,* edited by Jérôme de Lalande. Because her work was so closely tied with that of her husband and cousin, it is difficult to evaluate her achievements. At the very least, however, it is evident that she was a competent calculator and observer—one who made astronomical data more accessible.   JH/MBO

SECONDARY SOURCES
Du Deffand, Marquise Marie de Vichy Chamrond. *Correspondence complète de la marquise du Deffand avec ses amis le président Iténault, Montesquieu, d'Alembert, Voltaire, Horace Walpole.* Paris: H. Plon, 1865. Includes information about Lalande.
Lalande, Jérôme de. *Bibliographie astronomique avec l'histoire de l'astronomie depuis 1781 jusqu'à 1802.* Paris: Imprimerie de la République, 1803.

STANDARD SOURCES
DSB (under Lalande, Jérôme); *DFC;* Ogilvie 1986; Rebière.

LA MANCE, LORA SARAH (NICHOLS) (1857–?)
U.S. horticulturist. Born 1857. Death date unknown.

Lora La Mance was a horticulturist who published books on gardening in New York.   JH/MBO

PRIMARY SOURCES
La Mance, Lora S. *Beautiful Home Surroundings: A Book of Practical Information Regarding the Garden and Lawn.* Floral Park, N.Y.: J. L. Childs, 1892.
———. *House Plants: A Book of Practical Information Regarding the Culture of House and Greenhouse Plants.* Floral Park, NY: J. L. Childs, 1892.

LAMARCK, CORNELIÉ (fl. 1820)
U.S. naturalist. Flourished 1820s. Father J. B. Lamarck.

Corneliē Lamarck was the daughter of J. B. Lamarck, and worked with him for many years at the Muséum d'Histoire Naturelle after he became blind. She is mentioned by Etienne Geoffroy Saint-Hilaire, his colleague at the museum, in *Fragments Biographiques.*   JH/MBO

SECONDARY SOURCES
Geoffroy Saint-Hilaire, Etienne. *Fragments Biographiques.* Paris: F. D. Pillot, 1838. Corneliē Lamarck is mentioned on page 81.

STANDARD SOURCES
Rebière.

LAMBIN, SUZANNE (1902–)
French microbiologist. Born 1 August 1902 in Nantes, France, to Valentine (Perthuy) and René Lambin. Educated University of Nantes, School of Medicine and Pharmacology; University of Paris (Ph.D.). Professional experience: University of Nantes, School of Medicine and Pharmacology, assistant in physics; University of Paris, pharmacist (1925–1928), assistant in microbiology (1928–1945), department head (chef de travail) (1945), lecturer (agrégé) in natural sciences; University of Paris, Faculty of Pharmacy, professor of microbiology (1951–post-1968). Honors and memberships: French Association of Microbiologists, Académie de Pharmacie, Société de Biologie. Honors: Order of Public Health.

Suzanne Lambin was a French microbiologist who studied the evolution of bacterial cultures and the effects of different antiseptic agents. She was born in Brittany, in Nantes, and studied first at the University of Nantes, where she served as an assistant in physiology. In her early twenties, she went to Paris, where she studied microbiology and worked as pharmacist at the University of Paris, receiving her doctorate in microbiology (in 1928?). She served as an assistant in microbiology until she finished her agrégé thesis, entitling her to lecture in the university in natural sciences. At that point, she was made a department head (chef de travail) (which permitted her to run her own laboratory). In 1951, she became a professor of microbiology in the Paris Faculty of Pharmacy, where she remained until her retirement. Her research on bacterial evolution and antiseptic agents was recognized by a decoration, the Order of Public Health. She was also elected to the prestigious Academy of Pharmacy and was a member of the French Association of Microbiologists and the Société de Biologie.   JH/MBO

STANDARD SOURCES
Debus.

LAMME, BERTHA (1864–1943)
U.S. electrical engineer. Born 1864 in Springfield, Ohio. At least one brother. Married Russell S. Feicht. One daughter (1910). Educated Ohio State University (B.S. in mechanical engineering, 1893). Professional experience: Westinghouse, Pittsburgh, Pa., researcher (1893–?).

Bertha Lamme was the second U.S. woman to receive an engineering degree. She worked in Westinghouse's East Pittsburgh plant in the engineering department, where she designed motors and generators. In 1905 she married her supervisor, Russell S. Feicht. After she married, she gave up her profession. Her engineer brother lived with the couple. Her husband had designed the 2,000 horsepower induction motors for the 1904 St. Louis World's Fair, and her brother rose to the position of chief engineer at Westinghouse and designed the turbo generators at Niagra Falls. The couple had a daughter who displayed considerable mathematical abilities at an early age and who went on to become a physicist.   JH/MBO

SECONDARY SOURCES

Ohio State University Monthly 35 (December 1943): 13. Obituary notice, under Bertha Lamme Feicht.

Trescott, Martha. In *Women in Science and Engineering Professions*, ed. Violet B. Haas and Carolyn C. Perrucci. Ann Arbor: University of Michigan Press, 1984.

———. "Women in the Intellectual Development of Engineering." In Kass-Simon and Farnes.

STANDARD SOURCES

Rebière.

LAMONTE, FRANCESCA RAIMONDE (1895–?)

U.S. ichthyologist. Born 1895. Educated Wellesley College (B.A. and certificate of music). Professional experience: American Museum of Natural History, Department of Fishes and Aquatic Biology, associate curator (1947?–1968), curator emerita (1968). American Association for the Advancement of Science, Fellow. Honors and memberships: New York Zoological Society; Society for Systematic Zoology; Society of Icthyology and Herpetology. Death date unknown.

Francesca Raimonde LaMonte was trained in music as well as science. After receiving her bachelor's degree from Wellesley College, she became interested in folk legends and in her early thirties she published a book of folk legends about the Dolomite Alps with Karl Felix Wolff: *The Pale Mountains: Folk Tales from the Dolomites* (1927). Preserving wilderness areas was one of her early concerns.

LaMonte's work interest in ichthyology began later in her life. LaMonte participated in the World's Fair in 1939–1940 as a member of the Fisheries Commission. She was a delegate to the Eleventh International Congress of Zoologists in Padua, Italy, and attended other world congresses as her fame grew. Interested in writing for the public as well as producing scientific works, she wrote field guides and popular books on freshwater fish and on marine game fish. An associate curator of ichthyology at the American Museum of Natural History, she produced a guide to its collections in the 1940s in association with William K. Gregory.   JH/MBO

PRIMARY SOURCES

LaMonte, Francesca. *The Pale Mountains: Folk Tales from the Dolomites.* New York: Minton, Balch, 1927.

———. With M. R. Welch. *Vanishing Wilderness.* New York: Liveright Pub. Corp., 1934.

———. *North American Game Fishes.* New York: Doubleday, 1945.

———. With Brian S. Vesey-FitzGerald. *Game Fish of the World.* New York: Harper, 1949.

———. With William K. Gregory. *The World of Fishes: A Survey of the Habits, Relationships and History, and a Guide to the Fish Collection of the American Museum of Natural History.* New York: American Museum of Natural History, 1949.

———. With I. Gabrielson. *The Fisherman's Encyclopedia.* Harrisburg, Pa.: Stackpole and Heck, 1950.

———. *Marine Game Fishes of the World.* Garden City, N.Y.: Doubleday, 1952.

———. *Giant Fishes of the Ocean.* N.p., 1966.

STANDARD SOURCES

Bailey (as F. Raimond LaMonte); Debus (as F. Reymond La Monte); Hollis (as F. Raimonde LaMonte).

LAMPE, LOIS (1896–1978)

U.S. botanist, educator. Born 29 March 1896 to Gertrude Leslie (Hays) and Frederick Christian Lampe. Married Brenton C. Zimmerman, 1928(?). Educated Ohio State University (A.B.; B.S., 1919; M.S., 1922; Ph.D., 1927). Professional experience: Ohio State University, graduate teaching asistant (1920–1923); instructor (1923–1924, 1926–1940), assistant professor (1940–1966). Died 6 January 1978 in London, Ohio.

Although Lois Lampe's teaching career at Ohio State covered the years 1917 (when she was a student assistant) to 1966, the highest level that she reached was assistant professor. Since she held a doctoral degree and maintained a reputation for teaching excellence, it is difficult to understand her lack of promotion. Possible explanations may be her own diffidence and her sparse publication record. After forty-two years of service, she became assistant professor emerita in 1966. In her retirement, she married Brenton C. Zimmerman.

Lampe received a certificate of commendation in the field of science and education by a state representative to the Ohio House of Representatives. She was also a member of many scientific and honor societies, some of which she served as an officer. She was a Fellow and member of the council (1939–1940) of the American Association for the Advancement of Science. She was a member of the American Genetic Association, American Institute of Biological Sciences, Botanical Society of America, National Society of Arts and Letters, and the Ohio Academy of Science. She also belonged to several honorary societies such as Phi Epsilon Phi (National Honorary Botanical Fraternity); Phi Upsilon Omicron Honorary Society in Home Economics; Sigma Delta Epsilon Graduate Women's Scientific Fraternity (national president, 1940); and Sigma Xi.

Her research interests focused on the developmental anatomy of vascular plants. For her master's thesis, Lampe worked on twig abscission in cottonwood, and for her doctoral dissertation, the development of the endosperm of corn. She later became interested in cytology, studying the chromosome structure of *Trilium* and *Podophyllum*. She also studied the heritable variation in vascular plants as a basis for classification of the larger groups of flower plants. She was a disciple of John H. Schaffner and sought to preserve his ideas on phylogenetic taxonomy. An excellent artist, she contributed scientific illustrations for publications of her colleagues and also exhibited her art.   JH / MBO

PRIMARY SOURCES

Lampe, Lois. With Marion T. Meyers. "Carbohydrate Storage in the Endosperm of Sweet Corn." *Science* 61 (1925): 290–291.

———. "A Microchemical and Morphological Study of the Developing Endosperm of Maize." *Botanical Gazette* 91 (1931): 337–376.

SECONDARY SOURCES

Paddock, Elion F. "Lois Lampe (1896–1978)." *Genetics* 110, no. 3, pt. 2 (1985): 123.

Stuckey, Ronald L. "Lois Lampe." Unpublished notes. From the collection of Ronald L. Stuckey.

STANDARD SOURCES

AMS 5–8, B 9, P&B 10–12; Barnhart; Stuckey (with portrait).

LAMPL-DE GROOT, JEANNE (1895–1987)

Dutch psychiatrist. Born 16 October 1895 in Schiedam, Netherlands, to Henriette (Dupont) and M. C. M. De Groot. Third of four children. Married Hans Lampl, psychiatrist, on 7 April 1925 (he died in 1957). Two daughters, Henriette and Edith. Educated University of Leiden; University of Amsterdam (M.D., 1921); psychoanalytic training with Sigmund Freud (1922–1925). Professional experience: Wagner von Jauregg clinic, psychiatrist in training; Berlin Institute, psychiatrist, psychoanalyst (1925–1933); Institute of Psychoanalysis, Vienna, psychoanalyst and training analyst (1933–1938); Dutch Psychoanalytic Institute, Amsterdam, founder (with Hans Lampl). Honors and memberships: International Psychoanalytical Association, honorary vice-president (1963–?); Netherlands Society of Psychiatry and Neurology, honorary member (1971); University of Amsterdam (honorary doctorate, 1970). Died 1987.

Psychiatrist and psychoanalyst Jeanne de Groot received her medical education in the Netherlands. At age twenty-six, she approached Sigmund Freud for a training analysis, and thus began a long professional and social relationship with the renowned analyst and with his daughter Anna Freud. Her correspondence with Freud is extensive and filled with personal exchanges and gossip. Following her analysis, at Freud's suggestion, de Groot went to Berlin to work at the Berlin Institute before beginning her own analytic practice. In Berlin, she met and married Hans Lampl, a psychoanalyst from Freud's circle in Vienna and previously a suitor of Anna Freud. Their two daughters were born in Berlin.

The couple returned to Vienna when the National Socialist Party came to power under Adolf Hitler in the early 1930s. De Groot renewed her association with the Freuds, working to develop child analytic treatment and training with Anna Freud. In 1938, the political situation again forced the family to move; they settled finally in Amsterdam, where Lampl-de Groot became an important figure in Dutch psychoanalysis. She taught at psychoanalytic institutes in Berlin, Vienna, Amsterdam, and Frankfurt. She and Hans Lampl cofounded the Dutch Psychoanalytic Institute and established formal training procedures for analysts and psychotherapists.

Lampl-de Groot's early work was largely concerned with female sexuality. Her first paper read in Vienna was "The Oedupus Complex in Women" (1927), which Freud referred to in his own 1932 paper "Female Sexuality." In 1933, she published a second paper, "Problems of Femininity," which she reprinted in a collection in 1985. Her later research involved theoretical and practical problems of psychoanalysis, and its interaction with other branches of science. She was the author of numerous papers and publications, many of which have been collected in book form, first in *The Development of the Mind* (1965). Twenty years later, a second collection appeared as *Mind and Man: Collected Papers*.

                                                      JH / MBO

PRIMARY SOURCES

Lampl-de Groot, Jeanne. [Autobiographical memoir] in Hellstedt, *Autobiographies*.

———. *The Development of the Mind; Psychoanalytic Papers on Clinical and Theoretical Problems*. Foreword by Anna Freud. New York: International Universities Press, 1965.

———. *Mind and Man: Collected Papers*. New York: International Universities Press, 1985.

STANDARD SOURCES
Appignanesi; Debus.

LANCEFIELD, REBECCA CRAIGHILL
(1895–1981)

U.S. bacteriologist. Born 1895 on Staten Island, N.Y., to Mary Wortley Montague Byram and William Edward Craighill. Married Donald Lancefield. One child. Educated Wellesley College (B.A., 1916); Columbia University (M.A., 1918; Ph.D., 1925). Professional experience: Rockefeller Institute, researcher (1922–mid-1960s). Honors and memberships: T. Duckett Jones Memorial Award (1960); American Heart Association Achievement Award (1964); member, National Academy of Sciences (1970); New York Academy of Medicine medal (1973); Research Achievement Award from the journal Medicine *(1973); Research Achievement Award, Wellesley College (1973); Rockefeller University, honorary D.Sc. (1973); D.Sc. honoris causa, Wellesley College, honorary D.Sc. (1976); Royal College of Pathologists, honorary fellowship (1976). Died 3 March 1981.*

Rebecca Price Craighill majored in zoology at Wellesley College, though she had first intended to major in English and French. After graduation, she accepted a job teaching physical geography; she soon left that job, having received a graduate scholarship at Columbia University Teachers College. She decided to study bacteriology, and since she could not do so at Teachers College, she pursued her degree at Columbia. There she met Donald Lancefield, a fellow graduate student at Columbia. After she received her master's degree, she was offered a job as a technician on a streptococcus study proposed by O. T. Avery and A. R. Dochez. Lancefield, now her husband, finished his doctoral requirements in 1921 and was offered a position at the University of Oregon.

Rebecca Lancefield went with her husband, but returned to Columbia after a year to complete her doctoral degree there. Her advisor, Hans Zinsser, suggested that she accept a position at the Rockefeller Institute to study rheumatic fever with Homer Swift. She remained at that institution for the rest of her career. She spent the next three years working on *Streptococcus viridans,* a bacterium had been incorrectly linked with rheumatic fever. She finished her doctoral work on this organism and documented that it was not a causative agent of rheumatic fever in several publications.

Before she finished her doctoral degree, her early work as a technician was important enough that Avery and Dochez made her a coauthor of their 1919 paper. In this paper they presented the first documented evidence to indicate that specific streptococci caused specific infections. Lancefield later was able to show that the dominant strains of streptococci that cause infections vary from year to year.

Lancefield found evidence that countered the accepted belief that type-specific virulences were carbohydrates of polysaccharides. She challenged this theory, proposing that a specific protein, which she named the M protein, was responsible for virulence.

She published a major paper in 1933 on a method that she had devised that allowed her to classify more than sixty distinct strains of hemolytic streptococci. She continued her research on streptococcal antigens, using her classification system as a tool. She and Swift collaborated on a paper for the Second International Conference for Microbiology in London in 1936.

Lancefield preferred laboratory work to other duties. Her laboratory flourished and became the world source for the identification of streptococcus strains and for antisera. After Swift retired, Maclyn McCarty joined Lancefield's lab to continue the study of rheumatic fever. She took time out from her laboratory work to participate in professional activities. She was president of the Society of American Bacteriologists and the American Association of Immunologists.

Although Lancefield officially retired in the mid-1960s, she continued to participate in laboratory research. Lancefield found time to enjoy herself outside of the laboratory, as she, her husband, and daughter spent their summers at Cape Cod.

JH/MBO

PRIMARY SOURCES
Lancefield, Rebecca. With A. R. Dochez and O. T. Avery. "Antigenic Relationship Between Strains of *Streptococcus hemolyticus.*" *Transactions of the Association of American Physicians* 34 (1919): 63–67.
———. With J. H. Quastel. "A Note on the Antigenicity of Crystalline Egg Albumin." *Journal of Pathology and Bacteriology* 32 (1919): 771–773.
———. "Studies on the Biology of Streptococcus. I. Antigenic Relationship Between Strains of *Streptococcus haemolyticus.*" *Journal of Experimental Medicine* 30 (1919): 179–213.
———. "The Immunological Relationships of *Streptococcus viridans* and Certain of Its Chemical Fractions. I. Serological Reactions Obtained with Antibacterial Sera." *Journal of Experimental Medicine* 42 (1925): 377–395. Contains the results from her Ph.D. dissertation research.
———. "The Immunological Relationships of *Streptococcus viridans* and Certain of Its Chemical Fractions. II. Serological Reactions Obtained with Antinucleoprotein Sera." *Journal of Experimental Medicine* 42 (1925): 397–412. Contains the results from her Ph.D. dissertation research.
———. "Note on the Susceptibility of Certain Strains of Hemolytic Streptococcus to a Streptococcus Bacteriophage." *Proceedings of the Society of Experimental Biology and Medicine* 30 (1932): 169–171.
———. "A Serological Differentiation of Human and Other Groups of Hemolytic Streptococci." *Journal of Experimental Medicine* 57 (1933): 571–595.

———. "Specific Relationship of Cell Composition to Biological Activity of Hemolytic Streptococci." *Harvey Lectures* 36 (1941): 251–290.

SECONDARY SOURCES

McCarty, M. *Biographical Memoirs of the National Academy of Sciences* 57 (1987): 227–246.

O'Hern, Elizabeth Moot. "Rebecca Craighill Lancefield: Pioneer Microbiologist." *American Society for Microbiolgy News* 41 (1985): 805–810.

Wannamaker, Lewis W. "Obituary: Rebecca Craighill Lancefield." *American Society for Microbiology News* 47 (1981): 555–559.

STANDARD SOURCES

Annual Obituary 1981; Grinstein 1997 (article by Teresa T. Antony); *Notable;* Shearer and Shearer 1996 (article by Barbara I. Bond).

LANDES, RUTH (SCHLOSSBERG) (1908–1991)

U.S.-born Canadian cultural and linguistic anthropologist. Born in New York City 1908 to Anna (Grossman) and Joseph Schlossberg. Married (1) Landes (1929; divorced); (2) [?] Educated New York public schools. New York University (B.S., 1928); New York School of Social Work (certification, 1929); Columbia University (Ph.D. in anthropology, 1937). Field work: Harlem, New York; Objiwa tribe, Ontario (1933–1936); Bahia, Brazil (1938–1940). Professional experience: New York Children's Service Bureau (1929–1931); Fisk University, instructor in anthropology (1937–1938); Carnegie Corporation, research associate (with Gunnar Myrdal) (1939–1940); U.S. Office of Inter-American Affairs, research director (1941); U.S. Fair Employment Practices Commission (FEPC), President's Committee, field representative (1941–1945); American Jewish Committee, study director (1945–1959?); McMaster University, Ontario, Canada, professor of anthropology (1965–1978?). Honors and memberships: American Anthropological Association (AAA), Fellow. Died 1991.

Ruth Schlossberg Landes had a long and respected career in anthropology, but a difficult one, due to the political hysteria of the prewar period. She grew up in a secular Jewish household. Her father was a brillant man who had immigrated from Russia when he was in his teens, become an active union man, and then won and subsequently lost a graduate fellowship at Columbia because of his leftist and union sympathies. Schlossberg took an undergraduate degree from New York University and spent a year acquiring a certificate from the New York School of Social Work.

Not yet an anthropologist, but fascinated by the Garvey movement in Harlem that resulted in a black Jewry, she began to do research while working for the Children's Bu-reau as a social worker. Her resulting study would not be published for thirty-five years. Her investigations brought her into contact with RUTH BENEDICT and the aging Franz Boas, who encouraged her to study anthropology at Columbia. Her brief marriage foundered when her husband, a medical student, objected to her new work. Funded by a University Council Research Grant, Ruth Schlossberg Landes began her formal field work among the Objiwa tribe in Ontario resulting in her Columbia dissertation from which she produced two classic books as well as articles on Objiwa society and Objiwa women. Although she had by this point gained wide recognition from the anthropological community, her interest extended to sociology, and especially inherent problems in race relations. She was befriended by Robert E. Park, who was a founder of the Chicago School of Sociology. He invited her to teach anthropology for a year at Fisk University in Tennessee in order to understand the problems experienced by blacks in the United States while learning from Fisk about the different kinds of problems encountered by the poor black community in Brazil.

Again supported by a research grant, Ruth Landes went to Bahia to study the Afro-Brazilian candomble cults, following the successful work of another student of Fisk. As a woman, Landes found her position very difficult, requiring her to be escorted at all times in the evening. She fortunately was aided by an excellent scholar (more recently a renowned folklorist), Edison Caneiro, who helped her, encouraged her, and introduced her to places that would have been forbidden to her.

Perhaps the fact that her associate was a mulatto angered another Brazilian anthropologist, Arturo Ramos, who saw the cults as his own territory. Whatever the cause, he began to spread vehement accusations about Landes's sexual morals and left-wing politics. The result was that although her work was excellent, her professional career as an academic was for many years blocked by anthropologists such as Melville Herskovits and others who had received letters from Ramos. Landes herself wrote up this sad story in an autobiographical account in 1970. Her experiences bear some comparison with the experience of another woman anthropologist, GENE WELTFISH, whose studies on race resulted in accusations against her before the House Un-American Committee in the 1950s, blacklisting her from academic positions for nine years.

With the start of World War II, Landes began to work for the government, first as a director of research in the Office of Inter-American Affairs and soon after as a field representative for the President's Committee of the Fair Employment Practices Commission. After the war, Landes took a position as the study director of the American Jewish Committee, a position she held for some years. She began to publish her Brazilian studies. Her book *The City of Women* appeared first in 1947 and twenty years later in Brazil in a Portuguese translation. She went to California, married again, this time to a man of Spanish-American background, but again the marriage foundered.

Until 1965, Landes worked in California on issues involving race relations and school counseling. She helped develop an anthropology of education. In 1965, then fifty-four, she was finally offered a suitable position in an anthropological department when McMasters University invited her to Ontario. There she remained until her retirement in 1978, publishing an impressive series of books on the Latin Americans in the Southwest and on the American Indian tribes of the Ontario and Midwestern United States areas. JH/MBO

PRIMARY SOURCES

Landes, Ruth. *The Objiwa Woman.* New York: Columbia University Press, 1938.
———. *The City of Women.* New York: Macmillan, 1947.
———. "Negro Slavery and Female Status." *Afro-Americains Mémoires de l'Institut Français d'Afrique Noire* (Dakar) 27 (1953): 265–268.
———. *Culture in American Education.* New York: Wiley, 1965.
———. *The Latin-Americans of the Southwest.* St. Louis: McGraw Hill, 1965.
———. "Negro Jews in Harlem." *Jewish Journal of Sociology* (London) 1967.
———. *Objiwa Religion and the Midewiwin.* Madison: University of Wisconsin Press, 1968.
———. "A Woman Anthropologist in Brazil." In *Women in the Field: Anthropological Experiences,* ed. Peggy Golde, 117–139. Chicago: Aldine Pub. Co., 1970. Autobiographical account. Includes portrait.

STANDARD SOURCES

AMS 8, S&B 11, 12, P&B 13; Gacs (article by George and Alice Park).

LANE-CLAYPON, JANET ELIZABETH (1877–1967)

British epidemiologist and physiologist. Born 3 February 1877 in Boston, Lincolnshire. Married Sir Edward Rodolph Forber in 1929. Educated by private tutors; University College, London University (B.Sc., 1903; D.Sc., 1905); London School of Medicine for Women (M.B., 1907; M.D., 1910). Professional experience: University College, research assistant (1898–1905); Lister Institute for Preventative Medicine, research fellow (1908–1912); Ministry of Health, London Local Government Board, assistant health inspector; King's College, Dean of Women, lecturer in health (1916–1923); Ministry of Health, epidemiologist (1923–1931). Honors and memberships: British Medical Association Scholarship (1902–1903); Lister Institute, Jenner Research Scholar (1909–1911); University College, first-class honors in physiology and materia medica (1907); London School of Medicine for Women, exhibition and gold medals (1903). Died 17 July 1967 in Seaford, Sussex.

Janet Lane-Claypon was educated privately at home until she entered University College in 1898. She proved to be a brilliant student, studying physiology in the laboratory of Ernest H. Starling. Graduating with first-class honors, she also was awarded the exhibition and gold medals for her research on the rabbit ovary. Two years later, she received her doctorate of science following a thesis and the publication of further research with Starling and E. A. Sharper-Schafer on the rat ovary and on mammalian tissue. She then entered the London School of Medicine for Women, where she obtained a bachelor of medicine degree, and worked toward her doctor of medicine degree (which in England requires a thesis) while she was a fellow at the Lister Institute.

At the Lister Institute, Lane-Claypon began to do epidemiological studies of milk, indicating the presence of hemolytic factors in milk, and revealing the effects of heating on bacterial contamination. She wrote a paper that laid to rest the claim that heating destroyed the nutritional value of milk. Much of this work was later brought together in book form. She also investigated the effects of Poor Law legislation on the health of children, comparing British with German infant mortality. After touring facilities in Berlin, she recommended the adoption of the Berlin methods of "Kindersyl" or foster infant care linked with a first-class hospital for children. She was from this point on identified as a public advocate for child care reform. Subsequent papers dealt with infant welfare in England, its administrative organization, the biological properties of human and animal milk, and the economic aspects of midwifery.

Lane-Claypon's work on hygiene appears to have led to her selection as dean at King's College for Women in 1916 and her appointment as lecturer in household and social science. She produced two further books on hygiene during this period, one on the child welfare movement that emphasized the preventative nature of the work. Her next book on the hygiene of women and children emphasized an individual rather than public health approach, probably reflecting her teaching during this period. She resigned her position in 1923 and returned to scientific work.

In 1923, the Ministry of Health established a Departmental Committee on Cancer. One of the scientists with whom Lane-Claypon worked at the Lister Institute, Major Greenwood, subsequently professor of epidemiology and biostatistics at the London School of Hygiene and Tropical Medicine, was then a member of the ministry. At Greenwood's request and as part of a sequence of reports on cancer for the ministry, Lane-Claypon did a review of the literature on the surgical treatment of breast cancer the following year.

This was the beginning a series of classic epidemiological studies of cancer and its treatment that were regularly cited until the 1960s. In 1926, Lane-Claypon produced an important study of 367 pathologically confirmed primary cancers of the breast followed over ten years, the first to take into account competing risks and life-table survival analyses in an "end-results" study of cancer therapy.

Lane-Claypon later performed a careful world literature review on cancer of the uterus, analyzing the survival rates of cervical versus uterine cancer. She also produced a joint paper with Greenwood comparing breast and uterine cancer rate survival. This led to a further study of the success rate of surgical treatment of uterine cancer at one of the major cancer hospitals in London, the Samaritan Free Hospital, over a twenty-year period. She performed a similar analysis on surgical treatment of the breast in eight hospitals in England and Scotland. By 1930, she expanded her analysis to lip, tongue, and skin cancers, with a discussion of the descriptive epidemiology of the site-specific cancer and the antecedent conditions, as well as the success of various methods of treatment.

Lane-Claypon's final study was on incurable cancers studied in London hospitals. By this time, Lane-Claypon had married Sir Edward Rodolph Forber, and this final paper was published under her married name. There are some indications that her marriage to Forber followed a long-term relationship. Shortly after her marriage, although she was only in her fifties, her independent scientific life came to an end, not an uncommon consequence of marriage at this period. She died more than thirty years later in her nineties.

JH/MBO

PRIMARY SOURCES

Lane-Claypon, Janet Elizabeth. "On the Origin and Life History of the Interstitial Cells of the Ovary in the Rabbit." *Proceedings Royal Society* (London) 77, ser. B (1906): 32–52.

———. "Poor-Law Babies in London and Berlin." *Nineteenth Century and After* 68 (1910): 450–466.

———. *Milk and Its Hygienic Relations.* London and New York: Longmans Green and Co., 1916.

———. "Report on the Late Results of Operations for Cancer of the Breast." Reports on Public Health and Medical Subjects, no. 51. London: Ministry of Health, 1928.

———. "Report on Cancer of the Lip, Tongue and Skin: An Analysis of the Literature from a Statistical Standpoint with Special Reference to the Results of Treatment." Reports of Public Health and Medical Subjects no. 59. London: Ministry of Health, 1930.

Forber, Janet Elizabeth. "Incurable Cancer: An Investigation of Hospital Patients in Eastern London." Reports of Public Health and Medical Subjects no. 66. London: Ministry of Health, 1931.

SECONDARY SOURCES

Winkelstein, Warren. "Janet Elizabeth Lane-Claypon: Pioneer Epidemiologist and Protagonist for Women's and Children's Health." Unpublished paper presented at the American Epidemiological Society, 69th Annual Meeting, Atlanta, Ga., 21–22 March 1996. This paper includes a detailed critical bibliography that points out the important epidemiological conclusions of many of her reports.

STANDARD SOURCES

Creese 1991.

LANGDON, FANNY E. (fl. 1895)

U.S. invertebrate zoologist. Professional experience: studied the sense organs and nervous system of worms and other invertebrates.

Invertebrate zoologist Fanny E. Langdon probably worked with HARRIET RANDOLPH at Bryn Mawr. She published on the nervous system and sensory organs of the earthworm *Lumbricus.*

JH/MBO

PRIMARY SOURCES

Langdon, Fanny E. "The Sense Organs of *Lumbricus agricola,*" *Anatomische Anzeiger* (Jena) 10 (1895): 114–117.

———. "The Sense Organs of *Lumbricus." Journal of Morphology* 11 (1895): 193–234.

———. "The Peripheral Nervous System of *Nereis virens."* *Science* 5 (1897): 427–438.

STANDARD SOURCES

Mozans; *Catalogue Royal Society,* vol. 16, 1918.

LANGDON, LADEMA M. (1893–?)

U.S. botanist. Born 5 January 1893 in Arcade, N.Y. Educated Oberlin College College (A.B., 1916); University of Chicago (M.S., 1917; fellow, 1918–1919; Ph.D., 1919). Professional experience: Illinois public high school teacher (1920); Goucher College, instructor in biology (1920–1923), assistant professor (1923–1934), associate professor (1934–1944), professor (1944–1958), chair of chemistry department (1955–1957), emerita professor (from 1958); Baltimore Junior College, lecturer (1960–1964). Death date unknown.

After receiving her doctorate from the University of Chicago, LaDema M. Langdon spent most of her professional career at Goucher College, where she advanced to full professor after two years as instructor, eleven years as assistant professor, and ten years as associate. She was chair of the chemistry department for two years. Langdon held grants from the National Research Council and the American Philosophical Society. She did research on the stem anatomy of *Cycas* and of *Dioon spinulosum*. She also worked on the floral anatomy and embryology of the family Juglandaceae and the comparative morphology and taxonomy of the Fagaceae. She was a member of the Botanical Society, the Torrey Botanical Club, and the American Association for the Advancement of Science. JH/MBO

STANDARD SOURCES
AMS 4–8, B 9, P&B 10–11; Rossiter 1982.

LANGE, LINDA BARTELS (1882–?)

U.S. bacteriologist. Born 15 January 1882 in New York City. Educated Bryn Mawr College (A.B., 1903); Goucher College (1906–1907); Johns Hopkins University Medical School (M.D., 1911). Professional experience: Bryn Mawr School, Baltimore, assistant (1905–1907); New York Infirmary for Women and Children, intern (1911–1912); Rockefeller Institute, fellow in pathology and bacteriology (1912–1914); H. A. Kelly Hospital, Baltimore, pathologist and director (1914–1915); University of Wisconsin Medical School, instructor in pathology (1915–1916); Johns Hopkins Medical School, assistant and instructor (1916–1919), school of hygiene and public health, fellow, instructor, and associate in bacteriology (1919–1927), associate professor (1927–1937); Woman's Medical College of Pennsylvania, professor of bacteriology and immunology (1937–1940). Retired 1940. Death date unknown.

Linda Bartels Lange earned a medical degree from Johns Hopkins and then went into research. She worked in pathology and bacteriology, never practicing privately. Her research was on infectious diseases, bacteriology, malignant tumors, tuberculosis, and spirochetes. JH/MBO

STANDARD SOURCES
AMS 5–7.

LANGE, MATHILDE MARGARETHE (1888–?)

U.S. biologist. Born 14 March 1888 in New York City, N.Y. Educated University of Zurich (Ph.D., 1920). Professional experience: U.S. Department of Agriculture, researcher (1920–1921); Wheaton College (Mass.), professor of zoology (1921–1950), emerita professor (from 1950). Death date unknown.

After Mathilde Lange earned her doctoral degree from the University of Zurich, she worked for the U.S. Department of Agriculture for a year before she got a job at Wheaton College. She spent the rest of her career at Wheaton. Her research was on experimental embryology. She was a member

of the Genetic Association and the New York Academy of Growth. JH/MBO

STANDARD SOURCES
AMS 3–8, B 9, P&B 10.

LANGECKER, HEDWIG (1894–1989)

Bohemian/Czech/German pharmacologist. Born 29 January 1894 in Schluckenau, Bohemia. Father Leo Langecker, a merchant. Educated German University, Prague (Doctor of Medicine, 1920; additional doctorate, 1923), habilitated (1926). Professional experience: German university, Prague, assistant (1920–1930), extraordinary professor (1930–1934), professor (1934–1945); Freien Universität Berlin, professor (1945–1959); Schering-Werke company, scientific staff (1946); professor emerita (1959–1989). Honors and memberships: Freien Universität Berlin, honorary doctorate (1964); German Academy of Endocrinology, honorary member; Berlin Medical Society, member. Died 31 January 1989.

Hedwig Langecker was born in Bohemia and educated at the German University in Prague. Her father was a merchant. She spent the early part of her academic career at the German university in Prague, where she was an assistant, extraordinary professor, and professor. She habilitated in 1926 with her dissertation "Die Pharmakognosie des Polygonatum officinale und Polygonatum multiflorum." She left Prague in 1945 to become a professor in Berlin, where she remained until she retired. From 1946 she was also on the scientific staff of the Scherinug-Werke company. Her major research interst was in the field of the biochemistry of steroid hormones. She wrote over two hundred scientific articles. She was a contributor and coauthor of several textbooks in medicine and pharmacology. JH/MBO

STANDARD SOURCES
Strohmeier; *WW in Science in Europe.*

LANGFORD, GRACE (1871–?)

U.S. physicist. Born 27 June 1871 in Plymouth, Mass. Educated Massachusetts Institute of Technology (B.S., 1900); Columbia University (graduate study). Professional experience: Wellesley College, instructor in physics (1894–1905); Barnard College, Columbia University, instructor in physics (1908–?). Death date unknown.

Born in Plymouth, Massachusetts, Grace Langford studied physics first at Wellesley and then at MIT, where she received a bachelor of science degree. She taught as an instructor at Wellesley College even before she completed her degree and remained an instructor until 1905. She then began to study at Barnard College, Columbia University, in New York, where she did research on the selective reflection of phosphates in the infrared spectrum. She served as an instructor in physics at Barnard as well, but never completed her doctorate.   JH/MBO

STANDARD SOURCES
AMS 3; Rossiter 1982.

LANGSDORFF, TONI VON (1884–post-1976)

German obstetrician and gynecologist. Born 30 September 1884 in Prussia. Father Prussian army officer. Two siblings. Never married. Educated Cologne girl's high school (additional preparation for Abitur); University of Marburg, (preliminary medical exams, 1908) University of Heidelberg (M.D., 1910). Professional experience: medical clinic, Essen, physician (1910–1911); Essen Gynecological Clinic, physician (1911–1918); private obstetrics and gynecology practice (1918–1964). Honors and memberships: University of Heidelberg, Internal Medicine prize essay (1909); Medical Women's International Association, pioneer member. Died after her ninetieth year.

Toni von Langsdorff became a physician against significant opposition. Her father was a Prussian officer who himself had few objections but found his daughter's decision derided by his fellow officers. Her mother supported higher education for women. For von Langsdorff, the presence of a constant doctor in the house for her chronically ill mother and her sister with severe spinal tuberculosis made a medical career seem the path to an independent life.

In order to enter the university, girls had to take special preparation to qualify them for the Abitur, or matriculation examination. An organization in Cologne, where von Langsdorff was living at the time, encouraged and financially supported girls who wanted to prepare for and take the examination. In spite of some unpleasant opposition from teachers and examiners, von Langsdorff entered Bonn University to take courses in anatomy. She found Bonn difficult, since all women were treated as visiting students, and had to specially request treatment in advance.

After completing her first year, she moved to southern Germany, to the University of Heidelberg, where women were considered equal students with men. Fortunately, Germany had always supported the free movement of students between universities. She decided to attend the University of Marburg when she found that the Prussian government had given full matriculation rights to women. There she took her preliminary medical examinations in basic sciences in 1908, but returned to Heidelberg, where the interaction between men and women students was open and friendly. At Heidelberg, she won an essay prize in internal medicine, but the essay itself, which she hoped to use as the basis for her doctoral thesis, was mislaid. Again she encountered some unpleasantness in her final examinations from one of her professors, an opthalmologist who opposed women's medical education, but she passed and was awarded her degree.

Von Langsdorff again experienced problems when she sought a hospital appointment, the last requirement for her medical licence. With the strong recommendation of her thesis advisor, she obtained a year's placement at the municipal clinic in Essen as a gynecologist. She obtained her licence and continued for seven years at the Essen gynecological clinic. When an opening for a permanent post at a hospital fell open, the hospital board supported her application, but the surgeon adamantly refused to work with a woman.

Von Langsdorff went into private practice in obstetrics and gynecology in Essen. There she remained until she was eighty. She is recalled today outside her country for her participation in the International Medical Women's Association as a pioneer member.   KM

PRIMARY SOURCES
Langsdorff, Toni von. In Hellstedt, *Autobiographies.*

LANKESTER, PHOEBE (POPE) (1825–1900)

British botanist. Born 10 April 1825. Father Samuel Pope of Highbury. At least one brother. Married Edwin Lankester, Fellow of the Royal Society (1814–1874) in 1845. Eight children. Died 9 April 1900 in London.

Phoebe Pope was probably born in Highbury. Her father had been a Manchester mill owner. In 1845 she married the physician and scientist Edwin Lankester. In spite of the fact she had eight children (the eldest of whom was the noted biologist E. Ray Lankester [1847–1929]), she wrote a number of popular books on wildflowers, ferns, and parasitic plants. The Lankester family lived for many years in London, where her husband was professor at New College. Although early in Edwin Lankester's career he had been an active scientist and Fellow of the Royal Society, and editor for many years of the Royal Microscopic Society's journal, at the end of his life he turned to issues of public health. In the last ten years of his life he became a coroner for the city of London. The Lankesters received many famous scientists including Charles Darwin, Thomas Henry Huxley, and others at their home.
                                            JH/MBO

PRIMARY SOURCES
Boswell, J. T. I. *English Botany.* 3d. ed. 1863–1872. Lankester contributed the popular portion.
Lankester, Phoebe. *Plain and Easy Account of British Ferns.* London: R. Hardwicke, 1860; 1881.

———. "The Misteltoe and Parasitic Plants." *Popular Science Review* 2 (1863): 196–204.

———. *Talks about Plants.* London: Griffith and Farran, 1879.

SECONDARY SOURCES

Times, 14 April 1900. Obituary notice.

LANSDELL, KATHLEEN ANNIE (1888–1967)

South African botanical artist. Born 1888 in Durban, Natal, South Africa. Educated Government Art School, Durban; Royal College of Arts and Crafts, South Kensington, London. Professional experience: Natal Herbarium, illustrator (1915?–1917?); Division of Botany and Plant Pathology, Pretoria, illustrator (1917–1943). Died 1967 in Pietermaritzburg, Natal.

Kathleen Lansdell was born in Durban, South Africa. She was educated as an artist, and, after attending the Royal College of Arts and Crafts in London, was appointed to the Natal Herbarium. She completed a number of unfinished plates of natal plants that were being prepared for volume seven of Medley Wood's *Natal Plants.* She also worked on a number of watercolors of plants that hang in the Natal Herbarium. Beginning in 1917 until her retirement, she worked in the Division of Botany and Plant Pathology in Pretoria. She contributed numerous plates to the first few volumes of *Flowering Plants of South Africa.* Volume 35 of this set is dedicated to her. She also contributed plates to J. W. Bews's *Plant Forms and Their Evolution in South Africa.* In addition she both wrote the text and illustrated twenty-four plates for a series entitled "Weeds of South Africa," which appeared in the *Journal of Agriculture,* Pretoria. One of her major job-related tasks was to provide illustrations in black and white and color for official publications. Not only did she draw and paint plants, but she also made models in wax of healthy and diseased fruits and vegetables.

After she retired, Lansdell lived in Durban and continued to paint Natal plants. In 1962, she presented a folio of seventy-six plates to the Killie Campbell Library.   JH/MBO

PRIMARY SOURCES

Woods, Medley. *Natal Plants.* Durban: Bennett and Davis, 1899. Lansdell completed the plates.

Evans, Lllytd Buller Pole. *Flowering Plants of South Africa.* London: L. Reeve & Co., 1921–. Lansdell contributed illustrations to the first volumes.

Bews, J. W. *Plant Forms and Their Evolution in South Africa.* London: Longmans, Green, 1925. Lansdell contributed illustrations.

STANDARD SOURCES

Gunn and Codd.

LAPICQUE, MARCELLE (DE HEREDIA) (1873–ca. 1962)

French neurophysiologist. Born 17 July 1873 in Paris to Henriette (Hanaire) and Severiano de Heredia. Married Louis Edouard Lapicque, 14 May 1902. One son, Charles, born before marriage, 6 October 1898 in Theizé (Rhône). Educated French schools and University of Paris (D.Sc., 1903). Professional experience: Laboratoire de Physiologie, Ecole Pratique des Hautes Etudes, associate director (1904–1952); Laboratoire de Physiologie Générale, Ecole Pratique des Hautes Etudes, director (1952–?). Died around 1962.

Marcelle de Heredia Lapicque was the daughter of a landowner who was also a Paris municipal councilor. Her father believed in the education of women, and she studied science at the University of Paris, where she was a fellow student of Louis Lapicque. The two had a son, Charles, born out of wedlock in 1898. He was recognized by Lapicque before their marriage in 1902. Marcelle Lapicque did her dissertation under her husband in 1903 on the nerve impulse, and her later studies furthered her interest in the question of the electrical excitation of the nerve and the study of it as a wave form over time, which she and her husband termed "chronaxie" and investigated with their students for forty or more years. She worked closely with her husband, supervising his experimental physiology laboratory at the Sorbonne, publishing over eighty articles with him and with his students, often as first author.

When Louis Lapicque retired from the University of Paris, Sorbonne, in 1938, he continued to work with his wife on physiological problems, still working in his laboratory of general physiology. He was imprisoned by the Gestapo for a period of time during World War II for supporting the resistance, and, while in prison, wrote his last book, *La Machine Nerveuse* (1943). In this, his most accessible and popular book, he credited his wife with a collaboration of forty years "rich in important initiatives." At various points in the text, he cited their initial studies of chronaxie together in 1903, as well as her independent investigations in 1907 on the effect of poisons and other inhibiting substances on chronaxie (130–131; 167).

Their son, Charles René, trained in sciences as an engineer. Charles solidified the link between the Lapicques and the Paris scientific community when he married Aline Elise Thérèse Perrin, the daughter of the atomic scientist Jean Perrin. He became a painter in the 1920s and gave up engineering for art by the 1940s.

Marcelle and Louis Lapicque lived most of their lives in Paris but spent long periods after World War II vacationing in the Côtes du Nord. Husband and wife enjoyed sailing and more than once crossed the English Channel to attend neurophysiology conferences in their yacht, the *Axon.* They kept up a regular series of studies and publications until Louis

Lapicque's death in 1952. From the late 1930s, young physiologists, especially those in England working under A. V. Hill, sucessfully challenged the Lapicques's concept of chronaxie and by the mid-fifties the French had turned away from their increasingly unpopular theories.

Marcelle Lapicque has dropped out of history, and is not even mentioned in A. Monnier's biographical article on his teacher Louis Lapicque for the *DSB*, doubtless because her position in Lapicque's laboratory depended upon her husband in the same manner as MARGUERITE LWOFF depended upon her husband for her position in science. Unlike Lwoff, Marcelle Lapicque, by surviving her husband, continued to run the Laboratory of General Physiology as one of the Laboratoires des Hautes Etudes until her death around 1962. She was a member of the Société de Biologie and many of her individual publications, as well as those written with her husband and their students, appeared in the society's bulletins between 1907 and 1951.   JH

PRIMARY SOURCES

Lapicque, Marcelle. "Action de la strychnine sur l'éxcitibilité du nerf moteur." *Comptes Rendus des Seances, Société de Biologie* 62 (1907): 1062–1064.

———. "Chronaxies des principaux muscles striés de la Grenouille." *Comptes Rendus des Seances, Société de Biologie* 79 (1927): 933–934.

———. With M. Nattan-Larrier. "Influence du suc d'*Amanita muscaris* sur l'excitabilité du muscle et son imbibition." *Comptes Rendus des Seances, Société de Biologie* 79 (1927): 934–935.

———. With Louis Lapicque. "Sur la chronaxie des muscles squelettiques de la Tortue." *Comptes Rendus des Seances, Société de Biologie* 1 (1927): 1368–1376.

———. "Role des centres dans l'action periphique de la strychnine." *Comptes Rendus des Seances, Société de Biologie* 84 (1932): 957–959.

———. With Louis Lapicque. "Aptitude au galvanotonus dans les nerfs motrices de Batraciens sous l'influence des certaines actions experimentales." *Comptes Rendus des Seances, Société de Biologie* 145 (1951): 947–950.

SECONDARY SOURCES

Lapicque, Louis. *La machine nerveuse.* Paris: Flammarion, 1943. Mentions the importance of his wife's work.

"Louis Lapicque." Obituary articles 10 March 1953 at the Academie de Médécine by A. Giroudin, *Archives Biographiques Françaises.* These articles include a brief biography of Marcelle Lapicque.

STANDARD SOURCES

DSB (under Louis Lapicque).

LARSSON, ELISABETH (1895–?)

Swedish-U.S. obstetrician and gynecologist. Born 5 November 1895 in Grönviken, Bräcke, northern Sweden, to Erika and (?) Larsson. Eleven siblings. Educated: Adventist Academy at Nyhyttan, Järnboås (1920); Broadville College (1920–1926); College of Medical Evangelists (now Loma Linda), Calif. (M.D., 1931.) Professional experience: Los Angeles County Hospital, intern (1931–1932), resident (1932–1936); Loma Linda University assistant professor, (1935–1952); clinical professor of obstetrics and gynecology (1952–1963); emerita professor (1963). Concurrent experience: private practice (1952–1971). Honors and memberships: Fellow, American College of Obstetricians and Gynecologists (1952–1963); Fellow, American College of Surgeons; Fellow, American College of Obstetricians, Gynecologists; Swedish Medical Society (Hon. 1958); Swedish Gynecological Society (1965); Senior Citizen's Clinic, East Los Angeles, award (1971–1976); Medical Women's International Association, pioneer member. Death date unknown.

Elisabeth Larsson was a Swedish-born American physician, raised on a farm in Grönviken, northern Sweden. Elisabeth was the fourth child and first girl. Four of her siblings died before maturity, something that led Elisabeth to study medicine. She remained on the farm until after her father's death, when she began to study for her high school work first by correspondence and then at the Adventist Academy at Nyhyttan, Järnboås.

The family were strongly religious Lutherans, and Larsson determined to study in America, where she was able to obtain support for her high school, college, and premedical education from evangelical sources. She went on to the medical school at the College of Medical Evangelists (later Loma Linda College) where she would later teach obstetrics and gynecology.

Her placement in the Los Angeles County General Hospital for her internship in obstetrics and gynecology led to the rare opportunity for a woman to obtain a three-year residency in the hospital. She soon opened a private practice and took up a teaching position in medicine at Loma Linda College. She passed her boards in both surgery and obstetrics and gynecology. She remained at Loma Linda until she was made emerita professor at the age of sixty-eight. During that period she contributed a number of medical articles on prevention of cancer of the cervix, the premature infant, and the need for more women physicians.

Larsson continued in private practice until she was seventy-five. She calculated that she had delivered about sixteen thousand babies by the time she retired. At her last delivery she found she had delivered, years earlier, both the father and the mother as well as the anesthetist. She had a number of prestigious memberships in medical societies as well as her position as a pioneer member of the Medical Women's International Association.   KM

PRIMARY SOURCES.
Larsson, Elisabeth. In Hellestedt, *Autobiographies.*

LARTER, CLARA ETHELINDA (1847–1936)

British botanist. Born 27 June 1847 in Leeds, Yorkshire. Professional experience: Flora of Devon, editor in chief (1930–1936). Honors and memberships: Fellow of the Linnaean Society in 1912. Died 13 May 1936 in Torquay, Devon.

Clara Larter began to write seriously about the flora of North Devon in 1897. Following her second book, a manual on the Flora of Torquay, she was elected a Fellow of the Linnaean Society. Toward the end of her life, she was made the editor in chief of the *Flora of Devon,* which appeared only after her death. Her herbarium is at the Torquay Natural History Museum, and her plant collection is at Oxford.

JH/MBO

PRIMARY SOURCES
Larter, Clara. *Notes on the Botany of North Devon.* N.p., 1897.
———. *Manual of Flora of Torquay.* N.p., 1900.
———, ed. *Flora of Devon.* Arbroath: T. Buncle and Co., 1939.

SECONDARY SOURCES
"Clara Ethelinda Larter." *Botanical Society Exchange Club British Isles Reports* (1936): 212–213. Obituary notice.
"Clara Ethelinda Larter." *Proceedings Linnean Society* (1936–1937): 200–202. Obituary notice.
Martin, W. Keble, and Gordon T. Fraser. *Flora of Devon.* Arbroath: T. Buncle and Co., 1939. Discussion of Larter on pages 777–778.

STANDARD SOURCES
Desmond.

LA SABLIÈRE, MARGUERITE HESSEIN, MADAME DE (1640?–1693)

French student of natural philosophy. Probably born in 1640. Married Antoine de Rambouillet, Sieur de La Sablière. Three children. Died 1693 in Paris.

Little is known about Mme. de la Sablière's early life. She was a patron of artists, men of letters, and scientists. She found science especially interesting. Two members of the French Academy of Sciences, Joseph Sauveur (1653–1716) and Giles Persone de Roberval (1602–1675), taught her mathematics, physics, and astronomy; and the poet La Fontaine taught her natural history and philosophy. La Sablière and her husband, the financier and poet Antoine de Rambouillet, Sieur de La Sablière, had three children. Although Mar-

guerite did not engage in scientific research or writing herself, she maintained a popular salon frequented by many savants. She typifies the "scientific lady" in France on the eve of the Enlightenment.

The poet Boileau was annoyed by the intellectual pretensions of the women of La Sablière's circle, and in his *Satire contre les femmes,* portrayed her, astrolabe in hand, observing Jupiter and in the process weakening her sight and ruining her complexion. Charles Perrault defended her against Boileau's attacks. In his *Apologie des femmes* he claimed that she was not only very talented but sufficiently modest not to flaunt her abilities.

JH/MBO

SECONDARY SOURCES
Boileau-Despréaux, Nicolas. *Satire contre les femmes.* Includes the *Satire contre les maris* of Jean-François Regnard. Paris: George Birffaut, 1927. Satirizes learned women, including Mme. de La Sablière.

STANDARD SOURCES
NGB, vol. 29.

LASKEY, AMELIA (RUDOLPH) (1885–1973)

U.S. naturalist; ornithologist. Born 12 December 1885 in Bloomington, Ind., to Susan and Frank Rudolph. Married Frederick C. Laskey (1911). Educated elementary and secondary schools, Chicago. Honors and memberships: American Ornithologists' Union, Fellow; Tennessee Ornithological Society, member. Died 19 December 1973 in Nashville, Tenn.

Amelia Laskey's life indicates how an amateur can be an important contributor to science. Never formally educated in science, she, nevertheless, made important contributions. The daughter of German immigrants, Rudolph attended primary and secondary school in Chicago. She worked as a stenographer for the Oliver Typewriter Company before she met and married Frederick C. Laskey. The couple did not have any children. In 1921 they moved to a house outside of Nashville, Tennessee, where Amelia Laskey spent the remainder of her life. Like her mother, Amelia was an avid gardener. At first she created a wild garden in her back yard as a hobby. She was obsessively meticulous about both her house and garden, and the residence, named Blossomdell, thrived. Laskey was active in a garden club and read papers before members of a literary society. At one of her social events a friend suggested that she attend a Bird Club. She attended her first meeting of the Tennessee Ornithological Society in 1928 and immediately became fascinated with bird behavior. She obtained a bird-banding license and began a study of the migratory habits of several species, including the chimney swift, cowbird, and mockingbird. She was able to locate the swift's winter home, when one of her banded birds appeared in Peru. She caught a rare Gambel's sparrow, which had never before been recorded in Tennessee. She also studied the behavior of cowbirds and mockingbirds. For her research she set up hundreds of nesting boxes in a park where she was able to observe the nesting habits of bluebirds.

From 1933 to 1973, Laskey published papers on more than ten species of birds in different ornithological journals, *The Migrant* (104 papers), *Bird-Banding* (19 papers), *The Wilson Bulletin* (12 papers), the *Auk* (12 papers), *Bird Lore* (1 paper), *Journal of the Tennessee Academy of Science* (2 papers), *Inland News* (1 paper), the *Chicago Naturalist* (1 paper), and *The Volunteer Garden* (1). There is no doubt that she made important contributions to research on the development of song, defense of territory, and longevity in the cardinal. From 1931 to 1943, Laskey studied 1621 banded cardinals. The results of her research appeared in *The Wilson Bulletin* (1944). However, even more vital was her work on the mockingbird. She reported on the development of song, a seven-egg clutch, a nine-year-old wild bird and his five mates, the defense of territory, and mating behavior. Much of her information was gained from a captive bird, "Honeychile," a bird that lived for fifteen years and four months. She published three papers in the *Auk,* the last of which was a summary of her thirty-year study of this species. In another major study, Laskey noted only monogamous behavior in her study of numerous pairs of color-banded brown-headed Cowbirds. She did not observe defense of territory in the usual interpretation, but recorded other interesting displays that were part of the intimidation display of male cowbirds and to a lesser degree, females. Her study on cowbird behavior was published in *The Wilson Bulletin*.

Laskey corresponded with MARGARET MORSE NICE, who became her mentor through letters. Nice encouraged Laskey to publish her articles. Generous to her friends, Laskey shared her knowledge with others. She cared for wounded birds in her home, keeping a red-tailed hawk for over ten years and an albino Great Horned Owl for twenty-two years.

JH/MBO

PRIMARY SOURCES

Laskey, Amelia R. "The 1939 Nesting Season of Bluebirds at Nashville, Tennessee." *The Wilson Bulletin* 52 (September 1940): 183–190.

———. "Cowbird Behavior." *The Wilson Bulletin* 62 (1950): 157–174.

———. "Breeding Biology of Mockingbirds." *The Auk* 79 (October 1962): 596–605.

SECONDARY SOURCES

Goodpasture, Katharine A. "In Memoriam: Amelia Rudolph Laskey." *Auk* 92 (1975): 252–259.

STANDARD SOURCES

Bailey; Bonta.

LASKI, GERDA (1893–1928)

Austrian/German physicist. Educated University of Vienna (doctorate, 1917). Professional experience: Kaiser Wilhelm Institute for Fibers Research, researcher, Department of Infrared Radiation Research, director (1924–1928); Physikalisch-Technische Reichsanstalt (PTR), department head. Died 24 November 1928 in Berlin.

Originally from Austria, Gerda Laski was educated at the University of Vienna, and received her doctorate in 1917. She went to the Kaiser Wilhelm Institute for Fibers Research as the director of the Department of Infrared Radiation Research. In 1928, she went to the Physikalisch-Technische Reichsanstalt to build a new department of infrared radiation research.

JH/MBO

SECONDARY SOURCES

Tobies, Renate, ed. *Aller Männer-kultur zum Trotz.* Frankfurt: Campus Verlag, 1997.

STANDARD SOURCES

Vogt.

LASSAR, EDNA ERNESTINE (KRAMER) (1902–1984)

U.S. mathematician. Born 11 May 1902 to Sabine (Elowitch) and Joseph Kramer. Two siblings. Married Benedict Taxier Lassar. Educated Wadleigh High School, Manhattan; Hunter College (B.A. summa cum laude); Columbia University (M.A., 1925; Ph.D., 1930); New York University (postgraduate work, 1939–1940; 1965–1969); University of Chicago (postgraduate work, 1941). Professional experience: DeWitt Clinton High School, Bronx, N.Y., teacher (1922–1923); Wadleigh High School, teacher (1923–1929); New Jersey State Teachers College in Montclair, N.J., instructor (1929), assistant professor (1932). Thomas Jefferson High School, Brooklyn, N.Y., teacher (1933–1956); Brooklyn College, graduate instructor of methods courses (1935–1938); Brooklyn Polytechnic, instructor through professor (1948–1965). Died 9 July 1984 in Manhattan.

Antisemitism and the Depression affected the course of Edna Kramer's career. Her parents were Jewish immigrants from Rima-Sombad, Austria-Hungary, and encouraged their three children's intellectual interests. Her younger sister, Martha, and brother, Herbert, were all prize-winning students, all were elected to Phi Beta Kappa, and all became teachers. Kramer was somewhat of a prodigy, and when she arrived at Wadleigh High School in Manhattan, her high school mathematics teacher John A. Swenson encouraged her mathematical interests. Therefore when she went to Hunter College, she majored in mathematics. Her mathematical interests continued, and she earned master's and doctoral degrees.

Her first teaching jobs were in high schools; at her second school, Wadleigh High School, her former teacher, Swenson, arranged her teaching schedule so that she could continue her work at Columbia. After she received her degree, Swenson again helped her by recommending her strongly for a job as instructor of mathematics at the New Jersey State College in Montclair. She acquired the rank of assistant professor in 1932. The Depression was deepening and college positions were scarce, particularly for married women and Jews. Being both, Kramer was concerned about the stability of her job, especially because of the hostility of the prospective chairman of Montclair College. Therefore, she resigned her job and went back to public school teaching. While teaching at Thomas Jefferson High School, she also taught courses in the graduate division of Brooklyn College and at Columbia as a statistical consultant to the university's Division of War Research. From 1954 Kramer was affiliated with the New York Polytechnic Institute (then Brooklyn Polytechnic), where she began as adjunct instructor in 1948 and rose to adjunct professor in 1953. Kramer retired from the New York City school system in 1956 and from New York Polytechnic Institute in 1965. Kramer suffered from Parkinson's disease for the last ten years of her life and died of pneumonia at her home in Manhattan in 1984.

Kramer's dissertation, discussing the geometric properties of polygenic functions, extended the work of her thesis advisor, Edward Kasner, Georg Scheffers, and Edmond Laguerre. After this important theoretical work, she left pure mathematics and turned toward pedagogy and the history of mathematics. Her earliest pedagogical publication reflects the influence of her mentor John A. Swenson, and shows how prospective teachers can learn both content and method simultaneously. She recommends bringing appropriate college-level textbooks to the high school level and stresses the importance of concepts over memorization of facts. Some of her research was in statistics. She had taught educational statistics at Montclair College and from this knowledge she published her only textbook. This book described statistics in such a way that nonmathematicians could understand it. As a mathematician interested in history, she included many historical personages in her publications. She was especially interested in women in mathematics and wrote articles in *Scripta Mathe-*

matica describing the lives of women mathematicians. She also wrote the lives of several women in science for the *Dictionary of Scientific Biography.* Kramer's decision to teach in the public schools changed the direction of her research. When she first got her doctorate she had intended to do research in pure mathematics; however, after she had decided to make teaching her career, she modified her research to consider topics of importance to high school teaching. JH/MBO

PRIMARY SOURCES

Lassar, Edna Ernestine Kramer. "Polygenic Functions of the Dual Variable w = u + jv." *American Journal of Mathematics* 52 (1930): 370–376. Part 1 of Kramer's doctoral dissertation.

———. *Polygenic Functions of the Dual Variable w and the Laguerre Group.* Hamburg: Lütcke and Wulff, 1930. Part II of Kramer's doctoral dissertation combined with a reprint of Part I.

———. "Some Methods in Professionalized Subject Matter Courses in Mathematics for Teachers College." *Mathematics Teacher* 24 (1931): 429–435.

———. *A First Course in Educational Statistics.* New York: John Wiley and Sons, 1935.

———. "Six More Female Mathematicians." *Scripta Mathematica* 23 (1957): 83–95.

SECONDARY SOURCES

Lipsey, Sally Irene. "Edna Ernestine Kramer Lassar (1902–1984)." *Publishers Weekly* 226 (27 July 1984): 78. Obituary notice.

Robinson, D. "Women in Math Count for More Today." *Eugene* (Oregon) *Register-Guard,* 7 July 1963. Reprinted in Grinstein and Campbell. Includes bibliography.

LASTHENIA OF MANTINEA (5th century B.C.E.)

Greek student of philosophy. Born in Mantinea. Educated Plato's Academy.

Next to nothing is known about the life and work of Lasthenia. Until recently it was assumed that Lasthenia of Arcadia, mentioned by Iamblichus among the most famous of the female Pythagoreans, was identical with the Lasthenia of Mantinea, who, along with Axiothea, purportedly was a student of Plato. Although evidence from the available sources is inconclusive, it now appears likely that they were two different individuals. Lasthenia is remembered for her near uniqueness as a female student of Plato and Speusippus, rather than for any known intellectual accomplishments. If she did make any personal contributions to science or mathematics, the records are not available. JH/MBO

SECONDARY SOURCES

Athenaeus. *The Deipnosophists.* London: Bohn, 1907. Mentions the relationship between Speusippus and Lasthenia at 7.279e.

Diogenes Laertius. *Lives of Eminent Philosophers.* Trans. R. D. Hicks. 2 vols. Cambridge, Mass.: Harvard University Press, 1980. Reference to Lasthenia 3:46.

Jamblichus of Chalcis (Iamblichus). *De vita Pythagorica liber.* Ed. Ludwig Deubner. Leipzig: Teubner, 1937.

STANDARD SOURCES

Ogilvie 1986; Pauly-Wissowa.

LATHAM, VIDA ANNETTE (fl. 1887)

British/U.S. microscopist. Born in Lancashire, England. Educated University of London (M.Sc., 1889); University of Michigan (D.D.S., 1892); Northwestern University (M.D., 1895); Paris; Berlin; Hamburg. Professional experience: University of Michigan, demonstrator in pathological bacteriology and comparative dental anatomy and curator museum (1889–1892); Northwestern University, assistant secretary and registrar, medical school lecturer in stomatology and dental surgery (1892–1896); College of Pharmacy, lecturer (1892); College of Physicians and Surgeons, Chicago, extension lecturer (1893); Women's and Children's Hospital, oral surgeon (1892–1897); American Dental College, faculty member (1892–1898); College of Physicians and Surgeons, Milwaukee (1902); Edgewater Hospital, attending physician (1929–1931); practicing physician and microanalyst (from 1929). Honors and memberships: Stomatological Society; American Medical Association, Fellow; American Dental Association; Microscopical Society (vice-president and public health secretary, 1905); Society of Parasitology; Illinois Microscopic Society (secretary, 1893; president, 1932); New York Academy; Women's Medical Club, Chicago (vice-president, 1931; president, 1933); Women's Dental Association (past president); Royal Microscopical Society, Fellow; Manchester Microscopic Society, corresponding member; Quekett Microscopic Club, London, Fellow; Victoria Microscopical Society, Australia; and the International Stomatological Association.

Vida Annette Latham was both a dentist and a medical doctor. Born in London where she earned a master of science from the University of London, she moved to the United States, where she received medical degrees. She edited or coedited numerous publications, including the dental research section of the *Medical Woman's Journal,* the *Polk Dental Directory* (associate editor), and the *Standard Medical Dictionary.* For the Century of Progress Exposition in Chicago in 1933, she worked on the chemical exhibits. This very versatile woman published extensively and was an active member of an incredible number of organizations. Latham's dental research was on oral surgery, operative dentistry, and the

nerve supply of the pulp, teeth, and jaw. She worked on the pathology of tumors of the palate, cysts of the oral cavity, lead poisoning and fractures of the face. In addition she did research on aniline dyes and tissue reaction, tests for diabetic blood, the vasomotor system in teeth, and neoplasm in the pulp of teeth.   JH/MBO

PRIMARY SOURCES

Latham, Vida A. "Mounting Mosses." *Microscopical Society Journal* (1887): 843–844.

———. "Short Notes in Practical Biology: Amoeba." *American Microscopical Journal* 10 (1889): 151–155.

———. "The Use of Stains Especially with Reference to Their Value for Differential Diagnosis." *Proceedings American Society Microscopy* 13 (1891): 95–100.

———. "Reaction of Diabetic Blood to Some of the Aniline Dyes." *Transactions American Microscopical Society* 81 (1900): 31–40.

STANDARD SOURCES

AMS 5–8, B 9.

LATIMER, CAROLINE WORMELEY (1860–1930?)

U.S. physiologist. Born 28 March 1860 in Baltimore, Md. Educated Woman's Medical College of Baltimore (1890); Bryn Mawr (A.B.; A.M., 1896). Professional experience: Goucher College, instructor in biology (1897–1898); Maryland Medical and Chirurgical Faculty (1899?–1906?); Appleton's Medical Dictionary, associate editor (from 1915). Died ca. 1930.

Physiologist Caroline Latimer first trained in medicine in the 1880s, at the Woman's Medical College of Baltimore, a school that did not then require a bachelor's degree for matriculation. Feeling that her training in science was inadequate, she chose to study for both an undergraduate and graduate degree in biology at Bryn Mawr, publishing two articles on physiology in the year she completed her master's degree, one on the effect of muscle fatigue on rigor mortis in cold-blooded animals and the other on the salivary glands. She taught biology at Goucher and physiology at the Maryland Medical and Chirurgical Faculty. During this period, she wrote a number of popular books, including one on practical physiology for women and girls. In 1915, she became the associate editor of *Appleton's Medical Dictionary.*
                                                    JH/MBO

PRIMARY SOURCES

Latimer, Caroline Wormeley. "On the Modification of Rigor Mortis Resulting from Previous Fatigue of the Muscle in

Cold Blooded Animals." *American Journal of Physiology* 2 (1897): 29–46.

———. With Joseph W. Warren. "On the Presence of the Amylolytic Ferment and Its Synogen in the Salivary Glands." *Journal of Experimental Medicine* 2 (1897).

———. *Girl and Woman: A Book for Mothers and Daughters.* New York and London: D. Appleton & Co., 1910.

———, ed. *Appleton's Medical Dictionary.* New York: D. Appleton & Co., 1915.

STANDARD SOURCES
AMS 1–2, Bailey.

LAUBENSTEIN, LINDA (1947–1992)

U.S. physician noted for AIDS research. Born Boston, Mass., 21 May 1947 to Priscilla and George Laubenstein. Educated Barnard College (A.B.); New York University Medical School. Professional experience: New York University Medical Center, clinical professor; private physician (1982?–1992). Concurrent experience: first medical conference on AIDS, New York City, organizer (1983); Karposi's Sarcoma Research Fund, cofounder (1983); Multitasking (AIDS organization), founded with Jeffrey R. Greene (1989). Died 11 August 1992 in Chatham, Mass.

Linda Laubenstein became noted for her pioneer work in AIDS detection and treatment. She grew up in Rhode Island. In spite of the fact that she had polio as a child of five, which left her paraplegic, she went on to study at Barnard College, Columbia University. From there, in spite of asthma and being confined to a wheelchair, she went to medical school at the New York University School of Medicine, qualifying herself as a hematologist and oncologist. Working as a private physician in New York City, she was struck by the sudden rise in cases of the rare cancer Karposi's sarcoma among well-nourished young gay men whose immune systems had collapsed. In 1981, she coauthored the first paper on these patients, soon recognized as having symptoms of advanced AIDS at a period when AIDS sufferers could be numbered in the hundreds. One year later, she had treated sixty-two such cases of Karposi's sarcoma at a time when this represented one fourth of the then-known cases.

In 1983, Laubenstein organized the first national conference on AIDS at New York University with Alvin Friedman-Kien, with whom she had published her first cases. The same year she helped to found a research fund, Karposi's Sarcoma Research Fund to extend knowledge of this disease. She left the university to devote herself to the treatment of patients with AIDS, understanding that there was a need to establish a wide support system to those afflicted with this new and frightening disease. For this reason, she founded, with Jeffrey B. Greene (who later termed her "the ultimate AIDS physi-

cian"), Multitasking, a nonprofit organization that employed AIDS patients. After she called for the closing of gay bathhouses as focal areas of infection due to unsafe sex, she was criticized by militant gay groups. Nevertheless, the playwright Larry Kramer, an AIDS activist himself, saw in her the model for his very sympathetic character Dr. Emma Brookner in his Broadway play *The Normal Heart.* She died of undisclosed causes in 1992.   JH/MBO

PRIMARY SOURCES
Laubenstein, Linda J. With Alvin Friedman-Kien. *AIDS: The Epidemic of Kaposi's Sarcoma and Opportunistic Infections.* New York: Masson, 1984.

———. Papers, 1947–1993 (inclusive). Schlesinger Library, Radcliffe College. Collection includes photographs; autobiographical essays; a diary, 1969; and biographical information, correspondence, writings, videotapes, and audiotapes.

SECONDARY SOURCES
Kramer, Larry. *The Normal Heart.* New York: Plume, 1985. Play on the topic of AIDS. The character Dr. Emma Brookner based on Linda Laubenstein.

STANDARD SOURCES
Annual Obituary 1992.

LAUGHLIN, EMMA ELIZA (1866–1962)

U.S. educator, botanist, and librarian. Born 27 August 1866 in Guernsey County, Ohio, to Margaret J. (Cowden) and John Wilson Laughlin. Nine siblings. Educated Barnesville High School (graduated 1884); Steubenville Seminary. Professional experience: Barnesville High School, teacher; Sumerton High School, teacher. Died 5 June 1962 in Barnesville, Ohio.

Emma Eliza Laughlin was the oldest of ten children. She did not have a college degree or a position in a university, but spent most of her life as a botany teacher and as founder of the Barnesville Public Library. She was an amateur botanical collector and, without much formal training, published numerous papers on her plants. Her botanical collecting began as a project for her class. They collected many plants from Belmont County, which she sent to Professor William Kellerman for the State Herbarium at The Ohio State University. She began acquiring plants in 1904 and continued until 1942. Her large personal herbarium was given to Ohio State by one of her brothers. She published on the rare plants of Barnesville (1910) and the mustards of Ohio (1917). She was a founder of the Barnesville Public Library and served until 1948 with very little remuneration.

Her life had an important impact on the people of her small Ohio town, as well as on a larger population, because of the deposition of her herbarium at The Ohio State University.   JH/MBO

PRIMARY SOURCES
Laughlin, Emma Eliza. "Twenty-five Rare Plants at Barnesville, Ohio." *Ohio Naturalist* 10 (1910): 160–162.
———. "The Brassicaceae of Ohio." *Ohio Journal of Science* 17 (1917): 308–331.

SECONDARY SOURCES
Stuckey, Ronald L. "Emma Eliza Laughlin." Unpublished notes. From the collection of Ronald L. Stuckey.

STANDARD SOURCES
Stuckey.

LAURIE, CHARLOTTE LOUISA (d. 1933)

British botanist, teacher, and writer of botanical textbooks. Born in West Indies. Professional experience: Cheltenham Ladies College, teacher of botany (1880–1910). Died 1933.

Little is known about the life and education of the botanist and teacher Charlotte Louisa Laurie. She taught botany for thirty years at the Cheltenham Ladies College and served as secretary of the Cheltenham Science Society. Between 1903 and 1910 she published three textbooks on botany. She was mentioned in the *Flora of Gloucestershire* as a contributor.

                                    JH/MBO

PRIMARY SOURCES
Laurie, Charlotte Louisa. *Flowering Plants.* London: Allman and Son, 1903.
———. *Introduction to Elementary Botany.* London: Allman and Son, 1907.
———. *Textbook of Elementary Botany.* London: Allman and Son, 1910.

SECONDARY SOURCES
Riddlesdell, H. J. *Flora of Gloucestershire.* N.p., 1948. Laurie mentioned pages cxxxv–cxxxvi.

STANDARD SOURCES
Desmond.

LA VIGNE, ANNE DE (1684–?)

French student of natural philosophy. Born 1684 in Normandy. Father a physician. Death date unknown.

Anne de La Vigne was the daughter of a respected physician in Normandy. Better known for her poetry than for her sci-

ence, she was nevertheless interested in and knowledgeable about current developments in natural philosophy; she was particularly concerned with the work of Descartes and was representative of the coterie of informed women who were his disciples. She died when she was a very young woman.

                                    JH/MBO

STANDARD SOURCES
NBG, vol. 29.

LAVOISIER, MARIE ANNE PIERRETTE PAULZE (1758–1836)

French illustrator, editor, and assistant to chemist Antoine Laurent Lavoisier. Born 1758 to Claudine (Thoynet) and Jacques Paulze. Educated in a convent. Married (1) Antoine Laurent Lavoisier (he died in 1794); (2) Count Rumford. Died 1836 in Paris.

Marie Paulze's father, Jacques, a parliamentary lawyer and financier, was at one time the director of the French East India Company. He became a member of the Ferme Générale, a private consortium that collected taxes for the government. His wife was the niece of the Abbé Terray, who became France's controller general of finance in 1771. Paulze was educated in a convent, remaining there until 1771, when, at the age of thirteen, she was married to the twenty-eight-year-old Antoine Laurent Lavoisier (1743–1794), who had already achieved fame as a chemist and had been elected to the Academy of Sciences in 1768. The Lavoisiers had no children.

Both intelligent and interested in science, Marie Lavoisier quickly became involved in her husband's scientific pursuits. During the early years of their marriage, their home became a gathering place for members of the French intellectual community. When the revolution's fury overtook those who had held power in the days of the Old Regime, Lavoisier, who, like Marie's father, had been a member of the Ferme Générale, was especially vulnerable. He was arrested and imprisoned, and his property confiscated. During his imprisonment, Marie Lavoisier worked tirelessly but futilely to obtain her husband's release. Antoine Lavoisier was executed on 8 May 1794, during the last days of the Reign of Terror; Marie Lavoisier's father and many of her friends were also victims. Because certain incriminating documents had been found during a search of the Lavoisiers' home, Marie too was arrested, but she was released after a short period. With the execution of Robespierre in July 1794, the most violent of the revolutionary excesses came to an end. Eventually most of Lavoisier's confiscated property was returned to his widow.

In 1792 Lavoisier had begun work on his memoirs. At the time of his death only two volumes and part of a third, out of a projected eight, were completed. Lavoisier edited the finished portions and had them privately printed in 1805. As life in Paris became normalized under the directory and then Napoleon, Lavoisier again hosted a salon frequented by scientific leaders. Among her guests was the physicist Sir Benjamin Thompson, Count Rumford (1753–1814), whom she married in 1805. After the marriage, she insisted on being called the Countess Lavoisier-Rumford. However, the success of her first marriage to a scientist was not repeated, and after four years the mutually dissatisfied couple separated. Lavoisier died in Paris at the age of seventy-six.

Because Lavoisier's scientific work was so thoroughly interwoven with that of her husband, it is difficult to assess its originality. Nevertheless, certain achievements can be ascribed to her. Marie's artistic talent was especially useful to Lavoisier. She had learned to paint under the direction of Jacques Louis David and used her skill to make sketches of experiments and experimental apparatus. She drew the diagrams for Antoine Lavoisier's treatise *The Elements of Chemistry* (1789). Her husband's laboratory notebooks also included her contributions: numerous entries written by Marie Lavoisier are scattered throughout the books. Marie Lavoisier further contributed to science through her translations of English scientific works into French. Her translation of Richard Kirwan's 1787 *Essay on Phlogiston,* with a commentary by Antoine Lavoisier and his associates, was of particular significance. Through her drawings, translations, interpretations of notes, and skillful editing of Lavoisier's memoirs, she made some important additions to the body of scientific knowledge. Although there are indications that she made some theoretical contributions, the evidence is still uncertain.   MBO

PRIMARY SOURCES
Kirwan, Richard. *Essay on Phlogiston (Essai sur le phlogistique).* Trans. and ed. Marie Lavoisier. Paris: Rue et hôtel Serpente, 1788.
———. "Strength of Acids and the Proportion of Ingredients in Neutral Salts." *Annales de chimie* 14 (1792): 152, 211, 238–286.
Lavoisier, Antoine Laurent. *Traité élèmentaire de chimie.* Paris, 1789. Marie Lavoisier produced thirteen copperplate illustrations for this book.
———. *Mémoires de chimie.* Ed. Marie Lavoisier. Paris, 1805.

SECONDARY SOURCES
Aykroyd, W. R. *Three Philosophers.* Westport, Conn.: Greenwood Press, 1970. Concerns the lives of Lavoisier, Priestley, and Cavendish. Contains information on Marie.
Brody, Judit. "Behind Every Great Scientist—Madame Lavoisier Was Not Just the Wife of the Famous Chemist." *New Scientist* 116 (1987): 19–21. Discusses Marie Lavoisier's

roles as translator, collaborator, illustrator-engraver, and salon hostess. Continues with her life after Lavoisier's execution and her short marriage to Benjamin Thompson, Count Rumford.
Duveen, Denis I. "Madame Lavoisier." *Chymia: Annual Studies in the History of Chemistry* 4 (1953): 13–29. Brings to light previously ignored facts regarding Marie Lavoisier as a competent and contributing scientist in her own right.
McKie, Douglas. *Antoine Lavoisier: Scientist, Economist, Social Reformer.* London: Constable, 1952. Marie Lavoisier discussed on pages 67–71, 108, 138–139, 142, 162–163, 175, 184, 290–291, 298–299, 310, 313–320, and 322–326.
Rayner-Canham, G. W., and H. Frenette. "Some French Women Chemists." *Education in Chemistry* 22 (1985): 176–178.
Scheluer, Lucien. "Deux lettres inedité." In *Revue d'Histoire des Sciences* 38 (1985): 121–130.
Smeaton, William A. "Madame Lavoisier, P. S. and E. I. DuPont de Nemours and the Publication of Lavoisier's Memoires de Chemie." *Ambix: Journal of the Society for the History of Alchemy and Chemistry* 36 (1989): 22–30. Acknowledges the extensive help that Antoine Lavoisier received from his wife.
———. "Monsieur and Madame Lavoisier in 1798: The Chemical Revolution and the French Revolution." *Ambix: Journal of the Society for the History of Alchemy and Chemistry* 36 (1989): 1–4.

STANDARD SOURCES
DSB (under A. Lavoisier); Grinstein 1993; Ogilvie 1986.

LAW, ANNIE (d. 1889)
U.S. conchologist. Born in Carlisle, England. Father, John Law. Two siblings. Died in 1889.

Annie Law, the eldest of three children, was born in England but emigrated with her family to Tennessee about 1851. After spending much of her life in that area, she moved to California in 1874. Law collected mollusks in the mountains of Tennessee and North Carolina. Although she neither described new species nor wrote articles, she contributed to the field of conchology by providing material for the publications of others. Her work drew attention to a rich molluscan fauna that had previously been unknown; she discovered eleven new species and one new genus.   JH/MBO

SECONDARY SOURCES
"Law, Annie." *American Journal of Science.* 3d. ser. 37 (1889): 422. Obituary notice.

LAWDER, MARGARET (1900–1983)

Irish/South African botanist. Born 1900 in Ireland. Went to the Cape, South Africa, 1922. Professional experience: plant collector for National Botanic Gardens, South Africa. Died in South Africa, 1983.

Margaret Lawder was born and raised in Ireland. She left for the Cape of Good Hope in South Africa when she was twenty-two. There she began to collect plants for the National Botanic Gardens and to cultivate plants for conservation. She died at the age of eighty-three.   JH/MBO

SECONDARY SOURCES
"Margaret Lawder." *Veld and Flora* 69, no. 3 (1983): 126. Includes portrait. Obituary notice.

STANDARD SOURCES
Desmond.

LAWRENCE, BARBARA (1909–   )

U.S. zoologist and mammalogist. Born 30 July 1909 in Boston, Mass., to Theodora (Eldredge) and Harris Hooper Lawrence. Married William Edward Schevill (23 December 1938). Two children. Educated Vassar (B.A., 1931). Professional experience: Harvard University Museum of Comparative Zoology, staff (from 1931); associate and acting curator of mammals (1942–1952); curator of mammals (1952–1975?).

Barbara Lawrence was born in Boston and went to Vassar College. After she received her bachelor's degree she joined the staff of the Museum of Comparative Zoology at Harvard, where she began to do research in mammalian systematics, traveling to East Africa to study the howler monkey. Lawrence returned three years later as part of the expedition led by Glover Morrill Allen, who died a few years later. She married the scientist William Edward Schevill in the late 1930s and raised two children. In the late forties, the two scientists published a study of underwater communication by porpoises in *Science* and later the two did a study of the musculature of the porpoise. During World War II, she was appointed acting curator of mammals and then, by 1952, curator of mammals at the Concord Field Station of the museum.

In the 1950s, she formed part of the fifth Harvard expedition to study the mammals of Nyasaland and published on the results.   JH/MBO

PRIMARY SOURCES
Lawrence, Barbara. "Howler Monkeys of the Palliata Group." *Bulletin of the Museum of Comparative Zoology, Harvard College* 75, no. 8 (1933): 315–354.

———. With Glover Morrill Allen. "Scientific Results of an Expedition to Rain Forest Regions in Eastern Africa." *Bulletin of the Museum of Comparative Zoology, Harvard College* 79, no. 3 (1936): 31–126.

———. With William Edward Schevill. "Underwater Listening to the White Porpoise (*Delphinapterus leucas*)." *Science* 109 (1949): 143.

———. With Arthur Loveridge. "Mammals from Nyasaland and Tete, with Notes on the Genus Otomys." *Bulletin of the Museum of Comparative Zoology, at Harvard College* 110, no. 1 (1953): 1–80. Zoological results of a fifth expedition to East Africa.

———. "The Functional Anatomy of the Delphinid Nose." *Bulletin of the Museum of Comparative Zoology, Harvard College* 114, no. 4 (1956): 104–151. Thirty pages of plates.

———. With William Edward Schevill. "Gular Musculature in Delphinids." *Bulletin of the Museum of Comparative Zoology, Harvard College* 135, no. 1 (1965): 1–65. On dolphin musculature.

———. With Charles Pierson Lyman. *List of Mammals of Eastern Massachusetts.* Bedford, Mass.: Concord Field Station, Museum of Comparative Zoology, Harvard University, 1974. Guide to resources, Concord Field Station, no. 7.

STANDARD SOURCES
AMS 8, P&B 12–13; Debus.

LAWRENCE, PENELOPE (1856–1932)

British scientist and educator. Born 1876 to Charlotte (Bailey) and Philip Henry Lawrence. Educated Kohler's Institute in Gotha (Froebel Certificate, 1873); Newnham College, Cambridge (Natural Science Tripos, 1878). Professional experience: Newnham College, demonstrator (1879–1881); Tavistock Place, principal of the kindergarten college (later the Maria Grey Training College) (1881–1883); Fearegg school and Wimbledon High School, teacher (1883–1897); Roedean School, Brighton, founder and first headmistress (1897–1925). Died 3 July 1932.

Lawrence's father, Philip Henry Lawrence, belonged to an old Nonconformist family, and was descended from the Reverend Philip Henry, one of the clergy who left the established church on the passing of the Act of Uniformity in 1662. Philip Henry and his brother, Tertius, lost their parents when they were children and were raised by two maiden aunts who had a school for girls near Liverpool. They were friends of MARIA EDGEWORTH, and their upbringing probably influenced not only the boys but also their two daughters, Penelope and Susan. Penelope was raised by a stepmother, for her own mother died when Penelope was an infant. Her stepfamily was a loving one and she got along well with her sisters, Dorothy and Millicent.

Although Penelope Lawrence passed the Natural Science Tripos and was a demonstrator at Newnham for several years, her major importance was in founding an important girls' school, based on the idea that girls should have the same opportunities that their brothers had enjoyed for so long.

Lawrence was the third Newnham student to pass the Tripos. Once she had been appointed demonstrator, she had the responsibility of caring for the new chemical laboratory in the garden of the Old Hall. Since women could not use the Cambridge University laboratory facilities, they were forced to construct their own. Thus, what is now known as "The Old Laboratory" (now a structure for the performing arts) was then the "new" laboratory. Since the womens' college, Girton, had its own chemical laboratory, its students did not use this facility for chemistry. However, it soon served for practical work in biology, zoology, and physiology for both colleges. Material for dissection, and so on, was sent to Newnham from the men's laboratories after each lecture. Lawrence was known as an effective teacher.

Lawrence left Cambridge in 1881 and was principal of the kindergarten college in Tavistock Place for two years and taught at other schools for several years before she founded Roedean with her sisters. As headmistress, Lawrence's personality had a great impact on her students. One of her students recalled a current story that "the Misses Lawrence always vaulted over gates instead of opening them, or that we all played football in knickerbockers before breakfast, an incredible notion in the nineties!" (Gaskell). The same student noted that Lawrence's contention that games and hard work made for successful students was born out.   JH/MBO

SECONDARY SOURCES
Newnham Roll (Gaskell, C. S. "Penelope Lawrence.").
Newnham Roll (Sharpe, Julia. "Penelope Lawrence.").

LAWRENSON, ALICE LOUISA (d. 1900)
Irish botanical writer and gardener. Regular contributor to Gardener's Chronicle *and other journals. Died 14 March 1900 in Killiney, County Dublin.*

Alice Louisa Lawrenson was an Irish gardener who contributed articles on flower gardens under the pseudonym St. Brigid to the important journal *Gardener's Chronicle* and to *Garden.* She was a friend of Frederick W. Burbidge, the curator of the Trinity College garden, and himself a regular contributor to the journal *Garden* under the name of Veronica. An anemone variety (*Anemone coronaria* "St. Brigid") was named in honor of Lawrenson.   JH/MBO

SECONDARY SOURCES
"Alice Louisa Lawrenson" *Gardener's Chronicle* 1 (1900): 189.
Nelson, E. C. *Irish Flower Gardens* 1984, 150–151.
Walsh, W. and E. C. Nelson. *Irish Florilegium,* vol. 2. New York: Thames and Hudson, 1987. Laurenson mentioned on 14, 134, 136.

STANDARD SOURCES
Desmond.

LAWTON, ELVA (1896–1993)
U.S. botanist and bryologist. Born 3 April 1896 in West Middleton, Pa. Father, Ira Lawton. Educated: University of Pittsburgh (B.A., 1923; M.A., 1925); University of Michigan (Ph.D., 1932). Professional experience: Pennsylvania Public Schools, elementary school teacher (1915–1919); Crafton (Pa.) High School, teacher (1923–1925); University of Michigan, department of botany, laboratory assistant, Whittier Research Fellow (1925–1928); Hunter College, biology department, instructor (1928–1932), assistant professor through associate professor (1932–1959); University of Washington Herbarium, research associate and curator of bryophytes (1959–1979), lecturer on bryophytes (1959–1980). Field research: Cold Spring Harbor (1928–1932); Michigan Biological Station Summer Research (1949); University of Iowa, Lakeside Laboratory (summers, 1950–1953). Honors and memberships: Torrey Botanical Club (officer, 1947–1954; president, 1955). Commemorated by Rhacometrium lawtonae *Ireland and* Bryolawtonia. *Died in Seattle, Wash., 3 February 1993.*

Elva Lawton was an internationally recognized botanist and bryologist, teacher, taxonomist, and field biologist. She was born in West Middletown, Pennsylvania, and went to local schools. After graduating from high school in Washington, Pennsylvania, she followed the pattern of a number of other women from her state, teaching in rural elementary schools before she began her undergraduate education. When she was about twenty-three, she went to the University of Pittsburgh, obtaining first her bachelor's and then her master's in biology, becoming fascinated by the "alternation of generations" in the reproduction of nonvascular plants. For two years while pursuing her master's degree, she returned to teach biology and Latin at the high school level. Her master's thesis was on fern identification, and she continued her interest in ferns at the doctoral level when she went to the University of Michigan to continue her education. There she worked as laboratory assistant and was awarded a Whittier research fellowship for three years, working under the direction of Carl LaRue. While finishing her dissertation research, Lawton began to teach as an instructor at Hunter College in 1928. Four years later, she completed her dissertation on regeneration and induced polyploidy in ferns, published the same year in the *Journal of Botany*. She was made assistant and then associate professor at Hunter College, where she remained for about thirty-one years. She began to make a name for herself, working in the summers at Cold Spring Harbor, the University of Michigan Biological Station, and the Iowa Lakeside Laboratory, making good use of the New York Botanical Garden, and publishing regularly in the *Bulletin* of the Torrey Botanical Club, of which she was an active member. By the forties, she was an officer and she was elected president of the botanical society in 1955.

In the late fifties, Lawton was invited to study unidentified mosses from the western states at the University of Washington herbarium. Lawton and her colleague Grace Howard made an important field trip to Nevada to collect bryophytes and mosses, supported by a Washington University research grant.

Now almost sixty, Lawton decided to leave Hunter College and move to the Washington University Herbarium in order to work with the bryologist Theodore C. Frye, at his urging. Encouraged as well by the chair of the botany department, C. L. Hitchcock, she accepted the position of research associate and curator of bryophytes.

Between 1962 and 1971, Lawton regularly received grants from the National Science Foundation to study full time the bryophytes of the western states. At the end of this period, she published what she considered her crowning achievement, *Moss Flora of the Western States*, published by the Hattori Botanical Laboratory in Japan as part of its twenty-fifth anniversary. Lawton also regularly taught bryology at the University of Washington during the sixties and seventies, and supervised one graduate dissertation. She continued to be a presence at the herbarium until she was almost ninety. At ninety-five she went into a retirement home, and died little over a year later.   JH/MBO

PRIMARY SOURCES

Lawton, Elva, "Regeneration and Induced Polyploidy in Ferns." Ph.D. diss., University of Michigan, 1932. Papers from the Department of Botany of the University of Michigan no. 365. Reprinted from the *American Journal of Botany*, 19, no. 4 (April 1932): 303–333.

———. "Regeneration and Induced Polyploidy in *Osmunda regalis* and *Cystopteris fragilis*." *American Journal of Botany* 23 (1936): 107–114.

———. "A Revision of the Genus *Lescuraea* in Europe and North America." *Bulletin of the Torrey Botanical Club* 84 (1957): 281–307; 337–355.

———. "Mosses of Nevada." *The Bryologist* 61 (1958): 314–334.

———. *Moss Flora of the Pacific Northwest*. Nichinan, Miyazaki, Japan: The Hattori Botanical Laboratory, 1971. Suppl. no. 1, *Journal of the Hattori Botanical Laboratory*.

———. "Keys for the Identification of the Mosses of the Pacific Northwest." Nichinan, Miyazaki, Japan: The Hattori Botanical Laboratory, 1971. Suppl. no. 2, *Journal of the Hattori Botanical Laboratory*.

SECONDARY SOURCES

Denton, Melinda F. "Elva Lawton (1896–1993): Bryologist and Teacher." *Bulletin Torrey Botanical Club* 121 (1994): 84–86.

STANDARD SOURCES

AMS 6–8, B 9, P&B 10–12.

LAZARUS, HILDA MARY (1890–?)

Indian physician. Born 1890 in South India. Father school principal in Visakhapatnam. Eleven siblings. Educated London Mission High School and College, Visakhapatnam; Presidency College, Madras (A.B., 1912?); Andhra Medical College?, Visakhapatnam (M.D., 1917). Professional experience: Women's Medical Service, various posts (1917–1943), chief medical officer (1943–1947); Lady Hardinge Medical College Hospital, New Delhi, assistant in obstetrics and gynecology (1917); Dufferin Hospital, Calcutta, resident (1917–1918); Surat Hospital, Bombay, physician (1918–1922); Visakhapatnam Hospital, physician (1922–1927; 1933); Lady Willingdon Medical School, Madras, physician (1928–1932; 1935–1940), principal, superintendent of hospital (1940–1943); Christian Medical College, Vellore, principal (1947–1950); Andrha Medical College, Institute of Obstetrics and Gynecology, physician. Honors: Visakhapatnam, honorary director and professor (1950–1962). Legislative Council, Visakhapatnam (1962–1975). Death date unknown.

Born and brought up in Visakhapatnam, South India, Hilda Mary Lazarus was next to the youngest of twelve children, only nine of whom survived into adulthood. Her grandfather was a Brahmin who had converted to Christianity, to the anger of his community. Both her mother and her father had strong beliefs about education and had received excellent educations. One of her mother's sisters was a director of education in the principality of Madras and another had trained in medicine in Edinburgh. Her father was principal of the London Mission High School, which he had redesigned using the Montessori system of education. As a child, she was an excellent student, although she was always one of the few girls in her classes.

Lazarus went to a local college to prepare herself for medicine, but also decided to take a bachelor's degree in biology and botany should she decide to teach science. Her excellent performance in medical school meant that she was chosen to be appointed to the Women's Medical Service in India. As a member of the medical service, she was sent wherever she was needed for varying lengths of time, from New Delhi to

Calcutta and from there to Surat. In these hospitals, she found she had to expand her three languages to seven, including English and all the major Indian languages to deal with patients, midwives, and hospital staff of various backgrounds.

In many of the hospitals to which she was assigned, Lazarus was required to train midwives. In some cases, she found the caste system a hindrance in treating untouchables, and was able to obtain the cooperation of her staff only by setting an example. She also managed to expand teaching of nurses and midwives in regional languages, which markedly increased their competence, and introduced training of mothers in domestic hygiene and child-rearing skills in maternity and child-welfare centers with the cooperation of local governmental bodies.

For some years after she had worked throughout India, Lazarus was able to obtain a posting in her own city, at the Visakhapatnam hospital. There she remained until transferred to Madras, where she taught at Lady Hardinge Medical College, rising to principal by 1940. She also supervised the attached hospital. Three years later, she was made chief medical officer of the Medical Women's Service of India, where she remained until her retirement from the service in 1947.

At this point, Lazarus chose to become principal of the Christian Medical College in Vellore and then superintendent until she retired formally at the age of sixty. Her retirement did not affect her active work in medical education, since she took a position as professor of the Andrha Medical College in Visakhapatnam and honorary directory of the Institute of Obstetrics and Gynecology. She reorganized the institute, obtaining new clinical laboratories, library, lecture halls, living quarters and outpatient clinics for obstetrics and gynecology, as well as setting up an infertility clinic.

In her seventy-second year, Lazarus resigned, partly to give younger phsyicians a chance, but retained her tie to rural medicine until well past her eighty-fifth year by serving on the legislative council and sitting on the advisory staff of five hospitals.   K M

PRIMARY SOURCES
Lazarus, Hilda Mary. In Hellstedt, *Autobiographies.*

LEACH, MARY FRANCES (1858–1939)
U.S. chemist. Born 22 March 1858 in Payson, Ill. Educated: Mount Holyoke College (A.B., 1880); University of Michigan (B.S., 1893; fellow 1901–1905; Ph.D., 1903); University of Göttingen (postgraduate studies, 1897–1898); University of Zurich (postgraduate studies 1898–1900). Professional experience: Massachusetts public school teacher (1878–1879); Michigan public school teacher (1881–1885); Sedia(?), Mich., high school teacher

(1885–1889); Detroit, teacher (1889–1891); Mount Holyoke College, professor of chemistry (1893–1900); Western College of Women, assistant professor of hygiene (1906–1907), professor of chemistry and hygiene (1907–1921?). Died 1939.

Mary Frances Leach began her professional life like many American women who were born in the mid-nineteenth century, by teaching elementary school before she completed her undergraduate studies. She went on to Mount Holyoke College, but after obtaining her bachelor's degree, she moved to Michigan, where she taught elementary and then high school for ten years while she studied chemistry at the University of Michigan. When she completed her bachelor of science degree in chemistry, she returned to Mount Holyoke, where she taught chemistry for seven years while working on her doctorate at Michigan.

Again following the pattern of highly motivated American women scientists, Leach spent a period of postgraduate study in Germany, at the University of Göttingen, and then at the University of Zurich. Upon her return to the United States, she was appointed assistant professor of hygiene at Western College for Women, and then became professor of chemistry and hygiene by 1807. She remained in that position until her retirement.   J H / M B O

STANDARD SOURCES
AMS 1–6; Bailey.

LEACOCK, ELEANOR BURKE (1922–1987)
U.S. cultural anthropologist. Born 2 July 1922 in Weehawken, N.J., to Lilly Batterham and Kenneth Burke. Married (1) Richard Leacock, 27 December 1941 (divorced 1962), four children; (2) James Haughton, August 1966. Educated Barnard College (B.A., 1944); Columbia University (M.A., 1946; Ph.D., 1952). Professional positions: Cornell University Medical School, department of psychiatry, research assistant (1952–1955); Queen's College, lecturer (1955–1956); City College New York, lecturer (1956–1960); U.S. Department of Health, Education and Welfare, special consultant, behavioral sciences (1957–1958); Bank St. College of Education, faculty member (1958–1965); Washington Square College, lecturer (1960–1961); Polytechnic Institute, Brooklyn, associate professor of anthropology (1963–1967), professor (from 1967). Concurrent experience: research and publication on property relations among Eastern Canadian Indians; interracial neighborhoods; ethnicity and epidemiology of mental illness; anthropology. Honors and memberships: American Anthropological Association, Fellow; Ethnological Society, secretary-treasurer. Died 1987.

Eleanor Leacock made significant contributions on gender and society, ethnic factors in nutrition, and on epidemiology in mental illness. Born in the late twenties, she went to

Columbia University, studying first at Barnard, and then receiving her advanced degrees in anthropology at Columbia, even in the fifties an important training ground for women anthropologists. Although she studied an American Indian group for her doctorate, her later work was centered first on problems experienced by children of diverse ethnic background in the New York public schools, and later on women in colonial and developing societies.

Leacock married twice, first as an undergraduate to Richard Leacock, with whom she had four children, and next in her forties to James Haughton. By the time of her death in 1990, she was seen as a seminal figure in anthropological feminist scholarship. JH/MBO

PRIMARY SOURCES
Leacock, Eleanor Burke. "The Montagnais 'Hunting Territory' and the Fur Trade." *American Anthropologist* 56, no. 5 (1954): 50–59.

———. *Teaching and Learning in City Schools: A Comparative Study.* New York: Basic Books, 1969.

———. With Nancy Oestreich Lurie, eds. *North American Indians in Historical Perspective.* New York: Random House, 1971.

———. With Mona Etienne. *Women and Colonization: Anthropological Perspectives.* New York: Praeger, 1980.

———. With Leela Dube and Shirley Ardener. *Visibility and Power: Essays on Women in Society and Development.* Delhi and New York: Oxford University Press, 1986.

———. With Helen Icken Safen, eds. *Women's Work: Development and the Division of Labor by Gender.* South Hadley, Mass.: Bergin and Garvey, 1986.

SECONDARY SOURCES
American Anthropologist 92 (1990): 201–205. Obituary notice.

Sutton, Constance R., ed. *From Labrador to Samoa: The Theory and Practice of Eleanor Burke Leacock.* Arlington, Va.: Association for Feminist Anthropology/American Anthropological Association in Collaboration with the International Women's Anthropology Conference, 1993. These articles derive from presentations made at the 86th meeting of the American Anthropological Association, Chicago, 1987, and at the International Congress of Anthropological and Ethnological Sciences, held in Zagreb in 1988. Includes a bibliography of Eleanor Burke Leacock's published work (141–149).

STANDARD SOURCES
Debus.

LEAKEY, MARY DOUGLAS (NICOL) (1913–1996)

U.S. archeologist and anthropologist. Born 6 February 1913 in London to Cecilia Marion (Frere) and Erskine Edward Nicol. Married Louis Seymour Bazett Leakey, 1936 (d. 1972). Three sons. Educated private schools; University of Witwatersrand (D.Sc. with honors, 1968); University of Western Michigan (1980); University of Chicago (1981); Yale University (D.Sc., 1976); Oxford University (D.Litt., 1981). Professional experience: Early excavations in Kenya at the Olorgesailie and Rusinga Island in Lake Victoria sites (1937–1942); Olduvai Gorge Excavations, director. Honors and memberships: Geological Society of London, Prestwick Medal; National Geographic Society, Hubbard Medal; Society of Women Geographers, Gold Medal; Stockholm, Linnaeus Medal (1978); Geological Association, Stopes Medal (1980); Elizabeth Blackwell Award, Hobart and Smith College (1980); Royal Swedish Academy, honorary member; American Association for the Advancement of Science, Fellow. Died 10 December 1996.

Mary Leakey became interested in prehistory from childhood, when she visited prehistoric sites in southwestern France. She collected stone tools and visited the caves with paintings around Les Eyzies. She first met her future husband when she was illustrating his book, *Adam's Ancestors.* Mary was Louis's second wife. Shortly after they married, they left for Kenya, where she did ethnological and archeological research. She discovered *Proconsul africanus,* a fossil ape, in an island in Lake Victoria. This discovery brought the Leakeys to international attention and also brought them financial support. Mary Leakey worked at Olduvai Gorge in Tanzania from 1951. Beginning on a modest scale, the Leakeys expanded the scope of the excavation when they discovered the 1.75-million-year-old *Zinjanthropus* in 1959. Their funding increased when they found *Homo habilis* in 1960, a species contemporary with, but more advanced than *Zinjanthropus.* The description was published in 1964 amid considerable controversy. At Laetoli, thirty miles south of Olduvai, Mary discovered three trails of fossilized hominid footprints that demonstrated that human ancestors walked upright as long ago as 3.6 million years. Mary Leakey published numerous articles with Louis Leakey on their discoveries, while maintaining her own work on the ancient artifacts and art of the region. Many of the honors and awards listed for Mary Leakey were given to both Leakeys. JH/MBO

PRIMARY SOURCES
Leakey, Mary Douglas. With Walter Edwin Owen and L. S. B. Leakey. *Dimple-based Pottery from Central Kavirondo, Kenya Colony.* Nairobi, Kenya: Coryndon Memorial Museum, 1948. Cambridge: Cambridge University Press, 1948.

———. With L. S. B. Leakey. *Excavation in Beds I and II.* N.p., 1971.

———. *Olduvai Gorge: My Search for Early Man.* London: Collins, 1979. An account of her work with Leakey and others to find early fossil hominids.

———. *Africa's Vanishing Art: The Rock Paintings of Tanzania.* London: Hamish Hamilton/Rainbird, 1983.

———. *Disclosing the Past.* London: Weidenfeld and Nicolson, 1984. One of Mary Leakey's autobiographical accounts.

SECONDARY SOURCES
"Leakey, Mary Douglas, née Nicol." Chambers Harrap Ltd. 1993.

STANDARD SOURCES
Gacs; *Notable; WW in America,* vol. 136, 1984–1985.

LEAVITT, HENRIETTA SWAN (1868–1921)

U.S. astronomer. Born 4 July in Lancaster, Mass., to Henrietta (Kendrick) and George Leavitt. Six siblings. Never married. Educated public school, Cambridge, Mass.; Oberlin College (1885–1888); Society for the Collegiate Instruction of Women (later Radcliffe College) (1888–1892). Professional experience: staff member, Harvard Observatory (1902–1921). Died 12 December 1921 of cancer in Cambridge, Mass.

Henrietta Leavitt was one of seven children of a Congregationalist minister, who had a parish in Cambridge, Massachusetts, during most of Henrietta's childhood. She attended public school in Cambridge and, after the family moved to Cleveland, Ohio, studied at Oberlin College (1885–1888). Although her hearing was seriously impaired, this handicap did not impede her progress at school. In 1892, Leavitt completed her undergraduate education at Radcliffe College, then known as the Society for the Collegiate Instruction of Women.

Leavitt took a course in astronomy during her senior year at Radcliffe and developed an interest in the subject. After graduation, she took another course and then spent some time traveling before volunteering her services to the Harvard Observatory in 1895. Appointed to the permanent staff in 1902, she soon attained the position of chief of the photographic photometry department. She worked at the observatory until her death, of cancer, at age fifty-two.

Much of Leavitt's scientific work involved the accurate measurement of the brightnesses—and hence the magnitudes—of stars. During the first years of the century, visual photometry was superseded by photographic methods, because the photographic plate is more sensitive to light of certain wavelengths than the human eye. Edward Pickering, director of the Harvard Observatory, appointed Leavitt to execute his plan to establish a "north polar sequence" of magnitudes that would serve as a standard for the entire sky.

In 1913, the system of the north polar sequence was adopted by the International Committee on Photographic magnitudes for its projected astrographic map of the sky. Leavitt worked on this project until her death, at which time she had established sequences for 108 areas.

In the course of her observations, Leavitt made the important discovery that the fainter stars of a sequence were usually redder than the brighter stars. This phenomenon raised the question of whether the stars were actually more red or whether their light appeared red because of the effects of interstellar adsorption. Since Leavitt's discovery, photoelectric techniques have been developed that can distinguish between the two cases.

Leavitt's most important theoretical contribution was the establishment of the period-luminosity relation of the cepheid variable stars—stars that brighten and dim in a highly regular fashion. In her study of these stars, she noted that the longer the period of pulsation, the brighter the star. This relation was used by subsequent astronomers for determining the distances from the earth of similar stars within our own galaxy and in distant galaxies.   MBO

PRIMARY SOURCES
Leavitt, Henrietta. "Ten Variable Stars of the Algol Type." *Annals of the Harvard College Observatory* 60, no. 5 (1908): 109–146.

———. "1,777 Variables in the Magellanic Clouds." *Annals of the Harvard College Observatory* 60, no. 4 (1908): 87–108.

The records of astronomical work of Leavitt from 1912 to 1919 are held in the Harvard Archives for Harvard College Observatory under her name.

SECONDARY SOURCES
Krupp, E. C. "Astronomical Musings." *Griffith Observer* 39 (May 1975): 8–18. Includes information on Leavitt.

STANDARD SOURCES
DAB; Debus; *DSB;* Jones and Boyd; *NAW*(M); Ogilvie 1986; *Notable.*

LE BEAU, DÉSIRÉE (1907–1993)

Austro-Hungarian/U.S. chemist and inventor. Born 14 February 1907 in Teschen, Austria-Hungary (now Poland). Married Henry W. Meyer (1955). Educated University of Vienna (undergraduate degree); University of Graz, Austria (Ph.D., 1931). Professional experience: Austro-American Rubber Works, Vienna, researcher (1932–1935); Sociétè de Progrès Technique, consultant in Paris; Dewey and Alma Chemical Company, Massachusetts, research chemist (1936?–1940); MIT, Department of Chemical Engineering and Division of Industrial Cooperation, research associate (1940–1945); Midwest Rubber Reclaiming Company, Illinois

(1945–1950?); *Pennsylvania State College, Currie lecturer (from 1950). Died 1993.*

Born in Austria-Hungary, Désirée Le Beau earned an undergraduate degree from the University of Vienna and a doctorate in chemistry from the University of Graz, where she majored in chemistry and minored in physics and mathematics. She left Austria for Paris in 1935, and moved to the United States in 1936. In the United States, she first became a research chemist with a company in Massachusetts and then, during World War II, served as a research associate at MIT's department of chemical engineering. Le Beau was a colloid chemist who developed methods of reclaiming natural and synthetic rubbers. She mainly used old tires to produce new products. After the war, she was appointed director of research at the world's largest independent rubber reclaiming company, where she studied the structures of natural and synthetic rubbers and clays. She developed a tie pad for railroads using reclaimed rubber and patented this process. She held other patents for producing reclaimed rubber.

JH/MBO

PRIMARY SOURCES

Le Beau, Désirée. "Basic Reactions Occurring during Reclaiming of Rubber I." *Rubber Chemistry and Technology* 21 (1948): 895.

———. "Reclaiming Agents for Rubber: Solvent Naphtha I." *Rubber Age* (October 1950).

———. "Reclaiming of Elastomers." In *Colloid Chemistry*, vol. 7, ed. Jerome Alexander, 569–597. N.p.: Reinhold, 1950.

SECONDARY SOURCES

Society of Women Engineers Newsletter (June 1959): 1, 3.

STANDARD SOURCES

Notable (article by Karen Withem).

LEBEDEVA, NATALIIA IVANOVA (1894–1978)

Russian anthropologist and ethnographer. Born 19 July 1894 in Riazan' (Russia). Died 19 May 1978 in Riazan'.

Nataliia Lebedeva studied the material culture of East Slavic peoples. She was particularly interested in the spinning, weaving, and typology of the dress of Russians, Ukranians, and Belorussians. Her studies extended to an analysis of dwelling and work buildings of these ethnic groups. She was considered to be in the forefront of those using material culture as a source of information on the evolution of these people and their ethnic history. She worked extensively in the museums of Moscow and Raisan'.

JH/MBO

PRIMARY SOURCES

Lebedeva, Nataliia Ivanova. "Vostochnoslavianskii etnograficheskii sbornik: ocherki narodnoi material'noi kul'tury russkikh, ukraninisev i belorusov v XIX–nachale XX v." *Trudy Instituta etnografii AN SSSR* 31 (1956): 461–540.

———. With G. N. Maslova. "Ruskaiia krest'ianskaiia odeshda XIX—nache XX v." In *Russkie: Istoriko-Etnograficheskii atlas*, ed. P. I. Kushner, 193–267. Moscow, 1967.

SECONDARY SOURCES

Maslova, G. S., and M. N. Morosova, "Vydaiushciishia sovetski etnograf, N. I. Lebedeva." *Sovetskaia etnografiia* 6 (1979): 90–94.

STANDARD SOURCES

IDA (article by A. M. Reshetov).

LEBEDEVA, VERA PAVLOVNA (1881–1968)

Russian physician. Born 18 September 1881 in Nizhni-Novgorod. Father Pavel Livodonov. Six siblings. Married I. Lebedev-Polianskii. Educated at local gymnasium; Women's Medical Institute. Professional experience: Geneva, obstetrics and gynecology clinic, physician; Central Institute for Maternity and Child Protection, director; People's Commissariat of Social Security, deputy; People's Commissariat of Public Health in the Russian Republic, state inspector; Central Institute of Advanced Training for Physicians in Moscow, director. Died in 1968.

Vera Pavlovna Lebedeva was born in Nizhnii Novgorod (later Gorkii), daughter of Pavel Livadonov, a cook. In 1892, Livadonov died of cholera, leaving seven young children. The family was forced to take refuge in an almshouse, and the children went out to work. A charitable society found Vera a place in the gymnasium, from which she graduated with a gold medal. She then worked for two years as a rural schoolteacher.

In 1901, having saved up some money, she enrolled in the Women's Medical Institute. However, she soon became caught up in the political activity of the period and was twice expelled from the institute. She posed as the wife of the Bolshevik Lebedev-Polianskii in order to be able to visit him in prison and when he was released, she married him and went to Finland. Later Lebedev had to escape to Geneva, but Lebedeva returned to St. Petersburg to the Women's Medical Institute, from which she graduated in 1910.

She began work as a zemstvo (district) physician in Vladimir province, but was soon fired, again for political activity. In 1912, she went to Geneva, a haven for young people with revolutionary sympathies. There she worked in an obstetrics and gynecology clinic and engaged in underground revolutionary activity. In 1917, Lebedeva returned to Russia, where she joined the Bolsheviks.

After the Bolshevik coup of November 1917, Lebedeva found herself at last in a strong position. She had all the qualifications for a leadership position in the new society: she was of proletarian origin, she was a dedicated revolutionary personally acquainted with leading Bolsheviks, and a trained physician. She was appointed director of the Central Institute for Maternity and Child Protection with the responsibility for organizing a national system of maternal and child care.

Later, from 1931 to 1934, as deputy of the People's Commissariat of Social Security, Lebedeva was involved in research on the question of disability. From 1934 to 1938, she was a state inspector for the People's Commissariat of Public Health for the Russian Republic, and from 1938 to 1950, she was director of the Central Institute of Advanced Training for Physicians in Moscow. Lebedeva was awarded three Orders of Lenin and the Order of the Red Flag of Labor. She died in 1968.

Lebedeva was one of the first women appointed to high office in the newly created Soviet state and, over the years, she occupied a series of important positions in the health administration of the country.

Her most significant work was the creation of a network of creches (*iasli*) for children up to four years old and preschool nurseries (*detskie sady*) for children four to seven (seven being the age when children started school). In connection with the day nurseries, she set up consultation centers with resident pediatricians. These centers, besides looking after the health of the children, disseminated advice and information to their parents. The infant mortality rate dropped significantly. Reliable child care also made it possible for mothers to enter the labor force in the enormous numbers that rapid industrialization demanded.

The Soviet Union was the first nation to provide such services, and Lebedeva had no model to follow. Although implementation of the project involved many hundreds of people, its success was owing largely to her energy and dedication.

The medical relief program of the American Women's Hospitals Committee of the American Medical Women's Association, which was active in the 1920s in the Caucasus and other areas, was also under her authority. In 1924, Lebedeva took part in a Congress of the Medical Women's International Association in London. ACH

SECONDARY SOURCES
Kovrigina, Mariia D. *V neoplatnom dolgu*. Moscow: Politizdat, 1985.

STANDARD SOURCES
Tuve.

LEBOUR, MARIE VICTOIRE (1876–1971)

British marine biologist. Born 20 August 1876 in Goodburn, Northumberland, to Emily Nora (Hodding) and George Alexander Louis Labour. Educated Armstrong College (in art). Durham University (A.Sc. in zoology, 1903; B.Sc., 1904; M.Sc., 1907; D.Sc., 1917). Professional experience: Durham University, staff (1904–1906). University of Leeds, Department of Zoology, junior demonstrator (1906–1908), demonstrator (1908–1909), assistant lecturer and demonstrator (1909–1915); Marine Biological Laboratory, Plymouth, research staff and marine biologist (1915–1946); honorary staff member (1946–1964). Honors and memberships: Linnaean Society, Fellow; Zoological Society, life Fellow; Marine Biological Association, United Kingdom, member. Died 2 October 1971.

As a young woman, Marie Lebour accompanied her father, a professor of geology at Durham College of Science, on his geological excusions. It was only in her late twenties that she began her formal education in science, having first studied art at Armstrong College. She received her bachelor of science in zoology at Durham University in 1904. Even before she formally turned to science, she had already begun to make an extensive collection of land and freshwater molluscs and had published her first paper on that topic in 1900. She continued on for a master's degree that she earned three years later (1907), by which time she had begun to publish on the larval stages of trematodes, parasites on molluscs, as well as investigating the larval stages of molluscs, on which she eventually published more than one hundred papers.

Although she was on the staff at Durham University until she received her master's degree, Lebour then took up an appointment as demonstrator and then assistant lecturer at Leeds University under Walter Garstang until the beginning of World War I. Through an arrangement with her department, she went to Plymouth to work with E. J. Allen at the Plymouth Marine Biological Laboratory at the start of the war to supplement the depleted staff. She found the situation so congenial to her work and interests that she chose to remain there for the rest of her scientific career. She received her doctorate of science shortly after she joined the staff in Plymouth.

Lebour began to investigate microplankton in Plymouth, soon after her arrival, and published two classical papers on this topic in 1917. Her subsequent work on taxonomy of plankton species resulted in her first book, *Dinoflagellates of the Northern Seas,* and in a subsequent volume in 1930. She identified no fewer than twenty-eight new species.

Her interest in the larva of Crustacea led her to develop the use of the plunger jar to study the euphausiid larvae of the North Atlantic in the early twenties, contributing heavily to the research done in this field by Robert Gurney, with whom she also published. In the late twenties, her work included a study of the Antarctic species. Later, after her retirement, she extended her research to include studies of the species found around Bermuda.

Lebour also made some important contributions to the study of eggs and larvae of fish species, especially sprat, pilchard, and herring, considered to be among the most accurate and detailed descriptions. As she had in studying the larvae of Crustacea, she employed the plunger jar to research the feeding of young fish. In this as in all her researches, her detailed and artistic sketches enhanced her publications. The marine biologist MIRIAM ROTHSCHILD remembered that her first impression was of the sound of the creaks and tinkles of Marie Lebour's plunger jars and the miniature world that these contained, not to speak of the happy expressions of those who left her laboratory, owing in part to her kindness and her infectious love of nature.

When Lebour's father died in 1918, her mother and one of her sisters came to live with her in Plymouth. Although her mother's subsequent illness meant that Lebour could not continue to spend a full day at the laboratory, she managed to turn out an enormous number of publications and research over the subsequent fifteen years, until she was able to return to full-time work following her mother's death. Only at this time was she able to travel to Bermuda, West Africa, and other locations to expand the geographical range of her research. Although she retired in 1946, her love of science kept her in her laboratory for almost twenty more years. At the age of eighty-eight, she began to find the travel into the laboratory too difficult and her increasingly poor vision made microscopical work impossible. She died at the age of ninety-five, having produced more than 175 publications, the last one when she was in her mid-eighties.   JH

PRIMARY SOURCES

Lebour, Marie Victoire. "Larval Trematodes of the Northumbrian Coast." *Transactions of the Natural History Society, Northumberland* 1 (1907): 437–453.

———. "The Larval and Post-larval Stages of the Pilchard, Sprat and Herring from Plymouth District." *Journal of the Marine Biological Association, United Kingdom* 12 (1921): 427–457.

———. *The Dinoflagellates of Northern Seas.* Plymouth: The Marine Biological Association of the United Kingdom, 1925.

———. "The Larval Stages of the Plymouth Brachyura." *Proceedings of the Zoological Society, London* (1928): 473–560, pls. 1–16.

———. Studies of the Plymouth Brachyura. I, II. *Journal of the Marine Biological Association* 14 (1927): 795–821; 15 (1928): 109–123.

———. *The Planktonic Diatoms of Northern Seas.* London: The Ray Society, 1930. Publication no. 116 of the Ray Society.

———. "The Larval Stages of Caridion, with a Description of a New Species, *C. Steveni.*" *Proceedings of the Zoological Society, London* (1930): 181–194.

———. *The Planktonic Decapod Crustacea and Stomatopoda of the Benguela Current.* Part 1, first survey, R.R.S. 'William Scoresby,' March 1950. Cambridge: Cambridge University Press, 1954. Series of discovery reports issued by the National Institute of Oceanography.

SECONDARY SOURCES

Russel, F. S. "Marie Victoria Lebour." *Journal of the Marine Biological Association, United Kingdom* 52 (1972): 777–788. Obituary notice with two portraits. This also includes her bibliography and an extensive tribute from Miriam Rothschild.

LE BRETON, ELAINE (1897–?)

French physiologist. Born 18 March 1897. Death date unknown.

Although Elaine Le Breton's degrees are not listed in the available biographical source, we do know that she worked on cellular nutrition and the mechanisms of transformation of a normal cell into a cancerous cell. She worked at the Faculté des Sciences in Paris and Rennes as well as the University of Strasbourg, as a member of the Faculté de Médecin and director of research.   JH/MBO

PRIMARY SOURCES

Le Breton, Elaine. *Variations biochimiques du rapport nucleoplasmatique au cours du developpement embryonnaire . . .* Paris: Masson, 1923. Published as part of the publications of the Institute of Physiology, Faculty of Medicine of the University of Strasbourg.

———. With Georges Schaeffer. *L'action dynamique specifique des protides; theories anciennes, theorie nouvelle.* Paris: Hermann, 1938.

———. With G. Popjak, eds. *Biochemical Problems of Lipids; Proceedings of the Second International Conference on the Biochemistry of Lipids.* New York: Interscience Publishers, 1956. International Conference held at the University of Ghent, 27–30 July 1955, organized with the collaboration of the Vlaamse Chemische Vereniging of Belgium, under the presidency of Professor R. Ruyssen.

STANDARD SOURCES

Turkevich and Turkevich.

LECLERCQ, SUZANNE (CÉLINE) (1901–)

Belgian paleobotanist and paleontologist. Born 28 March 1901. Educated University of Liège (Ph.D.); visits to University College, London; the British Museum (Natural History); the Geological Survey, London; Cambridge University; Glasgow University; Manchester University. Professional experience: University of Liège (Belgium), professor of paleophytology and stratigraphy (1928); Société d'Anthropologie, foreign member (1930s). Honors and memberships: Botanical Society of America, corresponding member (1952); Paleobotanical Society of India, foreign honorary member (1957); Geological Society of Belgium (president 1953–1954).

Suzanne Céline was a paleobotanist who worked on the Devonian flora preserved by petrification and the formation of impression and petrifaction. She got her doctorate from the University of Liège and made numerous trips to English universities and museums to study their collections. She belonged to many scientific societies in different parts of the world. JH/MBO

PRIMARY SOURCES
Céline, Suzanne. With Henry N. Andrews, Jr. "Calamophyton bicephalum: A New Species from the Middle Devonian of Belgium." *Annals of the Missouri Botanical Garden* 47 (1960): 1–23.
———. With H. Banks. "Pseudosporocchnus Nodosus sp. Nov., a Middle Devonian Plant with Cladoxylalean Affinities." *Palaeontographie* 110, issue B (1962).

STANDARD SOURCES
Turkevich and Turkevich.

LEDINGHAM, UNA CHRISTINA (GARVIN) (1900–1965)

British physician. Born 2 January 1900 to Christina (Wilson) and James Louis Garvin. Married John Ledingham (1925). One son; one daughter. Educated South Hampstead High School; University of London (M.B.; B.S., 1923); London School of Medicine for Women (later the Royal Free Hospital of Medicine) (M.D., 1927). Professional experience: Brompton, the Royal Free and Royal Northern Hospitals, house posts (to 1925); London School of Medicine for Women, medical registrar (1925–1931; staff room physician, 1931); Hampstead General Hospital, staff; Marie Curie Hospital, staff (from 1931). Honors and memberships: London University, senior examiner; Royal Free Hospital, board of governors (1957–1960); Fellow of the Royal College of Physicians (1942). Died 19 November 1965.

Una Ledingham was a brilliant, opinionated woman who was feared as well as respected by her students. Her hard exterior concealed the real sympathy she felt for her patients.

While she was at the Hampstead General Hospital and the Marie Curie Hospital, she developed an interest in diabetes and became an expert on the problems of the pregnant diabetic woman. During World War II, she managed her husband's medical practice while keeping up with her own medical work. The Ledinghams had two children. Their son became a physician to Westminster Hospital. JH/MBO

SECONDARY SOURCES
British Medical Journal 2 (1965): 1314. Obituary notice.
Lancet 2 (1965): 1136–1137. Obituary notice; includes portrait.

STANDARD SOURCES
Europa; Munks Roll.

LEE, JULIA SOUTHARD (1897–?)

U.S. textile chemist. Born 29 September 1897 in Southard, Mo. Married 1937. Educated University of Missouri (B.S., 1926); Kansas State University (M.S., 1929); University of Chicago (Ph.D., 1936). Professional experience: Purdue University, instructor in textiles and clothing (1934–1937); Iowa State University, associate professor (1939–1946); Washington State University, associate professor of home economics, chair of textiles and clothing department (1946–1950); New Mexico State University, professor of home economics (from 1953). Death date unknown.

Julia Southard Lee was twenty-nine years old when she earned her bachelor of science degree at the University of Missouri. She continued at Kansas State University, where she got a master's degree and then went to the University of Chicago, where she began work on a doctorate. Between 1929 and 1933 she had an ELLEN H. RICHARDS fellowship from the American Home Economics Association (1930–1931) and another from the University of Chicago (1931–1933). During the time that she was completing her doctorate, she took a position at Purdue University as an instructor in textiles and clothing. After she received her doctorate, she took a position as associate professor at Iowa State University, where she remained for seven years. She became chair of the textile and clothing department at Washington State University, where she remained for five years. At that point she went to New Mexico State University as professor of home economics.

Lee's research involved protein fibers, X-ray studies on cellulose, and service qualities of textile materials. She was a member of the Chemical Society, the Association of Textile Chemists and Colorists, and the American Home Economics Association. JH/MBO

STANDARD SOURCES
AMS 7–8, B 9, P&B 10–11; Bailey.

LEE, REBECCA (1840–1881)

U.S. physician. Born in 1840. First African-American woman to obtain a university medical degree. Educated New England Female Medical College, Boston (M.D., 1864). Professional positions: Richmond, Va., private practice (1865?–1881). Died in 1881.

Rebecca Lee was the first African-American woman to obtain a university medical degree, but nothing is known of her early life. She attended the New England Female Medical College during the period that MARIE ZAKRZEWSKA, brought from the New York Infirmary for Women and Children as professor of obstetrics and diseases of women and children, became dissatisfied with the level of teaching there and threw her energy into the newly founded New England Hospital for Women and Children. We have no information whether Lee followed her there. Soon after, Lee went to Richmond, Virginia, where she practiced privately until her death at the young age of forty-one. Lee has been confused recently with Rebecca Lee Crumpler, who published a book on women's diseases in Boston in 1883. Crumpler's birthdate, 1858, makes the identification highly unlikely.

KM

SECONDARY SOURCES

Sammons, Vivian. *Blacks in Science and Related Disciplines.* Washington, D.C.: Science Reference Section, Science and Technology Division, Library of Congress, 1990.

STANDARD SOURCES

LKW; Lovejoy; O'Neill.

LEE, ROSE HUM (1904–1964)

U.S. sociologist. First Chinese-American university chair. Born 20 August 1904 in Butte, Mont., to Lin (Fong) and Wah-Lung Hum. Married (1) Ku Yong Lee (1923?, later divorced); (2) Glenn Ginn (1951). One adopted daughter. Educated Butte High School; Carnegie Institute of Technology (B.S., 1942); University of Chicago (A.M., 1943; Ph.D., 1947). Professional experience: Chinese government secretary (1928–1937); Roosevelt University, assistant professor (from 1945), chair (1956), professor (1959–1964); Phoenix College, visiting professor (1962–1963). Died 25 March 1964 in Phoenix, Ariz.

Rose Hum Lee was born in Butte, Montana, to an energetic Chinese father who immigrated from Kwangtung Province, China, to California. He then worked in Montana as a ranch hand, miner, and laundry worker. Her mother, also from Kwangtung, continued her husband's business after his death despite the fact that she was illiterate. She also encouraged her children to get an education. Rose was the second oldest of seven and attended the local high school, training as a sec-

retary. She married a young Chinese student in Philadelphia whom she met while working, and the two went to China to work both for the new republican government and for American corporations stationed there.

During the Japanese invasion of China in 1937, Rose Hum Lee helped the government organize emergency social services for widows and children. She was to adopt one of these children as her one daughter. She returned to the United States just before the beginning of World War II with her daughter.

Lee then began to study for an undergraduate degree at Carnegie Institute of Technology, financing herself with the help of her mother and by lectures and freelance writing about the situation in China. She continued on for graduate degrees at the University of Chicago in sociology, finishing her doctorate two years after the end of the war. She drew upon her own knowledge of the Chinese-American communities in the West for her thesis, "The Growth and Decline of Chinese Communities in the Rocky Mountain Region." During this period, she also wrote children's plays, including one about a little Chinatown detective, produced by the well-known Chicago children's theater, Goodman Theatre.

Upon graduation, Rose Hum Lee was appointed to the sociology department of the newly formed Roosevelt University in Chicago, where she remained for the rest of her professional career. She continued to write on issues of urbanization and the Chinese-American. She was appointed chair of the department in 1956 and was made full professor of sociology three years later.

Lee was married for the second time in 1951 to Glenn Ginn, a Chinese-American lawyer from Phoenix, Arizona. Although she continued to go back and forth between Chicago and Phoenix, she decided to take a year as a visiting professor at Phoenix College in the early sixties. The following year she died from a stroke while visiting Phoenix. There is a file on her with a portrait at Roosevelt University.

JH/MBO

PRIMARY SOURCES

Lee, Rose Hum. *The City: Urbanism and Urbanization in Major World Regions.* Chicago: Lippincott, [1955?].

———. *The Chinese in the United States of America.* [Hong Kong]: Hong Kong University Press, 1960.

———. *The Growth and Decline of Chinese Communities in the Rocky Mountain Region.* New York: Arno Press, 1978. Reprint of the author's thesis, University of Chicago, 1947.

SECONDARY SOURCES

Chicago Sun Times, 26 March 1964. Obituary notice.
New York Times, 27 March 1964. Obituary notice.

STANDARD SOURCES
AMS 8, S&B 9–10; *NAW*(M) (article by William Burr).

LEE, SARAH WALLIS BOWDICH (1791–1856)

British popularizer, amateur geologist, author, and artist. Born 10 September 1791 in Colchester. Father John Wallis. Married (1) Thomas Edward Bowdich (1812, he died in 1824); (2) Robert Lee (1829). Died 22 September 1856 at Erith.

Sarah Wallis married naturalist Thomas Edward Bowdich when she was twenty-two years old. She shared his interests and accompanied him on field trips to Africa. Armed with a letter of introduction to Baron Cuvier in 1817, she and her husband went to visit Cuvier at the Museum d'Historie Naturelle. He received both husband and wife kindly and allowed them to study his collections. They remained in Paris until 1823, when they set off on a second trip to Africa. Bowdich, however, died on the Gambia River on 10 January 1824. His account of that expedition was completed by his wife, who published it along with a natural history appendix. Sarah continued her researches aided by Cuvier. In 1829, she married Robert Lee, and subsequently devoted much of the rest of her life to popularizing natural science, illustrating many of her books herself. Her manual on taxidermy went through multiple editions, as did her best-known book on freshwater fish, beautifully illustrated by herself. She wrote a paper on paleontology in 1831, and published her recollections of Cuvier in a biographical work, the *Memoirs of Baron Cuvier,* in 1833. At the end of her life, she produced a literary romance describing adventures in West Africa based on her own experiences.   JH/MBO

PRIMARY SOURCES
Bowdich, Sarah Wallis. *Taxidermy: or the Art of Collecting, Preparing, and Mounting Objects of Natural History. For the Use of Museums and Travelers.* London: Longman, Hurst, Rees, Orme, and Brown, 1820. This manual went through six editions.
Bowdich, Thomas Edward. *Excursions in Madeira and Porto Santo. During the Autumn of 1823, While on His Third Voyage to Africa.* London: G. B. Whittaker, 1825. "To which is added, by Mrs. [Sarah] Bowdich, 1. A narrative of the continuance of the voyage to its completion . . . 2. A description of the English settlements on the river Gambia. 3. Appendix: containing zoological and botanical descriptions, and translations from the Arabic."
Bowdich, Sarah Wallis. *The Freshwater Fishes of Great Britain.* London: Printed for the authoress and R. Ackermann, 1828–1838. This may be her most important work. It was published in eleven parts, although a twelfth part was planned but was not published because of insufficient funds. The fish

were caught for Lee who was able to reproduce their exact colors before they faded.

Lee, Mrs. R. [Sarah Wallis Bowdich]. *Memoirs of Baron Cuvier.* London: Longman, 1833. Published simultaneously in Paris and New York.
———. *The African Wanderers, or The Adventures of Carlos and Antonio. Embracing Interesting Descriptions of the Manners and Customs of the Western Tribes and the Natural Productions of the Country.* London, Grant and Griffith, 1847.
———. *Adventures in Australia; or, The Wanderings of Captain Spencer in the Bush and the Wilds. Containing Accurate Descriptions of the Habits of the Natives, and the Natural Productions and Features of the Country.* London: Grant and Griffith, 1851.
———. *Anecdotes of the Habits and Instincts of Birds, Reptiles, and Fishes.* London, Grant and Griffith, 1853.
———. *Trees, Plants, and Flowers: Their Beauties, Uses, and Influences.* London: Grant and Griffith, 1854. Continued through a number of editions, even after Lee's death.

STANDARD SOURCES
Creese and Creese; *DNB.*

LEEBODY, MARY ELIZABETH (d. 1911)

Irish botanist. Born at Portaferry in County Down. Married Professor J. R. Leebody of Foyle College, Londonderry. Died 1911.

Field biologist Mary Elizabeth Leebody added greatly to botanical knowledge of two Irish counties, Derry and Donegal. She added to the range of the American orchid *Spiranthes romanzoffiana* (Kilrea), and discovered, among others, *Dryas octopetala* on Muckish, and *Teesdalia nudicaulis* on Lough Neagh, and *Malaxis* on Slieve Snacht.   JH/MBO

PRIMARY SOURCES
Leebody, Mary. "*Spirathes Romanzoviana* in County Londonderry." *Irish Naturalist* 2 (1893): 228.
———. "*Stachys betanica in Donegal.*" *Journal of Botany* 87 (1899): 273.

SECONDARY SOURCES
Britten, James, and George Simonds Boulger, ed. *A Biographical Index of British and Irish Botanists.* Vol. 2. London: West Newman, 1893.
Irish Naturalist 20 (1911): 218. Obituary notice.

STANDARD SOURCES
Desmond; Praeger.

LEES, FLORENCE SARAH (1840–1922)

British nurse, pioneer of district nursing. Born 31 March 1840 in Blandford, Dorset to Mathilda and Henry Lees (a physician). Married Dacre Craven in 1879. Two sons. Educated Secondary School, London; St. Thomas' Nursing School (1866); Kaiserwerth Institute on the Rhine (Germany) (1867); King's College Hospital School of Nursing (1868); Paris Hospital (1869–1870). Professional experience: Royal Reserve Hospital, Hamburg, Germany, superintendant of nurses (1870–1871); Metropolitan and National Nursing Association, superintendent-general (1874–1887); Queen's Nursing Institute, council member and advisor on training (1889–1918). Honors and memberships: Prussian war medal; Prussian Ordre de la Merité (1871). Jubilee medal. Cross of St. John of Jerusalem. Died 24 October 1922 at Walton-on-the-Naze, England.

Florence Lees was the only daughter of a physician in Dorset who deserted his family when she was a child. She went to school in London and then began to study nursing in both London and Germany. After studying at King's Hospital, she went to study nursing in the great hospitals in Paris when the Franco-Prussian war broke out. Her loyalty was to the Prussian side, and after volunteering her skills as a nurse, was sent by Crown Princess Fredericka of Prussia (the eldest daughter of Queen Victoria) to serve as the superintendent of nurses at the Royal Reserve Hospital, Hamburg.

When Lees returned to London, she embarked on a tour of American nursing education, where she was influenced by the American ideas that nurses needed to be trained in the same manner as medical students. FLORENCE NIGHTINGALE and William Rathbone then asked her to survey the nursing needs of London, a request that resulted in her review of nursing in 1874. Subsequently she was appointed superintendent-general of nurses at the newly formed Metropolitan and National Nursing Association. She pursuaded her board to develop a district nursing system.

She married Reverend Dacre Craven, a supporter of her work, and had two sons. Craven later became secretary to the Home for District Nurses in London. With the cooperation of Florence Nightingale, both Cravens successfully pursuaded Queen Victoria to create a new nursing school in her jubilee year, the Queen's Nursing Institute. Lees, writing under her married name, then produced an important *Guide to District Nurses*. Even in retirement, she continued to have an influence on the development of district nursing as a consultant to the Nursing Institute.   JH/MBO

PRIMARY SOURCES
Lees, Florence S. *Handbook for Hospital Sisters*. London: Isbister, 1874.
———. [as Craven, Mrs. Dacre]. *A Guide to District Nurses and Home Nursing*. New York: Macmillan, 1889.

SECONDARY SOURCES
Baly, Monica. *A History of Queen's Nursing Institite*. London: Croom Helm, 1987.
Stocks, Mary. *A Hundred Years of District Nursing*. London: Allen & Unwin, 1960.

STANDARD SOURCES
DNB Missing Persons.

LEFROY, HELENA (TRENCH) (1820–1908)
Irish botanist. Born 1820. Died 1908.

Helena Lefroy is known for a single discovery at Garraris Cove near Tramore in Waterford in 1839. There she found the last survivor of a native colony of the southern spurge, *Euphorbia peplis*. This specimen was the only one found in Ireland.   JH/MBO

SECONDARY SOURCES
Colgan, Nathaniel, and Reginald W. Scully. *Cybele hibernica*, 2nd ed. Dublin: Edward Personby, 1898. Lefroy mentioned on page 52.
Mackay, James Townsend. *Proceedings of the Dublin University Zoological and Botanical Association* 1 (1859).
Natural History Review (1859): 6.

STANDARD SOURCES
Desmond; Praeger.

LEHMANN, INGE (1888–1993)
Danish seismologist and geologist. Born 13 May 1888 in Copenhagen to Ida (Torsleff) Lehmann and Alfred Georg Ludvig Lehman. One sibling. Never married. Educated Newnham College, Cambridge (1910–1911, no Tripos); University of Copenhagen (master's in mathematics and physics, 1920; M.S. in geodesy, 1928; D. Phil., 1968); Columbia University (Sc.D., 1964). Professional experience: Danish Geodetic Institute, staff member (1925); state geodesist (1928); chief of the seismological department (1928–1953). Died 21 February 1993 in Copenhagen.

Inge Lehmann's father was a psychology professor at the University of Copenhagen. Inge attended the school of Hanna Adler, Niels Bohr's aunt, where boys and girls did the same lessons and played the same games. She entered Newnham College during the Michelmas term of 1910 and stayed for four terms. She attended mathematical lectures but did not take her Tripos. She graduated from the University of Copenhagen with a degree in mathematics and physics. Much later, after she began working for the Danish Geodetic Institute, she returned and received a master of science degree in geodesy; after retirement, she earned additional degrees at Copenhagen and Columbia. After a brief stint as an actuarial scientist, Lehmann obtained a position with the Danish Geodetic Institute, where she remained for her entire career. As a staff member in 1925, she accidentally became interested in seismology when she and three young men, none of whom had previously encountered a seismograph, were given the task of installing it. Her success in this undertaking led her to read in this area, and in 1927 she took a leave of absence to study with leading European seismologists. After her return (with a master's degree from Copenhagen), she was made chief of the seismological department of the institute, a post she retained for the rest of her career.

Lehmann was a member of a number of learned societies and received some important honors. She was a founding member of the Danish Geophysical Association and president of that organization from 1941 to 1944, an associate of the Royal Astronomical Society (1957), an honorary Fellow of the Royal Society of Edinburgh (1959), a foreign member of the Royal Society of London (1969), an honorary member of the European Geophysical Society (1973), and an honorary member of the Seismological Society of America (1973). Her honors include the Emil Wiechert Medal of the Deutsche Geophysikalische Gesellschaft (1964), the Gold Medal of the Royal Danish Academy of Science and Letters (1965), the Harry Oscar Wood Award in Seismology (1960), and the William Bowie Medal of the American Geophysical Union (1971).

Lehmann visited a number of remote outposts to supervise the installation of seismograph stations. During this time she published prolifically, including a paper that added a new discontinuity, which divided the core into inner and outer parts. After she was no longer responsible for the routine operation of the seismological stations, she continued to publish, particularly emphasizing the upper mantle of the earth's crust. She published over fifty-six papers on geophysical subjects, mainly in Danish periodicals from 1926 to 1970.

JH/MBO

PRIMARY SOURCES

Lehmann, Inge. "'P' Waves." *Union Géodésique et Géophysique Internationale, Série A, Travaux Scientifiques* 14 (1936): 87–115.

SECONDARY SOURCES

Birch, Francis. "Thirty-third Presentation, William Bowie Medal to Inge Lehmann: EOS." *American Geophysical Union Transactions* 52 (1971): 537–538.
Elder, Eleanor S. "Women in Early Geology." *Journal of Geological Education* 30, no. 5 (1982): 287–293.

STANDARD SOURCES

Current Biography 1962; *Newnham*, vol. 1.

LEHMUS, EMILIE (1841–1932)

German physician. Born 30 August 1841 in Fürth to mother (with a maiden name of Heinlein) and pastor and church administrator Eduard Lehmus. Five sisters. Never married. Educated Paris, teacher education; Zurich, studied medicine (M.D., 1874). Professional experience: Marienstift in Fürth, teacher; University birthing clinic, Prague, volunteer under Professor Weber; Königlich Sächsischen Entbindungsanstalt in Dresden (birthing center), intern under Professor Franz V. Winckel; Berlin, physician for women and children (1876); Polyclinic for women, Berlin, founder with FRANZISKA TIBURTIUS (later the "Klinik weiblicher Ärte") (1878). Died 17 October 1932 in Gräfenberg/Erlangen.

Emilie Lehmus was the first German woman to receive a medical degree in a Swiss university. Two years later, she was followed by the better known FRANZISKA TIBURTIUS, with whom she later joined for thirty-one years in her practice.

The Lehmus family originally came from Silesia and later settled in southern Germany in Rothenburg an der Tauber. Lehmus's ancestors for several generations were churchmen. Her father, Eduard Lehmus, was a church official. He became a minister in Fürth and married a woman from this city from the merchant family Heinlein. Since they had no sons, Lehmus's parents decided to give their six daughters a superior education, and one that catered to their individual talents, a most unusual decision for those times. The gifted Emilie was sent to Paris for her education. Back in Fürth she found employement as a teacher at the Marienstift. Four of her sisters were already married to theologians. After a long visit with her older sister in Berlin, Lehmus came to the conclusion that she wanted to study medicine. Her sister introduced her to the first German female dentist in Berlin, HENRIETTE HIRSCHFELD-TIBURTIUS. The latter convinced her on the occasion of an excursion to the Spreewald to study medicine in Switzerland, an adventurous idea at that time. Her father agreed, and immediately started to teach his ambitious daughter Latin.

In October 1870 she matriculated in the medical school at Zurich. Since 1864, women had attended medical lectures there. At first it was Russians. In 1868–1869 there were eight female medical students. Discounting the United States, the first decision to allow women to study in scientific disciplines occurred in Zurich in 1868–1869. A female foreigner first asked to be allowed to matriculate into natural history and medical lectures at Zurich University. After the door was opened for female students, the openminded Swiss continued to offer places for those who were qualified. There were still problems related to the proper role of women. It was necessary to register for matriculation, for this was the only way that a student could be promoted. However, registration was only available for men and not for women. The directorate took a more or less "wait and see" stance on this question.

The then rector of the university interpreted the university rules, which neither forbade nor permitted female study, in favor of women. Thus in 1867 the first female doctor of medicine could leave the university after finishing her studies with the blessing of the administration.

This success inspired others to try as well. In 1870–1871 there were nineteen students who registered, and in the summer semester of 1872 there were sixty-three women students, of whom only two came from Switzerland, four from Germany, two from Austria, one from the United States, and fifty-four from Russia. Of these sixty-three women students, fifty-one were registered for medicine and the others in the philosophical faculty. The fact that the women preferred medical studies was based not only on the role of women as nurturer of the healthy and the sick. Women considered it a necessity to educate women about gynecological problems. Women were hesitant to seek help from male doctors because of embarrassment. There were numerous young women who during puberty started to have problems in the lower abdomen and knowingly or unknowingly suffered the consequences because they were afraid to be examined by a male doctor. When they subjected themselves to medical examinations after they married it was often too late. After marriage, men often infected their mostly virgin wives with sexually transmitted diseases.

The Würzburg faculty in 1870 asked what complications flowed from the admission of females to medical school. They especially questioned the presence of women in coeducational lectures that could prove difficult because of female modesty. However, the experience of Zurich University with female students was good. Not even in physiology or anatomy did embarrassing situations arise. The medical faculty of Zurich University replied to Würzburg that the presence of female students in the theoretical and practical courses had not resulted in any problems and lectures were given without regard to the ladies present.

In Germany they decided the study by females was dangerous and against nature. Even twenty years later, a scientifically talented school principal at the Friedrich-Wilhelms-Universität in Berlin was prevented by a privat-doztin (assistant professor) of dermatology from attending his lecture "Prostitution in Ethical, Legal, and Health Issues." In 1903 when the German women's movement association submitted to the Reichstag a petition to allow women to study bearing sixty thousand signatures they were ignored. Therefore, there was a great increase of female students in Switzerland which culminated in the years 1905–1909. Later the numbers were steadily reduced, because in the middle of the 1890s the universities in all countries began to grapple with the question of admitting women and girls.

At the beginning of her third semester in Zurich, Lehmus met Franziska Tiburtius, from Berlin, who had already corresponded with her. Lehmus graduated in Zurich *summa cum laude* in her ninth semester. Her dissertation was "Erkrankung der Macula lutea bei progressiver Paralyse" (Illness of the Macula Lutea with Progressive Paralysis). After her studies, she found a job with Professor Weber at the University Lying-In Hospital in Prague. Afterward, she accepted a ten-month position as "interne Ärtzin" (intern) with the gynecologist Franz V. Winckel at the Königlich Sächsischen Entbindungsanstalt (Royal Saxon birthing center) of the Dresden women's clinic. Franziska Tiburtius followed her to this clinic. It was extremely difficult even for a graduate woman to be able to further her education after her initial studies in a German clinic. When Lehmus and Tiburtius moved to Berlin in 1876, they were refused recognition as women doctors and could not take the state medical examination. They were not even allowed to take the midwife examination. According to the law, they could practice but they were looked upon as "charlatans."

Lehmus established herself as a doctor for women and children. She and Tiburtius were for more than fifteen years the only female doctors in Berlin and held their place in the fight against colleagues and prejudice. In the 1880s, they both established their practices despite all resistance. They were denounced several times because they allegedly used the title "Doctor" without being entitled to it. Their prescriptions had to be signed by male colleagues. Their joint goal, because of their experiences in Zurich and Dresden, was to found a clinic for working women. Aided by a grant and with active help from Henriette Hirschfeld-Tiburtius, who was the first female dentist in Germany and sister-in-law of Franzisca Tiburtius, they opened the Poliklinik für Frauen in 1887 in the Alten Schönhauser Strasse. The treatment cost only ten pfennig. Women who were not insured and could not afford this amount were treated for free. In no time at all, the two medical doctors had more patients than they could handle. Soon a small hospital was opened which later developed into the Klinik weiblicher Ärzte (Clinic of Female Physicians) in Karl-Schrader-Strasse.

Around the turn of the century, Lehmus gave up her practice because of illness. She suffered twice from influenza-caused pneumonia, which she had trouble shaking off. It forced her to change climate. She went to southern Germany, where she spent the rest of her life close to her family.

In contrast to the gregarious nature of Tiburtius, Lehmus was not very sociable. She was in and out of the home of her sister's family in Berlin. All of the sisters played excellent piano and played music daily, but very rarely did Emilie participate in the Tiburtius household's Saturday open house (*offenen Sonnabenden*). Emilie Lehmus pretended to be harsh, so that the outside world would not cause her hurt. Her reluctance to openly assert herself reflects a deep religious feeling that came from generations of clergymen in the Lehmus family. All of her life, Lehmus was interested in theological questions. She loved to discuss theology with her brother-in-law, who was unable to follow her ideas.

Though she was a pioneer of German female medical education, Lehmus's contributions have been largely forgotten.

G V L

PRIMARY SOURCES

Lehmus, Emilie. *Die Erkrankung der Macula lutea bei progressiver Paralyse.* Zurich: Zürcher and Furrer, 1875. A reprinted version of her 1874 dissertation.

SECONDARY SOURCES

Bluhm, Agnes. "Ein Gedenktag der deutschen Medizinerinnen." *Die Ärztin* 17 (1941): 337–339. This article was written on the occasion of Lehmus' hundredth birthday "the first female doctor of the Second Reich." The woman doctor Agnes Bluhm, who studied medicine in Zurich a little later, described the life path of Emilie Lehmus and her personal encounters with Lehmus and Tiburtius. She explained why Tiburtius is better known than Lehmus, "her director."

Heischkel, Edith. "Die Frau als Ärztin in der Vergangenheit." *Die Ärztin* 16 (1940): 59–61.

STANDARD SOURCES

Lexikon der Frau.

LEHR, MARGUERITE (ANNA MARIE) (1898–?)

U.S. mathematician. Born 22 October 1898 in Baltimore, Md. to Margaret Kreuter and George Lehr. Educated Goucher College (A.B., 1919); University of Rome (1923–1924); Bryn Mawr College (Ph.D., 1925). Professional experience: Bryn Mawr College, faculty (1924–1955; professor, 1955–retirement); Johns Hopkins, honorary Fellow (1931–1932); Swarthmore College, lecturer (1944); Institut Poincaré, Paris, researcher (1950); Princeton University, visiting Fellow (1956–1957). Death date unknown.

After mathematician Marguerite Lehr received her bachelor's degree at Goucher College, she received an American Association of University Women Fellowship to attend the University of Rome. She also was the recipient of the M. Carey Thomas European Fellowship during 1923–1924. Obtaining her doctoral degree from Bryn Mawr, she became a part of its faculty until she was made professor in 1955. During this period, she also had associations with other universities, including the Institut Poincaré in Paris. Toward the end of her career she spent a year as a Fellow at Princeton University and served as a member of the Woodrow Wilson Fellowship Award Committee for ten years (1956–1965). Her undergraduate college, Goucher, gave her a distinguished citation

for her work in mathematics in 1954. She was a member of both French and American mathematics associations and a Fellow of the American Association for the Advancement of Science. She was a consultant on curriculum and the teaching of mathematics for state and private organizations. Lehr was a Protestant.

Lehr published on algebraic geometry and the humanistic aspects of mathematics. She was the author of articles in algebraic geometry in numerous mathematical journals.

J H / M B O

PRIMARY SOURCES

Lehr, Marguerite. *The Plane Quintic with Five Cusps . . .* Baltimore: N.p., 1927. First written as her 1925 doctoral dissertation, Bryn Mawr College.

STANDARD SOURCES

American Women; AMS 4–8, P 9, P&B 10–11; Debus.

LEIGHTON, DOROTHEA (CROSS) (1908–1989)

U.S. social psychiatrist and medical anthropologist. Born 2 September 1908 in Lunenberg, Mass., to Dorothea (Farquhar) and Frederick Cushing Cross. Married Alexander Leighton, 1937 (divorced 1965). Two children. Educated Bryn Mawr College (A.B., 1930); Johns Hopkins University (M.D., 1936); Columbia University, anthropology course work (1939). Professional positions: Johns Hopkins Hospital, chemistry technician (1930–1932); Phipps Clinic, Baltimore, Md., psychiatric residency; field work, Navajo tribe, Ariz. (1940); U.S. Bureau of Indian Affairs (with University of Chicago), Indian Personality Research Project, special physician (1942–1945); Yoruba tribes, Nigeria, Africa, fieldwork (1960?); Cornell University, professor of child development and family relations (1949–1952); University of North Carolina, professor of mental health (1965–1974); University of California, San Francisco, lecturer (1977) University of California, Berkeley, visiting professor (1981–1982); Society for Medical Anthropology, founder. Died 15 August 1989 in Fresno, Calif.

Dorothea Cross Leighton was one of the founders of medical anthropology. Her mother encouraged her, as a young woman from a small town in Massachusetts, to enter her alma mater, Bryn Mawr College. Like her father, who had attended MIT, she was interested in science and majored in chemistry and biology. Upon graduation, she worked for two years as a chemical technician at Johns Hopkins Hospital, where she decided to enter medical school. At Johns Hopkins Medical School, she met her future husband, Alexander Leighton, and began a collaboration that lasted for many years. They both decided to study psychiatry, and went as residents to the Phipps Clinic in Baltimore. Here they were encouraged by the head of the clinic to adopt anthropological interviewing techniques for which purpose they attended seminars at Columbia University. From there they went to do field work among the Navajo in New Mexico and then went to Alaska.

When the couple returned to Johns Hopkins, only Alexander Leighton received a staff appointment. In the fall of 1942, the Bureau of Indian Affairs (BIA) invited the Leightons to work with the Navajo to study concepts of illness and treatment. This task fell mainly to Dorothea since her husband was in the United States Navy. The result of her study was a book, *The Navaho Door*, which contrasted Anglo and Navajo concepts of health and disease. As research physician she began to collect data for the personality project sponsored by the BIA. As a part of a team, her work led to important publications with leading anthropologists such as Clyde Kluckhohn and John Adair.

After World War II, the Leightons moved from Washington, D.C., to Cornell with their two small children. There Dorothea Leighton held a part-time position. Nevertheless, the couple continued their research together and developed a multi-year study of Stirling County in Nova Scotia intended to examine psychiatric disorders in a rural population. This research was considered a classic study, and the Leightons were asked to develop comparative studies in Sweden and Nigeria modeled on their Stirling County studies. These large research projects required a great deal of supervision and preparation by Dorothea Leighton, involving a staff of forty people in the first Stirling County studies.

When the Leightons' marriage broke up in 1965, the divorce enabled her to accept her first full-time appointment in anthropology and public health at the University of North Carolina. She held this position for the following ten years, during which time she founded the Society for Medical Anthropology. She served as chair of her department for the final two years of her tenure, retiring in 1974. Subsequently, she moved to Berkeley and then to Fresno, as she followed her daughter who had settled in California. She taught briefly at the California universities in her mid-seventies, and died in Fresno at the age of eighty-one.

JH/MBO

PRIMARY SOURCES

Leighton, Dorothea. With Alexander H. Leighton. *The Navaho Door: An Introduction to Navaho Life.* Cambridge, Mass.: Harvard University Press, 1940.

———. With Clyde Kluckhohn. *The Navaho.* Cambridge, Mass.: Harvard University Press, 1946.

———. With Clyde Kluckhohn. *Children of the People.* Cambridge, Mass.: Harvard University Press, 1947.

———. With Alexander Leighton. *Gregorio, the Hand Trembler.* Cambridge, Mass.: Harvard University Press, 1949.

———. With Alexander Leighton, et al. *The Character of Danger: Psychiatric Disorder among the Yoruba.* New York: Basic Books, 1963.

———. With others. "Psychiatric Findings of the Sterling County Study." *American Journal of Psychiatry* 119 (1966): 1021–1026.

The Leighton papers on the Navajo personality research project are in the National Anthropological Archives, Smithsonian.

STANDARD SOURCES

AMS P&B 10–14; Gacs (article by Joyce Griffin); *IDA.*

LELAND, EVELYN (ca. 1870–ca. 1930)

U.S. astronomer. Born circa 1870. Staff member, Harvard College Observatory (1889–1925). Died circa 1930.

Evelyn Leland was one of the low-paid female assistants ("computers") who worked for Edward Pickering at the Harvard College Observatory. As part of the observatory's work on stellar spectra, numerous photographs were shipped from the Arequipa Station in Peru to Cambridge, Massachusetts. Leland was at the observatory from 1889 to 1925, and was one of those who examined the plates and studied the spectra in detail, in the course of this examination discovering new variable stars and other objects with peculiar spectra. Although not a theorist, Leland was a competent observer. She was representative of Pickering's group of women assistants and was involved in the publications of the observatory.

JH/MBO

STANDARD SOURCES

Jones and Boyd; Mozans.

LE MAÎTRE, DOROTHÉE (1896–1990)

French paleontologist. Born 1896 in Angers(?). Educated Angers Free University; Catholic Univeristy of Lille (graduated 1926; Ph.D., 1934). University of Lille, free faculty of sciences, assistant to the laboratory of geology (from 1926). Honors and memberships: Prix Fontannes (1941); Grand Prix Bonnet from the Académie des Sciences (1959); Kuhlmann Prize (1956). Died 26 January 1990 at Loudéac (Côtes-du-Nord).

Dorothée Le Maître was devoted throughout her life to her native Angers and the area around Lille, in the north of France. Her first paper was published in 1926 in the *Annales de la Société géologique du Nord* and twenty-three years later she became president of the society.

Her scientific interests centered around the Devonian in France and the geology of North Africa. Her thesis was on the Devonian fauna of the basin of Ancenis. Between 1935 and 1937, she did original research on the Spongiomorphides. Since she was known as an expert on the Devonian, the Service des Mines sent her on two missions to northern Africa (1938–1939) and the center of Saharan research sent her on three other missions, this time to the Valley of Saoura in 1947, 1949, and 1952.

From 1946 Le Maître was a "collaborateur" to the Geological Service of Algeria. She published numerous papers on North African and sub-Saharan Devonian fauna. Between 1954 and 1956 she was called to Algeria three times to help identify paleontological specimens for petroleum research. She compared the Devonian fauna of Africa to that of the Ardenne, the Massif, Asturia, Bohemia, and Austria, which underlined the originality of certain African fauna. She was the first to establish affinities between Devonian fauna of North Africa, the Sahara, and faunas of North America. By preference, she studied the area of the Massif armoricain around the area of her birth. She was named adjunct "collaborateur" of the Service de la carte (1946). From 1950 she was appointed head of research of the Centre National de la Recherche Scientifique, and later became a scientific director.

Among her honors were the Prix Fontannes in 1941 and the Grand Prix Bonnet in 1959 from the Académie des Sciences. She was awarded the Kuhlmann prize in 1956.

JH/MBO

PRIMARY SOURCES
Le Maître, Dorothée. "La faune des couches à *Spirifer cultrijugatus* à Fourmies." *Annales Société Géologique du Nord* 54 (1929): 27–74.
———. "La faune des calcaires dévoniens du Bassin d'Ancenis." *Comptes rendus Société Géologique de France* (1931): 188–190.
———. "Etude sur la faune des calcaires dévoniens du Bassin d'Ancenis. Calcaire de Chaudefons et Calcaire de Chalonnes (Maine et Loire)." *Memoires Société Géologique du Nord* 12 (1934): 1–261.
———. "Nouveaux éléments communs avec l'Amé dans la faune de l'Afrique du Nord." *Comptes rendus Académie des Sciences* (1950): 253–256.

SECONDARY SOURCES
Brice, Denise. "L'oeuvre de Dorothée Le Maître (1896–1990)." *Annales de la Société du Nord* 1, no. 1 (1991): 15–18.

LEMMON, SARAH PLUMMER (1836–1923)

U.S. botanist. Born 1836 in New Gloucester, Maine. Married John Gill Lemmon. Educated Female College, Worcester, Mass.; Cooper Union, New York City. Died in Stockton, Calif., 1923.

Although now known as a botanist, during the Civil War, Sarah Plummer served as a hospital nurse. In 1869, she moved to California, where in 1880 she married botanist John Gill Lemmon (1832–1909). Through her husband, Lemmon became interested in botany. She produced watercolor paintings of the flora of the Pacific slope; her collection of more than eighty sketches of flowers made in the field took a prize at the World's Exposition in New Orleans in 1884–1885. She discovered a new genus of plants in 1882, named *Plummera floribunda* by Asa Gray (1810–1888) in her honor. Lemmon published three scientific papers and was a skilled collector and painter of plants. JH/MBO

PRIMARY SOURCES
Lemmon, Sarah Plummer. *A Record of the Red Cross Work on the Pacific Slope, including California, Nevada, Oregon, Washington with Their Auxiliaries.* Oakland, Calif.: Pacific Press Publishing, 1902. The preface is signed "Mrs. J. G. Plummer, Chairman." It also includes reprots from Nebraska, Tennessee, and "far-away Japan."
Lemmon, John Gill. *How to Tell the Trees and Forest Endowment of the Pacific Slope . . . and Also Some Elements of Forestry with Suggestions by Mrs. Lemmon. The Cone-Bearers,* 1st ser. Oakland, Calif., 1902.

SECONDARY SOURCES
Barnhart, John Hendley, comp. *Biographical Notes upon Botanists.* 3 vols. G. K. Hall, 1965.
Ewan, Joseph. "Bibliographical Miscellany—V. Sara Allen Plummer Lemmon and her Ferns of the Pacific Coast." *American Midland Naturalist* 33 (September 1944): 513–518.

STANDARD SOURCES
Appleton's Cyclopaedia; Bailey.

LEONTIUM (4th and 3d century B.C.E.)

Greek Epicurean philosopher. Either the wife or concubine of Metrodorus. One son and one daughter. Follower of Epicurus.

The place of Leontium in history is very unclear. She was a hetaera or courtesan. Athenian citizens often found their lawful wives boring and uninterested in ideas. Since they could not leave their wives, they often turned to the well-educated hetaerae who were seldom from Athens and most often from a city-state where the women had a better chance of getting an education. Many of the salons were presided over by the well-educated, interesting hetaerae.

The sources are unclear about Leontium's place. Ménage alleges that she was Epicurus's courtesan. As Epicurus's mistress and presumably his pupil, she apparently was acquainted with Epicureanism. According to Castner, Epicurus made her president of his school for a day. Castner also reported that Leontium married Metrodorus and that they had a son and daughter. However, Diogenes Laertius reported that Metrodorus took Leontium as his concubine. The problem is further complicated by a painting by Aristides of Thebes that led biographers to assume that she was involved in philosophical thinking, for she was pictured in a pose of meditation. Recently a statue in the Vatican Library has been identified as female, and one researcher is convinced that it is Leontium, whereas another argues that it is Themista.

JH/MBO

SECONDARY SOURCES

Castner, Catherine J. "Epicurean Hetairai as Dedicants to Healing Deities?" *Greek, Roman and Byzantine Studies* 23 (1982): 51–57.

Diogenes Laertius. *Lives of Eminent Philosophers.* Trans. R. D. Hicks. Cambridge, Mass.: Harvard University Press, 1925. Leontium mentioned in book 10, 4 ff.

STANDARD SOURCES

Alic; Ménage; Mozans; Rébière.

LEOPARDA (ca. 340 C.E.)

Roman physician. Professional experience: Court of Gratian (359–383).

Our information about Leoparda's medicine comes through Priscian, the emperor Gratian's physician. He wrote a book for women doctors that contained quotations from Soranus, Cleopatria, and Aspasia. Some of it was in rhyme so that the women could remember it. He dedicated the book to three woman physicians, Leoparda, Salvina, and Victoria. In this book he noted that Leoparda was a respected gynecologist, but that her remedies were no more scientific than those of the Greek Dioscorides.

JH/MBO

SECONDARY SOURCES

Priscianus Theodorus. *Ad Timotheum fratrem. Book 3: Gynaecea ad Slavinam.* Basel: In Officina Frobeniana, 1532. Book 3 discusses Leoparda.

STANDARD SOURCES

Dorland; Hurd-Mead 1938; Mozans.

LEPAUTE, NICOLE-REINE HORTENSE (ETABLE DE LA BRIÈRE) (1723–1788)

French astronomer. Born 5 January 1723 in Paris. Married Jean André Lepaute (27 August 1748). Died 6 December 1788 at Saint-Cloud.

According to the astronomer Joseph Jérôme Lalande (1732–1807), Nicole-Reine (called Hortense) Lepaute was the most distinguished female astronomer France had produced. She was born in the Luxembourg Palace in Paris, where her father, Etable de la Brière, was a member of the entourage of Elizabeth d'Orléans, the queen of Spain. As a child she gained a reputation for intelligence and "spirit." Although she devoured all available books and attended a variety of lectures, she was also known for her social gifts. This agreeable young woman was married in 1748 to Jean André Lepaute (1720–1789), who became the royal clockmaker of France. Through helping her husband and through her association with his friends, Hortense Lepaute became interested in mathematics and astronomy. Much of her adult life was spent in perfecting her skills in these areas. Although Lepaute had no children of her own, she encouraged and assisted in the education of two young men from her husband's family. His poor health and her own failing eyesight cut short her career in astronomy. Her death in 1788 was a great loss to Lalande, who wrote, "Cette femme intéressante est souvent présente à ma pensée, toujours chère à mon coeur" (This interesting woman has been often in my thoughts and always dear to my heart) (Lalande, 681).

Lepaute made several important scientific contributions. In 1757 the mathematician and astronomer Alexis Claude Clairaut (1713–1765) enlisted the help of Lalande and Lepaute in determining the exact time when Halley's comet would reappear in 1759. The chief problem was to assess the influence of the gravitational attraction of Jupiter and of Saturn on the movement of the comet. Lepaute was, according to Lalande, an essential link in the entire operation, performing most of the laborious calculations. Her abilities were tested again in 1762, when an annular eclipse of the sun was predicted for France in two years' time. She calculated the time and percentage of eclipse for all of Europe and published a map showing the progress of the eclipse at quarter-hour intervals. From these calculations, she compiled a table for the *Connaissance des temps* of 1763. During the years 1760 to 1776, while Lalande was editor of the *Connaissance des temps* (an almanac published by the Academy of Sciences for the use of astronomers and navigators), Lepaute helped him with the production of ephemerides—tables listing the positions of various celestial bodies for each day of the year—for that publication. She was also interested in her husband's work on pendulums, joining him and Lalande in writing a *Traité d'horlogerie* (1775). For this book, published under her husband's name, Lepaute calculated a table of the number of oscillations per unit of time made by pendulums of various lengths.

Although only one of Lepaute's publications is cited in the catalogue of the French Bibliothèque Nationale, she was more productive than this single entry indicates. Most of her work consisted of tables that formed part of the published work of other scientists.   MBO

PRIMARY SOURCES

Lepaute, Nicole-Reine. *Explications de la carte qui représente le passage de l'ombre de la lune au travers de l'Europe dans l'eclipse du soleil centrale et annulaire du I Avril 1764, présenté au Roi, le 12 aoü 1762, par Mme Le Paute.*

SECONDARY SOURCES

Krupp, E. C. "Astronomical Musings." *Griffith Observer* 39 (May 1975): 8–18.

STANDARD SOURCES

Bibliographie astronomique; Biographie universelle, vol. 24; *DSB; DFC;* Ogilvie 1986; Rebière (includes portrait).

LEPESHINSKAIA, OL'GA BORISOVNA (1871–1963)

Russian biologist and revolutionary. Born 18 August 1871 in Perm, daughter of Boris Protopopov. Married Panteleimon N. Lepeshinskii. One daughter, Ol'ga. Educated in St. Petersburg; University of Lausanne, Switzerland; Moscow University (M.D., 1915). Professional experience: Tashkent and Moscow, teacher, researcher; Timiriazev Biological Institute, staff; All-Union Institute of Experimental Medicine, research staff; Institute of Experimental Biology, researcher. Stalin Prize 1950. Died 2 October 1963 in Moscow.

Ol'ga Borisovna Lepeshinskaia was born into a wealthy family. Accounts vary as to her education as, although enrolled in various institutions, her political activities seem to have been more important to her than her studies. She first became involved in the revolutionary struggle as a medical student in St. Petersburg. In 1894, she participated in the work of the St. Petersburg Union for the struggle to emancipate the working class, and in 1898, she joined the Social Democratic Party. Her revolutionary pseudonym was Galia. In 1897, Lepeshinskaia followed her husband into exile in Siberia, where she worked for a time as a feldsher or surgeon's assistant (something akin to a nurse practitioner). In this period she was among those exiles who signed Lenin's protest against the manifesto (known as the Credo) put out by the Economists (a revolutionary faction that supported the struggle for better labor conditions and social improvements within the framework of the existing order). Later she took part in ef-

forts to organize a group in Pskov to cooperate with Lenin's Iskra group. She was thus associated with the Bolshevik wing of the revolutionary movement from the beginning.

Lepeshinskaia then went to Switzerland to continue her medical education at the University of Lausanne. In 1902 she returned briefly to Russia to organize her husband's flight from Siberia, before returning again to Switzerland. In 1906, she came back to Russia and worked as a physician in Moscow and the Crimea, at the same time playing an active role in Communist Party work. At the time of the Revolution of 1917, she was a member of the Revolutionary Committee of the Podmoskovnaia station.

After the revolution, Lepeshinskaia worked as a teacher and researcher in Tashkent and then Moscow. In 1926, she joined the staff of the histological laboratory at the Timiriazev Biological Institute. In 1936, she was on the staff of the cytology laboratory of the All-Union Institute of Experimental Medicine of the Soviet Academy of Medical Sciences, and in 1949 she became associated with the Institute of Experimental Biology of the Soviet Academy of Medical Sciences.

Although her higher education was deficient, her status as an Old Bolshevik and friend of Lenin helped her to find research work in scientific institutions. In 1931, Lepeshinskaia reported that she had discovered animal cell membranes that differed from those previously described, and in 1934, she reported a process by which nonliving matter turned into living matter. Her work was criticized by a number of specialists and would undoubtedly have died a natural death if Lepeshinskaia had not managed to use her revolutionary connections to get Stalin's approval of the manuscript in which she described her experiments. In 1945, the Academy of Sciences published a book in which these experiments were described in detail. This book, which was highly praised by the agronomist Trofim D. Lysenko, the promoter of an obscurantist pseudoscience known as, among other things, "Michurinist biology," was submitted to the Stalin Prize Committee, but was almost unanimously voted down. A year or two later, Lepeshinskaia published another similar book which was again criticized by the scientific community.

By now, however, Lysenko, who had gained the support of the political establishment, had seen the usefulness of Lepeshinskaia's work as support for his own theories. If, as she claimed, cells could arise from noncellular matter, perhaps one species could turn into another by passing through a stage of this "cell-free" material. Lysenko and his supporters began to promote Lepeshinskaia. Her book was resubmitted for the Stalin Prize, which she was awarded in 1950.

Lepeshinskaia was celebrated and glorified in various ways: a film, *Court of Honor* and a play, *Taking Up the Cudgels,* were written in her honor. Her eightieth birthday in 1951 was marked by many celebrations. She became a deputy of the Supreme Soviet and was appointed to many scientific commissions.

By the early 1950s, the foundations of Lysenko's "Michurinist biology" were beginning to crumble, and Lepeshinskaia's theories became increasingly challenged. One of her more fantastic notions was the idea that bicarbonate of soda taken internally or in the form of baths would promote longevity and cure many ailments. Unfortunately for Lepeshinskaia, this venture into practical medicine was too easily tested and popular disillusionment set in.

On 5 March 1953, Stalin died, and with his death, criticism of Lepeshinskaia and Lysenko became increasingly vocal. Within a few years, references to her theories quietly disappeared.

It is difficult to know to what extent Lepeshinskaia believed in her own pseudo discoveries in which wishful thinking probably played a part. There is no doubt that she and her daughter, Ol'ga Panteleimonovna, who assisted her, were careless, sloppy experimenters, but she was also ambitious and had no hesitation denouncing her critics. To her, even such a revered scientist as Louis Pasteur was a reactionary and a bourgeois idealist. In support of the new "science," textbooks were rewritten, scientists were persecuted and disastrous agricultural experiments were undertaken. Lepeshinskaia's fatuous egotism made her a perfect tool in the hands of Lysenko, who, for his own personal ends, had no hesitation in destroying genuine scientists and setting Soviet life sciences back thirty years.

Ol'ga Borisovna Lepeshinskaia's name is inextricably linked to this shameful and tragic episode in the history of Russian science.   ACH

PRIMARY SOURCES

Lepeshinskaia, Ol'ga Borisovna. *Proiskhozhdenie kletok iz zhivogo veshchestva i rol' zhivogo veshchestva v organizme.* Moscow: Izd-vo Akademii nauk SSSR, 1945.

———. *Vnekletochnye formy zhizny.* Moscow: Izd-vo Akademii pedagogicheskikh nauk RSFSR, 1952.

SECONDARY SOURCES

Bol'shaia sovetskaia entsiklopediia. 3d. ed. Moscow: Izd-vo "Sovetskaia entsiklopediia," 1973.

Medvedev, Zhores A. *The Rise and Fall of T. D. Lysenko.* Trans. I. Michael Lerner. New York: Columbia University Press, 1969.

Soyfer, Valery N. *Lysenko and the Tragedy of Soviet Science.* Trans. Leo and Rebecca Gruliow. New Brunswick, N.J.: Rutgers University Press, 1994.

Wieczynski, Joseph L., ed. *The Modern Encyclopedia of Russian and Soviet History.* Gulf Breeze, Fla.: Academic International Press, 1976–1994.

STANDARD SOURCES

Debus; Grinstein 1997 (article by John Konopak); *Great Soviet Encyclopedia,* vol. 14; *WWW (USSR).*

LEPIN, LIDIIA KARLOVNA (1891–?)

Russian physical chemist. Born 4 April 1891. Educated Moscow Higher Women's Courses. Professional experience: Plekhanov Institute of Popular Economy, staff (1917–1930); Moscow Higher Technical School, researcher (1920–1932); Voroshilov Academy of Chemical Defense, researcher (1932–1941); Moscow University, researcher (1920–1930; 1942–1946); Latvian University and Chemistry Institute of Latvian Academy of Sciences, researcher. Death date unknown.

Lidiia Karlovna Lepin (or Liepinia) graduated from the Higher Women's Courses in Moscow in 1917. From 1917 to 1930, she worked at the Plekhanov Institute of Popular Economy. She was also on the staff of Moscow University (1920–1930) and at the Moscow Higher Technical School (1920–1932). From 1932 to 1941, Lepin was on the staff of the Voroshilov Academy of Chemical Defense. In 1942 she returned to Moscow University where she remained until 1946.

In 1946 Lepin moved to Riga in Latvia, where she was on the staff of the Latvian University and the Chemistry Institute of the Latvian Academy of Sciences.

Lepin's principal research has been in the field of physical and colloidal chemistry, particularly on the action of chemical colloids in retarding corrosion, on hydride formation, absorption in solids, surface reactions, and dispersion of solutes.   JH/MBO

PRIMARY SOURCES

Lepin, Lidiia Karlovna. With coauthor. *Inorganic Chemistry: An Introduction to Preparative Inorganic Chemistry.* N.p., 1932.

———. *Surface Compounds and Surface Chemical Reactions.* N.p., 1940.

STANDARD SOURCES

Debus.

LERMONTOVA, EKATERINA VLADIMIROVNA (1899–1942)

Russian paleontologist. Born 11 February 1899 in St. Petersburg. Educated Women's Pedagogical Institute; University of St. Petersburg. Professional experience: Geological Committee; All-Union Scientific Research Institute of Geology. Died 9 January 1942 in Leningrad.

Ekaterina Vladimirovna Lermontova was born in St. Petersburg in 1899. She was a member, on her father's side, of the Lermontov family, which included the poet Mikhail I. Lermontov and the chemist IULIIA VSEVOLODOVNA LERMONTOVA. Lermontova graduated from the Women's Pedagogical Institute in 1910 and from the University of St. Petersburg in 1912.

Beginning in 1921, Lermontova worked on the Geological Committee and later in the All-Union Scientific Research Institute of Geology. She died in the blockade of Leningrad in the terrible winter of 1942.

Lermontova was the first researcher of Cambrian trilobite fauna on the territory of the USSR and the creator of the first Cambrian stratigraphic scheme of Siberia.

Her main area of research was the trilobites of the southern Urals, Siberia, Middle Asia, and Kazakhstan. Several fossil animals, algae, and biostratigraphic divisions of the Cambrian have been named after her.   ACH

PRIMARY SOURCES

Lermontova, Ekaterina Vladimirovna. *Kembriiskaia sistema.* Moscow: N.p., 1965.

SECONDARY SOURCES

Bol'shaia sovetskaia entsiklopediia. 3d ed. Moscow: Izd-vo "Sovetskaia entsiklopediia," 1973.

LERMONTOVA, IULIIA VSEVOLODOVNA (1847–1919)

Russian chemist. Born 2 January 1847 in St. Petersburg, daughter of a general. One sister. Educated Heidelberg University; Berlin University; Göttingen University (Ph.D., 1874). Professional experience: worked in Moscow with V. V. Markovnikov; St. Petersburg with A. M. Butlerov. Died December 1919 in Petrograd.

Iuliia Vsevolodovna Lermontova came of a distinguished family: her father, a general and director of the Moscow Cadet Corps, was a second cousin of Mikhail I. Lermontov, the poet. Her family was enlightened and although puzzled by Lermontova's early interest in chemistry, did not discourage it, and even engaged private tutors for her. At first she thought of studying medicine, but the sight of corpses and the sufferings of the patients horrified her. Instead she applied to the Petrovskaia Agricultural Academy (later the Timiriazev Academy), which had an excellent chemistry program. Although she had the support of several professors, her application was turned down, and she decided to go abroad.

Through her cousin Anna Evreinova (later to become Russia's first woman doctor of laws), Lermontova made the acquaintance of the mathematician SOFIA KOVALEVSKAIA, who was also planning to study abroad. Kovalevskaia came to Moscow, where she persuaded Lermontova's reluctant parents to allow her to leave. In the autumn of 1869, Lermontova arrived in Heidelberg, and took up residence with the Kovalevskis. With typical forcefulness, Kovalevskaia intervened with the university authorities to overcome obstacles and Lermontova was allowed to attend some lectures and to work in the laboratory of the German chemist R. W. Bunsen. They were joined by Anna Evreinova who, unable to obtain her parents' permission to leave Russia, had simply walked over the border, under fire from the border patrol.

In 1871, Lermontova and Kovalevskaia left Heidelberg for Berlin. There Lermontova worked in the laboratory of August W. Hofman and published her first research paper. By the beginning of 1874, Lermontova had completed her dissertation, which she successfully defended in Göttingen.

Returning to Russia in 1874, Lermontova was greeted cordially by Dmitri I. Mendeleev and other chemists. For a time she worked in the laboratory of V. V. Markovnikov in Moscow, but later returned to St. Petersburg, where she worked in the university laboratory with A. M. Butlerov and M. D. L'vov.

In 1877, Lermontova's father died and family business kept her in Moscow. Butlerov tried to persuade her to return to St. Petersburg to teach at the recently opened Higher Women's Courses, but she hesitated: she feared the minister of education would not approve the appointment and she also cited other personal reasons. Butlerov was not satisfied and he put the blame, not without reason, on Kovalevskaia, whom he accused of exploiting Lermontova, leaving her daughter in Lermontova's care while she went gadding abroad (as he put it).

In 1880, still in Moscow, Lermontova was asked to take part in a study of petroleum. This fuel, which had been discovered in large quantities in the Baku area, was beginning to be exploited in Russia at this time, and there had been little native research on the subject. Lermontova joined the Russian Technical Society and until 1888 worked in its chemical-technical group.

Lermontova had inherited the family estate, Semenkovo, and was in the habit of passing a few summer months there. Ultimately she took up permanent residence there and, abandoning chemistry, turned her attention to scientific agriculture. Her cheeses achieved great success and were sold in Moscow and the Ukraine.

Lermontova never married but she had the nearest thing to a daughter in her goddaughter, "Fufa" Kovalevskaia, to whom she was "Mama Iulia."

After the October Revolution of 1917, there was an attempt to dispossess Lermontova from her estate, but A. B.

Lunacharskii, the Commissar of Education, intervened, and she was left in peace. She died in 1919.

Lermontova never held an official post. Her working life was devoted to research and can be divided into roughly three periods, in all of which she made valuable contributions to chemistry. Her earliest research was done at Heidelberg in Bunsen's laboratory. There she investigated methods of separating the platinum metals.

More important work was done by Lermontova in the field of organic chemistry. This research was conducted in Hofman's laboratory in Berlin and later in Moscow and St. Petersburg. She was the first to study the alkylation of olefins by halogen derivatives and the first to obtain 1,3-dibromobutane and dimethylacetylene and to demonstrate the structure of 4,4-diaminohydrazobenzene.

Lermontova's last period of research was devoted to her work for the petroleum industry. In the 1870s and 1880s, this was a rapidly expanding field in which many of the foremost chemists of the day were involved. She was the first woman to undertake research in this area. At Markovnikov's suggestion, Lermontova studied catalytic cracking and the pyrolysis of petroleum. In 1883, she presented a report to the Moscow division of the Russian Technical Society on this subject. Much of her work had a practical character: she developed an original apparatus for the continuous distillation of petroleum, which was highly praised by her contemporaries. In the period before her voluntary retirement, she was considered one of the foremost chemists of the day.   ACH

PRIMARY SOURCES

Lermontova, Iuliia Vsevolodovna. "Über die Zusammensetzung des Diphenins." *Berichte* 5 (1872): 231–235.
———. "O poluchenii normal'nogo bromistogo propilena trimetilenbromida." *Zhurnal Russkogo khimicheskogo obshchestva* 8 (1876): 281–283.
———. "Poluchenie krotonilena." *Zhurnal Russkogo khimicheskogo obshchestva* (1881): 13.

SECONDARY SOURCES

Bol'shaia sovetskaia entsiklopedia. 3d ed. Moscow: Izd-vo "Sovetskaia entsiklopedia," 1973.
Musabekov, Iusuf S. *Iuliia Vsevolodovna Lermontova, 1846–1919.* Moscow: Izd-vo "Nauka," 1967.

LESCHI, JEANNE (fl. 1958)

French physical anthropologist. Never married. Educated University of Paris (licenciée en sciences). Professional experience: Museum National d'Histoire Naturelle, Laboratoire de Physiologie. Centre National Recherches Scientifique, chargée de recherches (1956). Memberships: Société d'Anthropologie (1945).

Jeanne Leschi, who obtained her doctorate in science, first worked in the Physiology Laboratory at the Museum National d'Histoire Naturelle, the great natural history museum in Paris, later supported by her position with Centres Nationales Recherches Scientifiques. She published articles on fingerprints of West African peoples in 1948; on the stature of the Ouolof of West Africa (1948); and on skull measurements of members of the Dogon tribe in 1958 and 1959.

JH/MBO

PRIMARY SOURCES

Leschi, Jeanne. *Pigmentation and Fonctionnement Cortico-Surrenalien.* Paris: Masson, 1952.
———. "Fingerprints of West African People." *Bulletin et Memoires Société d'Anthropologie de Paris* 48.
———. "Stature of the Ouolof." *Bulletin et Memoires Société d' Anthropologie de Paris* 48.
———. "Craniometry of the Dogon." *Bulletin et Memoires Société Anthropologie de Paris* (1958; 1959).

LESLIE (BURR), MAY SYBIL (ca. 1887–1937)

British chemist. Possibly from Glasgow. Married Alfred Hamilton Burr (1922?). Educated University of Leeds, Britain (B.Sc., 1908; M.Sc., 1909; D.Sc., 1918). Professional experience: Radium Institute, Paris, researcher (1909–1911); University of Manchester, researcher (1911–1912); University of Leeds, honorary demonstrator, department of physical chemistry (1909, and summer 1910); Municipal High School for Girls, West Hartlepool, science mistress (1912–1914); University College of North Wales, Bangor, junior assistant lecturer and demonstrator (1914–1915); H. M. Factory, Messrs. Brotherton's, Ltd., Liverpool, research chemist (1916–1917); director of laboratory (1916–1918); University of Leeds, demonstrator in chemistry (1918–1919); assistant lecturer and demonstrator in chemistry (1919–1924); assistant lecturer and demonstrator in physical chemistry (1926–1927). Probably remained on the Leeds faculty until her death. Died in Bardsey, England, near Leeds, 3 July 1937.

May Sybil Leslie registered at the University of Leeds in October 1905 at age eighteen with the intent of becoming a teacher. An excellent student in all her courses, she graduated with first-class honors in chemistry. After receiving a university research scholarship in physical chemistry, Leslie studied the reaction mechanism between iodine and acetone under Harry M. Dawson. She also investigated abnormal ionization phenomena in organic media, including the anomalous electrical conductivity of solutions of iodine in nitrobenzene.

Leslie was awarded the 1851 Exhibition Science Scholarship for 1909–1910, and with her master of science work completed, she went to Paris to work in MARIE CURIE's laboratory. There she searched (unsuccessfully) for new radioactive elements in the mineral thorite. She then investigated thorium and its decay products, and used diffusion to find the molecular weight of thorium emanation (later known as radon). Leslie enjoyed Paris and her work, and succeeded in obtaining a second year on the scholarship. During the summer of 1910, she returned briefly to England and served as honorary demonstrator for her former chemistry professor Arthur Smithell's domestic science class, held at Scarborough.

During 1911–1912, Leslie continued working with radioactive gases in Rutherford's laboratory at Manchester. She found that the emanations from actinium and thorium diffused at about the same rate. This meant that their atomic weights must be similar, as predicted by Rutherford and Soddy's theory of radioactivity.

For the next three years, Leslie taught at University College of North Wales, where she installed a physical chemistry laboratory and organized a course in physical chemistry for honors students. In 1915 she began work as an industrial research chemist for the war effort. Leslie received a doctorate of science in 1918 for her researches, particularly those on radioactive substances and on production of explosives and use of their by-products.

Leslie returned to Leeds, where she apparently spent the rest of her career. During this time, she married and became known as Dr. Burr. Her husband died a few years after the marriage. Leslie seems to have enjoyed literature, such as the works of Jane Austen and Charlotte Brontë. JH/MBO

PRIMARY SOURCES

Leslie, May Sybil. With Harry M. Dawson. "Dynamics of the Reaction between Iodine and Acetone." *Transactions of the Chemical Society* 95 (1909): 1860–1870.

———. With Harry M. Dawson. "Ionization in Non-aqueous Solvents." *Transactions of the Chemical Society* 99 (1911): 1601.

———. "Sur le poids moléculaire de l'émanation du thorium." *Comptes rendus* 153 (1911): 328–330.

———. "Le thoriun et ses produits de désagrétion." *Le radium* 8 (1911): 356–363.

———. "Sur la période du radiothorium et le nombre des particules α données par le thorium et ses produits." *Le radium* 9 (1912): 276–277.

———. "A Comparison of the Coefficients of Diffusion of Thorium and Actinium Emanations, with a Note on their Periods of Transformation." *Philosophical Magazine* 24 (1912): 637–647.

Letters from Leslie to Arthur Smithells, 1909–1911. Leeds University Library.

SECONDARY SOURCES

Badash, Lawrence. *Radioactivity in America.* Baltimore and London: Johns Hopkins University Press, 1983.

Davis, J. L., "The Research School of Marie Curie in the Paris Faculty, 1907–14." *Annals of Science* 52 (1995): 321–355.

Rutherford, Ernest. *Radioactive Substances and Their Radiations.* Cambridge: Cambridge University Press, 1913.

STANDARD SOURCES

Rayner-Canham 1997.

L'ESPERANCE, ELISE DEPEW STRANG (1878–1959)

U.S. pathologist. Born 1878 (1879?) in Yorktown, N.Y., to Kate (Depew) and Albert Strang. One sister. Married David L'Esperance, lawyer. Educated St. Agnes Episcopal School in Albany; Woman's Medical College of the New York Infirmary for Women and Children (M.D., 1899); Babies Hospital, N.Y., resident (1900–1902). Professional experience: private practice in pediatrics (1900–1908); Cornell Medical College, assistant in pathology (1910–1912), instructor in pathology (1912–1920), assistant professor (1920–1932), professor of preventive medicine (1950–1959); New York Infirmary for Women and Children, New York, pathologist and laboratory director (1910–1936); Strang Cancer Prevention Clinic, director (1932–1959); Memorial Hospital for Cancer, assistant pathologist; New York Hospital, assistant pathologist; Pathological Institute, Munich, Mary Putman Jacobi Fellow (1914); Bellevue Hospital, instructor in surgical pathology (1918–1932). Honors and memberships: American Woman's Association Friendship Award for Eminent Achievement (1946); New York City Cancer Committee Clement Cleveland Medal (1948); Elizabeth Blackwell Citation (1950), New York Academy of Medicine, Fellow. Died 21 January 1959.

Elise Strang and her sister grew up in the home of a physician, Albert Strang. Their mother, Kate Depew Strang, died of cancer, and Elise decided early in her life to follow her father's career. She entered the Woman's Medical College of the New York Infirmary at age sixteen, just after graduating from St. Agnes Episcopal School. After receiving her medical degree, she practiced for several years in pediatrics before becoming interested in tuberculosis research. She became a member of the Tuberculosis Research Commission of the research laboratory of New York City, directed by William H. Park. This, plus bacteriology work for the New York City Department of Health, drew her increasingly into pathology as a specialty. In 1910, she was accepted as an assistant to James Ewing, cancer specialist at Cornell University Medical School, who had previously refused to hire women assistants. From this introduction, she remained at Cornell forty years, retiring as full professor—the first woman in this position in preventive medicine.

When an uncle, Chauncey Depew, left a sizable inheritance to L'Esperance and her sister, they established the Kate

Depew Strang Tumor Clinic at the New York Infirmary for Women and Children, in honor of their mother (1932). They eventually assisted with the establishment of two additional preventive and treatment clinics, which became the models for similar centers elsewhere in the United States. L'Esperance's interest in tumor pathology led her to Munich, Germany, and to years of cancer research at Cornell, out of which came several important papers. In 1948, she added services for the detection of diabetes to those for early detection of cancer at her clinics. She was also interested in early detection of tuberculosis and Hodgkin's disease. L'Esperance published around thirty peer-reviewed papers.

As an alternative to her intense professional work, L'Esperance made a home with her sister in suburban Westchester County, raising horses and cats and racing harness ponies. She was known for the unusual hats she wore on every possible occasion.   JH/MBO

PRIMARY SOURCES

L'Esperance, Elise. "Primary Atypical Malignant Hepatomia." *Journal of Medical Research* (1915).
———. "Early Carcinoma of the Cervix." *American Journal of Obstetrics and Gynecology* (October 1924).
———. "Influence of the New York Infirmary on Women in Medicine." *Journal of the American Medical Women's Association* (1949).

STANDARD SOURCES

AMS 5–8, B 9; Bailey; *Current Biography* 1950, 1959; *NAW*(M) (article by Deborah Dwork); Shearer and Shearer 1996; *WW in America*, vol. 26, 1950–1951.

LEVERTON, RUTH MANDEVILLE (1908–)

U.S. nutritionist. Born 23 March 1908 in Minneapolis. Educated University of Nebraska (B.S., 1928); University of Arizona (M.S. 1932); University of Chicago (Ph.D., 1937). Professional experience: Nebraska high school, teacher (1928–1930); University of Arizona Experimental Station, assistant (1932–1934); University of Nebraska, assistant professor (1937–1940), associate professor (1941–1949), professor (1949–1954); United States Department of Agriculture, Bureau of Home Economics (1940–1941); Oklahoma Agricultural and Mechanical College, professor of home economics and assistant director, agricultural experimental station (1954–1958); Agricultural Research Service, associate director, institute of home economics (1958–1961), assistant department administrator (1961–1971), science advisor (1971–1974). Retired 1974. Concurrent experience: University of the Philippines, Fulbright Professor (1949–1950). Honors and memberships: Bordon Award (1953); University of Nebraska honorary degree (1961); University of Nebraska Institute for Nutritional Research; American

Dietetic Association; American Home Economic Association; American Public Health Association.

Ruth Leverton received her bachelor's degree from the University of Nebraska and returned to that institution to teach after she earned her doctoral degree. She took a year off from Nebraska and worked at the United States Department of Agriculture, but returned to Nebraska, where she climbed the academic ranks to professor. She moved to Stillwater, Oklahoma, in 1954, where she remained for four years, after which she returned to the USDA for a position in the human research division and the institute of home economics. She remained in this position until she retired. According to Rossiter, the home economics units were reduced in size and some were eliminated. The three remaining divisions were combined to form an institute of home economics under HAZEL STIEBELING and Ruth Leverton. She was a member of many societies and published papers on human metabolism, mineral requirements, the nutritive value of Nebraska food products, and blood regeneration and prevention of anemia.   JH/MBO

PRIMARY SOURCES

Leverton, Ruth. *Food Becomes You*. Lincoln: University of Nebraska Press, 1952.
———. With Floyd Leslie Rogers. *Your Diabetes and How to Live with It*. Lincoln: University of Nebraska Press, 1953.

STANDARD SOURCES

AMS 8, B 9, P&B 10–13; Bailey; Rossiter 1995.

LEVI, HILDE (1909–)

German-born Danish physicist. Born 1909 in Frankfurt am Main, Germany to Claire Reis and Adolf Levi. Educated Victoria School in Frankfurt; University of Munich; University of Berlin (D.Phil., 1934). Professional experience: Kaiser Wilhelm Institute for Physical Chemistry (under Hans Beutler), researcher (1932–1934); Danish Institute for Theoretical Physics (Niels Bohr), researcher (1934–1939?). Stockholm Wennergren Institute for Experimental Biology, researcher (1939?–1946); University of Copenhagen? Laboratory of Zoological Physics, researcher (1946–1954), amanuensis (1954–1960), docent (1960–1979), professor emerita (from 1979). Honors and memberships: Tagea Brandts award (1955); George Hevesy Foundation Gold Medal (1975).

Hilde Levi was born and raised in Frankfurt am Main in Germany. She attended the Victoria School and studied physics at the universities of Munich and Berlin. She obtained her doctorate from the University of Berlin in 1934, working at the Kaiser Wilhelm Institute for Physical Chemistry under Hans Beutler. With the anti-Jewish laws, she was forced to emigrate and went first to Denmark where she worked with August Krogh and Niels Bohr on radioactive isotopes and, most important, with George (Gyorgy) Hevesy. In 1936, Hevesy and Levi together published a significant article detailing a method of neutron activation analysis, now one of the most important microanalytic procedures. They also worked on isotope tracer techniques. Hevesy would receive the Nobel Prize for this and earlier work in 1946.

As the Nazi army approached Copenhagen, Levi and Hevesy fled to Stockholm, where Levi worked in the Wennergren Institute for Experimental Biology, while Hevesy was at the university. After the war, she continued to work in the field of radioactive physics in the University of Copenhagen[?] Laboratory of Zoological Physics, retiring as an emerita professor in 1979.

In 1947–1948, Levi came briefly to the United States to work with Willard F. Libby at the University of Chicago on methods of carbon 14 dating. In the 1950s, she helped develop the use of artificial radioactive isotopes for biology and medicine. She was a consultant on radioactivity from 1954 to 1971. She was awarded the George Hevesy Foundation's gold medal in 1975, and wrote biographical accounts of Hevesy's life and work.   JH/MBO

PRIMARY SOURCES
Levi, Hilde. "Die Spektren der Alkalihalogenide." D.Phil. diss., University of Berlin, 1934.
———. "George de Hevesy". *International Journal of Applied Radiation and Isotopes* 16 (1965): 512–524.
———. *George de Hevesy, Life and Work: A Biography.* Copenhagen: Rhodos, 1985.

SECONDARY SOURCES
Schmidt-Nielson, Bodil. *August and Marie Krogh.* New York: American Physiological Society, 1995. This biography of Schmidt-Nielson's parents includes some discussion of Hilde Levi's work in the late 1930s.

STANDARD SOURCES
Dansk Biografisk, vol 9.

LEVI-MONTALCINI, RITA (1908–)
Italian/U.S. neuroscientist. Born 22 April 1908 in Torino (Turin), Italy to Adele Montalcini and Adamo Levi. Three siblings. Educated public elementary school in Turin; Girls' High School, Turin; tutored privately for university entrance examinations; University of Turin (M.D. 1936). Professional experience: Institute of Anatomy, University of Turin, research assistant (1936–); Turin Clinic for Nervous and Mental Disorders, medical practitioner (1936–1938);

Neurology Institute, Brussels, researcher (1939); Washington University, St. Louis, researcher and eventually full professor (1946–1979); Center for Neurobiology, Rome, director of research concomitantly (1961–1979). Honors and memberships: Elected member of National Academy of Sciences (1968); William Thompson Wakeman Award of the National Paraplegic Foundation (1974); Lewis S. Rosenstiel Award of Brandeis University for Distinguished Work in Medical Research (1982); Louisa Gross Horowitz Prize of Columbia University (1983); Nobel Prize in medicine and physiology (1986); with Stanley Cohen, the Albert Lasker Medical Research Award (1987); National Medal of Science (1987); honorary doctorates from University of Uppsala (Sweden), the Weizmann Institute (Israel), St. Mary's College, and Washington University School of Medicine.

Rita Levi-Montalcini's Sephardic Jewish parents' families had settled in the Piedmont region of Italy for many generations. Both her mother's and father's families had a strong tradition of education, particularly for the boys. Although the family was Jewish, they were "free-thinkers." Nevertheless, Levi-Montalcini later became a victim of antisemitism and left Italy.

One of four children (one older brother, Gino, an older sister, Anna, and a fraternal twin sister, Paola), Rita Levi-Montalcini showed an early interest in intellectual subjects. Although Adamo Levi stressed the importance of education for his sons, he believed that too much education for the girls would make them unhappy. Despite the fact that she showed ability in mathematics and science, Levi attended a middle school and high school that lacked courses in mathematics, science, and the classics. Thus, though she graduated from the girls' high school in Turin with an excellent record, Levi-Montalcini was not prepared to attend the university. After graduation, she remained at home and spent much of her time reading. The death of her former governess, Giovanna Bruatto, from stomach cancer, made her determined to study medicine. Although her mother supported her, her father was skeptical. Eventually, he was convinced, and provided the tutors necessary to prepare her to sit for the university entrance examinations.

Levi-Montalcini and her cousin, Eugenia, prepared for the examinations together for eight months; at the end of that time, they made the highest scores on the entrance examination for the University of Turin. In 1930, they both entered the faculty of medicine. Levi-Montalcini was fortunate to come under the tutelage of Professor Guiseppe Levi at the Institute of Anatomy of the Turin Medical School. Although notorious for his outrage at incompetent students, he was a fine role model for the bright and hard-working ones. Levi-Montalcini fell into the latter category, and after passing her first-year examinations with honors was invited to be an intern in his laboratory. This experience led to her life-long study of the nervous system.

After she received her medical degree in 1936, Levi-Montalcini worked for two years as a research assistant for Professor Levi and began practice at the Turin Clinic for Nervous and Mental Disorders. Antisemitism in Italy caused Jews to be dismissed from their positions, and both she and Professor Levi lost theirs. During her last years in medical school, she met and became engaged to a young student who graduated with her. Germano R. Raising, her fiancé, was in poor health; he died in 1939 of tuberculosis.

Levi-Montalcini left Turin for Brussels, where she continued her research at the laboratory of Professor L. Laruelle. She worked there for less than a year and then returned to Turin. In Turin, she clandestinely helped those who were ill and could not afford a physician. However, she was unable to write prescriptions and the situation became more restrictive as Italy entered the war in 1940. During the war years, she worked out of her house using histologic techniques she had gleaned from the work of Santiago Ramon y Cajal for studying the nervous system. Turin became too dangerous for her to keep up the research, so she and her mother and sister moved to a farmhouse in Asti, where she again set up a makeshift laboratory. After the resignation of Benito Mussolini and the invasion of the German army in 1943, the family fled to Florence, where they lived under assumed identities until the end of the war. After the British entered Florence, Levi-Montalcini volunteered her service to the Red Cross. The helplessness she felt when faced with impossible conditions served to stimulate her to return to research.

During the summer of 1945, she returned to work in Levi's laboratory at the Institute of Anatomy in Turin, and enrolled in a course of biological studies, an area she had not yet studied. Late in this same year, she received an invitation from Victor Hamburger through Levi to come to Washington University, St. Louis, to continue work on spinal cord and ganglion development. Her first position at Washington University was as a visiting research associate, but her importance was recognized and she was made a full professor in the zoology department. She returned to Italy many times during her time at Washington University, keeping in close contact with her family. She also established a Center for Neurobiology in Rome that originally was supported by the National Science Foundation and later by institutes in Italy. After the establishment of the center, she spent six months of each year directing the center and the other six months doing research at Washington University. She retired from active teaching in 1979.

Levi-Montalcini's primary interest was in the development of the nervous system, neurogenesis. A major question was whether neurogenesis was genetically programmed or environmentally driven. The project assigned to Levi-Montalcini by Victor Hamburger prepared her to work on this question and others, which drove her research through her career. The first problem involved a tedious task of counting the number of neurons in the spinal ganglia of mice. The goal was to find out if all mice from the same litter had the same number of ganglia and if the number varied with mice from different litters. In other words, did all mice have the same number of neurons in their spinal ganglia. The second project was not a success, but the third one became the subject of her doctoral dissertation. She developed a new technique of tissue culture that made it possible to grow tissues *in vitro*. Thus, her two successful early projects introduced her to the two dominant facets of her research, neurogenesis and tissue culture.

Her experience at the Clinic for Nervous and Mental Disorders in Turin produced what she considered to be one of her most rewarding projects. There she worked with Fabio Visintini, who implanted electrodes into chick embryos. Through this technique he could stimulate specific neural centers of the embryos at different developmental stages. By using histological techniques, Levi-Montalcini studied the experimentally manipulated nervous system. Using Visintini's results, Levi-Montalcini could correlate specific stages of neurological development with the initiation of specific types of neurological responses. The paper that resulted from this research was published in 1939 in Switzerland, after being refused publication in Italy for political reasons.

During the time that Levi-Montalcini was working at home, she read Victor Hamburger's 1934 paper on the degeneration of ganglia and nerve columns in chick embryos whose limbs had been removed. Hamburger postulated that the cause of the degeneration was "induction" from a signal, probably chemical, sent from the peripheral tissues. Of course, if there was not peripheral tissue, then no outgrowth of nerves from the spinal cord and neural crest going into the tissues would occur. After extensive experimentation, Levi-Montalcini postulated an alternative hypothesis. She observed that the neurons actually do grow toward the stump of the amputated limb. However, the limb cannot be innervated because it is missing, and the nerve fibers and cell bodies then degenerate. She replaced Hamburger's idea of induction with a new postulate. She presumed that the peripheral tissue supplied a "trophic" factor that was necessary to keep the neuron from degenerating. She concluded that the relationship between the neuron and the innervated cells was one of mutual dependency. Although the neuron allows the peripheral cell to function, if it is not supplied with the "trophic" factor by the peripheral cell, then the neuron will die. Professor Levi, also without a job in 1942, worked with Levi-Montalcini on this project and published several papers on this research. Hamburger was intrigued by their papers and this interest caused him to invite Levi-Montalcini to Washington University.

At Washington University, Levi-Montalcini continued her tedious work on chick embryos, work that shed light on the relationship between genetics and the environment in the development of the nervous system. She noticed a pattern in the migration of the neurons in developing spinal cords that was the same in animals of the same species, thus indicating the importance of genetic programming. However, she also had demonstrated that environmental factors played a role in the development of the central nervous system. Using chick embryos was extremely time-consuming, so as she considered other models for her research, she thought about her earlier research on tissue culture. After a series of *in vitro* experiments, she and her collaborator, Stanley Cohen, identified a nerve growth factor (NGF). NGF demonstrated that the earlier ideas of both Hamburger and Levi-Montalcini were important. Both induction and trophic relationships are involved in neurogenesis and NGF chemically signalled both effects. In 1986, the partnership of Cohen and Levi-Montalcini shared the $290,000 Nobel Prize for medicine and physiology.

The importance of this work cannot be overemphasized. Scientists now had the tools to investigate and manipulate the development of the nervous system. The discovery of NGF and the development of antibodies to it opened up the whole area of neurosciences.   JH/MBO

PRIMARY SOURCES

Levi-Montalcini, Rita. With F. Visintini. "Relationship between the Functional and Structural Differentiation of the Nerve Centers and Pathways in the Chick Embryo." (In Italian and French). *Archives Suisses de Neurologie et de Psychiatrie* 43 (1939): 381–393; 44 (1939): 119–150.

———. With G. Levi. "The Consequences of Destruction of a Peripheral Innervation Territory on Development of Corresponding Central Nervous System Neurons in the Chick Embryo." (In French). *Archives de Biologie* 53 (1942): 537–545.

———. With G. Levi. "Developmental Correlations between the Parts of the Nervous System. The Consequences of Destruction of a Limb Bud on Development of the Corresponding Region of the Central Nervous System in the Chick Embryo." (In Italian). *Commentaries, Pontifical Academy of Science* 8 (1944): 527–568.

———. With V. Hamburger. "Proliferation, Differentiation, in the Spinal Ganglia of the Chick Embryo under Normal and Experimental Conditions." *Journal of Experimental Zoology* 3 (1949): 457–501.

———. With S. Cohen. "Purification and Properties of a Nerve-Growth-Promoting Factor Isolated from Mouse Sarcoma 180." *Cancer Research* 17 (1957): 15–20.

———. "The Nerve Growth Factor 35 Years Later." In *Les Prix Nobel, 1986,* 276–299. Stockholm: Nobel Foundation, 1987.

———. *In Praise of Imperfection: My Life and Work.* Trans. Luigi Attardi. New York: Basic Books, 1988.

SECONDARY SOURCES

"Collaborators Cohen and Levi-Montalcini Win the Medicine Nobel Prize." *Science News* 130 (1986): 244.

STANDARD SOURCES

Grinstein 1997 (article by Mary Clarke Miksic); *Notable.*

LEVINE, LENA (1903–1965)

U.S. gynecologist; psychiatrist. Born 17 May 1903 in Brooklyn, N.Y., to Sophie and Morris H. Levine. Six siblings. Married Louis Ferber (1929). Two children. Educated Girls High School Brooklyn; Hunter College (A.B., 1923); University and Bellevue Hospital Medical College (M.D., 1927). Professional experience: Private practice (1930–1965). Died 9 January 1965 in New York City of a stroke.

Lena Levine's career evolved from obstetrics and gynecology to gynecology and psychiatry and finally to marriage counseling and planned parenthood issues. After she received her medical degree she married Louis Ferber, a fellow student, and they did their residencies together at Brooklyn Jewish Hospital. Levine retained her maiden name. The couple started a practice together in Brooklyn, with Ferber serving as a general practitioner and Levine, as gynecologist and obstetrician. They had two children, a daughter, Ellen Louise (born 1939), and a son, Michael Allen (born 1942), who became severely retarded after a bout with viral encephalitis when he was an infant. Ferber died suddenly of a heart attack in 1943, causing Levine to change her lifestyle. She limited her practice to gynecology because of the irregular hours that were involved in obstetrics. She retrained as a Freudian psychologist, undergoing analysis at the Columbia Psychoanalytic Institute. This experience prompted her to place new emphasis on women's psychological health and freedom. She opened a separate psychiatric practice on Fifth Avenue while maintaing a small gynecological practice at her home. After her daughter left for college, she moved her practice to Greenwich Village.

While her children were growing up, Levine had been working for legalized birth control. She worked for the Birth Control Federation of America in both the U.S. organization and later as the medical secretary for the international organization. She also did marriage counseling and organized group counseling programs on sexual problems and contraception. Both on the individual and on the organizational levels, Levine was an effective advocate of birth control, lecturing widely in the United States and abroad. With her medical training, she was able to help women who had physical and emotional problems.   JH/MBO

PRIMARY SOURCES
Levine, Lena. *The Doctor Talks with the Bride.* New York: Planned Parenthood Federation of America, 1938.
———. With Beka Doherty. *The Menopause.* New York: Random House, 1952.
———. With Abraham Stone. *The Premarital Consultation.* New York: Grune and Stratton, 1956.
———. *The Emotional Sex: Why Women are the Way They Are Today.* New York: Morrow, 1964.

SECONDARY SOURCES
Gordon, Linda. *Woman's Body, Woman's Right: A Social History of Birth Control in America.* New York: Grossman, 1976.
New York Times, 11 January 1965. Obituary notice.

STANDARD SOURCES
Bailey; *NAW*(M) (article by Linda Gordon).

LEVYNS, MARGARET RUTHERFORD BRYAN (MICHELL) (1890–1975)

South African botanist. Born 24 October 1890 in Cape Town. Married John Levyns (1923). Educated South Africa College (B.A., 1911); Newnham College, Cambridge (1912–1914); John Innes Institute (1914–1916); Cape Town University (D.Sc., 1933). Professional experience: South Africa College (now Cape Town University), lecturer in botany (1916–1945). Honors and memberships: South African Association for Advancement of Science, president of section B (1952–1953); South African medal (1958); Royal Society of South Africa, president. Died 1975.

Margaret Rutherford Bryan Levyns was born in Cape Town, South Africa. She studied first at South Africa College (later Cape Town University), and after winning both the Queen Victoria scholarship and the 1851 Exhibition Memorial Scholarship she went for two years to Newnham College, Cambridge. After two years, she was awarded another scholarship to study genetics at the John Innes Institute near Cambridge.

Upon her return to South Africa, she obtained a position at her former university as lecturer in botany, a post she held until her obligatory retirement at the age of sixty-five. She married John Levyns, later assistant provincial secretary for the Cape Province, when she was in her mid-thirties. He shared her botanical interests, serving on the council of the Botanical Society of South Africa and joining her in her plant collecting. In 1933, Cape Town University awarded

her a doctorate in science for her study of the genus *Lobostemon.* She and her husband collected some twelve thousand plant specimens, which are in collections throughout South Africa and reflect her interest in phytogeography. Her work resulted in the revision of many South African plant genera, particularly *Muraltia.*

Even after her retirement, Margaret Levyns continued to be a very active scholar, writing a major part of the *Flora of the Cape Peninsula, Cape Town,* which appeared in 1950. She was awarded the South African medal in 1958 and served as president of the Royal Society of South Africa in 1962–1963. She was also honored with a special issue of the *Journal of South African Botany* (volume 38) dedicated to her in her seventy-eighth year. She died at the age of eighty-five.
                                                        JH/MBO

PRIMARY SOURCES
Levyns, Margaret Rutherford Bryan. *A Guide to the Flora of the Cape Peninsula.* Cape Town: Juta and Co. 1929.
———. *A Botanist's Memoirs.* Cape Town: University of Cape Town, 1968.

SECONDARY SOURCES
Levyns, John. *Insnar'd with Flow'rs.* Cape Town: 1977. Includes discussion of Margaret Levyns.
"Margaret Rutherford Levyns." *Veld and Flora* 61 (1975). Obituary notice.

STANDARD SOURCES
Gunn and Codd; Stafleu and Cowan.

LEWIS, FLORENCE PARTHENIA (1877–?)

U.S. mathematician and astronomer. Born 24 September 1877 in Ft. Scott, Kans. Educated University of Texas (A.B., 1897); Radcliffe (A.M., 1926); Johns Hopkins (Ph.D., 1913). Professional experience: Goucher College, professor of mathematics (1928–1938). Honors and memberships: Astronomical Society; Astronomical Society of the Pacific; Mathematical Society, councilor (1919–1922). Death date unknown.

Florence Parthenia Lewis was born in Kansas, but attended the University of Texas, where she received her undergraduate degree. Always interested in mathematics, she went to study both astronomy and mathematics at Johns Hopkins, where she received her doctorate sixteen years later. A member of the Mathematical Society, she was a councilor of the society for three years. After she went to Radcliffe College to do further work for which she was awarded a master's degree, she taught mathematics at Goucher College for ten years until she retired at the age of seventy. Her mathematical studies focused on geometrical interpretation of algebraic invariants.   JH/MBO

PRIMARY SOURCES
Lewis, Florence P. *A Geometrical Application of the Theory of the Binary Quintic.* [Baltimore, 1914]. Reprinted from *American Journal of Mathematics* 36 (3 July 1914). Originally her Johns Hopkins University doctoral thesis (1913). Includes biographical sketch.

STANDARD SOURCES
AMS 6; Rossiter 1982.

LEWIS, GRACEANNA (1821–1912)

U.S. ornithologist. Born 1821 in West Vincent Township, Chester County, Pa., to Esther (Fussell) and John Lewis. Educated at home; Kimberton Boarding School for Girls (1839). Professional experience: Boarding school, York, Pa., teacher of astronomy and botany (1842–1844); Friends' school, Philadelphia, teacher (1870–1871); Foster School for Girls, Clifton Springs, N.Y., teacher (1883–1885). Died 25 February 1912 in Media, Pa.

Graceanna Lewis was born on a farm in Chester County, Pennsylvania. Her father died when she was three. She and her three sisters were left in the care of their mother, who defeated an attempt to appoint trustees to administer the estate left to her unconditionally by her husband. This experience and the nurturing example of their mother probably helped to make the daughters zealous advocates of women's suffrage. Esther Lewis became a successful businesswoman. A teacher before her marriage, she directed the early education of her daughters at home. The household was a refuge for fugitive slaves.

Although the boarding school that Graceanna Lewis attended included astronomy, botany, and chemistry in its curriculum, she obtained most of her scientific education informally. Interested in science from an early age, she also showed talent as a painter, especially of birds and other animals. John Cassin, volunteer curator of birds at the Academy of Natural Sciences, Philadelphia, directed her progress in ornithology. In 1877, she presented a paper on the development of the animal kingdom at a meeting of the Association for the Advancement of Woman, published by its committee on science that included MARIA MITCHELL and MARY PUTNAM JACOBI and headed by ANTOINETTE BROWN BLACKWELL.
                                                                JH/MBO

PRIMARY SOURCES
Lewis, Graceanna. *The Development of the Animal Kingdom: A paper Read at the Fourth Meeting of the Association for the Advancement of Woman.* Nantucket: Hussey & Robinson, 1877.

SECONDARY SOURCES
Warner, Deborah Jean. *Graceanna Lewis: Scientist and Humanitarian.* Washington, D.C.: Smithsonian Institution Press, 1979.

STANDARD SOURCES
NCAB, vol. 9; Rossiter 1982.

LEWIS, HELEN GENEVA (1896–?)

U.S. chemist. Born 22 October 1896, in New Haven, Conn. Educated Mount Holyoke College (A.B., 1921); Yale University (honorary scholar, 1922–1923; Ph.D., 1923); University of Paris, postgraduate studies (1926–1927); Claremont College, postgraduate studies (1928). Professional experience: Connecticut College (1925); Long Beach Junior College, instructor (1928–1929); Stanford College, research associate in biochemistry (1931–1934); Miss Harker's School, Palo Alto, academic principal (1934–1935); Beverly Hills High School, instructor in mathematics (1935–1936); College of Osteopathic Physicians and Surgeons, Los Angeles, Calif. (1937–?). Death date unknown.

Helen Geneva Lewis was born in New Haven, Connecticut, just before the end of the last century. She went to Mount Holyoke, where she became interested in chemistry. She went to Yale as an honorary scholar, and received her doctorate only two years after her undergraduate degree. She spent a year teaching at Claremont College and then went to Paris for a postgraduate year in the late twenties. On her return, she moved to California and began to teach chemistry at Long Beach Junior College. She then, in the early thirties, took a research position in biochemistry at Stanford University, where she remained for four years. Lewis was offered an opportunity to serve as academic principal of one girls' high school and then as instructor of mathematics in another. She returned to biochemistry studies at the College of Osteopathic Physicians and Surgeons in the late thirties. Lewis did research on vapor pressure of aqueous salt solutions, on protein metabolism, and on the specific dynamic action of amino acids.   JH/MBO

STANDARD SOURCES
AMS 6.

LEWIS, ISABEL (MARTIN) (1881–?)

U.S. astronomer. Born 11 July 1881 in Old Orchard Beach, Maine. Married (1912). One child. Educated Cornell University (A.B., 1903; M.A., 1905). Professional experience: astronomical computer (for Simon Newcomb) (1905–1907); Naval Observatory, Nautical Almanac Office, astronomical computer (1908–1927), assistant scientist (1927–1930), astronomer (1930–1951). Retired 1951. Concurrent experience: astronomical writer, magazines and newspapers (1916–1949); Solar Eclipse Expeditions to Russia (1936), Peru (1937). Honors and memberships: Astronomical Society, Royal Astronomical Society, Canada; Astronomical Society, Pacific. Death date unknown.

Isabel Martin Lewis was born in Maine and educated at Cornell University, where she received a bachelor's and a master's degree. From her graduation she worked as an astronomical computer, first for Simon Newcomb and then at the Nautical Almanac Office of the Naval Observatory. She married in 1912 and had one child. She continued at the Nautical Almanac Office for her whole career, while also writing popular articles on astronomy for magazines and newspapers beginning in 1916, some of which were later collected into a popular book on astronomy.

Lewis rose to the position of assistant scientist by the late twenties and in 1930 she was finally designated astronomer, a position she held until her retirement in 1951. She was a member of two Solar Eclipse Expeditions, one to Russia in 1936 and one the following year to Peru. Her research focused on solar eclipses and occultations.   JH/MBO

PRIMARY SOURCES
Lewis, Isabel Martin. *Splendors of the Sky.* New York: Duffield & Company, 1919. First published as a series of articles in the *New York Evening Sun.*
———. *A Handbook of Solar Eclipses.* New York, Duffield & Company, 1924.

STANDARD SOURCES
AMS 4–8, P 9.

LEWIS, LILIAN (BURWELL) (1904–)
U. S. zoologist. Born 13 August 1904 in Meridian, Miss. Married (1934). One child. Educated Howard University (B.S., 1925); University of Chicago (M.S., 1931; Ph.D., 1946). Professional experience: State Agriculture and Mechanics College, S.C. (1925–1929). Morgan College, assistant–associate professor (1929–1931); Tillotson College, associate through professor of zoology (1931–1947); Winston-Salem Teachers College, professor (from 1947). Honors and memberships: Rosenwald Fellow (1931–1932); Rosenwald Scholar (1943–1943).

Lilian Burwell was an African-American biologist who studied as an undergraduate with the cell biologist Ernest Everett Just. After teaching at State Agricultural and Mechanics College of South Carolina for four years, she moved to Morgan College, where she rose to associate professor. With the encouragement and advice of Just, she followed his other outstanding woman student, ROGER ARLINER YOUNG, to study with Frank Lillie at the University of Chicago, where she

received her master's. degree in 1931. Just recommended Burwell for a Rosenwald Fellowship to pursue further research in biology, but she also needed to teach to earn a living. She returned to South Carolina, where she taught zoology at Tillotson University before returning to University of Chicago to complete a doctorate in her field. Young's disastrous experience with her oral examination at Chicago may explain Burwell's fifteen-year delay. Her marriage to [?] Lewis in 1934 and the birth of her child may have also slowed her research. She obtained another fellowship to return to Chicago, and after completing her dissertation in endocrinology, she was hired as a full professor at Winston-Salem Teachers College, where she remained to the end of her career. Burwell's research interests, like those of Just and Young, were in embryology. She also worked on sex hormones and development, and, more specifically, on the early differentiation of duck gonads.   JH/MBO

SECONDARY SOURCES
Manning, Kenneth R. *Black Apollo of Science: The Life of Ernest Everett Just.* New York: Oxford University Press, 1983. Although there is only a brief mention of Burwell as Just's student, she is listed (as Burwell-Lewis) as one of those encouraging Manning in his study of Just. This helps to place her life in context.

STANDARD SOURCES
AMS 7–8, B 9, P&B 10, 11–12.

LEWIS, MADELINE DOROTHY (KNEBERG) (1903–)
U.S. archeologist. Born 18 January 1903 in Moline, Ill. Married Thomas M. N. Lewis (1961). Educated University of Chicago (B.A., 1933; M.A., 1947). Professional experience: Beloit College, instructor (1937–1938); University of Tennessee, director of archeology laboratory (1938–1942), department of anthropology, assistant professor (1940–1946), associate professor (1946–1949), professor (1949–?); Cherokee Historical Association, consultant, (1953–?); Tennessee Archaeologist, cofounder, coeditor. Honors and memberships: American Association for the Advancement of Science fellow, American Anthropological Association, Fellow. Society of American Archaeology, vice president, 1952.

Madeline Kneberg was born in Illinois and went to the University of Chicago for both a bachelor's and master's degree. While working on her doctorate (never completed), she began to teach for a year at Beloit. Although her early work was in physical anthropology, at the recommendation of her Chicago professors, William Krogman and Fay-Cooper Cole, she joined the New Deal's Works Progress Administration's archeological project in the Tennessee Valley, headed by Thomas M. N. Lewis. Shortly therafter, she took over the direction of the archeological laboratory. The sole support of her sister and mother, she brought her family to live with her in Knoxville.

Kneberg became a crucial part of the team working on the Chickamauga Basin project. She began a collaboration with Thomas Lewis that was life-long, resulting in their eventual marriage, which took place only on upon their retirement. Kneberg was hired as an assistant professor of anthropology at the university after two years, teaching as well as directing the lab. By 1942, the WPA project was ended, and the war ended their field archeology, but the two archeologists began a long series of important publications based on the enormous amount of material excavated.

Thomas Lewis, with Kneberg's help, began to promote archeology in the state through the founding of the Tennessee Archaeological Society. Welcoming the amateur as well as the professional, they began to publish a journal, *Tennessee Archaeologist,* which educated the public about the importance of the information that could be derived from excavations.

In their more scholarly publications, they also were careful to associate the prehistoric and historic people producing the artifacts with the objects that they manufactured. Kneberg and her Chicago-trained associates used the taxonomic methods developed by the Chicago school, developing elaborate trait lists for identifying new archeological complexes. According to her biographers, Kneberg's analysis formed the basis for much subsequent work on what came to be known as the Southern Ceremonial complex. While certain aspects of the work of Kneberg and Lewis have since been set aside through better dating methods, many other conclusions have proven viable and have stimulated further research.

JH/MBO

PRIMARY SOURCES

Kneberg, Madeline. With Thomas M. N. Lewis. *The Prehistory of the Chickamauga Basin in Tennessee: A Preview.* [Knoxville]: Division of Anthropology, University of Tennessee, 1941. Tennessee anthropology papers no. 1. Sponsored by the University of Tennessee, assisted by the Tennessee Valley Authority.

———. With Thomas M. N. Lewis. "The Archaic Horizon in Western Tennessee." *University of Tennessee Record* ext. ser. 23 (1947): 1–39.

———. "The Tennessee Area." In *Archaeology of Eastern United States,* ed. James B. Griffin, 190–198. Chicago: University of Chicago Press, 1952.

———. With Thomas M. N. Lewis. *Tribes That Slumber: Indians of the Tennessee Region.* Knoxville: University of Tennessee Press, 1958.

———. With Thomas M. N. Lewis. *Eva: An Archaic Site.* Knoxville, University of Tennessee Press, 1961.

SECONDARY SOURCES

Sullivan, Lynne P. "Madeline Kneberg Lewis: An Original Archaeologist." *Women in Archaeology* 110–119.

STANDARD SOURCES

AMS 8 (under Kneberg), S&B 9–10.

LEWIS, MARGARET ADALINE REED (1881–1970)

U.S. anatomist and physiologist. Born 9 November 1881 in Kittaning, Pa., to Martha Adaline (Walker) and Joseph Cable Reed. Married Warren Harmen (1910). Three children. Educated Goucher College (A.B., 1901). Professional experience: New York Medical College for Women, lecturer (1904–1907); Barnard College, lecturer (1905–1906); Columbia University, preparator in zoology and assistant to T. H. Morgan (1906–1907), instructor in biology (1907–1909); Carnegie Institute of Washington, collaborator, department of embryology (1915–1926), research associate (1927–1946). Honors and memberships: Pathological Society of Philadelphia, William Wood Gerhard Gold Medal, joint recipient with her husband (1938); Goucher College, honorary LL.D. (1938); Wistar Institute of Anatomy and Biology, Philadelphia, guest investigator (1940–1946), member. Died 20 July 1970.

Although Pennsylvania-born Margaret Reed Lewis attended several universities after she received her bachelor's degree (including Bryn Mawr College and the universities of Zurich, Paris, and Berlin), she never completed a graduate degree. After 1901, when she received her bachelor's degree, and before 1915, when she joined the Carnegie Institute of Washington, she held a number of teaching and research positions as well as periodically attending graduate schools. She joined the institute as a collaborator in the department of embryology, later becoming a research associate. She remained at the institute until 1946, but in 1940 she became affiliated with the Wistar Institute of Anatomy and Biology in Philadelphia. In 1946, she became a member of the institute and remained there until 1964. She retired in 1958, but continued to do research at the Wistar. Many of her summers were spent doing research in other laboratories, including Woods Hole, the Harpswell Laboratory and the Mt. Desert Island Biological Laboratory in Maine, and Stanford University.

Early in her research career, Reed worked on regeneration in crawfish and on the embryology of amphibians. She was a pioneer in culturing cells *in vitro,* a feat that had first been done by Ross G. Harrison in 1907. During 1908, in Berlin, she worked with RHODA ERDMANN, who cultured amoebae on agar supplemented with physiological salt solution. Following Erdmann's techniques, Reed cultured guinea pig bone marrow and spleen cells. She was probably the first person successfully to cultivate mammalian tissue.

In 1910, Reed married Warren Harmon Lewis, and the two began to collaborate on mammalian tissue culture research. Together, they formulated different culture media for different purposes. The clear medium that they developed to investigate cell structure became known as the Locke-Lewis solution, and their method of culturing by suspending the cells in a drop of medium hanging from the underside of a cover slip and suspended in a hollow on the microscope slide was known as the Lewis culture. Cells would grow on the underside of the cover slip and allow the viewer to observe many hard-to-see cell organelles, including mitochondria. This method also allowed the observation of certain physiological processes such as the contraction of smooth muscle cells.

During the second decade of the twentieth century, biologists, including Lewis, were recognizing the importance of pH to living systems. She and a colleague, Lloyd D. Felton, investigated the effects of different pH values in the tissue culture media and published a paper in *Science* in 1921, "The Hydrogen-Ion Concentration of Tissue Growth *in vitro*." From this research and additional work by Warren Lewis, they were able to determine the circumstances under which a particular type of white blood cell, the monocyte, became transformed into macrophages, or scavenger cells, thus disproving the commonly held idea that monocytes and macrophages were two different types of cells.

Later in her life, Lewis became interested in the study of immunity and cancer, still collaborating with her husband on occasion. Especially interested in the chromosomes of malignant cells, the Lewises noted that although malignant cells sometimes contained an aberrant number of chromosomes, this was not always the case—in some cases the chromosomes were completely normal. From these observations, Lewis and colleagues investigated the effects of various chemical agents on tumor inhibition.

Lewis published around 150 papers during her lifetime. Because of their importance in the field, the Lewises contributed the chapter on tissue culture for the book *General Cytology*. They also made motion pictures of cellular processes to be used in school classrooms.

Lewis received a number of honors during her life, including a star by her name in the sixth edition of *American Men of Science*. Lewis not only was an important scientist, she also juggled her time between work and her husband and three children, Margaret Nast Lewis, Warren Reed Lewis, and Jessica Helen Lewis Myers.   JH/MBO

PRIMARY SOURCES

Lewis, Margaret Reed. "Development of Connective-Tissue Fibers in Tissue Cultures of Chick Embryos." *Contributions to Embryology* 6, no. 17 (1917): 45–60. Publications of Carnegie Institution of Washington, no. 226.

———. With Lloyd D. Felton. "The Hydrogen-Ion Concentration of Cultures of Connective Tissue from Chick Embryos. *Science* 54 (23 December 1921): 636–637.

———. With Warren Lewis. Chapter in *General Cytology: A Textbook of Cellular Structure and Function for Students of Biology and Medicine,* ed. Edmund V. Coudry. Chicago: University of Chicago Press, 1924.

STANDARD SOURCES

American Women; AMS 2–8, B 9, P&B 10; Bailey; *NCAB;* Rossiter 1982; Shearer and Shearer 1996 (article by Kimberly J. Wilcox); Siegel and Finley.

LEWIS, MARY BUTLER (1903–1970)

U.S. archeologist. Born 1903. Married Clifford Lewis (1942). Two children. Educated Vassar College (A.B., 1925); University of Paris (Sorbonne), postgraduate study (1926); Radcliffe College (Harvard University) (M.A., 1930); University of Pennsylvania (Ph.D., 1936). Professional experience: Hunter College; Vassar College; Bryn Mawr College, instructor; University of Pennsylvania Museum, American Section, research assistant (1930–1939), research associate (1940–1970). Field work: Mesoamerican Expediton to Guatemala (1931–1936); Hudson Valley Archaeological Survey, director (1939–1941); Pennsylvania, historical archeologist (1943–1970). Honors and memberships: American Philosophical Association funding (1930–1936). Carnegie Institution Award (1939–1941); American Anthropological Association, Fellow. Died 1970.

Mary Butler was born in 1903. After studying at Vassar College and spending a year of postgraduate work at the Sorbonne in Paris, she returned to teach French in the United States. She soon decided to work in the new and exciting field of anthropology. She received a master's from Radcliffe College, and then went on to the University of Pennsylvania, where she was the first woman to receive a degree in anthropology from the university. This began a life-long connection with the university museum.

In the period 1931 through 1936, while she worked on her dissertation, Butler was highly productive both in the field, studying pottery types at Mesoamerican sites in Guatemala and publishing the results in the University of Pennsylvania Museum bulletins. In 1939, she received a five-year grant from the Carnegie Corporation to lead an archeological survey of the Hudson Valley. Her field crew, a third of whom were women, succeeded in investigating forty-five sites. In spite of their productivity, after two years the Carnegie discontinued its support with the advent of World War II. Although she published a brief survey report and discussed her results at the Eastern States Archaeological Federation, some antagonism with the official New York State archeologist prevented her contributions from being recognized, nor were her final site reports even published.

During the war, Butler married Clifford Lewis. Her marriage and the birth of her children soon after did not interrupt her archeological work, but it restricted her to what some commentators have called "backyard archeology," working on local historical sites. She directed an excavation in Broomall, Pennsylvania, when her first child was eleven weeks old. She continued to do historical archeology in Pennsylvania until her death in 1970, when she was working on the restoration of a nineteenth-century house, the Mortenson House, near Philadelphia.   JH/MBO

SECONDARY SOURCES

Keur, Dorothy. "Mary Butler Lewis, 1903–1970." *American Anthropologist* (1971): 255.

Levine, Mary Ann. "Creating Their Own Niches." In *Women in Archaeology*, ed. Cheryl Claassen, 23–24. Philadelphia: Walker, 1981. A series of biographical sketches of strategies of women archeologists.

LEYEL, HILDA WINIFRED IVY (WAUTON) (1880–1957)

British herbalist. Born 16 December 1880 in Uppingham, Rutland. Father: Edward Brenton Wauton. Educated Halliwick Manor. Married Carl Leyel (1900). Professional experience: Society of Herbalists and Culpepper Shops, founder. Honors and memberships: French Palme Académique; St Mary's Hospital, life governor; Royal Orthopedic Hospital, West London Hospital. Died 15 April 1957 in London.

Hilda Winifred Leyel was trained as an actress, had a few parts in shows and then married at the age of twenty. She then devoted her life, first to setting up fancy dress balls and lotteries on behalf of hospitals, and then to herbalism. Her charity work led to her appointment as a life governor of a number of hospitals in London.

Although Leyel had little scientific training, she had studied with a well-known botanist, Edward Thring, as a child. Her books on diet and herbs became very popular, and she founded the Society of Herbalists. She also published new editions of the herbal of the seventeenth-century physician Nicholas Culpepper, under the imprint of the company she founded, Culpepper House.   JH/MBO

PRIMARY SOURCES

Leyel, Hilda. *Magic of Herbs.* New York: Harcourt, Brace, 1926.

———, ed. *A Modern Herbal: The Medicinal, Culinary, Cosmetic and Economic Properties, Cultivation and Folk-Lore of Herbs, Grasses, Fungi, Shrubs & Trees with All Their Modern Scientific Uses.* By Maud Grieve. 2 vols. London: J. Cape, 1931.

———. *Herbal Delights.* London: Faber, 1937.

———. *Compassionate Herbs.* London: Faber, 1946.

———. *Hearts-ease.* London: Faber, 1949.

———. *Green Medicine.* London: Faber, 1952.

———. *Truth about Herbs.* London: Culpepper Press, 1954.

SECONDARY SOURCES

Macleod, Dawn. *Down-to-Earth Women.* N.p., 1982. Leyel discussed on pages 57–64.

STANDARD SOURCES

DNB; Europa; WWW, vol. 5, 1951–1960.

LIBBY, LEONA WOODS MARSHALL (1919–1986)

U.S. chemist and physicist. Born 9 August 1919 in La Grange, Ill., to Mary (Holderness) Woods and Wreightstill Woods. Four siblings. Married (1) John Marshall, Jr. (divorced 1966); (2) Willard Frank Libby. Two sons by Marshall. Educated University of Chicago (B.S. in chemistry, 1938; Ph.D., 1943). Professional experience: Chicago Metallurgical Laboratory, researcher (1942–1944); Hanford, Wash., plutonium production project, researcher (1944–1945?); Institute for Nuclear Studies, University of Chicago, research associate (1947–1954), assistant professor (1949–1957); Institute of Advanced Studies, Princeton, N.J., Fellow (1957–1958); Brookhaven National Laboratory, visiting scientist (1958–1960); New York University, associate and full professor (1960–1963); University of Colorado, Boulder, associate professor (1963–1972); University of Los Angeles, visiting professor of engineering (1970–1972); R&D Associates, staff member (from 1972). Died 10 November 1986 in Santa Monica, Calif.

Leona Woods Marshall Libby had several careers throughout her life. Her first career was as a chemist. Born in La Grange, Illinois, a suburb of Chicago, she attended college at the University of Chicago, where she obtained her degree in chemistry. She continued as a graduate student at Chicago, where she was introduced to quantum research in a seminar given by James Franck, who had come to Chicago in 1938 to introduce quantum research to the chemistry department. Although Franck accepted her as a graduate student, he warned her that she might starve to death as a woman in a man's field. For her dissertation, Woods worked under Robert S. Mulliken on diatomic molecular spectroscopy. She was also advised by physics professor Stanislaw Mrozowski, who had come to the United States from Poland. In 1942, a secret project known as the Chicago Metallurgical Laboratory—part of the Manhattan Project and led by Enrico Fermi—required a molecular spectroscopist to construct the neutron detectors needed to monitor the progress of a chain reaction. Mulliken hurried his graduate student along on her route to the doctoral degree so that she could supply her expertise in this field. Woods actually began work with Fermi's group before she had completed the degree. Excitement characterized the group of young physicists who were working on the project, and they both worked and socialized together. As the only woman on the team, Woods enjoyed the attention of the young men who worked there. She soon fell in love with John Marshall, Jr., a physicist who moved from experimental work at Columbia, where he was hired by Leo Szilard, to Chicago with Fermi. The couple continued to work on nuclear reactors, although their work moved to Argonne, Illinois, away from Chicago. They had two sons, one born in 1944 and the second in 1949. During this time, Woods Marshall had left chemistry behind and moved more completely into physics. Peter, their first son, was born in Chicago, and his mother returned to work a week after his birth. John Marshall had gone to work on the plutonium production reactors at Hanford, Washington, and Leona and baby Peter soon followed, accompanied by John's mother, who was to take care of the baby. Woods Marshall's major responsibility during the final days of the Manhattan Project were with the production reactors at Hanford.

After the war, the Marshall family returned to Chicago, where Leona accepted a fellowship at the University of Chicago's Institute for Nuclear Studies. Enrico Fermi, the head of the institute, influenced her scientific development. A second son, John, was born in 1949, two years after Leona became a research associate at the institute and five years before she became an assistant professor.

After Fermi's death in 1954, his research group dispersed, and Leona held a fellowship for a year at the Institute of Advanced Studies in Princeton, N.J. After leaving Princeton, she held a number of positions. Her marriage to John Marshall ended in divorce in 1966, and later that year she married a former colleague on the Manhattan Project, Willard Frank Libby. At the time of her second marriage, she was an associate professor at the University of Colorado, and Willard Libby was on the faculty of the University of California at Los Angeles. In 1960, Libby had won the Nobel Prize in chemistry for his work on the techniques of radiocarbon dating. Although Leona Libby continued her research on particle physics, she became increasingly interested in Willard Libby's work on the determination of ancient climates by observing tree rings, or dendochronology. She

moved to California and held an adjunct professorship of engineering at UCLA. She continued her work on ancient climates. Upon the death of Willard Libby in 1980, she edited and published his collected papers. She also became an outspoken advocate for nuclear power.　　JH/MBO

PRIMARY SOURCES

Marshall, Leona Woods. With Enrico Fermi. "Interactions between Neutrons and Electrons." *Physical Review* (1947): 1139–1146.

———. With E. Courant. "Mass Separation of High-Energy Particles in Quadruple Lens Focusing Systems." *Review of Scientific Instruments* 3 (1960): 193–196.

———. "Elements in the Region of Platinum Formed by Fusion in Fission Explosions." *Physical Review* 129 (1963): 740–743.

Libby, Leona Woods Marshall. With G. P. Fisher, V. Domingo, et al. "Hyperon Production in Interactions of 2.7-GeV/c Antiprotons on Protons." *Physical Review* 161 (1967): 1335–1343.

———. "Repulsive Core and Interaction Energy in Proton-Proton Scattering." *Physics Letters* B 29 (1969): 345–347.

———. With H. G. Jackson and H. R. Lukens. "Measurement of Oxygen-18/Oxygen-16 Ratio Using a Fast Neutron Reactor." *Journal of Geophysical Research* 78 (1973): 7145–7148.

———. With W. F. Libby. "Vulcanism and Radiocarbon Dates." In *Proceedings of the International Conference Radiocarbon Dating,* 8th ed., ed. T. A. Rafter and T. Grant-Taylor. Vol. 1, A72–A75. Royal Society of New Zealand, 1973.

———. With W. F. Libby. "Geographical Coincidence of High Heat Flow, High Seismicity, and Upwelling, with Hydrocarbon Deposits, Phosphorites, Evaporites, and Uranium Ores." *Proceedings of the National Academy of Sciences* 71 (1974): 3931–3935.

———. With L. J. Pandolfi. "Temperature Dependence of Isotope Ratios in Tree Rings." *Proceedings of the National Academy of Sciences* 71 (1974): 2482–2486.

———. *The Uranium People.* New York: Crane, Russack, and Co., 1979.

———, ed. *Willard L. Libby Collected Papers.* 4 vols. Los Angeles: UCLA Press, 1981.

———. *Past Climates: Tree Thermometers, Commodities, and People.* Austin, Tex.: University of Texas Press, 1983.

SECONDARY SOURCES

Burgess, P., ed. *The Annual Obituary 1986.* Chicago: St. James Press, 1989.

Folkart, B. A. "Leona Marshall Libby Dies: Sole Woman to Work on Fermi's First Nuclear Reactor." *Los Angeles Times* (13 November 1986). Obituary notice.

STANDARD SOURCES

AMS 12–14; Grinstein 1993 (article by Ruth H. Howes with
bibliography); *WW in America* 1984–1985.

LIBERT, MARIE-ANNE (1782–1865)

*Belgian botanist. Educated girls' school in Prüm. Professional expe-
rience: contributed studies on both phanerograms and cryptograms.
Died 1865.*

Marie-Anne Libert, born in Belgium in the late eighteenth
century, was first interested in mathematics but soon devoted
her energies to botany. She was encouraged by the Swiss
botanists Augustin Pyramus de Candolle and his son Al-
phonse. She published on cryptogams between 1820 and
1829. Her name is memorialized by two genera, *Libertia* and
Libertella. Her herbarium and notes are in the Botanical Garden, Brussels.

JH/MBO

PRIMARY SOURCES

Libert, M. A. "Sur un genre nouveau d'hepatique." *Annales
Générales des Science Physiques* 6 (1820): 372–374.
———. "Illustration du genre Inoconia, dans la famille des
Algues." *Memoires Société Linéenne* (Paris) 5 (1827): 402–403.
———. "Observations sur le genre Asteroma, et description de
deux espèces appartnenat à ce genre." *Memoires Société
Linéenne* (Paris) 5 (1827): 404–406.
———. "Description d'un nouveau genre de Champignons
nommé Desmazierella." *Annals des Sciences Naturelles* 18
(1829): 82–86.

SECONDARY SOURCES

Dumortier, Eugene. "Notice sur Marie-Anne Libert." *Bulletin
de la Société de la Botanique de Bruxelles* (1865): 403–411.
Morren, Charles. "Prologue a la mémoire de Marie-Anne
Libert." *Belgique horticole* (1868): v–xv. Includes portrait.

STANDARD SOURCES

Rebière.

LIEBER, CLARA FLORA (1902–1982)

*U.S. chemist. Born 10 July 1902 in Indianapolis, Ind., to Clara
(Becker) and Robert Lieber. One sibling, Louise. Married Otto
Nothacksberger. Educated Shortridge High School, Indianapolis;
Smith College (A.B., 1923); University of Chicago (summer 1924);
University College, London (B.Sc., 1936). Professional experience:
Kaiser-Wilhelm Institut für Chemie, Berlin-Dahlem, guest chemist
(1936–1939). Honors and memberships: Phi Beta Kappa. Died
14 December 1982 in Indianapolis.*

Clara Lieber was born in Indianapolis, where her father's
family owned an art firm. Robert Lieber was in charge of
the company's photographic department, then became involved in the production and distribution of motion pictures. Lieber graduated *magna cum laude* from Smith with a
concentration in geology. The next summer she studied at
the University of Chicago. From 1931 to 1936, Lieber attended University College, London, graduating in chemistry
with second-class honors.

Lieber entered the Kaiser-Wilhelm Institute on 15 September 1936 as an unpaid worker, intending to prepare a
doctoral dissertation. Using a method developed by Otto
Hahn, Lieber investigated the process of dehydration in barium and strontium compounds, obtaining information useful for analytical radiochemical studies. She showed that
dehydration of halogen compounds of barium proceeds in
well-defined stages. Lieber worked with Hahn and Fritz
Strassmann on the research leading to the discovery of fission, and then on fission products. In addition to several isotopes of barium, she found three isotopes for strontium,
which indicated that uranium could split into strontium and
xenon as well as barium and krypton.

Lieber returned to the United States at the end of 1939,
apparently without receiving a degree. She lived in Indianapolis and in the New York City area, where her father
had done business. After the war, Lieber served on the Committee of Resettlement for Japanese-Americans. During this
period she married her husband. Later she spent time in
Paris and in Salzburg.

JH/MBO

PRIMARY SOURCES

Lieber, Clara Flora. "Über die stufenweise Entwässerung von
Erdalkalihalogeniden, geprüft nach der Emaniermethode."
Zeitschrift für physikalische Chemie 182 (A) (1938): 153–166.
———. "Über strukturelle Veränderungen von entwässertem
Bariumchlorid beim weitern Erhitzen." *Zeitschrift für
physikalische Chemie* 42 (B) (1939): 240–248.
———. "Die Spaltprodukte aus der Bestrahlung des Urans mit
Neutronen: die Strontium-Isotop." *Die Naturwissenschaften*
27 (1939): 421–423.
Records in Archiv zur Geschichte der Max-Planck
Gesellschaft, Berlin; University College London; Smith
College Archives.

SECONDARY SOURCES

Hahn, Otto. *A Scientific Autobiography.* Trans. and ed. Willy Ley.
New York: Charles Scribner's Sons, 1966.
Krafft, Fritz. *Im Schatten der Sensation: Leben und Wirken von Fritz
Strassmann.* Weinheim, Deerfield Beach, Fla., and Basel:
Verlag Chemie, 1981.

McGrayne, Sharon Bertsch. *Nobel Prize Women in Science.* New York: Birch Lane Press, 1993.

Sime, Ruth. *Lise Meitner: A Life in Physics.* Berkeley, Los Angeles, and London: University of California Press, 1996.

Strassmann and Hahn expressed thanks for Lieber's assistance in several of their papers.

LIEU, K. O. VICTORIA (fl. 1930s–1940s)

Chinese entomologist. Educated College of Agriculture, National Szechuen University, Chengfu, China; Ohio State University, graduate fellow. Professional experience: Board of Trustees for the Administration of the Boxer Indemnity Fund Remitted by the British Government, research fellow (1933–1944); Musie Heude, Shanghai, honorary research fellow.

Victoria Lieu authored papers on Chinese Aegeriidae and Cerambycidae (mulberry borers and citrus borers).

JH/MBO

STANDARD SOURCES
Osborn.

LIN QIAOZHI (LIN CHIAO-CHI) (1901–1983)

Chinese physician. Born 23 December 1901 in Amoy in Fukien Province. Educated Peking Union Medical College (PUMC) (graduated 1929); Manchester University, England (1932–1933); London University (1939–1940); University of Chicago (1939–1940). Professional experience: PUMC, staff (1929–1942); Zhonghe Hospital, staff (1942–1948); PUMC, Department of Obstetrics and Gynecology (1948–1983). Honors and memberships: Chinese National Committee of Protection for Children, member (1954); Birth Control Guidance Committee, member (1957); Birth Control Standing Committee, deputy, member (1960); Chinese Academy of Biological Sciences, Fellow (1955); Democratic Women's Association, Beijing chapter, vice-president (1953, 1963); Chinese National People's Congresses (1954, 1958, 1964, 1975, and 1978); Chinese Academy of Medical Sciences, vice-chairman (1964); National Women's Association, member (1978); Family Planning Association, founding member, vice-president (1980). Died 23 April 1983.

When she was twenty years old, Lin Qiaozhi entered the Peking Union Medical College. This college, supported by the Rockefeller Foundation, was known for its education of a medical elite in Western medicine. Lin was this college's first female enrollee. Graduating in 1929, she joined the Department of Obstetrics and Gynecology as its first woman Chinese doctor. During Lin's life, China was engulfed in political turmoil. She lived through the days of the demise of the monarchy, civil war, revolution, the Japanese occupation,

and the final Chinese upheaval that resulted in the creation of a new socialist society. PUMC was also a victim of the political and social turmoil, closing during World War II and reopening in 1948. Lin spent most of her professional career at PUMC, although in 1942, after it was closed down, she joined the staff of Zhonghe Hospital, where she founded the Department of Obstetrics and Gynecology. However, once PUMC reopened after the war, Lin returned as head of obstetrics and gynecology.

Lin was trained under the PUMC philosophy that it was vital for China's well-being to train a corps of elite physicians, who in turn would serve as resources to less well-trained doctors in the provinces. Ideally, this "trickle-down" effect would be in the interest of China's masses. However, this method was found lacking, for the number of doctors was woefully inadequate to serve China's vast medical problems. Lin, as well as many others, supported the Barefoot Doctors movement, a program developed to train rural citizens in routine medical procedures.

Lin's medical activities in the realm of public health and public service left her little time for research. Her list of activities is daunting. She was twice vice-president of the Democratic Women's Association, Beijing Chapter (1953–1963); deputy or member of five National People's Congresses (1954, 1958, 1964, 1975, and 1978); member Chinese National Commmittee of Protection for Children (1954); fellow, Chinese Academy of Biological Sciences (1955); vice-chairman, Chinese Medical Association (1957); member, Birth Control Guidance Committee (1957); vice-president, Peking's Municipal Committee; deputy and member Standing Committee (1960); vice-chairman, Chinese Academy of Medical Sciences (1964); vice-chairman, National Women's Association (1978); vice-president and founding member, Family Planning Association of China (1980). JH/MBO

PRIMARY SOURCES
Lin Qiaozhi. "Why the Party Keeps Me Young." In *New Women in China,* 21–30. Beijing: Foreign Language Press, 1972.

SECONDARY SOURCES
Bullock, Mary B. "A Brief Sketch of the Role of PUMC Graduates in the People's Republic of China." In *Medicine and Society in China,* ed. John Z. Bowers and Elizabeth F. Purcell. New York: Josiah Macy, Jr., Foundation, 1974.

Ferguson, Mary E. *China Medical Board and Peking Union Medical College: A Chronicle of Fruitful Collaboration, 1914–1951.* New York: Rockefeller Foundation, 1970.

Meschel, Susan V. "Teacher Keng's Heritage: A Survey of Chinese Women Scientists." *Journal of Chemical Education* 69 (September 1992): 723–730.

Rosenbaum, Thomas. *The Archives of the China Medical Board and the PUMC at the Rockefeller Archive Center: Some Sources on the Transfer of Western Science, Medicine, and Technology to China during the Republican Period.* New York: Rockefeller Archive Center, 1989.

STANDARD SOURCES
Shearer and Shearer 1996 (article by Grace Foot Johns).

LINCOLN, ALMIRA HART (1793–1884)

See Phelps, Almira Hart Lincoln.

LIND-CAMPBELL, HJÖRDIS (1891–?)

Swedish physician. Born 27 June 1891 in Sweden. Father [?] Lind. Three siblings. Married [?] Campbell, later professor of ethnology, University of Uppsala (ca. 1918). Four children. Educated local girl's school, Karolinska Institute, Stockholm, basic science courses (1911–1914); University of Lund (M.D., 1922). Professional experience: University of Lund Hospital, physician (1918); Västerås Sanitorium, temporary assistant doctor to acting chief physician (1922–1940); private medical practice, school doctor in Västerås (1940–1973). Concurrent experience: Västerås and rural areas, various medical positions (1922–1940); Västerås City Council, member; National Swedish Association for Sexual Information, Stockholm, medical advisor (for twenty years). Honors and memberships: Medical Women's International Association, pioneer member. Death date unknown.

Hjördis Lind-Campbell was a Swedish physician involved in sanitorium care, the provision of sexual information, and the creation of an adoption agency in connection with a home for unmarried women. As a young woman growing up in a middle-class family, Lind had become interested in medicine through friendship with a Stockholm nurse who treated women with venereal disease. She worked in a maternity home while still in school, and then decided to apply for premedical study at the Karolinska Institute in Stockholm. Here she acquired an excellent background in science, enjoying the work, although she found herself at first to be the only female student among twenty male students.

For her further work, Lind was assigned to a hospital attached the the University of Lund, and had intense clinical experience for six months. She then took university courses, and chose to follow the psychology lectures at the university. At this time, she met her future husband, an ethnologist, [?] Campbell, then at the university museum. The two married and she had two children before she finished her medical studies in 1922.

Lind-Campbell then took temporary positions, filling in for a physician at the Västerås Sanitorium, something she continued to do for the follwing eighteen years. The city was conveniently located west and equidistant from both Stockholm and Uppsala. This proved to be a useful decision, since her husband obtained a position as professor of ethnology at University of Uppsala. Since Lind-Campbell had two further children, she found it convenient to take various temporary medical positions in the city and in surrounding rural areas, including a position at the children's hospital, as a doctor in the medical ward (which gave her specialist competence in pulmonary disease), as a doctor in an outpatient clinic for gynecology, and also as a rural visiting doctor.

By 1940, Lind-Campbell opened a private practice while serving as a school physician, serving ten years on the local city council, and acting as a member of the local hospital board and the Maternity Assistance Board over the next thirty-threee years.

During this same period, she became active in the National Swedish Association for Sexual Information with Elsie Ottesen-Jensen. Once a week, she traveled to Stockholm to serve as medical advisor to women with sexual problems. They also consulted on abortions (then heavily restricted), and provided maternity care for young single women. In connection with the assocation, Lind-Campbell founded an adoption agency that worked closely with welfare agencies, arranging adoptions for healthy infants. She retired from her medical practice at the age of eighty-two. Two of her children followed her example and went into medicine.   K M

PRIMARY SOURCES
Lind-Campbell, Hjördis. In Hellstedt, *Autobiographies.*

LINDEN, MARIA GRÄFIN VON (1869–1936)

German bioloigist. Born 18 July 1869 to Edmund and Eugenie (Hiller von Gaertringen) von Linden at the family castle, Burberg bei Heidenheim / Württemberg. One brother. Never married. Educated privately; boarding school for girls in Karlsruhe; Realgymnasium for boys in Stuttgart (baccalaureate 1891); University of Tübingen (Dr.rer.nat., 1896). Professional experience: assistant to zoologist professor Theodor Eimer in Tübingen (1896–1899); assistant, Institute of Hygiene, Bonn University (1900–1908); newly founded Institute of Parasitology in Bonn, head (1908–1910); professor without the right to give lectures (from 1910). Died on 26 August 1936 in Schaan near Vaduz / Leichtenstein.

Maria von Linden was born in 1869 at the family castle Burgberg, Württemberg, where she was brought up together with her brother, Wilhelm, in close contact with nature. She was taught French by Swiss nannies. Her interest in biology was aroused by her mother, Eugenie. From 1883 until 1887 she attended the boarding school for girls in Karlsruhe

(Viktoriapensionat), where she received the education of a young upper-class lady. The other students could not keep up with her in physics and mathematics. After returning to Burberg, she made her first mineralogic discovery. Her paper on chalk sediments (Indusienkalke) in the river Hürbe was read at the assembly of the geologists' society at Karlsruhe by a man. In 1888 her uncle Joseph von Linden demanded permission from the ministry of education for a young well-educated lady to get her degree at Tübingen University, provided that she presented a good thesis. In summer 1891 Maria passed the baccalaureate examination at the *Realgymnasium* for boys in Stuttgart, without ever having attended the lessons. In spring 1892 she demanded permission to attend lectures at the scientific faculty of Tübingen University. She was encouraged by the feminist Mathilde Weber, a supporter of women's studies. In October 1892 the senate agreed to Maria's demand. From November 1893 on, Maria attended lectures in mathematics, chemistry, zoology, and physiology. The only lady student at Tübingen, she wore lady's suits with stiff collars and gentleman's hats. The huge shape and style of her shoes resembled men's shoes. After her father's death in January 1894, she received a scholarship of the feminist movement (Allgemeiner Deutscher Frauenverein), so that she could finish her studies. In 1896 she passed the doctor's examination and got her degree (Dr.rer.nat.). Her doctoral professor, Theodor Eimer, was a supporter of the Lamarckian theory of evolution. She wrote her thesis on the evolution of the drawing and formation of sea snails. She stayed as Eimer's assistant at Tübingen until he died in 1898. In 1899 she became an assistant at the Institute of Hygiene at Bonn University. Even when the Prussian ministry of Education refused her the right to qualify to teach university, she became head of the newly founded Institute of Parasitology in Bonn in 1908. In 1910, she was made the first woman professor in Germany, however, without the right to give lectures.

She discovered that copper salts could be used as disinfectants in surgery and had her invention patented. The Paul Hartmann company later produced sterile bandages and surgical wool using her discovery. Her main interest was research on lung diseases. She was convinced that copper therapy was the way to treat tuberculosis, an urgent medical problem of her time. Copper therapy was replaced as a treatment for tuberculosis, whereas, in accordance with the terms of her patent, copper was still used in surgery.

After the National Socialists came to power, von Linden had to leave the university. She had to sell the family castle for financial reasons and went to Leichtenstein with Frau von Altenburg, who had been her companion in Bonn. Von Linden died of pneumonia in August 1936 in Leichtenstein.

SNS

PRIMARY SOURCES

Linden, Maria von. "Die Entwicklung der Skulptur und der Zeichnung bei den Gehäuseschnecken des Meeres." *Zeitschrift für wissenschaftliche Zoologie* 61 (1895–1896): 261–317.

———. "Die entwicklungshemmende Wirkung von Kupfersalzen auf Krankheit erregende Bakterien." In *Medizinisch-hygienische Bakteriologie, Virusforschung und Parasitiologie.* Part 1, *Zentralblatt für Bakteriologie, Parasitenkunde, Infektionskrankheiten und Hygiene.* N.p.: 1920–1921.

SECONDARY SOURCES

Junginer, Gabriele, ed. *Maria Gräfin von Linden: Erinnerungen der ersten Tübingen Studentin.* Tübingen: Attempo Verlag, 1991.

Kretschmer, Johanna. "Maria von Linden: die erste Studentin an der Universität Tübingen." *Attempo.* 33/34 (1969): 78–88.

LINDSTEN-THOMASSON, MARIANNE (1909–)

Swedish physician. Born 6 October 1909 in Göteborg (?) Sweden. Father [?] Lindsten, teacher. Three siblings. Married [?] Thomasson (1950). Two children, five stepchildren. Educated Landskrona gymnasium (1927); University of Lund (M.D., 1936). Professional experience: Landskrona Hospital, assistant locum tenens; Gällivare Hospital, assistant doctor (1939–1945); Tranas, physician locum tenens; Vilhelmina (Southern Lapland), district general practitioner (1946?–1956); Lycksele, district medical officer (1956–1973). Retired 1973. Private practice 1973–post-1977. Memberships and honors: Medical Women's International Association, pioneer member.

Marianne Lindsten-Thomasson was the oldest daughter of a teacher whose ancestors had all been farmers in Småland, Sweden, except for the occasional university-trained minister. She early determined to be a physician, and after attending the local *gymnasium,* she studied medicine at the University of Lund.

Rather than study for a specialty, Lindsten decided to become a distict general practioner. It proved difficult to find a permanent position, and for some years she filled in for doctors on leave. Finally she obtained a permanent position in Vilhelmina in Southern Lappland that she held for the next ten years. At the age of forty-one, she met and married a widower, the district judge in a city some 120 kilometers away. Although he had five children, she took over their care (with the help of a competent housekeeper), continued her own practice, had two children of her own, and commuted between the two towns.

When Lindsten-Thomasson was in her late forties, the rural district officer in the town of Lycksele retired and she was able to take over his position, finally having her medical practice and her family in the same area. At the age of sixty-three, she retired on full pension, and opened a small private practice that she continued to run for some years. She was a pioneer member of the Medical Women's International Association, an organization that brought together eminent women physicians from all parts of the world.   KM

PRIMARY SOURCES
Lindsten-Thomasson, Marianne. In Hellstedt, *Autobiographies.* With portrait.

LINES, DOROLYN (BOYD) (1901–1975)
U.S. engineer for canal and irrigation systems. Born 24 October 1901 in Baldwin, Kans. to Jenny S. and George A. Boyd. Three sisters. Married Marion B. Lines (1924; he died in 1934). Three daughters. Educated Colorado public schools; University of Kansas, School of Engineering (B.S., 1923). Professional experience: Hassell Iron Works, Colorado Springs; University of Kansas School of Engineering, instructor (for one year); U.S. Bureau of Reclamation, Canals Branch of Design and Structures, canals engineer (1934–1966). Died 17 January 1975.

Dorolyn Boyd was the youngest of four girls. The family moved to Colorado when she was young and she attended local public schools. She went to study at the University of Kansas School of Engineering, an unusual step for a young woman at that period, and graduated with a bachelor of science in mechanical engineering in 1923. She held a position at the Hassell Iron Works, Colorado Springs, and was instructor for a year at the University of Kansas School of Engineering. She declined an associate professorship in order to marry Marion B. Lines, an engineering classmate. After his accidental death in 1934, she began to work for the federal government to support her three daughters. She became a canals engineeer in the Canals Branch of Design and Structures, U.S. Bureau of Reclamation, from 1934 until her retirement in 1966.

Lines assisted in the design of large western canal and irrigation systems (Friant-Kern and Coachella Valley canal systems in California, and Wellton-Mohawk near Yuma); Missouri River basin, Columbia River basin, and design work for modernizing the Lower Rio Grande in Texas. Her last project was a feasibility study of the irrigation system for ninety-six thousand acres near Pendleton, Oregon.

She retired in 1966 and received the Certificate of Merit from the Bureau of Reclamation that year. She died 17 January 1975 in Denver, Colorado. She was survived by three daughters, ten grandchildren, and three great-grandchildren. Her obituary writers mention her cheerful personality and the help she provided in gaining respect for women engineers. She also supported the Engineering Society.

JH/MBO

SECONDARY SOURCES
SWE Newsletter 21, no. 4 (1975): 3. Obituary notice.

STANDARD SOURCES
NAW unused.

LINTON, LAURA ALBERTA (1853–1913?)
U.S. school teacher, chemist, mineralogist, and physician. Born 1853 in Ohio to Christina and Joseph Linton. Educated Minnesota State Normal School, at Winona (graduated 1872); University of Minnesota (B.A., 1879; M.D., 1898?); MIT, advanced study. Professional experience: Lombard University, Galesburg, Ill., science professor; Minneapolis Central High School, head, science department; University of Michigan, chemical researcher; Rochester State Hospital, physician to mentally ill women patients. Died circa 1913.

Laura Linton led a varied and active life. She was born in Ohio to a Quaker family. Her parents moved to Wabasha County, Minnesota, and she attended the University of Minnesota. She made a brief excursion into mineralogy and chemistry during her senior year at the University of Minnesota, when, in a chemistry class, she conducted the analysis that established a green semiprecious stone, a rare zeolite found only on the shores of Lake Superior. This analysis showed that its chemical composition was similar in composition and specific gravity to thomsonite without the latter's crystalline structure. It varied enough from thomsonite to make its discoverers assume it to be a new mineral. They named it lentonite, after the student who had analyzed it.

Linton later took advanced courses at MIT, after which she served as science professor at Lombard University in Galesburg, Illinois. She left Lombard to become head of the science department in Minneapolis Central High School, where she remained for ten years. After this time, she resigned in order to do chemical research at the University of Michigan for two years.

When Linton was in her early forties, she returned to Minneapolis and enrolled in the university's medical school. She received her medical degree and spent the last fifteen years of her life as a physician to Minnesota's mentally ill women patients at Rochester State Hospital.   JH/MBO

PRIMARY SOURCES
Linton, Laura. With Stephen Farnham Peckham. "On Trinidad Pitch." *American Journal of Science* ser. 4, no. 1 (1896): 193–207.

SECONDARY SOURCES
Dahlberg, Jean C. "Laura A. Linton and Lentonite." *Earth Science* 18, no. 1 (1965): 18–19. Originally published in *Minnesota History.*

Peckham, S. F., and C. W. Hall. "On Lentonite and Other
Forms of Thomsonite: A Preliminary Notice of the Zeolites
of the Vicinity of Grand Marais, Cook County, Minnesota."
American Journal of Science 19 (February 1880): 122–130.

STANDARD SOURCES
Sarjeant.

LIPINSKA, MÉLANIE (fl. 1920s)
Polish/French physician.

Mélanie Lipinska was Polish-born, although she lived the
later part of her life in France. She trained in Polish and then
Parisian hospitals. She worked closely with the Polish physician and physiologist JOSÉPHINE JOTEYKO. She is best known
as a historian of women physicians.   JH/MBO

STANDARD SOURCES
DFC; Hurd-Mead 1938 (as Lepinsky); Lipinska 1900; Lipinska
1930.

LISITSIAN, SRBUI STEPANOVA (1893–1979)
*Soviet Armenian ethnographer, folklorist. Born 28 June 1893 in
Tbilisi, Georgia, Russia. Father Stepan Danilovich Lisitsian. Educated Insitut Istorii (Armenian Institute of History), Armenia,
USSR (Ph.D.). Professional experience: Institut Arkheologii I Et-
nologii (Armenian Institute of Archeology and Ethnology), ethnologist. Editor of father's ethnographic books (1969). Died 1979.*

Srbui Stepanova Lisitsian was the originator of a new field of
ethnochoreography, developing precise tools for recording
folk dance. She began with film analysis of movement and
developed a mathematical description of each position. Her
work built on the important studies of Armenian ethnography done by her father, Stepan Danilovich Lisitsian, who
was professor at the Institute of History under the Academy
of Sciences, Armenian S.S.R.

It was Lisitsian's belief that her analysis would penetrate
the essence of "primitive" thought, clarified by the seman-
tics of the language of movement. She also edited her father's work, especially his monograph *Armiane Zangezura*
(1969), published twenty-two years after his death. One year
after her death, the Institute of Archeology and Ethnography in Armenia was renamed in honor of her and her father.
    JH/MBO

PRIMARY SOURCES
Lisitsian, Srbui Stepanova. *Starinnye pliaski I teatral'nye pred-
stavleniia armianskogo naroda.* Erevan: Izd-vo Academia Nauk
Armianskogo SSR, 1959–1972. 2 vols.

———. *Armianskie starinnye pliaski.* Erevan: Izd-vo An Armi-
anskoi i SSR, 1983.

SECONDARY SOURCES
"S. Lisitsian." *Sovetskaia Etnografiia* 2 (1980): 188–189.

STANDARD SOURCES
IDA.

LISOVSKAIA, SOFIYA NIKOLAIEVNA (1876–1951)
*Russian physician. Born 1876. Father Nikolai Lisovski. Educated
Petersburg Women's Medical Institute (graduated 1902; M.D.,
1911). Professional experience: Petersburg Women's Medical Institute Hospital Surgical Clinic, surgeon (1904–1917), head (from
1917); Leningrad Medical Institute, chair of operative surgery and
topographical anatomy (1919–1937), chair of urology (1933–
1951). Died 1951.*

Sofiya Lisovskaia was a Russian surgeon and urologist
trained at the prerevolutionary Petersburg Women's Medical
Institute. After graduation she worked under A. Kad'yan at
the Hospital Surgical Clinic. During this period she prepared
and defended her doctoral thesis on the transplantation of
the thyroid gland. After 1917, she was head of the Hospital
Surgical Clinic of the same institute (now renamed the Petrograd Women's Medical Institute). She then became the
chair of operative surgery for the next eighteen years and
chair of urology until her death. During this period it was
renamed the Leningrad Medical Institute.

Lisovskaia devised a modification of the Debré-Pareff reaction for the diagnosis of gonorrhea, which involved an
immune reaction. She also devised and introduced Pavlovian
techniques for the treatment of enuresis. She published
eighty-six works on a variety of immunological and urologi-
cal topics.   ACH

PRIMARY SOURCES
Lisovskaia, Sofiya. "Kucheniyu o peresadke shchitovidnoy
zhelezy" (The theory of the transplantation of the thyroid
gland). Petersburg Women's Medical Institute, doctoral diss.,
1911.
———. *K voprosu O syvorotochnoy anafilaksii* (Serum anaphy-
laxis). N.p., 1911.
———. *O glukozurii pri khirugicheskikh zabolevaniyakh bryushnoy
polosti* (Glucosuria in surgical diseases of the abdominal
cavity). N.p., 1922.
———. *Tripper i sposoby bor'by s nim* (Gonorrhea and how to
combat it). N.p., 1929.

STANDARD SOURCES
WWW (USSR), 1972.

LISTER, GULIELMA (1860–1949)

British botanist and mycologist. Born 28 October 1860 in Leytonstone, Essex, to an artist mother and Arthur Lister, Fellow of the Royal Society Six siblings. Educated at home; Bedford College (one year). Professional experience: British Mycological Society, president (1912; 1932); Essex Field Club, president (1916–1919); Fellow of the Linnean Society (1904); council member (1915–1917; 1927–1931); vice president (1929–1931). Died 18 May 1949 in Leytonstone.

Born into the eminent Quaker Lister family, Gulielma Lister was the daughter of botanist Arthur Lister, Fellow of the Royal Society. Her grandfather, J. J. Lister, F.R.S., was a much respected physicist and one of her uncles was Lord Lister, the surgeon. Although her father was a wine merchant by trade, his real interest was in natural history. He was especially interested in the Mycetozoa and published the standard monograph on the subject in 1894. Gulielma Lister's mother was a talented amateur artist. Most of Lister's education was at home, although she did spend one year at Bedford College.

Working alongside her father on his *Monograph of Mycetozoa* (1894), she produced some of the plates for this work. Arthur Lister wrote in the preface of this book that throughout his studies, he had been assisted by his daughter. She revised this work for the second and third edition (1911 and 1925) and included new specimens collected from many places. She became the world expert on this group.

In 1903, Lister joined the British Mycological Society, and participated enthusiastically in its activities. She was president of the society twice, and was made an honorary member in 1924 in recognition of her service. She also participated in the activities of the Essex Field Club. In 1904, she was elected to the Linnaean Society, and was a council member from 1915 to 1917 and again from 1927 to 1931. She was a vice-president from 1929 to 1931.

Like her father, Gulielma was a good general naturalist, showing a special interest in birds and coniferous trees. She did the figures for the *Handbook of the Coniferae* by Dallimore and Jackson and the colored plates in F. J. Hanbury's *Illustrated Monograph of the British Hieracia*.

Always painstakingly accurate in her observations and records, Gulielma Lister carried on the scientific traditions of her illustrious family. JH/MBO

PRIMARY SOURCES
Lister, Gulielma. "*Elatine hydropiper L.* in Surrey." *Journal of Botany* 36 (1898): 400.
———. "Notes on the Mycetozoa of Linnaeus." *Journal of Botany* 51, n.s., no. 42 (1913): 160–164.
———. "Mycetozoa of Australia and New Zealand." *Journal of Botany* 53 (n.s. 44) (1915): 205–212.
———. "Notes on Malaysian Mycetozoa." *Journal of Botany* 69 (1931): 42–43.
———. Revised Arthur Lister's *Monograph of the Mycetozoa*. 2d and 3d ed. London: British Museum of Natural History, 1911, 1925.
Drawings at British Museum of Natural History, letters and manuscripts at Kew, and herbaria at Bedford College, London, and the Essex Field Club.

SECONDARY SOURCES
Essex Naturalist (1950): 214. Obituary notice; includes portrait.
London Naturalist (1949): 141–142. Obituary notice.
Nature 164 (1949): 94; (1960): 362–363. Obituary notice.
Times, 6 June 1949. Obituary notice.
W., E .M. "Miss Gulielma Lister." *Transactions of the British Mycological Society* 33 (1950): 165–166. Includes portrait.

STANDARD SOURCES
Desmond.

LITCHFIELD, HENRIETTA EMMA (DARWIN) (1843–1927)

British editor. Born September 1843 in Downe, Kent, England, to Emma (Wedgwood) and Charles Robert Darwin. Seven surviving siblings. Married Richard Litchfield (1871; he died in 1903). No children. Educated privately at home. Professional experience: edited chapters of Charles Darwin's Descent of Man *(1870); collected materials for Darwin's* Expression of the Emotions in Man and Animals *(1867–1869); published mother's and some of father's letters (1915), memoir of her husband (1905?). Died 1927.*

Henrietta Emma Darwin was not a scientist, nor was she an advocate of scientific studies. Nevertheless, she assisted her father, Charles Darwin, by serving as the first audience for his book describing the mutual accommodation of insect and flower, *Orchids* (1862), and editing chapters of *Descent of Man* (1871). She also collected information for him from among her friends between 1867 and 1870 on the contraction of certain eye and face muscles in young children for *Expression of the Emotions in Man and Animals* (1873).

The second daughter of Darwin, Henrietta felt herself inferior to her brilliant older sister, Annie, who died at the age of nine. Her father mourned this loss over many years, and Henrietta preserved almost intact a small chest of drawers belonging to Annie containing her labeled shell collection, some handwritten notes, and other odds and ends. Henrietta was often ill when a child and in her adolescence, and joined her father in his visits to various watering places in her search to improve her health.

Partly for the reason of ill health, her education was spotty, and the various governesses hired to teach her and her younger brothers seem to have been resented and disliked by Henrietta. She expressed a keen resentment at the education she had been given in an autobiography written in her old age, but she also criticized the unfashionable scientific education of all her brothers except for William, the eldest, who attended Rugby. After she was married in 1871 to Richard Litchfield, who had been the corresponding secretary for F. D. Maurice's Working Men's College, her health improved remarkably. After his death, she published a memoir on Litchfield's life.

Although she did not write the *Life and Letters* of her father, a task taken on by her botanist brother, Francis, she did attempt to enlarge the amount of space allotted to her mother, Emma Darwin. In the first volume of *Emma Darwin: A Century of Letters*, Litchfield celebrated the Wedgwood women in the late eighteenth century and the early nineteenth century through the charming letters written by and to Emma's mother and aunts as well those of Emma and her sisters. In the second volume, she focused on Emma as Darwin's wife. She included family letters from her father to his children, including those to herself. One lacuna is any mention of her sister, Elizabeth, other than a reference to her birth. This sister, called Lizzy or Bessie, though odd in some ways and never able to live independently, was not retarded as many writers have surmised. A group of interesting letters that Bessie wrote to Henrietta in 1868 (while Henrietta was in Italy) survive in the Darwin correspondence, the only written record by this little-known Darwin daughter.

In Litchfield's editing of the letters written by her mother, she eliminates discussions of Darwin's science with a few exceptions, whether these were included in letters to herself or relayed by Emma on Darwin's behalf to his sons. Nor does she indicate Emma's heavy involvement in Darwin's daily scientific correspondence, and her daily tasks copying manuscripts and translating to and from French. She even avoids discussing the information-collecting she did on behalf of her father for *Expression of the Emotions*.

Archival sources indicate that Litchfield, supported by her husband, expressed much stronger opposition to the publication of Darwin's admission of free thought in his autobiography than did her mother. In her depiction of the religious side of Emma Darwin, as well as in other pieces of selective editing, Henrietta Litchfield shaped the popular view of Emma Darwin as a rather strict, even puritanical figure, suppressing the humorous side so evident in her mother's

letters to her eldest son, William, not included in Henrietta's edition. An affectionate although eccentric portrait of Henrietta Litchfield is to be found in *Period Piece* (1952), written by her niece Gwen Ravarat. JH

PRIMARY SOURCES

Litchfield, Henrietta Emma. *Richard Buckley Litchfield: A Memoir Written for his Friends by His Wife.* Cambridge: privately printed at Cambridge University Press, 1910.
———, ed. *Emma Darwin: A Century of Family Letters 1792–1896.* 2 vols. London: John Murray, 1915. Includes portraits of Darwin and his family.
Henrietta Darwin Litchfield's unpublished autobiography can be found in the Richard Litchfield papers in the British Library. The Darwin Archive contains extensive correspondence between Charles Darwin, Emma Darwin, and Henrietta. Correspondence between Henrietta and her father numbers more than forty letters. The archive also includes letters to Henrietta later in life, notably from Professor Dicey of Oxford. The extensive Emma Darwin letters are also in the Darwin archive.

SECONDARY SOURCES

Browne, Janet. *Charles Darwin: Voyaging.* New York: Alfred Knopf, 1995. This first volume of Darwin's life gives a lively picture of the Darwin household before 1859.
Burkhardt, Frederick H., et al. *Correspondence of Charles Darwin, (1842–1862).* Cambridge: Cambridge University Press, 1993–1998. Vols 5–10. Portraits of Henrietta Darwin as a young girl are included in these volumes. These also include correspondence and editorial appendices that illuminate her early years.
Burkhardt, Frederick, and Sydney Smith, eds. *A Calendar of the Correspondence of Charles Darwin 1821–1882 (with supplement).* Cambridge: Cambridge University Press, 1994.
Ravarat, Gwen. *Period Piece: A Cambridge Childhood.* London: Faber and Faber, 1952. Ravarat was the daughter of George Darwin, the second oldest son of Charles Darwin. Contains amusing descriptions and drawings of Henrietta later in life.

LITVINOVA, ELIZAVETA FEDOROVNA (1845–1919?)

Russian mathematician. Born 1845 near Tula. Father Fedor Ivashkin. At least one sister. Married a Dr. Litvinov. Educated Mariinskaia gymnasium in St. Petersburg; Zurich Polytechnic Institute (B.A., 1876); Bern University (Ph.D., 1878). Professional experience: teacher in schools. Died probably in 1919.

Elizaveta Fedorovna Litvinova was born into the landed gentry and educated in St. Petersburg. There she became drawn into radical circles concerned with the advancement of natural sciences and women's rights. Litvinova wished to continue her studies, but at that time universities in Russia were closed to women as officially enrolled students. Hopeful that the situation would change, many young women continued to prepare themselves for further study with the help of sympathetic professors. When, after several years, it became clear that the authorities had no intention of opening the doors of the universities to women, many went abroad to foreign universities, Zurich being a particular favorite.

Litvinova also wished to go to Zurich but her husband, Dr. Litvinov, whom she had married in 1866, would not permit her to leave Russia. At that time, women could not obtain passports without permission of their fathers or husbands. Litvinova continued to study privately, acquired a certificate of competency in 1870, and by 1872 managed to emancipate herself from her husband and leave for Zurich.

Unlike most of the women students in Zurich, Litvinova chose to study at the polytechnic rather than the university. She was often the only woman in the class. Her instructors were helpful, though, and she expected to finish her studies in four years.

However, in 1873, fearing that the women in Zurich were becoming too radical, Tsar Aleksandr II issued a decree ordering all Russian women to leave. The penalty for noncompliance was forfeiture of future admission rights to Russian educational establishments and exclusion from licensing examinations and civil service posts (none of which at that time were open to women). Many women left Zurich for other universities, and some returned to Russia, but Litvinova decided to defy the tsar's ban and remained in Zurich until 1876, when she completed her undergraduate studies. She then went to Bern, where she received her doctoral degree *summa cum laude* in 1878. Her dissertation was on function theory.

Litvinova then returned to Russia only to find that the penalties laid down in the tsar's decree were not idle threats. She was not allowed to take the examinations to teach in a *gymnasium* or to obtain a post, and she was forbidden to take the magister degree which would have qualified her to teach at university level. By this time the Higher Women's Courses had opened and women instructors (although not professors) were being hired.

Eventually Litvinova found a post teaching in the lower classes of a girls' academy. This post was paid by the hour and carried with it no benefits. Ultimately, after nine years, she was allowed to teach mathematics in the upper division of the *gymnasium,* the first woman in Russia to do so, but even then her conditions of employment were not equivalent to those of male teachers.

To earn money, Litvinova wrote popular biographies of mathematicians and philosophers, published in the series *Zhizn' zamechatel'nykh liudei.* She also wrote articles for the *Bulletin de l'Union universelle des femmes* and was a delegate to the 1897 International Women's Congress in Brussels.

Over time, Litvinova became interested in the teaching of mathematics and wrote numerous articles on this subject. After she retired, she went to live with her sister in the country. It is not certain whether she died in the famine of 1919 or whether she survived for several years longer.

In a sense, Litvinova's career as an original mathematician was nipped in the bud by the penalties that arose from defying the Tsar's decree. However, even under difficult circumstances, her influence made itself felt. Litvinova's contribution to mathematics was twofold: as a proponent of advanced pedagogical methods and an inspiration to her students, some of whom went on to become scientists, and as a disseminator of information about cultural, social, and other issues, which, in an era of heavy censorship, she introduced into her biographical works.   JH/MBO

PRIMARY SOURCES
Litvinova, Elizaveta Fedorovna. *Lösung einer Abbildungsaufgabe.* St. Petersburg: Buchdruckerei der Kaiserlichen Akademie der Wissenschaften, 1879. Doctoral thesis.

———. *F. Becon, ego zhizn', nauchnye trudy i obshchestvennaia deiatel'nost'.* St. Petersburg: Izd. F. Pavlenkova, 1891.

———. *S. V. Kovalevskaia: zhenshchina-matematik: eia zhizn' i uchenaia deiatel'nost.* St. Petersburg: P.P. Soikin, 1894.

STANDARD SOURCES
Grinstein and Campbell (article by Ann Hibner Koblitz).

LITZINGER, MARIE (1899–1952)

U.S. mathematician. Born 14 May 1899 in Bedford, Pa. Educated Bryn Mawr (A.B., 1920; A.M., 1922); European fellow (Rome) (1923–1924); University of Chicago (Ph.D., 1934). Professional experience: Devon Manor, mathematics teacher (1920–1922); Greenwich Academy, mathematics teacher (1924–1925); Mount Holyoke College, instructor (1925–1928), assistant professor (1928–1937), associate professor (1937–1942), professor (1942–1952), chair, department of mathematics (1937–1949), emerita professor (1951). Memberships: American Association of College Professors; American Mathematical Society; Mathematical Association; Association of Teachers of Mathematics in New England (president, 1940–1941).

Born in Bedford, Pennsylvania, and educated at Bryn Mawr College and the University of Chicago, mathematician Marie Litzinger progressed through the academic ranks at Mount Holyoke to professor and chair of the mathematics department. Her research was in number theory, substitution quantics, and residual polynomials for composite moduli.
                                    JH/MBO

PRIMARY SOURCES

Litzinger, Marie. "A Basis for Residual Polynomials in n Variables." *Transactions of the American Mathematical Society* 37 (1935): 216–225. Litzinger's thesis.

———. "Real Numbers for Freshman." *Mathematical Magazine* 22 (1949): 263–264.

SECONDARY SOURCES

New York Times, 8 April 1952. Obituary notice.

STANDARD SOURCES

AMS 6–8; Debus; Grinstein; Grinstein and Campbell.

LLOYD, DOROTHY JORDAN (1889–1946)

See Jordan-Lloyd, Dorothy.

LLOYD, RACHEL (1830–1900)

U.S. chemist. Born 1830. Educated private schools; Harvard summer school; University of Zurich (Ph.D., 1886). Professional experience: University of Nebraska, faculty (1888–1900), assistant professor (1891); Nebraska Agricultural Experiment Station, assistant chemist (1888–1900). American Chemical Society member (elected), 1891.

Rachel Lloyd was educated in science in private schools, and attended some of the Harvard summer schools in science open to female as well as male schoolteachers. She presented two papers at a meeting of the Boston division of the American Chemical Society in 1880 with another woman, Helena Stallo. Realizing that she would not be able to obtain an advanced degree in chemistry in the United States at that time, she traveled to Zurich, where she completed her doctorate at the university. Her dissertation was on the high-temperature chemistry of aromatic compounds. Returning to the United States, she worked with the Nebraska Agricultural Experiment Station analyzing the constitution of the sugar beet.

Along with her experimental research, she held a full-time faculty position at the University of Nebraska from 1888 to 1900. The American Chemical Society, which only elected one woman, RACHEL BODLEY, in the 1880s, elected Lloyd to membership after she was appointed assistant professor at Nebraska. She also served as head of the department of chemistry during this time. JH/MBO

SECONDARY SOURCES

Tarbell, D. Stanley, and Ann T. Tarbell. *Journal of Chemical Education* 59 (1982).

STANDARD SOURCES

Bailey; Rossiter 1982; Siegel and Finley.

LLOYD-GREEN, LORNA (1910–)

Australian physician. Born 4 February 1910 in Australia to a schoolteacher mother and a veterinarian father. Three siblings. Never married. Educated medical school in Australia. Professional experience: obstetrics and gynecology.

Australian Lorna Lloyd-Green was encouraged to select the career of her choosing. Her veterinarian father, although he allowed her to help him in his practice, was opposed to her medical education. Her mother financed her medical education completely through some property that she owned, and her father contributed nothing toward it. Her teachers in secondary school were convinced that she would return to study music because the courses would be "too much" for her. Although she did not have the prerequisite medical subjects, she worked extraordinarily hard and eventually got the degree. She did her residency in obstetrics and gynecology and, after two years in general practice, worked in this area. She was president of the Medical Women's International Association from 1968 through 1970. KM

PRIMARY SOURCES

Lloyd-Green, Lorna. In Hellstedt, *Autobiographies.*

LOCHMAN-BALK, CHRISTINA (1907–)

U.S. invertebrate paleontologist. Married Robert Balk (1947). Educated Smith College (A.B., 1929; A.M., 1931). Johns Hopkins University (Ph.D., 1933). Professional experience: Smith College, assistant (1929–1931); Mount Holyoke, instructor (1935–1940), assistant professor (1940–1946), associate professor (1946–1947); University of Chicago, lecturer (1947); New Mexico Institute of Mining and Technology, Department of Geology, lecturer (1954), professor; head of department (1957–1972), emerita (1972); New Mexico Bureau of Mines and Mineral Resources, consultant (1955–1957).

Christina Lochman earned her first two degrees from Smith College in geology. While she was working on her master's degree, she was an assistant in the department. After she received her doctorate from Johns Hopkins, she went to teach geology at Mount Holyoke College, where she rose through the ranks to associate professor. After she married Robert Balk in 1947, there was a break in her career. She moved with her husband to the University of Chicago, where he was professor of geology, but where she could be appointed only as lecturer because of the contemporary nepotism rules.

Urged by a colleague and fellow geologist in New Mexico, the couple moved to Socorro, New Mexico, where, after a few years, Lochman-Balk began to teach at the New Mexico Institute of Mining. After her husband's death in a plane crash in 1955, the geology department offered her a tenured position; in 1957, she was made full professor and head of the department. She remained there except for a brief period until she retired as an emerita professor in 1972.

Lochman-Balk's research interests were in invertebrate paleontology and stratigraphy, chiefly on Cambrian faunas of the western United States, including Wyoming and Montana. She served on the subcommittee on nomenclature for the National Research Council from the late 1930s with a number of important geologists. Lochman-Balk was a Fellow of the Geological Society of America and the American Association for the Advancement of Science.   JH/MBO

PRIMARY SOURCES
Lochman, Christina. "Fauna of the Basal Bonneterre Formation of Missouri." Baltimore, 1933. Ph.D. diss., Johns Hopkins University, 1933.
———. With Donald Duncan. *Early Upper Cambrian Faunas of Central Montana.* GSA Special Papers no. 54. [New York]: Geological Society of America, 1944.
Papers (1918–1985) at the American Heritage Center, University of Wyoming, Laramie.

STANDARD SOURCES
Debus; Sarjeant.

LOEWE, LOTTE LUISE FRIEDERICKE (1900–)
German chemist. Born 7 November 1900 in Breslau, Germany, to Helene (Druey) Loewe. Educated University of Breslau (D.Phil. 1927). Professional experience: University of Breslau, assistant in chemistry (1927–1933); University of Zurich, Chemical Institution, science collaborator (1934); University of Istanbul, Turkey (1934–1955); University of Basel, Switzerland (1955–1961); J. R. Geigy AG, Basel, researcher (from 1961); University of Freiberg, privat dozent (assistant professor) in chemistry (from 1956).

Lotte Loewe earned her doctoral degree from the University of Breslau. After receiving her degree, she stayed on at the university for four years as an assistant in chemistry. She worked as a science collaborator at the University of Zurich for a year and then went to the University of Istanbul, where she remained for twenty-one years. After leaving Turkey, she went to the University of Basel for six years and then worked for the J. R. Geigy AG firm in Basel.

Loewe was a member of a number of professional organizations, including the German and Swiss chemical societies, the German and Swiss Academic Unions, and the Swiss Microanalytic Society. She was the recipient of the Bundesverdienstkreuz in 1955. She collaborated on articles in organic chemistry, including work on uric acid, carotinoids, keto-enol-tautomery, diazomethane reactions, and the kinetics of ascorbic acid.   JH/MBO

STANDARD SOURCES
Debus.

LOGAN, MARTHA DANIELL (1704–1779)
U.S. horticulturist. Born 29 December 1704 in St. Thomas Parish, S.C., to Martha and Robert Daniell. Married George Logan, Jr. Six children. Died 28 June 1779.

Martha Daniell's father was the deputy governor of South Carolina and with his land, ships, and slaves was apparently very well-off. Her mother, Martha, was Daniell's second wife. All that we know of the daughter's education was that she was taught to read and write and that she knew something of horticulture and gardening. After her father's death when she was fourteen years old, Daniell married George Logan, Jr. Of the couple's eight children, six survived. The couple apparently encountered financial difficulties, for Martha placed an advertisement in the *South Carolina Gazette* in 1742, offering to board children and teach them to read and write. Later she offered her estate for sale and opened a school in Charleston. We know that her son Robert advertised imported seeds, flower roots, and fruit stones. This event apparently marked the beginning of her nursery business.

Reputedly, Daniell was the author of the "Gardener's Kalendar," first published in John Tobler's *South Carolina Gazette* in 1751. She is mainly remembered for her association with the botanist John Bartram, for some of their letters to each other were saved. She supplied him with seeds and cuttings and he called her "my facinated widow." In her letters to Bartram she mentioned botanist Dr. Alexander Garden none too favorably, for he apparently forgot to deliver letters from Bartram to her.   JH/MBO

PRIMARY SOURCES
Logan, Martha Daniell. *A Gardener's Kalendar Done by a Colonial Lady.* Ed. Alice Logan White. Charleston: National Society of the Colonial Dames of America in the State of South Carolina, 1976.
———. "Letters of Martha Logan to John Bartram, 1760–1763." Ed. Mary Barbot Prior. *South Carolina Historical Magazine* 1 (1958): 38–46.

SECONDARY SOURCES
Hollingsworth, Buckner. "Martha Logan, 1704–1779. John Bartram's 'Facinated Widow'—and a Notable Early American Florist." In *Her Garden Was Her Delight.* New York: Macmillan, 1962.
Spruill, Julia C. *Women's Life and Work in the Southern Colonies.* Chapel Hill: University of North Carolina Press, 1938.

STANDARD SOURCES
AMS 6–8, B 9, P&B 10–14; *NAW* (article by George F. Frick); Shearer and Shearer 1996 (article by Carol W. Cubberly).

LOGAN, MYRA ADELE (1908–1977)

U.S. anatomist and physician. Born 1908 in Tuskegee, Ala., to Adella (Hunt) and Warren Logan. Seven siblings. Married Charles Alston (1943). Educated Atlanta University, Ga. (B.A., 1927); Columbia University (M.S. in psychology); New York Medical College (M.D., 1933). Professional experience: Harlem Hospital, N.Y., resident, associate surgeon; Sydenham Hospital, visiting surgeon; Upper Manhattan Medical Group, practice (1960s). Honors and memberships: Board Certified American College of Surgeons. Retired 1970. Died 13 January 1977 in New York City of lung cancer.

African-American physician Myra Adele Logan was the first woman to perform open-heart surgery. She grew up in Tuskegee, Alabama, as the eighth and youngest child of a trustee and treasurer of the Tuskegee Institute. Her mother was involved in both the health care and the suffrage movements. Logan had a sister who was involved in health care and her brother became a physician. She was valedictorian of her class at Atlanta University. After she received her bachelor's degree, she went to Columbia University, where she studied psychology. Before she decided to go into medicine, she worked for a few years on the staff of the YWCA in Connecticut. She won the first Walter Gray Crump scholarship, which paid for her four years at the New York Medical College. She took a residency in Harlem Hospital, where she worked in the emergency room and on the ambulances, and then stayed on as an associate surgeon. She also had visiting privileges at Sydenham. Hospital. She married a recognized painter, Charles Alston, but had no children.

Not only was Logan a pioneer in performing open-heart surgery, she published the results of her research on the new antibiotic drugs. She worked on new diagnostic techniques for breast cancer in the 1960s. During this period, she retained a private practice as well as working in a group practice.

Logan's social and professional concerns were shown by her membership on Governor Dewey's New York State Commission on Discrimination from which she resigned in disgust. Her activities extended to Planned Parenthood, the National Association for the Advancement of Colored People, and the New York State Workmen's Compensation Board. Among her other achievements was her ability as a classical pianist. JH/MBO

SECONDARY SOURCES
Flint, Peter R. "Dr. Myra Logan, 68: Physician in Harlem." *New York Times Biography Service,* 15 January 1977: 100–101.

Hine, Darlene Clark, ed. *Black Women in America—An Historical Encyclopedia.* Brooklyn, N.Y.: Carlson, 1993.
Journal of the National Medical Association (July 1977): 527. Obituary notice.
Sammons, Vivian Ovelton. *Blacks in Science and Medicine.* Hemisphere Publishing, 1990. Logan discussed on page 156.

STANDARD SOURCES
Haber; *Notable* (article by J. Sydney Jones).

LOGSDON, MAYME (IRWIN) (1881–?)

U.S. mathematician. Born 1 February 1881 in Elizabethtown, Ky., to Nan Belle (Farmer) and James David Irwin. Married Augustus H. Logsdon (1900). Educated University of Chicago (Ph.B., 1913; S.M., 1915; Ph.D., 1921. Professional experience: Hastings College, professor of mathematics and dean of women (1913–1917); Northwestern University, instructor (1917–1919); University of Chicago, assistant professor (1921–1925), associate professor (1930–1946); University of Miami, professor (1946–1961), emerita professor (from 1961). Honors and memberships: Phi Beta Kappa, Sigma Xi, Sigma Delta Epsilon. Death date unknown.

Mayme Logsdon returned to school after the death of her husband and earned all of her degrees from the University of Chicago. After teaching for four years at Hastings College, she returned to Chicago, where she advanced to associate professor. She remained at that rank for sixteen years without being promoted to professor. In 1946, she took a job as professor at the University of Miami and remained there until retirement. She was a dean of the college at Chicago from 1922 to 1925 and was an International Education Board Fellow in Rome from 1924 to 1925. She was a member of the American Association for the Advancement of Science, the Mathematical Society, and the Mathematical Association. Her research interests were algebraic geometry and the problems of mathematics teaching.

Logsdon was a Baptist and a Democrat. Her many hobbies included bird watching, travel, swimming, and golf. She was the director of American Association of University Women from 1929 to 1935. JH/MBO

PRIMARY SOURCES
Logsdon, Mayme. *The Equivalence and Reduction of Paris of Hermitian Forms.* Ph.D. diss., University of Chicago, 1921.
———. *Elementary Mathematical Analysis.* 2 vols. New York: McGraw-Hill, 1932–1933.
———. *A Mathematician Explains.* Chicago: University of Chicago Press, 1936.

STANDARD SOURCES
American Women; AMS 4–8, P 9, P&B 10–11; Grinstein and
Campbell.

LOMAX, ELIZABETH ANNE (SMITHSON) (1810–1895)

British botanist. Born 22 February 1810 in Pontefract, Yorkshire. Married Robert Lomax (1842). Professional experience: Botanical Exchange Club. Died 16 March 1895 in Torquay, Devon.

Elizabeth Lomax was an amateur botanist who worked with the Botanical Exchange Club and collected plants. Her herbarium is at Manchester. JH/MBO

SECONDARY SOURCES
Journal of Botany (1895): 160.

STANDARD SOURCES
Desmond.

LONGFIELD, CYNTHIA (1896–1989?)

Anglo-Irish entomologist. Born 1896 in London, England, to Alice (Mason) and Mountifort Longfield. Two sisters. Privately tutored. Professional experience: Royal Army Service Corps, driver (1914–1916); Aeroplane factory worker (1916–1918). St. George Expedition, assistant entomologist (unpaid) (1924–1925); Moto Gross Expedition, Brazil, researcher (1927–1928); field trip to Kenya, Uganda, Congo, Rhodesia, South Africa (December 1933–May 1934); British Museum, Natural History, Entomology Department, assistant (unpaid) (1927–1948), honorary associate (1948–1956). Honors and memberships: Fellow, Royal Entomological Society (1925); Royal Geographical Society (1925), Fellow; London Natural History Society, Fellow (president 1934, 1935, 1936). British Dragonfly Society, first Honorary Fellow (1983) Died ca. 1989.

Cynthia Longfield was an Anglo-Irish entomologist for many years attached to the zoological and then the entomological department of the British Museum of Natural History. She never held a paid position, but devoted her life to the systematic collection and study of dragonflies, becoming an international authority on the Odonata.

Longfield's father had inherited a large estate in Ireland, which would be gradually dismantled and sold over the decades. Since the family went to its Irish home, Castle Mary, Cloyne, in County Cork for the winter months of every year, returning only to Belgravia in London for the summer, Longfield had an opportunity as a child to study natural history. She was a keen Girl Guide, remaining involved in the movement until the age of forty. Somewhat

sickly, she was often sent during hot months to the seaside, where Phillip Gosse's books guided her early studies. Cynthia was very attracted to children's books on science, such as those by ARABELLA BUCKLEY, as well as to Lyell's books on geology, T. H. Huxley's essays, and Darwin's *Voyage of the Beagle.*

As a young woman, Longfield's life was interrupted by World War I. She went to work as a driver for the Royal Army Service Corps until a man took over her job. She then went to work in an airplane factory, making army planes (she was in charge of the glue). After the war, she traveled with her cousin and a diplomat friend of her mother to South America on a sea voyage of three months. She developed a sense of insect diversity while crossing Argentina by railroad to the Chilean and Bolivian coast and back through the Panama canal to the Caribbean islands.

Her taste for the study of insects whetted, Longfield began to collect Irish varieties of butterflies, dragonflies, and moths. Back in England she began to raise caterpillars. Her interests led her to jump at the opportunity to go as a companion to LUCY EVELYN CHEESMAN, the woman keeper of the Insect House at the London Zoological Society, on a scientific expedition to the South Pacific leaving in April 1924 on board the St. George. She saw herself as retracing Darwin's Beagle voyage. With her family's consent and the approval of Cheesman, who needed another woman on the expedition, she made a voyage that turned her from an interested amateur into a serious entomologist.

One of the organizers of the expedition was Cyril Collenette, a professional entomologist only eight years older than she was. Since he was interested in beetles, butterflies, and moths, Longfield soon began to assist him rather than Cheesman, who was collecting mosquitos. C.L.C. (as Longfield came to call Collenette) was experienced in collecting in the tropics. They began in Trinidad, moved to Panama, where they found wonderful butterflies, and then through the Canal to Balboa, collecting wherever they stopped. They collected in Colombia, went on to the Galapagos Islands, and then steamed to the South Seas.

On her return, Longfield joined the London Natural History Society, the Royal Entomological Society, and the Royal Geographical Society with her new qualifications as a member of an expedition. She also began to work in the British Museum, Natural History Department (now the British Museum of Natural History) on the insects she and C.L.C. had collected. She was assigned to work under Douglas Kimmins, who was in charge of Neuroptera, which then included the dragonflies. She was assigned this group, now classified as Ondonata, which was relatively unresearched. Not dependent on a salary from the museum, she could throw herself into the work.

Her friendship with Collenette grew; he dedicated his book on the expedition to Longfield. He also invited her to set off on another collecting expedition to Matto Grosso, Brazil, in 1927. This time she needed a woman companion to share her cabin, and she soon settled on a friend who was an excellent artist as well. Returning to the museum after almost six months with exciting new specimens, she found that she was now assigned a regular desk in the entomological department. In 1929, she read her first paper on Odonata to the Entomological Society, published soon after in its journal.

Longfield and Collenette were soon working together at the museum on their new collections and lunching together every day. Although it looked for a while as though Collonette and Longfield might marry, the differences in their social position, and some hesitation on her part upon hearing that he had left a common-law wife and child in Malaysia, resulted in a decision to stay good friends, even when he married a few years later. Financially free and independent, following the death of her father, Longfield set off on another expedition.

Longfield made a collecting trip in 1929 to Southeast Asia with another woman friend, possibly influenced by Collenette's stories about the insects to be found there. She returned with almost one thousand specimens, significantly 368 Odonata. One new species, sent to a fellow entomologist for identification, was named in her honor, *Agrionoptera insignis cynthiae* Lieftinck. She returned to find that C.L.C. had brought her additional dragonfiles from British Somaliland, on which she published the following year.

In 1932, Longfield took a trip to Canada. Soon after her return, she set off, this time alone for Africa, traveling through Kenya, Uganda, Congo, Rhodesia, and South Africa for six months. On her return, she settled down to serious work on her African collections and to enjoy her position as president of the London Natural History Society. She collected and systematized the records of British dragonflies, and published an attractively illustrated handbook, *The Dragonflies of the British Isles,* accepted immediately as the authoritative guide.

Again anxious to travel, Longfield returned to South Africa, this time with a niece of Cecil Rhodes. By the time she returned and wrote up her collection, World War II had started, and she was involved in the Auxiliary Fire Service in charge of one hundred other women. When a bomb fell on the botany department of the museum, within the range of the Brompton Fire Station where Longfield was stationed, she helped save it from destruction by insisting on the use of the turntable ladder.

At the end of the war, Longfield returned to her work on dragonflies, serving also as a member of the Council of the Entomological Society and again as an officer of the London

Natural History Society. She put out a new edition of her book and began to correspond widely, while training new students of Odonata. She was made an honorary associate of the museum, and continued her field trips in Britain and Europe. In 1956, however, she retired from the museum and went to live in County Cork. She continued to be interested in her subject and traveled to international congresses throughout the world, combining them with collecting expeditions. In 1986, she celebrated her ninetieth birthday, having survived many of her colleagues, including her friend C.L.C., whose obituary she wrote for the *London Naturalist* in 1959. Dragonflies had become a major interest of entomologists, and the British Dragonfly Society was formed in 1983, with Cynthia Longfield as its first Honorary Fellow.   JH/MBO

PRIMARY SOURCES

Longfield, Cynthia. "A list of the Odonata of the State of Matto Grosso, Brazil." *Transactions of the Entomological Society of London* 77 (1929): 125–139.

———. "Studies on the African Odonata with Synomy and Descriptions of New Species and Subspecies." *Transactions of the Entomological Society of London* 85 (1936): 467–498.

———. *The Dragonflies of the British Isles.* London: Frederick Warne, 1939. 2d enlarged ed., 1949.

———. "Nomenclature of the European Species of Odonata (Dragonflies)." *Entomological Monthly Magazine* 90 (1954): 145–148.

———. "Some Distribution Records of the British Dragonflies (Odonata) for the Years 1962 and 1963." *Entomologist* 97 (1964): 145–146.

SECONDARY SOURCES

Hayter-Haymes, Jane. *Madam Dragonfly: The Life and Times of Cynthia Longfield.* Edinburgh: Pentland Press, 1991. Biography written by a grandniece includes many photographs from her expeditions and quotations from her unpublished letters.

LONGSHORE, HANNAH E. (MYERS) (1819–1902)

U.S. pioneer woman physician. Born 30 May 1819 in Sandy Spring, Md., to Paulina (Oden) and Samuel Myers. Six siblings. Married Thomas Ellwood Longshore in 1841. One son; one daughter. Educated private medical training; Woman's Medical College, Philadelphia (M.D., 1851). Professional experience: Female Medical College (Woman's Medical College of Pennsylvania), demonstrator of anatomy (1851–1852); New England Female College, demonstrator (1852–1853); Pennsylvania Medical University (female department), demonstrator in anatomy (1853–

1857); Private practice (1858–1892). Died 19 October 1901 in Philadelphia.

Hannah (Myers) Longshore was among the first women to be admitted to the Female Medical College of Pennsylvania and the first to be listed as a faculty member, although she never became a professor. Like ANN PRESTON, she was brought up in a Quaker family with a commitment to women's education. Many of her own opportunities appear to have come from a supportive husband and brother-in-law.

Hannah Longshore's first medical training, after her two children were born, was in private classes taught by Dr. Joseph Longshore, her brother-in-law. His interest in training female physicians was demonstrated by his instruction of Ann Longshore, his own sister, at the same time. Joseph Longshore was fired by the interest and enthusiasm of his women students and the difficulties of obtaining formal medical education for them. Shortly afterward, he played an important role by helping to found the Female Medical College of Pennsylvania (later renamed the Woman's Medical College) with a group of other determined male physicians.

When the Female Medical College was opened, Hannah Longshore, then thirty-one, entered the first class along with Ann Preston. At her graduation, it was her brother-in-law, by then a member of the board of trustees, who was the first commencement speaker. Upon graduation she was the first woman appointed to a position on the faculty, with the title of demonstrator of anatomy. This position as demonstrator was not followed by an appointment as professor, possibly because the anatomy professorship was held by a widely respected male physician, Nathaniel Moseley, who had been Ann Preston's first teacher. Longshore held a similar position as demonstrator at the New England Female Medical College the following year and then returned for another year of teaching to Philadelphia.

Following a schism betweeen two groups on the Women's Medical College faculty, Longshore followed Joseph Longshore to the female department of the Pennsylvania Medical University, and served as demonstrator of anatomy there for an additional four years.

Two of Hannah Longshore's sisters, Jane Myers and Mary Frame Myers Thomas, also became physicians. Longshore was compelled to give up teaching and lecturing as she found herself increasingly busy with a private practice. She continued to be a successful physician until her retirement forty years later. She died of uremia at the age of eighty-two.

JH/MBO

SECONDARY SOURCES
Abram, Ruth. "Will There be a Monument?: Six Pioneer Women Tell Their Own Stories." In *"Send Us a Lady Physi-*

cian": Women Doctors in America (1835–1920), ed. Ruth Abrams, 71–106. New York: Norton, 1984.
Alsop, Gulielma Fell. *History of the Woman's Medical College, Philadelphia, Pennsylvania, 1850–1950.* Philadelphia: J. B. Lippincott Co., 1950.

STANDARD SOURCES
Hurd-Mead 1933; Lovejoy; *NAW* (article by Patricia Spain Ward).

LONGSTAFF, MARY JANE (DONALD) (1856–1935)

British naturalist and invertebrate paleontologist. Born 1856. Father M. H. Donald of Carlisle. Three siblings. Married Dr. G. B. Longstaff. Died 19 January 1935.

Mary Jane Donald was the oldest of four children, and from an early age was interested in natural history, although she had little formal education. Land and freshwater mollusks especially fascinated her, and she became an authority on these groups. She married a well-known entomologist, Dr. G. B. Longstaff, and traveled all over the world with him.

Since, as a woman, she was obliged to be an amateur, she was never connected with a museum or other institution. The lack of a formal institutional home made it difficult for her to access the literature and study materials. Nevertheless, she managed to do so and became quite proficient at interpreting the material on gastropod systematics.

During her free time, Longstaff worked on Carboniferous fossil gastropods for over fifty years. She began by describing a series of fossils that she collected at Penton, in Cumberland, but soon progressed to a systematic revision of different genera and families. The papers that she produced from her studies are thorough and accurate. Most of them were published by the Geological Society, and she received an award from the Murchison Fund in 1898. Longstaff joined the Geologists' Association in 1883, and when she died was one of its oldest members. Her nephew, M. H. Donald, presented her collections of recent and fossil shells to the British Museum (Natural History).

JH/MBO

SECONDARY SOURCES
Cox, Leonard R. "Mrs. Mary Jane Longstaff." *Proceedings of the Geological Society of London* (1935): xcvii–xcviii.
[Cox, Leonard R.]. "Mrs. Mary Jane Longstaff (née Donald)." *Proceedings of the Geologist's Association* 47 (1935): 97.

STANDARD SOURCES
Sarjeant.

LONSDALE, KATHLEEN (YARDLEY)
(1903–1971)

British crystallographer. Born 1903 in Newbridge, Ireland, to Jessie Cameron and Harry Frederick Yardley. Married Thomas Jackson Lonsdale. Three children. Educated Bedford College for Women, London (B.S. in physics, 1922). Professional experience: University College London, researcher (1922–1923), reader in crystallography (1946–1949), professor of chemistry and head of the department of crystallography (1949–1968); The Royal Institution, researcher (1923–1946). Honors and memberships: International Union of Crystallography (1960–1966; vice president, president, 1966); British Association for the Advancement of Science, president (1968); Atomic Scientists Association, vice-president; Women's International League for Peace and Freedom, British section, president. Honors: universities of Wales, Leicester, Manchester, Lancaster, Oxford, and Bath, honorary doctorates; Fellow of the Royal Society (1945); Royal Society, Davy Medal (1957); Dame Commander of the Order of the British Empire (1956). Died 1 April 1971 in London.

Kathleen Yardley was born in Newbridge, Ireland, south of Dublin. She was one of ten children born to Jessie Cameron and Harry Frederick Yardley, a postal worker. When Kathleen was five, her parents were separated, and her mother relocated the children to Essex in England. She attended the County High School for Girls at Ilford, and also was allowed to take physics, chemistry, and higher mathematics at the High School for Boys, since these subjects were not offered at the girls' school.

Attending Bedford College for Women in London, Yardley initially studied mathematics. She later changed her field of study to physics, because of her strong interest in experimentation. When she received her degree with honors in 1923, she was offered a research position at University College, London, by William Henry Bragg, Nobel laureate in physics. Under Bragg, Yardley began to study a series of organic compounds using X-ray crystallography techniques. She followed Bragg to the Royal Institution in 1923, as part of a team of young international students.

In 1927, she married Thomas Jackson Lonsdale, whom she had met as a fellow research student at University College, and moved briefly to Leeds, where she took a part-time demonstratorship at the University of Leeds, supplementing the Tate scholarship from Bedford College (1927–1929). The first of her three children (two daughters and one son) was born during this period. When the family returned to London, she did mathematical work on structure analysis at home, but returned to the laboratory at Royal Institution at the urging of Bragg. Here she remained as his research assistant until his death in 1942, paid by a series of grants and fellowships. She then worked under Sir Henry Dale and was named a Dewar Fellow 1944 to 1946. She began to teach

only in her forties, as reader in crystallography and then professor of crystallography and head of department (1949) at University College, London. In 1945 she was elected among the first women Fellows of the Royal Society, and she was honored with the society's Davy Medal in 1957.

Lonsdale's scientific work had begun with the relationship of the mathematical theory of space groups to X-ray reflections, and resulted in a paper with W. T. Astbury published in the *Philosophical Transactions of the Royal Society* in 1924. She began to work with an international group to prepare tables of crystal structures that appeared in 1934. Part of this work on ethane derivatives served as the thesis for her doctorate of science. This was updated in 1951 with additional volumes on mathematical, physical, and chemical data in 1959, 1969, and 1974, with Lonsdale serving as the chair of the new Commission on Tables for the International Union of Crystallography.

Lonsdale was strongly attracted to experimentation and considered the best work to be that work done alone. In 1929, she published a remarkable paper on the first aromatic compound to be examined by crystallography, hexamethylbenzene; the paper is considered to be a classic in the field. She followed this up with a study of hexachlorobenzene. In the same year, she analyzed the evidence for the planarity of aromatic molecules. Taking time for the birth of her second and third child, she returned to the laboratory in 1934 to find the X-ray apparatus occupied. She then turned to the study of molecules, using a huge old electromagnet in the laboratory to establish the existence of molecular orbitals. She went on to use divergent X-ray beams to measure the distance between carbon atoms. Her first popular book on crystallography, *Crystals and X-Rays,* appeared in 1948.

In 1949, Lonsdale began to work with a woman student from South Africa, Judith Grenville-Wells (later Milledge), studying natural and artificial diamonds under high temperature and pressure. Earlier, she had studied diamond structure, concluding that the anomolies of the structure were due to imperfections in the crystal lattice. Together, she and Milledge began to reevaluate earlier studies. Milledge became her literary executor after her death, carrying on much of her work. Lonsdale also became interested in bladder stones, urged to study them by Dr. D. A. Anderson, who had an extensive collection. By 1969, she had expanded her observations to over one thousand with the help of crystallographer June Sutor and a grant from the Medical Research Council. She expected that commonalities of constituents and crystal growth would prove of medical importance. The investigation has continued after her death, with the hope that she shared to find some useful inhibitor.

A peace activist with her husband, Lonsdale became a Quaker along with her husband in 1936. She opposed nuclear testing after World War II, as a founding member of the Association of Atomic Scientists. She served as its vice-president, and published a book, *Is Peace Possible,* in 1957 at the height of the Cold War. She also was president of the British Section of the Women's International League for Peace and Freedom. She advised the founders of the Pugwash movement and attended a number of their conferences. Lonsdale also served as a member of the East-West Committeee of the Society of Friends. She also felt that scientists from technologically advanced countries were responsible to those who had come from developing nations, and that in encouraging the intellectual exodus, the advanced country owed financial support to schools and colleges in return. Her sense of obligation to young scientists led her to foster the creation of the Young Scientists section of the British Association.

As a woman scientist, Lonsdale was a pioneer not only as an early member of the Royal Society but as the first woman president of the International Union of Crystallography (1966) and the first woman president of the British Association for the Advancement of Science (1968). Conscious of the difficulties of being a productive woman scientist, she commented that for a married woman scientist it was necessary above all to have "chosen the right husband" and to learn to concentrate "in any available moment." She was named Dame Commander of the Order of the British Empire in 1956. In 1965, a rare artifically created mineral was named "lonsdalite" in her honor.

Although they had lived in London for most of her married life, following her husband's retirement from the Ministry of Transport, the Lonsdales retired to Bexhill-on-Sea which she found very pleasant. There for the next ten years, her husband assisted her in handling the floods of correspondence on peace and prisons, while she continued to work in the laboratory, although this required her to travel for five hours a day. Kathleen Lonsdale died of cancer, 1 April 1971, in London, leaving unfinished a study of thermal expansion of crystals. Some autobiographical notes on her international travels are held in the archives of the Royal Society.

JH/MBO

PRIMARY SOURCES

Yardley, Kathleen. With William Thomas Astbury. "Tabulated Data for Examination of the 230 Space-Groups by Homogenous X-Rays." *Philosophical Transactions of the Royal Society* 224A (1924): 221–257.
Lonsdale, Kathleen. *Simplified Structure Factor and Electron Density Formulae for the 20 Space-Groups of Mathematical Crystallography.* London: G. Bell & Sons, 1936.
———. "Diamonds, Natural and Artificial." *Nature* (London) 153 (1944): 669–672.
———. *Crystals and X-Rays.* London: G. Bell and Sons, 1948.
———. With N. F. M. Henry. *International Tables for X-Ray Crystallography.* Birmingham, England: Kynboch Press, vol. 1, 1952; vol. 2, 1959; vol. 3 (with G. H. MacGillavry and G. D. Reich), 1962.

SECONDARY SOURCES

Hodgkin, Dorothy M. C. "Kathleen Lonsdale." *Biographical Memoirs of Fellows of the Royal Society* 21 (1975): 447–489.
Julian, Maureen M. "Profiles in Chemistry: Dame Kathleen Lonsdale (1903–1971)." *Journal of Chemical Education* 59 (1982): 965–966.
Mason, Joan. "The Admission of the First Women to the Royal Society of London." *Notes and Records of Royal Society of London* 46 (1992): 279–300.

STANDARD SOURCES
DNB; Notable.

LOSA, ISABELLA (1473–1546)

Spanish theologian and hospital founder. Born 1473 in Cordova. Educated University of Cordova in theology. Founded Hospital of Loretta in Italy. Died in 1546 in Italy(?).

Isabella Losa was a doctor both of theology and of medicine. She founded a hospital in Italy. JH/MBO

STANDARD SOURCES
Hurd-Mead 1938; Rebière.

LÖSER, MARGARET SIBYLLA VON (ca. 1665)

German chemist. Born mid-seventeenth century, probably in Dresden.

All that is known about Margaret Sibylla von Löser is that she studied medical authors zealously. She died at the age of thirty but during her lifetime was celebrated for "her learning in all the four faculties." All of the sources say essentially the same thing.

STANDARD SOURCES
Harless; Hurd-Mead 1938; Rebière.

LOUDON, JANE (WEBB) (1807–1858)

British botanist and writer on horticulture. Born 1807 near Birmingham. Father Thomas Webb. Married John Loudon. Died 1807 in London.

Forced to make her own living after the death of her father, Jane Webb wrote a science fiction romance, *The Mummy: A*

Tale of the Twenty-Second Century (1827). The book came to the notice of John Loudon, a well-known landscape gardener and horticultural writer, who published a favorable review in a journal he then edited. Loudon sought out the author, whom he presumed to be a man, and eventually met Webb in 1830. They were married later that year. Jane Loudon accompanied her husband on his landscaping assignments, learned about plants, and served as his amanuensis. In order to extricate them from debt, she began to write books on popular botany. The books sold very well, particularly *The Ladies' Companion to the Flower Garden* (1841).

JH/MBO

PRIMARY SOURCES
Loudon, Jane. *The Young Naturalist's Journey; or, The Travels of Agnes Merton and Her Mama.* London: William Smith, 1840.
———. *Modern Botany; or, a Popular Introduction to the Natural System of Plants, According to the Classification of De Candolle.* 2d ed. London: J. Murray, 1851. First published in 1842.

STANDARD SOURCES
DNB; Ogilvie 1986; Shteir.

LOVEJOY, ESTHER POHL (1869–1967)

U.S. physician and medical administrator. Born 17 August 1869 near Seabeck, Wash., to Annie (Quinton) and Edward Clayson. Five siblings. Married (1) Emil Pohl (1894, he died in 1911), one son (b. 1901; d. 1908); (2) George A. Lovejoy (1913; divorced 1920). Educated University of Oregon Medical School (1894); postgraduate study, Chicago West-side Postgraduate School (1896); Vienna obstetrics and gynecology clinic (1904); Berlin (1910–1911). Professional experience: Skagway, Alaska, private practice and Union Hospital (1897–1899); Portland, Ore., private practice (1899–1904, 1909, 1911–1913); Portland Board of Health member, then director (1905–1909); Red Cross physician (in France) (1917–1919); American Women's Hospitals, director (1919–1959), corporation president (1959–1967). Honors and memberships: Medical Women's International Association, founder (1919), president (1919–1924); American Medical Women's Association, president (1932–1933); Legion of Honor (France); Gold Cross of the Holy Sepulcher (Jerusalem); Gold Cross of the Order of George I (Greece); Gold Cross of Saint Sava (Yugoslavia); AMWA Elizabeth Blackwell Medal (twice). Died 16 August 1967 in New York City.

Esther Pohl Lovejoy had a long career as a physician, public health officer, advocate of women's medical education, director of the American Women's Hospitals and spokesperson for the Medical Women's International Association. Her parents, Edward and Annie Clayson, were English immigrants who had come to the Washington Territory in the 1860s with her oldest brother. Esther was born a few years later in a logging camp near Seabeck. When she was twenty, her mother moved to Portland to help her children find positions. After a year's work in a department store, Clayson entered the University of Oregon Medical School. Although she had to borrow and even drop out for a year to earn more money, she managed to graduate four years later with a medal for academic achievement.

Soon after she graduated, Esther married a Czech-born fellow student, Emil Pohl, who had trained as a surgeon. The two set up in private practice in Portland, but Esther Pohl shortly afterward went for further training in Chicago in obstetrics and gynecology. Within a year, the two went to Alaska to join Esther Pohl's brothers in the Klondike. There they set up their practice and helped found a hospital in Skagway. When her brother Frederick was found murdered, Pohl chose to return to Portland, joining her husband only in the summers. In 1901 her only son was born and she entrusted his care to her mother while she continued her practice. He died at the age of seven from septic peritonitis after drinking contaminated milk. Pohl had by this time spent time at both a Viennese clinic and in Berlin furthering her medical skills.

On her return to Portland from abroad in 1905, Pohl became a member of the Portland Board of Health and, two year's later, its director. She was the first woman to hold the directorship of a board of health in any major American city. Her major accomplishments were in fighting tuberculosis, regulating the milk supply, funding school nurses, and instituting high sanitation standards—too late, however, to protect her own son. Her husband died in Alaska, three years after her son, while she was studying in Berlin.

Pohl made the first of her moves into politics in the early teens, supporting women's suffrage and prohibition. She met and married a local businessman, George Lovejoy, whom she divorced seven years later on the grounds that he was misusing her name to support dubious business projects. Her interest in a political career ended in 1920, with her failure to win a seat in Congress on the Democratic ticket—before women had won the right to vote.

During World War I, Lovejoy went to France as a Red Cross physician in Paris, volunteering at a charity hospital in the evenings, as described by her in her first book *House of the Good Neighbor* (1919). She also helped raise funds for the American Medical Women's Association to support the American Women's Hospitals (AWH) in Europe, which emphasized civilian support rather than the model of military support hospitals established by the British women's organization headed by ELSIE INGLIS. Lovejoy returned to France as the head of the organization. After the war, Lovejoy worked tirelessly to expand the work of this organization, later called the American Women's Hospitals Service, as its chair, until shortly before her death in her late nineties.

At the end of the war, Lovejoy was one of the founders of the Medical Women's International Association, and served as its head for the first five years. Her interest in and contacts with women around the world are reflected in her books on women physicians that record the biographies of many otherwise neglected medical women.

Lovejoy's AWHS organization assisted many people around the world, offering medical aid to war refugees and those fleeing natural disasters in Japan, Greece, Turkey, and the United States and during World War II throughout Europe. It expanded into South America during in the postwar period. Throughout her life, she had supported women in medicine and women's rights. Before Lovejoy died, she set up a scholarship award in her first husband's and her son's names at the University of Oregon Medical School, stipulating that one-third must go to women students.   JH/MBO

PRIMARY SOURCES

Lovejoy, Esther. *The House of the Good Neighbor.* New York: Macmillan, 1919.

———. *Certain Samaritans.* New York: Macmillan, 1927, 1933. Describes Lovejoy's work with the AWH, later the American Women's Hospital Service.

———. *Women Physicians and Surgeons.* Livingston, N.Y.: Livingston Press, 1939. Includes Lovejoy's portrait.

———. *Women Doctors of the World.* New York: Macmillan, 1957. Includes brief biographies of famous women physicians and some of the women associated with the Medical Women's International Association.

———. "My Medical School, 1890–1894." *Oregon Historical Quarterly* (March 1974): 7–35. Taken from Lovejoy's autobiographical writings, this work includes an introduction by Bertha Hallam.

Archival materials, letters, and photographs in the University of Oregon Health Services Center Library, Oregon Historical Society and American Women's Hospital Association, New York City.

SECONDARY SOURCES

Burt, Olive W. *Physician to the World.* New York: J. Messner, 1973.

"Esther Pohl Lovejoy." *New York State Journal of Medicine* 77 (1977): 1161–1165.

STANDARD SOURCES

Hurd-Mead 1933; *NAW*(M) (article by Elizabeth H. Thompson).

LOVELACE, AUGUSTA ADA BYRON, COUNTESS OF (1815–1852)

See Byron, Augusta Ada, Countess of Lovelace.

LOVELESS, MARY HEWITT (1899–1991)

U.S. physician, allergist, immunologist. Born 28 April 1899 in Clovis, Calif. Married 1925. Educated Stanford University (A.B., 1921; M.D., 1925). Professional experience: Roosevelt Hospital, New York, Department of Allergy, fellow (1935–1938); Cornell University, Medical College, instructor (1938–1940), research associate (1940–1944), assistant professor of medicine (1944–1947), associate professor of clinical medicine (1948–?); New York Hospital Department of Medicine, assistant physician to outpatients (1938–1940), physician (1940–1952), assistant attending physician (1952–?), consultant in allergy to inpatients (1944–1950), director of labs for allergen preparation (1940–?), allergy clinic, director of testing (1945–1950). Honors and memberships: Marcelle Award (1945); Academy of Allergy, Fellow; Immunological Association, member; Harvey Society, member. Died 1991.

After Mary Loveless received her medical degree from Stanford, she moved to New York, where she had various positions in hospitals and at Cornell University Medical College. Her specialty was allergies, and she directed a laboratory for allergen preparation and later became the director of testing in an allergy clinic.

She worked with antibodies and antigens involved in hay fever and in its control. She also studied insulin resistance, the immunology of serum disease, the purification of pollen allergens, and the purification of sensitizing and blocking antibodies.   JH/MBO

SECONDARY SOURCES

"Mary Hewitt Loveless." *Allergy Proceedings* 12 (1991): 357–359.

STANDARD SOURCES

AMS 7–8, B 9, P&B 10–11.

LOWATER, FRANCES (ca. 1871–?)

British/U.S. physicist. Born Stoke-sub-Hamdon, England. Educated University College, Nottingham (1889–1891; 1892–1893); Newnham College, Cambridge (1891–1892); Bryn Mawr (1896–1897; Ph.D., 1906). Professional experience: Bryn Mawr College, assistant demonstrator, physics (1894–1898), acting secretary (1898–1899), demonstrator (1899–1910); Western College, acting associate professor (1910–1911); Rockford College, instructor (1911–1915); Wellesley College, instructor (1915–1918), assistant professor (1918–1921), associate professor (from 1921). Death date unknown.

Born in England, physicist Frances Lowater attended universities in that country before coming to the United States. She earned a doctorate from Bryn Mawr, and then remained in several capacities until she took a teaching position at Westfield(?) College for a year. She then went to Rockford

College, where she remained for four years before going to Wellesley, where she moved up the ranks from instructor to associate professor. She drops out of *American Men of Science* after the fourth edition, and the further course of her career is unknown. During the summers, she was a research assistant at the Yerkes Observatory. She was a member of the Physical Society, a Fellow of the Royal Astronomical Society, and a Fellow of the London Physical Society. She was interested in spectroscopy, particularly the absorption spectrum of sulphur dioxide. She did spectrographic observations of Mira Ceti, R Leonis, T Cephei, and R. Serpentis.

JH/MBO

STANDARD SOURCES
AMS 2–4; Rossiter 1982.

LOWELL, FRANCES ERMA (1886–?)

U.S. educational psychologist. Born 12 October 1886 in Minneapolis, Minn. Educated University of Minnesota (A.B., 1915; A.M., 1917; Ph.D., 1919). Professional experience: Minnesota schools, teacher (1904–1909, 1915–1916); State School for Feeble-Minded, assistant psychologist (1917–1918); University of Minnesota, instructor in psychology (1918–1920); Rochester, N.Y., public school psychologist (1920–1921); Indianapolis Normal School, department of psychology, head (1922–1925); Cleveland Board of Education, clinical psychologist (1925–1952). Honors and memberships: American Psychological Association; Ohio Association of Applied Psychology. Death date unknown.

Born in Minneapolis, Frances Lowell earned all three of her degrees from the University of Minnesota. Lowell taught for five years in the Minnesota schools before she attended the university, and then for an additional year after she received her bachelor's degree. Her first position after she earned her master's degree was as an assistant psychologist at the State School for the Feeble-Minded. Many of her positions were for a short amount of time. After spending a year at this school, she spent two years at the University of Minnesota as an instructor before she went to Rochester, New York, as a public school psychologist, again for a short stay. She moved to Indianapolis as head of the department of psychology for the state normal school, this time for three years. Her last position was as a clinical psychologist for the Cleveland Board of Education. She stayed at this position for twenty-seven years, and retired from it in 1952.

Her research interests were in child psychology, anatomical versus mental age, intelligence, and school placement on basis of mental age.

KM

STANDARD SOURCES
AMS 3–8, S&B 9.

LOZIER, CLEMENCE SOPHIA (HARNED) (1813–1888)

U.S. physician. Born 11 December 1813 in Plainfield, N.J., to Hannah (Walker) and David Harned. Married (1) Abraham Lozier (1830; he died in 1837); (2) John Baker (1844; divorced 1863). One surviving son. Educated Syracuse Medical College (1853). Professional experience: New York City, private lecturer in medicine and physiology; New York Medical College and Hospital for Women, founder (1863), president and clinical professor of diseases of women (1863–1867), dean and professor of gynecology (1867–1888); private practice (1853–1888). Honors and memberships: New York City Suffrage League, president (1873–1883); National Women's Suffrage Association, president (1877–1878). Died New York City, 26 April 1888.

Clemence Harned was born in Plainfield, New Jersey. An orphan from a young age, she met and married Abraham Lozier at the age of seventeen. A number of her children died in infancy (only one son survived). Since her husband was in poor health, Lozier opened a girls' school in her home and began to teach physiology and hygiene, part of the reform movement of the day. She was a strong Methodist and found support and encouragement from her church.

After her husband's death, Lozier became involved in the New York Female Moral Reform Society, working with "fallen" women. Her earlier interest in physiology and hygiene led her to study medicine in her late thirties and she began that education with her brother, a physician. During this period she married again, to John Baker, about whom little is known.

Lozier (now Baker) began to study at an eclectic medical school in Rochester, but then finished her medical training at Syracuse Medical College, from which she graduated with high honors at the age of forty. She then moved to New York City, where she opened a private practice. By 1861, her marriage had proven unhappy, and she divorced her husband, returning to the name Lozier.

Ten years after she had obtained her degree, Lozier established a homeopathic medical college and hospital for women that opened even before the better-known New York Woman's Medical School of the New York Infirmary founded by ELIZABETH and EMILY BLACKWELL. First she took the position of president and clinical professor of diseases of women and children. Later, as the college experienced difficulties, she reorganized it, taking over the positions of Dean and professor of gynecology and obstetrics. She was reputed to be a good surgeon, even operating on women for tumors. Lozier wrote one pamphlet on sensible measures for childbirth, but was neither a scholar nor research scientist like MARY PUTNAM JACOBI.

Although the allopathic physicians of New York did not recognize this medical college, the homeopathic physicians embraced it. Her son, Abraham, also became a homeopathic physician. The student body grew from seven students and eight faculty members to over two hundred graduates by the time Lozier died twenty-five years later. The development of the college was at the cost of her own financial security, and she declared bankruptcy in 1878. The school survived, and Jennie de la Montagnie Lozier, her son's second wife, who was a physician like her son, became professor of physiology. It was eventually absorbed into a hospital medical school in the second decade of the twentieth century.

Lozier was deeply involved in reform movements of her era, an abolitionist in the sixties, offering her hospital as an asylum for African-Americans at the time of the draft riots during the Civil War. She also was a supporter of women's suffrage with her money from her lucrative practice as well as her personal energy. She was praised by Elizabeth Cady Stanton and underwrote Susan B. Anthony's suffrage weekly. In the early 1870s, Lozier was president of the New York City Suffrage League and later in the decade became president for two years of the National Women's Suffrage Association. Lozier was active politically in other directions, with the Women's Christian Temperance Union (W.C.T.U.) and the National Working Women's League, and women's groups supporting prison and Indian reform. She was an active member and president of the influential woman's club Sorosis, to which the anthropologists ERMINNIE SMITH and ALICE FLETCHER belonged. Lozier died in 1888 from fatty degeneration of the heart.   JH/MBO

PRIMARY SOURCES
Lozier, Clemence. *Childbirth Made Easy.* Pamphlet. N.p., 1870.

STANDARD SOURCES
Debus; *NAW* (article by Milton Cantor).

LU GWEI DJEN (1904–1991)

Chinese/British biochemist and historian of science. Born 1 September 1904 in Nanjing, China, to Lu Hsiu-Ying and Lu Mou T'ing. Married Joseph Needham (1989). Educated Ming-Te School, Nanjing; Ginling College, Nanjing (B.A.); Beijing Union Medical College; and Cambridge University (Ph.D., 1939). Professional experience: St John's University, Shanghai, lecturer in physiology and biochemistry; Lester Institute of Medical Research, Shanghai, researcher; University of California, Berkeley, research fellow (1939); College of Physicians and Surgeons, New York, staff; Sino-British Science Cooperation Office, British Embassy, Nanjing; Ganling College, Nanjing, professor of nutritional science (1947–?); UNESCO, Natural Sciences Division, Paris (1946–1956); Science and Civilization Series, collaborator with Joseph Needham (1957–1991); Joseph Needham Institute, East Asian History of Science Library, cofounder, director (1976–1991). Honors and member-

ships: Academia Sinica, China, honorary professor (1990); Chinese Medal for Literature; Cambridge University, Robinson College, fellow (1979–1980), emerita fellow (1980–1991). Died 28 November 1991 in Cambridge, England.

Lu Gwei Djen was the collaborator and, shortly before her death, the second wife of biochemist and historian of science Joseph Needham. Her fluency and skill in using ancient Chinese texts allowed him to develop an important new survey of ancient Chinese science in the 1970s. Lu was born into middle-class, Westernized family in Nanjing, China; her father's knowledge as a pharmacist in both Western and traditional Chinese herbal remedies would later serve her well. She acquired a good understanding of Chinese scholarship while she was learning science at Ginling College, Nanjing. Lu then studied clinical pathology at Bejing Union Medical College and began to lecture on physiology and biochemistry at St. Johns University in Shanghai. At the same period she did medical research at the Lester Institute of Shanghai into causes of the nutritional disorder beriberi.

With the beginning of the Japanese invasion in 1937 and the shelling of Shanghai, Lu fled to England where she worked toward her doctorate at the Cambridge Biochemical Laboratories under the biochemist DOROTHY NEEDHAM. Here she also met Joseph Needham, then married to Dorothy. Her knowledge of ancient Chinese science intrigued Joseph Needham, and her father later presented him with an encyclopedia of Chinese science.

Just before World War II, in 1939, Lu had an opportunity to do further research in nutritional studies at University of California, Berkeley, then briefly at Birmingham City Hospital, Alabama, and finally at Columbia University in New York, where she was on the staff of the College of Physicians and Surgeons. At the end of the war, she went for a short period back to China, where she was attached to the Sino-British Scientific Mission and taught nutritional science at her old college, Ganling. Here she reencountered the Needhams, who had spent part of the war in China as part of the British Scientific Mission.

When Joseph Needham went to Paris as part of UNESCO, Lu also joined the organization and was a staff member in the Natural Sciences Division in Paris for ten years, returning to Cambridge in 1957. In the late fifties and continuing until her death, the two began a long-term collaboration on the *Science and Civilization in China* series of books.

As the volumes began to appear, the contribution of Lu's scholarship was gradually recognized. She was primarily responsible for the volume on acupuncture and moxa entitled *Celestial Lancets* (1980). She helped to found and manage the East Asian Library Trust and Library and the Joseph Needham Institute at Cambridge. In 1979, she was made a fellow of Robinson College, Cambridge. As Dorothy Needham became more and more debilitated with increasing illness, Lu became a personal and emotional support to Joseph Needham as well. Upon the death of Dorothy Needham in 1987, Lu and Needham were finally married when they both were in their eighties.

At the end of her life, Lu was honored in China as well with an honorary professorship in the Academia Sinica and a medal for literature. She saw herself as the arch sustaining the bridge built between the civilization of the West and the East by Joseph Needham. On his side he recognized her contribution in his dedication to her in his book of essays *The Grand Titration: Science and Society in East and West* as the "explainer, the antithesis" and the "link that no separation can break."

JH/MBO

PRIMARY SOURCES

Lu Gwei-Djen. *Epicure in China.* 1942.

———. With Joseph Needham and others. *Clerks and Craftsmen in China and the West.* Cambridge: Cambridge University Press, 1970.

———. With Joseph Needham and others. *Science and Civilization in China.* Vol. 1, pt. 3; vol. 5, pts. 2–5, 7; vol. 6, pts. 1,3,4. Cambridge: Cambridge University Press, 1976.

———. With Joseph Needham. *Celestial Lancets: A History of Acupuncture and Moxa.* Cambridge: Cambridge University Press, 1980.

———. With Joseph Needham. *Listening Once Again.* Cambridge: Cambridge University Press, 1985.

———. With Joseph Needham. *Chemistry and Chemical Techology.* Cambridge: Cambridge University Press, 1986.

STANDARD SOURCES

Annual Obituary 1991 (Lu noted pages 687–688).

LUBINSKA, LILIANA (1904–1990)

Polish neuroscientist. Born 1904. Married Jerzy Kornorski. Educated University of Paris, Sorbonne (B.A., 1927; doctor of natural sciences, 1932). Professional experience: University of Paris, Sorbonne, Laboratory of Physiology (Lapicque), assistant (1927–1932); Nencki Institute of Experimental Biology (Warsaw), Department of Physiology, researcher (1932–1939?); Institute of Experimental Medicine, Sukhumi (Caucasus), researcher (1940?–1945); Nencki Institute of Experimental Biology (Warsaw), Department of Physiology, researcher (1945–1982). Died November 1990.

Considered by her colleagues to be one of the best-known and best-loved Polish neurobiologists, Liliana Lubinska had decided from her early youth to study animal physiology. Like many Polish scientists, she went to Paris to study natural sciences in 1924, obtaining a degree from the Sorbonne in

biological chemistry and general physiology. After obtaining her degree, she began to work in the physiology laboratory of Louis Lapicque and his wife, MARCELLA H. LAPICQUE, as an assistant. Working on her doctorate, she investigated a topic related to that of the Lapicques, on chronaxie and non-iterative reflexes. This work was awarded the Solange Coemme prize by the Académie de Médecine, Paris. Completing her doctorate in natural sciences in 1932, Lubinska returned to Warsaw, working in the Department of Physiology of the Nencki Institute of Experimental Biology. With her husband, Jerzy Kornorski, also a neuroscientist, she went to the Caucasus during World War II to work at the Institute of Experimental Medicine in Sukhumi. Here they studied regeneration of peripheral nerves.

Returning to Warsaw immediately after the war, Lubinska helped to rebuild the Nencki Institute. She worked on the physiology of the peripheral nervous system, investigating nerve fibers, neurotubules, and the axoplasm. Her studies of axoplasmic transport were extremely important, and she used acetylcholinesterase (AChE) as a marker in these studies to elucidate its bidirectional movement. The resulting work brought her to the forefront of the field of axoplasmic transport studies. She published a total of about eighty papers, two of which were important reviews of her field.

Her friends remembered her as a humane person, deeply committed to art and literature as well as science. She was on the editorial board of the journal *Neuroscience* from 1976 until her death and was a foreign member of the German Academy of Natural Scientists, Leopoldina, an honorary member of the International Brain Research Organization (IBRO), and a member of many Polish and foreign scientific societies.

JH/MBO

PRIMARY SOURCES

Lubinska, Liliana. "Contribution à l' étude des reflexes non-iteratifs." Ph.D. diss., University of Paris, Sorbonne, 1932.

———. "Axoplasmic streaming in Regenerating and in Normal Nerve Fibres." *Progress in Brain Research* 13 (1964): 1–71.

———. "On Axoplasmic Flow." *International Review of Neurobiology,* 17 (1975): 241–296.

SECONDARY SOURCES

Neuroscience 42 (1992): iii–iv. Obituary notice with portrait.

Niemierko, Stella, and Jirina Zelena. *Acta Neurobiologiae Experimentalis* 51 (1991): 1. Obituary notice.

LUKANINA, ADELAIDA N. (1843–1908)

Russian physician. Born in 1843. Educated courses in pedagogy; Helsingfors University; University of Zurich; Woman's Medical College in Philadelphia (1876). Died in 1908.

Little is known about Adelaida Lukanina's early life. As a young woman, she took courses in pedagogy but decided to become a physician instead. To this end, she started to study with Aleksandr P. Borodin (1834–1887). Although better known in the West as a composer, Borodin was also a chemist and, as one of the foremost supporters of women's education, welcomed a number of women students in his laboratory.

Borodin considered Lukanina his most able student; while in his laboratory, she conducted some noteworthy research on the oxidation of albumen to produce urea and also on the action of succinyl chloride on benzoin, correcting the results of the German chemist Limpricht. She published several papers, one in the bulletin of the Petersburg Academy of Sciences, apparently the first chemical work to be published by a woman in that academy's publication.

Lukanina became involved in political activity and was detained for a short time by the police. In 1870 she went to Helsingfors in Finland, which in that year began to admit women. In 1872, she was accepted in the medical school in Zurich.

By this time, Zurich had become a center for revolutionary activity and an arena for lively discussion among anarchists, populists, Marxists, and others. Many young women students became involved. In 1873, Tsar Aleksandr II issued a proclamation ordering all women students to leave Zurich. Those who remained would not be allowed to take licensing examinations or hold civil service posts in Russia if, in the future, they became open to women. Lukanina was among those who decided to defy the decree and stay on in Zurich. By 1875, only her dissertation remained to be written and Lukanina made up her mind to go to America to try to complete her degree there. A desire to get further away from the tsarist police seems to have played a role in this decision.

In America, Lukanina was befriended by MARIE ZAKRZEWSKA and, for a time, worked in the New England Infirmary for Women in Boston. She described her experiences in articles she wrote for *Vestnik Evropy* in 1881 and 1882. Later, she attended Woman's Medical College in Philadelphia where she successfully passed the final examinations in 1876.

Although Zakrzewska offered her a position at the New England Infirmary, Lukanina declined and went back to Europe. Little is known of her career after she left the United States. She did not return to Russia until after the Revolution of 1905, by which time she was ill. She died in 1908.

Lukanina was by all accounts a brilliant student both in chemistry and in medicine, but she was a casualty of the politics of the time and could not, perhaps, make the contribution to science that, under other circumstances, she could have made. Nevertheless, her early chemical research main-

tains its value and her later writings give an unusual insight into the American medical practices of the day.   A C H

PRIMARY SOURCES

Lukanina, Adelaida N. "Okislenie belka khameleonom." *Zhurnal Russkogo khimischeskogo obshchestva* 3 (1871).

———. "O deistvii khloristogo suktsinila na benzoin." *Zhurnal Russkogo khimischeskogo obshchestva.* 1874, 4.

———. "God v Amerike." *Vestnik Evropy* 16, no. 8 (1881): 621–666; 16, no. 9 (1881): 31–78; 17, no. 4 (1882): 503–545.

SECONDARY SOURCES

Musabekov, Iusuf S. *Iuliia Vsevolodovna Lermontova, 1846–1919.* Moscow: Izd-vo "Nauka," 1967.

STANDARD SOURCES

Tuve.

LUNN, KATHARINE FOWLER (1902–1997)

See Fowler-Billings, Katharine Stevens.

LUOMALA, KATHARINE (1907–)

U.S. anthropologist. Born 10 September 1907 in Cloquet, Minn., to Eliina (Forsness) and John Erland Luomala. Educated University of California (A.B., 1931; M.A., 1933; Ph.D., 1936). Professional experience: Bernice P. Bishop Museum, Honolulu, honorary associate (1941–retirement); U.S. Office of Strategic Services, researcher (1942–1945?); University of Hawaii, professor of anthropology (1946–retirement), chair (1954–1957; 1960; 1964). American Anthropological Association, Fellow. Honors and memberships: Anthropological Society of Hawaii; Polynesian Society; Phi Beta Kappa; Sigma Xi.

Born in Minnesota, Katharine Luomala went to the University of California, Berkeley, for all of her degrees, obtaining her doctorate in anthropology. This was the period when Alfred Kroeber was developing Berkeley into a great center for ethnology. As did many of the women anthropologists who preceeded her (ELISE CLEWS PARSONS, RUTH UNDERHILL, RUTH BENEDICT), Luomala did her field work in the Southwest, publishing on the changing Navajo Indian people. Her first position was as an associate in the Bishop Museum in Hawaii where she came in contact with the artifacts and the legends of Oceania, continuing her interest in comparative mythology.

During World War II, Luomala, along with anthropologist Rosalie Wax, worked with a team under Dorothy Swaine Thomas, a sociologist from her university. One of their assignments was the assessment of the effects of Japanese American relocation for the Office of Strategic Services.

Returning to Hawaii after World War II, Luomala was professor of anthropology at the University of Hawaii, serving a number of times as chair of her department. She published on the legends of the Hawaiian Islands and in the 1950s she began to examine the ethnobotany of the Gilbert Islands and to expand her studies of mythology.   JH/MBO

PRIMARY SOURCES

Luomala, Katharine. *Navaho Life of Yesterday and Today.* Berkeley: Western Museum Laboratories, United States Department of the Interior, National Park Service, 1938.

————. *Oceanic, American Indian, and African Myths of Snaring the Sun.* N.P., 1940.

————. *Menehune and Other Little People of Oceania.* Honolulu: Bernice P. Bishop Museum, 1951.

————. *Ethnobotany of the Gilbert Islands.* Honolulu: The Museum, 1953.

————. *Voices on the Wind.* Honolulu: Bishop Museum Press, 1955.

STANDARD SOURCES

Debus; Rossiter 1995.

LUTWAK-MANN, CECELIA (fl. 1938)

German-British physiologist, endocrinologist. Born in Germany in 1900(?). Married Thaddeus Mann. Went to Britain in 1934, one of many German-Jewish refugee scientists.

Cecelia Lutwak was born in Germany. She married Thaddeus Mann (an endocrinologist who discovered inhibition of carbonic anhydrase), who studied biocemistry of male reproduction and who was sometimes facetiously referred to as the "king of sperm." Lutwak-Mann, working on biochemical factors in female reproduction, showed that progesterone controls synthesis of carbonic anhydrase in the placenta. She worked also with Feldberg and D. K. Keilin on cell respiration.   JH/MBO

SECONDARY SOURCES

Davenport, Horace V. "Carbonic Anhydrase or the Strange Case of the Disappearing Scientist." *The Physiologist* 23, no. 2 (1980): 11–15.

Keilin, D. K. *The History of Cell Respiration and Cytochrome.* Cambridge: Cambridge University Press, 1960.

LWOFF, MARGUERITE (BOURDALEIX) (1905–1979)

French microbiologist and virologist. Married André Lwoff (5 December 1925). Educated University of Paris. Professional experience:

Pasteur Institute, research associate (1929–1959); Kaiser Wilhelm Insitute, visiting researcher (with Andre Lwoff) (1933–1934). Died 1979.

Marguerite (Bourdaleix) Lwoff worked closely with her husband, the microbiologist and virologist André Lwoff, at the Pasteur Institute, Paris. In the twenties, the two were close colleagues when they worked with Edouard Chatton at the Roscoff Marine Biological Station, studying parasitical ciliates, and later with Chatton at the marine station Banyuls-sur-Mer. During 1928, when André Lwoff was away fulfilling his military duty, Chatton turned to Marguerite Lwoff to take over her husband's work on a monograph on the Apostomes. When André Lwoff first headed his own laboratory at the Pasteur in 1929, his wife was his major colleague. She began to publish not only with him, but in her own right and with other members of the lab. The first publications of Jacques Monod in the 1930s were with both André and Marguerite Lwoff. (Monod would later win a Nobel Prize with André Lwoff and François Jacob in 1965 for their work on molecular biology).

In the 1930s, husband and wife traveled to a number of laboratories, exchanging their methods and expertise with others. They went to London to do research at the Middlesex Hospital bacterial chemistry unit. There they became involved in the question of protozoan and bacterial nutrition, and "growth factors" and presented a paper that bore both their names to the Royal Society of London identifying cosymase 1 or 2 as the so-called V factor for *Hemophilus.* They spent time at Cambridge with David Keilin learning new biochemical techniques. They traveled to Heidelberg, Germany, to work as scientific guests in the Institute of Physiology of the Kaiser Wilhelm Institute of Medical Research under the direction of Nobel Prize–winner Otto Meyerhof.

Marguerite Lwoff published alone in 1940 a significant monograph on the role of hematin in the oxygen-linked respiration of trypanosomes, a study that related to the Lwoffs' joint research on microbial cellular metabolism. The question then is why does the joint work of husband and wife diminish in importance? The influence of André Lwoff was steadily growing as a teacher and a central figure for what would develop into molecular biology, while the role of Marguerite Lwoff, still important for her husband's experiments, was no longer that of an equal colleague. Instead, Jacques Monod, who had joined the laboratory during World War II, was soon a major figure in focusing research, leading seminars, and pushing work on viruses. In the postwar era, the studies of Lwoff and Monod (and Lwoff's student François Jacob) on bacteriophage and lysogeny would help to change the look of biology. In this, Marguerite

Lwoff had more of an enabling role. Husband and wife still worked together, still published together, but the significant citations of André Lwoff bore the names of other colleagues.

Evidence for the changing status of Marguerite Lwoff is given in the accounts of laboratory life in the reminiscences of former colleagues in a book written to honor André Lwoff, edited by Monod and Borek. Those writing about the thirties and even the early forties invariably speak of the Lwoffs as a team of researchers. Those writing about the fifties and sixties depict her almost as a laboratory assistant, completing virus assays begun by her husband. The exception to this is when husband and wife travel abroad to work in a foreign laboratory, but even in those accounts, André, not Marguerite, is the featured scientist. Renato Dulbecco, for example, talks of the two scientists coming to work with him at the California Institute of Technology in the early sixties, but discusses Marguerite Lwoff only in reference to the labeling of glassware by two competing Marguerites, his own research associate, Marguerite Vogt, and Marguerite Lwoff. By the sixties, when André Lwoff was made the head of the cancer laboratory, Marguerite had come to be perceived (perhaps by herself as well as by others) as a supportive figure in the laboratory, working with the great scientist but no longer a major player in science.   JH

PRIMARY SOURCES

Lwoff, Marguerite. With Edouard Chatton and André Lwoff as first authors. "Les *Photophyra* n.g. Ciliés Foettingériiodee, hyperparisites des *Gymnodinioides, Foetingeriiidae* parasites des Crustacés." *Comptes Rendus Académie des Sciences* (1930).

———. With André Lwoff as first author. "Sur la nature du facteur V. Studies on codehydrogenasess I & II." *Proceedings of the Royal Society of London* ser. B 122 (1937): 352.

———. *Recherches sur le pouvoir de synthèse des flagellés trypanosomides.* Paris: Masson, 1940.

———. With N. Groman, and André Lwoff as first authors. "Recherches sur un variant dit 'froid' du virus de la poliomyelite." *Annales Institute Pasteur* 98 (1960): 351–359.

SECONDARY SOURCES

Monod, Jacques, and Ernest Borek, eds. *Of Microbes and Men (Les Microbes et la Vie).* New York and London: Columbia University Press, 1971. Written by a group of European, English, and American scientists to honor Lwoff, and the source for many anecdotes about the work of André and Marguerite Lwoff, including photographs.

STANDARD SOURCES

Vogt (describes the Lwoffs in Meyerhoff's laboratory, citing *Tätigkeitsberichte* (annual reports) of *Die Naturwissenschaften* (1933–1935).

LYELL, KATHARINE MURRAY (HORNER) (1817–1915)

British botanist. Born 1817 in London. Father Leonard Horner. Five siblings. Married Henry Lyell. Privately educated. Died 19 February 1915.

Katharine Horner, like her older sister MARY, was brought up in a household unusually devoted to science. Her father, Leonard Horner, took his daughters to meetings of the British Association for the Advancement of Science, where they had the opportunity to meet and listen to the great scientists of the day. She met her future husband, Henry Lyell, at the home of her sister Mary, who had married his brother, the great geologist Charles Lyell. Later, following the death of her brother-in-law, she would compile and edit his life and letters. Twenty-five years later, she edited the life and letters of another brother-in-law, Charles Bunbury.

Katharine Lyell became interested in botany, particularly ferns, and compiled a geographical handbook of fern distribution in 1870. Traveling with her husband to India, she collected plants in the Ganges Delta, Assam, and Khasia Hills. Her plants were given to the British Museum, where they still can be found, but her fern collection was given to the Royal Botanical Gardens at Kew.   JH/MBO

PRIMARY SOURCES

Lyell, Katharine Murray. *Geographical Handbook of All the Known Ferns.* London: J. Murray, 1870.

———, ed. *Life, Letters, and Journal of Sir Charles Lyell.* 2 vols. London: Murray, 1881.

———. *Life and Letters of Sir Charles J. F. Bunbury.* 2 vols. London: Murray, 1906.

SECONDARY SOURCES

Huxley, Leonard. *Life and Letters of Sir Joseph Dalton Hooker.* 2 vols. London: J. Murray, 1918. Lyell discussed throughout.

LYELL, MARY ELIZABETH (HORNER) (1808–1873)

British geologist and conchologist. Born 1808 in London. Father Leonard Horner. Five siblings. Married Charles Lyell. Privately educated. Died London(?) 1873.

Mary Horner, the eldest of six remarkable daughters of the geologist Leonard Horner, later president of the Geological Society of London, became the wife of a geologist in 1832. Her husband, Charles Lyell (1797–1875), later the president of the Geological Society like her father, was the author of the influential *Principles of Geology* (1830–1833), a work essential to Darwin in the development of his evolutionary theory.

Lyell, who was knighted in 1848, traveled widely in Europe and North America; throughout her life, Mary Lyell traveled with him whenever possible. She read both French and German fluently and translated scientific papers for him. Because Sir Charles's eyesight was poor, she frequently read to him, and managed much of his correspondence. Exposed to science first in her childhood by her father and then through her assistance with her husband's research, Mary Lyell became an accomplished conchologist. Her death before that of her husband meant that it was her sister, KATHARINE MURRAY LYELL, who edited his letters.   JH/MBO

SECONDARY SOURCES
Bailey, Edward. *Charles Lyell.* Garden City, N.Y.: Doubleday, 1963.
Lyell, Katharine Murray. *Life and Letters of Charles Lyell.* London: Murray, 1881.

STANDARD SOURCES
DNB; DSB; Ogilvie 1986.

LYNN, MARY JOHNSTONE (1891–?)

Irish botanist. Born 1891 at Carrickfergus. Educated Queen's University, Belfast (B.Sc., 1914; D.Sc., by thesis 1937); Manchester University, post-graduate work. Professional experience: Belfast, senior lecturer in botany. Death date unknown.

Mary Johnstone Lynn's research was on the phyto-ecology of the tidal zone in Northern Ireland. She published regularly in the *Irish Naturalists Journal* in the 1930s.   JH/MBO

PRIMARY SOURCES
Lynn, Mary J. "The Scarcity of *Zostera marina* (Slitch, Eelgrass or Grass-Wrack) in Strangford, Lough." *Irish Naturalists' Journal* 6 (1936): 106–117.

STANDARD SOURCES
Desmond; Praeger.

LYON, MARY (1797–1849)

U.S. educator. Born 28 February 1797 in Buckland, Mass., to Jemima (Shepard) and Aaron Lyon. Seven siblings. Educated Sanderson Academy in the village of Ashfield (1817); Amherst, Mass., Academy (1818); Amherst College, attended Amos Eaton's chemistry lectures; New Rensselaer School (1825). Professional experience: village schools, teacher (from 1814); Byfield, Mass., Female Seminary, teacher (1821); different female seminaries including the Ipswich Seminary in Philadelphia, teacher (to 1834); Wheaton Female Seminary, Norton, Mass., consultant (1835); Mount Holyoke Female Seminary (later Mount Holyoke College), founder (1836), principal (1836–1848). Died 5 March 1849 at Mount Holyoke.

Mary Lyon was born in Buckland, Massachusetts, the sixth of eight children. She grew up on a farm and attended one-room schools. After her father died in 1802, her mother remarried and moved to Ashfield, Mass., a short distance away. Thirteen-year-old Mary stayed on the farm and kept house for her brother Aaron. He paid her a dollar a week toward her education. She later more than repaid him by paying off a mortgage that he had on another farm to which he and his family moved. In 1814 she began her teaching career—teaching young children during the summers. She began a pattern of alternating studies with teaching in 1817 when she enrolled in the new Sanderson Academy in the village of Ashfield. This academy was coeducational, and Lyon was exposed to more advanced subjects. This year was a good one not only academically but socially: Lyon lived in the house of Thomas White whose daughter, Amanda, became Mary's lifelong friend.

In 1818, Lyon spent a term at Amherst Academy, where she studied Latin, science, and history. School again produced a good friend, this time Orra White, the preceptress. Since people were planning to form a college, Lyon listened to their plans and observed that the citizens were attempting to fund the project themselves. She returned to Sanderson to study and again alternated her academic experience with teaching. When she returned to school she studied at Byfield, Mass., Female Seminary, where Joseph Emerson was headmaster. Emerson respected the girls and acted as though they had intelligence. Lyon absorbed some of his ideas, particularly the need for permanent educational institutions for women. At Byfield, she met Zilpah Grant, the preceptress, who became a good friend.

In 1823, Lyon returned to teach at Sanderson and at a school in Conway, Massachusetts. At the school in Conway, she boarded with the Reverend Edward Hitchcock and his wife, Orra (White) Hitchcock. The three took geological expeditions. By this time Lyon had had considerable teaching experience and opened a girls' school in Buckland in the winter and in the summers worked with Zilpah Grant at the new Adams Female Academy in what is now East Derry, New Hampshire. Lyon's academy was a success, and she found the innovative teaching methods that she had invented worked. However, after Zilpah Grant was forced out of the Adams Academy, Grant established a new academy, the Ipswich, Massachusetts, Female Seminary. Lyon devoted herself to the Ipswich school, and left the Buckland Seminary in other hands (it ultimately disbanded). Much of her energy went into an attempt to convince people of the importance of an endowment. Amid all of the happenings, Lyon still found time to attend lectures at Amherst College by Amos Eaton, the lawyer who stressed the importance of the laboratory in science teaching. In 1824 she also studied at the New Rensselaer School (later the Rensselaer Polytechnic Institute where Eaton was senior professor).

During the summer of 1934, Lyon went on a long trip and formulated plans for a new school. The dream that was to become Mount Holyoke began during those travels. Her radical plan involved the seminary owning its own property with trustees dealing with the financial affairs. It was to be a Christian institution both founded and supported by this community. The seminary was to be residential and affordable for the students were to perform the domestic work. In 1834 she resigned from Ipswich to plan her own institution. However, her dream did not come immediately, for she spent a year as a consultant in the planning of the Wheaton Female Seminary. She planned for her own institution. Three western Massachusetts communities requested that the seminary come to their town.

South Hadley, Massachusetts, won the right to house the new institution, Mount Holyoke Seminary. The seminary was an immediate success. Lyon was principal of the school for twelve years and remained there until her death. Her health became increasingly worse, and as the fifty-two-year-old woman was beginning to recover from erysipelas, she became totally distraught at news of the suicide of a nephew and died.

Lyon was responsible for the emphasis on science at Mount Holyoke, the institution that she founded. She had studied chemistry with Amos Eaton and stressed the importance of science teaching in schools.   JH/MBO

PRIMARY SOURCES

Lyon, Mary. *A Missionary Offering.* Boston: Crocker & Brewster, 1843. Lyon's only full-length book.

SECONDARY SOURCES

Fisk, Fidelia. *Recollections of Mary Lyon: Manuscript Reminiscences of Early Students at Mount Holyoke Seminary.* Mount Holyoke, Mass., 1866.

Gilchrist, Beth Bradford. *The Life of Mary Lyon.* Washington, D.C.: National Education Association, 1910.

Green, Elizabeth Alden. *Mary Lyon and Mount Holyoke.* Hanover, N.H.: University of New Hampshire Press, 1979.

Hitchcock, Edward, comp. *The Power of Christian Benevolence, Illustrated in the Life and Labors of Mary Lyon.* 2d ed. Northampton, Mass.: Bridgman, 1851.

Lansing, Marion, ed. *Mary Lyon through Her Letters.* Boston: Books, Inc., 1937. See chapter 9: "Science with Professor Eaton."

Lyon's papers are found at Mount Holyoke College.

STANDARD SOURCES

NAW (article by Sydney R. MacLean); Rossiter 1982.

LYUBIMOVA, YELENA ALEKSANDROVNA (1925–1985)

Soviet geologist. Born 1925 in Moscow. Educated Moscow State University, faculty of physics (graduated 1949). Professional experience: Institute of Earth Physics (then the Geophysical Institute), researcher (1949–1985). Died 22 April 1985.

Yelena Aleksandrovna Lyubimova obtained her higher education at the Faculty of Physics, Moscow State University, where her advisor was A. N. Tikhonov. Tikhonov considered her one of his most capable students. She also studied under O. Yu. Schmidt. She graduated in 1949 and joined the Geophysical Institute, where she worked for the rest of her life.

Lyubimova received international recognition as one of the founders of the International Committee for Heat Flow and served as its president from 1971 to 1979, was vicepresident of the Scientific Council for Geothermal Research, and was the coordinator for the project "Heat Model of the Lithosphere."

During her over thirty-five years of scientific activity at the Institute of Physics, she supervised numerous doctoral candidates. She considered the important problems of geophysics and geothermics such as the thermal evolution of the earth and moon, the study of the physical nature of heat and of the mechanism of heat exchange in the earth's interior, electroconductivity, elastic stresses, the analysis of the relationship of observed values of heat flow to the processes in the earth's crust and mantle, the nature of observed anomalies of heat flow, the interpretation of heat fields along geotraverses, zones of subduction and spreading along the Kola trench, and measurements of heat flow along the continents and oceans and in the Arctic. She was one of the first Soviet woman geophysicists to take part in scientific research voyages in the Atlantic. She is the author of numerous scientific papers.   CK

PRIMARY SOURCES

Lyubimova, Yelena Aleksandrovna. "The Influence of Radioactive Decomposition of the Heat Regime of the Earth." *Izvestiya Akademii Nauk SSSR. Serriya Geofizicheskiy* (1952): 3–14.

———. "Termika zemli i luny" (Thermic conditions of the earth and moon). Moscow: Akademii Nauk Institut Fizika Zemli, 1968.

———. "Teplovyye potoki i radiogennoye teplo iz kori i mantii" (Heat flow and radiation from the crust and mantle). In

Glubinnyy teplovoy potok yevropeyskoy chasti SSSR, ed. S. I. Subbotin, 130–142. Kiev Izdjanak Nauk, Dumka, 1974.

————. With V. M. Lyuboshits and V. N. Nikitina. "Ob interpretatsii anomaliy teplovogo potoka v osevykh zonakh sredinno-okeanicheskikh khrebtov" (Interpretation of heat flow anomalies within the axial zones of mid-ocean ridges). In *Geotermicheskiye issledovaniya na dne akvatoriy* (Geothermal investigations of submarine environment), ed. Yu. M. Puscharovskiy and V. I. Kononov, 11–21. Moscow: Nauka, 1988.

SECONDARY SOURCES

"In Memoriam; Yelena Aleksandrovna Lyubimova." *Physics of the Solid Earth* 21, no. 11 (1985): 895.

M

MAASS, CLARA LOUISE (1876–1901)

U.S. nurse who died serving as an experimental subject for yellow fever. Born 28 June 1876 in Beauville, N.J. Eight siblings. Educated German Hospital of Newark (R.N., 1898?). Professional experience: military hospitals in Florida, Cuba, Philippines; Las Animas Hospital, Havana, Cuba. Died 27 September 1901 in Havana of yellow fever.

Clara Louise Maass was one of nine children of a German immigrant family that settled in New Jersey. When she was in her teens, she began to study nursing at the German Hospital of Newark (later renamed the Newark Hospital and then the Lutheran Memorial Hospital). At the beginning of the Spanish-American War, she served under contract to military hospitals in Florida, Cuba, and the Philippines. While in the Philippines, she contracted dengue fever and was sent back home. Once she was well, she was assigned to a Havana hospital by General Gorgas, head of the Cuban department of public health.

At Las Animas Hospital in Havana, Maass began to work with John Guiteras, who, under the Yellow Fever Commission directed by Walter Reed, was trying to understand the effect of previous inoculations of yellow fever on the course of the disease. He subjected eight volunteers to light infections in the hope of preventing a serious attack. Maass was one of the volunteers. Having nursed hundreds of men successfully, she appears to have believed that she was immune. Although she recovered from the first inoculation on 24 June 1901, suffering only a light fever, the second challenge in September resulted in her death at the age of twenty-five. It was in 1901 that Walter Reed and others managed to identify the agent carried by the mosquito as a filterable virus, verifying earlier conclusions.

Maass was regarded as a medical martyr, and her body was returned to New York at the beginning of the following year. She was commemorated with a portrait and a room named in her honor in 1910 at her old hospital in Newark, but during the anti-German furor of World War I, the memorial was removed. In recent years, the hospital has been renamed Clara Maass Memorial Hospital. Two stamps have been issued in her honor: one in Cuba in 1951, a second in the United States in 1979.   JH/MBO

SECONDARY SOURCES

Arvys, Lucie. "Clara Louise Maass (1874–1901) et la fièvre jaune." *Clio Medica* 13 (1979): 277–282. Includes images of the two stamps bearing Maass's likeness. The Cuban stamp shows the hospital in which she trained and the Havana hospital in which she died.

MACAULAY, CATHARINE (SAWBRIDGE) (1731–1791)

British social scientist. Born 1731. Married (1) George Macaulay (1760; he died); (2) William Graham. One daughter by Macaulay. Educated at home.

Catharine Sawbridge received a good education at home, where she read Roman history and became convinced that a republic was the best form of government. She and her Scottish physician husband settled in London and had one daughter. After her husband's death, she remarried, this time to a man of lower social class from Berkshire, losing the support of many of her admirers. In the 1770s, she and her husband visited France, where they met Benjamin Franklin and Anne Robert Jacques Turgot. They also visited the United States in 1785, where she met George Washington and subsequently corresponded with him. An ardent advocate of liberty, she supported both the French and American revolutions. Her works also inspired support of the American women's movement.

Before her first husband died, Macaulay had published the first volume of her *History of England.* The last volume appeared in 1783. Her histories were popular in Britain and were available in French translation. However, after her unconventional second marriage, her histories began to sink into obscurity. She also published numerous pamphlets, among which one excoriated Hobbes's views and another sought legislative relief for authors through the copyright laws. Her espousal of Lockean empiricism was clear from her earliest historical writings to her most famous work, *Letters on Education.* She affirmed in the latter that "as the senses . . . are the only inlets to human knowledge, consequently human knowledge can only be gained by experience and observation." The importance of the senses obviously affected the way that science should be conducted. Macaulay was convinced that the mind is more often in error than the body. Through experience we would gain knowledge of relations and causation, making reason more valuable. Macaulay clearly did not believe in the existence of innate ideas. She applied these ideas to her philosophy of history, where her empirical "facts" were meticulously documented. She concluded that war and slavery were not justified from the facts.

In her *Letters on Education,* she presents an eloquent defense of empiricism as well as a demand for educational reform. Rejecting the body/mind dualism, she shared the empiricist view that animals were on a continuum with human life. It was also a key to her advocacy of women's rights. She even rejected the gendering of God, referring to God as the "universal parent." From these basic ideas, she rejected the utilitarian principle that the utility principle (of which she generally was an advocate) applied only to the human species. She insisted that virtue was a general property, not one that supplied only human advantage. Consistent with her philosophical views, she insisted that education should be similar for both sexes. Girls' education should not be confined to the ornamental arts, as boys' education should also include handicrafts. JH/MBO

PRIMARY SOURCES

Macaulay, Catharine. *History of England from the Accession of James I to that of the Brunswick Line.* 8 vols. London: Nourse, 1763–1783.

———. *Loose Remarks on Hobbes's Philosophical Rudiments.* London: Davies, 1767.

———. *A Modest Plea for the Property of Copy Right.* London: Dilly, 1774.

———. *An Address to the People of England, Scotland, and Ireland.* Bath: Cruttwell, 1775.

———. *The History of England from the Revolution to the Present Time.* London: Cruttwell, 1778.

———. *A Treatise on the Immutability of Moral Truth.* London: Hamilton, 1783.

———. *Observations on the Reflections of the Rt. Hon. Edmund Burke on the Revolution in France.* London: Dilly, 1790.

———. *Letters on Education.* 1790. New York: Garland Reprint, 1974.

SECONDARY SOURCES

Donnelly, Lucy Martin. "The Celebrated Mrs. Macaulay." *William and Mary Quarterly* 6 (1949): 173–207. A negative critique of Macaulay's work.

Hill, Bridget. *The Republican Virago: The Life and Times of Catharine Macaulay, Historian.* Oxford: Clarendon Press, 1992.

McDonald, Lynn. *Women Founders of the Social Sciences.* Ottawa, Canada: Carleton University Press, 1994.

Stenton, Doris Mary. *The English Woman in History.* London: Allen and Unwin, 1957.

Titone, C. *Catherine Sawbridge Macaulay: Feminist Philosopher on Education.* Qualifying papers, Harvard University Graduate School of Education, 1992.

Todd, Janet. "Catherine Macaulay." *Dictionary of British Women Writers.* London: Routledge, 1989.

MACCALLUM, BELLA DYTES (MACINTOSH) (ca. 1886–1927)

New Zealand / British botanist. Born in New Zealand. Married Dr. P. MacCallum. Educated Canterbury College, N.Z. (B.A., 1908; M.A., 1909); University of New Zealand (D.Sc., 1915?); Cambridge Medical School (course in bacteriology, 1919). Professional experience: National Research Scholarship (1900–1911); St. Mary's College, Christ-Church (1911–1913); New Plymouth High School, assistant (1913–1915); Edinburgh University, Department of Botany, assistant (1920–1921). Died 1927.

Bella MacCallum was born in New Zealand and received her bachelor's and master's degrees from Canterbury College in that country. While living on a National Research Scholarship and holding several jobs, she earned her doctorate with a thesis entitled "*Phormium* with Regard to Its Economic Importance." She came to England in 1919 and took a course in bacteriology at the Cambridge Medical School. After this course, she did research at the Mycological Department at the University of Edinburgh, which resulted in the publication of "Some Wood-Staining Fungi," 1920. The next year she served as an assistant in the botany department of the university, and in 1921 was elected a Fellow of the Linnean Society. MacCallum returned to Australia with her husband, Dr. P. MacCallum, when he was appointed professor of pathology at the University of Melbourne. JH/MBO

SECONDARY SOURCES

Wilson, Malcolm. "Mrs. Bella Dytes MacIntosh MacCallum." *Proceedings of the Linnean Society* (1930–1931): 180–181.

STANDARD SOURCES
Desmond.

MACDONALD, ELEANOR JOSEPHINE (1909–)

U.S. epidemiologist. Born 4 March 1909 in West Somerville, Mass., to Catharine (Boland) and Angus Alexander Macdonald. Five siblings. Educated Radcliffe College (A.B., 1928); Harvard School of Public Health, postgraduate work (1928–1929). Professional experience: Massachusetts Department of Public Health, staff member (1930–1940); Connecticut State Health Department, researcher (1940–1948); University of Texas M.D. Anderson Hospital, Houston, Tex., professor of epidemiology (1948–1974). Honors and memberships: American Radium Society; New York Academy of Sciences; Public Health Cancer Association; American Statistics Association; Biometric Society. Honors: Phi Beta Kappa; Myron Gordon award for research into pigment cell growth in melanoma (1973); American Cancer Society, Outstanding Service Award (1973).

Eleanor Macdonald's degree from Radcliffe was in music and history of literature and English. For two years after her graduation, she performed as a professional cellist, following her mother's musical career. She became interested in epidemiology when a physician friend of her father asked her help in writing a research paper. Largely self-taught except for postgraduate work at the Harvard School of Public Health, she was hired by the Massachusetts Department of Public Health to study the incidence of cancer in individuals over forty years of age. She directed a five-year door-to-door survey that resulted in the first reliable biostatistical study of cancer incidence. She followed this up with a project involving a group of physicians and more than three hundred Massachusetts communities, alerting the public to early symptoms of cancer through diagnostic clinics and self-examination. Recognized from this point on as one of the first cancer epidemiologists, Macdonald spoke on public health issues in a weekly radio program emphasizing cancer awareness.

Throughout the forties, Macdonald and a volunteer assistant continued to follow up all cases of cancer with a population-based cancer registry for the state of Connecticut. While checking hospital records for patients with cancer they found that many patients were still alive whom physicians had assumed were dead. The system of tracing developed by Macdonald has served as a model for other cancer registries. During the weekends, Macdonald set up and ran the statistical department at Memorial Sloane Kettering hospital, an institution that specializes in cancer. During the same period she was a consultant to the National Advisory Cancer Council in Washington, D.C.

In 1948, Macdonald went to Houston, Texas, as a professor of epidemiology. She was a full professor in spite of her lack of advanced degrees. At Texas, Macdonald created a comprehensive pilot cancer registry, including data from hospitals, clinics, laboratories, nursing homes, and various other places such as doctor's offices where cancer patients might have been seen. Comparative data showed for the first time that cancer incidence for Hispanics was lower than in whites. She also determined that exposure to intense sunlight was linked to the occurrence of skin cancer. Macdonald's accumulated data inspired clinical trials to check the effectiveness of various forms of therapy. The first chemotherapy trials for leukemia patients were the direct result of Macdonald's organizational skills.   JH/MBO

PRIMARY SOURCES
Macdonald, Eleanor. "Fundamentals of Epidemiology." *Radcliffe Quarterly* (February 1936): 19–22.
———. With Evelyn B. Heinze. *Epidemiology of Cancer in Texas: Incidence Analyzed by Type, Ethnic Group, and Geographic Location.* New York: Raven Press, 1978.
———. "Present Directions in the Epidemiology of Lung Cancer." In *Thoracic Oncology,* ed. N. C. Zhoi and H.C. Grillo, 1–22. New York: Raven Press, 1983.

STANDARD SOURCES
Debus; *Notable.*

MACDOUGALL, MARY STUART (1885–?)

U.S. zoologist. Born 7 November 1885 in Laurinburg, N.C. Educated Randolph-Macon Woman's College (A.B., 1912); University of Chicago (M.S., 1916); Columbia University (Ph.D., 1925); Montpelier (D.Sc., 1935). Professional experience: Athens College, head, department of science (1912–1914); Shorter College, zoology (1914–1917); Winthrope College (1917–1919); Agnes Scott College, professor of biology and head of department (1920–1952); Barnard College, Columbia, assistant (1922–1923); Johns Hopkins, School of Hygiene, research associate (1926); Guggenheim Memorial Foundation, fellow, Kaiser Wilhelm Institute (1931–1932). Death date unknown.

From Randolph-Macon Woman's College, where she earned her bachelor's degree, MacDougall went to the University of Chicago, where she earned a master's degree and then to Columbia, where she earned her doctorate. She later received a doctor of science degree from Montpelier, in France. After she had received her bachelor's degree, she went to Athens College, where she was head of the science department. She held positions at two other small colleges before she went to Agnes Scott College, where she remained as professor of biology and head of the department until she retired and became emerita in 1952. During her career she held several concurrent positions at Barnard, Columbia, and

Johns Hopkins. She held a Guggenheim Memorial Fellowship at the Kaiser Wilhelm Institute from 1931 to 1932. She was a member of the Society of Zoologists. Her research included work in protozoology and cytology. In the latter field, she worked on the diploid and tetrapoloid forms of *Chilodonella uncinatus,* the inheritance of mutations in *C. uncinatus* obtained by ultraviolet rays, and the chromosomes of *Plasmodium.* She also studied bird malaria and the neuromotor apparatus of *Chlamydodon.* JH/MBO

STANDARD SOURCES
AMS 7–8, B 9, P&B 10; Rossiter 1982.

MACGILL, ELSIE GREGORY (1908–1980)

Canadian aeronautical engineer. Born 27 March 1908 in Vancouver, B.C., to Helen Gregory MacGill and a barrister father. Married E. J. Soulsby. Educated University of Toronto (bachelor's degree in electrical engineering, 1927); University of Michigan (master's degree in aeronautical engineering); Massachusetts Institute of Technology (two years of work toward doctorate). Professional experience: Austin Aircraft Company in Pontiac, Mich.; Fairchild Aircraft Company, Montreal (to 1937); Canadian Car and Foundry Company, chief aeronautical engineer (1937–1943); Toronto, aeronautics consulting firm (from 1943). Honors and memberships: Canadian Aeronautics and Space Institute, Fellow; United Kingdom's Royal Society of Arts, Fellow; Royal Aeronautical Society, Fellow; Society of Women Engineers Achievement Award (1953); Order of Canada (1971); Julian C. Smith Award from the Engineering Institute of Canada (1973). Died in 1980.

Elsie Gregory MacGill's maternal relatives were involved in feminist causes. Her mother was British Columbia's first woman judge of the juvenile court. Both her mother and grandmother were active suffragists. Thus it was appropriate that Elsie MacGill was the first woman to design, build, and test an airplane and was the first woman named chief aeronautical engineer of a North American firm. She was the first female fellow of the Canadian Aeronautics and Space Institute and the first female member of the Association of Consulting Engineers of Canada.

At the University of Toronto, MacGill was the first woman to receive a degree in electrical engineering. After graduation, she obtained a position with Austin Aircraft Company in Pontiac, Michigan. During her time there, she attended graduate school at the University of Michigan. However, right before she was due to take her examination for a master's degree in aeronautical engineering, she contracted polio and was unable to walk. She completed her examinations from her hospital bed. Again, MacGill had attained a first—this time, the first woman to complete a master's degree at the University of Michigan.

After receiving this degree, she returned home to Vancouver, where she earned money to pay the expenses of her hospitalization by writing articles on airplanes for popular magazines. She designed a flying boat while convalescing in a wheelchair, and, after she had recovered sufficiently to walk on crutches, completed two years of doctoral work on air currents at the Massachusetts Institute of Technology.

When MacGill left MIT, she found a position with the Fairchild Aircraft Company in Montreal, where she applied stress analysis to the structure of airplane wings and fuselages. Presenting the results of this research, she became the first woman to read a paper before the Canadian Engineering Institute, and became its first woman member. As chief aeronautical engineer for the Canadian Car and Foundry Company, her first project was designing the Maple Leaf Trainer II plane for the Mexican Air Force. She had another first—the first woman to design, build, and test a trainer plane.

During the early part of World War II, MacGill directed the conversion of a boxcar factory into a facility to produce the United Kingdom's four-hundred-mile-per-hour Hawker Hurricane fighter planes. It took MacGill and 120 employees, including housewives, lumbermen, and other nontechnical workers, only a year to convert the plant. At the height of production, the plant employed 5,600 employees, 700 of whom were women. Accuracy was essential, for the parts had to be interchangeable with their British equivalents. She later became involved in the production of the Curtiss Wright SB2C Helldiver fighter planes, which were flown from U.S. naval aircraft carriers.

In 1943, MacGill began her own aeronautics consulting firm in Toronto. After the war, she was the Canadian Technical Advisor to the United Nations Civil Aviation Organization and also chaired the Stress Analysis Committee. Carrying on her family's feminist tradition, she was an early advocate of equal pay for equal work and in 1967 was appointed to the Royal Commission on the Status of Women. MacGill did not marry until 1943, when she married E. J. Soulsby. JH/MBO

PRIMARY SOURCES
MacGill, Elsie Gregory. *My Mother, the Judge.* Toronto: Ryerson Press, 1955. Rpt., Toronto: PMA Books, 1981. A chronicle of MacGill's mother's life.

SECONDARY SOURCES
Goff, Alice C. *Women Can Be Engineers.* Youngstown, Ohio: Edwards Brothers, 1946. MacGill discussed on pages 45–49.

STANDARD SOURCES
Notable (article by Karen Withem); O'Neill.

MACGILLAVRY, CAROLINA HENRIETTE (1904–)

Dutch crystallographer and chemist. Born 22 January 1904 in Amsterdam to Ida (Matthes) and Donald MacGillavry. Educated University of Amsterdam (doctor's degree with honors, 1937). Professional experience: University of Amsterdam, researcher (1927–1933; 1937–?), professor (1950); University of Leiden, Netherlands, assistant (1937). Honors and memberships: Royal Netherlands Chemical Society (1937); Royal Netherlands Academy of Sciences; International Union of Crystallography, executive committee (1954–1960).

Caroline H. MacGillavry was the first woman elected to the Royal Netherlands Academy of Science. A colleague of J. M. Bijvoet at the University of Amsterdam, MacGillavry studied the properties of crystals of all types. Although her interest in X-ray crystallography was extensive, she was especially intrigued by disorder and twinning studies in crystals. (Disorder results from the degree to which a crystal departs from its regular geometry; twinning results when an "error" in crystal growth occurs.) She also was interested in absorption studies, the mathematical techniques of "direct methods" and the derivation of the Harker-Kasper inequalities (those mathematical inequalities related to the fact that the electron density can never be negative but is near zero). MacGillavry coauthored the standard crystallographic text in the Netherlands, *Roentgenanalyse von Krystallen*. She was a part of a small but active group that attracted overseas visitors to the Netherlands.   JH/MBO

PRIMARY SOURCES

MacGillavry, Caroline H. With J. M. Bijvoet and N. H. Kolkmeijer. *Roentgenanalyse von Krystallen*. Berlin: Springer, 1940.

———. With H. J. Vos. "Anomale Untergrundschwarzung in Weissenberg Diamrammen." *Zeitschrift für Kristallographie*. A105 (1943): 257–267.

———. With B. Strijk. "Determination of Order Parameters from the X-ray Diffraction Effect." *Nature* 157 (1946): 135–136.

———. With B. Strijk. "X-ray Determination of Order Parameters in Lattices Showing Order-Disorder Transition." *Physica* 11 (1946): 369.

———. With B. Strijk. "X-ray Determination of Order Parameters in Lattices Showing Order-Disorder Transition." *Physica* 12 (1946): 129.

———. "On the Derivation of Harker-Kasper Inequalities." *Acta Crystallographica* 3 (1950): 214–217.

———. "Phase Limiting Relations Following from a Known Maximum Value of the Electron Density." *Acta Cryst.* 4 (1951): 284.

———. *Fantasy and Symmetry: The Periodic Drawings of M. C. Escher*. New York: Harry N. Abrams, Inc., 1976.

STANDARD SOURCES
Kass-Simon and Farnes (article by Maureen M. Julian).

MACINTYRE, SHEILA SCOTT (1910–1960)

Scottish mathematician. Born 23 April 1910 in Edinburgh to Helen Myers (Meldrum) and James Alexander Scott. Married Archibald James Macintyre. Two living children. Educated Trinity Academy; Edinburgh Ladies' College (now the Mary Erskine School) (graduated 1926 as joint Dux [top student] and Dux in mathematics); University of Edinburgh (M.A., 1932); Girton College, Cambridge (B.A., 1934); University of Aberdeen (Ph.D., 1949). Professional experience: succession of teaching jobs (1934–1939); University of Aberdeen, assistant (1941–1957); University of Cincinnati, visiting professor (1958–1960). Died 21 March 1960.

Sheila Scott received her early education in her native Edinburgh. However, after she received her master's degree in 1932 from the University of Edinburgh, her professors recommended that she study at Cambridge, where she was a member of Girton College and ended up with a bachelor's degree—she sat for the Mathematical Tripos and was a Wrangler (first-class honors) in mathematics and natural philosophy. Although this seems backwards, the Scottish degree was more general, and so she went to Cambridge to gain more in-depth knowledge. After doing research for a year, she apparently decided that she did not wish to continue, so she took a succession of teaching jobs instead. Professor Edmund Whittaker introduced Scott to a Cambridge-educated lecturer at Aberdeen, Archibald James Macintyre. The couple married on 27 December 1940. She was appointed in the same department as her husband in March 1941. She taught special War Office and Air Ministry courses, and took on the duties of staff who were directly involved in the war. She held this job until October 1943, when she was pregnant with their first child, Alister William. She was absent from teaching for only a year, for she began teaching again in October. She was appointed assistant lecturer on a permanent basis in October 1945 and was elected to a lectureship in 1949. She also began a thesis that was published in 1948. Their second baby, Douglas Scott, died of enteritis in March 1949. They had one more child, Susan Elizabeth, who was born in March 1950. Macintyre continued to teach and to care for her family. Her husband accepted a position at the University of Cincinnati in 1958, where Macintyre became a visiting professor. She died of cancer in Cincinnati at the age of fifty.

Macintyre was elected a Fellow of the Royal Society of Edinburgh in 1958. She was active in the Mathematical Association and the Edinburgh Mathematical Society. She is best known for her research on the Whittaker constant and interpolation series of different kinds of integral functions. Her major interest was the theory of functions of a complex variable. Her thesis extended some of the previous ideas, although it included some errors and omissions. Her supervisor, Edward M. Wright, mentioned that although her research was good, there would have been more of it if it were not for her family responsibilities. She published a second paper in 1947 and another in 1949. Before 1956 she published six more papers, including one joint work with her husband. She also published a German-English mathematical dictionary with a member of the German department.

JH/MBO

PRIMARY SOURCES

Scott, Sheila. "On the Asymptotic Periods of Integral Functions." *Proceedings of the Cambridge Philosophical Society* 31 (1935): 543–554.

Macintyre, Sheila. "Overconvergence Properties of Some Interpolation Series." *Quarterly Journal of Mathematics* (Oxford Series) 2, no. 2 (1951): 109–120.

———. With A. J. Macintyre. "Theorems on the Convergence and Asymptotic Validity of Abel's Series." *Proceedings of the Royal Society of Edinburgh* A 63 (1952): 222–231.

SECONDARY SOURCES

Cartwright, Mary L. "Sheila Scott Macintyre." *Journal of the London Mathematical Society* (1961): 254–256.

Cossar, J. "Sheila Scott Macintyre." *Edinburgh Mathematical Notes* 43 (1960): 19. In *Proceedings of the Edinburgh Mathematical Society* 2, no. 12 (1960–1961): 112.

STANDARD SOURCES

Grinstein and Campbell (article by Florence D. Fasanelli; includes bibliography).

MACK, PAULINE BEERY (1891–1974)

U.S. chemist. Born 19 December 1891 in Norborne, Mo., to John Perry and Dora (Woodford) Beery. Married Warren B. Mack. Two children, Oscar and Anna. Educated at Missouri State University (B.A., 1913); Columbia University (M.A., 1919); Penn State College (Ph.D., 1932). Professional experience: Norborne (Mo.) High School in Missouri, science teacher, chair of science department (1913–1915); Webb City High School, teacher, chair of science department (1915–1918); Springfield High School, teacher (1918–1919); Penn State College, faculty member (1919–1952); Philadelphia Mass Studies in Human Nutrition, Director (1940–1945); Penn Mass Studies, director (1935–1952); Ellen H. Richards Institute, College of Chemistry and Physics, director (1940–1952); College of Household Arts and Sciences, Texas Women's University, dean and director of research (1952–1962). Honors and member-

ships: Distinguished Daughters of Pennsylvania (1949); Garvan Medal, American Chemical Society (1950); Moravian College for Women (honorary D.Sc., 1952); Western College (honorary D.Sc., 1952); "Silver Snoopy" by American astronauts (1970); American Association of Textile Technology, American Association of Physical Anthropologists, Royal Society of Health, Society of Chemical Industry, American Ordinance Association, American Chemical Society, American Association of University Women, American Dietetic Association, Sigma Xi. Died 20 October 1974 in Texas.

Pauline Mack was a leader in the field of nutrition and an inspiration to many of her students. As Pauline Beery, she acquired her first research experience while at Missouri State University. After earning her bachelor's degree with a major in chemistry and a minor in biology, Beery went on to teach science in Missouri high schools and also served as a chairperson of the science departments in these schools. Being a woman chemist made it difficult for her to find a position after she received her master's from Columbia University. Beery would have preferred a university research position in physical chemistry, but universities did not accept ideas and input from women chemists. However, she was offered a position as a teacher of elementary and applied chemistry at Penn State College. There she taught freshmen chemistry for students in home economics and liberal arts and household chemistry for sophomores in home economics.

While teaching at Penn State, Beery met Warren B. Mack. They were married on 27 December 1923 and subsequently had two children, Oscar and Anna. Working with the students at Penn State, Mack realized the need to promote science to younger adults, for they were capable of gaining and developing scientific insights on how chemical processes and products influenced their lives. Through her efforts, a pocket-sized magazine entitled *Chemistry Leaflet* began in 1927. This magazine, which was later known as *Chemistry,* was published by Science Service. Because of her efforts, Mack was asked to serve as editor of what was to become one of the most innovative and informative science magazines of its time. Mack was the editor for the first seventeen years of *Chemistry's* existence.

Being the editor was not easy for Mack. The Chemical Foundation, an organization that had been a generous donor to the *Chemistry Leaflet,* withdrew its financial support. This action led to a meeting to determine the fate of the *Chemistry Leaflet.* During the meeting, Mack convinced the committee to return ownership of the *Chemistry Leaflet* to her. She contended that she could continue its publication through other financial means. She won and took over ownership of the magazine, which was renamed *Science Leaflet* in 1933. It retained this name until the end of Mack's editorship, when it once again became the *Chemistry Leaflet.* This magazine catered to high school students, encouraging them to take an interest in science. After the end of Mack's editorship, she served as a contributing editor, hoping to continue to influence students.

After going to Penn State, Mack began the research that she continued for most of her life. Her doctorate from Penn State was a part of this research. Her dissertation was entitled, "A Quantitative Study of the Effects of Radiant Energy from Different Parts of the Spectrum on Ossification and Growth." The research focus was to develop a method for measuring calcium retention in the bones of living organisms through Roentgenograms. She developed the methodology based on the scanning of X-ray pictures of standardized bone areas by means of a photometric technique.

Mack made other contributions to Penn State. She worked on various research problems, all of which involved the application of chemistry to food, clothing, and shelter. Mack originated studies in human nutrition in 1935. Her research activities in nutrition were later supported by the state of Pennsylvania and eventually led to the establishment of the Penn Mass Studies in Human Nutrition. This all came about as Mack was its director from 1935 to 1952. The nutrition research staff initially was very small, but by 1950, sixty-five people were working on the project.

A departmental research organization, the Ellen H. Richards Institute, was established as a result of Mack's emphasis on research. It was named in honor of the first woman graduate in chemistry from the Massachusetts Institute of Technology. Mack became the institute's first director (1940–1952). During her years as director, the institute performed studies in three general areas: (1) chemistry of food and nutrition, (2) chemistry of textiles and detergents, (3) chemistry and physics of household equipment and materials. The research and the institute were kept alive by Mack's efforts in obtaining grants and aid from various sources. The research Mack did in those three general areas did not go unnoticed by her community. In 1949 Mack received the Distinguished Daughters of Pennsylvania Medal. This medal is the highest honor that a private citizen of Pennsylvania could receive, "for having made exemplary personal and professional contributions and demonstrated leadership to the local community, to the general public, the scientific and educational community, to the state and at large."

Mack also received the Garvan Medal at the 117th American Chemical Society meeting in 1950. She was awarded this honor for her work in the calcium chemistry of bone density. She was introduced by ACS president E. H. Volwiler as "one of the most outstanding women scientists of our time." This medal reflected her relentless dedication and hard work in the development and validation of a quantitative method for bone density measurement. Two years later,

Mack received honorary degrees from Moravian College and the Western College for Women in Oxford, Ohio for her continued research and contributions.

In 1952, Mack moved from Penn State to Texas Women's University in Denton, Texas. Here she accepted an administrative and teaching position, became the new dean of the College of Household Arts and Sciences, and continued her research in nutrition, textiles, and detergents. Ten years later Mack became the director of Texas Women's University Research Institute. Her research in these years focused mainly on bone density studies, particularly the tendency of men to lose calcium during their time in space. Working on this research with NASA earned her the "Silver Snoopy" Award for her professional excellence. It was presented to her by the American Astronauts in 1970.

Mack was a member of more than twenty professional societies and organizations, most notably Phi Beta Kappa Associates. She was a fellow of the American Public Health Association, the American Institute of Chemists, and the American Association for the Advancement of Science. Noteworthy was her membership in the American Association of Textiles and Technology, the Royal Health Society (Great Britain), and the Texas Academy of Sciences.

Mack died on 22 October 1974 in Texas. She left numerous contributions and detailed research that improved human living standards in a variety of ways. Her lifetime of research provided a great deal of information about human nutrition, as well as methods for testing and refining commercial products.

NR

PRIMARY SOURCES

Mack, Pauline Beery. "An Investigation of the Essential Oil from Eucalyptus Cneorifolia, D.C." *Transactions and Proceedings of the Royal Society of South Australia* 46 (1922): 207–221. Her first research paper related to nutrition.

———. *Chemistry Applied to Home and Community.* Philadelphia: J. B. Lippincott Company, 1929. Focuses on the importance of chemistry to everyday living. Provides the groundwork for many of the areas of her research.

———. "The First Year Chemistry Course." *Journal of Chemical Education* 8 (1931): 1781–1816. Discusses the type of course she taught and provides insights into her teaching philosophy.

———. "Progress in Textile Research from the Consumer Point of View." *American Dyestuff Reporter, Proceedings of the American Association of Textile Chemists and Colorists* 24 (1939): 696–699. Highlights the importance of much of her research in textiles, dyes, and cleaning.

———. "The Contributions and Potentialities of Household Chemistry." *25th Anniversary Priestley Lectures.* Pennsylvania State College, Phi Lambda Upsilon, Department of Chemistry, 1951. 1–28. Discusses the many areas in which she worked, and points out the importance of chemistry to the household.

SECONDARY SOURCES

Dallas Morning News, 25 October 1974. Obituary notice.
"Garvan Medal to Pauline Mack." *Chemical & Engineering News* 28 (1950): 1032.
The Iotan Newsletter 9 (1975): 6. Obituary notice.
Roscher, Nina Matheny. "Chemistry's Creative Women." *Journal of Chemistry Education* 64z (1987): 748–752.
Roscher, N. M., and P. L. Ammons. "Early Women Chemists of the Northeast." *Journal of the Washington Academy of Science* 71 (1981): 177–182.

STANDARD SOURCES

AMS 8, P 9, P&B 10–14; *Current Biography* 1950; *WW in America,* 1950–1951.

MACKAY, HELEN MARION MACPHERSON (1891–1965)

British physician and pediatrician. Born in Inverness, Scotland, in 1891 to Marion G. C. (Wimberley) and Duncan L. M. Mackay. Educated Cheltenham Ladies College; London (Royal Free Hospital) School of Medicine for Women (B.S. and M.B., 1914; M.D., 1917). Professional experience: Medical Research Council, staff; Mothers' Hospital, Clapham and Hackeny Hospital, pediatrician; General Lying-In Hospital; Infants Hospital, Westminster, physician; Royal Free Hospital, house physician and assistant pathologist; London School of Medicine for Women Magazine, *editor. Honors and memberships: Beit Memorial Research Fellow, Vienna and Lister Institute Preventative Medicine (1919–1922); British Medical Association, Ernest Hart Memorial Research Scholar; Dawson Memorial Prize (Pediatrics); Royal College of Physicians, Fellow (London), 1934. Advisory Committee of Pediatricians, chair; Royal Society of Medicine, Section of Disease in Children, president; Queen Elizabeth Hospital for Children, honorary consultant. Died 15 July 1965.*

Helen MacPherson Mackay was born in Inverness, Scotland, but she was sent as a young woman to the prestigious English girl's school, Cheltenham Ladies College. Making a decision to study medicine, she attended the women's medical school at the Royal Free Hospital in London where she first obtained her bachelor's and master's degree and three years later her medical degree. During this period, she served as both house physician and as assistant pathologist at the hospital and edited a women physician's magazine of the women's medical school.

Mackay developed an intense interest in nutrition, which led to her award of a Beit Research Fellowship and her investigations of nutritional disease, especially rickets in the postwar period in Vienna. The publication that resulted appeared as a special pamphlet in the series sponsored by the Medical Research Council. She continued to study preventive medicine in children for which she was awarded a research fellowship by the British Medical Association and the Dawson Prize in Pediatrics.

In the 1930s, after publishing some important studies on nutritional anemia, Mackay was elected a Fellow of the Royal College of Physicians, the first woman to be elected to this position. She continued her work on dietary deficiency diseases and studied the health of children fed on bottle and breast milk, writing an important chapter on dietary deficiency diseases for the *Encyclopedia of Medical Practice.* In her later years, she served on the advisory board of pediatrics and headed the section on diseases of children for the Royal Society of Medicine. She was an honorary consultant for the Queen Elizabeth Hospital for Children.   JH/MBO

PRIMARY SOURCES

Mackay, Helen Marion MacPherson. With others. *Studies of Rickets in Vienna (1919–1922),* Special Report Series no. 77. London: Medical Research Council, 1923.
———. *Nutritional Anaemia in Infants.* Special Report Series no. 157. London: Medical Research Council, 1931.
———. "Dietetic Deficiency Diseases." *Encyclopedia of Medical Practice.* N.p., 1937.
———. With others. *Weight Gains, Serum Protein Levels and Health of Breast Fed and Artificially Fed Infants.* Special Report Series no. 296. London: Medical Research Council, 1959.

STANDARD SOURCES

Concise Universal Biographies; Munks Roll, vol. 5, 1968; *WWW,* vol. 6, 1961–1970.

MACKLIN, MADGE (THURLOW) (1893–1962)

U.S. physiologist. Born 6 February 1893 in Philadelphia, Pa. Married Charles C. Macklin. Three daughters. Educated Goucher College (A.B., 1914); Johns Hopkins University, fellow (1914–1915); American University, fellow (1916–1919); Goucher College, Dean Van Meter Fellow (1918–1919; M.D., 1919). Professional experience: Johns Hopkins University Medical School, assistant physiologist (1915–1916); University of Pittsburgh Medical School, instructor of gross anatomy (1918); Johns Hopkins University, School of Hygiene and Public Health, physiologist (1919–1920); University of Western Ontario, faculty of medicine, instructor of histology and embryology (1921–1929), assistant professor (1929–1945); Ohio State University, National Research Council, Fellow and research associate (1945–1959). Retired 1959. Honors and memberships: McLane Lecturer, Goucher College (1937); Gibson Memorial lecturer, Buffalo (1942); Richards Memorial lecturer, Ontario Cancer Treatment and Research Foundation (1958); Eliz-

abeth Blackwell Award (1957); President American Society of Human Genetics (1959). Died 4 March 1962.

After receiving her primary and secondary education in Baltimore, Maryland, Madge Thurlow attended Goucher College, where she received her bachelor's degree. She received several scholarships while attending college and medical school. After she earned her medical degree, she married Charles C. Macklin, with whom she had three daughters. In 1920, she worked as instructor of physiology at Johns Hopkins University, but in 1921 the Macklins moved to the University of Western Ontario. She was appointed part-time instructor in histology and embryology (1922) when her husband was appointed professor of histology and embryology. In 1930, Macklin was promoted to part-time assistant professor and remained at that rank until she was dismissed in 1945. During this time she taught embryology to first-year students and assisted her husband in his histology course. A gifted teacher and meticulous experimenter, she collaborated with her husband on histological research. By 1961, she had published over two hundred papers in the field of medical genetics.

She insisted that human genetics should be taught in medical schools, and was interested in the fact that the incidents of stomach and breast cancer were higher in individuals who had relatives with cancer. With her views that heredity was the major causative factor in cancer, she embraced the eugenics movement that was at its apex in the 1920s and 1930s. Macklin was not rewarded for her many publications and excellent teaching by the University of Western Ontario. Husband and wife professors on the same faculty and in the same department were forbidden. Her appointments were for each session, and she was underpaid or, during the Depression, not paid at all. Many people found her views in the area of eugenics offensive. She was relieved when the National Research Council offered her a research associateship in 1946. She conducted cancer research for the council at Ohio State University, where she was a research associate. She worked with Lawrence Snyder at Ohio State and taught a course in human genetics. Macklin remained at Ohio State until her retirement in 1959, and then returned to Canada, where her husband had remained to teach and do research. He died that same year, and Macklin moved to Toronto to be near her three married daughters. She died at the age of sixty-nine of coronary thrombosis. Macklin was a member of many scientific organizations, including the American Association for the Advancement of Science; Society of Naturalists; Human Genetics Society; Physiologists' Society; Association of Anatomists; and the Canadian Genetics Society. JH/MBO

PRIMARY SOURCES

Macklin, Madge. "Medical Genetics: An Essential Part of the Medical Curriculum from the Standpoint of Prevention." *Journal of the Association of American Medical Colleges* 8 (1933): 291.

———. "The Need of a Course in Medical Genetics in the Medical Curriculum: A Pivotal Point in the Eugenic Programme." *Edinburgh Medical Journal* 40 (1933): 20.

———. *The Role of Inheritance in Disease.* Baltimore: William and Wilkins Co., 1935.

———. "Comparison of Number of Breast Cancer Deaths Observed in Relatives of Breast Cancer Patients, and in the Number Expected on the Basis of Mortality Rates." *Journal of the National Cancer Institute* 22 (1959): 927.

———. "Inheritance of Cancer of the Stomach and Large Intestine in Man." *Journal of the National Cancer Institute* 24 (1960): 551.

SECONDARY SOURCES

Soltan, Hubert C. "Madge Macklin—Pioneer in Medical Genetics." *University of Western Ontario Medical Journal* 38 (October 1962): 6–11.

STANDARD SOURCES

AMS 5–8, B 9, P&B 10; Bailey; *NAW*(M) (article by Barry Mehler); Shearer and Shearer 1996 (article by Margaret A. Irwin); Siegel and Finley.

MACKOWSKY, MARIE-THERESE (1913–1986)
German mineralogist. Born 7 December 1913 in Koblenz, Germany. Never married. Educated universities of Freiburg, Königsberg, and Bonn (doctorate, 1938). Professional experience: Verein für die bergbaulichen Interessen (Syndicate for Mining Interests), Essen, researcher (1940–1978). Died 4 August 1986 in Bad Mergentheim.

Marie-Therese Mackowsky was born in Koblenz, qualified for university in 1933 in Hanover, and studied science at the universities of Freiburg, Königsberg, and Bonn, increasingly specializing in mineralogy. In 1938 she received a doctoral degree and wrote her dissertation on the optical and chemical properties of garnets. She began her professional employment in 1940 at the Verein für die bergbaulichen Interessen (Syndicate for Mining Interests) in Essen. In January 1965, she was promoted to director of the section for mineralogy and petrology, and remained in that position until her retirement on 31 December 1978. Mackowsky also taught at the university level. She completed her inaugural dissertation in 1944, received the *venia legendi* in 1951, and became visiting professor at Münster in 1957. She lectured in technical mineralogy and coal petrography and supervised numerous doctoral students until her death. She had a number of outside interests, including offices in the Soroptimists; she was president of the German Union of Soroptimists International.

Although during her graduate studies Mackowsky did her research on garnets, she moved, in her professional employment, to coal geology. Her early crystallographic work was more theoretical in nature and her work with coal was more practically oriented applied mineralogy. She used microscopic measuring techniques to solve problems that arose from the mining, uses, and preparation of hard coal. She produced 107 publications, including contributions to textbooks, handbooks, and encyclopedias. Her language skills served her well in translating works.

Mackowsky received a number of honors, including an appointment as Fellow of the Institute of Fuel in Great Britain; the Reinhardt-Thiessen Medal of the International Committee for Coal Petrology (1971); the Carl-Engler Medal of the Deutsche Gesellschaft für Mineralölwissenschaft und Kohlechemie e.V. (1978); and the Georg Agricola Medal bestowed by the Deutsche Mineralogische Gesellschaft. A member of many professional organizations, Mackowsky was especially active in the Kohlenpetrographische Arbeitsgemeinschaft, a working group for German coal petrologists. She presided over the Kommission für Technische Mineralogie der Deutschen Mineralogischen Gesellschaft (Commission for Technical Mineralogy of the German Mineralogical Society).

JH/MBO

PRIMARY SOURCES

Mackowsky, Marie-Therese. "Ueber die chemisch-physikalischen Zusammenhaenge in den Granatsystemen Grossular-Melanit und Melanit-Titanmelanit unter dem Einfluss des Eisens bzw. Titan." *Chemie der Erde* 12, no. 2 (1939): 123–157.

———. "Mineralogie und Petrographie als Hilfsmittle für die rohstoffliche Kohlenforschung." *Archiv für Bergbau und Huettenwesen.* 5, no. 6 (1947): 1–13.

———. "Neuere Anschauungen über den Inkohlungsvorgang." *Fortschritte der Mineralogie* 28 (1949): 38–46.

———. "Der Sedimentationsrhytmusder Kohlenflöze." *Neues Jahrbuch fur Geologie und Paläontologie Monatshefte* 10 (1955): 438–449.

———. "Fortschritte auf dem Gebiet der Kohlenpetrographie." *Fortschritte der Mineralogie* 45 (1967): 52–94.

———. "Die Bedeutung der Kohlenpetrographie in Geowissenschaften und Technologie." *Fortschritte der Mineralogie* 55 (1977): 172–196.

SECONDARY SOURCES

Otte, Margrit-Ursula. "In Memoriam Marie-Therese Mackowsky." *International Journal of Coal Geology* 9 (1987): 1–3. Portrait and bibliography.

MACLAUGHLIN, FLORENCE EDITH CAROTHERS (1895–?)

U.S. psychologist. Born 1 October 1895 in Norwich, N.Y. Married 1926. One child. Educated Columbia University (A.B., 1916; A.M., 1917; Ph.D., 1920). Professional experience: Columbia University, assistant and instructor in psychology (1917–1921); New York high schools, psychologist (1921–1926); domestic relations court, Brooklyn, counselor (1922–?). Honors and memberships: New York State Association of Applied Psychology; Metropolitan New York Association of Applied Psychology. Death date unknown.

Florence MacLaughlin was an applied psychologist who earned all three of her degrees at Columbia University. While she was working on her doctoral degree, she was an assistant and instructor at Columbia. Her experience from this time (1921) was largely practical. She served as a psychologist in New York City high schools and worked in a domestic relations court.

McLaughlin's interests were in mental testing and psychological examinations of college and high school students.

KM

STANDARD SOURCES
AMS 5–8, S&B 9–12.

MACLEAN, IDA (SMEDLEY) (1877–1944)

British biochemist. Born 14 June 1877 in Birmingham to Annie Elizabeth Duckworth and William T. Smedley. At least one sibling, a sister. Married Hugh MacLean (1913). One son (b. 1914); one daughter (b. 1917). Educated by mother until nine; King Edward VI High School, Birmingham; Newnham College, Cambridge (1896–1899; Natural Science Tripos, Part I, class 1, 1898; Part II, class 2 [chemistry and physiology], 1899; M.A., 1944; Bathurst studentship, 1901–1903); Central London Technical College, London, research (1903–1906); London University under H. E. Armstrong (D.Sc., 1905). Professional experience: Manchester University, assistant lecturer in chemistry department (1906–1910); Lister Institute for Preventive Medicine, London, Beit Research Fellow (1910–1914); Admiralty, research worker (1914–1918); Lister Institute, Gas Warfare Department under Department of Scientific and Industrial Research (1918–1932); Lister Institute, Biochemistry Department, member of staff (1932–?). Honors and memberships: Ellen Richards Prize (1915); London Chemical Society, first woman to be accepted as a member; Council Member (1931–1934); Cambridge University Appointments Board (1941–1944). Died 2 March 1944.

A native of Birmingham, Ida Smedley grew up in a home where her gifted parents devoted themselves to their children's interests and those of their children's friends. They filled their leisure time with literature, theatricals, music, and languages. The children were encouraged to be independent. After attending King Edward's School, Birmingham, under Miss Creak, one of the original five Newnham students, she went to Newnham College, Cambridge, for her university education. She held a series of jobs, including work at the Lister Institute in London, where she held several different posts. She held one of the first Beit Research Fellowships and at the institute worked on the metabolism of fats, a subject on which she became a recognized authority. It was at the Lister Institute that she met, collaborated with, and later married Hugh Maclean, later professor of medicine at St. Thomas's Hospital. Her marriage was a happy one and she was devoted to her children and husband.

MacLean was a member of a number of organizations, including the Committee of Food Investigation Board (1918–1928) and the Committee of the Biochemical Society (1925–1928; chair, 1926–1927). She was awarded the Ellen Richards Prize of the American Federation of University Women for the most outstanding contribution to science during 1913. She was one of the founders of the British Federation of University Women (1907) and held many offices in this organization, including president (1929–1935). She contributed numerous papers to the *Transactions* and *Proceedings of the Chemical Society*.

JH/MBO

PRIMARY SOURCES

MacLean, Ida Smedley. With Sibyl Taite Widdows. "The Action of Magnesium Phenyl Bromide on Derivatives of Phenyl Styrl Ketones." *Transactions of the Chemical Society* 105 (1915): 2169.

STANDARD SOURCES

DNB Missing Persons; Newnham, vol. 1; *Newnham Roll.*

MACLEOD, ANNIE LOUISE (1898–?)

U.S. chemist. Born 1883 in Canada. Educated McGill University (B.A., 1904; M.Sc., 1905; Ph.D., 1910). Professional experience: McGill University, chemistry teacher (1905–1908); Barnard College, Columbia, fellow (1908–1909); Bryn Mawr College, fellow (1909–1912; reader, 1912–1914); Vassar College, staff member in chemistry (1914–1919), associate professor (1919–1924), professor and director of euthenics (1924–1928); Syracuse University, dean, college of home economics (1928–1948). Retired 1948. Death date unknown.

A native Canadian, Annie MacLeod earned all three of her degrees at McGill University. She then came to Barnard College on a fellowship and from 1910 to 1928 held positions at Bryn Mawr and Vassar colleges. During this period she worked in organic chemistry, especially the vital factors

of food, euthenics, and chemistry and cooking. Her career changed directions in 1928, when she accepted a deanship at Syracuse University, a post that she held for twenty years, until retirement.

JH/MBO

STANDARD SOURCES

AMS 3–8, P 9, P&B 10.

MACLEOD, GRACE (1878–1962)

U.S. nutritionist. Born 6 August 1878 in Rothesay, Scotland, to Jessie MacGregor and Joseph MacLeod. Several siblings, including two sisters, Sarah and Florence. Educated Massachusetts Institute of Technology (B.S., 1901); Columbia University Teachers College (A.M., 1914; Ph.D., 1924). Professional experience: Massachusetts schools, teacher (1901–1910); Pratt Institute, teacher (1910–1917); Journal for Industrial and Engineering Chemistry, assistant editor (1917–1919); Columbia University Teachers College, advanced from instructor to professor (1919–1944). Concurrent experience: Carnegie Institution, cooperating investigator, nutrition laboratory (1922–1928). Honors and memberships: American Chemical Society; American Institution of Nutrition, charter member; Society of Biological Chemists; Society for Experimental Biology and Medicine; American Association for the Advancement of Science; American Home Economics Association; American Dietetic Association. Died 16 November 1962.

Best known for her research on energy metabolism, Grace MacLeod spent twenty-five years working at Columbia University Teachers College, where she rose through the academic ranks.

MacLeod was only four years old when she arrived in the United States with her mother, who followed her father who had already established himself in Cambridge, Massachusetts. Her family encouraged Grace by providing her with the best education they could afford. Her education in the public schools of Cambridge was excellent, and her high school teacher recognized her abilities in science and mathematics and encouraged her to enter the Massachusetts Institute of Technology, where she would major in chemistry. One of her professors was ELLEN SWALLOW RICHARDS. Richards helped supply her with some needed books and supplies. When MacLeod offered to repay her, Richards remarked that although you cannot repay people who help you, you can pass along the kindness. She always remembered this incident. MacLeod's first teaching position was at the Mount Hermon School for Boys in Massachusetts, a position she enjoyed greatly. After two years, she took a job at the Technical High School in Springfield, Massachusetts, where she taught for seven years. While she was at Pratt, she took advanced courses in chemistry at Columbia University. She registered for a seminar with Henry C. Sherman and

MARY SWARTZ ROSE and, partly because of her excellent background in German, was able to contribute to the course. This course formed the basis of her interest in nutrition as a science, and she went on to get both her master's and doctoral degrees from Columbia.

She became the assistant editor of the *Journal of Industrial and Engineering Chemistry,* a position she held for two years until she obtained an instructorship in nutrition at Teachers College. She worked with Rose, and the pair provided inspirational teaching to their nutrition students. After she obtained her doctorate in 1924, she was appointed to assistant professor, and was promoted eventually to professor, a position which she held until her retirement, in 1944. After Rose retired in 1940, MacLeod assumed the chief responsibility for the nutrition program at Teachers College.

MacLeod was a conscientious teacher, always willing to spend as much time as necessary to assure that each student succeeded. She was also a skillful, thorough, and conscientious researcher. Most of her studies related to energy metabolism. Her dissertation set the stage for subsequent studies carried out by the nutrition laboratory at Teachers College. She chaired numerous doctoral projects on the energy metabolism of children, including basal metabolism studies of children of different ages and mechanical efficiency studies. She published research papers with Rose and others, on other areas of research, including the supplementary values of foods, calcium utilization, vitamin B, availability of iron, and protein utilization. She published in the *Journal of Biological Chemistry, Journal of Nutrition, Journal of the American Home Economics Association,* and the *Journal of the American Dietetic Association.* She also wrote semipopular articles. After Rose's death, MacLeod was responsible for the fourth revision of *Rose's Foundation of Nutrition.* She was the coauthor with Clara Mae Taylor of the fifth edition, published in 1956. She also coauthored the fifth edition of *Rose's Laboratory Handbook for Dietetics.*

During World War II, MacLeod, as were many other nutritionists, was involved in organizations established to foster good nutrition in both the United States and overseas. She was chair of the Food and Nutrition Council of Greater New York and of the Nutrition Committee of the Greater New York Area, serving on the National Nutrition Program of the War Food Administration. She was also chair of the Nutrition Advisory Board of the New York chapter of the American Red Cross. In addition she was a member of the Executive Committee of the New York City Food and Nutrition Program, and cochair of the Planning Committee, member of the Nutrition Advisory Committee for the Henry Street Visiting Nurse Service, and a member of the Advisory Board of the Interstate Dairy Council in Philadelphia.

MacLeod was also a member of numerous professional organizations, including the American Chemical Society, the American Institution of Nutrition (charter member), the Society of Biological Chemists, the Society for Experimental Biology and Medicine, the American Association for the Advancement of Science, the American Home Economics Association, and the American Dietetic Association. She also was an associate editor of the *Journal of Nutrition,* and she served on its editorial board (1940–1945), as well as on the editorial board of the *Journal of the American Dietetic Association.* Upon her retirement, the Columbia nutrition students established a scholarship in her honor, the Grace MacLeod Scholarship, to provide financial assistance to graduate students.

In 1958, MacLeod closed her apartment in New York City and moved to Knoxville, Tennessee, to live with her sister Florence, who was head of the nutrition department at the University of Tennessee. She died on 16 November 1962 after a short illness and was buried in the family plot in the Cambridge Cemetery, Cambridge, Massachusetts.

JH/MBO

PRIMARY SOURCES
MacLeod, Grace. "Studies of the Normal Basal Energy Requirements." Ph.D. diss., Columbia University, 1924.
———. With Mary Swartz Rose and Clara Mae Taylor. *Foundations of Nutrition.* 4th ed. New York: Macmillan, [1944]. MacLeod and Taylor revised Rose's earlier work.

SECONDARY SOURCES
Taylor, Clara Mae. "Grace MacLeod, a Biographical Sketch." *Journal of Nutrition* 95 (1968): 3–7.

STANDARD SOURCES
AMS 4–8, B 9, P&B 10; Bailey; Rossiter 1982.

MACRINA (b. early 4th century C.E.)

Greek physician. Probably born in Cappadocia. Sister of St. Basil of Cappadocia. Educated in Athens. Professional experience: built three hospitals with her brother.

Although the exact date of Macrina's birth is unknown, we know that her brother, Basil, was born in 329 C.E. Brother and sister studied medicine in Athens, learning Hippocratic medicine. Together, they built a large hospital in Caesarea. It has been described as being as large as a walled city or the pyramids. The hospital included pavilions for treating different kinds of diseases, houses for physicians and nurses, and medical schools. This hospital (and the two others that they built) was clean, the physicians and nurses wore white clothes, and the rooms were airy. Macrina was described as a great organizer.

JH/MBO

SECONDARY SOURCES
Nutting, Adelaide, and Livinia L. Dock. *History of Nursing*. Vol.
1. New York: G. P. Putnam's Sons, 1907–1912. Macrina
discussed on pages 123–126.

STANDARD SOURCES
Hurd-Mead 1938.

MACROBERT, RACHEL (WORKMAN), LADY OF DOUNESIDE AND CROMAR (d. 1954)

U.S. mineralogist and igneous petrologist. Married. Died 1954.

Rachel MacRobert studied the occurrence of calcite in igneous rocks of the alkaline rocks of Alnö Island in southern Norway. She also worked on the petrography of the Eildon Hills, Roxburghshire, Scotland.   JH/MBO

SECONDARY SOURCES
[Smith, W. Campbell]. "Lady (Rachel Workman) MacRobert
of Douneside and Cromar." *Proceedings of the Geological Society of London* no. 1529 (1955): 146.

STANDARD SOURCES
Sarjeant.

MADDISON, ADA ISABEL (1869–1950)

British mathematician. Born 13 April 1869 in Cumberland, England, to Mary and John Maddison. Never married. Educated Miss Tallies School in Cardiff, South Wales; University of South Wales (1885–1889); Girton College, Cambridge (Mathematical Tripos, class 1, but no degree, 1892); Bryn Mawr (attended graduate lectures 1892–1893; Ph.D., 1896); University of London (B.S. with honors, 1893); University of Göttingen (1894–1895); University of Dublin (B.A., 1904). Professional experience: Bryn Mawr College, assistant to the president (1896), secretary to the president and reader in mathematics (1897–1904), associate professor and assistant to the president (1904–1910), administrator (1910–1926). Died 22 October 1950 in Pennsylvania.

Ada Isabel Maddison had a checkered academic career. She first went to school in Wales, then to Girton College, Cambridge, where she sat for the Mathematical Tripos. Even though she passed her examination with a score equal to that of the twenty-seventh Wrangler, Cambridge did not award her a degree because she was a woman. At Girton she met fellow mathematician GRACE CHISHOLM YOUNG, who entered Girton at the same time. After her Girton examinations, she went to Bryn Mawr, where she attended the graduate lectures of CHARLOTTE ANGAS SCOTT, who was very

impressed by her intelligence. In the meantime, the University of London conferred a bachelor of science degree with honors upon her in 1893. Awarded the Mary E. Garrett Fellowship from Bryn Mawr for study abroad, Maddison went to the University of Göttingen and attended the lectures of such stellar mathematicians as Felix Klein and David Hilbert. She was awarded a doctoral degree from Bryn Mawr in 1896, after which, the University of Dublin conferred a bachelor's degree upon her. Her studies at Girton were deemed all that was necessary for the degree. Maddison's professional career was entirely at Bryn Mawr where she became increasingly involved in administrative duties. She began as assistant secretary to the president of the college, M. Carey Thomas. After her degree was awarded, she became secretary to the president and reader in mathematics. In 1904, she was appointed associate professor and assistant to the president. By 1910, her duties were almost entirely administrative. After retiring from Bryn Mawr, she returned to England. She later returned to Pennsylvania where she died in 1950. She left ten thousand dollars in her will in memory of President Thomas, stipulating that it be used as a pension fund for nonfaculty members of the college staff.

After a promising start to a research career, Maddison became so involved in administrative matters that she had little time to continue her research. Her dissertation was published in 1896 and was in the area of differential equations. She published a translation of Felix Klein's 1895 address before the Royal Academy of Science at Göttingen. During the 1890s, she reviewed several textbooks.   JH/MBO

PRIMARY SOURCES
Maddison, Ada Isabel. "On Certain Factors of c- and p-
Discriminants and Their Relation to Fixed Points on the
Family of Curves." *Quarterly Journal of Pure and Applied Mathematics* (1893): 307–321.
———. "On Singular Solutions of Differential Equations of
the First Order in Two Variables and the Geometric Properties of Certain Invariants and Covariants of Their Complete
Primitives." *Quarterly Journal of Pure and Applied Mathematics* 28 (1896): 311–374. Doctoral dissertation.
———, trans. "The Arithmetizing of Mathematics." By Felix
Klein. *Bulletin of the American Mathematical Society* 2 (1896): 241–248.

SECONDARY SOURCES
New York Times, 24 October 1950. Obituary.
Whitman, Betsey S. "Women in the American Mathematical
Society before 1900." *Association of Women in Mathematics
Newsletter* 13, no. 5 (September-October 1983): 7–9.

STANDARD SOURCES
Grinstein and Campbell (article by Betsey S. Whitman); Siegel and Finley.

MAHLER, MARGARET SCHÖNBERGER (1897–1985)

Hungarian/U.S. child psychologist. Born 10 May 1897 in Sopron (Oedenburg), Hungary, to Eugenia Wiener and Gusztav Schönberger. One sister. Married Paul Mahler (1936). Educated Höhere Töchterschule; Vaci Utcai Gimnazium, Budapest (1913–1916); University of Budapest (1916–1919); University of Munich (1919–1920); University of Jena (graduated magna cum laude in 1922); Vienna qualifying examination (1923); Vienna Psychoanalytic Institute, certification (1926–1933). Professional experience: von Pirquet's [pediatric] Clinic, apprentice (1922–1926), analyst (1936–1938); New York State Psychiatric Institute, analyst (1941–1949); Albert Einstein College of Medicine, analyst (from 1949); Masters Children's Center, analyst (from 1959). Died 1985.

Margaret Schönberger's life began in a climate of anti-Semitism, developed as fascism gained in power during her medical school days, and reached its maturity during Hitler's Anschluss in Austria. After the Anschluss, Mahler fled to London and then to the United States. She was born in a town in western Hungary only forty miles from Vienna; her father spoke Hungarian as his first language and her mother, German. Her father was a prominent physician and had an active social life not shared by her mother. Schönberger found her beautiful, narcissistic mother to blame for many of her own problems and turned to her father. She always considered her pretty, feminine younger sister her mother's favorite and was jealous. Her father treated her like the son that he did not have and supported her desire to leave Sobron and go to the *gymnasium* in Budapest. In Budapest she stayed with an aunt who also preferred her sister, but found support from a friend's family. Her good friend was Alice Szekely-Kovacs, whose mother, Vilma Kovacs, was not only a *grande dame* of Budapest society, but was a distinguished Hungarian psychoanalytic training analyst. With her friends, she read and discussed Freud. The Budapest circle was very important to her future development.

After leaving the *gymnasium*, Schönberger went to the University of Budapest, where she decided to study medicine. The decision was not an easy one, and she vacillated, but in January 1917 she was admitted to the medical school. She planned to pursue psychoanalysis through medical study. After three semesters of premedical courses at the University of Budapest, she decided to transfer to the University of Munich to begin clinical training and study pediatrics. In Munich, hostility toward Jews was increasing, and life became very difficult. The situation became intolerable, and in

spite of the pleas of her sister who wanted to stay in Munich but whose parents would not allow her to stay alone, Schönberger moved to Jena and her sister returned to Vienna. While still in medical school she studied two diseases of infants, and she began to consider the possibility of a psychological cause for the physical manifestations.

Schönberger began to suffer the same kind of anti-Semitism that she had found in Munich. In spite of protests, she was allowed to graduate. However, she completed her Jena degree at Heidelberg.

After completing her degree, Schönberger moved to Vienna, where she took a position in von Pirquet's clinic. Although von Pirquet was opposed to having women in any position of authority, he liked Schönberger and gave her numerous statistical and research projects to complete. He refused to promote her, stating that he would never have a woman as an assistant. Schönberger, nevertheless, worshipped him, and was upset when he and his wife committed suicide in 1928. Although she had a high regard for von Pirquet and his associates, she was appalled by the detached way in which they treated sick children. The "nem system" of feeding infants, created by von Pirquet, was especially disturbing to her. Infants were placed in a sterilized cubicle with glass panels for walls. The baby was bottle-fed by means of a nipple inserted into the cubicle. The food was measured in "nems," units of nutrition that corresponded to the caloric value of one gram of breast milk. She preferred Leopold Moll's Institute for Mother and Child Care, where "mothering" was considered essential if a sick baby was to get well.

From the time she first arrived in Vienna, Schönberger began a transition from pediatrics to child psychiatry and psychoanalysis She heard lectures by ANNA FREUD and HELENE DEUTSCH. In 1926, Deutsch began the process of analyzing Schönberger. After about thirteen or fourteen months, Deutsch cancelled her analysis and declared that she was "unanalyzable." Because of Deutsch's conclusions, Anna Freud, the secretary of the Vienna Psychoanalytic Institute, informed her that she was dismissed from "candidate" status, but could reapply for admission if she would undertake a therapeutic analysis with another analyst. She rejected the choice of Deutsch for an analyst and turned to August Aichhorn, who had been her mentor. She and Aichhorn fell in love during the three-year period of analysis. She was readmitted into the program, but both she and Aichhorn realized that she should complete her training analysis with some else. That person was Willi Hoffer. She began doing analyses and did very well. Many of the best-known psychoanalysts supervised her training, including JEANNE LAMPL-DE GROOT, GRETE BIBRING, Edward Bibring, and Willi Hoffer. However, she still felt like an outsider, and the mutual animosity with Helene Deutsch continued. In 1933, her formal psychoanalytic training was over, and she certified by the committee on education of the Vienna Psychoanalytic Institute. During her training analysis with Hoffer, she met Paul Mahler, a junior partner of a Viennese cordial factory, whom she married in 1936.

With the Anschluss of 1938 (the annexation of Austria by Nazi Germany), most of the psychoanalytic community immigrated to Britain or the United States. Mahler sought temporary asylum in Britain and then left for the United States in October 1938. Friends including Ernest Jones helped the almost penniless couple to live in the United States. In New York, Mahler faced the hurdle of obtaining a state medical license. She passed the state medical board on the first try, after repeating the English examination a second time, and was licensed at the end of 1939. She unwittingly became involved in the division within the New York Psychoanalytic Society. In addition to the New York Psychoanalytic Society, she was a member of CAROLINE ZACHRY's Institute of Human Development where Benjamin Spock was also a nonsalaried member of the staff. She worked with clients and did research that resulted in publications.

Mahler's father had died, and in 1945 she learned that her mother had been deported and murdered in Auschwitz in 1944 by the Nazis. Although this period of time was marked by personal tragedy, her professional career blossomed. Her psychoanalytic work fell into two broad categories during this time, studies of tics and childhood psychosis. She accepted a position on the new Albert Einstein College of Medicine faculty. In 1950, Mahler expanded her teaching activities to Philadelphia, where she accepted the chairmanship of the child analysis training program of one branch of the recently split Philadelphia Psychoanalytic Institute. Philadelphia became the focus of her teaching and New York, her research. In 1955 she and Dr. Furer got a grant from the National Institute of Mental Health to study the natural history of symbiotic childhood psychosis. Because she felt that Einstein did not have the facilities to do the research, she returned the grant money to NIMH. However, in 1956, the master's school received a donation of two buildings in Greenwich Village. These buildings were ideal for her project, but they lacked funding. To their surprise, in 1959 they received a five-year grant from NIMH. This study provided the basis for numerous papers and her 1968 book, *On Human Symbiosis and the Vicissitudes of Individuation: Infantile Psychosis.*

During the latter part of her career, Mahler moved away from abnormal development to study normal development. In 1962 she began a study comparing seriously disturbed babies and their mothers with normal babies and their mothers. She considered this date as the beginning of her formal transition from psychosis research to research into normal development. She was especially interested in separation-individuation.

Mahler died in 1985, and about eight years before her death she made arrangements for the interment of her ashes and those of her late husband, Paul, in the Jewish Cemetery in Sopron beside the grave of her father. At the time of the burial of the ashes, there were only sixteen Jews living in Sopron. She always affirmed her Jewishness, but was nonobservant throughout her life. JH/MBO

PRIMARY SOURCES
Mahler, Margaret S. "Pseudoimbecility: A Magic Cap of Invisibility." *Psychoanalytic Quarterly* 11 (1942): 149–164.
———. With L. Rangell. "A Psychosomatic Study of Maladie des Tics (Gilles de la Tourette's Disease)." *Psychiatric Quarterly* 17 (1943): 579–603.
———. *Selected Papers of Margaret S. Mahler.* New York: Jason Aronson, 1979.
———. *The Memoirs of Margaret S. Mahler.* Ed. by Paul E. Stepansky. New York: Free Press, 1988.

STANDARD SOURCES
O'Connell and Russo 1990; Stevens and Gardner.

MAHOUT, COUNTESS OF ARTOIS (d. 1329)

French healer. Lived thirteenth century in Paris. Great-niece of Saint Louis; mother-in-law of Kings Philip IV and Charles V. Educated by scholars in Paris. Professional experience: built hospitals. Died 1329.

Mahout, Countess of Artois was a great-niece of Saint Louis and the mother-in-law of Philip IV and Charles V. She went to Paris in 1402 to consult with scholars about the best architecture for her hospitals. In Paris, she studied with the best available medical scholars. Thirty lazarettos (leper hospitals) and eighty hospitals were built according to her wishes. One hospital had a large ward 160 by 35 feet in size with 16-foot-thick walls, a gabled roof, and large windows on each end where the sick could be laid beside open windows on sunny days. She made provisions for a special ward for confinement cases, a chapel, a kitchen, a room for the matron, and one for herself. Apparently Mahout was knowledgeable in several languages and collected medical books. She left her library to the hospital when she died. JH/MBO

SECONDARY SOURCES
Franklin, Alfred. *La vie privée d'autrefois.* Paris: E. Plon, 1887.
Richard, Jules Marie. *Une petite-nicè de Saint Louis Mahout, Comtesse d'Artois et de Bourgegne.* Paris: H. Champion, 1887.

STANDARD SOURCES
Hurd-Mead 1938.

MAIR, LUCY PHILIP (1901–1986)

British anthropologist. Born Banstead, Surrey, 18 January 1901 to Jessy (Philip) and David Beveridge Mair. Educated St. Paul's School for Girls; Newnham College, Cambridge University (Tripos in Classics, Class I, with distinction in philosophy, 1923; M.A., 1927); London School of Economics, University of London (Ph.D., 1933). Professional experience: London School of Economics, assistant in international studies (1927), assistant lecturer (1931), lecturer in colonial administration (1932), reader (1947–1952), applied anthropology reader (1952–1963), professor (1963–1968); Foreign Research Service, Royal Institute of International Affairs, research worker (1939–1943); Ministry of Information, research worker (1943–1944); Australian Land H Q Civil Affairs School, lecturer (1945–1946); University of Kent, honorary professor (1969–1979); field research, Uganda (1931), Papua, New Guinea. Died 1 April 1986 in London, England.

Lucy Philip Mair, the British anthropologist, was known for her studies of applied anthropology, and for her clear analysis of the field of anthropology. Born into an active family in which her mother worked in university administration and her father as a civil servant, Lucy Philip went to St. Paul's School for Girls and then to Newnham College, where she read classics. She passed the Tripos examinations with first-class degrees, the second part with distinction in Philosophy in 1923. For some years following this, she worked for Sir Gilbert Murray, and during this period wrote on the protection of minorities under the League of Nations (1929). Studying at the London School of Economics from 1927, she attended seminars given by the dynamic anthropologist Bronislaw Malinowski, and decided to become an anthropologist. For her field work, she went to Uganda, Africa, in 1931–1932, returning to East Africa in 1937–1938, and 1949. Here she studied local systems of land tenure, which she incorporated into her dissertation, and her doctoral degree was awarded in 1932. She began to lecture at the LSE on colonial administration in 1932, and after further publishing studies on native policies in Africa (1936), she worked in Foreign Research of the Royal Institution for International Affairs during the period of World War II, 1939–1943. She joined the Ministry of Information in 1943, then trained Australian administrators to work in New Guinea (1945–1946). Returning to the LSE in 1946, she was reader in colonial administration and then reader in applied anthropology from 1952, and professor from 1963 until her retirement in 1968.

Mair never married, but she wrote on the function of African marriage in the life of that society, and a more general book on marriage in 1972 that contained an ironic chapter headed "What Are Husbands For?" After she retired, she continued to teach as an honorary professor at University of Kent and to publish extensively on theoretical and applied anthropology. Some of her most interesting work comes from this late period, including a discussion of various forms of patronage and their role in state formation (*Primitive Government*, 1962). One of her students, John Davis, has commented on her commitment to intellectualism, her dedication to rationality in public affairs, but observes her touch of irony that qualified her dedication to work for human betterment and her sense that justice was attained only against heavy odds. Others have seen her greatest contribution to be her recognition of the part that anthropologists play in providing an understanding of cultures to local and international governments.   JH/MBO

PRIMARY SOURCES
Mair, Lucy Philip. *The Protection of Minorities.* London: Christophers, 1923.
———. "Native Land Tenure in East Africa." *Africa* 4 (1931): 314–329.
———. *An African People in the Twentieth Century.* London: Routledge, 1934. Mair's Ph.D. thesis.
———. "What Anthropologists Are After." *Uganda Journal* 7 (1939): 85–92.
———. *Australia in New Guinea.* 1948. 2d ed. London: Christophers, 1968.
———. *Studies in Applied Anthropology.* London: Athlone Press, 1957. London School of Economics Monographs no. 16. London: 1972.
———. *Primitive Government.* Baltimore: Penguin, 1962.
———. *Witchcraft: An Introductory Survey.* London: Weidenfeld & Nicholson, 1969.
———. *Anthropology and Development.* London: Macmillan, 1984.

SECONDARY SOURCES
Davis John, ed. *Choice and Change: Essays in Honor of Lucy Mair.* London: Athlone, 1974. Includes a bibliography of her work.

STANDARD SOURCES
Annual Obituary 1986; IDA; *Newnham*.

MAKEMSON, MAUDE (WORCESTER) (1891–?)

U.S. astronomer. Born 16 September 1891 in Center Harbor, N.H., to Fannie Malvins (Davisson) and Ira Eugene Worcester. Married Thomas Emmet Makemson (1912); divorced. Three children. Educated Boston Girls' Latin School (graduated 1908); Radcliffe College (1908–1909); University of California, Berkeley (B.A., 1925; Ph.D., 1930). Professional experience: Sharon, Conn., public school teacher (1909–1911); Bisbee (Ariz.) Re-

view, *proofreader (1917–1918); Phoenix (Ariz.) Gazette, reporter (1918–1922); Southern California, public school teacher (1923–1924); University of California, Berkeley, instructor in astronomy (1930); Rollins College, Fla., professor of mathematics (1931–1932); Vassar College, associate professor of astronomy (1933–1957), chair (from 1941), emerita professor (from 1957); Bishop Museum, HI, research (summer 1935); University of Arizona, Kinishba Pueblo Archaeological Expedition, researcher (summer 1936); University of California, Los Angeles, consultant in lunar astrodynamics (1959–1964), lecturer (1960–1964). Honors and memberships: Guggenheim fellowship (1941); Fulbright lecturer in Japan (1953–1954), Pakistan (1957–1958). American Association for the Advancement of Science, Fellow.*

Maude Worcester was born in New Hampshire, but her parents sent her to the prestigious Girl's Latin School in Boston. She claimed that she was first exposed to astronomy at this school, but paid little heed because she was extremely nearsighted and could only see the moon and a few bright stars and planets. After she saw an oculist, her world was transformed. From the Latin School she went for one year to Radcliffe College, but left in 1909 in order to teach public school in Connecticut. Two years later she married William Makemson from Pasadena, California, and they moved to a small ranch in Arizona where their children were born.

Desiring her own profession, she served first as a proofreader for a Bisbee Arizona paper and then worked as a reporter for the *Phoenix Gazette* for an additional three years. She became interested in returning to college, and entered the University of California, Berkeley, earning the money for this by teaching in a public school in Southern California. Her interest and proficiency in astronomy led to her pursuing a doctorate at Berkeley, serving as instructor in astronomy in the final year of her doctoral studies. After receiving her degree, Makemson took a position for a year in a small Florida college, teaching mathematics. From there, she went to Vassar College as an associate professor in astronomy, a position she maintained until her retirement as emerita professor in 1955. During this period, she also directed the Vassar observatory.

Makemson pursued summer research in Hawaii, and in the southwestern pueblos to investigate archeological evidence for ethnoastronomy. In 1941, she was awarded a Guggenheim fellowship to pursue research on Polynesian astronomy. The book that resulted, *The Morning Star Rises: An Account of Polynesian Astronomy,* was soon followed by another, *The Astronomical Tables of the Maya,* studying the Maya astronomical tables in the Dresden Codex.

Makemson's three children shared her interests in ethnology, archeology, and the American Southwest. Her daughter became an archeologist and one of her sons wrote on the Apache. Toward the end of her career at Vassar, she took the

opportunity to lecture as a Fulbright professor in Japan. After her retirement in the late fifties, she went to Pakistan as a Fulbright professor for two years and then moved to California where she was affiliated with University of California, Los Angeles, as a research associate and as a lecturer in astronomy. She continued to publish books and articles into her sixties, including a coauthored volume on astrodynamics, and articles in *Astronomical Journal, Popular Astronomy, Sky and Telescope,* and *American Anthropologist.* She retired to Santa Ana in the 1960s. JH/MBO

PRIMARY SOURCES

Makemson, Maude Worcester. *The Morning Star Rises: An Account of Polynesian Astronomy.* New Haven: Yale University Press, 1941.

———. *The Astronomical Tables of the Maya.* Washington: Carnegie Institution, 1943.

———. *The Maya Correlation Problem.* Poughkeepsie, N.Y.: Vassar College Observatory Publications, no. 5, 1946.

———. *The Book of the Jaguar Priest.* New York: Schuman, 1951.

———. With Robert M. L. Baker. *An Introduction to Astrodynamics.* New York: Academic Press, 1960.

STANDARD SOURCES

AMS 5–8, P 9, P&B 10; Bailey; *Current Biography* 1941; Debus; Rossiter 1982.

MALING, HARRIET FLORENCE (MYLANDER) (1919–1986?)

U.S. pharmacologist. Born 2 October 1919 in Baltimore, Md., to Mathilda (Hopf) and Walter Conrad Mylander. Married Henry Forbes Maling, Jr. (1943). Four children. Educated Goucher College (A.B., 1940); Radcliffe College (A.M., 1941; Ph.D., 1944). Professional experience: Harvard Medical School, faculty (1944–1946); George Washington Medical School, faculty (1951–1955), assistant research professor (1952–1954); National Heart Institute, National Institutes of Health Laboratory of Chemistry and Pharmacology, researcher (1954–retirement), head of physiology section (1962–retirement). Died 1986?

Harriet Florence Maling spent her research career investigating the physiology of the heart and the effects of various drugs upon the heart as well as the autonomic and sympathetic nervous system. Trained as an undergraduate at Goucher, she went to Harvard Medical School to continue her studies in physiology. At that period, all advanced degrees in science that women earned were awarded by Radcliffe College, although Mylander worked with the pharmacologists at the medical school. While she was preparing her dissertation, she met and married Henry Forbes

Maling, Jr. For two years following her degree, she worked as an assistant pharmacologist and instructor at the Harvard Medical School. The couple moved to the Washington, D.C., area, and after her four children (Joan, Walter, Anne, and Charles) were born, Maling took a position on the faculty of George Washington University as an assistant professor in the medical school, and then as an assistant professor in research.

After three years at the university, she moved to the National Institutes of Health, where she obtained a research position in the laboratory of chemistry and pharmacology of the National Heart Institute. There she began to investigate the effects of a variety of drugs on heart function, experimenting with artificially created myocardial infarction. She also became interested in the role that various substances had upon fat and carbohydrate metabolism.   JH/MBO

STANDARD SOURCES
Bailey; Debus.

MALLESON, ELIZABETH (1828–1916)

British educator and pioneer of rural district nursing. Born 29 October 1828 in Chelsea to Frances Ann (Maguire) and Henry Whitehead. Ten siblings. Married Frank Rodbard Malleson (1857) (he died 1903). Three daughters; one son. Educated at home; dame school; Unitarian school in Clapton. Professional experience: amanuensis and governess; experimental Portman Hall School (from 1854); Working Woman's College, founder (1864); Rural Nursing Association, founder (August 1889), secretary (until 1894), consultant (1897); local nursing association, manager (1889–1916). Died 27 December 1916 at home in Dixton Manor from influenza.

Elizabeth Malleson was not a scientist in the usual sense of the word, yet she was important in providing a scientific education to others and organizing local nursing associations. The oldest of eleven children, her own education was woefully lacking and she vowed to help others. Her parents were politically active and were often away attending political rallies. At fifteen, she was caring for her younger siblings. Thinking about the deficiencies in her own education, she worked out her own educational theory by studying available books on the subject. When she was twenty-four she found work outside the home, first as an amanuensis and governess. However, in 1854, she was appointed to a post as teacher at Barbara Leigh Smith's (later Bodichon) experimental school. She embraced enthusiastically the school's coeducational policies and its mixing of middle- and working-class children. Ill health forced her to resign from this position. In 1857 she married the son of a Unitarian minister and a partner in a firm of vintners. The couple eventually

had four children. Malleson became involved in Frederick Maurice's Working Men's College, and decided to open a similar institution for women. Her Working Women's College opened in Queen Square, Bloomsbury, in 1864. This school offered a variety of course subjects at very low fees. Malleson recruited university teachers who were willing to donate their time. Still impressed with the idea of coeducation, she attempted to get the Men's and Women's Colleges to merge. Failing that, she converted her Working Women's College to a coeducational institution in 1874. While she was in London, she worked for many other causes.

In 1882, the Mallesons moved to Dixton Manor near Winchcombe. Malleson set up workers' colleges in Cheltenham and organized technical education in the Winchcombe district. She and her husband started reading rooms and libraries in nearby villages. Recognizing that one of the most urgent needs of the area was district nurses, she launched her Rural Nursing Association in 1889, after winning backing from many doctors and nurses. (FLORENCE NIGHTINGALE was opposed to the idea.) Malleson ran the branch as secretary until 1894, remained as consultant until it was absorbed into the institute in 1897, and also managed a local nursing association from 1889 to 1916.   JH/MBO

PRIMARY SOURCES
Malleson, Elizabeth. *Notes on Early Training of Children.* 1884.
    Autobiographical notes and letters.

SECONDARY SOURCES
Malleson, Hope, ed. *Elizabeth Malleson.* Privately printed. 1926.

STANDARD SOURCES
DNB Missing Persons.

MALLORY, EDITH (BRANDT) (1901–)

U.S. psychologist. Born 28 November 1901 in Philadelphia, Pa., to Lida (Roberts) and Frank Burke Brandt. Married Tracy Burr Mallory (1925). Two children. Educated Wellesley College (A.B., 1923); Columbia University (A.M., 1924; Ph.D., 1925). Professional experience: Wellesley College, assistant in psychology (1927–1928), instructor (1928–1929), assistant professor (1933–1941), associate professor (1941–1958), chair of department (1954–1963), emerita professor (from 1964); Brown University, lecturer (1943–1945). Honors and memberships: American Psychological Association member; American Association for the Advancement of Science member.

Edith Mallory earned her two advanced degrees at Columbia University, where she majored in psychology. She spent most of her career at Wellesley, the college she had attended as an undergraduate. She worked with THELMA G. ALPER on the Wellesley Spelling Scale. Her research interests were in memory, voice cues to personality, college level psychological tests, and attitude changes. She also worked on the memory value of color in advertising.   JH/MBO

PRIMARY SOURCES

———. "The Memory Value of Advertisements with Special Reference to the Use of Color." *Archives of Psychology* 79 (1925): 69.

STANDARD SOURCES

AMS 6–8, S&B 9–11; Debus; O'Connell and Russo 1988.

MALTBY, MARGARET ELIZA (1860–1944)

U.S. physicist. Born 1860 in Bristolville, Ohio, to Lydia (Brockway) and Edmund Maltby. Two siblings. Never married. Educated Oberlin College (B.A., 1882; M.A., 1891); Art Students' League, New York City (1882–1883); Massachusetts Institute of Technology (1887–1893; B.S., 1891); Göttingen University (Ph.D., 1895). Professional experience: Wellesley College, instructor in physics (1889–1893, 1896); Lake Erie College, Painesville, Ohio, instructor, physics and mathematics (1897–1898), instructor in chemistry (1900–1903); Barnard College, professor of physics (1903–1931); Died 1944 in New York City.

Born on a farm in Ohio, Margaret Maltby was the youngest of three daughters. She graduated from Oberlin College in 1882, where she demonstrated her talent in both science and art. After graduation, she spent a year in New York City to study at the Art Students' League and then returned to Ohio. Before she attended college, she taught school for four years. She attended the Massachusetts Institute of Technology, earning a bachelor's in chemistry and physics and then remaining as a graduate student. During her years at MIT, she taught physics at Wellesley College.

In 1893 Maltby traveled to Germany on a research fellowship, and after two years of study became the first American woman to receive a doctorate from Göttingen University. She remained in Germany for a postdoctoral year, supported by a second grant, and, after a brief teaching interval in the United States (1896–1898), returned to Germany as the research assistant of her dissertation adviser, Friedrich Kohlrausch (1898–1899).

After she returned to the United States, Maltby engaged in research in theoretical physics with A. G. Webster at Clark University for a year before settling into her long career as a teacher at Barnard College in New York (1900–1931). Her research suffered at Barnard, because teaching and administration consumed so much of her time. She was known for her effectiveness in procuring scholarships for women in graduate and postdoctoral studies. She was a member of the

fellowship committee of the American Association of University Women from 1912 to 1929 (serving as its chairman from 1913 to 1924), and in 1929 published a *History of the Fellowships Awarded by the American Association of University Women, 1888–1929*, a volume that includes carefully researched biographical sketches of the fellows. In 1926 the American Association of University Women established the Margaret E. Maltby Fellowship in her honor.

Most of Maltby's significant research occurred before she began teaching at Barnard. The subject of her doctoral dissertation was the measurement of high electrolytic resistances; the results of her postdoctoral work with Kohlrausch, involving the measurement of the conductives of aqueous solutions of alkali chlorides and nitrates, were published in Germany in 1899 and 1900. A capable physicist, Maltby allowed her creative energy to be diverted from research into teaching and administration during her Barnard years.

MBO

PRIMARY SOURCES

Maltby, Margaret. "On the Number of Vibrations Necessary to Determine Pitch." B.S. thesis, Massachusetts Institute of Technology, 1891.

———. *Methode zur Bestimmung Grosser Elektrolytischer Widerstand*. Leipzig: Englemann, 1895. Ph.D. thesis.

SECONDARY SOURCES

Barr, E. Scott. "Anniversaries in 1960 of Interest to Physics." *American Journal of Physics* 28 (May 1960): 462–475.

"Maltby, Margaret." *New York Times,* 5 May 1944. Obituary notice.

Reimer, Marie. "Margaret E. Maltby." *Barnard College Alumnae Magazine* 33 (June 1944): 21. A short obituary tribute to Maltby.

STANDARD SOURCES

AMS 1–6; *NAW* (article by Agnes Townsend Wiebusch); Ogilvie 1986.

MAN, EVELYN BROWER (1904–   )

U.S. biochemist. Born 7 October 1904 in Lawrence, Long Island, N.Y., to Mary (Hewitt) and Edward Man. Educated Wellesley College (B.A., 1925); Yale University (Ph.D., 1932). Professional experience: Yale University faculty (1934–1961); Brown University, Institutes of Health Sciences (1961–post 1968); Providence Lying-In Hospital, director, thyroid laboratory (from 1961).

Evelyn Man did her undergraduate work at Wellesley College and earned her doctorate from Yale University. After she completed her doctoral degree, she joined the Yale University faculty, where she remained for twenty-seven years. She left Yale for Brown University in 1961. During the same period she was the director of the thyroid laboratory at the Providence Lying-In Hospital. Man published on lipidemia and iodemia in health, disease, infancy, and pregnancy.

JH/MBO

STANDARD SOURCES
AMS 6–8, P 9, P&B 10–14; Debus.

MANGOLD, HILDE (PROESCHOLDT) (1898–1924)

German embryologist and physiologist. Born 20 October 1898 in Gotha Thuringia, an east-central German province, to Gertrude (Bloedner) and Ernest Proescholdt. Two sisters, one older and one younger. Married Otto Mangold (1921). One son. Educated University of Jena (1918–1919); University of Frankfurt (1919–1920); Zoological Institute of Freiburg (Ph.D., 1923). Died 4 September 1924.

After a short stint at the universities of Jena and Frankfurt, Hilde Mangold heard a lecture by Hans Spemann on experimental embryology. Fascinated by his talk, she resolved to pursue her studies at the Zoological Institute of Freiburg under Spemann, the leader in embryological research. She married Spemann's chief assistant, Otto Mangold, and the couple had one son. After they were married, Mangold completed her doctoral degree in zoology with the thesis, "On the Induction of Embryonic Transplants by Implantation of Organizers from Different Species." The next year, 1924, she, her husband, and infant son moved to Berlin where Otto Mangold had been made director of experimental embryology at the Kaiser Wilhelm Institute for Biology. An accident on 4 September 1924, when the gas heater in their apartment exploded, ended her short life. Her only son was killed in World War II.

Mangold's dissertation supplied the foundation on which her adviser, Spemann, won the Nobel Prize in 1935. Although he had designed the experiment, she performed the detailed work and was the codiscoverer of the "organizer." The organizer was the chemical that directs the embryonic development of tissues and organs. RITA LEVI-MONTALCINI used these results in her research. Because the model organism was an amphibian, the newt *Triturus cristatus*, the experiments could only be performed during the brief breeding season. All of the difficult, delicate experiments were performed during the springs of 1921 and 1922. Mangold transplanted a piece of the upper blastoporal lip of the gastrula of *Triturus cristatus*, to the flank of a gastrula of the common newt, *Triturus taeniatus*. She produced an embryo that displayed on its flanks a large secondary neural tube.

Spemann included her results in a paper that he had previously prepared and introduced the term "organizer," composed of migratory cells that invaginated from the surface and induced the development of the neural tube.

Because the work was so delicate, Mangold only produced six viable embryos. From the transplanted tissue neural tubes, notochords, intestines, and kidney tubules were induced, producing an embryo composed of cells from both the donor and the host. She showed that the organizer substance was responsible for the induced development of the neural tube. Unfortunately, Mangold did not live to see her paper published or to witness the impact that her experiments had on experimental embryology.

JH/MBO

PRIMARY SOURCES
Mangold, Hilde Proescholdt. "Über Induktion von Embryonalanlagen durch Implantation artfremder Organisatoren." Ph.D. diss., Zoological Institute of Freiburg, 1923.
———. With H. Spemann. "Über Induktion von Embryonalanlagen durch Implantation artfremder Organisatore." *Archiv für Mikroskopische Anatomie und Entwicklungsmechanik* 100 (1924): 599–638.
———. "Organisatortransplantationen in verschiedenen Kombinationen bei Urodelen." *Archiv für Entwicklungsmechanik der Organismen* 117 (1929): 697–710. Paper published posthumously by her husband in her name.

SECONDARY SOURCES
Hamburger, Victor. *The Heritage of Experimental Embryology.* Oxford: Oxford University Press, 1988. Mangold discussed on pages 173–180.

STANDARD SOURCES
Grinstein 1997 (article by Veronica Reardon Mondrinos).

MANN, HARRIET (1831–1918)
See Miller, Olive Thorne

MANNING, ANN B. (HARNED) (ca. 1790–1870s)

U.S. inventor. Born circa 1790 probably in Plainfield, N.J., to Hannah Walker Harned and David Harned. Twelve siblings. Married William Manning. Professional experience: developed mower, reaper, and clover cleaner.

Little is known about Ann Harned Manning, and the little that is reported of her accomplishments is contradictory. We know that she was born Ann or Anne Harned in about 1790. She may have been the oldest of the thirteen children of a Methodist farmer of Huguenot descent and a mother who was from English Quaker stock. The family supported liberal causes. Her sister was a well-known reformer, physician CLEMENCE HARNED LOZIER. This sister joined others in petitioning the New York legislature for women's right to vote in presidential elections. Although the date of her marriage is unknown, Ann married William Henry Manning, a member of an important Baptist pioneer family in the Plainfield region; the couple had three children, James, Ann Eliza, and Hannah. Ann may have moved to New York to be near her sister Clemence.

H. J. Mozans reports that Manning had invented the earliest reaper and that a neighbor had robbed her of credit for the invention. Autumn Stanley contends that this is a mistake: Indeed she was robbed of credit for inventing the reaper and the clover cleaner, but by her husband. The reaper, known as the Manning reaper, was an extremely important invention.

Matilda Gage, the suffragist, is the source of much of the extant information on Manning. She apparently knew Manning and gives Ann sole credit for both the reaper and the cleaner.   JH/MBO

PRIMARY SOURCES
Gage, Matilda Joslyn. *Woman as Inventor.* Fayetteville: New York State Woman Suffrage Association, 1870. There is a revision in the *North American Review* 136 (May 1883).

STANDARD SOURCES
Mothers and Daughters; Mozans.

MANSON, GRACE EVELYN (1893–?)
U.S. psychologist. Born 15 July 1893 in Baltimore, Md. Educated Goucher College (A.B., 1915); Columbia University (A.M., 1919); Carnegie Institute of Technology (Ph.D., 1923). Professional experience: National Research Council, assistant in human migrations; University of Michigan, researcher (1923–1926), research associate (1926–1930); Northwestern University, associate professor of psychology and director bureau of personnel research (1930–1944); Adjunct General Office, personnel technician, personnel research section (1944–1945); Veterans Administration, vocational psychologist (1945–1949); Social Security Administration, Bureau of Old Age Survivors Insurance, chief personnel psychologist (from 1949).

After psychologist Grace Evelyn Manson received her doctoral degree from the Carnegie Institute of Technology, she worked for several years doing research. Then for fourteen years she was an associate professor of psychology at Northwestern and the director of the bureau of personnel research. She left academia for government work in 1944, and spent the remainder of her career in government service. She was a member of the Psychological Association. She worked in personnel research, vocational and differential psychology, and selection techniques.   KM

STANDARD SOURCES
AMS 5–8, S&B 9–10.

MANTELL, MARY ANN (WOODHOUSE) (1795–ca. 1855)
British fossil collector. Married Gideon Mantell. Three surviving children. Died ca. 1855.

Mary Ann Woodhouse was born 9 April 1795. In 1816 Woodhouse married surgeon-geologist Gideon Mantell. The couple lived in the town of Lewes in Sussex, and it was at this time, while he was a busy surgeon and accoucheur, that he supposedly made his discoveries of the fossils *Hylaeosaurus, Iguanodon,* and other lizards in the Weald of Sussex. Gideon Mantell was very eager to extend his practice to those who were involved with the Court, so he moved his family to Brighton. However, he became so involved in his nonpaying avocation, geology, that he neglected his practice, which soon failed. He turned his house with its collection of fossils into a public museum, and his wife and children had to find shelter elsewhere. He sold his fossil collection to the British Museum and bought a practice at Clapham Common, which was reasonably successful. It allowed him access to London, where he could attend the meetings of the various scientific societies of which he was a member. His last move was in 1844 to Chester Square in Pimlico.

Gideon Mantell kept a journal between 1818 and 1852. During the first years, he refers to his wife as "my dear." However, in the later years he refers to her less and less. In the introduction to the journal, the editor noted that "Mantell, though disappointed in his wife—perhaps through his own fault—was devotedly attached to his children and suffered intensely when he lost them through death or emigration" (Mantell, 1:iii).

It has been said that Mary Ann actually discovered the *Iguanadon* fossils that her husband, Gideon, described before the Royal Society in 1825. He reported in his journal that "a paper of mine on the Iguanodon was read before the Royal Society last month." He also described it in his books on the older rocks of England. At this time, it is impossible to be certain about Mary Ann's role. In the early days, she accompanied him on his fossil collecting trips. She apparently also helped in illustrating his books, for he remarked that he had "assisted Mrs. Mantell in engraving the plates for my work" (Mantell, 1:19).   JH/MBO

SECONDARY SOURCES

Mantell, Gideon. *The Journal of Gideon Mantell*. Ed. E. Cecil Curwen. 3 vols. London: Oxford University Press, 1940.

Simon, Cheryl. "Dinosaur Story—Who Found the Tooth?" *Science News* 124 (1983): 312.

STANDARD SOURCES

Kass-Simon and Farnes (article by Michele L. Aldrich).

MANTON, IRENE (1904–1988)

British botanist and cytologist. Born 17 April 1904 in Kensington, England, to Milana Angele Terese (d'Humy) and George Sidney Frederick Manton. One sister (Sidnie Milana Manton). Educated Froebel Educational Institute; St. Paul's School for Girls; Cambridge University, Girton College, (National Sciences Tripos, Parts I and II, first class, 1926; Ph.D., 1930); University of Stockholm, postgraduate study in cytology (1927). Professional experience: University of Manchester, assistant lecturer (1929–1946), demonstrator in botany (1929–1941); University of Leeds, chair of botany (1946–1969). Honors and memberships: Linnean Society, Trail Award and Medal (1950), Gold Medal (1959), president (1973–1976); Leopoldina (East Germany), Schleiden Medal (1972); McGill University (1959), University of Oslo (1961), University of Durham (1966), University of Lancaster (1979), University of Leeds (1984), honorary doctorates; Fellow of the Royal Society (1961); multiple honorary and foreign memberships and fellowships of scientific societies. Died in Lancaster, England, 13 May 1988.

Irene Manton, like her older sister, the zoologist SIDNIE MILANA MANTON, grew up in an unusual household in which both mother and father were skilled, highly regarded craftspeople. Her father carved furniture and had many apprentices, while her mother created designs for the Liberty company. She and her sister both attended Froebel Educational Institute, and then went for their final years of schooling to St. Paul's School for Girls. Their parents arranged to teach them by the sea during the summer term, giving worries about their fragile health as an excuse. Their experiences in school and their parents' teaching resulted in unusual training for both girls in natural history. Irene, an excellent violinist, never developed the drawing and watercolor skills of her sister, but all her life had a strong, well-developed appreciation of art.

In 1923, in spite of some doubts expressed by her teachers at St. Paul's, Manton won a scholarship to Cambridge and followed her sister to Girton College with the intention of studying cytology and genetics. Unlike her sister, who found a place for herself at Girton in both sports and academic life, Irene Manton was unhappy with her years there. In spite of this discontent, she passed her Natural History Tripos examinations with first-class honors in both parts.

At the suggestion of two botanists, she took a postgraduate year in the laboratory of a Swedish cytologist (Otto Rosenberg) and studied the cytology of the Cruciferae. She continued this work for a further year in Cambridge, paid for by a fellowship (the Yarrow Bursary) and then wrote up her dissertation, which included the examination of the cytology (and chromosomes) of some 250 species. This formed the basis of her first published paper in 1932, which appeared in the *Annals of Botany*.

During her doctoral examination, a challenge by one of her examiners on the discrepant chromosome numbers of some of her species, some of which varied by multiples of 2 or 4, caused her to begin to study polyploidy in plants. In 1929, she was offered an assistant lectureship in botany at the University of Manchester, where she began to work with W. H. Lang, professor of cryptogamic botany. He urged her to move to a study of ferns (his own topic), and she also served as his demonstrator for the next twelve years. Throughout her research, Manton made it an axiom to photograph microscopical observations rather than use drawings, to increase objective records. During this period, she studied a number of important subjects, including a demonstration of the spiral form of the chromosomes and their changing dimension during cell division. She introduced a new method of chromosome counting (the "squash" method) which used the stain acetocarmine and displayed all the chromosomes on one plane, following a variation of a method used very successfully on corn by BARBARA McCLINTOCK.

Manton's description of her groundbreaking work on chromosome structure at a lecture at Leeds led to an offer of a recently empty chair of botany. Some of the faculty hoped that she would form a partnership with W. Astbury, the molecular biologist, but she was too deeply involved in pursuing her own research, setting up greenhouses and equipment, and reorganizing the teaching of biology.

Always receptive to new technical advances, Manton worked first with an excellent ultraviolet microscope and then, from 1950 on, with the electron microscope. The distinguished marine botanist MARY PARKE came to work with her and this new instrument, as did E. C. Cocking. Manton was the first botanist to work on cell organelles in plants, and she maintained an exchange of visits with other scientists in America (with Keith Porter at the Rockefeller Institute), in Switzerland (with the Nobel Prize–winning chemist Tadeus Rieichstein), G. Vida in Hungary, H. E. Holttum in Malaya, and a Danish taxonomist, T. Christensen, in Copenhagen.

Her work on polyploidy allowed her to use her understanding of the basic numbers of species and distinguish parallel evolution from true relationships of fern species. She also developed methods of hybridization in ferns to analyze chromosome pairing for clues to ancestral species. Although she began by working with ferns under the electron microscope, her work with Mary Parke led her to emphasize marine algal flagellates and to study their cellular chloroplasts and organelles membranes. With Parke she published a total of eleven papers on marine flagellates. From this topic she moved to nanoplankton, which she studied extensively after she formally retired from Leeds in 1969.

Manton's retirement was the beginning of new and extensive researches and an incredible itinerary. Although she based her office in two ground-floor rooms provided by the physics department, she traveled regularly to Nottingham, London, Lancaster, and even to Canada and Marburg, Germany, to use new electron microscopes and other new techniques. She also went on collecting expeditions to obtain further samples of nanoplankton from Denmark to South Africa and from Alaska to the Galapagos Islands from 1970 to 1974. She lectured everywhere she went.

Manton also developed her interest in the arts throughout her life. While at Manchester, she had played violin with a chamber music group, and her playing was said to be of concert quality. She made a fine collection of abstract painting and Chinese art, bequeathed by her to Leeds University, and used her understanding of these to give lectures on "Other Ways of Looking at Nature." During her retirement, she also became interested in the links between science and art, and searched the archives of the Linnean Society for excellent examples of plant illustration by scientists.

Among her many honors, Manton was made a Fellow of the Royal Society in 1961. Because her sister, Sidnie, had been a member since 1949, this created a stir, since the two women were the only sisters to be thus honored. It is interesting that both of them pursued problems of phylogenetics and evolution using microscopical analysis, each from the point of view of her own speciality. From 1973, Manton became president of the Linnean Society, which had awarded her its Trail Medal and Gold medal in the 1950s. From 1959, she was awarded a number of honorary doctorates from Britain, Europe, and North America, and she was awarded a number of honorary memberships from important scientific societies throughout the world. In all, Manton published over 150 papers. She died in 1988, outliving her sister by nine years.   JH

PRIMARY SOURCES

Manton, Irene. "Introduction to the General Cytology of the Cruciferae." *Annals of Botany* 46 (1932): 509–556. Manton's first published paper.

———. *Problems of Cytology and Evolution in the* Pteridophyta. Cambridge: Cambridge University Press, 1952. This book represents the pulling together of much of Manton's work on ferns.

———. With Mary W. Parke and B. Clarke. "Studies on Marine Flagellates." (II) *Journal of the Marine Biological Association,*

U.K. 34 (1954): 579–609; (III) 35 (1956): 387–414; (IV) 37 (1958): 209–228; (V) 38 (1959): 169–188. A series of studies on marine flagellates made with Mary Parke (at the Plymouth Marine Biological Station) and Barbara(?) Clarke.

SECONDARY SOURCES

Preston, R. D. "Irene Manton." *Biographical Memoirs Fellows of the Royal Society* 35 (1990): 247–261.

"Irene Manton." *Watsonia* 17, no. 3 (1989): 379–380. Obituary notice.

Times, 8 June 1988. Obituary notice.

STANDARD SOURCES

Desmond; *DNB.*

MANTON, SIDNIE MILANA (1902–1979)

British zoologist. Born 4 May 1902 in London, England, to Milana Angele Terese (d'Humy) and George Sidney Frederick Manton. One sister. Married John Philip Harding (1937). One daughter, one adopted son. Educated Froebel Educational Institute; St Paul's School for Girls; Girton College, Cambridge University (National Sciences Tripos, Part I and II, first-class honors, 1925; Ph.D., 1928; D.Sc., 1934); University of London, Imperial College, Yarrow Research Studentship (1925–1926). Professional experience: Cambridge University, demonstrator in comparative anatomy (1927–1935); Girton College, supervisor in zoology (1927–1928), staff fellow (1928–1945), director of studies (1935–1942), research fellow (1945–1948); University of London, Kings College, reader (1949–1960); British Museum, Natural History, honorary associate. Honors and memberships: Fellow of the Royal Society; Leverhulme and Department of Science and Industry Research Fellowships; Linnean Society Gold Medal (1963); Zoological Society of London, Frink Medal (1977). University of Lund (Sweden), honorary degree. Died 2 January 1979.

One of the outstanding zoologists of her day, Sidnie Manton was known for her work first on crustacean morphology and later for work on arthropod embryology, locomotion, and evolution, producing significant work in all these subjects. Her early education, like that of her younger sister, the botanist and cytologist IRENE MANTON, was unusual. Her parents, both involved in highly skilled crafts, sent the two girls to the Froebel Educational Institute, where they remained until their mid-teens, having an opportunity to study natural history. The two girls then were sent to St. Paul's School for Girls, where again they had excellent teachers in biology. Every summer term, their parents arranged for them to study away from the school to the seashore, where they developed their skills as artists and as natural historians.

Sidnie Manton was awarded a series of scholarships that allowed her to attend Girton College, Cambridge, where she studied botany, zoology, and physiology. She obtained the Montifiore Prize for Part I of the Natural Sciences Tripos, and received the highest marks for Part II in zoology, although, as a woman, she could not receive the university prize. At Girton she was also active in sports, as swimming captain and a hockey blue. In 1926, after completing her undergraduate work, she went to Imperial College to work with H. Graham Cannon, a distinguished investigator of the Crustacea, and published two pioneering studies with him on feeding and excretory mechanisms in members of this group. Returning to Cambridge for her doctorate, she worked with J. S. Gardiner, who helped her obtain a position as university demonstrator in comparative anatomy in 1927, the first woman to hold the post. She began to explore the embryology of crustaceae and their evolution. She also held the position of supervisor in zoology at Girton, and was named a staff fellow the following year. After receiving her doctorate in 1928, she joined the Great Barrier Reef Expedition in the Low Isles, Queensland, accomplishing a great deal in the four months she spent there. A number of her studies from this period were published as part of the Great Barrier Reef scientific reports.

Returning to Cambridge, Manton taught, served as demonstrator, and did her research, while producing an important laboratory manual in vertebrate morphology, illustrated by her, that went through many editions to 1969. In 1934, she was the first woman to be awarded a doctorate of science from Cambridge University; the degree was for her work on crustacean embryology, which was published that year in the *Philosophical Transactions* of the Royal Society. Appointed director of studies at Girton until 1942, she continued as a staff member and then a research fellow at the college.

In 1937, Manton married John Phillip Harding, who later became an important zoologist. Skilled with his hands, like her father, he provided her assistance by developing microdissecting tools and aiding her with photography. They had a daughter, born in 1939, and later adopted a son. Harding moved to the British Museum, where he later became keeper of zoology. Manton was elected as a Fellow of the Royal Society, one of the first women to be elected, and began to lecture at University of London and Birkbeck. She then accepted a post as reader at Kings College, London, in 1949, which she held for the next eleven years. During this period, her research and publication on arthropod evolution enhanced her reputation, with major reviews of the affinities of Arthropoda developing alternative interpretations of them as a polyphyletic assemblage, through an examination of their locomotion and the independent development of the compound eye.

In the mid-fifties, Manton went to the Soviet Union, particularly to Central Asia, and was impressed by the science there, although not uncritical of other aspects of life. Later she brought the ecological and embryological studies by Russian scientists to the attention of the British scientists. She continued her studies on arthropods until her death, focusing on myriapods, and publishing her final papers in the year of her death.

Increasing arthritis and cataracts reduced her active lifestyle and her microscopical analyses in her retirement years. Manton became interested in the breeding of color-point Himalayan cats and wrote a delightful and useful book on cat breeding that described the basic genetics of this group. Her energy and the high level of her work continued to amaze all of her friends and associates until her death. She had served the Linnean Society as vice-president and received its Gold Medal in 1963, while the Zoological Society awarded her the Frink Medal two years before her death, in 1977.

JH/MBO

PRIMARY SOURCES

Manton, Sidnie Milana. "On the embryology of the mysid crustacea, *Hemimysis lamornae*." *Philosophical Transactions of the Royal Society of London* B 216 (1928): 363–463.

———. With J. T. Saunders. *A Manual of Practical Vertebrate Morphology.* Oxford: Oxford University Press, 1931. 2d ed., 1949; 3d ed., 1959; 4th ed. (with Margaret Brown), 1969.

———. *The Soviet Union Today: A Scientist's Impression.* London: Lawrence and Wishart, 1952.

———. "The Evolution of Arthropodan Locomotory Mechanisms, 2. General Introduction to the Locomotory Mechanisms of Arthropoda." *Journal of the Linnean Society (Zool.)* 42 (1952): 93–117.

———. With O. W. Teigs. "The Evolution of the Arthropoda." *Biological Reviews* 33 (1958): 255–337.

———. *Colourpoint, Longhair and Himalyan Cats.* London: Allen and Unwin, 1971.

———. "Arthropod Phylogeny—A Modern Synthesis." *Journal of Zoology, London* 171 (1973): 111–130.

———. *The Arthropoda: Habits, Functional Morphology, and Evolution.* Oxford: Clarendon Press, 1977.

SECONDARY SOURCES

Fryer, G. "Sidnie Milana Manton." *Biographical Memoirs of the Royal Society of London* B 26 (1980): 327–356. Remarkable for its detailed analysis of her contributions to evolution of Arthropoda and other scientific areas, with a complete bibliography; it also provides a sense of her personality. With portrait.

STANDARD SOURCES

Debus; *DNB; Notable.*

MANZOLINI, ANNA MORANDI (1716–1774)

Italian anatomist. Born 1716 in Bologna to Rose (Giovanni) and Charles Morandi. Married Giovanni Manzolini (1736). Six children. Self-educated. Professional experience: University of Bologna, lecturer in anatomy (1755); professor of anatomy (1760–1774). Honors and memberships: Italian Royal Society; Russian Royal Scientific Association; the Royal Society of London; bust placed in Pantheon in Rome; portrait in wax which she modeled herself in museum at the University of Bologna. Died 1774 in Bologna.

Little is known about Anna Morandi's early life. We know that she married her childhood sweetheart, Giovanni Manzolini, when she was twenty years old and he twenty-four. Manzolini was a professor of anatomy at the University of Bologna and an expert in the construction of anatomical models. Although Anna had an almost pathological fear of dead things, she overcame her aversion and studied specimens in order to develop skill in the molding of wax models. The arrival of six children in five years did not deter her. After her husband became ill with tuberculosis and was unable to lecture, Anna Manzolini, with the blessing of university officials, lectured in his place. On her husband's death in 1760 she was elected professor of anatomy with the added title of *modellatrice* (model maker). Her fame spread throughout Europe; the emperor Joseph II of Austria bought several of her models, Catherine II invited her to Russia to lecture (while there, she was elected to the Russian Royal Scientific Society), and she lectured in London. After her death, at age fifty-eight, her bust was placed in the Pantheon in Rome and in the museum of the University of Bologna.

An excellent teacher and a skilled craftsman, Manzolini's skill at dissection resulted in anatomical discoveries, including the termination of the oblique muscle of the eye. Her models were displayed all over Europe and became the archetypes of later models. After her death, the Medical Institute of Bologna acquired the collection of models that she had constructed, and the collection is now at the Institute of Science in Bologna.   JH/MBO

SECONDARY SOURCES

Fantuzzi, Giovanni. *Notizie degli scrittori bolognesi, raccolte da Giovanni Fantuzzi.* 9 vols. Bologna: S. Tommasco d'Aquino, 1781–1794.
Schiebinger, Londa. *The Mind Has No Sex?* Cambridge, Mass.: Harvard University Press, 1989.

STANDARD SOURCES

Hurd-Mead 1938; Grinstein 1997 (article by Connie H. Nobles); Lipinska 1930; Ogilvie 1986.

MARACINEANU, STEFANIA (1882–1944)

Romanian physicist. Born 18 June 1882 in Bucharest. Educated physical and chemical sciences (degree 1910); Radium Institute, Paris (1919 or 1920–1926?; doctorate 1924). Professional experience: Central School for Girls, Bucharest, teacher; Meuden and Paris Astronomical Observatories, researcher (1926?–1930). Died 1944.

In Marie Curie's laboratory, Maracineanu investigated the half life of polonium and developed a method for measuring alpha ray intensity. She believed some of her results showed that polonium's alpha rays could change some atoms into radioactive isotopes. Although these observations were not confirmed, Maracineanu later claimed priority for the discovery of artificial radioactivity. She also thought that sunlight could induce radioactivity, a hypothesis she investigated with the astronomer Deslandres. This work was hotly contested by other researchers.

Maracineanu returned to her homeland in 1930, where she investigated supposed connections between radioactivity and rainfall (performing experiments in Algeria) and between rainfall and earthquake activity. She died in 1944.

                                                          MM

PRIMARY SOURCES

Maracineanu, Stefania. *Recherches sur la constante du polonium et sur la pénétration des substances radioactives dans les métaux.* Paris: Presses Universitaires de France, 1924.
———. "Actions spéciales du Soleil sur la radioactivité du plomb et de l'uranium." *Comptes rendus* 181 (1925): 774–776.
———. "La radioactivité du globe, les radiations et les tremblements de terre." *Académie des Sciences de Roumanie, Comptes rendus* 6 (1942): 72–75.

SECONDARY SOURCES

Records in archives of the Institut Curie, assembled by Mme. Monique Bordry.

STANDARD SOURCES

Meyer and von Schweidler; Rayner-Canham 1997.

MARCELLA (fl. late 4th century C.E.)

Roman healer. Born in Rome. Mentioned by St. Jerome. Died in Bethlehem.

Marcella was one of the Christian women healers praised by St. Jerome for their care of the sick. Along with Fabiola and Paula, Marcella read Homer in Greek, studied Hebrew, sang hymns and prayed, and constantly cared for her patients.

                                                          JH/MBO

STANDARD SOURCES
Hurd-Mead 1938.

MARCET, JANE HALDIMAND (1769–1858)

British writer on natural philosophy. Born 1769 in London. Father Anthony Francis Haldimand. Eleven siblings. Married Alexander Marcet. Two children. Died 1858.

Biographical information is scarce on Jane Marcet. Her father, Anthony Francis Haldimand, was a wealthy Swiss merchant residing in London. Jane's childhood was divided between her London home and visits to relatives in Geneva. One of twelve children and the only female to survive infancy, fifteen-year-old Jane took over the management of the household, including the supervision of her siblings, after the death of her mother. As a young girl she was interested in art, but there are no indications of an interest in writing or in science until after her marriage in 1799 to Alexander Marcet, a physician who preferred to spend his time on his hobby, chemistry, rather than on his profession. As his medical practice became more financially rewarding, Marcet was able to devote more time to his scientific interests. He was elected a Fellow of the Royal Society after publishing several scientific papers. He also was a member of literary and scientific circle that included the historian Henry Hallam (1777–1858), the political economists Thomas Malthus (1766–1834) and HARRIET MARTINEAU (1802–1876), the novelist MARIA EDGEWORTH (1767–1849), and the naturalists Augustin-Pyramus de Candolle (1778–1841) and Auguste de la Rive (1823–1873). Jane Marcet became involved in the activities of this group and, with the encouragement of her husband and friends, began a writing career.

Jane Marcet indulged the taste for "popular science" that had developed in the late eighteenth century. She produced a number of introductory science books, especially intended for women and young people. Although, as she assured her readers, she neither pretended to be a scientist nor sought a depth of knowledge that might be "considered by some . . . as unsuited to the ordinary pursuits of her sex," she did believe that "the general opinion no longer excludes women from an acquaintance with the elements of science" (*Conversations on Chemistry*, iii).

Conversations on Chemistry was enthusiastically received, largely appealing to a new audience created by Sir Humphry Davy (1778–1829) at the Royal Institution. Handsome, debonair, and an intriguing lecturer, Davy mesmerized the young English society ladies who flocked to his lectures. Although Marcet addressed her book to the general public, it was designed particularly to appeal to these women. In the preface she admitted that when she had first attended these lectures, she had found it difficult to understand them be- cause each point had been presented or demonstrated so rapidly that she could not follow the discussion. After discussing the lectures with a friend and repeating some of the experiments, she had begun to comprehend the lectures. When she again attended lectures at the Royal Institution, she found it a great advantage to have discussed the material previously. Since she had found discussion a useful tool in understanding chemistry, she presumed that others would respond in the same way and therefore presented her subject in the form of conversations. The three protagonists—Mrs. B., the teacher, and Caroline and Emily, the students—took part in a dialogue, in the course of which Mrs. B. expounded current ideas in chemistry. The conversation approach was so successful that Marcet continued in it numerous books.

Marcet's *Conversations on Chemistry* had a great impact on one future scientist, Michael Faraday (1791–1867). Throughout his life he praised this book, which, as a young apprentice bookbinder with little formal education, he read in 1810. The *Conversations* introduced him to electrochemistry. After reading it, he recognized that the electrical forces that had already intrigued him were of fundamental importance as regulators of chemical change.

Although Marcet was isolated from the mainstream of literary women because she chose science as her subject, her importance as a teacher was great. Through her popularizations she simplified the important scientific ideas of her time so that the layperson could understand them. Although the most conspicuous testimonial to the influence of her work comes from Michael Faraday, it is probable from the wide circulation of her books that they influenced a large audience.

MBO

PRIMARY SOURCES

Marcet, Jane. *Conversations on Chemistry In Which the Elements of That Science Are Familiarly Explained and Illustrated by Experiments and Plates. To Which are Added: Some Later Discoveries on the Subject of the Fixed Alkalies, by H. Davy, Esq., of the Royal Society,—and a Short Account of Artificial Mineral Waters in the United States. With an Appendix Consisting of Treatises on Dyeing, Tanning and Currying.* New Haven: Sidney's Press, for Increase Cooke and Co., Booksellers, 1809.

———. *Conversations on Natural Philosophy, in Which the Elements of That Science Are Familiarly Explained and Adapted to the Comprehension of Young Pupils.* 4th ed. London: Longman, Hurst, Rees, Orme, Brown, and Green, 1824.

———. *Conversations on Vegetable Physiology; Comprehending the Elements of Botany, with Their Application to Agriculture.* 2 vols. London: Longman, Rees, Orme, Brown, and Green, 1829.

SECONDARY SOURCES

Allibone, Samuel Austin. *A Critical Dictionary of English Literature and British and American Authors, Living and Deceased. From the*

Earliest Accounts to the Latter Half of the Nineteenth Century. Containing Over Forty-Six Thousand Articles (Authors), with Forty Indexes of Subjects. 3 vols. Philadelphia: Lippincott, 1874.

Armstrong, Eva. "Jane Marcet and Her 'Conversations on Chemistry.' " *Journal of Chemical Education* 15 (February 1938): 53–57.

De la Rive, Auguste. "Madame Marcet." *Bibliothèque revue Suisse et étrangère* 64, no. 4 (1859).

Derrick, M. Elizabeth. "Jane Marcet, Early Textbook Author." *The Hexagon* (Summer 1985): 38–41.

Fussell, G. E. "Some Lady Botanists of the Nineteenth Century. V. Jane Marcet." *The Gardener's Chronicle. A Weekly Illustrated Journal of Horticulture and Allied Subjects* 3d ser. 130 (22 December 1951): 238.

The Gentleman's Magazine and Historical Review n.s. 5 (July-December 1858): 204. Obituary notice.

Williams, L. Pearce. *Michael Faraday.* New York: Basic Books [1965].

STANDARD SOURCES
DNB; DSB; Ogilvie 1986.

MARCHE, MARGUERITE DU TERTRE DE LA (1638–1706)
See De la Marche, Marguerite du Tertre.

MARGERY (fl. 1300–1306)
British healer. Flourished 1300–1306.

Margery was a "leech" in Wales in County Worcester. She probably practiced marginally on locals. Margery appeared in manorial court several times for various offenses and reputedly was once thrown into a river to determine whether or not she was a witch.   JH/MBO

SECONDARY SOURCES
Talbot, Charles H., and Eugene Ashby Hammond. *Medical Practitioners in Medieval England: A Biographical Register.* London: Wellcome Medical Historical Library, 1965. Margery mentioned on 209.

MARGULOVA, TEREZA KRISTOFOROVNA (1912–)
Soviet nuclear scientist. Born 1912.

Tereza Kristoforovna Margulova worked in nuclear research. Her book on nuclear power stations is the only English source on her.   MM

PRIMARY SOURCES
Margulova, Tereza Kristoforovna. *Nuclear Power Stations.* Moscow: Mir, 1978.

SECONDARY SOURCES
Rayner-Canham, M. F., and G. W. Rayner-Canham. "Pioneer Women in Nuclear Science." *American Journal of Physics* 58 (1990): 1036–1043.

MARIC, MILEVA (1875–1948)
See Einstein-Maric, Mileva.

MARILLAC, LOUISE DE (1591–1671)
French nurse and pharmacist. Born 1591. Married LeGras. Educated privately. Professional experience: established Sisters of Charity. Died 1671.

Louise de Marillac was well educated and from a noble family. Her husband, LeGras, was the secretary of the queen, Maria de Medicis, and he was a physician who taught his wife medicine and surgery. After her husband died, she vowed to commit her life to medicine, but not in a convent. She prepared medicines and organized a group of helpers who became the first Sisters of Charity. Her followers adopted a gray dress and a veil. They visited prisoners in the jails, slaves in the galleys, the sick in "pest houses" (hospitals for those with communicable diseases), and other places where nursing was needed.   JH/MBO

STANDARD SOURCES
Hurd-Mead 1938.

MARINOV, EVELINA (1929–1984)
Bulgarian engineering geologist. Born 2 September 1929 in Dalgodeltzi, Bulgaria. Married Ivan Marinov in 1956. Two children. Educated high school in Berkowiza; Higher Technical Teaching Academy in Sofia (certificate 1951). Professional experience: Offices of the head administration for the department of street and bridge construction at the ministry in Sofia (1951); "Energo hydro project" on energy-efficient building materials, researcher (1953–1996); Institute for Hydroproblematics of the Bulgarian Academy of Sciences, researcher (1960–1964); Federal Geological Institute, researcher. Prepared geological maps. Died 16 January 1984.

Evelina Marinov essentially had two careers, one in her native Bulgaria and a second in Vienna, Austria. She was awarded a certificate as an engineering geologist in 1951. She went to work for the ministry in charge of bridge and street construction and worked in several other areas of practical application until she married Ivan Marinov in 1956. They had two children, Theodor, born in 1957, and Angelina, born in 1963. The year after Angelina's birth, the family emigrated to Vienna where she gave up her career and dedicated herself to her family until 1975, when she resumed her professional activities. Marinov became an Austrian citizen in 1973. She was employed by the Federal Geological Institute, where her duties included preparing technical maps and preparing bibliographical files for automated processing.

Marinov was not an original researcher. However, the quasi-clerical work that she did in Vienna illustrates one of the near-scientific careers that women could successfully engage in. JH/MBO

SECONDARY SOURCES
Schnabel, Wolfgang. "Evelina Marinov. 2 September 1929–16 Jänner 1984." *Jahrbuch der Geologischen Bundesanstalt Wien* 127, no. 2 (1984): 149.

MARKS, HERTHA (1854–1923)
See Ayrton, Hertha (Marks).

MARLATT, ABBY LILLIAN (1869–1943)
U.S. home economist. Born 7 March 1869 in Manhattan, Kans., to Julia Ann (Bailey) Marlatt and Rev. Washington Marlatt. Four siblings. Educated local district school; Kansas State Agricultural College, Manhattan (B.S., 1888; M.S., 1890); Brown University, special student; Clark University, Worcester, Mass., summer sessions. Professional experience: Utah State Agricultural College, professor of domestic economy (1890–1894); Manual Training High School (later Technical High School), Providence, R.I., faculty member (1894–1909); University of Wisconsin, organized home economics department (1909), director of home economics (1913–1939). Honors and memberships: Kansas State Agricultural College, honorary degree (1925); Utah State Agricultural College (1938), honorary degree. Died 23 June 1943 in Madison, Wisc., of cancer.

Abby Marlatt was the youngest of the five children of Reverend Washington Marlatt, of French Huguenot descent, and his wife, Julia. After Rev. Marlatt moved to Kansas, he traded farming for the ministry. Abby attended a local district school and then attended Kansas State Agricultural College in Manhattan where the family lived. After receiving her bachelor's degree, she taught while working on the master's degree. After obtaining the master's degree in chemistry, she went to a new institution in Logan, Utah, the Utah State Agricultural College, as professor, and organized a new department of domestic economy. After four years, she left Utah to again pioneer a home economics program, this time

at Manual Training High School, Providence, Rhode Island. At the 1900 session of the Lake Placid Conference on Home Economics established by ELLEN SWALLOW RICHARDS, Marlatt reported on her successful work in Providence, where she was correlating home economics with the sciences. She served as chairman (1903) and vice-president (1907) of the conference. This conference evolved into the American Home Economics Association, and Marlatt was vice-president from 1912 to 1918.

In 1908, the University of Wisconsin's home economics department was moved to the agriculture college. The college was not a respected part of the university, and its dean brought Marlatt in to rectify the situation. She developed a curriculum that not only included basic science and technical courses but English and a foreign language. Prodigiously energetic herself, she had trouble understanding why others could not be productive in research and carry a full teaching load as well.

Marlatt participated in a number of conferences during World War I, and was chair of a committee on state participation in the Division of Food Conservation. Later, in 1930, Hoover appointed her chair of the Committee on Kitchens and Other Works Centers of the President's Conference on Home Building and Home Ownership.

Her students were sometimes in awe of Marlatt, for she was a demanding teacher. However, they soon recognized that she was a caring person, who was deeply interested in their success. She was also an active suffragist. JH/MBO

SECONDARY SOURCES
Jones, Nellie Kedzie. "Abby L. Marlatt." *Journal of Home Economics* (October 1943).
"Resolution in Honor of Abby Lillian Marlatt." Minutes of the General Faculty, University of Wisconsin, Madison, 4 October 1943. The most complete account of Marlatt's career.

STANDARD SOURCES
AMS 5–6; Bailey; *NAW* (article by Mary Tolford Wilson); Rossiter 1982; Siegel and Finley; *WW in America*, 1920–1921, 1930–1931.

MARRIOTT, ALICE LEE (1910–1992)
American anthropologist and ethnologist. Born 8 January 1910 in Wilmetter, Ill., to Sydney Kenner (Cunningham) and Richard Goulding Marriott. Educated Central High School, Oklahoma City, Okla.; University of Oklahoma (B.A., 1935). Professional experience: Muskogee (Okla.) Public Library, cataloguer; Department of Anthropology, University of Oklahoma, graduate assistant; U.S. Department of Interior, Bureau of Indian Affairs, consultant, museum consultant. Honors and memberships: Sigma Xi (1935); Phi

Beta Kappa (1945); Oklahoma Outstanding Woman of 1945. Died Oklahoma City, Okla., 18 March 1992.

Alice Marriott moved with her family from Illinois to Oklahoma City when she was seven years old. Her father had come to the United States from England as a boy and her mother was from a prerevolutionary southern family. She received her education in Oklahoma, and was granted a bachelor's degree in anthropology in 1935. She studied American Indians, especially those from Oklahoma, and wrote with a deft and sensitive style that has made her books very popular. Although she considered herself chiefly a research anthropologist and not a writer, some critics often reverse the two, stressing her ability to sympathetically portray the people among whom she lived. She promoted a wider understanding of the rich and complex culture of the Indians. She was also modest: when she was honored as the State's Outstanding Woman of 1945, she replied "they were hard up for women that year."

Marriott's literary output was broad and varied. She produced scholarly ethnological reports, novels, short stories, and popular nonfiction. She contributed to periodicals such as *Mademoiselle, Harper's, American Mercury,* and the *Southwest Review.* She published more than ten books. Her story of *Maria the Potter* was the selection of the Natural History Book Club for July 1948.   JH/MBO

PRIMARY SOURCES
Marriott, Alice Lee. *Winter-Telling Stories.* New York: Crowell, 1947.
————. *Indians on Horseback.* Eau Claire, Wis.: Hale, 1948.
————. *Maria the Potter of San Ildefonson.* Norman: University of Oklahoma Press, 1948.
————. *The Valley Below.* Norman: University of Oklahoma Press, 1949.

SECONDARY SOURCES
Kobler, Turner S. *Alice Marriott.* Austin, Tex.: Steck-Vaughn, 1969.
New York Times, 21 March 1992. Obituary notice.

STANDARD SOURCES
Current Biography, 1992; *Current Biography Yearbook,* 1950.

MARSH, MARY ELIZABETH (1895–?)

U.S. nutritional physiologist. Born 12 December 1895 in Bliss, N.Y. Educated University of Rochester (B.A., 1916; M.S., 1923; Ph.D., 1927). Professional experience: University of Rochester, assistant in physiology (1921–1923), instructor (1923–1928); Trudeau Foundation research fellow (1930–1931); School of Medicine and Dentistry, University of Rochester, assistant physiologist (1931–1933), instructor (1933–1935), assistant professor (1935–1937); Killian Research Labs, Inc., assistant director (1937–1950). University of California, San Francisco, research assistant, school of medicine (1951–1954), assistant research pathologist (1955–1961). Retired 1961. Honors and memberships: Physiological Society and Institute of Nutrition. Death date unknown.

Elizabeth Marsh, an American nutritional physiologist, was born in upstate New York and spent her entire academic training period and the first half of her professional life at the University of Rochester. When in her forties she still had only an assistant professorship, she took the opportunity to join the Killian Research Laboratories as an assistant director, remaining there until 1950. Following this period, she became a research assistant at the University of California School of Medicine, San Francisco, and then assistant research pathologist.

Marsh's research focused on tissue metabolism and nutritional studies in animals. She examined tissue enzymes in deficiency diseases, especially vitamin B6 deficiency. Following her retirement at the age of sixty-five, she remained in San Francisco.   JH/MBO

STANDARD SOURCES
AMS 5–8, *P&B* 10–11.

MARSHALL, CLARA (1847–1931)

U.S. physician. Born 8 May 1847 in Chester County, Pa., to Mary (Phillips) and Pennock Marshall. Never married. Educated Woman's Medical College of Pennsylvania (1875); Philadelphia College of Pharmacy (1875–1876, postgraduate year). Professional experience: public school teacher (before 1871); Woman's Medical College of Pennsylvania, demonstrator in materia medica (1875), professor of materia medica and therapeutics (1876–1905), dean of medical school (1886–1917), emerita professor (1917–1923). Concurrent experience: Philadelphia Hospital, demonstrator in obstetrics (1882–1906); Philadelphia House of Refuge, Girls' Department, attending physician (from 1886); private practice (1886–1923?). Died 13 March 1931 in Bryn Mawr, Pa., of arteriosclerosis.

Clara Marshall came from Quaker parentage and grew up in a privileged Pennsylvania family born in Chester County, Pennsylvania, just a block from the home of ANN PRESTON, the pioneer woman physician who would serve as a model to young Clara. After a preliminary education, Marshall briefly taught school, but by 1871, she decided to attend the Female Medical College (later the Woman's Medical College) in Philadelphia, founded some ten years earlier.

Marshall studied chemistry under RACHEL BODLEY, physiology under Ann Preston, obstetrics under EMELINE HORTON

CLEVELAND, and anatomy under Mary Scarlett-Dixon. She soon showed her skill in diagnosis and therapy and was made a demonstrator of materia medica at the medical college by the first dean, Ann Preston. She decided to spend a year of postgraduate study at the Philadelphia College of Pharmacy, where her ancestor had been one of the first presidents.

Returning to the Woman's Medical College, Marshall was appointed professor of materia medica and therapeutics. Although the Woman's Medical College had a close tie to the Woman's Hospital, founded by Ann Preston, Marshall recognized the need to forge close ties to other Philadelphia hospitals. She became a demonstrator in obstetrics at Blockley Medical College for Men, part of Philadelphia Hospital, and an attending physician at the Philadelphia House of Refuge, both part of the complex of "Blockley."

When Rachel Bodley, dean of faculty, died suddenly in 1888, the Board of Corporators chose Clara Marshall as the next dean, seeing in her the necessary qualities of leadership and statesmanship that the college needed. As dean, Marshall realized that laboratory training in bacteriology was a significant part of medical practice, and set up both a laboratory and a professorship in the field in 1896, the first in the country. She also recognized that it was necessary to expand the clinical experience of young women physicians as interns and residents. By 1904, she helped open the Pavillion Hospital for General Surgery and Medicine, which provided opportunities for the graduates of the medical school. In 1907, this became the much larger College Hospital built floor by floor between 1907 and 1913. As dean, Marshall also initiated an entrance examination; increased the faculty to sixty-six, forty-five of whom were women; increased subjects taught from the basic five or six of 1888 to twenty-two; and spearheaded the building of the first hospital directly under the control of the college board and faculty. When her private practice became too large for her to keep along with her deanship and professorship, she resigned from teaching.

Like MARY PUTNAM JACOBI, Marshall was a strong supporter of woman's suffrage, and in 1898 spoke at the National Woman's Suffrage Association conference on women in medicine, following in Putnam Jacobi's footsteps there as well. She had fought successfully ten years earlier for women's admission to the County Medical Society.

Marshall retired from her position at the medical school in 1917, and later resigned her emerita professorship following the unwelcome reforms introduced by Dean MARTHA TRACY. She lived in Bryn Mawr toward the end of her life, dying there of arteriosclerosis.
JH/MBO

PRIMARY SOURCES

Marshall, Clara. *The Woman's Medical College of Pennsylvania: An Historical Outline.* Philadelphia: Blakiston, 1897.

SECONDARY SOURCES

Abram, Ruth, ed. *"Send Us a Lady Physician": Women Doctors in America (1835–1920).* New York: Norton, 1984. There is a portrait of Clara Marshall on page 150 and a quotation from her commencement address of 1879 on page 151.

Alsop, Gulielma F. *The History of the Woman's Medical College, Philadelphia, Pennsylvania 1850–1950.* Philadelphia: J. B. Lippincott Co., 1950.

STANDARD SOURCES

Morantz-Sanchez; *NAW* (article by Gulielma F. Alsop).

MARSHALL, SHEINA MACALISTER (1896–1977)

Scottish marine biologist. Born 20 April 1896 in Rothesay, Scotland, to Jean Colville (Binnie) and John Nairn Marshall, M.D. Two sisters. Educated St. Margaret's School, Polmont; Glasgow University (B.Sc., 1919; D.Sc., 1934). Professional experience: Glasgow University, Carnegie Fellowship (1922–1923); Marine Biological Station, Millport (Isle of Cumbrae, Scotland), naturalist (1922–1964), deputy director (1962–1963); expedition to the Great Barrier Reef (Queensland, Australia) (1927); Ministries of Health and Supplies, consultant (1939?–1945). Honors and memberships: Edinburgh Royal Society, Fellow (1949); Royal Society, Fellow (1963); Edinburgh Royal Society, Niels Prize (1971); Order of the British Empire (1966); University of Uppsala, honorary doctorate, (1977). Died 7 April 1977.

Sheina Marshall dedicated her life to marine biology, particularly to the understanding of animal and plant plankton, especially the copepod Calanus. She grew up in a household in Scotland that valued both music and science. Ill for two years with rheumatic fever, she spent her time in bed reading Charles Darwin's books. Her father, a physician keenly interested in natural history, encouraged his three daughters to keep a freshwater aquarium and produce a collection of dried wild flowers for the Rothesay Museum.

Sheina Marshall went to Glasgow University, where she studied science, taking off one year at the beginning of World War I to work in her uncles' instrument-making factory. Returning to the university, she completed courses in physiology, zoology, and botany, earning an honors degree. She then spent two additional years at the university on a Carnegie fellowship.

An opportunity arose that allowed Sheina to join the Millport Marine Biological Station on the Isle of Cumbrae as a naturalist. The same year, A. P. Orr was hired as a biochemical assistant. They became close friends and lifelong collaborators, using the ship *Nautilus* for surveys of the coast through regular tow-nettings and water sampling. They joined their areas of expertise: he studied physical and chemical conditions and she studied plankton distribution over the lochs of the Clyde Sea. Her attention focused on the marine copepod Calanus. Together they analyzed pollution levels and the seasonal growth of diatoms and published their classic investigations on the biology of phytoplankton.

In 1928–1929, Marshall and Orr took a leave of absence to join the expedition to the Great Coral Reef off Queensland in Australia. Here, with other internationally renowned marine biologists, Marshall studied living corals, observing the liberation of planulae from corals. With Orr, she studied the coral reef sediments and produced a number of joint papers for the Philosophical Society of Edinburgh as well as for expedition publications.

Just before World War II, Marshall made a study of herring growth along the Clyde, but this work was put aside for more urgent concerns. Marshall sat with Orr on a number of ministry committees during the war years, suggesting, for example, some practical replacements for the seaweed agar-agar that was no longer available.

In the postwar period, Marshall and Orr put together their many studies on the copepod Calanus into a book form, and also produced a delightful book on the seashore for popular consumption.

Marshall was elected to the Royal Society of London some thirteen years after her admission to the Royal Society of Edinburgh. Soon after her election, her close friend Orr died. Although she served as deputy head of the Marine Station the year following his death, the early sixties marked the end of her formal position. She chose, however to continue working informally at Millport, now under the control of Glasgow and Edinburgh universities, continuing to publish some of the work that she and Orr had begun together. She also began to collaborate with other scientists with whom she published through the late sixties. A bout with pneumonia in the early seventies and, a few years later, the weakening of her eyesight by cataracts, diminished her remarkable scientific production. Among her honors, she deeply appreciated the Niels Prize of the Royal Society of Edinburgh and the honorary doctorate from a Swedish university just before her death.

JH/MBO

PRIMARY SOURCES

Marshall, Sheina Macalister. "Observations on the Behavior and Stricture of Hydra." *Quarterly Journal of the Microscopical Society* 67 (1923): 593–616.

———. With A. P. Orr. "The Recent Expedition to the Great Barrier Reef of Australia." *Proceedings of the Royal Philosophical Society of Glasgow* (1930): 58–100.

———. With A. G. Nicholls and A. P. Orr. "On the Growth of the Larval and Post-Larval Stages of the Clyde Herring." *Journal of the Marine Biological Association U.K.* 20 (1935): 427–455.

———. With A. Nichols, et al. *Seaweed Utilization.* London: Sampson and Low, 1951.

———. With A. P. Orr. *The Biology of a Marine Copepod, Calanus finmarchicus (Gunnerus).* Edinburgh and London: Oliver and Boyd, 1955.

———. With E. D. S. Corner and C. B. Cowry. "On the Nutrition and Metabolism of Zooplanton. III. Nitrogen Excretion by Calanus." *Journal of the Marine Biological Association U.K.* (1964): 429–444.

SECONDARY SOURCES

Barnes, Harold. *Some Contemporary Studies in Marine Science.* London: Allen & Unwin, 1966. This book on the contemporary work in marine biology was presented to her. It discusses (as do all the other sources) her close association and collaboration with A. P. Orr.

Mills, Eric. *Biological Oceanography: An Early History, 1870–1960.* Includes portrait.

Russell, Frederick. "Sheina Macalister Marshall." *Biographical Memoirs of the Royal Society* 24 (1978): 369–389.

STANDARD SOURCES
Debus.

MARTIN, ELLA MAY (1892–?)

U.S. botanist. Born 4 May 1892 in Kansas(?). Educated Lawrence College (B.A., 1915); University of Wisconsin (M.A., 1920; Ph.D., 1924). Professional experience: University of Wisconsin, assistant in botany (1918–1921, 1923–1924); Kansas Wesleyan University, professor of biology (1921–1923, 1945–1946); Illinois Wesleyan, assistant professor (1924–1926); Greensboro College, professor (1926–1932); Newcomb College, Tulane (1932–1934); Chicago, botanical research, DePaul University, professor of botany (1935–1937); University of Wisconsin, Extension Division, botany instructor (1937–1938), research (1938–1941); West Maryland College, instructor in biology (1941–1942); Hood College, assistant professor of botany and bacteriology (1944–1945); Wisconsin State Board of Health, bacteriologist (1944–1945); Wisconsin State College, associate professor of biology (1946–1955), professor (1955–1962), emerita professor (1962–). Death date unknown.

Ella May Martin was educated first at Lawrence College and then served as assistant in botany while getting her advanced degrees. She went on to teach at Kansas Wesleyan, Greensboro, Newcomb, and De Paul, and then spent two years as bacteriologist at the Wisconsin State Board of Health during World War II. In the postwar period, she was appointed first as associate professor at Wisconsin State College, Platteville, rising through the ranks to professor. She was made emerita at the time of her retirement in the early 1960s. Her research specialty was on the morphology and cytology of *Taphrinas.*

JH/MBO

STANDARD SOURCES
AMS 5–8, B 9, P&B 10–11.

MARTIN, EMILIE NORTON (1869–1936)

U.S. mathematician. Born 30 December 1869 in Elizabeth, N.J. Educated Bryn Mawr College (A.B., 1894); Mary E. Garrett Fellow, Göttingen (1897–1898; Ph.D., 1901). Professional experience: private tutor (1899–1902); Pennsylvania schools, mathematics teacher (1900–1902); Mount Holyoke College, instructor (1903–1911), associate professor (1911–1925), professor (from 1925). Died 1936.

While Emilie Martin completed her doctorate, she worked as a private tutor and as a mathematics teacher. Much of her research for her doctorate was done at Göttingen while she held a Mary E. Garrett fellowship. After she got her degree, she accepted a position at Mount Holyoke, where she slowly proceeded up the academic ladder. She completed an index to the first ten volumes of the *Bulletin of the American Mathematical Society.* She was a member of the American Association for the Advancement of Science, the American Mathematical Society, and the Mathematical Association. Her research was on imprimitive substitution groups of degree fifteen and the primitive substitution of degree eighteen. JH/MBO

STANDARD SOURCES
AMS 1–5; Bailey; Grinstein and Campbell; Siegel and Finley.

MARTIN, LILLIEN JANE (1851–1943)

U.S. psychologist. Born 7 July 1851 in Olean, N.Y., to Lydia (Hawes) and Russel Martin. Educated Olean Academy; Vassar College (B.A., 1880); University of Göttingen (Ph.D., 1898); postgraduate studies at Würzburg (1907) and Bonn (1908). Professional experience: teacher of physics and chemistry, Indianapolis High School (1880–1889); Girls' High School, San Francisco, vice-principal and head of science department (1889–1894); Stanford University, assistant professor of psychology (1899–1909), associate professor (1909–1911), professor (1911–1916). Died 1943 in San Francisco.

The eldest of four children, Lillien Martin grew up in a single-parent family because her father, a merchant, left his family when Lillien was a child. Her mother struggled to provide the children with a good education. Lillien began earning her living as a schoolteacher at about age sixteen, saving what she could in order to put herself through col-

lege. In 1876 she entered Vassar College, where she excelled in science. After she graduated in 1880, she spent fourteen years teaching high-school science, mostly physics and chemistry. At age forty-three, Martin abruptly changed her career, resigning her position as vice-principal and head of the science department at Girls' High School in San Francisco to study psychology at the University of Göttingen with G. E. Müller. She received a doctoral degree from Göttingen in 1898. Over the next two decades she spent several summers doing additional research in Germany, publishing most of her work there.

Martin joined the staff at Stanford University in 1899 as an assistant professor of psychology, progressing through the academic ranks. During her last year there (1915–1916), she was chair of the psychology department—the first woman to be made a department head at Stanford.

Martin, unhappy with retirement, embarked on a new career at age sixty-five, becoming a consulting psychologist. She founded and worked in mental health clinics in San Francisco. After she worked with preschool children for several years, she turned her attention to gerontology, establishing in 1929 what may have been the first counseling center for the elderly. Martin was chiefly occupied with this work during her last years. Her own old age was exceptional: she learned to drive a car in her seventies, and made an auto trip across America at age eighty-one. She traveled alone to Russia at seventy-eight, and to South America at eighty-seven.

Martin's work as an experimental psychologist covered a variety of subjects. She devised a classic series of experiments on the psychophysics of lifted weights, and developed an experimental method that was held to measure imageless thought and hence to support the hypothesis that there are elements in thinking that are neither sensory nor derived from sensory images. Her clinical work with the elderly was of at least equal significance. JH/MBO

PRIMARY SOURCES
Martin, Lillien Jane. *Die Projektionsmethode und die Lokalisation visueller und anderer Vorstel-lungsbilder.* Leipzig: J. A. Barth, 1912.
Archives, Stanford University. Includes newspaper clippings and thirteen articles by Martin.

SECONDARY SOURCES
Stanford University Register, 1915–1916. Lists degrees and professional positions. Martin listed on page 27.

STANDARD SOURCES
AMS 1–6; Bailey; *DSB; NAW* (article by John Chynoweth Burnham); Ogilvie 1986; *Psychological Register,* vol. 3, 1932.

MARTINEAU, HARRIET (1802–1876)

British sociologist. Born 1802 in Norwich, U.K. Seven siblings. Never married. Educated at home. Died 1876.

Radical reformer Harriet Martineau was the sixth of eight children. Although her brothers attended the university, Harriet was educated at home. She became fluent in French and Latin. The death of her father left the family with little money, and Harriet began to earn her living as a writer and journalist. She published more than fifty books and over sixteen hundred feature articles.

Her first book on methodology, "Essays on the Art of Thinking," written in 1829–1832, was published in 1836 in an anthology, *Miscellanies.* Her empirical methodology was applicable for scientific investigation as well as decisions on political problems, household economy, and the raising of children. Problems in all areas resulted from deficient observation and poor judgment. She stated that the proper process was to induce theories from facts.

Martineau continued her interest in methodology when she embarked on a visit to the United States after Alexis de Tocqueville had returned and was writing up his impressions of the United States. Unlike de Tocqueville, who had only spent nine months there, Martineau lived in the United States for over two years. During her voyage across the ocean, she developed a methodology for her study of Americans, entitled *How to Observe Morals and Manners.* This book may have been the first account of a methodology of social research in the embryonic disciplines of sociology and anthropology. The volumes published from the trip, *Society in America,* recognized not only the evils of slavery but the separate issue of racism, remarking on the discrimination that northern blacks faced.

Martineau is better known for her translation of Auguste Comte's *Cours de philosophie positive* than for her earlier, more original works. Her three methodological books appeared before Comte had coined the term "sociology" in 1838.

Her first popularly successful book was on economic principles, *Illustrations of Political Economy.* This book outsold John Stuart Mills's *Principles of Political Economy.* The style of writing in this book is popular. She used fictional characters to demonstrate the major aspects of economic theory.

Martineau became involved in mesmerism after she had suffered from a long illness. Certain that she was cured by mesmerism, she described her experiences in *Letters on Mesmerism.* An activist throughout her life, she worked for women's suffrage, and rights to education, divorce, and jobs. JH/MBO

PRIMARY SOURCES
Martineau, Harriet. *Illustrations of Political Economy.* 9 vols. London: Charles Fox, 1834.

———. "Essays on the Art of Thinking." In *The Miscellanies.* 2 vols. Boston: Hilliard, Gray, 1836.
———. *How to Observe Morals and Manners.* London: Knight, 1837.
———. *Society in America.* [1837.] Ed. S. M. Lipset. Garden City, N. J., 1962.

SECONDARY SOURCES
Hoecker-Drysdale. *Harriet Martineau: First Woman Sociologist.* Oxford: Berg, 1991.
McDonald, Lynn. *The Women Founders of the Social Sciences.* Ottawa, Canada: Carleton University Press, 1994.
Webb, R. K. *Harriet Martineau: A Radical Victorian.* New York: Columbia University Press, 1960. Includes a discussion of her later involvement in mesmerism.
Wheatley, Vera. *The Life and Work of Harriet Martineau.* London: Secker & Warburg, 1957.

STANDARD SOURCES
DNB.

MARTINEZ-ALVAREZ, JOSEFINA (1890–?)

Puerto Rican physician. Born 1890. Educated Peabody Conservatory of Music, Baltimore; Woman's Medical College of Pennsylvania (graduated with honors, 1911). Professional experience: Puerto Rico, private practice, medical college teacher. Honors and memberships: American Association of Women Doctors, honorary medical diploma (1961). Death date unknown.

Josefina Martinez-Alvarez's first interest was music, and she studied at the Peabody Conservatory of Music in Baltimore. However, the fate of the poor in Puerto Rico haunted her, and she enrolled at the Woman's Medical College of Pennsylvania, graduating with honors in 1911. She became one of the first women physicians from Puerto Rico. After graduation, she completed additional medical studies in New York and Baltimore. Returning to Puerto Rico to practice, she became obsessed with the high incidence of tuberculosis among the peasants. She is credited with developing a method for its detection. While working at her private practice, she taught at a medical college and other institutions. Active in the women's movement and an avid proponent of women's suffrage, she was instrumental in helping Puerto Rican women obtain the right to vote in 1932. She received numerous awards for her contributions. She remained active in the women's movement at the age of ninety-five.

JH/MBO

SECONDARY SOURCES

Torres, Lola Kruger. "Martinez-Alvarez, Josefina." *Enciclopedia Grandes Mujeres de Puerto Rico.* Hato Rey, Puerto Rico: Ramollo Brothers, 1975.

Waters, Bertha, comp. *Women's History Month in Pennsylvania.* Philadelphia: Pennsylvania Department of Education, 1988.

STANDARD SOURCES
LKW.

MARY THE JEWESS (1st or 2d century C.E.)

Alexandrian alchemist. Born in Alexandria in first or second century C.E.

Alchemists cultivate secrecy, making it difficult to extricate the factual from the fanciful in their lives and works. Alchemical practitioners couched their works in obscure symbolic and metaphorical terms in order to place themselves in exalted positions. They also complicated the task of the historian by appropriating historical names such as Moses, Cleopatra, and Adam. Ben Jonson responded to this tradition in *The Alchemist,* writing of the so-called sister of Moses, identified with the alchemist known variously as Mary, Maria, or Miriam the Jewess. Although no books by Mary remain, and no biographical information exists, enough fragments of her writings are available to establish her historicity.

The seething, homogenizing society of Alexandria in the first few centuries after Christ was the perfect climate for the appearance of a female alchemist. Philo's ideas had merged with those of the mystery cults and Christianity. The liberalization in Egypt of the strict patriarchal attitudes of rabbinical Judaism toward women established an environment compatible with the existence of a female Jewish alchemist. Such an environment of magic, philosophy, astrology, and religion was appropriate for the development of alchemy.

Mary understood alchemy to represent a fusion of the rational, mystical, and practical. Although this combination would have been impossible in classical Greece, it was not unusual in an eclectic Hellenistic society. For example, Mary is credited with inventing a three-part still, described by the alchemist Zosimos. His description notes this amalgamation of the practical, technological facet of her alchemy merging with the imagery of the "above and below" that pervaded Hermetic philosophy. Mary is not, however, remembered for her mystical or theoretical contributions, but for the invention or the elaboration of apparatus that proved basic for the development of chemistry: the three-armed still, the *kerotakis,* the hot-ash bath, the dung bed, and the water bath. Mary's name was given to the latter device, the *bain-marie,* a

name first used by Arnald of Villanove in the fourteenth century.

Although as a historical person, Mary will always remain out of focus, she was important to science because she incorporated the empirical-sensory elements of science within an explanatory-theoretical framework—one of the few women in antiquity to attempt it.   JH/MBO

SECONDARY SOURCES

Berthelot, Marcellin Pierre Eugène. *Collection des anciens alchimistes grecs.* Paris: G. Steinheil, 1887.

Jonson, Ben. *The Alchemist.* In *The Complete Plays of Ben Jonson,* vol. 2. London: J. M. Dent and Sons, 1910. Mary is mentioned on page 19.

Lindsay, Jack. *The Origins of Alchemy in Graeco-Roman Egypt.* New York: Barnes and Noble, 1976.

Read, John. *Prelude to Chemistry: An Outline of Alchemy, Its Literature and Relationships.* London: G. Bell and Sons, 1936.

Stapleton, H. E. "The Antiquity of Alchemy." *Ambix* 5 (October 1953): 33–36.

Taylor, F. Sherwood. *The Alchemists: Founders of Modern Chemistry.* New York: Henry Schuman, 1949.

STANDARD SOURCES
Ogilvie 1986.

MASON, CAROL Y. (1902–1956)

U.S. geologist and geographer. Born 1902 in Watertown, Mass. One sister, Mrs. LeBaron Riggs. Never married. Educated Wellesley College (A.B., 1924); University of Chicago; Clark University (M.A., 1925; Ph.D., 1936). Professional experience: University of Illinois, graduate teaching assistant (1925); Milwaukee-Downer College, assistant professor of geography (1928–1938); Northwest State College, Marysville, Mo., faculty member (1938–1943); University of Tulsa, associate professor (1943–1956). Honors and memberships: American Association for the Advancement of Science; National Council of Geography Teachers; American Meteorological Society; Association of American Geographers; American Geographical Society; Tulsa Audubon Society; Tulsa Geographical Society; Oklahoma Academy of Sciences. Died 26 November 1956.

Carol Mason was an excellent teacher and a skilled advisor of students. Born in Massachusetts, she earned her undergraduate degree at Wellesley College, but spent her career in the Midwest. Her last teaching position was at the University of Tulsa, a position she held at the time of her death.

She was a member of Sigma Xi, Sigma Delta Epsilon, Mortar Board, and Delta Kappa Gamma. She was active in civic affairs—president of the Tulsa Town Club (1950–1951) and a member of the Oklahoma UNESCO Council.

She held memberships in numerous scientific societies, including the American Association for the Advancement of Science, National Council of Geography Teachers, American Meteorological Society, Association of American Geographers, American Geographical Society, Tulsa Audubon Society, Tulsa Geological Society, and the Oklahoma Academy of Sciences.

Most of her scientific research was on geographical subjects. She published numerous articles on the subject.　CK

PRIMARY SOURCES
Mason, Carol Y. *The Geography of Allegany State Park*. Albany: New York State Museum, Circular no. 16, 1936.

SECONDARY SOURCES
Murray, Albert Nelson. "Carol Y. Mason." *Tulsa Geological Society Digest* 25 (1957): 31.

MASON, MARIANNE HARRIET (1845–1932)

British botanical artist. Born February 1845 in Nottinghamshire. Professional experience: collected plants in South Africa. Died 7 April 1932 in Rondebosch, South Africa.

Although born in England, Marianne Mason went to South Africa in 1910 as the first official woman inspector of boarded-out children. She was a plant collector and botanical artist and made journeys to the Cape, Rhodesia, and Uganda on collecting trips. A plant, *Indigofera masoniae*, was named for her.　JH/MBO

PRIMARY SOURCES
Mason, Marianne Harriet. "Some Flowers of Eastern and Central Africa." *Journal of the Royal Horticultural Society* (1913): 8–16.
Mason's drawings, letters, and plants are at Kew Gardens.

SECONDARY SOURCES
Kew Bulletin (1932): 203–204. Obituary notice.
Times, 9 April 1932. Obituary notice.

STANDARD SOURCES
Desmond; Gunn and Codd.

MASSEE, IVY (fl. 1910s)

British botanist. Father G. E. Massee (1850–1917). Professional experience: collected and painted plants.

Ivy Massee's father, George Edward Massee, was the first president of the British Mycological Society. Ivy was also a mycologist, and actively collected in the field. She also painted plants. With her father, she produced a book. She also executed a series of drawings of poplars for Augustine Henry that are now at Glasnevin.　JH/MBO

PRIMARY SOURCES
Massee, Ivy. With G. E. Massee. *Mildews, Rusts, and Smuts*. London: Dulau, 1913.

SECONDARY SOURCES
Naturalist (1961): 62.
International Dendrology Society Yearbook (1985): 101–105.

STANDARD SOURCES
Desmond.

MASSEVITCH, ALLA GENRIKHOVNA (1918–　)

Russian astrophysicist. Born 9 October 1918 in Tbilisi to Nataliia A. Zhgenti, a nurse, and Genrikh C. Massevich, a lawyer. Married Joseph N. Friedlander. One daughter, Natasha. Educated Moscow University; Sternberg State Astronomy Institute; Kuibyshev Institute of Physics. Professional experience: Kuibyshev Teacher's College, staff; Moscow University, assistant professor, professor; Astronomical Council, Soviet Academy of Sciences, vice-president; Section Satellite Tracking for Geodesy, president; UNISPACE, deputy general secretary. Honors and memberships: Royal Astronomical Society, International Academy of Astronautics, State Prize, 1975.

Alla Genrikhovna Massevitch (or Masevich) was the eldest child of a professional family. She was attracted to science at the age of thirteen when she discovered the popular scientific works of Ia. Perelman of the Leningrad Polytechnical Institute. She initiated a correspondence with him which became a guide to her education in astronomy, mathematics, and physics. After graduating from secondary school in 1936, Massevitch entered the Moscow Industrial Pedagogical Institute at Moscow University, majoring in physics, and earned her degree in 1940. Postgraduate studies at the same institute were cut short by the German attack on Russia in the summer of 1941.

In November 1941, Massevitch married Joseph N. Friedlander, a metallurgical engineer she had met in a bomb shelter not long before. Friedlander worked at the Institute of Physics and Metals, which was being evacuated to Kuibyshev, and Massevitch followed him there, leaving Moscow University, which was being evacuated to another area. At Kuibyshev, Massevitch worked at the Institute of Physics and also taught astronomy at Kuibyshev Teacher's College, while studying English in the evenings.

When the institute returned to Moscow in 1942, Massevitch enrolled in the Sternberg State Astronomy Institute to work on her doctorate. She specialized in the internal structure of stars and stellar evolution. In 1946, she earned her candidate's degree (similar to a doctorate) and accepted a position as assistant professor of astrophysics at Moscow University, becoming a full professor in 1948.

In 1952, Massevitch was appointed vice-president of the Astronomical Council of the Soviet Academy of Sciences and became closely involved with space research. Six months before the launching of Sputnik I in 1957, she was given the task of tracking space vehicles. She developed a network of optical tracking stations, which functioned flawlessly on launch date. Besides organizing and administering the network, she was responsible for publishing the data collected by the stations. In 1988, Massevitch became the chief scientist for the council in charge of tracking space vehicles, and she maintained her own experimental station near Moscow.

Massevitch is best known for her work in space research and was the first in the field in the optical tracking of space vehicles. However, her earlier work on stellar evolution and the structure of red giants is also significant. Altogether she published 147 papers as well as three books on stellar evolution, one on satellite geodesy, and several popular books on astronomy.

Massevitch was also prominent on the international scene. She chaired a working group for the Committee on Space Research of the International Council of Scientific Unions (1961–1966), and was president of the section on satellite tracking for Geodesy (1968–1989). In 1982 she served as deputy secretary general to the United Nations Conference on the Exploration and Peaceful Uses of Outer Space (UNISPACE).

She was elected a foreign member of the Royal Astronomical Society in 1963 and was also a member of the Austrian and Indian academies of science and the International Academy of Astronautics (since 1964). She was awarded the USSR State Prize in 1975.   ACH

PRIMARY SOURCES

Massevitch, Alla Genrikhovna. *Istochnik energii solntsa i zvezd.* Moscow: Izdvo Akademii nauk SSSR, 1949.

———. *Sovremennye problemy fiziki i evoliutsii zvezd.* Moscow: "Nauka", 1989.

STANDARD SOURCES

Notable (article by Sebastian Thaler); *The International Who's Who.*

MASSEY, PATRICIA (1905–)

South African physician. Born 5 July 1905 in Graff-Reinet, South Africa. Father a physician. Three siblings. Never married. Educated University of Cape Town. Professional experience: private practice; part-time consultant appointments at teaching hospitals and at the University of Cape Town.

Patricia Massey grew up in the fourth oldest town in South Africa under the foothills of the Sneeuwberg, a very large range of mountains. The plains were very hot in the summer and bitterly cold in the winter. Her father was a general practitioner who had come from Ireland in 1902. Her mother was of German descent but born in Graff-Reinet, South Africa. Since many of the members of her family were physicians, Massey decided that she wanted to carry on the tradition.

Although her father strongly supported higher education for women, he was less than enthusiastic when his eldest daughter wanted to study medicine. He insisted that being a physician was too difficult a life for his daughter. He eventually supported her and she entered the University of Cape Town, where women constituted 25 percent of the class. She specialized in obstetrics and gynecology and did not encounter prejudice as a woman.   KM

PRIMARY SOURCES

Massey, Patricia. In Hellstedt, *Autobiographies.*

MASSY, ANNE L. (d. 1931)

Irish conchologist. Professional experience: Fisheries Department, temporary post (1906–1931). Died 1931.

Anne Massy became very involved with the Dublin Field Club, where she acquired an excellent knowledge of birds and marine mollusks. Because of her in-depth knowledge of the latter group, she was offered a "temporary" post in the fisheries department. This temporary post continued until her death in 1931. She produced a series of important monographs on the molluscan fauna of the Irish coasts. She also worked on the Holothurians and Brachiopods of different parts of the world. Her taxonomic work on Antarctic molluscans was also important. Massy continued her interest in Irish birds, being the secretary of the Irish Society for the Protection of Birds. She served on its committee until her death.   JH/MBO

PRIMARY SOURCES

Massy, Anne L. *Mollusca.* Part 1. London: British Museum, 1915.

———. *Mollusca: Cephalopoda.* Part 2. London: British Museum, 1916.

———. *Mollusca: Eupteropoda.* Part 3. London: British Museum, 1920.

———. *Mollusca: Gastropoda Thecosomata Gymnoaomata.* Cambridge: Cambridge University Press, 1932.

SECONDARY SOURCES
Nature 128 (1931): 59. Obituary notice.

STANDARD SOURCES
Praeger.

MASTERS, SYBILLA (RIGHTON) (d. 1720)

U.S. inventor. Born to Sarah and William Righton. Six siblings. Lived in Burlington, colony of West New Jersey. Married Thomas Masters (between 1693 and 1696). Four children: Sarah, Mary (Mercy?), Thomas, and William. Professional experience: invented a maize-stamping mill and a new way of working in straw and palmetto leaf. Died 23 August 1720, probably in Philadelphia.

Little is known of Masters's early life. She may have been born in Bermuda, for her Quaker father emigrated from there in 1687. It is thought that she spent her early life on her father's plantation in Burlington Township of the banks of the Delaware. She married a prosperous Quaker merchant. The couple moved to Philadelphia, where he was an alderman, mayor, and provincial councilor. In addition to raising her four children, she made numerous inventions. She apparently went to London in 1712 to obtain patents on two of her inventions. In 1715, letters of patent were granted to Thomas Masters for Sybilla's invention for cleaning and curing Indian corn. Her second patent, again in her husband's name, was granted on 18 February 1716, for a new way of working in straw.

Sybilla Masters's inventions of a maize-stamping mill and a new way of working in straw and palmetto leaf do not sound as significant today as they were in the eighteenth century. Straw hats and bonnets were important articles of clothing for both women and men. After the War of 1812, straw hats and bonnets became a very important commercial venture. Sybilla's husband was well-known, and his prominence accounts for the fact that her British patents of 1715 and 1716 were issued in his name. Not only was Masters an inventor, she was an entrepreneur as well. She gained a monopoly on importing palmetto leaf to England. She also marketed her patented hats and bonnets in London.

JH/MBO

STANDARD SOURCES
Mothers and Daughters; NAW (article by Frederick B. Tolles).

MATEER, FLORENCE EDNA (1887–?)

U.S. psychologist. Born 6 December 1887 in Lancaster, Pa. Educated Clark University (A.M., 1914; Ph.D., 1916). Professional experience: public schools of Delaware and Pennsylvania, teacher (1906–1910); New Jersey Training School for Feeble Minded Boys and Girls, assistant psychologist (1911–1913); Massachusetts School for the Feeble Minded, psychologist (1916–1918); Ohio Bureau of Juvenile Research, psycho-clinician (1918–1921); laboratory school, Columbus, psychologist, and clinical practice (1921–1927); Merryheart Schools, director and consulting psycho-clinician (1927–1946); Claremont College Graduate School, professor of clinical psychology (1947–1955), emerita professor (from 1955); Pomona, Calif., public schools, clinical psychologist (from 1947). Honors and memberships: American Psychological Association, Fellow; Ohio Academy; International Council of Women Psychologists; Association of Psychologists, Southern California. Death date unknown.

Florence Mateer taught school for four years to support herself in college. While she was working on her master's degree, she served as a psychologist at the Massachusetts school for the feeble-minded. Once she earned her doctorate she worked in a number of schools in a variety of positions. In 1947, she became professor of clinical psychology at Claremont College Graduate School, where she remained until her retirement.

Mateer's research was on somato-behavioral syndromes, hypothyroidism, hypocalcemia myotomia, and hypopituitarism.

JH/MBO

PRIMARY SOURCES
Mateer, Florence. *Child Behavior.* New York: R. G. Badger, 1918.

———. *The Unstable Child.* New York: Appleton, 1924.

———. *Glands and Efficient Behavior.* New York: Appleton-Century, 1935.

STANDARD SOURCES
AMS 3–8, S&B 9.

MATEYKO, GLADYS MARY (1921–1968)

U.S. biologist. Born 22 August 1921 in Brooklyn, N.Y. Married (1960). Two children. Educated Hunter College (A.B., 1932); Mount Holyoke College (M.A., 1944); New York University (Ph.D. in zoology, 1953). Professional experience: Mount Holyoke, assistant in plant science (1942–1944); American Cyanamid Company, Lederle Laboratory, microbiologist in analysis department (1944–1945); Hunter College, instructor (1946–1948); Brooklyn College, instructor (1947–1948); New York University, fellow (1948–1950); Brookhaven National Laboratory, research associate in radiation biology (1950–1951); New York University, cancer cytologist (1952; 1955–1956); Runyon fellow, cancer research (1952–1955); New York University, assistant professor in biology (1956–1961), associate professor (1961–1965), professor (1965–1968); Lerner Marine Lab, American Museum Natural History, researcher (summers); Marine Biological Laboratories, Woods Hole, researcher (summers, 1957–1966). Honors and memberships: New York Academy of Sciences, Fellow; American Association for the Advancement of Science; American Microscopic Society; American Society of Cell Biology; American Association for Cancer Research; Society of General Physiologists; Growth Society; Sigma Xi; Phi Beta Kappa; Phi Sigma. Died 1968.

Much of Gladys Mateyko's work involved cancer research. She was a microbiologist in industry after she earned her master's degree at Mount Holyoke College. She left the American Cyanamid Co. to become an instructor at Hunter College. For two years she did not have a job; in 1950, she became a research associate in radiation biology at the Brookhaven National Laboratory. She then worked in cancer cytology at New York University and was a Runyon fellow in cancer research. In 1956, Mateyko was appointed assistant professor and from then progressed up the academic ladder to professor in nine years.

Mateyko spent her summers working at biological stations and marine laboratories. She studied the cytophysiology of living tumor cells, intracellular stratification, isolation, and isopycnic cushioning. She also worked on colchicine-induced tumors and chimeras of tomato plants. In addition, she studied radiation effects on hypophyseal cytology and hormones and the cytology of Lucke tumor. Mateyko was a Fellow of the New York Academy of Sciences and a member of the American Association for the Advancement of Science, American Microscopic Society, the American Society of Cell Biology, the American Association for Cancer Research, the Society of General Physiologists, the Growth Society, Sigma Xi, Phi Beta Kappa, and Phi Sigma.

JH/MBO

STANDARD SOURCES
AMS P&B 10–11; Debus.

MATHER, SARAH (fl. 1845)
U.S. inventor. Flourished 1845. Married. At least one daughter. Professional experience: patented submarine telescope and lamp.

Sarah Mather's patent on a submarine telescope and lamp was one of fourteen issued to women from 1841 to 1851. She patented these devices in 1845. They were intended to allow ship's hulls to be examined so that defects could be diagnosed without removing the ship from water. The benefits from such an invention are obvious: both labor and money

would be saved. Matilda Gage observed that Mather's telescope for viewing the depths of the ocean was even more wonderful than the invention of the astronomical telescope for viewing the heavens.

JH/MBO

SECONDARY SOURCES
Gage, Matilda. *Woman as Inventor.* Fayetteville: New York State Woman Suffrage Association, 1870.
Tarbell, Ida C. "Women as Inventors." *The Chautauquan* 7, no. 6 (March 1887): 355–357.

STANDARD SOURCES
Mothers and Daughters; Mozans.

MATHIAS, MILDRED ESTHER (1906–)
U.S. botanist. Born 19 September 1906 in Sappington, Mo., to Julia Hannah (Fawcett) and John Oliver Mathias. Married Gerald L. Hassler (1930). Four children. Educated Washington University, St. Louis (A.B., 1926; M.S., 1927; Ph.D., 1929). Professional experience: Missouri Botanical Garden (1929–1930); New York Botanical Garden Research Associate (1932–1936); University of California, Berkeley (1937–1942); University of California, Los Angeles, faculty (1947), professor of botany (from 1962). Honors and memberships: Woman of Science Award, University of California; Los Angeles Medical Auxiliary (1963); Nature Conservancy, national award (1964); Washington University Alumni Association Award (1966); American Society of Plant Taxonomists; Western Society of Naturalists; International Association for Plant Taxonomy; International Society for Horticultural Science; American Institute for the Biological Sciences; American Society of Naturalists; Botanical Society of America; Organization for Tropical Studies (Board of Directors); Nature Conservancy (Board of Governors).

Mildred Mathias moved from a small Missouri town to New York and then California. This move represented an important change for Mathias, for she grew up in Missouri, earned all of her degrees there, and had her first professional position there. After she married in 1930, she did not hold a position for two years, but then got a job at the New York Botanical Garden as a research associate. Although she and her husband had four children, she continued to work outside of the home. The family moved to California, where she worked at the University of California, Berkeley. They then moved to the University of California, Los Angeles, where she was on the faculty and promoted to professor of botany in 1962. From 1956, she was also the director of the University of California Botanical Gardens. Her talent with botanical gardens was in great demand. She was a member of the advisory committee for the Hunt Botanical Library (from 1961), Santa Barbara Botanical Garden (1951), and the

Huntington Botanical Gardens (1964). She was also on numerous boards and committees.

Mathias's major research was on the taxonomy of flowering plants of the family Umbelliferae. She concentrated on those plants that grew in the western hemisphere. She published numerous papers on these plants.   JH/MBO

STANDARD SOURCES
AMS 6–8; Debus.

MATHISEN, KAROLINE (1898–?)

Norwegian physician. Born 5 January 1898 in Troms, Norway. Eleven siblings. Educated Oslo University (pharmacy examination, 1919; medical degree, 1925). Professional experience: worked in pharmacy (1919–1925); assistant physician (locum tenens) for district physicians (from 1925). Death date unknown.

Karoline Mathisen, the eleventh of twelve children, was born north of the Arctic Circle in the capital of northern Norway, Troms. Her father was a teacher and later a banker in Troms, a town that had a long tradition of musical and cultural interests. Especially fond of the sciences and mathematics in secondary school, Mathisen decided to study pharmacy rather than medicine at Oslo University because her brother-in-law was a pharmacist in Hammerfest and this would allow her to study pharmacy free. After she passed her examinations in 1919, she worked in a pharmacy, but began to study medicine as well. Although it was a difficult time for her financially, Mathisen graduated from medical school in 1925. Her first position was as *locum tenens* for a district physician. In this job she had to travel by boat and horse and trap to visit her patients who lived along two long fjords and eight valleys. She later was *locum tenens* for a coastal district where travel was by boat on the open sea. Her next position was on the Oslo fjord in a little town of Vestfold. She became interested in various techniques to treat tuberculosis at this time.   KM

PRIMARY SOURCES
Mathisen, Karoline. In Hellstedt, *Autobiographies.*

MATIKASHVILI, NINA (fl. early 20th century)

Russian protozologist and veterinary surgeon. Professional experience: Georgia Zooveterinary Research Institute, head.

Nina Matikashvili was an expert on ixoliid ticks and wrote more than fifty works on the subject. She was a veterinary surgeon who became head of the Arachnology and Protozoology Laboratory at the Georgia Zooveterinary Research Institute.

SECONDARY SOURCES
Macksey, Joan, and Kenneth Macksey. *The Book of Women's Achievements.* New York: Stein and Day, 1976.

MATILDE (fl. ca. 1232)

British healer. Flourished 1232 in Wallingford, Berkshire.

All that is known about Matilde la Leche is that she was assessed in 1232 at twenty pence. As this assessment was rather high, she apparently had a good trade.   JH/MBO

SECONDARY SOURCES
Talbot, Charles H. and Eugene Ashby Hammond. *Medical Practitioners in Medieval England: A Biographical Register.* London: Wellcome Medical Historical Library, 1965. Matilde mentioned on page 211.

MAUNDER, ANNIE SCOTT DILL RUSSELL (1868–1947)

Irish/English astronomer. Born 1868 in Strabane, County Tyrone, Ireland, to Rev. William Andrew Russell and Hester Nesbitt Dill. Brother, J. Dill Russell. Married Edward Walter Maunder. No children. Educated Victoria College, Belfast; Girton College, Cambridge (Senior Optime, Mathematical Tripos, 1889; Pfeiffer Student for Research, 1897–1898). Professional experience: Royal Observatory, Greenwich, computer (1891–1895, 1915–1920); Journal of the British Astronomical Association, editor (1894–1896, 1917–1930).

Annie Russell was born in Strabane, County Tyrone in northern Ireland. Details are missing about her early life, but her interest in astronomy may have stemmed from her childhood, for her brother, J. Dill Russell, also became an astronomer. Her early education at home and at the Victoria School and College, Belfast, left her unprepared for the rigorous courses at Girton College, where she matriculated in 1886. By studying hard, she overcame her deficit and won the highest mathematical honor available to women, Senior Optime in the Mathematical Tripos.

When Russell left Girton, she took a position as a mathematics teacher at the Ladies' College, Jersey, but found teaching school faintly disagreeable. She learned of a possible vacancy for a "lady computer" at the Royal Greenwich Observatory and, although the pay was discouragingly low, she took the position. While she was employed as a lady computer in the Greenwich Observatory, examining and measuring daily sunspot photographs, she met Edward Maunder, head of the solar photography department and founder of the British Astronomical Association (BAA). They worked together on the association's journal; she was its first editor, from 1894 to 1896, and served again as editor from 1917 to 1930. Russell and Maunder married in 1895 and worked together on astronomical projects. The BAA encouraged amateur astronomers, including women, and Maunder was as enthusiastic about its potential as was her husband.

Maunder made many contributions to astronomy, including a photographic survey of the Milky Way (with support from a research grant from Girton College) and eclipse observations and photographs, made during BAA eclipse expeditions. Although much of her work was in collaboration with her husband, she worked independently of him as well. The sun was her favorite subject. She theorized that the earth influences the numbers and the areas of sunspots and that sunspot frequency decreases from the eastern to the western edge of the sun's disk as viewed from the earth. She postulated that changes in the sun trigger climatic changes on the earth. Maunder was also interested in the history of astronomy, particularly in early records of the constellations, and published numerous papers.

In 1892 Annie Russell and two other women had been proposed for fellowship in the Royal Astronomical Society. They failed, however, to receive the necessary three-fourths vote for election. When the BAA, a national organization of amateur astronomers, was formed, it welcomed female members, making it possible for Russell to participate in an astronomical organization. Annie Russell Maunder's career illustrates the involvement of nineteenth-century British women in astronomy. She was far from typical, however, in that she worked at Greenwich in a paid position.   MBO

PRIMARY SOURCES

Maunder, Annie. "Some Experiments on the Limits of Vision for Lines and Spots as Applicable to the Question of the Actuality of the Canals on Mars." *Journal of the British Astronomical Association* (1903).

———. With E. W. Maunder. *The Heavens and Their Story.* London: R. Culley, [1908].

———. "An Apparent Influence of the Earth on the Numbers and Areas of Sun-Spots in the Cycle 1889–1901." *Monthly Notices of the Royal Astronomical Society* 67: 451–475.

———. "Iranian Migrations before History." *Scientia* 19 (1916): 115–124.

Maunder's papers are located in the Archives of the British Astronomical Association, the Archives of the Royal Astronomical Society, and the Archives of the Royal Greenwich Observatory.

SECONDARY SOURCES

Kidwell, Peggy Aldrich. "Women Astronomers in Britain, 1780–1930." *Isis* 75 (1984): 534–546.

"Maunder, Annie Russell." *Journal of the British Astronomical Association* 57 (1947): 238. Obituary notice.

McKim, Richard, ed. *The History of the British Astronomical Association: The First Fifty Years.* 2d ed. London: The British Astronomical Association, 1989.

Meadows, A. J. *Greenwich Observatory.* Vol. 2: *Recent History, 1836–1975.* London: Taylor and Francis, 1975.

STANDARD SOURCES

Notable; Ogilvie 1986.

MAURY, ANTONIA CAETANA DE PAIVA (1866–1952)

U.S. astronomer. Born 1866 in Cold Springs, N.Y., to Virginia (Draper) and Rev. Mytton Maury. Two siblings. Educated at home; Vassar College (B.A., 1887). Professional experience: Harvard College Observatory, staff member (1888–1896, 1918–1935); Draper Park Observatory Museum, Hastings-on-Hudson, N.Y., curator (1935–1938). Died in Dobbs Ferry, N.Y.

Antonia Maury was born in Cold Springs, New York, the oldest of three children. Although her father was a minister, by avocation he was a naturalist and editor of a geographical magazine. Maury also inherited an interest in science from the other side of the family, for her mother, Virginia Draper, was the sister of Henry Draper (1837–1882), an amateur astronomer who made major contributions in the field of astronomical photography and spectroscopy. Her younger sister, CARLOTTA, became a noted paleontologist. When Maury graduated from Vassar College, her father asked Edward Pickering, director of the Harvard College Observatory, to provide employment for her. Doubting that a Vassar graduate would be satisfied with twenty-five-cent-an-hour pay, Pickering, nevertheless, offered her a job. Her first task was to classify the bright northern stars according to their spectra.

Pickering seemed satisfied with Maury's work, for he wrote to MARY ANNA PALMER DRAPER, widow of Henry Draper and benefactor of the Harvard Observatory, commending her niece's skill. Maury, as Pickering had predicted, became bored with the routine of the work and dissatisfied with the existing system of classification. She left the observatory in 1891 for a teaching position, but did not stay away for long, because she had left some of her work unfinished. She wanted to receive credit when the results of the project in which she was involved were published, so she returned to the observatory periodically.

Maury chafed under the constant supervision of Pickering. Her aunt Draper regarded Maury as a prima donna, and urged Pickering "to treat her as if she were a stranger, on a strictly business basis." Draper predicted that once she had finished her research, "we will bid her goodbye without regret" (Jones and Boyd, 398). Eventually Maury finished her star catalogue, which was published in 1897 in volume 28, part 1, of the *Annals of the Harvard College Observatory*. For the next twenty years she avoided the Harvard Observatory. She was a visiting teacher and lecturer in various cities and colleges, and tutored private students.

In 1918, Maury returned to the observatory as a research associate and resumed work on a subject that had always fascinated her, the spectroscopic binaries. After Pickering died in 1919, she found a more congenial superior in Harlow Shapley, director from 1920 to 1952. Volume 84, parts 6 and 8, of the Observatory *Annals* (1933) contains the results of her later research. After her retirement from Harvard in 1935, Maury served for three years as curator of the museum that had been created from her uncle Henry Draper's home in Hastings-on-Hudson, New York. More time was available for the pursuit of her other interests, ornithology, natural history in general, and conservation. Maury died at Dobbs Ferry, New York, at the age of eighty-five.

Pickering and Maury had personal differences that hindered her creativity. Pickering wanted meticulous followers, not innovators, and Maury, who was a free spirit, irritated him. Free spirit though she was, there was nothing careless about her methods as an astronomer. In her work on stellar spectra, she discovered deficiencies in Pickering's system and invented a scheme of classification of her own. The Danish astronomer Ejnar Hertzsprung (1873–1967) praised Maury's 1897 catalogue and wrote to Pickering that her system of subdivisions represented a major advance. Pickering refused to acknowledge its value. In 1943 the merits of Maury's system were at last recognized. She received the Annie J. Cannon Prize from the American Astronomical Society for her contribution, now considered an essential step in the development of theoretical astrophysics.

Maury's later work on spectroscopic binaries also became a classic study. A highly skilled observer, she made important contributions to sidereal astronomy. Her very quick mind was capable of going beyond observation; and with additional training in mathematics and more freedom, she might have been a creator of theories.   JH/MBO

PRIMARY SOURCES

Maury, Antonia. *Spectra of Bright Stars Photographed with the 11-Inch Draper Telescope as a Part of the Henry Draper Memorial and Discussed by Antonia C. Maury under the Direction of Edward C. Pickering. Annals of the Astronomical Observatory of Harvard College* 28, pt. 1 (1897).

———. *The Spectral Changes of Beta Lyrae. Annals of the Astronomical Observatory of Harvard College* 84, no. 8 (1933).

SECONDARY SOURCES

Hoffleit, Dorrit. *Sky and Telescope* 11 (March 1952): 106. Obituary notice.

STANDARD SOURCES
AMS 1–8; *DSB;* Jones and Boyd; *Notable;* Ogilvie 1986.

MAURY, CARLOTTA JOAQUINA (1874–1938)

U.S. paleontologist. Born 6 January 1874 at Hastings-on-Hudson, N.Y. to Virginia (Draper) and Rev. Mytton Maury. Two siblings. Educated Radcliffe College (1891–1894); Cornell University (Ph.B., 1896; Schuyler Fellow, 1898; Ph.D., 1902); Columbia University (special work, various times); Jardin des Plantes, Paris (1899–1900). Professional experience: Erasmus High School, Brooklyn, N.Y., teacher (1900–1901); Columbia University, Department of Paleontology, assistant (1904–1906); Louisiana Geological Survey, paleontologist (1907–1909); Barnard and Columbia Colleges, lecturer in geology (1909–1912); Huguenot College, University of the Cape of Good Hope, South Africa, professor of geology and zoology (1912–1915). Died 3 January 1938 in Yonkers, N.Y.

The younger sister of the astronomer ANTONIA MAURY, Carlotta Maury was a vivacious, outgoing woman whose interests were not confined to science. She was active in the Episcopalian Church, fond of philosophy (particularly the works of Plato), and an entertaining writer.

Maury was of the sixth generation of Maurys in the United States and the fourth child born to her parents. Her father, Reverend Mytton Maury, was an Episcopalian priest and the editor of *Maury's Geographical Series* (1875–1895). She had two siblings who survived infancy, Antonia Caetana Maury and John William Draper (his birth name was John Draper Maury; he later took the name of his maternal grandfather). Many of Maury's relatives were well known, including her first cousin twice removed, Matthew Fontaine Maury (1806–1873), the famous American hydrographer, and John William Draper (1811–1882), her maternal grandfather, who was a pioneer physicist.

Maury's father took daily walks with the children and, according to daughter Antonia, taught Carlotta the names of all the trees before she could talk plainly. He was fascinated by natural objects and taught his children to respect and be in awe of nature. Virginia Draper, her mother, was talented artistically and also transmitted a love for nature to her children, who were taught at home until they were in their teens. Maury had a varied university experience. She attended Radcliffe College, Columbia University, the University of Paris, and Cornell University, where she received the degrees of bachelor of philosophy and doctor of philosophy.

After teaching in several universities, Maury got involved in her real love, paleontological expeditions. She remained active in paleontological research for much of her life. She was paleontologist for Arthur Clifford Veatch's geological expedition to Venezuela (1910–1911), organized and conducted the

Maury expedition to the Dominican Republic (1916), was consulting paleontologist and stratigrapher for the Venezuelan division of the Royal Dutch Shell Petroleum Company (intermittently from 1910 until her death), and was official paleontologist to Brazil (from 1914 until her death). She specialized in the study of Antillean, Venezuelan, and Brazilian fossil faunas and determined the ages and relationships of the various formations.

Maury produced numerous papers and reports during her career, most of which were concerned with her specialty, Antillean, Venezuelan, and Brazilian stratigraphy and fossil faunas. Many of her specimens were sent to the American Museum of Natural History. She was a Fellow of the Geological Society of America, a member of the American Association for the Advancement of Science and of the American Geographical Society, and a corresponding member of the Brazilian Academy of Sciences.   JH/MBO

PRIMARY SOURCES

Maury, Carlotta. *A Comparison of the Oligocene of Western Europe and the Southern United States.* Ithaca, N.Y.: Cornell University Press, 1902. "A thesis presented to the Faculty of Cornell University for the degree of Doctor of Philosophy."

———. "New Oligocene Shells from Florida." *Bulletin of American Paleontology* 21 (1910). This forty-six-page report challenged the fossils attributed to the Oligocene by Dr. Dall and the United States Geological Survey. After Maury's work they were attributed to the Miocene.

———. "Santo Domingo Type Sections and Fossils. Part I. Description of the Maury Expedition and of the Species Collected." *Bulletin of American Paleontology* 29 (1917): 251 pp. Includes three photo engravings of localities, thirty-seven plates of fossils, and many new species. This expedition was carried on when Maury was a Sarah Berliner Fellow in Geology.

———. "Santo Domingo Type Sections and Fossils." Part II. Stratigraphy. *Bulletin of American Paleontology* 30 (1917): 43 pp. This paper describes three formations in the Yaqui Valley in descending geological order. It includes the first differentiation of Oligocene and Miocene beds in the Antillean area.

———. "Recent Mollusca of the Gulf of Mexico and Pleistocene and Pliocene Species from the Gulf States." *Bulletin of American Paleontology* 38 (1922): 142 pp.

———. "New Genera and New Species of Fossil Terrestrial Mollusca from Brazil." *American Museum Novitates* 764 (1935): 15 pp. Includes fifteen figures.

SECONDARY SOURCES

Elder, Eleanor S. "Women in Early Geology." *Journal of Geological Education* 30, no. 5 (1982): 287–293.

Moraes, Luciano Jacques de. "Dra Carlotta J. Maury." *Mineração e metalurgia* 12 (1938): 375–376. Includes silhouette.

Reeds, Chester A. "Memorial to Carlotta Joaquina Maury." *Proceedings of the Geological Society of America* (May 1939): 157–168. Includes a bibliography of Maury's work and a portrait.

STANDARD SOURCES

AMS 1–5; *Cyclopaedia; Notable.*

MAVER, MARY EUGENIE (1891–1975)

U.S. biochemist. Born 25 September 1891 in Detroit, Mich. Educated University of Chicago (B.S., 1914; Ph.D. in organic chemistry, 1926). Professional experience: Sprague Memorial Institute, researcher (1914–1924); Smith Fellow in biochemistry (1926–1930); National Cancer Institute, biochemist to senior biochemist (1930–1961); civilian researcher with U.S Army (1918). Died 1975.

Mary Maver earned both her bachelor's and doctoral degrees from the University of Chicago. Her research interests were in biochemistry, and she did research on the isolation of proteinase cathepsin from tissues. She also worked on serodiagnostic tests for cancer, and nuclear metabolism of tumor tissues. She was a member of the Biological and Chemical societies and the New York Academy of Sciences. She lived in Washington, D.C., after retirement.   JH/MBO

STANDARD SOURCES

AMS 5–8, P 9, P&B 10–11.

MAXWELL, MARTHA DARTT (1831–1881)

U.S. naturalist. Born 1831 in Dartt's Settlement, Tioga County, Pa., to Amy and Spencer Dartt. Two half-sisters. Married James Maxwell. Six stepchildren; one daughter. Educated Oberlin College (1851–1852); Lawrence College, Wis.; MIT (ca. 1876). Professional experience: collected and studied habits of birds and mammals; taxidermy. Died 31 May 1881.

In response to a letter from mammalogist E. Raymond Hall asking for the name of the first woman mammalogist, HILDA GRINNELL answered that if one eliminated the qualification of publication it would be Martha Maxwell. The life of this independent woman was full of adventure as well as tragedy. She came by her independence naturally, from her grandmother, Abigail, who had purchased a farm in Tioga County, Pennsylvania, and refused to return to her husband for several years. Abigail's daughter, Amy, married Spencer Dartt, and they had one child, Martha. Shortly after Martha's birth, Spencer Dartt died of scarlet fever. Martha's mother, weakened both emotionally and physically by the experience, left Abigail to raise Martha in her early years. Amy married Josiah Dartt, her late husband's cousin, when Martha was nine years old, and the family, including Abigail and three of her brothers, went west. However, they only made it as far as Baraboo, Wisconsin, where the family settled. Along with other pioneers, the independent Abigail succumbed to malaria. Martha's stepfather encouraged Martha to attend college. She went to Oberlin College, where her courses included Latin grammar and arithmetic. However, the cost proved prohibitive, and she was forced to drop out of school after a year. She returned to her family in Wisconsin, where she attended Lawrence College. At Lawrence, she met her future husband, the wealthy widower father of one of her friends. James Maxwell had six children, some of whom were as old as she, and she at first declined his offer of marriage. She eventually agreed, but the marriage was never a happy one. James Maxwell lost his fortune, and in order to make ends meet, the Maxwells went to Colorado to seek their fortune in the gold fields; they left their two-year-old daughter, Mabel, behind in Wisconsin. Bad luck seemed to plague this enterprise. In Denver, the boarding house that Martha had built was destroyed in a fire that consumed much of the town. She was able to buy some land with the small savings she had accumulated, and she and James moved to a cabin on the property. However, a German claim jumper occupied the property while they were gone. When she went to try to convince him to leave, she saw his collection of taxidermy specimens and asked him to teach her how to stuff birds. He refused, fearing that she would do a better job than he because women were considered better with their hands. In a letter to her family, she asked them to send her books on taxidermy. Returning to Wisconsin to be with Mabel, Maxwell accepted a position at the Baraboo Collegiate Institute, where her job was to assist in preparing mounted specimens of birds and mammals for the zoology department. She remained there for five years and then returned to Colorado to begin applying the skills she had learned.

Maxwell began a correspondence with a number of scientists, including secretary of the Smithsonian, Joseph Henry, whom she wrote in 1869 about textbooks that might help her in identifying specimens, and naturalists Robert Ridgeway and Elliot Coues. She sent Ridgeway a specimen of screech owl for identification that she had shot in her yard. She confirmed the existence of the black-footed ferret that had been described much earlier by Audubon.

Although her collecting never was done in a systematic manner, Maxwell managed to acquire and prepare so many specimens that they could no longer be accommodated in her home. In order to house these specimens and to make money for Mabel's college expenses, she opened a museum. This museum was not a financial success, but she saw an opportunity in the 1876 Centennial. The Colorado legislature asked her to exhibit as a part of the Colorado pavilion. Although the legislature had offered to reimburse her for transporting the specimens, it failed to live up to its promise. She had hoped to make money by selling postcards and minerals, but financially the operation was a failure. Nevertheless, her exhibit secured her reputation. In her panorama the specimens varied from the smallest birds to the largest mammals from Colorado, all of which she had mounted herself, grouped in a diorama of naturalistic surroundings. Both Coues and Ridgeway prepared annotated lists of the birds and mammals shown in the exhibition. The fate of the specimens was unfortunate. Since she could not afford to have them returned or properly cared for they fell into the hands of an individual who allowed them to disintegrate. Once she was able to salvage the collection, she found that they had been hopelessly damaged. At that point, estranged from her husband, with a daughter who showed no interest in natural history and who had resented her mother's involvement in the field, she, too, seemed to disintegrate. She died 1881 of blood poisoning, supposedly from an ovarian tumor.

JH/MBO

SECONDARY SOURCES

Benson, M. *Martha Maxwell: Rocky Mountain Naturalist.* Lincoln: University of Nebraska Press, 1986.

Dartt, Mary. *On the Plains and among the Peaks; or, How Mrs. Maxwell Made Her Natural History Collection.* Philadelphia: Claxton, Remsen, and Hoffelfinger, 1879.

DeLapp, M. "Pioneer Woman Naturalist." *Colorado Quarterly* 13 (1964): 91–96.

Henderson, J. T. "A Pioneer Venture in Habitat Grouping." *Proceedings of the American Association of Museums* 9 (1915): 87–91.

Schantz, Violet S. "Mrs. M. A. Maxwell, a Pioneer Mammalogist." *Journal of Mammalogy* 24 (1943): 464–466.

Stein, Barbara R. "Women in Mammalogy: The Early Years." *Journal of Mammalogy* 77, no. 3 (1996).

STANDARD SOURCES
Bonta.

MAY, CAROLINE REBECCA (1809–1874)

British botanical artist. Born 1809. Lived in South Petherton, Somerset. Professional experience: drew Guernsey plants (between 1858 and 1862). Died December 1874.

Amateur botanist and painter Caroline May drew plants of Guernsey. Her drawings are found in D. McClintock's *Wild Flowers of Guernsey* and R. Mabey's *Flowers of May: Selected from Unpublished Flora of Caroline May.* Her drawings are in the possession of her family.
JH/MBO

PRIMARY SOURCES

Mabey, R. *Flowers of May: Selected from Unpublished Flora of Caroline May.* N.p.: Collins and Brown, 1990.

SECONDARY SOURCES

Country Living (November 1990): 111.

STANDARD SOURCES

Desmond.

MAYER, MARIA GOEPPERT (1906–1972)

See Goeppert Mayer, Maria Gertud Käte.

MAYO, CLARA ALEXANDRA (WEISS) (1931–1981)

Austrian/U.S. social psychologist. Born 13 September 1931 in Linz, Austria, to Maria and Joseph Weiss. Married (1953; divorced 1978). Educated New York City public schools; Hunter High School; Cornell University (B.A., 1953); Wellesley College (M.A., 1955); Clark University (Ph.D., 1959). Professional experience: Veterans Administration Hospital, Brockton, Mass., social psychology trainee (1959–1960); Boston Veterans Administration Hospital, research social psychologist (1960–1964); Boston University, lecturer (1961), assistant professor (1964–1968), associate professor (1968–1974), director of graduate program in social and personality psychology (1970–1974), professor (from 1974), Afro-American studies, director of graduate program (from 1978). Died 21 November 1981.

Even though her mother was Catholic and her father only part Jewish, Clara Weiss's family recognized that they must leave Austria immediately in 1938. Clara and her mother went to Paris to wait for Joseph Weiss to catch up with them. They stayed as refugees in southern France for a while trying to obtain help to immigrate to the United States. Clara learned French in school and subsequently learned English when they arrived in the United States. They settled in New York City, where Clara attended public school. After graduating from Hunter High School, she went to Cornell University, where she majored in philosophy. However, she was a research assistant to Urie Bronfenbrenner, who introduced her to psychology. As Clara Mayo, she further explored psychology through a master's program at Wellesley. After she received her master's degree, Mayo was admitted to the excellent social psychology department at Clark University, where she earned her doctorate.

After working for several years at Veterans Administration hospitals, Mayo finally returned to the university setting that she loved. While working at the Boston Veterans Administration Hospital, she became a part-time lecturer at Boston University. She progressed through the academic ranks, and held several administrative positions.

Mayo's research was based on the postulate that knowledge must produce usable findings. She believed that social psychology had the potential to redress social problems. Her own work addressed racism and sexism. She always considered herself on the margins of her field—an outsider, although others would probably not agree.

Mayo was president of the New England Psychological Association for 1966–1967, a Fellow of the American Psychological Association from Division 9, and president of the Society for the Psychological Study of Social Issues for 1981–1982. She died suddenly before she was able to give her presidential address to the American Psychological Association. She was married for twenty-five years and then divorced. She had no children.   KM

PRIMARY SOURCES

Mayo, Clara. With J. Teele and E. Jackson. *Family Experiences in Operation Exodus: The Bussing of Negro Children.* New York: Community Mental Health Journal, monograph 3, 1967.

———. "Achievement and Self-Concept in Women." In *Women Today! Tomorrow?*, ed. E. T. Nickerson and E. S. Williams. Dubuque, Iowa: Kendall/Hunt, 1975.

———, ed. With H. Henley. *Gender and Nonverbal Behavior.* New York: Springer-Verlag, 1981.

———. "Training for Positive Marginality." In *Applied Social Psychology Annual*, ed. L. Bickman. Vol. 3. Beverly Hills, Calif.: Sage, 1982.

STANDARD SOURCES

AMS 10–13; O'Connell and Russo 1990.

MCAVOY, BLANCHE (1885–1976)

U.S. plant ecologist and educator. Born 11 September 1885 in Mitchell Lawrence County, Ind., to Mary (McIntire) and George McAvoy. Educated University of Cincinnati (B.A., 1909); The Ohio State University (M.A., 1912); University of Chicago (Ph.D., 1930). Professional experience: Kennedy Heights elementary school, teacher (1909–1911); Watterman Hall high school, Sycamore, Ill., teacher (1914–1915); Mt. Healthy high school, teacher (1915–1918); Wyoming, high school teacher (1918–1921); The Ohio State University, fellow in department of botany (1911–1914); Ball State Teachers College, instructor (1921–1925); Illinois State Normal University, instructor (1926–1931), assistant professor (1931–1945), associate professor (1945–1951), professor (1951–1954), professor emerita (1954–1976). Died 23 October 1976 in Tulsa, Okla.

Blanche McAvoy spent most of her teaching career at Illinois State Normal Institution, where she progressed through the academic ranks to professor. Her research interests were in ecology, cytology, and the taxonomy of spermatophytes, especially roses and their history. On retiring from Illinois Normal Institution she moved to Cincinnati and then to Tulsa, Oklahoma, where she died. She held memberships in a number of professional societies.

McAvoy had a varied research career. Her master's thesis was on reduction division in *Fuchsia* (1912). While she was a teaching fellow, she published a paper on reduction division in *Oenothera bienni*. She also assisted John Schaffner on his flora of Ohio project, preparing papers on the Liliales and the panicums. For her dissertation at the University of Chicago under Henry C. Cowles, she studied the Bella Coola region in the coast mountains of British Columbia.

JH/MBO

PRIMARY SOURCES
McAvoy, Blanche. "The Reduction Division in *Fuchsia*." *Ohio Naturalist* 13 (1912): 1–18.
———. "The Reduction Division in the Microsporocytes of *Oenothera biennis*." *Ohio Naturalist* 14 (1913): 189–197.
———. "Liliales of Ohio." *Ohio Naturalist* 13 (1913): 109–130; 14: 204.
———. "An Ecological Study of the Bella Coola Region." *Botanical Gazette* 92 (1931): 141–171.

SECONDARY SOURCES
Stuckey, Ronald L. "McAvoy, Blanche." Unpublished notes.

STANDARD SOURCES
AMS 5–10; *DIB; Leaders in American Science,* vol. 7; Stuckey; *WW in American Education,* vol. 23; *WW of American Women; WW in the Midwest,* vol. 9.

MCBRIDE, KATHARINE ELIZABETH (1904–1976)

U.S. psychologist and educator. Born 14 May 1904 in Philadelphia, Pa., to Sally Hulley (Neals) and Thomas Canning. Educated Bryn Mawr College (A.B., 1925; A.M., 1927; Ph.D., 1932); Columbia University, graduate work in neurology (1928). Professional experience: Bryn Mawr College, part-time reader in psychology (1925), lecturer in psychology (1935–1936), assistant professor (1936–1938), associate professor (1938–1940), president (1942–1970); psychology research worker with Theodore Weisenburg (1929–1934); Radcliffe College, dean (1940–1942). Died 7 April 1976.

Katharine McBride earned all three of her degrees at Bryn Mawr College and held all of her teaching positions (except for a two-year period as dean at Radcliffe) there as well. McBride went on to become the fourth president of Bryn Mawr. She continued to do psychological research even after she became an administrator.

McBride's first major research project was with Dr. Theodore Weisenburg and resulted in a coauthored book, *Aphasia.* She published a second book with ANNE ROE and Weisenburg in 1936. She was a member of the American Psychological Association, the American Association of Applied Psychology, and the American Association of University Women.

JH/MBO

PRIMARY SOURCES
McBride, Katharine. With Theodore Weisenburg. *Aphasia.* New York: Commonwealth Fund, 1935.
———. With Anne Roe and Theodore Weisenburg. *Adult Intelligence.* New York: Commonwealth Fund, 1936.

STANDARD SOURCES
Current Biography 1942; *WW in America; WWW(A),* 1977–1981.

MCCARTHY, DOROTHEA AGNES (1906–1974)

U.S. psychologist. Born 4 March 1906 in Minneapolis, Minn., to Mary (Malloy) McCarthy and Francis D. McCarthy. Married 1934. One child. Educated University of Minnesota (B.A., 1925; Ph.D., 1928). Professional experience: Minnesota Institute of Child Welfare, assistant (1926–1928); National Research Fellow (1928–1929); Bureau of Juvenile Research, California, clinical psychologist (1929–1930); University of Georgia, Department of Child Development, associate professor of psychology and child psychologist (1930–1932); Georgia State College, director of nursery school (1931–1932); Fordham University, associate professor educational psychology (1932–1941), graduate school psychologist (1941–1947), professor (1948–1971), emerita professor of psychology (from 1971); Westchester County children's court psychologist (1939–1940); Columbia University Teachers College, associate professor (summers 1941, 1943, 1944). Honors and memberships: American Psychological Association, Society for Research in Child Development; Eastern Psychological Association; New York State Psychological Association; New York Academy (secretary, 1941; vice-president, 1942). Died 1974.

Dorothea McCarthy moved comfortably between the practical and theoretical worlds of psychology. After many jobs, she went to Fordham in 1932 as an associate professor and graduate school psychologist and was promoted to professor in 1948. She spent the remainder of her career there.

McCarthy did research on both child and clinical psychology and worked with language development and disorders. She also worked with measures of musical talent.

KM

PRIMARY SOURCES

McCarthy, Dorothea. *The Language Development of the Preschool Child*. Minneapolis: University of Minnesota Press, 1929.

———. *McCarthy Scales of Children's Abilities*. Cleveland: Psychological Corporation, 1972.

STANDARD SOURCES

AMS 5–8, S&B 9–12; Stevens and Gardner.

MCCLINTOCK, BARBARA (1902–1992)

U.S. geneticist. Born 16 June 1902 in Hartford, Conn., to Sara (Handy) and Thomas Henry McClintock. Three siblings. Never married. Educated Cornell University (B.S., 1923; M.A., 1925; Ph.D., 1928). Professional experience: Cornell University, instructor in botany (1927–1931), research associate (1934–1936); National Research Council, fellow (1931–1933); Guggenheim Foundation, fellow (1933–1934); University of Missouri, assistant professor (1936–1941); Carnegie Institute of Washington, Cold Spring Harbor, N.Y., staff member (1942–1967); California Institute of Technology, visiting professor (1954); Rockefeller Foundation, consultant, Agricultural Science Program (1963–1969); Cornell University, Andrew D. White Professor at Large (1965–1974). Honors and memberships: American Association of University Women, Achievement Award (1947); University of Rochester, honorary Sc.D. (1947); Western College for Women, honorary Sc.D. (1949); Botanical Society of America, Merit Award (1957); Smith College, honorary Sc.D.; National Academy of Sciences, Kimber Genetics Award (1967); Carnegie Institution of Washington, Cold Spring Harbor, N.Y., Distinguished Service Member (1967–1992); University of Missouri, honorary Sc.D. (1968); National Medal of Science (1970); Williams College, honorary Sc.D. (1972); Lewis S. Rosensteil Award for Distinguished Work in Basic Medical Research (1978); Louis and Bert Freedman Foundation Award for Research in Biochemistry; Rockefeller University, honorary Sc.D. (1979); Harvard University, honorary Sc.D. (1979); Genetics Society of America, Salute (1980); Genetics Society of America, Thomas Hunt Morgan Medal (1981); Society for Developmental Biology, honorary member (1981); Wolf Prize in Medicine (1981); Albert Lasker Basic Medical Research Award (1981); MacArthur Prize Fellow Laureate (1981); Georgetown University, honorary LL.D.; Genetical Society [of Great Britain], honorary member (1982); Louisa Gross Horwitz Prize for Biology or Biochemistry (1982); Académie des Sciences, Institut de France, Charles Leopold Mayer Prize; Yale University, honorary Sc.D. (1982); University of Cambridge, honorary Sc.D. (1982); Nobel Prize for Medicine (1983); Bard College, honorary Sc.D. (1983); State University of New York, honorary Sc.D. (1983); New York University, honorary Sc.D. (1983); Albert A. Michelson Award (1984); American Medical Women's Association, honorary member (1984); State University of New York, Regents Medal of Excellence (1984); La faculté des sciences Agronomiques de l'etat à Gambloux, Belgium (1985); American Society of Naturalists, honorary member (1985); New York Academy of Sciences, honorary member (1985); 16th International Congress of Genetics (Ontario, Canada), honorary vice-president (1985); National Women's Hall of Fame Award (1986); Royal Society of London, foreign member (1989); University of California, San Francisco, 125th Anniversary Medal (1990); Indian Society of Genetics and Plant Breeding, honorary fellow (1991). Died 2 September 1992.

Barbara McClintock's mother's parents were descended from New England stock whereas her father's parents were Celtic immigrants. Sara McClintock, Barbara's mother, was somewhat of an iconoclast who was overwhelmed by the responsibility of rearing four children. Barbara's grandfather on her mother's side was a stern Congregationalist minister who was horrified with the thought that Sara intended to marry the son of immigrant parents. Nevertheless, Sara married Thomas Henry McClintock in 1898. With a small inheritance, Sarah helped her husband pay his medical school debts. Their four children were born in rapid succession. Barbara was originally named Eleanor (considered by her parents to be a feminine and delicate name), but they changed it to Barbara (which they considered a more masculine name), because it seemed to fit the child better. From the first, there was tension between Barbara and her mother. When she was little more than a toddler, she was shipped off to live with her paternal aunt and uncle in Massachusetts. Periodically during her childhood she lived with this aunt and uncle. Barbara grew up with a lack of overt affection, becoming an independent child. Her love for solitude concerned her parents, particularly her mother. The family moved to Brooklyn in 1908, where Barbara attended elementary school and then Erasmus Hall High School.

The McClintocks allowed the children a great deal of autonomy. If school did not appeal to them, they were not forced to go. If they needed equipment for a particular sport, it was provided. Music was an exception. Sara McClintock felt that Barbara was obsessive about the piano, practicing interminably. She also loved sports, playing various games that were thought to be solely for boys. Sara McClintock began to change her mind about nontraditional roles for her children when they reached adolescence. Thomas McClintock served in Europe during World War I, and Sara made the family decisions. She was able to dissuade her two oldest daughters from going to college, although they were both very bright. Both girls were accomplished musicians and entertained the thought of going on the stage; however, both married and bowed to tradition. Barbara, on the other hand, discovered that learning about science could replace the sports she was forced to leave behind. She enrolled at Cornell, where she blossomed socially as well as intellectually. Although she dated during her college years, she felt no need for a personal attachment to anyone, and had difficulty understanding the institution of marriage.

McClintock received all three of her degrees from Cornell. Early in her career she decided to work on linkage groups (characteristics that are on the same chromosome and are inherited together). Most of the early work had been on the fruitfly, *Drosophila,* and McClintock proposed to do the same thing on maize, *Zea.* In order to pursue this path, McClintock needed to collaborate with people actually working in the field of corn breeding, something that hadn't been done before. As she stayed on at Cornell to pursue this research, she met a young graduate student, Marcus Rhoades, who was fascinated by her studies. She also met George Beadle (known with Edward Tatum for the "one gene, one enzyme" theory). These people were brought to Cornell by Rollins A. Emerson, the foremost corn geneticist of the time. Emerson's research was confined to breeding experiments, and McClintock brought a cytological perspective to bear upon the genetics.

The years from 1931 through 1936 were trying ones for McClintock. She did not have a regular position at Cornell, and most of her options for fellowships had run out. She had been awarded a fellowship from the National Research Council from 1931 to 1933, where she divided her time between the University of Missouri, the California Institute of Technology, and Cornell, with Cornell remaining her home base. In 1933, she went to Germany on a Guggenheim Fellowship and was repelled by the political situation she encountered there. When she returned, the Depression had deepened to the point that few research scientists were able to get regular positions. With the help of her male colleagues, she was awarded a Rockefeller stipend. It was clear to these colleagues individually that she was a brilliant geneticist. However, institutionally the idea of a female scientist was less palatable. Nevertheless it was during this period that she demonstrated her intuitive scientific creativity, as well as her acute observational skills. While observing the nucleolus in the nucleus of a cell, she noticed a minute structure near this body, and postulated that it was important. No one else had presumed its importance or even remarked upon its presence. McClintock postulated that it was the organizer necessary to reform the nucleolus after it disappears in late prophase. Earlier, she had postulated and then observed the occurrence of the ring chromosome, which she interpreted as a special case of broken chromosome. This ability to look at one thing and see another characterized McClintock as a scientist.

One of her collaborators and supporters, Lewis Stadler, worked hard to find McClintock a job. He had been at the University of Missouri since 1919 and on the faculty since 1921. He was able to persuade the university administration to offer her a position as assistant professor in 1936. How-

ever, for a variety of reasons, the appointment was not a success. She was never promoted and left in 1941. Again without a job and disenchanted with the university scene, she contemplated giving up genetics. Still doubting if she really wanted a job, she considered a position at the Carnegie Institution at Cold Spring Harbor. Impressed with Vannevar Bush, the president of the Carnegie Institution, she accepted the position. She again had a salary, a laboratory, and a place to grow her corn. In 1944, she was able to demonstrate again her observational skills and her theoretical acumen. Invited to Stanford by George Beadle, she supplied the cytological work on the bread mold, *Neurospora,* necessary to confirm Beadle and Tatum's "one gene, one enzyme" hypothesis.

In 1944, McClintock was elected to the National Academy of Sciences, the third woman to be so honored (the other two were FLORENCE SABIN and MARGARET WASHBURN). By the early 1940s, molecular biology was just beginning. McClintock was not a part of that beginning, but her investigation of mutations produced by the breakage-fusion-bridge cycle was a revolution in itself. She grew a culture of seedlings that were produced by self-pollination of plants in which in early development one of both chromosome 9s had been newly broken. These seedlings including a number of variants of the basic green culture. They might be white, light green, or pale yellow. However, the astounding result of these experiments indicated that the colors of the plants were apparently unstable within the plants' individual lifetimes. She noted anomalies in the color of irradiated corn leaves which seemed to indicate genetic instability of a undescribed sort. However, this apparent instability seemed to follow a pattern. To explain the pattern, McClintock postulated "controlling elements" which provided a way for the genes to regulate themselves. These controlling elements enabled pieces of chromosomes to move spontaneously, her so-called jumping genes. It took McClintock six years to develop an explanation that she was convinced was correct. She published a brief account of transposition in 1951, and presented a paper at the annual Cold Spring Harbor Symposium. Some of her colleagues ridiculed her, whereas others simply admitted that they did not understand what she was doing. She presented several seminars and five years later gave another presentation at the 1956 Cold Spring Harbor Symposium with an equally disturbing reception. She became increasingly isolated from the scientific community.

Discoveries in molecular biology in the 1950s solved the vexing questions of how genes made exact copies of themselves and how those copies were translated into proteins. However the problem of how cells deriving from a single fertilized egg differentiate into the organs of the organism was still unsolved. McClintock listened to and participated in the general excitement surrounding these discoveries. She thought that transposition could help explain differentiation.

After reading a paper by Jacques Monod and François Jacob that proposed that protein synthesis was regulated not by the gene that codes for the protein but by two genes lying adjacent to the protein coding gene, she was elated, for they provided a satisfying molecular model for how a gene functions in the cell. Monod and Jacob had worked on bacteria, but McClintock saw similarities to the systems that she had worked on in maize. Recognition of her work did not come even after she again tried to explain it at another seminar at Cold Spring Harbor. Taking time out to train local cytologists in Central and South America in techniques that would help them preserve the population of indigenous maize that was becoming increasingly scarce, she returned to her work on transposition. Although she was recognized for much of her work in the late 1960s and early 1970s, her most important work on transposition was still largely ignored. The situation began to change in the middle to late 1970s as molecular biology became increasingly complex. Others began to see what she had been describing for years in corn. The idea of transposable elements and genome regulation were eventually accepted into mainstream science. When the importance of McClintock's work was finally acknowledged, she won many prizes, culminating in the Nobel Prize in 1983.

Although McClintock hated publicity and was always something of a rogue scientist, she did have a life outside of the laboratory. She was an ardent gardener and amateur botanist. She had a number of friends whom she would talk to for long periods of time both inside and outside the laboratory. JH

PRIMARY SOURCES

McClintock, Barbara. "A Cytological and Genetical Study of Triploid Maize." Ph.D. diss., Cornell University, 1927.

———. With G. W. Beadle. "A Genic Disturbance of Meiosis in *Zea Mays.*" *Science* 68 (1928): 56.

———. With H. B. Creighton. "A Correlation of Cytological and Genetical Crossing-Over in *Zea Mays.*" *Proceedings of the National Academy of Sciences* 17 (1931): 492–497.

———. "Mutable Loci in Maize." *Carnegie Institution of Washington Yearbook* 47 (1948): 155–169.

———. "Mutable Loci in Maize." *Carnegie Institution of Washington Yearbook* 53 (1954): 227–237.

———. *The Discovery and Characterization of Transposable Elements: The Collected Papers of Barbara McClintock.* New York: Garland Press, 1987.

SECONDARY SOURCES

Craig, Patricia Parratt. *Jumping Genes.* Washington, D.C.: Carnegie Institution of Washington, 1994.

Federoff, Nina, and David Botstein, eds. *The Dynamic Genomes: Barbara McClintock's Ideas in the Century of Genetics.* Plainview, N.Y.: Cold Spring Harbor Laboratory Press, 1992.

Keller, Evelyn Fox. *A Feeling for the Organism: The Life and Work of Barbara McClintock.* San Francisco: W. H. Freeman, 1983.

Opfell, Olga S. *The Lady Laureates.* 2d ed. Metuchen, N.J.: Scarecrow Press, 1986.

Shields, Barbara. *Women and the Nobel Prize.* Minneapolis: Dillon Press, 1985.

Torrey Botanical Club. *Index to American Botanical Literature, 1886–1966.* Boston: G. K. Hall, 1969.

STANDARD SOURCES

Grinstein 1997 (article by Virginia L. Buckner); *LKW;* McGrayne; *Notable;* Shearer and Shearer 1996 (article by Nathaniel Comfort); *WW in America,* 1984, 1985.

MCCONNEY, FLORENCE (1894–?)

Canadian physician. Born 20 September 1894 in Lindsay, Ont., Canada, to Annie Florence Everett and Edwin Austin Hardy. One sister. Married Garnet McConney. Four children: two sons and two daughters. Educated Moulton Ladies' College, Toronto; Jarvis Collegiate (1910–1913); University College of the University of Toronto (graduated in arts, 1917); University of Toronto (M.D., 1920). Professional experience: St. Michael's Hospital, Toronto, intern; Women's College Hospital, staff; private practice. Death date unknown.

Born into a family of teachers, Florence McConney decided at the age of seven to become a doctor. The family moved to Toronto when Florence was nine, and after finishing primary school she went to the Moulton Ladies' College, from which she graduated at the age of fifteen. She could not be admitted to the University of Toronto until she was eighteen so she spent the intervening three years at Jarvis Collegiate. She entered University College studying biological and physical sciences, including two years of premedical studies. She married Garnet McConney in 1917, before she graduated and before he went overseas during World War I. Florence entered medical school while Garnet was away, and when he returned they lived with her family until she graduated in 1920. He was very supportive of her need for a career.

After her internship, McConney joined the staff of the Women's College Hospital and remained associated with it for fifty years. She became associate chief and the chief in medicine. She retired as chief at age fifty-five. However, she really did not retire. She became director for the Cancer Detection Clinic, modeled after the Strang Memorial Clinic in New York. For fifty years she had a vibrant private practice.

McConney's four children were born beginning in 1921. With the help of her husband, she was able to spend time on both her profession and her family. Always interested in learning more about her subject, she attended a postgraduate course offered by the American College of Physicians. She became a fellow of this college in 1950 and her thesis was on chronic mercurial poisoning from diuretics. In 1944 she received certification as a specialist in internal medicine from the Royal College of Physicians and Surgeons of Canada and from the Ontario College of Physicians in 1945.   KM

PRIMARY SOURCES
McConney, Florence. In Hellstedt, *Autobiographies.*

MCCRACKEN, EILEEN MAY (1920–1988)
Irish botanist and historian of botany and Irish gardens. Born 16 February 1920 in Lisburn, County Antrim. Educated University of Belfast (B.Sc.; Ph.D.) Professional experience: schoolteacher; University of Witwatersrand, South Africa, lecturer in geography. Died in Durban, South Africa, 12 November 1988.

Eileen May McCracken was an Irish botanist who trained in science, receiving both her undergraduate and graduate degrees from the University of Belfast. She became a schoolteacher and moved to South Africa, lecturing on geography at the University of Witwatersrand. In the 1970s, she produced a series of interesting books on the changing landscape of Ireland from the Tudor period to the present day, on the Botanic Garden, Belfast, and on the National Botanic gardens of Glasnevin. In spite of the heavy emphasis in her writings on Irish landscapes, McCracken continued to live in South Africa, dying in Durban in 1988.   JH/MBO

PRIMARY SOURCES
McCracken, Eileen May. *Irish Woods since Tudor Times.* Newton Abbott: David & Charles, 1971.
———. *Palm House and Botanic Garden, Belfast.* Belfast: Ulster Architectural Heritage Society, 1971.
———. With E. C. Nelson. *Brightest Jewel: History of the National Botanic Gardens, Glasnevin.* Kilkenny: Boetnius, 1987.
———. With D. McCracken. *The Way to Kirstenbosch.* Capetown: National Botanic Gardens, 1988.
Papers are in the Botanic Gardens, Glasnevin.

STANDARD SOURCES
Desmond.

MCCRACKEN, ELIZABETH (UNGER) (1908–)
U.S. cytogeneticist. Born 28 October 1908 in Clearfield, Pa. Educated Wellesley College (A.B., 1929; M.A., 1932); University of California (Ph.D., 1937). Professional experience: Wellesley College, assistant in botany (1929–1932); Kansas State University, assistant in botany and instructor (1938–1949), instructor in botany and zoology (1939–1942); University of California, assis-

tant in botany, lecturer (1944–1946); Wesleyan, Ohio, instructor in botany and zoology (1942–1943); U.S. Department of Agriculture, Vermont, instructor in botany and assistant (1943–1944). Kansas State University, assistant professor of zoology (1946–1950); Agricultural Experimental Station, associate professor of botany and assistant in cytogenetics (1950–post-1966).

Elizabeth McCracken earned her doctorate from the University of California. After holding positions at other institutions, she moved to Manhattan, Kansas, where she became an assistant professor at Kansas State University. In 1950, she was promoted to associate professor and assistant cytogeneticist at the Agricultural Experimental Station. She was a member of the American Association for the Advancement of Science, the Botanical Society, the Genetics Society, the Society for Agronomy, and the Crop Science Society. Kansas State is an agricultural college, and her research was geared along those lines. She worked on the cytogenetics of nicotiana, viola, and wheat.   JH/MBO

STANDARD SOURCES
AMS 7–8, B 9, P&B 10–12.

MCCRACKEN, MARY ISABEL (1866–1955)
U.S. entomologist. Educated Stanford University (A.B., 1904; M.A., 1905; Ph.D., 1908); University of Paris, postgraduate studies (1913–1914). Professional experience: Oakland, Calif., schools, teacher (1890–1900); Stanford University, assistant (1903–1904), instructor (1904–1909), assistant professor (1909–1918), associate professor (1918–1930), professor (1930–1931), professor emerita (1931–1955). Died 1955.

Isabel McCracken began her career as a public school teacher for ten years in the Oakland, California schools. At the age of thirty-four, she returned to college, Stanford University, to obtain her undergraduate degree. Obtaining an assistantship in entomology and physiology, she continued her education, earning her master's degree in 1905. After she received her first advanced degree she was made an instructor in entomology and bionomics for the next five years, while she worked for her doctoral degree. A year after she received her doctoral degree, she was promoted to assistant professor. During this period she took a year's leave to study at the University of Paris, returning at the beginning of World War I. She carried on research on economic entomology, especially on bees and silkworms. Among her other research interests were studies on California mosquitoes and inheritance in beetles and silkworms. McCracken rose to associate professor, a position she held until the year before she retired, when she was promoted to professor. After her retirement, she remained active as a research associate of the California

Academy of Sciences from 1931 to 1942. At this point she had shifted her interests to the relationship between birds and insects.

McCracken's research was varied and often was related to her teaching. Along these lines, she kept bees in a special demonstration hive and made an extensive study of silkworms.   JH/MBO

SECONDARY SOURCES
"In Memoriam, 1955. McCracken." *Stanford Review* 57 (December 1955): 28.
Vickery, Robert K. "Dr. Isabel McCracken." *Stanford Illustrated Review* 32 (June 1931): 412–413. Includes photograph. Written at the time of her retirement.

STANDARD SOURCES
AMS 1–10; Bailey; Osborn; Siegel and Finley.

MCCREA, ADELIA (1880–?)

U.S. botanist. Born 1880. Educated University of Michigan (A.B., 1919; Ph.D., 1930). Professional experience: Public school teacher (1897–1899; 1904–1919); Parke, Davis and Company, research mycologist (1919–1942). Death date unknown.

Adelia McCrea, like MARY ISABEL McCRACKEN, began her career as a schoolteacher, finishing an undergraduate degree after she had taught for many years. Upon completing her undergraduate degree at the University of Michigan, she was hired by Parke, Davis and Company as a research mycologist. While working for the pharmaceutical company, she pursued her doctoral degree. Her research interests were closely connected to her position at Parke Davis, for she studied dermatrophytic fungi and respiratory mycoses. She was a member of the Botanical Society of America and the American Mycological Society.   JH/MBO

STANDARD SOURCES
AMS 5–8, B 9, P&B 10, Bailey; Barnhart.

MCDONALD, JANET (1905–)

U.S. mathematician. Born in 1905. Educated Belhaven College (B.A., 1925); Tulane University (M.A., 1929); University of Chicago (Ph.D., 1943). Professional experience: high school teacher (1925–1928); Mississippi Synodical College, mathematics department, head (1929–1932); Hinds Junior College, head of mathematics department and registrar (1932–1941); University of Chicago, instructor (1943–1944); Vassar College, instructor (1944–1946), assistant professor (1946–1953), associate professor (1953–1959), professor (1959–1971), chair (1962–1966; 1969–1971), professor emerita (from 1971).

Janet McDonald taught mathematics for three years in high school after she received her bachelor's degree. She earned her master's degree from Tulane and then accepted positions in two small southern colleges, where she served as head of the mathematics departments. At the beginning of World War II, McDonald went to the University of Chicago to work on her doctorate. After two years as a doctoral student, she became an instructor at this university. When she completed her doctoral degree, she was hired by Vassar College, where she moved through the ranks to professor. In mathematics, her specialty was geometry.   JH/MBO

STANDARD SOURCES
AMS 8, P 9, P&B 10–14; Bailey; Debus.

MCDOWELL, LOUISE SHERWOOD (1876–1966)

U.S. physicist. Born 29 September 1876 in Wayne, N.Y., to Francis Marion and Eva (Sherwood) McDowell. Educated at Penn Yan (N.Y.) Academy; Wellesley College (A.B., 1898); Cornell University (A.M., 1907; Ph.D., 1909). Professional experience: Northfield Seminary, teacher (1898–1901); Warren High School, Ohio, teacher (1901–1906); Wellesley College, instructor (1909–1910), associate professor (1910–1912 or 1913), professor and chair of department (1913–1945), emerita professor (from 1945); National Bureau of Standards, assistant physicist (1918); associate physicist (1918–1919); Radio Research Laboratory, Harvard, research associate (1945–1946). Honors and memberships: American Physical Society, section chair (1937); American Association for the Advancement of Science, fellow; Optical Society of America; American Association of Physics Teachers, associate editor (1933–1937), vice-president (1944); Association of Collegiate Alumni; Phi Beta Kappa; Sigma Xi. Died 6 July 1966 in Wellesley, Mass.

McDowell grew up in rural upstate New York. She studied at Wellesley's excellent physics department under SARAH FRANCES WHITING. After graduation, she taught high school students for eight years, first in science and English, then in science and mathematics. In 1905 McDowell was admitted to Cornell University, where the chairman of the physics department, Edward L. Nichols, was supportive of women in physics. There she worked with Ernest G. Merritt on short-wave radiation. She also worked with FRANCES WICK, who became a good friend.

After receiving her doctorate, McDowell took an instructorship at Wellesley, where her former teacher Whiting chaired the physics department. She became chair upon Whiting's retirement. Soon afterward a fire destroyed the physics facilities. McDowell spent many years rebuilding the department. She was determined to give her students the best education, and devoted much energy to providing them laboratory resources and lectures by renowned physicists.

A demanding teacher, yet thoughtful and kind, McDowell encouraged her students to pursue science. She received much support from women during her life, and gave much in return. McDowell enjoyed mountain climbing until she was well into her seventies. During the last years of her life, McDowell was bedridden, but she remained good natured and alert.

McDowell's dissertation on the electrical properties of selenium was one of the early studies of semiconductors. She investigated crystal detectors for the Signal Corps during World War I. Her determinations of power loss in dielectrics provided much useful information on properties of different insulators, especially glass. McDowell also researched the topic of luminescence when subjected to high temperatures and when bombarded by cathode rays, working with Wick, Nichols, Merritt, and others. During World War II she taught electronics classes. During 1945–1946 McDowell worked on radar at Harvard for the U.S. Office of Scientific Research and Development.

McDowell was active in many professional organizations, including the American Association of Physics Teachers (associate editor, 1933–1937; executive committee 1939–1944; vice-president, 1944); the American Physical Society (section chair, 1937); the Institute of Electrical and Electronics Engineers; and the Institute of Radio Engineers. She was a fellow of the American Physical Society and the American Association for the Advancement of Science, and a member of the Optical Society of America, the American Association of Physics Teachers (vice-president, 1944), the Association of Collegiate Alumnae, Phi Beta Kappa, and Sigma Xi. MM

PRIMARY SOURCES

McDowell, Louise. "The Fluorescence and Absorption of Anthracene." *Physical Review* 26 (1908): 155–168.

———. "Some Electrical Properties of Selenium." *Physical Review* 29 (1909): 1–36; 30 (1910): 474–481; 31 (1910): 524–535.

———. With F. G. Wick. "A Study of the Law of Response of the Silicon Detector." *Physical Review* 8 (1916): 133–141.

———. With F. G. Wick. "A Preliminary Study of the Luminescence of the Uranyl Salts under Cathode Ray Excitation." *Physical Review* 11 (1918): 421–429.

———. "The Power Loss in Condensers with Liquid Dielectrics." *Physical Review* 23 (1923): 507–516.

———. With H. L. Begeman. "Behavior of Glass as a Dielectric in Alternating Current Circuits." *Physical Review* 31 (1928): 476–481; 33 (1929): 55–65.

SECONDARY SOURCES

Baly, E. C. C. *Spectroscopy.* Vol. 2. New York: Longmans, Green and Co., 1927.

Guernsey, Janet B. "The Lady Wanted to Purchase a Wheatstone Bridge: Sarah Frances Whiting and Her Successor." In *Making Contributions: An Historical Overview of Women's Role in Physics,* ed. B. Lotze, 65–90. College Park, Md.: American Association of Physics Teachers, 1984.

Physics Today 19 (19 August 1966): 97. Obituary notice.

STANDARD SOURCES

AMS 5–8, P 9, P&B 10; Grinstein 1993 (article by Janet B. Guernsey); *Woman's Who's Who of America.*

MCGEE, ANITA (NEWCOMB) (1864–1940)

U.S. military physician. Born 4 November 1864. Father Simon Newcomb, a professor. Married W. J. McGee (1888). Two children: one son, Eric, and one daughter, Klotho. Educated University of Geneva; University of Berlin (1882–1885); George Washington University (M.D., 1892). Professional experience: U.S. Army, acting assistant surgeon (1898–1900); Army Nurse Corps, superintendent (1898–1900); Japanese army, supervisor of nurses, with officer's rank (1904); University of California, Berkeley, lecturer in hygiene (1911). Honors and memberships: Imperial Order of the Sacred Crown; Decorations from the Japanese Emperor and Empress. Died 1940.

Anita Newcomb was the daughter of Simon Newcomb, the distinguished astronomer who was assigned to the U.S. Naval Observatory in Washington and then the American Nautical Almanac Office. Both her husband and father were scientists, and she took a medical degree at Columbian (George Washington) University. Six years after she got her medical degree, she served as acting assistant surgeon of the United States Army during the Spanish-American War. During the Philippine insurrection and the Boxer campaign she served as a military physician. She was an officer in the Japanese army during Japan's war with Russia. She organized and trained nurses, inspected hospitals in Japan and Manchuria, and was a supervisor of nurses at Hiroshima and aboard hospital ships.

McGee was a fellow of the American Association for the Advancement of Science and secretary of section H in 1897 and was a lecturer in hygiene at the University of California, Berkeley. She also contributed to magazines. KM

PRIMARY SOURCES

McGee, Anita Newcomb. "The Women's Anthropological Society of America." *Science* 3 (29 March 1889): 240–242. McGee discusses the women who formed the group. This paper shows her wide interests.

STANDARD SOURCES
AMS 1–6; Bailey; Hurd-Mead 1933; Ireland; Rossiter 1982; Siegel and Finley.

MCGLAMERY, JOSIE WINIFRED (1887–1977)

U.S. geologist and paleontologist. Born 26 July 1887 in Churchville, Augusta County, Va., near Staunton. Educated University of North Carolina; Goucher College, Baltimore (A.B., 1919); Johns Hopkins (M.A., 1925). Professional experience: American Museum of Natural History, staff paleontologist; Humble Oil Co., micropaleontologist; the Museum of the University of Rochester, researcher (1927–1928); Alabama State Geological Survey, paleontologist (1931–1961). Honors and memberships: Geological Society of America, Fellow; Paleontological Society of America, member; American Association of Petroleum Geologists, member; American Malacological Union, member; Alabama Academy of Science, member; Society of Economic Geologists, member. Died 1977.

Josie Winifred McGlamery was born in Virginia and first attended the University of North Carolina. She transferred to Goucher College, where she majored in English. In 1922, she enrolled as a graduate student at the Johns Hopkins University. Here she met Walter B. Jones, who was then a graduate student but in 1927 became state geologist of Alabama. This contact with Jones was important in McGlamery's later career with the Alabama State Geological Survey. After she received her master's degree, she worked for Humble Oil and Refining Company and was a paleontologist in the museum at the University of Rochester.

McGlamery was a Fellow of the Geological Society of America, and a member of the Paleontological Society of America, American Association of Petroleum Geologists, American Malacological Union, Alabama Academy of Science, and the Society of Economic Geologists.

Most of McGlamery's career was with the Alabama State Geological Survey. With Walter B. Jones, she developed collections of core samples from oil and water drilling in Alabama. She then used these reference materials to describe the geological sequences of the subsurface formations. McGlamery collected fossils in the field in order to build up the survey's collection. The useful nature of her research is shown by the fact that the materials cataloged and described by McGlamery and Jones remain the major baseline data for oil geologists in the Gulf area. The research is also used by scientists interested in reconstructing the geologic and evolutionary history of the area.

Although she is best known for her contributions to the stratigraphy and paleontology of Alabama through her well descriptions and fossil collections, McGlamery also coauthored three publications with the micropaleontologist J. A. Cushman.

CK

PRIMARY SOURCES
McGlamery, Josie Winifred. "Subsurface Stratigraphy of Northwest Alabama." *Alabama Geological Survey Bulletin* (1955): 64.
———. With J. A. Cushman. "Oligocene Foraminifera near Choctaw Bluff, Alabama." *U.S. Geological Survey Professional Paper* 189-D (1938): 103–119.
———. With J. A. Cushman. "Oligocene Foraminifera Near Millry, Alabama." *U.S. Geological Survey Professional Paper* 197-B (1941): 65–84.

SECONDARY SOURCES
Copeland, Charles W. "Memorial to Josie Winifred McGlamery, 1887–1977." *Geological Society of America Memorials* 9 (1979): 3 pp. Includes a selected bibliography.

STANDARD SOURCES
Kass-Simon and Farnes (article by Michele L. Aldrich).

MCGRAW, MYRTLE BYRAM (1899–1988)

U.S. psychologist. Born 1 August 1899 in Birmingham, Ala. Married R. F. Mallina (1936). One child. Educated Ohio Wesleyan (A.B., 1923); Columbia University (A.M., 1925; fellow, 1929–1930; Ph.D., 1931). Professional experience: Columbia University Teachers College, Institution of Child Development, research assistant (1925–1927); Florida State College for Women, assistant professor of psychology (1928–1929); Babies Hospital, New York City, research psychologist and director, normal child development study (1930–1942); Child Education Foundation, New York City, teacher training (from 1948). Died 1988.

Although Myrtle McGraw became a research psychologist she was also a teacher and an administrator. Born near Birmingham, Alabama, she grew up in an area still suffering from the aftermath of the Civil War. After the sixth grade she left public school and registered in a local business school to learn typing and shorthand. Upon completing this course, she secured a position with a lawyer who encouraged her to continue her formal education. With his help, she was admitted to a Methodist boarding school, the Snead Seminary. During her second year at Snead, she read an article about John Dewey who was, at that time, a professor at Columbia University. The article so impressed McGraw that she wrote him an admiring letter to which he replied. They continued corresponding for over a year.

McGraw graduated from Snead and went on to Ohio Wesleyan University where she earned a bachelor's degree. Upon graduation she went to Columbia University Teachers College, intending to major in religious education. After less than a year she realized that she had made a mistake. She left Columbia for a year to teach in Puerto Rico. When she returned to Columbia in 1925, she had decided to major in psychology. While continuing graduate studies she worked at the Institute of Child Development at Teachers College under the direction of Dr. Helen Woolley. Although her position was research assistant much of her time was spent in baby-sitting the children who were used as experimental subjects. During her time with the Institute, she continued taking classes. However, in 1927 the secretary general of the General Education Board of the Rockefeller Foundation offered her a Laura Spelman Rockefeller fellowship so that she could complete the course requirements for the Ph.D. degree without working full-time. In September of 1927, she left New York to take a position in the psychology department at Florida State College for Women, where she conducted her thesis research while teaching.

After completing her degree she accepted a position with Dr. Frederic Tilney, director of the Neurological Institute at Columbia-Presbyterian Medical Center. He was extending his research operation and arranged with the director of Babies Hospital for a place to set up a laboratory there. Because they had a grant from the Rockefeller Foundation's General Education Board, the laboratory thrived during the Depression.

McGraw's research interests involved the controversial supposed dichotomy between maturation and learning. This study involved bringing babies, preferably twins, to the laboratory for several years. In 1935, she published *Growth: A Study of Johnny and Jimmy.*

The year after *Johnny and Jimmy* was published, McGraw married Rudolph Mallina. The wedding took place in the home of John Dewey, his son, and daughter-in-law. After the birth of a daughter in 1937, Myrtle McGraw faced a dilemma. Funding institutions were not as willing to support academic research as previously because of the imminent advent of war. She also felt the pull between family and career and decided after 1942 to dedicate herself to the former.

JH/MBO

PRIMARY SOURCES

McGraw, Myrtle. *Growth: A Study of Johnny and Jimmy.* New York: Appleton, 1935.
———. *The Child in Painting.* Greystone, [1941].
———. "Let Babies Be Our Teacher." *March of Medicine.* New York Academy of Medicine, 1943.
———. "Maturation of Behavior." In *Manual of Child Psychology,* ed. L. Carmichael. New York: Wiley, 1946.
———. *Neuromuscular Maturation of the Human Infant.* New York: Hafner, 1963.

SECONDARY SOURCES

"McGraw, Dr. Myrtle Byram (Mrs. R. F. Mallina)." *Journal of the History of Behavioral Science* 25 (1989).

STANDARD SOURCES

AMS 6–8, S&B 9–12; O'Connell and Russo 1988 (autobiography).

MCGUIRE, RUTH COLVIN STARRETT (1893–?)

U.S. plant pathologist. Born 1893. Married (1) (1925); (2) (1940). Educated Indiana University (A.B., 1914; M.A., 1916); Northwestern University (1917); George Washington University (1923); University of Maryland (1930). Professional experience: Indiana University, assistant (1915–1916); high school teacher (1916–1919); Bureau of Plant Industry, U.S. Department of Agriculture, assistant (1919–1923), junior plant pathologist (1923–1925), assistant cytologist (1925–1948), associate cytologist (from 1948). Death date unknown.

Ruth McGuire taught high school for three years after she received her master's degree. Although she took additional courses from several universities, she never earned a doctoral degree. Once she accepted a position with the U.S. Department of Agriculture, she moved through the academic ranks, retiring as an associate cytologist. After her retirement, she worked as a research associate at the California Academy of Sciences (1931–1942), where she concentrated on her interest in birds and their relationships to insects.

McGuire published papers in the USDA's *Journal of Agricultural Research.* Her research involved work on sugar beets and sugar cane. She was a member of the Botanical Society of Washington and the International Society of Sugar Cane Technologists. In addition to her work on sugar, she also did research on a number of topics including bees and silkworms. As a member of the Entomological Society of America, her research was on mosquitoes in California and inheritance in beetles and silkworms.

JH/MBO

STANDARD SOURCES

AMS 8, B 9; Bailey; Barnhart.

MCHALE, KATHRYN (1889–1956)

U.S. psychologist. Born 22 July 1889 in Logansport, Ind., to Margaret (Farrell) and Martin McHale. One brother. Educated Columbia University (B.S., 1919; A.M., 1920; Ph.D., 1926). Professional experience: Goucher College, Baltimore, instructor in education (1920–1922), assistant professor (1922–1926), associate professor (1926–1927), professor (1927–1935), nonresident professor (from 1935). Honors and memberships: American Association for the Advancement of Science, Fellow; American Association of University Professors; American Psychological Association; National Society for the Scientific Study of Education; National Society of College Teachers of Education; Kappa Delta Pi; Delta Kappa

Gamma; Alfred I. du Point Radio Committee on Education, the United States Office of Education (1947–1950) National Foundation for Education in American Citizenship, Board of Educational Advisers; American Association for Adult Education; Brown University, honorary degree (1941); Russell Sage College, Troy, N.Y., honorary degree (1942); MacMurray College, honorary degree (1946). Died 8 October 1956.

Kathryn McHale received her three degrees from Columbia University. She was appointed an instructor in education after she received her master's degree and rose through the ranks to professor at Goucher College. While she was teaching at Goucher, she taught in the summer at Columbia University and fulfilled the requirements for a doctorate.

McHale modified parts of the Thorndike Intelligence Tests to make them more applicable to women. Edward L. Thorndike, after hearing of her work, modified his tests along the lines that she had suggested. The first form of the McHale Vocational Interest test was given to a population of Goucher students in 1922, and a revised form was published by the American Association of University Women in 1933.

In addition to her teaching and research activities, Kathryn McHale was active in professional organizations and in national education agendas. She became executive and educational secretary of the American Association of University Women in 1929; her title changed to general director in 1931.

McHale was a member of numerous government committees and private groups. Among these was an appointment to the Subversive Activities Control Board in 1950 and reappointment in 1952. From 1936 to 1946 she served as a trustee for Purdue University (the first woman to be a trustee). From 1946 to 1948, she was a member of the U.S. National Committee for UNESCO and from 1946 to 1948, a member of its executive committee. She participated in numerous forums and national committees. JH/MBO

PRIMARY SOURCES

McHale, Kathryn. "Psychology and Hygiene of the Overweight Child." Ph.D. diss., Columbia University Teachers College, 1926.
———. "An Information Test of Interests." *The Psychological Clinic* 19 (April 1930) [53]–62.
———. With Elizabeth Moore Manwell. *The Infant.* Washington, D.C.: National Headquarters [American Association of University Women], 1931.
———. With others. For the American Association of University Women. *Changes and Experiments in Liberal Arts Education,* ed. Guy Montrose Whipple. 31st Yearbook. Bloomington, Ill.: National Society for the Study of Education, 1932.
———. With Frances Valiant Speek and Harriet Ahlers Houdlette. *Adolescence: Its Problems and Guidance.* Washington, D.C.: National Headquarters [American Association of University Women], 1932.

STANDARD SOURCES
AMS S&B 9; *Current Biography,* 1947.

MCKEAG, ANNA JANE (1864–1947)

U.S. psychologist and educator. Born 13 March 1864 in West Finley, Pa. Educated Wilson College (A.B., 1895); University of Pennsylvania (Ph.D., 1900). Professional experience: public and private schools, teacher (1881–1892); Wilson College, instructor in philosophy (1892–1894), professor (1894–1902); Wellesley College, instructor in education (1902–1903), associate professor (1903–1909), professor (1909–1912; 1915–1932), professor emerita (from 1932); Wilson College, president (1912–1915). Died 1947.

Before she received her bachelor's degree, Anna McKeag was a school teacher for two years and an instructor in philosophy at Wilson College, the school where she later became president. After obtaining this degree from the small Wilson College, she went to the University of Chicago where she earned a Ph.D. degree and during the time that she was working on this degree was advanced to professor at Wilson. Upon the completion of this degree she accepted a position at Wellesley College, where she rose through the ranks to professor. However, for three years she left Wellesley to become the president of Wilson College. She then returned to Wellesley where she remained for the remainder of her career.

Although her research was in educational psychology, she was better known for her teaching. JH/MBO

PRIMARY SOURCES
McKeag, Anna Jane. *The Sensation of Pain and the Theory of the Specific Sense Energies.* Boston: Ginn, 1902. McKeag's doctoral dissertation research.

STANDARD SOURCES
AMS 1–7; Bailey; *Psychological Register,* vol. 3, 1932; Rossiter 1982; Siegel and Finley; Stevens and Gardner.

MCKINNEY, RUTH ALDEN (1898–?)

U.S. bacteriologist, cytologist. Born 8 February 1898 in Garnett, Kans. Educated University of Chicago (B.S., 1923; Ph.D. in bacteriology, 1933). Professional experience: Michigan North End Clinic, laboratory director (1933–1936); West Pennsylvania Hos-

pital, research bacteriologist (1936–1943); U.S. Navy, Hospital Corps (1943–1946); California State Department of Health, virus laboratory (Rockefeller foundation), researcher (1946); U.S. Army Chemical Corps, Camp Detrick, bacteriologist (1946–1951); U.S. Naval Medical Research Unit, researcher (1951–1953); Imperial Valley Tuberculosis Sanatorium, laboratory director (1955–1960). Honors and memberships: Influenza Committee, fellow (1929–1931); Rockefeller Foundation, fellow (1946). Death date unknown.

Ruth Alden McKinney was an American bacteriologist who worked on biological warfare during the 1950s. She was born in Kansas and attended the University of Chicago in the 1920s, obtaining her doctorate ten years later, after first obtaining a fellowship from the Influenza Committee from 1929 to 1931. Her initial professional positions after receiving her degree were in hospitals, first working as the laboratory director of the Michigan North End Clinic and the West Pennsylvania Hospital.

During World War II, McKinney served in the U.S. Navy Hospital Corps. With a research grant from the Rockefeller Foundation, she returned to research to work in the California State Department of Health virus laboratory. Her major research was on bacterial nutrition in relation to virulence and microbic-cytologic host response to infection as part of biological warfare defense, carried out first at the U.S. Army Chemical Corps at Camp Detrick and then with the U.S. Navy Medical Research Unit. There is a lapse in her work record from 1953 to 1955, which may indicate a period of ill health. She returned to clinical bacteriology to work as the laboratory director of the Imperial Valley Tuberculosis Sanatorium in California. She retired in 1960 at age sixty-two, remaining in California. Her birthdate is given erroneously as 1900 in the earlier edition of *AMS*. JH/MBO

STANDARD SOURCES
AMS 6–8, B 9, P&B 10–11.

MCLAREN, AGNES (1837–1913)
Scottish physician. Born 1837. Educated Women's Medical College, Edinburgh (1875); University of Montpellier Medical School, France (M.D.). Professional experience: Cannes, France, private practice. Dominican missionary order, Third Order, medical instructor. Died 1913.

At age thirty-eight, Agnes McClaren attended the Women's Medical College at Edinburgh where she became friends with the founder of the college, SOPHIA JEX-BLAKE. Like Jex-Blake, she found it necessary to go abroad to obtain a medical degree, which she received from the University of

Montpellier with her thesis "Flexions of the Uterus." She began to practice privately in Cannes, France.

In 1898 she converted to Catholicism, joining the Third Order of Dominicans. She began her life's work to train women doctors for Catholic missions (even though the Roman Catholic canon law forbade women from becoming doctors until 1936). One of her students, Elizabeth Bielby, began the Open Hospital in Rawalpindi, India, which Agnes visited at the age of seventy-two. Another pupil, the Austrian medical missionary ANNA DENGEL, founded the Society of Catholic Medical Missionaries in 1925 with Joanna Lyons. JH/MBO

SECONDARY SOURCES
Burton, Katherine. *According to the Pattern: The Story of Dr. Agnes McLaren and the Society of Catholic Medical Missionaries.* New York: Longmans, Green, 1946.

STANDARD SOURCES
Uglow 1982.

MCLEAN, HELEN (VINCENT) (1894–?)
U.S. psychoanalyst. Born 27 May 1894 in Sandusky, Ohio, to Lucy (Hall) Vincent and Clarence A. Vincent. Married Franklin C. McLean (1923). One son. Educated Mount Holyoke College (B.S., 1915); MIT (Ellen Richards Fellow, 1917–1918); Johns Hopkins (M.D., 1921). Professional experience: Peking Union Medical College, resident physician, obstetrics and gynecology (1922–1923); Social Hygiene Council, Chicago, lecturer (1923–1930); Infant Welfare Society and Birth Control Clinic, counselor (1925–1930); School Social Service Administration, University of Chicago, lecturer (1926–1930); Staff Institute for Psychoanalysis, Chicago, member (from 1932); Michael Reese Hospital, Chicago, consulting psychiatrist (1944–1948); American Psychoanalytic Association, Illinois, Society for Mental Health, director (1954–1955); Planned Parenthood Association, director (1954–1955). Honors and memberships: Elizabeth Blackwell Centennial Citation (1949); Chicago Psychoanalytic Society, president (1938–1940). Death date unknown.

Helen Vincent McLean displayed an interest in social medicine as well as psychoanalysis through most of her life. Born in Ohio, Vincent went east to Mount Holyoke for her undergraduate degree in science, after which she received the Ellen Richards Fellowship to study nutrition and food analysis at Massachusetts Institute of Technology. Her experiences there convinced her to study medicine, for which purpose she went to Johns Hopkins Medical School. The recently established Peking Union Medical College, supported by the Rockefeller Institute, was drawing young men and women physicians and scientists to China. Vincent was offered a residency there as an obstetrician and gynecologist. She stayed only a year, leaving China upon her marriage to Franklin Chambers McLean, who had been both director and professor of medicine in Peking since 1916.

Returning with her husband following his appointment to a professorship in medicine at the University of Chicago, she first obtained a position as a lecturer at the Social Hygiene Council. In the mid-twenties, McLean began to divide her time between the Infant Welfare Society Birth Control Clinic and the state Public Health Institute as a staff physician. After two further years teaching in the Social Service Administration, she became interested in Freudian psychoanalysis, studying and then joining the staff of the Institute for Psychoanalysis in Chicago. Some time during this period she had her only child, a son, who died young.

McLean began to divide her time between the Institute for Psychoanalysis and her work first as a consulting psychiatrist at Michael Reese Hospital in the forties and then in the fifties as director of the Illinois Mental Health Association and the Planned Parenthood Association. These directorships allowed her to combine her long-term interests in both social medicine and psychiatry. She was recognized for her contributions to medicine with the Elizabeth Blackwell Centennial citation in 1949. Like her husband, whose work in human relations was honored in the 1950s, McLean published on race relations. She also conducted research and published on psychoanalytic education, even applying her knowledge of psychoanalysis to a study of Greek drama.

JH/MBO

STANDARD SOURCES
Debus.

MCNAB, CATHERINE MARY (1809–1857)

British botanical popularizer. Born 13 February 1809 in Richmond, Surrey. Father, William McNab. Educated privately. Died in Dailly, Ayrshire, 1857.

Catherine Mary McNab was the eldest daughter of William McNab, a gardener at the Royal Botanical Gardens, Kew. She was born near the gardens and had an interest throughout her life in botany. Soon after she was born, the family moved to Scotland, where William McNab took the position of superintendent of the Royal Botanic Gardens, Edinburgh. He wrote a number of books and articles on propagating and cultivating plants in Scotland when McNab was in her twenties; she may have assisted him in preparing them. She wrote *Botany of the Bible* when she was in her early forties, and prepared the sheets for *Object Lessons in Botany*.

JH/MBO

PRIMARY SOURCES
McNab, Catherine Mary. *Botany of the Bible*. 1850–1851.

SECONDARY SOURCES
Notes from Royal Botanical Garden, Edinburgh 3 (1908): 323. This article, on pages 293–324, is on her father, William McNab, and includes a portrait of him.

STANDARD SOURCES
Barnhart; Desmond.

MCVEIGH, ILDA (1905–)

U.S. biologist and botanist. Born 12 February 1905 in Fulton, Mo., to Emma Carrant and Joseph F. McVeigh. Educated Synodial College (A.A., 1925); University of Missouri (B.S. in education; M.A., 1933; Ph.D., 1937). Professional experience: University of Missouri, faculty (1937–1940); Northwest State College, Alva, Okla. (1940–1941); Connecticut College (1942–1943); Yale University, research assistant (1941–1942; 1943–1945); New York Botanical Garden, researcher (1945–1948). Vanderbilt University, associate professor of biology (1948–1966), professor (1966–post-1968). Honors and memberships: Fellow American Association for the Advancement of Science; member, Sigma Xi; member, Sigma Delta Epsilon, member, various mycological and microbiological societies; member, Torrey Botanical Club.

Born and raised in Missouri, Ilda McVeigh earned her doctorate from the University of Missouri. After short terms at various universities, McVeigh went to Vanderbilt and remained there during the rest of her career, rising to professor in 1966. She studied vegetative reproduction, nutrition and growth factors of microorganisms, and the effects of antibiotics.

JH/MBO

STANDARD SOURCES
AMS 7–8, B 9, P&B 10–14.

MEAD, MARGARET (1901–1978)

U.S. anthropologist. Born 16 December 1901 in Philadelphia, Pa., to Emily (Fogg) and Edward Sherwood Mead. Married (1) Luther Cressman (1923; divorced 1928); (2) Reo Fortune (1928; divorced 1935); (3) Gregory Bateson (1936–1950). One daughter, Mary Catherine Bateson Kassarjian (born 1939). Educated Barnard College (B.A., 1924); Columbia University (Ph.D., 1929). Professional experience: American Museum of Natural History, assistant curator (1926–1942), associate curator (1942–1964), curator (1964–1969), curator emerita (1969–1978). Died 1978.

Best known for her field research on gender and sex roles, Margaret Mead was the first anthropologist to study child rearing and women in a cross-cultural perspective. During her career, Mead conducted twenty-four field trips with major expeditions. She first worked with the people on the island of T'au in American Samoa (1925 to 1926). On several different occasions, she studied the Manus of the Admiralty Islands in Papua, New Guinea. Her first trip was in 1928–1929, then again in 1953, 1965, and 1975. From December 1931 to August 1932 she worked with the Arapesh and in the autumn of 1932 with the Mundugumor for three weeks. For the first few weeks of 1933 she studied the Tchambuli or Chambri and the Iatmul of New Guinea in 1938–1939. She conducted additional field work in Bali (1936–1939) and among the Omaha. Mead developed a working knowledge of the languages involved, with the exception of Omaha. She also used pidgin or Neo-Melanesian. She published numerous articles on her field work.

Mead's professional home was the American Museum of Natural History, where she remained for almost fifty years. She collaborated with her last two husbands in her field work in New Guinea and Bali. Such partnerships made it possible for a woman to work in remote, often dangerous areas. She found that as a woman, she was able to include women and children in her studies. After her divorce from Bateson, she continued to collaborate with others, finding it a fruitful approach.

Her training under Franz Boas at Columbia prepared Mead for the work that she did. She also came in contact with Boas's other female students such as ELSIE CLEWS PARSONS, GENE WELTFISH, RUTH UNDERHILL, RUTH BUNZEL, GLADYS REICHARD, and ERNA GUNTHER. She also met RUTH BENEDICT there when Benedict was Boas's teaching assistant. Mead's interpretations reflected Boas's ideas, both his older and newer agendas. As Boas changed, Mead adopted the new ideas. She was also influenced by the British anthropologists such as A. R. Radcliffe-Brown. He considered the idea of "culture" outside of scientific inquiry and instead focused on the concrete study of kinship. Her early works *Coming of Age in Samoa* and *Growing Up in New Guinea* emphasized the development of individual female adolescents in Samoa and of individual children in New Guinea. In the *Social Organization of Manu'a* she used the configuralist approach that she had absorbed from her talks with Ruth Benedict. However, after her marriage to Reo Fortune, who was strongly influenced by the British school, those views are reflected in her study "Kinship in the Admiralty Islands."

Gregory Bateson met Mead and Fortune in New Guinea in 1932. By this time she had already managed to blend the two schools together. From Mead's extended conversations with Bateson before their marriage, she expressed her ideas in *Sex and Temperament in Three Primitive Societies*. In Bali from 1936 to 1939, Mead studied the relationship of trance, dance, ritual, and child rearing practices to character forma-

tion. At the same time Bateson proposed testing his theory of the dynamics of social interaction by connecting child development and character formation. They both attempted to develop methods that would make their observations more objective. From her Bali studies, Mead realized that there could be a wide variation of cultural expression of maleness and femaleness, as documented in a later book, *Male and Female*.

During World War II, Mead worked for the federal government as an anthropologist. The war changed many of her ideas. She has been criticized for clinging to the importance of culture over the biological basis for sex-typed behavior. However, in the face of Hitlerism, she did not want to stress biology over culture. After the war, she explored the biological determinants of gender as well, arriving at a holistic determination. In the 1950s, she revisited the cultures that she had previously studied, concerned that "progress" would have changed them.

Mead's accomplishments were recognized in her later years. She became adjunct professor at Columbia University (1954) and then chair of the department of social sciences and professor of anthropology at Fordham University (1968–1970). She held several visiting lectureships. She was the second woman and the first anthropologist since Franz Boas to become president of the American Association for the Advancement of Science. She was elected to the National Academy of Sciences (1973). Mead received twenty-eight honorary degrees and forty distinguished awards for science and citizenship including the Viking Medal in general anthropology and the Kalinga Prize for the popularization of science. Posthumously, she was awarded the Presidential Medal of Freedom.

Mead's work has generated considerable controversy. Her field work has been criticized as too subjective. Others note that she was extremely fortunate in locating three New Guinea tribes that support her hypothesis about the cultural determination of sex roles. One of the most virulent criticisms was by the Australian anthropologist Derek Freeman, who excoriated her Samoan research for ignoring the biological boundaries of human behavior. This controversy is by no means settled. Mead created a great deal of interest in anthropology through her popularizations.   JH

PRIMARY SOURCES

Mead, Margaret. *Coming of Age in Samoa: A Psychological Study of Primitive Youth for Western Civilization*. New York: William Morrow, 1928.

———. *Growing Up in New Guinea: A Comparative Study of Primitive Education*. New York: William Morrow, 1930.

———. *Social Organization of Manu'a*. Bulletin 76 of the Bernice P. Bishop Museum. Honolulu: Bishop Museum, 1930.

————. "Kinship in the Admiralty Islands." *Anthropological Papers of the American Museum of Natural History* 34 (1934): 183–358.

————. *Sex and Temperament in Three Primitive Societies.* New York: William Morrow, 1935.

————. *Male and Female: A Study of the Sexes in a Changing World.* New York: William Morrow, 1949.

————. *Blackberry Winter: My Earlier Years.* New York: William Morrow, 1972.

SECONDARY SOURCES

Freeman, Derek. *Margaret Mead and Samoa: The Making and Unmaking of an Anthropological Myth.* Cambridge, Mass.: Harvard University Press, 1983.

Goodman, R. A. *Mead's Coming of Age in Samoa: A Dissenting View.* Oakland, Calif.: Pipperine Press, 1983.

Gordan, Joan. *Margaret Mead: The Complete Bibliography, 1925–1975.* The Hague: Mouton, 1976.

Mark, Joan T. *Margaret Mead, Anthropologist: Coming of Age in America.* New York: Oxford University Press, 1998.

Modell, Judith S. *Ruth Benedict: Patterns of a Life.* Philadelphia: University of Pennsylvania Press, 1983.

STANDARD SOURCES

AMS 1–8, S&B 9–12, P&B 13–14; Bailey; Gacs (article by Virginia Yans-Mclaughlin).

MEASHAM, CHARLOTTE ELIZABETH (COWPER) (1863–1937)

British botanist. Born 2 July 1863 probably in Cambridge. Professional experience: Rochester, science teacher; Newcastle-upon-Tyne, science teacher; Leicester, science teacher. Died 17 March 1937.

Charlotte Measham taught science in three different cities. She botanized in Leicestershire.   JH/MBO

SECONDARY SOURCES

Primavesi, A. L. and P. A. Evans. *Flora of Leicestershire.* Leicester: Leicestershire Museums, Art Galleries, and Records Service, 1988. Measham discussed on pages 73–75.

STANDARD SOURCES

Desmond.

MECHTHILD OF MAGDEBURG (1212–1282)

German healer. Born 1212 in Hackedorn or Magdeburg. Educated nunnery of Helfta. Professional positions: uncloistered nun; cared for the sick. Died 1282.

Mechthild of Hackedorn and Magdeburg was born of the nobility. Educated in the nunnery of Helfta, she was an uncloistered nun who devoted her life to teaching and visiting patients. At night, she wrote her visions in a poetic style. She was both a mystic and a practical woman of the world. Her advice on caring for the sick involved cleanliness, preparation of ointments for healing sores, cooling lotions, and sweet smelling flowers to brighten their rooms. She was quite critical of the clergy. She retired to the convent at Einsiedeln where her superior was the abbess Gertrude of Helfta, who also recorded her visions. Some authorities claim that it was Mechthild whom Dante saw in *Paradiso,* Canto 28.   JH/MBO

STANDARD SOURCES

Eckenstein; Hurd-Mead 1938.

MEDAGLIA, DIAMANTE (fl. 17th century)

Italian mathematician. Flourished seventeenth century. Professional experience: wrote dissertation on the importance of mathematics to women.

Diamante Medaglia was one of several Italian women mathematicians of the Renaissance, such as MARIA ARDINGHELLI, Cristina Roccati, CLELIA BORROMEO, and, later, MARIA GAETANA AGNESI. Medaglia wrote a dissertation on the importance of mathematics in the curriculum of studies for women.   JH/MBO

SECONDARY SOURCES

Boccaccio, Giovanni. *Delle donne illustri.* Florence: Filippo Giunti, 1596.

STANDARD SOURCES

Mozans.

MEDES, GRACE (1885–1967)

U.S. chemist. Born 9 November 1886 in Keokuk, Iowa, to Kate (Hagney) and William Medes. Educated University of Kansas (B.A., 1904; M.A., 1913); Bryn Mawr College (Ph.D., 1916). Professional experience: Vassar College, instructor in zoology (1916–1919), assistant professor of physiology (1919–1922); Wellesley College, associate professor of physiology (1922–1924); University of Minnesota Medical school, Fellow (1924–1925), assistant professor of clinical chemistry school (1925–1932); Lankenau Hospital Research Institute (later merged with Institute for Cancer Research), research faculty (1932–1952); Institute for Cancer Research, senior member (1954–1960); Department of Metabolic Chemistry, Institute for Cancer Research, emerita chair

(1960–1967). Honors and memberships: Garvan Medal (1955); American Academy of Arts and Scientists, Fellow (1955); University of Kansas, Distinguished Service Citation (1955); Bryn Mawr College, Distinguished Service Citation (1960). Died 31 December 1967.

Born in a small Iowa town, Grace Medes moved to Lawrence, Kansas, for both her bachelor's and master's degrees in zoology. She then moved to Bryn Mawr, Pennsylvania, where she completed a doctoral degree. After earning this degree, she served as an instructor and then assistant professor at Vassar College. Medes moved to Wellesley as an associate professor and remained there for two years before becoming a fellow and then an assistant professor at the University of Minnesota Medical School.

She remained at Minnesota for seven years before she went as department head of metabolic chemistry to the Lankenau Hospital Research Institute. During her time in Minnesota she made an important discovery, a human metabolic disorder known as tyrosinosis.

In 1932, Medes moved to private industry as a member of the cancer research staff of the Lankenau Hospital Research Institute in Philadelphia. Pathologist Samuel P. Reichmann was the institute's director. Medes limited her research on tyrosinosis and joined Reichmann's group in its study of the relationships of different sulphur groups in compound in stimulating and retarding cell proliferation. Her work at Lankenau began with her attempt to decipher the pathway that produces inorganic sulfate from the amino acids cystine and methionine, found in numerous body proteins. Because of the scarcity of experimental animals, Medes reputedly used herself as a guinea pig.

When carbon isotopes became available and isotope tracer studies were feasible, Medes turned to the study of fatty acid metabolism in the body. From her work she published a series of papers that showed that acetyl groups participated in acetoacetate synthesis. This work became the basis in the later discovery of coenzyme A. When Lankenau Hospital Research Institute merged with the Institute for Cancer Research in 1950, Medes remained with the new institute until she retired in 1956. Two years before retirement, she became a senior member of the institute.

In 1955 Medes won the coveted Garvan Medal of the American Chemical Society recognizing the outstanding achievements of a woman chemist. Her research on tyrosinosis was further honored by a symposium in Oslo, Norway, in 1965. After she retired in 1956, she resumed her research on tyrosinosis at the Fels Research Institute, Temple University.

JH/MBO

PRIMARY SOURCES

Medes, Grace. "A Study of the Causes and the Extent of Variations in the Larvae of Arbacia punctulata." Ph.D. diss., Bryn Mawr, 1916. Published in *Journal of Morphology* 30, no. 1 (December 1917): 317–432.

———. "A New Error of Tyrosine Metabolism: Tyrosinosis." *Biochemical Journal* 26 (1932): 917–940.

———. "Metabolism of Sulfur. III." *Biochemical Journal* 31 (1937): 12–16. She published numerous articles on the metabolism of sulfur, of which this article is one.

———. "Cancer Isotopes in the Study of Cancer." *Clinics* 4 (1945): 128–134.

———. "Production of Ketone Bodies." *Proceedings of the American Diabetes Association* 7 (1948): 85–93.

———. "Fat Metabolism." *Annual Review of Biochemistry* 19 (1950): 215–234.

———. With A. Allen and S. Weinhouse. "The Effects of Growth Hormone on Fatty Acid Metabolism in vitro." *Journal of Biological Chemistry* 221 (1956): 333–345.

SECONDARY SOURCES

"Deaths—Grace Medes." *Chemical and Engineering News* 46 (4 March 1968): 68.

STANDARD SOURCES

American Women 1974; *AMS* 3–8, B 9, P&B 10–11; Grinstein 1993 (article, with excellent bibliography, by Paris Sivronos); Shearer and Shearer 1997 (article by Stefanie Buck).

MEDVEDEVA, NINA BORISOVNA (1899–1969)

Russian pathophysiologist. Born 1899 in Saratov. Educated Saratov University, medical department (graduated 1921). Professional experience: Saratov University, staff (1921–1925); Second Moscow Medical University, assistant, then lecturer (1925–1931); Institute of Experimental Biology and Pathology, Ukrainian Academy of Sciences, senior associate (1931–1952); Bogomolets Institute of Physiology, Kiev, department head (from 1953). Honors and memberships: Ukrainian Academy of Sciences, corresponding member; Order of Lenin. Died in 1969.

Nina Borisovna Medvedeva graduated from the medical department of Saratov University in 1921. From 1921 to 1925 she worked as an assistant in the department of general pathology at Saratov University. She then moved to Moscow, where she worked as an assistant and then as a lecturer in the department of pathological physiology at the Second Moscow Medical University until 1931. From 1931 to 1952, she was a senior assistant at the Institute of Experimental Biology and Pathology of the Ukrainian Academy of Sciences.

In 1953, she became head of a department at the Bogomolets Institute of Physiology in Kiev. Medvedeva died in 1969.

Medvedeva conducted research in various areas of pathological physiology and was the author of numerous publications, whose topics include effect of tiredness on tissue metabolism under normal and various abnormal conditions; blood transfusion; autocatalytic function of lungs, liver, spleen, and lymph nodes; and changes in tissue proteins in old age. She established limits of permissible muscle loading in liver and kidney deficiency and proved experimentally that antireticular cytotoxic serum affects change in tissues' nitrogen and protein composition. Medvedeva isolated cortical hormone from the adrenal cortex and also suggested that presence of desoxydative carbonuria be regarded as an early symptom in the diagnosis of cancer.

Medvedeva also compiled a bibliography on pathological physiology and endocrinology. She was elected a corresponding member of the Ukrainian Academy of Sciences. She was also a member of the editing board of the *Medical Journal* and was awarded the Order of Lenin.   ACH

PRIMARY SOURCES
Medvedeva, Nina Borisovna. *Eksperimental'naia endokrinologiia.* N.p., 1946.

STANDARD SOURCES
Debus.

MEE, MARGARET URSULA (BROWN) (1909–1988)

British botanist and botanical artist. Born 22 May 1909 in Chesham, Buckinghamshire. Married Greville Mee (1953). Educated St. Martin's School of Art; Camberwell School of Art. Professional experience: expeditions to the Amazon to paint flowers. Died 30 November 1988 in Leicester.

Although she had received training in art when she was young, Margaret Mee's importance to the field came later. When she was forty-seven years old she first visited the Amazon forests, traveling with her husband. When she was fifty-seven, she settled in Brazil and traveled extensively in the Brazilian Amazon, where she collected and painted new species of plants. Her work is especially important, because some of the species she collected or painted have since become extinct. She was an outspoken ecological advocate and was angry at the destruction of Amazonia. The Margaret Mee Amazon Trust was set up in 1988 to draw attention to the ecological crisis in the area.   JH/MBO

PRIMARY SOURCES
Mee, Margaret Ursula. *Flowers of the Brazilian Forests,* [London]: Tryon Gallery, [1968].
———. *Flores do Amazones.* Rio de Janeiro: n.p., 1980.

SECONDARY SOURCES
Hortus no. 10 (1989): 111–117.
Journal of the Bromeliad Society 30 (1980): 253–255.

STANDARD SOURCES
Desmond.

MEEK, LOIS HAYDEN (1894–1984)

U.S. psychologist. Born 19 October 1894 in Washington, D.C., to Fannie Virginia (Price) and Alexander Kennedy Meek (lawyer). Married Herbert R. Stoltz (1938). One child. Educated George Washington University (A.B., 1921); Columbia University Teachers College (A.M., 1922; fellow, 1922–1923; Ph.D., 1924). Professional experience: Washington, D.C., public school teacher (1912–1917); Columbia University Teachers College, assistant in education (1922–1923); American Association of University Women, education secretary (1924–1929); Columbia University Teachers College, associate professor of education and associate director of child development institute (1929–1930), division of individual development and guidance, professor (1930–1940), director (1930–1937), chairman (1938–1939); Institute of Child Welfare, Palo Alto(?), Calif., research associate (1940–1943); Stanford University, lecturer in psychology (1943–1946), professor (from 1947); San Francisco State College, lecturer (from 1941); state coordinator, care of children in wartime, San Francisco(?), Calif. (1942); Kaiser Company, Inc., director of child service centers (1943–1945); summer instructor at many different universities. Died 1984.

Lois Meek had a variety of academic and nonacademic positions. Her first academic positions were at Columbia University Teachers College, where she had earned her master's and doctoral degrees, eventually becoming a full professor and director of the child guidance clinic. She gave up the position that she had at Columbia and moved to California, possibly following her husband. She got a research associate job at the Institute of Child Welfare in California, and a job as lecturer at Stanford. She was soon promoted to professor but moved again, this time to San Francisco, where she began again as a lecturer at San Francisco State College. After San Francisco State, she essentially left teaching, although she taught at several different universities during the summer. She had a variety of public service positions and also worked in industry.

Meek was a member of the National Advisory Committee on Education (1929–1931) and was the associate chairman for child development for the American Council of Education (1939–1940). She worked for the Office of Indian Affairs (from 1947). She belonged to numerous professional organizations, including the Society for Study of Education, Society for Research in Child Development, Progressive Association, and the American Psychological Association.

Her research was in the areas of child development, child guidance, and education.   KM

STANDARD SOURCES
AMS 4–8; O'Connell and Russo 1988; Stevens and Gardner.

MEIGLER, MARIE J. (1851–1901)

German/U.S. gynecologist. Born 18 May 1851 in Main Stockheim, Bavaria. Father Francis R. Meigler. Educated Cook County, Ill., Normal School; State Normal School, Oswego, N.Y. (1871, classics); Woman's Medical College, Chicago (M.D., 1879); postgraduate study in Zurich (1880). Professional experience: Woman's Medical College, surgical assistant, later chair of gynecology (1890); Cook County General Hospital, staff physician (from 1882); Woman's Hospital in Chicago, attending surgeon (1886–1901); Wesley Hospital, Chicago, gynecologist (1890–1901); Mary Thompson Hospital, Chicago, head physician and surgeon; Northwestern Woman's Medical School, dean (1897); Medical School of Chicago (postgraduate school), professor of gynecology. Honors and memberships: Illinois State Medical Society; Chicago Medical Society, member. Died 18 May 1910 in Chicago of pernicious anemia.

Marie Meigler gained wide distinction as a gynecologist, diagnostician, and surgeon. She was born in Bavaria of old German stock and moved with her family to Illinois in 1853. There she attended local normal schools and entered Woman's Medical College in 1876. She graduated class valedictorian in 1879 and applied to take the examinations for interns at Cook County Hospital. Met with boos and hisses at the examination, none of the women who applied were accepted. Nevertheless, Meigler applied again a year later and was told she passed the exam successfully but would not receive an appointment because of her sex. Meigler then returned to the Woman's Medical College as surgical assistant to her professor, William H. Byford. Upon his death, Meigler was appointed chair of gynecology.

Meigler held numerous appointments in gynecology and surgery, including staff appointment at Cook County Hospital (where she had been snubbed earlier). Her appointment as head physician and surgeon at the Mary Thompson Hospital was met with unanimous support of the Chicago Gynecological Society and a majority of the members of the medical profession of Chicago. She was lauded for her success in abdominal surgery, which had, at this time, a poor

success rate. She contributed to professional journals and held an editorship with the *Woman's Medical Journal of Chicago.* She died in California, on her fiftieth birthday, of pernicious anemia.   KM

PRIMARY SOURCES
Meigler, Marie. "A Guide to the Study of Gynecology." *Woman's Medical Journal of Chicago* (1892).
———. "History of the Woman's Medical College of Chicago." *Woman's Medical Journal of Chicago* (1893).
———. With Charles W. Earle. "Diseases of the New-born." *American Textbook of Obstetrics,* N.p., n.d.

STANDARD SOURCES
Cyclopaedia.

MEITNER, LISE (1878–1968)

Austrian physicist. Born 7 November 1878 in Vienna to Hedwig (Skowran) and Philipp Meitner. Seven siblings. Never married. Educated at local schools; University of Vienna (doctorate 1906); University of Berlin, habilitation (1922). Professional experience: Berlin, research scientist (1907–1912); Max Planck's assistant (1912–1915); Kaiser Wilhelm Institute for Chemistry, scientific associate and professor (1913–1938); University of Berlin, adjunct professor of physics (1926–1933). Nobel Institute for Experimental Physics, Stockholm (1938–1947); Royal Institute of Technology, Stockholm, professor (1947–1954). Honors and memberships: Silver Leibniz Medal (1924), Ignaz Lieben Prize (1925), Ellen Richards Prize (1928), National Women's Press Club (U.S.) Woman of the Year (1946), Vienna Prize for Science and Art (1947), Max Planck Medal (1949), Otto Hahn Prize (1955), Orden pour le mérite (1957), Wilhelm Exner Medal (1960), Dorothea Schlözer Medal (1962); numerous Nobel nominations, honorary degrees. Died 27 October 1968 in Cambridge, England.

Lise Meitner was the third child (third daughter) of a cultured Viennese family of Jewish origin that emphasized music, politics, and social concerns. Judaism played essentially no role in the children's upbringing, and all eventually converted, Lise to Protestantism in 1908. Typical of public education for Austrian girls, Lise's schooling was mediocre and brief, ending at age fourteen. When Austrian universities were opened to women in 1897, however, she took intensive private lessons and entered the University of Vienna in 1901. From 1902 to 1905, she studied physics under the theoretical physicist Ludwig Boltzmann, a charismatic teacher who also seems to have been an enthusiastic early supporter of women's education. Meitner's doctoral research was done under the experimental physicist Franz Exner, and in 1906 she became the second woman to receive a doctorate in physics from the University of Vienna.

In 1907 Meitner went to Berlin to attend the lectures of the theoretical physicist Max Planck. Although Prussian universities were closed to women until 1908, Planck became her mentor and friend, and she joined Otto Hahn, a chemist just her age, for radioactivity research. Their collaboration was immediately successful, but as a woman Meitner was without hope for a position or pay. Meitner was shy by nature; her early struggles for education and work left her with a deep insecurity, which she overcame at the height of her career, but which returned later during her difficult exile in Sweden.

Meitner's association with Hahn is a remarkable example of an extended interdisciplinary partnership. They worked under the same roof for thirty-one years, together in radioactivity until about 1920, then independently when Meitner turned to nuclear physics, then together again from 1934 to 1938 for the investigation that culminated in the discovery of nuclear fission. Compared to other female/male collaborations, Meitner was fortunate at first, in that her work as a physicist was evaluated and recognized independently of Hahn's.

Once underway, Meitner's career provided milestones for the inclusion of women in German science. In 1912 Planck made her his assistant, the first woman to hold that position in Prussia, and in 1913 she was appointed a paid associate in the newly established Kaiser Wilhelm Institute for Chemistry (KWI). From 1915 to 1916 she volunteered as an X-ray nurse in Austrian military hospitals. Upon her return to Berlin, she was given her own section for physics in the KWI in 1917, and in 1919 she was appointed professor in the institute. In 1922, she was the first woman physicist in Prussia to undergo *habilitation,* the first step on the traditional academic ladder, and in 1926 she was appointed adjunct professor at the University of Berlin, making her the first woman physics professor in Germany. In the 1920s and early 1930s Meitner was internationally recognized for her pioneering work in nuclear physics, a successful scientist and an assertive professor, secure in her friendships with some of the great physicists of the time, including, among others, Planck, Einstein, Niels Bohr, James Franck, Max von Laue, Erwin Schrödinger, and Max Born.

In 1933 the National Socialists rescinded Meitner's university professorship but as an Austrian citizen she was protected, and she did not lose her position in the KWI. After the Austrian *Anschluss* of March 1938, however, she knew her dismissal was imminent, and in the summer of 1938 she secretly fled Germany with the help of Dutch colleagues by way of Holland to Stockholm.

Meitner's forced emigration shattered her career and clouded her scientific reputation. Five months after she left Berlin, the remaining members of her team, Hahn and the chemist Fritz Strassmann, announced the splitting of the uranium nucleus, a discovery in which she should have fully shared. For political reasons, she could not share authorship with Hahn and Strassmann, and Hahn soon distanced the discovery from Meitner and physics, a stance he maintained the rest of his life. Although Meitner and her nephew, the physicist Otto Frisch, gave the first theoretical interpretation for the process (and named it fission), the 1944 Nobel Prize in chemistry was awarded to Hahn alone. Meitner's exclusion from the Nobel award can be attributed, at least in part, to her marginality as an émigré woman scientist with no real position in Sweden.

After World War II, Meitner was briefly a celebrity, especially in the United States. In Sweden she was made a research professor in 1947 and participated in the development of Sweden's first nuclear reactor. In West Germany she was honored as a person, but never rehabilitated as a scientist: references either omit her entirely or portray her as Hahn's subordinate, two common fates for women in science. Late in life she lectured on issues of science and world peace, the control of nuclear weapons, and the status of women in the professions. In 1960 she moved to Cambridge, England, where she died in 1968, a few days before her ninetieth birthday.

Meitner's experimental work spanned the development of atomic physics from the early years of radioactivity to nuclear physics to the discovery of nuclear fission and beyond. Under the formative influence of her two great teachers, Boltzmann and Planck, she chose her most important work at the point where theory and experiment progress together. In 1906–1907 she studied alpha particle scattering and the absorption of beta radiation; with Hahn she developed radioactive recoil for the separation of radioactive species (1908–1909) and with Hahn and Otto von Baeyer she began the first systematic studies of beta spectra (1910).

In the new KWI for chemistry, Meitner and Hahn studied weakly radioactive species and in 1918 they discovered protactinium (^{231}Pa), element 91. After World War I she entered nuclear physics with precision studies of beta-gamma spectra. Convinced that the nucleus is quantized, she engaged in a extended controversy with British physicist C. D. Ellis over the sequence of radioactive decay and the reality of the continuous primary beta spectrum. In 1825 she proved her contention that the emission of nuclear gamma radiation follows alpha and beta decay, and in 1929 she verified Ellis's measurement of the continuous beta spectrum with an improved experiment, after which Wolfgang Pauli proposed the existence of the neutrino in 1930. Her measurements of high-energy gamma radiation (1930) verified the Klein-Nishina formula and Dirac's relativistic electron theory. In an effort to establish whether neutrons were fundamental or complex, she determined neutron mass using neutron-induced reactions (1933). She was the first to describe the radiationless transitions now known as the Auger effect (1923), and the first to identify positrons from a non-cosmic source and to recognize positron-electron pair formation (1933).

In 1934, intrigued by Enrico Fermi's experiments indicating that transuranic elements were produced by the neutron irradiation of uranium, Meitner recruited Hahn, and later Strassmann, for the investigation that resulted in the discovery of nuclear fission. Meitner was the team's leader, interpreting the data from chemistry, radiochemistry, and her own physical measurements into the context of nuclear physics. In Swedish exile she corresponded closely with Hahn, playing a crucial role by insisting on the rigorous experiments that led directly to the finding of barium and the realization that uranium had split. Had Meitner been in Berlin, the discovery would have been regarded as an interdisciplinary achievement in which she would have fully shared. Instead, the chemists announced the finding of barium and the physicists, Meitner and Frisch, separately provided the first theoretical interpretation of the fission process, including a calculation of the energy released. Although Meitner and Frisch's work was regarded as seminal and became the starting point for further nuclear theory, particularly by Bohr, and Bohr and John Wheeler in 1939, the fission discovery itself was ascribed to chemistry and, after the Nobel Prize, primarily to Hahn. The misperception distorted the history of the discovery and for many years diminished Meitner's scientific reputation overall.   RLS

PRIMARY SOURCES
Meitner, Lise. With Otto Hahn. "Die Muttersubstanz des Actiniums." *Physikalische Zeitschrift* 19 (1918): 208–218.
Meitner, Lise. "Die y-Strahlung der Actiniumreihe und der Nachweis, dass die y-Strahlen erst nach erfolgtem Atomzerfall emittiert werden." *Zeitschrift für Physik* 34 (1925): 807–808.
———. With H. Kösters. "Uber der Streuung kurzwelliger y-Strahlen." *Zeitschrift für Physik* 84 (1933): 137–144.
———. With K. Philipp. "Die bei Neutronenanregung auftretenden Elektronenbahnen." *Naturwissenschaften* 21 (1933): 286–287.
———. With O. R. Frisch. "Disintegration of Uranium by Neutrons: A New Type of Nuclear Reaction." *Nature* 143 (1939): 239–240.
———. "Wege und Irrwege zur Kernenergie." *Naturwissenschaftliche Rundschau* 16 (1963): 167–169.
———. "Looking Back." *Bulletin of the Atomic Scientists* 20, no. 11 (1964): 2–7.

SECONDARY SOURCES
Crawford, Elisabeth, Ruth Lewin Sime, and Mark Walker. "A Nobel Tale of Wartime Justice." *Nature* 382, no. 6590 (1996): 353.

Ernst, Sabine, ed. *Lise Meitner an Otto Hahn: Briefe aus den Jahren 1912 bis 1924, Edition und Kommentierung.* Stuttgart: Wissenschaftliche Verlagsgesellschaft, 1992.
Frisch, Otto Robert. "Lise Meitner, 1878–1968." *Biographical Memoirs of Fellows of the Royal Society* 16 (1970): 405–420.
Frisch, Otto Robert. *What Little I Remember.* Cambridge: Cambridge University Press, 1979.
Krafft, Fritz. *Im Schatten Der Sensation: Leben und Wirken von Fritz Strassmann.* Weinheim: Verlag Chemie, 1981.
Rife, Patricia. *Lise Meitner: Ein Leben für die Wissenschaft.* Trans. Peter Jacobs. Düsseldorf: Claassen, 1990.
Sime, Ruth Lewin. *Lise Meitner: A Life in Physics.* Berkeley: University of California Press, 1996.

STANDARD SOURCES
DSB; Grinstein 1993 (article by Sallie Watkins); *Notable.*

MELISSA (ca. 6th century B.C.E.)
Greek mathematician and natural philosopher.

Very little is known about Melissa. She may have belonged to the original Pythagorean sect and been a contemporary of THEANO, MYIA, and DAMO. Since most of the early Pythagoreans were mathematicians, it is assumed that she probably had interests in that area. In Thesleff's *Pythagorean Texts of the Hellenistic Period* there is a letter in Doric purportedly written by Melissa to Clareta. The letter is about clothing. It says that the only red color which should be worn is that which comes from modesty, that is, blushing.   JH/MBO

PRIMARY SOURCES
Melissa. Letter in *The Pythagorean Texts of the Hellenistic Period,* ed. Holger Thesleff. Acta Academiae Aboensis, Ser. A. Humaniora 30, no. 1. Abo: Abo Akademi, 1965.

STANDARD SOURCES
Ménage.

MELLANBY, MAY (TWEEDY) (1882–1978)
British physiologist. Born 1882. Married Edward Mellanby (1914). Educated in London; Girton College, Cambridge; Natural Science Tripos I and II (2nd class) (1905, 1906). Professional experience: Bedford College, research fellow; lecturer (1906?–1914); Medical Research Committee (then Council), Brown Animal Sanatory Institution, member (1914–1919); Medical Research Council, University of Sheffield, member (1920–1933). Honors and memberships: University of Sheffield (D.Sc., 1933); University of Liverpool (D.Sc., 1934); Cambridge University (Sc.D.); Girton College, Cambridge, honorary fellow. Died 1978.

May (Tweedy) Mellanby, like her sister Nora (Tweedy) Edkins made a name for herself as a physiologist. Born in imperial Russia, where her father was helping to develop the oil industry, she was educated in schools in London and then at Girton. She sat both Natural Tripos exams, achieving the equivalent of a second-class degree. Tweedy then went to Bedford College for Women, London as a research fellow where she collaborated with her head of department, J. S. Edkins, who would later marry her younger sister, Nora. Edkins, later recognized as the discoverer of gastrin, was then trying to prove his controversial ideas about the chemical mediation of gastric secretion.

After a few years, Tweedy began to teach physiology at Bedford College, helping to educate a series of remarkable women physiologists, including her own sister. In 1914, Tweedy married Edward Mellanby, whom she had met in Cambridge, who then was teaching physiology at King's College for Women, London. She subsequently resigned her position at Bedford and devoted herself to research.

During World War I, May Mellanby began to conduct animal research at the Brown Animal Sanatory Institute. Working on a problem related to her husband's research in the nutritional causes of rickets, she discovered that structural abnormalities appeared in the teeth of dogs with rickets in 1919. She continued to explore the relationship between nutrition and teeth formation, collaborating with her husband on work that was published in a variety of journals and then incorporated into chapter two of his important book *Nutrition and Disease* (1934).

When the couple moved to the University of Sheffield, she continued animal experiments on this topic well into the thirties, exploring the development of jaw and teeth in a number of species as well as these implications for human development. She was supported by a series of grants from the Medical Research Council.

In the thirties, Mellanby was honored for her important work with honorary doctorates in science from Sheffield, Liverpool, and Cambridge. She was also an honorary fellow of her alma mater, Girton College. Following her husband's death, she was belatedly admitted to the Physiological Society of London. (Similarly Augusta Déjerine-Klumpke was admitted to the Société de Biologie in France only as a widow.) At the age of ninety-two, Mellanby's work on nutritional research was recognized by the Science Award from the International Association for Dental Research, which had earlier recognized her as an honorary member.   JH/MBO

PRIMARY SOURCES
Tweedy, May. With J. S. Edkins. "The Natural Channels of Absorption Evoking the Chemical Mechanisms of Gastric Secretion." *Journal of Physiology* (London) 38 (1909): 263–267.

Mellanby, May Tweedy. "An Experimental Study of the Influence of Diet on Tooth Formation." *Lancet* 2 (1919): 767–770.

———. "Diet and the Teeth: An Experimental Study." Part I, Medical Research Council Special Report Series No. 140. London, 1929.

———. "Diet and the Teeth: An Experimental Study." Part II, Medical Research Council Special Report Series No. 153. London, 1930.

———. "Diet and the Teeth: An Experimental Study." Part III, Medical Research Council Special Report Series No. 191. London, 1934.

Personal and scientific papers in Edward Mellanby Archive, Contemporary Medical Archive Centre, Wellcome Institute for the History of Medicine.

SECONDARY SOURCES
Mellanby, Edward, *Nutrition and Disease: The Interaction of Clinical and Experimental Work*. Edinburgh: Oliver and Boyd, 1934. Chapter two, on diet and the teeth, contains a description of May Mellanby's scientific work.

STANDARD SOURCES
Women Physiologists.

MEMMLER, RUTH LUNDEEN (1900–)

U.S. physician. Born 26 August 1900 in North Dakota. Five siblings. Married (1929). One daughter. Educated teachers college (graduated); University of California, Berkeley (B.A.); University of California Medical School; College of Medical Evangelists (now Loma Linda University) (M.D.). Professional experience: elementary school teacher; secondary school teacher (two years); Pasadena, Calif., high school, biology and physiology teacher; Los Angeles City College, teacher (to 1941); Los Angeles County Hospital, teacher (1941–1945); East Los Angeles College, developed new programs in the health fields; later professor of life sciences and coordinator of health and paramedical courses (1945–1965).

Ruth Lundeen Memmler was born of Norwegian and Swedish stock. Her parents had a wheat ranch in North Dakota and the severe winters with inadequate medical care impressed Ruth as a child. In 1907 her father sold his homestead and they moved to California, where she helped with the ranch work and walked three miles to school each day. After she completed elementary school, Memmler's father exchanged the ranch for an orange grove in southern California. After she graduated from high school, she went to a teachers' college in Los Angeles. Her practical work was a nightmare, for she had a hard time maintaining discipline.

She taught for a year in a country school near her home.

During this year, her oldest brother was struck by a car while riding his bicycle. He recovered, but Memmler's dream of becoming a physician was strengthening. She saved her money and with her mother's encouragement was admitted to the University of California, Berkeley, with the immediate goal of pursuing a bachelor's degree and obtaining general secondary credentials. Secondary school teachers' pay was much higher than elementary. She also studied zoology and chemistry, subjects that she would need later in medical school. After two strenuous years of high school teaching, Memmler had saved enough money to go to medical school.

The requirements had been upgraded, so Memmler had to spend an extra year doing premedical work. She encountered sexism in her first two years of medical school. Finances forced her to give up medical school and she got a job teaching biology and physiology to high school students in Pasadena. At this school she met a young graphics art teacher and they were married the next year. In order to be near her husband, who continued to teach, Memmler transferred to the College of Medical Evangelists (now Loma Linda University). She purchased a Model A Ford, which made it easier for her to go to clinics and hospitals. She did her internship at the Los Angeles County Hospital. When she applied for a residency at the Children's Hospital, she was told that they did not plan to accept any female doctors. She taught again, frustrated with the sexism that was prevalent in the medical profession. While teaching at the Los Angeles City College, she took her students to observe the variety of medical careers available.

World War II changed Memmler's life. She taught at the Los Angeles County Hospital and then drove about twenty miles to the Douglas Aircraft Medical offices, where she examined women applicants for work in the plant. Her husband worked as an efficiency expert at Douglas Aircraft during the day and in the evenings in a printing plant doing photographic work for navy manuals. Their daughter was born in January 1945. During that same year, Memmler took the job that she was to keep until retirement. She went to East Angeles College, where she articulated her views that required courses in health should be taught by registered nurses with special training in teaching. She published a successful textbook that went through at least three editions. Designed for nurses, it integrated elementary anatomy and physiology with some disease discussion. The third edition included chapters on matter, elements of chemistry and physics, and additional material on the cause of disease.

Memmler retired from her position as professor of the life sciences in 1965. In retirement she worked with her husband on his project of supplying high-quality slides for use in the classroom. This project involved traveling all over the world. Both Memmler and her husband were supporters of the

Equal Rights Amendment and she served in several official positions in the local branch of the National Women's Party.

JH/MBO

PRIMARY SOURCES
Memmler, R. L. In Hellstedt, *Autobiographies.*
Memmler, Ruth L. *The Human Body in Health and Disease.* Philadelphia: Lippincott, [1959].
———. With Ruth Byers Rada. *Structure and Function of the Human Body.* Philadelphia: Lippincott, [1970].

MENDENHALL, DOROTHY (REED) (1874–1964)

U.S. research and clinical physician. Born 22 September 1874 in Columbus, Ohio, to Grace (Kimball) and William Pratt Reed. Two siblings. Married Charles Elwood Mendenhall (1912). Four children (two surviving). Educated privately; Smith College (B.L., 1895); Massachusetts Institute of Technology (1895–1896); Johns Hopkins Medical School (M.D., 1900). Professional experience: Johns Hopkins Medical School, fellow in pathology (1901–1902); New England Hospital for Women and Children (resident, June 1902–January 1903); Babies Hospital, New York (1903–1906?); University of Wisconsin, Department of Home Economics, field lecturer (1914–1936). Concurrent experience: Wisconsin State Board of Health, epidemiologist; United States Children's Bureau, medical officer (intermittent 1917–1936). Died 31 July 1964 in Chester, Conn., of arteriosclerotic heart disease.

Dorothy Reed was noted for her research on Hodgkin's disease and for her work in organizing maternal and child welfare clinics. Raised in a prosperous family in Columbus, Ohio, where her father was a shoe manufacturer, she was educated first privately and then attended Smith College. Although she initially planned to work as a journalist, she became interested in biology. After graduation, Reed went to Massachusetts Institute of Technology to study with ELLEN SWALLOW RICHARDS and acquire the necessary sciences to enter medical school.

In 1896, Reed entered Johns Hopkins Medical School and soon became proficient as a pathologist and bacteriologist. Two years into her medical school years, she spent a summer working in a U.S. naval hospital laboratory as a bacteriologist and an operating hospital assistant. After obtaining her degree, she spent a year as an intern with William Osler.

When Reed was offered a fellowship in pathology with William Henry Welch in 1901, she began to teach bacteriology and to do research into Hodgkin's disease. Her research resulted in a remarkable discovery that this was not a form of tuberculosis but a separate disorder with its own pathological cell changes. This finding was published in *Johns Hopkins Hospital Reports* in 1902 and won her international attention.

In spite of this success, there seemed little future for her in pathology, and rather than take the slow and frustrating road of her fellow student FLORENCE SABIN, she took the opportunity to expand her knowledge of obstetrics and early childhood diseases as a resident first at New England Hospital for Women and Children and then in the newly opened Babies Hospital of New York as its first resident physician. Her marriage three years later to Charles Elwood Mendenhall, an academic physicist, appeared to end this part of her career.

For some years, Mendenhall remained at home with her children. The death of her first and only daughter a few hours after birth due to bungled obstetrical problems, and the death of a son at the age of five meant that after her subsequent two children were born, Mendenhall determined to return to medicine to study maternal health and welfare. In 1914, she had the opportunity to serve as a field lecturer for the Department of Home Economics of the University of Wisconsin, where her husband had obtained a professorship. By 1915, she organized the first infant welfare clinic in the state, in Madison. During her lecture tours through the state, she began to compile statistics on prenatal conditions and infant mortality for the Wisconsin State Department of Health, publishing a report on her findings in the state medical journal.

Mendenhall prepared pamphlets on children's nutrition for the U.S. Children's Bureau during World War I and then traveled through Europe to study the nutritional condition of children in orphanages. She spurred the drive of the bureau to measure and weigh all children under six as an indication of malnutrition, and represented the Children's Bureau at the International Child Welfare Conference in 1919, which set minimum standards for health centers. Her study of midwifery in Denmark in 1926 led to conclusions (not taken seriously at the time) that less medical interference during childbirth and more training of midwives would lower the infant mortality rate.

In addition to her work for the Children's Bureau, which she continued on an intermittent basis through 1936, Mendenhall developed a correspondence course for new and prospective mothers for the Department of Agriculture at the University of Wisconsin, and created the first course in sex hygiene. After her husband died in 1935, she began to withdraw from her work in medicine and traveled throughout Mexico and Central America. She settled first in North Carolina and then in Connecticut, where she died at the age of eighty-nine.

Smith College honored Mendenhall's memory by naming a hall after her and her classmate Florence Sabin (the Sabin-Reed Hall). A scholarship was given in her name for women medical students at Johns Hopkins by family members. One of her mother's cousins, the critic and author Edmund Wilson, included a chapter on her in his own memoir entitled *Upstate.*

JH/MBO

PRIMARY SOURCES

Reed, Dorothy. "On the Pathological Changes in Hodgkin's Disease with Especial Reference to Its Relation to Tuberculosis." *Johns Hopkins Medical Reports* 10 (1902): 113–196.

Mendenhall, Dorothy Reed. "Prenatal and Natal Conditions in Wisconsin." *Wisconsin Medical Journal* (March, 1917): 353–369.

———. *Milk: The Indispensable Food for Children.* Washington D.C.: U.S. Children's Bureau, 1918.

———. (with others). *Child Care and Child Welfare.* Washington D.C. U.S. Children's Bureau, 1921. Six chapters of this were written by Mendenhall.

———. *Midwifery in Denmark.* Washington D.C.: U.S. Children's Bureau, 1929.

Papers in the Sophia Smith Collection, Smith College, contain an autobiography.

STANDARD SOURCES

Bailey; *NAW*(M) (article by Elizabeth Robinton); *Notable; Uneasy Careers* (article by Regina M. Morantz-Sanchez).

MENDREZ-CARROLL, CHRISTIANE (1937–1978)

See Carroll, Christiane (Mendrez).

MENTEN, MAUD L. (1879–1960)

Canadian biochemist and pathologist. Born 20 March 1879 in Port Lambton, Ontario. Mother postmistress at Harrison Mills, British Columbia. Educated University of Toronto (B.A., 1904; M.B., 1907); University of Toronto (M.D., 1911); University of Chicago (Ph.D., 1916). Professional experience: demonstrator in physiology (1904–1907); Rockefeller Institute for Medical Research, research fellow; New York Infirmary for Women and Children, intern (one year); Krankenhaus am Urban, Berlin, researcher (1912–1913); Western Reserve University with George Crile, researcher (1915–1916); Barnard Skin and Cancer Hospital pathologist; E. S. Magee Hospital in Pittsburg, pathologist (1916); University of Pittsburgh, demonstrator in pathology (1918), assistant professor (1923), associate professor (1925), professor (1949); British Columbia Medical Research Institute, research (1950–1954). Died 26 July 1960.

Maud Menten was a Canadian biochemist who worked for most of her life in the United States. She is noted for her research on cancerous cells, on enzyme kinetics, on the bacterial toxins, and for her work on nucleic acids of bone marrow and cancerous cells. She also helped to open up the field of enzyme histochemistry. Born in Port Lambton, Ontario, on 20 March 1879, she moved with her family to Harrison Mills, where her mother was postmistress. She went to the University of Toronto in 1900, obtaining her degree in 1904. She stayed on to do her mater's degree in physiology, serving as demonstrator in that subject from 1904 to 1907. In that year she obtained a research fellowship from the Rockefeller Institute for Medical Research in New York City, and worked with Simon Flexner and J. V. Jobling on the effects of radium bromide on cancerous tumors in the white rat. This was published as the first monograph of the institute. The following year, she served as an intern at the New York Infirmary for Women and Children and then returned to the University of Toronto for her medical degree in 1911. She followed this up with further research at the Berlin Krankenhaus am Urban with Leonor Michaelis (1911–1912), studying enzyme kinetics, and defining the Michaelis-Menten constant. She further expanded her research into cancer by studying at Western Reserve University with George Crile, working from 1915 to 1916 at the Barnard Skin and Cancer Hospital. She obtained a doctoral degree in biochemistry at the University of Chicago in 1916. In that same year she went to Pittsburgh, where she worked as a pathologist at the E. S. Magee Hospital. By 1918, she was demonstrator in pathology at the University of Pittsburgh, remaining there as assistant professor, associate professor, and finally full professor of pathology in 1949 at the age of seventy, a year before her retirement.

Menten's work continues to have important significance. With Helen Manning she discovered the hyperglycemic effects of salmonella toxins in 1924. In 1944 (with Andersch and Wilson) she determined sedimentation constants and electrophoretic mobilities of both adult and fetal carboxylhemoglobin. According to her colleagues, this work antedated Linus Pauling's use of eletrophoretic mobility to determine differences in human hemoglobin. Menten developed an azo-dye coupling reaction for the demonstration of alkaline phosphatase in the kidney with Junge and Green, which has been called a stroke of genius in first edition of A. G. Pearse *Histochemistry* because of its influence in opening up a new field of enzyme histochemistry. She published on oxidases and vitamin C with C. G. King and with O. Bessey on streptococcal toxins, and on the histochemistry of glycogens and nucleic acids in bone marrow.

Apart from her research, Menten had extensive interests in languages, music, and art. She was a fine painter and several of her canvases hung in art exhibitions. She also took time to work on behalf of sick children. She was remembered by her colleagues at the University of Pittsburgh for her keen mind, unobtrusive modesty, and enthusiasm for research. Returning to Canada at age seventy-one, she continued to do research into nucleic acids in cancer cells at the British Columbia Medical Research Institute, Vancouver, before ill health forced her final retirement. She then moved to Leamington, Ontario, until her death in 1960. Although she lived and worked in the United States for most of her life, Menten retained her Canadian citizenship and is buried in Oddfellow's Cemetery, Chilliwack, British Columbia. She was memorialized by her former colleagues at University of Pittsburgh in *Nature* in 1961.

JH/MBO

PRIMARY SOURCES

Menten, Maud L. With A. B. Macakkum. "On the Distribution of Chlorides in Nerve Cells and Fibers." *Proceedings of the Royal Society,* 1906.

———. "Experiments on the Influence of Radium Bromide on a Carcinomatous Tumor of the Rat." *Monograph of the Rockefeller Institute of Medical Research* 1 (1910): 73–80.

———. With Leonor Michaelis. "Die Kinetik der Invertinwirkung." *Biochemische Zeitschrift* 49 (1913): 333–369.

———. With M. A. Andersch and D. A. Wilson. "Sedimentation Constants and Electrophoretic Mobilities of Both Adult and Fetal Carboxylhemoglobin." *Journal of Biological Chemistry* 153 (1944): 301–305.

———. With J. Junge and M. H. Green. "Distribution of Alkaline Phosphatase in Kidney Following the Use of Histochemical Azo Dye Test." *Proceedings of the Society for Experimental Biology and Medicine* 57 (1944): 82–86.

SECONDARY SOURCES

Stock, Aaron H., and Anna-Mary Carpenter. "Professor Maud Menten." *Nature* 189 (25 March 1961): 965.

STANDARD SOURCES

NAW unused; Rayner-Canham 1998.

MENTUHETEP, QUEEN (fl. 2300 B.C.E.)

Egyptian physician. Flourished 2300 B.C.E., probably in Thebes. Queen of the eleventh dynasty.

Little is known about this Egyptian queen. An artifact found in her tomb yields some information about her. The Berlin museum owns what is probably Mentuhetep's traveling medicine kit. The large cedar chest covered with a bamboo case and enveloped in a wicker chest holds five large alabaster jars for ointments. It also includes a large serpentine jar for tinctures, two measuring spoons, a mixing dish, and several dried herbs. It is thought to have been buried with the queen for use in the next life. JH/MBO

STANDARD SOURCES
Hurd-Mead 1938.

MERCURIADE (14th century)

Italian physician. Born 14th century in Salerno(?). Teacher, medical school at Salerno.

Nothing is known about Mercuriade's early life. She was both a surgeon and a physician and taught at Salerno. She wrote on crises in fevers, on ointments, and on the cure of wounds. She is representative of a class of female physicians who taught at Salerno during the fourteenth century.

JH/MBO

SECONDARY SOURCES
Harington, John. *The School of Salernum: Regimen sanitasis salernitarium.* New York: August M. Kelley, 1970.

STANDARD SOURCES
Hurd-Mead 1938; Lipinska 1930.

MEREDITH, LOUISA ANNE (TWAMLEY) (1812–1895)

British/Australian botanist. Born 20 July 1812 in Birmingham. Professional experience: collected and drew plants; wrote popular books. Died 21 October 1895 in Melbourne.

Louisa Meredith was born in England but went to Australia and Tasmania. She illustrated her own works. JH/MBO

PRIMARY SOURCES
Meredith, Louisa Anne. *The Romance of Nature.* London: C. Tilt, 1836.
———. *Our Wild Flowers.* London, 1839.
———. *Some of My Bush Friends in Tasmania.* London: Day & Son, 1860.

SECONDARY SOURCES
Blunt, Wilfrid. *The Art of Botanical Illustration.* 3rd ed. London: Collins, [1955]. Meredith discussed on page 220.
Mennell, Philip, comp. *The Dictionary of Australian Biography.* London: Hutchinson & Co., 1892. Meredith cited on page 320.

STANDARD SOURCES
Desmond.

MERGLER, MARIE (1851–1901)

U.S. physician. Born 1851 in Chicago(?). Educated Woman's Hospital Medical College (M.D.). Professional experience: Woman's Hospital Medical College, Chicago, faculty member. Died 1901.

Marie Mergler was one of several women who were educated at the Woman's Hospital Medical College in Chicago, which was founded in 1870, and who later became a faculty member at that institution. JH/MBO

STANDARD SOURCES
Morantz-Sanchez.

MERIAN, MARIA SIBYLLA (1647–1717)

German naturalist. Born 2 April 1647 in Frankfurt am Main. Father Mathaeus Merian. At least one sibling, brother Matthew. Married Andreas Graf. Two daughters, Johanna Sibylla and Dorothea Maria Henrietta. Educated by stepfather, artist Jacob Marell; studied with artist Abraham Mignon. Joined Labadist community. Professional experience: insects and other fauna of South America; fauna of Surinam. Died 1717.

Depending on the source, Maria Merian is described as the daughter of a physician-naturalist of Frankfurt am Main or as the child of an etcher named Mathaeus Merian, of Basel, Switzerland. Maria Merian married an artist by the name of Andreas Graf by whom she had two daughters, both of whom were given a medical education and were also artists. A popular flower painter, Maria Sibylla painted flowers on tablecloths and made copperplate engravings. Flower painting was much in vogue, but Maria Sibylla began to paint insects on the flowers. She had begun a journal in 1660 that reported accurate observations of the metamorphosis of the silkworm. In 1685, Merian and the two girls joined the Labadist community, a group that demanded celibacy. Leaving husband and father, they went to live in Holland. This move accelerated their studies in natural history. Maria Sibylla was also able to learn Latin at this time. When the community broke up in 1688, she went to Amsterdam. When she was fifty-two years old, Merian and her daughter Johanna Helena left Europe for South America, where they painted and wrote about the insects that they encountered. Upon returning, they traveled to see the principal European specimen collections. With the financial help of the City of Amsterdam, Merian collected funds for trips to India and Surinam that resulted in an extensive study of the flora and fauna of these areas—particularly the insects. In 1705 they published *Dissertatio de generatione et metamorphosibus insectorum surinamensium.* The sketches and paintings done for this book, together with its information on the flora and fauna of the areas studied, constituted a valuable resource for European naturalists.   JH/MBO

PRIMARY SOURCES
Merian, Maria. *Dissertatio de generatione et metamorphosibus insectorum surinamensium.* Amsterdam: J. Oosterwijk, 1719.

SECONDARY SOURCES
Guentherodt, Ingrid. "Dreyfache Verenderung und Wunderbare Verwandelung: Zu Forschung und Sprache der Naturwissenschaflerinnen Maria Cunitz (1610–1664) und Maria Sibylla Merian (1647–1717)." In *Deutsche Literatur von Frauen.* Volume 1: *Vom Mittelalter bis zum ende des 18. Jahrhunderts,* ed. Gisela Brinker-Gabler, 197–221. Munich: C. H. Beck, 1988.
Hoerner, Wilhelm. *Die Schmetterling: Metamorphose und Urbild. Eine naturkundliche Studie mit eine Lebensbeschreibung und Bildern aus dem Werk der Maria Sybilla Merian.* Stuttgart: Rachhaus, 1991.
Stearn, William T. "Maria Sibylla Merian (1647–1717) as a Botanical Artist." *Taxon* 31 (1982): 529–534.
Valiant, Sharon D. "Questioning the Caterpillar." *Natural History* 101 (1992): 46–59. Biographical article. Beautiful color illustrations from Merian's works. Concentrates on her work on caterpillars.
———. "Maria Sibylla Merian: Recovering an Eighteenth-Century Legend." *Eighteenth Century Studies* 26 (1993): 467–479.

STANDARD SOURCES
DSB; Hurd-Mead 1938; Ogilvie 1986; Shearer and Shearer 1996 (article by Diane M. Calabrese).

MERITT, LUCY TAXIS (SHOE) (1906–)
U.S. archeologist. Born 7 August 1906 in Camden, N.J., to Mary Esther (Dunning) and William Bonaparte Shoe. Married Benjamin Dean Meritt (7 November 1964). Educated Bryn Mawr College (A.B., 1927; M.A., 1928; Ph.D., 1935). Professional experience: American School of Classical Studies, Athens, fellow (1929–1932); American Academy in Rome, fellow (1936–1937), research fellow (1949–1950); Mount Holyoke College, assistant professor, then associate professor, of art, archaeology, and Greek (1937–1950); Princeton University, Institute for Advanced Studies, member (1948–1949); Washington University, St. Louis, visiting professor (1958; 1960); Princeton University, visiting lecturer (1959); American School of Classical Studies, editor of publications (from 1950). Honors and memberships: excavation staff at Cosa (1950); Morgantina (1957); American School of Classical Studies, managing committee (from 1937), executive committee (1948–1952); Archaeological Institute of America (acting general

secretary, 1962; recorder, from 1960); Society of Architectural Historians; Historical Society of Princeton.

Lucy Taxis Shoe Meritt was a classical archeologist who was very active in the numerous organizations of which she was a member. She studied full-size profiles of Greek architectural mouldings. This work provided new criteria for dating Greek architecture, which led to new historical observations. It was especially important in discovering the relationships between Greece and the western colonies. Her study of Etruscan and early Roman mouldings established the independence of Etruscan architecture from the Greek and emphasized the dependence of Republican Roman architecture on the Etruscan.   JH/MBO

PRIMARY SOURCES
Meritt, Lucy T. Shoe. *Profiles of Greek Mouldings.* Cambridge, Mass.: Harvard University Press, 1936.
———. *Profiles of Western Greek Mouldings.* [Rome]: American Academy in Rome, 1952.
———. *Etruscan and Republican Roman Mouldings.* [Rome]: American Academy in Rome, 1965.

STANDARD SOURCES
Debus.

MERRIAM, FLORENCE (1863–1948)
See Bailey, Florence Augusta (Merriam).

MERRIFIELD, MARY PHILADELPHIA (WATKINS) (19th century)
U.S. translator of scientific works.

Little is known of Merrifield's life. She produced an abstract of an important work written in Swedish by V. B. Wittrock. The abstract appeared in *Nature* 20 July 1882.   JH/MBO

PRIMARY SOURCES
Merrifield, Mary. "On Monostroma, a Genus of Algae." *Nature* 26 (20 July 1882): 284–286.

MERRILL, HELEN ABBOT (1864–1949)
U.S. mathematician. Born 30 March 1864 in Llewellyn Park, Orange, N.J., to Emily Abbot and George Dodge Merrill. At least three siblings. Educated Newburyport High School; Wellesley College (B.A., 1886); University of Chicago (1896–1897); Göttingen and Yale universities (1901–1903; Yale Ph.D., 1903). Professional experience: Classical School for Girls, New York City, instructor (1886–1889); Dutch Reformed Church, New Brunswick, N.J.,

teacher for mill girls (1889–1891); Walnut Lane School, German-town, Philadelphia, Pa. (1891–1893); Wellesley College, instructor (1893–1901), associate professor (1902–1915), professor (1915–1932); professor emerita on retirement. Died 1 May 1949.

Helen Abbot Merrill took advantage of the newly opened women's college, Wellesley, and was in one of its first graduating classes. Although her original intention was to study classical languages, she changed her mind after taking a class in mathematics during her freshman year. She had previously spent most of her life in Newburyport, where she lived with her very religious parents, two brothers (who later became Presbyterian ministers), and one sister. After graduating from Wellesley (which had a very positive influence on her), she taught in several schools until Helen Shafer asked her to return to Wellesley as an instructor in the mathematics department. The salary was almost insultingly low, three hundred dollars per year, but she also received housing. She progressed as might be expected up the academic ladder, although she remained at the associate level for thirteen years. In order to get her doctoral degree, Merrill took time off from Wellesley. She went to the University of Chicago and studied the theory of functions with Heinrich Maschke. She went to the University of Göttingen, where she studied descriptive geology with G. F. Schilling. At Yale, where she earned a doctorate in 1903, she studied with James Pierpont.

Merrill was a good administrator so she was called upon to hold several administrative positions, including chair of the mathematics department from 1916 until she retired. She was vice-president of the Mathematical Association of America in 1920 and was on its board of trustees from 1917 to 1919. Other organizations to which she belonged included the American Association for the Advancement of Science, American Association of University Women, American Mathematical Society, Mathematical Association of America, Deutsche Mathematiker Vereinigung, Phi Beta Kappa, and Sigma Xi.

Merrill's research was in the area of analysis and primarily in the theory of functions. Teaching was her chief interest and she wrote several textbooks, two coauthored with CLARA E. SMITH. She wrote an amusing book for the general reader, *Mathematical Excursions.*   JH/MBO

PRIMARY SOURCES

Merrill, Helen Abbot. "On Solutions of Differential Equations which possess an Oscilation Theorem." *Transactions of the American Mathematical Society* 3 (1903): 423–433.
———. With Clara E. Smith. *Selected Topics in College Algebra.* Norwood, Mass.: Norwood Press, 1914.
———. With Clara E. Smith. *A First Course in Higher Algebra.* New York: Macmillan, 1917.

———. "Why Students Fail in Mathematics." *Mathematics Teacher* 11 (1918): 45–46.
———. *Mathematical Excursions.* [New York]: Dover, [1933].

SECONDARY SOURCES
New York Times, 3 May 1949. Obituary notice.
Young, Mabel. "Helen Abbot Merrill." *Wellesley Magazine* (1932): 405–406.

STANDARD SOURCES
Grinstein and Campbell (article by Claudia Henrion).

MERRILL-JAMES, MAUD AMANDA (1888–1979)

U.S. psychologist. Born 30 April 1888 in Owatonna, Minn. Educated Oberlin College (A.B., 1911); Stanford University (A.M., 1920; Ph.D., 1923). Professional experience: Minnesota Bureau of Research (1921?–1929); Stanford University, instructor in psychology (1920–1924), assistant professor (1924–1931), associate professor (1931–1947), professor (1947–1953), emerita professor (from 1953). Died 1979.

Maud Merrill-James had a career trajectory that many women would have envied. After earning her doctoral degree from Stanford, she steadily received the promotions that made her full professor in 1947. Her research interests were in individual and clinical psychology, tests, and mental defectives and delinquents. Merrill-James was a member of the National Advisory Committee on Education from 1929 to 1931.

She was a member of numerous professional organizations including the Society for Study of Education, Society for Research in Child Development, Progressive Association, American Psychological Association, the National Advisory Committee on Education from 1929 to 1931, and the American Council of Education.   KM

STANDARD SOURCES
AMS 4–8, S&B 9.

SECONDARY SOURCES
American Psychologist 34 (1979): 176. Obituary notice.

MESSINA, ANGELINA ROSE (1910–1968)

U.S. micropaleontologist. Born 23 April 1910 in New York City to Josephine and Angelo Messina. Never married. Educated public schools of New York City; Columbia University; New York University. Professional experience: American Museum of Natural History, associate curator (1940–1968), chairman (1968), curator (1968). Died 20 November 1968 in New York City.

Angelina Rose Messina was born in New York City, the daughter of Sicilian immigrants who had come to New York in the early twentieth century. Science was her life. In addition to her work at the American Museum of Natural History, she taught at Brooklyn College and later at Rutgers University as adjunct professor of geology. Traveling always interested Messina, and she visited countries where micro-fossil research was happening.

The societies of which Messina was a member include the American Association of Petroleum Geologists, the Geological Societies of France and Germany, and the Paleontological Societies of Italy and Japan. She was a Fellow of the Geological Society of America and president of the Eastern Section of the Society of Economic Paleontologists. She was awarded an honorary doctorate from the University of Basel, Switzerland.

Messina edited *Micropaleontology* and published several important catalogues. In 1934 she worked on a New York University–sponsored project to systematize the literature of the Foraminifera. She soon became the supervisor of the project and remained in that position until it was taken over by the American Museum of Natural History, which cosponsored it with New York University. She was a recognized international authority in micropaleontology as co-author of the sixty-nine-volume *Catalogue of Foraminifera;* the twenty-eight volume *Catalogue of Ostracoda;* a three-volume *Catalogue of Index Larger Foraminifera;* and a three-volume *Catalogue of Index Smaller Foraminifera.*

Messina died suddenly at the American Museum of Natural History in 1968.   JH/MBO

PRIMARY SOURCES

Messina, Angelina Rose. With Brooks F. Ellis. *Catalogue of Foraminifera.* 69 vols. New York: American Museum of Natural History, 1940–1987.

———. With Brooks F. Ellis. *Catalogue of Ostracoda.* 28 vols. New York: American Museum of Natural History, 1952–.

———. With Brooks F. Ellis. *Catalogue of Index Smaller Foraminifera.* 3 vols. New York: American Museum of Natural History, 1968–1969.

SECONDARY SOURCES

Amor, J. Menéndez. "[Dra. Angelina R. Messina]." *Col-Pa.* University of Madrid no. 14 (1968): 15.

Ellis, Brooks F. "Angelina Rose Messina (1910–1968)." *Bulletin of the American Association of Petroleum Geologists* 53, no. 3 (1969): 694–695.

STANDARD SOURCES

Sarjeant.

METCHNIKOVA, OLGA (BELOKOPYTOVA) (1858–1944)

Russian-French biologist and biographer of her husband, Elie Metchnikov. Born in Odessa (?), Russia, in 1858. Father Nicholai (?) Belokopytov. Two sisters, three brothers. Married Elie Metchnikov (his second wife) (1875). Educated Odessa girls' lycée (graduated 1875) and privately. Professional experience: Pasteur Institute, and Naples Biological Station, assistant to Elie Metchnikov (1879–1904). Died in Paris, 1944.

Olga Nikolevna Belokopytova was born in Odessa to a well-to-do landowner from Kiev. She was the second oldest of a family of six children. While she was studying at the girls' lycée, she encountered Elie Metchnikov, who was teaching natural history in the university and at one of the local schools, and who had rented rooms on a floor below her family. He became attracted to her and offered to teach her natural history. As he grew to know this young girl, he fell in love with her, and supported by her young mother, he married her when she was only seventeen, before she completed her courses at the lycée. She recalled that the first time she wore long skirts was at her wedding. As a married woman, Metchnikov was compelled to take her examinations before a special committee. Her husband continued to instruct her in biology and she soon began to assist him in the laboratory.

In 1878, the couple moved to Naples to Anton Dohrn's famous Naples Biological Station. Here Elie Metchnikov studied the mesodermic cells of the larvae of insects, and the process of digestion, while Olga Metchnikov assisted him and studied as well the sterilization of the alimentary canal of tadpoles. She also did an independent study of cartilaginous fish morphology, published the following year in a German journal. Unfortunately, on return to Odessa, she fell ill with typhoid fever that she contracted in Naples. Her husband was disturbed enough by the near death of his second wife (his first had died of tuberculosis soon after marriage) that he experimented on himself with blood infected with relapsing fever, partly to see if it was possible for humans to catch the disease in that manner and partly out of a suicidal wish. His subsequent illness resulted in jaundice and a weakened heart.

When Olga's father and then her mother fell ill and died, the Metchnikovs had charge of the large family who came to live with them in Odessa. Fortunately, the inheritance from the landed property allowed her husband to resign from the university and do independent research in Messina, Italy, taking the entire family with him. There, Elie Metchnikov first observed phagocytosis that would lead him to study the process of immunity and eventually win him the Nobel Prize.

When the Odessa Bacteriological Institute was formed, Elie Metchnikov was made director and remained there for almost three years until he decided to leave Russia permanently for Paris, France. Pasteur had offered him laboratory space in the Pasteur Institute in 1888, hoping to encourage his work on immunity, and Olga Metchnikov began to serve as her husband's assistant. She also began to pursue her interests in painting and sculpture. In a letter written to Elie on 17 August 1890, Pasteur spoke of the work of the Metchnikovs as a couple. Commenting on Elie's refusal of a good offer to head up a bacteriological institute in St. Petersburg, he expressed his confidence that destiny would reward them with new and remarkable discoveries. Adding a comment on his hopes for the success of Olga Metchnikova's work, probably her art in this context, he wrote that she provided a beautiful example to everyone.

For many years, the couple lived in the vicinity of the Pasteur Institute. For many years she assisted her husband in his work. In 1898, they bought a small villa in Sevres for weekend stays and summers. There for the first time, Olga built her own studio and got to know both the sculptor Rodin and one of Tolstoy's sons, who had a studio in Paris. By 1905, they moved to the villa from Paris and Elie Metchnikov began to commute to the suburbs. They returned to Russia for a number of notable visits. One long visit following the award of the Nobel Prize to Elie Metchnikov in 1908 took them to Iasnaïa Poliana (Yasnya Polyana) to meet Leo Tolstoy, who welcomed both Metchnikovs very warmly. Three years later, they went on a special bacteriological expedition with members from the Pasteur Institute to the Kalmuk steppes, where Metchnikov hoped to discover whether there was a natural immunity to tuberculosis among the population.

With the beginning of World War I, the scientific investigations in the Pasteur Institute were interrupted. Elie Metchnikov, who had had a heart attack, moved with Olga into an apartment in the Pasteur Institute where his doctors and his colleagues could see him daily. After his death in 1916, Olga began to work on her husband's biography at the urging of his friends and former colleagues. Unfortunately, her modesty prevented her from detailing her own scientific work, which is mentioned only in passing or in comments later offered by her husband's colleagues. Among other assistance, her ability to translate English had, according to E. Ray Lankester, been of great help to him. When her book appeared, it was heralded and immediately translated into a number of other languages, including English. Olga sent many of her husband's papers to Moscow, where a Metchnikov Museum was founded in 1926. She died in Paris in 1944.   JH/MBO

PRIMARY SOURCES

Metchnikova, Olga. "Zur Morphologie des Bechen–und Schulterbogens der Knorpelfische." *Zeitschriften für Wissenschaften Zooologie* 33 (1879): 423–438.

———. *Vie d'Elie Metchnikoff 1845–1916.* Paris: Hachette, 1920.

———. *Life of Elie Metchnikoff 1845–1916.* Preface by Sir Ray Lankester. London: Constable and Co., 1921. The preface to the translation contains some observations by Lankester on the life and work of Olga.

SECONDARY SOURCES

Metchnikov, Elie. *Souvenirs: Recueil d'articles autographiques.* Edited with commentaries by A. Gaissinovitch. Moscow: Editions en Langues Etrangères, 1959. The footnotes and biographical index contain material on the life of Olga Metchnikov. There is a portrait of her with her husband facing page 144.

METRODORA (1st or 2d century B.C.E.)
Greek midwife. Practiced during the first or second century B.C.E.

Although little is known about her, an unedited manuscript by the midwife Metrodora exists in Florence. Entitled *Extracts from the Works of Metrodora Concerning the Diseases of Women,* it consists of 263 leaves of parchment. Conclusions about Metrodora's contributions to medicine must await examination of this manuscript.   JH/MBO

STANDARD SOURCES

Lipinska 1930; Ogilvie 1986; Pauly-Wissowa.

METZGER, HÉLÈNE (BRUHL) (1889–1944)
French chemist and historian of chemistry. Born 26 August 1889 near Paris to Eugénie Emilie (Adler) and Paul Bruhl. One sister, Louise. Married Paul Metzger (1913). Educated high school (Brevet Supérieur); Sorbonne (Ph.D., 1918). Professional experience: published numerous books and papers on the history of chemistry. Honors and memberships: Académie Internationale d'Histoire des Sciences, administrator-treasurer (1929); Centre International de Synthèse, head, history of science library (1939); Groupe Français d'Historiens des Sciences, secretary; French Academy of Sciences Binoux Prize. Died 10 March 1944 in Auschwitz.

Hélène Metzger's mother died in childbirth when her daughter was only two years old. Her father, Paul Bruhl, remarried when Hélène was eight years old, and the child always felt alienated from her stepmother. Her father did not want his daughters to pursue careers, but Metzger risked his wrath and obtained a higher-level high-school diploma (Brevet Supérieur) and attended the Sorbonne. At the Sorbonne, she studied the structures of crystals with Frédéric Wallerant. Her interest in this subject probably came from her father's family business in diamonds, pearls, and precious stones. She received a diploma for advanced studies based on her crystallographic analysis of lithium chlorate. Her marriage in 1913 to Paul Metzger was a very short one, for he was killed in an early battle in World War I.

Metzger submitted her doctoral thesis on the origins of crystallography in 1918, showing how the study of crystals slowly became differentiated from mineralogy, physics, and chemistry to become a separate science. From this beginning, Metzger began her focus on the history of chemistry, particularly French history in the seventeenth and eighteenth centuries. She moved away from the "great man" idea of science and focused instead on the importance of lesser-known figures who often held "false" theories. In her study of Nicholas Lémery's alchemical research, she demonstrated that this scientist's overlooked work played an important role in the development of modern chemistry. She continued to write the history of ideas as they existed within their particular timeframe. During the 1930s, she wrote a series of articles and books on the history of early modern chemistry.

Metzger was active in history of science organizations. She moved from Paris, which was controlled by the Germans, to Lyon, controlled by the Vichy government. Instead of keeping a low profile in Lyon, she called attention to her Jewish ancestry, and began a study of Jewish monotheism. On 8 February 1944 she was arrested and eventually was transferred to Auschwitz, where she was taken to the gas chambers on 10 March 1944.   JH

PRIMARY SOURCES
Metzger, H. *Chemistry.* Trans. and annotated by C. V. Michael. West Cornwall, Conn.: Locust Hill Press, 1991. Most recent edition of this work.

SECONDARY SOURCES
Boas, Marie. "Notice Nécrologique: Hélène Metzger (1889–1944)." *Archiv Internationale d'Histoire des Sciences* 8 (1955): 433–434.
Freudenthal, Gad. "Hélène Metzger: Eléments de biographie." In *Études sur Hélène Metzger*, ed. Gad Freudenthal. Leiden, Germany: E. J. Brill, 1990.
Golinski, Jan. "Hélène Metzger and the Interpretation of Seventeenth Century Chemistry." *History of Science* 25 (1987): 85–97.
Sarton, George. "Notes and Correspondence: Hélène Metzger (1889–1944)." *Isis* 36 (1946): 133.

STANDARD SOURCES
DFC; DSB; Rayner-Canham 1998.

MEURDRAC, MARIE (fl. 1666)
French chemist. Professional experience: published a treatise on chemistry.

The only information available on the life of French chemist Marie Meurdrac is gleaned from her book. In her discussion of essence of rosemary she mentioned that it is efficacious against many maladies and wrote that she had used it with good results. The fact that she offers specific examples of its use suggests that she was either a medical doctor or had practiced medicine.

Her book, published in 1666, may have been the first treatise on chemistry written by a woman. The book is divided into six parts: Part one considers principles and operations, vessels, lutes, furnaces, fires, characteristics, and weights; part two, the properties of simples (medicinal herbs or the medicines made from these herbs); part three, animals; part four, metals; part five, instructions on making medicines; and part six, addressed to ladies, concerns cosmetics. Meurdrac informs her readers that the information she includes is true, and that she has tested all of the remedies. The book was popular; it went through several editions and was translated into German and Italian.   JH/MBO

PRIMARY SOURCES
Meurdrac, Marie. *La chymie charitable et facile, en faveur des dames. Par Damoiselle M. M.* Paris: 1666.
———. *La chymie charitable et facile, en faveur des dames.* 2d ed. Lyon: Jean Baptiste Deville, 1680.

SECONDARY SOURCES
Bishop, Lloyd O., and Will S. DeLoach. "Marie Meurdrac— First Lady of Chemistry?" *Journal of Chemical Education* 47 (1970): 448–449.

STANDARD SOURCES
Alic; Grinstein 1993 (article by Will S. DeLoach); Hurd-Mead 1938.

MEXIA, YNES (1870–1938)
U.S. botanist. Born 24 May 1870 in Georgetown, Washington, D.C., to Sarah R. Wilmer and Enrique Antonio Mexia. Married 1897; husband died 1904; second marriage ended in divorce. Educated Saint Joseph's Academy, Emmitsburg, Md.; natural science classes University of California, Berkeley; course in flowering plants, Hopkins Marine Station, Pacific Grove, Calif. Professional experience: expeditions to western Mexico (1925–1926); Mount McKinley, Alaska (1928); Brazil (1929); Ecuador (1934); from Peru south to the Straits of Magellan (1935); southwestern Mexico (1937). Died 12 July 1938 in Mexico.

Ynes Mexia's childhood and early adult life were fraught with trauma. When her mother, Sarah, married Enrique Mexia, an agent for the Mexican government, she already had six children from a previous marriage. Her parents separated when Ynes was three years old, and her mother and all of the children moved to Texas. When Ynes was fifteen, she returned East to attend St. Joseph's Academy in Maryland. After leaving St. Joseph's, she went to Mexico and spent the next ten years on her father's hacienda in Mexico City. She had bad luck in her two marriages. She married her first husband in 1897; he died seven years later. Upon his death, Mexia began a successful poultry and pet stock-raising business on the hacienda. However, she soon embarked on a disastrous second marriage to a man sixteen years her junior. He nearly bankrupted the business while Mexia was in San Francisco seeking treatment for a medical problem. When she returned, she divorced her husband and sold her business.

An interest in botany snapped her out of the depression that she had been enduring. She began to take trips with the local Sierra Club, enrolled in a natural science class at the University of California, Berkeley, and went on a collecting trip to southwestern Mexico. During this trip, she fell from a cliff and was injured. While she was recuperating in San Francisco, she decided to finance future botanical trips by selling specimens to institutions and to collectors. From her 1925–1926 trip to western Mexico, she collected over thirty-three thousand specimens, including fifty new species and one new genus, *Mexianthus mexicanus*. After this trip, she collected in Alaska and all over South America. She died in 1938 of lung cancer. JH/MBO

PRIMARY SOURCES
Mexia, Ynes. "Three Thousand Miles up the Amazon." *Sierra Club Bulletin* (February 1933): 88.
———. "Camping on the Equator." *Sierra Club Bulletin* (February 1937): 85.

SECONDARY SOURCES
Goodspeed, T. Harper. *Plant Hunters in the Andes.* Berkeley and Los Angeles: University of California Press, 1961.
Moore, Patricia Ann. "Cultivating Science in the Field: Alice Eastwood, Ynes Mexia and California Botany, 1890–1940." Ph.D. diss., University of California, Los Angeles, 1996.

STANDARD SOURCES
Bonta; *LKW; NAW;* Shearer and Shearer 1996 (article by Rebecca Lowe Warren).

MEYER, MARGARET THEODORA (ca. 1862–1924)

British mathematician and astronomer. Born ca. 1862 in Ulster (Northern Ireland). Father Reverend Theodore Meyer. One sister. Educated North London Collegiate School for girls; Girton College, Cambridge (honors in Mathematical Tripos 1882). Professional experience: Notting Hill High School, teacher (1882–1888); Girton College, resident lecturer in mathematics (1888–1901; 1901–1918); Air Department, calculator (1918–1919); University College, London, lecturer (1919–1924). Died 27 January 1924.

Margaret Theodora Meyer took honors in the Mathematical Tripos, and was a lecturer and director of studies at Girton for many years. She was an amateur astronomer, and was elected a Fellow of the Royal Astronomical Society on 11 February 1916. During the last year of World War I, she assisted in the calculating section of the Air Department. After the war, she coached students at University College, London, but was gradually cutting down on her work when she was killed suddenly in 1924. Her bicycle collided with a bus.

In addition to astronomy, cycling, and mountain climbing, Meyer's great interest was in Girton College. She carved panels or directed students in carving them for the chapel, and bequeathed to the college a collection of mathematics books and two thousand pounds. The interest on the money was to be given either to a student in her second or third year or to someone who intended to do mathematics research.

JH/MBO

SECONDARY SOURCES
Maunder, Annie. "Margaret Theodora Meyer." *Monthly Notices of the Royal Astronomical Society* 85 (February 1925): 314.

MEYER-BJERRUM, KIRSTINE (1861–1941)

Danish physicist. Born 12 October 1861 in Skaerbaek, North Schleswig to Christine (Degn) and Niels Janniksen Bjerrum. Married Adolph Constantin Meyer (7 November 1885). Educated University of Copenhagen (M.S. 1886, Ph.D. 1909). Professional experience: secondary schools and teacher preparation institutes, Copenhagen (1882–1930); Fysik Tidsskrift, co-founder (1902), publisher and co-publisher (1902–1912), editor (1902–1910). Honors and memberships: Examination Board for Teachers, member, director (1909–1940); Scientific Society in Denmark, gold medal (1889); gold medal for service awarded by the King of Denmark (1920). Died 12 October 1941 in Hellerup.

Kirstine Meyer-Bjerrum's interest in thermochemistry led her to investigate the historical development of ideas about heat and temperature, the subject of her doctoral dissertation. She published a number of articles and monographs on the work of Danish scientists, including the astronomer Ole

Rømer and the physicist Hans C. Ørsted. Meyer-Bjerrum also wrote a book on radioactivity. In 1902 she cofounded a Danish physics journal, *Fysik Tidsskrift,* which she published and edited for many years.

Several members of Meyer-Bjerrum's family distinguished themselves in the sciences, including her brother, opthalmology professor Jannick Bjerrum, and her nephew, chemist Niels Bjerrum.   JH/MBO

PRIMARY SOURCES
Meyer-Bjerrum, Kirstine. "Zur Geschichte der Antiperistasis."
    Annalen der Naturphilosophie 3, ca. 1903: 143–.
———. *Radium og radioaktive Stoffer samt nyere opdagelser an-*
    gaaende Straaler. Copenhagen: Glyldendalske boghandel
    nordisk forlag, 1904.
———. *Die Entwickelung des Temperaturbegriffs im Laufe der*
    Zeiten. Trans. Irmgard Kolde. Brunswick: Friedrick Vieweg
    & Son, 1913.
———. "Scientific Life and Works of H. C. Ørsted." In *H. C.*
    Ørsted: Scientific Papers. Vol 1. Ed. the Royal Danish Society
    of Sciences. Copenhagen: A. F. Host and Son, 1920.

STANDARD SOURCES
Poggendorff 5, 6, 7b; *Dansk Biografisk* 15.

MEYLING-HYLKEMA, ELISABETH (1907–)
Dutch physician. Born 1907 in Friesland to a midwife mother and a father who was a clerk. Two siblings. Married a veterinarian (1941). Two daughters. Educated University of Groningen (1925–1932); medical degree (1940); training psychoanalysis (1940?). Professional experience: Psychiatric-Neurological clinic in Groningen, assistant (1932–1936); mental hospital, head of department (1936–1941?); consultant (from 1941); private practice and child-guidance clinic (to 1945); Mental Health Sanatorium, psychoanalyst? (1945–1958).

Elisabeth Meyling-Hylkema was born in Friesland in the north of Holland. Meyling's mother was a midwife and her father a clerk who was an avid socialist. Her brother was diagnosed with multiple sclerosis when she was thirteen years old. His disease and her mother's midwife practice made her decide to be a physician. However, because of her parents' many expenses for her brother, she was forced to receive scholarships if she was to pursue her dream. Meyling attended the University of Groningen for seven years, graduating in 1932. After graduation, she applied for an assistantship at the psychiatric neurological clinic in Groningen. After assuring her that no woman would become an assistant, the head of the department relented, and she became the first female assistant. This training period lasted for four years; in 1935, she became chief assistant. In 1936, she be-

came the head of a department in a mental hospital, along with her social-psychiatric duties.

Her major interest was in active therapy, a technique that she had learned as an assistant. Two weeks before the Nazis attacked Holland, she was awarded a medical degree. Her thesis was "A Contribution to the Knowledge of Narcolepsy." After a year undergoing psychoanalysis training, she married a veterinarian, and the couple had two daughters. While the children were young, Meyling-Hylkema worked only part time.

During the war, Meyling-Hylkema had a private practice for several years. She left the hospital because the superintendent was a Nazi. In 1945, she took a full-time job at the new modern sanatorium, retiring in 1958. By that time both her health and that of her husband were precarious. Her husband died in 1969, and after that time she felt that she was too old to practice.   KM

PRIMARY SOURCES
Meyling-Hylkema, Elisabeth. In Hellstedt, *Autobiographies.*

MEZNERICS, ILONA (1906–1977)
See Csepreghyné-Meznerics, Ilona.

MICHAEL, HELEN CECILIA DESILVER ABBOTT (1857–1904)
U.S amateur chemist and dentist. Born 23 December 1857 in Philadelphia, Pa., to Caroline (Montelius) and James Abbott. At least one brother. Married Arthur Michael (1888). Educated privately; studied music in Paris; Woman's Medical College (Philadelphia) (1882–1883, no degree); Tufts College (M.D., 1903). Professional experience: practice in a free hospital; no permanent position or formal association with a research institution. Honors and memberships: American Philosophical Society (1887); American Association for the Advancement of Science; Academy of Natural Sciences; Franklin Institute of Philadelphia; Deutsche Chemische Gesellschaft in Berlin. Died 29 November 1904 in Boston of "the grippe."

For most of Helena Abbott Michael's life she worked as an amateur, earning a formal degree only in 1903. Only one year after she earned her doctoral degree from Tufts, she died from an infection contracted from one of her patients.

Her family was apparently wealthy enough to assure her education through private tutors and governesses. Displaying considerable musical talent, Abbott studied the piano in Philadelphia with Mary F. Howell. By 1878 she was sufficiently accomplished to participate in a concert on the Isle of Wight—an event that won her favorable newspaper reports. However, her family's assumption that she would continue with her music was in error, for in 1881 she discovered her real interest, science. Through reading H. L. F. Von Helmhotz's *Handbuch der Physiologisches Optik* (1867), Abbott was introduced to science. From this beginning she broadened her interests to include zoology, anatomical dissections of animals, and medicine. The study of medicine became her most compelling interest, and she applied for admission to the Woman's Medical College of Philadelphia in 1882. However, after two years she dropped out of school as a result of a serious fall.

During her lengthy recovery, Abbott continued to work with Philadelphia scientists, but took no formal courses. Her family's position probably provided useful contacts for her. She became interested in the chemical analysis of plants. Reputedly, this interest came about when she read about children who had been poisoned by eating the roots of what was purported to be wild carrots. In 1887, she went on a scientific journey to Europe, armed with a letter of introduction from the secretary of the Smithsonian Institution, Samuel P. Langley. Returning from Europe late in 1887 she began to study at Tufts College with organic chemist Arthur Michael. They were married in June 1888 and began a world tour together. They returned to the United States in 1890, when they moved to Worcester, Massachusetts, and then to the Isle of Wight, where they set up a private laboratory. They returned to Boston and Tufts in 1895. Upon their return, Helen Michael became very concerned over the condition of the poor. She also occupied herself with writing poetry and philosophical speculations. She reentered medical school at Tufts in 1900 and in 1903 earned her medical degree. She assumed that she could put her social ideals into practice by becoming a physician. However, she was only able to practice for one year (in a free hospital that she had created for the poor), when she contracted "the grippe" and died.

Michael's most important work involved the determination of the chemical composition of plants. She was able to estimate quantitatively the various oils and resins in *Yucca angustifolia*. She worked on several other species of plants as well. Through her detailed studies, she drew a picture of the relationship between the chemical composition of plants and their morphology. She was one of the first to appreciate the usefulness of a biochemical classification in the plant kingdom. She recognized a connection between her studies and Charles Darwin's ideas. While she was on the Isle of Wight, she published four papers describing research in synthetic organic chemistry. An excellent lecturer, her talents were in demand. As she grew older and her health declined, she turned more to the arts and humanities and their relation to the sciences.

JH/MBO

PRIMARY SOURCES

Abbott, Helen Cecilia DeSilver. "Certain Chemical Constituents of Plants Considered in Relation to Their Morphology and Evolution." *Botanical Gazette* 11 (1886): 270–272.

———. "The Chemical Basis of Plant Forms." *Journal of the Franklin Institute* 124 (1887): 161–185.

———. "Comparative Chemistry of Higher and Lower Plants." *American Naturalist* 21 (1887): 719–730.

Michael, Helen Cecilia DeSilver Abbott. *Studies in Plant and Animal Chemistry and Literary Papers.* Ed. N. H. Dole. Cambridge, Mass.: Riverside Press, 1907. A collection of Michael's reprints together with autobiographical notes and a photograph.

SECONDARY SOURCES

Tarbell, A. T., and D. S. Tarbell. "Helen Abbott Michael: Pioneer in Plant Chemistry." *Journal of Chemical Education* 59 (July 1982): 548–549.

STANDARD SOURCES

Grinstein 1993 (article by K. Thomas Finley and Patricia J. Siegel); Reyner-Canham.

MICHELET, ATHÉNAÏS (MIALARET) (1826–1899)

French memorialist and writer on natural history; Darwin correspondent. Born 19 October 1826 in Léojac near Montauban, France, to Marguerite-Emma Becknell and Yves-Louis-Hippolyte Mialaret. Five siblings. Educated privately; University of Toulouse, teaching certificate in primary education (1845). Married Jules Michelet (1798–1874), 12 March 1849. One son (died soon after birth). Professional experience: governess in Vienna, Austria to children of Princess Cantacuzène (house of Esterhazy) (1846–1848); wrote natural history essays with husband and memoirs; corresponded with Charles Darwin (1872–1874) and with other scientists; edited husband's works after his death. Honors and memberships: Officer of the Academy (before 1893). Died of pneumonia, Easter day (end of March), 1899.

Athénaïs Mialaret was the second daughter in a household full of sons in an upper-middle-class household near Montauban. Her father had been a secretary of Touissant L'Overture in Santo Domingo, a supporter of Napoleon in exile, and finally a teacher in Louisiana where he met his beautiful and rich wife. Mialaret's account of her early childhood and education vividly depicts the expectations and difficulties of rural upper-class life in early-nineteenth-century France. She spent her early years as an almost forgotten child farmed out to a nurse; she was then required to spend hours learning needlework, considered at the time to be the most appropriate female occupation. Her father, who had retired, was fascinated by natural history and Enlightenment philosophy. Educated by her father until his death when she was fourteen, Mialaret determined to continue her education by obtaining the only degree available to women, a teaching certificate.

She then went to Vienna as a governess in her early twenties. She was inspired by the writings of the historian Jules Michelet, who held the chair of history at the College de France and directed the historical section of the Archives de France. The two began a literary, philosophical, and political correspondence in 1847 and shared their enthusiasm about the Revolution of 1848 in both Paris and Vienna. Mialaret left Vienna at the end of that year and went to Paris to meet Michelet. A strong believer in democratic and republican ideas, he had been a widower for eight years and was then in his early fifties. They were married just before the fall of the Second Republic, after which he lost his position because of his unfailing opposition to Louis Napoleon's Third Empire. The couple had a son, Yves-Jean-Lazare Michelet, who died after seven weeks. Athénaïs Michelet's decision to have her dying child given extreme unction by a priest troubled her husband, who was a strong anticleric. She was in poor health for sometime afterward and never had another child.

The marriage was successful and happy in other ways, and the couple began to collaborate in the 1850s (some authors who regretted his departure from the field of history depict her as forcing her collaboration upon him). She urged him to return to his early interest in natural history and cowrote *L'Oiseau* (1856), *La Mer* (1861), *L'Insecte* (1857), and *La Montagne*. Their collaboration was unacknowledged in the first editions but cited by the historian in the preface of later editions. Her letters include her observations of living insects and birds, and Jules Michelet more than once credited her with introducing him to the study of birds. The natural history books were popular successes in their day. During the Franco-Prussian War and the Commune, the couple were in Italy, working on behalf of the French and Garibaldi's army. They also supported amnesty for the Communards in spite of the historian's anger at the burning of archives at Paris city hall.

In 1872, Athénaïs Michelet and her husband sent Charles Darwin a copy of a beautifully illustrated book in English, *Nature,* extracted from their earlier writings and published in London that year. Jules Michelet had just had the first of a series of strokes that would kill him two years later, but he expressed his pleasure in Darwin's work in shaky handwriting. His wife continued the correspondence on her own account, asking Darwin for assistance and advice on the study she had begun on domestic cat behavior. He replied with helpful suggestions, and the correspondence continued for two years. Although she also collected materials on cat behavior and reproduction from Georges Pouchet and other

scientists, the resulting book (*Les Chats,* 1905) was published only after her death, along with her correspondence on this topic, edited by the historian Gabriel Monod, pupil and biographer of her husband.

When royalties were not awarded to her in 1876, following her husband's death, Michelet successfully sued the publishers for her share of profits of their collaborative natural history books. She continued to edit and publish posthumous works of Michelet, releasing a regular flow of his memoirs and diaries, although her intrusive editing later caused concern among historians. Although she spent the greatest part of the year in a country house in Vélizy, she maintained an apartment in Paris, where she died from pneumonia on Easter day, 1899, leaving some pictures and objects to museums and libraries, and their personal papers to the historian Gabriel Monod. Her letters to Charles Darwin are in the Darwin Archive, Cambridge University Library, and are listed in the *Calendar of the Correspondence of Charles Darwin* (1985; 1994).   JH

PRIMARY SOURCES

Michelet, Athénaïs (Mialaret). With Jules Michelet. *L'Oiseau.* Paris: Hachette, 1856.
———. With Jules Michelet. *L'Insecte.* Paris: Hachette, 1859.
———. With Jules Michelet. *La Mer.* Paris: Hachette, 1861.
———. With Jules Michelet. *La Montagne.* Paris: Libraire internationale, 1867.
———. *Memoirs d'une enfant.* Paris, 1867.
———. With Jules Michelet. *Nature.* London, 1872.
———. *La Mort et les funerailles de Michelet.* Paris: Flammarion, 1876.
———. *Revendication des droits de Mme Michelet; pour sa collaboration aux ouvrages de M Jules Michelet, L'Oiseaux, L'Insecte, La Mer, La Montagne.* Paris, 1876.
———. *Les Chats.* Paris: Flammarion, 1905. Edited by the historian Gabriel Monod.

SECONDARY SOURCES

[Archives de France]. *Michelet: Sa vie, son oeuvre (1798–1874).* Paris: Archives de France, 1961. Although this is a catalogue of the work of Jules Michelet, it includes a portrait of Athénaïs Michelet, as well as a description of a number of other portraits and photographs. This catalogue includes a list of her writings, as well as the best summary biography of her life, documents significant letters, and her editorial work on Jules Michelet's papers after his death.
Halévy, Daniel. "Le mariage de Michelet." *Revue de Paris* (August 1902): 557–579.
Ledrain, E. "Madame Michelet: Lettres et Souvenirs inédits." *La Revue* (1 October 1907): 311–331. An account of the later years and death of Athénaïs Michelet with some letters to Ledrain.

Monod, Gabriel. "Comment furent composé memoires d'une enfant." *La Revue* 1908: 385–394. Monod looks at the early life of Athénaïs Michelet through the accounts of the exploration of her childhood home as described by Jules Michelet in his journal in preparation to writing her memoir.

———. "Michelet (Jules)." In *La Grand Encyclopédie*. Vol. 23. Ed. Andre Berthelot. Paris: Société anonyme de la Grande Encyclopédie, [1886–1902].

STANDARD SOURCES
DFC (not completely reliable).

MILDMAY, GRACE SHERRINGTON (1552–1620)

British physician, alchemist, and general scholar. Born 1552. Related to physician Lady Anne Clifford. Married Sir Anthony Mildmay (1567). At least one daughter. Died 1620.

Grace Sherrington was a relative of the Cliffords who, before she married Sir Anthony Mildmay, already had a good knowledge of medicine and surgery. She spent her time studying herbals and medical books and ministering to the health needs of her friends and acquaintances. Her daughter reported that Mildmay spent much of her time preparing medicines, studying the signs of disease, and applying that knowledge. A 1613 portrait of Mildmay shows her holding a prayerbook with an open book on simples and two retorts and stills beside her on a table.   JH/MBO

PRIMARY SOURCES
Mildmay, Grace. "Medical Papers." In Pollack.

SECONDARY SOURCES
Pollack, Linda. *With Faith and Physic: The Life of a Tudor Gentlewoman, Lady Grace Mildmay, 1552–1620.* London: Collins and Brown, 1993. Includes her medical papers that describe causes and symptoms of diseases, appropriate treatment, and manufacture of medications.

STANDARD SOURCES
Hurd-Mead 1938.

MILES, CATHERINE COX (1890–?)

U.S. psychologist. Born 20 May 1890 in San Jose, Calif., to Lydia Shipley Bean and Charles Ellwood Cox. One sister, Anna. Married Walter Richard Miles. Educated Stanford University (A.B., 1912; A.M., 1913; fellow, 1923–1924; Ph.D., 1925). Professional experience: Stanford University, assistant in physical education (1912–1913); College of the Pacific, assistant professor of German (1914–1915), professor (1915–1920); Stanford, instructor (1920–1923); California Bureau of Juvenile Research, Whittier, Calif., director (1924–1925); Central Mental Hygiene Clinic, Cincinnati, Ohio, psychologist (1925–1927); Stanford University, research associate in psychology (1927–1930); Yale University, institute of human relations, research associate and professor of psychiatry and psychology (1930–1931), clinical professor of psychology (from 1931); New Haven Hospital and New Haven Dispensary, attending psychologist (from 1932); General Hospital, Cincinnati, assistant attending psychologist (1925–1927); Children's Hospital, psychologist (1926–1927); U.S. Veterans Bureau Diagnostic Center No. 1, psychologist (1926–1927). Honors and memberships: American Psychological Association; Association of Consulting Psychology. Death date unknown.

Between the time Catherine Miles got her master's degree and her doctorate, she went to Germany. She became proficient in German, after spending a year in Jena (1913) and another in Berlin (1914). Upon her return, she worked as an assistant professor in German at the College of the Pacific and rose to professor in 1915 where she stayed until 1920. She returned to Stanford as an instructor for three years and then accepted a fellowship to work on her doctoral degree. She had several positions while working on her thesis. Armed with a new doctorate, she accepted a position as psychologist for the Central Mental Hygiene Clinic in Cincinnati for two years. She returned to Stanford for a three-year stint as a research associate in psychology. After leaving the West Coast, Miles took a position at the Yale University institute of human relations, where she was a research associate and professor of psychiatry and psychology. After working as a psychologist at the New Haven Hospital and New Haven Dispensary, she moved to Cincinnati's General Hospital, where she worked as a psychologist.

Her research interests were in the psychology of genius, sex differences, personality measurement, and behavior deviations.   KM

STANDARD SOURCES
AMS 5–8, S&B 9–10.

MILL, HARRIET HARDY TAYLOR (1807–1858)

British social scientist. Born 8 October 1807 to Harriet (Hurst) and Thomas Hardy, surgeon. Six siblings. Married (1) John Taylor (14 March 1826; he died in 1849); (2) John Stuart Mill (1851). Three children by Taylor, two sons and one daughter. Educated at home largely through own efforts. Professional experience: collaborated with John Stuart Mill. Died 3 November 1858 in Avignon, France, of "congestion."

Harriet Hardy married John Taylor when she was only eighteen, and soon had three children. By the time she was twenty-three she was bored with her Unitarian husband, a successful merchant. She was introduced to John Stuart Mill by a Unitarian minister to whom she had confided her plight. Soon after she became pregnant with her third child and only daughter, she fell in love with Mill. She began to work with him and separated from her husband, commencing a twenty-year platonic affair with Mill. The two began to spend much time together, inciting a considerable amount of scandal. The three finally reached an accommodation, but the rest of Taylor's family continued to be bitter until the death of her first husband in 1849. A recent commentator, Jo Ellen Jacobs, has suggested that John Taylor may have contracted syphilis and passed it on to her, something that might explain her long years of physical suffering, her semiparalysis, and the failure of her second marriage to be consummated.

Mill and Taylor began to inspire each other's ideas and often they worked together on a text. Taylor looked after her first husband during his last illness, and when he died he left her the life interest on his fortune. She and Mill did not marry until 1851; they finished *The Enfranchisement of Women* on their honeymoon. The tract on women's rights was published anonymously, but it was initially attributed to John Stuart Mill. Later, the couple worked together closely on many other manuscripts, including revisions of his *Principles of Political Economy*. They revised J. S. Mill's autobiography when they thought that they both were dying of tuberculosis, recovering to continue their work. Mill and his stepdaughter Helen Taylor described his famous appeal "On Liberty" as a joint production, and Mill published it after Harriet died with a dedication to her. Helen Taylor continued her mother's work as John Stuart Mill's secretary and associate until his death in 1873. J. S. Mill and Helen Taylor worked together in the suffrage movement and organized the Society for the Representation of Women.

The extent of Harriet Taylor Mill's collaboration with Mill has often been debated. She published nothing in her own name after they began to work together. Although Mill himself praised her lavishly, his statements must be taken with some caution. However, there is little doubt that she was the source of his feminism. J. S. Mill called "The Enfranchisement of Women" a joint production in his autobiography. When he included the essay in his anthology, *Dissertations and Discussions*, Taylor Mill was listed as the sole author. Mill claimed that she was a joint author on *The Principles of Political Economy* and the essay "On Liberty." Her first husband had been upset when Mill dedicated a limited edition of *Principles of Political Economy* to her. Mill stated that he was only responsible for the "abstract and purely scientific parts" and credited Taylor Mill with noting the distinction between the laws regulating the production of wealth and the modes of its distribution. This distinction was very im-

portant, for she insisted that the real laws of nature were involved in production, dependent on the properties of objects, whereas the modes of its distribution were dependent upon human will. Previously, economists had merged the two.

In spite of Mill's protestations to the contrary, many critics have discounted her part in the collaboration. Others, such as Lynn McDonald, find it very credible that she contributed important methodological ideas to Mill, and Jo Ellen Jacobs insists on her extensive collaboration.   JH/MBO

PRIMARY SOURCES

Mill, H. T. With Mill, J. S. "The Enfranchisement of Women." In *Essays on Sex Equality,* ed. Alice Rossi. Chicago: University of Chicago Press, 1970.

———. *The Complete Works of Harriet Taylor Mill.* Ed. Jo Ellen Jacobs. Bloomington and Indianapolis: Indiana University Press, 1998. Includes her portrait and those of her parents, husbands, sons and daughter. It also includes drafts of her writings and all known correspondence.

Harriet Taylor Mill's papers and those of her daughter are with the John Stuart Mill/Harriet Taylor collection in the British Library of the London School of Political and Economic Sciences.

SECONDARY SOURCES

Hayek, F. A. *John Stuart Mill and Harriet Taylor.* London: Routledge and Kegan Paul, 1951.

McDonald, Lynn. *The Woman Founders of the Social Sciences.* Ottawa, Canada: Carleton University Press, 1994.

Mill, John Stuart. *Autobiography of John Stuart Mill.* Contains extensive discussions of Harriet Taylor.

Packe, Michael St. John. *The Life of John Stuart Mill.* London: Secker and Warburg, 1954. Includes material on Harriet.

STANDARD SOURCES

DNB Missing Persons.

MILLER, BESSIE IRVING (1884–?)

U.S. mathematician. Born 1884 in Baltimore, Md. Educated Goucher College (A.B., 1907; fellow, 1907–1908); Johns Hopkins University (fellow, 1913–1914; Ph.D., 1914). Professional experience: Kemper Hall, Wis., instructor in mathematics (1911–1913); Rockford College, Ill., head, physics and mathematics department (1915–1920); head, mathematics department from 1920. Death date unknown.

Bessie Irving taught mathematics at Kemper Hall for two years before returning to Johns Hopkins on a fellowship. She earned her doctoral degree in 1913, and in 1915 took a position as head of the physics and mathematics department at

Rockford College. She remained in this position for five years. The two departments apparently split in 1920, and Irving became head of the mathematics department. It is not known how long she remained in that position. She was a member of the Mathematics Society and the Mathematical Association (secretary of the Illinois section, 1924). Her research was on the canonical form of elliptic integrals.

JH/MBO

STANDARD SOURCES
AMS 3–4.

MILLER, ELIZABETH CAVERT (1920–1987)

U.S. biochemist and oncologist. Born 2 May 1920 in Minneapolis, Minn., to Mary Elizabeth (Mead) and William Lane Cavert. One sister. Married James A. Miller (1942). Two daughters, Linda Ann and Helen Louise. Educated University of Minnesota (bachelor's degree, 1941; M.S., 1943; Ph.D., 1945). Professional experience: University of Wisconsin, Carl Baumann's laboratory, research worker; McArdle Laboratory for Cancer Research, postdoctoral fellow (1945–?), associate director (1973–1987).

The career of Elizabeth Cavert Miller illustrates the importance to a woman scientist of having a male advocate. Miller's parents were well educated: her mother was a graduate of Vassar, and her father the director of research in agricultural economics at the Federal Land Bank in Minneapolis. Elizabeth graduated from the University of Minnesota Phi Beta Kappa in biochemistry and then went to the University of Wisconsin, where she began graduate work in a joint biochemistry and home economics program. Although she had applied for admission to the biochemistry program, permission was denied. However because her future husband, James Miller, pleaded her case with Carl Baumann, he agreed to take her on as a biochemistry graduate student. It was a fortuitous decision, for she obtained both a master's and a doctoral degree in a short time and went on to a very successful research career.

The advocacy of a well-positioned male continued to help Elizabeth. James Miller joined the McArdle Laboratory for Cancer Research and continued his study of experimental chemical carcinogenesis. In 1945, Elizabeth received a postdoctoral fellowship to work in the laboratory with James Miller, whom she had married in August 1942. They began an effective collaboration on chemical carcinogenesis that lasted throughout their careers.

Together the Millers became the first researchers to show that a foreign chemical caused cancer in rats by binding with proteins in the liver—a process known as covalent binding. After the structure of DNA was discovered in 1953, the Millers realized that DNA was important in the binding of chemical carcinogens. They and others in the laboratory recognized that the initiation of carcinogenesis depended on metabolic reactions of carcinogenic chemicals with DNA. Their work stimulated research on the binding of carcinogens to DNA, the mechanisms of mutagenesis, the activation of proto-oncogenes, and the inactivation of tumor suppressor genes, all vitally important in understanding cancer. Their findings on carcinogenesis was significant in opening up a new field involving drug interactions in metabolic studies in toxicology and pharmacology. They also demonstrated that chemical carcinogens were potential mutagens. This work set the stage for testing substances that were potentially mutagenic and assessing the risk for humans.

Elizabeth Miller served as editor of *Cancer Research* between 1954 and 1964, was president of the American Association for Cancer Research from 1976 to 1978 and served on its board of directors twice, and was president of Carter's Cancer Panel of the National Cancer Institute from 1970 to 1980. She remained as associate director of the McArdle Laboratory until her retirement in 1987. Both she and her husband were appointed Senior Distinguished Research Professors of Oncology and Emeritus Professors of Oncology. When they retired, the Millers had written over three hundred papers in chemical carcinogenesis and mentored forty-two McArdle researchers. They received a number of awards including the Papanicolaou in 1975, the First Founder's Award from the Chemical Industry Institute of Toxicology in 1978, and the Mott Award from General Motors Cancer Research Foundation in 1980. Elizabeth Miller died of kidney cancer in 1987.

JH/MBO

PRIMARY SOURCES
Miller, Elizabeth C. With James Miller. "The Presence and Significance of Bound Aminoazo Dyes in the Livers of Rats Fed p-Dimethylaminoazobenzene." *Cancer Research* 7 (1947): 468–480.

———. "Some Current Perspectives on Chemical Carcinogenesis in Humans and Experimental Animals." *Cancer Research* 38 (1978): 1479–1496. Her presidential address.

———. With James Miller. "Milestones in Chemical Carcinogenesis." *Seminars in Oncology* 6 (1979): 445–460.

———. "Some Historical Perspectives on the Metabolism of Xenobiotic Chemicals to Reactive Electrophiles." In *Bioactivation of Foreign Compounds,* ed. M. W. Anders. Orlando, Fla.: Academic Press, 1985.

SECONDARY SOURCES
Conney, A. H. "Introduction of Elizabeth C. Miller and James A. Miller." In *Accomplishments in Cancer Research,* ed. J. G. Fortner and Jonathan E. Rhoads. Philadelphia: Lippincott, 1980.

Fogel, S. "The Landmark Interviews: In Search of the Ultimate Carcinogen." *Journal of NIH Research* (February 1992): 66.

Kadlubar, F. F. "Obituary: Elizabeth Cavert Miller." *Carcinogenesis* 9 (1988): 517–518.

STANDARD SOURCES

Grinstein 1993 (article by J. A. Miller); *Notable* (article by Laura Newman); *WWW*, vol. 9, 1985–1989.

MILLER, OLIVE THORNE (1831–1918)

U.S. nature writer. Born Harriet Mann, 1831, in Auburn, N.Y., to Mary (Hollbrook) and Seth Mann. Three siblings. Married Watts Miller. Four children: Harriet, Charles, Mary, Robert. Died 1918 in Los Angeles, Calif.

Harriet Mann was the eldest of four children born to a banker who moved around constantly. Thus, Harriet spent her childhood in Ohio, Wisconsin, Illinois, and elsewhere, and her schooling was fragmented. The shy child compensated for her imagined inadequacies by reading and writing stories.

In 1854 Mann married Watts Miller, a businessman. While their four children (born between 1856 and 1868) were young, she gave up writing. Beginning in 1870, however, she published a series of children's stories, mainly about animals. Written under the pen name Olive Thorne Miller, most of her children's fiction has been forgotten, but her nature sketches, both for children and for adults, are still read. She became interested in bird watching in 1880 and avidly pursued this hobby for the rest of her days. After her husband's death in 1904 she moved to Los Angeles, where she continued to write until her death at age eighty-seven.

Olive Thorne Miller wrote books on birds that reflected a close observation of their habits. Although her treatment was sometimes anthropomorphic, most of her facts were accurate, and her works were useful in stimulating popular interest in natural history. JH/MBO

PRIMARY SOURCES

Miller, Olive Thorne. *The Bird Our Brother: A Contribution to the Study of the Bird as He Is in Life.* Boston: Houghton Mifflin, 1908.

STANDARD SOURCES

DAB; NAW; Ogilvie 1986.

MINOKA-HILL, LILLIE ROSA (1876–1952)

U.S. physician. Born 30 August 1876 on the St. Regis Mohawk Indian Reservation in New York State. Mother died after childbirth. Father, Joshua G. Allen, a Quaker physician from Philadelphia.

Married Charles Abram Hill (1905; he died 1916). Six children: Rosa Melissa, Charles Allan, Norbert Seabrook, Alfred Grahame, and twins Jane Frances and Josephine Marie. Educated by father; Grahame Institute; Quebec to study French; Woman's Medical College of Pennsylvania (graduated 1899). Professional experience: Woman's Hospital, Philadelphia, intern (1899); Woman's Clinic, attended indigent and immigrant women (from 1899); private practice with Frances Tyson; Lincoln Boarding School; Oneida, Wis., physician (1917–1952). Honors and memberships: Indian Council Fire in Chicago, American Indian of the Year (1947); adopted by Oneida Tribe. Died 1952 in Fond du Lac, Wis., of a heart attack.

Lillie Rosa Minoka-Hill was born to a Mohawk Indian mother and a Quaker physician father. After Rosa's birth, her mother died. Her father left her with her mother's family until she was five years old. At that age she was old enough to attend school. Her father took her to Philadelphia and then sent her to a boarding school, the Grahame Institute. Minoka absorbed the Quaker ethic of the importance of doing good and decided to become a nurse. However, her father discouraged her and encouraged her to study to become a physician. He sent Rosa to Quebec for a year to learn French. During that year she lived in a convent and, impressed by the piety of the sisters, converted to Catholicism. After she returned to Philadelphia, she entered the Woman's Medical College of Pennsylvania, where she earned her medical degree. She did her internship at the Woman's Clinic, a dispensary for immigrant and indigent women that was connected with the college. She and a fellow physician, Frances Tyson, established a private practice. While working at a government boarding school for Native Americans, she met an Oneida student, Anna Hill, who introduced her to her brother Charles Abram Hill, whom she married in 1905. She moved to his farm in Oneida, Wisconsin, and gave up her medical practice to be a farmwife. Within nine years, she had six children.

Her resolution to give up medicine soon began to waver. The Oneidas began to ask her for help with their medical problems. She learned much about herbal medicine from the medicine men and combined it with "scientific" medicine. The town physician was not respected, so they went to Minoka-Hill for their problems, even though she was not licensed to practice in Wisconsin. Charles Hill died in 1916 and when the town's sole physician left in 1917, she became its only trained doctor. She kept a "kitchen-clinic" stocked with herbals and medicines, traveled long distances to deliver babies, and treated the diseases common to reservation life, such as tuberculosis. The Depression wiped out the small trust fund left to Minoka-Hill by her father, and she was in serious financial straits. Since she did not have a Wisconsin medical license, she had never been able to admit patients to the hospital. However, in 1934, Green Bay physicians loaned her the hundred-dollar examination fee, she passed the test, and received her Wisconsin license. She remained in Oneida, where she practiced for the rest of her life.

In addition to her medical practice, Minoka-Hill also taught nutrition, sanitation, and preventive medicine. In 1946 she had a heart attack that prevented her from making house calls, although she still kept her kitchen clinic open and helped those who came for advice.

The State Medical Society of Wisconsin awarded her a lifetime membership and financed her trip to the American Medical Association national convention and her fiftieth college reunion in 1949. Three years later, another heart attack killed Lillie Rosa Minoka-Hill, who had given her life to serve others through medicine.   JH/MBO

SECONDARY SOURCES
Brown, Victoria. "Dr. Rosa Minoka Hill." *Uncommon Lives of Common Women: The Missing Half of Wisconsin History.* Madison, Wis.: Wisconsin Feminists Project Fund, Inc., 1975.

Edeen, Susan. *Women Scientists.* Palo Alto, Calif.: Dale Seymour Publications, 1992. Contains portraits for classroom bulletin boards. Discusses Lillie Minoka-Hill.

Gridley, Marion E. *American Indian Women.* New York: Hawthorne Books, 1974.

Archival material is found in the Archives Division of the State Historical Society of Wisconsin and the Alumnae Office, Medical College of Pennsylvania.

STANDARD SOURCES
NAW(M) (article by Rima D. Apple).

MINOR, JESSIE ELIZABETH (1880–?)
U.S. chemist. Born 17 April 1880. Educated Drury College (B.S., 1904); University of Pennsylvania (fellow, 1908–1910); Bryn Mawr College (Ph.D., 1917). Professional experience: Rogers Academy, Ark., science teacher (1904–1906); Drury College, substitute professor of chemistry (1906–1908); Huguenot College, South Africa, professor and chief of the department (1910–1914); Goucher College, associate professor (1917–1918); Hammersly Manufacturing Co., N.J., chief chemist in paper mill laboratory (1918–1920); Emersom laboratory, paper mill consultant (1920–1922); Collins Manufacturing Company, Mass., chief chemist (1922–1928); Rag Paper Manufacturers, research chemist (1928–1932), consulting chemist (1932–1941); Hurlbut Paper Company, director of the laboratory (1941–1955). Retired 1955. Death date unknown.

Jessie Elizabeth Minor taught in Arkansas immediately after she got her bachelor's degree from Drury College. She returned to Drury for two years as a substitute professor of chemistry before she went to South Africa as professor and

departmental chair of Huguenot College. She returned to the United States and earned her doctoral degree in organic chemistry from Bryn Mawr College. After finishing this degree, she seemed to be heading toward an academic career. However, she resigned her position at Goucher College after a year and from that time on worked in industry as a chemist. Her research interests were in cellulose structure and reactivity, the nature of paper sizing, the permanence of paper, and photographic paper features.   JH/MBO

STANDARD SOURCES
AMS 3–8, P 9, P&B 10.

MINOT, ANN STONE (1894–?)
U.S. biochemist and physiologist. Born 25 April 1894 in Bath, N.H. Educated Smith College (A.B., 1915); Radcliffe College (Ph.D., 1925). Professional experience: Massachusetts General Hospital, laboratory assistant (1915–1920); Harvard Medical School, researcher (1923–1926); Wellesley College, instructor in physiology (1925–1926); Vanderbilt University School of Medicine, research associate in pharmacology (1926–1930), assistant professor of pediatric research (1930–1940), associate professor (1940–1943), associate professor of biochemistry (in charge of clinical chemistry) (1943–1950), professor (1950–1960), emerita professor (1960–post-1968), research associate in endocrinology (1960–post-1968).

Born in a small town in New Hampshire, Ann Stone Minot attended Smith College, graduating in 1915. Upon leaving college, she remained in Massachusetts, taking a position as a laboratory assistant at Massachusetts General Hospital. Here her interest in clinical studies of biochemistry and physiology was stimulated. After five years, she returned to graduate work, eager to study clinical aspects of lead poisoning, an important topic of the day. Of course, all advanced degrees from Harvard University were officially granted by Radcliffe College, although the actual research was in a Harvard department. As Ann Minot began to do research on lead poisoning for her doctorate, she must certainly have been influenced by the groundbreaking work of the great industrial hygienist ALICE HAMILTON, who came to lecture at Harvard Medical School from 1919 to 1927. Minot must have worked with Joseph Aub, with whom her work was published, in his physiological laboratory at Harvard Medical School. This laboratory had been well funded by grants provided by the lead companies (with no strings attached), arranged by Hamilton. Minot remained as a researcher from 1923 until a year following the completion of her dissertation.

With her doctorate in hand, Minot then moved to Vanderbilt University in Tennessee, where she worked as a research associate in pharmacology until 1930, when she began to teach at the university as assistant professor of pediatric research. At this time, she became interested in hormonal effects on bone growth and fluid balance on infant diarrhea. She also became very interested in progressive muscle diseases, especially myasthenia gravis and muscular dystrophy. She was first to use guanadine in treatment of myasthenia gravis in 1938. In 1943, she was made associate professor in biochemistry, rising to full professor in 1950. Upon retirement in 1960, she was appointed an emerita professor, continuing her research as a research associate in endocrinology.   JH/MBO

PRIMARY SOURCES

Minot, Annie *(sic)* Stone. "Distribution of Lead in the Organism in Acute and Chronic Lead Poisoning." Ph.D. diss., Radcliffe College, 1923.

———. With Joseph C. Aub, T. Fairhall, and Alice Hamilton. *Lead Poisoning.* Baltimore: Williams and Wilkins, 1926.

MIRCHINK, MARIA E. (1887–1978)

Soviet geologist. Born 1887 in Smolensk. One sibling. Married G. F. Mirchink. Children. Educated Smolensk Women's Gymnasium; Highest Women's Courses (completed 1910). Professional experience: Professor M. V. Pavlova, assistant (1913–1918); Moscow Government Oil Institute, researcher (1918); Geologic Institute of Academy of Sciences of the USSR, researcher. Died 1978.

Maria E. Mirchink was Professor M. V. PAVLOVA's assistant until 1918. Pavlova lectured at Shanyavskiy University. Mirchink was not merely an assistant, for Pavlova had assigned her the problem of describing the Jurassic corals of the Crimea. Mirchink published descriptions of many of these fossils. She worked with Pavlova until 1918, when she joined the Moscow Government Oil Institute. Mirchink later moved to the Geologic Institute of the Academy of Sciences of the USSR.

Mirchink was assigned to work in the Urals under E. D. Soshkina. Afterward she studied the Permian North of the Russian Platform. In 1938, her second article appeared dedicated to Zechstein of Pinega and its brachiopods. Her productive scientific days were cut short, for after her children were born she left scientific work.

Fluent in German, she translated A. Wegener's *The Origin of Continents and Oceans.* She also translated a geology text by the then popular Professor Kaizer..   JH/MBO

PRIMARY SOURCES

Mirchink, M. E. "Some New Data on the Study of the Spirifer Horizon (Kasanian Stage) and the Development of the Groups of *Spirifer rugulatus* Kut and *Sp. schrenki* Keys" (in

Russian). *Byulleten' Moskovskogo Obshchestva Ispytateley Prirody, Otdel Geologicheskiy* 43, no. 13 (1935): 356–383.

———. "On the Paleogeography of the Kazan Basin in the European Part of the USSR." *Problems in Soviet Geology* 6, no. 11 (1936): 1010–1012. In Russian. The historical geology and paleography of the Kazan basin.

———. With D. M. Rauzer-Chernousova. *Société des naturalistes de Moscou.* n.s. 45 (1937): 475–477. In Russian. A brief account of the conference on the study of Permian deposits of the USSR, held in connection with the meetings of the 17th International Geological Congress in Russia.

———. "Corals from the Jurassic Beds of the Environs of Koktebel in the Crimea" (in Russian). *Byulleten' Moskovskogog Obshchestva Ispytateley Prirody, Otdel Geologicheskiy* 45, no. 15 (1937): 62–80.

———. *Anna Boleslavovna Missuna (1869–1922).* Moscow, 1940. In Russian. Biography and list of writings of the Lithuanian-born geologist Anna Missuna, much of whose work was in the field of glacial geology.

SECONDARY SOURCES

Nalivkin, Dmitry V. *Our First Women Geologists.* Leningrad: Nauka, 1979.

MISES, HILDA GEIRINGER von (1893–1973)

See Geiringer, Hilda.

MISSUNA, ANNA BOLESLAVOVNA (1868–1922)

Polish/Russian geologist, paleontologist, and mineralogist. Born 12 November 1868 in Vitebsk province, settlement Bykoshizna, to Polish parents. Educated at home; Riga, private gymnasium "School of Daughters" (completed 1887); Moscow, Highest Women's Courses (1893–1896). Professional experience: gymnasium at Riga, Polish and arithmetic teacher (1887–1890); other teaching positions. Died May 1922.

Anna Boleslavovna Missuna was born into a Polish family. She received her primary education at home, but then went to a private *gymnasium* in Riga, whose name, "School of Daughters," may have referred to "daughters of the Polish people." An avid opponent of the tsar's regime, her father participated in the revolt of 1863.

At the *gymnasium,* Anna learned to speak, read, and write German fluently. As a result, she was able to write her papers in German as well as in Russian or her native language, Polish. She remained in Riga after she finished her course. However, in 1890, after the death of her father, she returned to her homeland to take care of her mother and younger brothers. She studied avidly at home and became interested in natural sciences. She ordered books and made contacts with the Warsaw Society of Natural Scientists. She later gave them the large collection of plants and insects that she made during that time. Her first publication (1895) was a list of the plants with short remarks about them written in Polish.

In 1893 Anna received a small private scholarship to attend the Highest Women's Courses in Moscow. At this time, she began to feel that Moscow was her second homeland. Even after numerous opportunities to return to Poland, she remained in Russia. In Moscow the private courses' professors were well known in their fields and they gave all of their time to their students.

After graduation, Missuna decided to dedicate her life to geology and at first worked on mineralogy with V. E. Vernadskiy. He assigned her several mineralogical questions to study and probably introduced her to the crystallographer E. S. Federov. Fedorov assigned L. V. Yakovleva to study the crystal forms of ammonium sulphate. In 1898 Missuna and Yakovleva wrote an article on this topic in the *Protocols* of the Moscow Naturalist Society. This work was Missuna's first geological publication.

Much of Missuna's work was with V. D. Sokolov. Their friendship had an important effect on her scientific work, for under him she started to study the Quaternary deposits to which she dedicated many years of her life.

Missuna grew up in a country where glacial moraine was abundant. Her first work, published in 1899, was on the finite moraines of Poland. In 1902 she published a large work on the glacial deposits of Belarus and Latvia, and in the same year published it in German. She turned her attention to the Crimea and Tversk province in 1904, where she continued to work on Quaternary deposits; her work was published in a German glaciology magazine.

Although Missuna is best known for her studies of the Quaternary deposits that extended over twenty years, she was interested in many different geological subjects. Before she became involved in Quaternary freezing, she worked in botany and entomology. Simultaneously while working with the Quaternary, she studied Jurassic corals and Mesozoic magmatic rocks, which are important for stratigraphy and paleogeography.

When she went to the province of Tversk with V. D. Sokolov, she studied Carboniferous fish and glacial deposits. She worked in this province for three years and in 1910 returned to her favorite subject, finite moraines. Her important series on Quaternary deposits was published then, but in 1913, she changed topics and wrote an article on South Russian diatoms. At the time of World War I and after the October Revolution, Missuna returned to Quaternary deposits, but, to help her country, concentrated on studying the minerals related to these deposits.

Although not known as a teacher, Missuna was an assistant professor in the chemistry department with A. E. Konovalov,

but without pay. When the geology department was established in the Moscow Highest Women's Courses, V. D. Sokolov invited Missuna to be his assistant professor (1906). At first there were not enough professors and Missuna often had to teach practical petrography, paleontology, and historical geology. Later she taught only historical geography. In an obituary article, her fellow geologist MARIA MIRCHINK wrote that her scientific interests were evident in her teaching and that this helped interest her students in serious scientific work. She encouraged students in a first course to attend scientific society meetings. She led students to find answers. Missuna died when she was only fifty-three years old.

JH/MBO

SECONDARY SOURCES

Mirchink, Maria E. *Société des naturalistes de Moscou, Historical* Ser. no. 6, 15, 1940. An account of the life and work of Anna Boleslavovna Missuna. A bibliography of her works is appended. Includes two plates, portraits.

Nalivkin, D. V. *Our First Women Geologists.* Leningrad: Nauka, 1979. In Russian.

MITCHELL, ANNA HELENA (1794–1881)

Swedish/British botanist. Born 22 May 1794 in Gothenburg, Sweden. Died 14 January 1882 in Montrose, Angus Co., Scotland.

Swedish-born Anna Mitchell was a lichenologist and algologist. She worked with botanists Alexander Croall and James Gilchrist, and her plants are at the Montrose Museum.

JH/MBO

STANDARD SOURCES

Desmond.

MITCHELL, EVELYN GROESBEECK (ca. 1884–?)

U.S. zoologist and psychiatrist. Born East Orange, N.J. Educated Cornell University (A.B., 1902); University of Pennsylvania (A.M., 1911; fellow, 1912–1914; Ph.D., 1913); George Washington University (M.S., 1906); Howard University (M.D., 1913). Professional experience: Louisiana, laboratory, field assistant, and artist to Dr. Dupree (1904); George Washington University, assistant in zoology (1904–1906); U.S. National Museum, zoological artist (unofficial) (1904–1912); Woman's Hospital, Philadelphia, intern (1913–1914); practicing physician (from 1914); Howard University, lecturer in neurology (1917–1921); Freedmen's Hospital, visiting neurologist (1915–1921); Park Hospital, Stoneham, Mass., superintendent (1921–1922); Boston City Hospital, outpatient department (1923–1924); Ring Sanitarium, medical director (1924–1925). Death date unknown.

African-American zoologist and psychiatrist Evelyn Mitchell had a varied career. In 1913 she received a doctoral degree from the University of Pennsylvania. Her research was on insects (particularly the Diptera). She also worked on the life histories of Culicidae and Chironomidae. However, she could not be called just an entomologist, for she also worked in ichthyology (specifically the morphology of fish), herpetology, and mammalogy. From 1909 to 1912 she attended medical school at Howard University. She held a number of short jobs in medicine, particularly in psychiatry and neurology. As the result of her medical interests, she also studied dream states.

JH/MBO

STANDARD SOURCES
AMS 2–5; Dorland.

MITCHELL, HELEN SWIFT (1895–?)

U.S. physiologist and nutritionist. Born 21 September 1895 in Bridgewater, Conn., to Minnie (Swift) and Walter L. Mitchell. Education: Mount Holyoke College (B.A., 1917); Yale University (Ph.D., 1921). Professional experience: Battle Creek College, research professor of physiology and nutrition (1921–1935). University of Massachusetts, research professor of nutrition (1935–1941). U.S. Office of Health and Welfare Service, Washington, D.C., chief nutritionist (1941–1943); U.S. Office of Foreign Relief Rehabilitation, chief nutritionist (1943–1944); University of Massachusetts, School of Home Economics, dean (1946–1960); Hokkaido University, Sapparo, Japan, exchange professor (1960–1962). Harvard School of Public Health, research consultant (1964–1967); U.S. Office of Economic Opportunity, Head Start, administrator (1964–1967). Death date unknown.

Helen Swift Mitchell pursued nutrition research, working on the quantitative relations of iron and copper in nutritional anemia. After receiving her bachelor's degree from Mount Holyoke College, she taught high school for several years. After she received her doctorate, she was appointed as professor of nutrition at Battle Creek College, and then accepted a position as a research professor. During World War II, she served as the principal nutritionist for the Office of Defense, Health, and Welfare, and then became the chief nutritionist for a state department program. After the war, she returned to academe, this time as a professor at Carnegie Institute of Technology. She remained at this university for only one year before she was appointed dean of home economics at the University of Massachusetts in 1946. After retirement, she received an honorary degree from the University of Massachusetts.

In addition to her work on the quantitative relations of iron and copper in anemia, she studied experimental galactose cataracts in rats and the relation of protein to human

adolescent growth. One of her special interests involved the cause and prevention of nutritional anemia and cataracts.

JH/MBO

PRIMARY SOURCES
Mitchell, Helen Swift. With Lenna F. Cooper and (after 1938) others. *Nutrition in Health and Disease.* Philadelphia: Lippincott, 1938–1968.

STANDARD SOURCES
AMS 6–10; Bailey; Debus.

MITCHELL, MARIA (1818–1889)

U.S. astronomer. Born 1 August 1818 on Nantucket Island, Mass., to Lydia (Coleman) Mitchell and William Mitchell. Nine siblings. Never married. Educated private elementary schools; William Mitchell's school (1827–1833); Cyrus Peirce's school for young ladies (1833–1834). Professional experience: Nantucket Atheneum, librarian (1836–1856); Vassar College, professor of astronomy and director of the observatory (1865–1888). Died 1889 in Lynn, Mass.

Maria Mitchell's childhood included a Quaker background, a mother who had worked in two libraries in order to read all the books they contained, a gentle father with a love for astronomy, and a geographical location that stimulated the study of natural phenomena. She wrote that her love of mathematics was "seconded by my sympathy with my father's love for astronomical observations." She claimed that on Nantucket, people often made astronomical observing a hobby, and it was not uncommon to find sextants in their houses. She credited this interest in the heavens to the flat, monotonous landscape, claiming that the heavens were far more attractive.

Maria was the third of ten children. Although the Mitchell children had few luxuries, Maria Mitchell later wrote that "our want of opportunity was our opportunity—our privations were our privileges, our needs were our stimulants—we are what we are partly because we had little and wanted much, and it is hard which to tell which was the more powerful leader" (Wright, 4). Her father, William Mitchell, had a variety of careers, but most important to Maria's future, he was a highly respected amateur astronomer. Nantucket whalers employed him to check the accuracy of their chronometers by means of stellar observation.

Maria attended local private elementary schools from the age of four at which time she enrolled in her father's schools: he was first a public school master, but in 1827 established a free school of his own, where he stressed field work—the collecting of stones, shells, seaweed, and flowers. When William Mitchell gave up his school, Maria was sent to

Cyrus Peirce's school for "young ladies." Peirce, who later became principal of the first normal school in the United States, was intrigued by Maria's mathematical abilities and encouraged her in this area. Although she later insisted that she "was born of only ordinary capacity, but of extraordinary persistency," Peirce "saw in her the quality of self-discipline together with the rare insight which makes the difference between a creative life and the prosaic existence of a mere fact collector." (Kendall, 7).

When she was sixteen years old, Maria Mitchell's formal education ended. On her own she labored over Bridge's *Conic Sections,* Hutton's *Mathematics,* and Bowditch's *Practical Navigator;* she studied the works of Lagrange, Laplace, and Legendre in French; and she carefully considered Gauss's *Theoria motus corporeum coelestium.*

William Mitchell used his children as his assistants in his nightly observations, "counting seconds by the chronometer, during the observations." Their astronomical equipment consisted of a sextant (which Maria learned to operate at an early age) and a clumsy reflecting telescope. They gradually added more sophisticated tools.

After first assisting Cyrus Peirce at his school, the seventeen-year-old Mitchell opened her own school in 1835. She seems to have used her father's methods, for she espoused an unconventional approach to education. She sometimes convened school before dawn so that the students could watch birds. On other occasions it extended late into the evening so that they could observe the planet and stars. In 1836, Mitchell was offered the post of librarian at the new Nantucket Atheneum, which allowed her time to study and also enabled her to influence the reading of the young people in town. "If she saw that boys were eagerly reading a certain book, she immediately read it; if it were harmless she encouraged them to read it; if otherwise she had a convenient way of *losing* the book. In November when the trustees made their annual examination, the book appeared upon the shelf, but the next day after it was again lost" (Kendall, 11). She continued as librarian until 1856.

On 1 October 1847, Mitchell observed a new comet. Her father immediately wrote to William Cranch Bond at the Harvard Observatory to tell him of the discovery, but the mails did not go out of Nantucket until October 4. In the meantime the comet was reported by an observer in Rome and another in England. A gold medal had been offered by the king of Denmark for the discovery of a comet, with the stipulation that the discovery be communicated by the first post after the observation. After numerous letters had passed back and forth among all the concerned parties, Mitchell's right to the medal was acknowledged one year after the discovery.

This medal led to Mitchell's being acknowledged as a leading astronomer in both the United States and Europe.

She was elected the first woman member of the American Academy of Arts and Sciences (1848) and of the newly founded American Association for the Advancement of Science (1850) and became the subject of numerous magazine articles. From her point of view, however, the most important result of the discovery was a lifelong friendship with physicist Joseph Henry (1797–1878), director of the newly founded Smithsonian Institution in Washington, D.C., to whom she had sent a report of the comet.

In 1849 Mitchell became a computer for the *American Ephemeris and Nautical Almanac* (a post she held for nineteen years) and began to work for the United States Coast Survey, making measurements that helped in the accurate determination of time, latitude, and longitude. Nantucket was often visited by famous people, like the writer Herman Melville, who mentioned that he visited Mr. Mitchell and his daughter, "the discoverer of comets."

In 1857 Mitchell was asked to chaperone the daughter of a wealthy Chicago banker on a trip through Europe. Armed with letters of introduction, she visited observatories in England and on the Continent. Although her duties as chaperone were cut short when her charge was forced to return home because of family financial losses, Mitchell continued her tour. She met, among others, the author Nathaniel Hawthorne, the astronomer George Biddell Airy, the dour philosopher of science William Whewell, and the geologist Adam Sedgwick—"an old man of seventy-five" who "is said to be fond of young ladies even now." She also met the hospitable aging physicist and astronomer John Herschel and the philosopher-explorer-naturalist Alexander von Humboldt, author of *Kosmos.* One of the high points of her trip was a meeting with the seventy-seven-year-old physicist and astronomer MARY SOMERVILLE: "I could not but admire Mrs. Somerville as a woman. The ascent of the steep and rugged path of science had not unfitted her for the drawing room circle; the hours of devotion to close study have not been incompatible with the duties of wife and mother; the mind that has turned to rigid demonstration has not thereby lost its faith in those truths which figures will not prove" (Kendall, 113–119).

After her mother died in 1861, Mitchell moved with her father to Lynn, Massachusetts, where one of her sisters lived. They remained in Lynn for four years (1865), when Mitchell accepted an invitation to become professor of astronomy and director of the observatory at the newly founded Vassar College in Poughkeepsie, New York. For the rest of her life, Mitchell was committed to the cause of higher education for women. She considered ridiculous the prevalent view that women were innately unsuited to mathematics and other sciences. On the contrary, she postulated, women would be *more* competent astronomical observers than men, because "the perceptive faculties of women" are "more acute than those of men." Women would "perceive the size, form and color of an object more readily and would catch an impression more quickly." She reflected that "the training of girls (bad as it is) leads them to develop these faculties. The fine needlework and the embroidery teach them to measure small spaces. The same delicacy of eye and touch is needed to bisect the image of a star by a spider's web, as to piece delicate muslin with a fine needle. The small fingers too come into play with a better adaptation to delicate micrometer screws" (Maria Mitchell Association, 5). Mitchell's experiences with the young women at Vassar convinced her that women could also excel in areas beyond mere "stargazing"—that they could penetrate to the heart of the subject, mathematics.

Mitchell's teaching methods remained unorthodox. She dispensed with lectures and stressed the importance of small classes and individual attention. She also believed that elaborate, expensive equipment was unnecessary, for students could make the necessary observations with simple instruments. As for the rest, "all their book learning in astronomy should be mathematical. The astronomy which is not mathematical is what is so ludicrously called 'Geography of the Heavens'—is not astronomy at all" (Kendall, 171).

In 1873 Mitchell made a second European tour. Her visit to the Russian observatory at Pulkova highlighted this trip. In the same year she helped found the Association for the Advancement of Women, a moderate feminist group, of which she was president for two years (1875–1876) and chairman of the science committee until her death.

Throughout her life, Mitchell was plagued by religious conflicts. Although she accepted the doctrines of love and peace advocated by the Quaker religion in which she had been raised, she despised the joyless, confining discipline imposed by the more unbending members of the sect. Her doubts were not tolerated by these people, and in 1843 in Nantucket, after a visit by two female church members during which she told them of her uncertainty, she was "disowned" by the church. For the rest of her life she attended the Unitarian church, but never became a member. As she grew older she continued to seek, asking the opinions of her friends as to the existence of God and immortality but was never satisfied with their answers. Institutionalized Christianity never appealed to her. Once when the regular chapel service at Vassar threatened to interfere with her observations of Saturn, she wrote to the president of the college asking him to shorten his prayer.

Mitchell retired on Christmas Day, 1888, after teaching for twenty-three years at Vassar Although she was offered a home in the observatory for the remainder of her life, she returned to Lynn, where she died in 1889. As death approached, she murmured, "Well, if this is dying, there is nothing very unpleasant about it" (Maria Mitchell Association, 5–6).

As "the female astronomer," Mitchell was respected by scientific colleagues, toasted by writers in popular magazines, and honored by award-giving groups. Yet Mitchell herself was uncomfortably aware of her limitations. Throughout her career she was hampered by inadequate equipment. Lacking the fine micrometer necessary for accurate measurements, she was unable to trust her own comet observations, and even during her tenure at the Vassar observatory she was unable to get a poorly structured telescope improved. She was an exacting self-critic and suspected that she might not meet the standard for scientific creativity: "The best that can be said of my life so far," she wrote, "is that it has been industrious, and the best that can be said of me is that I have not pretended to what I was not" (Wright, 76).

The comet discovery in 1847 that catapulted her to fame in the eyes of others did not give Mitchell the kind of satisfaction that might be expected. Years after the discovery she wrote,

I have just gone over my comet computations and it is humiliating to perceive how very little more I know than I did seven years ago when I first did this kind of work. To be sure, I have only once in the time computed a parabolic orbit, but it seems to me that I know no more in general. I think I am a little better thinker, that I take things less on trust, but that the same time I trust myself much less. (Wright, 76)

Mitchell's publications corroborate her image of herself as observer and teacher rather than theoretical astronomer. Observational records appeared in *Silliman's Journal* and in numerous reports in the *Nantucket Inquirer*. Popular accounts appeared in *Hours at Home,* the *Century,* and the *Atlantic.* During her tenure at Vassar she edited the astronomical column of the *Scientific American.* Although these publications indicate the breadth of her interests in observational astronomy, in the history of science, and in education, their composition did not require a mastery of theoretical astronomy.

Mitchell's unpublished papers reveal a number of astute statements about the nature of science. An observer herself, she recognized the limits of observation and the importance of creativity in science. Mitchell firmly believed that astronomy transcended observation. Even her beloved mathematics could not explain the universe. Although she once remarked that "a mathematical formula is a hymn of the universe and therefore a hymn of God," she believed that "we especially need imagination in science. It is not all mathematics, nor all logic, but is somewhat beauty and poetry" (Kendall, 164, 205). These philosophical perspectives enticed Mitchell away from pure science and into the consideration of the relationship of poetry to astronomy. Especially fascinated by Milton, she observed that *Paradise Lost* reflected "through a poet's lens but with considerable learning, the state of astronomical knowledge in his time." Her voluminous notes on this epic were converted into a paper by her sister, Phebe Mitchell Kendall, and published posthumously.

Mitchell's contributions to theoretical astronomy may be found in the undeveloped speculations that accompany many of her descriptions of the astronomical features that most interested her: the sun, Jupiter and Saturn, the dark bodies between these planets, the nebulae, and the colors of stars. As for many nineteenth- and early-twentieth-century astronomers, the sun was a special object of Mitchell's observations. During her lifetime she observed several total eclipses, sometimes traveling many miles with bulky equipment in order to do so. She also followed the fate of sunspots, speculating about their origin and mutations. Although no fully developed theory about their nature emerged in her published papers, partial explanations were included among the observations. She postulated that changing sunspots indicated that they were rotating vortices in the solar surface.

Her novel interpretations of observational data on Jupiter also suggest that she was interested in interpreting as well as recording. Most astronomers assumed that they were viewing a cloud-shrouded surface, whereas Mitchell postulated that the body of the planet itself was composed of clouds—clouds that were seething upward and downward and moving at different rates. Because the brilliant white spots appeared to cast shadows, she concluded that they were at higher levels than the shadowless darker areas. Jupiter's satellites, she suggested, differed from each other in composition. Whereas three of them (the first, second, and fourth) appeared to be icy—similar to the polar region of Mars—the third satellite did not reflect light like the others, leading her to conclude that it was qualitatively different.

In observing Saturn she noted variations in the light of the rings and of the planet itself. From her observations, without the benefit of spectroscopic analysis, she concluded that the rings and the globe must be of different composition. As for the tiny bodies lying between Saturn and Jupiter, from her study of these Mitchell postulated that there were many "dark bodies" in the universe, bodies that perhaps formed the centers of systems. The presence of such "unseen centers" would explain the irregular orbits of certain heavenly bodies.

Along with other nineteenth-century astronomers, Mitchell was intrigued by the nature and cosmological significance of the nebulae. Her observations suggested that they were variable; yet variable nebulae were unlikely if the nebulae were considered to be unresolvable stars. Mitchell's observations of the double nebulae in the Great Bear reminded her of the dissimilarity of size in double stars. She speculated that one might revolve around the other. Finally,

Mitchell considered the subtle color variations among stars. Distance, she speculated, might account for some of the differences, but not all; the chemical constitution of a star must play a part.

Although there is no evidence that Maria Mitchell developed a systematic framework for celestial phenomena, she certainly sought explanations for her astronomical observations. Mitchell apparently made a deliberate choice to commit herself to teaching rather than to theoretical astronomy. At a time when higher education for women was in its infancy, she decided that her talents would be of most use in this area. And because she was a devoted teacher, her research time was sharply limited. Recognizing an essential conflict between teaching and research, she asserted that

the scientist should be free to pursue his investigations. He cannot be a scientist and a schoolmaster. If he pursues his science in all his intervals from his class-work, his classes will suffer on account of his engrossments; if he devotes himself to his students, science suffers; and yet we all go on, year after year, trying to work the two fields together, and they need different culture and different implements. (Kendall, 223)

Mitchell became increasingly committed to the idea of higher education for women. In 1876, in a paper read at the fourth congress of the Association for the Advancement of Women, she suggested that because so few women had been given the educational opportunities that would have fully developed their abilities in science, it was unfair to compare the scientific achievements of men and women. She elaborated on this theme in a paper read at the 1880 congress, this time stressing the need for the endowment of women's colleges.

In addition to her gold medal from the king of Denmark and the other honors that followed upon her comet discovery, Mitchell received numerous distinctions. She was given three honorary degrees, from Hanover College in Indiana (1853), Columbia University (1887), and Rutgers Female College (1870). A crater on the moon was named for her, as was a public school in Denver. Her name appears on the front of the Boston Public Library, and a society to honor her, the Maria Mitchell Association of Nantucket, was established after her death.   MBO

PRIMARY SOURCES

Mitchell, Maria. "Mary Somerville." *Atlantic Monthly* 5 (May 1860): 568–571.
———. "Eclipse of the Sun of 1869." *Hours at Home* 9: 555–560.
———. "The Collegiate Education of Girls." Paper read at the Congress for the Advancement of Women held in Boston,

October 1880. In *Women and the Higher Education,* ed. A. Brackett, 76–77. New York: Harper and Brothers, 1893.

———. "The Astronomical Science of Milton as Shown in *Paradise Lost.*" *Poet-Lore* 6 (June 1894): 313.

SECONDARY SOURCES
Botsford, Amelia H. "The Mother of the Stars." *Ladies Home Journal* (January 1900): 13.

Kendall, Phebe Mitchell, ed. *Maria Mitchell: Life, Letters, and Journals.* Boston: Lee and Shepard, 1896. A biography written by Mitchell's sister, containing portraits and other illustrations.

Kohlstedt, Sally Gregory. "Maria Mitchell: The Advancement of Women in Science." *New England Quarterly* 51 (1978): 39–63.

Maria Mitchell Association. Philadelphia: Ferris & Leach, 1909. Includes a list of Mitchell memorabilia in the Maria Mitchell Library, brochures about Mitchell and her birthplace, her works, annual reports of the association, and various biographical publications.

Wright, Helen. *Sweeper in the Sky: The Life of Maria Mitchell, First Woman Astronomer in America.* New York: Macmillan, 1949.

STANDARD SOURCES
Bailey; *DAB; DSB; NAW;* Ogilvie 1986; Shearer and Shearer 1997.

MITCHELL, MILDRED BESSIE (1903–)

U.S. psychologist. Born 25 December 1903 in Rockford, Ill. to Bessie (Warner) and Louis Biglow Mitchell. Five siblings. Married Ira Spear 1947. Educated: Rockford College (B.A., 1924); Radcliffe College (M.A., 1927); Yale University (fellows 1930–1931; Ph.D., 1931). Professional experience: Lees College, Ky., professor of education and math (1927–1928); George School, Pa., psychologist (1931–1933); New Hampshire State Hospital, chief psychologist (1933–1936); U.S. Employment Service, N.H., vocational director (1936–1937); Bellevue Hospital, New York City, psychologist (1937–1938); Psychopathic Hospital, Iowa, chief psychologist (1938–1939); Mt. Pleasant and Independence State Hospitals, Iowa, psychologist (1939–1941); Bureau Psychological Services, Ft. Snelling, Minn., clinical psychologist (1941–1942); Veterans Guidance Center, College City, N.Y., vocational appraiser (1945–1946); Domestic Relations Court, New York, psychologist (from 1946); U.S. Veterans Administration Mental Hygiene Clinic, Ft. Snelling, Minn., chief psychologist (1947–1958); Wright Patterson Air Force Base, clinical psychologist (1958–1960); University of Tampa, Fla., research psychologist (1960–1965), associate professor of psychology (1965–1967). Retired 1967. U.S. Navy (1942–1945), reserves (1945–1964, Lt. Comdr.).

Although Mildred Mitchell both taught and applied psychology, most of her positions and her research were in the applied area. At Harvard she ran up against Edwin G. Boring, who was notorious for his treatment of women. She earned a master's degree from Harvard (Radcliffe) but then went to work on her doctorate at Yale, where the climate was more favorable. After she got her doctoral degree she held a number of jobs as a psychologist. During World War II, she entered the U.S. armed forces and was in the navy from 1942 to 1945. She spent from 1945 to 1964 in the reserves, where she reached the rank of lieutenant commander. After the war, she served as a psychologist for the U.S. Veterans Administration and then the Wright Patterson Air Force Base. She returned to academia when she accepted a position at the University of Tampa, where she became both a research psychologist and an associate professor in psychology.

Mitchell received the Distinguished Technical Achievement Award of the U.S. Air Force in 1962 and 1964 and was a Fellow of the American Psychological Association. She also belonged to the American Association for the Advancement of Science, the Midwest Psychological Association, the Metropolitan New York Association of Applied Psychology (committee chairman, 1945), and the International Council of Women Psychologists (secretary, 1946).

Her research was on projective techniques, psychological tests, hypnosis and waking suggestion, and learning and memory. She also worked on the selection of personnel for unusual missions, including astronauts. She also published over forty journal articles and chapters in books. KM

PRIMARY SOURCES
Mitchell, Mildred. *Time Disorientation and Estimation in Isolation.* U.S. Air Force, 1962.

STANDARD SOURCES
AMS 5–8, S&B 9–12; O'Connell and Russo 1988.

MIYAJI, KUNIE (1891–?)

Japanese physician. Born 1 March 1891 in Suzaki, Kochi prefecture, Japan. Two siblings. Married Katsuro Miyaji. At least one daughter. Educated prefectural girls' high school, Kochi, boarding school (graduated 1909); Tokyo Women's Medical School (graduated 1914); Kyushu University, further training; Tokyo Imperial University School of Medicine (doctorate, 1945). Professional experience: medical practice in Burma (1916–1919); practice in Kochi (ca. 1922–1941). Death date unknown.

Kunie Miyaji got her education during two world wars. Born in the small fishing village of Kochi into a medical family, her aspirations were to become a doctor. After getting permission from her parents, she entered Yaoi Yoshioka's Tokyo Women's Medical School. At that time women were not allowed to enter the many national and private medical colleges. The only way that a woman could become a physician was by passing the national licensing examination. In 1914, Miyaji graduated from medical school and passed the examination. She remained at the medical school for two more years studying gynecology.

The Burmese requested some Japanese women physicians to care for their women, and Miyaji, another physician, and two midwives were chosen to go. She worked for three years in Burma. After she returned home she married Katsuro Miyaji. She was allowed to enter the gynecology department of Kyushu University for further training. After a year, she returned to her home town of Kochi to open a practice and to build a modern hospital. After practicing for twenty years, Miyaji decided to study at the gynecological department of the Tokyo Imperial University School of Medicine. By now she was fifty years old, and her friend and teacher Yayoi Yoshioka reprimanded her for giving up a good practice and her family for research. During 1941 the Japanese entered World War II, and it became very difficult to work on her degree. She earned her doctorate in 1945. After the war, she noted that great changes occurred in the educational system. Women were allowed to enter the universities that formerly were closed to them. She was active in the formation of the Japanese Women's Medical Association which was closed down during the war but was revived in 1955.   KM

PRIMARY SOURCES
Miyaji, Kunie. In Hellstedt, *Autobiographies.*

MOCKERIDGE, FLORENCE ANNIE
(ca. 1889–1958)
British botanist. Born circa 1889. Educated University of London (B.Sc., 1909; D.Sc., 1917). Professional experience: King's College, London, demonstrator and lecturer in botany (1917–1922); University College, Swansea, lecturer (1922–1935?), professor (1936–1954). Honors and memberships: Linnean Society, Fellow. Died 18 December 1958.

Florence Annie Mockeridge earned first-class honors in the pass and honors degrees of the University of London and was awarded the Carter Gold Medal. From 1911 to 1917 she worked under W. B. Bottomley on nitrogen fixation by *Azotobacter* and on the auximones of natural manures. Using peat as a medium, she organized numerous trials. This research earned her a doctor of science degree. She remained on the staff of King's College for five years and produced some important work on growth-promoting substances.

Mockeridge left London in 1922 to go to the newly established University College of Swansea as an independent lecturer in biology. During her thirty-two years at Swansea, she was dean of the faculty of science twice, vice-principal from 1949 to 1951, and the first professor of botany in 1936. One of her accomplishments was to establish separate departments of botany and zoology with honors degrees in each. This occurred shortly before she retired in 1954, when the new Natural Sciences Building, which she had planned, was completed. During her career, Mockeridge was also the editor of the *Proceedings of the Swansea Field Naturalist Society.* She died in 1958, at the age of sixty-nine.   JH/MBO

SECONDARY SOURCES
Newton, Lily. *Proceedings of the Linnean Society* 171 (1959–1960); 135. Obituary notice.

MOFFAT, AGNES K. (1905–   )
Canadian physician. Born 11 January 1905 in the village of Weston, near Toronto, to Janet Catherine (McNish) and Frederick William Moffat. Four siblings. Married Dr. Magee. Four children, two adopted. Educated McGill University, Montreal (graduated 1931); Banting Institute (M.A. in pathological chemistry, 1934?). Professional experience: Toronto General Hospital, intern; Children's Hospital, Detroit, senior intern; St. Joseph's Hospital, Guelph, Ontario, first resident; London, resident (1934–1936); Women's College Hospital, Toronto, outpatient work (1936); Standard Medical and Surgical Clinic of Peterborough, physician; on staff at two hospitals (1936–1972). Retired 1972.

Agnes K. Moffat grew up in a strict, authoritarian Presbyterian home. She had two older brothers and a younger brother and sister. She and her younger brother, Fred, had an especially good relationship. Fred enrolled in medicine at the University of Toronto, but Moffat succumbed to her parents' suggestion that she get a diploma in physical education. Fred was killed in an automobile accident, removing the one family support person in whom she could confide. She was accepted at McGill University in Montreal where she was one of two women in a class of 125. After graduating from McGill, she was accepted as one of two women interns at the Toronto General Hospital for one year. There she met her future husband, Dr. Magee, who was a senior intern. After they were married, they had a difficult time, for there were no salaries nor living quarters supplied for married interns and residents. They found rooms near the hospital, and Moffat did outpatient work at the Women's College one afternoon a week. At the same time, she was working on a degree in pathological chemistry, which she received after a year.

The couple went to London, where Magee studied for an advanced degree in surgery, and Moffat held residencies in various hospitals there. She met many well-known physicians, including MAUDE ABBOTT. Moffat returned to Canada before her husband, and set up an office in Toronto. After he returned, they accepted appointments with the Standard Medical and Surgical Clinic of Peterborough, the first partnership clinic in Canada. They were on the staff of two hospitals in Peterborough. During the Depression, they worked long hours under rather primitive conditions.

Magee joined the medical corps during World War II and spent from 1942 to 1946 overseas. His absence and that of many other Canadian physicians meant that those who remained at home shouldered the entire burden.

Before the war, Moffat had two children. She took four to five weeks off after their births. Their son died of cancer at the age of six and a half. After the war they adopted two children. Magee was always supportive of Moffat's desire to continue to practice. She practiced full time until 1972, when his health began to fail; he died in November 1972.   KM

STANDARD SOURCES
Moffat, Agnes K. In Hellstedt, *Autobiographies.*

MOHR, ERNA W. (1894–1968)

German zoologist. Born 1894 in Hamburg, Germany. Educated University of Munich (Dr. H.C.). Professional experience: Hamburg, Zoologisches Museum und Institut, curator of mammals. Died 1968.

Erna Mohr spent most of her career curating mammals at the Zoologisches Museum und Institut, Hamburg. She was a lifelong member of the American Society of Mammalogists. Immediately following World War II, she was dropped from the society's membership for failing to pay her dues, since she was unable to send money from Germany. After a poignant exchange of letters with Remington Kellogg, then president of the society, she was reinstated. Mohr published more than four hundred works during her lifetime. Mohr was named an honorary member of the society in 1966, the only woman to be so named.   JH/MBO

PRIMARY SOURCES
Mohr, Erna. "The Muskrat, *Ondatra zibethica* (Linnaeus), in Europe." *Journal of Mammalogy* 14 (1933a): 58–63.
———. "The Status of the Wisent on December 31, 1932." *Journal of Mammalogy* 14 (1933b): 260–262.

SECONDARY SOURCES
Kaufman, Dawn M., Donald W. Kaufman, and Glennis A. Kaufman. "Women in the Early Years of the American

Society of Mammalogists (1919–1949)." *Journal of Mammalogy* 77, no. 3 (1996): 642–654.
Taylor, J. M., and D. A. Schlitter. "Awardees." In *Seventy-five Years of Mammalogy (1919–1994),* ed. E. C. Birney and J. R. Choate, 71–109. Special Issue, The American Society of Mammalogists, 11 (1996).

MOLESWORTH, CAROLINE (1794–1872)

British botanist. Born 4 November 1794 in Pencarrow, Cornwall, to Caroline Treby (Ourry) and Sir William Molesworth, sixth baronet of Pencarrow. Never married. Professional experience: meteorological, natural history, and geological observations (1823–1858). Died 29 December 1872 in Cobham, Surrey.

Caroline Molesworth was the youngest daughter of Sir William Molesworth, sixth baronet of Pencarrow, Cornwall, and Caroline Treby Ourry. After the death of Sir William, Cobham Lodge and its estate, near Esher, Surrey, was left first to Lady Molesworth (d. 1842) and afterward to Caroline. No information is available as to why Caroline became interested in making extensive observations on the estate. However, it is noted that she became interested in botany as a young person.

Molesworth lived in London until 1823 when they moved to Cobham. Immediately upon arriving, she began the series of observations that she continued with only occasional lapses until 1858, when her failing health forced her to entrust a part of them to others. However, she did not completely abandon the observations until 1867.

Personally, Molesworth was described by her friends as kind to the poor and generous to her relatives. Small of stature, disdainful of fashion, and an entertaining companion, she was well informed in many different areas. She was also a meticulous observer. According to her letters, she was in contact with other observers and with scientists.

Molesworth's journals consisted of daily records arranged in nineteen parallel columns with their appropriate headings, such as the day of the month; day of the week; time of sunrise and sunset; phase of the moon; hour of observation; barometer; thermometer in the vestibule (adjacent to the barometer); thermometer "on the post"; thermometers maximum and minimum; south aspect; modifications of the clouds; general appearance of the weather; direction of the wind; rain; miscellaneous observations; observations relating to animals; observations relating to plants; and Tagliabue's storm glass. The instruments that she used for her measurements are described in the introduction by ELEANOR A. ORMEROD to the abridged version of *The Cobham Journals.*   JH/MBO

PRIMARY SOURCES

Molesworth, Caroline. *The Cobham Journals. Abstracts and Summaries of Meteorological and Phenological Observations Made by Miss Caroline Molesworth, at Cobham, Surrey, In the Years 1825 to 1850.* Introduction by Eleanor A. Ormerod, F.M.S. London: Edward Stanford, 1880.

Molesworth's herbarium and letters are at Kew Gardens.

SECONDARY SOURCES

Journal of Botany (1874): 209.

Journal of Botany (1882): 28.

Sowerby, James, and John Edward Smith. *English Botany.* London: J. Davis, 1900.

STANDARD SOURCES

Desmond.

MOLZA, TARQUINIA (1542–1617)

Italian student of natural philosophy. Born 1542 in Modena. Died 1617.

Tarquinia Molza was a typical woman polymath of the Italian Renaissance, who excelled both in poetry and fine arts and in astronomy and mathematics. The Senate of Rome conferred upon her the honor of Roman citizenship transmissible in perpetuity to her descendants.   JH/MBO

STANDARD SOURCES

Alic; Mozans; Ogilvie 1986.

MONIN-MOLINIER, MADELINE (fl. 1917–1921)

French physicist. Flourished 1917–1921. Professional experience: Carnegie Institution fellowship (1917–1918); Marie Curie's laboratory at the Radium Institute, researcher (1917–1918; 1920–1921).

Monin-Molinier worked in Paris in Marie Curie's laboratory at the Radium Institute during 1917–1918 and 1920–1921, apparently marrying sometime after her first year. She held a Carnegie fellowship during 1917–1918.   MM

SECONDARY SOURCES

Records in Institut Curie archives, assembled by Mme Monique Bordry.

MONSON, LADY ANNE VANE (ca. 1714–1776)

British natural history collector. Born around 1714 to an aristocratic family. Married twice (divorced once). Educated privately. Professional experience: collected insects and plants; worked on botanical books and collected in India; correspondent of Linnaeus. Died 1776.

Lady Anne Vane Monson was a great-granddaughter of Charles II. She collected both insects and plants in Britain. In her forties, she worked with the nurseryman James Lee on his book *Introduction to Botany,* published in 1760, but wished to remain anonymous. After she obtained a divorce from her first husband, she married a colonial officer with a regiment based in Calcutta. While in India, she began to collect plants and insects and had them illustrated by native artists. She corresponded with Linnaeus, who named the genus *Monsonia* in her honor. On her way to India, she also visited Linnaeus's pupils in Cape of Good Hope and collected with them. Shteir sees her as a "bridging figure," linking aristocrats who had an interest in natural history with the developing passion for botany among the middle class.   JH/MBO

SECONDARY SOURCES

Britten, James, "Lady Anne Monson." *Journal of Botany* 56 (1918): 147–149.

STANDARD SOURCES

Desmond; Shteir.

MONTAGUE, LADY MARY WORTLEY (1689–1762)

British writer, popularizer of smallpox inoculation. Baptized 26 May 1689 in London. Born to Mary (Feidling, daughter of earl of Denbigh) and Evelyn Pierrepont (fifth Earl of Kingston, then marquis of Dorchester and duke of Kingston). Three siblings. Married Edward Wortley Montague, 12 August 1712. One son, one daughter. Educated private tutors. Friend of Alexander Pope and other literary figures. Died 12 August 1762 in England.

Now chiefly known as a correspondent and friend (then enemy) of Alexander Pope and for her support of smallpox inoculation, Lady Mary Wortley Montague was born the oldest daughter of Evelyn Pierrepont, then the earl of Kingston. Her mother, also an earl's daughter, died when Montague was five, leaving three other children. At the age of nineteen Montague demonstrated her ability in Latin by translating a work of Epictetus, which she sent to Bishop Burnet.

Even before she was married, she was a friend of MARY ASTELL, a defender of women's rights, who later wrote a preface to Lady Montague's *Letters from the East* (1724). A close friend of hers, Anne Montague, was a regular correspondent, and after her friend's death she married her friend's brother, Edward Wortley Montague, with whom she had one son and one daughter. Lady Mary Montague was popular both at court and among the wits of the day. She wrote poetry, and was especially admired by Alexander Pope.

When she was twenty-seven, Lady Montague accompanied her husband, who was an ambassador, to Turkey. In Adrianope in 1717, on her way to Constantinople, she learned of the practice of smallpox inoculation, described by her in a famous letter to Sarah Chiswell, 1 April 1717. Since she herself had been badly marked by smallpox, she had her son inoculated and strongly advocated the practice when she returned to England, performed under her patronage. Her daughter's inoculation in 1721 was widely discussed, although Lady Montague attacked the medical community for the more "dangerous" manner in which they performed the inoculation. The procedure of Turkish smallpox inoculation, adapted from Greek folk medicine, was being widely discussed at the Royal Society from 1713. Lady Montague is owed some credit for introducing it to the British population, although quite independently the American colonists, Cotton Mather and Zabdiel Boylston, performed an extensive and notable series of inoculations in Boston during a smallpox epidemic in 1721.

After she returned to England, Lady Montague continued to make her name known in English society and among men of letters. For some time, Pope and she were neighbors and close friends, until a quarrel resulted in a series of satires and libels on both sides. Other writers besides Pope, including Henry Fielding, spoke of her with admiration. In 1739, she went abroad and did not return again to England until shortly before her death, corresponding extensively with her children and friends. She settled first in Avignon, then in Brescia, and finally in Venice. She became a close friend of Horace Walpole and then the political economist James Denham Stuart. She returned to England in 1762, a year after the death of her husband, to live at his family seat. After her death at the age of seventy-three, her charming letters were published in three volumes.　　　　　JH/MBO

PRIMARY SOURCES

Montague, Lady Mary Wortley. *Letters of Lady Mary Montague.* Ed. Robert Hasbland. 3 vols. Oxford: Oxford University Press, 1960–1967.

SECONDARY SOURCES

Hasbland, Robert. *Life of Lady Mary Montagu.* Oxford: Clarendon Press, 1956.

Miller, Genevieve. "Putting Lady Mary in Her Place: A Discussion of Historical Causation." *Bulletin History of Medicine* 55 (1981): 2–16.

Moulin, Anne-Marie, and Pierre Chuvin. *L'Islam au Peril des Femmes: Une Anglaise en Turquie au XVIIIe siècle.* Paris: Maspero (La Découverte), 1983.

STANDARD SOURCES

DNB.

MONTEL, ELIANE (fl. 1927–1931)

French researcher in radioactivity. Professional experience: École de Sèvre, researcher (Agrégée); Institut Curie, researcher (1927–1932); secondary school, teacher (1929–1930); Rothschild Fellowship (1931).

Eliane Montel was at the Institut Curie from 1927 to 1928. Although she published only one paper on her research, all of the references in this paper are to the work by other women: Stefania Maracineanu, ELISABETH RÓNA, IRÈNE JOLIOT-CURIE, and CATHERINE CHAMIÉ. After she left the institute, Montel taught at a secondary school from 1929 to 1930. The following year she held the Rothschild fellowship. According to Robert Reid, Montel had a son by the physicist Paul Langevin.　　　　　JH/MBO

PRIMARY SOURCES

Montel, Eliane. "Sur la pénétration du polonium dans le plomb." *Journal de Physique* 10 (1929): 78–80.

SECONDARY SOURCES

Records in Institut Curie archives, assembled by Mme. Monique Bordry.

Reid, Robert. *Marie Curie.* New York: The New American Library, Inc., 1974.

STANDARD SOURCES

Rayner-Canham 1997.

MONTESSORI, MARIA (1870–1952)

Italian physician and psychologist. Born 31 August 1870 in Chiaravalle, Ancona to Renilde (Stoppani) and Alessandro Montessori. No siblings. Never married; one son, Mario. Educated University of Rome (engineering classes 1884; M.D., 1896); audited courses in pedagogy (1897); studied physical anthropology, experimental psychology, educational philosophy (1901–?). Professional experience: San Giovanni Hospital, Rome, assistant (1896–1897); private practice (1896–1899); Regio Istituto Superiore di Magistero Femminile, lecturer in hygiene and anthropology (1899–1916); Scuola Magistrele Ortofrenica, co-director (1900–1901); University of Rome, instructor and member of Board of Examiners (1904–1908); Children's House, director (1907–?). Died 6 May 1952 at Noordwijk, aan Zee, the Netherlands.

Maria Montessori is best known for her pedagogical methods. Her method was known as psychopedagogy, a strategy for educating young children.

Her army officer father discouraged her from getting an education, but in spite of his opposition, Montessori became the first woman in Italy to earn a medical degree. She became a co-director, with Guiseppe Montesano, of the Scuola Magistrele Ortofrenica, an institute for training teachers of "deficient" children. During her time at this institution she had a child, Mario, with Montesano. However, he married another woman, and Montessori resigned this post in 1901 and began working with normal children.

Montessori's interests were in the realm of human behavior, and she saw a particular need in the area of education of "backward" children. She worked in La Casa dei Bambini crèche in the San Lorenzo slums and developed some practical methods of dealing with the children.

In defiance of contemporary educational theories, Montessori believed in a spontaneous learning process without formal rewards or punishments, paced by the normal speed of development in each individual child. She discovered that certain methods of teaching would enable the subnormal child to learn to read and write like a normal child. She used the same methods on normal underprivileged children in her Casa dei Bambini school. Among her educational theories was her postulate that children go through "sensitive periods" during which they are more apt to learn certain things. She assumed that children prefer to work with creative materials rather than play with toys and that they are capable of extreme concentration if the situation is properly structured. Children love orderliness and she felt that under proper conditions discipline was unnecessary.

Montessori's educational methods were tried with success in England, the United States, and elsewhere. She traveled, lectured, and organized training courses at colleges during the 1920s and 1930s. In the United States, her methods were repopularized in the 1950s when many new schools were opened. They continue to function.   JH/MBO

PRIMARY SOURCES

Montessori, Maria. *Pedagogical Anthropology.* New York: Frederick C. Stokes, 1913.
———. *The Montessori Method.* New York: Schocken, 1964.
———. *The Secret of Childhood.* New York: Schocken, 1966.
———. *The Absorbent Mind.* New York: Dell, 1967.
———. *From Childhood to Adolescence.* New York: Schocken, 1973.

SECONDARY SOURCES

Kramer, R. *Maria Montessori: A Biography.* New York: G. P. Putnam's Sons, 1976.
Standing, E. M. *Maria Montessori: Her Life and Work.* New York: Mentor Omega, 1962.

STANDARD SOURCES

AMS 5–8, S&B 9-12; Kass-Simon and Farnes (article by Patricia Farnes); O'Connell and Russo 1990; Uglow 1982; Zusne.

MOODY, AGNES CLAYPOLE (1870–1954)

See Claypole, Agnes Mary.

MOODY, MARY BLAIR (1837–?)

U.S. physician and anatomist. Born 8 August 1837 in Barker, N.Y. Educated Medical College in Buffalo, N.Y. (M.D., 1876). Professional experience: Women's and Children's Dispensary, Buffalo, founder and senior physician (1882–1886). Honors and memberships: Society of Naturalists; Association of Anatomists; the American Medical Association; Forestry Association; the Association for the Protection of the Adirondacks. Death date unknown.

Mary Blair Moody got her medical degree during the years in which it was a very difficult feat for a woman. In 1882 she founded the Women's and Children's Dispensary in Buffalo and was also the senior physician. Moody had many interests involving reviewing and editing. She was a book reviewer for the *Buffalo Medical and Surgical Journal* and association editor of the *Bulletin of the Buffalo Naturalist Field Club.* Her research was in general medicine, natural science, household economics, and the rearing and education of children and youth.

JH/MBO

STANDARD SOURCES

AMS 1–2.

MOONEY-SLATER, ROSE CAMILLE LEDIEU (1902–)

U.S. physicist and X-ray crystallographer. Born 23 October 1902 in New Orleans, La. Married twice (1923, 1954). Educated Tulane University (B.S., 1926; M.S., 1929); University of Chicago (fellow, 1921–1923; Ph.D., 1932). Professional experience: Sophie Newcomb College, Tulane University, New Orleans, instructor (1926–1930), assistant professor (1933–1935), associate professor (1935–1941), professor and head of department (1941–1952); National Bureau of Standards, physicist (1952–1956); MIT, research physicist (from 1956).

Rose Mooney-Slater was born in Louisiana and earned her first two degrees from Newcomb (Tulane University). After finishing her doctorate at the University of Chicago she returned to Newcomb, where she steadily moved through the academic ranks until, in 1941, she became professor and head of the physics department. She left academia in 1952 to work at the National Bureau of Standards as a physicist. After four years in that position, she became a research physicist at MIT. In 1939–1940, she was a Guggenheim fellow. She was a Fellow of the Physical Society and of the Crystallographic Association. Her research was on the structure of crystals and crystalline materials using X-ray diffraction.   JH/MBO

STANDARD SOURCES
AMS 6–8, P 9, P&B 10–11.

MOORE, ANNE (1872–?)

U.S. physiologist. Born 1872 in Wilmington, N.C., to Eugenia (Beery) and Roger Moore. Educated St. Mary's School, Raleigh, N.C.; Vassar College (B.A., M.A.); University of Chicago (Ph.D.). Death date unknown.

Anne Moore worked on the effects of solutions of electrolytes upon muscle tissue. She was a strong supporter of women's suffrage.   JH/MBO

PRIMARY SOURCES
Moore, Anne. "On the Effects of Solutions of Various Electrolytes and Non-Conductors upon Rigor Mortis and Heat Rigor." *American Journal of Physiology* 7 (April 1902). From Moore's Ph.D dissertation.
———. *Physiology of Man and Other Animals.* New York: Holt, 1909.

STANDARD SOURCES
AMS 1–6; *Woman's Who's Who of America.*

MOORE, CHARLOTTE EMMA (1898–1990)

See Sitterly, Charlotte Emma (Moore).

MOORE, EMMELINE (1872–1963)

U.S. icthyologist and aquatic biologist. Born 29 April 1872 in Batavia, N.Y. Educated Cornell (A.B., 1905; fellow, 1912–1914; Ph.D. 1914); Wellesley College (A.M., 1906). Professional experience: public schools, teacher (1895–1903); normal school, instructor in biology (1906–1910); Huguenot University, South Africa, substitute professor of botany (1911); Vassar College, instructor and assistant professor (1914–1919); New York Conservation Department, State Biological Survey, from research biologist to chief aquatic biologist and director of the biological survey (1920–1944); Yale University, Bingham Laboratory of Oceanography, assistant (1944–1945). Honors and memberships: Boston Society of Natural History, Walker Prize (1909, 1915); American Fisheries Society, president (1928); Hobart College, honorary Sc.D., 1939.

Memorialized by New York State marine research vessel, Emmeline M. *(1958). Died 12 September 1963.*

Famous for her many articles on fish diseases and for her work in conservation combating water pollution, Emmeline Moore followed the path of many other young women born in the 1870s, and taught after her graduation from high school in various elementary schools until she could earn enough to study at the college level. She went to Cornell, where she trained in botany, and went on to pursue a master's degree at Wellesley College. With a master's degree, she taught biology at normal schools for four years and then accepted a position in South Africa for a year as a substitute professor of botany at Huguenot College, on the Cape. Upon her return, she entered Cornell for her doctorate in aquatic botany, serving as a teaching assistant at the same time.

From 1914 to 1919, Moore taught biology at Vassar College, rising to the level of assistant professor. During the summers, she worked at the Bureau of Fisheries, and became interested in pursuing a research life. She then entered the New York Conservation Department, where she worked first as a research biologist then as chief aquatic biologist and director of the New York State Biological Survey. She produced what is said to be possibly the best of the early state surveys of aquatic resources.

For twenty-four years, Moore worked with the New York State Conservation Department, studying river and lake pollution and fish diseases. Moore's research on fungus diseases in fish were extensive and won her significant attention. She was the first woman elected president of the American Fisheries Society.

As a young woman, Moore had twice been honored with the Walker Prize from the Boston Society of Natural History. While she was director of the Biological Survey, she was awarded an honorary degree from Hobart College. After her retirement, she continued to do research at the Laboratory of Oceanography at Yale for a few years. In her late eighties, she christened a New York State oceanographic research ship named in her honor.   JH/MBO

PRIMARY SOURCES
Moore, Emmeline. With Russell Suter. *Stream Pollution Studies.* Albany, N.Y.: J.B. Lyon Co., 1922.
———. *Studies on the Marine Resources of Southern New England.* New Haven: Peabody Museum of Natural History, Yale University, 1947.

SECONDARY SOURCES
"Emmeline Moore." *New York Times,* 14 September 1963. Obituary notice.

Seamen, E. "Emmeline Moore." In *Leaders of American Conservation*, ed. H. Clepper. Washington, D.C.: Smithsonian Institution, 1971.

Stroud, Richard ed. *National Leaders of American Conservation*. Washington, D.C.: Smithsonian Institution, 1985.

STANDARD SOURCES
AMS 4–8, B 9, P&B 10; Bailey; *NAW;* Rossiter 1982.

MOORE, LILLIAN MARY (1887–?)

U.S. physiologist. Born 14 February 1887 in Las Vegas, N.M. Educated University of California (B.S., 1914; M.S., 1915; Ph.D., 1918). Professional experience: University of California, assistant in physiology (1915–1916), instructor (1916–1924), assistant professor (from 1924). Death date unknown.

Lillian Moore was twenty-seven years old when she got her bachelor's degree. Once she began college, she progressed very rapidly. After earning her doctoral degree, she stayed at the University of California, where she rose to the rank of assistant professor. She is listed only in volumes three and four of *American Men of Science;* she may have left science or she may merely have been left out of subsequent editions.

Moore was a member of the Physiological Society. Her research was on temperature centers in the brain, regulation of body temperature, and periodic variations in physiological processes in women. JH/MBO

PRIMARY SOURCES
Moore, Lillian Mary. "Experimental Studies on the Regulation of Body Temperature." University of California, Ph.D diss., 1918.

———. "Note on the Reliability of the Martin Muscular Efficiency Test." *American Physical Education Review* 29 (December 1924): 572–578.

STANDARD SOURCES
AMS 3–4.

MOORE, MARY MITCHELL (1892–?)

U.S. physiologist. Born 1 May 1892 in Raleigh, N.C. Educated Bryn Mawr College (A.B., 1915); University of Pennsylvania (fellow, 1915–1916); Rutgers University (Ph.D., 1918). Professional experience: New Jersey College for Women, instructor in chemistry (1918–1919); Rutgers, research fellow in physiology (1924–1926); University of Oregon, research associate (from 1926). Death date unknown.

The later career of Mary Mitchell Moore is unknown. After earning her doctoral degree at Rutgers, she taught for a year at the New Jersey College for Women and returned to Rutgers as a research fellow for two years. She then moved to the Northwest, where she was a research associate at the University of Oregon. She worked on the American Woman's Table at the Naples Zoological Station. During the summers, she assisted Jacquest Loeb at Woods Hole (1915–1918). Her research was on temperature coefficients, tropistic responses of cerianthus, and the reactions of cerianthus to light. She was a member of the Society for Experimental Biology.

JH/MBO

STANDARD SOURCES
AMS 4–7.

MOORE, RUTH ELLA (1903–   )

U.S. bacteriologist. Born 19 May 1903 in Columbus, Ohio. Educated Ohio State University (B.S., 1926; M.A., 1927; Ph.D., 1933). Professional experience: Tennessee State College, instructor (1927–1930); Howard University College of Medicine, instructor (1933–1939), assistant professor (1939–1948), acting head of bacteriology, preventive medicine, and public health (1948–1955), head of the department (1955–1960), associate professor (1960–1973).

As an African-American woman, making a name for herself as a scientist was doubly difficult for Ruth Moore. She, however, became the first African-American woman to earn a doctoral degree in bacteriology from Ohio State University. She spent her entire teaching career, with the exception of her graduate student days, at the Howard University College of Medicine, rising to the rank of associate professor.

Moore's major interests were in public health problems. Her dissertation focused on the bacteriological aspects of tuberculosis. She was a member of the American Public Health Association and the American Society of Microbiologists. JH/MBO

SECONDARY SOURCES
Sammons, Vivian O. *Blacks in Science and Medicine.* New York: Hemisphere, 1990. Moore noted on page 176.

STANDARD SOURCES
Notable (article by Leonard C. Bruno).

MOREHOUSE, KATHLEEN M. (1912–1975)

British botanist. Born 1912. Educated Leeds University. Professional experience: Doncaster Technical College (from 1941). Honors and memberships: Doncaster Naturalists' Society, president. Died 1975.

Kathleen Morehouse was educated at Leeds University and then taught at the Doncaster Technical College. She made extensive plant collections, which can be found at the Doncaster Museum.

JH/MBO

SECONDARY SOURCES
Naturalist no. 936 (1976): 18.

STANDARD SOURCES
Desmond.

MORGAN, AGNES FAY (1884–1968)

U.S. home economist, biochemist, and nutritionist. Born 4 May 1884 in Peoria, Ill., to Mary (Dooley) and Patrick John Fay. Married Arthur I. Morgan (1908). One son, Arthur. Educated University of Chicago (B.S., 1904; M.A., 1905; Ph.D., 1914); University of Montana (fellow, 1907–1908). Professional experience: Hardin College, instructor (1905–1907); University of Washington, Seattle, instructor (1910–1913); University of California, assistant professor of nutrition (1915–1919), associate professor of household science (1919–1923); professor (1923–1928), professor of home economics (1938–1954), emerita professor (from 1954). Honors and memberships: American Chemical Society, Garvan Medal (1949); Borden Award (1954); University of California, Berkeley, LL.D. (1959); the Home Economics building at Berkeley named for her (1961).

After Agnes Morgan received her doctoral degree from the University of Chicago, she accepted a position in the new Department of Household Science and Arts at the University of California, Berkeley. She advanced quickly to associate professor and to professor, when she was also appointed department chair. Morgan was one of the first home economists to make chemistry an integral part of the curriculum. She founded Iota Sigma Pi, a national society for women in chemistry.

Morgan was proud of her administrative abilities. The department she founded ran very smoothly. She also had an excellent record in teaching and research. Her research was on the biochemistry of vitamins. One of her projects involved the graying of hair; she was able to demonstrate that it was caused by a vitamin deficiency. She also worked on the effect of heat on the biological value of proteins and the mechanism of the action of vitamins.

JH/MBO

PRIMARY SOURCES
Morgan, Agnes Fay. *Course in Food Preparation and Tests.* Berkeley: University of California Press, 1919.
———. ed. *Nutritional Status U.S.A.* Berkeley: Agricultural Experiment Station, 1959.

STANDARD SOURCES
AMS 3–8, P 9, P&B 10–11; Bailey; Debus; Kass-Simon and Farnes; Rossiter 1982.

MORGAN, ANN HAVEN (1882–1966)

U.S. zoologist. Born 6 May 1882 in Waterford, Conn., to Julia Douglass and Stanley Griswold Morgan. Two siblings. Educated Wellesley College (1902); Cornell University (bachelor's degree, 1906; Ph.D., 1912). Professional experience: Mount Holyoke College, assistant and instructor (1906–1909), instructor (1912), associate professor (1914), professor (1918); Cornell University, assistant and instructor (1909–1911); Marine Biological Laboratory, Woods Hole, Mass. (1918); Harvard University, visiting fellow (1920); Yale University, visiting fellow (1921). Retired 1947. Died 5 June 1966.

Ann Haven Morgan was christened Anna, but changed her name to Ann around 1911. Her interest in living things came early, as she explored the woods and waters around her Connecticut home when she was a child. After a brief encounter with Wellesley, Morgan went to Cornell, where she earned her bachelor's and doctoral degrees. For her doctorate, Morgan studied with James G. Needham in the Limnological Laboratory. Pleased with her work, Needham proposed her name to the Entomological Society. After receiving her doctoral degree, Morgan returned to Cornell, where she remained throughout her professional career. She advanced steadily up the academic ladder, becoming a full professor in 1918. During the summers she conducted research and taught courses on echinoderms at the Marine Biological Laboratory, Woods Hole. Although she carried on most of her research in the northeastern United States, she spent the summer of 1926 working in British Guiana at the Tropical Laboratory in Kartabo.

Although limnology was her special subject—on which she wrote a useful book, *Field Book of Ponds and Streams* (1930)—Morgan was also interested in many other facets of zoology, particularly hibernating animals. Her *Field Book of Animals in Winter* (1939) reflected this interest. In 1949, the *Encyclopaedia Britannica* made it into an educational film. She was also interested in conservation and ecology. Her last book, *Kinship of Animals and Man* (1955), reflects that interest.

In addition to her research, Morgan was interested in educational reform, particularly in the sciences. This pursuit was inspired by CORNELIA CLAPP, who was a friend of Morgan's. She, in turn inspired other women at Mount Holyoke, in particular, Elizabeth Adams. Research, teaching, educational reform, and conservation were all areas of great importance to Morgan.

JH/MBO

PRIMARY SOURCES

Morgan, Ann Haven. "May-Flies of Fall Creek." *Annals of the Entomological Society of America* 4 (1911): 93–126.

———. "A Contribution to the Biology of May-Flies." Ph.D. diss., Cornell University, 1912.

———. "The Temperature Senses in the Frog's Skin." *Journal of Experimental Zoology* 35 (1922): 83–114.

———. *Field Book of Ponds and Streams: An Introduction to the Life of Fresh Water.* New York: G. P. Putnam Sons, 1930.

———. *Field Book of Animals in Winter.* New York: G. P. Putnam Sons, 1939.

———. With Catherine H. Fales. "Seasonal Conditions and Effects of Low Temperature in the Thyroid Glands of Amphibians. I. Adult *Triturus viridescens*." *Journal of Morphology* 71 (1942): 257–389.

———. With Barbara J. Johnson. "Seasonal Conditions and Effects of Low Temperature in the Thyroid Glands of Amphibians. II. Terrestrial Phase of *Triturus viridescens*." *Journal of Morphology* 70 (1942): 301–321.

———. *Kinships of Animals and Man: A Textbook of Animal Biology.* New York: McGraw-Hill, 1955.

SECONDARY SOURCES

Alexander, Charles P. "Ann Haven Morgan, 1882–1966." *Eatonia* 8 (15 February 1967): 1–3.

"Deaths, Dr. Ann Haven Morgan, Prominent Conservationist, Dies at 84." *Holyoke (Mass.) Transcript Telegram,* 6 June 1966.

"Professor Ann Morgan, Taught Zoology at Mt. Holyoke." *New York Times,* 6 June 1966.

STANDARD SOURCES

Bonta; Grinstein 1997 (article by Susan J. Wurtzburg); *NAW*(M); Shearer and Shearer 1996 (article by Stefanie Buck); Siegel and Finley.

MORGAN, ELIZABETH FRANCES (1843–1927)

British physician. Born 1843. Married Dr. George Hoggan (1874). Educated Wales; Paris; Dusseldorf; and London; studied medicine with private teachers in England; University of Zurich (M.D., 1870). Professional experience: St. Mary's Dispensary for Women and Children, physician; joint practice with husband. Died 1927.

Elizabeth Morgan studied medicine with private tutors in order to pass the preliminary examinations for an apothecary's license. She passed her examinations before the Council of Apothecaries Hall passed a resolution barring women from licensure. She entered the University of Zurich, where she emerged as a prodigious worker, taking as many as sixty hours of class each week and finishing her medical work in three years (rather than the usual five). On 12 March 1870, she became the second woman to defend her thesis before the entire faculty. Her topic, directed by a Professor Biermer, was progressive muscular atrophy. As the discussion opened, Biermer launched a lengthy attack on her principal conclusions, which differed from his own. Morgan responded cooly and clearly, citing British and American sources unavailable to Biermer. After further student questions, Biermer announced his satisfaction with her responses, and she was awarded the doctoral degree.

Morgan returned to London and began working at St. Mary's Dispensary for Women and Children. In 1874, she married Dr. George Hoggan and they began a joint practice (the first husband and wife medical team in Britain). After her husband's death, Morgan gave herself wholly to social causes, including women's rights, education, women and India, and lepers in the Middle East.   JH/MBO

STANDARD SOURCES

Bonner.

MORGAN, LILIAN VAUGHAN SAMPSON (1870–1952)

U.S. embryologist, geneticist. Born 1870 in Hallowell, Maine, to Isabella (Merrick) and George Sampson; two sisters. Married Thomas Hunt Morgan (6 June 1904). Four children. Educated Bryn Mawr College (B.A., 1891; M.A., 1892). Professional experience: T. H. Morgan's laboratory, Columbia University, researcher in genetics (1921–1928); Kershoff Biological Laboratory, California Institute of Technology, research associate (from 1946). Died 1952 in Los Angeles.

Lilian Vaughan Sampson lost both of her parents and baby sister, Grace, to tuberculosis. Edith and Lilian were raised by their maternal grandparents. The loss of her family (including Edith, who later also died of tuberculosis) probably influenced Lilian to give up research and stay home with her own four children, Howard Key (b. 1906), Edith Sampson (b. 1907), Lilian Vaughan (b. 1910), and Isabel Merrick (b. 1911), while they were young.

Encouraged by her grandparents, Lilian and Edith studied biology at Bryn Mawr College. Bryn Mawr was an excellent place for a budding young biologist to study, for cytologist Edmund B. Wilson and geneticist Thomas Hunt Morgan were both there. In 1891, Sampson graduated at the top of her class. As were many of the top students, including NETTIE MARIA STEVENS and ALICE BORING, she was awarded the European Fellowship. After graduation, she spent the first of many summers at the Marine Biological Laboratory and then went to Switzerland on her fellowship to study with Arnold Lange at the University of Zurich. She received a master's degree in biology in 1894 under Thomas Hunt Morgan.

Lilian Sampson and Thomas Hunt Morgan were married in 1904. Morgan left Bryn Mawr to become professor of experimental zoology with E. B. Wilson at Columbia University. The couple spent the first summer after they were married at Stanford University, where Lilian later published two papers on planarian regeneration. Although from 1905, Lilian Morgan did not actively do research, she retained her interest in science and understood the astounding new developments that were occurring in the field. She worked with her husband after her children were grown, returning to research in heredity before 1920, while her husband was still at Columbia running the *Drosophila* laboratory (usually termed the "fly room"). She published important works with both Thomas Morgan and his student Alfred R. Sturtevant. When Thomas Morgan moved to the California Institute of Technology in 1928, she received the title of research associate in the Kershoff Biological Laboratory where he was director. Although she worked in the laboratory from the time they arrived, Lilian Morgan did not have an academic appointment until after the death of her husband. Her major work was the discovery of the attached X and ring X chromosomes of *Drosophila*. Her later work developing a vaccine for polio in primates has recently been called a crucial step in developing the human vaccine.   JH/MBO

PRIMARY SOURCES

Sampson, Lilian Vaughan. "The Musculature of Chiton."
    Journal of Morphology 11, 1895: 595–628. Published as
    L.V. Sampson.

Morgan, Lilian Vaughan Sampson. "Incomplete Anterior Regeneration in the Absence of the Brain in *Letoplana littoralis*."
    Biological Bulletin 9 (1905): 187–193.

———. "Regeneration of Grafted Pieces of Planarians." *Journal of Experimental Zoology* 3 (1906): 269–294.

———. "Non-Criss-Cross Inheritance in *Drosophila melanogaster*." *Biological Bulletin* 42 (1922): 267–274.

———. "A Closed X Chromosome in *Drosophila melanogaster*." *Genetics* 18 (1933): 250–283.

———. "Origin of Attached-X Chromosomes in *Drosophila melanogaster* and the Occurrence of Non-Disjunction of X's in the Male." *American Naturalist* 72 (1938): 434–446.

———. "A Spontaneous Somatic Exchange between Non-homologous Chromosomes in *Drosophila melnogaster*." *Genetics* 24 (1939): 747–752.

———. "A Variable Phenotype Associated with the Fourth Chromosome of *Drosophila melanogaster* and Affected by Heterochromatin." *Genetics* 32 (1947): 200–219.

SECONDARY SOURCES

Allen, Garland. *Thomas Hunt Morgan: The Man and His Science.*
    Princeton: Princeton University Press, 1978.

Keenan, Katherine. "Lilian Vaughan Morgan (1870–1952)."
    American Zoologist 23 (1983): 867–976.

STANDARD SOURCES

DAB suppl. 3 (under T. H. Morgan); Grinstein 1997 (article by Katherine Keenan); *NAW* unused.

MORIARITY, HENRIETTA MARIA
(fl. 1803–1813)

British botanical illustrator and novelist. Married and widowed. Four? children. Professional experience: published bowdlerized books on plants for young women.

There seems to be little information about the life of Henrietta Moriarity, although she is thought to have been a governess and then a teacher. The widow of an army colonel, she turned to writing and illustrating in order to make living. Her illustrated book of botany avoided separate illustrations of the stamens and pistils of plants, and explicitly avoided the Linnean classification system that depended on the sexual reproductive system. She assured her readers that this avoidance made her illustrations suitable for young ladies. Her books included the major greenhouse plants and suggested methods of cultivation. In one of her novels, she described a woman much like herself who turns to writing and publishing small books of botany to provide a living for herself.
                                                JH/MBO

PRIMARY SOURCES

Moriarity, Henrietta Maria. *Viridarium*. London: printed by Dewick and Clarke for the author, 1806. Reissued as *Fifty Plates of Green-House Plants*. London: printed for the author by T. Bensley, 1807.

———. *Brighton in an Uproar*. N.p., 1811.

STANDARD SOURCES

Shteir.

MOROZOVA, VALENTINA GALAKTIONOVNA
(1910–1989)

Soviet geologist and paleontologist. Born 13 March 1910 in Leningrad. Married; divorced (1943). One daughter. Educated School No. 190, the former Lentovskaya Gymnasium; Leningrad University (graduated 1933; postgraduate course, 1937). Professional experience: All-Union Research Institute of Geological Prospecting, researcher paleontological laboratory; Volga-Bashkiria Expedition, researcher (1941–1943); Geological Institute of the USSR Academy of Sciences (from 1949). Died 28 December 1989 in Moscow.

The political situation in the Soviet Union had an important impact on Valentina Galaktionovna Morozova's career. Her life was difficult, like that of many talented people of her generation. Her father was a railroad engineer and her mother worked in a textile factory. She attended the former Lentovskaya Gymnasium, known for fine teachers, and made many lifelong friends. Talented, she drew beautifully, sang professionally, played the piano, and spoke four European languages fluently.

She and a group of her school friends were arrested. She was convicted but was released on probation and prohibited from living in seven cities. The group had apparently engaged in "subversive" activities.

Morozova became a paleontologist due to circumstances. Music and art were emphasized in the Morozov family, but she was unable to get into a Higher Art College even with very good examination scores, because, at that time, children of intellectuals were rejected for political reasons. She was denied admission to a medical university, as well. Finally, in 1929, Valentina was admitted into Leningrad University. She enrolled in this university to study geomorphology and graduated in 1933. Her first position was with the Paleontological Laboratory of the All-Union Research Institute of Geological Prospecting, which employed the Soviet Union's best known micropaleontologists. She took postgraduate courses at Moscow University, and in 1937 defended her thesis on the turnover of the foraminifera of the Cretaceous/Tertiary boundary. She was awarded a medal "for Courageous Work during the Great Patriotic War," for her work in studying the stratigraphy of oil-bearing Paleozoic sediments in the Bashkirian Cisurals.

After defending her thesis, Morozova worked as a geologist at the Mineralovodskaya Expedition of Scientific Research of the Moscow Institute of Geological Exploration. From 1941 to 1943, she was a scientific researcher on the Volga-Bashkir expedition, studying the stratigraphy of oil-bearing Paleozoic deposits of the Bashkirian Pre-Urals. In 1938, she became a member of the Moscow Naturalist Society, and of the All-State Paleontological and Geographical Societies.

In 1949, she began her work with the Geological Institute of the USSR, Academy of Sciences, studying Mesozoic and Cenozoic stratigraphy in the southern part of the USSR and on the Russian Platform. Politics again intervened in 1950, when the ministry of state security brought up the old charges against her. She was summoned to the KGB, which demanded that she inform on her colleagues. She refused, but this experience on top of losing her father to starvation during the siege of Leningrad and her twenty-year-old brother on the Leningrad front was too much for her to bear, and she became gravely ill, never to completely recover. Her short-lived marriage ended in divorce. She had one daughter who, in turn, had two sons.

Morozova's work on the Paleozoic and Cretaceous deposits of the Emba region involved strenuous field work. She worked in the Talysh Mountains, on the Soviet-Iranian border, as well as the Lenkoran Lowland, where she contracted malaria. Her geological interests were diverse, including biostratigraphy, paleoecology, phylogenesis of foraminifera, and methods of flushing and selecting samples of microfauna. She was one of the first to speak of the influence of cosmic factors on foraminiferal evolution, including the catastrophic disappearance of Mesozoic plankton at the Cretaceous/Tertiary boundary. Although much of her work was theoretical, it was also valuable for oil prospecting and geological surveys.

Morozova published over fifty scientific works, including four monographs and ten reports.   CK

PRIMARY SOURCES

Morozova, Valentina G. "On the Age of the Lower Foraminiferous Beds of the North Caucasus." *Comptes rendus (Doklady) de l'Academie des Sciences de l'URSS* 54, no. 1 (1946): 53–55. Also in Russian.

———. "The Cretaceous/Tertiary Boundary in Light of the Study of Foraminifers." *Comptes rendus (Doklady)de L'Academie des Sciences de l'URSS* 54, no. 2 (1946): 153–155. Also in Russian.

———. "K sistematike i morfologii paleogenovykh predstavitelei nadsemeistva Globigerinidea." *Voprosy Mikropaleontologii* 2 (1958): 27–58. In Russian. A review of the systematic relationships and morphologic variations of lower Tertiary globigerines, based in large part on a study of planktonic foraminiferal faunas of the USSR. It concludes that secondary modifications of morphologic features reflect adaptation to environmental conditions permitting definition of series or groups of species within genera and subgenera.

———. With R. M. Davidzon and G. P. Kreidenkov. "Biostratigrafiia paleotsenovykh otlozhenii Tadzhikskoi depressii (Biostratigraphy of Paleocene deposits of the Tadzhik Depression)." *Biulleten Moskovskogo obshchestva ispytatelei prirody: Otdel geologicheskii* 40, no. 3 (1965): 23–29.

SECONDARY SOURCES

Keller, N. B., and M. Ya Serova. "Valentina Galaktionovna Morozova, Her Life and Work, 1910–1989." *Micropaleontology* 37, no. 1 (1991): 98–100.

———. "Losses of Science. Valentina G. Morozova—Life and Scientific Activity (1910–1989)." *Moscow Naturalist Society Bulletin, Geological Department* 66, no. 2 (1991): 128–131.

MORRIS, MARGARETTA HARE (1797–1867)

U.S. entomologist. Born 3 December 1797 probably in Philadelphia, Pa., to Ann (Willing) and Luke Morris. Never married. No formal education. Professional experience: published on entomology.

Without any kind of formal education, Margaretta Hare Morris managed to study insects' life histories. She published studies of the Hessian fly and of the seventeen-year locust, insects with great agricultural significance.

She carefully worked out the life history of these insects. For the Hessian fly, she concluded that eggs were laid on the grain rather than the stalk and also described its main predator. She apparently investigated fungi as enemies of plants. She prepared illustrations for a paper by W. Gambel in 1848 and with her mother attended lectures on science in Germantown. She sent her papers to various scientific societies where male members would read them for her.

Morris lived with her mother and unmarried sister. Her sister, Elizabeth Carrington Morris (1795–1865), was interested in botany and is reported to have corresponded with Asa Gray.   JH/MBO

PRIMARY SOURCES

Morris, Margaretta Hare. "Observations on the Development of the Hessian Fly." *Proceedings of the Academy of Natural Sciences, Philadelphia* 1 (1841–1843): 66–68.

———. "On the Cecidomyia destructor, or Hessian Fly." *Transactions of the American Philosophical Society* n.s. 8 (1843): 49–52.

———. "On the Discovery of the Larvae of the Cicada septemdecim." *Proceedings of the Academy of Natural Sciences, Philadelphia* 3 (1846–1847): 132–134.

———. "On the Cecidomyia culmicola." *Proceedings of the Academy of Natural Sciences, Philadelphia* 4 (1848–1849): 194.

———. "On the Seventeen Year Locusts." *Proceedings of the Boston Society of Natural History* 4 (1851): 110.

STANDARD SOURCES

Bailey; Bonta; Elliott; Rossiter 1982; Siegel and Finley.

MORSE, ELIZABETH EATON (1864–1955)

U.S. mycologist. Born 31 December 1864 in Framingham, Mass. Educated Ashland (Mass.) High School (1882); Wellesley College (diploma from the school of art, 1891; A.B. in botany, 1926); University of California (graduate studies). Professional experience: elementary schools, teacher (1882–1889); Castle School, Tarrytown-on-the-Hudson, teacher (1891–1894); Murdoch High School, Winchester, Mass., art instructor and school supervisor (1894–1902); New York City schools, teacher (1902–1922); mycologist (1926–1955). Died 13 November 1955 at Berkeley, Calif.

Elizabeth Eaton Morse had two very different careers. After she graduated from high school she taught elementary school for seven years before she went to Wellesley to earn a diploma from the school of art. She returned to teaching for a total of about thirty-one years. In 1924 she initiated a second career, this time studying botany. She earned a bachelor's degree in 1926 and gave up teaching forever. Her interests were in cryptogamic botany. Although she attended the University of California, Berkeley, as a part-time graduate student, she never worked toward an advanced degree. Morse organized the California Mycological Society with herself as its secretary. She used it as a mechanism for the exchange of specimens. During the summers she went on collecting trips. Mainly interested in macroscopic fungi, she still collected myxomycetes, lichens, mosses, and some flowering plants. Between collection trips, she identified, catalogued, and distributed her collections. She also photographed plants and contributed a selection of 364 mounted illustrations to the Mycological Herbarium of the University of California, Berkeley, with the stipulation that they be kept together.

Morse gave her mycological collections to the Mycological Herbarium of the University of California. She contributed money toward the salary for an assistant. She anonymously donated three gifts totaling $2,100 to the Mycologia Endowment Fund.   JH/MBO

PRIMARY SOURCES

Morse, Elizabeth Eaton. "Trailing the Sierran Puffball." *Sierra Club Bulletin* 14 (1929): 61–63.

———. "A New Chanterelle in California." *Mycologia* 22 (1930): 219–220.

———. "A Study of the Genus *Podaxis*." *Mycologia* 25 (1933): 1–33.

———. "A New Puffball." *Mycologia* 27 (1935): 96–101.

———. "*Geaster limbatus*: A New Variety." *Mycologia* 33 (1941): 139–141.

———. "Study of a New *Tricholoma*." *Mycologia* 35 (1943): 573–581.

———. "Some Western Discomycetes, *Gyromitra esculenta*, *Helvella lacunosa*." *Mycologia* 37 (1945): 414–424.

———. "Variations in *Montagnites arenarius* (DC)." *Mycologia* 40 (1948): 255–261.

SECONDARY SOURCES

Bonar, Lee. "Elizabeth Eaton Morse." *Mycologia* 48 (1956): 439–442. Obituary notice. Includes portrait.

STANDARD SOURCES

Debus.

MORSE, MEROË MARSTON (1923–1969)

U.S. engineer, inventor, photographic scientist. Born 1923 to Celeste Osgood and Marston Morse. Never married. Educated Smith College (A.B., 1945). Professional experience: Polaroid Corporation, director of special photographic research (1945–1969). Died 29 July 1969.

Meroë Marston Morse held numerous sole or joint patents on the development of fast black and white films using the diffusion transfer process. The daughter of a physicist at the Institute of Advanced Studies, Princeton, she grew up around brilliant scientists. She also studied music seriously. After attending Smith College, graduating with a bachelor of arts in 1945, she was able to enter Polaroid Corporation in Cambridge, Massachusetts, as director of a laboratory of photographic research, a position she held until her early death at the age of forty-six. She received the outstanding graduate award from Smith College in 1968. The following year, May 1969, she was honored as the first woman elected fellow of Society of Photographic Scientists and Engineers. Multitalented, she was both a harpist and an artist. She also encouraged young photographers. She helped her community by serving as director of the Cambridge Neighborhood House, where she taught photography and art to local children. She died 29 July 1969.   JH/MBO

SECONDARY SOURCES

Boston Herald Traveler, 29 July 1969. Obituary notice.
Rogers, Hovis. "Eulogy of Meroë Marston Morse." Delivered on 15 August 1969, Harvard Memorial Chapel. Rogers directed the color photographic lab at Polaroid.

MORTON, EMILY L. (1841–1917?)

U.S. entomological artist. Born 1841. Professional activities: studied and collected insects.

Emily L. Morton was an amateur insect collector and an entomological artist. No information is available about her life except that she and a sister lived in the family home at New Windsor, New York. Nothing is known about her education, but she apparently became interested in insects when she was a young child. When she was thirteen years old, she was given a scientific work on insects with their Latin names. She began to collect books on insects, including the agricultural reports of the state of New York. She later read books at the Astor Library in New York City. She met other collectors through articles and advertisements in the journal *Canadian Entomologist*. The only money that she made from her collecting was from an extensive collection of Lepidoptera in which she had hybridized several forms. She sold eight specimens to an English collector. She is not known to have

published her research results and her collection was dispersed in 1904 among the American Museum of Natural History, the Boston Society of Natural History, and private collectors.   JH/MBO

SECONDARY SOURCES

Newcomb, H. H. "Emily L. Morton." *Entomological News* 28 (1917): 96–101.
Entomological Society of Washington Proceedings 21 (1921): 92. Includes a portrait.

STANDARD SOURCES

Bailey.

MORTON, ROSALIE SLAUGHTER (1876–?)

U.S. physician and surgeon. Born 1876 in Lynchburg, Va., to Mary Haines (Harker) and John Flavel Slaughter. Five brothers, one sister (two other sisters and a brother died in childhood). Married George R. Morton, Jr. No children. Educated locally; Baltimore finishing school; Woman's Medical College of Philadelphia (M.D.); graduate studies, Berlin, Vienna, Paris and London. Professional experience: Philadelphia City Hospital, intern; Massachusetts State Hospital at Tewksbury; Alumnae Hospital and Dispensary, resident physician; British Government Laboratory, Bombay, physician; private practice in medicine and surgery, Washington D.C. (ca. 1903–?); George Washington Hospital, attending surgeon; 13th Street Clinic, clinical staff; Pan American Medical Congress, delegate (1905); Public Health Education Committee of the American Medical Association, chairman (1907–1910); New York Polyclinic Hospital, clinical assistant and instructor; New York Post-Graduate Hospital, adjunct professor of gynecology; College of Physicians and Surgeons, Columbia University, associate professor of surgery; Battle Harbor Hospital of the Grenfell Mission, Labrador, director (summer 1915); Serbian front hospitals, physician (1915–1916); founder of two hospitals in Yugoslavia; League of Nations, delegate (1924); Medical Board of National Council of Defense, member. Honors and memberships: Rollins College, honorary doctor of humanities (1929); Rutgers University, honorary doctor of science (1939); New York Academy of Medicine, Fellow; Academy of Science, Fellow; Cross of Czar Nicholas II, Russia; Commander of the Order of St. Sava of the Royal Red Cross (and others), Yugoslavia; Conspicuous Service Cross, State of New York; Joan of Arc Medal, Medaile d'Honneur, Palme Academique, France. Death date unknown.

Rosalie Slaughter was descended from John Slaughter, who settled in Virginia in 1620. Mary Harker was a northern Quaker who met her husband, John Flavel Slaughter, on vacation in Lynchburg and had to adjust to the large extended family and plantation life of the pre–Civil War South. Rosalie had five brothers and a sister and was educated locally, then sent to a "finishing school" in Baltimore. As a young lady in a prominent, well-to-do family, she was expected to marry well and become a model wife. Instead, she chose to follow her grandfather's and two older brothers' footsteps and become a doctor. She entered the Woman's Medical College of Philadelphia in 1893.

After graduation, Slaughter was appointed resident physician of the Alumnae Hospital and Dispensary, which was run in conjunction with the obstetrical hospital. In 1899, after she had accumulated some savings, she traveled to Germany, stopping first in Gottingen for two months to learn the language. In Berlin, she took courses in surgery, microscopic diagnosis, and obstetrics. She then traveled to Vienna, where she was allowed to assist the hospital interns, follow grand rounds, observe surgery, and attend autopsies. In Paris, she was particularly interested in studying the relation of circulatory, respiratory, and digestive conditions to gynecology, believing that diagnosis of female conditions and disease should include considerations of mental, social, and economic conditions. A champion of women's rights, Slaughter wrote several papers concluding that the health, energy, and endurance of women is equal to that of men. Finally, in London, she finished her European education with studies of gynecological surgery and obstetrics and brain surgery and neurology.

As Slaughter finished her term in London, Sir Victor Horsley, a celebrated brain surgeon and her instructor, suggested she return to the States via India and the British Government Laboratory at Bombay, where she would work on a new prophylactic against three forms of the plague. After six months, she returned to the United States, visiting several missionary hospitals in India on her way. Anxious to begin her medical practice, Slaughter considered several locations, then settled on Washington, D.C. She opened an office and arranged for surgical privileges at George Washington Hospital.

Because of her knowledge of tropical disease, she was chosen as a delegate to the Pan-American Medical Congress in Panama and the American Public Health Association meeting in Havana that followed in January 1905. In 1906 (1907?) she married George B. Morton, Jr., a practicing New York attorney who had studied medicine before turning to law.

Rosalie Morton soon passed the New York Boards and began a new medical practice. For several years, she worked for the city as examiner of applicants for city employment; she was on the medical staff of the Teacher's Retirement System. In 1909, the American Medical Association approved the organization of a Public Health Education Committee, with Morton as its chairman. The work of educating the public in personal health and hygiene, child care, the value of regular physical examinations by a professional, and so on, spread across the nation, with the assistance of the Federated

Women's Clubs, the Young Women's Christian Associations, Mothers' Clubs, United Charities Association, and many other organizations. After the sudden death of her husband, Morton became clinical assistant and instructor at the Polyclinic Hospital of New York and, two years later, was appointed a professor of gynecology. She lectured at several other universities and was professor of applied physiology during the summer at the University of Vermont, operating at Burlington Hospital.

In 1915, Morton took a leave of duty and sailed to Labrador to work in the Mission Hospitals. Her experiences there made her determined to volunteer for war service and in 1916 she went to Washington, D.C., to request service in Serbia. She was made a special commissioner of the Red Cross to take supplies from Paris to the Salonica Front. While waiting for the supplies, she attended the wounded French soldiers and learned all she could about management of field hospitals. In Serbia, she chose to work at the field hospital at Sedes in Macedonia, a vast tent hospital serving three thousand patients. She worked with the Serbs until the armistice.

On her return to New York, Morton's first priority was to establish a means of establishing American hospitals in Europe. She worked through the Medical Women's National Association and with others began the American Women's Hospitals in 1917. Morton was chosen as first chairman of the War Service Committee and was designated to join the General Medical Board of the National Council of Defense. One of the aims of the War Service Committee was to recognize women physicians for medical duty equal with men. Morton presented to the General Medical Board in Washington a list of over a thousand medical women who had volunteered for foreign service with an outline of the work they could do. Because of opposition in Congress and the Surgeon General's office to enlisting women physicians, Morton and her cohorts began a national fundraising drive for the American Women's Hospitals, and within ten days had over three hundred thousand dollars.

For many years, Morton ran her practice, worked in support of the European hospitals, and tried to establish channels for education of the young men and women, especially of Yugoslavia and Serbia, whose lives she had personally witnessed being so traumatically disrupted by the war. In 1924 she went to Lyon, France, as a delegate from the American Society for the Promotion of the League of Nations. A serious bout of pneumonia in the early 1930s prompted a move from New York City to Winter Park, Florida. Morton quickly passed the Florida medical exam and began a small clinical practice. She had time to research her newest interests, arthritis and endocrinology. In 1934, the American Medical Association presented her with a special award in recognition of her work as founder of the American Women's Hospitals.   JH/MBO

PRIMARY SOURCES

Morton, Rosalie Slaughter. *A Woman Surgeon: The Life and Work of Rosalie Slaughter Morton.* New York: Frederick A. Stokes Co., 1937.

SECONDARY SOURCES

Alsop, Gulielma Fell. *History of the Woman's Medical College, Philadelphia, Pennsylvania 1850–1950.* Philadelphia: J. B. Lippincott Co., 1950.

Fabricant, Noah. *Why We Became Doctors.* New York: Grune and Stratton, 1954. Morton discussed on pages 9–12.

Rosen, George. *Four Hundred Years of a Doctor's Life.* New York: Schuman, 1947. Morton discussed on pages 124–127.

STANDARD SOURCES

Hurd-Mead 1933; *WWW*(A).

MOSER, FANNY (1872–1953)

German zoologist. Born 27 May 1872 in Badenweider to Fanny Freiin von Sulzer-Wart and Johann-Heinrich Moser, an engineer. One sister. Married Jaroslav Hoppe. Educated Boys Preparatory High School in Lausanne, Switzerland. University studies in Freiburg, Zurich, and Munich (doctorate, 1902). Professional experience: Prussian Academy of Sciences in Berlin, independent scientific work (from 1903); parapsychology and occultism, foundational research. Died February 1953 in Schloss Au am Zürichsee, Switzerland.

Fanny Moser grew up in a very wealthy home. She and her younger sister, Mentona, were heavily influenced by their intelligent and well-educated mother, Swiss-born noble-woman Fanny von Sulzer-Wart. Fanny Moser's father was a prominent engineer who became well known for his work on the Moser dam in Schaffhausen. He died young and left his young widow such a vast fortune that she was considered one of the richest women in Europe in her time. As Fanny Moser decided at eighteen to pursue a preparatory education for university study, a violent conflict erupted between mother and daughter. Until that time she had been taught by private tutors. The famous Sigmund Freud, who was a family friend, was consulted on the matter. He observed in the young woman "an ambition inappropriate to her meager talent." It was not until she was twenty-one that Fanny Moser was able to overcome her mother's opposition and enter a boys' preparatory high school in Lausanne. In 1896 Fanny Moser became the first female student until 1900 to register at the University of Freiburg. She first studied medicine and took the first preliminary medical exam in Zurich in 1899. Afterward she began studies in zoology in Munich and received her doctorate there in 1902 with the topic of developmental history of the vertebrate lung.

In 1903, Moser married the Czechoslovakian musician and composer Jaroslav Hoppe and moved with him to Berlin, where she began her international research work. It is proof of her extraordinary scientific qualifications that work was commissioned to her even though she was a woman. At the Museum of Natural History in Berlin, for example, she worked on material from the South Pole expedition of 1901–1903. The Prussian Academy of Sciences sent her to do research in France and Italy and the prince of Monaco commissioned her to work on his richly varied zoological deep sea collection.

Due to an occult experience and her husband's nerve disorder, Fanny Moser became involved exclusively with parapsychology and occultism from 1914 on. After the death of her husband in 1927 she resided permanently in Munich. Her work on occultism, which spanned 1,000 pages, appeared in Munich in 1935 and is still regarded today as the standard work for German parapsychological research. In 1950 Moser released an investigation into the subjects of spirits with a preface by C. G. Jung. During her work on the second volume, Moser died at the age of eighty at the family estate, Schloss Au on Lake Zurich (Zürichsee), Switzerland.

SNS

PRIMARY SOURCES

Moser, Fanny. *Okkultismus—Täuschungen und Tatsachen.* Zurich: O. Füssli, 1935.

———. *Das grosse Buch des Okkultismus.* Munich: E. Reinhardt, 1935.

———. *Spuk. Irrglaube oder Wahrglaube.* Freiburg: Baden bei Zürich, Gyr-Verlag, 1950.

———. *Spuk, ein Rätsel der Menschheit.* With a foreword by C. G. Jung. Baden bei Zürich: Gyr, 1950.

MOSHER, CLELIA DUEL (1863–?)

U.S. physician and physiologist. Born 16 December 1863 in Albany, N.Y. Educated Stanford University (A.B., A.M., 1894); Johns Hopkins University (M.D., 1900). Professional experience: Stanford University, assistant in hygiene (1893–1894), instructor (1894–1896), assistant professor of personal hygiene (1910–1923), associate professor of hygiene (1923–1928), professor (1928–1929), emerita professor (from 1929); medical adviser of women (1910–1929); Hopkins Hospital, H. A. Kelly sanitarium and external dispensary, assistant (1900–1901); American Red Cross, Paris, France, medical investigator, children's bureau and associate medical director, refugee bureau (1917–1919). Honors and memberships: Mills College honorary LL.D. (1934); American Medical Association, member. Death date unknown.

Clelia Mosher got her first two degrees from Stanford and worked there until she went to Johns Hopkins to work on her medical degree. After obtaining this degree she continued in academia, continuing at Stanford as assistant professor of personal hygiene, moving through the ranks to professor. She was professor for only one year before she retired as emerita professor. During her teaching career, she served as a medical adviser to women. During World War I, she worked for the American Red Cross in Paris as a medical investigator. She also was associate director of the refugee bureau (1917–1919).

Mosher's research was on the physiology of women, blood pressure, respiration, menstruation, and dysmenorrhea. She developed a schematograph for recording posture. Her other research was on gallstones, muscular strength, and the height of college women.   JH/MBO

STANDARD SOURCES
AMS 3–6; *WWW*(A), vol. 1.

MOTTL, MÁRIA (1906–1980)

Hungarian speleologist and vertebrate paleontologist. Born 1906 in Budapest to a successful Oberbaurat *(head of a planning department). Educated gymnasium; Universities of Vienna, Berlin, and Budapest (Ph.D., 1932). Professional experience: Royal Hungarian Geological Institute, field paleontologist (1936–1945); WW II at the Joanneum, Graz, Austria. Died 1980.*

After receiving her doctoral degree in paleontology *summa cum laude,* with minors in geology and geography, Mária Mottl joined the Geological Institute in Budapest. After two years she became field paleontologist, a position that involved administrative work at the institute as well as actual field work. This institute was a headquarters for the archeological and paleoanthropological aspects of speleology. Mottl began to produce a series of publications about caves and cave bears. Her abilities were evident in the periodic reports in which she concisely presented her research. Her publications demonstrate her growing interest in the last Ice Age and its inhabitants. They reflect an expansion of her work to include an evaluation of that epoch, based, in part, on the chronology of technical innovations of existing ice-age tools in Moustèien, Aurignacien, Solutrèen, and Magdalènien.

Following World War II, Mottl relocated to a new home in Steiermark in Austria. At this time, Steiermark was in an occupied country with an uncertain economic, political, and cultural future in which even the availability of food was an issue. Moving away from the theoretical problems that had previously occupied her, Mottl became involved in a very practical pursuit for war-torn Austria. Her knowledge of caves led her to locate deposits of cave guano, the material from which phosphate fertilizer can be produced. Finding these guano caves was especially important at this time, for

fertilizer could not be imported because of border restrictions. It was necessary to rely on local sources, even when production was economically impractical. The practical search for fertilizer, however, often led to finding the fossils of large vertebrates in the caves. For example, the thirty-five-meter cave Repolust was discovered in a sunny cliff near Badlgraben and was planned as a site for the mining of guano. Luckily, the mining never took place, so the artifacts under the deposits remained intact for later use. After the end of World War II, Mottl, with a team of local workers, uncovered and documented the remains of Ice Age inhabitants, which yielded a wealth of information. This 100,000-year-old cave provided a rest station for Ice Age hunters of southern Austria and is still the site of the most richly varied tool inventory which the Austrian Alps ever produced. In 1947, Mottl led a productive excavation.

Mottl was devoted not only to her research but to her family as well. The sources do not indicate the name of her husband or the number of her children. Her interests were in the cave mammals, not just in the human artifacts. Her discoveries, including the artifacts, were often exhibited in museums and special collections. However, more important, she attempted to publish everything and share it with the scientific world. She did not hesitate to reevaluate her own findings. When she found data that contradicted her hypotheses, she did not hesitate to admit that she was wrong.   JH/MBO

PRIMARY SOURCES
Mottl, Mária. "Zur Morphologie der Hehlenbaerenschaedel aus der Igric-Hoehle." *Instituti Regii Hungarici Geologici Annales* 29 (1933): 197–246.
———. "Jelentes az 1936/1938. Evi astasok eredmenyerol es az osgerinces osztaly mukoedeserol." Magyar Kiralyi Foeldtani Intezet 1945 (1936–1938): 1513–38.
———. "Faunen, Flora und Kultur des ungarischen Solutreen." *Quartaer* 1 (1938): 36–54.
———. "Hipparion-Funde der Steiermark." *Mitteilungen das Museums für Bergbau, Geologie und Technik am Landesmuseum Joanneum* 13 (1954): 43–71.
———. "Die jungtertiaeren Saugetierfaunen der Steiermark, Suedost-Oesterreichs." *Mitteilung das Museums für Bergbau, Geologie und Technik am Landesmuseum Joanneum* 31 (1970): 1–92.

SECONDARY SOURCES
Modrijan, Walter von. "Laudatio für Dr. Maria Mottl." *Steierm Arkisches Landesmuseum Joanneum. Jahresbericht* 2 (1972): 109–113.
Szekely, Kinga. "Mottl, Mária 1906–1980." *Karszt és Barlong* 2 (1980): 118.

STANDARD SOURCES

Sarjeant.

MOUFANG, RUTH (1905–1977)

German mathematician. Born 10 January 1905 in Darmstadt, Germany, to Else (Fecht) and Eduard Moufang. One sister. Educated Bad Kreuznach Realgymnasium; University of Frankfurt, teaching degree (1929; Ph.D., 1931). University of Rome, fellowship (1931–1932; habilitation, 1936). Professional experience: University of Königsburg, instructor (1933); University of Frankfurt, instructor (1933–1935), lecturer to associate professor (1947–1957), professor (1957–1967); Krupps Research Institute, Essen, industrial mathematician (1937–1946). Died 26 November 1977.

Ruth Moufang was a German mathematician noted for the development of algebraic analysis of projective planes, later called Moufang planes and Moufang loops. She was the first German woman to be made full professor at the University of Frankfurt. Her father, Eduard Moufang, was a scientific consultant for the chemical industry. While her older sister, Erica, pursued a career as an artist, Ruth became fascinated by mathematics.

Moufang entered the University of Frankfurt in 1925 to study mathematics. She received a teaching certificate in 1929, and then went on to complete a doctoral dissertation on projective geometry under Max Dehn. She was awarded a fellowship in mathematics and studied in Rome, returning to Germany to take up a teaching position at the University of Königsburg. It was during this period, from 1931 to 1934, that she produced her most significant work, writing papers that would establish a new specialty in mathematics, the algebraic analysis of projective planes. Her work was taken up by other mathematicians in the 1950s and resulted in the analysis of what would be called "Moufang planes" and "Moufang loops."

Although Moufang received her habilitation degree, which should have qualified her for an academic post, in February 1937 the Nazi government rewrote the rules and refused to recognize that her preparation was sufficient, as a woman, to teach in a university. Instead she obtained a position in the Krupps research facility at Essen as an industrial mathematician, working on applied elasticity theory. After the war, her qualification to teach in the university was recognized and she returned to the University of Frankfurt for the rest of her career. She was named the first female full professor at the university in 1957. Although she continued to develop her work on Moufang planes and loops, she ceased to publish important papers in the fifties and sixties. Her most important influence in the last years of her life was on her graduate students.

JH/MBO

PRIMARY SOURCES

Moufang, Ruth. "Zur Struktur der projektiven Geometrie der Ebene." *Mathematische Annalen* 105 (1931): 536–601. Her first classic paper derived from her dissertation on what became known as Moufang planes. Also appeared as a book published by J. Springer in Berlin, 1931.

———. "Die Schnittpunktsätze des speziaellen Fünfecksnetzes in ihrer Abhängigkeit voneinander." *Mathematische Annalen* 106 (1932): 755–795.

———. "Alternativkörper und der Satz vom vollständingen Vierseit (D_9)." *Abhanglungen aus dem Mathematischen Seminar der Hamburgischen Universität* 9 (1933): 207–222.

——— "Zur Structur von Alternativkörpern." *Mathematische Annalen* 110 (1934): 416–430. Her paper on what would become known as Moufang loops.

SECONDARY SOURCES

Chein, Otto. *Moufang Loops of Small Order*. Providence, R.I.: American Mathematical Society, 1978. A description of the mathematics of Moufang loops.

Srinivasan, Bhama. "Ruth Moufang 1905–1977." *Mathematical Intelligencer* 6, no. 2 (1984): 51–55. Includes biography and list of publications.

STANDARD SOURCES

DSB; Notable Mathematicians (includes portrait).

MUELLER, KATE HEUVNER (1898–?)

U.S. psychologist. Born 1 November 1898 in Derry, Pa. Married 1935. Educated Wilson College (A.B., 1920); Columbia University (A.M., 1923); University of Chicago (fellow, 1926–1928; Ph.D., 1928). American Board of Professional Psychologists, diplomate in counseling psychology (1949); Rockefeller Foundation grant, Indiana University (1967–1971); Indiana University Foundation grant (1972–1973). Professional experience: Wilson College, instructor of psychology (1923–1926); University of Minnesota, assistant professor (1928–1935); Indiana University, Bloomington, lecturer, extension division (1936–1938), dean of women (1937–1949), associate professor of counseling psychology (1949–1952); professor of higher education (1952–1969), emerita professor of higher education (from 1969). Concurrent experience: High Commission for Germany, Frankfurt, specialist in women's education (summer 1951); Florida State University, visiting professor of higher education (1970). Death date unknown.

Kate Mueller worked at the University of Indiana from 1936 to 1969, when she retired. She began as a lecturer in the extension division, then became successively dean of women, associate professor of counseling psychology, and professor of higher education. She was a member of the American Psychological Association, the American Association of University

Women, the American Association of Higher Education, the American Society of Aesthetics, and the National Association of Women Deans and Counselors.

Much of her research was on aesthetics, specifically on music expressiveness and appreciation. She also worked on psychometrics, counseling for mental hygiene, and the influence of social backgrounds. Mueller wrote more than seventy-five books and articles.   JH/MBO

PRIMARY SOURCES

Mueller, Kate. *Appreciation of Music and Tests for Appreciation of Music.* University of Oregon, 1934.
———. *Educating Women for a Changing World.* Minneapolis: University of Minnesota, 1954.
———. *Student Personnel Work in Higher Education.* Boston: Houghton, 1961.

STANDARD SOURCES

AMS 7–8, S&B 9–13.

MUIR-WOOD, HELEN MARGUERITE (1896–1968)

British invertebrate paleontologist and historian of paleontology. Born 1896 in Hampstead. Never married. Educated Bedford College, University of London. Professional experience: British Museum of Natural History (1922–1965). Died 16 January 1968.

Helen Muir-Wood was educated at Bedford College, University of London. After the end of World War I, she joined a talented group of young paleontologists at the British Museum of Natural History. She spent her career at the British Museum of Natural History and became an authority on the fossil brachiopods of the British Isles, India, Malaysia, Iran, Iraq, Israel, Jordan, and Somalia. Younger researchers found her somewhat formidable, although they had a great respect for her knowledge. She was known as a person who would not tolerate sloppy work, and who demanded the utmost accuracy in bibliographic and observational matters. Neither could she abide what to her were "dilettante" branches of paleontology—those that departed from the rigorous discipline of systematic description.

Muir-Wood's work was done on specimens sent to the museum from all parts of the world, so it is understandable that she was known as a "splitter" in taxonomic terms for she did not do the field work herself. She pioneered the classification of Mesozoic forms on their internal structure and wrote a history of the study of these fossils. However, even though she was the recognized expert on the phylum Brachiopoda, she never attempted a synthetic work that would trace its evolution from the simplest shell-bearing phase to its state of near extinction today. She was an extremely careful scholar who refused to generalize when she was not sure that the evidence was totally certain—both a strength and a weakness.

Muir-Wood was awarded the Lyell Fund by the Geological Society of London in 1930 and Lyell Medal in 1958 for her contributions to the study of the Brachiopoda. When she retired from the Museum of Natural History, she was awarded the Order of the British Empire in recognition of her services to that great institution. She also served on the councils of the leading geological and paleontological societies and attended meetings when subjects of paleontological interest were presented.   JH/MBO

PRIMARY SOURCES

Muir-Wood, Helen. "On the Internal Structure of Some Mesozoic Brachiopoda." *Philosophical Transactions of the Royal Society of London,* ser. B, Biological Sciences 505, no. 223 (1934): 551–567.
———. "A Monograph on the Brachiopoda of the British Great Oolite Series. Part I. The Brachiopoda of the Fuller's Earth." London: Palaeontographical Society 144, 1936.
———. "Notes on British Eocene and Pliocene Terebratulas." *Journal of Natural History* 2 (1938): 154–181.
———. "Some Jurassic Brachiopoda from the Lincolnshire Limestone and Upper Estuarine Series of Rutland and Lincolnshire." *Proceedings of the Geologists' Association* (1952): 113–142.
———. "On the Morphology and Classification of the Brachiopod Suborder." *British Museum of Natural History* (1962): 132.

SECONDARY SOURCES

[Ager, Derek V.] "Helen Marguerite Muir-Wood." *Proceedings of the Geologists' Association* 80, no. 1 (1969): 122–124.
Owen, Ellis F. "Dr. H. M. Muir-Wood." *Nature* 217, no. 5135 (1968): 1294–1295.
Hayes, Pamela D., and T. C. Davenport. "Muir-Wood, Helen M. 1896–1965." In *Biographies of Geologists: Materials for the Study of the History of Geology, Prepared in Geology 851, a Seminar in the History of Geology, 1853–1958.* Sixth supplement, ed. Aurèle LaRogue, 12–13. Columbus, Ohio: Ohio State University, Department of Geology, 1961.
[Williams, Alwyn]. "Helen Marguerite Muir-Wood." *Proceedings of the Geological Society of London* 1655 (1969): 123–125.

STANDARD SOURCES

Sarjeant.

MULLER, MARIE CLAIRE EIMMART (1676–1707)

See Eimmart, Marie Claire.

MURPHY, LOIS BARCLAY (1902–)

U.S. child and social psychologist. Born March 1902 in Lisbon, Iowa, to May (Hartley) and Wade Crawford Barclay. Two brothers; two sisters. Married Gardner Murphy, 1926 (he died 1979). One son; one daughter. Educated Vassar College (A.B., 1923); Union Theological Seminary (B.D., 1928); Columbia University (Ph.D. in child psychology, 1937); Topeka Psychoanalytic Institute, certificate in psychoanalytic training (1960). Professional experience: Sarah Lawrence College, instructor in comparative religion (1928–1929), instructor, assistant professor, professor in psychology (1931–1952); Menninger Foundation, research psychologist (1952–1971); Children's Hospital, Washington, D.C., Infant-Rearing Study, researcher (1967–1971). Concurrent positions: Bank St. College, lecturer, research associate (1937–1952); William Alanson White Institute, psychiatrist (1949–1971); Institute of Child Development, India, researcher (1950–1960); Chicago Institute of Psychoanalysis, researcher (1954–1956); National Institutes of Child Health and Human Development, director of research project (1966–1968); North Topeka Day Care Center, researcher (1966–1970). Honors and memberships: Conference Early Childhood, National Institutes of Mental Health (1964–1966); White House Task Force on Infancy & Early Childhood (1967–1968); American Orthopsychiatry Association; Society of Personality Assessment; Society for the Psychological Study of Social Issues; New York Academy of Sciences.

Lois Barclay Murphy was born in Iowa and raised in Cincinnati, where her father was active as a leader in the Methodist Federation for Social Service, which shared some of the ideals of figures like JANE ADDAMS. She went as an undergraduate to Vassar, where she studied economics as well as studying the psychology of delinquent girls, on which she wrote her undergraduate thesis. For her study she spent a few months replacing the matron in a training school. She had already demonstrated her interest in the problems of factory workers, spending a summer break punching holes in clock faces when she was eighteen.

After graduating *magna cum laude,* she spent four years learning about child psychology under Helen Thompson Woolley and Mabel Fernald at the Psychological Laboratory of the Cincinnati Board of Education. Possibly because of the involvement of her father in religious social service, Barclay briefly moved away from her interest in social problems to earn a degree in comparative religion at Union Theological Seminary in New York City.

Lois Barclay's roommate, who was attending Columbia, introduced her to Gardner Murphy. He had already begun to explore fields of social psychology and was teaching as a young instructor in psychology at Columbia. The two were married two years later in 1926. After her marriage, much of Lois Murphy's professional as well as personal life was intertwined with that of her husband, although she maintained

an independent teaching career at Sarah Lawrence College. After an initial year of teaching comparative religion at Sarah Lawrence, Lois Murphy was fired because she and a group of other professors insisted that the college live up to its constitution and give the faculty a major share in administration. When the president was herself let go, Murphy was hired back by the new administration and began to teach psychology.

During the year when she was not teaching, Murphy's first child was born. She also worked on the book her husband was preparing, analyzing data on children and cowriting the pioneering new study *Experimental Social Psychology* (1931). In preparation for the volume, they both sat in on the course given by the anthropologist RUTH BENEDICT and talked to MARGARET MEAD upon her return from Samoa. Their volume had a considerable impact on the field of social psychology and established Gardner Murphy as a major figure in psychology.

Lois Murphy had begun to work toward her doctorate at Columbia, studying personality in young children, spending an hour or so every morning at the Sarah Lawrence Nursery School. Her dissertation was published as a book, *Social Behavior and Child Personality* (1937). Her husband had, by then, moved to City College of New York, where he was head of the department.

In the late thirties and forties, personality theory had become a major theme for psychologists. Gardner Murphy, who had been teaching a course on personality since 1931, wrote his second major book summarizing the enormous growth of the field of personality. His integration of a wide range of interdisciplinary studies, according to Lois Murphy, was probably her husband's most important contribution to psychology. Although she minimized her participation in this study, her husband recognized it in his autobiography. After the two psychologists moved in the fifties to the Menninger Clinic, Lois Murphy would develop her ideas further in a two-volume book, *Personality in Young Children* (1956), stimulated by her clinical work.

The Murphys also traveled to India in 1950 for UNESCO, to study growing social tensions over a six-month period, just after the partition of India and Pakistan, when both Hindu and Moslem as well as intercaste tensions were running high. The two were impressed by the active participation of women in the professional and governmental life of the country. The work of the two psychologists was greeted warmly by Indian psychologists, and they returned a number of other times to India during that decade.

Both husband and wife chose research over academic psychology, when they chose to move to Topeka, Kansas, to the Menninger Foundation, where Gardner pursued more clinically oriented work and Lois worked with the Menninger Children's Service staff while serving as a consultant on the newly started Head Start project. She also trained in child psychoanalysis at the Topeka Psychoanalytic Institute under analysts who had worked with ANNA FREUD.

Lois Murphy began a longitudinal study of normal children, termed by her the Coping Study, funded by the National Institutes of Mental Health and the Menninger Foundation. She directed the study, which involved an important team of pediatricians, psychologists, psychotherapists, and others. During the sixties, participation in the writing of a series of booklets for Head Start (published by the Office of Child Development) delayed her analysis of the Coping Project, which finally appeared only in 1976 as *Vulnerability, Coping and Growth,* with Alice Moriarity.

Lois Murphy was also slowed in her work by her husband's developing Parkinson's disease and spent much of the seventies assisting her husband as he became increasingly disabled. Her experience with his hospitalizations and his home health care resulted in her writing a popular book on how to deal with catastrophic illness in the home.

The two psychologists also shared a lifelong interest in parapsychology, although Lois Murphy was only peripherally involved in this aspect of her husband's work. Gardner Murphy was a leading officer in the American Society for Parapsychology, trying to establish the society on a scientific basis according to William James's ideas in the nineteenth century, and J. B. Rhine's more recent studies at Duke.

After her husband's death in 1979, Lois Murphy undertook a series of studies of her husband's work, resulting in a definitive biography published when she was eighty-eight.

KM

PRIMARY SOURCES

Murphy, Lois. With Gardner Murphy. *Experimental Social Psychology.* New York: Harpers, 1931.

———. *Social Behavior and Child Personality.* New York: Columbia University Press, 1937.

———. *Personality in Young Children.* 2 vols. New York: Basic Books, 1956.

———, ed. With Gardner Murphy. *Asian Psychology.* New York: Basic Books, 1968.

———, ed. With Gardner Murphy. *Western Psychology: From the Greeks to William James.* New York: Basic Books, 1969.

———. With Alice Moriarity. *Vulnerability, Coping and Growth.* New Haven: Yale University Press, 1976.

———. *The Home Hospital: How a Family Can Cope with Catastrophic Illness.* New York: Basic Books, 1982.

———. *Gardner Murphy: Integrating, Expanding and Humanizing Psychology.* Jefferson, N.C., and London: McFarland, 1990. This biography of her husband presents a great deal of material on her own life.

STANDARD SOURCES

AMS 7–8, S&B 10–12; Debus; O'Connell and Russo 1988; Stevens and Gardner.

MURRAY, AMELIA MATILDA (1795–1884)

British botanist. Born 1795 to Anne Charlotte and Lord George Murray. At least three siblings. Professional experience: maid of honour to Queen Victoria; botanist and artist. Died 7 June 1884 in Glenberrow, Hereford.

Amelia Matilda Murray spent much of her childhood at court, when her mother was appointed a lady in waiting to the Princesses Augusta and Elizabeth. She became a friend of Lord Byron. In 1837, she became a maid of honour to Queen Victoria. In July, 1854, she traveled to the United States, Cuba, and Canada, returning home in 1855. This trip reinforced her previous antipathy toward the institution of slavery. She refused to suppress her opinions after she was told that court officials were not allowed to publish anything redolent of politics. She subsequently resigned her post, but was later made extra woman of the bedchamber. She was an excellent botanist and botanical artist. In 1855, she collected *Asplenium verecundum* in Florida.

JH/MBO

PRIMARY SOURCES

Murray, Amelia Matilda. "Remarks on Education in 1847." London: T. Varty, 1847.

———. "Letters from the United States, Cuba, and Canada." 2 vols. London: G. P. Putnam, 1856.

———. "Recollections from 1803–1837, with a Conclusion in 1868." London: Longmans, Green, 1869.

STANDARD SOURCES

Desmond; *DNB.*

MURRAY, LADY CHARLOTTE (1754–1809)

British botanist. Born 1754. Professional experience: wrote on the Linnean system of classification suitable for young ladies. Died 1808 at Bath, Somerset.

Lady Charlotte Murray is best known for her book *The British Garden,* in which she explains how the Linnean system may be used to discover the name of an unknown plant. She encouraged others to study botany, considering it more accessible than the other sciences. Never stepping across the boundaries of propriety, Lady Charlotte does not pretend to be an expert in the area. As Ann Shteir notes, she wrote within the polite culture of botany and targeted an audience of young people.

JH/MBO

PRIMARY SOURCES

Murray, Lady Charlotte. *The British Garden: A Descriptive Catalogue of Hardy Plants, Indigenous, or Cultivated in the Climate of Great Britain. With Their Generic and Specific Characters, Latin and English Names, Native Country, and Time of Flowering.* 2 vols. Bath: S. Hazard, 1799.

SECONDARY SOURCES

Fussell, G. E. "The Rt. Hon, Lady Charlotte Murray." *Gardners Chronicle* 128 (1950): 238–239.

STANDARD SOURCES

Desmond; Shteir.

MURRAY, MARGARET ALICE (1863–1963)

British archeologist, folklorist. Born 13 July 1863 in Calcutta, India, to Margaret Carr and James Charles Murray. One sister. Never married. Educated privately, Calcutta General Hospital, nurse probationer (1883); University College, London (course work in Egyptology, archeology, ethnology, 1894–1901?). Professional experience: University of London, University College, assistant to Flinders Petrie (1898–1909), junior lecturer in Egyptology (1899–1909), lecturer (1910), senior lecturer (1922–1924), assistant professor (1924–1935). Lectured Oxford (1910), Finland, Norway, Sweden, Estonia. Field expeditions to Abydos (1902–1903, 1903–1904), Malta (1921–1923), Minorca (1931–1935), Palestine (1935, 1936), Petra (1937), Tel Ajjul (1938). Honors and memberships: University College Fellow (1922); honorary D. Litt. (1931); Folklore Society, president (1953–1955). Died 13 November 1963 in London, England.

Margaret Alice Murray became a remarkable Egyptian archeologist and scholar and an important authority on European witchcraft without formal degrees. She was born and raised for most of her childhood in Calcutta, India, where her father was a colonial businessman. Her mother, whose family had lived for a number of generations in India, devoted herself to missionary and social work. Margaret Murray was educated privately in England and in Germany.

As a young woman, Murray was interested in medicine and decided to enter the Calcutta Hospital as a "lady probationer," where she assisted during a cholera epidemic. On her return to England with her family in 1886, her small stature prevented her meeting the height requirement for admission to English nursing schools.

Murray's sister, Mary, who married a man who moved to Madras, India, called her attention to the lectures offered by the great Egyptologist Flinders Petrie. Murray's attendance at Petrie's courses led her to throw herself into the task of learning hieroglyphics, and she soon became an invaluable assistant. She was to devote herself to Petrie as disciple and as-

sociate for the rest of her life. She soon began to lecture in Egyptology at University College, teaching elementary courses in hieroglyphics. Soon her teaching became an invaluable part of Petrie's Egyptology department, and she rose through the ranks to the level of assistant professor.

Continuing her course work with C. V. Seligman and others, Murray prepared herself for field work in archeology. She went on field expeditions to important ancient Egyptian sites with Petrie and his wife and to Abydos at the turn of the century. She then put her field work aside as she did administrative work in the university department and catalogued the Egyptian antiquities in museums in Ireland, Scotland, Oxford, and Manchester.

Murray began to produce guides to museum collections, introductory textbooks on Egyptian grammar, as well as more general works, some of which were criticized for uncritically adopting Petrie's chronology of archaic dynasties. Nevertheless, her some eighty books were well regarded for their acute observation. She returned to field expeditions in the twenties, publishing on her work in Malta, Minorca, and Palestine. When Petrie in his old age found it difficult to obtain funding for his last expeditions to Palestine, Murray and other former students obtained the necessary backing for him in 1938, and assisted him in studying Hyksos culture.

Murray also obtained fame as a student of European witchcraft, publishing her study of the witch cult in 1921. Some of her conclusions were challenged, especially her claim that Joan of Arc was the leader of a pagan cult.

Murray had a longtime interest in woman's suffrage, working to improve the position of women at University College and assisting women students. Her long life was celebrated by an autobiography that she wrote in her hundredth year with the challenging title *My First Hundred Years*. She died four months after the book was published.   JH/MBO

PRIMARY SOURCES

Murray, Margaret. *The Osireion at Abydos.* London: B. Quaritch, 1904.

———. *Elementary Egyptian Grammar.* London: B. Quaritch, 1905.

———. *Saqqara Mastabas.* London: B. Quaritch, 1907.

———. *Witch Cult in Western Europe.* Oxford: Clarendon Press, 1921.

———. *Petra, The Rock City of Edom.* London: Blackie and Son, [1939].

———. *The Splendour That Was Egypt.* New York: Philosophical Library, [1949].

———. *The Genesis of Religion.* London: Routledge & Paul, [1963].

———. *My First Hundred Years.* London: W. Kimber, 1963. An autobiography written when Murray was one hundred years old. With portraits.

STANDARD SOURCES
DNB Missing Persons; IDA (article by David Lonergan).

MURRAY, MARGARET MARY ALBERTA (1874?–1974)

British physiologist. Born 1874. Educated Bedford College (first-class honors, 1921); University of London (M.Sc., 1926; D.Sc., 1937). Professional experience: Bedford College, demonstrator in physiology (1947–1959), head of the department (1974), chair, University of London (1974), emerita professor (1959–1974). Died 6 March 1974.

A born teacher, Margaret Murray earned her degrees from Bedford College and returned to teach there for the rest of her career. The physiology department at Bedford had a good reputation, even though the facilities were poor, because J. S. Edkins, known for the discovery of gastrin, was the first head of the department (1896–1930). Edkins's wife, NORA EDKINS, later became head of the department and Margaret Murray carried on the tradition when she was appointed chair. After graduation, Edkins invited Murray to stay on as a demonstrator in the physiology department. She left Bedford for a short stay at Chelsea Polytechnic, where she taught physiology. She return to Bedford and collaborated with J. S. Edkins (who was very impressed by her abilities) for about thirty years. Her first publication was a joint production with Nora Edkins dealing with the influence of alcohol on the gastric absorption of carbon dioxide and of glucose.

Murray was also interested in the formation of dental caries. She and her colleagues carried out careful chemical analyses of healthy teeth, establishing the base line proportions of these compounds in the dentine and enamel so that they could compare the compositional changes that occur in teeth with caries. They also did comparative experiments on various types of teeth, such as molars and incisors, and those of different animals such as dogs and rodents. She also worked on the effect of fluorine on the teeth. Murray's work had a great influence on public health controversies regarding fluorine.

Murray was an original member of the Board of Studies in Biochemistry in 1929 and a member of the Physiological Society. She served on the committee and the editorial board of the society's *Journal of Physiology.*

A demanding but dedicated teacher, Murray was very generous with her time. Students were sometimes put off by her gruff manner, but they soon realized that she cared for them deeply. She published more than forty papers.

JH/MBO

PRIMARY SOURCES
Murray, Margaret Mary Alberta. "The Diuretic Action of Alcohol and Its Relation to Pituitrin." *Journal of Physiology* 76 (1932): 379.
———. With J. H. Bowes. "Variations in Chemical Composition in Relation to Dental Structure." *Biochemical Journal* 30 (1936): 977–984.
———. With J. H. Bowes. "Calcium, Magnesium and Phosphorus Content of Teeth in Different Animals. The Mechanisms of Calcification." *Biochemical Journal* 30 (1936): 1567–1571.
———. With Bowes. "Chemical Study of 'mottled teeth.'" *British Dentistry Journal* 60 (1936): 556–562.
———. "Maternal Transference of Fluorine." *Journal of Physiology (London)* 87 (1936): 388–393.
———. With others. "Study of Development of Dental Enamel in Dogs." *Journal of Dental Research* 21 (1942): 183–199.
———. *Thyroid Enlargement and Other Changes Related to the Mineral Content of Drinking Water with a Note on Goitre Prophylaxis.* London: Medical Research Council (memorandum no. 18), 1948.

STANDARD SOURCES
Women Physiologists; WWW, vol. 7.

MURRAY, MARGARET RANSONE (1901–)

U.S. cell biologist, neuroscientist. Born 14 November 1901 near Yorktown, VA, to Harriet (Ransone) and Archibald Campbell Murray. Married Burton Le Doux (1941). Educated Goucher College (A.B., 1922); Washington University (M.S., 1924); University of Chicago (Ph.D., 1928). Professional experience: Florida State College for Women, associate professor of biology and physiology (1928–1929); Columbia College of Physicians and Surgeons, instructor in surgery (1929–1930), assistant (1930–1946), assistant professor (1947–1953), associate professor (1953–1959), professor of anatomy (1959–1970), emerita professor (1970); National Institutes of Health, research and senior scientist (1973–1976?). Honors and memberships: NIH research career award (1962–1972); Goucher College, science citation (1954); University of Brussels, science medal (1964); National Multiple Sclerosis Society, Golden Hope Chest award (1964); Commonwealth Fund, traveling fellow (1963–1964); National Multiple Sclerosis research advisory commission (1963–1968); Tissue Culture Commission (1946–1950); National Institutes of Health, fellowship awards panel (1960–1963); New York Academy of Sciences, Fellow. Tissue Culture Association, honorary member (secretary, 1946–1950; president, 1953–1959); Japanese Tissue Culture Society, honorary member.

Margaret Ransone Murray was a cell biologist and neuroscientist who developed a successful method of nerve cell tissue culture and later studied degeneration in the nervous system. She was born and brought up in Virginia and went to Goucher College for her undergraduate education. She obtained a master's degree from Washington University in St. Louis, where she studied under Coswell Grove and did research on a method for observing secretion in insect egg follicule cells. She attributed her technique for tissue culture to MARGARET REED LEWIS, at the Carnegie Foundation. Lewis, like Murray, had been an undergraduate at Goucher some twenty years previously. Murray's work for her master's degree resulted in her first publication, completed only after she began to work toward her doctorate at the University of Chicago, studying with Frank R. Lillie, a renowned physiologist.

Murray spent the year after obtaining her doctoral degree as an associate professor of biology and physiology in the Southeast at Florida State College for Women. In 1929, intent on continuing her research, Murray moved to New York and began to work in a laboratory of the College of Physicians and Surgeons at Columbia. She married Burton Le Doux at the beginning of the forties, but retained her own name. Although for fifteen years she was only an assistant in a research laboratory, shortly after the end of World War II she was appointed assistant professor of anatomy at Columbia and began to rise through the ranks to full professor some thirteen years later. At the time she was made full professor, she was one of a handful of women in science at this academic level.

Murray developed a tissue culture method which allowed organized portions of the nervous system to be maintained for periods of months. The recognition of this work resulted in a number of awards and citations, including one from her undergraduate college, Goucher, in 1954. She was an active member of the research committee of the National Multiple Sclerosis Society and was awarded its Golden Hope award for her research work on degenerative neuromuscular diseases.

In the 1960s, she obtained a Commonwealth Fund award, which allowed her to travel to Britain and other countries in Europe and the Far East. She was made an affiliate of the British Royal Society of Medicine and recognized by the Japanese Tissue Culture Society and the University of Brussels for her tissue culture work in the 1960s. She served the Tissue Culture Association as both secretary and president and was eventually made an honorary member.

Murray was also elected a Fellow of the New York Academy of Science. By the 1970s, she began to consider herself a neurobiologist, describing her research interests as including not only degenerative diseases of the nervous system but functional differentiation of nerve and muscle in vitro.

Following Murray's retirement from teaching at the College of Physicians and Surgeons, she retained her National Institutes of Health career research grant for the next two years and continued her research at the Laboratory for Cell Physiology. At the age of seventy-one, Murray moved to Bethesda, Maryland, where she continued her research as a senior scientist at the National Institutes of Health, studying active transport in the cerebrovascular system. JH/MBO

PRIMARY SOURCES
Murray, Margaret Ransone. "Secretion in the Amiototic Cells of the Cricket Egg Follicule." *Biological Bulletin* 50 (1926): 210–228.
———. With (?) Kopech. *A Bibliography of Tissue Culture Research, 1884–1950.* New York: Academic Press, 1953.

STANDARD SOURCES
AMS 11–12; Debus; Rossiter 1995.

MURRELL, CHRISTINE MARY (1874–1933)

British physician. Born 1874. Educated London University (M.D., 1905). Professional experience: general practice; Women's Emergency Corps (WWI), physician. Member St. Marlybone Health Society; General Medical Council of Great Britain (first woman); Council of the British Medical Association; Medical Women's Federation. Died 1933.

Christine Murrell graduated from the London University medical school in 1905 and went into general practice, becoming a member of the St. Marlybone Medical Society. During World War I, she served in the Women's Emergency Corps. She was active in professional organizations and became the first woman member of the General Medical Council of Great Britain (1933). Her book, *Womanhood and Health,* was published in 1923. JH/MBO

PRIMARY SOURCES
Murrell, Christine Mary. *Womanhood and Health.* London: Mills & Boon, 1923.

SECONDARY SOURCES
Uglow 1982.

MURTFELDT, MARY (1848–1913)

U.S. entomologist. Born 1848 in New York City. Educated Rockford (Ill.) College (1858–1860). Died 1913.

Although she was born in New York City, Mary Murtfeldt spent her early years in Rockford, Illinois. She lived most of her life in Kirkwood, Missouri, with her father and sister. As the result of an early illness she used crutches in order to walk and was unable to complete her schooling because of poor health. Murtfeldt became interested in entomology after her father accepted a position as editor of *Colman's Rural World* in 1868. Through this channel she met Charles Valentine Riley, the state entomologist, who recommended her for a position in the Bureau of Entomology of the United States Department of Agriculture as a local assistant. This position allowed her to attend scientific meetings, and to present numerous papers. As Riley's assistant from 1868 until 1877, Murtfeldt accomplished some important work. Her knowledge of both entomology and botany enabled her to unravel cases involving the relationship of insects to the pollination of plants and to follow the life histories of newly discovered or little-known insects upon their host plants. One of her more important contributions was an understanding of the details of the pollination of *Yucca*. In 1885 the botanist S. M. Tracy published a list of the plants of Missouri ("Flora of Missouri," *Missouri State Horticultural Society Report*), in which Murtfeldt was named as the collector of many species from the St. Louis area.   J H / M B O

PRIMARY SOURCES

Murtfeldt, Mary. *Outlines of Entomology: Prepared for the Use of Farmers and Horticulturists at the Request of the Secretary of the State Board of Agriculture and the State Horticultural Society of Missouri*. Jefferson City, Mo.: Tribune Printing Co., 1891.

SECONDARY SOURCES

Spalding, Perley. "A Biographical History of Botany at St. Louis, Missouri, IV." *Popular Science Monthly* 74 (March 1909): 240–258.

STANDARD SOURCES

Ogilvie 1986; Osborn; *Woman's Who's Who of America*.

MUSZHAT, ANIELA (fl. 1920s)

Polish researcher in radioactivity. Flourished 1920s. Never married. Professional experience: Warsaw Society of Scientists, radiology laboratory.

Aniela Muszhat worked at the radiology laboratory of the Warsaw Society of Scientists. She investigated the recoil due to emission of beta particles, a particularly difficult phenomenon to detect. She also showed that fluctuations in alpha particle emission followed the Gaussian distribution and confirmed that radium A and polonium were isotropic. In each case, the studies were done to improve the methods and results of previous experimenters.   M M

PRIMARY SOURCES

Muszhat, A. "*On the B-Recoil*." *Philosophical Magazine* 39 (1920): 690–694.

———. With H. Herszfinkel. "Sur l'isotropie du radium A et du polonium." *Journal de physique et la Radium* 2 (1921): 15–18.

———. With Louis Wertenstein. "Sur les fluctuations du rayonnement alpha." *Journal de physique et la Radium* 2 (1921): 119–128.

STANDARD SOURCES

Meyer and von Schweidler.

MYERS, MABEL ADELAIDE (1900–   )

U.S. bacteriologist, natural historian. Born 8 October 1900 in Indianapolis, Ind., to Bertha Helen (Klusman) and William Park Myers. Educated: Fullerton Junior College (A.A., 1919); Pomona College (B.A., 1921; M.A., 1922); Cornell University (Ph.D., 1926). Professional experience: Palo Verde High School, teacher (1922; 1924); Fullerton Union High School, teacher (1926–1928); Fullerton Junior College, faculty biological sciences and geology (1926–1946); San Diego State College, Life Sciences division, faculty (1946–1950), professor (1952–post-1968), Department of Bacteriology, chair (1955–1960); coordinator of graduate studies in biology (1960–post-1968). Concurrent experience: Board of Directors, San Diego Biomedical Research Institute; President, Orange County Health and Welfare Council (1945–1946). Honors and membership: Fellow, San Diego Society of Natural History (past president). Sigma Delta Epsilon (past president, national board).

Mabel Adelaide Myers conducted research on the tonsilar structure of Anurans. She also worked on the life history of the moth and control of pear slug, leafhopper, and slime bacteria.   J H / M B O

PRIMARY SOURCES

Myers, Mabel Adelaide. "A Study of the Tonsillar Developments of the Lingual Region of Anurans." *Journal of Morphology and Physiology* 45 (June 1928): 399–439. From Myers's Ph.D. dissertation.

STANDARD SOURCES

Debus.

MYIA OR MYA (late 6th century B.C.E.)

Greek natural philosopher. Said to be the daughter of the mathematician Pythagoras and THEANO, *his disciple.*

Myia was one of the female Pythagoreans about whom little is known. She is said to have written on the nourishment of the child.   J H / M B O

STANDARD SOURCES

Rebière.

N

NANCE, NELLIE WARD (1893–?)

U.S. plant pathologist. Born 16 December 1893 in Leesville, Va. Educated George Washington University (A.B., 1931; M.A., 1938). Professional experience: U.S. Department of Agriculture, Bureau of Plant Industries, Soils and Agricultural Engineering, personnel worker (1922–1930), senior science aide (1930–1936), junior pathologist, plant disease survey, division of mycology and disease survey (1936–1943), assistant pathologist (1943–1949), Division of Agricultural Research Services, crops protection research, Bureau of Crops Research (from 1950). Death date unknown.

Nellie Ward became one of the many women who made a career at the U.S. Department of Agriculture. Beginning as a personnel worker before she earned either of her college degrees, she was promoted to senior science aide after she earned her bachelor's degree. After that, she received regular promotions in the department.   JH/MBO

PRIMARY SOURCES
Nance, Nellie Ward. "Revegetation of a Denuded Area of Widewater, Maryland, below the Great Falls of the Potomac after the Flood of March 19, 1936." George Washington University, M.A. thesis, 1938.

STANDARD SOURCES
AMS 7–8, B 9, P&B 10.

NAPPER, DIANA MARGARET (1930–1972)

British botanist. Born 23 August 1930 in Woking, Surrey. Educated Exeter University (B.Sc., 1951). Professional experience: Coffee Research Station, Kenya, laboratory assistant (1954); East African Herbarium, Nairobi, assistant (1955); Kew Herbarium, staff (1965). Died 31 March 1972 in London.

Three years after Diana Napper received her degree from Exeter University, she accepted a position at the Coffee Re-search Station in Kenya as a laboratory assistant and the next year worked at the East African Herbarium, Nairobi. She spent much of her time collecting and wrote on her research. After she returned to England, she was on the staff of the Kew Herbarium for a short time. Her studies included the Acanthaceae, Cyperaceae, and Gramineae of East Africa.
          JH/MBO

PRIMARY SOURCES
Napper, Diana Margaret. *Grasses of Tanganyika.* Dar es Salaam: Government Printer, 1965.
———. "Cyperaceae of East Africa." Reprinted from the *Journal of the East Africa Natural History Society and Natural Museum* 24, no. 2: 106.
———. "Dipsacaceae." In *The Flora of Tropical East Africa.* [London]: Crown Agents for Oversea Governments and Administrations, 1968.
———. "Flagellariaceae." In *The Flora of Tropical East Africa.* [London]: Crown Agents for Oversea Governments and Administrations, 1971.
———. "Typhaceae." In *The Flora of Tropical East Africa.* [London]: Crown Agents for Oversea Governments and Administrations, 1973.

SECONDARY SOURCES
Journal of the Kew Guild (1972). Obituary notice with portrait.
Kew Bulletin (1973). Obituary notice with portrait.

STANDARD SOURCES
Desmond.

NASYMUTH, DOROTHEA CLARA (MAUDE) (1879–1919?)

British physician. Born 26 February 1879. Father A. H. Maude. Married G. C. H. Nasmyth, 1909. One son. Educated Cheltenham Ladies College; Somerville College, Oxford (1898–1902;

honors in natural sciences, physiology, class 1, 1902); University of Dublin (M.A., 1905); University of London (M.B.; B.S., 1906; M.D.). Professional experience: Hull Nottingham Children's Hospital, house physician (1907); Royal Free Hospital, physician (1907); Hospital for Women, Liverpool, house surgeon (1908); WWI service in Belgium, Serbia, France, Corfu, Macedonia; medal 1914; Governor Warneford Asylum, consultant; Oxford, first woman general practioner. Died 1919 in Oxford.

Dorothea Nasymuth earned first-class honors in physiology at Somerville College, Oxford. After a year studying at the University of Dublin, she went to London University, where she earned bachelor of medicine, bachelor of science, and doctor of medicine degrees. Oxford did not grant degrees to women at that time. She worked at several hospitals, was in the service during World War I, and became the first woman general practioner in Oxford.   JH/MBO

SECONDARY SOURCES
Somerville College, Oxford. *Register* (1871–1917).

NAUMOVA, SOFIYA NICKOLAEVNA (1902–1974)

Soviet palynologist. Born 1902. Professional experience: Central Geologo-Prospecting Institute, Leningrad, organizer and chief of laboratory (1930s); All-Union Research Institute of Mineral Products in Moscow; Moscow Geologo-Prospecting Institute, the Institute of Mines, and the Academy of the Oil Industry, docent; Geological Institute of the Academy of Sciences, USSR (1946). Died 1974.

Sofiya Nickolaevna established the first classification system of the fossil spores and pollens of the Paleozoic (the Seventeenth Session of the First International Geological Congress). At the Geological Institute of the Academy of Sciences of the USSR, she organized and headed the laboratory studying Mesozoic and Paleozoic spores and pollen in the Department of Stratigraphy. She trained an entire generation of palynologists working in the Soviet Union and was a member of permanent commissions of the International Committee on Paleozoic microflora, a member of the editorial board of the journal *Pollen et Spores,* and a member of the editorial board charged with publishing the transactions of the Third International Palynological Conference.

Much of Sofiya Nickolaevna's work was taxonomic, and she devised a system of classification of pollen that is still considered very useful. She developed useful techniques for isolating the fossil membranes and pollen from metamorphosed rocks and collected her own materials in the USSR, England, China, Romania, Poland, India, and Czechoslovakia. Devonian coals were her special interest and she produced a monograph on them devoted to the classification of Devonian

spores. After World War II, she spent less time on her classification system of spores and pollen and more on the study of microfossils.

Naumova saw more than a practical use for her system of classification. She wanted to show a link that would connect the flora of the Precambrian with that of the early Paleozoic. She produced over seventy publications and left a number of unpublished manuscripts.   CK

PRIMARY SOURCES
Naumova, Sofiya Nickolaevna. "Etude pétrographique des houilles des mines de Bobrik du bassin de la banlieue de Moscou." *Trudy Vsesoyuzny Geologorazved. Obshchestva: Akademiya Nauk SSSR* 355 (1934): 46 pp. In Russian.
———. "The Spores from Cambrian and Silurian Deposits." *Akademiya Nauk SSSR, Vestnik Geologicheskayha Seriya* 10 (1946): 121–124. In Russian.
———. "Spore and pollen Assemblage from the Upper Devonian of the Russian Platform and their Stratigraphic Significance." *Akademiya Nauk SSSR Trudy Geologicheskogo Instituta* 143, no. 60 (1953): 1–204. In Russian.

SECONDARY SOURCES
"In Memoriam. Sofiya Nickolaevna Naumova (1902–1974)." *Review of Palaeobotany and Palynology* 21, no. 2 (1976): 135–139.

NAYLOR, BERTHA (fl. 1922)

British physicist. Educated (B.Sc. degree). Professional experience: National Physical Laboratory, England, research.

Although little is known about Bertha Naylor, it is known that she had at least a bachelor of science degree and worked in research in England.

Radium salts were often sealed in platinum or silver tubes, which afforded safety and convenience, but absorbed some of the radiation. Working in England at the National Physical Laboratory, Naylor and E. A. Owen developed correction tables which allowed researchers to determine the true radium content of these tubes.   MM

PRIMARY SOURCES
Naylor, Bertha. With E. A. Owen. "On the Measurement of the Radium Content of Sealed Metal Tubes." *Physical Society of London, Proceedings* 34 (1922): 92–97.

STANDARD SOURCES
Meyer and von Schweidler.

NEAL, MARIE CATHERINE (1889–1965)

U.S. conchologist and botanist. Born 7 December 1889 in South-ington, Conn., to Eva W. (Chedney) and Linus B. Neal. Educated Lewis High School; Smith College (B.A., 1912); Yale University (M.S., 1925); Hartford, business course. Professional experience: Travelers Insurance, stenographer; Children's Aid Society, stenographer; Yale University, geology department, secretary (1915?); Bishop Museum (affiliation with Yale), part-time botanist (1920–1926), full-time botanist (1926–1930); director of herbarium (from 1930).

Although Marie Catherine Neal never was awarded a doctoral degree, she earned a master's degree from Yale, and worked as a botanist in its affiliate Bishop Museum for thirty-five years. She wrote her thesis on Hawaiian marine algae. She began to work at the Bishop Museum herbarium part-time in 1926 and eventually took charge of the herbarium. In this capacity, she catalogued many specimens (both shells and botanical). She was a Bishop Museum botanist for thirty-five years. Her major work, *In Gardens of Hawaii,* discussed, illustrated, and described two thousand species of plants belonging to about one thousand different genera and 188 families.

JH/MBO

PRIMARY SOURCES
Neal, Marie Catherine. *In Honolulu Gardens.* Honolulu, Hawaii: The Museum, 1928.
———. With Henry Augustus Pilsbry and C. Montague Cook, Jr. *Land Snails from Hawaii, Christmas Island, and Samos.* Honolulu, Hawaii: The Museum, 1928.
———. *In Gardens of Hawaii.* Honolulu, Hawaii: The Museum, 1948.

SECONDARY SOURCES
Bulletin of the Torrey Botanical Club 93 (1966): 199–206. Obituary notice.
Taxon 14 (October 1965): 250–253. Includes an extensive publication list. Obituary notice.

STANDARD SOURCES
NAW unused.

NECKER, SUSANNE (CURCHOD) (1739–1817)

Swiss/French writer and philanthropist. Born 1739 at Crassier (Pay du Vaud). Father a Protestant minister, Curchod. Married Jacques Necker, banker and politician (1764). One daughter, Germaine, later Madame de Staël. Founded a hospital in 1776. Author of several books. Died 1817.

Susanne Curchod was the daughter of a Protestant minister in Switzerland. She met and almost married the English his-

torian Edward Gibbon while he was living in Lausanne. A beautiful and well-educated young woman, she was taken to Paris by Mme. de Vermenou, who negotiated her marriage in 1764 to banker and politician Jacques Necker. The two became devoted to each other. Her husband soon became the finance minister of Louis XVI. She established a salon which was frequented by some of the brightest in literature, the arts, and politics (such as Diderot, Buffon, Marmontel, LaHarpe, and Grimm). Well educated herself in Latin, English, and German, she passed her love of learning and writing on to her daughter Germaine, later MADAME DE STAËL.

Necker was an active reformer and a strict Calvinist with a special interest in providing for the sick poor. She visited Paris hospitals and studied medicine and architecture in order to improve conditions she found in hospitals of her day. In 1776, she obtained permission to convert a disused convent into a charity hospital, Hôpital Charité, later renamed Hôpital Necker after her death. Under her direction it was modern, clean, and efficiently administered and became, in the nineteenth century, a leading center for pediatric medicine and research. She wrote a book, *Memoire sur l'etablissement des hospices* (1786), explaining her methods.

In 1790, Susanne Necker and her husband were forced into exile in Switzerland by the events of the French Revolution. She continued to keep in close touch with the administrators of her hospital until her death four years later. She also wrote other books, one on premature burials and another on divorce, both reflecting her strong opinions.

JH/MBO

PRIMARY SOURCES
Necker, Susanne. *Memoire sur l'etablissement des hospices.* Paris, 1786.
———. *Mélanges extraits des manuscrits de Mme. Necker.* 3 vols. Paris: C. Pougens, [1798].
———. *Reflexions sur la divorce.* Lausanne: Aubin, 1794.

SECONDARY SOURCES
Bertholet, A., et al., eds. *La Grande Encyclopédie.* Vol. 24. Paris: Société Anonyme La Grande Encyclopédie, n.d.

STANDARD SOURCES
Cyclopaedia; Lipinska 1930; Uglow 1989.

NEEDHAM, DOROTHY MARY (MOYLE) (1896–1987)

British biochemist. Born 22 September 1896 in London to Ellen (Daves) and John Moyle. Married Joseph Needham (1924). Educated Clarement College, Stockport; Girton College, Cambridge (D.Sc.); postgraduate study, Europe and the U.S. Professional experience: Cambridge University, biochemical laboratory, research worker (1920–1963); Girton College, Cambridge, instructor and researcher (1928–1940); Ministry of Supply (Chemical Defense), research worker (1940–1943); Sino-British Science Co-operation Office, Chungking, China, chemical adviser and acting director (1944–1945); Medical Research Council, research worker (1946–1952); Cambridge University, Broodbank fund, research grantee (1952–1955). Agricultural Research Council, research grantee (1955–1962). Honors and memberships: Beit Memorial Research Fellow (1925–1928); Royal Society, Fullerton Award (1961–1962); Leverhulme Award (1963); Cambridge University, Gonville and Caius College, honorary fellow (1979); Fellow of the Royal Society (1948). Died 22 December 1987 in Cambridge.

Dorothy Moyle was born in London and educated at Clarement College. She then went to Girton College, Cambridge, where she studied toward a doctor of science degree and began to work in the biochemical laboratory. Here she met and married Joseph Needham and continued to conduct studies of muscle and nerve response. In the late 1920s she also began to teach and do research at Girton College, supervising the work of promising young researchers like Lu Gwin-Djen. She also traveled to various research laboratories in Europe and the United States.

With the outbreak of World War II, Dorothy Needham was assigned to the Chemical Defense branch of the Ministry of Defense. In 1944, she went with her husband to Chungking, China, as a chemical advisor to the Sino-British Science Cooperation Office, serving as its acting director in 1945. On her return to Cambridge, she obtained funding for her research on muscle biochemistry from the Medical Research Council and a series of other funds. During this period, she became one of the first women elected to the Royal Society of London.

In her seventies, she began to study the history of biochemical research, especially on the biochemistry of muscle, publishing her book *Machina Carnis.* Fifteen years later, in her eighties, she published a source book on biochemistry. In increasing poor health, she died in Cambridge at the age of ninety-one.   JH/MBO

PRIMARY SOURCES

Needham, Dorothy Mary. *Biochemistry of Muscle.* Cambridge: Cambridge University Press, 1932.
———. With Joseph Needham, ed. *Science Outpost.* London: Pilot Press, 1948.
———. *Machina Carnis: The Biochemistry of Muscle in Its Historical Development.* Cambridge: Cambridge University Press, 1971.
———. *A Documentary History of Biochemistry, 1770–1940.* [Leicester?]: Leicester University Press, 1991.

SECONDARY SOURCES

New York Herald Tribune, January 2, 1941. Obituary notice.

STANDARD SOURCES

Biographical Memoirs; Current Biography, 1941; *WWW,* vol. 8, 1981–1990.

NEIBURG, MARIA FEODOROVNA (1894–1962)

See Neuburg, Maria Feodorovna.

NELSON, KATHERINE GREACEN (1913–1982)

U.S. petroleum geologist and invertebrate paleontologist. Born 9 December 1913 in Sierra Madre, Calif. At least one brother, Robert A. Greacen. Married Frank H. Nelson. Educated Vassar College (A.B., 1934); Rutgers University (Ph.D., 1938). Professional experience: Milwaukee-Downer College, Milwaukee, Wis., teacher and curator (1938–1943, 1945–1956); Shell Oil, Hunt Oil, petroleum geologist (1943–1945); University of Wisconsin, Milwaukee, researcher (1956–1982). Died 29 December 1982 in Milwaukee, Wis.

Katherine Greacen Nelson was the first woman to earn a doctorate at Rutgers University. Upon receiving this degree she began teaching at Milwaukee-Downer College. In addition to teaching, she curated the geologic collections in the Greene Memorial Museum on campus. She left teaching to accept a job as a petroleum geologist and paleontologist first with Shell Oil and then with Hunt Oil Company. Following this time in the oil fields during World War II, she returned to Milwaukee-Downer as professor of geology and geography and curator of the Greene Museum. She had brief additional teaching experience at the Milwaukee-Downer Seminary, the YWCA, and Wisconsin State College in Milwaukee.

In 1956, Nelson joined the faculty of the University of Wisconsin, Milwaukee, where she continued to work until her final illness. Nelson was important in establishment of the Department of Geological and Geophysical Sciences, acting as its first chair. She was a good citizen of the university, serving on many committees. Nelson convinced the university to buy the Greene Museum from Milwaukee-Downer. After this purchase, Nelson initiated a public education program at the museum. Teaching students about the earth was Nelson's most lasting contribution to geology.

Nelson was a member of and held offices in many professional associations. She was a Fellow of the Geological Society of America and the American Association for the Advancement of Science. Always a dedicated worker, she held many different positions in the Wisconsin Academy of Sciences, Arts, and Letters. In 1952–1953, she was its first woman president. She was a member of the National Association of Geology Teachers and president of the Central Section in 1968–1969. She also held memberships in the Paleontological Society and the American Association of Stratigraphic Palynologists. She was named Educator of the Year in 1982 by the Midwest Federation of Mineralogical and Geological Societies.

Although she published scholarly papers, she had the capability of inspiring people of all ages to be interested in the earth and its geological contents.   JH/MBO

PRIMARY SOURCES

Greacen, Katherine F. "A Bryozoan Fauna as a Criterion for the Correlation of the Vincentown Formation with Descriptions of Some New Species of Bryozoa." Ph.D. diss., Rutgers University, 1938.

———. "The Stratigraphy, Fauna and Correlation of the Vincetown Formation." *New Jersey Department of Conservation Geology Series* 52 (1941).

———. With John Rich Ball. "Silurian Invertebrate Fossils from Illinois in the Thomas A. Greene Memorial Museum at Milwaukee-Downer College." *Milwaukee-Downer College Bulletin* (1946).

———. With John Rich Ball. "Catalog of the Egan Collection of Silurian Invertebrate Fossils." Chicago: Chicago Academy of Sciences, 1946.

Nelson, Katherine G. With Norman P. Lascan. "Milwaukee, Its Geologic Setting." *Geotimes* 15, no. 8 (1970): 12–15.

SECONDARY SOURCES

Kluessendorf, Joanne, Donald G. Mikulic, Rachel K. Paull, and Richard A. Paull. "Katherine Greacen Nelson (1913–1982)." *Bulletin of the American Association of Petroleum Geologists* 68, no. 6 (1984): 786–787.

STANDARD SOURCES
Sarjeant.

NEMCOVÁ-HLOBILOVÁ, JINDRISKA (1916–)
Czech mineralogist and igneous and metamorphic petrologist. Born 19 November 1916. Educated University of Olomouc.

Jindriska Nemacová-Hlobilová did research on Czechoslovak minerals, pegmatites, and basic and ultrabasic rocks.
                    JH/MBO

PRIMARY SOURCES

Nemcová, Jindriska. "Prspevek k exotickym horninam Chribua." *Sbornik Praci Prirodovedecke Fakulty Univerzity Palackeho v Olomouci* 26, no. 9 (1967): 61–81.

———. With F. Nemec. "Petrografie nekterych

bazickych a intermediarnich hornin Staromestskeho svoroveho pasma." *Sbornik Praci Prirodovedecke Fakulty Univerzity Palackeho v Olomouci* 70 (1981): 65–84.

———. With F. Nemec. "Pkontaktni horniny hadcoveho telesa u Habartic." *Sbornik Praci Prirodovedecke Fakulty Univerzity Palackeho v Olomouci* 70 (1981): 57–64.

———. With F. Nemec. "Petrographie der ultrabasischen und basischen Gesteine in der sudelichen Haelfte der Stare Mesto p. Sn-Glimmerschieferzone." *Sbornik Praci Prirodovedecke Fakulty Univerzity Palackeho v Olomouci* 54, no. 16: 117–154.

SECONDARY SOURCES

Gába, Zdeněk, and Ilja Pek. "Sedesát let doc. RNDr. Jindrisky Nêmocové, Csc." *Zpravy. Vlastivedny Ustav v Olomouci. Odbor prirodnich ved* 181 (1976): 29–31.

Kudelasek, Vladimír. "Padesátiny doc. RNDr. Jindrisky Nemocové-Hlobilové, CSc" (Fiftieth Birthday of Jindriska Nemcová [née Hlobilová]). *Sbornik Praci Prirodovedecke Fakulty Univerzity Palackeho Olomouci*, 26, no. 9 (1967): 5–7.

STANDARD SOURCES
Sarjeant.

NEMIR, ROSA LEE (1905–)
U.S. physician. Born 16 July 1905 in Waco, Tex., to Emma and David Nemir. Five siblings. Married Elias J. Audi (1934). Three children. Educated Texas University (B.A., 1926); Johns Hopkins (M.D., 1930); Johns Hopkins, postgraduate medical school (1950–1953). Professional experience: Medical College, New York University, instructor of pediatrics (1933–1939), assistant professor (1939–1950), associate professor (1950–1953), professor (from 1953); Columbia University, College of Physicians and Surgeons, visiting professor (1958–1959); Bellevue Hospital, School of Nursing, lecturer (1934–1949); University Hospital, attending pediatrician (from 1950); Children's Medical Service, visiting physician, director of chest unit (from 1960); Governour Hospital, New York City, attending pediatrician (1950–1958), consultant (from 1958); New York Infirmary, consultant (1954). Honors and memberships: Society of Pediatric Research; Medical Women's Association; New York Academy of Medicine.

Rosa Nemir was an academic pediatrician who worked not only in research but also with sick children while she held her academic posts. Her special interests were pneumonia and tuberculosis in children, nutrition, and virology.

When she was fourteen years old, Nemir declared her intentions to study medicine to her biology teacher in Austin, Texas. A series of good teachers with whom she could identify, a happy childhood in Austin, and a healthy relationship with church and the out-of-doors, helped her achieve what she wanted. She attended the University of Texas, and when it was time to enter medical school went to Johns Hopkins in Baltimore, which she had heard had a liberal attitude toward women students. Her experience at Hopkins was not all positive, due to her father's financial problems and her own difficulties with her eyes. After graduation she interned in San Francisco and then moved to Bellevue Hospital in New York as an intern and assistant resident in pediatrics. At that time she met Elias J. Audi, whom she married. She made choices in favor of her family, although she continued with her medical career. She was active in the American Medical Women's Association.   K M

PRIMARY SOURCES
Nemir, Rose L. In Hellstedt, *Autobiographies.*

STANDARD SOURCES
AMS B 9, P&B 10–14.

NETRASIRI, KHUNYING CHERD-CHALONG (1909–)

Thai physician. Born 27 August 1909. Married Arun Netrasiri (1940). One daughter. Educated Phuket Girls' School (1914); Assumption Convent, Bangkok (1916–1918); St. Joseph's Convent; Rajinee School (secondary school diploma); Chulalongkorn University, Faculty of Arts and Sciences (passed examination 1929); Siriraj Hospital Medical School (M.B., 1933); postdoctoral work in Germany, Alexander von Humboldt Fellowship (1938). Professional experience: Siriraj Hospital, house officer in medical department (1933), permanent post (1934–1969), department of pediatrics, head (1968–1969). Retired 1969.

Khunying Cherd-Chalong was in the first coeducational class in Thailand. In a conversation with Princess Chandranipa Decakul, after Cherd-Chalong graduated from high school, she informed the princess that she wanted to study medicine, but feared it was impossible. The princess spoke to her husband and in 1927 coeducation began with the admission of seven undergraduates into the Faculty of Arts and Sciences. After studying basic science for two years, Cherd-Chalong passed an examination and entered the Siriraj Medical School. She became one of the first three medical graduates in Thailand.

In 1938 Cherd-Chalong was awarded an Alexander von Humboldt Fellowship to pursue further studies in Germany. She worked for a year at the Leipzig University Hospital under a prominent pediatrician. She then applied for admission to the Institute of Tropical Medicine, but was told that Germany was not in a position to admit foreign students. She stopped in the United States and spent a month observing at the Children's Hospital in Philadelphia.

She married Arun Netrasiri, a colleague at Siriraj Medical School whom she had met thirteen years earlier. The couple had one daughter. Netrasiri had also studied in Germany where he spent eleven years and obtained a medical degree specializing in pediatrics. The couple worked together at the Siriraj Medical School until his retirement in 1968. She succeeded her husband as head of the department of pediatrics. She earned several honors, including an honorary doctor of medicine. She became Companion of the Most Illustrious Order of Chula Chom Klao, which gave her the title Khunying.   K M

PRIMARY SOURCES
Netrasiri, Cherd-Chalong. In Hellstedt, *Autobiographies.*

NEUBURG, MARIA FEODOROVNA (1894–1962)

Russian paleobotanist and stratigrapher. Born 1894. Educated (Ph.D. 1948). Professional experience: Institute of Geology, Academy of Sciences, Moscow, researcher. Died 1964.

Maria Feodorovna Neuburg studied Lycopodiales, Ginkogoales, and other groups from the Upper Paleozoic and Triassic of the USSR. One of her first contributions was on the stratigraphy and the age of the carboniferous deposits of Kuznetsk. She came out in opposition to the traditional view of the age and constitution of these deposits, finding that the sedimentary sequence had elements of the Carboniferous, Permian, Triassic, and Jurassic. She published a paper on this subject in 1929.

For her doctoral thesis (which was not published until 1948), she studied the flora of the Upper Paleozoic of Kuznetsk, a solid descriptive work with stratigraphic significance. During 1944, Neuburg began a study on other aspects of the flora of the vast sedimentary Upper Paleozoic of Siberia, especially the Lycopods and the Ginkgos. From working on mummified fossil Bryophytes, she recognized that the similarities between fossil and modern forms in Argentina were applicable worldwide.   J H / M B O

PRIMARY SOURCES
Neuburg, M. F. "On the Stratigraphy of the Coal-Bearing Deposits of the Kuznetsk Basin." *Academiya Nauk URSS Instytut Geologii Serie Geologichnykh* 4 (1936): 469–510.
———. "K stratigrafii i vozrastu uglenosnykh otlozhenii Tannu-Tuvinskoi Narodnoi Respublike." *Academiia Nauk URSS Institute Geologicheskikh. Trudy* 5 (1936): 129–159.
———. "On the Flora and Stratigraphy of the Upper Paleozoic of the North of Siberia." *Subsurface of the Arctic* 1 (1946): 155–171.
———. "Opyt fitostratigraficheskogo sopostavleniya verkhnepaleozoiskikh otllozhenii Angaridy i Gondvany

(Indiya)." *Voprosy Geoloii Azii (Akademia Nauk SSSR)* 1 (1954): 765–797.

———. "Permian True Mosses of Angaraland." *Journal of the Palaeontological Society of India* 3 (1958): 22–29.

SECONDARY SOURCES
Archangelsky, Sergio. "Maria Feodorovna Neuburg (1894–1962)." *Ameghiniana* 2, no. 2 (1963): 56.

STANDARD SOURCES
Sarjeant.

NEUMANN, ELSA (1872–1902)

German physicist. Born 1872 in Berlin. Educated University of Berlin; Max Planck Institute (Ph.D. cum laude, 1899). Died 1902.

Little is known about Elsa Neumann's life. It is known that she attended the University of Berlin and then studied physics at the Max Planck Institute, where she earned her doctorate. Her doctoral thesis was "Über die Polarisationscapacität umkehrbarer Elektroden." In order to collect her doctorate, she had to receive special permission from the Ministry of Education, becoming, on 18 February 1899, the first German woman physicist to obtain a Ph.D. The Deacon of the University, a Professor Schwarz, was of the opinion that women should be high priestesses of the home, that they should be wives and mothers. Nevertheless, he was also of the opinion that scientific work was not necessarily incompatible with women's most important work and that Neumann was a person who could do both.   JH/MBO

PRIMARY SOURCES
Neumann, Elsa. *Über der polarisationscapacität Umkehrbarer Elektroden.* Leipzig: J. A. Barth, 1899. Dissertation, including vita.

STANDARD SOURCES
Strohmeier.

NEUMANN, HANNA (VON CAEMMERER) (1914–1971)

German/British mathematician. Born 1914 in Germany. Married Bernhard H. Neumann. Five children. Educated Berlin and Göttingen; Oxford University (Ph.D.). Immigrated to England (1938). Professional experience: University of Hull, senior lecturer. Died 1971.

Born in Germany, Hanna von Caemmerer emigrated to England in 1938 in order to marry Bernhard H. Neumann, an abstract algebraist of Jewish extraction. Since Hanna was classified as an Aryan, the Nuremberg laws of 1935 made it illegal for the two "races" to intermarry. In England, she was given credit for her previous work at Berlin and Göttingen and her research in England led to a doctoral degree at Oxford University. She became senior lecturer at the University of Hull and her husband became a reader at the University of Manchester.

The Neumanns had a very productive career and a stable, loving family life. Although they often collaborated, they worked on different aspects of abstract algebra. However, they were both fascinated by "group theory," and jointly wrote a book on "free groups." When working independently, they often referred to the works of the other. In 1956, Bernhard Neumann wrote a paper entitled "On a Conjecture of Hanna Neumann." Hanna Neumann was able to write about very abstract topics in a clear fashion.
                                            JH/MBO

PRIMARY SOURCES
Neumann, Hanna. "On Some Finite Non-Desarguesian Planes." *Archiv der Mathematik* 6 (1955): 36–40.

SECONDARY SOURCES
Kramer, Edna B. "Six More Female Mathematicians." *Scripta Mathematica* 23 (1957): 83–95.
Neumann, Bernhard. "On a Conjecture of Hanna Neumann," *Proceedings of the Glasgow Mathematics Association* 3 (1956): 13–17.

NEVILL, LADY DOROTHY FRANCES (WALPOLE) (1826–1913)

British horticulturist and plant collector. Born 1 April 1826 in London to Mary (Fawkener) and Horatio Walpole, third Earl of Orford. Four siblings. Married Reginald Henry Nevill (1847; he died in 1878). Six children, four of whom survived past childhood. Educated by a governess in French, Greek, and Latin; no other formal education. Professional experience: took charge of twenty-three-acre garden. Died 24 March 1913 in London.

Lady Dorothy Nevill came from an illustrious family. Her father was Horatio Walpole, the third earl of Oxford, and her mother was the daughter of the envoy extraordinary at St. Petersburg and a close friend of Empress Catherine. Although Dorothy received no formal education, she was taught Italian, Greek, and Latin by a governess. A lively girl, she was interested in many things. In 1847 she married a distant relative twenty years her senior and the couple had six children, four of whom survived to adulthood.

In 1851, the Nevills acquired an estate in Sussex, Dangstein, in addition to their London House. Whereas Reginald looked after the estate, Lady Dorothy managed the garden.

This garden soon became famous in horticultural circles, particularly for its collection of exotics. Lady Nevill housed them in seventeen hothouses, and they were the subject of at least twelve articles in horticultural journals. She became friends with Sir William Hooker at Kew as well as his son Sir Joseph Hooker. She provided Charles Darwin with a number of rare plants. In addition to the exotics, the garden at Dangford had one of the earliest herbaceous borders, various exotic birds and animals, a silkworm farm, and a museum with some of her numerous collections. She even had a flock of pigeons with Chinese whistles attached to their tails.

Politically, she was a conservative. However, she was a good friend of both conservative Benjamin Disraeli and the radical Richard Cobden. After her husband's death she moved to Stillyans in East Sussex, where she also had a garden. She died at her home in Charles Street, London.

JH / MBO

PRIMARY SOURCES
Nevill, Lady Dorothy Frances. *The Reminiscences of Lady Dorothy Nevill*. London: E. Arnold, 1906.
———. *Leaves from the Notebooks of Lady Dorothy Nevill*. London: Macmillan, 1907.
———. *Under Five Reigns*. London: Methuen, 1910.

SECONDARY SOURCES
Gosse, E. "Lady Dorothy Nevill." *Fortnightly Review* 101 (1914): 277–287.
Trotter, W. R. "The Glasshouses at Dangstein and Their Contents." *Garden History* 16 (1988): 71–89.

STANDARD SOURCES
DNB Missing Persons.

NEWBIGIN, MARION ISABEL (1869–1934)

British / Scots biologist, geographer, and editor. Born 1869 in Alnwick. Father James Lesslie Newbigin. Seven siblings. Educated Edinburgh Association for the University Education of Women; University College, Aberystwyth; Extramural School of Medicine for Women, Edinburgh; University of London (B.Sc., 1893; D.Sc., 1898). Professional experience: School of Medicine for Women, Edinburgh, lecturer in biology and zoology. Died 20 July 1934 in Edinburgh.

Many of the specifics of the life of Marion Isabel Newbigin are unknown. We do know that her father was a pharmacist and that she was one of five girls and three boys. After studying in Scotland she took both a bachelor's and a doctorate of science from the University of London. She and her four sisters were all strong feminists. At the School of Medicine for Women in Edinburgh, she was greatly influenced by a teacher, J. Arthur Thompson. She succeeded Thompson as lecturer in biology and zoology. Her studies on coloration in plants, crustaceans, and fish resulted in several publications.

She became editor of the *Scottish Geographical Magazine* in 1902 until her death in 1934. Her interests in geography were very broad, and she published widely in the area. She was an examiner in geography for many institutions and served as president of the geographical section of the British Association in 1922.

JH / MBO

PRIMARY SOURCES
Newbigin, Marion Isabel. *Life by the Sea Shore*. London: Swan, Sonnenschein & Co., 1901.
———. *An Introduction to Physical Geography*. London: J. M. Dent, 1912.
———. *Animal Geography: The Faunas of the Natural Regions of the Globe*. Oxford: Clarendon Press, 1913.
———. *Ordnance Survey Maps*. Edinburgh: W. and A. K. Johnston, Ltd., 1913.
———. *Geographical Aspects of Balkan Problems*. London: Constable, 1915.
———. *Southern Europe*. London: Methuen, 1932.

SECONDARY SOURCES
Geographical Review 24 (1934): 676. Obituary notice.
Scottish Geographical Magazine 1 (1934): 331–333. Obituary notice.

STANDARD SOURCES
DNB Missing Persons.

NEWSON, MARY FRANCES WINSTON (1869–1959)

U.S. mathematician. Born 7 August 1869 in Forreston, Ill., to Caroline (Mumford) and Thomas Winston. Three siblings. Married Henry Byron Newson. Three children. Educated University of Wisconsin (classical degree with honors in mathematics, 1889); Bryn Mawr College (1891–1892); University of Chicago (1892–1893); University of Göttingen (Ph.D. magna cum laude, 1897). Professional experience: Downer College, Fox Lake, Wis., teacher (1889–1890); Kansas State Agricultural College, Manhattan, Kans., faculty member (1897–1900); Washburn College, Topeka, Kans., faculty member (from 1913); Eureka College, faculty member (to 1942). Died 5 December 1959.

Mary Frances Winston was tutored by her mother, because she was dissatisfied with the education the children received at public schools. Caroline Winston even taught herself Greek and Latin so that she could prepare the children for college. After receiving her bachelor's degree with honors in mathematics, Mary Frances taught at Downer College for two years. After the first year, she applied for a mathematics fellowship to study at Bryn Mawr but was unsuccessful. Charlotte Angas Scott encouraged her to reapply the next year. She received the fellowship and studied at Bryn Mawr from 1891 to 1892. According to Scott, Winston was a diligent but not a brilliant student. Although she was invited to remain at Bryn Mawr, she returned to Chicago and studied at the university for another year. A new opportunity opened up for her in the summer of 1893, when she met Göttingen mathematician Felix Klein at the International Mathematical Congress at the World's Columbian Exposition in Evanston, Illinois. He encouraged her to go to Göttingen to study, but warned her that she might not be admitted. Although she applied for a fellowship from the Association of Collegiate Alumnae (later the American Association of University Women), she did not receive it. However she did hear from Christine Ladd-Franklin, who had met her at the exposition and deemed her worthy of support, and offered her five hundred dollars for study abroad.

During her last year of three at Göttingen, Winston was awarded a European Fellowship from the Association of Collegiate Alumnae. Although she had completed most of the requirements for the degree in 1896, she could not comply with the German stipulation that the dissertation be published, because she could not find a printer in the United States who could print the German diacritical markings. She, therefore, had to wait until 1897 after the dissertation was printed in Germany. During the interim, she taught high school in Missouri. In 1897 she accepted a position teaching in the mathematics department at Kansas State Agricultural College (now Kansas State University), where she stayed for three years.

In 1900 she married Henry Byron Newson, acting head of the mathematics department at the University of Kansas. The couple had three children: a daughter, Caroline, born in 1901, a second daughter, Josephine, born in 1903, and a son, Henry Winston, born in 1909. Henry Newson died of a heart attack at the age of forty-nine. Now a single mother who had not worked for a number of years with three small children, Newson would have been desperate if her parents had not lived nearby and helped the family. Not until 1913 did she find a job, at Washburn College in Topeka. She left her children with her parents and rented an apartment in Topeka, where she stayed during the week. Eventually the children moved there. Newson was one of eight Washburn faculty members to sign a petition to support a political science professor who had been dismissed for talking freely with his students about his political views. This case was one of the first involving academic freedom to be investigated by the American Association of University Professors. All eight of the petition signers found other jobs. Newson went to

Eureka College in Illinois as department head, where she remained until she retired in 1942 when she was seventy-three years old. She died at age ninety.

Newson was one of twenty-two women who became members of the American Mathematical Society. She was also a member of the Mathematical Association, president of the Kansas Association of Teachers of Mathematics, and an alumna member of the Phi Beta Kappa chapter at the University of Wisconsin. Her three children started a fund to support a lecture series at Eureka College—the Mary Winston Newson Memorial Lecture on International Relations.

More of a teacher than a research mathematician, Newson did little research after she received her doctorate. At Göttingen, she studied the area of differential equations. She published one paper and her dissertation while she was there. However, after she returned to the United States she published only one more article, and that was a translation.   MM

PRIMARY SOURCES

Newson, Mary Frances Winston. "Eine Bemerkung zur Theorie der hypergeometrischen Function." *Mathematische Annalen* 46 (1895): 159–160.

———. Über den Hermite'schen Fall der Lamé'schen Differentialgleichungen." Ph.D. dissertation, Göttingen University. Hanover, Germany: 1897.

———. "Mathematical Problems." Translation of lecture delivered before the International Congress of Mathematicians in Paris in 1900 by Professor David Hilbert. *Bulletin of the American Mathematical Society* 8 (1901/1902): 437–479.

SECONDARY SOURCES

"Miss Mary F. Winston." *The Industrialist* (Manhattan, Kans.) 22, no. 40 (15 June 1897): 166.

Washington Post, 6 December 1959. Obituary notice.

Whitman, Betsey S. "Mary Frances Winston Newson: The First American Woman to Receive a Ph.D. in Mathematics from a European University." *Mathematics Teacher* 76 (1983): 576–577.

STANDARD SOURCES

Grinstein and Campbell (article by Betsey S. Whitman).

NEWTON, MARGARET (1887–?)

Canadian plant pathologist. Born 20 April 1887. Educated McGill University (B.S.A., 1918); National Research Council of Canada (studentship, 1918–1919; M.Sc., 1919); Saskatchewan, National Research Fellowship (1919–1921; B.A., 1920); University of Minnesota (Ph.D., 1922). Professional positions: Saskatchewan, associate professor of biology (1922–1925); Dominion Laboratory of Plant Pathology, senior plant pathologist (1925–

1945); retired 1945. Honors and memberships: Royal Society of Canada, Flavelle gold medal (1948);University of Minnesota, gold medal (1956). Death date unknown.

Plant pathologist Margaret Newton pursued all of her academic work in Canada with the exception of her doctorate, which she received from the University of Minnesota. After she attained this degree, she returned to Canada, where she became an associate professor of biology at the University of Saskatchewan. After three years there, she became senior plant pathologist in the Dominion Laboratory of Plant Pathology, where she remained until she retired. She was a member of the Phytopathology Society, the Royal Society of Canada, the Canadian Phytopathology Society, the Arctic Institute of North America, and the Agricultural Institute of Canada. Her research was on physiological specialization in the cereal rusts, the genetics of wheat and oat stem rust, and mildew of wheat and barley.   JH/MBO

PRIMARY SOURCES

Newton, Margaret. "Studies in Wheat Stem Rust (*Puccinia graminis tritici*)." *Proceedings and Transactions of the Royal Society of Canada* ser. 3, vol. 16, section 5, 1922. Ph.D. diss., University of Minnesota, 1922.

STANDARD SOURCES

AMS 4–7, P&B 10–11.

NICE, MARGARET MORSE (1883–1974)

U.S. ornithologist. Born 6 December 1883 in Amherst, Mass., to Margaret Duncan (Ely) and Anson Daniel Morse. Six siblings. Married Leonard Blaine Nice. Five children. Educated Mount Holyoke College (A.B., 1906); Clark University (1915). Honors and memberships: American Ornithologists' Union, Fellow (1937); Wilson Ornithological Club, president (1938); American Ornithologists' Union, Brewster Medal (1942); Mount Holyoke College, honorary D.Sc. (1955). Died 26 June 1974.

Ornithologist Margaret Morse Nice is best known for her work on the behavior of the song sparrow. In spite of numerous impediments, including the lack of institutional support and the rearing of five children, she became well enough known for her research that Nobel Prize–winning ethologist Konrad Lorenz once credited her with founding the science of ethology (behavior).

Morse's father was a history professor at Amherst College who encouraged his children to enjoy nature; her mother was a graduate of Mount Holyoke College, who led the children on Sunday nature walks. Margaret began keeping a nature journal when she was nine years old, concentrating

on birds. In spite of this seemingly liberal environment, her parents discouraged their three daughters from pursuing professions. However, Margaret was able to attend Mount Holyoke, because a college education was considered important to a homemaker. At Holyoke she majored in French. She complained that her zoology courses emphasized taxonomy and dissection. She saw this as a distortion of what an animal really was. Her bird watching days were severely limited during those years. After receiving her bachelor's degree, she went home to her parents. However, after hearing a lecture at Amherst by Clifton Hodge of Clark University, who studied the economic impact of animals on humans, she saw an opportunity to study live birds. She convinced her parents to allow her to attend graduate school at Clark. As a part of her preparation for a master's degree, she worked on the food habits of bobwhite quail. Although she had planned to pursue a doctorate at Clark, she met and married Leonard Blaine Nice, a graduate student. She abandoned her plans to complete her doctorate and kept house for her husband as he finished his degree.

When Margaret Nice's husband moved, she followed him to each new academic post. They moved to Norman, Oklahoma, after two years at Harvard, where Leonard Nice became a professor of physiology and pharmacology at the University of Oklahoma. Margaret managed to streamline her housework in order to have more time for her real interests. She published the results of her bobwhite research and embarked on new research on her daughter's language development. Clark University awarded her a master's degree in psychology for her thesis work, which concerned environmental influences on the development of children's vocabulary. Nice's interest in birds was rekindled by an article she read in the *Daily Oklahoman*, which reported that hunters wanted to open the mourning dove season in late summer, declaring that nesting was completed. She began a study of the nesting behavior of these doves, and determined that the doves nest into October. She became interested in Oklahoma birds after the dove study and published articles on many local birds in ornithological journals. She and her husband published the first complete bird survey, *The Birds of Oklahoma*, in 1924. Blaine Nice supported his wife's research, caring for the five children and paying for expenses. However, when her husband received a new academic appointment in Columbus, Ohio, she was torn from her research on Oklahoma birds. To make matters worse, one of their five daughters died during the winter of 1927. Life began to look brighter in the spring of 1928. After witnessing a battle between two male song sparrows, Nice decided to decipher little-known aspects of these birds' territorial behavior. An invention of hers made it possible to recognize individual birds in the field. Although other ornithologists marked birds with numbered leg bands to study migration patterns of populations, Nice used colored celluloid bands to identify individual birds in the field. This enabled her to study the behavior of individuals.

Nice received accolades from ornithologists for her research on the song sparrow. The American Ornithologists' Union elected her to membership, the fifth woman to be elected. Since the local Wheaton Ornithological Club excluded women, she kept in the mainstream by reviewing papers for the journal *Bird Banding,* including European works. Because of her language skills, she was able to bring the results of European research to the United States.

Nice's first major publication on the song sparrow was published in *Journal für Ornithologie* to international acclaim. She published additional articles in American journals as well as a popular book, *The Watcher at the Nest.*

Public gardens replaced much of Nice's research site and her husband took a new job in Chicago. In Chicago, she switched to studying captive birds, but she continued writing papers and reviews. She was elected a Fellow of the American Ornithologists' Union and in 1938 became the first woman president of the Wilson Ornithological Club. Her international reputation expanded. During her trips to Europe in the 1930s, she worked with Konrad Lorenz. She kept in contact during World War II. Horrified at the condition of her European colleagues after the war, she organized American ornithologists to supply food and clothing to the Europeans. She continued to be interested in social concerns, campaigning against pesticide misuse, dam construction in Dinosaur National Monument, the development of the Indiana sand dunes outside of Chicago, and for the protection of the Wichita National Wildlife Refuge in Oklahoma. She described her dedication to science in her posthumously published autobiography, *Research Is a Passion for Me.* JH/MBO

PRIMARY SOURCES

Nice, Margaret Morse. "Food of the Bobwhite." *Journal of Economic Entomology* 3 (1910): 295–313.

———. "The Development of a Child's Vocabulary in Relation to Environment." Master's thesis, Clark University, 1915. Published in *Pedagogical Seminary* 22 (1915): 35–64.

———. "The Speech Development of a Child from Eighteen Months to Six Years." *Pedagogical Seminary* 24 (1917): 2044–2243.

———. With G. F. Miller and M. D. Miller. "A Boy's Vocabulary at Eighteen Months." *Proceedings of the Oklahoma Academy of Science* 3 (1923): 140–144.

———. "Nesting Records from 1920–1922 from Norman, Oklahoma." *University of Oklahoma Bulletin* 3 (1923): 61–67.

———. With L. B. Nice. "The Birds of Oklahoma." *University of Oklahoma Bulletin,* n.s. 286 (1924): 1–122.

———. "Observations on Shorebirds in Central Oklahoma in 1924." *Wilson Bulletin* 37 (1925): 199–203.

———. "An Analysis of the Conversation of Children and Adults." *Child Development* 3 (1932): 240–246.

———. "Studies in the Life History of the Song Sparrow. I. A Population Study of the Song Sparrow." *Transactions of the Linnaean Society of New York* 4 (1937): 1–247. Rpt., New York: Dover, 1964.

———. *The Watcher at the Nest.* New York: Macmillan, 1939.

———. With R. W. Allen. "A Study of the Breeding Biology of the Purple Martin (*Progne subis*)." *American Midland Naturalist* 47 (1952): 606–665.

———. *Research Is a Passion with Me.* Toronto: Consolidated Amethyst Communications, 1979.

SECONDARY SOURCES

Bonta, Marcia Myers. "Song Sparrow Lady." *Birder's World* 7 (August 1993): 24–28.

Gibbon, Felton, and Deborah Strom. *Neighbors to the Birds: A History of Birdwatching in America.* New York: Norton, 1988.

Trautman, Milton B. "In Memoriam: Margaret Morse Nice." *Auk* 94 (July 1977): 430–441.

STANDARD SOURCES

Ainley; Bonta; Grinstein 1997 (article by Alan Contreras and Milton Bernhard Trautman); *Notable;* Shearer and Shearer 1996 (article by Julie Dunlap).

NICERATA, SAINT (4th century C.E.)

Greek physician. Lived fourth century.

Saint Nicerata was a Christian martyr who reputedly cured Saint John Chrysotom of a stomach ailment. Although nothing is known about her specific medical contributions, she is representative of a category of Christian women who took care of the medical needs of the poor. JH/MBO

STANDARD SOURCES

Hurd-Mead 1938; Mozans.

NICHOLS, MARY LOUISE (1873–1953)

U.S. zoologist. Born 19 February 1873 in Brookville, Pa. Educated University of Pennsylvania (Ph.D., 1901). Professional experience: Philadelphia Normal School, zoology teacher (1893–1902); zoology and geography teacher (1902–1916); South Philadelphia High School for Girls, teacher (from 1916).

After completing a certificate in biology in 1893, Mary Louise Nichols earned a doctoral degree in 1901. She spent summers at the Woods Hole Laboratory, working on her research. Her research was on diverse topics such as comparative studies of Crustacean spermatogenesis, the development of pollen in *Sarracenia,* and nesting habits of the burrowing bee.   JH/MBO

PRIMARY SOURCES

Nichols, Mary Louise. "The Spermatogenesis of *Oniscus asellus* Linn. With Especial Reference to the History of the Chromatin." *Proceedings of the American Philosophical Society* 41, no. 168 (1901?): 77–112. Ph.D. diss., University of Pennsylvania, 1901.

———. *Science for Boys and Girls.* Chicago: J. B. Lippincott, [1934].

STANDARD SOURCES

AMS 1–8; *American Women;* Siegel and Finley; *Woman's Who's Who of America.*

NICHOLS, MARY SARGEANT NEAL GOVE (1810–1884)

U.S. health reformer. Born 10 August 1810 in Goffstown, N.H., to Rebecca R. Neal and William A. Neal. Three siblings. Married (1) Hiram Gove (1831; divorced ca. 1847); (2) Thomas Low Nichols. One child who reached adulthood. Professional experience: opened girl's school in Lynn, Mass. (ca. 1837); lectured to women on anatomy, physiology, and hygiene; Ladies Physiological Society in Boston, delivered course of lectures to members (1838); developed health reform regimen; established water-cure house; wrote stories and novels under pseudonym Mary Orme. Died 30 May 1884 of cancer.

As a child, Mary Sargeant Neal was characterized by the phrase, "as odd as Mary Neal" (Blake, 627). And the older she got, the odder she became! Converting to Quakerism at the age of fifteen, she married an abusive Quaker hatter who did poorly in business. The couple had only one child, Elma Penn, who survived to adulthood, and four subsequent pregnancies were aborted or stillborn. Mary opened a girl's school, but then became inspired by dietary reformer Sylvester Graham. She began lecturing on anatomy, physiology, and hygiene to a new Ladies Physiological Society in Boston. Although her husband appropriated the proceeds, the lectures themselves were very successful.

Mary Gove became increasingly involved in regimens for healthy living that included fresh air and exercise, cleanliness, daily cold bathing, and whole wheat bread. She believed one should never eat meat, or drink alcohol, coffee, or tea. In 1840, she edited the *Health Journal and Advocate of Physiological Reform* and published her *Lectures to Ladies on Anatomy and Physiology.* She left her autocratic husband and concentrated on new fields of interest, including the water cure system of

Vincent Priessnitz. She became enamored by Henry Gardiner Wright, who came from England to join Bronson Alcott in the establishment of a Utopian community. There is evidence that she and Wright had an affair. In 1843, she established the *Health Journal and Independent Magazine,* which folded after one issue. In a fit of pique, Hiram Gove seized their child, Elma, for three months.

Gove contracted tuberculosis and after going to several water-cure centers decided to establish her own water-cure house. She stressed the importance of a vegetarian diet, as well as the importance of mutual love for the begetting of healthy children. She began to write short stories for *Godey's Lady's Book* and novels under a pseudonym. She developed what might be the equivalent of a French salon on Saturday nights in her New York home. Writers, musicians, and artists all came.

Because he wanted to remarry, Hiram Gove divorced Mary, much to her joy. She had met Thomas Low Nichols in 1847 and he had liberal views regarding women. They were married by a Swedenborgian clergyman and had one daughter, who died of bronchitis at the age of thirteen. Nicholson finished medical school and he and Mary opened a new water-cure establishment in New York City. They established several schools, the American Hydropathic Institute (1851), and a girls' summer school at Port Chester, N.Y. (1852). They planned a controversial School of Life, characterized by perfect freedom. They advocated free love, and espoused the view that marriage was the root of all evil. This school never opened, and their views alienated them from other members of the water-cure committee. They now received messages from the spirit world, and moved to Cincinnati in 1855 where they continued to lecture and published *Nichols' Journal.* The school that they established was a new School of Life, the Memnonia Institute.

Reversing their earlier teachings, the Nicholses established a dictatorship at their school, based on strict chastity, confession, and penance. Various saints began to appear to them at the seances instructing them in the rudiments of Catholicism. Both Nicholses, Elma Gove, and loyal followers were baptized into the Roman Catholic Church. They went to England in 1861 and continued to write on health reform and operated a water-cure institution at Malvern. Increasingly obsessed by mysticism, Mary Nichols, who was nearly blind with cataracts, claimed that she could heal by the laying on of hands. She died in London of cancer.   JH/MBO

PRIMARY SOURCES

Nichols, Mary Sargeant Gove. *Lectures to Ladies on Anatomy and Physiology.* Boston: Saxton and Peirce, 1842.

———. *Experience in Water-Cure: A Familiar Exposition of the Principles and Results of Water Treatment in the Cure of Acute and Chronic Diseases.* New York: Fowlers and Wells, [1849].

———. *A Woman's Work in Water Cure and Sanitary Education.* London: Nichols, [1874].

SECONDARY SOURCES

Blake, John B. "Mary Gove Nichols, Prophetess of Health." *American Philosophical Society Proceedings* (June 1962).

Gleason, Philip. "From Free Love to Catholicism. Dr. and Mrs. Thomas L. Nichols at Yellow Springs." *Ohio Historical Quarterly* (October 1961).

Stearns, Bertha-Monica. "Two Forgotten New England Reformers." *New England Quarterly* 6 (March 1933): 59–84.

STANDARD SOURCES

NAW (article by John B. Blake).

NICHOLSON, BARBARA EVELYN (1906–1978)

British botanist/botanical artist. Born 15 November 1906 in Surrey. Educated Royal College of Art.

Barbara Nicholson was trained as an artist and illustrated a number of botanical books.   JH/MBO

PRIMARY SOURCES

Nicholson, Barbara E., illus. *Oxford Book of Wild Flowers.* By S. Ary and M. Gregory. London: Oxford University Press, 1960.

———, illus. *The Oxford Book of Garden Flowers.* By E. B. Anderson. London: Oxford University Press, 1963.

———, illus. *The Oxford Book of Flowerless Plants.* By Frank H. Brightman. London: Oxford University Press, 1966.

———, illus. *Oxford Book of Trees.* By A. R. Clapham. London: Oxford University Press, 1975.

———. *Barbara Nicholson's Plants of British Isles.* London: Oxford University Press, 1982. Includes biographical data.

STANDARD SOURCES

Desmond.

NICKERSON, DOROTHY (1900–   )

U.S. physicist. Born 5 August 1900 in Boston, Mass. Professional experience: Munsell Research Laboratory, assistant and assistant manager (1921–1926); United States Department of Agriculture, color technologist (1927–1964). Retired 1964. Concurrent experience: Munsell Color Foundation (from 1942; president, 1973–1975); International Commission on Illumination (1956–1967). Honors and memberships: USDA, Superior Service Award (1951); American Horticultural Council, Gold Certificate (1957); International Society of Color Council, Godlove Award (1961); Illumination Society of England, gold medal (1970).

Nothing has been found on Dorothy Nickerson's early life or education. She spent her career working in color science. She conducted research on color measurement related to grade standards for agricultural products, colorimetry, color tolerances, and small color-differences specification, color spacing, automatic cotton colorimeter, color rendering properties of light souces, and color-fan chart for horticulture. She was a member of the American Association for the Advancement of Science, the Optical Society of America, and the International Society of Color Council (secretary, 1938–1952; president, 1954). She published a number of works listed in the National Union Catalog of Pre-1956 Imprints under U.S. Agricultural Marketing Service.   JH/MBO

PRIMARY SOURCES

Nickerson, Dorothy. *A Method for Determining the Color of Agricultural Products.* Washington, D.C.: U.S. Government Printing Office, 1929.

———. *Color Measurement and Its Application to the Grading of Agricultural Products: A Handbook on the Method of Disk Colorimetry.* Washington, D.C.: U.S. Government Printing Office, 1946.

STANDARD SOURCES

AMS 5–8, P 9, P&B 10–14.

NICKERSON, MARGARET (LEWIS) (1870–?)

U.S. histologist and embryologist. Born 8 December 1870 in Akron, N.Y. Married. Educated Smith College (A.B., 1893); Radcliffe College (A.M., 1897); University of Minnesota (M.D., 1904). Professional experience: University of Minnesota, instructor in histology and embryology (1898–1906); Public Schools, Minneapolis, physician (from 1912). Death date unknown.

Margaret Nickerson may have had a short career as a research scientist. After she earned her doctor of medicine degree she began a private practice in medicine. Sources do not indicate how long she continued practicing, but we do know that she was married and is not included in *American Men of Science* past the fifth edition.   JH/MBO

STANDARD SOURCES

AMS 1–5.

NICOSIA, MARIA LUISA (1922–1977)

Italian geologist. Born 9 April 1922 in Messina. Educated University of Rome. Professional experience: Servizio Geologico (Geological Service) (1956–1977?). Died 1 September 1977.

After graduating from the University of Rome in the geological sciences, Maria Luisa Nicosia began working with the Servizio Geologico. At some point in her career she evidently completed a doctorate. She first worked as a volunteer and in 1956 secured the position which she made into her career. Her first major project with the service was a paleontological survey of Isole Egadi on Mount Peloritani in 1956–1957. Her next major task (1957–1970) was to produce geological maps of Italy. She continued her survey work by reviewing the paleozoic fauna (trilobites) around Sardegna. Because of her years doing survey work, Nicosia collaborated with a museum of geological sciences (in Rome?). Her collaboration with the museum was invaluable.

Nicosia participated in many national and international meetings, conventions, and congresses. In 1970 she became a member of the Associazione Geo-archeologica Italiana.

JH/MBO

PRIMARY SOURCES

Nicosia, Maria Luisa. *Bibliografia del paleozoico italiano.* Rome: Olimpica, [1971].

Desio, Ardito. With many others. *Geologia dell'Italia.* Turin: Unione tipografico-editrice torinese, [1973]. Nicosia contributed to this volume.

SECONDARY SOURCES

Zanfrà, Silvana. "Maria Luisa Nicosia (1922–1977)." *Servizio Geologico Bollettino* 98 (1978): 196–197.

NIEH CHUNG-EN (1907–   )

Chinese physician. Born 2 August 1907 in Anking, Anhwei Province, China, to a Christian family. Six siblings. Married Chang Hsien-lin (1936). Two sons. Educated primary school; St. Hilda's Girls' School, Wuchang (1917–1922); St. Mary's Shanghai (1922–1923?); missionary high school in Changsha (1923); Ginling Women's College, Nanjing (1927–?); Peking Union Medical College (PUMC) (graduated 1936); Brown Medical Center, Houston, Tex., for training and then New York. Professional experience: Babies' Hospital Columbia Medical Center; Shanghai Children's Hospital in the French Concession, physician (1937); Kweiyang, lecturer on infectious diseases to army officers in the Medical Training School (to 1944); Chungking (1944–1945); National Defense Medical College, Taipei, associate professor (from 1949).

Nieh Chung-en got her medical training in spite of the turmoil in China. Born on the Chinese mainland to an Episcopalian family, she decided when she was sixteen years old that she wanted to study medicine. She transferred to the missionary high school in Changsha, which offered more science courses, but both Communist political activity and the death of her mother at the age of forty-two and at the end of her twelfth pregnancy made it necessary for Nieh to return home. She stayed at home to care for her younger siblings. Her father remarried, freeing Nieh to enter Ginling Women's College at Nanjing for premedical training. Nieh was an excellent pianist, and her teacher tried to get her to stay at Ginling and teach music.

Peking Union Medical School, a Rockefeller Institution, was the premier medical school in China. It had very rigorous entrance standards, but Nieh was accepted. There she met her future husband, Dr. Chang Hsien-lin, a fourth-year assistant resident in surgery. The couple married in Shanghai in 1936, after Hsien-Lin graduated from medical school, and the couple took a luxury liner for San Francisco. Hsien-lin was awarded a scholarship at Columbia Medical Center, and Nieh worked at Babies' Hospital. She became pregnant and son Raymond was born in 1937.

While Hsien-lin remained in the United States, Nieh and baby Raymond returned to Shanghai. War with the Japanese had broken out and she worked in the Shanghai Children's Hospital. Hsien-lin returned and was promoted to assistant professor at PUMC, but he took over the Red Cross Medical Corps, going first to Hankow and then to Changsha, while Nieh and the baby remained in Shanghai. As the war became more serious, they went to the interior—first to Kweilin and then to Kweiyang, the headquarters of the Chinese Red Cross Medical Corps. It was very cold and food was scarce. Nieh gave lectures on infectious diseases to army officers in the Medical Training School. When Raymond was three years old, Nieh became pregnant, but at Hsien-lin's insistence had an abortion. She later had another child, Norman, born in July 1943. Undergoing great hardships during the last days of the war, they stayed in Chungking, where they had fled from the Japanese.

After V-J Day, Nieh left the boys with their father and went to the United States for further training. Hsien-lin and the boys came later.

Returning to Taipei, Nieh taught pediatrics in the National Defense Medical College. In 1951, when her son was sixteen, she sent him back to the United States to school, but remained in Taiwan herself, where she continued to practice medicine.

Nieh Chung-en was active in the Medical Women's International Association and founded the Taiwan Medical Women's Association and was elected its first president.   KM

PRIMARY SOURCES

Nieh Chung-en. In Hellstedt, *Autobiographies.*

NIGHTINGALE, DOROTHY VIRGINIA
(1902–)

U.S. chemist. Born 21 February 1902 in Fort Collins, Colo., to Jennie (Beem) and William David Nightingale. Educated University of Missouri (A.B., 1922; A.M., 1923); University of Chicago (Ph.D. 1928). Professional experience: University of Missouri, instructor (1923–1939), assistant professor (1939–1948), associate professor (1948–1958), professor (1958–1972), emerita professor (from 1972); Office of Scientific Research and Development, researcher (1942–1945). Honors and memberships: Committee on Medical Research (1943–1945); American Chemical Society, Garvan Medal; American Chemical Society, vice-president and treasurer for the Missouri section; Phi Beta Kappa, local chapter vice-president; Sigma Delta Epsilon, local chapter president).

Dorothy Nightingale was born and had her early education in Colorado. However, when she was seventeen years old, her family moved to Columbia, Missouri. While at the University of Missouri, she planned to major in foreign languages and history (where she held a job as a grader in the German department), and intended to take only one course in chemistry. Encouraged by her professor, Herman Schlundt, she first wanted to teach high school chemistry. Schlundt, an outstanding teacher, suggested that she attend graduate school and then teach at the college level. One year after receiving her bachelor's degree, she earned a master's degree at the University of Missouri. Her thesis was on the determination of the spectra of organomagnesium halides and other luminescent compounds. After she received this degree, Nightingale remained at the University of Missouri as an instructor, the second woman to hold that position. She attended the University of Chicago as a university fellow, and completed her doctoral degree under the supervision of Julius Stieglitz. Her doctoral thesis was "Studies in the Merexide and Alloxantine Series."

After a year as an honors fellow at the University of Minnesota (1938), Nightingale was advanced to assistant professor. During World War II, she performed antimalarial research for the Office of Scientific Research and Development on the Committee on Medical Research. After the war, in 1946, she was a research associate at the University of California, Los Angeles. She was promoted to associate professor in 1948 and in 1958 became a full professor. She received the Garvan Medal of the American Chemical Society for distinguished service to chemistry in 1959. Before she retired, she was director of graduate studies at the University of Missouri. Nightingale did research on the lack of opportunity for women chemists. Her own career was an excellent case study, for it took her thirty years rather than the usual ten to fifteen to become a full professor.

Nightingale was apparently an excellent teacher and advisor. Twenty-three of her students earned doctoral degrees and twenty-seven earned master's degrees. She encouraged her students to publish.

Her research was in the field of synthetic organic chemistry. In her early work, she studied the chemiluminescence of organomagnesium halides, resulting from light emissions given off from a chemical reaction. She worked with Friedel-Crafts reaction. There are two main types of these reactions, alkylation and acylation of aromatic hydrocarbons catalyzed by anhydrous aluminum chloride. Alkylation is the introduction of alkyl groups into aromatic hydrocarbons. This process had industrial significance in the production of such items as high-octane gasoline, cumene (a solvent used to produce phenol and acetone), and ethylbenzene (a solvent used to produce styrene). Other useful results include making better cleaning detergents, synthetic rubber, and plastics and elastomeres. In her research she noted that a variety of reactions can occur to the alkylbenzene or the alkyl radical.

Nightingale was interested in wildflower photography, mountain climbing, and traveling. After she retired in 1972, she moved back to Boulder, Colorado. JH/MBO

PRIMARY SOURCES

Nightingale, Dorothy Virginia. With R. T. Dufford and S. Calvert. "Luminescence of Organomagnesium Halides." *Journal of the American Chemical Society* 45 (1923): 1058–1072.

———. "Alkylation and the Action of Aluminum Halides on Alkylbenzenes." *Chemical Reviews* 25 (1939): 329–376.

———. "Anomalous Nitration Reactions." *Chemical Reviews* 40 (1947): 117–140.

———. With O. L. Wright and H. B. Hucker. "The Anomalous Acylation of Some Monoalkylbenzenes." *Journal of Organic Chemistry* 18 (1959): 244–248.

STANDARD SOURCES

American Women; AMS 5–8, P 9, P&B 10–14; Bailey; Grinstein 1993 (article by Adriane P. Borgias); Shearer and Shearer 1996 (article by Jill Holman).

NIGHTINGALE, FLORENCE (1820–1910)

British nursing pioneer. Born 12 May 1820 in Florence, Italy, to Frances (Smith) and William Edward Nightingale. One sister. Never married. Educated privately at home by father and governess; Kaiserworth Institute of Protestant Deaconessess, Germany, course in nursing (1851). Professional experience: Harley Street Nursing Home for Sick Gentlewomen in Distressed Circumstances, superintendent of nursing (1853); Middlesex Hospital, nursing (early 1854); nursing establishment of English Hospitals (Turkey and Crimea), superintendent of nursing (1854–1856); studies on British military hospitals (1857–1870s); St. Thomas Hospital, Nightingale Training School for Nurses, London, founder and patron (1860–1881); Royal Commission on the Health of the Army in India, organizer (1859–1865); advisor on hospital organization, construction, and hygiene (1865–1905). Honors and memberships: Queen Victoria's Crimean brooch (1854); City of London, Order of Merit (1907); Keys to the City of London (1908). Died 13 August 1910 in Emberly Park, Hampshire.

Florence Nightingale has become a legend around which has formed the image of the nurse as humane, hygienic, and caring, as well as properly deferential to doctors and supervisors. She was born in Florence and named after that city by her parents who loved Italy, just as her sister was earlier named Frances Parthenope after the ancient name of Naples. Her father had inherited a fortune while young, but he was of broad education; her mother was the daughter of a famous abolitionist and financier, William Smith, who had another illegitimate family that included Barbara Smith (later Bodichon).

Nightingale was educated by her father in ancient and modern languages and she was interested enough in mathematics to ask for further tutoring in mathematics. She found it difficult to expand her life outside the usual life of a Victorian woman, in spite of the fact that her mother had an active social life that placed her in contact with both men and women of power. Her mother also wrote novels on the side and Florence's sister was a fine social observer and commentator on the French village. In her early years, Nightingle saw herself as a rebel against Victorian restrictions and the domestic sphere. She wrote a piece, "Cassandra," that recently has been widely cited as a feminist tract because of its depiction of the inability of women to control their own time.

She decided to obtain training in nursing, and visited many hospitals throughout Europe, unhappy at the state of hygiene and the low level of nursing standards, but excited by the republican revolutions occurring in Italy and France. On returning home, however, she again found the restrictions of her domestic life almost unbearable and began to expand her *Suggestions for Thought*. In the early 1850s, she finally settled on a training course for four months at the Kaiserworth Institute of Protestant Deaconessess, near the Rhine. Upon returning home, Nightingale obtained a position as a supervisor at a Harley Street nursing home for sick gentlewomen "in distress." She took the opportunity to completely revise the organization of the nursing home with excellent effect.

The Crimean War broke out in 1853, and Great Britain joined its allies in 1854 against the Russian armies moving into Moldavia, then part of the Ottoman Empire. A friend of Nightingale, Sidney Herbert, held an important position in the Ministry of War. He wrote to her to ask for her help in the improvement of military hospitals for the wounded in the Crimea at the same time that she was organizing nurses for the same purpose. She left for the Crimea with much

public acclaim. She also obtained the offices of a cook who had been trained in France who was capable of making the army rations palatable for large groups of men, and who proved his ability to create baking ovens and large regimental-sized teapots. The work of her nurses focused on making the injured soldier's life more hygienic, more physically endurable, and also more humane by listening to them, and helping them write letters home. Her system was followed closely by DOROTHEA DIX some years later in the Civil War hospitals. But Florence Nightingale's own work was also extensively administrative, as she dealt with the organization and issuing of supplies, kept track of the voluntary contributions from England, wrote letters about the sick and dying, and communicated with Sidney Herbert about conditions. It was this for which Nightingale had a genius. She would eventually direct some 125 nurses in a variety of hospitals from the Crimea to Turkey.

Although she fell seriously ill more than once, Nightingale remained key to the running of the hospital service during the war and returned to England to international acclaim. From this point on, she never served again as nurse or supervisor of nurses but played a seminal and extremely important role in creating training schools for nurses, advising the government on the building, organizing, and staffing of the army hospitals in England and India, and writing major papers on lying-in hospitals. She continued to work very closely with Sidney Herbert until his death from kidney disease in 1860. He regretted that he was not going to live to see some of their hoped-for reforms take place, and felt he had let Nightingale down.

From her return to England until her death, Nightingale conducted all her business from her sickbed. She rarely saw her visitors, even her cousin Henry Bonham Carter, who acted as her secretary. But she was prodigious in her correspondence and in her ability to stay on top of governmental decisions.

One of her first actions was to establish a school of nursing at St. Thomas Hospital in London. This was paid for by a fund raised on her behalf, and the training school consequently bore her name when it was opened in 1860. There has been some discussion in recent years as to whether she was blocking the request by ELIZABETH GARRETT ANDERSON, one of the early women pioneer physicians, to establish this school at King's Hospital instead. Nightingale reviewed all the applications for nurses for twenty years, until her increasing illness prevented this. The Nightingale model became the standard by which most nurse training was developed, although critics have pointed out that she never described special nursing, such as that for young children or the insane.

Florence Nightingale began to get requests from all over the world to suggest new designs for hospitals and nurse training. In the United States, the nursing profession still sees itself as deriving from her stipulations. Curiously, she was not always supportive of some innovations. When antisepsis instead of asepsis was introduced into hospital hygiene, Nightingle opposed it for fear that carbolic acid and other antiseptics would make nurses less careful in their cleaning. She also objected in her later life to the British Nursing Association because of its demands for certification, something that she did not regard as necessary, and acted indirectly to block its recognition.

She was honored throughout her life with many awards. Queen Victoria had awarded her a Crimean brooch for her work during the war and welcomed her at Balmoral on her return. King Edward VII awarded her the Order of Merit when she was eighty-seven, a decoration never before awarded to a woman. She died in her ninetieth year, and her family at her request refused the offer for burial in Westminster Abbey. Instead she is buried in the Hampshire family plot with only her initials and birth and death dates on the stone.   JH/MBO

PRIMARY SOURCES

Nightingale, Florence. *Cassandra and Other Selections from Suggestions on Thought.* Ed. Mary Poovey. NYU Women's Classics. New York: New York University Press, 1992. This work had been written much earlier but was privately printed in 1860.

———. *Notes on Matters Affecting the Health, Efficiency and Hospital Administration of the British Army.* London: Harrison and Sons, 1858.

———. *Notes on Nursing: What It Is and What It Is Not.* London: Harrison, [1859].

———. *Observations on the Evidence Contained in the Stational Reports Submitted to Her by the Royal Commission on the Sanitary State of the Army in India.* London: E. Stanford, 1863.

———. *Introductory Notes on Lying-In Institutions: Together with a Proposal for Organizing an Institution for Training Midwives and Midwifery Nurses.* London: Longmans, Green, & Co., 1871.

———. *A Calendar of the Letters of Florence Nightingale.* Ed. Sue Goldie and W. J. Bishop. Oxford: Oxford Microform Publications for the Wellcome Institute for the History of Medicine, 1983. Includes summaries of all the known letters and a listing of libraries that hold them.

SECONDARY SOURCES

Herbert, Raymond G. *Florence Nightingale: Saint, Reformer or Rebel?* Malabar, Fla.: Robert E. Kreiger Publishing Company, 1981. Incorporates essays written from 1855 to 1932 on Nightingale including that of Lytton Strachey, with some excerpts from Nightingale's own writings.

Hobbs, Colleen A. *Florence Nightingale.* New York and London: Twayne Publishers, Simon and Schuster and Prentice Hall

International, 1997. Takes a feminist approach to her early writings.

Smith, F. B. *Florence Nightingale: Reputation and Power.* New York: St. Martin's Press, 1982. Reevaluates her influence on modern nursing, and analyzes her manipulation of political power.

STANDARD SOURCES
DNB; Europa; Uglow 1988.

NIHELL, ELIZABETH (1723–post-1772)
British midwife. Born 1723 in London. Married Edward Nihell. At least one child. Educated Hôtel Dieu in Paris (late 1740s). Professional experience: practiced midwifery near the Haymarket in London until at least 1772.

After working diligently to be accepted at the great school for midwives, the Hôtel Dieu in Paris, Elizabeth Nihell studied midwifery under Marie-Claude Pour for two years. We know that she was back in London by 1754 where she lived with her surgeon husband near the Haymarket. During this time male midwives were usurping the traditional position of women. In *A Treatise on the Art of Midwifery* (1760), Nihell deplored the situation, insisting that the men unnecessarily resorted to metal instruments when they were not needed, causing needless infant deaths. She also complained that male midwives charged higher fees than women. While criticizing William Smellie for teaching midwifery to surgeons using a leather model, she also claimed that it was unethical to force poor women in charitable institutions to give birth in the presence of male medical students. A former student of Smellie's, Tobias Smollett, wrote an essay in the *Critical Review* (1760) ridiculing her arguments, yet implying that her husband must have written her book. An updated version of her book was translated into French and published in 1771. We know that Nihell was still alive and practicing in 1772, for her name appears on a list of London midwives published that year.   JH/MBO

PRIMARY SOURCES
Nihell, Elizabeth. *A Treatise on the Art of Midwifery.* London: A. Morley, 1760.

———. *An Answer to the Author of the Critical Review, for March 1760. Upon the Article of Mrs. Nihell's Treatise on the Art of Midwifery.* London: A. Morley, 1760.

SECONDARY SOURCES
Aveling, J. H. *English Midwives: Their History and Prospects.* London: Churchill, 1872.

Donnison, Jean. *Midwives and Medical Men.* New York: Schocken, 1977.

Klukoff, "Smollett's Defence of Dr. Smellie in *The Critical Review.*" *Medical History* 1970, xiv.

London Evening Post, 21–23 February 1754.

[Nihell, Edward?]. *The Danger and Immodesty of the Present too General Custom of Unnecessarily Employing Men-Midwives.* 2d. ed. London: J. Wilkie, 1772.

STANDARD SOURCES
DNB Missing Persons.

NODDACK, IDA EVA TACKE (1896–1978)

German chemist. Born 25 February 1896, Lackhausen bei Wesel, then part of Rhenish Prussia, on the shores of the Rhine River. Married Walter Noddack. Educated Technical University of Berlin; University of Berlin, Charlottenberg (doctorate in engineering, 1921). Professional experience: Physico-Technical Research Agency in Berlin, researcher (1921?-1935); University of Freiburg, researcher (1935–1943); University of Strasbourg, researcher (1943–1956); State Research Institute for Geochemistry, Bamberg, researcher (1956–1968). Honors and memberships: Spanish Society of Physics and Chemistry, honorary member; International Society of Nutrition Research, honorary member; honorary doctorate of science, University of Hamburg; High Service Cross, German Federal Republic (1966). Died 24 November 1978 in Bad Neuenahr.

Born in Germany, Ida Tacke earned a doctor of engineering degree from the University of Berlin, Charlottenburg. She and the German chemist Walter Noddack were codiscoverers in 1925 of the elements rhenium and masurium. Tacke and Noddack married in 1926. Walter Noddack became director of the chemistry laboratory of the PTR under Rudolf Nernst in 1922, director of the new Photochemistry Laboratory in Berlin (1927), chair of the department of physical chemistry at the University of Freiburg (1935), and director of both the physical chemistry department and the Research Institute for Photochemistry at the University of Strasbourg. After the war, he worked at the Philosophische-Theologische Hochschule in Bamberg and from 1956 to 1960 he was director of new research institute for geochemistry in Bamberg. The couple worked together until Walter's death in 1960.

In 1934 Ida Noddack expressed scepticism at Enrico Fermi's transuranic elements, pointing out that the products of neutron bombardment of uranium had not been tested for elements below lead in the periodic table. The notion of uranium breaking into elements of approximately equal size conflicted with contemporary understanding of nuclear physics, and Noddack's suggestion was dismissed. When Otto Hahn and Fritz Strassmann announced the discovery of nuclear fission in 1938, Noddack objected that they had not cited her 1934 remark, published as "Über das Element 93." Noddack was the loser in the resulting brief priority dispute.

According to Irving, she herself did not pursue her idea, and the world of physics ignored it. As a physicist, Enrico Fermi saw little point in making comparisons with elements below lead, for he worked under the assumption of chipping off fragments under bombardment.

Noddack, on the other hand, was convinced that it was necessary to compare the chemistry with the chemistry of all known elements because it would be conceivable that the nucleus could break into several large fragments. She was ahead of her time, however. The liquid drop model had not yet been devised, and thus there was no way to calculate whether breaking up into large fragments was energetically allowed. Her suggestion was chemically sound, but she was up against the establishment. Perhaps if she had had the courage of her convictions, she would have performed the Hahn and Strassmann chemistry five years before they did.

After they discovered rhenium, the Noddacks were regarded as the leading authorities on the chemistry of the rare earths. In 1934 they received a red salt from a Czech chemist, Koblic, and showed that his assumption of a transuranic element was incorrect. Likewise, Noddack asserted that Fermi had not submitted convincing chemical evidence. Fermi, however, did not take this criticism seriously, for a neutron exhibited a force less than one volt, yet the nucleus could withstand millions of volts. He was all the more convinced when Hahn agreed with him. Noddack reported that she had just as strong doubts about Hahn's and Strassmann's identification of the separate transuranics. Both Noddacks had known Hahn well for decades, and he often inquired about the progress of their work. Walter Noddack suggested in 1935 or 1936 that Hahn refer to Ida Noddack's suggestion. Hahn replied that he did not want to make her look ridiculous, for her assumption was "absurd."

Fermi's group may have been distracted from clear thinking and scientific self-criticism during the Italy-Abyssinia conflict. This excuse did not work for the other physicist who ignored Ida Noddack's work. Fritz Krafft agreed with Fermi that Noddack's assumption of disintegration was nothing but a chance hit, and fission does not produce a number of approximately equal fragments. Hahn and Meitner were very critical and unbelieving of all statements of the Noddacks for the results for "masurium" were not reproducible. They also claimed to have broken the X-ray proof on the trip. The result of the skepticism was that the name of Ida Noddack became taboo at the Berlin Institute. They were also skeptical of the research of Gottfried von Drostes, who calculated the Po (as alpha emitter), also discussed by Ida Noddack, as a folgeprodukte (resulting product) of radiated uranium.

Politics also entered into the mix. The Noddacks were positive about National Socialism and this also played a role in Hahn's and Strassmann's evaluation of their science. Hahn explained that Noddack did not have many friends within their group, but apparently had some in others. Karl von Frisch, for example, thought the criticism of the Noddacks was pointless, since no reason was given for why the criticism was valid.

The Noddacks were awarded the Liebig medal from the Geochemical Institute of Bamberg. In their notable discovery of the element rhenium (named after the river Rhine), they used X-ray spectroscopy. They were assisted by Otto Berg. They expected a new element from examination of empty spaces in the periodic table, predicted its properties, then searched for it, first in platinum ores, then in sulfide ores and columbite. They mistakenly thought they also found element 43, naming it masurium. Element 43, named technetium by its discoverers (E. Fermi and C. Perrier), was found to be produced only artificially.   MM

PRIMARY SOURCES
Tacke, Ida. With Walter Noddack and Otto Berg. "Die Eka-mangane: Chemischen Teil." *Naturwissenschaften* 13 (1925): 567.
———. "Eka- and Divi Manganese: Chemical Part." *Chemical News* 131 (7 August 1925): 84–87.
———. "Zur Auffindung der Ekamangane." *Zeitschrift für angewandte Chemie* 38 (1925): 794, 1157–1160.
Noddack, Ida Tacke. With Walter Noddack. "Über den Nachweis der Ekamangane." *Zeitschrift für angewandte Chemie* 40 (1927): 250–254.
———. With Walter Noddack. "Die Sauerstoffverbindungen des Rheniums." *Zeitschrift für anorganischee Chemie* 181 (1929): 1–37.
———. With Walter Noddack. *Das Rhenium.* Leipzig: Leopold Voss, 1933.
———. "Das Periodische System der Elemente und seine Lücken." *Zeitschrift für angewandte Chemie* 47 (1934): 301–305.
———. "Über das Elemente 93." *Zeitschrift für angewandte Chemie* 47 (1934): 653 ff.
———. "Bemerkung zu den Untersuchungen von O. Hahn, L. Meitner und F. Strassmann über die Produkte, die bei der Bestrahlung von Uran mit Neutronen entstehen." *Die Naturwissenschaften* 27 (1939): 212 ff.

SECONDARY SOURCES
Archives for the History of Quantum Physics, College Park, Maryland. Interviews of Georg von Hevesy, Lise Meitner, Hevesy, 25 May 1962. Discusses the controversy between Noddack and other physicists about the existence of weak X-ray lines from Manganeses' homologue, #43.

Bunte, E. H. *Die atomare Herausforderung.* Munich: Markus, 1968. See pages 56–60, Ida Noddack's Vorhersage.
Center for the History of Physics, College Park, Maryland. Interviews of Aristid von Grosse.
Graetzer, H. G. and D. L. Anderson. *The Discovery of Atomic Fission, A Documentary History.* New York: Van Nostrand Reinhold, 1971. See pages 15ff.
Habashi, Fathi. "Ida Noddack, 75 and Element 75." In *Element Profiles.* Washington, D.C.: American Chemical Society, 1972. Collection of articles selected from those appearing in *Chemistry* during 1964–1972.
Irving, David. *The Virus House.* London: William Kimber and Co., 1967. See page 18.
Krafft, Fritz. *Im Schatten der Sensation. Leben und Wirken von Fritz Strassmann.* Weinheim, Deerfield Beach, Fla., and Basel: Verlag Chemie, 1981. See pages 10, 49f, 54, 96, 125, 209f, 305, 314–322, 458f, 476, 528, 530, 532.
Libby, Leona Marshall. *The Uranium People.* New York: Crane, Russak & Company, Charles Scribner's Sons, 1979. See pages 43–44, 46.
Rhodes, Richard. *The Making of the Atomic Bomb.* New York: Simon & Schuster, 1986. See pages 230–232.
Sciascia, Leonardo. *The Moro Affair; and, the Mystery of Majorana.* New York: Carcanet, 1987.
Segre, Emilio. *From X-Rays to Quarks: Modern Physicists and Their Discoveries.* San Francisco: W. H. Freeman, 1980. See page 207.
———. *Enrico Fermi, Physicist.* Chicago & London: University of Chicago Press, 1970. See page 76.
Starke, Kurt. "The Detours Leading to the Discovery of Nuclear Fission." *Journal of Chemical Education* (December 1979): 771–775.
Weeks, Mary Elvira. *Discovery of the Elements.* Easton, Pa.: Journal of Chemical Education, 1956.

STANDARD SOURCES
Kass-Simon and Farnes; *Notable.*

NOEL, EMILIA FRANCES (d. 1950)

British botanist. Probably born in Rutland. Father Honorable Henry Lewis Noel. At least three siblings. Educated Somerville College, Oxford; Swanley Horticultural College. Professional experience: collected and described plants on her many foreign travels. Died 19 March 1950.

Emilia Noel's family homes were in Rutland and Lincolnshire. She was the youngest child and the third daughter of the Honorable Henry Lewis Noel, whose father was the first earl of Gainsborough. He was the first cousin of the third earl of Gainsborough, who was an amateur botanist and who collaborated with A. R. Horwood in writing the *Flora of Rutland and Northamptonshire.*

Emilia Noel attended Somerville College, Oxford, and then went to the Swanley Horticultural College as an advanced student living in private rooms. At Swanley, Noel received prizes for the best diary of garden work and the best notebook of advanced botany. Before her college career was completed, she began her travels by going to Egypt (1892). After she finished college, she went to India (including Kashmir) and in about 1938 visited the Canaries and West Africa. In between these trips she traveled throughout Europe and to North Africa. She also went to the Middle East and ventured even farther to the United States, South Africa, Ceylon, Australia, New Zealand, Java, and Lombok. She kept elaborate diaries of the plants that she encountered in all of these places.

During World War I, Noel registered for Women's War Service and during and between the two wars she traveled extensively in England. Her field diary begun in 1919 includes names of many British plants.

Noel's extensive diaries complete with sketches are in the Royal Geographical Society. She also made numerous gifts to libraries and museums. In 1905 she published a book with a list of plants found in Kashmir and some notes on the country. Later she published a volume of historical letters and sketches belonging to her family, many dating from the eighteenth century. JH/MBO

PRIMARY SOURCES
Noel, Emilia Frances. *Some Wild Flowers of Kashmir.* Nottingham, England: J. & H. Bell, 1903.
———. *Some Letters and Records of the Noel Family.* London: St. Catherine Press, Ltd., 1910.
Noel's Kashmir plants are at Liverpool University and her drawings are at the Linnean Society.

SECONDARY SOURCES
Whiting, M. Muriel. Obituary notice. *Proceedings of the Linnean Society* 162 (1949–1950): 232.

STANDARD SOURCES
Desmond.

NOETHER, AMALIE EMMY (1882–1935)

German mathematician. Born 23 March 1882 in Erlangen, Germany, to Ida (Kaufmann) and Max Noether. Three brothers. Never married. Educated University of Erlangen (1900–1902; 1904–1907; Ph.D., 1907); University of Göttingen (1903–1904). Professional experience: University of Erlangen, unpaid instructor (1908–1915), unpaid lecturer (1915–1922); University of Göttingen, unofficial associate professor (1922–1933); Bryn Mawr College, visiting professor (1933–1935); Institute for Advanced Study, Princeton, N.J., lecturer (1933–1935). Died 14 April 1935 of complications following surgery in Bryn Mawr, Pa.

Emmy Noether was born into a distinguished German-Jewish family of scientists: her father was a research mathematician at the University of Erlangen, one of her three brothers became a physicist and another a mathematician. Her mother was a talented musician. As a child, Emily attended the Städtischen Höheren Tochterschule in Erlangen, took piano lessons, and enjoyed dancing. After passing her examinations, she considered teaching French and English at female educational institutions, but decided instead to study mathematics at the University of Erlangen. Noether and one other woman had to content themselves with attending lectures as auditors only, for women were prohibited at this time from matriculating at the University of Erlangen. In 1898, two years before Noether sought to enter, the academic senate had reaffirmed its policy, declaring that the admission of female students would "overthrow all academic order." After two years at Erlangen, Noether registered at the University of Göttingen, again as a nonmatriculated student. She remained there only one semester, however, for during her absence Erlangen changed its policy and allowed women to matriculate and take examinations with the same privileges as men. At Erlangen (1904–1907), she studied under the algebraist Paul Gordan (1837–1912), a longtime friend of the family. In 1907 she received her doctorate, *summa cum laude,* for a dissertation on algebraic invariants.

It was virtually impossible for a German woman to obtain a paid position. From 1908 to 1915 Noether worked without compensation at the Mathematical Institute at Erlangen. The mathematician David Hilbert (1862–1943) invited Noether to Göttingen to lecture in 1915. Hilbert tried, unsuccessfully, to obtain a university appointment for her. In 1922, she was at last given the title of "unofficial associate professor" and a small salary. She remained at Göttingen until 1933. Twice during this time she held visiting professorships—at Moscow (1928–1929) and at Frankfurt (summer, 1930).

Along with other Jewish faculty members, Noether received, on 7 April 1933, a communication that read, "I hereby withdraw from you the right to teach at the University of Göttingen." Offered positions at both Somerville College, Oxford, and by Bryn Mawr College in the United States, Noether decided to accept Bryn Mawr's invitation, partly because of its tradition of eminent female mathematicians, including CHARLOTTE SCOTT and ANNA PELL WHEELER. Beginning in the autumn of 1933, Noether lectured and did research at both Bryn Mawr and the Institute for Advanced Study in Princeton, New Jersey. In April 1935 she underwent surgery for an ovarian cyst; complications developed, and she died four days after the operation.

The mathematician Hermann Weyl divided Noether's mathematical career into three epochs: relative dependency (1908–1919), investigations around the theory of ideals (1920–1926), and noncommunicative algebras (1927–1935). During the first epoch, the ideas of Paul Gordan and David Hilbert were the dominant influences on her thinking. In this period her most important achievement was the devising of mathematical formulas for several concepts found in Einstein's general theory of relativity; she was intrigued by the connections between invariant theory and Einstein's theory. Throughout World War I, Noether continued to work on differential invariants.

The second epoch in Noether's development as a mathematician involved investigations grouped around the general theory of ideals. During this time she was influenced by the work of Richard Dedeking (1831–1916). It was during this period that Noether's investigations profoundly changed the appearance of algebra. In a joint paper written with W. Schmeidler in 1920, "Modulin in nichtkommutativen Bereichen, insbesondere aus Differential-und Differenzenausdrücken" (*Mathematische Zeitschrift* 8:1–35), she presented her new approach.

In the third epoch, Noether was interested in noncommunicative algebras, especially as represented by linear transformations and as applied to commutative number fields. During this time she produced two major publications, "Hyperkomplexe Grössen und Darstellungstheorie" (1929) and "Nichtkommutative Algebra" (1933), both in the *Mathematische Zeitschrift* (30: 641–692 and 37: 514–541).

Emmy Noether's mathematics was both original and creative. Her work in abstract algebra, in which she concentrated on formal properties such as associativity, commutativity, and distributivity, has inspired so many successors that mathematicians speak of the "Noether school" of mathematics. JH/MBO

PRIMARY SOURCES
Noether, Emmy. *Gesammelte Abhandlungen*. Ed. N. Jacobson. Berlin: Springer, 1983. These collected papers contain all of Noether's published mathematical papers.

SECONDARY SOURCES
Brewer, James W., and Martha K. Smith, eds. *Emmy Noether: A Tribute to Her Life and Work*. New York: Marcel Dekker, 1981. A commemoration of Noether's 100th birthday.
Dick, August. *Emmy Noether, 1882–1935*. Trans. H. I. Blocher. Boston: Birkhauser, 1981.
"Emmy Noether in Bryn Mawr." *Proceedings of a Symposium Sponsored by the Association of Women in Mathematics in Honor of Emmy Noether's 100th Birthday*. Ed. Bhama Srinvasan and Judith D. Sally. With contributions by Armand Borel. New York: Springer, 1983.

Osen, Lynn M. *Women in Mathematics*. Cambridge, Mass.: MIT Press, 1975.
Perl, Teri. *Math Equals: Biographies of Women Mathematicians and Related Activities*. Menlo Park, Calif.: Addison-Wesley, 1978.

STANDARD SOURCES
DSB; Notable; Ogilvie 1986.

NOLTE, MARGARETHE (1895–1967)

German botanist and scientific editor. Born 1895 in Germany. Educated University of Berlin-Dahlen (Ph.D., 1952). Professional experience: Mufindi, Tanganyika (German East Africa), plantation manager (1934–1939); Excerpta Botanica, Section A, editor (1958–1967). Honors and memberships: International Botanical Congress. Died in Berlin 9 September 1967.

Margarethe Nolte became interested in botany in her forties while managing a plantation in Mufindi, Taganyika, then part of German East Africa. Upon her return to Germany, at the end of World War II, she began to work toward a doctorate in botany at the University of Berlin, completing a dissertation at the Botanical Museum under Professor R. Pilger when she was fifty-seven.

In the late 1950s, then over sixty years old, Nolte took on the editorship of the reference journal *Excerpta Botanica, Section A*, which surveyed and abstracted botanical articles and reports from around the world on systematics. She described her reference work at the International Botanical Congress in Edinburgh in 1964. Displaying a great deal of energy and a gift for organization, Nolte continued her work until illness forced her to resign her position at the age of seventy-two. She died six months later in Berlin. JH/MBO

PRIMARY SOURCES
Nolte, Margarethe. "Rhizomzerfall mit vegetativer Verhmehrung bei Rumex." Ph.D. diss., University of Berlin, Dahlen, 1952.

SECONDARY SOURCES
Melchior, H. "Margarethe Nolte, 1895–1967." *Taxon* 16 (1967): 572.

NORSWORTHY, NAOMI (1877–1916)

U.S. psychologist. Born 29 September 1877 in New York City. Educated Trenton State Normal School (diploma 1896); Columbia University (B.S., 1901; Ph.D., 1904). Professional experience: public schools, teacher (1896–1899); Columbia University Teachers College, assistant in psychology (1901–1902), tutor (1902–1904), instructor (1904–1909), adjunct professor (1909–1916). Honors and memberships: American Psychological Association; Society for Sanitation and Moral Prophylaxis. Died 1916.

Naomi Norsworthy is considered to be the first woman faculty member at Columbia University Teachers College, where she earned both a bachelor's and a doctoral degree. After she completed her doctorate, she became an instructor but was promoted to adjunct professor in 1909. It is unclear what is meant by this promotion, since there are no intermediate steps on the academic ladder noted, and the professorship she held was an adjunct position.

Norsworthy's research was on the effect of special training in school on the general abilities of children. She was especially interested in studies of the "feebleminded."   KM

PRIMARY SOURCES

Norsworthy, Naomi. *How to Teach*. New York: Teachers College, Columbia University, 1917.

————. *The Psychology of Childhood*. New York: Teachers College, Columbia University, 1918.

STANDARD SOURCES

AMS 1–2; Bailey; *DAB;* Siegel and Finley; Rossiter 1982.

NORTH, MARIANNE (1830–1890)

British botanical artist and botanist. Born 1830 at Hastings Lodge, Hastings, Sussex, to Mrs. North (previous married name, Shuttleworth) and Frederick North. Three siblings (Charley and Catherine; half-sister Janet). Never married. Educated at home by governesses and through European travels as a young woman, with eighteen months at a girls' boarding school in Norwich, Norfolk, and some professional singing and painting lessons. Died 30 August 1890 of liver disease at Alderley, Gloucestershire.

The most important person in Marianne North's life was her father. North was irritated by her mother's lack of education and her weak health. Her mother was annoyed by Marianne's energetic spirit and adventurous nature and told her that her singing and painting were a waste of time. In later life, North would write scathingly of her mother's life to a close friend; in her *Recollections*, she simply noted: ". . . my mother died. . . . She did not suffer, but enjoyed nothing, and her life was a dreary one" (*Recollections*, 29–30). Her father, in contrast, was her "one idol and friend of my life, and apart from him I had little pleasure and no secrets" (*Recollections*, 5). Her earliest memories were of her father, traveling and walking with him and later learning from him. She was educated, ostensibly, by governesses, and was devastated when her father sent her to a girls' boarding school for a term in an attempt to curb her spirit. He relented by traveling on horseback to visit her whenever he could and soon

withdrew her from the school. North did not have a close relationship with her siblings. Her elder half-sister, Janet, later to marry the famous Dr. Kay, was significantly older than North. Her younger brother was sent away to school and later married. Her younger sister, Catherine, later to marry John Addington Symonds, spent much time with North, but never on the best of terms. Catherine could not understand her penchant for wandering the globe and not settling down. North, on the other hand, took Catherine's ill-fated marriage as a warning sign of the pitfalls of marriage and avoided it for herself.

Her interest in botany began after her mother's death, when her father decided to build a greenhouse. North began nurturing plants there and began to learn the rudiments of botany. She had noted an earlier interest in botany in her enjoyment of a Mrs. Hussey's volumes on British fungi. Now she was learning more, both from her own experience and from books. Her botanical artistry did not truly begin until after the death of her father in 1869. She was devastated by his death and felt isolated and deserted. However, she was unwilling to accept the company of friends or family and set off to Mentone in the company of a maidservant. After spending several months there, she decided to visit women artist friends in Rome. She enjoyed her visit with these women immensely. From the age of thirty-nine, she decided to travel, to paint, and to live for herself.

Marianne North's travels were extensive, both in terms of the number of places she visited and in terms of their long duration. Although she kept an apartment in Victoria Street, London, she was rarely there. Her travels took her to Canada and the United States in 1871 and down to Jamaica and Brazil in 1872–1873. By 1875, North was venturing to Japan, Hong Kong, Saigon, Cambodia, and, by 1876, to Singapore. During this trip, she stayed at Government House in Borneo with the Rajah and Rani of Sarawak and then moved on to Ceylon in 1877. Later that year, beginning a tour through India, she met the Indian scholar Dr. Arthur Coke Burnell (1840–1882), with whom she became close friends. The two worked together on a book of Hindu sacred plants; however, the manuscript was never published. The early 1880s brought a trip to Australia and New Zealand and a return to the United States. By 1882 she was off to Africa. Her last two trips were to the Seychelles in 1883 and to Chile in 1884. North sometimes found herself in fine surroundings, but more often than not she was in very rough accommodations that were usually more to her liking, as they were free of tiresome, high society ladies who rarely ventured beyond their verandas.

Marianne North's botanical art is unique within this art tradition. Using oils, instead of watercolors, painting out-of-doors under various and often extreme weather conditions, placing her flowers in a context of landscape and even wildlife on occasion, her paintings were to some degree interpretive as well as being, to some degree, imitations of life. North's flowers and plants were rooted, living entities, and not disconnected matter floating on a white background. Botanists at Kew Gardens, London, while scolding her for her artistic license, were nevertheless impressed. Not only could they almost always identify the species she had drawn, but North's oils also rendered the species' conditions for life—their natural environment—often previously unknown to botanists. As she observed and painted, year after year, country after country, North taught herself the intricacies of botany. She learned to identify specimens, to dissect them, and to preserve them. She sent many specimens to Kew Gardens for their collections, both living and dead, and contributed to the discovery of new species, including a pitcher plant, *Nepenthes northiana,* named for North.

On the occasions when she did return to London, North began to move not only in the artistic and literary circles to which her father had introduced her, but also in scientific circles. She became friends in her own right with the Hookers of Kew, the Owens, the Huxleys, Herbert Spencer, and even Alfred Russel Wallace and Charles Darwin. In fact, Darwin convinced her that she must travel to Australia and New Zealand so that the world might see that unique part of the globe through her eyes.

As the number of paintings she produced increased with her travels and as she was inundated at her home when in London with visitors who insisted on seeing her paintings, she opened a gallery for her work in Conduit Street in London. The *Pall Mall Gazette,* in its favorable review, suggested that a more permanent gallery of her work ought to be on display to the nation. Although her proposal for this idea was quickly accepted by Sir Joseph Hooker, then director at Kew, North faced frustrating negotations with Kew Gardens. She eventually got permission from the Board of Governors and from the British Government to build a gallery in the gardens. She paid for the building herself, and employed a favorite achitect, James Fergusson (1808–1886) to design a Greek-style gallery in which to display her work. She spent a great deal of time arranging, ordering, labeling, and helping to write a pamphlet for visitors to the gallery. North believed in the importance of her own work not only to the scientific community but also for educating the general public, whom, she felt, were sadly ignorant about the flora and fauna of the world. The gallery, which still stands at Kew, is a testament to her artistry and to her fortitude. Sir Joseph Hooker commented about North's work that she was recording for posterity landscapes that were often disappearing under the encroachment of "civilization." Although today it is easy to be critical of the lighting and display techniques of the nineteenth-century gallery, the paintings cannot fail to make an impact on curious visitors.

North was also intent on leaving a written record of her journeys. This writing, which she began in 1880, gave her much joy in recalling her lifetime of travels. (Unfortunately a publisher was not found for her *Recollections* until after her death. Her journals and her manuscripts were left in trust to her sister, Catherine, who eventually did find a publisher and allowed two volumes of North's travels to be published in an extremely edited format. Surprised by their success, she allowed a further volume to be published dealing more specifically with North's early years before the death of her father.)

Gradually, North's body began to feel the toll of constant work and travel. She suffered greatly from rheumatism, made worse by painting and living in damp and cold conditions. She slowly found herself becoming deaf, and she was plagued by constant buzzing noises in her head. On a couple of occasions, she had nervous breakdowns. Catherine tried incessantly to stop her sister from traveling, but even at the height of her complaints, North still insisted on planning more trips. Eventually North realized that she had no choice but to retire and she settled in Adderley House, West Gloucestershire, in 1886. While she had extensive plans to build impressive gardens, which were begun, her health finally gave out and she died at the age of fifty-nine. North is buried in the churchyard at Adderley.   SLS

PRIMARY SOURCES

North, Marianne. *Further Recollections of a Happy Life. Selected from the Journals of Marianne North Chiefly Between the Years 1859–1869.* New York: Macmillan and Co., 1892.

———. *Recollections of a Happy Life: Being the Autobiography of Marianne North.* 2 vols. New York: Macmillan and Co., 1893.

Paintings are in the North Gallery, Royal Botanial Gardens, Kew.

SECONDARY SOURCES

Brenan, J. P. M., Anthony Huxley, and Brenda E. Moon, eds. *A Vision of Eden: The Life and Work of Marianne North, 1830–1890.* New York: Holt, Rinehart and Winston, 1980.

Morgan, Susan. *Recollections of a Happy Life: Being the Autobiography of Marianne North.* Charlottesville: University Press of Virginia, 1993.

———. *Place Matters: Gendered Geography in Victorian Women's Travel Books about Southeast Asia.* London: Routledge & Kegan Paul, 1996.

Ponsonby, Laura. *Marianne North and Kew Gardens.* Exeter: Webb and Bower in association with the Royal Botanic Gardens, Kew, 1990.

———. "Marianne North." *The Kew Magazine* 7 (1990): 138–139.

STANDARD SOURCES

DNB.

NORTHRUP, ANN HERO (1875–?)

U.S. chemist. Born 21 April 1875 in New Orleans, La. Educated Vassar College (A.B., 1896; A.M., 1897). Professional experience. Pratt Institute, instructor in chemistry (1898–1903); Sophie Newcomb College, Tulane, acting professor (1904–1905), professor (from 1905). Death date unknown.

Information regarding Ann Northrup's early life, her professional experiences after leaving Sophie Newcomb College, and her research is unavailable.   JH/MBO

STANDARD SOURCES
AMS 3–4.

NOVOSELOVA, ALEKSANDRA VASIL'EVNA (1900–1986)

Russian inorganic chemist. Born 24 March 1900 at Veresino. Educated secondary school, Rybinsk; Moscow University, physical-mathematical faculty (degree 1925). Professional experience: Moscow University, docent (1935), professor (1946). Honors and memberships: Soviet Academy of Sciences, corresponding member, later academician; two state prizes; three Orders of Lenin. Died 27 September 1986.

Aleksandra Vasil'evna Novoselova was born at Veresino, a village in the Kashinskii region of Kalinin province, and finished secondary school in Rybinsk. Her first position was as a governess in an orphanage. In 1925 she completed a degree at the physical-mathematical faculty of Moscow University. She remained in Moscow University on the staff of the chemistry department, becoming docent, then professor, and later (from 1948 to 1955) head of the department. After 1955, she continued in the department as head of a laboratory. Novoselova was also active in community affairs as a deputy of the Moscow Regional Soviet.

Novoselova's work was in the field of inorganic chemistry, particularly that of the compounds of beryllium and other rare metals. She was the first scientist in the Soviet Union to use chemical gas transport reactions in synthesizing refractory compounds. She and B. P. Sobolev were also the first to obtain single crystals of silicates of beryllium, zinc, aluminum, and manganese.

In 1953, Novoselova was elected corresponding member of the Soviet Academy of Sciences; she became an academician in 1970. She was a member of numerous editorial boards and societies. Apart from two state prizes, she received the Order of Lenin three times, as well as other orders and medals.   ACH

PRIMARY SOURCES
Novoselova, Aleksandra Vasil'evna. "Ftoristyi berillii i ftorober-illaty." *Usphekhy khimii* 28 (1959): 1.
————. With L. R. Batsanova. *Analiticheskaia khimiia berilliia.* Moscow: Izd-vo "Nauka," 1966.
————. With others. "Physico-chemical Study of the Germanium, Tin, Lead Chalcogenides." *Progress in Solid State Chemistry* 7 (1972): 85.

SECONDARY SOURCES
Bol'shaia sovetskaia entsiklopedia. 3d ed. Moscow: Izd-vo "Sovetskaia entsiklopedia," 1973.
Vestnik Akademii nauk 12 (1986): 92–93. Obituary notice.

NOYES, MARY CHILTON (1855–1936)

U.S. physicist. Born 13 January 1855. Educated University of Iowa (Ph.B., 1881; A.M., 1884); Cornell University (M.S., 1894); Western Reserve University (Ph.D., 1895). Professional positions: Lake Erie College, teacher of mathematics, physics, and astronomy (1886–1900); Minneapolis Academy, instructor of mathematics, physics, and astronomy (from 1900). Died 13 September 1936 in Pasadena, Calif.

The sources are contradictory as to where Mary Chilton Noyes earned her doctoral degree—at Western Reserve or at Cornell. She then taught physics and astronomy as well as mathematics in Lake Erie College and the Minneapolis Academy. According to the Cornell University Alumni Records, she retired in Pasadena, California, and died there. Her research interests were in the relationship between heat and elasticity.   JH/MBO

STANDARD SOURCES
AMS 1; Siegel and Finley.

NUTTALL, GERTRUDE (CLARKE) (1868–1929)

British botanist. Born 1868. Married. Educated at an unknown university (B.Sc.). Professional experience: wrote popular books on botany. Died 4 May 1929 in Hertfordshire.

Although we know that Gertrude Clarke Nuttall was one of the first women to take a bachelor of science degree from a British university, we do not know which university. She published at least three popular books.   JH/MBO

PRIMARY SOURCES
Nuttall, Gertrude (Clarke). *Wild Flowers as They Grow.* 7 vols. London: Cassell and Co., 1911–1914.
————. *Trees and How They Grow.* London: Cassell and Co., 1913.

———. *Beautiful Flowering Shrubs.* London: Cassell and Co., [1922].

SECONDARY SOURCES
Journal of Botany 1929: 183. Obituary notice.
Horwood, Arthur Reginald, and C. W. F. Noel. *Flora of Leicestershire.* London: Oxford University Press, 1933. See page ccxxx.

STANDARD SOURCES
Desmond.

NUTTALL, ZELIA MARIA MAGDALENA (1858–1933)

U.S. archeologist and anthropologist. Born 6 September 1858 in San Francisco, Calif. Educated private schools, Paris and Dresden; Bedford College, London (1864–1876). Professional experience: Peabody Museum, Cambridge, Mass., honorary special assistant (from 1887); National Museum of Mexico, honorary professor of archeology; Crocker archeological researches, Mexico and California, field director (from 1904); Department of Anthropology, University of California, advisory council; scientific mission to Russia and Transylvania, member (1894); Columbian Exposition, international jury awards (1893); Louisiana Purchase Exposition, researcher (1904); Columbian Exposition, researcher (1893); Pan American Exposition, researcher (1901–1915). Honors and memberships: Historical Exposition, Madrid, medal (1892). Died 1933.

Although Zelia Nuttall was born in the United States, she was educated in Europe. She had several honorary affiliations, but most of her work was on a volunteer basis. She may have been paid for her work on the Crocker archeological research areas in Mexico and California, for she was the field director of the expedition. Nuttall was a member of many scientific societies, including the Anthropological Association (Fellow); the Ethnological Society; the American Geographic Society; the Philosophical Society; the Hispanic Society; the Geographic Society of Philadelphia (corresponding member); the Royal Anthropological Society (Fellow). Her research was on ancient and colonial history, calendar systems, religions and languages of the inhabitants of Mexico and Central America, ancient manuscripts and picture writings, and documents relating to expeditions of Sir Francis Drake and John Hawkins. She also worked on the botany of Mexico.   JH/MBO

PRIMARY SOURCES
Nuttall, Zelia. "The Terracotta Heads of Tetihuacan." *American Journal of Archaeology* (1886): 37 pp.
———. *Standard or Head-Dress? An Historical Essay on a Relic of Ancient Mexico.* Cambridge, Mass.: Peabody Museum of American Archaeology and Ethnology, 1888.

———. *Some Unsolved Problems in Mexican Archeology.* Lancaster, Pa.: The New Era Printing Co., 1906.

STANDARD SOURCES
AMS 1–5.

NUTTING, MARY ADELAIDE (1858–1948)

Canadian/U.S. nurse. Born 1 November 1858 in Waterloo, Quebec, Canada, to Harriet Sophia Peasley (earlier Peaselee) and Vespasian Nutting. Four siblings. Never married. Educated village academy; convent school; Bute House, a private school at Montreal; studied music in Ottawa; Johns Hopkins Hospital Training School for Nurses (1889–1891). Professional experience: Cathedral School for Girls, music teacher (1882–1883); Johns Hopkins Training School for Nurses, head nurse (1891–1894), superintendent of nurses and principal of the training school (1894–1907); Columbia University Teachers College, professor of institutional management (1907–1925). Honors and memberships: National Institute of Social Sciences, Liberty Service Medal; Yale University, honorary M. A. (1922); National League of Nursing Education, Mary Adelaide Nutting Medal established in her honor (1944); Florence Nightingale International Foundation (1934). Died 3 October 1948 in White Plains, N.Y.

Born in Canada to an intellectual mother and a gentle father who had difficulty providing for his family, Adelaide Nutting studied music in Ottawa and taught music in the Cathedral School for Girls in St. John's, Newfoundland. Since she felt that her mother's potential had been stifled, she decided against marriage. Hearing about the new Johns Hopkins Hospital Training School for nurses, she applied for admission and entered the school on 31 October 1889, one day before her thirty-first birthday. She was one of seventeen in the first class. After graduation, she remained at Hopkins and advanced rapidly. Hopkins was in the forefront of medical education and hospital administration and included such well-known people as William H. Welch, William Osler, Simon Flexner, Henry M. Hurd, and Daniel Coit Gilman (president). The atmosphere was electric, and new ideas were welcome.

Nutting, as head of the training school, revised the curriculum, and improved the conditions under which the nurses lived and worked. She added personnel to the graduate staff, created a library, and instituted scholarships.

Nutting was also active in the larger profession and worked to establish professional standards. She was president (1896) of the American Society of Superintendents of Training Schools for Nurses of the United States and Canada (later the National League of Nursing Education). She held other offices in this society and was a very active member. At the 1896 meeting, she began a crusade to establish the education of nurses within universities. To aid communication, she helped establish the *American Journal of Nursing* (1900) and was the first president of the State Association of Graduate Nurses in 1903. In 1904, she helped draft the state's first nurse-practice law.

As a solution to the problem of expanding medical care needs, the Society of Superintendents appointed a committee whose members included Nutting to recommend ways to prepare teachers and administrators in the nursing field. This result of this committee was an experimental program in hospital economics at Columbia University Teachers College, where the college's new dean agreed to admit nurses to existing courses in psychology and household economics if the society would supply financial support and teachers for new courses. Nutting traveled back and forth from Hopkins to Columbia. In 1907, she left Hopkins to accept a full-time professorship in institutional management at Teachers College. This appointment made her the first nurse to be appointed to a university chair. She supplied leadership for many new programs at Columbia. She continued to be active in national and international committee work. Among other innovations, she led a three-year project which resulted in the *Standard Curriculum for Schools of Nursing* (1917). Nutting worked constantly for the creation of endowment funds for nursing schools.

JH/MBO

PRIMARY SOURCES

Nutting, Mary Adelaide. With Lavinia L. Dock. *A History of Nursing: The Evolution of Nursing Systems from the Earliest Times to the Foundation of the First English and American Training Schools for Nurses.* 2 vols. New York: G. P. Putnam's Sons, 1907. This book later grew to four volumes and became a standard work.

———. *Educational Status of Nursing.* Washington, D.C.: U.S. Government Printing Office, 1912.

———. *A Sound Economic Basis for Schools of Nursing.* New York: G. P. Putnam, 1926.

Personal and professional files are in the archives at Columbia University Teachers College, New York City.

SECONDARY SOURCES

Goostray, Stella. "Mary Adelaide Nutting." *American Journal of Nursing* (November 1958).

Johns, Ethel, and Blanch Pfefferkorn. *The Johns Hopkins Hospital School of Nursing, 1889–1949.* Baltimore, Md.: Johns Hopkins University Press, 1954.

Marshall, Helen E. *Mary Adelaide Nutting: Pioneer of Modern Nursing.* Baltimore, Md.: Johns Hopkins University Press, 1972. A full-length biography of Nutting. Includes a bibliography of Nutting's works.

New York Times, 5 October 1948. Obituary notice.

STANDARD SOURCES

NAW (article by Virginia M. Dunbar); *Woman's Who's Who of America.*

O

O'BRIEN, CHARLOTTE GRACE (1845–1909)

Irish horticulturist. Born 23 November 1845 in Cahirmoyle, Col Limerick, Ireland. Died 3 June 1909 in Foynes, County Limerick.

Charlotte O'Brien was a poet as well as a horticulturist and plant collector. She created a well-known garden at Foynes and collected plants in counties Clare and Limerick. She contributed articles to *Irish Gardening*. Her plants are at the National Botanical Gardens, Glasnevin, and in the Limerick Museum.   JH/MBO

PRIMARY SOURCES
O'Brien, Charlotte. With M. C. Knowles. "Flora of Barony of Shanid." *Irish Naturalist* (1907): 185–201.
———. Contributed plant records to R. L. Praeger's "Additions to Irish Topographical Botany in 1902." *Irish Naturalist* (1903): 23–40.

SECONDARY SOURCES
Crone, John Smyth. *A Concise Dictionary of Irish Biography.* Rev. and enlarged ed. Dublin?: Nendeln, Liechtenstein, Kraus, 1970.
Gwynn, S. T. "Charlotte Grace O'Brien, 1845–1909." *Irish Gardening* (1909): 104–106.
Irish Naturalist 12 (1903): 249–253.

STANDARD SOURCES
Desmond.

O'BRIEN, RUTH (1892–?)

U.S. chemist, nutritionist, and home economist. Born 19 September 1892 in Taylorville, Ill. Educated University of Nebraska (B.S., 1914; M.A., 1915); George Washington University (Ll.B., 1931). Professional experience: Iowa State College, instructor in Textile Chemistry (1917–1918), assistant professor (1918–1921), associate professor (1921–1923); Bureau of Human Nutrition and Home Economics, U.S. Department of Agriculture, researcher (1923–1944), assistant chief (from 1944). Death date unknown.

Ruth O'Brien spent the first part of her career in academia, advancing from instructor to associate professor at Iowa State College. At Iowa State, she worked in textile chemistry. She spent the remainder of her career working for the U.S. Department of Agriculture's Bureau of Human Nutrition and Home Economics. She was a member of the U.S. International Textile Research group, the Home Economics Association, the Association of Textile Chemistry and Colorists, and advisory editor for the *Journal of the Chemical Society.*   JH/MBO

PRIMARY SOURCES
O'Brien, Ruth. With Esther C. Peterson and Ruby K. Worner. *Bibliography of the Relation of Clothing to Health.* Washington, D.C.: U.S. Department of Agriculture, 1929.
———. *Selection of Cotton Fabrics.* Washington, D.C.: U.S. Department of Agriculture, 1931.

STANDARD SOURCES
AMS 4–8, P 9; P&B 10.

OBRUTSHEVA, A. (fl. 1924)

Russian chemist. Flourished 1924.

Obrutsheva worked with the radiochemist Georg von Hevesy at the Universitetets Institut for Teoretisk Fysik, Copenhagen, on radioactive indicators. She and Hevesy determined the rate of self-diffusion of solid metals. They worked on radioactive elements including polonium, and concluded that the atoms of polonium loosen the lattice of the individual lead crystals and diffuse as if through "amorphous" lead. In their paper they noticed that the discrepancy between the values of the period of polonium's decay found by different investigators could be explained by MARIE CURIE's explanation that during the long time of observation the polonium in some cases diffused into the metal on the surface of which it was collected.   MM

PRIMARY SOURCES
Obrutsheva, A. With Georg von Hevesy. "Self-Diffusion in Solid Metals." *Nature* 115 (1924): 674–675.

STANDARD SOURCES
Meyer and von Schweidler.

OCCELLO OF LUCANIA
(5th or 4th century B.C.E.)
Greek natural philosopher and mathematician.

Both Ocello and Ecello are mentioned by Gilles Ménage in his *History of Women Philosophers*. They are probably the same person as both are from Lucania and both Pythagorean scholars.   JH/MBO

STANDARD SOURCES
Kersey; Ménage.

O'CONNELL, MARJORIE (1900–)
U.S. paleontologist. Born 15 August 1900 in Newark, N.J. Married William Shearon. Educated Columbia University (A.B., 1911; A.M., 1912; Ph.D., 1916). Adelphi College, lecturer in geology (1913–1914); Columbia University, curator of paleontology (1914–1916); Sarah Berliner Fellow (1917–1918); American Museum of Natural History, expert assistant paleontologist (1918–1919), research assistant (1920). Honors and memberships: Boston Natural History Society, Walker First Prize (1914); Paleontological Society, Fellow; American Geographic Society, member; Geological Society, member; New York Academy, member.

Marjorie O'Connell was a student of paleontologist Amadeus Grabau at Columbia and wanted to do research in geology. She opted against teaching in women's colleges because she thought it would take away from her research. While waiting for a research position, she did various clerical and sales jobs until she was hired for a paleontological job at the American Museum of Natural History, where she made much less money than the men doing equivalent tasks. Since she was estranged from her family and had only herself to depend upon for support, she gave up on the profession and went to work for a bank. She married William Shearon and completely changed careers again, this time to social work and public health during the Depression.

O'Connell apparently was a paleontologist of much promise. She worked on invertebrate paleontology and stratigraphy and the Jurassic of Cuba. She won the Walker First Prize of the Boston Natural History Society in 1914, was a Fellow of the Paleontological Society, and a member of the American Geographic Society, the Geological Society, and the New York Academy.   JH/MBO

PRIMARY SOURCES
O'Connell, Marjorie. "Jurassic Ammonite Fauna of Cuba." *Bulletin of the American Museum of Natural History* 42 (14 December 1920): 643–692.
———. "Phylogeny of the Ammonite Genus Ochetoceras." *Bulletin of the American Museum of Natural History* 46 (12 July 1922): 387–411.

SECONDARY SOURCES
Aldrich, Michele L. "Women in Geology." In Kass-Simon and Farnes.

STANDARD SOURCES
AMS 3–5.

ODLUM, DORIS (1890–?)
British physician. Born 26 June 1890. Educated Oxford University (1909; honors degree, 1912; M.A., 1919); London School of Medicine for Women (1915); St. Mary's Hospital, Paddington (M.D., 1924); diploma (1927). Professional experience: Workers' Education Association, lecturer (1912); Lady Chichester Hospital, resident medical officer (1924–1925), honorary consultant (1925–1927?); Royal Victoria General Hospital in Bournemouth, formed psychiatric department (from 1928); consultancies and private practice. Honors and memberships: British Medical Women's Federation, president (1950–1952); Medical Women's International Association, serving at different times as vice-president and treasurer. Death date unknown.

Doris Odlum was the only child in a close family. Her father was an accountant and her parents first managed hotels and eventually became the proprietors of a hotel. Her parents were religiously and politically liberal. During her early years in school, Doris had trouble getting along with the other children and her father home-schooled her for a year. She was happier in the next day school that she attended and by the time she was eleven enjoyed being with other children. At the age of fourteen, she passed with honors an exam usually taken by fifteen-year-olds. With the encouragement of her headmistress, she prepared to go to Oxford. In 1908 she passed the London University intermediate degree in arts, with honors in English, thus qualifying for admission to Oxford. After leaving Oxford in 1912, she had an opportunity to spread her liberal ideas. She lectured for the Workers' Education

Association, which put her in contact with women all over the country. She took part in the suffrage campaign and also promoted pacifism.

With the consent of her parents, Odlum decided to study medicine. She began her studies in October 1915 at the London School of Medicine for Women, which was attached to the Royal Free Hospital. World War I interrupted her education, and she joined a volunteer reserve corps of women in London. She became a captain in charge of a company and later in the war did full-time work as commander of a forage guard in the New Forest for eighteen months (1917–1919). In 1920, she returned to medical school, this time at St. Mary's Hospital, Paddington, which had opened its doors to women. Odlum claimed to have an undistinguished medical school experience, but managed to qualify in 1924. After qualifying, she became interested in "psychological medicine" (the word *psychiatry* had not been invented). She took her diploma in 1927 while working part-time at Maudsley hospital. In 1928, Odlum was invited by the senior surgeon and physician of the Royal Victoria General Hospital in Bournemouth to join in forming a psychiatric department. After she applied for a position as consultant, she came up against her first example of prejudice against women in medicine, for she was told that there was no precedent for hiring a woman in that position.

The National Association for Mental Hygiene had recently been established, and Odlum became an honorary secretary. This organization gave her access to people in both the United Kingdom and Europe who were interested in mental health. She also paid an important role in the development of social work and occupational therapy.

Odlum worked in a number of organizations involved in mental health, including the Psychological Medicine Committee of the British Medical Association. She was the only woman member of this organization, and was elected chair in 1940. She became a Fellow in 1958. She also worked in the Samaritan movement, which was a volunteer organization for suicide prevention.

Odlum was an early member of the British Medical Women's Federation (president, 1950–1952), and joined the Medical Women's International Association in 1926. She was vice-president in 1929, treasurer between 1940 and 1945, and was later vice-president again.   K M

PRIMARY SOURCES
Odlum, Doris. In Hellstedt, *Autobiographies.*

OGILVIE, IDA HELEN (1874–1963)

U.S. stratigrapher, Quaternary geologist, and glaciologist. Born 12 February 1874 in New York City to Helen Slade and Clinton

Ogilvie. Educated Bryn Mawr (A.B., 1900); Columbia University (Ph.D., 1903). Professional experience: Barnard College (Columbia University) Department of Geology, faculty (1903–1941). Honors and memberships: Geological Society of America, member; Sigma Xi, member; American Association for the Advancement of Science, vice-president. Died 13 October 1963 in Germantown, N.Y.

Ida Ogilvie's wealthy parents had expected their daughter to be socially prominent and allowed her to travel extensively before she attended college. Both of her parents were artists, and they taught her drawing as a very young child. She attended the Brearley School in New York as well as other schools in Europe that emphasized art education. However, by the time she reached Bryn Mawr, she had no intentions of pursuing the life of a society matron. She studied geology with FLORENCE BASCOM, then went to Columbia University to complete a doctoral degree (1903).

After receiving this degree, she took a position at Barnard College, where she founded the department of geology. Not content with working only with undergraduates, she wanted to teach graduates at Columbia as well. However, they were well stocked with professors in her areas of expertise. She found, nevertheless, that they had no one to teach glacial geology. Interested in the subject since her time at Chicago, she read extensively and prepared herself to teach it. Ogilvie was an excellent lecturer and spent a considerable amount of time organizing and preparing for her classes. She worked extensively on the geology of New York State and the glaciers of Alberta, Canada. The second woman to be admitted to the Geological Society of America, one of the three women first admitted to the Columbia Chapter of Sigma Xi, and a vice-president of the American Association for the Advancement of Science, Ogilvie was active professionally. She used a portion of her inherited wealth to support geology students at Bryn Mawr, Columbia, and Barnard.

Geology was not Ogilvie's only interest. She and a close friend, Delia Marble (curator of the geology department's collections), had been involved in the Woman's Land Army during World War I. The two spent weekends and holidays on a farm called Airlie (so named because the Ogilvies are the dukes of Airlie in Scotland). During World War I, it became "Bedford Camp," the first Woman's Land Army unit in America. Since most of the men were needed for direct wartime service, women were needed to keep the farms going. Ogilvie toured colleges throughout the United States attempting to pursuade young women to take part in this program. Some of the girls stayed on after the emergency passed, and the farm was moved to Germantown, New York, where the main house was named the Hermitage. Administering the farming operation took a great deal of time. Both farms had registered Jersey cattle, and Ogilvie's hobby was breeding collies, cocker spaniels, percheron horses, Peking ducks, Persian kittens, Shetland ponies, and tropical fish.   JH/MBO

PRIMARY SOURCES

Ogilvie, Ida Helen. "Glacial phenomena in the Adirondacks and Champlain Valley." *Journal of Geology* 10 (1902): 397–412.

————. "An Analcite-Bearing Camptonite from New Mexico." *Journal of Geology* 10 (1902): 500–507.

————. "Some Igneous Rocks From the Ortiz Mountains, New Mexico." *Journal of Geology* 10 (1902): 397–412.

————. "Geology of the Paradox Lake Quadrangle, N.Y." *New York State Museum Bulletin* no. 96 (1905): 461–508. Ogilvie's Ph.D. dissertation.

————. "A Contribution to the Geology of Southern Maine." *Annals of the New York Academy of Sciences* 17 (1907): 519–558.

————. "Some Igneous Rocks from the Ortiz Mountains, New Mexico." *Journal of Geology* 16 (1908): 230–238.

SECONDARY SOURCES

Elder, Eleanor S. "Women in Early Geology." *Journal of Geological Education* 30, no. 5 (1982): 287–293.

Wood, Elizabeth A. "Memorial to Ida Helen Ogilvie." *Bulletin of the Geological Society of America* (February 1964): 35–39.

STANDARD SOURCES

Notable (article by Sydney J. Jones); Sarjeant.

OGILVIE-GORDON, DAME MARIA MATILDA (1864–1939)

Scottish geologist. Born 30 April 1864 in Monymusk, Aberdeen, Scotland, to Maria Matilda (Nicol) and Reverend Alexander Ogilvie. Six siblings. Married John Gordon, physician. Three children, two daughters and one son. Educated Merchant Company School's Ladies College, Edinburgh; Royal Academy of Music, London (1882); Heriot-Watt College, Edinburgh; University College, London (B.S., 1890; D.Sc., 1893); University of Munich (1891–1895, Ph.D. 1900). Honors and memberships: English National Council of Women, vice-president and president; International Council of Women, vice-president. Died 1939.

Maria Mathilda Ogilvie was born in Monymusk, Aberdeenshire, in northeastern Scotland. Her oldest brother, Sir Francis Ogilvie, was a natural scientist and director of the Science Museum in London and sat on the Geological Survey Board. Another brother, the Very Reverend James N. Ogilvie, produced some controversial theological writings on the history of the Christian missions in India. One other brother was an army officer and one a physician. She spent her childhood in Edinburgh, where she attended Merchant Company School's Ladies College boarding school from age nine to age eighteen. During this time she spent vacations at her parents' country house near Balmoral Castle. She and her brother Francis hiked around the area and she became interested in natural history. However, when she graduated from middle school at age eighteen, she did not immediately go into science, but studied music. Realizing that she would never be a superb musician, she decided that her real interests lay in natural science.

For a young nineteenth-century woman, it was still difficult to get admitted to a program in higher education. Ogilvie studied chemistry and botany at Edinburgh and was eventually admitted to University College, London, to study zoology with the famous zoologist Ray Lancaster. Her London doctorate of science (1893) was the first such degree awarded to a woman. She went to Berlin to continue her studies, but her efforts to be admitted to the university were unsuccessful. However, she was allowed to study at Munich, under two sympathetic and well-known professors, the paleontologist Konrad Zittel and the zoologist Oskar Hertwig. One professor, the mineralogist Groth, however, closed his laboratory to her. She received her doctorate in geology from the University of Munich—the first woman to receive that degree.

In 1891, Ogilvie had a life-changing experience. She had been working on fossil corals when the Baron and Baroness Richthofen invited her to join them on an excursion to the Dolomites. She found the magnificence of the mountains overwhelming and vowed to study them. In the autumn of the same year until the end of the following summer (1892), she began a field study. She isolated and identified a group of fossils in the Cassianer formation. She would later reminisce about the difficulties she encountered in her first field work without direction.

This field work became the basis of her dissertation, which earned her a degree from the University of London. She returned to the Dolomites in 1893 to study tectonic appearances, to which little previous attention had been paid. The field work involved was very difficult. Researchers rose at 2:00 A.M. and returned before dark. There were no facilities for staying at a site, so all of the work had to be done in one day. In 1894 and 1895, Ogilvie devoted herself to her scientific studies. In Munich she seems to have encountered some jealousy, possibly because of her beauty and ambition.

In the fall of 1895, Ogilvie returned to Aberdeen and married her patient suitor, John Gordon. Her two monographs on corals, the result of her earlier work, appeared in 1897. After her marriage, she was occupied with domestic activities and became very involved in the women's movement. However, she continued to work on her scientific projects, spending her summers in the Tyrol. The results of her studies of the South Tyrol were collected into a two-volume monograph that was almost ready for publication in 1914. World War I, however, intruded on her plans and the text manuscript plus part of the engravings for her diagrams and maps, which she had left in Munich, were lost. During the war, she took on various patriotic tasks in Britain.

In 1919, Gordon died, a blow from which she found it difficult to recover. Ogilvie-Gordon moved her young family to London and became involved in civic affairs. She served as justice of the peace and later as first woman chair of a London borough court. She continued to work on reconstructing the destroyed materials. She brought out her old notes and compared it to the new manuscript she had completed. The work was published in 1927 and was well received, proving wrong those people who thought that after her successful publication she would leave geology for social and political activism. Two years later, she revised the work.

In 1931, Ogilvie-Gordon had a life-threatening operation which left her in poor health for the rest of her life. Some of her interpretations were criticized by younger geologists, particularly the 1927 presentation of the Langkofel group. She made a last trip to the Dolomites in 1936 and developed a new description of this group. Her interpretations were in large part confirmed, and it was her wish to see this explanation of the tectonics of this group published. In the fall of 1938, she spent a long time in Vienna, talking through the work. There were many disagreements, and she tired quickly. Many factors prevented timely publication, and a few days before her death, an editor looked through only the drawings. When she returned to London, her strength continued to ebb and she died there 24 June 1939 at age seventy-five.

She left three children. Her older daughter and her son lived in India and the younger daughter, wife of a doctor and mother of two children, in London.

She received a number of honors, including the diploma of honorary membership at the University of Innsbruck, honorary correspondent of the Geological Survey of Austria, the Lyell Medal of the London Geological Society, an honorary doctorate from the University of Edinburgh, and she was named Dame of the British Empire in 1935. She published over thirty original works. Another important contribution to geology was her translation into English of Zittel's *History of Geology and Palaeontology* (1901).

The special contribution of Ogilvie-Gordon to geology was her interpretation of the tectonic structure of the South Tyrol. She questioned her mentor von Richthofen's explanation of the cause of the irregular disposition of the Triassic dolomites in the southern Tyrol. She suggested—instead of von Richthofen's interpretation, which drew on Darwin's theory of coral atolls—a better theory would explain the irregularities by folding movements cut by thrusts. She published a series of papers on this subject and in 1927 brought together the results of this work in a comprehensive two-volume monograph. The bulk of her work consists of detailed descriptions of individual mountain groups with large-scale maps. Although there are errors in some of her many geological maps, it is understandable because of the large quantitity that she produced. Other geologists with less to do than Ogilvie-Gordon also made mistakes. One must also consider that the publications spanned forty years. Clearly, she was the most productive woman field geologist of the nineteenth century.

Maria Ogilvie-Gordon was active in the women's movement. She was president and vice-president of the English National Council of Women and vice-president of the International Council of Women. In opposition to the radical group that opposed all special treatment for women, she represented the group that advocated the necessity of legal protection for working women. Her other activity in the area of social concern was organizing events about child and youth care and public health questions. JH/MBO

PRIMARY SOURCES

Ogilvie, Maria. "Coral in the 'Dolomites' of South Tyrol." *Geological Magazine* 1, no. 4 (December 1894): 1, 49.

Ogilvie-Gordon, Maria. "Microscopic and Systematic Study of Madreporian Types of Corals." *Philosophical Transactions* B 187 (1896): 83–345.

———. "The Thrust-Masses in the Western District of the Dolomites." *Transactions of the Edinburgh Geological Society* 9 (1909–1910): Appendix.

———. *Das Grödener-, Fassa-, und Ennerberggebiet in den Südtiroler Dolomiten. Geologische Beschreibung mit besonderer Berucksichtigung der Überschiebungscheinungen.* Vienna: Geologische bundesanstalt, 1927.

———. *Geologisches Wanderbuch der westlichen Dolomiten.* Vienna: G. Freytag & Berndt. 1928.

SECONDARY SOURCES

Creese, Mary R. S. "Maria Ogilvie Gordon (1864–1939)." *Earth Sciences History* 15, no. 1 (1996): 68–75.

[Garwood, Edmund J.]. "Dame Maria Mathilda Ogilvie Gordon." *Proceedings of the Geological Society, London.* (1946): xl–xli.

Pia, Julius. "Maria Mathilda Ogilvie Gordon." *Mitteilungen der geologischen Gesellschaft in Wien* 32 (1939): 173–186. Includes bibliography.

STANDARD SOURCES

Creese and Creese 1994; Sarjeant.

OGINO, G. (fl. 1880s)
Japanese physician. Flourished 1880s.

In the late 1800s, the Japanese government passed a law that only those physicians who passed a strict examination would be allowed to obtain a medical license. This examination was closed to women, in spite of the fact that women had been working as doctors for centuries, some with great success. G. Ogino, who graduated from a medical school opened for men, petitioned (with others) the head of the board of health to allow women access to the examination and licensing. The petition was rejected, but Ogino persisted and persuaded and was finally allowed to take the exam. She passed with a high grade and was licensed to practice in 1884, opening the way for her medical sisters.   K M

SECONDARY SOURCES
Tomo Inouye. *Medical Women's International Journal* (June 1931).

STANDARD SOURCES
Lovejoy.

OHNESORGE, LENA (1898–?)
German physician. Born 17 June 1898 in Prenzlau, in the province of Brandenburg. One brother. Married. Five children. Educated Prenzlau, teachers' seminary; University of Berlin, medical training (from 1918); University of Kiel (doctorate, 1923). Professional experience: Prenzlau, clinical work; social welfare institution, physician (from 1928); private practice. Death date unknown.

Lena Ohnesorge's experiences in World War II encouraged her to be a political activist and a pacifist. She was born in Prenzlau in Brandenburg in the heart of Prussia. During World War I, she was educated at the teachers' seminary in Prenzlau. Her mother was involved in an attempt to win the franchise for women. During World War I, her brother was killed by a bomb. In 1918 and 1919, she cared for the wounded and gave aid to many in the disenfranchised classes. She also cared for friends and neighbors during the influenza epidemic. During her first postwar term at the university, some of the male students were displeased at having women classmates, but for the most part they were accepting, and good friendships were formed. She planned to devote herself to hygiene and bacteriology. She also studied many nonmedical subjects, such as history, social economy, and fine arts and literature, just for the love of learning. She put her scientific goals away when she met her future husband. The couple had five children, but one died shortly after birth in an air raid. Ohnesorge helped in the hospital, working carefully with the refugees.

In 1939 her husband was drafted into the army as a medical officer. The treatment of Jews was becoming increasingly bad. In 1945, the entire city was bombed and the family was separated. After they got back together, Ohnesorge's practice grew, but she became increasingly involved in political work. She was appointed minister of labor, social work, and refugees in Schleswig-Holstein in 1957, forcing her to give up her medical practice. She stayed in this position until about 1967.

Social work seemed to Ohnesorge a vitally important task, for so many people were uprooted during the war. She also became more involved in encouraging women to participate in social and public life.   K M

PRIMARY SOURCES
Ohnesorge, Lena. In Hellstedt, *Autobiographies.*

OKEY, RUTH ELIZA (1893–?)
U.S. biochemist. Born 13 September 1893. Educated Monmouth College (B.S., 1914); University of Illinois (M.S., 1915; fellow, 1917; Ph.D., 1918). Professional experience: University of Illinois, instructor of physiological chemistry (1918–1919); University of California, assistant professor of household science (1919–1921, 1922–1926); University of Iowa, assistant professor of home economics (1921–1922); Experimental Station, University of California, Berkeley, associate professor and associate biochemist (1926–1944), professor and biochemist (1944–1961), emerita professor (from 1961). Awards: Borden Award (1961). Honors and memberships: American Association for the Advancement of Science; Chemical Society; Society for Biological Chemistry; Society for Experimental Biology; Home Economics Association; Dietetic Association; Institute of Nutrition. Death date unknown.

Ruth Okey was educated in the Midwest, but spent most of her professional career in California. She rose to the rank of professor and biochemist at the University of California, Berkeley's experimental station. Active in a number of professional organizations, she was honored by the Borden Award of the Home Economics Association. Her research was on emodin containing drugs, insulin metabolism, menstrual variations in blood constituents, and fat and cholesterol metabolism. She also conducted research on achieving adequate nutrition at low cost.   JH/MBO

PRIMARY SOURCES
Okey, Ruth Eliza. *A Proximate Analysis of the Alcoholic Extract of the Root of Rumex crispus, and a Comparison of the Hydroxy-methyl-anthraquinones Present with Those from Certain Other Drugs.* Easton, Pa.: Eschenbach Printing Co., 1919. University of Illinois, Ph.D. dissertation.
———. *The Foods Chosen by Dependent Families: An Analysis of the Food Purchased by 25 Dependent on the Berkeley Welfare*

Society in May 1932. Berkeley: University of California Press, 1933.

―――. *Nutritive Value of Foods Purchased by Dependent Families: a Study of Grocery Orders of 233 Families on Relief in Alameda County, California.* Berkeley: University of California Press, 1934.

STANDARD SOURCES
AMS 3–8, B 9, P&B 10–11.

OLYMPIAS OF THEBES (1st century B.C.E.)

Greek midwife. Lived first century B.C.E. in Thebes.

Olympias of Thebes was a practicing midwife who wrote of her experiences. Parallel quotations make it probable that the herbalist Dioscorides (born circa C.E. 20) was familiar with her works. Pliny described Olympias's knowledge of the curative properties of a number of plants. He reported that "the Theban lady Olympias" said that mallows "with goose grease . . . cause abortion" (20.84.226); and that she could cure a certain kind "of barrenness . . . by bull's gall, serpents' fat, copper rust and honey, rubbed on the parts before intercourse" (28.27.253).   JH/MBO

SECONDARY SOURCES
Pliny. *Natural History.* See 28.77.253 and 20.84.226.

STANDARD SOURCES
Ogilvie 1986.

O'MALLEY, LADY EMMA WINIFRED (HARDCASTLE) (1847–1927)

British botanist. Born 1847 in Essex. Married Sir E. L. O'Malley. Professional experience: collected and described plants. Died 25 June 1927 in Oxford.

Emma Hardcastle married Sir. E. L. O'Malley, the attorney general for Jamaica from 1876 to 1880 and of Hong Kong from 1880 to 1889. As was often the case when the husband was working in the colonies, Lady Emma became interested in plants as a hobby. In particular, she was fascinated by the ferns of Jamaica and Hong Kong. She contributed an account of Chinese plants to *Scientific Gossip.*   JH/MBO

PRIMARY SOURCES
O'Malley's plants are at the British Museum (Natural History).

SECONDARY SOURCES
Botanical Exchange Club of the British Isles, Report (1927): 379–380. Obituary notice.

STANDARD SOURCES
Desmond.

ONSLOW, MURIEL (WHELDALE) (1880–1932)

British plant biochemist. Born 31 March 1880 at Birmingham. Married the Honorable Huia Onslow (3 February 1918); Educated King Edward VI high school, Birmingham; Newnham College, Cambridge (Natural Science tripos Pt. I, class 1, 1902; Pt. II, botany, class 1, 1904; M.A., 1923). Professional experience: Cambridge University, Newnham College, Bathurst Student (1904–1906); research fellow (1909–1914); college research fellow (1914–1915); Cambridge, Bristol University, University College, London, and John Innes Horticultural Institute, various positions; Newnham College, teacher (1911–1912), associate (1909–1932); University Biological Laboratory, assistant; later biochemistry lecturer in plant biochemistry (1918–1927); Cambridge University, lecturer in plant chemistry (1927–1932). Died 19 May 1932.

Distinguished plant biochemist Muriel Onslow (then Muriel Wheldale) was educated during her undergraduate years at Newnham College, Cambridge. Earning firsts on both parts of her Tripos examination, she was awarded a Bathurst studentship and then became a research fellow and associate of her college. For two years she was a research worker at the John Innes Horticultural Institution. Onslow went on to become a Cambridge University lecturer in plant biochemistry.

Onslow's research involved two major types of studies. In the first line of investigation, she was concerned with the chemistry of anthocyanins with special reference to the behavior of these pigments in the genetics of flower color. The second line involved the nature of the oxidase system of plants. From 1903 to 1909, she studied color inheritance in *Antirrhinum majus.* She developed a theory that anthocyanins are formed from the glucosides of flavones. At that time she thought that the conversion was due to the action of an oxidase. She isolated and studied the antirrhinum pigments in 1913–1914. Although she was not correct in all of her details, she was a pioneer in the subject and was one of the first to discuss the factors of inheritance from a chemical point of view.

In her second line of research, the study of plant oxidase systems, Onslow made one particularly interesting contribution. It had been shown that the tissues of some plants held extracts that could directly induce certain oxidations, while others could do so only after a peroxide is added. Onslow showed that one of the factors is a catechol derivative and found that it was present in all plants. She also worked on a project upon the respiration of apples.   JH/MBO

PRIMARY SOURCES

Onslow, Muriel. *Anthocyanin Pigments of Plants.* Cambridge: Cambridge University Press, 1916.

———. *Practical Plant Biochemistry.* Cambridge: Cambridge University Press, 1920.

———. *Principles of Plant Biochemistry.* Cambridge: Cambridge University Press, 1931.

Onslow's plants are at the Pharmaceutical Society.

SECONDARY SOURCES

Nature 129 (1932): 859. Obituary notice.

Times, 20 May 1932. Obituary notice.

STANDARD SOURCES

Desmond; *WWW,* vol. 3, 1929–1940.

OPPENHEIMER, ELLA HUTZLER (1897–?)

U.S. pathologist. Born 9 September 1897 in Baltimore, Md. Educated Goucher College (A.B., 1918); Johns Hopkins Medical School (M.D., 1924). Professional experience: Johns Hopkins Medical School, assistant pathologist to associate professor (1925–1963), emerita associate professor (from 1963). Death date unknown.

Ella Oppenheimer taught and conducted research at the Johns Hopkins Medical School, where she had earned her doctor of medicine degree. After thirty-five years at Hopkins, she was still an associate professor. She also worked at the University Hospital, moving from assistant to associate pathologist (1925–1949). She became a pathologist in 1949. Her research was on epituberculosis, vaccinia virus, gout, Marfans disease, endocardial fibroelastosis, and pediatric pathology.

JH / MBO

STANDARD SOURCES

AMS B 9; P&B 10–12.

OPPENHEIMER, JANE MARION (1911–1996)

U.S. embryologist and historian of biology. Born 19 September 1911 in Philadelphia, Pa., to Sylvia (Stern) and James H. (Harry) Oppenheimer. Educated Bryn Mawr (A.B., 1932); Yale University (Ph.D., 1935), postgraduate research (1935–1938). Professional experience: Yale University, fellow (1936–1937); Rochester University, department of biology, research fellow in embryology (1937–1938); Bryn Mawr, department of biology, instructor (1938–1942), Guggenheim fellow (1942–1943), assistant through full professor (1943–1974), graduate program, professor of history of science (1974–1980); emerita professor (1980–1996). Concurrent experience: Bryn Mawr Graduate school, acting dean (1946–1947); Rockefeller Foundation, fellow (1950–1951); Guggenheim fellow (1952–1953); Johns Hopkins University, visiting pro-

fessor of biology (1966–1967); National Science Foundation, senior fellow (1959–1960); University of Paris, Faculty of Science, exchange professor (1969). Honors and memberships: Yale Graduate Alumni Association, Wilbur Lucius Cross medal; American Association History of Medicine, Otto H. Haffner award; National Aeronautics and Space Administration Group Achievement Award; Kosmos Achievement Award (USSR); National Science Foundation, History of Life Sciences study section (1966–1970); American Society of Zoologists (treasurer, 1957–1959; president, 1974); American Association for the History of Medicine, council member (1970–1974); History of Science Society, council member (1974–1977); College of Physicians, Pa., honorary member; International Association History of Science, corresponding member; Yale Graduate School Association, executive committee; Fellow, American Association for the Advancement of Science. Died 19 March 1996.

Jane Oppenheimer was remarkable in combining important work in embryology with major studies in the history of science and medicine. She studied as an undergraduate at Bryn Mawr, which had been an important center for training women in biology early in the century. After graduation, she went on to work toward a doctorate in embryology at Yale, where she studied under Ross Harrison and John Spangler Nicholas. Her studies on killifish (*Fundulus hereoclitus*) embryos at Yale were inspired by the work of Nicholas, who had pioneered a method for dechorionating the embryo nervous system. GRACE PICKFORD, who was studying at Yale during those same years, later made killifish endocrinology her specialty. Many years later, Oppenheimer would write the biographical memoir on Nicholas for the National Academy of Sciences.

Oppenheimer received a series of grants to continue postgraduate work, including a Sterling fellowship from Yale and a Sarah Berliner fellowship from the American Association for University Women. In 1937, she went for a year to the University of Rochester as a fellow. Invited back to teach biology at Bryn Mawr, Oppenheimer would remain there for the rest of her academic career, with occasional visiting professorships to other universities in the United States and Europe.

While at Yale, Oppenheimer studied the history of biology, and became interested in early experimental studies on teleosts. She published the historical part of her dissertation in *Osiris,* commencing an outstanding career as both a biologist and a historian of biology and medicine.

In the 1940s, she became interested in the early experimental work of the eighteenth-century anatomist John Hunter, and published a study of his experiments and the work of his brother William during her year as a Guggenheim fellow. While continuing to teach and do research in embryology, Oppenheimer investigated the history of her field, publishing articles on Haeckel, Spemann, Driesch, and others, later collected into a book. In the late forties, she began to teach the history of science at Bryn Mawr in association with the geologist Dorothy Wyckoff, while continuing to be an important professor of biology.

Oppenheimer became involved in the cooperative space venture between the United States and USSR (Apollo-Soyuz) and designed an embryological experiment to be carried out in space. By the 1970s, she was a significant figure in establishing a cooperative graduate program in the history of science with Bryn Mawr, University of Pennsylvania, and the American Philosophical Society. Unfortunately this lapsed after her retirement.

Although Oppenheimer retired in 1980 from Bryn Mawr as professor emerita, she returned as visiting professor of history for a year in 1983 to 1984. Oppenheimer was active in many organizations both scientific and historical, serving on councils and as an officer, and referring papers and grants on the boards of a number of journals and foundations. She was recognized extensively with awards and other honors throughout her life, including membership in the American Philosophical Society and the American Academy of Arts and Sciences and an honorary doctorate from Brown University.

JH/MBO

PRIMARY SOURCES

Oppenheimer, Jane. "Experiments on Early Developing Stages of *Fundulus.*" and "Processes of Localization in Developing *Fundulus.*" *Proceedings National Academy of Sciences* 20 (1934): 536–538; and 21 (1935): 551–553.

———. "Historical Introduction to Teleostean Development." *Osiris* 2 (1934): 124–148.

———. *New Aspects of John and William Hunter.* London: Heinemann, 1946.

———. With B. H. Willier. *Foundations of Experimental Embryology.* Englewood Cliffs, N.J.: Prentice Hall, 1964.

———. *Essays in the History of Embryology and Biology.* Cambridge, Mass.: MIT Press, 1967.

SECONDARY SOURCES

Fullmer, June S. "Jane Oppenheimer." *Isis* 88 (1997): 181–183.

STANDARD SOURCES

AMS 7–8, B 9, P&B 10–19; Debus.

ORDAN, LAURA G. (1951–1984)

See Buchbinder, Laura G. Ordan.

O'REILLY, HELEN (1922–1987)

Irish botanist. Born 24 March 1922. Educated University of Dublin (B.Sc., 1943; Ph.D., 1945). Professional experience: University College, Dublin, senior lecturer (1947–1961). Died 3 June 1987.

Helen O'Reilly earned both a bachelor's degree and a doctorate from the University of Dublin. After getting her doctorate she became a senior lecturer at that institution. O'Reilly studied the Coniferae and the ecology of salt-marshes. She was the president of the Dublin Naturalists Field Club in 1981.

JH/MBO

SECONDARY SOURCES

Irish Naturalists Journal 22 (1988): 461–463. Obituary notice.

ORENT-KEILES, ELSA (1904–)

Russian/U.S. nutritionist. Born 31 October 1904 in Proskuroff, Russia. Educated Tufts College (B.S., 1925); Johns Hopkins (Sc.D., 1930). Professional experience: Jewish Hospital, Brooklyn, assistant biochemist, pediatrics research laboratory (1925–1927); Johns Hopkins, school of hygiene and public health, national research fellow (1930–1932), instructor then assistant professor of biochemistry (1932–1940); U.S. Department of Agriculture, bureau of human nutrition and home economics, researcher (1940–1942), nutrition, chemistry, and physiological research laboratories, director (from 1941).

As a child, Elsa Orent-Keiles left Russia for the United States, where she received her education. She appeared to begin a career in academe after she received her doctorate of science from Johns Hopkins University, but in 1940, she took a position in the U.S. Department of Agriculture, where she became director of the nutrition, chemistry, and physiology laboratories. It is not known when she married and how long she remained at the USDA. The last account of her in *AMS* is in the eighth edition (1949). She belonged to a number of professional organizations, including the Chemical Society, Chemical Institute (Fellow); Nutrition Institute; the Society for Experimental Biology; the Society for Biological Chemistry; the Public Health Association (Fellow); and the Animal Nutrition Research Council.

Orent-Keiles's research was on the biochemistry of calcification, trace elements (boron, manganese, magnesium, sodium, and potassium) in animal nutrition, and physiological availability and interrelationships among nutrients.

JH/MBO

STANDARD SOURCES

AMS 7–8.

ORIGENIA (b. 2d century C.E.)

Greek healer.

Galen of Pergamum, a second-century physician, mentioned Origenia along with several other medical women. He praised her for her remedies for hemoptysis and diarrhea.

JH/MBO

STANDARD SOURCES
Hurd-Mead 1938.

ORMEROD, ELEANOR ANNE (1828–1901)

British economic entomologist. Born 11 May 1828 at Sedbury Park, West Gloucestershire, to Sarah (Latham) and George Ormerod. Nine siblings. Never married. Educated at home by her mother (honorary LL.D. from University of Edinburgh, 1900). Professional experience: Royal Agricultural Society of England, consulting entomologist (1882–1892); Royal Agricultural College, Cirencester, special lecturer in economic entomology (1881–1884); Board of Agriculture, advisor (1885–1890); University of Edinburgh, examiner in agricultural entomology (1896–1898). Honors and memberships: Royal Meteorological Society, London, Fellow; Entomological Society, London, Fellow; Association of Official Economic Entomologists, Washington and the Eastern Province Naturalists' Society, Cape Colony; Field Naturalists' Club of Ontario, corresponding member; Entomological Society, Stockholm, the London Farmer's Club, the Royal Agricultural and Horticultural Society of South Australia, and the Entomological Society of Ontario, honorary member; Royal Horticultural Society, England, Floral Medal (1872); Victoria Medal of Honor in Horticulture (1901). Died 19 July 1901 of malignant disease of the liver at Torrington House, St. Albans, Hertfordshire.

Eleanor Anne Ormerod began work on her annual *Reports on Injurious Insects* at the age of forty-nine. Until the age of forty-five, she had lived at her parents' home, Sedbury Park, an 800-acre country estate in West Gloucestershire. Ormerod was the last of ten children. Her father, George Ormerod, a landed gentleman, magistrate for the counties of Cheshire, Gloucester, and Monmouth, with a penchant for antiquarian interests, preferred the isolation of country life to the society of town living. Likely as a result of their isolation, the Ormerods were a close-knit family. Only three of Eleanor Ormerod's brothers married and then only late in life.

Eleanor Ormerod was educated by her mother, Sarah, the eldest daughter of John Latham, of Cheshire, Fellow and sometime president of the Royal College of Physicians. Sarah Ormerod was an intelligent woman and an exceptional artist, much interested in botany. She oversaw all her children's education and was praised for the early education of her sons by Dr. Thomas Arnold. Both George and Sarah

Ormerod took the home education of their daughters very seriously, although the nature of the education fit firmly within the expected norms for upperclass women. The girls were given lessons in biblical knowledge and moral precepts, geography, French, and English, as well as modeling, music, sewing, and drawing. All the children were permitted access to their father's extensive library, of which Eleanor Ormerod made much use. Supplementing her mother's training, which Ormerod herself also praised, Eleanor pursued her own interest in science, urging her brothers to let her help them in their own scientific explorations, observations, and experiments. In this way, Ormerod learned the basics of anatomy and classification and had practice using a microscope. She struggled with her entomological studies, choosing the difficult Stephen's *Manual of British Coleoptera, or Beetles* as her earliest guide. These studies were to be of much use to Ormerod in her later career, yet in these early years her family insisted that such endeavors be kept strictly private and to the order of a hobby.

Ormerod's interest in scientific pursuits remained of amateur status until, between the years 1868 and 1870, she helped to arrange an entomological collection for the Royal Horticultural Society in England for which she was awarded the Floral Medal in 1872. In the same year, she also won the gold medal of honor from Moscow University for a collection of plaster models of plants, fruits, leaves, and reptiles. These awards were the earliest glimmerings of the scientific career upon which Ormerod was shortly to embark. During this period in her life, Ormerod's education was broadened to include the running of her father's estate. Sedbury Park, consisting as it did of a variegated landscape, taught Ormerod much about agriculture and insects as well as about the relationships between landowner, farmer, and laborer. Her father's death in 1873 caused the break-up of the Ormerod family, since her brother moved onto the estate with his family. Her mother had died thirteen years earlier. The remaining Ormerods were expected to find new accommodations. Eleanor, with her sister Georgiana Elizabeth Ormerod (1823–1896), settled down at Torrington House, St. Alban's, Hertfordshire, in September 1877. The sisters lived on a comfortable inheritance from their father, and later, Eleanor would receive another inheritance from their brother Arthur. Neither Eleanor nor Georgiana Ormerod were ever to marry.

Eleanor Ormerod was now the ostensible "head" of her own household. Emotionally and intellectually supported by her sister, best friend, and helpmate, Georgiana, Eleanor began her scientific endeavors in earnest. She wasted no time. In 1873 she published her first article in the *Journal of the Linnean Society,* and by 1877 she had begun her well-known, annual *Reports,* although they would not take firm shape until 1881. Her publications of a strictly scientific nature and her publications in economic entomology were numerous indeed. However, both in her own time and today, Eleanor Ormerod is best known for her annual *Reports*. She was interested in promoting agricultural education among young children and among the general public, not to mention farmers, land agents, and landowners. Publishing pamphlets, lectures, guides, handbooks, and textbooks, often at her own expense, and replying to thousands of pieces of correspondence upon entomological matters, Ormerod became the agriculturalists' godsend. Ormerod's work was particularly admired because she paid special attention to making her popular works readable and accessible and succeeded in this endeavor. In the words of the dean of the faculty of law at Edinburgh University, Ormerod was "entitled to be hailed as the protectress of agriculture and the fruits of the earth—a beneficent Demeter of the 19th century" (*Times* [London], 20 July 1901). Ironically, then, Eleanor Ormerod, childless spinster, was nevertheless considered responsible for the fertility of the English soil, mother of the Earth.

Ormerod's contribution to economic entomology went beyond her publications. In 1882 she was invited by the House of Lords to become a member of the Committee of the Council on Education to advise in improving the collections of economic entomology in the South Kensington and Bethnal Green Museums. From 1881 to 1884, Ormerod gave six addresses at the Royal Agricultural College in Cirencester. She also read a paper at the Farmer's Club in 1889. Ormerod enjoyed receiving anyone of a scientific persuasion at Torrington House, and held evening "at homes," during which she lectured to her guests on entomological topics. Ormerod was an enthusiastic supporter of formal, agricultural education and supported the establishment of agricultural lectureships at the universities that were hesitant to create chairs in this area. In her will, Ormerod bequeathed five thousand pounds to the University Court of the University of Edinburgh, "upon trust for the benefit of that University." While Ormerod, as a woman, was never permitted to hold a permanent teaching post at a university or college, she appreciated the irony of holding the post of examiner in Agricultural Entomology for two years for the University of Edinburgh—examining what she could not teach.

As a member, or honorary member, of numerous scientific societies around the world, Eleanor Ormerod was a well-respected scientific figure in her day, particularly in entomological circles. She was best known, however, for her work as a consulting entomologist to the Royal Agricultural Society of England from 1882 to 1892. On the day of her interview with the Royal Agricultural Society, she was hit by a carriage on her way home, which caused her permanent lameness thereafter. She took up the position as an unpaid one. The society had, initially, offered Ormerod a salary; however, she had declined so that she could negotiate the terms under which she would work. She was particularly eager to avoid any and all travel away from home, and the society accommodated her in this request. She officially resigned from the consultant position in 1892, claiming ill health and overwork. Yet her own letters to Robert Wallace in 1892 and remarks in her *Times* and *Nature* obituaries allude to another reason for her resignation. According to an anonymous note in *Nature* in 1891, Ormerod had been accused by the Society of "us[ing] . . . information in her possession beyond what the terms of her engagement granted." While Ormerod was permitted to use information gathered from society correspondents in her own annual publications as well as in her "Reports" for the Royal Agricultural Society's *Journal,* the society accused Ormerod of overstepping the bounds of their agreement in this matter. While the accusation was withdrawn, bad feeling between Ormerod and the society likely continued as Ormerod refused to return to work.

In the last years of her life, Ormerod continued her high productivity, despite the loss of her sister in 1896, which deeply depressed her. In 1900, the University of Edinburgh awarded her an honorary doctorate for her life's work in economic entomology, of which she was extremely proud. In the last year of her life, Ormerod received the Victoria Medal of Honor in Horticulture from the Royal Horticultural Society. She was the third woman to receive this medal in 1901 and was the last woman to be so honored until 1931.

SLS

PRIMARY SOURCES

Ormerod, Eleanor Anne. "The Cutaneous Exudation of the 'Triton cristatus.'" *Journal of the Linnean Society* (1873).

———. *A Manual of Remedies and Means of Prevention for the Attacks of Insects on Food Crops, Forest Trees, and Fruit.* London: W. S. Sonnenschein & Allen, 1881.

———. *Guide to Methods of Insect Life, and Prevention and Remedy of Insect Ravage, Being Ten Lectures Delivered for the Institute of Agriculture, December, 1883.* London: Simpkin, Marshall, 1884. Republished as *A Text-Book of Agricultural Entomology Being a Plain Introduction to the Classification of Insects and Methods of Insect Life.* London: Simpkin, Marshall, Hamilton, Kent, & Co., 1892.

———. *The Hessian Fly,* Cecidomyia destructor, *in Great Britain: Being Observations and Illustrations from Life. With Means of Prevention and Remedy from the Reports of the Department of Agriculture, U.S.A.* London: Simpkin, Marshall, and Co., 1886.

———. *Report of Injurious Insects and Common Farm Pests, with Methods of Prevention and Remedy.* 3 vols. London: Simpkin, Marshall, Hamilton, Kent & Co., 1885–1890, 1891–1894, 1895–1898, and Index. The year these reports were bound together is not given.

———. *Handbook of Insects Injurious to Orchard and Bush Fruits, with Means of Prevention and Remedy.* London: Simpkin, Marshall, Hamilton, Kent & Co., 1898.

———. *Eleanor Ormerod, LL.D.: Economic Entomologist. Autobiography and Correspondence.* Ed. Robert Wallace. London: John Murray, 1904.

For references to Ormerod's scientific publications, other than her first, listed above, see the *Catalogue of Scientific Papers* for 1864–1873, 1847–1883, 1884–1900. Compiled by the Royal Society of London.

SECONDARY SOURCES

McDiarmid Clark, J. F. "Eleanor Ormerod (1828–1901) as an Economic Entomologist: 'Pioneer of Purity Even More than of Paris Green.'" *British Journal for the History of Science* 25 (1992): 431–452.

"Ormerod, Eleanor Anne." *Times,* 20 July 1901. Obituary notice.

Wallace, Robert, ed. *Eleanor Ormerod, LL.D., Economic Entomologist: Autobiography and Correspondence.* New York: Dutton, 1904. The editor used Ormerod's own words, whenever possible, so this biographical source is mainly autobiographical.

Woolf, Virginia. "Miss Ormerod." *The Dial* 77 (1924): 466–474.

STANDARD SOURCES
DNB; Ogilvie 1986.

ORR, MARY (1867–1949)
See Evershed, Mary Orr.

O'SHEA, HARRIET EASTABROOKS (1895–1986)

U.S. psychologist. Born 27 October 1895 in Buffalo, N.Y. Three siblings. Educated University of Wisconsin (B.A., 1916; M.A., 1917), Brackett fellow (1919–1920); Columbia University (fellow, 1920–1921; Ph.D. in psychology, 1930); University at Strasbourg, fellow. Professional experience: Children's University School, New York City, school psychologist (1917–1919, 1922–1925) and principal (1923–1925); Bellevue Hospital, New York City, psychologist (1919–1920); Bryn Mawr College, lecturer in education (1922–1923); Mills College, assistant professor (1925–1927), associate professor of psychology and education, student personnel consultant, (1927–1931), director of preschool laboratory (1927–1930); Purdue University, associate professor of psychology (1931–1937), consulting psychologist for women (1937–1945), associate professor of psychology (1931–1964), emerita professor (from 1964). U.S. War Department, statistician (1918); Newark, N.J., statistician (1926); State of Mississippi, advisory staff state school survey (1926); L. S. Ayers, Indianapolis, consulting psychologist (1937). Died 25 January 1986.

Harriet Eastabrooks was born into a family of cultural and educational achievement in which the children were encouraged to develop a wide range of interests. After receiving her bachelor's and master's degrees from the University of Wisconsin, she held a variety of jobs, often wearing more than one hat. At Children's University School in New York City, she was head of the English department, school psychologist, and principal. At Mills College, she was student personnel advisor and director of the preschool laboratory. Along with these diverse and overlapping responsibilities, she took classes and finished a doctorate in psychology at Columbia University (1931). For over thirty years, Harriet O'Shea devoted herself to the students and programs of Purdue University, advancing from associate professor to professor emerita. She was able to juggle multiple tasks and taught courses in child and adolescent development, clinical psychology, and the usual introductory, general educational courses, while developing or improving related programs. She organized and directed the nursery school; served as Women's Personnel Director; was therapist and psychologist in the University Psychological Services. She organized and actively participated in the clinical psychology program, developed along the Boulder Conference model. A hands-on, dynamic practitioner, she published little, leaving research and the development of theory to others.

Always concerned with the mental health of children, she continually sought ways of identifying and treating early adjustment problems, emphasizing the interdependence of parents, educators, counselors, and psychologists in caring for the needs of the developing child. Among her special interests were parent-child relationships, the characteristics and needs of brilliant children, and the mental health of college students. She worked to develop and strengthen organizations that united academic and applied psychologists, and to make those organizations more effective in areas of legislation and public policy development. To that end, she was active in her chosen profession's organizations, promoting the merger of the American Psychological Association and the American Association for Applied Psychology in the 1940s, and advocating separate divisions for school, educational, and child psychology in the APA. She played a key role in defining and evaluating school psychology.

In Indiana, O'Shea was a principal organizer of the Indiana Psychological Association. She supported high standards of training and professionalization for psychologists. She was active in organizing the International Council of Women Psychologists and served as its president several terms. She also held memberships in the Association for Nursery Education, the Society for Research in Child Development (Fellow), and others.

After retirement from Purdue, O'Shea continued to share her experience and expertise in private practice and through community programs in her new home in Massachusetts. She joined a mental health program and an educational collaborative program, staying active past age eighty-five. Her creative approach to problems and her encouragement to both staff and clients made her an excellent mentor. She died 25 January 1986. JH/MBO

PRIMARY SOURCES

O'Shea, Harriet Eastabrooks. *A Study of the Effect of the Interest of a Passage on Learning Vocabulary.* New York: Teachers College, Columbia University, 1930.

SECONDARY SOURCES

Crissey, Marie Skodak. "Harriet Eastabrooks O'Shea (1895–1986)." *American Psychologist* 43 (January 1988): 71. Obituary notice.

STANDARD SOURCES

AMS 6–8, S&B 9–11.

OSTERHAUT, MARIAN IRWIN (1889–?)

See Irwin, Marian.

OSZAST, JANINA CELINA (1908–1986)

Polish palynologist and botanist. Born 2 February 1908 in Cracos. Educated Jagellonian University Faculty of Philosophy and Natural Sciences (master's degree, 1934); Institute of Botany, Polish Academy of Science (Ph.D., 1960). Professional experience: Ursuline grammar school, Cracow, teacher; Jagellonian University Department of Pharmacognosy, assistant (1946–1950), department of paleobotany, researcher (1950–1956?); Polish Academy of Sciences, Institute of Botany (1956–1978). Died 7 October 1986.

Janina Celina Oszast spent her entire life in Poland. After receiving her master's degree, she taught at the Ursuline school until it was closed by the Germans at the outbreak of World War II. During the occupation, she was involved in underground activities and also taught clandestine courses. She was promoted to the rank of captain in the home army, awarded the Gold Cross of Merit and the Cross of Valor. After the war ended, she returned to Jagellonian University, where she was first an assistant in the department of pharmacognosy and then was connected with the department of paleobotany. She worked at the Institute of Botany from 1956 until she retired in 1978. After her official retirement, she continued her research work.

Oszast participated in national and international conferences and conventions of the Polish Botanical Society. She did not like to deliver papers before a group. She was awarded a Wladyslaw Szafer medal on the occasion of the Jubilee Session in connection with the centenary of her mentor Professor Szafer's birth and the thirtieth anniversary of the Institute of Botany.

Oszast's scientific interests were focused largely on the Quaternary deposits. In her study of the Late Glacial and Holocene deposits from Zuchowo, she was the first in Poland to identify pollen from a broad range of herbaceous plants. She was also interested in the influence of prehistoric humans on vegetation from the palynological profile that she created. She was also the first in Poland to find pollen grains of *Ephedra* in the deposits of the last glaciation. During the late 1960s and early 1970s, simultaneously with studies of the Quaternary, Oszast began to investigate the Tertiary. This work resulted in a doctorate in natural sciences based on the results of a pollen analysis of Miocene clays from Stare Gliwice in Upper Silesia. Much of her attention was given to a study of deposits from Mizerna, where the Pliocene-Pleistocene border was defined. She attempted to reconstruct the changes in vegetation that occurred in southern Poland at the decline of the Tertiary and the beginning of the Quaternary. She also did some important palynological work that helped determine the boundary between the Miocene and Pliocene in the Western Carpathians. CK/MBO

PRIMARY SOURCES

Oszast, Janina. "Historia klimatu i flory Ziemi Dobrynskiej w Póznym glacjale i w holocenie" ("History of the Climate and Flora of the Dobrzyn region [northern Poland] in the Late Glaciation and Holocene"). *Biuletyn Instytutu Geologicznego* 118, Z Badan Czwartorzedu w Polsce, no. 8 (1957): 179–232.

———. With W. Szafer. "The Decline of Tertiary Plants before the Maximal Glaciation of the West Carpathians." In *Report of the VIth International Congress on Quarternary, Warsaw 1961.* 2 (1964): 479–482.

———. "O wieku stozka Domanskiego Wierchu na podstawie badan palynologicznych" (Age of the Domanski Wierch Based on Palynologic Studies). *Kwartalnik Geologiczny* 14, no. 4 (1970): 843–846.

———. "The Pliocene Profile of Domanski Wierch near Czarny Dunajec in the Light of Palynological Investigations (Western Carpathians, Poland)." *Palaeobotanica* 14, no. 1 (1973): 42 pp.

———. With L. Stuchlik. "Roslinnosc Podhala w neogenie" (The Neogene Vegetation of the Podhale [West Carpathians, Poland]). *Acta Palaeobotanica* 18, no. 1 (1977): 45–86.

Materials are in the Archives of the Cracow Division of the Polish Botanical Society at the W. Szafer Institute of Botany, Polish Academy of Sciences, ul. Lubica 46: 31–512 Cracow, Poland.

SECONDARY SOURCES
Zastawniak, Ewa. "Dr. Hab. Janina Oszast 1908–1986." *Acta Palaeobotanica* 29, no. 1 (1989): 5–9. Photograph with others and bibliography.

OWEN, LUELLA AGNES (ca. 1855–1932)

U.S. geologist and speleologist. Born circa 1855 in St. Joseph, Mo., to Agnes (Cargill) and James Owen. Six siblings. Never married. Educated St. Joseph High School (graduated 1872). Educated in the eastern U.S. Died 31 May 1932.

Born to a pioneer St. Joseph, Missouri lawyer and a staunch Presbyterian mother, Luella Agnes Owen spent her life in St. Joseph, except for a period when she went East to study geology. She was one of seven children in a stimulating family environment and salutatorian of her high school class of 1872. Two of her sisters, Juliette and Mary, had distinguished careers of their own. The youngest, Juliette, was an ornithologist, and the eldest, Mary, was a fiction writer, historian, and an expert on voodoo. Luella's interest in geology probably stemmed from her childhood, when she reputedly became excited after finding fossils in front of her house when the street was being graded. In the East, her geological interests were spurred on by Yale geologist N. H. Winchell. Since both Juliette and Mary were graduates of Vassar College, it seems probable that Luella also received a college education in the East, but contemporary biographies do not report her education.

Although some writers claim that Owen worked for the Missouri Geological Survey, there is no confirmation of this; in fact, the reports of the State Geologist do not refer to her employment. She became an expert on the Pleistocene loess deposits on the hills along the Missouri and Mississippi Rivers and became one of the country's foremost speleologists. She is probably best known for the latter contribution, partially because it was unusual for a woman to explore caves. Her fame was assured when she published a book about her travels to caves in southern Missouri, the Black Hills, and Yellowstone Park. In this book she proposed a unique theory of the origin of geyser speleogenesis of Black Hills caves. This book is long out of print, though parts of the book concerned with Missouri caves have been reprinted by the Missouri Speleological Survey with new illustrations.

Owen was a Fellow of both the American Geographic Society and the American Association for the Advancement of Science. She also had a membership in the American Forestry Association and was the only woman member of the French Societé de Speleologie. She traveled widely, going to Europe several times, and made a trip around the world in 1908. Owen died of pneumonia in 1932 and her body was interred in the Owen mausoleum in Mount Mora Cemetery, St. Joseph.   CK/MBO

PRIMARY SOURCES
Owen, Luella Agnes. *Cave Regions of the Ozarks and Black Hills.* Cincinnati, Ohio: The Editor Publishing Co., 1898.
———. *The Bluffs of the Missouri River.* Berlin: W. Greve, 1900.

SECONDARY SOURCES
Vineyard, Jerry D. "Louella Agnes Owen." *Missouri Speleology* 10, no. 2 (1968): 22–26.

OWENS, MARGARET (1892–?)

Canadian physician. Born 11 January 1892 in Lachute, Quebec, near the Ontario border. Married Alfred Waite (1939). Educated Ontario High School; Ottawa Normal School; Toronto University Medical School (M.D., 1923); Montreal General Hospital, internship (1924); Royal Victoria Hospital, internship in pharmacology and gynecology (1925); Philadelphia Hospital postgraduate work in pathology and radium treatment (1926–1928). Professional experience: Ontario public schools, teacher; Ottawa public schools, teacher (until 1918); Alberta Public Health Department, Edmonton, rural physician (1929–1936); Winnipeg, Manitoba, private practice of obstetrics and gynecology (1936–1976); founded Winnipeg Planned Parenthood Clinics. Honors and memberships: Medical Women's International Association, pioneeer member; Federation of Medical Women of Canada, secretary, treasurer, president; Recipient of Arnham Medal, Netherlands for Federation. Death date unknown.

Margaret Owens was brought up on a farm in Quebec near the Ontario border. She went to school in Ontario and then to normal school in Ottawa, teaching before and after her training. By the time she was twenty-six, she determined to give up teaching and study medicine. She attended University of Toronto Medical School, where she met and worked with MAUDE ABBOTT. She interned at Montreal General Hospital and the following year at Royal Victoria Hospital, studying obstetrics and gynecology as well as pharmacology.

Owens's interest in pathology as well as in the use of radium treatment in cervical cancer sent her to Philadelphia for a year. On her return, she entered the Alberta Public Health Service and spent the next seven years traveling though rural areas treating difficult cases and consulting for district nurses. Her experiences included many very challenging deliveries under very primitive conditions. Every summer she was part of a traveling clinic that examined and treated all the children in rural areas, offering dental; ear, nose, and throat; and general medical care.

In 1936 Owens was forced to leave Alberta because of a change of government that disliked women physicians. She went to Manitoba, where she established a private practice in obstetrics and gynecology in Winnipeg. There she remained for nearly forty years. She established a number of Planned Parenthood clinics, dispensing contraceptive advice. She married Alfred Waite, an aircraft pilot, when she was in her mid-forties.

Owens became very much interested in the Federation of Medical Women of Canada, serving that body as secretary, treasurer and president. While president, she received the Arnhem Medal for the Federation from Queen Wilhelmina of the Netherlands. She also became a pioneer member of the Medical Women's International Association.   KM

PRIMARY SOURCES
Owens, Margaret, in Hellstedt, *Autobiographies.*

OWENS-ADAIR, BETHENIA (1840–1926)

U.S. physician. Born 1840 in Missouri. Married, divorced, remarried. Two children. Educated informally until high school; eclectic medical school in Philadelphia (medical degree, 1874); University of Michigan medical school (M.D., 1880). Private medical practice until retirement (1905). Died 1926.

Born in Missouri, Bethenia moved with her pioneer parents across the plains to Oregon in a covered wagon, enduring many hardships during the journey and early years in the West. Informally educated, Bethenia taught school, married at age fourteen, had her first child at age sixteen, divorced at nineteen, then started her formal education. She graduated from high school and opened a millinery shop in Portland. At age thirty-three, she decided to become a doctor and left her shop to attend an eclectic medical school in Philadelphia. She received her degree in 1874 and returned to Portland, Oregon, to begin practice. Because the medical school she had attended had a dubious reputation, Owens-Adair reinforced her medical education by obtaining a degree from the University of Michigan medical school in 1880 and resumed her practice, specializing in the treatment of eye and ear diseases. In 1884, she remarried, and at age forty-seven became a mother for the second time. She retired from medical practice at age sixty-five and died in 1926.   KM

SECONDARY SOURCES
LKW; Lovejoy.

P

PABST, MARIE B. (1909–1963)

U.S. paleobotanist and ornithologist. Born 1909 in Chicago, Ill. Educated University of Minnesota (B.S.); University of California (M.A.; Ph.D., 1962). Professional experience: Chicago Museum of Natural History, researcher (1936–1943); U.S. Naval Reserves, lieutenant senior grade (1943–1945); Western Washington State College, Bellingham, faculty member (1948–1963). Died 8 February 1963 in Bellingham, Wash.

Born in Chicago, Marie Pabst went to Minnesota and then to California for her education. Her teaching career was entirely at Washington State College, where she was known as an excellent teacher. Pabst studied the paleobotany of the northwestern United States.   JH/MBO

PRIMARY SOURCES

Pabst, Marie B. "Ferns of the Clarno (Eocene and Oligocene Formation (Oregon)." Master's thesis, University of California, Berkeley, 1948.

———. With Robert Christman. "Status of Teaching of Earth Science in Washington." *Northwest Science* 36, no. 4 (1962): 127.

———. "The Flora of the Chuckanut Formation of Northwestern Washington; the Equisetales, Filicales, Coniferales." *University of California Publications in Geological Sciences* no. 76, 1985. This title is the same as that of her doctoral thesis accepted in 1962 at the University of California, Berkeley.

SECONDARY SOURCES

Christman, Robert A. "Marie B. Pabst (1909–1963)." *Journal of Geological Education* 11, no. 3 (1963): 94.

STANDARD SOURCES

Sarjeant.

PACAUD, SUZANNE (1902–)

Polish-born French psychologist. Born 1902 in Cracow, Poland. Educated University of Cracow. Married. Professional experience: Institut de Psychologie, University of Paris, professor (1967). Honors and memberships: Société Française de Psychologie (president); Société d'Ergomonie de Langue Française (vice president); Société Française de Gerontologie (vice-president).

Suzanne Pacaud was a Polish-born French psychologist who was educated at the University of Cracow. Her research interests at the Institut de Psychologie at the University of Paris included the psychology of work, the problems of gerontology associated with genetic psychology, and the problems of ergonomics in visual and auditory perception, psychomotility, and information. As of 1967, she was professor of psychology at the University of Paris.   JH/MBO

STANDARD SOURCES

WW in Science in Europe.

PAGE, MARY MAUD (1867–1925)

British colonial botanist. Born in London, 21 September 1867. Father Nathaniel Page. Never married. Professional positions: Bolus Herbarium, Cape Town, botanical artist (1917–1925). Died 8 February 1925 in Cape Town.

Mary Maud Page was born in London. She attended the School of Art at Caldrons until her failing eyesight led her to woodcarving and working with metals and enamels. In poor health, she moved to Cape Town, South Africa, in 1911 after the death of her father, who had been for a time the mayor of Croydon. After traveling through parts of Africa, including Botswana and Rhodesia, she then visited Pretoria, where she became interested in botany. She assisted a friend (Mrs. Beaumont) form a teaching herbarium for the education of children in botany at Morija.

The botanist HARRIET BOLUS encouraged her to work as a botanical artist in the herbarium established by Bolus. She was attached to the Bolus Herbarium for the subsequent nine years until her death. As a member of the Royal Horticultural Society, she wrote a handbook on culinary herbs that the Society later published.   JH/MBO

PRIMARY SOURCES
Page, Mary. *Culinary Herbs.* London: Royal Horticultural
    Society, 1974.

STANDARD SOURCES
Desmond; Gunn and Codd.

PAGE, WINIFRED MARY (1887–1965)

British botanist and mycologist. Born 11 November 1887. Honors and memberships: Linnean Society, Fellow (elected 1951). Died 9 March 1965.

Winifred Page was a mycologist who was made a Fellow of the Linnean Society when she was in her early sixties. She contributed papers on mycology to the *Transactions of the British Mycological Society.*   JH/MBO

SECONDARY SOURCES
"Winifred Mary Page." *Proceedings of the Linnean Society* 1966:
    121. This obituary includes only two lines about Page.

STANDARD SOURCES
Desmond.

PAGET, DAME MARY ROSALIND (1855–1948)

British nursing reformer. Born 1855 in England to Elizabeth (Rathbone) and John Paget. Educated Westminster Hospital. Professional experience: British Lying-In Hospital; founded Midwives Institute, Royal College of Midwives (1881). Honors and memberships: Dame of the British Empire (DBE) (1935). Died 1948.

Descended from a long line of social reformers, Mary Rosalind Paget was the daughter of a well-known Whig author and police magistrate. Her parents encouraged her in a life of public service. FLORENCE NIGHTINGALE was her inspiration as she trained to be a nurse at the Westminster Hospital. She later worked at the British Lying-In Hospital, where she became convinced of the importance of better training in midwifery. Therefore in 1881, she became one of the founders of the Midwives Institute, later the Royal College of Midwives. She worked for the Midwives Act of 1902, which provided for the registration of midwives. She also was involved in district nursing and participated in the founding of the Chartered Society of Physiotherapy. In recognition of her work in providing improved training for nurses and midwives, she was named a Dame of the British Empire in 1935.   JH/MBO

STANDARD SOURCES
Europa; WWW, vol. 4, 1961–1970.

PAGET, ROSE ELIZABETH (ca. 1868–?)

British physicist. Born circa 1868 in Cambridge, England. Father Sir George Paget. Educated Newnham College, Cambridge; Cavendish Laboratory, Cambridge. Married J. J. Thomson (2 January 1890). One son; one daughter.

Rose Paget's father was a prominent physician, Sir George Paget, Regius Professor of Physics at Cambridge University. She attended classes at Newnham College and lectures at the Cavendish Laboratory. Paget began research at the Cavendish in the fall of 1888 on the stationary vibrations produced in soap films by audible sound waves, a topic suggested by the director, J. J. Thomson. This research does not seem to have been published by either Paget or Thomson. On 2 January 1890, Rose Paget married J. J. Thomson. She did not continue her work in physics after her marriage. The couple had a son, George, born in 1892, and a daughter, Joan, born in March 1903. J. J. Thomson was credited with the 1897 discovery of the electron. George P. Thomson later became an eminent physicist.   MM

PRIMARY SOURCES
Letters from Rose Paget Thomson and J. J. Thomson to Ernest
    Rutherford. Rutherford correspondence, Cambridge
    University.

SECONDARY SOURCES
Eve, Arthur S. *Rutherford: Being the Life and Letters of the Rt. Hon.
    Lord Rutherford, O.M.* New York and Cambridge: Macmillan
    and Cambridge University Press, 1939.
Thomson, George Paget. *J. J. Thomson and the Cavendish Laboratory in his Day.* London and Edinburgh: Thomas Nelson and
    Sons Ltd., 1964.
Wilson, David. *Rutherford: Simple Genius.* Cambridge, Mass.:
    MIT Press, 1983.

PAINE, MARY ESTHER (TRUEBLOOD) (1879–1939)

U.S. mathematician. Born 1879. Married Robert Paine (1911). Educated Earlham College (Ph.B., 1893); University of Michigan (Ph.M., 1896); University of Göttingen (graduate work, 1900–1901). Professional experience: Earlham College, instructor (1897–

1899); *Mount Holyoke College, mathematics instructor (1902–1910); University of California, Berkeley, Extension School, head of mathematics (1914–1939). Honors and memberships: American Woman's Educational Association, fellowship (1900–1901). Died 1939.*

Mary Esther Trueblood did an undergraduate degree at Earlham College and went on to the University of Michigan for a graduate degree in mathematics in 1896. After receiving her master's degree, she taught as an instructor at her undergraduate college, and in 1900 was awarded a fellowship to study in Germany for a year, traveling to the University of Göttingen. Upon her return, she taught mathematics at Mount Holyoke College for eight years. After her marriage to Robert Paine in 1911, she moved to the San Francisco area, eventually obtaining a position with the extension school at the University of California, Berkeley. She remained there for the rest of her career, serving as head of the extension school department of mathematics. Her contemporaries considered her to be a very competent mathematician.
JH/MBO

PRIMARY SOURCES

Paine, Mary Esther. *John Dee and His "Fruitful Preface."* New York: n.p., [1910]. Reprinted from *Popular Science Monthly* (September 1910): 236–241.

STANDARD SOURCES

AMS 3–4 (as Trueblood), 5–6 (as Esther Paine); Bailey.

PAJCHLOWA, MARIA LEOKADIA (1919–1996)

Polish geologist. Born 1919. Died 1996.

Maria Pajchlowa published on Devonian fossils of Poland. She was the editor of a large work on the geology of Poland.
CK/MBO

PRIMARY SOURCES

Pajchlowa, Maria. "Le devonien de la Pologne." In *International Symposium on the Devonian System*, vol. 1: 311–327. N.p., 1967. Indicates that Devonian deposits crop out only in the southern part of Poland, but have been recognized in wells drilled in Pomerania, the Lublin plateau, and the Carpathians. All stages of the Devonian are represented in Poland.

———. With Lech Milaczewski. "Dewon gorny; fran, 1:2,000,000." (The Upper Devonian; Frasnian, 1:2,000,000). In *Atlas litologiczno-paleogeograficzny obszarow platformowych Polski, czesc proterozoik i paleozoik,* ed. J. Czerminski. Sheet 15, map. Warsaw: Wydawnictwa Geologiczny, 1974.

———. With others. "Dewonu w Polsce" ("The Devonian of Poland"). *Kwartalnik Geologiczny* 24, no. 1 (1980): 141–153.

———, ed *Geology of Poland, Volume 3: Atlas and Guide and Characteristic Fossils. Part 1a, Paleozoic (including Upper Proterozoic). Atlas of Fossils.* Warsaw, Poland: House Wydawnictwa, 1991.

PALLIS, MARIETTA (1882–1963)

Greek/British botanical artist and ecologist. Born 1882 in Greece to Greek parents. Educated Newnham College, Cambridge (1910). Professional experience: field trips along Danube (1911–1913), Greece (1936), and Near East (1956–1957). Plants at Royal Botanical Gardens, Kew. Died in Norwich, Norfolk, 30 August 1963.

Marietta Pallis was born in Greece to Greek parents, but came to England at the age of twelve. She studied at Newnham College, Cambridge, and began to make a name for herself as a botanical artist and ecologist, studying aquatic vegetation in river valleys of East Norfolk, publishing on that topic in 1911. She studied the reed swamps of the Danube delta. Towards the end of her life, she published on the permeability of peat and the status of the fens. Her plants are at Kew. She died in Norwich at the age of eighty-one. She is memorialized by the plant name *Fraxinus pallisiae* Wilmott.
JH/MBO

PRIMARY SOURCES

Central Committee for the Survey and Study of British Vegetation. "River Valleys of East Norfolk." In *Types of British Vegetation,* ed. A. G. Tansley, 214–245. Cambridge: Cambridge University Press, 1911. Pallis was a member of the survey committee.

Pallis, Marietta. "Structure and History of Plav." *Journal of the Linnean Society* 43 (1916): 233–290.

———. *The General Aspects of the Vegetation of Europe.* London: Taylor and Francis, 1939.

———. *The Impermeability of Peat.* Glasgow: Robert Maclehose and Co., 1956.

———. *An Attempt at a Statement Concerning a Vital Unit as Shown by the Reed in the Delta of the Danube.* Glasgow: Robert Maclehose and Co., 1958.

———. *The Status of the Fen and the Origin of the Norfolk Broads.* Glasgow: Robert Maclehose and Co., 1961.

SECONDARY SOURCES

Annales Musei Goulandris 7 (1986): 157–173. Obituary notice.

STANDARD SOURCES

Desmond; Sarjeant.

PALMER, ALICE W. (fl. 1878)
U.S. chemist.

Biographical information on Alice W. Palmer is lacking. She, however, worked in the Women's Laboratory at the Massachusetts Institute of Technology with ELLEN SWALLOW RICHARDS. Palmer spoke on antimony tannate in 1878 before the American Association for the Advancement of Science. Like Richards, she was one of the few women speakers at the meetings.

JH/MBO

PRIMARY SOURCES

Palmer, Alice W. "Note on Antimony Tannate." *Proceedings of the American Association for the Advancement of Science.* 1878.

STANDARD SOURCES

Rossiter 1982.

PALMER, DOROTHY BRYANT (KEMPER) (1897–1947)
U.S. petroleum geologist. Born 14 April 1897 in Chicago, Ill. Married Robert H. Palmer (1923). Educated University of California, Berkeley (B.A., 1920; M.A., 1922). Professional experience: University of Washington, instructor (1928–1929); Rio Bravo, geologist (1924–1930); Atlantic Refining (1930–1933; 1940–1947). Died 16 June 1947.

Dorothy Palmer was born in Chicago. She completed her secondary education in Los Angeles and entered the University of California in 1918 as one of the first three women geology majors of that university, receiving her bachelor's degree in 1920 with honors in paleontology. Subsequently, she was assistant to Bruce L. Clark (1921–1922). In 1922 she received a master's degree. She married paleontologist Robert H. Palmer on 3 January 1923, and thenceforth the couple often collaborated on research. In 1928, the Palmers went to Washington State to do geological work, and Dorothy Palmer took graduate work and taught at the University of Washington. She worked for both Rio Bravo and Atlantic Refining.

Palmer's first publications resulted from her work with Clark on fossil Mollusca. In 1923 her thesis on a dwarf fauna from the Eocene near Vacaville, California, was published, and shortly thereafter she and Clark published a joint paper on a revision of the Eocene *Rimella*-like gastropods. When she began working for the Rio Bravo Oil Company in Houston in 1924, she began to study the economic use of the Foraminifera. During 1925–1926, her husband was working on his doctorate at Stanford University and Dorothy Palmer contributed articles to the first and third issues of *Micropaleontology Bulletin.*

While the Palmers were in Washington state, Dorothy Palmer collected and began investigating the Astoria Miocene Foraminifera. Although this paper was to have been published with C. C. Church, it was never completed. Under the guidance of T. Wayland Vaughan at the Scripps Institute of Oceanography, she published her first paper on a foraminiferan species. The Palmers moved to Cuba, where she and her husband studied the fossils and formations of the Caribbean region. The Palmers were popular in Cuba, and many of her papers were published in the *Memorias de la Sociedad Cubana de Historia Natural.* She assisted both in exploring for petroleum and in understanding the geology of the region.

CK/MBO

PRIMARY SOURCES

Palmer, Dorothy K. With B. L. Clark. "Revision of the *Rimella*-like gastropods from the West Coast of North America." *University of California Publications in Geological Science* 14, no. 7 (1923): 277–288.

———. "A Fauna from the Middle Eocene Shales near Vacaville, California." *University of California Publications in Geological Science* 14, no. 8 (1923): 289–318.

———. "The Upper Cretaceous of the Orbitoidal Genus *Gallowayina* Ellis." *Journal of Paleontology* 8, no. 1 (1934): 68–70.

———. "Cuban Foraminifera of the Family Valvulinidae." *Memorias de la Sociedad Cubana de Historia Natural* 12, no. 4 (1938): 281–301.

———. "Notes on the Foraminifera from Bowden, Jamaica." *Bulletin of American Paleontology* 29, no. 115 (1945): 1–82.

SECONDARY SOURCES

Palmer, K. V. "Dorothy K. Palmer, 1897–1947." *Journal of Paleontology* 22 (1948): 518–519.

STANDARD SOURCES

Kass-Simon and Farnes (article by Michele L. Aldrich).

PALMER, ELIZABETH DAY (1872–1945)
American ornithologist. Born 30 November 1872 in Oakland, Calif., to Jane (Day) and Henry Austin Palmer. Educated University of California (A.B., 1894). Professional experience: Claremont Public Schools, teacher; Los Angeles High School, teacher (1894–1937). Honors and memberships: Cooper Ornithological Club; American Ornithologists' Union, life associate (1918). Died 4 December 1945, Los Angeles, Calif.

Elizabeth Day Palmer was born and educated in California. After receiving her undergraduate degree she taught in the Claremont Public Schools and then in a Los Angeles High School as a science teacher until her retirement at the age of sixty-five. She was a dedicated ornithologist, joining the Cooper Ornithological Club and becoming a life associate of the American Ornithologists' Union in 1918. She was an enthusiastic traveler, and reported on her bird sighting in her travels from Fiji to the Arctic Circle.   JH/MBO

SECONDARY SOURCES

Palmer, T. S. "Elizabeth Day Palmer." *Auk* (1950): 429. Obituary notice.

———. *Biographies of Members of the American Ornithologists' Union.* Reprinted from the *Auk,* 1883–1954. Washington, D.C.: Lord Baltimore Press, 1954.

PALMER, KATHERINE EVANGELINE HILTON (VAN WINKLE) (1895–1982)

U.S. geologist. Born 4 February 1895. Married Ephraim Laurence Palmer. Two sons. Educated University of Washington (B.S., 1918); Cornell University (Goldwyn Smith Fellow in Geology, 1918–1920; assistant in paleontology and historical geology, 1921–1925; Hecksher Fellowship, 1925–1927. Professional experience: Cornell University, special lecturer in paleontology (1942–1945); University of Washington, assistant professor (1922); Oberlin College, curator of the paleontologic collections (1928); New York State Museum, technical expert in zoology (1945); McGill University, special technical assistant (1950); Provincial Museum of Quebec, special technical assistant (1951); Paleontological Research Institution, Ithaca, N.Y., director and emerita director (1952–1982). Honors and memberships: Sigma Delta Epsilon, president (1938), honorary member (1971); Geological Society of America, Fellow (1935); Cushman Foundation, secretary-treasurer (1954–1961), vice-president (1958), president (1960); Western Society of Malacologists award (1974); Society of Economic Paleontologists and Minerologists, honorary member. Died 12 September 1982.

Katherine Van Winkle Palmer took many short-term positions before she finally settled in as director of the Paleontological Research Institution, Ithaca, New York. Her reputation as a Tertiary geologist began in 1918 with a publication on the Oligocene of the Chehalis Valley, in Washington. She was Charles E. Weaver's student and laboratory assistant; he was well known for his research into the Tertiary. She left the West Coast to go to Cornell for graduate work. While there, she met and married Ephraim Laurence Palmer, a professor of nature study at that institution. They had two sons, one of whom was an invalid. She, on occasion, received appointments for special work in nature study at Cornell and the Utah Agricultural College in support of her husband's work. She was appointed director of the Paleontological Research Institution, Ithaca, New York, from 1952 to 1978, when she retired. Palmer became emerita director

from 1978 until her death. This institute was founded by a group of G. D. Harris's former paleontology students to house his collections and library and to continue his work of publishing the *Bulletins of American Paleontology* and *Palaeontographica Americana.* Katherine Palmer was a founding member and life trustee. Under Palmer's leadership from 1952, the collections grew, funds for curating were established, and a new headquarters was built.

Palmer received many honors, including the Paleontological Society Medal (1972) for distinguished work on Tertiary Mollusca. She also received the Western Society of Malacologists award (1974) and an honorary doctor of science degree from Tulane (1978). She held memberships and offices in many organizations. She was president of Sigma Delta Epsilon, women's graduate scientific fraternity (1938), and designated an honorary member in 1971. She was a charter member and president of Chi Upsilon, women's geological sorority. She served as secretary-treasurer of the Cushman Foundation (1954–1961), as well as vice-president (1958) and president (1960). In 1935, she was designated a Fellow of the Geological Society of America. A Geological Society of America Special Paper was dedicated to her in 1976. She was an honorary member of the Society of Economic Paleontologists and Mineralogists. These are only a few of the organizations in which she was a Fellow or member.

During her research career, Palmer was often supported by grants, but on the occasions when she was not, she continued her research on the Tertiary. She had many opportunities for field studies and collected recent fossil mollusks from many parts of the world, including in the Gulf of Mexico, New Zealand, and the West Indies. Until her death she was involved in active research. She authored more than sixty publications.   CK

PRIMARY SOURCES

Palmer, Katherine Van Winkle. "Paleontology of the Oligocene of the Chehalis Valley, Washington." *University of Washington Publications in Geology* 1, no. 2 (1918): 69–97.

———. With G. D. Harris. "New or Otherwise Interesting Tertiary Molluscan Species from the East Coast of America." *Bulletins of American Paleontology* 8, no. 33 (1919): 32 pp.

———. "A New Fauna from the Cook Mountain Eocene near Smithville, Bastrop County, Texas." *Journal of Paleontology* 2, no. 1 (1928): 20–31.

———. "The Claiborne Scaphopoda, Gastropoda and Dibranchiate Cephalopoda of the Southern United States." *Bulletins of American Paleontology* 7, no. 32 (1937): 1–730.

———. "Paleozoic Nonmarine Bivalve from a Deep Well in Georgia." *Bulletin of the Georgia Academy of Science* 28 (1970): 45–54.

SECONDARY SOURCES

Caster, Kenneth E. "Memorial to Katherine Van Winkle Palmer, 1895–1982." *Journal of Paleontology* no. 5 (1983): 1141–1144. Portrait and bibliography.

Dockery, David T. III. "Research in Gulf Coastal Plain Tertiary Mollusks and the Role of Katherine V. W. Palmer—Remembered on the 100th Anniversary of Her Birth." *Mississippi Geology* (16 December 1995): 69–73.

PALMER, MARGARETTA (fl. 1900s)

U.S. astronomer. Educated Yale University (Ph.D.). Professional experience: Yale University Observatory, computer.

Margaretta Palmer was a Yale-educated astronomer who worked at the Yale University Observatory.   JH/MBO

PRIMARY SOURCES

Palmer, Margaretta. *The G.F.H.* Northfield, Minn.: N.p., 1923. First published in *Popular Astronomy* 31 (1923): 78–82.

SECONDARY SOURCES

Mack, Pamela Etter. "Women in Astronomy in the United States, 1875–1920." B.A. thesis, Harvard University, 1977.

STANDARD SOURCES

Rossiter 1982.

PALMER, MIRIAM AUGUSTA (1878–?)

U.S. entomologist. Educated University of Kansas (A.B., , 1903; A.M., 1904); Colorado Agricultural (later State) College (M.S., 1925). Professional experience: Colorado Agricultural (State) College, instructor in zoology and physiology (1904–1922), assistant professor in entomology (1922–1927), associate professor (1927–1947). Concurrent positions: Colorado State Experimental Station, delineator (1904–1947). Honors and memberships: Colorado State College, honorary D.Sc. (1959); Entomological Society of America, Fellow. Death date unknown.

Miriam Augusta Palmer was educated at the University of Kansas, where she obtained both an undergraduate and a master's degree. From the time she obtained her master's degree in 1904, she taught at the Colorado Agricultural College and worked in the state experimental station there. An authority on aphids, Palmer conducted her major study on these insects when she was seventy-four years old. This study covered the area of Colorado and Utah and the border areas of those states including southern Wyoming, southeastern Idaho, and northern New Mexico. In this work she discussed most of the aphid species that have an economic impact on North America. In 1959, she was honored by Colorado State College by an honorary doctorate.   JH/MBO

PRIMARY SOURCES

Palmer, Miriam Augusta. "On the Dorsal Glands as Characters of Constant Specific Value in the Coccid Genus Parlatoria." *University of Kansas Science Bulletin* 3, no. 5 (1905): 131–146.

———. *Aphids of the Rocky Mountain Region.* [Baltimore, Md.]: Thomas Say Foundation, 1952.

SECONDARY SOURCES

Osborn, Herbert. *Fragments of Entomological History.* Columbus, Ohio: the author, 1937. Includes a photograph of Palmer.

STANDARD SOURCES

AMS 5–8, B 9, P&B 10; Bailey.

PALMER, SOPHIA FRENCH (1853–1920)

U.S. nurse, nursing educator, and administrator. Born 26 May 1853 in Milton, Mass., to Maria Burdell (Spencer) and Simeon Palmer. Four sisters; five brothers. Never married. Adopted daughter (1906). Educated Boston Training School for Nurses (later Massachusetts General School of Nursing) (R.N., 1878); Massachusetts General Hospital (postgraduate training, 1888). Professional experience: Philadelphia Hospital for Nurses, associate of Dr. S. Weir Mitchell; private psychiatric nurse (1878–1884); St. Luke's Hospital, New Bedford, Mass., supervisor of nurses (1884–1886?); Garfield Memorial Hospital (Washington, D.C.) Nursing School, founder and administrator (1889–1895); Rochester City (N.Y.) Hospital and Training School, superintendent (1896–1900); American Journal of Nursing, editor-in-chief (1900–1920). Concurrent experience: New York State Board of Nurse Examiners. Died 27 April 1920 at Forest Lawn, N.Y. (near Rochester) of a cerebral hemorrhage.

Sophia French Palmer was born in Milton (near Boston), Mass., as the youngest of ten children. Her decision to study nursing in her early twenties appears to have been opposed by her family, who never visited her at the Boston Training School of Nursing during her period of training. After graduation, she went to Philadelphia to work with S. Weir Mitchell, noted for his treatment of women with nervous diseases. (He was famous, or infamous, for the treatment described by Charlotte Gilman in her book *The Yellow Wallpaper*). After a few years, Palmer began to work as a private nurse in this field.

By 1884, Palmer moved back to Massachusetts, taking over as superintendent of nursing at St. Luke's Hospital in New Bedford. She left after a few years when the hospital cut back on the number of nurses and then worked for a time as a private nurse while doing postgraduate work at Massachusetts General Hospital. By the end of the 1880s, she took the opportunity to establish a school for nurses in a hospital in the Washington, D.C., area. Although this proved to be quite successful, she left to become superintendent of nurses at the Rochester City Hospital in upstate New York.

Palmer began to edit a journal established at the Buffalo Training School and this led some years later to the appointment as editor-in-chief of the *American Journal of Nursing,* established by the Nurses Associated Alumnae of the United States (later the American Nurses Association). She had already proven her administrative ability as one of the founding members of the American Association of Superintendents of Training Schools for Nurses founded in 1893, for which she drafted the constitution. She represented this group in the organization of a national nurses association.

As editor of the nursing journal, Palmer became known for her vigorous editorials, speaking out on a number of professional and social issues. She was aware of the need to rally more general support and obtained the help of the women's clubs in New York State to push through laws regulating training and practice of nurses. Palmer was made one of the first members of the Board of Nurse Examiners in New York State when the law was passed. She used the same strategy on a national level, using editorials and articles in the *American Journal of Nursing* to educate and stimulate her colleagues to push through other nursing reforms.

Although she never married, Palmer adopted and raised a girl of eight when she was fifty-two. This daughter died at age twenty, two years before Palmer's own death. Palmer was active until her sudden death in 1920. Her colleagues testified to her importance in a series of articles in the nursing journal. She was memorialized by having two libraries named in her honor, one at the offices of the *American Journal of Nursing* and the other at the Massachusetts General Hospital School of Nursing.   JH/MBO

SECONDARY SOURCES
[Article on Sophia French Palmer]. Parts 1 and 2. *American Journal of Nursing* (April 1920); (June 1920).

STANDARD SOURCES
Notable (article by Stella Goostray).

PALMIE, ANNA HELENE (1863–1946)

U.S. mathematician. Born 21 May 1863 in Brooklyn, N.Y. Educated Cornell University (Ph.B., 1890; fellow, 1890–1891); University of Chicago (graduate studies, summers? 1896–1898?); Göttingen University (graduate studies, 1898–1899). Professional experience: high school teacher (1891–1892); Western Reserve University College for Women, instructor (1892–1893), associate

professor (1893–1895), professor (1895–1928), emerita professor (1928–1946). Died 1946.

Anna Helene Palmie was trained in mathematics at Cornell University, where she received a bachelor's degree and remained for a fellowship year. After teaching German at a high school for a year, she obtained a position at Western Reserve's College for Women (then called the Flora Stone Mather College) teaching mathematics. She remained there for the rest of her professional career, taking time out to do graduate work at the University of Chicago and then at Göttingen University, famous for its achievements in mathematics. Her mathematical studies and her teaching were of sufficient quality to ensure her position at the college, and she rose to the rank of professor in 1895 at the age of thirty-two. Two years later, she was made a member of the American Mathematical Society. She retired to Brooklyn in 1928 and continued her mathematical studies as an emerita professor.   JH/MBO

PRIMARY SOURCES
Palmie, Anna Helene. "The Fringes of Shadows." Ph.B. diss., Cornell University, 1890.

STANDARD SOURCES
AMS 1–7; Bailey.

PANAJIOTATOU, ANGELIKI (1875–1954)

Greek physician and microbiologist. Born in Greece in 1875. Educated University of Athens (1896–?); Medical School in Germany. Professional experience: University of Athens Medical School, lecturer, later professor (from 1938); Cairo University, Egypt, professor of microbiology; General Hospital, Alexandria, Egypt, director. Died 1954.

Angeliki Panajiotatou was the first woman to be accepted at the medical school of the University of Athens. She received additional medical education in Germany. After graduation, she was appointed lecturer in the medical school but was forced to resign due to students' uproar and refusal to attend her classes because of her sex. She received an appointment as professor in microbiology at Cairo University. She also became director of the general hospital in Alexandria.

Panajiotatou's special interest was as a microbiologist in tropical diseases, especially cholera and typhus. Her research revealed ways of eliminating lethal epidemics. Her home in Egypt was a gathering place for Greek and foreign artists and intellectuals. In 1938, she returned to Greece as professor at Athens University Medical School, where she remained for the rest of her career. She died in 1954.   JH/MBO

PRIMARY SOURCES

Panajiotatou, Angeliki. *The Hygiene of the Ancient Greeks I.* Paris: Vigot Frères, 1923.

———. "Dysentery and Enteritis in Tropical Countries." *Grammata* 27 (1932): 737–783.

STANDARD SOURCES

Notable (article by Margo Nash); Uglow 1982.

PAPHNUTIA THE VIRGIN (fl. 300 C.E.)

Egyptian alchemist. Flourished 300 C.E.

In extant fragments of his letters to his sister Theosebeia (probably an alchemist), the alchemist Zosimos chastised her for conversing with the virgin Paphnutia and "other uneducated persons." He was concerned that Theosebeia's alchemy would be corrupted by one (presumably Paphnutia) who incorrectly practiced alchemy. He wrote that Paphnutia was laughed at for her ideas. Because of the secrecy surrounding the alchemists it is impossible to determine whether Zosimos was upset because Paphnutia belonged to another school of alchemy or if he despised her because she was a priestess.

JH/MBO

SECONDARY SOURCES

Berthelot, M. P. *Collecions des anciens alchimistes Grecs.* Osnabruck: Otto Zeller, 1967.

Houlihan, Sherida, and John H. Wotiz. "Women in Chemistry before 1900." *Journal of Chemical Education* 52, no. 6 (June 1975): 362.

Meislich, Estelle K. "The Eve of Chemistry." *Chemtech* 8, no. 9 (September 1978): 588–592.

Taylor, F. S. *The Alchemists.* New York: Heinemann, 1951. See pages 45–47.

PARIS, MARIE-LOUISE (1889–1969)

French engineer. Born 1889. Ecole Polytechnique Feminine, cofounder (1925–1945). Died 1969.

Marie-Louise Paris was one of the founders of the short-lived Ecole Polytechnique Feminine, which taught women engineering in Paris from 1925 to 1945.

JH/MBO

SECONDARY SOURCES

Grelor, André. "Marie-Louise Paris et les debuts de l'Ecole Polytechnique Féminine (1925–1945)." *Bulletin Histoire Electricité* 19–20 (1992): 133–155.

PARKE, MARY WINIFRED (1908–1989)

British botanist. Born 23 March 1908, Bootle, Lancashire, to Mary Magdalene and William Aloysius Parke. Five siblings. Never married. Educated Notre Dame Convent, Liverpool. University of Liverpool (B.Sc. with honors, 1929; Ph.D., 1932; D.Sc., 1950). Professional experience: University of Liverpool Marine Station, Port Erin, Isle of Man, algologist (1930–1939); Marine Biological Association, Plymouth Marine Laboratory, botanist (1941–1973); British Phycological Journal, editor (concurrent). Honors and memberships: Fellow of the Royal Society (1972); University of Liverpool (honorary D.Sc., 1986); Norwegian Academy of Sciences, Fellow; Netherlands Royal Botanical Society, corresponding member; British Phycological Society, founding member, president (1959–1960). Died 17 July 1989.

The British botanist and phycologist Mary Winifred Parke was born in Liverpool, the second of six children. Her father was a partner in a company that ran barges along the Manchester Canal. Her interest in botany was evident from her early youth. She attended a Catholic convent school, where her mother had to argue with the headmistress to provide her daughter with an adequate biological training for the university. Parke entered Liverpool University, graduating with a bachelor of science in botany. She spent a postgraduate year at Liverpool and then joined the University of Liverpool Marine Station at Port Erin on the Isle of Man, where she worked as an "algologist" (phycologist) compiling species lists. She worked on detailed life histories of algae under Margery Knight and did her research for her doctorate. Knight was noted for her careful description of the cytology of brown algae (Endocrapales family) and the demonstration of its alternating haploid and diploid generations. Together they published a handbook describing the algae of the area, *Manx Algae,* which appeared in 1931.

After Parke received her doctorate from Liverpool, she continued to work at the Port Erin station, turning her attention to the small flagellates that oysters fed upon. Her success in identifying one of these, *Isochrysis galbana,* as an important food source for larval oysters, led to a paper with the former director of the marine station, the zoologist J. H. Orton, in *Nature* and subsequent attention from the press in 1938 as the process was developed successfully. She continued to be interested in culturing minute marine flagellates and was highly successful both in cultivating and describing these organisms.

During World War II, Parke and Knight were both involved in the project to develop agar sources for bacteriological work and alginate for "national service requirements." As a result, Parke was moved to the Plymouth Marine Laboratory under the Marine Biological Association, where she and E. Clay worked on brown algae, publishing a sequence of articles with Knight on seaweeds. She was appointed botanist with the MBA, and remained at Plymouth for the rest of her professional career.

Her interest returned to marine flagellates in the postwar period, stimulated by the work being done in electron microscopy by IRENE MANTON, with whom she began to collaborate very successfully, producing a total of fourteen important papers with her and (later) her students. Since both Parke and Manton were strong-minded women, their arguments over details led bystanders to retire "to cover," according to Parke's obituary. They described unusual details of structure including extracellular scales and an organelle capable of attaching itself to solid substrates. They also described the role of other organelles that could form and package material for extracellular transport. They carefully decribed the importance of these organisms in rock-building as well as in the pelagic food chain.

Parke provided important cultures of marine flagellates to other scientists, playing a notable part in developing the use of these microorganisms. She enforced rigorous standards of cleanliness and screening for toxicity of materials that allowed her to cultivate flagellates that others could not grow. Her own culture collection of flagellates, known as the Plymouth Culture Collection, is still maintained by the Plymouth Marine Laboratory as an important resource.

She was a founding member (with eight others) of the British Phycological Society in 1951, serving as a council member for many years and as the chair of a committee to produce a new flora, *Seaweeds of the British Isles.* She was also president of the society, 1959–1960. For a number of years, she served as editor of the journal of the society, the *British Phycological Society,* overseeing the printing quality as well as the content. Her own skill as a botanical illustrator came in handy in this work. Although she worked closely with foreign scientists, she hesitated about the formation of the International Phycological Society, fearing it would diminish the work of the national societies.

In the 1970s and 1980s, Parke received a number of national and international honors, including election as a Fellow of the Royal Society in 1972. Three years before her death, her university, Liverpool, conferred an honorary doctorate upon her. Since she had already earned a doctorate from Liverpool for her research, she expressed some unhappiness that they did not come up with some "new combination of letters" for this distinction. She remained at Plymouth until her death, working in the Plymouth laboratory until physical incapacity made this impossible. JH/MBO

PRIMARY SOURCES

Parke, Mary W. With Margery Knight. *Manx Algae.* Liverpool: Liverpool Marine Biological Commission, no. 30 (1931).

———. "Algological Records for the Manx Region." *Reports of the Marine Biological Station, Port Erin* 46 (1933): 35–49; 47 (1934): 29–36.

———. With J. H. Orton and W. C. Smith. "Breeding of Oysters at Port Erin." *Nature* 131 (1933): 26.

———. "Studies on Marine Flagellates." *Journal of the Marine Biological Association, UK* 28 (1949): 255–286. The first of a series of six papers on this topic published in this journal over the next ten years, most of the subsequent papers with Irene Manton.

———. "A Preliminary Check List of British Marine Algae." *Journal of the Marine Biological Association, UK* 32 (1953): 497–520.

———. "Recent Planktonic and Benthic Algae Related to Fossil Forms Used by Micropaleontologists for Oil Detection and Rock Dating." *Proceedings of the Challenger Society* 4 (1973): 155–161.

SECONDARY SOURCES

Boalch, G. T., and G. E. Fogg. "Mary Winifred Parke." *Biographical Memoirs of the Royal Society of London* 37 (1991): 381–398.

STANDARD SOURCES

Desmond.

PARKER, IVY MAY (1907–)

U.S. chemist and engineer. Born 11 September 1907 in Quay County, N.M. Educated West Texas State Teachers College (1928); University of Texas (M.A., 1931; Ph.D., 1935). Professional experience: Mary Hardin-Baylor College, assistant professor, chemistry (1934–1935); Shell Oil Company, Houston, Tex., analytical chemist (1936–1943); J. S. Abercrombie Company, senior research chemist (1943–1945); Plantation Pipe Line Company, Atlanta, Ga., field technologist (1945–1946), research engineer (1956–1972), senior engineer (from 1972). Concurrent experience: University of Houston, assistant professor (1939–1940, 1942–1943). Honors and memberships: American Association for the Advancement of Science; American Chemical Society; Electrochemical Society; American Institute of Chemistry, Fellow.

Ivy Parker earned her doctorate in organic chemistry and began a short-lived academic career. She left academia to work for Shell Oil Company and later Plantation Pipe Line Company in Atlanta, Georgia. She used her chemistry to become a specialist in research on the causes and prevention of corrosion of pipelines and published numerous papers on this subject. A systems thinker, she made contributions to the development of pipeline technology as it expanded after World War II. She did research on "quality of product" flowing through the pipeline. She also worked on corrosion protection, innovations in both water and oil-soluble inhibitors. In 1944 she was appointed the first editor of *Corrosion,* the official publication of the National Association of Corrosion Engineers, and remained in that position until 1965. Her research also included ways to keep the pipeline clean, filtration, and tank painting and tank seals.   JH/MBO

STANDARD SOURCES
AMS 6–8, P 9; P&B 10–13; Kass-Simon and Farnes.

PARKINS, PHYLLIS VIRGINIA (1908–)

U.S. biologist and information scientist. Born April 1908. Married William Parkins (1933). Two children. Educated Goucher College (A.B., 1929). Syracuse University (A.M., 1930). Professsional experience: Goucher College, assistant instructor in biology (1930– 1931); Carnegie Institution, research assistant in genetics (1931– 1933); Philadelphia Zoological Society, Penrose Pathology Laboratory, staff (1942–1944); University of Pennsylvania, instructor in zoology (1943–1947); Bryn Mawr College, biology instructor (1947–1948); Harrison School of Medicine, Department of Surgical Research, research fellow (1951–1953); Biological Abstracts, assistant editor (1953–1954), editor (1954–1961), assistant director of educational affairs (1961–1964), trustee and director (1964– retirement).

Phyllis Parkins was trained as a biologist and obtained her degrees first at Goucher College and then at Syracuse University, where she was a fellow and where she obtained a master's degree. As a research assistant in genetics at the Carnegie Institution, she met and married Iowa-born William Milton Parkins, a Princeton-trained physiologist who had a brief position with the Long Island Biological Association.

For the first five years of their marriage, the couple remained in New Jersey while William Parkins continued to work as a research endocrinologist at Princeton and Phyllis Parkins raised their two children. For two years they traveled to Kentucky where he obtained a position as an assistant professor of physiology at the medical school in Louisville. In 1940 they returned to Princeton, where he again did research in endocrine physiology until he received a position at the University of Pennsylvania School of Medicine, first in surgical research, then rising through the ranks to a full professorship.

By 1942, Phyllis Parkins returned to her science, working in the pathology laboratory of the Philadelphia Zoo, then as instructor of zoology at the University of Pennsylvania. The antinepotism laws that were enforced in the late 1940s seem to have affected her position, for she then moved to Bryn Mawr to teach for a year.

In the 1950s, she was a research fellow in the Department of Surgical Research of the Harrison School of Medicine until she had an opportunity to serve as one of the first editors of *Biological Abstracts* and recreate herself as an information specialist. She remained with *Biological Abstracts,* becoming both a director and trustee in the 1960s until her retirement.
                                                                        JH/MBO

SECONDARY SOURCES
Steere, William. *Biological Abstracts Biosis: The First Fifty Years.* New York: Plenum Press, 1976. See pages 132–134.

STANDARD SOURCES
AMS B 9; P&B 10–12.

PARLOA, MARIA (1843–1909)

U.S. writer and lecturer on home economics and food preparation. Born Massachusetts in 1843. Professional experience: owner of cooking school (1877–1887); Boston Cooking School, teacher (1879–1887); writer and lecturer (1887–1909). Died 1909.

Maria Parloa, a native of Massachusetts, made her home in Bethel, Connecticut. She lectured on the topic of home economics and wrote a number of articles and books on food preparation and household management intended for the middle-class woman. She also ran a school for cooking. She was a charter member of the Lake Placid Conference that founded the American Home Economics Association. In addition to her books, she published numerous articles in the *Ladies Home Journal.* Notice appeared in *Science* at the time of her death.   JH/MBO

PRIMARY SOURCES
Parloa, Maria. *Kitchen Companion.* Boston: Clover Publishing Co., [1887].
———. *First Principles of Household Management and Cookery.* Boston: Houghton Mifflin, [1888].
———. *Home Economics.* New York: Century Co., 1898.

SECONDARY SOURCES
"Maria Parloa." *Science* 30 (1909): 403. Obituary notice.

STANDARD SOURCES
Bailey; Barr; *WWW(A),* vol. 1 (1897–1942).

PARMELEE, RUTH A. (1880–?)

U.S. physician and missionary. Born 1880 in Turkey of missionary parents. Never married. Educated University of Illinois (M.D., 1912). Professional experience: missionary to Turkey; American Women's Hospitals, Greece, physician (1922–1941), director in Greece (1928–1941); American Women's Hospital School of

Nursing, Salonika, founder and director (1922–1925); American Women's Hospital School of Nursing, Kokkinia, director (1925–1934); Greek War Relief, Distribution Committee, representative of AWH (1934–1941). Death date unknown.

Ruth Parmelee was born in Turkey of missionary parents. After she received her medical degree at the University of Illinois, she returned to Turkey as a medical missionary. She worked in Greece with the American Women's Hospitals. In 1922, she and her nurses set up a tent hospital on the beach of Macedonia to care for deportees of war-stricken Black Sea countries and helped establish an American Women's Hospital in Salonika within the year. Recognizing the need to train nurses locally, Parmelee recommended the founding of a school, and in 1923, she opened the American Women's Hospital School of Nursing. In 1925, the hospital was turned over to the city and AWH extended its services to the interior of Macedonia and Thrace. Parmelee directed the AWH service in Greece from 1928 to 1941.

Parmelee went from the hospital at Salonika to the Kokkinia hospital, where she stayed until 1934. The nursing school, which was suspended in Salonika in 1925, was reestablished at Kokkinia. Parmelee headed the teaching staff and worked under difficult conditions to provide teaching materials where there were literally no Greek nursing texts and lessons were translated and copied on a Greek typewriter for each student. The AWH nursing school graduates served to upgrade nursing service throughout the country.

When Greece was invaded by the Italian Fascists in 1940, Parmelee, as director of the American Women's Hospitals in Greece, supervised the evacuation of several city hospitals to safer rural areas and expanded her field of activity to civilian relief. She was appointed representative of the AWH to the Greek War Relief in Athens. American relief activities were cut short in 1941 when the Nazi-Fascist regime took charge and Parmelee returned to New York.   KM

PRIMARY SOURCES
Parmelee, Ruth A. *A Maternal and Child Health Program for Greece Prepared for the Co-ordinating Committee of American Agencies in Greece.* New York: Near East Foundation, 1943.

SECONDARY SOURCES
Lovejoy, Esther C. Pohl. *Women Physicians and Surgeons: National and International Organizations.* [Livingston, NY]: Livingston Press, 1939.

PARRISH, REBECCA (1869–1952)
U.S./Philippino physician. Born 1869. Educated Medical College of Indiana. Manila, Philippines, physician (from 1906).

Rebecca Parrish departed for the Philippines in 1906 and became the first woman doctor to practice there. She established a free dispensary at Manila to treat the destitute. A small hospital for women and children was built with the financial help of an American philanthropist who named it the Mary Johnston Hospital in memory of his wife. Over the years, the hospital grew and became an important medical center. When it burned down during World War II, it was rebuilt (1950) and dedicated with a plaque honoring Dr. Parrish and her years of work in the Philippines.   KM

PRIMARY SOURCES
Parrish, Rebecca. *Iligatos ang mga bata* (Save the Babies). Manila: P. I. Ikatlong Pagkapaimbag, 1922.

STANDARD SOURCES
Lovejoy.

PARRY, ANGENETTE (1858?–1939)
U.S. physician. Born 1858?. Professional experience: Committee on American Women's Hospitals (ca. 1917–1937); American Women's Hospitals, Kokkinia, Greece (ca. 1925–1929). Died 1939.

Agenette Perry served on the Committee of the American Women's Hospitals for twenty years. She spent four years of volunteer service at the AWH in Kokkinia, Greece, with RUTH PARMELEE. Parry represented the American Women's Hospitals at the dedication of the medical center at the Résidence Sociale in Levallois-Perret (on the outskirts of Paris).   KM

STANDARD SOURCES
Lovejoy.

PARSONS, ELOISE (1895–?)
U.S. physiological chemist and physician. Born 7 July 1895 in Roswell, N.M. Married William J. Baker. Educated Randolph-Macon Woman's College (A.B., , 1917); University of Chicago (M.D., 1923); Rush Medical College, Chicago (M.D., , 1925). Professional experience: Mayo Foundation, Minnesota, fellow (1925–1926); University of Chicago, clinical assistant in medicine (1928–1929), assistant professor of gynecology and obstetrics (1929–1934); private practice (from 1934). Honors and memberships: American Medical Association, member; College of Surgeons, Fellow. Death date unknown.

Eloise Parsons was trained in medicine at both the University of Chicago and Rush Medical College. She held positions as a fellow of the Mayo Foundation and served as clinical assistant in medicine at the University of Chicago, where she was later assistant professor of gynecology and obstetrics. Although she turned to private practice in 1934, she continued to do research on a variety of topics, publishing on histamine as a constituent of secretin preparations, on hemorrhage and shock in traumatized limbs, on the treatment of diabetes during pregnancy, and on the treatment of cystic cervicitis by cauterization.   JH/MBO

PRIMARY SOURCES

Parsons, Eloise. *Histamine as a Constituent of Secretin Preparations.* Baltimore: 1925. University of Chicago, Ph.D. thesis. Private edition distributed by the University of Chicago libraries. Reprinted from *The American Journal of Physiology*, 71, no. 3 (February 1925).

SECONDARY SOURCES

Hall, Diana Long. *Academics, Blue Stockings and Biologists: Women at the University of Chicago, 1892–1932,* Annals of the New York Academy of Sciences, vol. 23. New York, 1979.

STANDARD SOURCES

AMS 5–7.

PARSONS, ELIZABETH INGERSOLL (1894–?)

U.S. immunologist. Born 8 September 1894 in Colorado Springs, Colo. Educated Vassar (A.B., 1917); Johns Hopkins University (Sc.D., 1925). Professional experience: American Museum of Natural History, department of public health, staff (1918–1919); Johns Hopkins University, research fellow (1925–1927); West Virginia State Hygienic Laboratory, director (1928–?). Death date unknown.

Elizabeth Parsons was born in Colorado, but went east to New York State to study at Vassar. After she received her undergraduate degree, she spent a brief period at the short-lived public health department of the American Museum of Natural History.

Parsons began to work toward an advanced degree in immunology at Johns Hopkins Medical School. After two postgraduate years as a research fellow at Hopkins, she was hired by the West Virginia State Hygienic Laboratory, where she remained as director from 1928. Like many women in the early half of the twentieth century, (for example, ANNA WESSELS WILLIAMS) she found career advancement and scientific satisfaction in a public health laboratory.   KM

STANDARD SOURCES

AMS 4–8, B 9.

PARSONS, ELSIE WORTHINGTON (CLEWS) (1875–1941)

U.S. pioneer anthropologist, ethnologist, and folklorist. Born 27 November 1874 in New York City to Lucy (Worthington) and Henry Madison Clews. Married Herbert Parsons, 1 September 1900 (he died in 1925). Six children (two died in infancy): three sons, one daughter. Educated by private tutors; Miss Ruel's School; Columbia University, Barnard College (A.B., 1896; A.M., 1897; Ph.D. in sociology, 1899). Professional experience: Barnard College, Harley House Fellow (1899–1902), lecturer in sociology (1902–1905); New School for Social Research, founder and lecturer (1919); Journal of American Folklore, associate editor (1918–1941); anthropological field work in U.S. Southwest (1915–1939), Oaxaca, Mexico (1932), Ecuador (1937–1938); Folklore research in Haiti, Dominican Republic, Barbados, Bahamas, Bermuda (1916–1928). Honors and memberships: American Folklore Society (president, 1919–1920); American Anthropological Society (president-elect, 1940). Died 19 December 1941 in New York City.

Born into a privileged New York family, Elsie Clews reacted against the restrictions of her family. She was educated at home by tutors and then sent to a socially acceptable girls' school in New York City. When she insisted on entering Barnard College to study further, her mother objected, but she obtained her father's consent. As an undergraduate, she was interested in philosophy, but went on to obtain first a master's and then a doctorate in sociology under Franklin Giddings. For the following four years, she lectured in the department of sociology, although this was also the period in which she married Herbert Parsons, and bore her first three children.

Although Parsons was devoted to her husband, she nevertheless expressed strong feminist sentiments in her early books, insisting for example that women had a subordinate position as a carryover from primitive society, and that women should live with prospective husbands before they decided to marry and have children. She was also a strong pacifist, objecting to World War I in such radical publications as *The Masses* and the *New Republic*. She advocated the birth-control movement led by MARGARET SANGER and supported her publicly before Sanger's trial in 1916.

Influenced by the growing field of anthropology, and particularly by Franz Boas, with whom she corresponded from 1907, she became interested in doing field work among the American Indians, realizing the importance of examining social organization. In 1919, after teaching a course at the newly founded New School for Social Research where she introduced RUTH BENEDICT to anthropology, she went with Franz Boas to the Southwest, intoducing him to research in this area. He later dedicated his *Keresan Texts* to her. Over a period of twenty-five years, she researched and published major texts on the New Mexican pueblos of Zuni, Laguna, Isleta, and Acoma, and among the Hopi in Arizona. This work culminated in a seminal synthesis, *Pueblo Indian Religion,* showing the close tie between religion and social organization among the pueblos.

Interested in comparisons with Central American pueblos, Parsons then began to do field research in Oaxaca, Mexico (looking at the Mitla, an Aztec people) and among the Andean Indians of Ecuador.

Her interest in folklore began at around the same time as her research in anthropology, and she began to collect folktales, spirituals, and other materials at Franz Boas's urging, among Afro-American and Afro-Caribbean people, traveling from Virginia to Florida, noting the great richness of the folklore of the Sea Islands of South Carolina. She extended these studies in regular trips to the Caribbean islands. Her work appeared posthumously in a three-volume collection, *Folk-Lore of the Antilles, French and English* (1943). Elsie Parsons was able to support other people's research as well, enabling research expeditions to be made to Guiana, Brazil, and elsewhere.

As a patron, Parsons supported the *Journal of American Folklore* financially while also functioning as the associate editor. She also subsidized further Pueblo research and other expeditions and publications through money contributed to the American Museum of Natural History. Although her patronage was highly important to many folklorists and anthropologists, her donations may have obscured the major importance of her own work and prevented appropriate honors. She was, however, president of the American Folklore Society in the early period of her folklore research. At the end of her life, she was president-elect of the American Anthropological Society, but before she could take up her office as the first woman president, she died in December 1941, following an appendectomy.   JH

PRIMARY SOURCES

Parsons, Elsie Clews. "The Educational Administration and Legislation of the Colonies." Ph.D. diss., Columbia University, Barnard College, 1899.
————. *The Family.* New York: G. P. Putnam's Sons, 1906.
————. "Interpreting Ceremonialism." *American Anthropologist* 17 (1915): 600–603.
————. *Isleta, New Mexico.* Bureau of Ethnology, Forty-Seventh Annual Report. Washington, D.C.: Bureau of Ethnology, 1932.
————. *Pueblo Indian Religion.* 2 vols. Chicago: University of Chicago Press, 1939.
————. "Folklore of the Antilles." In *Memoirs of the American Folklore Society.* New York: The American Folklore Society, 1943. Published posthumously.

SECONDARY SOURCES

Hare, Peter. *A Woman's Quest for Science: Portrait of the Anthropologist Elsie Clews Parsons.* New York: Prometheus Books, 1985. Written by a philosopher who is the great nephew of Parsons.
Rosenberg, Rosalind. *Beyond the Domestic Sphere: Intellectual Roots of Modern Feminism.* New Haven: Yale University Press, 1982. Includes portraits.
Zumwalt, Rosemary Levy. *Wealth and Rebellion: Elsie Clews Parsons, Anthropologist and Folklorist.* Urbana: University of Illinois Press, 1992. The most recent full-scale biography of Parsons, one of a series of publications by the American Folklore Society.

STANDARD SOURCES

AMS 3–6; Bailey; Debus; Gacs (article by Judith Friedlander); *IDA; NAW.*

PARSONS, EMILY ELIZABETH (1824–1880)

U.S. Civil War nurse and hospital founder. Born 8 March 1824 in Taunton, Mass., to Catherine Amory (Chandler) and Theophilus Parsons. Educated Cambridge High School; Massachussetts General Hospital Nursing School (1860–1862). Professional experience: Fort Schuyler Military Hospital (Long Island), nurse (October 1862–January 1863); Lawson Hospital, St. Louis, Mo., nurse (January 1863); Western Sanitary Commission Transport, head nurse on a steamship (February–March 1863); Benton Barrack Hospital, St. Louis, supervisor of nurses (April 1863–August 1864). Founded Cambridge (Mass.) Hospital (later Mount Auburn Hospital) (1871). Died 19 May 1880 in Cambridge Mass., of apoplexy (stroke).

Emily Elizabeth Parsons overcame physical disabilities in her life to become an important Civil War nurse and establish a hospital in Cambridge, Massachusetts. After studying at Cambridge High School, she had no further education until the beginning of the Civil War. In spite of impaired vision, deafness from scarlet fever, and a bad ankle, she determined to become a nurse at the outset of the war, although she was thirty-seven at the time. With the recommendation of Jeffries Wyman, professor of comparative anatomy at Harvard University, she was accepted for training at Massachusetts General Hospital, where she studied and served as a volunteer nurse for eighteen months. She was then given charge of a ward of fifty patients on Long Island at Fort Schuyler Military Hospital.

After a few months, Parsons's health began to deteriorate; while recuperating, she found a position with the Western Sanitary Commission in St. Louis, Missouri. There she worked first at Lawson Hospital and then as head nurse on the *City of Alton,* a steamboat used to transport wounded and ill soldiers. She contracted malaria, and from this period on had recurrent bouts of fever. Nevertheless, she was made supervisor of nurses at the Barracks Hospital near St. Louis. This hospital was the largest in the West. Under her efficient management, it soon had the lowest death rate in the region. She continued there after the hospital was changed to serve black refugees, the new "freedmen." By August 1864, Parsons's recurrent malaria required that she return to Cambridge, although she continued to send back clothes and provisions to St. Louis.

Determined to open her own hospital in Cambridge after the war, Parsons raised money to this end, and in 1871 obtained a charter for the Cambridge Hospital (now the Mount Auburn Hospital), which she set up in a rented house. She served as the first matron as well as nurse, but the hospital soon closed. After her death in 1880 from apoplexy, or stroke, friends and family rallied to support the hospital and reopen it six years later. Her correspondence detailing her experiences as a war nurse was published by her father in the year of her death. She was buried in Mount Auburn Cemetary, along with many other famous figures from the area.   JH/MBO

PRIMARY SOURCES
Parsons, Emily Elizabeth. *Cambridge Hospital for Women and Children.* Cambridge, Mass.: John Wilson and Son, 1868.
———. *Memoir of Emily Elizabeth Parsons.* Boston: Little Brown, 1880. Includes the correspondence of Parsons concerning her experiences in the Civil War, as edited by her father.

STANDARD SOURCES
NAW (article by George Adams).

PARSONS, HELEN TRACY (1886–?)

U.S. biochemist and nutritional chemist. Born 26 March 1886 in Arkansas City, Kans. Educated Kansas State College (B.S., 1911); University of Wisconsin (M.S., 1916); Yale University (Ph.D., 1928). Professional experience: University of Wisconsin, assistant and instructor (1913–1916); Johns Hopkins School of Hygiene and Public Health, instructor and research worker (1916–1920); University of Wisconsin, associate professor of home economics (1920–1938), professor (1938–retirement). Death date unknown.

Helen Tracy Parsons, like other important women nutritionists such as MARY SWARTZ ROSE and FLORENCE SEIBERT, trained with Lafayette B. Mendel at the Yale Physiological Chemistry Laboratory. First obtaining her undergraduate degree at Kansas State College, she received her master's degree at the University of Wisconsin. She then went to Johns Hopkins to do research with FLORENCE SABIN for four years until she obtained a position with ABBY MARLATT at the

University of Wisconsin as an associate professor in the home economics department. In the late 1920s, she returned for graduate work at Yale, where her research in the physiological chemistry laboratory focused on the effect of nephrectomy on the rat's kidney during reproduction and lactation, when the animal was fed high protein diets. Returning to Wisconsin, she was in charge of Purnell Research Laboratory in Nutrition at the university, where she studied the effects of various vitamins, especially vitamin C. She rose to full professor by 1938.

Although an excellent teacher and researcher, Parsons was not honored as fully as some of her contempory physiological nutritionists. She was suspicious of such honors, and refused at one point to sit on a committee of the American Institute of Nutrition to award the Borden Prize because of her sensitivity to the political nature of such awards and the resulting jealousies among colleagues.   JH/MBO

PRIMARY SOURCES
Parsons, Helen Tracy. With Arthur H. Smith, T. S. Mosie, and Lafayette B. Mendel. "Diet and Tissue Growth VII Responses to High Protein Diets and Unilateral Nephrectomy During Reproduction and Lactation in the Rat with Particular Reference to Kidney Changes in Both Mother and Offspring." *Archives of Pathology* 10 (1930): 1–22. The title page indicates that the data were taken from Parsons's Yale dissertation, 1928.
———. Oral history, University of Wisconsin archives. Quoted in Rossiter 1982.

STANDARD SOURCES
AMS 5–8, B 9; *P&B* 10; Rossiter 1982.

PARSONS, MARY, COUNTESS OF ROSSE (1813–1885)

English/Irish pioneer photographer. Born 23 July 1813 at Heaton near Bradford, England, to Anne Wharton-Myddelton and John Wilmer Field. One sister. Educated at home by governess. Married William Parsons, third earl of Rosse, Birr Castle, County Offaly, Ireland. Eleven children; four sons reached adulthood. Died 1885 at her house in Connaught Place, London.

Mary Field enjoyed the life of the privileged of the nineteenth century. She was fortunate to ally herself with a husband vitally involved with intellectual progress and the foremost scientists of his time, who condoned and encouraged her interests as well. After her mother's death, when she and her sister Delia were very young, Field was tutored by Susan Lawson, who recognized her artistic talent and stimulated its development. In 1836, she married William Parsons, third earl of Rosse, government official, and amateur astronomer, whose chief contribution to science was in astronomical instrumentation, particularly the design and construction of large telescopes. Parsons first occupied her time with designing furniture for Birr Castle and redesigning the surrounding grounds, adding heraldic entrance gates and a drawbridge tower, for which she made beautiful scale models.

Turning her hand to photography, she quickly mastered the chemical processes of development and experimented with both the "wet collodian" process and "daguerreotype" photos (apparatus given to her by her husband in 1842). Her first daguerreotype photographs were of her husband's great six-foot telescope. The earl sent the photos to W. H. Fox Talbot, developer of the first negative-positive process in photography, who immediately requested permission to have them framed and exhibited at what was to be the first exhibition of the London Photographic Society (later the Royal Photographic Society). The countess outfitted her own large darkroom and perfected a form of the "waxed paper" process. Her pictures were exceptionally artistic in technique and composition and were exhibited widely in Ireland and England. She won the silver medal of the Photographic Society of Ireland (1859) and was specially mentioned by the jury of the Dublin International Exhibition in 1865. She was an active member of the Amateur Photography Association and gradually collected a wide range of cameras, including one for making stereoscoptic views.

In 1845, William, as peer and Irish representative, entered the English House of Lords and set up residence in Connaught Place, London, where he and the countess entertained the leading scientists of the era and hosted showings of Talbot's "photoglyphic engravings" and the world's first news photograph. Mary Parsons took portrait photographs of family and visitors, which are wonderfully spontaneous considering the long negative exposure time required. When her husband died in 1867, she seems to have completely lost interest in photography, and in 1870 she moved out of Birr Castle and back to London, where she died in 1885. She was buried in Birr beside her husband.   JH/MBO

SECONDARY SOURCES
Mollan, Charles, William Davis, and Brendan Finucane, eds.
  More People and Places in Irish Science and Technology. Dublin:
  Royal Irish Academy, 1990.

STANDARD SOURCES
DSB (under Parsons, William).

PARTHENAY, CATHERINE DE (DAME DE ROHAN) (1554–1631)

French philosopher and mathematician, later Princess de Rohan. Born 1554. Mother Antoinette d'Aubterre. Educated by tutor, François Viète. Died 1631.

Catherine de Parthenay was noted in her day as an unusually proficient mathematician. Her mother encouraged her to learn mathematics and had her tutored as a young girl by outstanding mathematicians. A strong Calvinist, she acted as a patron to her former tutor, François Viète, one of the founders of modern algebra. He dedicated to her his work, *In artem analyticen izagoge ou Introduction à l'art de l'analyse.* In the dedication, he recognized her love for the science of mathematics.

After she became Princess of Rohan, she also translated Socrates and published an apology for Henri IV, the Protestant noble who accepted Catholicism in order to ascend the French throne.   JH/MBO

PRIMARY SOURCES
Parthenay, Catherine de. *Ballets allégoriques en vers 1592–1593.*
  Paris: E. Champion, 1927.

STANDARD SOURCES
Mozans; Rebière.

PASTERNAK, LYDIA (1902–1989)

Russian psychiatrist. Born 1902. Married Eliot Trevor Oakeshott Slater. Four children. Professional experience: Munich, Kaiser Wilhelm Institute for Psychiatry, researcher (1901–?). Died 1989.

Lydia Pasternak was the sister of Boris Pasternak, the Nobel Prize winner in literature. She worked at the Kaiser Wilhelm Institute for Psychiatry in the chemical department of Irvine H. Page. She met her future husband there, and the couple had four children. They moved to Oxford, and in her later years she translated her famous brother's poems.   JH/MBO

PRIMARY SOURCES
Pasternak, Lydia. *Beitrag zur kenntnis der algogenierten tyrosinderivate.* Berlin: Innaugural dissertation, 1926.

SECONDARY SOURCES
Vogt, Annette. "The Kaiser-Wilhelm-Gesellschaft and the
  Career Chances for Female Scientists between 1911
  and 1945." Paper presented for the International Congress for the History of Science, Liège, Belgium, 23
  July 1997.
———. "Vom Hintereingang zum Hauptportal—Wissenschaftlerinnen in der Kaiser-Wilhelm-Gesellschaft." *MPI für*

Wissenschaftsgeschichte, Berlin: Preprint 67 (1997): 32–43. Includes biographical information on Pasternak and Cécile Vogt.

PASTEUR, MARIE (LAURENT) (1826–1910)

French assistant to and wife of Louis Pasteur. Born 15 January 1826 in Clermont-Ferrand, France, to Amélie (Huet) and [?] Laurent. Married Louis Pasteur (29 May 1849). Four children (two survived to adulthood). Educated Pension Lamotte. Died 23 September 1910 in Paris. Buried in Pasteur Institute, Paris.

Marie Laurent met Louis Pasteur while he was serving as a professeur suppléant (assistant professor) at the Academy (later the University) of Strasbourg, where her father had just been appointed rector. She became interested in his scientific work and served as his amanuensis, assisting his experiments and helping him to raise silkworms when he was studying their diseases. Although she had three daughters and one son, only one daughter and her son survived to adulthood.

Marie Pasteur followed with great interest the experiments of her husband. She took care of the children attacked by rabid animals brought to him for his famed experimental treatment. After the founding of the Pasteur Institute, she lived with him in specially built quarters, where she continued to live after his death until she died at the age of eighty-four. Pasteur's students and collaborators considered her an important factor in Pasteur's success. She was buried with her husband in a tomb in the basement of the institute.

JH/MBO

SECONDARY SOURCES
Vallery-Radot, René. *Madame Pasteur.* Paris: Ernest Flamarion. 1941. This includes some letters by Marie Pasteur describing her husband's work.

STANDARD SOURCES
DFC; Mozans.

PASTORI, GIUSEPPINA (1891–?)

Italian physician. Born 12 October 1891 in Milan, Italy. Seven siblings. Never married. Educated public schools to age thirteen; tutored by her sister for secondary exams; University of Milan; University of Pavia (M.D., 1921). Professional experience: Primary school teacher; New Catholic University of Milan, research assistant; hospital in Milan, volunteer house officer; nursing home for chronic patients, house officer; Catholic University, Milan, lecturer in histology; lecturer in biology; Institute of Physiology, University of Turin, research. Death date unknown.

Giuseppina Pastori's father was a groundskeeper at a religious institution and her mother was a lacemaker who bore eight children, six of whom survived. Giuseppina was the second oldest and second girl, followed by two sisters and two brothers. She was frail and often ill as a child. The Pastori children were encouraged to attend school beyond the required age of eight; following primary school, they each attended a technical school to learn a trade. When Giuseppina told her mother of her desire to study medicine, she was scolded and forbidden even to think of it, but she continued to dream of becoming a doctor. Her younger sister MARIA was exceptionally intelligent and was allowed to continue her schooling, eventually becoming a professor of mathematics at the University of Milan and a member of three academies, including the Academia Nazionale dei Lincei. Mary taught Giuseppina mathematics, physics, chemistry, and other subjects so that Giuseppina was able to take the degree examinations as an external candidate and pass. Thus she was able to get a job teaching while she studied Latin and Greek for the *maturita classica* degree necessary for attendance at the university. She was awarded a scholarship to the university at Pavia, where she could study medicine.

In an autobiographical account, she tells of her frustration with the requirement that candidates for the obstetrical examination assist at two deliveries beforehand. The overnight sleeping area for interns was for men only and all the babies seemed to prefer coming at night. After weeks of waiting for a day birth, she asked to be allowed to sleep in the ward with the patients, so she would be available for the nighttime deliveries. After six years, Pastori received her degree in medicine and surgery (1921) and was offered a job as assistant at the new Catholic University of Milan, and there began her research in histology. To gain experience, Pastori volunteered as house officer in the hospital in Milan. She was finally given a paid job as house officer in a nursing home for chronic patients. Her job as practitioner was in addition to her university duties and research, for which she was awarded a scholarship by the Italian Medical Women's Association, which permitted her to frequent the histological laboratory of the Neurological Institute at the University of Rome. In 1930 she became a fully invested lecturer in histology and taught biology in the faculty of philosophy at Catholic University. This appointment came with the stipulation that she receive the *nihil obstat* (permission) of the Holy See. This was at first refused, but the refusal was reversed when she cited the precedent of MARIA GAETANA AGNESI of Milan, who was called to the University of Bologna by an apostolic brief.

In addition to her teaching and research, Pastori gave public lectures and wrote articles and books. After World War II, she began research on the vital functions of protozoa. In

1961, soon after the Catholic University opened its faculty of medicine in Rome, she retired, but published and gave lectures into her seventies.   KM

PRIMARY SOURCES
Pastori, Giuseppina. In Hellstedt, *Autobiographies*.

PASTORI, MARIA (1895–1975)

Italian mathematician. Born 10 March 1895 in Milan. Seven siblings. Educated Milan public schools ending at age thirteen; magisterial school; baccalaureate examination; Scuola Normale Superiore Pisa, University of Pisa (Ph.D., 1920). Professional experience: elementary school near Milan, teacher; secondary school, teacher; University of Milan, assistant, assistant professor (libera docente) through professor, chair of rational mechanics (1939–1965), Prof fuori ruola (extraordinary professor) (1965–1970), emerita professor, 1971. Died 17 April 1975 in Milan.

Maria and her sister GIUSEPPINA came from a working-class family of eight children with no academic tradition, yet they both were inspired to go beyond the minimal education that the family could afford. In the Milan public schools, Maria showed mathematical talent that was noted by a teacher. Recognizing that the family could not afford any higher education, she assisted Maria in obtaining a scholarship to a magisterial school, the equivalent of a U.S. teacher-education institution. After achieving this minimal amount of additional education, she became an elementary school teacher in a small town near Milan. However, both she and Giuseppina recognized the importance of additional education and studied together early in the morning before Maria took the commuter train to her teaching job. When Maria was twenty, they took the state examination for the baccalaureate and passed with highest honors.

Maria then took the entrance examination for the Scuola Normale Superiore of Pisa and scored so well that she received a small scholarship. She sustained herself during the four years that it took her to get her doctorate by supplementing her scholarship by tutoring. Her thesis advisor was the geometer Luigi Bianchi, and her dissertation was awarded laureate status. After earning her degree, she did well enough on her examinations to be appointed assistant at the University of Milan and moved quickly up the academic ladder to professor. The promotion system in Italian universities is based on examination scores and Maria always performed well on examinations.

Pastori's publications were numerous. Much of her research involved the absolute differential calculus, developed in Italy by Ricci and his pupil Levi-Civita. This mathematical instrument (tensor calculus) was vital in Einstein's con-

cept of the physical universe as well as in the theoretical treatment of classical physics. In her research, Pastori extended the usefulness of Ricci's calculus. She wrote many articles in which she applied mathematics to electromagnetism and other physical principles.   JH/MBO

PRIMARY SOURCES
Pastori, Maria. With Bruno Finzi. *Calcolo tensoriale e applicazioni*. Bologna: N. Zanichelli, 1949.
———. "Sullo spazio della recente teoria unitaria di Einstein." *Convegno Internazionale di Geometrica Differenziale* (1953): 107–113.
———. With Bruno Finzi. *Instituzioni di matematica*, 3d. ed. Milan: F. Mariani, [1954].
———. "Sul significato meccanico della seconda forma fondamentale per una superficie forma fondamentale per una superficie e delle forme analoghe per un sistema olonomo." *Rendiconti Instituto Lombardo di Scienze e Lettere* A 95 (1961): 1012–1023.

SECONDARY SOURCES
Kramer, Edna. "Six More Women Mathematicians." *Scripta Mathematica* 23 (1957): 83–95.

STANDARD SOURCES
Poggendorff, vol. 73.

PATCH, EDITH MARION (1876–1954)

U.S. entomologist. Born 1876 in Worcester, Mass., to Salome (Jenks) and William Patch. Educated University of Minnesota (B.S., 1901); University of Maine (M.S., 1910); Cornell University (Ph.D., 1911). Professional experience: Maine Agricultural Experimental Station, Orono (affiliated with the University of Maine), head of the department of entomology (1904–1937). Died 1954 in Orono, Maine.

Edith Patch graduated from the University of Minnesota in 1901 and taught school in that state for some years. Entomology rather than school teaching intrigued her, and she applied to agricultural stations in many states. On the grounds that "it was not a work for women" (Ogilvie 1986), she received numerous rejections. In 1903, Charles Dayton Woods, director of the Agricultural Experimental Station of the State of Maine, at Orono, offered her the unsalaried job of organizing a department of entomology. In 1904, Patch became head of the department she had organized. The agricultural station appointment made her the second woman on the university faculty. Her position at Maine was not universally accepted, as seen by the remarks of agricultural writers, one of whom pronounced it a mistake to appoint a woman as an entomologist because "a woman could not climb a tree" (Ogilvie 1986) while another noted that she would "have a hard time catching grasshoppers" (Ogilvie 1986). Dr. Woods replied to the last critic by asserting that "it would be a fairly lively grasshopper that could get away from Miss Patch" (Ogilvie 1986).

Patch, recognizing that she needed further formal training, returned to the university. She received a master's degree from the University of Maine (1910) and a doctorate from Cornell University (1911), where she studied under John Henry Comstock. In 1927 she accepted an invitation to do research at the Rothampsted Experimental Station in Harpendon, Hertfordshire, England.

Patch was recognized for her contributions. In 1930 she was chosen as the first woman president of the Entomological Association of America, and in the same year became president of the American Nature Study Society. The University of Maine awarded her an honorary doctorate in 1938. She was included in *Who's Who in Entomology, Who's Who in the World, Who's Who in the U.S.A., Who's Who in the East,* and *Who's Who in Education.* She retained her early interest in literature and, along with her scientific works, wrote a number of nature books for children.

Patch's major scientific interests were in the areas of economic and ecological entomology. Particularly concerned with the insect family Aphidae, she discovered and described habits, characteristics, food preferences, and variations in this group. One new genus and several species have been named after her. Her technical publications included fifteen books and nearly one hundred published papers. Among her publications are a short history of early women entomologists and a paper entitled "Entomology as a Vocation for Women," the latter written in 1939. MBO

PRIMARY SOURCES

Patch, Edith Marion. "Aphid Pests of Maine." "Food Plants of the Aphids." "Psyllid Notes." Bulletin 202. Orono: Maine Agricultural Experiment Station, 1912.

———. *Food-Plant Catalogue of the Aphids of the World, Including the Phylloxeridae.* Annual report 55. Orono: Maine Agricultural Experiment Station, 1955. Includes compilation of aphid literature up to and including 1955 and a bibliography.

Cornell University Library Archives contain some materials on Patch.

SECONDARY SOURCES

Mallis, Arnold. [Biography of Patch.] In *American Entomologists.* New Brunswick, N.J.: Rutgers University Press, 1971.

STANDARD SOURCES

AMS; Ogilvie 1986; *Woman's Who's Who of America.*

PATRICK, RUTH (1907–)

U.S. limnologist, botanist, and ecologist. Born 26 November 1907 in Topeka, KS to Myrtle Moriah (Jetmore) and Frank Patrick. Married Charles Hodge IV (1931). One child, Charles Hodge V. Educated University of Kansas (1925); Coker College, South Carolina (graduated 1929); University of Virginia (M.A., 1931; Ph.D., 1934). Professional experience: Academy of Natural Sciences, Philadelphia, unpaid researcher (1933); Leidy Microscopical Society (1937–1947); Microscopy Department, associate curator (1939–1947; Pennsylvania School of Horticulture, botany teacher (1935–1947). Academy of Natural Sciences, microscope section, head (1945–1947); Limnology department, founder and chair (1947–1972), Francis Boyer Chair of Limnology (1973–1997); University of Pennsylvania, lecturer in botany (1950–1970), adjunct professor (1970). Honors and memberships: National Academy of Sciences (Fellow, elected 1970); Second International John and Alice Tyler Ecology Award (1975); Ecological Society of America, Eminent Ecologist Award (1972); American Academy of Arts and Sciences (Fellow, elected 1976); Society of Environmental Toxicology and Chemistry, founder's award (1982); American Philosophical Society, Benjamin Franklin Award for Outstanding Scientific Achievement (1993); National Medal of Science (1996); twenty-four honorary degrees from various universities.

Ruth Patrick's father, Frank, was probably the major influence on her future career. Frank Patrick's father had insisted that his son study law, fearing that he could not support a family as a scientist. Frustrated in his own ambitions to become an algalogist, he enjoyed natural history as a hobby. Ruth Patrick, in turn, became intrigued with the diatoms that her father studied. However, her mother was concerned mostly that her daughter should marry well. Patrick's older sister, Catherine, who was afflicted by polio and required the attention of their mother while they were children, eventually earned a Ph.D. in psychology from Columbia University.

As a child, Ruth Patrick spent time wading in streams collecting algae, fishing beside her father, and looking at specimens through her microscope, the first of which she received when she was seven years old. There was little doubt that she would pursue a career in biology.

After one year at the University of Kansas, she left to attend Coker College in South Carolina. Her father arranged for her to spend the summers at biological stations such as Woods Hole Oceanographic Institution and the Cold Spring Harbor Laboratory on Long Island. After earning her bachelor's degree in botany, Patrick attended the University of Virginia, where she received both a master's and a doctoral degree. While at Virginia, she met and married an entomologist, Charles Hodge IV, but with her father's encouragement elected to retain her maiden name. Patrick and Hodge moved to the Philadelphia area, where he had family ties, and he taught zoology at Temple University. Patrick completed her doctoral degree by taking courses at the University of Pennsylvania and returning to Virginia to take examinations and write her thesis. In her early forties, Patrick gave birth to her only child, Charles Hodge V (b. 1951), who became a physician.

Positions were difficult to find in Philadelphia and Patrick worked at unpaid positions and part-time teaching positions until 1945 when, funded by grant monies, she joined the Academy of Natural Sciences, Philadelphia, to head the microscope section. She founded the Limnology Department, which she chaired until 1973, when she was given the Francis Boyer Chair of Limnology, a position she still had in 1997. She also taught at the University of Pennsylvania, first as a lecturer then as an adjunct professor. She led limnological expeditions to Mexico (1947), Peru, and Brazil (1955).

In her early work, Patrick studied the taxonomy and ecology of diatoms. After acquiring this basic knowledge she moved toward applied limnology studying the problems of aquatic pollution, river systems, and groundwater. Diatoms differ from other algae by having a silica shell. In the mid-1940s she presented a paper about diatom communities in which she postulated that diatoms might be useful for studying water constituents because they require different nutrients. An executive of the Atlantic Refining Company in Philadelphia recognized that diatoms could help industries concerned with pollution problems. He raised funds for Patrick to head a study on diatoms as determiners of water pollution. In spite of the scepticism of her colleagues at the Academy of Natural Sciences, she approached the problem by studying the Conestoga Basin. She became the first scientist to use a team approach of people from different disciplines. She determined that the distribution of living organisms was the true measure of whether or not a body of water was healthy. She found that in a healthy stream there was great biodiversity, but as pollution increased, the more sensitive species disappeared and more individuals of the remaining species were found.

Patrick discovered not only that diatoms yielded important information on pollution, but that they were useful in providing answers to other scientific questions. For example, as a graduate student she showed that the identification of diatoms in sediment could help reconstruct ancient environments.

Unlike many of her colleagues, Patrick has gotten along well with industry and recognized the importance of cooperation for all sectors. She has served on a large number of advisory boards and environmental organizations. She has published more than 175 works, and a look at her bibliography makes it clear with what ease she moves back and forth from theoretical to applied concerns.   JH/MBO

PRIMARY SOURCES

Patrick, Ruth. "The Diatoms of Siam and the Federated Malay States." Ph.D. diss., University of Virginia, 1934.

———. "Factors Affecting the Distribution of Diatoms." *Botanical Reviews* 14, no. 8 (1948): 473–524.

———. "A Proposed Biological Measure of Stream Conditions." *Proceedings of the International Association of Theoretical and Applied Limnology* 11 (1951): 299–307.

———. "Diatoms as an Indicator of River Change." In *Proceedings of the 9th Industrial Waste Conference, Purdue University Engineering Bulletin* 878, 325–330. West Lafayette, Ind.: Purdue University, 1954.

———. "Aquatic Communities as Indices of Pollutions." In *Indicators of Environmental Quality,* ed. W. A. Thomas, 93–100. New York: Plenum, 1972.

———. "The Potential of Various Types of Thermal Effects on Chesapeake Bay." *Journal of the Washington Academy of Sciences* 62, no. 2 (1972): 140–144.

———. "Use of Algae, Especially Diatoms, in the Assessment of Water Quality." In *Biological Methods for the Assessment of Water Quality,* eds. J. Cairns, Jr., and K. L. Dickson. Special Technical Publication 528, 76–95. Philadelphia: American Society for Testing and Materials, 1973.

———. "The Formation and Maintenance of Benthic Diatom Communities." *Proceedings of the American Philosophical Society* 120, no. 6 (1976): 475–484.

———. With V. Pye. "Groundwater contamination in the United States." *Science* 221 (1983): 713–718.

———. *Surface Water Quality: Have the Laws Been Successful?* Princeton: Princeton University Press, 1992.

———. With J. Hendrickson. "Factors to Consider in Interpreting Diatom Change." *Nova Hedwigia* 106 (1993): 361–377.

———. *Rivers of the United States.* 2 vols. New York: John Wiley and Sons, 1994–1995.

SECONDARY SOURCES

Holden, C. "Ruth Patrick: Hard Work Brings Its Own Reward." *Science* 188 (1975): 997–999. Includes an excellent bibliography.

Steinmann, M. "Ruth Patrick." In *Science Year 1986: The World Book Science Annual,* 351–362. Chicago, World Book, 1985.

Woods, M., and L. J. Forristal. "The River Doctor." In *The World and I,* 340–347. Washington, D.C.: Washington Times, 1989.

STANDARD SOURCES

AMS 6–14; Bailey; Grinstein 1997 (article by Barbara Mandula); *Notable;* Rossiter 1995.

PATTERSON, FLORA WAMBAUGH (1847–1928)

U.S. botanist. Born 1847 in Columbus, Ohio, to Sarah (Sells) and Rev. A. B. Wambaugh. Married. Two sons. Educated by private tutors; Antioch College (1860); Cincinnati Wesleyan College (M.L.A., 1865; M.A., 1883); Radcliffe College (1892–1895); University of Iowa (M.A., 1895). Professional experience: Gray Herbarium, Harvard University, assistant (1895); Division of Physiology and Pathology, U.S. Department of Agriculture, assistant pathologist in charge of herbarium (1896–1901); Division of Vegetable Pathology, Bureau of Plant Industry, mycologist in charge of pathological collections and inspection work (from 1901). Died 1928.

Patterson's research was primarily on fungal disease of plants and animals. One of many women to work for the Bureau of Plant Industry in the United States Department of Agriculture, she published on edible and poisonous mushrooms and on fungus diseases of economic importance, working and publishing with the mycologist VERA CHARLES. She was also interested in systematic mycology. JH/MBO

PRIMARY SOURCES

Patterson, Flora (Wambaugh). With Vera K. Charles and Frank J. Veihmeyer. *Some Fungous Diseases of Economic Importance.* Washington, D.C.: U.S. Government Printing Office, 1910.
———. With Vera K. Charles. *Mushrooms and Other Common Fungi.* Washington, D.C.: Government Printing Office, 1915.
———. With Vera K. Charles. *Some Common Edible and Poisonous Mushrooms.* Washington, D.C.: U.S. Government Printing Office, 1917.

SECONDARY SOURCES

"Flora Wambaugh Patterson." *Mycologia* 21 (1929): 1–4. Obituary notice.
"Flora Wambaugh Patterson." *Phytopathology* 18 (1928): 877–879. Obituary notice.

STANDARD SOURCES

AMS 1–4; Dorland; Rossiter 1982; *Woman's Who's Who of America.*

PATTULLO, JUNE GRACE (1921–1972)

U.S. oceanographer. Born 30 June 1921 in Newark, N.J., to Loraine Louise (Taylor) and David Harry Pattullo. Educated University of Chicago (B.S., 1948); University of California, Los Angeles (M.S., 1950; Ph.D., 1957). Professional experience: Scripps Institution of Oceanography, staff (1948–1960); Oregon State University, Corvalis, associate professor (1960–1963), professor of oceanography (1963–1972). Honors and memberships: International Association of Physical Oceanography, committee on mean sea level; American Society of Limnology and Oceanography, Pacific Coast Division secretary-treasurer (1964–1967); Sigma Xi; Phi Beta Kappa. Died 1972.

June Grace Pattullo received her undergraduate education at the University of Chicago, but went to the University of California to study oceanography and work at the Scripps Institution of Oceanography. She remained at Scripps as a staff member until 1960, while working for her master's and doctoral degrees in oceanography. In 1960, she moved to Corvallis, Oregon, where she was appointed associate and then full professor of oceanography by 1963.

Pattullo's research interests included the heat and water budgets of oceans; determinations of temperature, salinity, and water mass variations; the current shear across oceanic fronts. She proposed explanations for the large-scale seasonal variations in sea level. JH/MBO

PRIMARY SOURCES

Pattullo, June Grace. *Mixed Layer Depth Determined from Critical Gradient Frequency.* La Jolla, Calif.: Scripps Institution of Oceanography, 1952.

STANDARD SOURCES

AMS P&B 10, 11; Debus.

PAULA (347–404 C.E.)

Roman healer. Born 347. Died 404.

Paula followed St. Jerome's views that celibacy was the ideal, and developed a system of education for girls that, although exalting virginity and otherworldliness, also stressed scholarly achievement. Paula was the friend and colleague of FABIOLA. Jerome, writing to pagans in Rome, asked them how they could wear silks and permit themselves to be carried around by eunuchs when Paula was wearing sackcloth, trimming lamps, providing medical treatments, and bathing the sick. JH/MBO

STANDARD SOURCES

Hurd-Mead 1938; Lovejoy; Ogilvie 1986.

PAULSEN, ALICE ELIZABETH (1890–?)

U.S. psychologist. Born 15 February 1890 in New York City, N.Y. Educated Mount Holyoke College (A.B., 1913); Columbia University (M.A., 1914; Ph.D., 1924). Professional experience: New York Postgraduate Hospital, psychologist (1914–1920); Neurological Institute, New York City, psychologist (1922–1925); New York Children's Court, psychologist (1920–1930); National Committee for Mental Hygiene, psychologist (1922–1923); Cor-

nell University Clinic, psychologist (1923–1924); New York Academy of Medicine, Public Health Committee, assistant executive secretary (1925–1937); St. Luke's Hospital, New York City, psychologist (1925–1930; 1937–?). Death date unknown.

Alice Paulsen received her master's and doctoral degrees from Columbia University. The same year, her dissertation on the motor and mental effects of intestinal toxemia was published in R. S. Woodward's journal *Archives of Psychology*. Two years after she received her degree, she prepared a preliminary report on religious healing for the American Medical Association. She held a number of posts as a psychologist. Paulson was a member of the Psychological Association and the Association of Applied Psychologists (secretary-treasurer, 1930).

One of her main interests was in public health medicine. She was the assistant executive secretary for the Public Health Committee of the New York Academy of Medicine for twelve years.   JH/MBO

PRIMARY SOURCES
Paulsen, Alice. "The Influence of Treatment for Intestinal Toxemia on Mental and Motor Efficiency." Ph.D. diss., Columbia University, 1924.
———. "Religious Healing: Preliminary Report." *Journal of the American Medical Association* 86 (1926): 1519–1524; 1617–1623; 1692–1697.

STANDARD SOURCES
AMS 5–7.

PAULUCCI, MARIANNA, MARCHESA (1835–1919)

Italian botanist, malacologist, and ornithologist. Born 3 February 1835 to Giulia (De Saint Seigne) and Marchese Ferdinando Panciatichi Ximenes d'Aragona in Florence, Italy. Married Marchese Alessandro Paulucci 1853 (he died in 1887). Educated Collegio di Ripoli (Secondary School). Died 7 December 1919 in Florence.

Marianna Paulucci was born Marianna Panciatichi Ximenes d'Aragona in Florence and attended a school for the daughters of nobility, the Collegio di Ripoli. When she was eighteen, she married a titled botanist, Alessandro Paulucci. She began to study natural history and, by 1873, she and her husband had collected a large group of rare molluscs. S. P. Woodward, a malacologist who published a catalog of this collection, described her as more erudite than many scientific men, praising her willingness to use both her fortune and her intelligence in the service of science.

Paulucci began to publish her own observations in numerous notes to scientific journals and in small pamphlets published in Paris and Siena. Her first publication, in 1866, was on a fossil gastropod, *Murex veranyi*. She displayed her collection at the Paris Universal Exposition in 1878, and it was signaled out for special distinction.

By the 1880s, she had begun to publish on a regular basis, primarily on Italian gastropods, in the bulletin of the Italian Malacological Society. She described new species and multiple varieties. Ten species were named after her, and she carried on intensive correspondence with many distinguished scientists in France, England, and Germany.

By the late 1880s, Paulucci's interest had turned to ornithology. She published notes on her observations in the journal of the Florence Ornithological Society, the last note appearing in 1911. She gave her malacological collection, her library, and a legacy to the Natural History Museum at Florence. The museum then named a room after her, displayed a bust of her, and struck a gold medal in her honor. After her death, two of her manuscripts summarizing her observations on Mediterranean shells were placed in the Florence museum.   JH/MBO

PRIMARY SOURCES
Paulucci, Marianna. "Description d'une Murex fossile du terrain subappenin de la vallée de l'Elsa (Toscane)." *Journal de Conchyologie* (January 1866).
———. *Matériaux pour servir à l'étude de la Faune malacologique terrestre et fluviatile de l'Italie et de ses Îles.* Paris: Librarie F. Savy, 1878.
———. "Fauna italiana, articulo VII. Descrizione di una nuova specie del genere *Acme.*" *Bolletin Societa Malacologia Italiana* 7 (1881): 221.
———. "Contributo ornitologico sulla Toscana." In *Primo Resocento Inchiesta della Ornitologica in Italia.* Vol. 3. Ed. Enrico Hillyer Giglioli. Florence: Le Monnier, 1891.

SECONDARY SOURCES
Arrigoni degli Oddi, E. "Della vita e delle opere della Marchesa Marianna Paulucci, malacologie italiana." *Atti Reale Istituto Veneto Scienze Lettere ed Arti* 80, no. 2 (1920–1921): 59–70.

STANDARD SOURCES
Sarjeant, vol. 3.

PAVENSTEDT, ELEANOR (1903–)

U.S. psychiatrist and psychoanalyst. Born 16 March 1903 in New York City. Educated University of Zurich (1925–1926); University of Geneva (M.D., 1929). Professional experience: Massachusetts General Hospital, Boston, assistant child psychiatrist (1934–1937); James Jackson Putman Children's Center, staff psychiatrist (1943–1954); Boston Psychoanalysis Society and Institute, Inc., training analyst (1947–?); Boston University School of Medicine, assistant professor of psychiatry (1954–1958), associate professor (1958–1959), professor of child psychiatry (1960–?); Massachusetts Memorial Hospital, associate visiting psychiatrist (1955–?); Boston City Hospital, visiting physician (1957–?). Honors and memberships: American Orthopsychiatric Association, Fellow; American Psychological Association, Fellow; American Academy of Child Psychiatry, Fellow.

Eleanor Pavenstedt was born in New York City, but trained in Europe at the University of Zurich and obtained her doctorate at the University of Geneva in 1929. On her return to the United States, she became interested in psychoanalysis and after training, served as a child psychiatrist at Massachusetts General Hospital in the thirties and early forties.

In the 1940s, Pavenstedt joined the James Jackson Putnam Child Center as a staff psychiatrist, while also serving as a training analyst at the Boston Psychoanalytic Society and Institute. In the late forties, she began to serve as the director of child psychiatry at Boston University School of Medicine and soon was appointed as an assistant professor of Psychiatry, becoming a full professor of clinical psychiatry by the mid-1960s. In 1965 she expanded her association to Tufts Medical Center and became the staff child psychiatrist at the Tufts-Columbia Point Medical Center.

Pavenstedt served as an editor with Louise Jessner of a standard text on child psychiatry. Later, she and coauthor Charles A. Malone examined the children of seriously deprived and disorganized families in *The Drifters* (1967). Pavenstedt was a Fellow of the American Orthopsychiatric Association, the American Academy of Child Psychiatry, and the American Psychological Association. She was interested in problems associated with child psychoses and her research included both severe early disturbances and longitudinal studies of child development.   JH/MBO

PRIMARY SOURCES

Pavenstedt, Eleanor, ed. With Louise Jessner. *Psychopathology of Childhood.* New York: Grune & Stratton, 1959.

———. With Charles A. Malone. *The Drifters: Children of Disorganized Lower-Class Families.* Boston: Little, Brown and Co., [1967].

STANDARD SOURCES

AMS 10–12; Appignanesi; Debus.

PAVLOVA, MARIIA VASIL'EVNA (1854–1938)

Russian geologist and paleontologist. Born 27 June 1854 in Kozel'sk. Father V. S. Gortynskii, a district physician. Married (1) Illych Shishatskiy (d. 1880); (2) Aleksei P. Pavlov. Educated University of Kiev; Sorbonne; and Museum of Natural History in Paris.

Professional experience: Lubianskii Women's Courses, teacher; Shaniavskii People's University; Moscow University, professor. Honors and memberships: Ukrainian Academy of Sciences, member; Soviet Academy of Sciences, honorary member. Died 23 December 1938 in Moscow.

Mariia Vasil'evna Gortynskiia was born at Kozel'sk in Chernigovsk province. Her father was a zemstvo (district) doctor. She graduated from the Kiev Women's Institute in 1870 and began work as a teacher. However, she soon became aware of her lack of knowledge in the natural sciences, an area in which she was becoming particularly interested.

At an early age, she married a much older man, who died in 1880. As higher education was not open to women in Russia at that time, Gortynskiia went to Paris where she attended lectures in botany, zoology, and paleontology, and studied under the French paleontologist Albert Gaudry. In Gaudry's laboratory, she worked with a French paleontologist, Charles Jean Julian Deperet, and an American, Henry Fairfield Osborn, the director of the American Museum of Natural History. Osborn and Gortynskiia corresponded after he returned to the United States. In one letter, he told Gortynskiia that he had been happy when he received her letter and picture, "which I right away put into a frame so I could put it on my table where I keep the pictures of outstanding paleontologists." He congratulated her on becoming a member of the Kiev Academy of Sciences and the Petrograd Academy of Sciences. He sent her some of his most important papers.

Returning to Russia in 1885, Gortynskiia began to work at the Lubianskii Women's Courses, which had only just opened. There she became acquainted with the geologist Aleksei Petrovich Pavlov; in 1886, they were married. Apparently, she inherited money from her first husband, although little information is available about this. In this period, her first work was published. This was on the subject of ammonites, and was closely connected with Pavlov's work on the Mesozoic of the Povolzh'ia region.

Soon Pavlova turned her attention to the study of fossil mammals. As a woman, Pavlova encountered various difficulties in pursuing her research. It required the influence of her husband and Moscow University professor Vladimir I. Vernadskii for her to gain access to the paleontological materials in the collection of Moscow University. Thanks to her energy and her ability to popularize the subject, fossils began flowing in from all parts of the empire. Pavlova scoured the provincial museums, unearthing specimens and encouraging the search for more.

In 1910, Pavlova began teaching at the Shaniavskii People's University. In 1919, after the Revolution of 1917, she became a professor and head of the department of paleontology at Moscow University, where she remained until 1930.

In her obituary, Pavlova is described as "a whole stage" in Russian paleontology. As a student of Gaudry, she brought European evolutionary thinking as applied to fossils to Russia and pursued her studies and collecting activities with great vigor. She was particularly interested in hoofed mammals and also those with trunks: horses and elephants were her favorites.

Pavlova also did much to popularize paleontology with the general public, translating and writing a series of popular works. Together with her husband, she founded a geological museum with a large paleontology section at Moscow University (now the A. P. and M. V. Pavlov Museum of the Moscow Geological Research Institute). Materials that she collected formed the basis for the exhibitions of vertebrates there.

For her work on fossil animals of the Ukraine she was elected a member of the Ukrainian Academy of Sciences in 1921. In 1929, she was elected a corresponding member of the Soviet Academy of Sciences and, in 1930, made an honorary member. ACH

PRIMARY SOURCES
Pavlova, Mariia Vasil'evna. *Mamifières Fossiles de Russie.* Moscow: Kouchne'reff, 1910–1914.
———. *Prichiny vymiraniia zhivotnykh v proshedshie geologicheskie epokhi.* Moscow: 1924.
———. *Paleozoologiia.* Chaps. 1–2. Moscow: 1927–1929.

SECONDARY SOURCES
Bol'shaia sovetskaia entsiklopediia. 3d ed. Moscow: Izdvo "Sovetskaia entsiklopediia," 1973.
Borisiak, A. A., and V. V. Menner. "Mariia Vasil'evna Pavlovna." *Vestnik AN SSSR* 6 (1939): 78–80.

STANDARD SOURCES
Nalivkin.

PAYNE, NELLIE MARIA DE COTTRELL (1900–)

U.S. physiologist and entomologist. Born Cheyenne Wells, Colo. Educated Kansas College (B.S., 1920; M.S., 1921); University of Minnesota (Ph.D., 1925). Professional experience: Kansas State[?] College, assistant zoologist and entomologist (1918–1922); Lindenwood College, instructor of science and mathematics (1921–1922); University of Minnesota, department of entomology, assistant and librarian (1925–1930); National Research Council, fellow in zoology, University of Pennsylvania (1925–1927). Biological Abstracts, scientific staff (1927 to 1930s); Boston and Vienna, research investigator (1930, 1931); Plymouth, Marine Biological Laboratory, guest investigator. Honors and memberships: Zoological Society of America, member; Entomological Society of America, member.

Nellie de Cottrell Payne was born in Colorado, but did her undergraduate work and a master of science degree at Kansas State[?] College. She remained there as an assistant in zoology and entomology until she obtained her master's degree in 1921. She then went to Lindenwood College while she worked on her doctorate in invertebrate zoology at the University of Minnesota. After obtaining this degree, she remained in the university department, as assistant in entomology and as a librarian. From 1925 to 1927, she was a National Research Council fellow at the University of Pennsylvania. From 1927 to well into the 1930s she was on the scientific staff of *Biological Abstracts.*

In 1930 and again in 1931, she went to Boston and then to Vienna as a research investigator. She also was a guest investigator at the Plymouth (England?) Biological Laboratories. Her research interests included the life histories of alfalfa insects and hydroid pigments. JH/MBO

PRIMARY SOURCES
Payne, Nellie Maria de Cottrell. "Freezing and Survival of Insects at Low Temperature." *Quarterly Review of Biology* 1, no. 2 (April 1926): 270–282. Ph.D. dissertation.
———. "The Differential Effect of Environmental Factors upon Microbracon hebetor Say (Hymenoptera: Braconidae) and Its Host, Ephestia kuhniella Zeller (Lepidoptera: Pyralidae)." *Ecological Monographs* 4 (1934): 1–46.

STANDARD SOURCES
AMS 3–12; Bailey; Rossiter 1995.

PAYNE, ROSE MARISE (1909–)

U.S. immunologist, hematologist. Born 5 August 1909 in Lake Bay, Wash. Married 1942. Educated University of Washington (B.S., 1932; M.S., 1933. Ph.D. in bacteriology, 1937). Professional experience: Oklahoma Agricultural and Mechanical College, assistant professor of bacteriology (1937–1938); Seattle College, lecturer (1939–1942), research assistant and research associate (1948–1964), senior scientist (1964–1972); Stanford University Medical School, professor of medicine (1972–1982?). Concurrent positions: University of Washington, McDermott Foundation, tuberculosis research fellow (1938–1939); World Health Organization, hematology and immunology panel member (1967–1974).

Rose Marise Payne was born and educated in the state of Washington. After receiving her undergraduate and advanced degrees in bacteriology at the University of Washington, she went for one year to Oklahoma, where she taught as assistant professor of bacteriology. Returning to Seattle in 1938 to spend a year as a McDermott tuberculosis research fellow at the University of Washington, she remained at the university, first as a lecturer, until 1942. That year she married and did not take up a research or teaching positon for the following six years. She worked on various research projects in hematology and immunology at Seattle College, until she was appointed a senior scientist in 1964. She was soon serving as a consultant to the World Health Organization on leuckocyte antigen terminology, and she sat on the expert advisory panel on immunology until 1974.

When hiring professional women to major posts in academia became part of public policy in the early seventies, Rose Payne for the first time was made a full professor, moving to Stanford University School of Medicine as professor of medicine, where she remained until retirement. JH/MBO

STANDARD SOURCES
AMS 12–15.

PAYNE, SYLVIA MAY (MOORE) (1880–1976)

British psychiatrist and psychoanalyst. Born 6 November 1880 in Wimbledon, England. Father Rev. E. W. Moore. Married John Ernest Payne, Fellow, Royal College of Surgeons, 1908. Three sons. Educated Wimbledon High School; Westfield College (London University); London (Royal Free) School of Medicine for Women (M.B., B.S., 1908). Professional experience: Royal Free Hospital, house surgeon and assistant anesthetist (1907–1908); Red Cross Hospitals, Torquay, staff (1914–1918); London Clinic of Psychoanalysis, psychiatrist (1926); Institute of Psychoanalysis, honorary secretary (1929), honorary training secretary (1939), chairman of directors (1944–1947). Honors and memberships: British Psychoanalytic Society, president; Royal Society of Medicine, Fellow; British Psychological Society, Fellow (Medical Section, chairman, 1936); British Psychoanalytic Society, honorary member (1962); Commander of the British Empire (1918). Died 30 May 1976.

Sylvia May Payne was a medically trained psychoanalyst who was an important member of the British Psychoanalytic Society, along with Ernest Jones, ANNA FREUD, MELANIE KLEIN, and JOAN RIVIERE. The daughter of a Wimbledon clergyman, she was educated first in Wimbledon and then attended Westfield College, part of London University, before she went on to study medicine at London School of Medicine (then Royal Free Hospital), serving in her last year as house surgeon and assistant anesthetist. She was awarded a joint bachelor of science and bachelor of medicine degree. In the same year, she married the surgeon John Ernest Payne.

Over the next twelve years, while her three sons were young, Payne held no professional positions. At the beginning of World War I, Payne took up a medical career as Commandant and Medical Officer in charge of the Torquay Red Cross Hospital which she continued over the course of the war. In 1918, she was honored for this work by being made a Commander of the British Empire.

With the establishment of Freudian psychoanalysis in London by Ernest Jones, she trained and then began to practice as a psychiatrist at Jones's London Clinic of Psychoanalysis (later the Institute of Psychoanalysis). At the beginning of World War II, Jones, who chose not to remain in London, entrusted Payne with the administration of the institute and the British Society for Psychoanalysis. As tension began to grow in the early 1940s between the rival Freudian camps of Melanie Klein and Anna Freud, Payne was seen as a moderating force, although she sympathized with Klein. As a member of the training committee of the institute, she managed to broker an agreement between the two camps that would allow a choice between training along one line or another. She served as president of the British Psychoanalytic Society, and was made a Fellow of the Royal Society of Medicine, and a Fellow of the British Psychological Society. At the age of eighty-two, she was made an honorary member of the British Psychoanalytic Society.

JH/MBO

PRIMARY SOURCES
Payne, Sylvia May. "Observations on the Formation and the Function of the Super-Ego in Normal and Abnormal States." *British Journal of Medical Psychology* 7, no. 1 (1927).
———. "The Myth of the Barnacle Goose." *The International Journal of Psycho-analysis* 10, nos. 2 and 3 (1929).
———. "A Conception of Femininity." *The British Journal of Medical Psychology* 15, no. 1 (1935).
———. "Post-War Activities and the Advance of Psychotherapy." *The British Journal of Medical Psychology* 16, no. 1 (1936).
———. With Jack Marsh Payne. *The Metabolic Profile Test.* Oxford: Oxford University Press, 1987.

STANDARD SOURCES
Appignanesi; Uglow 1982; *WWW*, vol. 7, 1971–1980.

PAYNE-GAPOSCHKIN, CECILIA HELENA (1900–1979)

British/U.S. astronomer. Born 10 May 1900 in Wendover, Buckinghamshire, to Emma Leonora Helena (Pertz) and Edward John Payne. Three siblings. U.S. citizenship (1931). Married Sergei Ilarionowitsch Gaposchkin (1934). Three children: Edward Michael (1935), Katherine Lenora (1937), and Peter (1940). Educated London girls school; St. Paul's Girls' School (1918–1919); Newnham College, Cambridge (1919–1923); Bathurst Scholarship (A.B., 1923); Radcliffe College (Ph.D., 1925). Professional experience: Harvard College Observatory staff (1927–?), astronomer, then Phillips Astronomer; Harvard University, Department of Astronomy, professor and chairman (1956–1979). Died 7 December 1979 in Cambridge, Mass.

Cecilia Helena Payne's father, a solicitor and historian, and mother, a painter, believed in providing their three children with the best education possible. Cecilia first attended a small school in the suburbs of London and then transferred to a London girls' school, where she studied classical languages and religion. Edward Payne died in 1904, leaving the education of the children to her mother. When it came time to make a decision about further education, Cecilia, with the blessings of her mother and inspiration from one of her mother's relatives, Dorothea Horner, decided to attend Newnham College, Cambridge. At Newnham, she held a Bathurst Studentship, studied under Edward A. Milne, and received a bachelor's degree in 1906. At Cambridge, she admired astronomer Arthur S. Eddington's work, and he regarded her as a promising astronomer. Unable to find a position for Payne in England, Eddington and Leslie J. Combrie encouraged her to apply for National Research Fellowship, which allowed her to pursue astronomy at Radcliffe College and the Harvard College Observatory. She expressed an interest in studying astrophysical problems and was awarded the Mary Ewart and Arthur Hugh Clough scholarships. In 1925, she earned her doctoral degree in astronomy, becoming the first Radcliffe student to earn a doctorate in this field. Although she had previously worked at the Harvard Observatory, in 1927 she became a member of its permanent staff. Her freedom was curtailed when she was an actual employee of the observatory, and she was expected to follow its research program. After marrying the Russian-born astronomer Sergei Ilarionowitsch Gaposchkin in 1934, she became known as Payne-Gaposchkin. The couple had three children, one girl and two boys.

In 1938 Payne-Gaposchkin was appointed Phillips Astronomer and lecturer in astronomy. After a period of low pay and little recognition, Payne-Gaposchkin was credited with many "firsts" in astronomy. She was appointed full professor at Harvard, the first woman to achieve that rank. She also became the first woman chairperson of a department at Harvard University (1956–1960). In 1965, she was appointed astronomer at the Smithsonian Astrophysical Observatory. Wilson College (1942), Cambridge University (1950), Smith College (1951), and the Western College for Women (1953) all awarded her honorary degrees. In addition she received the Award of Merit from Radcliffe, the Annie Jump Cannon medal of the American Astronomical Society, and the annual achievement award of the American Association of University Women (AAUW). She was an active member of the Society of Friends and interested in music, painting, and fiction writing. She wrote an autobiographical account entitled "The Dyer's Hand." Payne-Gaposchkin was a successful astronomer in a culture where combining marriage and professional life was seldom done. An unconventional spouse and sympathetic employers made

it possible for this arrangement to work. Payne-Gaposchkin died in Cambridge, Massachusetts, on 7 December 1979.

Payne's Radcliffe dissertation, "Stellar Astrophysics," was published as a monograph. In this work she applied Meghnad Saha's ionization theory to the determination of stellar temperatures and chemical abundances. At the Harvard Observatory, she became interested in the spectroscopy of supergiants, Wolf-Rayet stars, and variables. From this work, she published another classic monograph, *The Stars of High Luminosity* (1930). After these two promising pieces of research, she undertook, at Harlow Shapley's suggestion, a study of photographic stellar photometry. Since this work was both tedious and time-consuming, although important, she was convinced that it took up too much of her time. However, it did lead her into variable star research, the field for which she is best known. After marriage, she and her husband collaborated on variable star research. They jointly published *Variable Stars* in 1938. After the publication of this work they analyzed all known variable stars recorded in the Harvard Observatory photographic plate collection. Payne-Gaposchkin went beyond merely analyzing the plates. She used her understanding of variable stars to place them in perspective, as indicators of the structure of the galaxy, as playing a role in stellar evolution, and in their relationships to each other. She published over 150 papers and two semipopular books, in addition to the monographs previously mentioned.

JH/MBO

PRIMARY SOURCES

Payne-Gaposchkin, Cecilia. "Stellar Atmospheres: A Contribution to the Observational Study of High Temperature in the Reversing Layers of Stars." Ph.D. diss., Radcliffe College, 1925.

———. With Harlow Shapley. "Photographic Magnitudes of Bright Stars Between +25° and +15°." Harvard Observatory Monographs 1, no. 2 (1935).

———. With Sergei Gaposchkin. "Variable Stars: A Study Completed." *Science* 107 (1948): 590.

———. "Variable Stars and Galactic Structure." *Nature* 170 (1952): 223–225.

———. *Variable Stars and Galactic Structure.* London: Athlone Press, University of London, 1954.

———. *Cecilia Payne-Gaposchkin: An Autobiography and Other Recollections.* Ed. Katherine Haramundanis. Cambridge: Cambridge University Press, 1984. Includes complete bibliography.

SECONDARY SOURCES

Gingerich, Owen. "Obituaries. Cecilia Payne-Gaposchkin." *Quarterly Journal of the Royal Astronomical Society* 23 (1982): 450–451. Obituary notice.

Kidwell, Peggy A. "Cecilia Payne-Gaposchkin: The Making of An Astrophysicist." In *Making Contributions: An Historical Overview of Women's Role in Physics,* ed. B. Lotze, 43–63. College Park, Md.: American Association of Physics Teachers, 1983.

Smith, Elske V. P. "Cecilia Payne-Gaposchkin." *Physics Today* 33 (June 1980): 64–65. Obituary notice.

STANDARD SOURCES

Grinstein 1993 (article by Soraya Svoronos); *Newham Roll; Notable* (article by Mindi Dickstein); Poggendorff, vol. 6; *Uneasy Careers* (article by Peggy Kidwell).

PEAK, HELEN (1900–1985)

U.S. psychologist. Born 17 May 1900 in Dallas, Tex. Educated University of Texas (B.A., 1921); Radcliffe University (M.A., 1924); Yale University (Ph.D., in psychology, 1930). Postdoctoral fellowships and grants: Yale University, Sterling fellowship (1932–1933); University of Michigan, Ann Arbor, Office Naval Research grant (1955–1959); Center for Advanced Study, fellow (1958–1959); University of Michigan, Ann Arbor, Social Science research council faculty, fellow (1964–1965); Ford Foundation Behavioral Science Research Fund, fellow (summer 1960); Rackham faculty research grant (1960–1961). Professional experience: Girls' Training School, Texas, clinical psychologist (1924–1926); Southern Methodist University, instructor in psychology (1926–1927); Yale University, research assistant (1929–1932); Randolph-Macon Woman's College, professor and chair, psychology department (1933–1949); War Production Board, psychologist (1944–1945); U.S. Strategic Bombing Survey, Office of War Information, bombing analyst (1945–1946); Connecticut College, professor of psychology and chair of psychology department (1946–1950); University of Michigan, Ann Arbor, Kellogg Professor (1950–1970), emerita professor of psychology (1970–?). Honors and memberships: American Board of Examiners of Professional Psychologists, vice-president (1951); Journal of Experimental Social Psychology, member, board of editors (1965–1971); American Psychological Association Board of Directors, Policy and Planning Board, Publications Board, member. Died 28 October 1985.

Helen Peak did her undergraduate work at the University of Texas, then traveled east for her master's degree at Radcliffe College (1924). For a time, she returned to Texas to work as a clinical psychologist at a girls' training school (1924–1926), and as instructor in psychology at Southern Methodist University (1926–1927), before returning for a doctorate at Yale University (1930). While at Yale, she combined studies with a job as research assistant, and received a Sterling fellowship (1932–1933), which enabled her to continue her training in scientific methodology. She was one of the early group to approach problems and variables of social behavior using precise laboratory measurement and experimentation. Like so many other women seeking a place in the profession during this period, Helen Peak had to overcome blatant discrimination due to her sex, ranging from William McDougall's barring her from his seminar at Harvard to inequities in research and job opportunities. A charming and gracious southern woman, she also possessed the Texas pioneer determination and independent spirit that enabled her to succeed. When a national organization of women psychologists was formed, Peak refused to join, preferring to receive recognition as an equal within the male-dominated establishment.

Prior to World War II, Peak was professor and chair of the psychology department at Randolph-Macon Woman's College (1933–1949). With the war came additional opportunity for behavioral research and Peak's skills in the study of personality and interpersonal relations were used by the War Production Board (1944–1945), the Office of War Information (1945–1946), and the U.S. Strategic Bombing Survey. Her publications from the Likert bombing survey were among the few technical reports to appear in psychological journals.

After the war, Peak continued her research with an Office of Naval Research grant (University of Michigan, Ann Arbor, 1955–1959) and a fellowship from the Center for Advanced Study (1958–1959). Her projects were concerned with attitudinal structure and change. She and her students developed techniques for measuring the strength of values and goals and the perceived relevance of means for reaching these goals. Her experiments showed how attitudes could be changed and led her to the development of a general activation theory of both motivational processes and the properties of structure.

From 1946 to 1950, Peak served as professor of psychology and chair of the department at Connecticut College; then she accepted the position of Kellogg Professor, University of Michigan, Ann Arbor (1950–1970), becoming an emerita professor of psychology in 1970. Highly respected by her colleagues and students, Helen Peak contributed significantly to behavioral psychology and helped reunite social psychology with individual psychology through her research and overarching general theories on attitude change in relation to attitude structure and cognitive structure.   JH/MBO

PRIMARY SOURCES

Peak, Helen. *Modification of the Lid-Reflex by Voluntary Induced Sets.* Princeton, N.J.: Psychological Review Co., [1931]. Monograph taken from her doctoral dissertation.

———. *Research Methods in Behavioral Science.* Dryden, N.Y.: N.p., 1953.

————. *Observations on the Characteristics and Distribution of German Nazis.* Washington, D.C.: American Psychological Association, 1945.

————. *Nebraska Symposium on Motivation.* Lincoln: University of Nebraska Press, 1955.

————. *Person Perception and Interpersonal Behavior.* Stanford, Calif.: Stanford University Press, 1958.

————. *Theories of Cognitive Consistency.* New York: Rand McNally, 1968.

SECONDARY SOURCES

Katz, Daniel. "Helen Peak (1900–1985)." *American Psychologist* 42 (1987): 510. Obituary notice.

Tolman, Ruth. "Helen Peak." *Journal of Consulting Psychology* 1933. Obituary notice.

STANDARD SOURCES

AMS 5–8, S&B 9–12.

PEARCE, LOUISE (1885–1959)

U.S. pathologist and physician. Born 5 March 1885 in Winchester, Mass., to Susan Elizabeth (Hoyt) and Charles Ellis Pearce. One younger brother. Never married. Educated Girls' Collegiate School, Los Angeles (1900–1903); Stanford University (A.B., 1907); Boston University (1907–1909); Johns Hopkins University (M.D., 1912). Professional experience: Rockefeller Institute, assistant pathologist and bacteriologist (1913–1915), associate (1916–1923), associate member (1923–1951). Honors and memberships: Belgium Order of the Crown (1920); National Research Council, member (1931–1933); Princeton Hospital, trustee (1940–1944); Woman's Medical College, Pa., Board of Corporators, member (from 1941; president, 1946–1951); New York Infirmary for Women and Children, Blackwell Citation (1951); Belgian Officer of Royal Order of Lion (1953). Died 9 August 1959 in New York City.

Born in Winchester, Massachusetts, Louise Pearce grew up in California, where her family began ranching. Louise attended high school in Los Angeles. After four years at Stanford University, she received a bachelor's degree in physiology and histology. She then moved to Boston, where she studied and worked at the Boston University School of Medicine as an instructor in embryology and assistant in histology. Although she was offered a scholarship from the Woman's Medical College of Pennsylvania, she declined because of financial constraints.

In 1909, she was admitted to the Johns Hopkins University School of Medicine with advanced standing. After graduating third in her class in 1912, Pearce was appointed as a fellow by the Rockefeller Institute in 1913, advancing to assistant then associate. Although she remained at the institute until she retired in 1951, she was never promoted to full member. Simon Flexner cited economic depression as the reason.

In 1919, while working with the pathologist Wade Hampton Brown at the Rockefeller Institute, Pearce discovered tryparsamide to be an effective agent against sleeping sickness in rabbits. The two published their results in 1919. From 1920 to 1921, she conducted the African Sleeping Sickness Mission in the Belgian Congo, investigating the effectiveness of tryparsamide in human beings. The spectacular success of the drug therapy resulted in an award from the Belgians, the Order of the Crown of Belgium (1920). For the next two years, Pearce was visiting professor of Medicine at the Peking Union Medical College.

Returning to New York and the Rockefeller Institute, Pearce continued important work with Brown on syphilology and cancer research. The two researchers began to study in a systematic way the development of malformations in the rabbit. They also identified a small scrotal tumor in rabbits, which proved to be a very useful tool in cancer research, the Brown-Pearce tumor. She and her colleagues also isolated an important rabbit virus that was decimating their rabbit colony.

The laboratory was then moved to Princeton, New Jersey, but after Brown's death in 1942, Pearce began to wind up the research, ending the breeding program and writing up their research on hereditary malformations.

Pearce had achieved a reputation as a distinguished researcher in the United States and abroad. She was a trustee of the New York Infirmary for Women and Children and, in 1940, she became trustee of Princeton Hospital, Princeton, New Jersey, and a member of the Board of Corporators of the Woman's Medical College, Pennsylvania.

In the mid-forties, Pearce was appointed president of the Woman's Medical College of Pennsylvania, a position she held while continuing her research on resistance and susceptibility to disease. At the time of her retirement from both the Rockefeller Institute and her presidency, she received the Blackwell Citation, given by the New York Infirmary for Women and Children. A Women's Medical College Citation followed the next year. Other honors included two further awards from Belgium: the Leopold II First Laureate Prize and Officer of the Royal Order of the Lion in 1953.

Pearce retired to Trevenna Farm, in Skillman, New Jersey, where she lived with the novelist Ida A. J. Wylie. While returning from a trip abroad, she became ill and died in New York City soon after. She was a member of the Society for Experimental Pathology; the Association of Pathologists and Bacteriologists; the Society of Experimental Biologists; the Society of Pharmacology; the Association for Cancer Research; the Social Hygiene Association; Society of Tropical

Medicine; the Genetics Association; the Harvey Society; New York Society of Tropical Medicine; the New York Academy of Medicine; and the Pathologists' Society of Great Britain and Ireland. She also held honorary memberships in other international societies. JH/MBO

PRIMARY SOURCES

Pearce, Louise. With J. H. King and J. E. Bigelow. "Experimental Obstructive Jaundice." *Journal of Experimental Medicine* 14 (1911):159–178.

———. With W. H. Brown. "Multiple Infections with *Treponema pallidum* in the Rabbit." *Proceedings of the Society for Experimental Biology and Medicine* 18 (1921): 258.

———. With T. M. Rivers. "Effects of a Filterable Virus (Virus III) on the Growth and Malignancy of a Transplantable Neoplasm of the Rabbit." *Journal of Experimental Medicine* 46 (1927): 81–99.

———. *The Treatment of Human Trypanosomiasis with Tryparsamide: A Critical Review.* Monograph no. 23. New York: Rockefeller Institute for Medical Research, 1930.

———. With P. D. Rosahn and C. K. Hu. "Experimental Transmission of Rabbit-Pox by a Filterable Virus." *Proceedings of the Society for Experimental Biology and Medicine* 30 (1932–1933): 894–896.

———. "Experimental Syphilis: Transmission to Animals and the Clinical Reaction to Infection." In *Syphilis,* ed. F. R. Moulton. Publication no. 6, 58–71. Washington, D.C.: American Association for the Advancement of Science, 1938.

———. With A. E. Casey and P. D. Rosahn. "The Association of Blood Cell Factors with the Transplantability of the Brown-Pearce Tumor." *Cancer Research* 2 (1942): 284–289.

SECONDARY SOURCES

Alsop, Gulielma Fell. *History of the Woman's Medical College, Philadelphia, Pennsylvania, 1850–1950.* Philadelphia: J. B. Lippincott Co., 1950.

Rockefeller Archives Center Newsletter. (Summer 1989): 12.

STANDARD SOURCES

AMS 3–8, B 9; Bailey; Debus; Grinstein 1997 (article by Anne-Marie Scholer); *NAW*(M) (article by George W. Corner).

PEARL, MAUD DEWITT (fl. 1923)

U.S. biological editor. Married Raymond Pearl.

Maud Dewitt Pearl assisted her husband, Raymond Pearl, in editing the journal *Human Biology,* serving as the journal's book review editor. After Raymond Pearl's death, she prepared his scientific papers for publication. She bemoaned the low caliber of the men elected to the National Academy of Sciences. JH/MBO

PRIMARY SOURCES

Pearl, Maud Dewitt, ed. With Raymond Pearl. *Man, the Animal.* Bloomington, Ind.: Principia Press, 1946.

STANDARD SOURCES

Rossiter 1982.

PECHEY-PHIPSON, MARY EDITH (1845–1908)

British physician. Born 1845 near Colchester, England. Sixth of seven children. Married Herbert Phipson (1889 in Bombay, India). Educated University of Edinburgh; Bern University (M.D., 1877). Professional experience: Birmingham and Midlands Hospital for Women, house surgeon (1875–1876); private practice, Leeds, Yorkshire (1877–1883); Medical Women for India Fund, founder; secretary (1880s); Kama Hospital for Women and Children, Bombay, director; private practice, Bombay (from 1884). Died 1908 at Folkestone, England, of breast cancer.

Mary Edith Pechey was the daughter of a Baptist minister and was educated as a governess. Wanting to do more with her life and frustrated by English society's imposed limitations, she helped initiate the struggle for women's education in medicine when, along with SOPHIA JEX-BLAKE and others, she applied to the University of Edinburgh. There, in competition, she won the Chemistry Prize, which awarded the Hope Scholarship and 250 pounds, but they were withdrawn because she was a woman and therefore ineligible. The women at Edinburgh were also denied certificates of attendance for the classes they had completed. Both decisions were appealed and the University Senate agreed to issue the certificates but not to reconsider the issue of Pechey's scholarship. Pechey and the other women attending classes at Edinburgh were subjected to extreme harassment and threats, but garnered a considerable body of support among the press and public. Eventually, the courts upheld Edinburgh's refusal to give medical degrees to women, and Pechey, along with Jex-Blake, transferred to Berne University in Switzerland and completed her medical degree there in 1877. In 1879, she became one of the founding members of the Medical Women's Federation, an organization to help bond the growing numbers of medical women in the face of educational and professional opposition.

Pechey was appointed House Surgeon at the Birmingham and Midlands Hospital for Women in 1875. She gave educational lectures on physiology to women's groups in Yorkshire during the 1870s. Following the Enabling Act of 1876, she went to Berne, Switzerland, to complete her medical degree. Returning to Leeds, she set up a private practice.

In the 1880s, Pechey founded the Medical Women for India Fund to help women physicians practice abroad. Pechey herself went to India in 1883 for her work in the Medical Women for India movement. She ran a dispensary and started a private practice in Bombay in 1884 and was appointed senior medical officer of the new Kama Hospital for Women and Children. In 1889 she married Herbert Phipson, who also worked with the fund. Pechey learned Hindustani and established a nursing school and campaigned for improved health services and the banning of child marriages. She was elected to the senate of the University of Bombay.

In 1905, Pechey-Phipson returned to England via Australia and Canada and became an active speaker for women's and children's rights and suffrage. Before her death, she established and endowed the Pechey-Phipson Sanitorium for Women and Children near Nasik in India. She died in 1908 at Folkestone of breast cancer. JH/MBO

PRIMARY SOURCES

Pechey-Phipson, Edith. *Upon the Constitutional Causes of Uterine Catarrh, with Notes of Personal Observation.* Brighton: M. Sickelmore, 1877.

————. *Inaugural Address Delivered October 1st, 1877 [at the] London School of Medicine for Women.* London: McGowan, 1878.

SECONDARY SOURCES

Blake, Catriona. *Charge of the Parasols: Women's Entry to the Medical Profession.* London: Women's Press Ltd., 1990.

Lutzker, Edythe. *Edith Pechey-Phipson, M.D.* New York: Exposition Press, 1973.

STANDARD SOURCES

Uglow 1982.

PECKHAM, ELIZABETH (GIFFORD) (1854–1940)

U.S. arachnologist and entomologist. Born 1854 in Milwaukee, Wis., to Mary (Child) and Charles Gifford. Married George Peckham. Three children. Educated Vassar College (B.A., 1876; M.A., 1888); Cornell University (Ph.D., 1916).

Elizabeth Peckham did research on the behavior and taxonomy of spiders and wasps. She coauthored many works with her entomologist husband and published a paper by herself on protective resemblance in spiders. JH/MBO

PRIMARY SOURCES

Peckham, Elizabeth. *Protective Resemblances in Spiders.* Milwaukee, Wis.: Natural History Society of Wisconsin, 1889.

————. With George Peckham. *Spiders of the Homolattus Group of the Family Attidae.* Milwaukee, Wis.: Natural History Society of Wisconsin, 1895.

————. With George Peckham. *On the Instincts and Habits of the Solitary Wasps.* Madison, Wis.: State of Wisconsin, 1898.

STANDARD SOURCES

AMS 2–3. *Woman's Who's Who of America.*

PEEBLES, FLORENCE (1874–1956)

U.S. biologist. Born 1874 in Pewee Valley, Ky., to Elizabeth (Cummins) and Thomas Peebles. Never married. Educated Girls' Latin School, Baltimore; Woman's College of Baltimore (Goucher College) (B.A., 1895); Bryn Mawr College (1895–1896; Ph.D., 1900); University of Munich and University of Halle (1899); University of Bonn (1905); University of Würzburg (1911); University of Freiburg (1913). Professional experience: Bryn Mawr College, demonstrator in biology (1897–1898), acting head of biology department (1913), associate professor of biology (1917–1919), Goucher College, instructor in biology (1899–1902); Miss Wright's School, Bryn Mawr, Pa., instructor in science (1906–1912); Sophie Newcomb College, Tulane University, head of biology department (1915–1917); California Christian (now Chapman) College, professor of biological sciences (1928–1942). Died 1956 in Pasadena, Calif.

Florence Peebles was a competent research biologist, an outstanding teacher, and a sensitive humanitarian. She had several careers in her long life, the first involving teaching and research. She taught biology for thirty-three years at Goucher, Bryn Mawr, and Sophie Newcomb Colleges. Kentucky-born Peebles, along with other outstanding women scientists of her day, studied under Thomas Hunt Morgan at Bryn Mawr College. Her research reflected Morgan's early interest in regeneration; much of it involved marine specimens. Between 1895 and 1924 she spent much time doing research at the Marine Biological Laboratory at Woods Hole, Massachusetts. She held the American Women's Table at the Naples Zoological Station in Italy five times between 1898 and 1927.

After retiring from teaching in 1928, Peebles began her second career, establishing a bacteriology department at Chapman College in California, where she became professor of biology. Her second retirement ended when she founded the biology laboratory, named in her honor, at Lewis and Clark College in Portland, Oregon. She received an honorary degree from Goucher College. At eighty, Peebles became an authority on gerontology, stating that "grandma and grandpa should be rehabilitated—not scrapped." Her last "retirement" occurred in 1946, when she moved to Pasadena,

California. During this retirement she was active in community service, particularly as a counselor for the aged.

Florence Peebles touched the lives of many people through her commitment to teaching and general humanitarian pursuits. In 1956 she sponsored a young Japanese woman who wished to study in the United States. Her unfinished Christmas letter of 1956, reporting to friends on the year's events, noted "the arrival of my little Japanese girl after five months of dickering with the American Consul in Tokyo." Peebles entered her protégée at Pasadena City College, where, "although she was two months later than the class in starting, she passed second from the top in the final exam." In August 1956 Peebles suffered a stroke and dictated the letter from a convalescent home in Pasadena, where she died in December. Peebles is thought to have written an unpublished autobiography.   MBO

PRIMARY SOURCES

Peebles, Florence. *Some Experiments on the Primitive Streak of the Chick*. Leipzig: Engelmann, 1898.

———. *Experiments in Regeneration and in Grafting of Hydrozoa*. In *Bryn Mawr College Biological Laboratory Monographs*. Reprint Series. Bryn Mawr, Pa., 1901.

———. *The Influence of Grafting on the Polarity of Tubularia*. In *Bryn Mawr College Biological Laboratory Monographs*. Reprint Series. Bryn Mawr, Pa., 1908.

———. With Dennis L. Fox. *The Structure, Functions, and General Reactions of the Marine Sipunculid Worm Dendrostoma zostericola*. Berkeley: University of California Press, 1933.

SECONDARY SOURCES

Rossiter, Margaret. "Women Scientists in America before 1920." *American Scientist* 62 (May–June 1974): 212–323. Peebles is discussed on pages 247–248.

STANDARD SOURCES

AMS 1–8, B 9; Ogilivie 1986; *Woman's Who's Who of America*; *WWW(A)*, vol. 5, 1969–1973.

PELL, ANNA JOHNSON (1883–1966)

See Wheeler, Anna Johnson Pell.

PELLETIER, MADELEINE (1879–1939)

French physician and feminist. Born 18 May 1874 in Paris to Anne (Passavy) and Louis Pelletier. Number of siblings uncertain, but references indicate an older brother and a younger sister. Christened Anne. Never married. Educated primary school, Paris (1881–1886); University of Paris (passed baccalaureate July 1897; PCN July 1898); Paris Medical Faculty (graduated 1903). Professional experience: Paris hospitals, emergency night duty (1903–1906); *Salpetrière, psychiatric intern (1903–1906); private practice (1903–1914; 1918–1938); French Mental Health Service, medical officer (from 1904); Postes et Télégraphes, medical officer (1911?–1918?). Died 1939.*

Madeleine Pelletier is best known for her feminist views, but she both trained and published in medicine. Her feminism pervaded all of her work.

Pelletier's early home life was extremely difficult. Her father was paralyzed by a stroke and her illegitimate mother was slovenly, of poor moral character, a monarchist, and a religious zealot. The exact number of her siblings is unknown, but Pelletier later mentioned that her mother had had eleven miscarriages. Although her father taught her to read, Pelletier did not begin to attend school until she was seven. When she went to school, the other children made fun of her because of her untidiness. She was clearly intelligent, but had trouble with written work. In spite of the fact that the nuns encouraged her to continue with school, she left at the age of thirteen and began attending evening meetings of feminist and anarchist groups. A nonconformist in dress as well as ideas, Pelletier wore men's clothes.

Her enjoyment of her association with the bohemian anarchists and feminists began to wane, and when she was in her mid-twenties, Pelletier decided that the way to success was through the intellect. Thus she decided to resume her studies. She prepared for her baccalaureate by herself, a very difficult task. She passed the examination, was awarded a scholarship, and passed the preparatory certificate in physics, chemistry, and natural sciences, and qualified to enter medical school. In 1898 she began studying medicine and passed her examinations adequately but not brilliantly in 1903. However, her thesis, also submitted in 1903, was an excellent piece of research.

Anthropology was a major interest of Pelletier from the time of her baccalaureate studies. Both medicine and anthropology seemed to confirm her positivist scientific biases and legitimize her reaction against her mother's religious mysticism. The French neurologist and anthropologist Paul Broca claimed that women's brains were smaller and less developed than men's and would only increase with improved education. This had been taken still further by one of his disciples, the sociologist Gustave Le Bon, who insisted that women's social roles must be limited. Still, Pelletier was drawn to Broca's Paris Anthropological Society for its materialistic, positivistic, evolutionary, and freethinking approach—all very attractive to her. Her first work in anthropology was in craniometry, the assumption that a correlation exists between the size and shape of the skull and intelligence. At the time when Pelletier began her research, craniometry was losing its respectability. Under the direction of Léonce Manouvrier, who had challenged Le Bon's views, she published three research articles, one of which suggested modifications of Broca's scale; the other two were analyses of fifty-five Japanese skeletons to determine the relationship between skull capacity and body size in different races and sexes. She also worked with a Romanian, Nicholas Vaschide. The paper that resulted from their collaboration, "Les Signes physiques de l'intelligence," began with the assumptions of the racial evolution of the brain. They attempted to correlate skull shape to intelligence in a group of primary school children in a working-class suburb of Paris. Their results showed that there was little difference, based on a method of measuring auricular height, between previously denoted intelligent and unintelligent children. There was an obvious contradiction between her feminism and her work, which might support the theory of the intellectual inferiority of women. The interesting result of her research was that it was demolished by biometrician Karl Pearson, a socialist, a freethinker, and a believer in the emancipation of women. He indicated that the statistical methods employed by craniometer were flawed. The discounting of her work probably saved her from a contradiction between her feminism and science. However, Pelletier's experiences in the Anthropological Society enabled her to educate herself in the scientific arguments for women's inferiority.

When Pelletier finished her medical training in 1903, she found that it was difficult for a woman doctor to attract patients. Her early work involved emergency night duty and a three-year posting as a psychiatric intern. Pelletier intended to make psychiatry her career but immediately ran into difficulties. After she successfully registered for the examination, she was denied permission to take it because she was a woman. She appeared at the examination as a protest, knowing she would be turned away. After a successful public relations campaign, she was allowed to take the examination. She successfully passed the competitive examination on 3 December 1903 after a first, thwarted attempt. Even though she found the French asylum environment hostile, it allowed her to do research in psychiatry. In this period she produced four papers and her doctoral thesis. She also produced her first clearly feminist pamphlets, offering a critique of the scientific community within which she moved. Her entire career became a conscious focusing on feminist goals. Although she agreed with her fellow socialists that women were oppressed by class, she added that women were oppressed regardless of class by men. She joined La Solidarité des Femmes, a support group for feminist ideas and political activism. Pelletier was somewhat dismissive of Solidarité's militance, considering many of the women as members of the bourgeoisie.

During the course of her career, Pelletier campaigned on a wide range of feminist issues, many focused on votes for women. Between 1906 and 1912, Pelletier had lost the chance to rise in the psychiatric service and limited her

medical career to a small private practice. She spent her energies on both socialism and feminism. An inevitable conflict arose between Pelletier's socialism and her feminism. However, she attempted to resolve it by broadening the socialist agenda to include women. Practically and tactically, she appropriated socialist electoral machinery for feminist ends. She did not win any position she sought as a socialist candidate. Since socialism had many factions, she found one in which she could work, the Guesdistes. Although a far-left socialist herself, she believed that it was essential for feminists to cooperate across class lines and that socialist women should keep links with bourgeois feminists. After the defeat of two resolutions on women's rights sponsored by the Guesdistes, she moved to a further left group, the Hervéistes, in which she worked from 1907 to 1911. During this period, she wrote a number of militant articles in *La guerre sociale.*

Between 1911 and 1914, Pelletier published a series of books and pamphlets on sexual emancipation, abortion, female education, and social justice. During this period she earned most of her meagre income from a position that she held as a medical officer for the Postes et Télégraphes. Her private medical practice brought in negligible earnings. At the outset of World War I, she closed her surgery and moved to the *pension* of Elizabeth Renaud, a feminist and socialist militant. During this period she kept a war diary, which was both a personal record and a psychosocial study. She suffered from intense depression as she found her socialist dreams and personal expectations thwarted.

In 1918, Pelletier reopened her surgery, this time in the Latin Quarter. She was heartened by the situation in Russia, for it seemed to be the revolution that she and the other socialists had long awaited. She enthusiastically allied herself with the Bolshevik cause and in 1921 made a pilgrimage to the Soviet Union. On this trip she was forced to confront the implications of revolution and to attempt to square pacifism with revolutionary ideas. Even though conditions were abysmal, she found many things of which she approved, including a woman soldier and women in many hitherto all-male professions. In spite of these "advances," the women seemed to accept their inferior status—few were in the highest levels of government.

Pelletier's medical practice began to expand in the 1920s and 1930s. One of her major disappointments came during this period—the defeat of the women's suffrage campaign by the Senate in 1922. She became less active in organized feminism. In 1925 she became disillusioned with the Communist Party and left it. From 1925 to 1935, she moved from publishing political and social works to fiction. Pelletier's choice of costume was seen by her contemporaries as somewhat eccentric, since she adopted men's clothing. This represented a strong political as well as social comment on her part.

In April 1939 the police raided Pelletier's surgery and arrested her cleaning woman and her midwife on the charge of performing abortions under Pelletier's direction. Pelletier was released, for at that time she was partially paralyzed. In June after the initial investigation, she was declared mentally incompetent and was committed to the insane asylum of Perray-Vaucluse. Her friends were convinced that she was as mentally competent as ever and that her incarceration in the asylum was politically motivated. After six months in the asylum, Pelletier died. JH

PRIMARY SOURCES

Pelletier, Madeleine. *Le féminisme et la famille.* Paris: n.d.

———. "Sur un nouveau Procédé pour obtenir l'indice cubique du crâne." *Bulletins de la Société d'Anthropologie de Paris* (7 March 1901): 188–193.

———. "Étude de la phylogenèse du maxillaire inférieur." *Bulletins de la Société d'Anthropologie de Paris* (1 May 1902): 537–545.

———. With N. Vaschide. "Les signes physiques de l'intelligence." *Revue de Philosophie* (1 October 1903); reprinted (1 February 1904).

———. With Dr. Marie. "Le sérum marin dans la thérapeutique des aliénés." *Archives de biothérapie* (May 1905): 49–74.

———. *L'éducation féministe des filles.* Paris: 1914.

SECONDARY SOURCES

Gordon, Felicia. *The Integral Feminist: Madeleine Pelletier, 1874–1939.* Minneapolis: University of Minnesota Press, 1990. An excellent biography that includes a complete bibliography of Pelletier's works. It also includes a discussion of her novels, an area only alluded to in this account.

Hause, Steven C. With Anne R. Kenney. *Women's Suffrage and Social Politics in the French Third Republic.* Princeton, N.J.: Princeton University Press, 1984. See pages 48–50.

STANDARD SOURCES

DFC.

PENDLETON, ELLEN FITZ (1864–1936)

U.S. college president and mathematician. Born Westerly, Mass., 7 August 1864, to Mary Ette (Chapman) and Enoch Burrows Pendleton. Never married. Educated Westerly High School; Wellesley College (A.B., 1886; A.M., 1891). Newnham College, Cambridge University (1888–1890). Professional experience: Wellesley College, tutor in mathematics, Latin, and Greek (1886–1888), instructor of mathematics (1888–1897), associate professor of mathematics (1901–1911). Wellesley College, secretary (1897–1901), dean (1901–1910), acting president (1910–1911), president (1911–1936). Honors and memberships: Brown University (Litt.D., 1911); Mount Holyoke (LL.D., 1912); Smith

College (LL.D., 1925); University of Toronto (LL.D., 1927); Williams College (LL.D., 1931). Died 26 July 1936 of a cerebral hemorrhage.

Ella Fitz Pendleton, mathematician and fifth president of Wellesley College, was born in Westerly, Massachusetts, where her father was a prominent member of the new Republican Party just before the Civil War, and postmaster upon President Lincoln's election. As a young girl, she attended Westerly High School where she was valedictorian of her class. She then attended Wellesley College, where she studied mathematics under Helen Shafer, who later became the third president of Wellesley and whose protégée she became. After receiving her undergraduate degree, she was hired at her alma mater as a tutor in mathematics, Latin, and Greek. After two years, she was made instructor of mathematics. She then took the unusual step of spending a year at Newnham College, Cambridge, during the same year that the young woman mathematician PHILLIPA FAWCETT passed the Mathematical Tripos at Cambridge with a mark above that of the highest male student. Upon her return to Massachusetts, Pendleton completed a master's degree, while continuing to teach mathematics. She was an excellent administrator as well, serving as secretary of the college in 1897, then appointed dean of the college in the same year that she was made associate professor of mathematics. While dean, she proposed a scholarship for Chinese students after the visit of the Chinese minister of education in 1906. When President Caroline Hazard became ill in 1910, Pendleton served as acting president of Wellesley, and then was appointed president the following year in spite of the desire of some members of the trustees to see a male president elected. That same year, she was awarded an honorary doctorate at Brown University, followed by an honorary degree the next year at Smith. A disastrous fire at Wellesley in 1914, which destroyed much of the administrative offices and science laboratories along with the library and dormitories, led to Pendleton's lengthy struggle to raise money and to rebuild the college during her term of office. Her strong support for academic freedom issues in the face of attacks on pacifists during World War I, and her opposition to the Massachusetts bill to require loyalty oaths in 1935, characterized her presidency. She also supported a wide liberal education, independent study and freedom in choosing electives by the undergraduates while expanding the size of the faculty.

Pendleton supported women's scientific research as a member of the Naples Table Association. She was a member of the College Examination Board, where she helped to liberalize the structure of those examinations and served as the only woman juror for the American Peace Prize founded by Edward Bok. She was also a member of the American Academy for Political and Social Science. She was widely honored not only by other women's colleges but by the University of Toronto and Williams College. Within a month of her retirement from office, she died of a cerebral hemorrhage at the home of a niece in Newton, Massachusetts, shortly before her seventy-second birthday. JH/MBO

SECONDARY SOURCES

Converse, Florence. *Wellesley College: A Chronicle of the Years.* Wellesley, Mass.: Hathaway House, 1939.

Hackett, Alice P. *Wellesley: Part of the American Story.* New York: Dutton, 1949.

STANDARD SOURCES

AMS 3–5; *NAW* (article by Kathryn Preyer); Rossiter 1982; *WWW(A),* vol. 1, 1897–1942.

PENNINGTON, MARY ENGLE (1872–1952)

U.S. chemist. Born 8 October 1872 in Nashville, Tenn., to Sarah (Molony) and Henry Pennington. One sibling. Never married. Educated University of Pennsylvania (Ph.D., 1895; fellow in botany, 1895–1897); Yale University (fellow in physiological chemistry, 1897–1898). Professional experience: Philadelphia Clinical Laboratory, director (1898–1907); Woman's Medical College of Pennsylvania, lecturer (1898–1906); Philadelphia Health Department, bacteriological laboratory, director (1898–1906); Bureau of Chemistry, U.S. Department of Agriculture, Food Research Laboratory, director (1908–1919); American Balsa Company, director of research and development (1919–1922); consultant on food preservation, based in New York City (1922–1952). Died 27 December 1952 in New York City.

Although Mary Pennington was born in Nashville, Tennessee, her family moved to Philadelphia soon after her birth. Mary was the older of two daughters whose father was a businessman and an avid gardener. When she was twelve years old, Mary borrowed a book on medical chemistry from the library. This book established the direction she was to take, and her supportive family made it possible for her to pursue it. In 1890 she enrolled in the Towne Scientific School of the University of Pennsylvania. After two years of study in chemistry and biology, she completed the requirements for the bachelor's degree—which was not, however, awarded to her because she was a woman; instead she received a certificate of proficiency. She continued at the university as a graduate student and received a doctoral degree in 1895. After two additional years as a fellow in botany, she studied for a year at Yale as a fellow in physiological chemistry.

Pennington returned to Philadelphia in 1898 and established her own business, the Philadelphia Clinical Laboratory, where she conducted bacteriological analyses for local physicians. Because of her success at this enterprise, she was appointed lecturer at the Woman's Medical College of Pennsylvania. She soon became head of the Philadelphia Health Department's bacteriological laboratory, where she developed methods of preserving dairy products and standards for milk inspection that came to be employed throughout the country.

On the advice of Harvey Wiley, a family friend and chief of the Bureau of Chemistry of the United States Department of Agriculture, Pennington took the civil service examinations as "M. E. Pennington," so that if she passed, the Department of Agriculture would not realize that it was about to hire a woman. She succeeded, and in 1907 became a bacteriological chemist for the department. Wiley appointed Pennington chief of the Food Research Laboratory (1908), a new division of the Bureau of Chemistry. For her convenience, the laboratory was established in Philadelphia, and for eleven years Pennington supervised the laboratory's research on food handling and storage. During World War I, she devised standards for railroad refrigerator cars; her war work on perishable foods earned her the Notable Service Medal.

Pennington left the USDA in 1919 for a job in private industry as the director of the research and development department of the American Balsa Company, manufacturers of insulating materials, in New York City. After three years there she established her own consulting office in New York City, advising packing houses, shippers, and warehousers on food handling, storage, and transportation, as well as doing original research on frozen foods.

Pennington's early work in devising methods of preventing spoilage of eggs, poultry, and fish, as well as her later research on the freezing of various foods, resulted in many practical techniques for the preparation, packaging, storage, and distribution of perishables. She published her conclusions in technical journals, government bulletins, and magazines. Pennington also worked on the physiology of *Spirogyra nitela,* on the chemicobacteriology of milk, and on diphtheria. JH/MBO

PRIMARY SOURCES

Pennington, Mary Engle. *A Bacteriological and Chemical Study of Commercial Eggs in the Producing Districts of the Central West.* Washington, D.C.: U.S. Government Printing Office, 1914.

———. With H. M. P. Betts. *How to Kill and Bleed Market Poultry.* Washington, D.C.: U.S. Government Printing Office, 1915.

———. With Paul Mandeville. *Eggs.* Progress Publications, 1933.

SECONDARY SOURCES

Rossiter, Margaret. "Women Scientists in America before 1920." *American Scientist* 62 (May–June 1974): 312–323.

STANDARD SOURCES
AMS 1–8; *NAW* (article by Vivian Wiser); *Notable* (article by Kimberlyn McGrail); Ogilvie 1986; Siegel and Finley.

PENSA-JOJA, JOSIPA (d. 1982)
Yugoslav stratigrapher and structural geologist. Died 1982.

The only information available on Josipa Pensa-Joja is from Sarjeant and from an obituary notice in a Slavic journal. She was a Yugoslav stratigrapher.   JH/MBO

SECONDARY SOURCES
Jagacic, Terezija. "Josipa Pensa-Joja." *Geoloski Vjesnik* 36 (1983): 308.

STANDARD SOURCES
Sarjeant.

PENSTON, NORAH LILIAN (1903–1974)
British botanist. Born 20 August 1903 to Louise Mary and Andrew Joseph Penston. One sister. Educated Bolton School; St. Anne's College, Oxford (B.A., 1927); Oxford University (D. Phil., 1930). Professional experience: Oxford University, demonstrator in botany (1929–1933); University of London, Kings College, Department of Botany, assistant lecturer (1933–1936), lecturer (1936–1945), acting head (1940–1944). University of London, Wye College, vice-principal and head of biological sciences (1943–1951); University of London, Bedford College, principal (1951–1964). Honors and memberships: British Federation of University Women, Academic Sub-Committee (1944–1972); University of London, Senate member (1951–1964); Hilda Martindale Educational Trust, exhibition trustee (1953–1970). International Federation of University Women, Membership Committee for International Fellowships (1953–1958); University of London, chairman of collegiate council (1957–1959); Dominion Students Hall Trust, governor (1965–1974); Wye College, University of London, honorary fellow. Died 1 February 1974.

Norah Penston remained at Oxford University as a demonstrator in botany after she earned a doctor of philosophy degree from that institution. She spent the remainder of her career at London University, later becoming the principal of Bedford College, London University.   JH/MBO

STANDARD SOURCES
WWW, vol. 7.

PERCEVAL, ANNE MARY (FLOWER) (1790–1876)
British horticulturist. Born 1790. Father Sir Charles Flower (Lord Mayor of London 1809). Married Michael Henry Perceval. Professional experience: raised and collected new American species. Plants in Biosystematics Research Institute, Ottawa, and the Academy of Natural Sciences, Philadelphia. Died at Stornoway, Isle of Lewis, 23 November 1876.

Anne Mary Flower was the daughter of Sir Charles Flower, who became Lord Mayor of London in 1809. Her husband, Michael Henry Perceval, was sent to Quebec, Canada, as Collector of Customs in 1810. In 1810, her husband and she began to lay out an important garden of American species at Spencer Wood, near Quebec City. She collected in the area around the wood, and brought her plants to the attention of William Hooker, who acknowledged around 150 new American species in her collection. She died at Stornoway, Isle of Lewis, at the age of eighty-six. Her plants are preserved in Canadian and American natural history collections.   JH/MBO

PRIMARY SOURCES
Perceval, Anne Mary. *Miscellaneous Thoughts, Maxims, Essays, Aphorisms, and Extracts.* 4th ed. Printed for private circulation, 1874.
Her plants are in Biosystematics Research Institute, Ottawa, Canada, and the Academy of Natural Sciences, Philadelphia.

SECONDARY SOURCES
Hooker, William J. *Flora Boreali-Americana.* This flora attributes 150 species to Perceval.

STANDARD SOURCES
Desmond.

PEREIASLAVTSEVA, SOF'IA MIKHAILOVNA (d. 1903)
Russian marine biologist. Daughter of a colonel. Educated University of Zurich (Ph.D., 1875). Professional experience: Sebastopol Biological Research Station, director; biological research stations, Roskov and Naples. Honors and memberships: prize from Congress of Naturalists (1893). Died in 1903.

Beyond the fact that Sof'ia Mikhailovna Pereiaslavtseva was the daughter of a colonel, little is known about her birth or early education. She received a doctorate from the University of Zurich in 1875. From 1881 to 1891, she was the director of the Sebastopol Biological Research Station and later worked at biological research stations at Roskov and Naples. She explored the Gulf of Naples and the coasts of

France. In 1893, she received a prize from the Congress of Naturalists for her large and beautifully illustrated work *Monographie des turbellaries de la Mer Noire* (Odessa, 1892).

Pereiaslavtseva was also the author of a number of other publications on marine biology that are still in use today.

ACH

PRIMARY SOURCES

Pereiaslavtseva, Sof'ia Mikhailovna. Vorlaufige Mittheilungen. "Uber die Nase der Fische." Zurich: Zurcher und Furrer, 1876. Inaugural dissertation.

———. *Etudes sur le dévelopement des Amphipodes.* Moscow, 1888–1889. 8 vols.

———. *Monographie des turbellaries de la Mer Noire.* Odessa: A. Schultze, 1892.

SECONDARY SOURCES

Andreevskii, I. E., ed. *Entsiklopedicheskii slovar'.* St. Petersburg: Tip. I. A. Efron, 1890–1906.

STANDARD SOURCES

Mozans; Rebière (includes portrait).

PEREIRA DE QUEIROZ, CARLOTA (1892–?)

Brazilian physician. Born 13 February 1892 in São Paulo, Brazil. Three siblings. Never married. Educated public schools; teacher's training (diploma 1909); Faculty of Medicine of São Paulo (1920–1923); Medical School of Rio de Janeiro (1923–1926?); Artur Bernardes Hospital, resident intern and director of school for young mothers (M.D., ?, Miguel Couto Prize); additional courses in Paris, Italy, Switzerland, and Germany. Professional experience: Charity Hospital of São Paulo, Pediatrics Clinic, laboratory chief (1928–?); Chamber of Deputies, Brazil, congresswoman; Commission on Health and Education, member (ca. 1932–1937); private practice in surgery, private laboratory in hematology (1937–1940s); Faculty of Medicine of São Paulo, technical assistant in hematology (ca. 1946–?); retired 1965. Honors and memberships: Brazilian Association of Medical Women, member and president (1961–1967), honorary president (1967). Society of Medicine and Surgery of São Paulo, honorary member; Brazilian Academy of Medicine and National Academy of Medicine of Buenos Aires (first woman elected in each academy); Medical Women's International Association, member; Legion of Honor of France (1950). Death date unknown.

Carlota Pereira de Queiroz was born into a well-to-do family in São Paulo, Brazil. Her interest in medicine began in childhood, but a financial reversal led her to take teacher's training in order to contribute to the family income. While teaching kindergarten, she became especially interested in children's health. When the family's economic situation improved, Pereira took private lessons in languages, music, and painting and was active socially in an effort to offset her feeling of dissatisfaction with her job and life. While higher education was available to women, the majority of professions were completely dominated by men.

In 1920, having been encouraged by a nationally known physician and scientist Miguel Couto, Pereira took and passed the entrance examination at the Faculty of Medicine of São Paulo. In 1923, she transferred to the Medical School of Rio de Janeiro where she was able to intern with her mentor, Couto. During this time she began work in hematology and began research for her thesis on cancer. This thesis, "Studies on Cancer," passed the examining board with distinction and was awarded the Miguel Couto Prize and honorary mention from the Cancer Institute. For a time, Pereira traveled and took courses in several countries. She was made a member of the French Society for Studies on Cancer.

Returning to São Paulo in 1928, Periera opened a consultation clinic with three male associates. She was appointed laboratory chief of the pediatrics clinic at the Charity Hospital of São Paulo and continued her work in hematology. The next decade was a time of revolution in Brazil. Pereira was caught up in support of the Constitutionalist revolution in São Paulo in 1932 and became part of the organizational commission of the Department of Assistance to the Wounded. This was disbanded by the federal government, but a new constitution was drafted, which granted the vote to women. In the new elections, Pereira was nominated by the Federation of Volunteers and became the first woman in the Brazilian congress (also the first congresswoman in South America). As a member of the Commission on Health and Education, she was able to initiate several projects for the improvement of conditions for mothers and children. Among her creations were social service schools, a laboratory for child biology in Rio de Janeiro, and the establishment of Child Welfare Week.

In 1937, a new dictatorial regime shut down the congress, and Pereira reopened her surgical practice and research laboratory in hematology in São Paolo and added a clinical laboratory for preoperative testing. She was elected honorary member of the Society of Medicine and Surgery of São Paulo in 1941 and was elected first woman member of the Brazilian Academy of Medicine (1942) and the National Academy of Medicine of Buenos Aires (1944). She continued to participate in the movement to establish a constitutional government, which succeeded in 1945. When a teaching hospital was added to the Faculty of Medicine in São Paulo, Pereira transferred there as technical assistant in hematology. Active in the formation of the Brazilian Association of Medical Women, she was elected its first president, then reelected twice and finally given the title of Honorary President in 1967. Serious health and vision problems led to a reduction in professional activities and retirement from practice in 1965.   JH/MBO

PRIMARY SOURCES

Pereira de Queiroz, Carlota. In Hellstedt, *Autobiographies*.

——. *Vida e morte de um capitao-mor*. São Paulo: Conselho Estadual de Cultura, 1969.

PERETTE OF ROUEN (1360–ca. 1411)

French midwife. Born 1360.

Perette of Rouen was a sage-femme, a midwife and/or surgeon of Rouen. She was prosecuted in Paris for witchcraft and for practicing medicine as an unlicensed physician. Although she was imprisoned for some time, she was later acquitted by an order of King Charles VI. Alternate forms of her name are "Peretta" and "Peronne."   JH/MBO

STANDARD SOURCES

Echols and Williams; Hurd-Mead 1938.

PERETTI, ZAFFIRA (fl. 1780)

Italian physician and anatomist. Mother Maria Pettracini. Educated University of Bologna (degree ca. 1800). Professional experience: University of Ferrara, anatomy teacher and medical practitioner; Ancona, head of the school of the levatrici *(midwives) (after 1780).*

Like her mother MARIA PETTRACINI, Zaffira Peretti received a degree from an Italian university. She taught anatomy at the University of Ferrara and practiced medicine there until sometime after 1780, when she went to Ancona to be the head of the school of *levatrici* (midwives) there.   JH/MBO

STANDARD SOURCES

Hurd-Mead 1938.

PEREY, MARGUERITE CATHERINE (1909–1975)

French radiochemist. Born 19 October 1910 in Villemomble, France, to Anne Jeanne (Ruissel) and Emile Louis Perey, a mill owner. Four siblings. Never married. Educated École d'Enseignement Technique Féminine (Diplôme d'État de Chimiste, 1929); Université de Paris (Sorbonne) (license; D.Sc., 1946). Professional experience: Institut du Radium, Paris, researcher (1929–1949), préparateur (assistant to M. Curie); Centre National de la Recherche Scientifique (CNRS), Maître de Recherches (1946–1949); University of Strasbourg, professor, director of laboratory (later under the auspices of the CNRS) (1949–?). Honors and memberships: Grand Prix of the City of Paris; Académie des Sciences (Lavoisier Prize, Laureate, corresponding member); Silver Medal, Société Chimique de France; officer, Legion of Honor; National Order of Merit and Order of Academic Palms, commander (academic decoration). Died 13 May 1975, in Paris.

Perey was born near Paris into a Protestant family of Swiss and Alsatian descent. Her father died when she was very young (in 1914), leaving the family in difficult financial circumstances. Perey and her older siblings, Jacques, Jean, Paul, and Madeleine, had no funds for higher education. Perey was trained as a chemical technician, and upon graduation began work under MARIE CURIE at the Institut du Radium. Curie acted as a mentor to the young technician, making Perey her personal assistant and helping her to develop her chemical knowledge and skills.

In 1939 Perey discovered the elusive element 87, which she named francium after her native country. Eventually she completed studies at the Sorbonne. After receiving her diploma, Perey submitted her work on element 87 ("L'élement 87: Actinium K"), for which she received a doctorate in physics in 1946. In 1949 she was appointed to a newly created chair of nuclear chemistry at the University of Strasbourg. There she developed a program in radiochemistry and nuclear chemistry, as well as a laboratory (later the Laboratory of Nuclear Chemistry of the Center of Nuclear Researches, Strasbourg-Cronenbourg). Perey received many honors for the discovery of francium, including election to the Academy of Sciences—its first female corresponding member. She died from cancer resulting from exposure to radiation.

In Curie's laboratory, Perey first worked to purify actinium, a difficult and painstaking process. After several years her source was sufficiently concentrated to give a measurable spark emission spectrum. After Curie's death in 1934 Perey worked under André Debierne and I. Joliot-Curie, both of whom suggested that she continue purifying actinium. While doing so, Perey found previously unnoticed beta radiation from her actinium, which she concluded came from a new radioelement. Her tests showed that the new substance behaved like an alkali metal. Further study indicated that it was the long sought-after element number 87, which fit into the periodic table above cesium. This turned out to be the last of the missing elements which exists in nature (those discovered later can only be produced artificially.)

The discovery of francium made Perey famous. Not yet thirty years old and lacking a university degree, she had succeeded in a task that had confounded many experienced researchers. Perey finally obtained her undergraduate degree and doctorate after the war. She continued to investigate francium's properties and determined that it tended to concentrate in cancerous tissues in laboratory rats.   MM

PRIMARY SOURCES

Perey, Marguerite. With S. Rosenblum and M. Guillot. "Sur l'intensité des groupes de structure fine des spectres magnétiques α du radioactinium et des descendants." *Comptes rendus* 202 (1936): 1274–1276.

———. "Sur un élement 87, dérivé de l'Actinium." *Comptes rendus* 208 (1939): 97–99.

———. "L'Élément 87" and "Propriétés chimiques de l'élément 87: Actinium K." *Journal de Chimie Physique et de Physico-Chimie Biologique* 43 (1946): 152–168, 262–268.

———. With Jean-Pierre Adloff. "Séparation chromatographique du Francium." *Comptes rendus* 236 (1953): 1163–1165.

———. With A. Chevallier. "Sur la répartition de l'élément 87: francium dans le sarcome expérimental du rat." *Comptes rendus société biologie* 145 (1951): 1208–1211.

SECONDARY SOURCES

Adloff, J. P. "Marguerite Perey, 1909–1975." *Radiochemical and Radioanalytical Letters* 23, no. 4 (1975): 189–193.

Kastler, A. "Marguerite Perey." *Comptes rendus* 280 (1975, Supplement 19): 124–128.

Kauffman, G. B., and J. P. Adloff. "Marguerite Perey and the Discovery of Francium." *Education in Chemistry* 26 (1989): 135–137.

"Marguerite Perey." *New York Times,* 15 May 1975. Obituary notice.

Reid, Robert. *Marie Curie.* New York: New American Library, 1974.

Weeks, Mary Elvira. *Discovery of the Elements.* Easton, Pa.: Journal of Chemical Education, 1956.

STANDARD SOURCES

Grinstein 1993; Ireland; *Notable;* Shearer and Shearer 1997; Uglow 1989.

PERICTIONE (4th century B.C.E.)

Greek natural philosopher. Lived in the fourth century B.C.E.

Two extant documents are attributed to the late Pythagorean philsopher Perictione. Evidence seems to indicate that there are two different Perictiones, who are identified in Waithe as Perictione I, who wrote *On the Harmony of Women* and Perictione II, who wrote *On Wisdom.* Often no distinction is made between the two. Some identify Perictione I with Plato's mother, Perictione. Even if the two are not one and the same, it seems probable that she lived about the time of Plato and that she was an Athenian. The text of Perictione I deals with moral philosophy and the social and moral status of women in society. In agreement with Pythagorean doc-

trine, Perictione I sets forth *harmonia* as the normative principle for a virtuous woman.

Perictione II, on the hand, comtemplates and analyzes as a human enterprise the way all things have reference to one principle. She states that humankind came into being in order to contemplate the principle of the nature of the whole. Geometery, arithmetic, and other theoretical studies are a part of this contemplation. The natural sciences contemplate those attributes that are universal to most things whereas separate sciences are concerned with the more particular. She explains that wisdom searches for the basis of all things, natural science for the principles of natural beings, and geometry, music, and arithmetic for both numerical quantity and harmony.

There are numerous theories as to whether these women really existed.
JH/MBO

PRIMARY SOURCES

Perictione I and II. Fragments found in Thesleff, Holger. "Pythagorean Texts of the Hellenistic Period." *Acta Academiae Aboensis.* Humanoira, ser. A, vol. 30, no. 1 (1965). See Waithe for fragments and commentary.

STANDARD SOURCES

Kersey; Waithe.

PERLMANN, GERTRUDE ERIKA (1912–1974)

Czechoslovakian-born U.S. biochemist. Born 20 April 1912 in Liberec (Reichenberg), Czechoslovakia. Naturalized 1945. Educated German University of Prague (D.Sc., 1936). Professional experience: Carlsberg Foundation and Carlsberg Laboratory, Copenhagen, Denmark (1937–1939); Harvard Medical School, researcher (1939–1941); Massachusetts General Hospital, researcher (1941–1945); Rockefeller Institute, assistant visiting investigator (1947–1951), associate visiting investigator (1951–1957), assistant professor of biochemistry (1957–1958), associate professor of biochemistry (1959–1973), professor of biochemistry (1973–1974). Honors and memberships: Grand Prix de la Ville de Paris, France (1960); Société Chimique de France, silver medal, Legion of Honor, officier (1960); Académie des Sciences (France), corresponding member (1962); American Chemical Society, Garvan Medal (1965). French National Order of Merit, Commandeur (1974). Died 9 September 1974 in New York City.

Gertrude Erika Perlmann was a biochemist who did significant work on phosphoproteins and the structure and action of pepsin and pepsinogen. She was born in Czechoslovakia and educated at the German University of Prague, where she obtained a docotorate in chemistry and physics. Since she was of Jewish descent, she fled to Denmark in 1936 as the Nazis threatened her homeland, to work at the Carlsberg Laboratory in Copenhagen. In 1939, at the beginning of the war in Europe, she emigrated to the United States and began work in the laboratories of Harvard Medical School and then at Massachusetts General Hospital in Boston, Massachusetts.

After becoming a U.S. citizen following World War II, Perlmann moved to New York City and accepted an offer by the Rockefeller Institute to work as a visiting investigator. At the Rockefeller, she began to use the new techniques of electrophoresis to study egg albumin, determining electrophoretic patterns of phosphoproteins and relating the structure to their biological activity. She was made an assistant professor in the 1950s and then an associate professor of the Rockefeller Institute, but was made full professor only a year before her death.

The French scientists honored Perlmann in the 1960s with the silver medal of the Chemical Society and the Legion of Honor. She was also one of the first women corresponding members of the Académie des Sciences. In 1965, the American Chemical Society awarded her the Garvan Medal for women in chemistry. Shortly before her death, she received the French Order of Merit.   JH/MBO

PRIMARY SOURCES

Perlmann, Gertrude E. "The Specific Reactive Increment of Some Purified Proteins." *Journal of the American Chemical Society* 70 (1948): 2719–2724.

———. "Enzymic Dephosphorylation of Pepsin and Pepsinogen." *Journal of General Physiology* 41 (1958): 441–450.

———. "Relation of Protein Conformation to Biological Activity." *Biochemical Journal* 89 (1963): 45.

———. "Correlation between Optical Rotation, Fluorescence and Biological Activity of Pepsinogen." *Biopolymers,* Symposium no. 1 (1964): 343–347.

Gertrude Perlmann's papers are at the Rockefeller Archive Center, Tarrytown, New York.

SECONDARY SOURCES

"Garvan Medal." *Chemical and Engineering News* 43 (April 1965): 94.

Nature 251 (1974): 363. Brief obituary notice.

New York Times, 10 November 1974.

STANDARD SOURCES

AMS 8–12; Shearer and Shearer 1996 (includes portrait); Rossiter 1995.

PERNELL (ca. 1350)
British healer. Birth date unknown. Married physician Thomas de Rasyn, Sidmouth, county Devon. Death date unknown.

Although known as respected physician, Pernell and her husband were accused of causing the death of a local miller. However, they received a royal pardon for the offence and were freed without further waiver and continued to practice.   JH/MBO

SECONDARY SOURCES

Talbot and Hammond. *Medical Practitioners in Medieval England: A Biographical Register.* London: Wellcome Medical Historical Library, 1965. See page 241.

PÉRONELLE (1292–1319)
French espicière. A seller of herbs and spices and a renowned herbalist. Born 1292. Died 1319.

In Paris in 1292, Dame Péronelle paid a very large tax, indicating that she was very prosperous in her business. She probably was the herbalist recorded as traveling from Paris to Artois in 1319 to take herbal medicines and proffer advice to the Countess Mahaut.   JH/MBO

STANDARD SOURCES

DBF, vol. 2, 1933; Echols and Williams; Hurd-Mead 1938.

PERRETTE, BERTHE (fl. 1920s)
Probably French chemist and physicist who worked on radioactivity.

Little is known about Berthe Perrette's life, but we do know that she devised an improved method for obtaining spectra, which required only minute quantities of the material to be tested. She then used her apparatus to compare the spectra of ordinary lead and lead produced from radioactive substances. She also compared the densities of these isotopic samples, finding consistent differences.   MM

PRIMARY SOURCES

Perrette, Berthe. "Sur un dispositif d'arc dans le vide permettant d'obtenir les spectres des métaux avec de très faibles quantités de matière." *Comptes rendus* 177 (1923): 876–879.

———. "Contribution à l'étude de l'isotopae de plomb." *Comptes rendus* 180 (1925): 1589–1591.

STANDARD SOURCES

Meyer and von Schweidler.

PERTZ, DOROTHEA FRANCES MATILDA (1859–1939)

British botanist. Born 14 March 1859 to a daughter of geologist Leonard Horner and George Heinrich Pertz. One sister. Educated privately; Newnham College, Cambridge (1882–1885, Natural Science Tripos, Part I, class 2, 1885; M.A., 1932). Professional experience: research worker in Cambridge on plant physiology under Francis Darwin and William Bateson; Newnham College, teacher; correspondence courses, teacher; Botany School under Dr. F. F. Blackman, cataloguer and indexer of pamphlets. Honors and memberships: Linnean Society, Fellow. Died 6 March 1939.

Dorothea (or Dora, as she was known) Pertz came from an honorable scholarly lineage. Her father was Royal Librarian at Berlin, and her mother was one of the brilliant daughters of Leonard Horner, Fellow of the Royal Society and President of the Geological Society. She grew up surrounded by her well-educated aunts, one of whom married Charles Lyell and the other, KATHARINE (Horner) LYELL, who was a botanist in her own right and who wrote the life and letters of her brother-in-law, Charles Lyell. Dora recalled going to the zoo with Lyell and visiting Charles Darwin at Down.

As a young girl, Pertz lived primarily in Berlin, but after her father's death, her mother (who was preparing a number of translations from Italian and later published on her tours of Florence and Naples) brought her children to live for a time in Florence, then returned to London and finally settled in Cambridge. Dora entered Newnham College, Cambridge, at the age of twenty-three, where she took the Natural Science Tripos, with botany as one of her subjects, and received honors. This was later converted to a regular bachelor's degree. Following her degree, she worked under Francis Darwin, Charles Darwin's son, professor of botany at Cambridge, doing research in physiological botany. She published a number of papers with him on movement in plants. During this same period, she also worked with the geneticist William Bateson on a paper on inheritance, published in *Veronica*. She also produced her own independent papers. In 1905, she was elected a Fellow of the Linnean Society, one of a group of women first admitted as full fellows. For the rest of her life, she remained attached to the Botanical Laboratory, although this was not a paid position.

F. F. Blackman, who was professor of plant physiology after Darwin's death, urged Pertz to reproduce the work reported by De Vries on an ephermeral phase of starch formation in the meristematic tissue. Her year of observations on germinating seeds was inconclusive, and as happens with most negative findings, was never published. As botany and genetics became more complex, Pertz chose to move out of research and into indexing of botanical literature. At the urging of Blackman, she prepared an elaborate index of the plant physiological literature in German, especially the hun-

dreds of volumes of the *Biochemische Zeitschrift* and the *Zeitschrift der Physiologischen Chemie,* a task completed only shortly before her death.

Pertz prepared illustrations for a series of papers on floral anatomy, written between 1923 and 1936 by her close friend, the botanist EDITH R. SAUNDERS. Saunders later wrote the obituary on Pertz for the Linnean Society in which she highlighted her charitable work as well as her science. Most of Pertz's work was unpaid labor contributed for the love of science, according to AGNES ARBER, who memorialized her for *Nature*. Arber characterized her work as "true to the family tradition handed on to her by Horner, Lyell and Bunbury," an amateur "in the basic sense of that much mishandled word." Pertz died in Cambridge after a long period of illness some days before her eightieth birthday.

JH / MBO

PRIMARY SOURCES

Pertz, Dorothea. With Francis Darwin. "Artificial Production of Rhythm in Plants." *Annals of Botany* 6 (1892): 245–264.
———. "On the Dispersal of Nutlets in Certain Labiatae." *Natural Science* (1894).
———. With Frances Darwin. "On a New Method of Estimating the Aperture of Stomata." *Proceedings of the Royal Society* 84B (1911): 136–154.

SECONDARY SOURCES

Arber, Agnes. "Miss Dorothea F. M. Pertz." *Nature* 143 (1939): 590–591. Obituary notice.
Saunders, E[dith] R. "Dorothea Frances Mathilda Pertz." *Proceedings of the Linnean Society* (1938–1939): 245–247. Obituary notice.

STANDARD SOURCES

Desmond.

PÉTER, RÓZSA (1905–1977)

Hungarian logician and mathematician. Born 17 February 1905 in Budapest, Hungary, to Irma Klein and Dr. Gusztav Politzer. Two brothers. Never married, but changed her name from Politzer to Péter. Educated Eötvös Loránd University (graduated 1927); University of Zurich (Ph.D., 1935); Hungarian Academy (higher doctoral degree, 1952). Professional experience: Pedagógiai Förskola, Budapest (teachers' college), faculty (1945–1955); Eötvös Loránd University (1955). Died 1977.

Rózsa Péter was well known for her research. She was born and received her early education in Budapest. When she first went to the university she studied chemistry; however, she soon realized that her real interest lay in mathematics. She had internationally known teachers, including Lipót Fejér,

József Kürschák, and László Kalmár. Kalmár, in particular, was important to her future achievements and called her attention to the subject of recursive functions. Having a degree did not guarantee her a job. She was unemployed (except for part-time jobs) for eighteen years. However, during this dry period, she did research in mathematical logic. By 1930 she was a world-renowned logician. In 1932 she lectured on recursive functions at the International Congress of Mathematicians in Zurich, and in 1935 defended her dissertation and was awarded a doctorate *summa cum laude*. She gave talks on "higher-order" recursion and was invited to join the editorial boards of several leading international mathematical journals. She was happy at the teachers' college, where she taught from 1945 until 1955, and continued to publish prolifically. However, in 1955 this college closed and she moved to another university that she never liked as well, but she remained until she retired in 1975. She had little time to enjoy retirement, for she died of cancer in 1977.

Péter received several awards including the Manó Beke Award of the János Bolyai Mathematical Society for popularizing mathematics. She was a corresponding member of the Hungarian Academy of Sciences (1973).

Péter was a creative theoretical mathematician, and was known as one of the founders of the branch of mathematical logic called recursive function theory. She wrote two books and more than fifty papers on this subject. In 1976 she wrote an important book on the connections between recursive function theory and computer programming languages. She also saw the importance of making the public aware of the nature of mathematics. She was especially concerned about female students. To this end she gave popular lectures and wrote popular books and articles. JH/MBO

PRIMARY SOURCES

Péter, Rózsa. "Rekursive Funktionen." *Proceedings of the International Congress of Mathematicians.* Zurich 2 (1932): 336–337.

———. "Über rekursive Funktionen der zweite Stufe." *Proceedings of the International Congress of Mathematicians.* Oslo 2 (1936): 267.

———. *Playing with Infinity: Mathematical Explorations and Excursions* (in Hungarian). Budapest: Dante Könyvkiadó, 1945. This book has been translated into many languages, including English.

———. *Rekursive Funktionen in der Komputer-Theorie.* Budapest: Akadémiai Kiadó, 1976. English translation: *Recursive Functions in Computer Theory.* Trans. I. Juhász. New York: Halsted, 1981.

SECONDARY SOURCES

Csázár, A. "Rósa Péter: February 17, 1905–February 16, 1977." (In Hungarian). *Matematikai Lapok* 25 (1977): 255–258.

STANDARD SOURCES

Grinstein and Campbell (article by Hajnal Andréka); *Notable* (article by Sally M. Moite); *Notable Mathematicians.*

PETERMANN, MARY LOCKE (1908–1975)

U.S. biochemist and physiological chemist. Born 25 February 1908 in Laurium, Mich., to Anna Mae Grierson and Albert Edward Petermann. Two siblings. Educated Calumet High School (graduated 1924); Massachusetts preparatory school (1924–1925); Smith College (graduated 1929); University of Wisconsin (Ph.D., 1939). Professional experience: Yale University, technician (1929–1931?); Boston Psychopathic Hospital (1931–1935?); University of Wisconsin, department of physical chemistry, postdoctoral researcher (1939–1945); Memorial Hospital, New York City, researcher (1945–1946); Sloan-Kettering Institute, Finley-Howell Foundation Fellow (1946–1960); associate member (1960–1963), member (1963–1973), member emerita (1973–1975); Sloan-Kettering Division, Graduate School of Medical Sciences, professor (1966). Honors and memberships: Sloan Award (1963); Garvan Medal of the American Chemical Society (1966); Smith College, honorary doctorate; American Academy of Achievement, Distinguished Service Award. Died 13 December 1975 of intestinal cancer.

Mary Petermann was one of three children. Both of her parents were college-educated, and her Cornell-educated father was first a lawyer and later president and general manager for Calumet and Hecla Consolidated Copper Company in Calumet, Michigan. The family had considerable status in the community. After graduating from Calumet High School and spending a year at a Massachusetts preparatory school, Petermann entered Smith College, graduating Phi Beta Kappa with high honors in chemistry. After graduation, she spent a year at Yale University as a technician and then investigated the acid-base balance of mental patient at the Boston Psychopathic Hospital.

Petermann returned to the University of Wisconsin to complete her education. Her doctoral degree was in physiological chemistry and her thesis on the role of the adrenal cortex in ion regulation. After receiving her degree, Petermann became the first woman chemist on the staff of the department of physical chemistry at Wisconsin. She remained at Wisconsin as a postdoctoral fellow for six years.

During her years at Wisconsin, Petermann worked with Alwin M. Pappenheimer on the physical chemistry of proteins. While doing this research, she discovered cell organelles that were named ribosomes at a 1958 meeting of the Biophysical Society; they were first named "Petermann's particles." These ribosomes are the site of protein synthesis in the cell. She later studied antibodies, and her research contributed to the award of a Nobel Prize to Rodney Porter in 1972 for his work delineating the structure of immunoglobulins.

After a short time as a chemist at the Memorial Hospital in New York City, Petermann moved to the newly founded Sloan-Kettering Institute, where she worked on the role of nucleoproteins in cancer. She also taught biochemistry at the Sloan-Kettering Division of the Graduate School of Medical Sciences, Cornell University, becoming the first woman at the university to be appointed full professor.

The author or coauthor of approximately one hundred scientific papers, Petermann was known for her fundamental work on the cell ribosome and for stressing the importance of a knowledge of proteins and nucleoproteins in understanding abnormal growth of cancers. After she received the Sloan Award, she used the award money to work for a year in the laboratory of Nobel laureate Arne Tiselius and lectured in several European countries.

Petermann organized the Memorial Sloan Kettering Cancer Center Association for Professional Women and served as its president in 1975. The year after her death, the Educational Foundation of the Association for Women in Science named one of its graduate scholarships after her.　JH/MBO

PRIMARY SOURCES
Petermann, Mary Locke. *The Physical and Chemical Properties of Ribosomes.* New York: Elsevier Publishing Company, 1964.

STANDARD SOURCES
AMS 7–8; P 9; P&B 10–12; Debus; Grinstein 1993 (article by Mary L. Moller); *Notable* (article by Jill Carpenter); O'Neill.

PETERSON, EDITH (RUNNE) (1914–1992)

U.S. medical researcher. Born 24 June 1914 in Brooklyn, N.Y., to Else Helmke and Hermann Runne. One sister. Married Charles Peterson (1941). One son, Wesley; One daughter, Rhonda Lea. Educated Barnard College (B.S., 1937); Columbia University (M.A., 1939). Professional experience: Columbia University, laboratory of Margaret Murray, research worker (early 1940s to 1966); Albert Einstein College of Medicine of Yeshiva University in the Bronx (1966–1990). Died 15 August 1992 of a stroke.

Edith Runne's German-born father, the co-owner of a restaurant and catering establishment in New York, died when Edith was six years old. Her mother, her sister, and she were in Germany when he died and they remained there for six years before returning to the United States. Her mother became a custom dress designer in New York. Runne married Charles Peterson in 1941, after which she worked in MARGARET MURRAY's laboratory at Columbia. Her major accomplishment was her ability to grow functional nerve cells using cultures containing chicken embryos. In doing this she

was able to grow myelin, the sheath that surrounds nerve cells. This discovery was important in research on multiple sclerosis, a disease that involves the degeneration of the myelin sheath in the brain and spinal cord.

When she moved to the Albert Einstein College of Medicine, Peterson worked with Murray Bornstein on muscular dystrophy. She applied her method of culturing cells, the "organotype" culture that involves having cells simulate the actual structure and functions of the organs from which they have been taken, to this disease.

Peterson only lived for two years after she retired in 1990. A first stroke hindered her ability to use her right hand. She and her husband moved to Middletown, New York, where Peterson died of a second stroke.　JH/MBO

SECONDARY SOURCES
Edelson, Edward. *The Nervous System.* Philadelphia: Chelsea House, 1991.
"Edith Peterson, 78, Studied Cell Cultures." *New York Times,* 18 August 1992. Obituary notice.
Rosner, Louis, and Shelley Ross. *Multiple Sclerosis.* Englewood Cliffs, N.J.: Prentice-Hall, 1987.

STANDARD SOURCES
Notable (article by Francis Rogers).

PETERSON, RUTH DIXON (1906–　)

U.S. biochemist. Born 15 May 1906 in Diamond, Wash. Married 1926. Two children. Educated Washington State College (B.S., 1926); University of Oregon (M.S., 1948; Ph.D., 1950). Professional experience: University of Oregon Medical School, instructor (1950–1953), instructor, biochemistry (1953–1955); assistant professor (1955–1961), associate professor (1961–1963); Primate Research Center, assistant scientist (1960–1962), associate scientist (1962–1963); Tulane University school of medicine, associate professor (1963–1970), professor (1970–1971); retired 1971.

Biochemist Ruth Dixon Peterson was born and educated in the Pacific Northwest. After earning a doctorate in biochemistry from the University of Oregon, she taught at that institution, progressing from instructor to associate professor. Concurrently she was first an assistant then an associate scientist at the primate research center. Leaving Oregon in 1963, Dixon went to the Tulane Medical School as an associate professor. The year before she retired she was promoted to professor. Peterson was married and had two children.

Peterson's research was on muscle metabolism during growth and development, protein synthesis, and high energy phosphates. She was a member of the American Society of Biological Chemistry and the British Biochemical Society.

JH/MBO

PRIMARY SOURCE
Peterson, Ruth D. "Studies in Glutatione." Ph.D. diss., University of Oregon, 1950.

STANDARD SOURCES
AMS 9, P&B 10–12.

PETRAN, ELIZABETH IRENE (1906–)

U.S. bacteriologist and parasitologist. Born a U.S. citizen, 25 July 1906 in Aguascalientes, Mexico. Educated Goucher College (A.B., 1928); University of Chicago (Ph.D., 1933). Professional experience: State Department of Health, Minnesota, assistant bacteriologist (1928–1930); University of Chicago, laboratory assistant (1931–1933); State Department of Health, Maryland, assistant bacteriologist (1933–1935), from bacteriologist to principle bacteriologist (1935–1961), chief, division of microbiology (1961–?).

Elizabeth Petran was born in Mexico but was an American citizen. After a bachelor's degree at Goucher, she earned a doctorate from the University of Chicago. She spent most of her career in public health service, beginning in Minnesota, then moving to Maryland. At Maryland she moved through the ranks and eventually became principal biologist. In 1961, she became chief of the division of microbiology. Her research was on methods used in diagnostic bacteriology and parasitology, especially in the laboratory diagnosis of tuberculosis and diptheria. She also worked on hemolytic streptococci. She was a Fellow of the Society of Microbiology, the Public Health Association, and the Academy of Microbiology.

JH/MBO

PRIMARY SOURCES
Petran, Elizabeth Irene. "Intestinal Flora of Monkeys and Dogs during Digestion and Following the Direct Introduction of Food Substances into the Cecum and into Isolated Segments of Bowel." *Journal of Infectious Diseases* 57 (November/December 1935) 296–314. From Petran's Ph.D. dissertation.

STANDARD SOURCES
AMS 8, B 9, P&B 10–12.

PETROVA, MARIA KAPITONOVNA (1874–1948)

Russian physiologist. Born 6 April 1874 in Tbilisi. Educated St. Petersburg Women's Medical Institute. Professional experience: Clinic of St. Petersburg Medical Institute, on staff; Institute for Experimental Medicine; I. P. Pavlov Institute of Physiology of the Soviet Academy of Sciences; Leningrad Institute for the Advanced Training of Physicians, professor. Honors and memberships: Academy of Sciences, I. P. Pavlov Prize (1940); Russian Soviet Federated Socialist Republic (RSFSR), honored scientist (1945); State Prize (1946); Badge of Honor. Died 14 May 1948 in Leningrad.

Maria Kapitonovna Petrova graduated from the St. Petersburg Medical Institute in 1908 and until 1931 worked at the institute's clinic. From 1910 to 1936 she was a student and coworker of the physiologist I. P. Pavlov. In 1910, she began working at the Institute for Experimental Medicine and then at the I. P. Pavlov Institute of Physiology of the Soviet Academy of Sciences where, in 1946, she became head of a laboratory. From 1935 to 1944, she was also a professor and head of the subdepartment of physiology and pathophysiology of higher nervous activity at the Leningrad Institute for Advanced Training of Physicians.

Petrova's research was devoted primarily to the physiology and pathology of higher nervous activity and to the study of experimental neuroses caused by overstrain, the interaction of excitation and inhibition in the cerebral cortex, and the dependence of these processes on the animal's type of nervous system. Petrova demonstrated the dependence of skin and other diseases on pathological states of the cerebral cortex in animals. She also did research on the use of bromine salts as a treatment for neuroses.

Petrova was named an Honored Scientist of the Russian Soviet Federated Socialist Republic (RSFSR) in 1945. She was also awarded the I. P. Pavlov Prize in 1940 and the State Prize in 1946 as well as the Badge of Honor and various medals.

ACH

PRIMARY SOURCES
Petrova, Mariia Kapitonovna. *Sobranie trudov,* vols 1–2. Moscow, 1953.

STANDARD SOURCES
Debus.

PETTERSSON, DAGMAR (fl. 1924)

Swedish physicist. Flourished 1924.

Although some information is available on Dagmar Pettersson's work, nothing is known about her life. We know that she was at the Institut für Radiumforschung, Vienna, in 1924. While there, she searched for long-range alpha particles. She also investigated methods for improving viewing of low intensity scintillations produced by alpha particles on a fluorescent screen. This was important for research that required counting of alpha particles.

MM

PRIMARY SOURCES

Pettersson, Dagmar. "Über die maximale Reichweite der von Radium C ausgeschleiderten Partikeln." *Akademie der Wissenschaften, Vienna. Sitzungsberichte 2a* 133 (1924): 149–162. See also *Nature* 113 (1924): 263, 641–642; *Die Naturwissenschaften* 12 (1924): 389–390.

SECONDARY SOURCES

Bol'shaia sovetskaia entsiklopediia. 3d ed. Moscow: Izd-vo "Sovetskaia entsiklopediia," 1973.

STANDARD SOURCES

Meyer and von Schweidler.

PETTIT, HANNAH STEELE (1886–?)

U.S. astronomer. Born 6 November 1886 in Catesville, Pa. Educated Swarthmore College (A.B., 1909; M.A., 1912); University of Chicago (Ph.D., 1919). Professional experience: Sproul Laboratory, observer (1912–1916); Yerkes Observatory, assistant (1916–1920); Carnegie Institution, Mount Wilson Observatory, assistant (1920–1930s?); expeditions to Solar Eclipse, Matheson Colorado (1918), Point Loma (1923), Honey Lake (1930), Lancaster, N.H. (1932). Honors and memberships: Astronomical Society. Death date unknown.

Hannah Steele Pettit was a U.S. astronomer interested in solar eclipses, astrophysics, and stellar parallax. She was born in Pennsylvania and studied for both her undergraduate and master's degrees at Swarthmore College. After receiving her master's degree, she worked as an astronomical observer from 1912 to 1916 at the Sproul observatory. She was hired as an assistant at Yerkes Observatory while working toward her doctorate at the University of Chicago. Once she had her degreee, she moved to the Mount Wilson Observatory, under the Carnegie Institution, where she remained for the rest of her professional life.

With her interest in solar eclipses, she joined expeditions to observe this phenomenon in 1918, in Colorado, the Honey Lake expedition in 1923, and the Point Loma (California) expedition in 1930. The final solar expedition she participated in was to Lancaster, New Hampshire, in 1932.

JH/MBO

STANDARD SOURCES

AMS 3–8, P 9, P&B 10; Rossiter 1982.

PETTIT, MARY DEWITT (1908–)

U.S. physician. Born 1 January 1908 in Philadelphia, Pa. Educated Bryn Mawr College (A.B., 1928); University of Pennsylvania (M.D., 1932). Professional experience: Albany Medical College, Union College, Albany, New York, staff (1938–1939), from instructor to assistant professor (1939–1946); Medical College of Pennsylvania, professor of gynecology and obstetrics (1946–?). Concurrent experience: U.S. Veterans Administration, consultant.

Mary Dewitt Pettit earned her bachelor's degree at Bryn Mawr College and her medical degree from the University of Pennsylvania. Her last position was professor of gynecology and obstetrics at the Medical College of Pennsylvania. She was a Fellow of the American Medical Association and the American College of Obstetrics and Gynecology.

JH/MBO

STANDARD SOURCES

AMS 8, B 9, P&B 10–14.

PETTRACINI, MARIA (fl. 1780)

Italian anatomist and physician. Educated University of Florence (medical degree, 1780). Teacher of anatomy, University of Ferrara.

Little is known about the scientific work of Maria Pettracini. According to the brief accounts, Maria and her daughter, ZAFFIRA PERETTI, taught anatomy at the University of Ferrara. First Salerno and then Bologna were centers of medical education in Italy and known as the locations where most female anatomists and physicians taught. The careers of Maria Pettracini and her daughter indicate that Ferrara also encouraged female students and teachers.

JH/MBO

STANDARD SOURCES

Hurd-Mead 1938; Ogilvie 1986.

PFEIFFER, IDA (REYER) (1797–1858)

Austrian geographer and naturalist. Born 1797 in Vienna. Married. At least two sons. Died 1858.

Ida Pfeiffer was one of the nineteenth century's most intrepid travelers. It seemed unlikely that she would be able to indulge her peripatetic interests, because she was married, had children, and lacked financial resources. Nevertheless, she managed to save a small sum yearly, and when her husband died and her children were on their own (we do not know the exact number of children, but we know that she spent much time on the education of two sons), she set out on her first journey in 1842. She traveled to Turkey, Palestine, and Egypt, using the money she had carefully saved over the past twenty years. She kept a diary on this trip and published it in two volumes. In 1845 she went to Scandinavia and Iceland, publishing an account on her return. When she was fifty-one years old, she left Vienna on 1 May 1846 and undertook a trip around the world. She met an elderly gentleman companion in Hamburg, Count Berchthold, who was to accompany her. They got only as far as Brazil together, for she found him a useless encumbrance. Her many adventures included an attack by an assailant in Brazil, but, undaunted by this incident, she continued through the Brazilian forests, visiting the native inhabitants and taking notes, moving through swamps and forests on a mule, and moving through the trackless llanos. She slept in the wigwams of the natives, attended their ceremonies and dances, and took elaborate notes on what she observed.

From Brazil Pfeiffer took a small sailing vessel, went around Cape Horn, stopped in Chili, and headed for China via Tahiti. In China, she encountered prejudice against both the English and women. She traveled from China to India, and in a steamer bound for Bassora she had an attack of fever. She recovered and continued to Bagdad and continued home by way of Russia, Constantinople, and Athens. She arrived in Vienna on 4 November 1848. After returning home she spent three years resting and recovering from this journey. During this time she prepared her journal for publication.

Not satisfied with her circumnavigation of the globe, Pfeiffer visited London, and from there set sail to the Cape of Good Hope, intending to explore the African continent. However, she ran short of money and cut this project short. She did explore the Sunda Island and in the beginning of 1852 she reached Sarawak and from there penetrated into the interior of Borneo and then to Java and Sumatra, which Europeans had reported was peopled by cannibals. She went from the Molaccas to California, down the western coast of North America, visited the source of the Amazons, crossed the Andes, and then traversed the length and breadth of England.

Her books are important for naturalists because of her graphic power of description, illustrating a considerable amount of scientific knowledge, which enabled her to make correct geogoraphical observations and accurately describe the plants, animals, and people that she encountered.

JH/MBO

PRIMARY SOURCES
Pfeiffer, Ida. *A Lady's Journey Round the World, from Vienna to Brazil, Chili, Tahiti, China, Hindostan, Persia, and Asia Minor.* Trans. from the German. London: Office of the National Illustrated Library, [1850].
———. *Visit to Iceland and the Scandinavian North.* Trans. from the German. London: Ingram, Cooke, and Co., 1853.

STANDARD SOURCES
Cyclopaedia; DFC; Dorland; Mozans.

PFEIFFER, NORMA ETTA (1889–1989)

U.S. botanist. Born Chicago, Ill. in 1889. Educated University of Chicago (B.S., 1909; Ph.D., 1913; fellow 1910–1911). Professional experience: University of North Dakota, instructor, assistant professor, associate professor of botany (1912–1923). Boyce Thompson Institute, Yonkers, N.Y., research morphologist (1923–1954). Retired 1954. Honors and memberships: Massachusetts Horticultural Society Silver Medal; Torrey Botanical Club, second vice-president (1947); Botanical Society, North Dakota Academy of Science, president (1922). Died 12 September 1989.

Norma Pfeiffer was born and educated in Chicago. She earned both her bachelor's degree and her doctorate at the University of Chicago and remained as a fellow for an additional year after completing her dissertation in 1911. She then went to the University of North Dakota, where she remained for eleven years, rising to the position of professor of botany. She joined the North Dakota Academy of Science, where she served as president of the botanical section in 1922. In spite of this unusual record of academic success, she moved to the Boyce Thompson Institute at which she, like a number of other women of the period, found a situation that enabled her to focus on botanical research. She remained there as research morphologist until her retirement in 1954. She was awarded the silver medal of the Massachusetts Horticultural Society and served the Torrey Botanical Club as vice-president in 1947. She died in 1989, almost reaching her hundredth year. Her research interests included microchemistry, morphological and chemical differences effected by light, Isoetes, and plant breeding.   JH/MBO

PRIMARY SOURCES
Pfeiffer, Norma Etta. "Morphology of *Thismia americana.*" *Botanical Gazette* 57, no. 2 (1913). University of Chicago. Ph.D. dissertation.
———. *Monograph of the Isoetaceae.* St. Louis, Mo.: Missouri Botanical Garden, 1922.
———. *New Hybrids of Lilium auratum and L. Superbum as Seed Parents.* Yonkers, N.Y.: Bryce Thompson Institute for Plant Research, [1942].

SECONDARY SOURCES
"Norma Etta Pfeiffer." *New York Times,* 12 September 1989. Obituary notice.

STANDARD SOURCES
Rossiter 1995.

PFIESTER, LOIS ANN (d. 1992)

U.S. botanist and phycologist. Born in Louisville, Ky. Married Dee Fink (1978). Two adopted children, one son and one daughter. Educated Catherine Spaulding University, Louisville, Ky. (A.B., 1965); Murray State University (M.A., 1970); Ohio State University (Ph.D., 1974). Professional experience: University of Oklahoma, assistant through full professor of botany (1974–1992). Associate editor of Phycology *(1980–1988). Died 28 September 1992 in Norman, Okla.*

Lois Pfiester was born in Louisville, Kentucky. After attending Catherine Spaulding University and Murray State University, she went to Ohio State University for her doctoral work in botany and wrote her dissertation under Clarence Taft. She obtained a position in the department of botany at the University of Oklahoma in Norman, moving from assistant to full professor of botany. She taught large numbers of undergraduates and directed sixteen master's theses and four doctoral dissertations. She published more than seventy-five journal articles (including abstracts, a book, and four invited chapters). Her last paper was published posthumously in the *Transactions of the American Microscopical Society.* She conducted major research on dinoflagellate sexual reproduction. She worked in algal ecology and assisted business, industry, and others on problems of water quality.   JH/MBO

PRIMARY SOURCES

Pfiester, Lois A. With I. Kelly. "Sexual Reproduction in the freshwater Dinoflagellate *Gloeodinium montanum." Journal of Phycology* 36 (1990): 167–173.

———. With Joe F. Highfill. "Sexual Reproduction of *Hemidinium nasutum,* alias Gloeodinium montanum." *Transactions of the American Microscopical Society* 112 (1993): 69–74. Published posthumously.

SECONDARY SOURCES

Highfill, Joe F. "Lois A. Pfiester." *Transactions of the American Microscopical Society* 112, no. 2 (1993): 120. Includes portrait.

PHELPS, ALMIRA HART LINCOLN (1793–1884)

U.S. science educator. Born 1793 in Berlin, Conn., to Lydia (Hinsdale) and Samuel Hart. Sixteen siblings and half-siblings. Married (1) Simeon Lincoln (he died 1823); (2) John Phelps. Four children: Emma, Jane, Charles, Almira. Educated district schools; girls' academy in Pittsfield, Mass. (1812–1813). Professional experience: Berlin, Conn. (1813–1816) and Sandy Hill, N.Y., schoolmistress (1816–1817); Troy (N.Y.) Female Seminary, teacher (1823–1831); Rahway (N.J.) Female Institute, principal (1839–1841); Patapsco Female Institute, Ellicott's Mills, Md., principal (1841–

1856). Honors and memberships: American Association for the Advancement of Science, second woman elected to membership. Died 1884 in Baltimore, Md.

Almira was the youngest of Samuel Hart's seventeen children and the tenth child of his second marriage (to Lydia Hinsdale). The Phelps's home represented a politically liberal enclave within a conservative environment. Family discussions of books and political issues supplemented the children's formal education at the district schools. Almira continued her studies at the Berlin Academy and in 1809 taught in a rural school district near Hartford.

Her sister, EMMA WILLARD (1787–1870), the well-known educator, and her sister's husband, Dr. John Willard, were influential in Almira's education. She lived with them in Middlebury, Vermont, for two years. Her cousin, Nancy Hinsdale, operated a school for girls in Pittsfield, Massachusetts, which Almira attended in 1812. She returned in 1813 to her home town to teach in the Berlin Academy and in the district school. In 1814 she opened a small boarding school in her home, and in 1816 she became head of an academy in Sandy Hill, New York. In 1817, she married Hartford newspaperman Simeon Lincoln.

Hart became a widow when Lincoln died in 1823, leaving her with two small daughters to support. Consequently, she returned to teaching and joined the staff at her sister Emma's boarding school, the Troy Female Seminary. It was at this time that she became interested in natural science, encouraged by Amos Eaton, a Rensselaer Polytechnic Institute professor. Shortly after meeting Eaton, she began work on her first science textbook, *Familiar Lectures on Botany* (1829), which enjoyed great popularity. Although a series of science books followed, none was as successful with the public as the first had been. She edited *The Child's Geology* by Samuel Griswold Goodrich and translated and revised Louis Vauquelin's *Dictionary of Chemistry.* Her version added a history of chemistry, an introduction, abridgments of the long sections on manufacturing, and additions of the latest ideas in chemistry from French, English, and American writers.

In 1831 Almira Lincoln married John Phelps, a lawyer and widower with six children. Almira occupied herself with caring for her stepchildren and her own children, born in 1833 and 1836, in Phelps's home in Guilford, Vermont. In spite of her domestic responsibilities, she continued to write and revise her previous works. She was invited to become principal of a new seminary for girls in West Chester, Pennsylvania, in 1838. The school soon closed due to a lack of funds. A brief tenure (1839–1841) at another new seminary in Rahway, New Jersey, ended when John and Almira Phelps were asked to take joint charge of the Patapsco Female Institute at Ellicott's Mills, Maryland: she as principal and he as business manager. (John Phelps held this position until his death in 1849.) Almira Phelps developed a strong curriculum, emphasizing the sciences.

Following the death of her daughter Jane in 1856, Phelps retired and moved to Baltimore and continued to write textbooks. She was elected the second woman member of the American Association for the Advancement of Science in 1859. Although she supported educational equality for women, Phelps was opposed to women's suffrage. In fact, she was active in the Woman's Anti-Suffrage Association and wrote several articles on the subject.

Phelps's major contribution to the history of science was in the area of science education. Both as a teacher and as the author of a widely used school text, *Familiar Lectures on Botany*, she furthered the cause of science instruction.

JH/MBO

PRIMARY SOURCES

Phelps, Almira Hart Lincoln. *Familiar Lectures on Botany. Including Practical and Elementary Botany, with General and Specific Descriptions of the Most Common Native and Forcing Plants, and a Vocabulary of Botanical Terms. For the Use of Higher Schools and Academies.* Hartford, Conn.: H. and F. J. Huntington, 1829.

———. *Dictionary of Chemistry.* New York: Carvill, 1830. A translation of *Le Dictionnaire de Chimie of Louis Vauquelin.*

———. *The Child's Geology.* Brattleboro, Vt.: G. H. Peck, 1832.

———. *Botany for Beginners.* Hartford, Conn.: F. J. Huntington, 1833.

———. *Lectures to Young Ladies, Comprising Outlines and Applications of the Different Branches of Female Education.* Boston: Carter, Hendee, 1833.

———. *Chemistry for Beginners.* Hartford, Conn.: F. J. Huntington, 1834.

———. *Familiar Lectures on Natural Philosophy.* New York: F. J. Huntington, 1837.

———. *Natural Philosophy for Beginners.* New York: F. J. Huntington, 1838.

———. "History and Defence of Emma Willard's Theory of Circulation by Respiration." In *Reviews and Essays on Art, Literature, and Science.* Philadelphia: Claxton, Remsen, and Haffelfinger, 1873.

———. "Woman's Duties and Rights." *National Quarterly Review* 29 (1874): 29–54.

SECONDARY SOURCES

Bolzau, Emma L. *Almira Hart Lincoln Phelps: Her Life and Works.* Philadelphia: University of Pennsylvania Press, 1936.

Weeks, M. E., and F. B. Dains. "Mrs A. H. Lincoln Phelps and Her Services to Chemical Education." *Journal of Chemical Education* 14 (1937): 53–57.

STANDARD SOURCES

DAB; Grinstein 1997 (article by Robert M. Hendrick); Kass-Simon and Farnes; *NAW* (article by Frederick Rudolph); Ogilvie 1986.

PHELPS, MARTHA AUSTIN (1870–1933)

U.S. chemist. Born 1870 in Georgia, Vt. Married Isaac K. Phelps (1904). Educated Smith College (B.S., 1892); Yale University (Ph.D., 1898). Professional experience: Saratoga, N.Y., high school teacher (1892–1893); Holyoke, Mass., teacher (1893–1896); Rhode Island Experimental Station, analyst (1900–1901); high school substitute teacher (1901–1903); Wilson College, chemistry and physics teacher (1903–1904); Bureau of Standards, analyst (1908–1909). Died 1933.

Martha Austin Phelps is interesting because even after earning a doctoral degree from Yale, she worked as a substitute teacher in high schools. Her other positions were short-term, but she appeared to do a considerable amount of research. She married in 1904 and published papers with her husband, Isaac King Phelps, in the *American Journal of Science* on the quantitative analysis of several elements, including double ammonium phosphates in the analysis of magnesium, zinc, and cadmium, the gravimetric determination of phosphoric acid, and the salts of manganese in analysis. She also worked on the quantitative determination of organic chemistry, the formation of amides and esters, and catalysis in organic relations. Phelps was one of the first women to work for the U.S. Bureau of Standards.

JH/MBO

STANDARD SOURCES

AMS 1–3; Bailey; Siegel and Finley.

PHILIP, ANNA-URSULA (1908–   )

German/British biologist and geneticist. Educated Kaiser Wilhelm Gesellschaft Biological Institute (now the Max Planck Institute for Biology) (Ph.D., 1934). Professional experience: Kaiser Wilhelm Gesellschaft Biological Institute, visiting researcher (1932–1934?); University of London, research scientist (1934–?).

Anna-Ursula Philip was one of the doctoral students at the Kaiser Wilhelm Gesellschaft Biological Institute (now the Max Planck Institute for Biology) who served as a "scientific guest" or visiting researcher at the institute. After receiving her doctoral degree she emigrated to England, where she worked in J. B. S. Haldane's research group.

JH/MBO

STANDARD SOURCES

Vogt.

PHILLIPS, MELBA NEWELL (1907–)

U.S. physicist. Born 1 February 1907 near Hazelton, Ind., to Elida (Meehan) and Virgil B. Phillips. Three siblings. Educated one-room school (graduated from 8th grade, 1919); Union, Ind. high school (graduated 1923); Oakland City (Ind.) College (A.B., 1926); Battle Creek (Mich.) College (M.A., 1928); University of California, Berkeley (Ph.D., 1933). Professional experience: Union (Ind.) High School, mathematics, physics, and English teacher (1926–1927); Battle Creek College, instructor (1928–1930); University of California, Berkeley, researcher (1933), intern (1934–1935); Bryn Mawr College, Helen Huff Research Fellow (1935–1936); Institute for Advanced Study in Princeton, American Association of University Women Margaret Maltby Fellow (1936–1937); Connecticut College for Women (now Connecticut College), instructor (1937–1938); Brooklyn College, instructor (1938–1941), assistant professor (1944–1952); University of Minnesota, lecturer (1941–1944); Washington University, St. Louis, associate director of the Academic Year Institute for secondary school physics teachers (1957–1962); University of Chicago, professor (1962–1972); State University of New York at Stony Brook, visiting professor (1972–1975); Graduate School of the University of Science and Technology, Chinese Academy of Science, Beijing. Honors and memberships: American Association of Physics Teachers, Oersted Medal (1973); American Institute of Physics, Karl Taylor Compton Award "for distinguished statesmanship in science" (1981); American Association of Physics Teachers, Melba Newell Phillips Award (1981); Vanderbilt University's Guy and Rebecca Forman Award for Outstanding Teaching in Undergraduate Physics; AIP governing board (1965–1968; 1975–1977); American Philosophical Society, member; AAPT (member of executive board, 1962–1965; president, 1966–1967; acting executive officer, 1975–1977); American Association for the Advancement of Science, council (1976–1983); Commission of College Physics (1960–1968).

Melba Phillips grew up on a family farm in Indiana and attended a one-room schoolhouse through the eighth grade, when she went to Union, Indiana, to attend high school. After graduating at age sixteen, although she passed the examinations that qualified her to teach in elementary school, she could not find a teaching job, so she entered Oakland City College (Indiana). She alternated her education with teaching or research positions, ending up at the University of California as a physics doctoral candidate in 1930. She began her research with J. Robert Oppenheimer in 1931 and earned her doctoral degree in 1933. The job market for women physicists was very lean. Phillips was fortunate to be able to stay at Berkeley for two postdoctoral years and then to receive two research fellowships, one at Bryn Mawr College and the other, the American Association of University Women's Maltby Fellowship, at the Institute for Advanced Study in Princeton. After the end of her fellowship, Phillips was an instructor at the Connecticut College for Women for one year, after which she joined the physics department at Brooklyn College as an instructor in 1938. She had a leave of absence during the war years, when she served as a lecturer at the University of Minnesota. She also spent five months during 1944 at the Harvard Radio Research Laboratory at Cambridge, Massachusetts, where she produced two articles after the war on applied physics. After the rather heady experience of teaching superior students at the University of Minnesota, she returned to Brooklyn College. She also held a part-time appointment at the Columbia University Radiation Laboratory, where she worked with graduate students.

In 1952, Phillips came up against another employment barrier, this time a political one. She refused to testify before Senator Joseph McCarthy's anticommunist committee, and was fired from her positions. During this enforced leave, she wrote an advanced textbook on electricity and magnetism. In 1957, the chairperson of physics at Washington University, St. Louis, hired her and she served for five years as associate director of the Academic Year Institute for secondary school physics teachers. She finally reached full faculty appointment status in 1962, when she became a full professor at the University of Chicago. She taught physical science to non-science majors and contributed to graduate examinations. She reached the mandatory retirement age in 1972, but until 1975 she worked at the State University of New York and five years later was a visiting professor in the graduate school of the University of Science and Technology, Chinese Academy of Science, Beijing.

Phillips's research was on the theory of complex atomic spectra. She was involved in attempting to explain the energy levels of atoms containing more than hydrogen's one electron.

Phillips was active in a number of professional organizations, and was a member of the Commission on College Physics from 1960 to 1968.

JH/MBO

PRIMARY SOURCES

Phillips, Melba Newell. "Photoionization Probabilities of Atomic Potassium." *Physical Review* 39 (1932): 905–912. Based on her doctoral dissertation.

———. "Inversion of Doublets in Alkali-Like Spectra." *Physical Review* 44 (1933): 644–650. Based on her doctoral dissertation.

———. With E. Feenberg. "Structure of Light Nuclei." *Physical Review* 51 (1937): 597–608.

———. With W. E. Lamb, Jr. "Space Charge Frequency Dependence of Magnetron Cavity." *Journal of Applied Physics* 18 (1947): 230–238.

SECONDARY SOURCES

Ford, K. W. "Melba Newell Phillips: Øersted Medalist for 1973." *American Journal of Physics* 42 (1974): 357.

STANDARD SOURCES

AMS 6–8, P 9, P&B 10–14; Bailey; Grinstein 1993 (article by Francis T. Bonner); Kass-Simon and Farnes; Rossiter 1982.

PHILPOT, ELIZABETH (1780–1857)

British fossil collector. Born 1780. Two sisters, Mary and Margaret Philpot; one brother. Never married. Died 1857 in Lyme Regis.

In 1805, Elizabeth Philpot and her two sisters, MARY and MARGARET PHILPOT, moved to Lyme Regis, where they settled in a home given to them by their brother, a London solicitor. They lived in Lyme for the rest of their lives. Little information is available about the three sisters. Surviving correspondence is scant, but it is probable that Elizabeth was the sister who kept up the contacts with geologists such as William Buckland, Conybeare, and De La Beche, who used their collections. The sisters apparently knew and encouraged MARY ANNING, who also was from Lyme Regis.

The Philpot sisters collected fossils and accumulated an excellent "cabinet" of fossils, which was used by many geologists and paleontologists. Elizabeth's nephew gave a museum building in Lyme Regis in honor of the three sisters.

JH/MBO

SECONDARY SOURCES

Edmonds, J. M. "The Fossil Collection of the Misses Philpot of Lyme Regis." *Proceedings of the Dorset Natural Historical and Archaeological Society* 98 (1978, for 1976): 43–48.

Elder, Eleanor S. "Women in Early Geology." *Journal for Geological Education* 30, no. 5 (1982): 287–293.

STANDARD SOURCES

Sarjeant.

PHILPOT, MARGARET (d. 1845)

British fossil collector. Two sisters, Mary and Elizabeth Philpot; one brother. Never married. Died 1845 in Lyme Regis.

Much of the same information applies to Margaret as to her sisters ELIZABETH and MARY. The three sisters were involved with fossil collecting in the region around Lyme. (See account of Elizabeth Philpot.)

JH/MBO

SECONDARY SOURCES

Edmonds, J. M. "The Fossil Collection of the Misses Philpot of Lyme Regis." *Proceedings of the Dorset Natural Historical and Archaeological Society* 98 (1978, for 1976): 43–48.

STANDARD SOURCES

Sarjeant.

PHILPOT, MARY (1777?–1838)

British fossil collector. Born 1777. Two sisters, Margaret and Elizabeth Philpot; one brother. Never married. Died 1838 in Lyme Regis.

Much of the known information on Mary Philpot is the same as for her sisters. She was a fossil collector. (See account of Elizabeth Philpot for additional information.) JH/MBO

SECONDARY SOURCES

Edmonds, J. M. "The Fossil Collection of the Misses Philpot of Lyme Regis." *Proceedings of the Dorset Natural Historical and Archaeological Society* 98 (1978, for 1976): 43–48.

STANDARD SOURCES

Sarjeant.

PHISALIX, MARIE (PICOT) (1861–1946)

French histologist, embryologist, and physiologist. Born in 1861. Married [?] Phisalix. Educated Museum d'Histoire Naturelle, University of Paris (degree in science, 1900). Professional experience: Museum d'Histoire Naturelle, Paris, associate (1906–1946); service de vaccination, associate (1914–1919?). Died 1946.

Marie Picot married a scientist who worked at the Muséum d'Histoire Naturelle, collaborating with him to develop antivenoms against the bites of vipers. Determined to qualify herself, she studied natural history at the Museum d'Histoire Naturelle and presented a thesis for an advanced degree in science at the University of Paris on the subject of the histology, embryology, and physiology of the venomous glands of the terrestrial salamander. For this thesis, she was awarded a medal.

When her husband died prematurely in 1906, Marie Phisalix continued their joint research on her own, publishing a sequence of articles on the venomous apparatus of spiders, frogs, venomous lizards, and snakes. She also began to branch out into related problems, such as that of immunity, and methods for developing vaccinations against venom. She became interested in examining protozoa as examples of primitive parasitic animals who could be regarded as simple venomous beings. She pulled her research together in a large two-volume work, *Animaux venimeux et venins*, illustrated with both black and white and color plates.

During World War I, she organized at the Muséum d'Histoire Naturelle, a medical service where children in the neighborhood could be brought for vaccination. She also worked during this period in the hospitals of Paris.

Phisalix's work was recognized by honors and diplomas from the scientific societies with which she was associated. She was also awarded the cross of chevalier of the Legion of

Honor under the patronage of the Pasteur Institute. She died
soon after World War II in 1946.   JH/MBO

PRIMARY SOURCES
Phisalix Picot, Marie. *Recherches embryologiques, histologiques,
physiologiques sur les glandes à venin de la Salamandre terrestre.*
Paris: Schleicher frères, 1900.
———. *Répartition des glandes cutanées et leur localisation progres-
sive, en fonction de la disparition des écailles chez les batraciens
apodes.* In *International Congress on Zoology VIII, Graz: 1910;
Proceedings.* Jena, 1912.
———. *Animaux venimeux et venins.* 2 vols. Paris: Masson and
Co., 1922.
———. *Vipères de France.* Paris: Stock, [1940].

STANDARD SOURCES
DFC; Lipinska 1930.

PIAZOLLA-BELOCH, MARGHERITA (1879–?)

*Italian mathematician and mathematical physicist. Born 12 July in
Frascati, Rome, Italy. Educated University of Rome (Ph.D., 1908).
Professional experience: University of Rome, assistant (1919–
1927); University of Palermo, postdoctorate (Lib. Doc., 1924–
1927); University of Ferrara, professor ordinario (associate professor) (1927–1949), professor fuori ruolo (adjunct professor) (1949–
1954), emerita professor (1954–?). Death date unknown.*

Born in Frascati, the Italian mathematician Margherita
Piazolla-Beloch was educated at the University of Rome.
There she obtained a position as an assistant in mathematics
for eight years, with a joint appointment at the University of
Palermo. From the late 1920s on, she obtained a position at
the University of Ferrara as professor ordinario (associate
professor), a position she held for the next twenty-two years.
During this period, she published widely in prestigious
mathematical, physical mathematical and other important
journals, including the Academy Lincei (to which Galileo
had belonged) and the Paris Academy of Sciences.

In the late 1930s, Piazolla-Beloch became interested in
the topological problems including the mathematical analysis
of photographs. Although she at first applied this to aerial
photographs, she soon shifted her interest to an analysis of
X-rays and made this a specialty. By the mid-fifties, she was
appointed full professor at the University of Ferrara, four
years before her retirement as emerita professor. In the late
1960s, an edition of selected articles by her on her photographic analyses, topography, and geometrical algebra was
published, at which time she was eighty-six.   JH/MBO

PRIMARY SOURCES
Piazolla-Beloch, Margherita. "Sur une famille remarquables de
courbes topologiques planes." *Comptes rendus hebdodomaire
Académie des Sciences, Paris* 196 (1933): 1193–1196.
———. *Roentgenfotogrammetria.* Milan, 1936.
———. "Topologia delle curve situate sopra superficie generali
del 3° ordine con meno di 27 rette reali." *Atti Reale Acacade-
mia Nazionale dei Lincei* 8 (1950): 183–185.
———. *Lezioni di matematica complementare (La matematica
elementare vista dall'alto).* Ferrara, 1953.
———. *Opere Scelte* [Selected Works]: *Fotogrammetria, Geometria
Algebrica, Topologia.* Padova, 1967.

STANDARD SOURCES
Poggendorff, vol. 7B.

PICCARD, SOPHIE (ca. 1906–)

*Russian/Swiss mathematician. Born St. Petersburg to Eulalie Güée
and [?] Piccard. Educated University of Smolensk; University of
Lausanne (Licence-ès-Sciences, 1927; Doctorat-ès-Sciences, 1928).
Professional experience: actuary; Feuille d'avis de Neuchâtel, newspaper, administrative secretary (1932–1938); University of Neuchâtel, assistant in geometry (1936–1938), professeur extraordinaire
(adjunct professor) (1938–1943), full professor mathematics
(1943–?).*

Sophie Piccard came from a distinguished family. Her father
was a professor at the University of Smolensk and her
mother a respected literary personage, who wrote, among
other things, a series of five books on the Bolshevik revolution, and the novel *Galia.* Eulalie Piccard had been a language professor at the Russian lycée Sophie attended. The
teachers at the school informed her of her daughter's exceptional mathematical abilities. Sophie's father's ancestors were
Swiss and her mother's French Huguenot, so when the situation in Russia became increasing uncomfortable in the
1920s, the family emigrated to Switzerland. Sophie entered
the University of Lausanne, where her doctoral thesis, under
the supervision of Professor Mirimanoff, was in the field of
probability. After the death of her father, Sophie and her
mother were in dire financial straits. Her mother worked as a
dressmaker and Sophie, in spite of her advanced degrees,
worked as an actuary then as administrative secretary for a
newspaper. During this period, she continued to study and
do research. In 1936, she became assistant in geometry to
Professor Gaberel of the University of Neuchâtel and succeeded to his position after his death in 1938. From 1943,
Piccard held the chair of higher geometry and probability
theory.

Her research interests were set theory and group theory.
She published papers in other areas as well: function theory,

the theory of relations, probability theory, and actuarial science. Her set-theory treatises resulted into comprehensive treatises. JH/MBO

PRIMARY SOURCES

Piccard, Sophie. *Sur les ensembles de distances des ensembles de points d'un espace Euclidien.* Neuchâtel: Secrétariat de l'Université, 1939.

————. *Sur les ensembles parfaits.* Neuchâtel: Secrétariat de l'Université, 1942.

SECONDARY SOURCES

Kramer, Edna. "Six More Women Mathematicians." *Scripta Mathematica* 23 (1957): 83–95.

PICKETT, LUCY WESTON (1904–)

U.S. chemist. Born 19 January 1904 in Beverly, Mass., to Lucy (Weston) and George Ernest Pickett. One brother. Educated Mount Holyoke College (A.B., 1925; M.A., 1927); University of Illinois (Ph.D., 1930). Royal Institution, London (fellowship, 1932–1933); University of Liège and Harvard, Educational Foundation Fellowship (1939). Professional experience: Goucher College, instructor (1927–1928); Mount Holyoke, instructor of chemistry (1930–1935), assistant professor (1935–1940), associate professor (1940–1945), professor of chemistry (1945–1968), chair of Department of Chemistry (1954–1962); University of California, visiting professor (1947–1948). Honors and memberships: American Chemical Society, Garvan Medal, 1957; memorialized by Lucy Pickett Fund, Mount Holyoke (1968).

Lucy Pickett pioneered the use of spectroscopy for the investigation of molecular structure. She was born in Beverly, Massachusetts, and attended Mount Holyoke College, where she became interested in chemistry, graduating *summa cum laude* in both chemistry and mathematics in 1925. She stayed on to take a master's degree in chemistry two years later. She then went to teach as an instructor of chemistry for a year before moving to the University of Illinois, where she studied for her doctoral degree.

Having done her research on X-ray effects on chemical compounds and X-ray investigation of organic compounds, she continued to be intrigued by the new field of X-ray crystallography. She accepted a position to teach at her undergraduate college, but within two years took the opportunity to spend a year doing postdoctoral research under the Nobel Prize–winner William Bragg at the Royal Institution in London. On return to Mount Holyoke, she realized the new techniques required equipment not available in the college and turned to spectroscopy in collaboration with her colleagues EMMA PERRY CARR and MARY SHERRILL. She remained at Mount Holyoke as an assistant professor, associate

and full professor by 1945 until her retirement in 1968 as Mary Lyon professor of chemistry.

By 1939, Pickett had a further opportunity to develop her research techniques by using an educational fellowship to travel to the University of Liège to work with the Belgian spectroscopist Victor Henri, then returning to Massachusetts to work with George Kistiakowsky at Harvard. Her participation in a conference on spectroscopy placed her in contact with the organizer Robert S. Mulliken at the University of Chicago, with whom she would later work during the summer of 1952 on interpretations of the spectrum of the benzenium ion. The two published a paper on their theoretical analysis a few years later. Mulliken would later receive a Nobel Prize.

Other opportunities outside the college included a short stint as a visiting professor at University of California, Berkeley, followed by a month during which she worked in the laboratory of another Nobel laureate, this time, Linus Pauling.

Pickett had both a happy and successful career as a teacher as well as a researcher. She published an article about new methods of teaching analytical chemistry in the 1940s. She also published a number of articles on her studies of molecular structure using spectroscopy. She was awarded the Garvan prize of the American Chemcial Society in 1957 and received two honorary degrees, one from Mount Holyoke. When a chemistry lecture series was created in her name, she requested the use of the funds to bring women chemists to the campus, and expressed pleasure in the results. JH/MBO

PRIMARY SOURCES

Pickett, Lucy. "Some New Experiments on the Chemical Effects of X-Rays and the Energy Relations Involved." *Journal of the American Chemical Society* 52 (1930): 465–479.

————. "Developments in the Teaching of Analytical Chemistry." *Journal of Chemical Education* 20 (1943): 102.

————. With others. "Molecular Complexes of Tetracyanoethylene with Tetrahydrofuran and P-Dioxane." *Journal of Physical Chemistry* 66 (1962): 1754–1755.

STANDARD SOURCES

AMS 3–8, P 9, P&B 10–13; Grinstein 1993 (article by George Fleck); Shearer and Shearer 1997.

PICKFORD, GRACE EVELYN (1902–1986)

British/U.S. biologist, endocrinologist. Born 24 March 1902 in Bournemouth, England, to Evelyn May (Flower) and William Pickford. One brother. Married G. Evelyn Hutchinson (divorced). Educated Bournemouth Collegiate School for Girls; Bournemouth Municipal College; Newnham College, Cambridge University (1921–1925), Natural Sciences Tripos Pt. I, class 2; Yale Univer-

sity (Ph.D., 1931). *Professional experience: Yale University, department of biology, research fellow (1931–1933), lecturer (1957–1959), associate professor (1959–1969), professor (1969–1970), professor emerita (1970); Albertus Magnus College, instructor through assistant professor (1934–1948); Hiram College, Ohio, department of biology, distinguished scientist in residence (1970–1986). Concurrent experience: Yale University Bingham Oceanographic Laboratory, research assistant through research associate (1931–1966). Honors and memberships: Newnham College Exhibitioner (1921–1922); Mary Ewart Traveling Scholarship for South Africa (1925–1927); Wilbur Cross Medal; Pickford Medal (endocrinology) named after her in 1980. Memorialized by cephalopod* Pickfordiateuthis Voss *in 1953. Died 20 January 1986 in Ohio.*

Grace Pickford was a British-born biologist and endocrinologist who did most of her noted work on oligochaete systematics, cephalopod biology, and fish endocrinolgy in the United States. Her father was a journalist and editor of the *Bournemouth Guardian* and later the head of a printing firm. Both her father and mother encouraged her interest in science, particularly in natural history. She went to local schools and then to Cambridge, where she entered Newnham College on an exhibitioner's scholarship. She took the first part of the Natural History Tripos but fell ill after studying for the second part and was unable to take the examination.

After graduating from Newnham, Pickford went to South Africa, where she worked with G. Evelyn Hutchinson on his early studies of limnology. She married Hutchinson soon after, but the marriage ended in divorce after a few years. Pickford then went to Yale, where Hutchinson had begun to teach, and enrolled as a graduate student in biology. There she completed her dissertation on South African acanthodriline earthworms, later published as a long monograph. She began to teach biology at Albertus Magnus College, which must have been an exciting place at the time, since MARCELLA BOVERI was also teaching there. Many Yale-trained women biologists found part-time teaching positions at this college.

Pickford's work at the Bingham Oceanographic Laboratory attached to Yale led her to the study of cephalopods. She used the extensive collection at Yale's Peabody Museum to develop her knowledge of cephalopod systematics; she became an authority in this field. She would later join the Danish-sponsored deep-sea *Galathea* expedition in 1951 to study rare octopods in the Indo-Malayan region.

In the 1940s, Pickford became interested in the endocrinology of the killifish, an organism that John Nicholas had used at Yale in nervous system research and on whose embryology JANE OPPENHEIMER, a fellow graduate student, had written her dissertation. Pickford, in later years, attributed the start of her own interest in this "trash" fish to the interest of the head of the Bingham Laboratory in exploring

its use as a food source during World War II. The fish, *Fundulus heteroclitus*, became the experimental organism on which Pickford established her outstanding work in fish endocrinology. She became interested in the growth rings on fish scales, and examined the effects of the newly developed growth hormone upon the endocrine system of the fish. In the process, she developed a number of techniques adapted from pediatric research and her earlier work on invertebrates. Pickford published a seminal monograph, *The Physiology of the Pituary Gland of Fishes* (1957), which soon became the bible for scientists working on the endocrinology of lower vertebrates. She continued this research for another twenty years, focusing on hormome research and osmoregulation. After the publication of this important work, Yale invited her to join the faculty as associate professor, and she remained there until she retired as emerita professor at the age of sixty-eight.

Pickford's retirement was far from the end of her research or her teaching career. A former student invited her to come to Hiram College in Ohio as distinguished scientist in residence. There she continued to teach and do research on a number of topics, publishing up to the time of her death in her eighties. The endocrinological society named their medal after her, and she had the honor of twice presenting it in person to younger scientists who had made outstanding contributions.

JH/MBO

PRIMARY SOURCES

Pickford, Grace E. *A Monograph of the Acanthodriline Earthworms of South Africa.* Cambridge, England: Heffner and Sons, 1937.

———. *Studies on the Digestive Enzymes of Spiders.* New Haven, Conn.: Connecticut Academy of Arts and Sciences, [1942].

———. With Bayard H. McConnaughey. *The Octopus bimaculatus Problem: A Study in Sibling Species.* New Haven, Conn.: Peabody Museum of Natural History, 1949.

SECONDARY SOURCES

Ball, J. N. "In Memoriam, Grace E. Pickford (1902–1986)." *General and Comparative Endocrinology* 65 (1987): 162–165.

Slack, Nancy. "Grace Pickford: Eminent Scientist, Uncredited Wife, and Research Advisor." Paper presented at the History of Science Society meeting, Kansas City, Mo., October 1998.

STANDARD SOURCES

AMS 5–8, B 9, P&B 10–14; *Creative Couples;* Newnham.

PICKFORD, LILIAN MARY (1902–)

British physiologist. Born 1902 in Jubbalpore, India. Educated privately in England (1907–1915); Wycombe Abbey School (1915–1921); Bedford College (B.Sc. in physiology, 1925). University

College Hospital (M.B.). Professional experience: University College, London, instructor of history of science and medicine (1925–1926?); University College, London, department of pharmacology, research assistant and demonstrator; Stafford General Infirmary, house physician; Cambridge University, department of pharmacology, research fellow (1936–1939); University of Edinburgh, lecturer in physiology (1939–1952), reader (1952–1966), professor (1966–1972), retired (1972); University of Nottingham, special professor of endocrinology, department of physiology and pharmacology (1972–1977); University of Brisbane, Australia, visiting professor (1977). Honors and memberships: Royal Society of Edinburgh, Fellow (1977); Royal College of Physicians, Fellow (1977). Retired to Edinburgh in 1982.

Lilian Mary Pickford, the daughter of a successful colonial businessman, spent the first five years of her life in India. She was educated in England, under the care of her uncle and aunt, initially with a governess and then at the Wycombe Abbey School, graduating in 1921. She entered Bedford College that year, and graduated in physiology in 1925. Unable to find a position in research, she taught part time at University College, London, teaching history of science and medicine. Through her uncle's influence, she managed to obtain a position in the department of pharmacology at University College, working with E. B. Verney on renal circulation, supported part-time by a Medical Research Council grant. She was elected a member of the Physiological Society in 1928.

Pickford's work with Verney on the physiology of the kidneys led her to continue related research. She was inspired to continue in research and she determined to first obtain a medical degree at University College Hospital, which she partly funded through teaching in pharmacology. She then took a position as house physician at Sheffield General Infirmary, where she had wide clinical experience in minor surgery. She was encouraged by one of her former teachers, T. R. Elliott at University College Hospital, to return to scientific research. In 1935 she was the first woman elected to the Pharmacology Society.

Continuing her successful collaboration with Verney from 1936 to 1939, she moved with him to his department at Cambridge University, where she began to study the role of acetycholine in regulating urine flow in dogs, and she began to focus on the release of the antidiruretic hormone, ADH. She developed new surgical techniques to expose the posterior pituitary in dogs so that she could assure the injection of substances directly into the supra-optic nucleus. This allowed her to demonstrate a central role for acetylcholine in 1947. In 1945 she was able to show, with V. C. Abrahams, that oxytocin and ADH were separate substances even though they were released together, by measuring urine flow and uterine activity simultaneously.

From Cambridge, Pickford went to the University of Edinburgh in 1939 as a lecturer in physiology, where she carried a heavy load of both teaching and research at the outbreak of World War II. In the summers, she returned to London, where she served as a relief physician for general practioners and inspecting the air-raid shelters during the Blitz. Noted as an excellent teacher, she rose from reader in 1952 to professor in 1966 at University of Edinburgh until her retirement in 1972. Her retirement was only nominal, since she went from Edinburgh to being a special professor in endocrinology at University of Nottingham 1972 to 1977, and in 1977 spent six months as a visiting professor in Australia at the University of Brisbane. That same year she was made Fellow of the Royal Society of Edinburgh and Fellow of the Royal College of Physicians. In 1982 Pickford finally retired and returned to Edinburgh. In 1987 she was made an honorary member of the Physiological Society. By the mid-seventies, she was recognized as a pioneer of neuroendocrinology.

JH/MBO

PRIMARY SOURCES

Pickford, Mary. "Experiments on the Hypothalamic and Pituitary Control of Water Excretion." *Journal of Physiology* 104 (1945): 105–128.

———. "The Action of Acetylcholine in the Supraoptic Nucleus of the Chloralosed Dog." *Journal of Physiology* 106 (1947): 264–270.

———. "Antidiruretic Substances." *Pharmacological Review* 4 (1952): 254–283.

———. "Stimuli That Release Hormones of the Pars Nervosa." In *Pioneers of Neuroendocrinology,* ed. J. Meiles, et al., 205–216. New York: Plenum Press, 1975.

STANDARD SOURCES
Women Physiologists.

PICOTTE, SUSAN (LA FLESCHE) (1865–1915)

U.S. (Native American) physician. Born 17 June 1865 on the Omaha reservation (later Thurston County) in Nebraska to Chief Joseph La Flesche (Iron Eye) and Mary (One Woman). Four siblings. Married Henry Picotte 1894 (he died 1905). Two sons. Educated Elizabeth (N.J.) Institute for Young Ladies; Hampton Institute (Va.) (graduated 1886); Woman's Medical College of Pennsylvania (M.D., 1889). Professional experience: Woman's Hospital, Philadelphia, intern (1889–1890); Omaha Indian School, physician (1890–1894); Barcroft, Nebr., private practice (1894–1915); Presbyterian Missionary hospital (later Susan Picotte Hospital) at Walthill, Nebr., founder (1913). Died 15 September 1915 in Walthill of bone infection.

Susan La Flesche was one of five remarkable children of the Omaha chief Joseph La Flesche, also known as Iron Eye. Her older sister, Susette (later Tibbles, known as Bright Eyes) became noted as an educator and reformer, and her half brother Joseph became an important anthropologist working closely with ALICE FLETCHER at the Smithsonian Bureau of Ethnology, publishing on the Omaha Indians. La Flesche was brought up on the reservation and attended reservation and Presbyterian mission schools. At the age of fourteen she was sent, as was her sister Susette, to the Elizabeth (New Jersey) Institute for Young Ladies and from there to the government Indian school, Hampton Institute, in Virginia where she graduated at the top of her class.

Attracting the attention of the leaders of the Woman's National Indian Association which had close ties to Alice Fletcher, Susan La Flesche received financial support that enabled her to attend the Woman's Medical College of Pennsylvania. Again she proved to be a remarkable student, and graduated at the top of her class in 1889. After a year as an intern in the Woman's Hospital in Philadelphia, she returned to the reservation, where she worked for four years as a physician to the government reservation schools and also for a time as a medical missionary for the Woman's National Indian Association. After her marriage to Henry Picotte, half Sioux and half French, she went into private practice, establishing herself in Bancroft and then in Walthill, Nebraska. Nursing her husband through a long illness (until his death five years later), she successfully raised two sons, both of whom went on to college. One son later became a lieutenant colonel during World War II.

Susan Picotte was noted as a spokesperson on behalf of her tribe at the same time that she established the county medical society and served as chair of the local board of health. Her close link to the Presbyterian Board of Home Missions led to her position as a medical missionary and the subsequent establishment by that body of a hospital in Walthill under her direction. Two years after the hospital was founded in 1913, she died from a longstanding infection of the facial bones. The hospital was renamed in her honor.

JH/MBO

SECONDARY SOURCES
Mathes, Valerie Sherer. "Susan La Flesche Picotte: Nebraska's Indian Physician, 1865–1915." *Nebraska History* 63 (1982): 502–530.

STANDARD SOURCES
NAW (article by Norma Kidd Green).

PIERCE, MADELENE EVANS (1904–1989)

U.S. zoologist. Born 7 November 1904 in Boston, Mass. Educated Radcliffe College (A.B., 1926, A.M., 1927; Ph.D., in zoology, 1933). Professional experience: Smith College, instructor in zoology (1927–1929); Vassar College, instructor (1931–1938), assistant professor (1938–1944), associate professsor (1944–1950), professor of experimental zoology (1950–1970), emerita professor (1970–1989). Concurrent experience: Woods Hole Marine Biological Station, summer instructor (1943–1952). Honors and memberships: MBL Corporation, member; Society of Zoologists, member. Died early September 1989.

Madelene Pierce was born in Boston and earned her undergraduate degree and her master's degree at Radcliffe College. Working at the Museum of Comparative Zoology, Harvard, she did a doctoral degree in zoology, writing a dissertation in experimental embryology in which she examined the role of the chick amnion as an independent effector. She was appointed as an instructor in zoology at Smith College, where she remained for two years, and then moved to Vassar College, where she moved up in the ranks to full professor in 1950. During the summers in the 1940s through the early fifties, she taught at the Marine Biological Station, Woods Hole, eventually becoming a member of the Marine Biological Laboratory Corporation.

Pierce's research included studies of melanophore activity in cold-blooded vertebrates, skin grafting in amphibia, and invertebrate ecology, especially of mollusks.   JH/MBO

PRIMARY SOURCES
Pierce, Madelene Evans. "The Amnion of the Chick as an Independent Effector." Ph.D. diss., Radcliffe College, 1933.

SECONDARY SOURCES
New York Times, 12 September 1989. Obituary notice.

STANDARD SOURCES
AMS 6–8, B 9, P&B 10–15; Debus; Rossiter 1995.

PIERCE, MARION (ARMBRUSTER) (1910–1988)

U.S. chemist. Born 17 March 1910 in Folsomdale, N.Y. Married Robert H. H. Pierce 1947. Two children. Educated Mount Holyoke College (A.B., 1930) Bryn Mawr (scholar, 1930–1931; fellow, 1931–1933; A.M., 1933, Huff fellow, 1933–1934; Ph.D., 1934). Professional experience: Barnard College, assistant in chemistry (1934–1935), instructor (1943–1944), assistant professor (1945–1946); U.S. Steel Corporation research laboratory, research chemist (1934–1943). Du Pont de Nemours and Company, Arlington, N.J., chemist (1946–1982?).

Marion Armbruster was born in New York State and educated at Mount Holyoke College in Massachusetts, moving then to another of the Seven Sisters colleges, Bryn Mawr, for her master's and doctoral degrees. While she was working on her advanced degreees, she held a number of prestigious fellowships. Although she seemed destined for an academic career, she chose to work as an industrial research chemist for U.S. Steel for nine years following one year as an instructor in chemistry at Barnard College.

During World War II, Marion Armbruster returned to Barnard College as an instructor, rising after a year to assistant professor. Her marriage in 1947 again interrupted her academic career. She met her husband, H. H. Pierce, while they both were working for U.S. Steel in New Jersey in the 1930s and 1940s. Exactly the same age as Marion, he was also interested in the properties of metals and later of polymers. Her husband was associate director of cryogenic lab at Ohio State when they married, but following Marion, who had gone to work for Du Pont in Arlington, New Jersey, he left the university for a research position at Du Pont in 1949, moving to the Delaware research group while she continued to list Arlington as her office until 1982. The couple had two children. Marion Pierce's interests were in chemical thermodynamics, electrochemistry and the properties of metals. She later focused on high polymers.   JH/MBO

SECONDARY SOURCES
"Marion Armbruster Pierce." *New York Times,* 1 June 1988. Obituary notice.

STANDARD SOURCES
AMS P&B 10–15.

PIERRY, LOUISE ELIZABETH DU (1746–?)
French astronomer. Born 1746. Death date unknown.

For all the esteem she apparently commanded among her contemporaries, little biographical information is available on du Pierry. The astronomer Joseph Jérôme Lalande dedicated his *Astronomie des dames* (1790) to her, praising her talent, good taste, and courage, and suggesting that other women might well emulate her. He noted that du Pierry had presented a course in astronomy for women in 1789. Although, he explained, many of the students had feared that the course material would be too difficult for them, the course was successful.

In addition to teaching, du Pierry computed most of the eclipses used by Lalande in his investigations of lunar motions; she collected historical data on their occurrences during the past hundred years. She computed tables for the lengths of day and night, and tables of refraction in right ascension and declination for the latitude of Paris.   JH/MBO

SECONDARY SOURCES
Davis, Herman S. "Women Astronomers, 100 A.D.–1750." *Popular Astronomy* 6 (May 1898): 128–138.
Lalande, Jérôme de. *Bibliographie astronomique avec l'histoire de l'astronomie depuis 1781 jusqu'à 1802.* Paris: Imprimerie de la République, 1803.

STANDARD SOURCES
Ogilvie 1986; Rebière.

PILLIET, BLANCHE EDWARDS (1858–1941)
See Edwards-Pilliet, Blanche.

PINCKNEY, ELIZA (LUCAS) (1722–1793)
U.S. horticulturist and agronomist. Born 8 December 1722 in the West Indies to Ann and George Lucas. Three siblings. Married Colonel Charles Pinckney. Three children. Educated in England. Professional experience: Managed Wappoo Creek plantation, Garden Hill plantation, and 3,000 acres of rice along the Waccamaw River near Charles Town, S.C., for her father. Returned to England, 1753. Returned to South Carolina on her husband's death (1758) and managed his plantation. Died 26 May 1793 in Philadelphia of breast cancer.

Born in 1722 in the West Indies, Eliza was educated in England. The oldest of four children, she moved to South Carolina with her father, mother, and younger sister in 1738. Her father owned three plantations, and she quickly became integrated into the social life of the town. When the War of Jenkins Ear (between England and Spain) erupted, George Lucas went to fight. In his absence, Eliza managed the three plantations when she was just eighteen years old, and also acted as a schoolteacher for her younger sister. While taking care of the business side of plantation ownership, Eliza began experimenting with a number of crops. She was most successful in cultivating indigo. She began experimenting with it in 1740 and became the first person to successfully cultivate the plant on a large scale and produce a quality dye for the marketplace. She received seeds for the indigo plant from her father in the West Indies. Her father secured the help of a neighboring planter and a dye-maker. However, her first efforts were a dismal failure. The dye-maker sent by her father sabotaged the process. After hiring a new dye-maker, Lucas began to have success. Following her successful cultivation of indigo, Lucas married Charles Pinckey, a wealthy landholder twice her age. The couple had three children. In 1753, the family returned to England, where Charles Pinckney served as an agent to South Carolina merchants. He died of malaria in 1758, so Eliza again managed the plantation and nurtured her three children. Eliza Pinckney supported the Revolution by loaning money to South Carolina. After he was elected president, George Washington visited Pinckney and her daughter. He also served as a pallbearer at her funeral.   JH/MBO

PRIMARY SOURCES

Pinckney, Eliza Lucas. *The Letterbook of Eliza Lucas Pinckney, 1739–1762.* Ed. Elise Pinckney with Marvin R. Zahniser. Chapel Hill: University of North Carolina Press, 1972.

SECONDARY SOURCES

Bird, Caroline. *Enterprising Women.* New York: W. W. Norton, 1976.

Booth, Sally S. *The Women of '76.* New York: Hastings House, 1973.

Ravenel, Harriott Horry. *Eliza Pinckney.* New York: Charles Scribner's Sons, 1896.

Williams, Frances Leigh. *Plantation Patriot: A Biography of Eliza Lucas Pinckney.* New York: Harcourt, Brace, and World, 1967.

STANDARD SOURCES

Grinstein 1997 (article by Virginia Pezalla; *NAW* (article by James Harvey Young); Shearer and Shearer 1996 (article by Heather Martin).

PINK, OLIVE MURIEL (1884–1936)

Australian anthropologist and botanist; activist for aboriginal rights. Born 17 March 1884 in Hobart, Tasmania, to Eveline Fannie Margaret (Kerr) and Robert Stuart Pink. Never married. Educated Julien Ashton School of Art, Sydney. University of Sydney (studied anthropology from 1932). Professional experience: Railways Commission, Sydney, draftswoman; Australian National Research Council, Canberra, research expeditions to Alice Springs (1934–1938); independent research (1939–1946); museum (now Olive Pink Museum of Anthropology), Alice Springs, founder; Arid Region Flora Reserve, Alice Springs, honorary curator (1957–1975). Died 1975 in Alice Springs, Central Australia.

Olive Muriel Pink was an Australian anthropologist who was an activist for aboriginal rights and a strong advocate of land preservation. She had been born in Tasmania and trained first at the School of Art in Sydney. Her first positions were as a draughtswoman for the Railways Commission in Sydney. She became interested in aboriginal rights in her thirties and with the encouragement of the anthropologist Ray-

mond Firth, she began to study anthropology as a non-degree student at the University of Sydney. At first encouraged by her professors, especially A. P. Elkin, she eventually took issue with him as a practicing minister of the Church of England. He, however, drafted a proposal to establish an Aboriginal Reserve that would not be religiously based, that would have adequate water and fertile soil, and that would exclude police and settlers and be administered by a woman. From her earliest studies, Pink was outspoken in her dislike of the manner in which the Australian aboriginal tribes had been treated and she actively opposed racism.

Unlike other Australian anthropologists, such as PHYLLIS KABERRY, she did not wish to limit her research to the concerns of aboriginal women and refused to follow Elkin's advice about this. As a woman in her mid-forties by the time she began her work, she felt that her interests, as she put it, in "things,—ideas—& beliefs," were closer to those of the men she was studying. In the field, she studied the native plants as well as the people and sketched many of the wildflowers in the area.

In 1934, with the support of Elkin and J. B. Cleland, a professor of pathology at the University of Adelaide, Pink obtained a reseach grant from the Australian National Research Council in Caberra to study "culture contact" among the Arrente and Warlpiri tribes. However, her advocacy of the political rights of these tribes and her strong criticism of both mission and government practices brought criticism from local settlers as well as her fellow anthropologists. Although she had small research grants until 1939, and had helped other visiting anthropologists in the Alice Springs area, tension between her and her former supporters led to an end to her research support. She left all of her anthropological notes to the Australian National Research Council, sealed for fifty years.

When in her fifties, Pink continued to work for the establishment of a museum for the Alice Springs area and to agitate on behalf of a Flora reserve that was eventually established, with Pink as the honorary curator, when she was seventy-three. She continued to live in the area, and speak out on behalf of the Aboriginal tribes of the region until her death when she was turning ninety. After her death, the Olive Pink Society was established to carry out the aims for which she had worked so hard throughout her life.   JH/MBO

PRIMARY SOURCES

Pink, Olive. "Spirit Ancestors in a Northern Aranda Horde Country." *Oceania* 4 (December 1933): 176–186.

———. "The Landowners of the Northern Division of the Aranda Tribe, Central Australia." *Oceania* 6 (March 1936): 275–305.

SECONDARY SOURCES

Marcus, Julie. "Yours Truly, Olive M. Pink." Canberra: Olive Pink Society, 1991.

———. "Olive Pink and the Encounter with the Academy." *Mankind* 17, no. 3 (1987) 185–197.

———, ed. *First in Their Field: Women and Anthropology in Australia*. Melbourne: Melbourne University Press, 1993.

PIOZZI, HESTER LYNCH (1741–1821)

British writer and traveler. Born 16 January 1741 at Bodvel near Pwllheli, Carnarvonshire, to Hester Maria (Cotton) and John Salusbury. No siblings. Married (1) Henry Thrale (he died in 1781), and (2) Gabriel Piozzi. Twelve children by Thrale; five survived. Died 2 May 1821.

Hester Lynch Piozzi is remembered by geologists for her vivid description of an Italian earthquake. She was educated in Latin and modern languages by tutors. She began to write essays when she was fifteen years old. Her marriage to Henry Thrale was unhappy and Hester complained that she was not allowed to ride or to manage the household. Her only way of entertaining herself was with literature and her children. Thrale also had a number of affairs. She became friends with Samuel Johnson and published several works about him, although their relationship later soured. When Thrale died in 1781, Hester fell in love with Gabriel Piozzi, an Italian musician. Her family disapproved, as did Johnson. Nevertheless, she married Piozzi on 23 July 1784. The couple traveled through Italy and lived in Wales until Gabriel Piozzi died in March 1809. Hester Piozzi adopted his nephew, to whom she left everything.

During her travels in Italy, Hester Lynch Piozzi published a description of an earthquake, reporting the experiences of an Italian woman who survived the disaster but whose son did not. Extracts were reprinted in at least four American magazines. JH/MBO

PRIMARY SOURCES

Piozzi, H. L. "Affecting Picture of of an Earthquake Scene." *Lady's Magazine and Repository of Entertaining Knowledge* 2 (1793): 187–188. A reprinted extract from the original work.

———. *Observations and Reflections Made in the Course of a Journey through France, Italy, and Germany*. 2 vols. London: Printed for A. Strahan and T. Cadell, 1789.

STANDARD SOURCES

DNB; Kass-Simon and Farnes.

PIRAMI, EDMEA (1899–?)

Italian physician. Born 27 June 1899 in Ascoli Piceno, Italy, to a homemaker mother and a teacher father. Four sisters. Married a physician (1932). One daughter, Alberta. Educated Livorno; Bologna gymnasium (matriculation exam, 1916); University of Bologna, Faculty of Medicine and Surgery (graduated 1922; examination in pediatrics, 1927; course in child welfare, honors, 1933). Professional experience: Pediatric Clinic, Bologna, assistant professor at institute; second professor of hospitals (1922–1933); private practice (1933–post-1972). Honors and memberships: Premio della Bontà (Prize of Goodness) (1968); Order of Physician (1972). Death date unknown.

Edmea Pirami was born in a small Italian town into a family interested in education. One of her sisters became a drawing teacher, another took a degree in chemistry, and the oldest became a physician. Pirami passed her matriculation examination in 1916, and entered the Bologna University Faculty of Medicine and Surgery. When she was twenty-two years old she graduated in medicine with a thesis on celiac disease in infants and children. During her fourth year, she became interested in Carlo Francioni's lectures on pediatrics and upon graduation joined his institute as an assistant professor. She stayed at the Pediatric Clinic in Bologna until 1933, in the meantime passing her examination in pediatrics with highest honors and completing a course in child welfare.

Pirami married a physician in 1932 and the two had a daughter. After she left the clinic, she went into private practice, where she remained for the rest of her long career. Many things changed with the advent of World War II. Her work was often interrupted by sirens and bombings, and she was often called to venture out to attend those in shelters. Though in constant fear for the lives of her small daughter and her husband, who was in the army, she still continued with her medical practice. She and her family had moved to a small village for safety but returned to Bologna when conditions bettered. She gave six Jewish children a temporary home during the worst of the conflict.

After the war her husband helped to reorganize the reconstruction. Pirami was the first woman to be elected councilor of the Order of Physicians of Bologna, was the president of the Medical Women's Association of Bologna for several terms, and president of the Italian Medical Women's Association. She attended all of the congresses of the Medical Women's International Association and was vice-president for southern Europe in Manilla (1962). She was a founding member of the Soroptimists of Bologna and was president for two terms.

Pirami's published papers were concerned with celiac disease in children and historical studies on medical women.

JH/MBO

PRIMARY SOURCES

Pirami, Edmea. In Hellstedt, *Autobiographies.*

PIRIE, ANTOINETTE (1905–1991)

British biochemist and researcher in opthalmology. Born 4 October 1905. Married N. W. Pirie. One son. Educated Cambridge University (first-class degree; Ph.D.); Imperial Cancer Research Fund Laboratories at Mill Hill, postdoctoral research. Professional experience: research with Ida Mann on the responses of the eye to war gases (1938 or 1939–1942); Nuffield Laboratory of Opthalmology, Oxford, research assistant to Mann (1942–1947); Margaret Ogilvie Reader in opthalmology and Somerville College, professorial fellowship (1947–1971 or 1972). Died 11 October 1991.

Antoinette Pirie actually had two careers, one as a biochemist and a second involving malnutrition. However, they both converged in her research on preventing eye disease that would result in blinding.

She earned a first-class degree in biochemistry at Cambridge and later a doctorate. For her postdoctoral work, she studied tumor viruses at the Imperial Cancer Research Fund Laboratories at Mill Hill.

Toward the beginning of World War II, she was seconded to work with Ida Mann on the responses of the eye to war gases. This experience initiated a collaboration that was to continue until Mann's retirement in 1947. In 1942 the Nuffield Laboratory of Opthalmology at Oxford was formed. Mann and Pirie worked as a team on problems of ocular development, metabolism and toxicology. In 1946 they collaborated on *The Science of Seeing.* Even though Pirie had a doctoral degree, she always felt that she was treated as a second-class citizen at Oxford.

Pirie succeeded Mann in 1947 as the Margaret Ogilvie Reader in Opthalmology and at the same time was elected to a professorial fellowship at Somerville College, Oxford. During her years at Oxford, she built a team of researchers to unravel the major eye diseases by studying the basic biochemical processes of the eye. They made fundamental discoveries in the areas of lens metabolism, enzymes, and lens proteins. They especially did important work on cataracts. In 1956, Pirie published a classic text with Ruth van Heyningen, *The Biochemistry of the Eye.* Pirie organized a symposium in 1962 in Oxford on "Lens Metabolism in Relation to Cataracts." She also established the International Committee for Eye Research, the forerunner of the International Society for Eye Research. In 1968 she became the first woman to receive the Proctor award.

In 1971, shortly before she retired from Oxford, Pirie went to India at the request of the Royal Commonwealth Society to investigate vitamin deficiency in Tamil Nadu in southern India. She was concerned especially with vitamin A deficiency, which causes xerophthalmia. At Madurai, Tamil Nadu, she set up a nutrition center with the goal of preventing childhood blindness due to keratomalacia, a disorder causing corneal scarring or perforation and caused by a deficiency of vitamin A. Her pragmatic approach was to identify vegetables seldom used but rich in vitamin A and encourage people to plant kitchen gardens containing these vegetables. Experimentally, she was able to show the role of white cell–derived proteolytic enzymes in this process.

Pirie was married and had one son. She was socially active, at one time standing for Labour Councillor for Cambridge. She also spoke at rallies about the hazards of radiation and nuclear fallout. She edited the book *Fallout* (1957).

JH/MBO

PRIMARY SOURCES

Pirie, Antoinette. With Ida Mann. *The Science of Seeing.* Harmondsworth: Penguin Books, 1946.

———. With Ruth van Heyningen. *The Biochemistry of the Eye.* Springfield, Ill.: Thomas, [1956].

———, ed. *Fall Out: Radiation Hazards from Nuclear Explosions.* London: MacGibbon and Kee, 1957.

SECONDARY SOURCES

"Antoinette Pirie." *Times,* 21 October 1991. Obituary notice.

PIRIE, MARY (1821–1885)

Scottish botanist. Born 1821 in Aberdeen, Scotland. Died 8 February 1885.

Mary Pirie, a nineteenth-century Scottish botanist, published one book on flowers, grasses, and shrubs in 1860.

JH/MBO

PRIMARY SOURCES

Pirie, Mary. *A Popular Book on Flowers, Grasses and Shrubs with Anecdotes and Poetical Illustrations.* London: Blackwood, [1860].

SECONDARY SOURCES

Aberdeen Journal. "Notes and Queries" 1 (1908): 15.

STANDARD SOURCES

Desmond.

PIRRET, RUTH (ca. 1874–?)

Scottish physicist. Born circa 1874. Educated University of Glasgow, (B.Sc. with honors in science, 1898). Professional experience: Arbroath, Scotland (near Dundee), teacher; research with F. Soddy (1909–probably April 1911). Death date unknown.

Little is known about Ruth Pirret's life. We do know that after earning a bachelor's degree in science from the University of Glasgow, she taught at Arbroath, Scotland. She then worked with the physicist Frederick Soddy for six months, and during that short time she coauthored two papers with him. After this six months, nothing is heard of her.

Pirret and Soddy worked with the ratio of radium to uranium in uranium-bearing minerals. The disintegration theory of radioactivity predicted a constant ratio of radium to uranium in uranium-bearing minerals, and Soddy and Pirret were two of the researchers who determined this ratio.

In their first paper, they wrote an account of the ratio of radium to uranium in Ceylon thorianite and a specimen of Portuguese autunite. Their preliminary result seemed to confirm those of ELLEN GLEDITSCH in that the ratio in autunite was considerably lower than that in pitchblende. However, the results with thorianite were less conclusive. In their second paper they worked further on these substances. They became very skeptical of Gleditsch's hypothesis that the equilibrium ratio of radium to uranium is less in a geologically recent mineral like Joachimsthal pitchblende than in an ancient mineral like thorianite.   MM

PRIMARY SOURCES

Pirret, Ruth. With F. Soddy. "The Ratio Between Uranium and Radium in Minerals." *Philosophical Magazine* 20 (1910): 345–349.

———. With F. Soddy. "The Ratio Between Uranium and Radium in Minerals II." *Philosophical Magazine* 21 (1911): 652–658.

SECONDARY SOURCES

Fleck, Lord Alexander. "Early Work in the Radioactive Elements." *Proceedings of the Chemical Society of London* (1963): 330.

Howarth, Muriel. *Pioneer Research on the Atom.* London: New World Publications, 1958.

Rayner-Canham, M. F., and G. W. Rayner-Canham. "Pioneer Women in Nuclear Science." *American Journal of Physics* 58 (1990): 1036–1043.

Rutherford, Ernest. *Radioactive Substances and Their Radiations.* Cambridge: Cambridge University Press, 1913.

PISAN, CHRISTINE DE (1364–1429)

Italian/French scholar and natural philosopher. Born 1364 in Italy. Father Thomas of Pisano. Married Etienne de Castel (circa 1380); three children. Excellent education at court. Died 1429.

The daughter of Thomas of Pisano, Christine was born in Italy but went with her father to the Parisian court of Charles V of France in 1365. Her father was a court astrologer and physician from whom she received an excellent education. She married Etienne de Castel around 1380; he died nine years later, leaving her with three young children to support. She began her career as a writer, often extolling the value of honorable women playing the traditional roles of teacher, nurturer, and healer to their families. She condemned the antifeminist literature of the time and wrote of the virtue of the pious wife and mother playing an active role in the prosperity of family and nation. She lauded Joan of Arc, but did not hold her as an example for every woman to follow. In later life, around 1418, she retired to the convent at Poissy.   JH/MBO

PRIMARY SOURCES

Pisan, Christine de. *Le Livre des fait d'armes et de chevalerie.* Westminster: William Caxton, 1489.

———. *Here Begynneth the Boke of the Cyte of Ladyes the Whiche boke is deuyded in to iij partes.* London: H. Pepwell, 1521. Translated from the French.

———. *The Book of Deeds of Arms and of Chivalry.* Ed. Charity Cannon. Trans. Sumner Willard. University Park, Pa.: Pennsylvania State University, 1999.

STANDARD SOURCES

Echols and Williams.

PISCOPIA, HELENA LUCRETIA CORNARO (d. 1685)

See Cornaro (Cornero), Elena (Helena) Lucretia.

PITT-RIVERS, ROSALIND VENETIA (HENLEY) (1907–1990)

British biochemist. Born 4 March 1907 in London, to the Honorable Sylvia (Stanley) and the Honorable Anthony Henley. Two younger sisters. Married George Pitt-Rivers (1931); divorced (1937). One son (Anthony). Educated privately and at Notting Hill High School; University of London, Bedford College (B.S., class 1, 1930; M.S., 1931); University of London (Ph.D., 1939); Professional experience: University College Hospital Medical School (London), research faculty (1939–1940; 1941–1945); South-East Blood Transfusion Unit in Maidstone, Kent (1940–1941); Medical Research Council, National Institute for Medical Research, Division of Chemistry, researcher (1945–1969), head (1969–1972). Honors and memberships: Mickle Prize (1952); Royal Society, Fellow (1954); London Thyroid Club, president (1965); European Thyroid Association (1971); Bedford College, Fellow (1973); Royal College of Physicians, honorary member (1986). Died 14 January 1990 in the village of Hinton St. Mary, Dorset.

Rosalind Pitt-Rivers came from a liberal aristocratic family, related to the Mitfords and Pitt-Rivers. Her education began privately with a French governess, but the greatest pleasure of her childhood was making stink bombs and explosions with a chemistry set in the stables with one of her cousins. She attended Notting Hill High School for her secondary education, and went on to Bedford College for Women, which was educating other remarkable scientists in the 1920s like the physiologist LILIAN MARY PICKFORD. She studied chemistry with E. E. Turner (with whom she later published a number of articles) and MARGARET M. MURRAY, graduating at the top of her class. She remained to finish a master's degree in chemistry, but then ended further academic studies following her marriage the same year to her cousin, George Pitt-Rivers. He soon proved to be a difficult man with eccentric and extreme scientific and political beliefs, as a vocal supporter of the English facist leader, Sir Oswald Mosley.

After her marriage ended in 1937, she returned to study biochemistry at University College, London, impressed by the work Charles Harington was doing on thyroid hormones. She worked with him as a research student at the Department of Pathological Chemistry, University College Hospital Medical School. Although Harington was to become her mentor, the research for her doctoral degree was with Albert Neuberger on methyl glucosaminides, studying their hydrolysis by enzymes produced by snails. After completing her degree, she moved to Harington's laboratory and continued to work under him and then in association with him for most of her professional career, as he moved from University College to the National Institute for Medical Research.

Pitt-Rivers managed to extend Harington's groundbreaking work on thyroid hormones by preparing thyroxine from iodinated casein and by developing an improved method for iodination and analysis of iodoproteins. These studies were published and attracted some attention. World War II interrupted the research, and Pitt-Rivers worked at a blood transfusion unit in Kent and then at the Maudsley Hospital. She rejoined Harington to work on artificial iodoproteins, a scheme to increase milk yield in cows. At the end of the war, in 1945, she joined JANET VAUGHAN to make a survey of the malnourished state of released prisoners of war, which included three weeks at Bergen-Belsen concentration camp at the time of its liberation, an experience whose horrors she never forgot and to which she attributed her heavy smoking.

Back at Harington's laboratory, his increasingly heavy administrative duties allowed her to have an independent life in her own laboratory. She also aided him in his continuing research by setting up experiments for him so that he could spend brief but productive periods in the laboratory, leaving her to complete the work-up. The availability of radioactive isotopes and the new technique of paper chromatography

opened up new avenues of exploration. Pitt-Rivers's most significant work came from her collaboration with a young man trained in these new techniques, Jack Gross. He was a postdoctoral student, a Canadian anatomist and endocrinologist who had trained at McGill under a former colleague of Frederic and IRENE JOLIOT-CURIE using radioactive iodine to investigate thyroid function. The NIMR was at the time a center for the new technique of paper chromotography which would prove crucial for their work.

Spurred by a competition with the French laboratory of J. Roche to find new isotopes of thyroid hormones that would have application to human disease, Pitt-Rivers and Gross identified a new substance that they labeled "unknown 1." This soon proved to be a new thyroid hormone, triiodothyronine or T_3, which later was found to have significant physiological activity in rats and later humans. They immediately published a series of articles in *Lancet* in 1952. Although Pitt-Rivers and Gross were hailed as the first to describe this thyroid hormone, Pitt-Rivers in later years downplayed the rivalry between the work of the French and English groups, since their research proved to be complementary. The French group under Roche had emphasized the biosynthesis and secretion of both T_3 and T_4 (described much earlier by Harington), while Pitt-Rivers and Gross analyzed the physiological activity of T_3 and its occurrence in the blood.

The impact of this discovery was immediate, with almost simultaneous publications in multiple journals, the Mickle prize for Pitt-Rivers, many invitations to lecture, and people requesting to work in their laboratory. Pitt-Rivers was also asked to write a number of important reviews on thyroid hormones during the next two years. She was elected to the Royal Society only two years after the discovery, a rare endorsement for women at that time. She continued to work on triiodothyronine, and numerous patents were taken out by the Medical Research Council with subsequent valuable royalties as it was proven to be widely useful for diagnosis and treatment of thyroid disorders.

Although some of her subsequent work proved to be a disappointment immediately after (especially the collaborative work with Odille Thibault at the Sorbonne physiology laboratory), Pitt-Rivers spent a productive sabbatical year in U.S. laboratories in 1954, notably with the Nobel Prize–winner, Fritz Lippmann at Massachusetts General Hospital in Boston. Her work continued to expand into studies of the derivatives of triiodothyroxine, but only the acetic acid analogues proved to have significant physiological activity.

For the final twelve years of her work at the National Institute of Medical Research, Pitt-Rivers examined the structure of thyroglobulin and its formation in the thyroid gland. In the late fifties and early sixties, she spent some time at the National Institutes of Health in the laboratories of Ed Rall and Harold Edelhoch pursuing studies on the structure of thyroglobulin. Back at the NIMR, she worked in close collaboration with the immunologist N. A. Mitchinson, then head of the Division of Experimental Biology, identifying and preparing iodine-containing synthetic determinants, particularly NIP (4–hyroxy-3-iodo-5-nitrophenylacetic acid) to track antibodies in mouse tissues. This opened up an entire field of immunology, so that many compounds she developed became part of the immunologist's repertoire without the younger scientists even knowing her name. As Mitchison was reported to have said, "that is real fame" (*Biographical Memoirs*, 342).

Pitt-Rivers was made head of the Division of Chemistry at the very moment that the decision was made to disband it, in spite of its enormous earlier successes, and she had the difficult task of relocating the staff and laboratories with the minimum of upset between 1969 and 1972. She herself moved to Mitchison's immunological laboratory at University College, and again to the Department of Pharmacology under Sir James Black in 1975, where she continued to work, produce excellent experiments, and meet old friends, until failing health forced her to leave University College in 1985. She then left London for Hinton St. Mary to be close to her married son Anthony, who had inherited the Pitt-Rivers Dorset estate, where she spent her early married life.

Rosalind Pitt-Rivers was casual and friendly with her colleagues and staff except with her mentor Harington with whom she always maintained formalities. She was noted for her wit, and she loved the lively discussion of scientific ideas and the latest novels. She was always helpful to younger colleagues and generous with her time and occasionally financial assistance. She had many students, both men and women, among them Valerie Galton. Pitt-Rivers published over one hundred articles and book chapters and her final years were filled with honors. She was made a Fellow of Bedford College and an honorary member of a number of medical and endocrinological societies, as well as a Fellow of the Royal Society of Physicians just four years before her death. JH

PRIMARY SOURCES
Pitt-Rivers, Rosalind. With Jack Gross. "The Identification of 3: 5: 3′ Triiodothyronine in Human Plasma." *Lancet* 1 (1952): 429.
———. Physiological Activity of 3: 5: 3′ triiodothyronine." *Lancet* 1 (1952): 593.
———. "Metabolic Effects of Compounds Structurally Related to Thyroxine *in vivo*: Thyronine Derivatives." *Journal of Clinical Endocrinology* 14 (1954): 1444–.
———. With Odette Thibault. "Immediate Effects of Thyroxine Analogues on Biological Oxidations *in vitro*." *Lancet* 1 (1955). See also *Comptes Rendus Academie des Sciences, Paris* 240 (1955) 668.
———. With J. R. Tata. *The Thyroid Hormones.* Oxford: Pergamon Press, 1959.
———. With R. H. Cavaliere. "The Effects of Drugs on the Distribution and Metabolism of Thyroid Hormones." *Pharmacological Review* 33 (1981): 55.

STANDARD SOURCES
Biographical Memoirs, vol. 39 (1994): 327–348.

PITTMAN, MARGARET JANE (1901–)

U.S. bacteriologist. Born 20 January 1901 in Prairie Grove, Ark. Educated Hendrix College (A.B., 1923); University of Chicago (M.S., 1926; Ph.D., 1929). Professional experience: Galloway Women's College, principal (1923–1925); Metropolitan Life Insurance Company, influenza commission (1926–1928). Rockefeller Institute, research assistant (1928–1934); New York State Department of Public Health, assistant bacteriologist (1934–1936); National Institutes of Health, U.S. Public Health Services, associate bacteriologist (1936–1941); bacteriologist (1941–1947); senior bacteriologist (1948–1954); principal bacteriologist (1954–1958); National Institutes of Health, Division of Biological Standards, bacteriologist and chief of laboratory of bacterial production (1958–1967); World Health Organization, consultant (1958; 1959; 1962). Honors and memberships: Society of Microbiology, Academy of Microbiology; Society of Experimental Biology; Harvey Society; British Society of General Microbacteriology; New York Academy of Sciences; Hendrix College (Hon. LL.D., 1954); American Board of Bacteriologists, diplomate (1962).

Margaret Pittman was born in Arkansas and went from a small college to the University of Chicago for advanced degrees in biology and bacteriology. She began by teaching for a few years in the early 1920s, but soon returned to research, studying respiratory diseases and influenzal meningitis for the Metropolitan Life Insurance Company. After two years she moved to the Rockefeller Institute, where she worked as a research assistant for four years. She then moved to the New York State Department of Health, where she held a position as assistant bacteriologist during the period when ANNA WESSELS WILLIAMS served as William H. Park's associate.

During the mid-thirties, Pittman obtained a position with the National Institutes of Health, where she remained for most of her professional career, moving up through the ranks to principal bacteriologist. Although her first research was on bacterial classifications, she later worked on vaccine standardization, sensitization to pertussis histamine, and contaminants of biological products. Toward the end of her career, she became chief of the Laboratory of Bacterial Productions, which studied the standardization of biological products. She was a consultant to the World Health Organization and was honored by her undergraduate college, Hendrix College, with an honorary degree. She was a diplomate of the American Board of Bacteriologists from 1962.

JH/MBO

PRIMARY SOURCES

Pittman, Margaret. "The Pathogenesis of Experimental Pneumococcus Lobar Pneumonia." Ph.D. diss., University of Chicago, 1929. Typescript at the University of Chicago.

———. *The Protection of Mice Against Hemophilus Influenzae (Non-Type-Specific) With Sulfapyridine.* Washington, D.C.: U.S. Government Printing Office, 1939.

———. *A Comparison of the Precipitation Reaction in Immune Serum Agar Plates with the Protection of Mice by Antimeningococcus Serum.* Washington, D.C.: U.S. Government Printing Office, 1940.

———. *A Study of Certain Factors Which Influence the Determination of the Mouse Protective Action of Meningococcus Antiserum.* Washington, D.C.: U.S. Government Printing Office, 1941.

STANDARD SOURCES

AMS 5–14; Bailey; Debus; Rossiter 1982.

PLATT, JULIA BARLOW (1857–1935)

U.S. comparative embryologist and neuroscientist. Born 14 September 1857 in San Francisco, Calif., to Ellen Loomis (Barlow) and George King Platt. Educated University of Vermont (Ph.B., 1881); Harvard University, Radcliffe College (graduate studies, 1887–1889; 1895–1896); Bryn Mawr College (graduate studies, 1889–1890); Munich University (graduate studies, 1893–1894; 1896–1897); University of Freiburg (Ph.D., 1897); Marine Biological Laboratory, Woods Hole, Mass. (summers 1889, 1890). Professional experience: independent researcher; mayor of Pacific Grove, Calif. (1931–1935). Died 1935.

Julia Barlow Platt has been hailed as one of the first women neuroscientists, although she never held a professional position in science. She was born in California; her father was a lawyer who served as state's attorney for Vermont in the 1840s and married Ellen Loomis Barlow from Burlington. She was raised in the Unitarian Church. Since her father died soon after her birth, she appears to have been brought up in Vermont and attended undergraduate college at the University of Vermont. Following her degree, she managed to acquire an unusually thorough training in experimental embryology through advanced graduate studies in both American and German universities. She was willing to seek out important scientists with whom to study: Howard Ayers at Harvard, then Charles Otis Whitman at Woods Hole, Chicago, and Clark University, and E. B. Wilson at Bryn Mawr. She published research on embryological segmenta-

tion of head segments of chick embryos, amphioxus, and other vertebrates.

Traveling to Europe, Platt took advantage of the opportunity to move from university to university while working toward a doctorate at the University of Freiberg, to which she was only the second woman ever admitted. Although she first planned to work with Anton Dohrn at the Naples zoological station, at Whitman's suggestion, she instead collected specimens of amphioxus in Sicily, which she took to analyze in Freiberg, using some of the new staining techniques to determine the neuronal origin of a set of processes between the central nervous system and the openings of the notocord. She conducted research under Wiedersheim at Freiberg on the development of the nervous system of the spiny dogfish, *Squalus acanthius.* She studied under and worked with Richard Hertwig and Carl Wilhelm von Kupffer at Munich on the morphogenesis of the neural crest of *Necturus,* returning to Freiberg to take lectures on evolution given by August Weismann. Her work on embryological segmentation, particularly of the head segments of *Necturus maculosus,* the mud puppy, and their relation to the formation of the cartilaginous skull, formed the major part of her doctoral dissertation, successfully defended in 1898 with Weismann as the major referee. During this period, she also returned to Harvard to attend Charles B. Davenport's lectures.

Platt's work proved to be very stimulating and widely discussed, although its challenges to some aspects of the germ layer theories of the time also made it controversial. She argued at length with Dohrn over some of her findings in 1891. He reported these arguments to Whitman in America, although he later praised other aspects of her work in his written papers. During her graduate studies, she published a total of twelve papers, many of which are still cited and evaluated today.

Sadly, upon her return to the United States, Platt was unable to obtain an academic position, perhaps due to the fact that she had no strong ties to the women's colleges on the East Coast, which offered some of the few places for women biologists. It would not have helped that her determination about the valuable nature of her work made her appear argumentative to some of her male colleagues. Some stories about practical jokes played upon her at Woods Hole may explain her decision not to continue to study there during the summers. Her work was extremely specialized, a virtue for productive research, but perhaps a hindrance for undergraduate teaching.

Platt moved to Pacific Grove, California, where, in 1899, after hearing a lecture by David Star Jordan, the new president of Stanford, she wrote to him expressing her frustration at not obtaining a teaching position in the United States. Although she may have intended to continue research at the nearby Hopkins Marine Station, there is no record of such research, nor did she publish further papers except for a study of geotaxis in Paramecium and the tadpole in *American Naturalist* in 1899. She did maintain a friendship with the comparative anatomist and embryologist Harold Heath, attached to the station, to whom she expressed her hope that her research would continue to be used and verified.

Platt was a member of the American Society of Morphologists (one of the first three women members, along with CORNELIA CLAPP and HARRIET RANDOLPH). She was also elected a lifelong member of the Anatomische Gesellschaft, the important German anatomical society.

Failing to find a position that offered her a chance to develop her science, Platt settled in Pacific Grove, adopted a son, Harold, worked actively in civic affairs, and became the first woman mayor of the city in 1931. She died at the age of seventy-eight.   JH/MBO

PRIMARY SOURCES

Platt, Julia B. "Studies on the Primitive Axial Segmentation of the Chick." *Bulletin Museum Comparative Zoology* 17 (1889): 171–190.

———. "Fibres Connecting the Central Nervous System and Chordata in *Amphioxus*." *Anatomischer Anzieger* 7 (1892): 282–284.

———. "Ontogenetische Differenzirung des Ektoderms in *Necturus*." *Archiv fur Mikrosckopische Anatomie* 43 (1894): 911–966.

———. "The Development of the Thyroid Gland and of the Suprapericardial Bodies of *Necturus*." *Anatomischer Anzieger* 11 (1896): 557–567.

———. "The Development of the Cartilaginous Skull and of the Branchial and Hypoglossal Musculature in *Necturus*." *Morphologische Jahrbuche* 25 (1898): 377–464.

SECONDARY SOURCES

Zotolli, Steven J, and Ernst-August Seyforth. "Julia B. Platt (1857–1935): Pioneer Comparative Embryologist and Neuroscientist." *Brain Behavior and Evolution* 43, no. 2 (1994). Includes two portraits, and is the only extensive biographical source on her life, along with an analysis of her significance.

Northcutt, R. G. "The Phylogenetic Distribution and Innervation of Craniate Mechanoreceptive Lateral Lines." In *The Mechanosensory Lateral Line—Neurobiology and Evolution,* ed. S. Coombs, et al., 17–78. New York: Springer-Verlag, 1989. Discusses the significance of her work.

STANDARD SOURCES

AMS 3–5; *Woman's Who's Who of America*.

PLEHN, MARIANNE (1836–1946)

German zoologist. Born 30 October 1863 in Lubochen, West Prussia. Father manor lord and lieutenant colonel. Five siblings. Educated Eidgenössische Technische Hochschule (Zurich); passed exam as special instructor for natural sciences (1893); doctorate in zoology (1896). Professional experience: Bavarian Biological Experimental Institute, School for Veterinary Medicine, Munich, assistant lecturer; with Bruno Hofer founded the science of "fish pathology"; first female titular professor in Bavaria (1914). Honors and memberships: University of Munich, Faculty of Veterinary Medicine, honorary doctorate (1929). Died 18 January 1946 in Grafrath near Munich.

The third of six children, Marianne Plehn was born in 1863 into a manor lord's family in Lubochen, West Prussia. The example provided by her older brothers, who did medical research, likely inspired Plehn to study as well. It was not until she reached the age of twenty-seven, after the death of her parents, however, that Plehn went to Zurich to take up studies in zoology, botany, and geology. There, with support from her uncle, she studied at the Eidgenössische Technische Hochschule. In 1896, she received her doctor of philosophy degree in zoology from this institution, the first woman to do so. At that time, the natural sciences still belonged to the philosophy faculty. During her studies she met the writer Riccharda Huch, with whom she formed a lifelong friendship, maintained through lively correspondence. In 1898 she became the assistant for the Bavarian Biological Experimental Institute (Bayerische Biologische Versuchsanstalt) at the School for Veterinary Medicine in Munich. This assignment was to have a far-reaching impact in her life. Together with Bruno Hofer, she is considered today as the founder of fish pathology. Even so, she always acted in the shadow of her academic teachers and superiors.

Modest and unassuming, Plehn dedicated herself with untiring diligence to the intense research she carried out in the silence of her laboratory and in the field. She set aside her own desires and left public appearances to her director. Plehn turned down a position in Vienna that would have allowed her to work in a completely independent environment. Nevertheless, her work received due recognition.

Although Marianne Plehn never acquired qualification as a lecturer—in Germany this was first possible for women in 1919—she was awarded the title "royal professor" in 1914 by King Ludwig III for her great contribution to fish pathology. A teaching certificate was not linked to this title. On the occasion of her retirement she was given honorary doctoral status of the Faculty of Veterinary Medicine at the University of Munich (she was the first woman to be so honored). She was not given a leading position until male researchers were taken into the military in World War II. When she was almost eighty years old, Plehn took over the management of the Bavarian Biological Experimental Institute, which was then bombed out in 1943. Not quite one year after the end of the war she died in Grafrath near Munich.   SNS

PRIMARY SOURCES
Plehn, Marianne. *Die Fische des Meeres und der Binnengewässer.* Esslingen, Germany: J. F. Schieber, 1906.

———. *Praktikum der Fischkrankheiten.* Stuttgart: Schweizerbart (E. Nagle), 1924.

———. "Briefwechsel zwischen Marianne Plehn und Riccharda Huch." Ed. Gabriele Junginger. In *Frauenleben in München.* Munich: Buchendorfer Verlag, 1993.

SECONDARY SOURCES
Brunner, Gertrud. "Die Mitbegründerin der Fischpathologie. Frau Professor Dr. Marianne Plehn—80 Jahr." *Zeitschrift für Fischerei und deren Hilfswissenschaften,* vol. 48 (1944).

Junginger, Gabriele. "Marianne Plehn. Ein Leben in der Stille des Laboratoriums." In *Dokumentation des 18. Bundesweiten Kongresses Frauen in Naturwissenschaft und Technik.* Bremen: N. 1992.

"Marianne Plehn." In *Bussmann, Hadumod: Stieftöchter der Alma mater? 90 Jahre Frauenstudium in Bayern.* Ed. Hadumod Bussman. Munich: 1993.

PLUES, MARGARET (ca. 1840–1903)

British botanist. Brought up in Ripon, Yorkshire. Professional experience: Roman Catholic convent, Weybridge, Surrey, nun; mother superior (ca. 1880–1903). Died 1903 in Weybridge, Surrey.

Margaret Plues published a number of popular accounts of her botanical rambles in her early twenties. Some years later, she published more formal accounts of British ferns and grasses that have recently attracted attention. In middle age, she entered a Roman Catholic convent, where she became mother superior. Her correspondence with the British botanist Christopher Edmund Broome is in the British Museum of Natural History.   JH/MBO

PRIMARY SOURCES
Plues, Margaret. "British Fungi." *Popular Science Review* 2 (1862): 322–333.

———. "Rambles in Search of Flowerless Plants." *Journal of the Horticulture and Cottage Gardener Office* (London) (1864).

———. *British Ferns: An Introduction to the Ferns, Lycopods and Esquiseta Indigenous to the British Isles.* London: L. Reeve, 1866.

———. *British Grasses: An Introduction to the Study of the Gramineae of Great Britain and Ireland.* London: L. Reeve, 1867.

———. *Rambles in Search of Wild Flowers and How to Distinguish Them.* London: G. Bell, 1870.

SECONDARY SOURCES
Hawksworth, D. L., and M. R. D. Seaward. *Lichenology of the British Isles: 1568–1975.* Richmond, Surrey: Richmond Publishing, 1977.

STANDARD SOURCES
Desmond; Stafleu and Cowan.

PLUMMER, HELEN JEANNE (SKEWES) (1891–1951)

U.S. micropaleontologist. Born 7 May 1891 in Muskegon, Mich. Married Frederick Byron Plummer. Educated Evanston High School, Evanston Ill.; Northwestern University (B.A., 1913; M.A., 1925). Professional experience: Illinois Geological Survey, micropaleontologist (1914–1917); Roxana Petroleum Co., Tulsa, Okla., geologist (1917–1918); Northwestern University, special lecturer on micropaleontology (1930 and 1932); Bureau of Economic Geology, Austin, Tex., consulting geologist (1933–1948). Died 11 January 1951 in Austin, Tex.

Helen Plummer's career indicates the choices a woman scientist who is married must sometimes make. After her marriage to Frederick B. Plummer most of her work was on a part-time basis. She completed a master's degree at Northwestern after their marriage, but thereafter moved with her husband, taking jobs that permitted her to work part-time. They traveled to many different places, including The Hague and the Dominican Republic. She spent much of her energy in working with her husband—editing his manuscripts, preparing the drawings, and checking data. When he died suddenly in 1947, she never fully recovered from the loss.

Plummer was a member of the American Association of Petroleum Geologists, the American Geophysical Union, the Paleontological Society of America, the Geological Society of America, the American Association for the Advancement of Science, Sigma Xi, and the Texas Academy of Science.

Plummer worked on the foraminifera and published numerous papers on this group. She garnered an international reputation for her work.   JH/MBO

PRIMARY SOURCES
Plummer, Helen Jeanne. "Foraminifera of the Midway Formation in Texas." *University of Texas Bulletin* no. 3201. Austin: University of Texas, 1926.

———. *Calcareous Foramifera in the Brownwood Shale Near Bridgeport, Texas.* Austin: University of Texas, 1930.

———. "Some Cretaceous Foraminifera in Texas." *University of Texas Bulletin* no. 2644. Austin: University of Texas, 1931.

———. "Texas Pennsylvanian Conodonts and Their Stratigraphic Relations." *University of Texas Bulletin* no. 3102. Austin: University of Texas, 1932.

———. "Structure of Ceratobulimina." *American Midland Naturalist* 17, no. 2 (1936): 460–463.

———. "Smaller Foraminifera in the Marble Falls, Smithwick, and Lower Strawn Strato Around the Llano Uplift in Texas." *Bureau of Economic Geology Publication* no. 4401 (1945): 209–271.

SECONDARY SOURCES

Adkins, Mary G. Muse. "Helen Jeanne Plummer (1891–1951)." *Bulletin of the American Association of Petroleum Geologists* 38, no. 8 (1954): 1854–1857. Includes a portrait.

Marks, Edward. "The Helen Jeanne Plummer Collections." *Micropaleontologist* 6, no. 4 (1952): 30–47.

Moore, Raymond Cecil. "Helen Jeanne Plummer, 1891–1951." *Micropaleontologist* 5, no. 2 (1951): 28–30.

STANDARD SOURCES

AMS 3–5; Rossiter 1982; Sargeant.

POCKELS, AGNES (1862–1935)

German physicist. Born 14 February 1862 in Venice, Italy. Father Theodor Pockels. One brother. Educated Municipal German High School for Girls, Brunswick (Braunschweig), 1872. Honors and memberships: Laura Leonard Prize, Leipzig (1931); Polytechnical University of Brunswick (Braunschweig) (honorary doctorate, 1932). Died 1935 in Brunswick.

Agnes Pockels was born in Venice, where her father was garrisoned as a captain in the Royal Austrian Army. He was released from the army because of ill health and the family moved to Brunswick in Lower Saxony when Agnes was nine. She graduated from the Municipal High School for Girls in Brunswick where she developed an enthusiasm for physics. Although she wished to continue her education, her parents forbade her to do so, and, as an unmarried daughter, she managed the house for her sickly parents.

Pockels began to teach herself, first with a textbook and later through books provided to her by her younger brother, Friedrich, who was studying at the Univesity of Göttingen. Oily dishwater was her first inspiration for her observational and finally scientific research. In 1881 she made her first observations of surface tension. She constructed an apparatus from a can which she mounted on the apothecary's balance that had belonged to her grandfather. Instead of a balance pan she used a wire ring that she dropped into the liquid contained in a brass vessel. This whole construction consisted of an ingenious "slide trough," a surface film balance technique that was later exhibited in a museum founded by Professor Oswald in Leipzig. This was a forerunner of the Langmuir trough developed by the American physicist and chemist Irvin Langmuir, who later received the Nobel Prize

for his work on surface tension in 1932. Pockels's apparatus is still known in Germany as a Pockelscher Trog (Pockels trough).

Pockels considered publication impossible at the time (she was only twenty), and did not know whether her observations in question were already known. Her brother, Friedrich, beginning to study physics at the University of Göttingen, recognized the value of his sister's research. He received a doctorate in 1888 and a year later was appointed assistant in the Physical Institute in Göttingen.

In 1890, an article in the *Naturwissenschaftlichen Rundschau* to which the Pockels subscribed, mentioned similar studies made by the English physicist Lord Rayleigh. He had been the Cambridge Professor of Experimental Physics and later Director of the Davy-Faraday Research Laboratory of the Royal Institution in London. One of the aims of this institution was the popularization of science. With this in mind, Agnes Pockels wrote to Lord Rayleigh, encouraged by her brother, briefly describing her research on surface films and her new measurement technique. Rayleigh was uncertain as to her gender, and replied, "I do not find a sign in your interesting letter that it does not come from a man although the signature in England could only be from a lady" (Pockels, 1891, 437).

Rayleigh's wife took it upon herself to translate Pockels's letter, which appeared with an introduction by Lord Rayleigh in *Nature*, commending the valuable results accomplished with simple methods "by this German lady." He explained that the first part agreed with "my own newer work," adding that: "The later parts seem to be very original and they might really answer many important questions completely. I hope to have the opportunity soon to repeat some of Miss Pockel's [sic] experiments" (Pockels, 1891, 437).

Agnes Pockels had laid the foundation for quantitative research on surface films that would soon open up a new field of science. At first, German physicists took little notice of Agnes Pockels, nor could she have accepted the offer of the use of the physics laboratory in Göttingen. Her family responsibilities now included keeping house for her brother, Friedrich, appointed professor of theoretical physics at Heidelberg. In spite of this, a series of her articles was published in *Nature* between 1891 and 1894. She also published in popular scientific German journals such as *Naturwissenschaftlichen Rundschau*, occasionally appearing as well in more specialized journals. The opportunity to investigate elasticity, light reflection, and surface tension properties of surface films, spurred the investigation of molecular structure using her technique. She corresponded with physicists such as Quincke, Teubner, Sommerfeld, and Charles G. Darwin, and translated Darwin's *Tides* (as *Ebbe und Flut*). In 1909 she wrote a natural philosophical treatise, "Das Willkürliche in der Welt." Even after 1913, when Pockels's brother died, she continued to publish her research in scientific journals almost yearly. After 1918, she ceased to be in the same position to obtain scientific literature or do research, although she did publish a report in 1926 and another discussion about the adherence of solids in 1933.

When Agnes Pockels turned seventy, the importance of her work began to be recognized in Germany. In 1932, she received an honorary doctorate in engineering from the Department of Mathematics and Physics of the Polytechnical University of Brunswick, as the inventor of the quantitative method for measuring surface tension. She was the first woman to receive an honorary degree, signifcantly with the unanimous support of the department. That same year, she also received the Laura Leonard Prize (with H. Devaux) from the Colloid Society (Kolloid-Gesellschaft). An issue of *Kolloid-Zeitschrift* included an article testifying to the importance of her work by the physicist Wolfgang Ostwald, accompanied by her autobiographical account and a photograph. Pockels expressed delight in finding that her method was known in Germany, France, and England. "Knowing that my work has been used by others to do new research has given me great pleasure" (Ostwald, 1932, 1). In 1936, FLORENCE SABIN commemorated Pockels in a speech on "Women in Science," while accepting an award for her own work.

Over time, Pockels has been more or less forgotten except by chemists. Until the recent research on women scientists revived her name, she was in no current biographical dictionary. A small exhibit on Pockels's life was displayed in the library of the Polytechnic University of Brunswick in which she was celebrated as a remarkable woman who, without formal education and without institutional connections, become an internationally known scientist.   JH/MBO

PRIMARY SOURCES
Pockels, Agnes. "Surface Tension." *Nature* 43 (1891): 437–439.
———. "Untersuchung von Grenzflächenspannungen mit der Kohässionswaage." *Annalen der Physik* 67 (1899): 668–681.
———. "Über das spontane Sinken der Oberflächenspannung von Wasser, wässerignen Lösungen und Emulsionen." *Annalen der Physik* 8 (1902): 854–871.
———. "Das Wilkürliche in der Welt." *Annalen der Naturphilosophie* 8 (1909): 321–328.
———. "Zur Frage der sitlichen Veränderung der Oberflächenspannung." *Physikalische Zeitschrift* 17 (1916): 441–446.
———. The Measurement of Surface Tension with the Balance." *Science* 64 (1926): 304.

SECONDARY SOURCES
Beisswanger, Gabriele. "Das Portrait: Agnes Pockels und die Oberflächenchemie-Sauberkeiten nicht nur herzzustllen,

sondern sogar zu messen." *Chemie unserer Zeit* 25, no. 2 (1991): 97–101.
Giles, C. H., and S. D. Forrester. "The Origins of the Surface Film Balance." *Chemistry and Industry* (1971): 43–53.
Ostwald, Wolfgang. "Die Arbeiten von Agnes Pockels über Grenzschichten und Filme." *Kolloid-Zeitschrift* 58 (1932): 1–8.

STANDARD SOURCES
Grinstein 1993 (article by M. Elizabeth Derrick); Poggendorff, vol. 6.

POCOCK, MARY AGARD (1886–1977)
South African phycologist. Born 31 December 1886. Educated University of London (B.S., 1908); Cambridge University (B.S., 1921); University of Cape Town (Ph.D., 1932). Professional experience: Cheltenham Girl's School, teacher (1909–1912); Wynberg (Cape) Girl's High School, teacher (1913–1917); Cambridge University, assistant to A. C. Seward (1919–1921); Rhodes University, Department of Botany, temporary lecturer (1924; 1929; 1938; 1942 and 1950s), acting head of department (1942). Honors and memberships: Fellow Linnean Society, FLS Crisp Medal (1967); Royal Society of South Africa, Fellow; Rhodes University, honorary D.Sc. (1967). Died 10 July 1977 in Grahamstown, Cape Province.

Mary Agard Pocock studied botany at the University of London. After receiving her undergraduate degree in 1908, she taught at various girls schools, first in London and then in the Cape. Eleven years after obtaining her first degree, she worked with A. C. Seward while she studied for an additional honors degree in botany at Cambridge. From 1924 and sporadically throughout the rest of her career, she was a temporary lecturer at Rhodes University. From 1925 to 1926, she collected a large number of flowering plants on a six-month expedition on foot from Rhodesia across Angola to Luanda, along with the botanist Dorothea Bleek. She then went to England the following year to study these Angolan plants at the Royal Botanical Gardens at Kew and in the British Museum. On her return to South Africa, she became interested in algae and studied freshwater algae, especially *Volvox*. She obtained a doctorate for this work from the University of Cape Town at the age of forty-six. During one of her teaching stints in 1942, while serving as acting head of the Rhodes University Department of Botany, she established the University herbarium.

In her early eighties, Pocock was recognized by the Crisp Medal of the Linnean Society and an honorary doctoral degree by Rhodes University. Her plants are in a number of South African herbaria and especially the Rhodes University Herbarium, which also holds her paintings, notebooks, and manuscript notes.   GVL

SECONDARY SOURCES

"Mary Agard Pocock." *Phycologia* 17 (1978): 440–445. Includes a portrait.

STANDARD SOURCES

Gunn and Codd; Stafleu and Cowan.

POGSON, ISIS (fl. 19th century)

See Kent, Elizabeth Isis Pogson.

POKROVSKAIA, IRINA MITROFANOVNA (1902–1970)

Soviet palynologist and geologist. Born 1902. Professional experience: Ministry of Geology of the USSR, research geologist (1931–1970); Leningrad State University, Faculty of Geography, professor in the geomorphology department, concurrently. Died 3 May 1970.

Irina Mitrofanovna Pokrovskaia was one of the founders of the Soviet school of palynology. She spent her entire professional career working for the Ministry of Geology of the USSR. In addition, she taught in the geomorphology department of the faculty of geography at Leningrad State University, delivering lectures on palynology and geomorphology.

A gifted scientist, she pursued a wide range of subjects. Her seventy-five papers dealt with geomorphology, the stratigraphy of Mesozoic and Cenozoic formations of various Soviet regions, the history of the evolution of the flora during Mesozoic and Cenozoic times, floral zoning, taxonomy and nomenclature of spores and pollen grains, and methods of determination of the age of sediments with the help of palynological data. In her early work, she was concerned with the study of Quaternary sediments in the northern regions of the European part of the Soviet Union. She was among the first Soviets to apply spores and pollen analysis to the stratigraphic subdivision of Cenozoic sediments. Following this early work, she studied Mesozoic sediments of the Urals and the West Siberian plains, the Turgai plains and the Bashkir Pre-Urals region, the Baltic region, and the Ukraine. From her results she and others compiled stratigraphic and correlation schemes using paleobotanical criteria.

An important reference book, *Pollen Analysis,* resulted from her work. It was translated into French and Chinese and won her the USSR State Prize for her contribution.

A fine administrator and organizer, Pokrovskaia became chair of the palynological section of the All-Union Botanical Society, formed from her initiative. She also was a member of the Inter-Departmental Stratigraphic Committee of the USSR, a member of the editorial board of different

jornals, and the editor of numerous published works. Participating in international conferences and symposia on problems of palynology, she became internationally known. Well-liked and highly respected by her students and colleagues, Pokrovskaia was an important research geologist and teacher.   CK/MBO

PRIMARY SOURCES

Pokrovskaia, I. M. "The Flora from the Interglacial Deposits of the Polomet River [Russia]." *Byulleten Moskovskogo Obshchestva Ispytateley Prirody Otdel Geologichesky* 44, no. 14 (1936): 261–276.

———. *Atlas miotsenovykh sporovo-pyltsevykh kompleksov razlichnykh raionov SSSR.* Moscow: Vsesoyuznyi Nauchno-Issledovatelskii Geologicheskii Institut Informatsionnyi Sbornik: Materialy, Monaya Seriya Trudy (Paleontlogiya i Stratigrafiya) 13, 1956.

———, ed. *Pyltesevoi analiz.* Moscow: Vsesoynuzanyi Nauchno-Issledovatgelskii Geologicheskii Institut, 1958. A French translation by Eugene Boltenhagen: *Analyse pollinique.* Paris: Bureau Rechereches Geologiques, Geophysiques et Minieres, Publications, Service d'Information Geologique Annales 24, 1958.

———. *Atlas verkhnemelovykh, paleotsenovykh i eotsenovykh sporovo-pyltsevykh kompleksov nekotorykh raionov SSSR.* Moscow: Vsesoynuzunyi Nauchno-Issledovatgelskii Geologicheskii Institut Trudy. New Series 30, 1960.

———. *Paleopalinologiya.* 3 vols. St. Petersburg: Vsesoyuznogo Nauchno-Issledovatel'skogo Geologorazvedochnogo Neftyanoyh Institut (VNIGRI), 1966.

SECONDARY SOURCES

Boitsova, E. P., et al. "In Memoriam. I. M. Pokrovskaya (1902–1970)." *Review of Palaeobotany and Palynology* 11 (1971): 163–164.

Boitsova, E. P., L. A. Panova, G. M. Romanovskaia, A. I. Moiseyeva, and Z. I. Glezer. "Irina Mitrofanovna Pokrovskaia (1902–1970)." *Paleontologicheskiy Zhurnal* (1970): 127–128.

"Pamyati Iriny Mitrofanovny Pokrovskoy." *Sovetskaya Geologiya* 12 (1970): 149–150.

POKROVSKAIA, MARIIA IVANOVNA (1852–post-1917)

Russian physician and feminist. Born 1852 in Nizhnii-Lomov near Penza. Educated at home; St. Petersburg Women's Medical Courses. Zemstvo (district) physician in Pskov province; private practice in St. Petersburg. Died sometime after 1917.

Personal details of Mariia Ivanovna Pokrovskaia's life are almost entirely unavailable. She was born in 1852 in Nizhnii-Lomov in the Penza province and educated at home. In

1870 she passed an examination to qualify as a tutor, but in 1876 she enrolled in the Women's Medical Courses in St. Petersburg and, upon graduation (around 1882), took a post as a zemstvo (district) physician in the Glubokov district of the Pskov province. In 1888, Pokrovskaia returned to St. Petersburg, where she practiced medicine and, more important, wrote on public health issues. She died sometime after 1917.

Even in her first post as a zemstvo doctor, Pokrovskaia showed a bent for statistical observation and analysis. Her first study was concerned with the living conditions of peasants and the influence of water and ventilation on their health. She attempted to identify the factors at work in causing eye diseases such as trachoma, which were widespread among the peasantry. Some of her observations pointed the way to later research in that area.

After moving to St. Petersburg, Pokrovskaia turned her attention to the appalling housing conditions. She investigated building regulations and studied those of cities in other parts of Europe and America.

Pokrovskaia was interested also in the subject of prostitution and made a comparison between the prostitutes of St. Petersburg and those of Paris. In her report, she made recommendations for the elimination of prostitution in Russia.

She was also concerned with the working conditions of women physicians and expressed her criticisms of contemporary medicine in the form of a novel, *How I was a City Doctor for the Poor,* published in 1903. Pokrovskaia's heroine concludes that attention to hygiene would have better results than medical treatment, and that society was not ready to give women doctors the support they needed.

Pokrovskaia was a leading feminist. In 1904, she started a journal, *Women's Messenger,* and during the Revolution of 1905 she organized the Women's Progressive Party, which called for equality for women and women's suffrage.

Pokrovskaia's feminism was similar to the feminism of the West, but it was at odds with the increasingly Marxist tendencies of the Russian revolutionary movement with its emphasis on class struggle, and the feminist movement did not survive the Revolution of 1917. At that time, Pokrovskaia's journal ceased publication and her writing career ended, though she left behind a significant body of work.   ACH

PRIMARY SOURCES

Pokrovskaia, Mariia Ivanovna. *Sanitarnyi nadzor nad zhilishchami i sanitarnaia organizatsiia v razlichnykh gosudarstvakh.* St. Petersburg: Soikin, 1897.

———. *Vrachebno-politseiskii nadzor za prostitutsiei sposobstvuet vyrozhdeniiu naroda.* St. Petersburg: S. Peterburgskaia elektropechatnia, 1902.

———. *Kak ia byla gorodskim vrachem dlia bednykh.* St. Petersburg: Soikin, 1903. Novel.

STANDARD SOURCES

Tuve.

POLENOVA, YELENA NIKOLAYEVNA (1915–1987)

Soviet micropaleontologist. Born 15 August 1915 in Moscow. Guardian B. K. Polenov. Married V. S. Sokolov. Educated Leningrad University (graduated with distinction, 1937); Vsesoyuznogo Neftyanogo Nauchno-Issledovtel'skogo Geologofazvedochnogo Instituta (graduate work, 1938–1941?). Professional experience: USSR Academy of Sciences, Institute of Geology and Geophysics, Siberian Division, micropaleontologist (1962–1978). Geological Institute, Moscow, micropaleontologist (1978–1987). Honors and memberships: Commission on Micropaleontology, deputy chair; USSR Academy of Sciences, Subcommission on Ostracodes, chair; Interdepartmental Stratigraphic Commission, bureau member; International Union of Geologists, corresponding member; International Association of Ostracodologists, vice-president. Died 1987.

Yelena Nikolayevna Polenova's father died early, and she spent her childhood in the household of B. K. Polenov, a well-known geologist. He was also a student of Siberia, a professor in Kazan University and founder of the first geology department at the University of Perm. In Yelena Nikolayevna's student years, she studied micropaleontology in the departments of paleontology and historical geology in Leningrad University. She also had interests in biology. After graduating in 1937, she began graduate work under the micropaleontologist A. V. Fursenko in 1938, though it is unclear whether she finished a graduate thesis or not. Until 1941, her research was on the Jurassic foraminifera from the Emba oil-bearing region. She did field work in western China, middle Asia, and Kazakhstan, returning to Leningrad after the war in 1945. She married V. S. Sokolov, a member of the Presidium of the USSR Academy of Science.

Polenova had a number of disciplinary responsibilities. She was a deputy chair of the Commission on Micropaleontology, Chairman of the Subcommission on Ostracodes of the Problematic Council of the USSR Academy of Sciences on "paths and patterns of evolution of animal and plant organisms," a member of the Bureau of the Standing Commission of the Interdepartmental Stratigraphic Commission on the Stratigraphy of the Devonian System, Corresponding Member of the International Subcommission of IUGS on the Devonian System, vice-president of the International Association of Ostracodologists, and represented Soviet Paleontology at many foreign symposia, conferences, and congresses.

During World War II, petroleum exploration was a vital concern. The commercial worth of petroleum from Devonian sediments was established and the development of the

Devonian stratigraphy of the entire Russian Platform was an important scientific problem. Micropaleontology was the most effective way of determining the oil-bearing strata. Polenova was selected to work on this problem, and she proceeded to study the biostratigraphy of regions of the Platform, using ostracodes as identifiers. This seems to be the first time that ostracodes were used in geological practice. Her research was generalized to include many different areas. Over a seventeen-year period, a Soviet school of ostracodologists developed, and its work embraced the entire country. In 1962 she moved to the Soviet Academy of Sciences at Novosibirsk, where she began another sixteen years of work on the Jurassic sequence in Siberia, the Soviet Arctic, and part of Middle Asia. A series of monographs that gave her worldwide acclaim resulted from this work. In addition to her regional paleontological biostratigraphic studies, she also worked on the revision of ostracode taxa, as well as other subjects. CK/MBO

PRIMARY SOURCES

Polenova, Yelena Nikolayevna. "Ostrakody srednego devona severo-zapada Russkoy platformy." *Trudy Vsesoyuznogo Neftyanogo Nauchno-Issledovtel'skogo Geologorazvedochnogo Instituta* 250 (1960): 5–49.

———. "Ostrakody nizhnego devona Salaira: Tom'chumyskskiy gorizont." Akademiya Nauk SSSR Sibirskoe Otedelenie Institut Geologii i Geofizikii (1968).

———. "Devonskiye ostrakody SSSR: Obshchiy obzor." *Trudy Instituta Geologii i Geofiziki (Novosibirsk)* 71 (1970): 22–37.

———. "Skafinomorfnyye ostrakody razlichnykh privintskiy rannego devsna Tablitsy i ob yasneniya k nim." *Voporsy Mikropaleontologii* 22 (1979): 188–197.

———. "O granitse nizhnego i srednego devona: ostrakodovyye assotsiatsii." In *Biostratigrafiya paleozoya Zapadnoy Sibiri*, ed. V. N. Dubatolov and A. V. Kanygin, 99–119. Novosibirsk: Nauka Sibirskoye Otdeleniiye Instituta Geologii i Geofiziki, 1985.

———. "Skafinomorfnyye ostrakody nizhnego devona: ikh rasprostraneniye i korrelyatsionnyye svyazi." *Vosporsy Mikropaleontologii* 27 (1985): 170–187.

SECONDARY SOURCES

Krashenninikov, V. A., V. V. Menner, D. M. Rauzer-Chernousova, M. N. Solovyeva, A. V. Kanygin, and P. S. Lyubimova. "Yelena Nikolayevna Polenova (1915–1987)." *Paleontological Journal* 21, no. 2 (1987): 113–114.

POLLACK, FLORA (fl. 1900)

U.S. physician. Professional experience: Johns Hopkins Hospital, Gynecology Clinic, medical assistant (ca. 1909).

Flora Pollack worked in Howard Kelly's gynecology clinic at Johns Hopkins Hospital in the early 1900s. Kelly, a senior professor at Johns Hopkins Medical School, began to use women assistants following women's admission to the medical school in the 1890s.

Concerned about the large number of children who contracted venereal disease through sexual assault, Pollak undertook a five-year study of the city's police and hospital records. From this research, she advanced an "infectionist theory." Pollak suggested that the rise in cases of child venereal disease was due to the common myth among infected men that the only certain cure for syphilis or gonorrhea was to pass it on to a virgin. She also noted that the pregnancy of a syphilitic woman usually terminated in miscarriage or premature birth, discovering as well that these women often believed the baby took away their disease. She took this ignorance and misinformation among both men and women to be a primary source of danger to their children.

Pollack enlisted the Charity Organization Society to study an effective means to reach the community as a whole. They inaugurated a lecture series for civic and church groups, which received vigorous public support. Courses in social hygiene focused as well on teachers and playground directors. Because of the campaign sparked by Pollack, Hugh Cabot, urologist at the Massachusetts General Hospital, spearheaded new national legislation to reform the treatment and prevention of venereal disease. KM

PRIMARY SOURCES

Pollack, Flora. "The Acquirement of Venereal Infections in Children." *Johns Hopkins Hospital Bulletin* 20 (May 1909): 143–144.

SECONDARY SOURCES

Taylor, Lloyd C., Jr. *The Medical Profession and Social Reform, 1885–1945.* New York: St. Martin's Press, 1974.

POLUBARINOVA-KOCHINA, PELAGEYA YAKOVELEVNA (1899–?)

See Kochina, Pelageia Iakovlevna.

PONSE, KITTY (1897–?)

Swiss endocrinologist. Born in Bindley, West Indies, 1897. Educated University of Geneva, Faculty of Sciences (doctorate, 1924). Professional experience: University of Geneva, assistant, privat dozent, professor of endocrinology (1947 to retirement). Death date unknown.

Kitty Ponse, a Swiss endocrinologist, came from a Dutch family living in the Dutch West Indies at the time of her birth. When she was eight, they moved to Geneva, Switzerland. She studied science at the University of Geneva, and worked for her doctorate under Emile Guyénot. Her dissertation topic was on secondary sexual characters in the toad. After she received her doctorate in the mid-twenties, she remained at the University of Geneva, teaching for the next forty years first as an assistant, then as *privat dozent* (lecturer), and finally as professor of endocrinology.

Her research topics focused on genetics and endocrinology, particularly hormones responsible for sexual differentiation in vertebrates. In her experimental work, she studied the functional inversion of sexual characters in adult vertebrates, writing a number of significant monographs on the topic, her best known being on sexual differentiation and intersexuality, published in 1949. JH/MBO

PRIMARY SOURCES

Ponse, Kitty. *La Différenciation du Sexe et l' Intersexualité des Vertébrés: Facteurs Héréditaires et Hormones.* Lausanne: F. Rouge, 1949.

STANDARD SOURCES
DFC.

POOL, JUDITH GRAHAM (1919–1975)

U.S. physiologist. Born 1 June 1919 in Queens, N.Y., to Nellie (Baron) and Leon Wilfred Graham. Married (1) Ithiel de Sola Pool (1938; divorced 1953). Two sons; one daughter. Married (2) Maurice Sokolow (1972, divorced 1975). Educated University of Chicago (A.B., 1939; Ph.D. in physiology, 1946). Professional experience: University of Chicago, assistant in physiology (1940–1942), toxicity laboratory, assistant (1946); Hobart and William Smith Colleges (1943–1945); Stanford Research Laboratory, research associate (1950–1953); Stanford School of Medicine, research fellow (1953–1956), research associate (1957–1960), senior research associate (1960–1975?). Honors and memberships: Fulbright research scholar, Norway (1958–1959); Physiological Society; New York Academy of Sciences; International Society of Hematology. Died 13 July 1975 of a brain tumor.

Judith Graham was born in Queens, New York, into a well-to-do Jewish family. Her mother was a schoolteacher and her father (born in England) was a stockbroker. She was an excellent student, and after attending Jamaica High School, she went to the University of Chicago, where she studied physics. In her junior year she married Ithiel da Sola Pool, a political scientist, and the two young people both continued their undergraduate studies and went on to graduate work. Judith Pool also served as an assistant in her department. While writing her dissertation on the electrophysiology of

muscle fibers under the neurophysiologist Ralph Waldo Gerard, she taught physics as an instructor at Hobart College in Geneva, New York. Her work was further interrupted by the birth of her two sons in the 1940s. She eventually completed her work for the degree in 1946, producing a remarkable study of the electropotential of a single isolated muscle fiber.

Following her doctoral degree, Pool worked in a variety of research and even secretarial positions, until the family moved to California, where her husband was offered a position in the Hoover Institution on War, Revolution and Peace at Stanford University. She obtained a research position at the Stanford Research Institute, and in 1953 began to do blood coagulation studies at the Stanford School of Medicine as a research fellow supported by a Bank America-Giannini Foundation grant. Once her own work began to be recognized, her marriage broke down, ending in divorce.

In 1958–1959, Pool went to Oslo, Norway, on a Fulbright research fellowship. But with this exception, she remained at the Stanford Medical School. Twenty years after the birth of her second son, she had a daughter. In 1972, she married Maurice Sokolow, professor of medicine and hematology, but this marriage ended three years later.

Pool's work on blood coagulation resulted in the development of a cold-insoluble protein fraction of blood plasma, cryoprecipitate, which contains an antihemolytic factor (AHF) soon to be used widely in blood banks. She was heralded for this discovery, receiving awards like the Murray Thelin Award of the National Hemophilia Foundation in 1968 and the Elizabeth Blackwell Award from Hobart and William Smith Colleges in 1973. Pool delivered an important lecture, the Paul M. Anggeler Memorial Lecture, in 1974 and then was awarded the Professional Achievement Award the next year. Pool held no professorship until she was made a full professor at Stanford belatedly in the early seventies, a time when many women were suddenly raised to professorships following the establishment of affirmative action.

Aware of the problems of women in science, Pool devoted her last years to studying and extending opportunities to young women in science. She was copresident of the Association of Women in Science, soon after its founding in 1971, and served as the chair of the Stanford Medical School Professional Women's organization the previous year.

When she was diagnosed with a brain tumor that progressed rapidly, Pool expressed no regrets, only her appreciation for a life that had been so rewarding. She died at the age of fifty-six at the Stanford University Hospital. Her archives are at Stanford University Medical Center. JH/MBO

PRIMARY SOURCES
Pool, Judith Graham. With Ralph W. Gerard. "Membrane Potentials and Excitation of Impaled Single Muscle Fibers."

Journal of Cellular and Comparative Physiology 28 (1946). This study derived from her dissertation at Chicago.

————. With T. H. Spaet. "Ethonionine-Induced Depression of Plasma Antihemophiliac Globulin in the Rat." *Proceedings of the Society for Experimental Biology and Medicine* 87 (1954): 54. Pool's first paper on blood coagulation.

————. With E. J. Hershgold and A. B. Papenhagen. "High Potency Antihemophiliac Concentrate Prepared from Cryo-globulin Precipitate." *Nature* 203 (18 July 1964): 312. Her major paper on Cryoprecipitate.

————. "Cryoprecipitate: Its Preparation and Clinical Use." In *Handbook of Hemophilia*, ed. K. M. Brinkhous and H. C. Henker. Chapel Hill: University of North Carolina Press, 1975. Pool's last communication.

SECONDARY SOURCES

Brinkhous, K. M. "Judith Graham Pool (1919–1975): An Appreciation." *Thrombosis and Haemostasis* (30 April 1976). Obituary notice.

STANDARD SOURCES

AMS 8, B 9, P&B 10–12; Bailey; Debus; *NAW* (article by K. M. Brinkhous); *Who's Who in America* (1974–1975).

POPE, CLARA MARIA (LEIGH) (ca. 1768–1838)

British flower painter. Born around 1768. Married (1) Francis Wheatley before 1788; (2) Alexander Pope (the actor and artist) 1808. Professional experience: exhibited flower paintings at Royal Academy, 1796–1838; watercolors of Paeonia *at British Museum of Natural History. Died 24 December 1838 in London.*

Clara Maria Leigh was born around 1768. She first married Francis Wheatley, an artist and member of the Royal Academy, before she was twenty. Ten years after her marriage, she began to exhibit flower paintings regularly at the Royal Academy. She also illustrated S. Curtis's *Beauties of Flora* (1806, 1820) and *Monograph on Genus Camilla*. After Wheatley's death, she married another artist and actor, Alexander Pope (not the poet). She continued exhibiting her work until her death in 1838.   JH/MBO

PRIMARY SOURCES

Curtis Samuel. *A Monograph on the Genus Camellia*. London: I. & S. Arch, 1819. Original drawings by Clara Maria Pope.
————. *Beauties of Flora*. 1806, 1820; rpt., Gamston: S. Curtis, 1920. Contains Pope's illustrations.

STANDARD SOURCES

Desmond; Stafleu and Cowan.

POPENOE, DOROTHY K. (HUGHES) (1899–1932)

British archeologist. Born 19 June 1899 in Ashford, England. Married Wilson Popenoe (17 November 1923). Two sons; two daughters. Educated Welsh Girls' School (Ashford); University College, London (no degree). Women's Land Army (1914–1916). Professional experience: Royal Botanical Gardens, Kew, student-assistant and illustrator (1918–1923); United States Bureau of Plant Industry, Herbarium, botanist (1923–1925); United Fruit Corporation, plant introduction station, Tela, Honduras, botanist (1925–1927); Peabody Museum Ulua River Expedition to Playa de los Muertos, Honduras (1927–1929). Died in Tela, Honduras, 30 December 1932, following an operation.

Although Dorothy Hughes Popenoe had a short life in archeology, her work was considered important by a number of American archeologists. Hughes was born in Ashford, England, at the very end of the nineteenth century; her studies were interrupted by World War I. She joined the Women's Land Army, but became ill and was forced to retire. In 1918, she was trained as a student assistant at the herbarium at the Royal Botanical Gardens. Working under the guidance of Otto Stapf, she combined the work with studies in botany at University College, London. She soon became an authority on African grasses, and described new species for the *Kew Bulletin*.

In 1923, she was offered a position at the United States Herbarium in Washington, D.C., by MARY AGNES CHASE, under the Bureau of Plant Industry. Here she studied and did taxonomic studies of cultivated bamboo and met and married a fellow botanist, Wilson Popenoe, who worked for the United States Department of Agriculture. Two years later, when her first child was a year old, her husband accepted a position running a field station for the United Fruit Company in Lacentilla, Honduras, near Tela. Here the two botanists became intrigued by the remnants of Mayan culture and published some observations on them in the United Fruit magazine. In spite of the fact that Dorothy Popenoe had three more children during this period and was assisting her husband in agronomic research, she became fascinated by the little-known Mayan ruins of Honduras.

Obtaining small grants from the Peabody Museum at Harvard, she traveled with Jorge Benitez, her Ecuadorian assistant, to the prehistoric site of Tenampua, high in the mountains. Here she mapped and described the site.

From 1927 on, she was in regular communication with Alfred Tozzer at the Peabody Museum. She became intrigued with the pottery from sites along the Ulua River, especially with the ancient cemetary called Playa de los Muertos, and began a systematic study of the plain and poly-chrome pottery and the skeletons found there. Undoutedly her training as a systematist in botany was of great help to her in establishing an important sequence for the area recognized by both Tozzer and George Valliant.

In 1930, the Popenoe family was transferred to Guatemala, but she continued to work on her materials from Honduras. When in 1932, they were transferred back to Tela, she again began to work on the Ulua valley polychrome ware. She died at the end of that year from intestinal problems and an operation necessitated presumably from accidentally eating the poisonous stage of the akee fruit (*Blighia sapia*).

JH/MBO

PRIMARY SOURCES

Dorothy Popenoe Collection: unpublished notes and photographs, accession files, letters of Popenoe to Alfred Tozzer 1929–1932. Peabody Museum, Harvard University.

Popenoe, Dorothy. "Two Expeditions in Search of Painted Pottery." Unpublished Report, March 1930. Harvard University, Peabody Museum of Archaeology and Ethnology, accession files.

———. With Wilson Popenoe. "The Human Background of Lancetilla." *Unifruitco Magazine* (August 1931): 6–10.

———. "Some Excavations at Playa de Los Meurtos, Ulua River, Honduras." *Maya Research* 1 (1934): 62–86. Published posthumously.

SECONDARY SOURCES

Joyce, Rosemary A. "Dorothy Hughes Popenoe." *Women in Archaeology*, ed. Cheryl Claassen, 51–64. Philadelphia: University of Pennsylvania Press, 1994.

Tozzer, Alfred. "Dorothy Hughes Popenoe." *Maya Research* (1935).

PORADA, EDITH (1912–1994)

Austrian/U.S. archeologist. Born 22 August 1912 in Vienna. At least one sister, Hildegard Randolph. Educated University of Vienna (Ph.D., 1935). Professional experience: American Schools of Oriental Research, research at Metropolitan Museum of Art, N.Y. on bas-reliefs of Assurnasirpal II; Pierpont Morgan Library, research supported by American Philosophical Society and the Bollingen Foundation, studied and cataloged seals; Guggenheim Fellowship to Turkey and Iran (1950); City University of New York, Queens College, assistant professor of art history (1950–1958); Columbia University, associate professor, professor (1958–1973), Arthur Lehman Professor of Art History and Archaeology (1973–1984), emerita professor (1984). Honors and memberships: Archaeological Institute of America, 12th annual Gold Medal Award for distinguished archeological achievement. Died 24 March 1994 in Honolulu, Hawaii.

Born in Austria, Edith Porada earned her doctorate at the age of twenty-three from the University of Vienna. Although she was first interested in the Minoan and Mycenaean civilizations, she was encouraged to work on the ancient Near East. She wrote her dissertation under Victor Christian on glyptic art of the Old Akkadian period. Two years after receiving her doctoral degree, she went to Paris to study the seal impressions on Old Assyrian tablets in the Louvre.

Because of the political climate in Austria, in 1938, Porada and her sister and later her father left that country for the United States. In the United States she worked at the Metropolitan Museum of Art in New York, where she published on the bas-reliefs of Assurnasirpal II. Her first support was from the American Schools of Oriental Research. With this support, she was able to continue the research on seals that she had begun in Paris. This times she analyzed more than one thousand sealings impressed on tablets by five generations of merchants found at Nuzi. She also studied and cataloged the collection of cylinder seals in the Pierpont Morgan Library. The support of the American Philosophical Society and the Bollingen Foundation enabled her to publish a comprehensive catalog of the library's seals. This two-volume study became the first part of a series presenting the seals in North American collections.

In 1950, Porada was awarded a Guggenheim Fellowship. She traveled from Istanbul to Baghdad and then met another archeologist, Barbara Parker, and together they went from Basra to Susa and Tehran.

When she returned, Porada took a job teaching art history at Queens College of the City University of New York. She stayed there for eight years before accepting a position at Columbia University, where for the first time she was able to teach in her area of expertise. She became the Arthur Lehman Professor of Art History and Archaeology, and developed the program at Columbia as the center of the study of the ancient Near East.

In addition to being an excellent teacher, Porada was a superb scholar. She completed seven comprehensive systematic studies considered to be classics in the field, including *The Collection of the Pierpont Morgan Library (Corpus of Ancient Near Eastern Seals in North American Collections I*; *Seal Impressions from Nuzi*; *The Art of Ancient Iran*; and *Chronologies in Old World Archaeology*. She published over eighty scholarly papers. The review articles that she produced brought archeologists up to date on the literature. She also published many short notes.

Porada's greatest strength was in the analysis of the style and iconography of works of art, applying the fundamental tenets of archeology to these works. Therefore, she insisted that her students gain exposure to field work.

JH/MBO

PRIMARY SOURCES

Porada, Edith. "Seal Impressions of Nuzi" (Mesopotamia)." New Haven: American Schools of Oriental Research, 1947.

————. *The Collection of the Pierpont Morgan Library (Corpus of Ancient Near Eastern Seals in North American Collections I)*. Washington, D.C.: N.p., 1948.

————. With Mogens Weitemeyer and Paul Lampl. *Some Aspects of the Hiring of Workers in the Sippar Region at the Time of Hammurabi. With a Chapter on Seal Impressions*. Copenhagen: Munksgaard, 1962. The chapter on seal impressions is by Porada.

————. With Hetty Goldman and George M. A. Hanfmann. *Excavations at Gozlu Kule, Tarsus*, ed. Hetty Goldman. 3 vols. Princeton: Princeton University Press, 1950–1963.

————. *The Art of Ancient Iran: From the Prehistoric to the Sasnian Period*. Washington, D.C.: Smithsonian, 1964.

————. *Man and Images in the Ancient Near East*. Wakefield, R.I.: Moyer Bell, 1995.

SECONDARY SOURCES

Pittman, Holly. "Edith Porada, 1912–1944." *American Journal of Archaeology* 99 (1995): 143–146.

Kelly-Buccellati, Marilyn, ed., with Paolo Matthiae and Maurits Van Loon. *Insight through Images: Studies in Honor of Edith Porada*. Malibu, Calif.: Undena Publications, 1986.

PORTER, GENE STRATTON (1863–1924)

See Stratton Porter, Gene.

PORTER, HELEN KEMP ARCHBOLD (1899–1987)

British physiologist and biochemist. Born 10 November 1899 at Place Hall, Farnham, Surrey, to Caroline Emily (Whitehead) Broghton and George Kemp Archbold. One older sister. Married (1) William Kemp Porter in 1937 (died); (2) Arthur St. George Huggett in 1962 (died 1968). Two step-daughters. Educated at home; Clifton High School for Girls, Bristol (1914–1917); University of London, Bedford College (A.B., 1921); Imperial College (postgraduate study); University of London (D.Sc., 1932). Professional experience: University of London, Food Investigation Board, research assistant (1922–1932); Imperial College, Research Institute of plant physiology, staff (1932–1959); Swanley Horticultural College, visiting lecturer in Biochemistry (1932?–1946?); Imperial College, reader in enzymology (1957–1959), professor of plant physiology (1959–1964), emerita professor (1964–1987); Agricultural Research Council, second secretary (1969–1971), scientific advisor to the secretary (1971–1972). Honors and memberships: Royal Society, Fellow (1956); Agricultural Research Council Society, honorary member (1964); Imperial College of Science and Technology, Fellow (1966).

Helen Kemp Archbold was born to a schoolmaster in Surrey who later became a partner in a private school (Aysgarth Preparatory School) in Yorkshire. When she was two years old, the family moved to Bristol, where she was tutored at home until the beginning of World War I. At that point, she was sent to the local Clifton Girls' High School, where she developed skills in biology, passing the Cambridge Examinations with distinction in biology and English at the age of seventeen. She entered Bedford School for Women (which had become part of the University of London), where she undertook a four-year course in chemistry, physics, and mathematics, graduating with honors in chemistry and physics.

Upon graduation, Archbold obtained one of the few postgraduate positions for women, working in Professor Thorpe's chemistry laboratory at Imperial College of Science and Technology (also part of University of London), working under MARTHA WHITELEY studying barbituate derivatives. In 1922, Helen Archbold was recommended to work with V. H. Blackman, head of the department of plant physiology and plant biochemistry at Imperial College. She was appointed to work as a research assistant with a group analyzing the organic acids and sugars in apples in order to study cold storage of the fruit. Not having taken any biology since her undergraduate days, she took evening courses at Birkbeck College. As she worked on this problem of biochemistry, she also expanded her study of that field at Chelsea Polytechical College.

Her interest in apple maturation resulted in her first publication on apple sugars, pectin, and apple metabolism, depending as well on her careful chemical analyses. When this project came to an end, she was transferred by Blackman to another research group, which was based both at the Research Institute of Plant Physiology at Imperial College and in a field station at Rothamsted Experimental Laboratories, where her research focused on barley. Here she began to work with the physiologist Frederick Guggenheim Gregory, who became her friend and mentor. In 1937, she met and married a physician, William George Porter, who died a few years later. During this period, she also lectured in biochemistry at Swanley Horticultural College until after World War II.

Porter's work on apples and barley served as the basis for her later important studies on polysaccharide synthesis, especially that of starch and fructosans. After spending her war years at the experimental station at Rothamsted, Porter continued her work on starch metabolism, and began to acquire a wider reputation. This led to an invitation in 1945 to spend six months in the laboratory of Stanley Peat at Bangor, Wales, where she managed to demonstrate the presence of starch phosphorylase in barley. Porter then went to Washington University, St. Louis, to work in the laboratory of Carl and GERTY CORI who won their Nobel Prize during the year she spent there (1947). There she studied the enzyme techniques that they used to study glycogen metabolism.

Returning to London, Porter was finally offered an important grant from the Nuffield Foundation in 1953, which enabled her to set up her own research group with a small staff at Imperial College. Reluctant to continue to study polysaccharide metabolism with conventional techniques, she began to use both radioactive tracers and chromatography in her work. This allowed her to study metabolism in living plant tissues with autoradiography and counting techniques.

Helen Porter was elected as a Fellow of the Royal Society in 1956 for her innovative work, and the following year she was appointed reader in enzymology in the botany department of Imperial College. Two years later, she was named the first woman professor in the history of Imperial College. She also married for the second time, a physiologist and Fellow of the Royal Society, Arthur St. George Huggett. Soon after, she followed her colleague Frederick Guggenheim Gregory as head of the department of plant physiology. She retired from the chair as an emerita professor a few years later, in 1964, and four years later her second husband died.

Although she retired from teaching, she continued her interest in the Biochemical Society in a number of administrative roles. She also encourged changes in the *Biochemical Journal*. She became a public servant in her seventies, working as second secretary to the Agricultural Research Council and then as scientific advisor to the secretary. Helen Kemp Porter had an artistic side as well, rendering scientific photographs as dramatic tapestries. She died a month after her eighty-eighth birthday.   JH/MBO

PRIMARY SOURCES

Porter, Helen Kemp. "The Nitrogen Content of Stored Apples." *Annals of Botany* 39 (1925): 97–107.

———. "The Chemical Composition of Mature and Developing Apples and Its Relationship to Environment and to the Rate of Chemical Change in Store." *Annals of Botany* 42 (1928): 541–565.

———. "Ripening Processes in the Apple and the Relation of Time of Gathering to the Chemical Changes in Cold Storage." *Annals of Botany* 46: 407–459.

———. "Fructosans in the Monocotyledons: A Review." *New Phytologist* 39 (1940): 189–219.

———. "Some Factors Concerned in the Starch Storage of Barley Grain." *Nature* 156 (1945): 70–76.

———. With L. H. May. "Metabolism of Radioactive Sugars by Tobacco Leaf Disks." *Journal of Experimental Botany* 6 (1955): 43–63.

———. "Synthesis of Polysaccharides of Higher Plants." *Annual Review of Plant Physiology* 13 (1961): 303–328.

STANDARD SOURCES

Biographical Memoirs, vol. 37, 1991, 399–410; *WWW* 8.

PORTER, LILIAN E. (BAKER) (1885–ca. 1966)

British botanist. Born 21 September 1885 in Airdrie, Lanarkshire. Father J. G. Baker. Married [?] Porter. Educated Liverpool University (M.Sc., 1909). Professional experience: University College, Bangor (Ireland), lecturer in botany (1913–1916); University of Cork (Ireland), demonstrator in biology (1916–1919); National University of Ireland, assistant examiner in botany for matriculation examination (1921–1945). Died around 1966.

Lilian Baker was born in Lanarkshire and educated at Liverpool University in England where she received a master of science degree in botany. She then taught for a number of years, first botany at University College, Bangor, and then biology at the University of Cork. She continued to serve as an examiner in botany for the matriculation examination for the National University of Ireland until the mid-1940s when she was in her early sixties. Her research in botany was on the lichens, and she prepared a supplement on this topic to M. C. Knowles's monograph on the lichens of Ireland. Her collection of lichens is held at the National Botanical Gardens, Glasnevin, Ireland. She died around her eightieth year.   JH/MBO

PRIMARY SOURCES

Porter, Lilian E. "Supplement to M.C. Knowles's Lichens of Ireland." *Proceedings of the Royal Irish Academy* 51 (1948): 345–386.

STANDARD SOURCES

Desmond; Stafleu and Cowan.

PORTER, MARY WINEARLS (1886–1980)

British/U.S. crystallographer. Born 1886 in London. Father Robert Porter, journalist. Educated at home and (unofficially) at Oxford University; University of Munich (graduate studies); Bryn Mawr; Heidelberg (graduate studies); Oxford University (D.Sc., 1932). Professional experience: Oxford University, Somerville College, research fellow in crystallography. Died 1980.

Mary Porter was born in England into a family that did not believe in educating their daughter. Although she exhibited an early interest in classical archeology, her parents refused to allow her a formal education, even when urged to do so by her brothers and Sir Henry Miers, Waynflete Professor of Mineralogy at Oxford. They did agree to allow her to study at Oxford to assist Miers in rearranging and cataloging the Corsi Collection of Italian ornamental marbles in the Oxford Museum. When in the summer of 1911 Porter's family left Oxford for the United States, Porter had a chance during that year and the next (1911 to 1912) to catalogue the collection of building and ornamental stones at the Smithsonian

Museum. This opportunity ended when her family moved from Washington to Munich. Here she studied at the university during the spring semester of 1913, returning to the United States in the summer of 1913 to prepare a small collection of perfect crystals from the mineral collection at Bryn Mawr for crystallographic studies. At Bryn Mawr she met FLORENCE BASCOM, who, from this point on, served as her mentor. This experience spurred Porter's interest in crystallography. Bascom wrote on behalf of Porter to Victor and Leontine Goldschmidt, who offered Porter the opportunity to study at the University of Heidelberg. A series of letters between Porter, the Goldschmidts, and Bascom (collected by Lois Arnold) clarifies Porter's scientific progress as well as her personal relationships.

Porter studied in Heidelberg at a period when it was difficult for women to be admitted to German universities and even more difficult for a woman to receive a degree. (A few American women managed to do so in the biological sciences in the late nineteenth century, such as JULIA B. PLATT and IDA HYDE.) Porter pursued her studies with Victor Goldschmidt between June 1914 and April 1915, at a time when he was undergoing both a mental and physical breakdown. Instead of proceeding to the University of Geneva to continue her studies as she had planned, she returned to England and to Oxford. She received a five-year research scholarship at Somerville College, Oxford, renewed for a second five years in 1924, which allowed her some measure of financial security as well as the opportunity to continue her research.

In 1929, Porter was named an Honorary Research Fellow at Somerville College and in 1932 was awarded a doctor of science degree. Mary Porter later published with R. C. Spiller the three-volume *Barker Index of Crystals*. She continued to work at Somerville College where she met DOROTHY HODGKIN, a future recipient of the Nobel Prize (1964) for her studies on the structure of certain important biochemical compounds. Porter died in 1980.   JH/MBO

PRIMARY SOURCES

Porter, Mary W. *What Rome was Built With: A Descripion of the Stones Employed in Ancient Times for Its Building and Decoration.* London: H. Fowde, 1907.
———. With R. C. Spiller and L. W. Codd. *The Barker Index of Crystals: A Method for the Identification of Crystalline Substances.* 3 vols. Cambridge: W. Heffer and Sons, [1951–1965].
Sophia Smith Women's History Archive at Smith College, Northampton, Mass., contains the correspondence between Florence Bascom, Helen Porter, and Victor and Leonine Goldschmidt.

SECONDARY SOURCES

Arnold, Lois B. "The Bascom-Goldschmidt-Porter Correspondence 1907–1922." *Earth Sciences History* 12 (1993): 196–223. An excellent source built around the correspondence of three scientists.

POTTER, BEATRIX (1866–1943)

British natural historian and children's story writer. Born 28 July 1866 in Bolton Gardens (Kensington), London, to Helen (Leech) and Rupert Potter. One brother. Married William Heelis. Educated by governess; Art Student's Certification, second grade. Professional experience: published over 25 children's books. Died 22 December 1943 in Castle Cottage, Sawrey of bronchitis and heart failure.

Born to a well-to-do Victorian family, Beatrix spent most of her time away from her aloof parents in a third-story nursery with her brother, Bertram. A shy child, Beatrix enjoyed collecting all kinds of natural history objects. Although both Beatrix and Bertram were artists, Beatrix was interested in minute details whereas Bertram drew bold overviews. She kept careful notes, and made drawings of caterpillars, fungi, beetles, and everything else she could find to study. With Bertram when they were on holiday, she skinned dead rabbits and boiled them until only the bones remained and then drew the skeleton. She also caught rabbits, tamed them, drew them, and brought them back to London as pets.

Beatrix was without companionship after Bertram went away to school. Her minimal education was with a governess, and her studies included French, German, and needlework. She studied with a Miss Cameron from age twelve to seventeen and completed her only education requirement, the Art Student's Certification, second grade, in July 1881.

As she grew older, her shyness became more acute. When she was nineteen years old, she visited the British Museum of Natural History and drew many of the objects in the collections there. She became interested in fungi when her family went on a vacation to Scotland, where she collected, drew, and studied numerous specimens, eventually producing over three hundred drawings. She recorded her observations in a coded journal. An attempt to study at the Royal Botanic Gardens at Kew was brokered by her uncle. She also shared some of her research on the germination of spores with the Linnean Society of London. After being discouraged in her work on fungi by the keeper of botany at the Museum of Natural History, she returned to the picture letters that she had sent to the children of her last governess, Annie Moore. These letters became the basis of her children's books. *The Tale of Peter Rabbit*, based on her own bunny, Benjamin Bouncer, was rejected by a succession of publishers. The Frederick Warne publishing company advised her to publish in color, however and the books became a great success. Potter became engaged to Norman Warne, her editor, but he died suddenly at the age of thirty-seven.

Potter cared for her aging parents at Bolton Gardens and then bought a farm, Hilltop House, in the Lake District, where she continued to write children's stories. She bought additional land in Sawrey, and when she was forty-seven years old, married the solicitor in her land purchases. She ceased writing until 1916, when the Warne publishing firm was in difficulty. To help them out, she wrote *Appley Dapply's Nursery Rhymes.*

Potter was a farmer for the last thirty years of her life, with enough money from her royalties for buying enough farms and cottages to be certain that urban life would not encroach on her privacy.

Potter's work on fungi deserves more attention than it has gotten. A self-taught botanist, and a meticulous observer, she described the symbiotic relationship existing between algae and fungi in lichens. A Swiss botanist had previously described lichens as two organisms, but British botanists did not accept his theories. Potter used the term *symbiosis,* a term coined by a German botanist to describe the relationship between algae and fungi in lichens. Her manuscript that indicated this idea was burned after her death, and it was not until her encoded notebooks were deciphered by Leslie Linder that this knowledge became available. During the Scottish holiday when she studied the Scottish fungi so relentlessly, she met Charles McIntosh, who was an amateur mycologist, and he validated her illustrations. However, Sir William Flower of the British Museum of Natural History failed to acknowledge her work. Her chemist uncle, Sir Henry Roscoe, suggested tests to determine that the fungus contributed minerals taken from the air and water that the algae needed to survive. Sir Henry introduced her to the director of the Royal Botanic Gardens at Kew, Sir William Turner Thiselton-Dyer, but he was uninterested in her explanation of the symbiotic relationship in the lichen and thought her drawings "too artistic" to meet scientific criteria. Although she obtained a student pass to study at Kew, she was met with indifference. After receiving a rude letter from Thiselton-Dyer, her uncle reviewed Potter's work and encouraged her to prepare a paper for the Linnean Society. On April 1, 1897, her paper "On the Germination of the Spores of Agaricineae" was read by George Massee of the Royal Society. Before the paper could be published, Potter withdrew it in order to conduct additional research. Her spore research remains unpublished.   JH/MBO

PRIMARY SOURCES
Potter, Beatrix. "On the Germination of the Spores of Agaricineae." Paper read at the meeting of the Linnaean Society, London, 1 April 1897.

———. *The Tale of Peter Rabbit.* London: Frederick Warne, 1902.

SECONDARY SOURCES
Battrick, Elizabeth. *The Real World of Beatrix Potter.* Norwich, England: Jarold and Sons, 1987.

Linder, Leslie. *Beatrix Potter 1866–1943: Centenary Catalog.* London: National Book League, 1966.

———. *A History of the Writing of Beatrix Potter.* London: Frederick Warne, 1971.

———. *The Journal of Beatrix Potter from 1881 to 1897.* London: Frederick Warne, 1966.

———. With E. Linder. *The Art of Beatrix Potter.* London: Frederick Warne, 1955.

Noble, Mary. "Beatrix Potter, Naturalist and Mycologist and Charles McIntosh, the Perthshire Naturalist." *Notes from the Royal Botanic Garden Edinburgh* 44 (1987): 607–627.

———. With R. Davis. "Cup Fungus or Basidiomycetes and Potterism." *Bulletin of the British Mycological Society* 20 (October 1986): 145–147.

STANDARD SOURCES
Grinstein 1997 (article by Edna May Duffy).

POTTER, EDITH LOUISE (1901–)

U.S. pathologist. Born 26 September 1901 in Clinton, Iowa, to Edna Rugg (Holmes) and William Harvey Potter. Married Alvin Meyer (17 June 1944). One stepdaughter. Educated University of Minnesota (B.S.; M.D., 1926; M.S., 1932; Ph.D., 1934). Professional experience: Minneapolis General Hospital, intern (1925); private practice (1927–1931); University of Chicago, instructor and assistant professor (1934–1947); Department of Obstetrics and Gynecology, associate professor of pathology (1947–1956), professor (1956–1967), emerita professor (1967–?); University of Brazil, São Paolo (1949); National Association of Retarded Children, distinguished scholar (1960–?). Honors and memberships: American Pathological Society, diplomate board; American Gynecological Society, Adair Award (1963); University of Minnesota, Award of Achievement; New York Infirmary, Blackwell Award; University of Brazil, honorary doctorate (1953).

Edith Louise Potter was an American pathologist who built her reputation on her studies of the Rh factor as a cause of fetal death. After studying medicine at the University of Minnesota, she was an intern for a year and then started general practice for five years. She returned to the university to obtain a doctoral degree and then began to teach pathology in the department of obstetrics and gynecology at the University of Chicago, where she remained until her retirement as emerita professor.

In her early forties, she married Alvin Meyer, who had one daughter. She spent a year as guest lecturer at the University of Brazil in São Paolo, which later awarded her an honorary degree. She also served as a consultant to the

Armed Services Institute of Pathology and the Surgeon General of the Army in the Far East.

Her work on the role of the Rh factor and hemolytic disease of the newborn brought her a wide fame, and she published a number of standard texts on the pathology of the fetus and the newborn. In the 1960s she retired to Fort Myers, Florida. JH/MBO

PRIMARY SOURCES

Potter, Edith Louise. With F. L. Adair. *Fetal and Neonatal Death.* Chicago: University of Chicago Press, [1940].

———. *Fundamentals of Human Reproduction.* New York: McGraw-Hill, 1948.

———. *Rh: Its Relation to Transfusion Reactions and Hemolytic Diseases of the Newborn.* Chicago: Year Book Publisher, 1947.

———. *Pathology of the Fetus and Newborn.* Chicago: Year Book Publisher, 1952.

STANDARD SOURCES

AMS 6–8, B 9, P&B 10–11; Debus; O'Neill.

POTTER, ELLEN CULVER (1871–1958)

U.S. public health physician. Educated Woman's Medical College of Pennsylvania. Professional experience: Philadelphia General Hospital, obstetrical assistant; Woman's Medical College of Pennsylvania, medical director of the college hospital (1917–?); Bryn Mawr College, consulting physician (1915–1918); Philadelphia medical inspector of schools (1915–1918); Philadelphia Bureau of Municipal Research, medical staff; Bureau of Children (Child Health Division), chief (1920–1922); state of Pennsylvania, secretary of welfare (1922–?); New Jersey State Department of Institutions and Agencies, director of medicine (1930s?); U.S. Committee on Governmental Relief Methods (1933–?). Honors and memberships: Rutgers University, New Jersey College of Women (honorary D.LL., 1936).

Ellen Culver Potter studied at the Woman's Medical College of Pennsylvania. After graduating, she spent fifteen years in private practice, with various faculty assignments at the college and at Bryn Mawr. She was a member of the medical staff of the Philadelphia Bureau of Municipal Research, as medical inspector of public schools of Philadelphia and supervising inspector of public schools. She worked as assistant to the obstetrical staff at Philadelphia General Hospital and consulting physician at several institutes and colleges for girls, becoming medical director of the Woman's Medical College of Pennsylvania college hospital in 1917.

When the state of Pennsylvania formed a Department of Welfare in 1920, the Commissioner of Health, Edward Martin, asked Potter if she would become chief of the bureau of children (Child Health Division), a position she accepted with

many reservations, having had no training in public health. Her passionate interest in children's health and public education as well as her administrative expertise were sufficient. In 1922 she was made a member of the governor's staff as secretary of welfare of the Commonwealth of Pennsylvania.

She moved to New Jersey in the 1930s, where she accepted a new position as director of medicine in the New Jersey State Department of Institutions and Agencies. In this post she was instrumental in the reorganization and modernization of such programs as the State Home for Girls, and became involved in the system of classification of inmates in the penal, correctional, and charitable institutions. Potter was consultant to the Wickersham Commission on Prisons and Parole. She was called in by the federal government to direct development of national policy in relation to transients, and served on the pathfinding Committee on Governmental Relief Methods and the steering committee of the Social Work Conference on Federal Action (1933).

During the New Deal, Potter was involved in the recruiting program for the Civilian Conservation Corps, and was a member of the Division of Medicine and Inspection of Private Institutions. She was awarded an honorary doctor of laws in 1936 by the New Jersey College for Women, part of Rutgers University. JH/MBO

PRIMARY SOURCES

Potter, Ellen Culver. *How Can a Program for Care of the Chronically Ill and Aged Be Integrated?: A Case Report of Experience in One State.* Chicago: American Public Welfare Association, 1943.

SECONDARY SOURCES

Alsop, Gulielma Fell. *History of the Woman's Medical College, Philadelphia, Pennsylvania, 1850–1950.* Philadelphia: J. B. Lippincott Co., 1950.

STANDARD SOURCES

Lovejoy.

POTTS, ELIZA (1809–1873)

British amateur botanist. Born 11 March 1809 in Chester, Chestershire. Died 6 December 1873 in Funchal, Madeira.

Eliza Potts was a British botanist who lived in Chestershire but collected plants for T. B. Halls's *Flora Liverpool* (1839). Later she moved to Glanyr Afon. She was a friend of the botanist William Wilson, who did extensive collecting of British plants, especially mosses. Her plants are at the Natural History Museum, London. JH/MBO

SECONDARY SOURCES

Hall, T. B. *Flora Liverpool*. London: Whitaker & Co., 1839. Includes Potts's plants.

Warren, J. B. *Flora Chestershire*. N.p., 1899. See page lxxxvii.

"Eliza Potts." *Journal of Botany* (1910): 41; 4, suppl. 1 (1911): 4.

STANDARD SOURCES

Desmond.

POVITSKY, OLGA RAISSA (1877–1948)

Russian/U.S. bacteriologist. Born 1877, Maryampol, Russia. Educated Girls' Gymnasium (Russia); Woman's Medical College of Pennsylvania (M.D., 1901); New York University (Ph.D., 1924). Professional experience: New York State Health Department, laboratories, bacteriologist (1912–1947?). Honors and memberships: Society of Bacteriologists; Association of Immunology; Public Health Association; Women's Medical Association; New York Academy of Medicine. Died New York City in 1948.

Olga Povitsky was a Russian bacteriologist who came to the United States after her teen years. She obtained her medical degree from the Woman's Medical College of Pennsylvania at the turn of the century. Her interest in bacteriology led her in 1912 to take a position with the New York State Department of Health, where she remained until her death, working as a colleague of ANNA WESSELS WILLIAMS. In the 1920s, she took an advanced degree in public health from New York University.

Her research interests were connected to her work for the New York State Department of Health: studies of influenza, pertussis, scarlet fever, diphtheria, toxins, antitoxins, and the Ramon flocculation test. Her memberships in the Association of Immunologists as well as the Society of Bacteriology testify to her interests. She died in New York City at the age of seventy-one.

JH/MBO

STANDARD SOURCES
AMS 5–7.

POWDERMAKER, HORTENSE (1896–1970)

U.S. anthropologist. Born 24 December 1896 in Philadelphia, Pa., to Minnie Jacoby and Louis Powdermaker. One sibling. Never married. Foster son, Won Mo Kim. Educated Western High School; Goucher College (B.A., 1919); London School of Economics, University of London (Ph.D., 1928). Professional experience: union organizer (1919–1924); Institute of Human Relations, Yale University, research associate (1930–1937); Hunter College, instructor in anthropology (1938–1954), professor of anthropology (1954–1968), University of California, Berkeley, Yale University, University of Chicago, Columbia University, Stanford University, visiting professor; field studies in Lesu, New Ireland (1929), American South (1932–1934), California Japanese-American detention camps (1942?), Northern Rhodesia (Zambia) (1953–1954). Died 15 June 1970.

Hortense Powdermaker, U.S. anthropologist, made her name as both a keen observer of class and race prejudices in widely different social settings in America, from American black churches in the American South to Japanese-American detention camps during World War II to the film industry in Hollywood in the 1960s. She also made more traditional field studies in Lesu, New Ireland, a small island in the Southwest Pacific, and in Rhodesian mining camps in Africa. Born into a middle-class business family in Philadelphia, with strong ties to the Jewish community, she moved with her family first to Reading, Pennsylvania, and then to Baltimore, Maryland. She attended Western High School and then majored in history at Goucher College in 1919. She threw herself into union organizing when she graduated, working for Amalgamated Clothing Workers, first in New York City, and then in Cleveland and Rochester.

Her interest in social theory led her to the London School of Economics in 1924, where she attended a seminar in anthropology taught by Bronislaw Malinowski. She became one of his first graduate students, and spent her summers in the Tyrol, not far from the Malinowski summer home, adopting his ideas of functionalism and a psychoanalytic approach to anthropology. The fact that her older sister, Florence Powdermaker, had become a psychiatrist may have stimulated her interest in this approach. She would later enter into psychoanalysis in order to understand herself and others. She finished her doctoral dissertation in 1928 and then went the following year to do the obligatory anthropological field work in a small village in the southwest Pacific, on the small island, New Ireland, supported by a grant from Australia. The result was her first book, *Life in Lesu* (1933).

Moving back to the United States, Powdermaker became a research associate at the Institute of Human Relations at Yale University, where her interest in culture and personality was stimulated by the linguist Edward Sapir. Powdermaker, with support from Sapir, received a Social Science Research Council grant to study southern black and white relations in Mississippi. Her book on the topic, *After Freedom* (1938), included an important section on the importance of black churches to the African-American community, and is now seen as classic.

Appointed an instructor of anthropology at Hunter College, New York, in 1938, Powdermaker remained there for the rest of her teaching career, but took short leaves and summer positions, to lecture at many universities throughout the United States. She became full professor at Hunter in 1954. During World War II, she became involved in government work like many other anthropologists. She assisted the government by lecturing in the Army Specialized Training Program for the southwest Pacific and studying the Japanese-Americans placed into detention camps in California. She wrote about the latter experience in a feeling manner in her autobiographical book, *Stranger and Friend: The Way of an Anthropologist* (1966).

Because she was aware of the importance of the mass media on society, she decided in the immediate postwar year (1946–1947) to do research on the social structure of the film industry in Hollywood, California, then in its heyday. The result was *Hollywood, the Dream Factory* (1950), which brought her to national and international notice beyond the anthropological community and provoked some hostile criticism as well. She extended this interest in media and society in her next study of a mining town in northern Rhodesia, 1953–1954, picking this location at the suggestion of a friend, the British anthropologist Audrey Richards, with whom she had attended the London School of Economics. She felt some dissatisfaction with the limitations imposed on her direct observation in this area. This appeared as a book (*Copper Town*) nine years later (1962), and received mixed reviews because of her use of psychological concepts and her dependence on her major male informant and translator.

Just before Powdermaker's retirement, the success of her autobiographical description of her many field experiences in *Stranger and Friend* led to her write the classic article on field work for the *International Encyclopedia of Social Sciences* in 1968. After retiring from Hunter College, she moved to Berkeley, California, where she became interested in studying the rising youth culture, and role of women in society. Never married, she had a number of intense relationships with men. At the end of her life, she shared an apartment with her foster son, the violinist Won Mo Kim. She died suddenly of a heart attack 15 June 1970.

Although she felt that empathy was more important than age or gender in field work, she also felt her marked achievements did not bring with them the same status she would have achieved as a man. She had received a number of honors in the last decades of her life, including an honorary degree from her alma mater, Goucher College, in 1957 and a distinguished teaching award from the Alumni of Queens College. She served one term as president of the American Ethnological Society.   JH/MBO

PRIMARY SOURCES

Powdermaker, Hortense. *Life in Lesu: The Study of a Melanesian Society in New Ireland.* New York: W. W. Norton; London: Williams and Norgate, 1933.

———. *After Freedom: A Cultural Study in the Deep South.* New York: Viking, 1938. Rpt., New York: Atheneum Press, 1968.

———. *Hollywood, the Dream Factory: An Anthropologist Studies the Movie Makers.* Boston: Little, Brown, 1950.

———. *Copper Town: Changing Africa. The Human Situation on the Rhodesian Copperbelt.* New York: Harper and Row, 1962.

———. *Stranger and Friend: The Way of an Anthropologist.* New York: W. W. Norton, [1966].

———. "Field Work." *International Encyclopedia of the Social Sciences,* vol. 5, 418–424. New York: Macmillan, Free Press, 1968.

SECONDARY SOURCES

Traeger, George. "Hortense Powdermaker, a Tribute." *American Anthropologist* 73 (1971): 786–787.

Wolf, Eric. "Hortense Powdermaker, 1900–1970." *American Anthropologist* 73 (1971): 783–786.

STANDARD SOURCES

AMS 6–8; S&B 9–11; Gacs (article by Sydel Silverman); NAW(M) (article by Joan Mark).

POZARYSKA, KRYSTYNA (MALISZEWSKI) (1914–1989)

Polish paleontologist. Born 29 October 1914 in Warsaw to Wanda and Wladyslaw Maliszewski. Two siblings, Zbigniew and Barbara. Married Wladyslaw Pozaryski. Two children. Educated Cecylia Plater-Zyberkowa's school (finished 1921); Warsaw University, Faculty of Mathematics and Natural Sciences (graduated 1937; M.Sc.?; Ph.D., 1956). Professional experience: Warsaw University, junior lecturer, geology and paleontology; State Institute of Geology, paleontologist (1937?–1945); Polish Academy of Sciences, Institute of Paleozoology, faculty (1953–1980; professor, 1970); Warsaw University, teacher (1954–1969). Died 21 October 1989 in Warsaw.

Krystyna Maliszewski's parents were well educated; her mother, Wanda, was a music and foreign language teacher and her father a self-educated ethnographer and geographer. All of Maliszewski's higher education was at Warsaw University. Her master's thesis was entitled "The Evolution of the Pilica River Valley." Her first position after graduation was as a junior lecturer in geology at Warsaw University; she was also commissioned by the State Institute of Geology to do the geological mapping of the Quaternary. During World War II, Krystyna Pozaryska (she had married Wladyslaw Pozaryski by this point) continued working privately on her research—the stratigraphy of the Pleistocene of the Kamienna River Valley, based on material collected from 1937 to 1939.

In 1945, Pozaryska resumed work for the State Institute of Geology. After the separation of the chair of paleontology from that of geology at Warsaw University, Roman Kozlowski, paleontolology chair, was a great influence of Pozaryska's research. She was transferred to the Institute of Paleozoology of the Polish Academy of Sciences in 1953. She also lectured in paleontology at the evening engineering school and (from 1954) taught geology at Warsaw University for fifteen years.

The majority of Pozaryska's professional work was linked with the Institute of Paleozoology, later the Institute of Paleobiology. In 1956, she received her doctoral degree and in 1970 was made full professor.

Pozaryska was active in a number of professional organizations, including the Belgian Geological Society, the German Paleontological Society, and the German Academy of Sciences in Halle. She also was a member of the Scientific Council of the Polish Academy of Sciences, the Scientific Council of the Geological Publishing House in Warsaw, and she worked on the editorial boards of *Acta Palaeontologica Polonica*, and *Revista Española de Micropaleontologia*.

During the period between 1936 and 1939, Pozaryska's research involved the mapping of the Quaternary. The early results of this field work were published before the war and the final ones, after the war, including an important monograph on the Kamienna River Valley (1948). After the war and until 1957, inspired by Kozlowski, Pozaryska worked on the Late Cretaceous microfauna of Poland. Her first major publication in this area was a 1952 monograph on sedimentological questions of the Maastrichtian and Danian of the Pulawy region. This was a pioneer work which provided data for the interpretation of the ecology of the Late Cretaceous foraminifera. She published several papers that were widely used in geological prospecting in Poland. Her doctoral thesis was published in French in 1957. It described 180 species of foraminifera from the Upper Cretaceous and the Lower Tertiary of the Polish Lowlands, deterined their paleoecological and stratigraphical significance, and recognized their facies relations. In order to complete this research, she was awarded a scholarship to Sweden. In the third period of her research, 1957–1968, Pozaryska worked on the microfauna from the boundary layers between the Cretaceous and Tertiary of the Polish Lowlands. This research resulted in two major monographs, one of which, "Foraminifera and Biostratigraphy of the Danian and Montian of Poland," earned her the State Prize. The period from 1968 to 1986 was devoted to further work on the Paleocene, a study of the Eocene, and to summing up already achieved results in several synthetic papers.

In addition to her research, Pozaryska spent a considerable amount of time reviewing doctoral theses, tutoring young scientists, and advising her colleagues. Popularizing science was another major interest of Pozaryska's. Early in her career, she read public lectures on the natural resources of Poland and later wrote articles for daily newspapers and for the radio.

JH/MBO

PRIMARY SOURCES

Pozaryska, Krystyna. "Stratygrafia plejstocenu w dolinie dolnej Kamiennej." *Panstowowy Instytut Geologiczny* (Poland) *Biuletyn* 52 (1948): 5–91.

———. "Lagenidae du Crétacé supérieur de Pologne." *Palaeontologia Polonica* 8 (1957): 1–190.

———. With J. Szczechura. "On Some Warm-Water Foraminifera from the Polish Montian." *Acta Paleontologia Polonica* 15, no. 1 (1970): 95–115.

———. "O gornym eocenie w Polsce." *Kwartalnik Geologiczny* 21 (1977): 59–72.

———. With Ehrhard Voigt. "Bryozoans as Substratum of Fossil Fistulose Foraminifera (Fam. Polymorphinidae)." *Lethaia* 2 (1985): 155–165.

SECONDARY SOURCES

Szczechura, Janina. "Krystyna Pozaryska (1914–1989)." *Acta Palaeontologica Polonica* 35, nos. 3–4 (1990): 99–107.

PRÁDACOVÁ, MARCELLA (1912–1972)

Czechoslovakian invertebrate paleontologist and coal petrologist. Born 1912. Died 1972.

Marcella Prádacová published prolifically on invertebrate fossils as indicators of the presence of oil. However, information about her life and education is not available.

JH/MBO

PRIMARY SOURCES

Prádacová, Marcella. "Celed' Favositidae z celechovvickeho devonu." *Ceska Akademie ved a Umeni. Trida II Rozpravy* 48, no. 25 (1939): 168–179.

———. With others. "Vyzkum radvanickeho sousloji ve vnitrosudetske panvi v oblasti Chvalce, Hodkovic, Radvanic, Janovic a Jivky." *Vyber Praci-Geoindustria* 3 (1970): 24–60.

SECONDARY SOURCES

Sindelár, Jiri. "Za RNDr. Marcellou Pradácovou." *Casopis pro Mineralogii a Geologii* 18, no. 4 (1973): 429–430.

STANDARD SOURCES

Sarjeant.

PRANKERD, THEODORA LISLE (1878–1939)

British botanist. Born 21 June 1878 in London. Educated University College, London (B.Sc., 1903; D.Sc., 1929). Professional experience: London, schoolteacher (1904–1911); Bedford College, lecturer in botany (1912–1917); University College, Reading, lecturer in botany (1917–1939). Died 11 November 1939, Reading, Berkshire, in a bus accident.

Theodora Prankerd was born in South Hackney, London. After attending Brighton High School, she went for two years to the Royal Holloway College on a Founder's Scholarship and was then awarded a Driver Scholarship. She moved from there to University College, London, where she obtained first-class honors in botany in 1903.

Teaching school in London, she continued to do research in botany at the botanical laboratory of the University of London. She also took the opportunity to visit her cousin, Professor Soares, who was at the University of Chicago, and published a paper for the *New Phytologist* (1908) on her observations of the botanical laboratory there. Returning to London, at the suggestion of F. E. Fritsch, she studied the structure of the two species of *Hottonia,* becoming interested in the sensitivity of that genus to geotropism and other aspects of graviperception. She determined to study the relationship of this sensitivity to the amount of statolith starch. The result was published eventually in *Annals of Botany* and led to her appointment as a part-time lecturer in botany at Bedford College.

Prankerd then began to study the structure of a fossil seed, *Lagenstoma ovoides,* obtaining fifty-one examples to study. Although she published only this one paper on fossil botany, she returned to this topic in the late thirties. Bedford College soon raised her to a full-time position as lecturer in botany, and she taught there until 1917. She then moved to the University of Reading, where she was a lecturer in botany for the rest of her career.

Prankerd continued her work on geotropism, extending it to a study of ferns, the first to do so extensively in spite of the difficulties the work entailed. She published numerous articles in *Annals of Botany,* the *Botanical Gazette,* the *New Phytologist,* and the *Journal of the Linnean Society* from 1911 through 1935. Her students at Reading included a number of future Fellows of the Linnean Society, who continued her studies of geotropism in plants with some important publications.

In her earliest years, Prankerd was a strong advocate of women's suffrage. Later she also supported the League of Nations, and was the local secretary of the Reading Branch. She died suddenly after she was hit by a bus close to her home in Reading at the age of sixty-one. Her mother, who lived with her, endowed a research scholarship in her name at Reading. JH/MBO

PRIMARY SOURCES

Prankerd, Theodora Lisle. "On the Structure and Biology of the Genus *Hottonia.*" *Annals of Botany* (January 1911).

———. "The Fossil Seed, *Lagenostoma ovoides.*" *Journal of the Linnean Society* (1912).

SECONDARY SOURCES

Stiles, W. "Theodora Lisle Prankerd." *Proceedings of the Linnean Society* 152 (1939–1940): 371–372.

"Theodora Lisle Prankerd." *Nature* 144 (1939): 932–933.

STANDARD SOURCES

Desmond.

PRATT, ANNE (1806–1893)

British botanical popularizer. Born 1806 in Strood, Kent. Married John Pearless in 1866. Educated Eastgate School, Rochester. Professional experience: published popular books on botany (1838–1890). Died at Redhill, Surrey, 1893.

Anne Pratt, the daughter of a grocer in Kent, received some education at a school in Rochester. Since her own health was poor, and she was lame, she enlisted her older sister in her botanical enterprises. Her sister brought her specimens and enabled her to form a herbarium. She also provided plants for Anne to illustrate.

Although she published her first book on field and garden plants anonymously when she was still living at home at the age of thirty-two, her most important work (a five-volume study of flowering plants and ferns) appeared under her own name some twenty-three years later. Like many women popularizers of botany in the Victorian period, she included religious elements in her writings.

Although her works were appreciated by women readers, the botanists of her day were anxious to point out that Pratt was not a botanist, and that her knowledge was incomplete. Shteir judges that Pratt's popularizing of botany enabled her to "shape and work the codes of early Victorian literary and botanical culture in order to carve out authorial sphere for herself." In her sixties, Pratt married a man she had known for some time, but continued to publish her books under her birth name. She lived for a time in East Grimstead, Sussex, but spent the last years of her life in Redhill, Surrey. Her books remained in print until some years after her death.

JH/MBO

PRIMARY SOURCES

Pratt, Anne. *The Field, the Garden and the Woodland, or Interesting Facts Respecting Flowers and Plants in General.* London: Charles Knight, 1840.

———. *Wild Flowers.* London: Society for Promoting Christian Knowledge, 1852–1853. This book was intended for children and included block prints; it was her most widely reprinted.

———. *Flowering Plants and Ferns of Great Britain.* 5 vols. London: Society for Promoting Christian Knowledge, 1855.

———. *The Ferns of Great Britain and Their Allies the Club-Mosses, Pepperworts and Horsetails.* London: Society for Promoting Christian Knowledge, [1855?]. 41 plates.

———. *The British Grasses and Sedges.* London: Society for Promoting Christan Knowledge, [1859]. Includes 20 leaves of colored plates.

———. *Flower Folk.* New York: Frederick A. Stokes Co., 1890.

STANDARD SOURCES
DNB; Europa; Shteir.

PRESSEY, LUELLA (COLE) (1893–?)

U.S. psychologist. Born 1 April 1893 in Haverhill, Mass. Married Sidney Leavitt Pressey. Educated Vassar (A.B., 1916); Indiana University (A.M., 1919, Ph.D., 1920; research fellow, 1920–1921). Professional experience: Ohio State University, instructor in psychology (1921–1926), assistant professor (1926–?). Honors and memberships: American Psychological Association, member; Educational Research Association, member. Death date unknown.

Luella Pressey earned her two advanced degrees from the University of Indiana. After receiving her doctoral degree, she was a research fellow at the university for a year. She took a position at Ohio State University as an instructor, then assistant professor in psychology. She was a member of the American Psychological Association and the Education Research Association. Her interests were in mental and educational tests and in scientific curriculum building. She also studied the psychological difficulties of college students.

JH/MBO

PRIMARY SOURCES
Cole, Luella. With Sidney Pressey. *Methods of Handling Test Scores.* Yonkers-on-Hudson, N.Y.: World Book Co., 1926.
———. With Sidney Pressey. *Introduction to the Use of Standard Tests: A Brief Manual in the Use of Tests of Both Ability and Achievement in the School Subjects.* Rev. ed. Yonkers-on-Hudson, N.Y.: World Book Co., 1931.
———. *The Improvement of Reading.* New York: Farrar and Rinehart, Inc., 1940.

STANDARD SOURCES
AMS 4–5.

PRESTON, ANN (1813–1872)

U.S. pioneer physician. Born 1 December 1813 in West Grove, Pa., to Margaret (Smith) and Amos Preston. Eight siblings. Never married. Educated private study (1847–1849); Female Medical College (Woman's Medical College) of Pennsylvania (M.D., 1851). Professional experience: schoolteacher; Woman's Medical College, *professor of physiology and hygiene (1853–1872), dean (1866–1872). Died 18 April 1872 in Philadelphia.*

Ann Preston was a pioneer woman physician, one of the first women who attended the Female Medical College of Pennsylvania (later the Woman's Medical College). She served both as a professor of physiology and hygiene and as its first woman dean. Raised as a Quaker, and surrounded by a strong Quaker community, Preston began as a schoolteacher and then was able to study medicine privately with a sympathetic physician, Nathaniel Moseley. Unable to find a male medical school that would admit her, as ELIZABETH BLACKWELL had been able to do, Preston was almost forty before she was able to obtain a medical degree.

Inspired by the determination of Preston and others, the first medical school for women was founded in 1850 by a group of physicians and public-spirited men including Joseph Longshore, William Mullen, and Nathaniel Moseley. Unlike that of the medical school that Elizabeth and EMILY BLACKWELL founded some ten years later, the first faculty at the Female Medical College was entirely male. Longshore's sister-in-law HANNAH LONGSHORE, like Ann Preston, had studied privately with a sympathetic physician and entered the medical school for women with her. Both women were credited for their previous two years of study, and graduated in 1851 with five other women. Preston's medical thesis endorsed the growing objection to the practice of purging and bloodletting and proposed a more natural method of healing.

Upon graduation, Preston visited Elizabeth Blackwell in New York City. Blackwell was experiencing difficulties obtaining clients, and Preston informed her about the Philadelphia success, which inspired Blackwell to continue her own work. Preston returned the following fall to Philadelphia for an additional postgraduate year and then began a series of lectures for women on hygiene and what was termed "physiology" in 1852. She was appointed the following year as professor of hygiene and physiology at the Woman's Medical College of Pennsylvania.

When certain groups of doctors in the Pennsylvania Medical Society resolved not to recognize the school and excluded women students from the clinics of the major Philadelphia hospitals, Preston began a campaign to preserve clinical teaching by founding the Woman's Hospital in 1861. Seven years later she obtained the admission of women to teaching clinics of the Philadelphia Hospital ("Blockley") and then Pennsylvania Hospital, although not to internships or residencies. Preston was named dean in 1866, the first woman in that position, and remained in that post until her death six years later from articular rheumatism at the age of fifty-six. Her will left her books, instruments, and an endowment to the medical college.

JH/MBO

PRIMARY SOURCES

Preston, Ann. "Valedictory Address to the Graduating Class of the Female Medical College of Pennsylvania for the Session of 1857–58." Philadelphia: Ketterlinus, 1858.

SECONDARY SOURCES

Abram, Ruth. "Will There Be a Monument?: Six Pioneer Women Tell Their Own Stories." In *Send Us a Lady Physician: Women Doctors in America (1835–1920),* ed. Ruth Abrams, 71–106. New York: W. W. Norton, 1984.

Alsop, Gulielma Fell. *History of the Woman's Medical College.* Philadelphia: Lippincott, 1950.

Foster P. P. "Ann Preston: A biography." Ph.D. diss., University of Pennsylvania, 1984.

Kelly, Howard A. *Cyclopedia of American Medical Biography.* Vol. 2. Philadelphia: W. B. Saunders, 1911.

STANDARD SOURCES

Hurd-Mead 1933; Lovejoy; Morantz-Sanchez; *NAW* (article by Gulielma Fell Alsop); Uglow 1982.

PRESTON, ISABELLA (1881–1965)

British-born Canadian botanist. Born 4 September 1881 in Lancaster, England. Educated Swanley Horticultural College; Ontario Agricultural (?) College (ca. 1912). Professional experience: Ontario Central Experimental Farm (1921?–retirement). Died 31 December 1965 in Ottawa, Canada.

Isabella Preston was a British-born botanist who was trained at Swanley Horticultural College but moved to Ontario, Canada, in 1912. There she continued her education in horticulture, joining the Ontario Central Experimental Farm, where she became an authority on plant hybridization, particularly of lilies. Her portrait is at the Hunt Library in Pittsburgh.   JH/MBO

PRIMARY SOURCES

Preston, Isabella. *Garden Lilies.* London: K. Paul, Trench, Trubner and Co., Ltd., 1929

———. *Lilies for Every Garden.* New York: Orange Judd, 1947.

SECONDARY SOURCES

Canadian Horticultural History 1 (1987): 125–175.
Lily Yearbook. 1967. 129–131.

STANDARD SOURCES

Desmond.

PRESTWICH, GRACE ANNE (MILNE) M'CALL (1832–1899)

British scientific biographer, illustrator, popular science writer, and novelist. Born 18 December 1832 in Findhorn, Morayshire, Scotland, to Louisa (Falconer) and James Milne. Married (1) George M'Call, 18 October 1854 (died March 1856), no surviving children; (2) Joseph Prestwich, 26 February 1870 (died 1896). Educated at boarding schools and London girls' schools and privately. Professional experience: assisted uncle Hugh Falconer and husband, Joseph Prestwich; published two novels, popular essays on geology, biographical articles on scientists, biography of Sir Joseph Prestwich. Honors and memberships: Shoreham Nursing Association (1893–1899), secretary. Died 31 August 1899 at Darent-Hulme near London.

Grace Anne Milne was born in Scotland. Her father was a justice of the peace. Her mother's brother, the botanist and paleontologist Hugh Falconer, took an interest in her from a young age. After learning to read at an early age, she went as a school boarder at the age of six. She was said to be able to write down an entire sermon from memory at the age of twelve and also developed excellent drawing skills. As a young prwoman, she carried on a long correspondence with her uncle Hugh Falconer, then head of the Botanic Gardens in Calcutta, India, on the nature of knowledge and evidence. At the age of twenty-two, she married a young lawyer from Glasgow, who died only eighteen months later. Soon after, her only infant died.

To help her recover from her grief, her uncle took her with him on a paleontological and botanical tour of Europe from fall 1858 through June 1859, during which they met the archeologist Boucher de Perthes in Abbeville, France (about whom she later wrote a short biographical article), and various geologists, botanists and anthropologists in Montpellier, Paris, Vesuvius, Palermo, Florence, Rome, and Sicily. During this tour, the young Grace M'Call sketched fossils and geological sections for Falconer. The following year, she traveled again with her uncle, this time with her sister as well, along the Rhone and then to Genoa and Turin, where they met the famous Italian revolutionary and general Garibaldi, and finally to Milan, where she served as her uncle's secretary at the Museum of Natural History, taking notes on a fossil rhinoceros skull. Keeping careful records in a diary, she noted not only the scientists and important political figures and the usual travelers' experiences, but interesting botanical specimens and geological sites they encountered along the way. This proved to be a marvelous education for her future life.

On the return of the party to London, Grace M'Call deeply impressed a close friend of Falconer, the geologist Joseph Prestwich, some twenty years older than she, who at that time worked as a banker while pursuing his geology as an avocation. In early 1865, Falconer died suddenly on a trip with his friend, the scientist George Busk. Almost five years later, Prestwich and Grace M'Call were married and the couple went to live at Darent-Hulme, near Sevenoaks, some miles outside London. Within four years, Prestwich was named professor of geology at Oxford University, and Grace Prestwich began to help her husband prepare his lectures, his scientific papers, and the illustrations for his geological texts. She traveled with Prestwich on his geological excursions in Great Britain as well as through Europe, meeting and talking with many of the same geologists she had met many years before. Grace Prestwich made many friends among the wives of the scientists at Oxford. She also became an active member of the council of the first woman's college at Oxford, Somerville Hall (later Somerville College), named after MARY SOMERVILLE whom she had met in Italy with Falconer and later with her husband.

Grace Prestwich began to publish her own work as well, writing two novels about Scotland that were published anonymously by Macmillan, *The Harbour Bar: A Tale of Scottish Life* (1875) and *Egna* (1880), the first of which attained some popular success. She then wrote a series of popular geological articles published in *Every Girl's Magazine, Good Words,* and *Leisure Hours* between 1879 and 1888. One of these descrbed the parallel roads of Glen Roy about which both her husband and Charles Darwin had written. She also wrote lively recollections of Boucher de Perthes and Mary Somerville. Her husband relinquished his chair at Oxford in 1887 at the age of seventy-five and after that time, the couple lived at their home in Darent-Hulme, often going up to London. During this period, she served as secretary of the Shoreham Nursing Association from 1893 to 1899. Joseph Prestwich was knighted for his contributions to science in 1896, but died soon after, at the age of eighty-four, leaving his wife the task of organizing his papers and writing his biography. *The Life and Letters of Joseph Prestwich* appeared in 1899, but Grace Prestwich became ill and died the same year after a period of illness. Her sister, Louisa E. Milne, collected her popular science essays and biographical sketches into a little volume, *Essays Descriptive and Biographical,* with a biographical memoir of Grace Prestwich's life, which appeared two years after her death. JH/MBO

PRIMARY SOURCES

Prestwich, Lady Grace Milne. *Essays Descriptive and Biographical. With a Memoir by Her Sister, Louisa E. Milne.* Ed. Louisa E. Milne. Edinburgh and London: Wm. Blackwood & Sons, 1901. Includes a portrait of Grace Prestwich. The description of her meetings with Mary Somerville and Boucher de Perthes, as well as her geological sketches, are reprinted in this volume.

———. *Life and Letters of Sir Joseph Prestwich Written and Edited by His Wife.* Edinburgh and London: Wm. Blackwood & Sons, 1901. Includes an account of Hugh Falconer as well.

SECONDARY SOURCES

Milne, Louisa E. "Memoir." In *Essays Descriptive and Biographical, with a Memoir by Her Sister, Louisa E. Milne,* by Lady Grace Milne Prestwich. Edinburgh and London: Wm. Blackwood & Sons, 1901. Some of the letters of Falconer to Grace Prestwich are included here.

STANDARD SOURCES

DNB (under Joseph Prestwich).

PRICE, DOROTHY (1899–?)

U.S. endocrinologist. Born 12 November 1899 in Aurora, Ill. Educated University of Chicago (B.S., 1922; Ph.D. in zoology, 1935). Professional experience: University of Chicago, Department of Zoology, assistant (1923–1935), research associate (1935–1947), assistant professor (1947–1950), associate professor (1950–1958), professor (1958–?). Honors and memberships: Endocrine Society; Society of Naturalists; Association of Anatomists; International Society for Cellular Biology and Endocrinology. Death date unknown.

Dorothy Price was born in Illinois and attended the University of Chicago, where she spent her entire professional career. Although she was a research associate for twelve years after receiving her doctorate, she obtained an assistant professorship in 1947 and rose to full professor eleven years later in 1958. Her research interests in endocrinology included the physiology of reproduction, interaction of hormones and growth, development, and differentiation of mammalian reproductive system. She served as a department editor for *Encyclopedia Britannica* from 1958 and in that same year she edited the studies from a Developmental Biology conference on the dynamics of proliferating tissues held in Upton, New York. JH/MBO

PRIMARY SOURCES

Price, Dorothy. "Normal Development of the Prostate and Seminal Vesicles of the Rat with Study of Experimental Postnatal Modification." *American Journal of Anatomy* 60 (1936): 79–127.

———, (ed.) *Dynamics of Proliferating Tissues.* Chicago: University of Chicago Press, 1958. Published as part of the Developmental Biology conference series.

STANDARD SOURCES

AMS 6–8, B 9, P&B 10–11.

PRICE, DOROTHY (STOPFORD) (1890–1954)

Irish physician. Born 8 September 1890 in Clonskeagh, County Dublin, Ireland, to Jemmeth Stopford and Constance Kennedy Stopford. Two older siblings. Married Liam Price 1925. Educated St. Paul's Girls School, London; Dublin University (M.D., 1921). Professional experience: Meath Hospital; pediatrics; Kilbrittain, County Cork, researcher; private practice, Dublin; St. Ultan's Hospital for Infants, cofounder; Royal City of Dublin Hospital, children's specialist (1932–?); National Bacille Calmette et Guerin Committee, chair (1949–1950). Died 30 January 1954 after a long illness.

Dorothy Stopford was born at Newstead, Clonskeagh, County Dublin, the third child of an accountant. Her mother's father was a physician, and her aunt, Alice Stopford Green, a distinguished historian. When she was twelve, Dorothy's father died, and the family moved to London, where she was educated at St. Paul's Girls School. After graduation, Dorothy worked for some years with the Charity Organisation Society and was involved in the movement for Irish independence. Eventually she applied for admission to Dublin University to study medicine and received a medical degree. She married Liam Price in 1925. Within a few years, Dorothy Price had an active practice in Dublin and was one of the founders of St. Ultan's Hospital for infants.

Working in her specialty of children's medicine, she found she needed to know more about the lethal disease tuberculosis and taught herself German before visiting clinics in Germany, Sweden, and Denmark to learn more. She was introduced to the tuberculin skin test, which enabled physicians to ascertain whether a tuberculous infection had occurred and helped gauge the prevalence of infection in particular groups. In 1932, Price was appointed children's specialist to the Royal City of Dublin Hospital. Alarmed at the number of children infected with tuberculosis at an early age when their resistance was often inadequate to fight off the disease, Price espoused the vaccination method developed in France by A. Calmette and C. Guerin (Bacille Calmette et Guerin, or BCG). In this method, an attenuated tubercle bacillus was used to produce immunity. Price initiated a pioneering vaccination project at St. Ultan's, injecting thirty-five children with BCG in 1936. Her book *Tuberculosis in Childhood* was published in 1942. The success of the St. Ultan project led to Dublin Corporation's BCG scheme of 1948 and Price was named chairperson of the BCG Committee in 1949. Unfortunately, in 1950, Dorothy Price became seriously ill; she died 30 January 1954, too soon to see the dramatic drop in the incidence of lethal tuberculosis in Ireland due in part to widespread BCG vaccination.

JH/MBO

PRIMARY SOURCES

Price, Dorothy. *Tuberculosis in Childhood*. Bristol: Wright, 1942.

SECONDARY SOURCES

Mollan, Charles, William Davis, and Brendan Finucane, eds. *Some People and Places in Irish Science and Technology*. Dublin: Royal Irish Academy, 1985. See pages 70–71.

PRICHARD, MARJORIE MABEL LUCY (1906–)

British physiologist. Born 11 February 1906 in Oxford, England, to Mabel Henrietta (Ross) and Harold Arthur Prichard. Educated St. Anne's College, Oxford (B.A., 1926, M.A., 1928, D.Phil, 1950; D.Sc., 1968). Professional experience: field archeologist and educator (1928–1936); Oxford University, Nuffield Instutute for Medical Research, personal assistant to radiologist (1937–1941), graduate assistant (1941–1955), senior research officer (1955–1968); St. Anne's College, research fellow (1955–?). Honors and memberships: Physiological Society, member; Anatomical Society of Great Britain and Ireland, member.

Marjorie Prichard was born in Oxford and remained there for her educational and professional life. She attended St. Anne's College and after receiving her degree, spent some time doing field archeology and teaching. She became personal assistant to the radiologist at Nuffield Research Institute, which brought her back into science. She began a doctor of philosophy degree at Oxford, and served as a graduate assistant in physiology, continuing in that position for five years after obtaining her degree. During that period she worked on a book detailing fetal circulation, and another on renal circulation.

In 1955, Prichard obtained a position as a senior research fellow in the Nuffield Institute and was made a research fellow of her undergraduate college, St. Anne's. She continued to produce significant articles, studying the circulation in the pituitary gland, and its effects on growth. In her later years, she began to focus on experimental studies of mammary cancer.

JH/MBO

PRIMARY SOURCES

Prichard, Marjorie. With A. E. Barclay and K. J. Franklin. *The Fetal Circulation and Cardiovascular System and the Changes That They Undergo at Birth*. Oxford: Blackwell Scientific Publications, 1944.

———. With others. *Studies of the Renal Circulation*. [Oxford?]: [Blackwell?], 1947.

STANDARD SOURCES

Debus.

PRINCE, HELEN WALTER (DODSON) (1905–)

U.S. astronomer. Born 31 December 1905 in Baltimore, Md. Father [?] Dodson. Married Edmond L. Prince, 1956. Educated Goucher College (B.A., 1927); University of Michigan (M.A., 1932; Ph.D. in astronomy, 1934). Professional experience: University of Maryland, Department of Education, assistant statistician (1927–1931); University of Michigan, Department of Astronomy, assistant (1932–1933); Wellesley College department of astronomy, instructor through assistant professor (1933–1945); Goucher College, associate professor, professor of mathematics and astronomy (1945–1950); University of Michigan, McMath/Hulbert Observatory, astronomer (1949–1957), associate director (1962–1976), associate professor of astronomy (1950–1957), professor of astronomy (1957–1976). Concurrent experience: Maria Mitchell Observatory, Nantucket, summer observer (1934; 1935); Observatoire de Paris, Section d'Astrophysique, Meudon, summer research assistant (1938, 1939); Massachusetts Institute of Technology, Radiation Laboratory, staff member (1943–1945). Honors and memberships: Goucher College (honorary Sc.D., 1952); Annie J. Cannon Prize (1955); University of Michigan Distinguished Achievement Award (1974); American Astronomical Society, Fellow; American Geophysical Union, member.

Helen Walter Dodson was born in Baltimore, Maryland. She went to Goucher College for undergraduate training in mathematics. Immediately upon graduation, she began to use her mathematical skills as an assistant statistician for the Maryland Board of Education. Her interest in astronomy took her to the University of Michigan, where she completed first a master's and then a doctoral degree in the field, completing a thesis on solar flares, focusing on the spectrum of 25 Orionis. In 1933, a year before she completed her dissertation, Dodson began to teach astronomy as an instructor at Wellesley College. She spent two subsequent summers at the Maria Mitchell Observatory on Nantucket Island, and, just before World War II, she spent two more summers outside Paris at the astrophysical observatory connected with the Paris Observatory at Meudon. There she continued her work on solar flares, publishing the results of her six years of observations the following year in the *Astrophysical Journal*.

Dodson remained at Wellesley until the end of the war, working part-time on radar problems at the famous "Rad Lab," the Radiation Laboratory at MIT. In 1945, she took an associate professorship of mathematics and astronomy at her undergraduate college, Goucher, where she remained until 1950. Her growing interest in working at the new McMath/Hulbert Observatory attached to the University of Michigan soon prompted her to move to the university. In the mid-fifties, she published with her long-term colleague E. Ruth Hedeman and with the director and founder of the observa-

tory, Robert R. McMath, on the photometry of solar flares. Around this same time, now in her fifties, she married Edmond Lafayette Prince.

By the early sixties, Dodson (now Prince) had become both full professor of astronomy at the University of Michigan and associate director of the McMath/Hulbert Observatory. She continued working and teaching with great energy, eventually publishing more than one hundred articles on her subject. An important article with Hedeman on the solar mimimum (the years of comparatively quiet solar flares) appeared in *Science*. In 1975, Prince and her colleagues published their studies of solar particle events observed over fifteen years.

Although Prince retired in 1976, she continued until 1979 to be active at the observatory as professor emerita. She had demonstrated her abilities as both astronomer and administrator. She had worked with a number of important astromers, including, for over twenty years, radio astronomer Arthur Covington, based in Canada. In 1952, Goucher College had awarded her an honorary doctorate and in 1955, she received the Annie Jump Cannon Medal from the American Astronomical Society.   JH/MBO

PRIMARY SOURCES

Dodson, Helen W. "The Spectrum of 25 Orionis, 1933–1939." *Astrophysical Journal* 91 (1940): 126. Extends Dodson's observations for her thesis.

———. With E. Ruth Hedeman. "The Frequency and Position of Flares within a Spot Group." *Astrophysical Journal* 110 (1949): 242.

———. With E. Ruth Hedeman and R. R. McMath. "Photometry of Solar Flares." *Astrophysical Journal* supp. 20 (1956): 241–270.

———. With E. R. Hedeman et al. *Catalogue of Solar Particle Events 1955–1969.* Dordrecht, Holland: Reidel, 1975.

STANDARD SOURCES

AMS 6–8; P 9, P&B 10–13; Bailey (under Dodson); Debus; O'Neill; Shearer and Shearer 1997 (article by Rebecca Roberts).

PRINGLE, ELIZABETH WATIES (ALLSTON) (1845–1921)

U.S. horticulturist. Born 29 May 1845 at Canaan Seashore near Paley's Island, S.C., to Adele (Petigru) and Robert Withers Allston. Four siblings surviving childhood. Married John Pringle. Educated by a governess; Madame Acelie Togno's boarding school, Charleston (until 1863). Professional experience: school founded by her widowed mother in Charleston, teacher (1865?); purchased and managed a plantation (the White House plantation); managed

Pringle, Mia Lilly (Kellmer)

Chicora Wood plantation (1896). Died 5 December 1921 at Chicora Wood.

Elizabeth Pringle is an example of a woman forced by circumstances to do a "man's work" who made a success of it. Part of the reason was her willingness to experiment in methods of horticulture and animal husbandry. Born before the Civil War on the Chicora Wood plantation, on the Peedee River in South Carolina to aristocratic parents, Elizabeth learned proper aristocratic codes of behavior. After originally being taught by a governess, she was sent to a boarding school in Charleston. Her father, Robert Withers Allston, was a wealthy plantation owner and had at one time served in the state legislature for twenty-eight years and as governor of South Carolina for two years. In 1863, Union gunboats on the Peedee River convinced Elizabeth's father to transfer his family to another farm eighty miles inland, while he remained at the plantation. The women were forced to care for themselves for the first time in their lives. Robert Allston died in 1864. Although he left each of his children a plantation and one hundred slaves, debt and the emancipation of the slaves left them nothing but the Chicora Wood plantation.

Elizabeth's mother, Adele, founded a school in Charleston after the war and Elizabeth taught there until 1868 when she, her mother, her sister Jane, and her younger brother, Charles, moved back to Chicora Wood. In 1870, she married John Julius Pringle, the owner of the White House plantation. Elizabeth had several reasons to grieve in the later 1870s. She lost an infant son, and her husband died in 1877. At this point, in spite of the skepticism of family and friends, Pringle managed the White House plantation while she lived at Chicora Wood. She experimented with different kinds of crops and kept livestock and poultry. She used an incubator to hatch chicks and she used inoculated alfalfa seed to improve both quality and production. After her mother died, Pringle inherited Chicora Wood and managed it as well. After eighteen years of struggle, taxes, bad weather, and high labor costs finally defeated her efforts. One of her goals was to be a writer, and from 1904 to 1907 the *New York Sun* published excerpts from her diary under the pseudonym Patience Pennington. These excerpts and others were collected to form the book *A Woman Rice Planter* (1913). This book and another, *Chicora Wood,* published after her death, portray graphically the passing of an old way of life.   JH/MBO

PRIMARY SOURCES

Pringle, Elizabeth. *Chronicles of Chicora Wood.* New York: Charles Scribner's Sons, 1922.

———. *A Woman Rice Planter.* Columbia: University of South Carolina Press, 1992.

STANDARD SOURCES

NAW; Shearer and Shearer 1993 (article by Silvia Nichols).

PRINGLE, MIA LILLY (KELLMER) (1920–1983)

British child psychologist. Born 20 June 1920 in Vienna to Sophie Sobel and Samuel Kellmer. One sibling. Married (1) William Joseph Somerville Pringle (1946; he died 1962); (2) William Leonard Hooper (1969). Educated State Humanistic Gymnasium, Vienna (matriculated with distinction); Birbeck College, London (first-class honors; B.A. in psychology, 1944); University of London (Ph.D., 1950); London Child Guidance Training Centre, educational and clinical psychologist (qualified Dip.Ed., 1945). Professional experience: primary school teacher; Hertfordshire, educational psychologist (1945–1950); University of Birmingham, lecturer, senior lecturer, deputy head of the Remedial Education Centre (later the Department of Child Study) (1950–1963); National Children's Bureau, director (1963–1981). Honors and memberships: Commander of the British Empire (1975); Henrietta Szold Award for services to children (1970); honorary doctorates from the universities of Bradford (1972), Aston (1979), and Hull (1982); Manchester Polytechnic, honorary fellow (1972), College of Preceptors (1976), Birbeck College, London (1980). Died February 1983.

Mia Pringle was an educational psychologist and child welfare expert who became the first director of the National Children's Bureau. Born and educated in Vienna, she came to England in 1938. Without an income and speaking very little English when she first arrived with her mother, she supported herself and her mother by teaching primary school while she was attending Birbeck College, London. At Birbeck she took a Dip.Ed. in 1945. She worked as an educational and clinical psychologist for the Hertfordshire Child Guidance Service from 1945 to 1950. During this time, Pringle was working on her doctorate, which she received in 1950 from the University of London. After obtaining her doctorate, she became a lecturer in educational psychology at Birmingham University, advancing to senior lecturer (1960–1963). She was also deputy head of the Department of Child Study (1954–1963).

The position for which she is best known was director of the National Children's Bureau, which she headed until her retirement in 1981. She had four major goals for the bureau: bringing together different professionals concerned with children, publicizing research knowledge about children, improving services for children and pioneering new ones, and carrying out policy-related research about children. The best known, and probably most important, of the bureau's research projects was the National Child Development Study, a longitudinal study of 17,000 children born in 1958.

Pringle was a fine scholar with an interest in detail. She had no time, however, for research that had no practical bearing on a problem. A very effective administrator, she was sometimes authoritarian. Nevertheless, her charm carried her along.

Pringle married twice. Her first husband was an analyical chemist. Seven years after he died, she married William Leonard Hooper, who died in 1980. According to Barbara Tizard in the *DSB*, she sometimes seemed to be deeply depressed. She had no children. In 1983 she committed suicide in her London flat.   JH/MBO

PRIMARY SOURCES
Pringle, Mia Kellmer. *The Emotional and Social Adjustment of Physically Handicapped Children.* London: Information Service of the National Foundation for Educational Research in England and Wales, 1964.
———. *The Challenge of Thalidomide.* N.p.: Harlow, Longmans, 1970.
———. *The Needs of Children: A Personal Perspective.* New York: Schocken Books, 1975.

STANDARD SOURCES
DNB; Europa; WWW, vol. 8.

PRINS, ADA (1879–1977)
Dutch physical and analytical chemist. Born 18 September 1879 in Amsterdam, Netherlands. Educated University of Leiden (ca. 1908). Professional experience: Höheren Bürgerschule and then Lyceum, Der Haag; University of Leiden, privat dozent (lecturer) (1920–1936). Died 20 July 1977 in Leidschendam.

Ada Prins was a Dutch chemist who, like MILDA PRYTZ in Norway, made her name by writing well-accepted textbooks on qualitative chemical analysis and inorganic and organic chemistry. After some thirty-odd years of teaching in high schools and a lyceum, she was appointed privat docent (lecturer) at the University of Leiden.   JH/MBO

PRIMARY SOURCES
Prins, Ada. "Sur la difficulté d'obtenir une idée du méchanisme d'une réaction par la détermination de la vitesse." *Receuil Travaux Chimiques Pays-Bas* 51 (1932): 576–578.
———. *Beknopte leidraad voor de qualitative chemische analyse.* Amsterdam: Scheltiema and Hokema, 1942.
———. With G. P. de Groot. *Leidraad voor de anorganische en organische scheikunde met torpassing in industrie en huishoulding.* Amsterdam: N.p., 1935, 1942, 1947, 1952.

SECONDARY SOURCES
"Ada Prins." *Chemisch Weekblad* 73 (1977): 76. Obituary notice.
Chemisch Weeklt. 78, no. 36 (1977). A group portrait that includes Ada Prins.

Van der Kolkf, M. C. *Seventig Jaar Vrowenstudie.* Rotterdam: N.p., 1959. See page 51.

STANDARD SOURCES
Poggendorff, vol. 7B.

PROCTOR, MARY (1862–?)
U.S. popular writer on astronomy. Born 1862. Published popular books on astronomy 1906–1937. Death date unknown.

Mary Proctor was an American popular writer on astronomy who began to publish a series of books on the solar system in 1906. She included star charts in some of her later books, and outlined the origin of comets, meteors, and shooting stars.   JH/MBO

PRIMARY SOURCES
Proctor, Mary. *Giant Sun and His Family.* New York, Boston: Silver, Burdett and Co., [1906?].
———. *Half-Hours with the Summer Stars.* Chicago: A. C. McClung, 1911.
———. *Evenings with the Stars.* New York and London: Harper & Brothers, 1925.
———. *Our Stars Month by Month.* New York: F. Warne, [1937]. Included star charts in separate folders.
———. *Comets: Their Nature, Origin and Place in the Science of Astronomy.* London: Technical Press, 1937.

STANDARD SOURCES
AMS 1–3; Bailey; Mozans.

PROSKOURIAKOFF, TATIANA (1909–1985)
Russian-born U.S. archeologist. Born 23 January 1909 in Tomsk, Siberia, to Alla (Nekrassova) and Avenir Proskouriakoff. Educated Philadelphia Public Schools; Pennsylvania State University (B.S., 1930). Professional experience: Museum of the University of Pennsylvania, research assistant (1934–1938); field work to Honduras and Yucatan (1939, 1940); Carnegie Institution of Washington, staff member (1940–1958); Harvard University, Peabody Museum of Ethnology, staff member and honorary curator of Mayan art (1958–1977). Honors and memberships: American Anthropological Association Alfred V. Kidder Medal (1962); University of Pennsylvania, honorary doctorate (1971?); Tulane University, honorary doctorate (1972?); Guatemala Order of the Quetzal (1984). Died 1985.

Tatiana Proskouriakoff became renowned for her archeological architectural drawings of Mayan monuments and her successful interpretation of Mayan hieroglyphics. Her work resulted in the first successful dating of Mayan dynasties.

Proskouriakoff's father was a Russian chemist who came with his family to the United States to inspect munitions for the tsar just before the Bolshevik revolution. Her mother had been trained as a physician in Russia, and the two daughters spent their early years in Siberia.

Proskouriakoff grew up in a White Russian community in Philadelphia, and attended the public schools there. She then went to Pennsylvania State University, where she majored in architecture, but found no positions in the field upon graduation. An opportunity at the museum of the University of Pennsylvania opened up for an architecture student to make reconstructions of the Guatemalan Mayan ruins. She began to work with the archeologist Linton Satterthwaite, and soon became an indispensable part of his team. Another colleague, Sylvanus G. Morley at the Carnegie Institution, found funds to send her to a number of Mayan sites in Honduras and the Yucatan, Mexico. The result was a series of unusual perspective drawings that she published in 1950, which made her name.

Attached from the 1950s to the Carnegie Institution of Washington, Proskouriakoff began her studies of the hieroglyphic texts found on Mayan monuments, and succeeded in decoding the pattern of dates and dynasties of the Mayan rulers. Her interpretation changed the understanding of the portraits and hieroglyphics, which were thought to be purely calendrical. She also pointed out that the women depicted represented mothers.

When the Carnegie ceased to fund archeology in the late fifties, Proskouriakoff moved to Harvard's Peabody Museum of Ethnology, where she continued her work on Mayan cities and eventually was named honorary curator of Mayan art. In the early 1970s, she received two honorary degrees, and one year before her death, she was honored with an award from the Guatemalan government, the Order of the Quetzal.

JH/MBO

PRIMARY SOURCES

Proskouriakoff, Tatiana. *An Album of Mayan Architecture.* Washington, D.C.: Carnegie Institution of Washington, 1946.

———. *A Study of Classic Maya Sculpture.* Washington, D.C.: Carnegie Institution, 1950.

———. "Historical Implications of a Pattern of Dates at Piedras Negras, Guatemala." *American Antiquity* 25, no. 4 (1950): 454–474. Her classic study of hieroglyphic texts.

———. "Portraits of Women in Maya Art." In *Essays in Pre-Columbian Art and Archaeology,* 81–99. Cambridge, Mass.: Harvard University Press, 1961.

———. *Jades from the Cenote of Sacrifice, Chichenitza, Yucatan.* Cambridge, Mass.: Peabody Museum of Archaeology and Ethnology Memoirs (vol. 10), 1974. Includes color plates.

———. With Rosemary A. Joyce. *Maya History.* Austin: University of Texas Press, 1993. Published posthumously.

Proskouriakoff's papers are in the Harvard Archives. A scrapbook of drawings, letters, notes, and diplomas is held in Harvard's Tozzer Library.

SECONDARY SOURCES

"Proskouriakoff, Tatiana." *American Antiquity* 55 (1990): 6–11. Obituary notice.

STANDARD SOURCES

Gacs (article by Joyce Marcus).

PRUETTE, LORINE LIVINGSTON (1896–?)

U.S. psychologist. Born 3 November 1896 in Millersburg, Tenn. Educated Chattanooga University (B.S., 1918); Clark University (M.A., 1920); Columbia University (Ph.D., 1924). Professional experience: Brooklyn YMCA, tester (1920–1922); Smith College, instructor (1922–1923); University of Utah, instructor (1923–1924); R. H. Macy Department Store, research psychologist (1925–1926); New York University, lecturer, graduate school (1926–1927); Committee on Social Attitudes, director of research (1928–1929); National Council of Women, consulting psychologist and lecturer (1929–1932), director of study (1932–1933); American Woman's Association, education personnel study (1934–1935); Progressive Education Asociation, consultant to committee on human relations (1936–1938); National Bureau of Economic Research, consultant (1931–1943); Office of War Information, supervisor overseas radio (1943–1945), consulting psychologist (1945–?). Honors and memberships: recipient, Parents Magazine annual medal; associate, American Psychological Association. Death date unknown.

Lorine Pruette first trained as a psychologist at Clark University, where she studied under the well-known psychologist G. Stanley Hall, whose biography she later wrote. During this period, Pruette served briefly as an instructor in psychology at Smith College and at the University of Utah.

Moving to Columbia University in the 1920s for her doctoral work, she focused her study on the lack of appropriate gainful employment for middle-class women. Her dissertation, "Women and Leisure," was subtitled "A Study of Social Waste" and was published in 1924. Her work as a research psychologist at Macy's department store the following year grew out of her study. There is some question whether she was married briefly at this time, since one copy of her Columbia dissertation bears the attribution "Louise Pruette Fryer."

In the thirties, Pruette began to work with national women's organizations and education associations as a consulting psychologist. Her book *The Parent and the Happy Child* came out of this work, joining other parental advice books on this topic. She also took a position with the government

Bureau of Economic Research as a research psychologist researching vocational psychology, a position she held into the first years of World War II.

Pruette's skills proved useful to the Office of War Information, and she began to supervise the overseas radio broadcasts, studying the psychological impact of radio on its listeners. Her interest extended to the psychology of prejudice, an important topic in the post-war period.   K M

PRIMARY SOURCES
Pruette, Lorine. *Women and Leisure: A Study of Social Waste.* New York: E. P. Dutton, 1924. Ph.D. dissertation.
————. *G. Stanley Hall: A Biography of a Mind.* New York: D. Appleton, 1926.
————. *The Parent and the Happy Child.* New York: Holt, 1932.
————. *Women Workers through the Depression: A Study of White Collar Employment.* New York: Macmillan, 1934.

STANDARD SOURCES
AMS 5–8, S&B 9–11.

PRYTZ, MILDA DOROTHEA (1891–1977)
Scottish-Norwegian chemist. Born 1891 in Leith, Scotland. Educated University of Oslo and University of London; University of Oslo (doctorate, 1908). Professional experience: University of Oslo, Chemical Insitute, scientific assistant (1918; 1925–1948), amanuensis (1919–1924), docent (1948–1957).

Milda Dorothea Prytz was educated as a chemist in both London and the Unversity of Oslo, where she obtained her doctorate. Although for many years she was only a scientific assistant and amanuensis at the Chemical Institute of the university, she published regularly in both Norwegian and German scientific journals on polarographic analyses of hydroxamic acids, and on electrolytic reduction of mono- and polyvalent cations. Her textbooks, *Quantitative Analysis* and *Inorganic Chemistry*, went through many editions.   JH/MBO

PRIMARY SOURCES
Prytz, Milda Dorothea. "Electrolytic Reduction of Cations from Transition Elements." *Achiv foer Matematik og Naturvidenskab* 49 (1947): 157–170.
————. "Polarographic Investigation of Oximes as an Indication of the Polarographic Behavior of Hydroxamic Acids." *Acta Chemica Scandinavica* 10 (1956): 451–458.
————. With R. A. Minken. *Pratisk veiledung i kvalitativ analyse.* Oslo: N.p., 1957, 1967.
————. With T. Osterud. *Uorganisk kjemi.* Oslo: N.p., 1946, 1959, 1971.

SECONDARY SOURCES
Osterud, T. "Milda Dorothea Prytz." *Tidsskrift Kjemi, Bergvesen og Metallurgi* 21 (1961): 96. In honor of her seventieth birthday. Includes portrait.

STANDARD SOURCES
Poggendorff, vol. 7B.

PUFFER, ETHEL DENCH (1872–1950)
See Howes, Ethel Dench Puffer.

PULCHERIA, EMPRESS (399–453 c.e.)
Byzantine empress. Born 399. Married Theodesius II. Died 453.

Pulcheria was a Lombard princess who supposedly performed medical miracles.   JH/MBO

SECONDARY SOURCES
Lemoyne, Pierre. *Gallerie of Heroick Women.* Trans. Marquess of Winchester, 1652.
Teetgen, Ada B. *The Life and Times of the Empress Pulcheria, A.D. 399–A.D. 452.* London: S. Sonnenschein, 1907. Discusses her life as empress of the Byzantine court as wife of Theodesius II.

STANDARD SOURCES
Hurd-Mead 1938.

PUTNAM, HELEN CORDELIA (1857–1951)
U.S. physician and health educator. Born 14 Sept 1857 in Stockton (now part of Winona), Minn., to Celintha T. Gates and Herbert Asa Putnam. Educated Vassar College preparatory school; Vassar College (A.B., 1878); Radcliffe College, Sargent School of Physical Training; Women's Medical College of Pennsylvania (M.D., 1889). Professional experience: New England Hospital for Women and Children, Boston (1890–1891); Vassar, director of physical education (1880–1890); medical practice (1892–1935); editor of "Child Hygiene," in Journal of Child Welfare. *Honors and memberships: Western Reserve University, honorary LL.D. degree (1913); Helen Putnam Fellowship for Advanced Research, Radcliffe College, founder (1944); American Medical Association, Fellow. Died 3 February 1951 of an intestinal obstruction and arteriosclerotic heart disease.*

Helen Cordelia Putnam's family were among the early settlers in Minnesota. Her father took charge of iron ore mines for his father, who operated similar mines in New York. Although her early local education was in a one-room schoolhouse, she went on to secondary school at Vassar College preparatory school, and graduated from Vassar College in 1878. She then studied at Radcliffe College, and the Sargent School of Physical Training.

From 1880 until 1890, Putnam held the position as director of Physical Education at Vassar. At the end of this period, she decided to expand her understanding of medicine, and attended the Woman's Medical College of Pennsylvania, where she received a medical degree in 1889. She spent an internship year at the New England Hospital for Women and Children, where MARIE ZAKRZEWSKA was director.

After she received her medical degree, Putnam left Vassar and became concerned with child health. She began to demand cooperation between physicians and schools, claiming that educators should work side by side with physicians and dentists in every school. Even the school janitors, she added, should pass an examination in housewifery. Putnam inaugurated a major conference on infant mortality in 1908. This became her major concern, and she helped to found the American Association for the Study and Prevention of Child Mortality (publishing the journal *Mother and Child*, later renamed *Child Health Bulletin*. Her articles in *Child Welfare Magazine* were collected in her book *School Janitors, Mothers and Health* (1913). She also wrote on school gymnastics and later on the teaching of hygiene and biology in the schools. She also worked with the American pediatrician Abraham Jacobi, widower of MARY PUTNAM JACOBI, to develop the American Child Health Association, and served as editor of "Child Hygiene" for the journal *Child Welfare*. She was awarded an honorary degree from Western Reserve in 1913. A member of the National Council of Playground Associates and National Recreation, a vice-president of American Academy of Medicine, and the U.S. delegate to the International Conference on Tuberculosis and the International Conference on School Hygiene (1907), she also served as delegate to the Second International Conference on Eugenics.

Putnam maintained a private practice in Providence, Rhode Island, for more than forty-three years, emphasizing first infant health and then gynecology. An active woman, she also worked on the home gardening movement taken up by the Rhode Island Horticultural Society. She founded Helen Putnam Fellowship for advanced research at Radcliffe College in 1944. She remained opposed to the idea of separate medical education for women and recommended to MARTHA TRACY the merging of the Woman's Medical College with the University of Pennsylvania in the 1940s. Putnam left money in her will to Western Reserve to honor her former colleague Marie Zakrzewska.　　　JH / MBO

PRIMARY SOURCES

Putnam, Helen Cordelia. *Supervision of School Gymnastics by Medical Specialists.* Providence, R.I.: Snow and Farnham, 1892.

————. "Well Being of Children as Determined by Education of Women." *Rhode Island Medical Society Journal* 4 (1917): 404–405. Proceedings of the Second Pan-American Scientific Congress, 1915–1916.

SECONDARY SOURCES

JAMA 145 (21 April 1951): 1281. Obituary notice.
New York Times, 5 February 1951. Obituary notice.
Providence Sunday Journal, 4 February 1951. Obituary notice.
Thomas, E. K. "Brief sketch of life of Dr. Helen C. Putnam M.D." Rhode Island Medical Society offprint, 1951.

STANDARD SOURCES

DAB, supp. 5; *NAW* unused; *WW* vol. 7, 1928–1929.

PUTNAM, MARIAN CABOT (1893–1972)

U.S. psychiatrist. Born 1893 to Marian (Cabot) Putnam and James Jackson Putnam. Never married. Educated Johns Hopkins Medical School (M.D., 1921); Children's Hospital (Boston) (1923–1925); Henry Phipps Psychiatric Clinic, Johns Hopkins, intern (1925–1927). Professional experience: Yale Clinic of Child Development, research associate (1927–1930); Yale School of Medicine, assistant professor of medicine (1930–1940); Baker Guidance Clinic, psychiatrist (1940–1941); The Children's Center (later the James Jackson Putnam Children's Center), psychiatrist, later codirector and president of trustees (1941–1970). Died 1972.

Marian Putnam was a daughter of James Jackson Putnam, the psychiatrist and neurologist based in Boston, Massachusetts. He was an admirer and close friend of William James, Morton Prince, and others, corresponding extensively with Sigmund Freud. As a young girl, Putnam traveled with her father to Europe and met Freud, Jung, Ernest Jones, and other members of the Psychoanalytic Congresses. She was educated at Johns Hopkins Medical School, where she received her medical degree in 1921. She then studied at the Children's Hospital (Boston) and served as an intern at Henry Phipps Psychiatric Clinic at Johns Hopkins. In the late twenties she spent three years studying under Arnold Gesell at the Yale Clinic of Child Development.

In 1930, Putnam was named assistant professor of medicine at Yale School of Medicine, a position she held for ten years. She returned to Boston to work at the Baker Guidance Clinic and then became associated with the newly created Children's Center (later the James Jackson Putnam Children's Center), where she spent the rest of her active life serving as its codirector and as trustee. She died in 1972 and left her papers and some of her father's papers to the Countway Library, Harvard Medical School.　　　JH / MBO

PRIMARY SOURCES

Putnam, Marian Cabot. With Bronson Crother. "Cord Birth Injuries." Part 2 of *Birth Injuries of the Central Nervous System*, ed. Frank Rudolph Ford. Baltimore: Williams and Wilkins, 1927.

SECONDARY SOURCES

A short biography appears in the finding guide to her papers, which include her correspondence with Anna Freud, at Countway Library, Harvard Medical School.

PUTNAM, MARY LOUISE (DUNCAN) (1832–1903)

U.S. scientific philanthropist. Member of Davenport (Iowa) Academy of Natural Sciences. Born 1832. Father [?] Duncan was second governor of Illinois. Married Charles E. Putnam. One son (?). Professional experience: Davenport (Iowa) Academy of Natural Sciences, founder, supporter, and administrator; president (1879). Died 1903.

Mary Louise Duncan Putnam was an early member of the Davenport Academy of Natural Sciences, whose president at the time was the botanist Charles Christopher Pratt. She was the first woman member elected, at the insistence of her thirteen-year-old son, J. Duncan Putnam, who later became an entomologist. Her support of the society was primarily financial and administrative. She organized a woman's society to publish the *Proceedings*, arranged for the rental and furnishing of an additional room, and obtained financial support to purchase a lot on which the society stood. Her son became secretary of the society at age fifteen, although his developing tuberculosis made it impossible for him to attend Harvard University as he had intended. Instead, he studied extensively and became the major authority on the invertebrate genus *Galeodes* (part of the family Solpugidae), a group related to spiders and scorpions.

Mary Putnam became president of the society in 1879. Her son, although fatally ill, was elected president in 1881 at the age of twenty-five. After his death at the end of that year, she found additional funds to support the *Proceedings*, the second volume of which came out as a memorial volume to him. She then donated to the society her son's entomological collection, consisting of twenty-five thousand specimens representing eight thousand species, along with his scientific library. Her husband, Charles E. Putnam, was named president of the society from 1885 to 1886. Upon the death of her husband, she encouraged philanthropist Mary P. Bull to set up a memorial in the name of J. Duncan and Charles E. Putnam as a permanent publication fund in 1895. When she died some seven years later, she was noticed in the journal *Science*.   JH/MBO

SECONDARY SOURCES

Science 17 (1903): 399: 622–623. Obituary notice.
Starr, Frederick. "Davenport Academy of Natural Sciences." *Popular Science Monthly* 51 (1897): 83–98. Includes a portrait.

STANDARD SOURCES

Barr.

PYE, EDITH MARY (1876–1965)

British midwife and international relief organizer. Born 20 October 1876 to Margaret Thompson and William Arthur Pye. Never married. Educated as nurse and midwife. Professional experience: London, superintendent of district nurses; Quaker Society, relief work; Hospital Chalons, founder. Honors and memberships: Legion d'Honneur; Women's International League; Friends' Service Council France and Switzerland Committee; German Emergency Committee, chair and vice-chair. Died 1965.

Daughter of a wine merchant and niece of an eminent surgeon, Edith Pye trained as a midwife and a nurse. She is best remembered for the Quaker Society relief work done after she became a member of the Society of Friends in 1908. Her friend Hilda Clark organized the Friends War Victims Relief in 1914 and together they devised an international scheme to supply milk to millions starving in Vienna. In France, they organized a maternity hospital within the war zone itself and helped women and children war victims. The hospital was permanently established in Chalons after the war. Pye was awarded the Legion d'Honneur for her work. She continued relief work in the Ruhr in 1923 and in China, associated with the Women's International League.

Pye organized the Friends' work in Spain during the Spanish Civil War and was involved with the International Commission for the Assistance of Child Refugees and in the Women's International League for Peace and Freedom. She argued for the partial lifting of the Allied blockade during World War II so that food and medical supplies could be sent to the starving in Europe. A leading member of the Famine Relief Committee, she lobbied the Ministry of Economic Warfare for compassionate aid. She worked in France and Greece between 1941 and 1955 and continued her efforts for peace and war relief until she was quite old.   JH/MBO

PRIMARY SOURCES

Pye, Edith. *Infant Welfare Work in Austria*. N.p., 1921.
———. *Feeding Spain's Children*. London: Friends Service Committee, [1936?].
———, comp. *Food Conditions in Europe*. London: Family Relief Committee, 1942.
———. With Dingle M. Foot and Roy Walter. *Food Relief for Occupied Europe*. London: National Peace Council, 1942.

Clark, Hilda. *War and Its Aftermath: Letters from France, Austria, and the Near East, 1914–1924*. [Well, Somerset, England]: printed by Clare, 1956.

STANDARD SOURCES
DNB Missing Persons; Uglow 1982.

PYTHIAS OF ASSOS (fl. 330 B.C.E.)
Greek biologist and embryologist. Married Aristotle.

Pythias, the wife of Aristotle, supposedly worked with him on an encyclopedia from the material they gathered on their honeymoon on Mytilene. She is reputed to have collected specimens of all sorts of living things. Hurd-Mead suggests that they collaborated in the study of generation. Of course, her name is not on *De generatione animalium* or the *Historia animalium*.

JH/MBO

STANDARD SOURCES
Hurd-Mead 1938.

QUEIROZ, CARLOTTA PEREIRA DE (1892–?)

See Pereira de Queiroz, Carlotta.

QUIGGLE, DOROTHY (1903–)

U.S. chemist and chemical engineer. Born 21 August 1903. Educated Massachusetts Institute of Technology (B.S., 1926; M.S., 1927); Pennsylvania State College (Ph.D., 1936). Professional experience: MIT, assistant in applied chemistry (1927–1929); Pennsylvania State College, Petroleum Research Laboratory (1929–1935), chemical engineering instructor (1935–1937), assistant professor (1937–1939), associate professor (1939–1949), associate research professor, chemistry and chemical engineering (1949–1953), research professor (1953–?).

Dorothy Quiggle earned her bachelor's and masters of science degrees from MIT and her doctorate from Pennsylvania State College. She spent her academic career at Penn State, except for civilian work during World War II with the Office of Scientific Research and Development. Her research was important for the war effort. It dealt with catalysis, high-pressure reactions, petroleum refining technology, fractionation, composition and knock-rating of gasoline, cracking of oils and gases, oxidation of hydrocarbons, and selective absorbents for gases. JH/MBO

PRIMARY SOURCES
Quiggle, Dorothy. "Oxidation of Synthetic Rubber." B.S. thesis, Massachusetts Institute of Technology, [1926].
———. "Catalytic Decomposition of Methanol by Zinc Oxide and Copper." M.S. thesis, Massachusetts Institute of Technology, 1927.

STANDARD SOURCES
AMS 6–8, P 9, P&B 10–12.

QUIMBY, EDITH SMAW (HINCKLEY) (1891–1982)

U.S. biophysicist. Born 10 July 1891 in Rockville, Ill., to Harriet and Arthur Hinckley. Married Shirley Quimby (1915). Educated Boise High School; Whitman College, Walla Walla, Wash. (B.S., 1912); University of California, Berkeley (M.A., 1917). Professional experience: Memorial Hospital for Cancer and Allied Diseases, N.Y.C., physician (1919–1942); Cornell University Medical College, assistant professor (1941–1942); Columbia University, College of Physicians and Surgeons, associate professor (1943–1954), professor (1954–1961), professor emerita (1961–1978). Honors and memberships: American Radium Society, Janeway Medal (1940); Radiological Society of North America, gold medal (1941); International Women's Exposition, Scientific Achievement Medal (1947); Lord and Taylor, American Design Award (1949); Indian Radiological Society, Jagadish Bose Memorial Gold Medal (1952); American Cancer Society, medal (1957); Memorial Hospital for Cancer and Allied Diseases, Judd Award (1962); American College of Radiology, gold medal (1963); American Medical Association, Scientific Achievement Award (1973); Radiological and Medical Physics Society, Distinguished Service Award (1976); American Association of Physicists in Medicine. Died 11 October 1982 in New York.

Child of a peripatetic architect and farmer, Edith Hinckley was born in Rockford, Illinois, and then moved to Alabama, Idaho, and finally to California. She was encouraged by her father and inspired by a high school teacher to study science. She earned a four-year scholarship to Whitman College, where she majored in mathematics/physics, the first woman at Whitman to take this particular major. After graduation, Hinckley took a position teaching chemistry and physics in Nyssa, Oregon. She received a teaching fellowship in physics at the University of California, Berkeley, where she earned her highest degree, a master's. At Berkeley, she met her future husband, Shirley L. Quimby, who was also a physics graduate student. After they married, they moved to Antioch, California, where Shirley taught science and Edith appeared satisfied with housewifely chores. Shirley joined the navy during World War I, and while he was gone she took over his position teaching science at the high school. Shirley remained in the military for an additional year working on submarine detection, and Edith followed him to Connecticut. After her husband was discharged from the navy, he began to work on his doctoral degree at Columbia. In order to support them, Edith went back to work in 1919 as an assistant physicist to Giocchino Failla, chief physicist at the New York City Memorial Hospital for Cancer and Allied Diseases. Quimby got in on the ground floor of medical radiation physics. She conducted studies on both living patients and cadavers to measure the amount of radiation piercing various parts of the body, so that appropriate doses of radiation could be given to patients without damaging healthy body parts. She worked in the area of radiotherapy, writing fifty technical articles in this field. She received many honors, including the Janeway Medal, the highest honor of the American Radium Society. She recieved honorary degrees from Whitman College and from Rutgers University.

Quimby was offered a position as assistant professor of radiology at the Cornell University Medical College and then went to the College of Physicians and Surgeons at Columbia University. It was very unusual for a teacher without a doctoral degree to be a respected teacher at a medical school of graduate physicians. During World War II, Quimby did research for the Manhattan Project, which involved learning about radioactive isotopes. From her research, recommendations emerged for the safe handling of isotopes and the safe disposal of radioactive wastes. She also became an expert in procedures for cleaning up radioactive spills. This work resulted in a position on the Atomic Energy Commission's Committee for the Control and Distribution of Radioactive Isotopes and the National Committee for Radiation Protection. In 1954, she was made full professor at Columbia. Quimby's total output was impressive; she published over seventy articles and four books. Her work did much to establish the field of radiation physics.

Quimby's nonprofessional interests included sports, theater, bridge, cooking, traveling, and reading detective stories. She was a member of the Democratic Party and the League of Women Voters.

JH/MBO

PRIMARY SOURCES

Quimby, Edith Smaw Quimby. With G. Failla and A. Dean. "Some Problems of Radiation Therapy." *American Journal of Roentgenology* 9 (1922): 479–497.

———. "A Method for the Study of Scattered and Secondary Radiation in X-Ray and Radium Laboratories." *Radiology* 7 (1926): 211–217.

———. With G. Failla, F. Adair, et al. "Dosage Study Relative to the Therapeutic Use of Unfiltered Radon." *American Journal of Roentgenology and Radium Therapy* 15 (1926): 621–625.

———. "Measurement of Tissue Dosage in Radiation Therapy." *Radiology* 32 (1939): 593–590.

———. With B. C. Smith. "The Use of Radioactive Sodium as a Tracer in the Study of Peripheral Vascular Disease." *Radiology* 45 (1945): 335–346.

———. With S. C. Werner and C. Schmidt. "Influence of Age, Sex, and Season upon Radioiodine Uptake by the Human Thyroid." *Proceedings of the Society for Experimental Biology and Medicine* 75 (1950): 537–540.

———. With H. Speert and S. C. Werner. "Radioiodine Uptake by the Fetal Mouse Thyroid and Resultant Effects in Later Life." *Surgery, Gynecology and Obstetrics* 93 (1951): 230–242.

———. With S. C. Werner and B. Coelho. "Ten Year Results of I-131 Therapy of Hyperthyroidism." *Bulletin of the New York Academy of Medicine* 33 (1957): 783–806.

———. With E. Hiza. "Evaluation of the Resin Uptake of I-131 Triiodothyronine as a Test for Thyroid Function." *Journal of Nuclear Medicine* 5 (1964): 489–499.

SECONDARY SOURCES

Emberlin, Diane. *Contributions of Women: Science.* Minneapolis: Dillon Press, 1977.

Noble, Iris. *Contemporary Women Scientists of America.* New York: Julian Messner, 1979.

STANDARD SOURCES

AMS 5–8, P 9, P&B 10–12; *Annual Obituaries,* 1982; *Current Biography,* 1949; Debus; Grinstein 1997 (article by Margaret Ott); *LKW; Notable;* Rossiter 1982; Shearer and Shearer 1996.

QUIRK, AGNES (fl. 1920s)

U.S. plant pathologist. Professional experience: United States Department of Agriculture, Bureau of Plant Industry, assistant to senior plant pathologist (1901–1927?), head of laboratory (1928?–1948?) Death date unknown.

Agnes Quirk was hired by Dr. B. T. Galloway, chief of the Bureau of Plant Industry. There she became an assistant to Erwin Frink Smith, who was proud of his record of appointing women to work at the Department of Agriculture. The first woman that he appointed was Effie A. Southworth (later EFFIE SOUTHWORTH SPALDING). After Southworth's appointment, many others followed, including Quirk. Although Quirk had not been prepared for this work as a student, Smith recognized her abilities and prescribed a course of reading and study. Quirk remained at the bureau until retirement, and for many years was head of one of its main laboratories.

Among many research papers, Quirk published studies with Smith on hydrogen ion concentration of crown gall fluids versus normal juice of sugar beet and sunflower. With another woman, E. H. Fawcett, she published on the hydrogen-ion concentration of culture media as compared with Fuller scale readings. In this paper they considered the approximate ranges of growth (acid-alkaline) of more than twenty-four bacteria pathogenic to plants. Another publication that resulted from her work with Smith was on *Begonia lucerna.* They were attempting to determine why *Bacterium tumefaciens,* which produced tumors in many plants, did not do so in begonias. The paper that resulted from this study was published in 1926: "A Begonia Immune to Crowngall: With Observations on other Immune or Semi-immune Plants." It seemed that the plants that contained oxalic acid were resistant to crowngall inoculations. These studies are samples of what a woman who was not especially educated in phytopathology could do when placed in a supportive environment.   JH/MBO

PRIMARY SOURCES

Quirk, Agnes. With Edna H. Fawcett. "Hydrogen-Ion Concentration vs. Titratable Acidity in Culture Mediums." *Journal of Infectious Diseases* 33, no. 1 (July 1923): 4.
———. With Erwin Frink Smith. "Hydrogen-Ion Content and Total Acidity in Crown-Gall Tumors." *Journal of Cancer Research* 8 (1924): 525–516; 537 ff.
———. With Nellie A. Brown. "Influence of Bacteriophage on *Bacterium tumefaciens,* and Some Potential Studies of Filtrates." *Journal of Agricultural Research* 39, no. 7 (1929): 503–530. Considers the work of F. D'Hérelle on the bacteriophage.

SECONDARY SOURCES

Baker, Gladys. "Women in the United States Department of Agriculture." *Agricultural History* 50 (1976):190–201.
Rodgers, Andrew Denny. *Erwin Frink Smith: A Story of North American Plant Pathology.* Memoirs of the American Philosophical Society, 31. Philadelphia: American Philosophical Society, 1952.

STANDARD SOURCES

Rossiter 1982 (includes portrait).

QUIROGA, MARGARITA DELGADO DE SOLIS (fl. 1926–1957)

See Solis Quiroga, Margarita Delgado de.

R

RABINOFF, SOPHIE (1889–1957)

Russian-born U.S. public health physician. Born 19 May 1889 in Mogileff, Russia, to Rose (Horwitz) and Louis Rabinoff. Came to N.Y.C. as infant (1889). Educated public schools New York; Hunter College (1906–1908); Woman's Medical College, Philadelphia (M.D., 1913); Columbia University, DeLamar Institute Public Health (M.S.P.H., 1945); Diplomate in Preventive Medicine and Public Health. Professional experience: Beth Israel Hospital, New York, first woman intern (1913), resident in pediatrics (1914–1917); pediatric clinic Mount Sinai Hospital, physician (1925–1934); New York Infirmary for Women and Children, cardiologist (1930); Union Health Center, physician; New York City Department of Health, part-time pediatrician (1919–1934); New York Medical College, clinical instructor in public health (1939), professor of public health and preventive medicine, director (1941–1956). Died 2 October 1957 in New York City.

Sophie Rabinoff came to New York City as an infant in 1889 with her parents who had emigrated from Russia. Educated in New York public schools and then at Hunter College, she went on to the Woman's Medical College of Pennsylvania, obtaining her medical degree in 1913. She was the first woman intern at Beth Israel Hospital in New York and went on to become a resident in pediatrics. While she was associated with Alfred F. Hess she did important research on rickets and scurvy. She worked on the first large-scale project on the use of diptheria toxin, antitoxin, and toxoid from 1918 to 1919. She joined the American Zionist Medical unit in Palestine serving with British forces, where she helped to organize hospitals and clinics for Arab and Jewish children.

On her return to New York City, she maintained a private medical practice, specializing in pediatrics, from 1919–1934, she also ran the pediatric clinic at Mount Sinai Hospital and, for a period of time in the 1930s, was the cardiologist for the New York Infirmary for Women and Children. She began in the thirties to work with the New York City Department of Public Health first part time and then full time. In 1934 she began to organize health center programs on the Lower East and Lower West Side. She was health officer for the East Harlem Health District in 1938 and six years later in the Bronx where she instituted chest X-rays for visitors to Bronx Park.

In 1939, she taught as a clinical instructor in Public Health for the New York Medical College. Rabinoff extended her qualifications to include a master's degree in public health from Columbia University in 1945, and then progressed to professor of public health and preventive medicine, finally retiring as director in 1956. Politically liberal, she continued after retirement to be active on the East Harlem Council for Community Planning and Public Health Committee of New York County Medical Society. She led the campaign to reduce infant mortality in East Harlem (1946) for the New York Department of Public Health. Rabinoff also raised money for various Jewish philanthropies.

Rabinoff received many honors and awards, including the Achievement Award of the Alumnae Association of the Woman's Medical College, Philadelphia. She was a Diplomate of the American Board of Preventive Medicine and Public Health and a member of many other local and national medical associations. JH/MBO

PRIMARY SOURCES

Rabinoff, Sophie. "Prophylactic Vaccination for Varicella." *Archives of Pediatrics* 34 (April 1918).

———. "Nutrition Problems in Community Health Programs." *Medical Women's Journal* 46 (May 1939).

———. "Progress in Public Health in the Last Half Century." *Journal of the Americal Medical Women's Association* 10 (February 1955).

———. With others. "Development of a Family Health Teaching Program." *New York State Medical Journal* (December 1957).

SECONDARY SOURCES

Knapp, Sally. *Women Doctors Today.* New York: Crowell, [1947].

Lovejoy, Esther Clayson Pohl. *Women Physicians and Surgeons: National and International Organizations.* Livingston, N.Y.: Livingston Press, 1939.

STANDARD SOURCES

NAW unused; *NCAB.*

RABINOVITCH-KEMPNER, LYDIA (1871–1935)

Lithuanian/German bacteriologist. Born 22 August 1871 in Kaunas, Lithuania. Married Walter Kempner (ca. 1901). At least one son, Walter (b. 1903). Professional experience: Woman's Medical College of Pennsylvania, presided over the first bacteriologic laboratory (1896–1898); Berlin University–Moabit Hospital, director of bacteriology; University of Berlin, associate professor of pathology (1898). Died 3 August 1935 in Berlin.

Born in Lithuania, Lydia Rabinovitch-Kempner received her education in Berlin with Robert Koch, with whom she studied bacteriology. Lydia Rabinovitch came to the United States, where she established the first bacteriology laboratory at the Woman's Medical College of Pennsylvania. Soon after she returned to Germany, she married Walter Kempner, with whom she had at least one child. She became associate professor of pathology and director of the bacteriological department of Berlin University-Moabit Hospital. She was the first woman to receive Prussian professorial rank. She was a colleague of the pioneering bacteriologist, Robert Koch, who discovered, among other other things, the transmission of bubonic plague. She worked with Koch until his death in 1910. Her research included work on plague, human and animal tuberculosis, sleeping sickness, and other parasitic diseases. After her death her son, a physician and physiologist, emigrated to the United States to Duke Medical Center.

JH/MBO

PRIMARY SOURCES

Rabinovitch, Lydia. *Beiträge zur Entwickelungsgeschichte der Fruchtkörper einiger Gastromyceten.* Munich: Val. Höfling, 1894.

SECONDARY SOURCES

Alsop, Gulielma Fell. *History of the Woman's Medical College, Philadelphia, Pennsylvania, 1850–1950.* Philadelphia: Lippincott, [1950].

STANDARD SOURCES

Debus; Hurd-Mead 1933; Ireland.

RADEGONDE (ca. 520–587)

French/German physician. Princess of Thuringia. At least one brother. Married Clotaire (497–561), son of Clovis I. Fled to convent in Poitiers (542). Professional experience: built hospital and cared for sick (550). Died 587 in Poitiers.

One of three sixth-century medical queens, Radegonde was the fifth living wife of Clotaire, the son of Clovis I. Clotaire seized her against her will and married her in a fight to unite his father's kingdom, Burgundy, with Thuringia. She had her own palace where she collected those who were ill, studied their diseases, and prescribed treatment for them. She depended at first on the court's learned men as her teachers, but she soon became skilled in diagnosis herself. Her husband, angered that she was as cold to him as she was warm to her patients, killed her brother. She fled to a convent in Poitiers founded by a friend, Cesaria, where she later became abbess. She sold all her jewels and built a hospital where she cared for the sick and trained two hundred nurses to follow her example. At the hospital, they set bones, dressed wounds, prepared remedies, and made bandages. Whatever spare time they had was spent in copying manuscripts. Apparently Clotaire's anger dissipated, for her husband saw to it that she always had what she needed for the hospital. Rich women also contributed to its support.

JH/MBO

SECONDARY SOURCES

Kavanagh, Julia. *The Women of Christianity.* London: Smith, Elder, 1852.

STANDARD SOURCES

Hurd-Mead 1938.

RADNITZ, GERTY (1896–1957)

See Cori, Gerty Theresa Radnitz.

RAFATDJAH, SAFIEH (1903–)

Iranian physician. Born 26 June 1903 in Moscow of Iranian parents. Four siblings. Married. Two children. Educated public school, Moscow; Moscow University (medical degree). Professional experience: south of Russia, physician; Tehran, physician (1932); health department (20 years); Medical Women's Association, assistant to Dr. Kia and treasurer.

Safieh Rafatdjah had a peripatetic career. Although specific dates for her various moves are not available, the general pattern of her career shows her to be an excellent example of what happens to a woman's career when she marries a strong-minded man. Born in Moscow of Iranian parents, her father was a professor. He became a linguist after graduating from the university in Alexandria, and ended up in Moscow. Safieh learned to read Persian when she was five years old, and then mastered Russian, German, and French. Her pleasant childhood was disrupted by the Russian Revolution. Although she had passed her matriculation examination, she went to work as a typist as soon as she received her certificate. The family moved to Vienna in 1921, but, as a foreigner, her father was unable to get work. Consequently, the family returned to Moscow, where Safieh studied for her entrance examination for medical school. During her first year at medical school, she fell in love with a Polish engineering student, but did not accept his proposal of marriage because it would have meant breaking with her family for good. She later married an Iranian diplomat who agreed to allow her to finish her medical studies at the university. She became pregnant during her second year at medical school and had an abortion.

After Rafatdjah received her medical degree, she joined her husband, who had been appointed consul in a town in southern Russia. Here she began practicing medicine. Again, she became pregnant; this time she carried a little girl to term. She began minor surgery on her own. However, her husband was ordered to close the consulate and to leave immediately for Tehran. While her husband went to Tehran, she went to Russia to live with her parents. Rafatdjah's husband was unable to get a position in Russia so she and her daughter went to live in Iran for the first time; there she gave birth to a boy. In Tehran, she practiced medicine until her husband got another appointment—this time in Iraq. After two years there, they returned to Tehran. Shortly thereafter, he was appointed consul-general to India, where the family moved for five years. During this time, Rafatdjah's main exposure to medicine was reading medical journals. They returned to Iran at the beginning of World War II. In Iran, she began to practice medicine again, working in a maternity hospital and running a private practice. Her young son became ill with a condition called Meckel's diverticulum, and the operation that might have saved his life was unsuccessful. After his death and after the marriage of her daughter, Rafatdjah worked for twenty years in the national health department. After the formation of the Medical Women's Association in Iran, she became its secretary and later treasurer. After becoming a trustee for her younger brother's estate, she was charged with donating the money to a charitable cause. She decided to build a clinic and to donate it to the Medical Women's Association.

In her later years, Rafatdjah suffered from glaucoma, losing the sight in one eye. During her career, she recognized the great need for women physicians in Iran and did what she could to remedy the situation. She noted that the nature of her husband's profession stifled her work in the career that she loved.

KM

PRIMARY SOURCES
Rafatdjah, Safieh. In Hellstedt, *Autobiographies.*

STANDARD SOURCES
Ireland.

RAGINS, IDA (1894–?)
See Kraus Ragins, Ida.

RAISIN, CATHERINE ALICE (1855–1945)
British igneous and sedimentary petrologist and botanist. Born 24 April 1855 in Camden, New Town, London. Father a pannierman at the Inner Temple. Never married. Educated North London Collegiate School and University College, London (entered 1873; B.Sc., 1884; D.Sc., 1898). Professional experience: Botany Department, Bedford College for Women, head (1890–1920). Died 12 July 1945 in Cheltenham.

Catherine Raisin was born in Camden, New Town, to a father who was a pannierman at the Inner Temple. At University College she attended lectures on geology and mineralogy, the first woman to do so. She left the college for a short time and undertook club work. She also studied botany and zoology and earned a special certificate in botany in 1877, a year before degrees were open to women. In 1878, London University degrees were opened to women, and in 1879 she passed the intermediate examination and returned to University College to work toward a degree. She attended Professor Bonney's lectures as well as T. H. Huxley's lectures on zoology at the Royal School of Mines. She was the first woman to study geology at University College, the second woman to be awarded the London doctor of science in geology, the first woman to receive an award from the Geological Society of London (1893), and one of the first women to be admitted to this society (1919).

Known for her teaching, Raisin was an important mentor to the next generation of British women geologists, including DORIS LIVESEY REYNOLDS. She supervised her teaching assistants carefully. Raisin was a physically strong, psychologically powerful, and somewhat intimidating woman who was considered eccentric by her colleagues and students (they nicknamed her "the Raisin" and called her "the Sultana" behind her back). She did not tolerate "unauthorised perambulation" in the geology department. However, she was kind and helpful to her students. Raisin died at the age of ninety at Cheltenham.

Most of Raisin's geological research was in microscopic petrology and mineralogy. Raisin published twenty-four papers between 1887 and 1905, including collaborative works with Bonney. The majority of these papers were published in three journals: the *Quarterly Journal of the Geological Society; Geological Magazine;* and the *Proceedings of the Geologists' Association.* She studied chert and its microstructures, serpentines, spilites from Jersey and other rocks from Wales, Switzerland, Belgium, Africa, and the Karakorum Himalayas. She was especially interested in the microscopic structure of serpentines, and published an important collaborative paper on the subject with Bonney.   JH/MBO

PRIMARY SOURCES

Raisin, Catherine Alice. "On the Nature and Origin of the Rauenthal Serpentine." *Quarterly Journal of the Geological Society* 53 (1897): 246–268.

———. "Petrological Notes on Rocks from Southern Abyssinia (Collected by Dr. R. Kottlitz)." *Quarterly Journal of the Geological Society of London* 59 (1903): 292–306.

———. With T. G. Bonney. "The Microscopic Structure of Minerals Forming Serpentine and Their Relation to Its History." *Quarterly Journal of the Geological Society of London* 61 (1905).

SECONDARY SOURCES

[Garwood, Edmund J.]. "Dr. Catherine Raisin." *Proceedings of the Geological Society of London* (1946): xliv–xlv.

[Hawkes, Leonard]. "Catherine Alice Raisin, D.Sc., F.G.S." *Proceedings of the Geologists' Association* 57, no. 1 (1946): 53–54.

Reynolds, Doris L. "Catherine Alice Raisin." *Nature* 156, no. 3959 (1945): 327–328.

Spencer, Leonard J. "Raisin, Catherine Alice (1855–1945)." In "Biographical Notices of Mineralogists Recently Deceased" (eighth series)," 216. *Mineralogical Magazine* 28, no. 199 (1947): 175–229.

STANDARD SOURCES

Creese and Creese; *DNB Missing Persons;* Sarjeant.

RAMART-LUCAS, PAULINE (1880–1953)

French chemist. Born 22 November 1880 in Paris. Father: (?) Lucas. Educated University of Paris, Sorbonne (licence, 1909; doctorate in sciences, 1913). Professional experience: University of Paris, Sorbonne; laboratory manager (1918?–1925); lecturer (1925–1930); professor (1930–1953). Honors and memberships: Legion of Honor, Knight (1928), Officer (1938), Commander (1953); Ellen Swallow Richards Research Prize of the American Association

of University Women (1928); Consultative Assembly, vice-president of the educational section (1944–?); Palais de la découverte, National Science Museum, and the École de physique et de chimie. Died 13 March 1953.

Pauline Ramart was from a poor family in Paris. In order to study for her baccalaureate, she made artificial flowers during the daytime and took courses in the evening. Working close to the Sorbonne, she resolved to attend the university. In order to prepare herself, she took evening courses and obtained the equivalent of a secondary-school diploma. When she was twenty-nine years old, she completed the *licence* in physical sciences. Recognized as a brilliant scientist, she went on to obtain a doctoral degree in organic chemistry at the University of Paris, Sorbonne.

After working in the laboratory of Albin Haller for her degree, she left academia for a short time during World War I to work in radiology. Haller called her back to his laboratory; with the exception of the years between 1941 and 1944, she spent her entire career working at the Sorbonne. As a woman, she encountered prejudice, but eventually she became the second woman (after MARIE CURIE) to become a full professor at the University of Paris.

Her career was divided into two parts. During the first part, from 1908 to 1924, she concentrated on the molecular changes that occur when alcohols are dehydrated. She successfully accomplished the synthesis of alcohol following her research on molecular transpositions accompanying alcohol dehydration. During the second part of her career, she studied the relationships between structure, chemical reactivity, and the spectrum of ultraviolet and visible absorption in organic compounds, publishing more than one hundred memoirs and scientific notes.

Ramart-Lucas never married. Her work was her life; her students and colleagues were her family. She was the recipient of numerous honors.   JH/MBO

PRIMARY SOURCES

Ramart-Lucas, Pauline. With M. Haller and M. Bauer. "Action de l'amidure de sodium sur cétones aromatiques et mixtes." *Bulletin de la Société chimique de France* 4, no. 3 (1908): 1155.

———. "Déshydratation du pseudobutyldiphénylcarbinols." *Comptes rendus l'academie des sciences* 153 (1911): 1771.

———. "Contribution à l'étude de l'action des organomagnésiens sur les trialcoylacétophénones." *Annales de chimie,* 8th ser., 30 (1913): 349.

———. With M. Haller. "Synthèses au moyen de l'amidure de sodium. Préparation des ò-aminocétones des 2-phényl-3–3.3 dialcoyltétrahydropyridines." *Annales de chimie,* 9th ser., 8 (1917): 5.

———. "Transpositions moléculaires dans la série du pseudobutyldiphénylcarbinol." *Comptes rendus l'academie des sciences* 176 (1923): 684.

———. "Transpositions moléculaires, préparation et déshydratation du triphényl-1, 1, 3 diméthyl-2,2 propanol-1. *Comptes rendus l'academie des sciences* 179 (1924): 276.

———. "Sur le mécanisme des transpositions moléculaires I." *Comptes rendus l'academie des sciences* 185 (1927): 561.

———. "Sur le mécanisme des transpositions moléculaires II." *Comptes rendus l'academie des sciences* 185 (1927): 718.

———. With M. Hoch. "Stabilité comparée des isoméres éthyléniques etnsynthèses par l'ultraviolet." *Comptes rendus l'academie des sciences* 189 (1931): 1696.

———. With M. M. Naik and Trivédi. "Sur la structure des arylamides maloniques." *Bulletin de la Société chimique* 1 (1934): 158.

SECONDARY SOURCES

Denis, Paul. "Madame Pauline Ramart-Lucas." *Bulletin de la Société chimique de France* 21 (1954): 269–271.

Martynoff, Modeste. "L'oeuvre scientifique de Pauline Ramart-Lucas." *Bulletin de la Société chimique de France* 21 (1954): 272–280. Includes a bibliography of 111 of Ramart-Lucas's publications.

STANDARD SOURCES
DFC; Notable.

RAMIREZ, ROSITA RIVERA (1906–)

Philippino physician. Born 3 May 1906 in Cabangan, Zambales, Philippine Islands. Father Don Benito Rivera. Six siblings. Married Adolfo Ramirez (1942). One child, died in infancy; one adopted son, Raymond; two foster daughters. Educated Iba elementary and secondary schools; Zambales Provincial Farm School (graduated valedictorian); University of the Philippines College of Medicine (M.D., 1930); St. Teresita Hospital, Manila, resident (1930–1940). Professional experience: purchased the hospital and established the St. Teresita General Hospital and the School of Nursing and Midwifery (1948–1974). Honors and memberships: Philippine Medical Women's Association, president (1956–1961); Medical Women's International Association, representative at congresses in Italy and England; Philippine Medical Association, Philippine Obstetrical and Gynecology Society, the Philippine Hospital Association, and the Philippine Federal and Private Medical Association, boards; outstanding physician in Quezon City, Philippine Medical Association (1965); National Radio and Television trophy for one of ten outstanding hospital directors (1966); CAWP Presidential Medal of Merit for Community Service presented by President Ferdinand Marcos.

Although Rosita Rivera Ramirez was not a research physician, she did outstanding medical work in the community in the Philippines. After the death of her father, who was an important citizen of Zambales, her mother was responsible for the support of her and her six siblings. During her childhood, she decided on a medical career after observing the pain and misery around her. However, this goal seemed financially impossible until a well-to-do uncle volunteered to send her to the University of the Philippines College of Medicine. She returned to her home during vacations to care for the sick. After graduating with a medical degree, she was accepted as a resident physician at the St. Teresita Hospital in Manila, where she spent ten years being trained in a number of medical fields. During World War II, she was in charge of the hospital. She married Adolfo Ramirez, a lawyer and a pharmaceutical chemist. The couple's one son died in infancy, and they adopted a boy who became a physician. They had two foster daughters, one of whom became a physician and the other a hospital administrator.

St. Teresita closed after the war, and the Ramirezes purchased it. They established a school of nursing and midwifery and a division to care for indigent patients. From 1948 to 1974, during its years of service, this hospital had thousands of admissions, and the School of Nursing had 666 graduates, all receiving high marks on board examinations. The School of Midwifery had over 880 graduates.

Rosita Ramirez made a great difference in health care for Philippinos. She stressed full care, including food, medicine, and clothing, and stressed the importance of civic organizations. She received many honors.   K M

PRIMARY SOURCES
Ramirez, Rosita. In Hellstedt, *Autobiographies.*

RAMSAY, CHRISTINA (BROUN), COUNTESS OF DALHOUSIE (1786–1839)

Scottish botanist. Born 28 February 1786 in Coalstoun, East Lothian. Married the ninth earl of Dalhousie. Died 22 January 1839.

Christina Ramsay married the ninth earl of Dalhousie. She went with him to Nova Scotia where she collected plants from 1816 to 1828. When he was made Commander in Chief of the East Indies, she again accompanied him between 1829 and 1832. She collected plants in the Simla region of India and Panang. She is mentioned in Joseph Dalton Hooker and T. Thomson's *Flora Indica* (1855). Her herbarium is at the Royal Botanic Gardens, Edinburgh, and her letters are at the Royal Botanical Garden at Kew. She was honored by having the plant genus *Dalhousia* Graham named for her.   J H / M B O

SECONDARY SOURCES

Curtis's Botanical Magazine Dedications, 1827–1927 London: Royal Horticultural Society, 1931.

Gardener's Magazine (1826): 255. Obituary notice.

Transactions of the Botanical Society of Edinburgh (1836–1837): 40; (1837–1838): 40; (1839–1840): 52.

STANDARD SOURCES

Desmond; Gunn and Codd.

RAMSEY, ELIZABETH MAPELSDEN (1906–)

U.S. physician and pathologist. Born 17 February 1906 in New York City to Grace Keys and Charles Cyrus Ramsey. Married Hans Alexander Klagsbrun (1934). Educated Mills College (B.A., 1928); University of Hamburg (1928–1929); Yale University (M.D., 1932). Professional experience: Yale University, assistant pathologist (1933–1934); Carnegie Institution Department of Embryology, guest investigator (1934–1949), research associate (1949–1951), staff member placentology and pathology (1951–post-1968). George Washington University, associate pathologist (1934–1941), professorial lecturer (1941–1945); National Research Council, assistant information officer, office of medical information (1942–1945). Honors and memberships: Woman's College of Pennsylvania (honorary D.Sc., 1965); Association of Anatomy, member.

Elizabeth Ramsey received her bachelor's degree at Mills College, studied at the University of Hamburg for a year, and earned her doctor of medicine from Yale. She then held several research positions. She worked on placental circulation, the implantation of the human embryo, and the vasculature of the pregnant endometrium. She studied the treatment for shock and researched Kaposi's disease.   JH/MBO

PRIMARY SOURCES

Ramsey, Elizabeth Mapelsden. *Venous Drainage of the Placenta of the Rhesus Monkey (Macaca mulatta).* Washington: Carnegie Institution of Washington, 1954.

———. With John W. S. Harris. *Comparison of Uteroplacental Vasculature and Circulation in the Rhesus Monkey and Man.* Washington: Carnegie Institution of Washington, 1966.

STANDARD SOURCES

AMS 8, B 9, P&B 10–14; Debus.

RAMSTEDT, EVA JULIA AUGUSTA (1879–1974)

Swedish physicist. Born 15 September 1879 in Stockholm to Henrika Charlotta (Torén) and Johan Olof Ramstedt, a civil servant, later mayor of Stockholm. Several siblings. Never married. Educated in Stockholm; University of Uppsala (B.A., 1904; licentiate, 1908; Ph.D., 1910). Professional experience: Radium Institute, Paris, researcher (1910–1911); Nobel Institute of Physical Chemistry, researcher (1911–1914), assistant (1913–1914); Stockholm Academy (later Stockholm University), associate professor in radiology (1915–1932), professor of physics (1919–1920), associate professor of physics (1927–1928); Teacher Training College, Stockholm, lecturer in mathematics and physics (1919–1945). Honors and memberships: Illis Quorum (medal from Swedish government)(1942). Died 11 September 1974 in Stockholm.

Eva Ramstedt grew up in a prominent and cultured family. She was educated in Stockholm at the Åhlinska School, then at Uppsala University, where she presented a dissertation on behavior of fluids. She studied radium decay products at MARIE CURIE's laboratory during 1910–1911, finding that the behavior of the solid products depended on the surface upon which they were collected, and that the solubility of radium emanation (radon) varied with the solvent used and the temperature. Also working at the Radium Institute was the Norwegian chemist ELLEN GLEDITSCH, with whom Ramstedt later coauthored several works.

Ramstedt returned to Sweden and worked at the Nobel Institute under Svante Arrhenius, publishing "On the activity of the undissociated molecule in ester catalysis." She also measured atmospheric electricity while on an expedition to study the 1914 solar eclipse.

Well known for her pedagogical ability, Ramstedt was liked and admired by her students. She was active in the Society Nya Idum (secretary, 1921–1937; auditor, 1952–1962) and the Federation of University Women (vice-president, 1922–1930; president of International Committee, 1920–1945). She served as vice-president and president of the board for the Stockholm upper elementary school for women's education (1920–1939) and on the state study loan panel (1943–1950).   MM

PRIMARY SOURCES

Ramstedt, Eva. *Om vatskors forhallande vid uttanjning.* University of Uppsala, Ph.D. diss., 1910.

———. "Sur la solubilité de l'émanation du radium dans les liquides organiques." *Le Radium* 8 (1911): 253–256.

———. "Sur la solubilité du dépôt actif du radium." *Le Radium* 10 (1913): 159–165.

———. With E. Gleditsch. *Radium och radioaktiva processer.* Kristana: Aschehoug, 1917.

———. *Marie Curie och Radium.* Stockholm: P. A. Norsted & Söner, 1932.

———. "Marie Sklodowska Curie." *Svenska Fysikersamfundets Kosmos* 12 (1934): 10–44.

SECONDARY SOURCES

Beckman, Anna. "Eva Ramstedt." In *Svenska män och kvinnor* 6 (1949): 210–211.

Davis, J. L. "The Research School of Marie Curie in the Paris Faculty, 1907–14." *Annals of Science* 52 (1995): 321–355.

Levin, Hjördis. "Eva Ramstedt." In *Svenskt Biografiskt Lexikon* 29 (1997): 647–649.

Lindgvist, Svante, ed. *Center on the Periphery: Historical Aspects of 20th-Century Swedish Physics.* Canton, Mass.: Science History Publications, 1993.

Róna, Elisabeth. *How It Came About: Radioactivity, Nuclear Physics, Atomic Energy.* Oak Ridge, Tenn.: Oak Ridge Associated Universities, 1978.

Rutherford, Ernest. *Radioactive Substances and Their Radiations.* Cambridge: Cambridge University Press, 1913.

Records in Institut Curie archives, assembled by Mme Monique Bordry.

STANDARD SOURCES

Meyer and von Schweidler; Rayner-Canham 1997.

RANCKEN, SAIMA TAWAST (1900–)

Finnish physician. Born 9 October 1900 in Pieksämäki, Finland, to Maria Henrika (Varis) and August Tawast. Married Professor Rancken (died 1935). One adopted son, Risto (1941). Educated University of Helsinki, Gymnastic Institute (teaching degree, 1923); University of Helsinki, (M.D.). Professional experience: University of Helsinki Hospital Department of Physical Therapy, lecturer in physical therapy (1935–1944), chief of department (1944–1964), professor of physical therapy (1964–1968).

Saima Tawast Rancken grew up in the small town of Mikkeli. She began to study gymnastics at Helsinki Gymnastic Institute the same year that her father died. Three years later she graduated as a gymnastics teacher one year after her mother had died. She became interested in medicine and decided to study the scientific basis of exercise, possibly stimulated by the death of her parents. She wrote her medical thesis on physical therapy and after she received her doctor of medicine degree she took a modest position in the surgical department of the university hospital. About this time, she married her former physiology teacher. The marriage was short-lived because of his early death. She subsequently adopted her cousin's infant child orphaned by the war.

Her interest in physical therapy was greatly increased by World War II, and Rancken trained many physical therapists for military hospitals. By the last year of the war she was chief of the new department of physical therapy, her field was recognized as a bonafide specialty, and she was raised to professorial rank. A new building was dedicated to physical therapy, just two years before she retired. Rancken had been an important figure in the development of physical therapy in Finland.

KM

PRIMARY SOURCES

Rancken, Saima Tawast. In Hellstedt. *Autobiographies.*

RAND, MARIE GERTRUDE (1886–1970)

U.S. psychologist. Born 29 October 1886 in Brooklyn, N.Y., to Mary Catherine (Moench) and Lyman Fiske Rand. Third child of a large family. Married Clarence E. Ferree (1918). Educated Girls High School in Brooklyn (1904); Cornell University (A.B., 1908); Bryn Mawr College (A.M.; Ph.D., 1911). Professional experience: Bryn Mawr College, fellow (1911–1913), associate (1913–1927); Wilmer Institute, School of Medicine, Johns Hopkins University, associate professor (1928–1932); Research Laboratory of Physiological Optics, Baltimore, Md., associate director (1936–1943); Knapp Foundation of the Columbia University College of Physicians and Surgeons, research associate (1943–1957). Honors and memberships: Illuminating Engineering Society, first woman Fellow (1952), Gold Medal (1963); Optical Society of America, Edgar D. Tillyer Medal for outstanding research in vision (1959). Died 30 June 1970.

Gertrude Rand studied psychology at Bryn Mawr College under the experimental psychologist Clarence Errol Ferree, who directed her dissertation on the sensitivity of the retina to color. After receiving her degree, she continued at Bryn Mawr as a postdoctoral fellow and a Sarah Berliner Research Fellow until 1913. At this time she was appointed an associate in experimental psychology. She continued to collaborate with Ferree, and in 1918 they married, but she retained her maiden name professionally. She left Bryn Mawr with her husband in 1928, to join the Wilmer Ophthalmological Institute of the Johns Hopkins University School of Medicine, where she taught as an associate professor, first research ophthalmology and then physiological optics. In 1935, she became associate director of the Research Laboratory of Physiological Optics in Baltimore. Clarence Ferree died in 1943, at which time Rand moved to New York City to become a research associate at the Knapp Foundation of the Columbia University College of Physicians and Surgeons. In 1957 she retired, leaving an important legacy behind her.

An unassuming woman, Rand was respected as an advisor to doctoral and medical students. Her abilities were also in demand as a consultant for the government and military during World War II.

When Rand was at Bryn Mawr, she collaborated with Ferree on the effects of general illumination on color perception. They also developed techniques for measuring the light sensitivity and color discrimination of different parts of the retina. The results of their research led to the Ferree-

Rand perimeter, which mapped the retina for its perceptual abilities. This map became important in diagnosing visual problems. Much of Rand's work involved developing new instruments and lamps for ophthalmologists. After Ferree died, she returned to her early work on color perception, where, in collaboration with Legrand Hardy and M. Catherine Rittler, she determined experiments for the detection and measurement of color blindness. Their work made it possible not only to identify color blindness qualitatively, but to determine type and degree of color blindness for each subject. Rand contributed more than one hundred single author and coauthored papers to the literature.   JH/MBO

PRIMARY SOURCES

Rand, Gertrude. With C. E. Ferree. *Radiometric Apparatus for Use in Psychological and Physiological Optics.* Princeton, N.J.: Psychological Review Company, [1917].

————. With LeGrand H. Hardy and M. Catherine Rittler. *AO H-R-R Pseudoisochromatic Plates.* Buffalo, N.Y.: American Optical Co., 1954.

————. *The Factors That Influence the Sensitivity of the Retina to Color.* [New York]: Johnson Reprint Corp., 1970.

Materials in Cornell University Library.

SECONDARY SOURCES

Ogle, Kenneth N. "Gertrude Rand: Edgar D. Tillyer Medalist for 1959." *Journal of the Optical Society of America* 49 (October 1959): 937–941. Includes select bibliography and a photograph.

"Rand, Marie Gertrude." *New York Times,* 3 July 1970. Obituary notice.

STANDARD SOURCES

AMS 4–8, B 9, P&B 10; Bailey; Debus; *NAW*(M) (long article by Elizabeth Garber); Rossiter 1982.

RANDOIN, LUCIE GABRIELLE (FANDARD) (1888–1960)

French biologist and nutritionist. Born 11 May 1888 in Bouers-en-Othe (Yonne), France. Married Alfred Randoin (1914). Educated Ecole Normale Supérieure, Paris; Natural Sciences fellowship (1911); University of Clermont-Ferrand; University of Paris, Faculty of Science (doctorate in sciences, 1918). Professional experience: assistant to Dr. A. Dastre (1917–1918?); Oceanographic Institute in Paris, researcher (1918–1920?); Physiology Laboratory of the Research Center of the Ministry of Agriculture, researcher (1920–1923), director (1924–1954); Institut Superieur d' Alimentation, director (1942–1960); Ecole Diététique, director (1951). Honors and memberships: Legion of Honor (1958). Died 13 September 1960.

Lucie Gabrielle Randoin was a French physiologist and nutritionist. Her family was from the Yonne valley, but she pursued her secondary studies at the prestigious Ecole Normale Supérieure in Paris. She was the first woman to compete for a Natural Sciences fellowship. In the same year, 1911, Lucie's future husband, Alfred Randoin, also received a fellowship. She then went on to study science at the Faculty of Science at the University of Clermont-Ferrand, studying general physiology and the physiology of nutrition under the biologist Albert Dastre. At the beginning of World War I, she married Randoin.

Working as Dastre's assistant, Lucie Randoin began research around 1917 on vitamins. The existence of vitamins had already been established, but she was intrigued by how vitamins affect human metabolism.

After receiving her doctorate and becoming eligible to teach at the university by passing her *agrégation* examinations, Randoin first took a position in the laboratory of the Oceanographic Institute in Paris, where she continued her work on vitamins. In 1920, she moved to the Physiology Laboratory of the Research Center of the Ministry of Agriculture and became its director in 1924. Her research on vitamins escalated at this time and in the 1920s she demonstrated how vitamins B and C affect the body's use of sugars and other chemicals. She also studied the composition of vitamins, and this research helped scientists understand the function of these substances.

Although she remained at the Agricultural Research Center until 1953, she was also the director of the Institute of Nutritional Science, a position she held from 1942 until her death. Her important work on blood sugars and vitamins established the therapeutic role of a balanced caloric diet and the relationship between poor nutrition and alcoholism.

Not only did she help found a national school for dietary studies to train students to become dieticians in hospitals and cafeterias, but she also created a set of quality standards for vitamins used in foods and formed a nutritional information service. Her preeminence in the field of vitamins and nutrition was obvious in 1931 and 1934, when she was the official French representative to international conferences on vitamin standardization. A member of several prestigious scientific organizations, Randoin served as president of the French Society of Biological Chemistry and was the general secretary of the Institute of Nutritional Hygiene. Randoin was made a member of the Académie de Medecin in 1946 and commander of the Legion of Honor in 1958, a time in which few women were so honored. She died in Paris in 1960.   JH/MBO

PRIMARY SOURCES

Randoin, Lucie Gabrielle. With Henri Simmonet. *Les donnees et les inconnues du problème alimentaire.* Paris: Les presses universitaires, 1927.

————. With Henri Simmonet. *Les vitamines.* Paris: A. Colin, 1937.

————. *Equilibre d'alimentation et de nutrition.* Paris: Hermann and Co., 1937–1942.

————. With Alfred Rossier. *Regimes, vitamines et équilibre alimentaire.* Paris: Baillière, 1942.

SECONDARY SOURCES

Fabre, René. "Nécrologie: Lucie Randoin." *La Presse Medicale* 68, no. 54 (3 December 1960): 2109–2110.

STANDARD SOURCES

DFC; Notable (article by George Milite); Poggendorff, vol. 7B.

RANDOLPH, HARRIET (1856–?)

U.S. invertebrate zoologist and embryologist. Born 27 October 1856 in Philadelphia, Pa. Educated Bryn Mawr College (A.B., 1889); University of Zurich (Ph.D., 1892). Professional experience: Bryn Mawr College, demonstrator in biology (1892–1893), reader in biology (1893–post-1910). Honors and memberships: Society of Zoologists; Breeder's Association. Death date unknown.

Harriet Randolph grew up in Philadelphia, so it is not surprising that she chose Bryn Mawr for her undergraduate work at a time when the dynamic Margaret Carey Thomas was president of the college. She studied biology under, among others, the cell biologist Edmund Beecher Wilson. She followed the example of other women of her time by acquiring further training in Europe. Randolph went to Zurich to do a thesis on spermatogenesis in insects. On her return she was hired by Bryn Mawr as a demonstrator and then a reader in biology. She disappeared from *American Men of Science* in 1910 and information is lacking on her after that date.

JH/MBO

PRIMARY SOURCES

Randolph, Harriet. *Observations and Experiments on Regeneration in Planarians. Archiv fur Entwickelungsmechanik der Organismen* 5 (1897): 352–372.

————. *Laboratory Directions in General Biology.* New York: H. Holt, 1898.

————. "Chloretone (acetonchloroform): An Anaesthetic and Macerating Agent for Lower Animals." *Zooligischen Anzeiger* 23 (1900): 436–439.

STANDARD SOURCES

AMS 1–2.

RASSKAZOVA, YELENA STEPANOVNA (1911–1969)

Russian geologist and paleobotanist. Born 18 May 1911 in Moscow, the daughter of a civil servant. Educated teacher training college (graduated 1930); further study 1932?–1934. Professional experience: school teacher (1930–1931); Moscow Institute of Geological Prospecting, teacher (1934–1939); Institute of Geology, USSR Academy of Sciences, paleobotanist (1937–1969) simultaneously with teaching. Died 12 February 1969.

Yelena Stepanovna Rasskazova was born and educated in Moscow. After graduating from teacher training college, she became a school teacher. She was sent, under the auspices of the Komsomol (the Communist youth organization), to assist in the building of Karaganda in Kazakhstan. She contributed to the organization of schools, the eradication of illiteracy, and the promotion of child welfare. For this work she was awarded a diploma and sent back to Moscow for further study. She taught at the Moscow Institute of Geological Prospecting and simultaneously did research at the Institute of Geology at USSR Academy of Sciences, where she spent the rest of her career.

Rasskazova's research was on the flora and stratigraphy of the Upper Paleozoic. Originally interested in the tectonics and stratigraphy of the eastern Urals, she transferred to the Division of Stratigraphy and specialized in paleobotany under the direction of M. F. NEUBURG. She spent several seasons collecting fossils from the difficult-to-work-in Pechora basin, providing Neuburg with material for her three-volume monograph on the Permian flora of the Pechora basin. After taking part in the institute's eastern Siberian expedition in 1950, she became interested in the flora and stratigraphy of the Upper Paleozoic of the Tunguska basin. She made several expeditions to this difficult-to-access basin and carefully collected fossil material. She summarized the results in several papers, including a major monograph which provided geologists with the accepted picture of the stratigraphy, age, and paleobotany of many of the Tunguska geologic sections. She produced monographic descriptions of many groups of fossil plants. One of her last research projects was a study of the Jurassic flora of the Irkutsk basin. However, she became ill while working on this subject and published only one paper jointly with Ye. L. Lebedev.

CK/MBO

PRIMARY SOURCES

Rasskazova, Yelena Stepanovna. "The Fossil Flora of the Kata Suite of the Tunguska Basin." In Russian. Moscow: Akademiya Nauk SSSR, 1958.

————. *Novyy rod mezozoyskikh paporotnikov, Lobifolia.* In Russian. Moscow: Nauka, 1968.

SECONDARY SOURCES

Doludenko, M. P., and S. V. Meyyen. "Yelena Stepanovna Rasskazova (1911–1969)." *Paleontological Journal* 3, no. 3 (1969): 436–437.

RATHBONE, MARY MAY (1866–1960)

British physician and botanist. Father Theodore Rathbone. Born in 1866 in Backwood, Neston, Cheshire. Educated Society of Apothecaries (licentiate in medicine and surgery before 1908). Professional experience: Botanical Research Fund, founder and governor. Honors and memberships: Linnean Society, Fellow (1908). Died 15 November 1960 at Chipping Campden, Gloucestershire.

Mary May Rathbone was a physician and botanist who qualified as a licentiate in medicine and surgery with the Society of Apothecaries before 1908. She was the daughter of a justice of the peace in Cheshire. Since botany was an accepted part of the medical curriculum in the nineteenth and early twentieth centuries, Rathbone may have developed her taste for botany in the course of her medical training.

Four years before she was made a Fellow of the Linnean Society, Rathbone worked for a period at the British Museum under the direction of ETHEL SAREL GEPP and published her first and only botanical paper, an examination of the structure of two brown algae.

A friend of the distinguished botanist, ETHEL SARGANT, she joined her and twenty-five other women in founding the Linnean Society Botanical Research Fund in 1913–1914. Continuing her interest in this fund, she sat on its board as a governor. She continued to meet with her fellow governors until the last two or three years of her life.

For many years, Rathbone spent her holidays in Norway, and presented a manuscript to the Linnean Society containing a Norwegian glossary of botanial terms and names. She died in Chipping Campden at the age of ninety-four, one of the society's oldest members. Her botanical library was given to the Linnean Society by her executors.   JH/MBO

PRIMARY SOURCES

Rathbone, Mary May. "Notes on *Myriactus areschougii* and *Coilodesme californica*." *Journal of the Linnean Society* 35 (1904): 670–675.

SECONDARY SOURCES

Delf, E. M. "Mary May Rathbone." *Proceedings of the Linnean Society* 173 (1960–1961): 66.

STANDARD SOURCES

Desmond.

RATHBUN, MARY JANE (1860–1943)

U.S. marine zoologist. Born 1860 in Buffalo, N.Y. to Jane (Furey) and Charles Rathbun. Four siblings. Educated Buffalo public schools (graduated from Buffalo Central School, 1878); George Washington University (Ph.D., 1917). Professional experience: U.S. National Museum, Washington, D.C., division of marine invertebrates, staff member (1884–1914), assistant curator from 1907. Died 1943 in Washington, D.C.

Mary Jane Rathbun, the youngest of five children, grew up in Buffalo, New York. Both Mary Jane and her brother Richard, who later became assistant secretary of the Smithsonian Institution and director of the U.S. National Museum, developed an interest in zoology from a fascination with the fossils found in the rocks of the several large stone quarries that their father operated. When Mary Jane was only one year old, her mother died, and she was raised by an elderly nurse. Although her formal education ended when she graduated from the Buffalo Central School in 1878, she was awarded an honorary master's degree by the University of Pittsburgh in 1916 and in 1917 received a doctoral degree from George Washington University for a study on marine crabs.

Richard Rathbun began to work as an assistant to Spencer Baird, head of the U.S. Fish Commission, in 1873, and in 1880 became curator of marine invertebrates at the National Museum in Washington, D.C. Beginning in 1881, Mary Jane spent the summers with her brother at the Marine Biological Station at Woods Hole, Massachusetts, helping him examine and catalogue specimens. Baird hired her as a full-time employee of the Fish Commission in 1884. She was assigned to the division of marine invertebrates at the National Museum, where her responsibilities included organizing and cataloging the museum collections. In 1886, Rathbun became a museum staff member. Richard Rathbun's preoccupation with his Fish Commission duties allowed his sister to be, in effect, the curator of the marine invertebrate division. Although her official status was that of a clerk, her functions ranged from clerical work to research. Her self education in marine biology continued, and in 1891 she began to publish. Remaining at the National Museum until 1939, she eventually became assistant curator, a position she held from 1907 to 1914. After 1914 she remained at the museum as an honorary associate, a position that allowed her more time for research.

Rathbun's scientific studies centered around recent and fossil decapod crustaceans. During her lifetime, she published 158 works. She emphasized taxonomy in all of her work, clarifying and standardizing many of the categories in the Crustacea, and establishing principles of nomenclature for these groups. Her research papers and extensive notes have provided a descriptive basis upon which later students of the Crustacea have built.   JH/MBO

PRIMARY SOURCES

Rathbun, Mary Jane. "Les Crabes d'Eau." *Nouvelle archives muséum d'histoire naturelle* 6–8 (1904–1906).

———. *The Brachyura.* Cambridge, Mass.: printed for the National Museum, 1907.

———. *The Grapsoid Crabs of America.* Bulletin 97 of the United States National Museum, 1918. The work for which she received her Ph.D.

———. *The Fossil* Crustacea *of the Atlantic and Gulf Coastal Plain.* Special Paper No. 1, Geological Society of America, 1935.

———. *The Oxystomatous and Allied Crabs of America.* Bulletin 166 of the United States National Museum, 1937.

SECONDARY SOURCES

Journal of the Washington Academy of Sciences 33 (15 November 1943). Obituary notice.

Science 33 (May 1943). Obituary notice.

STANDARD SOURCES

AMS 1–6; *NAW* (article by Waldo Schmitt); Ogilvie 1986.

RATNAYAKE, MAY (1892–?)

Sri Lankan physician. Born 31 May 1892 in Kandy, Ceylon (now Sri Lanka). Father John de Livera. Six siblings. Married (?) Ratnayake (ca. 1927). One daughter; one son. Educated local schools in Kandy and Matara; Ceylon Medical College, Columbo (M.D., 1916); Royal Free Hospital for Women, postgraduate work (1925–1927?); University of Edinburgh Medical School (1932–1933). Professional experience: American Mission Hospital, Jaffna, attending physician (1916–1921); Lady Havelock Hospital, Columbo, house officer and assistant female medical officer, outpatient department (1921–1925), surgeon (1927–1931); chief surgeon (1933–?); University of Ceylon, medical school, faculty of medicine (1934–?). Death date unknown.

May de Livera's father was a physician who worked at the general hospitals in both Columbo and Kandy. She was one of seven children. As a young girl she prepared for the Cambridge Local Examinations. Her mother wanted her to become a physician. She applied at Ceylon Medical College in 1911 and in spite of some resistance she was permitted to take the entrance examination. For the first year she was the only woman student (in 1896 a young Sinhalese woman had attended the medical school, but died soon after and never qualified). Livera was soon joined by two other young women. When she qualified as a physician she was told that in spite of her good qualifications there was no vacancy for a woman doctor. She was finally offered a post at the American Mission Hospital at Jaffna working under another woman doctor.

When a vacancy for a house officer occurred at Lady Havelock Hospital, Livera took the post in order to work with a brilliant surgeon, Catherine Anderson. Alice DeBoer, her chief, created a position for her as assistant female medical officer in the outpatient department, which gave her an hour for private practice two days a week. In 1925 she went for further postgraduate training at the Royal Free Hospital for Women, where she worked in the laboratory and had opportunities for ward experience. She succeeded DeBoer as the medical officer of the female outpatient department and took over her private patients. It was during this time that she met her husband, a lawyer, through his sister and niece who were her patients. In 1932 at the urging of her husband and Catherine Anderson, she went to Edinburgh on a fellowship. On her return in 1933, she took over Anderson's position as surgeon in the outpatient department. Both Ratnayake's daughter and son went into medicine, although her daughter practiced medicine only after the doctor she had married died.

There was a change in Ceylon after the university took over the staffing of the children's hospital. For the first time, women doctors were appointed to the teaching staff as professors, with the resulting appointing of Ratnayake to the faculty of the medical school in the mid-thirties. Ratnayake had a long and productive life. She was an active member of the Medical Women's International Association.   KM

PRIMARY SOURCES

Ratnayake, May. In Hellstedt, *Autobiographies.*

RATNER, SARAH (1903–   )

U.S. biochemist. Born 9 June 1903 in New York City to Hannah and Aaron Ratner. Four siblings (one twin brother). Educated Cornell University (A.B., 1924); Columbia University (M.A., 1927; Ph.D., 1937). Professional experience: Columbia College of Physicians and Surgeons, assistant biochemist (1930–1934); Macy Research Fellow (1937–1939), instructor and assistant professor (1939–1946); New York University College of Medicine, assistant professor of pharmacology (1946–1953), associate professor (1953–1954), adjunct associate professor of biochemistry (1954–?); Division of Nutrition and Physiology, Public Health Research Institute of New York, associate member (1954–1957); Schoenheimer Lecturer (1956); Public Health Research Institute of New York, member, department of biochemistry (1957–?). Honors and memberships: American Society of European Chemists and Pharmacists, Carl Neuberg Medal (1959); American Chemical Society, Garvan Medal (1961); New York Academy of Sciences, L. and B. Freedman Foundation Award (1975); National Institutes of Health (1978–1979); Northwestern University (D.Sc., 1982).

Best known for her studies on amino acid metabolism and the clarification of features of the urea cycle, Sarah Ratner also made key contributions to the use of heavy nonradio-active isotopes in metabolic studies.

Sarah and her twin brother were born into a family of Russian Jewish immigrants in New York City. A self-educated man, her father, Aaron Ratner, had a manufacturing business in the United States. He was an avid reader who loved not only books but inventing. Sarah, his only daughter, was given the same education as his four sons, but turned out to be the only one of the children to pursue an academic career. Her favorite courses in high school were the sciences and mathematics. After receiving a scholarship to Cornell University, she studied chemistry and found that all of her peers were male. After graduating with a bachelor's degree in chemistry, she worked in a laboratory doing analytical chemistry, but found the job dull. She found her second job, doing research in pediatrics in a clinical laboratory, much more interesting.

She was attracted to physiological chemistry, and began to explore the literature and research in this field. She began to attend graduate courses at Columbia University, where she was accepted as a student by Hans T. Clarke, the talented organic chemist, at Columbia College of Physicians and Surgeons. Clarke proved to be an excellent mentor and role model for Ratner. She was supported financially through a part-time job as an assistant in biochemistry. In Clarke's laboratory, she became part of the pioneer work on studies of follicular hormones and on a uterine-contracting substance, later identified as a prostaglandin. Her thesis was on the interaction of formaldehyde with cysteine, an amino acid, and established the structure of its product, thiazolidine carboxylate. Through this project, she learned a good deal about the chemistry of amino acids and became interested in nitrogen metabolism and urea synthesis.

After she earned her doctoral degree, Ratner had a difficult time finding a suitable position. At that time, most positions for women involved teaching in the women's colleges and were not in research. Through persistence, she was able to find a research position away from New York City. However her father's sickness and eventual death forced her to return to New York City to care for her mother.

She broke the typical female teaching mold when she was offered an appointment as a Macy Research Fellow at the College of Physicians and Surgeons to work with Rudolph Schoenheimer. She was involved in the fascinating study of amino acid metabolism with isotope tracers. These experiments pioneered the use of nonradioactive, "heavy" isotopes to study the metabolic process.

During her seven years as instructor and assistant professor at the College of Physicians and Surgeons she moved from her work with Schoenheimer to David Clarke, another distinguished biochemist. From her research at this time, she learned to trace the metabolic pathways of nitrogen iso-topes—this procedure became the basis of her lifetime work on nitrogen metabolism in the urea cycle. In 1942, Ratner began to work with biochemist David Greene in amino acid oxidases research, an especially important subject for enzymology. She worked with Greene until 1946, when she accepted an appointment to the Department of Pharmacology at the New York University Medical School. In addition to teaching pharmacy, she synthesized the pieces of biochemical evidence for the urea cycle. Through designing experiments to test her hypotheses, she was able to propose a new intermediate for urea synthesis, a compound called argininosuccinate. Moving from New York University to the Public Health Research Institute of New York City, she helped elucidate the Krebs (or citric acid) cycle, which is vital to understanding the biochemistry of life.

As a woman, Ratner found that her opportunities for postdoctoral positions were limited. However, she soon became so well-known that gender was not a problem. Perhaps her gender was not the only reason for her lack of opportunity. In the mid-1950s, after the discovery of the double helix, the focus in biochemistry had shifted from metabolism toward the understanding of molecular form and function. Even after her reputation was assured she still headed a small research group with modest funding relative to the importance of her work. In addition to the medals that she won, Ratner received honorary doctorates from three universities, the University of North Carolina, Northwestern University, and the State University of New York at Stony Brook. She also was a Fogarty Scholar in Residence at the National Institutes of Health from 1978 to 1979. JH/MBO

PRIMARY SOURCES

Ratner, Sarah. With Hans T. Clark. "The Action of Formaldehyde upon Cysteine." *Journal of the American Chemical Society* 59 (1937): 200–206. Based on Ratner's thesis.

———. With N. Weissman and R. Schoenheimer. "Metabolism of D-lysine Investigated with Deuterium and Heavy Nitrogen." *Journal of Biological Chemistry* 147 (1943): 549–556.

———. "Urea Synthesis and Metabolism of Arginine and Citrulline." *Advances in Enzymology* 15 (1954): 319–387.

———. "A Long View of Nitrogen Metabolism." *Annual Review of Biochemistry* 14 (1977): 1–24.

SECONDARY SOURCES

Pullman, Maynard E., ed. *An Era in New York Biochemistry: A Festschrift for Sarah Ratner.* New York: New York Academy of Sciences, 1983.

STANDARD SOURCES
AMS 6–8, P 9, P&B 10–14; Bailey; Debus; Grinstein 1993
(article by Nancy M. Tooney); *Notable;* Shearer and Shearer
1997 (article by Kathleen Palombo King).

RAUZER-CHERNOUSOVA, DAGMARA (MAXIMILIANOVNA) (1895–1996)

Russian / Soviet geologist and paleontologist. Born 1895 in Moscow to a music teacher mother and engineer father. Married K. N. Chernousov. One daughter, Irina. Educated gymnasium (silver medal, 1913); Highest Women's Course Moscow (completed 1918); Geology Institute, Moscow (Ph.D., 1945). Professional experience: Sevastopol Biology Station, Academy of Sciences, volunteer research worker (1925–1927); Moscow State University, assistant professor in geological department (1927); department of historical geology, assistant (1930); Ural Oil and Research Geological Oil Institute, micropaleontologist (1931); Geology Institute of the Academy of Sciences of the USSR, micropaleontologist and geologist (until her death). Died June 1996.

Dagmara Rauzer's talent was recognized early by Professor A. A. Chernov, who invited her to go on the Pechora geological expedition. After completing her studies at the Highest Women's Courses (already reorganized into the second Moscow University), she married K. N. Chernousov, an accounting instructor. The couple had a daughter, Irina. After her husband contracted tuberculosis, they moved to the Crimea. She continued her scientific work by volunteering as a research worker in a Sevastopol Biological Station of the Academy of Sciences and combining it with teaching. She was accepted as an assistant professor in the geological department of Moscow State University in 1927.

When Rauzer-Chernousova moved back to Moscow, she worked as an assistant in the department of historical geology in Moscow State University and then in a pedagogic institute. From 1931, she specialized in the new field of micropaleontology, working in a trust of "UralOil" and then in a Research Geological Oil Institute. She relocated to Leningrad and became a research worker in the Geology Institute of the Academy of Sciences of the USSR, where she worked until the end of her life.

At the onset of World War II, she was in the Urals. She worked in Bashkir Autonomous Soviet Socialist Republic and lived in Ishimbay and Ufa until 1944 when she returned to Moscow. She then continued her work in the Geology Institute as head of a micropaleontological laboratory. In 1945, she defended a thesis for a doctoral degree in geologo-mineralogical sciences.

Rauzer-Chernousova was an important specialist on Paleozoic foraminfera. Until the 1950s, her work consisted chiefly of factual paleontological stratigraphic information.

However, in the 1950s and 1960s, she turned to social, theoretical, and biological questions. She produced an interesting series of theoretical works. These began in 1948 with *About Periodicity in Development of Foraminifera;* in 1949 she published an article about the ontogenesis of foraminifera, and in 1950 she published one about facies.

She began to work on a very important and difficult question about lower classification singles of foraminifera and connected upper fraction stratigraphic subdivisions with them. In 1954 to 1956, she published a series of articles on the subject. In 1960, she moved to geographical natural habitat, history of development, appearance of new kinds, and finally she wrote a small but important article, "Stages and Periodicity in Development of Fasulinids" (1965).

She continued to publish and wrote fourteen works after 1965, not including small articles, reviews, and chronicles. Half of these works have a biostratigraphic content; these are articles about zones, borders of the Carboniferous and Permian, the Kasimovian stage, and the distribution of foraminifera in Sakmarian and Asselian seas. The other half of these works involved paleontological research, especially the evolution of foraminifera of the Upper Paleozoic and the classification in the paleoecology of the foraminifera.

Rauzer-Chernousova was especially interested in changes in foraminiferal walls, and the meaning of these changes to classification. Together with A. A. Gerke, she published a *Terminological Reference Book.* This proved to be a gargantuan task, but her research on the literature enabled her to write a paper about the historical development of the wall shell and its taxonomic meaning. She considered this subject to be very important for the classification of the foraminifera.

Often under appreciated, Dagmara Rauzer-Chernousova's pedagogical work deserves special attention. She almost completely dropped this interest when she became more involved in actual research. However, she was known for her skill in organization work.

Foraminifera are extremely important as indicators. They change very quickly from strata to strata. Each stratigraphic horizon has its own foraminiferal fauna. Just a small piece of the fossil is enough to determine its age. This discovery was very important for drilling on the Russian Platform. The drilling was for coal, different salts, and (most important) for oil and gas. The oil industry seized upon this new method, which saved it hundreds of thousands and even millions of rubles. Oil Geo-Explorational organizations opened a series of Micropaleontological laboratories. New specialists were needed, and Rauzer-Chernousova and her laboratory associates actively took part in training young specialists. Many micropaleontologists now consider themselves students of Dagmara M. Rauzer-Chernousova.

She became the head of the Commission of Micropaleontology, a commission that organizes academic conferences, seminars, and state meetings, and has its own magazine, *Questions of Micropaleontology*. Irreplaceable records are available in her collection of thin sections and her card index on which all famous Paleozoic foraminifera are registered. These records take up a special building and are constantly used.

Rauzer-Chernousova received the Lenin Prize, the highest scientific award of the Soviet Union. She also received an honorary title of Honored Science Worker of Science and Technology of the USSR. In honor of her hundredth birthday, her colleagues from the Russian Academy of Sciences organized a gala event, an All-Russian Micropalaeontological Conference, to which she contributed her own recollections. Unfortunately, Rauzer-Chernousova did not live to see the publication of the proceedings; she died at the age of 102 before the volume was published.   C K

PRIMARY SOURCES

Rauzer-Chernousova, Dagmara M. With V. N. Krestovnikov. "On the Foraminifera from the Transitional Beds between the Devonian and the Carboniferous (Etroeung zone) of Kazakkhstan, South Urals, and Samarskaya Luka" (in Russian). *Doklady Akademii Nauk SSSR* 20, nos. 7–8 (1938): 587–589.

———. *About Periodicity in Development of Foraminifera* (in Russian). Moscow: Izd-vo Akademii nauk SSSR, 1948.

———. With others. *Srednekamennougol'nye fazulinidy Russkoi platformy i sopredel'nykh oblastei: spravochnik-putevoditel'.* Moscow: Izd-vo Akademii nauk SSSR, 1951.

———. *Stages and Periodicity in Development of Fasulinids* (in Russian). Moscow: Nauka, 1965.

———, ed. With B. I. Chuvashov, ed. *Biostratigrafiia artinskogo i kungurskogo iarusov Urala.* Sverdlovsk: UNTS AN SSSR, 1980. On Permian biostratigraphy in the Ural Mountains.

———. "Memories of My Childhood and Student Years." In *Biostratigraphy and microorganisms of the Phanerozoic of Eurasia; Rauzer-Chernousova Memorial Volume,* eds. V. M. Podobina, et al. Moscow: Izdat. GEOS, 1997. This volume also includes a summary by Rauzer-Chernousova of her life's work on Paleozoic foraminifera, as well as an obituary article. English translations in appendix.

SECONDARY SOURCES

Nalivkin, D. V. *Nashi pervye zhenshchiny-geologi* (Our First Women Geologists). Leningrad: Nauka, 1979.

RAY, DIXY LEE (1914–1994)

U.S. marine biologist and zoologist. Born 3 September 1914 in Tacoma, Wash., to Frances (Adams) and Alvis Marion Ray. Four sisters. Educated Stadium High School, Tacoma (1933); Mills College, Oakland, Calif. (B.A., 1937; M.A., 1938); Stanford University (Ph.D., 1945). Professional experience: Oakland High School, biology teacher (1938–1942); University of Washington, assistant professor and associate professor (1945–1976); National Science Foundation, special assistant to the assistant director for the Division of Biological and Medical Science (1960–1962); National Academy of Sciences, Committee on Oceanography and its Committee on Postdoctoral Fellowships, member (1960–1963), Subcommittee on International Biological Stations, member (1962–1965); Subcommittee on Productivity of Marine Communities, member; Pacific Science Center, Seattle, director (1963); American Association for the Advancement of Science, Fellow (1962); Stanford University, visiting faculty and chief scientist for the International Indian Ocean Expedition (1964); Smithsonian Institution's Advisory Council for the National Museum Act, member; Smithsonian Research Awards Committee, member; Atomic Energy Commission (member, 1972; chairman, 1973–1975); Assistant Secretary of State for Oceans and International Environmental and Scientific Affairs (1975); governor of Washington State (1977–1981); KVI-radio, consultant; Greater Tacoma Community Foundation, board member and treasurer; Los Alamos National Laboratory and the Lawrence Livermore National Laboratory, consultant; Washington Institute for Policy Studies, founding board member, consultant, and columnist for its publication, Counterpoint; *Brookhaven National Laboratories, member, Board of Directors; Science Research Advisory Committee for the U.S. Coast Guard, member; the Defense Science Board, member; the Visiting Committee for Nuclear Engineers, Massachusetts Institute of Technology; Americans for Energy Independence, member. Died 2 January 1994 on Foxtrot Farm, Fox Island (Puget Sournd), of a bronchial infection and viral pneumonia.*

Few women scientists have managed such a public-spirited life as Dixy Lee Ray. The girl who felt that she would never marry because "I'm too ugly," and whose childhood was dominated by her father's disappointment that she was not a boy, became the chair of the Atomic Energy Commission, governor of the state of Washington, and was on inumerable boards and commissions. She was the second of five daughters. Rejecting her given name, Margaret, she legally changed it to Dixy Lee when she was sixteen years old. Her response when asked why she changed her name was that it was no one's business. At the age of twelve, she became the youngest girl to climb Mount Rainier.

She attended Mills College in Oakland, California, and earned both a bachelor's (Phi Beta Kappa) and master's degree in zoology from that institution. Knowing that she would be unable to afford additional education unless she worked to earn it, she got a teacher's certificate. She taught for four years after receiving her master's degree and was able to pay off most of her educational debt. During her last two years of teaching high school, she was a weekend employee at the Hopkins Marine Biological Station, Stanford University. At this station she developed a substance that trapped bacterial flagella and worked with soil amoebae.

After receiving a John Switzler fellowship (1942) and a Van Sicklen fellowship (1943–1945) at Stanford, Ray was able to pursue her doctoral degree. Her scientific career was distinguished by its emphasis on public service. She wanted to build bridges between science and the public. When a vacancy arose at the AEC, President Nixon appointed Ray who developed three goals for the agency: public education, the creation of a moderate governmental policy toward the environment and nuclear energy, and the encouragement of further research in nuclear medicine. Ray was convinced that nuclear energy was safe, but that the government needed more stringent safety rules. The AEC was disbanded in 1975, and Ray was appointed to another important post by Nixon. In 1977, she campaigned and won the governorship of the state of Washington, and became the state's first female governor. Although she ran for reelection, she was defeated.

Although Ray produced numerous papers in pure science, her most important work was in public science. She was convinced that nuclear energy was an important source of energy and put a great deal of effort into propagandizing for it.

JH/MBO

PRIMARY SOURCES

Ray, Dixy Lee. "The Peripheral Nervous System of *Lampanyctus leucopsarus*: With Comparative Notes on Other *Iniomi*." Ph.D. diss., Stanford University, 1945.

———. "Peripheral Nervous System of *Lampanyctus leucopsarus*." *Journal of Morphology* 87 (1950): 61–178.

———. "Digestion of Wood by *Limnoria lignorum* (Rathke)." *Proceedings XIV International Congress of Zoology* [Copenhagen] (1953): 279.

———. With D. E. Stuntz. "Possible Relation between Marine Fungi and *Limnoria* attacks on Submerged Wood." *Science* 129 (1959): 93–94.

———. "Some Marine Invertebrates Useful for Genetic Research." In *Perspectives in Marine Biology,* ed. Adriano A. Buzzati-Traverso. Berkeley: University of California Press, 1960.

———. With Louis R. Guzzo. *Trashing the Planet: How Science Can Help Us Deal with Acid Rain, Depletion of the Ozone, and Nuclear Waste (among Other Things).* Washington, D.C.: Regnery Gateway, 1990.

———. With Louis R. Guzzo. *Environmental Overkill: Whatever Happened to Common Sense?* Washington, D.C.: Regnery Gateway, 1993.

SECONDARY SOURCES

"AEC Former Head Runs for Governor." *New York Times,* 16 March 1976.

Gillette, R. "A Conversation with Dixy Lee Ray." *Science* 189 (1975): 124–127.

———. "Ray Nominated to AEC." *Science* 186 (1974): 612–613.

———. "Ray's Shift to State Department Will Test Kissinger's Interest in Science." *Science* 186 (1974): 612–613.

Noble, Iris. *Contemporary Women Scientists of America.* New York: Julian Messner, 1979.

Stead, Elizabeth, and Kathleen Waugh. *Dixy Lee Ray 1977–1981, Guide to the Governor's Papers, vol. 6.* Olympia, Wash.: Office of the Secretary of State, 1993.

STANDARD SOURCES

AMS 8, B 9, P&B 10–13; *Current Biography* 1973; Grinstein 1997 (article by Janet Newlan Bower); *Notable.*

RAYMOND-SCHROEDER, AIMEE J. (1857–1903)

U.S. physician. Born 21 August 1857 in Montreux, Switzerland. Father Henry J. Raymond. Married Henry Harmon Schroeder in 1893. Educated in France and Italy; Woman's Medical College (M.D., 1889). Professional experience: private practice; New York Infirmary, outpatient clinic, staff physician; New York Medical Record and American Journal of Obstetrics, editorial board. Died 25 December 1903 following an operation for appendicitis.

Born in Switzerland to a socially active and affluent family, Aimee Raymond was schooled informally during travels in France and Italy and did not receive a formal diploma until she graduated from the Woman's Medical College. Her father, Henry J. Raymond, was founder and editor of the *New York Times* and was a strong supporter of ELIZABETH and EMILY BLACKWELL in their struggles for the medical education of women. No doubt he encouraged his intelligent and altruistic daughter in her choice of career.

Raymond practiced in New York, being associated with the New York Infirmary outpatient clinic for several years. When she married in 1893, she gave up her practice for health reasons and spent the succeeding years as an active student of medicine and as an editor for the *New York Medical Record* and the *American Journal of Obstetrics.* She wrote only one book but translated many medical articles from French and Italian.

JH/MBO

PRIMARY SOURCES

Schroeder, Aimee Raymond. *Health Notes for Young Wives.* New York: Wood, 1895.

SECONDARY SOURCES

Kelly, Howard A. *Cyclopedia of American Medical Biography.* Vol. 2. Philadelphia: W. B. Saunders, 1912.

RAYNER, MABEL MARY CHEVELEY (ca. 1888–1948)

British botanist. Born ca. 1888. Married W. Nielson Jones (1912). Educated University of London (B.Sc., 1908; D.Sc., 1915). Professional experience: University College, Redding, head, botany department. Died 17 December 1948 at Wareham, Dorset.

Mabel Rayner was an authority on mycotrophy in plants. She was married to W. Nielson Jones, who was also interested in this topic. Both began by investigating the ecology of *Caluna vulgaris* on the Wiltshire and Berkshire Downs. This work resulted in a classic paper, "Obligate Symbiosis in *Caluna vulgaris*," which earned her a doctor of science degree. In this paper she studied its association with its fungus endophyte. Twenty years later she published a monograph on endophytic mycorhiza of heath plants. Following a discussion at the British Association meeting of 1926, she began to work on ectophyte associates of forest tree roots. The forestry commission provided Rayner with a research nursery at Wareham Heath in Dorset to study this problem.

Her series of papers along with those of her husband were reprinted in *Problems of Tree Nutrition* (1944). Her subject engendered a heated conflict among botanists, because she indicated that the endophytic mycorrhiza association had beneficial as well as deleterious effects. She extended her study to include a wide variety of plants, both tropical and temperate. She traveled widely in pursuit of examples. She shared a laboratory at Bedford College with her husband. Their collaboration was an example of a true symbiotic relationship, both finding it beneficial and happy. She died after a round of visiting her plants at Wareham Heath in Dorset.

JH/MBO

PRIMARY SOURCES

Rayner, Mabel Mary. With Sir F. Keeble. *Practical Plant Physiology.* London: G. Bell and sons, Ltd., 1912.

———. With W. Nielson Jones. *Textbook of Plant Biology.* London: Methuen & Co., Ltd., [1920].

———. *Mycorrhiza: An Account of Non-pathogenic Infection by Fungi in Vascular Plants and Bryophytes.* London: Wheldon and Wesley, Ltd., 1927.

———. *Trees and Toadstools.* London: Faber and Faber, 1946.

SECONDARY SOURCES

Forestry 22 (1948): 241–244. Obituary notice.

Garrett, S. D. *Nature* 163 (19 February 1949): 275–276.

Times, 31 December 1948.

STANDARD SOURCES

WWW 1941–1950.

REA, MARGARET WILLIAMSON (1875–?)

Irish botanist. Born 1875 in Belfast. Educated Belfast (B.Sc., 1919; M.Sc., 1921). Death date unknown.

Margaret Williamson Rea published botanical papers in the *New Phytologist* and *Protoplasma.* She published two of these papers with Professor J. Small in 1921 and 1927 and was the sole author on the others. Her special interest was in collecting the Mycetozoa. Her plants are at University College, Galway.

JH/MBO

PRIMARY SOURCES

Rea, Margaret W. "Stomata and Hydathodes in *Campanula rotundifolia,* L., and Their Relations to Environment." Master's thesis, University of Belfast, Queen's College, 1921.

STANDARD SOURCES

Desmond; Praeger.

REAMES, ELEANOR LOUISE (1883–?)

U.S. botanist and physics teacher. Born 18 February 1883 in New Orleans, La. Educated Tulane University (A.B., 1905; A.M., 1907; Ph.D., 1913); University of Chicago, postdoctoral studies (1914–1915). Professional experience: Tulane University, Newcomb College, Department of Physics, instructor (1909–1927), assistant professor (1927–1954?). Honors and memberships: New Orleans Academy. Death date unknown.

Eleanor Louise Reames was raised in New Orleans and educated at Tulane University. She taught there in Newcomb College, the women's college, in the physics department after receiving her doctoral degree. Her only experience outside Tulane was a brief period of postdoctoral studies at the University of Chicago. In spite of her training and teaching in physics, she did research in botany, specializing in freshwater algae. She retired as assistant professor after 1954. She was a member of the New Orleans Academy.

JH/MBO

STANDARD SOURCES

AMS 3–8, P 9, P&B 10.

REDDICK, MARY LOGAN (1914–1966)

U.S. neuroembryologist. Born 31 December 1914 in Atlanta, Ga. Educated Spelman College (B.A., 1935); Atlanta University (M.S., 1937); Radcliffe College (M.A., 1943; Ph.D., 1944). Professional experience: Spelman College, laboratory assistant (1933–1939), Morehouse College, teacher (1939–1942, 1944–1952); Cambridge University, Department of Anatomy, fellow (1951–1952); University of Atlanta, professor (1953–1966). Honors and memberships: Radcliffe College, General Education Board fellow

(1942–1944); Ford Foundation fellow (1951–1952). Died October 1966.

Mary Logan Reddick was an early African American doctoral student in biology at Radcliffe College, Harvard, in 1944, only four years after ROGER ARLINER YOUNG had obtained her doctorate at the University of Pennsylvania. Reddick studied nerve cell differentiation in the medulla of chick embryos and went on to do further research in neuroembryology.

Reddick had spent her undergraduate and early graduate years at black colleges in the South. She attended Spelman College, working there as a laboratory assistant before and for four years after receiving her degree, while studying at Atlanta University towards a master's in biology. She moved to another black college, Morehouse, to teach biology, but they awarded her no higher position than "teacher," even after she completed her advanced degrees.

In 1942, during World War II, Reddick was awarded a General Education Board fellowship from Radcliffe College, to study embryology in the Harvard Department of Biology. She remained there for two years, obtaining first a second master's and then a doctorate for her study of chick embryo nerve cell differentiation.

Reddick was not likely to have the opportunity to teach at any large research university. She returned to Morehouse. Again she was offered a fellowship, this time by the Ford Foundation, and went to Cambridge University in the early fifties to work in the Department of Anatomy pursuing her research on embryonic nerve cells. On her return in 1953, she was appointed as a professor of biology at Atlanta University, where she remained until her early death at the age of fifty-five.   JH/MBO

PRIMARY SOURCES

Reddick, Mary Logan. "The Differentiation of Embryonic Chick Medulla in Corioallantoic Grafts." Ph.D, thesis, Radcliffe College (Harvard, Department of Biology), 1944.

SECONDARY SOURCES

Jet Magazine (5 November 1966): 7. Obituary notice.
"Mary Logan Reddick." *Atlanta Journal,* October 1966. Obituary notice.
Morgan State College. *The Negro in Science.* Ed. Julius H. Taylor, et al. Baltimore: Morgan State College Press.
Sammons, Vivian O. *Blacks in Science and Medicine.* New York: Hemisphere Publishing, 1990.

STANDARD SOURCES

AMS 8, B 9, P&B 10–11; Rossiter 1982; Rossiter 1995; *Who's Who of American Women.*

REDER, RUTH ELIZABETH (1898–?)

U.S. biochemist. Born 21 December 1898 in Logansport, Ind. Married (?) St. Julian. Educated Oberlin College (A.B., 1920); University of Illinois (M.A., 1927; Ph.D., 1929). Professional experience: Oklahoma Agricultural and Mechanical College (now Oklahoma State University), Stillwater, Okla., associate professor and research chemist (1929–retirement). Death date unknown.

Ruth Elizabeth Reder attended Oberlin College, Ohio, and after she got her doctorate in physiological chemistry moved to Stillwater, Oklahoma, where she spent her academic career. She studied the relationship of soil and climatological factors on vitamin and mineral contents of plants.   JH/MBO

STANDARD SOURCES
AMS 5–8; P9.

REDFIELD, HELEN (1900–)

U.S. geneticist. Born 5 May 1900 in Archbold, Ohio. Married Jack Schultz (1927). Two children. Educated Rice Institute of Technology (A.B., 1920); University of California, fellow (1920–1924; Ph.D., 1924). Professional experience: Rice, assistant in mathematics (1917–1920); National Research Council, fellow, Columbia University (1925–1928); New York University, teaching fellow in biology (1929); California Institute of Technology, Kirchoff Laboratory, geneticist (1939–1942); Institute for Cancer Research, Philadelphia, Pa., research associate (1951–1961).

In spite of her excellent training at many of the top institutions in the United States, Helen Redfield never progressed beyond the level of research associate, although she received several research fellowships. Born in Ohio, she did her undergraduate work in Texas and then went to the University of California, where she had a research fellowship while working on her doctoral degree in zoology. After she obtained her degree, she received a fellowship at Columbia University, where she worked in genetics, probably in the laboratory of Thomas Hunt Morgan. Marrying and raising two children probably slowed down her academic progress, for she held no research position between 1929 and 1939. During the first part of World War II, she worked as a geneticist at the Kirchoff Laboratory at California Institute of Technology. From 1942 until well after the war, she held no formal position, although she worked as a laboratory scientist at Cold Spring Harbor during the summers. In the postwar period, she was able to find a position as a research associate at the Institute for Cancer Research where her husband, the geneticist Jack Schultz, headed the Division of Biology. There she remained during the last ten years of her career. She presented her husband's papers to the American Philosophical Society in 1983.   JH/MBO

PRIMARY SOURCES

Redfield, Helen. "The Maternal Inheritance of a Sex-Limited Lethal Effect in Drosophila melanogaster." Ph.D. thesis, University of California, 1924. Published in *Genetics* 11, 1926.

SECONDARY SOURCES

Glass, Bentley. "Finding Aid to Jack Schultz Papers." In Schultz, Jack. Papers (1920–1971), Manuscript Collections, American Philosophical Society. Discusses an innovative paper by Redfield and Schultz on *Drosophila* chromosomes.

Kitty Warren Scrapbook. Cold Spring Harbor Laboratory archives. Photograph of Helen Redfield Schultz with her husband, summer 1950, among the "laboratory people."

STANDARD SOURCES

AMS 4–8, P 9, P&B 10.

REED, EVA M. (d. 1901)

U.S. botanist. Educated University of Wisconsin. Professional experience: Missouri Botanical Gardens, indexer (1894–1901); University of Chicago, botanical department, researcher on plant ecology. Died 7 July 1901 near Louisiana, Mo.

American botanist Eva Reed was deeply interested in botanical pursuits, particularly mosses. She also published on winter characteristics of trees. She had been at the University of Wisconsin and went from there to work as an indexer in the library of the Missouri Botanical Gardens, St. Louis, Missouri. In 1901 she began to work on plant ecology under the direction of the plant department of the University of Chicago. While investigating plants in the field, she was killed by a train while walking on the tracks near Louisiana, Missouri.   JH/MBO

PRIMARY SOURCES

Reed, Eva M. *The Shaw Garden Library.* St. Louis, Mo.: Missouri Botanical Garden, Library, [1898]. Found in *Public Library Magazine* 5, no. 4 (1898): 233–239.

SECONDARY SOURCES

Annual Report of the Missouri Botanical Gardens 13: 22–23.
Science 14 (1901): 158. Obituary notice.

REES, FLORENCE GWENDOLEN (1904–1995)

British invertebrate biologist, parasitologist. Born 3 July 1906 in Abercynon, Glamorganshire, Wales, to Elizabeth Agnes (Jones) and Ebenezer Rees. One sister. Never married. Educated University College of Wales, Cardiff (B.S., 1927; Ph.D., 1930). Professional experience: University College of Wales, Aberystwyth, faculty
(1930–1973). Honors and memberships: University College of Wales, personal chair in zoology (1973); Fellow, Royal Society. Died 4 October 1995 in Aberystwyth, Wales.

The parasitologist Florence Gwendolen Rees (always called Gwendolen or Gwen) was born in Wales, near Cardiff, and grew up in Aberdare, where her father was the superintendent of police. In Gwen's teen years, her mother died of cancer and she and her older sister, Mary, had to adjust to the care of a kind housekeeper. Gwen had already developed a fascination with zoology, and her marked academic ability resulted in the award of a number of scholarships that enabled her to attend the University of South Wales, in Cardiff.

Gwen decided in her third year to specialize in parasitology, a subject that she had to pursue primarily on her own. Receiving a second class honors degree in zoology, she worked toward an education certificate, a requirement of one of her scholarships. Her college, Aberdare Hall, then offered her a scholarship that allowed her to enter the Department of Zoology to work toward her doctorate in parasitology.

Joining a team that included an agricultural zoologist, H. W. Thompson, and another woman scientist, Anne Bryant, Rees investigated liver fluke disease in sheep. In order to investigate the parasitic trematodes, she began to collect snails, the intermediate host. With Bryant, she collected over five thousand snails from one hundred localities in Glamorgan and Monmouthshire. Rees completed her investigations within eighteen months and obtained her doctoral degree on the resulting analysis, which was remarkable for the fifty detailed plates that accompanied her study. The later publication of only a few of these in the *Proceedings of the Zoological Society of London* did not do her plates justice.

One of the readers of her dissertation, R. T. Leiper, a Fellow of the Royal Society, recommended that she be appointed as assistant lecturer at the University of Wales in Aberystwyth under Douglas Laurie. Rees began to take on heavy teaching responsibilities at all levels of undergraduate zoology. Her own research was conducted primarily in vacation time and during the field courses that she led to museums and research stations in Britain and Europe. She remained an assistant lecturer until 1937, when she was appointed as lecturer. Her teaching always included field work as well as careful technical training.

In her first years of teaching, Rees published papers based on her dissertation and on hookworm in rabbits. The hookworm (cestodes) became one of the major focuses of her later research. Rees expanded her investigations on the trematode, examining the host–parasite system in detail, using as her subject the digenetic trematode *Perorchis acanthus* (called *Cercaria purpurea I* in its larval stage) that had as its intermediate host the dog whelk, which in turn parasitized the herring gull. She and her students became skilled at collecting whelks and hatching gull eggs for experimental infection.

During World War II, Rees served as an Air Raid Warden and found research difficult to continue, although she continued to study helminthic infection of sheep, with the idea of improving agricultural yield. During this period she was aided by the appointment of T. A. Stephenson, a marine ecologist, to the zoology chair. He, like Rees, had a precise, technical approach to zoology, coupled with a fine draftsmanship and devotion to invertebrate zoology, and he facilitated her independent research. She was awarded an honorary doctorate in science by her university during this period. Following the war, she was raised to senior lecturer and then, in the mid-sixties, to a readership.

In the late 1950s, the Department of Zoology moved into new quarters that included an aquarium, and they purchased important pieces of equipment, including an electron microscope. By the end of the sixties, Rees began to use microcinematography to study the movement of the body and tail of trematodes. Over the years, she directed many undergraduate and postgraduate students, and many of her students went on to distinguished research and teaching careers.

Rees was a founding member of the British Society of Parasitology, regularly attending the meetings of that organization and those of the International Congress of Parasitology. But in spite of her research visits abroad, she was reluctant to leave Wales. She accepted only temporary positions, teaching at the University of Aligarh in India and later supervising research in helminthology at the University of Ceylon. Her research visits, such as her trip to the inner and outer reefs of Bermuda to study helminths of fish, were for brief periods.

The appointment of Rees to a personal chair in her department came on the heels of her election as a Fellow of the Royal Society in 1971. She was made an honorary member of the British Society of Parasitology. She was elected a Fellow of the Institute of Biology and a Fellow of her college in Cardiff. In 1990, her lifetime contribution to zoology and to the understanding of the evolution of the host-parasite association was recognized by the award of the Linnean Medal. Rees was also photographed by *Vogue* as one of Britain's interesting and influential women of 1975.

Rees never married, in part because of a rule that required women faculty to resign their posts upon marriage. She died at the age of eighty-eight in a hospital in Aberystwyth, after a short illness.   JH/MBO

PRIMARY SOURCES

Rees, Gwendolen. "An Investigation on the Occurrence, Structure and Life Histories of the Tremetode Parasites in Four Species of Lymnaea." *Proceedings of the Zoological Society of London* 1 (1932): 1–32.

SECONDARY SOURCES

Beverly-Burton, M. "Obituary: Gwendolyn Rees F.R.S." *International Journal of Parasitology* 25 (1995): 1145–1148.
Williams, H. "Gwendolen Rees, FRS, Fifty-Six Years (1930 to date) in Research." *Parasitology* 92 (1986): 483–498

STANDARD SOURCES

Biographical Memoirs, vol. 43, 1997.

REES, MINA SPIEGEL (1902–1997)

U.S. mathematician. Born 2 August 1902 in Cleveland, Ohio, to Alice Louise (Stackhouse) and Moses Rees. Three siblings. Married Leopold Brahdy. Educated Hunter High School; Hunter College (graduated summa cum laude, 1923); Columbia University (M.A., 1925); University of Chicago (Ph.D., 1932). Professional experience: Hunter High School, teacher (1923–1925); Hunter College, instructor, assistant professor (1932–1940), associate professor (1940–?), professor (1953–1961); Applied Mathematics Panel, Office of Scientific Research and Development, technical aid and executive assistant to Warren Weaver (1943); Office of Naval Research, deputy director of mathematics and science (1946–1952); Deputy Science Director (1952–1953); City University of New York, dean of graduate studies (1961–1968), provost (1968, 1969–1972), president of the Graduate School and University Center (1972). Died 25 October 1997 at the Mary Manning Walsh Home in Manhattan.

Mina Rees's brilliance in mathematics was surpassed only by her organizational and administrative abilities. She was the youngest child of an insurance salesman father who was generous to a fault with his friends. The family moved to the Bronx where Mina attended elementary school and made straight A's on her report card. A teacher recommended that she attend Hunter High School, an adjunct of Hunter College that was designed to educate bright girls. She graduated valedictorian of her class and then entered tuition-free Hunter College. She graduated summa cum laude, made Phi Beta Kappa, was president of the student body, and was yearbook editor. Although she was asked to remain at Hunter to teach, Rees preferred to teach at Hunter High School while she worked on a master's degree in mathematics at Columbia University. She obtained a sabbatical in 1929 and went to the University of Chicago to study for a doctoral degree in mathematics. After she finished her dissertation in division algebras under L. E. Dickson, she returned to Hunter to teach until 1943, when she took a leave to become technical aide and executive assistant to the chief of the Applied Mathematics Panel of the Office of Scientific Research and Development. After the war, the Office of Naval Research (ONR) played an important role in establishing its mathematics program and Rees stayed on to become its deputy science director. The policies that she developed for the ONR are said to have influenced the policies for the National Science Foundation. She returned to Hunter in 1953 as professor of mathematics and dean of the faculty, but continued to participate in numerous policy-making committees for the government. She was invited to become the first dean of graduate studies at the newly created City University of New York and created a graduate school based on a consortium of the colleges of the university with an independent graduate center. She became provost in 1968 and from 1969 the president of the Graduate School and University Center. Her interest in graduate education expanded to the national scale, where she became chair of the Council of Graduate Schools in the United States (1967–1971).

Rees received a number of honors, including the President's Certificate of Merit and the (British) King's Medal for Service in the Cause of Freedom, the first Award for Distinguished Service to Mathematics of the Mathematical Association of America. She was a member of the National Science Board (1964–1970). She was active in the American Association for the Advancement of Science, serving as vice-president, member of the board of directors, president-elect, president, and chairman of the board. Her election as president was especially important, for she was the first woman to hold that office.

Although she clearly had the ability to excel in pure mathematics, Rees turned to applied mathematics, where she felt her skills would be of the greatest use. Her work during World War II showed the importance of applied mathematics to the war effort. JH/MBO

PRIMARY SOURCES

Rees, Mina. "Division Algebras Associated with an Equation Whose Group has Four Generators." *American Journal of Mathematics* 54 (1932): 51–65.

———. "The Nature of Mathematics." *Science* 138 (5 October 1962): 9–12.

———. "The Mathematical Sciences and World War II." *American Mathematical Monthly* 87 (1980): 607–621.

———. "The Computing Program of the Office of Naval Research, 1946–1953." *Annals of the History of Computing* 4 (1982): 102–120.

SECONDARY SOURCES

"Rees Awarded Medal." *Association for Women in Mathematics Newsletter* 3 (May–June 13 1983): 9–10.

Weyl, F. Joachim. "Mina Rees, President-Elect 1970 (AAAS)." *Science* 167 (10 February 1970): 1149–1151.

STANDARD SOURCES

AMS 6–8, P 9, P&B 10–14; Bailey; Grinstein and Campbell (article by Phyllis Fox); *Notable; Notable Mathematicians*.

REFSHAUGE, JOAN JANET (1896–c. 1979)

Australian physician. Born 3 December 1906 in Australia to a Scottish mother and an English/Danish father. Four siblings. Married M.W. Bergin (1937; divorced 1948). One son. Educated Wangarett State School; educated at home; tutoring college (intermediate certificate); conservatorium (senior certificate); University of Melbourne (M.Sc. in chemistry, 1929; M.B.B.S., 1939); University of Sydney (M.P.H., 1953); Royal Children's and Queen Victoria hospitals, refresher course. Professional experience: University of Melbourne, tutor and teacher, chemistry and math; Working Man's College, lecturer in mathematics to engineering students; Alfred Hospital, resident; Queen Victoria Hospital for Women, resident; Chronic and Incurable Diseases Hospital, resident; Mildura Base Hospital, senior medical officer; Royal Women's Hospital, Melbourne; Army Medical Corps (1943–1946); Territory of Papua and New Guinea, medical officer to the Public Health Department (1947–1963); Queensland Public Health Department, medical officer in the Maternal and Child Welfare Service (1964–1968), deputy director (1968–1974). Retired 1974.

Australian physician Joan Refshauge told the story of her life in medicine, but without providing specific dates. Her father, a headmaster of an agricultural high school, was twenty-two years older than her mother. He was authoritarian, with very decided ideas about the education of his children. He retired when Joan was eight years old, and the family moved to Melbourne from the country. Her father was sick much of the time. Because of a serious eye problem that the doctors thought could cause blindness, Refshauge was taken out of school when she was twelve years old and left to "run wild." During this time she helped run the household. She took music lessons and did well on the examination at the university conservatorium. She was allowed to continue at the conservatorium and was even sent to a tutoring college to learn the subjects that her father could not teach her. She passed eight subjects in the intermediate certificate, and the doctors could see no deterioration in her sight. She returned to the conservatorium and earned honors in the senior certificate. However, after the death of her music teacher her father decided that she had become unstable and forced her to study mathematics and science—"stabilizing subjects"—at the university.

She entered a science program at the university and majored in mathematics and chemistry. Her father refused to allow her to study medicine, although the idea was very appealing to her. She had worked as a demonstrator in chemistry and had tutored in various subjects. She later taught chemistry and mathematics at the university. After her father's death, she was able to enter medical school. She went immediately into second-year medicine, while still teaching and tutoring. Before she finished her medical degree she married and soon had a son. Her first residency at Alfred

Hospital was rather unpleasant because of the views of the male graduates about women and the views of the female graduates about married women. Forced to resign from her second residency at Queen Victoria Hospital because of morning sickness, she took another at the Chronic and Incurable Diseases Hospital. She left to give birth to her son.

At the beginning of World War II, Refshauge's husband was sent to New Guinea as a civilian. After several jobs, she enlisted in the Army Medical Corps and was responsible for the health of the women in the army stationed in and around Melbourne. After demobilization, she took a refresher course at the Royal Children's and Queen Victoria hospitals and then became the first woman to be appointed medical officer to the Public Health Department in the Territory of Papua and New Guinea. Her husband was in Port Moresby, Papua, where she moved and began work as a general practioner. She then pioneered the Infant, Child and Maternal Health Service.

After retiring from the position on Papua, Refshauge joined the Queensland Public Health Department as a medical officer in the Maternal and Child Welfare Service. She retired nine years later. Although Refshauge was pleased with her medical career, she was upset with the way that women physicians were treated in Australia. Her papers are deposited in the National Library of Australia.   JH/MBO

PRIMARY SOURCES

Refshauge, Joan. In Hellstedt, *Autobiographies.*

Records of Dr. Joan Refshauge, National Library of Australia.

   Includes records of her work in Papua New Guinea as well as personal papers and a short biography.

REICHARD, GLADYS AMANDA (1893–1955)

U.S. anthropologist. Born 17 July 1893 in Bangor, Pa., to Minerva Ann (Jordan) and Noah W. Reichard. Educated Swarthmore College (A.B., 1919). Columbia University (M.A., 1920; Ph.D., 1925). Professional experience: Pennsylvania Public Schools, elementary school teacher (1909–1915); Columbia University, Barnard College, assistant in anthropology (1921–1923), instructor (1923–?), assistant professor, professor of anthropology (1951–1955). Died 25 July 1955 after a brief illness.

Gladys Reichard, the American anthropologist and linguist, was one of the most dedicated of Franz Boas's women students, who included RUTH BENEDICT and ELSIE CLEWS PARSONS. Her studies of the Navajo, which generated controversies with the Harvard anthropologist Clyde Klukhohn, are currently read with renewed appreciation.

Reichard came from a Quaker family of Pennsylvania Dutch extraction. Her father was a physician and both her mother and father supported her early intellectual endeavors.

At sixteen she went for two years to teach in a rural school and then taught elementary school for four further years in the Bangor public schools.

After working as a teacher, Reichard went to Swarthmore to study classics, but soon she became interested in anthropology. When she graduated Phi Beta Kappa, she was awarded a Lucretia Mott fellowship to study anthropology at Columbia University. After receiving her master's degree in 1920 and working as Franz Boas's assistant at Barnard College, she obtained a research fellowship at the University of California under Alfred Kroeber to study a northeastern California Indian language. Doing field work among the Wiyot Indians for two years, she prepared a grammar of their language as her dissertation. Kroeber was later to complain that she was so strongly influenced by Boas even then that she absorbed little of what the California school had to offer.

When Reichard returned to New York, Boas offered her a full-time instructorship at Barnard College in anthropology, even before she finished her dissertation. Although he passed over Ruth Benedict in making this choice, she seems to have felt no resentment. Reichard remained at Barnard for the rest of her career until her retirement in 1955, although she was appointed full professor only four years before.

Reichard began a series of field trips to the American Southwest, the first before she completed her doctorate, many of them financed by Clews Parsons. On her first trip to Arizona to research the social life of the Navajo, she traveled as the companion of her mentor, Pliny Earle Goddard, then curator at the American Natural History Museum in New York. Returning for many summers to Arizona beginning in the early 1930s, she lived in close proximity to the family of a famous Navajo medicine man and chanter, learning not only the genealogies of the people she studied and their religion but also the women's weaving techniques. She is one of the few anthropologists who not only studied Navajo weaving but became a good weaver herself. Her books on social organization, life histories, and finally her great work on Navajo religion made her a notable authority on the Navajo.

Though best known for her work on the Navajo, Reichard studied Melanesian design as well, and obtained a Guggenheim fellowship to study a famous Melanesian collection in Hamburg, Germany. The resulting book on Melanesian design won her the A. Creesy Morrison prize in Natural Sciences from the New York Academy of Sciences in 1932.

In New York, Reichard remained a close friend of Boas, sometimes living as a daughter in his household. After the death of his wife, she helped him with his children, and as he aged, assisted him in other ways. To her, he was always "Papa Franz." She never married, but seems to have had close male companions including Goddard.

Although Reichard as a teacher at a woman's undergraduate college had limited effect on graduate students, she was remebered warmly by those who did work with her. She also kept Parsons regularly informed by letter about her studies and her impressions while in the field. Not a feminist like Benedict or Parsons, she celebrated the success of her fellow women anthropologists, including Benedict and Parsons, and helped others, like Kate Peck Kent and Ruth Underhill.

Reichard was active in many organizations. She was secretary of the American Folk-Lore Society for eleven years (1924–1935) and served also as its editor. She was a Fellow of the American Anthropological Association and acted as program director for a year in 1945.   JH

PRIMARY SOURCES

Reichard, Gladys. "Wiyot Grammar and Texts." *University of California Publications in American Archaeology and Ethnology* 22 (1925): 1–215. Reichard's Ph.D. dissertation.

———. *Social Life of the Navajo Indians.* New York: Columbia University Press, 1928.

———. *Melanesian Design.* 2 vols. New York: Columbia University Press, 1932.

———. *Spider Woman: A Story of Navajo Weavers and Chanters.* New York: Macmillan, 1934.

———. *Dezba, Woman of the Desert.* New York: J. J. Augustin, 1939.

———. *Navajo Medicine Man: Sandpaintings and Legends of Miguelito.* New York: J. J. Augustin, 1939.

———. *Navaho [sic] Religion: A Study in Symbolism.* 2 vols. New York: Bollingen Foundation, 1950.

SECONDARY SOURCES

Lamphere, Louise. "Gladys Reichard." In *Hidden Scholars: Women Anthropologists and the Native American Southwest*, ed. Nancy Parezo, et al. Albuquerque: University of New Mexico Press, 1993.

STANDARD SOURCES

Gacs (article by Eleanor Leacock); *IDA* (article by Nathalie Woodbury); *NAW* (article by Joan Mark).

REID, ELEANOR MARY (WYNNE EDWARDS) (1860–1953)

British botanist and geologist. Born 1860 in Denbigh. Married Clement Reid (1897). Educated Westfield College (B.Sc., 1892). Professional experience: Cheltenham, mathematics teacher. Honors and memberships: Geological Society, Murchison Fund (1919); Fellow (1920); Lyell Medal (1936). Died 28 September 1953 of a cerebral thrombosis at Milford-on-Sea, Hampshire.

Paleobotanist Eleanor Mary Reid was not educated to be either a geologist or a paleontologist. Her only paid position was as a mathematics teacher at Cheltenham. However, she met and married paleobotanist Clement Reid and immediately began to collaborate with him. Clement mentioned in his paper, "Origin of the British Flora" (1899) that the two of them had collected ninety-four plants (from fruits and seeds) from a Pleistocene deposit at West Wittering. They published a joint paper in 1907 and between that time and 1915 they jointly published twelve papers on fossil plants several of which were of significant importance. For example, one on the preglacial flora of Britain nearly doubled the number of species known in 1899 from the Cromer Forest Bed. Another, on the lignite of Bovey Tracey, greatly enlarged the knowledge of Tertiary fauna. Eleanor Reid prepared for the study by devising or improving techniques for extracting plant remains from peats and other deposits and preserving the specimens.

When he retired, Clement Reid moved to Milford-on-Sea in Hampshire. However, he only lived three years after his retirement. Eleanor outlived Clement forty years, and her house became a paleobotanical research center. In 1919, she received the Murchison Fund and in 1920 was elected a Fellow of the Geological Society. She published two papers in 1920 in the *Quarterly Journal*. Realizing the need for an assistant, Reid met Marjorie Chandler, which led to an important collaboration. Although the working conditions were less than ideal, particularly for Chandler, the two made important contributions. Together they published the monograph *London Clay Flora* (1933). For twenty years after this publication (Reid was seventy-three when it was published), she continued to maintain an interest and an extensive correspondence in the subject. She also published a few short papers. Reid was awarded the Lyell Medal by the Geological Society in 1936.   JH/MBO

PRIMARY SOURCES

Reid, Eleanor Mary. With Clement Reid. "The Preglacial Flora of Britain." *Linnean Society,* 1908.

———. With Clement Reid. "Lignite of Bovey Tracey." *Philosophical Transactions* (1910).

———. With Marjorie Chandler. *Bembridge Flora.* London: British Museum (Natural History), 1926.

———. With Marjorie Elizabeth Jane Chandler. *London Clay Flora.* London: Trustees of the British Museum, 1933. Plants are at the Royal Botanical Gardens, Kew and Trinity College, Dublin.

SECONDARY SOURCES

Andrews, Henry Nathaniel. *Fossil Hunters: In Search of Ancient Plants.* Ithaca: Cornell University Press, 1980. See pages 374–381. Includes portrait.

Edwards, W. N. "Eleanor Mary Reid." *Proceedings of the Geological Society of London* no. 1515 (1954): cxl–cxlii.

Nature 173 (1954). Obituary notice.
Times, 9 October 1953. Obituary notice.

STANDARD SOURCES
Desmond; Stafleu and Cowan.

REID, MARY ELIZABETH (1885–1968)

U.S. nutritionist. Born 30 May 1885 in Ocomowoc, Wis. Educated University of Wisconsin (B.S., 1910; fellow, 1920–1922; Ph.D. in plant physiology, 1923). Professional experience: Appleton, Wis., high school teacher (1910–1917); University High School, Madison, teacher (1917–1919); University of Wisconsin, assistant instructor of botany (1923); Boyce Thompson Institute, New York, fellow in plant physiology (1923–1926); Yale University, Sterling fellow in biochemistry (1926–1929); U.S. Golf Association, plant physiologist, green section (1929–1934); National Institutes of Health, research physiologist (1936–1955). Died 1968.

After receiving her bachelor's degree in biology, Mary Elizabeth Reid taught for nine years in two Wisconsin high schools in order to save money for her graduate studies. Returning to the university, she served as an assistant instructor in botany while working toward her doctoral degree. After she received this degree she worked at the Boyce Thompson Institute for Plant Research in New York. She spent three years at this institute, after which she accepted a postdoctoral fellowship as a Sterling fellow. After the completion of this fellowship she worked for five years as a plant physiologist for the U.S. Golf Association. In 1934, she went to work at the National Institutes of Health under the physiologist Lafayette B. Mendel, who worked on the interaction between plant and animal physiology and nutrition. She worked at the NIH until she retired, and then continued for several years as a guest researcher.

Reid's major research was on the effect of environmental factors on accumulation of vitamin C in plants, on the interrelations of calcium and vitamin C in plants and animals, and nutritional requirements and deficiencies in the guinea pig (an important laboratory animal). JH/MBO

PRIMARY SOURCES
Reid, Mary Elizabeth. "Histology of the Leaves of the Genus Begonia." Bachelor's thesis, Cornell University, 1898.
———. *Growth of Seedlings in Light and in Darkness in Relation to Available Nitrogen and Carbon.* N.p., 1929. Reprinted for private circulation from *Botanical Gazette* 87, no. 1 (February 1929).
———. "The Quantitative Relations of Carbohydrates to Nitrogen in Tomato Cuttings in Determining the Regeneration of Roots and Shoots." Ph.D. thesis, University of Wisconsin, Madison, 1923.

STANDARD SOURCES
AMS 7–8; B 9; P&B 10–11; *NAW* unused.

REIMER, MARIE (1875–1962)

U.S. organic chemist. Born 1875 (1874?) in Northumberland, Pa. Educated Vassar (A.B., 1897); Bryn Mawr College (Ph.D., 1904); University of Berlin, postdoctoral studies (1902–1903). Professional experience: Vassar College, assistant in chemistry (1898–1899); Columbia University, Barnard College, instructor (1904–1909), adjunct professor (1909), associate professor (1910–1921), professor (1921–1945), emerita professor (1945–1962). Honors and memberships: American Chemical Society, honorary member; New York Academy of Sciences, Fellow. Died 1962.

Marie Reimer was born in Pennsylvania and attended Vassar. After finishing her undergraduate degreee, she continued to teach as an assistant in the chemistry laboratory for a year. She then went on to study for her doctoral degree at Bryn Mawr, spending a postgraduate year in Berlin, as did a number of other women at the time.

Upon her return, she taught at Barnard College as an instructor, remaining there for the rest of her academic career. She was made associate professor in 1910 and full professor eleven years later.

During this period, Reimer continued to do research, primarily on the influence of light upon addition reactions. She also published on new methods of unsaturated organic compounds. Reimer retired as emerita professor at the age of seventy. JH/MBO

PRIMARY SOURCES
Reimer, Marie. "Reaction of Organic Magnesium Compounds with Cinnamylidene Esters." *American Chemical Journal* 38 (1907): 11S and 39 (1908): 14S.
———. "Action of Light on Esters of Alpha-Cyanancinnamylidenacetic Acid." *American Chemical Journal* 45 (1911): 19S.
———. "Action of Sunlight on Crystalline Methanyl Benzalpyruvate." *Journal of the American Chemical Society* 46 (1924): 8S.
———. "Addition Reactions of Unsaturated Alpha-Ketonic Acid." *Journal of the American Chemical Society* 55 (1933): 4643–4648; 57 (1935): 211–215; 60 (1938): 2469–2471.

STANDARD SOURCES
AMS 3–8, P 9, P&B 10; Poggendorff, vols. 6, 7B.

REINHARDT, ANNA BARBARA (fl. 1750)

Swiss mathematician. Born in Winterthur, Switzerland. Educated privately.

Anna Reinhardt was a friend of the mathematician Jean Bernoulli, the father of Daniel Bernoulli. According to Jean Bernoulli, her mathematical ability was superior to the well-known French natural philosopher GABRIELLE-EMILIE DU CHÂTELET. She extended and improved the solution of a problem on which French mathematician Pierre Maupertuis, then living in Switzerland, was working.   JH/MBO

STANDARD SOURCES
Mozans; Rebiére.

REMOND, SARAH PARKER (1826–1887?)

U.S. anti-slavery activist and physician. Born 6 June 1826 in Salem, Mass., to Nancy (Lenox) and John Remond. Seven siblings. Married (?) Pintor. Educated Salem Public Schools; Bedford College (1859–1861); Santa Maria Nuova Hospital, Florence, Italy (1866–1868). Died ca. 1887.

Sarah Parker Remond was from a prominent African American family that was active in the Salem Anti-Slavery Society and the Essex County and Massachusetts antislavery societies. Although she received her formal education in the public schools of Salem, most of her education was informal, at home. She read widely, and listened to political discussions by her parents and their numerous visitors. Since her home was a meeting place for both black and white abolitionists, she was exposed early to accounts of the Underground Railway. She became an avid reformer and lectured in many places in the United States on the evils of slavery and appeared before the National Woman's Rights Convention in New York City in May 1858.

Remond went to England, where her lectures on the abolitionist movement were well received. While in London, she enrolled in the Bedford College for Ladies, studying history, mathematics, geography, French, Latin, English literature, elocution, and vocal music. Twice she was denied a passport to travel to France, but with the help of British friends, she managed to visit the continent.

In 1866, Remond left London for Florence. In this city, she became a medical student, studying for two years at the Santa Maria Nuova Hospital. No official record is available to indicate that she received a medical degree, but it is said that she pursued a regular medical course including clinical hospital experience, receiving a diploma certifying her for professional medical practice.

When Elizabeth Buffum Chace, a Rhode Island reformer, visited Italy, she noted that Sarah Remond was earning an excellent income in Florence as a physician in spite of some unsympathetic Americans who attempted to use their influence against her. Other old friends recorded their visits to Remond, including the great orator and abolitionist, Freder-ick Douglass. As late as 1887 she was still in Italy, but nothing more is known about her later life or death. Some conflicting evidence suggests she married, since a note in her hand on the back of a photograph from this later period adds Pintor to her name. Her legacy is found in summaries of her lectures in newspapers and magazines, which record her remarks on slavery, and her criticism of Christianity for condoning both slavery and colonialism.   JH/MBO

PRIMARY SOURCES
Remond, Sarah Parker. "The Negroes & Anglo-Africans as Freedmen and Soldiers. Tract no. 7." London: Emily Faithfull, Ladies' London Emancipation Society, 1864.
———. "Colonization." *Freed-Man* (1 February 1866): 162–163.

SECONDARY SOURCES
Porter, Dorothy B. "Sarah Parker Remond, Abolitionist and Physician." *Journal of Negro History* (July 1935).
Tuke, Margaret J. *A History of Bedford College for Women, 1849–1937*. London: Oxford University Press, 1939.
Venet, Wendy Hamand. *Neither Ballots Nor Bullets: Women Abolitionists and the Civil War*. Charlottesville: University Press of Virginia, 1991.

RENOOZ, CÉLINE (1849–1926?)

Belgian-born French editor and writer on popular science. Born 7 January 1849 in Liège. Married (?) Muro (divorced). Three daughters. Professional experience: Organizer of lecture series (1877–1878?). Revue Scientifique des Femmes, editor (1888). Honors and memberships: Société d'Ethnographie, member; Société de Botanique Française, member. Died 1920s in Paris.

Céline Renooz was a Belgian-born writer who married a Spanish diplomat and lived for approximately the first ten years of her married life in Spain. She moved to Paris and became estranged from her husband. Intrigued by the world of science, she joined the two scientific societies in Paris that welcomed women without a scientific background: the Botanical Society and the Ethnological Society.

Picking up on the interest of the French public in a reformulated evolutionism in the late 1870s, she managed to persuade the prestigious publishing house Baillière to publish a very unscientific book that adopted an antievolutionary comparative embryology. This may have been produced with some private funds from her own resources, since the publishers later claimed they had never read the text before publication.

In 1888, she interested a number of women in joining her in editing a new review to discuss the role of women in science and medicine, *Revue Scientifique des Femmes*. Although she enrolled some eager young women, including Jacques Bertillon's future wife, the young physician CAROLINE SCHULTZE, and covered the triumphs of women physicians and scientists throughout the world, the journal soon foundered and ceased publication at the end of a year. In her memoirs she blamed women scientists like CLÉMENCE ROYER for this failure, but the real cause was more likely to have been her attacks on the scientific establishment, including Jean Baptiste Charcot, and the regular publication of sections of her own rather mystical book on force later self-published as *La Nouvelle Science*. In it she described oxygen as the great "God Oxygen," incorporating a trinity opposed by the "evil enemy" nitrogen. She also included descriptions of various forces as "goddesses." She attacked Darwinism although she commended Royer, Darwin's first French translator, for her opposition to Newtonian physics.

Toward the end of her life, Renooz rejected science and became a theosophist. She wrote extensive memoirs, which are preserved along with her correspondence in Paris. She has been recently revived by French feminists as a nineteenth-century feminist precursor.   JH

PRIMARY SOURCES

Renooz, Céline. "Charcot devoilé." *Revue Scientifiques des Femmes* 1, no. 245 (1888). Prefigures modern feminist attacks on Charcot's clinics on hysteria.

———. *L'Evolution de l'Homme et des Animaux*. Paris: Adimin-istration de la Nouvelle Science, 1890.

———. *La nouvelle science*. Paris: Librairie nationale, 1890.

Céline Renooz Correspondence, Fonds Bouglé, Bibliothèque Historique de la Ville de Paris, Paris. This archive includes her memoirs as well as extensive correspondence.

SECONDARY SOURCES

Harvey, Joy. *Almost a Man of Genius: Clémence Royer, Feminism and Nineteenth Century Science*. New Brunswick, N.J.: Rutgers University Press 136 (1997). See pages 162–163.

Bard, Christine. *Les Filles de Marianne: Histoires des Feminismes, 1914–1940*. Paris: Fayard, 1995. A revisionist account of Renooz as a feminist and advanced thinker.

"Céline Renooz." *Archives biographiques contemporaires*. Vol. 1. Paris: n.p., 1906.

STANDARD SOURCES

Barnhart.

REYNOLDS, DORIS LIVESEY (1899–1985)

British geologist. Born 1 July 1899 to Margaret (Livesey) and Alfred Reynolds. Married Arthur Holmes, 1939. Educated Palmer's School, Grays, Essex; Bedford College, London University (B.S.; D.Sc.). Professional experience: Queen's University, Belfast, assis-tant in geology (1921–1926); Bedford College, demonstrator in ge-ology (1927–1931); University College, London University, lec-turer in petrology (1931–1933); Durham College, Durham University, lecturer (1933–1943); University of Edinburgh, hon-orary research fellow (1943–1960); Bedford College, honorary re-search fellow (1962–1985). Honors and memberships: Fellow, Royal Society of Edinburgh; Fellow, Geological Society; Geological Society of London, Lyell medallist (1960). Died 10 November 1985.

Doris Reynolds received one of British geology's most cherished awards, the Lyell Medal. The medal was awarded in recognition of the importance of her research in petrology that extended over a period of more than thirty years. Her geological training was from two outstanding women geologists, CATHERINE RAISIN and GERTRUDE ELLES at Bedford College. Raisin encouraged her interest in geology and stimulated her interest in petrology. Her interest in the structural setting of crystalline rocks was stimulated by Elles, another great geologist, whose exposition on Caledonian tectonics inspired her.

Reynolds's earliest work was on the Triassic sandstones of northeastern Ireland when she discovered authigenic potash feldspar. In her other work on petrology, she worked with albite-schists and discovered that albite was of metasomatic origin and could be correlated with an increase of soda. Most of her contributions to petrology involved the geochemical and structural conditions that attended the production of rock-forming minerals by metasomatism. When she was working on the island of Colonsay she found that xenoliths of quartzite found on Colonsay in a hornblendite were transformed metasomatically into micropegmatite.

Reynolds is probably best known to petrologists for her writings on granitization—especially for her development of the doctrine of "fronts." She proposed the idea of basification in advance of granitization and analyzed the complicated sequence of migration of ions believed to have accompanied the driving ahead of unwanted elements to give origin to granite. These articles appeared in the *Quarterly Journal of the Geological Society*, the *Proceedings of the Royal Irish Academy*, the *Proceedings of the Royal Society of Edinburgh* and the *Geological Magazine*.

Little is known of her personal life. She was educated at a girls' school in Essex and then went on to study at Bedford College and the University of London. She subsequently taught at Queen's University, Belfast, at Durham College, returned for some years to University College, London, and then accepted an honorary research post at Edinburgh. For some years before her death, she was an honorary research fellow at her undergraduate college, Bedford, by then part of the University of London system, while finishing an important textbook on geology. While teaching at Durham College just before World War II, she married the geologist Arthur Holmes. After his death in 1965, she published two versions of his textbook on physical geology under her married name. CK/MBO

PRIMARY SOURCES

Reynolds, Doris Livesey. "Catherine Alice Raisin." *Nature* 156 (1945): 327–328.

Holmes, Doris L. *Elements of Physical Geology.* New York: Ronald Press Co., 1969. An adaptation of Arthur Holmes' *Principles of Physical Geology* (1965).

———, ed. *Holmes' Principles of Physical Geology.* New York: Wiley, 1978.

SECONDARY SOURCES

"Presentation of the Lyell Medal to Dr. Doris Reynolds." *Proceedings of the Geological Society of London* 1580 (4 July 1960): 95–96.

STANDARD SOURCES

WWW, vol. 8, 1981–1990.

RHINE, LOUISE ELLA (WECKESSER) (1891–?)

U.S. psychologist and parapsychologist. Born 9 November 1891 in Sanborn, N.Y. Married Joseph Banks Rhine (8 April 1920). Three daughters; one son. Educated University of Chicago (B.S., 1919; M.S., 1921; Ph.D., 1923). Professional experience: Boyce Thompson Plant Institute, New Jersey, assistant plant pathologist. Duke University, Department of Psychology, fellow (1927–1928), Department of Botany, instructor (1928–1948?); Institute for Parapsychology, staff member (1948–1962), director of research (1962–post-1968); Journal of Parapsychology Research, co-editor. Death date unknown.

The education and career of Louise Weckesser Rhine is intimately tied to that of her husband, the parapsychologist Joseph Banks Rhine. She met him first in Ohio as an intense young neighbor, four years younger than she, interested in philosophy. The two young people resolved on forestry as a career and both became students and then graduate students in plant biology at the University of Chicago. She finished her dissertation early and with his master's and her doctorate, they began to work as assistant plant physiologists at the Boyce Thompson Plant Institute in New Jersey. Joseph Rhine soon after was offered a position as instructor in botany at the University of West Virginia in Morgantown, where he remained while completing his dissertation. Inspired by accounts of psychic phenomena and by a lecture by A. Conan Doyle, then touring the United States, he resolved to study the scientific evidence for parapsychology.

Husband and wife went to Boston in the hope that J. B.

Rhine could study with the Harvard professor William McDougall, an English-born psychologist who had written a significant book on the mind-body problem. While in the Boston area, they participated in the Boston-based Society for Psychical Research in which William James had been active. They were dismayed to find McDougall on the verge of moving to a new position at Duke University in North Carolina. He offered them both fellowships, and the two agreed to join him. J. B. Rhine with the help of his wife began to do a series of experiments on parapsychology in McDougall's lab from 1927 to 1930. In 1930, McDougall invited J.B. to stay on to work in the newly established parapsychology lab, while Louise raised four children and taught botany.

After some years developing experimental tests to demonstrate parapsychological phenomena in the laboratory, J. B. published his wildly successful book on Extra Sensory Perception (ESP was a term he coined), published in 1934 under imprint of Boston Psychic Research. His new prominence helped establish him as director of the parapsychology lab from 1940. During the forties, Louise Rhine devoted herself to raising their four children. Aside from occasionally teaching botany, Louise held no formal position until eight years later. By 1948 she became a staff member of the parapsychology laboratory at Duke, regularly conducting research on such problems as telekinesis. Following the publication of her first major book on parapsychology, *Hidden Channels of the Mind,* she was named director of research for the Institute for Parapsychology and placed on the board of her husband's Foundation for Research on the Nature of Man. JH/MBO

PRIMARY SOURCES

Rhine, Louisa Ella. *Hidden Channels of the Mind.* New York: W. Sloane Associates, 1961.

———. *ESP in Life and Lab; Tracing Hidden Channels.* New York: Macmillan, [1967]. Includes biographical details of the life of the Rhines.

———. *Mind over Matter: Psychokinesis.* New York: Macmillan, 1970.

———. *The Invisible Picture: A Study of Psychic Experiences.* Jefferson, N.C.: McFarland, 1981.

———. *Something Hidden.* Jefferson, N.C.: McFarland, 1983. Includes further biographical information.

SECONDARY SOURCES

Sheehy, Noel, Antony J. Chapman, and Wendy A. Conroy, eds. *Biographical Dictionary of Psychology.* New York: Routledge, 1997. Includes biography of James B. Rhine.

STANDARD SOURCES

AMS S&B 11–13; Debus.

RHODES, MARY LOUISE (1916–1987)

U.S. geologist. Born 5 April 1916 in Clinton, Mo. Two sisters. Never married. Educated Humansville High School; University of Missouri (bachelor's degree with distinction, 1938; master's degree, 1939). Professional experience: Standard Oil Company of Texas (SOTEX), production department staff (1942–1946); exploration department staff (1946–1977). Died 26 June 1987 in Midland, Tex.

Mary Louise Rhodes was born in a small town in Missouri and was educated in a different small town. She attended the University of Missouri, where she received bachelor's and master's degrees in geology. Her first professional job was with Standard Oil of Texas (SOTEX) in the production department. In this position, she examined well samples and constructed sample logs, prepared subsurface maps and cross sections and recommended well locations to production management. She transferred into the exploration department in 1946 and for the rest of her career worked in a variety of exploration assignments. Her outside interests included traveling throughout the world. She died of cancer in 1987.

Mary Rhodes was active in professional societies throughout her career. She was awarded honorary life memberships in the Permian Basin Section of SEPM (1974) and to the West Texas Geological Society (1978).

She became an excellent carbonate stratigrapher and was an expert on several of the Permian basin rock units. She and coworker John Emery Adams shared an interest in the Permian basin and were coauthors with others of two classic papers.

CK

PRIMARY SOURCES

Rhodes, Mary Louise. With John Emery Adams and others. "Starved Pennsylvanian Midland Basin." *American Association of Petroleum Geologists Bulletin* 35 (1951): 2600–2607.

———. With John Emery Adams and others. "Dolomitization by Seepage Refluxion." *American Association of Petroleum Geologists Bulletin* 44 (1960): 1912–1920.

SECONDARY SOURCES

Reese, Donald L., and N. Cheatham Bruce. "Mary Louise Rhodes (1916–1987)." *American Association of Petroleum Geologists Bulletin* 72, no. 1 (1988): 92–93.

RICE, ELSIE (GARRETT) (1869–1959)

British/South African botanical artist. Born 25 November 1869 in Elton, Derbyshire, England. Father Reverend Feydell Garrett. At least one brother, Edmund Garrett. Married Charles Rice. Educated Slade School of Art, London; Florence, studied art. Professional ex-

perience: Bedales School, art teacher. Died 27 April 1959 at Cape Town.

Elsie Garrett was born in England and studied in London and Florence. After she completed her studies in Florence, she became an art teacher at Bedales School, where she met a science and mathematics master, Charles Rice, who qualified as a physician in 1918. The couple married and in 1933 they emigrated to South Africa and settled in Cape Town. Elsie Rice began painting wildflowers. One set of her paintings were published in *Wild Flowers of the Cape of Good Hope.* The text was written by Professor R. H. Compton. She also provided the illustrations for Harry Hall's book, *Common Succulents* (London, 1955).

JH/MBO

PRIMARY SOURCES

Rice, Elsie Garrett. With Robert Harold Compton. *Wild Flowers of the Cape of Good Hope.* Kirstenbosch: Botanical Society of South Africa, 1950. Rice contributed the illustrations.

Hall, H. *Common Succulents.* London: Longmans, Green, 1955. Rice contributed the illustrations.

SECONDARY SOURCES

"Elsie Garrett Rice." *Journal of the Botanical Society of South Africa* 45, no. 6 (1959).

Heesom. *Journal of the Botanical Society of South Africa* 63, no. 1 (1977): 23–26.

Letty, Cythna, and Mary Gunn. *The Transvaal Gardener* 45, no. 65 (1975).

STANDARD SOURCES

Gunn and Codd.

RICE-WRAY, EDRIS (1904–)

U.S. physician. Born 21 January 1904 in Newark, N.J., to Mabel (Simon) and Theron Canfield Rice-Wray. Married Robert Carson (30 March 1929; divorced, 1943). Two daughters. Educated Vassar College (A.B., 1927); Northwestern University (M.D., 1932); University of Michigan (M.P.H., 1950). Professional experience: Chicago, practiced medicine (1935–1947); Puerto Rico Health District, director (1948–1949); Public Health Training Center, Rio Piedras, Puerto Rico, director (1950–1956); University of Puerto Rico, professor of preventive health (1950–1956); Planned Parenthood Association, medical director (1950); World Health Organization, medical officer (1957–1958); Asociación Pro-salud Maternal, Mexico City, founder and director (1959–1975); University of the Americas, professor of population studies (1975-retirement). Honors and memberships: University of Michigan, 150th Anniversary Award (1967); American College of Preventative Medicine, Fellow;

Planned Parenthood Federation of America (PPFA); Margaret Sanger Award (1978).

Although she had practiced for a number of years in Chicago, Edris Rice-Wray began her most important life work in public health after her divorce. She went with her young daughters to Puerto Rico to work as the director of the health district there. After she received her master of public health degree, she was made director of the public health training center in Rio Piedras. At the same time, she was professor at the university in preventive medicine. She became interested in Planned Parenthood and began research on oral contraceptives. She published the first field study on these contraceptives in Puerto Rico, studying their availability, acceptability, and hazards. In 1956 or 1957 she went to Mexico City and founded and directed the Association for Maternal Health there. Both of her daughters married Mexican men. Her final position was as professor of population studies in Pueblo, Mexico. She sat on the council of the Planned Parenthood Federation of America and received their Margaret Sanger Award in 1978.   KM

STANDARD SOURCES
AMS P&B 11–14; Debus.

RICH, MARY FLORENCE (1865–1939)

British botanist. Born 1865 in Weston-Super-Mare. Educated Haberdasher's Aske School, Hatcham; Somerville College, Oxford University. Professional experience: Roedian, Sussex, teacher; Granville School, Leicester, established and directed (1900?–1923); Queen Mary College, London, honorary research assistant in botany. Died 20 April 1939 in Ruislip, Middlesex.

Florence Rich contributed to knowledge about fresh water algae. After graduating from Haberdasher's Aske School, she obtained a Clothworker's College scholarship to attend Somerville College, Oxford. She began to teach at the Roedian Girls' School and then established a girls' school, the Granville School, at Leicester. She began to study freshwater algae in 1903 in Leicester, and before 1923 published a series of articles with Felix E. Fritsch, who was then at Queen Mary College. For the last fifteen years of her life, she produced a long series of papers on the freshwater algae of Africa, including those collected by the Cambridge Expedition to East African Lakes, that were published in the English journals *Annals of Botany* and *Journal of Botany,* as well as in the *Transactions of the Royal Society of South Africa.* In recognition of this work she was made a Fellow of the Linnean Society in 1926. Her assistance to the research workers in the

department at Queen Mary College was recognized by her appointment as a fellow six months before her death.

                    JH/MBO

PRIMARY SOURCES
Rich, Florence. "Scientific Results of the Cambridge Expedition to the East African Lakes, 1930–1: The Algae." Part 7. *Journal of the Linnean Society: Zoology* 38, no. 259 (1933): 26.
———. With Mary Agard Pocock. "Observations on the Genus Volvox in Africa." *Annals of the South African Museum* 16 (1933): 427–471.

SECONDARY SOURCES
"M. Florence Rich." *Journal of Botany* 74 (1939): 184. Obituary notice.
Fritsch, Felix E. "Miss M. F. Rich." *Nature* 143 (20 May 1939): 845. Obituary notice.

STANDARD SOURCES
Desmond.

RICHARDS, AUDREY ISABEL (1899–1984)

British anthropologist. Born 8 July 1899 in London to Isabel (Butler) and Henry Erle Richards. Educated privately in India and in English public schools; Newnham College, Cambridge (Natural Science Tripos, 1921; M.A., 1928); London School of Economics, University of London (Ph.D., 1929). Field work: Bemba, Northern Rhodesia (Zambia) (1932–1934); (1957); Tswana of Northern Transvaal (1939–1940); Uganda (1950–1955). Professional experience: Bedford College, assistant lecturer in social anthropology (1928–1930); London School of Economics, lecturer, social anthropology, (1931–1932, 1935–1937); Witwatersrand University, South Africa, senior lecturer (1937–1940); British Colonial Office, researcher (1940–1945); University of London, lecturer and reader in anthropology (1945–1949); East African Institute for Social Research, Makerere University, Kampala, Uganda, founder and director (1949–1956); Studies in Archaeology and Anthropology, Newnham College, director (1957); Newnham College, vice-principal (1958–1960); Cambridge University, Smuts Reader in Anthropology (1961–1966); Cambridge University African Studies Centre, founder (1965–1966). Retired 1967. Honors and memberships: Commander of the British Empire (1955); Fellow of the British Academy (1967); first woman president of the Royal Anthropological Institute (1959–1961); second woman president of African Studies Association (1963–1966); Wellcome Trust gold medalist, Rivers medalist for field work. Died 1984.

One of the outstanding British women anthropologists trained by Bronislaw Malinowski at the London School of Economics, Audrey Richards was born in London into a family with numerous social connections among academics and colonial bureaucrats. Her father held a position as a lawyer with the viceroy of India, and later was a professor of law at Oxford University. Richards spent her early years in India, but returned to England for her secondary education. She went to Newnham College, Cambridge, where she received her undergraduate degree in natural science in 1921. She continued to maintain a loyalty to her college and to the education of young women for the rest of her life.

After she received her master's degree in anthropology from Newnham, she lectured in anthropology at Bedford College for Women in London and attended the London School of Economics. There she studied anthropology with Malinowski, whose functionalism Richards adopted for her study of food habits. She received her doctorate in 1929 with a dissertation on the southern Bantu tribes and then lectured at the London School of Economics. By 1932–1934 she was doing field work among the Bemba of Northern Rhodesia (Zambia), investigating biological and cultural needs, stressing food culture, agriculture, and land use. She continued to return to the Bemba over subsequent years, and also studied the Tswana of the Northern Transvaal (1939–1940). She taught as senior lecturer, Witwatersrand University, South Africa, until 1940, when her teaching and her field work were interrupted by World War II.

Richards returned to England to do research for the Colonial Office during the war, but found the bureaucrats suspicious of anthropologists, particularly social anthropologists. She lectured for four years at University of London following the war. Then in 1949, she went to Uganda to do part-time field work and there she founded and directed the East African Insitute for Social Research, Makerere, Uganda, from 1949 to 1956. Returning to England once more, she was made director of studies in archeology and anthropology at Newnham College in 1957. The following year she was made vice-principal of Newnham College (1958–1960) and then Smuts Reader in Anthropology at Cambridge University (1961–1966). She founded the African Studies Centre, Cambridge University (1965–1966), and became principal of Newnham, but she was never made full professor at Cambridge in spite of her unusual role as scholar and lecturer.

Although Richards never married, she had a deep attachment to her teacher and mentor Malinowski, with whom she had a romance following the death of his wife. She became guardian of his children and was said to fulfill this role admirably. Throughout her life she published important studies on African groups focusing on political tribal organization. Her writings on women's roles, economic transition, and nutritional studies in East and Central Africa have become classics.

JH

PRIMARY SOURCES

Richards, Audrey. *Hunger and Work in a Savage Tribe: A Functional Study of Nutrition among the Southern Bantu.* London: Routledge, 1932.

———. *Land Labor and Diet in Northern Rhodesia: An Economic Study of the Bemba Tribe.* Oxford: Oxford University Press, 1939.

———. *Bemba Marriage and Modern Economic Conditions.* Rhodes-Livingstone Papers no. 4. Rhodesia (Zambia): Rhodes Livingstone Institute, 1940.

———. "Some Types of Family Structure amongst the Central Bantu." In *African Systems of Kinship and Marriage,* ed. A. R. Radcliffe-Brown and D. Forde. Oxford: International African Institute, Oxford University Press, 1950.

———. *Chisingu: A Girl's Initiation Ceremony among the Bemba of Northern Rhodesia.* London: Faber; New York: Crove, 1956.

———, ed. With Ford Sturrock and Jean M. Fortt. *Subsistence to Commercial Farming in Present-Day Buganda: An Economic and Anthropological Survey.* Cambridge: Cambridge University Press, 1973.

SECONDARY SOURCES

Firth, Raymond. "Obituary of Audrey Richards." *Man* 20, no. 2 (1984): 341–343.

Gladstone, Josephine. "Audrey I. Richards (1899–1984): Africanist and Humanist." In *Persons and Powers of Women in Diverse Cultures: Essays in Commemoration of Audrey I. Richards, Phyllis Kaberry, and Barbara E. Ward,* ed. Shirley Ardener. New York: Berg, 1992.

Gulliver, P. H. "Bibliography of the Principal Writings of Audrey Richards." In *The Interpretation of Ritual,* ed. J. S. LaFontaine, 285–289. London: Tavistock, 1972.

Werbner, Richard P. "Audrey I. Richards." *International Encyclopedia of Social Sciences,* ed. David L. Sills. Vol. 18. New York: Macmillan, 1968.

STANDARD SOURCES

Gacs (article by Stella Silverstein).

RICHARDS, CLARICE AUDREY (1887–1953)

U.S. forest pathologist. Born 1887. Educated Miami University, Ohio (A.B., 1912; M.A., 1914); University of Wisconsin (Ph.D., 1922). Professional experience: public schools, teacher (1906–1909); Miami University, Ohio, assistant in botany (1912–1914); Ohio Biological Survey, assistant (1915); University of Wisconsin, assistant botanist (1915–1917); U.S. Forest Service, pathologist (1917–1929); Madison branch, pathologist in charge (1929–1943), forest pathologist (1943–1947), senior pathologist (1947–1952). Died 1953.

Clarice Audrey Richards credited her early interest in botany, forests, and forest products to her carpenter father. She explained that he took his children on long walks in the woods and described the different plants and trees. Before Richards completed her bachelor's degree, she taught school. It was financially necessary for Audrey to work her way through college, but despite this impediment she completed her undergraduate degree in three years and was elected to Phi Beta Kappa. After she received her master's degree, she worked for the Ohio Biological Survey as an assistant and then as an assistant botanist at the University of Wisconsin.

Most of Richards's professional career was spent with the U.S. Forest Service. After working at the service for a number of years, she was named acting director of the Madison branch. She was a great success and was named director in 1928. As chief of the Madison branch, she held the highest position of authority achieved by a woman in the bureau. In the early part of her career, she had many opportunities for research and publications, but as she gained more responsibility, her work became almost entirely administrative.

While Audrey Richards was working for the U.S. Forest Service she did fundamental work on causes and prevention of decay, stain, and mold in wood products. She also pioneered subjects such as the relation between durability and the effect of decay on the chemical composition of wood and the comparative resistance of wood-destroying fungi to various preservatives. She and her colleagues explored the properties of over two hundred chemicals that might help prevent blue stain in lumber. The result was the industry's adoption of the mercurial dip treatment. Especially interesting was her work on the physiology of wood-inhibiting fungi. She was active in the Botanical Society of America, the American Forestry Association, the Phytopathoological Society, the Forest Products Research Society, and the American Association for the Advancement of Science.

JH/MBO

PRIMARY SOURCES

Richards, C. Audrey. "Defects in Cross Ties Caused by Fungi." In a report, "Railroad Tie Decay," American Wood Preservers' Association, 1939.

SECONDARY SOURCES

McDonald, John K. "Clarice Audrey Richards." *Journal of Forestry* 49 (December 1951): 918–919. Includes photograph.

STANDARD SOURCES

AMS 3–8; Bailey (with portrait).

RICHARDS, ELLEN HENRIETTA SWALLOW (1842–1911)

U.S. chemist and home economist. Born 1842 in Dunstable, Mass., to Fanny (Taylor) and Peter Swallow. Married Robert Hallowell Richards. Educated at home; Westford (Massachusetts) Academy (1859–1863); Vassar College (1868–1870; B.A., 1870; M.A., 1873); Massachusetts Institute of Technology (special student in chemistry, 1870–1875; B.S., 1873). Professional experience: Women's Laboratory, MIT, instructor (1876–1883); private and government organizations on pollutants and toxic chemicals, consultant (1870s and 1880s); MIT, instructor in sanitary chemistry (1884–1911). Died 1911 in Boston, Mass.

Ellen Swallow Richards was the only child of schoolteacher parents. Her father was both a teacher and a farmer, and Ellen helped him with the farmwork and her mother with the housework. Although the Swallows wanted to provide the best possible education for their only child, they had limited financial resources. In spite of the financial burden they moved to Westford, Massachusetts, which had a fine school, the Westford Academy, where Ellen began to study in 1859. In order to earn a better living, Peter Swallow opened a village store. In addition to managing a strenuous academic workload, Ellen helped her father in the store, tutored other students, and collected plants and fossils. During this time she showed the interest in applied science that later caused her to be known as the founder of the science of home economics. She observed the buying habits of the women at the store and became aware of issues of product purity and air and water contamination.

After Ellen graduated from the Westford Academy in 1863, the family moved to Littleton, Massachusetts, where her father again operated a store. Beginning in 1864, Ellen worked to save money for her future education. She taught school, tutored, "hired out" to other families as a cook, cleaning woman, or nurse, and helped in the store. As soon as she had saved enough from her earnings, she left home for the larger city of Worcester, Massachusetts, to attend school.

In order to maintain her independent existence, Swallow worked very hard. She wrote of her exhaustion, combined with the apparent hopelessness of her ambitions for further education, and blamed them for both physical illness and mental depression. Describing this time as two years in purgatory, she recognized that the money she saved eventually provided the means for this education. A newly opened institution for women—Vassar College, in Poughkeepsie, New York—provided her with the opportunity for further studies.

With the three hundred dollars she had saved, the twenty-five-year-old Swallow entered Vassar in September 1868. She was first admitted as a special student but joined the senior class her second year and received a bachelor's degree in 1870. An excellent student, Swallow was particularly influenced by astronomy teacher Maria Mitchell and chemistry teacher Charles Farrar. Swallow was predisposed toward a field that would have useful applications, thus she decided to continue in chemistry rather than astronomy.

In the autumn of 1870, Swallow was accepted as a special student in chemistry at the Massachusetts Institute of Technology, which, like Vassar, was a young institution (both had opened in 1865). She was the first woman to be accepted at any "scientific school." Since she was admitted free, she at first assumed that financial need motivated the admissions officers. She soon found, however, that it was so that the president could deny that she was a student if any of the trustees or students complained. She claimed that if she had realized the situation, she would not have gone. In 1873 Swallow received a bachelor's degree from MIT, as well as a master's from Vassar, to which she had submitted a thesis on the chemical analysis of iron ore. Although she remained at MIT for two more years as a graduate student, she was never awarded a doctorate, because the heads of the department wanted to avoid having a woman receive the first doctor of science in chemistry. Swallow's interest in practical chemistry was strengthened during these years by her association with Professor William Nichols, who analyzed public water supplies for the Massachusetts Board of Health, and Professor John Ordway, an industrial chemist.

In 1875 Swallow married Robert Hallowell Richards, a professor of mining engineering and head of MIT's new metallurgical laboratory. Both physically and in their personalities, Richards and Swallow were very different. He was physically good looking and she, not particularly pretty. She was quick to act and he moved very deliberately. In spite of the disruptive presence of Swallow's mother, who moved in with them after a year of marriage, the merger of opposites was successful. Since the couple had no children they were able to devote considerable energy to supporting each other's scientific endeavors.

Economically secure with an understanding husband, Ellen Richards was able to apply herself during the period 1875–1885 to furthering the cause of scientific education for women. These efforts resulted in the establishment of the Woman's Laboratory at MIT, which offered training in chemical analysis, industrial chemistry, mineralogy, and biology. Richards organized the science section of the Society to Encourage Studies at Home. This society, actually a correspondence school, was begun in 1882 by Anna Ticknor. Richards personally communicated with the students of the school and soon found her work expanding from an effort to teach women science to an attempt to help them solve problems in many areas. She was concerned with the prevalence of ill health among middle-class housewives, and stressed the

importance of healthful foods, comfortable dress, and both physical and mental exercise. She was one of the founders, in 1882, of the Association of Collegiate Alumnae, which later became the American Association of University Women. The new organization helped fight the myth that extensive study was detrimental to the health of young women. To counter this, the members conducted a survey of the health of college-educated women and concluded that no ill effects were seen that could be attributed to their studies.

Richards's strategy of discretion was successful, for the young female science students at the Woman's Laboratory at MIT were soon admitted to regular courses and by 1882 four women had received degrees. Because it was no longer needed, the Woman's Laboratory was closed in 1883. In its place, a new building was erected, equipped with a parlor and reading room for female MIT students. Although it looked at first as though Richards had worked her way out of a job (in 1879 MIT had recognized her as an "assistant instructor," probably without pay), she received in 1884 an appointment as instructor in sanitary chemistry in the new MIT laboratory for the study of sanitation, an appointment she held for the rest of her life. From 1887 to 1889 she supervised a highly influential survey of Massachusetts inland waters and for many years taught techniques of water, air, and sewage analysis to students in the MIT sanitary engineering program. During the years she worked in the Woman's Laboratory, she also took on consulting work for government and industry, testing commercial products as well as the air, water, and soil for harmful substances.

Richards's conviction that the family should be the civilizing institution led her to consider ways to make the home an ideal environment. She looked at methods of systematizing and simplifying housework and of providing nutritious meals at reasonable cost. This new field of study came to be known as home economics. It had many practical ramifications, one of the first being the opening of the New England Kitchen in Boston in 1890. This demonstration kitchen offered nourishing foods for sale at a low price, with the cooking area open to the public so that methods of food preparation could be demonstrated. The idea burgeoned and spread to other cities. School systems and hospitals became interested in the project, and the U.S. Department of Agriculture sought Richards's advice in the preparation of its bulletins on nutrition.

The term "home economics" emerged from a series of summer conferences at Lake Placid, New York. Richards organized and chaired these sessions, which prepared courses of study for public schools, colleges, and extension schools, syllabi for women's clubs, and so on. Ellen Richards insisted that it be based on a foundation of economics and sociology. She was involved in the formation of the American Home Economics Association in 1908 and provided both the inspiration (and the funds) for the founding of this association's *Journal of Home Economics.* She lectured and wrote books on the subject, and was appointed (1910) to the council of the National Education Association, with the responsibility of supervising the teaching of home economics in schools. She died at age sixty-eight in Boston, of heart disease.

As an applied scientist, Ellen Swallow Richards observed the physical and societal effects of rapid industrialization, such as polluted air and water, impure products, and social decay. She used her skills as a chemist to devise methods to improve physical conditions, assuming that the result would be the elimination of social evils. Richards hoped to achieve success through the education of the individuals who were in charge of the home, insisting that women's ignorance must be remedied for the universal good. Presaging both the consumer and the environmentalist movements, her proposals included the formation of associations for homemakers where they could have suspect substances analyzed. She urged women to arm themselves with some knowledge of chemistry, and of "mechanical and physical laws."

Richards's picture of the relationships between organisms and their physical and social environments accorded with the ideas of the ecology movement then being established by Ernst Haeckel (1834–1919). She perceived the interrelatedness of all forms of life and called for the education of women to correct the imbalances in the system caused by ignorance and greed. The home could serve as the primary agency for preventing abuses perpetrated on consumers because of their ignorance. By focusing on the home, Richards avoided the opprobrium attached to "scientific women." By studying home economics, women accepted their traditional role in the home while exploring methods of making the home a better and safer place.   MBO

PRIMARY SOURCES

Richards, Ellen H. *The Chemistry of Cooking and Cleaning: A Manual for House-keepers.* Boston: Estes and Lauriat, 1882.

———. With Alpheus G. Woodman. *Air, Water, and Food from a Sanitary Standpoint.* New York: Wiley, 1900.

SECONDARY SOURCES

Bevier, Isabel, and Susannah Usher. *The Home Economics Movement.* Boston: Whitcomb and Barrows, 1912.

Clarke, Robert. *Ellen Swallow: The Woman Who Founded Ecology.* Chicago: Follett, 1973.

Henderson, Janet K. "Four 19th-Century Professional Women." *Dissertation Abstracts International* 43 (1982): 698.

Hunt, Caroline L. *The Life of Ellen H. Richards.* Boston: Whitcomb and Barrows, 1912.

STANDARD SOURCES

AMS 1; *DAB; NAW; Notable;* Ogilvie 1986.

RICHARDS, MARY ALICE ELEANOR (STOKES) (1885–1977)

British botanist. Born 1885 in Dolseran near Dolgellau, Wales. Father Frederick Stokes. Married Henry Richards (1907). One son; two daughters. Educated privately; Mason College (later University of Birmingham), studied part-time. Professional experience: Royal Botanical Gardens, Kew, field collecting (1950–1973). Honors and memberships: University of Wales (honorary M.Sc., 1964); West Wales Field Society, Merioneth branch, founder and president (1953); Order of the British Empire (OBE) (1969). Died 1977.

Mary Alice Eleanor Richards, always interested in botany, became a remarkable field collector of herbarium specimens in Africa. She was brought up both in Litchfield and in Wales where her grandmother lived. She was not permitted to study botany at the university, but managed only to attend part-time classes. She studied under William Hillhouse, professor of botany at Mason College, Birmingham. She married her cousin and settled in Wales near her grandmother's house. She began to travel around the world collecting botanical specimens with her army officer husband. They visited India, Malaya, China, Japan, some Pacific islands and North America. During World War I she turned her home into a Red Cross hospital and helped to run it, for which she got the Royal Red Cross Medal. She was a councilor on the Merioneth County Council and became active in many social and public health concerns.

In the early 1920s, Richards returned to field botany and began to study the botany of Wales, as a life member of the Botanical Exchange Club. Although she took time out to work with the Red Cross again in World War II, she returned to botany after the end of the war. She found a number of unusual specimens of Welsh flora.

After her husband died and her children married, she set up her own bog garden and rock garden. At sixty-five Richards went to stay with friends in Northern Rhodesia (Zambia) and was asked to do collecting for Kew. She spent a part of each year for the next twenty years collecting numerous specimens for Kew. On the recommendation of President Kenneth Kaunda, she was elected OBE. Richards died at the age of ninety-two.   JH / MBO

PRIMARY SOURCES

Richards, Mary. "An Account of an Excursion in Wales." *Botanical Society of the British Isles Yearbook* (1950): 44–51.

———. With Peter Benoit. "A Contribution of a Flora of Merioneth." *Nature in Wales* 7 (1961): passim. Republished in a 69-page booklet, 1963.

Herbarium of Welsh plants at the National Herbarium of Wales.

SECONDARY SOURCES
Milne-Redhead, E. "Mary Alice Eleanor Richards." *Watsonia* 12 (1978): 187–190.

RICHARDS, MILDRED HOGE (ALBRO) (1885–?)

U.S. geneticist and zoologist. Born 7 July 1885 in Baltimore, Md. Married Aute Richards (19 December 1917). Two sons. Educated Goucher College (A.B., 1908); Columbia University (M.A., 1912; Ph.D. in genetics, 1914). Professional experience: high school teacher (1908–1911); Indiana University, instructor in zoology (1914–1918); Rocky Mountain Biological Laboratory, summer teaching; University of Oklahoma, associate professor (1947–1948). Retired 1948. Death date unknown.

Mildred Hoge Albro was well trained as a geneticist and zoologist. She and Aute Richards, her future husband, both had a connection with the Rocky Mountain Biological Laboratory. He was teaching at Wabash College in Indiana when they married. They came to Oklahoma in 1920, where he was a professor of zoology from 1920 to 1950. He was also director of the Oklahoma Biological Survey and the Oklahoma Museum of Zoology. Probably because of nepotism rules, Mildred Richards was unable to hold a position, in spite of her education. She finally got an appointment as an associate professor one year before she retired in 1948. The couple spent the rest of their lives in Tucson, Arizona.

JH/MBO

PRIMARY SOURCES
Richards, Mildred Hoge. *The Descendants of Samuel Hogg of Wilmington, Delaware.* Tucson, Ariz.: N.p., 1959.
———. Correspondence in Fernandus Payne Papers, Indiana University Archives.

STANDARD SOURCES
AMS 3–8, B 9, P&B 10.

RICHTER, EMMA (HÜTHER) (1888–1956)

German paleontologist. Born 4 May 1888. Married to Rudolf Richter. One daughter. Senckenburg Museum, paleontolological volunteer (ca. 1845–1888). Died 15 November 1956.

Emma Richter, the wife of paleontologist Rudolf Richter, spent about forty-five years working as a volunteer in the Senckenburg Museum. She worked side-by-side with her husband, and particularly concentrated on the relationships between various trilobites. She was known for her sharp eyes, which could pick up minor differences between specimens.

In 1934 Richter became an honorary member of the Paleontological Society of America. She received an honorary doctorate from the University of Tübingen in 1949.

CK/MBO

PRIMARY SOURCES
Richter, Emma. With Rudolf Richter. "Neue Beiträge zur Kenntnis der Geologie, Palaeontologie un Petrographie der Umgegend von Konstantinopel; 4, Trilobiten aus dem Bosporus-Gebiet." *Preussische Geologische Landesanstalt, Abhandlungen* 190 (1939).
———. With Rudolf Richter. "Das Kambrium am Toten Meer und die älteste Tethys (Studien im Palaeozoikum der Mittelmer-Laender), 7." *Abhandlungen der Senckenbergischen Naturforschenden Gesellschaft* 460 (1941).
———. With Rudolf Richter. "Die Trilobiten der Erdbach-Zone (Kulm) im Rheinischen Schiefergebirge und im Harz; 1, Die Gattung Phillibole." *Senckenbergiana* 30, nos. 1–3 (1949): 63–94.
———. With Rudolf Richter. "Die Frage der Saukianda-Stuff (Kambrium, Spanien); studium im Palaeozoikum der Mittelmer-Länder, 9." *Senckenbergiana* 30, nos. 4–5 (1949): 217–240.
———. With Rudolf Richter. "Die Trilobiten des Ebbe-Sattels und zuvergleichende Arten (Ordovizi, Gotlandium/Devon)." *Abhandlungen der Senckenbergischen Naturforschenden Gesellschaft* 488 (1954).

SECONDARY SOURCES
Kegel, W. "Nachruf für Rudolf Richter—Emma Richter." *Zeitschrift deutsche Geologische Gesellschaft* 10, pt. 3 (1958): 637–642.
Schmidt, Herta. "Emma Richter 4.3.1888–15.11.1956." *Natur und Volk* 86, no. 12 (1956): 428–429.
Simom, Wilhelm. "Rudolf und Emma Richter." *Palaeontologische Zeitschrift* 31, nos. 3–4 (1957): 111–115.
Teichert, Curt. "From Karpinsky to Schindewolf—Memories of Some Great Paleontologists." *Journal of Paleontology* 50 (1976): 1–12.

STANDARD SOURCES
Current Biography, 1940; Sarjeant.

RICHTER, GRETE (fl. 1919)

Austrian (?) physicist. Professional experience: Vienna Institute for Radium Research, researcher.

Nothing is known of Richter's life. Her research, however, was of note. When measuring the ionization produced by alpha particles in order to determine their total energy, a significant portion of the energy may be absorbed by the walls of the ionization chamber. Working at the Vienna Institute for Radium Research, Richter developed mathematical corrections to account for this energy loss, and compared the accuracy of three different formulas for calculating ionization. MM

PRIMARY SOURCES

Richter, G. "Messungen im Schutzringplattenkondensator mit RaF nebst eingehender diskussion der Verwendung des Binanten-oder Quadrantenelektrometers als Strommessinstrument." *Akademie der Wissenschaften, Vienna. Sitzungsberichte 2a.* 128 (1919): 539–569.

STANDARD SOURCES

Meyer and von Schweidler.

RIDDLE, LUMINA COTTON (1871–1939)

U.S. botanist. Born 18 March 1871 to Ida (Carlton) and George Riddle. At least two siblings. Married Bernard Bryan Smyth. Educated Ohio State University (B.S., 1897; M.S., 1898; Ph.D., 1905). Professional experience: Akeley Institute, Mich., teacher (1899–1900); Altoona, Kans., high school teacher (1901–1902); Munden, Kans., high school teacher (1917–1918), superintendent (1918–1920). Washburn College, Topeka, Kans., curator of natural history (1901; 1903–1904; 1917); Kansas State Museum, Topeka, staff (1906–1913), curator (1913–1915); Ottawa University, Ottawa, Kans., assistant professor, biology (1921–1924). Died 2 February 1939 in Cleveland, Ohio.

Lumina Cotton Riddle, a direct descendant of John Cotton of New England historical fame, was the first student to receive a doctorate in botany from The Ohio State University and the second student in the university to receive a doctoral degree. She held a number of teaching and curatorial positions. In 1906 she married Bernard Bryan Smyth, curator of the herbarium and ornithological collections at the Kansas State Museum. Known for a fine singing voice, Riddle gave public performances on occasion.

She was a member of the American Association for the Advancement of Science, Agassiz Association, Britton and Brown Botanical Club, and the Ohio and Kansas Academies of Science.

Riddle published her research on the embryological life histories of flowering plants in the genera *Alyssum, Elodea, Staphylea,* and *Ranunculus.* She also worked on the morphology of plants. She published a list of the algae recorded from Sandusky Bay and listed the algae and protozoa from Brush Lake, a naturally formed glacial kettle lake. After Riddle married, she assisted her husband in research on the vascular flora of Kansas. JH/MBO

PRIMARY SOURCES

Riddle, Lumina Cotton. "The Embyology of *Alyssum.*" *Botanical Gazette* 27 (1899): 314–323.

———. "Development of the Embryo Sac and Embryo of *Staphylea trifolia.*" *Ohio Naturalist* 5 (1905): 353–363.

Smyth, Lumina C. Riddle. With Bernard B. Smyth. "Catalogue of the Flora of Kansas, Part I." *Transactions of the Kansas Academy of Science* 23/24 (1911): 273–295.

SECONDARY SOURCES

Stuckey, Ronald L. "Lumina Cotton Riddle." From the collection of Ronald L. Stuckey.

STANDARD SOURCES

Barnhart; Stuckey.

RIDENOUR, NINA (1904–)

U.S. psychologist and administrator. Born 12 December in Vincennes, Ind., to Ada (Allen) and Horace Daniel Ridenour. Married Maximilian Arnold Boll (26 August 1941). Educated Vincennes public schools, high school; Balboa High School (1922); Harvard University, Radcliffe College (A.B., 1926); Colorado College (M.A. in sociology, 1930); New York University (Ph.D., 1941). Professional experience: Dennison Manufacturing Company, Detroit, assistant to staff psychologist (1926–1929); Colorado College, instructor in sociology (1929–1930); Detroit Children's Center, chief psychologist (1931–1937); State Charities Aid Association, New York City and State Committees on Mental Hygiene, assistant executive secretary (1937–1947); National Committee for Mental Hygiene, director division of world affairs (1947–1949), director of education (1949–1952); Ittelson Family Foundation, executive director (1952–1967). Concurrent experience: Wayne State University, Graduate School of Public Affairs, instructor; New York University, School of Education, instructor (1946–1947); International Committee for Mental Hygiene, executive officer (1947–1949); Mental Health Materials Center, editorial consultant (1949–1952). Honors and memberships: American Orthopsychiatry Association, secretary (1944–1948); Psychological Association.

Nina Ridenour's expertise was primarily in the field of mental health administration. She came to prominence as the director of education of the National Association for Mental Health. After studying psychology at Radcliffe, she went to Colorado Springs to take a position in a child guidance clinic. She taught briefly at Colorado College, and then finished a master's degree in sociology.

Moving to Detroit, she again began to work as a psychologist at a child guidance clinic over the following six years, teaching briefly at Wayne State in the Public Affairs Division. From Detroit, Ridenour went to New York where she became assistant executive secretary for the committees on mental hygiene of the State Charities. She also began to study toward a doctorate at New York University. In 1941 she completed this degree, writing her dissertation on the educational use of mental hygiene literature.

As director of education for the Mental Hygiene Committee, she helped organize the joint participation of the American organization, the National Committee for Mental Health and the National Mental Health Association of Great Britain to hold the first postwar International Congress of Mental Hygiene, which took place in London in 1948. She began to set up commissions of professional associations throughout the United States to formulate international mental health guidelines. The result was resoundingly successful and the United Nations Educational, Scientific, and Cultural Organization gave the international association that developed from this congress, the World Federation for Mental Health, its formal recognition as a consulting organization. The National Committee for Mental Hygiene represented the federation in the United States.

Ridenour also wrote and produced a number of widely distributed pamphlets for mental health education. In the 1950s, she continued to play an influential role in the organization of conferences on children and youth for the White House and served on international advisory boards associated with the World Federation for Mental Health abroad. For the last fifteen years of her career she was the executive director of the Ittleson Foundation, which under her leadership focused on mental health and the mental, physical, and social well-being of children.   JH/MBO

PRIMARY SOURCES

Ridenour, Nina. "Mental Hygiene Literature: The Preferences of Instructors in Mental Hygiene as Related to Clincial Experience." Ph.D. diss., New York University, 1941.

———. "Signposts for Social Psychiatry from the International Congress on Mental Health." *American Journal of Orthopsychiatry* 20 (June 1950).

———. *Mental Health in the United States: A Fifty-Year History.* Cambridge, Mass.: Commonwealth Fund and Harvard University Press, 1961.

———. *Mental Health Education: Principles in the Effective Use of Materials.* New York: Mental Health Materials Center, 1969.

STANDARD SOURCES

AMS S&B 9–12; *Current Biography* 1951.

RIGAS, HARRIETT B. (1934–1989)

Canadian/U.S. electrical engineer. Born 30 April 1934 in Winnipeg, Manitoba. Married (1959). Educated Queen's University in Ontario (bachelor's degree, 1956); University of Kansas (M.S., 1959; Ph.D., 1963). Professional experience: Mayo Clinic, engi-

neer (1956–1957); Ventura College, instructor (1957–1958); Lockheed Missile and Space Company, senior research engineer (1963–1965); Washington State University, research associate (1965–1967), manager of the hybrid facility (1968–1980), professor of electrical engineering (1976–1987); Michigan State University, professor and chair of the department of electrical engineering (1987–1989). Died 26 July 1989.

Although engineer Harriett Rigas was born in Canada, she spent her entire career in the United States. She married in 1959. Her specialties were computer technology, automatic patching, control system stability, and logic design. She established the computer engineering program at Washington State University and made advances in computer coding theory. In her research she concentrated on improving methods for creating the digital code that allowed computers to store and manipulate data. Her theories helped reduce computer memory requirements and helped facilitate the discovery of software errors.

After only two years as professor and chair of the department of electrical engineering at Michigan State University, Rigas died at the age of forty-five. She was a board member of the Institute for Electrical and Electronic Engineers (IEEE) and was its representative on the Accreditation Board for Engineering and Technology.   JH/MBO

STANDARD SOURCES

Notable (article by Karen Withem).

RING, BARBARA TAYLOR (1879–1941)

U.S. psychiatrist, dramatist, and administrator. Born 2 April 1879 in Scotland. Six siblings, three brothers; three sisters. Married Arthur Hallam Ring (1900); one son, Hallam T. Ring. Educated Boston College of Liberal Arts; Boston University School of Medicine (M.D.). Professional experience: Ring Sanatorium and Hospital, administrator and psychiatrist (1920?–1941). Concurrent experience: Arlington Training School for Nurses (later Ring Psychiatric School of Nursing), administrator. Died 31 August 1941 in Arlington Heights, Mass.

Although Barbara Ring was a psychiatrist and administrator of the Ring Sanatorium in Arlington, Massachusetts, she is best known for the plays and pageants that she produced. Born in Scotland, she came to the United States when very young and her family settled in Sullivan, Maine. In order to prepare herself for the Boston College of Liberal Arts, she attended a seminary at Bucksport. She then went to the Boston University School of Medicine, where she received a medical degree. What began as an avocation, writing and producing pageants, developed into a major part of her life. She attended a well-known course at Harvard, Professor

George Pierce Baker's English 47 Workshop to prepare herself. Her best-known plays are *Esculapius, Three Plays under Three Flags,* and *Psyche Lights Her Lamp.*

In 1900, she married psychiatrist Arthus Hallam Ring. Professionally she was a psychiatrist and administrator of the Ring Sanatorium, and held executive positions at the Arlington Training School for Nurses and at the Ring Psychiatric School of Nursing. In addition to her dramatic writings, Ring also produced medical papers.   JH/MBO

PRIMARY SOURCES
Ring, Barbara. *Three Plays under Three Flags.* Boston: Baker, 1928.
Ring Sanatorium and Hospital. *Diagnosis and Therapeutics* (*Purpose*). Arlington Heights, Mass.: [Ring Sanatorium and Hospital], 1937.

SECONDARY SOURCES
"Barbara Taylor Ring." *New York Times,* 1 September 1941.

STANDARD SOURCES
Current Biography 1941.

RIOCH, MARGARET J. (1907–)

U.S. psychologist. Born 24 January 1907 in Paterson, N.J. Married David McKenzie Rioch, 1938. Educated Bryn Mawr; Wellesley College (A.B., 1929?); University of Frankfurt-am-Main; University of Berlin; University of Basle (graduate study); Washington University, St. Louis (M.A. in psychology, 1942?). Professional experience: Wilson College, instructor in German; Wellesley College, instructor in German (to 1938). Community Mental Hygiene Clinic, Rockville, Md., psychologist; Chestnut Hill Lodge, psychologist; private practice; National Institutes of Mental Health researcher (1960–1962); A. K. Rice Institute, executive director. Died 25 November 1996 in her home in Chevy Chase, Maryland.

Psychologist and psychotherapist Margaret J. Rioch's father died when she was one year old, and her mother moved in with her grandmother and her two unmarried teacher aunts. Educated at Wellesley and Bryn Mawr, she did graduate studies in Germany and Switzerland. Having acquired great facility in German, her first positions were teaching German at Wilson College and at Wellesley. In the late thirties, she married David McKenzie Rioch, a neuropsychiatrist who had trained at Johns Hopkins and who was then an assistant professor of neuroanatomy at Harvard Medical School. The young couple moved to St. Louis where he was made professor of neurology and chairman of the department of neuropsychiatry at Washington University.

With her husband's involvment in psychiatry, Rioch gradually became interested in psychology and worked toward a master's degree in clinical psychology from Washington University, St. Louis, with a thesis on the Rorschach test. She prepared for this work by taking private lessons from Emil Oberholzer on Rorschach interpretation. Her interest in projective testing later led her to take private lessons with Sylvan Tomkins in 1958–1959 on the Thematic Apperception Test and its interpretation at Princeton during her husband's year at the Institute for Advanced Studies.

Rioch moved with her husband to the Washington, D.C., area when he took a job as staff psychiatrist and director of research at the Chestnut Lodge Sanitarium in Rockville, Maryland, during the war years. After the war, he moved to the Walter Reed Army Institute for Research. Rioch began working at the Community Mental Hygiene Clinic in Rockville, but she later worked as a part-time psychologist at Chestnut Lodge while retaining a private practice.

Rioch's interest in psychotherapy increased as she studied with Frieda Fromm-Reichmann and Harry Stack Sullivan. Her research interests led her to conduct a study for the National Institutes of Mental Health (1960–1962) to develop a pool of professional psychotherapists by recruiting women of middle age whose families were already grown to return to graduate work and develop professional careers. She encouraged A. Kenneth Rice to expand his group relations conferences from England to the U.S. Rice had adopted the Tavistock approach—the premise that individual issues relating to social interaction will result in a microcosm of actual social dynamics. This connection resulted in the establishment of the A. K. Rice Institute, which became a national organization. Rioch was the first executive director and chairman of the executive committee of the Washington-Baltimore Center.   JH/MBO

PRIMARY SOURCES
Rioch, Margaret J. With others. *Pilot Project in Training Mental Health Counselors.* Washington, D.C.: U.S. Department of Health, Education, and Welfare, Public Health Service, 1965.
———. *Group Relations and Psychotherapy.* Fort Lee, N.J.: Sigma Information, 1972. Spoken recording.
———. *Dialogues for Therapists.* San Francisco: Jossey-Bass, 1976.

SECONDARY SOURCES
"Dr. Margaret J. Rioch, 89, Psychotherapist." *New York Times,* 16 December 1996. Obituary notice.
Evans, F. Barton III. "Margaret Jeffrey Rioch (1907–1996)." *American Psychologist* 53, no. 11 (November 1998).

STANDARD SOURCES
AMS 13 (under David McKenzie Rioch); O'Connell and Russo 1988 (includes portrait).

RIPLEY, MARTHA (ROGERS) (1843–1912)

U.S. homeopathic physician. Born 30 November 1843 in Lowell, Orleans County, Vt., to Esther Ann (George) and Francis Rogers. Four siblings. Married William Warren Ripley (25 June 1867) in Decorah, Iowa. Three daughters. Educated Lansing, Iowa, High School (no diploma); Boston University Medical School (M.D., 1883). Professional experience: Lansing Elementary Schools, teacher (seven terms); medical practice, Minneapolis, Minn. (1883–1912?); Maternity Hospital, established; Homeopathic Medical College, professor of children's diseases. Died 18 April 1912.

Although she was born in New England, Martha Rogers's family moved to northeastern Iowa, where she grew up. Brought up by a Free-Will Baptist mother and a father who was noted for being litigious (he also helped escaping slaves), Martha had a fitful public school education. Although she did not graduate from Lansing High School, she taught elementary school for seven terms. She married a Massachusetts man, William Warren Ripley, and returned to Massachusetts, where her three daughters were born. She joined the woman's suffrage movement in 1875. Concern about illness among the mill girls in Lawrence, Massachusetts, led her to study medicine. One of her sisters had already graduated from the Boston University Medical School. The year she got her medical degree, her husband was severely injured in a mill accident. They moved to Minneapolis, Minnesota, where she began her medical practice. Ripley was elected president of the Minnesota Women's Suffrage Association. She was president for six years and continued on the medical board for the next six years.

Ripley specialized in children's diseases. She established a maternity hospital, which catered both to married and unmarried women. She was professor of children's diseases at the Homeopathic Medical College in Minneapolis. She was also interested in many social and public health issues concerning women.

Ripley died of complications from a rheumatic heart. After her death a plaque in her honor was installed in the rotunda of the state capitol in Minneapolis in 1939.   JH/MBO

SECONDARY SOURCES

Willard, Frances E., and Mary A. Livermore. *A Woman of the Century: Fourteen Hundred-Seventy Biographical Sketches Accompanied by Portraits of Leading American Women in All Walks of Life.* Buffalo, N.Y.: Moulton, 1893.

STANDARD SOURCES

NAW (article by Winton Solberg).

RISING, MARY MEDA (1889–1997)

See Stieglitz, Mary Rising.

RISSEGHEM, HORTENSE VAN (1889–1974)

Belgian organic chemist. Born 20 October 1889 in Ixelles. Educated Université Libre de Bruxelles (1908–1913; D.Sc. in chemistry, 1913); Agrégée de l'Ensignement Supériere (qualification to teach in higher education) (1937). Professional experience: Ecole Normale Emile André, Brussels, professor of chemistry and physics (1919–1933); Université Libre de Bruxelles, Chef de travaux (research head) (1937–1959), Chargé de Cours (instructor) (1959–1960). Honors and memberships: Prix Jean Stas (1913); Prix Henri van Laer (Société Chimique Belgique). Died 3 January 1974 in Brussels.

Hortense van Risseghem was an organic chemist who both studied and conducted research at the Université Libre de Bruxelles. She was awarded a prize for her dissertation and soon after began to teach chemistry and physics at the Ecole Normale Emile André in Brussels while pursing her career as a research chemist. She was an assistant in chemistry at the Université Libre until she qualified as agregée, allowing her to teach at the university level, in the late 1930s. She was then made chef de travaux, research supervisor, and in 1959, was chef de cours at the university for one year before she reached retirement age.

Throughout her research career, Risseghem published widely, alone and with her colleagues in both Belgian and French chemical journals and in the journal of the Académie des Sciences, Paris. Much of her work focused on ethyl isomers. She also illuminated the action of oxidizing bacteria on the gycols and the effect of microorganisms on hexanes. In 1921, the Chemical Society of Belgium (Société Chimique Belgique) awarded her its Henri van Laer prize. She continued to produce significant research on the physical structure of organic compounds until the age of seventy. She died in her early eighties in Brussels.   JH/MBO

PRIMARY SOURCES

Risseghem, Gertrude van. "De l'action de microorganismes sur les formes diastéréomères de l'hexane -3,4,-diol." *Bulletin Société Chimique Belgique* 45 (1936): 21–35.

———. "Préparation et l'étude de l'hexéne-3." *Bulletin Société Chimique Belgique* 47 (1938): 194–215; 221–240; 261–286.

———. "Nouvelle contribution à l'étude du 3-methyl-pentène-2." *Bulletin Société Chimique France* 19 (1952): 177–182.

———. With B. Gredy. "Isomerie allylique dans le cas des bromohexénes." *Comptes rendus Académie des Sciences, Paris* 202 (1931): 489–491.

STANDARD SOURCES

Poggendorff, vol. 7B (includes more than twenty articles by van Risseghem).

RITTER, MARY ELIZABETH (BENNETT) (1860–1949)

U.S. physician. Born 7 June 1860 in Salinas, Calif., to Abigail (Noble) and William Bennett. Married William E. Ritter (23 June 1891). No children. Educated Gilroy School (1877); San Jose Normal School, premedical studies (1882–1883); Cooper Medical College (M.D., 1886); Children's Hospital, Berkeley, Calif. (internship, 1886–1887). Professional experience: Peachtree and Fresno, Calif., public schools, teacher (1877–1883); Berkeley, Calif., private medical practice (1887–1909); University of California, Berkeley, medical examiner and advisor of women (1892–1909); University of California, San Diego, lecturer in social hygiene (1914–1919?). Honors and memberships: University of California, San Diego, honorary LL.D. (1935). Died 1949 in Mountain View, Calif.

Mary Elizabeth Bennett was born in 1860 in Monterey County, where her parents had been pioneers and about which she later wrote. She graduated from Gilroy School at the age of seventeen. She then taught in the public schools of Peachtree and Fresno, California, until she decided to take classes at the San Jose Normal School in chemistry with a Professor Norton and study as a medical apprentice with a woman physician, Euthausia S. Meade. After this year, she entered Cooper Medical College (later Stanford Medical School), as one of only two women in her class. With the encouragement of CHARLOTTE BLAKE BROWN, who had graduated from Woman's Medical College of Pennsylvania and founded the Pacific Dispensary (soon expanded to Children's Hospital), she spent almost a year as an intern in the Children's Hospital. Before she completed the year, she was offered the practice of another woman physician, Sarah I. Shuey, who was moving to Sierra Madre. She then practiced privately for the following twelve years.

During her internship year, she met her future husband, William Emerson Ritter, who was studying zoology. He performed a careful autopsy on a dog whose kidney had been excised by Brown and who had been carefully observed by Mary Bennett. After their continued correspondence during his year as a master's student at Harvard University, he returned to Berkeley as assistant professor at the University of California, Berkeley, in the new zoology department headed by Joseph LeConte. Shortly after he returned, Mary Bennett and he were married. He later became head of the zoology department.

Like many scientific couples, the honeymoon was also a scientific expedition; the two were almost drowned when their sailboat capsized as they were searching for blind "Goby" fish. Back in Berkeley, Mary Bennett Ritter continued her medical practice. She also took on the position as medical examiner and advisor to the young women students at the University of California, serving as the first woman's

"dean" (in fact if not in name), established a residential system for the women, and set up gymnasium privileges. Later she was honored for this work.

One of the founding members of Scripps Institution of Oceanography (later part of the University of California, San Diego), William Ritter was appointed its first director. Husband and wife moved to La Jolla to become residents in 1909. As wife of the director, Mary Ritter put aside her own medical practice and assisted him, and also established the first women's club of La Jolla and served on many boards. During World War I, she also lectured on social hygiene at the University of California. After her husband's retirement, she wrote a book on the early experiences of her family in California, *More Than Gold in California* (1933). Her husband died in 1944, but Mary Bennett Ritter lived for an additional five years, dying at the age of eighty-nine.   JH/MBO

PRIMARY SOURCES

Ritter, Mary Bennett. *More Than Gold in California*. Berkeley, Calif.: n.p., 1933. A historical memoir of the life of the Bennett family as California pioneers.
——— . With George Blumer, and Luis and Walter Alvarez. *Recollections of Cooper Medical College (1883–1905)*. Palo Alto, Calif.?: Stanford Medical School, 1964. Contains Mary Ritter's recollections of her life as medical student and intern.

SECONDARY SOURCES

"Mary Elizabeth Bennett Ritter." Biographical Files, Scripps Institute of Oceanography.
"Mary Elizabeth Bennett Ritter." Biographical files, La Jolla Historical Society.

RIVIERE, JOAN (VERRALL) (1883–1962)

British psychoanalyst. Born 9 July 1882 in Brighton, Sussex, to Anna Hodgson and Hugh John Verrall. Oldest surviving child. Married Evelyn Riviere. One daughter, Diana. Educated Wycombe Abbey; Germany; Ernest Jones, analysis (1916–1921); Sigmund Freud, analysis (1922). Professional experience: firm of Nettleship, court dressmaker.

Joan Verrall became one of Britain's first lay analysts, a practicing member of the newly formed British Psycho-Analytical Society. Born in Sussex to an intellectual and literary family, Joan Hodgson Verrall attended Wycombe Abbey and then studied in Germany, where she became very proficient in the language, a facility that later became very important in her career. Her talents appeared to be concentrated along artistic and design lines so she did not attend the university. She used these skills for a time as a court dressmaker with the firm of Nettleship. However, through her uncle's Cambridge circle and the Society for Psychical Research, she began to become interested in Freud. Verrall was considered arrogant and was not well-liked among her peers. She married a barrister, Evelyn Riviere, when she was twenty-three; they had their only child two years later. Joan Riviere's beloved father died shortly after daughter Diana was born, and she suffered a breakdown, leading her to seek help from the analyst Ernest Jones. She continued to see Jones for almost five years and was won to the cause of psychoanalysis. Her analysis with Jones ended after Riviere fell in love with him, a good example of "transference love." He confessed that his analysis of Riviere was his worst failure. He handed her over to Sigmund Freud for analysis in 1922. Freud criticized Jones's handling of the case and stood up for Riviere, although by 1927 the tables were turned.

Riviere met MELANIE KLEIN at the Hague Congress of 1920 and again at the Salzburg Congress of 1924. The two got along well and when the British criticized ANNA FREUD, Riviere supported Klein. At this time Sigmund Freud attacked Riviere and Jones defended her. For her part, although she was an advocate of Klein, Riviere never turned away from Sigmund Freud. She, however, was critical of his inability to see new facts, something at which she excelled. Several important papers resulted from her ability to analyze rigorously, without recourse to prior hypotheses. She published "Womanliness as a Masquerade" in 1929, in which she explored the intellectual woman. She concluded that womanliness could be worn as a mask to both hide masculinity and to avert reprisals if found to have it. In "Jealousy as a Mechanism for Defence" (1932), she postulated a deep primal envy in the child resulting in the child's desire to despoil and ravage the mother.

Joan Riviere may best be remembered as one of the first English translators of Freud. She also is known for her translation of Melanie Klein's works into English. JH/MBO

PRIMARY SOURCES
Riviere, Joan. *The Inner World and Joan Riviere: Collected Papers: 1920–1958.* Ed. With a biographical chapter by Athol Hughes. London: Karmac, 1991.

STANDARD SOURCES
Appignanesi.

ROB, CATHERINE MURIEL (1883–1962)

British botanist. Born 21 February 1906 at Catton Hall near Thirsk, Yorkshire. Educated at home by governesses. Professional experience: Yorkshire Naturalists' Union, recorder of flowering plants in North Riding, secretary (1958), president (1969). Honors and memberships: Linnean Society, Fellow (1946). Died 1962.

Catherine Rob (known as Kit) was an experienced amateur field botanist. Working in North Yorkshire, Rob was the unequaled authority on the distribution of the region's vascular plants. She collected the North Yorkshire records for the *Atlas of the British Flora.* Her section was one of the most complete ones in this work. She also published an account of the plants in the Forestry Commission Guide, *North Yorkshire Forests,* and made numerous contributions to *The Naturalist.*

Rob was educated privately by governesses and had no formal training in botany. During World War II, she served as a cook at the Catterick Military Hospital and was employed full time by the Yorkshire Rent Assessment Panel.

Active in local natural history organizations, she joined the Wild Flower Society when she was only seventeen years old and became secretary of its lower section in 1930 and of its upper section in 1949. She also was a long-term member of the Botanical Society of the British Isles and was local secretary for North Yorkshire, and later served this organization in different positions. She served on the Council of the BSBI for many years. In 1934 she joined the Yorkshire Naturalists' Union and held many important offices in that organization. She was the plant recorder for North Yorkshire from 1938 to 1971, and was responsible for the publication of Yorkshire plant records from 1957 to 1965. In 1969, she became the third woman to be elected president of the union. Rob also had a keen interest in conservation. She was active in the Yorkshire Naturalists' Trust, held numerous offices, and served it in many ways.

Rob was generous in disseminating information. She shared her fine herbarium and her library with beginning botanists. Her generosity with information and her warm personality all contributed to her reputation as one of Yorkshire's most valuable botanists. She was elected a Fellow of the Linnean Society, and was honored by having a plant *Rubus robii* named for her. JH/MBO

PRIMARY SOURCES
Rob, Catherine. With F. Pering and J. G. Dony. *English Names of Wild Flowers.* London: Butterworth for the Botanical Society of the British Isles, 1974.

SECONDARY SOURCES
Annual Report of the Yorkshire Philosophical Society (1975): 7. Obituary notice.
Crackles, F. E. "Catherine Muriel Rob." *Naturalist* (1975): 67–68. Obituary notice.
Watsonia 11, no. 1 (1976): 89–90. Obituary notice.

ROBB, JANE (SANDS) (1892–?)

U.S. physiologist, pharmacologist. Born 20 November 1893 in Corning, N.Y. Married Robert Cumming Robb (1928). Two

children. Educated Syracuse University (A.B., 1915); Woman's Medical College of Pennsylvania (M.D., 1918); University of Pennsylvania (D.Sc., 1925); Philadelphia General Hospital, internship (1919–1920). Professional experience: Philadelphia General Hospital, assistant resident physician (1921–1923); Woman's Medical College of Pennsylvania, assistant and instructor in medicine and cardiology (1921–1923), acting professor (1925–1926); professor (1926–1930); Syracuse Medical School, associate professor of pharmacology (1930–1948), acting professor and department head (1942–1945); Syracuse, Department of Cardiovascular Research (1946–?). Concurrent experience: Bryn Mawr College, physician (1920–1921); University of Pennsylvania, instructor (1922–1924). Honors and memberships: American Medical Association, bronze medal (with Robert Robb) (1935); National Science Research Fellow (1923–1925); New York Infirmary for Women and Children, Blackwell Citation (1954); Woman's Medical College of Pennsylvania, honorary D.Sc. (1950); Physiological Society, Fellow; Society for Experimental Biology and Medicine, Fellow. Death date unknown.

Jane Sands went to Syracuse University for her undergraduate degree and continued for a medical degree at the Woman's Medical College of Pennsylvania, interning at Philadelphia General Hospital ("Blockley"). Although she obtained a position soon after as a physician for a year at Bryn Mawr, she returned for her residency at the hospital while teaching cardiology and medicine at the Woman's Medical College.

Sands's research interests in pharmacology and physiology inspired her to travel to Cambridge and Edinburgh as well as to Western Reserve on a medical National Research Fellowship in the early 1920s while working toward a doctorate at the University of Pennsylvania. She returned to Philadelphia to teach as a professor at the Woman's Medical College, a position she held for four years.

Awarded a Berliner fellowship, Sands continued her research in physiology. During this period, she met and married Robert Cumming Robb, a physiologist ten years younger than she, who was finishing his doctor of science degree at Harvard and doing research as an exhibition scholar. The couple went to Syracuse Medical School in 1930, when she obtained a position as associate professor in the pharmacology department and he began to work toward a medical degree. They worked together on experiments in cardiovascular physiology that earned them a joint bronze medal from the American Medical Society in 1935. The couple had two children, but this does not appear to have slowed Jane Robb's career.

During World War II, Robb was acting head of the pharmacology department, but after the war she moved into the department of cadiovascular research, where she remained for the rest of her career. In her early sixties, she began to re-

ceive a number of awards in recognition for her work, including an honorary degree from the Woman's Medical College of Pennsylvania and the Blackwell Citation (named after ELIZABETH BLACKWELL) from the New York Infirmary for Women and Children.   JH/MBO

PRIMARY SOURCES
Robb, Jane Sands. *Comparative Basic Cardiology.* New York: Grune and Stratton, 1965.

STANDARD SOURCES
AMS 5–8, B 9, P&B 10–11; Rossiter 1982.

ROBB, MARY ANNE (BOULTON) (1829–1912)

British horticulturist. Born 1829 in Tew Park. Married [?] Robb (1856). Educated privately. Professional experience: garden at Liphook; collected plants in Greece. Died 1912.

Mary Anne Robb lived in Tew Park until her marriage in 1856. She then moved to Liphook where she established a garden that displayed a notice to deter trespassers which stated "Beware of the Lycopodium!" She was a friend of the botanists W. Robinson and E. A. Bowles. She collected plants in Greece in 1891 and introduced *Euphorbia robbiae,* "Mrs. Robb's Bonnet," to British gardens.   JH/MBO

SECONDARY SOURCES
"Mary Anne Boulton Robb." *Kew Bulletin* (1912): 203.
"Mary Anne Robb." *Journal of the Royal Horticultural Society* (1973): 306–310. Includes portrait.
Morley, B. D. *Wild Flowers of the World.* New York: Putnam, 1970.

STANDARD SOURCES
Desmond.

ROBERTS, CHARLOTTE FITCH (1859–1917)

U.S. chemist. Born 13 February 1859 to Mary (Hart) and Horace Roberts. Educated Wellesley College (A.B., 1880); Cambridge University, England (1886–1887); Yale University (Ph.D., 1894); University of Berlin, Germany (1899–1900). Professional experience: Wellesley College, instructor (1881–1887), assistant professor (1887–1892), associate professor (1892–1896), professor and head of chemistry department (1896–1917). Honors and memberships: Wellesley College, fellow; American Association for the Advancement of Science. Died 5 December 1917.

Charlotte Roberts is best known for her 189-page monograph *The Development and Present Aspects of Stereochemistry.* Although the ideas presented in Roberts's book were superseded by the electronic theory of chemical bonding, it was an important textbook for a number of years. Today it serves as a historical record of ideas current one hundred years ago.

After spending her early years in Greenfield, Massachusetts, Roberts earned her bachelor's degree at Wellesley (entering in that institution's first class) and then served as an instructor for six years. During that period, she went to Cambridge University, attended the lectures by the Scottish chemist Sir James Dewar, and became interested in stereochemistry. She returned to Wellesley as an associate professor. In 1892 she was given a leave of absence for graduate work at Yale University where she earned her doctoral degree. After obtaining this degree, she was promoted to full professor and head of the department.

Rather than attempting laboratory work, Roberts worked on the development of ideas in chemistry. During her career at Wellesley, she had three study leaves in Europe during which time she concentrated on keeping current rather than on doing original research. JH/MBO

PRIMARY SOURCES
Roberts, Charlotte Fitch. "On the Reduction of Nitric Acid by Ferrous Salts." *American Journal of Science* 46 (1893): 126–134.
———. *The Development and Present Aspects of Stereochemistry.* Boston: D. C. Heath, 1896.

SECONDARY SOURCES
Burrell, E. L. "Charlotte Fitch Roberts." *Wellesley Alumnae Quarterly* 2, no. 2 (1918): 80–81.
Creese, Mary R. S., and Thomas M. Creese. "Charlotte Roberts and Her Textbook on Stereochemistry." *Bulletin for the History of Chemistry* 15–16 (1994): 31–36.

STANDARD SOURCES
AMS 2; *WWW*(A), vol. 1, 1897–1942.

ROBERTS, DOROTHEA KLUMPKE (1861–1942)

U.S. astronomer. Born 9 August 1861 in San Francisco, Calif., to Dorothea (Tolle) and John Klumpke. Married Isaac Roberts. Educated public and private schools, San Francisco; studied in Germany, Switzerland, and France; Paris Observatory; Sorbonne (B.S., 1886; Matt. D., 1893). Professional experience: Paris Observatory, assistant (1887–1901); Bureau of Measurements, Paris, director (1891–1901). Died 5 October 1942 in San Francisco, Calif.

Dorothea Klumpke Roberts spent most of her career in Europe, although she remained a citizen of the United States. After she completed her studies at the Sorbonne, Klumpke worked at the Paris Observatory. She married Isaac Roberts, a Welsh astronomer who had a private observatory at Crow-

borough, Sussex, and spent the years 1901–1904 with him in Sussex. Upon his death in 1904 she returned to France and lived with her mother and sister, continuing her astronomical work.

As director of the Paris Bureau of Measurements, Klumpke supervised the charting and cataloguing of stars to the fourteenth magnitude. She gained worldwide recognition for her work on the Congress of Astronomy and Physics held in Chicago during the World's Columbian Exposition of 1893. The paper she presented at this meeting on the charting of the heavenly bodies earned her a $300 award from the French Académie des Sciences in 1893 and the Prix des Dames from the Société Astronomique de France in 1897. In 1928 Roberts published *Celestial Atlas* as a memorial to her husband. She produced a supplement to this volume in 1932. She received another prize from the Académie des Sciences in 1932 for this project. The many scholarly societies of which she was a member included the Royal Astronomical Society, the American Astronomical Society, the American Association for the Advancement of Science, the Société Astronomique de France, the British Astronomical Association, and the International Astronomical Union. In 1934 the French government presented her with the Cross of the Legion of Honor for forty-eight years of service to French astronomy. She returned to California in 1932; she died in San Francisco ten years later. MBO

PRIMARY SOURCES
Roberts, Dorothea Klumpke. *Contribution à l'étude des anneaux de Saturne.* Paris: Gauthier-Villars et Fils, 1893.

SECONDARY SOURCES
Bracher, Katherine. "Dorothea Klumpke Roberts: a Forgotten Astronomer." *Mercury* 10 (1981): 139–140.
Kidwell, Peggy Aldrich. "Women Astronomers in Britain, 1780–1930." *Isis* 75 (September 1984): 534–546.
Meadows, A. J. *Science and Controversy.* London: Macmillan, 1972. Information on Roberts within this biography of J. Norman Lockeyer.

STANDARD SOURCES
NCAB; Ogilvie 1986; Rebière.

ROBERTS, EDITH ADELAIDE (1881–?)

U.S. botanist. Born 28 April 1881 in Dover, N.H. Educated Smith College (A.B., 1905); University of Chicago (M.S., 1911; Ph.D., 1915). Professional experience: Mount Holyoke College, instructor to associate professor of botany (1915–1917); U.S. Department of Agriculture, extension worker with women (1917–1919); Vassar College, associate professor (1919–1921), professor (1921–1950), emerita professor (1950–?); Massachusetts Insti-

tute of Technology, department of food technology, guest scientist (1951–?). Honors and memberships: American Association for the Advancement of Science; Botanical Society of America. Death date unknown.

Edith Roberts is known for her work in plant physiology. After earning her doctorate from the University of Chicago, she took a position for two years at Mount Holyoke College. She left academia for time when she joined the U.S. Department of Agriculture, where she was probably involved in war work projects. After two years at the USDA, she took a position at Vassar College, where she spent the remainder of her career. She conducted research on the appearance of starch grains of potato tubers of plants grown under constant light and temperature conditions, the relationship of the microphysical and microchemical structure of starch grains to that of the plastid in which it is formed, and the comparative effect of ionizing radiations and heat upon the starch-containing cells of the potato tubers. She also did work on the germination of seeds and propagation of native plants.

JH/MBO

PRIMARY SOURCES
Roberts, Edith Adelaide. With Elsa Rehmann. *American Plants for American Gardens: Plant Ecology, the Study of Plants in Relation to Their Environment.* New York: Macmillan, 1929.
———. *American Ferns: How to Know, Grow and Use Them.* New York: Macmillan, 1935.
———. With Helen Wilkinson Reynolds. *The Role of Plant Life in the History of Dutchess County.* Poughkeepsie, N.Y.: Lansing Bros., 1938.

STANDARD SOURCES
AMS 3–8; B 9; P&B 10–13; Bailey; Barnhart.

ROBERTS, LYDIA JANE (1879–1965)

U.S. nutritionist and home economist. Born 30 June 1879 in Hope Township, Barry County, Mich., to Mary (McKibbin) and Warren Roberts. Three siblings. Educated public grammar and high school, Martin, Mich.; Mt. Pleasant Normal School (later Central Michigan University), one-year course (1899); (life certificate, 1909); University of Chicago (M.S., 1919; Ph.D., 1928). Professional experience: school teacher (1899–1915); University of Chicago, assistant professor of home economics (1919–1928), associate professor (1928–1930), professor and department chair (1930–1944); University of Puerto Rico, chair home economics department (1944–1952). Died 28 May 1965 in Rio Piedras of a ruptured abdominal aneurism.

Lydia Roberts was a specialist in the nutrition of children. After obtaining her teaching credentials she taught in a vari-

ety of schools throughout the United States until 1915 when at age thirty-six she entered the University of Chicago with advanced standing. Chicago was an excellent choice of a school for Roberts, for there she was able to work with KATHARINE BLUNT, a biochemist. During her teaching experience she had become interested in the relation between diet and health, and felt it was important to continue her education in order to better understand the nutritional needs of children. After earning both a master's and a doctoral degree from this institution, she remained at Chicago, where she moved up the academic ladder to professor. She remained at Chicago until mandatory retirement, at which time she accepted a faculty appointment at the University of Puerto Rico. During her time at Chicago, she had a heavy schedule of administration, teaching, and research on nutritional needs of children. Her research was geared to practical applications.

Roberts was chair of the home economics department at the University of Puerto Rico from 1946 to 1952. Even after her second retirement she was active in programs to improve the nutrition of Puerto Rican families. In Puerto Rico she studied the food habits of the people; the results of this study were published in 1949.

Roberts served on three committees of the White House Conference on Child Health and Protection and was a longtime member of the Council on Foods and Nutrition of the American Medical Association. She was also a member of the Food and Nutrition Board of the National Research Council, where she played an important role in setting up recommendations for the addition of selected vitamins and minerals to food materials to assure improved nutrition during the war.

JH/MBO

PRIMARY SOURCES
Roberts, Lydia Jane. "A Malnutrition Clinic as a University Problem in Applied Nutrition." *Journal of Home Economics* 11 (March 1919). A revised version of Roberts's master's thesis.
———. *Nutrition Work with Children.* Chicago: University of Chicago Press, 1927.
———. With Rosa Luisa Stefani. *Patterns of Living in Puerto Rican Families.* Rio Piedras: University of Puerto Rico Press, 1949.
———. *The Doña Elena Project: A Better Living Program in an Isolated Rural Community.* Rio Piedras: University of Puerto Rico Press, 1963.

SECONDARY SOURCES
Bing, Franklin C. "Lydia Jane Roberts—a Biographical Sketch." *Journal of Nutrition* 97 (September 1967): 1–13.
Martin, Ethel Austin. "Lydia Jane Roberts, June 30, 1879–May 28, 1965." *Journal of the American Dietetic Association* 49 (August 1965): 127–128.

STANDARD SOURCES
AMS 5–8, B 9, P&B 10; Bailey; *NAW*(M) (article by Aaron J. Ihde); *WWW(A)*, vol. 4, 1961–1968.

ROBERTS, MARY (1788–1864)

British botanist and author. Born 18 March 1788 in Homerton, London, to Ann (Thompson) and Daniel Roberts. Grandfather T. Lawson (1630–1691). At least one sibling, brother Oade. Professional experience: wrote popular books on natural history. Died 13 January 1864 in Brompton, London.

Mary Roberts was probably educated at home. Little is known about her early life, although we know that she and her family moved to Painswick, Glocestershire, in 1790. Her grandfather, the Quaker botanist Thomas Lawson, was the so-called father of Lakeland Botany. Lawson was a correspondent of John Ray and his plant records were used by John Wilson in his *Synopsis of British Plants in Mr. Ray's Method* (1744). Although Roberts would not have known her grandfather, his reputation may have sparked her interest in botany. Her brother, Oade (1786–1821) contributed to a botanical work as well.

Although Roberts was brought up a Quaker, she left the Society when her father died. After his death she moved with her mother to Brompton Square, London, where she remained until her death in 1864. She wrote many popular nature books.   JH/MBO

PRIMARY SOURCES
Roberts, Mary. *Wonders of the Vegetable Kingdom Displayed in a Series of Letters.* London, 1822.
———. *Annals of My Village, Being a Calendar of Nature for Every Month in the Year.* London: G. and W. B. Whittaker, 1831.
———. *The Seaside Companion: or Marine Natural History.* London: Printed for Whitaker, 1835.
———. *Flowers of the Matin and Evensong; or Thoughts for Those Who Rise Early, in Prose and Poetry.* London: Grant, 1845.
———. *Voices from the Woodland, Descriptive of Forest-Trees, Ferns, Mosses, and Lichens.* London: Reeve and Benham, 1850.
———. *A Popular History of the Mollusca.* London: Reeve and Benham, 1851.

STANDARD SOURCES
Desmond; *DNB.*

ROBERTSON, FLORENCE (1909–1954)

U. S. geophysicist. Born 11 November 1909 in Paris, Tex. Never married. Educated high school in Bonham, Tex. (graduated 1927); Paris, Tex., Junior College (graduated 1929); Texas Technological College, Lubbock (B.A., 1935; M.A., 1936); St. Louis University (Ph.D., 1945). Professional experience: St. Louis University, instructor in Geophysics (1939–1945); St. Louis University, Institute of Technology, assistant professor (1945–1948), associate professor (1948–1951), professor (1951–?). Died 18 November 1954 in Wichita Falls, Tex.

Born in Paris, Texas, Florence lost her father at an early age. Her mother remarried and there was one child of this second marriage who died of diptheria. After attaining her early education in Texas, including a master's degree from Texas Technological College in Lubbock, Texas, in physics and mathematics with a thesis on geophysics, she entered graduate school at St. Louis University as a graduate fellow in geophysics, receiving a doctoral degree from this institution. She climbed the academic ladder at the newly founded Institute of Technology and was made full professor in 1951. She died at the age of forty-five from lymphatic cancer.

Robertson was active in professional and scientific societies, including the Society of Exploration Geophysicists, the American Institute of Mining and Metallurgical Engineers, and the Seismological Society of America (served as secretary, vice-chairman, and chairman of its eastern section). She was secretary of the Section of Seismology of the American Geophysical Union and active on the Executive Committee of this organization. She was a Fellow of the American Physical Society and the Geological Society of America and a member of Pi Mu Epsilon, Sigma Xi, and the American Society for Engineering Education.

Robertson took an active part in developing the curriculum in geophysical education. Her contributions were largely in the area of education.   CK

SECONDARY SOURCES
Heinrich, Ross Raymond. "Florence Robertson." *Geophysics* 21, no. 2 (1956): 503–504.

STANDARD SOURCES
AMS 8, P 9.

ROBERTSON, JEANNIE (SMILLIE) (1878–?)

Canadian physician. Born 10 February 1878 in Tuckersmith Township, Huron County, Ontario. Six siblings. Married Alex Robertson (1936). Educated local schools (teacher's certificate, 1896); Woman's Medical School in Toronto; University of Toronto (M.D., 1909); Woman's Medical College of Pennsylvania hospital, intern (1909). Professional experience: Toronto, private practice (1910–?); Woman's College Hospital, Toronto, surgeon (1911?–1951). Death date unknown.

Jeannie Smillie was born and raised in Canada of Canadian parents of Irish and Scottish descent. Although they never went beyond grammar school, both of her parents were interested in education. She was the third child in a family of seven. At an early age, Jeannie decided to study medicine. The family lived on a farm and the children had to walk two and a half miles each day to the nearest school. She then attended public school in Hensall, and then in Seaforth, where she paid three dollars a week for room and board.

Smillie taught until she was twenty-five in order to earn enough money to attend medical school. She began her medical education at the Women's Medical School in Toronto. However, at the end of her first year the women's school closed, and the women were admitted to Toronto University. Internships were difficult for women to obtain in Canada, so she went to the Woman's Medical College of Pennsylvania to intern. After a year in the United States, she went back to Toronto and opened a practice. She soon realized the importance of becoming a surgeon, so she returned to the Woman's Medical College of Pennsylvania for six months in order to have a concentrated learning experience. When she returned, women were not able to do surgery in a hospital, and she performed her first operation on a kitchen table. More Canadian women were becoming physicians and they wanted to have their own hospital. The Women's College Hospital resulted, and Smillie spent her forty years of practicing doing abdominal and especially gynecological surgery.

She was a charter member of the Federation of Medical Women of Canada and active in liberal causes. She was a member of the Women's Liberal Association and eventually became its president. Late in life Smillie married Alex Robertson, a widower whom she had met forty years previously. KM

PRIMARY SOURCES
"Robertson, Jeannie Smillie." In Hellstedt, *Autobiographies.*

ROBERTSON, MURIEL (1883–1973)

British microbiologist and immunologist. Born 8 April 1883 in Glasgow, Scotland, to Elizabeth (Ritter) and Robert Andrew Robertson. Eleven siblings. Educated at home (governesses); Glasgow University (arts degree; M.A., 1905; D.Sc., 1922). Professional experience: Carnegie Fellowships (1907–1910); study in Ceylon (1907–1909); Lister Institute of Preventive Medicine, London, post-doctoral fellow (1910–1914); staff (1910–1961); Protozoologist to the Protectorate of Uganda (from 1915). Died 1973.

Born in Glasgow into a family of twelve children, Muriel Robertson lived in a cultivated and stimulating atmosphere. The house echoed with exciting discussions of Darwin's ideas. She had a good deal of freedom and was interested in many subjects (including horseback riding and astronomy).

Because the family could afford good governesses and tutors, Muriel had an excellent early education at home. When she was about thirteen, her mother found a tutor who would teach her and one of her sisters Latin and mathematics. After her father's death when she was sixteen years old, the family's financial situation was reduced. Muriel planned to study medicine, but at the insistence of her mother took an arts degree first. The science courses required for that degree were the first formal sciences courses that she had ever had. Fortunately she had excellent professors in zoology and botany, including Graham Kerr, a Fellow of the Royal Society who introduced her to what was later to become her specialty. As an undergraduate, she was provided with a bench in a chilly laboratory to work on the life cycle of *Pseudospora volvocis,* an organism that has both an ameboid and a flagellate stage of development. This work was published in 1905, and by that time she had forgotten her desire to study medicine.

A Carnegie Fellowship awarded in 1907 allowed her to go to the tropics (Ceylon) to study blood parasites of reptiles, particularly trypanosomes. She returned to Glasgow in 1908, and then spent the last two years of her fellowship at the Lister Institute of Preventive Medicine in London as an assistant to E. A. Minchin, Fellow of the Royal Society, who held an endowed chair of protozoology there. In 1910, Muriel Robertson was appointed to the staff of the Lister Institute. The experience she had gained in Ceylon with the protozoan *Trypanosoma,* which causes sleeping sickness, and her work on trypanosomiasis in fish and reptiles was useful in the early twentieth-century battle against this disease in Uganda, where an epidemic was raging. She was offered a temporary appointment by the Colonial Office to go to Uganda as protozoologist. She went to Uganda by herself, learned Luganda, studied the trypanosomes, and made herself popular among the Ugandans. Her most important work was her study of the life cycle of *T. Gambiense.* She described her observations in five papers published in 1912 and 1913.

Returning to the Lister Institute after the beginning of World War I, Robertson and HARRIETTE CHICK worked on making tetanus antitoxin for the army. She was assigned the task of investigating the bacterial causes of gas gangrene. At the end of the war, Robertson returned to work on protozoans with an occasional foray into bacteriology.

During World War II she was sent to Cambridge, where she again began to work on the gas gangrene bacillus and searched for a prophylactic vaccine. She remained at Cambridge, where she became a friend of MARJORY STEPHENSON. At the Lister Institute she continued the research on *Trichomonas* in cattle that she had begun earlier.

After having an eye removed because of a severe case of glaucoma she moved to Cambridge. She continued to work in Cambridge with Alan E. Pierce, whose doctoral work she had supervised. She remained in Cambridge for eighteen months before she decided that her work was not as good as it should be. She joined her sister, Dorothy, in the family home in Limavady in Northern Ireland where she remained until her death at the age of ninety.

Although she studied immunology and bacteriology at different times in her career, her major interest was in protozoology, where she made her most important contributions. However, the two world wars accounted for her incursions into the realm of bacteriology, where she worked on anaerobic organisms of the genus *Clostridium*. After working with immunological techniques on bacteria, she later applied these techniques to protozoa. Her major work in immunology was a collaborative work with W. R. Kerr on the infection of cattle by *Trichomonas foetus*. By combining Kerr's experimental and veterinary talents with Robertson's protozoological and serological expertise, they were able to clarify the features of the immunopathology of the disease.

Robertson was sometimes a rather prickly person willingly confronting colleagues whenever she disagreed with them. She looked upon the pre–World War I times as the halcyon days when life was civilized. After the two world wars, she found the world a different and much less pleasant place to be. Although critical of the Royal Society until the election of its first two women Fellows, Marjory Stephenson and KATHLEEN LONSDALE in 1945, she was happy with her own election in 1947.

JH/MBO

PRIMARY SOURCES

Robertson, Muriel. "Studies on Ceylon Haematozoa. No. 1. The Life Cycle of *Trypanosoma vittatae*." *Quarterly Journal of Microscopical Science* 53 (1909): 665–695.

———. "Transmission of Flagellates Living in the Blood of Certain Freshwater Fishes." *Philosophical Transactions of the Royal Society of London* B 202 (1911): 29–50.

———. "Notes on the Polymorphism of *Trypanosoma gambiense* in the Blood and Its Relation to the Exogenous Cycle in *Glossina palpalis*." *Proceedings of the Royal Society* B 85 (1912): 527–539.

———. "Notes on the Life-History of *Trypanosoma gambiense*, with a Brief Reference to the Cycles of *Trypanosoma nanum* and *Trypanosoma precorum* in *Glossina palpalis*." *Philosophical Transactions of the Royal Society* B 203 (1913): 161–184.

———. "Pathology." In *Medical Services: Diseases of the War*, ed. William Grant MacPherson, 97–118. London: H.M. Stationary Office, 1922.

———. With J. Keppie. "The *in vitro* Production of Toxin from Strains of *Cl. Welchii* Recently Isolated from War Wounds and Air Raid Casualties." *Journal of Pathological Bacteriology* 53 (1941): 95–104.

———. With W. R. Kerr. "An Investigation into the Infection of Cows with *T. Foetus* by Means of the Agglutination Reaction." *Veterinary Journal* 97 (1941): 351–363.

———. With J. Keppie. "Gas Gangrene. Active Immunization by Means of Concentrated Toxoids." *Lancet* 2 (1943): 311–318.

———. "Antibody Response in Cattle to Infection with Trichomonas foetus." In *Immunity to Protozoa: A Symposium of the British Society of Immunology*, ed. P. C. C. Garnham, A. E. Pierce, and I. Roitt, 336–345. Oxford: Blackwell Scientific Publications, 1963.

STANDARD SOURCES
Biographical Memoirs, vol. 20, 1974; *WWW*, vol. 7, 1971–1980.

ROBESON, ESLANDA CORDOZA (GOODE) (1896–1965)

U.S. anthropologist and chemist. Born 15 December 1896 in Washington, D.C., to Eslanda (Cordoza) and John Goode. Married Paul Robeson (1921); one son, Paul, Jr. Educated New York City public schools; University of Illinois (1912–1914); Columbia University Teachers College (B.S., 1920); University of London (1935–1937); London School of Economics (1938); Hartford Seminary (doctoral student, 1945–?). Professional experience: Presbyterian Hospital of Columbia University, surgical technician and chemist (1920–1925); anthropological studies of African societies; political activist. Died 13 December 1965 of cancer.

Most of Eslanda Robeson's career was devoted to political and social issues rather than science. However, she originally was trained as a chemist and later worked on a doctorate in anthropology. It was in the descriptive anthropology of African societies where most of her creative scientific work appeared.

Born to a father of West Indian descent and a mother from a Sephardic Jewish family, Eslanda experienced discrimination throughout her life. After attending the University of Illinois, she transferred to Columbia University Teachers College, where she earned a bachelor's degree in chemistry. Upon graduation she worked as a chemist and surgical technician at the Presbyterian Hospital of Columbia University for five years. At Columbia she met Paul Robeson, a student at Columbia University Law School, and they married. Eslanda convinced Paul that his future was in acting rather than law. She quit her job and accompanied Paul to London for his famous performance in Eugene O'Neill's *Emperor Jones*. Their only child, Paul Jr., was born in 1927. She booked tours for Paul and managed the finances. Convinced that racial discrimination was less virulent in England than in the United States, the Robesons settled in London in 1928 and remained there for twelve years.

Robeson became interested in Africa while she was in England, where a mass of information on the continent and its people was available. In 1935 she enrolled at the University of London to take anthropology classes. She then studied at the London School of Economics. Meanwhile, in 1936 she and her son toured Africa for six months and gathered information for a book.

Throughout the 1930s, Robeson's ideas became increasingly radical. She traveled through Europe and made several trips to the Soviet Union. With her husband she went to Spain during the Spanish Civil War to demonstrate her support for the Republicans. World War II forced the Robesons to return to the United States. After settling in Connecticut, Robeson became a doctoral student at Hartford Seminary in Anthropology, but did not complete her degree. In 1945 her book *African Journey,* based on her earlier travels to Africa, was published. She applied her anthropological education in this basically descriptive book. She described the living habits, customs, and lifestyle of different tribes, illustrating them with her own photographs. She stressed the need for reform by the colonial powers. During the 1940s she became a popular lecturer on African topics.

After the war, she continued her interest in colonialism. She saw the United Nations as a potential mediator between the colonial powers and the rising tide of nationalism in Asia and Africa. Highly critical of the United States government for invoking the issue of communism whenever confronted by national problems, she was sympathetic to the Soviet Union. She was active in the establishment of the Progressive Party and campaigned for Henry A. Wallace for president. She ran as the candidate for secretary of state in Connecticut for the Progressive party in 1948 and in 1950 for congresswoman-at-large for Connecticut. Their political stands led to hardships for both Robesons. Eslanda was called before the House Un-American Activities Committee, where she refused to discuss her political ideas. She cited not only the fifth amendment but the fifteenth, which guarantees equal rights regardless of race and color, as well, which infuriated Joseph McCarthy. She expanded on her views of democracy's failure in postwar America in the book, *An American Argument,* which was a dialogue with Pearl Buck. She was an early believer that change would not come without a strong black protest movement. She participated in many of the early civil rights protests, including Martin Luther King, Jr.'s, Prayer Pilgrimage to Washington, D.C. She lived abroad for five years from about 1958 to 1963.

JH/MBO

PRIMARY SOURCES
Robeson, Eslanda. *Paul Robeson, Negro.* New York: Harper, 1930.
———. *African Journey.* New York: John Day Co., [1945].

STANDARD SOURCES
Current Biography 1965; Gacs; *NAW*(M) (article by Patricia A. Sullivan).

ROBINSON, DAISY MAUDE (ORLEMAN) (1869–1942)

U.S. biologist and physician. Born 6 November 1869. Married Andrew R. Robinson. Educated Columbia College (later George Washington University) (M.D., 1890; M.S., 1894); University of Zurich (1892–1894). Professional experience: teacher (1885– 1887); U.S. Pension Bureau, medical examiner (1890–1893); private school, surgeon and associate principal (1895–1904); New York Polyclinic Medical School, lecturer; woman's auxiliary board, president; North West Dispensary, N.Y.; New York State Department of Health, lecturer and diagnostician. Honors and memberships: American Public Health Association, member; American Medical Association, member. Retired 1938. Died 12 March 1942.

Although in the first edition of *American Men of Science* (1906), Robinson is listed as having interests in biology and medicine, she does not seem to have used her biology professionally. After receiving her medical degree from Columbia College (later George Washington University), she studied for two years at the University of Zurich before returning to Columbia to work toward her master of science degree.

During World War I Robinson joined the medical corps of the French Army and transferred to the American army when the United States entered the war. She received decorations from both countries. After the war, she worked in the New York State Department of Health and later the United States Public Health Service. She had a private practice in dermatology. She even was an Acting Surgeon General for a short time.

Robinson was married to Andrew Rose Robinson, one of the founders of the Polyclinic Hospital in Washington. Her research was on the injurious effects of roentgen rays, and the diagnosis and treatment of herpes, cancer, gonorrhea, and syphilis. She also worked on treating leprosy with X-rays.

JH/MBO

SECONDARY SOURCES
"Dr. Daisy Robinson, A Noted Surgeon." *New York Times,* 14 March 1942.

STANDARD SOURCES
AMS 1–6; Bailey; Siegel and Finley.

ROBINSON, GERTRUDE MAUD (WALSH) (1886–1954)

British organic chemist. Born 6 February 1886 in Winsford(?), England. Married Robert Robinson, future Nobel laureate (1912). Two children. Educated University of Manchester (M.Sc., 1908). Professional experience: University of Manchester, research chemist (1908–1912, 1922–1928); University of Sydney, Australia, research chemist (1915–1920); University of Liverpool, research chemist (1921–1922); St. Andrews University, chemist (1928–1930); University College, University of London, research chemist (1928–1930); Oxford University, research chemist (1930–1954). Oxford University, honorary M.A. (1953). Died 1 March 1954 in Oxford.

Gertrude Maud Robinson, like MURIEL WHELDALE ONSLOW, was a British organic chemist who worked extensively on plant anthocyanins. She studied at the University of Manchester, where she received a master of science degree in chemistry. She began to do research in chemistry at Manchester, where she met her future husband, Robert Robinson, then an assistant lecturer in chemistry. The year they married, the couple went to Sydney, Australia, then to St. Andrews in Scotland, to University College, London, and finally to Oxford, where Gertrude Robinson did her most significant work, taking over half of his laboratory. The two published collaboratively from 1915 until the early 1940s. Her positions, however, were always dependent upon his funding. They were both enthusiastic mountain climbers and in her younger days Robinson accompanied him in the Alps and in the mountains around Sydney. They were also keen gardeners, and produced a profusion of flowers every spring. The couple had two children, first a daughter and a later a son, who was disabled.

In the 1930s, Robinson published extensively with her husband and others, including the Nobel laureate Peter B. Medawar. Rose Scott-Montcrieff (later Meares), who also collaborated with her, recalled the vibrant atmosphere of the early years when the field of "classical chemical genetics" was being developed. Gertrude Robinson's articles and reviews on anthocyanins in flower pigments appeared in numerous prestigious chemical and biochemical journals as well as in *Nature* and the *Philosophical Transactions of the Royal Society.*

Her husband was awarded the Nobel Prize in 1947 for chemistry and continued to obtain every significant British award, including presidency of the Royal Society. Although the significance of her work was recognized by colleagues and friends, her only honor was an honorary master of arts from Oxford a year before her death. Robert Robinson retired the year after his wife died although he was officially past retirement age. He remarried three years later and continued a long and prestigious career for twenty years after her death. JH/MBO

PRIMARY SOURCES

Robinson, Gertrude M. With R. Robinson. "A Survey of Anthocyanins." *Biochemical Journal* 25 (1931): 1687–1705; 26 (1931): 1647–1664.

———. With R. Robinson. "Developments in the Chemistry of the Anthocyanins." *Nature* 130 (1932): 21.

———. "A Synthesis of Certain Higher Aliphatic Compounds. 4: Synthesis of n-triacontanoic Acid from Stearic Acid." *Journal of the Chemical Society, London* (1934): 1543–1545.

———. With G. H. Beale, R. Robinson, and R. Scott-Moncrieff. "Genetics and Chemistry of Flower Colour Variations in *Lathyrus odoratus.*" *Journal of Genetics* 37 (1939): 375–388.

———. With P. B. Medawar and R. Robinson. "A Synthetic Growth Inhibitor." *Nature* 151 (1943): 193.

SECONDARY SOURCES

Baker, W. "Gertude Maud Robinson." *Nature* 173 (1954): 566 ff. Obituary notice.

Scott-Moncrieff, Rose [Mrs. O. M. Meares]. "The Classical Period in Chemical Genetics. Recollections of Muriel Wheldale Onslow, Robert and Gertrude Robinson and J. B. S. Haldane." *Notes and Records of the Royal Society* 36 (1981): 125–154. Discusses Robinson and her husband along with Onslow, J. B. S. Haldane, P. B. Medawar, and others.

Simonsen, J. L. "Gertude Maud Robinson." *Journal of the Chemical Society.* (1954): 2667 ff.

Synge, R. L. M. "How the Robinsons Nearly Invented Partition Chromatography in 1934." *Notes and Records of the Royal Society* 46, no. 2 (1993): 309–312.

Todd, Lord, and J. W. Cornworth. "Robert Robinson." *Biographical Memoirs of the Royal Society* 22 (1976): 415–527. Includes details of the life of Gertrude and Robert Robinson.

STANDARD SOURCES

Poggendorff, vols. 6, 7B.

ROBINSON, HARRIET MAY SKIDMORE (ca. 1888–1962)

British botanist. Born ca. 1888 in Bewdley, Worcestershire, England. Never married. Educated Girls' High School, Kidderminister; Birmingham University (B.A., 1912?). Professional experience: Wolverhampton Girls' School, teacher of biology; Durban Ladies College, Natal, South Africa, headmistress (1924–1932); Herschel Girls' School, near Cape Town, head (1924–1948); St. James Girls' School, Malvern, England, headmistress (1948); St. Mary's Hall, Brighton, principal (1949–1950?). Honors and memberships: Linnean Society, Fellow (1915). Died 13 April 1962 in Bewdley, Worcestershire.

Harriet Robinson was trained at Birmingham University and was elected a Fellow of the Linnean Society within three years of receiving her bachelor's degree. She taught biology and science at a series of girls' schools first in England and then in Natal and Cape Town. Serving as headmistress and principal at most of the schools where she taught, she managed to instill a love of science and especially botany in her pupils, although she had little time to do her own research.

Toward the end of her life, after retiring from teaching in South Africa, she returned to England where she served as principal at St. Mary's Hall, Brighton, rebuilding the schoool which had been taken over by the military during World War II. She then returned to Natal, occassionally teaching botany and biology in Pietermaritzburg until her sister asked her to return to England. There, in the town where she was born, she died in her seventy-fifth year.   JH/MBO

SECONDARY SOURCES
Pocock, M. A. "Harriet May Skidmore Robinson." *Proceedings of the Linnean Society* 175 (1962–1963): 95.

STANDARD SOURCES
Desmond.

ROBINSON, JULIA (BOWMAN) (1919–1985)

U.S. mathematician. Born 8 December 1919 in St. Louis, Mo., to Helen (Hall) and Ralph Bowers Bowman. One sibling. Married Raphael M. Robinson. Educated San Diego High School (graduated 1936); San Diego State College (now San Diego State University) (1936–1939); University of California, Berkeley (graduated 1939; Ph.D., 1948). Professional experience: Rand Corporation in Santa Monica (1949–1950). Died 30 July 1985.

Julia Bowman's childhood was traumatic. Her mother died after her second birthday and her father remarried and retired first to Arizona and then to San Diego. Julia suffered rheumatic fever when she was nine years old, after an attack of scarlet fever, and her heart was severely damaged and she was never very strong thereafter. She missed several years of school, but after tutoring was able to make up the lost time and entered the ninth grade with her age group. She had difficulty understanding why the other girls shunned mathematics, her favorite subject. At graduation she received honors in mathematics and in the sciences which she had elected to take. She also won the Bausch-Lomb medal for all-around excellence in science.

By the time she entered college (San Diego State), her father had used up the savings with which he could have supported his family. Despondent, he committed suicide. Because of the low tuition, Bowman was able to continue with her education. She spent three years at San Diego State, but was able to transfer to the University of California, Berkeley, because her older sister supplied her with money from her teaching job with the San Diego school system. At Berkeley, she met assistant professor Raphael M. Robinson, from whom she took a number theory course and whom she married in 1941.

The fact that she could find people who were actually enthused by modern mathematics delighted her. Although she had a mathematics department teaching assistantship, nepotism rules forbade husband and wife from teaching at the same institution. She joined other faculty wives and worked in the Berkeley Statistical Laboratory on secret projects for the military. She was unconcerned about the nepotism situation because she wanted to begin a family. However, she became pregnant and lost the baby. She was told that she must never have children because of the buildup of scar tissue in her heart caused by the rheumatic fever. Depressed, Raphael suggested that they go to Princeton during the year 1946 and 1947, and that she should take up mathematics again.

When they returned to Berkeley in 1947, she began to work toward a doctoral degree with Alfred Tarski, a logician, who had joined the Berkeley faculty during the war. She received her doctoral degree in 1948. Raphael had a sabbatical in 1949–1950, and Julia worked for Rand corporation during that year. In 1961, her heart had deteriorated to such an extent that surgery to remove the scar tissue on the mitral valve was essential. After the operation, her health improved dramatically. In 1975 she was elected to the National Academy of Sciences and full professor at Berkeley. Since she tired easily, her duties included only a one-quarter-time teaching load. In 1982 she became the first woman president of the American Mathematical Society. While she was presiding over the 1984 summer meeting of the American Mathematical Society she found out that she had leukemia. She died the following year.

Many honors came her way in addition to those already mentioned. In 1979 she was awarded an honorary degree by Smith College. The following year, she was invited to deliver the Colloquium Lectures of the American Mathematics Society, the second time a woman had been so honored. She was awarded a MacArthur Fellowship of sixty thousand dollars for five years. And finally she was elected to the American Academy of Arts and Sciences.

Robinson's thesis was "Definability and Decision Problems in Arithmetic." Her major professor asked whether the arithmetic of the rational numbers is decidable or undecidable. Robinson proved the undecidability in her thesis by providing an arithmetical definition of the intergers in the field of rational numbers. The work done in her thesis showed that her main interest lay on the borderline between logical and number theory. However, she wrote two papers outside of this field, one on statistics and another on game theory. Her most interesting contribution was providing the vital foundation for the solution of the Tenth Problem on mathematician David Hilbert's list—to find an effective method for determining if a given Diophantine equation is solvable in integers. When Yuri Matijasevic solved Hilbert's Tenth Problem in 1970, Robinson's work on the solution was recognized. She soon gained fame and honors in mathematical circles.   JH/MBO

PRIMARY SOURCES

Robinson, Julia Bowman. "Definability and Decision Problems in Arithmetic." *Journal of Symbolic Logic* 14 (1949): 98–114. Doctoral dissertation.

————. "An Iterative Method of Solving a Game." *Annals of Mathematics* 54 (1951): 296–301.

————. "Existential Definability in Arithmetic." *Transactions of the American Mathematical Society* 72 (1952): 437–449.

————. With Yuri Matijasevic. "Reduction of an Arbitrary Diophantine Equation to One in Thirteen Unknowns." *Acta Arithmetica* 27 (1975): 521–553.

SECONDARY SOURCES

Feferman, Soloman. "Julia Bowman Robinson." *Biographical Memoirs, National Academy of Sciences* 63 (1994): 453–478.

Gaal, Lisl. "Julia Robinson's Thesis." *Association for Women in Mathematics Newsletter* 16, no. 3 (May–June 1986): 6–8.

"Julia Bowman Robinson: 1919–1985." *Notices of the American Mathematical Society* 32 (1985): 739–742.

Kelley, Loretta. "Why Were so Few Mathematicians Female?" *The Mathematics Teacher* 89 (October 1996): 592–596. Short sketches of women mathematicians.

STANDARD SOURCES

Grinstein and Campbell (article by Constance Reid and Raphael M. Robinson); *Notable; Notable Mathematicians.*

ROBINSON, MARGARET (KING) (1906–   )

U.S. oceanographer. Born 23 February 1906 in Provo, Utah, to Maynetta (Bagley) and Samuel Andrew King. Married Arthur G. Robinson (24 May 1937). One son; one daughter. Educated University of Utah (B.A., 1928); University of California, Berkeley (1928–1930); Scripps Institution of Oceanography and the University of California (M.S., 1951). Professional experience: Consul-Vultee Aircraft Co., San Diego, Calif., tool designer (1943–1945); Pacific Beach High School, San Diego, teacher (1945–1946); Scripps Institution of Oceanography, staff (1946–1957), bathythermograph data processing and analysis section, head (1957–post-1968). Concurrent experience: industry consultant (1952-retirement); United Nations Educational, Scientific, and Cultural Organization oceanography expert to Bangkok, Thailand (1962–1963); U.S.-Japan Cooperative Science Program, physical oceanography (1964). Honors and memberships: Arctic Institute of America; American Geophysical Union; American Society for Limnology and Oceanographics.

Margaret King was born in Provo, Utah, and received her undergraduate degree from the University. Seven years later she married Arthur G. Robinson and had two children, a girl and a boy. During World War II, she followed many other women into the workforce and took a job as a tool design consultant for a small aircraft company in San Diego.

At the war's end, she began to teach in the public school system, but soon became interested in oceanography, and a year later joined the Scripps Institution of Oceanography as a staff member. There she worked with LAURA HUBBS, the wife and associate of Carl Hubbs, director of Scripps who arrived in the mid-forties. Robinson became a member of the staff and obtained a master of science degree in physical oceanography from Scripps and the University of California in 1951.

By 1957, Robinson was the head of the bathythermograph data analysis and processing and analysis section of the Oceanic Research Division of Scripps. In the early sixties, she traveled to Bangkok, Thailand, as a UNESCO oceanographic expert, and participated in the major Japan–U.S. Cooperative Program on Physical Oceanography. Her research work on ocean temperature distribution and variability, based on data from the bathythermograph, was supported from the late forties by the Office of Naval Research and in the sixties by the Naval Oceanographic Office and the Naval Undersea Research and Development Center as well as the National Science Foundation. She served as a consultant to UNESCO, and various corporations including Lockheed in the 1960s.   JH/MBO

PRIMARY SOURCES

Robinson, Margaret K. "Physical Oceanography: Plans for U.S.-Japan Co-operation." *Science* 146 (1964): 1371–1372. This article and a few biograpical excerpts are in a biographical file at Scripps.

STANDARD SOURCES

Debus.

ROBINSON, PAMELA LAMPLUGH (1919–1994)

British geologist. Born 1919. Educated University College, London (matriculated, 1947; Ph.D., 1957). Professional experience: University College, London, assistant lecturer in zoology (to 1955), lecturer in zoology (1955–1956), reader in paleozoology (1966–1982). Died 24 October 1994 in London.

Pamela Robinson spent her entire career, including both graduate and undergraduate education, at University College, London. She began her undergraduate work at the age of twenty-eight, embarking on a degree in geology. Her education had previously been interrupted by her war service in munitions work from 1942 to 1945. After receiving her first degree, she remained at University College as an assistant lecturer in zoology and then as a lecturer. She earned her doctoral degree from this institution in 1957. Her mentors at University College were J. B. S. Haldane, Walter Kühne, and D. M. S. Watson. She supervised three doctoral students, Beverly Halstead, who worked on pliosaurs, Barry Hughes, who studied a Karroo reptile, and Steven Rewcastle. Robinson worked in Calcutta until 1966, and supervised numerous students there. When she returned to England, she was appointed reader in paleozoology at University College, which she remained until retirement. After retirement she devoted her time to Indian philosophy and gardening in east London.

During the fall of 1972, Robinson was Alexander Agassiz Visiting Professor at Harvard University, and in the following year was awarded the Wollaston Fund of the Geological Society.

In Robinson's doctoral dissertation, she studied the formation, stratigraphy, and faunal assemblages of the Triassic and Early Jurassic vertebrate-bearing fissure sediments from the Mendip Hills and Gloucestershire. This work was published by the Linnean Society in 1957. She produced a major monograph on the Triassic reptile, *Kuehneosaurus,* which has never been published.

In 1957, she made the first of many visits to India upon the invitation of Professor Mahalonobis, the head of the Indian Statistical Institute in Calcutta. J. B. S. Haldane, who influenced Robinson during her early years at University College, recommended her. In India, she established the Geological Studies Unit at the Indian Statistical Institute. She began her contributions to vertebrate paleontology and Gondwana stratigraphy by initiating these programs in India. She published a major review of the stratigraphy of the Pranhita-Godavari Valley, which has become a major reference on this subject. Her published legacy, although modest, contributed to knowledge of Mesozoic paleontology. In the 1970s her research changed course, and she became involved in the young discipline of paleoenvironmental studies and paleoclimatic modelling.   JH/MBO

SECONDARY SOURCES

Milner, Angela, and Barry Hughes. "Pamela Lamplugh Robinson, 1919–1994." *Society of Vertebrate Paleontology* 164 (June 1995): 54–55.

ROBOZ-EINSTEIN, ELIZABETH (ca. 1902–)
See Einstein, Elizabeth Roboz.

ROBSCHEIT-ROBBINS, FRIEDA SAUR (1893–1973)
German-born U.S. biologist. Born 8 June 1893 in Euskirchen, Germany. Father [?] Robscheit-Robbins. Naturalized 1932. Mar-

ried Oscar V. Sprague (1915). One child. Educated University of Rochester (Ph.D., 1934). Professional experience: Hooper Foundation for Medical Research, assistant (1917–1922); University of Medicine and Dentistry, Rochester, N.Y., research associate in pathology (1922–1955?), extension division, lecturer (1932–1933); Oswaldo Cruz Institut, Rio di Janeiro, Brazil, guest. Honors and memberships: Society for Experimental Pathology, secretary-treasurer (1946–1949), president (1951); Physiological Society, Fellow; New York Society for Medical Research (president, 1952). Retired in 1955. Died in Rochester 20 December 1973.

Frieda Robscheit-Robbins was born in Germany. She married Oscar V. Sprague when she was twenty-two and had one child. Two years later she was an assistant in the research division of the Hooper Foundation, where she first began to work with George Hoyt Whipple. He soon found her skill at the bench indispensable and brought her with him when he moved to the University of Rochester, where she was made a research associate in pathology. In her thirties she began to work toward a graduate degree at the university.

Although Robscheit-Robbins never obtained a formal position above that of research associate, she coauthored many of the articles written by Whipple on liver disease and worked with him for thirty-six years. When he received the Nobel Prize in 1934 with two other colleagues, he publicly expressed some embarrassment that she did not share in the award. He then divided the money from the prize with Robscheit and his other assistants. Robscheit-Robbins herself denied the importance of such awards, stating that the success of the work was all that one needed.

Robscheit-Robbins was recognized by her colleagues in other ways. She was a Fellow of the Physiological Society. She traveled to Brazil to spend a year at the Oswaldo Cruz Institute. She also served as secretary-treasurer and then president of the Society for Experimental Pathology. She also served as president of the New York Society for Medical Research in the mid-fifties, just before her retirement.

JH/MBO

PRIMARY SOURCES

Robscheit-Robbins, Frieda Saur. With George Hoyt Whipple. "Blood Regeneration in Severe Anemia." Parts 1–3. *American Journal of Physiology* 72 (1925): 395–430.

SECONDARY SOURCES

"Frieda Robscheit-Robbins." *Rochester Times,* 20 December 1973. Obituary notice.

STANDARD SOURCES

AMS 6–8, B 9, P&B 10; Rossiter 1982.

ROCKLEY, LADY ALICIA MARGARET (AMHERST) (1865–1941)

British botanist. Born 30 July 1865 in Poole, Dorset. Father First Baron Amherst of Hackney. Married Evelyn Cecil, later First Baron Rockley (1898). One son; two daughters. Professional experience: Collected plants in South Africa and Mozambique (1899), Rhodesia (1900), Ceylon, Australia, New Zealand, Canada (1927). Honors and memberships: Freedom of the Worshipful Company of Gardeners (1896); Freedom of the City of London; Overseas Settlement of British Women, vice-chairman; Member of the British Empire (1918); Commander of the British Empire (1920); Dame Grand Cross of the Order of St. John of Jerusalem; Board of Agriculture, food production department, honorable assistant director of horticulture (1917–1919). Died Poole, Dorset, 14 September 1941.

Lady Alicia Margaret Rockley had an early interest in gardening, writing her first book, the *History of Gardening,* in 1895. She went with her husband to Africa the year after they were married and collected plants for Kew Gardens. She later traveled with her husband to other parts of the British Empire where she continued collecting plants. She also received recognition for her work in horticulture and her work during World War I. JH/MBO

PRIMARY SOURCES

Rockley, Alicia Margaret. *A History of Gardening in England.* London: Bernard Quaritch, 1895.

——. *Children's Gardens.* New York: Macmillan, 1902.

——. *London Parks and Gardens.* New York: Dutton, 1907.

——. *Wild Flowers of the Great Dominions of the British Empire.* London: Macmillan and Co., Ltd., 1935.

——. *Some Canadian Wild Flowers: Being the First Part of Wild Flowers of the Great Dominions.* Toronto: Macmillan, 1937.

——. *Historic Gardens of England.* London: Country Life, Ltd., 1938.

Rockley's manuscripts are at the Chelsea Physic Garden and her plants are at Kew.

SECONDARY SOURCES

Times, 15 September 1941.

STANDARD SOURCES

Gunn and Codd; Stafleu and Cowan, vol. 4, 1983; *WWW,* vol. 4, 1941–1950.

ROCKWELL, ALICE JONES (1898–?)

U.S. child psychologist. Born 16 August 1898 in Philadelphia, Pa. Educated University of Pennsylvania (B.S., 1918; A.M., 1922; Ph.D., 1924). Professional experience: University of Pennsylvania Psychological Clinic, recorder (1922–1924); Beaver County, Pa.,

Child Study Bureau (1924–1928); Baltimore Mental Hygiene Clinic, psychologist (1929–?). Death date unknown.

Although Alice Rockwell was listed in only three editions of *American Men of Science,* it is known that she earned a doctorate in psychology from the University of Pennsylvania, where she had also earned her first two degrees. She held several positions as a psychologist and was a member of the American Psychological Association and the Orthopsychiatric Association. Her interests were in clinical psychology, and she worked mainly with children. She did research on the superior child, the problem child, and the mental hygiene of childhood. KM

STANDARD SOURCES

AMS 5–7.

ROCKWELL, MABEL MACFERRAN (d. 1979)

U.S. electrical and aeronautical engineer. Born in Philadelphia, Pa., to Mabel (Alexander) and Edgar O. MacFerran. Married Edward W. Rockwell. One daughter. Educated Bryn Mawr College; Massachusetts Institute of Technology (B.S., 1925); Stanford University (B.S. in electrical engineering). Professional experience: Southern California Edison Company, technical assistant (1925–?); Metropolitan Water District in Southern California, assistant engineer; Lockheed Aircraft Corporation, plant electrical engineer (1937?–1940), production research engineer (1940–?); Westinghouse, research engineer (1945?–?). Honors and memberships: Society of Women Engineers, Achievement Award (1958). Died June 1979.

Mabel Rockwell may have been the first woman aeronautical engineer in the United States. She was one of the designers of the control system for the Polaris missile and for the Atlas guided missile launcher. She also helped design and install electrical power systems for facilities on the Colorado River.

Little material is available on Rockwell's early life. Although she attended Bryn Mawr College, she transferred to Massachusetts Institute of Technology and received her bachelor's degree in science, teaching, and mathematics from that institution. She moved to California the next year, where she was awarded a second degree in electrical engineering. In 1935 she married engineer Edward W. Rockwell and the couple had one daughter.

Rockwell was one of the women whose career was given a boost by World War II. Before the war, she was a technical assistant with the Southern California Edison Company, where she was a pioneer in the application of the method of symmetrical components to transmission relay problems in power systems. Her work made it easier to diagnose system malfunctions and to make multiple-circuit lines more reliable. In her second position she was a member of the team that designed the Colorado River Aqueduct's power system and the only woman to participate in the creation of electrical installations at Boulder Dam.

During the early days of the war effort, Rockwell joined Lockheed Aircraft Corporation as plant research engineer and was soon named production research engineer. This position involved the oversight of engineers and technicians in an attempt to enhance the aircraft manufacturing process. She made many innovations at Lockheed, including refining the process of spotwelding and developing techniques for maintaining cleaner surfaces in order to ensure that the metals completely fused during welding. She also worked with electrical and mechanical problems in aircraft manufacturing. Rockwell's research led to the replacement of riveting with the less expensive and quicker spotwelding.

By the end of the war, Rockwell's reputation made her eligible to work at Westinghouse, where she designed the electrical control system for the Polaris missile launcher. Later, at Convair, she developed the launching and ground controls for the Atlas guided missile system. She was recognized for these accomplishments by President Dwight D. Eisenhower, who named her Woman Engineer of the Year in 1958.

Rockwell served as an engineer at McClellan Air Force Base in California, the Mare Island Naval Installation, the U.S. Bureau of Reclamation, and the Naval Ordnance Test Station in Pasadena, California. She was also a consulting technical editor at Stanford University's electrical engineering department.

JH/MBO

SECONDARY SOURCES

Goff, Alice C. *Women Can Be Engineers.* Edwards Brothers, 1946. See pages 94–112.

"Mabel M. Rockwell." *MIT Technology Review* (June/July 1980): B-7.

STANDARD SOURCES

Notable (article by Karen Withem).

RODDE, DOROTHEA VON (SCHLÖZER) (1770–1825)

German scholar, natural philosopher, and artist. Born 10 August 1770 in Göttingen. Father A. L. von Schlözer. Married von Rodde (1792). Three children. Educated at home and by tutors; studied art in Paris. Died 12 July 1825 in Avignon.

Dorothea von Rodde was a general scholar. Encouraged by her professor father to learn languages at an early age, she learned Plattdeutsch (at age three) followed by French, English, and Italian. She later became proficient in Latin,

Greek, and Hebrew. At the age of six, she studied mathematics with Professor Kästner, who was amazed by her mathematical ability. She studied mineralogy with Professor Gmelin and attained a practical knowledge of mining and mineralogy. She also delved into natural history, botany, chemistry, and materia medica.

On one of her many trips, she met a merchant, Senator von Rodde, whom she married, and by whom she had three children. On another of her journeys, she went to Paris, where her artistic sense was developed. She was in the first class of the National Institute. She painted important individuals, including Kaiser Franz. Toward the end of her life she moved to the south of France, where she died.

JH/MBO

SECONDARY SOURCES

Allgemeine Deutsche Biographie. Duncker & Humboldt, 1967–1970.

ROE, ANNE (1904–1991)

U.S. psychologist. Born 20 August 1904 in Denver, Colo. Mother Edna Roe. Three siblings. Married (1) Cecil Brolyer (1927; divorced 1936); (2) George Gaylord Simpson (1938). Four stepdaughters. Educated University of Denver (B.A., 1923; M.A., 1925); Columbia University (Ph.D. in experimental psychology, 1933); American Board of Professional Psychology (diplomate, 1947). Professional experience: Commonwealth Fund Grant, psychologist (1931–1933); Worcester State Hospital, assistant psychologist (1933–1934); Work Projects Administration, New York Infirmary for Women and Children, resident psychologist (1935–1936); Yale University, assistant, research studies (1941–1942), director of the study on alcohol education in public schools (1941–1942), laboratory of applied physiology, research assistant (1943–1946); U.S. Public Health Service, Study of Scientists, director (1946–1951); Guggenheim Fellow (1952–1953); Veterans Administration Hospital, Montrose, N.Y., chief of psychology training unit (1955–1957); New York University, adjunct professor, research and psychology (1957–1959); Harvard University, Graduate School of Education, research associate and lecturer (1959–1963); professor (1963–1967), emerita professor (1967–1991). Concurrent experience: Veterans Administration, New York, chief of clinical psychology, Branch 2 (1946–1947); American Board of Professional Psychologists, trustee (1953–1959); Harvard Center for Research on Careers, founder and director (1963–1966), emerita director (1966–1991); University of Arizona, lecturer in psychology (1967–?). Honors and memberships: Harvard Graduate School Educational Association Award (1967); American Psychological Association, Richardson Creativity Award (1968); Distinguished Contribution to Clinical Psychology Award (1972); Columbia University Teachers College, Medal for Distinguished Service (1977); American Psychological Association Division 17,

Roe, Anne

Leona Tyler Award (1984); APA, Fellow in four divisions (President, Division 12, 1957); APA Board of Directors, member; American Board of Examiners in Professional Psychology, trustee; New England Psychological Association, cofounder and second president; Harvard University, honorary M.A. (1963); Lesley College, honorary LHD (1965); Kenyon College, honorary Sc.D. (1973). Died 29 May 1991 in Tucson, Ariz.

Anne Roe was the second of four children in a supportive family where the roles of occupational choice and necessity were demonstrated to her at an early age. Her father's transport company went bankrupt and the bulk of financial support for the family fell to Anne's mother, Edna, who was a teacher and national secretary for the Parent Teacher Association. The job as national secretary led to much travel, during which Anne was largely responsible for her home and siblings. Anne's mother showed her that women could achieve, excel, and assert themselves in a patriarchal society and Anne's self-confidence was bolstered by this example and by handling the household chores and associated emergencies in her mother's absence. She was extremely bright, read voraciously, finished her bachelor of arts degree at the University of Denver (1923) at age nineteen and assumed she would become an English teacher. Luckily, Thomas Garth, an educational psychologist, convinced Anne to accept a graduate assistantship in psychology and complete a master's degree (1925). Further, he arranged a job for her in E. L. Thorndike's office at Columbia University, and she began doctoral studies under Robert S. Woodworth.

During research projects at Columbia, Roe became intrigued with the interaction between occupation and healthy life function in normally intelligent persons. She was able to alternate between doing experimental research projects and conducting clinical work in child guidance clinics and in hospital settings. As an undergraduate, she studied ways of assessing differences between students in dental school who would become "good" dentists and those who would not. She worked with Garth studying southwestern ethnic groups and her master's thesis focused on a critical analysis of Native American intelligence test scores. Her doctoral dissertation concerned musical aptitudes and the kinds of errors people make in sight reading. She interviewed hospital patients with different medical diagnoses to assess intellectual functioning. Her experiences at Worcester State Hospital following graduation led to some collaborative research with David Shakow on the intellectual functioning of schizophrenic patients. Shakow became a close friend and the two collaborated on papers later in her career. Her early work was periodically interrupted by bouts of brucellosis (undulant fever) that would disable her for weeks at a time until finally diagnosed and cured in the 1940s.

Throughout her life, Roe's capacity to shift roles in response to opportunities as well as to the expectations of others (husband, family, colleagues) served her well and enabled her to accomplish an astounding amount professionally while integrating a traditional dedication to husband and children. She had become close friends with George Gaylord Simpson in childhood, as he was her older brother's best friend. Following brief first marriages, the two resumed their friendship, were married (1938), and began a life of intellectual support and collaboration that began with the major work *Quantitative Zoology* (1939). Roe subordinated her work in psychology to his in paleontology on several occasions during their marriage but was able to take advantage of associative opportunities which she incorporated into the mainstream of her own research. During a trip to Venezuela where her husband studied the Kamarakoto Indians at Ayantapui, Roe collected fossil mammals and prepared specimens of local animals for the American Museum of Natural History in New York City (Simpson's employer). When Simpson moved to Yale University, Roe was able to get a grant to study the effect of alcohol on artists. Believing that work is an expression of personality, she approached the study from the point of view of the artists' perceptions of reality and discovered close correlations between what and how they painted and personality structure variables. A grant from the National Institute of Public Health (1947–1951) to study the life choices of scientists allowed Roe an opportunity to contribute to psychological research and (incidentally) to the history of science. This study was published in her 1953 book *The Making of a Scientist,* based on interviews with well-known scientists. During the late 1940s and early 1950s, Roe's personality research on artists and scientists led her to develop a classification system that focused on interests and interpersonal relationships tied directly to Abraham Maslow's personality theory. She published *Psychology of Occupations* in 1956, the first in-depth treatment of the relationship between occupational choice and personality correlates.

When Simpson was invited to Harvard in 1959, Roe inquired of her friend and Harvard psychology faculty member David McClelland about job opportunities in Boston or Cambridge. She was pleased to be invited to join the faculty of the Graduate School of Education. Starting as lecturer in education, she was appointed full professor in 1963, making Simpson and Roe the first husband-wife professorial team at Harvard. Being honored academically at Harvard did not shelter Roe from the blatant sexual discrimination that abounded there. The Harvard Faculty Club limited its main dining room to men. Women faculty, faculty wives, and men accompanied by women had to use a small side room. Some undergraduate libraries also retained restricted access by women. Roe was certainly cognizant of the problems faced by women of her generation pursuing careers, though she was not rebellious herself, finding ways to overlay her professional aspirations onto the role of traditional wife and mother. In articles such as "Satisfactions in Work" (1962), "Women in Science" (1966), "Women and Work"(1966), and "Womanpower: How is it Different?" (196?), Roe discusses the problems, inequalities, and deterrents to achieving eminence in their fields faced by women. After her death, the Harvard Graduate School of Education instituted an Anne Roe Award for Outstanding Research in Occupational Psychology. JH/MBO

PRIMARY SOURCES

Roe, Anne. *A Study of the Accuracy of Perception of Visual Musical Stimuli.* Ph.D. thesis, Columbia University, 1933.

———. With George Gaylord Simpson. *Quantitative Zoology: Numerical Concepts and Methods in the Study of Recent and Fossil Animals.* New York: McGraw-Hill, 1939.

———. With David Shakow. *Intelligence in Mental Disorder.* New York: New York Academy of Sciences, 1942.

———. *A Survey of Alcohol Education in Elementary and High Schools in the United States.* New Haven, Conn.: Quarterly Journal of Studies on Alcohol, 1943.

———. With Barbara Stoddard Burks. *Studies of Identical Twins Reared Apart.* Washington: American Psychological Association, 1950.

———. *The Making of a Scientist.* New York: Dodd-Mead, 1953. Rpt., Westport, Conn.: Greenwood Press, 1973. The original questionnaires by scientists on which this study was based are in the American Philosophical Society Library.

———. *The Psychology of Occupations.* New York: Wiley, 1956. Rpt., New York: Arno Press, 1977.

———. "Early Determinents of Vocational Choice." *Journal of Counciling Psychology* (1957).

———. With George Gaylord Simpson. *Behavior and Evolution.* New Haven, Conn.: Yale University Press, 1958.

———. *The Origin of Interests.* Washington, D.C.: American Personnel and Guidance Association, 1964.

Many of Roe's papers are at the American Philosophical Society.

SECONDARY SOURCES

Wrenn, Robert L. "Anne Roe (1904–1991)." *American Psychologist* 47 (1992): 1052–1053.

STANDARD SOURCES

AMS, S&B 9–13; Debus; O'Connell and Russo 1990 (article by Elizabeth Leonie Simpson); Stevens and Gardner.

ROE, JOSEPHINE ROBINSON (1858–1946)

U.S. mathematician. Born 5 May 1858 in Meredith, N.H. Educated Oberlin College (A.B., 1894); Dartmouth College (A.M., 1911); Syracuse University (Ph.D., 1918). Professional experience: New Hampshire high school principal (1880–1882); Literary Institute, New Hampton, N.H., instructor (1882–1890); Kimball Union Academy, N.H., preceptress (1894–1897); Berea College, dean of women (1897–1907), professor of mathematics (1897–1911); Syracuse University, assistant professor (1920–?). Died 1946.

Much of Josephine Roe's academic career occurred before she earned her bachelor's degree. After obtaining this degree she became a preceptress and then dean of women and professor of mathematics at Berea College. She then went to Syracuse University as an assistant professor, the highest rank that she received. JH/MBO

PRIMARY SOURCES

Roe, Josephine Robinson. *Interfunctional Expressibility Tables of Symmetric Functions.* Syracuse, N.Y.: Distributed by Syracuse University and by the author, 1931.

STANDARD SOURCES
AMS 3–7.

ROGER, MURIEL (1922–1981)

U.S. molecular biologist. Born 6 October 1922 in New York City. Married Charles O. Beckmann (1958; he died in 1968). Educated Evander Childs High School, N.Y.C.; City College of New York (1938–1947); Columbia University (B.S.; Ph.D. in physical chemistry, 1952). Professional experience: Columbia University, Department of Chemistry, research assistant (1947–1950), teaching assistant (1950), research fellow (1950–1952), postdoctoral research fellow (1952–1954). Corn Industries Research Foundation, research scientist (1954–1955); Rockefeller Institute (later Rockefeller University) postdoctoral fellow (1955–1956), research associate (1956–1960), assistant professor, genetics laboratory (1960–1970), senior research associate (1970–1981). Died 24 December 1981 in Bayville, N.Y.

Muriel Roger was trained as a physical chemist but made significant contributions to the study of the structure of DNA, perfecting techniques for separating genes and introducing them into bacterial cells. She had an unconventional education, finishing her college degree as a mature student of twenty-eight. After high school, she had continued her education part-time at City College while working as a secretary. Moving to Columbia University, she served as secretary to the chemistry department from 1945 to 1947. When she received a research assistantship to work with Charles O. Beckmann in 1947 (whom she married ten years later), she was able to attend college full-time, receiving a bachelor of science degree in 1950. Two years later, she obtained a doctorate in physical chemistry, completing her dissertation on the structure of starches.

After a short period as a postdoctoral fellow and as a research scientist at the Corn Industries Research Foundation, she joined the staff of the Rockefeller Institute for Medical Research (later Rockefeller University) and became involved in studying the structure of DNA, following the tradition at the Rockefeller that had been developed by Oswald T. Avery and his associates. Her husband, Charles O. Beckmann, joined her in the laboratory headed by Rollin D. Hotchkiss. By the early 1960s she demonstrated that DNA's high viscosity was due to the enormous length of the molecule, although her results were not at first accepted. By mid-1960, she and her associates published internationally recognized work on the genes of pneumonia bacteria that she showed could be differentiated according to their different heat sensitivities. Her research team then demonstrated that they could bind different genes on a strand to basic protein owing to their acidity, publishing an account of this technique in 1966. Roger was one of the first researchers who was able to isolate single genes.

By 1970, Roger was senior research associate of the genetics laboratory at Rockefeller University, studying the alteration and separation of bacterial genes. After heating and separating them, she reassembled them in the test tube and then introduced them into recipient bacteria. Her work demonstrated that bacteria can correct or ignore molecular mismatches in their genetic structure. Unfortunately, her work using recombinant DNA techniques on bacteria was interrupted by her death from a heart attack at the age of fifty-nine.

JH/MBO

PRIMARY SOURCES

Roger, Muriel. "Evidence for Conversion of Heteroduplex Transforming DNAs to Homoduplexes by Recipient Pneumococcal Cells." *Proceedings of the National Academy of Sciences* 69, no. 2 (1972): 466–470.

STANDARD SOURCES
Annual Obituary 1981.

ROGERS, AGNES LOWE (1884–1943)

Scottish/U.S. psychologist. Born 1884 in Dundee, Scotland. Educated St. Andrews, Scotland (M.A., 1906); Cambridge University (1908–1911); Columbia University (Ph.D., 1917). Professional experience: St. Andrews, assistant (1906–1908); Aberdeen, lecturer (1911–1914); Columbia University, assistant (1916–1917), lecturer (1917–1918); Goucher College, professor of education (1918–1923); Smith College, professor of psychology and education (1923–1925); Bryn Mawr College professor of education and psychology (1925–?). Honors and memberships: Psychological Association, member; British Association of Educational Psychologists, member. Died 1943.

Although Agnes Rogers grew up in Scotland and attended universities there, she moved to the United States, where she earned a doctorate. She stayed on as a lecturer at Columbia for two years after she finished this degree. She held a series of teaching positions at universities. When she got a job at Bryn Mawr College in 1925, she remained there for the rest of her career.

Rogers's research interests were in educational psychology, especially in the measurement of mathematical intelligence. She also devised mental tests for college entrance.

JH/MBO

STANDARD SOURCES
AMS 3–6; *Psychological Register*, vol. 3.

ROGERS, JULIA ELLEN (1866–ca. 1958)

U.S. botanist and popular scientific writer. Educated Iowa State University (A.B.); Cornell University (M.A., 1902). Professional experience: Des Moines, Iowa, high school teacher (1881–1887); Cedar Rapids, Iowa (1892–1900); New Jersey, public lecturer (1903–1915?); Long Beach Shell Club (to 1957). Died ca. 1958.

Julia Ellen Rogers was educated in botany at Iowa State University and Cornell University. Before and after she received her bachelor's degree, she taught high school in Iowa. After she received her master's degree at Cornell, she moved to New Jersey where she began to write books and lecture on natural history and civic improvement.

Rogers soon established a reputation as a popular lecturer on trees and garden plants. Her book on trees, originally published in 1905, with 160 photographs, was reprinted in 1908, and reissued again in 1935. She was noted enough to be listed in the 1908–1909 *Who's Who in America* and again in 1914–1915. She moved to Long Beach, California, where she lived for the remainder of her life. A clipping from an unidentified Long Beach newspaper (ca. 1958) held by the California Academy of Science refers to her as the "tree and shell lady" and gives her age at death as ninety-two.

JH/MBO

PRIMARY SOURCES

Rogers, Julia. *The Tree Book: A Popular Guide to a Knowledge of Trees of North America.* Garden City, N.Y.: Doubleday, 1905.

———. *The Shell Book: A Popular Guide to a Knowledge of the Families of Living Mollusks, and an Aid to the Identification of Shells Native and Foreign,* Boston: Charles T. Branford Co., 1908 (reissued 1936).

———. *The Book of Useful Plants.* Garden City, N.Y.: Doubleday, Page and Co., 1913.

California Academy of Science Archives. Edwin Hand Collection. Scattered cards and notices. Includes obituary.

STANDARD SOURCES

Barnhart; Stafleu and Cowan; *WW in America*, vol. 5, 1908–1909, vol. 8, 1914–1915.

ROGERS, MARGUERITE MOILLET (1915–1989)

U.S. physicist and engineer. Born 6 November 1915 in Minatitlan, Mexico. Educated Rice University (A.B.; M.A.; Ph.D., 1940?). Married Fred Rogers (died 1956). Five children (two sons; three daughters). Professional experience: University of Houston, instructor (1940–1943); Rice Institute, assistant (1942–1943); U.S. Naval Ordnance Plant, Naval Avionics Facility, Indianapolis, optics section, manager (1943–1946); University of North Carolina, research associate (1947–1948); Oak Ridge National Laboratory, senior physicist (1948–1949); Naval Ordnance Test Station (later Naval Air Warfare Center Weapons Division), electronics scientist (1949–1953), head of various divisions (1957–1966); Columbia College, South Carolina, professor and chair of physics (1953–1957). Died 1989.

Marguerite M. Rogers was raised in Texas and attended Rice University for both her undergraduate and advanced degrees. She taught for two years at the University of Houston immediately after receiving her doctorate, but like many women scientists she decided to contribute her expertise to the war effort during World War II, joining the optics section of the Naval Avionics facility in Indianapolis for the final three years of the war. Soon afterward, she took a position as a research associate at the University of North Carolina, but again turned to weapons research at the Oak Ridge National Laboratory in Tennessee, subsequently joining the Naval Ordnance Test Station (NOTS) in California.

By 1953, she again returned to academia and was appointed professor of physics and chair of the department at Columbia College in South Carolina. After four years, she returned once more to the NOTS (later the Naval Air Warfare Division), where she worked on the development of fire-control and navigational systems. Even the start of the Vietnam War had no effect on her decision to work in this field, and she was soon the head of a division developing fire-control systems and air-to-surface weapons. She became responsible for the analysis of the effectiveness of such systems as the "eye" weapons series used in Vietnam.

Rogers eventually managed a division of a hundred and fifty people. She was honored with a series of awards and citations by the Naval Weapons Center, including its highest honor, the L. E. T. Thompson Award (1966). The same year she received the Naval Air Systems Command Superior Civilian Service Award. She received the Federal Women's Award in 1976 and in 1981, the Department of Defense Distinguished Civilian Service Award. Her husband died in 1956 and she raised her children while pursuing weapons research. Her two sons followed her example as physicists in the military weapons area.   JH/MBO

STANDARD SOURCES

AMS 8, P 9, P&B 10–13; *Notable* (article by Karen Withem).

ROGICK, MARY DORA (1906–1963)

U.S. invertebrate zoologist. Born 1906 in East Sandy, Pa., 1906. Educated University of Nebraska (B.Sc., 1929; M.Sc., 1930); Ohio State University (Ph.D., 1934). Professional experience: College of New Rochelle, zoology department, assistant professor, associate professor, professor and chair (1935–1963). Died 26 October 1963 at New Rochelle, N.Y.

Little is known about the personal life of Mary Dora Rogick except that her family originally spelled her name Rogic. She was born in Pennsylvania but went to Nebraska for her undergraduate and master's degrees. There she became interested in marine biology, writing her thesis on the comparative histology of the digestive tract of teleost fish, especially the minnow. This thesis was published in the *Journal of Morphology and Physiology* (1931). Moving to the University of Ohio, she worked under Raymond C. Osburn, and wrote her doctoral dissertation on freshwater Bryozoa of Lake Erie, doing research at the University of Ohio summer biological station at Put-in Bay, Ohio. She also assisted her advisor by preparing illustrations for his book on Bryozoa.

After she received her doctoral degree, Rogick sent out over two hundred letters to colleges looking for a position. She was successful in finding a position teaching invertebrate biology at the College of New Rochelle. Although she carried a heavy teaching load at New Rochelle, she managed to remain a very productive scientist. Her area of specialty was freshwater and marine Bryozoa. She was funded from 1954 to 1961 by the National Science Foundation to study Antarctic Bryozoa.

Rogick contributed articles to the *Encyclopedia Britannica* and McGraw Hill *Encyclopedia of Science and Technology*. She was a sectional editor for *Biological Abstracts*. Almost every summer she devoted herself to research at one of the major marine biological stations, such as the Marine Biological Laboratory (MBL) at Woods Hole, and the Maine Biological Laboratory (1943–1947). Some summers she taught at the University of New Hampshire. During the school year she taught a wide variety of biological courses at New Rochelle.

An excellent artist, Rogick illustrated some of her own articles. She also illustrated *Are You Your Garden's Worst Pest?* by Cynthia Wescott (Doubleday, 1961). In letters and notes, her watercolor illustrations of her trials and tribulations as a bryologist amused and informed her scientific colleagues and friends.

Sixteen of Rogick's scientific notebooks, the personal property of Thomas J. M. Schopf (Department of Geophysical Sciences, University of Chicago), have been analyzed in an unpublished manuscript by Judith (Dudley) Winston now held in the Schlesinger archives at Radcliffe College (*Notable American Women* unused files). Rogick published over 60 scientific articles. She gave her excellent collection of 386 books and reprints on bryozoology to MBL, Woods Hole, maintained there as the Rogick Collection. She was a corporation member of the MBL, 1944–1964. She was also a Fellow of the American Association for the Advancement of Science, New York Academy of Sciences, the Academy of Antartic Bryozoa, Phi Beta Kappa, and Sigma Xi.   JH/MBO

PRIMARY SOURCES

Rogick, Mary Dora. "Studies on Comparative Histology of the Digestive Tract of the Minnow, *Campostoma anomalum.*" *Journal of Morphology and Physiology* 52 (1931): 1–25.

———. "Studies on Fresh water Byrozoa. I. Occurrence of *L. carteri*"; "II. Bryozoa of Lake Erie." *Transactions of the American Microscopical Society* 53 (1934): 416–424; 54 (1935): 245–263.

———. "Studies on Fresh Water Bryozoa XII. A Collection from Various Sources." *Annals of the New York Academy of Sciences* 43, no. 2 (1942): 123–144.

———. "Studies on Marine Bryozoa III. Woods Hole Marine Bryozoa Associated with Algae." *Biological Bulletin* 96 (1949): 32–69.

———. "Bryozoa of the U.S. Navy's 1947–48 Antarctic Expedition I–IV." *Proceedings of the U.S. National Museum* 105 (1956): 221–317. Includes 35 plates.

Rogick's unpublished scientific notebooks are held privately in Chicago. An analysis of these in an unpublished manuscript is held in the Schlesinger Library archives (*Notable American Women*, unused files).

SECONDARY SOURCES

Ohio Journal of Science 65, no. 4 (1965): 238. Obituary notice.

STANDARD SOURCES

AMS 6–8; B 9, P&B 10.

ROHDE, ELEANOUR SINCLAIR (1881–1950)

British horticulturist and popular gardening writer. Born 9 August 1881 in Allepy, Travancore to Isabel (Crawford) and John Rohde. Educated Cheltenham Ladies' College; St. Hilda's College, Oxford. Professional experience: Heather & Heath Ltd., horticultural advisor. Died 23 June 1950 in Reigate, Surrey.

An only child, Rohde first attended the prestigious Cheltenham Ladies' College for her secondary education and then went to St. Hilda's College, Oxford. She began to write gardening articles for a number of popular magazines and served as horticultural advisor to a nursery specializing in herbs.

JH/MBO

PRIMARY SOURCES

Rohde, Eleanour Sinclair. *Garden of Herbs.* London: P. L. Warner, 1920.

———. *Old English Herbals.* London: Longmans, Green and Co., 1922.

———. *Old English Gardening Books.* London: M. Hopkinson and Co., 1924.

———. *Oxford's College Gardens.* London: H. Jenkins, 1932.

———. *Herbs and Herb Gardening.* London: Medici Society, 1936.

———. *Uncommon Vegetables and Fruits.* London: Country Life, Ltd., 1943.

SECONDARY SOURCES

"Eleanour Sinclair Rohde." *Gardeners' Chronicle* 2 (1950): 12; 164 (1968): 18–19.

"Eleanour Sinclair Rohde." *Herbal Review* 9 (1983): 3–6. Includes portrait.

Macleod, D. *Down-to-Earth Women: Those Who Care for the Soil.* Edinburgh: Blackwood, 1982. See pages 64–70. Includes portrait.

STANDARD SOURCES

Desmond; *WWW,* vol. 4, 1941–1950.

RÓNA, ELISABETH (1890–1981)

Hungarian/U.S. radiochemist and geophysicist. Born 20 March 1890 in Budapest, Hungary, to Ida (Mahler) Róna and Samuel Róna, a physician. One sibling. Educated local schools; University of Budapest (B.A.; Ph.D., 1916); Technical University of Karlsruhe, Germany, and University of Budapest, postgraduate work. Professional experience: Institute of Physiology and Biochemistry, University of Budapest, instructor (1918–1920); Kaiser Wilhelm Institute for Chemistry, Berlin, fellow (1922–1924); Kaiser Wilhelm Textile Institute, research fellow; researcher at a textile mill in Hungary (1927). Institute for Radium Research, Vienna (1927–1938); Institute of Radium, Paris (1926–1927, one month); oceanographic station at Bornö, Sweden, summers (1928–1940); Cavendish Laboratory, Cambridge, researcher; University of Oslo, chemistry division, visiting researcher; Trinity College, Washington, D.C., associate professor of chemistry (1941–1946?); University of Washington, associate professor (1947–1950); Carnegie Institute, Washington, D.C., geophysical laboratory (1941); University of Rochester, war work (ca. 1942); Argonne National Laboratory, research scientist (1947–1951); Civilian with Office of Scientific Research and Development; Oak Ridge Institute of Nuclear Studies (later Oak Ridge Associated Universities), senior research scientist

(1950?–1965); Institute of Marine Sciences, University of Miami, senior scientist (1965–1972). Honors and memberships: Haitinger Prize, 1933. Emigrated to the United States in 1941 and naturalized in 1948. Died July 1981.

Elisabeth Róna grew up with her sister Marie in a cultured environment, where the children mingled with their father's multinational group of assistants and collaborators at the family's summer home. She learned French from playmates, and developed a love for nature. Róna became interested in science at an early age through her father, a prominent Budapest physician and researcher. Although she wished to study medicine, her father believed a medical career was too hard emotionally for a woman. After his premature death, Róna deferred to his wishes, and elected to study chemistry and physics. She received a doctorate in chemistry, physics, and geophysics from the University of Budapest.

Róna decided to do postgraduate work at the Technical University, Karlsruhe. She joined the laboratory of Kasimir Fajans, who introduced her to radioactivity. Róna enjoyed working under this young, informal mentor who did not discriminate against women. Her knowledge and skills in radioactivity were enhanced by working with Georg von Hevesy at the University of Budapest, founder of the method of radioactive tracers; with Otto Hahn and LISE MEITNER at the Kaiser Wilhelm Institute in Berlin; with MARIE CURIE, IRÈNE CURIE, and others in Paris; and with Stefan Meyer and colleagues in Vienna. Róna also visited Rutherford and his students at the Cavendish Laboratory in Cambridge. She collaborated with numerous other scientists during her career, including many women.

In 1919 the Communists took over Hungary, instituting a reign of terror. After several months they were overthrown in a bloody counterrevolution. When Otto Hahn offered her a position at the Kaiser Wilhelm Institute, Róna quickly left Budapest. Conditions soon deteriorated in Germany, and Róna was transferred to the Textile Institute, which was considered more important for Germany's economy than radiochemical research. She returned to Hungary in 1923, where she applied her new experience to textile manufacturing. Róna then went to Vienna's Radium Institute, where she spent the greater part of her career. After the Nazis annexed Austria in 1938, Róna accepted an invitation from ELLEN GLEDITSCH (whom she had met in Paris) to take a temporary position in the chemistry division of the University of Oslo. Afterward she returned to Hungary. Reluctant to leave her homeland, Róna did not emigrate to the United States until 1941.

Róna was a member of the American Chemical Society and the American Physical Society, the American Institute of Physics, and the American Association for the Advancement of Science.

In her first researches in radioactivity, Róna verified the existence and radioactive properties of uranium Y. She also found the diffusion constant and atomic radius of radium emanation (radon), and worked with the new radioactive tracer method. At Berlin she determined ionium content of radium residues and separated a thorium isotope from uranium ores. Róna arrived at the Radium Institute in Vienna in the midst of a controversy between researchers at Cambridge and Vienna on the disintegration of medium weight elements by α rays. In order to learn how to prepare polonium sources needed for these experiments, Róna (after turning down an offer to work with the Cambridge group) went to the Institute of Radium in Paris. She developed an improved method for producing these α-emitting sources, and soon became known as an expert in preparing them. Back at Vienna, Róna measured absorption, range, and ionization of hydrogen (proton) beams and determined ranges of α particles from different radioelements. She also investigated the thorium series and took part in experiments bombarding rare earth elements and thorium with neutrons. During World War II Róna worked on separation of polonium and lead isotopes.

Róna began work in oceanography in 1928 with the Swedish physicist Hans Pettersson. She measured the radium content of ocean sediments during the summers of 1928–1940, first at Vienna, then at the oceanographic station in Bornö, Sweden. After she came to the United States, Róna worked at the Carnegie Institute in Washington to determine the uranium content of seawater she collected from the Woods Hole Oceanographic Institute. In 1950 Róna went to Oak Ridge to teach nuclear theories and methods to scientists, where her fluency in a number of languages was particularly useful. She also collaborated with Texas A & M University on the geochronology of marine sediments. In 1965 Róna joined the marine scientist F. F. Koczy at the Institute of Marine Sciences at the University of Miami, where she determined the ages of sediment cores.   MM

PRIMARY SOURCES

Róna, Elisabeth. "Diffus grösse & Atomdurchmesser der Radiumemantion." *Zeitschrift für physikalische Chemie* 92 (1916/1918).

———. With E. A. W. Schmidt. "Meth zur Herstellung von hochkonz Poloniumpräpar." *Sitzungsberichte der Kaiserlichen Akademie der Wissenschaften zu Wien* 2A 137 (1928).

———. With Ernst Föyn, Berta Karlik, and Hans Pettersson. "Radioactivity of Sea Water." *Göteborgs Vetenskaps-och Vitterhets-Samhälles Handingar* 6 (1939): 1–44. See also *Nature* 143 (1939): 275 ff.

———. With William D. Urry. "Radioactivity of Ocean Sediments, 8: Radium and Uranium Contents of Ocean and River Waters." *American Journal of Science* 250 (1952): 241–262.

―――. *How It Came About: Radioactivity, Nuclear Physics, Atomic Energy.* Oak Ridge, Tenn.: Oak Ridge Associated Universities, 1978. Includes autobiographical material.

SECONDARY SOURCES

Krafft, Fritz. *Im Schatten der Sensation. Leben und Wirken von Fritz Strassmann.* Weinheim, Deerfield Beach, Fla., and Basel: Verlag Chemie, 1981.

STANDARD SOURCES

AMS 8, P 9, P&B 10–14; Meyer and von Schweidler; Poggendorff, vols. 6, 7a; Rayner-Canham 1997; *Who's Who of American Women.*

RONZONI, ETHEL (BISHOP) (1890–?)

U.S. chemist. Born 21 August 1890 in California. Married (1923). Educated Mills College (A.B., 1913); Columbia University (M.S.); University of Wisconsin (Ph.D., 1923). Professional experience: Washington University, St. Louis, assistant professor (1923–1943), associate professor (1943–?). Death date unknown.

After chemist Ethel Ronzoni earned a doctorate from the University of Wisconsin, she went to Washington University, where she remained at the rank of assistant professor for twenty years. She finally was promoted to associate professor in 1943. Her research was in muscle biochemistry and steroid hormones. She was a member of the Society of Biological Chemistry.   JH/MBO

PRIMARY SOURCES

Ronzoni, Ethel. "Acid Base Equilibrium of the Blood in Exercise." Ph.D. diss., University of Wisconsin, Madison, 1923.
―――. *Ether Anesthesia.* Washington University: School of Medicine, Laboratory of Biological Chemistry, 1923. Reprinted from *Journal of Biological Chemistry* (1923): 741–788.

STANDARD SOURCES

AMS 6–8, P 9, P&B 11.

ROPER, IDA MARY (1865–1935)

British botanist. Born 25 August 1865 in Bristol, England. Never married. Honors and memberships: Linnean Society, Fellow (1909); Bristol Naturalists Society, honorary secretary and librarian, president (1913–1916); Bristol and Gloucestershire Archaeological Society, council member; British Association for the Advancement of Science; Somersetshire Archaeological and Natural History Society. Died 8 June 1935 in Bristol.

Although little is known of Ida Mary Roper's personal life, she was widely respected as an active field botanist and later

in life as a historical archeologist. She was for nineteen years the honorary secretary and librarian of the Bristol Naturalists Society, and was the first woman member to serve as president of that society. She was also the first woman member to sit on the council of the Bristol and Gloucestershire Archaeological Society and wrote an interesting pamphlet on the monumental effigies of the region. She contributed well-selected dried specimens to the Botanical Society and Exchange Club of the British Isles. An authority on *Viola*, she also discovered or rediscovered a number of plants in the early 1900s, most notably *Nitella muronata* var. *gracillina* in 1917. Roper reported most of these in the *Journal of Botany* and the *Proceedings of the Bristol Naturalists Society.* She also had a keen interest in mosses and ferns and was an active member of the British Bryological Society, enjoying their excursions and the excursions of the British Association.

Roper was credited as being of great assistance to the botanist J. W. White in his compilation of the *Flora of Bristol* (1912) for her field work, library research, and for seeing the volume through the press. For eighteen years she was largely responsible for the exhibition of wildflowers at the Bristol Museum and Art Gallery. Her herbarium of dried British flowering plants and ferns was given to the University of Leeds. Her plants are at Oxford. She died in a nursing home in Bristol, the city where she had been born.   JH/MBO

PRIMARY SOURCES

Roper, Ida M. "Some Historical Associations of Flowers." Presidential Address. *Proceedings of the Bristol Naturalists Society* 4–6 (1914).
―――. *Monumental Effigies of Gloucestershire and Bristol.* Gloucester: Privately printed for the author by H. Osborne, 1930.

SECONDARY SOURCES

H. S. T. "Miss Ida M. Roper." *Nature* 136 (1935): 134–135.
"Ida Mary Roper." *Proceedings of the Linnean Society* (1935–1936): 212–213. Obituary notice.
"Ida M. Roper." *Proceedings of the Bristol Naturalists Society* 8 (1935): 25–26. Includes portrait.

STANDARD SOURCES

Barnhart; Desmond; Stafleu and Cowan.

ROPER, MARGARET (1505–1544)

British healer. Father Sir Thomas More. Educated in medicine and in the Scriptures. Professional experience: healed the sick. Died 1544.

Margaret Roper was one of the three daughters of Sir Thomas More, all of whom were well educated. Margaret became a famous scholar and was her father's close companion. Both Erasmus and Pole claimed that she was one of the best scholars they had known. She and her husband lived in Canterbury where she was respected for her knowledge of medicine.   JH/MBO

SECONDARY SOURCES
Kavanagh, Julia. *Women of Christianity*. London: Smith, Elder, 1852.

STANDARD SOURCES
Hurd-Mead 1938; Uglow 1989.

ROSE, FLORA (1874–1959)

U.S. home economist. Born 13 October 1874 in Denver, Colo. Educated Kansas State College (B.S., 1904); Columbia University (A.M., 1909); New York State College for Teachers (Ped.D.); Kansas State College (Sc.D., 1937). Professional experience: Kansas State College, instructor (1903–1906); Cornell University, lecturer (1907–1911), college of home economics, professor (1911–1940), emerita professor (1940–1959). Died 1959.

Flora Rose had a career in home economics, becoming a full professor at Cornell in 1911. In 1907 a deparment of home economics was formed within the College of Agriculture at Cornell. Rose and MARTHA VAN RENSSELAER were selected as cochairs of the new department. The two women shared the administrative responsibilities. Rose concentrated on resident teaching and research and Van Rensselaer on administration and extension work.

Rose's research was on nutrition. She conducted a survey on the nutrition of Belgian school children and was a member of the Committee for Relief in Belgium in 1923. She was director of the food conservation program in New York from 1917 to 1919. She also did research on weight and how to control it.   JH/MBO

PRIMARY SOURCES
Rose, Flora. "A Page of Modern Education: Forty Years of Home Economics at Cornell University." Ithaca, N.Y.: New York State College of Home Economics, *Fifteenth Annual Report*, 1940.

SECONDARY SOURCES
A Growing College: Home Economics at Cornell University. Ithaca, N.Y.: New York State College of Human Ecology, 1969.

STANDARD SOURCES
AMS 6–8, B 9; Bailey; Rossiter 1982.

ROSE, GLENOLA BEHLING (fl. 1918–1935)

U.S. chemist. Professional experience: Dupont Chemical Company, chemist (1918–1935?).

Glenola Behling Rose was a chemist at the Dupont Company, Delaware Branch, from 1918, but she lost her job in the late thirties. She was asked to form a women's committee of chemists within American Chemical Society in 1926. As chair of the Women's Service Committee, she was faced with the difficult situation during the Depression when many women lost their jobs. Her colleague Lois Woodford was an active and concerned member of the women's committees as a letter from Lois Woodford to Glenola Rose concerning the work of this ACS committee in 1928 indicates.   JH/MBO

PRIMARY SOURCES
Rose, Glenola Behling. [Responses to] Questionnaire for Chemists (1920). Bureau of Vocational Information papers, Schlesinger Library, Radcliffe College.
Woodford, Lois, to Glenola Rose, 20 July 1928, Charles Holmes Herty Papers, Robert W. Woodruff, Emory University.

STANDARD SOURCES
Rossiter 1982.

ROSE, MARY DAVIES SWARTZ (1874–1941)

U.S. chemist and physiologist. Born 31 October 1874 in Newark, Ohio, to Martha Jane (Davies) and Hiram Buel Swartz. Four siblings. Married Anton Richard Rose (15 September 1910). One son, Richard Collin Rose (b. 1915). Educated Wooster High School, Wooster, Ohio; Shardson College (later part of Denison University), Granville, Ohio, preparatory course (1893), college course (1894–1897; 1900–1901; bachelor of letters degree, 1901); College of Wooster (1898–1899); Mechanical Institute, Rochester, N.Y., studied home economics (1902); Columbia University Teachers College, household arts (B.S., 1906); Yale University (Ph.D., 1909). Professional experience: Font du Lac, Wis., high school teacher (1902–1905); Columbia University Teachers College, assistant professor of nutrition (1910–1918), associate professor (1918–1921), professor (1921–1940). Honors and memberships: American Institute of Nutrition (president, 1937–1938); Journal of Nutrition (associate editor, 1928–1936); American Dietetic Association (honorary member, 1919). Died 1 February 1941 in New York City of cancer.

Mary Davies Swartz was born in Newark, Ohio, but grew up in the town of Wooster, Ohio, where her lawyer father became mayor and later probate judge. Her mother was educated at Shepardson College, which Swartz later attended and where she received a classical degree. After teaching home economics for three years, Swartz returned to Columbia University Teachers College, as a student in household arts, and received her bachelor of science degree. Her interest in the chemistry of food and nutrition was stimulated after she became an assistant in the department the year after she received her bachelor's degree. Columbia granted her a traveling fellowship for advanced study, which she used to study physiological chemistry at Yale University under Professor Lafayette B. Mendel. Mendel's laboratory was friendly to women scientists; several women, including MARY ELIZA-BETH REID, studied there.

In 1910, Mary Swartz married Anton Richard Rose, Yale graduate student in biochemistry and three years her junior. He received his doctoral degree from Columbia. In 1915, their only child was born. The family moved from Edgewater, New Jersey, to Manhattan in 1920. Anton Rose had been on the faculty at Fordham University, but he resigned to take a position with the Prudential Insurance Company of Newark. He was very supportive of his wife's career.

In 1910, the year of her marriage, Mary Rose was appointed assistant professor of nutrition at Columbia University Teachers College, where the previous year she had established a department of nutrition. She rose through the ranks at Columbia, and because of her, its excellent nutrition program became well known throughout the country.

Although most of her own scholarly papers involved the practical aspects of nutrition, some of her interests were theoretical. She published more than forty papers and authored two frequently reprinted textbooks. During World War I, she published *Everyday Foods in War Time* and was the deputy director for the New York City Bureau of Conservation of the United States Food Administration. She was one of the three American members appointed to a commission by the League of Nations' Health Committee in 1935 to study the physiological bases of nutrition, and in 1940 she was one of five advisors on nutrition to the Council of National Defense. In addition she was a member of the Council on Foods of the American Medical Association. Rose was especially interested in nutrition in the public schools and wrote a book entitled *Teaching Nutrition to Boys and Girls*. She was honored by a prize established by the Nutrition Foundation, and awarded annually by the American Dietetic Association, the Mary Swartz Rose Fellowship for graduate study in nutrition or allied fields.   JH/MBO

PRIMARY SOURCES

Rose, Mary Swartz. *A Laboratory Hand-book for Dietetics.* New York: Macmillan, 1912.
———. *Everyday Foods in War Time.* New York: Macmillan, 1918.
———. *The Foundations of Nutrition.* New York: Macmillan, 1927.
———. *Teaching Nutrition to Boys and Girls.* New York: Macmillan, 1932.

SECONDARY SOURCES

Eagle, J. A. *Mary Swartz Rose, Pioneer in Nutrition.* New York: Teachers College Columbia, 1979.
Sherman, Henry C. *Journal of Nutrition* (March 1941): 209–211. Obituary notice.
———. *Journal of Biological Chemistry* (September 1941): 687–688.
New York Times, 2 February 1941. Obituary notice.

STANDARD SOURCES

AMS 3, 6; Bailey; NAW (article by Clara Mae Taylor); Rossiter 1982.

ROSENFELD, EVA (1892–1977)

Austrian psychoanalyst. Born 1892 on Manhattan's Fifth Avenue. Mother "Omi." Married Valentin (Valti) Rosenfeld. Four children; only one survived to adulthood. Educated Berlin Institute of Psychoanalysis, psychoanalytic course (1933?–1936); analyzed by Sigmund Freud and Melanie Klein. Professional experience: the Schloss Tegel, Ernst Simmel's psychoanalytic sanatorium, analyst (1931). Died 1977.

A member of ANNA FREUD's circle, Eva Rosenfeld was born in the United States because her father, a theatrical impresario, was there to introduce dramatist Gerhardt Hauptmann to the New York theater.

Rosenfeld had a longstanding connection with Freud. Before marrying Valentin, a first cousin, she asked Freud's advice on the advisability of cousin marriage. With Freud's blessing the couple married. Although Rosenfeld gave birth to four children, only the youngest son survived. A daughter, Maedi, was killed in a mountaineering accident and the other children died very young in a diptheria epidemic.

Rosenfeld met Freud through his daughter Anna, whom she had met in 1924. Anna Freud became very close to Rosenfeld's family until the arrival of the Burlinghams in Vienna. Rosenfeld, fearing that DOROTHY BURLINGHAM was supplanting her in Freud's affections, grew jealous, although the three families were always together. Anna Freud tried to reassure Rosenfeld, particularly after the tragic death of Maedi. Rosenfeld threw herself into building a school, the Matchbox school, in her back yard. To reassure Rosenfeld of her friendship, Freud offered her a free analysis with Sigmund Freud. She went through an intensive time of analysis with Freud.

Rosenfeld moved with her son, Victor, to Berlin, where she was a matron at Ernst Simmel's Psychoanalytic Sanatorium. The sanatorium closed in July and Rosenfeld went to

Russia as the Nazi threat increased in Germany. Her experiences in Moscow were unpleasant and she returned home. Upon returning, Rosenfeld continued her psychoanalytic training at the Berlin Institute of Psychoanalysis and was seeing patients. Rosenfeld and her family moved to London in 1936, where Ernest Jones appointed her secretary of the Rehabilitation Fund. Eva Rosenfeld did much of the work necessary to bring Jewish analysts out of Austria.

Understandably disturbed by the uncertainty in her life, Rosenfeld decided to be analyzed by MELANIE KLEIN rather than undergo another analysis by Sigmund Freud. Freud was not unhappy about the change, although Anna Freud may have felt betrayed. When the Freuds arrived in London, Rosenfeld appeared to be pulled between the Kleinian and Freudian camps and tried to be a peacemaker. She worked as a Middle Group analyst until she died in 1977.　　JH/MBO

PRIMARY SOURCES
Rosenfeld, Eva. "Dream and Vision: Some Remarks on Freud's Egyptian Bird Dream." *International Journal of Psychoanalysis* 37 (1956): 97–105.

STANDARD SOURCES
Appignanesi.

ROSS, JOAN MARGARET (1889–?)

British pathologist and physician. Born 1889 in Rutherford, Roxburgh, England, to Emily Harriet (Johnson) and Richard Ross. Educated St. Leonards School, St. Andrews; University of Cambridge, Girton College (1908–1911, Natural Science Tripos); University of London (B.S., 1922; M.D., ?) Professional experience: St. Mary's Hospital house surgeon, (1919–1920); assistant pathologist. Death date unknown.

An early graduate of Girton College, Cambridge, Joan Margaret Ross continued her education at the University of London, where she earned both a bachelor's and a medical degree. She then worked at St. Mary's Hospital.　　JH/MBO

STANDARD SOURCES
Girton.

ROSS, MARION AMELIA SPENCE (1903–)

Scottish physicist. Born 4 September 1903 in Edinburgh, Scotland, to Marion (Thomson) and William Baird Ross. Educated Edinburgh University (M.A., 1925; Ph.D., 1943). Professional experience: Edinburgh University, faculty (1923–1941; 1946–1957) reader (1957–post-1968); Admiralty, mine design department (1942–1946). Honors and memberships: Fellow Royal Society of Edinburgh; Physical Society of London, member; British Acoustical Society, member.

Marion Ross was born and educated in Edinburgh. After she received her master's degree in 1925, she began to teach at Edinburgh University, where she remained for most of her active life. For four years during World War II, she was attached to the Admiralty mine design department, working on acoustical problems.

When she returned to university teaching, she still held only a lectureship, even after she received her doctoral degree at the age of forty, almost twenty years after her undergraduate work. Finally in 1957, she was appointed a reader in physics. Ross's research interests included the yields from L-shells of heavy atoms, underwater acoustics, and low-speed wind tunnel studies of boundary layers.　　JH/MBO

STANDARD SOURCES
Debus.

ROSS, MARY G. (1908–)

U.S. aerospace engineer. Born 1908 in Oklahoma. Educated Northeastern State College in Tallequah, Okla. (graduated 1928); Colorado State Teachers College, Greeley, Colo. (M.A., 1938); University of California, Los Angeles (courses in aeronautical and mechanical engineering, 1942–1943?). Professional experience: public schools, mathematics teacher (1928–1937); Lockheed Aircraft Corporation, Burbank, Calif. (1942–1973). Honors and memberships: Society of Women Engineers, Fellow (1982); Silicon Valley Engineering Hall of Fame (1992).

Mary G. Ross's background was Cherokee Indian, a source of great pride. Her great-great-grandfather, John Ross, was the principal chief of the Cherokee Nation between 1828 and 1866. Mary Ross was convinced that the Cherokee idea of equality of education for girls and boys made it possible for her to succeed in a "man's field." With this kind of support from the community, she did not mind that she was the only girl in her mathematics class. After graduating from high school, she attended Northeastern State College, graduating when she was twenty years old. Teaching was the obvious career for someone with her interests, so she taught mathematics and science for nine and a half years in the public schools. During this time she also served as a girls' advisor at a Navajo school for boys and girls.

Ross returned to college to work on a master's degree in mathematics. The growth of the aviation industry during the earliy part of World War I opened other options for her. She accepted a position as an assistant to a consulting mathematician with Lockheed Aircraft Corporation in Burbank, California. Lockheed financed her continued education at the University of California, Los Angeles, where she studied aeronautical and mechanical engineering. In 1954 Lockheed selected Mary Ross as one of the first forty employees and the only woman for its Missiles Systems Division. As the program matured, she became involved in research into the feasibility and performance of ballistics missiles and other defense systems. Her research also involved studying the distribution of pressure caused by ocean waves and how it affected submarine-launched vehicles.

Beginning in 1958, she concentrated on satellite orbits and the Agena series of rockets important in the Apollo moon program during the 1960s. She also worked on the Polaris reentry vehicle and engineering systems for manned space flights. She also did research on flyby space probes to study Mars and Venus.

Although she retired from Lockheed in 1973, Ross continued to share her knowledge by giving lectures to high school and college groups. She was especially interested in working with women and Native American young people, encouraging them to prepare for technical careers.

Many of Ross's publications were classified, because they involved national defense. She was a charter member of the Society of Women Engineers, which made her a Fellow in 1982. She won the *San Francisco Examiner*'s award for Woman of Distinction, and the Woman of Achievement Award from the California State Federation of Business and Professional Clubs. Ross was a fellow and life member of the Society of Women Engineers, and the Santa Clara Valley Section established a scholarship in her name. The American Indian Science and Engineering Society and the Council of Energy Resources Tribes honored her with their achievement awards. In 1992, she was inducted into the Silicon Valley Engineering Hall of Fame.   JH/MBO

STANDARD SOURCES
Notable (article by Karl Preuss).

ROSSE, MARY, COUNTESS OF (1813–1885)

See Parsons, Mary, Countess of Rosse.

ROTHSCHILD, MIRIAM (1908–)

British zoologist and parasitologist. Born 5 August 1908 at Ashton Wold near Peterborough, England, to Rozsika (von Wertheimstein) and Nathaniel Charles Rothschild. Three siblings. Married George Lane (1943; divorced 1957). Four children. Educated at home with tutors and in evening classes at a local polytechnic school; Marine Biological Station in Plymouth, continued her education (1932–?). Professional experience: University of London, Biological Station in Naples, Italy, researcher (late 1920s). Honors amd memberships: Fellow of the Royal Society (1985); Commander of the British Em-
pire (CBE); Dame of the British Empire (DBE); honorary doctorates from Oxford, Gothenberg, and Hull Universities; Essex University (Hon. D.Sc., 1999); Cambridge University (Hon. D.Sc., 1999).

Miriam Rothschild was educated at home by a series of tutors. She first learned about her chosen fields of entomology and parasitology from her father and, even more important, from her uncle Walter, a physician. She was born into the famous Rothschild banking family, the oldest of four children; her banker father Nathaniel Charles Rothschild thought that a formal education would stifle Miriam's creativity, so he gave her books to read and stimulated her natural curiosity. His avocation was zoology, and he founded the Society for the Promotion of Nature Preserves. He also studied moths, butterflies, and fleas. Her Hungarian-born mother was an astute businesswoman as well as a champion in women's lawn tennis.

When she was a child, Miriam spent six months of each year with her grandparents and uncle Walter at their estate outside London. Walter Rothschild was an amateur zoologist who collected and prepared birds, insects, and other animals. Miriam was initially fascinated by all of these specimens. However, after her father's suicide, she lost interest in natural history for a time. At seventeen, she enrolled in several evening classes at a local polytechnic institute.

After a fourteen-year marriage to George Lane, a British soldier who had emigrated from Hungary, and four biological and two adopted children, the couple divorced in 1957.

With the recommendation of a naturalist from the British Museum of Natural History, Rothschild was accepted for study at the Biological Station in Naples, founded in the nineteenth century by Anton Dohrn. While there, she developed a strong interest in parasitology, noting that the mollusks with which she was working were infected with flatworms. After studying at Naples, she went to the Marine Biological Station in Plymouth in 1932, where she collected the parasites, their hosts, and other related marine animals.

Rothschild's laboratory was destroyed when the Germans bombed the research station during World War II, and Rothschild returned to her childhood home, Ashton Wold, which had been converted to a military hospital and air field during the war.

Rothschild was active in British secret war work with mathematician Alan Turing on the British project, *Enigma,* that resulted in cracking the German code. During this period, she opened the family home to European refugees. In addition to her active war work, she continued with her natural history investigations, cataloging her father's collections and studying human and animal parasites, especially fleas. She studied flea reproduction, their host preferences, and the mechanics of flea leaping. In collaboration with Nobel laureate Tadeus Reichstein, she demonstrated the manner in which the monarch caterpillar's diet of milkweed plants protects it from birds and other predators through the presence of glycosides in the milkweed that act as an emetic.

In addition to science, Rothschild was interested in travel, reading, and philanthropy. She continued her research at Ashton Wold. She published more than three hundred scientific articles in addition to her very popular science books. In August 1999, she presented 2,000 microscope slides of sections of fleas to the British Natural History Museum. One of her non-biological accomplishments was her claim that she was the first person to put seatbelts in a car (1940).

JH/MBO

PRIMARY SOURCES

Rothschild, Miriam. *Fleas, Flukes and Cuckoos: A Study of Bird Parasites.* New York: Macmillan, [1952].

———. *Dear Lord Rothschild: Birds, Butterflies, and History.* American Institute of Physics. Philadelphia: Balaban, 1983.

———. With Clive Farrell. *The Butterfly Gardner.* London: Michael Joseph/Rainbird, 1983

———. *Animals and Man.* Oxford: Clarendon Press, 1986.

SECONDARY SOURCES

Fraser, Kennedy. "Mariam Rothschild." *New Yorker* (1987).
Gibson, Helen. "Britain's Quirky Samaritans." *International Wildlife* (July–August 1993): 38–43.
Holloway, Margaret. "Profile: Miriam Rothschild. Natural History of Fleas and Butterflies." *Scientific American* (May 1996).
Scientific American (August 1990): 116.
Sullivan, Walter. "Miriam Rothschild Talks of Fleas." *New York Times,* 10 February 1984.

STANDARD SOURCES
Notable (article by George A. Milite).

ROUPELL, ARABELLA ELIZABETH (PIGGOTT) (1817–1914)

British botanist. Born 23 March 1817 in Newport, Shropshire, England. Father Reverend John Dryden Piggott. Married Thomas Boone Roupell (16 September 1840). At least one son, Norton Aylmer. Educated privately. Professional experience: Cape of Good Hope, husband's service leave, painted local flora (1843–1844). Died 1914.

Arabella Elizabeth Roupell is known for her accurate and attractive botanical drawings. Born in England, Arabella Piggott married an official in the East India Company. During his service leave in South Africa, she made paintings of the local flora. Her paintings impressed Nathaniel Wallich, su-perintendent of the botanic gardent in Calcutta, who was also on leave in South Africa. He took a selection of her paintings to England where he showed them to Sir William Hooker of the Royal Botanic Gardens, Kew, who recommended the publication of a portfolio of ten plates. Nine plates were from South Africa and the tenth was a drawing from Sierra Leone, included because of its scientific name, *Roupellia grata.* Processed by the well-known French lithographer M. Gauci, they were issued anonymously in 1859 (1849 on the title page) with the title *Specimens of the Flora of South Africa by a Lady.* The text was written by William Harvey. The portfolio was well received in England (Queen Victoria headed the list of subscribers) and on the Continent, where Roupell was elected a member of the Regensburg Society of Arts. She donated a copy to the public library, Cape Town.

It was not until the 1930s that the remaining plates were traced. Once located, they were presented by South African prime minister General Jan Smuts's son, Jan, to the University of Cape Town and are now housed in the library of the Bolus Herbarium. Eleven of these paintings were printed by Allan Bird under the title *More Cape Flowers by a Lady* and in 1975 reproduced with photographs and biographical information about the artist under the title *Arabella Roupell* (Johannesburg, 1975). JH/MBO

PRIMARY SOURCES

Roupell, Arabella Elizabeth. *Specimens of the Flora of South Africa by a Lady.* London: N.p., 1849. Published anonymously. Includes text by botanist William Harvey.

———. *More Cape Flowers by a Lady: The Paintings of Arabella Roupell.* Text by Allan Bird. Johannesburg: The South African Natural History Publication Company, 1964.

———. *Arabella Roupell: Pioneer Artist of Cape Flowers.* Johannesburg: The South African Natural History Publication Company, 1975.

SECONDARY SOURCES

Hyams, Edward. "Arabella Roupell." *Illustrated London News,* 19 December, 1964.
Richings. *Quarterly Review of South African Libraries* 27 (1972): 4–13.

STANDARD SOURCES
Desmond; Gunn and Codd.

ROYER, CLÉMENCE (1830–1902)

French science writer, economist, philosopher, first French translator of Darwin's Origin of Species. *Born Augustine-Clémence Royer 21 April 1830, Nantes, Brittany, to Josephine-Gabrielle Audouard and Augustin-René Royer. Lifelong companion of Pascal Duprat*

BIOGRAPHICAL DICTIONARY OF WOMEN IN SCIENCE 1129

(died 1885). One son. Educated privately; briefly at Sacre Coeur, Le Mans; Hotel de Ville teaching certificates in French, music, and mathematics. Professional experience: Haverfordwest (Wales) private school, teacher (1853–1854); Touraine (France) private teacher (1854–1856); private lecturer (1859–1863); journalist, woman of letters (1859–1902); columnist for newspaper La Fronde *(1897–1902). Scientific memberships: Société d' Ethnologie; Société d'Anthropologie. Honors and memberships: Canton de Vaud economics prize (1862); Academie des Sciences Morales et Politiques, prize for essay on poverty (1888); award for essay on history of atomism (1893); Banquet in her honor sponsored by* La Fronde *(March 1897); Legion of Honor (1900). Died 1902 in Neuilly-sur-Seine.*

Clémence Royer was born in Nantes, Brittany, to a Breton mother, Josephine-Gabrielle Audouard, and a father, Augustin-René Royer, who was an army captain from Le Mans. Throughout her life she believed children "belonged to their mothers" and therefore considered herself to be a true daughter of Brittany although she had never lived there except for the first months of her life. Royer had learned needlework and lace making from her mother in the Breton manner and her small height, dark hair, and blue eyes gave her a strongly Breton appearance. Royer's grandfather had been a distinguished naval captain who had fought in the Napoleonic wars and continued to serve in the merchant marine in Brittany throughout the peace. Her father participated in the royalist uprising of 1832 that had been heavily supported by the Bretons. The result was that her father and his family fled to Switzerland for four years. On their return, Royer spent a short and disastrous period of education in a convent school, after which she was educated at home, learning mathematics from her father.

Royer became interested in republicanism during the Revolution of 1848 that led to the short-lived Second Republic in France. Following her father's death in 1849, she trained as a secondary school teacher, obtaining certificates in French, music, and mathematics, and went for a year (1853–1854) to Haverfordwest in Wales to teach and to learn English. On her return, she found herself in a state of turmoil over her shaken religious beliefs, and after a short period of teaching, left suddenly for Lausanne, Switzerland, determined to make a new life for herself.

Royer spent two years educating herself in science and philosophy in the Lausanne public library, and with the encouragement of the women of Lausanne began to lecture on science to women in 1859. In these remarkable lectures, she emphasized the need of women to embrace science as a source of knowledge and transform it by making it their own. The following year she began to write for the political science journal *Le Nouvel Economiste,* edited by Pascal Duprat, a former French republican deputy in exile. Duprat

would shortly become her lover and the father of her child. During this period in Switzerland, Royer won a prize offered by the Canton of Vaud for her book on the income tax, and began to write reviews and articles for the widely read *Journal des Economistes.* She also wrote the first draft of a melodramatic novel that contained some interesting claims about the future role of women in society, and included one section of scientific and psychological insights.

Royer, lecturing on Lamarck, read Darwin's *Origin of Species* and immediately recognized its importance as an evolutionary theory that incorporated modern economic theories, notably those of Malthus. She then obtained the consent of her publisher, Guillaumin, to publish a translation of Darwin (although he was primarily a publisher of social science and economics books and journals). Obtaining help on the science from the naturalist Edouard Claparède, who had enthusiastically reviewed Darwin for a Swiss journal, she produced a translation accompanied by long explanatory notes and a lengthy preface in 1862. In her preface, she challenged religious authority and suggested that human beings were unwittingly influencing the normal course of human evolution in a negative manner through the preservation of the weak and sick, and marriage choices that favored passive and less intelligent women.

Although Darwin had authorized the translation, he had some objections to her notes and was both amused and startled by her preface. For the second edition in 1866, he made some significant changes of language; for example, he changes the word *election* that she had borrowed from Claparède to *selection,* although he could not suppress her preface, which she reprinted with modifications to her severe eugenic claims. She finally finished her novel, *Les Jumeaux d'Hellas,* set in Italy and Switzerland. It was published to no great success by Victor Hugo's publishers, although she was to claim that her anticlerical and revolutionary sentiments had placed it on the Index of the Catholic Church and prevented its sale under Napoleon III's empire.

In 1865, Royer went to live openly with Duprat in Italy. There she continued to lecture on Darwinism, wrote a book on the evolution of human society, continued to contribute to various journals and reviews, published a series of articles on Lamarck, and gave birth to her child, René. She also prepared a third edition of Darwin's *Origin,* but made the mistake of adding a new preface that criticized Darwin's hereditarian theory, pangenesis. Darwin took the opportunity to reject her edition and to obtain a new French translation that, for various reasons, did not appear until three years later. Just before his death, in 1882, Darwin allowed her to publish a new popular edition that would incorporate the changes he had made in his subsequent editions. As the political climate improved in France, Royer and Duprat were able to return to Paris, where Duprat reentered politics and established a short-lived newspaper to which Royer contributed.

Royer was elected to the all-male scientific society, the influential Société d'Anthropologie headed by Paul Broca that was engaged in a debate on Darwinism in 1870, and she added her views on evolution to the debate. Years later a colleague, Charles Letourneau, recalled the uproar accompanying the election of this woman who had "shattered the windows" with her Darwin translation. She continued to contribute a large number of papers and discussions before the anthropological society over the following years, most of which were published in the society's bulletins and Broca's own *Revue d'Anthropologie*. One remarkable discussion of the place of women in French society and of women's decision to reduce the number of their children, "Sur la Natalité," was suppressed by the society and has only recently come to light.

Royer wrote a series of other books, including one on ethics and society, *Le bien et la loi morale,* but began to lose her audience. After the death of her companion, Duprat, in 1885, she raised her son herself, sending him to the prestigious Ecole Polytechnique to train as an engineer. The Société d'Anthropologie honored her with an honorary membership in the late 1880s and asked her to give a series of lectures on mental evolution as part of its newly inaugurated conferences on evolution. Although threatened by increasing poverty, aided only by a small grant from the Ministry of Public Education, she submitted a number of lengthy monographs on scientific and political questions to various branches of the Institut de France, but won minor awards only. Royer was rescued from her poverty in the 1890s by a husband and wife journalist team who drew attention to the manner in which she was "knocking at the door of the Institut de France" (Harvey 1997, 167).

After Royer obtained a position in a retirement home in a genteel suburb of Paris with the help of her friends, she found herself surrounded by a new community of feminist supporters who enlisted her aid in the formation of the new feminist newspaper, *La Fronde,* for which she began to write a regular column on scientific and political themes. She continued to publish on science and the structure of matter, corresponding with mathematicians and philosophers on these topics. In 1900, she pulled together her writings on the structure of matter and on cosmology in a massive volume, *La constitution du monde,* for which she prepared theoretical models of atomic structures and suggested a preintelligence in the action of atoms. She died in 1902, having been celebrated twice by the feminist and scientific community and awarded the Legion of Honor in 1900. The bulk of her surviving archives are in the feminist library Bibliothèque Marguerite Durand, Paris.

Royer's central ideas, repeated in her articles for scientific, economic, and feminist journals, emphasized a number of themes common to her and the lay republicans of the late nineteenth century. Among these were her pacifism, her anticlerical beliefs, her strong feminism that did not necessarily endorse women's suffrage. Above all, she insisted upon the importance of science as a basis for philosophy and as a guide to personal and social morality.   JH

PRIMARY SOURCES

Royer, Clémence. "Preface à la Première Edition." Charles Darwin, *De l'origine des espèces,* trans. Royer. Paris: Guillaumin and V. Masson, 1862. This translation went through four editions.

———. *Theorie de l'Impôt.* Paris: Guillaumin, 1862. Royer's prize-winning essay on the income tax in two volumes.

———. *Origine de l'homme et des sociétés.* Paris: Guillaumin, 1870. Written before Darwin wrote his *Descent of Man,* this book focuses on the evolution of society and attacks Rousseau's view of natural man.

———. "L'evolution mentale dans la série organique: Conferences transformistes." *Revue Scientifique* 39 (1887): 749–758; 40 (1887): 70–79. Royer's essay on the development of the brain and the evolution of animal intelligence.

———. *Le bien et la loi morale.* Paris: Guillaumin, 1881. An essay on ethics in science, written in response to Herbert Spencer.

———. *La constitution du monde: Natura rerum.* Paris: Schleicher, Frères, 1900. Royer's cosmological book, complete with illustrations of models of molecular structures and theories of the intelligent atom.

SECONDARY SOURCES

Bertholet, A., ed. *La Grande Encyclopédie.* Vol. 28. Paris: Larousse, 1900.

Blanckaert, Claude. "Clémence Royer (1830–1902): L'anthropologie au feminin." *Revue de synthèse* 109 (1982): 23–39.

———. "'Les bas-fonds de la science française': Clémence Royer, l'Origine de l'Homme et le Darwinisme social." *Bulletin et Mémoires de la Société d'Anthropologie de Paris,* new series 3 (1991): 115–130.

Clark, Linda. *Social Darwinism in France.* Tuscaloosa, Ala.: University of Alabama Press, 1984.

Fraisse, Geneviève. *Clémence Royer: Philosophe et femme de sciences.* Paris: La Découverte, 1985.

Harvey, Joy. *Almost a Man of Genius: Clémence Royer, Feminism and Nineteenth Century Science.* New Brunswick, N.J.: Rutgers University Press, 1997.

Miles, Sarah Joan. "Evolution and Natural Law in the Synthetic Science of Clémence Royer." Ph.D. diss., University of Chicago, 1988.

Millice, Albert. *Clémence Royer et sa doctrine de la vie.* Paris: J. Peyronnet, 1926.

STANDARD SOURCES
DFC; Mozans; Rivière; *Uneasy Careers* (articled by Joy Harvey).

ROZANOVA, MARIIA ALEKSANDROVNA
(1885–1957)

Russian botanist. Born 17 August 1885 in Moscow. Father Aleksandr Konstantinov, a railway official. Educated Moscow gymnasium; Petersburg Higher Women's Courses. Professional experience: Higher Women's Courses, teacher; Petrograd (later Leningrad) University, professor. Died 27 October 1957 in Leningrad.

Mariia Aleksandrovna Rozanova was the daughter of a Moscow railway official. In 1902, she graduated from a Moscow gymnasium with a gold medal. Although she wished to continue her education, she met with opposition from her family, who thought that higher education was not necessary for women. For a time, Rozanova taught evening classes for adults and studied on her own.

In 1912, Rozanova moved with her husband to St. Petersburg and enrolled in the natural history department of the Bestuzhev Higher Women's Courses. Having completed the course with a first-class diploma, she remained at the faculty of botany for further study. In 1916, she passed the state examinations at Petrograd University and in the same year became an assistant at the faculty of botany.

In 1919, the Higher Women's Courses became part of Petrograd University (later Leningrad University) and Rozanova remained on the staff. She taught there until 1944, becoming a professor in 1933. From 1925 to 1940, she also worked as a specialist on fruit culture and was head of the section of berry culture at the All-Union Institute of Plant Industry (VIR) of the Soviet Academy of Sciences.

Rozanova obtained her master's degree from Moscow University in 1926 and in 1940, she was awarded the degree of doctor of biological sciences. She also became a research associate at the Lenin All-Union Academy of Agriculture.

Rozanova survived the blockade of Leningrad in the terrible winter of 1941–1942. By the time she was evacuated to Saratov with the rest of the faculty of Leningrad University, her health had been severely undermined and she was very ill. When she recovered, she went to work as a consultant at a fruit-growing station in Saratov. In 1943, she was called to Moscow to work at the All-Union Vitamin Research Institute. She also lectured at Moscow University and was a senior research associate at the Main Botanic Garden (1944–1950).

In 1946, Rozanova returned to Leningrad as professor of the botanical faculty at the Herzen Pedagogical Institute, remaining at the same time a consultant at the Botanical Garden.

In 1948, Rozanova left the Herzen Pedagogical Institute and returned to the Botanical Garden in Moscow. However, her health worsened and she retired in 1950, although she continued to write. Among her interests at this time was the history of botanical gardens in Russia.

Rozanova published more than eighty works on various aspects of fruit and berry breeding and genetics. Her earliest work was devoted to various forms of fungi but soon she turned to fruit and berry breeding. Over the course of her career she was responsible for the development of numerous commercially useful hybrids.

Rozanova was also a dedicated teacher: besides lecturing, she organized expeditions, helped her students find good placements, and even gave them financial assistance.

Although much of her work had a practical character, Rozanova was particularly interested in wider theoretical questions relating to the formation of species, phylogeny, and the principles of taxonomy of the higher plants, and she was a convinced adherent of experimental genetic methods of research. Her first major work, "Sovremennye metody sistematiki rastenii" (Modern Methods of Plant Systematics) was published in 1930.

The period between the mid-1930s and 1960s was not a good time to be a botanist in the Soviet Union. Early in the 1930s, traditional life sciences came increasingly under attack by the agronomist Trofim D. Lysenko and his followers, who promoted an obscurantist pseudoscience known, among other things, as "Michurinist biology" (after the plant breeder Ivan V. Michurin). This doctrine in essence rejected much modern biology and particularly the science of genetics and in time received official sanction as dogma with which it became dangerous to disagree. Lysenko's greatest triumph occurred at the so-called August Session of the Lenin All-Union Academy of Agricultural Sciences in 1948, after which the study of genetics was banned. Textbooks were rewritten and many scientists who had escaped previous purges were dismissed or arrested. Although cracks started to appear in the Lysenkoist front in the 1950s after Stalin's death, the situation in Soviet biology was not fully normalized until late in the 1960s. The science of genetics had been set back thirty years.

As a geneticist, Rozanova was very much in the line of fire but, unlike many of her colleagues who gave at least lipservice to Lysenko's ideas, remained uncompromising in her defense of her subject in spite of being in real danger of repression. Her close colleague at VIR, the geneticist Nikolai I. Vavilov, was arrested in 1940 and died in prison of malnutrition in 1943. Another colleague, Georgii D. Karpechenko, a geneticist and head of department at Leningrad University, was also arrested in 1941 (died 1942). It was undoubtedly very difficult for Rozanova to carry on her work under these circumstances and it took great courage to do so. It is remarkable that, in such a dark period, she managed to make a substantial contribution to her science.　　　ACH

PRIMARY SOURCES

Rozanova, M. A. "Sovremennye metody sistematiki rastenii." *Trudy po Prikladnoi botanike, genetike i selekts,* no. 1941 (1930): 1–184.
——. *Eksperimental'nye osnovy sistematiki rastenii.* Moscow: Izdvo AN SSSR, 1946.

SECONDARY SOURCES

Joravsky, David. *The Lysenko Affair.* Cambridge: Harvard University Press, 1970. Includes partial list of repressed scientists.
Strelkova, O. C. "Pamiati Marii Aleksandrovny Rozanovoi." *Botanicheskii zhurnal* 43, no. 10 (1958): 1502–1509. Contains list of publications. This obituary, published at a period when Lysenko was still powerful, is very carefully written. "Intense emotional suffering" is given as one of Rozanova's reasons for leaving the Botanical Gardens in 1950. It is also obviously not coincidental that she left VIR in 1940 (after Vavilov's arrest) or the Herzen Pedagogical Institute in 1948 after the August Session in which Lysenko triumphed. It is interesting to note that the editorial board of *Botanicheskii zhurnal* was disbanded at the end of 1958 and replaced with followers of Lysenko.

ROZOVNA, EVDOKIA ALEKSANDROVNA (1899–?)

Russian seismologist. Educated Leningrad University (graduated 1929); Doctor of Physical-Mathematical Science. Professional experience: Seismological Institute (later Geophysical Institute) of the Soviet Academy of Science (1935–1952); Kirghizia (Kirghiz) Academy of Science, head, department of seismology (1952–?); professor (1955–?). Honors and memberships: Communist Party (1952–?); Kirghizia Academy of Science, full member (1954–?). Death date unknown.

Russian seismologist Evdokia Aleksandrovna Rozovna began her career studying regional earthquakes in Central Asia. To do this, she used data from the USSR seismological stations. In 1952 she became a member of the Communist Party and during the same year became head of the Kirghizia Academy of Science's department of seismology. She probably received her doctorate at about that time although the exact date is unknown. After being made a full member of the Kirghizia Academy in 1954, she became a full professor in 1955. Rozovna published extensively.　　CK/MBO

PRIMARY SOURCES

Rozovna, Evdokia Aleksandrovna. *Sostavlenie godografa i opredelenie osnovnykh seysmologicheskikh elementov diya Sredney Azii* (Compilation of a Hodograph and the Determination of the Basic Seismological Elements for Central Asia). Moscow: Akademiia nauk SSSR, Seismological Institute, 1936.
——. *Zemletryaseniya Sredney Azii* (The Earthquakes of Central Asia). Akademiia nauk SSSR, Seismological Institute, 1947.
——. *Raspolozhenie epitsentrov i gipotsentrov zemletryaseniy Srednry Azii* (The Distribution of Epicenter and Seismic Centers in the Earthquakes of Central Asia). Moscow: Akademiia nauk SSSR, Seismological Institute, 1950.

SECONDARY SOURCES

Who's Who in the USSR. Ed. Heinrich E. Schulz and Stephen S. Taylor. Montreal: Intercontinential, 1961–1962.

RUBIN, VERA (DOURMASHKIN) (1911–1985)

Russian-born U.S. cultural anthropologist. Born 9 August 1911 in Moscow to Jennie (Frankel) and Elias Dourmashkin. Married Samuel Rubin. One son; one daughter. Educated New York public schools; New York University (B.A., 1930); Columbia University (Ph.D., 1952). Professional experience: Hunter College, part-time instructor (1952–1954?); New York University, instructor (1952–1954?); University Medical School, Midtown Manhattan Health Project, research assistant (unpaid) (1952?); Columbia University, Department of Anthropology, research associate (1954–1955); Columbia Univiersity, Research Institute of the Study of Man in the Tropics (later Reseach Institute for the Study of Man (RISM), founder and director (1955–1985). Honors and memberships: Society for Medical Anthropology, founding member; Transcultural Psychiatry, founding member; Society for Applied Anthropology, president; New York Academy of Sciences, anthropology section, chair; Brooklyn College, honorary L.H.D. (1981); University of the West Indies, honorary Litt. D. (1985). Died 1985.

Vera Rubin is remembered for her studies and her support for Caribbean studies in the United States. Born in Russia, her father brought her to this country as an infant when he emigrated to New York after her mother died in childbirth. Her father was a journalist and her uncle a physician. She grew up in the Jewish culture of the Lower East Side of New York City. Although she attended New York University, she did not immediately consider further education. Instead she married soon after college, had two children, and threw herself into civic affairs.

When she was in her forties, she began to do graduate work in anthropology, taking courses with RUTH BENEDICT and MARGARET MEAD. Mead became a good friend. Her mentor and advisor was Julian Steward, who had developed a concept of "cultural ecology" that emphasized environmental and technological effects on forms of labor and consequently on society. She applied these ideas in her dissertation study of the acculturation of an immigrant Italian group. After completing this work in 1951 (when it was published, a year before the degree was awarded), she worked as a research associate at Columbia and studied an Irish American group as part of an ethnicity and mental health study being pursued by Cornell Medical School in New York.

She began to teach a seminar with Charles Wagley on the Caribbean and soon became fascinated by the English-speaking area of the West Indies. In one of these early seminars, she influenced a student, Lambros Comitas, who took this topic as his dissertation research, became her associate, and later succeeded her in the institute she would shortly found.

In the mid-fifties, with the cooperation of the Columbia Department of Anthropology, Rubin decided to create a new organization that would provide research space and financial support for studies of the Caribbean. This became the Research Institute of the Study of Man in the Tropics (later abbreviated to Research Institute for the Study of Man or RISM). It began as a training project for graduate students, but soon expanded into research on interdisciplinary concerns about health and social problems in the Caribbean area. Her organization was soon funding major conferences and sponsoring the exchange of scholars.

Rubin developed close ties to the University of the West Indies and to the Caribbean Foundation of Mental Health. She focused as well on education and postcolonialism, and later (with Comitas) on sociocultural causes and effects of marijuana smoking in Jamaica. The conferences she organized had a significant effect on anthropology. Her research interests began to widen beyond the Caribbean and a curiosity about Russia, her birth place, led her to organize an investigation of comparative longevity in Soviet Georgia and Kentucky. She was praised for opening up closer communication between the United States and the USSR before the end of the Cold War.

Rubin was an excellent organizer and was important in her willingness to support as well as to organize important anthropological journals, especially those linked to applied anthropology. She was a founder of the Society for Medical Anthropology and the journal *Transcultural Psychiatry*. She gave financial support to the journal *Human Organization* and was president for a time of the Society of Applied Anthropology. Toward the end of her life she was given honorary degrees by Brooklyn College and the University of the West Indies. She died at the age of seventy-four, and was commemorated in a memorial sketch by her successor and friend, Lambros Comitas.   JH/MBO

PRIMARY SOURCES

Rubin, Vera. *Fifty Years in Rootville: A Study in the Dynamics of Acculturation of an Italian Immigrant Group in a Rural Community.* Boston: Eagle Enterprises, 1951. A published version of her dissertation for Columbia.

————, ed. *Caribbean Studies: A Symposium.* Mona, Jamaica: University College of the West Indies, 1957.

————. "The Adolescent: His Expectations and His Society." *Proceedings of the Third Caribbean Conference for Mental Health,* Jamaica 1961: 56–71.

————. "Culture, Politics and Race Relations." *Social and Economic Studies* 11 (1962): 433–455.

————. With Lambros Comitas. *Ganja in Jamaica.* The Hague: Mouton, 1974.

STANDARD SOURCES

AMS 10–12, P&B 13; Gacs (article by Lucie Wood Saunders includes Lambros Comitas's biographical sketch of Rubin); *IDA* (article by David Lonergin).

RUCKER, AUGUSTA (1873–1963)

U.S. invertebrate zoologist and physician. Born 24 May 1873 in Paris, Tex. One foster daughter. Educated University of Texas (A.B., 1896; A.M., 1899); Johns Hopkins University (M.D., 1911). Professional experience: University of Texas, fellow (1896–1897), instructor of biology (1899–1900); Hospital for the Ruptured and Crippled in New York, physician; pediatric private practice. Honors and memberships: Texas Academy of Medicine, Fellow. Died 26 December 1963 in Hyannis, Mass., of arteriosclerosis and cerebral thrombosis.

Augusta Rucker was trained in biology at the University of Texas. She continued in biology for a master's degree, pursuing the study of arachnids. After teaching as an instructor in biology, she decided to obtain a medical degree that would guarantee her a profession and income. Rucker went to Johns Hopkins University from which she received her medical degree in 1911. She returned to Paris, Texas, where she opened a private practice and was eventually made a Fellow of the Texas Academy of Medicine. She was considered to be a pioneer in the field of pediatrics.

Rucker's research interests in invertebrate zoology focused on *Peripatus eisenii* and the Texan *Koenenia*. She was especially interested in the anatomy of *Koenenia* and its position among the Arachnida. She retired to West Dennis, Massachusetts, and died in a rest home in nearby Hyannis at the age of ninety.   JH/MBO

SECONDARY SOURCES

"Augusta Rucker." *New England Journal of Medicine* 28 (March 1964). Obituary notice.

"Dr. Augusta Rucker." *San Francisco Examiner,* 27 December 1963. Obituary notice.

STANDARD SOURCES

AMS 1–8.

RUDNICK, DOROTHEA (1907–1990)

U.S. embryologist. Born 17 January 1907 in Oconomowoc, Wis. Two brothers. Educated University of Chicago (Ph.B., 1928; Ph.D., 1931). Professional experience: Yale University, Seessell Fellow (1931–1932), research fellow (1932–1933), National Research Council, fellow (1933–1934); University of Rochester, research fellow in embryology (1934–1937); University of Connecticut, Storrs Agricultural Experiment Research Station, instructor in genetics (1937–1939); Wellesley College, Department of Zoology, instructor (1939–1940); Albertus Magnus College, department of biology, assistant professor (1940–1948), professor (1948–1977), emerita professor (1977). Honors and memberships: Guggenheim Fellow (1952–1953); U.S. Public Health special fellow (1965–1966); Society for Study of Growth and Development, symposia editor; Connecticut Academy of Sciences, secretary (1948–1953); International Institute of Embryology, member; Albertus Magnus (Hon. D.Sc., 1977). Died 10 January 1990 at Los Alamos, New Mexico.

Dorothea Rudnick grew up in a household in Chicago that emphasized science. Her father was a chemist with Armour Laboratories and her two brothers, one older and one younger, would become physicists. At first she had no interest in becoming a scientist. Although she studied mathematics and found it fun, she did not have any desire to learn physics or chemistry. At the age of fifteen, she entered the University of Chicago, where she studied languages but dropped out for two years to work in a bank in order to finance a trip to Europe.

On her return, Rudnick became interested in embryology at Chicago and began to work on a problem of thyroid development in the chick under Benjamin H. Willier, who had made a specialty of chick embryology. She decided to go to graduate school to pursue these questions under Willier. She continued throughout her research to use the chick embryo as her preferred experimental organism.

Like JANE OPPENHEIMER, Rudnick chose to continue her postdoctoral study at Yale with the embryologist John S. Nicholas, who was an associate editor of the *Journal of Morphology* with Willier. She began her long association with the Osborn Laboratory of Zoology at Yale. After three years of postdoctoral study, Rudnick went to the University of Rochester, where Willier had relocated, to continue her research on chick embryology. Willier had already begun to switch his interest to developmental genetics, and Rudnick followed him in that direction.

By the late thirties, after remaining at Rochester for more than three years, Rudnick had an opportunity to teach genetics at the Storrs Agricultural Experiment Station, part of the University of Connecticut. From there she went to teach at Wellesley for a year. She wanted an opportunity both to teach and do her own research, and decided that a position at

the woman's college Albertus Magnus would be more suitable. MARCELLA BOVERI had returned to America from Germany some twelve years before to establish an active program in biology there. She had already hired the Yale-trained biologist GRACE PICKFORD as an assistant professor. Then in her eighties, Boveri was looking for other women biologists interested in both teaching and research to succeed her. Another advantage of this college was the proximity of the Yale Osborn Zoological Laboratory, where Rudnick could set up her own experimental research projects.

Rudnick remained at Albertus Magnus for the rest of her career, rising to full professor by 1948. She edited the yearly seminar series issued by the Society for the Study of Growth and Development. Again this put her in contact with her old professor, Willier, who was president of the society in the 1940s. She continued to publish on chick development and also began to use rat embryos to study limb grafting. She retired in 1978 as emerita professor. After retirement, she joined her brother in Los Alamos, New Mexico, where she died at the age of eighty-three. Albertus Magnus College honored her with a special memorial service a month after her death.   JH

PRIMARY SOURCES

Rudnick, Dorothea. "Bilateral Localization of Prospective Thyroid in the Early Chick Blastoderm. Studied in Chorio-Allantoic Grafts." *Proceedings of the Society for Experimental Biology and Medicine* 28 (1930/1931): 132–134.

———. "Differentiation of Prospective Limb Material from Creeper Chick Embryos in Coelomic Grafts." *Journal of Experimental Zoology* 100 (October 1945): 1–18.

———, ed. *Aspects of Synthesis and Order in Growth.* Princeton, N.J.: Princeton University Press, 1954.

———, ed. *Developmental Cytology.* New York: Ronald Press, 1959.

———, ed. *Synthesis of Molecular and Cellular Structure—The 19th Symposium, Society of Development and Growth.* New York: Ronald Press, 1961.

———, ed. *Regeneration.* New York: Ronald Press, 1962.

———. "Madame Boveri and Professor Boveri." *Albertus Magnus Alumna* 4 (1967): 8–11, 14.

Dorothea Rudnick file. Albertus Magnus College Archives. Includes her curriculum vita and the program of her memorial service.

SECONDARY SOURCES

"Dorothea Rudnick." *Albertus Magnus News,* 5 Febuary 1990.

"Albertus Plans Service for Dorothea Rudnick." *New Haven Register,* 15 February 1990.

STANDARD SOURCES

AMS 6–8, B 9, P&B 10–14; Bailey; Yost.

RUMBOLD, CAROLINE (THOMAS) (1877–1949)

U.S. plant pathologist. Born 27 July 1877 in St. Louis, Mo. Educated Smith College (L.B., 1901); Washington University, St. Louis (A.M., 1903; Ph.D., 1911). Professional experience: U.S. Department of Agriculture, Bureau of Plant Industry, assistant (1903–1905), expert and collaborator (1911–1917), assistant pathologist (1917–1919), plant pathologist (1919–1924); University of Missouri, assistant in botany (1908–1910); Missouri Botanical Garden, fellow (1910–1911); Office of Forest Pathology, Madison, Wis., assistant pathologist (1924–1929), associate pathologist (1929–1942). Died 1949.

Caroline Rumbold's major research interest was in forest pathology. She worked for the U.S. Department of Agriculture both before and after she earned her doctorate. After rising to the position of plant pathologist in 1919, she remained at the USDA for only five years in that rank before moving to Wisconsin, where she was first assistant pathologist and later associate pathologist. She published extensively in the USDA *Journal of Agricultural Research*. Rumbold was a member of the Phytopathological Society, the American Society of Plant Physiologists, and the Botanical Society of Washington. Her research was on fungus diseases of trees, blue stain of wood, and results from the injection of chemicals into chestnut trees.   JH/MBO

PRIMARY SOURCES
Rumbold, Caroline. *Sugar Beet Seed Disinfection with Formaldehyde Vapor and Steam.* New York: n.p., 1924.
———. *Two Blue-Staining Fungi Associated with Bark-Beetle Infestation of Pines.* Washington, D.C.: Government Printing Office, 1932.

STANDARD SOURCES
AMS 3–8; Bailey; Barnhart.

RUSSELL, ANNA (WORSLEY) (1807–1876)

British botanist. Born November 1807 in Arno's Vale, Bristol. Married [?] Russell. Educated privately. Died 11 November 1876 at Kenilworth, Warwick.

Born in Bristol, Anna Worsley spent most of her life after she married at Kenilworth. She became interested in fungi, which she studied and drew. Her drawings are at the British Museum (Natural History). She corresponded with Hewett Cottrell Watson on botanical matters. Watson was the botanist aboard the *HMS Styx* during its survey of the Azores in 1842, known as the father of British topographical botany, and the person for whom the botanical journal of the Botanical Society and Exchange Club of the British Isles,

Watsonia, was named. Russell was a member of the Botanical Society of London.   JH/MBO

PRIMARY SOURCES
Russell, Anna Worsley. *Catalogue of Plants, Found in the Neighbourhood of Newbury.* [Speenhamland]: n.p., 1839.
Russell, Anna. "Note on a List of Newbury Plants." *Phytologist* 3, no. 1 (1849): 716.
Russell, Anna Worsley. "List of Some of the Rarer Fungi Found Near Kenilworth." *Journal of Botany* 6 (1868): 90–91.

SECONDARY SOURCES
"Anna Worsley Russell." *Journal of the Society for the Bibliography of Natural History* 9 (1979): 134–135.
Watson, H. C. *Topographical Botany.* London: n.p., 1883.

STANDARD SOURCES
Desmond.

RUSSELL, ANNIE (1868–1947)
See Maunder, Annie Russell.

RUSSELL, DOROTHY (1895–1983)

British physician and pathologist. Born 27 June 1895 in Sydney, Australia, to Alice Louisa (Cave) and Philip Stuart Russell. Orphaned at eight years. Never married. Educated Perse School for Girls, Cambridge; Girton College, Cambridge (Natural Science Tripos, Part I, class 1, 1918); Gilchrist Studentship, 1918; London Hospital Medical College (M.B.; B.S., 1923; M.D. 1930); Cambridge University (D.Sc., 1943). Professional experience: London Hospital, Bernhard Baron Institute of Pathology (1922–1932), director (1946–1960); Medical Research Council, scientific staff (1933–1942); Nuffield Department of Surgery (1940–1944); London Hospital Medical College, professor of morbid anatomy (1946–1960), emerita professor (1960–1983). Honors and memberships: Junior Beit Fellow (1922–1923); Rockefeller Traveling Fellowship to Boston and Montreal; Association of Clinical Pathologists, president (1953); Royal College of Physicians, Fellow; Sutton Prize in Pathology (1921); Clinical Obstetrics and Gynecology Prize (1921); Royal College of Surgeons, John Hunter Medal and Triennial Prize 1934. Died 19 October 1983.

Dorothy Russell was a British pathologist noted for her study of nervous system tumors, hydrocephalus, and the histology of the nervous system. Orphaned at eight years of age, she was sent to the prestigious Perse School for Girls in Cambridge, and from there went to Girton College, Cambridge, where she completed the first part of the Natural Science Tripos with first-class marks. At the end of World War I, women were urged to enter the medical field, and for this reason she went to London Hospital Medical College in 1919 and soon won awards in both pathology and clinical obstetrics and gynecology.

Russell's major interest was pathology, not clinical medicine, however. She worked under the noted pathologist M. H. Turnbull, serving as his assistant and then his associate in the Bernhard Baron Institute of Pathology. In 1928, Russell traveled to North America on a Rockefeller fellowship, working first with Frank B. Mallory in Boston and then with Wilder Penfield at the Montreal Neurological Institute in order to develop her knowledge of neuropathology, and upon her return completed a doctoral thesis on the classification of Bright's disease. She received various grants from the Medical Research Council, becoming a member of its scientific staff from 1933 to 1942. During this period she also developed her knowledge of histological techniques, applying them to the study of the nervous system.

During World War II, Russell worked with Hugh Cairns at Oxford in the Nuffield Department of Surgery in the military hospital he established there for head injuries. There she began the work on her book on the *Pathology of Hydrocephalus,* a classic work on the subject. In 1946, she replaced Turnbull on his retirement as professor of morbid anatomy at the London Hospital School of Medicine, becoming the director of the Bernhard Baron Institute of Pathology there until her retirement in 1960. Just before her retirement, she published a definitive study of the tumors of the nervous system that she had begun with Hugh Cairns, establishing her position as one of the world authorities on the topic. Russell was also a pioneer in the application of tissue culture techniques to the study of intracranial brain tumors. She was a Fellow of the Royal Society of Medicine, the Royal Microscopical Society, and the Royal College of Physicians. She continued to be active following her retirement, being awarded the Oliver Sharpey Prize by the Royal College of Physicians in 1968, remaining as emerita Professor at the London Hospital until her death at age eighty-eight.

JH/MBO

PRIMARY SOURCES

Russell, Dorothy. "A Classification of Bright's Disease." M.D. thesis, London Hospital School of Medicine, 1930.

————. *Histological Technique for Intracranial Tumours.* London: Oxford University Press, 1939.

————. *Observations on the Pathology of Hydrocephalus.* London: H. M. Stationery Office, 1949.

————. With Lucien Rubenstein. *Pathology of Tumours of the Nervous System.* London: Arnold, 1959.

STANDARD SOURCES

Annual Obituary 1983; *Munk's Roll,* vol. 7, 1984.

RUSSELL, JANE ANNE (1911–1967)

U.S. biochemist and endocrinologist. Born 9 February 1911 in Los Angeles County, Calif. (now Watts) to Mary Ann (Phillips) and Josiah Howard Russell. Four older siblings (two sisters and two brothers). Married Alfred Ellis Wilhelmi (1940). Educated Polytechnic High School, Long Beach, Calif. (1928); University of California, Berkeley (B.A., 1932; Ph.D., 1937). Professional experience: University of California, Berkeley, department of biochemistry, technician; California Fellowship in Biochemistry (1934); Rosenberg Fellowship (1935); Department of Pharmacology, Washington University School of Medicine, St. Louis, Mo., research associate (1936); Institute of Experimental Biology, University of California, research fellow (1937); Yale University, postdoctoral fellow, Department of Physiology (1938–1941), instructor (1941–1950); Emory University, assistant professor (1950–1953), associate professor (1953–1965), professor (1965). Honors and memberships: CIBA Foundation Award of the Endocrine Society (1945); National Institutes of Health, peer review committee for research grant applications (1949); Endocrine Society, vice-president (1950–1951); National Research Council, committee for the evaluation of postdoctoral fellowships; National Science Foundation, board member (1958–1964); Upjohn Award of the Endocrine Society (shared with her husband) (1961). Died 12 March 1967.

Jane Anne Russell was a fine student, ranking second in her graduating class at Polytechnic High School, and first in her class at the University of California, Berkeley, where she received the Kraft Prize, a Phi Beta Kappa key, a Steward Scholarship, and the University Gold Medal. Russell was accepted into the Institute of Experimental Biology at the University of California for her doctorate, where she worked under Leslie L. Bennett on the investigation of the role of pituitary hormones in carbohydrate metabolism. While she was still working on her dissertation, she went to the Washington University School of Medicine to work for three months with the Nobel laureates Carl and GERTY CORI. She had published six papers on pituitary hormones by the time she finished her doctorate. Supported by a Porter Fellowship from the American Physiological Society, she remained for an additional year at the Institute of Experimental Biology. She received a postdoctoral fellowship to do research at Yale University where she worked with C. N. H. Long. At this time she married a research collaborator, Alfred Ellis Wilhelmi, but continued to use her birth name professionally. The couple moved to Emory University in Atlanta in 1950, where Wilhelmi was appointed professor and chairman of the department of biochemistry. Russell was appointed assistant professor, but was supported by the National Institutes of Health. Although she was nationally recognized and held numerous honors, she was not appointed to associate professor until 1953, and spent twelve years at that rank before she was finally promoted to professor. Although she had developed breast cancer in 1962, she cared for her mother who lived with her. She edited manuscripts for the *American Journal of Physiology* up until the time of her death.

Russell's main area of research was to demonstrate the relationship between pituitary extracts and glucose utilization, publishing sixteen articles on the subject. In addition, she published a review article. During her research at Yale, she discovered that if carbohydrate deprivation occurred, an unknown pituitary factor was necessary in order to keep adequate levels of blood glucose and tissue carbohydrates. This factor was later discovered and named somatotropin. In her carefully designed experiments she discovered that the growth hormone that was isolated by Evans et al. in 1943 and 1944 contained the carbohydrate regulator. While she was still at Yale, she worked on the adrenal hormones, and found that their effect on carbohydrate metabolism was different from that of the pituitary. At Emory, Russell and her husband studied nephrectomized animals and the effect of the growth hormone in reducing urea formation. Her continued work on the growth hormone indicated that it could affect cardiac and skeletal muscles and have a role in starvation and hypoglycemia. From her extensive work on the growth hormone and metabolism, she postulated that the growth hormone is necessary in order to prevent the breakdown of essential structural proteins.   JH/MBO

PRIMARY SOURCES
Russell, Jane Anne. "Carbohydrate Metabolism in the Hypophysectomized Rat." Ph.D. diss., University of California, Berkeley, 1937.
———. With L. L. Bennett. "Carbohydrate Storage and Maintenance in the Hypophysectomized Rat." *American Journal of Physiology* 118 (1937): 196–205.
———. With G. T. Cori. "A Comparison of the Metabolic Effects of Subcutaneous and Intravenous Epinephrine Infusions in Normal and Hypophysectomized Rats." *American Journal of Physiology* 119 (1937): 167–174.
———. "The Relation of the Anterior Pituitary to Carbohydrate Metabolism." *Physiological Review* 18 (1938): 1–27.
———. "The Adrenals and Hypophysis in the Carbohydrate Metabolism of the Eviscerated Rat." *American Journal of Physiology* 140 (1943): 255–270.
———. With E. G. Frame. "Effects of Insulin and Anterior Pituitary Extracts on the Blood Amino Nitrogen in Eviscerated Rats." *Endocrinology* 39 (1946): 420–429.
———. "Hormonal Control of Glycogen Storage." In *Hormonal Factors in Carbohydrate Metabolism. Ciba Foundation Colloquia on Endocrinology* 6, ed. G. E. W. Wolstenholme, et al., 193–206. Boston: Little, Brown, 1953.

SECONDARY SOURCES
Long, C. N. H. "In Memoriam: Jane A. Russell." *Endocrinology* 81 (1967): 689–692.
Tepperman, Jay. "Jane Anne Russell (Wilhelmi)." *Physiologist* 10 (1967): 443–444.
———. "The Use of Isotopic Tracers in Estimating Rates of Metabolic Reactions." *Perspectives in Biology and Medicine* 1, no. 2 (1957): 404–416.

STANDARD SOURCES
Grinstein 1997 (article by David R. Stronck).

RUYS [RUIJS], ANNA CHARLOTTE (1898–1977)

Dutch microbiogist and physician. Born 1898. Educated University of Utrecht Medical School (M.D., 1925). Professional experience: University of Amsterdam Medical School, faculty member (1940–1944; 1945–1950?), professor of medicine, dean of medical faculty (post-1950). Honors and memberships: Medical Women's International Association, president (1948).

A. Charlotte Ruys was born in the Netherlands in 1898. She graduated from the University of Utrecht Medical School in 1925, where she had been a favorite pupil of Catherine van Tusschenbroek, who trained her in microbiology as well as medicine. Ruys was appointed to the faculty of the University of Amsterdam Medical School at the beginning of World War II, but when the Nazi government took over, she was discharged and then imprisoned for underground activities. She was released by the Allied Forces, and returned to the medical school. In 1948, she was elected president of the Medical Women's International Association.

With her commitment to public health as well as microbiology, Ruys was appointed director of the Public Health Laboratories of Amsterdam. In the 1950s, she was made professor of microbiology and dean of the medical faculty in Amsterdam.   JH/MBO

PRIMARY SOURCES
Ruys, A. Charlotte. "Pioneer Medical Women in the Netherlands." *Journal of the American Medical Women's Association (JAMWA)* 7 (1952): 99–101.
Biografisch Woordenboek van Nederland. J. Charite ed. S'-Gravenhage: Nijhoff, 1979–1994. III, 508. Listed under Ruijs.
Schaper, W. B. F. *In het eerste gelid: twaalf vooraangaande Nederlanders.* Meppel: Roelofs van Goor, [1955].

STANDARD SOURCES
Lovejoy.

RUYSCH, RACHEL (1664–1740)

Dutch anatomical preparator and flower painter. Born ca. 1662 in The Hague, Netherlands, to Maria (Post) and Frederik Ruysch. Married Jurriaan Pool. Ten children. Educated privately. Professional experience: assisted father with anatomical preparations; flower painter.

Rachel Ruysch was a Dutch anatomical preparator and flower painter who assisted her father, the well-known physician, anatomist, and botanist Frederik Ruysch (1638–1731). Her talents came from both sides of her family, since her mother was a daughter of the architect to Prince Frederik of Orange.

The significant and celebrated anatomical preparations of Ruysch used a secret recipe of talc, white wax, and cinnabar injected into the tissues by a syringe. The specimens were displayed in a special cabinet in houses rented for the purpose in a romantic, even pathetic manner, intended to demonstrate different ailments. One striking example was a hydrocephalic child sitting on a cushion holding his placenta in his hand. Peter the Great visited this cabinet and was very impressed by the lifelike quality of the figures and bought the collection in 1717, some skeletons of which still remain in the Leningrad Academy of Sciences.

When her father was seventy-nine, he began a second collection, in the preparation of which Rachel Ruysch appears to have been most involved. This was sold after his death to August II (John Sobieski), King of Poland, who gave it to the University of Wittenberg. Her brother, Henrik, a physician, anatomist, and botanist like her father, also assisted in preparing specimens, and although a practicing obstetrician, was more interested in natural history. Rachel Ruysch later married a well-known painter, Jurriaan Pool, and became noted for her own paintings of flowers, which were bought by the elector palatinate, Johann Wilhelm. Her reputation as an important Dutch artist has increased in recent years. Her paintings are held in the Netherlands, London, England, and the National Museum of the Women in the Arts and the Detroit Institue of Art in the United States.

JH/MBO

SECONDARY SOURCES

Hazen, A. T. "Johnson's Life of Frederic Ruysch." *Bulletin for the History of Medicine* 7 (1939): 324–334. No mention of Rachel Ruysch, but article describes embalming process her father used.

Lindeboom, G. A. *Dutch Medical Biography: A Biographical Dictionary of Dutch Physicians and Surgeons, 1475–1975.* Amsterdam: Rodopi, 1984. Includes some additional information on Rachel Ruysch under Frederick and Henrik Ruysch.

STANDARD SOURCES

DSB (under Frederik Ruysch).

RYDH, HANNA (1891–?)

Swedish archeologist. Born 1891 in Stockholm. Educated Stockholm Hogskola (kandidatexamen, 1915; Ph.D., 1919). Death date unknown.

Hanna Rydh was the first woman in Sweden to earn a doctorate in archeology. She was involved in several important archeological excavations in Sweden and participated in a Swedish excavation in Suratgarh in India.

She published the results of her work and also popularized archeology, particularly for children.

JH/MBO

SECONDARY SOURCE

Ryberg, Av Ewa. "Hanna Rydh—fömedlare av förhistorien." *Fornvannen* 85 (1990).

S

SABIN, FLORENCE RENA (1871–1953)

U.S. anatomist and histologist. Born 9 November 1871 in Central City, Colo., to Serena (Miner) and George Kimball Sabin. One surviving sibling, Mary. Educated Wolfe Hall, Denver; Vermont Academy, Saxtons River, Vt. (graduated 1889); Smith College (B.A., 1893); Johns Hopkins Medical School (M.D., 1900). Professional experience: faculty member, Johns Hopkins Medical School (assistant in anatomy, associate professor, 1902–1917; professor of histology, 1917–1925); research scientist, Rockefeller Institute (1925–1938); chairman, subcommittee on public health, Colorado governor's Postwar Planning Committee (1944–1947); manager, Denver Health and Welfare Department (1947–1951). Honors and memberships: Smith College, honorary Sc.D. (1910); American Association of Anatomists, president (1924); National Academy of Sciences, first woman member (1925); University of Michigan, honorary Sc.D. (1926); Mount Holyoke College, honorary Sc.D. (1929); named one of America's twelve most eminent living women (1931); Goucher College, honorary LL.D.; New York University, honorary Sc.D. (1932); Wilson College, honorary Sc.D. (1932); Syracuse University, honorary Sc.D. (1934); M. Carey Thomas Prize at the 50th anniversary of Bryn Mawr College (1935); Oglethorpe University, honorary D.Sc. (1935); University of Colorado, honorary Sc.D. (1935); University of Pennsylvania, Honorary Sc.D. (1937); Oberlin College, honorary Sc.D. (1937); Russell Sage College, honorary Sc.D. (1938); Trudeau Medal, National Tuberculosis Association (1945); Jane Addams Medal for distinguished service by an American woman (1947); Colorado State College of Education, honorary Sc.D. (1947); Elizabeth Blackwell Award, Hobart and William Smith Colleges (1949); Woman's Medical College of Pennsylvania, honorary Sc.D. (1950); Lasker Award for outstanding service in the field of public health administration (1951); University of Colorado, Distinguished Service Award (1953); Elizabeth Blackwell Citation (1953). Died 3 October 1953 in Denver, Colo.

Florence Sabin was born in Central City, Colorado, and spent her early years in that state. Her parents had both moved from the East, where a lack of money thwarted her father's dream of attending medical school. He made his way to Colorado in 1860, hoping to make his fortune in mining. He met Serena Miner, who had arrived by stage in 1867, and the couple married. Florence, the second of their two surviving children, was left motherless when she was four years old. When Serena Miner died, the family was living in Denver, where Florence and her sister, Mary, were placed in a boarding school, Wolfe Hall, by their father, who felt that he was unable to care for them himself. Missing a family life, the girls were pleased when their uncle, Albert Sabin, offered to take them into his family in Chicago. Florence spent four happy and intellectually stimulating years with these relatives.

When she was twelve, Florence went to live with her grandparents in Vermont. Upon graduating from the Vermont Academy in Saxtons River, she entered Smith College, where her sister was already a student. Not long after she arrived at Smith, Sabin decided that she wanted to be a doctor. The newly opened Johns Hopkins Medical School was the obvious choice for an aspiring woman physician, for it had been financed by a group of Baltimore women who had attached to their gift the stipulation that women be admitted on the same terms as men. Financial shortages forced Sabin to find an interim profession, so she taught mathematics for two years at her old school in Denver, Wolfe Hall (1893–1895), and zoology for a year at Smith (1895–1896).

Having saved enough money for her tuition, Florence Smith entered Johns Hopkins in 1896. She soon became a favorite of the anatomist Franklin Mall, who encouraged her to go into research. As an undergraduate, she constructed a three-dimensional model of the medulla, pons, and midbrain, and in connection with this project wrote a laboratory manual, *An Atlas of the Medulla and Midbrain*. This manual was published in 1901 and became a popular textbook. Her professional detachment earned her the respect of her male colleagues; one of them noted that "Florence Sabin was the first woman I ever met who was free from prudery in sex anatomy and physiology" (Bluemel, 46–47).

Sabin's lifelong interest in social issues began during her medical school years. Public health became a particular passion, as well as, to a lesser extent, women's rights. She attended suffragist meeings and produced the Maryland *Suffrage News.*

In 1900, Sabin received her medical degree and began a one-year internship in internal medicine at Johns Hopkins Hospital. The following year, she was awarded a fellowship in anatomy. With this appointment, she began a twenty-five-year research and teaching association with Johns Hopkins. She became the university's first woman faculty member in 1902, as an assistant in anatomy, and progressed through the academic ranks, receiving an appointment as professor of histology in 1917—the first full professorship awarded to a woman at Hopkins. This last promotion was tainted, for she was passed over for promotion after the death of her mentor, Franklin Mall, in 1917. Sabin was considered the obvious candidate to succeed him as professor of anatomy, but a man was appointed instead. Her students and colleagues who urged her to refuse the histology professorship and to resign from Hopkins in protest had to be satisfied with her answer that of course she would stay because she had research projects in process.

Sabin changed her research focus during the latter part of her stay at Johns Hopkins. Moving from the descriptive study of cell morphology to the functional physiology of living connective tissue and blood cells, she became interested in immunology and, specifically, in the reaction of body cells to tuberculosis and the body's ability to build up an immunity to the bacterium. It was this interest in immunity that recommended her to Simon Flexner in the department of cellular studies at the Rockefeller Institute in New York. A long-term cooperative research study of tuberculosis was initiated under Sabin's direction. It integrated the Rockefeller faculties with those of research institutes, universities, and research divisions of pharmaceutical companies. With Flexner, she developed a collaborative arrangement whereby her basic work on the cell could complement his interest in humoral theories of immunology. Sabin's research goal was to correlate cellular ideas with the serological. The study of tuberculosis seemed to be an ideal research topic, because she could combine her interest in public health with her findings about cellular morphology and physiology.

Sabin resigned from the institute in 1938 and returned to Denver to live with her sister, Mary. However, her "retirement" was actually the beginning of a new career in public health. In 1944, she accepted an appointment from the governor of Colorado, John Vivian, to be a member of a postwar planning committee whose immediate task was to aid the return of soldiers to civilian society. Vivian, who thought

that he was appointing a nice little old lady who, having spent her entire life in a laboratory, wouldn't know anything about medicine and wouldn't give any trouble, soon had second thoughts. Elected chairman of the public health subcommittee, Sabin demonstrated her willingness to fight for adequate public health legislation, supervising the drafting of a program for reorganization of the state health department and stumping the state to gain support for her reform bills. By 1947, she had achieved passage of most of them.

Sabin was still not satisfied, because, under a home-rule principle, the city of Denver remained outside the health unit. In 1947, she undertook local reforms under the title of Manager of Health and Charity for Denver. She donated her salary to the University of Colorado for medical research. She retired once more in 1951 to care for her sister, who had become both physically and mentally incapacitated. Sabin spent the last years of her life alone and died in her Denver home a few weeks before her eighty-second birthday.

During her lifetime, Sabin received many awards and honorary degrees. She was the first woman president of the American Association of Anatomists (1924–1926) and the first woman elected to the National Academy of Sciences (1925). When MARIE CURIE visited the United States, Sabin was chosen to welcome her on behalf of the women in science of America.

Sabin's research career was long and varied. It spanned anatomy, histology, physiology, embryology, and public health science. Her research on the lymphatics was original, although controversial at the time. Her idea that the lymphatics represented a one-way system closed at the collecting ends, where the fluids entered by seepage arising from preexisting veins instead of independently was later proved correct. She eventually published seven papers on the lymphatics.

Sabin found the study of the origin of the blood vessels and the development of blood cells in embryos fascinating. She wrote that one of the most exciting incidents in her life was the time she stayed up all night to watch the "birth" of the bloodstream in a chick embryo. After she observed the blood vessels form, she saw the beginning of the cells from which the red and white blood cells were derived and finally watched the heart make its first beat. Sabin discovered that blood plasma is developed by liquefaction of the cells that form the walls of the first blood vessels.

During her last years in Colorado, Sabin's contributions were mainly to applied science and its political ramifications. She used both her knowledge of science and her ability to manipulate human beings to spearhead the passage of vital public health legislation. MBO

PRIMARY SOURCES

Sabin, Florence. *An Atlas of the Medulla and Midbrain: A Laboratory Manual.* Ed. Henry M. E. Knower, Baltimore: Friedenwald, 1901.

———. "Tuberculous Pericarditis with Effusion; Repeated Tappings; Bacilli in the Exudate; Recovery." *American Medicine* 3 (1902): 388–389.

———. *The Origin and Development of the Lymphatic System. Johns Hopkins Hospital Reports.* Baltimore: Johns Hopkins Press, 1913.

———. "The Method of Growth of the Lymphatic System." *Harvey Lectures, Series* (1915–1916): 124–145.

———. "Discrimination of Two Types of Phagocytic Cells in the Connective Tissues by the Supravital Technique." *Contributions to Embryology* 16, no. 82 (1925): 125–162.

———. "Experimental Studies on the Origin and Maturation of Avian and Mammalian Red Blood Cells." Carnegie Institution of Washington, *Contributions to Embryology* 16, no. 83 (1925): 219–220.

———. "Bone Marrow." *Physiological Reviews* 8 (1928): 191–244.

———. *Franklin Paine Mall: The Story of a Mind.* Baltimore: Johns Hopkins University Press, 1934.

SECONDARY SOURCES

Bluemel, Elinor. *Florence Sabin: Colorado Woman of the Century.* Boulder: University of Colorado Press, 1959.

Downing, Sybil. *Florence Rena Sabin, Pioneer Scientist.* Boulder: Pruett Publishing, 1981.

Kaye, Judith. *The Life of Florence Sabin.* New York: Henry Holt and Co., 1993.

Kronstadt, Janet. *Florence Sabin, Medical Researcher.* New York: Chelsea House, 1990.

McMaster, Philip D., and Michael Heidelberger. "Florence Rena Sabin." In *Biographical Memoirs, National Academy of Sciences* vol. 34. Washington, D.C.: National Academy of Sciences, 1960.

Rossiter, Margaret W. "Florence Sabin: First Woman in the National Academy of Sciences." *American Biology Teacher* 39 (1977): 484–486 and 494.

STANDARD SOURCES

AMS 2–8; *DAB* supplement; *DSB*; Grinstein 1997 (article by Linda H. Keller); *Notable;* Ogilvie 1986; Shearer and Shearer 1996 (article by Gail M. Golderman); Yost.

SABLIÈRE, MARGUERITE (HESSEIN) DE LA (1640–1693)

French learned woman and natural philosopher. Born 1640 in Paris to Gilbert Hessein and his wife of the Menjot family. At least one brother. Educated informally. Married Antoine de Rambouillet de la Sablière (15 March 1654; separated 1668). Three children. Died 6 January 1693 in Paris.

Marguerite de la Sablière came from a successful bourgeois Huguenot family. Her father, Gilbert Hessein, was a wealthy businessman whose father dealt in the saffron, diamond, precious stone, and natron (sodium carbonate) trade. When Gilbert's wife, who was also a Huguenot, died, Gilbert wanted to remarry but hesitated because he declared that he did not want his daughter raised by a stepmother. Consequently, he arranged for her marriage at age fourteen, to Antoine de Rambouillet, the son of a prominent financier. Antoine was the second of eleven children of Nicolas de Rambouillet. The name Sablière (sandpit) came from a piece of land that Nicolas gave to his son and his wife. The marriage was unsuccessful and, after having three children, the couple agreed to a separation.

It was after the separation that Marguerite established her salon in a hotel on the Rue Neuve des Petits-Champs. Her salon became famous as important visitors from different scholarly areas flocked there. Many famous people visited, including John Sobieski, the king of Poland. She studied mathematics, physics, and astronomy with two of her visitors, both members of the Académie des Sciences, Gilles de Roberval (1602–1675) and Joseph Sauveur (1653–1716). John Bernier (1622–1698) tutored her in natural history and anatomy and also piqued her interest in speculative natural philosophy, particularly the works of Pierre Gassendi (1592–1655).

Although Marguerite de la Sablière showed an early aptitude for physics and astronomy, her most compelling claim to fame is as a friend of the poet Jean de la Fontaine (1621–1695) and as the object of Boileau's satire on scientific women, *Satire contre les femmes.* In this book, he portrayed Sablière with an astrolabe in her hand making observations of the planet Jupiter. He proclaimed that this occupation had the effect of weakening her sight and ruining her complexion. La Fontaine, who lived at her house, spoke of Sablière as his muse, who combined manly beauty and feminine grace. On 8 January 1693, she died of cancer.

Marguerite de la Sablière belonged to a class of seventeenth- and eighteenth-century French women who were intelligent, fascinated by ideas, and also social beings. After she separated from her husband, she was able to combine these attributes within the institution of the salon. Forbidden entrance to the universities and academies, she plied her talents through studying mathematics and the sciences (with the help of well-known scholars) and participating in discussions with the *cognoscenti.*

JH/MBO

SECONDARY SOURCES

Hallays, André. "Le Salon de Madame de la Sablière." In *Les Grands Salons Littéraires.* Paris: Payot, 1928.

STANDARD SOURCES

Mozans; *NBG.*

SABUCO BANERA D'ALCARAZ, OLIVIA (1562–1588)

Spanish Physician. Born 1562 in Alcaraz, Spain. Educated by her father. Died 1588 in Spain.

Olivia Sabuco was taught medicine by her physician father. Her book, the *New Philosophy of Man,* published a year before her death, was greeted with opprobrium by other Spanish doctors. The first edition was destroyed, but the later editions, published in the late sixteenth, seventeenth, and eighteenth centuries, made her name widely known.

Her ideas on medicine were unacceptable to establishment physicians not only because she was a woman, but because she based her medicine on psychosomatic concepts, attributing to the passions the source of many diseases, and even death. Her book was later condemned by the Inquisition. She died at the age of twenty-six. JH/MBO

PRIMARY SOURCES

Sabuco de Nantes y Barerra, Olivia. *Nueva filosofia de la naturaleza del hombre, no conocida ni alcanzada de los grandes filosofos antiquos, la qual mejora la vida y salud human, con las adicciones de la segunda impression.* 4ᵗʰ impression. Madrid: En la imprenta de D. Fernandez; a costa de F. Lopez Fernandez, 1728.
Castro, Adolfo de, ed. *Obras escogidas de filosofos con un discurso preliminar del excelentisimo e ilustrisimo senor. Biblioteca de autores espanoles.* Madrid: M. Rivadeneyra, 1873. Includes work by Sabuco de Nantes.

STANDARD SOURCES

DFC.

SACKVILLE-WEST, VICTORIA MARY (1892–1962)

British poet, novelist, and horticulturist. Born 1892 in Knole House, Kent, daughter of the third Baron Sackville. Married Harold Nicolson (1913). Educated privately. Died 1962.

Privately educated, Victoria Sackville-West (known as Vita) published poetry and novels. One of her novels, *The Land,* expressed sympathy with those who earned their livings from the soil. She was an ardent gardener and established a spectacular garden at Sissinghurst, Kent, her married home.

She wrote a weekly gardening column for the *Observer.* Sackville-West is probably best known for her private life. She married Harold Nicolson and the couple stayed together in spite of his homosexuality and her own lesbian affairs with Violet Trefusis and Virginia Woolf. JH/MBO

PRIMARY SOURCES

Sackville-West, Victoria. *Orchard and Vineyard.* London: J. Lane, 1921.
———. *The Land.* New York: G. H. Doran, 1927.
———. *The Garden.* London: M. Joseph Ltd., 1946.
———. *The Letters of Vita Sackville-West to Virginia Woolf.* London: Hutchinson, 1984.
———. *The Illustrated Garden Book.* New York: Atheneum, 1986.

SECONDARY SOURCES

Brown, Jane. *Vita's Other World: A Gardening Biography of V. Sackville-West.* Harmondsworth, Middlesex, England; New York: Viking, 1985.
Glendinning, Victoria. *Vita: The Life of V. Sackville-West.* New York: Knopf, 1983.

STANDARD SOURCES

DNB; DFC.

SAFFORD, MARY JANE (1834–1891)

U.S. nurse; physician. Born 31 December 1834 in Hyde Park, Vt., to Diantha (Little) and Joseph Safford. Four siblings. Married James Blake of Boston (probably ended in divorce). Two adopted daughters, Margarita and Gladys. Educated at home and with tutors; school in Bakersfield, Vt. (ca. 1852); nursing with Mary Ann Bickerdyke on Civil War battlefields; New York Medical College for Women (M.D., 1869); further medical training in Europe (1869–1872). Professional experience: school teacher; volunteer nurse (1860–1862); private practice in Chicago (1872–1873); Boston University School of Medicine, professor of women's diseases (1873–1886). Died 8 December 1891 in Tarpon Springs, Fla.

The second daughter and youngest of five children, Mary Jane Safford lived with her family in Crete, Illinois, near Chicago, where her father was a farmer. Her mother died in 1849, and Mary Jane was sent to Bakersfield, Vermont, to attend school. After graduation she spent a year in Montreal studying French and then lived in the family of an educated German to learn the language. For a time she lived with an older brother, and after she moved to Shawneetown, Illinois, he advanced her the money to establish a public school. However, the outbreak of the Civil War made Mary Jane want to contribute more to the war effort, and she began to visit the sick and the injured. In the summer of 1861, she began working with a volunteer nurse, MARY ANN BICK-ERDYKE, who taught her to care for the wounded. No matter how unpleasant the circumstances, Safford could be depended upon to handle the situation calmly. However, she became ill, and in 1862 joined a party of friends for an extended tour of Europe. During this time, she visited numerous European hospitals, which increased her desire to become a physician. When she returned, she entered the New York Medical College for Women, from which she graduated in 1869. During the fall of 1869, she returned to Europe for nearly three years of surgical training. At the University of Breslau, she was credited with being the first woman to perform an ovariotomy.

When she returned to the United States, she began her practice in 1872 in Chicago. She was an advocate of women's suffrage, and dress reform. In this same year she married, but the marriage probably ended in divorce. In 1873, she joined the faculty of the Boston University School of Medicine as professor of women's diseases. During this time, she also was engaged in private practice, served on the staff of the Massachusetts Homeopathic Hospital, and wrote pamphlets on women's hygiene, dress, and exercise. Safford retired in 1886 and moved with her two daughters to Tarpon Springs, Florida, where another of her brothers lived.

JH/MBO

SECONDARY SOURCES

Baker, Nina Brown. *Cyclone in Calico: The Story of Mary Ann Bickerdyke.* Boston: Little, Brown, 1952.

Brockett, L. P., and Mary C. Vaughan. *Woman's Work in the Civil War.* Philadelphia: Hubbard Brothers, 1888.

Cleaves, Egbert. *Biographical Cyclopedia of Homeopathic Physicians and Surgeons.* Chicago: American Homeopathic Association, 1893.

STANDARD SOURCES

NAW (article by Le Roy Fischer).

SAGER, RUTH (1918–1997)

U.S. geneticist. Born 7 February 1918 in Chicago to Deborah (Borovik) and Leon B. Sager. Two sisters. Married (1) Arthur B. Pardee; (2) Seymour Melman. Educated New Trier High School, Winetka, Ill. (graduated 1934); University of Chicago (A.B., 1938); Rutgers University (M.S., 1944); Columbia University (Ph.D., 1948). Professional experience: Rutgers University, research and teaching assistant (1942?–1944); National Research Council, Merck Fellow (1949–1951). Rockefeller Institute for Medical Research, staff (1951–1955); Columbia University, research associate (1955–1960), senior research assistant (1960–1966); City University of New York, Hunter College, professor of biology (1966–1975); Dana Farber Cancer Institute, chief of cancer genetics (1975–1988); Harvard Medical School, professor of cellular genetics (1975–1988), emerita professor (1988–1997). Concurrent experience: University of Edinburgh, Institute of Animal Genetics, non-resident fellow (1962–?). Honors and memberships: Guggenheim Fellowship; National Academy of Sciences, Fellow; National Academy of Arts and Sciences, Fellow; NAS Gilbert Morgan Smith Medal; National Cancer Institute, Outstanding Investigator Award. Died 29 March 1997 in Brookline, Mass., of bladder cancer.

Ruth Sager was an American geneticist renowned for her work on nonchromosomal genetics and cancer genetics. Born in Chicago, she attended the University of Chicago for her bachelor's degree. The University of Chicago at this time had a Great Books curriculum, and Sager appreciated the liberal arts education that she received there. She found that her favorite courses were in science and changed her major from liberal arts to biology, intending to go to medical school. She realized that she preferred research to practice and, after graduating Phi Beta Kappa with a bachelor of science degree in physiology, she moved to Rutgers University, where she earned a master of science degree in plant physiology. Her master's thesis, "Nutritional Status of the Tomato Seedling in Relation to Successful Transplanting," was never published, but was a part of a wartime research project. Her interest in research was intensified when she went to Columbia University to work on her doctoral degree. At Columbia she worked under Marcus M. Rhoades and with BARBARA McCLINTOCK.

As a Merck Fellow appointed by the National Research Council, Sager joined the staff of the Rockefeller Institute, where she remained for four years. After moving to Columbia University in various research positions, she wrote a successful textbook, *Cell Heredity* (1961), with zoology professor Francis Ryan. In 1966, she was appointed profesor of biology at Hunter College (part of the City University of New York), where she remained for ten years. She met and married Arthur Pardee, a biochemist and professor of biochemistry at Princeton University, a supportive partner. In 1972, she wrote her second book, *Cytoplasmic Genes and Organelles.*

Leaving Hunter in 1975, Sager moved with her husband to Boston, where they both began to do research at the Dana-Farber Cancer Institute and to teach at the Harvard Medical School (affiliated with the institute). She had the foresight to employ recombinant DNA techniques in her research as early as 1975. At the same time she was chief of the division of cancer genetics, Dana-Farber Cancer Institute. She remained at the Harvard Medical School until her death in 1997.

As early as the 1950s, Sager began to work on the fragments of genetic material that were located in the cell cytoplasm, outside the cell nucleus, and within the cellular organelles. She began to suspect that an increasing number of human diseases resulted from mutations in genes in respiratory organelles, and turned her attention to human genetics, especially the genetics of cancer.

Ruth Sager was a pioneer in a new kind of genetics. The prevailing view stated that in eukaryotes (cells containing structures such as nuclei), the genes occur only in the nucleus on the chromosomes. While she was at the Rockefeller Institute, Sager began to suspect the existence of genetic material outside the nucleus. In order to test her hypothesis, she began to hunt for the ideal organism for her Merck fellowship research. She found it in a genus of Algae, *Chlamydomonas,* which has two mating types (allowing classical genetics experiments to be carried out), and which could be grown in the dark as well as in light, allowing her to do experiments on the cell organelle, the chloroplast. While performing classical breeding experiments, she used a chloroplast inhibiting agent (streptomycin). When she crossed parents with contrasting traits, streptomycin-sensitive and streptomycin-resistant, she found that the offspring showed the characteristics of only one parental type, showing that the mutants did not exhibit Mendelian segregation. This pattern resembled maternal cytoplasmic inheritance in higher plants. She then mapped the nonchromosomal genes by performing crosses and identifying recombinants. After she found that the nonchromosomal genes were especially stable, she suggested that they represent a second genetic system that provide the organism with stability, and perhaps represented the existence of an earlier genetic system that existed before the chromosomes.

Other important research by Sager and her coworkers resulted in identifying many factors involved in tumor suppression.

Among the many honors during her life, Sager was made a member of the National Academy of Sciences, and received their Gilbert Morgan Smith medal, and the National Cancer Institute recognized her with its Outstanding Investigator award. JH/MBO

PRIMARY SOURCES
Sager, Ruth. "Mutability of Waxy Locus In Maize." Ph.D. diss., Columbia University, 1948.
———. "On the Mutability of the Waxy Locus in Maize." *Genetics* 36 (1951): 510–540.
———. "The Architecture of the Chloroplast in Relation to its Photosynthetic Activities." *Brookhaven Symposia in Biology* 11 (1958): 101–117.
———. With Francis J. Ryan. *Cell Heredity.* New York: John Wiley, 1961.
———. With M. G. Hamilton. "Cytoplasmic and Chloroplast Ribosomes of *Chlamydomonas*: Ultracentrifugal Characterization." *Science* 157 (1967): 709–711.

———. With R. Wells. "Denaturation and Renaturation Kinetics of Chloroplast DNA from *Chlamydomonas reinhardi.*" *Journal of Molecular Biology* 58 (1971): 611–622.
———. *Cytoplasmic Genes and Organelles.* New York: Academic Press, 1972.
———. "Patterns of Inheritance of Organelle Genomes: Molecular Basis and Evolutionary Significance." In *Genetics and Biogenesis of Mitochondria and Chloroplasts,* ed. C. W. Birky, Jr., 252–257. Columbus: Ohio State University Press, 1975.
———. "Transposable Elements and Chromosomal Rearrangements in Cancer—a Possible Link." *Nature* 282 (1979): 447–449.
———. With N. Howell. "Cytoplasmic Genetics of Mammalian Cells, Conditional Sensitivity to Mitochondrial Inhibitors and Isolation of New Mutant Phenotypes." *Somatic Cell Genetics* 5 (1979): 833–846.
———. With B. L. Smith. "Genetic Analysis of Tumorigenesis. XXI. Suppressor Genes in CHEF Cells." *Somatic Cell and Molecular Genetics* 11 (1985): 25–34.
———. "Tumor Suppression Genes." *Journal of Cellular Biology* 32 (1988): 353–357.
———. "Tumor Suppressor Genes in the Cell Cycle." *Current Opinions in Cell Biology* 4 (1992): 155–160.

SECONDARY SOURCES
New York Times, 4 April 1997. Obituary notice.

STANDARD SOURCES
Grinstein 1997 (article by Carol A. Biermann); *Current Biography* 1967; Debus.

SALBACH, HILDE (fl. 1922)
German (?) physicist. Educated Physical Institute of the Agricultural College, Berlin (doctorate). Professional experience: research.

Salbach completed her doctoral dissertation under Otto von Baeyer at the Physical Institute of the Agricultural College, Berlin. She used the apparatus and facilities of the Berlin School of Technology to determine whether the blackening of photographic plates by alpha and beta rays followed the same quantitative laws as for light. Salbach's findings were useful for researchers who wished to determine intensities of particle beams from their photographic effects. JH/MBO

PRIMARY SOURCES
Salbach, Hilde. "Das Schwärzungsgesetz für α- und β-Strahlen." *Zeitschrift für Physik* 11 (1922): 107–128.

SECONDARY SOURCES
Hevesy, George and Fritz Paneth. *A Manual of Radioactivity.* London: Oxford University Press, 1926.

STANDARD SOURCES
Meyer and von Schweidler.

SALE, RHODA (fl. 1923)

British physicist. Professional experience: research with Charles Glover Barkla.

Sale held a master's degree. She worked with the physicist and Nobel Laureate Charles Glover Barkla, professor at the University of Edinburgh from 1913, to clarify the relationship between wavelength and scattering for X-rays. Barkla and Sale also searched unsuccessfully for a new type of characteristic X radiation.   MM

PRIMARY SOURCES
Sale, Rhoda R. C. With Charles G. Barkla. "Notes on X-ray Scattering and on J Radiations." *Philosophical Magazine* 45 (1923): 737–750.

SECONDARY SOURCES
Siegbahn, Manne. *The Spectroscopy of X-Rays.* Trans. George A. Lindsay. London: Oxford University Press/Humphrey Milford, 1925. Siegbahn explains in the preface that he includes later references but did include a discussion of the "new topic" of X-ray scattering.

SALMON, ELEANOR SEELY (1910–1984)

U.S. geologist and editor. Born 16 February 1910 in Rochester, N.Y., to Flora Seely Salmon and William Harry Salmon. Never married. Educated Columbia Preparatory School in Rochester and St. Agatha's School, New York; Smith College (graduated magna cum laude in 1932); Columbia University (Ph.D., 1942). Professional experience: Socony-Vacuum Oil Company Technical Service Laboratory, Brooklyn, N.Y., chemist and analytical tester (1942– 1943), specialties department, chemist (1944–1946); American Museum of Natural History, Works Project Administration project, junior supervisor (1940?–1942), department of micropaleontology, assistant curator, Catalog of the Foraminifera, *managing editor;* Quarterly Journal Micropaleontology, *managing editor and editor (1946–1959); American Petroleum Institute Central Abstracting and Indexing Service, New York, indexer (1959–1975). Died 30 September 1984.*

Eleanor Seely Salmon was born in Rochester, New York. When she went to Smith College, she intended to major in French, but was converted to geology by Howard Meyerhoff, her geology instructor. An excellent student, she was elected to Phi Beta Kappa. She earned her doctoral degree in geology from Columbia University and, while she was a graduate student, worked at the American Museum of Natural History on the Works Project Administration project *Catalog of the Foraminifera.* After she got her degree, Salmon was unable to find a position in geology, so she accepted a job as an analytical chemist at the Socony-Vacuum Oil Company. She remained there until 1946, when she returned to the American Museum of Natural History. She left the museum for an abstracting and indexing service in 1959 and remained there until her retirement. At first she was an abstracter for the *Drilling and Exploration Bulletin* and worked from French, German, Italian, and Russian sources. After this bulletin was discontinued in the early 1960s, Salmon went to the *Refining Bulletin* and became its editor in 1966. She was also editor of a biweekly bulletin on alternative sources of energy for the American Petroleum Institute. Emphysema took a toll on her health, but after retirement she continued to do freelance abstracting and translating.

Salmon was a Fellow of the American Association for the Advancement of Science and the Geological Society of America. She was a member of Sigma Xi, and the American Association of Petroleum Geologists. She also was a member of civil liberties organizations such as the National Organization for Women, the American Civil Liberties Union, and conservation organizations such as the Nature Conservancy.

Salmon's contributions to geology were largely in the area of editing. She only published a few signed works.   CK

PRIMARY SOURCES
Salmon, Eleanor Seely. With H. N. Coryell. "A Molluscan Faunule from the Pierre Formation in Eastern Montana." *American Museum Novitates* no. 746 (1934).
———. "Mohawkian rafinesquinae." *Journal of Paleontology* 16, no. 5 (1942). From her doctoral dissertation from Columbia University Teachers College.

SECONDARY SOURCES
Phelps, Miriam E. "Memorial to Eleanor Seely Salmon, 1910–1984." *Geological Society of America Memorials* 17 (1987). With portrait.

SALPE (1st century B.C.E.)

Greek midwife.

Salpe was a midwife from Lemnos. Pliny reported on her methods of curing different ailments. Salpe contended that saliva had the power to restore sensation to a numbed limb if one would spit "into the bosom or if the upper eyelids are touched by saliva" (Pliny, 28.7.38). In order to strengthen the eyes, Salpe recommended the application of urine. Urine could also be used to relieve sunburn if applied for two hours at a time, "adding the white of an egg, by preference that of an ostrich" (Pliny, 28.18.66). She also suggested a remedy for rabies and intermittent fevers (Pliny, 28.23.82). Barking dogs would stop their yapping if fed with live frogs, and boys would be more beautiful if they would try her medications.

All that can be said for certain about Salpe, is that she was a midwife who had become well enough known to bring her to the attention of Pliny, the one original source on her.

JH/MBO

SECONDARY SOURCES
Pliny. *Natural History,* 22.48, 22.52, 28.7, 28.18, 28.23.

STANDARD SOURCES
Ogilvie 1986; Pauly-Wissowa.

SAMPSON, KATHLEEN SAMUEL (1892–1980)
British botanist. Born 23 November 1892 in Derbyshire. Educated Royal Holloway College (M.Sc., 1917). Professional experience: Leeds University, assistant lecturer in agricultural botany (1915–1917); University College, Aberystwyth, lecturer (1919–1945). Honors and memberships: British Mycological Society, president (1938).

Most of Kathleen Sampson's professional experience was at University College, Aberystwyth, where she spent twenty-six years. Her research specialty was fungal diseases of British grasses and herbaceous plants.

JH/MBO

PRIMARY SOURCES
Sampson, Kathleen. With J. H. Western. *Diseases of British Grasses and Herbage Legumes.* Cambridge, England: University Press, 1941. This book went through a second edition (1954).
———. With Geoffrey Clough Ainsworth. *The British Smut Fungi.* Kew, Surrey: Commonwealth Mycological Institute, 1950.

SECONDARY SOURCES
Transactions of the British Mycological Society 75 (1980): 353–354.

STANDARD SOURCES
Desmond.

SANBORN, ETHEL (d. 1952)
U.S. botanist and paleobotanist. Never married. Educated South Dakota State College (B.S., 1903); University of South Dakota (B.A., 1904; M.A., 1907); Stanford University (Ph.D., 1927). Professional experience: University of Oregon, faculty (1914– *1932); Oregon State College, faculty (1932–1948). Died 31 October 1952 in Vancouver, Wash.*

A successful teacher, botanist and paleobotanist Ethel Sanborn enjoyed her students at the University of Oregon and at Oregon State College. Her botanical interests included studies of algae, mosses, and liverworts. Worthy of special note are her monographs on the Hepaticae and Anthocerotes of western Oregon, on the moss flora of the Willamette Valley (with Clara J. Chapman), and on the marine algae of the Coos Bay-Arago region (with Maxwell S. Doty). When she observed fossil leaves in a highway cut near Goshen, Lane County, Oregon, she and Ralph Chaney of the University of California prepared a monograph on these flora. After looking at over one thousand specimens, they described specimens belonging to forty-nine species, all but five of which were new. The modern equivalents of these plants are found in Mexico, Central America, and other tropical areas. This implied that the climate was different during the upper Eocene or possibly the lower Oligocene than it is today. After this first study, she studied the Comstock flora of the middle Eocene, and the Scio flora of upper Oligocene or lower Miocene from Franklin Butte in Linn County, Oregon.

Sanborn held memberships in Sigma Xi, Phi Beta Kappa, Oregon Academy of Science, Pi Lambda Theta, Delta Kappa Gamma, and American Association of University Women. The Oregon Academy of Sciences awarded her a Citation of Merit at its annual meeting on 23 February 1952. Some scattered material, including a photograph of Ethel Sanborn, appears in the Oregon State University archival files.

JH/MBO

PRIMARY SOURCES
Sanborn, Ethel. *Hepaticae and Anthocerotes of Western Oregon.* University of Oregon Publications, Plant Biology Series, 1, no. 1 (1929).
———. With Ralph Chaney. *Goshen Flora of West Central Oregon.* Washington, D.C.: Carnegie Institute of Washington, Publ. 439, 1933.
———. *The Comstock Flora of West Central Oregon.* Washington, D.C.: Carnegie Institute of Washington, Publ. 465, 1937.
———. With Clara Chapman Hill. *Moss Flora of the Willamette Valley, Oregon.* Oregon State monographs. Studies in Botany, 34. Corvallis: Oregon State College, 1941.
———. *The Scio Flora of Western Oregon.* Oregon State Monographs, Studies in Geology, no. 4. Corralis: Oregon State College, 1947.

STANDARD SOURCES
AMS 5–7.

SANDFORD-MORGAN, ELMA (LINTON) (1890–?)

Australian physician. Born 22 February 1890 in Adelaide, South Australia. Five siblings. Married Captain Harry Morgan (1921). Two children. Educated "dames' school"; private girls' school; Cheltenham Ladies College (1905); University of Sydney (M.D., 1917). Professional experience: Royal Prince Alfred Hospital, senior medical registrar (1918?–1919); Bhiwani mission women's hospital in the Punjab, physician (1919–1920); Baghdad, hospital for women and children and private practice (1921–1923); private practice, Hobart, Australia (1923–1926); private practice, Sydney (1926–?); Public Health Department, assistant and then director of maternal and baby welfare (1928–1937); Adelaide, Mothercraft Training School, director and developer (1937–?); member, parliamentary commission to investigate health services in South Australia; Commonwealth Immigration Camp in New South Wales (1940–1951); general practice, Adelaide; University of Adelaide, neoplasm registrar to the Anticancer Foundation (1954–1965); Red Cross Blood Transfusion Service, phlebotomist (1964–?). Death date unknown.

Elma Sandford-Morgan's peripatetic career illustrates the difficulty women physicians encountered as they attempted to pursue their careers. She was a child of Scottish emigrants from South Australia and the youngest of six children. Her father had died in 1905; her mother encouraged her when she decided to enter medical school. Problems with sexism in medicine did not surface until later in her career. After graduating from medical school, she was appointed a resident medical officer at the Royal Alexandra Hospital for children in Sydney where she stayed for six months and then became a senior medical registrar at the Royal Prince Albert Hospital. At this time she became interested in opthalmology and went to England to get additional experience in London hospitals.

Finding that eye disease was rampant in the Punjab, she went to India for experience. Instead of returning immediately to Australia, she heard about a post in Baghdad, where the British were about to open a hospital for women and children. During this time she met and married Captain Harry Morgan, a British army officer seconded to the Arab army.

Sandford-Morgan found the conditions at the hospital unsatisfactory, so when they returned to Baghdad she opened a private practice until her daughter was born in 1922. Eventually they returned to Australia. After giving birth to a son, she tried private practice in a number of Australian cities but never seemed to be satisfied. However, she did accept several positions with the Public Health Service. The marriage disintegrated and Sandford separated from her husband and moved to Adelaide with the children. At the outbreak of World War II, she enlisted in the Royal Aus-

tralian Air Force Medical Service, but the medical personnel authorities banned her from leaving South Australia. She compromised by working with one partner of a three-person medical practice while the other two were absent for medical service. At the close of the war, she was appointed as the only woman member to investigate the health services in South Australia and to recommend desirable innovations.

Sandford-Morgan was interested to revisiting Europe. She answered an advertisement in the *Australian Medical Journal* for a post as a medical officer at the Commonwealth Immigration Camps in Australia, since a European posting was the reward for service. Finding herself the lone officer for five thousand migrants, she applied for a European post after a year. At this point she was told that the European reward for service applied only to male doctors. She went to Europe on her own, but had little luck breaking the sex barrier. Returning to Australia, she substituted in several general practices and finally got a permanent position as neoplasm registrar to the Anticancer Foundation of the University of Adelaide. She worked there until she was seventy-four, compulsory retirement, and then continued to work with the Red Cross Blood Transfusion Service.

Sandford-Morgan was convinced that there was a bias against women in the Australian medical world, and did all that she could to right the situation. At one time she was president of the Medical Women's Society of South Australia, and worked for the equal treatment of women in medicine.   JH/MBO

PRIMARY SOURCES

"Sandford-Morgan, Elma Linton." In Hellstedt, *Autobiographies.*

SANDHOUSE, GRACE ADELBERT (1896–1940)

U.S. entomologist. Born 1896. Educated University of Colorado (A.B., 1920; A.M., 1923); Cornell University (1924–1925). Professional experience: Federal Horticulture Board, U.S. Department of Agriculture, senior scientific aide (1925–1926); U.S. Bureau of Entomology, Division of Insect Identifications, USDA (1926–1928), assistant entomologist (1928–1937), associate entomologist (1937–1940). Died 1940.

Grace Sandhouse was a native of Monticello, Iowa, and worked for the Division of Insect Identification of the Bureau of Entomology and Plant Quarantine on bees and sawflies. She first studied zoology under T. D. A. Cockerell at the University of Colorado, where she found his interest in bee taxonomy compelling. After receiving her master's degree, Sandhouse joined the U.S. Department of Agriculture, where she advanced through the ranks to associate entomologist. She published several papers on the Hymenoptera, and a major monograph of the genus *Osmia*.   JH/MBO

PRIMARY SOURCES

Sandhouse, Grace. With Theodore D. A Cockerell. "Some Eocene Insects of the Family Fulgoridae." *Proceedings of the U.S. National Museum* 59 (1921): 455–457.

———. *The North American Species of Bees Belonging to the Genus Halictus.* Washington, D.C.: Government Printing Office, 1924.

———. With Theodore D. A Cockerell. "Parasitic Bees (Epeolinae and Melectinae) in the Collection of the California Academy of Sciences." *Proceedings of the California Academy of Sciences,* 4th ser., 13, no. 19 (21 November 1924): 305–324.

———. "The North American Bees of the Genus *Osmia* (Hymenoptera: Apoida)." Entomological Society of America, *Memoir* 1 (1939).

SECONDARY SOURCES

"In Memoriam." *Proceedings of the Entomological Society of Washington* 42 (1940): 186–189. Includes a bibliography of her works as well as a photograph.

STANDARD SOURCES

AMS 5–7; Bailey; Bonta; Osborn.

SANDIFORD, IRENE (1899–?)

U.S. biochemist. Born 30 June 1889 in St. Charles, Minn., to Ellen (Burns) and Benjamin Sandiford (farmer). Educated Cambridge Latin School; Radcliffe College (A.B., 1913); University of Minnesota (Ph.D. in chemistry, 1919). Professional experience: Mayo Clinic and Mayo Foundation, Rochester, Minn., assistant director metabolism laboratory (1916–1930); University of Chicago, assistant professor of medicine (1930–1954). Death date unknown.

A member of the Society for Biological Chemistry with a doctorate in chemistry from the University of Minnesota, Irene Sandiford became an assistant professor at the University of Chicago. Later information on her is not available, but she remained at Chicago until the mid-1950s. Her research interests were in metabolic studies and in endocrinology.

JH/MBO

PRIMARY SOURCES

Sandiford, Irene. With Walter M. Boothby. *Laboratory Manual of the Technic of Basal Metabolism Rate Determinations.* Philadelphia: Sanders, 1920.

STANDARD SOURCES

AMS 5–8, P 9.

SANFORD, VERA (1891–1971)

U.S. mathematician. Born 1 October 1891 in Douglaston, N.Y., to Anna Eugenia (Munson) and Edgar Lewis Sanford (clergyman). Educated St. Agnes School, Albany, N.Y.; Radcliffe College (A.B., 1915); Columbia University (M.A., 1922; Ph.D., 1927). Professional experience: Masters School, N.Y., teacher (1915–1916); Shippen School, Pa., teacher (1916–1918); St. Mary's School, N.J., teacher (1918–1919); Berkeley Institute, N.Y.C., teacher (1919–1920); Lincoln School, Columbia University Teachers College, teacher (1920–1929); Western Reserve University, assistant professor (1929–1933); State University of New York College at Oneonta, head of mathematics department (1933–1943), professor (1943–1959), emerita professor (1959–?). Died 28 December 1971.

Vera Sanford taught in the public schools of New York, Pennsylvania, and New Jersey for about five years and then for nine more at the laboratory school for Columbia University Teachers College. After this experience, she went to Western Reserve University for four years and finally to the State University of New York College at Oneonta where she spent the remainder of her professional career. She was a member of the History of Science Society and the Mathematical Association. Her research interests were in the history of mathematics, particularly of algebra. JH/MBO

PRIMARY SOURCES

Sandford, Vera. *Manual of Directions for Schorling-Sanford Achievement Test in Plane Geometry.* New York: Teachers College, Columbia University, 1925.

———. *The History and Significance of Certain Standard Problems in Algebra.* Teachers College, Columbia University, Contributions to Education, no. 251. New York: Teachers College, Columbia University, 1927.

———. *A Short History of Mathematics.* Boston: Houghton Mifflin Co., [1930?].

STANDARD SOURCES

AMS 5–8, P 9, P&B 10–11.

SANGER, MARGARET HIGGINS (1879?–1966)

U.S. nurse, birth control advocate. Born 14 September 1879? in Corning, N.Y. to Anne (Purcell) and Michael Hennessey Higgins. Ten siblings. Married (1) William Sanger (1902; divorced 1920; three children); (2) J. Noah Slee (1922; he died in 1943). Educated Corning schools; Claverack College, Hudson, N.Y.; White Plains (N.Y.) Hospital Nursing School. Professional experience: New York's Lower East Side, home health nurse; Brownsville, N.Y., established clinic (1916); founded the American Birth Control League (later the Planned Parenthood Federation); opened the first doctor-staffed birth control clinic in the United States: Birth Control Clinical

Research Bureau, New York City (1923); formed Committee on Federal Legislation for Birth Control; helped found the International Planned Parenthood Federation (1952). Concurrent experience: published the journals Woman Rebel *(1914),* Birth Control Review *(1917–1940),* Human Fertility *(1940–1948). Died 6 September 1966 of congestive heart failure.*

The sixth of eleven children (and the third of five daughters), Margaret Sanger knew firsthand the effects of poverty and uncontrolled reproduction. Daughter of a stonemason, she managed with her older sisters' help to attend Claverack College, a private coeducational school. After a period of caring for her tubercular mother, who died at age forty-nine, Margaret trained as a nurse at White Plains Hospital. In 1902 she married an architect, William Sanger, and was soon pregnant. Her son Stuart was followed by another son, Grant (1908) and a daughter, Margaret (1910) who died of pneumonia at age five.

Increasingly dissatisfied with life as a housewife, Sanger turned to radical politics and, when the family moved to Manhattan, a job as home nurse on the Lower East Side. She became an activist in the International Workers of the World (IWW) efforts to organize textile workers in the Northeast. Gradually she saw the important connection between issues of economic and social justice and feminist demands for the right of women to control their bodies. She became convinced that sexual reform for women was the first step to liberation and the ability to command higher wages and control in the workplace.

During this period, Sanger and her husband became increasingly alienated, and she experimented with her own sexual liberation and expression. She found the double standard for sexual behavior repressive and insulting. She began publishing articles in the socialist weekly *The Call,* hoping to disseminate information on venereal diseases, abortion dangers, and contraception, but found her efforts thwarted by the Comstock Act of 1873. This broadly inclusive legislation banned from the U.S. mails any material considered obscene and also any information on contraception and abortion. Sanger determined to remove the stigma of obscenity from contraception and to find a safe, effective, female-controlled form of birth control. In 1914, she traveled to Europe to study the methods in use in that more liberal environ. She returned to the States prepared to mobilize a demand for legalization of birth control through publication of her journal *The Woman Rebel.* She was soon indicted for violation of the Comstock Act and left again for Europe. Her pamphlet *Family Limitation,* which provided the most in-depth information on women's physiology and contraceptive technique available in America, was distributed widely by her followers.

While in Europe, Sanger became an intimate friend of Havelock Ellis, who influenced the slant and tone of her later propaganda. In the Netherlands, Sanger found contraceptive advice centers staffed by midwives and learned about the spring-loaded vaginal diaphragm popularized by that country's first woman physician, ALETTA JACOBS. She took the Mensinga vaginal diaphragm back to the United States, and it remained the only contraceptive officially approved by national and international birth control organizations for many years. Two deeply disturbing events occurred during Sanger's year in Europe: her husband, William, was entrapped and arrested by a Suppression of Vice agent for handing out *Family Limitations*; and their daughter died of pneumonia. Sanger returned to the United States in October 1915 and submerged herself in her cause, beginning with a nationwide tour. In October 1916, she and her younger sister, Ethel Byrne, opened the Brownsville clinic and managed to counsel 488 Brooklyn women before the clinic was closed by the police and Sanger was put in jail. The trial of the "birth control sisters" was highly publicized and gave Sanger the opportunity to win a clarification of the New York law that forbade distribution of birth control information. Judge Frederick Crane ruled that the statute was reasonable, but expanded the clause that allowed doctors to prescribe condoms to men for venereal disease to include the right of doctors to provide women with contraceptive advice for "the cure and prevention of disease." Sanger interpreted the Crane decision as a mandate for doctor-staffed birth control clinics. She began lobbying for bills removing prohibitions on medical advice given by physicians.

Following the advice of Havelock Ellis, Sanger gradually separated herself from militant feminism and her own radical past and stressed social and eugenic arguments for birth control. Her slogan was "Every child a wanted child." She soon had financial backing from prominent socialites and philanthropists, which allowed her to organize (1921) the American Birth Control League, a national lobbying organization which later became the Planned Parenthood Federation of America (1942). Sanger divorced William in 1920 and married millionaire J. Noah Slee in 1922. He agreed to respect her autonomy and fund her cause and, in spite of Sanger's intimate friendships with other men, the marriage lasted until his death in 1943.

The New York Birth Control Clinical Research Bureau (later the Margaret Sanger Research Bureau, which operated until 1973), opened in 1923, was the first doctor-staffed birth control clinic in the United States. Sanger appointed Hannah Stone as medical director and a careful clinical record was established demonstrating the safety and effectiveness of contraceptive practice. Not without opposition, the bureau gave instruction in contraceptive technique to hundreds of physicians and became a model for the network of over three hundred birth control clinics established by Sanger and her coworkers between 1923 and 1938.

One of Sanger's greatest achievements came at the end of a long and bitter lobbying and legal battle to reverse the Comstock Act's classification of birth control as obscenity. In 1936 a federal court ruled that new clinical data (mainly collected through the careful documentation of the birth control clinic network) forced reinterpretation of the 1873 law to permit the mailing of contraceptive materials intended for physicians. This made possible the 1937 resolution of the American Medical Association recognizing contraception as a legitimate medical service that should be taught in medical schools.

After this achievement, Sanger took a lesser role in the movement and moved with Slee to the home they built in Tucson, Arizona, for their retirement. In 1952, after World War II, Sanger played a role in the founding of the International Planned Parenthood Federation and served as first president. She applied to go to Japan to help in the effort to introduce family planning to the Japanese, but was denied permission. In 1952, she met with Clarence Gamble, well-known family planning philanthropist and advocate through the research/medical route, in Bombay, India. Though the two had never met before, they knew and respected each other's work for family planning, coming from different directions and sometimes at odds with each other. That same year, having long sought a female-controlled contraceptive more effective than the diaphragm, Sanger brought the work of biologist Gregory Pincus to the attention of Katherine Dexter McCormick, who partially subsidized the final development and testing of the birth control pill. Sanger died of congestive heart failure in 1966 at a Tucson nursing home

JH/MBO

PRIMARY SOURCES

Sanger, Margaret. *Family Limitation*. New York: M. H. Sanger, 1914. Pamphlet. Provided the most detailed and informed discussion of contraceptive technique then available in English.

——. *Women and the New Race*. New York: Eugenics Publications, 1920.

——. *The Pivot of Civilization*. New York: Brentano's, 1922.

——. *Happiness in Marriage*. New York: Brentano's, 1926.

——. *Motherhood in Bondage*. New York: Brentano's, 1928.

——. *My Fight for Birth Control*. New York: Farrar and Rinehart, 1931. Autobiography.

——. *An Autobiography*. New York: W. W. Norton, 1938.

SECONDARY SOURCES

Chesler, E. *Woman of Valor: Margaret Sanger and the Birth Control Movement in America*. New York: Simon & Schuster, 1992.

Coigney, V. *Margaret Sanger: Rebel with a Cause*. Garden City: Doubleday, 1969

Dash, J. *A Life of One's Own: Three Gifted Women and the Men They Married*. New York: Harper & Row, 1973.

Douglas, E. *Margaret Sanger: Pioneer of the Future*. New York: Holt, Rinehart & Winston, 1970.

Foster, M. *Significant Sisters: The Grassroots of Active Feminism*. New York: Knopf, 1984

Gray, M. *Margaret Sanger: A Biography of the Champion of Birth Control*. New York: R. Marek, 1970.

Kennedy, D. *Birth Control in America: The Career of Margaret Sanger*. New Haven: Yale University Press, 1970.

Moore, G., and R. Moore. *Margaret Sanger and the Birth Control Movement: A Bibliography 1911–1984*. Metuchen, N.J.: Scarecrow, 1986.

Reed, James. *From Private Vice to Public Virtue: The Birth Control Movement and American Society*. Princeton, N.J.: Princeton University Press, 1984.

Williams, Doone, and Greer Williams. *Every Child a Wanted Child: Clarence James Gamble, M.D., and His Work in the Birth Control Movement*. Boston: Harvard University Press, 1978.

STANDARD SOURCES
NAW(M); Uglow 1989.

SARA OF SAINT-GILLES (fl. 1326)
French Jewish healer. Fl. 1326.

Sara practiced and also taught medicine to other women. In 1326, she was licensed to train a male apprentice.

STANDARD SOURCES
Echols and Williams.

SARA OF WÜRZBURG (15th century)
German physician of the fifteenth century.

Sara of Würzburg was a Jewish physician who was forced to pay ten florins a year to practice medicine because of her Judaism. According to Hurd-Mead, this fee was reduced to two florins after she had bought a new house in town.

JH/MBO

STANDARD SOURCES
Echols and Williams; Herzenberg; Hurd-Mead 1938.

SARGANT, ETHEL (1863–1918)
British botanist. Born 1863 in London to Catherine (Beale) and Henry Sargant. Never married. Educated North London Collegiate

School; Girton College, Cambridge (tripos, 1884). Professional experience: botanical research at home. Died 1918.

Ethel Sargant was a barrister's daughter who was interested in plants from childhood. After attending the North London Collegiate School, she studied natural science at Girton College, Cambridge, where in 1884 she took the two-part Natural Science Tripos examination. Sargant never had a professional position. She carried out most of her research at home, first in a laboratory built on the grounds of her mother's house at Reigate and eventually at her own home in Girton Village, Cambridge. She spent one year (1892–1893) at Kew Gardens studying under D. H. Scott, where she gained invaluable training and experience in general methods of research and in the specific methods of plant anatomy. In 1897 she visited several laboratories on the Continent, including that of Adolf Strasburger (1844–1912) at Bonn. Sargant became an unofficial advisor to botany students who came to her laboratory for instruction. Although never proficient in lecturing and demonstrating, Sargant was an excellent research adviser to her students.

One of these students was AGNES ARBER. Sargant assigned her various tasks, including sectioning and staining plant material for microscopic examination. Sargant never attempted to get a teaching post partly because she felt it would stifle original thought. She also felt the need to care for her mother and her mentally handicapped sister.

Sargant was elected to an honorary fellowship at Girton College in 1913, became a Fellow of the Linnean Society and the first woman to serve on its council, and was president of the Botanical Section at the 1913 meeting of the British Association. At the time of her death, at age fifty-four, she was serving as president of the Federation of University Women.

Ethel Sargant studied both the cytology and the morphology of plants. Her earliest research was cytological and was involved with the presence of centrosomes in higher plants. She then progressed to a general study of oogenesis and spermatogenesis in *Lilium martagon*. During this time (the late nineteenth century), some investigators suspected that the synaptic stage in cell division was merely an artifact caused by new staining procedures. Sargant confirmed the existence of this stage by examining unstained specimens of the anthers of the Turk's-cap lily, in which synapsis was evident as well as in the stained specimens.

After she had completed the studies of *Lilium martagon*, Sargant discontinued her cytological work. Although the strain on her weak eyes from constant use of the microscope was partly accountable, she also had become unhappy with the direction in which she perceived cytological research to be moving. She complained that the tendency of investigators "to obscure cytological issues by presenting the facts

colored beyond recognition by some preconceived theory" (Arber, 122) was deplorable.

While pursuing her cytological research, Sargant had become interested in plant embryology. In 1895 she studied the seedlings of wild arum. After her study of *Arum*, she investigated the life history of monocotyledons and especially their method of lowering themselves into the soil. Phylogenetic questions intrigued her. She wrote about the vascular systems of monocotyledons near the end of her life, saying that she had looked upon the number and arrangement of vascular bundles (axial or lateral) as a useful guide to descent. This conviction indicated that these characters are slow to alter and, therefore, often betray ancestry. By studying monocotyledonous seedlings, particularly of the Liliaceae, she made some startling conclusions about the evolutionary origin of this group. She reported to a colleague in 1902, "My seedlings have suddenly turned up trumps. Did I ever tell you that for some years I have been convinced that the single 'cotyledon' of monocotyledons is not homologous with one, but with both the cotyledons of a dicotyledon?" (Arber, 125). She discussed the implications of her findings on monocotyledons in three papers, "A Theory of the Origin of Monocotyledons Founded on the Structure of Their Seedlings," "The Evolution of Monocotyledons," and "The Reconstruction of a Race of Primitive Angiosperms." JH

PRIMARY SOURCES

Sargant, Ethel. "The Formation of the Sexual Nuclei in *Lilium martagon*: I. Oogenesis." *Annals of Botany* 10 (1896): 445–477.

———. "The Formation of the Sexual Nuclei in *Lilium martagon*: II. Spermatogenesis." *Annals of Botany* 2 (1897): 187–222.

———. "The Origin of the Seed-Leaf in Monocotyledons." *New Phytologist* 1, no. 5 (1902).

SECONDARY SOURCES

Arber, Agnes. "Ethel Sargant." *New Phytologist* 18 (March-April 1919): 120–128.

"Ethel Sargant." *Nature* 100 (31 January 1918): 428–429.

Packer, Kathryn. "A Laboratory of One's Own: The Life and Works of Agnes Arber, F.R.S. (1879–1960)." *Notes and Records of the Royal Society of London* 51, no. 1 (1997): 87–104.

STANDARD SOURCES

DNB Missing Persons; Ogilvie 1986.

SARGENT, WINIFRED (1905–1979)

British mathematician. Born 8 May 1905 at Ambergate in Derbyshire. Educated at home; school for Friends' children; Friends boarding school at Ackworth (near Pontefract) (1916–1919);

Mount School, York (from 1919); Herbert Strutts' School, Belper (higher school certificate) (1923); Newnham College, Cambridge, first-class degree (1924–1927); Mary Ewart traveling scholarship and a Goldsmiths Company Senior Studentship (1928); Cambridge University (Sc.D., 1954). Professional experience: research work (1928); Bolton High School, teacher (1928?–1931); Westfield College, assistant lecturer (1931–1936); Royal Holloway College, assistant lecturer? (1936–1941), lecturer (1941–1948); Bedford College, lecturer (1948–1954), reader (1954–1967). Died October 1979.

Winifred L. C. Sargent came from a Quaker family and was the only child of her father's second marriage. She was brought up in the Quaker Community of Fritchley, and her father provided her early education. She then attended a small private school for Friends' children, followed by a Friends boarding school. After a Joseph Rowntree entrance scholarship, she next went to the Mount School at York on a scholarship. However, this school was not strong in mathematics, so she transferred as a day girl at the Herbert Strutts' School, Belper, a school with a high academic reputation. She was awarded a Derby Scholarship in 1923 and a state scholarship and Mary Ewart scholarship to Newnham College, Cambridge, in 1924. After attaining a first-class degree there, she remained at the university to conduct research. A perfectionist, she was unhappy with her results, and left Cambridge to teach at Bolton High School until 1931.

For the next years, Sargent was an assistant lecturer at Westfield and Royal Holloway colleges. In 1939, she became a research student of Professor Bosanquet and in 1954 was awarded the degree of doctor of science by Cambridge University. In 1967 she left Bedford College, where she had advanced to reader.

Sargent's research was based on the theory and applications of Lebesgue integration, which by the 1930s was well established. She worked on the elucidation of the exact relations and properties of new integrals and derivatives. She also contributed to the theory of fractional integration and differentiation. In her last three papers she worked on the properties of BK-spaces, spaces of complex sequences in which the mapping from a sequence to one of its terms is continuous.

Sargent's lucid work was recognized for its exactness and for the decisiveness of her results. She was absolutely dedicated to mathematics, and had few interests outside the field. She seldom addressed seminars and did not attend mathematical conferences.

JH/MBO

PRIMARY SOURCES

Sargent, Winifred L. C. "On Young's Criteria for the Convergence of Fourier Series and Their Conjugates." *Proceedings of the Cambridge Philosophical Society* 25 (1929): 26–30.

———. "On the Integrability of a Product." *Journal of the London Mathematical Society* 23 (1948): 28–34.

———. "On Linear Functionals in Spaces of Conditionally Integrable Functions." *Quarterly Journal of Mathematics* (Oxford) 2, no. 1 (1950): 288–298.

———. "Some Summability Factor Theorems for Infinite Integrals." *Journal of the London Mathematical Society* 32 (1957): 387–396.

———. "On Sectionally Bounded BK-Spaces." *Mathematische Zeitschrift* 83 (1964): 57–66.

SECONDARY SOURCES

Eggleston, H. G. *Bulletin of the London Mathematical Society* 13 (1981): 173–176. Reprinted in *Association for Women in Mathematics (AWM) Newsletter* 11, no. 1 (January-February 1983): 7–10.

STANDARD SOURCES

Høyrup.

SATUR, DOROTHY MAY (1902–   )

Indian physician. Born 28 May 1902 in Madras, India. Fourteen siblings; ten survived infancy. Educated Queen Mary's College, Madras (graduated 1920); Presidency College, Madras (B.A., 1923?); Madras Medical College (M.B.; B.S., 1928); specialized in obstetrics in Britain (1934–1936). Professional experience: Women's Medical Service, deputy medical superintendent; medical superintendent; Calcutta, Visakhapatam, Lucknow, New Delhi, and Gaya, professor of obstetrics and gynecology (1936–1946); various colleges, professor of obstetrics and gynecology (1946–1961); Bangalore, professor of obstetrics and gynecology (1961–1968), professor emerita (1968–?).

Dorothy Satur, although an Indian national, came from a multiethnic background. Her paternal grandfather was Armenian and his wife was of mixed French-Indian origin; her mother's father was Portuguese and her mother was a Dutch burgher from Kandy, Ceylon. Both of Satur's parents were devout Roman Catholics. Although her father was a self-made man and her mother married before she had an opportunity to go further in her education (she passed the higher local examination at the Trinity College of Music in London), both parents passed on an educational work ethic as well as a love for music, writing, and sports to their ten surviving children.

During her school days, Satur was interested in science and mathematics. In order to prepare herself to study medicine, she attended Queen Mary's College in Madras until she was eighteen years old, after which she went to Presidency College, where she obtained her bachelor's degree. In 1923, she was admitted to the Madras Medical College and completed her degrees in 1928.

Satur did not immediately enter the Senior Women's Medical Service of India, for she was told that marriage might cause her service to be terminated. Even though she had no plans to marry, she thought the terms of the contract unfair and went to Britain where she specialized in obstetrics. She was, however, "drafted" into the Women's Medical Service in 1936, and remained there until it was dissolved in 1949. During her time with the service, she held many positions, including professorships in obstetrics and gynecology in hospitals all over India. After additional studies in the United Kingdom and the United States in 1947, she eventually got a post as professor of obstetrics and gynecology at Bangalore, where she settled in 1961.

Satur was a member of many medical societies and was on the Advisory Committee for Maternity and Child Welfare of the Indian Council of Medical Research. She was a fellow of the Royal College of Obstetrics and Gynecology, on the Advisory Committee for Maternity and Child Welfare of the Indian Council of Medical Research, and an examiner for science and medical degrees.   KM

PRIMARY SOURCES
"Satur, Dorothy May." In Hellstedt, *Autobiographies.*

SAUNDERS, EDITH REBECCA (1865–1945)

British botanist and geneticist. Born 14 October 1865 in Brighton, England, to Jane Rebecca Whitwell and John Saunders. Educated Handsworth Ladies College; Newnham (1884–1888), Birmingham Scholar, Natural Science Tripos Part I, class 2; Part II, class 1; Bathurst studentship (1888–1889). Professional experience: Newnham College, demonstrator in botany (1889–1902), lecturer (1892–1925); Girton College, lecturer (1904–1914); Newnham, associate (1893–1918), president (1917–1918), member of council (1903–1907, 1915–1919). Research in botany (from 1888), with William Bateson in genetics (1895). Honors and memberships: Banksian Medalist of the Royal Horticultural Society (1906); President of the Botanical Section, British Association for the Advancement of Science (1920); Genetical Society, president (1936); Linnean Society, Fellow; Horticultural Society, Fellow (1925–1945). Concurrent experience: YMCA, Cambridge offices; honorary treasurer of the WVS Services Club (1941–1945). Died 6 June 1945 in a bicycle accident.

Edith Rebecca Saunders has been called the mother of British plant genetics. Her research was in two areas, plant genetics and floral morphology. She was educated at Handsworth Ladies College and at Newnham College, Cambridge, where she took both parts of the Natural Sciences Tripos (1887, 1888) and obtained first-class honors. In 1889 she was appointed demonstrator in botany at Newnham

College. Along with her colleague MARION GREENWOOD, she organized the Balfour laboratory, whose direction she took over in 1899. She taught natural sciences for more than twenty years to women, at both Newnham and Girton Colleges.

Saunders's first research was a study of the structure and function of the septal glands of *Kniphofia.* Early in her career, however, she worked collaboratively with William Bateson on plant breeding experiments of dominant and recessive characters on *Biscutela laevigata,* the results of which were published in 1897 and 1902. From this time on, she and Bateson were the leading proponents of plant genetics in Britain. Saunders published twenty-two papers studying the complex genetic interactions in *Matthiola incana.* During these investigations, she became interested in some of the morphological peculiarities found in her specimens, particularly the lines of hairs on the stems of some *Matthiola* and abnormalities of the gynoecium in others. Since neither of these phenomena could be explained by current morphological ideas, she attempted to determine the cause. She developed her "leaf-skin" theory to explain the structure of the stem of flowering plants and the theory of carpel polymorphism to explain the abnormal gynoecium. Many of her papers on these subjects are found in the *Annals of Botany,* the publications of the Linnean Society, and the *New Phytologist.* In 1938 and 1939 her two-volume *Floral Morphology* was published. These volumes summarized and integrated her work. Although her genetics work was ignored after World War II, her important work in floral anatomy continued to be cited.

At the outbreak of World War II, Saunders abandoned her research work and filled a full-time war post until 1945. She had just begun to return to active scientific work when she was killed in a bicycle accident at the age of nearly eighty.

Saunders was one of the first women to be elected a Fellow of the Linnean Society (1905). She later served on its council and was its vice-president (1912–1913). The esteem in which her scientific colleagues held her was indicated by her election to the presidency of the Botanical Section of the British Association in 1920 and to the presidency of the Genetical Society in 1936. In 1906 the Royal Horticultural Society awarded her the Banksian medal. She traveled to meetings of the British Association in all the Commonwealth countries, Australia, New Zealand, South Africa, and then to China, Japan, and North America. During World War II she was active in many volunteer activities.

                                        JH/MBO

PRIMARY SOURCES
Saunders, Edith Rebecca. With William Bateson. *Experiments [in the Physiology of Heredity].* London: Harrison, 1902.

———. "The History, Origin and Characters of Certain Interspecific Hybrids in *Nolana* and Their Relation to *Nolana paradoxa.*" *Journal of Genetics* 29 (1934): 387–419.

———. "Floral Anatomy and its Morphological Interpretation." *New Phytologist* 33 (1934): 127–169.

———. "On Certain Features of the Gynoecium in Nolanaceae." *New Phytologist* 35 (1936): 423–431.

———. *Floral Morphology: A New Outlook with Special Reference to the Interpretation of the Gynaeceum.* 2 vols. Cambridge: W. Heffer & Sons, 1937; 1939.

———. "Floral Anatomy: Bibliography and Index to Families Studied." *Botanical Journal of Linnean Society* 74 (February 1977): 179–187.

SECONDARY SOURCES

Schmid, Rudolf. "Edith R. Saunders and Floral Anatomy: Bibliography and Index to Families She Studied." *Botanical Journal of the Linnean Society* 74 (1977): 179–187.

STANDARD SOURCES

DNB Missing Persons; Newnham, vol. 1; Newnham Roll.

SAVULESCU, OLGA (1905–)

Rumanian mycologist and plant pathologist. Born 16 October 1905 in Oltenita, Rumania, to Jeannette and Jancu Savulescu. Married Traian Savulescu. Educated University of Bucharest (1924–1929); Columbia University (Ph.D., 1934). Professional experience: Plant Pathology Institute of Tobacco Cultivation and Fermentation, assistant (1929–1931); Institute of Agricultural Research, principle research worker, plant pathology section (1934–1939); head of lab (1939–1949), head of plant pathology section (1949–1957); Institute of Biology, Rumanian Academy of Sciences, assistant director, head of section of microbiology and general phytopathology, teacher of doctoral students (1950–?).

Plant pathologist Olga Savulescu was married to Traian Savulescu, the founder of phytopathology in Rumania. She worked on fungal and viral diseases in plants and methods of controlling them. She was especially interested in black spot in roses, rusts of cereals and their control, and diseases of potatoes (particularly black wart disease). The work on rusts led her to to study host-parasite relationships. She also studied diseases of ornamental plants and fruit trees. She published numerous articles on these subjects.

She was a member of many societies, including the Rumanian Academy of Sciences (corresponding member, 1952; member, 1962) and the New York Academy of Sciences.

JH/MBO

PRIMARY SOURCES

Savulescu, Olga. With Traian Savulescu. *Tratat de patologie vegetala* (Plant Pathology: A Guide to Crop Zonation). Bucuresti, editura academiei republicii populare romine, 1959.

STANDARD SOURCES

Debus; Turkevich and Turkevich.

SAWIN, MARTHA (1815–1859)

U.S. physician. Educated Woman's Medical College, Philadelphia. Died 1859.

Martha Sawin was a member of the first graduating class of the Woman's Medical College in Philadelphia.   JH/MBO

SECONDARY SOURCES

Alsop, Gulielma F. *History of the Woman's Medical College, Philadelphia, Pennsylvania.* Philadelphia: J.B. Lippincott, 1950.

STANDARD SOURCES

Bonner 1992; Hurd-Mead 1933.

SAY, LUCY (SISTARE) (1801–1885)

U.S. scientific illustrator. Born 1801 in New London, Conn., to Nancy and Joseph Sistare. Married Thomas Say. Died 1885 in Lexington, Mass.

Lucy Sistare was born in New London, Connecticut, and grew up in New York City. She married the entomologist and conchologist Thomas Say of Philadelphia in 1827. At that time they were members of New Harmony, a communistic colony in Indiana, which had become a scientific and cultural center with the first kindergarten, first free public school, first free library, and first fully coeducational school in the United States. Lucy Say's responsibilities in connection with the schoolchildren and the household at New Harmony included spinning wool, knitting stockings, and making winter clothing for the boys.

Say moved back to New York City to live with her sister after her husband died in 1834. She presented Thomas Say's entomological cabinet and library to the Academy of Natural Sciences of Philadelphia and was made the first woman member of this society (1841).

Lucy Say was a superb illustrator, whose drawings of invertebrates were included in many of her husband's published works. She also corresponded with other naturalists. Through her illustrations she was able to contribute to science.   JH/MBO

PRIMARY SOURCES

Say, Lucy Way Sistare. Five Drawings for Thomas Say's *American Conchology*. New Harmony, Ind.: School Press, 1832. Five drawings in pencil and crayon. Located in Houghton Library, Harvard University.

Say, Thomas. *Correspondence between Thomas Say and Others.* Includes correspondence from Lucy Way Sistare Say. In Museum of Comparative Zoology, Harvard University.

SECONDARY SOURCES

Weiss, Harry B., and Grace M. Ziegler. *Thomas Say: Early American Naturalist.* Springfield, Ill.: Charles C. Thomas, 1931.

STANDARD SOURCES

Bailey; Ogilvie 1986.

SCARPELLINI, CATERINA (1808–post 1872)

Italian meterorologist, astronomer, mathematician, and geologist. Born 1808. Professional experience: Meteorological Ozonometric Station, Rome, founder. Honors and memberships: Italian gold medal (1872).

Caterina Scarpellini organized the Meteorological Ozonometric station in Rome. Born in 1808, she discovered a comet in 1854. In 1872, a gold medal honoring her work in statistics was struck in her honor in Italy.   JH/MBO

PRIMARY SOURCES

Scarpellini, Caterina. *Biografia dell'astronomo Don Ignazio Calandrelli.* Rome: Tip. Delle Belle Arti, 1866.
———. *Un omaggio alla memoria di Benedetto Trompeo.* Rome: Tip. Eredi Botta, 1872.
———. With Paolo Peretti. *La sabbia caduta in Roma nelle notti del 21 e 23 febbraio 1864 confrontata con la sabbia del deserto di Sahara: investigazioni fisico-chimiche.* Rome: Tip. Delle Belle Arti, 1865.

SCHAFFNER, MABEL (BROCKETT) (1869–1906)

U.S. botanist. Born 15 April 1869 in Kansas, to Mary A. and Henry P. Brockett. Four siblings. Married John Henry Schaffner (1895). Educated Baker University, Baldwin City, Kans. Died 6 May 1906 in Columbus, Ohio.

Mabel Schaffner was the wife of John Henry Schaffner, assistant professor in the department of botany at The Ohio State University. The couple met at Baker University, where she completed her degree and was an assistant for five years. After leaving Kansas, the two spent one academic year at the University of South Dakota and the University of Chicago before they came to Ohio State. John Schaffner hired his wife as his assistant. He acknowledged his debt to her in a paper of March 1906 on chromosome reduction in *Lilium triginum*. She prepared the majority of the slides on which the paper was based. However, she was a skilled botanist in her own right. Her paper on the embryonic development of the shepherd's purse, *Capsella bursa-pastoris,* was published after she had died at age thirty-seven; her husband had to complete some of the illustrations.   JH/MBO

PRIMARY SOURCES

Schaffner, Mabel. "Key to the Ohio Sumacs in the Winter Condition." *Ohio Naturalist* 5 (1905): 293.
———. "Free-Floating Plants of Ohio." *Ohio Naturalist* 6 (1905): 420–421.
———. "The Embryology of the Shepherd's Purse." *Ohio Naturalist* 7 (1906): 1–8. Addendum by John H. Schaffner.

SECONDARY SOURCES

Stuckey, Ronald L. "Mabel (Brockett) Schaffner." Unpublished notes.

STANDARD SOURCES

Stuckey.

SCHANTZ, VIOLA SHELLY (1895–1977)

U.S. zoologist. Born 1895 in Quakertown, Pa. Educated Perkiomem Seminary (1911–1913); Muhlenburg College (summers, 1915–1916). Professional experience: Pennsylvania public school teacher (1913–1918); U.S. Biological Surveys, U.S. Department of Agriculture biological aide (1918–1929), senior biological aide (1929–1944); U.S. Fish and Wildlife Service, systematic zoologist (1949–1961). Retired 1961. American Society of Mammalogists, charter member, officer, and member, board of directors. Died 1977.

Viola Shelly Schantz was the first female charter member of the American Society of Mammalogists and later became a life member of the society. Her service to her discipline was without peer. She was the first female officer of the society as treasurer from 1930 to 1953 and, by virtue of this position, was the first woman to serve on the board of directors. She was also the first woman elected to the board of directors, serving from 1953 to 1957 and from 1959 to 1963. She served as chair of the local committee for the annual meeting of the American Society of Mammalogists in 1959. Schantz also served nineteen years as chair of the index committee (1948–1966), and coordinated the first three multiyear indices of the *Journal of Mammalogy* (1919–1939; 1940–1949; and 1950–1959). The 1970–1989 index was dedicated to her.

Schantz contributed thirty-two articles, notes, histories, and obituaries to the *Journal of Mammalogy.* Her early papers were published as Viola Schantz Snyder. While she was serving the society, she continued with her own research. One of her most important contributions to mammalogy was the catalog of type specimens in the United States National Museum.   JH/MBO

PRIMARY SOURCES

Poole, A. J. and V. S. Schantz. With A. J. Poole. "Catalog of the Type Specimens of Mammals in the United States National Museum, Including the Biological Surveys' Collection." *Bulletin of the United States National Museum* 178 (1942): 1–705.

———. "The Rice Rat, *Oryzomys palustris palustris,* in Delaware." *Journal of Mammalogy* 24 (1943): 104.

———. "A New Race of Badger (*Taxidea*) from Eastern Kansas." *Journal of Mammalogy* 31 (1950): 346–347.

———. "Record of an Albino Pine Vole." *Journal of Mammalogy* 42 (1960): 129.

SECONDARY SOURCES

Kaufman, Dawn M., Donald W. Kaufman, and Glennis A. Kaufman. "Women in the Early Years of the American Society of Mammalogists (1919–1949)." *Journal of Mammalogy* 77, no. 3 (1996): 642–654.

STANDARD SOURCES

AMS P&B 10–11.

SCHARLIEB, DAME MARY ANN DACOMB (BIRD) (1845–1930)

British physician and surgeon. Born 1845. Educated Madras Medical School, the London School of Medicine for Women; London University (M.D., 1888). Professional experience: London University, Women's Medical School, faculty; New Hospital for Women, senior surgeon; Royal Free Hospital, Madras, gynecologist; Victoria Hospital for Cast and Gosha Women, founder. Honors and memberships: Named Dame of the British Empire in 1926. Died 1930.

Dame Scharlieb was not only an outstanding physician, gynecologist, and surgeon, she also wrote prolifically on health issues vital to women and children. Her books include those on welfare of the expectant mother, child care, sexual problems and venereal disease, and women in medicine. Married before the age of twenty, she accompanied her husband, a barrister, to India in 1866 and immediately became aware of the suffering of women there. She entered the Medical School of Madras with three other women, in spite of hostility of the superintendent. She returned to England to complete her medical degree, specializing in gynecology and surgery. ELIZABETH GARRETT ANDERSON helped Scharlieb set up practice and later obtain the position of chief surgeon at the New Hospital for Women. Scharlieb was listed on the medical faculty of the University of London women's medical college after 1900.

Alternating between England and India, Scharlieb concerned herself with aspects of women's physical and mental health from birth through "the seven phases of woman's life" to death. Her efforts to control venereal diseases in women and children through education led to her association with the National Council for Combating Venereal Diseases. She founded the Victoria Hospital for Cast and Gosha Women and lectured at Madras Medical College. She was an early proponent of sex education and helping women understand the physical and sexual phases of development from menstruation through menopause.

During World War I Scharlieb helped form a Women's Medical Service for India. Her work was recognized formally with the bestowal of the Order of the British Empire and then Dame of the British Empire (1926). She was one of the first women magistrates in England. Her final book, *The Bachelor Woman and Her Problems,* was published a year before her death in 1930.   JH/MBO

PRIMARY SOURCES

Scharlieb, Mary Ann Dacomb Bird. *A Woman's Words to Women: On the Care of Their Health in England and India.* London: Sonnenschein, 1895.

———. *The Mother's Guide to the Health and Care of Her Children.* London: George Routledge and Sons, 1905.

———. *The Seven Ages of Woman: A Consideration of the Successive Phases of Woman's Life.* London: Cassell & Co, Ltd., 1915.

———. *The Hope of the Future: The Management of Children in Health and Disease.* London: Chapman & Hall, 1916.

———. *Venereal Diseases in Children and Adolescents: Their Recognition and Prevention: Notes of Three Lectures Addressed to Schoolmistresses, at the Royal Society of Medicine, London, September, 1916.* London: National Council for Combating Venereal Diseases, 1916.

———. *What Mothers Must Tell Their Children.* London: National Council for Combating Venereal Diseases, 1917.

———. *Notes on Venereal Diseases for Nurses and Midwives.* London: The Scientific Press, 1918.

———. *Reminiscences.* London: Williams and Norgate, 1924.

———. *Health and Sickness in the Nursery.* London: Williams and Norgate, 1926.

———. *The Psychology of Childhood, Normal and Abnormal.* London: Constable, 1927.

———. *The Bachelor Woman and Her Problems.* London: Williams and Norgate, [1929].

———. *Change of Life: Its Difficulties and Dangers.* Rev. ed., London: Faber and Faber, 1941.

SECONDARY SOURCES

Attar, Dena. *Bibliography of Household Books Published in Britain 1800–1914.* London: Prospect Books, 1987. See page 335.

STANDARD SOURCES

DNB; Europa; Lovejoy; Siegel and Finley; Uglow 1989.

SCHARRER, BERTA (VOGEL) (1906–1995)

German zoologist and professor of anatomy and neuroscience. Born 1 December 1906. Father Karl Philipp Vogel, judge. Mother, Johanna Greis. Two siblings (Karl and Charlotte). Married to Ernst Scharrer 1934 (d. 1965). Luisengymnasium Munich (baccalaureate, 1926); University of Munich (Ph.D. in zoology, 1930). Professional experience: Research Institute of Psychiatry, University of Munich, assistant (1932–1934); Neurological Institute in Frankfurt am Main, guest investigator (1934–1937); University of Chicago, department of anatomy, visiting researcher (1937–1938); Rockefeller Institute, visiting researcher (1938–1940); Western Reserve University, senior instructor (1940–1946); University of Colorado, instructor and assistant professor (1946–1954); Albert Einstein Medical College, Yeshiva University, New York, profesor of anatomy and neuroscience (1955–1978), emerita professor (from 1978). Honors and memberships: Israel Society of Anatomy, honorary member; International Society of Neuroendocrinology, member; American Academy of Arts and Sciences; University of Giessen, honorary doctor of medicine (1976); Max Plank Institute, Munich, Kraepelin Gold Medal in Microbiology (1978); German Academy of Sciences Leopoldina, Schleiden Medal (1983); U.S. National Medal of Science (1985). Died 23 July 1995 in New York.

There are very few scientists whose discoveries have marked the advent of a new discipline. Berta Scharrer was one of these pioneers. Her scientific career was crowned with great success. The concept of neurosecretion developed by Ernst and Berta Scharrer between 1928 and 1937 formed the foundation for contemporary neuroendocrinology, particularly the concept of peptidergic neurons in vertebrates and invertebrates. Today we know that secretory nerve cells are widely distributed over the whole nervous system. The neuropeptides serve to maintain the organism and preserve the species.

Berta Vogel was the eldest of three children, born in December 1906 in Munich. Her father was a judge. Her early scientific work in the Munich University laboratory of zoologist Karl von Frisch (Nobel laureate, 1973) was concerned with chemoreception in bees. Soon after receiving her doctorate in 1930, she became research associate at the Research Institute for Psychiatry in Munich, where her scientific activities were focused mainly on the microbiology of spirochetes and their occurrence in the central nervous system. Another disciple of von Frisch, Ernst Scharrer, who had dis-

covered manifestations of endocrine activity, was at the institute at the same time. After their marriage in 1934, Ernst and Berta Scharrer became associated with the Neurological Institute (Erdinger Institut) in Frankfurt am Main, where they began their career as a congenial research team. The years in Frankfurt were of extraordinary importance for the development of the concept of neurosecretion. In 1937, Berta Scharrer published a representative paper on neurosecretion in the central nervous system of invertebrates. It was followed by a comprehensive review by Ernst and Berta Scharrer on neurosecretory organs in vertebrates and invertebrates. These two papers may be regarded as the conceptual bases of neuroendocrinology.

The Scharrers left Germany in 1937 for Chicago. Ernst had a scholarship at the department of anatomy at the University of Chicago for one year, and Berta could continue her work as a research associate there. The political developments in Nazi Germany made them decide to stay in the United States. New York, Cleveland, and Denver became their academic and scientific homes.

The idea of a secretory activity of nerve cells was so revolutionary that it originally met with considerable opposition in the United States as well as Germany. The breakthrough for their theories occurred during their Denver period (1947–1955). In 1943 Berta Scharrer published with her husband several important surveys on neurosecretion and hormones produced by neurosecretory cells. These papers soon became the classics in neuroendocrinology. In 1963, they finished a seminal, comprehensive monograph, *Neuroendocrinology.*

Due to nepotism rules at most institutions, Scharrer was unable to get a full-time faculty appointment until 1955. In several interviews, she described this situation as favorable, because she could concentrate on research without the burden of administrative responsibilities.

In 1955 Ernst and Berta Scharrer founded the department of anatomy at the Albert Einstein College of Medicine in New York. In the following twenty-two years as a professor, she was a highly devoted and respected teacher. In 1978 she became Distinguished Professor Emeritus of Anatomy and Structural Biology and of Neuroscience. After the sudden death of Ernst Scharrer in 1965, Berta continued to interpret the role of neurosecretory cells in the central nervous system. She extended the concept of neurosecretion to an overall concept of peptidergic neurons. She continued her research work long past retirement age; her last paper, dealing with neuroimmunological questions, was submitted for publication two days before her death.

The international recognition for the scientific achievements of Berta Scharrer was mirrored by the honors she received. Eleven universities, including Harvard, bestowed honorary doctorates upon her. Among her numerous medals and prizes were the Kraepelin Gold Medal of the Max Planck Society, the Schleiden Medal of the German Academy of Sciences Leopoldina, and the National Medal of Science of the United States of America.　　　　SNS

PRIMARY SOURCES

Scharrer, Berta. With Ernst Scharrer. *Neuroendocrinology.* New York: Columbia University Press, 1963.

———. *Aspects of Neuroendocrinology.* With W. Bargmann. Berlin and New York: Springer-Verlag, 1970.

———. *An Evolutionary Interpretation of the Phenomenon of Neurosecretion.* New York: American Museum of Natural History, 1978. James Arthur lecture on the evolution of the human brain.

———. "The Concept of Neurosecretion and its Place in Neurobiology." In *The Neurosciences: Paths of Discovery,* ed. Frederic G. Worden, Judith P. Swazey and George Adelman, 232–243. An autobiographical account of her scientific life and her work with her husband, Ernst Scharrer. With portraits.

———. "Neurosecretion: Beginnings and New Directions in Neuropeptide Research." *Annual Review of Neuroscience* 10 (1987).

SECONDARY SOURCES

Oksche, Andreas. "In memoriam Berta Scharrer (1906–1995)." *Annals of Anatomy* 178 (1996).

———. "In memoriam Berta Scharrer." In *The Peptidergic Neuron,* ed. B. Kirsch and R. Mentlein. Basel: Birkhauser Verlag, 1996.

STANDARD SOURCES

AMS 8, B 9, P&B 10–16; Bailey; Debus; Grinstein 1997 (article by Birgit H. Satir and Peter Satir); *Notable; Who's Who of American Women.*

SCHIEMANN, ELISABETH (1881–?)

German plant geneticist. Born 15 August 1881 in Fellin, Livonia (now Latvia and Estonia). Father a professor of history. At least one sibling. Educated in girls' schools and a teacher training college in Berlin; Paris (1903–1904); University of Berlin (Ph.D., 1912); Stockholm (1922); England (1920; 1947). Professional experience: Institute for Research in Genetics and Plant Cultivation, Agricultural Hochschule, Berlin, assistant, then senior assistant (1914–1931); University of Berlin, temporary associate professor (1930–1940); Botanical Museum, Dahlem (Berlin), visiting scholar (1930–1943); Kaiser Wilhelm Institute for Plant Cultivation Research, director, division for history of plant cultivation (1943–1949); Deutsche Forschungshochschule (1949–1952); Max-Planck Gesellschaft, researcher (1952–1956); University of Berlin, professor (1945–1956). Honors and memberships: Max-

Planck Gesellschaft, elected member; Deutsche Akademie der Naturforscher Leopoldina, elected member. Death date unkown.

Elisabeth Schiemann moved to Berlin in 1887 when her father became a professor there. During 1903–1904, she studied French in Paris. She began her studies at the University of Berlin in 1906, but could not officially enroll until 1908, when Prussian universities were opened to women.

Schiemann believed strongly in the importance of a humanistic education and valued the opportunity to study philosophy and logic at the university. She found these subjects exciting and pertinent to her field, particularly since biology was then in the midst of philosophical and ethical disputes stemming from Darwinism. After she received her doctorate, Schiemann took the state examination that qualified her for a teaching position (in 1913).

Schiemann developed a close friendship with the physicist LISE MEITNER, who worked at the nearby Kaiser Wilhelm Institute. Meitner became a regular visitor at Schiemann's family home. She shared Schiemann's love of nature, and the two scientists took many outings and hiking trips together.

Schiemann became interested in genetics when the field was just beginning to explode. Working under Erwin Baur, who became Germany's first professor of genetics in 1912, she earned her doctorate for a dissertation on mutation in a type of mold ("Über Mutation bei *Aspergillus niger*"). Schiemann then took a position at the Agricultural Hochschule. In addition to lecturing on the origin and history of cultivated plants, the biology of reproduction, and other subjects, she prepared and assisted with student exercises and set up and maintained the bookstore. She also received a professorship for teaching the science of seeds, which involved training for nurserymen.

Schiemann's research concerned genetics and the history of cultivated plants, particularly grains, as well as questions on the classification and genetic relationships of strawberry plants. In her inaugural address for the University of Berlin ("Die Bedeutung der Genetik für die systematische Botanik," 1931) she recommended applying genetics to systematic botany, so that cultivated plants would be included in a comprehensive system. During much of her career, Schiemann evaluated plant materials from excavations in Europe and Asia in order to elucidate the origin and phylogeny of cultivated plants.

An outspoken opponent of the Nazis, Schiemann lost her university position in 1940. After the war, Schiemann continued to investigate problems in genetics and the theory of heredity.　　　　JH/MBO

PRIMARY SOURCES

Schiemann, Elisabeth. *Geschlechts und Artkreuzungsfragen bei Fragaria.* Jena: G. Fischer, 1931.

————. *Entstehung der Kulturpflanzen.* Berlin: Gebrüder Born-
traeger, 1932.

————. *Weizen, Roggen, Gerste: Systematik, Geschichte und
Verwendung.* Jena: G. Sischer, 1948.

————. "Die Pflanzenfunde in den neolithischen Siedlungen
Mogetorp . . ." In *Vråkulturen, stenåldersboplatserna vid Mogetorp . . .* , ed. Sten Florin. Stockholm: Almqvist & Wiksell,
1958.

————. "Autobiographie." *Nove Acta Leopoldina* 21, no. 143
(1959): 291–292.

————. "Freundschaft mit Lise Meitner." *Neue Evangelische
Frauenzeitung* 3, no. 1 (1959): 3pp.

————. "Erinnerungen an meine Berliner Universitätsjahre."
In *Sonderdruck aus Studium Berolinese. Gedenkenschrift.* Berlin:
Walter de Gruyter & Co., 1960.

Papers at the Archiv zur Geschichte der Max-Planck Gesellschaft, Berlin.

Correspondence in the Meitner Collection, Churchill College,
Cambridge, England.

SECONDARY SOURCES

Darrow, George M. *The Strawberry: History, Breeding, and Physiology.* New York: Holt, Rinehart & Winston, [1966]. Contains
detailed information on Schiemann's genetic research on the
strawberry.

Deichmann, Ute. *Biologen unter Hitler: Vertreibung, Karrieren,
Forschung.* Frankfurt: Campus Verlag, 1992.

Krafft, Fritz. *Im Schatten der Sensation: Leben und Wirken von Fritz
Strassmann.* Weinheim, Deerfield Beach, Fla., and Basel:
Verlag Chemie, 1981.

Scheich, Elvira. "Science, Politics, and Morality: The Relationship of Lise Meitner and Elisabeth Schiemann." *Osiris*
12 (1997): 143–168. (*Women, Gender, and Science Issue.*)

Sime, Ruth. *Lise Meitner: A Life in Physics.* Berkeley, Los Angeles, and London: University of California Press, 1996.

SCHLIEMANN, SOPHIA (KASTROMENOS) (1852–1932)

*Greek archeologist and philanthropist. Born 1852 in Athens to Vic-
toria (Gheladaki) and George Engastromenos (born Kastromenos).
Married Heinrich Schliemann, September 1869. One son, one
daughter. Educated Arsakeion Girls' School, Athens. Professional
experience: Excavations at Hissarlik, Turkey (Troy II) (1871–
1873); Mycenae (1874, 1876); Skripa, Greece (1880); supported
further Troy excavations (1890–1893); Founder of Soteria Hospital; patron of Greek orphanages. Honors and memberships: Greek
Archaeological Society, honorary member (1874); Royal Archaeological Institute of Great Britain and Ireland, honorary member
(1877); Royal Historical Society, Fellow (1877). Died 1932 in
Phaleron, Greece. Buried with state honors in Athens.*

Sophia Kastromenos was a girl of seventeen when the German businessman turned archeologist Heinrich Schliemann
came to Athens to find a second wife. He had just divorced
his first wife, a Russian, and hoped that a young woman
from Greece would help to inspire his archeological research
on the history of the Trojan War. Introduced to Kastromenos by a cousin of her family, he immediately proposed
and was accepted. She began to accompany him on his excavations, and soon joined him as an equal partner, supervising
the workmen and overseeing separate areas of the archeological excavation.

Sophia Schliemann helped to find the unusual golden
treasure at Hissarlik, Turkey (called Troy II) supervising the
excavation at Lion's Gate. She also assisted her husband in
smuggling the gold treasure out of the country, and in excavating the rich gold treasury at Mycenae (including the spectacular golden mask Heinrich Schliemann called "the mask
of Agamemnon"). One of these treasuries she excavated on
her own. Although she took time out to have two children
(a daughter named Andromache in 1873 and a son named
Agamemnon in 1877), she soon joined him again in the field.

When the public, as well as the Greek and British archeological societies, began to celebrate Heinrich Schliemann in
1877, they honored Sophia as well, making her an honorary
member of a number of societies along with her husband.
When she was unable to attend the award ceremony because
of illness due to her pregnancy, the Royal Archaeological Institute held another special day in her honor, at which she
made a speech about ancient Greece and her own part in the
excavations.

From this point on, her husband, for a variety of reasons
including his close association with the German scientist
Rudolf Virchow, began to downplay Sophia's part in the expeditions. After she assisted him in the Orchomenus excavations at Skripa in Greece and made the major discovery of
the inner tomb in 1880, Schliemann failed to credit her as he
previously had done. Nevertheless, she translated his book
on Orchomenus into Greek. Husband and wife were soon in
some conflict over the disposition of the Troy materials.
While he wanted them to go to Britain, and then settled on
Germany, Sophia begged him to place them in Greece. The
Mycenae materials did remain in Greece, but he chose the
Berlin Museum for the Troy treasures. As a result, he was
awarded various honors by the Prussian state, including an
honorary citizenship for himself and his wife.

Sophia Schliemann settled into an impressive house that
her husband built for the family in Athens, decorated with
statuary. She chose to be actively involved in only one more
excavation, at Marathon not far from Athens, where presumably the Mound of the Dead held soldiers slain in the
Persian Wars. Their search failed to reveal any skeletal material. Her husband then went to Tiryns not far from Mycenae,

where he excavated with the German archeologist Wilhelm Dörpfeld, who continued important excavations at Troy after Heinrich Schliemann's death.

Heinrich Schliemann began to suffer from severe earaches and was rendered deaf. He failed to obtain necessary surgery because of his sense of the urgency of his work and his defense from attacks on the veracity of his reports on the excavations. He died in Naples in 1890 and was buried with great honors in a mausoleum he had designed in Athens.

Sophia Schliemann, then only thirty-eight, continued to publicize her husband's work, editing his autobiography for publication and subsidizing the further work of Dörpfeld at Troy. She turned her attention to founding orphanages and establishing the tuberculosis sanitarium and research center, Soteria. She lived an active life until her eightieth year.

JH/MBO

PRIMARY SOURCES
Schliemann, Sophie Kastromenos. "On the High Culture of the Ancient Greeks." *Journal of the Royal Archaeological Institute* 1877. Reprinted in Poole and Poole, 285–290.
———, trans. Schliemann, Heinrich. *Orchomenos: hypomnema epi ton en to Voiotiko Orchomeno anaskaphon autou.* By Heinrich Schliemann. Athens, ek ton katastematon Andreou Koromela, 1883. English text in the *Journal of Hellenic Studies, London* 2 (1881): 122–163. Account of the Orchomenos excavation.
———. With Heinrich Schliemann and Alfred Bruckner. *Heinrich Schliemann's Selbstbiographie: Bis zu seinem Tode vervollstandigt.* Leipzig: F. A. Brockhaus, 1892.

SECONDARY SOURCES
Poole, Lynn, and Gray Poole. *One Passion, Two Loves: The Story of Heinrich and Sophia Schliemann, Discoverers of Troy.* New York: Thomas Y. Crowell Co., 1966. Based on previously unpublished letters between the Schliemanns. Includes portraits.

STANDARD SOURCES
Debus (under Heinrich Schliemann); Mozans.

SCHMID, ELISABETH (1912–1994)

German archeologist; osteologist. Born 1912 in Freiburg i Brisgau (Germany). Educated University of Freiburg (Ph.D.); habilitated Freiburg and Basel. Professional experience: Universities of Breslau, Bonn, Köln, and Freiburg, assistant (1937–1962); University of Freiburg and Basel, teacher; laboratory of prehistory, laboratory head, Swiss Archaeological Society, founder with R. Laur-Belart (1953); Basel University, professor (1960), ordinary professor (1972–1976); Natural Sciences Faculty, first woman dean (1972). Died 27 March 1994.

Elisabeth Schmid worked on the osteology of central European mammals. She also did research on sedimentary deposits in excavation as aids in dating. She published over two hundred papers and two books, including the *Atlas of Animal Bones* and another on cave sedimentology. In addition to her research and teaching, she prepared the permanent exhibit devoted to European prehistory in the Basel Ethnographical Museum and published a guide to it. She was active in the Swiss Prehistoric Society and became an honorary member in 1987.

JH/MBO

PRIMARY SOURCES
Schmid, Elisabeth. *Hohlenforschung und Sedimentanalyse: ein Beitrag zur Datierung des Alpinen Palaolithikums.* Basel: Verlag des Institutes fur Ur-und Fruhgeschichte der Schweiz, 1958.
———. *Knochenatlas: Für Prahistoriker, Archaeologen und Quartargeologen* (Atlas of Animal Bones: For Prehistorians, Archaeologists and Quaternary Geologists). Amsterdam: Elsevier, 1972.

SECONDARY SOURCES
Schibler, and L. Chaix. "In Memoriam Prof. Dr. Elisabeth Schmid." *Archaeozoologia* 7, no. 1 (1994): 77–78.

STANDARD SOURCES
IDA.

SCHMIDEBERG, MELITTA (KLEIN) (1904–)

Austrian-born English psychoanalyst. Born 19 January 1904 in Rosenberg, Austria, to Melanie (Reizes) and Arthur Klein. Two brothers. Married Walter Schmideberg, April 1924 (he died in 1954). Educated University of Berlin (M.D., 1927); Berlin Psychoanalytic Society, psychoanalytic training (1929–1930); Berlin Psychoanalytic Society, training analysis (1930–1933); Professional experience: British Psychoanalytic Institute, member (1933–1945; formally resigned 1962); private psychoanalyst, New York (1945–1961); Association Psychiatric Treatment of Offenders, N.Y.C., founding psychiatrist (1950–1961). Returned to Britain, 1961.

The daughter of the famous psychoanalyst MELANIE KLEIN, Melitta was born in the Hungarian city of Rosenberg (then part of Austria). She was analyzed by her mother when she was in her teens and taken by her to early meetings of the Berlin Psychoanalytic Society when she was fifteen. She determined to study medicine and then psychoanalysis, which first required that she take her matriculation in Slovak rather than German.

When she was twenty, she married Walter Schmideberg, an aspiring psychoanalyst who suffered from alcoholism. Personable and well connected, he was sixteen years older than she. No children resulted from the marriage. During the early years, she studied medicine at the University of Berlin. When her mother went to London in 1928, she stayed with her while she wrote her medical dissertation on the history of homeopathy in Germany. On return to Berlin, she began a training analysis with KAREN HORNEY.

After Schmideberg moved to England, she trained at the British Psychoanalytic Institute, where her mother was a member. There she again entered into analysis as part of her training under the direction of Edward Glover, president of the British Institute, who started as an advocate of Klein's theories and had become her opponent. Schmideberg, whose publications initially drew upon her mother's ideas, joined Glover as one of her most vocal opponents, attacking not only her mother but ANNA FREUD (who also was in opposition to Klein). Her angry denunciations eventually led to a permanent break with both her mother and the British Freudians.

In 1945, she left England and moved to New York City, where she became interested in adolescent delinquents, and spent the next fifteen years working in that field. Schmideberg is best known in the United States for founding the Association for the Psychiatric Treatment of Offenders, and its journal, now called the *International Journal of Offender Therapy and Comparative Criminology*. She worked successfully to have prisoners released into custody for treatment by her or her associates prior to trial. She moved back to London in early 1961, and broke permanently with the British Psychoanalytic Society the next year, while continuing her own work with disturbed criminals. When her mother died, internationally recognized, Schmideberg deliberately avoided her funeral.   JH/MBO

PRIMARY SOURCES

Schmideberg, Melitta. "A Contribution to the Psychology of Persecutory Ideas and Delusions." *International Journal of Psycho-Analysis* 12 (1931): 331–367.
———. "Bad Habits in Childhood: Their Importance in Development." *International Journal of Psycho-Analysis* 16 (1935): 455–461.
———. "After the Analysis." *Psychoanalytic Quarterly* 7 (1938): 122–142.
———. "Psychotherapy with Failures of Psycho-Analysis." *British Journal of Psychiatry* 116 (1970): 195–200.
———. "A Contribution to the History of the Psycho-Analytical Movement in Britain." *British Journal of Psychiatry* 118 (1971): 61–68.

SECONDARY SOURCES

Grosskuth, Phyllis. *Melanie Klein: Her World and Her Work.* Cambridge: Harvard University Press, 1986. Includes portraits of Melitta Schmideberg as child and adult.

SCHMIDT, JOHANNA GERTRUD ALICE (1909–)

German topographer. Born 7 August 1909 in Leipzig to Alice (Fiedler) and Fritz Schmidt. Educated Greifswald, Fribourg/Brisgau, Munich, Berlin (Ph.D.). Professional experience: University of Greifswald (also University of Berlin), reader in classical languages, assistant for historical geography; Leipzig, professor in the Institute for Educational Sciences; Leipzig, instructor Diesterweg College and W. Berlin College of education; Institut für Kultur und Heimatkunde, director.

Johanna Schmidt earned a doctorate at the University of Berlin. She published numerous articles on the topography of Mediterranean countries. She was also interested in geographic history and European history.   JH/MBO

PRIMARY SOURCES

Schmidt, Johanna Gertrud Alice. *Ethos.* Leipzig: R. Noske, 1941.
———. *Mass und Harmonie.* Berlin: Institut für Kultur und Heimatkunde, 1968.
———. *Heimat und Kultur.* Berlin: Fontane-Buchandlung, 1955.

STANDARD SOURCES

Debus.

SCHMIDT-FISCHER, HILDEGARD (1906–)

German physician. Born 13 May 1906 in Danzig. Married Fischer, a forester. Two stepchildren, Ingeborg and Peter. Educated Berlin University (M.D., 1945). Professional experience: Niedersachsen, private practice (1946–1976).

Hildegard Schmidt-Fischer was thirty-three years old when she began to study medicine. As a child during World War I, she played doctor to her wounded dolls. The postwar inflation ruined her chances of matriculating in a university, so her ambition to be a doctor was thwarted at this time. Instead, she married at the age of nineteen and raised her husband's two small children. His first wife, who had died in childbirth, had been Jewish, and Hildegard and her family were ostracized as antisemitism became increasingly more rampant. After World War II broke out, a number of circumstances made her decide to study medicine. She was accepted at Berlin University and at the time of her premedical examination learned that her stepson, Peter, had been killed in action. Because Berlin was being bombed incessantly, the students were evacuated. She went to Danzig for the last clinical terms and passed in the state examinations in 1945. She remained in Danzig long enough to pick up her medical license and then was evacuated by ship.

It was not until 1946 that Schmidt-Fischer was able to open a medical practice. She practiced for thirty years in Niedersachsen, where she was the only woman doctor for a large area. Her home was in the country, in Lauenstein in the Weserbergland, where the nearest hospital and specialists were miles away. At this point she realized the importance of going beyond her medical training, understanding that empathy as well as technical skills were vital in the care of patients.

Schmidt-Fischer developed a personal rapport with her patients, stemming from her own emotional feelings about the importance of life, probably because she had so much experience with wartime losses.   KM

PRIMARY SOURCES
"Schmidt-Fischer, Hildegard." In Hellstedt, *Autobiographies.*

SCHOENFELD, REBA WILLITS (1906–1971)

Canadian physician. Born 22 June 1906 in Kelowna, British Columbia to Ellen Carrie (Bailey) and Palmer Brooks Willits. One sister. Married Henryk Schoenfeld. Educated public schools, Kelowna; University of Toronto (M.D., 1931); diploma in public health (1940). Professional experience: Vancouver General Hospital, rotating internship (1931–1933); private practice, Kelowna (1934–1939?); War Wound Commission to study streptococcal infections in war wounds (1940–1941); Metropolitan Health Committee of Vancouver, health unit director (1941–1942); School Health Services, associate director; Metropolitan Health Committee, director of medical services (1941–1964). Died March 1971.

Reba Willits Schoenfeld was born in a small town in British Columbia, where her pharmacist father owned a drugstore. As is the case with many women physicians, Reba developed an interest in medical subjects as a child and was encouraged by physicians who were family friends. As was not often the case, her father pushed her into going into medicine from the time she was in high school, although her mother disapproved. After passing her junior matriculation examination at age sixteen, she was too young to enter the medical courses at the University of Toronto. During the following year, she was privately tutored in chemistry, a course that was not taught in Kelowna High School. At seventeen, she traveled two thousand miles to Toronto, where she spent the first year enrolled in the arts course, because she had not been able to take the senior matriculation in Kelowna. After this year, she entered the six-year medical program at the university.

Reba Willits's first paying position was as an intern at Vancouver General Hospital. Instead of remaining for a third year, she went home to Kelowna in the spring of 1934, where she set up practice with the doctor who had delivered her and had encouraged her to go to medical school. She did not like maternity work and its irregular hours but enjoyed much more the "well-baby clinic" she conducted, which was sponsored by the Women's Institute. She found that she liked the preventive medicine aspect much more than the therapeutic. When World War II began, she gave up her practice and went back to Toronto to study public health. After she received her diploma, the first woman from the University of Toronto to receive one in public health, she had two opportunities for a job. One, however, was soon eliminated, for the provincial health officer told her that he would never employ a woman. Therefore, she accepted the second job, a National Research Fellowship to work with Ronald Hare on the War Wound Commission.

After a year working on this grant, she became a health unit director for the Metropolitan Health Committee of Vancouver. In this position she supervised public health nurses, nursing staff, and clerical workers. She was also responsible for examining schoolchildren and was a consultant for well-baby clinics. When the director of School Health Services retired, Willits became acting director of both the School Health Services and of mental hygiene. At the end of the war and the return of physicians, her work was confined to the School Health Services and her title was changed to associate director. In this position, she coordinated various aspects of health care with the outpatient department staffs of the Children's Hospital and the Health Center for Children at the Vancouver General Hospital. She also conducted medical examinations of students at the University of British Columbia. Part of her work was as a liaison to the Provincial School for the Deaf and Blind. Around 1955, she was transferred to the Metropolitan Health Committee and her title was changed to director of medical services.

Willits retired at the age of fifty-eight after she found a suitable replacement. She became involved in numerous volunteer activities including Meals on Wheels and the Vancouver United Way.

During her many years as a public health physician, Willits had never married. However, she met a Polish chemical engineer, Henryk Schoenfeld, at the Unitarian Fellowship and they married six months after they met. The marriage was happy but of a short duration; Henryk died of a brain tumor in March 1971.   KM

PRIMARY SOURCES
Schoenfeld, Reba Willits. In Hellstedt, *Autobiographies.*

SCHOENTAL, REGINA (1906–)

Polish/British physician. Born 12 June 1906 in Dzialoszyce, Poland, to Dina (Eisenberg) and Gershon Schoental. Educated Jagiellonian University, Cracow (D.Phil., 1930); University of

Glasgow (Scotland) (D.Sc., 1950). Professional experience: Oxford University, school of pathology, researcher (1938–1946); University of Glasgow, department of chemistry, researcher (1945–1952); Royal Beatson Memorial Hospital, cancer research department, researcher (1952–1954); University of Chicago Medical School, department of oncology, researcher (1952–1953); Medical Research Council, Carshalton, Surrey, England, toxicology researcher (from 1955). Memberships and fellowships: Chemical Society of London, Fellow; Biochemical Society of Cambridge.

Polish by birth and early education, Regina Schoental went to Scotland, where she earned a doctor of science degree. From that time on, she worked on cancer research, publishing works on the identification and synthesis of metabolites of polycyclic aromatic hydrocarbons. She found research into natural products present in plants and fungi in the aetiology of human cancer to be a fruitful study. She also discovered the carcinogenic actions of pyrrolizidine alkaloids, diazomethane, n-methyl-N-nitrosourethane.   JH/MBO

STANDARD SOURCES
Debus.

SCHOFIELD, BRENDA MURIEL (1926–1968)

British physiologist. Born 1926 to a colonel. Educated Windermer; Queen Anne's School, Reading (left 1944); St. Andrews University (first-class degree, 1948), postgraduate scholarship (Ph.D., 1951). Professional experience: Oxford University, demonstrator in the pharmacology department (1951–1952); Baltimore, Md., Smith-Mundt Fellow (1952–1953); Carnegie Fellow (1953–1954); Royal Veterinary College, London, lecturer (1954–1968). Died 1968 in London of cancer.

Brenda Schofield's research life was ended by cancer when she was just forty-two years old. From the time she wrote her doctoral dissertation, "The Physiology of the Cervix and Cornu Uteri," her research revolved around the physiology of the cervix. After earning her doctoral degree from St. Andrew's University and working as a demonstrator in the pharmacology department at Oxford, she accepted a fellowship in the United States. She remained in the United States for a second year with a Carnegie fellowship. When she returned to England, she accepted a position as lecturer in the physiology department of the Royal Veterinary College in London, a post she retained until her death.

Schofield's first publication was in 1949, and was based on a presentation to the Physiological Society entitled "The Action of Isopropylnoradrenaline on the Cornu and Cervix Uteri." Although she worked in pharmacology for a time, her main interest remained in uterine physiology. Working on the rabbit myometrium, she contributed to the under-

standing of the influence of ovarian hormones on the myometrium and was the first to demonstrate *in vivo* that the relative amounts of estrogen and progesterone determine the response of the myometrium. Through demonstrating the relationship of these two hormones to each other she traced hormonal dominance during pregnancy in the rabbit. She showed that estrogen was dominant during mating (lasting only twenty-four hours) and occurred again on the last day of pregnancy. The estrogen rose steadily from mid-pregnancy until birth.

A careful designer of experiments, Schofield proved that many earlier conclusions were based on faulty research techniques. In 1966, on a leave of absence from the Royal Veterinary College, Schofield returned to the United States to work with D. G. Porter. Their work resulted in a collaborative paper demonstrating that there was very little change in the intrauterine pressure until around thirty-one hours before delivery.

Schofield also investigated the mechanism of parturition and the failure of the cervix to dilate. Some of her work was carried on collaboratively with veterinary surgeons. In the year that she died she was notified that she had received an honorary doctorate of science from the University of London.

During her short life, Schofield produced fifty-seven publications. She was the sole author of thirty-five papers and contributed eleven more to the *Journal of Physiology*. She attended every International Physiological Congress between 1950 and 1968.

Not only was Schofield an outstanding, creative research physiologist, she was also an enthusiastic teacher. St. Andrews University established a Brenda Schofield Prize in physiology.   JH/MBO

PRIMARY SOURCES
Schofield, Brenda Muriel. "The Hormonal Control of Myometrial Function During Pregnancy." *Journal of Physiology* 138 (1957): 1–10.
——. *"Effect of the Synthetic Oestrogen Stilboestrol on Pregnancy in the Rabbit."* Nature 182 (1958): 58–59.
——. "The Physiology of the Myometrium." In *Recent Advances in Physiology,* ed. R. Crease. 222–251. London: Churchill, 1963.
——. With C. Wood. "Length-Tension Relation in Rabbit and Human Myometrium." *Journal of Physiology* 175 (1964): 125–133.
——. With J. C. Hindson. "Notes on Parturition in the Sheep." *Journal of Reproductive Fertility* 18 (1969): 355–357.

SECONDARY SOURCES
Nature 221 (1969): 221; 885. Obituary notice.
Veterinary Record (14 December 1968). Obituary notice.

STANDARD SOURCES
Women Physiologists (article by Susan Wray).

SCHRADER, SALLY PERIS HUGHES (1895–?)

See Hughes-Schrader, Sally Peris.

SCHRADERS, CATHARINA GEERTRUIDA (1656 or 1666–1746)

Dutch midwife. Born 1656 or 1666 in Bentheim, Germany, to a court tailor. Eldest daughter. Married (1) Ernst Cramer (1683, died 1692; six children); (2) Thomas Hight (1713; he died in 1721). Died 1746.

After Catharina Schraders married surgeon Ernst Cramer, they moved to Hallum, Friesland, where she worked as wife and mother to six children until Cramer's death in 1692. She then began working as a midwife to support her family. Moving to nearby Dokkum, she built up a large practice. In 1713, she married the mayor of Dokkum, a gold and silversmith, Thomas Hight. He died in 1721 and Catharina returned full-time to midwivery, specializing in difficult deliveries. She wrote a *Notebook* of instruction, which stressed traditional skills, avoidance of instruments, and detailed manual manipulation of the fetus in assisting difficult delivery. She advocated greater training for midwives and cooperated with male doctors and surgeons.   JH/MBO

PRIMARY SOURCES
Schrader, Catharina Geertruida. *Mother and Child Were Saved: The Memoirs (1693–1740) of the Frisian Midwife Catharina Schrader.* Amsterdam: Rodopi, 1987. This English edition was published to coincide with the 21st International Congress of the International Confederation of Midwives held in the Hague in August 1987.

SECONDARY SOURCES
Nuyens, B. W. Th. "Mrs. Schraders' Diary: A Contribution to the History of Midwifery in the Seventeenth and Eighteenth Centuries." In Dutch. *Bijdr. Gesch. Geneesk.* 6 (1926): 93–104.

STANDARD SOURCES
Uglow 1989.

SCHROEDER, EDITH VON (fl. 1922)

German (?) chemist. Professional experience: School of Mining in Clausthal, Germany; published with Gustav Hüttig.

Working with Gustav F. Hüttig at the School of Mining in Clausthal, Germany, von Schroeder investigated the chemical behavior of uranium. Her experiments determined con-

ditions needed to create certain uranium compounds, and showed that other compounds did not exist.   MM

PRIMARY SOURCES
Schroeder, Edith von. With Gustav F. Hüttig. "Über die Hydrate des Urantetroxyds und Urantrioxyds." *Zeitschrift für anorganische und allgemeine Chemie* 121 (1922): 243–253.

STANDARD SOURCES
Meyer and von Schweidler.

SCHUBERT, ANNA (1881–?)

Swiss psychologist.

Schubert presented an inaugural dissertation in Zurich on the psychological theories of the eighteenth-century natural historians Charles Bonnet and Johan Nicolas Tetens in 1909.   KM

PRIMARY SOURCES
Schubert, Anna. *Die psychologie von Bonnet und Tetens mit besonderer berücksichtigung des methodologischen verfahrens derselben; historisch-psychologische studie.* Zurich: J. J. Meier, 1909.

SCHULTZ, HELEN REDFIELD (1900–)

See Redfield, Helen.

SCHULTZE, CAROLINE M. (BERTILLON) (1867–1900s)

See Bertillon, Caroline Schultze.

SCHURMAN, ANNA MARIA VAN (1607–1678)

Dutch/German artist and scholar. Born in 1607 in Cologne. Educated at home by her father; studied with tutors in Utrecht. Died 1678 in Wivert in Friesland.

Although Anna Maria van Schurman was born in Germany her father moved to Utrecht when she was a baby. She exhibited great talent at an early age and became known for her drawings of flowers, vocal and instrumental music, painting, sculpture, and engraving. Her father, noting that when she was eleven she prompted her brothers on their Latin exams, saw to it that she studied not only Latin, Greek, and Hebrew, but several Asian languages as well. She also understood and spoke French, English, and Italian. Anna Maria became interested in the sciences and studied geography, astronomy, and natural philosophy. Her mother continued with her education after the death of her father in 1623. Although modest about her accomplishments, she attained a considerable fame, so much so that such celebrated personages as Cardinal Richelieu came to visit her.

As she grew older, Schurman became more interested in religion and theology and became a disciple of Jean de Labadie. JH/MBO

PRIMARY SOURCES
Schurman, Anna Maria van. *Nobilissimae virginis Annae Mariae a Schurman Dissertatio, de ingenii muliebris ad doctrinam, et meliores litteras aptitudine: accedunt quaedem Epistolae, ejusdem argumenti.* [Leiden]: Ex Officina Elseviriana, 1641.
———. *Nobilissimae virginis Annae Mariae a Schurman Opuscula hebraea, graeca, latina, gallica, prosaica et metrica.* 2d ed. [Leiden]: Ex Officina Elseciriorum, 1650.
———. *The Learned Maid; or, Whether a Maid May Be a Scholar?: A Logick Exercise.* London: John Redmayne, 1659. A translation of *Dissertatio de ingenii muliebris.* Pierre Gassende is listed as one author.

SECONDARY SOURCES
Pope-Hennessy, Una. *Anna van Schurman, Artist, Scholar, Saint.* London: Longmans, Green, 1909.

STANDARD SOURCES
Cyclopaedia.

SCHWIDETSKY, ILSE (1907–1997)

German physical anthropologist. Born 18 March 1907. Married [?] Rösing. Two children. University of Breslau (D.Phil., 1934?; habilitation, 1938). Professional experience: Institute of Anthropology, University of Breslau, research assistant, research associate (1934?–1945); University of Leipzig, Department of Anthropology, director (1945–1946); Johannes Gutenberg University, Mainz, Institute of Anthropology, lecturer (1946–1961), professor and chair (1961–1975), emerita professor (1975–1997); Homo, editor (1961–1997); Collegium Anthropologium, Zagreb, consulting editor. Honors and memberships: International Union of Anthropological and Ethnological Sciences, council member, vice-president (1974); Mainz Academy of Science, Fellow; Société d'Anthropologie de Paris; recipient of the Société's Broca award, 1980; German Society of Anthropology and Human Genetics, secretary (1948–1968), chair (1968–1970). Died 6 September 1997 in Mainz, Germany.

Ilse Schwidetsky was a well-known physical anthropologist whose writings just before and during the Nazi period made her a controversial figure later in life. Although her biographers tell little about her personal life, she was educated at the University of Breslau where she wrote her dissertation on a historical topic. Working as an assistant to the director of the Institute of Anthropology, her habilitation dissertation (qualifying her to teach at a university level) was firmly on a topic in physical anthropology: "Racial Knowledge of the Ancient Slavs." The director, Egon von Eickstedt, had begun a series of volumes on the scientific study of race (Rassenkunde), and Schwidetsky wrote on his theortical formulae and on methods of differential diagnoses of skeletons of "Nordic" and "Mediterranean" types for his journal *Zeitung für Rassenkunde und ihre Nachbargebiete,* which some have called the single most important journal of the Nazi period. Although these terms were in wide use since the nineteenth century, her use of them in 1935 carries an unpleasant burden given the adoption of Nordic and Aryan theories by the Nazis.

Like her mentor, Eickstedt, Schwidetsky does not seem to have joined the Nazi party, nor were either of them vocally in favor of Nordic or Aryan theories. (Eickstedt was however sympathetic to the Nazis in 1933 and attempted to join the party but was turned down, possibly because, as his supporters later claimed, he did not adhere to their antisemitic racial philosophy.) Nevertheless, Schwidetsky continued to produce regular articles on skeletal analysis and racial diagnosis until 1944, including an article on dark complexions as a racial indicator. Proctor has published a photograph from a book by Eickstedt and Schwidetsky showing a group of anthropologists taking head measurements as part of a racial survey in Upper Silesia in 1940.

The only discussion of this period by her German biographers is the comment that Schwidetsky's husband was killed in the war leaving her with two small children, and this was a difficult period for her. Nevertheless, she seems to have quickly regained her feet, since she briefly held the directorship of the Ethnological-Anthropological Institute in Leipzig, but left it when Eickstedt was refused a position and many of the books and journals were confiscated by the occupying forces.

Eickstedt carried his library with him to Mainz and was soon joined by Schwidetsky. The two set up an Institute of Anthropology in the Johannes Gutenburg University at Mainz, and there Schwidetsky remained first as lecturer, and then after the death of Eickstedt in 1961, as full professor and director. The two anthropologists were also important in reestablishing the German anthropological society in 1948 (Deutsche Gesellschaft für Anthropologie) with Eickstedt as chair and Schwidetsky as secretary. They also established a new journal in that year representing the society, *Homo: Internationale Zeitschrifte für die vergleichende Biologie der Mensche.* It is to Eickstedt's credit that when the United Nations Educational, Scientific, and Cultural Organization statement on race was presented to the German anthropologists, he was one of the few who accepted it without qualification. Schwidetsky, however, began to follow the curious practice of publishing articles that included the term *Rassen* or *Ras-*

senkunde in German, but carefully speaking only of "physical anthropology" in her English or French articles.

In the early fifties and then again in the sixties, Schwidetsky began to ask what the future was for racial science in the modern period. She published new editions and further volumes of Eickstedt's series on *Rassenkunde* after his death and took over the editorship of the journal *Homo*. On the occasion of her sixty-fifth birthday, the journal published a celebration of her accompanied by her extensive bibliography. However, in spite of the fact that she was well regarded by many German and European physical anthropologists, there were public protests when the French Anthropological Society (Société d'Anthropologie de Paris) awarded her a prize on the occasion of the Broca Centennial in Paris in 1980. Some of her racial statements from the thirties and forties were quoted in the left-wing press in France at that time. To her credit, she did publish an article on race theories during the Nazi period in a German journal for the history of medicine when she was in her eighties, but the focus was not on her own work. She died a few months before her ninetieth birthday.   JH

PRIMARY SOURCES

Schwidetsky, Ilse. *Das Menschnibild der Biologie—Ergebnisse und Probleme der naturwissenschaftlichen Anthropologie.* Stuttgart: G. Fischer, 1959.

———. *Die vorspanische Bevölkerung der Kanarischen Inseln.* 1. Beiheft zu Homo. Göttingen: Musterschmidt, [1963].

———. "Wissenschaften Arbeiten von Ilse Schwidetzky." *Homo* 23 (1970): 300–305. Her bibliography from 1935 to 1970.

SECONDARY SOURCES

Bernhard, Wolfram. "In Memoriam: Ilse Schwidetzky." *Collegium Anthropologium* (Zagreb) 21 (1997).

Bernhard, W., R. Knussmann, and F. W. Rösing. "Nachruf: Ilse Schwidetzky." *Homo* 48 (1997): 203–212. Includes a portrait and her bibliography from 1970 to 1992.

Proctor, Robert. In *Bones, Bodies, Behavior: Essays on Biological Anthropology,* ed. George W. Stocking. Madison: University of Wisconsin Press, 1988.

STANDARD SOURCES

Turkevich and Turkevich.

SCOTLAND, MINNIE (BRINK) (1891–1984)

U.S. entomologist; ornithologist. Born 12 August 1891 in Cohoes, N.Y. One brother, A. Donald Scotland. Educated New York State Normal College (later New York State College) (B.S., 1913); Columbia University (A.M., 1921); Cornell University (Ph.D. in entomology, 1933). Professional experience: New York high schools, *teacher (1913–1914; 1915–1918); Connecticut (1914–1915); New York State College (later part of State University of New York, Albany), instructor (1918–1929), assistant professor of biology (1929–1948), professor (1948–1956), emerita professor (from 1956). Honors and memberships: Entomological Society of America, member; American Ornithological Union, member; American Association of University Professors, Albany chapter, president; State University of New York, Distinguished Alumni Award (1968). Died 5 October 1984 in the Westley Nursing Home in Saratoga Springs, N.Y.*

Minnie Scotland received her bachelor's degree at the State University of New York and returned to teach in that institution. She moved up the academic ladder to professor. Her research interests were in both entomology and ornithology.
                                    JH/MBO

PRIMARY SOURCES

Scotland, Minnie. "The Periodic Distribution of Plant Forms in the Albany Drinking Water." Master's thesis, Columbia University, 1921.

———. "The Animal Population of Lemna Minor." Ph.D. diss., Cornell University, 1933.

SECONDARY SOURCES

"Minnie Brink Scotland" *Times Union,* Albany, N.Y., 10 October 1984. Obituary notice.

STANDARD SOURCES

AMS 6–8, B 9, P&B 10–11.

SCOTT, CHARLOTTE ANGAS (1858–1931)

British/U.S. mathematician. Born 1858 in Lincoln, England to Eliza Ann (Exley) and Rev. Caleb Scott. Never married. Educated private tutors; Girton College, Cambridge (honors degree, 1880); University of London (B.S., 1882; D.Sc., 1885). Professional experience: Girton College, lecturer in mathematics (1880–1884); Bryn Mawr College, professor and chair of mathematics department (1885–1925). Died 1931 in Cambridge, England.

Charlotte Scott was born in Lincoln and received her early education from private tutors. Her father was an educator and a prominent Congregationalist minister. She entered Girton College, Cambridge, in 1876, and received an honors degree in 1880. At that time women could not receive Cambridge degrees and could take the Cambridge examinations only on an informal basis. Scott won eighth place in the mathematics examinations, an unprecedented achievement for a woman. Her sex, however, prevented her from receiving the title "eighth wrangler" that would have been hers had she been a man, nor was she allowed to be present at the commencement ceremony. A minor protest resulted when the name of the official male eighth wrangler was read aloud in the University Senate House as Girton women and their supporters shouted "Scott of Girton! Scott of Girton!"

At the same time she was doing graduate work at the University of London, Scott remained at Girton as resident lecturer in mathematics from 1880 to 1884. She received the bachelor of science degree in 1882 and in 1885 the doctorate. In 1885, the newly established Bryn Mawr College in Pennsylvania offered her a position as the one female member of a faculty of six. She established the graduate program and undergraduate mathematics programs at Bryn Mawr and was considered an excellent teacher; a large number of her students went on to distinguished academic careers. Scott was also active in the development of the New York Mathematical Society, which reorganized as the American Mathematical Society in 1894–1895; she served as its vice-president in 1906. She retired from Bryn Mawr in 1925 and returned to Cambridge, England, where she died at age seventy-three.

Charlotte Scott's special interest was in the developing field of algebraic geometry, where she worked with the problem of analysis of singularities for algebraic curves. She published thirty papers in various mathematical journals. In 1922 she was honored when seventy members of the American Mathematical Society and seventy former students met at Bryn Mawr to pay tribute to her. The main address was given by philosopher Alfred North Whitehead, who had come from England especially for the purpose.   MBO

PRIMARY SOURCES
Scott, Charlotte Angas. *An Introductory Account of Certain Modern Ideas and Methods in Plane Analytical Geometry.* London: Macmillan and Co., 1894.
———. *Analytical Conics.* London: J. M. Dent, 1907.

SECONDARY SOURCES
Kenschaft, Pat. "Charlotte Angas Scott, 1858–1931." *Association for Women in Mathematics Newsletter* 7 (November–December, 1977): 9; 8 (April 1978): 11–12.

STANDARD SOURCES
AMS 1–4; *NAW* (article by Marguerite Lehr); Ogilvie 1986; *Woman's Who's Who of America.*

SCOTT, FLORA MURRAY (1891–1984)

Scottish/U.S. botanist, plant anatomist. Born 6 September 1891 in Craig, Scotland, to Mary Jobson and Robert Scott. Educated St. Andrews University, Scotland (M.A., 1911; B.Sc., 1914); Stanford University (Ph.D., 1925). Professional experience: Constantinople College for Women, associate professor (1919–1921) League of Red

Cross Societies, Geneva, Switzerland, instructor in biology (1921–1922). Stanford University, faculty (1922–1925); UCLA, faculty (1925–1950), professor of botany (1950–1959), professor emerita (1959). Concurrent experience: UCLA Botanical Garden, assistant director. Honors and memberships: UCLA Association of Faculty Women, founder and first president. Died 24 March 1984 in Los Angeles.

Although Flora Murray Scott was born in Scotland and educated at St. Andrews University, she soon showed her interest in distant lands by taking a position for a year in Constantinople at the College for Women. The following year, she left for California, to study at Stanford University, where she received her doctoral degree acting as a teaching assistant during her student years. She remained in California, joining the faculty of UCLA in 1925, finally being named professor of botany in 1950. Her research centered on plant anatomy, especially on the structure of the plant cell wall. By 1950, the development of the electronic microscope enabled more detailed descriptions of the cell wall on which she published. While at the University of California, she served as chair of the department of botany, as plant anatomist at the Agricultural Experiment Station, and as assistant director of the Botanical Garden. She founded and served as the first president of the Association of Faculty Women at the university. She retired as professor emerita in 1959. She was awarded a medal by the UCLA faculty.   JH/MBO

PRIMARY SOURCES
Scott, Flora Murray. *Introduction to the Limnology of Searsville Lake.* Palo Alto, Calif.: Stanford University Press, 1927.
Flora Murray Scott Papers (Collection 395). Department of Special Collections, University Research Library, University of California, Los Angeles. Includes a short bibliography as well as a finding guide.

STANDARD SOURCES
AMS 4–8, B 9; P&B 10–11; Debus.

SCOTT, HENDERINA VICTORIA (KLAASSEN) (d. 1929)

British botanist and paleobotanist. Birthdate and place unknown. Married Dukinfield Henry Scott (1887). Educated Royal College of Science (1886). Honors and memberships: Linnean Society, Fellow (February 1905). Died Oakley, Hants, 18 January 1929.

Henderina Victoria Klaassen married paleobotanist Dukinfield Henry Scott in 1887. The two met when she was a student at the Royal College of Science in 1886 and attended an advanced class in botany held at the Jodrell Laboratory, Kew, by Scott. The following year they married. They worked together as a team, and their home was a place where botanists gathered. Scott worked with her husband, but also did research on her own, although the publication often bore the name of a collaborator. Her first investigation (before they married) was on the nucleus-like bodies in the cells of the blue-green algae *Oscillaria* and *Tolypothrix;* D. H. Scott acknowledged Klaassen with the contributions. She published several papers in the field of fossil botany. In addition to those listed in the bibliography, she published on the sporangial bodies called *Tracquairia* in *Annals of Botany* (1911) and collaborated with ETHEL SARGANT in an investigation on the development of *Arum maculatum* from the seed, published in *Annals of Botany* (1898). Scott also worked in physiology, making a detailed study of the movements of the flowers of *Sparmannia africana* (*Annals of Botany,* 1903), demonstrating by means of the cinematograph the movements. One of the first to use these techniques, she demonstrated at the Linnean Society the opening and closing of flowers and other plant movements. She prepared the illustrations for her husband's *Introduction to Structural Botany* (1894–1896) and *Studies in Fossil Botany* (1900).

Both Scott and her husband were delegates to the International Botanical Congress in 1905. She also attended the annual meetings of the British Association for the Advancement of Science. Scott was one of the earliest "Lady-Fellows" of the Linnean Society, elected in 1905.

In addition to her botanical interests, Scott was active in local affairs; she was elected to the Wootton St. Lawrence Parish Council in 1913, and became chair of that council in 1924. She was a manager of the Oakley and Deane School, and as treasurer, raised funds for the building of a new schoolroom.

JH/MBO

PRIMARY SOURCES

Scott, Dukinfield Henry. *Journal of the Linnean Society* 24 (1888). Illustrations by Henderina Victoria Scott.

———. *Introduction to Structural Botany.* London: A. & C. Black, 1894–1896. Illustrations by Henderina Victoria Scott.

———. *Studies in Fossil Botany.* London: A.& C. Black, 1900. 151 illustrations by Henderina Victoria Scott.

Scott, Henderina Victoria. "On the Megaspore of *Lepidostrobus foliaceus.*" *New Phytologist,* 1906.

———. "On *Bensonites fusiformis.*" *Annals of Botany* 22 (October 1908): 683–687.

SECONDARY SOURCES

A. B. R. "Mrs. Henderina Victoria Scott." *Journal of Botany* (1929): 57. Obituary notice.

Botanical Society Exchange Club of the British Isles (1929): 98. Obituary notice.

"Mrs. D. H. Scott." *Nature* 123 (1929): 287.

Oliver, F. W. "Mrs. Henderina (Rina) Victoria Scott." *Proceedings of the Linnean Society* 141 (1928–1929): 146–147. Obituary notice.

STANDARD SOURCES

Desmond.

SCUDDER, IDA SOPHIA (1870–1960)

U.S. physician. Born 1870 in Ranipet, Madras Presidency, India, to Sophia (Weld) Scudder and John Scudder II. Five siblings. Educated Dwight Moody's Northfield Seminary (left without graduating); Woman's Medical College of Pennsylvania and Cornell University Medical School (M.D., 1899). Professional experience: Vellore, India, Mission Post Physician; Mary Taber Schell Memorial Hospital, developed hospital (1902–1918?); Vellore Christian Medical College, South India, founder (from 1918). Died 1960 at her home near Kodaikanal, India.

Both of Ida Scudder's parents were medical missionaries. Ida Scudder's father, John Scudder II, was the youngest of seven sons and two daughters born to the first American medical missionary to India. Ida was the sixth and youngest child and only daughter. Born at the mission in Ranipet, Ida's early years set her against missionary work. The family was returned to the United States for respite in 1878, where they lived four years on a farm near Creston, Nebraska, but her father resumed his duties in India in 1882 and was followed by her mother. They left Ida under the care of an uncle, Reverend Henry Martyn Scudder, and his wife in Chicago. This couple also abandoned the then thirteen-year-old Ida in order to join the mission service in Japan, leaving her in the Dwight Moody Northfield Seminary in Massachusetts to continue her education. When her mother became ill in 1890, Ida left the school before graduating to help at her parent's post in Tindivanam, determined to return to the United States as soon as possible. One night, she was called on to help deliver the babies of three different Indian women whose husbands refused to allow the more experienced John Scudder to attend delivery. All three died. This tragedy determined Ida's future, for she returned to the States to achieve her goal of a medical degree and to raise funds for developing a hospital in India. She took her final year of medical school at Cornell for the superior clinical training there, and received her medical degree in 1899.

In 1900, she returned to India with a Northfield classmate and friend, Annie Hancock, who stayed in India as an evangelistic worker until her death in 1924. An even closer companion and coworker was Gertrude Dodd, who joined Scudder in 1916 as an unofficial Reformed Church missionary. Dodd lived off her own money and contributed much of her inheritance to support students at the medical college founded by Scudder and for emergency needs. The two lived and traveled together until Dodd's death in 1944. Ida Scudder's mother was also part of the team, spending the last twenty-five years of her life as her daughter's unofficial hostess, assistant, and adviser.

Ida Scudder treated thousands of cases in a tiny missionary bungalow and on outpatient rounds, while also constructing the small Mary Taber Schell Hospital, which opened in 1902. At the hospital, she was the only surgeon until 1932. Convinced that the medical needs of India's women could not be met by government or mission facilities, Scudder added a nursing school to Schell Hospital in 1909. Her next project was the Union Mission Medical School for Women, partially funded by interdenominational support and subsidies from the Madras government. The school opened in 1918 and was expanded significantly over the next twenty years. In 1938, a change in government regulations requiring university affiliation for the granting of medical degrees seemed to doom the school, and the seventy-year-old Scudder returned to the United States to raise funds and support. In spite of wartime depression and personal sorrow at the loss of her friend Gertrude Dodd, Scudder persisted and the newly coeducational school was granted permanent affiliation with the University of Madras in 1950. After fifty years of service in India, Ida Scudder retired, remaining quite active into her eighties. She died at her bungalow home in the Palani Hills in her ninetieth year. The medical school (renamed the Christian Medical College in 1940) continued, acquired more Indian personnel, and grew to over two thousand staff members in the 1970s.   JH/MBO

PRIMARY SOURCES

Scudder, Ida Sophia Scudder. *Papers.* Ida Sophia Scudder Papers, Schlesinger Library, Radcliffe College.

SECONDARY SOURCES

Wilson, Dorothy Clarke. *Dr. Ida: The Story of Dr. Ida Scudder of Vellore.* New York: McGraw-Hill, 1959.

STANDARD SOURCES

Lovejoy; *NAW*(M) (article by Valentin Rabe); Uglow.

SEAMAN, ELIZABETH COCHRANE (1865–1922)

U.S. newspaper reporter and world traveler. Known as Nellie Bly. Born 5 May 1865 at Cochran's Mills, Pa. Father, Michael Cochran. Nine siblings. Married Robert L. Seaman (1895). Professional experience: Pittsburgh Dispatch, *reporter; (1885–1887);* World, *reporter (1887–1895?);* Iron Clad Manufacturing Company, *co-manager with her husband (1896–1922);* New York Journal, *reporter. Died 1922.*

Elizabeth Cochran was born at Cochran's Mills, the third child of her father's second marriage. As a child, she was called "Pinky," because her mother dressed her in pink most of the time. Her family moved to a small mining town, Apollo, Pennsylvania, but her father died shortly after the move, leaving a wife, ten children, and a small estate. Elizabeth was always a rebel, and was determined not to spend the rest of her life in Apollo. After talking her mother into moving to Pittsburgh, she eventually landed work at the *Pittsburgh Dispatch.* Her first work proceeded from a response she had written to an article in this newspaper entitled "What Girls Are Good For." The gist of the article was that married women should have children, raise them, and run the house. If they were unfortunate enough not to find a husband, they should live at home and work as housekeepers and nurses for children. Cochrane (she had added an "e" to her name), issued a clever, accurate, and commonsensical rebuttal of this article. The editor of the paper was impressed and advertised for the author of the piece. Cochrane emerged and the editor asked her to write a series of articles. She chose the delicate topic of divorce. Her editor then hired her as a regular reporter at five dollars a week. The editor suggested that she chose a *nom de plume.* She chose the name Nellie Bly (after the Stephen Foster song) and used it for the rest of her career. Her journalistic career expanded when she was sent to Mexico to write about the people. After writing her successful articles on Mexico, Bly moved to New York and got a job with Joseph Pulitzer's *World.* She was a part of an exposé on the treatment of inmates at an insane asylum on Blackwell's Island in the East River. Posing as an inmate, she observed the horrors that the inmates endured. After she was released, she wrote a series on Blackwell's Island, entitled "Behind Asylum Bars." She continued her work at the *World,* but also became involved in writing fiction. After reading *Around the World in Eighty Days,* Nellie decided that she would like to do the same, and was convinced that she could better this record. Although the *World* was against it at first, assuming that only a man could make such a journey, they eventually decided it was a good idea. Beating Phineas Fogg's record, she returned in seventy-two days. Her reporting continued to stress a wide range of subjects, including many other exposés involving investigative reporting. In 1895, on a train trip to Chicago, the twenty-eight-year-old Bly met the seventy-two-year-old manufacturer Robert L. Seaman, and married him several days later. In 1896, as a birthday gift, he gave her one of his companies. This company, the Iron Clad Manufacturing Company, did well during the period the Seamans managed it jointly. However, after Robert Seaman died in 1904, unscrupulous employees forged her name to checks. Bly was forced to declare bankruptcy, but refused to turn over the company's books as she was ordered. She left the country for Europe in 1914 where she was trapped during World War I. Cleared of the indictment, she returned to the United States, where her company had few assets. She worked for a short time for the *New York Journal*, but her style of writing was no longer in vogue. She died of pneumonia in 1922.

Although Nellie Bly was certainly not a scientist, her work was important to science. First, as a reporter she exposed conditions in mental hospitals and made public other examples of social injustice. Her stories publicized the abuses to psychiatrists and social workers, so that they could attempt to correct them. Second, she was very important to the petroleum industry. In 1904, she observed some small metal containers on the docks of a French port. Discovering that glycerine was shipped in them, she made sketches, and after she returned home, had her engineers prepare the details of a metal container. After the death of Robert Seaman, she perfected and patented a prototype metal oil drum, beginning a revolution in packaging, transporting, and handling of many petroleum products. The Nellie Bly Formation (Pennsylvanian) of Oklahoma is named after her.   JH/MBO

PRIMARY SOURCES

Bly, Nellie. *Ten Days in a Mad-House, or, Nellie Bly's Experience on Blackwell's Island*. New York: Munro, 1887.

———. *Around the World in Seventy-Two Days*. New York: The Pictorial Weeklies, 1890.

SECONDARY SOURCES

Baker, Nina B. *Nellie Bly*. New York: Holt, 1956.

[Meyers, John]. *The Story of Nellie Bly*. New York: American Flange and Manufacturing Co., 1951.

Miller, Ernest C. "A Very Fast Woman." *Early Daze in Oil*. Philadelphia: Dorrance, 1974.

Noble, Iris. *Nellie Bly, First Woman Reporter (1867–1922)*. New York: Messner, 1956.

Rittenhouse, Mignon. *The Amazing Nellie Bly*. New York: Dutton, 1956.

Ross, Isabel. *Charmers and Cranks: Twelve Famous American Women Who Defied the Conventions*. New York: Harper & Row, 1965.

STANDARD SOURCES

Sarjeant.

SEARS, PAULINE SNEDDEN (1908–1993)

U.S. educational psychologist. Born 5 July 1908 in Fairlee, Vt. Married Robert Richardson Sears (1932). Two children. Educated Stanford University (A.B., 1930); Columbia University Teachers College (M.A., 1931); Yale University (Ph.D. in psychology, 1939). Professional experience: Yale University, clinical instructor (1936–1942); University of Iowa, research fellow (1942–1949); *Harvard University, research associate in education (1949–1953); Stanford University, assistant professor of education (1953–1958), professor (1958–1974), professor emerita (1974–1993). Honors and memberships: APA Gold Medal (with husband, Robert Sears, 1980); Society for Research in Child Development; American Psychological Association (president, Division of Developmental Psychology, 1959–1960); American Ethic Research Association. Died 14 March 1993.*

Respected for her innovative accomplishments in the fields of developmental and educational psychology, Pauline Snedden Sears is best known for her research on aggression in children as manifested by doll-play and for studies on aspiration levels. She and Robert Richardson Sears made up one of the most successful husband-wife research teams in the field, inspiring each other intellectually from their undergraduate days.

Pauline Snedden was born on 5 July 1908 to David Snedden, an educational administrator, later professor at Columbia University Teachers College, and Genevra (Sisson) Snedden, a schoolteacher and author. She was the fourth child (third girl) of five children and lived in Brookline, Massachusetts, until the family moved to Yonkers, New York, when David Snedden began teaching at Teachers College. She attended high school at private Lincoln school, New York City, then according to family tradition, went to Stanford University, California, to earn her bachelor's degree (1930). At Palo Alto, Pauline met Robert Sears in an introductory psychology class, and the two began the intellectual interaction that would dominate their lives. She returned east to study at Columbia University Teachers College for a master's degree (1931) in clinical psychology.

After graduation, Pauline Snedden moved to New Haven, where Robert Sears was a graduate student in psychology at Yale, and took an assistantship doing comprehensive testing of psychiatric patients. When Robert Sears completed his doctorate in 1932, they were married and Robert accepted a position as instructor of psychology at the University of Illinois, Urbana. Due to the university's nepotism rules, Pauline "retired" from pursuing a career to devote her time to her family, which eventually included two children (David born in 1935 and Nancy born in 1938). She found time to take a few classes and, more important, began her reading and research on levels of aspiration.

Robert Sears was invited back to Yale as assistant professor in 1936, and Pauline enrolled in graduate school to complete her doctorate (1939). During her clinical training she began the testing and data collection for her innovative studies on levels of aspiration. A paper based on her thesis was published in 1940 ("Levels of Aspiration in Academically Successful and Unsuccessful Children" in *Journal of Abnormal and Social Psychology*) and an additional, more clinical paper in

1941 ("Level of Aspiration in Relation to Some Variables of Personality: Clinical Studies" in *Journal of Social Psychology*).

Pauline Sears began her studies of aggression in children during an observational study of a five-month-old conducted with Robert Sears at Yale, published in the book *Frustration and Aggression* in 1939. Her research on various aspects of the concept of aggression in children was very important, especially following her development at Iowa of the doll-play technique for testing aggression levels in children. The papers she authored and coauthored on the subject between 1939 and 1951 include "Effect of Father Separation on Preschool Children's Doll-Play Aggression" (1946), "Sex-Difference in Doll-Play Aggression" (1947), and "Doll-Play Aggression in Normal Young Children: Influence of Sex, Age, Sibling Status, Father's Absence" (1951).

As was typical of dual-career families of the time, Robert Sears's career had priority and Pauline followed along, taking whatever lower-ranking positions were available to her. She filled a series of these positions for over twenty years, despite an excellent research and publishing record. When Robert Sears was offered the directorship of the Iowa Child Welfare Research Station, Pauline was told by a colleague there that she would receive an appointment on the psychiatry staff—only to find when they moved that antinepotism rules forbade her appointment. She was an unpaid research associate for the seven years they were there, yet she and Robert Sears did important joint research focusing on aspects of parental behavior that were expected to affect sex-typing and interpersonal motives such as dependency and aggression. Coworkers at Iowa included Kurt Lewin, TAMARA DEMBO, and Leon Festinger, with whom Sears coauthored the important theoretical chapter on level of aspiration in J. V. Hunt's *Personality and the Behavior Disorders,* volume 1 (1944).

When Harvard invited Robert Sears to teach, Pauline was appointed lecturer and research associate, this time with pay. Her research involved patterns of childrearing and the launching of the cross-cultural study of socialization (with Beatrice and John Whiting). She continued her interest in levels of aspiration with a study of preschool children.

In 1953 the family made its final move, this time to Stanford University with Robert Sears as professor and chair of the department of psychology and Pauline Sears as an assistant professor of education with possibility of tenure. She began studies on self-esteem and achievement motivation and their relation to school performance; on psychological effects of accelerated mathematics programs; on computer-assisted instruction. She administered the Elementary Teacher Training Program for several years and organized the program in child development in the School of Education. Her research also included studies on teaching techniques in the nursery school; self-concept in children; childrearing practices; plus a monumental project designed to examine interrelations among six desired outcomes of elementary education and the classroom conditions or situational variables associated with each. Case studies from this massive project constituted the material for *In Pursuit of Self-Esteem,* which she wrote with V. Sherman (1964). Sears was promoted to associate professor in 1958 and to full professor in 1966.

The team of Sears and Sears collaborated again in the 1970s on a follow-up study of the Terman sample of gifted children. From their data came Pauline Sears and A. Barbee's chapter "Career and Life Satisfactions among Terman's Gifted Women" in *The Gifted and the Creative: A Fifty-Year Perspective* (1977) and Robert Sears's "Sources of Life Satisfaction of the Terman Gifted Men" (*American Psychologist* 32 [1977]). The American Psychological Association Gold Medal was presented to Pauline and Robert Sears jointly in 1980 for their lifelong contributions to the field of psychology in the study of human development and applications of knowledge to the educational and social betterment of children. The couple lived in Menlo Park, near Stanford University, after retiring.   JH/MBO

PRIMARY SOURCES

Sears, Pauline Snedden. *Doll-Play Aggression in Normal Young Children: Influence of Sex, Age, Sibling Status, Father's Absence.* Washington, D.C.: American Psychological Association, 1951.

———. *The Effect of Classroom Conditions on the Strength of Achievement Motive and Work Output on Elementary School Children.* Palo Alto, Calif.: Stanford University Press, 1963.

———. With Vivian Sherman. *In Pursuit of Self-Esteem.* Belmont, Calif.: Wadsworth, 1964.

STANDARD SOURCES

AMS 7–8, S&B 12; O'Connell and Russo (article by Judy F. Rosenblith); Stevens and Gardner.

SEEGAL, BEATRICE CARRIER (1898–?)

U.S. immunologist. Born 29 January 1898 in Santa Barbara, Calif. Educated University of California, Berkeley (B.A., 1918; M.A., 1921); Johns Hopkins University (M.D., 1924). Professional experience: Harvard University School of Medicine, fellow, pathology (1924–1926), instructor in bacteriology (1927–1930), assistant through associate professor (1931–1958); professor (1959–1966); Columbia University, emerita professor of microbiology, College of Physicians and Surgeons (from 1966). Death date unknown.

Beatrice Seegal advanced through the academic ranks at the Harvard University School of Medicine, taking thirty-two years to arrive at the rank of professor. Upon retirement, she became emerita professor of microbiology at Columbia. Seegal was a member of the American Association of Experimental Pathologists, the Society of Experimental Biology and Medical Research, the American Association for the Advancement of Science, and the American Association of Pathologists and Bacteriologists.

Seegal's research was immunological studies of allergic and immune-complex diseases. She used fluorescein-labeled antibodies. She applied her studies to benign and malignant human tumors, indicating the importance of the immune system in malignancies.   JH/MBO

PRIMARY SOURCES
Seegal, Beatrice Carrier. With Deborah Locatcher-Khorazo.
    Microbiology of the Eye. St. Louis: Mosby, 1972.

STANDARD SOURCES
AMS 5–8, B 9, P&B 10–13.

SEIBERT, FLORENCE BARBARA (1897–1991)

U.S. biochemist. Born 6 October 1897 in Easton, Pa., to Barbara (Memmert) and George Peter Seibert. One brother; one sister. Educated Easton High School; Goucher College, Towson, MD (A.B., 1918); Yale University (Ph.D., 1923). Professional experience: Hammersley Paper Mills, Garfield, N.J., laboratory worker (1918–1920); University of Chicago, American Philosophical Society, Porter Fellowship (1923–1924); Otho S. A. Sprague Memorial Institute, Chicago, instructor in pathology and assistant to Dr. Esmond R. Long (1924–1932); Henry Phipps Institute of the University of Pennsylvania, through academic ranks to professor (1932–1959), emerita professor (1959–1991). Honors and memberships: Uppsala University, Guggenheim Fellowship (1937–1938); National Tuberculosis Association, Trudeau Medal (1938); American Chemical Society, Garvan Medal (1942); American Association of University Women, first Achievement Award (1943); Chi Omega, National Achievement Award (1944); Gimberl Award (1945); John Scott Award (1947); National Women's Hall of Fame (1990); Association of Blood Banks, John Elliot Award (1962). Honorary doctorates: Goucher College (LL.D., 1938); University of Chicago (Sc.D., 1941); Lafayette College (1947); Woman's Medical College of Pennsylvania (1950). Died 23 August 1991.

Florence Seibert and her older brother contracted polio as small children; Florence was only three, and needed leg braces thereafter. She graduated first in her class at Easton High School and won a scholarship to Goucher College. She had three additional scholarships to support her undergraduate studies. Intending to be a physician, she took the required premedical courses. However, in her senior year, her chemistry professor, Jessie Minor, suggested that they work together at the Hammersley Paper Mills laboratory in Garfield, New Jersey. After she received her bachelor's degree in biol-ogy, she worked as a chemist at the mill. The experience was gratifying to her, and she realized that she did not want to practice medicine but work as a biochemical researcher. After saving enough money, Seibert began graduate school at Yale University, where she won the Dean Van Meter Scholarship (1923). After she earned her doctoral degree, she received the coveted Porter Fellowship, which supported her during the years 1923–1924. She worked at the University of Chicago during these years and in 1924 became an instructor in pathology and assistant to Esmond R. Long. When Long went to Philadelphia as director of the Henry Phipps Institute of the University of Pennsylvania, Seibert went with him, and rose through the academic ranks to professor.

A Guggenheim Fellowship gave Seibert an opportunity to join Nobel laureate Theodor Svedberg at Uppsala University. The Guggenheim year with Svedberg established her reputation as a leading scientist. She received numerous honors and awards and died at the age of ninety-three at a nursing home in St. Petersburg, Florida.

Although Seibert published her first three papers on the chemistry of pulps and papermaking, it was Esmond Long's support that directed her scientific research along its path. Through his grant from the National Tuberculosis Association, Long supported her research. In her early research, Seibert observed that successive distillations failed to kill all of the bacteria and that fever in patients could be caused by the survivors. She invented a distillation apparatus that eliminated the fever-producing chemical, thus providing a safer water distillate. For her discovery she won the University of Chicago's Ricketts Prize.

Seibert is best known for building on Robert Koch's initial skin test for tuberculosis. Koch's method was notoriously inaccurate, for the evaporated solution used in the test contained numerous impurities. Even people with a serious case of tuberculosis sometimes failed to get a positive test. Seibert worked for ten years on methods of isolating pure tuberculin by filtration, by using a guncotton membrane of a specific thickness. The result was a creamy white powder which was the purified protein derived from the tuberculosis bacillus, known as PPD. Never patenting the process (which would have made her rich), she furnished the National Tuberculosis Association with a large quantity of pure tuberculin.

While she was in Uppsala, she worked with Arne Tiselius, who had invented the electrophoresis apparatus for separating molecules by passing them through an electric field. At Long's instigation, she asked for and received an apparatus to use when she returned to the United States. Her most important work was on tuberculosis, although she conducted research in several other areas, including cancer.   JH/MBO

PRIMARY SOURCES

Seibert, Florence Barbara. "Febrile Reactions Following the Injection of Non-specific Agents into Rabbits." Ph.D. diss., Yale University, 1923.

————. *Pebbles on the Hill of a Scientist.* St. Petersburg, Fla.: N.p., 1968. Autobiography. Includes Seibert's complete bibliography.

SECONDARY SOURCES

"Dr. Florence B. Seibert, Inventor of Standard TB Test, Dies at 93." *New York Times,* 31 August 1991.

"Dr. Florence Seibert." *Newsday,* 2 September 1991.

Hall, D. L. "Academics, Bluestockings, and Biologists: Women at the University of Chicago, 1892–1932." In *New York Academy of Sciences,* ed. A. M. Briscoe and S. M. Pfafflin, 300–320. New York: New York Academy of Sciences, 1993.

Handbook of Scientific and Technical Awards. New York: Special Library Association, 1956.

STANDARD SOURCES

AMS 4–8, B 9, P&B 10–14; Grinstein 1993 (article by Ariel Hollingshead); Grinstein 1997 (article by Paris Svoronos); *Notable;* Yost.

SELIGMAN, BRENDA ZARA (1882–1965)

British anthropologist. Born 1882 in London to Sarah and Myer Salaman. Thirteen siblings. Married Charles Gabriel Seligman in 1905 (died 1940). One daughter (died aged thirteen). Educated at home; Roedean School; Bedford College (premedical, no degree). Professional experience: assistant to C. G. Seligman; Notes and Queries in Anthropology, editor; Royal Anthroplogical Institute, C. G. Seligman Endowment Fund, founder. Field research: Vedda of Ceylon (1907); Sudan expeditions (1909–1910; 1911–1912; 1921–1922). Honors and memberships: Royal Anthropological Institute, Patron's Medal, 1963; Association of Social Anthropologists, President (1959). Died 2 January 1965, probably in London.

Brenda Seligman was educated at Roedean School and then at Bedford College, where she followed a premedical course. She left school when she married Charles G. Seligman, a medical colleague and friend of her brother Redcliffe. When they married, Charles was a research pathologist, but as an avocation wrote up the results of the Cooke-Daniels 1904 expediton to New Guinea. Although she was never educated in anthropology or ethnology, Brenda became interested in the subject when she helped Charles with his paper. She became thoroughly involved when she reluctantly (hesitating to leave her young daughter, born soon after their marriage)

accompanied her husband on an expedition to the Vedda of Ceylon (Sri Lanka). On this expedition she began as Charles Seligman's general assistant. Her diaries and notebooks presaged her future work. Whereas Charles was most interested in the physical anthropology, archeology, and history of the people they studied, Brenda became increasingly interested in kinship and social organization. This division of labor continued throughout their collaboration. In Ceylon and then on a series of expeditions to the Sudan, she was a joint author on subsequent publications while establishing herself as an independent investigator in social anthropology, specializing in kinship studies.

While her husband held the position of professor of anthropology at the University of London, Brenda Seligman never held an equivalent post, though she was his full collaborator. She was made a Fellow of the Royal Anthropological Institute and later served as vice-president of the society. Their home at Toot Baldon in Oxfordshire was sought out by both anthropologists and colonial administrators, who found her both a mentor and, at times, a patron.

After her husband died in 1940, Brenda Seligman opened her house to children escaping the London bombardment during World War II. She continued her independent research and served as editor of the revived *Notes and Queries on Anthropology.* She founded and worked for the funding of an endowment that bore her husband's name. The Royal Anthropological Institute awarded her its patrons medal for her quiet patronage of many anthropologists. In 1959, she was made president of the Association of Social Anthropologists in recognition of her significant contributions.   JH

PRIMARY SOURCES

Seligman, Brenda Z. With Charles G. Seligman. *The Veddas.* Cambridge: Cambridge University Press, 1911.

————. With Charles G. Seligman. "The Kababish, a Sudan Arab Tribe." *Harvard African Studies.* Vol. 2, Cambridge: Harvard University Press, 1918.

————. "Bilateral Descent and the Formation of Marriage Classes." *Journal of the Royal Anthropological Institute* 57 (1927): 349–375.

————. "Asymmetry in Descent, with Special Reference to Pentecost." *Journal of the Royal Anthropological Institute* 58 (1928): 533–558.

————. "Incest and Descent: Their Influence on Social Organization." *Journal of the Royal Anthropological Institute* 59 (1929): 231–272.

————. "The Incest Barrier: Its Role in Social Organization." *British Journal of Psychology* (General) 22, no. 3 (1932): 250–276.

————. With C. G. Seligman. *Pagan Tribes of the Nilotic Sudan.* London: G. Routledge & Sons, 1932.

———. "The Part of the Unconscious in Social Heritage." *Essays Presented to C. G. Seligman.* London: K. Paul, Trench, Trubner & Co., 1934.

———. "The Incest Taboo as a Social Regulation." *Sociological Review* 27, no. 1 (1935): 75–93.

———. "The Problem of Incest and Exogamy: A Restatement." *American Anthropologist* 50 (1952): 305–316.

———, ed. *The Ainu Creed and Cult.* New York: Columbia University Press, 1962. Based on N. G. Munro's field records. In addition to editing the volume, Seligman contributed a chapter.

SECONDARY SOURCES
Fortes, Meyer. "Brenda Zara Seligman, 1882–1965: A Memoir." *Man* 216 (1965): 177–181.
Oriental Art 11 (Autumn 1965): 189. Obituary notice.
Schapera, Issac, and E. E. Evans-Pritchard, eds. *Studies in Kinship and Marriage.* London: Royal Anthropological Institute, 1963. Dedicated to Brenda Z. Seligman on her 80th birthday.
Times, 6 January 1965. Obituary notice.

STANDARD SOURCES
IDA.

SEMIKHATOVA, SOFIA VIKTOROVNA (KARPOVA) (1889–1973)

Russian geologist and paleontologist. Born 1889 in St. Petersburg. Married Alexander Semikhatov. Two sons; one daughter. St. Petersburg Highest Women's Courses, law department (1909–1916); Moscow Highest Women's Courses, natural sciences department (1916–1918). Professional experience: Geological Committee, research scientist (1924–1930); Moscow Geological Oil Institute, senior paleontologist (1930–1934); Oil Institute, consultant (1934–1936); Paleontological Institute, researcher (from 1936); Uzbek Geological Administration, researcher (1942–1944); Oil Institute Moscow, gas development researcher (1944?; 1946–1953); All Union Scientific Geological Oil Institute, researcher (1953–1973). Died 1973.

St. Petersburg native Sofia V. Karpova first studied law in the Highest Women's Courses of that city. She lived independently and earned money by giving private lessons. In 1916 she finished law school by correspondence because she had moved to Moscow when she married Alexander Semikhatov in 1913. She studied in the natural sciences department in Moscow Highest Women's Courses until 1918, when she left because of the birth of her first son. She continued to study geology by correspondence and later in the department of Y. V. Samoilov.

In 1921, her second child, a daughter, was born. By 1924,

she had gone back to work, first as a research scientist in the Geological Committee and then at the Moscow Geological Oil Institute as a senior paleontologist. However, in 1932, she had a third child, another son, and found it difficult to work full time with the three children. Thus, she left her regular job and worked on a part-time arrangement, first at the Oil Institute and from 1936 in the Paleontological Institute.

The family evacuated to Tashkent in 1942, where she worked in the Uzbek Geological Administration until 1944. When they returned to Moscow she went to work at the Oil Institute and in 1946 moved into the system of establishing gas development. In 1953, she went to the All-Union Scientific Research Geological Oil Institute, where she worked until the end of her life.

Her major scientific work involved the biostratigraphy of the Carboniferous, mainly in the Volga-Ural province. She was extremely important to the understanding of the geology of this petroleum-bearing region of the USSR. During her lifetime, she published ninety works; her last monograph, *Carboniferous Deposits of Volga-Ural Area,* was published in 1970 when Semikhatova was eighty-one years old. Her works were printed in Germany, England, and in the United States.

One of her most important achievements was the separation of the Bashkirian stage in the base of the Middle Carboniferous. Her careful analysis of the development of the region's fauna, especially brachiopods, made this possible. Semikhatova's basic scientific topics involved the study of Carboniferous cross-sections and the analysis of brachiopod evolution. These research topics, which she pursued throughout her life, gave a stability to her research that enabled her to succeed. She also researched the Russian Platform and the areas adjacent to it in the western inclination in the Urals and in Donbas. She not only separated the Bashkirian stage, but used infinite detail to study its brachiopod fauna. This allowed her to break up stages into horizons.

Unlike other leading women geologists, Semikhatova never taught in establishments of higher education. Nevertheless she spent much time and effort in preparing young scientists for their future careers. CK/MBO

PRIMARY SOURCES
Semikhatova, Sofia. "Some Results of Investigation of the Internal Structure of Carboniferous Brachiopods." *Doklady Akademii Nauk SSSR* 21, no. 4. Moscow: Akademiya Nauk SSSR, 1938. In English.
———. *Brachiopods of Bashkirian Beds of USSR; 1, Genus Choristites Fischer.* Academy of Science USSR, Inst. Paleont. 55, no. 4 (1941). In Russian. A monographic study of brachiopods belonging to the genus Choristites (including new

species and varieties) from Bashkirian beds (Carboniferous) of the west slope of the Urals, USSR.

———. "The Group of *Spirifer trigonalis* Martin from the Lower Carboniferous Supra-coalbearing Beds of Moscow Basin." *National Academy of Sciences, USSR, Institute Paleontologica,* 12 (1941). In Russian. Descriptions of several species of *Spirifer* from the lower Carboniferous of the Moscow basin, whose external features resemble those of representatives of *S. trigonalis.* Makes special reference to the internal structure.

———. "Ietapy razvitiya brakhiopod i voprosy stratigrafii namyura." *Byulleten' Moskovskogo Obshchestva Ispytateley Prirody, Otdel Geologischeskiy* 41 (1966): 73–101. Explains that the Carboniferous (Namurian) of Western Europe is equated with the Tarussk-Protvinsk stage of brachiopod development in the Russian platform.

———, ed. With A. A. Ryzhova. "Kamennougol'nyye otlozheniya Volgo-Ural'skoy neftegazonosnoy oblasti" (Carboniferous Deposits of the Volga-Ural Oil and Gas Regions). *Trudy-Vsesoyuznyy Nauchno-Issledovatel'skiy Geologorazvedochniy Neftyanoy Institut (VNIGRI).* Moscow: Vsesoyuznyy Nauchno-Issledovatel'skiy Geologorazvedochniy Neftyanoy Institut, 1970.

SECONDARY SOURCES
Nalivkin, Dmitriy V. *Our First Women Geologists.* Leningrad: Nauka, 1979.
Solovyeva, M. N. "Sof'ya Viktorovna Semikhatova; k 100-letiyu so dnya rozhdeniya" (Sof'ya Viktorovna Semmikhatova; 100th birthday). Moscow, Russian Federation, *Byulleten' Moskovskogo Obshchestva Ispytateley Prirody, Otdel Geologischeskiy* 66, no. 3 (1991): 103–109.

SEMPLE, ELLEN CHURCHILL (1863–1932)

U.S. geographer. Born 1863 in Louisville, Ky., to Emerine (Price) and Alexander Semple. Four siblings. Never married. Educated private tutors; Vassar College (B.A., 1882; M.A., 1891); University of Leipzig (1891–1892; 1895). Professional experience: Semple Collegiate School, Louisville, founder and history teacher (1893–1895); University of Chicago, lecturer (1906–1924); Oxford University (1905; 1912); Wellesley College (1914–1915); University of Colorado (1916); Columbia University (1918); Clark University, lecturer in anthropogeography (1921–1923); professor of anthropogeography (1923–1932). Died 1932 in West Palm Beach, Fla.

Ellen Semple, the youngest of five children, was raised by her mother when her father, a successful Louisville merchant, died when Semple was twelve. After studying with private tutors, Semple attended Vassar College and was graduated as valedictorian (1882).

A European tour in 1887 sparked Semple's interest in geography. On this trip she was introduced to and impressed by the work of the German anthropogeographer Friedrich Ratzel, of Leipzig University. On her return to Louisville, she read geography and related subjects such as sociology, economics, and history. She prepared herself for a return to Europe with the goal of studying under Ratzel. After this intensive study period, she took an examination that resulted in the granting of a master's degree by Vassar College (1891). She then returned to Leipzig, where she was given special permission to attend Ratzel's classes, for women were not allowed to enroll at the university. Ratzel postulated that the characteristics of human societies are determined by their physical environments, a thesis that Semple accepted. Semple became Ratzel's favorite student and a close friend of his family. After a year's study in Leipzig, she and her recently divorced sister founded a girls' school, where she taught for two years. She revisited Leipzig in 1895 and then devoted herself to research and writing in her native town.

In order to study the influence of geographic isolation on a population, Semple traveled into the remote Kentucky highlands on horseback and lived among the people there. In 1901, she published a paper based on this study, which established her scholarly reputation. After this initial study, her career blossomed; in 1903, she published a book on the geographical influences on American history and in 1904 she was invited to read a paper before the International Geographical Society in London. During this visit to England, Semple taught a summer course at Oxford. From 1906 to 1924, she lectured at the University of Chicago every other year; during these years she also lectured at Wellesley, Columbia, and the University of Colorado. During the summers she camped out in the Catskill Mountains and wrote.

In 1911, Semple's major work, *The Influences of Geographic Environment, on the Basis of Ratzel's System of Anthropo-geography,* was published. After its publication and its favorable reception by scholars, Semple and two friends went on an eighteen-month world tour. During the summer of 1912 she again lectured at Oxford.

Semple served as a consultant for The Inquiry, a government group constituted to study problems that might arise at the Versailles peace conference in 1918, and President Wilson made use of her reports on the Austro-Italian frontier and on the history of the Turkish empire. In 1921, Semple was invited to join the faculty of Clark University, Worcester, Massachusetts, which had a new graduate school of geography. She was first a lecturer, then became professor of anthropogeography. She taught (with frequent semesters off for writing) at Clark for the rest of her life. Her last book, *The Geography of the Mediterranean Region: Its Relation to Ancient History,* was completed a few months before her death in 1932 at West Palm Beach, Florida.

As did her mentor, Ratzel, Semple assumed that the physical environment determined the ways in which people developed their institutions. In her first book she portrayed American expansion as the inevitable product of geographic factors. In her *Influences* of 1911, she classified types of geographic conditions and explained how each influenced mankind at various stages of historical development. Semple's ideas became unfashionable toward the end of her career, as antideterministic approaches became ascendant in the study of geography. Still by focusing attention on the deterministic approach, and by the excellence of her scholarly methods, she made an important contribution to geography as an academic discipline.   MBO

PRIMARY SOURCES

Semple, Ellen Churchill. *Influences of Geographic Environment, on the Basis of Ratzel's System of Anthropo-geography.* New York: Holt, 1911.

STANDARD SOURCES

DAB; Debus; *NAW*; Ogilvie 1986.

SERMENT, LOUISE-ANASTASIA (1642–1692)

French student of natural philosophy. Born 1642 in Grenoble. Died 1692.

Louise-Anastasia Serment was born in Grenoble but spent most of her life in Paris. Although Serment was not a scientist, she was interested in and knowledgeable about contemporary ideas in natural philosophy. As a student of Descartes, she typified his group of female followers.   JH/MBO

STANDARD SOURCES

Bibliographie universelle; Ogilvie 1986.

SESSIONS, KATE OLIVIA (1857–1940)

U.S. horticulturist and agriculturist. Born 8 November 1857 in San Francisco, Calif., to Harriet (Parker) and Josiah Sessions. One brother. Educated Oakland public schools; University of California, Berkeley (Ph.B., 1881). Professional experience: Oakland primary schools, substitute teacher (1881–1883); San Diego, Calif., Russ School (later San Diego High School), instructor and vice-principal (1983–1985); Coronado, San Diego, Pacific Beach, Calif., nursery owner and retail florist (1885–1940); developed what later became San Diego's Balboa Park (1892). Died 24 March 1940 of bronchial pneumonia.

Kate Olivia Sessions was interested in plants from an early age. Her father, Josiah, bred Hambletonian trotting horses, and moved his family to a farm in Oakland. Kate was able to explore the Oakland area on her pony and became familiar with California wildflowers and those in her mother's garden. After graduating from the Oakland public schools, she took a trip to Hawaii, where she was fascinated with the exotic plants there. She earned a bachelor's degree in chemistry from the University of California, Berkeley.

After a short career as a high school teacher, Sessions left teaching to open a nursery in Coronado, California, with retail outlets in San Diego. In 1892, the city of San Diego gave her a lease for thirty acres of undeveloped land in the city park at Sixth and Upas streets to use as a temporary nursery on the condition that she plant one hundred trees there yearly and donate three hundred more to the city. This tract later became San Diego's Balboa Park, where many exotic plants for the city's streets and parks were introduced.

Sessions's greatest importance to science is to be found in the new plants that she introduced into the horticultural trade as she constantly searched for better cultivars. She made numerous collecting trips to places such as Baja, California, returning with more introductions. She introduced such plants as the queen palm, flame eucalyptus, camphor trees, and many different varieties of acacias. She was the first woman to receive the Meyer Medal of the American Genetic Association (1939) for distinguished service in the field of foreign plant introduction.

Sessions was one of the leaders in the foundation of the San Diego Floral Association and served as an officer or board member for over twenty years. She contributed some 250 popular articles and brief notes on plants to its journal. She was also the founder of Arbor Day celebrations in San Diego.

Sessions sold her retail flower shop in 1909, but continued to operate a nursery business until her death. Among her other activities, she was the supervisor of agriculture for the San Diego grammar schools between 1915 and 1918 and conducted a class for the University of California Extension Division in 1939, entitled Gardening Practice and Landscape Design. An elementary school (1956) and a memorial park in Pacific Beach, California (1957) were named after her.   JH/MBO

PRIMARY SOURCES

Sessions, Kate Olivia. *The Complete Writings of Kate Sessions in California Garden, 1909–1939.* San Diego, Calif.: San Diego Floral Association, 1998.

SECONDARY SOURCES

"Two Meyer Medals Awarded During 1939." *Journal of Heredity* 30 (December 1939): 531–532.

STANDARD SOURCES
Bailey; Barnhart; *NAW* (article by Mildred Mathias); O'Neill; Siegel and Finley; Uglow 1982.

SÉVIGNÉ, FRANÇOISE MARGUERITE DE (1646–1705)

See Grignan, Françoise Marguerite de Sévigné, Comtesse de.

SEWALL, LUCY ELLEN (1837–1890)

U.S. physician. Born 26 April 1890 in Boston to Louisa Maria (Winslow) and Samuel Edmond Sewall. Professional experience: New England Hospital for Women and Children, resident physician (1863–1869), attending physician (1869–1886). Died 13 February 1890 of valvular disease of the heart.

Lucy Sewall's specialty was obstetrics and diseases of women. Sewall was first the student and then the trusted colleague of DR. MARIE ELIZABETH ZAKRZEWSKA. With the financial assistance of her father and other socially concerned Bostonians, the New England Hospital for Women and Children was founded in 1862, and Sewall soon became resident physician and then one of the two attending physicians. She met SOPHIA JEX-BLAKE when Blake came to Boston, and Sewell influenced her decision to study medicine and fight for the rights of women physicians in England and Scotland.

The maternity building at the New England Hospital is named Sewall Maternity, after her. She influenced the founding of the Massachusetts Infant Asylum. Semi-invalid in her later years due to organic heart disease, she took up the study of mineralogy.   JH/MBO

SECONDARY SOURCES
Drachman, Virginia G. *Hospital with a Heart: Women Doctors and the Paradox of Separatism at the New England Hospital, 1862–1969.* Ithaca: Cornell University Press, 1984.
Todd, Margaret. *Life of Sophia Jex-Blake.* London: Macmillan, 1918. Includes letters between Sewall and Jex-Blake.

STANDARD SOURCES
Cyclopedia of American Medical Biography; NAW (article by Shirley Phillips Ingebritsen).

SEWARD, GEORGENE HOFFMAN (1902–1992)

U.S. psychologist. Born 21 January 1902 in Washington, D.C., to Georgene (Geddes) and Carl Henry Hoffman. Educated Barnard College (B.A., 1923); Columbia University, Curtis Scholar (M.A., 1924; Ph.D., 1928). Married John Perry Seward, Jr. (7 September 1927). Two daughters. Professional experience: Hunter College, instructor in psychology (1929–1930); Barnard College, instructor (1930–1937); Connecticut College, assistant professor (1937–1945); University of Southern California, assistant professor through professor (1946–1971), emerita professor of psychology (1971–1992). Concurrent experience: Los Angeles Psychiatric Service, Veterans Administration Hospital, and Didi Hirsch Mental Health Clinic, Los Angeles, consultant (from 1948); Kaiser Permanente Medical Group, attending consultant psychiatric services (1961–1965). Honors and memberships: American Psychological Association, Fellow; California State Psychological Association; California State Psychological Association, distinguished psychologist award (1987). Died 19 September 1992 in Los Angeles.

Although Georgene Janet Hoffman was born in Washington, D.C., she was reared in New York City by her grandfather and great aunt after her mother died and her father remarried and moved away. She received a baccalaureate degree in psychology from Barnard College, was elected Phi Beta Kappa, and entered Columbia University to work toward a doctoral degree. There she met and married John Perry Seward, Jr., and a partnership ensued that lasted a lifetime. Their friends at Columbia included faculty members Robert Woodworth, Harry and LETA HOLLINGWORTH, Otto Klineberg, and Gardner and LOIS MURPHY. After receiving two advanced degrees, Georgene Seward taught a year at Hunter College, then returned to Barnard, where she taught from 1930 to 1937, while John Seward instructed at Columbia College. In her seven years at Barnard, Seward was passed over for advancement and promotion repeatedly in deference to men who were often less experienced and competent.

Together the Sewards shared responsibility for the psychology department at the Connecticut College for Women, from 1937 to 1944, and again Georgene Seward left at the same level at which she was hired. She became incensed by the differential treatment of women and was an outspoken feminist, involved in research on issues relevant to women and concerned with psychology's response to and treatment of female patients. Five of her books dealt with feminism or related issues; her husband was equally dedicated to the cause of feminism and social justice.

During the years she was at Connecticut College, Georgene Seward made friends with many psychiatrists and psychologists (including Alfred Adler, Max Wertheimer, Karl and CHARLOTTE BÜHLER, Eva and Kurt Goldstein, Fritz Weiss, Wolfgang Köhler, and Heinz Hartmann) who emigrated to the U.S. from Nazi-occupied Europe. A staunch antifascist and avowed socialist, Seward became an acknowledged "Hebrewphile" with a profound sympathy and admiration for the Jews.

John and Georgene Seward both were devoted teachers and researchers and began publishing jointly during their early postdoctoral years. They formed a close association with G. N. Papanicolaou (developer of the Pap test), resulting in a series of experimental articles on reproductive processes and the influence of hormones on behavior. In 1944, she published a study showing that the menstrual cycle had little direct effect on working women despite the existence of a "code of menstrual invalidism." This was a prelude to her important first book, *Sex and the Social Order* (1946), a pioneering summary of sex differences and related studies.

In 1946, the Sewards moved to California, he to UCLA and she to the University of Southern California. She taught social psychology, personality, and clinical child psychology and directed the clinical psychology training program. She became a diplomate in clinical psychology and began a private practice of individual and group therapy. She also served as a consultant at the Veterans Administration Hospital, Metropolitan State Hospital, and the Didi Hirsch Mental Health Clinic. In 1956 she published *Psychotherapy and Culture Conflict* and a companion volume, *Clinical Studies in Culture Conflict,* which explore neurotic tendencies and other stresses accompanying minority group membership. Politically liberal, the socialist Sewards were caught up in the McCarthy-era persecutions because of the Loyalty Oath controversy and allegations about their perceived radicalism. Another difficult period followed their older daughter, Barbara's, death in 1958. In 1959, the Sewards coedited a Festschrift entitled *Current Psychological Issues: Essays in Honor of Robert S. Woodworth* in tribute to their friend and mentor. With Robert Williamson, she published *Sex Roles in Changing Society* (1970).

Georgene Seward left the University of Southern California in 1972 as professor emerita and continued her private practice and community service for another fifteen years. She and John enjoyed traveling and were devoted to their surviving daughter, Joan, and grandchildren. In the 1970s, Georgene Seward finally began receiving the recognition she had long deserved for her accomplishments and steady championing of women in the profession. She was one of the first to suggest that women should be treated by female psychotherapists; she emphasized the role of social variables in the treatment process and in the etiology of neurosis; she focused her investigations on sex behavior and sex roles. John Seward died in 1985. When Georgene Seward died on 19 September 1992, she had become a favorite of new militant feminist psychologists. JH/MBO

PRIMARY SOURCES

Seward, Georgene H. With John P. Seward. *Effect of Repetition on Reactions to Electric Shock; with Special Reference to the Menstrual Cycle.* New York: N.p., 1934.

———. With John P. Seward. *Alcohol and Task Complexity.* New York: N.p., 1936.

———. *Sex and the Social Order.* New York and London: McGraw-Hill, 1946.

———. *Psychotherapy and Culture Conflict.* New York: Ronald Press, 1956. Reprinted in 1972 as *Psychotherapy and Culture Conflict in Community Mental Health.*

———. *Clinical Studies in Culture Conflict.* New York: Ronald, 1958.

———, ed. With John P. Seward. *Current Psychological Issues: Essays in Honor of Robert S. Woodworth.* New York: Holt, 1958.

———, ed. With Robert Williamson. *Sex Roles in Changing Society.* New York: Random House, 1970.

———. With John P. Seward. *Sex Differences: Mental and Temperamental.* Lexington, Mass.: Lexington Books, 1980.

SECONDARY SOURCES

Sargent, S. Stansfeld, and Robert C. Williamson. "Georgene H. Seward (1902–1992)" *American Psychologist* 48 (1993): 1089. Obituary notice.

STANDARD SOURCES

AMS 5–8, S&B 10–13; Stevens and Gardner.

SHABANOVA, ANNA NIKOLAEVNA (1848–1932)

Russian pediatrician. Born 1848 in Smolensk province. Father a lieutenant. Educated at boarding school; Helsingfors University; St. Petersburg Women's Medical Courses. Professional experience: Nikolaevskii Hospital, worked at children's clinic; Prince Oldenburg Children's Hospital. Died in 1932.

Anna Nikolaevna Shabanova, the daughter of a lieutenant, was born in Smolensk and was educated in a girls' boarding school there. When she was fifteen, her parents lost their money and she was forced to support herself by giving lessons and doing translations. However, she wished to continue her education and managed to change her residence to Moscow. Here she soon became involved with a radical circle of young people who were modelling their lives on that described in Chernyshevskii's influential novel *What Is to Be Done?*. Like the characters in the novel, Shabanova and her friends set up a cooperative sewing workshop to support themselves.

In 1866, the cooperative was broken up by the police, and Shabanova was imprisoned for six months and then sent back to Smolensk. Her attempt in 1868 to enter the Medical Surgical Academy in St. Petersburg was unsuccessful.

Shabanova did not have the resources to go abroad as some other young women did but she succeeded in gaining admittance to Helsingfors University in Finland (at that time a part of the Russian empire), where she was the first woman medical student. She was assisted financially by the writer Mikhail E. Saltykov-Shchedrin and the physiologist Ivan M. Sechenov.

Meanwhile in Russia, steps had been taken in the direction of women's medical education, and in 1872, a four-year training course disguised as a course for "scientific midwives" was opened in St. Petersburg.

Although many women scorned this course, it was a godsend to those for whom European training was out of the question. Some of the women who had been studying in Zurich enrolled in the course after Tsar Aleksandr II's decree of 1873 ordered them to leave Zurich. Shabanova also gladly returned to St. Petersburg. Entrance was competitive and the courses, taught by faculty of the Medical Surgical Academy, were of high quality. In 1876, the courses were extended to five years and the name changed to Women's Medical Courses.

Shabanova graduated with the first class in 1877 and specialized in pediatrics. From 1878 to 1884, she worked with Dr. Raukhfus in the children's clinic at the Nikolaevskii Hospital and also at the Prince Oldenburg Children's Hospital with which she retained a connection her whole life, working up from intern to consultant.

Shabanova was a prolific writer and wrote on many topics connected with children's health. Her first paper was published in 1878. She also promoted first aid courses, which ultimately became a required subject in women's schools. She was instrumental in founding the Society for the Treatment of Chronically Ill Children and for establishing a hospital for chronically ill children at Gatchina, the first of its kind (1883). She also tried to find good homes and educational opportunities for children who recovered.

Shabanova was active in many medical societies and was an ardent feminist. In 1895, she founded the Russian Women's Mutual Benevolence Society, a deceptively named women's right's organization, and in 1905 she established a suffrage division, the Electoral Department, which she led until 1917. She also campaigned with another doctor, MARIIA POKROVSKAIA (leader of the Women's Progressive Party) against legalized prostitution. She organized a National Women's Congress in 1908 and was active in the international women's movement and in the peace movement which was shattered by World War I. During the war she organized voluntary agencies and worked with the War Industries Committee. Shabanova managed to avoid revolutionary politics and continued to work through the Revolution and the turmoil that followed it. After the Revolution, Shabanova returned to her practice in pediatrics, publishing her last work on the subject in 1926. She died in 1932.

Shabanova dedicated her whole life to the cause of children's health and women's rights. She was also a tireless proponent of women's medical education. In 1923, she was honored by the Leningrad Society of Pediatricians and was elected to the Court of Honor by the Union of Doctors of Leningrad.

ACH

PRIMARY SOURCES
Shabanova, Anna Nikolaevna. *Obzor deiatel'nosti detskoi lechebnitsy v Gatchine.* St. Petersburg: Golike, 1887.
———. *K bor'be s khronicheskimi nedugami detei.* St. Petersburg: Suvorin, 1897.

STANDARD SOURCES
Tuve; Uglow 1982.

SHAKESPEAR, DAME ETHEL MARY READER (WOOD) (1871–1946)

British invertebrate paleontologist. Born 17 July 1871 at Biddenham, near Bedford. Educated Bedford High School; Newnham College, Cambridge (Natural Science Tripos, Part I, class 2, 1894; Part II, class 1, 1895); Birmingham University (D.Sc., 1906). Professional experience: Birmingham, research assistant to Charles Lapwirth (1896? to 1906). Died 17 January 1946.

Ethel Wood was born at Biddenham near Bedford, and was educated at Bedford High School, Newnham College, Cambridge, and Birmingham University. She studied under Thomas McKenny Hughes and John Edward Marr at Cambridge and was especially interested in field work. During her college days at Newnham, she was a tennis champion, active in liberal politics, and a fine piano player. At Newnham she met her lifelong friend and colleague, GERTRUDE ELLES. At Marr's request the two geologists conducted a field study on some rocks in the Lake District, which was published in the *Geological Magazine.* The next year they published a more extensive joint work on the project. In 1906, after receiving her doctorate from Birmingham, she married a lecturer in physics there, G. A. Shakespear.

Ethel Wood Shakespear was named Member of the British Empire (1918) and became a Dame of the British Empire (1920) in recognition of her humanitarian service during World War I. She worked with untiring energy on securing adequate pensions for servicemen, and from 1917 to 1926 was a member of the Special Grants Committee of the Ministry of Pensions. Shakespear never really returned to geology after the war and continued her public work, becoming a justice of the peace for Birmingham, and taking an interest in women's rights. She was president of the Birmingham branch of the National Council of Women (1929–1932), the Midland branch of the Women's Electrical Association (1932–1935), and the Birmingham and Midlands branch of the Federation of University Women.

She and her husband left Birmingham in 1922, and

moved to Bromsgrove (Caldwell Hall) where they farmed. She, however, did not give up her outside activities, attending meetings of various organizations as regularly as before. During World War II, her farm duties increased, and her strength was taxed.

After Wood and Elles published their first two papers, Wood published three major works. The first two were published in the *Quarterly Journal of the Geological Society* and were concerned with the graptolite fauna of the Lower Ludlow Formation and the Tarannon series. These works are illustrated by beautiful plates using a technique devised by Lapworth and mastered by Wood. Her last major work was a joint monograph by Wood, Elles, and Lapworth. This work involved clarifying the nomenclature of the graptolites which was in disarray. Although Lapworth was the inspiration for this major project, much of the actual "spade work" was done by Elles and Wood. Wood's two previous papers were especially important in preparing this monographic synthesis.

The Council of the Geological Society recognized the importance of this work and awarded her the Wollaston Fund. She became a Fellow of the Geological Society and was awarded the Murchison Medal in 1920.   JH/MBO

PRIMARY SOURCES
Wood, Ethel. "On the Llandovery and Associated Rocks of
    Conway." *Quarterly Journal of the Geological Society* 52 (1896).
———. "The Lower Ludlow Formation and Its Graptolite
    Fauna." *Quarterly Journal of the Geological Society* 56 (1900).
———. "The Tarannon Series of Tarannon." *Quarterly Journal
    of the Geological Society* 62 (1906).
———. With Elles and Charles Lapworth. *Monograph of British
    Graptolites.* London: Printed for the Palaeontolographical
    Society, 1901–1918.

SECONDARY SOURCES
[Elles, Gertrude L.]. "Dame Ethel Mary Reader Shakespear
    (née Wood)." *Proceedings of the Geological Society of London*
    (1946): xvli–xvii. Obituary notice.
———. *Quarterly Journal of the Geologists Society* 102 (1946): 37,
    38. Obituary notice.
Nature 157 (1946): 256–257. Obituary notice.

STANDARD SOURCES
Newnham Roll; Sarjeant.

SHARP, EMILY KATHARINE (DOORIS) (1846–1935)

Irish/British/U.S. traveler and writer. Born 18 February 1846 in Glasmullagh, Ireland, to Margaret (Dejoynstyn) and John Dooris. Seven siblings. Married Henry James Sharp in 1872. Five children,

two daughters who died young and three sons who survived to adulthood. Died 19 September 1935.

Emily Sharp's contribution to botany is contained in the book *Summer in a Bog.* This book consisted of a collection of botanical topics written in a popular style about the native plants, their habits, and their habitats in the vicinity of London, Madison County, Ohio, where she lived. She also published novels and poems.   JH/MBO

PRIMARY SOURCES
Sharp, Emily Katharine. *Summer in a Bog.* Cincinnati: Stewart
    and Kidd, 1913.

SECONDARY SOURCES
Stuckey, Ronald L. "Emily Katharine (Dooris) Sharp." Unpub-
    lished notes.

SHARP, JANE (fl. 1671)
British midwife. Flourished 1671.

The only clue that we have about Jane Sharp's birth date is that she wrote in 1671 that she had been "a practitioner in the art of midwifery about thirty years." She complained about the inadequacy of female education when she noted that "women cannot attain so rarely to the knowledge of things as many may, who are bred up in universities."

Sharp's *The Midwives' Book; or, The Whole Art of Midwifery Discovered,* went through several editions. It consisted of six parts and discussed anatomy, signs of pregnancy, and postpartum disease. Because she actually wrote a book, Jane Sharp is set apart from most seventeenth-century practitioners. Her book, a practical manual, reflects the state of knowledge in midwifery as well as the restrictions on the medical education of women in England at this time. During the seventeenth century, male midwives were becoming more common, and Sharp's work defends women's dominant role in childbirth and pregnancy care. She insisted that midwifery was a female preserve.   JH/MBO

PRIMARY SOURCES
Sharp, Jane. *The Complete Midwife's Companion; or, The Art of
    Midwifery Improv'd.* London: J. Mansell, 1725.

STANDARD SOURCES
AMS 4–8, B 9, P&B 10–14; *Europa;* Hurd-Mead 1938; Jex-
    Blake.

SHARSMITH, HELEN KATHERINE (1905–1982)

U.S. botanist. Born 26 August 1905 in Oakland, Calif. Married Carl William Sharsmith. Educated University of California (A.B., 1927; M.A., 1928; Ph.D., 1940). Professional experience: high school and junior college teacher (1928–1931); University of California, Berkeley, assistant in botany (1931–1934); Mills College, biology teacher (1936–1937); Carnegie Institution, general assistant, secretary of the division of plant biology (1947–1950); University of California, Berkeley, senior herbarium botanist (1950–1969). Retired 1969. Died 10 November 1982.

Helen Sharsmith was educated in botany at the University of California, Berkeley. She taught botany briefly at Berkeley after she obtained her master's degree and then moved to Mills College to teach until she returned to Berkeley to complete her doctorate. She married Carl W. Sharsmith who was a long-time naturalist at Yosemite Park who later combined this work with teaching as professor of botany at San Jose State University. In the 1940s, she did extensive field research on California wild flowers. She moved to the Carnegie Institution of Washington as the secretary of the division of botany and ended her career as the senior herbarium botanist at the University of California, Berkeley, during which period she published a major book on wild flowers of the San Francisco area. She died at the age of seventy-seven. A number of biographies of her husband have recently appeared.   JH/MBO

PRIMARY SOURCES

Sharsmith, Helen. "Notes on *Navarretia abramsii* of the Polemoniaceae." *American Midland Naturalist* 32, no. 2 (1944): 510–512.

———. "The Native California Species of the Genus Coreopsis Linn." *Madrono* 8 (October 1945): 209–231.

———. "Flora of the Mount Hamilton Range of California." *American Midland Naturalist* 34 (1945): 289–367.

———. "A New Species of Linum from the Coast Ranges of California." *Madrono* 8 (October 1945): 143, 144.

———. *Spring Wildflowers of the San Francisco Bay Region.* Berkeley: University of California Paress, 1965.

SECONDARY SOURCES

Sharsmith, John and Allan Shields, eds. *Climb Every Mountain: A Portrait of Carl Sharsmith.* Mariposa, Calif.: Jerseydale Ranch Press, 1994.

Taxon 32 (May 1983): 346. Obituary notice.

STANDARD SOURCES

AMS 8, B 9; P&B 10–11.

SHATTUCK, LYDIA WHITE (1822–1889)

U.S. botanist, natural history biologist, and chemist. Born 19 June 1822 in East Landaff (now Easton), N.H., to Betsey (Fletcher) and Timothy Shattuck. Five siblings (only one brother survived). Educated Mount Holyoke Seminary, South Hadley, Mass. (graduated 1851). Professional experience: Mount Holyoke, faculty member (1851–1889). Died 2 November 1889.

Raised in a highly religious but tolerant family, Lydia was the fifth child and the first to survive infancy. Her younger brother, William, was a friend with whom she played and hiked in the hills surrounding their New Hampshire farm. From both of her parents she learned a love of nature, and from her own experiences, she learned about the plants surrounding her. After her early schooling, she taught in district schools from 1836 to 1848, when she entered Mount Holyoke Seminary. This institution was founded on the principles of Mary Lyon, who stressed the importance of science in the curriculum. Shattuck paid her own way through Holyoke by working as a domestic.

Shattuck graduated from the seminary with honors and was hired to teach there immediately. She remained at Holyoke for the rest of her life. She was first recognized as a botanist and later as a chemist, being one of the founders of the American Chemical Society. She taught a variety of courses, including algebra, geometry, physiology, natural philosophy, astronomy, and physics. Shattuck became a friend of the Harvard botanist Asa Gray, and invited him to lecture at Holyoke.

Shattuck was a devout Methodist, but had no problem in reconciling her faith with her equally strong belief in evolution. In her lecture notes, she refers to religion as the "human way of looking at Divine actions" (Segal, 497). She believed strongly in the social gospel aspect of Methodism.

It was as a science teacher rather than a research botanist that Lydia Shattuck shone. Although she did research on the classification of plants, she did not publish her results. However, she did teach a generation of women who became active research scientists and science educators. The Mount Holyoke College archives contain many of her papers, including her lecture notes. She described many experiments that she used for her students in the laboratory.

In 1783, Shattuck attended the Anderson School of Natural History on Penikese Island off the coast of Massachusetts. This school, run by Louis Agassiz with the help of his wife, ELIZABETH AGASSIZ, was an important educational institution helping women improve science teaching.

A fine teacher, a curious researcher, and an active professional (she was not only a founder of the ACS, but a corresponding member of the Torrey Botanical Club), her innovations produced such future women scientists as CORNELIA CLAPP. A new chemistry and physics building was named in her honor, but was later demolished, and her name was transferred to a new physics building.   JH/MBO

PRIMARY SOURCES

Shattuck, Lydia White. "Notebooks and other Papers of Lydia Shattuck." South Hadley, Mass.: Mount Holyoke College Archives.

SECONDARY SOURCES

Cole, A. *A Hundred Years of Mount Holyoke College.* New Haven, Conn.: Yale University Press, 1940.

Hooker, H. "Miss Shattuck as a Student and Teacher of Science." In *Memorial of Lydia W. Shattuck*, 25–31. Boston: Beacon Press, 1890.

Shmurak, C., and B. Handler. "Lydia Shattuck: 'A Streak of the Modern.'" *Teaching Education* 3 (1991): 127–131.

STANDARD SOURCES

Grinstein 1997 (article by Philip Duhan Segal); *NAW* (article by C. Haywood).

SHAW, HESTER (1586?–1660)

British midwife. Probably baptised 11 April 1586 in Allhallows parish, London. Father Nicholas Essex, gentleman. Married John Shaw. At least one daughter. Professional experience: Practiced midwifery in London (1610), licensed by Bishop of London before 1634. Buried 18 June 1660.

Little is known about the life of Hester Shaw except that she married John Shaw sometime before 1 April 1610, when her daughter was born. During this period, Peter Chamberlain, the elder, a male midwife, wanted the female midwives under his governance. A Mrs. Shaw and Mrs. Whipp led a petition of sixty midwives opposing the change Chamberlain proposed. Although the petition to the king and to the college of physicians was successful, it did not change the Episcopal licensing.

In 1650, Shaw took both her son-in-law and grandchildren into her house. The controversy had cost her over three thousand pounds in earnings. She published complaints against her clergyman who she said had taken her remaining earnings. She was buried in Allhallows, 18 June 1660.

JH/MBO

PRIMARY SOURCES

Shaw, Hester. *A Plaine Relation of My Sufferings by That Miserable Combustion Which Happened in Tower-Street through the Unhappy Firing of a Great Quantity of Gun-Powder, There the 4 of January 1650: Now Printed That the World May See What Just Cause I Had to Complain of the Injuries Then Done to Me. . . .* London: N.p., 1653.

SECONDARY SOURCES

Aveling, J. H. *The Chamberlens and the Midwifery Forceps.* London: J. & S. Churchill, 1882.

Donnison, Jean. *Midwives and Medical Men.* N.p.: Historical Publications, 1977.

STANDARD SOURCES

DNB Missing Persons; Europa.

SHELDON, JENNIE ARMS (1852–?)

U.S. zoologist and geologist. Born 1852 in Bellows Falls, Vt. to Eunice (Moody) and Albert Arms. Married George Sheldon. Educated Greenfield (Mass.) High School; Massachusetts Institute of Technology (special student, 1877–1879); laboratory of the Boston Society of Natural History (special student of natural sciences, 1879–1880). Professional experience: Museum of the Boston Society of Natural History, staff member (1890–1894). Death date unknown.

From 1877 to 1879, Jennie Arms was a special student at Massachusetts Institute of Technology. In 1879 she participated in a special student laboratory operated by the Boston Society of Natural History. She worked for the Boston Society's museum for four years, from 1890 to 1894. From 1878 to 1897, she taught zoology and geology in Boston and lectured in natural science at Saratoga during the summers from 1886 to 1888. When she married historian and writer George Sheldon in 1897, she gave up her lecturing responsibilities.

Though most of her publications were of a general and popular nature, Sheldon also published scholarly works on the concretions of the Champlain clays of the Connecticut Valley and on the behavior and systematics of insects, as well as an insect book written with Alphaeus Hyatt.   JH/MBO

PRIMARY SOURCES

Sheldon, Jennie Arms. With Alpheus Hyatt. *Insecta.* Boston: D. C. Heath & Co. 1893.

———. *Concretions from the Champlain Clays of the Connecticut Valley.* Boston: N.p., 1900.

———. With George Sheldon. *Newly Exposed Geological Features within the Old '8000' Acre Grant.* New York: Hart & von Arx, printers, 1903.

STANDARD SOURCES

AMS 2–5; Woman's Who's Who of America.

SHEPARDSON, MARY (THYGESON)
(1906–1997)

U.S. anthropologist. Born 26 May 1906 in St. Paul, Minn. One sister. Married Dwight Shepardson in 1943. Educated Stanford University (A.B., 1929; M.A., 1956); University of California, Berkeley (Ph.D., 1960). Professional experience: National Science Foundation, fellow in anthropology (1960–1961); National Institute of Mental Health Research Association of the University of Chicago (from 1961); Mills College, instructor (1960–?); San Francisco State University, professor to professor emerita (196?–1977). Honors and memberships: Anthropological Association, Fellow; Ethnological Association, Fellow. Died 30 March 1997 in Palo Alto, Calif.

Although Mary Shepardson published extensively in anthropology both before and after she earned her doctorate, biographical information on her is scarce. She earned her first two degrees at Stanford University but did not receive her master's degree until twenty-seven years after her A.B. degree. After her master's degree, it took only four years at the university of California at Berkeley for her to complete her doctorate. Shepardson also studied at the Sorbonne and the London School of Economics.

Shepardson's research interests were on acculturation, social organization, and comparative politics. She did field work in the Southwest, concentrating on the Navajo. She was particularly interested in methods of handling dispute cases. She taught anthropology at Mills College, and retired in 1977 as professor emerita from San Francisco State University. After retirement she wrote a memoir on her fieldwork among the Navajo. She died in Palo Alto, California, at the age of ninety after a long illness.   JH/MBO

PRIMARY SOURCES

Shepardson, Mary. *The Jemez Pueblo of Unshagi, New Mexico, with Notes on the Earlier Excavations at "Amoxiumqua" and Giusewa.* Albuquerque: University of New Mexico Press, 1938.
———. "The Symmetry of Abstract Design with Special Reference to Ceramic Decoration." Contributions of American Anthropology and History, no. 47. Washington, D.C.: Carnegie Institution of Washington, 1948.
———. *Ceramics for the Archaeologist.* Published in Carnegie Institution of Washington Publication, 609. Washington, D.C.: Carnegie Institution of Washington, 1956.
———. *Navajo Ways in Government: A Study in Political Process.* American Anthropological Association, memoir 96. Menasha, Wisc.: American Anthropological Association, 1963.
———. *Beginnings of Ceramic Industrialization: An Example from the Oaxaca Valley.* Washington, D.C.: Carnegie Institution of Washington, 1963. Revision of thesis, University of California, Berkeley.
———. *The Navajo Mountain Community: Social Organization and Kinship Terminology.* Berkeley: University of California Press, 1970.
———. With others. Suffragists Oral History Project. *Transcripts of Oral History Project, 1959–1974* (inclusive). Held in Schlesinger Library, Radcliffe College.

SECONDARY SOURCES

"Mary Thygeson Shepardson." *San Francisco Chronicle,* 4 April 1977.
"Mary Thygeson Shepardson." *American Anthropological Association News,* September–October, 1997. Obituary notice.

STANDARD SOURCES
AMS S&B 10–13.

SHEPS, MINDEL (CHERNIACK) (1913–1973)

Canadian/U.S. biostatistician. Born 20 May 1913 in Winnipeg, Manitoba, Canada. Naturalized U.S. citizen. Married Cecil George Sheps (1937). One child. Educated University of Manitoba (M.D., 1936); University of North Carolina (M.P.H., 1950). Professional experience: government of Saskatchewa, secretary health service planning commission (1944–1946); North Carolina College, Durham, director student health service (1950–1952); visiting lecturer, North Carolina School of Public Health (1948–1953); Simmons College, special lecturer community health organization (1953–1954); Harvard, school of public health, research associate in biostatistics (1954–1957); assistant professor of preventive medicine (1957–1960); University of Pittsburgh, associate research professor of biostatistics (1960–1961), research professor (1961–1965); Columbia University, school of public health and administrative medicine, professor (from 1965). Concurrent experience: Beth Israel Hospital, consultant (1958–1961); Lemuel Shattuck Hospital, consultant (1959–1961). Died 1973.

Equipped with a Canadian medical degree and a master's in public health from North Carolina, Mindel Sheps's career evolved from the directorship of the public health service in Durham, North Carolina, to professor of biostatistics at Columbia University. She was a member of the Biometrics Society, the Public Health Association, the Statistics Association, the Teachers of Preventive Medicine, the Endocrine Society, the Population Association, the Society of Pharmacology, and the New York Academy of Science. Shelps researched demography, mathematical models, fertility studies, epidemiology, and clinical trials.   JH/MBO

PRIMARY SOURCES
Sheps, Mindel C., ed. With Jeanne Clare Ridley. *Symposium on Research Issues in Public Health and Population Change. Public*

Health and Population Change: Current Research Issues. Pittsburgh: University of Pittsburgh Press, [1965?].

———. *Mathematical Models of Conception and Birth.* Chicago: University of Chicago Press, 1973.

SECONDARY SOURCES
Notes in Schlesinger Library, Radcliffe College.

STANDARD SOURCES
AMS P&B 10–11, S&B 12.

SHERBOURNE, MARGARET DOROTHEA (WILLIS) (1791–1846)

British botanist. Born 3 October 1791 in Prescot, Lancastershire. Died 6 November 1846 in Prescot.

Little information is available on Margaret Sherbourne other than that she was an avid plant collector. She was the first to collect the flower *Sherbournia foliosa* in England.   JH/MBO

SECONDARY SOURCES
Willis, Margaret. *Back Gardens: A Survey Made among Tenants in Houses in the County of London.* London: County Council, Architects Deptartment, [1960].
Sherbourne's letters are at Kew Gardens.

SECONDARY SOURCES
Curtis's Botanical Magazine, Dedications, 1827–1927 69 (1843): 63–64.
Hadfield, M., et al. *British Gardeners.* London: Zwemmer/ Condé Nast, 1980. 261. Includes a portrait.

SHERIF, CAROLYN (WOOD) (1922–1982)

U.S. psychologist. Born 26 June 1922 in Loogootee, Ind. Married Muzafer Sherif (1945). Three children, Sue, Joan, and Ann. Educated Purdue University (B.S., 1943); State University of Iowa (M.A., 1944); University of Texas (Ph.D. in psychology, 1961). Professional experience: University of Iowa, assistant psychologist (1943–1944); Audience Research, Inc., assistant to research director (1944–1945); Princeton University, assistant to M. Sherif (1945–1947); University of Oklahoma, researcher and writer (1949–1958); Instructional Group Relations, researcher (1959–1965); Pennsylvania State University, visiting associate professor (1965–1966), associate professor (1966–1969), professor (from 1970). Died 1982.

Carolyn Sherif's career depended on that of her husband, social psychologist and author Muzafer Sherif. Before her marriage she had earned a master's degree and had a position at the University of Iowa as an assistant psychologist. After her marriage, she moved to Princeton, New Jersey, where Muzafer was a U.S. State Department fellow. In Princeton, she served as her husband's assistant. In 1949 the couple moved to Oklahoma, where Muzafer was a research professor. During this time, Carolyn both conducted research and wrote. In 1958–1959, Muzafer was a visiting research professor at the University of Texas, and Carolyn probably worked on her doctoral degree from that university. In 1965, the year after she received her doctoral degree, the couple moved to Pennsylvania, where Muzafer became a distinguished visiting professor. At that time Carolyn moved up the ranks at Pennsylvania State University, becoming a full professor in 1970. She held several concurrent positions, including consulting assistant professor, University of Oklahoma Medical School (1963–1965), and associate professor of sociology (1963–1965). She was a visiting professor of psychology and sociology at Cornell University (1969–1970).

Sherif was a member of the American Psychological Association and the American Sociological Association. Her research was on group and intergroup processes, attitudes, social judgment, and adolescence. She was also interested in methodology.   JH/MBO

PRIMARY SOURCES
Sherif, Carolyn Wood. With Muzafer Sherif. *Groups in Harmony and Tension.* New York: Harper, 1953; New York: Octagon Books, 1966.
———. *Reference Groups: Exploration into Conformity and Deviation of Adolescents.* New York: Harper, 1964; Nagoya: Kyoto University, 1968.
———. *Attitude and Attitude Change.* Philadelphia: W. B. Saunders, 1965.
———. *Problems of Youth: Transition to Adulthood in a Changing World.* Chicago: Aldine, 1965.

STANDARD SOURCES
AMS S&B 10–13; O'Connell and Russo.

SHERMAN, ALTHEA ROSINA (1853–1943)

U.S. ornithologist. Born 1853 in National, Iowa. Two siblings. Educated college as art teacher. Died 1943.

Althea Rosina Sherman did not become involved in scientific ornithology until she was almost fifty years old. College educated as an art teacher, she scuttled her plans to become a professional artist and returned home to care for her elderly parents. Her general interest in nature became scientific in the early part of the twentieth century. After the death of her parents, she began to conduct serious research on the nesting biology of birds. Her artistic training helped her, as she recorded detailed observations. Her laboratory was her "Iowa dooryard," where she became particularly interested in the life history of cavity-nesting birds such as woodpeckers.

Sherman's location in Iowa was especially hospitable for bird observations because this former prairie land contained a variety of habitats. Many species of birds nested there year after year. An astute observer, Sherman was diligent in her work. She joined the American Ornithologists' Union as an associate in 1907 in order to keep abreast of ornithological research. In 1912, she was elected a member. She attended scientific meetings and presented papers and exhibited her bird art. One of her best-known studies was on the chimney swift. In order to attract swifts to her property she had a twenty-eight-foot tower built. It had an artificial chimney inside with windows permitting observations of the swifts. She observed them from 1918 to 1936 and carefully documented their activities.

Though it might seem as if Althea Sherman was in an ideal situation to work on her research projects, she felt that the many distractions of living in the country kept her away from the work she loved. One of her worst problems came from sharing the ownership of the house with her domineering and miserly older sister, Amelia, who refused to modernize the homestead. Althea claimed that she would have left if it were not for the chance to study the birds.

JH/MBO

PRIMARY SOURCES

Sherman, Althea. "At the Sign of the Northern Flicker." *Wilson Bulletin* 22 (1910): 135–171.
———. "Nest Life of the Screech Owl." *Auk* 28 (1911): 155–168.
———. "Experiments in Feeding Hummingbirds During Seven Summers." *Wilson Bulletin* 25, no. 4 (December 1913): 459–468; reprinted in *Smithsonian Annual Report* 1913.
———. *Birds of an Iowa Dooryard.* Ed. F. J. Pierce. Boston: Christopher Pub. House, 1952.

SECONDARY SOURCES

Bonta, Marcia. "The Chimney Swift Lady." *Bird Watcher's Digest* (March-April 1985): 36–40.
Taylor, H. J. "Iowa's Woman Ornithologist: Althea Rosina Sherman, 1853–1943." *Iowa Bird Life* 13 (1943): 19–35.

STANDARD SOURCES

AMS 3–7; *Uneasy Careers* (article by Marianne G. Ainley).

SHERMAN, IRENE CASE (1894–?)

U.S. psychiatrist. Born 7 October 1894 in Peoria, Ill. Married (1919). Educated University of Chicago (Ph.B., 1916; Ph.D. in psychology, 1924); Rush Medical School, Chicago (1932). Profes-

sional experience: Children's Memorial Hospital, Chicago, psychologist (1924–1928); American Association of Museums, investigator (1925–1926); Northwestern University Medical School, psychologist (1926–1928); George Washington University, lecturer (1928–1929); Rush Medical College, Chicago, instructor (1929–1931); Frances Willard Hospital, instructor (1931–1932); Psychiatric College of Medicine, Ill., instructor (1934–1937), associate (1937–1942), assistant professor (1942–1952), associate professor (1952–1955); Emergency Clinic, Associate Professor (from 1955). Death date unknown.

First a psychologist, then a psychiatrist, Irene Case Sherman had a variety of positions. In 1934 she started her climb up the academic ladder. Her career took an interesting turn when she concurrently became assistant alienist (hypnotist) in the Department of Public Welfare, Illinois, from 1941 to 1949. She was also acting chief of the mental hygiene section of the Chicago Board of Health from 1949 to 1957.

Sherman's special research interest was in the suggestibility of normal and defective children. She was a member of the Psychiatric Society, the American Medical Association, and the Illinois Psychiatric Society.

JH/MBO

PRIMARY SOURCES

Sherman, Irene Case. *The Suggestibility of Normal and Mentally Defective Children.* Baltimore: Williams and Wilkins, [1924?].
———. With others. "The Behavior of the Museum Visitor." *Publications of the American Association of Museums,* new ser. 5 (1928).
———. With Mandel Sherman. *The Process of Human Behavior.* London: Williams and Norgate, Ltd., [1930].

STANDARD SOURCES

AMS 5–8, B 9, P&B 10–11; *Psychological Register,* vol. 3, 1932.

SHERRILL, MARY LURA (1888–1968)

U.S. chemist. Born 14 July 1888 in Salisbury, N.C. Educated Randolph-Macon Women's College (A.B., 1909); University of Chicago (A.M., 1911; Ph.D., 1923). Professional experience: Randolph-Macon Women's College, instructor (1909–1916), adjunct professor (1917–1918); North Carolina College for Women, associate professor (1918–1920); Edgewood Arsenal, associate chemist (1920–1921); Mount Holyoke College, assistant professor (1921–1924), associate professor (1924–1931), professor (1931–1954), emerita professor (from 1954). Honors and memberships: University of North Carolina, honorary D.Sc. (1948); Garvan Medal of Chemical Society (1947). Died 1968.

Mary Lura Sherrill earned her doctoral degree from the University of Chicago just before she was promoted to associate professor at Mount Holyoke College. She spent the latter part of her academic career in this institution. Her achievements were rewarded when she was selected for the prestigious Garvan Medal of the Chemical Society and also for an honorary degree at the University of North Carolina. She became a Fellow of the Committee on Relief for Belgium of the Educational Foundation in 1928–1929 and a Berliner Fellow of the American Association of University Women. During World War II, she was a civilian with the Office of Scientific Research and Development, and the Committee on Medical Resources.

Sherrill's research was chiefly in organic chemistry. She worked on organic, unsaturated hydrocarbons and olefins and diolefins. She also worked on infrared absorption of unsaturated hydrocarbons, quinazoline derivatives, and 1-diethylamino-5-aminohexane.

JH/MBO

STANDARD SOURCES
AMS 4–8, P 9, P&B 10; Grinstein (1993); Shearer and Shearer (1997).

SHIELDS, MARGARET CALDERWOOD (1883–?)

U.S. physicist. Born 1883 in St. Johnsbury, Vt. Educated Mount Holyoke College (A.B., 1905); University of Chicago (Ph.D., 1917). Professional experience: Mount Holyoke, instructor in physics (1907–1911), associate professor (1918–1925); Wellesley College, instructor (1911–1914); Wilson College, professor (1925–1927). Death date unknown.

Two years after physicist Margaret Shields received her bachelor's degree from Mount Holyoke she became an instructor of physics at her alma mater. She left Holyoke to become an instructor at Wellesley. Her tenure at Wellesley was short, because she went to the University of Chicago to work on her doctoral degree. After obtaining this degree she returned to Holyoke, where she was an associate professor. She became a full professor at Wilson College for two years, but no information is available after she left this post in 1927. She was not included in later editions of *American Men of Science*.

JH/MBO

PRIMARY SOURCES
Shields, Margaret. "A Determination of the Ratio of the Specific Heats of Hydrogen at 18° and −190°." Ph.D. diss., University of Chicago, 1917. A private edition distributed by the University of Chicago libraries.

STANDARD SOURCES
AMS 3–4.

SHINN, MILICENT WASHBURN (1858–1940)

U.S. psychologist. Born 15 April 1858 in Niles, Calif. Educated University of California, Berkeley (A.B., 1880; Ph.D., 1898). Professional experience: public schools, teacher (1875–1876; 1881–1882); San Francisco Commercial Herald, editor (1879–1881); Overland Monthly, editor (1883–1894). Died 1940 of heart disease.

Milicent Shinn entered the University of California, Berkeley, at age sixteen, but left to teach and earn money to continue school. After receiving her bachelor's degree, she left school again to teach and then to become an editor, contributor, and writer of prose and poetry for the *San Francisco Commercial Herald* and the *Overland Monthly*. In 1894 she sold her interest in the *Overland Monthly* to enroll in the doctoral program at the University of California.

Shinn is known for her systematic and detailed study of child development. While she worked on her doctorate, she kept a record of the physical and mental development of a young niece. Her published notes on this study formed the basis of her thesis. Her observations were especially important, for they were the only such systematic observations published in English at that time. The reports were later published in a popular form, *The Biography of a Baby*.

After she published this book she retired to the family ranch and was involved in community work on prohibition, forest conservation, and women's suffrage. Her research on mental and physical development included the development of the senses in infancy, development of instinctive movement, primary education, and development of memory and association in infants.

Shinn was involved in advisory council educational congresses, the Columbia exposition of 1893, and was chair of the child study congress of the Midwinter Fair, San Francisco, in 1894. She was a member of the Women's Anthropological Society and the American Association for the Advancement of Science.

In her short working career as a psychologist, she became an authority on child psychology and innovator of the "diary method" of data analysis. She exemplified a pioneer woman psychologist who had great promise and potential but who dropped out after an initial significant contribution and was scarcely heard from again.

JH/MBO

PRIMARY SOURCES
Shinn, Milicent. *Notes on the Development of a Child*. Vol. I. Berkeley: The University Press, 1893–1899.
———. *The Biography of a Baby*. Boston: Houghton, Mifflin and Company, 1900.
———. *Notes on the Development of a Child*. Vol. 2. *The Development of the Senses in the First Three Years of Childhood*. Berkeley: The University Press, 1907.

————. Correspondence (1890–1938) Lick Observatory Archives, University of California, Santa Cruz.

Some of Shinn's letters are also held by the California Historical Society.

SECONDARY SOURCES

Scarborough, E., and L. Furumoto. *Untold Lives: The First Generation of the American Women Psychologists.* New York: Columbia University Press, 1987.

STANDARD SOURCES

AMS 1–6; Bailey; *NAW*; Rossiter 1982; Siegel and Finley; Stevens and Gardner; Vare and Ptacek.

SHIRLEY, MARY MARGARET (1899–?)

U.S. psychologist. Born 7 February 1899 in Orleans, Ind. Educated University of Indiana (A.B., 1922); University of Minnesota (A.M.; Ph.D., 1927). Professional experience: public school teacher (1918–1924); University of Minnesota, psychologist (1926–1929), instructor of child welfare (1927–1929), assistant professor (1929–1932); Randolph-Macon Women's College, professor (1932–1933); National Council Parent Educators, Spelman Fellow (1933–1934); Smith College, research fellow in social work (1938–1943); University of Indiana, assistant professor in psychology (from 1943). Death date unknown.

Psychologist Mary Margaret Shirley returned to her home state of Indiana after spending time in Minnesota, Georgia, and Massachusetts. In addition to her regular positions, she held concurrent positions at the University of Indiana (assistant professor of psychology, 1943); Institute of Child Welfare (assistant professor and fellow, 1939–1940); Children's Aid Society in Pennsylvania (clinical psychologist, 1941–1942); and Wellesley College (lecturer, 1943).

Shirley was a member of the Society for Research in Child Development, the Orthopsychiatric Association, the American Psychological Association, and the Society of Clinical Psychologists. She worked on motor sequences, intellectual and personality manifestations during the first two years, methods of teaching psychology, the impact of family life on children's personalities, and casework and the work of social agencies.   JH/MBO

PRIMARY SOURCES

Shirley, Mary Margaret. *The First Two Years: a Study of Twenty-Five Babies.* Minneapolis: University of Minnesota Press, [1931–1933?].

STANDARD SOURCES

AMS 5–7; *Psychological Register,* vol. 3, 1932.

SHISHKINA, OLGA VASIL'YEVNA (1916–1983)

Russian marine geologist and geochemist. Born 24 May 1916 in Moscow. Educated Mendeleyev Moscow Chemico-Technology Institute (1940); USSR Academy of Sciences, candidate thesis (1955); doctorate (1970). Ordzhonikidze Works, engineering technician (1940–1947); Caspian Commission of the USSR Academy of Sciences, junior scientific associate (1947–1948); Shirshov Institute of Oceanology, researcher (1949–1983). Died 17 April 1983.

Olga Vasil'yevna's doctoral dissertation foretold the direction that her career would take. This work, on the silty waters of the ocean, pointed out new directions in marine geochemistry. She published more than one hundred papers, including two monographs. In these papers she studied the composition of the silty waters of open ocean sediment and marginal and closed seas. She investigated saline composition, ion diffusion, exchange processes at the water-bottom interface, and many other problems.

Her colleagues praised her ability to distill the essence from a huge fund of facts and link the vital ingredients together in a meaningful way. Young scientists often used her for an advisor.   CK/MBO

PRIMARY SOURCES

Shishkina, Olga Vasil'yevna. *Geokhimi'i'a morskikh i okeanicheskikh ilovykh vod* (Geochemistry of Sea and Ocean Silty Waters). In Russian. Moscow: Nauka, 1972.

SECONDARY SOURCES

Colleagues of the Shirshov Institute of Oceanology, USSR Academy of Sciences. "In Memory of Olga Vasil'yevna Shishkina (May 24, 1916–April 17, 1983)." *American Geophysical Union* 23, no. 4 (1984): 544.

SHORT, JESSIE MAY (1873–1947)

U.S. statistician and mathematician. Born 5 June 1873 in College Springs, Iowa. Educated Beloit College (A.B., 1900); Carleton College (A.M., 1911); University of Chicago (fellow, 1914–1916); University of California (1925). Professional experience: high school in Minnesota, principal (1901–1909); Carleton College, instructor in mathematics (1909–1914); dean of women (1911–1914), Rollins College, instructor (1917–1918); National Workmen's Compensation Service Bureau, office supervisor (1918–1920); Reed College, instructor in mathematics (1920–1926), assistant professor (from 1926). Honors and memberships: Mathematical Association Astronomical Society, Fellow. Died 1947.

Jessie Short was born in the Midwest and spent the early part of her career there. In 1920, she moved to Oregon, where she taught at Reed College. She was active in political affairs in Oregon: she was a member of its board of education from

1934 and was involved in a cost-of-living survey for the Housing Administration of Portland. She was also interested in teachers' salaries compared with living costs and general community standards, and women in the teaching profession. Her research was on mathematics and photographic distortion of the reflector field. JH/MBO

PRIMARY SOURCES
Short, Jessie M. "Cost of Living Survey." *Reed College Bulletin* 4, no. 1 (January 1925): 2–16.

STANDARD SOURCES
AMS 3–7.

SHOVE, ROSAMUND FLORA (ca. 1878–1954)

British botanist. Born ca. 1878. Never married. Educated Girton College, Cambridge (1889–1896). Professional experience: Maria Grey Training College, Isleworth, Middlesex (1921–1938). Died 17 October 1954 in Richmond, Surrey.

Rosamund Shove attended Cambridge long before it granted degrees to women. She was trained in research by A. C. Seward. She published a long, detailed paper in *Annals of Science* in 1900, in which she described the anatomical structure of the stem of *Angiopteris evecta*. In this paper, she included two plates. Her professional career consisted of seventeen years of science teaching in the schools followed by twenty years of university and training college teaching in biology and hygiene.

From 1943 to 1947 Shove served on the council of the Linnean Society. In 1937 she became honorary secretary of the School Nature Study Union and edited its journal, *School Nature Study,* from 1940–1953. A faithful member of a volunteer panel that viewed natural history films from many sources, she contributed many film and book reviews to *School Nature Study.* She also produced illustrated articles based on her observations, including a life history of a pink-flowered weed, *Oxalis.* Her collection of plants was accepted for the Royal Botanic Gardens, Kew.

Shove died after a long illness in the hospital at the age of seventy-six. She remained interested in science and intended to return to its practice until a few months before her death. JH/MBO

PRIMARY SOURCES
Shove, Rosamund F. "On the Structure of the Stem of *Angiopteris evecta.*" *Annals of Botany* 55 (December 1900): 497–525.

SECONDARY SOURCES
Munro, Madeline. *Nature* 174 (1954): 995–996. Obituary notice.
School Nature Study 50 (1955): 1–2. Obituary notice.

STANDARD SOURCES
Desmond.

SHTERN, LINA SOLOMONOVNA (1878–1968)

Russian physiologist. Born 26 August 1878 in Libava, now Liepaia, Latvia, to Elena and Solomon Shtern, a businessman. Six siblings. Educated at local gymnasium; Geneva University. Professional experience: University of Geneva, professor; Department of physiology of second Moscow Institute, director; Institute of Physiology of the Soviet Academy of Sciences, director; department of physiology of Biophysics Institute of the Soviet Academy of Sciences, director. Honors and memberships: Soviet Academy of Sciences and Soviet Academy of Medical Sciences, academician; State Prize (1943); University of Geneva, honorary doctorate. Died 7 March 1968 in Moscow.

Lina Solomonovna Shtern, born in Libava in 1878, was the daughter and oldest child of an enterprising but not always successful businessman. Jewish in origin, the family did not observe religious practices.

In 1888, Lina and her sister Anna entered the city *gymnasium,* where Lina became interested in literature and history. She also excelled in natural history and languages. In 1895, she graduated from the gymnasium and decided to continue her education. At that time, her ambition was to become a doctor, and she applied for admission to the medical department of Moscow University. However, the competition was great, places were few, and Shtern had the disadvantage of being Jewish.

Failing Moscow, Shtern enrolled instead in the medical department of the University of Geneva in 1898. There she attended lectures by Jean Louis Provost, a leading physiologist, and became interested in his work, performing several experiments in his laboratory. In 1903 she obtained her medical diploma. However, at that time faculty posts were not given to women, and Shtern went to Moscow to take the state examinations that would allow her to practice medicine in Russia.

Shtern was looking for a post when unexpectedly she received a letter from Provost inviting her to return to the department of physiology at the University of Geneva as an assistant. During the next fourteen years, Shtern did important work, much of it in conjunction with the Italian physiologist F. Battelli, and when, in 1917, the department of physiological chemistry was created, she was appointed its director.

Shtern had always followed events in Russia closely and sympathized with the Revolution. In 1924, she accepted an invitation from A. N. Bakh, an old friend and former revolutionary, later academician, to return to Russia to direct the department of physiology at the Second Moscow Medical

Institute. In addition, in 1929, she was appointed director of the newly created Institute of Physiology of the Soviet Academy of Sciences. The years that followed were busy and productive ones for Shtern. She added teaching to her research, joined the Communist Party in 1938, and, in 1939, she became the first woman to be elected an academician of the Soviet Academy of Sciences.

In 1948, Shtern's life suddenly changed. At this time there was tremendous upheaval in all biological sciences resulting from the temporary triumph of Trofim Lysenko's so-called "Michurinist biology," acceptance of which became ideologically necessary. This, combined with a deeply antisemitic campaign against "internationalism," "cosmopolitanism," and other code words signifying various forms of Western influence, created a wave of purges in which many scientists lost their jobs or were sent to the Gulag. Suspect in any case because of her international associations and Jewish descent, Shtern was not spared. Her work was attacked in a book entitled *Against Universalism and Oversimplification in Medicine.* Other criticisms followed, and Shtern was dismissed from both her positions.

Shtern spent the years between 1949 and 1954 in the Gulag and in exile at Dzhambul, Kazakhstan. In 1954, after Stalin's death, she returned to Moscow, where she became head of the department of physiology at the Institute of Biophysics of the Soviet Academy of Sciences. She remained there until her death in 1968.

In Russia, Shtern is considered to be one of the founders of modern chemical physiology. She conducted research on the chemical basis of physiological processes in humans and animals and on such diseases as tubercular meningitis and encephalitis. Her earliest research concerned biological oxidation. She was also interested in respiration of the skin. Experiments with curare led her to believe that a barrier existed between the blood and the brain and also between other organs. Much of her work was devoted to the pursuit of this line of inquiry. Further, she postulated the existence of biologically active by-products of metabolism which play a role in various functions of the organism, thus paving the way for the later discovery of neuropeptides, endorphins, and similar chemicals. In 1943, she received a State Prize for her work on the bloodbrain barrier.

Shtern also worked on electric impulse methods for stopping fibrillation of the heart and methods for treating shock. Between 1902 and 1963, she published more than five hundred papers on various aspects of physiology.   ACH

PRIMARY SOURCES

Shtern, Lina Solomonovna. "Neposredstvennoe khimicheskoe vozdeistvie na nervnye tsentry: teoreticheskoe obosnovanie i prakticheskie rezultaty primeneniia." *Vestnik AN SSSR* 7 (1948): 39–48.

———. *Neposredstvennaia pitatel'naia sreda organov i tkanei.* Moscow: USSR AS, 1960.

———. *Gisto-gematicheskie bar'ery. Institut biologicheskoi fiziki.* Moscow: Akademiia nauk SSSR, 1961. Concerned with the blood/brain barrier.

SECONDARY SOURCES

"Akademik L. S. Shtern." *Vestnik AN SSSR* 5 (1968): 118. Obituary.

Rosin, Iakov A., and Viktor B. Malkin. *Lina Solomonovna Shtern, 1878–1968.* Moscow: "Nauka," 1987.

SHUBNIKOVA, OL'GA MIKHAILOVNA (1884–1955)

Russian mineralogist. Born 7 July 1884 in Moscow. Father Mikhail D. Lebedev, a physician. Several siblings. Married Aleksei M. Shubnikov. Educated at local gymnasium; Moscow Pedagogical Courses; Moscow Higher Women's Courses; Moscow University (Ph.D., 1936; D.Sc., 1952). Professional experience: Higher Women's Courses, lecturer; Shaniavskii People's University; Sverdlovsk College of Mines; Sverdlovsk University; Leningrad Mineralogical Museum, staff; Institute of Geological Sciences of the Soviet Academy of Sciences in Moscow, staff. Died 16 November 1955.

Ol'ga Mikhailovna Shubnikova was born into the family of a well-known and enlightened doctor, Mikhail D. Lebedev, in 1884. She had several brothers and their Moscow home was a gathering place for revolutionary young people.

In 1901, Shubnikova finished the *gymnasium* and entered the Moscow Pedagogical Courses. At the same time, she directed a Sunday school for working women. Later, she completed the Higher Women's Courses and stayed on to work in the faculty of mineralogy and crystallography taught by the geologist Vladimir I. Vernadskii. In this period (1912–1920), she also taught in schools and at the Shaniavskii People's University.

In 1913 Shubnikova passed the state examinations at Moscow University in the natural history section of the physical-mathematical department as an external student. In 1920, she and her husband Aleksei Mikhailovich Shubnikov, also a geologist, went to work in Sverdlovsk. There she taught mineralogy and crystallography at the College of Mines and the university, but in 1925, on the invitation of the Academy of Sciences, she moved with her family to Leningrad to take up a position in the Mineralogical Museum. In 1934, Shubnikova went to Moscow to work in the Institute of Geological Sciences of the Academy of Sciences.

Shubnikova was greatly influenced in her choice of career by Vernadskii, who was head of the department of mineralogy and crystallography at Moscow University. At Sverdlovsk, Shubnikova taught mineralogy and helped organize a laboratory, a museum, and a science library.

Later, in Moscow, Shubnikova and her husband developed a statistical method for studying the forms of crystals. She wrote a number of general articles about various minerals, including augite, adular, tantalite, and schungite. One of her greatest contributions was the compilation of a comprehensive bibliography of the rapidly expanding literature on mineralogy in the form of a card index. This contained, by 1950, over three hundred thousand entries, and formed a basis for the monograph *Minerals of the USSR*. She also periodically published surveys of data on new minerals.

Shubnikova's work was so greatly respected that, in 1936, she received the degree of kandidat without writing a dissertation; in 1952, she became a doctor of geological-mineralogical sciences.

Shubnikova edited many important works published by the Academy of Sciences including the collected works of V. I. Vernadskii and works by A. E. Fersman and F. V. Chukhrov. She was awarded the order of the Red Banner of Labor, the Badge of Honor, and other medals. ACH

PRIMARY SOURCES
Shubnikova, Ol'ga Mikhailovna. *Mineraly redkikh zemel' i ikh diagnostika.* [Moscow?]: 1945.

SECONDARY SOURCES
Petrovskaia, N. V. "Pamiati O.M. Shubnikovoi: k 100 letiiu so dnia rozhdeniia." *Izvestiia Akademii nauk SSSR, seriia geologicheskaia* 5 (1985): 127–128.

SHULGA-NESTERENKO, MARIA I. (1891–1964)

Soviet geologist and paleontologist. Born 1891 in Kiev to a soldier father and a housewife mother. Married first Nesterenko, then Chernov. Educated Kiev gymnasium; Highest Women's Courses (1919); Paleontological Institute (defended dissertation successfully). Professional experience: Moscow University, Department of Geology, assistant professor; Moscow Institute of Geological Exploration, assistant professor (1930–1938); Paleontological Institute, researcher (1938–1960?).

Born and raised in Kiev, Maria I. Shulga was a Ukranian like M. V. PAVLOVA, but after she entered the Highest Women's Courses, her life was connected with Moscow. Her early professional positions were teaching. She taught in the *gymnasia* of Kiev in 1917, but once she studied in Moscow, she became an assistant professor in the geology department of Moscow University. The Moscow Institute of Geological Exploration was established in 1930, and Maria worked there as an assistant professor. She taught paleontology, a special course (Methods of Paleontological Research) she planned herself, and worked with postgraduate students.

However, she left her teaching career in 1938 when she was invited to join the Paleontological Institute.

Shulga was something of a scientific prodigy. Her first geological work, questioning the periodicity of glaciers, was written when she was only in the eighth grade. She published her first paleontological work (on the parapronorites of the Urals) as her diploma work in 1916. Although she continued to study Permian ammoneis, she found that she was no longer interested in simple descriptions, but in theoretical questions. She published one work in 1925, *About Spiral ammoneis* and another in 1926, *Inner Structure of Shell Ammoneis* (both in Russian).

During this period, she took part in expeditions led by A. A. Chernov as a paleontologist. Chernov advised her to study bryozoans rather than ammoneis because of their importance for stratigraphy; from 1928, all of her works were on bryozoans. At that time V. P. Nehoroshev and A. I. K. Nikiforova began to use the new microscopic method to study bryozoans. Shulga became interested in this method, broadened its application, and published an interesting series of works on the data she collected using it.

From 1928 to 1931, Maria was a member of the Geological Committee in the Department of Monographic Work, headed by A. A. Borisyak. In 1937, she was invited to the Paleontological Institute by Borisyak and this determined the direction of her future research. She devoted all of her efforts to a study of the bryozoa. At Borisyak's suggestion she concentrated more on this work and generalized her observations in a monograph, *Lower Permian Bryozoans of the Urals,* which she defended as her doctoral dissertation. She published one work after another, and became universally recognized as the leading specialist on Upper Paleozoic bryozoans.

Beginning in 1949, Shulga's works were published in five volumes of the Paleontological Institute's works. The last large monograph, *Carboniferous Bryozoans of the Russian Platform,* came out in 1955. Her last two works were small articles published in 1960. CK/MBO

PRIMARY SOURCES
Shulga-Nesterenko, M. I. *Lower Permian Bryozoan of the Urals* (In English.) Vol. 5. Moscow: Academy of Sciences of the USSR, Institute of Paleontology, 1941. Descriptions of new species and varieties.
———. *Funktsionalnoe, filogeneticheskoe i stratigraficheskoi znachenie mikrostruktury skeletnykh tkanei mshanok.* Trudy Paleontologicheskogo Instituta 23. Moscow: Rossiyskaya Akademiya Nauk, Paleontologicheskiy Institut, 1949. A detailed study of the microstructure of bryozoans with special reference to the function and significance of the capillar tube system present in the skeleton.
———. Trudy Paleontologicheskogo Instituta 32. Moscow: Rossiyskaya Akademiya Nauk, Paleontologicheskiy Institut,

1951. A monographic study of fenestellids from Carboniferous deposits of the Russian platform region.

———. *Novye nizhnepermskie mshanki Priuralya.* Trudy Paleontologicheskogo Instituta 37. Moscow: Rossiyskaya Akademiya Nauk, Paleontologicheskiy Institut, 1952. Description of bryozoans, most of which are new species from the lower Permian deposits of the Ural region.

———. *Kamennougolnye mshanki Russkoi platformy.* Trudy Paleontologicheskogo Instituta 57. Moscow: Rossiyskaya Akademiya Nauk, Paleontologicheskiy Institut, 1955. A monographic systematic study of bryozoans from Carboniferous localities of the Russian platform.

STANDARD SOURCES
Nalivkin.

SIBELIUS, HELENA (1905–)
Finnish physician. Born 24 April 1905 in Finland to a mother from St. Petersburg and a father, Harry Fabritius, from Finland. One surviving sister. Married Jussi Sibelius (1929). Educated University of Helsinki (B.S. in chemistry, 1928; M.D., 1947); specialist certificate in psychiatry (1950). Professional experience: a chemistry laboratory, Helsinki, Finland, researcher; National Board of Health, medical counselor (1952–1968).

Harry Fabritius, Helena's father, interested his daughter in the study of medicine. She went with him to the hospitals and even was allowed to view autopsies being performed. Her interest in medicine was also piqued by a woman who was one of the first female physicians in Finland and who lived in their home. When she was five years old, her father was granted a scholarship to study abroad for three years. The family first went to Berlin, where Helena entered a German school. In 1912, they moved to Vienna, where her father continued his studies (including the lectures of Sigmund Freud) and where she entered an Austrian school. After returning to Finland in 1913, she was entered in a Finnish-language school.

When it came time to decide on a career, Helena decided to become a physician. Although she was not encouraged by her father, he did not object, so she matriculated at the University of Helsinki. However, at the university she met her future husband, Jussi Sibelius, the composer Jean Sibelius's nephew. They decided that it would be difficult for her to combine marriage and medicine, so she compromised by getting a bachelor's in chemistry. She worked in chemical laboratories for several years.

Jussi Sibelius volunteered for active service in World War II and was killed on 9 March 1940. Helena Sibelius decided to go back to medical school. She was forty-two years old when she obtained her medical degree. After doing psychiatric specialist studies in her father's clinic she received her specialist certification in psychiatry in 1950.

After her father's death in 1948, Sibelius and her mother set up housekeeping together in a new home. She got a position as head of the psychiatric department at the National Board of Health. Her civil-service title was "medical counselor." In this job she was responsible for the development and implementation of hospital and noninstitutional therapy. She was the only woman to hold the post of department chief in the National Board of Health.   KM

PRIMARY SOURCES
"Sibelius, Helena." In Hellstedt, *Autobiographies.*

SICHEL, ELSA MARIE (KEIL) (1906–)
See Keil, Elsa Marie.

SIDGWICK, ELEANOR (BALFOUR) (1845–1936)
British electrochemist. Born 11 March 1845 to Lady Blanche Gascoigne Cecil and James Maitland Balfour. Married Henry Sidgwick (1876). Educated at home; studied mathematics. Professional experience: Newnham College, Michelmas term (1875); Cambridge, honorary treasurer. Honors and memberships: Association for Promotion of Higher Education of Women (1878); Newnham College Association (1879–1920), vice-principal (1880–1882), Governing Body and Council, life member. Died 10 February 1936; buried at Terling, Essex.

Eleanor Balfour married Henry Sidgwick, fellow and later honorary fellow of Trinity College, Cambridge, in 1876. Two years later she became the honorary treasurer for the Association for the Promotion of Higher Education in Cambridge and the next year the previous organization was merged into the Newnham College Association. She remained treasurer of this organization, later Newnham College, until January 1920. She and Henry Sidgwick lived in North Hall from 1880 to 1882, and Eleanor was vice-principal. In 1892 she became principal, still retaining the office of treasurer. In 1894 she and her husband moved into the new Pfeiffer Buildings. As a founder, she was a life member of the Governing Body and Council.

Eleanor Sidgwick was involved in spiritualism, and joined in sessions with Lord Rayleigh, who later became her brother-in-law, and others including her husband. She was a founding member of the Society for Psychical Research in 1881, was secretary from 1907 to 1932, president from 1908 to 1909, and president of honor in 1932. She edited the society's journal from 1888 to 1897.

Sidgwick worked in the Cavendish Laboratory with a

professor of experimental physics from 1880 to 1885 on the redetermination of electrical standards of measurement.

JH/MBO

PRIMARY SOURCES

Sidgwick, Eleanor. With Baron John William Strutt. *On the Electro-Chemical Equivalent of Silver.* London, 1884.

————. *Health Statistics of Women Students of Cambridge and Oxford and of Their Sisters.* Cambridge: University Press, 1890.

————. With Arthur Sidgwick. *Henry Sidgwick.* London: Macmillan, 1906.

————. *The International Crisis in Its Ethical and Psychological Aspects: Lectures Delivered in February and March, 1915.* London: H. Milford, 1915.

STANDARD SOURCES

Newnham, vol. 1, 1871–1923.

SIEBOLD, CHARLOTTE MARIANNE HEIDENREICH VON (1788–1859)

German physician. Mother Josepha Henning von Siebold; stepfather, Damien Siebold. Educated University of Giessen (M.D. in obstetrics, 1817). Professional experience: private practice with her mother. Died 1859.

Charlotte's father died when she was very young and she was greatly influenced by her mother, JOSEPHA HENNING VON SIEBOLD. Charlotte was adopted by her stepfather, Damien Siebold, a physician. She was educated at the University of Giessen and obtained her doctorate in obstetrics in 1817, just two years after her mother had become the first woman in Germany to do the same. After assisting in her mother's practice for some years, she married a military surgeon in 1829. She worked with her mother in obstetrics and later was attending obstetrician for eminent people in various countries.

JH/MBO

STANDARD SOURCES

Uglow 1989.

SIEBOLD, JOSEPHA (HENNING) VON (1771–1849)

German physician. Trained to manage her uncle's large agricultural holdings; Würzburg (practical tutoring in obstetrics); Archducal Medical College at Darmstadt (licensed, 1807); University of Giessen (doctorate in obstetrics, 1815). Married [unknown]; at least one daughter, Charlotte. Married Damian Siebold, physician (1795). Worked as midwife and assistant to D. Siebold; private practice in obstetrics. Died 1849.

Josepha von Siebold was the first woman to gain a doctorate in obstetrics from a German university (University of Giessen in 1815); her daughter, CHARLOTTE VON SIEBOLD, would obtain the same degree just two years later. Siebold began to practice medicine when her physician husband became unable to continue to practice. She determined to study obstetrics and first trained under her brother-in-law and later was licensed to deliver babies and vaccinate for pox by the Archducal Medical College at Darmstadt (1807). Siebold found that she had difficulty getting her patients to pay and reasoned that a university degree would verify her credentials and bring her the respect of her patients. After taking her doctorate at Giessen, she built a charitable practice, assisted by her daughter.

JH/MBO

STANDARD SOURCES

Uglow 1989.

SIEGEMUND, JUSTINE DITTRICH (1630–1705)

Silesian midwife. Born 1630 in Rohnstock. Father a pastor. Married Renth-Schrieber Siegemund, a master of horse. Educated by reading on her own. Professional experience: practiced, taught, and wrote on midwifery. Died 1705.

Justina Dittrich's pastor father died when she was four years old and, thus, her education was very sparse. She married a master of horse, Siegemund, and was under the impression that she was pregnant for two years. After seeing a series of midwives who declared that she was in labor, she eventually met one who denied that she was even pregnant. This experience prompted her to learn about female reproductive anatomy and physiology. After she read Regnier De Graaf's book on generation in 1672, she began her career on scientific midwifery.

Siegemund began her practice among the poor, and began to teach others her craft. Moving from working with peasant women to upper-class women, she eventually was appointed midwife to the royal family of Prussia and to the family of the Kurfürst of Brandenburg. In 1688 she went to Berlin to attend the wife of Frederick I of Prussia. She was not only a practitioner but a recorder of data as well; in 1689, she published a textbook of midwifery with copious illustrations. In this book, she proposed ways to turn an infant in the uterus including a sling around the foot of the fetus to bring the feet down; she also used a blunt hook in especially difficult cases. This book went through six editions and a Dutch translation.

JH/MBO

PRIMARY SOURCES

Siegemund, Justine Dittrich. *Die chur-brandenburgische hoff-wehe-mutter. Das ist: Ein höchst-nöthiger unterricht. Von schweren und unrecht-stehenden geburten.* Cölln an der Spree: Liebperten, 1690.

STANDARD SOURCES
Hurd-Mead 1938.

SIEVERTS, HERTHA (1899–1991)
See Doreck, Hertha.

SIGNEUX, JEANNE (1902–1987)
French paleontologist. Born 1901. French National Museum of Natural History, Institute of Paleontology, assistant (1942?–1967). Died 20 August 1987.

Jeanne Signeux was Professor Camille Arambourg's assistant in the Institute of Paleontology for twenty-five years. Although she officially retired in 1967 she remained at the institute until Arambourg's death in November 1969. With Arambourg's guidance, Signeux became very knowledgeable about Cretaceous and Lower Cenozoic Selachii. She collaborated with Arambourg on his memoir about vertebrate fossils in phosphate deposits in Algeria and Tunisia. She also studied sharks and rays from the Upper Cretaceous in Lebanon, fish remains from the Upper Cretaceous and Lower Eocens of Iraq, Jordan, and Syria, and Upper Cretaceous teleosts from Bolivia.

She published over a dozen scientific papers in which she created several new genera of sharks, teleosts, and a clupeiod.

JH/MBO

PRIMARY SOURCES
Signeux, Jeanne. "Les poissons néogènes de la Bretagne, d'l'Anjou et de la Touraine: Revu et complété par Jeanne Signeux Avant-propos de Georges Lecointre." Paris: N.p., 1957.

SECONDARY SOURCES
Gaudant, Jean. "Jeanne Signeux, 1902–1987." *News Bulletin of the Society of Vertebrate Paleontologists* 149 (1990): 95–96.

SILBERBERG, RUTH KATZENSTEIN (1906–1997)
German/U.S. pathologist. Born 20 March 1906 in Kassel, Germany, to Kathe Plaut and Ludwig Katzenstein. Married Martin Silberberg (1933). Educated University of Freiburg (1925) and University of Berlin (1926); University of Göttingen (M.D., 1927); University of Breslau, postdoctoral work (1930). Professional experience: University of Breslau, staff (1932–1934); University of Dalhousie, Nova Scotia (1934–1936); Washington

University, medical school faculty (1944–1967); professor of pathology (1968–1975 retirement); University of Jerusalem, visiting professor (1976–1997). Concurrent hospital experience in St. Louis. Research and publications on tissue growth, carcinogenesis, aging of skeleton, and arthritis. Died in 1997 in Jerusalem, Israel.

Ruth Katzenstein Silberberg trained at a number of German universities, attending the University of Freiberg in 1925, the University of Berlin in 1926, and completing her medical studies at the University of Göttingen in 1927. She subsequently did a postdoctoral year at the University of Breslau and was appointed to the staff in 1932, but held this position only until the rise of Nazi Germany made it impossible as a Jew to continue. She came to Nova Scotia where she did research for two years at the University of Dalhousie, and then was appointed to the medical school at Washinton University, St. Louis, Missouri, until the beginning of World War II. She spent the war years at New York University from 1941 to 1944, and during this period she became a naturalized American citizen (1943). She returned to Washington University in 1944 until the end of her career, rising to the position of professor of pathology in 1968. She held concurrent hospital positions as a senior pathologist at the St. Louis City Hospital (1938–1959) and Pacific Hospital (1956–1959). She published a series of important papers on tissue growth, carcinogenesis, skeletal aging, and arthritis. She was a member of the American Association of Pathologists and Bacteriologists, the Society of Experimental Pathologists, the Society for Experimental Biology and Medicine, the American Association for Cancer Research, the American Gerontological Society, and the Human Genetics Society, as well as Sigma Xi. She retired in 1975 and moved the following year to Israel, teaching at the University of Jerusalem until her death in 1997.

JH/MBO

PRIMARY SOURCES
Silberberg, Ruth Katzenstein. *Untersuchungen über die Umwandlungsfahig—keit der Lymphzellen.* Berlin: Julius Springer, 1931.
———. A portrait, personal papers, oral history, and photomicrographs are held at the Becker Medical Library, Washington University, St. Louis.

STANDARD SOURCES
Debus; *WW in America* 1958–1959.

SILLIMAN, HEPSA ELY (d. 1883)
U.S. geologist. Married. At least one son, Augustus Ely. Flourished 1859. Died 1883.

Hepsa Ely Silliman of Brooklyn, New York, published a theory of the origin of meteorites. She postulated that particles of dust in the atmosphere clumped together. Silliman clearly had read much of the contemporary scientific literature, citing Faraday's work on chemical affinity and electromagnetism to explain the forces that caused the dust to agglomerate. She also included a list of the recorded meteors.

After her death in 1883, her children, particularly her son Augustus Ely Silliman, presented eighty thousand dollars to Yale University to establish a series of Hepsa Ely Silliman Memorial Lectures (now called the Silliman Memorial Lecture Series). When these began in 1901, it was with the intent of illustrating "the presence and wisdom of God as manifested in the natural and moral world." Dr. William Osler, an early speaker in the series, emphasized that her son wished to give "special prominence to astronomy, chemistry, geology, and anatomy" (Osler 1921, *Preface*). JH/MBO

PRIMARY SOURCES
Silliman, H. E. *On the Origins of Aerolites.* New York: W. C. Bryant, 1859.

SECONDARY SOURCES
Osler, William. *The Evolution of Modern Medicine: A Series of Lectures Delivered at Yale University on the Silliman Foundation, in April 1913.* New Haven: Yale University Press, 1921.

STANDARD SOURCES
Kass-Simon and Farnes (article by Michele L. Aldrich).

SIMONS, LAO GENEVRA (1870–?)

U.S. mathematician. Born 29 March 1870. Educated Columbia University (A.M., 1912; Ph.D., 1925). Professional experience: Hunter College, assistant professor mathematics (1916–1925), associate professor (1925–1928), professor and head of department (1928–1940), emerita professor (1940–?). Death date unknown.

Although Lao Genevra Simon's professional positions were in mathematics, her research interests were primarily in history of mathematics. She published on the introduction of algebra into American schools in the eighteenth century and worked on a bibliography of early American textbooks on algebra. She was a member of the Mathematical Society, the Mathematical Association, and the History of Science Society. JH/MBO

PRIMARY SOURCES
Simons, Lao Genevra. *Bibliography of Early American Textbooks on Algebra Published in the Colonies and the United States through 1850.* Scripta Mathematica Studies no. 1. New York: Scripta Mathematica, Yeshiva College, 1936.
———. *Short Stories in Colonial Geometry.* Bruges (Belgium): St. Catherine Press, [1936]. Reprinted from *Osiris* 1 (January

1936). Deals with the influence of French mathematics at the end of the eighteenth century.
———. *Fabre and Mathematics, and Other Essays.* Scripta Mathematica Studies no. 4. New York: Scripta Mathematica, Yeshiva College, 1939.

STANDARD SOURCES
AMS 4–7.

SIMPSON, ANNE ROE (1904–1991)
See Roe, Anne.

SINCLAIR, MARY EMILY (1878–1955)

U.S. mathematician. Born 1878 in Worcester, Mass., to Marietta S. (Fletcher) and John Elbridge Sinclair. Two siblings. Never married. Two adopted children. Educated Oberlin College (graduated 1900); University of Chicago (M.A., 1903; Ph.D., 1908). Professional experience: Woodside Seminary in Hartford, Conn., mathematics teacher (1900–1901); Painesville, Ohio, school teacher (spring 1903); University of Nebraska, Lincoln, instructor (1904–1907); Oberlin, instructor (1907), associate professor (1908–1925), professor (1925–1941), head of mathematics department (1939–1941?), Clark Professor of Mathematics (1941–1942); Berea College, Kentucky (1942–1947). Died 1955 in Belfast, Maine.

Mary Emily Sinclair was born into a family that valued education. Her father was a mathematics professor at Worcester Polytechnic Institute and her two sisters, Helen and Alice, attended college at Mount Holyoke and Oberlin respectively. Mary Emily was the middle daughter. She was a member of Phi Beta Kappa and Sigma Xi at Oberlin, where she earned her undergraduate degree. For graduate work, she went to the University of Chicago, where she developed an interest in the calculus of variations under the tutelage of Oscar Bolza. While she was working on her degrees, she taught at various institutions. She finished her doctorate in 1908 and was immediately promoted from instructor to associate professor. In 1914 she adopted a baby girl, Margaret Emily, and in 1915 a son, Richard Elbridge. Sinclair continued to climb the academic ladder, was promoted to full professor in 1925, and became head of the mathematics department until she retired in 1944. While at Oberlin, Sinclair had several sabbaticals that she used for further study and for travel. During 1914–1915 she had her first sabbatical and studied at Columbia and Johns Hopkins. In 1922–1923, Sinclair received a Julia C. G. Piatt Fellowship from the American Association of University Women, and traveled to the University of Chicago and Cornell University. She considered this year her most productive for research. During her sabbatical of 1925–1926, she studied at the University of

Rome and at the Sorbonne. She taught at the University of Miami from 1927 to 1928, on leave from Oberlin, because of her daughter Margaret's health. During the Depression, her salary at Oberlin was reduced drastically. Her last sabbatical was in the spring of 1942. For a time after her retirement she taught at Berea College, but returned to Oberlin. In her will she left five thousand dollars to Oberlin College with the remainder to be divided between her daughter and Oberlin. Her son was not mentioned nor was anything specified about an estrangement. In May 1950, she was attacked and beaten severely by a man who took her purse and car. She left Oberlin and bought a house with her daughter-in-law in Belfast, Maine, where she died two years later.

JH/MBO

PRIMARY SOURCES

Sinclair, Mary Emily. "Minimum Surface of Revolution in the Case of One Variable End Point." *Annals of Mathematics* 8 (1906/1907): 177–188.

———. "Absolute Minimum in the Problem of the Surface of Revolution of Minimum Area." *Annals of Mathematics* 9 (1907/1908): 151–155.

———. "Concerning a Compound Discontinuous Solution in the Problem of the Surface of Revolution of Minimum Area." *Annals of Mathematics* 10 (1908/1909): 55–80. Doctoral dissertation.

SECONDARY SOURCES

Maltby, Margaret. "Mary Emily Sinclair." In *History of the Fellowships Awarded by the American Association of University Women: 1888–1929,* ed. Margaret Maltby, 65–66. Washington, D.C.: American Association of University Women, 1930.

STANDARD SOURCES

Grinstein and Campbell (article by Laurel G. Sherman).

SINSKAIA, EVGENIIA NIKOLAEVNA (1889–1965)

Russian botanist. Born 25 November 1889 in Velikii Luki, daughter of a teacher. Educated at local school, Petrov Academy of Agricultural Sciences in Moscow. Professional experience: Saratov Land Department, staff; Saratov University, laboratory assistant; Petrograd Bureau of Applied Botany, head of section; All-Union Institute of Plant Industry, Leningrad, specialist; Leningrad Agricultural Institute, professor; All-Union Institute of Oil Plants, Krasnodar, staff; Zakataly Experiment Station; All-Union Institute of Plant Industry, head of division. Died 4 March 1965.

Evgeniia Nikolaevna Sinskaia was educated at a girl's school and entered the Petrov Academy of Agricultural Sciences in Moscow in the department of plant growth. She received her diploma in 1917, her studies having been interrupted at intervals by lung disease and by the necessity of earning a living. As a student Sinskaia worked as an assistant at the Bezenchuk Experiment Station (1910), at the Novozybkovskaia Experiment Station (1915–1916) and at the Department of Turkestan Land Improvement (1917). She took part in a series of expeditions to Central Asia, Northern Territory, and other regions of Russia.

In 1919 Sinskaia began working at the Saratov Province Land Department and simultaneously as a laboratory assistant at the department of plant production of the agronomical faculty of Saratov University under the geneticist Nikolai I. Vavilov. She conducted research in meadow cultivation on the Volga meadows during 1919–1921 and organized experimental farms in this region for meadow and fodder production.

At this time Sinskaia became interested in the family Cruciferae, and she continued studies in this area after she moved to Petrograd with the rest of Vavilov's group in 1921. Here she became head of the Cruciferae plant section and in 1923 head of the oleiferous, spinning, and root crops section.

When Bureau of Applied Botany was reorganized into the All-Union Institute of Plant Industry (VIR) in 1925, Sinskaia was appointed a specialist. Later she held the posts consecutively of chief of the oleiferous crops division, forage crops division, and plant ecology. In 1940 she was appointed professor at the Leningrad Agricultural Institute.

In March 1942, as a result of the German invasion, Sinskaia was evacuated to Krasnodar, where she worked at the All-Union Research Institute of Oil Plants as head of the plant physiology division. When this institute was evacuated to the Transcaucasus owing to the progress of the war, Sinskaia moved to the experiment station at Zakataly.

In 1945, Sinskaia returned to Leningrad and was in charge of the taxonomy, ecology, and geography division, and also the division of forage crops at VIR. In her later years at this institute, she retained only the taxonomy, ecology, and geography division.

Sinskaia made numerous expeditions: to the Altai in 1924, to Japan in 1928–1929, and across the Caucasus and to central Asia. In the last years of her life she went to the forest-steppe regions of the European part of the Soviet Union.

Sinskaia published over 140 works in the fields of ecology, taxonomy, speciation, and other aspects of Cruciferae, Leguminosae, cereals, and other families. She left a number of articles in manuscript after her death including a biography of N. I. Vavilov (who died in prison in 1943, a victim of the purges of Russian biologists initiated by Trofim D. Lysenko).

Sinskaia was a member of the All-Union Botanical Society and the Geographical Society. She was awarded the Order of Lenin.

ACH

PRIMARY SOURCES

Sinskaia, Evgeniia Nikolaevna. "Oleiferous and root crops of the family Cruciferae." *Trudy po Prikladnoi Botanike Genetiki i Selektsii* 19, no. 3 (1928):1–645.

———. *Vidoobrazovanie u liutserny i drugikh rastenii.* Leningrad: Izd. Vsesoiuznoi akad. c.-kh. nauk im V. I. Lenina, 1935.

———. *Vospominaniia o N. I. Vavilova.* Kiev: Naukova dumka, 1991.

SECONDARY SOURCES

Bakhteyev, F. K., et al. "Evgenija Nikolaevna Sinskaya, 1889–1965." *Taxon* 5 (1966): 169176. Includes bibliography.

SITTERLY, CHARLOTTE EMMA (MOORE) (1898–1990)

U.S. astrophysicist. Born 24 September 1898 in Ercidoun, Pa., to Elizabeth Palmer (Walton) and George Winfield Moore. Educated at Swarthmore College (A.B., 1920); University of California, Berkeley (Ph.D., 1937). Married Bancroft Walker Sitterly, 30 May 1937. Professional experience: Princeton Observatory, computer (1920–1925; 1928–1929), research assistant (1931–1936), research associate (1936–1945); Mt. Wilson Observatory, computer (1925–1928); National Bureau of Standards, physicist (1945 to the end of her career). Honors and memberships: Annie Jump Cannon Prize (1937); the Annie Jump Cannon Centennial Medal (1963); and honorary doctorate of science from Swarthmore (1962). Died 1990.

Born in a small town in Pennsylvania, Charlotte Moore Sitterly attended Swarthmore College, graduating in 1920. Her strong interest in astronomy was shown by her immediately taking a position as a computer at Princeton Observatory. After five years she left to spend a few years as a computer at Mount Wilson Observatory, returning as an assistant spectroscopist to Princeton, where she did research on the solar spectrum, looking at atomic lines produced by the sunspot spectrum, a study that resulted in her first publication (1932). She rose to the level of research assistant by 1931. She returned to California to do a doctorate in astronomy at University of California, Berkeley, completing it by 1936. Now a research associate at Princeton Observatory, she left that position to work as a physicist at the National Bureau of Standards, where she worked on tables of atomic energy levels and continued her work on the ultraviolet and infrared spectrum. In 1968 she moved to the Office of Standard Reference Data. She then moved to the Naval Research Laboratory, where she remained until her retirement in 1978. During her government work, she received a series of awards. She was a Fellow of the American Optical Society, the American Physics Society, and the Washington Academy of Science, as well as holding memberships in many other scientific organizations. She was recognized by Wellesley College with the Annie Jump Cannon Centennial medal in 1963, and received an honorary doctorate from her undergraduate college, Swarthmore, in 1962.   JH/MBO

PRIMARY SOURCES

Sitterly, Charlotte. *Atomic Lines in the Sun-Spot Spectrum.* Princeton, N.J.: Princeton University Press, 1933. Published by Princeton University Observatory and the Mount Wilson Observatory of the Carnegie Institution of Washington with the help of a grant from the National Academy of Sciences.

———. With Henry Norris Russell. *The Masses of the Stars, with a General Catalogue of Dynamical Parallaxes.* Chicago: University of Chicago Press, [1940].

———. With Henry Norris Russell. "The Arc Spectrum of Iron (Fe 1). Part I. Analysis of the Spectrum Based on the Work of Many Investigators and Including Unpublished Studies." *Transactions of the American Philosophical Society,* new ser. 34, pt. 2 (1944): 111–207.

———. *A Multiplet Table of Astrophysical Interest.* Rev. ed. Princeton, N.J.: The Observatory, 1945.

———. *Atomic Energy Levels as Derived from the Analyses of Optical Spectra.* 3 vols. Washington, D.C.: U.S. Department of Commerce, National Bureau of Standards, 1949–1958.

———. With M. G. J. Minnaert and J. Houtgast. *The Solar Spectrum 2935A to 8700A.* Washington, D.C.: National Bureau of Standards, 1966.

SECONDARY SOURCES

Vissher, Stephen S. *Scientists Starred 1903–1943 in American Men of Science.* New York: Amo Press, 1975.

STANDARD SOURCES

AMS 5–18; Bailey; Debus.

SKEAT, ETHEL GERTRUDE (1865–1939)

See Woods, Ethel Gertrude (Skeat).

SKOCZYLAS-CISZEWSKA, KAMILA (1902–1971)

Polish stratigrapher and structural geologist. Born 1902. Died 1971.

Much of Skoczylas-Ciszewska's work was concerned with the Miocene of the Carpathians.   JH/MBO

PRIMARY SOURCES

Skoczylas, Kamila. With M. Ksiazkiewicz. "Comparaison du flish du Wienerwald avec celui des Carpathes." *Materialy i Prace-Polska Akademia Nauk, Instytut Geofizyki* 6 (1937).

———. "Problem rzekomej kredy dolnej w Pogwizdowie dolo Bochni." *Prace Panstwowego Instytutu Geologiczny Prace* 7 (1951): 187–197.

———. With Tadeusz Tyniec. "O pegmatycie turmalinowym z fliszu okolicy Zegociny; on tourmaline pegamatite from the Flysch Around Zegocina." *Archiwum Mineralogiczne* 2 (1954): 187–210.

———. With Marian Kamienski. "O skale wzbogaconej w P (Sub 2) O (Sub 5) w Karpatach Fliszowych." *Archiwum Mineralogiczne* 19 (1956): 161–180.

———. With J. Poborski. "Tectogenesis of the Miocene Evaporite Deposits at the Margin of the Carpathians East of Cracow." In *Report of the Session—23rd International Geological Congress. Report Section 3, Proceedings* (1968): 281–286.

SECONDARY SOURCES
Kamienski, Marian. "Wspomnienie o Kamili Skoczylas-Ciszewskiej zasluzonym geologu i wychowawcy mlodziezy. [Kamtila Szoczylas-Ciszewska (1902–1971)]." *Rocznik Polskiego Towarzystwa Geologicznego* 41, no. 4 (1971): 623–632.

STANDARD SOURCES
Sarjeant.

SLATER, IDA LILIAN (1881–1969)

British geologist. Born 30 June 1881 at Hampstead, London, to Mary Emily Wilkins and John Slater. Two sisters, Winifred M. and J. Mabel W. Slater. Married M. D. Lees (1912). One daughter. Educated South Hampstead High School; Newnham College, Cambridge (1900–1904), Natural Science Tripos, Part I, class 1 (1903), Part II class 1 (1904). Professional experience: Bedford College, London, demonstrator in geology (1910–1912). Died 7 August 1969.

Although Ida Slater showed academic promise when she received two firsts in the natural science and geology tripos successively, her actual contributions to her chosen field were not impressive in number. She published jointly with Gertrude Elles in the *Quarterly Journal of the Geological Society* (1906) and in the *Journal of the Palaeontological Society* in 1907. She was a Winkworth Scholar, a Bathurst Student (1904–1905), a Harkness Scholar (1905–1906), and a demonstrator in geology at Bedford College until her marriage in 1912. Following her marriage, she did little professionally in geology.   JH/MBO

PRIMARY SOURCES
Slater, Ida L. *A Monograph of British Conularioe.* London: Printed for the Palaeontological Society, 1907.

STANDARD SOURCES
Newnham.

SLATER, JESSE MABEL WILKINS (1879–1961)

British physicist. Born 24 February 1879 in Hampstead, England. Married Harold Baily (1926). Educated Newnham College, Cambridge University (1899–1903); Bathhurst College, Cambridge (1903–1905); University of London (B.Sc., 1902; D.Sc., 1906). Professional experience: Cheltenham Ladies College (1909–1913); Newnham College, lecturer in physics and chemistry (1914–1926); part-time nurse (1914–1917); Military Hospital, France, radiographer (1918). Died 25 December 1961.

Slater had a distinguished undergraduate career at Newnham College, Cambridge, from 1899 to 1903, and was one of the earliest women to earn a doctorate in science at the University of London in 1906. She returned to Newnham as science lecturer in 1914 after a period of teaching in schools. She was elected an associate in the same year. In 1926 Slater married Harold Baily and thereafter devoted herself to local work on charities and school care committees. She was mayor of Hampstead from 1930 to 1932 and was active in the Council of Unitarian and Free Christian Churches.

While at Cambridge, Slater worked under J. J. Thomson on the effect of temperature on thorium decay products and the electricity emitted by thorium and radium decay products. Upon heating a mixture of thorium products to a high temperature, she found the components volatilized at different temperatures. This property made it possible to separate them, thereby clarifying some details of the thorium series. The method of separating radioactive decay products by their differences in volatility became quite useful. Slater also showed that thorium and radium decay products emitted the slow-moving electrons then known as δ rays (later determined to be a type of secondary radiation), which Thomson had discovered. Slater discontinued professional work after her marriage.   JH/MBO

PRIMARY SOURCES
Slater, Jessie Mabel Wilkins Baily. "On the Excited Activity of Thorium." *Philosophical Magazine* 9 (1905): 628–644.

———. "On the Emission of Negative Electricity by Thorium and Radium Emanations." *Philosophical Magazine* 10 (1905): 460–466.

SECONDARY SOURCES
Rayner-Canham, M. F. and G. W. Rayner-Canham. "Pioneer Women in Nuclear Science." *American Journal of Physics* 58 (1990): 1036–1043.

Rutherford, Ernest. *Radio-activity.* Cambridge: Cambridge University Press, 1905. See pages 354–355.

———. *Radioactive Substances and Their Radiations.* Cambridge: Cambridge University Press, 1913. See pages 171, 537.

Trenn, Thaddeus J. "Rutherford and Recoil Atoms: The Metamorphosis and Success of a Once Stillborn Theory." *Historical Studies in the Physical Sciences* 6 (1975): 513–547.

STANDARD SOURCES
Newnham Roll; Rayner-Canham 1997.

SLAVIKOVA, LUDMILA (KAPLANOVA) (1890–1943)

Czechoslovak mineralogist, crystallographer, and economic geologist. Born 23 February 1890 in Prague. Married Frantisek Slavik (1917). Educated Charles University, Prague (Ph.D.). Professional experience: National Museum, keeper of minerals (1921–1939). Died 18 February 1943 in concentration camp in Rajsko (Birkenau).

Ludmila Slavikova studied the minerals of Bohemia and other parts of Czechoslovakia. For her doctoral thesis, she produced a crystallographic study on Bohemian pyragyrite.

Slavikova married fellow mineralogist Frantisek Slavik in 1917, and in that same year collaborated with him on the publication of a monograph on the structures and genesis of the Ordovician iron ores of Bohemia. Although she published some of her work with her husband, she also published independently. Her papers were concerned with the crystallography of some organic compounds, new occurrences of minerals in Czechoslovakia, a description of the Bohumilice meteorite, and historical notes on the mineral collection of the National Museum on the occasion of its centenary. She was keeper of minerals in the National Museum from 1921 to 1939, when the problems with the Germans escalated. Slavikova was taken to a German concentration camp in Poland, where she died in 1943.

JH/MBO

PRIMARY SOURCES
Slavikova, Ludmila. "Druhy kus bohumilickeho meteorickeho zeleza v Narodnim Museu." *Casopis Narodni Muzeum. Oddil Prirodovedny* 107, nos. 3–4 (1933): 82–85.

———. "Vyznacne prirustky cs. Sbirky nerostne v poslednich peti letech: Acquisitions of Czechoslovak minerals, New for the Collections of the Narodni Museum in the Last Five Years." *Casopis Narodni Muzeum. Oddil Prirodovedny* 113, no. 2 (1939): 43–54.

SECONDARY SOURCES
Spencer, Leonard J. "Biographical Notices of Mineralogists Recently Deceased." *Mineralogical Magazine* 28, no. 199 (1947): 175–229.

Tucek, Karel. "Ludmila Slavikova." *Vestnik Statniho Geologickho Ustavu Ceskoslovenske Republiky* (1946, for 1945): 3–5.

STANDARD SOURCES
Sarjeant.

SLOSSON, ANNIE TRUMBULL (1838–1926)

U.S. entomologist. Born 1838 in Stonington, Conn., to Sarah and Gurdon Trumbull. Married Edward Slosson. Educated schools of Hartford, Conn. Died 1926.

Annie Trumbull Slosson was a popularizer who wrote about the insects she collected in Florida at her winter home and in the White Mountains of New Hampshire where she spent her summers. She spent the intervening time in New York City. In 1867, she married Edward Slosson.

She wrote descriptions of the habits and anatomy of the insects she collected and studied. Most of her publications were popularizations of natural history. She turned over many of the specimens she captured to specialists for analysis. She was well enough known to have many new species named after her. A photograph of Annie Slosson is held among the collection of World Diptera Taxonomists at Bishop Museum, Hawaii.

JH/MBO

PRIMARY SOURCES
Slosson, Annie. "Aunt Randy: An Entomological Sketch." *Harpers* 75 (1887): 303.

SECONDARY SOURCES
Dougherty, V. "Annie Trumbull Slosson." *American Entomologist* 36, no. 2 (1990): 126–127.

STANDARD SOURCES
Ogilvie 1986; Rossiter 1982; *Woman's Who's Who of America.*

SLYE, MAUD (1869–1954)

U.S. medical researcher and pathologist. Born 8 February 1869 in Minneapolis, Minn., to Florence Alden (Wheeler) and James Alvin Slye. Two siblings. Educated public schools in Des Moines and Marshalltown, Iowa; University of Chicago (1895–1898; 1908–1911); Brown University (A.B., 1899). Professional experience: University of Chicago, clerk for William Rainy Clerk, president of the university (1895–1898); Rhode Island Normal School, staff (1899–?); Sprague Memorial Institute, University of Chicago, institute staff, instructor (1911–1922), assistant professor (1922–1926), associate professor (1926–1944), Cancer Laboratory, director (1936–1944), emerita professor (1944–1954). Honors and memberships: American Medical Association, Gold Medal (1914); University of Chicago, Ricketts Prize (1915); Radiological Society,

Gold Medal (1922); Brown University, honorary D.Sc. (1937). Died 17 September 1954.

Born in Minnesota, Maud Slye moved with her well-educated but poor family to Iowa. Although Maud could not really afford college, she was determined to get a college degree. She enrolled at the University of Chicago and worked as a clerk for the president of the university while she was taking a full load of classes. After three years at the university, she suffered a "nervous breakdown" and was asked to leave the university. For two months she rested, after which she took courses at the Woods Hole Laboratory. She had recovered sufficiently to enter Brown University in the fall of 1898, where she earned a bachelor's degree. After graduation, she worked at the Rhode Island Normal School, a two-year teacher-training institution, where she became interested in genetics—especially human heredity. She returned to the University of Chicago, where she became a graduate assistant to Professor Charles Otis Whitman. In her laboratory, she studied the Japanese waltzing mice. Slye was fortunate to get a position at the newly established Sprague Memorial Institute at the University of Chicago. Appointed to the institute staff in 1911, the highest academic rank that she achieved was associate professor, although she became director of the Cancer Laboratory of the Sprague Memorial Institute.

Slye never married, but had a close relationship with an artist in her early years. After he died, she devoted most of her time to science, although she also enjoyed writing poetry.

Slye's work with the waltzing mice (a nervous disorder) inspired her to do similar breeding experiments to provide data on the heritability of cancer. At that time (as today), there was a great deal of controversy over the cause of cancer. Those who thought it was inherited needed a controlled study on a group of animals to support their contentions. As Slye bred her mice, she found a mouse with breast cancer with others soon following. Using controlled breeding techniques she found that certain mice were susceptible to cancer whereas others were not. It was when Slye attempted to extrapolate her mouse result to humans that she became controversial. Few of her colleagues accepted the possibility of the transfer. In order to confirm her hypothesis, Slye suggested that a cancer statistics collection bureau be established to trace the genetics of cancer, but the bureau was never established.　　　　　　　　　　　　　　　　　　JH/MBO

PRIMARY SOURCES

Slye, Maud. "The Incidence and Inheritability of Spontaneous Cancer in Mice. Preliminary Report." *Zeitschrift für Krebsforschung* 13 (1913): 500–504.

———. "The Incidence and Inheritability of Spontaneous Tumors in Mice. Second Report." *Journal of Medical Research* 30, no. 3 (1914): 281–298.

———. "The Inheritability of Spontaneous Tumors of the Liver in Mice." *Journal of Cancer Research* 1 (1916): 503–522.

———. With H. F. Holmes and H. G. Wells. "Primary Spontaneous Tumors of the Ovary in Mice." *Journal of Cancer Research* 6 (1920): 205–226.

———. "Cancer and Heredity." *Annals of Internal Medicine* 1 (1928): 951–976.

SECONDARY SOURCES

McCoy, J. J. *The Cancer Lady: Maud Slye and Her Heredity Studies.* Nashville, Tenn.: Thomas Nelson, 1977.

STANDARD SOURCES

Grinstein 1997 (article by Jeanie Strobert Payne); *NAW*(M) (article by John Parascandola); *Notable.*

SMART, HELEN EDITH (FOX) (1891–?)

U.S. bacteriologist. Born 23 October 1891 in Westfield, Mass. Married (1927). Educated University of Michigan (A.B., 1918). Professional experience: U.S. Department of Agriculture, bureau of plant industry, junior pathologist, plant pathology laboratory (1918–1928), division of fruit and vegetable crops and diseases, assistant pathologist (1928–1936), associate pathologist (from 1947), bureau of agricultural chemistry and engineering, assistant bacteriologist (1936–1943); War Food Administration, special commodities branch, fish products division, marketing specialist (1943–1947). Death date unkown.

Upon receiving her bachelor's degree from the University of Michigan, Helen Edith Smart went to work for the U.S. Department of Agriculture, where she remained in different positions throughout her career. Although she never obtained a higher degree, the department advanced her steadily. During World War II, she worked for the War Food Administration, but returned to the division of fruit and vegetable crops and diseases in 1947. Her research was on the bacteriology of foods, microbiology of frozen foods, and storage diseases of fruits and vegetables.　　JH/MBO

PRIMARY SOURCES

Smart, Helen Edith Fox. "A New Bacterial Species Isolated from Strawberries." *Journal for Agricultural Research* 51 (1935): 363–364.

STANDARD SOURCES

AMS 5–8.

SMEDLEY, IDA (1877–1944)
See MacLean, Ida (Smedley).

SMIRNOVA-ZAMKOVA, ALEKSANDRA IVANOVNA (1880–1962)

Ukrainian pathologist and microbiologist. Born 31 May 1880 in Pereiaslav, Ukraine. Father a physician. Educated at medical faculty of Montpellier University, France. Professional experience: Kiev Bacteriological Institute, assistant professor; Kiev Higher Women's Medical Courses, assistant professor; Kiev Medical Institute, assistant professor; Institute of Clinical Physiology of the Ukrainian Academy of Sciences, staff, later head of department; Institute of Physiology, head of laboratory (1933–1941); concurrently 2nd Kiev Medical Institute, head of department. Honors and memberships: corresponding member, later academician, Ukrainian Academy of Sciences; Order of Lenin; Badge of Honor. Died 22 September 1962 in Kiev.

Aleksandra Ivanovna Smirnova-Zamkova graduated from the medical faculty of Montpellier University in France. From 1907 to 1908 she was assistant professor at the Kiev Bacteriological Institute. From 1908 to 1920, she worked at the Higher Women's Medical Courses in Kiev and from 1920 to 1930 in the Kiev Medical Institute. In 1931, she began work in the Institute of Clinical Physiology of the Ukrainian Academy of Sciences, becoming head of department in 1938. She remained there until 1953. During part of this period (1933 to 1941) she was also head of the department of pathological anatomy at 2nd Kiev Medical Institute. From 1953 until her death in 1962, she was director of the laboratory of the Institute of Physiology of the Ukrainian Academy of Sciences.

Smirnova's principal scientific research was devoted to the study of the pathological anatomy of radiation sickness, infectious diseases, and various precancerous conditions. While studying scarlet fever, she was the first to describe privascular infiltrates in many organs and the abnormal changes of the blood vessels, indicating early infection of the mucous lining of the stomach. She also introduced the use of reduced silver-staining methods in the study of neural tissues and connections.

In 1939 she was elected a corresponding member of the Ukrainian Academy of Sciences, becoming a full member in 1951. She was named an Honored Scientist of the Ukrainian Republic in 1944 and was also awarded the Order of Lenin, the Badge of Honor, and the medal "For Valiant Labor During the Great Fatherland War." ACH

PRIMARY SOURCES
Smirnova-Zamkova, Aleksandra Ivanovna. "Les recherches sur les lésions et le parasite de l'actinomycose." Doctoral dissertation, 1906.

———. *Problema osnovnogo mezhutochnogo veshchestva.* N.p.: 1955.

STANDARD SOURCES
Strohmeier; *WWW(USSR).*

SMITH, ADELIA CALVERT (fl. 1885–1905)
See Calvert, Emily (Adelia) Smith.

SMITH, ALICE EMILY (fl. 1850–1905)

British chemist. Educated University College, Bangor (B.Sc.); Owens College, Manchester. Professional experience: University College, Bangor, demonstrator in chemistry.

Alice Emily Smith was an 1851 exhibition scholar at University College, Bangor. She later worked as a demonstrator there. She went to Owens College, Manchester, where she did research in organic chemistry. During this time, she collaborated with W. H. Perkins, Jr., and K. U. P. Orton. Between 1902 and 1904 she published four important papers resulting from this research. Her three publications with Perkins were on structural determinations and new synthetic routes in organic chemistry. Her collaboration with Orton was on reaction mechanism studies. JH/MBO

STANDARD SOURCES
Creese 1991.

SMITH, ANNE MILLSPAUGH (COOKE) (1900–1981)

U.S. anthropologist. Born 20 October 1900 in New York City. Married (1) Chauncey Cooke (1922? divorced 1930s); (2) Eastburn Smith (1939). Two sons, Eastburn H. and Jeffrey M. Smith. Educated Cornell University (B.A., 1922); Yale University (M.A., 1937; Ph.D., 1940). Professional experience: University of New Mexico Field School (summers of 1937–1938); special lecturer (until 1941); War Relocation Authority, Rivers, Ariz., acting director of community services (1940?–1943); volunteer and homemaker (1943–1957); Museum of New Mexico, Santa Fe, curator (1957–1960; 1962–1965); New Mexico Health Project, research associate (1960–1962). Died 18 June 1981 in Santa Fe, N.M.

Anne Millspaugh (Cooke) Smith, known as Nan, had a divided career. Shortly after receiving her bachelor's degree from Cornell, she married and lived a conventional life as a housewife. However, when the couple divorced, she went to work as a docket clerk for a New York law firm and in 1935 enrolled in the graduate program in anthropology at Yale University. She became the second woman to receive a doctorate in anthropology at Yale and was elected to both Phi Beta Kappa and Sigma Xi.

Her first field work (1936) was among the the Northern Ute of Utah and Colorado. For this project (which lasted three or four months) she set out with a sleeping bag and three hundred dollars. During this experience she interviewed the oldest Northern Utes about their lives before the reservations. From this project she wrote her master's thesis, "The Material Culture of the Northern Ute." Her doctoral thesis analyzed the basin mythology. The work was strongly influenced by her mentor, Leslie Spier. This important ethnographic study was not prepared for publication until 1974, when the project was financed by a fellowship from the American Association of University Women.

Returning to the Southwest every summer, she became a faculty member during the summers of 1937 and 1938 and continued as a special lecturer until 1941 at the University of New Mexico Field School.

Her career took a different turn in 1939 when she married Eastburn Smith. At that time he was the regional director of the Bureau of Land Management of New Mexico and later a New Mexico State Park commissioner. During the early days of World War II, he was appointed director of the War Relocation Authority, and Nan Smith served as acting director of community services. After a year they both resigned in protest, finding the conditions under which the Japanese interns were forced to live intolerable. She spent from 1943 to 1957 raising her sons and becoming active in community events. She was active in the League of Women Voters, spearheaded a study of the Santa Fe Public Schools, and was a founding member of the Santa Fe County Association for mental health.

In 1957 she returned to anthropology, becoming a curator at the Museum of New Mexico, a post which she held from 1957 to 1960 and again in 1962 to 1965 when she retired; she remained a research associate in the museum until her death. During the period from 1960 to 1962, she joined the New Mexico Health Project as a research associate.

Smith's accomplishments were chiefly in applied anthropology. After the mid-1930s, she was involved with the legal rights, education, and community health of the Indians of the Great Basin and the Southwest. She was an expert witness and research consultant in the Ute Land Claims case from 1950 to 1957. She was a consultant for the U.S. Solicitor's Office in Albuquerque on Indian water rights and an expert witness in the field of Indian education in the case of the Ramah Navaho vs. the Gallup-McKinley School Board in 1969. During this same time, she lectured to teachers of Pueblo and Apache children. From 1968 to 1971 she was a member of the Follow Through Programs in Santa Fe and in 1970 was appointed by the U.S. Commissioner of Indian Affairs to a six-person panel to evaluate the program at the In-

stitute of American Indian Art. When she was seventy-five years old, Smith was appointed to the New Mexico Commission on Indian Affairs, where she served until her death.

Smith's unpaid positions involving her anthropological expertise were legion. From 1970 to 1971 she was a member of the Public Health Task Force, NORCHAP. She was a founder of the New Mexico Civil Liberties Union and a contributing editor to the *New Mexico Review* and the *Legislative Journal*. An active member of the Democratic Party, she worked at getting out the vote for issues involving minority groups in New Mexico as well as many other liberal political causes.

JH/MBO

PRIMARY SOURCES

Smith, Anne Millspaugh. With Sam Schulman. "The Concept of 'Health' among Spanish-Speaking Villagers of New Mexico and Colorado." *Journal of Health and Human Behavior* (1964).

———. *Ethnography of the Northern Utes.* Santa Fe: Museum of New Mexico, 1974.

SECONDARY SOURCES

Whiting, Beatrice B. "Anne Millspaugh (Cooke) Smith (1900–1981)." *American Anthropologist* 84 (1982): 395–396.

SMITH, ANNIE LORRAIN (1854–1937)

British botanist. Born 25 October 1854 in Halfmorton, Dumfriesshire. Father Reverend Walter Smith. At least three brothers and one sister. Professional experience: governess to private families; British Museum of Natural History, worked on fungi and lichens (1892–1933); Royal Agricultural Society, assistant. Died 7 September 1937 in London.

Annie Lorrain Smith came from a talented family, with three of her brothers becoming professors, two in philosophy and one in pathology. She became a governess to private families and as such was able to visit Orléans and Tübingen. She spent her entire scientific career as a volunteer at the British Museum of Natural History. Smith was a woman who might be called an obligatory amateur, for although she was trained in botany by Dr. Scott at the Royal College of Science, she was unable to choose whether to become a professional or remain an amateur. Scott brought his students to the Department of Botany at the Natural History Museum, where Smith became acquainted with the Cryptogamic Herbarium. Since women were not admitted to the museum staff, she had no choice but to work for free if she wanted to work at all. She volunteered to remount a collection of recently purchased microscopical slides, and through this experience was able to prepare an exhibit of microfungi for the public gallery.

From this time on she was connected with the Cryptogamic Herbarium as an unofficial worker almost continuously up to the time of her eightieth birthday. She had a short break from 1899 to 1901 when she acted as an assistant to William Carruthers in his work as Consulting Botanist to the Royal Agricultural Society. Among other things, they tested farm seeds for germination, and Smith wrote an account of the fungi found on the seeds during germination in the *Journal of the Royal Microscopical Society* in 1901. Another interruption in her work at the museum occurred when she traveled to the United States to visit family. She also went on a British Association trip to Australia in 1914.

Although her earliest work was on seaweeds, she soon became fascinated with the fungi. She joined the British Mycological Society and contributed notes on new records and other papers to the Society's *Transactions*. After James Crombie, who was producing a monograph on British lichens, died in 1906, Smith undertook the completion of the work. After she prepared the second volume, she reworked the first, Crombie's original work; this two-volume set became a standard work. She also prepared a small *Handbook* in 1921 and in the same year produced her encyclopedic volume on lichens, which was one of the Cambridge Botanical Handbooks.

Just before her eightieth birthday she was given "A Civil List Pension" and the Order of the British Empire. Although she was given a small salary paid from a special fund, she remained unofficial for all of the time that she worked in the museum.

Smith's publishing record was outstanding. She became a Fellow of the Linnean Society (1904) and was twice president of the British Mycological Society (1907; 1917).

JH/MBO

PRIMARY SOURCES

Smith, Annie Lorrain. *A Monograph of Lichens Found in Britain: Being a Descriptive Catalogue of the Species in the Herbarium of the British Museum.* Vol. 2. London: Printed by Order of the Trustees of the British Museum, 1894–1911.

———. "British Mycology." *British Mycological Society, Transactions* 1 (1897–1898): 68–75.

———. "Fungi New to Britain," *British Mycological Society, Transactions* 1 (1898–1899): 113–116; 1 (1899–1900): 150–158; 1 (1900–1901): 192–201; 2 (1902): 31–41; 2 (1906): 167–172.

———. *A Monograph of the British Lichens, a Descriptive Catalogue of the Species in the Herbarium of the British Museum.* London: Printed by Order of the Trustees of the British Museum, 1918.

———. *Handbook of British Lichens.* London: Printed by Order of the Trustees of the British Museum, 1921.

———. *Lichens.* Cambridge: Cambridge University Press, 1921.

SECONDARY SOURCES

Gepp, A., and A. B. Rendle. *Journal of Botany* (1937): 329–330. Obituary notice.

Hawksworth, D. L., and M. R. D. Seaward. *Lichenology in the British Isles.* Richmond, Surrey: Richmond Publishing Co., 1977. See pages 25–28.

Irish Naturalists Journal 16 (1968): 111–112; 17 (1971): 48.

Kew Bulletin (1937): 442–443. Obituary notice.

Times, 14 September 1937. Obituary notice.

STANDARD SOURCES

Desmond.

SMITH, ANNIE MORRILL (1856–?)

U.S. botanist. Born 13 February 1856 in Brooklyn, N.Y. Educated Packer Collegiate Institute (1874). Honors and memberships: Genealogy Society; Sullivant Moss Society (president 1920); Wild Flower Preservation Society; Long Island Historical Society; Brooklyn Institute of Mosses. Death date unknown.

Annie Smith was a self-educated botanist, who became very interested in studying mosses. She was a member of numerous societies, and exchanged specimens and ideas with associates. She published several plant lists and edited *The Bryologist* in 1856. JH/MBO

PRIMARY SOURCES

Smith, Annie Morrill. "List of Plants Found on the Adirondack League Club Tract." *Adirondack League Club Year Book* (1898): 59–71.

———. *Corrected and Enlarged List of Plants Found on the Adirondack League Club Tract.* New York: P. F. McBreen, [1898].

STANDARD SOURCES

AMS 2–4.

SMITH, AUDREY U. (1915–1981)

British physiologist. Born 21 May 1915. Educated King's College, London (first-class B.Sc., 1935); Bedford College for Women (first-class B.Sc. in physiology, 1936); registered for a Ph.D. degree at King's College (1937); Vassar College (1937–1938); Marine Biological Institute at Woods Hole; King's College (M.D., 1956). Professional experience: King's College Hospital, house physician (1942), clinical pathologist (1943–1944); Epsom, public health laboratory, pathologist (1944–1945); Emergency Public Health Laboratory Service, Nottingham, pathologist (1945–1946); National Institute for Medical Research, then at Hampstead, researcher (1946–1970); Royal National Orthopaedic Hospital at Stanmore, staff (1970–1981). Died 1981 in Stanmore.

Little is known of Audrey U. Smith's early family life or education. After earning two bachelor's degrees she had plans to earn a doctoral degree. However, she spent one year in laboratory work and then went to the United States to study at Vassar College and the Marine Biological Institute. When she returned to England, she decided to study medicine. She began her professional career during World War II. In 1946 she began her research at the National Institute for Medical Research.

Smith's successes in cryobiology should have made her a recognized figure; however, she did not receive the credit she deserved. She began this research with her discovery of a method to preserve living cells at very low temperatures. She first worked with Alan Parkes, who had been attempting to find ways to freeze human semen and keep it viable. He tried many combinations of techniques on bull semen, but without success. After working with Parkes, she worked with Chris Polge, a recent graduate in agriculture. They tried another method: they partially dehydrated fowl spermatozoa in a sugar solution before freezing. This method also failed. After realizing that membranes within cells were affected by changes other than crystallization of ice during freezing and thawing, they hypothesized that these changes could be prevented in the presence of glycerol. The result of this idea had a tremendous practical significance. Bull semen could be frozen in glycerol and stored for as long as one year and still be used to fertilize cows. They had a 75 percent conception rate.

Smith modified her technique and tried it on red blood cells. They, too, could be stored for a long time by using glycerol. The method was especially useful for storing rare blood types, although it was too expensive and complicated for storing common types.

She moved on to research on freezing ovarian and other endocrine tissues. She published the first report on the freezing of bone-marrow stem cells and blood lymphocytes. She also worked on the separation of chondrocytes from the cartilage matrix, followed by freezing so that articular cartilage could be banked.

She was appointed head of the Division of Low Temperature Biology of the Clinical Research Centre in 1967. However, when the center moved to Harrow in 1970, she did not move with it. Her major reason was apparently ethical. She feared experimentation on human subjects and thought that this was the direction that the laboratory was taking. When she was head of the laboratory she made it clear that she was against *in vitro* human fertilization. She worked with the pioneers in this subject, Robert Edwards and Patrick Steptoe, whose research later led to the conception and birth of Louise Brown, the first person born from this method. While Smith was laboratory head, however, she insisted that *in vitro* fertilization of humans was unethical and went to the

director of the institute, Sir Charles Harrington, who banned research on humans.

Audrey Smith combined a knowledge of the characteristics of the organism with great creativity in order to answer questions about the cells and tissues with which she worked.

JH / MBO

PRIMARY SOURCES

Smith, Audrey U. With C. Polge and A. S. Parkes. "Revival of Spermatozoa after Vitrification and Dehydration at Low Temperatures." *Nature* 164 (1949): 666.

———. "Prevention of Haemolysis during Freezing and Thawing of Red Blood Cells." *Lancet* 2 (1950): 910–911.

———. With A. S. Parkes. "Freezing of Ovarian Tissue at Low Temperature." *Lancet* 2 (1951): 570–572.

———. "Twenty-Five Years of Research in Low Temperature Biology." *Koeltechniek* 67 (1974): 91–100.

SECONDARY SOURCES

Bindman, Lynn. "Audrey U. Smith (1915–1981)." In *Women Physiologists. An Anniversary Celebration of their Contributions to British Physiology.* London: Portland Press, 1993.

SMITH, CLARA ELIZA (1865–1943)

U.S. mathematician. Born 20 May 1865 to Georgiana and Edward Smith in Wellesley, Mass. Educated Mount Holyoke College (A.B., 1885); Yale University (Ph.D., 1904). Professional experience: Wellesley College, acting instructor in mathematics (1906–1907); West College for Women, instructor (1907–1908); Wellesley College, assistant (1908–1909), instructor (1909–1914), associate professor (1914–1924), professor (1924–1934), emerita professor (from 1934). Honors and memberships: Mathematical Association of America, council member (1923–1925), vice president (1927). Died 12 May 1943.

Women's colleges made it possible for Clara Smith to have a career as a mathematician. After she received her doctoral degree from Yale, she held a one-year position at Wellesley as an acting instructor. After a year at another college, she returned to Wellesley, where she spent the rest of her academic career. Her only time away from Wellesley was in 1918–1919, when she was an exchange professor at Goucher College. She was a member of the Mathematical Society and the Mathematical Association. She sat on the council of the latter society and served as its vice president in the late 1920s. Her research was on the theory of functions of real variables.

JH / MBO

PRIMARY SOURCES

Smith, Clara Eliza. "Representation of an Arbitrary Function by Means of Bessel's Functions." Ph.D. diss., Yale University, 1907.

———. *A Brief Course in Trigonometry.* Ann Arbor, Mich.: Edwards Brothers, 1927. Papers in Mount Holyoke Archives.

SECONDARY SOURCES

Grinstein, Louise. "Some 'Forgotten' Women of Mathematics: A Who Was Who." *Philosophia Mathematica* 13/14 (1976/77: 73–78.

STANDARD SOURCES

AMS 2–6.

SMITH, ELIZABETH (HIGHT) (1877–?)

U.S. plant pathologist. Born 12 January 1877 in Brookline, Mass. Educated Smith College (A.B., 1900); Massachusetts College (M.S., 1905). Professional experience: Mount Holyoke College, assistant botanist (1901); Connecticut high school, teacher (1902–1903); Massachusetts, teacher (1904); University of California, assistant plant pathologist (1910–1915), instructor (1910–1915), assistant professor (1915–1922). Death date unknown.

Interested in the diagnosis of plant diseases, Elizabeth Smith taught at the University of California and did research at the Experimental Station. She was a member of the Phytopathology Society. JH/MBO

PRIMARY SOURCES

Smith, Elizabeth H. "The Blossom End Rot of Tomatoes." *Massachusetts Experimental Station Technical Bulletin* 3 (1907). Offprint.

———. With Ralph E. Smith. "California Plant Diseases." *Bulletin California Agricultural Experiment Station* (Berkeley), no. 218 (1911): 1040–1193.

———. With Edith H. Phillips and Ralph E. Smith. "Fig Smut." *Bulletin California Agricultural Experiment Station,* no. 387 (1925). Offprint.

STANDARD SOURCES

AMS 3–5.

SMITH, EMILY ADELIA (PIDGEN) (fl. 1870s)

U.S. entomologist. Professional experience: Illinois assistant to Cyrus Thomas, state entomologist of Illinois.

Little information is available on Emily Adelia Smith's life. We know that she, along with G. H. French and D. W. Coquillet were employed to help Cyrus Thomas share in the work of the U.S. Entomological Commission, appointed after destructive outbreaks of the western locust. JH/MBO

PRIMARY SOURCES

Smith, Emily A. "Biological and Other Notes on *Pseudococcus aceris.*" *North American Entomologist* 1 (1880): 73–87.

SECONDARY SOURCES

Mallis, Arnold. *American Entomologists.* New Brunswick, N.J.: Rutgers University Press, 1971.

Osborn, Herbert. *A Brief History of Entomology.* Columbus, Ohio: The Spahr and Glenn Company, 1952.

Osborn, H., and Pamela Gilbert. *A Compendium of the Biographical Literature on Deceased Entomologists.* London: British Museum (Natural History), 1977.

SMITH, ERMA ANITA (1895–?)

U.S. physiologist and physician. Born 20 September 1895 in Larned, Kans. Educated University of Kansas (A.B., 1920); Vassar College (M.A., 1922); University of Chicago (Ph.D. in physiology, 1926); Rush Medical School (M.D., 1933). Professional experience: Vassar College, instructor (1920–1922); Iowa State College, associate professor (1928–1945); Duke University, student health officer and physician (1946–1949); Veterans Administration Hospital, physician, Framingham, Mass. (1950–1952); Hines, Ill. (1952–1955); Cleveland, Ohio (1955–1961); private practice (1961–?). Death date unknown.

Erma Smith began her professional career as a physiologist, but then got her medical degree and gradually moved away from physiology to medical practice. She was a member of the Physiological Society, the Society for Experimental Biology, the American Medical Association, and the Academy for Physical Medicine and Rehabilitation. Her research interests were also divided between physiology and medicine. Her first interest was in physiological chemistry and later physical medicine and rehabilitation. JH/MBO

STANDARD SOURCES

AMS 5–8, P&B 10.

SMITH, ERMINNIE ADELE (PLATT) (1836–1886)

U.S. geologist and ethnologist. Born 26 April 1836 in Marcellus, N.Y., to Ermina (Dodge) and Joseph Platt. Married Simeon H. Smith. Four sons. Educated Troy (N.Y.) Female Seminary (1850–1853); Heidelberg; School of Mines, Freiberg. Professional experience: research in geology, ethnology, and anthropology. Died 9 June 1886, in Jersey City, N.J.

Erminnie Platt was born in New York and attended the Troy Female Seminary. At this seminary, she became interested in science courses. In 1855, two years after she left school, she married Simeon H. Smith, who was a wealthy Chicago lumber dealer and merchant. During the years in Chicago, she helped classify and label mineral collections, pursuing an interest in geology that she had maintained since childhood. The family moved from Chicago to Jersey City, New Jersey, in 1866. The Smiths had four boys whom they sent to Germany for school. Erminnie accompanied them, and while she was there received more formal training in geology. She studied crystallography at Strassburg and graduated from a two-year course in mineralogy at the School of Mines in Freiberg. When she returned home, she became known for popularizing science. She became interested in ethnology and anthropology and was elected secretary of the anthropology division of the American Association for the Advancement of Science. She was the first woman Fellow of the New York Academy of Sciences. She died at the age of fifty, and two years later (1888) an annual award in geology was established in her name at Vassar College.

Smith was a gifted amateur. She did much of her work in geology while raising her family. However, her work in ethnology, done later, is often thought to be more important. She became the first woman to do field ethnography (she spent summers from 1880 to 1885 traveling and compiling an Iroquois dictionary) and is well known for her work on the language and culture of the Six Nations of the Iroquois Federation. Partial support for this work came from the Smithsonian Institution's Bureau of Ethnology, which she began under the tutelage of the anthropologist Lewis Henry Morgan. Like ALICE FLETCHER, who also relied on an educated informant, she was aided in this work by the Tuscorora ethnologist John N. B. Hewitt, who later joined the U.S. Bureau of Ethnology.   JH/MBO

PRIMARY SOURCES

Smith, Erminnie Adele Platt. *Myths of the Iroquois.* Washington, D.C.: Government Printing Office, 1883.

———. *Life among the Mohawks in the Catholic Missions Quebec Province.* Washington, D.C.: Government Printing Office, 1883.

SECONDARY SOURCES

Elder, Eleanor S. "Women in Early Geology." *Journal of Geological Education* 30 (1982): 287–293.

Elliott. *American Science.*

Saybders-Lee, Sara L. *In Memoriam. Mrs. Erminnie A. Smith. Marcellus, N.Y., 26 April 1837 [sic]–Jersey City, N.J., June 9, 1886.* Boston: Lee and Shepard, [1890].

STANDARD SOURCES

DAB (article by Nancy Oestreich Lurie); *NAW.*

SMITH, ISABEL FOTHERGILL (1890–1990)

U.S. geologist. Born 15 November 1890 in Greeley, Colo. Father educated at Cornell. Three siblings who survived past childhood. Never married. Educated Bryn Mawr College (A.B., 1915; A.M., 1919; Ph.D., 1922). M. Carey Thomas European Fellowship (1920–1921). Professional experience: Marcy C. Wheeler School, R.I., teacher (1915–1917); Concord (Mass.) Academy, teacher (1922–1923); Smith College, instructor of geology (1923–1925), assistant professor (1925–1928); Scripp's College, class dean (1928–1929), professor (1929–1954), emerita professor (1954–1990). Died September 1990.

Born in Greeley, Colorado, Isabel Fothergill Smith was the youngest of four living girls. Her family moved to Los Angeles when she was in her early teens. Since her father was a graduate of Cornell University and her sisters attended the University of Colorado, Stanford, and Columbia University Teachers College, Isabel assumed that she would have the same opportunities. However, her father was killed in a horse-and-buggy accident and her mother was unable to find funds for her education. A cousin came to the rescue and provided Isabel an oppportunity to study at Bryn Mawr, where she joined FLORENCE BASCOM's circle. Bascom appeared to be an ideal mentor for Fothergill both personally and because of her exceptional knowledge of both regional geology and crystallographic techniques.

After receiving her bachelor's degree in 1915, she continued for master's and doctoral degrees. From her research for her master's thesis, Smith published "A Columbite Crystal from Boothwyn, Pennsylvania." Upon Bascom's recommendation, Smith received an M. Carey Thomas European Fellowship from Bryn Mawr (1920–1921). At Paris she studied mineralogy with A. Lacroix and studied the methods and materials collected by the early crystallographer René-Just Haüy. When she returned, she completed her doctoral degree, which was also published.

After teaching for six years at Smith College, Smith left the East to become the first dean at Scripps College. At Scripps she became involved with interdisciplinary programs. However, she resigned her deanship so that she could return to teaching. In order to prepare herself to teach a course in the history of science, Smith took her sabbatical year to study this subject first at Columbia and then at Harvard with Professor George Sarton. She was committed to the value of a truly liberal education. Smith retired from Scripps as professor emerita of geology and the history of science. In 1979 a scholarship was established in her name with a gift of one hundred thousand dollars from an anonymous donor. After retirement, Smith wrote a biography of her mentor, Florence Bascom, *The Stone Lady*. Smith died in September 1990. JH/MBO

PRIMARY SOURCES

Smith, Isabel Fothergill. "A Columbite Crystal from Boothwyn, Pennsylvania." *American Mineralogist* 4 (1919): 132–123. From her master's thesis.

———. "Genesis of anorthosites of Piedmont, Pennsylvania," *Pan-American Geologist* 38 (1922): 29–50.

———. "Anorthosite in the Piedmont Province of Pennsylvania." Doctoral thesis accepted by Bryn Mawr College, 1923.

———. *The Stone Lady: A Memoir of Florence Bascom.* Bryn Mawr, Pa.: Bryn Mawr College, 1981.

Smith's papers are at the Denison Library, Scripps College.

SECONDARY SOURCES

Schneiderman, Jill Stephanie. "Growth and Development of a Woman Scientist and Educator." *Earth Sciences History* 11 (1992): 37–39.

SMITH, ISABEL SEYMOUR (1864–?)

U.S. botanist. Born 22 October 1864 in Hillsdale, Mich. Educated Oberlin College (A.B., 1901); University of Chicago (M.S., 1905; Ph.D., 1922). Professional experience: public high school, Ohio, teacher (1891–1895); Oberlin College, assistant botanist (1897–1902); Illinois College, instructor in biology (1903–1905), assistant professor (1905–1909), professor (1909–1927); emerita professor (from 1927). Death date unknown.

In addition to her teaching positions, Isabel Seymour Smith was assistant curator of the Oberlin College herbarium from 1928 to 1934. She was a resident at the Marine Biological Laboratory, Woods Hole, in 1903 and again in 1910. An active member of the Botanical Society of the Illinois Academy of Sciences, Smith served as vice-president in 1919. She worked on the nutrition of the egg in *Zamia*, native trees of Morgan County, Ill., and seedling anatomy of *Nelumbo lutea*. She also did herbarium work on flowering plants and fungi. JH/MBO

STANDARD SOURCES
AMS 1–7.

SMITH, JANICE MINERVA (1906–)

U.S. nutritionist. Born 13 October 1906 in Osco, Ill. Educated University of Illinois (A.B., 1930; M.S., 1932; Ph.D. in biochemistry, 1937). Professional experience: University of Illinois, assistant nutritionist (1930–1936); Pennsylvania State College, associate professor of human nutrition research (1937–1943); War

Food Administration, United States Department of Agriculture, nutritionist (1943–1944); University of Illinois, Urbana, professor (1944–1975), head of home economics department (1950–1971), emerita professor (from 1975).

Janice Minerva Smith was a nutritionist who spent most of her professional career at the University of Illinois. Concurrently, she was a member of the community-family work group of the United States Department of Agriculture from 1963 to 1964 and a member of the National Advisory Committee on Food and Fiber from 1965 to 1967. She was a member of the American Association for the Advancement of Science, the American Home Economic Association, the American Dietetic Association, the American Institute of Nutrition, and the New York Academy of Science.

Smith's research was on the protein requirements of adults, calcium requirements of adolescents and preschool children, the nutritional status of selected populations in Pennsylvania and Illinois, riboflavin and thiamine needs of preadolescents, and energy and dietary needs of the aging. JH/MBO

STANDARD SOURCES
AMS 8, B 9, P&B 10–14.

SMITH, MARGARET KIEVER (1856–1934)

Canadian/U.S. psychologist. Born 1856 in Amherst, Nova Scotia, Canada. Educated Oswego, N.Y., Normal School (diploma, 1883); universities of Jena, Thuringen, Göttingen; University of Zurich (Ph.D., 1900). Professional experience: State Normal School at New Paltz, N.Y., instructor (from 1901), professor and director of psychology and geography. Died 1934.

Born in New York but educated in Germany, Margaret Kiever Smith's research interests included the psychology of rhythm and work, reaction time as a measure of physical condition, and the value of Latin as a normal school subject. KM

PRIMARY SOURCES

Smith, Margaret K. *Rhythmus und Arbeit.* Leipzig: Engelmann, 1900. Ph.D. diss., University of Zurich.

STANDARD SOURCES
AMS 1–5; Siegel and Finley; *Woman's Who's Who of America.*

SMITH, MARIAN WESLEY (1907–1961)

U.S. anthropologist. Born 10 May 1907 in New York City. Married H. Farrant Akehurst (1952). Educated Columbia University (A.B., 1934; Ph.D., 1938); London School of Economics, Department of Anthropology, part-time academic staff (ten years).

Honors and memberships: American Ethnological Society, secretary-treasurer, vice-president, president, and editor; Royal Anthropological Institute, honorary secretary (1956). Died 1961.

When Marian Smith was three years old she had a severe case of poliomyelitis, which left one leg partially paralyzed. In spite of this handicap, she was able to do field work in northwest Wasington State and the adjacent parts of British Columbia. She studied at Columbia University, claiming to be the last student of Franz Boas. When she married H. Farrant Akehurst, a senior executive of British Insulated Callender's Cables, Ltd., she became closely involved with British anthropology. Their home at Bickenhall Mansions and later in a penthouse on the Marylebone Road became the gathering point of a circle of anthropologist friends. Since her husband's business took her to many different parts of the world, she went with him and pursued her anthropological interests. Her work in Australia was especially noteworthy.

She became associated with the department of anthropology of the London School of Economics for ten years. She worked part time, because of her commitment to numerous other activities, but regularly lectured on psychology and social anthropology and on current trends in American anthropology. In these courses she maintained a balance between her American cultural anthropology and British social anthropology.

Smith was always active in professional organizations. While she was in the United States, she was secretary-treasurer, vice-president, president, and editor of the American Ethnological Society.

Her most important research was in the ethnology of the Americas and Asia and the archeology and folklore of North America, Europe, the Near and Middle East, and India. She did field work on the Indians of Washington State and British Columbia. JH/MBO

PRIMARY SOURCES
Smith, Marian Wesley. "The Cultural Development of the Northwest Coast." *Southwestern Journal of Anthropology* 12 (1956): 272–294.

SECONDARY SOURCES
De Laguna, Frederica. "Marion Wesley Smith." *American Antiquities* 27 (April 1962): 567–569.
Mourant, A. E. "Dr. Marian W. Smith." *Nature* 192 (9 December 1961): 917.
"Obituary, Marion Wesley Smith." *Man* 61 (October 1961): 176–178. Obituary notice. Includes portrait.

STANDARD SOURCES
IDA.

SMITH, MATILDA (1854–1926)

British botanical artist. Born Bombay 30 July 1854. Professional experience: Kew, botanical artist.

As a botanical artist, Matilda Smith contributed to *Curtis's Magazine,* and illustrated the plants for other botanical books. JH/MBO

PRIMARY SOURCES
Balfour, Isaac Bayle. *Balfour's Botany of Socotra.* Edinburgh: R. Grant and Son, 1888. Plates by Matilda Smith.
Cheeseman, Thomas Frederick. *Illustrations of the New Zealand Flora.* Wellington, N.Z.: J. Mackay, government printer, 1914. Illustrations by Matilda Smith.
Hemsley, William Botting. *Report on the Scientific Results of the Voyage of H.M.S. Challenger during the Years 1873–1876.* London: Printed for H.M. Stationary Office, 1885–1886. Plates by Matilda Smith.
Hooker, William Jackson. *Icones Plantarum.* Codicote, Hertfordshire: Wheldon and Wesley, 1881–1923. Plates by Matilda Smith.
Smith, Matilda. With others. *Enumeration of All the Plants Known from China Proper, Formosa, Hainan, the Corea, the Luchu Archipelago, and the Island of Hongkong: Together with Their Distribution and Synonymy.* London: The Linnean Society, Longmans, Green, Williams and Norgate, 1886–1905. One of three authors of this work which was orginally published as volumes 23, 26, and 36 of the *Journal of the Linnean Society.* The first author is Francis Blackwell Forbes.

SECONDARY SOURCES
Gardener's Chronicle (1927): 40.
Journal of Botany (1927): 57–58.
Journal of the Kew Guild (1916): 265. Portrait.
Journal of the Kew Guild (1922): 83.
Journal of the Kew Guild (1927): 527–528. Portrait.
Kew Bulletin (1920): 210
Kew Bulletin (1921): 317–318.
Kew Bulletin (1927): 135–139.
Proceedings of the Linnean Society (1926–1927): 100–101.

STANDARD SOURCES
Desmond.

SMITH, OLIVE WATKINS (1901–1983?)

U.S. biochemist and endocrinologist. Born 29 April 1901 in Worcester, Mass. Married George Smith (1930). Two children. Educated Vassar College (A.B., 1923); Radcliffe College (Ph.D., 1928). Professional experience: Wellesley College, assistant chemist (1923–1925); Harvard Medical School, assistant biochemist (1925–1929); Fearing Research Laboratory, Free Hospital for

Women, Brookline, Mass. (1929–1943), associate director of research (1943–1947), director (1947–1963), associate director and consultant in research (1963–1967); Boston Hospital for Women, consultant in biochemistry (1968–1971); Fearing Research Laboratory, Boston Hospital for Women, director (1971–1980). Honors and memberships: Smith College, honorary Sc.D. (1951); Radcliffe College, Award of Merit (1960); American Association for the Advancement of Science. Death date unknown.

Biochemist Olive Watkins Smith and her husband, gynecologist George Smith, studied together toxemias of pregnancy, diseases of female reproductive organs, and the reason many pregnancies end in miscarriages. She spent her career at the Free Hospital for Women in Brookline, Massachusetts. Her husband became a professor of gynecology at the Harvard Medical School and she succeeded him as director of the Fearing Research Laboratory until 1960. She returned to the hospital in 1970 and served until 1980. In spite of all of the help the two Smiths provided pregnant women, they are too often remembered for their advocacy of a medication that had tragic implications. DES (diethylstilbestrol) had been shown to be effective in preventing miscarriages in women who were prone to them. What they did not realize at the time was that the "cure" that they prescribed widely was shown to cause vaginal cancer in the patients' daughters and other effects in their sons. JH/MBO

PRIMARY SOURCES
Smith, Olive Watkins. "The Occurrence of Lactose in the Urine, with Especial Reference to Pregnancy and Lactation." Ph.D. diss., Radcliffe College, 1928.
———. "The Men in My Life." *Radcliffe Quarterly* 67, no. 2 (June 1981): 25–27.

SECONDARY SOURCES
Harvard Magazine 85 (July-August 1983): 95. Obituary notice.
Meyers, Robert. *DES: The Bitter Pill.* New York: Seaview/ Putnam, 1983. See chapters 5 and 6.
Radcliffe Quarterly 69, no. 3 (September 1983): 33. Obituary notice.

STANDARD SOURCES
AMS 5–8, B9, P&B 10–14; Rossiter 1995.

SMITH, PLEASANCE (REEVE) (1773–1877)
British botanical benefactor. Born 11 May 1773 in Lowestoft, Suffolk. Married J. E. Smith. Benefactor of the Linnean Society. Died 3 February 1877 in Lowestoft.

Pleasance Smith is important in the history of botany because of her marriage to Sir James Edward Smith, one of the founders of the Linnean Society, who purchased Linnaeus's collections. She wrote and edited the memoirs and correspondence of her husband. JH/MBO

PRIMARY SOURCES
Smith, Pleasance, ed. *Memoir and Correspondence of Sir J. E. Smith.* 2 vols. London: Longman, Rees, Orne Browne, Green and Longman, 1832.

SECONDARY SOURCES
Journal of Botany (1877): 95–96.

SMITH, WINIFRED (1858–1925)
British botanist. Born 5 November 1858 in Mortlake, Surrey. Educated University of London (B.Sc., 1904). Professional experience: University College, London, lecturer in botany.

Winifred Smith was educated at the University of London and later became a lecturer in botany at that institution. She was a Fellow of the Linnean Society from 1908. JH/MBO

PRIMARY SOURCES
Smith, Winifred. "*Macaranga triloba.*" *New Phytologist* 2 (1903): 79–82.
———. "Anatomy of Sapotaceous Seedlings." *Transactions of the Linnean Society of Botany* 7 (1909): 189–200.

SECONDARY SOURCES
Journal of Botany (1926): 56.

STANDARD SOURCES
Desmond.

SNELLING, LILIAN (1879–1972)
British botanical artist. Born 8 June 1879 at St. Mary Cray, Kent. Professional experience: Royal Botanic Garden, Edinburgh, staff (1916–1921). Died 12 October 1972 in St. Mary Cray.

Lilian Snelling was a botanical artist at the Royal Botanic Garden, Edinburgh. She published illustrations in *Curtis's Botanic Magazine* from 1922 to 1952. JH/MBO

PRIMARY SOURCES
Snelling, Lilian. Illus. A. Grove, *A Supplement to Elwes' Mongraph of genus Lilium.* London: Dulau, 1933–1962. Illustrations by Lillian Snelling.
———, illus. F. Stoker. *Study of Genus Paeonia.* 1946.
———, illus. Frederick Claude Stern, *A Study of the Genus Paeonia.* London: Royal Horticultural Society, 1946.

Snelling's drawings are at Kew and the British Museum, Natural History.

SECONDARY SOURCES

Blunt, Wilfred. *The Art of Botanical Illustration*. London: Collins, [1950]. See page 251.

Curtis's Botanical Magazine (1952–1953). Portrait.

Hunt Library. *Artists from the Royal Botanical Gardens, Kew.* Pittsburgh: The Hunt Institute for Botanical Documentation, 1974. See pages 56–57.

Hunt Library. *Catalogue, 3rd International Exhibition of Botanical Art and Illustration*. Pittsburgh: The Hunt Institute for Botanical Documentation, 1972. 159 portraits.

Journal of the Royal Horticultural Society 1973.

"Miss Lillian Snelling." *Gardener's Chronicle* 139 (1956): 7. Portrait.

Times, 17 October 1972.

STANDARD SOURCES

Desmond.

SNETHLAGE, EMILIE (1868–1929)

German ornithologist. Born 1868 in Kratz, Westphalia. Professional experience: director of the zoological section, Brazilian Museum (1907–1929). Died 1929 in Amazonia, Brazil.

Although Emilie Snethlage was born in Germany, she spent most of her life in Brazil. She traveled extensively in Brazil to collect birds. She became director of the zoological section of the Brazilian Museum in 1907. The British Ornithologists' Union conferred an honorary membership on Snethlage in 1915 even though England and Germany were at war. She also had honorary memberships in the Berlin Geographical Society and the Academy of Sciences of Brazil.

JH/MBO

PRIMARY SOURCES

Snethlage, Emilie. "Über die Frage vom Muskelansatz und der Herkunft der Muskulatur bei den Arthropoden." Thesis, University of Freiburg, 1905. Harvard's Museum of Comparative Zoology has a copy.

———. *Catalogo das aves amazonicas, contendo todas as especies descriptas e mencionadas ate' 1913*. Para, Brazil: Museu Goeld; printed by Hopfer, Bung, German, 1914.

STANDARD SOURCES

Ogilvie 1986.

SNOW, JULIA WARNER (1863–1927)

U.S. botanist. Born 1863 in La Salle, Ill., to Charlotte (Warner) and Norman Snow. Never married. Educated Cornell University (B.S., 1888; M.S., 1889); University of Zurich (Ph.D., 1893). Professional experience: American College for Girls, Constantinople, science teacher (1894–1896), assistant in botany (1897), instructor (1898–1900); University of Michigan, instructor; Rockford College, instructor (1900–1901); Smith College, assistant (1901–1902), instructor (1902–1906), associate professor (from 1906). Died 24 October 1927.

Little biographical information is available on Julia Snow. However, from the twenty-eighth Official Circular of Smith College, 1901–1902, we know that she was an assistant in the biology department under Professor William Francis Ganong. She taught General Botany, Morphology and Ecology of the Groups, and Classification. The twenty-ninth Official Circular of Smith College, 1902–1903, reported that she had been promoted to instructor and taught General Botany, Morphology and Ecology of the Groups from the Algae and Fungi to the Phanerogams, and Bacteriology. In 1902, she was the first at the college to teach bacteriology.

Julia Snow worked on plant conductive tissue and on freshwater algae. She was a part of the U.S. Fish Commission's biological survey of Lake Erie during the summers of 1898 through 1901.

JH/MBO

PRIMARY SOURCES

Snow, Julia W. *The Conductive Tissues of the Monocotyledonous Plants*. Zurich: F. Lohbauer, 1893.

STANDARD SOURCES

AMS 1–4; Ogilvie 1986; *Woman's Who's Who of America*.

SNOW, MARY (PILKINGTON) (ca. 1902–1978)

British botanist. Married G. R. S. Snow. Professional experience: Oxford University, tutor in botany. Died 13 November 1978 in Perpignon.

Although the particulars of her education are unknown, Mary Snow was a tutor at Oxford and probably received a portion of her education at that institution. She married George Robert Sabine Snow, Fellow of the Royal Society, a botanist with special interests in geotropism and phyllotaxis. Mary collaborated with her husband in studies on phyllotaxis. She made many benefactions, including one that made possible the development of Oxford Botanic Gardens arboretum at Nuneham Courtney.

JH/MBO

SECONDARY SOURCES
Times, 22 November 1978. Obituary notice.

STANDARD SOURCES
Desmond.

SODDY, WINIFRED MOLLER (BEILBY) (1885–1936)

Scottish researcher in radioactivity. Born 1 March 1885 in Edinburgh to Sir George Beilby and Lady Emma (Clarke) Beilby. One brother. Married Frederick Soddy in 1908; no children. Died 17 August 1936 at Oxford, England.

Winifred M. Beilby's father was a prominent industrial chemist. Through her paternal grandmother she was descended from the Mollers, an aristocratic Danish family. The Beilbys moved from Edinburgh to Glasgow in 1900. Winifred Beilby was educated at home, then studied art in Paris around 1902. She married Frederick Soddy, codiscoverer of atomic transmutation and later of isotopy, while he was at the University of Glasgow. Some of his research at Glasgow was supported by Sir G. Beilby, who had published a paper on the luminescence produced by beta and gamma rays in 1905, possibly sparking his daughter's interest in these radiations.

W. M. Beilby Soddy worked with her husband, coauthoring one publication in 1910 with Soddy and his student A. S. Russell on the absorption of gamma rays from radium. From the mostly exponential absorption they observed in a number of materials, the team concluded that the rays were initially homogeneous, which would mean they were not related to beta emission. (Later it was shown that gamma radiation is generally inhomogeneous.) In further studies to determine the relations between β and γ rays, she compared the relative intensities of these radiations from two minerals. Winifred Soddy also assisted F. Soddy with researches that led to the concept of isotopy, making many accurate measurements and laboriously separating radium from barium.

JH/MBO

PRIMARY SOURCES
Soddy, F., W. M. Soddy, and A. S. Russell. "The Question of the Homogeneity of the γ Rays." *Philosophical Magazine* 19 (1910): 725–757.
Russell, A. S., and F. Soddy. "The γ-Rays of Thorium and Actinium." *Philosophical Magazine* 21 (1911): 130–154.
Notes and letters concerning W. M. Beilby Soddy at the Bodleian Library, Oxford.

SECONDARY SOURCES
Howarth, Muriel. *Pioneer Research on the Atom.* London: New World Publications, 1958.

Kent, Andrew, "Frederick Soddy (1877–1956)." *Proceedings of the Chemical Society of London* (1963): 327–331. Includes Lord Fleck, "Early Work in the Radioactive Elements," p. 330.
Malley, Marjorie. *From Hyperphosphorescence to Nuclear Decay: A History of the Early Years of Radioactivity, 1896–1914.* Berkeley, 1976; Ann Arbor, University Microfilms. See page 282.
Rayner-Canham, M. F. and G. W. Rayner-Canham. "Pioneer Women in Nuclear Science." *American Journal of Physics* 58 (1990): 1036–1043.
Rutherford, Ernest. *Radioactive Substances and Their Radiations.* Cambridge: Cambridge University Press, 1913. See pages 260, 299.
Letters from F. Soddy to E. Rutherford, Rutherford Correspondence, Cambridge, England.
Wise, Leonard. *Frederick Soddy.* London: Holborn Publishing and distributing Co., 1934. See for information concerning his wife.

SOKOL'SKAYA, ANNA NIKOLAYEVNA (1901–1971)

Russian geologist. Born 3 July 1901 in Moscow. Father a teacher in the Moscow Conservatory. Three children. Educated secondary school; Moscow University (finished geology course 1926). Professional experience: Moscow Department of the Committee for Geology, geologist (1928–1936); Paleontological Institute, geological researcher (1936–1971). Died 3 October 1971 in Moscow.

Little information is available on Anna Sokol'skaya's life. Although an obituary notice mentions that she had three children, it does not allude to a husband or other family members. We know that her interests in nature surpassed her strictly scholarly interests, perhaps evinced by the fact that all three of her children became natural scientists. She had a great love for literature and music as well.

Sokol'skaya began her geological work while she was still a student at Moscow University. She began work in the Moscow Land Department and the hydrogeologic section of the Moscow Public Health Department. Under the supervision of Professor A. P. Ivanov, she surveyed the geology and fauna of the southern flank of the Moscow Basin. She began full-time work in the Moscow Department of the Committee for Geology as a geologist in 1928. She headed geologic teams that produced geologic and hydrogeologic maps in the Moscow Basin. During her work as a geologist, she was interested in paleontology. When the Paleontological Institute was organized in 1936, she transferred there. Originally educated in geology and stratigraphy, she now taught herself the biology necessary for a paleontologist. Her research centered on brachiopods, with meticulous attention to their morphology, ontogeny, and systematics. Sokol'skaya was the first person in the Soviet Union to study large groups of brachiopods and to attempt to find both temporal and geographic phylogenetic links between groups.

She published several monographs and papers on this subject as well as serving as a major coauthor on team studies and summaries made by the Paleontological Institute on Paleozoic brachiopods.

Known for her tireless work on expeditions, Sokol'skaya not only was a careful observer but was a skilled interpreter of these data. CK/MBO

PRIMARY SOURCES

Sokol'skaya, Anna Nikolayevna. "Geologicheskoye stroyeniye doliny r. Moskvy mezhdu s. Srasskini i Shelepikhoy." *Moscow Geological Trust* 5 (1937): 3–27.

———. *Evolution of the Genus Productella and Related Forms in the Paleozoic of the Moscow Basin.* Moscow: N.p., 1948.

———. "Chonetidae Russkoi platformy." *Trudy Paleontologicheskogo Instituta* 27 (1950).

———. With T. G. Sarycheve. "Opredelitel paleozoiskikh brakhiopod Podmoskovnoi kotloviny." *Trudy Paleontologicheskogo Instituta* 32 (1952).

———. "Strophomenids of the Russian Platform." *Trudy Paleontologicheskogo Instituta* 51 (1954).

SECONDARY SOURCES

Grigor'yeva, A. D., Ye. A. Ivanova, and T. G. Sarcheva. "Anna Nikolayevna Sokol'skaya 1901–1971." *Paleontological Journal* 6, no. 1 (1972): 134–135.

SOLIS QUIROGA, MARGARITA DELGADO DE (fl. 1926–1957)

Mexican physician. Professional experience: University of Mexico, Faculty of Medicine, professor of physiological and biological research. Honors and memberships: Mexican Medical Women's Association, vice-president (1926); Pan American Medical Women's Alliance (1953).

Margarita Delgado de Solis Quiroga's birth and death dates are unknown. She was a physiologist and physician at the University of Mexico's Faculty of Medicine. In 1926, she was vice-president of the Mexican Medical Women's Association and in 1957, the president of the Pan American Medical Alliance.

STANDARD SOURCES
Lovejoy.

SOLLAS, IGERNA BRÜNHILDA JOHNSON (1877–1965)

British natural scientist and geologist. Born 16 March 1877 at Dawlish. Father William Johnson Sollas. One sister, Hertha B. C. Sollas. Never married. Educated Alexandra School and College, Dublin; Newnham College (Natural Science Tripos, Part I class 1, 1899; Part II (zool), class 1, 1901); Bathurst Student and demonstrator (1901–1902). Professional experience: Newnham College, lecturer in zoology (1903–1904; 1906–1913); College Research Fellow (1904–1906). Died November 1965.

Igerna Sollas, commonly known as Hilda, was the younger daughter of a geology professor at Oxford. She attended Newnham College and came to this college with her sister Hertha from Alexandra College, Dublin. She was associated with Newnham until 1913, when she resigned her lectureship and went to live with her father in Oxford. She later became interested in Christian Science and became a practitioner. As her sister pointed out, this made further experimental work on animals impossible. She took up gardening and ran her father's large house and garden, taking possession of it when he died in 1936. She occasionally published articles in Christian Science journals.

Sollas collaborated with her father in attempting to determine the internal structures of fossils. She also worked on methods of separating minerals for chemical analysis. She published several papers on paleontology and in zoology on cross-breeding in moths and guinea pigs. She published in the *Proceedings of the Royal Society* and in the *Philosophical Transactions of the Royal Society.* JH/MBO

PRIMARY SOURCES

Sollas, Igerna B. J. With William Johnson Sollas. "An Account of the Devonian fish *Palaeospondylus gunni,* Traquair." *Royal Society of London, Philosophical Transactions,* Series B 196 (1904): 267–294. *Proceedings* 72 (1904): 98–99.

———. "Porifera (Sponges)." In *Cambridge Natural History,* vol. 1, 163–242. London: Macmillan and Co., Ltd., 1906; 1922.

———. With William Johnson Sollas. "Lapworthura: a Typical Brittlestar of the Silurian Age, with Suggestions for a New Classification of the Ophiuroidea." *Royal Society of London, Philosophical Transactions,* Series B 202 (1912): 213–232.

———. "On Onychaster, a Carboniferous Brittle-Star." *Royal Society of London, Philosophical Transactions,* Physical and Engineering B 204 (1913): 51–62.

———. With William Johnson Sollas. "A Study of the Skull of a *Dicynodon* by Means of Serial Sections." *Royal Society of London, Philosophical Transactions* Series B, 204 (1914): 201–225.

STANDARD SOURCES
Creese and Creese; *Newnham,* vol. 1; *Newnham Roll.*

SOLOMKO-SOTIRIADIS, EVGENIIA (fl. 1887)

Russian geologist. Born 1862 in Yaroslavl, Russia. Married Greek philosopher Sotiriadis. Educated Catherine Women's University, Moscow (graduated 1878); Highest Women's Courses, St. Petersburg (finished 1883); University of Munich (studied with Karl Zittel); and University of Zurich (Ph.D., 1887). Professional experience: St. Petersburg University, Department of Geology and Paleontology, researcher. Died 1898.

Evgeniia Solomko-Sotiriadis died when she was only thirty-six years old. First educated at home, she next attended the Moscow Catherine Women's University, where she won an award upon graduation. After leaving Moscow, she studied in the physics/mathematics department at the Higher Courses for Women in St. Petersburg. Showing herself to be an excellent student, she stayed on after graduation in the department of geology and paleontology of St. Petersburg University, led by a famous geologist and petrographer, A. A. Inostrantsev. The assistant professor was P. N. Venukov, a scholar of Devonian fauna. She first worked in petrography under Inostrantsev, participating in geological field trips around the province of Olen in the Caucasus, and in the Ukraine. She also taught practical lessons in petrography in women's courses. Her first published work was a detailed description of volcanic rocks near the settlement of Isachki Poltavskaya province (1884). Her interests, however, were more in paleontology, so she worked with the demanding assistant professor, paleontologist Venukov. He studied Devonian brachiopods and mollusks, which were both interesting and easy to identify groups. However, he gave Solomko the group which he had immense problems identifying, the Devonian stromatopors. In order to tackle this assignment, Solomko had to start at the very beginning. It was helpful that she knew German well, for many of her sources were in that lanaguage. She consulted Professor Grevink at Derpt University (Tartu) who helped her identify successfully this Devonian stromatopor.

Venukov assigned her another even more difficult task. She was to describe a collection of Jurassic and Cretaceous corals of the Crimea. She went to Germany to work with Karl von Zittel on this problem. Von Zittel was sympathetic in his treatment of women geologists in general and especially of Solomko. He allowed her both to identify corals in the paleontological museum and to listen to his lectures. At this point, she realized that she needed a professional degree, but it was impossible to obtain one in Imperial Germany. Therefore, Solomko left Munich and went to Zurich, where she earned her doctoral degree in philosophy and geology. In 1887, she married a Greek man who was the director of the Odessa School of Commerce. After marrying Sotiriadis, she left her scientific career. She died ten years later, when she was only thirty-six years old.

Solomko-Sotiriadis published two important monographs—one on stromatoporoids and the other on Jurassic and Cretaceous corals.   CK/MBO

PRIMARY SOURCES

Solomko-Sotiriadis, Evgeniia. "Stromatopora des Devonischen System Russlands." *Verhandlungen der Russisch-Kaiserlichen Mineralogischen Gesellschaft zu St. Petersburg* 93 (1887): 1–48.

———. "Die Jura-und Kreidekorallen der Krim." *Verhandlungen der Russisch-Kaiserlichen Mineralogischen Gesellschaft zu St. Petersburg* 24 (1888): 67–231.

STANDARD SOURCES

Creese and Creese; Nalivkin.

SOMERVILLE, MARY (FAIRFAX) GREIG (1780–1872)

Scottish writer on science. Born 1780 at Jedburgh, Roxburghshire, Scotland, to Margaret (Charters) and Sir William Fairfax. Six siblings. Married (1) Samuel Greig; (2) William Somerville. Six children, three of whom survived to maturity: Woronzow Greig, Martha Somerville, Mary Somerville. Educated Miss Primrose's Boarding School, Musselburgh (ca. 1791); self-taught. Died 1872 in Naples, Italy.

Mary Fairfax, the fifth of seven children of Vice-Admiral Sir William Fairfax and his second wife, Margaret Charters, was born at the home of an aunt, Martha Charters Somerville. She later noted the she was born in the house of her future husband and nursed by his mother. Mary's childhood was spent at Burntisland, a seaport town across the Firth of Forth from Edinburgh. During these years, she spent much of her time outdoors, roaming and exploring. In recalling these times, she noted that she never cared for dolls and had few playmates. To amuse herself, she learned the habits and flight patterns of the birds in the garden.

This idyllic life came to a halt when Mary was eight and her father returned from one of his frequent long periods of sea duty and found that she read poorly and did not know how to write. Appalled at her ignorance, her father made her read a chapter of the Bible and part of the *Spectator* aloud every morning, after breakfast. The final indignity occurred when Mary was sent for a year to Miss Primrose's fashionable boarding school at Musselburgh, a period during which she was "utterly wretched." She reported that a few days after her arrival, "although perfectly straight and well-made, I was enclosed in stiff stays with a steel busk in front, while above my frock, bands drew my shoulders back till the shoulder blades met. Then a steel rod, with a semi-circle which went under the chin, was clasped to the steel busk in my stays. In this constrained state I, and most of the younger girls, had to prepare our lessons" (Somerville, *Recollections,* 21–22).

Mary was taken out of this expensive school, but sent to another when she was thirteen. She had developed a taste for reading by this time, and over the next few years she studied French and taught herself some Greek and Latin. She also attended to the usual feminine accomplishments such as practicing the pianoforte, painting, needlework, cooking, and reading poetry. Mary's uncle, Thomas Somerville, a historian and clergyman, was one of the few people who encouraged her intellectual aspirations.

When she was fourteen, Fairfax encountered algebra in an unorthodox way. She discovered a problem in a ladies' monthly magazine that seemed to be an ordinary problem in arithmetic. However she found the xs and ys in the answer puzzling. After being told that it was kind of arithmetic called algebra, she could discover nothing about it in the family library. Her drawing teacher, Alexander Nasmyth, finally provided Mary with the mathematical information she desired. After overhearing a conversation in which Nasmyth claimed that a knowledge of Euclid was essential to astronomy and mechanical science as well as to perspective, Mary acquired copies of both Euclid's *Elements* and Bonnycastle's *Algebra,* books used in the schools at that time. Fascinated by their contents, she began to spend long hours in study. Since her father discovered her new interest and forbade her to pursue it, she had to study in secret.

She married Samuel Greig, who was a captain in the Russian navy and a cousin on her mother's side in 1804. Greig, however, had a low opinion of the intellectual capabilities of women, and Mary was severely handicapped in continuing her mathematical studies. Greig died three years after their marriage, leaving her with two small sons, Woronzow, who grew up to be a successful barrister, and David, who died in infancy. She returned with the boys to her parents' home in Scotland.

Mary soon became popular in Edinburgh intellectual circles and became friends with many important figures, including the liberal statesman and educational reformer Henry Brougham (1778–1868), the scientist John Playfair (1748–1819), and Sir Walter Scott (1771–1832), author of the Waverly novels. William Wallace, who later became professor of mathematics at the University of Edinburgh, tutored her in mathematics. At this time she read Newton's *Principia.*

Mary's second marriage was more successful than the first. In 1812, she married her first cousin, William Somerville. Somerville approved of education for women and supported Mary in her mathematical and scientific work. Somerville was a widely read and well-traveled former army doctor. In 1816, he was appointed to the Army Medical Board, and the Somervilles moved to London. The invigorating intellectual and social climate provided an environment in which Mary flourished. Popular hosts, the Somervilles were a part of a social circle that included scientists John Herschel, Thomas Young, Roderick Murchison, Charles Babbage, and William Wollaston. In 1817, Mary Somerville traveled to Europe, where she met, among others, the scientists Dominique Arago, Jean Baptiste Biot, Georges Cuvier, Joseph Gay-Lussac, Pierre Simon, Marquis de Laplace, and Augustin de Candolle. In other words, she talked with many of the most important natural philosophers of her time.

Somerville was concerned with the care and education of her children, of whom one son, Woronzow Greig, and two daughters, Martha and Mary Somerville, survived to maturity; one child died at the age of ten, another at nine, and a third as a baby. When her husband accepted a post as physician at the Royal Hospital in Chelsea in 1824, Somerville was forced to make her home at a less convenient location on the outskirts of London. Moreover, she regularly attended the theater and the opera and gave frequent parties. In spite of these numerous interruptions Somerville began contributing to the literature of science. Her first paper, "On the Magnetizing Power of the More Refrangible Solar Rays," was presented to the Royal Society by her husband in 1826 and published in the *Philosophical Transactions.* Somerville's subsequent series of work on astronomy, physics, mathematics, chemistry, and geography earned her the respect of the leading scientists of the day.

Henry Brougham asked Somerville in 1827 to provide an English version of Laplace's *Mécanique céleste* for the library of his Society for the Diffusion of Useful Knowledge. She agreed to try, but insisted that if the manuscript were found unsatisfactory, it would be burned. Published in 1831 as *The Mechanism of the Heavens,* it was an immediate success and served as a college textbook for nearly a century. The high acclaim that it received encouraged Somerville to continue writing. She subsequently published *On the Connexion of the Physical Sciences* (1834), and articles on comets in the *Quarterly Review* (December 1835), *Physical Geography* (1848), and *On Molecular and Microscopic Science* (1869), as well as two more papers on the results of experiments with light rays (1836 and 1845).

For the sake of William Somerville's health, the Somervilles moved to Italy in 1838. They made many friends, and Mary Somerville was made a member of several Italian scientific societies. Although she outlived most of her friends and relatives—her husband died in 1860 and her son in 1865—she maintained her interest in life and kept herself informed about the latest developments in science to the very end. At the time of her death she was engrossed in a study of two recent mathematical texts, William Hamilton's *Lectures on Quaternions* and Benjamin Peirce's *Linear Associate Algebra.*

Somerville received many honors during her lifetime. Her

bust was placed in the Great Hall of the Royal Society in 1831; she and CAROLINE HERSCHEL became the first female honorary members of the Royal Astronomical Society in 1835; she was awarded the Royal Geographical Society's Victoria Gold Medal in 1870; and she had numerous other memberships and medals, from European and American scientific organizations. After her death, Oxford University named one of its first two women's colleges after her.

Mary Somerville's earliest published work was experimental. She designed a series of experiments that appeared to demonstrate that the sun's rays possessed magnetizing properties. Although the effects that she described were later shown to be attributable to factors other than the violet rays as she claimed, her results were widely accepted when her paper describing them appeared in 1826. She reported on further experiments with solar rays in a letter to Dominique Arago, who in 1836 presented the account to the French Academy of Sciences, which published it in its *Comptes rendus*. Her third and last venture into the experimental realm, an investigation of the effects of the rays of the solar spectrum on various plant juices, was described in a paper submitted to the Royal Society in 1845 and published in its *Philosophical Transactions.*

In spite of her early success, Somerville was skeptical about both her own creativity and of that of women in general. She wrote

In the climax of my great success, the approbation of some of the first scientific men of the age and of the public in general, I was highly gratified, but much less elated than might have been expected; for although I had recorded in a clear point of view some of the most refined and difficult analytical processes and astronomical discoveries, I was conscious that I had never made a discovery myself, that I had no originality. I have perseverance and intelligence but no genius; that spark from heaven is not granted to the sex. We are of the earth. Whether higher powers may be allotted to us in another existence, God knows; original genius, in science at least, is hopeless in this. (Patterson, 318.)

Mary Somerville's talent was a capacity to analyze, synthesize, and evaluate conflicting ideas. James Clerk Maxwell appreciated this ability and noted that she was able to understand and write clearly about the ideas on which scientists were working but could not clearly express.

Somerville's four books, *The Mechanism of the Heavens, On the Connexion of the Physical Sciences, Physical Geography,* and *On Molecular and Microscopic Science,* were models of clarity.

Even though Mary Somerville may have lacked scientific originality, as she was the first to admit, she was able to comprehend and synthesize the work of her contemporaries and to render it approachable for both general readers and more advanced students. Moreover, because of her cordial relations with so many of the leading scientists of her time, she was able to enlist their comments and suggestions in the preparation of her works. MBO

PRIMARY SOURCES

Somerville, Mary. "On the Magnetizing Power of the More Refrangible Solar Rays." *Philosophical Transactions of the Royal Society* 116 (1826): 132–139.

———. The Mechanism of the Heavens. London: John Murray, 1831.

———. *A Preliminary Dissertation on the Mechanism of the Heavens.* London: John Murray, 1832.

———. *On the Connexion of the Physical Sciences.* London: John Murray, 1834.

———. "Extrait d'une lettre de Mme Sommerville [*sic*] à M. Arago, Expériences sur la transmission des rayons chimiques du spectre solaire, à travers différents milieux." *Comptes rendus hebdomadaires des séances de l'Académie des Sciences* 3 (1836): 473–476.

———. "On the Action of the Rays of the Spectrum on Vegetable Juices." *Philosophical Transactions of the Royal Society* 5 (1845): 569–570.

———. *Physical Geography.* London: John Murray, 1848.

———. *On Molecular and Microscopic Science.* 2 vols. London: John Murray, 1869.

SECONDARY SOURCES

Basalla, George. "Mary Somerville: A Neglected Popularizer of Science." *New Scientist* 17 (March 1963): 531–533.

Eisberg, Joann. "Mary Somerville: Queen of Nineteenth-Century Science." Bachelor's thesis, Harvard University, 1982.

McKinlay, Jane. *Mary Somerville, 1780–1872.* Edinburgh: Scotland's Cultural Heritage, University of Edinburgh, 1987.

Osen, Lynn M. *Women in Mathematics.* Cambridge, Mass.: MIT Press, 1975.

Patterson, Elizabeth C. "The Case of Mary Somerville: An Aspect of Nineteenth-Century Science." *Proceedings of the American Philosophical Society* 118 (1974):169–275.

———. "Mary Somerville." *British Journal for the History of Science* 4 (December 1969): 311–339.

Pearl, Teri. *Math Equals: Biographies of Women Mathematicians and Related Activities.* Menlo Park, Calif.: Addison-Wesley, 1978.

Somerville, Martha. *Personal Recollections from Early Life to Old Age, of Mary Somerville. With Selections from her Correspondence.* Boston: Roberts Brothers, 1876.

STANDARD SOURCES

DNB; DSB; Ogilvie 1986.

SOMMER, ANNA LOUISE (1889–?)

U.S. plant nutritionist, botanist, and soil chemist. Born 9 January 1889 in Cucamonga, Calif. Educated University of California (B.S., 1920; M.S., 1921; Ph.D., 1924). Professional experience: University of California, teaching fellow in botany (1922; 1924) and plant nutrition (1924), assistant (1924–1926); University of Minnesota, research fellow (1926–1929); Alabama Polytechnic Institute, associate professor of plant nutrition and associate professor of soil chemistry (from 1930). Death date unknown.

Anna Sommer was born and educated in California. Her career developed, however, in Alabama (Alabama Polytechnic Institute), where she rose through the academic ranks. Her research was in general inorganic chemistry, inorganic nutrition of plants, and plant metabolism. She was a member of the Society of Plant Physiologists, the Soil Science Society, and the International Society for Soil Science.   JH/MBO

STANDARD SOURCES
AMS 4, B 9.

SOPHIA, ELECTRESS OF HANOVER (1630–1714)

Hanoverian student of philosophy, friend of Leibniz. Born 1630 to Elizabeth, daughter of James I of England, and Frederick V, elector of the Rhine Palatinate and later king of Bohemia. Eleven siblings. Married Ernest Augustus, elector of Hanover. Three sons, Georg Ludwig (later George I of Englnad), Friedrich August, and Ernst August. One daughter: Sophia Charlotte. Died 1714 in Herrenhausen.

The twelfth child of Frederick V, elector Palatine from 1610 to 1623 and briefly king of Bohemia (1619–1620), and Elizabeth Stuart, Sophia was the younger sister of Elizabeth of Bohemia who corresponded with Descartes. She married Ernest Augustus, a duke of Brunswick who became the first elector of Hanover in 1658. Ernest Augustus died in 1692. The English Parliament passed the Act of Settlement in 1701, making Sophia and her heirs the successors to James II's daughter Anne (who had no surviving children). Sophia's son was crowned George I of England, establishing Hanoverian (and Protestant) succession.

Sophia is known for the extensive correspondence she carried on with Gottfried Wilhelm von Leibniz (1646–1716), the German philosopher and mathematician. In this correspondence it is evident that she was well versed in both his physical and his metaphysical ideas. Her daughter, SOPHIA CHARLOTTE, also became a friend of Leibniz.   JH/MBO

PRIMARY SOURCES
Sophia, Electress of Hanover and Brunswick. With Leibniz, Gottfried Wilhelm. *Correspondence de [Gottfried Wilhelm] Leibniz avec l'electrice Sophie de Brunswick-Lunebourg.* Hanover: Klindworth, [1874].
Correspondence de Leibnitz avec l'électrice Sophie. Ed. O. Klopp. Hanover: N.p., 1864–1875.

SECONDARY SOURCES
Carr, Herbert Wilson. *Leibniz.* London: Bouverie House, 1929. See pages 60–66.

STANDARD SOURCES
Encyclopedia Britannica; Ogilvie 1986.

SOPHIA CHARLOTTE, QUEEN OF PRUSSIA (1668–1705)

Hanoverian, Prussian student of philosophy, friend of Leibniz. Born 1668 to Electress Sophia and Elector Ernest Augustus of Hanover. Married Prince Frederick (later King Frederick I) of Prussia. Died 1705.

Sophia Charlotte was the daughter of Elector Ernest Augustus and Electress Sophia of Hanover. In 1684 she became the second wife of Prince Frederick of Prussia, who became King Frederick I in 1701. As did her mother, Sophia Charlotte corresponded with the philosopher and mathematician Leibniz, who came to Berlin in 1700 at her invitation. In Berlin, Leibniz founded and became life president of the Berlin Academy of Sciences. Sophia Charlotte was known for her erudition and her patronage of arts and letters. Her interest in Leibniz's ideas influenced the intellectual character of the Prussian court.   JH/MBO

STANDARD SOURCES
DSB; Mozans; Ogilvie 1986.

SOROKIN, HELEN PETROVNA (BERATYNSKAIIA) (1894–?)

Russian/U.S. cytologist. Born 11 July 1894 in St. Petersburg, Russia. Married (1917); two children. Educated Petrograd (1912–1917); University of Minnesota (Ph.D., 1925). Professional experience: Petrograd University, instructor (1917–1922); Prague University, assistant (1922–1924); Minnesota Experimental Station, researcher (1925); botany research (1925–1930); Harvard University, Bussey Institute, researcher (1931–1932); private research (from 1936). Death date unknown.

A native of Russia, Helen Petrovna came to the United States where she became a naturalized citizen in 1929, after she had earned her doctorate from the University of Minnesota. She held several positions in both Russia and the United States. After 1936, she did private research. She was a member of the Botanical Society and did research in cytology.

JH/MBO

PRIMARY SOURCES
Sorokin, Helen P. "Experimental Production of Filaments and Network in Cytoplasm of Cichorieae." *Report on Experimental Cell Research* 9 (1955): 510–522.

STANDARD SOURCES
AMS 4–8, B 9; *NAW* unused.

SOSHKINA, ELIZABETH D. (1889–1963)

Soviet geologist, paleontologist, and biologist. Born 1889 in Ryazan. Educated Women's Gymnasium, Ryazan (completed 1909, gold medal); Highest Women's Courses in physics-mathematics department (diploma of first degree; special work in paleontology); Moscow Highest Women's Courses, paleontology department (1916–1918); candidate of geological mineralogical sciences (1937); Ph.D. in biological sciences (1946). Professional experience: natural sciences and geography, teacher public night courses (1913–1915); women's gymnasia, Moscow, teacher (1915–1922); Moscow State University, assistant professor (1919–1930); Moscow Institute of Geological Exploration, assistant professor (1930–1942); Petroleum Institute, researcher; Institute of Mineral Resources, researcher; Paleontological Institute, researcher (1936–1955). Died in 1963 in Ryazan.

During Elizabeth Soshkina's education for her first degree at the Highest Women's Courses in physics and mathematics, her specialty was paleontology. As a postgraduate in Moscow Highest Women's Courses in the department of paleontology, she could concentrate on her chosen field. She taught night courses in Ryazan and then taught in the *gymnasia* of Moscow. She began her professional work by teaching geology as an assistant professor at Moscow State University, but in 1930, the geology department was transferred to the Moscow Institute of Geological Exploration, where she taught as an assistant professor.

Her teaching career did not last long, for in 1942, she refused to teach geology and insisted on concentrating on paleontology. After this professional change, she worked for a time on corals in the Petroleum Institute and in the Institute of Mineral Resources. However, these institutes did not do the type of work that interested her. Finally she got a position in the Paleontological Institute where she worked with T. A. DOBROLUBOVA for twenty years. During this time she wrote a series of large monographs and articles.

Soshkina became one of the most important specialists on Devonian and Silurian corals in the Soviet Union. Her works moved from the descriptive to the ecological. She worked in ecology long before it became fashionable. During World War II (August 1941–April 1943) she worked in a group from the Paleontological Institute in a Bashkir expedition of the Academy of Sciences of the USSR, studying oil deposits of Ishimbaev. In 1946, she received a doctoral degree in biological sciences for her work on Devonian corals of the Urals. Although she became a professor in 1948, she did not teach for long. Her last scientific work was devoted to Paleozoic rugoses. In 1956, she retired and returned to her birthplace, where she died in 1963.

CK

PRIMARY SOURCES
Soshkina, E. D. *Devonskie chetyrekhluchevye korally Russkoi platformy.* Trudy Paleontologicheskogo Instituta 52. Moscow: Rossiyskaya Akademiya Nauk, Paleontologicheskiy Institut, 1954. A systematic study of tetracorals from Devonian localities of the Russian platform.

———. *Opredelitel devonskikh chetyrekhluchevykh korallov; sostavlen po materialam iz devona Urala, Timana, Armenii i tsentralnogo devonskogo poly Russkoi platformy.* Trudy Paleontologicheskogo Instituta 39. Moscow: Rossiyskaya Akademiya Nauk, Paleontologicheskiy Institut, 1952. Monographic study of Devonian rugose corals, based on material from Devonian deposits of the Ural, Timan, Armenian, and central Russian platform regions.

———. *Devonskie korally Rugosa Urala.* Trudy Paleontologicheskogo Instituta 15, no. 4. Moscow: Rossiyskaya Akademiya Nauk, Paleontologicheskiy Institut, 1949. A monographic systematic study of rugose corals from Devonian localities of the Ural region, USSR.

———. *Sistematika srednedevonskikh Rugosa Urala: Die Systematik der mitteldevonischen Rugosa des Urals.* Trudy Paleontologicheskogo Instituta 10, no. 4. Moscow: Rossiyskaya Akademiya Nauk, Paleontologicheskiy Institut, 1941. A systematic revision of rugose corals from middle Devonian localities of the Urals.

STANDARD SOURCES
Nalivkin.

SOTIRA (1st century B.C.E.)

Greek physician.

According to Pliny, Sotira had the ability to accomplish remarkable cures. She may be the author of a manuscript entitled *Gynaeciai*, presently in Florence.

JH/MBO

SECONDARY SOURCES
Pliny. *Natural History* 23.23.83.

BIOGRAPHICAL DICTIONARY OF WOMEN IN SCIENCE ❧ 1217

STANDARD SOURCES
Lipinska 1930; Ogilvie 1986.

SOUCZEK, HELENE (fl. 1910)

Worked in Austria on radioactivity. Professional experience: University of Vienna, Physical Institute, research.

Working at the University of Vienna's Physical Institute, Souczek determined the radium content of pitchblende residues by measuring the ionization they produced.

JH/MBO

PRIMARY SOURCES
Souczek, Helene. "Messungen des Radiumgehaltes der bei der Verarbeitung von St. Joachimsthaler Uranpecherzrückständen resultierenden radiumarmen Produkte." *Akademie der Wissenschaften, Vienna, Sitzungsberichte* 119 (1910): 371–376.

STANDARD SOURCES
Meyer and von Schweidler.

SOUTH, LILLIAN HERRALD (1880–?)

U.S. bacteriologist. Born 1880 in Bowling Green, Ky. Married H. H. Tye. Educated Woman's Medical College of Pennsylvania (M.D., 1904). Professional experience: State Board of Health of Kentucky, director of the bureau of bacteriology (1911–1954). Retired 1954. Death date unknown.

Lillian Herrald spent her entire career working for the State Board of Health in Kentucky's bureau of bacteriology. Her research interests were leprosy and hookworm in Kentucky. She endowed a fund at Cumberland College, Williamsburg, Kentucky, as the Lillian South Tye Endowed Loan Fund.

JH/MBO

STANDARD SOURCES
AMS 5–8, B 9, P&B 10.

SOWTON, SARAH C. M. (fl. 1928)

British medical and psychological researcher.

Sarah Sowton investigated the effects of menstruation on mental and muscular alertness and efficiency as a member of the Medical Research Council's Industrial Fatigue Research Board in the 1920s.

JH/MBO

PRIMARY SOURCES
Sowton, Sarah C. M., Charles S. Myers, and E. M. Bedale. *Two Contributions to the Experimental Study of the Menstrual Cycle.*

I. Its influence on mental and muscular efficiency. London: H. M. Stationery Office, 1928. Report no. 45.

SPALDING, EFFIE SOUTHWORTH (1860–?)

U.S. botanist and plant pathologist. Born 29 October 1860 in North Collins, N.Y. Educated University of Michigan (B.S., 1885); Bryn Mawr College, fellow (1885–1887); Barnard College, Columbia, fellow (1893–1895); University of Southern California (M.S., 1923). Professional experience: Bureau of Plant Industry, United States Department of Agriculture, assistant pathologist (1888–1893); University of Southern California, assistant professor (1920–1926).

Effie Spalding was one of many women who worked for the United States Department of Agriculture. After this experience she taught at the University of Southern California, but apparently remained as an assistant professor. JH/MBO

PRIMARY SOURCES
Spalding, Effie S. With Daniel Trembly Macdougal. *The Water Balance of Succulent Plants.* Carnegie Institution of Washington Publication 141. Washington, D.C.: Carnegie Institution of Washington, 1910.

STANDARD SOURCES
AMS 4–7.

SPENCE, ELIZA JANE (EDMONDSON) (1832–1917)

U.S. field botanist. Born 7 March 1832 in Dayton?, Ohio, to Ruth (Richards) and Edward Edmondson. Four siblings. Married George Smith. Two children. Educated Cooper Female Seminary in Dayton, Ohio. Died 1917.

Eliza Jane Edmondson began preparing herbarium specimens while she visited near Leipsic, Delaware, her tanner father's boyhood home. She continued to collect and prepare plant specimens from different parts of the United States. Her lists were used by other botanists and incorporated into their works. JH/MBO

SECONDARY SOURCES
Stuckey, Ronald L. "Eliza Jane (Edmondson) Spence." Unpublished notes.

SPENCER, ADELIN ELAM (1872–?)

U.S. chemist. Born 31 December 1872 in Natchez, Miss. Educated Newcomb (A.B., 1890); Tulane University (A.M., 1894); Cornell (M.S., 1896). Professional experience: high school Monroe,

La., teacher; Newcomb, instructor of chemistry (1901–?). Death date unknown.

Little is known about Adelin Spencer's life and career, except that after receiving two master's degrees and teaching high school chemistry, she went to Sophie Newcomb College as an instructor. Her research was on Zirconium tetraiodid.

JH/MBO

STANDARD SOURCES
AMS 1–2.

SPERRY, PAULINE (1885–1967)

U.S. mathematician. Born 5 March 1885 in Peabody, Mass., to Henrietta Leoroyd and Willard G. Sperry. Educated Smith College (B.A., 1906; M.A., in music); University of Chicago (M.S. in mathematics, 1914; Ph.D., 1916). Professional experience: Smith College, assistant in mathematics (1908–1911), instructor (1911), traveling fellowship (1912–1913), assistant professor (1916–1917); University of California, Berkeley, instructor (1917), assistant professor (1923), associate professor (1932), dismissed for not signing loyalty oath (1950), emerita associate professor (1956). Died 24 September 1967.

Pauline Sperry was a politically active mathematician who refused to sign the loyalty oath and forfeited her university position. In 1952, when the California Supreme Court declared the oath unconstitutional, it ordered the reinstatement of eighteen faculty members who had refused to sign the oath. Sperry was among those reinstated; her back salary was paid, and she was given the title of emerita associate professor. She was born in Peabody, Massachusetts, where her father was a Congregational minister. She attended Smith College and the University of Chicago, where she earned her master's and doctoral degrees. Her major professor was Ernest Julius Wilczynski, who created a new school of geometers known as the American school of projective differential geometers. Sperry used Wilczynski's work as a basis for her dissertation.

She was assistant professor at Smith for the year 1916–1917, but accepted a position at the University of California, Berkeley, the next year. She remained at Berkeley for the remainder of her career. After she retired from Berkeley, she continued to be politically active. She was a member of the Monterey Peninsula Friends Meeting and it formed the focal point for her actions, which included petitioning for a ban to nuclear weapons testing, and supporting the American Civil Liberties Union and the League of Women Voters. She served on the executive council of the Friends Committee on Legislation of Northern California, the Fellowship of Reconciliation, the American Friends Service Committee, and the Committee for a Sane Nuclear Policy. She also founded a school in Port-au-Prince, Haiti, to minister to the needs of children.

Sperry's doctoral dissertation marked the end of her research publications. She did, however, write two trigonometry textbooks.

JH/MBO

PRIMARY SOURCES
Sperry, Pauline. "On the Theory of a One-to-One and One-to-Two Correspondence with Geometric Illustrations." Master's thesis, University of Chicago, 1914.
———. "Properties of a Certain Projectively Defined Two-Parameter Family of Curves on a General Surface." *American Journal of Mathematics* 40 (1918): 213–224.
———. *Short Course in Spherical Trigonometry.* Richmond: Johnson Publishing Company, 1928.

STANDARD SOURCES
Grinstein and Campbell (article by Florence D. Fasanelli).

SPIEGEL-ADOLF, MONA (1893–?)

Austrian/U.S. biochemist. Born 23 February 1893 in Vienna, Austria. Educated University of Vienna (M.D., 1918). Professional experience: Medical School, Vienna, assistant in medical and colloid chemistry (1920–1930); Temple University School of Medicine, professor of colloid chemistry and head of department (1930–1966), emerita professor (1967–1969); National Parkinson Institute, director in charge of biochemistry (1968–1969). Death date unknown.

Born and educated at the University of Vienna, Mona Spiegel-Adolf came to the United States, where she took a position at the Temple University Medical School, eventually advancing to professor and head of the department. She was a Fellow of the American Association for the Advancement of Science, and a member of the American Chemical Society, the Optical Society of America, and the American Crystallographic Association. Her research was in physical chemistry of proteins and lipids, X-ray diffraction in biology and medicine, cancer, and amaurotic familial idiocy.

JH/MBO

STANDARD SOURCES
AMS 6–8, B 9, P&B 10–12.

SPONER-FRANCK, HERTHA DOROTHEA ELISABETH (1895–1968)

German/U.S. physicist. Born 1 September 1895 in Neisse, Schlesien, Germany. Two brothers and two sisters. Married James Franck (1946). Naturalized U.S. citizen (1941). Educated local schools in

Neisse and Zittau (1901–1910); women's secondary school courses (Gymnasialfrauenkurse) in Berlin (1910–1912); governess's seminary in Hannover and Heidelberg; Göttingen University (Ph.D., 1920; habilitation, 1925). Professional experience: governess (1913–1915); Kaiser-Wilhelm-Institute of Physical Chemistry, Berlin, researcher (1920–1921); Göttingen University, scientific assistant (1921–1925); adjunct professor of physics (privat docent) (1925–1932); associate professor (professor extraordonarius) (1932–1934); Oslo University, guest professor (1934–1936); Duke University, faculty (1936–1965); emerita professor (from 1965). Honors and memberships: Guggenheim Fellow (1952–1953); Physical Society, Fellow; New York and North Carolina academies of science; German Physical Society; Optical Society. Died 17 February 1968 in Ilten, near Hannover, Germany.

Hertha Sponer was the oldest of five children from a middle class family. Her shopkeeper father valued learning and enabled Hertha and her siblings to acquire an education. Although Hertha was ambitious and planned to attend a university, she first had to become independent by passing through the traditional female roles as a governess and primary school teacher. She studied physics, mathematics, and chemistry at Tübingen University for one year and at Göttingen for two years. She wrote her doctoral thesis in physics with Peter Debye (1884–1966) "Über ultrarote Absorption zweiatomiger Gase." This thesis was one of the first studies that used methods of quantum theory for the spectrum caused by the rotation of molecules. Debye gave her the grade *gut* (*cum laude*), and *sehr gut* (*magna cum laude*) in the doctoral examination. From 1920 to 1921 she worked on electronic impact experiments in the physical department of the Kaiser-Wilhelm-Institute of Physical Chemistry with James Franck. At the same time she was an assistant to Arthur Wehnelt (1871–1944) in the physics institute of Berlin University. She helped carry out the beginners' courses in practical physics training.

When James Franck got a professorship at Göttingen University in 1921, Hertha Sponer went with him as one of his assistants. She continued her work on electronic impact and on spectroscopic problems. In November 1925 she acquired the *venia legendi* in physics with the *Habilitationsschrift* "Anregungspotentiale der Bandenspektren des Stickstoffs." From October 1925 until October 1926 she had a Rockefeller fellowship at the University of California, Berkeley, granted by the International Education Board.

Around that time Sponer published a lot of articles by herself and with coauthors from Germany and from abroad. She gave her lectures at Göttingen University for about eighty students and founded a special private seminar in theoretical physics. She was the heart of this communication center of young Göttingen physicists, where Friedrich

Hund (b. 1896) participated and Werner Heisenberg (1901–1976) first spoke about quantum mechanics (see Hentschel and Tobies 1996). Hertha Sponer's talents were appreciated, and the Göttingen department of mathematics and sciences proposed her appointment as professor. In the application to the Prussian ministry the Göttingen department wrote that Hertha Sponer was qualified to hold a full professorship, but at this time women could only become unofficial adjunct professors in Prussia. She was awarded the position of professor extraordonarius (associate professor) in February 1932.

Although Hertha Sponer did not dread racist persecution when the Nazi dictatorship arrived, she could not keep her scientific position in Germany. Her Jewish chief James Franck and other Göttingen physicists left Germany; Robert Pohl (1884–1976), who remained in Göttingen, was less than sympathetic to women scientists.

In October 1934, Hertha Sponer left Germany and accepted a guest professorship at Oslo University, Norway. It was difficult to continue her research in Oslo; she used the time to finish the final stages of the publication of her two-volume book, published in 1935 and 1936. In 1936 she was appointed to a chair in the physics department of Duke University in Durham, North Carolina.

Hertha Sponer was a creative scientist and was a popular student adviser. Her two-volume *Molekuelspektren und ihre Anwendungen auf chemische Prozesse* was used by many physicists and chemists after 1945. Most of the later users in Germany did not know that these volumes were written by a woman because only the first letter of her first name was on the publication. Sponer published more than ninety articles. About forty of these contributions came out before 1936. Twelve of these were jointly published. After coming to the United States in 1936, she published more than sixty additional papers, fifty of which were jointly published.

From 1940 to 1943 and from 1947 to 1950, Sponer was an associate editor of the *Journal of Chemical Physics.* She received a Guggenheim fellowship at Uppsala University in 1952–1953 to do research on "A Theoretical Study of Quantum Mechanical Methods for Calculating Structural Properties of Complex Molecules." This work resulted in invitations to present her results to international congresses. Hertha Sponer was a member of the American Physical Society, the Optical Society, Sigma Xi, the American Association for the Advancement of Science, the New York Academy of Science, and the German physical society.

After retirement Sponer, now a widow, moved back to Germany to be near relatives. She died in Ilten, near Hannover, after being ill for several months.   RT

PRIMARY SOURCES

Sponer, Hertha. "Über ultrarote Absorption zweiatomiger Gase." *Jahrbuch der philosophischen Fakultaet in Göttingen, Teil 2* 34 (1921): 153–160.

———. *Molekuelspektren und ihre Anwendung auf chemische Probleme.* Vol. 1, *Tabellen;* Vol. 2 *Text mit 87 Abb.* Berlin: Julius Springer, 1935–1936.

SECONDARY SOURCES

Beyerchen, Alan D. *Scientists under Hitler.* New Haven and London: Yale University Press, 1977.

Elasser, Walter M. *Memoirs of a Physicist in the Atomic Age.* New York: Science History Publications; Bristol: Adam Hilger, 1978.

Hentschel, Klaus, and Renate Tobies. "Zum 100. Geburtstag von Friedrich Hund." *NTM-International Journal of History and Ethics of Natural Sciences, Technology and Medicine,* n.s. 4 (1996): 1–18. Interview.

Rosenow, Ulf. "Die Universität at Göttingen unter dem Nationalsozialismus." In ed. Heinrich Becher, Hans-Joachim Dahms, and Cornelia Wegeler, 374–409. Munich: K. G. Saur, 1987.

Tobies, Renate. "Zu den Anfaengen einer wissenschaftlichen Karriere von Frauen in Mathematik und Naturwissenschaften. Literaturbericht und erste Ergebnisse." In *Frauenforscherinnen stellen sich vor. Ringvorlesung Teil I,* ed. Ilse Nagelschmidt, 99–139. Leipzig: Universtaetsverlag, 1995.

———. "Physikerinnen und spektroskopische Forschungen. Zum 100. Geburtstag von Hertha Sponer (1.9.1895– 17.2.1968)." In *Geschlechterverhaeltnisse in Medizin, Naturwissenschaft und Technik,* ed. Chritoph Meinel and Monika Renneberg. Stuttgart: GNT-Verlag, 1996.

SECONDARY SOURCES

Marie-Ann Maushat. *"Um mich nicht zu vergessen": Hertha Sponer. Ein Frauenleben für die Physik im 20. Jahrhundert.* Bassum: GMT Verlag, 1997. A review of this in English by Karen Johnson with a summary of Sponer's life, includes a portrait of her with Franck. *Isis* 90 (March 1999): 145–146.

STANDARD SOURCES

AMS 6–8, P 9, P&B 10–11.

SPRAGUE, MARY LETITIA (GREEN) (1886–1978)

British botanist. Born 27 November 1886 in Breconshire. Married Thomas Archibald Sprague (1938). Educated University College, Aberystwyth. Professional experience: Kew Gardens, botanist and bibliographer (1912–1945). Died 15 January 1978 in Cheltenham in Gloucester.

Mary Letitia Green married the Deputy Keeper of the Kew Herbarium, an authority on Loranthaceae, plant nomenclature, and old herbals. She also worked at Kew and was involved in both botanical work and in producing the *Index Kewensis* and the *Index Londinensis.* JH/MBO

PRIMARY SOURCES

Sprague, Mary Letitia Green. *Standard-Species of Nomina Conservanda.* Kew, England: Royal Botanic Gardens, [1926?].

———. "Rules of Botanical Nomenclature." *Empire Forestry Journal* 19, no. 1 (1931).

———. "Proposal No. 23." *Taxon* 2 (1953): 113–114.

Her plants are at Kew and the National Museum of Wales.

SECONDARY SOURCES

Huntia 8, no. 1 (1988): 194.

Proceedings of the Cotteswold Naturalists Field Club 37, no. 4 (1977–1978): 18.

STANDARD SOURCES

Desmond.

SPRATT, ETHEL ROSE (1887–1970)

British botanist. Born 23 April 1887 in Bedford. Professional experience: King's College, London, lecturer. Died 29 June 1970.

Ethel Rose Spratt was elected a Fellow of the Linnean Society in 1920 and held a position as lecturer in King's College, London. JH/MBO

PRIMARY SOURCES

Spratt, Ethel Rose. *Chemistry and Physics for Botany Students.* London: W. B. Cliver, University Tutorial Press, 1924.

———. With Amy Vera Spratt. *Biology for Schools.* 5th ed. London: University Tutorial Press, 1946.

STANDARD SOURCES

Desmond.

STACKHOUSE, EMILY (1811–1870)

British botanist. Born 1811 in Modbury, Devon. Died 1870 in Truro, Cornwall.

Emily Stackhouse contributed plants from Truro and mosses from Cornwall to the *Journal of the Royal Institute of Cornwall* from 1865 to 1867. She also illustrated C. A. Johns's *Week at the Lizard.* JH/MBO

PRIMARY SOURCES

Stackhouse, Emily, illus. C. A. Johns, *Week at the Lizard*. London: Society for Promoting Christian Knowledge, 1848.

———, illus. C. A. Johns, "List of Musci, Natives of Cornwall." *Journal of the Royal Institute of Cornwall* no. 3 (1865): 58–62.

Letters are in the Wilson correspondence at the British Museum (Natural History).

SECONDARY SOURCES

Davey, F. Hamilton. *Flora of Cornwall*. Penryn: F. Chegwidden, 1909.

STANDARD SOURCES

Desmond.

STADNICHENKO, TASIA MAXIMOVNA (1894–1958)

Soviet/American geochemist. Born 9 October 1894 in Taganash, Crimea, to Anna and Maxim Stadnichenko. Two sisters. Never married. Educated Vladivostock Gymnasium (completed 1912); Petrograd University (completed 1917). Professional experience: Russian Geological Survey, Island of Sakahalin, chemist (1917); University of Illinois, research fellow (1918–1919); Far East Geological Survey, chemist (1919–1922); Vassar College, instructor (1922–1935); National Research Council and American Petroleum Institute, research associate (1925–1931); U.S. Geological Survey, associate geologist (1931–1950), geologist (1950–1958). Died 26 November 1958 of a heart ailment.

Tasia Stadnichenko spent her early life in Russia. After her education at Petrograd University, she joined the Russian Geological Survey as a chemist and made an expedition to survey the Island of Sakahalin in 1917. During World War I, she came to the United States as an intepreter for the Russian Mission and then remained as a representative to the Washington Disarmament Peace Conference after WWI. She became a research fellow at University of Illinois where she remained for two years. She then took part in the Far East Geological Survey, 1919–1922. After several jobs in the United States, she became a naturalized citizen in 1931, and in that same year took a position with the U.S. Geological Survey, eventually rising to the position of geologist in 1950. Unmarried, she lived with her mother in Washington.

She was considered the foremost geochemist investigating the origin, constitution, and microscopic structure of coal and other carbonaceous sedimentary deposits. She also worked on the geochemistry of minor elements in coal ash.

JH/MBO

SECONDARY SOURCES

Washington Star, 27 November 1958. Obituary notice.

STANDARD SOURCES

Debus; *NAW* unused.

STAËL-HOLSTEIN, ANNE LOUISE GERMAINE NECKER (1768–1817)

See De Staël Holstein, Anne Germaine Necker.

STANLEY, LOUISE (1883–1954)

U.S. chemist and home economist. Born 8 June 1883 in Nashville, Tenn. Educated George Peabody College (B.A., 1903); University of Chicago (B.Ed., 1906); Columbia University (A.M., 1907); Yale University (Ph.D., 1911). Professional experience: University of Missouri, instructor of home economics (1907–1911), assistant professor (1911–1914), associate professor (1914–1917), professor and chair of the division (1917–1923); U.S. Department of Agriculture, chief of the bureau of home economics (1923–1943); Agricultural Research Administration, special assistant to research administrator (from 1943). Died 1954.

Louise Stanley's career was divided between academia and government. After she received her doctoral degree from Yale University, she went to the University of Missouri, where she proceeded through the academic ranks from instructor through professor and chair of the division. However, she left the university to work for the United States Department of Agriculture, where she was chief of the bureau of home economics for twenty years. Finally, she concluded her governmental career at the Agricultural Research Administration.

She researched food chemistry, organic and inorganic phosphorus, and purine enzymes. In addition, she worked on the best temperatures for baking various foods.

In 1940, Stanley received an honorary doctorate from the University of Missouri. She was a member of the Chemical Society and the Home Economics Association. JH/MBO

PRIMARY SOURCES

Stanley, Louise. "The Preservation of Food in the Home." *University of Missouri Bulletin* 15, no. 7. Extension Series 6, 1914.

———. *Foods: Their Selection and Preparation*. Boston: Ginn and Company, 1935.

———. *From Tradition to Science*. U.S. Department of Agriculture. Yearbook Separate No. 1670. Washington: Government Printing Office, 1940.

STANDARD SOURCES

AMS 3–8.

STANTON, HAZEL MARTHA (1890–?)

U.S. psychologist. Born 16 July 1890 in Stromsburg, Neb. Educated University of Nebraska (A.B., 1912); University of Iowa (A.M., 1918; Ph.D., 1921). Eastman School of Music, Rochester, N.Y., music psychologist; University of Rochester, professor of psychology (1930–1933); Psychological Corporation, consulting psychologist (1933–1941); Daniel Starch and Staff, New York City, northwest regional manager (1944–?). Death date unknown.

Psychologist Hazel Stanton was especially interested in psychological tests of musical talent. She also worked in the area of the interitance of specific musical capacities. Her positions at the Eastman School of Music and as professor of psychology allowed her the opportunity for research in this area. In addition to her musical work, she also did research on controlling human behavior.

Stanton was a Fellow of the American Psychological Association, and a member of the American Association for the Advancement of Science and the International Council of Women Psychologists.   JH/MBO

PRIMARY SOURCES
Stanton, Hazel Martha. *The Inheritance of Specific Musical Capacities.* Cold Spring Harbor, N.Y.: N.p., 1922.
———. *Psychological Tests of Musical Talent, Eastman School of Music.* Rochester, N.Y.: Eastman School of Music the University of Rochester, [1925?].
———. *Musical Capacity Measures of Children Repeated after Musical Training.* University of Iowa Series on Aims and Progress of Research, no. 42. University of Iowa Studies. New Series, no. 259. Iowa City: University of Iowa, 1933.
———. *Measurement of Musical Talent: The Eastman Experiment.* Iowa City: University of Iowa, 1935.

STANDARD SOURCES
AMS 4–8, S&B 9–10.

STAUDINGER, MAGDA (WOIT) (1902–1997)

Latvian-German biochemist. Born 1902 in Elwa, Estonia. Father Oskar Woit. Married Hermann Staudinger (1927). Educated University of Berlin, doctorate in natural sciences. Professional experience: University of Riga, botanical laboratory, assistant; University of Freiburg, Brelsgau, chemistry laboratory associate (with husband) (1927–1961). Died 21 April 1997.

Magda Woit Staudinger was the daughter of Latvian diplomat and physician Oskar Woit with whom she traveled throughout Germany, Hungary, and Switzerland as a young girl. (He was ambassador to Germany from 1920 to 1932.) She then attended the University of Berlin, where she studied under the plant physiologist Gottlieb Haberlandt and ob-

tained her degree in natural sciences. Following her degree, she spent some years as an assistant to Professor Malta in the botanical laboratory at the University of Riga.

In 1927, she married Hermann Staudinger, a brilliant chemist almost ten years her senior. She studied the chemical structure of macromolecules with him and then collaborated closely in his laboratory for many years, publishing both jointly and independently. By the time that Hermann Staudinger was awarded the Nobel Prize for chemistry for his discovery of ketene in 1953, her contribution was freely acknowledged. He mentioned the importance of her work in his Nobel Prize address.

Magda Staudinger became interested in applying the study of macromolecules to biology in the 1940s and published on the role of macromolecules in protoplasmic development in the 1950s. After her husband died in Freiberg in 1965, she continued to live and work there. Elected an honorary member of the Latvian Academy of Sciences in 1990, she established the Magda and Hermann Staudinger Fund at the academy in 1995. The following year she was awarded their grand medal. Active to the end, she died at the age of ninety-five. Only the year before, she had written a letter to the journal *Terminology* complaining about the misuse of the words *macromolecule* and *polymer* originated by her husband.
JH/MBO

PRIMARY SOURCES
Staudinger, Magda Woit. With Hermann Staudinger. *Die Makromolekular Chemie und ihre Bedeutung fuer die Protoplasmaforschung.* Vienna: Springer, 1954.
———. "Das Lebensproblem im Licht macromolecular Forschung." 1956.
———, ed. *Das Wissenschaftliche Werk von Hermann Staudinger. Gasammelte Arbeiten nach Sachgebieten geordnet.* Basel, Huthig and Wepf, 1969–1976.
———, ed. With Ernst Jostkleigrewe. *Makromolekulare Chemie: das Werk Hermann Staudingers in seiner heutigen Bedeutung.* Munich: Schnell and Steiner, 1987.
———. "Letter from Dr. Staudinger Woit." *Terminology* 3, no. 2 (1996): 343–347.

SECONDARY SOURCES
Staudinger, Hermann. *From Organic Chemistry to Macromolecules: A Scientific Autobiography Based on My Scientific Papers.* Translated from the German with a foreword by Herman F. Mark. New York: Wiley-Interscience, 1970. This work mentions some of Magda Staudinger's collaborative and independent work, provides a short biographical comment on her, includes her references, and credits her with stimulating his work on the connections between biology and macromolecules. The book is dedicated to her. Includes portrait of husband and wife.

STANDARD SOURCES

Debus (under H. Staudinger); *DFC; Notable* (article, on
H. Staudinger, by Gail B. C. Marcella).

STEARNS, GENEVIEVE (1892–?)

*U.S. chemist. Born 24 December 1892 in Zumbrota, Minn., to
Clara (Beierwalter) and Clayton Henry Stearns. Educated Carleton
College (B.S., 1912); University of Illinois (M.S., 1920); University of Michigan (Ph.D., 1927). Professional experience: high
school teacher (1912–1919); University of Illinois, assistant chemist
(1918–1920); Child Welfare Research Station, Iowa, research
associate (1920–1925); University of Michigan, assistant in biochemistry (1926–1927); University of Iowa, associate in pediatrics
(1927–1930), research assistant professor (1930–1931), research
associate professor (1931–1943), research professor (1943–1954);
ORTHOP (1954–1958), emerita research professor (from 1958).
Honors and memberships: Home Economics Association, Borden
Award (1942); American Institute of Nutrition, Fellow; American
Society of Biological Chemists; Sigma Xi, Omicron Nu. Death date
unknown.*

Genevieve Stearns spent the greater part of her career at the
University of Iowa, rising through the ranks to professor.
She was a Fulbright professor at Ein Shams University in
Cairo from 1960 to 1961 and was a member of the U.S.
team for World Health Organization seminars in infant nutrition in Leiden in 1950. With others, she was the recipient
of the Borden Award of the Home Economics Association
in 1942 and the award of the American Institute of Nutrition with P. C. Jeans.

Much of her research was on nitrogen, mineral, and vitamin metabolism. Her special interests involved the ways in
which these substances were metabolised in healthy and in
sick infants. She published numerous papers on the subject.
She was especially concerned with metabolism in diseases affecting bone. Stearns was a Fellow of the American Institute
of Nutrition, a member of the American Society of Biological Chemists, Sigma Xi, and Omicron Nu.   JH/MBO

PRIMARY SOURCES

Stearns, Genevieve. *Studies on the Intermediary Metabolism of
Cystine.* Baltimore: Waverly Press, 1930.

———. "Philip Charles Jeans (1883–1952)." *Journal of Nutrition*
64 (1958): 1–12.

World Health Organization. *Infant Metabolism.* New York:
Macmillan, 1956. Stearns was a participant.

STANDARD SOURCES

AMS 5–8, P 9, P&B 10–11; Debus.

STEED, GITEL POZNANSKI (1914–1977)

*U.S. anthropologist. Born 3 May 1914 in Cleveland, Ohio, to Sara
Auerbach and Jakob Poznanski. Two sisters. Married Robert Steed
(1947). One son, Andrew Hart (1953). Educated New York University (B.A. in sociology); Columbia University (Ph.D., 1960).
Professional experience: Yale University, Institute of Human Relations, senior editor of information (1941–1943); Hunter College,
N.Y.C., teacher (1945, 1947); Fisk University, teacher; managing
editor of* Race Relations: A Monthly Summary of Events and
Trends; *Columbia University, research in contemporary cultures
project, researcher (1947–1949); Columbia University research in
contemporary India field project, researcher (1949–1951); Hofstra
College (now Hofstra University) (from 1962). Died 1977 of a
heart attack.*

Cultural anthropologist Gitel Poznanski Steed (born
Gertrude), is best known for her research in India. Although
she was not religious, Gertrude adopted the Yiddish name
Gitel to celebrate her heritage. After a checkered career at
New York University, in which she became involved in the
Greenwich Village artistic and political life, she dropped out
of school to take a job as a writer for the Works Progress Administration. In the 1930s in New York she met her future
husband, painter Robert Steed. She returned to the university and finished a bachelor's degree with honors in sociology and anthropology. Offered a graduate fellowship by
RUTH BENEDICT, whom she had met, Poznanski went to
Columbia. She held the fellowship from 1938 to 1940. Although she began her dissertation then, she did not complete
a doctorate until 1969, when she was fifty-five years old.

Steed became senior editor of information at Yale University's Institute of Human Relations from 1941 to 1943.
She left conventional anthropology for a while to join the
Jewish Black Book Committee, a group of writers who documented the crimes agains the Jews during World War II.
Steed taught anthropology courses at Hunter College in
1945 and 1947. During the intervening year, she taught at
Fisk University, where she taught a course on Africa. She
also was managing editor of *Race Relations: A Monthly Summary of Events and Trends.* In 1947 she became a part of Columbia University's Research in Contemporary Cultures
Project directed by Benedict and MARGARET MEAD. She was
part of the group studying the Chinese community in New
York; as the group coordinator, RUTH BUNZEL spoke very
highly of her work. The project ended in 1949, and Steed
proposed a plan to continue her research in China. However,
the project was aborted after the 1948 revolution in China.

After the end of the China project, Steed proposed another one in India, teaching herself photography in order to
document her field work. Her research team was funded by a
U.S. Navy Department grant. Steed's goal was to show the
relation of village structure and culture to personal careers.

To get at this interrelationship she studied social structure, kinship, social organization, and culture, and measured the individual lives against the "sociological horizon."

Professionally the Indian experience was excellent for Steed; she returned with many photographs and pages of notes. However, the trip left her with malaria and other health problems. She had no university affiliation for eleven years after she returned from India. During this period she gave birth to a son and taught English at a Manhattan private school, Jefferson School. She did retain her anthropological contacts, and in 1962 she was employed by Hofstra College, later Hofstra University.

Steed continued to work on her India material. Many of her photographs were published. Her many notes are unpublished and are in the special collections of the University of Chicago libraries. Although her reputation was not made by published materials, her undergraduate teaching, her oral presentations, and her photographs assure her reputation. She even wrote a screenplay, *Devgar* (never filmed) based on the character of a Hindu temple sexton she had met.

JH/MBO

PRIMARY SOURCES
Steed, Gitel. "Interview on Chinese Friendship. In *The Study of Culture at a Distance,* ed. Margaret Mead and R. Metraux, 192–198. Chicago: University of Chicago Press, 1953.
———. "Notes to an Approach to a Study of Personality Formation in a Hindu Village in Gujarat." In *Village India: Studies in the Little Community.* Memoirs of the American Anthropological Association no. 83, ed. McKim Marriott, 102–144. Chicago: University of Chicago Press, 1955.
———. "Caste and Kinship in Rural Gujarat: The Social Uses of Space." Ph.D. diss., Columbia University, 1960.

SECONDARY SOURCES
American Anthropologist 81 (1979): 88–91. Obituary notice.

STANDARD SOURCES
Gacs (article by Riva Berleant-Schiller).

STEFANESCU, SABBA (1857–1931)

Rumanian invertebrate and vertebrate paleontologist and stratigrapher. Born 1857. University of Bucharest. Died 1931.

Sabba Stefanescu's research was on the Tertiary geology of Rumania. Her vertebrate paleontology was on fossil elephants. Sabba Stefanescu was one of the successors of the great Romanian geologist Gregoriu Stefanescu at the Department of Mineralogy-Geology-Paleontology of the University of Bucharest. The Institute of Geodynamics in Bucharest is named after her.

JH/MBO

SECONDARY SOURCES
Protesco, O. "Sabba Stefanescu (1857–1931)." *Anuaire Institut de Geologie et de Geophysique* (Rumania) 15 (1932 for 1930): IX–XV. Includes a summary in French.

STANDARD SOURCES
Sarjeant.

STEIN, EMMY (1879–?)

German geneticist. Born 21 June 1879 in Düsseldorf. Death date unknown.

Stein investigated the effects which radium radiation produced on snapdragon plants and seeds. She observed that exposures greater than five hours stopped plant growth. Plants formed from radiated seeds displayed a wide variety of deformations, and usually were sterile. No genetic effects were observed in the isolated descendants of these plants. Emmy Stein's papers are held in the Archiv zur Geschicte der Max-Planck Gesellschaft (Archive for the History of Max-Planck Institute) in Berlin.

MM

PRIMARY SOURCES
Stein, Emmy. "Über den Einfluss von Radiumbestrahlung auf Antirhinum." (Summary.) *Die Naturwissenschaften* 11 (1923): 308.

STANDARD SOURCES
Meyer and von Schweidler.

STEINHARDT, EDNA (fl. 1910)

U.S. immunologist, public health researcher. Professional experience: New York Dept. of Public Health and Pathology laboratory, Bellevue Hospital. Honors and memberships: Society for Experimental Biology and Medicine.

Edna Steinhardt worked with the bacteriologist ANNA WESSELS WILLIAMS in the New York Public Health Laboratory in the early decades of the twentieth century. She studied the effectiveness of various vaccines on experimental animals.

JH/MBO

PRIMARY SOURCES
Steinhardt, Edna, and Thomas Flournoy. "The Effect of Specific Vaccines in the Typhoid of Rats and Mice." *Proceedings of the Society of Experimental Biology Medicine* 8 (1911): 109–110.

SECONDARY SOURCES
Anna Wessels Williams Papers in Schlesinger Library, Radcliffe College, makes some mention of Steinhardt.

STELFOX, MARGARITA DAWSON (MITCHELL) (1886–1971)

Irish botanist. Born 1886 at Lisburn, County Antrim. Married Arthur Wilson Stelfox. Died 1971.

Margarita Dawson Mitchell Stelfox was the wife of Arthur Wilson. He was trained as an architect but changed careers when he obtained an assistantship in the National Museum in Dublin in 1920, where he specialized in mollusks and hymenopterans. His wife worked in conjunction with M. W. Rea on Slime molds, Mycetozoa. She was one of the few Irish naturalists to work in that field. She published on this group in the *Irish Naturalists Journal*.   JH/MBO

SECONDARY SOURCES
Irish Naturalists Journal 249 (1973): 296–302.

STANDARD SOURCES
Desmond; Praeger.

STENHOUSE, CAROLINE (1900–)

New Zealand physician. Born 14 January 1900 in Otago, New Zealand. Two sisters. Educated local primary and secondary schools; Otago Medical School, Dunedin (1918–1924). Professional experience: Invercargill Hospital, house surgeon (1924?–1925); Moorsfields Hospital, London, physician (1925–1926?); India (the Punjab), physician (1926?–1930?); Christchurch, eye specialist (from 1930?).

Caroline Stenhouse knew from childhood that she wanted to be a physician. Both of her Scots parents had medical training—her father was a physician and her mother had been a nurse. Both parents encouraged their three daughters, of whom Caroline was the oldest, to pursue a profession. One sister earned an arts degree, and the other became a dentist. Caroline's father was delighted when she chose medicine. After pursuing her secondary education during World War I, she accumulated a good academic record and went to Otago Medical School in Dunedin as a first-year student. She considered herself naive and unsophisticated at the beginning of her medical schooling. However, she found that many of the students, particularly the women, were in the same situation. She found little discrimination or hostility toward women doctors. Out of a total of thirty-four medical students, about six were women. She credited the egalitarian outlook of New Zealand society for both the number of women and the general acceptance of them in medicine.

However, after she graduated she found it more difficult to get a position because of the soldier physicians returning from World War I. She also discovered that she had inherited otosclerosis from her mother. This disorder prevented her from hearing anything with a stethoscope. After looking for a specialty that would not require this, she settled on ophthalmology. Her experience was enhanced by the practical experience she got in London's Moorsfields Hospital. In London she was persuaded to go to India, where she worked for several years. She returned to New Zealand and took a position as an eye specialist at Christchurch, where she remained for the rest of her career.

After World War II ended, she and other women doctors in Christchurch formed a local branch of the New Zealand Medical Women's Association.   JH/MBO

PRIMARY SOURCES
"Stenhouse, Caroline." In Hellstedt, *Autobiographies.*

STEPHENS, JANE (1879–?)

Irish zoologist. Born 1879 in Dublin. Married Robert Francis Scharff (1920). Educated Royal University of Ireland (B.Sc.). Professional experience: National Museum in Dublin, technical assistantship, 1905; assistant naturalist (to 1920). Death date unknown.

Jane Stephens did most of her natural history work before she was married in 1920. Her husband spent his working life at the Dublin Museum of Science and Art, later the National Museum. He would have been Stephens's superior, for he was Keeper. It is probable that nepotism practices made it impossible for her to continue with her work. This work, however, was very significant, because she provided much of the early knowledge of the Irish sponges. Although she specialized in the freshwater and marine sponges of Ireland, she also worked on coelenterates.   JH/MBO

PRIMARY SOURCES
Stephens, Jane. "A List of Irish Coelenterata, including the Ctenophora." *Proceedings of the Royal Irish Academy* 25 (1905): 25–92.
———. "Alcyonarian and Madreporarian Corals of the Irish Coast." Department of Agriculture and Technical Instruction for Ireland. Fisheries Branch. Scientific Investigations, 1907, 5. Dublin: Printed for H.M. Stationery Office by A. Thom, 1909.

STANDARD SOURCES
Praeger.

STEPHENS, JOANNA (fl. 1740)
British physician and pharmacist.

Little is known about Joanna Stephens except for her use of an alternative to the common treatment of removing stones by surgery (lithotomy). Instead, she used a "medicine" called a lithontriptic which was taken orally or injected directly into the bladder. Although the use of lithontriptics was known in ancient times it was not the treatment of choice in the 1700s. Joanna Stephens's treatment represented a revival of the technique in the eighteenth century. Her empirical remedy was successful in a number of cases.

Her medicine consisted of a pill, decoction, and powder. Soap and calcined eggshells were the main ingredients. Although many accounts excoriate Stephens as a quack, there is evidence that the soaps and calcined shells that she used contained a high proportion of lime, a substance which could dissolve certain varieties of stone *in vitro*.

In 1738, Newtonian David Hartley published a small treatise in which he praised Stephens's remedy. He had used it himself and was cured. For her remedy, Stephens had demanded five thousand pounds, to be raised by contribution and collected by two bankers. As the money accumulated, the bankers were to invest the money. After the money had been collected she would present her remedy to the public and receive the interest. After sufficient time, she was to get the principal if the treatment worked. If not, the money would be returned to contributors. To convince the public, Hartley accumulated 155 case histories, which he published. After presenting the cases, Hartley provided a series of chemical experiments with both Joanna Stephens's medicine and other solvents. These experiments were followed by five conclusions: they must in general be safe; the medicines can be taken by the aged and infirm; that those who took the medicines voided whole stones or flakes from stones proves the healing power of the medicines; those who were healed were cured by her medicines only because no one had voided whole stones or flakes from stones who had not tried her treatment; and, again, that her medicine had worked.

Parliament decided in favor of the resolution to award her the five thousand pounds. Even before she actually got the money, numerous other people claimed it was a fraud. In addition to Hartley and Stephen Hales in England, S. F. Morand and C. J. Geoffroy also investigated her medicine. Hales, after many experiments, singled out lime as the effective agent.   JH/MBO

PRIMARY SOURCES
Stephens, Joanna. *A Most Excellent Cure for the Stone and Gravel.* London: N.p., [1740].

SECONDARY SOURCES
Hales, Stephen. *An Account of Some Experiments and Observations on Mrs. Stephens' Medicine for Dissolving the Stone: Wherein their Dissolving Power Is Inquired into, and Shown.* London: Printed for T. Woodward, Printer to the Royal Society, [1740].

Hartley, David. *A View of the Present Evidence for and against Mrs. Stephens's Medicines, as a Solvent for the Stone. Containing a Hundred and Fifty-Five Cases. With Some Experiments and Observations.* London: Printed for S. Harding, J. Robinson, and J. Roberts, 1739.

Rutty, John. *An Account of Some New Experiments and Observations on Joanna Stephens's Medicine for the Stone: With Some Hints for Reducing it from an Empirical to a Rational Use. With Remarks on Dr. Hales's Experiments on the Same Subject, and Some Additional Experiments on the Comparative Efficacy of Divers Other Medicines as Lithontripticks.* 2d ed. London: Printed for R. Manby and H. S. Cox, 1974.

Viseltear, Arthur J. "Joanna Stephens and the Eighteenth-Century Lithontriptics: A Misplaced Chapter in the History of Therapeutics." *Bulletin of the History of Medicine* 42 (1968): 199–220.

STEPHENSON, MARJORY (1885–1948)
British biochemist. Born 24 January 1885 in Burwell, near Cambridge, England, to Sarah Rogers and Robert Stephenson. Three siblings. Educated Berkhampsted High School for Girls (1897–1903); Newnham College (Natural Science Tripos, Part I, in chemistry, physiology, and zoology, class 2, 1906). Cambridge University, titular D.Sc., 1936. Professional experience: Gloucester County Training College in Domestic Science and Kings College of Household Science, London (1906–1911); University College, London, research assistant (1911–1913); Beit Memorial Fellowship for medical research (1913–1922?); Cambridge, research with Frederick G. Hopkins (1919–1929); Medical Research Council, annual grants (1919–1929); Cambridge, permanent research staff (1929–1947?); First Reader in Chemical Microbiology (1947–1948). Honors and memberships: Royal Society, first woman Fellow (1945). Died 12 December 1948 in Cambridge.

Marjory Stephenson, the first woman Fellow of the Royal Society, was born near Cambridge. Although her father never attended a university himself, he had an excellent secondary school education, and he and Marjory's mother were committed to educating their four children. A farmer, Robert Stephenson applied scientific theories to his farming and introduced fruit orchards to Cambridgeshire. Marjory was the youngest child, and she spent much of her early childhood alone. She had a governess who influenced her greatly and encouraged her parents to send her to Berkhampsted High School for Girls. She won a scholarship to the school and remained there for six years. She went to Newnham College in 1903. At that time women could not receive Cambridge degrees. She took a Part I Natural Science

Tripos in chemistry, physiology, and zoology and received a class 2 pass. The Part II Tripos was not available to women at that time, but later Stephenson worked to make it so. She continued her association with Newnham long after she graduated, and became a member of the governing body in 1931 and of the council in 1944.

She could not afford to attend medical school as she wanted. For five years she taught domestic science and household science. Nutrition opened the door for women research scientists who were interested in physiological chemistry during the first part of the twentieth century. R. H. A. Plimmer, a nutritional biochemist, recognized her talents and provided her with a position as a research assistant at University College, London. With Plimmer, she worked on lipid metabolism and metabolic disease. She published the first of many papers in the *Biochemical Journal* in 1911. After 1913 she was able to devote her entire time to biochemistry, first with a grant from Newnham College and then, in 1914, a Beit Memorial Fellowship.

When World War I erupted, she interrupted her research work to help in the war effort. From 1914 to 1918, she served in the British Red Cross, using her knowledge of diet and nutrition in the war effort. For her war service, she was made an associate of the Royal Red Cross and awarded the Member of the Order of the British Empire (MBE).

After the war ended, Stephenson returned to Cambridge, where she worked with a group of students who gathered around Frederick G. Hopkins. Hopkins made Cambridge the center of biochemical thought in Britain, and was well known for his research on vitamins. Stephenson began to follow in his footsteps, but her research on vitamin A deficiency in keraomalacia did not work out. When Hopkins changed his research from vitamins to the chemistry of biological oxidation, Stephenson also changed her research to bacterial biochemistry, a subject in which she had long had an interest.

When a young chemist left Hopkins's laboratory at Cambridge for industry, a position was open for Stephenson, who became one of the few women to work at Cambridge at the time. Free to establish her own research goals, she was by 1922 publishing papers on bacterial metabolism, the field that she defined as her life's work. Her monograph *Bacterial Metabolism,* first published in 1930, was almost the only book on the subject and was very widely read. In 1936, Stephenson took her doctor of science degree.

In her early years, Stephenson was a strong advocate for women's suffrage; however, as she grew older she was less interested in women's issues. She remained, however, a staunch supporter of education for women.

She built a house in Cambridge where she lived for fourteen years before her death, after a long illness, in 1948.

It would be unfair to view the number of Stephenson's published papers as a measure of her influence on the field. This scientist was intent on the quality of her research, not the quantity; she insisted on completing every project thoroughly. Her early interest in fat-soluble vitamins led her to study fat metabolism in bacteria. She demonstrated that growth could continue after the glucose had been depleted. She discovered that the relative amounts of nitrogen and lipoid substances differed depending on whether the carbonaceous food in a synthetic inorganic medium was supplied in the form of lactic acid or glucose. She found that the nitrogen/lipoid ratio was higher in the glucose medium, meaning that the lipoids were used while the protein remained stable. She worked on anaerobic metabolism in a variety of bacteria. Stephenson also developed an important technique, the washed suspension technique.

Stephenson and L. H. Stickland began a series of investigations on the transfer of hydrogen. They found an enzyme they called hydrogenase, which activated hydrogen in a mixed bacterial culture obtained from the river Ouse in the fenlands. After discovering hydrogenase, she and Stickland studied the factors that control the formation of enzymes in bacteria. They found that when the enzyme hydrogenase was present, formate was reduced by certain organisms to methane and sulphate was reduced to sulfide. They found that three enzymes are involved in hydrogen transfer when formate is present: formic dehydrogenase, formic hydrogenlyase, and hydrogenase. From these studies they investigated the growth conditions that led to the production of formic hydrogenlyase within the cell. They concluded that the enzyme was formed only when growth occurred on a medium containing the substrate or substances from which the substance was probably formed as an intermediate during degradation. They also found that enzyme formation could occur without significant cell division.

Stephenson was involved in numerous research projects. With her student John Yudkin, she demonstrated that galactozymase is an adaptive enzyme and that adaptation can occur as a direct response to the environment. Working with E. F. Gale, she studied the factors that controlled the formation of enzymes involved in the deamination of amino acids. She became interested in nucleic acids after working with A. R. Trim on the metabolism of adenine compounds in *E. coli*. World War II interrupted her research; during the war years she studied the fermentation of *Cl. acetobutylicum*. This research provided information useful for subsequent studies in fermentation. During the last years of her life, Stephenson returned to the study of nucleic acids of bacteria and of their breakdown by enzymes within cells, but her final illness prevented her from completing her investigation.

Stephenson is best known for establishing bacterial chemistry as a distinct discipline within biochemistry. Biochemists remember her for the discovery of a new kind of enzyme whereas molecular biologists remember her for her work on adaptive enzymes.   JH/MBO

PRIMARY SOURCES

Stephenson, Marjory. With M. D. Whetham. "Studies in the Fat Metabolism of the Timothy Grass Bacillus." *Proceedings of the Royal Society* 93 (1922): 262–280.

———. *Bacterial Metabolism. Monographs on Biochemistry.* London: Longmans, Green, 1930.

———. With L. H. Stickland. "Hydrogenase: A Bacterial Enzyme Activating Molecular Hydrogen. I. The Properties of the Enzyme." *Biochemical Journal* 25 (1931): 205–214.

———. With L. H. Stickland. "Hydrogenase. II. The Reduction of Sulphate to Sulphide by Molecular Hydrogen." *Biochemical Journal* 25 (1931): 215–220.

———. With L. H. Stickland. "Hydrogenalyses. Bacterial Enzymes Liberating Molecular Hydrogen." *Biochemical Journal* 26 (1932): 712–724.

———. With J. Yudkin. "Galactozymase Considered as an Adaptive Enzyme." *Biochemical Journal* 30 (1936): 506–514.

———. With A. R. Trim. "The Metabolism of Adenine Compounds by *E. coli.*" *Biochemical Journal* 32 (1938): 1740–1751.

———. With E. Rowatt. "The Bacterial Production of Acetylcholine." *Journal of General Microbiology* 1 (1947): 279–298.

———. With J. Moyle. "Nucleic Acid Metabolism in *Escherichia coli.*" *Biochemical Journal* 42 (1949): iv.

SECONDARY SOURCES

Kohler, Robert E. "Innovation in Normal Science: Bacterial Physiology." *Isis* 76 (June 1985): 162–181.

Needham, Dorothy. "Women in Cambridge Biochemistry." In *Women Scientists: The Road to Liberation,* ed. Derek Richter, 161–163. London: Macmillan, 1982.

Robertson, Muriel. "Marjory Stephenson, 1885–1948." *Obituary Notices of the Fellows of the Royal Society* 6 (1948): 563–577.

Woods, D. D. "Obituary Notice of Marjory Stephenson, 1885–1948." *Biochemical Journal* 46 (1950): 377–383.

STANDARD SOURCES

Grinstein 1997 (article by Rebecca Meyer Monhardt); Newnham.

STERN, CATHERINE (BRIEGER) (1894–?)

Polish/U.S. mathematician. Born 1894. Death date unknown.

Cathern Stern was born in Poland and came to the United States. She published a book on structural arithmetic and two textbooks for children.   JH/MBO

PRIMARY SOURCES

Stern, Catherine. *Children Discover Arithmetic: An Introduction to Structural Arithmetic.* New York: Harper, [1949].

———. *Structural Arithmetic.* Boston: Houghton Mifflin Co., 1962.

———. *Children Discover Reading: An Introduction to Structural Reading.* New York: Random House, [1965].

SECONDARY SOURCES

Fuller, Renee. "The Brain-Compatible Way of Teaching Humans." *The Link: A Homeschool Newspaper.* 3, no. 7 (1999): 1–2. Cites Stern's method of teaching arithmetic within a story context.

STERN, FRANCES (1873–1947)

U.S. dietician; nutritionist. Born 3 July 1873 in Boston, Mass., to Caroline (Oppenheimer) and Louis Stern. Six siblings. Educated Garland Kindergarten Training School, Boston (graduated 1897); Massachusetts Institute of Technology, courses in food chemistry and sanitation (1909, 1911–1912); London School of Economics, special student (1922). Professional experience: MIT, secretary and research assistant to Ellen Swallow Richards; Boston Association for the Relief and Control of Tuberculosis and later Boston Provident Association, developed visiting housekeeping program (1911–1912); State Board of Labor and Industries, industrial health inspector (1912–1915); Boston Dispensary, established food clinic; Division of Home Conservation of the United States Food Administration and Department of Agriculture, investigator of the adequacy of food for the industrial worker (1915–1918); American Red Cross and Child and Family Welfare Association in Paris, head worker (1918–1922); Boston Dispensary Food Clinic, founder and director (1922–1947). Died 23 December 1947 in Newton, Mass., of congestive heart disease. Died 1947.

Frances Stern's interest in social problems came from her early experience. Her German-born Jewish parents inculcated in her an ethic of service. She was moved when she saw inadequately fed and clothed small immigrant children. Possessing only a grammar school education, she rented an area in a tenement in Boston's South End, and opened the Louisa Alcott Club to teach homemaking to the young slum children. She soon recognized that she needed additional education, so she enrolled in the Garland Kindergarten Training School in Boston. She met ELLEN SWALLOW RICHARDS, the founder of home economics, and worked for her as secretary and research assistant. Inspired by Richards, she took courses at Massachusetts Institute of Technology, and after Richards's death in 1911, developed two visiting housekeeping programs. She worked for three years as industrial health inspector for the State Board of Labor and Industries, and in 1917, with Gertrude Spitz, published a book, *Food for the*

Worker, to show the importance of an integrated scientific, social, and economic approach to nutrition.

At the outbreak of World War I, Stern went to Washington, D.C., and in 1918 went to France to work for the American Red Cross and then as head worker for the Child and Family Welfare Association in Paris. When she returned to the United States in 1922, she began what was to be her life work, the Boston Dispensary Food Clinic. In this clinic, brightly decorated to give a homelike setting, she advised outpatients and gave them individual counseling on diets. Many of her clients were immigrants, so she developed plans for low-cost national dishes that would be healthful. She also began to train U.S. and foreign doctors, dentists, and nurses in dietetics.

Stern was both idealistic and practical. She worked as a member of the Welfare Committee of the Federated Jewish Charities and urged them to replace outdated practices with new ones. She was a member of the boards of numerous educational and philanthropic organizations. She worked actively in the American Public Health Association, the American Home Economics Association, and the American Dietetic Association. She taught nutrition and dietetics at various times at the Simmons College School of Social Work, Tufts College, Medical School, MIT, and the State Teachers College at Framingham. For the last years of her life, Stern was physically incapacitated by congestive heart disease, but she was still alert and managed the food clinic until her death.

JH/MBO

PRIMARY SOURCES

Stern, Frances. *Food for the Worker: The Food Values and Cost of a Series of Menus and Recipes for Seven Weeks.* Boston: Whitcomb and Barrows, 1917.

———. *Applied Dietetics: The Planning and Teaching of Normal and Therapeutic Diets.* Baltimore: Williams and Wilkins, 1936.

———. With Helen Rosenthal. *Diabetic Care in Pictures: Simplified Statements with Illustrations Prepared for the Use of the Patient.* Philadelphia: J. B. Lippincott, [1946].

SECONDARY SOURCES

Pfaffman, Mary. *Journal of the American Dietetic Association* (February 1948). Obituary notice.

STANDARD SOURCES

NAW (article by Mary F. Handlin).

STEVENS, NETTIE MARIA (1861–1912)

U.S. cytogeneticist. Born 7 July 1861 in Cavendish, Vt., to Julia (Adams) and Ephraim Stevens. One surviving sister, Emma Julia. Educated public schools, Westford, Mass.; Westford Academy (graduated 1880); Westfield (Mass.) Normal School (1881–1883);

Stanford University (B.A., 1899; M.A., 1900); Bryn Mawr College (Ph.D., 1903). Professional experience: Bryn Mawr College, research fellow in biology (1903–1904), reader in experimental morphology (1904–1905), associate in experimental morphology (1905–1912). Died 4 May 1912 in Baltimore, Md.

Both of Nettie Maria Stevens's parents were from old New England families. Of the three other children in the family only one, her sister Emma Julia who was born 14 January 1863, survived to maturity. Their mother died about six months after Emma was born and Stevens's father was remarried to Ellen C. (Thompson) in 1865. After the second marriage, the family moved to Westford, Massachusetts, where the father worked as a carpenter, joiner, and general handyman. By 1875, he had accumulated enough property to guarantee his family freedom from poverty. Stevens's early education was in the public schools of Westford, where she demonstrated exceptional ability quite early. She then attended the Westford Academy, from which she graduated in 1880. She spent three terms teaching Latin, English, mathematics, physiology, and zoology at the high school in Lebanon, New Hampshire, before she continued her education, this time at Westfield (Massachusetts) Normal School. At Westfield, she concentrated on the sciences and graduated (1883) with the highest scores in her class of thirty, demonstrating special proficiency in geometry, chemistry, and algebra.

From 1883 to 1896 Stevens earned her living as a schoolteacher and librarian in the towns of Westford, Chelmsford, and Billerica, Massachusetts. Lured to Stanford University by the school's reputation as a youthful, innovative enterprise, Stevens decided to pursue a degree. Beginning in September 1896 as a special student, Stevens was awarded regular freshman standing in January 1897, and three months later was admitted to advanced standing. Her father and sister followed her to California in 1899.

In 1897–1898, Stevens became the student of Frank Mace MacFarland, under whose tutelage she concentrated increasingly on histology. Stevens spent four summer vacations at the Hopkins Seaside Laboratory at Pacific Grove, California, pursuing histological and cytological problems. During the summers of 1898 and 1899 MacFarland was instructor; Jacques Loeb, a physician and associate professor of physiology at the University of Chicago, held the Investigator's Chair in 1898. Stevens probably became acquainted with Loeb at this time. She received the bachelor's degree from Stanford in 1899 and the master's in 1900; her master's thesis, *Studies on Ciliate Infusoria,* was published in 1901.

In 1900, Stevens returned to the East to study at Bryn Mawr College, an excellent choice for a potential cytologist or histologist, because of the presence of two well-known biologists, Edmund Beecher Wilson and Thomas Hunt

Morgan, on its faculty. Wilson left before Stevens arrived, but his thinking and reputation still saturated the biology department. During her first six months at Bryn Mawr, Stevens impressed her teachers enough by her ability that she was given a fellowship to study abroad (1901–1902). She studied at the Naples Zoological Station and at the Zoological Institute of the University of Würzburg, Germany, under Theodor Boveri (1862–1915). In 1903, Stevens was awarded a doctoral degree by Bryn Mawr. Her dissertation, *Further Studies on the Ciliate Infusoria, Licnophora and Boveria,* was published the same year.

Throughout her life, Stevens was affiliated with Bryn Mawr. From 1903 to 1905, her research there was funded by a grant from the Carnegie Institution. In 1905 she was awarded the Ellen Richards Prize for her paper, "A Study of the Germ Cells of *Aphis rosae* and *Aphis oenotherae*." The highest academic rank she attained was that of associate in experimental morphology (1905–1912). In 1908–1909 she again studied at Würzburg with Boveri. Although the trustees of Bryn Mawr eventually created a research professorship for her, her death, of breast cancer, came before she could occupy it. She died at the Johns Hopkins Hospital in Baltimore in 1912.

During her lifetime, Nettie Stevens published approximately thirty-eight papers. While most of her work was in cytology, she was also concerned with experimental physiology. Her chiefly descriptive early work dealt with the morphology and taxonomy of ciliate protozoa. The interest that she developed in the regenerative processes of two genera, *Licnophora* and *Boveria,* expanded into work on the regeneration of other forms, particularly hydroids and planarians. Although these studies were carefully conceived and superbly executed, Nettie Stevens is seldom remembered for them. In order to understand the importance of her greatest contribution to science, the demonstration that sex is determined by a particular chromosome, the general context of the history of genetics must be examined. During the period of Stevens's research, investigators were exploring the relationship between chromosomes and heredity. Although the behavior of the chromosomes had been described and explained, speculations about their relation to Mendelian heredity had not been experimentally confirmed. The problem was that no trait had been traced from the chromosomes of the parent to those of the offspring, nor had a specific chromosome been linked with a specific characteristic. When Stevens was doing her research there were hints that the inheritance of sex might be related to a morphologically distinct chromosome. This possibility suggested that perhaps this trait, sex, might be connected to a specific chromosome. If sex were shown to be inherited in a Mendelian fashion, then a chromosomal basis for heredity would be supported. An elegant connection between two heretofore parallel strands of information—one from breeding data and the other from cytological observations—would then be suggested.

Although it is not known exactly when Stevens became interested in the problem of chromosomes and sex determination, the question was certainly in her mind by 1903, when, in her first inquiry to the Carnegie Institution about a grant, she described one of her research interests as "the histological side of the problems of heredity connected with Mendel's Law." Since Edmund Beecher Wilson was doing research on the same problem at the same time, the issue of priority is sometimes raised regarding the studies by Stevens and Wilson. However, the evidence clearly indicates that the two arrived at their corresponding discoveries quite independently.

Stevens described the important breakthrough in her paper "Studies in Spermatogenesis with Especial Reference to the 'Accessory Chromosome'" (1905) resulting from her study of the common meal worm, *Tenebrio molitor*. She observed that in this species, while the egg pronuclei always contained ten large chromosomes, pronuclei of the spermatocytes could have either ten large chromosomes or nine large ones and one small one. Since the unreduced somatic cells of the female of *Tenebrio molitor* contained twenty large chromosomes while those of the male possessed nineteen large ones and one small one, Stevens concluded that this situation represented a case of sex determination by a difference in the size of a particular pair of chromosomes. Postulating that the spermatoza containing the small chromosome determine the male sex and that those containing ten chromosomes of equal size determine the female sex, she suggested that sex may in some cases be determined by a difference in the amount or quality of the chromatin.

Because the results in other species were so variable, Stevens, like Wilson, hesitated to make an unequivocal generalization about sex determination by chromosomes. She decided that it was prudent to wait until the spermatogenesis of many more forms had been worked out. "There appears," she wrote, "to be so little uniformity as to the presence of the heterochromosome, even in insects, and in their behavior when present, that further discussion of their probable function must be deferred until the spermatogenesis of many more forms has been carefully worked out" (Ogilvie 1986, 169). Stevens sought confirmation of her tentative theory by doing as she advised, investigating the gametogenesis of additional species—including the aphids, in which she found a perfect correlation between sex and chromosome composition. Her theory was by no means universally accepted by biologists at the time, and she herself constantly questioned her assumption of a Mendelian basis for the inheritance of sex.

MBO

PRIMARY SOURCES

Stevens, Nettie. *Studies in Spermatogenesis with Especial Reference to the 'Accessory Chromosome.'* Washington, D.C.: Carnegie Institution Publication 36, part 1, 1905.

———. "A Study of the Germ Cells of *Aphis rosae* and *Aphis oenotherae.*" *Journal of Experimental Zoology* 2 (1905): 313–333.

———. *Studies in Spermatogenesis: A Comparative Study of the Heterochromosomes in Certain Species of Coleoptera, Hemiptera and Lepidoptera, with Especial Reference to Sex Determination.* Washington, D.C.: Carnegie Institution Publication No. 36, part 2, 1906.

———. "A Study of the Germ Cells of Certain Diptera, with Reference to the Heterochromosomes and the Phenomena of Synapsis." *Journal of Experimental Zoology* 5 (1908): 359–374.

SECONDARY SOURCES

Brush, Stephen G. "Nettie M. Stevens and the Discovery of Sex Determination by Chromosomes." *Isis* 59 (June 1978): 163–172.

Morgan, Thomas Hunt. "The Scientific Work of Miss N. M. Stevens." *Science* n.s. 36, no. 928 (11 October 1912): 468–470.

Ogilvie, Marilyn Bailey, and Choquette, Clifford J. "Nettie Maria Stevens (1861–1912): Her Life and Contributions to Cytogenetics." *Proceedings of the American Philosophical Society* 125 (August 1981): 292–311. Includes a complete bibliography of Stevens's works.

STANDARD SOURCES

AMS 1–2; DSB; NAW; Notable.

STEVENSON, MATILDA COXE (EVANS) (1850–1915)

U.S. anthropologist and ethnologist. Born 12 May 1849 in Washington, D.C., to Maria (Coxe) and Alexander H. Evans. Married Colonel James Stevenson (18 April 1872; died 1888). Educated privately at home; Miss Annable's Academy, Philadelphia (1861–1868); studied law with father, geology and chemistry with N. M. Mew (1868–1872). Professional experience: assisted husband on Hayden Geological Survey (1872–1878); Smithsonian, Bureau of Ethnology, Southwest Indian surveys, volunteer coadjutor in ethnology (1879–1888); government anthropologist (1888–1890; 1890–1915). Honors and memberships: Woman's Anthropological Society of Washington, founder, president (1885); World's Fair Columbian Exposition, anthropology section, judge (1893). Died 1915.

Matilda Coxe Stevenson was the first woman to be hired as an anthropologist by the U.S. Bureau of Ethnology. She grew up in an upper-middle-class household in Washington, D.C., encouraged by her attorney and journalist father to go beyond the usual expectations for a young woman and train in both law and science. She studied geology and chemistry with N. M. Mew, a friend of her father, with the idea of becoming a government mineralogist. Instead she married Colonel James Stevenson from Kentucky when she was twenty-three.

James Stevenson was the executive officer of the Hayden Geological Survey that had as its mission the collection of fossils, natural history specimens, as well as the examination of the geology of the southwest territories. In the process, the survey was required to provide useful information on the local Indian tribes. The expedition traveled through Colorado, Idaho, Wyoming, and Utah between 1872 and 1878. During this period, Matilda Coxe Stevenson assisted her husband in the field and in preparing reports. His work on the geysers of Yellowstone made his name well known to the public.

When John Wesley Powell, a government geologist, took over as head of the new Bureau of Ethnology, the Stevensons went back into the field to investigate the life and customs of American Indians of the Southwest, especially in New Mexico and Arizona, investigating the material culture and lives of the Hopi, Zuni, and other Pueblo Indians. With Frank Hamilton Cushing, they also surveyed and collected from ancient archeological sites.

Matilda Stevenson began to collect material on women's ceremonies and games, talking to the women in the villages while the men obtained the more esoteric material for men's ceremonies. She also began to publish under her own name. Her husband became ill and died in 1888. Powell, as head of the Bureau of Ethnology, first hired Stevenson to finish her husband's work, but soon hired her in her own right, making her the first woman government anthropologist.

Stevenson had already written on Zuni. She returned to New Mexico determined to investigate further and insisted that the men allow her into the kivas and other sacred places from which women were ordinarily excluded. She generally got her own way, although the result was a feeling of ill will on the part of the Indians as well as her bureau colleagues. She produced a massive and thorough publication on Sia (Zia) Pueblo followed some years later by a comprehensive study of Zuni and other New Mexican Pueblo people. Her dream was to finish a comparative monograph of Pueblo religion, but she was never able to complete her study.

Stevenson also founded and became the first president of the Women's Anthropological Society of Washington with ALICE FLETCHER and other women in medicine and government after women were excluded from membership in the Anthropological Society of Washington. The fact that strong and articulate women had run their own organization with some success guaranteed a place for them on the executive board of the American Anthropological Association when that organization was formed from the merging of the two societies. JH

PRIMARY SOURCES

Stevenson, Matilda Coxe. "The Religious Life of the Zuni Child." *Bureau of Ethnology Fifth Annual Report, 1883–84,* 533–555. Washington, D.C.: U.S. Government Printing Office, 1887.

———. *The Sia: Bureau of Ethnology Eleventh Annual Report 1889–1890.* Washington, D.C.: U.S. Government Printing Office, 1891.

———. *The Zuni Indians: Their Mythology, Esoteric Fraternities, and Ceremonies. Bureau of American Ethnology Twenty Third Report, 1901–1902.* Washington, D.C.: U.S. Government Printing Office, 1904.

———. *The Zuni Indians and Their Use of Plants: Bureau of American Ethnology, Thirtieth Annual Report, 1908–1909.* Washington, D.C.: U.S. Government Printing Office, 1915. Includes bibliographical references.

SECONDARY SOURCES

Holmes, William H. "Matilda Coxe Stevenson." *American Anthropologist* 18 (1916): 552–559. Obituary notice.

STANDARD SOURCES

Gacs (article by Nancy J. Parezo); *NAW* (article by Nancy Ostreich Lurie); Rossiter 1982 (includes a discussion of the Women's Anthropological Society of Washington).

STEVENSON, SARA (YORKE) (1847–1921)

U.S. archeologist. Born 19 February 1847 in Paris. Married Cornelius Stevenson (1870). Educated privately. Professional experience: University of Pennsylvania, museum and department of archeology, helped in development (from 1892), secretary (1894–1902), president (1902–1905); American Exploration Society, staff (1894–1905), secretary (1894–1901); Philadelphia Museum, staff (1894–1901); curator (1906); Pennsylvania Museum and school of industrial art, lecturer. Honors and memberships: American Philosophical Society; American Archaeological Institute; American Oriental Society; American Association for the Advancement of Science. Died 14 November 1921.

Sara Yorke was born in Paris and lived with her family in Mexico for five years, from 1862 until 1867. During this time she wrote her book *Maximilian in Mexico.* In 1870 she married Cornelius Stevenson; she lived in Philadelphia for the rest of her life. Although without formal education, Stevenson had read widely and was deeply involved in the study of antiquities. She was active in the creation of the de-

partment of archeology at the University of Pennsylvania and helped to establish the Free Museum of Science and Art, now the university museum. She used her public relations skills to obtain large collections, which she catalogued and displayed herself.

At the request of the university and the American Exploration Society, Stevenson went to Rome in 1897 and Egypt in 1898. She published several scholarly papers on aspects of Egyptian archeological research along with popular articles. At the 1893 Columbian exposition she was vice-president of the jury for ethnology and was a director of the National Export Exposition in 1899.

Stevenson received two honorary degrees, one from the University of Pennsylvania and the other from Temple University. She was the first woman to receive such a degree from the University of Pennsylvania. During that same year she became the first woman lecturer on the Harvard calendar when she spoke at the Peabody Museum.

Stevenson was important in other civic ventures. She was the first president of the Equal Franchise Society of Pennsylvania, president of the Civic Club, and chair of the French war relief committee. For the latter activity she was awarded academic palms as Officier d'Instruction Publique (1916) and made a Chevalier du Legion d'Honneur (1920).

JH/MBO

PRIMARY SOURCES

Stevenson, Sara Yorke. *Maximilian in Mexico: A Woman's Reminiscences of the French Intervention, 1862–1867.* New York: Century, 1899.

SECONDARY SOURCES

Meyerson, Martin, and Dilys Pegler Winegrad. *Gladly Learn and Gladly Teach: Franklin and His Heirs at the University of Pennsylvania, 1740–1976.* Philadelphia: University of Pennsylvania Press, 1978.

STANDARD SOURCES

AMS 1–3 (under Mrs. Cornelius Stevenson); Bailey; *DAB*; Gacs (article by Christine Moon Van Ness); *NCAB*; Siegel and Finley.

STEVENSON, SARAH ANN (HACKETT) (1841–1909)

U.S. physician. Born 2 February 1841 in Buffalo Grove (later Polo), Ogle County, Ill., to Sarah T. Hackett and John Davis Stevenson. Educated Mt. Carroll, Ill., Seminary; State Normal University, Normal, Ill. (graduated 1863); Woman's Hospital Medical College of Chicago (M.D., 1874); South Kensington Science School, London. Professional experience: Bloomington, Ill., school-teacher (1863–1867); Mount Morris, Ill., and Sterling, Ill., teacher and principal; private practice (from 1875); Cook County Hospital in Chicago, staff (1881); Illinois State Board of Health, member (1893); Woman's Medical College in Chicago, teacher (1875–1894), professor of physiology and histology (1875–1880), professor of obstetrics (1880–1894); Illinois Training School for Nurses, founder (1880). Died 14 August 1909 in Chicago.

Sarah Stevenson was involved in many "firsts" in medicine. She was the first woman physician granted membership in the American Medical Association, the first woman on the staff of Cook County Hospital in Chicago, and the first woman appointed to the Illinois State Board of Health. Stevenson orginally trained as a teacher and spent many years in that profession before she became involved in medicine. She went to Chicago with the apparent intention of doing scientific writing, but began studying anatomy and physiology at the Woman's Hospital Medical College of Chicago. After beginning the medical courses, she broke up her training with a year in London at the Kensington Science School. She studied with Thomas Henry Huxley and was considered one of his brightest students. She wrote a high school text, *Boys and Girls in Biology,* based on his lectures. When she returned to Chicago she completed her medical degree in 1874 as class valedictorian. After attaining her degree she again went to Europe to visit hospitals and clinics.

Her series of "firsts" began shortly after she opened her private practice in Chicago in 1875. In 1879 she joined the faculty of the Woman's Medical College as professor of physiology and histology and then of obstetrics. She continued with her successful private practice and was a consultant at Woman's and Provident hospitals and an attending physician at the Mary Thompson Hospital. She later became involved in founding the Illinois Training School for Nurses.

Stevenson was also an active Methodist, a social reformer, and a member of the Woman's Christian Temperance Union (first superintendent, 1881–1882). She was a member of the Fortnightly, Twentieth Century, and Chicago Woman's clubs.

JH/MBO

PRIMARY SOURCES

Stevenson, Sarah Hackett. *Boys and Girls in Biology: or, Simple Studies of the Lower Forms of Life Based on the Latest Lectures of Prof. T. H. Huxley, and Published by His Permission.* Illus. M. A. I. Macomish. New York: D. Appleton and Co., 1875.

———. *Physiology of Woman, Embracing Girlhood, Maternity and Mature Age.* Chicago: Cushing, Thomas & Co., 1880. With essays on "Coeducation of the Sexes in Medicine," "The Physiological Basis of Education," "Temperance from a Physician's Point of View," and "A Plea for Moderation."

———. With Pye Henry Chavasse. *Wife and Mother: Or, Information for Every Woman.* Chicago: H. J. Smith and Co., 1887.

———. *Woman's Adviser for Maiden, Wife, and Mother: Containing Facts of Vital Importance to Every Woman.* Adapted from the writings of Pye Henry Chavasse together with an introduction by Sarah Hackett Stevenson. Chicago: W. B. Conkey Co., 1899. A manual of health care and hygiene for children and of health, hygiene, and beauty for women.

SECONDARY SOURCES

Jacobi, Mary Putnam. "Women in Medicine." In *Woman's Work in America,* ed. Annie Nathan Meyer. [New York: 1891.]

Waite, Lucy. *Distinguished Physicians and Surgeons of Chicago.* N.p., n.d.

STANDARD SOURCES

Cyclopedia of American Medical Biography; LKW.

STEWART, GRACE ANNE (1893–1970)

Canadian invertebrate paleontologist, micropaleontologist, and stratigrapher. Born 4 August 1893 on a farm near Minnedosa, Manitoba. Four siblings, two brothers and two sisters. Never married. Educated University of Alberta (B.A., 1918; M.A., 1920); University of Chicago (Ph.D., 1922). Professional experience: summers with the Geological Survey of Canada, 1921 and 1922; Ohio State University, instructor through professor (to 1954). Died 15 October 1970.

Grace Anne Stewart was born on a farm near Minnedosa, Manitoba. Stewart was a geology major and the first woman to obtain a geology degree at the University of Alberta. While she was working on a graduate degree, she was an assistant in the department of geology from 1918 to 1920, when she was awarded a master's degree. After successfully completing this degree, she won a fellowship at the University of Chicago. She worked there in paleontology under Stuart Weller and earned a doctoral degree in 1922. Her summer jobs were with the Research Council of Alberta and the Geological Survey of Canada working at the National Museum. Gender discrimination was rife in the male protectorate of the Geological Survey. Stewart joined the staff of Ohio State University, proceeding up the academic ladder to become a professor in 1946. She was a solid teacher and researcher, but her contributions were not limited to academic geology. She was a member of several faculty committees and was a good citizen of the university community. She apparently became discouraged with her long teaching career and retired in 1954 and moved to Arizona. However, she returned to Calgary to work again professionally, this time with the Strategic Service of Canada Ltd., Alta Canada, as paleontologist. She disliked the Canadian winter and soon returned to Tucson. In March 1969 she suffered a stroke and had to be placed in a nursing home. She continued to fail physically and mentally and died on 15 October 1970.

Stewart's research was mainly on the medial Paleozoic faunas of Ohio, with special concentration on Silurian and Devonian microfossils. She also studied Devonian ostracods, crinoids, and corals. She presented papers before the Paleontological Society, the American Association for the Advancement of Science, and the Ohio Academy of Science. She was chair of the Geological Section of the Ohio Academy in 1937. She was a Fellow of the Geological Society of America, the Paleontological Society, and the Ohio Academy of Science.   JH/MBO

PRIMARY SOURCES

Stewart, Grace Anne. "The Fauna of the Little Saline Limestone in St. Genevieve County." *Missouri Bureau of Geology and Mines* 2d ser., 17 (1924): 213–279. Same title as her dissertation accepted in 1923 by the University of Chicago.

———. "Ostracodes of the Silica Shale, Middle Devonian, of Ohio." *Journal of Paleontology* 10, no. 8 (1936): 739–763.

———. "Middle Devonian Corals of Ohio." *Geological Society of America Special Paper* 8 (1938).

———. "Ostracoda from Middle Devonian Bone Beds in Central Ohio." *Journal of Paleontology* 6 (1950): 652–666.

———. "Age Relations of the Middle Devonian Limestones in Ohio." *Ohio Journal of Science* 55, no. 3 (1955): 147–181.

SECONDARY SOURCES

Hayes, Pamela D. "Stewart, Grace Anne (1893–1970)." In *Biographies of Geologists. Materials for the Study of the History of Geology, Prepared in Geology 851, a Seminar in the History of Geology, 1853–1958. Sixth supplement,* ed. Aurèle LaRocque, 15–16. Columbus, Ohio: Ohio State University, 1971.

La Rocque, Aurèle. "Grace Anne Stewart." *Ohio Journal of Science* 71, no. 4 (1971): 254.

Spieker, Edmund M. "Memorial to Grace Anne Stewart 1893–1970." *Geological Society of America Memorials* 2 (1973): 110–114.

STANDARD SOURCES

Sarjeant.

STEWART, ISABEL MAITLAND (1873–1953)

U.S. nursing educator. Born 14 January 1878 in Raleigh, Ontario, Canada to Elizabeth (Farquharson) and Francis Beattie Stewart. Eight siblings. Never married. Educated Pilot Mound, Manitoba; Chatham, Ontario; Winnipeg General Hospital School of Nursing (graduated 1903); Columbia University Teachers College, hospital economics program (B.S., 1911; A.M., 1913). Professional experience: private nurse (1903–1905); Winnipeg General Hospital, *nurse supervisor (1905–1907); Columbia University Teachers College, assistant, instructor, assistant professor, Helen Hartley Jenkins Foundation Professor of Nursing Education and director of the department (1925–1947). Honors and memberships: National League of Nursing Education, Mary Adelaide Nutting Award (1947); government of Finland, medal (1946); several honorary degrees; Columbia University Teachers College, established the Isabel Maitland Stewart Research Professorship in Nursing Education (1961). Died 5 October 1963 in Chatham, N.J., of a heart attack.*

Canadian-born Isabel Stewart came from a Scottish family on both sides. Her father was a farmer and sawmill owner in Fletcher, Ontario, but when Isabel was in her early teen years, his business failed and finances became difficult. The fourth of nine children, Isabel was independent and proud of her pioneer heritage. She and her friends disdained marriage and planned careers for themselves. Encouraged by her parents to get a good education, she attended school and qualified for teaching certificates. She supported her own education by teaching others in the local schools. Although her parents assumed that she would become a teacher, Isabel was convinced that she wanted to be a nurse. Risking her parents' disapproval, she entered the Winnipeg General Hospital School of Nursing. Always interested in the theoretical aspects of her subject, Stewart was dismayed that her only education was on the wards. After graduation, she spent two years in private nursing, was a relief nurse in Winnipeg for several months, and then returned to Winnipeg general hospital where she was a nursing supervisor.

Finding Canadian nursing education inadequate, in 1908 Stewart enrolled in ADELAIDE NUTTING's hospital economics program at Columbia University Teachers College. She stayed on at Columbia after earning both a bachelor's and a master's degree, discarding her earlier goal—to return to Canada to establish a preparatory course for nurses. She moved up the academic ladder and in 1925 became the Helen Hartley Jenkins Foundation Professor of Nursing Education and director of the department. Between the time that Stewart entered Columbia and 1910, the program had changed greatly. At first the emphasis was on training nurse administrators. After Helen Hartley Jenkins provided an endowment in 1910 for an expanded nursing education department, the potential for the kind of nursing education that Stewart had dreamed of existed. Stewart convinced Nutting to allow her to devise a program to train nurses. Working together, the two women established the most advanced nursing education course in the country. Stewart was able to meld the all-important theoretical component into the curriculum.

Stewart was active in many professional organizations, especially those that were involved in nursing education. As chair of the education committee of the National League of

Nursing Education she was important in designing the national curricula published by the League in 1917, 1927, and 1937. She also initiated the first standardized tests in nursing which prepared the way for a system of voluntary accreditation (1939). She worked to improve the standards of nursing education through several different organizations. She also held leadership roles in both world wars. During World War I, she chaired the curriculum committee of the Vassar Training Camp. This organization recruited college graduates to serve as nurses and provided preliminary training; she also wrote much of the literature designed to recruit nurses for the war effort. From 1940 to 1942 she chaired the committee on educational policies and resources of the National Nursing Council for War Service.

Whereas many nurses emphasize the practical aspect of their craft, Stewart was well known for her many publications and for her research. A liberal politically, she was interested in politics, education, and economic equality for women.   JH/MBO

PRIMARY SOURCES

Stewart, Isabel Maitland. With Lavinia L. Dock. *A Short History of Nursing from the Earliest Times to the Present Day.* New York: G. P. Putnam's Sons, [1920]. The first four editions were written in collaboration with Lavinia L. Dock and the fifth with Anne L. Austin.

———. "Developments in Nursing Education since 1918." *Bulletin/Department of the Interior Bureau of Education, no. 20.* Washington, D.C.: Government Printing Office, 1921.

———. *The Education of Nurses: Historical Foundations and Modern Trends.* New York: Macmillan, 1943.

———. *Reminiscences.* Glen Rock, N.J.: Microfilming Corporation of America, 1972. Microfiche.

Stewart's papers are in the archives of the nursing education department at Columbia University Teachers College.

SECONDARY SOURCES

Goostray, "Isabel Maitland Stewart." *American Journal of Nursing* (March 1954).

New York Times, 7 October 1963. Obituary notice.

STANDARD SOURCES

NAW(M) (article by Anne L. Austin).

STEWART, MAUDE (1866–?)

U.S. physicist. Born 5 March 1866 in Elgin, Minn. Educated Carleton College (B.L., 1888); Columbia University (A.M., 1913). Professional experience: high school, Illinois, instructor (1892–1903); Salem College, head of department of science (1906–1912); Faribault, Minn., high school, teacher (1912–1920); Pipestone, *Minn., teacher (1920–1922); Farmington, Minn. (1922–1925); Northfield, Minn. (from 1925). Death date unknown.*

Maude Stewart spent most of her career teaching high school physics. She was, however, interested in research in radioactivity and was a member of the physical society.

                                        JH/MBO

STANDARD SOURCES

AMS 3–7.

STEWART, SARAH ELIZABETH (1906–1976)

U.S. bacteriologist and oncologist. Born 16 August 1906 in Tecalitlán, Mexico. Educated New Mexico Agricultural College (B.S., 1927); Massachusetts State College (M.S., 1930); University of Chicago (Ph.D. in bacteriology, 1939); Georgetown University (M.D., 1949). Professional experience: University of Colorado Experimental Station, assistant bacteriologist (1930–1933); National Institutes of Health, from assistant bacteriologist to bacteriologist (1936–1944); Georgetown University School of Medicine, instructor in bacteriology (1944–1947), assistant professor (1948–1955), professor of pathology (from 1955); National Cancer Institute, Section Chief Viral Biology (from 1960). Died 1976 of cancer.

Sarah Elizabeth Stewart earned a doctorate in bacteriology and then a medical degree. Most of her later work was in pathology and especially oncology. She held positions as senior assistant surgeon and senior surgeon at the National Cancer Institute from 1950 to 1960, posts she held concurrently. Her research was on oncogenic viruses, specifically polyoma viruses that cause multiple tumors in rodents. The research of Sarah Stewart, with her friend and collaborator BERNICE ELAINE EDDY, showed that the polyoma virus, with its tumor-forming capacity, could be transferred between individuals and even across species. The name *SE polyoma virus* memorializes both their names. Georgetown University instituted a memorial lecture series in her honor.   JH/MBO

PRIMARY SOURCES

Stewart, Sarah Elizabeth. "Studies on the Toxins and Antitoxins of *Clostridium perfringens.*" *Public Health Reports* 55 (1940): 753–775.

———. Papers. Special Collections. Georgetown University.

STANDARD SOURCES

AMS 7–8, B 9, P&B 10–13; *Mothers and Daughters.*

STIEBELING, HAZEL KATHERINE (1896–?)

U.S. food chemist and nutritionist. Born 20 March 1896 in Haskins, Ohio. Educated Columbia University (B.S., 1919; M.A.,

1924; Ph.D., 1928). *Professional experience: Ohio, supervisor home economics (1915–1918); Kansas State Teachers College, Emporia, Kans., supervising teacher (1919–1923); Columbia University, instructor of nutrition (1924–1926), assistant food chemist (1926–1930); U.S. Department of Agriculture food economics sections bureau of home economics, senior food economist (1930–1934), assistant chief (1943–1944); Bureau of Human Nutrition and Home Economics, chief (1944–1953); Agricultural Research Service, director of research for human nutrition and home economics (from 1954); Institute for Home Economics, director (1957–1962). Death date unknown.*

Hazel Stiebeling had a distinguished career in food chemistry and nutrition. As chief of the U.S. Department of Agriculture's Bureau of Human Nutrition and Home Economics she participated in the wartime task of extension work, or "nutrition education." This bureau advised housewives, businesses, and other institutions on how to reduce purchases and make substitutions. She was probably the first to adapt her menus for four income levels, providing each section of the population with an affordable nutritious diet. Hazel Stiebeling was one of the women biochemists who headed the Bureau of Home Economics, but its separate existence ended in 1953 when all the USDA research bureaus were consolidated into the Agricultural Research Service. The three remaining home economics divisions were combined to form an Institute for Home Economics in 1957, headed by Stiebeling. This nutrition section was phased out in 1962 and the clothing and textile research section in 1965.

Stiebeling's research interests were on the composition and nutritive values of food, energy metabolism, and food consumption habits of population groups. She was the recipient of numerous honors and awards, including honorary doctorates from Skidmore College (1943), Iowa State (1947), and Michigan State (1955). She received the USDA's distinguished service award (1952), the President's Gold Medal Award for Distinguished Federal Civilian Service (1959), and the Chemical Society's Borden Award (1943). She was a member of the food and nutrition board of the National Research Council, nutritional committees of the Food and Agricultural Organization and the World Health Organization, and a U.S. delegate for the conference of food and agricultural organizations of the United Nations (1946–1959).

JH/MBO

PRIMARY SOURCES

Stiebeling, Hazel K. *The Iron Content of Vegetables and Fruits.* Circular, U.S. Department of Agriculture, no. 205. Washington, D.C.: U.S. Department of Agriculture, 1932.

———. *Diets at Four Levels of Nutritive Content and Cost.* Circular, U.S. Department of Agriculture, no. 296. Washington, D.C.: U.S. Department of Agriculture, 1933.

———. *Diets of Families of Employed Wage Earners and Clerical Workers in Cities.* Circular, U.S. Department of Agriculture, no. 507. Washington, D.C.: U.S. Department of Agriculture, 1939.

———. *Are We Well Fed? A Report on the Diets of Families in the United States.* U.S. Department of Agriculture, miscellaneous publication, no. 430. Washington, D.C.: U.S. Department of Agriculture, 1941.

———. *Family Food Consumption and Dietary Levels: Five Regions.* U.S. Department of Agriculture, miscellaneous publications, nos. 405, 452. 2 vols. Washington, D.C.: U.S. Government Printing Office, 1941.

———. Papers (1982–1994). USDA Special Collections. The National Agricultural Library.

STANDARD SOURCES
AMS 5–8, B 9, P&B 10–11; Rossiter 1995.

STIEGLITZ, MARY RISING (1889–1977)

U.S. chemist. Born 21 July 1889 in Ainsworth, Nebr. Married Julius Oscar Stieglitz (1934). Educated Mount Holyoke (A.B., 1912); University of Chicago (Ph.D., 1920). Professional experience: University of Chicago, instructor to associate professor of chemistry (1920–1934), research associate (1934–1937). Died 5 January 1977.

Mary Meda Rising was the second wife of the chemist Julius Oscar Stieglitz. Twenty years older than Mary, he was a distinguished chemist trained in Germany. He was the head of the chemistry department at the University of Chicago from 1915 until the death of his first wife in 1933. Mary completed her doctorate at Chicago during the time Stieglitz was head of the department; she was first Stieglitz's student and then his colleague. On the death of his first wife, Anna Stiefel, he married Mary Rising. After he married her he left the department, perhaps to enable her to be made an associate professor. She remained with the university until his death in 1937, after which she disappears from the historical record. However, it is known that she died 5 January 1977 in Claremont, California.

JH/MBO

PRIMARY SOURCES

Stieglitz, Mary Rising. "The Behavior of Phenylacetonitrile and alpha-Phenylbutyronitrile with Sodium Ethylate." *Journal of the American Chemical Society* 54 (1932): 2021–2025.

———. "The Synthesis of Colored Derivatives of Phenobarbital." *Journal of the American Chemical Society* 55 (1933): 2817–2820.

———. "The Biuret Reaction." *Journal of Biological Chemistry* 99 (1933): 755–765.

SECONDARY SOURCES

McCoy, Herbert Newby. "Julius Stieglitz, 1867–1937: A Biographical Sketch." *Journal of the American Chemical Society* 60 (1938).

STANDARD SOURCES

AMS 4–8, P 9; Poggendorf, vol. 7B (under Rising and Stieglitz); Rossiter 1982.

STIMSON, BARBARA BARTLETT (1898–?)

U.S. physician and orthopedic surgeon. Born 14 February 1898 in New York City to Alice (Bartlett) and Henry A. Stimson. Three sisters, three brothers. Never married. Educated Vassar College (B.A., 1919); Columbia University (M.D., 1923; D.Sc. in medicine, 1934); Presbyterian Hospital, intern (1923–1925), medical research council fellow (1925–1927), surgery fellow (1927–1928). Professional experience: Presbyterian Hospital, assistant attending surgeon (1928–1945), associate attending surgeon (1945–1947); Columbia University College of Physicians and Surgeons, instructor (1928–1934), associate in surgery (1934–1945), assistant professor of orthopedic surgery (1945–1947); assistant clinical professor (from 1959); Vanderbilt Hospital, assistant attending surgeon (1945–1947); St. Francis Hospital, director of orthopedic service (from 1954); private practice in surgery, Poughkeepsie, N.Y. (from 1947); Mid-Hudson workshop for the disabled, director (from 1948); Royal Army Medical Corps, Major (1942–1945). Trustee alumnae Vassar College (1934–1941). Honors and memberships: Elizabeth Blackwell Citation, New York Infirmary (1950); Diplomate, American Board of Surgery; Fellow, American College of Surgeons and New York Academy of Medicine; American Association of Surgery Trauma, British Orthopedic Association, New York Surgical Society, Duchess County Medical Society, Officer of St. John of Jerusalem, Military Division Order of British Empire. Death date unknown.

Barbara Stimson was the daughter of a minister and one of seven children in a remarkable family that valued education and equality of opportunity. All seven children received college degrees. The girls were encouraged to excel, whether their interests were suitable in the eyes of nineteenth-century society or not. When Stimson's sister Lucille chose to take her master's degree in chemistry at Columbia University, she was seated at a separate table in a separate room apart from the male students. Stimson majored in chemistry at Vassar and chose the College of Physicians and Surgeons, Columbia University, for her medical degree because of its nearness to home. She was one of twelve women and ninety men in her class. Long interested in surgery, Stimson was led to fracture surgery by a senior doctor who sensed her special ability. She interned at Presbyterian Hospital and stayed to become a full-time staff surgeon. An outstanding pioneer in the area

of "internal fixation" of fractures, she developed a procedure that greatly shortened the patient's period of forced inactivity.

When Britain asked the United States for male doctors to supplement their dwindling medical resources during the war years (1940–1941), their plea went unanswered due to the U.S. armed forces' need for medical personnel. In June 1941, Britain asked for American women doctors and Stimson responded. She began at a London hospital in the Emergency Medical Service. After her commission as an officer in the Royal Army Medical Corps, she went to a hospital near London as an orthopedic surgeon. In 1943, she was sent to North Africa to a base hospital where she set up and directed an orthopedic center consisting of two doctors, two aides, four masseurs, and one occupational therapist. Her team stayed together a year and a half before being moved to Pompeii. From there, the Stimson team was sent to a large hospital in Naples and then to Rome where she served until her return to the States.

Stimson returned to Columbia-Presbyterian Hospital and set up a private surgical practice in Poughkeepsie, New York. She also worked at the Columbia University College of Physicians and Surgeons as assistant professor of orthopedic surgery (1945–1947) and as assistant clinical professor (from 1959). She held other positions at Vanderbilt Hospital (assistant attending surgeon) and at St. Francis Hospital (director of orthopedic service). The long hours spent in surgery or teaching were fulfilling for Stimson but she was not a one-dimensional personality. Her choice of career without marriage was based on careful thought and a sense of fairness. She did not rule out the combination for others but felt that a doctor with her own office and a specialty with definite hours had a better chance of a successful marriage than a general practitioner or hospital staff member. She did not feel that she suffered from male prejudice within her profession, although she admitted that a woman might have to be slightly better than a man applying for the same job. Her advice was to accept the professional disadvantages as a given, then forget them and apply oneself with determination and absolute dedication.

JH/MBO

PRIMARY SOURCES

Stimson, Barbara. *A Manual of Fractures and Dislocations.* Philadelphia: Lea and Febiger, 1939. Went through at least three editions.

SECONDARY SOURCES

Knapp, Sally. *Women Doctors Today.* New York: Thomas Y. Corwell Co., 1947. See pages 153–164. Includes a sketch.

STANDARD SOURCES

Who's Who of American Women.

STINCHFIELD, SARA MAE (1885–?)

U.S. psychologist. Born 29 September 1885 in Auburn, Maine. Married C. L. Hawk. Educated University of Pittsburgh (A.B., 1914); University of Iowa (A.M., 1920); University of Wisconsin (Ph.D., 1922); Vienna and London, postgraduate study (1931). Professional experience: University of Iowa, research assistant (1918–1920); University of Wisconsin, assistant (1920–1922); Mount Holyoke College, instructor in psychology (1922–1924), assistant professor (1924–1927), associate professor (1927–1932); University of Southern California, lecturer (from 1932). Honors and memberships: American Speech-Language-Hearing Association, Honors of the Association (1953). Death date unknown.

Sara Stinchfield had an interesting career trajectory, probably linked to her husband, C. L. Hawk's, positions. After rising to associate professor at Mount Holyoke, she moved to California and accepted a position as a lecturer at the University of Southern California. During her time in California, she was a psychologist for the Polytechnical Elementary and junior high schools in Pasadena and worked at the speech clinic in the Orthopedic Hospital, Los Angeles. During the summers of 1922–1924, 1926–1929, and 1937 she served on the staff at the Pennsylvania State College. She was assistant editor for the *Quarterly Journal of Speech Education* from 1922. As a member of several professional organizations she was active in the Psychological Association, the Society for the Study of Disorders of Speech (secretary, 1925–1930), and the American Academy of Speech Correction (past president). JH/MBO

PRIMARY SOURCES
Stinchfield, Sara Mae. "The Formulation and Standardization of a Series of Graded Speech Tests." Psychological Review Publications. *Psychological Monographs* 33, no. 2. Princeton, N.J.: Psychological Review Company, [1923].
———. *Speech Pathology with Methods in Speech Correction.* Boston: Expression Co., 1928.
———. *Speech Disorders: A Psychological Study of the Various Defects of Speech.* London: Kegan Paul, Trench, Trubner & Co., 1933.

STANDARD SOURCES
AMS 4–7.

STOKES, MARGARET MCNAIR (1832–1900)
Irish archeologist. Died 1900.

Little is known about the life of Margaret Stokes. She worked chiefly on Irish archeology, and one of her books, *Early Christian Architecture in Ireland,* went through many editions. Letters from her (as Miss Margaret Stokes) and her father,

William Stokes, to the Third Earl of Dunraven (1864–1871) are found among the archeological papers of the Third Earl in the Dunraven Papers, Public Record Office of Northern Ireland. JH/MBO

PRIMARY SOURCES
Stokes, Margaret. With Sir Samuel Ferguson. *The Cromlech on Howth: A Poem.* London: Day, 1861.
———. With George Petrie. *Christian Inscriptions in the Irish Language.* Dublin: Printed at the University Press for the Royal Historical and Archaeological Association of Ireland, 1872–1878.
———. *Early Christian Architecture in Ireland.* London: G. Bell and Sons, 1878.
———. "Carte montrant la distribution des principaux dolmens d'Irlande, avec rémarques sur les monuments funéraires préhistoriques de ce pays et un liste de ces monuments." Excerpt from *Revue archeologique,* July 1882. Paris: Didier, 1882.
———. *Six Months in the Apennines; or, A Pilgrimage in Search of Vestiges of the Irish Saints in Italy.* London: George Bell and Sons, 1892.
———. *Three Months in the Forests of France: A Pilgrimage in Search of Vestiges of the Irish Saints in France.* London: G. Bell, 1895.

SECONDARY SOURCES
McDonnell, Hector. "Margaret Stokes and the Irish Round Tower: A Reappraisal." *Ulster Journal of Archaelogy* 57, third series (1994): 70–80.

STOKEY, ALMA GRACEY (1877–1968)
U.S. botanist, fern specialist. Born 17 June 1877 in Canton, Ohio, to Margaret Purvines and Charles Frederick Stokey. Educated Oberlin College (B.A., 1904); University of Chicago (Ph.D., 1908). Professional experience: Canton public schools, teacher; Oberlin College, assistant in botany (1904–1906), instructor (plant science) (1908), associate (1911); Mount Holyoke College, professor and head of department of plant science (1916–1942), emerita professor (1942–1968); Women's Christian College, Madras, India, head of botany (1929–1931; 1936). Honorary D.Sc., Oberlin College (1955). Died 18 March 1968.

Alma Gracey Stokey was born in Canton, Ohio, to Margaret Purvines and Charles Frederick Stokey. She attended the local public schools and also taught in these schools before she went to Oberlin College, where she earned her bachelor's degree in botany. She remained as an assistant in botany after her graduation for two years before she went to the University of Chicago to study under John M. Coulter and W. J. G. Lan. She received her doctoral degree in 1908. From

Chicago, she went as instructor in plant science to Mount Holyoke College in Massachussetts, from which her sister Eva had earlier graduated.

Already interested in ferns, Stokey had been urged by F. O. Bower in Glasgow to fill in the gaps in the knowledge of these plants. She was particularly interested in prothallia of ferns and their role in the production of gametophytes for reproduction. She was the head of the Department of Plant Science at Mount Holyoke from 1916 to 1942. For two years she took leave to help set up botany at the Women's Christian College, Madras, India, a sister college of Mount Holyoke, returning there again in 1936. As a teacher, she involved her graduate students in her surveys of ferns. She went most summers to Woods Hole to do research and she built a house near Woods Hole where her sister Eva Evans and other relatives joined her from Atlanta, Georgia. She was a member of the Corporation of the Marine Biological Laboratories, Woods Hole, from 1917 until her death. In an article written for her alumnae magazine, she explained the crucial importance of opportunities for research provided for students at Woods Hole.

Stokey continued her research after her retirement, publishing a further thirty articles. In the first issue of *Phytomorphology*, she published her analysis of the contribution of gametophyte to classification of homosporous ferns (1950?). Stokey received an honorary degree from her undergraduate college, Oberlin, in 1955.   JH/MBO

PRIMARY SOURCES

Stokey, Alma Gracey. "The Roots of Lycopodium pithyoides." *Botanical Gazette* (1907).

———. "The Anatomy of Isoetes." *Botanical Gazette* (1909).

———. "The Sporangium of Lycopodium pithyoides." *Botanical Gazette* (1910).

———. With Anna M Starr. "*Lycopodium prothallia* in Western Massachusetts." *Botanical Gazette* (1924).

———. "The Prothallia of the Cyatheaceae." *Botanical Gazette* (1930).

———. "The Importance of Science at Woods Hole." *Mount Holyoke Alumnae Quarterly* 26 (1942).

———. With L. R. Atkinson. "The Gametophyte of Didymochlaena sinuata." *Phytomorphology* (November 1954).

———. "Multicellular and Branched Hairs on the Fern Gametophyte." *American Fern Journal* 50 (1960): 78–87.

SECONDARY SOURCES

American Fern Journal 58 (1968): 145–152. Obituary notice.

Atkinson, Geoffrey. "Alma Gracey Stokey." *Mount Holyoke Alumnae Quarterly* 26 (1942): 54–55.

Mount Holyoke Transcript Telegram, 19 March 1968. Obituary notice.

STANDARD SOURCES

NAW unused.

STONE, EMMA CONSTANCE (1856–1902)

Australian physician and feminist. Born 4 December 1856. Educated Woman's Medical College of Pennsylvania and University of Trinity College, Toronto, Canada (M.D., Ch.M., 1888); New Hospital for Women, London, licentiate of the Society of Apothecaries (1889); Medical Board of Victoria (1890). Professional experience: private practice in Victoria. Honors and memberships: Victorian Medical Women's Society, founding member (1895). Died 29 December 1902.

Constance Stone was the first woman to practice medicine in Victoria. She was active in community affairs and was elected to the local school board and ran the Victoria Vigilance Society, which campaigned for the age of consent (and therefore of legal prostitution) to be raised to sixteen. She helped establish the Queen Victoria Hospital for the Melbourne poor.   JH/MBO

STANDARD SOURCES

Uglow 1989.

STONE, DORIS ZEMURRAY (1909–1994)

U.S. anthropologist and archeologist. Born 19 November 1909 in New Orleans, La., to Sarah (Weinberger) and Samuel Zemurray. One younger brother. Married Roger Thayer Stone, 1930. One son. Educated Newman School; Radcliffe College (B.A., 1930); Harvard University (graduate courses in anthropology). Professional experience: Harvard University, Peabody Museum, Center for American Archaeology and Ethnology, research associate (1942–1994); Tulane University, researcher. Honors memberships: Andean Institute, member; Tulane University, honorary LL.D. (1957); Harvard University, Radcliffe College, honorary D.Sci. (1994); Union College, honorary degree (1973);Nicaragua, Comendador, Order of Ruben Darfo (1955); Honduras, honorary citizen (1956); Comendador, order of Francisco Morazon (1957); Panama, Caballero, Order of Vasco Nunez de Balboa (1957); France, Chevalier Legion de Honor (1958); Harvard Medal (1993); Society of American Archaelogy, Fellow; American Ethnological Society, Fellow; Royal Anthropological Institute of Great Britain and Ireland, Fellow; Mexican Anthropological Society, Fellow. Died 21 October 1994.

The life of Doris Zemurray Stone presents an example of an archeologist and ethnologist who, although she held no paid professional positions, had a considerable influence on her field, through both her research and the high quality of her analysis. She produced pioneering studies of the archeology of Honduras and Costa Rica and contributed extensively to the studies of the ethnohistory of indigenous Central American peoples.

Born in New Orleans, she spent much of her life traveling to and from Honduras and Costa Rica where her father had considerable business interests (he was later the president of United Fruit). She attended Radcliffe College, where she majored in anthropology and took two graduate archeology courses, which required special permission from Harvard. As an undergraduate she traveled through Finland and the Soviet Union. She married a physics student soon after graduation and took her honeymoon in Central America. Although they lived in New Orleans for the first nine years, they moved to San Jose, Costa Rica, before the outbreak of World War II, and remained there and on a coffee plantation in Curridabat until the retirement of her husband. Her marriage did not result in her relinquishing her interests, and her first articles and monographs on the archeology and ethnology of Central America began to appear in 1940. She was supported in her studies by Alfred Tozzer at Harvard, who praised and published her work in the Peabody Museum series.

In the post-war era, Stone established a society to protect the native Indian tribes (Council for the Protection of Indigenous Races). She also supported the Costa Rican revolution and persuaded its leader, Jose Figueres Ferrier, to convert the Bellevista Fortress that housed more than five thousand troops into the National Museum of Costa Rica. She also received the support of the Communist leader in spite of his opposition to her father, president of United Fruit, and the museum was soon built with the help of these leaders and many volunteers.

Stone produced the first comprehensive overviews of prehistoric Costa Rica. She established the accepted tripatriate cultural subdivision in Costa Rica that has been widely used; she also stressed the importance betwen tool assemblages and the subsistance culture. While accepting that Central America was a melting pot for anicent cultures in the south and the north, she insisted on the presence of a complex of features native to Central America, with South American ethnographic features. She studied plant diffusion, and the cultural diffusion of metallurgy, jade, and ceramics. Her work is still widely cited.

Stone contributed to the *Handbook of South American Indians* for the Smithsonian Institution, and the *Handbook of Middle American Indians*. A major figure in establishing Costa Rican institutions, she also organized and ran the 33rd International Congress of Americanists, held in San Jose in 1958, and served on the permanent council of the Congress as well as on the boards of many educational organizations and institutions.   JH

PRIMARY SOURCES

Stone, Doris Zemurray. "Archaeology of the North Coast of Honduras." *Papers of the Peabody Museum of Archaeology and Ethnology,* 9, no. 1 (1941).

———. "The Talmacan Tribes of Costa Rica." *Papers of the Peabody Museum of Archaeology and Ethnology* 43, no. 2 (1962).

———. "Pre-Columbian Man Finds the Archaeological Bridge." *Papers of the Peabody Museum of Archaeology and Ethnology.* Cambridge, Mass.: Peabody Museum Press, 1972.

———. *Pre-Columbian Man in Costa Rica.* Cambridge, Mass.: Peabody Museum Press, 1977.

SECONDARY SOURCES

Andrews, E. Wyllys, and Frederick W. Lange. "In Memoriam: Doris Zemurray Stone." *Ancient Mesoamerica* 6 (1995): 95–100. Obituary with portrait.

Andrews, E. Wyllys, ed. *Research and Reflections in Anthropology and History: Essays in Honor of Doris Stone.* New Orleans: Tulane University Press, 1986. Includes bibliography compiled by Stephen Williams, pages 203–209.

STANDARD SOURCES

AMS 8, S&B 9–12, P&B 13.

STONE, ISABELLE (1868–ca. 1934)

U.S. physicist. Born 1868 in Chicago to Harriet (Leonard) and Leander Stone. Never married. Educated Wellesley College (B.A., 1890); University of Chicago (M.S., 1896; Ph.D., 1897). Professional experience: Bryn Mawr Preparatory School in Baltimore, Md., teacher (1897–1898); Vassar College, instructor (1898–1906); Misses Stone's School for American Girls, Rome, Italy, principal (from 1907). Died ca. 1934.

Isabelle Stone received degrees from Vassar and Columbia. She taught at the Bryn Mawr Preparatory School in Baltimore and was an instructor at Vassar College.

Stone was one of the founders of the American Physical Society. Her research was on the electrical resistance of thin films, color in platinum films, and the properties of films when deposited in a vacuum. In 1934, Isabelle Stone left a bequest to Phi Beta Kappa for the establishment of a fellowship for women scholars.   JH/MBO

PRIMARY SOURCES

Stone, Isabelle. "On the Electrical Resistance of Thin Films." Ph.D. diss., University of Chicago, 1897.

SECONDARY SOURCES

Rossiter, Margaret. "Women Scientists in America before 1920." *American Scientist* 62 (May-June 1974): 312–323.

STANDARD SOURCES

AMS 1–7; *Woman's Who's Who of America.*

STOPES, MARIE CHARLOTTE CARMICHAEL (1880–1958)

British paleobotanist. Born 15 October 1880 in Edinburgh. Father Henry Stopes. Married (1) R. Ruggles Gates (annulled); (2) H. V. Roe. Educated London (D.Sc., 1905); Munich (Ph.D., 1909). Professional experience: Manchester University, scientific staff (1904–1907), lecturer in paleobotany (1909–1914); University College, London (1914–1920). Died 2 October 1958 at Norbury Park, Surrey.

Marie Stopes was the daughter of the archeologist and anthropologist Henry Stopes. In 1946 the Geologists' Association established a medal bearing his name for his work in human prehistory. Marie Stopes earned a chemistry scholarship to University College, London, where she won the Gold Medal in Junior and Senior Botany, graduating under F. W. Oliver. She then went to Munich where she pursued a doctoral degree, working on the morphology of living cycad seeds.

She published her first paper on a fossil plant in 1903, and for the next twenty years paleobotany was her major interest. Stopes became a lecturer in paleobotany at Manchester University, the first woman on the scientific staff. In 1907 she went to Japan to spend two years collecting fossil plants in the less frequented parts of the country. She was definitely an oddity, in this country of tradition where the role of women was distinctly defined. Her *Journal from Japan* (1910) describes her experiences in that culture. Deploring the impact of Western ideas on the old Japanese culture she and J. Sakurai wrote a book on the *Plays of Old Japan,* eulogizing the old culture. When she returned to Manchester, she published a popular account entitled *Ancient Plants.* In 1911, she went to the United States and Canada to study the Carboniferous "Fern Ledges" flora of New Brunswick, publishing on this subject in 1914. This paper offered evidence confirming the age of the plants and the identity of the Canadian plants with already known European ones.

During the three years before she went to Japan, Stopes published on coal-ball plants and on the nature of coal-balls themselves. She also published on the Scottish Inferior Oolite flora. While in Japan she explored many of the less populated areas and published a number of papers on her findings.

Returning to England again, Stopes resumed her studies of Cretaceous plants and published a two-volume catalog of Cretaceous Flora. She described the petrified woods from the British Lower Greensand. They were important because although they were the earliest angiosperms known from northwest Europe, they were essentially modern, apparently confirming the sudden rise of the flowering plants early in the Cretaceous. After working on Cretaceous flora, Stopes turned to the composition of coal. She published a number of papers between 1919 and 1923, both on her own and with R. V. Wheeler, on the origin and petrography of coal.

Stopes joined the Geologists' Association in 1911 and was elected an honorary member in 1946. She became more involved with her social interests later in her life; she wrote several books on those subjects and founded birth-control clinics. She was a pioneer of both birth control and sex education.

JH/MBO

PRIMARY SOURCES

Stopes, Marie. "Scottish Inferior Oolite flora." *Quarterly Journal of the Geological Society of London* 123 (1907): 63.

———. *Study of Plant Life for Young People.* London: A. Moring, 1907.

———. *Ancient Plants: Being a Simple Account of the Past Vegetation of the Earth and of the Recent Important Discoveries Made in This Realm of Nature Study.* London: Blackie & Son, Ltd., 1910.

———. "The Internal Anatomy of *Nilssonia orientalis.*" *Annals of Botany* 24 (1910): 389–394.

———. *Catalogue of the Mesozoic Plants in the British Museum (Natural History), The Cretaceous Flora.* London: Trustees of the British Museum (Natural History), 1913–1915.

———. "British Lower Greensand." *Philosophical Transactions of the Royal Society of London* B (1912): 85.

———. *Contraception (Birth Control): Its Theory, History and Practice; A Manual for the Medical and Legal Professions.* London: J. Bale, Sons & Danielsson, 1924.

Papers are at the British Library.

SECONDARY SOURCES

Brett, D. W. "Dr. Marie C. Stopes." *Nature* 182, no. 4644 (1958): 1201–1202.

Briant, Keith. *Marie Stopes: A Biography.* London: Hogarth Press, 1962.

Fox, Adam. *Marie Stopes.* London: The Poetry Society, 1959.

Hall, Ruth. *Passionate Crusader.* London: Quality Book Club, 1977.

STANDARD SOURCES

DNB; Desmond; Europa; WWW, vol. 5, 1951–1960.

STOPPEL, ROSE (1874–1970)

German botanist and plant physiologist. Born 26 December 1874 in Bündkin in East Prussia. Seven siblings. Educated locally; Abitur (university entrance exam, 1904) in Stuttgart; studied in Berlin, Strasbourg, Freiburg, and Basel. University of Freiburg (doctorate 1910). Professional experience: University of Hamburg, professor (1924), director of scientific expedition to Iceland, professor (1928); honorary professorship (1950). Died 20 January 1870 in Harburg.

Even as a young East Prussian country girl, Rose Stoppel showed an early interest in nature's processes. For twelve years she worked as domestic help, then completed an apprenticeship as a horticulturalist. She found work in Berlin doing botanical drawings. At the age of twenty-nine, this youngest of seven siblings finally received her dying mother's blessing to study. In 1904 she belonged to the first female graduating class of Stuttgart. After graduation she took up studies in Berlin, Strasbourg, Freiburg, and Basel. She was once thrown out of a lecture by a physics professor, probably because she had not asked for permission to attend.

She discovered a microscopic fungus which had been reported only once in Breslau in 1874. She submitted a work on the subject, *Eremascus fertilis Stoppel*, in 1904. She made a further important observation that plants exhibit certain nocturnal rhythms. She completed her doctoral work, "Über din Einfluss des Lichts auf das Öffnen und Schliessen einiger Blüten," and received her doctorate in 1910. In World War I she served as bacteriologist for the Red Cross. Her first assistantship in Hamburg paid only thirty marks. With the aid of the *Notgemeinschaft der Deutschen Wissenschaft* she was able to organize and equip an expedition to Iceland to observe the behavior of plants during the polar nights and extended summer days. She served as the technical director of the expediton. In 1924 she submitted her professorial work on this topic and was awarded a professorship at the University of Hamburg. She was the first female professor of botany in Germany. Her areas of scientific interest and expertise included the appearance of rhythms in plants; fungus research; and mycology in Iceland and South America. Rose Stoppel was an honorary member of the Verein für Rhythmik der Pflanzen.   GVL

PRIMARY SOURCES

Stoppel, Rose. "Über den Einfluss des Lichts auf das Öffnen und Schliessen einiger Blüten." Ph.D. diss., Freiburg, 1910.
———. *Beitrag zum Problem der Perzeption von Licht-und Schwerereiz durch die Pflanze.* Hamburg: Habilitationsschrift, 1924.
———. *Pflanzenphysiologische Studien.* 1926.
———. "Zahlreiche Publikationen in Fachzeitschriften und Mitarbeit." *Handbuch der normalen und pathologischen Physiologie* 17 (1926).
———. "Jahreszeitlicher und tageszeitlicher Rhythmus der Lebewesen im Lande der Mitternachtssonne." *Deutsche Islandforschung* (1930).

SECONDARY SOURCES

Brabec, F., H. Engel, and Söding. "Rose Stoppel. 26.12.1874 bis 20.1.1970." *Berichte der Deutschen Botanischen Gesellschaft* 84 (1971): 351–361.
Informationen für die Frau 2 (1970): 8.
Köppel, Anna-Pia. *Frauen in den Naturwissenschaften vom Mittelalter bis zur Neuzeit.* Hamburg: Begleitheft zur Ausstellung an der Universität Hamburg, 1985. (neu bearbeitet 1987 von Vera Stober für eine Ausstellung an der Universität Karlsruhe.)

STANDARD SOURCES

Lexikon der Frau.

STOSE, ANNA ISABEL (JONAS) (1881–1974)

U.S. igneous and metamorphic petrologist and structural geologist. Born 1881 near Cape May, N.J. Married George W. Stose. Educated Bryn Mawr (A.B., 1904; A.M., 1905; Ph.D., 1912). Professional experience: American Museum of Natural History, researcher (1916–1917); Maryland and Pennsylvania Geological Surveys, researcher (between 1919 and 1937); the Virginia Geological Survey, researcher (1926–1945); U.S. Geological Survey, researcher (1930–1954). Died 1974.

Anna Isabel Jonas Stose was a student of FLORENCE BASCOM. She received three degrees from Bryn Mawr College. She and ELEANORA BLISS KNOPF wrote a joint dissertation and continued to collaborate for many years. Both women followed a similar career pattern. Anna Jonas, like Knopf, served as a demonstrator in the geological laboratories (1905–1906) and assistant curator of Bryn Mawr's Geological Museum (1908–1909). After leaving Bryn Mawr, Jonas became a staff member at the American Museum of Natural History. Again the careers of the women overlapped as Jonas began work for the U.S. Geological Survey. Although Jonas was a disciple of Bascom, she and Knopf broke with her over the dating of the Wissahickon formation. In two major papers, they indicated that what Bascom and E. B. Mathews had referred to as Paleozoic were actually Precambrian. At that time, Anna Jonas began to collaborate with George Stose, who was very direct in his letters of disagreement with Bascom. The break with her students was complete. In 1938, Jonas and Stose married.

Jonas and Stose also had conflicts with others, including Benjamin Miller, head of the department of geology at Lehigh University. Miller was especially knowledgeable about local geology. After reviewing his data, he became convinced that Stose and Jonas were wrong regarding the Reading Hills Thrust. At a meeting of the Geological Society of America, Jonas presented a paper and refused to stop at the request of the chairman after the allotted time was up.

In the afternoon, Miller gave his paper and was adamant that the Reading Hills Overthrust did not exist. An acrimonius dispute resulted, and it was not until many months later that Miller was vindicated.

For most of her career, Anna Stose worked for the U.S. Geological Survey. She made major contributions to the unraveling of the structure of the Appalachians in Maryland, Pennsylvania, Virginia, North Carolina, and Tennessee.

JH/MBO

PRIMARY SOURCES

Stose, Anna I. Jonas. With Eleanor F. Bliss. "Relation of the Wissahickon Mica Gneiss to the Shenandoah Limestone and Octoraro Schist of the Doe Run and Avondale Region, Chester County, Pennsylvania." U.S. Geological Survey Professional Paper 98. *Shorter Contributions to General Geology, 1916* (1917): 9–34.

———. "Stratigraphy of the Crystalline Schists of Pennsylvania and Maryland." *American Journal of Science* 5th series, 5 (1923): 40–62.

———. *Geologic Map of Virginia.* [Washington, D.C.]: U.S. Geological Survey; Charlottesville, Va.: Virginia Geological Survey, 1928.

———. "Structure of the Metamorphic Belt of the Southern Appalachians." *American Journal of Science* 24 (1932): 230–231.

SECONDARY SOURCES

Arnold, Louis B. "The Wissahickon Controversy: Florence Bascom vs. Her Students." *Earth Science History* 2, no. 2 (1983): 130–142.

Dietrich, Robert V. "Memorial to Anna I. Jonas Stose 1881–1974." *Geological Society of America, Memoirs* 6 (1977).

Whitcomb, Lawrence. "The Reading Hills Overthrust: Jonas vs. Miller at the GSA Annual Meeting, Rochester, N.Y., 1935." *Pennsylvania Geologist* 14, no. 6. Rpt., *Earth Sciences History* 2, no. 2 (1983): 142–144.

STANDARD SOURCES

AMS 7–8, P 9, P&B 10; Sarjeant.

STOTT, ALICIA (BOOLE) (1860–1940)

Irish mathematician. Born December 1860 in Cork, Ireland, to Mary (Everest) and George Boole. Four siblings. Married Walter Stott. Two children. No formal education. Died 17 December 1940.

Alicia Boole was the daughter of George Boole, a professor of mathematics at Queen's College in Cork, Ireland. He was awarded a gold medal and a silver duplicate. He met an early death from a fever, leaving his widow and five daughters with very little money. Alicia's mother, Mary, was the niece of Sir George Everest, after whom the mountain was named.

To make ends meet, Mary worked as a matron at Queen's College, and the children saw little of their mother. Her mother and uncle agreed to let him keep one of the five children, and they selected Alicia. She suffered from boredom and loneliness, and when she was eleven returned home to London. She lived there for seven years with her mother, who was now an invalid, and sisters. The conditions under which they lived were abysmal, with the five girls sleeping in one room. When she was sixteen years old, Alice returned to Ireland to be a probationer in a children's hospital in Cork. She then returned to London where the son of her mother's friend James Hinton, Howard, stimulated her interest in geometry. In 1890, Alice married Walter Stott, an actuary, and they had two children, Mary and Leonard.

Howard Hinton had aroused Stott's interest in regular and semiregular polytopes. She constructed the solid sections by a sequence of three-spaces parallel to the three-space that contains one facet, for each of the six convex regular four-dimensional polytopes, analogous to the five Platonic solids. Walter Stott in 1895 drew Alice's attention to a paper written by Pieter Hendrik Schoute of the University of Groningen, in which he described the central sections of the same polytopes. Alice Stott sent photographs of her sequence of parallel sections. Schoute was impressed, came to England, and began a fruitful collaboration that lasted for over twenty years. They had a symbiotic relationship, for Stott's visualization supplemented Schoute's more orthodox methods of using coordinates. Schoute arranged for the publication of Stott's two papers. She received an honorary degree from the University of Groningen, which exhibited her models.

JH/MBO

PRIMARY SOURCES

Stott, Alicia Boole. "On Certain Sections of the Regular Four-Dimensional Hypersolids." *Verhandelingen der Koninklijke Akademie van Wetenschappen* 7, no. 3 (1900): 1–21.

———. "Geometrical Deduction of Semiregular from Regular Polytopes and Space Fillings." *Verhandelingen der Koninklijke Akademie van Wetenschappen.* 11, no. 1 (1910): 1–24.

STANDARD SOURCES

Grinstein and Campbell (article by H. S. M. Coxeter); *Notable.*

STOVIN, MARGARET (ca. 1756–1846)

British botanist. Born ca. 1756 in Doncaster, Yorkshire. Professional experience: collected plants. Died 16 February 1846 in Chesterfield, Derbyshire.

Margaret Stovin was a member of the Botanical Society of London and was both a plant collector and investigator. Little is known about her life.

JH/MBO

PRIMARY SOURCES
Her herbarium is at Middlesborough Museum.

SECONDARY SOURCES
Journal of Botany (1914): 321.
Naturalist (1979): 155–163.
Sorby Record 19 (1981): 21–23.

STANDARD SOURCES
Desmond.

STOWE, EMILY HOWARD (JENNINGS) (1831–1903)

Canadian physician. Born 1831 in South Norwich, Upper Canada (now Ontario). Married John Stowe. Educated public schools; New York College of Medicine for Women (M.D., 1867); College of Physicians and Surgeons, Ontario (1880). Professional experience: schoolteacher; private medical practice. Organized the Dominion Woman Suffrage Association (1893). Died 1903.

The first woman authorized to practice medicine in Canada, Emily Stowe had to fight for the privilege, even after she had been granted a medical degree from the New York College of Medicine for Women. Not surprisingly, she was a strong suffragist, and while furthering her medical practice also worked to improve opportunities for other women of Canada.

JH/MBO

STANDARD SOURCES
Uglow 1989.

STRACHEY, ALIX (SARGANT-FLORENCE) (1892–1973)

British psychoanalyst. Born 1892 in New Jersey to a British mother and American father. Elder brother, Philip. Married James Strachey (4 June 1920). Educated Bedales school, England; Slade School of Art (1910); Newnham College, Cambridge (1911–?); psychoanalyzed by Sigmund Freud (1921) and Karl Abraham (1924). Professional experience: psychoanalyst. Died 28 April 1973 at Lord's Wood.

Although Alix Sargant-Florence was born in New Jersey, her British mother returned to England after the drowning death of her American father. Her mother had a bohemian lifestyle, and Alix's early schooling was haphazard. Eventually she was enrolled in a preparatory school and from there attended Bedales. Mary Sargant imposed her own musical and artistic interests on Alix and insisted that she attend the Slade School of Art. Finding that her interests were more in philosophy and anthropology than in becoming a practicing artist, she left Slade after one year and attended Newnham College, Cambridge, where she read modern languages. She became especially close to her brother, Philip, at that time—he was a scholarship student at Caius College—and joined him on the editorial committee of the *Cambridge Magazine*. She also became involved in the rationalist Heretics Society and spent many evenings engaged in debates with the mostly male membership.

During her Cambridge years, Sargant-Florence developed a condition that transformed her from a rather large girl into the gaunt, unhealthy looking woman later described by Virginia Woolf. She was diagnosed with "degeneration of the heart," but it seems possible that she suffered from a form of anorexia. She became melancholic and had no real direction in her life.

She was in St. Petersburg during the outbreak of World War I but returned to London in January 1915, moving into her brother's flat in Bloomsbury. She became involved with the Bloomsbury group, and at that time met James Strachey, who also was a regular. When Sargant-Florence became attracted to Strachey, he was involved with the poet Rupert Brooke and then with Noel Olivier. Surprising all of their friends, Strachey and Sargant-Florence suddenly married. Shortly after their marriage, James Strachey had positive news from Sigmund Freud, who had agreed to analyze him. At first, it was only he who was to be analyzed, but Alix Strachey convinced him to approach Freud on her behalf. To Freud the double analysis was fascinating; James too, found it fulfilling, but Alix was dissatisfied. She later continued her analysis with Karl Abraham, whom she found to be a much better analyst.

Before their double analysis was terminated, the couple translated collaboratively what became known as the *Case Histories,* or volume three of the *Collected Papers of Sigmund Freud.* Most of the work on the *Case Histories* was completed in 1924, at which time Alix went to Berlin to be analyzed by Abraham. In Berlin she attended lectures at the Polyclinic and met most of the important people in psychoanalysis there, including LOUISE ANDRÉAS-SALOMÉ, HELENE DEUTSCH, and MELANIE KLEIN. Convinced that Klein was brilliant, but that her writing was too abstruse, Alix Strachey ended up writing as well as translating many of her works. Strachey took patients of her own as well as continuing analysis with Edward Glover and later SYLVIA PAYNE. She continued to edit and translate a growing psychoanalytic canon including Abraham's *Selected Papers.*

During World War II, the Stracheys retreated to her mother's former home at Lord's Wood, where they continued their translations. Alix Strachey found war particularly abhorrent and used her psychoanalytic knowledge to write *The Unconscious Motives of War.* She later wrote *The Psychology of Nationhood.* James Strachey died in April 1967, and Alix

Strachey lived by herself at Lord's Wood for the six years remaining in her life. JH/MBO

PRIMARY SOURCES

Strachey, Alix. *A New German-English Psycho-analytical Vocabulary.* Baltimore: Published for the Institute of Psycho-Analysis by William and Wilkins, 1943.

————. *The Unconscious Motives of War: A Psycho-analytical Contribution.* London: Allen & Unwin, [1957].

————. *Bloomsbury/Freud: The Letters of James and Alix Strachey, 1924–1925.* New York: Basic Books, 1985. Contains Alix Strachey's correspondence.

STANDARD SOURCES

Appignanesi.

STRANG, RUTH MAY (1895–1971)

U.S. psychologist. Born 3 April 1895 in Chatham, N.J. to Anna (Bergen) and Charles Garrett Strang. Two brothers. Never married. Educated Adelphi Academy, Brooklyn (graduated 1914); Pratt Institute (1914–1916); Columbia University (B.S., 1922; M.A., 1924; Ph.D., 1926). Professional experience: New York public schools, home economics teacher (1917–1920); Columbia University Teachers College, research assistant in nutrition (1923–1924), instructor and supervisor of health education, student personnel administrator (1926–1929), assistant professor, education (1929–1936), associate professor (1936–1940), professor (1940–1960), professor emerita (1960–1971); University of Arizona (from 1960). Honors and memberships: American Association for Gifted Children, founder (1946). Died 1971.

During her lifetime, Ruth Strang published thirty-six books, as well as hundreds of journal articles. She also produced a film series. After receiving her doctorate in education, she held a series of temporary teaching positions, until she was appointed assistant professor of education at Columbia. For several years she taught summer school at Women's College in Greensboro, North Carolina. She taught full time during both the school year and summers. Promoted to associate professor in 1936, she progressed to full professor in only four years.

Strang's major resarch areas were in child and adolescent psychology. She also worked in the area of guidance and the improvement of reading. A fellow of both the American Association for the Advancement of Science and the American Psychological Association, Strang was recognized for her work. She did consultant work for the Woods School for Exceptional children. In 1946, she and her good friend Pauline Williamson founded the American Association for Gifted Children. In the late 1950s, under the sponsorship of that organization, she published and distributed guidelines designed for parents, teachers, administrators, and students. After her death the National Association for Women in Education inaugurated the Ruth Strang award for graduate students and professionals doing research in women's studies. JH/MBO

PRIMARY SOURCES

Strang, Ruth May. *An Introduction to Child Study.* New York: Macmillan, 1930.

————. *Behavior and Background of Students in College and Secondary School.* New York: Harper and Brothers, [1937].

————. *Problems in the Improvement of Reading.* New York: McGraw-Hill, 1946.

————. *Diagnostic Teaching of Reading.* New York: McGraw, 1964.

————. *Helping Your Child Develop His Potentialities.* New York: Dutton, 1965.

STANDARD SOURCES

AMS S&B 9–11; Stevens and Gardner.

STRASSMANN-HECKTER, MARIA CAROLINE (1888–1956)

German chemist. Born 29 August 1898 in Hannover to Heinrich Wilhelm and Emilie Heckter. No siblings. Married Fritz Strassmann. One son, Martin. Educated University of Göttingen, Institute of Technology, Hannover (diploma, 1928; engineering doctorate, 1934). Professional experience: Institute of Technology, Hannover, Laboratory for Glass Technology and Ceramics, researcher (1928–1930?); Kaiser Wilhelm Institute for Silicate Research, Berlin, assistant (1930–1937?). Died 4 April 1956 in Mainz.

Maria Heckter was the only child of a professor of writing at the School of Arts and Crafts in Hannover. She studied mathematics in Göttingen, then switched to chemistry in the School of Technology in Hannover, receiving her diploma on 9 March 1928. Heckter worked in Gustav Keppeler's private Laboratory for Glass Technology and Ceramics at the School of Technology, then at the Kaiser Wilhelm Institute for Silicate Research in Berlin. She published a paper with Keppeler, then received the doctorate of engineering under him. Her dissertation, a radiochemical examination of important technical methods for determining the quality of glasses, was carried out at the Kaiser Wilhelm Institute for Silicate Chemistry in Berlin-Dahlem.

On 20 July 1937 Heckter married a fellow analytical chemist, Fritz Strassmann, who later (end of 1938) became codiscoverer of nuclear fission. Soon afterward she gave up her position because of her first pregnancy, which ended in a miscarriage in 1938. Maria Strassmann-Heckter and her husband regularly discussed his research, which makes it likely that she contributed to Fritz Strassmann's work in some way.

The Strassmanns collaborated on an article on barium for an analytical chemistry handbook. This extended project required Strassmann-Heckter to perform laboratory researches as well as to assemble relevant literature. In April 1940 the Strassmanns' son, Martin, was born. Strassmann-Heckter supported her husband's refusal to join the Nazi party, in spite of the professional and financial difficulties entailed.

After the war, Strassmann-Heckter hoped to resume chemical work with her husband. This was not to be. In August 1955 she underwent surgery for breast cancer. However, the cancer was already well advanced, and after a long and painful illness she died on 4 April 1956.   JH/MBO

PRIMARY SOURCES

Heckter, Maria. With G. Keppeler. "Temperaturabhängigkeit der Alkalität von Glasoberflächen." *Glastechnische Berichte* 10 (1932): 37–40.

———. "Radiochemische Oberflächenbestimmungen an Glas." *Glastechnische Berichte* 12 (1934): 156–172. Doctoral dissertation submitted to the Technische Hochschule, Hannover, 1934.

Strassmann-Heckter, Maria. With F. Strassmann. "Barium." In *Handbuch der Analytischen Chemie,* 365–402. Dritter Teil: Quantitative Bestimmungs- und Trennungsmethoden; IIa: Elemente der zweiten Hauptgruppe. Berlin: Springer, 1940.

SECONDARY SOURCES

Krafft, Fritz. *Im Schatten der Sensation. Leben und Wirken von Fritz Strassmann.* Weinheim, Deerfield Beach, Fla., and Basel: Verlag Chemie, 1981.

STRATTON PORTER, GENE (1863-1924)

U.S. science popularizer, natural history writer and photographer, and novelist. Born 17 August 1863 in Wabash County, Ind., to Mary (Shallenberger) and Mark Stratton. Eleven older siblings. Married Charles Dorwin Porter (21 April 1886). One daughter. Educated Wabash High School. Professional experience: McCall's magazine, editorial writer. Published multiple articles for many magazines, books on natural history, and novels with a natural historical component; film production company, founder. Died 6 December 1924, in Los Angeles, of fractured ribs and spine following an automobile accident.

Gene Stratton Porter was born Geneva Stratton on a farm in Wabash County, Indiana, the youngest of twelve children. At the age of twenty-three, she married Charles Dorwin Porter, thirteen years older than she. Later she would repeatedly give her age as younger than she was and list her husband's first two names more dramatically as Charles Darwin.

As a young child, she had become interested in the life of birds, raising a number of injured ones, and her house was always filled with the results of her wildlife excursions. Her daughter, the only child of her marriage, later wrote about her early childhood surrounded by birds, cocoons, and animals of various sorts. She was taught by her mother to handle all creatures with care and respect.

In her early forties, following some reverses experienced by her husband, who was a pharmacist and banker, Stratton Porter began to write and send out her observations to popular magazines. She found that she was constantly asked for illustrations, but she had no drawing abilities. She began to make photographs of the birds she loved, teaching herself the skill, and using her appreciation for birds and animals within their own environment. At a time when Americans were turning to the rapidly changed landscape to recapture a feeling for the wilderness, Stratton Porter's articles and photographs were greeted enthusiastically.

Given the popular response to her articles, she rewrote some of them as books: *What I Have Done with Birds* (1907), *Friends in Feathers* (1917), and *Homing with the Birds* (1919) are only some of her books that described wildlife areas such as the wilderness swamp area in Indiana near her home called the Limberlost. She also began to write sentimental, even melodramatic, but immensely popular novels, dramatizing versions of her own life story, sometimes including birds as commenters on the scene, but always incorporating her love of nature. The most famous of these novels was *Girl of the Limberlost* (1909), later made into an equally popular film. Since her heroine collected moths as a way to pay for her education, Stratton Porter followed this some years later with a book that described and illustrated the unusual moths of the area, *Moths of the Limberlost* (1912).

Stratton Porter was also an avid creator of bird sanctuaries. After she had become comparatively wealthy through her writing, she hired a naturalist and tree surgeon, Frederick Wallace, to supervise a crew to plant four thousand botanical specimens, including trees, vines, and wildflowers, on her property by Sylvan Lake, Indiana. From 1913 to 1919, she worked to transform this area. Fifty species of birds were nesting in the area as a result. Soon after, her growing fame meant her privacy was too easily invaded, and she moved to California, asking the state of Indiana to take the property over as a wildlife preserve. She asked for a return of her own investment, which was considerable, and the project was pigeonholed until after her death. It is now a state historic site.

Building a new home in what is now the Bel Air section of Los Angeles but was then open land, Stratton Porter again began to create an unusual home using dramatic collections of regional plants and striking local stones. Unfamiliar with the regional botany, she relied on the expertise of others for her new novels set in California. She also published regular editorials in *McCall's* magazine that echoed the eugenic language of the day. After two earlier films had been made from her novels, she became interested in film production and began to work with the director James Leo Meehan, who had married her daughter, Jeanette. Stratton Porter spent long days on the set of the silent film *Girl of the Limberlost.* She continued to write novels, but now with the intention of turning them immediately into films. In early 1924, she established a film production company. She died in December of the same year as the result of an automobile injury when her chauffeur-driven car was hit by a streetcar in Los Angeles. She was honored a few years after her death by a number of tree planting events at schools in the Los Angeles area and by the naming of a New York State pine forest in her name. Two historic sites associated with her in Indiana have been preserved.   JH/MBO

PRIMARY SOURCES

Stratton Porter, Gene. *The Song of the Cardinal.* Indianapolis: Bobbs Merrill, 1903.

———. *What I Have Done with Birds.* Indianapolis: Bobbs Merrill, 1907.

———. *At the Foot of the Rainbow.* Garden City, N.Y.: Doubleday and Page, 1908.

———. *A Girl of the Limberlost.* Garden City, N.Y.: Doubleday and Page, 1909.

———. *Birds of the Bible.* Garden City, N.Y.: Doubleday and Page, 1909.

———. *Moths of the Limberlost.* Garden City, N.Y.: Doubleday and Page, 1912.

———. *Homing with Birds.* Garden City, N.Y.: Doubleday and Page, 1919.

SECONDARY SOURCES

Long, Judith Reich. *Gene Stratton-Porter, Novelist and Naturalist.* Indianapolis: Indiana Historical Society, 1990. Includes multiple photographs and a complete bibliography

Meehan, Jeanette Porter. *The Lady of the Limberlost: The Life and Letters of Gene Stratton Porter.* Garden City, N.Y.: Doubleday and Doran, 1928. An account by her daughter.

Plum, Sydney, ed. *Coming through the Swamp: The Nature Writing of Gene Stratton Porter.* Salt Lake City: University of Utah Press, 1996.

STANDARD SOURCES

Bailey; *WWW*(A), vol. 1, 1897–1942 (information not accurate for dates).

STROBELL, ELLA CHURCH (1862–?)

U.S. cytologist. Born 26 June 1862. Educated private schools and tutors. Death date unknown.

Ella Strobell was a cytologist. About all that is known of her is that she coauthored papers with KATHERINE FOOT and that she was a member of the Society of Zoologists.   JH/MBO

PRIMARY SOURCES

Strobell, Ella. With Katherine Foot. *Cytological Studies.* 1894–1917. Variously paged. Reprints from various scientific periodicals.

———. With Katherine Foot. "A New Method of Focussing in Photomicrography." *Zeitschrift für Wissenschafte Mikroskopie und für Mikroscopische Technik* 18 (1901): 421–426.

———. With Katherine Foot. "Further Notes on the Cocoons of *Allolobophora foetida.*" *Biological Bulletin* 3 (1902): 206–213.

———. With Katherine Foot. "The Spermatozoa of *Allolobophora foetida.*" *American Journal of Anatomy* 1 (1902): 321–327.

———. With Katherine Foot. "A Study of Chromosomes in the Spermatogenesis of *Anasa tristis.*" *American Journal of Anatomy* 7 (1907): 279–316.

STANDARD SOURCES

AMS 1–2; Ogilvie 1986.

STRONG, HARRIET WILLIAMS (RUSSELL) (1844–1929)

U.S. agriculturist and environmentalist. Born 23 July 1844 in Buffalo, N.Y., to Mary Guest (Musier) and Henry Pierpont Russell. Six siblings. Married Charles Lyman Strong. Four daughters: Harriet, Mary, Georgina, and Nelle. Educated Young Ladies' Seminar of Mary Atkins, Benicia, Calif. (1858–1860). Professional experience: agriculture; environmental concerns. Died 16 September 1929 in Whittier, Calif., in an automobile accident.

The fourth daughter of seven children, Harriet Russell was born in Buffalo, New York, to a family that had trouble making ends meet. Harriet's father moved his family to California when she was about eight years old. A spine ailment caused her to be a semi-invalid for several years. During the time that she was incapacitated she studied in various fields. The family raised enough money to send her to the Young Ladies' Seminar at Benicia, California, where she remained for two years and studied music, French, and English literature. After Harriet finished at Benicia, her family moved to Carson City, Nevada, where her father became involved in the discovery of silver on the Comstock Lode. Shortly thereafter, she married Charles Lyman Strong, who was a superintendent of one of the great mines there. The couple had four children. Charles Strong was almost twice Harriet's age. A very hard worker, he suffered from periodic emotional and physical disabilities. He committed suicide in 1883 after one of his investments failed, leaving Harriet with a badly encumbered estate.

Harriet claimed that treatment by the neurologist S. Weir Mitchell, allowed her to become a new person—her previous semi-invalidism was replaced by energetic good health. Using a ranch that her husband owned in California (near what is now Whittier), she began planting walnuts and other plants. She studied marketing, irrigation, and flood control in order to make her investments succeed. She was very successful and became the first woman elected to the Los Angeles Chamber of Commerce. Her recognition became more than local when she exhibited water storage schemes and pampas grass at the World's Columbian Exposition at Chicago in 1893. After she gave a speech on the importance of business training for women, she was chosen president of a feminist Business League of America. She was also interested in numerous cultural opportunities for women. Insisting that women should study public affairs, she founded the Hamilton Club to encourage women's participation.

Strong became an important advocate of water supply measures to help Los Angeles County. She also advocated flood control. Her ideas were not always beneficial. In 1918 she appeared before a Congressional Committee urging the damming of the Colorado River in the Grand Canyon.

JH/MBO

PRIMARY SOURCES
Strong, Harriet. "Erythronium." *Chicago Naturalist* 5 (1942): 8–11.

STANDARD SOURCES
NAW (article by Rodman Wilson Paul).

STRONG, HELEN MABEL (1890–1973)

U.S. geographer. Educated University of Chicago (S.B., 1917; Ph.D., 1921). Professional experience: United States Department of Agriculture, assistant agricultural geographer (1918–1919); University of Missouri, assistant professor (1921–1923); U.S. Department of Commerce, trade in agricultural products, special survey (1923–1924); Bureau of Foreign and Domestic Commerce, geographer (1924–1933); U.S. Coast and Geodesic Survey, geographer (1933–1935); National Resources Committee, associate geographer (1935–1936); USDA, Soil Conservation Service, soil conservationist (1936–1941); U.S. War Department, military intelligence service, consultant (1941–1943); Foreign Economic Administration, analyst (1943–1946); U.S. Department of the Army, geographer (1946–1953); Elmhurst College, lecturer in geography (1953–1959). Retired 1959. Died 1973.

Helen Mabel Strong used her geography training in a career that varied from teaching to government work. She was a member of the American Association for the Advancement of Science, the Association of American Geographers, a Fellow of the Geographic Society, and the Society for Women Geographers (secretary treasurer). Her research interests were in economic, regional, and military geography. JH/MBO

PRIMARY SOURCES
Strong, Helen M. "Distribution of Agricultural Exports from the United States." U.S. Bureau of Foreign and Domestic Commerce (Dept. of Commerce) *Trade Information Bulletin,* no. 177. Washington, D.C.: Government Printing Office, 1924.
———. "Relation between Value and Volume of Agricultural Products." U.S. Bureau of Foreign and Domestic Commerce. *Trade Information Bulletin,* no. 271. Washington, D.C.: Government Printing Office, 1924.

STANDARD SOURCES
AMS 4–8, S&B 9–10.

STRONG, MIRIAM CARPENTER (1899–?)

U.S. botanist. Born 21 May 1899 in Lansing, Mich. Married 1928. Educated University of Michigan (B.S., 1922; M.S., 1924). Professional experience: Michigan State University, assistant plant pathologist (1922–1940), assistant research professor of botany and plant pathology (from 1940). Death date unknown.

Miriam Carpenter's career was typical of a woman scientist who never got her doctoral degree. Although she did some excellent research, she remained an assistant plant pathologist for eighteen years. In 1940, her talents were recognized somewhat, and she was promoted to assistant research professor.

Strong was active in the Mycological Society and the Phytopathology Society. Her research centered around the physiological and biological relations in the genus *Fusarium.* She also worked on pathogenicity in *Fusarium lycopersici* and diseases and disease control in the tomato. JH/MBO

STANDARD SOURCES
AMS 6–8, B 9, P&B 10–11.

STROZZI, LORENZA (1515–1591)

Italian student of natural philosophy. Born 1515 in Capalle. Never married. Died 1591.

Born into a prominent Florentine family, Lorenza Strozzi was educated in a convent, and took the Dominican habit. She remained in the convent of San Niccolo del Parto throughout the wars that devastated Tuscany during the reign of Cosimo I de' Medici. Noted for her piety and learning, she wrote sacred songs, developed a "profound knowledge of science and art," and became proficient in Latin and Greek.   JH/MBO

SECONDARY SOURCES

Coste, Hilarion de. *Les eloges et vies des reynes, princesses, dames et damoiselles illustres en pieté, courage et doctrine, qui ont fleury de nostre temps, et du temps devises, emblemes hyerogliphes, et symboles.* Paris: Sebastien Cramoisy, 1630. See volume 2, page 97.

STANDARD SOURCES

Mozans.

STUART, MIRANDA (1795–1865)

U.S. physician. Alias James Barry. Educated Edinburgh College (M.D., 1812). Professional experience: military service (from 1813). Died 1865.

An orphan, Miranda Stuart may have been reared as a boy, but it is probable she resorted to dressing as a male in order to practice medicine. After receiving her doctoral degree disguised as a male, Stuart as James Barry entered military service in 1813. She was made Staff Surgeon in Canada and also served in South Africa, the West Indies, and the Crimea.

Military records indicate that she made controversially strict administrative decisions about health care, sanitary conditions, and the diet of the sick. She also presented a significant report on a plant from the Cape of Good Hope which could be used to treat syphilis and gonorrhea.

She progressed through the ranks to become inspector-general of all British hospitals in Canada. The registrar-general heard rumors of her sex and requested an autopsy at the time of her death. When she was found to be a woman her previously arranged military funeral was countermanded.
                                                              KM

SECONDARY SOURCES

Rose, June. *The Perfect Gentleman: The Remarkable Life of Dr. James Miranda Barry, the Woman Who Served as an Officer in the British Army from 1813 to 1859.* London: Hutchinson, 1977.

STANDARD SOURCES

Uglow 1982.

STULL, OLIVE GRIFFITH (1905–)

See Davis, Olive Griffith Stull.

SULLIVAN, BETTY JULIA (1902–)

U.S. chemist. Born 31 May 1902 in Minneapolis, Minn. Educated University of Minnesota (B.S., 1922); Ph.D. in biochemistry

(1935). Professional experience: Russell Miller Milling Co., assistant chemist (1922–1924), chief chemist (1927–1947), vice-president and director of research (1947–1955); Peavey Co. Flour Mills, from vice-president to president (1967–1973), vice-chairman of the board (from 1973).

With a doctorate in chemistry from the University of Minnesota, Betty Sullivan began a career in industry that culminated in the presidency and vice-presidency of the board of Peavey Flour Mills. Never involved in academia, she began her career immediately after she received her bachelor's degree. Her research was on the chemistry of wheat and flour and fermentation.   JH/MBO

PRIMARY SOURCES

Sullivan, Betty Julia. "The Lipids of the Wheat Embryo." *Journal of the American Chemical Society* 58 (1936): 383–393. Based on Ph.D. diss., University of Minnesota, 1935.

STANDARD SOURCES

AMS 6–8, P 9, P&B 10–13.

SULLIVAN, ELIZABETH TERESA (1874–?)

U.S. psychologist. Born 6 January 1874 in Los Angeles. Educated California State Normal School (graduated 1895); University of California (1901–1903); Stanford University (A.B., 1905; A.M., 1918); Columbia University (Ph.D., 1922). Professional experience: Los Angeles public schools, teacher and principal (1895–1901); Los Angeles, high school and junior college teacher (1908–1913), vice-principal and dean of women (1913–1919); city schools, supervisor, department of psychology and educational research (1922–1923); University of California, extension division, instructor (1922–1925), lecturer (1925–1933); University College, Southern California, lecturer (1933–1944). Death date unknown.

Psychologist Elizabeth Sullivan spent most of her career in the Los Angeles schools. While she was working at the University of California extension division and University College, Southern California, she was also a psychologist at the Santa Rita Clinic (1925–1944). Other concurrent positions included being an instructor at Immaculate Heart College from 1928 to 1930 and professor and director of school education from 1930 to 1932. From 1937, she served as a psychologist for the Los Angeles County Schools.

Sullivan was a member of the Psychological Association, the Western Psychological Association, and the Southern California Society for Mental Hygiene (director, 1923–1929). She had numerous research interests, including elementary education in the United States previous to 1800, mood in relation to performance, and a comparison of accelerated, average, and retarded children. Other research projects included English in foreign schools and tests of mental maturity.   JH/MBO

PRIMARY SOURCES

Sullivan, Elizabeth Teresa. "Mood in Relation to Performance." *Archives of Psychology* 53 (1922). Also published as Ph.D. diss., Columbia University, 1922.

STANDARD SOURCES

AMS 4–8; *Psychological Register,* vol. 3, 1932.

SULLIVAN, ELLEN BLYTHE (1888–?)

U.S. psychologist. Born 20 October 1888 in Moberly, Mo. Educated University of Southern California (A.B., 1915); Stanford University (Ph.D., 1924). Professional experience: California State Normal School, Los Angeles, instructor in psychology (1912–1918); University of California at Los Angeles, assistant professor through professor of psychology (1918–1925); Whittier State School, Bureau of Juvenile Research, director (1925–1929); Children's Hospital, director of education and psychology clinic (from 1925); Los Angeles Health Department, organizer and director, mental hygiene clinic (1930–1932); Civil Service, Los Angeles County, adviser on test construction and examining (1933–1942?); Los Angeles Psychiatric Service, director (1942). Death date unknown.

Although she spent some years at a university, most of Ellen Sullivan's work was practical and administrative rather than theoretical. From 1925 to 1929, she was the editor of the *Journal of Delinquency.* She was also involved in veterans clinical training. Sullivan was a member or fellow of many organizations, including the Society of Research for Child Development; the Southern California Psychological Association; International Society for the Prevention of Epilepsy Diseases, and the California Academy of Social Science.

Her research interests include child delinquency; adult crimes, psychodiagnosis and psychotherapy. She also worked with readjustment in brain drainage and aphasia.   JH/MBO

PRIMARY SOURCES

Sullivan, Ellen B. *Attitude in Relation to Learning.* Princeton, N.J.: The Psychological Review Company, [1927].

———. *On Intelligence of Epileptic Children; From the Department of Psychology of the University of California at Los Angeles.* Worcester, Mass.: Clark University, 1935.

STANDARD SOURCES

AMS 4–8; *Psychological Register,* vol. 3, 1932.

SUMMERSKILL, EDITH CLARA (1901–1979)

British physician. Born 19 April 1901 to Edith and William Summerskill. Two siblings. Married Jeffrey Samuel (1925). Two children, one son and one daughter. Educated King's College, London; Charing Cross Hospital, London (1918–1924). Professional experience: practiced with her physician husband (1924–1945); Middlesex County Council Labour candidate (1931–1941); Member of Parliament for West Fulham (1938–1955); Parliamentary Secretary to the Ministry of Food (1945–1950); Minister of National Insurance (1950–1951); named Baroness Summerskill of Ken Wood. Died 1979.

Edith Summerskill was the youngest of three children. Her father was a physician, a radical politician, and a feminist. He took his children to visit poor families, and Edith, like her father, was appalled at the unsanitary and generally squalid conditions in which these people lived. Encouraged by her father, she entered King's College, London to study sciences and then to read medicine. She met her future husband, Jeffrey Samuel, when they were students at Charing Cross Hospital. The couple married in 1925, the year after she qualified as a physician. They had two children, a son, Michael, who became a barrister, and a daughter, Shirley, who became a physician. Summerskill and Samuel opened a practice together.

Summerskill was an advocate for liberal causes, antagonizing many in the conservative community. She understood that the best way to promote her causes was through liberal politics. She began on the local level by winning a place on the Middlesex County Council. She remained on the council until 1941 when work pressures became too great. Her first two attempts to stand for national office as a member of Parliament were unsuccessful. However, in 1938, on her third attempt, she won the seat from the Conservatives and became a member of Parliament for West Fulham. As a member of Parliament she espoused many liberal causes. At the onset of World War II, she established a women's consultative committee to advise the government on the wartime employment of women, and sat on a committee that inquired into the conditions of women in the services and one on equal compensation for civilian war injuries. She also campaigned for the admission of women to the Home Guard.

After the war, when the Labour government came to power, she was given junior ministerial rank as Parliamentary Secretary to the Ministry of Food. Up until 1945, she had continued with her regular medical practice. In 1949 she was made a member of the Privy Council and in 1950 became the first married woman to become a member of the British Cabinet. Because of the fall of the Labour government, her tenure lasted only one year.

Summerskill remained a member of the House of Commons until 1960. In 1961, she was elevated to the peerage, a move that strengthened Labour's presence in the House of Lords. She continued to press her humanitarian agenda, especially in the case of the health care system. She was a superb advocate for preventive medicine, National Insurance, and the Health Service. She was a champion of women's issues throughout her life.   JH/MBO

PRIMARY SOURCES

Summerskill, Edith. *Babies without Tears.* London: Hutchinson, 1941.

————. *Letters to my Daughter.* London: Heinemann, [1957].

————. *A Woman's World.* London: Heinemann, 1967.

SECONDARY SOURCES

Knapp, Sally. *Women Physicians Today.* New York: Crowell, 1947.

STANDARD SOURCES

Current Biography 1943, 1962; *Europa.*

SUNDQUIST, ALMA (ca. 1880–1940)

Swedish physician. Born ca. 1880. Educated Karolinska Institute of Stockholm University (M.D., 1900). Professional experience: Free Clinic in Stockholm, director. Died January 1940.

Alma Sundquist was an internationally known physician who specialized in venereal diseases. Through the League of Nations and the Swedish government she became associated with the international effort to fight venereal disease as well as the traffic in women and children. She attended the International Conference of Women Physicians in New York City in 1919 and was a member of the Committee of Twelve that organized the Medical Women's International Association. She presided at the congress held in Edinburgh in 1937 as its president.   KM

PRIMARY SOURCES

Sundquist, Alma. With Julia Kinberg-von Sneidern. *Sex Hygiene: the Anatomy, Physiology, and Hygiene of the Sex Organs.* New York: Henry Holt and Co., [1926].

SECONDARY SOURCES

Journal of the American Medical Women's Association 16 (1951): 33.

STANDARD SOURCES

Lovejoy.

SUNNE, DAGNY (ca. 1880–?)

Norwegian/U.S. psychologist. Born ca. 1880 in Norway. Educated University of Minnesota (A.B., 1901; A.M., 1905); University

of Chicago (Ph.D., 1909). Professional experience: Woman's College of Alabama, psychologist; Wellesley College, instructor; Oxford College and Western College, professor of psychology and education (1912–1914); Tulane University, assistant professor (1915–1931); Commonwealth Fund, grant-in-aid fund director (from 1931). Death date unknown.

Although she was born in Norway, Dagny Sunne received all of her higher education in the United States. In addition to her main professional responsibilities, she was the director for education research in the public schools of New Orleans from 1923 to 1924. She belonged to the Psychological Association, the Mental Hygiene Association, and the Southern Society of Philosophy and Psychology.

Sunne's research involved comparative studies of African Americans and white Americans and the psychological and sociological development of young children. She also did research in educational, vocational, and clinical psychology.   JH/MBO

PRIMARY SOURCES

Sunne, Dagny Gunhilda. *Some Phases in the Development of the Subjective Point of View during the Post-Aristotelian Period.* Philosophic Studies, Issued under the Direction of the Department of Philosophy of the University of Chicago, no. 3. Chicago: University of Chicago Press, [1911]. This was her University of Chicago Ph.D. dissertation.

STANDARD SOURCES

AMS 4–6.

SUSLOVA, NADEZHDA PROKOF'EVNA (1843–1918)

Russian physician. Born 1843 at Panino. Father Prokofii Suslov, agent for Count Sheremet'ev. Two siblings. Married (1) Frederick F. Erisman; (2) A. E. Golubev. Educated at boarding school in Tver; Petersburg Institute for Young Noblewomen; Zurich University (M.D., 1867). Professional experience: Petersburg Medical Surgical Academy, auditor; private practice in St. Petersburg and Crimea. Died 1918 at Kastel (Crimea).

Nadezhda Prokof'evna Suslova was the daughter of a freed serf, Prokofii Suslov, who was a trusted agent of Count Sheremet'ev. Posts of increasing responsibility led the family from the country to Moscow and later to St. Petersburg. The patronage of Count Sheremet'ev enabled Nadezhda and her brother and sister Apollinaria (later to become the mistress of the writer Dostoevsky) to attend schools from which their low rank would normally have barred them. Her parents supported her desire for education and she was further inspired by her acquaintance with other young women with ambitions beyond marriage, particularly Mariia Obrucheva, later to become a physician under the name BOKOVA-SECHENOVA.

Suslova was interested in literature and wrote several stories while pursuing medical studies. In 1861 she enrolled as an auditor in the Medical Surgical Academy in St. Petersburg, where the question of whether or not to admit women students was still under consideration. There Suslova worked with such professors as the physiologist Ivan M. Sechenov and Alexander Borodin (better known as a composer).

In 1863 the decision was made to close the universities to women and eventually, on Sechenov's advice, Suslova went to the University of Zurich, where she successfully defended her doctoral dissertation in December 1867. She was probably the first woman doctor to receive a degree in continental Europe and certainly the first Russian woman to do so.

During her stay in Zurich, Suslova met a Swiss medical student, Frederick Erisman, whom she married in 1868. She then returned to St. Petersburg while Erisman continued his studies in Heidelberg and Berlin.

Although Suslova now had her degree, she had yet to receive permission from the Russian government to practice. Eventually, having passed a special examination, permission was granted and she opened a private practice in St. Petersburg. For a time Erisman joined her but by 1873, difficulties began to arise in the marriage and in 1874, they were divorced.

In 1885 Suslova married A. E. Golubev, a professor of histology, and moved with him to Kastel, his estate in the Crimea, where she continued to practice medicine. She died there in 1918.

Apart from her pioneering role in medicine as a career for women, Suslova had many solid achievements. Her first research project while an auditor at the Medical Surgical Academy was on the influence of light stimulation of electricity on the skin published in 1862. The research for her doctoral dissertation, undertaken under Sechenov at Graz in Austria, was concerned with the connection between the nervous system and reflex muscle mechanisms (using frogs). However Suslova was primarily interested in treating and preventing illnesses and in hygiene and aspects of mother and child health. At a time when wet nurses were common, she supported breast feeding by the mother.

She was the first to suggest that infection with gonorrhea was the cause of inflammation of the eyes of newborn infants. Unlike Erisman, who was attracted to Marxism and political activism as a way to relieve the sufferings of the poor, Suslova preferred a personal approach. Not only did she treat the poorest patients for nothing, as the law required, but she frequently provided them with food and medicine out of her own resources. During her years in Kastel, she built an elementary school and a library and gave generous donations of money to worthy causes. Compassion and usefulness were her ideals both as a woman and as a physician.

JH/MBO

PRIMARY SOURCES

Suslova, Nadezhda Prokof'evna. "O vospitanii detei v pervye gody zhizni." *Archiv sudebnoi meditsiny i obshchestvennoi gigieny* 6, no. 4 (1870): 21–31.

SECONDARY SOURCES

Bonner, Thomas Neville. "Rendezvous in Zurich: Seven Who Made a Revolution in Women's Medical Education, 1864–1874." *Journal of the History of Medicine* 44, no. 1 (January 1989): 7–27.

STANDARD SOURCES

Tuve.

SUTTER, VERA LAVERNE (1924–1993)

U.S. microbiologist. Born 2 April 1924 in Los Angeles, Calif. Educated University of California at Los Angeles (A.B., 1946; M.A., 1947; Ph.D., 1950). Professional experience: University of California at Los Angeles, assistant bacteriologist (1945–1950); Veterans Administration General Hospital, chief bacteriologist, clinical laboratory (1950–1962); University of California, San Francisco, assistant research microbiologist, school of dentistry (1962–1967); Veterans Administration Wadsworth Hospital Center, director of anaerobic bacteria research (from 1967). Honors and memberships: American Board of Microbiology, diplomate; American Society of Microbiology; American Public Health Association, Fellow; New York Academy of Sciences. Died 1993.

Vera Sutter spent her entire career in California, earning all three of her degrees from the University of California at Los Angeles. In addition to her main positions as a bacteriologist, she was a laboratory director of bacteriology and parasitology and lecturer at St. Mary's College from 1952 to 1962. Sutter did research on clinical bacteriology, the epidemiology of hospital acquired infections, anaerobic bacteria in pathologic and pathophysiologic processes, and normal intestinal flora.

JH/MBO

PRIMARY SOURCES

Sutter, Vera. *Wadsworth Anaerobic Bacteriology Manual.* 3d ed. St. Louis, Mo.: Mosby, 1980.

———. With Sydney M. Finegold. *Anaerobic Infections.* 6th ed. Kalamazoo, Mich.: Upjohn, 1986.

SECONDARY SOURCES

Review of Infectious Diseases 13 (1991): 528. Obituary notice.

STANDARD SOURCES
AMS B 9, P&B 10–14.

SVARTZ, NANNA CHARLOTTA (1890–?)

Swedish physician. Born 1 August 1890 in Västerås, Sweden, to Anna Moxen and a Latin and Greek teacher. Four siblings. Married Nils Malmberg (1918). One daughter. Educated Stockholm University Medical School (1911–1918, license; doctoral thesis, 1927). Professional experience: Serafimerlasarettet Department of Medicine, assistant to head of central laboratories (1918–1927?), assistant professor of medicine (1927–1937), professor (1937–1970?). Death date unknown.

Nanna Svartz's parents were first cousins, and she was the fifth child in the family. Her father had a doctorate in Latin and was the senior teacher of Latin and Greek in the local secondary school. Svartz was exposed to death and illness as a child. Three brothers and one sister died as children, apparently of tuberculosis. The illnesses of her brothers and sister formed the basis of her interest in biology and medicine. In spite of her father's disapproval, Svartz was determined to study medicine. There were only two girls in her first-year class, and Svartz was the only one who graduated.

Svartz married her childhood sweetheart, who had also gone into medicine, keeping her maiden name at a time when this was not legally sanctioned. Some of her colleagues complained that she was not eligible for a promotion because she was living with a man to whom she was not married. The couple had one daughter, Gunvor Svartz-Malmberg, who also became a physician.

Although sexism was a problem with promotions, she was eventually selected over her male competitors as professor of medicine. The hospital moved from Serafimerlasarettet to the new university hospital (Karolinska Hospital) in 1940. Svartz had to organize the move and plan the new research institute in collaboration with the architect. Jealousy from male colleagues involved accusations of monetary wrongdoing, of which she was cleared.

Svartz was four times a member of the committee who would prepare judgments on scientists proposed for the Nobel Prize and also was the founder of an international society of medicine. Although she had proposed it during World War II, her colleagues convinced her to postpone its formation until 1948.

Svartz published over four hundred papers. Her work also encouraged the introduction of the drug salicylazosulfapyridine in 1938. Her interest focused on the primary cause of rheumatoid arthritis. She theorized that in the drug (also called "salazopyrin") sulphur would sort out an infective agent and the salicylate would act as an anti-inflammatory. The drug was forgotten as a therapy for arthritis but was used successfully for inflammatory bowel disease. It has been rediscovered for arthritis in recent years. In Sweden, grants and lectures in gastroenterology bear her name. She stated that her research gave her the greatest pleasure in life other than her family. Even after she retired from her chair, she carried on a restricted private practice. JH/MBO

PRIMARY SOURCES
Svartz, Nanna. *Arbeten from medicinska kliniken i karolinska sjukhuset.* Vol. 1. Stockholm: Almkvis & Bengstssons, 1940.
———. *Steg for steg: En sjalvbiografi.* Stockholm: Bonnier, 1968.
———. Letters (1954–1978). T. Grier Miller Collection, College of Physicians, Philadelphia.
"Svartz, Nanna." In Hellstedt, *Autobiographies.*

SVIHLA, RUTH DOWELL (1897–1974)

U.S. zoologist. Born 1897 in Rhode Island. Married Arthur Svihla. Educated Smith College (A.B., 1920); University of Illinois (M.S., 1923); University of Michigan (Ph.D., 1930). Professional experience: University of Washington, research associate of zoology and botany (from 1940). Died 1974.

During the early part of her career, Ruth Dowell Svihla was chiefly a mammalogist. She joined the American Society of Mammalogists in 1927, and published fourteen papers in the *Journal of Mammalogy.* Six of these papers were published with her husband. At that time, her research revolved around the natural history and ecology of several different rodents. Her single presentation at an annual meeting (1929) of the ASM was the first one given by a woman. Arthur Svihla was on the faculty at the University of Washington, and in 1940, Ruth took a position as a research associate of zoology and botany at that institution. Her research had shifted to bryology by that time, and she dropped her membership in the ASM. In 1952, she received a Fulbright Award to do bryological research in Burma. Some of her letters and notes on bryology addressed to the bryologist E. B. Bartram from this period are held in the Farlow Reference Library of Cryptogamic Botany at Harvard. JH/MBO

PRIMARY SOURCES
Svihla, Ruth D. "Mammals of the Uinta Mountain Region." *Journal of Mammalogy* 12 (1931): 256–266.
———. "Notes on Desert and Dusky Harvest Mice (*Reithrodontomys megalotis megalotis* and *R. m. nigrescens*)." *Journal of Mammalogy* 12 (1931): 363–365.
———. "Breeding and Young of the Grasshopper Mouse (*Onychomys leucogaster fuscogriseus*)." *Journal of Mammalogy* 17 (1936): 172–173.

SECONDARY SOURCES
Kaufman, Dawn M., Donald W. Kaufman, and Glennis A. Kaufman. "Women in the Early Years of the American Society of Mammalogists (1919–1949)." *Journal of Mammalogy* 77, no. 3 (1996): 642–654.

STANDARD SOURCES
AMS 7–8, B 9, P&B 10–12.

SWAIN, CLARA A. (1834–1910)

U.S. physician. Born 1834. Educated Woman's Medical College of Philadelphia. Professional experience: medical missionary. Died 1910.

A graduate of the Woman's Medical College of Philadelphia, Swain applied to a missionary society for a position as physician in a foreign country, but she was refused because she was not married. In 1869–1870 she was finally sent to Bareilly, India, where women of all classes clamored for her services. Her career flourished for thirty years; she built hospitals, taught nurses, and trained native midwives. She also introduced Christianity wherever she found women willing to listen. In 1871, His Highness, Mohammed Kallub Ali Khan, although opposed to the Christianity she espoused, presented Swain with an estate adjoining the mission premises as a site for a woman's hospital.   JH/MBO

PRIMARY SOURCES
Swain, Clara A. 1909. *A Glimpse of India.* New York: Garland, 1987. A reprint of *A Glimpse of India: Being a Collection of Extracts from the Letters of Dr. Clara A. Swain, First Medical Missionary to India of the Woman's Foreign Missionary Society of the Methodist Episcopal Church in America.* New York: J. Pott and Co., 1909.

SECONDARY SOURCES
Alsop, Gulielma Fell. *History of the Woman's Medical College, Philadelphia, Pennsylvania, 1850–1950.* Philadelphia: J. B. Lippincott Co., 1950.

STANDARD SOURCES
Hurd-Mead 1933; Lovejoy.

SWALLOW, ELLEN (1842–1911)

See Richards, Ellen Swallow.

SWANSON, PEARL PAULINE (1895–?)

U.S. nutritionist. Born 13 September 1895 in Cokato, Minn., to Maria Sigfridson and Frank Swanson. Educated Carleton College (B.S., 1916); University of Minnesota (M.S., 1924); Yale University (Ph.D., 1930). Professional experience: Fairbault, Minn., teacher (1916–1918); Carleton State College, faculty (1920–1922); Montana State College, faculty (1924–1927); Iowa State University, faculty, then professor of nutrition (1930–1967); Agricultural and Home Economics Experimental Station, assistant director (1944–1961). Honors and memberships: U.S. Department of Agriculture, member national commission (1948–1958); North Central Home Economics Research Administration, member advisory committee. New York Academy of Science, Fellow; Borden Award (1955); Universtiy of Minnesota Outstanding Achievement Award (1951); Journal of Nutrition, associate editor (1949–1953). Death date unknown.

Pearl Pauline Swanson studied the role of proteins and fat in nutrition. Born in Minnesota, she went to Carleton College, where she trained as a chemist. Upon completing her bachelor's in chemistry, she taught high school science in Fairbault, Minnesota, to earn enough money to return to graduate work at the University of Minnesota for a master's degree in nutrition. Again, she returned to teaching, this time as junior faculty at Carleton College and Montana State College until 1927. She next went to Yale University for her doctorate, and was awarded a Sterling fellowship and then a Bourne Cox fellowship (1928 and 1929). After earning her degree, she accepted a faculty appointment at Iowa State University at Ames, Iowa, where she became professor of nutrition in 1936, remaining in that position until her retirement in 1965. She also was assistant director of the experimental station in agriculture and home economics from 1944 to 1961, and served as a member of the National Commission of the U.S. Department of Agriculture. She was on the editorial board of *Nutritional Status U.S.A.* and associate editor of the *Journal of Nutrition* from 1949 to 1953. She received a number of prizes and honors including the Outstanding Achievement Award from the University of Minnesota, 1951, and the Borden Award in 1955.   JH/MBO

PRIMARY SOURCES
Swanson, Pearl Pauline. *Calcium in Nutrition.* Chicago: National Dairy Council, [1963].

STANDARD SOURCES
Debus.

SWIFT, MARY (fl. mid-19th century)

U.S. naturalist and children's writer.

Little is known about Mary Swift, except that she wrote books for children on natural philosophy.   JH/MBO

PRIMARY SOURCES
Swift, Mary A. *First Lessons on Natural Philosophy for Children*. 2 vols. Hartford: Belknap and Hamersley, 1840–1849.

SWINDLER, MARY HAMILTON (1884–1967)

U.S. archeologist. Born 3 January 1884 in Bloomington, Ind., to Ida M. (Hamilton) and Harrison T. Swindler. Two siblings. Educated Bloomington High School; Indiana University (A.B., 1905; A.M., 1896); Bryn Mawr College (1906–1912; Ph.D., 1912); University of Berlin (1909); American School of Classical Studies, Athens (from 1910?). Professional experience: Bryn Mawr College, rose to rank of professor (1931), post-retirement positions (1953–1956); retired 1949; University of Pennsylvania, faculty (1949–1950); University of Michigan, faculty (1950–1953). Honors and memberships: Indiana University, honorary LL.D. (1941); American Association of University Women, achievement award (1951); one of three outstanding scholars in the humanities awarded a grant from the American Council of Learned Societies (1959); Royal Society of Arts, London, Fellow; German Archaeological Institute, Fellow. Died 16 January 1967 in Haverford, Pa., of bronchopneumonia.

Mary Swindler spent most of her long career as a classicist and archeologist at Bryn Mawr College. Swindler earned both a bachelor's and master's degree in Greek from the University of Indiana. Awarded a Greek fellowship at Bryn Mawr in 1906, she soon began establishing her reputation when she wrote an article published in 1909 in the *American Journal of Archaeology*. In this article she analyzed a Greek vase exhibited at the Academy of Natural Sciences in Philadelphia. During the time that she was working on her doctorate she studied in Berlin, aided by the Mary E. Garrett European Fellowship. After Berlin, she went to the American School of Classical Studies in Athens. She earned her doctoral degree in 1912 and remained at Bryn Mawr, rising through the ranks to professor of classical archeology, in 1931.

Swindler's dissertation, "Cretan Elements in the Cults and Ritual of Apollo," was a masterful work. Always interested in the recently discovered Cretan or Aegean world, she published a major work, *Ancient Painting,* in 1929. She began another major project to be entitled "The Beginings of Greek." She planned for this book to follow the evolving creativity in Greece from Neolithic times through the Bronze and Dark Ages until a preclassical style emerged in the seventh century B.C. A perfectionist, Swindler never completed the manuscript.

Swindler was a challenging teacher and held seminars in her apartment. When she retired from Bryn Mawr in 1949, Swindler found that her modest pension was insufficient. Therefore, she returned to teaching. When she finally retired she continued to read extensively and helped students informally.   JH/MBO

PRIMARY SOURCES
Swindler, Mary H. *Ancient Painting: From the Earliest Times to the Period of Christian Art*. New Haven: Yale University Press, [1929].

SECONDARY SOURCES
New York Times, 18 January 1967. Obituary notice.
Thompson, Dorothy Burr. "Mary Hamilton Swindler." *American Journal of Archaeology* (October 1950): 292–293.

STANDARD SOURCES
NAW(M) (article by Emily Vermeule and Sara Anderson Immerwahr).

SWOPE, HELEN GLADYS (ca. 1909–   )

U.S. chemist. Born in Detroit, Mich. Educated University of Chicago (B.S., 1929). Professional experience: Sanitation district, Chicago, Ill., assistant chemist (1925–1932); National Aluminate Corporation, research chemist (1932–1935); State Board of Health, Kansas (1935–1937); North Shore Sanitation Division, Ill., district chemist (1937–1944); Mellon Institute, fellow (1944–1946); Allegheny Sanitation Authority, Pennsylvania, chief chemist (1946–1948); Argonne National Laboratory, chemical engineering division, senior chemist (from 1948); University of Kansas, assistant professor (1935–1937); University of Pittsburgh, special lecturer (1947–1949).

For a woman without an advanced degree, Helen Gladys Swope had an outstanding career. Her positions required not only technical expertise but also the ability to manage a laboratory. Only a skilled scientist would be asked, as she was, to be a section editor for *Chemical Abstracts* (from 1959). She was the secretary for the section on air and stream pollution for the XIIth International Congress for Pure and Applied Chemistry. Swope was also active in scientific societies, including the Chemical Society, the Nuclear Society, the Research Society, and the Water Works Association. Her research interests were in water, sewage, industrial and radioactive waste treatment, ion exchange, and radiation dosimetry.
                                           JH/MBO

STANDARD SOURCES
AMS P 9, P&B 10–11.

SWOPE, HENRIETTA (HILL) (1902–1982)

U.S. astronomer. Born 26 October 1902 in St. Louis, Mo. Educated Columbia University (A.B., 1925); Radcliffe College (A.M., 1928). Professional experience: Harvard College Observatory, assistant (1928–1942); Massachusetts Institute of Technology, staff radiation laboratory (1942–1943); U.S. Department of the Navy, hydrographic office, mathematician (1943–1947); Barnard College, Columbia, associate astronomer (1947–1952); Mt. Wilson and Mt. Palomar Observatories, assistant (1952–1962), research fellow (1962–1968). Retired 1968. Honors and memberships: American Astronomical Society, Cannon Prize (1968); Royal Astronomical Society, member.

For a person without a doctoral degree, Henrietta Hill Swope had a very successful career in astronomy. After she earned her highest degree, a master's from Radcliffe, she immediately went to work at the Harvard Observatory as an assistant. World War II enabled her to expand her competencies. In 1942 she accepted a position in the Massachusetts Institute of Technology staff radiation laboratory and then spent four years working as a mathematician for the Department of the Navy. She returned to academia in 1947 and after five years at Barnard became an assistant at the Mt. Wilson and Mt. Palomar Observatories until she retired. Her research interests were in photometry and variable stars.

JH/MBO

PRIMARY SOURCES

Swope, Henrietta Hill. With Harlow Shapley. "New Variable Stars in Low Galactic Latitudes." *Annals of the Harvard College Observatory* 90, no. 5 (1934).

———. "A Peculiar Variable with Changing Period and Light Curve." *Annals of the Harvard College Observatory* 105, no. 26 (1937).

———. *Papers* (1917–1982). Henrietta Hill Swope Papers; Schlesinger Library, Radcliffe College.

STANDARD SOURCES

AMS 5–8, *P* 9, *P&B* 10–14.

SYKES, MARY GLADYS (ca. 1884–1943)

British botanist. Born 1884. Married David Thoday (1910). Educated Girton College, Cambridge (first-class honors in both Part I and Part II of the Natural Sciences Tripos). Professional experience: Bathurst student; Newnham College, fellow; University of Manchester, honorary research fellow; studied flora of South Africa; University College of North Wales, honorary lecturer. Died 9 August 1943.

Mary Gladys Sykes had a distinguished record at Girton College, obtaining first-class honors in both parts of her Natural Sciences Tripos. She conducted research in botany as a Bathurst student and later as a fellow of Newnham College.

Her early research was in cytology, and she published on the structure and the division of the nucleus in *Funkia*. Sykes also wrote accounts of the histology of several Laminariacea

and worked on the histological relations between *Cuscuta* and its hosts. A versatile botanist, she became interested in the anatomy and morphology of vascular cryptogams, including *Psilotum, Tmesipteris,* and some of the Gnetaceae. She published important papers in the *Annals of Botany* and the *Philosophical Transactions* on this research.

Sykes married one of her Cambridge collaborators, David Thoday, in 1910. The couple moved to Manchester, where Thoday was appointed lecturer in plant physiology. She continued her research and was elected an honorary research fellow in the university. In addition to her research, she taught botany. When Thoday was appointed professor of botany at Capetown, South Africa, she followed him in 1918. She again collaborated with her husband, but this time on the flora of South Africa. She continued her investigation of the Gnetales and completed an authoritative book on this subject that H. W. Pearson had left unfinished.

When the Thodays returned to Britain, Mary Sykes Thoday was appointed honorary lecturer in botany at the University College of North Wales. She went to Canada with the British Association in 1924 and collected work on the mistletoe *Arceuthobium pusillum,* and began an investigation along the same lines as her earlier work on *Cuscuta,* but left it unfinished because she suffered from a serious illness.

During World War I, she became an active advocate of women's suffrage, and while she was in South Africa, became involved in the complex racial problems in that country. As she grew older she devoted more and more of her time to social issues, especially the promotion of international understanding and good will. In the 1930s, as the situation in Europe deteriorated, she devoted much of her time to organization work and public speaking. JH/MBO

PRIMARY SOURCES

Sykes, Mary G. "Note on the Nuclei of Some Unisexual Plants." *Annals of Botany* 23 (1909): 341.

———. With David Thoday. "Preliminary Observations on the Transpiration Current in Submerged Water-Plants." *Annals of Botany* 23 (1909): 635–637.

———. With W. Stiles. "The Cones of the Genus *Selaginella*." *Annals of Botany* 24 (1910): 523–536.

Thoday, Mary Sykes. "On the Histological Relations between Cuscuta and Its Host." *Annals of Botany* 25 (1911): 655–682.

———. "The Female Inflorescence and Ovules of *Gnetum africanum,* with Notes on *Gnetum scandens.*" *Annals of Botany* 25 (1911): 1101–1135.

———. "Anatomy of the Ovule and Seed in *Gnetum Gnemon,* with Notes on *Gnetum funiculare.*" *Annals of Botany* 35 (1921): 37–53.

SECONDARY SOURCES

Weiss, F. E. "Mrs. Thoday." *Nature* 152 (1943): 406. Obituary notice.

STANDARD SOURCES

Desmond.

SYNIEWSKA, JANINA (1893–1951)

Polish geologist and micropaleontologist. Born 1893. Died 1951.

Janina Syniewska conducted research in Tertiary micropaleontology. JH/MBO

PRIMARY SOURCES

Syniewska, Janina. "O faunie otwornicowej paleogenskiego fliszu z Koniuszy kolo Dobromil: sur la faune de foraminiferes du flysch paleogene de Koniusza pres de Dobromil." *Rocznik Polskiego Towarzystwa Geologicznego* 22, no. 4 (1954 for 1952): 522–523.

SECONDARY SOURCES

Kamienski, Marian. "Janina Syniewska (1893–1951)." *Rocznik Polskiego Towarzystwa Geologicznego* 22, no. 4 (1954): 522–523.

STANDARD SOURCES

Sarjeant.

SZEMINSKA, ALINA (fl. 1935)

Polish psychologist.

Little information is available on psychologist Alina Szeminska. She was one of the primary editors for a series *Cahiers de pedagogie experimentale et de psychologie de l'enfant*. She edited number 7 of this series, "Essai d'analyse psychologique du rassonement mathematique" (1935). Although she cowrote *The Child's Conception of Number* in 1941 with Jean Piaget, her name was left off subsequent translations so she was largely uncredited. She was incarcerated at Auschwitz during World War II and afterward became a popular speaker.

JH/MBO

PRIMARY SOURCES

Szeminska, Alina, ed. "Essay d'analyse psychologique du raisonnement mathematique." In *Cahiers de pedagogie experimentale et de psychologie de l'enfant.* N.p., 1935.
———. With Jean Piaget. *The Child's Conception of Number.* 1941. New York: Humanities Press, 1952.
———. With Jean Paget and others. *The Child's Conception of Geometry.* London: Routledge and K. Paul, [1960].

SZEPAROWICZ, MARIA (fl. 1920s)

Austrian physical chemist. Professional experience: Institute for Radium Research, Vienna, research (1920s).

Szeparowicz investigated the effect of temperature on the solubility of radium emanation (radon), and showed that some of the dissolved gas was captured in precipitates. This research was performed in Vienna at the Institute for Radium Research. MM

PRIMARY SOURCES

Szeparowicz, Maria. "Untersuchungen über die Verteilung von Radiumemeanation in verschiedenen Phasen." *Akademie der Wissenschaften, Vienna. Sitzungsberichte 2a* 129 (1920): 437–454.

STANDARD SOURCES

Meyer and von Schweidler.

SZMIDT, JADWIGA (1889–1940)

Polish-Russian physicist. Born 8 September 1889 in former Polish territory under Russian occupation, to Ryszard Szmidt. Married A. A. Tshernyshev (1923). Educated Warsaw; Pedagogical Institute for Girls, St. Petersburg (1905–1909); Curie Laboratory, Paris (1911); Manchester University (1913–1914); University for Men, St. Petersburg (1915–1916); Polytechnical Institute, St. Petersburg (1916). Professional experience: Secondary School for Girls, St. Petersburg, physics teacher (1909–1911); Leningrad Polytechnical Institute, lecturer (after WWI); Electro-vacuum Laboratory, director (ca. 1930); scientific translator. Died April 1940 in Leningrad.

Jadwiga Szmidt was born to a Polish family. After studying in Warsaw and Petersburg she taught physics at a girls school. In Paris she took a teachers' class at the Sorbonne, then worked in MARIE CURIE's laboratory. Returning to her teaching position in St. Petersburg, Szmidt began research there. She then went to Rutherford's laboratory in Manchester, where she investigated energy relationships between soft and hard gamma rays emitted from radium decay products. After returning to Russia she studied at the University for Men in St. Petersburg, earning the first-class grade in mathematics in 1915.

During the war Szmidt assisted refugees and organized Polish schools for them. Afterward she participated in the organization of the State Physico-Technical and Radiological Institute in Petersburg. There she worked on the Röntgen (X) rays under the institute's first director, Abram Joffé, who had studied under Röntgen.

In 1923 Szmidt married the physicist A. A. Tshernyshev, deputy director of the institute. She began work in electrotechnology, her husband's specialty. Together they did research on television, and received a patent for an oscillograph (a device for recording the wave forms of varying electrical quantities) in 1927. Later Szmidt, who was fluent in six languages, translated numerous scientific works.

Tshernyshev's organizational work for the Academy of Science led him to move to Moscow around 1938. Szmidt remained in Leningrad, and the couple continued their relationship by mail. During this time Szmidt became seriously ill. She died in April 1940.   MM

PRIMARY SOURCES

Szmidt, Jadwiga. "On the Distribution of Energy in the different Types of γ Rays Emitted from Certain Radioactive Substances." *Philosophical Magazine* 28 (1914): 527–539.

———. "Note on the Excitation of γ rays by β Rays." *Philosophical Magazine* 30 (1915): 220–224.

———. "X-ray Absorption." *Vestnik Rentgenologii i Radiologii Tr. Sov. Fiz. Tekhnol. Otd.* 1 (1919): 6–12. In Russian.

———. With A. A. Tshernyshev. "A Long-Distance Vision Apparatus." *Collection of Works in Applied Physics* (1926): 13–18. In Russian.

SECONDARY SOURCES

Birks, J. B., ed. *Rutherford at Manchester.* London: Heywood & Co., 1962; New York: W. A. Benjamin, 1963. Rutherford's student E. N. da C. Andrade later mentioned a laboratory accident involving a foreign student, most likely Szmidt. See pages 330–331 for the incident of "Natasha Bauer."

Golonka, M. Cielak, J. Róziewicz, J. Starosta, and K. G. Tokhadze. "Jadwiga Szmidt (1889–1940), a Pioneer Woman in Nuclear and Electrotechnical Sciences." *American Journal of Physics* 62 (1994): 947–948.

Records in Institut Curie archives, assembled by Monique Bordry.

Rutherford Correspondence, Cambridge University Library. Four letters from Szmidt to Rutherford.

STANDARD SOURCES

Meyer and von Schweidler; Rayner-Canham 1997.

SZWAJGER, ADINA BLADY (1918–1993)

Polish physician and author. Born 1918 in Poland to Jewish family. Married (1) Stefan Szwajger in 1939 (he died in 1943); (2) Wlsadyslav Swidowski. Two children. Educated University of Warsaw (M.D., 1939). Professional experience: Warsaw Children's Hospital, physician (1938–1942); Jewish resistance (1942–1945); pediatric practice, specializing in tuberculosis (1945–retirement). Died 13 February 1993 in Lodz, Poland.

Adina Blady Swajger was educated at the University of Warsaw medical school. She obtained her medical degree at the age of twenty-one and held her first post at the Warsaw Children's Hospital. She soon found herself tending to dying Jewish children afflicted with tuberculosis, typhus, and malnutrition. When the children were about to be sent to the death camps, she made the decision first to inject her crippled mother and then the fatally sick children with overdoses of morphine. This action she knew to be merciful for both her mother and the children but it chilled her for the rest of her life. She kept her actions a secret until the publication of her memoir many years later.

With false papers, she escaped the ghetto and joined the resistance. Her husband, Stefan Szwajger was not so lucky. He was transported to and died in Auschwitz. Later pregnant by a friend in the Resistance, she chose to abort the child rather than have it be born during the Holocaust period. After the war, she returned to medicine, setting up a pediatric practice and specializing in the treatment of tuberculosis. She married for a second time and had two daughters. Her story first was told in a Solidarity underground magazine and then translated into English in 1988.   JH/MBO

PRIMARY SOURCES

Szwajger, Adina Blady. *Remember Nothing More: The Warsaw Children's Hospital and the Jewish Resistance.* N.p., 1988. Memoir, first published by Polish Solidarity movement.

STANDARD SOURCES

Annual Obituary 1993.

T

TAEUBER, IRENE BARNES (1906–1974)

U.S. demographer. Born 25 December 1906 in Meadville, Mo., to Lilly Keller and N. C. Barnes. Educated University of Missouri (A.B., 1927); Northwestern University (M.A., 1928); University of Michigan (Ph.D., 1931). Married Conrad Taeuber (26 July 1929). Two sons. Professional experience: Office of Population Research, Princeton University, researcher (1936–1961), senior research demographer and professor (1962–retirement). Honors and memberships: American Sociological Association, Fellow; American Statistical Association, president; Population Association of America, vice-president; U.N. World Population Conference (1966); Smith College, honorary LL.D. (1960); Western College for Women, honorary D.Sc. (1965). Died 24 February 1974 of complications from emphysema.

Born and educated in the Midwest, Irene Barnes Taeuber focused on the field of population and demographic change. Three years before she completed her doctoral degree at the University of Michigan, she married fellow graduate student Conrad Taeuber and had two sons, Richard Conrad and Karl Ernst. Her marriage was characterized by the close partnership and collaboration between her and her husband. Conrad Taeuber also became a noted demographer, who worked on agricultural economics, was chief statistician for food and agriculture in the United Nations, and later served as associate director of the U.S. Bureau of the Census.

From 1936 to 1961, Irene Taeuber was employed in the Office of Population Research at Princeton University; she rose to senior research demographer and professor of sociology by 1962. Her research centered on population change and its consequences throughout the world. Even when she published on other topics, such as hereditary mental disease (1938), she set them within the context of population problems. She published studies on the Americas (1943), Europe and the Soviet Union (1944), the Far East (1949), on Tanganyika, on Japan (1958), and, in association with her husband, on changes in demographics in the United States (1958

and 1971). She also served as editor of the bibliographic journal *Population Index* for the first seventeen years of its publication (1937–1954).

Tauber's most important work was her study of Japan that detailed its expansionist years, the war years, defeat and transition to a rising economy, described by her biographer as unequalled in demographic literature in the depth of its research, focus and detailed analysis. Her and her husband's 1958 and 1971 studies of demographic change had a decided impact on governmental thinking. Her later work centered on the growth, formation, and modernization of the Chinese in the western Pacific, including the People's Republic of China. Unfinished at the time of her death in 1974, this study was expected to have an impact comparable to her work on Japan.

Taeuber was active in her professional associations as a Fellow of the American Sociological Association and the American Statistical Association. She was a major founder of the science of demography in the United States. She served as vice president of the international United Nations Conference on Population in 1966. Smith College and the Western College for Women awarded her honorary doctorates. Her work was characterized by a feminist humanism, influenced by an early training in anthropology.   JH/MBO

PRIMARY SOURCES

Taeuber, Irene Barnes. "Hereditary Factors in Mental Disease." In *The Problems of a Changing Population,* ed. National Resource Committee, 156–171. Washington, D.C.: Government Printing Office, 1938.

———. *General Censuses and Current Vital Statistics in the Americas.* Washington, D.C.: U.S. Government Printing Office, 1943.

———. *Population of Tanganyika.* New York: Lake Success, 1949. United Nations publication.

———. With Marshall C. Balfour and others. *Public Health and Demography in the Far East:* Report of a Survey Trip, September 13–December 13, 1948. New York: Rockefeller Foundation, 1950.

———. With Conrad Taeuber. *The Changing Population of the United States.* New York: Wiley, in cooperation with the U.S. Bureau of the Census, 1958.

———. With Conrad Taeuber. *People of the United States in the 20th Century.* Washington, D.C.: Government Printing Office, 1971.

SECONDARY SOURCES

Burkman, Sarah-Alicia W., comp. *Population Index* 44 (1978): 5–17. Full bibliography of Irene B. Taeuber.

Dudley, Kirk. "Irene B. and Conrad Taueber." *International Encyclopedia of Social Sciences: Biographical Supplement.* New York: Free Press, 1979.

STANDARD SOURCES

Debus; *NAW* (M) (article by Nathan Keyfitz); Rossiter 1995.

TAFT, JESSIE (1882–1960)

U.S. psychologist and teacher of social work. Born Julia Jessie, 24 June 1882 in Dubuque, Iowa, to Amanda May (Farrell) and Charles Chester Taft. Educated West Des Moines High School; Drake University (A.B., 1904); University of Chicago (Ph.B., 1905; fellow, 1909–1912; Ph.D., 1913). Professional experience: New York State Reformatory for Women, assistant superintendent (1913–1915); State Charities Aid Association, New York City, social services director (1915–1918); Children's Aid Society of Pennsylvania, director of child study (1918–1933); University of Pennsylvania School of Social Work, lecturer (1918–1933), associate professor of social case work (1933–1946), professor of social work (1946–1952), emerita professor (1952–1960). Honors and memberships: American Orthopsychiatric Association, Fellow; North American Social Workers. Died 7 June 1960 in Philadelphia, Pa., of a stroke.

After earning a doctorate from the University of Chicago, Jessie Taft went to New York City to work in various institutions. After being the director of child study for the Children's Aid Society of Pennsylvania, she rose through the academic ranks at the University of Pennsylvania to become a professor.

Otto Rank was a major influence upon Taft from the first time she met him in 1924. She underwent analysis with him and later wrote his biography with notes on her own connection to his life and work.

In the mid-1930s she took a position at the School of Social Work, where she began to apply Rank's theories to social work. She defined the interaction between the client and the social worker in Rank's terms, placing the client in the center and describing functional analysis in which the

social worker assisted the client's internal and self-determined development. Her writings influenced the professional identification of the social worker. She died from stroke in a Philadelphia hospital, just before her seventy-eighth birthday.

K M

PRIMARY SOURCES

Taft, Jessie. *The Dynamics of Therapy in a Controlled Relationship.* Gloucester, Mass.: P. Smith, 1973.

———. *A Functional Approach to Family Case Work.* Philadelphia: University of Pennsylvania Press, 1944.

———. *Otto Rank: A Biographical Study Based on Notebooks, Letters, Collected Writings, Therapeutic Achievements, and Personal Associations.* New York: Julian Press, 1958. Includes some autobiographical notes.

———. *Jessie Taft: Therapist and Social Work Educator, a Professional Biography.* Ed. Virginia P. Robinson. Philadelphia: University of Pennsylvania Press, [1962]. Memorial volume drawn from Taft's papers.

STANDARD SOURCES

AMS 4–8; S&B 9; *NAW* (M) (article by June Axinn).

TAKEUCHI, SHIGEYO (IDE) (1881–?)

Japanese physician and first woman member of Parliament. Born 3 August 1881 in Shinshu, Japan. Five siblings. Married Kohei Yakeuchi (1913). Educated Tokyo Women's Medical School (M.D., 1908). Tokyo University, postdoctoral studies (1916?). Professional experience: Tokyo Medical College, assistant to director (1908–1913); private practice (1913–1965); Member of Parliament (1945). Honors and memberships: Tokyo Women's Medical School, president of alumni association (1959–?); awarded Third Order of the Sacred Treasure (1964). Retired 1964.

Shigeyo Ide grew up as the oldest child of six children in a privileged Japanese family in the central highlands of Japan. She was the only girl in her primary school, since education was not ordinarily extended to girls, but she had to discontinue public schooling to help with her siblings when her mother became ill. Her father took responsibility for her education, and she studied long hours at home. In her adolescence, she developed alopecia, and was sent to a hospital in Tokyo where she met two women doctors: a Japanese woman physician and a visiting woman physician from America. She was inspired to go to Tokyo Women's Medical School which had just been opened a few years before, and after much insistence, she was allowed to enter at the age of twenty-one.

After five years of study under the pioneering director of the school, Yayoi Yashioka, Ide graduated and passed her national examination in medicine. Her accomplishment was celebrated with the attendance of the former prime minister of Japan, who praised her publicly. She then became Yashioka's assistant at the school before she opened her own private practice. After about five years, she met and married a young pathologist, Kohei Takeuchi. When her husband finished his studies, she took the opportunity to enter Tokyo University to do postdoctoral studies while carrying on her own private practice.

Takeuchi also was active in women's rights organizations, working for women's suffrage. She was the first woman elected to the Japanese parliament in 1945, but after the war she was excluded from public office because her volunteer war work had made her politically undesirable to the new government. She continued with her medical practice and was rehabilitated in 1959, which allowed her to take over the presidency of the alumni association of her medical school. Her husband had died of lung cancer, a disease that had been his specialty, some eight years earlier. When she was eighty-three, the Japanese government awarded her its Third Order of the Sacred Treasure. She retired from medical practice the following year, but continued to be mentally active well into her mid-nineties.   JH/MBO

PRIMARY SOURCES
"Takeuchi, Shigeyo." In Hellstedt, *Autobiographies*.

TALBOT, DOROTHY AMAURY (1871–1916)

British botanical collector. Born 20 December 1871. Married Percy Amaury Talbot. Professional experience: collected plants with husband in Nigeria (1909–1916). Died 28 December 1916 in Degama, Nigeria. Died 1916.

Dorothy Amaury Talbot married a surveyor who was sent as a district officer to Southern Nigeria. From 1909 until her death the couple collected plants in Southern Nigeria, subsequently sent to the British Museum (Natural History). A catalogue of the plants was published a year after her death in the *Journal of Botany*.   JH/MBO

SECONDARY SOURCES
Rendle, A. N., et al. *Catalogue of Plants Collected by Mr and Mrs P. A. Talbot in Oban District, S. Nigeria*. Printed by order of the Trustees [British Museum], 1913.

STANDARD SOURCES
Desmond.

TALBOT, MARION (1858–1948)

U.S. home economist and university dean. Born 31 July 1858 in Thun, Switzerland, to Emily (Fairbanks) and Israel Tisdale Talbot.

Educated Chauncey Hall School and Girl's High School, Boston; Boston University (B.A., 1880); Massachusetts Institute of Technology (B.S., 1888). Professional experience: Wellesley College, Department of Domestic Science, instructor (1890–1892); University of Chicago, Department of Social Science and Anthropology, assistant professor to full professor (1892–1925), dean of undergraduate women (1895–1925); Constantinople, Turkey, Woman's College, acting president (1928–1929; 1931–1932). Honors and memberships: American Association of University Women, founding member; American Home Economics Association, founding member (1908). Died 20 October 1948 in Chicago of chronic myocarditis.

Marion Talbot came from a family deeply involved in education in Boston. Her father was the first dean of medicine at Boston University, and her mother was a leading figure in the establishment of Girl's Latin School that offered public school college preparation to girls. Raised as a Unitarian, Marion attended private school and the less demanding public high school. She then entered Boston University and graduated three years later. The following year, she entered the new Woman's Laboratory, established by ELLEN SWALLOW RICHARDS at Massachusetts Institute of Technology. The laboratory was then studying the adulteration of foods and the chemical constituents of common household materials. She left after a term, but reentered a few years later after MIT established pleasant quarters for the women students and made them full-fledged students.

Richards had succeeded in establishing a new chemical laboratory to study sanitation, although she ostensibly worked under the direction of William Nichols. Talbot worked closely with Richards, and a year before she graduated published with her a book on sanitation in the home. She then taught domestic science at Wellesley College for two years.

Alice Freeman Palmer, Talbot's close friend, then president of Wellesley, had been asked to organize women's instruction at the University of Chicago. In her early thirties, Talbot moved to the University of Chicago as an assistant to Palmer and as an assistant professor in home economics in the Department of Social Science and Anthropology. After three years, Palmer resigned the deanship, which she had held virtually in absentia, in favor of Talbot.

At Chicago, Talbot actively investigated the nutritional requirements of college women and wrote a second book with Richards on this topic. She also developed a house system for the women and helped establish a woman's student union with a hall that included a gymnasium and pool. Ten years earlier, she had worked with her mother and Richards to establish the American Association of University Women (at first named the Association of Collegiate Alumnae). In the first decade of the twentieth century, she joined Richards at Lake Placid to found the American Home Economics Association.   JH/MBO

PRIMARY SOURCES

Talbot, Marion. With Ellen H. Richards. *Home Sanitation: A Manual for Housekeepers.* 1887. Boston: Home Science Publishing Co., 1898.

———. With Ellen H. Richards. *Food as a Factor in Student Life.* Chicago: University of Chicago Press, 1894.

———. *The Education of Women.* Chicago: University of Chicago Press, 1910.

———. *More Than Lore; Reminiscences of Marion Talbot, Dean of Women, the University of Chicago, 1892–1925.* Chicago: University of Chicago Press, [ca. 1936].

SECONDARY SOURCES

"Marion Talbot 1858–1948." *University of Chicago Magazine* 40 (1948). With photographs.

Morriss, Margaret S. "Our Professional Debt to Marion Talbot." *Journal of Home Economics* 41 (1949): 185–186.

STANDARD SOURCES

AMS 1–7; Bailey. *NAW* (article by Richard J. Storr).

TALBOT, MARY (1903–)

U.S. zoologist and entomologist. Born 30 November 1903 in Columbus, Ohio, to Paulena (Smitz) and Paul Thresher Talbot. Educated Denison University (B.S., 1925), Ohio State University (M.A., 1927); University of Chicago (Ph.D., 1934). Professional experience: University of Omaha, instructor (1927–1928); Stephens College, Columbia, Mo., instructor (1928–1930); Mundelein College, Chicago (1935–1936); Lindenwood College, St. Charles, Mo., Department of Biology, assistant professor through professor (1936–after 1968), departmental chair. Honors and memberships: L'Union Internationale pour l'Etude des Insectes Sociaux; Kansas Entomological Society; American Institute for Biological Research.

Born in the Midwest, Mary Talbot received degrees from both Denison and Ohio State universities before she went to the University of Chicago to complete her doctorate. She taught in Missouri and Illinois colleges before completing her degree and then took a position at Lindenwood College, where she rose to full professor and chair in the biology department.

Talbot published articles on social insects, especially slave-making ants, their daily behavior, their nuptial flights, raids, and population fluctuations. She was a member of a number of American and international entomological and research societies, including the Union Internationale pour l'Etude des Insectes Sociaux. JH/MBO

PRIMARY SOURCES

Talbot, Mary. "Distribution of Ant Species in the Chicago Region with Reference to Ecological Factors and Physiological Toleration." Ph.D. diss., University of Chicago, 1934.

STANDARD SOURCES

AMS 6–8, B 9, P&B 10–13; Debus.

TALBOT, MIGNON (1869–1950)

U.S. invertebrate and vertebrate paleontologist. Born 1869 in Iowa City, Iowa. Never married. Educated Ohio State University; Yale University (Ph.D., 1904). Professional experience: Mount Holyoke College, instructor (1904), assistant professor, associate professor, professor and chair of the department (1908), professor of geology and geography and chair of the combined departments (1929). Died 1950.

Mignon Talbot was born in Iowa City and did her undergraduate work at Ohio State University. She then attended Yale, where she received a doctoral degree. She spent her entire career at Mount Holyoke College and rapidly progressed up the academic ladder, becoming professor and, when the geology and geography departments were combined, chair of the joint department until her retirement in 1935. Even after retirement she actively pursued her profession.

Talbot worked on the paleontology of both vertebrates and invertebrates. Her contributions to invertebrate paleontology included a revision of the Helderbergian crinoids of New York State and the investigation of the faunas of Stafford limestone, also in New York State. Her discovery of the approximately eighteen-centimeter dinosaur, *Podokesaurus holyokensis,* in the Triassic sandstone near Mount Holyoke, established her reputation in vertebrate paleontology. She postulated that this small dinosaur was a bipedal carnivore. During her thirty-one years at Mount Holyoke College, she amassed a large collection of invertebrate fossils and Triassic footprints and minerals. However, the museum burned down and the specimens were destroyed, including the one extant skeleton of her *Podokesaurus.* JH/MBO

PRIMARY SOURCES

Talbot, Mignon. "A Contribution to a List of the Fauna of the Stafford Limestone of New York." *American Journal of Science* 16 (1903): 148–150.

———. "Revision of the New York Helderbergian Crinoids." *American Journal of Science* 20 (1905): 17–34.

———. "Podokesaurus holyokensis, a New Dinosaur from the Triassic of the Connecticut Valley." *American Journal of Science* 31 (1911): 469–479.

SECONDARY SOURCES

Elder, Eleanor S. "Women in Early Geology." *Journal of Geological Education* 30, no. 5 (1982): 287–293. Talbot is discussed on pages 290–291.

STANDARD SOURCES

AMS 1–8; Bailey; Sarjeant.

TALIAFERRO, LUCY (GRAVES) (1895–1973?)

U.S. microbiologist, immunologist. Born 12 July 1895 in Cleveland, Ohio, to Clara (Walter) and Herbert Cornelius Graves. Married William Hay Taliaferro (6 June 1919). Educated Goucher College (A.B., 1917); Johns Hopkins University (Sc.D., 1925). Professional experience: University of Chicago, research associate in microbiology (1925–1960), professor (1959–1960); Argonne National Laboratories, research associate (1960–post-1968). Died ca. 1973.

Lucy Graves was born in Cleveland and studied at Goucher College. Two years after she obtained her undergraduate degree, she married the immunologist and microbiologist William Hay Taliaferro, who had just completed his doctorate at Johns Hopkins and was about to start teaching on the faculty. She began to work toward a doctoral degree in the same field, receiving it just after the couple moved to the University of Chicago where her husband began to teach microbiology. From this period until the end of the sixties, she worked closely with her husband. She produced excellent work, but her positions as research associate were unpaid, although just before she left Chicago she was given the formal title of professor. She, like her husband, focused on the serological responses to parasites (malarial, protozooan, and worm), particularly studying immunological response.

Taliaferro and her husband moved in 1960 to the Argonne National Laboratoy in Illinois, where they began to investigate the effect of ionizing radiation on the immune response. In the mid-sixties, she published an important book with her husband and another colleague on that topic.

JH/MBO

PRIMARY SOURCES

Taliaferro, Lucy Graves. With William Hay Taliaferro. "The Resistance of Different Hosts to Experimental Trypanosome Infections, with Especial Reference to a New Method of Measuring the Resistance." *American Journal of Hygiene* 2 (1922): 264–319.

———. "Infection and Resistance in Bird Malaria, with Special Reference to Periodicity and Rate of Reproduction of the Parasite." *American Journal of Hygiene* 5 (1925): 742–789.

———. With William H. Taliaferro and B. Jaraslow. *Radiation and Immune Mechanisms.* New York: Academic Press, [1964].

SECONDARY SOURCES

O'Hearn, Elizabeth M. "Women Scientists in Microbiology." *Bioscience* 23 (1973): 539–543.

STANDARD SOURCES

AMS 4–8, B 9, P&B 10–12; Debus.

TAMMES, JANTINE (1871–1947)

Dutch geneticist, known as Tine. Born 1871. Educated Middelbare Meisjesschool (MMS); private lessons in mathematics, physics, and chemistry; University of Groningen (matriculated 1890); honorary doctorate (1911). Professional experience: MMS, teacher; J. W. Moll, assistant (1851–1899); Biological Laboratory, researcher (1903–1912), extraordinary (adjunct) professor of heredity (1919–1937). Died 1947.

Tine Tammes was educated in Middelbare Meisjesschool, a secondary school for girls, which did not prepare her for university admission. Therefore, she took private lessons in mathematics, physics, and chemistry after which she enrolled at the University of Groningen. Although she was allowed to attend lectures and practicals, she was not allowed to take the academic examinations. Consequently in order to earn a living she obtained her first teaching certificate in physics, chemistry, and cosmography in 1892 and a second one in botany, zoology, mineralogy, and geology in 1897. The rules that kept Tammes from taking the official examinations were strictly enforced, so she was unable to obtain her doctorate. She taught at MMS until 1897, when she became the assistant of Groningen professor of botany J. W. Moll (1851–1933).

Moll served as a mentor to the talented Tammes and used his influence to help her meet important scientists including Hugo de Vries. Since Tammes was interested in de Vries' work on his mutation theory, Moll encouraged a reluctant de Vries to allow Tammes to assist him. Since she was unable to receive a doctorate in the Netherlands, Moll, who considered her 148–page monograph sufficient for a thesis, was able to negotiate a doctorate for her in Belgium.

Tammes was always reluctant to leave her home, often pleading ill health. Accordingly, she sometimes missed opportunities that would have advanced her professional life. For example, after she received her doctorate in 1900, she was awarded a scholarship by the Buitenzorg Fund of the Royal Dutch Academy of Sciences for research at the Botanical Garden of Buitenzorg on Java. This scholarship was an important honor and given once every two years to a promising young biologist. Later in 1900, she had an opportunity to broaden her experience and become a research assistant at an experimental research station in Wageningen.

Again, she pleaded ill health and the responsibility for the care of her parents.

Tammes remained Moll's assistant until 1899, at which time she continued her research at the Botanical Laboratory. Her investigation of the characters of cultivated flax, begun in 1903, resulted in an important monograph (1907) that garnered high praise from de Vries. Moll came to her assistance again in 1911 when he was instrumental in persuading the University of Groningen to award her an honorary doctorate (1911). After receiving this degree she was appointed to supervise botany practicals for students at the University of Groningen and finally obtained a position as extraordinary (adjunct) professor of heredity in 1919.

Although Tammes published many papers that would assure her place in the history of genetics, her most important contribution is the explanation of the inheritance of continuous characters as a Mendelian function. During the early twentieth century, geneticists were divided over the question of the applicability of Mendel's laws to continuous characters. Certainly the observational evidence appeared to support the idea that continuous characters had their own laws of heredity. Before Tammes's work, others had proposed that in the case of continuous characters, multiple alleles were involved. It was Tammes, building on the work of N. H. Nilsson-Ehle, who proved conclusively that Mendel's laws were applicable and that a multiple-allele hypothesis could explain the observations.

Thanks to current historians of science such as Ida Stamhuis, Tine Tammes's work is now being appreciated. During her lifetime, many factors combined to assure that her work was undervalued, not the least of which was her sex. Her extraordinary ability plus her mentor Moll's support helped her overcome many obstacles.   JH/MBO

PRIMARY SOURCES

Tammes, Tine. "Das Verhalten Fluktuierend Variierender Merkmale bei der Bastardierung." *Recueil des Travaux Botaniques Néerlandais* (Nederlandse Botanische Vereeniging Leyden) 8 (1911): 208–288.

———. "The Genetics of the Genus Linum." S'-Gravenhage: Martinus Nijhoff, 1928. Pamphlet, originally published in *Bibliographia Genetica,* 1928.

SECONDARY SOURCES

Stamhuis, Ida H. "A Female Contribution to Early Genetics: Tine Tammes and Mendel's Laws for Continuous Characters." *Journal of the History of Biology* 28 (1995): 495–531.

———. "Tine Tammes." In *Vrouwen Miniaturen: Biografische Schetsen uit de exacte Vakken,* ed. Marianne I. C. Offereins. Utrecht: Centrum Vrouwen en Exacte Vakken, 1996.

Wilde, Inge E. de. "Jantina Tammes (1871–1947), Nederlands Eerste Hoogleraar in de Erfelijkheidsleer." In "Om niet aan Onwetendheid en Barbarij te Bezwijken," ed. G. A. van Gemert et al., 234–247. *Groningse Geleerden 1614–1989.* Hilversum: Verloren, 1989.

TANNERY, MARIE ALEXANDRINE (PRISSET) (1856–1945)

French historian of science. Born 27 November 1856 in Brion-près-Thouet (Deux Sevres) France to Alexandrine Léopoldine Désirée (Roy) and René Prisset. Married Paul Tannery (1880) (d. 1904). Educated convent; no formal professional experience. Died 27 January 1945 at Geay (Deux Sevres).

Marie Alexandre Prisset was born in Poitiers to a local attorney. She married the well-known historian of science Paul Tannery in 1881, and subsequently collaborated closely with him. When the first chair in history of science in France was awarded to Gregoire Wybouroff, the Russian-born former collaborator of Emile Littré, there was (according to George Sarton) a vehement outcry from some quarters who felt it should have gone to Tannery.

Following Paul Tannery's death in 1906 of pancreatic cancer, Marie took on the task of editing his work on the history of science in seventeen volumes (*Mémoires scientifiques*) including his reviews and correspondence. She also began her own reseaarch on the work of Marin Mersenne, publishing the correspondence of Mersenne with C. de Waard in 1932. She died during World War II.   JH/MBO

PRIMARY SOURCES

Tannery, Marie, ed. Paul Tannery, *Mémoires scientifiques.* 17 vols. Toulouse: F. Privat, [1912–1930?].

———, ed. With Cornelius de Waard. *Correspondence du Père Marin Mersenne.* Paris: Beauchesne, 1932.

SECONDARY SOURCES

Sarton, George. "Paul, Jules, and Marie Tannery." *Isis* 38, no. 9 (1947): 33–49.

STANDARD SOURCES

DFC.

TAUSSIG, HELEN BROOKE (1898–1986)

U.S. physician. Born 24 May 1898 in Cambridge, Mass., to Edith (Guild) and Frank William Taussig. Three siblings. Attended Radcliffe College; University of California (B.A., 1921); Johns Hopkins University (M.D., 1927). Received Archibald Fellowship in medicine, Johns Hopkins University (1927–1928 and 1928–1930). Professional experience: Johns Hopkins Hospital, internship in pediatrics (1928); Johns Hopkins School of Medicine, instructor in pediatrics; cardiac clinic of the Harriet Lane Home for Invalid

Children, physician-in-chief (1930–1963); Johns Hopkins School of Medicine, associate professor (1946–1959); professor (1959–1963); emerita professor (1963–1986). Honors and memberships: Chevalier Legion d'Honneur, France (1947); American College of Chest Physicians, honorary medal (1953); Feltrinelli Award, Rome (1954); American Heart Association, award of merit (1957); American College of Cardiology, honorary fellowship (1960); American Association of University Women, Woman of Achievement Award (1963); Thomas River memorial research fellow award (1963–1969); Medal of Freedom of the United States (1964); Dedication of the Helen B. Taussig Cardiac Clinic, University of Göttingen; American Heart Association, president (1965); American Pediatric Society, Howland Award (1971); American College of Physicians, Mastership (1972); Johns Hopkins University, Milton S. Eisenhower Gold Medal; International Cardiology Foundation, member of board (from 1967). Died 20 May 1986 in an automobile accident near her home in Kennett Square, Pa.

Helen Taussig was born into a well-educated and relatively well-to-do family. Her mother was an early graduate of Radcliffe College, and her father was an eminent Harvard economist. However, her mother developed tuberculosis when Helen was nine and died two years later. Helen developed a mild case of the disease and could attend school only in the mornings for several years. She also suffered from dyslexia. Nevertheless, she was only one year behind her classmates when she graduated from high school. She began her college education at Radcliffe, but completed her bachelor's degree at the University of California, Berkeley. She returned to the East to attend classes Harvard Medical School, where she was not allowed to be a candidate for a degree. After studying bacteriology and histology at Harvard, she transferred to Boston University to study anatomy. Under Alexander Begg, she studied the muscle bundles of the ox heart, a study that resulted in her first publication (1925) and stimulated her interest in cardiology. Begg encouraged her to apply to Johns Hopkins University School of Medicine, where she could be admitted as a degree candidate.

After being edged out by another woman by two-tenths of a point for a medical internship, Taussig took a fellowship in cardiology. After this fellowship, she was put in charge of a new cardiac unit that dealt with rheumatic fever. From 1930 to 1963, Taussig served as chief of the children's section of Johns Hopkins, the Harriet Lane Home. Working with a new tool, the fluoroscope, on numerous "blue babies," she determined that a hole between the ventricles and/or a partial blockage of the pulmonary artery resulted in unoxygenated blood that resulted in the child's blue (or cyanotic) appearance. In conjunction with Alfred Blalock, chief surgeon at Johns Hopkins, Taussig developed a corrective surgery. The operation was first performed on humans in 1946 after numerous experiments on dogs.

Taussig's 1947 book, *Congenital Malformations of the Heart*, described methods of identifying congenital heart defects. This book provided the basis on which pediatric cardiology was built.

Taussig compensated for a problem with deteriorating hearing by using an amplified stethoscope and by training her hands to feel the heartbeats of babies with cardiac diseases. Surgery in 1971 improved her hearing, but she later developed nerve deafness.

In the early 1960s, she visited Germany to examine the epidemic of "seal limb" deformity (phocomelia). Her work helped keep thalidomide out of the United States and halted its use in Europe.

Up until her death in an automobile accident when she was eighty-seven years old, Taussig continued to do research and to publish her results. During her lifetime, she published 129 scientific papers, including forty-one after her retirement. Right before she died, she was testing a hypothesis, using avian hearts, that isolated cardiac malformations resulting from genetic variants rather than developmental errors.

Taussig advocated socialized medicine, malpractice reform, liberalization of abortion laws, and the prolongation of life under hopeless situations. She received many honors.

JH/MBO

PRIMARY SOURCES

Taussig, Helen B. With Alfred Blalock. "The Surgical Treatment of Malformations of the Heart in Which There is Pulmonary Stenosis or Pulmonary Atresia." *Journal of the American Medical Association* 128 (1945): 189–202.

———. *Congenital Malformations of the Heart*. New York: Commonwealth Fund, Harvard University Press, 1947.

———. "The Thalidomide Syndrome." *Scientific American* 207 (1962): 29–35.

———. "Evolutionary Origin of Cardiac Malformations." *Journal of the American College of Cardiology* 12 (1988): 1079–1088.

SECONDARY SOURCES

Baldwin, Joyce. *To Heal the Heart of a Child: Helen Taussig, M.D.* New York: Walker Publishing, 1992.

Clymer, Eleanor. *Modern American Career Women*. New York: Dodd, Mead, 1959. Includes portrait.

Harvey, W. Proctor. "A Conversation with Helen Taussig." *Medical Times* 106 (1978): 28–44.

Neill, Catherine A. "Profiles in Pediatrics: Helen Brooke Taussig." *Journal of Pediatrics* 125 (1994): 499–502.

Rowntree, Leopold. *Amid Masters of Twentieth Century Medicine*. Springfield, Ill.: C. C. Thomas, 1958. See pages 470–474.

STANDARD SOURCES

AMS P&B 12–14; Annual Obituaries, 1986; Bailey; *Current Biography,* 1946, 1966; Grinstein 1997 (article by Laura Gray Malloy); *Notable;* Shearer and Shearer 1996 (article by Clara A. Callahan); Uglow 1982.

TAUSSKY-TODD, OLGA (1906–1995)

German/U.S. mathematician and teacher. Born 30 August 1906 in Olmütz (now Olomouc in the Czech Republic). Two sisters. Married John (Jack) Todd 29 September 1938. Educated Mittelschule and gymnasium at Linz; University of Vienna (Ph.D., 1930). Professional experience: Göttingen, editor (1930–1932); Bryn Mawr fellow (1934–1935); Girton College-Cambridge University, Yarrow Fellowship (1935–1937); University of London, instructor? (1937–?); Queen's University, Belfast, research; intermittant teaching in London and Oxford (1940–1942); Ministry of Aircraft Production, research in aerodynamics (1943–1946); U.S. National Bureau of Standards West Coast field station, (Institute for Numerical Analysis at UCLA) (1947); National Bureau of Standards, Washington, D.C., consultant in mathematics (1950–1956); California Institute of Technology, professor of mathematics (1957–1971), emerita professor (1971–1995). Memberships and special assignments: American Mathematical Society, council (vice-president, 1986–1987); editor of four mathematical journals. Died 7 October 1995 in Pasadena, Calif.

Olga Taussky, often considered the torchbearer for matrix theory, lived through the advancement of mathematics from pencil, paper, and deep thinking to the era of high-speed computers. She associated with prominent mathematicians such as Gödel, Philipp Furtwängler, G. H. Hardy, David Hilbert, Richard Courant, AMALIE EMMY NOETHER, and Wilhelm Magnus. All three girls in the family (Olga was the middle one) followed scientific careers. At age three, Olga moved with her family from Olmütz to Vienna, then to Linz during World War I. In 1925, the year her father died, Olga enrolled at the University of Vienna, where she eventually majored in mathematics. Her adviser, Philipp Furtwängler, suggested a thesis problem in class field theory involving p-groups, which he had solved for p = 2; she succeeded in solving the problem for p = 3 and she showed that the case was different for every prime p.

After she received her doctorate in 1930, she went to Göttingen at the invitation of Richard Courant. There she coedited, with Wilhelm Magnus and Helmut Ulm, David Hilbert's work on number theory; edited Artin's 1932 lectures; and assisted Courant in his differential equation course. Her first trip to the United States was in 1934, at the invitation of Bryn Mawr. For two years she worked for and observed Emmy Noether, and did some work at Princeton on topological algebra with Wilhelm Magnus and Nathan Ja-

cobson. In June 1935, she began a Yarrow Fellowship at Girton College, Cambridge University, then left to take a teaching position at one of the women's colleges in the University of London. At one of the intercollegiate seminars she met John (Jack) Todd, an Irishman and mathematician working in analysis at another college. They were married 29 September 1938.

The war years were difficult; the couple moved to Belfast, where Todd taught at Queen's University and Taussky conducted research on finite groups and matrices, but the government soon assigned Todd to war work in London, and Taussky returned to her college teaching job there (later at Oxford). Her teaching assignments proved unrewarding and Taussky sought to broaden her horizons. Finally in 1943, she obtained a research position in aerodynamics with the Ministry of Aircraft Production, working on wing flutter, which involves the stability of the describing matrix. There she became captivated by matrix theory and began work in eigenvalues of sums and products of finite matrices and integral matrices, which occupied her the rest of her life.

In 1947, the couple was invited to the United States to work for a year at the National Bureau of Standards' West Coast field station (Institute for Numerical Analysis at the University of California, Los Angeles). During their stay, Taussky wrote several papers and lectured at the California Institute of Technology (Caltech), University of Vancouver, and the University of Wisconsin. After the year, they returned to London, where conditions were still depressed. When the National Bureau of Standards offered them jobs in Washington, D.C., they returned to the United States to remain permanently. Taussky was appointed consultant in mathematics. During the years in Washington, she contributed chapters on algebra, operator theory, and ordinary differential equations for the *Condon-Odishaw Handbook of Physics,* refereed papers, found problems in number theory for the SEAC (Standards Eastern Automatic Computer), and helped organize the first symposium in 1951 on the numerical aspects of matrix theory (forerunner of the Gatlinburg-Householder meetings).

In 1957, the couple was invited to return to Caltech, to research and teach, and Taussky became the first woman appointed to a professorship there. She remained affiliated with Caltech as emerita professor after mandatory retirement in 1971 and continued writing and editing. She also wrote reviews for *Mathematical Reviews.* For six years she served on the council of the American Mathematical Society. During her career she contributed over two hundred professional publications (averaging three papers a year for over thirty years) and three autobiographical works. Among the honors awarded her were the Ford Prize (1970); Woman of the Year (Los Angeles Times, 1963); Golden Doctorate, University of Vienna (1980); Golden Cross of Honor First Class of the

Austrian Republic; membership in the Austrian and Bavarian academies of sciences (1985). Olga Taussky lived and breathed mathematics, even wearing clothing that displayed numbers, and was acknowledged as one of the leading mathematicians of the twentieth century. She died at the age of eighty-nine as consequence of a broken hip, survived by her husband of fifty-seven years. JH/MBO

SECONDARY SOURCES

Clymer, Eleanor. *Modern American Career Women*. New York: Dodd, Mead, 1959. See pages 91–98 and portrait 82.
Schneider, H. "On Olga Taussky-Todd's Influence on Matrix Theory and Matrix Theorists." *Linear and Multilinear Algebra* 5 (1997/1998): 197–224.
Vargh, R. "Olga Taussky Todd." *SIAM News* 29 (1996): 6.
Weiss, Eric. "Obituary: Olga Taussky-Todd." *IEEE Annals of the History of Computing* 18, no. 3 (Fall 1996): 60–61.

STANDARD SOURCES

AMS P 9–P&B 10–14; Bailey; Debus; *Notable Mathematicians;* Grinstein and Campbell.

TAYLOR, CHARLOTTE DE BERNIER SCARBOROUGH (1806–1861)

U.S. entomologist. Born 1806 in Savannah, Ga., to Julia (Bernard) and William Scarborough. Married James Taylor (27 April 1829). Two daughters, one son. Educated Madam Binze's School, New York City. Professional experience: published in Harper's New Monthly Magazine *(1850s). Died 26 November 1861 on Isle of Man, United Kingdom, of pulmonary tuberculosis.*

Charlotte De Bernier Scarborough Taylor is said to have been one of the first woman entomologists in the world. She, like MARGARETTA HARE MORRIS, was educated through study in the field and informed by reading agricultural and zoological texts. As a young woman, she attended a private school in New York City and then took a tour of Europe before returning to Savannah, where she married James Taylor, a well-to-do merchant. Her life on a Southern plantation led her to study insect pests of all kinds, especially parasites of economically important crops like cotton and wheat. She was also interested the potential of cultivating silkworms in America. This investigation of insects that could spin led her to a thorough study of the anatomy and natural history of spiders.

Beginning her scientific studies as a young girl in Georgia, she later mentioned that an elderly neighbor introduced her to the exciting world of minute insects seen through a microscope. She began to publish only at the end of the 1850s with a series of around nineteen articles in literary and popular magazines, especially *Harper's New Monthly Magazine.*

Taylor's texts were lively and filled with keen observations. One distinctive characteristic of her articles was her careful description of the conditions under which the insects and spiders could be found, the experiments she performed upon them and an appreciation of even human pests such as the flea, mite, and mosquito. They were profusely illustrated with the help of her daughters who assisted her.

Although she made careful drawings of insects, with accurate depictions of body parts, eggs, larvae and internal organs, some writers have commented that her drawings of plants, possibly done by her daughters, were less reliable. As popular articles, they had little effect on the scientific community or on agricultural practice. She left for England just before the beginning of the Civil War and died on the Isle of Man from tuberculosis while working on a book about plantation life.

PRIMARY SOURCES

[Taylor, Charlotte]. "The Flea." *Harper's New Monthly Magazine* 19 (June–November 1859): 178–189. This article, along with her other early article on insect pests ("The Mosquito Family"), is unsigned as were all articles in the magazine until volume 20.
Taylor, Charlotte. "Insects Destructive to Wheat." *Harper's New Monthly Magazine* 20 (December 1859): 38–52.
———. "The Silkworm." *Harper's New Monthly Magazine* 20 (May 1860): 753–764.
———. "Insects Belonging to the Cotton Plant." *Harper's New Monthly Magazine* 21 (June 1860): 37–52.
———. "Spiders: Their Structure and Habits." *Harper's New Monthly Magazine* 22 (September 1860): 323–335; 461–477.

SECONDARY SOURCES

Elliot, Clark. Biographical Dictionary of American Science. Westport, Conn.: Greenwood Press, 1979.

STANDARD SOURCES

Bailey; Bonta; *DAB;* O'Neill; Siegel and Finley.

TAYLOR, CLARA MAE (1898–?)

U.S. nutritionist. Born 15 March 1898 in Vineland, N.J. Educated Columbia University Teachers College (B.S., 1920; M.A., 1923; Ph.D., 1937); Oxford University, postgraduate work (1931). Professional experience: Academy School, N.J., instructor (1920–1922); Rhode Island State College, instructor (1922–1926); Columbia University Teachers College instructor (1927–1939), assistant professor (1939–1943), associate professor (1943–1948), professor (1948–retirement). Concurrent experience: U.S. Department of Agriculture, research director (1944), project nutritional editor (1947–1953); Woman's Home Companion, consultant (1941–1949); Parents Magazine, consultant (1948–1949). Honors and mem-

berships: *American Nutritional Society, diplomate; Food and Nutritional Council, New York, vice-president, chairman of planning board (1961); Public Health Association, Fellow; Dietetic Association; Home Economcs Association; Institute of Nutrition; New York Academy of Sciences. Death date unknown.*

Born in New Jersey, Clara Mae Taylor was educated at Columbia University Teachers College. Although she obtained her first two degrees by the time she was twenty-five, she finished her doctoral degree in nutrition only at the age of forty, with one year spent at Oxford. She began to teach in a school in New Jersey, and went on to teach at Rhode Island State College until she returned to Teachers College as an instructor, rising through the ranks to associate professor in the mid-forties, and full professor by the late forties.

During World War II, Taylor directed a research project under the U.S. Department of Agriculture that investigated energy metabolism in children. She also studied metabolism in women at different ages. Her animal experiments on white rats and guinea pigs included dietary studies, an investigation of different levels of ascorbic acid on reproduction, and studies on lactation and survival rates. During the war and the immediate postwar period, she served as a nutritional consultant to two popular women's magazines, *Woman's Home Companion* and *Parents Magazine.*   JH/MBO

PRIMARY SOURCES

Taylor, Clara Mae. *Discovery of the Nature of Air, and of Its Changes during Breathing.* London: G. Bell and Sons, Ltd., 1923.

———. *Food Values in Shares and Weights.* New York: Macmillan, [ca. 1942].

———. Revised with Grace MacLeod. *Rose's Foundations of Nutrition.* New York: Macmillan, 1944.

———. With Juanita Archibald Eagles and Orrea Florence Pye. *Mary Swartz Rose, 1874–1941, Pioneer in Nutrition.* New York: Teachers College Press, [1979].

STANDARD SOURCES

AMS 7, 8, B9, P&B 10–11.

TAYLOR, CLARA MILLICENT (fl. 1903–1930)

British chemist. Educated University College, Bristol (B.Sc.). Professional experience: Cheltenham Ladies College, instructor in chemistry (1904?–1925?).

Little is known about the life and work of Clara Millicent Taylor. She was educated at University College, Bristol, and published research on organic synthesis, one of which appeared with F. E. Francis (1903–1904). She is known to have taught at Cheltenham Ladies College, a famous girls' school, as an instructor in chemistry. Her research continued until 1930.   JH/MBO

PRIMARY SOURCES

Taylor, Clara Millicent. *Elementary Chemistry for Students of Hygiene and Housecraft.* London: John Murray, 1930.

STANDARD SOURCES

Creese 1991.

TAYLOR, EVA GERMAINE RIMINGTON (1879–1966)

British geographer and historian of science. Born 22 June 1879 in Highgate, London, to Emily Jane (Nelson) and Charles Richard Taylor. One sister; one brother. Married. Three sons. Educated at home; Camden School for Girls; North London Collegiate; Royal Holloway College; University of London (B.Sc. in chemistry, 1903; D.Sc. in geography); Oxford University, School of Geography (Certificate of Regional Geography and Diploma, 1908?). Professional experience: Burton-on-Trent School for Girls, science teacher (1903–1906?); research assistant to A. J. Herbertson (1908–1910); geography textbook writer (with J. F. Unstead) (1910–1916); Clapham Teachers' College and Froebel Institute, lecturer (1916–1918); East London College, part-time lecturer (1920); University of London, Birkbeck College, geography, lecturer (1920–1930); Froebel Insitute, part-time lecturer (1920–1930); Birkbeck College, lecturer and chair in geography (1930–1944). Retired 1944. Honors and memberships: Royal Geographical Society (committee chair); Association for Planning and Regional Reconstruction, consultant (1939–1946); British Association for the Advancement of Science, Section E (president); Royal Geographical Society, Victoria Medal (1947), honorary Fellow (1965); Hakluyt Society, vice-president; Institute of Navigation, honorary member; Society for Nautical Research, honorary vice-president. University of Aberdeen (honorary LL.D.); Birkbeck College, fellow (1960). Died 5 July 1966 in Wokingham, England.

Eva Germaine Rimington was a brilliant geographer and historian of practical mathematics and navigation. She had an unhappy childhood, since her mother left when she was three, and she was raised by a severe stepmother, who allowed her and her older sister and brother neither toys nor pets. Although her early schooling was at home, she soon went to local private schools, and entered the prestigious North Collegiate School for Girls. She went on scholarship to the Royal Holloway College, and obtained a bachelor in science degree in chemistry from the University of London when she was twenty-three.

After teaching science in girls' schools for three years, she went to Oxford University, where she studied geography, obtaining a certificate in regional geography and a diploma of geography. Subsequently she worked for four years as a research assistant to A. J. Herbertson, then head of the School of Geography at Oxford. She married soon after, and spent the following six years in London, working on geography textbooks and maps while she had the first two of her three sons. After the second child died in infancy, she took a position lecturing at the Clapham Training College and the Froebel Institute. Four years later, while preparing for her doctor of science degree in geography at the University of London, she began to lecture first at East London College and then at Birkbeck, the college for returning adult students. By 1930, she competed successfully for the chair of geography of Birkbeck and remained there until her retirement in 1944 at the age of sixty-five.

By this time, Taylor had published two important studies on the geography of Tudor and Stuart England. She had also worked on a memorandum on the distribution of the industrial population for the Royal Geographical Society, and served as an advocate of a National Atlas. During World War II, she trained officers of the Eastern Command in map reading and interpretation and worked closely with a number of planning and land use committees.

Taylor was active in professional organizations, twice serving as president of Section E of the British Association for the Advancement of Science. She was awarded the Victoria Medal by the Royal Geographical Society and later made an honorary Fellow. She received an honorary doctorate from Aberdeen University and was honored with one of the first fellowships awarded by Birkbeck College.

Taylor became interested during retirement in the history of science, and began a thorough study of the history of navigation and practical mathematicians of the sixteenth and seventeenth centuries. She published a series of important books on these topics when she was already in her seventies and eighties. The Institute of Navigation recognized her contributions by making her an honorary member and asking her to give the first Duke of Edinburgh lecture. Although she was very active to the age of eighty-four, a stroke impaired both her vision and her mobility in 1964. She died two years later in Wokingham. JH/MBO

PRIMARY SOURCES

Taylor, Eva Germaine Rimington. *Tudor Geography 1485–1583*. London: Methuen, 1930.

———. *Late Tudor and Early Stuart Geography, 1583–1650*. London: Methuen, 1934.

———. *The Mathematical Practitioners of Tudor and Stuart England*. Cambridge, England: Institute of Navigation at the University Press, 1954.

———. *The Haven-Finding Art*. Amsterdam: Theatrum Orbis Terrarum, 1956.

———. *The Mathematical Practitioners of Hanoverian England*. London: Cambridge University Press, 1966.

STANDARD SOURCES
DNB (article by Ella M. J. Campbell).

TAYLOR, HELEN (1831–1907)

British social scientist. Born in 1831 to Harriet and John Taylor. Stepdaughter of John Stuart Mill. Died 1907.

Helen Taylor was the only daughter of HARRIET TAYLOR MILL and John Taylor. She worked closely with her mother until her death in 1858 and after that continued her mother's work as John Stuart Mill's secretary and associate until his death in 1873. J. S. Mill and Helen worked together in the suffrage movement and organized the Society for the Representation of Women. She served as an editor for Mill's famous self-investigation, the *Autobiography of John Stuart Mill*, published posthumously. JH

PRIMARY SOURCES

Taylor, Helen. ed. *The Autobiography of John Stuart Mill*. New York: H. Holt, 1873.

———. *The Complete Works of Harriet Taylor Mill*. Ed. Jo Ellen Jacobs. Bloomington and Indianapolis: Indiana University Press, 1998. Includes some correspondence between Helen and her mother, and Helen's portrait and those of her parents and stepfather, John Stuart Mill.

Helen Taylor's papers are included in the John Stuart Mill/Harriet Taylor collection in the British Library of the London School of Political and Economic Sciences.

STANDARD SOURCES
DNB.

TAYLOR, JANET (d. 1870)

British writer and teacher on navigation. Lived in London. Married George Taylor (d. 1845). Professional experience: Wrote on nautical astronomy and navigation; ran nautical academy and mathematical instrument making firm (1845–1858). Died January or February 1870.

Janet Taylor was married to George Taylor, founder of the Nautical and Mathematical Academy located in London's East End. Her husband also made navigational instruments there. Beginning in 1833, Janet Taylor demonstrated her mathematical skills by editing a series of books on nautical astronomy and navigation. After her husband died in 1845, she took over his teaching as well as his instrument-making firm, and continued to produce (among other works) a planisphere of the fixed stars with a book of directions, a guidebook of wind and current charts, a diurnal register for various scientific instruments, and a handbook for the examination for officers of the British merchant marine. In December 1859, she was granted a civil-list pension of fifty pounds per year in recognition of her "benevolent labours among the seafaring population of London." She was called the "Mrs. Somerville of the marine world" in recognition of her mathematical abilities.　　　　　JH/MBO

PRIMARY SOURCES

Taylor, Janet. *Luni-Solar and Horary Tables with Their Application to Nautical Astronomy.* London: G. Taylor, 1833. Final edition, 1851.

———. *Diurnal Register for Barometer, Sympiesometer, Thermometer and Hygrometer.* 2d ed. London: G. Taylor, 1844.

———. *Planisphere of the Fixed Stars, Accompanied By a Book of Directions.* London: G. Taylor, 1846.

———. *Epitome of Navigation and Nautical Astronomy with Improved Lunar Tables: The Questions Arranged to the Nautical Almanac for 1852.* 9th ed. London: Taylor, 1851.

———. *A Guide Book to Lieutenant Maury's Wind and Current Charts.* London: G. Taylor, 1855.

SECONDARY SOURCES

Allibone, Samuel Austen. *Critical Dictionary of English Literature and British and American Authors.* Philadelphia: J. P. Lippincott, 1902.

STANDARD SOURCES

Boase; Mozans; Rebière.

TAYLOR, LUCY BEAMAN (HOBBS)
(1833–1910)

U.S. dentist. Born 14 Mary 1833 in western New York to Lucy (Beaman) and Benjamin Hobbs. Nine siblings. Married James Myrtle Taylor (1867). Educated Franklin Academy, Malone, N.Y. (1845–1849); privately studied medicine; private instruction from Charles A. Cleaveland, professor of materia medica at the Eclectic College of Medicine, Cincinnati, Ohio (1859); Jonathan Taft, dean of the Ohio College of Dental Surgery in Cincinnati, private dental instruction; apprentice to Samuel Wardle; Ohio College of Dental Surgery (D.D.S., 1866). Professional experience: Brooklyn, Mich., teacher (1849–1859); private dental practice Cincinnati (1861); private dental practice, Bellevue, Iowa (1862); private dental practice, McGregor, Iowa (1862–1865); private dental practice, Chicago (1867); private dental practice, Lawrence, Kans. Died 3 October 1910 in Lawrence, Kans., of a cerebral hemmorhage.

Although Lucy Taylor was the first U.S. woman to earn a dental degree, she had a long struggle before it was awarded.

After graduating from the Franklin Academy in Malone, New York, Lucy Hobbs taught school for ten years in Brooklyn, Michigan. At the same time she studied medicine under a local physician and in 1859 moved to Cincinnati, Ohio, home of the Eclectic College of Medicine. Although she was refused admittance because she was a woman, the professor of materia medica and therapeutics, Charles A. Cleaveland, tutored her privately. At one point Cleaveland suggested that she might pursue dentistry because it was more suitable for a woman. She found that Jonathan Taft, dean of the Ohio College of Dental Surgery in Cincinnati, was willing to teach her temporarily. She then found a dentist, Samuel Wardle, who accepted her as an apprentice. In 1861 she applied for admission to the college, but was again refused because of her sex. However, since a privately practicing dentist was not required to graduate from a dental school, Hobbs opened a series of private practices.

In 1865 Hobbs was elected a member of the Iowa State Dental Society and sent as a delegate to the American Dental Association's convention in Chicago. In this same year she reapplied to the Ohio College of Dental Surgery and this time was admitted to its senior class. After four months of study she was granted the degree of doctor of dental surgery.

Hobbs next practiced in Chicago, where she married James Myrtle Taylor, who was a painter in the Chicago and Northwestern Railway car shops. After Lucy instructed him, he too became a dentist. In 1867, she sold her Chicago office, and the couple moved to Lawrence, Kansas. For the next twenty years they developed a large practice. Lucy specialized in the dentistry of women and children. After James Taylor died in 1886, Lucy semiretired and became active in a numer of organizations such as the Rebekah Lodge, the Independent Order of Odd Fellows, and the Order of the Eastern Star. A member of the Republican Party, she was president of the Ladies' Republican Club of Lawrence. Taylor supported the woman's rights movement.　　JH/MBO

PRIMARY SOURCES

Taylor, Lucy Hobbs. "The Early Women in Dentistry." Hobbs's unpublished autobiography in Schlesinger Library, Radcliffe College, gifted by Kansas Historical Society.

———. "The Early Women in Dentistry." *Dental Register* (January 1894).

SECONDARY SOURCES

"Lucy Hobbs Taylor." *Journal of the American Dental Association* 117 (1988): 443.

Marusco, Susan Ahern. "Lucy Hobbs Taylor." Master's thesis, University of Kansas, 1984.

STANDARD SOURCES

Alic; *NAW* (article by Madeleine B. Stern); Yost.

TAYLOR, MONICA (1877–?)

British entomologist and protozoologist. Born 1 November 1877 in St. Helens, England, to Agnes (Picton) and Joseph Taylor. Educated Mt. Pleasant College, Edinburgh (1898–1900); University of London (B.Sc., 1910); University of Glasgow (D.Sc., 1917; LL.D., 1973). Professional experience: joined Order of Notre Dame (1900); University of Glasgow, College of Education, lecturer in science (1901–1946); Carnoy Institute, Louvain, Belgium, visiting lecturer; American Catholic University, Trinity College, visiting lecturer. Honors and memberships: Royal Society of Edinburgh, Neill Medal (1958); Royal Society Glasgow, vice-president (1954–1957); British Association for the Advancement of Science, vice-president (1952–?). Death date unknown.

Monica Taylor joined the Order of Notre Dame as a nun when she was twenty-three. She went on to study science at the University of London and the University of Glasgow and taught for almost forty years in the School of Education in Glasgow with occasional stints as visiting lecturer in Belgium and the United States.

She published a popular biology textbook with the distinguished biologist C. H. Waddington in the 1930s. In her later life, she was recognized with a medal from the Royal Society of Edinburgh and served as vice-president of the Royal Society of Glasgow. The University of Glasgow awarded her an honorary degree in 1973.

Taylor's scientific research included an analysis of the development of the insect *Symbrachus*, a study of the chromosome complex of *Culex pipiens*. She also studied amoeba and polypoidy and the connection to evolution. On the technical side, she developed laboratory growth materials for protozoa.   JH/MBO

PRIMARY SOURCES
Taylor, Monica. *Sir Bertram Windle: A Memoir*. London: Longmans, Green, 1932.
————. With C. H. Waddington. *Principles of Biology*. London: John Murray, 1935. Waddington is the first author.

STANDARD SOURCES
Debus.

TAYLOR, ROSE H. (d. 1918)

U.S. botanist. Educated Michigan Agricultural College (M.S.). Professional experience: Michigan Agricultural College, instructor in botany. Died 6 December 1918 from influenza.

Botanist Rose H. Taylor earned a master's degree from Michigan Agricultural College and after graduation taught there for ten years. She died in the 1918 influenza epidemic.
                                                        JH/MBO

SECONDARY SOURCES
"Rose H. Taylor." *Science* 38 (1918): 616.

STANDARD SOURCES
Barr.

TEAGARDEN, FLORENCE MABEL (1887–1975)

U.S. psychologist. Born 5 September 1887 in Dallas, W. Va. Educated University of Pittsburgh (A.B., 1915; A.M., 1916); Columbia University (Ph.D., 1924). Professional experience: Pennsylvania schools, teacher (1908–1913); University of Pittsburgh, teaching fellow in psychology (1915–1916), instructor (1916–1919), assistant professor (1919–1929), associate professor (1929–1931), professor of psychology (1931–1957), emerita professor (from 1957); private practice (from 1957). Concurrent experience: Mills College, summer lecturer (1941). Fellowships: American Psychological Association, American Orthopsychiatry Association, Association for Child Development, Pennsylvania Psychology Association (president 1939). Died 23 April 1975.

Florence Teagarden taught school before she received her bachelor's degree in psychology at the University of Pittsburgh. She continued at this university for her graduate work. After earning her doctorate, she rose through the academic ranks at the same university, achieving the rank of professor in 1931. She retired in 1957, and went into private practice. Her research interests were in child and clinical psychology, human behavior, and intelligence.   JH/MBO

PRIMARY SOURCES
Teagarden, Florence Mabel. *A Study of the Upper Limits of the Development of Intelligence*. New York: Teachers College, Columbia University, 1924.
————. *Child Psychology for Professional Workers*. New York: Prentice-Hall, 1940.

STANDARD SOURCES
AMS 4–8, S&B 9–11.

TEBB, MARY CHRISTINE (1868–1953)

British physiologist. Born in 1868. Married Otto Rosenheim (1910). Educated Bedford College, London (1882–1887); Cambridge University, Girton College (1887–1893); Natural Sciences Tripos (Part I, class 1, 1890; Part II, class 1, 1891). Professional experience: Newnham College, physiology assistant (1891–1893); King's College, London, Chemical Physiology Laboratory (1894?–1910); Physiology Laboratory (1910–1916). Medical Research Council Laboratories, Hampstead (1920s). Honors and memberships: Newnham College Bathurst Studentship; London Chemical

Society; Royal Society funding; Medical Research Council funding. Died 1953.

Mary Christine Tebb was educated first at Bedford College, London, and then at Girton College, Cambridge. During this period she was a Bathurst scholar. She took both parts of her Natural Sciences Tripos examinations with first-class honors. One part of this examination was in physiology. After she finished her education, she was awarded a Bathurst Studentship for research at Newnham College where MARION GREENWOOD (later Bidder) was demonstrator in physiology. She then worked for two years as an assistant to Greenwood, who was producing important articles on digestion. During this period, Tebb published intersting work on enzymatic hydrolysis of complex carbohydates.

Tebb then went to work in the Chemical Physiology Laboratory directed by W. H. Haliburton at King's College, London. Her work on the structure of protein fibers placed her in opposition to the German authority, Siegfried. At King's, she began to collaborate with the German-born chemist Otto Rosenheim, with whom she published ten articles on physiological chemistry in three years. Their work on "protogon," a crystalline substance derived from the brain, indicated that this was not a single chemical compound as had been claimed.

In 1910, Tebb and Rosenheim were married. She moved to the Physiological Laboratory at King's College, and worked on cholesterol until 1916 with funding from the Royal Society. Husband and wife moved to the Medical Research Council laboratories at Hampstead, where they continued their collaboration, publishing on the nature of spermine.

JH/MBO

PRIMARY SOURCES

Tebb, Mary Christine. "On the Transformation of Maltose to Dextrose." *Journal of Physiology* 15 (1894): 421–432.

———. "Note on the Liver Ferment." *Cambridge Philosophical Society Proceedings* 8 (1895): 199–200.

———. "Hydrolysis of Glycogen." *Journal of Physiology* 22 (1897–1898): 423–432.

———. "Chemistry of Reticular Tissue." *Journal of Physiology* 24 (1899): x–xi.

STANDARD SOURCES

Creese 1991; Girton.

TELFAIR, ANNABELLA (CHAMBERLAIN) (d. 1832)

British botanical artist and collector. Married Charles Telfair. Collected and drew Mauritius plants. Died 23 May 1832 in Port Louis, Mauritius.

Annabella Chamberlain married the Irish-born naturalist Charles Telfair, who had trained as a surgeon. The couple moved to Mauritius where he practiced medicine, collected botanical and natural history specimens, and established botanical gardens at Mauritius and at Réunion. Later he was supervisor of the botanic garden in Mauritius.

Annabella Telfair collected Mauritius algae that she sent to William J. Hooker at the Royal Botanical Gardens at Kew along with her drawings. Her drawings of plants also appeared in *Curtis Botanical Magazine* between 1826 and 1830. Her letters to Hooker are at Kew. JH/MBO

SECONDARY SOURCES
Journal of Botany 1 (1834): 147–157.

STANDARD SOURCES
Desmond; *DNB* (under Charles Telfair); Shteir.

TELKES, MARIA (1900–1995)

Hungarian-born U.S. physical chemist and engineer. Born 12 December 1900 in Budapest to Maria (Laban) and Aladar de Telkes. Naturalized U.S. citizen (1937). Educated Budapest University (B.A., 1920; Ph.D., 1924). Professional experience: Cleveland, Ohio, Clinic Foundation, biophysicist (1925–1937); Westinghouse Electric, research engineer (1937–1939); Massachusetts Institute of Technology Solar Energy Conversion Project (1939–1953); New York University, solar energy researcher (1953–1958); Curtis-Wright Company, director of research (1958–1961); Cryo-Therm, researcher (1961–1963); MELPAR company, head of solar energy application lab (1963–1969); University of Delaware, Institute of Energy Conversion, professor and research director (1969–1977), emerita professor (from 1978). Died 2 December 1995 in Budapest. Honors and memberships: Society of Women Engineers, Achievement Award (1952); International Solar Energy Society, Charles Greely Abbot Award (1977?).

Although she was born and educated in Budapest, Telkes spent her professional life in the United States. After a visit to her uncle in Cleveland, she was offered a position as a biophysicist at the Cleveland Clinic Foundation, where they investigated the energy associated with living things. She was especially interested in energy changes when a cell dies and those that occur when a normal cell is transformed into a cancer cell. She became a naturalized U.S. citizen in 1937, and in the same year moved to the Westinghouse Electric Corporation, where she worked for two years performing research and patenting thermoelectric devices that converted heat energy into electrical energy.

Telkes changed positions with relative frequency, finding solar energy research the most interesting. During her time at Massachusetts Institute of Technology, she designed a new type of solar heating system—one that stored solar energy as chemical energy through the crystallization of a sodium sulphate solution. A prototype house was built in Dover, Massachusetts, using her system. She also worked for the United States government studying the use of solar energy to produce drinking water from seawater. Her research resulted in a solar still that could be installed on life rafts to provide fresh water. At New York University, Telkes continued her work on solar stills, heating systems, and solar ovens. While she was working at Cryo-Therm, she developed materials for use in protecting sensitive instruments from temperature extremes. The results of her research were used in the Apollo and Polaris projects. She spent the end of her research career at the University of Delaware, where she worked on materials for storing solar energy and designed heat exchangers for the efficient transfer of energy. Her research resulted in a number of patents.

Telkes's accomplishments were recognized by awards from the Society of Women Engineers (Achievement Award in 1952) and the Charles Greely Abbot Award from the American Section of the International Solar Energy Society. The National Academy of Science Building Research Advisory Board honored Telkes for her contributions to solar heated building technology.   JH/MBO

PRIMARY SOURCES

Telkes, Maria. "A Review of Solar House Heating." *Heating and Ventilation* (September 1949): 68–74.

———. With Eleanor Raymond. "Storing Solar Heat in Chemicals: A Report on the Dover House." *Heating and Ventilation* (November 1949): 80–86.

———. "Fresh Water from Sea Water by Solar Distillation." *Industrial and Engineering Chemistry* 45 (1953): 1108–1115.

———. "Solar Thermoelectric Generators." *Journal of Applied Physics* 25 (1954): 765–777.

———. "Thermodynamic Basis for Selecting Heat Storage Materials." In *Solar Materials Science,* ed. L. E. Murr, 405–438. New York: Academic Press, 1980.

Telkes's archives are held in the Solar Energy Collection, Arizona State University.

SECONDARY SOURCES

New York Times, 13 August 1996. Obituary notice.

STANDARD SOURCES

AMS 6–18; *Current Biography* 1950; *Current Biography Yearbook* 1996 (obituary); Ireland; *Notable* (article by Jerome P. Ferrance); O'Neill; Rossiter.

TENENBAUM, ESTERA (1904–1963)

Polish zoologist and geneticist. Born 1904 in Warsaw. Educated University of Berlin (Ph.D., 1929). Professional experience: Kaiser Wilhelm Institute for Brain Research, assistant (1929–1934); University of Jerusalem. Died 1963.

Estera Tenenbaum worked in the laboratory directed by Nikolai Vladimorovich Timofe'eff-Ressovsky along with ELENA ALEKSANDROVNA TIMOFE'EFF-RESSOVSKY. In 1933, the Nazis demanded that Tenenbaum be dismissed; however, with the support of the director of the Kaiser Wilhelm Institute, Oskar Vogt, and the Rockefeller Foundation, she worked on a grant at the institute until 1934. At that time she emigrated to Palestine, where she eventually got a position at the University of Jerusalem.   JH/MBO

SECONDARY SOURCES

Vogt, Annette. "Vom Hintereingang zum Hauptportal— Wissenschaftlerinnen in der Kaiser-Wilhelm-Gesellschaft." Preprint 67. Berlin: MPI für Wissenschaftsgeschichte, 1997, 26–32. The first biographical study of Estera Tenenbaum.

———. "The Kaiser-Wilhelm-Gesellschaft and the Career Chances for Female Scientists between 1911 and 1945." Paper presented for the International Congress for the History of Science, Liège, Belgium, 23 July 1997.

TERENT'EVA, LIUDMILA NIKOLEVNA (1910–1982)

Russian ethnographer and sociologist. Born 1910 in Barnaul, Altai. Professional experience: Ethnography of the Peoples of the Volga Region, the European North and the Baltic Region, director; Soviet Academy of Sciences, Institute of Ethnography, deputy director. Died 9 June 1982 in Moscow.

Liudmila Nikolevna Terent'eva was known as both an ethnographer and sociologist. She was an important Soviet specialist on the ethnography of the peoples of the Baltic, directing the work on a major historical and ethnographic atlas of the region (*Istoriko-ethnograficheskii atlas Pribaltiki*). In sociology, she was noted for her studies of the ethnography of family and marriage. During her lifetime, she produced more than one hundred publications. She died at the age of seventy-two in Moscow.   ACH

PRIMARY SOURCES

Terent'eva, Liudmila Nikolevna. "Opyt izuchenia seminongo byta latyshskogo kolkhoznogo krest'ianstva." *Sovetskaia etnografila* no. 3 (1958): 38–51.

———. With S. A. Pribaltiiskaia. *Voprosy etnicheskoi istorii nazodov Pribaltiki: po dannym arkheologii, etnografii i antropologii.*

Moscow: Izdvo Akademii nauk SSSR, 1959. Archeology, ethnography and anthropology of the Baltic States.

———. *Kolkhoznoe Krestianstvo Latvii: Istoriko-Ethnograpficheskaia monografia. SSR.* Moscow: Izd-vo Academii nauk SSSR, 1960.

———. *Kolkhoznoe krest'ianstvo Latvii: istoriko-etnograficheskaia monografiiapo materialam kolkhozov Ekabpilsskogo raiona Latviiskoi SSR.* Moscow: Izdvo Akademii nauk SSSR, 1960. On Latvian peasantry.

———. *Sem'ia i semeinyi byt kolkhoznikov Pribaltiki.* Moscow: Izdvo Akademii nauk SSSR, 1962. Social life and customs on the collective farms of Baltic States.

———. *Etnicheskie protsessy i sem'ia.* Moscow: In-t konkretnykh sotsial'nykh issledovanii AN SSSR, 1972.

———. "Kartografirovanie kul'tury nasalenia Latgali v sviazi s. istorei ee formirovania." In *Areal'nye issledovaniia v. iazyknanii i ethnografii,* ed. M. A. Borodina, 200–211. Leningrad: Nauk, 1977.

———. With Solomon Il'ich Bruk. *Istoriko-etnograficheskii atlas Pribaltiki: zemledelie.* Vil'nius: "Mokslas," 1985. Historical and ethnographic atlas of Baltic states.

SECONDARY SOURCES

"Liudmila Nikolevna Terent'eva (1910–1982)." *Sovetskaia etnografila* no. 5 (1982): 169–172. Obituary in leading Soviet ethnographic journal. Includes bibliography on 171–172.

STANDARD SOURCES

IDA.

TERRY, ETHEL MARY (1887–1963)

U.S. chemist. Born 10 February 1887 in Hamilton, N.Y. Married Herbert Newby McCoy, 13 June 1922 (he died 1945). Educated University of Chicago (A.B., 1907; Ph.D., 1913). Professional experience: University of Chicago, instructor in chemistry (1912–1918), assistant professor (1918–1927), research associate (1927–1938, summers). Died 23 May 1963 in California.

Ethel Mary Terry was born in upstate New York. She was educated at the University of Chicago, and after receiving her doctorate, she served on the Chicago faculty, first as an instructor in chemistry and then as assistant professor until 1927. She married the chemist and chemical engineer Herbert Newby McCoy, with whom she wrote an introductory textbook and laboratory manual. When her husband left for California in the late twenties to pursue his work on radioactive materials, she gave up her faculty position to move to Los Angeles. For the next eleven years she returned to Chicago each summer to work on research problems as a research associate of her former department. Her research in-

terests included catalysis, the hydrolysis of esters, fumaric and maleic acids, and oxidation. JH/MBO

PRIMARY SOURCES

Terry, Ethel M. With Herbert N. McCoy. *Introduction to General Chemistry.* New York: McGraw-Hill, 1919.

———. With Herbert N. McCoy. *A Laboratory Outline of General Chemistry.* New York: McGraw-Hill, 1920.

———. With Julius Stieglitz. "The Coefficient of Saponification of Ethylacetate by Sodium Hydroxide." *Journal of the American Chemical Society* 49 (1927): 2216–2222. Taken from her Ph.D. Thesis, University of Chicago.

———. With Stanley Davis Wilson. "The Effect of Neutral Salts on the Velocity of Saponification of Ethylacetate by Sodium Hydroxide." *Journal of the American Chemical Society* 50 (1928): 1250–1254.

SECONDARY SOURCES

Eichelberger, Lillian, "Ethel Mary Terry." In *American Chemists and Chemical Engineers,* ed. Myles D. Wyndham. Washington, D.C.: American Chemical Society, 1976. Discusses Terry's collaboration with her husband and her philosophy of life and work.

STANDARD SOURCES

AMS 3–8; P 9; Debus (under Herbert Newby McCoy); Siegel and Finley.

TERZAGHI, RUTH DOGGETT (1903–)

U.S. civil engineer. Married Karl Terzaghi (he died in 1963). Educated Harvard University, Radcliffe College (Ph.D., 1930).

Ruth Allen Doggett studied geology, taking her doctorate at Radcliffe College in 1930. She wrote her doctoral dissertation on the geology and petrology of the Columbia Falls region of Maine. While a graduate student, she met the well-known Austrian geologist and civil engineer Karl Terzaghi, who trained in Germany and was teaching at the Massachusetts Institute of Technology. He was making a reputation for himself as the leader in research on soil mechanics. She became his second wife and practiced civil engineering until the late 1980s. Husband and wife deposited an archive of diaries, correspondence papers, and other materials in the Terzaghi Library of the Norwegian Geotechnical Institute in Oslo. JH/MBO

PRIMARY SOURCES

Doggett, Ruth Allen. "The Geology and Petrology of the Columbia Falls Quadrangle, Maine." Ph.D. diss., Radcliffe College, 1930.

SECONDARY SOURCES

Goodman, Richard E. *Karl Terzaghi: The Engineer as Artist.*
   Reston, Va.: American Society of Civil Engineers, 1999.

STANDARD SOURCES

AMS 8, P&B 9–18; Debus (under Karl T. Terzaghi).

TESSIER, MARGUERITE (1895–1991)

*French biologist. Born 1895 in France. Member of the Société de
Biologie. Died 1991.*

Biographical information on Marguerite Tessier is lacking.
We know that she was a member of the Société de Biologie
and published in the *Comptes rendus* of that society.

JH/MBO

SECONDARY SOURCES

"Marguerite Tessier." *Comptes rendus Société Biologie Fil* 185
   (1991): 247–249.

TETSUO, TAMAYO (1888–?)

*Japanese obstetrician and gynecologist. Born 21 January 1888 in
Okayama. Father Chief Buddhist priest of Okayama Prefecture.
Married [?] Tetsuo. Educated Okayama Prefectural Teacher's School
for Girls (graduated 1906); Tokyo Women's Medical School (M.D.,
1918) ; Tokyo Imperial University, postdoctoral work in gynecology
(1918–1919). Professional experience: Selon Girls' School, teacher
(1906–1907?); Kuchinozu Girls' School, teacher (1907–1914);
Buddhist Medical Hospital, Azabu, chief of gynecology (1919–
1920); private practice (1920–?); Tetsuo General Hospital, Kuchinozu, founder and chief of gynecology and obstetrics (1920–?);
Kuchinozu School for Midwives and Nurses, founder and professor
of gynecology and obstetrics (1927–1941). Concurrent experience:
Kuchika High School, school doctor (1923–1962). Honors and
memberships: Japan Medical Women's Association, president (forty
years); Medical Women's International Association, delegate from
Japan (1960); Honorary Citizen of Kuchinozu (1968); Sixth
Order of the Sacred Treasure (1969). Death date unknown.*

Tamayo Tetsuo was born in the Okayama Prefecture, where
her father was chief Buddhist priest. She was an excellent
student, such that her teachers suggested she become a
teacher. She studied at the regional education school. For the
following seven years, she taught in girls' grammar schools,
first in Selon and then in Kuchinozu, to which her parents
had moved.

   After her brother entered medicine and her sister married
a gynecologist, Tamayo decided to study medicine at the
Tokyo Women's Medical School under the famous woman
physician Yakoi Yoshioka, much as SHIGEYO TAKEUCHI had

done twelve years earlier. Although her parents were initially
opposed to her plan, wishing her to marry, she successfully studied for the entrance examination and gained their
support.

   After graduating from medical school, she took a further
year at the Tokyo Imperial University to qualify herself in
gynecology. She then volunteered for a year at the Buddhist
Medical Hospital in Asabu and served as chief of gynecology. Having in the meantime married a surgeon, she, with
her brother and her husband, founded a hospital in Kuchinozu. She became the chief of gynecology and obstetrics in
the new hospital and found herself very busy as one of only
two specialists in her field in the entire region. Seven years
later, Tetsuo also founded a school for midwives and nurses,
which continued to grow until the start of World War II
closed down the nursing school. With all her other work,
she also took time to serve as a school doctor for thirty-nine
years.

   Tetsuo had always been interested in the general health of
her patients, and she became especially interested in nutrition and the early detection and prevention of infectious diseases as the war progressed. After the war, she continued her
medical practice, but also worked with the Japanese Medical
Women's Association in the evenings. In 1960, she was one
of nineteen delegates from Japan to the Medical Women's
International Association.

   In her eighties, a number of honors came her way; she
was made the first Honorary Citizen of Kuchinozu and the
following year, received her government's honor of the
Sixth Order of the Sacred Treasure. JH/MBO

PRIMARY SOURCES

"Tetsuo, Tamayo." In Hellstedt, *Autobiographies.*

THEANO (late 6th century B.C.E.)

*Greek philosopher, mathematician, and physician. Flourished in the
last part of the sixth century B.C.E. Father, Brontinus. Husband,
Pythagoras.*

According to one tradition Theano was the wife of Pythagoras and in another, his student. And in still another she
was Pythagoras's daughter and Brontinus's wife. Sometimes
she is reported to be a woman from Crete—the daughter of
Pythonax. Other sources indicate that she was a Crotonian
and the daughter of Brontinus or Brontinos, Pythagoras's
successor. Even more confusing, the number and names of
the children attributed to Theano and Pythagoras vary. Although no writings of Theano are extant, an apocryphal literature written in her name has emerged. These writings are
classified into three groups. The first group stems, at the latest, from the fourth to the third century B.C.E. and consists of

a collection of apothegms that do not possess any obvious mathematical Pythagorean ingredients. The Pythagorean ideas on the transmigration of souls and on the soul's immortality appear in one apothegm. The second group of writings presupposes the apothegms. The third group consists of pseudo-Pythagorean literature in her name. One work, *On Piety,* refers to her ideas on the nature of objects. In it she indicates that Pythagoras did not mean that numbers generated bodies, but that bodies imitate numbers. Tradition places medicine among her areas of knowledge.

Discerning what Theano did or did not know or do is as difficult as discovering the same information about Pythagoras himself. In addition to the cult of secrecy surrounding Pythagoreanism, the practice of ascribing all ideas of importance introduced by members of the school to Pythagoras himself carried over to Theano. Since the Pythagorean mathematical apocrypha surfaced much later than the earlier apothegms, it is dangerous to assume that they convey the words or even the ideas of Theano. That Theano continued to operate the school of Pythagoras after his death is often affirmed but not confirmed. Thus, it can only be stated that, according to tradition, Theano was a mathematician, a physician, and an administrator—someone who kept alive an important training ground for future mathematicians.

JH/MBO

SECONDARY SOURCES
Plutarch. "Advice to Bride and Groom." *Morals* 31.48. Refers to Theano.
Porphyrius. *Vita Pythagorae.* In *The Presocratic Philosophers: A Critical History with a Selection of Texts,* ed. G. E. Kirk and J. E. Raven. Cambridge: Cambridge University Press. Only fragments remain, but contains some information on Theano.

STANDARD SOURCES
Lipinska; Mozans; Ogilvie 1986; Pauly-Wissowa, vol. 5; Waithe.

THELANDER, HULDA EVELIN (1896–1988)

U.S. pediatrician. Born 11 January 1896 in Little Falls, Minn., to Ida (Olson) and John August. Educated University of Minnesota (M.A., 1924; M.D., 1925). Professional experience: private practice, China (1925–1926), San Francisco (1926–1968); University of California, San Francisco, clinical professor of pediatrics (1948–1963); Children's Hospital, San Francisco, chief of pediatrics (1951–1961). Concurrent experience: Stanford Medical School, clinical pediatric instruction. Honors and memberships: Muscular Dystrophy Association, muscular dystrophy award (1958); Varsity Club International, humanitarian award (1964); National Board of Pediatrics, diplomate; American Pediatrics Society; World Medical Asociation; American Association of Mental Deficiency. Died 15 February 1988, in San Francisco.

Born and educated in Minnesota, Hulda Thelander spent a single year in China soon after she finished her medical degree. The rest of her career, she practiced and taught pediatric medicine in San Francisco. After some twenty years in private practice, she was made clinical professor at the University of California, San Francisco, and later at Stanford Medical School, while serving as chief of pediatrics at the Children's Hospital.

Thelander's work on chronic mental and physical disorders was recognized by awards from the Muscular Dystrophy Association (for her study of that debilitating disease in children) and the Varsity Club International (for her work with children with chronic mental and physical disorders). She also published extensively in her field, particularly on child development, childhood diseases, and chronic and debilitating disorders. Thelander deposited her papers in the Baker Research Library of the California Historical Society.

JH/MBO

STANDARD SOURCES
Debus.

THELBERG, ELIZABETH (BURR) (1860–1935)

U.S. physician. Born 29 October 1860 in Bangor, Maine, to Sarah Buck (Morrill) and Joseph J. Burr. Married John Thelberg (25 December 1883). One daughter, Elizabeth. Educated Woman's Medical College, New York City (M.D., 1884). Professional experience: Woman's Medical College of the New York Infirmary, assistant professor of eye and ear and children's diseases (1885–1886); Infant Asylum and Nursery and Childrens Hospital, New York City, resident (1886–1887); Vassar College, professor of physiology and hygiene and resident physician (1887–1889; 1892–1930). Honors and memberships: American Women's Hospitals, founding member, board member; decorated by the French government for her war work (1924). Died 22 April 1935.

Elizabeth Burr Thelberg was an early professor of physiology at Vassar College. She trained at the Woman's Medical College of New York at the time that EMILY BLACKWELL and MARY PUTNAM JACOBI were teaching there. Like Mary Putnam Jacobi, she was interested both in children's diseases and in physiology.

Thelberg married when she was twenty-three, shortly before she finished her medical studies. She then taught diseases of the eye and ear and children's diseases at her medical school the following year, before she obtained a residency at the Infant Asylum and Nursery and Children's Hospital in New York City.

When Thelberg was twenty-seven, she was appointed resident physician and professor of hygiene at Vassar College. She remained there for the rest of her professional life, except for the period during World War I when she helped found the American Women's Hospitals and spent some time in France.

Thelberg was a student and admirer of Dr. ELIZABETH CUSHIER, and she edited Cushier's autobiography shortly before her own death.   JH/MBO

PRIMARY SOURCES
Thelberg, Elizabeth B., ed. "Autobiography of Elizabeth Cushier." *Medical Review of Reviews* 39 (1933): 121–131.

STANDARD SOURCES
Lovejoy; *WWW(A)*.

THELKA, SAINT (late 3d century C.E.)
Seleucian healer. Flourished late third century C.E.

Saint Thelka was a medical woman who reputedly was martyred during the Diocletian persecution of Christians.

STANDARD SOURCES
Hurd-Mead 1938.

THEODORA, EMPRESS (d. 548)
Empress and founder of hospitals. Wife of Justinian (483?–565), Emperor of Byzantine Empire.

While she was empress, Theodora founded hospitals for the sick throughout the Byzantine Empire. The plans for her hospitals were developed by others. She attempted to wipe out prostitution and had the household water for Constantinople collected and stored in large cisterns which she had built under the city to prevent pollution.   JH/MBO

SECONDARY SOURCES
Browning, Robert. *Justinian and Theodora*. London: Weidenfeld and Nicolson, 1971. Rev. ed., 1987.

THEODOSIA, SAINT (3d century C.E.)
Roman physician.

Saint Theodosia was a Christian martyr who practiced medicine in Rome and was killed during the persecutions of Diocletian. She is variously described as the mother and the "relative" of Saint Procopius of Gaza (465–528). She repre-

sents a class of early Christian female physicians who ministered to the poor.   JH/MBO

SECONDARY SOURCES
Nicephorus, Saint (Nicephorus Callistus Xanthopuli). "Ecclesiasticae historiae." In *Patrologiae cursus completus*, Series Graeca. Paris: Migne, 1856–1887. See volume 8, page 15.

STANDARD SOURCES
Hurd-Mead 1938; Mozans.

THEOSEBEIA (3d century C.E.)
Egyptian alchemist. Flourished third century C.E. Sister or friend of Zosimus of Panopolis. Professional experience: Collaborated with Zosimus on a chemical encyclopedia.

Because of the veil of secrecy surrounding alchemists, little is known of Theosebeia. She is sometimes considered to be the sister of the famous alchemist Zosimus, but elsewhere is known as his wife. She reputedly collaborated on a twenty-eight-book encyclopedia of chemistry, *Cheirokmeta*, based on the ideas of MARY THE JEWESS (Maria) and CLEOPATRA. Greek and Syrian translations of sections of this work are extant. Also extant are letters on alchemy from Zosimus to Theosebeia that include a diatribe against the female alchemist PAPHNUTIA.   JH/MBO

STANDARD SOURCES
Alic.

THISELTON-DYER, LADY HARRIET ANN (HOOKER) (1854–1945)
British botanist and botanical illustrator. Daughter of Frances (Henslow) and Joseph Dalton Hooker. Married William Thiselton-Dyer 23 June 1877. Died 1945.

Harriet Ann Hooker grew up in a family with a strong botanical history. Her father was the famous botanist Joseph Dalton Hooker, friend of Charles Darwin and head of the Royal Botanical Gardens at Kew. Her maternal grandfather was the botanist John S. Henslow and her paternal grandfather was the botanist William Hooker, whose wife was a member of the Turner family.

After her marriage to William Thiselton-Dyer (who succeeded her father as head of Kew), she began to follow in the tradition of women on both sides of her family who assisted their husbands in their botanical work with both observations and illustrations.   JH

SECONDARY SOURCES

Mea, Allan. *The Hookers of Kew, 1785–1911.* London: Michael Joseph, 1967.

STANDARD SOURCES

Debus (under Joseph Dalton Hooker and William Thiselton-Dyer); Desmond.

THODAY, MARY GLADYS SYKES
(ca. 1884–1943)

See Sykes, Mary Gladys.

THOMAS, CAROLINE (BEDELL) (1904–1997)

U.S. physiologist. Born 29 November 1904 in Ithaca, N.Y., to Mary (Crehore) and Frederick Bedell. Married Henry M. Thomas, Jr. (1934). Three children, Henry M., Jr., Eleanor Carey, and Mary Whitall. Educated Smith College (A.B., 1925); Johns Hopkins University (Smith alumnae fellow, 1925–1926; M.D., 1930). Professional experience: Johns Hopkins Hospital, house officer, department of medicine (1930–1931), assistant resident (1931–1933), assistant in medicine, Johns Hopkins School of Medicine (1931–1933); Harvard University, national research fellow, department of neuropathology (1933–1934); Hopkins Medical School, fellow in physiology (1934–1935), instructor of medicine, physiology division (1935–1941), assistant professor (1941–1952), associate professor (1952–1970), School of Hygiene and Public Health, instructor in preventive medicine (1947–1952), lecturer (from 1960). Died 14 December 1977.

Caroline Thomas did much of her professional work at Johns Hopkins Medical School. She received her medical degree in 1930 and married in 1934, after she had completed her internship, residency, and a fellowship at Harvard University. While raising three children, she rose through the academic ranks at the Johns Hopkins Medical School. Her highest rank was associate professor. She was a member of the American Foundation for High Blood Pressure and was civilian medical consultant for the Secretary of War from 1943 to 1945. She was a member of American Physicians, the Physiological Society, the American Heart Association, and the College of Physicians.

During World War II, Thomas was a consultant for the Surgeon General of the Army (1944–1946) and from 1959 a consultant for the Smith College Health Committee. Among her awards were the James D. Bruce Memorial Award in Preventive Medicine (1957) and the Elizabeth Blackwell citation of the New York Infirmary (1958). She was a diplomate of the American Board of Internal Medicine and a Fellow of the American Cardiac Physicians, the Association of American Physicians, the American Heart Association, the Council for High Blood Pressure Research, and the Council on Epidemiology. She was a member of the American Medical Association, the American Physiological Society, the American Society for Clinical Investigation, Phi Beta Kappa, and Sigma Xi.

Thomas's research involved cardiovascular problems, specifically cardiac arrhythmias and cerebral circulation. She worked on experimental hypertension, the precursors of human hypertension, and coronary artery disease. Since rheumatic fever often resulted in heart damage, she published pioneer work on the prevention of this disease.

An extensive collection of her papers and her portrait are held in the Alan Chesney Medical Archives, Johns Hopkins School of Medicine.   JH/MBO

PRIMARY SOURCES

Thomas, Caroline. *The Precursors of Essential Hypertension and Coronary Artery Disease: Characteristics of the Johns Hopkins Medical Students.* (Baltimore: Johns Hopkins School of Medicine) 4 vols (v.1. 1948–1959. v.2. 1959–1962. v.3. 1963–1970. v.4. 1971–1977).

———.With D. C. Ross and E. S. Freed. *An Index of Rorschach Responses.* Baltimore: Johns Hopkins Press, 1964.

———. With Donald C. Ross and Elaine S. Freed. *An Index of Responses to the Group Rorschach Test.* Baltimore: Johns Hopkins Press, 1965.

———. *An Atlas of Figure Drawings.* Baltimore: Johns Hopkins Press, 1966.

STANDARD SOURCES

AMS 6–8, B 9, P&B 10–11; Debus; *NAW* (article by Madeleine B. Stern).

THOMAS, DOROTHY SWAINE (THOMAS)
(1899–1977)

U.S. sociologist. Born 24 October 1899 in Baltimore, Md., to Sarah (Swaine) and John Knight Thomas. Married William Isaac Thomas (1935). Educated Columbia (A.B., 1922); University of London (Ph.D., 1924). Professional experience: Federal Research Bank, research assistant (1924); Social Science Research Council, fellow (1925–1926); Laura Spellman Rockefeller Fund, researcher (1926); Columbia University Teachers College, research assistant through assistant professor (1927–1930); Yale University, research associate through associate professor (1931–1935), director of research in social science (1935–1939); Carnegie Corporation, Study of Negro in America (1939–1940); University of California, lecturer in sociology (1940–1941), professor of rural sociology (1941–1948); University of Pennsylvania, professor (1948–1970); Georgetown University, Washington, professorial lecturer (1972–1977). Concurrent experience: University of Stockholm, visiting professor (1933, 1935, 1936); New York State Research Foundation for Mental Hygiene, consultant; Federal Emergency Relief Administration, special analyst (1935–1936). Honors and memberships: London School of Economics, Hutchinson Research Medal (1924); University of Pennsylvania, honorary D.Sc. (1970); American Statistical Association, Fellow; American Sociological Society (president, 1952); American Philosophical Society (council, 1966–1967). Died 1 May 1977.

Dorothy Swaine Thomas, the well-respected sociologist, obtained her first degree from Columbia University and then traveled to the London School of Economics, University of London, where she studied for a doctorate in economics. When she returned to the United States, she worked closely with the sociologist William Isaac Thomas, whom she married ten years later. Her position as lecturer at Columbia University Teachers College prepared her for a successful research and teaching career at Yale, where she rose from research associate to associate professor and then, in the late 1930s, to director of research in social science. Her study, with Richard S. Nishimito, of Japanese-Americans and their reaction to discrimination and internment during World War II (*The Spoilage*) has become a classic.

In 1948 she went to the University of Pennsylvania as professor of sociology, where she remained for twenty-two years. During this period she was also director of the Population Research Center. After leaving the University of Pennsylvania, Thomas spent five years at George Washington University. For three different years, she was a visiting professor at the University of Stockholm. Her research interests were social demography, population change and economic development, and migration studies.   JH/MBO

PRIMARY SOURCES

Thomas, Dorothy Swaine. *Social Aspects of the Business Cycle.* London: G. Routledge and Sons, Ltd., 1925.

———. With W. I. Thomas. *The Child in America.* New York: A. A. Knopf, 1928.

———. *Social and Economic Aspects of Swedish Population Movements.* New York: Macmillan, 1941.

———. With Richard S. Nishimito. *The Spoilage.* Berkeley: University of California Press, 1946.

———. With others. *Population Redistribution and Economic Growth, United States (1870–1950).* 3 vols. Ann Arbor, Mich.: Interdisciplinary Consortium for Political and Social Research, 1982. First published 1957–1964.

STANDARD SOURCES
AMS S&B 9–12; *WWW(A)*.

THOMAS, ETHEL NANCY MILES (1882?–1944)
British botanist. Born in London to Mary Emily Davies and David Miles Thomas. Married Hugh Henry Francis Hyndeman (ca. 1930; he died 1934). Educated Imperial College of Science and Technology; University College, University of London (B.A.; D.Sc., 1914). Professional experience: assistant to Ethel Sargent (1897–1901); Bedford College, lecturer (1908–1916); University College, Cardiff, Department of Botany, acting head (1918–1919); National Museum, Wales, keeper of botany (1919–1921); University College, Leicester (1923–1937). Concurrent experience: University College, reader (1912–1916); Woman's Land Army, inspector (1916–1918). Honors and memberships: Fellow of Linnean Society (1908), council member (1910–1915); University College, London, fellow; British Association for the Advancement of Science; University College, gold medal; Apothecaries Society Prize. Died 28 August 1944.

In spite of the importance of Ethel Nancy Miles Thomas as a botanist, very little is known of her early life. She was educated at Mays High School (Home and Colonial) and then studied at University College, London, and the Imperial College for Science and Technology.

After studying botany, Thomas was for four years an assistant to the distinguished botanist, ETHEL SARGANT. During this period, she published a paper of some significance that extended the findings of the French botanist Guignard on "double fertilization" in the embryo sac of the angiosperm, published in 1900 in the *Annals of Botany*. Thomas also worked as an assistant to A. G. Tansley, who introduced her to the problems of seedling anatomy. She carried out important work on the theory of the "double leaf trace," published in the *New Phytologist* in 1907, before she received her doctoral degree from University of London.

Soon after, Thomas began to lecture at Bedford College, like many other women scientists of her time. She held a concurrent position as reader in botany at the University of London. About this same time, Thomas was elected as one of the first women Fellows of the Linnean Society. She served on the council over a six-year period. She also was active in the British Association for the Advancement of Science and was remembered fondly by fellow members. University College, London, also recognized her with a fellowship.

During World War I, Thomas did pathological work for the War Office and the Medical Research Council. After her lectureship at Bedford College ended in 1916, she joined the Woman's Land Army for two years. After the war, following a year as acting head of the department of botany at the University of Cardiff, Thomas served for three years as the keeper of botany at the National Museum of Wales. Then she was offered a position at University College, Leicester, which she held for fourteen years. She was remembered as an excellent teacher who had unbounded enthusiasm.

Thomas was a strong feminist and deeply interested in supporting women's careers. She married a barrister, Henry H. F. Hyndman, when she was well into her academic career and was badly affected by his sudden death a few years later in 1934, a shock that appeared to have affected her memory and hastened her death. She retired three years later and had a complete breakdown in health in 1940. At that point, her slides and records were catalogued and placed in the Jodrell Laboratory at Kew.

JH/MBO

PRIMARY SOURCES

Thomas, Ethel N. "On the Presence of Vermiform Nuclei in a Dicotyledon." *Annals of Botany* 14 (1900): 318–319.

———. "Some Aspects of 'Double Fertilisation' in Plants." *Scientific Progress* 3 (1907). Printed first in *New Phytologist,* 1907.

———. "Seedling Anatomy of Ranales, Rhoeadales, and Rosales." *Annals of Botany* 38 (1914): 695–733. Thomas's thesis.

SECONDARY SOURCES

Delft, E.M. "Dr. E. N. Miles Thomas." *Proceedings of the Linnean Society* 136 (1944): 235–236. Obituary notice.

"Dr. E. N. Miles Thomas." *Nature* (14 October 1944).

STANDARD SOURCES

Barnhart; Debus; Desmond; *WW* 1926.

THOMAS, MARY FRAME (MYERS) (1816–1888)

U.S. pioneer physician and suffragist. Born 28 October 1816 in Bucks County, Pa., to Mary (Frame) and Samuel Myers. One sister, seven stepsiblings. Married Owen Thomas (1839). Three daughters. Educated at home in Silver Spring, Md., Washington, D.C., and at local district schools in Ohio. Studied medicine with her husband (1849–1853); Western Reserve College of Medicine (1853–1854); Female Medical School of Pennsylvania (later Woman's Medical College of Pennsylvania) (M.D., 1856). Professional experience: private practice in Richmond, Ind., assistant physician with husband (1856–1862), physician (1864–1885); Sanitary Commission, Civil War, physician (1862–1864). Honors and memberships: Wayne County (Ind.) Medical Society (1875; president, 1887); Indiana State Medical Society (1876); Indiana Woman Suffrage Association (1855–1861; 1869–1888), president (1881?–1885); American Woman Suffrage Association, president (1880); Woman's Christian Temperance (state superintendant of franchise). Died 19 August 1888 in Richmond City, Ind., of dysentery.

Like her stepsister, HANNAH E. LONGSHORE, Mary Frame Myers Thomas was a pioneer physician, one of the first to attend the Female Medical School of Pennsylvania, later the Woman's Medical College of Pennsylvania. Mary Myers was born at the home of her grandmother to the first wife of her father, Samuel Myers, a strong Quaker and active abolitionist. Growing up, she lived in the area around Washington, D.C., and then in Ohio. After her mother's death, her father married again and had five more daughters and two sons.

Educated by her father and then in local schools, Mary Myers married a young doctor, Owen Thomas, when she was twenty-three and began to study medicine privately with her husband soon after the birth of her first daughter. When the family moved to Indiana near Fort Wayne, Thomas determined to expand her medical education by entering the Female Medical School of Pennsylvania, from which her stepsister Hannah Longshore had recently graduated and where she was the demonstrator in anatomy. Although the illness and death of her oldest daughter interrupted her study, Thomas took her medical degree in 1856, along the way studying with her husband at the Western Reserve Medical School in Cleveland. The two then began to practice medicine in Richmond City, Indiana, with Thomas at first acting as an assistant to her husband.

At the beginning of the Civil War, both Thomas and her husband began to work with the Sanitary Commission under the army, helping to tend wounded soldiers, most memorably those wounded in the battle of Vicksburg. When her husband, as an army contract physician, moved to Nashville, Tennessee, to assist refugees there, Thomas accompanied him as assistant physician.

When the two returned to Richmond City, Indiana, Thomas began to work with African-Americans in the city hospitals. There, she also served for eight years on the city board of health and founded a Home for Friendless Girls. Although she took over the major part of the practice with her husband, while he began to restrict his practice to dentistry, she was admitted to the county medical society only in 1875, and to the state medical society the following year. Five years later, her contibutions were recognized in her election to the presidency of the state medical society. During this period, Thomas was active in placing women physicians in state hospitals to care for female patients.

From the time she was a young girl and heard Lucretia Mott speak on behalf of women's rights, Thomas was a strong supporter of women's suffrage. In the pre–Civil War years, she edited suffrage magazines. She represented Indiana in the Woman's Rights Association, was a delegate to the national suffrage conference, and even served as president for a year of the American Woman Suffrage Association in 1880. She resigned from the presidency of the state association five years later only because of her failing health. Her youngest daughter, Julia Josephine (Thomas) Irvine became the fourth president of Wellesley College.

Although brought up a Quaker, Thomas was active in the Methodist Church in later life, working through that church on behalf of various social movements. Members of the black sister church, the African Methodist Episcopal Church, attended her funeral as well as representatives of other groups for whom she had been an important figure.

JH/MBO

SECONDARY SOURCES
Waite, Frederick. "The Three Myers Sisters—Pioneer Women Physicians." *Medical Review of Reviews* (March 1933).

STANDARD SOURCES
NAW (article by Clifton J. Phillips).

THOME, FRANCES (d. 1916)

U.S. astronomer. Married John Thome. Worked at National Observatory, Córdoba, Argentina, then served as director. Died 1916.

Frances Thome married the astronomer John Thome, who moved from the United States to direct the National Observatory of Argentina at Córdoba. For over twenty years she worked in close association with him in residence at the observatory. She took part in recording her husband's star survey catalogue—*Córdoba Durchmusterung,* a visual survey of southern stars in specific declination zones. She was not only one of the scientific observers but prepared this major publication for the press. She also worked on the publication of the meridian results. Following the death of her husband in 1908, she took over the direction of the observatory until her own death in 1916.

JH/MBO

PRIMARY SOURCES
Thome, Frances. With John M. Thome. *Córdoba Durchmusterung: Zonas de Exploracion.* Buenos Aires: Coni, 1892–1914. The star survey continued after the deaths of Frances and John Thome, until 1930. It was republished in 1993 with additional data and corrections by the Astronomical Data Section of the U.S. National Aeronautics Space Administration.

SECONDARY SOURCES
"Mrs. Frances Thome." *Science* 43 (916): 710.

STANDARD SOURCES
Barr.

THOMPSON, CAROLINE BURLING (1869–1921)

U.S. zoologist. Born 27 June 1869 in Philadelphia, Pa. Never married. Educated University of Pennsylvania (B.S., 1898; Ph.D., 1901). Professional experience: private school teacher of zoology, mathematics, and science; Wellesley College, instructor (1901) to full professor (1916–1921); U.S. Department of Agriculture, Bureau of Entomology, collaborator (1917–1921). Memberships: Society of Zoology; Boston Society of Natural History. Died 5 December 1921.

Known for her excellence in teaching and for her originality and thoroughness in biological research, Caroline Burling Thompson influenced countless students during her years at Wellesley College. While she took part in research on marine life at Naples, Italy, and Woods Hole, Massachusetts, her most outstanding work was on termites. She published her first paper on termites in 1916 in which she proved, through study of the brain and frontal gland, that there was little differentiation between the brains of the different castes of termite and none between the sexes. In 1917, a paper on the origin of the castes of a common termite revealed that reproductive queens were "created" through special feedings by workers. Her paper of 1919 discussed the phylogeny of the termite castes and outlined breeding experiments that were in progress at the time of her death. Due to her expertise, Thompson worked with the Branch of Forest Entomology, Bureau of Entomology, U.S. Department of Agriculture (from 1917).

Caroline Thompson had planned an in-depth study of the honeybee, similar to her work with termites, but ill health interfered. She was also working with coauthors on a book on the termite for laypersons or students at the time of her death.

Thompson chose to open new fields and to look for scientific fact in place of popular fantasy regarding the social insects. She was not deterred by long-held theories but searched for her own answers.

JH/MBO

PRIMARY SOURCES
Thompson, Caroline. "The Structure and Development of Internal Phloem in *Geisenium sempervirens, Ait.*" *American Naturalist* 32 (1898): 110.
———. "Preliminary Description of *Zygeupolia litoralis,* a New Genus and New Species of Heteromertean." *Zoologischer Anzeiger* 23 (1900): 151–153.
———. "*Carinoma tremaphoros,* a New Mesonemertean Species." *Zool. Anzeiger* 23 (1900): 627–630.

SECONDARY SOURCES
T.E.S. "Caroline Burling Thompson, 1869–1921." *Science* 55 (1922): 40–41.

STANDARD SOURCES
AMS 1; Bailey; *Catalogue Royal Society;* Siegel and Finley.

THOMPSON, CLARA MABEL (1893–1958)

U.S. psychiatrist. Born 3 October 1893 in Providence, R.I., to Clara Louise (Medhery) and Thomas Franklin Thompson. Educated Classical High School (1908–1912); Brown University (A.B., 1916); Johns Hopkins University (M.D., 1920); studied with Sandor Ferenczi, Budapest (1929–1933). Professional experience: Phipps Psychiatric Clinic, Johns Hopkins Hospital, intern (1920–1921), resident in psychiatry (1923–1925); New York Infirmary for Women and Children, intern (1921–1922); Vassar College, Institute of Euthenics, physician (1928–1929); New York Psychoanalytic Institute, training analyst (1936–1941); Washington School of Psychiatry (New York branch), assistant executive director (1943–1946); William Alanson White Institute of Psychiatry, executive director (1946–1958). Honors and memberships: American Institute of Psychoanalysis (to 1943). Founded Washington School of Psychiatry, New York Branch (1943), later the William Alanson White Institute. Died 20 December 1958 in New York City of cancer.

Clara Thompson had a strict religious background, and even planned to take medical training to practice as a medical missionary. Her plans changed during her medical training. She met and was at first heavily influenced by Harry Stack Sullivan at Johns Hopkins. She began to study psychiatry and worked with Sullivan at the Phipps Psychiatric Clinic.

When Thompson decided to undergo psychoanalysis as part of her training, she went to Hungary to study with the Freudian psychoanalyst Sandor Ferenczi. On her return, she formed part of the "Zodiac" group in New York that welcomed both Eric Fromm and KAREN HORNEY. Thompson collaborated closely with Horney for some ten years; however when Fromm, who had no medical degree, was denied the right to practice psychoanalysis by the American Institute of Psychoanalysis, Thompson found herself in opposition to Horney. She joined Fromm in establishing a new psychoanalytic group, the New York Branch of the Washington School of Psychiatry, later renamed the William Alanson White Institute, and became the executive director.

Thompson's writings had particular significance for women. She wrote first for Harry Stack Sullivan on adolescent sexuality, and later in 1943 on "penis envy" in women, denying the biological basis for penis envy. She also wrote on the nature of the psychoanalysis she was in the process of developing.

In her early forties, Thompson met a Hungarian artist, Henry Major, with whom she established a long-term love relationship in spite of his marriage. She spent ten happy summers with him in Provincetown, Massachusetts, until his death in the late 1940s. She developed cancer in the late 1950s and died in her apartment in New York. JH/MBO

PRIMARY SOURCES

Thompson, Clara. "Notes on Female Adolescence." In *Personal Psychopathology*, ed. Harry Stack Sullivan, 245–264. Washington, D.C.: William Alanson White Psychiatric Foundation, 1965.

———. *Interpersonal Psychoanalysis: The Selected Papers of Clara M. Thompson.* Ed. Maurice R. Green. New York: Basic Books, 1964. Includes a collection of Thomas's later articles.

———. *Psychoanalysis: Evolution and Development.* New York: Thomas Nelson and Sons, 1950.

A bibliography of Thompson's earlier writings is found in *Psychiatry* (1947): 237–238, which includes her important "Penis Envy in Women" (1943).

STANDARD SOURCES

NAW (M) (article by Helen Swick Perry); *WWW(A)*, vol. 3, 1951–1960.

THOMPSON, HELEN (1897–1978)

U.S. psychologist. Born 14 March 1897 in Huntington, N.Y. Educated Vassar College (A.B., 1919); Columbia University (M.A., 1923; Ph.D., 1927). Professional experience: Kentucky College for Women, professor of mathematics (1919–1922); Columbia University Teachers College, assistant (1924–1925); Lincoln School, teacher (1925–1926); Yale University, psychological clinic, research associate in anthropometry and statistics (1926–1931), clinic for child development, researcher in biometry (1931–1941); Cannon Street Health Center, New York City, attending psychologist (1939–1947); Columbia University, lecturer in psychology (1947–1949), consulting psychologist (from 1949); Spence-Chapin Adoption Service, New York City, consultant (1941–1945); New York University Bellevue Medical Center, associate psychologist (from 1941), assistant attending psychologist (1946–1949), assistant clinical professor (from 1949). Died 12 January 1978.

Helen Thompson studied infant and child behavior. She found reading problems of deaf children particularly challenging and did an experimental study of the early reading by deaf-mutes. She also studied genetic and developmental psychology in twins, using her training and expertise in the area of statistics. Thompson did research in biometry in the 1920s and 1930s. In the forties and fifties she practiced clinical psychology in New York through the New York Bellevue Medical Center.

Thompson was a Fellow of the American Psychological Association, the Society for Research in Child Development, and New York State Psychological Association. She was an associate Fellow of the New York Academy of Medicine and a member of the Orthopsychiatric Association.

KM

PRIMARY SOURCES

Thompson, Helen. *An Experimental Study of the Beginning Reading of Deaf-Mutes.* New York: Columbia University Teachers College, 1927.

——. With Arnold Lucius Gesell. *Twins T and C from Infancy to Adolescence: A Biogenetic Study of Individual Differences by the Method of Co-Twin Control.* Provincetown, Mass.: Journal Press, 1941.

STANDARD SOURCES

AMS 5–8, S&B 9–11.

THOMPSON, LAURA (1905–)

U.S. anthropologist. Born 23 January 1905 in Honolulu, Hawaii, to Maud Balch and William Thompson. Married Sam Duker (1963). Educated Mills College (B.A., 1927); postgraduate year Radcliffe College (1928); University of California, Berkeley (Ph.D., 1933). Professional experience: Bishop Museum, Honolulu, assistant ethnologist (1929–1934); Government of Guam, consultant (1938–1940); Territory of Hawaii, social scientist (1940–1941); Bureau of Indian Affairs, coordinator, personality research (1941– 1947); Institute of Ethnic Affairs, Washington, D.C., consultant (1947–1954); City College of New York, professor of anthropology (1954–1956); University of North Carolina, faculty (1957); North Carolina State College, Raleigh, visiting lecturer (1959); Pennsylvania State College, visiting faculty (1962); Brooklyn College, City University of New York, lecturer (1964). Field work in Guam; Hawaii; Southwest U.S. among Hopi, Zuni, and Navaho; Iceland; West Saxony; and Fiji. Honors and memberships: Society for Applied Anthropology, founder; American Anthropological Association, Fellow; American Association for the Advancement of Science; New York Academy of Science.

Laura Thompson, the founder of the Society for Applied Anthropology, was born in Honolulu, Hawaii, in 1905. In 1928, she went to the anthropology department at University of California, then under Alfred Kroeber, and after completing her required resident year, went as assistant ethnologist to the Bishop Museum in Honolulu, 1929–1934, obtaining her doctorate in 1933. After two years of doing field work she became a consultant to the government of Guam, then an American territory, from 1938 to 1940. She then went to Fiji to observe the culture, publishing her first major book, *The Fijian Frontier,* in 1940. Thompson returned to what was then the Territory of Hawaii as a social scientist for a year, then left the area with the approaching war in the Pacific. During World War II, she was hired by U.S. government Bureau of Indian Affairs, and remained coordinator of personality research, working in the field among Hopi, Zuni, Navaho, and Papago people until 1947. In 1944, she published another major work, *The Hopi Way,* with Alice

Joseph. Moving to another government bureau, the Institute of Ethnic Affairs, she worked as consultant from 1947 to 1954, publishing studies of the Pacific with her books *Guam and Its People* (1947) and *Culture in Crisis* (1950). Now recognized as a major scholar, she was appointed professor of anthropology, City College of New York from 1954 to 1956. Subsequently she served on the faculty of North Carolina State College, Raleigh, Pennsylvania State College in 1962, and Brooklyn College of the City University of New York, between further field work in Iceland, Guam, and elsewhere. She founded the Society of Applied Anthropology, which reflected her lifelong commitment to working with indigenous people as they adapted to a changing society. Late in life, she married Sam Ducker, 7 June 1963.   JH/MBO

PRIMARY SOURCES

Thompson, Laura. *Fijian Frontier.* San Francisco: American Council, Institute of Pacific Relations, 1940.

——. With Alice Joseph. *The Hopi Way.* Chicago: University of Chicago Press, 1944.

——. *Guam and Its People.* New York: Greenwood Press, 1947.

——. *Culture in Crisis.* New York: Harper, 1950.

——. *Personality and Government.* Mexico City: Ediciones del Instituto Indigenista Interamericano, 1951.

STANDARD SOURCES

AMS 7–8, S&B 9–13; Bailey; Debus.

THOMPSON, MARY HARRIS (1829–1895)

U.S. physician, surgeon. Born 15 April 1829 to Calista (Corbin) and John Harris Thompson in Fort Ann, N.Y. Never married. Educated Troy Conference Academy, Vt.; Fort Edward (N.Y.) Collegiate Institute; New England Female Medical College (M.D., 1863); New York Infirmary for Women and Children, surgical internship (1862); Chicago Medical College, postdoctoral diploma (1869–1870). Professional experience: Fort Edward (N.Y.) Collegiate Institute, teacher; private medical practice in Chicago (1863– 1865); Chicago Hospital for Women and Children, founder and head of medical and surgical staff (1865–1895); Woman's Hospital Medical College, founder (with William H. Byford) (1870), professor of hygiene (1870–1877), professor of obstetrics and gynecology (1877–1895?). Honors and memberships: International Medical Association; Chicago Medical Society; Northwestern University and Chicago Medical College, honorary M.D.s; memorialized by Mary Thompson Women and Children's Hospital. Died 21 May 1895 in Chicago from cerebral hemorrhage.

Mary Thompson spent her early years in Fort Ann, New York, part of Washington County, where her father was the partner in an iron mine. She attended the country school and then a girl's school in Vermont, where she proved to have an apptitude for learning. She went on first to study and then to teach at the Fort Edward (New York) Collegiate Institute. Preparing herself to teach anatomy and physiology in the school, she entered the New England Female Medical College under MARIE ZAKRZEWSKA. She soon decided to become a physician, and after two years of study, she served a year as intern with EMILY BLACKWELL, specializing in surgery, before returning to receive her medical degree.

Thompson left New York and began to practice medicine in Chicago in 1863 during the Civil War. Like MARY FRAME THOMAS, she was active with the Sanitary Commission. There she met a number of other reformers and activists, who helped her to found the Chicago Hospital for Women and Children after the war.

Wishing to sharpen her skills, Thompson entered the Chicago Medical College for postdoctoral training with two other women just starting out in medicine. Although Thompson was allowed to complete her program, in 1870 the college reversed its policy of admission and excluded women.

In 1871, a major fire destroyed the hospital. Within twenty-four hours, the Relief and Aid Society offered to rebuild the hospital on condition that twenty-five patients every year would be treated free of charge. Thompson raised additional funds herself so that construction could begin in 1873. She worked as head of the medical and surgical staff at the Chicago Hospital for Women and Children until her death on 21 May 1895 after a brief illness.

Thompson was also an ardent supporter of women's suffrage. The Chicago Medical College Department of Northwestern University gave Thompson an honorary degree in recognition of her work, the first awarded to a woman. She was a member of the International Medical Association and of the Chicago Medical Society.   JH/MBO

STANDARD SOURCES
NAW (article by Thomas Neville Bonner); Appleton's *Cyclopaedia;* Hurd-Mead 1933; *LKW;* Lovejoy.

THOMPSON, RACHEL FORD (1856–1906)

British botanist and temperance activist. Born 31 August 1856 in York, England. Father Silvanus Thompson. Professional experience: studied Yorkshire flora (1882–1892); assisted F. J. Hanbury. Honors and memberships: Liverpool Botanical Society; Women's Temperance Union. Died 9 December 1906 in Southport, Lancashire.

Rachel Ford Thompson was the daughter of the Quaker botanist Silvanus Thompson, who was schoolmaster at the Friends' School, York. Before her birth, her father had collected and contributed plants and information for H.

Baines's *Flora Yorkshire* (1840). She assisted F. J. Hanbury with his studies and collection of Hieracia and contributed to the *Flora of West Yorkshire* by F. A. Lees, published when she was in her late twenties. Her later collections of Hieracia appeared in C. C. Babington's *Manual of British Botany* (1904). As an active member of the Women's Temperance Union, Thompson was remembered with an obituary at the time of her death by that organization.   JH/MBO

PRIMARY SOURCES
Babington, C. C. *Manual of British Botany.* London: Gurney and Jackson, 1904. Includes Thompson's contributions of *Hieracia,* 232–270.
Lees, F. A. *Flora of West Yorkshire.* London: Lovell, Reeve & Co., 1888. Includes contributions by Thompson.

SECONDARY SOURCES
Journal of Botany 45 (1907): 78.
Proceedings Liverpool Botanical Society 2 (1909): 93. Obituary notice.
Wings (Women's Temperance Union) 25 (1906): 17. Obituary notice; includes portrait.

STANDARD SOURCES
Desmond.

THOMPSON, ROSE ELIZABETH (PAGET) (ca. 1868–?)

See Paget, Rose Elizabeth.

THOMPSON, SYDNEY MARY (ca. 1870–1923)

See Christen, Sydney Mary (Thompson).

THOMS, ADAH B. (SAMUELS) (1863–1943)

U.S. nurse. Born 12 January 1863? in Virginia to Melvine and Harry Samuels. Married (1) [?] Thoms; (2) Harry Smith (1924?). Educated Richmond Va., public schools; normal school; Cooper Union (N.Y.C.); Woman's Infirmary and School of Therapeutic Massage (N.Y.C.) (graduated 1900); Lincoln Hospital Nursing School (R.N., 1905); New York School of Philanthropy (course work); Hunter College (course work); New York School for Social Research. Professional experience: Lincoln Hospital, operating nurse and surgical supervisor (1904–1905), assistant director of nurses (1905–1921), acting head of nurses. Retired 1925. Honors and memberships: National Association of Colored Nurses (1908), founding member, treasurer, president (1916–1925); International Council of Nurses, Cologne, Germany (1912); National Medical Association, Mary Mahoney Medal (1930). Died 21 February 1943 of arteriosclerotic disease and diabetes.

As an African-American growing up in Virginia, Adah Samuels had to overcome prejudices and opposition in her search for a career as a nurse. She first attended a normal school in Virginia with the intention of becoming a teacher, but changed her mind after her marriage to Thoms, who may have been a physician. Little is known about this period of her life. In her late thirties, she moved to New York City, where first she studied elocution at Cooper Union and then began to study nursing. She was accepted at the Woman's Infirmary and School of Massage, the only black woman in a class of thirty. Following her graduation, she worked in New York City and then in a hospital in Raleigh, North Carolina, where she rose to the position of head nurse.

Thoms was dissatisfied with her training and returned to New York to continue her education at the School of Nursing of the Lincoln Hospital and Home, a hospital that recently had moved from Manhattan to Brooklyn in order to treat the poor black population. Her previous training allowed her to work as head nurse at the hospital while finishing her nursing course. Soon she was made assistant director of the nursing school, a post she held for eighteen years. Although she often served as acting director, racial discrimination prevented her from rising to the position of director. She helped to institute the teaching of public health in the nursing school, and she took the course herself.

In 1908, Thoms helped to organize the National Association of Colored Graduate Nurses, sponsoring its first meeting at the Lincoln Hospital. She served as treasurer and later as president. She also attended the International Nursing Council in Cologne, Germany, where, with three other black delegates, she urged the admission of black nurses from Africa, South America, and the Caribbean.

During World War I, Thoms fought hard, as president of the National Association of Colored Graduate Nurses, to gain the admission of black nurses into the American Red Cross. Although the head of the Red Cross agreed, this was vetoed by the Surgeon General of the United States. By 1917, one African-American nurse was enrolled in the Red Cross but given no assignment. By 1918, the great influenza epidemic made the use of all available nurses urgent, and eighteen black nurses were enrolled in the Army Nurse Corps where, although they treated sick soldiers of all backgrounds, they themselves lived in segregated quarters.

After Thoms' retirement from the Lincoln Hospital in 1923, she married for the second time, but her husband died within the year. She continued her activities on behalf of black nurses in the American Nurses Association and the National Organization for Public Health, which eventually led to the incorporation of the National Association of Colored Graduate Nurses into these organizations. She wrote a history of the organization she helped found and was awarded their first medal. Living in Harlem, she continued to lead an active life working with many African-American organizations, including the Urban League. Severe diabetes led to her death from arteriosclerotic complications at age eighty.   JH/MBO

PRIMARY SOURCES

Thoms, Adah B. *Pathfinders: A History of the Progress of Colored Graduate Nurses.* New York: Printed at Kay Printing House, 1929. Includes preface by LILLIAN D. WALD.

SECONDARY SOURCES

Staupers, Mabel Keaton. *No Time for Prejudice: A Story of the Integration of Negroes in Nursing in the United States.* New York: Macmillan, [1961].

STANDARD SOURCES

NAW (article by Mabel Keaton Staupers).

THOMSON, AGNES C. (fl. 1870s–1890s)

British botanist. Niece of botanist Thomas Thomson. Professional experience: plant collector.

Agnes C. Thomson was the niece of the British botanist Thomas Thomson, who was superintendent of the Calcutta Botanic Garden. She corresponded with the botanist G. C. Druce. Agnes Thomson appears to have collected in both Britain and India, possibly while visiting her uncle. Her British and Indian plants are at Oxford.   JH/MBO

STANDARD SOURCES

Desmond.

THOMSON, JANE SMITHSON (ca. 1876–1972)

Irish botanist. Memberships: Dublin Naturalists Field Club; British Bryological Society. Died 29 January 1972 in Dublin.

There is little information on the Irish bryologist Jane Smithson Thomson. Her herbarium is at University College, Galway.   JH/MBO

STANDARD SOURCES

Desmond.

THRING, LYDIA ELIZA DYER (MEREDITH) (1830–1925)

British botanist. Born 4 August 1830 in Brockhurst, Hampshire. Professional experience: collected plants. Died 1925.

Lydia Thring collected and described plants. Her list of Rutland plants was published in the *Uppingham School Magazine* of 1864.

JH/MBO

SECONDARY SOURCES
Horwood, Arthur Reginald, and C. W. F. Noel. *Flora of Leicestershire*. London: Oxford University Press, 1933. Includes portrait of Thring.

STANDARD SOURCES
Desmond.

THURSTONE, THELMA GWINN (1897–1993)

U.S. psychologist. Born 11 December 1897 in Hume, Mo. Father a teacher and supertendent of schools; mother taught music. Two younger brothers. Married Louis Leon Thurstone (d. 1955) in 1924. Three sons. Educated University of Missouri (A.B. in German, 1917; B.S. in education, 1920); Carnegie Institute of Technology (M.A. in psychology, 1923); University of Chicago (Ph.D., 1926). Professional experience: American Council of Education, test editor (1924–1948); Chicago Teachers College, instructor in psychology (1938–1942); University of Chicago, research associate (1942–1952); Frankfurt, Germany, visiting professor of education (1948); Chicago public schools, director, division of child study (1948–1952); Psychometric Lab, University of North Carolina, Chapel Hill, director (1955–1957); Division of Special Education, director (1967–1968); University of North Carolina, Chapel Hill, professor of education (1952–1968); Kabul, Afghanistan, specialist in evaluation (1961); F. P. Graham Center, Child Development Institute, education advisor (1970–1984); Science Research Associates, Child Development Institute, project director (1970–1984). Honors and memberships: American Psychological Association; Psychometric Society; University of North Carolina at Chapel Hill, honorary degree (1979). Died 12 February 1993 in Chapel Hill, N.C.

A skilled psychometrician and creator of psychological tests for over fifty years, Thelma Gwinn Thurstone spent much of her professional life in the shadow of her better known husband, Louis L. Thurstone. In his autobiography, Louis Thurstone described his wife as a "genius in test construction." They were partners in all the research projects carried out in his psychometric laboratory before she became director of the Division of Child Study in the Chicago public schools in the late 1940s. Her recognition as an autonomous psychologist came only after her husband's death in 1955, when she chaired the department of special education at the University of North Carolina and briefly ran the Psychometric Laboratory.

Thelma Gwinn was the oldest of three children and the only girl. With teachers as parents—her father was also superintendent of schools—Thelma and her siblings were expected to excel academically. Thelma graduated from high school at age fifteen and continued her education at the University of Missouri, receiving a baccalaureate degree in German in 1917. For three years she taught high school while earning an additional bachelor's degree in education. She accepted a graduate scholarship at Carnegie Institute of Technology at the invitation of W. W. Charters, formerly at Missouri. Gwinn enrolled as a psychology major in the department in which Louis Leon Thurstone was chair. Gwinn also gained admittance to the previously all-male mathematics courses for engineers in order to improve her knowledge of statistical analysis. She earned her master of arts degree in psychology in 1923.

Gwinn and Thurstone first worked together at the Institute for Government Research in Washington, D.C. (1923–1924), and were married at the end of the year. The couple then moved to Chicago, where Louis Thurstone had accepted a faculty position in psychology. Thelma Thurstone continued to work toward a doctorate while she worked with the American Council of Education (ACE), developing psychological tests and serving as a statistician. She earned her doctorate in psychology in 1926 with a dissertation that was recognized as a pioneering effort in test theory to establish a basic relation between item difficulty and the discriminating power of the test. For the next twenty-five years she and her husband continued to develop tests for the American Council of Education. She also worked with her husband at the Psychometric Laboratory, wrote articles and books with him, served as hostess for guests and seminars at their home, and raised their three sons (born in 1927, 1930, and 1932).

From 1923 to 1948, Thelma and Louis Thurstone developed various the test batteries for the American Council of Education, notably the *ACE Psychological Examination for College Freshmen*, and the *ACE Psychological Examination for High School Students* (grades nine to twelve). In 1938, they constructed an experimental version of the *Chicago Tests of Primary Mental Abilities* that provided the first successful application of factor analysis to large-scale mental testing. In 1946, Science Research Associates (SRA) was formed as a vehicle for publishing the *Primary Mental Abilities* tests, which made possible identification of ability factors for three different age ranges. They also developed abbreviated versions of the ACE tests along with the *SRA Tests of Educational Ability* that provided short-term prediction of achievement for pupils in grades four to twelve.

Thelma Thurstone was the sole author of curricular materials and achievement tests for elementary classrooms. She created the *Learning to Think* series, first published in 1947 and then revised several times. Her *Reading for Understanding* provided materials to assist reading instruction in grades one to twelve.

In 1948, the Thurstones were visiting professors at the University of Frankfurt, Germany. On her return to the States, Thurstone accepted the position of full-time director of the Division of Child Study for the Chicago public schools. There she directed counseling services for students. She played an important role in improving special education in the schools.

When her husband was offered a professorship and invited to establish a psychometric laboratory at the University of North Carolina in the early 1950s, Thelma Thurstone moved with him. She soon found a position as professor in the department of education at UNC. Only three years later, Louis Thurstone died and Thelma Thurstone took over as director of the Psychometric Laboratory, a position that she held for only two years. She continued as project director and investigator in the laboratory.

Besides working on grant projects for the Psychometric Lab, Thurstone served as a Columbia University Teachers College consultant at the University of Kabul, Afghanistan. In the late 1960s, she became senior research scientist at the Frank Porter Graham Child Development Center. She was given an honorary degree and citation from the University of North Carolina at Chapel Hill in 1979. Thelma Thurstone died 12 February 1993 in Chapel Hill.   JH/MBO

PRIMARY SOURCES

Thurstone, Thelma G. With Leon I. Thurstone. *Tests of Primary Mental Abilities.* Chicago: University of Chicago Press, 1938. Thelma Thurstone appears to have prepared the tests for this publication.

———. With Louis Leon Thurstone. *Factorial Studies of Intelligence.* Chicago: University of Chicago Press, [1941].

———. *Learning to Think.* West Hartford: Connecticut Braille, Association, Thurstone Laboratories, 1947. Revised until 1981. For grades K–2.

———. *Reading for Understanding.* N.p.: Science Research Associates, 1958. Revised up to the mid-1980s.

———. *An Evaluation of Educating Mentally Handicapped Children in Special Classes and in Regular Classes.* Chapel Hill: School of Education, University of North Carolina: [ca. 1960].

SECONDARY SOURCES

Jones, Lyle V. "Thelma Gwinn Thurston (1897–1993)." *American Psychologist* 51 (1996), 416–417. Obituary notice.

Thurstone, Louis L. [Autobiography]. In *History of Psychology in Autobiography,* ed. E. Boring. Vol. 4. Worcester, Mass.: Clark University Press, 1930.

STANDARD SOURCES

AMS 5–7, S&B 9–12; Debus; O'Connell and Russo (article by Carolyn T. Bashaw and W. L. Bashaw); Stevens and Gardner.

TIBURTIUS, FRANZISKA (1843–1927)

German physician. Born 24 January 1843 in Bisdamitz in Rügen. Ninth child of a tenant farming family in Rügen. Never married. Educated private school in Stralsund (entered 1852); completed teacher's examination (1866); continued education in London; medical school in Zurich (1871–M.D., 1876). Professional experience: Frauenklinik, Dresden, intern; Berlin, opened practice (1876); Poliklinik für Frauen in Berlin, cofounded with Emilie Lehmus (1878). Retired from practice 1907. Service in welfare work (1914). Died 5 May 1927 in Berlin.

Franziska Tiburtius was the ninth and youngest child of a tenant farmer family on the Baltic Sea island of Rügen. As early as the age of four she was tutored for half an hour each day. In 1852 the family moved to Stralsund, where Franziska attended private school from age nine to age sixteen. After learning home management from her mother for one year, she began working as a governess in 1860. Six years later she graduated from a teacher's training institute and attended an academy for young women in London, where she studied English and tutored the daughter of an English clergyman.

In 1871 she decided to study medicine in Zurich. This decision was influenced by advice offered by her brother Carl and her sister-in-law, HENRIETTE HIRSCHFELD-TIBURTIUS (the first German female dentist). She corresponded with EMILIE LEHMUS of Fürth, who had already begun medical studies in Switzerland.

In 1876 Fransiska Tiburtius passed her medical examinations with a score of "excellent." Further education at a German university, however, seemed out of the question because of prejudices in Germany at the time against women physicians. After a brief internship at the Women's Clinic in Dresden, where Lehmus also worked as a doctor of internal medicine for ten months, Tiburtius opened a practice in Berlin. She was refused permission to receive qualification in medicine or midwifery. Under newly passed legislation regulating the practice of health care she was, however, able to practice "medical science."

Tiburtius, Lehmus, and a former colleague of Tiburtius's from Switzerland were the only women doctors in Berlin for fifteen years. After only a short time, they were seeing tremendous numbers of patients—something that irritated their male colleagues. An anonymous denunciation was made suggesting that Tiburtius's medical degree was invalid because it was not recognized in Prussia. This episode ended happily when she was able to present her Swiss doctorate of medicine. In an effort to avoid future denunciation she added "from the University of Zurich" to the title "Dr. med." on her sign. What her male colleagues had hoped would discourage patients from her practice served instead to impress them; many thought that the longer title reflected additional qualifications. In 1878 a foundation made possible the building of the Poliklinik für Frauen (Women's Polyclinic), founded by Tiburtius and Lehmus, with strong support from Hirschfeld-Tiburtius. Within a brief period both doctors had more patients than they could see. They had to limit their patients to forty a day. A fee of ten pfennige was charged per person and per appointment. A few years later the two doctors were able to add a small infirmary with three beds. The Klinik weiblicher Ärzte (Clinic of Women Physicians) grew from these beginnings.

Franziska Tiburtius's pioneering work was closely connected with the women's movement. She wrote articles for Helene Lange's *Die Frau* in 1898. In 1923 she published her memoirs, *Erinnerungen einer Achtzigjährigen,* which made her better known than her fellow pioneer in medicine, Emilie Lehmus. In 1927 she retired from the practice of medicine after thirty-one years.   G V L

PRIMARY SOURCES

Tiburtius, Franziska. *Erinnerungen einer Achtzigjährigen* (A Journey of Eighty Years) (Selbstbibliograhie). In *Weibliches Schaffen und Wirken* Vol. 1. Berlin: C. A. Schwetschke, 1923.

———. "Frauenuniversität oder gemeinsames Studium?" *Die Frau* (July 1898).

———. *Leprahauser in Osten un Westen.* Leipzig: n.p., 1902.

SECONDARY SOURCES

Berliner Frauen-Kulturinitiative. "Fundorte: 200 Jahre Frauenleben und Frauenbewegung in Berlin." In *Kastalog zur Austellung "Kein Ort nirgends?"* Berlin: Orlanda Frauenverlag, 1987.

Bluhm, Agnes. "Ein Gedenktag der deutschen Medizinerinnen." *Die Ärztin* 17 (1941): 338 ff.

Lück, Conradine. *Frauen: Acht Lebensschicksale.* 1937. Reprint, Neuauflage: Reutlingen, Ensslin & Laiblin, 1952.

[Franziska Tibertius]. Schönfeld, W. In *Pommersche Lebensbilder,* vol. 2. Stettin: L. Saunier, 1936.

STANDARD SOURCES

Lexikon der Frau.

TILDEN, EVELYN BUTLER (1891–?)

U.S. microbiologist. Born 28 March 1891 in Lawrence, Mass., to Harriette (Butler) and Howard Benjamin Tilden. Educated Brown University (A.B., 1913); Columbia University (M.S., 1926; Ph.D., 1929). Professional experience: Rockefeller Institute for Medical Research, assistant in bacteriology and immunology (1928–
1931); Colorado State College, assistant professor (1931–1932); Northwestern University Medical School, Department of Research Bacteriology, research associate (1932–1937); Northwestern University Dental School, Department of Microbiology, associate professor (1942–1948), professor (1948–1954), chairman (1942–1954); National Institutes of Health, Bethesda, Md., microbiologist (1937–1942); Chicago Brookfield Zoo, Animal Hospital, curator of laboratories (1954–1963), curator emerita (1963–post-1968). Honors and memberships: Sigma Xi, Sigma Delta Epsilon, American Society for Microbiology.

After studying microbiology at Columbia, Evelyn Tilden took a position as a researcher at the Rockefeller Institute. After a year in Colorado, she moved to Chicago, where she did research at the medical school; she then moved to Bethesda, Maryland, to continue her research at the National Institutes of Health as a microbiologist. She returned to Northwestern to teach microbiology at the dental school. There she remained for twelve years, rising to full professor and chairman of her department.

In her early sixties, Tilden returned to research as the head of the laboratories of Chicago's Brookfield Zoo. There she remained until her retirement some nine years later. Her research included studies of inclusion conjuctivitis, bacterial production of rare carbohydrates, oral bacteria, fungal endotoxins, and animal infections. She published a textbook on bacteriology in the 1940s.   JH/MBO

PRIMARY SOURCES

Tilden, Evelyn Butler. *Outline of Bacteriology.* Chicago: n.p., 1948.

STANDARD SOURCES

AMS 5–8, B 9, P&B 10–11; Debus.

TILDEN, JOSEPHINE ELIZABETH (1869–1957)

U.S. botanist. Born 1869 in Davenport, Iowa, to Elizabeth Aldrich (Field) and Henry Tilden. Educated University of Minnesota (B.S., 1895; M.S., 1896). Professional experience: University of Minnesota, professor of botany (to 1938); Minnesota Seaside Station, research (summers, 1901–1907); studied and collected algae in Yellowstone, western U.S., Hawaii, Society Islands, New Zealand, Australia, Japan. Honors and memberships: American Association for the Advancement of Science, Fellow; American Geographical Society, member; Torrey Botanical Club, member; Botanical Society; Florida Academy of Science. Died 1957 in Florida.

Josephine Tilden spent her life studying algae. She joined the University of Minnesota faculty soon after she finished her master's degree. Although she never obtained a doctorate, she was internationally recognized as an authority, not only

on local algae, but on the algal stalactites (algae found around thermal springs) in Yellowstone National Park. She expanded her investigations to the South Pacific and Japan. In the 1930s she took a group of ten graduate students around the world to collect algae, traveling to Australia, New Zealand, and Japan. She retired to Golden Bough Colony, Hesperides Lake Wales, Florida.
JH/MBO

PRIMARY SOURCES

Tilden, Josephine Elizabeth. "Note on the Development of a Filamentous Form of *Protococcus* in Entomostracan Appendages." *Botanical Gazette* 19 (1894): 334–335.

———. "List of Fresh-Water Algae Collected in Minnesota during 1893–1897." *Minnesota Botanical Studies* 1 (1894–1898): 25–31, 228–237, 597–600; 2 (1898–1902): 25–29.

———. "On the Morphology of Hepatic Elaters with Special Reference to Branching Elators of *Conocephalus conicus*." *Minnesota Botanical Studies* 1 (1894–1898): 43–53.

———. "A Contribution to the Bibliography of American Algae." *Minnesota Botanical Studies* 1 (1894–1898): 295–421.

———. "A New Oscillatoria from California." *Torrey Botanical Club Bulletin* 23 (1896): 58–59.

———. "Observations on Some West American Thermal Algae." *Botanical Gazette* 25 (1899): 89–105.

———. *Minnesota Algae: The Myxophyceae of North America and Adjacent Regions.* Minneapolis: Authority of the Board of Regents of the University, 1910.

———. *The Algae and Their Life Relations.* London: H. Milford, Oxford University Press, 1935–1937.

STANDARD SOURCES

AMS 1–8, B 9; Bailey; *WWW(A),* vol. 3, 1957–1960.

TIMOFE'EFF-RESSOVSKY, ELENA ALEKSANDROVNA (FIEDLER) (1898–1973)

Russian geneticist. Born 1898 in Russia. Married Nikolai Vladimirovich Timofe'eff-Ressovsky, ca. 1925. Two sons. Educated Moscow State University and Kol'tsov Institute of Experimental Biology. Professional experience: Kol'tsov Institute of Experimental Biology, researcher (1922–1925); Kaiser Wilhelm Institute for Brain Research, research scientist (1925–1948?). Died 1973 in Soviet Union.

Elena Aleksandrovna Fiedler was educated at Moscow State University. There she met her future husband, Nikolai Vladimirovich Timofe'eff-Ressovsky, who, like Fiedler, formed part of the original group of brilliant students who worked and studied in the Kol'tsov Institute of Experimental Biology under the geneticist Sergei Sergeevich Chetverikov. This group established population genetics through the study of the fruit fly, *Drosophila,* brought by H. J. Muller from T. H. Morgan's laboratory at Columbia University.

The couple spent intense summers at the institute's hydrobiological station at Zvenigorod and winters in the laboratory developing the field of population genetics and applying their investigations to evolutionary theory. Another of Chetverikov's students was Theodor Dobzhanksy, who left Russia for Columbia in 1927.

Helena (as she now called herself) Timofe'eff-Ressovsky went with her husband to Germany to Oskar Vogt's Kaiser Wilhelm Institute for Brain Research in 1925 at the request of Vogt, who wanted to add genetics to his institute. In Berlin they set up a department of genetics, although neither husband nor wife as yet had doctoral degrees. In an important experiment, the two collected seventy wild pregnant *Drosophila* and cross-bred them. This experiment, published with Helena as the first author, demonstrated that homozygous offspring of inbred populations could reveal deleterious mutations. According to Mark Adams, population genetics and the early form of evolutionary synthesis developed around students of Chetverikov, through the Timove'eff-Ressovskys in Germany and Dobzhansky in America. Both husband and wife did their most important work before 1940.

When Oskar Vogt and his wife and collaborator CÉCILE VOGT left the Brain Research Institute during the Nazi era, Nikolai Timofe'eff-Ressovsky succeeded Vogt as director. Helena Timofe'eff-Ressovsky had held a paid position until the Nazis came to power, at which point her salary was stopped. Although she continued her research in her husband's laboratory, the Nazis would not allow husbands and wives to work together and both draw salaries.

Although they both considered returning to the Soviet Union before the war, friends advised against it since his friends and her relatives had been arrested during the 1930s purges. The couple decided to remain in Germany rather than risk deportation to Siberia. They continued their research on the genetic load of populations and lethal mutants while managing to stay out of politics.

At the end of World War II, the Russians entered East Germany and at first confirmed Nikolai Timofe'eff-Ressovsky as head of the Brain Research Institute. He was subsequently deported to Russia on suspicion of being a German spy. After he spent some time in a prison camp, he was released to a hospital and then to the Ural Atomic Laboratory, where his work on genetics was recognized as important. Two years after he arrived in Russia, his wife joined him with their younger son, although Nikolai was still technically under arrest.

Two years after Stalin's death, Timofe'eff-Ressovsky was released and initiated a biophysics section within the USSR

Academy of Sciences. In 1956, the couple visited their teacher, the aging Chetverikov, a few years before his death. Chetverikov had been forcibly retired from Gorki University during the Lysenko period and had become partially blind.

The couple began to work at Gorki University, where Nikolai now held a position. Helena continued to work closely with her husband, whose eyesight had also deteriorated badly during his period of imprisonment. Genetics was still a suspect subject in the Soviet Union, and neither scientist received the recognition he or she deserved, although photographs from the early seventies show the couple in happy consultation with scientists from Eastern Europe.

JH/MBO

PRIMARY SOURCES

Timofe'eff-Ressovsky, Helena Alexandrovna. With Nikolai Vladimirovich Timofe'eff-Ressovsky. "Genetische Analyse einer freilebenden *Drosophila melaganogaster* population." *Wilhelm Roux Archiv für Entwicklungsmechanik der Organismen* 109 (1927): 70–109. Some photographs of the Timofe'eff-Ressovskys are in the Caspari Collection at the American Philosophical Society Library, Philadelphia.

SECONDARY SOURCES

Paul, Diane B., and Costas B. Krimbas. "Nikolai V. Timofe'eef-Ressovsky." *Scientific American* (February 1992): 64.

Satzinger, Helga and Annette Vogt. *Elena Aleksandrovna and Nikolaj Vladimirovic Timofe'eef-Ressovsky (1898–1973; 1900–1981).* Berlin: Max Planck Institute for the History of Science 1996. Offprint.

Vogt, Annette. "Elena Aleksandrovna Timoféeva-Ressovskaja (H. A. Timoféeff-Ressovsky)—weit mehr als die 'Frau ihres Mannes.'" In *Festschrift zum 75 Geburtstag von Ilse Jahn,* ed. Kaarl F. Wessel. 1997.

STANDARD SOURCES

DSB (under Sergei Chetverikov and Nikolai Timofe'eff-Ressovsky); Vogt.

TINDALL, ISABELLA MARY (1850–1928)

British botanist. Professional experience: plant collector. Died 1928.

Isabella Tindall collected plants, particularly the hepatics. She contributed to the *Journal of Botany* describing these plants and noting their locations. Tindall's herbarium is now at the Exeter Museum; her plants are at the British museum of Natural History.

JH/MBO

STANDARD SOURCES

Desmond.

TINNE, ALEXANDRINA PETRONELLA FRANCINA (1835–1869)

Dutch explorer, botanical and ethnological collector. Born 17 October 1835 in The Hague, Netherlands, to Harriet (Van Capellen) and Phillip Frederick Tinne. Never married. Educated in science (including botany, geology, and archeology), languages, and logic by governesses at home. Professional experience: White Nile expedition, organizer and leader (1860–1861); Gondokora expedition, organizer and leader (1862); Bahr-al-Gazahl expedition, organizer and leader (1866–1867); Sahara expedition (1869). Died August 1869 of lance wound near Murzuch, Tripoli, North Africa.

Alexandrina Tinne was the daughter of a wealthy Dutch merchant trader and his second wife who had close links to the Dutch court. Her father's first wife had been Scottish and he had moved to Liverpool to expedite his trading in the West Indies, adopting British nationality in order to privately own ships. After his wife's death he returned to The Hague where he married for the second time and remained in the Netherlands.

Alexine (as she was usually called) was well educated by a series of governesses, studying botany, geography (which she loved), archeology, and languages (including Arabic). After her father's death, she and her mother began a series of long journeys to Germany, Scandinavia, Italy, and Egypt. There they became fascinated by the area and spent time in the Holy Land, intrigued by the possibility of outfitting an elaborate expedition to explore the source of the Nile, a focus of many explorations of the time.

Beginning in 1860, Tinne, her mother, and her aunt, Adriana Van Capplen, planned an expedition up the Nile which they outfitted very elaborately. They first traveled to Khartoum and from there, supplied themselves for a voyage up the White Nile with soldiers, boats, animals, and baggage, including photographic equipment used by Tinne. As they traveled to the interior, they also collected large amounts of ethnological items as well as botanical specimens. Two German scientists, ornithologist Baron Theodor van Heuglin and botanist Hermann Steudner, joined their expedition, but some explorers, significantly J. H. Speke, who had just discovered the source of the Nile, warned them of the danger from traveling with so many people, too much baggage, and an excessive number of camels and horses.

The first expeditions were successful. One of the most famous was the Bahr-al-Gazahl Expedition; another one, to Godokora, reached almost to Lake Victoria, although Steudner died from fever in an advance expedition.

Tinne's travels brought her recognition throughout Europe. The Royal Geographical Society in London followed her adventures by presenting reports and letters about her expeditions. She published one large and beautiful book on the botany of the expedition.

Even after her mother died in Africa, Tinne continued her explorations. In an attempt to cross the interior of Africa from Tripoli into the Sahara, her group was set upon by rival Tuareg tribesmen, who struck her with a lance as she emerged from her tent. Her body was not recovered, although rumors continued for years that one of her servants had set up her tomb in a small mosque in an oasis close to where she had been killed.   JH/MBO

PRIMARY SOURCES

Tinne, Alexandrina P. F. *Plantes Tinnéennes: Ou description de quelques des plantes recueillies par l'expedition sur les bords du Bahr-el-Ghasel* [sic] *et ses affluents en Afrique centrale.* Vienna: C. Gerold, 1867. This large folio volume has twenty-seven plates of plants found in the area of Bahr-al-Gazahl, published by Tinne in Vienna.

SECONDARY SOURCES

Gladstone, Penelope. *Travels of Alexine.* London: Murray, 1970. Includes photographs of Alexandrina Tinne and her family as well as photographs of her associates taken by Tinne.

TINSLEY, BEATRICE MURIEL (HILL) (1941–1981)

British astronomer and cosmologist. Born 27 January 1941 in Chester, England, to Jean (Morton) and Edward O. E. Hill. Two sisters. Married Brian A. Tinsley (1961; divorced 1974). Two adopted children, Alan (1966); Teresa (1968). Educated New Plymouth Girls High School, New Zealand; University of Canterbury, New Zealand (B.Sc., 1961; M.Sc., 1963); University of Texas, Austin (Ph.D., 1967). Professional experience: University of Texas, Dallas, visiting scientist (1972–1974); Hale Observatories, California Institute of Technology, visiting associate (1972); University of Maryland, visiting assistant professor (1973); University of Texas at Austin, assistant professor (1973–1974); University of California at Santa Cruz, assistant research astronomer and lecturer (1975); Yale University, Department of Astronomy, associate professor (1975–1978), professor (1978–1981). Honors and memberships: Annie Jump Cannon Prize in astronomy (1974); Sloan Foundation Research Fellowship (1975–1977); American Astronomical Society, Beatrice Tinsley Medal established in her honor. Died 23 March 1981 in New Haven, Conn., of melanoma.

Beatrice Hill Tinsley was the middle daughter of Anglican minister Edward Hill and religious novelist Jean Morton Hill, granddaughter of a Scottish textile magnate. Beatrice was born in postwar England and raised in New Zealand, where her father became mayor of New Plymouth. She ex-

celled at the violin, but decided on a career in science and mathematics. Though she became interested in cosmology as an undergraduate, opportunities at Canterbury University obliged her to write her master's thesis in solid state physics.

In 1961 she married fellow physicist Brian Tinsley and, after he completed his doctorate, followed him to Dallas, Texas. Dallas offered few opportunities to study astronomy, so in 1964 Beatrice Tinsley enrolled in the astronomy department at Austin, where she finished her doctoral dissertation on the evolution of galaxies in late 1966. That year, the Tinsleys had adopted a son, Alan, and in 1968, they adopted a daughter, Teresa. With two small children and a husband whose research demanded frequent travel, Tinsley was tied to Dallas, where she could find no real astronomy job, and for several years she gave up research, occupying herself with political activism.

In about 1970, Tinsley restarted her stalled career. Securing a succession of temporary, part-time (and sometimes unpaid) positions, and receiving part-time National Science Foundation funding, she started to publish profusely. Her work attracted attention from the wider astronomical community, and she began to work with several astronomers who would prove to be long-term collaborators and friends, including James Gunn at Caltech and Richard Larson at Yale. Tinsley received the American Astronomical Society's 1974 Annie Jump Cannon Prize (open to female astronomers) and offers of positions at Cambridge, Chicago, and Yale. Still, the University of Texas did not regularize her appointment.

In late 1974 the Tinsleys divorced. Leaving the children with her husband, Tinsley departed for six months at the University of California, Santa Cruz, after which she became an assistant professor at Yale, her first full-time, tenure-track job. Promoted to full professor in 1978, Tinsley remained at Yale until her death of melanoma in 1981.

Beatrice Tinsley was the first person to make a realistic, computer-generated model of how the color and brightness of a galaxy change as the stars that make up the galaxy are born, grow old, and die. Before Tinsley's work, astronomers treated galaxies as static, unchanging objects; since her work, galaxies have been recognized as entities that develop and change. Previously, astronomers had modeled galaxies by population synthesis—assembling the population of stars of different ages, masses, and chemistry whose total light best matched the light of the galaxy. This procedure modeled a galaxy at a single moment.

Tinsley's models were specifically evolutionary because she postulated reasonable initial conditions for the birth of stars, then let each star develop according to astronomers' theories of the lives of stars. She added up the colors and luminosities of the evolving stars to trace the total color and luminosity of the whole galaxy as it developed. Because galaxies are the milestones astronomers use to measure the most distant parts of the universe, improved galaxy models, like those Tinsley originated, give better answers to questions such as: How fast is the universe expanding? Will it expand forever, or eventually collapse?

Tinsley is also known for mentoring and network building, especially hosting a watershed symposium at Yale in 1977 that effectively clinched the status of the study of the evolution of galaxies as a field of astronomy. Tinsley is commemorated by a biennial prize awarded by the American Astronomical Society for exceptionally creative or innovative research and by a visiting professorship of astronomy at the University of Texas at Austin.   JE

PRIMARY SOURCES

Tinsley, Beatrice M. "Evolution of the Stars and Gas in Galaxies." *Astrophysical Journal* 151 (1968): 547–565. Tinsley's doctoral dissertation; a substantial first contribution to her field.

———. With Richard J. Gott III, James E. Gunn, and David M. Scramm. "An Unbound Universe?" *Astrophysical Journal* 194 (1974): 543–553. Observation parameters, including ones derived from measurements of galaxies, applied to cosmological questions.

———. With Richard J. Gott III, James E. Gunn, and David M. Scramm. "Will the Universe Expand Forever?" *Scientific American* 234, no. 3 (March 1976): 62–73. A popular verson of the 1974 article.

———, ed. With Richard B. Larsons. *The Evolution of Galaxies and Stellar Populations.* New Haven: Yale University Observatory, 1977. The proceedings of the 1977 conference.

———. "Evolution of the Stars and Gas in Galaxies." *Fundamentals of Cosmic Physics* 5 (1980): 287–388. This review remains the most frequently cited of Tinsley's first-author publications. It was written soon before her death, and lays out her final understanding of the field and provides an extensive bibliography, including her most significant publications.

SECONDARY SOURCES

Hill, Edward. *My Daughter Beatrice: A Personal Memoir of Dr. Beatrice Tinsley, Astronomer.* New York: The American Physical Society, 1986. This father's-eye view quotes at length from letters from Tinsley to her parents. It includes an introduction by Sandra M. Faber, and a reprint of Larson and Stryker's obituary.

Larson, Richard B., and Linda Stryker. "Beatrice Muriel Hill Tinsley." *Quarterly Journal of the Royal Astronomical Society* 23 (1982): 162–165. Obituary notice by Tinsley's close colleague and her student.

Overbye, Dennis. "The Endless Good-bye." In *Lonely Hearts of the Cosmos: The Story of the Scientific Quest for the Secret of the Universe,* 174–189. New York: Harper Collins, 1991. Overbye's story puts Tinsley's life and work in the context of recent cosmology. Material from Hill's book is enlivened by materials from interviews with Tinsley's colleagues and friends, but some details are incorrect.

TIPPER, CONSTANCE FLIGG (ELAM) (1894–1995)

British engineer. Born 16 February 1894 at New Barnet, Hertfordshire, to Lydia Coombes and William Henry Elam. Married George Howlegg Tipper (1928). Educated St. Felix School, Southwold; Newnham College (1912–1915; Tripos Part I, third class, 1915; M.A., 1923; Sc.D., 1949); University of London (D.Sc., 1926). Professional experience: College Research Fellow (1930–1931), associate (1928–1944), associate fellow (1947–1954); National Physics Laboratory, scientific assistant (1915–1916); Royal School of Mines, South Kensington, research worker (1916–1929); Frecheville research fellow (1921–1923); Royal Society of Armourers and Braziers, research fellow (1926–1929); Leverhulme research fellow (1934–1936); Cambridge University Department of Engineering, lecturer (1939–1945); collaborator with J. F. Baker, university reader (1949–1960), reader emerita (from 1960). Died 14 December 1995.

Constance Elam's father was a surgeon in New Barnet, Hertfordshire, when she was born. Her early education was at St. Ronans, Hadley Wood, and St. Felix, Southwold. After a short period of war work at the National Physical Laboratory, Elam started research at the Royal School of Mines, holding research awards successively from that institution, the Royal Society, Newnham College, and the Leverhulme Trust. After she developed a method of preparing metal crystals, she worked with G. I. Taylor at Cambridge, accumulating data on the deformation of these crystals under strain.

George Howlett Tipper (d. 1947), whom she married in 1928, was superintendent of the Geological Survey in India and retired in 1929. The couple made their home in Cambridge, and she continued her work there for over thirty years. For some time, she had no official position at the university, but in 1939 many of the male lecturers went off to the armed services or other wartime jobs, leaving a considerable amount of teaching in the department of engineering available to Tipper. She also took charge of the Heat Treatment Laboratory, where much important work was carried out in connection with war contracts. From this time until her retirement, she was a member of the faculty of engineering, first as a lecturer and later as reader. She was the only woman to hold office in a traditionally male department. She had a full teaching and advising load of both undergraduate and graduate students, and continued her research work during the little remaining time.

Lord John F. Baker described the importance of her work in a letter to Mrs. A. B. White of Newnham College in 1962: He had brought an urgent problem with him to Cambridge. The Liberty ships were developing a tendency to break in two, with a crack running around the middle of the ship. Baker and many of his coworkers at first suspected the welding. However, Tipper suggested that the material used in the American ships was notch brittle at temperatures above the freezing point, so that under normal conditions at sea would behave more like cast iron than ductile mild steel. Although notch brittleness was a known property of steel, Tipper was the first to direct attention to its importance in the ship problems. Ships in the North Atlantic convoys were subjected to especially icy temperatures and were particularly vulnerable to brittle fractures. Tipper showed that the critical temperature at which steel became brittle would have to be lowered by shipbuilders to well below what had previously been thought. The "Tipper test," as it was known, became the standard method of determining this form of brittleness in steel.

In 1960 Tipper retired and became an emerita reader. She went to live with her brother in Cumbria. She became a Fellow of the Imperial College of Science and Technology in 1963.   JH/MBO

PRIMARY SOURCES
Tipper, Constance. *The Deformation of Crystals.* Oxford: Oxford University Press, 1935.
———. *Brittle Fracture Story.* Cambridge, England: Cambridge University Press, 1962.

SECONDARY SOURCES
Baker, Lord J. F. Letter to Mrs. A. B. White, 12 January 1962. Newnham College Archives.
"Constance Tipper." Chronology. Newnham College Archives.
"Constance Tipper." *Times,* 30 December 1995. Obituary notice.
Other materials can be found in the Newnham College Archives.

STANDARD SOURCES
Newnham, vol. 1; *Newnham Roll.*

TISSERAND, M. (fl. 1950s)

French physician, physical anthropologist. Married [?] Perrier (1952). Educated University of Paris [?] Medical School. Professional experience: Centre National de la Recherche Scientifique (CNRS), researcher and school medical inspector, 1950s. Member of Société d'Anthropologie until 1956.

M. Tisserand was trained as a physician but became interested in physical anthropology after writing her medical thesis on that topic. She joined the Paris Anthropological Society in 1946 and began to make statistical studies of physical variations in nails, skin coloration, and sensory discrimination. She married and changed her name to Perrier-Tisserand in 1952, remaining active in her profession as both a research physician for the Institut de Hygiene and medical inspector of schools. She continued her membership in the Paris Anthropological Society until the early sixties but ceased to publish on anthropological topics.   JH/MBO

PRIMARY SOURCES
Tisserand, M. "Les Variations d'insertion du lobule de l'oreille dans le population francaise." *Bulletin et Memoires Société d'Anthropologie de Paris,* 9th ser., 6 (1947): 122–130. On the insertion of the ear lobe in the French population.
———. "Morphologie du bord spinal de l'omplate. *Bulletin et Memoires Société d'Anthropologie de Paris,* 9th ser., 6 (1947): 131–145. On the morphology of the spinal edge of the shoulder blade.
———. "Appréciation de la pigmentation dans le population francaise. I. Présentation de deux echelles chromatiques pour l'analyses de la coloration de le peau, des musqueses, des ongles et des dents. II. Présentations de'echelles chromatiques." *Bulletin et Memoires Société d'Anthropologie de Paris,* 9th ser., 6 (1947): 24–47. On pigmentation in the French population.
———. "Donées statistiques sur l'aptitude à gouter la phénylthiocarbamide dans la population parisienne, examen critique de la vateur du test." *Bulletin et Memoires Société d'Anthropologie de Paris,* 10th ser., 2 (1951): 12–17. On the ability to taste phenylthiocarbamide.
———. "Note préliminaire sur l'aptitude à sentir le farnésol." *Bulletin et Memoires Société d'Anthropologie de Paris,* 10th ser., 2 (1951): 18–22. On the ability to smell farnesol.
———. "Etude statistique de la coloration des téguments et de leur annexes chez 4,000 adultes parisiens." *Bulletin et Memoires Société d'Anthropologie de Paris,* 10th ser., 2 (1951): 23–31. Statistics of skin coloration in adult Parisians.

TODD, EMILY SOPHIA (1859–1949)

British botanist. Born 19 May 1859 in London. Professional experience: collected plants in Wiltshire. Herbarium at Swindon Museum. Plants at Oxford. Died 16 April 1949 in Wantage, Berkshire.

Emily Sophia Todd lived in Aldebourne, Wiltshire. A dedicated amateur botanist, she formed a herbarium that is now at Swindon Museum. Her Wiltshire plants, now at Oxford, are discussed in D. Grose, *Flora of Wiltshire* (1957). She died at the age of ninety.   JH/MBO

SECONDARY SOURCES
"Emily Sophia Todd." *Watsonia* 1 (1949–1950): 325. Obituary notice.
Grose, D. *Flora of Wiltshire.* Devizes: n.p., 1957.

STANDARD SOURCES
Desmond.

TODD, MABEL LOOMIS (1856–1932)

U.S. author and popular science writer. Born 10 November 1856 to Mary Alden (Wilder) and Eben Jenks Loomis. Educated private school, Cambridge Mass.; Georgetown Seminary, Washington, D.C.; New England Conservatory of Music. Married David Todd (5 March 1879). One daughter. Professional experience: editor of Emily Dickinson's works; popular writer of science and travel books and one novel. Died 14 October 1932 in Hog Island, Maine, of a cerebral hemorrhage.

Although Mabel Loomis Todd is remembered primarily as an editor of Emily Dickinson's works, she also wrote scientific books for the general public. As the daughter and the wife of notable astronomers, she produced a series of books throughout her life on solar eclipses, on the phenomena of sunsets, and on her experiences in traveling to view the eclipses with her husband.   JH/MBO

PRIMARY SOURCES
Todd, Mabel Loomis. *Total Eclipses of the Sun.* Boston: Roberts Bros., 1894. Later editions included an introduction by David Todd.
———. *Corona and Coronet: Being a Narrative of the Amherst Eclipse Expedition to Japan, in Mr. James's Schooner Yacht Coronet, to Observe the Sun's Total Obscuration, 9th August, 1896.* Boston and New York: Houghton, Mifflin Co., 1898.
———. *A Cycle of Sunsets.* Boston: Small, Maynard & Co., 1910.

STANDARD SOURCES
Debus; *NAW* (article by David Higgins).

TODD, RUTH (1913–1984)

U.S. geologist. Born 22 October 1913 in Seattle, Wash. Four siblings. Educated University of Washington (B.S. and M.S., 1939).

Professional experience: Mount Holyoke College, teaching fellow; Cushman Laboratory, assistant (1940–1942); U.S. Geological Survey, research assistant (1940–1950), research geologist (1950–1984). Died 19 August 1984 on Martha's Vineyard, Mass.

Ruth Todd was the oldest of five children. Although she was born in the state of Washington, in 1925 the family moved to Gering Valley, Nebraska, in order to help Ruth's grandfather homestead a farm on 160 acres of land. In 1928, after her grandfather died, the family moved back to Mercer Island on Lake Washington. Both her bachelor's and master's degrees came from the University of Washington. She then became a teaching fellow at Mount Holyoke College, where she worked with CHRISTINA LOCHMAN-BALK.

After a seemingly fruitless search for a job, she contacted Joseph A. Cushman in Sharon, Massachusetts, for further training, and he gave her a position as his assistant. She was associated with the laboratory for a number of years, and most of her early papers were published as a junior author with Cushman. She lived with the Cushman family for ten years. After Cushman's death in 1949, his collection, consisting of a great number of identified specimens and twelve thousand type specimens, was added to the then U.S. National Museum's already existing foraminiferan collection.

In 1942, Todd joined the U.S. Geological Survey as a research assistant and was promoted to research geologist by the time the collections were transferred to Washington, D.C., in 1950. Her office served not only the survey's branch of paleontology and stratigraphy but also the Cushman Library in the U.S. National Library located adjacent to the foraminiferan collections. Although the museum's curator of foraminifera was officially in charge of the collection, Todd continued to oversee the library.

Todd was a Fellow of both the Geological Society of America and the Cushman Foundation. She donated the journals to which she subscribed to the Cushman Library, now renamed the Todd Library. Other honors include a dual award with Paul Blackmon of the Society of Economic Paleontologists and Mineralogists Best Paper Award in the *Journal of Paleontology* for 1959. This work has become a classic on the mineralogy of foraminiferan tests. She became one of seven trustees and the first secretary-treasurer of the Cushman Foundation for Foraminiferal Research when it was incorporated in 1950.

Todd conducted research on fossil and recent foraminifera from all over the world. She not only worked in systematics, but also expanded her research into paleoecology and stratigraphy. From 1954 to 1964 she published four chapters in the survey's Professional Paper 260 that led to her becoming the survey's acknowledged expert on the smaller foraminifera of the Pacific area. After Cushman's death, she authored an annotated bibliography entitled "Recent Literature on Fora-minifera," which is now known as the *Journal of Foraminiferal Research*. She continued this service until her death, mailing the last manuscript the day before she died.   CK/MBO

PRIMARY SOURCES

Todd, Ruth. With J. A. Cushman. "The Genus *Cancris* and Its Species." *Contributions from the Cushman Laboratory for Foraminiferal Research* 18 (1942): 72–94.

———. "The Smaller Foraminifera in Correlation and Paleo-ecology." *Science* 119, no. 3092 (1954): 448.

———. With R. Post. "Smaller Foraminifera from Bikini Drill Holes." *U.S. Geological Survey Professional Paper* 260-N (1954): 547–568.

———. With P. D. Blackmon. "Mineralogy of Some Foraminifera as Related to their Classification and Ecology." *Journal of Paleontology* 33 (1959): 1–5.

———. With Doris Low. "Foraminifera from the Bahama Bank West of Andros Island." *U.S. Geological Survey Professional Paper* 683-C: (1971): 22 pages.

SECONDARY SOURCES

Buzas, Martin A. "Memorial to Ruth Todd, 1913–1984." *Geological Society of America, Memorials* 16 (1986): 1–3. Includes portrait.

STANDARD SOURCES

AMS P&B 10–11.

TODTMANN, EMMY MERCEDES (1888–1973)

German glacial geologist. Born 1888. Died 1973.

Emmy Todtmann was known for her descriptive geology of Iceland and Spitzbergen.   JH/MBO

SECONDARY SOURCES

Niedermayer, J. "Emmy Mercedes Todtmann." *Nachrichten Deutsche Geologische Gesselschaft* 10 (1974): 1–2.

Schwarzbach, Martin. "Emmy Mercedes Todtmann." *Eiszeitalter Gegenwart* (Ohringen, Württenburg) 23–24 (1973): 444–445.

STANDARD SOURCES

Sarjeant.

TOLMAN, RUTH (SHERMAN) (1893–1957)

U.S. psychologist. Born 10 October 1893 in Washington, Ind., to Lillie (Graham) and Warren C. Sherman. Married Richard Chace Tolman (5 August 1924). Educated University of California, Los Angeles. Professional experience: UCLA department of psychology, associate (1927–1929), clinical professor of psychology (1953–

1957); Occidental College, instructor (1930–1932); Scripps College, lecturer in psychology (1934); Los Angeles County, probation department senior psychological examiner (1936–1940); U.S. Department of Agriculture, division of program surveys, associate social science analyst (1941–1942); Office of War Information, public opinion analyst (1942–1944); Office of Strategic Services, clinical psychologist (1944–1945); Veteran's Administration, Los Angeles, head of clinical psychology training (1946–1954). Concurrent experience: Veteran's Administration Mental Hygiene Clinic, Los Angeles (1954–1957). Honors and memberships: American Orthopsychiatric Society, Fellow; American Psychological Asssociation, Fellow; member of other local psychological associations; Phi Beta Kappa, Sigma Xi. Died 18 September 1957. Buried in Woods Hole, Mass.

Although Ruth Sherman was born in Indiana, she went to the University of California, Los Angeles, to study psychology. She met and married a physicist, Richard Chace Tolman, then dean of the UCLA graduate school, when she was thirty years old. Her brother-in-law was the important learning theorist Edward Chace Tolman. After she completed her doctorate, she held a series of positions in California, first as a research associate in her graduate department, then as an instructor at Occidental College and then at Scripps College. Her interest in clinical work led her to take a position with the Los Angeles Probation Department, performing clinical evaluations on prisoners. When her husband moved to Washington in 1940, she spent a year acting as a social science analyst for the program survey section of the Department of Agriculture.

With the begininning of World War II, Tolman moved into war work, first with the Office of War Information and then with the Office of Strategic Services, like many other psychologists and anthropologists. Her husband, Richard Tolman, was vice-chairman to Vannevar Bush's National Defense Research Committee and head of its armor and ordinance. Subsequently he was involved in the Manhattan Project (1943–1946) serving as scientific advisor to General Leslie Groves.

After the war, the couple returned to Los Angeles, where Ruth Tolman worked with the Veterans Administration, first directing training in clinical psychology and later directing the mental health clinic. After her husband's death, she was offered an opportunity to return to teaching at UCLA, where she was made professor of clinical psychology. She died at the age of sixty-four and was buried at Woods Hole, Massachusetts, a favorite summer research and recreational area for many scientists.   KM

PRIMARY SOURCES
Tolman, Ruth Sherman. "Differences between Two Groups of
Adult Criminals." University of California at Berkeley,
Ph.D. diss., 1937.
———. With Ralph G. Wales. *Juvenile Detention in California.*
Los Angeles: California Advisory Committee on Detention
Home Problems, 1946.

STANDARD SOURCES
AMS 8, S&B 9; Rossiter 1995; *WWW(A)*, vol. 3, 1951–1960.

TOMASZEWICZ-DOBRSKA, ANNA (1854–1918)

Polish physician. Born 1854. Married. Educated in Zurich, Vienna, Berlin, and Petrograd (Leningrad). Professional experience: practiced in Warsaw; chief of Lying-In Hospital no. 2 in Warsaw (1882–1911). Other experience: Society of Polish Culture, founding member. Died 1918.

Determined to become a doctor in opposition to her family's wishes, Anna Tomaszewicz-Dobrska studied from 1871 to 1877 in Zurich to gain her medical degree. After postgraduate work she returned to Warsaw, married a doctor, and became the first Polish woman doctor to practice in Poland. (One other Polish woman had gotten a medical degree but did not return to Poland to practice.) Despite the prejudice and disapproval of the male medical establishment, Dobrska was named chief of Lying-In Hospital no. 2 in 1882 and remained until it was closed in 1911. Besides her hospital work and private practice, she worked for women's rights and was involved in community and cultural activities.

JH/MBO

STANDARD SOURCES
Lipinska 1900; Uglow 1989.

TOMPKINS, SALLY LOUISA (1833–1916)

U.S. (Confederate) nurse. Born 9 November 1833 at Poplar Grove, Mathews County, Va., to Maria Boothe Patterson and Col. Christopher Tompkins. Three siblings; four half-siblings. Educated at home. Professional experience: operated Robertson Hospital (1861–1865). Died 25 July 1916 in Richmond of chronic interstitual nephritis.

After the death of Sally Louisa Tompkins' father, the family moved to Richmond and shortly thereafter the Civil War broke out. She established one of the first private hospitals in the Confederate capital. The hospital was located in a residence donated by its owner, Judge John Robertson, and held twenty-five beds. She organized as nurses a group of socially prominent women, known as the Ladies of Robertson Hospital, and of the regular staff four were slaves, one was a carpenter, and the other a gardener. The latter two were unfit for military service. Largely because of Tompkins's insistence on cleanliness, the hospital had an unprecedented record for cures. It was allowed to remain open after five military hospitals had been opened in the suburbs and other inner city private hospitals were closed. Tompkins was commissioned by Confederate president Jefferson Davis as a captain of cavalry on 9 September 1861.

The hospital remained open until 13 June 1865. After the war, she engaged in charities largely through Richmond's St. James Episcopal Church.

JH/MBO

SECONDARY SOURCES
Coleman, Dabney. "The Captain Was a Lady." *Virginia Cavalcade* (Summer 1956).

STANDARD SOURCES
NAW (article by H. H. Cunningham).

TONNELAT, MARIE-ANTOINETTE (BAUDOT) (1912–1980)

French theoretical physicist and historian of science. Born 5 March 1912 in Charolles (Saône et Loire), France, to Alix (Menetriex) and Louis Baudot. Married physicist Jacques Tonnelat (10 November 1936). Two daughters; one son. Educated Institut Catholique de Paris (Licence de philosophie); University of Paris (Licence és Sciences, Licence és Lettres, Doctorat és Sciences). Professional experience: Centre Nationale de la Recherche Scientifique (CNRS), researcher; Faculté des Sciences, titular professor; College de France, Cours Peccot, historian of science (1944); Université de Paris, Institut d'Histoire des Sciences, cours libre (1949–1979); Université de Paris, Centre de Physique Théorique (Henri-Poincaré Institute), researcher (1935–1980), director (1972–1980). Honors and memberships: Académie des Sciences Morales et Politiques, Prix du Budget, 1947 (shared prize); Académie des Science, Prix Henri-Poincaré (1971). Died August 1980.

Marie-Antoinette Baudot began her education in the Catholic Insitute of Paris and then took an advanced degree in theoretical physics while studying with the physicist and philosopher Gaston Bachelard in the Institute of the History of Sciences. She obtained a position with the Centre Nationale de la Recherche Scientifique (CNRS) which supported her position in Louis de Broglie's Center for Theoretical Physics in the Henri Poincaré Institute. She married a fellow physicist, Jacques Tonnelat, in 1936, and had three children while she prepared her advanced dissertation (doctorat d'état) in 1941 on the theory of the photon in Reimann space.

Tonnelat began her distinguished publications with a sequence of notes in *Comptes rendus* of the Académie des Sciences in the early forties. She began to teach both theoretical physics and some courses at Bachelard's history of science institute, where she taught regularly from 1949. She also held seminars at the Collège de France.

Tonnelat examined relativity theory and in 1950 she began to correspond with Schrödinger and Einstein. She visited Schrödinger and was invited to Princeton just before Einstein died. She spoke on this topic in the 1953 International Congress for the History of Sciences in Jerusalem. In 1950, she competed for a chair at the Collège de France on unitary theories and the work of Einstein and Schrödinger. Failing to receive the chair, she continued with the CNRS—she had been maitre de recherches (research scientist) since the late forties—and worked at the Henri-Poincaré Institute. Tonnelat was adjunct professor to Louis de Broglie, taking over some of his courses on theoretical physics. She became director upon his retirement in 1972.

One of Tonnelat's last lectures, given to a popular audience at the Palais des Decouvertes, was on Einstein. She entitled it "Science in Search of Ethics" ("La science à la recherche d'une ethique") but was too ill to give it herself. Later the same year (1980) she aggravated her illness by giving another important lecture in July, on the state of current thinking in physics and the links between science and humanism ("La Pensée physique en 1980: Science et Humanisme en Notre Temps"). She died not long after her lecture, leaving an unpublished book on history of theories of light and color.   JH/MBO

PRIMARY SOURCES

Tonnelat, Marie-Antoinette. "Théorie du photon dans un Espace Riemann." Thesis for the doctorat d'etat, University of Paris, 1941.

————. "Lien profond entre la théorie relativiste de la gravitation et celle de la particule de spin 2." *Annales de Physique*, 11th ser., 19 (1944).

————. "Quel est le sens exact de l'opposition entre réalisme et idéalisme au point de vue de la conception et de la méthode de la science" (Prix du Budget). *Comptes rendus Académie des Sciences Morales et Politiques* (1947).

————. *Histoire du Principe de Relativité*. Paris: Flammarion, 1971.

SECONDARY SOURCES

Costabel, P. "Marie-Antoinette Tonnelat (1912–1980)." *Revue histoire des sciences* 36 (1983): 329–330.

STANDARD SOURCES

Debus; Turkevich and Turkevich.

TOOPS, LAURA CHASSELL (MERRILL) (1893–?)

U.S. psychologist. Born 24 March 1893 in Sundance, Wyo. Married Herbert Anderson Toops, psychologist (1922). Five children. Educated Cornell College, Iowa (A.B., 1912); Iowa State Teachers College (M.Di., 1913); Northwestern University (A.M., 1914); University of Chicago (1915); Columbia University Teachers College, Margaret Hoe Scholar and American University Fellow (1917–1918; Ph.D., 1920). Professional experience: Illinois Women's College, instructor of education and English (1914–1915); Wisconsin State Normal School, LaCrosse, teacher of modern foreign languages (1915–1917); Columbia University Teachers College, assistant in educational psychology (1918–1919); Ohio State University, instructor in psychology (1920–1923); Scarborough School, educational measurements, educational psychologist (1918–1919); Methodist Episcopal Church, research worker, department head in education (1919); Horace Mann School, Columbia, special psychological examiner (1920); Eastern Kentucky State Teachers College, special instructor (1926); Columbia University, National Fellow (1927–1928). Death date unknown.

Laura Toops studied at a number of midwestern universities, including the University of Chicago, but she went to Columbia University to obtain her doctorate in psychology. After she taught for three years as an instructor in psychology at Ohio State University, she married a fellow Columbia graduate who was also teaching there. She was forced to give up her position because of nepotism rules, but her husband went on to become full professor at Ohio State University.

Following her marriage and the subsequent birth of five children, Toops held only a few formal posiitons. She taught for a year at Kentucky State Teachers College and the following year was awarded a National Fellowship at Columbia University.

Toops was deeply interested in methods to measure child development. She studied the training of young children and the motor difficulties of gifted children. She also developed measurement systems to determine what qualities were associated with academic success in college students. Other personality studies by Toops attempted to predict positive outcomes in marriage and parenting.   KM

PRIMARY SOURCES

Toops, Laura Chassell. "The Measurement of Success in Marriage and in Parenthood: A Research Program Outlining the Construction of Tests and Their Use." *Teachers College Record* (March 1929): 579–588.

STANDARD SOURCES

AMS 4–8.

TOWARA, HÉLÈNE (1889–?)

Russian chemist. Born 21 March 1899 in Maikop, Russia. Father was a merchant. Educated Moscow Commerce Institute (advanced diploma); University of Karlsruhe, summer 1914. Professional experience: University of Leipzig, researcher (1910–1914). Death date unknown.

Working with the chemist Kasimir Fajans at the University of Leipzig, Towara investigated radium decay products. At first these researchers believed, erroneously, that they had discovered a new product in the radium series. Their results were later shown to have been caused by a known substance.

MM

PRIMARY SOURCES
Towara, Hélène. With Kasimir Fajans. "Über ein neues langlebiges Glied der Wismut-plejade." *Die Naturwissenschaften* 2, 1914: 685–686.
———. With Kasimir Fajans. *Chem. Zeitung* 22, VIII, 1914: 1032–?.

STANDARD SOURCES
Meyer and von Schweidler; Rayner-Canham 1997.

TOWN, CLARA HARRISON (1874–?)

U.S. psychologist. Born 11 October 1874 in Philadelphia, Pa. Educated Temple University (B.S., 1907); University of Pennsylvania (Ph.D., 1909); Paris, France (1920–1921). Professional experience: Friends Asylum, Frankford, Pa., resident psychologist (1905–1910); University of Pennsylvania, assistant in psychological clinic (1909–1911); Lincoln State School and Colony, Lincoln, Ill., state psychologist (1911–1914); Rush Medical College, Chicago, psychologist, orthogenic clinic (1914–1916); Colorado State Teachers College, Greeley, Colo., professor of psychology (1916–1918); Kansas City, Mo., public schools, director of orthogenic clinic and classes (1919–1920); Children's Aid Society, Buffalo, N.Y., psychologic clinic (1922–1935), consulting psychologist (from 1935); University of Pittsburgh, summer instructor (1913, 1918, 1919); Lehigh College, visiting faculty (1922). Honors and memberships: American Psychological Association (chairman, clinical section); Association of Applied Psychology. Death date unknown.

Clara Town received a doctoral degree from the University of Pennsylvania after she had earned a bachelor's degree from Temple University. After completing her doctorate she took a job at the University of Pennsylvania as an assistant in the psychological clinic. Her research interests were in abnormal psychology and racial psychology. She also worked as a clinical psychologist.

JH/MBO

PRIMARY SOURCES
Town, Clara Harrison. "Analytic Study of a Group of Five- and Six-Year-Old Children." University of Iowa Studies, 1st ser. (1 May 1921).
———. With Grace Hill. *How the Feebleminded Live in the Community: A Report of a Social Investigation of the Erie County Feeble-Minded Discharged from the Rome State School.* Buffalo: Children's Aid Society and Society for the Prevention of Cruelty to Children of Erie County, N.Y., [1930].

STANDARD SOURCES
AMS 3–7.

TRACY, MARTHA (1876–1942)

U.S. physician, administrator, and hygienist. Born 10 April 1876 in Plainfield, N.J. to Martha Sherman (Greene) and Jeremiah Evarts Tracy. Educated Plainfield Seminary for Young Ladies and Children; Bryn Mawr College (A.B., 1898); Woman's Medical College of Pennsylvania (M.D., 1904); Cornell University Medical School, graduate studies; Yale University, Woman's Medical College of Pennsylvania Alumnae Fellowship (1911); University of Pennsylvania (D.P.H. 1917). Professional experience: Meningitis Commission, New York Board of Health, assistant (1905); Huntingdon Fund for Cancer Research, researcher (1904–1918); Woman's Medical College of Pennsylvania, associate professor of chemistry and director of laboratories (1909–1913), professor (1913–1917), professor of physiological chemistry and hygiene (1917–1920), professor of nutritional hygiene (1922–1923), professor of hygiene and preventive medicine (1923–1931), dean of faculty (1917–1940); Board of Health, Philadelphia, assistant director (1936). Fellow, College of Physicians, Philadelphia. Died 22 March 1942 of pneumonia.

Martha Tracy was born in Plainfield, New Jersey, to an old New England Puritan family that had close ties to well-known political figures. Having completed her secondary school work at Plainfield Academy and eager to study medicine, Tracy entered Bryn Mawr, where she designed her own premedical program, which included a biology course with T. H. Morgan and chemistry with E. P. Kohler. She was an able athlete and president of the Athletic Association of the college.

Graduating with high honors, she entered the Woman's Medical College of Pennsylvania two years later, delayed by illness. Her interest in physiological chemistry led her to work as a technician in the histological lab in addition to her regular studies. Tracy was at the top of the list of medical students who passed the Pennsylvania State Board examinations (men and women).

After receiving her medical degree, she entered as a graduate student in the medical school at Cornell, where she worked under William B. Coley as an assistant in experimental pathology, helping to develop a treatment for sarcoma called "Coley's fluid." At the end of three years, she took a position as an associate professor of chemistry at the Woman's Medical College, although she continued to pursue independent research on microchemical reactions and cancer cells and on experimental tumors. Shortly after she began to teach at the medical college, she took the opportunity for further study in physiological chemistry at Yale.

Upon her return to the Woman's Medical College, she converted the chemistry department into a department of physiological biochemistry and became a full professor. Her interest in public health led her to work toward a doctorate at the University of Pennsylvania in public hygiene.

When CLARA MARSHALL resigned as dean of the college in 1917, Martha Tracy was appointed by the faculty to the position. As dean, she was immediately faced with the effects of America's entrance into World War I. In 1918, nine faculty members left to take an active part in the war and a major reorganization of teaching assignments took place. Tracy opened special classes in hygiene and sanitation, nutrition and dietetics, and laboratory technique to prepare women for war service in Europe and America. When the Anna Howard Shaw chair of preventive medicine was endowed by the National American Woman Suffrage Association, Tracy was apppointed to the position.

During her twenty-three years of tenure as dean, Tracy faced a series of crises that threatened the existence of the Woman's Medical College. It survived due to her firm belief in the necessity of preserving a medical school that would offer more opportunities for women. When the college faced bankruptcy in 1921, friends and alumnae came forward to ease the debt and reorganize the Board of Corporations to manage both the hospital and college. Partly as a result of changes made by the new board, a bitter dissention within the faculty occurred in 1923, which resulted in a student strike and many resignations by faculty members. Tracy managed to weather the storm.

In 1935 an adverse finding by the American Medical Association, due to the lowered faculty salaries required by the building of a new college, threatened to close the school. Within two years, the president of the board led a successful fundraising campaign based on endowments in the name of famous early graduates like HANNAH LONGSHORE, and the college returned to its "Grade A" standing.

Tracy believed that a woman physician needed to extend her services beyond the classroom or hospital. She set an example by her activities in professional and community organizations. She was a Fellow of the College of Physicians of Philadelphia and on the Committee of Public Health of the College of Physicians. For many years she was the only female dean among the more than sixty male deans in the

Association of American Medical Colleges. As the number of female deans increased, she played an active part in the formation of the Pennsylvania Association of Deans of Women. In 1940, after her retirement as dean, she was appointed to Philadelphia's Board of Health as assistant director. She became ill on her way home from a Civilian Defense Organization meeting in 1942, and died of pneumonia a few days later.   JH/MBO

SECONDARY SOURCES
Alsop, Gulielma Fell. *History of the Woman's Medical College, Philadelphia, Pennsylvania 1850–1950.* Philadelphia: J. B. Lippincott Co., 1950.

STANDARD SOURCES
AMS 4–6; Debus; *NAW* (article by Gulielma Fell Alsop); Rebière.

TRAILL, CATHARINE PARR (STRICKLAND) (1802–1899)

British-born Canadian botanist. Born 9 January 1802 in London. Married T. Traill (1832). Emigrated to Canada (1832). Professional experience: published on Canadian plants. Died 29 October 1899 in Lakefield, Ontario.

Catharine Parr Strickland was born in London and raised in a family with strong interests in botany and natural history. She and her sister Agnes collected plants in Suffolk. When she was thirty, she married Lieutenant T. Traill and emigrated with him to Canada. Her experiences in the backwoods of Canada led her to publish accounts of emigrant life. Later, she renewed her interest in botany, developing an herbarium and writing on Canadian wildflowers. In 1857, her herbarium was destroyed by fire, but some of her specimens still remain in the Ottawa Herbarium and the Queens University, Kingston Herbarium. From her sixties on, she published popular books on Canadian plants. She died in her late nineties. One of the colleges of Trent University in Peterborough, Ontario, was named in her honor.   JH/MBO

PRIMARY SOURCES
Traill, Catharine Parr. *The Backwoods of Canada: Being Letters from the Wife of an Emigrant Officer, Illustrative of the Domestic Economy of British America.* London: C. Knight, 1836. Reprinted in Toronto in 1929 and again in Ottawa in 1997.
———. *Canadian Wild Flowers.* Montreal: J. Lovell, 1869.
———. *Studies of Plant Life in Canada.* Ottawa: A. S. Woodburn, 1885.
———. *Pearls and Pebbles: Or Notes of an Old Naturalist.* London: S. Low, Marston, 1894. Includes portrait.

———. *Forest and Other Gleanings: The Fugitive Writings of Catharine Parr Traill.* Eds. Michael Peterman and Carl Ballstadt. Ottawa: University of Ottawa Press, 1994. This includes some biographical material.

SECONDARY SOURCES

Ballstadt, Carl, Elizabeth Hopkins, and Michael A. Peterman, eds. *I Bless You in My Heart: Selected Correspondence of Catharine Parr Traill.* Toronto: University of Toronto Press, 1996.

"Catharine Parr Traill." *Journal of Botany* 37 (1899): 448. Obituary notice.

Eaton, Sara. *Lady of the Backwoods: A Life of Catharine Parr Traill.* Toronto: McClelland and Stewart, 1969.

STANDARD SOURCES

Desmond.

TREAT, MARY LUA ADELIA (DAVIS) (1830–1923)

U.S. botanist and entomologist. Born 7 September 1830 in Trumansville, N.Y. to Eliza (English) and Isaac Davis, a Methodist minister. Educated Ohio public and private schools. Married Joseph Burrell Treat (1863; separated 1874). Professional experience: experimented on sensitive and insectivorous plants; corresponded with Asa Gray, Charles Darwin, and other botanists and entomologists; published both popular and scientific articles in Harper's Monthly, American Naturalist, Atlantic Monthly, *etc.; published series of popular books on plants and insects. Died 11 April 1923 in New York; buried in Vineland, N.J.*

Mary Treat was a self-trained botanist and entomologist whose keen eye and capacity for experimentation made her exceptional. Her father was a Methodist minister who moved his family to Ohio when Treat was a child. After she married the physician Dr. Joseph Burrell Treat in 1863, she moved with him to Vineland, New Jersey. Treat began to study nature seriously, spurred by devastating destruction to the fruit orchards around Vineland. Although Harshberger (1899) described her as an exceedingly self-effacing woman, she kept up an extensive scientific correspondence with major American and English botanists and entomologists, including Charles Darwin, and published excerpts from that correspondence in her descriptions of her own experiments.

Traveling with her husband to the area near the St. John's River in Florida, about thirty-five miles north of Jacksonville, for six months of every year, she recorded the unusual plant and flower specimens she saw there, sending them to important botanists for identification. When she encountered nests of insects, she sent these as well for identification to the entomologist C. V. Riley. She triumphantly recorded her discovery of the beautiful yellow water lily in Florida

that had been depicted by James Audubon in association with the white swan, but that was not known by botanists in America. She provided specimens of these plants to nurserymen as well as to botanists. She also sent over three hundred bulbs of a beautiful amaryllis lily to the botanic garden at Harvard.

At Asa Gray's urging, in 1874 she sent Darwin accounts of her careful experiments on insectiverous plants including the pitcher plant. She continued to correspond with Darwin about the sundew, *Drosera,* and *Dionea,* upon which Darwin was also experimenting. Treat never hesitated to correct and extend Darwin's observations if she felt her data were more accurate. Her work pleased and delighted Darwin, and he urged her to continue.

These observations and other studies on natural history were published in *American Naturalist, Harper's Magazine, Atlantic Monthly, Science,* and the *New York Tribune* and later collected in *Home Studies in Nature* (1885). She conveyed her own sense of excitement in nature studies in a series of very popular books, including *Chapters on Ants* (1879) and *Injurious Insects of the Farm and Garden,* 1882.

Treat's books provided her with an income after the failure of her marriage in the 1870s. She also wrote a brief memoir of the botanist Asa Gray after his death. She died at her sister's home in New York City after a long illness in April 1923, and was buried in Vineland, New Jersey.

JH/MBO

PRIMARY SOURCES

Treat, Mary. *Chapters on Ants.* New York: Harper & Bros., 1879.

———. *Injurious Insects of the Farm and Garden.* New York: Orange Judd Co., 1882.

———. "Behavior of *Dolomedes tenebrosus.*" *Science* 3 (1884): 217–218.

———. *Home Studies in Nature.* New York: Harper & Bros., 1885. Includes some letters from Darwin.

———. *My Garden Pets.* Boston: D. Lothrop, 1887.

———. "*Arigope riparia var, multiconcha.*" *American Naturalist* 21 (1887): 1122.

———. "Evergreens in the New Jersey Pine Region." *Garden and Forest* 3 (1890): 546–547.

Mary Treat's archives are in the Vineland, New Jersey, Historical Society.

SECONDARY SOURCES

Burkhardt, Frederick, and Sydney Smith. *A Calendar of the Correspondence of Charles Darwin.* 1985. Cambridge, England: Cambridge University Press, 1994. Includes the list of letters between Treat and Darwin.

Caruso, Lorraine Abbiate and Terry Kohn. "Mary Davis Treat." In *Past and Promise Lives of New Jersey Women,* ed. Joan N. Burstyn. Syracuse, N.Y.: Syracuse University Press, 1997.

Harshberger, John W. *The Botanists of Philadelphia and Their Work*. Philadelphia: T. C. Davis & Sons, 1899.

"Mary Treat." *New York Times,* 13 April 1923. Obituary notice.

STANDARD SOURCES

Bailey (includes portrait); *Catalogue Royal Society;* Mozans; *WWW(A)*, vol. 1, 1897–1942.

TRIMMER, SARAH (KIRBY) (1741–1810)

British author and botanist. Born 1741 in Ipswich, Suffolk. Father, Joshua Kirby; cousin of botanist William Kirby. Professional experience: wrote popular books on natural history. Died 15 December 1810 in Brentford, Middlesex.

Sarah Trimmer had no formal education, but through reading she was able to prepare herself to write books. Many of her books were on subjects other than natural history, such as *A Little Spelling-Book for Young Children*. Many were about religion, and were geared to young people. She established the charity schools and schools of industry at Old Brentford, where children could be instructed according to her principles. JH/MBO

PRIMARY SOURCES

Trimmer, Sarah. *Easy Introduction to the Knowledge of Nature.* Boston: Printed by Manning and Loring for David West, 1796.

SECONDARY SOURCES

"Sarah Trimmer." *Gentleman's Magazine* 81, part 1 (1811): 86.

STANDARD SOURCES

Desmond.

TRISTRAM, RUTH MARY (CARDEW) (1886–1950)

British amateur botanist. Born 25 April 1886. Married Major G. H. Tristram (1919). Four children. Professional experience: studied Plantago. Honors and memberships: Fellow, Linnean Society (1911); Wild Flower Society. Died 22 October 1950.

Ruth May Tristram was a British amatuer botanist who made herself an authority on *Plantago*, which won her election as a Fellow of the Linnean Society in the first years that women were so honored. She became interested in botany at an early age, and in 1905 discovered an extended range of *Holosteum umbellatum* and thus brought herself to the attention of her fellow botanists.

She collaborated with E. G. Baker on a study of *Plantago* with the intention of writing an account of the genus for Moss's *Cambridge British Flora*. This resulted in joint papers in the *Report of the Botanical Society* and the *Journal of Botany*. When she was elected to the Linnean Society (7 December 1911), only six years had passed since it first admitted women. Only twenty-five at the time, she was proud of the honor all of her life. JH/MBO

SECONDARY SOURCES

Cardew, J. W., and J. E. Lousley, "Ruth Mary Tristram." *Watsonia* 2 (1951–1953): 139.

STANDARD SOURCES

Desmond.

TRIZNA, VALENTINA BORISOVNA (1892–?)

Russian geologist and paleontologist. Born 1892 in Kattakurgan of Samarkandan. Father an officer. Educated Women's Gymnasium, Tashkent (completed 1914); Higher Women's Courses, Moscow; Middle Asian State University (completed 1930); Leningrad Mining Institute (thesis, 1948; Ph.D., 1958?). Professional experience: paleontological party, laboratory assistant (1922–1923); hydrogeological party, geologist (1926); Department of Mineralogical Resources, geologist (1927–1929); geological survey, leader (1930); worked in hydrogeology in Moscow (1930–1932); Hydrological Institute, Leningrad, research scientist (1932–1934); All-Union Oil Scientific Research Geological Exploration Institute, paleontologist (1935–1949), senior paleontologist (1949–post-1958).

After beginning her higher education in Tashkent, Valentina Trizna entered the Highest Women's Courses in Moscow. However, family concerns forced her to return to Middle Asia, where she attended the Middle Asian University in Tashkent. Although she entered the university in 1922, the illness and eventual death of her mother caused her to drop out of school for three years, and she did not complete her course until 1930. During her time in Middle Asia, she participated in several geological studies, including one as a laboratory assistant for a paleontological party. From 1929 to 1930, she worked under A. L. Protodyakonov collecting data about oil and coal deposits from Middle Asia. During her last year at Middle Asian University, she led a geological survey under the leadership of V. G. Myhin.

After she finished her studies, Trizna moved to Moscow, where she worked in hydrogeology. She subsequently moved to Leningrad, where she worked for the Hydrological Institute. After leaving the institute, she had a variety of other jobs. It was not until 1935 that her lifelong career as a paleontologist really began.

As a paleontologist at the All-Union Oil Scientific Research Geological Exploration Institute, she studied the paleontology of Paleozoic, Carboniferous, and Permian bryozoans. In 1948, she defended a thesis in the Leningrad Mining Institute as a candidate for a degree in geological and mineralogical sciences.

Trizna became a senior scientific researcher in 1949. Her research interests for the next ten years were bryozoans from the Lower Carboniferous of Kuzbas. She published five large monographs and did everything that would have qualified her for a doctorate, but her excessive shyness kept her from defending this thesis, so she remained a candidate. After all, she had spent ten years doing independent work before she felt ready to present her preparatory thesis.

Trizna's work on the bryozoans of the Upper Carboniferous and Permian along the western Urals, starting at Bashkir and ending at the Polar Urals, represented her major contribution. She made a single map of the vertical spreading of these organisms in cross-section of the Upper Carboniferous and Permian.

She identified bryozoans for the Institute of Geology of the Arctic, for the All-Union Scientific Research Geological Institute, for the Fifth Geological Department, the Primorski Geological Department, the Leningrad Geological Department, Giprovostokneft, the Leningrad Non-Metallic Trust, the Azerbaijan Industrial Institute, as well as for many geologists from her own All-Union Oil Scientific Research Geological Exploration Institute. Trizna was also a fine mentor to young paleontologists. She participated in meetings on stratigraphy of the Upper Paleozoic, and wrote numerous reviews in addition to her scientific works.   CK

PRIMARY SOURCES

Trizna, V. B. "New Species of the Upper Paleozoic Fenestellidae and Acanthocladiidae from the Bashkirian Urals." *Geological Prospecting Institute* 1939: 102–144. Includes descriptions of many new varieties.

———. With others. *Mikrofauna SSSR, sbornik VIII, Foraminifery, mshanki i ostrakody Russkoi platformy, Donbassa, Tengizskoi vpadiny i Kuzbassa.* Moscow: Trudy-Vsesouznyy Nauchno-Issledovatelskiy Geologorazvedocnyy Neftanoy Institut, 1956. A compilation of data on Paleozoic and Mesozoic microfaunas of the USSR. Trizna's part dealt with the lower Carboniferous bryozoans of the Kuznetsk basin.

———. Rannekamennougol'nye mshanki Kuzhetskoi Kotloviny. Leningrad: Gostoptekhizdat, 1958. A book on fossil Bryozoa.

STANDARD SOURCES

Nalivkin.

TROTTER, MILDRED (1899–1991)

U.S. anatomist and physical anthropologist. Born 3 February 1899 in Monaca, Pa., to Jennie Bruce (Zimmerley) and James Robert Trotter. Three siblings. Educated local one-room grammar school; high school, Beaver, Pa.; Mount Holyoke College (A.B., 1920); Washington University, St. Louis (M.A., 1921; Ph.D., 1924); Oxford University, National Research Council Fellowship (1925–1926). Professional experience: Washington University, faculty member (1920–1927), assistant professor (1927–1946), professor (1946–1967). Died 23 August 1991 in St. Louis, Mo., of a cerebral hemorrhage.

Mildred Trotter made important contributions to the understanding of hypertrichosis (excessive hair growth) and to the knowledge of bone as a tissue. She developed a method for using the length of certain bones in the human to estimate the height of the individual in life, a tool that is very important to forensic experts.

Born on a farm in Pennsylvania into an active family of Democrats and Presbyterians, Trotter raised a furor when she chose to study geometry over home economics. For her undergraduate degree in zoology, Trotter attended Mount Holyoke College. Upon graduating, she chose to work as a research assistant to C. H. Danforth, associate professor of anatomy at Washington University in St. Louis. Danforth had received funding from a man whose wife and daughters suffered from excessive facial hair. Through this funding Trotter was able to earn a master's degree in anatomy, examining hair distribution. The anonymous donor pledged additional funds, and Trotter was able to finish her degree. Her individual papers on hair were collected and published in book form by the American Medical Association in 1925 under Danforth's name.

After Trotter finished her doctoral degree, Washington University made her an instructor. However, she soon accepted a National Research Council Fellowship to study physical anthropology at Oxford. At this time, her interests switched from hair to bone. She studied museum specimens from ancient Egypt and the Roman era in Britain. In order to assure Trotter's continued services (she had been offered an additional fellowship), Washington University promoted her to assistant professor. She was not promoted again until sixteen years later, when she demanded to know why she had been passed over for promotion. The results of a review committee in 1946 recommended that Trotter be promoted to full professor, the first woman to attain that rank at Washington University. Trotter maintained the skeletal collection at Washington University School of Medicine that had been begun by R. J. Terry. During the fifty-five years that she was associated with the university, she published numerous papers on the human skeleton, including studies of growth cycles, sexual and racial differences, and changes in mineral mass and density occurring with age.

Trotter took an unpaid sabbatical in 1948 to volunteer as director of the Central Identification Laboratory at Schofield

Barracks, Oahu, Hawaii. There she helped identify unknown war dead brought from the Pacific theater after the war. This experience with forensic anatomy gave her data that allowed her to devise a formula for estimating the height of a person based on the relative length of the long bones.

During the 1950s and 1960s, Trotter began to attract national and international attention for her work. She had helped form the American Association of Physical Anthropologists in 1930 and in 1955 was elected its president. In 1956 she became the first woman to receive the Wenner-Gren Foundation Viking Fund Medal. She produced numerous reference books, served as a consultant to the Rockefeller Foundation, lectured in London and Washington, D.C., and served as a visiting professor to Makerere University in Kampala, Uganda. She wrote entries on the skin and the skeleton for the 1953 and 1956 editions of the *Encyclopedia Britannica*.

Trotter sat on the St. Louis Anatomical board and the Missouri State Anatomical Board (president from 1955 to 1957). She also was a consultant on numerous missing person cases. Believing that the attitude of the prevailing culture toward death was absurd, she was active in assuring that the Missouri legislature passed a bill enabling Missourians to donate their bodies to universities for medical research. Trotter was a strict, demanding teacher, but one whom her students respected. She continued to conduct research after her retirement. She suffered a severe stroke and died in August 1991.

JH/MBO

PRIMARY SOURCES

Trotter, Mildred. With G. C. Gleser. "Estimation of Stature from Long Limb Bones of American Whites and Negroes." *American Journal of Physical Anthropology* no. 10 (1952).

———. With G. C. Gleser. "Corrigenda to 'Estimation of Stature from Long Limb Bones of American Whites and Negroes.'" American Journal of Physical Anthropology, 1952." *American Journal of Physical Anthropology* no. 47 (1977).

Trotter's papers are held in the Resource and Research Center for Beaver County and Local History, in the Carnegie Free Library in Beaver Falls, Pa., and in the Washington University School of Medicine Library Archives, St. Louis, Mo.

SECONDARY SOURCES

Kerley, Ellist R. "Forensic Anthropology: Increasing Utility in Civil and Criminal Cases." *Trial* (January 1983): 66–111.

Wood, W. Raymond, and Lori Ann Stanley. "Recovery and Identification of World War II Dead: American Graves Registration Activities in Europe." *Journal of Forensic Sciences* 34 (1989): 1365–1373.

STANDARD SOURCES

Debus; *Modern Scientists and Engineers; Notable* (article by Jennifer Kramer).

TROTULA (d. 1097?)
Italian physician. Married John Platearius. Two sons. Died 1097 (?).

Many scholars consider Trotula to be one of the most famous physicians of the medical school at Salerno. Although there is a question about her name (her followers knew her by a variety of names), there is little doubt that a woman physician practiced, taught, and gained renown at Salerno in the eleventh century. John Benton's scholarly article produces evidence for the existence of a historical "Trotula" despite some nineteenth-century scholars' denial of her historical reality. He considers three views of Trotula: that she is a well-documented historical figure who lived in the eleventh century, was a member of the medical school of Salerno, and became the first woman professor of medicine there; that there was an eleventh- or twelfth-century physician with a name like Trotula, but who was actually a man named Trottus; and finally, that the name Trotula is not that of a real person but is related to the French verb *trotter* (to run about). The evidence is not consistent with any of these three views. The best evidence indicates that a woman physician named Trota existed, but that she was not the author of the three treatises commonly attributed to her. Supposedly, she was the wife of a noted physician, John Platearius. It is said that they had two sons, Matthias and Johannes the Younger, both of whom became physicians and medical writers. The older son, Matthias (Matteo), addressed his mother as "learned mother Trocta" and "mater magistra Platearii." Although there are no records of her education, she was probably not an ordinary midwife but a "master" in her own right; her son stressed that his mother cared for sick women as a "magistra," not an "empiric." Although theory was subordinate to practice in Trotula's work, she recognized its importance. For example, she is reputed to have applied Hippocratic and Galenic ideas of the humors and the pulse to her own diagnoses and treatments. Her gynecological expertise was especially valued. Trotula's work must be evaluated within the context of its own time. Along with introducing an important surgical technique for the repair of a ruptured perineum, she described a method of determining the sex of an infant before birth: the mother's blood, or milk from her right breast, was placed in a glass of water; if the fluid sank, the baby would be a boy.

Foremost in Trotula's medicine was the idea of prevention. When this failed, she preferred the less radical treatments—baths, ointments, and massages—to surgery and violent purges. The *Regimen sanitatis salernitatum* (which went through twenty editions before 1500) contained many contributions from Trotula's work.

JH/MBO

PRIMARY SOURCES

Trotula. *The Diseases of Women*. Trans. Elizabeth Mason-Hohl. Los Angeles: Ward Ritchie, 1940. Trotula's manuscript, *Passionibus mulierum curandorum,* was originally printed by Paulus Manutius in Venice in 1547.

SECONDARY SOURCES

Benton, John F. "Trotula, Women's Problems, and the Professionalization of Medicine in the Middle Ages." *Bulletin of the History of Medicine* 59 (1985): 30–53.

Grant, Edward, ed. *A Source Book in Medieval Science*. Cambridge: Harvard University Press, 1974. Includes a brief biography of Trotula.

Packard, Francis R. In "History of the School of Salernum." With a note on the prehistory of the *Regimen sanitatis* by Fielding H. Garrison. In *The School of Salernum: Regimen salernitanum,* trans. John Harrington. New York: August M. Kelley, 1970.

Siebold, Eduard Casper Jacob von. *Versuch einter Geschichte der Geburtshülfe*. 2 vols. Berlin: Enslin, 1839–1845. See page 312. History of obstetrics containing information about midwives.

Stuard, Susan Mosher. "Dame Trot." *Signs* 1 (1975): 537–542.

Thorndike, Lynn. *A History of Magic and Experimental Science during the First Thirteen Centuries of Our Era*. 6 vols. London: Macmillan, 1923. Trotula is mentioned in volume 1, page 740.

STANDARD SOURCES

Hurd-Mead 1938; Mozans; Ogilvie 1986.

TROWER, CHARLOTTE GEORGIANA (1855–1928)

British botanist and botanical artist. Born 1855 in Stanstead Bury, Herts. At least one sister. Professional experience: illustrated botanical books. Honors and memberships: Botanical Society and Exchange Club of the British Isles. Died in Stanstead Bury, 8 November 1928.

Charlotte Trower and her slightly older sister, Alice (born 1853), were both dedicated botanists. Her sister did the field work, collecting plants for Trower to paint for botanical collections. Trower's illustrations for *British Brambles,* prepared for the Botanical Society and Exchange Club of the British Isles, appeared in the year after her death. Other illustrations, for M. Skene's *Flower Book for the Pocket* (1935), appeared seven years later. Her drawings of British plants are in Oxford.

JH/MBO

PRIMARY SOURCES

Botanical Society and Exchange Club of the British Isles. *British Brambles*. Illus. Charlotte Georgiana Trower. Arbroath: T. Buncle, 1929.

Skene, Macgregor. *Flower Book for the Pocket*. Illus. Charlotte Georgiana Trower. London: Oxford University Press, 1935.

SECONDARY SOURCES

"Charlotte Georgiana Trower." *Botanical Society and Exchange Club of the British Isles Reports* (1928): 851–855; (1929): 98–99. Obituary notice with portrait.

"Charlotte Georgiana Trower." *Journal of Botany* 31 (1929): 22.

TSVETAEVA, MARIA (1854–?)

Russian geologist. Born 1854. Educated First Moscow Gymnasium (completed 1872); Highest Lubyanskiy Natural History Science Women's Courses (1874–1877). Professional experience: Fourth Moscow Women's Gymnasium, instructor of natural sciences (1872–1882); First Gymnasium, instructor of variety of subjects (1882–?). Death date unknown.

Maria Tsvetaeva began her formal education at the First Moscow Gymnasium and finished at the Highest Lubyanskiy Natural History Science Women's Courses. After she completed her work at the Moscow Gymnasium, she became an instructor of natural sciences and later in the First Gymnasium taught different subjects. While teaching, she completed a full course of physics and mathematical sciences. Her courses included chemistry, physics, botany, zoology, mineralogy, paleontology, and geology.

She became especially interested in Carboniferous nautiloides and collected and studied them. The result was that, in 1888 and 1898, she had two large monographs published by the Geological Committee (Geolkom), the first state geological survey of Russia, instituted in Saint Petersburg in 1882. These monographs, still currently used, were published in the *Work of the Geological Committee,* and contained much new material.

Tsvetaeva was a member of the Mineralogical Society, the Moscow Naturalist Society, and the Society of Experimental Natural Scientists, St. Petersburg. She was also a member of the International Geological Congress of 1897 and participated in the Ural expedition led by A. P. Karpinskiy and F. H. Chernyshev. She was the first woman geologist who participated in the work of the Geological Congress. Her name is listed among the members of the Congress and along with M. V. PAVLOVA is found in the list of members of the Organizational Committee of the Congress. This was an important honor, and her election to it showed that she was highly respected by her fellow professionals.

CK

SECONDARY SOURCES
Egorov, S. V., et al. *VSEGEI v razvitii geologicheskoi nauki i mineral'no-syr'evoi bazy strany, 1882–1982* (VSEGEI and the Department of Geological Science and Mineral Raw Material Base of the Country, 1882–1982). Leningrad: Nedra, Leningradskoe otd-nie, 1982.

STANDARD SOURCES
Nalivkin.

TUMANSKAYA, OLGA G. (SHIROKOBRUHOVA) (1888–1970)

Soviet geologist and paleontologist. Born 1888 in Yalta to a military family. Married [?] Tumanskiy. Educated Yalta Women's Gymnasium (gold medal); Moscow Highest Women's Courses (entered 1908; Ph.D. in geologo-mineralogical sciences, 1923). Professional experience: geological bureau section, geology; Crimean University, Simferopol, senior assistant professor (1921–1923); Second Moscow University, assistant professor (1923–1930); Geological Committee, field work in Crimea (1924–1960); Central Scientific Research Institute of Geological Exploration (now the All-Union Scientific Research Geological Institute); Institute of Geology, senior geologist (1960–1970). Died 1970.

After her childhood in a military family in Yalta, Olga Shirokobruhova entered the Moscow Highest Women's Courses. She began her geological work in the Crimea, to which she returned all of her life, beginning with work on the Mesozoic and in 1914 moving to the Upper Paleozoic. Sickness then forced her to leave school temporarily. One of her first important works was published in 1916, when she proved that deposits formerly considered Upper Carboniferous were actualy Permian. In 1923, she finished the First Moscow University as a geologist and was invited to work as an assistant professor in the Second Moscow University. Her marriage to a wealthy man made it possible for her to do many things she could not have done otherwise, and his death made her life much more difficult.

She received money for the first time from the Geological Committee for field work in the Crimea in 1924. In 1929 she continued her work in the Crimea through what is now the All-Union Central Scientific Research Geological Institute. During World War II, she was forced to evacuate to the Urals, where her research was based on war themes. After the war, she returned to the institute and continued her works in the Crimea, sometimes going into the Transcaucasus to study the Upper Palezoic. During the last years of her life, she worked in Moscow in the Institute of Geology and Exploration of Combustible Fuels. She also continued to study her favorite Crimean groups.

Although she never taught nor was a member of the State Institute of Higher Education and Geological Facilities, she still received their help with her work. Her scientific work was concentrated under one short and clear title, the *Biostratigraphy of Permian Tethys*. Tumanskaya was unique because she did not have a mentor or a supervisor of studies even in the beginning of her scientific career. She always worked by herself, though she consulted others.

Her first work on the Crimean Permian came out in 1916. From that time, she studied only Crimean fauna. The first work on Permian ammoneis of the Pamirs was printed in 1963 and one about the Permian of Nakhichevan in 1966. From 1916 to 1963, almost half a century, she studied only Permian fossils. After three monographs, she finally became a doctor of geologo-mineralogical sciences. She also had a pedagogical career until 1930, when she gave up teaching for good.

CK/MBO

STANDARD SOURCES
Nalivkin.

TUM-SUDEN, CAROLINE (1900–1976)

U.S. neurophysiologist and neuropharmacologist. Educated Columbia University (M.A., 1927); Boston University (Ph.D., 1933). Professional experience: Sargent School of Physical Education (Boston), instructor (1934–1942), fellow; Boston University Medical School, instructor in physiology (1942–1945); Mount Holyoke College, assistant professor (1947–1950); Army Chemical Research and Development Laboratories (Medical Laboratories), Bethesda, neurophysiologist/neuropharmacologist (1950–1965?). Died 24 January 1976.

The neurophysiologist Caroline tum Suden was born in 1900. She was educated at Columbia, and received her master's degree in 1927. She then moved to Boston University, where she completed her doctorate in physiology. At first she could only find a position as an instructor at the Sargent School of Physical Education, where she taught for eight years. However, she remained affiliated with Boston University Medical School, working closely with Leland Wyman. Subsequently she became instructor in physiology at Boston University Medical School. She collaborated on twenty-six abstracts and papers with Wyman between 1929 and 1945. She was then appointed assistant professor at Mount Holyoke from 1947 to 1950.

In 1950, B. D. Dill recruited tum Suden as a member of his famed Medical Laboratories (the Army Chemical Research and Development Laboratories), where she worked on the effects of various substances on the nervous system for eleven years. She retired to Harford County (Maryland) badly crippled with arthritis. She died 24 January 1976. A member of the American Physiological Society from 1936, she left that organization over one hundred thousand dollars in her will.   JH/MBO

PRIMARY SOURCES

Tum Suden, Caroline. *"The Response of the Uterine Smooth Muscle of the Rat to Histamine and in Anaphylactic Shock."* Ph.D. diss., Boston University. 1933.

SECONDARY SOURCES

Dil, B. D. "Physiologists at Medical Laboratories 1946–1961." *The Physiologist* 25, no. 6 (1982): 474–478.

Loewe, Earl R. "Department of Physiology, Boston University School of Medicine (1873–1948)." *The Physiologist* 27, no. 1 (1984): 1–12.

TUNAKAN, SENIHA (HÜSNÜ) (1908–)

Turkish biologist and physical anthropologist. Born 14 March 1908. Father [?] Hüsnü. Married [?] Tunakan. Educated Frederick Wilhelm University, Berlin (Ph.D., 1941). Professional experience: Ankara University, Faculty of Languages, History and Geography, Anthropological Institute, anthropology faculty (1941–1973). Retired 1973.

Seniha Tunakan was a Turkish biologist and physical anthropologist who studied in Berlin, Germany. After receiving her advanced degree, she returned to Turkey and worked for the following thirty-two years at Ankara University in the Anthropological Institute, part of the Faculty of Languages, History and Geography (called the DTCF).

Tunakan began by studying skeletal remains of ancient peoples from important archeological excavations in Turkey in association with the internationally recognized Turkish physical anthropologist Sevket Aziz Kansu, director of the Anthropological Institute. Later comparative investigations by Tunaken of palm and fingerprints among various groups in Turkey (including criminals and children) and her twin studies were seen as pioneering publications on the genetics of the Turkish population.   JH/MBO

PRIMARY SOURCES

Tunakan, Seniha. With Sevket Aziz Kansu. "The Anthropology of the Remains of the Peoples of the Chalcolithic, Copper and Bronze Ages." *Belleten* 10 (1946): 539–555.

———. With Sevket Aziz Kansu. "An Anthropological Study of the Hittite, Phrygian, and Classic Period. Skeletons Found in the Tumulus at Karsogian." *Belleten* 12 (1948): 749–774.

———. "Research on the Four-Finger Line of the Palms of Turks and Criminal Turks." *Ankara University Faculty of Languages, History and Geography Dergisi* 12 (1955): 117–126.

———. "A Report on the Multitude of Twin Births in Turkey." *Ankara University Faculty of Languages, History and Geography Dergisi* 13 (1955): 17–19.

———. "A Comparative Palm Study of Turkish Criminals." *Antropologi* 12 (1985): 496–498.

STANDARD SOURCES
IDA.

TUNNICLIFF, RUTH (1876–1946)

U.S. bacteriologist and immunologist. Born 1 May 1876 in Macomb, Ill., to Sarah Alice (Bacon) and Damon G. Tunnicliff. Educated Kenwood Institute (1891); Vassar College (A.B., 1895); University of Chicago (premedical courses, 1898–1900); Northwestern University Woman's Medical School (medical course work, 1900–1902); Rush Medical College (M.D., 1903); Radcliffe College (Ph.D., 1926). Professional experience: John McCormick Institute for Infectious Diseases, intern (1903, 1904), research bacteriologist (1905–1935); Loyola University, Foundation for Dental Research, Chicago, researcher (1934–1940). Concurrent experience: U.S. Army, contract surgeon (clinical research) (1918). Honors and memberships: Chicago Pathological Society (president, 1926); American Association of Immunologists; Association of American Biologists; Chicago Institute of Medicine. Died 22 September 1946 in Chicago, Ill., of a heart attack.

Ruth May Tunnicliff was distinguished for the work she did on the causative agent of measles and a serum therapy for this childhood disease. She also did significant work on streptococci bacteria. Tunnicliff was born in a small town in Illinois where her father practiced law. Her mother had gone from Illinois to Vassar College, and urged her daughter to do the same. After studying at home and attending the Kenwood Institute in Chicago, Tunnicliff went to Vassar, where she became interested in social welfare.

On her return to Illinois, she began to prepare for medical training at the University of Chicago. Although she entered the Northwestern University Woman's Medical College in 1900, the school closed two years later, necessitating a shift to Rush Medical College, which granted her a degree. Like ALICE HAMILTON and other socially concerned women, she lived at Hull House, the innovative center for social service founded by JANE ADDAMS. It may have been the concern of these social activists about sanitation and public health that made Tunnicliff abandon clincal medicine for bacteriology. She began an internship at the hospital associated with the John McCormick Institute for Infectious Disease and joined its staff two years later.

Working closely with George H. Weaver, who was exploring the use of antistreptococcal serums, Tunnicliff did pioneering research on this topic and on the causes of meningitis. She studied fusiform bacteria over two decades and made useful contributions to this field. Tunnicliff published more than one hundred papers, dealing not only with bacteriology but also with immunity. In the mid-1920s, some twenty years after she had begun work as a professional bacteriologist, she spent a few years at Harvard University to study at the Medical School, receiving a doctorate from Radcliffe in 1926. She remained at the McCormick Institute until her retirement in 1934, but this did not end her research career. She moved to the Foundation for Dental Research in the Dental College of Loyola University, where for six more years she investigated bacteria in dental caries.

Tunnicliff led a quiet life with her sister Sarah near the University of Chicago. The two spent their summers in New Hampshire, where they gardened and sketched. She died of a sudden heart attack in 1946 at the age of seventy.

JH/MBO

SECONDARY SOURCES
Hektoen, Ludwig. "Ruth May Tunnicliff." *Proceedings of the Institute of Medicine of Chicago* 16 (1947): 298–299.

STANDARD SOURCES
American Women; ANB.

TURNBULL, PRISCILLA FREUDENHEIM (1924–1985)

U.S. geologist and paleontologist. Born 2 September 1924 in Chicago, Ill. Married William Turnbull in 1948. One son. Educated local schools, Hyde Park, Chicago; University of Chicago (B.S., 1945; M.S., 1946). Professional experience: Field Museum of Natural History, scientific assistant (1946–1954), fossil mammal field trips, Washakie Basin Wyoming (from 1956), Australia expeditions (1963–1964, 1966–1967, 1976–1977), Iraq expedition (1974), research associate in geology (1974–1985). Died 6 December 1985 in Chicago.

Priscilla Freudenheim was born and educated and spent her professional career in Chicago. Educated in public schools, she then received a bachelor's and a master's degree from the University of Chicago. After earning her master's, she went to work for the Field Museum of Natural History as a scientific assistant. It was at the museum that she met and then married William Turnbull, curator of fossil mammals. Her marriage slowed her career, but she did accompany her husband, and work in close association with him, on his field trips to study the Cenozoic fossils of Washakie Basin, Wyoming (beginning in 1956), Australia (1963–1964, 1966–1967, 1976–1977), and Iraq (1974). The field experience to Iraq resulted in her first major publication. She was a research associate from 1974 to 1985.

JH/MBO

PRIMARY SOURCES
Turnbull, Priscilla F. "The Fauna from the Terminal Pleistocene of Palegawra Cave, a Zarzian Occupation Site in Northeastern Iraq." *Fieldiana: Anthropology* (Field Museum of Natural History, Chicago) 63 (1974): 81–146.

STANDARD SOURCES
Sarjeant.

TURNER, ABBY HOWE (1875–1957)

U.S. physiologist. Educated Mount Holyoke College (A.B., 1896); universities of Pennsylvania and Chicago, graduate studies; Radcliffe (Ph.D., 1926); Wilson College, Chambersburg, Pa. (D.Sc.). Professional experience: Mount Holyoke, teacher (1922–1940), head of department (1926?–1940). Retired 1940. Wilson College, head, department of physiology (1943–1944). Died 26 November 1957. Buried in Nashua, N.H.

Abby Turner received an excellent science education at Mount Holyoke College. After she earned her bachelor's degree, she went to the University of Pennsylvania and the University of Chicago for graduate work. She then went to study at Harvard University, receiving her doctorate from Radcliffe in 1926. She was the first head of physiology at Mount Holyoke from 1926(?) until her retirement in 1940. In the early years, she worked in close association with the president, CORNELIA CLAPP, who was building up the science program at the college. After retirement, she was head of the physiology department at Wilson College during the war years 1943–1944.

During her years at Mount Holyoke, Turner studied blood circulation and made scientific observations on generations of undergraduates. A member of Phi Beta Kappa and Sigma Xi, she was awarded the Alumnae Graduate Medal in 1946. She died at age eighty-two, and was buried in Nashua, New Hampshire.

JH/MBO

PRIMARY SOURCES
Turner, Abby Howe. "Respiratory and Circulatory Tests of Physical Fitness in Healthy Young Women." Ph.D. diss., Radcliffe College, 1926.

STANDARD SOURCES
AMS 4, B9; *NAW* unused.

TURNER, MARY (PALGRAVE) (1774–1850)

British botanist and botanical artist. Born 16 January 1773. Father, William Palgrave of Coltishall, Norfolk. Married Dawson Turner. Six surviving children (one son, five daughters). Educated in watercolor and etching by John Sell Cotman. Professional experience:

Prepared botanical and antiquarian illustrations for husband. Died 1850.

After the marriage of Mary Palgrave to the botanist and antiquarian Dawson Turner, the couple persuaded the watercolorist John Sell Cotman to settle near them in 1812 and teach her and four of her daughters the art of drawing and painting. The Turner women then produced illustrations and etchings for Dawson's scientific and antiquarian books. They assisted Cotman in preparing illustrations of the architectural antiquities of Normandy. They also illustrated Turner's *Synopsis of the British Fuci* (Yarmouth, 1802) and the *Natural History of Fuci* with 258 figures, colored in some copies (1808–1819).

The botanical and artistic skills of Mary Turner were carried on by her daughter Mary, who married the botanist William Hooker. Following the death of Dawson Turner in 1858, his interleaved copy of *Muscologiae Spicilegium* with colored sketches of the leaves of all mosses mentioned by Sir William Hooker and illustrated by Mary Turner and her daughters, was donated to Kew Gardens.   JH/MBO

PRIMARY SOURCES
Turner, Dawson. *Synopsis of the British Fuci.* London: J. White and T. Longman and O. Rees, 1802. Illustrations and engravings by Mary Turner.
———. *Fuci, or Colored Figures, and Descriptions of the Plants Referred by Botanists to the Genus* Fucus. Printed by J. M'Creery, 1808–1819. With 258 figures colored in some copies prepared by Mary Turner and her daughters.

SECONDARY SOURCES
Journal of Botany 1912: 64. On the Turner women.

STANDARD SOURCES
Desmond; Shteir.

TWINING, ELIZABETH MARY (1805–1889)

British botanist. Born in 1805. Professional experience: Working Men's College, London, lectured on botany to young women; published on indigenous plants. Died 1889.

Elizabeth Twining produced a two-volume folio book of color plates of one hundred sixty indigenous plants. Intended to demonstrate the wonders of nature as "gifts of a heavenly Father," her botany carried a moral and religious message, as did that of many of her contemporaries.

In her fifties, Twining lectured to young women on botany at the Working Man's College, founded by the Christian Socialist F. D. Maurice. She died at the age of eighty-four.   JH/MBO

PRIMARY SOURCES
Twining, Elizabeth Mary. *Illustrations of the Natural Orders of Plants.* London: S. Low, 1849–1855.
———. *Short Lectures on Plants, for Schools and Adult Classes.* London: D. Nutt, 1858.

SECONDARY SOURCES
Stageman, P. "Elizabeth Mary Twining." *Garden* (London) 108 (1883): 115–117.

STANDARD SOURCES
Desmond; Steir.

TYLER, LEONA ELIZABETH (1906–1993)

U.S. psychologist. Born 10 May 1906 in Chetek, Wis., to Bessis (Carver) Tyler and Leon M. Tyler. Three younger brothers. Educated public schools; University of Minnesota (A.B., 1925; M.S., 1939; Ph.D., 1941). Professional experience: high school teacher (twelve years); University of Oregon, Eugene, Personnel Research Bureau, staff psychologist (1940–1942), department of psychology, assistant professor (1942–1947); associate professor (1947–1955); professor (1955–1971); dean of the graduate school (1965–1971); professor emerita and dean emerita (1971–1993). Concurrent experience: Veterans Administration, consultant (1940–1970s?); University of California, Berkeley, visiting professor (1957–1958). United States Office of Education, consultant (1959–1971). University of Amsterdam, Fulbright lecturer (1962–1963). Honors and memberships: American Psychological Association (president, 1972–1973); Oregon Psychological Association (president, 1956–1957); Western Psychological Association (president, 1957–1958); APA Counseling Division (president, 1959–1960); E. K. Strong Gold Medal for interest measurement; American Board of Professional Psychology (ABPP) award for Outstanding Contribution to Professional Psychology; Linfield College, honorary doctorate; Pacific University, Founder's Award; University of Oregon, Distinguished Service Award; University of Minnesota, Distinguished Achievement Award (1963); American Porphyria Foundation (APF) Gold Medal Award (1991). Died 29 April 1993 in Eugene, Ore. of congestive heart failure.

Leona Elizabeth Tyler, a noted psychologist, was the eldest of four children and the only daughter. Her mother had been a teacher and her father was a bookkeeper with interests in real estate. Her family moved when she was very young to a remote mining region in Minnesota, the Mesabi Iron Range, with a diverse European population and excellent schools. She attended local schools and entered the University of Minnesota, where she received her undergraduate degree in English.

After graduating, Tyler taught English in high schools for twelve years; in the classroom, she became interested in the psychology of adolescents, and she began to study psychology during the summers. She returned to the University of Minnesota, where she began graduate study after meeting with the prominent applied psychologist D. G. Paterson.

Tyler's first position in psychology was at the University of Oregon, in the Personnel Research Bureau. Attracted by the natural setting and spirit of Oregon, she remained associated with the department of psychology at the university for the rest of her career, rising through the ranks to a full professorship in psychology. She served as dean of the graduate school from 1971 until her mandatory retirement.

During her teaching career, she offered courses in psychometrics and on group and individual differences. She also taught courses on administering standardized tests such as the Stanford-Binet. She worked with the Veterans Administration from the 1940s, setting up counseling services and rehabilitation programs (later part of the University Counseling Center).

Tyler's first book, *The Psychology of Human Differences,* was published in 1947 and appeared in new editions in the fifties to some acclaim. Dissatisfied with the limitations of standard tests she developed the Tyler Choice Pattern Procedure, which allowed individual expression of preferences accompanied by reasons for those preferences. She served as consultant to the United States Office of Education from 1959 to 1971.

Tyler spent a sabbatical year in England (1951–1952) working with Hans Eysenck at the Maudsley Hospital in London. As a Fulbright lecturer at the University of Amsterdam ten years later, she carried out her first cross-cultural study on commonalities and differences in interests, values, and time perspectives among Dutch, Indian, Australian, and American adolescents. She was led to the conclusion that a very short time frame orientation—that is, when people are not able to imagine a future for themselves, thinking in terms of short or limited time periods—was a crucial element underlying many social problems. In most of her writings and research, Tyler focused on her theory of "multiple possibilities" to explain individual choice, arguing that whenever choices are required, opportunities are made as well as offered so that any individual can actualize only a fraction of his or her possibilities. Through her teaching, writing, and counseling, she attempted to help students realize their potential, and set and achieve their goals.

Tyler's publications—eleven books, fourteen book chapters, and more than fifty articles—deal primarily with individual differences and testing, counseling and clinical psychology, and overviews of psychological issues. One of her textbooks was written with the child psychologist FLORENCE GOODENOUGH and exerted a major influence on psychology students and instructors for the following four decades.

The doctoral training program that Tyler initiated at the University of Oregon, approved by the American Psychological Association in the late fifties, provided a model for other university programs. She supervised more advanced degree candidates at the University of Oregon than any other faculty member. Within the profession, she consistently urged the pursuit of excellence through assessment and the development of both scientific and professional aspects of psychology. She also stressed the necessity of serving the needs of the general population. Leona Tyler died in Eugene, Oregon, 29 April 1993, of congestive heart failure at age eighty-six.

JH/MBO

PRIMARY SOURCES

Tyler, Leona Elizabeth. *Psychology of Human Differences.* New York: D. Appleton-Century Co., [1947].
———. *Work of the Counselor.* New York: Appleton-Century-Crofts, 1953.
———. *Tests and Measurements.* Englewood Cliffs, N.J.: Prentice-Hall, 1963.
———. "The Antecedents of Two Varieties of Vocational Interests." *Genetic Psychology Monographs* 70 (1964): 177–227.
———. *Individual Differences: Abilities and Motivational Directions.* New York: Appleton-Century-Crofts, 1974.
———. *Individuality: Human Possibilities and Personal Choice in the Psychological Development of Men and Women.* San Francisco: Jossey-Bass, 1978.
———. *Thinking Creatively: A New Approach to Psychology and Individual Lives.* San Francisco: Jossey-Bass, 1983.
———. In O'Connell and Russo, 1988. Autobiography.

SECONDARY SOURCES

"Citation: Leona E. Tyler." *American Psychologist* 46 (April 1991): 330–332.
Sundberg, Norman D., and Susan K. Gilmore. "Leona E. Tyler (1906–1993), Counseling Pioneer (In Memoriam)." *The Counseling Psychologist* 22 (January 1994): 179.
Sundberg, Norman D., and Richard A. Littleman. "Leona E. Tyler (1906–1993). Obituary." *American Psychologist* 49, no. 3 (March 1994): 211.

STANDARD SOURCES

AMS 8–13; O'Connell and Russo 1990 (article by Suzanne M. Zilber and Samuel H. Osipow).

TYLER, MARTHA G. (fl. 1890s)

U.S. ornithologist. Flourished late nineteenth century. Lived in northern New England.

Although biographical information on Martha Tyler is unavailable, she was apparently an amateur ornithologist who managed to get a paper published in the *Auk*. We know from this paper that she studied barn owls.   JH/MBO

PRIMARY SOURCES

Tyler, Martha G. "The Barn Owl (*Strix pratincola*) in Northern Vermont." *Auk* 11 (1894): 253.

STANDARD SOURCES

Catalogue Royal Society.

TYNDALL, A. C. (fl. 1890s)

Canadian ornithologist. Lived in Ottawa. Never married.

Little is known about this late-nineteenth-century ornithologist who studied and wrote popular accounts of birds.   JH/MBO

PRIMARY SOURCES

Tyndall, A. C. "A Little Wood and Some of Its Feathered Denizens." *Ottawa Naturalist* 10 (1896): 54–57, 71–72, 113–116.

———. "The Birds of a Garden." *Ottawa Naturalist* 13 (1899): 137–139.

———. "My Feathered Jester." *Ottawa Naturalist* 13 (1899): 188–190.

STANDARD SOURCES

Catalogue Royal Society.

TYNG, ANITA E. (fl. 1878)

U.S. physician and surgeon. Educated Woman's Medical College of Pennsylvania. Professional experience: New England Hospital for Women and Children, surgeon (1864–1873?); practiced in Providence, R.I. (ca. 1874).

Anita Tyng was an early graduate of the Woman's Medical College of Pennsylvania and a student of Dean RACHEL BODLEY (chemistry). For two years Tyng worked in private practice as a surgical assistant to Horatio Storer. She then joined the staff of the New England Hospital for Women and Children, founded by MARIE ZAKRZEWSKA, and began to perform gynecological surgery. In 1866 she joined LUCY SEWALL in a famous appeal for admission to Harvard Medical School that was denied by Dean Lemuel Shattuck. Tyng's article on the dangerous condition of eclampsia in pregnancy was presented at the quarterly meeting of the Rhode Island Medical Society in September 1874. She ran a successful practice in Providence, Rhode Island, that included gynecological surgery, and her work was well-regarded by male as well as female physicians. In the late 1870s and early 1880s Tyng mentored a number of young women physicians.

In a paper delivered to the alumnae of the Woman's Medical College of Pennsylvania in 1880, Tyng called for a concerted effort by women physicians to investigate female health. Her talk galvanized women physicians, who began to monitor the health of college women, and show that higher education not only did not have an adverse affect on women's health, but could actually be beneficial.

Tyng, among other physicians, occasionally performed Battey's Operation, the removal of normal ovaries to "cure" gynecological and psychological complaints.   JH/MBO

PRIMARY SOURCES

Tyng, Anita E. "Eclampsia puerperalis." *Communications of the Rhode Island Medical Society* (1874): 407–422.

Tyng, Anita. "A Case of Clitoridectomy." *Woman's Medical College of Pennsylvania Transactions* (1878): 25.

———. "Case of Removal of Both Ovaries? (Battey's Operation)." *Woman's Medical College of Pennsylvania Transactions* (1880): 27.

STANDARD SOURCES

Morantz-Sanchez.

TYSKA, MARIA (1917–1974)

Polish stratigrapher. Born 7 March 1917. Member of Geological Institute, Warsaw. Died 29 April 1974.

In addition to her stratigraphic work, Maria Tyska did editorial and cartographic work at the Geological Institute, Warsaw.   JH/MBO

SECONDARY SOURCES

Piechulska-Slowanska, Barbara. "Maria Tyska 7.III.1917–29.IV.1974." *Rocznik Polskiego Towarzystwa Geologicznego* (Annales de la Société géologique de Pologne) 45, nos. 3–4 (1975): 451–454.

Walsh, Mary Roth. *Doctors Wanted, No Women Need Apply: Sexual Barriers in the Medical Profession, 1835–1975.* New Haven: Yale University Press, 1977.

STANDARD SOURCES

Sarjeant.

U

UBISCH, GERTA VON (1882–1965)

German geneticist. Born 3 October 1882 in Metz. Father, Prussian artillery captain. Educated Heidelberg; Freiburg; Berlin; Strassburg (graduated Ph.D. in physics, 1911); Heidelberg University (qualified to teach university botany, 1923). Professional experience: Land-wirtschaftlichen Hochschule with Erwin Baur, scientific assistant; Heidelberg, assistant (1921–1923), docent (lecturer) in genetics (1923–1933); Utrecht, traveling research grant (1933); Switzerland, traveling research grant stipend (1934); Sao Paolo, Brazil Schlangenseruminstitut (Snake Venom Institute), research scientist (1934–1938). Died 31 March 1965 in Heidelberg.

Gerta von Ubisch's mother was from a Jewish merchant family in Danzig, and her father was a Prussian artillery captain. A number of her relatives were physicians, physicists, and lawyers. She spent her childhood and youth in Metz, Leipzig, Dresden, and Berlin. When she finished school at sixteen years of age she wanted to study physics. Despite the opposition of her parents, she was permitted to attend the gymnasium, from which she graduated in 1904. She also was permitted to study physics at Heidelberg University, unusual for a woman at that time. Only a few female students were registered, and they could be, and often were, denied permission by the professors to attend their lectures.

Disappointed by Professor Georg Quincke's lectures in physics, von Ubisch went to Freiburg for two semesters. She was so taken by August Weismann's lectures about the continuity of the germ plasm that she toyed with the thought of studying zoology. Since she was told that there were more work possibilities for women in physics than in zoology, she stayed with physics and moved to Berlin in order to study with Emil Warburg. However, Warburg had just been made director of the Physikalisch-Technischen Reichsanstalt, so he gave up his professorship, and von Ubisch continued her studies first with Paul Drude and then, after his suicide, with Heinrich Rubens.

In Berlin she made friends with a number of physicists, among them James Franck, Gustav Hertz, and LISE MEITNER. Since the doctoral advisor did not look after the women students, and von Ubisch ran into unsolvable technical difficulties in her dissertation, she went to Strassburg, where she could live with relatives. She finished her studies in 1911. According to her own dictates, she did not do her dissertation independently enough in order to become a physicist; thus, she decided to change to biology. In her academic career she had attended lectures for several semesters in botany and therefore took botany as one of her secondary fields. After her graduation she had to return to Berlin for financial reasons. However, the botanist at Berlin University had no place in his graduate courses for her, so she took the advice of friends and went to Erwin Baur, who had just been made chair of botany at the Agricultural University (landwirtschaftlichen Hochschule). She became the first woman Baur accepted as a scientific coworker. Helped by a stipend, she began research on analyzing barley, but she did not get a permanent job in Baur's institute. Therefore, she conducted scientific research for several years with private plant-raising organizations.

At the beginning of the Weimar Republic, von Ubisch started to become politically engaged, and in 1920 she joined the newly formed Deutschen Demokratischen party. During the election before the Reichstagswahlen, she wrote an article that the women should take part in the bourgeois and not only in left-leaning parties. In 1921 she took an assistant's job with Ludwig Jost at the Institute for Botany at the University of Heidelberg. She habilitated (qualified to teach university) in 1923, examining botanical genetics, and she was entitled to rise to the level of extraordinary (associate) professor in 1929. She was the first woman to habilitate in Baden. Jost considered her thesis excellent and had no qualms about recommending her for the professorship. She was the only female docent in Heidelberg to teach genetics.

In the ten years that she worked as a docent she found it difficult to be promoted because of the male professors' hesitation to recommend her.

She conducted research on barley and found a genetic explanation for heterostyly, publishing her results in the journal *Zeitschrift für induktive Abstammungs-und Verersbunglehre* as well as other periodicals. In 1933, she lost the position at Heidelberg because of her "non-Aryan" descent. Since her father was an officer and was at the front during World War I, she was officially given back the *venia legendi* (right to lecture), but her lectures were boycotted by the National Socialist Student Association. She was over fifty years old, and it was difficult for her to find a position abroad. In the summer of 1933 she followed an invitation of a Dutch Akademikerinnenverbandes for one semester at Utrecht.

In 1934 von Ubisch got a stipend to go to Switzerland, and in December 1934, she got a position in the Schlangenseruminstitut (snake venom institute) in Sao Paolo. Her department was dissolved in 1938 and after another short job, she was without permanent employment from 1940. After the war, she looked for a job in Norway where her brother lived. She even tried doing housework and being a governess for acquaintances in Brazil. In 1952 she arrived, almost seventy years old and without money, in Heidelberg. Her request for restitution was denied with the explanation that she was not a tenured faculty member of the University of Heidelberg.

In 1955, when former Privatdozenten and other non-tenured faculty were awarded restitution, she finally was given a pension. She was seventy-three years old. However, the decision was reversed when the natural history faculty of Heidelberg University, on 25 June 1956, decided that von Ubisch would not be included in the personnel list of Heidelberg University. JH/MBO

PRIMARY SOURCES

Ubisch, Gerta von. "II Beitrag zu einer Faktorenanalyse von Gerste." *Zeitschrift für induktive Abstammungs-und Verersbunglehre* 20 (1919): 65–117.

SECONDARY SOURCES

Deichmann, Ute. "Frauen in der Genetik, Forschung und Karriere bis 1950." In *Aller Männer-kultur zum Trotz. Frauen in Mathematik und Naturwissenschaften,* ed. Renate Tobies. Campus: Frankfurt, 1997.

UNDERHILL, RUTH MURRAY (1883–1984)

U.S. anthropologist. Born 22 August 1883 probably in Ossining, N.Y., to Anna Murray and Abram Sutton Underhill. Two sisters and one brother. Married Charles Crawford (divorced). Educated Ossining School for Girls; Bryn Mawr Preparatory School; Vassar College (A.B., 1905); London School of Economics and University of Munich (1906–1908); Columbia University (Ph.D., 1939). Professional experience: Massachusetts Society for the Prevention of Cruelty to Children, social worker (1905); various social work agencies, social worker (from 1908); field work among Papago Indians; Barnard College, assistant in anthropology (from 1934); Hogan School, Bureau of Indian Affairs (BIA), experimental seminar, lecturer (1934); Soil Conservation Service (1935–1938), soil conservationist (1935–1937); BIA, associate supervisor of Indian education (1938–1944), supervisor of Indian education (1944–1948); retired 1948; University of Denver, Department of Anthropology, professor (1948–1952). Died 1984.

Ruth Underhill began her anthropological career late in life after a failed marriage. Born on a farm on the Hudson River north of New York City, she attended a girls' school nearby and then the preparatory school for Bryn Mawr. She attended Vassar rather than Bryn Mawr, majored in English, and was elected to Phi Beta Kappa. After a short stint working in Boston for a social agency, she went to Europe where she studied at the London School of Economics and the University of Munich, learning French, German, Italian, and Spanish. She later was proficient in Papago. When she returned to the United States, she held a number of jobs in social agencies, wrote a column for the *New York Sun,* and wrote for magazines. She published a novel, *The White Moth,* in 1920.

Underhill claimed that she had married the wrong man in Charles Crawford, and the couple divorced soon after they married. Immediately after the decree was finalized, she enrolled in the department of anthropology at Columbia where she was encouraged by RUTH BENEDICT. She always felt that Franz Boas, chair of the department, considered her marginal. He did, however, provide a small sum of money for her to do research with the Papago Indians, now called the Tohono O'odham. After this research, Boas was convinced that she was dedicated to anthropology. Her thesis, "Social Organization of the Papago Indians," made a significant contribution to anthropological literature.

While she was a Columbia graduate student she worked as an assistant in anthropology under GLADYS REICHARD. During the summer of 1934, she and Reichard became involved in a seminar known as Hogan School, under the auspices of the Bureau of Indian Affairs (BIA), with the purpose of teaching Navajos to write the Navajo languages. This began Underhill's often stormy relationship with the BIA. One of her tasks in her extended position was to present cross-cultural information that would sensitize non-Indians to the cultural needs of the tribes with which they were working. When the Papago constitution was constructed, Underhill found it to be at odds with the tribes' social organization and was outspoken in her criticism. She was thereafter banned from participating in government projects dealing with tribal matters.

In 1945, she took the Civil Service examination for ethnologists. She was hired not as an ethnologist but by the Soil Conservation Service, which was better funded. The BIA did not use her as head of the Papago survey team because of various personality conflicts. In 1936 the Soil Conservation Service seconded Underhill to the BIA for twelve months to complete her previously begun pamphlets on cross-cultural information. In 1937, she was officially transferred to the BIA and in 1938 was promoted to associate supervisor of Indian education. During this time she worked with curriculum development in Indian schools from her home base in Santa Fe, New Mexico. Underhill was promoted to supervisor of Indian education in 1944 and was transferred to Denver.

After the BIA was reorganized following World War II, Underhill's career was in danger. Because of a sympathetic supervisor, she held a series of temporary appointments followed by a six-month leave of absence to work at the University of Oklahoma, qualifying her for retirement. After retirement she began a second career as a teacher in the anthropology department at the University of Denver until 1952 and again at New York State Teachers College and Colorado Women's College.

Underhill spent much of her later life traveling. Her field work was honored in 1979 by the Papago Indians, and in June 1984 she was presented with the American Anthropological Association's special recognition citation.   JH/MBO

PRIMARY SOURCES
Underhill, Ruth. "Autobiography of a Papago Woman." *Memoirs of the American Anthropological Association* no. 46. Supplement to *American Anthropologist* 38, no. 3, part 2 (1936).
———. *The First Penthouse Dwellers of America.* New York: J. J. Augustin, 1938.
———. *Singing for Power: The Song Magic of the Papago Indians of Southern Arizona.* Berkeley: University of California Press, 1938.
———. "Social Organization of the Papago Indians." *Columbia University Contributions to Anthropology* 30. New York: Columbia University Press, 1939.
———. *Ceremonial Patterns in the Greater Southwest.* American Ethnological Society Monographs, 13. New York: J. J. Augustin, 1948.
———. *The Navajos.* Norman: University of Oklahoma Press, 1956.
———. *Red Man's Religion: Beliefs and Practices of the Indians North of Mexico.* Chicago: University of Chicago Press, 1965.

SECONDARY SOURCES
Babcock, Barbara A. and Nancy J. Parezo. *Daughters of the Desert: Women Anthropologists and the Native American Southwest, 1880–1980.* Albuquerque: University of New Mexico Press, 1988.

STANDARD SOURCES
AMS 8, *S&B* 9–11; Gacs (article by Joyce Griffen).

USHAKOVA, ELIZAVETA IVANOVNA (1895–?)

Soviet agronomist. Born 21 August (2 September by new Russian calendar) 1895. Educated Timiriazev Agricultural Academy in Moscow (degree, 1931). Professional experience: Grigov Vegetable Experiment Station in Moscow Oblast (1937–1962?). Honors and memberships: Communist Party (1920); Stalin Prize 1946; All-Union (Lenin) Academy of Agricultural Sciences, member (1948). Death date unknown.

Elizaveta Ushakova was born in tsarist Russia and joined the Communist Party three years after the Bolshevik revolution. She was educated in agronomy in the late 1920s, and she received a degree in 1931. For many years Ushakova worked at the Grigov Experiment Station. In 1946, she was awarded the Stalin Prize; she was elected to the Academy of Agricultural Sciences two years later.   JH/MBO

STANDARD SOURCES
Who's Who in Soviet Science.

UVAROVA, COUNTESS PRASKOV'IA SERGEEVNA (1840–1924)

Russian archeologist. Born 1840 to Princess Praskov'ia Borisovna (Chetvertinskaia) Shcherbatova and Prince Sergei Aleksandrovich Shcherbatov. Four siblings. Married Count Aleksei Sergeevich Uvarov. Six children: Aleksei, Sergei, Fedor, Ekaterina, Praskov'ia, Igor'. Professional experience: Moscow Archaeological Society, president. Russian Academy of Sciences, member. Died in the summer of 1924 in Yugoslavia.

Praskov'ia Sergeevna Shcherbatova (later Uvarova) came from an aristocratic family that could trace its ancestry back to Riurik. Her education, within certain "ladylike" limits, would have been excellent: the Shcherbatovs belonged to a circle of wealthy families which had wide intellectual interests. One acquaintance was Count Lev Tolstoi (Leo Tolstoy) who was apparently much smitten with the young princess and immortalized his impression of her in the character of Kitty Shcherbatskaia in his novel *Anna Karenina.*

In 1859 the princess married Count Aleksei Sergeevich Uvarov. At the time of their marriage, Uvarov was thirty-five years old and well established as an archeologist. His interest in the subject had begun in childhood, encouraged by his father and well-known historians of the period with whom his family was acquainted. By the age of twenty, he was already conducting research in the south of Russia. Besides his own work, he encouraged the work of others and offered prizes from his own resources. In 1851, he excavated 757 *kurgany* or burial mounds in Suzdal', and in 1853 and 1854 he was in charge of excavations in the Tauride province. In 1857 he established the Uvarov Prize in the Academy of Sciences and was appointed head of the section of Russian and Slavic archeology. Uvarova's career was, until he died, inseparable from his. She became totally committed to the study of archeology and, even while bringing up six children (the oldest, Aleksei, was born in 1859), devoted her life to it.

In 1864, Uvarov was instrumental in establishing the Moscow Archaeological Society, of which he was unanimously elected president. When he died in 1884, Uvarova was elected president in his stead and remained in that capacity until the Revolution of 1917. The Revolution destroyed the old aristocracy. Within a few years, many of those who survived had fled the country. Countess Uvarova and her family emigrated to Yugoslavia where she died in 1924.

To the Uvarovs, Russian archeology and the preservation and restoration of historic monuments were much more than an aristocratic entertainment. Both the count and the countess were dedicated to their own work and to encouraging that of others.

Uvarova accompanied her husband on his expeditions to the Caucasus, at that time not without some hazard, and later made expeditions on her own. She made valuable contributions to the study of the Koban bronze culture, spending much time on research in libraries and museums, both in Russia and abroad. Over her lifetime she published 174 articles on various aspects of archeology. Most important of all was her work as an organizer of science through the medium of the Archaeological Society, which she guided through the force of her personality for thirty-five years.

Among other efforts to promote interest in archeology and the preservation of antiquities, the Archaeological Society established a series of congresses to be held every three years at one of six historic locations. In addition to her other work, Uvarova edited the transactions of these congresses. She was an honorary member of many Russian and foreign societies. In 1895, she became a member of the Russian Academy of Sciences.

When Uvarova died, in spite of all the work she had done for her country, her only obituary was published in the emigré *Izvestiia Rossiiskaia Akademiia*. Interest in Countess Uvarova's work is reviving and a program of Uvarov Lectures, recreating those of the original Russian Archaeological Society, has been instituted in memory of these two eminent archeologists. ACH

PRIMARY SOURCES

Uvarova, Praskov'ia Sergeevna. *Kavkaz: putevyia zamietki, grafini Uvarovoi.* Moscow: A. A. Levenson, 188?–1904.

———. *Katalog riznitsy Spaso-Preobrazhenskago monastyria v Iaroslavlie.* Moscow: Mamontova, 1887.

SECONDARY SOURCES

Andreevskii, I. E., ed. *Entsiklopedicheskii slovar'.* St. Petersburg: I. A. Efron, 1890–1906.

Lukina, O. A., and B. Kupriashina, eds. *Uvarovskie chteniia.* Murom: Muromskaia gorodskaia, 1990.

V

VACHELL, ELEANOR (1879–1948)

Welsh botanist. Born 1879 in Cardiff, Glamorganshire, to Winifred and Charles Tanfield Vachell. Educated small school in Cardiff; The Manse, Malvern; St. John's, Brighton. Honors: Linnean Society, Fellow (1917). Died 6 December 1948.

Eleanor Vachell was introduced to field botany as a child by her father. She was given a copy of Charles A. Johns's *Flowers of the Field* (1851) and a botanical diary. Although she outgrew Johns's book, she continued to keep the diary. She collected plants around Cardiff and on the Glamorgan coast where her family went for holidays. She took botanical trips to Scotland, Ireland, Brittany, Norway, and Switzerland with her father. After identifying a plant, she would record it by coloring the illustrations in botanical field guides. Her method enabled her to have a superb knowledge of British plants in their natural habitats. She was a member of the British Exchange Club and was very active in the Cardiff Naturalists' Society. From 1903, at first jointly with her father, she was honorary secretary of the committee responsible for preparing the *Flora of Glamorgan*. After the book was published she became recorder and held that post until her death. She continued to publish articles throughout her life.

Vachell was a popularizer of field botany. From 1921 she published a weekly note on wild flowers in the *Western Mail*, dictating the last of these articles on her death bed. She gave lectures to societies and encouraged young field botanists.

Although botany was Vachell's most important interest, she was an active churchwoman and a supporter of the British Red Cross Society. She also devoted herself to war work during both world wars. A member of the Court of Governors of the National Museum of Wales from 1919 and of its Council from 1925, she also served on several of its committees. JH/MBO

PRIMARY SOURCES

Vachell, Eleanor. "Glamorgan Flowering Plants and Ferns." *Glamorgan County History* 1 (1936): 123–178.

Vachell's herbarium and manuscripts are at the National Museum of Wales.

SECONDARY SOURCES

Hyde, H. A. "Eleanor Vachell." *Watsonia* 1 (1949–1950): 325–327.

Proceedings of the Linnean Society 179 (1948–1949): 252. Obituary notice.

STANDARD SOURCES

Desmond.

VALENTINE, LILA HARDAWAY (MEADE) (1865–1921)

U.S. health reformer and suffragist. Born 4 February 1865 in Richmond, Va., to Kate (Fontaine) and Richard Hardaway Meade. Four siblings. Married Benjamin Batchelder Valentine (1886). Educated at home; private schools in Richmond. Professional experience: Richmond Education Association, founder with others (1900), president (until 1904); Richmond Training School for Kindergartners, founder (1901); Co-operative Educational Association of Virginia (1904); Instructive Visiting Nurse Association of Richmond (1904); Anti-Tuberculosis Auxiliary (1904); Equal Suffrage League of Virginia, president (1909). Died 14 July 1921 in Richmond, Va., after surgery for an intestinal obstruction.

Lila Valentine can hardly be called a scientist. She was, however, active in health-care organizations, particularly those involving children. Because of her own sparse education, she was adamant in her belief that education should be for all children regardless of race of gender, and founded numerous organizations to support her beliefs. As she worked with the schools, Valentine realized that many of the children were unhealthy, and needed public health facilities. She found a group of volunteer nurses who were teaching hygiene to indigent patients, gathered a group of interested women to hear them describe their work, and formed the Instructive Visiting Nurse Association of Richmond in 1904. As president of this organization she set up an anti-tuberculosis auxiliary in 1904 that was the first concentrated campaign against tuberculosis in Virginia.

Valentine's health had been poor since 1888, when she had a stillborn child. In 1904, she became ill and was told by her doctors to give up her public work temporarily. She went to England where she became involved in suffragist questions. When she returned to Virginia she became president of the Equal Suffrage League of Virginia in 1909. She remained president until 1920, during which time she worked unsuccessfully for a state suffrage amendment, made numerous speeches, and addressed the Virginia House of Delegates. Her support of such liberal causes as black education and membership in the National Child Labor Committee and the American Association for Labor Legislation made her suspect to conservative opponents. When she realized that the suffrage amendment would be ratified, she turned to the problem of women's ignorance of politics. She requested a three-day conference on government be held at the University of Virginia in April 1920 to address this concern. She also urged that civics be added to the school curricula.

After the death in June 1919 of her husband, Valentine went to Maine, where she lived with two sisters. However, eventually she returned to Richmond, where she died at the age of fifty-six.   JH/MBO

PRIMARY SOURCES
Valentine's papers are at the Valentine Museum, Richmond, and the Woman Suffrage manuscripts at the Virginia State Library, Richmond.

SECONDARY SOURCES
Glasgow, Ellen. *The Woman Within*. New York: Harcourt, Brace, [1954].

STANDARD SOURCES
NAW (article by Lloyd G. Taylor, Jr.); *Woman's Who's Who of America*.

VAN BEVERWIJK, AGATHE L. (1907–1963)
Dutch botanist and mycologist. Born 18 September 1907 in Amsterdam, Netherlands. One sibling. Educated University of Amsterdam (1925–1930); Commonwealth Mycological Institute (1946); Paris, studied with Langeron and Rivalier (1948). Professional experience: secondary school, Amsterdam, teacher; Cancer Institute, research worker (1932–1933?); International Quaker School, biology and English teacher (1934–1944); Centraalbureau voor Schimmelcultures, Baarn, assistant collaborator (with Professor Westerdijk) (1944–1958), director (1958–1963). Died 10 July 1963 in Austria.

As the oldest of two children, Agathe L. van Beverwijk lived and played along the canals that passed by her elegant upper-class home in Amsterdam. She was educated at the University of Amsterdam, studying biology and geology from 1925 until 1930, when she received her degree. After teaching biology for a few years in a secondary school in Amsterdam, she left to join the Cancer Institute in Amsterdam, but found herself unable to experiment on animals. She learned English and taught biology in English at an international Quaker school. When the school closed in 1944, she joined the Centraalbureau voor Schimmelcultures in Baarn, where she first assisted and collaborated with Professor Westerdijk, director of that organization. She remained there the rest of her professional life and soon became an authority on the fungus genera *Fusarium*, *Pythium* and *Phytophthora*.

In 1946 van Beverwijk went to Royal Botanic Gardens at Kew to the Commonwealth Mycological Institute to study mycology for two months, and took the opportunity to tour the other phytopathological institutes in England. She traveled to Paris in 1948 to study medical mycology under Langeron and Rivalier. She visited mycological institutes in the United States in 1957, and attended international congresses on her topic between 1947 and 1962. Her greatest interest was in the watermolds (the heliocosporous Hyphomycetes) that have a mycelium below water but produce spores above water. One group of these fungi was named after her in 1961 (*Vanbeverwijkia spirospora*).

Van Beverwijk was appointed director of the Centraalbureau voor Schimmelcultures in 1958 and began to reorganize the type cultures and other organizational systems. She corresponded with colleagues around the world and worked to promote international cooperation and exchanges between culture collection specialists. She planned a new modern laboratory building for the institute, but died before the building was completed. She died in the Austrian mountains, where she had gone for her health, in July 1963. In addition to Dutch organizations, she had been a member of the British Mycological Society and Mycological Society of America.   JH/MBO

PRIMARY SOURCES
Van Beverwijk, Agathe L. "Are Type Cultures Type Materia?" *Commonwealth Mycological Institute, Conference, (1960)*. Kew: Royal Botanic Gardens, 1960.

———. "Catalogues of Culture Collection." In *Reunion de
Collections du Microorganisms.* n.p., 1962.
———."Culture Collections, Why and Wherefore." In *Confer-
ence on Culture Collection*. Ottawa: n.p., 1962.

SECONDARY SOURCES

Mycologia 56 (1964): 641–44. Obituary notice. Includes portrait.

VAN BLARCOM, CAROLYN (CONANT)
(1879–1960)

*U.S. nurse and midwife. Born 12 June 1879 in Alton, Ill., to
Fanny (Conant) and Willam Dixon Van Blarcom. Five siblings.
Educated at home informally; Johns Hopkins Training School for
Nurses (graduated 1901). Professional experience: Johns Hopkins
Training School for Nurses, instructor in obstetrics and assistant su-
perintendent of nurses (1901–1905); St. Louis, Mo., reorganized a
training school for nurses (1905); Maryland Tuberculosis Sanato-
rium at Sibillisville, director (1908); sanatorium near New Bedford,
Mass., director; helped establish midwives' school affiliated with
Bellevue Hospital in New York City; retired during 1930s; briefly
resumed career during World War II, as director of nurses' aid program of the American Red Cross. Died 20 March 1960 in Arcadia,
Calif., of bronchopneumonia.*

Raised in a single-parent family because her father deserted
her mother and her five siblings, Carolyn Van Blarcom had a
difficult childhood. When she was six years old she had
rheumatic fever followed by rheumatoid arthritis. Consequently she was unable to attend school; what education she
got she absorbed at home. At age fourteen, after the death of
her mother, Van Blarcom was sent east to live her portrait-
painter grandfather, Alban Jasper Conant, and other relatives. Her primary goal was to enroll in the Johns Hopkins
Training School for Nurses. In spite of opposition from her
family, she enrolled in 1898. Her health again interfered and
she was unable to complete the course in the usual three-
year time period. However when she graduated in 1901 she
completed the course superbly and was invited to stay on as a
member of the nursing school faculty. She stayed at the
school for four years as instructor in obstetrics and assistant
superintendent of nurses.

In 1905 Van Blarcom left Hopkins and went to St. Louis
to help reorganize a training school for nurses. However, she
was again laid low by her health. An arthritic episode forced
her to give up work for three years. After her health improved she became director of the Maryland Tuberculosis
Sanatorium, where she was very successful in improving
conditions for patients. She moved to a similar post in New
Bedford, Massachusetts, and made startling improvements to
the physical plant.

Van Blarcom's organizational talents became recognized,
and she was appointed secretary of the New York State
Committee for the Prevention of Blindness in 1909. During
this time she found an opportunity to play a role in investigating the causes and prevention of blindness. She noted that
ophthalmia neonatorum, the leading cause of preventable
blindness in newborns, could be prevented by applying a solution of silver nitrate. However, midwives were not using
the simple procedure, obliging Van Blarcom to study midwifery practices in the United States, England, and fourteen
other foreign countries. She published the results of this investigation in *The Midwife in England*. In this book she reported that the United States was the only country that she
studied that did not train and license its midwives.

Van Blarcom became the first American nurse to become
a licensed midwife. She wrote many articles for both the
professional and popular press and adressed groups about the
problem. She established a midwives' hospital in conjunction
with Bellevue Hospital in New York City. She continued
her work on blindness; in 1916 she was was secretary of the
Illinois Society for the Prevention of Blindness, and during
World War I was director of the Bureau of Nursing Service
of the Atlantic Division of the American Red Cross. During
the 1920s, Van Blarcom accelerated her activities on behalf
of women and children. She published three books and became health editor for the *Delineator*. She wrote another
book, *Building the Baby*, which was published in 1929.

All through Van Blarcom's life, she experienced chronic ill
health. She retired during the 1930s and resumed her career
on a limited scale during World War II. During the postwar
years, her health continued to deteriorate.   JH/MBO

PRIMARY SOURCES

Van Blarcom, Carolyn. *The Midwife in England*. New York:
[Committee for the Prevention of Blindness], 1913.
———. *Obstetrical Nursing*. New York, Macmillan 1922.
———. *Getting Ready to Be a Mother*. New York: Macmillan,
1922.
———. *Building the Baby*. Chicago: The Public Service Office
of the Chicago Tribune, [1929].
Van Blarcom's papers are at the Alan Mason Chesney Medical
Archives, Johns Hopkins Medical Institutions, Institute of
the History of Medicine, and the headquarters of the Johns
Hopkins Nurses Alumni Association, Baltimore.

SECONDARY SOURCES

American Journal of Nursing 60 (June 1960). Obituary notice.
Homans, J. E., and L. E. Dearborn, eds. *The Cyclopedia of
American Biography. Supplementary edition*. New York: The
Press Association Compilers, 1918–1931.
Johns Hopkins Hospital School of Nursing *Alumnae Magazine*
59 (October 1960). Obituary notice.

Pennock, Meta Rutter, ed. *Makers of Nursing History.* New York: Lakeside Publishing Co., 1940.

STANDARD SOURCES
NAW (M) (article by Judy Barrett Litoff).

VAN DEMAN, ESTHER BOISE (1862–1937)

U.S. archeologist. Born 1 October 1862 in South Salem, Ohio, to Martha (Millspaugh) and Joseph Van Deman. Five siblings and half siblings. Never married. Educated South Salem Academy; University of Michigan (A.B., 1891; A.M., 1892); Bryn Mawr College (1892–1893); University of Chicago (Ph.D., 1898). Professional experience: Wellesley College, Latin teacher (1893–1895); Bryn Mawr School, Baltimore, teacher (1895–1896); Mount Holyoke College, instructor (1898–1901); American School of Classical Studies, Rome, fellowship (1901–1903); Goucher College, associate professor of Latin and archeology (1903–1906); Carnegie Institute of Washington, fellow (1906–1910), staff (1910–1930); Archaeological Institute of America, Charles Eliot Norton lectureship (1924–1925); University of Michigan, Carnegie Research Professor of Roman Archaeology (1925–1930). Died 3 May 1937 in Rome of cancer.

Born into a family of six children, Esther Van Deman was the youngest child. Her father, who had two sons by a previous marriage, was a farmer, and her mother was a devout Presbyterian who encouraged her children to follow in her path. Esther did not attend college until she was twenty-four, when she matriculated at the University of Michigan. She left after her first year but returned in 1889 and received a bachelor's degree in 1891 and a master's degree in 1892. She taught Latin for several years but then began graduate work at the University of Chicago, where she earned a doctorate in 1898. Although she taught at Mount Holyoke for three years after receiving her doctoral degree, she always preferred research to teaching. In 1901 she won a fellowship to the American School of Classical Studies in Rome; she returned to the United States as an associate professor of Latin and archeology at Goucher College. In 1906 she returned to Rome as a Carnegie Institution of Washington fellow and in 1910 joined the institution's staff. She remained in Rome for the next thirty years, with several breaks during which she returned to the United States.

Van Deman became the authority on ancient Roman building construction and established criteria for its dating. The first woman Roman field archeologist, she investigated the fundamental problems of the chronology of building materials and methods of construction. Another of her important contributions was a monograph on Roman aqueducts. This monograph absorbed so much of her time that she was unable to complete the work that she considered the

most important, the chronology of building materials and methods of construction. When she realized that she would be unable to complete this work because she had cancer, she arranged her notes for her colleague Marion E. Blake to complete.

She is buried in the Protestant cemetery in Rome.

JH/MBO

PRIMARY SOURCES
Van Deman, Esther Boise. *The Atrium Vestae.* Washington, D.C.: Carnegie Institution, 1909.
———. "Methods of Determing the Date of Roman Concrete Monuments." *American Journal of Archaeology,* 2d ser., 16 (April–June 1909). Offprint.
———. *The Building of Roman Aqueducts.* Washington, D.C.: Carnegie Institution, 1934.

SECONDARY SOURCES
American Journal of Archaeology 31 (April–June 1937). Obituary notice. Includes a bibliography of her writings.

STANDARD SOURCES
NAW (article by Lucy Shoe Merritt).

VAN HOOSEN, BERTHA (1863–1952)

U.S. surgeon and feminist. Born 26 March 1863 on a farm in Stony Creek, Mich., to Sarah Ann (Taylor) and Joshua Van Hoosen. One sister. Never married. Educated district public schools; Pontiac (Mich.) High School (graduated 1880); University of Michigan (A.B., 1884); University of Michigan Medical School (M.D., 1888). Professional experience: Woman's Hospital in Detroit, Kalamazoo, Mich., State Hospital for the Insane, and New England Hospital for Women and Children in Boston, resident (1888–1892); Chicago, private practice (from 1892); Northwestern University, Woman's Medical School, lecturer in anatomy and embryology (1892–1902); Illinois University Medical School (1902–1912); Loyola University Medical School, professor and head of obstetrics (1918–1937); Cook County Hospital, chief of the gynecological staff (1913–1920), chief of obstetrics (from 1920). Honors and memberships: American Medical Women's Association (AMWA), founder and first president (1915). Died 7 June 1952 in Romeo, Mich., of a stroke.

Bertha Van Hoosen was born on a farm in Michigan and attended public schools in that state. To her parents' dismay, she insisted on a medical education. Hoping to discourage her, they refused to pay her way to medical school, forcing her to teach school, do obstetrical nursing, and demonstrate in anatomy in order to finance her education. After she completed medical school (University of Michigan) she stated that she was not happy with the clinical training that she had received there. After a residency at three different hospitals, Van Hoosen opened a private practice in Chicago. It was several years before she earned enough to support herself, so she worked at several jobs at the same time. One of these extra positions was at the Woman's Medical School of Northwestern University, a facility that closed in 1902. She then became professor of clinical gynecology at the Illinois University Medical School. In 1918 she went to Loyola University as professor and head of obstetrics, becoming the first woman to head a medical division at a coeducational university. She was also on the staff at several Chicago hospitals and became the first woman physician to receive a civil service appointment; she was appointed chief of the gynecological staff at Cook County Hospital. In 1920 she became chief of the obstetrical staff there.

Throughout her career, Bertha Van Hoosen's major interest was in women's health. She was an excellent general surgeon, but she was particularly concerned with women and children. She pioneered in the use of scopolamine-morphine anesthesia for childbirth. Although this method, known as twilight sleep, had become popular in Germany, it was not used in the United States. She produced a book and two articles on her research in this area.

Fiery in temperament, Van Hoosen was a demanding and inspiring teacher. She resented the discrimination that she felt because she was a woman. Forbidden to join the Chicago Gynecological and Obstetric Society and uncomfortable at the American Medical Association conventions, she called a meeting in 1915 of Chicago medical women. From this meeting the American Medical Women's Association was formed. She became the first president of the new organization and fought for the right of women physicians to serve in the armed forces during World War I. Criticized for separatism, she explained that it was absolutely necessary as long as women physicians experienced discrimination.

Family was very important for Van Hoosen. She never married, but her widowed sister Alice and niece Sarah Van Hoosen Jones served as a substitute family. Her parents eventually became supportive of her career. Performing her last operation at the age of eighty-eight, she had to go to a convalescent home shortly thereafter and died there of a stroke.

JH/MBO

PRIMARY SOURCES

Van Hoosen, Bertha. *Scopolamine-Morphine Anaesthesia.* Chicago: The House of Manz, 1915.

———. "The New Movement in Obstetrics." *Woman's Medical Journal* 25 (June 1915): 121–123.

———. "Scopolamine Anesthesia in Obstetrics." *Current Researches in Anesthesia and Analgesia* 7 (May–June 1928): 151–154.

———. *Petticoat Surgeon.* Chicago: Pellegrini & Cudahy, 1947.

The AMWA Collection at Cornell University Archives has numerous references to Van Hoosen. Further archival material is held in the Bentley Historical Library, University of Michigan.

SECONDARY SOURCES

Gardner, Mabel E. "Bertha Van Hoosen, M.D." *JAMWA* 5 (October 1950): 413–414. Includes photograph.

Menendian, Rose V. "Bertha Van Hoosen: A Surgical Daughter's Impressions." *JAMWA* 20 (April 1965): 349–350.

STANDARD SOURCES

LKW; *NAW*(M) (article by Regina Markell Morantz).

VAN RENSSELAER, MARTHA (1864–1932)

U.S. home economist. Born 21 June 1864 in Randolph, Cattaraugus County, N.Y., to Arvilla A. Owen and Henry Killian Van Rensselaer. One sister. Never married. Educated Chamberlain Institute (1884); Cornell University (A.B., 1909). Professional experience: Chamberlain Institute and other schools (1884–1894); New York State Department of Public Instruction, Chautauqua Summer School, secretary and instructor (1894–1903); school commissioner of Cattaraugus County (1893–1899); College of Agriculture, extension program instructor, course for farmers' wives (1901–1932); Cornell University, teacher of homemaking (1906), offered first regular courses in home economics at Cornell (1908–1909), professor (1911). Died 26 May 1932 of cancer.

Martha Van Rensselaer was of Dutch and Welsh extraction. She was the second daughter of Henry Van Rensselaer and his second wife. Her Methodist, Republican, storekeeper, insurance agent father was a trustee of the coeducational school, Chamberlain Institute, that Martha attended. After graduation, Martha taught at this and other schools. She attended the Chautauqua Summer School and later worked there as secretary and instructor for the New York State Department of Public Instruction. Nominated as one of two school commissioners of Cattaraugus County by the Woman's Christian Temperance Union, she won two terms but lost a third in 1899.

The school commissioner position plus the lectures that she gave at teachers' institutes opened up a career for Van Renesselaer, who did not have a college degree. During these activities she met ANNA BOTSFORD COMSTOCK. Through her work as school commissioner, she encouraged the agricultural extension program. Comstock was trying to stimulate interest in farming through nature study, but Van Rensselaer realized that these programs were not reaching farmwives. Therefore, when asked by Liberty Hyde Bailey, professor of horticulture, she was agreeable to organizing an extension program for farmers' wives to complement the one already in place for farmers. With this step she began the program that was to occupy her for the rest of her career. It grew into the New York State College of Home Economics at Cornell University.

This program involved bulletins that were distributed to the farmers' wives about five times a year. The first bulletin was distributed to approximately five thousand women; soon enrollment had grown to over twenty thousand. They covered subjects such as interior decorating, nutrition, reading programs, dressmaking, sanitation, and child care.

When Liberty Hyde Bailey became dean of the College of Agriculture in 1903, home economic teaching on a resident and accredited basis began. Van Rensselaer offered a course in homemaking that year and in 1906 organized a course that included visiting experts and Cornell faculty members as lecturers. By 1907 a department of home economics was developed within the College of Agriculture. Van Rensselaer and FLORA ROSE served as cochairs, with Van Rensselaer concentrating on the administrative and extension work. Her connections with Bailey and his successor plus her own abilities made her a very effective administrator. By 1917, the program boasted a degree in home economics, monthly bulletins, approximately two hundred Cornell Study Clubs, extension courses, and work in the public schools. Due to the untiring work of Van Rensselaer, the department of home economics was removed from its former place in the College of Agriculture and became its own school on 24 February 1925. The New York State College of Home Economics gained in prestige and Rose and Van Rensselaer served as codirectors. A new home economics building named Van Rensselaer Hall was constructed in 1929–1930, with the backing of Governor Franklin Delano Roosevelt.

Van Rensselaer earned a belated bachelor's degree from Cornell in 1909, and in 1911 both she and Rose were promoted to professor. She was also involved in both world war efforts and was active in the American Home Economics Association, of which she was president from 1914 to 1916. She served as chair of the home economics section of the Association of Land-Grant Colleges and Universities from 1928 to 1929, and was assistant director of the White House Conference on Child Health and Protection.   JH/MBO

PRIMARY SOURCES

Van Rensselaer, Martha. Various bulletins of "Farmers's Wives Reading Course." Ithaca, N.Y.: The College, 1902–?

——, et al. *The Home and the Child: Housing, Furnishing, Management, Income, Clothing: Report of the White House Conference on Child Health and Protection, Subcommittee on Housing and Home Management.* Ed. Lisa Bane. New York: The Century Company, 1931.

SECONDARY SOURCES

Coleman, Gould P. *Education and Agriculture: A History of the New York State College of Agriculture at Cornell University,* [1963].

Rose, Flora. "A Page of Modern Education. Forty Years of Home Economics at Cornell University." New York State College of Home Economics, *Fifteenth Annual Report,* 1940, 63–145.

STANDARD SOURCES

NAW (article by Edith M. Fox).

VAN WAGENEN, GERTRUDE (1893–1978)

U.S. physiologist and endocrinologist. Born 23 May 1893 in Rock Rapids, Iowa. Educated University of Iowa (A.B., 1913; Ph.D., 1920). Professional experience: University of Iowa, assistant in anatomy (1913–1920); Stanford University, instructor in anatomy (1920–1921); University of California, Medical School, Department of Anatomy, instructor (1921–1927); Frankfurt (Germany) Municipal Hospital, instructor in vegetable physiology (1927–1928); Johns Hopkins School of Medicine, assistant in anatomy (1929–1930); Yale University School of Medicine, Department of Obstetrics and Gynecology, instructor (1931–1932), assistant professor (1932–1935), associate professor (1935–1938), professor (1938–1958); research associate (1951–1960), lecturer (1961–1976). Honors and memberships: Dr. Samuel L. Stegler award and lecture (1967); American Physiological Society, Fellow; Endocrine Society; Association of Anatomists; British Endocrinological Society.

Gertrude van Wagenen was educated at the undergraduate and graduate level at the University of Iowa. As an anatomist, she accompanied the Barbados-Antigua expedition in 1918. After serving as an assistant in anatomy duirng her graduate training, she moved to Stanford and then to the University of California Medical School in San Francisco as an instructor. In 1927, she went to work for two years in Germany as an instructor in plant physiology.

On return to the United States, she taught in Johns Hopkins Medical School. She was then brought by the physiologist John Fulton to Yale where she established a primate colony and pursued research on the endocrinology of reproduction in primates, maintaining a primate colony in her most active period. By 1938, she was made full professor. Toward the end of her career, she produced two major books on the ovary in human and macaque. Even after her retirement twenty years later, Van Wagenen continued to conduct research and to lecture on primate reproduction at Yale. She maintained an office in her former department into her eighties, completing what she called the "leftovers of research from when I had an active primate colony" (Reminiscences . . . , 1977).   JH/MBO

PRIMARY SOURCES

Van Wagenen, Gertrude. With Marian E. Simpson. *Embryology of the Ovary and Testes: Homo sapiens and Macaca mulatta.* New Haven: Yale University Press, 1965.

———. With Marian Simpson. *Post-Natal Development of the Ovary in Homo sapiens and Macaca mulatta and Induction of Ovulation in the Macaque.* New Haven: Yale University Press, 1973.

SECONDARY SOURCES

"Reminiscences of Gertrude Van Wagenen." *Physiologist* (February 1977): 30.

"Wagenen, Gertrude van." In *Zur Geschichte der Endokrinologie und Reproduktionsmedizen: 256 Biographen und Berichte,* ed. Gerhard Bettendorf. Berlin: Springer, 1995.

Zuckerman, Solly. *Monkeys Men and Missles: an Autobiography.* London: Collins, 1988. See pages 73–74.

STANDARD SOURCES

AMS 4–12; Rossiter 1982; Rossiter 1995.

VARSANOF'EVA, VERA ALEKSANDROVNA (1890–1976)

Russian geologist. Born 22 July 1890 in Moscow. Father a military officer. Educated at gymnasium in Riazan'; Higher Women's Courses in Moscow; 2d Moscow University (doctor of geological-mineralogical sciences 1935). Professional experience: Kalinin Pedagogical Institute, teacher; Ivanovskii Polytechnic, teacher; 2d Moscow University, professor; Lenin Pedagogical Institute in Moscow, professor. Honors and memberships: Moscow Society of Naturalists, vice-president; Academy of Pedagogical Science, corresponding member; Karpinskii Gold Medal of the Soviet Academy of Sciences; Order of Lenin and other medals. Died 29 June 1976 in Moscow.

Vera Aleksandrovna Varsanof'eva was born in Moscow into the family of a military officer. Her talented mother was French, and she taught her daughter foreign languages at an early age. She graduated from the gymnasium in Riazan' in 1907 and enrolled in the natural history section of the physical mathematical faculty of the Moscow Higher Women's Courses. Her choice of natural history was influenced by her reading, particularly the works of the geologist A. P. Pavlov. Even before she completed her courses in 1914, Varsanof'eva took part in an expedition to the Urals (1910) and her first publication appeared in 1911. In 1917–1918, she was a member of A. A. Chernov's expedition to the Tsil'ma River basin.

In 1918, Varsanof'eva began teaching as an assistant at the Higher Women's Courses in Moscow. In 1919, she became a docent in the geology department of Moscow University. Simultaneously she taught at the Kalinin Pedagogical Insti-

tute and the Ivanovskii Polytechnic. In 1921, she took part in an expedition to the Pechora River.

In 1925, Varsanof'eva was invited to become the head of the department of geology of the pedagogical faculty of the Second Moscow University (renamed Moscow State Pedagogical Institute in 1930), a position she held until 1955. In 1935 she was appointed a professor and received the degree of doctor of geological-mineralogical sciences, the first woman to do so.

In 1955, at the age of sixty-five, Varsanof'eva left Moscow and instead of retiring went to work at the Komi branch of the Academy of Sciences. This gave her greater opportunity to conduct field work in the area in which she was most interested.

Varsanof'eva was elected a corresponding member of the Academy of Pedagogical Sciences of the USSR in 1945, and in 1950 the Academy of Sciences awarded her the Karpinskii Gold Medal for her work on behalf of geology. She was honored further by having a peak in the Polar Urals named after her.

Varsanof'eva is known for her geological studies of the stratigraphy of Paleozoic sediments in the Upper Pechora basin and the geomorphology of the Northern Urals, particularly the Komi area. She published more than 120 papers on this subject. Varsanof'eva's other important achievement was to popularize geology with the general public, especially the younger generation. She did this both in her role as a teacher and as a writer of popular books on the history of geology.

ACH

PRIMARY SOURCES

Varsanof'eva, Vera A. *Proiskhozhdenie i stroenie Zemli.* Moscow and Leningrad, 1945. A popular textbook on the origin and structure of the earth. Chapters on the position of the earth in the cosmos, the origin of the earth, the physical properties of the earth's structure, the distribution of chemical elements, magnetic properties, and geological history are included.

———. *A. P. Pavlov i ego rol' v razvitii geologii.* 2d ed. Moscow, 1947.

———. "Uralskaia gornaia oblast', khrebet Pai-Khoi i Pechorskaia nizmennost'." *Geologiia SSSR* 2, pt. 1 (1963). Offprint.

———. *K. kharakteristike vizeyshikh otlozheniy basseyna Maloy Pechory* (Characterization of Visean sedimentary rocks of the Lesser Pechora Basin). Syktyvkar: Akademiya Nauk SSSR, Komi Filial, Institut Geologii, Komi knizhnoe izd-vo, 1970.

———. *Litologiia paleozoia I nizhnego mezozoia severo-vostoka Evropeiskoi chasti SSSR.* Syktyvkar: Komi knizhnoe izd-vo, 1970.

SECONDARY SOURCES

Bol'shaia sovetskaia entsiklopediia. 3d ed. Moscow: Izdvo "Sovetskaia entsiklopediia," 1973.

Durkin, G. F., ed. *Vera Aleksandrovna Varsanof'eva, 1890–1976: ukazatel' literatury.* Syktyvkar: Komi knizhnoe izdvo, 1977.

Shimanskiy, V. N., and V. F. Barskaya. "Vera Aleksandrovna Varsanof'yeva kak pedagog" (Vera Aleksandrovna Varsanof'yeva as a teacher). *Byulleten' Moskovskogo Obschestva Ispytateley Prirody, Otdel Geologicheskiy* 52, no. 6 (1977): 11–14.

"Vera Aleksandrovna Varsanof'yeva, glavnyy redaktor geologicheskogo otdela Byulletenya Moskovskogo obshchestva ispytateley prirody" (Vera Aleksandrovna Varsanof'yeva, editor-in-chief of the Geological Series of the Bulletin of the Moscow Society of Naturalists). *Byulleten' Moskovskogo Obshchestva Ispytateley Prirody, Otdel Geologicheskiy* 52 (1977): 6–10.

STANDARD SOURCES
Nalivkin.

VASILEVICH, GLAFIRA MAKAR'EVNA (1895–1971)

Russian ethnographer, folklorist, and linguist. Born 15 March 1895 in St. Petersburg, Russia. Ph.D. in historical sciences. Professional experience: taught Tungus-Manchurian ethnography and language in the higher educational instiutions of Leningrad. Soviet Academy of Sciences, Institute of Ethnography, research ethnographer. Died 21 April 1971 in Leningrad.

Glafira Makar'evna was interested in Siberian ethnography, and she began to study the language and culture of the Tungus-Manchurian people and the Altai, investigating problems of ethnography, material culture, social structure, and shamanism. She taught the language (Evenki) and literature as well as the ethnology of this group in Leningrad higher institutions, and published a number of textbooks. Vasilevich was a member of the Soviet Academy of Sciences, Institute of Ethnography, Siberian section, under which she did extensive and fundamental research on the Tungus.   ACH

PRIMARY SOURCES

Vasilevich, Glafira Makar'evna. *Uchebnik evenkiiskogo (tunguskogo) iazykaya: Dlia kursov po perepodgotovke uchitelei evenkiiskikh shkol.* Moscow: Gos. Uchebno-Pedagogik Izdvo, 1934.

———. *Sbornik materialov po étnograpfischeskomu (tuguskomu) fol'klosru.* Leningrad, 1936.

———. "Drevneischie Etnonimy Azii Nazvaniia Evenkiiskikh Rodov." *Sovetskaia Etnografiia* 4 (1946): 34–49.

———. "Evenki." *Narody Sibiri Moscow* (1956): 701–741.

———. *Evenki: Istoriko-étnografischeski Ocherki (XVIII–nachalo XX v).* Leningrad: n.p., 1969.

SECONDARY SOURCES
Taksami, C. M. "G. M. Vasilevich (nekrolog)." *Sovetskaia Etnografiia* 5 (1971): 184–187. Obituary notice.

STANDARD SOURCES
IDA.

VAUGHAN, DAME JANET (1899–1993)

British physiologist. Born 18 October 1899 in Clifton, Bristol to Margaret (Symonds) and William Wyamar Vaughan. Three siblings. Married David Goulay (1930). Two daughters (born 1934 and 1935). Educated privately; North Foreland Lodge; Somerville College, Oxford; University College Hospital Medical School (qualified 1924); resident, South London Hospital for Women. Professional experience: University College Hospital, assistant clinical pathologist; Rockefeller Traveling Fellowship (1929); Department of Morbid Anatomy, London Hospital, researcher (1930–1934); Research in Germany for Medical Research Council (1945–1946); MRC Unit of Bone Seeking Isotopes, head; Somerville College, Oxford, principal (1945–1967). Honors and memberships: Dame British Empire, 1957; Fellow Royal Society, 1979. Died 9 January 1993.

Janet Vaughan, a physician and experimental physiologist who studied blood diseases, blood transfusion, the treatment of starvation, and the effects of radioactivity on bone and bone marrow, was the daughter of a well-known educator, William Wyamar Vaughan, headmaster of the Rugby School. One of her aunts was a founder of Somerville College, Oxford. She was educated at home until she was fifteen. She then went to North Foreland Lodge and from there to Somerville College, entering after passing the entrance examinations on her third try.

At Somerville, Vaughan developed a strong interest in biological sciences and studied under Charles Sherrington. Profiting from private tutoring by J. S. Haldane, she obtained a first-class degree in physiology. She stayed on at Oxford for two further postgraduate years studying physiology and pharmacology until a Goldsmith's scholarship to University College Hospital Medical School in London led her to study medicine. She qualified as a physician in 1924. A resident at South London Hospital for Women, she decided against general practice or consultancy because she wanted to spend weekends with her father following the death of her mother in 1925. Obtaining a post as assistant clinical pathologist at University College Hospital, she began to investigate treatment of anemias with liver extracts, preparing the extract herself. The results were encouraging and she received a

Rockefeller traveling fellowship in 1929 that took her to Charles Minot's laboratory at Harvard Medical School, where she experimented on anemias in pigeons.

Returning to London, she married David Goulay, who encouraged her to continue research. Obtaining Medical Research Council and other grants, she began to work with the histopathologist H. M. Turnbull, extending her investigations of blood and bone marrow diseases at the Department of Morbid Anatomy, University College Hospital. She managed to produce her first major textbook, *The Anemias,* just before the birth of her first daughter in 1934. This was perhaps the first British book on hematology. She continued in clinical pathology at the Postgraduate Medical School in London, and in 1936, published an important paper arguing that the release of immature red and white blood cells into the blood marrow was associated with infiltrative bone disease.

Concerned about the possibility of war following the rise of fascism in Europe, Vaughan was stimulated to try experiments on stored blood by the physiologist Duran Jorda, head of the Barcelona Blood Bank, who had fled from Spain following the collapse of the Republic at the end of the Spanish Civil War. Her suggestion that blood be banked for transfusion in case of war was adopted by the Medical Research Council. From the beginning of the World War II, Vaughan was made director of the North West London Blood Supply, with great success. She was awarded an Order of the British Empire before the end of the war for this work.

At the request of the Medical Research Council, Vaughan went to Belgium with ROSALIND PITT-RIVERS and Charles Dent at the end of the war to investigate new treatments for starvation. Finding the British prisoners of war undernourished but not starving, Vaughan and her team continued on to Germany to the recently liberated concentration camp in Belsen and tried oral powdered milk rather than intravenous serum or hydrolysates.

In 1945, Vaughan was made principal of Somerville College, Oxford, a position she held until her retirement in 1967. She also brought up her two daughters during this period, held weekly medical clinics, and continued to have the support of her husband to advance her research. During this period, her experimental work was pursued in the department of pharmacology at Oxford. Reports from the United States suggested that strontium-90 was carcinogenic when incorporated into the bone, a question that Vaughan proposed to investigate with experiments on rabbits. With MRC grants, Vaughan made major studies that resulted in two books, published only after she retired from Somerville: *The Physiology of Bone* (1969) and *The Effects of Irradiation of the Skeleton* (1973).

Vaughan also was a significant voice for medical education for women since she sat on an important commission (the Goodenough Committee) reviewing selection procedures by British medical schools. She was made a Dame of the British Empire in 1957 and to her great delight was made a Fellow of the Royal Society in 1979 at the age of seventy-eight. She died in January 1993.　　　JH/MBO

PRIMARY SOURCES

Vaughan, Janet. *The Anaemias.* London: Oxford University Press, 1934.

———. "Leuco-erythoblastic Anemias." *Journal of Pathology and Bacteriology* 17 (1936): 541–64.

———. "Conditions at Belsen Concentration Camp." *British Medical Journal,* Physiology and treatment of Starvation ser. (1945): 819.

———. *The Physiology of Bone.* Oxford: Clarendon Press, 1969.

———. *The Effects of Irradiation of the Skeleton.* Oxford: Clarendon Press, 1973.

STANDARD SOURCES

Biographical Memoirs, vol. 41, 1995 (article by Maureen Owen); Debus; *Women Physiologists* (article by Helen Dodsworth).

VAVRINOVA, MILADA (1934–1973)

Czech economic and engineering geologist and geological bibliographer. Born 1934. Professional experience: Prague-based geologist. Died 1973.

Milada Vavrinova had a short career as an economic and engineering geologist and geological bibliographer. Two of her unpublished manuscripts on geology are held in the geological archives of the Czechoslovak Academy of Sciences in Prague.　　　JH/MBO

PRIMARY SOURCES

Vavrinova, M. "Zprava O Geologickem Mapovani na Listu Sumperk." *Vestnik Statniho Geologickeho Ustavu* (Prague) 23 (1948). Offprint.

———. "Zprava O Geologickem Pruzkumu Nekterych Lomu V Oblasti KSS V Ceskych Budejovicich." Czechoslovak Academy of Sciences, Library, Geological Archives, Prague, 1952.

———. "Zprara O Lomarsko-Geologickych Pomerech Lamprofyrovych zil v Okoli Malcic sz od Pisku." Czechoslovak Academy of Sciences, Library, Geological Archives, Prague, 1957.

SECONDARY SOURCES

Buzek, Cestmír. "Zivotn jubileum RNDr. Milady Vavrinové." *Vestnik Ustredniho ustav Geologickeho* 54, no. 1 (1979): 59–60.

STANDARD SOURCES
Sargeant.

VEIL, SUZANNE ZÉLIE PAULINE (1886–?)

French chemist. Born 28 April 1886 in Paris. Never married. Educated Sorbonne (1905–1911; D.Sc., 1920). Professional experience: Ecole Pratique des Hautes Etudes, Paris, Chef de Travaux (laboratory head); Caisse Nationale des Recherches, Paris, Chargée des Recherches (laboratory scientist), then Chef de Travaux (laboratory head); University of Paris, professor; Revue scientifique, editor. Death date unknown.

For her doctoral research, pursued in the Sorbonne's inorganic chemistry laboratory under the noted chemist Georges Urbain, Veil investigated physical-chemical properties of metallic oxides and hydroxides. Her studies of their electric conductibilities and magnetic susceptibilities revealed a number of previously unknown combinations and allotropic varieties, for which she determined the temperature ranges that allowed stability. Veil then examined the process of dehydration in metallic hydroxides, looking for changes in magnetic susceptibility. She found that magnetism of oxides and hydroxides sometimes depended upon previous chemical treatments, a phenomenon the Cahours Foundation regarded as "extremely curious, whose study . . . merits an encouragement."

Veil published numerous articles on various aspects of physical chemistry. She distilled some of her results into her 1934 publication on periodicities in chemistry. In addition to drawing inferences from a wide range of chemical phenomena, she included references to geology and biology in this work. Veil received the Cahours Prize and the Berthelot Medal from the Paris Academy of Sciences in 1924.

JH/MBO

PRIMARY SOURCES
Veil, Suzanne. "Alliages s'oxydes." *Comptes rendus Académie des Sciences* 170 (1920): 939–941.
———. *Recherches sur quelques propriétés physicochimiques des oxydes métalliques et de leurs mélanges . . .* Paris: University of Paris, 1920. Thesis.
———. "L'évolution de la molécule d'hydroxyde ferrique au sein de l'eau." *Comptes rendus Académie des sciences* 180 (1925): 211–213.
———. *Les phénomenes periodiques de la chimie. I: Les periodicites de structure. II: Les périodicités cinétiques.* Paris: Hermann & Cie., 1934.
———. "Etude de quelques effets physiologiques consécutifs à l'inhalation d'air chaud chez le lapin." *Journal de Physiologie* 46 (1954): 643.
———. "Contributions à l'étude de la physiologie des labrocytes. Réactions anaphylactiques et action d'un libérateur d'histamine." *Neerlandica* 6 (1957): 366.
———. "Le mécanisme d'action de la vitamine A sur le métabolisme de base." *Pathologie-Biologie* 9 (1961): 2285.

SECONDARY SOURCES
Comptes rendus Académie des Sciences 179 (1924): 1504–1505; 1529. Awards of the Priz Cahours and the Berthelot Medal.

STANDARD SOURCES
Turkevich and Turkevich.

VELEY, LILIAN JANE (NUTCOMBE) (1872–1936)

British zoologist and microscopist. Father Reverend J. Nutcombe. One sister. Married Victor Herbert Veley, Fellow of the Royal Society. Educated Oxford (first-class degree 1894). Honors: Linnean Society, Fellow. Died 2 December 1936.

Lilian Jane Veley was one of the original women Fellows of the Linnean Society. She earned a first-class degree from Oxford, although women were not allowed to be officially awarded a degree at that time. Her special field was animal morphology. She married Victor Herbert Veley, a Fellow of the Royal Society, and collaborated with him in microbiological research. She authored numerous papers for the *Quarterly Journal of Microscopical Science*, the *Transactions of the Entomological Society*, and the *Journal of the Linnean Society*.

JH/MBO

PRIMARY SOURCES
Veley, Lilian Jane. With Victor Herbert Veley. *The Micro-Organism of Faulty Rum.* London: H. Frowde, 1898.

SECONDARY SOURCE
Proceedings of the Linnean Society 149 (1936–1937): 218. Obituary notice.

VENNING, ELEANOR (HILL) (1900–)

Canadian biochemist and endocrinologist. Born 16 March 1900 in Montreal, Quebec, to Annette Kent and George W. Hill. Educated McGill University (B.A., 1920; M.Sc., 1921; Ph.D. in experimental medicine, 1933). Professional experience: McGill University, research fellow (1934–1944), faculty (1944–1960), professor of experimental medicine (1960–retirement). Honors and memberships: Royal Society; Canada, Fellow; British Society of Endocrinology; Canadian Physiological Society, president; Koch Medal of the Endocrine Society (1962).

Eleanor Venning was a Canadian biochemist and endocrinologist, educated at McGill University for all of her degrees. She married after she received her master of science degree, but before she finished her dissertation research. After she received her doctoral degree in experimental medicine, she joined McGill University as a research member, and became a faculty member in 1944. Venning was a research associate at the University Clinic, Royal Victoria Hospital in 1950s, conducting research on reproduction and adrenal physiology. Venning was active in the Canadian Physiological Society, serving as its president and later as the vice-president of the Endocrine Society. She was promoted to full professor of experimental medicine in 1960, two years before she received the Koch medal from the Endocrine Society. Eight years later, at the age of sixty-eight, she retired from the university. She was elected a fellow of Royal Society of Canada. JH/MBO

SECONDARY SOURCES
Venning, Eleanor H. *Evaluation of Adrenal Cortical Function in Man*. Medical Clinics of North America—Chicago Number, Endocrinology. London: W. B. Saunders, 1948.

STANDARD SOURCES
AMS 6–8, B 9, P&B 10–12; Debus.

VERDER, ADA ELIZABETH (1900–)

U.S. bacteriologist. Born 18 June 1900 in Davenport, Iowa. Educated University of Chicago (B.S., 1923; Ph.D., 1928). Professional experience: University of Chicago, instructor in bacteriology (1928–1932); George Washington University, school of medicine, assistant professor (1932–1935); Maryland State Department of Health assistant bacteriologist (1935); National Institutes of Health, associate bacteriologist (1936–1940), bacteriologist (1940–1954), senior bacteriologist (1954–1963); National Institutes of Allergy and Infectious Diseases, scientist administrator for extramural programs (1963–1970); University of Texas Medical School, San Antonio, assistant through administrator of the graduate program, department of microbiology (1971–1972).

Ada Verder began her career in academia after achieving the doctoral degree from the University of Chicago. She remained at Chicago for four years as an instructor before moving to George Washington University as assistant professor for another three years. She left George Washington in 1935 to begin a career in public health medicine, first on the state level and then at the National Institutes of Health, where she rose through the ranks from associate bacteriologist to senior bacteriologist. In 1963 she left NIH to become an administrator for the National Institutes of Allergy and Infectious Diseases. For her last year of work she was an administrator in the graduate program at the University of Texas Medical School, San Antonio. Verder was seventy-two years old when she finally retired.

Verder was a Fellow of the American Association for the Advancement of Science, the American Society of Microbiology, and the American Public Health Association. She was a member of the American Academy of Microbiology and the New York Academy of Sciences. Her research was on food poisoning, gastrointestinal flora, and the pseudococcus, pseudomonas, and pleuropneumonia organisms. JH/MBO

PRIMARY SOURCES
Verder, Ada Elizabeth. "The Effects of Diet Deficient in Vitamin A or B on Resistance to Organisms of the Paratyphoid Enteritidis Group." University of Chicago, Ph.D. diss., 1928.

STANDARD SOURCES
AMS 5–8, B 9, P&B 10–12; Rossiter 1982.

VERETENNIKOVA, ANNA IVANOVNA (1855–1888)

Russian physician. Born 1855 in Kazan to Anna Aleksandrovna (Blank) and Ivan Veretennikov. At least one sibling. Educated local secondary school; St. Petersburg Women's Medical Courses. Professional experience: zemstvo (district) physician; Belebei district, Ufimsk province, physician; St. Petersburg eye clinic, physician. Died 1888 at Kokushkino.

Anna Ivanovna Veretennikova was the daughter of a teacher and a granddaughter, on her mother's side, of Aleksandr Blank, a St. Petersburg physician, known for his strong and sometimes unusual views. Blank had hoped that his own daughter, Veretennikova's aunt, would follow in his footsteps and become a physician. However, she preferred teaching and ultimately married Il'ia Nikolaevich Ul'ianov, the father of Vladimir Il'ich Ul'ianov (later to be known as V. I. Lenin). The Veretennikovs and Ul'ianovs were very close and the cousins spent happy summers together at the family estate at Kokushkino.

Ivan Veretennikov died early and, after finishing secondary school in 1871, Veretennikova supported herself by teaching and office work.

In 1877, Veretennikova was admitted to the Women's Medical Courses in St. Petersburg, from which she graduated in 1882. Athough she could have remained in St. Petersburg as an assistant to a faculty member, she chose zemstvo (district) service in a remote Moslem, non-Russian-speaking area thirty-five miles from Belebei in the Ufimsk province.

This was an idealistic choice: the conditions were primitive in the extreme. Veretennikova took up residence in a one-room hut that also served as her office, and she was overwhelmed with patients. Apart from physical difficulties, her work was hampered by the stinginess and shortsightedness of the zemstvo council. Medical supplies were difficult to obtain and Veretennikova spent a large part of her own meagre salary on them. Her staff consisted of a feldsher (surgeon's assistant), a midwife, and a housekeeper.

Shortly after her arrival, Veretennikova had to deal with a serious smallpox epidemic. Owing to the lack of foresight on the part of the zemstvo council, Veretennikova had to order vaccine directly from St. Petersburg to undertake an adequate vaccination program.

Although Veretennikova was very popular with her patients, her difficulties with the council ultimately led to her resignation, and she returned to St. Petersburg. There she worked in an eye clinic but became ill and went to Kazan to stay with her relatives. She wrote her doctoral dissertation but was not allowed to defend it. In 1888, in her early thirties, she died at the family estate at Kokushkino.

Veretennikova was one of many highly-motivated and idealistic young people who, coming from a gentry background, felt a strong obligation to help the peasants. Some, like her cousins, Aleksandr Ul'ianov, hanged in 1887 for his part in an attempt on the life of the tsar, and his brother Vladimir (Lenin) became revolutionaries, convinced that only the overthrow of the government could improve the conditions in the country.

Veretennikova, brought up in the same milieu, chose a different route and, in doing so, also sacrificed herself. With the best intentions, she was not able singlehandedly to overcome the inertia of the provincial council whose help was vital to her success, and she was too far from a major center and too isolated to get the support that might have made her efforts more successful.   ACH

PRIMARY SOURCES
Veretennikova, Anna Ivanovna. *Zapiski zemskogo vracha*. Ufa: Bashkirskoe kn. izdvo, 1984.

STANDARD SOURCES
Tuve.

VERNON, MAGDALEN DOROTHEA (1901–1991)

British psychologist. Born 25 June 1901 in Oxford, England, to Katharine Dorothea (Ewart) and Horace Middleton Vernon. One brother. Educated Oxford High School; Cambridge University, Newnham College (M.A., 1926; Sc.D., 1953). Professional experience: Industrial Health Research Board, assistant investigator (1924–1927); Cambridge Psychological Laboratory (under Frederick Bartlett) (1927–1946); scientific staff member (funded by Med-

ical Research Council); University of Reading, lecturer (1946–1951), senior lecturer in Psychology (1951–1955), reader in psychology (1956–1967), reader emerita (1967–1991). Honors and memberships: founding member, Experimental Psychology Group (later Experimental Psychological Society), president (1952–1953); British Psychological Society, president (1958), honorary fellow (1970). Died 1 December 1991 in Beckenham, England.

Named after the college at Oxford where her father was a fellow, Magadelen Dorothea, like her brother Philip, chose to study psychology. She went to Oxford High School and then in 1919 entered Newnham College, Cambridge, on a scholarship. Following her father's interests in industrial psychology, she worked at first as an assistant invesigator to the Industrial Health Research Board in which her father was an important figure. Vernon returned to Cambridge after three years to carry out experimental research with Professor Frederick Bartlett at the Cambridge Psychological Laboraoratory, funded by the Medical Research Council. There she studied eye movements in proofreading and then moved into the broader area of of visual perception.

Vernon was internationally recognized for her experimental study of reading, published in 1931. After examining the flicker phenomenon in binocular fusion, she wrote a widely read book on visual perception toward the end of the decade. She also collaborated with Kenneth Craik on a study of dark adaptation.

By 1946, Vernon was offered a lectureship at Reading, rising to the rank of reader and head of department. She trained an important group of psychologists at Reading and she was noted for her good humor and her direct approach, never hesitating to give her opinions. Heavily influenced by her former professor, Bartlett, she extended his ideas of "effort after meaning," a term indicating the complex schemata used by the individual in perception of material. Her many books focused both on reading and on perception. Her last book, published when she was seventy, again examined reading difficulties. In her seventieth year, she was made an honorary Fellow of the British Psychological Society.   JH/MBO

PRIMARY SOURCES
Vernon, Magdalen Dorothea. *The Experimental Study of Reading*. Cambridge: Cambridge University Press, 1931.
———. *Visual Perception*. Cambridge: Cambridge University Press, 1937.
———. *Backwardness in Reading*. Cambridge: Cambridge University Press, 1957.
———. *Human Motivation*. Cambridge: Cambridge University Press, 1969.
———. *Readings and Its Difficulties*. Cambridge: Cambridge University Press, 1971.

SECONDARY SOURCES
Sheehy, Noel, Antony J. Chapman, and Wendy A. Conroy, eds. *Biographical Dictionary of Psychology.* London: Routledge, 1997.

STANDARD SOURCES
WWW, vol. 9, 1991–1995.

VESIAN, DOROTHY E. DE (1889–1983)

British botanist. Professional experience: Cheltenham Ladies College, head of biology (to 1950). Honors and memberships: Botanical Society of the British Isles, member (1953–1983); Cottswold Naturalists' Field Club; Cheltenham and District Naturalists' Society (later the Gloucestershire Naturalists' Society), founder, recorder, editor, vice-president (1968); Linnean Society, Fellow. Died 8 January 1983.

Although information about Dorothy de Vesian's education is unavailable, we know that she was head of biology at Cheltenham Ladies College until 1950. She was an active member of many botanical organizations. She attended field meetings of the Botanical Society of the British Isles both locally and overseas and was recorder for East and West Gloucestershire from 1955 to 1970. As a founding member of the Cheltenham and District Naturalists' Society, she edited the Botanical Reports for the five biennial reports that it published and in 1968 was its vice-president. She was also elected a Fellow of the Linnean Society and was a member of the British Bryological Society. She illustrated her lectures with her own slides.

De Vesian collected botanical specimens in Gloucestershire, and her herbarium is in the Gloucester Museum.

JH/MBO

SECONDARY SOURCES
Cotteswold Naturalists Field Club 39 (1982–1983): 11–12. Obituary notice.
Holland, S. "Dorothy E. De Vesian." *Watsonia* 15, no. 1 (1984): 57.

STANDARD SOURCES
Desmond.

VICKERS, ANNA (1852–1906)

British botanist. Born 28 June 1852 in Bordeaux, France. Professional experience: Canary Islands, collected plants (1895–1896); Antilles, collected plants (1898–1899). Died 1 August 1906 in Roscoff, Finisterre, Spain.

Anna Vickers was a French-born British algologist. She collected algae in the Canaries and in the Antilles. She pub-lished major papers on the algae she studied on these trips. Her surviving plants are found at the British Museum (Natural History). The plant *Vickersia* Karsakoff was named for her.

JH/MBO

PRIMARY SOURCES
Vickers, Anna. *Contribution à la flore algologique des Canaries.* Paris: Masson & Cie, [1896]. Excerpt from the *Annales des sciences naturelles.*
———. *Phycologia Barbadensis des algues marines récoltées à L'Ile Barbade (Antilles) (Chlorophycées et Pheophycées).* Paris: Librairie des sciences naturelles Paul Klincksieck, 1908. A biographical account by Mary Helen Shaw is found in this book.

SECONDARY SOURCES
Memoirs of the New York Botanical Gardens 19, no. 1 (1969): 104. Obituary notice.

STANDARD SOURCES
Barnhart; Desmond; Stafleu and Cowan.

VILAR, LOLA (1900–)

Spanish physician. Born 4 May 1900 in Castellón. Two sisters. Married Gerardo Vilar. One son, Ricardo (b. 1943). Educated general school (highest award in final examinations); University of Madrid (medical studies, valedictorian); specialty in pediatrics (M.D. degree); University of Paris (finished pediatrics specialty). Professional experience: private practice in Valencia. Honors and memberships: Medical Women's International Association.

Lola Vilar was the oldest daughter of a hard-working mother and a schoolteacher father. After a younger sister died at age six of meningitis the family was distraught until the birth of another little girl, Guillermina. An excellent student, Lola was encouraged to study medicine and went to the University of Madrid, where there was only one other female in medical school. However, she was well accepted and graduated valedictorian. She continued at Madrid for her doctorate and specialization in pediatrics. In order to complete her specialization, she went to Paris to work and study. She returned to Paris two years later to learn about new treatments for children with tuberculosis.

The number of patients coming to her began to increase. She married Gerardo Vilar, and shortly after their marriage the couple went to Germany to visit tuberculosis centers. They found a Germany under the sway of Hitler. When they returned to Spain, they found that the Spanish Civil War had broken out. Her uncle Julio, the priest who had married Gerardo and Lola, was killed because of his religion.

Vilar was a follower of Franco, stating that he was not a dictator as many foreigners said. Two years before the end of

World War II, their son, Ricardo, was born. He became a pediatrician, earning his medical degree in 1960.

Vilar's practice continued to grow, and she became active in the Medical Women's International Association, attending many of its conferences. KM

PRIMARY SOURCES
Vilar, Lola. In Hellstedt, *Autobiographies.*

VILMORIN, ELISA (BAILLY) (fl. 1850s–1860s)

French horticulturist, plant breeder. Educated privately. Married Louis de Vilmorin ca. 1843. Professional experience: assisted husband in significant breeding experiments; Vilmorin-Andrieux et Cie, the distinguished Paris seed company, head (1860–1866). Published on strawberry breeds.

Elisa Bailly Vilmorin has the distinction of having aided her husband, Louis de Vilmorin, in his important breeding experiments on varieties of wheat, lupines, and other flowering and economically important plants. A member of the prestigious scientific family Vilmorin, which founded the Vilmorin-Andrieux seed company in the mid-eighteenth century, Louis de Vilmorin assumed the position as head of the company upon his father's retirement in 1843. Louis de Vilmorin steered the company in the direction of careful scientific breeding, following the lead of important French scientists at the Jardin des Plantes of the Muséum d'Histoire Naturelle like Charles Naudin and Joseph Decaisne. Since Louis de Vilmorin had a serious physical handicap, he relied on the assistance of his wife for much of his research. She is said to have independently published her own researches on strawberry varieties. Following Louis de Villmorin's death in 1860, she successfully directed the company until 1866, when her son Henry took over as head of the firm.

JH/MBO

PRIMARY SOURCES
[Villmorin, Elsa]. Les fleurs de plein terre: comprenant la description et la culture des fleurs annuelles, bisannuelles, vivaces et bulbeuses de plein terre suivies de classements divers indiquant l'emploi de ces plantes. Paris: Vilmorin-Andrieux et cie, 1863. Although her name does not appear as author, this was published during the period when Elsa Villmorin was head of the company. Her husband and her son are credited as authors of similar publications during the period when they headed Villmorin.

SECONDARY SOURCES
Gayon, Jean, and Doris T. Zallen. "The Role of the Vilmorin Company in the Promotion and Diffusion of Experimental Science of Heredity in France 1840–1920." Paper presented at International Society for the History, Philosophy, and Social Sciences of Biology meeting, Brandeis University, in the session "Genetics in Agricultural Context," 15–18 July 1993.

VIVIAN, ROXANA HAYWARD (1871–?)

U.S. mathematician and astronomer. Born 1871 in Hyde Park, Mass., to Roxanna (Nott) and Robert Hayward Vivian. Educated Hyde Park Hight School; Wellesley College (B.A., 1894); alumna fellow, mathematics (1898–1904); University of Pennsylvania (Ph.D., 1901). Professional experience: Stoughton (Mass.) High School, teacher (1895–1898); American College for Girls, Constantinople, professor of mathematics (1906–1907); Wellesley College, associate professor of mathematics (from 1909). Death date unknown.

In her thesis, Vivian considered poles and polars with respect to higher plane curves and used analytic methods to discuss these problems. The thesis was entitled "The Poles of a Right Line with Respect to a Curve of Order n." JH/MBO

SECONDARY SOURCES
"Vivian, Roxana Hayward." *Science,* n.s. 14 (August 30, 1901): 33.

VOGT, CÉCILE (MUGNIER) (1875–1962)

French neurologist. Born 27 March 1875 in Annécy, France. Married Oskar Vogt (1899). Two daughters. Educated Paris Medical School (M.D., 1900). Professional experience: Neurobiological Institute, Berlin (later associated with University of Berlin) (1900–1931); neurological and psychiatric practice (1900–1931); Kaiser Wilhelm Institute for Brain Research (Berlin-Buch), research director (1931–1937); Brain Research Institute, Neustadt (Swarzwald), research director (1937–1959). Died 3 May 1962 in Cambridge, England.

Cécile Vogt worked in close collaboration with her husband, Oskar Vogt, during the entirety of her career. They met in Paris while he was training with the neurologist and neuroanatomist Jules Déjerine, who had provided an excellent model for this kind of marital collaboration with his own wife, AUGUSTA DÉJERINE-KLUMPKE. The Vogts (as they were referred to even in the scientific literature) established a private Neurobiological Institute in Berlin, financing it with their neurological and psychiatric practices. Their first notable publication in 1903 outlined their program to map the cryoarchitectonics of the cerebral cortex, linking cortical nerve cells to physiological areas of the monkey cortex. They believed that structure and function were intimately linked and that eventually all aspects of human intellect and behavior could be linked to specific brain structures. Eventually they delineated two hundred brain areas that they considered to have distinct cryarchitechtonic patterns. This highly particularistic view was challenged by Karl Lashley and others in the forties who believed that greater brain variability existed between individuals and even within the same individual over time.

In 1911, Cécile Vogt, working independently and with other neurologists, described the direct involvement of the corpus striatum in movement disorders in a case of erratic spasmodic movement disorders (choreo-athetosis) in a human patient. Although the striatum had been indicated as a focal point for such disorders, Vogt's description of bilateral atrophy of the area was an important demonstration of a direct link between loss of cells or a change in their myelination and a well-observed clinical case.

As the fame of the Vogts grew, the private laboratory became associated with the University of Berlin, in which Oskar Vogt taught. A number of notable brain researchers were trained in their laboratories, including the neuroanatomist Korbinian Brodmann. Cecile's two daughters, MARTHE and Marguerite VOGT, followed their mother's example. They first studied medicine and then came to work in their parents' laboratory. In 1929, the newly formed Kaiser Wilhelm Institute began to build a huge complex of laboratories for the Vogts and their associates, including living quarters for the Vogt family in the suburbs of Berlin. Completed in 1931, the Brain Research Institute included state-of-the-art electronics for recording the brain impulse, laboratories for genetics, neuropathology, neurophysiology, neurochemistry and even a sixty-bed neurological clinic.

With the rise of the Nazi state, the Vogts found themselves in increasing opposition. Considered persona non grata by 1937, they retired from the Brain Research Institute in Berlin and went to Neustadt in Southern Germany, again opening a private brain research institute. They continued to be active into their old age, and in the period following World War II, the Vogts began to study aging in nerve cells. After her husband's death in 1959, Cécile Vogt left Germany and went to live with her daughter in Cambridge, England, where Marthe had become a widely acclaimed neuropharmacologist. Cécile Vogt died there at the age of eighty-six.

JH/MBO

PRIMARY SOURCES

Vogt, Cécile. "Quelques considérations générales à propos du syndrome strié." *Journal für Psychologie und Neurologie* 18 (1911): 479–488.
———. With Oskar Vogt. "Zur anatomischen Gliederung des Cortex cerebri." *Journal für Psychologie und Neurologie* 2 (1903): 160–180. An initial statement of the cytoarchitectonic brain research program of the Vogts.
———. With Oskar Vogt. "Allgemeinere Ergebinesse unserer Hirnforschung." *Journal für Psychologie und Neurologie* 25 (1919): 273–462. The often-cited analysis of the Vogts' research.
Vogt, Cécile. With Oskar Vogt. "Ageing of Nerve Cells." *Nature* 158 (1946): 304.

SECONDARY SOURCES

Clarke, Edwin, and C. D. O'Malley. *The Human Brain and Spinal Cord: A historical Study Illustrated by Writings from Antiquity to the Twentieth Century.* University of California Press, 1968. See pages 453–457 for brief biographies of Oskar and Cécile Vogt with excerpts and analysis of two key papers.
Finger, Stanley. *Origins of Neuroscience: A History of Explorations into Brain Function.* Oxford and New York: Oxford University Press, 1994. Places work of Vogts in modern perspective and describes Cécile Vogt's 1911 case.
Haymaker, W. "Cécile and Oskar Vogt on the Occasion of Her 75th and His 80th birthday." *Neurology* 1 (1951): 179–204.
Hopf, A. "Cécile Vogt." *Journal Hirnforschung* 5 (1962): 245–248.
Jung, Richard. "Some European Neuroscientists: A Personal Tribute." In *Neurosciences, Paths of Discovery,* ed. F. O. Worden, J. Swazey, and G. Abrams. MIT Press, 1974. Includes a photograph of the buildings comprising the Kaiser Wilhelm Gesellschaft Brain Research Institute.
Satzinger, Helga. "Das Gehirn, die Frau und ein Unterschied in den Neurowissenschaften des 20. Jahrhunderts: Cécile Vogt (1875–1962)." In *Geschlecterverhältnisse in Medizin, Naturwissenschaft und Technik,* eds. Christoph Meinel and Monika Rennenberg, 75–82. Bassum and Stuttgart: Verlag für Geschichte der Naturwissenschaften und der Technik, 1995.

STANDARD SOURCES

Debus (under Oskar Vogt); Vogt.

VOGT, MARTHE LOUISE (1903–)

German-born British neuropharmacologist. Born 1903 in Berlin to Cécile (Mugnier) and Oscar Vogt. One sister. Educated at University of Berlin (M.D., 1928); Kaiser Wilhelm Institut für Biochemie (Ph.D., 1929); Cambridge University (Ph.D. in pharmacology, 1938). Professional experience: Kaiser Wilhelm Institute für Hirnforschung (Brain Research Institute), research scientist (1929–1935); department of pharmacology, Head, (1935); National Institute for Medical Research, Hampstead, England, Rockefeller Traveling Fellow (1935–1936); Cambridge University, department of pharmacology, research associate; Girton College, Cambridge, Alfred Yarrow Research Fellow (1937–1940); Pharmaceutical Society of London, research pharmacologist (1941–1946); University of

Edinburgh, department of pharmacology, lecturer and reader (1947–1960); Institute of Animal Physiology, Agricultural Research Council, Pharmacology Unit, head (1960–1968), emerita researcher (1968–1990?). Honors and memberships: Fellow of Royal Society (1952); honorary member British Pharmacological Society; British Physiological Society; British Association of Psychopharmacology; American Academy of Arts and Sciences; honorary Fellow, Royal Society of Medicine; Hungarian Academy of Sciences.

Marthe Vogt grew up in the remarkable family of two noted scientists in Berlin. Her French mother, CÉCILE VOGT, and her German father were both important neuroanatomists who collaborated throughout their lives and brought their daughters up in an atmosphere of intellectual stimulation. As young girls, Marthe and her sister Marguerite could speak three languages. She decided to follow her parents into medicine, attending the University of Berlin medical school, and then became intrigued by pharmacology, completing her doctorate in chemistry in 1929. Like EDITH BÜLBRING, who came to be a lifelong friend, Vogt went to study in the laboratory of Paul Trendelenburg. There she was a research assistant until 1935, studying nervous control of hormone release, research that was later seen as the beginning of neuroendocrinology.

She qualified and trained under outstanding scientists and in 1935 was given the position of head in the chemistry division of her father's Brain Research Institute. The times were unsettled in Berlin, however, as Hitler had come to power and her parents were not on good terms with the Nazi regime. She took the opportunity to study in England on a Rockefeller traveling fellowship and remained there not only through World War II, but for the rest of her life.

Upon arriving in England, Vogt worked at first with the physiologist and pharmacologist Sir Henry Dale in Hampstead, who was defining the role of chemical neurotransmitters. With Dale and Feldberg, she published a classic paper on the release of the neurotransmitter acetylcholine at the neuromuscular junction. During this period, she could work only on research grants, not being allowed to take formal employment. She went to the department of pharmacology at Cambridge University to do research under E. B. Verney. When she received the Yarrow fellowship at Girton College, Cambridge, she was able to further qualify herself with a British degree from Cambridge University.

At the beginning of World War II, Vogt was classified as an "enemy alien," but was still allowed to take a research post at the Pharmaceutical Society of London doing bioassays of medicinal products. In the time left for her own research, she continued to work on the endocrine system, investigating the control of adrenocortical secretion. Again her research led to significant publications.

In 1947, Vogt joined the pharmacology department of the University of Edinburgh and spent the following thirteen years there, first as lecturer and then as reader. The royal Society of London elected her as a Fellow in the early fifties, and a long series of honorary fellowships and other honors followed. She was appointed to the headship of the Pharmacology Unit of the Research Council Institute of Animal Physiology where she remained until she retired in 1968. After the death of her father in 1959, her mother joined her in Cambridge, dying there three years later. Marthe Vogt retained her research link with the unit and continued active research well into her eighties, recognized as one of the pioneers of neuropharmacology and neuroendocrinology.

In her nineties, Martha Vogt relocated to San Diego to live with her sister Marguerite. JH/MBO

PRIMARY SOURCES

Vogt, Marthe. "Zur Frage der nervösen Regulation Schilddrüs entatigkeit." *Archives für experimentelle Pathologie Pharmakologie* 162 (1931): 129.

———. "Cortical Lipids of the Normal and Denervated Supra Renal Gland under Conditions of Stress." *Journal of Physiology* 106 (1947): 394.

———. "The Concentration of Sympathin in Different Parts of the Central Nervous System under Normal Conditions and after the Administration of Drugs." *Journal of Physiology* (London) 123 (1954): 451–481.

———. "Nervous Influences in Endocrine Activity." In *Pioneers in Neuroendocrinology,* ed. Joseph Meites, Bernard Donovan, and Samuel M. McCann. New York: Plenum Press, 1975. Includes a thumbnail biography, an autobiographical article, and a portrait of Vogt with some primary references.

———. "Some Functional Aspects of Central Serotonergic Neurones." In *Biology of Serotonergic Transmission,* ed. N. N. Osborne. Chichester: John Wiley, 1982.

———. With H. H. Dale and W. Feldberg. "Release of Acetylcholine at Voluntary Nerve Endings." *Journal of Physiology* (London) 86 (1936): 353–379.

STANDARD SOURCES

Debus; *Women Physiologists* (article by Susan Greenfield).

VOLD, MARJORIE JEAN YOUNG (1913–1991)

U.S. chemist. Born 25 October 1913 in Ottawa, Ontario, to Whilhelmine (Aitken) and Reynold Kenneth Young. Naturalized U.S. citizen, 1921. Married Robert Donald Vold (1936). Three children: Mary Louise, Robert Lawrence, and Wylda Bryan. Educated University of California at Berkeley (B.S., 1934; Ph.D., 1936). Professional experience: University of Cincinnati, lecturer (1936–1937); Stanford University, research associate (1937–1941);

Union Oil Company, industrial chemist (1942–1946); University of Southern California, research associate and lecturer in chemistry (1947–1957); University of Utrecht, Netherlands, Guggenheim Fellow (1953–1954); Indian Institute of Science, Bangalore, India, honorary reader in physical chemistry (1955–1957); University of Southern California, adjunct professor (1958–1974). Honors and memberships: Phi Beta Kappa; valedictorian; American Chemical Society, Garvan Medal (1967); Los Angeles Times, "Woman of the Year." Died 4 November 1991.

Marjorie Vold was born in Canada into a family of scientists and science teachers. In 1918 she moved to the United States and three years later was naturalized as an American citizen. She graduated Phi Beta Kappa and valedictorian of her class at the University of California, Berkeley, and received the University Medal. Two years later she earned a doctorate in chemistry. She married a fellow graduate of the Berkeley chemistry doctoral program, Robert Vold, in 1936, and the couple had three children.

Her husband's position, her children, and her health kept Vold from holding a tenure-track position. After working as an industrial chemist during World War II, she became a research associate and lecturer in chemistry at the University of Southern California for ten years. For a year, both Volds went to the University of Utrecht, where they worked in the laboratory of colloid chemist J. T. G. Overbeek. Marjorie had a Guggenheim Fellowship and Robert, a Fulbright. In 1957 she became the first woman to address the Indian Institute of Science in Bangalore, India, where she was an honorary reader in physical chemistry.

In 1958, Vold was diagnosed with multiple sclerosis and from 1960 until her death was confined to a wheelchair. From 1958 until her retirement she held only an adjunct position at the University of Southern California.

Vold was an avid researcher and prolific writer. In the course of her career she published either individually or coauthored about 150 papers, many book chapters, and two books. Her research was in the area of colloid chemistry, and she spent most of her career working with the phase behavior and kinetic properties of soaps, liquid crystals, and colloidal suspensions. She and her husband established the Center for Surface and Colloid Chemistry at the University of Southern California's chemistry department. They collaborated on many projects, including an important textbook in colloid chemistry.

In spite of her disability, Vold continued to publish, deliver lectures, and do volunteer work for the Boy and Girl Scouts. She received many honors, including the prestigious Garvan Medal for outstanding work in chemistry. In 1974, the Volds were honored when members of the Division of Colloid and Surface Chemistry sponsored a symposium on colloid science at the 167th meeting of the American Chemical Society to pay tribute to their work. This year marked their retirement from the University of Southern California. During her last years, while confined to bed, Vold designed complex mathematical simulations on a computer. A month before her death at the age of seventy-eight, she submitted her last paper to the *Langmuir*, the journal of the American Chemical Society, on surfaces and colloids. It was published posthumously in 1992. JH/MBO

PRIMARY SOURCES

Vold, Marjorie J. With Robert D. Vold. *Colloid Chemistry: The Science of Large Molecules, Small Paraticles and Surfaces.* New York: Reinhold Publishing Group, 1964.

———. With Robert D. Vold. "A Third of a Century of Colloid Chemistry." In *Colloidal Dispersions and Micellar Behavior,* ed. K. L. Mittal. Washington, D.C.: American Chemical Society, 1975.

———. "Micellization Process with Emphasis on Premicelles." *Langmuir* 8 (1992): 1082–1085.

SECONDARY SOURCES

"Garvan Medal: Marjorie J. Vold." *Chemical and Engineering News* 45, no. 15 (1967): 87.

STANDARD SOURCES

AMS 7–8, P 9, P&B 10–14; Bailey; Debus; Shearer and Shearer 1977 (article by Sharon Sue Kleinman).

VOLKOVA, ANNA FEDOROVNA (d. 1876)

Russian chemist. Professional experience: worked with A. N. Engel'gardt and D. I. Mendeleev. Honors and memberships: Russian Chemical Society. Died 1876.

Anna Fedorovna Volkova was the first Russian woman ever to publish studies in chemistry. Her birth date is unknown, as are details of her childhood and education. As at that time there was no higher education for women in Russia, her early chemical education was probably acquired in a practical capacity in a laboratory. In 1869 she began working in the laboratory of the chemist and agronomist Aleksandr N. Engel'gardt, and in 1870 she moved to the laboratory of the Russian Technical Society, where she conducted her own experiments and, under the supervision of Dmitri I. Mendeleev, gave practical lessons to the female students of the St. Petersburg public schools.

For her research on sulfonic acid and the acid amides of the aromatic series she was accepted as a member of the Russian Chemical Society in 1870, the first woman to be admitted. She also became an editor of the *Journal of the Russian Chemical Society.* At the Third Congress of Russian

Naturalists in Kiev in 1871, she presented two reports and was elected president of the session.

Volkova was greatly respected by Mendeleev, A. M. Butlerov, and other chemists of the time, and they tried to assist her by finding paying work for her. However, she lived in great poverty and died at an early age.

Although undoubtedly other women worked in various capacities in chemical laboratories, Volkova was the first in Russia to be accepted as a chemist in her own right and to publish work under her own name.

Volkova published over twenty important articles in the *Journal of the Russian Chemical Society.* She was the first chemist to produce orthotoluenesulfonic acid and its acid chloride and amide in pure form and the first to obtain para-tricresol phosphate, a chemical now important in the production of plastics, from paracresol.　　ACH

PRIMARY SOURCES

Volkova, Anna Fedorovna. "Ob izomernykh sernotoluolovykh kislotakh." *Zhurnal Russkogo fiziko-khimicheskogo obshchestva* 2, nos. 5–6, (1870): 161–175.

SECONDARY SOURCES

Musabekov, Iusuf S. *Iuliia Vsevolodovna Lermontova, 1846–1919.* Moscow: Izd-vo "Nauka," 1967.

VYSSOTSKY, EMMA T. R. (WILLIAMS) (1894–1975)

U.S. astronomer. Born 23 October 1894 in Media, Pa. Married Alexander N. Vyssotsky (21 September 1929); one son. Educated Swarthmore College (A.B., 1916; 1924); University of Chicago (graduate study, 1926); Harvard University, Radcliffe College (Ph.D. in astrophysics, 1930). Professional experience: Smith College, department of astronomy, demonstrator (1916–1917); life insurance actuary (1917–1925); Swarthmore College, instructor in mathematics (1925–1927); McCormick Observatory, University of Virginia, research fellow (1929–1932), instructor in astronomy (1932–1944). Died 1975, probably in Florida.

Emma T. R. Williams was born in Pennsylvania and attended Swarthmore College. Interested in both mathematics and astronomy, she first took a position as demonstrator in astronomy at Smith Colelge and then entered a life insurance company, using her mathematical skills for actuarial work. After World War I, she went to Germany on a child-feeding mission over a period of three years, returning to her actuarial position. She then returned briefly to Swarthmore College, where she served as an instructor in mathematics for two years.

Her love of astronomy led her first to Chicago for a year and then to Radcliffe College, where she pursued a doctoral

degree in astronomy, doing her dissertation research at Harvard Observatory on A stars. She then went as a research fellow to the McCormick Observatory at the University of Virginia, where she met and married the Russian astronomer Alexander N. Vyssotsky, a professor at the university. She remained for the rest of her career at the University of Virginia, first as a research fellow and instructor in astronomy, and then, at age fifty, she began to work with her husband on a book on stellar motions, published four years later. The same year, her husband was made a full professor at the University of Virginia. After he retired as emeritus professor in 1958, they moved to Florida.　　JH/MBO

PRIMARY SOURCES

Vyssotsky, Emma T. R. Williams. "A Spectrophometric Study of A Stars." Ph.D. diss., Radcliffe College, 1929.
———. With A. N. Vyssotsky. *An Investigation of Stellar Motions.* Charlottesville: Publications of the Leander McCormick Observatory of the University of Virginia, vol. 10, 1948.

STANDARD SOURCES

AMS 5–8; P 9 (as Emma T.R. Williams, Mrs. Alexander Vyssotsky); Debus (under A. N. Vyssotsky).

VYTILINGAM, KAMALA ISRAEL (1901–)

Indian physician. Born 28 June 1901 in Tamil Nadu (formerly Madras state) in South India. Father S. Israel Pillai (originally Mangaan). Three siblings. Married (1928). One daughter. Educated medical school at Vellore (1919–1923); Madras University (Licensed Medical Practitioner degree, 1923; M.D. in general medicine, 1945). Professional experience: Lady Wellington Medical School for Women in Madras (1924–1926); Medical School at Vellore, tutor in anatomy and hospital assistant (1926–1967); Bangalore hospital, attending physician (1967). Honors and memberships: Association for European Paediatric Cardiology, honorary member.

Kamala Israel's father was a graduate of Tanjore Christian College, who had been baptized Israel. Her mother was from a respected family and reputed to be intelligent. When they were married, she demanded that Israel Pillai educate her at home. They had four children; the first son was a physician who specialized in leprosy, and Kamala, the second-born, also became a physician. She grew up with her four boy cousins who had lost their parents.

Kamala's determination to be a doctor was strengthened after the death of her mother from childbirth. She had refused to be attended by a male doctor. Her mother's last wish was that Kamala be educated as a doctor. Although her father soon remarried, he did not forget her mother's request even though her stepmother's family disapproved.

Kamala entered the medical school at Vellore, encouraged by IDA SCUDDER. After receiving her licensed medical practitioner degree from Madras University, she worked as resident doctor in a small women's hospital in 1923. In 1924, she became demonstrator in anatomy at the Lady Wellington Medical School for Women in Madras, and in 1926 returned to Vellore, this time as a tutor in anatomy and a hospital assistant. In 1928 she married her husband, who was very supportive of her desire for knowledge, and encouraged her when she wanted to specialize.

Although she wanted to specialize in thoracic diseases, she was discouraged by the male physicians. However, with the encouragement of Scudder and of her husband she earned a medical degree in 1945. She had a difficult time at Vellore, but the disparaging remarks from those who felt women had no place in specialty fields were overridden by those who encouraged her in developing a cardiology department. She went to Johns Hopkins Hospital for postgraduate studies twice, the first time from 1953 to 1954 and the second from 1962 to 1963. At Johns Hopkins, HELEN TAUSSIG was especially important to her development in her specialty.

Vytilingam remained at Vellore until retirement in 1967, at which point she joined the hospital at Bangalore, where she developed the medical department and began some work in cardiology. K M

PRIMARY SOURCES
"Vytilingam, Kamala Israel." In Hellstedt, *Autobiographies.*

W

WAELSCH, SALOME GLUECKSOHN (1907–)

German/U.S. developmental biologist and geneticist. Born 6 October 1907 in Danzig, Germany, to Nadia (Pomeranz) and Ilya Gluecksohn. At least one sibling. Married (1) Rudolf Schoenheimer (1932); (2) Heinrich Waelsch (1943). Two children from second marriage, Naomi Barbara and Peter Benedict. Educated University of Königsberg; University of Berlin; University of Freiburg (Ph.D., 1932). Professional experience: University of Berlin, research assistant in cell biology (1932); Columbia University, research associate (1936–1953); Columbia University, College of Physicians and Surgeons, research associate (1953–1955); Albert Einstein College of Medicine, faculty (from 1955), professor (1963), distinguished professor emerita in genetics (from 1988). Honors and memberships: National Academy of Sciences (1979); National Medal of Science (1993); Columbia University, honorary D.Sc. (1995).

Salome Gluecksohn grew up in post–World War I Germany. Her father died in the flu epidemic of 1918, and her mother lost her savings in the postwar inflation. Salome was subjected to antisemitic taunts in school. After she received her bachelor's degree, she moved to the University of Freiburg for her graduate work. At Freiburg, she worked with 1935 Nobel laureate Dr. Hans Spemann and his group. After receiving her degree in 1932, she returned to the University of Berlin where she worked as a research assistant. Fear of the Nazis stimulated Salome and her new husband, Rudolf Schoenheimer, a prominent biochemist, to leave Germany. Rudolf Schoenheimer got a position at the College of Physicians and Surgeons, but Salome was without a job for three years. She was offered a position in the laboratory of the renowned geneticist L. C. Dunn at Columbia in 1936; she remained as research associate for seventeen years. After her husband, Rudolf, died (1941) she remarried another Columbia University biochemist, Heinrich Waelsch (1943). The couple had two children both of whom became teachers. After she left Dunn's laboratory, she served as a research

associate in obstetrics and gynecology at the College of Physicians and Surgeons. She finally realized that she would have no chance of advancement at Columbia and in 1955 moved to the newly established Albert Einstein College of Medicine.

Gluecksohn had become acquainted with Hans Spemann's work in an embryology class. He accepted her as a graduate student, assigning her to a descriptive study of limb development for her doctoral dissertation. She worked with two species of salamanders having different types of limb development. She was assigned the task of describing the development of each species while a male student transplanted tissues between them. She considered Spemann to be a strong German nationalist with prejudices against women as scientists, an influential embryologist but one whose dogmatism limited his creativity. However, in Spemann's laboratory she met other eminent scientists, including Richard Goldschmidt, Walter Vogt, and most important to her, Viktor Hamburger, who supervised her experimental results. Hamburger, who left Germany in 1933, became one of the founders of modern neuroembryology.

When Gluecksohn Schoenheimer first arrived in the United States, she met Ross G. Harrison, who demonstrated that the nerve fiber arose as an outgrowth of a single neuronal cell. Her association with Leslie C. Dunn was important in her development, for Dunn stressed the significance of the gene in development and differentiation. At first, because of the lack of funds, she worked without a salary in Dunn's laboratory. In the late 1930s, the National Research Council was formed and it awarded Dunn money so that he could pay her. She became convinced of the overlap between genetics and embryology and spent most of her later research working on the genetic causes of differentiation.

Waelsch authored or coauthored more than one hundred papers on developmental genetics, was elected to the National Academy of Sciences in 1979, and awarded the National

Medal of Science by President Bill Clinton. She was recognized by the University of Freiburg, her alma mater, with a gold doctoral diploma in recognition of her life's work.

As of 1999, Waelsch was still the head of Molecular Genetics at Albert Einstein College of Medicine, studying the mechanism of cell and tissue differentiation and the genetic control and regulation of specific gene expression using experimental studies of chromosome deletions in abnormal liver cell differentiation of prenatal hepatocytes.   JH/MBO

PRIMARY SOURCES

Gluecksohn, Salome. "Aussere Entwicklung der Extremitäten und Stadieneinteilung der Larvenperiode von *Triton taeniatus Leyd.* und *Triton cristatus Laur.*" *Archiv für Entwicklungsmechanik der Organismen* 125 (1931): 341–405.

Schoenheimer, Salome Gluecksohn. With L. C. Dunn. "The Inheritance of Taillessness (Anury) in the House Mouse. II. Taillessness in a Second Balanced Lethal Line." *Genetics* 24 (1939): 587–609.

Waelsch, Salome Gluecksohn. "Physiological Genetics of the Mouse." *Advances in Genetics* 4 (1951): 1–51.

———. "Abnormalities in the Nervous System in the Mouse." In *Progress in Neurobiology, vol. 4. The Biology of Myelin,* ed. S. R. Korey, 108–121. New York: Harper and Brothers, 1959.

———. With A. S. Pai. "Developmental Genetics of a Lethal Mutation, Muscular Dysgenesis (MDG), in the Mouse. I. Genetic Analysis and Gross Morphology." *Developmental Biology* 11 (1965): 82–92.

———. With A. S. Pai. "Developmental Genetics of a Lethal Mutation, Muscular Dysgenesis (MDG), in the Mouse. II. Developmental Analysis." *Developmental Biology* 11 (1965): 93–109.

———. "Gene Regulation in Mammalian Cells." *Science* 167 (1970): 1524–1526.

———. "Genetic Control of Differentiation." In *Cold Spring Harbor Conferences on Cell Proliferation,* vol. 10, ed. Lee M. Silver, et al., 3–13. Cold Spring Harbor, N.Y.: Cold Spring Harbor Laboratory, 1983.

———. "In Praise of Complexity." *Genetics* 122 (1989): 721–725.

———. With M. Lia and D. Bali. "Regulatory Genes Linked to the Albino Locus in the Mouse Confer Competence for Inducible Expression on the Structural Gene Encoding Serine Dehydrase." *Proceedings of the National Academy of Sciences* 89 (1992): 2453–2455.

SECONDARY SOURCES

Beck, Phil. "Medal of Science Winners: Eight Pioneers of Research." *The Scientist* 7 (15 November 1993): 7–8.

Zuckerman, Harriet, et al. *The Outer Circle: Women in the Scientific Community.* New York: W. W. Norton, 1991.

STANDARD SOURCES

AMS B 9, P&B 10–18; Bailey; Debus; Grinstein 1997 (article by Paris Sovronos); *Notable.*

WAKEFIELD, ELSIE MAUD (1886–1972)

British botanist and mycologist. Born 3 July 1886 in Birmingham. Educated Swansea High School for Girls; Somerville College, Oxford (M.A.); Munich. Professional experience: Kew Herbarium, assistant (1910); Imperial Department of Agriculture, West Indies, Barbados, temporary mycologist (1920–1921); Kew herbarium, deputy keeper (1945–1951). Retired 1951. Honors and memberships: Linnean Society, Fellow (1911); Mycological Society, secretary (1918–1936), president (1929), honorary member (1941).

Elsie Wakefield became interested in the larger fungi during her school days, an interest that developed throughout her life. A talented artist, she made colored drawings of the different fungi. While she was at Somerville College, Oxford, she completed a course in botany and was awarded a Gilchrist Scholarship, which took her to Munich, Germany, to work under Professor von Tubeuf at the Forstliche Versuchsanstalt. While in Munich, she worked on the production of fruit bodies in cultures of Hymenomycetes, resulting in her first publication, *Über die Bedingungen der Fruchtkoeperbildung bei Hymenomyceten* (On the Condition of the Fruiting Bodies of the Hymenomycetes). When she returned to England, she was appointed an assistant in the herbarium at Kew. Wakefield remained at Kew until her retirement. In January 1910, she began her new position, working under G. Massee. Until Massee retired in 1915, her duties included responsibility for both the fungi and lichens combined with advisory work. Before 1915, the pathological work was also done at Kew, but afterward was confined to the newly founded Pathological Laboratory under the Ministry of Agriculture. The Imperial Mycological Institute was founded in 1921, and after that time, Wakefield's advisory duties lessened, enabling her to spend more time in fungi systematics. Short-handed, with only temporary help until 1944, she was still overworked.

Wakefield received a traveling fellowship from Somerville College and was able to use it to go to the West Indies. She was seconded to work with the Imperial Department of Agriculture for six months in order to learn about tropical fungi and the diseases of tropical crops first-hand.

Her later research involved mycological nomenclature, and she attended International Botanical Congresses at Cambridge (1930), Amsterdam (1935), and Stockholm (1950). Her services to the profession were recognized when she was made an honorary member of the Mycological Society, and in 1950 was honored by King George VI for her services to the Empire as a mycologist.

PRIMARY SOURCES

Wakefield, Elsie M. *Über die Bedingungen der Fruchtkoerperbildung bei Hymenomyceten, sowie das Auftreten fertiler und steriler Staemme bei denselben.* Stuttgart: Verlag von Eugen Ulmer, 1909.

———. "Australian resupinate Hydnaceae." *Transactions of the Royal Society of South Australia* 54 (1930): 155–158.

———. "Contributions towards the Fungus Flora of Uganda IX. The Uredinales of Uganda by E. M. Wakefield and C. G. Hansford." *Proceedings of the Linnean Society of London* 161, pt. 2 (1948–1949).

———. *Common British Fungi: A Guide to the More Common Larger Basidiomycetes.* [London]: P. R. Gawthorn, [1950].

———. *The Observer's Book of Common Fungi Describing Nearly 200 Species.* London: F. Warner, [ca. 1958].

———. "Some Extra-European Species of Tomentella." *Transactions of the British Mycological Society* 49, no. 3 (1966): 357–362.

———. "Tomentelloideae in the British Isles." *Transactions of the British Mycological Society* 53, no. 2 (1969): 161–206.

SECONDARY SOURCES

Blackwell, E. *Bulletin of the British Mycological Society,* 6, pt. 2 (1972): 81–82.

Bullock, A. A. "Miss Elsie M. Wakefield, O.B.E., M.A., F.L.S." *Taxon* 1 (1951): 113–114. Includes portrait.

Cotton, A. C. *Journal of the Kew Guild* 1944: 343–344. Biographical sketch and portrait.

Journal of the Linnean Society 5, no. 4 (1973): 392–393. Obituary notice.

STANDARD SOURCES

Barnhart; Desmond; Stafleu and Cowan.

WAKEFIELD, PRISCILLA (BELL) (1751–1832)

British writer for children on botany and natural history. Quaker philanthropist. Born 31 July 1751 in Tottenham, Middlesex, to Catharine (Barclay) and Daniel Bell. At least one younger sister. Married Edward Wakefield (1771). Two sons and one daughter. Professional experience: wrote popular books on botany. Died 1832 in Ipswich, Suffolk.

Priscilla Bell was the oldest daughter of Catharine and Daniel Bell of Stamford Hill, Middlesex. She married a merchant, Edward Wakefield, and was known for her philanthropic activities. She was an early promoter of savings banks and herself established several "frugality banks."

A liberal and a Quaker, Priscilla Wakefield began writing books when she was more than forty years old. Financial as well as ideological considerations motivated her to write, for her husband was a poor (or an unlucky) businessman and one of her sons had legal problems. Thus she chose to write her introductory botany book as well as a series of travelogues and natural history books because the subjects were popular and had the potential to be lucrative. Her *Introduction to Botany* was very popular and was reprinted so often than it became known as "Wakefield's Botany." It was translated into French and appeared in three American editions.

In her botany book, Wakefield used the correspondence between two teenage sisters to introduce children and young people to botany. In this book, she clearly explained the Linnaean system of classification and presented the essentials of plant morphology. She especially wanted to emphasize the virtues of botany as a suitable subject for girls, without challenging traditional mores regarding women.   JH/MBO

PRIMARY SOURCES

Wakefield, Priscilla. *Introduction to Botany in a Series of Familiar Letters, with Illustrative Engravings.* London: printed for E. Newberry, St. Paul's Churchyard; Darton and Harvey, Gracechurch Street; and Vernor and Hood, Birchin-Lane, 1796.

———. *An Introduction to the Natural History and Classification of Insects, in a Series of Letters.* London: Darton, Harvey, and Darton, 1816.

———. "[Various excerpts]." *Autograph Letters, Characteristic Extracts, and Signatures, from the Correspondence of Distinguished Women of Great Britain from the XIVth to the XIXth Century, Collected and Copied in Facsimilie from Original Documents,* ed. Joseph Netherclift. London: J. Netherclift, 1838.

SECONDARY SOURCES

Gentleman's Magazine 2 (1932): 650. Obituary notice.

Wheeler, A., and Price, J. H. *From Linnaeus to Darwin.* London: Society for the History of Natural History, 1985. See pages 29–36.

STANDARD SOURCES

Barnhart; Desmond; *DNB*, Shteir; Stafleu and Cowan.

WALCOTT, HELENE B. (STEVENS) (ca. 1868–?)

U.S. geologist. Married Charles Doolittle Walcott (1888). Four children (Charles, Helen, Sidney, and Stuart). Professional experience: collaborated with her husband on geographical research. Death date unknown.

Helene B. Stevens Walcott was the first wife of the paleontologist Charles Doolittle Walcott, and they collaborated on geological research. She had four children by him, but she died young. Charles Walcott then married MARY VAUX WALCOTT.   JH/MBO

SECONDARY SOURCES

Yechelson, Ellis L. *Charles Doolittle Walcott, Paleontologist.* Kent, Ohio: Kent State University Press, 1998.

STANDARD SOURCES

Debus.

WALCOTT, MARY MORRIS (VAUX) (1860–1940)

U.S. mountaineer, glaciologist, painter, dairy farmer, and artist. Born 1860. Married Charles Doolittle Walcott. Professional experience: collaborated with her husband on geological research. Died 1940.

Mary Walcott was associated with George and William S. Vaux, Jr., in studies of glaciers in the Canadian Rockies. She became the second wife of paleontologist (later director of the Smithsonian Institution) Charles Doolittle Walcott. Mary Walcott aided her husband in his stratographic works.

JH/MBO

PRIMARY SOURCES

Walcott, Mary Morris Vaux. *North American Wild Flowers.* Washington, D.C.: Smithsonian Institution, 1925.
———. *Illustrations of North American Pitcherplants.* Washington, D.C.: Smithsonian Institution, 1935. The text was by Edgar T. Wherry.
———. With Dorothy Falcon Platt and Harold William Rickett. *Wild Flowers of America.* New York: Crown Publishers, 1953. Includes 400 flowers in full color based on paintings by Vaux and published by the Smithsonian as noted in the previous citation.

SECONDARY SOURCES

Cavell, Edward. *Legacy in Ice: The Vaux Family and the Canadian Alps.* Banff, Alberta: The Whyte Foundation, 1983.
New York Times, 25 August 1940. Obituary notice.
Y., H. W. "Mary Vaux Walcott." *Canadian Alpine Journal* 27, no. 2 (1940): 236–237.

STANDARD SOURCES

AMS 6; Bailey; Barnhart; Sarjeant.

WALD, LILLIAN D. (1867–1940)

U.S. nurse and public health worker. Born 10 March 1867 in Cincinnati, Ohio, to Max D. and Minnie (Schwarz) Wald. Third of four children. Never married. Educated private schools; New York Hospital nurses training school (graduated 1891); Woman's Medical College, New York City. Professional experience: founded the Henry Street Nurses Settlement (Henry Street Visiting Nurses Service); cofounded the National Child Labor Committee (1904); established Department of Nursing and Health at Columbia University; established the Town and Country Nursing Service, Red Cross; founded American Union Against Militarism (later League of Free Nations Association). Died in Westport, Conn., in 1940 after a long illness brought on by a cerebral hemorrhage.

Lillian Wald grew up happily in a family that prospered from her father's business in optical goods. Having moved to Rochester, Lillian was enrolled in Miss Cruttenden's English-French Boarding and Day School and enjoyed music and reading. At sixteen, she applied for admission to Vassar but was turned down because she was too young. For a few years she lived the active social life of a lovely, intelligent, and privileged young lady until in 1889 she decided she was dissatisfied with the lack of "serious, definite work," and entered the New York Hospital training school for nurses. After graduation in 1891, she spent an unhappy year at the New York Juvenile Asylum, then enrolled in the Woman's Medical College to supplement her nurse's training. In 1893, she left the college to organize home nursing classes for immigrant families on the Lower East Side.

With her friend Mary Brewster, Wald moved into a tenement house on the East Side, determined to work within the community. With the financial backing of Mrs. Solomon Loeb and banker Jacob H. Schiff, the rapidly growing nursing service moved in 1895 to a permanent home at 265 Henry Street and became the Henry Street Nurses Settlement. Of the eleven residents, nine were trained nurses. By 1913, the service had grown to ninety-two nurses, divided into specialized staffs, who conducted over two hundred thousand visits annually from Henry Street and branches in upper Manhattan and the Bronx. This was the birth of the public health nursing profession, and it soon expanded across the country.

Extensions of public health nursing were initiated by Wald, such as public school nursing programs, nursing programs for industries, the Town and Country Nursing Service through the American Red Cross, and the establishment in 1910 of a department of nursing and health at Columbia University Teachers College, which was chaired by MARY ADELAIDE NUTTING. Wald's work extended to social services as well as medical, providing aid and work relief during the Depression of 1893–1894, so that by 1913 the Henry Street Settlement occupied seven houses on the street and two uptown branches. Vocational guidance and training, scholarships, neighborhood and housing improvement, child labor reform, and other civic improvement movements were addressed by the settlement personnel. Wald worked with Florence Kelley (director of the National Consumers League) to found the National Child Labor Committee, which was instrumental in creation of a Federal Children's Bureau. Appalled by the outbreak of war, as president of the American Union Against Militarism, she petitioned (with JANE AD-

DAMS, Kelley, and others) President Wilson to mediate with neutral nations to stop the hostilities. After the United States entered the war, Wald turned her attention to encroachments on civil liberties, and to nursing and vaccination of children, especially during the influenza epidemic of 1918. The postwar League of Free Nations Association was an outgrowth of her American Union Against Militarism. The Henry Street Settlement grew to include a leading experimental theater and a music school; the Visiting Nurses Service boasted over 250 nurses by 1929.

Wald's political allegiance was to whichever candidates could best serve her social reform agenda. She had close ties with Eleanor Roosevelt, and in 1936 they cochaired the Good Neighbor League, which rallied independent voters for the Democratic ticket. The depression of the 1930s further debilitated her health, which had begun to fail ten years earlier with anemia and heart problems. In 1933 she resigned from Henry Street Settlement and retired to Westport, Connecticut, where she wrote a sequel to her 1915 autobiography, *The House on Henry Street,* titled *Windows on Henry Street* (1934). She died in Westport in 1940 after a long illness brought on by a cerebral hemorrhage.   JH/MBO

PRIMARY SOURCES
Wald, L. *The House on Henry Street.* New York: Henry Holt, 1915.
————. *Windows on Henry Street.* Boston: Little, Brown, 1934.

SECONDARY SOURCES
Duffus, R. L. *Lillian Wald: Neighbor and Crusader.* New York: Macmillan Co., 1938.
"Nursing Research." *Nursing Times* 40 (1991).

STANDARD SOURCES
NAW (article by Robert H. Bremner); Uglow 1989.

WALKER, ELIZA (ca. 1845–?)
Scottish/British physician. Born in India. Educated Cheltenham Ladies' College; University of Zurich (M.D., 1868). Professional experience: Zurich cantonal hospital, first woman assistant (ca. 1867–1868). Death date unknown.

Biographical information is very sketchy on Eliza Walker. Some information is found in Thomas Bonner's *To the Ends of the Earth.* Bonner located a brief biography in the *Medical Women's Federation Newsletter,* 1925. We know that she was born in India and was educated at the Ladies' College in Cheltenham before she went to Zurich to study medicine. She was among the many women who went to Zurich, because they could study medicine there, whereas it was difficult, if not impossible, to do so in their home countries.

After four years in Zurich she passed her final examination with special distinction. Her thesis was on the blockage of the arteries of the brain, based on fourteen cases she had observed at the Zurich clinic, as well as a search of the literature. She was the first woman assistant in the Zurich cantonal hospital, working in the women's ward, while she was still a student. Information about her subsequent career is unavailable.   JH/MBO

PRIMARY SOURCES
Walker, Eliza. *Ueber Verstopfung der Hirnarterien.* Zurich, 1872.

STANDARD SOURCES
Bonner 1992.

WALKER, ELIZABETH (1623–1690)
British pharmacist. Married Anthony Walker. Died 1690.

Elizabeth Walker was known as the proprietor of a pharmacy stocked with many efficacious remedies.   JH/MBO

SECONDARY SOURCES
Walker, Anthony. *The Holy Life of Mrs Elizabeth Walker, Late Wife of A. W., D. D., Rector of Fyfield in Essex: Giving a Modest and Short Account of Her Exemplary Piety and Charity: Published for the Glory of God and Provoking Others to the Like Graces and Vertues: Chiefly Designed to be Given to Her Friends, Who Can Abundantly Testifie to the Truth of What Is Here Related: with Some usefull Papers and Letters Writ by Her on Several Occasions.* London: Printed by John Leake for the Author, 1690.

STANDARD SOURCES
Hurd-Mead 1933.

WALKER, HARRIET ANN (1845–1929)
U.S. botanist. Born 27 July 1845. Educated Mount Holyoke Seminary (A.B., 1870); New York State Library School (1890–1892). Professional experience: Wellesley College, curator of museum (1875–1877), botanical laboratory, assistant (1892–1903); missionary to New York City (1879–1892); University of California, herbarium assistant (1905–1927). Died 26 June 1929.

Born in eastern New York to a Congregational minister, Harriet Walker was educated at Mount Holyoke. There she received a bachelor's degree while it was still a seminary; she was twenty-five. No record exists for what happened during the five years after her graduation, but she spent twelve years as an assistant in the department of botany at Wellesley, and two years as the curator of the Wellesley College museum in the mid-1870s, while expanding her knowledge of botany.

For thirteen years, she left university work and her botanical studies to work as a missionary in New York City. In the early 1890s, however, she spent two years studying at the New York State Library School and then returned to Wellesley as assistant in the botanical laboratory.

By 1905, then sixty years old, Walker moved to San Francisco, where she worked on the Berkeley campus of the University of California as an assistant in the herbarium; she stayed until she retired at the age of eighty-three. During this time she made collections of the native plants for the herbarium and distributed duplicates to other institutions. Most of her excursions were in the San Francisco Bay region, but she sometimes went further afield to the Mendocino Range and to the Sierra Nevadas. She died two years after she retired, leaving property valued at about four thousand dollars to the University of California. The Regents of the University of California preserved the legacy intact to be used as an endowment for books for the botanical library.   JH/MBO

SECONDARY SOURCES

Hall, H. M. "Harriet Walker." *Madrono* 2 (1932): 55.

J., W. L. "Harriet A. Walker." *Madrono* 1 (1929): 261. Obituary notice.

STANDARD SOURCES

Barnhart.

WALKER, HELEN MARY (1891–1983)

U.S. statistician. Born 1 December 1891 in Keosauqua, Iowa. Educated Iowa Wesleyan College (Ph.B., 1912; LL.D., 1942); Columbia University (M.A., 1912; fellow, 1926–1927; Ph.D., 1928). Professional experience: University of Kansas, assistant professor of mathematics (1922–1924), associate professor (1924–1925); Columbia University Teachers College, lecturer (1925–1926); associate (1927–1929), assistant professor of education (1929–1936), associate professor (1936–1940), professor (1940–1957), emerita professor (from 1957). Honors and memberships: American Education Research Association (1940–1943; vice president, 1948; president, 1949); Statistical Association, fellow, president (1944); Institute for Mathematical Statistics, member. Died 1983.

Helen Walker began her career in mathematics. However, after leaving her position at the University of Kansas to work on her doctoral degree, she moved more completely into the realm of theoretical statistics. She rose through the academic ranks at Columbia University Teachers College. After she retired in 1957, she remained active, working as a Fulbright lecturer in Chile in 1958, at the International Christian University and Tokyo University, Japan, from 1958 to 1959, and as a consultant for the Agency for the International Development of India in 1961. Her research interests were in the history of statistical methods and statistical theory and method.   JH/MBO

PRIMARY SOURCES

Walker, Helen Mary. *Mathematics Essential for Elementary Statistics.* New York: Holt, 1934.

———. With U. G. Mitchell. *Algebra: A Way of Thinking.* New York: Harcourt, Brace, and Co., 1936.

———. *Elementary Statistical Method.* New York: Henry Holt and Co., 1943.

SECONDARY SOURCES

"Women in Statistics: Sesquicentennial Activities." *American Statistician* 44 (1990): 74–80.

STANDARD SOURCES

AMS 5–8, S&B 9–11.

WALKER, MARY EDWARD (1832–1919)

U.S. physician. Born 26 November 1832 in Oswego, N.Y., to Vesta and Alvah Walker. Four siblings, three sisters and one brother. Married Albert Miller (1855); divorced (1869). Educated Syracuse Medical College (1855). Professional experience: volunteer surgeon, Civil War (1861); United States Army, acting assistant surgeon (1864). Honors and memberships: Congressional Medal of Honor (1865; rescinded, 1917; restored, 1977). Died 21 February 1919.

Mary Edward Walker was an iconoclast during most of her life. In her early years, her farmer father became interested in medicine while recovering from a lingering illness. He became convinced that liquor, tobacco, and tight clothing were harmful to the health, and allowed his four daughters to go without corsets at home. He also believed that girls should be educated and encouraged his daughters to become involved in a profession. Mary Walker absorbed her father's ideas, and entered the first coeducational medical school in the United States, Syracuse Medical College.

Walker strongly disapproved of unequal pay for men and women physicians, asserting that since she had to surmount more obstacles than men, if there was to be inequality, she should receive more. She refused to wear the modish floor-length dresses with hoop skirts and replaced them with bloomers covered by a coat dress. She married Albert Miller in an unorthodox ceremony, not wearing a wedding dress, retaining her maiden name, and having "obey" removed from the liturgy. The marriage really lasted only five years, although the divorce was not made final until 1869.

Walker practiced in Columbus, Ohio, and New York state. During the Civil War, she went to Washington, where she petitioned to become a surgeon in the Union army. Her application for a commission in the army was refused several times. She worked as an assistant physician and surgeon without recognition or pay. She served in tent hospitals in the Virginia unit during the Civil War. In 1864, Walker was captured as a prisoner of war and spent time in Richmond, Virginia, incarcerated in Castle Thunder, a political prison. She was exchanged after four months under abominable circumstances. After her release she eventually was awarded a contract as acting assistant surgeon in the United States Army with a salary of one hundred dollars a month plus back pay. She was never commissioned as an officer, however. Her demand to be promoted to major was refused because she had never been an officer in the first place. To pacify her and to recognize her service, Congress eventually awarded her a Congressional Medal of Honor for bravery. However in 1917, this honor was withdrawn by a federal review board after Congress revised the Medal of Honor standards to include only actual combat with the enemy. After an army board appeal was unsuccessful, she still refused to give it up. In 1977, the medal was restored.

Strong-minded and quarrelsome, Walker alienated colleagues in all areas in which she worked—military, medicine, women's rights, and community. An ardent suffragist, she campaigned for women's rights. However, she withdrew from the suffrage movement when she decided the Constitution already guaranteed women the right to vote. Known for her eccentric dress (a legacy from her father's ideas), she wore trousers and a tunic to her medical practice and a regular army uniform while in service. She occasionally attended formal functions in men's full evening dress and a silk top hat (with curls to show her femininity). Several times she was arrested for masquerading in men's clothes.

After the war, she worked for a New York newspaper becoming one of the first woman journalists in the United States. Two books she wrote—*Hit* (1871) and *Unmasked or The Science of Immorality* (1878)—received little notice.

Walker retired to the family farm in 1890, and in 1897 she founded a colony for women called Adamless Eden. Cut off from the community by her abrasive personality and eccentric activities, she died alone and poverty-stricken in 1919.

JH/MBO

PRIMARY SOURCES

Walker, Mary Edward. *Unmasked, or the Science of Immorality.* Philadelphia: Wm. H. Boyd, 1878.
———. "Woman Suffrage. Hearings before the Committee on the Judiciary." Sixty-second Congress, Second Session, February 13, [March 13], 1912.

SECONDARY SOURCES

Lockwood, Allison. "Pantsuited Pioneer of Women's Lib, Dr. Mary Walker." *Smithsonian* 7, no. 12 (March 1977): 113–114, 116–119.
Snyder, Charles M. *Dr. Mary Walker—The Little Lady in Pants.* New York: Arno Press, 1974.

STANDARD SOURCES

LKW; Hurd-Mead 1938; Shearer and Shearer 1996 (article by Laurie A. Potter); Uglow 1982.

WALKER, NORMA (FORD) (1893–1969?)

Canadian biologist. Born 3 September 1893 in St. Thomas, Ontario to Margaret (Dyke) and Norman W. Ford. Married Edmund Murton Walker (1943). Educated University of Toronto (B.A., 1918; Ph.D., 1923). Professional experience: University of Toronto, assistant (1918–1923), instructor (1923–1925), lecturer (1925–1930), assistant professor (1930–1937), human biologist (1937–1943), associate professor (1943–1958), professor of human genetics (from 1958); Hospital for Sick Children, Toronto, department of genetics, director (1947–1963); Victoria College, University of Toronto, acting dean of women (1931–1934). Died 1969?

Norma Ford Walker's main scientific interest was in human genetics. She wrote numerous scientific articles and was a pioneer in genetic and heredity counseling. She put theoretical genetics to practical use when she directed the department of genetics of the Hospital for Sick Children in Toronto. She became a trustee of the Queen Elizabeth Canadian Fund Research in Children's diseases.

Walker's early research was on insect morphology and the behavior of *Wohlfahrtia vigil* and *Grylloblatta*. Later, she worked on the inheritance of physical characters in multiple births, dermatoglyphics, genetical studies of mental defects and diseases, Down's syndrome, and twins. She published numerous articles in journals.

JH/MBO

PRIMARY SOURCES

Walker, Norma Ford. With John W. MacArthur. *A Biological Study of the Dionne Quintuplets—An Identical Set.* In *Collected Studies of the Dionne Quintuplets.* University of Toronto Studies, Child Development Series, ed. William E. Blatz, nos. 11–16. Toronto: University of Toronto Press, 1937. Each study has its own title page and pagination.

SECONDARY SOURCES

Proceedings of the Royal Society of Canada (1969): 109–112. Obituary notice.

STANDARD SOURCES

AMS 8, B 9, P&B 10–11; Debus.

WALL, FLORENCE (1893?–)

U.S. chemist. Born ca. 1893 in Patterson, N.J. Educated St. Eliza-
beth College (B.A. and B.Ed., 1913); New York University
(M.A., 1938). Professional experience: high schools in New York,
assistant teacher (1913–1917); Radium Luminous Materials Cor-
poration, N.J. (1917–1918); Seydel Manufacturing Company
(1918); Fellows Medical Manufacturing Company, New York
(1918–1919); U.S. Motor Fuel Corporation, staff member in re-
search and development (1919–1921); private tutor in Havana,
Cuba (1922–1924); Inecto, Inc., from assistant chemist to director
of trade education and technical publicity (1924–1928); private
consultant (1929–1943); General Aniline and Film Corporation,
Pa., technical education research laboratory (1943–1945); R. L.
Evans Co., New York (1945–1947); private consultant (1947–
1961); Chemical Publishing Company, Inc., editor (1961–1967);
private consultant (from 1967). Honors and memberships: Society
for Cosmetic Chemistry (medal 1956); Society for Medical Jurispru-
dence; Institute of Chemistry, fellow; History of Science Society.

Twenty-five years after Florence Wall earned her bachelor's degree she earned her master's. In the interim and afterward she held numerous positions in industry that used her chemical expertise. Her special interests were in dyes, detergents, essential oils, and synthetic aromatics. She was also interested in the history of chemistry, medicine, and cosmetics, cosmetology in industrial education, and technical writing. She served as an editor for *The Chemist* from 1929 to 1931. From 1936 to 1943 she lectured at New York University's School of Education and in 1948 at its College of Medicine.

JH/MBO

PRIMARY SOURCES
Wall, Florence E. "Wilhelm Ostwald." *Journal of Chemical Educa-*
tion 25, no. 1 (1948). Offprint.

STANDARD SOURCES
AMS 7–8, P 9, P&B 10–11; Rossiter 1982.

WALLACE, LOUISE BAIRD (1867–1968)

U.S. zoologist. Born 21 September 1867 in Newville, Pa. Educated
Mount Holyoke College (A.B., 1898); Naples Zoological Station
(1901); University of Pennsylvania (A.M., 1904; Ph.D., 1908).
Professional experience: Mount Holyoke College, assistant zoologist
(1893–1896), instructor (1899–1903), associate professor (1904–
1912), professor (1927–1928); Smith College, assistant (1896–
1899); Constantinople College, professor of biology (1912–1925),
dean of faculty (1913–1924), vice-president (1924–1925); Spel-
man College, faculty (1928–1931).

Louise Baird Wallace graduated from Mount Holyoke College and was on its faculty until 1912. She returned to

Holyoke for one year (1927–1928) as a full professor. After leaving Mount Holyoke in 1912, she took a position as professor and dean of the faculty at Constantinople College, where she eventually became vice president. Wallace remained at Constantinople for thirteen years, returning to Mount Holyoke in 1927. In 1928 she accepted a position at Spelman College and worked there for four years. Her research was on toadfish and spiders. She worked on auxiliary glands of Batrachus and spermatogenesis and oogenesis of the spider.

JH/MBO

PRIMARY SOURCES
Wallace, Louise B. "The Spermatogenesis of Agalena Naevia."
Biological Bulletin 17 (1909): 120–160.
———. "A Tribute to Dr. Clapp." *Mount Holyoke Alumnae*
Quarterly 19 (May 1935): 4–5.

SECONDARY SOURCES
A student notebook of her lectures in zoology is held in the Ethel Breitenstein Robinson papers in the Archives and Special Collections, Mount Holyoke College Library.

STANDARD SOURCES
AMS 1–8, B 9; Bailey.

WALLIS, RUTH SAWTELL (1895–1978)

U.S. physical anthropologist and ethnographer. Born 15 March
1895 in Springfield, Mass., to Grace (Quimby) and Joseph Otis
Sawtell. Married Wilson D. Wallis (1931). Two stepchildren. Edu-
cated Vassar College (1913–1914); Harvard University, Radcliffe
College (A.B., 1919; M.A., 1923); Columbia University (Ph.D.,
1929). Professional experience: Harvard University, Peabody Mu-
seum, Harvard African Studies, editorial assistant; Andover Pecos
expedition, research assistant (1920–1923); Columbia University,
department of anthropology, research assistant (1926); New York
Bureau of Educational Experiments (later Bank Street College of
Education); University of Iowa, assistant professor of sociology
(1931–1932); Hamline University, St. Paul, Minn. (1932–1935);
Works Project Administration (WPA), researcher (1935–1937);
United States Department of Agriculture, Bureau of Home Econom-
ics, researcher (1937–1938); mystery writer (1943–1950); Am-
herst College, sociology department, from lecturer to full professor
(1960?–1974), emerita professor (1974–1978). Died 21 January
1978 in Connecticut.

Ruth Sawtell Wallis's life reflects both the challenges and successes of women in the academic world. Her career as an anthropologist included field work in France and publications on physical anthropology, writing mystery novels with a woman anthropologist as a heroine, conducting ethnographic research on Eastern Indians with her husband, and finally teaching as a university professor in sociology and anthropology.

Ruth Sawtell was born in Springfield, Massachusetts, where her father was a haberdasher. She went to college, first to Vassar, but shortly afterward, to Radcliffe College. There she majored in English, receiving her bachelor's degree in 1919 *cum laude,* and with election to Phi Beta Kappa. While a student, she had become interested in Earnest A. Hooten's work in physical anthropology at Harvard, and decided to work toward a master's degree. During this period, she was able to support herself by working at the Peabody Museum, as an editorial assistant with the publication series, Harvard African Studies, and then as research assistant with the Andover Pecos expedition. She was twenty-eight when she received her master's degree.

With a Radcliffe traveling fellowship, Sawtell was able to study and do research in England and Europe for two years. Most notably, she worked with a friend Ida Treat and her French husband excavating two Mesolithic Azilian sites in the French Pyranees, which indicated that Upper Paleolithic humans had experienced more gradual transition toward and greater similarities, both physically and culturally, with the Neolithic. She reported to the American Anthropological Association on her research and published with Treat both a detailed scholarly and a popular account.

Wallis decided to continue her work in anthropology under Franz Boas, who, like Wallis, had begun as a physical anthropologist, although he is far better known for his ethnographic work. He was analyzing changes in head form among immigrant populations in New York, and hired Wallis to do the measurements on Sicilian women. Boas's work on children's physical growth led her to focus her doctoral research on this topic, using a number of techniques, including radiography, to obtain evidence for rate of ossification, correlated with age, weight, and sex. During this period, she also worked with the Bureau of Educational Experiments, later to become the Bank Street College of Education. By 1930, the year after she completed her doctorate, she was elected as a charter member of the American Association of Physical Anthropologists, one of only two women to enter at that time. In 1932, she attended the Third International Congress of Eugenics, presenting a paper on "Harmonic Types among Western European Crania," a topic that would soon carry unpleasant overtones.

Her first teaching position was at the University of Iowa, where she was hired as an assistant professor of sociology. The same year, she met and married the well-known cultural anthropologist Wilson D. Wallis, a widower with two children. After her marriage, she joined her husband in St. Paul, Minnesota, where he taught at the University of Minnesota. Because of nepotism rules, she had to turn to a small college, Hamlin College, in the same city to find a position.

After teaching successfully for three years, she was fired because (she believed) of resentment on the part of the faculty toward a dual-income family at the height of the Depression.

Wallis then turned to working for the Works Project Administration during the Depression years, preparing a manuscript with her husband that drew on both ethnographic works and folk stories as sources for information on how different cultures perceived the natural world. Entitled "Primitive Science," this ran to seven volumes but was never published. By 1937, she was working for the United States Department of Agriculture, Bureau of Home Economics, compiling statistics on the rate of growth in children in order to develop a standard measurement for children's clothing sizes. Her study, which directed the measurement of ten thousand school-aged chldren, was the first major anthropometic study on this age group.

Starting in the 1940s, Wallis, who had always loved literature, began to write mystery novels. Her first mystery, *Too Many Bones,* featured a woman physical anthropologist as heroine, and won an award of a thousand dollars from Red Badge Mystery. She followed this book with four others, ending the series in 1950. Even during this period, the Wallises held informal discussion groups in anthropology at their home, and encouraged young scholars. In the early 1950s, Ruth Wallis began to work as an ethnographer in the field with her husband, studying some of the Eastern Dakota tribes in Manitoba. She brought some of her insights from working with children and her sensitivity to the changing status of women to an analysis of the fears expressed by Indian children. She also examined the different attitudes toward twins as a test of acculturation.

Wallis expanded her collaboration with her husband to a major ethnographic study of the Canadian Micmac people, on whom her husband had done research some forty years before. The two documented cultural changes and culture losses, and evaluated both their attitudes and their subjects' motivations. A husband and wife team proved to work better than Wilson Wallis alone, and they were able to communicate effectively with their informants. They also extended their ethnographic study to another Canadian tribe, the Malecite in New Brunswick.

When Wilson Wallis retired to Connecticut from the University of Minnesota, Ruth Wallis began to teach at Amherst College. Although she held her position as lecturer in sociology on a part-time basis during her husband's retirement years, she returned to academic teaching full time after his death, rising to full professor and retiring in 1974 as professor emerita, the first woman to hold that position at Amherst. She died four years later at the age of eighty-three.

JH/MBO

PRIMARY SOURCES

Wallis, Ruth Sawtell. With Ida Treat. *Primitive Hearths in the Pyrenees.* New York: D. Appleton and Co., 1927.

———. "Ossification and Growth of Children from One to Eight Years of Age." *American Journal of Diseases of Children* 37 (1929): 61–87.

———. "Azilian Skeletal Remains from Montardit (Ariege) France." *Papers of the Peaody Museum of American Archaeology and Ethnology* 11 no. 4 (1931): 217–253.

———. *How Children Grow: An Anthropometric Study of Private School Children from Two to Eight Years Old.* Iowa City: University of Iowa Press,1931.

———. *Too Many Bones.* New York: Dodd Mead, 1943.

———.With Wilson D. Wallis. *The Micmac Indians of Eastern Canada.* Minneapolis: University of Minnesota Press, 1955.

The unpublished, seven-volume manuscript "Primitive Science" by Wilson D. Wallis and Ruth Sawtell Wallis was deposited by the WPA in microfilm form at Tozzer Library, Harvard University.

SECONDARY SOURCES

"Ruth Sawtell Wallis, 1895–1978." *American Anthropologist* 81 (1979): 85–89. Obituary notice.

STANDARD SOURCES

AMS 5–7, S&B 9–13; Gacs (article by Patricia Case).

WALWORTH, ELLEN HARDIN (1832–1915)

U.S. popular science writer. Born 20 October 1932 in Jacksonville, Ill., to Sarah Ellen (Smith) and John J. Hardin. Married Mansfield Tracy Walworth (29 July 1852). Eight children (three died in childhood). Educated Jacksonville Academy. Professional experience: federal government clerk (1868–1870; 1886–?); founder of Saratoga Art and Science Field Club (1873?–1885); speaker on geology at American Association for Arts and Sciences. Other activities: founder of Daughters of American Revolution and editor of American Monthly Magazine. *Died 23 June 1915 from gallstone obstruction, Georgetown University Hospital, Washington, D.C.*

Although Ellen Hardin Walworth is best known for her club work as one of the founders of the Daughters of the American Revolution and the Monument Society, she also had a strong interest in science and was one of the few women of her time to present a paper to the American Association for the Advancement of Science. Born in Jacksonville, Illinois, she was the daughter of a lawyer who was later killed while serving as an officer in the Mexican War (when she was fifteen). When her mother married a distinguished judge, Reuben Hyde Walworth, the last chancellor of New York state, she accompanied her mother to Saratoga Springs. At the age of twenty, she married a stepson of Walworth in what proved to be a disastrous marriage, owing to her husband's violence. She rapidly had six children, two of whom died in childhood, and she left her husband temporarily, taking her children to live on her family's farm in Kentucky. Following a reconciliation with her husband, two more children were born, the second of whom died at a young age.

After Walworth was injured by her husband during her last pregnancy, she obtained a permanent separation or "limited divorce" in 1871. She moved to Washington, D.C. and Kentucky, then finally to Saratoga. There she opened a girl's boarding school in her home and also began to promote the study of geology and botany through a Field Club that brought young men and women together in field study trips around the Saratoga area in the mid-seventies. This organization also published a journal describing the studies of geological features. In 1876, she attended the American Association for the Advancement of Science, and at the Boston meeting in 1880, became one of the first women to speak before it, advocating the study of science by women, especially geology, and the creation of amateur field clubs throughout the United States.

A tragedy struck her household when her son, enraged by his father's threats against her, killed his father in a New York hotel room in 1873. Although he was sentenced to life imprisonment, Walworth was able to have him released on an insanity plea in 1877, and he returned to a quiet life in Saratoga. Walworth became involved in many other projects, including the Saratoga Monument Society, which helped raise funds to save Mount Vernon and protected the sites of famous Revolutionary War battles in the Saratoga area.

Her interest in the Revolutionary War led her to found with two other women the Daughters of the American Revolution. After she moved to Washington, D.C., in the early 1890s, she was struck by the manner in which professional women in both literary and scientific fields were able to come together in that city. She became the first secretary general of the organization and edited its journal, although arguments between the founders led to her resignation.

In 1893, Walworth was also active in setting up the Woman's Expositon at the Chicago World's Fair, and always considered herself active in the advancement of women, though she never formally joined a suffrage organization. One of Walworth's daughters, inspired by stories of nurses in war time, went to serve as a nurse during the Spanish-American War and died in Cuba(?) soon after her arrival from a tropical fever. Walworth raised a large monument in Saratoga to her memory. Walworth's former home has been turned into an historical museum, the Walworth Memorial Museum, in Saratoga Springs.

JH/MBO

PRIMARY SOURCES

Walworth, Ellen Hardin. "Washington a Literary Center" *Chautauquan* 13 (1891): 168–169. Walworth mentions Washington as an important center for professional women, including those in the sciences.

Some primary biographical material and issues of the Field Club for Art and Science of Saratoga are held at the Wallworth Memorial Museum in Saratoga Springs.

STANDARD SOURCES

NAW (article by Wallace Evan Davies); Rossiter 1982.

WANG CHI CHE (1894–?)

Chinese/U.S. biochemist. Born 30 October 1894 in Soochow to Jan Dan (Siah) Zone Wai Wang. Naturalized U.S. citizen (1947). Educated Wellesley College (A.B., 1914); University of Chicago (M.S., 1916; Ph.D., 1918); Johns Hopkins University, postgraduate work (1917). Professional experience: University of Chicago, assistant in nutrition (1918–1920); Michael Reese Hospital, Chicago, head department of chemistry in charge of clinical research (1920–1930); University of Cincinnati, faculty, and Children's Hospital Cincinnati, researcher (1931–1940); Northwestern Yeast Co., Chicago, research chemist (1940–1943); Northwestern University Medical School, Chicago, researcher (1943–1946); Mayo Clinic, Rochester, N.Y., researcher (1946–1947); Veteran's Hospital Hines, Ill., research biochemist in charge of Metabolic Laboratory (1947–1954); Veteran's Hospital, Topeka, Kans., biochemist in charge of research and clinical chemistry (1954–1960); Washburn University, Topeka, lecturer. Honors and memberships: American Association for the Advancement of Science, Fellow, Society for Research in Child Development; American Society of Biological Chemists; American Chemical Society; and more. Retired 1961. Death date unknown.

During a period of unrest in China, Wang Chi Che and her family came to the United States. She attended Wellesley College and the University of Chicago, where she eventually got her degree. In 1947, she became a naturalized citizen of the United States.

Wang had a rather peripatetic work career, finally ending up in Topeka, Kansas. Her research, resulting in numerous publications, was on the chemistry of biological fluids, food products, energy, mineral and protein metabolism of obese and undernourished children and adults. She was a member or fellow of numerous professional organizations, including the American Association for the Advancement of Science (Fellow), Society for Research in Child Development; American Society of Biological Chemists; American Chemical Society; American Association of Clinical Chemicals; Sigma Xi, Phi Beta Kappa; and Sigma Delta Epsilon.

JH/MBO

PRIMARY SOURCES

Wang Chi Che. "The Chemistry of Chinese Preserved Eggs and Chinese Edible Birds' Nests." Ph.D. diss., University of Chicago, 1921. Private edition. Distributed by the University of Chicago Libraries, Chicago, Ill., and Baltimore, 1921.

STANDARD SOURCES

Debus.

WANG ZHENYI (CHEN-I) (1768–1797)

Chinese mathematician and astronomer. Born 1768 in the Nanjing area. Father a prominent physician. Married (1793). Professional experience: wrote books on the positions of the heavenly bodies; attempted to measure humidity; collected data to allow her to make accurate forecasts. Died 1797.

Wang Zhenyi was one of the few Chinese women of the eighteenth century to defy society's strictures on the proper duties and responsibilities of women. Since childhood, Wang Zhenyi had been fascinated by mathematics and astronomy. Encouraged by her father, who was an enlightened man, she spent much of her time doing laboratory work and making astronomical observations.

She wrote a total of twelve volumes on astronomy and mathematics, but these books have been lost. The only works surviving are some essays on astronomy and thirteen volumes of poetry. Her first book was an extensive treatment of the positions of the stars (*Some Observations on Forms and Figures*). Through modeling in her house, she gained information for another book, *The Interpretation of the Eclipse of the Moon*. For the purpose of this book, she used a round table in the center of the room to represent the earth, a mirror for the moon, and a lamp suspended from a central roof beam for the sun. She spent years gathering data on the heavenly bodies and the clouds. The data gathered from her attempts to measure atmospheric humidity were used for weather forecasting and, purportedly, could predict floods and droughts.

Wang Zhenyi married when she was twenty-five years old and died four years later. She apparently realized that her situation was an unusual one for a woman, as she wrote, "I have traveled ten thousand *li* and read ten thousand volumes. Bold is my attempt to surpass men." JH/MBO

SECONDARY SOURCES

Gu Qian. *Departed but not Forgotten: Women of China*. Beijing: n.p. 1984. Illustration of Wang Zhenyi on page 134.

Meschel, S. V. "Teacher Keng's Heritage: A Survey of Chinese Women Scientists." *Journal of Chemical Education* 9 (September 1992): 723–730.

Needham, Joseph. *Science and Civilization of China*. Cambridge: Cambridge University Press, 1980.

WARD, MARY (KING) (1827–1869)

Irish microscopist, astronomer, naturalist, and artist. Born 27 April 1827 at Ballylin in Ferbane, King's County, Ireland. Educated at home by a governess. Married Henry William Crosbie Ward. Three sons, five daughters. Died 31 August 1869 at age forty-two, when she was bounced out of a steam carriage and crushed under a wheel.

Mary Ward was a multitalented woman who made contributions to natural science in several areas while staying within the bonds of propriety for a lady of the nineteenty century. Educated by a governess at home, she took advantage of kinship with William, the third earl of Rosse, whose scientifically oriented household she visited frequently to expand her knowledge. Her friend Mary, Countess of Rosse, was an artist, architect, and superb photographer and was hostess at Birr Castle to the most eminent men of science of the day. Mary Ward observed and chronicled the building of the giant telescope on Birr Castle grounds. She received a fine microscope at age eighteen, which she used all her life, becoming so adept at preparing slide specimens that Sir David Brewster asked her to prepare specimens for him. Ward was the first woman to publish a book on the microscope, *Sketches with the Microscope* (a difficulty for women of that time since most publishers refused their manuscripts). When republished in 1858 by Groomsbridge of London, it was called *The World of Wonders Revealed by the Microscope*. This edition was greatly expanded and became *Microscope Teachings* in 1864. *Telescope Teachings,* a companion volume, was published in 1859.

Ward was an exceptionally fine artist, and her illustrations graced all her own books and papers and those of other scientists as well. Some microscope specimens she drew and painted may be seen in the *Transactions of the Royal Society of Edinburgh,* (1864). She made the original drawings of Newton's and Lord Rosse's telescopes for Brewster's *Life of Newton,* and her painting of the natterjack toad (prepared for her own article, "Natterjack Toads in Ireland," published and later reprinted in *The Irish Times,* May 1864) was acquired by Sir Richard Owen for the British Museum. First writing as The Hon. Mrs. W., she completed three books on scientific subjects plus numerous articles for scientific journals while fulfilling her duties as wife and mother of eight chidren. On 31 August 1869, she was traveling with her husband and others on a steam carriage invented by her cousin Lord Rosse when a sudden jolt threw her to the ground and she was run over and killed instantly by one of the heavy wheels.

JH/MBO

PRIMARY SOURCES

Ward, Mary King. *Telescope Teachings: A Familiar Sketch of Astronomical Discovery.* London: Groombridge and Sons, 1859.

———. *Entomology in Sport.* London: Paul Jerrard & Son, 1859.

———. *Microscope Teachings: Descriptions of Various Objects of Especial Interest and Beauty Adapted for Microscopic Observation.* London: Groombridge and Sons, Paternoster Row, 1864. Originally published as *A World of Wonders Revealed by the Microscope* in 1858.

———. "A Windfall for the Microscope." *The Intellectual Observer* 5 (1864): 13–17.

SECONDARY SOURCES

Harry, Owen G. "The Honorable Mrs. Ward and 'A Windfall for the Microscope' of 1856 and 1864." *Annals of Science* 41 (1984): 471–482.

STANDARD SOURCES

Mollan and Finucane.

WARGA, MARY ELIZABETH (1904–1991)

U.S. physicist. Born 5 February 1904 in Donora, Pa., to Mary (Obruba) and John Warga. Educated University of Pittsburgh (B.S.; M.S., 1928; Ph.D., 1937). Professional experience: Mellon Institute for Industrial Research, Pittsburgh, staff (1929–1936); University of Pittsburgh, faculty (1936–1972), professor of physics and applied spectroscopy (1952–1962); adjunct professor of physics and engineering (1962–1972). Honors and memberships: Distinguished Daughter of Pennsylvania (1954); Woman of the Year in Scientific Research, Pittsburgh (1959); Distinguished Service Medal, New York Section of the Society for Applied Spectroscopy (1962); Optical Society of America, Fellow. Died 10 December 1991.

Mary Elizabeth Warga earned all three of her degrees from the University of Pittsburgh and spent most of her professional life at that institution. She received several fellowships before she was appointed instructor of physics. She rose to the rank of professor of physics and director of the spectroscopy laboratory.

Warga's research was concerned with optics and spectroscopy. She worked on optical absorption, upper atmosphere spectroscopy, spectrochemical analysis, and ultraviolet, visible, and infrared optical emission. After her distinguished teaching and research career, Warga became executive secretary of the Optical Society of America. Although when she first took this position she still directed the spectroscopy laboratory at the University of Pittsburgh, she eventually reduced her teaching load and became an adjunct professor of physics.

Well respected, Warga was a member or fellow of many important scientific institutions, including the Optical Society of America, Fellow (received a distinguished service award when she retired in 1972), the American Association for the Advancement of Science, American Physical Society,

Physical Society (London), American Chemical Society, the Washington Academy of Sciences, the American Association of Physics teachers, and the Groupement pour l'advancement des methodes spectrographiques (honorary, Paris). She was a member of the governing board of the American Institute of Physics (from 1960) and served as the secretary of the Joint Council on Quantum Electronics. In 1999, the fiftieth Pittsburg Conference on Analytical Chemistry and Applied Spectroscopy was dedicated to Warga's memory, in honor of her founding of the Spectroscopy Society of Pittsburg and her participation as an early organizer of the Pittsburg Conference. She was remembered by the conference for her work in training spectroscopists for government national defense during World War II. The University of Pittsburg offers a predoctoral fellowship in her name to an entering female graduate student in astronomy and physics.

JH/MBO

PRIMARY SOURCES
Warga, Mary E. *Magnesium Triplets in Arc and Solar Spectra.* Pittsburgh: University of Pittsburgh Press, 1929.
———. With J. W. Quinn. *Sample Examination Questions for the Intermediate Optics Course.* Sponsored by the National Science Foundation under grant no. GP1549. Washington, D.C.: Optical Society of America, 1966.

STANDARD SOURCES
AMS 5–12; Bailey; Debus.

WARING, SISTER MARY GRACE (1897–?)

U.S. chemist. Born 12 May 1897 in Oregon, Mo. Educated William Jewell College, Liberty, Mo. (B.A., 1921); Kansas State University (M.S., 1926); Catholic University (Ph.D., 1931). Professional experience: Marymount College, Salina, Kans., faculty (1922–). Death date unknown.

Sister Mary Grace Waring spent her entire teaching career at Marymount College. She received resident grants from the Kansas Division of the American Cancer Society (1963–1967) and the Kansas Heart Association (1963–1968). She participated in a summer residence conference on radioisotopes at the National Science Foundation in Maryland in 1959. During the summer of 1960, she taught a course on radioisotope techniques at the Philadelphia College of Pharmacy. She continued to spend summers increasing her knowledge of radioisotopes, and passing that knowledge on to others. She attended an institute at the University of Kansas in 1962 and Kansas State in 1963. Sister Mary Grace was a member of the Chemical Society Science Teachers Association and the Association of Physics Teachers.

JH/MBO

PRIMARY SOURCES
Waring, Mary Grace. *The Preparation and Study of 7,7'-Dimethyl-8,8'-diquinolyl, 6,6'-dinitro-2,2', 4,4'-tetramethyldiphenyl, 6,6'-diamino-2,2', 4,4'-tetramethyldiphenyl, and 5,5',7,7'-tetramethyl-8,8'-diquinolyl.* Washington, D.C.: Catholic University Press, 1900.

STANDARD SOURCES
AMS 6–7, P&B 10–12; Rossiter 1982.

WARREN, ELIZABETH ANDREW (1786–1864)

British botanist. Born 28 April 1786 in Truro, Cornwall. Died 5 May 1864 in Sussex.

Elizabeth Andrew Warren studied flowering plants in Cornwall and collected specimens for well-known botanists. She is cited by Davey in his *Flora of Cornwall.*

JH/MBO

PRIMARY SOURCES
Warren, Elizabeth. "Falmouth Algae." *Report of the Cornwall Polytechnic Society* (1849): 31–37.

SECONDARY SOURCES
Journal of Botany (1865): 101–103. Obituary notice.
Report of the Cornwall Polytechnic Society (1864): 11–14. Obituary notice.

STANDARD SOURCES
Barnhart; Desmond.

WARREN, MADELEINE (FIELD) (1903–)

U.S. physiologist. Born 9 March 1903 in Greenfield, Mass. Educated Oberlin College (A.B., 1925); Radcliffe College (Ph.D., 1931). Professional experience: Mount Holyoke College, assistant in physiology (1925–1927); Simmons College (1927–1928); Harvard School of Public Health, research fellow in physiology (1931–1932), instructor (1932–1935), associate (1935–1937), assistant professor (from 1941).

Physiologist Madeleine Warren began her professional career at Simmons College, but soon moved to the Harvard School of Public Health where she ultimately became an assistant professor. She was a Fellow of the American Association of University Women, and did research in Copenhagen in 1934–1935. Warren was a member of the Physiological Society and worked on the lymphatics.

JH/MBO

STANDARD SOURCES
AMS 7.

WASHBURN, MARGARET FLOY (1871–1939)

U.S. psychologist. Born 25 July 1871 in New York City to Elizabeth (Davis) and Francis Washburn. Educated Ulster Academy, Kingston, N.Y. (1883–1887); Vassar College (B.A., 1891); Columbia University (1891–1892); Cornell University (Ph.D., 1894; first woman Ph.D. in psychology). Professional experience: Wells College, professor of psychology, philosophy, and ethics (1894–1900); Sage College, warden; Cornell University, instructor in social psychology and animal psychology (1900–1902); University of Cincinnati, head of psychology department (1902–1903), associate professor (1903–1908); Vassar College, professor of psychology (1908–1937). Died 29 October 1939 in Poughkeepsie, N.Y.

Margaret Washburn's parents were both affluent and well educated. Her mother had inherited a comfortable fortune and her father had been a successful businessman. He later became a minister, first in the Methodist and then in the Episcopal Church. In 1878 he settled with his family in Kingston, New York, after accepting a parish in Walden, New York. Early in her life, Margaret developed an appetite for reading and a love of poetry and philosophy. She attended the Ulster Academy (1883–1887) in Kingston, and entered Vassar College in 1887 at age fifteen. There she found that her favorite courses were chemistry, biology, and philosophy. The new field of experimental psychology seemed to be a logical way of uniting her two favorite subjects, philosophy and science.

After she graduated from Vassar (1891) she applied to study at Columbia University with James McKeen Cattell. Cattell had been trained by Wilhelm Wundt at Leipzig. Although Columbia reluctantly admitted Washburn as an auditor, it refused to consider the possibility of a woman holding regular graduate-student status. Cattell supported Washburn's efforts but advised her, after a year at Columbia, to move on to Cornell which was much more friendly to women—not only admitting them but also giving them scholarships. At Cornell she studied under another disciple of Wundt, Edward Bradford Tichener, becoming his first female student. She earned a doctorate from Cornell with a dissertation on the influence of visual imagery on tactual judgments of distance and direction. The dissertation was published in Germany.

Washburn taught at three colleges: Wells College (1894–1900), Cornell (1900–1902), and the University of Cincinnati for one year (1902–1903) before accepting an appointment as associate professor of philosophy at Vassar. Promoted to full professor in 1908, she remained at Vassar until her retirement in 1937. Washburn established psychology as a separate department at Vassar and developed the rudimentary psychological laboratory into a professional operation out of which came a stream of data and interpretive publications. Washburn carried on a variety of experimental work, including studies of color vision in animals, the differences in preference for speech sounds between poets and scientists, and differences in the color preferences of students. She designed many of these studies as projects for the senior students in her classes, who conducted the data gathering and analysis. She then interpreted the results for publication under joint authorship in the series *Studies from the Psychological Laboratory of Vassar College.* Under her encouragement many of her students pursued advanced degrees after Vassar.

Washburn was especially intrigued by animal behavior. The most influential of her works was *The Animal Mind*, a compilation and analysis of the literature of animal psychology. First published in 1908 (subsequent editions in 1917, 1926, 1936), this became the standard comparative psychology text for twenty-five years and was translated into several other languages. The book met a critical need and presented systematically and clearly the results of experimental studies which had previously been scattered and largely inaccessible. It also dealt with research methodology, provided a systematic orientation for the theoretical problems of animal psychology and detailed a history of the movement. Washburn believed that consciousness and behavior were two different kinds of phenomena, and that both must be encompassed by the study of psychology. Thus she represented a force for compromise between the introspectionist and behaviorist factions. In her book *Movement and Mental Imagery* (1916) and in an article, "A System of Motor Psychology," contributed to Carl Murchison's *The Psychologies of 1930* (1930), she set forth her theory that all mental functions—all thoughts and perceptions—produce some form of motor reaction. Over her lifetime she published over two hundred titles and was one of the four coeditors of the *American Journal of Psychology* from 1925.

Washburn was an active member and held offices in major scientific societies. She was elected president of the American Psychological Association in 1921, of the New York Branch (now the Eastern Psychological Association) in 1932, and of the Society of Experimental Psychologists in 1931; and vice-president of the American Association for the Advancement of Science (1927). She received an honorary doctorate from Wittenberg University (1927); dedication of a commemorative volume of the *American Journal of Psychology* (1927); she was named one of the fifty most outstanding psychologists of the country in 1903, and was elected as the second woman member of the National Academy of Sciences (1931). Washburn's honors are testimony to the respect and high regard others felt for her.

A member of the first generation of leading American women in science and academics, Washburn exuded enthusiasm and confidence. Although she strongly supported educational equality for women, she never actively supported organized efforts for women's rights, including the suffrage movement. She had many friends, male and female, and professional contacts with whom she corresponded. In 1937 she suffered a debilitating stroke, and died two years later in Poughkeepsie, New York.

Her contributions were significant in several areas: production of basic experimental data (mainly through development of the psychology laboratory and program at Vassar); critique, interpretation and theory building; teaching and encouragement of students in psychology; and development of the profession. *The Animal Mind* is a classic in the development of comparative psychology.   JH/MBO

PRIMARY SOURCES

Washburn, Margaret. *The Animal Mind: A Textbook of Comparative Psychology.* New York: Macmillan, 1908.
———. *Movement and Mental Imagery: Outlines of a Motor Theory of the Complexer Mental Processes.* New York: Houghton Mifflin, 1916.
———. "The Psychology of Esthetic Experience in Music." *Journal of the Proceedings and Addresses of the National Education Association of the United States* (1916): 600–606.
———. "Motor Factors in Voluntary Control of Cube Perspective Fluctuations and Retinal Rivalry Fluctuations." *American Journal of Psychology* 45 (April 1933): 315–319.

SECONDARY SOURCES

Goodman, Elizabeth. "Margaret F. Washburn (1871–1939): First Woman Ph.D. in Psychology." In *Eminent Women of Psychology: Models of Achievement.* Special issue of *Psychology of Women Quarterly* 5, no. 1 (Fall 1980): 69–80.
Rossiter, Margaret. "Women Scientists in America before 1920." *American Scientist* 62 (May–June 1974): 312–323.
Woodworth, R. S. In *Biographical Memoirs of the National Academy of Sciences* (1949): 275–295. Obituary notice.

STANDARD SOURCES

AMS 1–6; Bailey; *DAB; NAW;* Ogilvie 1986; Zusne.

WASHBURN, RUTH WENDELL (1890–1975)

U.S. psychologist. Born 19 January 1890 in Northampton, Mass. to Miriam and Philip Washburn. Educated Vassar College (A.B., 1913); Radcliffe College (M.A., 1922); Yale University (Ph.D., 1929). Professional experience: Institute of Human Relations, Yale, research associate, clinic of child development (1929–1934), assistant (1937–1938), assistant professor of child development (1934–1938), consultant, child development (from 1938). Honors and memberships: American Association for the Advancement of Science; Psychological Association, Fellow. Died 1975.

After Ruth Wendell Washburn earned her doctoral degree at Yale, she stayed at that institution in various positions. She conducted research in child development and was especially interested in social behavior and the smiling and laughing of infants. A nursery school in Colorado Springs has been named for her.   JH/MBO

PRIMARY SOURCES

Washburn, Ruth. *Children Have Their Reasons.* New York: Appleton-Century, 1942.
———. *Children Know Their Friends.* New York: W. Morrow, 1949.
———. With H. M. Halverson. "A Study of the Smiling and Laughing of Infants in the First Year of Life." *Monographs on Infancy.* Classics in Child Development series. New York: Arno Press, 1975. The article was first published in 1929.
Ruth Washburn materials are held in the Philip Washburn papers, Colorado College, Tutt Library.

STANDARD SOURCES

AMS 5–8, S&B 9–12.

WASSELL, HELEN ERMA (1895–?)

U.S. chemist. Born 19 March 1895 in Pittsburgh, Pa. Educated Carnegie Institute of Technology (B.S., 1917). Professional experience: Koppers Co., Mellon Institute, chemist, coal and gas analyst, fellow (1918–1921), dry cleaning, junior research fellow (1921–1928); American Cleaning Company, researcher (1928–1929); Industrial Research, Carbide and Carbon Chemical Company, fellow (1930–1934; 1937). Honors and memberships: Chemical Society. Death date unknown.

Although Helen Wassell is listed in only one edition of *American Men of Science* and earned only a bachelor's degree, she is interesting to the extent that she shows an alternative career path for a woman chemist: she worked in industry. She was especially interested in dry-cleaning processes and materials, mothproofing compounds, and industrial research. She also worked on new uses for known organic chemicals and for new compounds in the fields of cosmetics, polishes, emulsions, and surfactants.   JH/MBO

STANDARD SOURCES

AMS P 9; Rossiter 1982.

WATKINS, DELLA ELIZABETH (INGRAM) (d. 1977)

U.S. botanist, phytopathologist. Married Harry E. Watkins 19 November 1913. Educated Washington State College (A.B. 1907); University of Nebraska (A.M. 1910). Professional experience: U.S. Department of Agriculture, Bureau of Plant Industry (1910–post-1929). Died April 1977.

Della Elizabeth Ingram was brought up in Dayton, Washington. She attended Washington State College and the University of Nebraska. After receiving her master's degree in biology, she worked in the U.S. Department of Agriculture in the Bureau of Plant Industry under the energetic Erwin Frink Smith, who made a point of hiring women as "scientific assistants." She met Harry E. Watkins, a botanist attached to the same bureau, and married him in 1913. Della Watkins published on plant pathologies.   JH/MBO

PRIMARY SOURCES
Ingram, Della E. "A Twig Blight of *Quercus prinus* and Related Species." *Journal of Agricultural Research* 1 (1914): 339–346.

SECONDARY SOURCES
Washington Evening Star, 12 April 1977. Obituary notice.

STANDARD SOURCES
Barnhart; Rossiter 1982.

WATSON, JANET VIDA (1923–1985)

British geologist. Born 1 September 1923 in Hampstead, London to Katherine Margarite and D. M. S. Watson, a Fellow of the Royal Society. At least one sister. Married John Sutton, F.R.S. Two daughters who died at birth. Educated Reading University (first-class general honors degree, 1943); Imperial College London (Ph.D., 1949). Professional experience: Imperial College London, faculty (1943–1985). Died 29 March 1985 at Ashtead.

Janet Vida Watson was undoubtedly one of the most influential geologists to work in the British Isles. Her father, David Meredith Seares Watson, a Fellow of the Royal Society, was a vertebrate paleontologist and professor of zoology and comparative anatomy at the University of London. Her mother was active in embryological research until her marriage.

After obtaining her first class general honors degree in biology and geology, Watson first worked on chicken growth and diet in a research institute. Restless at this tedious work, she tried teaching in a girls' school. Not find teaching particularly satisfying either, she decided to go to Imperial College and become a geologist. She became a student of H. H. Read, who suggested that she study one of his favorite topics, the migmatites of Southerland. He then sent her with another graduate student, John Sutton, to parts of the Lewisian complex of northwest Scotland, where migmatitic and igneous rocks were common. They were to test the concepts of place and time in plutonism that Read had postulated in his presidential addresses to the Geological Society of London in 1948 and 1949. The two young geologists went to the rocks of Northwest Scotland, where a distin-

guished team from the Geological Survey had previously developed ideas that had been so important at the turn of the century. Both of their theses were accepted in the summer of 1949. They married that same summer and honeymooned in the Channel Islands. For the next thirty years they published prolifically on this area and influenced the direction of the thinking in both the United Kingdom and abroad. Many papers carried both of their names; however, as time went by Sutton became more involved in administrative duties and Watson published more on her own. Watson was important in the expansion of the research school at Imperial College. Her students and colleagues were less impressed by her role in the expansion than they were by her role as a researcher to whom they could go for inspiration. Watson was also a popular speaker, and student associations through the United Kingdom consistently put her at the top of their speakers list.

The couple began their research collaboration a year before they were married. They set off on bicycles to look at the parts of the Lewisian Complex around Gruinard Bay. They tested their hypothesis that this complex contained the products of two separate orogenic (mountain building) episodes and that chronological subdivision could be made using basic dikes as time markers. The joint paper that Watson and Sutton published in 1951 had a great impact on geology in Britain. In the paper they postulated that the Precambrian (which was considered to be a fundamental complex and, thus, indivisible) could be chronologically subdivided using field observations. They also provided a model that could be tested. Although much of Watson's work was on the Lewisian complex, she became involved in other fields such as ore genesis and regional geochemistry. She also became very involved with the British geological survey.

Janet Watson was accorded numerous honors. She was the first woman president of the Geological Society of London (1982–1984). The society awarded her the Lyell Fund (1954), the Bigsby Medal (1965) jointly with her husband, and the Lyell Medal (1973). Her father had been awarded the Lyell Medal forty years earlier. She was awarded Clough Medal (1980) of the Edinburgh Geological Society. She was president of section C of the British Association for the Advancement of Science (1972) and elected a Fellow of the Royal Society of London (1979; member of the council and vice-president until 1985).   JH/MBO

PRIMARY SOURCES
Watson, Janet. With John Sutton. "The Pre-Torridonian Metamorphic History of the Loch Torridon and Scourie Areas in the North-West Highlands, and Its Bearing on the Chronological Classification of the Lewisian." *Quarterly Journal of the Geological Society of London* 106 (1951): 241–307.

———. With John Sutton. "Scourie Dykes and Laxfordian Metamorphism." *Geological Magazine* 88 (1951): 299–301.

———. With John Sutton. "The Structure of Sark, Channel Islands." *Proceedings of the Geological Association of London* 68 (1957): 179–203.

———. "Post-Scourian Metadolerites in Relation to Laxfordian Deformation in Great Bernera, Outer Hebrides." *Scottish Journal of Geology* 4 (1968): 53–67.

———. "Regional Geochemistry of the Northern Highlands of Scotland." In *The Caledonides of the Britishs Isles-Reviewed,* ed. A. L. Harris, C. H. Holland, and B. E. Leake, 117–128. Edinburgh: Scottish Academic Press for the Geological Society of London, 1979.

SECONDARY SOURCES
Bowes, D. R. "Janet Watson—an Appreciation and Bibliography." *Geological Society Special Publications* 27 (1987): 1–5. Includes bibliography.

"In Memoriam; Janet Watson." *American Journal of Science* 285, no. 8 (1985): 768.

STANDARD SOURCES
DNB.

WATT, HELEN WINIFRED BOYD (DE LISLE) (1879–1968)

British ornithologist, botanist, writer. Born 1879. Married Hugh Boyd Watt. Professional experience: writer; secretary to Julian Huxley; studied British birds and British flora. Honors and memberships: Royal Society of Literature; Wild Flower Society (1942); Bournemouth Natural History Society, founder and president (1949–1950); Selborne Society, founding member, president; Botanical Society of the British Isles (1946). Died 8 January 1968 in Bournemouth.

Helen Boyd Watt began her career with a keen interest in literature. After publishing a book of poems she was made a Fellow of the Royal Society of Literature. Her interest in nature, especially in birds and later plants, led her to the thorough study of her subject. She served for a time as the secretary to Sir Julian Huxley. During this early period, she was on the council of the Zoological Society of London. With her husband, Hugh Boyd Watt, she went to various bird sanctuaries.

Her husband's illness at the start of World War II sent the couple to Bournemouth, where she threw herself into the study of flowering plants, particularly after her husband died. Watt was intent on examining almost the entire British flora. To this end she traveled throughout Britain from the age of sixty-four almost to her death. Watt died shortly before her ninetieth birthday in Bournemouth. JH/MBO

SECONDARY SOURCES
Morgan, B. M. C., "Watt, Helen Winifred Boyd (De Lisle)." *Proceedings of the Bournemouth Natural History Society* 1968. Obituary notice.

"Watt, Helen Winifred Boyd (De Lisle)." *Proceedings of the Botanical Society of the British Isles* (1968): 624–625. Obituary notice.

WATT, MENIE (1871–1957)

British botanist. Born 2 April 1871 in Glasgow to Jessie (Archibald) and W. C. E. Jamieson. Married James Watt. Five sons; one daughter. Professional experience: collecting and arranging garden plants. Honors and memberships: Fellow of the Linnean Society. Died 13 December 1957.

Menie Watt became interested in plants through her uncles John, James, and Adam Archibald, who farmed Overshields, Stow, Midlothian. The uncles had a fine natural history library and John was a knowledgeable botanist. She read their books and collected plants. Although she found wild plants interesting, she was especially preoccupied with learning about the husbandry and aesthetic possibilities of domestic plants. JH/MBO

PRIMARY SOURCES
Watt, Menie. *Flowers in the Home.* London: A.&C. Black, Ltd., [1927].

SECONDARY SOURCES
Fletcher, H. R. *Proceedings of the Linnean Society* 169 (1956): 244–245. Obituary notice.

WATTS, BETTY (MONAGHAN) (1907–)

U.S. chemist. Born 4 June 1907 in Johnstown, Pa., to Anne (Young) and John H. Monaghan. Married Hilary Watts (1936). One son, Jeremy Alan. Educated Wilson College (B.S., 1928); Washington University (Ph.D., 1932). Professional experience: University of California, Berkeley, instructor, household science, and later assistant professor, home economics (1937–1943); Washington State College, associate professor (1943–1946); Syracuse University, professor, home economics (1946–1951); Florida State University, Tallahassee, Fla., faculty (1951–1968), Robert O. Lawton Distinguished Professor (1965–1968), emerita professor (from 1968). Awards: American Meat Institute Foundation, Vibrans Senior Scientist Award (1958); Borden Award, research in food sciences (1964).

Betty Monaghan Watts was a food chemist who taught and conducted research at Florida State University. Her research concerned the chemical and enzymatic mechanisms of flavor and color deterioration in animal and vegetable tissues used as foods. She was particularly interested in this subject as it related to the decomposition of unsaturated fatty acids. She developed control measures suitable for foods preserved by low or high temperatures, curing, freeze-drying, and irradiation.

She was a member of numerous organizations, some of which were honorary, including Phi Beta Kappa, Sigma Xi, and Phi Kappa Phi. Watts was a member of the U.S. Department of Agriculture's research advisory committee on human nutrition beginning in 1964.   JH/MBO

PRIMARY SOURCES

Watts, Betty Monaghan. *Stabilizing Irradiated Meats against Oxidative Changes during Storage.* Chicago: Quartermaster Food and Container Institute for the Armed Forces, Research and Engineering Command, Quartermaster Corps, U.S. Army, [1960].

———. *Proceedings of the Flavor Chemistry Symposium,* 1961.

———. *Lipids and their Oxidation.* 2d. Symposium on Foods, Oregon State University, 1961, ed. H. W. Schultz. Westport, Conn.: AVI Publishing Company, 1962.

———. "Correspondence and Published Material, 1937–1950." Records of Velma Phillips (Dean of the College of Home Economics), Special Collections, Washington State University Library.

STANDARD SOURCES

AMS 6–8, B 9, P&B 10–12; Bailey; Debus.

WAY, KATHARINE (1903–)

U.S. physicist. Born 20 February 1903 in Sewickley, Pa. Educated Columbia University (B.S., 1932; University of North Carolina (Ph.D., 1938). Professional experience: Bryn Mawr College, Huff residential fellow (1938–1939); University of Tennessee, physics instructor (1939–1941); U.S. Naval Ordnance Laboratory, physicist (1942); Manhattan Project, Oak Ridge National Laboratory, researcher (1942–1948); National Bureau of Standards, researcher (1949–1953); Nuclear Data Project, National Research Council, director (1953–1963); Oak Ridge National Laboratory, director (1964–1968); Duke University, adjunct professor of physics (1968–1988).

World War II gave Katharine (Kay) Way an opportunity for a career alternative to academia. Beginning as a research fellow at Bryn Mawr, Way became the first female faculty member in the University of Tennessee Physics Department. In 1942 she began working in the federal government laboratories. She edited the *Atomic Data and Nuclear Data Tables* and its predecessors *Atomic Data* and *Nuclear Data Tables,* essential to nuclear physicists. She was active in the Manhattan Project's efforts to develop an atomic bomb from 1942, when she first

became involved with the project at the Naval Ordnance Laboratory. She moved as the project required, to both the Oak Ridge National Laboratory and the National Bureau of Standards as part of the Nuclear Data Group. She was one of a group of colleagues who suggested linking the scientific and technical resources in Oak Ridge to graduate programs in southern universities. She went to work for the National Research Council in 1953, where she was involved in the nuclear data project that produced the three publications named above. After she left the project in 1982, she accepted a position with the National Institutes of Health, where she worked from 1981 to 1985.

After the bustle of the war and immediate postwar period, Way had an opportunity to teach as an adjunct professor at Duke University, which she did from 1968 to 1988.

JH/MBO

PRIMARY SOURCES

Way, Katharine, ed. With Dexter Masters. *One World or None: A Report to the Public on the Full Meaning of the Atomic Bomb.* New York: Whittlesey House, McGraw-Hill, 1946.

———. With L. Slack. *Radiations from Radioactive Atoms in Frequent Use.* Washington, D.C.: U.S. Atomic Energy Commission, 1959.

———. *Atomic and Nuclear Data Reprints.* New York: Academic Press, 1973.

STANDARD SOURCES

AMS 7–8, P 9; P&B 10–18; Bailey; Debus; O'Neill.

WEBB, JANE (1807–1858)

See Loudon, Jane (Webb).

WEBER, ANNE ANTOINETTE (VAN BOSSE) (1852–1943)

Dutch botanist. Born 1852 in Amsterdam to Jacquéline Jeanne (Beynvaan) and Jacob van Bosse. Four siblings. Married (1) Wilhelm Ferdinand Willink van Collen (d. 1877); (2) Max Weber. Educated at home; University of Amsterdam. Honors and memberships: University of Utrecht, honorary doctorate (1910); Knight of the Order of Orange-Nassau (1935). Died 1943.

Although Anne Antoinette van Bosse had always been fascinated by botany and the animals at the Amsterdam zoo, she did not do research in the area until much later. She was educated privately at home by a Swiss governess and married her first husband, a painter, in 1870. The marriage was a brief one, and when van Collen died in 1877, van Bosse returned to live with her father. Three years later she enrolled at the University of Amsterdam, where she was one of three female botany students. Studying with Hugo de Vries in plant physiology increased her interest, and in 1883 she began her life's specialty, the study of algae.

In that same year, she married Max Weber, a university lecturer in anatomy who later (1884) became professor of zoology and director of the zoological museum at Amsterdam. Her career and that of her husband worked well together. Although she never had a paid position she traveled with her husband on research trips.

One of her first projects was to study the algae that lived on the body of the South American sloth. During the research trips with her husband to Norway and Indonesia, Weber continued her work on algae. One of her major research topics involved the symbiotic relationship between algae and sponges. She also worked on the algae that live on the leaves of the plant *Pilea*. The material that she collected from an 1898 deep-sea oceanographical expedition on board the ship *Siboga* occupied both Webers for the rest of their lives. Although she often assisted her husband in his research, she analyzed the algae collected on the ship herself and published a popular account of the expedition. She donated her algae herbarium of fifty thousand specimens to the Royal Herbarium at Leiden.

Weber was interested in the Montessori movement in education. She was rewarded for her scientific work with an honorary doctorate and one of the highest honors in the Netherlands, a knighthead of the Order of Orange-Nassau.

JH/MBO

PRIMARY SOURCES
Weber, Anne Antoinette van Bosse. *Monographie des Caulerpes.* Leiden: E. J. Brill, 1898.
———. *Een jaar aan boord H.M. Siboga.* Leiden: E. J. Brill, [1904].
———. *Liste des algues du Siboga.* Leiden: E. J. Brill, 1928.

SECONDARY SOURCES
Koster, Joséphine Thérèse, and Tera S. S. van Benthem Jutting. *Blumea: Tijdschrift voor de systematiek en de geografie der planten,* supplement 2 [Leiden], 1942.
———. *Notes on Malay Compositae.* N.p., 1948.

STANDARD SOURCES
DSB (under Max Weber); *Notable* (article by Lewis Pyenson).

WEBSTER, MARY MCCALLUM (1906–1985)

British botanist. Born in Sussex, 31 December 1906. Educated privately and in private schools; Brussels, Belgium, finishing school. Professional experience: Army, 10th Batallion Gordon Highlanders, cook-sargeant, (1941?–1943); Field Marshall Montgomery Headquarters (Germany), staff captain (1944–1945); hotel chef (post-war); collected plants for Royal Botanical Gardens, Kew, in North Rhodesia and Tanganyika (1958); Royal Botanical Gardens, Kew, curatorial assistant (1959–1962); Cambridge University Botanical Garden, herbarium curator (1962–1966). Honors and memberships: Fellow of the Linnean Society, London (1960–1974). Plants are at the University of Aberdeen, Royal Botanic Gardens, Edinburgh, and University of Cambridge Botanical Gardens. Died 7 November 1985.

Mary McCallum Webster was brought up in England, the daughter of a Scottish mother and father. She was educated by a series of governesses, then in boarding school, and finally she went to finishing school in Brussels, Belgium. Her two main enthusiasms were botany and tennis. She had joined the Wild Flower Society at the age of nine and later demonstrated her tennis skills by qualifying for Wimbledon. Her grandmother, Mary Louise Wedgwood, was also a keen botanist and longtime member of the Botanical Society of the British Isles.

During World War II, Mary Webster was attached to a Highland unit as a cook, and gradually worked her way up until she was attached to Field Marshall Montgomery's headquarters in Germany by the end of the war, having reached the rank of staff captain. She continued to work as a chef in various hotels after the war, but botanized whenever she had an opportunity. Her knowledge of Scottish taxonomy was prodigious, and she collected over one hundred specimens for the new *Atlas of British Flora,* produced by the Botanical Society of the British Isles.

A visit to her brother in Natal when she was forty-two was followed by a botanical safari of seven months in Tanganyika and Northern Rhodesia that allowed her to collect over five thousand specimens for the Royal Botanical Gardens, Kew. The following three winters, beginning in 1962, were spent working through her African collection at Kew, and doing some general curating. She then spent four winters in Cambridge University, helping to reorganize their specimens. The level of productivity she managed not only to maintain herself but also to coax from the technicians and other scientists who worked with her has been described as "frightening" (Stewart, Sell).

She began to dedicate herself to Scottish botany, serving as the secretary for the Scottish branch of the Wild Flower Society, helping new members learn their plants. She was a member of the Botanical Society of Edinburgh in 1954, and the Linnean Society of London elected her a Fellow in 1960. Her *Flora of Moray, Mairn and East Inverness* was highly idiosyncratic, but outstanding. She included specimen locations, notes on specimens, and helpful keys. The book proved a success, and from the proceeds she was able to pay for two subsequent trips to Australia, where she did additional collecting. She was an ardent field botanist and believed in a conservationist attitude by those in the field as well as on the public debating platform. Toward the end of her life she lived in Dyke, Scotland, and led field trips for both the Botanical Society and the Wild Flower Society, thereby reaching the next generation with her knowledge.   JH/MBO

PRIMARY SOURCES

Webster, Mary McCallum. With Peter Marler. *Check List of the Flora of the Culbin State Forest,* 1975.

———. *Flora of Moray, Nairn and East Inverness.* Aberdeen: Aberdeen University Press, 1978. Her major contribution to Scottish botany, containing her own location guide.

SECONDARY SOURCES

Botanical Society of the British Isles. *Atlas of British Flora.* New York: T. Nelson for the Botanical Society of the British Isles, 1962. Includes the plants Webster collected for the Atlas.

Stewart, O. M. and Sell, P. D. "Mary McCallum Webster." *Watsonia* 16 (1987): 356–358. Obituary notice.

STANDARD SOURCES

Desmond.

WEDDERBURN, JEMIMA (1823–1909)

British artist, ornithologist, constructor of scientific toys. Born in Edinburgh, 1823, to the sister of John Clerk-Maxwell (father of James Clerk-Maxwell, 1831–1879). Six older siblings. Married Hugh Blackburn, professor of mathematics at Glasgow University (1849). Professional experience: illustrator and lithographer; collaborated with James Clerk-Maxwell on scientific toys; experimented with photography. Died 1909.

Jemima Wedderburn was an artist, ornithologist, constructor of scientific toys, and first cousin and close friend of James Clerk-Maxwell. She was born in Edinburgh six months after her father's death, the youngest of seven children. Her mother was a Clerk of Penicuik and sister of John Clerk-Maxwell, father of James Clerk-Maxwell (1831–1879). Their elder brother, Sir George Clerk, was Laird of Penicuik House.

The widowed Mrs. Wedderburn and her brother John Clerk-Maxwell were very close, as were James Clerk-Maxwell (an only child) and Jemima. In 1849, Jemima married Hugh Blackburn, professor of mathematics at Glasgow University, close friend and colleague of William Thomson (Lord Kelvin) who was professor of physics at Glasgow and a close associate of James Clerk-Maxwell.

Wedderburn was a self-taught artist. She had her studio in the garret on the top of the house. By the time she married she had exhibited her work (probably in the Royal Academy of Edinburgh) and obtained commissions as an illustrator and lithographer. She went on to a successful career as an il-

lustrator of books and as an artist of birds and animals. She did all her work from nature—most other wild-life artists used stuffed birds and animals. Her books include *Birds from Nature* (1862), *Birds of Moidart* (1896), *Illustrated Natural History for Children* (1857), and *Scenes from Animal Life* (1866, seven editions).

She collaborated with James Clerk-Maxwell in his youthful scientific experiments in constructing scientific toys, dating back to before 1839. These include a "magic disk," later called a zoescope or "wheel of life" (based on physiological optics, first invented about 1830 in the form of a cylinder), the precursor of the cinematograph. Jemima and James's version consisted of a series of drawings (like modern animation) on a circle, viewed through a slit. When the circle was spun the figures seemed to move. Jemima did the drawings, while James made the mechanical parts (some examples are preserved in Penicuik House). This was a serious instrument which Clerk-Maxwell improved in Cambridge by adding lenses. Another toy was a colored top, on which colors were mixed by spinning—another instrument perfected by Clerk-Maxwell at Cambridge.

Wedderburn was also involved in constructing a hot air balloon with the Blackburn children. On a more serious level, she did experiments in photography with her husband, Hugh, who was an early photographer. In one of their experiments she drew sketches on glass, which were then used to make contact photographic prints for illustrations; these prints have not survived, since in those days the method of fixing photos was not available; they would have become blackened in time.

In ornithology, Wedderburn was acclaimed not only as an artist but also as a recognized ornithologist for her knowledge and for the faithfulness of her paintings. She corresponded with many leading naturalists, and settled a previously unconfirmed question that baby cuckoos eject other chicks from their nests. She recorded this in one of her drawings, which survives, and reported the observation in the journal *Nature* in 1872.   MB

PRIMARY SOURCES

Blackburn, Jemima Wedderburn. *Scenes from Animal Life.* London: Griffith and Farran, [1858?].

———. *Birds from Nature.* Glasgow: J. Maclehose, 1868.

———. *The Pipits.* Glasgow: James Maclehose, [1872].

———. *Blackburn's Birds.* Edited and introduced by Rob Fairley. Edinburgh: Canongate Press, 1993.

WEDGWOOD, CAMILLA HILDEGARDE (1901–1955)

British social anthropologist. Born 25 March 1901 in Barlaston, England, to Ethel Bowen and Josiah Wedgwood IV. Six siblings

(third of seven). Educated Orme Girls' School, Staffordshire; Bedford College; Newnham College, Cambridge. Professional experience: department of social studies, Bedford College, teacher (1926–1927); University of Sydney, Australia, department of anthropology, faculty (1928–1929); University of Capetown, South Africa, department of African life and languages, faculty (1930); London School of Economics, lecturer and research assistant (1931–1932); Manam Island, New Guinea, field work (1933–1934); Sydney, Australia, government researcher (1934–1935); Women's College, University of Sydney principal (1935–1944), department of anthropology, honorary lecturer; Army Directorate of Research (ANGAU), lecturer? (1944–1945); Australian School of Pacific Administration, lecturer (1945–1947), senior lecturer (1948–1955). Died 17 May 1955 in Sydney, Australia.

Camilla Wedgwood, an important social anthropologist who worked for most of her life in Australia, was the third daughter in a family of seven children, a direct descendant of Josiah Wedgwood I, who created the famous pottery works, and a relative of Charles Darwin. She was born on the family estate in Barlaston, England. Her mother separated from her husband when Camilla Wedgwood was ten, but the children remained with their father, who went on to become a distinguished member of Parliament and Labour Party leader. Wedgwood was educated first at Orme Girls' School in Staffordshire, then at Bedford College in London and finally at Newnham College, University of Cambridge, where she studied with the anthropologist Alfred Cort Hadden.

Immediately after graduation, Wedgwood taught in the department of social studies at her old school, Bedford College, for a year (1926–1927). She then traveled to Australia and then to South Africa, lecturing first in the department of anthropology at the University of Sydney (1928–1929), and then at the department of African life and languages, at the University of Capetown. Returning to London, she worked from 1931 to 1932 as research assistant to the renowned anthropologist Bronislaw Malinowski. She went to study the Manam in New Guinea in 1932, with a fellowship from the Australian Research Council. She published the results of this work over the following six years, studying the treatment of disease and the role of women and children in Manam society. Eventually she would publish a major work on Manam kinship with Marie Reay in 1959. Her depiction of New Guinea women as "junior partners" of the men, of a partial equality, conflicted with the perspective of other women investigators and is still controversial. Wedgwood stressed that women needed to be studied with a perspective free of Western bias.

After completing her studies of Manam Island, Wedgwood went back to Sydney, Australia. Like many British and American anthropologists of her era, she became interested in what was termed "applied anthropology," although this often came as a stimulus from government agencies that had control over the lives of dependent peoples. The government of Nauru asked her to explore the possibilities of native cultural revivial through education and arts and crafts. Wedgwood also served as principal at the Women's College, University of Sydney, and was honorary lecturer in anthropology at the university from 1935 to 1944, supplementing the lectures of A. P. Elkin.

In 1944, toward the end of World War II, she joined the Australian Army and was made a lieutenant colonel in the women's services as part of the Army Directorate of Research, Australian New Guinea Administrative Unit (ANGAU), through which she influenced government policies concerning women and education in New Guinea. Her interest in the education of native women continued in her postwar work with the Australian School of Pacific Administration, and she helped organize technical and vocational training throughout Oceania.

For a year in 1947, Wedgwood returned to London to work with Margaret Reed at the Institute of Education at the University of London, expanding her ideas of native education. She returned to the School of Pacific Administration as senior lecturer in 1948–1954, successfully promoted her ideas, and participated in a United Nations Educational, Scientific, and Cultural Organization (UNESCO) seminar on the use of vernacular languages, as expert on Oceania. She died from lung cancer in Sydney, 17 May 1955. Her extensive work on Manam kinship was published after her death, in 1959.

According to her biographers, Nancy Lutehaus and Ute Gacs, Wedgwood had an ambivalent attitude toward feminism, condemning it as a political position but directly working to correct male bias in field studies, perhaps overzealously. Gacs points out her work on the importance of women in non-Western societies, her insistence on a female point of view in ethnographic studies, and her commitment to the involvement of women in native education.

JH/MBO

PRIMARY SOURCES

Wedgwood, Camilla H. "Girl's Puberty Rites in Manam Island." *Oceania* 4, no. 1 (1933): 132–155.

———. "Sickness and Treatment in Manam Island." *Oceania* 5, no. 1 (1934): 64–79.

———. "Women in Manam." *Oceania* 7, no. 4 (1937): 401–428; 8, no. 2, (1937): 72–192.

———. "The life of Children in Manam." *Oceania* 9, no. 1 (1938): 1–29.

———. "A Plan for Tackling Kinship." *The South Pacific* 6, no. 1 (1952): 291–293; 6, no. 2 (1952): 320–324; 6, no. 5 (1952): 390–406; 6, no. 6 (1952): 433–438.

———. With Ian Hogbin. "A Background Documentary Survey on the Education of Women and Girls in New Guinea." Mss., National Library of Australia, Canberra.

———. With Marie Reay. "Manam Kinship." *Oceania* 29, no. 4 (1959): 239–256.

SECONDARY SOURCES
Elkin, A. P. "The Hon. Camilla H. Wedgwood." *Oceania* 26 (1955): 172–180.
Firth, Raymond. "The Hon. Camilla H. Wedgwood." *Nature* 176 (1955): 144–145.
Lutekaus, Nancy. "She Was *Very* Cambridge: Camilla Wedgwood and the History of Women in British Anthropology." *American Ethnologist* 13, no. 4 (1986): 776–798.

STANDARD SOURCES
Gacs (article by Ute Gacs).

WEDGWOOD, MARY LOUISA (BELL) (1854–1953)
British botanist. Born 23 November 1854. Married (1) [?] Webster (2) [?] Wedgwood. Two sons (one from each marriage). Professional experience: formed important herbarium for Marlborough College. Honors and memberships: Botanical Society of the British Isles, council member. Died 17 April 1953 in Slough, Scotland.

Mary Louisa (Bell) Wedgwood was an active botanist, a member of the Botanical Society of the British Isles during its early years, and a good friend of the early head of that society, George Claridge Druce. Active in London intellectual life at the turn of the century, she had traveled widely in India and the Mediterranean long before she became interested in botany. She began a herbarium with the only child of her second marriage, Allen Wedgwood, who was keenly interested in plants. When he was killed in World War I at Gallipoli, she traveled throughout the British Isles, collecting specimens for the herbarium, intent on obtaining every species, variety, and hybrid listed in the *London Catalogue.* She also took care to verify every critical specimen with a botanical authority.

Wedgwood's formation of the herbarium brought her into contact with important British botanists. She then gave the collection to Marlborough College, her son's secondary school, along with a playing field. Later, during World War II, when Mary Wedgwood had to move from London to Marlborough because of the Blitz, she wrote and published a catalogue of the Wedgwood herbarium.

Mary Wedgwood was remembered by the older members of the Botanical Society as an imperious beauty and by the younger members as an outspoken and intelligent woman.

Her granddaughter by the first marriage, MARY McCALLUM WEBSTER, was also a member of the Botanical Society of the British Isles. Wedgwood died at Marlborough in her ninety-ninth year.

JH/MBO

PRIMARY SOURCES
Wedgwood, Mary Louisa. *A Catalogue of the Plants in the Wedgwood Herbarium at Marlborough College.* Arbroath [England]: Printed by T. Buncle & Co., 1945.

SECONDARY SOURCES
Sandwith, N. Y. "M. L. Wedgwood, 1854–1953." *Proceedings of the Botanical Society of the British Isles* 1 (1954–1955): 114–115.

STANDARD SOURCES
Desmond.

WEEKS, ALICE MARY (DOWSE) (1909–1988)
U.S. geologist. Born 26 August 1909 in Sherborn, Mass., to Jessie (Parker) and Charles Arthur Dowse. Three sisters (including a twin); married Albert Weeks, 1950. Educated Tufts (cum laude, 1930); Radcliffe College (M.A., 1934; Ph.D., 1949). Professional experience: Wellesley College, laboratory instructor in physical and historical geology (1936–1937), instructor (1936–?), assistant professor (?–1951); U.S. Geological Survey, researcher (1949–1962); Temple University, faculty (1960–1976). Died 29 August 1988 in Bryn Mawr, Pa.

Alice Mary Dowse and her twin sister, Eunice, were born in 1909. The girls were strongly encouraged to get an education and Alice, after receiving a diploma from Sawin Academy and Dowse High School, graduated from Tufts in 1930 *cum laude* in mathematics. After graduation she taught at the Lancaster School for girls (1930–1933?). With the aid of a small scholarship she was able to return to Tufts to take some geology courses. She then went to Harvard to work on a master's degree in geology, which she received in 1934. She could not afford to continue at Harvard so she accepted a year-long research fellowship at Bryn Mawr and then stayed for a second year as a laboratory instructor. She returned to Harvard in 1936 to start work on her doctorate. She began to teach at Wellesley at about this same time, first as a laboratory instructor, then as instructor, and finally as assistant professor. She taught a wide variety of courses. During the war she taught military map making to navy officers. Although she was working toward her doctorate while teaching at Wellesley she had a difficult time completing her dissertation. She finally completed her field work in 1947 and received her degree in 1949.

The next year she married petroleum geologist Albert

Weeks. She took leave from Wellesley in 1949 to work for the U.S. Geological Survey and in 1951 resigned from Wellesley to take a permanent position with the survey. During this time she became a project leader (1951) and studied the mineralogy of radioactive deposits. She did extensive field work and, in order to visit certain mines, had to disguise herself as a man. Weeks accepted a position at Temple University in 1962 to establish a viable degree program in geology. While she was at Temple, she continued her research on uranium mineralogy. She suffered from Alzheimer's (as did her twin sister) and died in 1988.

Weeks was active in professional organizations and attended many conferences. In 1976, when she retired from Temple, she was awarded emeritus status. In 1980 at the Northeast Section meeting of the Geological Society of America, a symposium on uranium was held in her honor. A strong supporter of women in geology, Weeks was a charter member of the American Geological Institute's Women Geoscientists Committee, formed in 1972.

Much of Weeks's important research was done on the mineralogy of radioactive deposits. From the time she joined the U.S. Geological Survey to the end of her research career she worked with uranium mineralogy, particularly that of the Colorado Plateau.   CK/MBO

PRIMARY SOURCES

Weeks, Alice Mary Dowse. "New Evidence on the Cambrian Contact at Hoppin Hill, North Attleboro, Massachusetts." *American Journal of Science* 248 (1950): 95–99.
———. With M. E. Thompson. "Identification and Occurrence of Uranium and Vanadium Minerals from the Colorado Plateau." *U.S. Geological Society Bulletin* 1009-B (1954).
———. "Mineralogy and Oxidation of the Colorado Plateau Uranium Ores." *U.S. Geological Survey Professional Paper* 300 (1956): 187–193.
———. With M. L. Lindberg, A. H. Truesdell, and Robert Meyrowitz. "Gransite, a New Hydrated Sodium Calcium Vanadate from New Mexico, Colorado, and Utah." *American Mineralogist* 49 (1964): 1511–1526.

SECONDARY SOURCES

Dowse, Mary Elizabeth. "Memorial of Alice Mary Dowse Weeks, August 26, 1909–August 29, 1988." *American Mineralogist* 74, nos. 5–6, (1989): 694–695. Partial bibliography. Complete bibliography available as Document AM-89-407 from the Business Office of the Mineralogical Society of America.

STANDARD SOURCES

AMS P 9, P&B 10–13.

WEEKS, DOROTHY W. (1893–1990)

U.S. physicist. Born 3 May 1893 in Philadelphia. Educated Wellesley College (B.A., 1916); Massachusetts Institute of Technology (M.S., 1923; Ph.D. in mathematics, 1930); Simmons College (S.M., 1925). Professional experience: U.S. Patent Office, assistant examiner (1917–1920); Massachusetts Institute of Technology, assistant in physics (1920–1921), research associate (1921–1922), instructor (1922–1924); Jordan Marsh Co., Mass., employment supervisor of women (1925–1927); Wellesley College, instructor of physics (1928–1929); Wilson College, professor and department head (1930–1943; 1945–1956); Pennsylvania Conference of College Physics Teachers (TPC-CPT), officer (1953–?); Army Ordnance Material Research Office, Watertown Arsenal, physicist (1956–1962); Harvard College Observatory, spectroscopist (1964–1976). Died June 1990 in Wellesley, Mass..

Dorothy Weeks was the first woman to obtain a doctorate in mathematics from the Massachusetts Institute of Technology, and she became a physicist with a variety of professional experiences. In addition to her regular positions she concurrently worked as an assistant at the National Bureau of Standards in 1920, as an instructor at Buckingham School, Cambridge University, from 1923 to 1924, and as a technical aide to the Office of Scientific Research and Development from 1943 to 1946. She was a Guggenheim fellow from 1949 to 1950 and held grants from the American Academy of Sciences (1938), and the American Philosophical Society (1940 and 1948). She was a consultant for the National Science Foundation from 1953–1956 and was a lecturer at the Newton College of the Sacred Heart from 1966 to 1971. She was a member of the American Physical Society, the Optical Society of America, and the American Association of Physics Teachers.

Weeks's main research interests involved atomic spectroscopy. She worked with Lande g values, vacuum ultraviolet, Zeeman patterns of Fe1 and Fe11, coherency matrices, and radiological shielding.

After her retirement, she moved to Massachusetts and for six years coordinated a program at the U.S. Army's arsenal at Watertown, where they were developing radiological shielding materials for use against nuclear weapons. At the age of seventy-one she became a spectroscopist studying solar satellites and worked at Harvard Observatory in Cambridge, Massachusetts, for the next twelve years. She died at her home in Wellesley at the age of ninety-seven.   JH/MBO

PRIMARY SOURCES

Weeks, Dorothy W. With Henry Norris Russell, Charlotte Emma Moore, and Miguel A. Catalan. "The Arc Spectrum of Iron (Fe1). Part 1. Analysis of the Spectrum, Based on the Work of Many Investigators and Including Unpublished

Studies." *Transactions of the American Philosophical Society* n.s. 34, pt. 2 (1944).

Weeks, Dorothy. "Women in Physics.: *Physics Today* 13 (August 1960): 22–23.

———. *Absorption Spectrum of Iron in the Vacuum Ultraviolet 2950–1588 Å.* Cambridge, Mass.: Harvard College Observatory, 1967.

"Dorothy Weeks, 97, A Physicist Who Led in a Variety of Careers." *New York Times,* 8 June 1990. Reprinted with comments in *MIT Tech Talk* (18 July 1990).

STANDARD SOURCES
AMS 5–8, P 9, P&B 10–14.

WEEKS, MARY ELVIRA (1892–?)

U.S. chemist. Born 10 April 1892 in Lyons, Wis. Educated Ripon College (A.B., 1913); University of Wisconsin (A.M., 1914); University of Kansas (Ph.D., 1927). Professional experience: University of Kansas, instructor (1921–1927), assistant professor (1927–1937); associate professor (1937–?). Honors and memberships: Chemical Society, Kansas Academy of Science, and History of Science Society. Death date unknown.

Mary Elvira Weeks earned her doctoral degree at the University of Kansas and spent her professional career there, moving from instructor to associate professor.

Weeks's research was in physical and analytical chemistry. She worked on the atmospheric oxidation of solutions of sodium sulfite in ultraviolet light, the role of hydrogen ion concentration in the precipitation of calcium and magnesium carbonates and the use of oxidation–reduction indicators in the determination of iron. She was also interested in the history of chemistry, particularly in the discovery of the elements. JH/MBO

PRIMARY SOURCES
Weeks, Mary Elvira. *The Discovery of the Elements: Collected Reprints of a Series of Articles Published in the Journal of Chemical Education by Mary Elvira Weeks.* Easton, Pa.: Mack Printing Co., 1933.

STANDARD SOURCES
AMS 5–8, P 9.

WEIGHTMAN, MARY (1883–1941)

British botanist. Born 30 July 1883 in Litherland, Lancashire. Never married. Educated Liverpool University (B.Sc., 1904). Professional experience: Birkenhead High School for Girls, teacher. Honors and memberships: Liverpool Botanical Society. Died 7 April 1941.

Mary Weightman was educated in Liverpool and taught at a girls' school there. She collected plants and was the secretary of the Liverpool Botanical Society. JH/MBO

SECONDARY SOURCES
North Western Naturalist (1941): 344–345. Obituary notice.

STANDARD SOURCES
Desmond.

WEINZIERL, LAURA (LANE) (1900–1928)

U.S. petroleum geologist and paleontologist. Born 28 July 1900 in Louisville, Ky. Married John F. Weinzierl. Educated German schools (1907–1911); public schools, Los Angeles; San Antonio High School (graduated 1917); University of Texas (B.A., 1923). Professional experience: Rio Bravo (early 1920s); Marland Oil Company (until 1928); Consulting micropaleontologist in association with Alexander Deussen. Died 28 September 1928 in Houston, Tex.

Laura Lee Lane was born in Louisville, Kentucky, and spent her early childhood on a ranch in west Texas. When she was seven years old, she accompanied her mother to Germany where they remained for four years while her mother studied music. In the early part of 1911, Laura and her mother moved to Seven Oaks, Kent, England, and in the latter part of that same year returned to the United States. After a brief stay in San Antonio, she and her mother moved to Los Angeles, where she attended public school for two years. Her family then returned to San Antonio, where she graduated from San Antonio High School in 1917.

During her first year at the University of Texas, she intended to major in English, but through the persuasion of a Professor Whitney decided to major in geology and specialize in paleontology. Upon the recommendation of Whitney and Esther Richards (later ESTHER APPLIN), Lane was hired by the Rio Bravo Oil company as a paleontologist during the summer of 1922. She wanted to acquaint herself with the practical details of the profession. She returned to the university in the fall of 1922, served as a student assistant, and graduated in 1923. After graduation, she moved to Houston, Texas, to work as paleontologist for Alexander Deussen. She married John F. Weinzierl, a geologist with the Marland Oil Company and later a consulting geologist in Houston. She conducted a laboratory for Marland until they moved from the Gulf Coast. She retained an office with the vice-president of Marland Oil, published with him, and did consulting work until her death. On 28 September 1928 she died of a heart attack. At the time of her death she was working on a paper, "The Yegua Formation of the Coastal Domes," with Applin. CK

PRIMARY SOURCES

Weinzierl, Laura Lane. "Subsurface Geology of the North Part of the Blackwell Field, Oklahoma." Master's thesis, University of Oklahoma, 1922.

———. With Alexander Deussen. "The Hockley Salt Dome, Harris Co., Texas." *American Association of Petroleum Geologists* 9, no. 7 (October 1924): 1031–1060. Also appeared in *Geology of Salt Dome Oil Fields: A Symposium on the Origin, Structure and General Geology of Salt Dome, with Reference to Oil Production and Treating Chiefly the Salt Domes of North America*, 570–599. Tulsa, Okla.: American Association of Petroleum Geologists, 1926.

———. With Esther Richards Applin. "The Claiborne Formation on the Coastal Domes." *Journal of Paleontology* 3, no. 4 (1929): 384–410.

SECONDARY SOURCES

Applin, E. R. "Memorial to Laura Lane Weinzierl." *Journal of Paleontology* 2 (1928): 383.

STANDARD SOURCES

Kass-Simon and Farnes (article by Michele L. Aldrich).

WEISHAUPT, CLARA GERTRUDE (1909–1991)

U.S. botanist. Born 29 July 1898 to Peter and Elizabeth Barbara (Weisflock) Weishaupt. Educated Bliss Business College, Columbus, Ohio (diploma in bookkeeping, shorthand, and typing, 1917); Ohio State University (B.S., 1924; M.S., 1932; Ph.D., 1935). Professional experience: State Teachers College, Jacksonville, Ala., assistant professor and later associate professor (1935–1946); Ohio State University, instructor (1946–1951), assistant professor (1951–1960), associate professor (1960–1968), curator of the herbarium (1949–1967); emerita associate professor (1968–1991). Honors and memberships: Ohio Academy of Science, Sigma Xi, Sigma Delta Epsilon, Ohio State University Alumni Distinguished Teaching Award, Ohio State Distinguished Service Award, Ohio Academy of Science Centennial Honoree.

Clara Weishaupt earned all three of her degrees at Ohio State University. She was born on an Ohio farm, attended a one-room elementary school, and graduated from the Lynchburg High School in 1916. After attending a business college, she went to Ohio State where she specialized in plant physiology. Her master's thesis was on the effects of ultraviolet light on plants; while her doctoral dissertation concerned the diffusion of water vapor through multiperforate septa. Her major professor for both degrees was Bernard S. Meyer. Upon completing her doctoral degree she went to the State Teachers College, Jacksonville, Alabama, where she progressed from assistant professor to associate. The only woman on the faculty, she taught a huge range of courses,

from botany to industrial arts. No doubt she was pleased when, in 1946, the opportunity arose for her to return to her alma mater to teach in the department of botany and plant pathology. She retired as emerita associate professor in 1991, never making it to full professor.

Weishaupt was a member of several scientific societies, including the Ohio Academy of Science, in which she was quite active. She was also a member of several honor societies including Sigma Xi, and Sigma Delta Epsilon, the National Honorary Society for Women in Science. Her honors include the Ohio State University Alumni Distinguished Teaching Award, the Distinguished Service Award from Ohio State University, and the Centennial Honoree of the Ohio Academy of Science.

When Weishaupt began to teach local flora at Ohio State University, she recognized the need for a new field and laboratory manual of Ohio plants. She and three other members of the deparment coauthored a *Guide to Ohio Plants*. Weishaupt then published a book that went through three editions and several subsequent reprintings. Although she was not trained as a plant taxonomist and had no experience as a curator, Weishaupt quickly learned how to restore a neglected facility. For the Ohio Flora project which began in 1951, Weishaupt wrote the systematic treatment of *Gramineae* (grasses). JH/MBO

PRIMARY SOURCES

Weishaupt, Clara G. *Vascular Plants of Ohio.* Dubuque, Iowa: Kendall/Hunt Publishing Co., 1960.

———. *Vascular Plants of Ohio: a Manual for Use in Field and Laboratory.* 3d ed. Dubuque, Iowa: Kendall/Hunt, [1971].

———. "A Descriptive Key to the Grasses of Ohio Based upon Vegetative Characteristics." *Bulletin of the Ohio Biological Survey* (1985).

SECONDARY SOURCES

Stuckey, Ronald L. "Obituary Clara Gertrude Weishaupt (1898–1991)." *The Michigan Botanist* 31 (1992): 109–110.

STANDARD SOURCES

AMS B 9, P&B 10–14; Stuckey.

WEISS, MARIE JOHANNA (1903–1952)

U.S. mathematician and educator. Born 21 September 1903. Never married. Educated Vassar College (A.B., 1925); Radcliffe College (M.A., 1926); Stanford University (Ph.D., 1928). Professional experience: University of Chicago, National Research Fellow (1928–1930); Tulane University, teacher (1930–1936); Vassar College, teacher (1936–1938); head of mathematcs department (1938–1952). Died 19 August 1952.

Marie Johanna Weiss was born in 1903 into a staunchly Lutheran family of German origin. Educated at Vassar College she earned a bachelor's degree and then continued her education at Radcliffe and Stanford. Her thesis at Stanford was on primitive groups that contain substitutions. From 1928 to 1930, she was a National Research Fellow at the University of Chicago. She taught at Newcomb College, Tulane, for a short period before going to Vassar in a similar position. She returned to Vassar in 1936 and in 1938 became head of the mathematics department.

Weiss wrote various articles on fundamental systems of units in normal fields on the limit of transitivity of a substitution group. She was very interested in the interaction between youth and genius in mathematics. Her one book, *Higher Algebra for the Undergraduate,* published in 1949, became an important text. She served as the governor-at-large of the Mathematics Association of America from 1950 to 1952.

JH/MBO

PRIMARY SOURCES

Weiss, Marie Johanna. "Primitive Groups Which Contain Substitutions of Prime Order p and of Degree 6p or 7p." Ph.D. thesis, Stanford University, 1928.

———. "The Limit of Transitivity of a Substitution Group." *Transactions of American Mathematics Society* 32 (1930): 262–283.

———. "Fundamental Systems of Units in Normal Fields." *American Journal of Mathematics* 46 (1936): 249–254.

———. "On Genius and Youth in Mathematics." Invited talk, Sigma Delta Epsilon to Women in Science, American Association for the Advancement of Science meeting, Columbus, Ohio, December 1950.

———. *Higher Algebra for the Undergraduate.* 2d ed. New York: Wiley [1962].

STANDARD SOURCES

AMS 3–8; Grinstein and Campbell; *NAW* unused.

WEISS, MARY CATHERINE (BISHOP) (1930–1966)

U.S. mathematician. Born 11 December 1930 in Wichita, Kans., to Helen and Albert Bishop. One brother, Errett. Married Guido Weiss. Educated University of Chicago Experimental Laboratory; University of Chicago (undergraduate degree; Ph.D., 1957); Cambridge University, National Science Foundation postdoctoral fellowship (1965–1966). Professional experience: University of Chicago, lecturer (from 1957?); University of Illinois, faculty (1966). Died 8 October 1966.

Mary Catherine Weiss had a short, productive career. She was born in Wichita, Kansas, her West Point–educated fa-

ther taught mathematics at the university level after he retired from the military. He died when Mary Catherine and her brother were young children and the family moved first to another part of Kansas to be closer to relatives, and then to Chicago, when Errett, her brother, entered the University of Chicago. Mary Catherine attended the university's laboratory school and then the university itself. As an undergraduate, she met and married a fellow student, Guido Weiss. Both husband and wife earned doctorates working under Antoni Zygmund.

Weiss's thesis served as the foundation for her future work on lacunary series. Apparently, Weiss remained at the University of Chicago as a lecturer after getting her degree. From 1960 to 1961, Weiss and her husband went to Buenos Aires and Paris. Both of them worked with Hardy spaces in the framework of classical mathematics. They extended the topic onto the complex or Gaussian plane and also into higher dimensions. Upon their return they worked with Zygmund and Alberto P. Calderón to write a paper on Calderón-Zygmund singular integral operators in higher dimensions. Her most important contribution was in proving the early Zygmund and Calderón.

In 1965 the couple went to Cambridge for a year. When they returned to the United States, Weiss began teaching at the University of Illinois but died a few weeks after the beginning of the semester. To honor her, the Edwardsville campus of Southern Illinois University held a symposium on harmonic analysis.

JH/MBO

PRIMARY SOURCES

Weiss, Mary Catherine Bishop. "The Law of the Iterated Logarithm for Lacunary Trigonometric Series." *Transactions of the American Mathematical Society* 91 (1959): 444–469.

———. With Guido Weiss. "A Derivation of the Main Results of the Theory of Hp Spaces." *Revista de la Union Matematica Argentina* 22 (1960): 63–71.

———. With Alberto P. Calderón and Antoni Zygmund. "On the Existence of Singular Integrals." In *Singular Intervals: Proceedings of Symposia in Pure Mathematics. Volume 10,* ed. by Alberto P. Calderón. Providence: American Mathematical Society, 1967.

———. "A Theorem on Lacunary Trigonometric Series." In *Orthogonal Expansions and Their Continuous Analogues,* ed. D. T. Haimo, 227–230. Carbondale: Southern Illinois University Press, 1968.

SECONDARY SOURCES

Zygmund, A. "Mary Weiss: December 11, 1930–October 8, 1966." In *Orthogonal Expansions and Their Continuous Analogues,* ed. D. T. Haimo, xi–xviii. Carbondale, Ill.: Southern Illinois University Press, 1968.

STANDARD SOURCES

Grinstein and Campbell (article by Guido Weiss); *Notable* (article by Jennifer Kramer).

WELCH, BETTY (1913–1985)

U.S. aeronautical engineer. Educated Cornell University (degree in mechanical engineering, 1936); Trinity College, Hartford, Conn. (master's in physics, 1964). Professional experience: United Aircraft Corporation and later Kaman Aircraft in Connecticut, aeronautical engineer (1936?–1966); University of Connecticut, Torrington branch (1964–1978). Honors and memberships: American Society of Mechanical Engineers, Centennial Medal (1980). Died 1985.

Betty Welch earned a Cornell degree in mechanical engineering and after graduating took a job as an aeronautical engineer at United Aircraft Corporation. She later moved to Kaman Aircraft. She remained in these positions for thirty years. While working at Kaman, she earned a master's degree and then took a teaching position at the Torrington branch of the University of Connecticut, where she remained until she retired in 1978. She was awarded the Centennial Medallion, the highest award given by the American Society of Mechanical Engineers. JH/MBO

STANDARD SOURCES

LKW.

WELCH, WINONA HAZEL (1896–?)

U.S. botanist. Born 5 May 1896 in Goodland, Ind., to Carrie Eliza Johnson Welch and Charles Alfred Welch. Educated DePauw University (A.B., 1923); University of Illinois (M.A., 1925); Indiana University (Ph.D., 1928). Professional experience: DePauw University, Greencastle, faculty (1930–1938), professor of botany (1939–1961), head of department of botany and bacteriology (1956–1961), emerita professor (from 1961); curator of herbarium (from 1964). Concurrent experience: Indiana University Summer School, visiting professor (1956, 1959, 1963); Field Biology Program, Pigeon Lake Field Station, Wisconsin State University, lecturer in cryptobotany (summer 1964). Honors and memberships: American Association for the Advancement of Science, Fellow; Indiana Academy of Science, Coulter Award (1951); DePauw University, Outstanding Woman Teacher Award (1964); Indiana Academy of Science, president; American Association of University Professors, president; Botanical Society of America, Society of Plant Taxonomists, International Association for Plant Taxonomy, member. Death date unknown.

Two years after getting her doctoral degree from DePauw University, Winona Welch became a faculty member at that institution, where she remained throughout her career. Her major research interest was in cryptogamic botany, and she wrote several important books and monographs in addition to numerous papers. JH/MBO

PRIMARY SOURCES

Welch, Winona Hazel. *Mosses of Indiana.* Indianapolis: Bookwalter, 1957.

———. *A Monograph of the Fontinaiaceae.* The Hague: M. Nijhoff, 1960.

STANDARD SOURCES

AMS 9–14; Debus.

WELD, JULIA TIFFANY (1887–?)

U.S. pathologist. Born 24 September 1887 in New York City to Louise and Louis Comfort Tiffany. Seven sisters. Married. Two children. Educated Columbia University (1909–1924, degree unknown). Professional experience: College of Physicians and Surgeons, Columbia, assistant pathologist (1924–1930), research associate (1930–1952); Cornell University Medical College, assistant (from 1953). Honors and memberships: Society for Experimental Biology; Society of Microbiology; Harvey Society; Association of Immunology; New York Academy of Sciences. Death date unknown.

Although Julia Tiffany Weld was born into the lavish home of Louis Comfort Tiffany, artist and producer of decorative arts, she, like her younger sister, the psychoanalyst DOROTHY BURLINGHAM, choise to follow a professional career. Under the influence of her intellectual mother, Louise Tiffany, who was a trustee of the New York Infirmary for Women and Children founded by ELIZABETH and EMILY BLACKWELL, she became interested in medicine and microbiology.

After obtaining at least one degree, Weld stayed on at Columbia for twenty-eight years until 1953, when she moved to Ithaca. Weld was married and had two children. Much of her research was on the microbiology of staphylococcus and diffusible products.

Weld donated some of the decorative pieces made by her father, including an elaborate Egyptian-style headdress made for her, to the Museum of the City of New York and the Metropolitan Museum of Art. JH/MBO

STANDARD SOURCES

AMS 8, B 9; P&B 10.

WELLMAN, BETH LUCY (1895–1952)

U.S. developmental psychologist. Born 10 June 1895 in Clarion, Iowa, to Hannah and Alonzo Wellman. Two sisters. Educated, Ames, Iowa, high school; Iowa State Teachers College, Cedar Falls, Iowa (B.A., 1920) State University of Iowa (Ph.D., 1925). Professional

experience: *Child Welfare Research Station, State University of Iowa (1921–1924); Lincoln School, Columbia University Teachers College (1924–1925); Child Welfare Research Station, Iowa City, Iowa, research associate professor (1925–1929), associate professor of psychology (1929–1937), professor of child psychology (from 1937). Honors and memberships: Psychological Association; Society for the Study of Education; Educational Research Association. Died 22 March 1952 after a long illness.*

Educational psychologist Beth Lucy Wellman researched developmental child psychology, especially the mental, motor, and language development of children. She also worked on sex differences in these areas and on intelligence and its measurement. In addition to her books, she published many journal articles.   JH/MBO

PRIMARY SOURCES

Wellman, Beth Lucy. "Development of Motor Coordination in Young Children." *University of Iowa Studies in Child Welfare* 3 (1926): 1–93.

———. *Speech Sound of Young Children.* Iowa City: University of Iowa Press, 1931.

———. With G. Stoddard. *Child Psychology.* New York: Macmillan, 1934.

———. *A Manual of Nursery School Practice.* Iowa City: University of Iowa Press, 1934.

———. *Factors Associated with Binet IQ Changes of Preschool Children.* Washington, D.C.: American Psychological Association, 1946.

STANDARD SOURCES

AMS 5–8; O'Connell and Russo 1990 (article by Marie Skodak Crissey); Stevens and Gardner.

WELLS, AGNES ERMINA (1876–1965)

U.S. astronomer and mathematician. Born 4 January 1876 in Saginaw, Mich. Educated Bryn Mawr College; University of Michigan (A.B., 1903; Ph.D., 1924); Carleton College (A.M., 1916). Professional experience: high school in Michigan, principal (1904–1905); Minn., teacher (1905–1906), head mathematics department (1907–1914); Carleton College, instructor (1915–1916), Helen Newberry residence, Mich., social director (1917–1918), acting dean of women (1917–1918); University of Indiana, dean of women (1918–1938), professor of mathematics (from 1918), professor of astronomy (from 1924). Honors and memberships: Astronomical Society; Indiana Academy of Sciences. Died 1965.

After attending Bryn Mawr College but not getting a degree, Agnes Wells went to the University of Michigan, where she earned a bachelor's degree. Immediately after she

graduated, Wells took a job as a high school principal for a year and taught in Minnesota for nine years. Feeling the need for an advanced degree, Wells went to Carleton College, where, in addition to working on her master's, she was an instructor and social director at a residence hall. She was also acting dean of women during this period. After attaining her degree she went to the University of Indiana as dean of women and professor of mathematics. She later became professor of astronomy. Her research was on radial velocities.

JH/MBO

PRIMARY SOURCES

Wells, Agnes Ermina. Papers, 1894–1959 (inclusive). Mss. Schlesinger Archives A/W45. Consists primarily of personal memorabilia, her thesis in astronomy, some correspondence, calendars, club and organization programs, and clippings related to Wells and her work. Also includes family photographs.

STANDARD SOURCES

AMS 5–7; Rossiter 1982.

WELLS, CHARLOTTE FOWLER (1814–1901)

U.S. phrenologist, author, and publisher. Born 14 August 1814 in Cohocton, N.Y. to Martha (Howe) and Horace Fowler. Married Samuel Robert Wells, 13 October 1843. No children. Educated local schools and Franklin Academy, Prattsburg. Professional experience: school teacher (1833–1837); Fowler Publishing House (later Fowler and Wells), editor, business manager (1837–1875), sole proprietor (1875–1901). Died 4 June 1901 in West Orange, N.J. from heart disease.

Charlotte Fowler was born in upstate New York, and grew up in a rural area. After her education in the local schools and for six months at the Franklin Academy, she began to teach in the public schools. When she was twenty-three, two of her brothers, Orson Squire and Lorenzo Niles Fowler, started an institute devoted to the study and popularization of phrenology, on which they had been lecturing for some years as a basis for educational, penal, and personal reform. They asked Charlotte to join them as proofreader, and business manager of the enterprise, which had grown into a lecture bureau, museum, and publishing house. In 1843, her future husband, Samuel Robert Wells, joined the phrenological institute and shortly thereafter became an equal partner. She married Wells the following year and the new firm, Fowler and Wells, soon became a success, publishing a large number of works on the water cure, diet, health, and even spiritualism. The *Phrenological Journal* published by their firm included regular features on important scientists and educators in Europe as well as America. Her brothers returned to lecturing, and by 1855, Charlotte and Samuel Wells bought out the business.

Phrenology continued to grow in the 1860s as a popular science while it ceased to be considered a serious science. Nevertheless, Fowler and Wells continued to be a highly influential publishing firm, and husband and wife soon founded the American Institute of Phrenology. After her husband's death in 1875, Charlotte Fowler Wells became sole proprietor and president of Fowler and Wells. The company was also one of the first to use the typewriter as part of its regular business. Although she was linked to Spiritualism, and even practiced as a medium, Wells also supported eclectic women physicians like CLEMENCE SOPHIA LOZIER, whose organizational meetings of the New York Medical College for Women were held at her offfice in the Phrenological Institute.

In her old age, Wells still wrote for the *Phrenological Journal,* including a study of the founding father of phrenology, the anatomist Franz Josef Gall. After an injury to her eye resulting from a fall in her eighty-second year, she still continued to lecture. Increasing heart disease led to her death at her home in West Orange, New Jersey, at the age of eighty-six.

JH/MBO

PRIMARY SOURCES
Wells, Charlotte Fowler. "Some Account of the Life and
Labors of Francis Joseph Gall." *Phrenological Journal.* New
York: Fowler and Wells, 1896.

SECONDARY SOURCES
Davies, John D. *Phrenology: Fad and Science.* New Haven: Yale
University Press, 1955. Discusses the development of Fowler
and Wells and the entire field of popular phrenology.
Fowler, Jessie. "Charlotte Fowler Wells." *Phrenological Journal*
(July 1901). Obituary notice.

STANDARD SOURCES
NAW (article by Ernest Isaacs).

WELLS, LOUISA D. (mid-19th century–?)
U.S. astronomer. Computer, Harvard University (1887–1933).

Louisa Wells joined the staff of the Harvard Observatory in 1887 and left in 1933. She was one of the original group of director Edward Pickering's "computers," who worked at the observatory for low wages. She assisted in cataloguing the plates and analyzing stellar spectra from photographs taken at the Arequipa station in Peru. Although she contributed to the observatory's publications, her name is not on any of them.

JH/MBO

STANDARD SOURCES
AMS 5–8, P9; P&B 10; Jones and Boyd; Mozans.

WELSER, PHILIPPINE (1527–1580)
Austrian/German herbalist. Born 1527 in Augsburg. Father Franz Welser. Married Ferdinand II, Archduke of Austria and Count of Tyrol (1548). Two sons; number of daughters unknown. Died 1580.

Phillipine or Phillipina Welser was the daughter of a wealthy burger family who had financed the Hapsburgs and, as a reward, were permitted to found colonies in the Caribbean and Venezuela. She met Ferdinand II, Archduke of Austria and Count of Tyrol, at the Diet of Augsburg in 1547, marrying him the following year. At first, the alliance was frowned upon by Ferdinand's father, the Emperor Ferdinand. Phillipine Welser's beauty and intelligence were legendary, and a number of books on cooking and herbal remedies are attributed to her. Her father-in-law relented in his opposition twelve years after her marriage, recognizing her two sons as margraves of Austria. One of these sons, Marc Welser, corresponded with Christoph Scheiner on sunspots and was elected to the Lyncean Academy, to which Galileo belonged. Phillipine Welser has an altar-tomb in the Silver Chapel of the Franciscan or Court Church, Innsbruck, near her husband's tomb.

JH/MBO

SECONDARY SOURCES
Boeheim, Wendelin. *Philippine Welser: eine Schilderung ihres
Lebens und ihres Characters.* Innsbruck: Verlag des Museum
Ferdinandeum, 1894.
Grossing, Sigrid-Maria. *Kaufmannstochter im Kaiserhaus: Philip-
pine Welser und ihre Heilkunst.* Vienna: Kremayr and Scheriau,
1992. Includes bibliographical references.

STANDARD SOURCES
Høyrup.

WELSH, JANE KILBY (b. 1783)
U.S. science writer for children.

Jane Kilby Welsh wrote a textbook for older children. Written in the form of a dialogue among family members, the father served as teacher. However, the mother and the girls participated in the experiments and the discussions. Volume one of this two-volume work was on crystallography and introduced the reader to the crystals through chemical groups rather than crystallographic features. Volume two was on geology, beginning with the oldest rocks, granite, and moving toward the younger formations. She used standard sources (English and French geologists), the latest findings of the state geological surveys, and reviews from New England geologists to assure accuracy.   JH/MBO

PRIMARY SOURCES

[Welsh, Jane K.] *A Botanical Catechism: Containing Introductory Lessons for Students in Botany . . . By a Lady*. Northampton, Mass.: Education Society, 1819.

——. *Familiar Lessons in Mineralogy and Geology Designed for the Use of Young Persons and Lyceums*. 2 vols. Boston: Clapp and Hull, 1832–1833.

——. *A View of the Heathen World and of Light Dispelling the Darkness: with Questions Adapting it to Sabbath Schools and Juvenile Associations*. Worcester: Dorr, Howland and Co., 1834.

STANDARD SOURCES

Kass-Simon and Farnes (article by Michele L. Aldrich).

WELSH, LILIAN (1858–1938)

U.S. physician. Born 6 March 1858 in Columbia Pa., to Annie Eunice (Young) and Thomas Welsh. Educated Pennsylvania State Normal School, Millerville (1875); Woman's Medical College of Pennsylvania (M.D., 1889); University of Zurich, postgraduate study (1889–1891). Professional experience: Columbia (Pa.) High School, teacher (1875–1880?), principal (1881–1886); Pennsylvania State Normal School, Millersville, instructor (1880–1881?); Pennsylvania State Hospital for the Insane, Norristown, physician (1890–1892); private practice (with Mary Sherwood) (1892–1894); Goucher College, physician for preventive health and professor of physiology and hygiene (1894–1924). Concurrent experience: Baltimore Evening Dispensary for Working Women and Girls, director (with Sherwood) (1893–1910). Honors and memberships: Baltimore Association for the Promotion of the University Education of Women, founding member (1897–1908), secretary (1901–1908); National American Women's Suffrage Association, member. Died 23 February 1938 in Columbia, Pa. of encephalitis lethargica.

Lilian Welsh was the daughter of a merchant and soldier, who died when Welsh was five years old of an illness following the siege of Vicksburg during the Civil War. She lived in her father's hometown of Columbia, Pa., and attended the local high school and then the State Normal College at Millersville. She then taught in the Columbia high school and went back to the Normal College as an instructor. Appointed as principal of the high school, she remained in that position until her interest in chemistry drove her to study medicine at the Woman's Medical College of Pennsylvania, where she received a medical degree. She then went to the University of Zurich for eighteen months to study physiological chemistry. There she met Mary Sherwood, also a student, who became her companion and lifelong friend.

Upon her return, her inability to find a teaching position

led her to accept a two-year stint as a physician to the State Hospital for the Insane while also continuing to study pathology in Johns Hopkins Hospital. She also began a private practice in Baltimore with Sherwood. Although this practice did not flourish, the two women took over the Evening Dispensary for Working Women and Children in Baltimore that had been founded by Kate Hurd-Mead a few years before. This groundbreaking dispensary distributed milk and cared for sick babies as well as provided obstetrical care and postnatal observation. It also introduced public health instruction into the home.

Goucher College appointed Welsh as a physician in charge of women's hygiene and later as professor of physiology and hygiene. She remained in this post for thirty years, writing about her experiences in Baltimore in an autobiographical account. She helped obtain privileges for graduate students at Johns Hopkins University in 1908 comparable to those obtained earlier for medical women through her active role as secretary of the Baltimore Association for the Promotion of the University Education of Women. She served in various women's clubs and in public health organizations and was a member of the National American Woman Suffrage Association, for which she marched in street parades. After her companion and colleague, Mary Sherwood, died in 1935, she left Baltimore to return to her home town of Columbia, Pennsylvania, and died there three years later.

JH/MBO

PRIMARY SOURCES

Welsh, Lilian. *Fifty Years of Women's Education in the United States*. Baltimore, [1923].

——. *Reminiscences of Thirty Years in Baltimore*. Baltimore: The Norman Remington, Co., 1925. Autobiography.

SECONDARY SOURCES

Moldow, Gloria. *Women Doctors in Gilded Age Washington*. Urbana: University of Illinois Press, 1987.

STANDARD SOURCES

Hurd-Mead 1933; Morantz-Sanchez; *NAW* (article by Genevieve Miller); Rossiter 1982.

WELTFISH, GENE (1902–1980)

U.S. anthropologist. Born 7 August 1902 to Eve Furman Weltfish and Abraham Weltfish. Older of two daughters. Married Alexander Lesser (1924; divorced 1940). One child. Educated Hunter College; Barnard College (Columbia University) (A.B., 1924); Social Science Fellowship (1931); Columbia University (Ph.D., 1950). Professional experience: Columbia University, lecturer in anthropology (1936–1944); Fairleigh Dickinson University, Madison, N.J., assistant professor (1961–1964), associate professor (1964), pro-

fessor (1968–1972), emerita professor (1972). Post-retirement experience: New School for Social Research and the Manhattan School of Music, lecturer; Rutgers University, Department of Gerontology, visiting professorship. Died 12 August 1980.

Although Gene Weltfish began her college studies at Hunter College in journalism, she soon transferred to Barnard, where she met her future husband, Alexander Lesser, in a senior class given by Franz Boas. Following her graduation in 1925, she enrolled in Boas's graduate program in anthropology at Columbia University, where she met and worked with RUTH BENEDICT and the other remarkable women surrounding her. In 1928 she went to Oklahoma to study kinship patterns in Siouan tribes and began linguistic studies among the Pawnee. She continued her study of the Pawnee in the summer of 1929, and in 1930 she spent the entire year living and working among the Pawnee under the sponsorship of a Social Science Research Fellowship.

In 1931, her only daughter was born. Only in 1935 could she return to the field, taking her young child with her. In the Southwest, she focused her field work on social relations and surviving customs and traditions among the Pawnee. At Boas's invitation she began to teach courses in linguistics, ethnology, and archeology in the graduate anthropology program at Columbia. Later she developed one of the first courses in the country on invention and technology in human culture and another on race problems. Although she completed all her degree requirements, including her dissertation, she was not awarded her formal degree until 1950 due to the high cost of publishing her dissertation.

Between the mid-1930s and early 1940s, Weltfish was a prolific writer on the topic of race equality, drawing from her ethnological background. She and Ruth Benedict collaborated on a famous 1943 pamphlet criticizing race concepts, "The Race of Mankind." Although originally written at the request of the U.S.O. to be used in the armed forces, it was then distributed worldwide until 1944, when the U.S. Army began to argue within its ranks about the "liberal" views on racial equality expressed in the pamphlet, and its implications. After the war it formed an important basis for the statements on race published by the United Nations.

In 1945 Weltfish was elected vice president of the Women's International Democratic Federation at a convention in Paris. Later that same year she was elected president of an affiliated organization, the Congress of American Women. In the early fifties, Weltfish was called to testify before Senator Joseph McCarthy's notorious Un-American Activities Committee, where she was questioned about her involvement in the two women's groups and her pamphlet on race, now considered subversive. This was sufficient to prompt a termination notice from Columbia University in spite of strong support from Ruth Benedict.

Unable to find a teaching position for the following nine years, Weltfish continued her scholarly research on her own. After her book *The Origins of Art* was published, a former Columbia colleague, John Champe, invited her to work on the Pawnee material at the University of Nebraska, which she did over the next four years. By 1958 she received a two year grant from Bollingen Foundation to work on her book *The Lost Universe* (1965) based in part on research that she had done in the 1930s. This received wide recognition. In 1961 Weltfish was appointed to a position as assistant professor at Fairleigh Dickinson University in Madison, New Jersey, rising within six years to full professor.

In her later years, Weltfish was instrumental in developing the American Civilization Institute, an important gerontological society, and also the Grey Panthers in New York City. Upon her compulsory retirement in 1972 she was made emerita professor, but also found a position as part-time faculty member in the graduate department at the New School for Social Research and at the Manhattan School of Music. She also held a visiting professorship at Rutgers University in its new gerontology program, teaching courses until the end of her life in 1980. Her last book, on aesthetics, came out that same year.   JH

PRIMARY SOURCES

Weltfish, Gene. "Problems in the Study of Ancient and Modern Basket-makers." *American Anthropologist* 34 (1932): 108–117.

———. *Preliminary Classification of Prehistoric Southwestern Basketry.* City of Washington: Smithsonian Institution, 1932.

———. *Caddoan Texts, Pawnee, South Band Dialect.* New York: G. E. Stechert, 1937.

———. With Ruth Benedict. *The Races of Mankind.* New York: Public Affairs Committee, 1944.

———. With Ruth Benedict. *In Henry's Backyard: The Race of Mankind.* New York: H. Schuman, [ca. 1948].

———. *The Origins of Art.* Indianapolis: Bobbs-Merrill, 1953.

———. *The Lost Universe.* New York: Basic Books, 1965. Rpt., New York: Ballantine, 1971.

———. "The Aims of Anthropology: An American Perspective." *Current Anthropology* 9 (1968): 305–306. In response to: "The Aims for Anthropology: A Scandinavian Point of View," by Åke Hultkrantz.

———. *Work: An Anthropological View.* Saratoga Springs, N.Y.: Empire State University of New York (S.U.N.Y.), 1974.

SECONDARY SOURCES

Margetson, Ann. "Anthropology Begins at Home: Reflections of a Daughter." In *Theory and Practice: Essays Presented to Gene Weltfish,* ed. Stanley Diamond, 351–356. The Hague: Mouton, 1980.

———. "A Memorial: A Tribute to Professor Emeritus Gene Weltfish." *Fairleigh Dickinson University Magazine* (Spring, 1981).

New York Times, 5 August 1980. Obituary notice.

STANDARD SOURCES
AMS 6–8, S&B 9–12.

WERTENSTEIN, MATHILDE (fl. 1920s)

Physical chemist who worked in Poland. Married. May be the wife of Louis/Ludwik Wertenstein, a Pole who worked at the Curie Institute during 1908–1913. Educated perhaps at Curie Institute and may have held a scholarship there around 1923. Last-name only entry could be her or her husband. Professional experience: Radiological Laboratory of the Warsaw Scientific Society, research.

Working at the Radiological Laboratory of the Warsaw Scientific Society, Wertenstein did research on the electrochemical properties of the radioelements. With Hilary Lachs, she also investigated the distribution of radioactivity in solutions of radium decay products, in order to determine the physical state of radioactive particles in solution. The experimental results suggested that these particles formed larger masses by adhering to dust particles, but did not form true colloids. Her husband[?] Ludwik Wertenstein (1887–1945) worked with her both at the Curie Institute and at the Radiological Laboratory of the Warsaw Scientific Society, of which he was the head. He was later professor of nuclear physics at the Free Polish University. Ludwik Wetenstein's archives, which include experimental notes, a diary, and correspondence with MARIE CURIE, are in the Archives of the Polish Academy of Science.   MM

PRIMARY SOURCES
Wertenstein, Mathilde. With Hilary Lachs. "Über die Verteilung radioaktiver Körper in Lösungen." *Physikalische Zeitschrift* 23 (1922): 318–322.

Ludwik Wertenstein papers, Archivum Poskiej Akademii Nauk (Archives of the Polish Academy of Science).

SECONDARY SOURCES
Fajans, Kasimir. *Radioaktivität und die neueste Entwicklung der Lehre von den chemischen Elementen*. Brunswick: Friedrick Vieweg & Sohn, 1920.

STANDARD SOURCES
Meyer and von Schweidler.

WESSEL, BESSIE (BLOOM) (1889–1969)

U.S. anthropologist. Born 22 April 1888 in the Ukraine. Married. One son, Morris A. Wessel. Educated Providence, R.I., public schools; Brown University (Ph.B., 1911); Columbia University (M.A., 1924; Ph.D., 1935). Professional experience: Immigrant Educational Bureau in Providence, director (1911–1915); Connecticut College for Women at New London, Conn., instructor (1918–1922); assistant professor (1922–1925), professor of sociology (1934–1945), professor and chair of the department of social anthropology (1945–1954). Honors and memberships: American Anthropological Association, Fellow; American Sociological Society; Eastern Sociological Society; National Association of Social Workers; American Ethnological Society; American Society of Applied Anthropology. Died 11 April 1869 in New Britain, Conn.

Born in the Ukraine, Bessie Bloom Wessel came to the United States at the age of two. She earned her two graduate degrees at Columbia University. Although her formal graduate education extended over a period of almost twenty-five years, during the intervening years she had established herself as a teacher and research worker, and published her most important work, *An Ethnic Survey of Woonsocket, Rhode Island*. Her academic career was spent at the Connecticut College for Women at New London, where she began in the Department of Economics and Sociology. She became chairman of the department of sociology and later chair of the department of social anthropology.

Wessel's research commitment from the beginning was in devising precise procedures for studying specific ethnic components that operate in any particular community setting. She obtained her information by submitting questionnaires to public and parochial school populations. She then traced the ethnic descent of each child through information taken from these questionnaires. Wessel was able to blend sociology and anthropology to study the concept of the melting pot, which interested her particularly as an immigrant herself.

While she was on leave of absence from Connecticut College from 1925 to 1928, she directed a study of ethnic factors in community life in Brown University's graduate school. This five-year project was funded by a Laura Spellman Rockefeller Memorial and Rockefeller Foundation grant first to Brown and then to Connecticut College. For this project, she conducted surveys in communities in Connecticut and Rhode Island. These studies were praised for their precise methodology and for providing a new approach to social research, especially regarding the concept of the melting pot.   JH/MBO

PRIMARY SOURCES
Wessel, Bessie Bloom. *An Ethnic Survey of Woodsocket, Rhode Island*. Chicago: University of Chicago Press [ca. 1931].

STANDARD SOURCES
AMS 8, S&B 9.

WEST, ETHEL (1870?–1939)

British botanist. Born about 1870 in London. Emigrated to South Africa. Married Thomas Anderson. Professional experience: plant collector. Died 1939 in Grahamstown, South Africa.

Although Ethel West was born in England, she emigrated to Port Elizabeth, South Africa, with her mother and brothers. She collected plants in the eastern Cape province. She was a member of the Eastern Province Naturalists Society. A plant, *Leonotis westiae* Skan, was named after her. Her plants are in the Bolus Herbarium and other South African herbaria.

JH/MBO

SECONDARY SOURCES
Bothalia 15 (1985): 653.

STANDARD SOURCES
Desmond.

WESTALL, MARY (1889–?)

U.S. botanist. Born 27 February 1889 in Asheville, N.C. Educated Randolph-Macon Woman's College (A.B., 1910); Columbia University (M.S., 1918); University of Chicago (Ph.D., 1925). Professional experience: Randolph-Macon Woman's College, instructor (1913–1918), adjunct professor (1918–1922); Agnes Scott College, assistant professor (1926–1930), associate professor (1930–1934). Retired 1934. Death date unknown.

Mary Westall was thirty-seven years old when she got a permanent teaching position. She had just earned a doctorate from the University of Chicago and while working on this degree held an adjunct position at Randolph-Macon Woman's College. At Agnes Scott College, she advanced to associate professor, but retired when she was only forty-five years old. Her research was on the tracheids in the Cycadales.

JH/MBO

STANDARD SOURCES
AMS 5–8, B 9.

WESTCOTT, CYNTHIA (1898–1983)

U.S. plant pathologist and rose expert. Born 29 June 1898 in North Attleboro, Mass., to Elizabeth (Tourtellot) and Frank Thomas Westcott. Educated Wellesley College (B.A., 1920); Cornell University (Ph.D., 1932). Professional experience: Northboro High School, science teacher (1920–1921); Cornell University, instructor, research assistant (1921–1931); New Jersey Experimental Station, horticulturist (1931–1933); U.S. Department of Agriculture, associate pathologist (1944–1945); Glen Ridge N.J., self-employed horticulturist, writer, lecturer (1931–1961); Springvale, Croton-on-Hudson, N.Y., writer, lecturer (1961–1983?). Honors and memberships: New Jersey Rose Society, president (1954–1956); American Rose Society, director (1954–1960); American Rose Society, gold medalist; American Society of Nurserymen, Garden Writers Award. Died 22 March 1983 in North Tarrytown, N.Y.

Cynthia Westcott, noted as a rose expert and an authority on diseases of garden plants, had an unusual career, in which she practiced plant pathology following the model of the family doctor, even hanging out a shingle. She was educated at Wellesley College, intending originally to teach science. Although she did teach for a year following her graduation, she soon decided to return to graduate work in the School of Agriculture at Cornell University. There she taught and served as a research assistant in plant pathology. She studied with Herbert Whetzel, and worked for him as well, putting in long hours every day for ten years. She often expressed the opinion that her training had been as rigorous and demanding as that of any medical doctor.

Shortly before and for a year after receiving her doctorate from Cornell in 1932, she followed the traditional track of women plant pathologists, working in the New Jersey Experimental Station. By 1933, however, hoping to develop a private clientele from home gardeners, she took the unusual step of setting up practice as a "plant doctor" in Glen Ridge, New Jersey, with the same code of ethics as a medical doctor, including the refusal to advertise. At the same time, she set up her own garden of both display flowers and diseased plants. In 1937, she published a widely hailed book on her work, *The Plant Doctor.* Westcott developed a number of effective chemical sprays against various plant fungi, notably one in 1944 for *Ovulinia azaleae*, a fungus that attacked azalea petals. At the same time, she was aware of the limitation of chemical sprays, realizing that many gardeners oversprayed their plants, killing them instead of protecting them. She also believed in thorough sanitation of gardens, removing moldy stems and leaves that could serve as a source for spores.

Westcott's greatest fame came from her work as a rose expert, publishing a book in the early 1950s on roses that listed three hundred available varieties. She formed the New Jersey Rose Society, served as its first president, and then directed the American Rose Society from 1954 until her retirement in 1960. She was awarded a citation by the American Horticultural Society in 1955 and a gold medal by the Rose Society on her retirement in 1960. She also had memberships in scientific societies, such as the American Phytopathological Society, and the American Entomological Society. Even after she retired to Croton-on-Hudson, she continued to cultivate a significant garden to which the public was invited yearly on her Rose Day Open House. She died of heart disease in 1983.   JH/MBO

PRIMARY SOURCES

Westcott, Cynthia. *The Plant Doctor: The How, Why and When of Disease and Insect Control in Your Garden.* New York: Frederick A. Stokes Co., 1937.

———. *The Gardener's Bug Book. 1,000 Insect Pests and their Control.* New York: The American Garden Guild and Doubleday & Company, 1946.

———. *Plant Disease Handbook.* New York: Van Nostrand, 1950.

———. *Anyone Can Grow Roses.* Princeton, N.J.: Van Nostrand, 1952.

———. *Plant Doctoring is Fun.* Princeton, N.J.: Van Nostrand, [1957].

SECONDARY SOURCES

Kinkhead, Eugene, "Physician in the Flowerbed." *New Yorker* 28 (26 July 1952): 26–43.

STANDARD SOURCES

AMS 7–8, B 9; *Annual Obituaries* 1983.

WESTOVER, CYNTHIA MAY (1858–1931)

U.S. inventor. Born 1858 probably in New York City. Married John Alden. No children.

Cynthia May Westover was a multitalented individual. She was a horsewoman, a language student, a mathematician, and a naturalist. She also held a wide array of jobs, from factory superintendent to geology and vocal music teacher; from a customs inspector to an employee in the New York City Street Commissioner's office. Westover then became interested in journalism and worked for the *Ladies' Home Journal* and wrote several books. Later in her life she became a philanthropist and founded the International Sunshine Society to benefit blind babies and children.

As an inventor, Westover obtained a patent in 1892 for a dumping cart with movable body and self-emptying derrick. She did this while working for the New York City Street Commissioner.   JH/MBO

PRIMARY SOURCES

Westover, Cynthia May. *Woman's Ways of Earning Money.* New York: Sully and Kleinteich, 1904.

STANDARD SOURCES

Mothers and Daughters.

WHARTON, MARTHA LUCILLE (1885–?)

U.S. biochemist. Born 30 August 1885 in Sturgeon Bay, Wis. Married (1932). Educated University of Wisconsin (B.A., 1907); Columbia University (Ph.D., 1925). Professional experience: Wisconsin high school, teacher (1907–1915); Columbia University, chemist (1918–1923); Vanderbilt Metabolic Clinic, assistant biological chemist (1925–1926); Jewish Hospital, Brooklyn, research associate in biology (1926–1929); Cold Spring Harbor, pharmacological biology laboratory (1929–1932); Medical College, Cornell, resident assistant in dermatology (1944–1947); Institute for Cancer Research, resident fellow in biochemistry (1948–1950); U.S. Quartermaster's Corps, biochemist, pioneering research laboratory (1953–1966). Retired 1966. Death date unknown.

Little information was found to explain the career trajectory of Martha Lucille Wharton. With a doctorate from Columbia University, she spent only a few years in each of her positions, and there is an unexplained gap in her work from 1950 to 1953. In 1953, she seems to have found a permanent position with the Quartermater's Corps.

Wharton's research is varied and interesting. She worked on the composition of bone, the effects of X-rays on dilute aqueous solutions, canine distemper, susceptibility and immunization of rabbits to trichophytosis, chemotherapeutic aspects of cancer, isolation of odorous attractant and investigation of population density of the American cockroach, radiobiology of the cockroach, and insect physiology and behavior.   JH/MBO

STANDARD SOURCES

AMS B 9; *P&B* 10–11.

WHEDON, FRANCES LOVISA (1902–)

U.S. meteorologist. Born 27 August 1902 in Provincetown, Mass. Educated Massachusetts Institute of Technology (S.B., 1924). Professional experience: Langley Memorial Laboratory National Advisory Committee for Aeronautics, laboratory assistant (1924–1927); Staten Island Academy, teacher (1933–1942); U.S. Department of the Army, meteorologist, chief of the meteorological section and member of staff, signal research officer, chief signal officer (1942–1959), meteorologist, geophysical research officer, chief of research and development (1959). Honors and memberships: Meteorological Society, Geophysical Union, American Association for the Advancement of Science, U.S. War Department Meritorious Civilian Service Award (1946, 1962).

Frances Whedon demonstrates through her career an alternative path that a woman scientist might pursue. She did not earn an advanced degree, but had a bachelor's degree from the Massachusetts Institute of Technology that prepared her well for the government career that she eventually pursued.

Before she entered federal service, she taught school for nine years. Perhaps the war made it easier for her to enter this field, but she made for herself an excellent career in meteorological research and later in administration.

Whedon was a member of the American Association for the Advancement of Science, the Meteorological Society, and the Geophysical Union. Her research was in astrophysics, artillery meteorology, upper air research, cloud physics, and atmospheric sciences. The United States War Department honored her with the Meritorious Civilian Service Award in 1946 and 1962.   JH/MBO

STANDARD SOURCES
AMS 10–11.

WHEELER, ANNA JOHNSON PELL
(1883–1966)

U.S. mathematician. Born 1883 in Calliope (now Hawarden), Iowa, to Amelia (Frieberg) and Andrew Johnson. Two siblings. Married (1) Alexander Pell; (2) Arthur Leslie Wheeler. Educated Akron (Iowa) High School (graduated, 1899); University of South Dakota (B.A., 1903); University of Iowa (M.A., 1904); Radcliffe College (M.A., 1905); University of Göttingen (1906); University of Chicago (Ph.D., 1910). Professional experience: Mount Holyoke College, instructor (1911–1918); Bryn Mawr College, associate professor (1918–1925), professor (1925–1948). Died 1966 in Bryn Mawr, Pa.

The youngest of three surviving children of Swedish immigrant parents, Anna Johnson's Swedish heritage remained important to her throughout her life. Her father was a furniture dealer and undertaker. Anna reportedly was a shy, delicate child. She graduated from the high school in Akron, Iowa, and entered the University of South Dakota in 1899; she received a bachelor's degree from there in 1903.

Johnson was encouraged in mathematics by one of her professors, Alexander Pell. Pell, whose real name was Sergei Degaev, had been a Russian double agent who was forced to flee from Russia both by the government and by his revolutionary compatriots. At Pell's urging, Johnson attended graduate school at the University of Iowa and at Radcliffe College, earning a master's degree from each. Wellesley College offered her a fellowship that enabled her to spend a year at Göttingen University, allowing her to study under the mathematicians Hermann Minkowski (1864–1909), Felix Klein (1849–1925), and David Hilbert (1862–1943). Alexander Pell joined her in Germany, and they were married in Göttingen in 1907. After an apparent conflict with Hilbert, she returned to the United States with a completed thesis but no degree.

The Pells left South Dakota in 1909 on his accepting a position at the Armour Institute of Technology in Chicago. In 1910 Anna Pell received a doctoral degree from the University of Chicago (for the thesis that had been unacceptable at Göttingen) and began to search for a teaching position. During the fall semester of 1910 she did teach a course at the University of Chicago. In 1911 Alexander Pell suffered a stroke, and Pell successfully substituted for him at the Armour Institute, persuading her colleagues that a woman was competent to teach technical subjects.

Pell taught at Mount Holyoke College from 1911 to 1918, carried on research, and cared for her semi-invalid husband. She resigned from Holyoke to accept a position at Bryn Mawr, where she remained, except for short periods, until her retirement in 1948. Alexander Pell died in 1921, and in 1925 she married a classics scholar from Bryn Mawr, Arthur Leslie Wheeler. Although the couple moved to Princeton, New Jersey, Anna Wheeler continued to teach at Bryn Mawr on a part time basis. When in 1932 Arthur Wheeler died suddenly of apoplexy, Anna Wheeler returned to Bryn Mawr to teach full time. She remained active after her retirement until she suffered a stroke in 1966. She died shortly thereafter, at the age of eighty-two.

Wheeler was an active participant in professional organizations (she served on the council and board of trustees of the American Mathematical Society and was active in the Mathematical Association of America) and an able administrator. She was starred in the 1921 edition of *American Men of Science;* received honorary doctorates from the New Jersey College for Women, now Douglass College of Rutgers University (1932), and from Mount Holyoke College (1937); and was one of the hundred women honored by the Women's Centennial Congress as succeeding in careers not open to women a hundred years before (1940). As head of the mathematics department at Bryn Mawr, Wheeler was instrumental in offering professional and political asylum to AMALIE EMMY NOETHER, the eminent German-Jewish algebraist, in 1933.

Much of her work was in the area of linear algebra of infinitely many variables. This interest stemmed from her years at Göttingen, where Hilbert had interested her in integral equations.   JH/MBO

PRIMARY SOURCES
Pell, Anna. *Biorthogonal Systems of Functions.* Lancaster, Pa.: The New Era Printing Co., 1911. Ph.D. thesis, University of Chicago.
The Bryn Mawr Archives contain materials on Wheeler.

SECONDARY SOURCES
Grinstein, Louise, and Paul J. Campbell. "Anna Johnson Pell Wheeler, 1883–1966." *Association for Women in Mathematics Newsletter* (September 1978): 14–16; (November 1978): 8–12.

———. "Anna Johnson Pell Wheeler: Her Life and Work." *Historia Mathematica* 42 (1982): 4753-A.

STANDARD SOURCES
AMS 4–8, B 9; *NAW*(M); Ogilvie 1986.

WHEELER, ELIZABETH LOCKWOOD (1907–)

U.S. public health worker and chemist. Born 30 May 1907 in Laingsburg. Married 1950. Educated Wayne State University (B.S., 1932); Cornell University (M.A., 1938); Harvard University (M.P.H., 1946; D.P.H., 1948). Professional experience: public schools in Michigan, teacher (1926–1945); Harvard, School of Public Health, director research study of nutrition education (1945–1949); National Foundation for Infantile Paralysis, field consultant, health education (1949–1950), associate director, department of public education (1950); University of Michigan, lecturer, public health and education extension services (1951–1957); Central Michigan University, visiting professor of health education (1953–1954), professor (from 1957); Wayne State University, teacher (1937–1950). Honors and memberships: American Association for the Advancement of Science; Public Health Association; Science Teachers Association; Association of Biology Teachers; Society for Public Health Education.

Elizabeth Lockwood Wheeler taught in the public schools before she went to Harvard to earn both a master's and a doctoral degree in public health. After she earned her degrees, her jobs all related to that subject. At Central Michigan University she implemented a program in public health education, and before her retirement she established a lectureship to discuss public health issues. She was a member of numerous professional organizations.   JH/MBO

STANDARD SOURCES
AMS B 9; P&B 10–12.

WHEELER-VOEGLIN, ERMINIE BROOKE (1902–1988)

U.S. folklorist and ethnohistorian. Born 1902. Married Charles Voeglin, anthropologist (1931; divorced 1956). Professional experience: Indiana University, history professor (1956–1970?); Ethnohistory, editor (1954–1963). Died 1988 in Virginia.

Erminie Brooke Wheeler-Voeglin, now known as a pioneer of ethnohistory, married the anthropologist Charles Voeglin in 1931. Although she served as editor of the *Journal of American Folklore* from 1942 to 1946, she was prevented by nepotism rules from holding a position at Indiana University where her husband taught until after her divorce in 1956. Subsequently she became a professor of history at Indiana, where she taught ethnohistory for about fourteen years. She edited the journal *Ethnohistory*, and helped to shape that field by both her teaching and her encouragement of other students and researchers.   JH/MBO

PRIMARY SOURCES
Wheeler-Voeglin, Erminie Brooke. *An Anthropological Report on the History of the Miamis, Weas, and Eel River Indians.* Bloomington: Indiana University, Great Lakes-Ohio Valley Research Project, [1957].
———. *An Ethnohistorical Report on the Wyandot, Potawatomi, Ottawa, and Chippewa of Northwest Ohio.* New York: Garland, 1974.
———. *Pitt River Indians of California.* New York: Garland, 1974.
An extensive bibliography is available in Human Resources Area Files (HRAF) Ethnographic Bibliography of North America.
Papers at Newberry Library, Chicago.

SECONDARY SOURCES
"Erminie Brooke Wheeler-Voeglin." *Journal of American Folklore* (1988). Obituary notice.

WHITE, EDITH GRACE (1890–?)

U.S. zoologist. Born 16 May 1890 in Boston, Mass. Educated Mount Holyoke College (B.A., 1912); Columbia University (M.A., 1913; Ph.D., 1918). Professional experience: Princeton University, assistant (1915–1916); Heidelberg College (Ohio), instructor of biology and head of department (1918–1920); Shorter College, professor and head of department (1920–1923); Wilson College, professor (1923–1958), emerita professor (from 1958); American Museum of Natural History, research associate (1935–1947). Death date unknown.

Edith Grace White spent most of her career teaching in small colleges. As was the case for many teachers in that situation, she did not have much time for research. However, she was interested in working in her specialties, ichthyology and herpetology. Her special field was the morphology and taxonomy of elasmobranch fishes. Her concurrent positions as a research associate at the American Museum of Natural History, the Imperial University of Tokyo and the Marine Laboratory, Misaki, and the Laboratorium, Batavia, Java, gave her an opportunity for research she would not otherwise have had.   JH/MBO

PRIMARY SOURCES
White, Edith Grace. *A Textbook of General Biology.* St. Louis, Mo.: C. V. Mosby, 1933.

———. *The Heart Valves of the Elasmobranch Fishes.* New York: By Order of the Trustees of the American Museum of Natural History, 1936.

———. *Principles of Genetics.* St. Louis: C. V. Mosby, 1940.

STANDARD SOURCES
AMS 3–8, B 9; P&B 10–11; Debus.

WHITE, ELIZA CATHERINE (QUEKETT) (1812–1875)

British botanist. Born 1812 in Langport, Somerset. Married C. F. White. Professional experience: botanical collector. Died 14 November 1875 in Ealing, Middlesex.

Eliza Quekett married the botanist Charles Frederick White. Charles drew mosses and worked with microscopic fungi. Eliza also collected mosses and microscopic fungi. Both husband and wife were members of the the Linnean Society.

JH/MBO

SECONDARY SOURCES
Proceedings of the Linnean Society (1896–1897): 72–73. Obituary notice for Charles discusses both Charles and Eliza.

STANDARD SOURCES
Desmond.

WHITE, ELIZABETH JUANITA (GREER) (1905–)

U.S. physical chemist. Born 1905 in Atlanta, Ga. Married T. S. White, 1935. One child. Educated Agnes Scott College (A.B., 1923); Johns Hopkins University (Ph.D., 1929). Professional experience: Agnes Scott College, assistant in chemistry (1924–1926); Mary Baldwin College, professor of biology and chemistry (1930–1935); Bennet Junior College, instructor in physiology (1935–1938); Twentieth Century Fox Film Corp. Deluxe Laboratories, technical staff (1943–1946); Willmantic State Teachers College, Conn., associate professor (1951–1952); Office of Scientific Research and Development, civilian staff (1944). Honors and memberships: Johns Hopkins University, scholar and fellow (1929); American Association of University Women, Boston alumnae fellow (1929–1930); Chemical Society, Fellow; New York Academy of Sciences, member; Society of Motion Picture and TV Engineers, member.

Elizabeth Juanita Greer was born in the South but educated in New England. She returned to the South to attend Agnes Scott College, and there became interested in chemistry, serving as an assistant in chemistry at the college for two years after her graduation. She then went to Johns Hopkins Uni-

versity where she received a doctoral degree. She was awarded a postdoctoral fellowship by the American Association of University Women. She then went to Virginia to take up an appointment at the woman's college, Mary Baldwin College, where she was professor of biology and chemistry for five years until her marriage to T. S. White in 1935. Following her marriage, she held a part-time position as an instructor in physiology at Bennett Junior College. With the birth of her child, she dropped out of science and teaching for almost five years.

When the United States joined World War II it became easier for women to obtain good positions. White found a post with the laboratories of Twentieth Century Fox, working on the development of color film for three years. She became a member of the Society of Motion Picture and TV Engineers, a membership she kept up even after she had left the laboratory. She also worked on sound film, exploring the use of sulfides.

During this same period, she taught at Hunter College in the evenings as a method of keeping up her teaching, She also held a civilian post under the army's Office of Scientific Research and Development in 1944. Following the war, she returned to full-time academic teaching at the Willmantic State Teachers College in Connecticut, not too far from her alma mater. Among her many research interests were the purification of benzene, the etching of quartz in hydrofluoric acid, and aluminium. She also began to work on programs in conservation education.

JH/MBO

STANDARD SOURCES
AMS 6–8, P 9.

WHITE, FLORENCE ROY (1909–)

U.S. chemist. Born 6 March 1909 in Newcastle, Pa. Married 1932. Four children. Educated University of Illinois (A.B., 1930; A.M., 1931); University of Michigan (Ph.D., 1935). Professional experience: University of Michigan School of Medicine, assistant in physiology (1935–1936), research fellow (1936–1938); Yale University School of Medicine, research assistant (1938–1939); U.S. Department of Agriculture, Bureau of Home Economics, assistant chemist (1942); National Institutes of Health, chemist (1942–1945); National Academy of Science, resident assistant (1956–1958); National Cancer Institute, National Institutes of Health, chemist (1958–1966); Biochemical Section of the Drug Evaluation Bureau, National Cancer Institute (from 1966).

Florence Roy White held a series of short term positions until 1958, with one interruption of eleven years. This pattern is not unusual for a woman scientist, especially one with children. After the children were older, she was able to get more involved in her research on the nervous control of respiration and the biochemistry of cancer. White was a member of the Society of Biological Chemistry and the American Association of Cancer Research.   JH/MBO

STANDARD SOURCES
AMS 6–8, P&B 10–14; Debus.

WHITE, FRANCES EMILY (1832–1903)

U.S. anatomist and physiologist. Born 1832. Educated Woman's Medical College of Philadelphia (1872). Professional experience: Woman's Medical College of Philadelphia, demonstrator in anatomy and instructor in physiology (1872–1876), professor of physiology (1876–1903); Franklin Institute of Philadelphia, lecturer; International Medical Congress in Berlin (1890), delegate. Honors and memberships: Philadelphia County Medical Society. Died 29 December 1903 at Jamaica Plain, Mass.

Frances Emily White graduated from the Woman's Medical College of Philadelphia in 1872 and remained at her alma mater as teacher for over thirty years. While a student she studied chemistry under RACHEL BODLEY, physiology under ANN PRESTON, obstetrics under EMELINE HORTON CLEVELAND, and anatomy under Mary Scarlett-Dixon. She started as a demonstrator in anatomy and instructor in physiology and was promoted to professor of physiology in 1876. She developed the first experimental physiologic laboratory at the college after studying at the laboratory at Cambridge with Michael M. Foster. White represented the WMC in 1893, with MARY PUTNAM-JACOBI, at the opening of the medical school at Johns Hopkins University. Besides teaching, White wrote scientific articles and was published in local and national journals. She was one of the first women to lecture before the Franklin Institute of Philadelphia and was the first woman delegate to the International Medical Congress (1890). Nationally known, White was lauded as being of scientific mind, logical, clear-headed, and an excellent teacher. She retired due to ill health in 1903 and died the same year.

White was one of the founders of the Alumnae Association in 1875. A woman of great personal charm and social gifts, she understood the value of membership in authoritative organizations and the power of a well-organized group to achieve a common goal. White was a lifelong advocate for women's education saying exceptional women are duty-bound, through the example provided by their individual lives, to elevate the achievements of the whole sex. Interested in preventive medicine (then covered by the term "personal hygiene"), White equipped a gymnasium for regular exercise for the students.   JH/MBO

PRIMARY SOURCES
White, Frances Emily. "Woman's Place in Nature." *Popular Science Monthly* 6 (January 1875): 292–301.
———. "Persistence of Individual Consciousness." *Pennsylvania Monthly* (1878).
———. "Relations of the Sexes." *Westminster Review* (1879).
———. "Blood, Is It a Living Tissue?" *New York Medical Record* 33 (1883).
———. "From Moner to Man." *Popular Science Monthly* 24 (March 1884): 577–587.
———. "Hygiene as a Basis of Morals: Address to Graduates at the Thirty-Fifth Annual Commencement of the Woman's Medical College of Pennsylvania, March 17, 1887." Published in *Popular Science Monthly* 31 (May 1887): 67–79.

SECONDARY SOURCES
Alsop, Gulielma Fell. *History of the Woman's Medical College, Philadelphia, Pennsylvania 1850–1950.* Philadelphia: J. B. Lippincott Co., 1950.
Cyclopedia of American Medical Biography. Vol. 1. Philadephia: W. B. Saunders, 1912.
Women's Medical Journal 1904. Obituary notice.

STANDARD SOURCES
Hurd-Mead 1933; Rossiter 1982.

WHITE, MARGARET PIRIE (fl. 1917)

Scottish (?) physicist. Married Robert T. Dunbar (1921). Educated Edinburgh University (graduated 1915).

Margaret White graduated from Edinburgh University in 1915. She worked on X-rays in Charles Barkla's laboratory, first as an assistant, then as a university lecturer. White abandoned research upon her marriage to Barkla's student Robert T. Dunbar, in 1921.   JH/MBO

PRIMARY SOURCES
White, Margaret. With Charles G. Barkla. "Absorption and Scattering of X-rays and the Characteristic Radiation of the J Series." *Philosophical Magazine* 34 (1917): 270–285.

SECONDARY SOURCES
Sir James Chadwick, ed. *The Collected Papers of Lord Rutherford of Nelson.* Vol. 2, plate. London: George Allen aand Unwin, 1963.

STANDARD SOURCES
Rayner-Canham 1997.

WHITE, MARIAN EMILY (1921–1975)

U.S. anthropologist and archeologist. Born 28 August 1921 in Hartland, N.Y. Educated Cornell University (A.B., 1942); University of Michigan (M.A., 1953; Ph.D., 1956). Professional experience: Rochester Museum of Arts and Science, research fellow (1956–1958); University of Buffalo, assistant professor, anthropology and assistant curator of the Buffalo Museum (1958–1962); Niagara Frontier Archaeological Project, director (from 1958).

Although Marian White's degree was in anthropology, she did research in both archeology and anthropology. Much of her research was on the Iroquois. JH/MBO

PRIMARY SOURCES

White, Marian E. *The Niagara Frontier Iroquois.* Buffalo, N.Y.: Buffalo Museum of Science, [1958].

———. *Prehistoric Hunting and Fishing Camp.* Buffalo, N.Y.: Buffalo Museum of Science, [1959].

———. *Iroquois Culture History in the Niagara Frontier Area of New York State.* Ann Arbor: University of Michigan, 1961.

———. *An Early Historic Niagara Frontier Iroquois Cemetery in Erie County, New York; Archaeology and Physical Anthropology of the Kleis Site.* Rochester, N.Y.: New York State Archeological Association, 1967.

WHITEHEAD, LILIAN ELIZABETH (1893–1979)

British botanist. Born 1893 probably in Northumberland. Married Peter Whitehead. Professional experience: nurse (1914–1918); Herefordshire Botanical Society, one of the founders (1951). Died 6 June 1979 in Hereford.

Lilian Elizabeth Whitehead spent her early life in remote country in Northumberland and later in Canada. During World War I she served as a nurse and met her future husband, Peter Whitehead. In 1925, the couple moved to Hereford when Peter took a position as director of education for Herefordshire. Lilian had always been interested in natural history and was a member of the Herefordshire Ornithological Club and the Council and Conservation Committee of the Herefordshire and Radnorshire Nature Trust from its formation in 1963 until her death. Her major interest, however, was in plants, particularly in wildflowers. In 1951, she and several others began the Herefordshire Botanical Society. Whitehead served as its recorder, and became involved in gathering data for the county to be contributed to the *Atlas of the British Flora.* As she worked during the 1950s and 1960s she acquired a superb knowledge of the plants of the area. When she was eighty-three years old she published the *Plants of Herefordshire.*

Age did not hinder Whitehead's enthusiasm for botanizing. She was said to have appeared on collecting expeditions armed with only a grapefruit and raisins as provisions. When she was eighty-five, she still climbed her fruit trees to harvest the crop. JH/MBO

PRIMARY SOURCE

Whitehead, Lilian Elizabeth. *Plants of Herefordshire: A Handlist.* Hereford, [England]: Herefordshire Botanical Society, 1976.

SECONDARY SOURCE

Thomson, P. and S. E. "Lilian Elizabeth Whitehead." *Watsonia* 13, no. 2 (1980): 163.

STANDARD SOURCES

Desmond.

WHITELEY, MARTHA ANNIE (1866–?)

British chemist. Born 1866. Death date unknown.

Little information is available on Martha Whiteley. She published several textbooks that were used in the schools. JH/MBO

PRIMARY SOURCES

Whiteley, Martha Annie. *A Student's Manual of Organic Chemical Analysis: Qualitative and Quantitative.* London: Longmans, Green, 1926.

———. With Jocelyn Field Thorpe, Hubert Meulen, and Jacob Heslinga. *A Student's Manual of Organic Chemical Analysis: Qualitatiave and Quantitative.* London: Longmans, Green, 1926.

———. With Jocelyn Field Thorpe. *Dictionary of Applied Chemistry.* 4th ed. London: Longmans, Green, [1937–1956].

WHITING, MARIAN MURIEL (1881–1978)

British botanist. Born 1881 in Hong Kong. Never married. Professional experience: Kew Herbarium, voluntary assistant. Died 24 February 1978.

Marian Whiting had a great interest in plants. She became a Fellow of the Linnean Society in 1940 and worked without pay at the Kew herbarium for many years. She arranged plants from India, China, and Morocco. JH/MBO

PRIMARY SOURCES

Whiting, Marian Muriel. "Early Collection of Plants in Prince Edward Island." *Kew Bulletin,* no. 2 (1948): 236.

Whiting's plants and papers are at Kew and additional plants are at the National Museum of Wales.

WHITING, SARAH FRANCES (1847–1927)

U.S. physicist and astronomer. Born 1847 in Wyoming, N.Y., to Elizabeth (Comstock) and Joel Whiting. Never married. Educated Ingham University, LeRoy, N.Y. (B.A., 1865). Professional experience: Ingham University and Brooklyn Heights Seminary classics and mathematics, teacher (1865–1876); Wellesley College, professor of physics (1876–1912), Whitin Observatory, director (1900–1916). Died 1927 in Wilbraham, Mass.

Sarah Whiting's father taught Greek, Latin, and mathematics as well as physics, and tutored his daughter in these subjects. It was through helping her schoolteacher father prepare demonstrations for his classes that Whiting became interested in physics. She earned a bachelor's degree from Ingham University, in LeRoy, New York. She taught classics and mathematics at this university and then at the Brooklyn Heights Seminary for girls. In 1876 Henry Durant, founder of Wellesley College, invited her to become professor of physics at his new institution.

Since Durant wished to establish a physics laboratory at Wellesley, he arranged for Whiting to attend classes at the Massachusetts Institute of Technology, where laboratory physics had been introduced, during the first two years following her appointment. She traveled to other New England colleges as well, to observe their physics programs. While she was doing this preparatory work, she met Edward Pickering, a physics professor at MIT who left to become director of the Harvard Observatory in 1877. Pickering invited her to observe some of the techniques of physics that were being applied to astronomy, particularly the use of the spectroscope in the investigation of stellar spectra. In 1878 Wellesley, under Whiting's direction, opened the second undergraduate teaching laboratory of physics in the United States. After learning from Pickering, Whiting decided to introduce astronomy courses at Wellesley. Her equipment was very primitive when she first taught astronomy from 1880 to 1900. However, in 1900 the Whitin Observatory—made possible by the generosity of a Wellesley trustee, Mrs. John Whitin—was opened. This observatory, which contained a spectroscopic laboratory, enabled Whiting and her students to conduct significant research.

In 1888–1889 and 1896–1897 Whiting had sabbaticals and spent them in Germany, England, and Scotland, where she learned of the newest developments in physics and astronomy. She retired from the physics department in 1912 and in 1916 from the directorship of the Whitin Observatory. She died at the age of eighty, in Wilbraham, Massachusetts, where she had spent her last years with her sister.

Although Sarah Whiting was not a research physicist, she was an inspiring teacher, training many women who later became influential in research areas. ANNIE JUMP CANNON, for example, was one of her students. Her publications were chiefly concerned with teaching methods.   JH/MBO

PRIMARY SOURCES

Whiting, Sarah. With William H. Niles and Marion E. Hubbard. "In Memoriam, Clara Eaton Cummings." *College News* 6, no. 1 (6 February 1907): 7. Obituary notice of Clara Eaton Cummings.

———. *Daytime and Evening Exercises in Astronomy for Schools and Colleges.* Boston: Ginn, 1912.

———. *Science* 42 (1915): 853–855. Obituary notice of Margaret Huggins.

STANDARD SOURCES

AMS 1–4; Bailey; *NAW* (article by Gladys A. Anslow); Ogilvie 1986.

WHITNEY, MARY WATSON (1847–1921)

U.S. astronomer. Born 1847 in Waltham, Mass., to Mary (Crehore) and John Whitney. Four siblings. Never married. Educated Waltham High School (graduated 1864); Swedenborgian academy, Waltham (1864–1865); Vassar College (B.A., 1868; M.A., 1872); University of Zurich (1873–1876). Professional experience: Vassar College, assistant to Maria Mitchell (1881–1888), professor of astronomy and director of the observatory (1888–1910). Died in Waltham, Mass.

The second of five children of a prosperous real estate dealer, Mary Whitney showed early on remarkable ability in mathematics. She was supported by her parents, who encouraged the intellectual pursuits of their daughters and sons alike. She spent a year after graduating from high school at a Swedenborgian academy in Waltham, awaiting the opening of Vassar College, a proposed new institution for women she had heard about in high school. She entered Vassar in 1865, its first year, and soon became an admirer and favorite pupil of the astronomer MARIA MITCHELL.

Shortly after her graduation from Vassar in 1868, Whitney returned to Waltham to live with her mother. Both her father and her older brother had died recently. She taught school, but studied mathematics and astronomy in her leisure time. She joined Maria Mitchell and a group of her students on a trip to Iowa to observe a solar eclipse (1869). She also attended Harvard mathematician Benjamin Pierce's lectures on quaternions in 1869–1870, took a postgraduate course in celestial mechanics with Pierce in 1870, and in the same year worked for some months at the Dearborn Observatory in Chicago. In 1872 she received a master's degree from Vassar, and from 1873 to 1876 she studied mathematics and celestial mechanics at the University of Zurich, where her sister was attending medical school.

Her experience in Switzerland did not help her find a university position. Whitney taught at Waltham High School until 1811, when Maria Mitchell invited her to become her assistant at Vassar. When Mitchell retired in 1888, Whitney succeeded her as professor of astronomy and director of the Vassar Observatory. Known both as an excellent teacher and as a competent investigator, Whitney vigorously promoted women's education. She was a member of the Association for the Advancement of Women and an active participant on its science committee. Whitney was a charter member of the American Astronomical Society (1899). In 1907 she was made president of the Maria Mitchell Association of Nantucket. After a serious illness and resulting partial paralysis forced her early retirement from Vassar in 1910, she spent her last years in Waltham. She is reported to have said not long before her death, "I hope when I get to Heaven I shall not find the women playing second fiddle" (*NAW* 3:604).

Mary Whitney is best remembered for her teaching abilities, but she also carried on research. For example, she determined the longitude of the new Smith College Observatory and recorded her observations of comets, asteroids, and double stars. In 1896 she signed a contract with Columbia University to undertake the measurement and reduction of a collection of photographic plates of star clusters made by Lewis Rutherford. Perhaps her most lasting influence, though, was in training future astronomers.   JH/MBO

PRIMARY SOURCES

Whitney, Mary. *Education: Scientific Study and Work of Woman.* N.p., n.d.

———. *Maria Mitchell.* N.p.: Printed by special contribution, on behalf of the Maria Mitchell Endowment Fund, 1889.

SECONDARY SOURCES

Davis, Herman S. "Women Astronomers." *Popular Astronomy* 6 (June 1898): 211–228.

Furness, Caroline E. "Mary W. Whitney." *Popular Astronomy* 30 (1922): 597–608; 31 (1923): 25–36.

STANDARD SOURCES

AMS 1–3; *DAB; NAW* (article by Helen Wright); Ogilvie 1986; Rebière.

WICK, FRANCES GERTRUDE (1875–1941)

U.S. physicist. Born 2 October 1875 in Butler, Pa., to Alfred and Sarah (Mechling) Wick. Father was a store clerk, an innkeeper, and an oil producer. Six siblings. Never married. Educated Wilson College (A.B., 1897); Cornell University (A.B., 1905; A.M., 1906, Ph.D., 1908). Professional experience: Butler High School, teacher (1898–1904); Simmons College, instructor in physics (1908–1910); Vassar College, instructor in physics (1910–1915), assistant professor (1915–1919), associate professor (1919–1922), professor (1922–1941). Concurrent experience: Cornell University, acting assistant professor (1918–1919). Honors and memberships: Wilson College, honorary D.Sc.; Sigma Xi; Sigma Delta Epsilon. Died 15 June 1941 in Poughkeepsie, N.Y.

Frances Wick became interested in physics while preparing herself to teach the physics class at Butler High School. She resigned in 1904 in order to study full time at Cornell University. There she worked with the physics department chair, Edward L. Nichols, and his former student Ernest Merritt. Nichols and Merritt were supportive of women students, and Wick continued to collaborate with them on studies of luminescence for many years. Wick also worked for a time with another Cornell student, Louise McDowell, who became a lifelong friend.

Facilities and resources for research were quite limited in the small women's colleges where Wick taught, so during summers she performed research in laboratories at General Electric, Harvard, Cornell, Cambridge, Berlin, and Vienna. Her researches and travel were supported by numerous fellowships and grants. During World War I Wick worked for the U.S. Signal Corps on gun sights and radio equipment.

In 1926 Wick bought a house near Vassar, which she shared with her older sister, Sarah Blanche Wick. In 1939 Wick became head of Vassar's physics department. She died at home two years later.

At Cornell Wick was introduced to the field of luminescence, which became her research specialty. For her master's degree she studied the relation between fluorescence and absorption in an organic compound. To avoid having too narrow a background, Wick selected her doctoral topic from a different area, the electrical properties of silicon. Nevertheless, this topic was related to luminescence, since some current theories of phosphorescence traced it to electron movements.

Wick next took part in comprehensive studies of the fluorescence of uranium compounds coordinated by Nichols and funded by the Carnegie Institution. During the remainder of her career, Wick investigated the luminescence produced by various agents, such as cathode, X, and radium rays; heat; and friction; as well as the effects of previous exposure to radiation on thermoluminescence. Several of her papers were published jointly with colleagues at women's colleges and with students.

Wick was known as an inspiring, enthusiastic teacher who loved her research. She was well respected for her extensive experimental researches on luminescence. Wick was a Fellow of the American Physical Society, the Optical Society of America, and the American Association for the Advancement of Science, and a member of the American Association of University Women, the American Association of Physics Teachers, the Association of College Professors, and the Cornell and Wilson clubs of New York City. She served as Alumnae Trustee and as Trustee for Wilson College.

JH/MBO

PRIMARY SOURCES

Wick, Frances Gertrude. "Spectro-photometric Study of the Absorbing Power and the Fluorescence of Resorufin." *Physical Review* 24 (1907): 356–378.

———. "Electromotive Force of Cells with Silicon." *Physical Review* 27 (1908): 238–250.

———. With E. L. Nichols, et al. *Fluorescence of the Uranyl Salts.* Washington, D.C.: Carnegie Institution, 1919.

———. "The Effect of X-rays upon Thermoluminescence." *Journal of the Optical Society of America and Review of Scientific Instruments* 14 (1927): 33–44.

———. "Über Triboluminescence." *Akademie der Wissenschaften in Wien, mathematisch-naturwissenschaftliche Klasse* 145, no. 11a (1936): 689–705.

SECONDARY SOURCES

Journal of the Optical Society of America 32 (July 1942): 431–432. Obituary notice.

New York Times, 16 June 1941; 22 January 1942. Obituary notices.

STANDARD SOURCES

AMS 2–6; *Current Biography* 1941; Grinstein 1993 (articles by Elizabeth M. Cavicchi and Janet B. Guernsey); *NCAB*; Poggendorff, vols. 6, 7b; Rossiter 1982.

WICKENS, ARYNESS JOY (1901–)

U.S. statistician and economist. Born 5 January 1901 in Bellingham, Wash. Married (1935). One child. Educated University of Washington, Seattle (A.B., 1922); University of Chicago (A.M., 1924). Professional experience: Mount Holyoke College, instructor and assistant professor economics and statistics (1924–1928); Board of Governors of the Federal Reserve System, member of resident staff (1928–1934); Office of Economic Advice, National Emergency Council, chief statistician (1934–1935); U.S. Centenary Statistical Board, chief economist and chief statistician (1935–1938); U.S. Department of Labor, assistant to the Commissioner of Labor Statistics (1938–1940), chief of Prices and Cost of Living Division (1940–1945), assistant commissioner of progressive operations (1945–1949), deputy commissioner (1949–1955), acting commissioner (1954–1955); Secretary of Labor, departmental as-

sistant (1956–1959); Economic Advisor to the Secretary of Labor (1959–1962); Consumer Programs Advisor (from 1962).

After a short career in academia, Aryness Joy Wickens began a very successful career in the federal government, using her knowledge of economics and statistics to reach a high position within the Department of Labor. She received the first Federal Woman's Award. She was a Fellow of the Statistical Association and its vice-president in 1935 and again in 1947. She was president in 1952.

JH/MBO

PRIMARY SOURCES

Wickens, Aryness Joy. Papers, 1936–1978 (inclusive), mss. Schlesinger Library, Radcliffe College. Includes biographical information, employment records, publications, and clippings.

———. *The Reminiscences of Mrs. A. J. Wickens.* New York: Oral History Research Office, Columbia University, 1957. Available in microfiche.

STANDARD SOURCES

AMS S&B 9–12.

WIDDOWSON, ELSIE MAY (1906–)

British physiologist. Educated Imperial College of Science and Technology (bachelor's degree; Ph.D., 1933); King's College of Household and Social Science, training in dietetics; University of London (D.Sc., 1948). Professional experience: Courtauld Institute of Biochemistry at the Middlesex Hospital, temporary appointment in human biochemistry; Medical Research Council, staff (1933–1937). Honors and memberships: University of Manchester (honorary D.Sc.); Fellow of the Royal Society (1976); Commander of the British Empire (1979); Bristol Myers award; Rank Prize Fund award; Nutrition Society, founder and president (1977–1980); Neonatal Society, founding member and president (1978–1980).

Although Elsie Widdowson was most interested in zoology, a chemistry mistress at her school near Dulwich persuaded her to study chemistry at the Imperial College of Science and Technology. In a class of one hundred, there were only three women. After earning her undergraduate degree, she remained at Imperial College to work with Helen Archbold (later HELEN PORTER), who was in charge of the chemistry and physiology of apples for the Department of Scientific and Industrial Research. Widdowson developed methods for separating and measuring the carbohydrate content of apples at various stages and in 1933 earned a doctorate with a thesis, "The Carbohydrate Content of Developing Apples." In order to gain experience in human biochemistry, she worked temporarily at the Courtauld Institute of Biochemistry at the Middlesex Hospital. Since she could not find a permanent research post, she decided to train as a dietician.

Since one of the requirements was preliminary experience with large-scale cooking, she went to King's College Hospital, where she met a young physician, R. A. McCance, who was studying the importance of various types of cooking on nutrient loss. She immediately perceived that his values for carbohydrates in fruits were wrong and told him so. He offered her a job on the Medical Research Council staff, where she remained until retirement in 1973.

Widdowson and McCance collaborated throughout his life. Their first results were published in special reports of the Medical Research Council. These early reports focused on the composition of fruits and vegetables and the effect of cooking on them. During the first five years of their collaboration, they did experiments on themselves and on volunteers on mineral metabolism.

When McCance took the readership in medicine under J. A. Ryle at Cambridge, Widdowson followed him there. During the early years of World War II, Widdowson and McCance engaged in an experimental study of rationing to see how self-sufficient in food production Britain could be. They designed a diet and formed part of the volunteer group of four women and four men who lived on the diet for three months.

After the war, Widdowson was part of a medical group sent to Germany by the Medical Research Council to study hunger edema and the influence of undernutrition on the civilian population. She returned to an early interest, the influence of growth and development on the chemical composition of the body and the variation between species. In the 1950s, the MRC set up the Infantile Malnutrition Research Unit in Kampala, Uganda, and Widdowson went there and was able to see the practical results of her experimental work.

Most of Widdowson's work had been on human subjects, but after McCance retired, she moved to the Medical Research Council's Dunn Nutrition Laboratory in Cambridge where she worked on animal subjects.

Although known as an excellent lecturer, Widdowson was best known for her research. She published over three hundred original papers, reports and review articles.   JH/MBO

PRIMARY SOURCES
Widdowson, E. M.With J. C. Mathers, eds. *The Contribution of Nutrition to Human and Animal Health.* Cambridge: Cambridge University Press, 1992.
———. With R. A. McCance. "The Absorption and Excretion of Iron Following Oral and Intravenous Administration." *Journal of Physiology* (London) 94 (1938): 148–154.
———. "A Study of Individual Children's Diets." *MRC Special Report Series* 257 (1947): 1–196.
———. With R. A. McCance. "Some Effects of Accelerating Growth. 1. General Somatic Development." *Proceedings of the Royal Society of London* ser. B 152 (1960): 188–206.

———. "Intrauterine Growth Retardation in the Pig. 1. Organ Size and Cellular Development at Birth and after Growth to Maturity." *Biology of the Neonate* 29 (1971): 329–340.
———. With V. E. Colombo and C. A. Artavanis. "Changes in the Organs of Pigs in Response to Feeding for the First 24 Hours after Birth." *Biology of the Neonate* 28 (1976): 272–281.

STANDARD SOURCES
WW in Science in Europe; Women Physiologists.

WIEBUSCH, AGNES (TOWNSEND) (1902–)

U.S. physicist. Born 27 March 1902 in Albany, N.Y. Married (1926). Educated University of Texas (B.A., 1923; M.A., 1924); Columbia University (Ph.D., 1935). Professional experience: University of Texas, tutor in physics (1923–1926); instructor (1926–1927); Barnard College, Columbia, assistant (1927–1930), lecturer (1930–1944), assistant professor (1944–1947); Douglas College, Rutgers, lecturer (1948–1953), from associate professor to professor (1953–1958), emerita professor (from 1958). Honors and memberships: Physical Society; Association of Physics Teachers.

After earning her first two degrees at the University of Texas, Agnes Wiebusch went to Columbia, where she earned a doctorate in physics. Before she went to New York, she served as a physics tutor and instructor at the University of Texas. Before she earned her doctorate, Wiebusch was an assistant at Barnard College and later a lecturer. She remained a lecturer until 1944 when she moved to assistant professor. In 1947 she went to Rutgers as a lecturer and advanced through the academic ranks to professor. Her research was on ferromagnetism and photography.   JH/MBO

STANDARD SOURCES
AMS 8, P&B 9–11; Rossiter 1982.

WIENHOLZ, EVA (1930–1969)

German geologist. Born 3 September 1930. Died 17 March 1969.

In her short life, German geologist Eva Wienholz published extensively on fossil Ostracods. Additional information on Wienholz is found in the biography by Gunter Kootz in the journal *Jahrbuch Geologische.*   JH/MBO

PRIMARY SOURCES
Wienholz, Eva. "Mikrobiostratigraphie an der Lias/Dogger-Grenze in Bohrungen noerdlich der mitteldeutschen Hauptscholle." *Jahrbuch für Geologie* 1 (1967): 537–571.
———. Neue Ostracoden aus dem norddeutschen Callov." *Frieberger Forschungshefte, Reihe C: Geowissenschaften, Mineralogie-Geochemie* 213 (1967): 23–29.

———. "Ostracodenfaunen der Jura/Kreide-Grenzschichten im Norden der Deutschen Demokratischen Republik." *Deutschen Gesellschaft für geologische Wissenschaften. Reihe A. Geologie und Palaontologie* 13, no. 2 (1968): 233–238.

———. With H. Kozur. "Drei interessante Ostracodenarten aus dem Keuper im Norden der DDR." *Geologie* 19, no. 5 (1970): 588–593.

SECONDARY SOURCES
Kootz, Gunder. "Eva Wienholz zum Gedenken, 3.9. 1930–17.3.1969." *Jahrbuch Geologische* 5–6 (1969–1970): 785–787.

STANDARD SOURCES
Sarjeant.

WILDER, INEZ (WHIPPLE) (1871–1929)

U.S. zoologist. Born 19 May 1871 in Diamond Hill, R.I. Married H. H. Whipple. Educated Brown University (Ph.B., 1900); Smith College (A.M., 1904). Professional experience: Rhode Island Normal School, biology teacher (1893–1897); Massachusetts high school, teacher (1900–1902); Smith College, instructor of zoology (1902–1914), associate professor (1914–1922), professor (from 1922). Died 1929.

After beginning her career as a normal school and a high school teacher, Inez Whipple Wilder went to Smith College as an instructor, a rank she retained for twelve years before finally moving up the academic ladder. She remained an associate professor for eight years and was finally promoted to full professor in 1922. Her husband, Harris Hawthorne Wilder, who had a doctoral degree from the University of Freiburg (1891), became professor of zoology at Smith College in 1892. Thus, he was already at Smith when Inez Whipple arrived on campus.

Inez Wilder's research involved the epidermal markings of mammalian palms and soles as well as the anatomy, embryology, and life history of amphibians.   JH/MBO

PRIMARY SOURCES
Wilder, Harris Hawthorne, and Inez Whipple Wilder. *The Early Years of a Zoologist: The Story of a New England Boyhood.* Northampton, Mass.: Private printing, Smith College; New York City: the Harbor Press, 1930.

Wilder, Inez Whipple. *Laboratory Studies in Mammalian Anatomy.* Philadelphia: P. Blakiston's Son & Co., [ca. 1914].

———. *The Morphology of Amphibian Metamorphosis.* Northampton, Mass.: Smith, 1925.

STANDARD SOURCES
AMS 2–4; Dorland; Rossiter 1982.

WILEY, GRACE OLIVE (1884–1948)

U.S. entomologist. Died 1948.

Although no information is available on Grace Olive Wiley, she published a number of papers on entomology.   JH/MBO

PRIMARY SOURCES
Wiley, Grace Olive. "Life History Notes of Two Species of Saldidae (Hemiptera) Found in Kansas." *University of Kansas Science Bulletin* 4, no. 9 (1922): 301–311.

———. "Some Notes on the Biology of Curicta from Texas." *University of Kansas Science Bulletin* 14, no. 20 (1922): 507–511.

———. "A New Species of Rheumataobates from Texas (Heteroptera, Gerridae)." *Canadian Entomologist* 55 (1923): 202–205.

WILKINSON, HELEN AVINA (HUNSCHER) (1904–?)

See Hunscher, Helen Avina.

WILLARD, EMMA (HART) (1787–1870)

U.S. educator. Born 23 February 1787 in Berlin, Conn., the daughter of Lydia (Hinsdale) and Samuel Hart. Nine full siblings. Married (1) Dr. John Willard; (2) Christopher Yates (divorced). One child, John Hart Willard. Educated Berlin Academy (1802–1806). Professional experience: Westfield Academy, Westfield, Mass., assistant (1807); Middlebury Academy, Middlebury, Vt., preceptress (summers 1807–1809); Middlebury Female Seminary, teacher (1814–1821); Troy Female Seminary, teacher (from 1821). Died 15 April 1870 in Troy, N.Y.

Emma Hart grew up on a farm. Her father was a political liberal and encouraged her intellectual interests by granting her freedom from domestic chores so that she could discuss philosophical questions with him. In 1802 she enrolled in the Berlin Academy; by 1804 she was teaching the younger children at the academy. Apparently a superb teacher, she continued teaching at the Berlin Academy while attending classes at schools in Hartford. During the spring of 1807, she was employed as an assistant at the Westfield Academy and the following summer became preceptress of the female academy there. While at Middlebury, the twenty-two-year-old Hart met and married a fifty-year-old physician, John Willard. Although Willard had four children from two previous marriages, the couple had only one son, John Hart Willard (born 1810) together. After her husband suffered financial reverses, she opened a school, the Middlebury Female Seminary, in her own home. Willard was convinced the women could learn the subjects previously open only to boys and men.

In order to gain support for her educational ideas, Emma Willard approached the New York legislature for support for female education. Although she received a favorable hearing, the state did not produce funds, but it did provide a charter. In order to be near the legislature Willard moved her school to Troy, New York, in 1921, where the council had voted four thousand dollars in tax dollars to subsidize a female academy. She supported teaching natural philosophy to girls, asking why they should be kept in ignorance of the "great machinery of nature." She continued by explaining its usefulness, for mothers could communicate its principles to their children. Further rationalizing the teaching of science, she noted that it is designed to heighten moral taste by imbuing girls with the majesty of God's creation. She did, however, note the advisability of editing some parts of science for girls. The school's enrollment soared, and by 1831 there were more than three-hundred students, both day students and boarders.

John Willard, who had been the school's physician and business manager, died in 1824. By 1938, Emma Willard turned over the management of the school to her daughter-in-law, Sarah Lucretia Hudson, and her son, John Hart Willard. In the same year, Willard made a disastrous second marriage to a physician who was a gambler and fortune hunter. The marriage ended in divorce in 1843. She returned to Troy in 1844 in order to be near the seminary.

Emma Willard is known for her importance in science education for women. She published *Ancient Geology* as a supplement to William Woodbridge's *System of Universal Geography*. This combined book went through ten reprintings in the next twenty years. It was commended by the *American Journal of Science* as having ordered a previous jumble of facts. Her section emphasized human geography in ordered civilizations but also included sections on rivers, mountains, volcanoes, and other geological phenomena that determined cultures in the ancient world.

Although Willard introduced many demanding subjects into her curriculum, including science, she still featured domestic subjects as well. Her strategy was a conservative one; while introducing radical reforms, she personally was socially conservative. As Rossiter noted, whether or not Willard recognized it, her school and others like it provided the starting point for women in science and in the professions.

JH/MBO

PRIMARY SOURCES

Willard, Emma H. With William C. Woodbridge. *Woodbridge and Willard's Universal Geography: Accompanied by Modern and Ancient Atlases*. Hartford, 1824–1844.

———. *Ancient Geography*. Hartford: (various publishers), 1824–1844.

———. *History of the United States, or, Republic of America*. New York: A. S. Barnes, 1845. Numerous abridged and non-abridged editions were published.

———. *Astronography: Or, Astronomical Geography, with the Use of the Globes*. Troy, N.Y.: 1854.

SECONDARY SOURCES

Lutz, Alma. *Emma Willard: Daughter of Democracy*. Boston: Houghton Mifflin, 1929. Includes a bibliography.

STANDARD SOURCES

Kass-Simon and Farnes (article byMichele L. Aldrich); *NAW*; Ogilvie 1986; Rossiter 1982.

WILLARD, MARY LOUISA (1898–?)

U.S. chemist. Born 19 May 1898 in State College, Pa., to Henrietta (Nunn) and Joseph Moody Willard. Educated Pennsylvania State University (B.S., 1921; M.S., 1923); Cornell University (Ph.D., 1927). Professional experience: Pennsylvania State University, University Park, faculty member (1920–?), professor of chemistry (1948–1964), emerita professor (from 1964). Honors and memberships: American Institute of Chemists, Fellow (honor award, 1955); American Association for the Advancement of Science; American Crystallographic Society; American Microscopic Society; American Microchemical Society; American Forensic Society. Death Date unknown.

Mary Louisa Willard was active in many professional societies. She did much of her research on advancing the then new field of chemical microscopy and its allied fields. She became associate editor of *Mikrochemie* in 1942, a position that she retained for many years.

JH/MBO

PRIMARY SOURCES

Willard, Mary Louisa. *Hydroxyhydroquinolsulfonephthalein, 2′, 4′, 5′-trihydroxybenzoylbenzene-ortho-sulfonic acid (the Intermediate Acid) and Some of their Derivatives*. Easton, Pa.: 1929. Ph.D. thesis from Cornell University, reprinted from the *Journal of the Americal Chemical Society* 51, no. 7 (May 1929).

———. *Pioneer Women in Chemistry*. State College, Pa., 1940? Reproduced from type-written copy.

———. *Introduction to Chemical Microscopy*. Ann Arbor, Mich., Edwards Brothers, 1949.

STANDARD SOURCES

AMS 5–11; Debus.

WILLCOCK, EDITH GERTRUDE (GARDINER) (1879–1953)

British biochemist. Born 7 January 1879 at Albrighton, Salop, England, to R. A. Willcock. Married John Stanley Gardiner (1909). Two daughters. Educated Newnham College, Cambridge (1900–1904); Bathhurst College (1904–1905); Bathhurst College, 'N' Research Fellow (1905–1909); University of Dublin (D.Sc.). Professional experience: Bathurst College, lecturer and associate (1908–1921); British Ministry of Agriculture, consultant. Died 8 October 1953.

Edith Willcock is an example of a promising scientist who gave up her career for marriage and children. When she was a research student at Newnham College, she was known for her beautiful singing voice as well as for her academic skills. Willcock lived in Cambridge for most of her life; her husband was professor of zoology at the Cambridge University. Their first child, Nancy, was born around 1910. Later a second daughter was born. The family enjoyed sailing and gardening, and Willcock also raised animals for food. As a talented watercolorist, Willcock helped her husband assemble a substantial art collection.

Willcock's early researches concerned influences on oxidation reactions of iodine and in a resin. Working with the chemist W. B. Hardy, she determined the chemical action of rays from radium on iodine solutions and compared these to the action of light and of X-rays. She also investigated the effects of radium rays on animals and on certain biochemical substances. Willcock pursued further studies of proteins and of amino acids. JH/MBO

PRIMARY SOURCES
Gardiner, Edith Gertrude. With W. B. Hardy. "On the Oxidizing Action of the Rays from Radium Bromide as shown by the Decomposition of Iodoform." *Proceedings of the Royal Society of London* 72 (1903): 200–204.
———. "Radium and Animals." *Nature* 69 (1903): 55.
———. "Note on the Influence of Certain Salts and Organic Substances on the Oxidation of Guaiacum." *Proceedings of the Chemical Society of London* 22 (1904): 197–198.
———. With W. B. Hardy. "Presence of Phosphorus in Crystalline Egg-Albumin." *Journal of the Chemical Society of London (Abstracts)* 1 (1908): 366.

SECONDARY SOURCES
Forster-Cooper, C. "John Stanley Gardiner." *Obituary Notices of Fellows of the Royal Society* 5 (1945–1948): 541–553.
Marx, Erich, ed. *Handbuch der Radiology.* Vol. 5. Leipzig: Akademische Verlagsgesellschaft, 1919. See page 268.
Rayner-Canham, M. F. and G. W. Rayner-Canham. "Pioneer Women in Nuclear Science." *American Journal of Physics* 58 (1990): 1036–1043.

Rutherford, Ernest. *Radio-activity.* Cambridge: Cambridge University Press, 1904; 1905. See page 175 (1904); 214 (1905).

STANDARD SOURCES
Newnham Roll.

WILLCOX, MARY ALICE (1856–1953)

U.S. zoologist. Born 24 April 1856 in Kennebunk, Maine. Educated Newnham College, Cambridge (1880–1883); University of Zurich (Ph.D., 1898). Professional experience: Massachusetts high school teacher (1876–1879); Wellesley College, professor of zoology and physiology (1883–1910), emerita professor (1910–1953). Died 1953.

Although she was born in Maine, Mary Alice Willcox went to England for her undergraduate education. Cambridge University did not grant degrees to women at that time. When she returned from Newnham, she was offered a position at the new Wellesley College. Interested in obtaining a doctorate and already well known for her study of mollusks, she attended lectures at the University of Zurich in 1896 and went to the Naples Zoological Station in 1898. She received her doctorate from the University of Zurich. Most of her research was on the comparative anatomy of mollusks, and the comparative anatomy of the Acmaeidae. She remained on Wellesley's faculty until 1910 when she retired. After retirement she became active in the League of Women Voters and the Federation of Women's Clubs. She was an active member of the National Audubon Society and the Boston Society of Natural History. JH/MBO

PRIMARY SOURCES
Willcox, Mary Alice. *Pocket Guide to the Common Land Bird of New England.* Boston: Lee and Shepard, [ca. 1895].
———. "Anatomy of the Grasshopper." *Observer* 7 (1896): 184–192.
———. "Anatomy of the May Beetle." *Observer* 7 (1896): 365–373.
———. "Directions for the Practical Study of the Grasshopper." *Observer* 7 (1896): 374–378.
———. *Zur Anatomie von Acmaea fragilis Chemnitz.* Jena, 1898.

STANDARD SOURCES
AMS 2–8; Bailey; Rossiter 1982.

WILLIAMS, ANNA WESSELS (1863–1954)

U.S. bacteriologist. Born 17 March 1863 in Hackensack, N.J., to Jane and William Williams. Five siblings. Educated at home; New Jersey State Normal School, Trenton (graduated 1883); Woman's Medical College of the New York Infirmary for Women and Children

(M.D., 1891); Universities of Vienna, Heidelberg, and Leipzig; intern in the Royal Frāuen Klinik of Leopold in Dresden (1892–1893). Professional experience: New York Infirmary, instructor in pathology (1891–1893); assistant to department chair, pathology and hygiene (1891–1895); New York City Department of Health, volunteer in diagnostic laboratory (1894), assistant bacteriologist (1895–1905); Pasteur Institute, Paris, researcher (1896); New York Infirmary, consulting pathologist (1902–1905); New York City, Department of Health Research Laboratory, assistant director (1905–1934). Retired 1934. Honors and memberships: Committee on the Standard Methods for the Diagnosis of Rabies, American Public Health Association (1907); Woman's Medical Association, president (1915); American Public Health Association, laboratory section, vice-chair (1931); chair (1932). Died 20 November 1954.

Anna Wessels Williams is best known for her contributions to the understanding of infectious diseases, diphtheria and rabies in particular. One of six children, she was taught at home by her father, a private school teacher, and her evangelically inclined mother, a supporter of the mission activities of the First Dutch Reformed Church. She attended New Jersey State Normal School, and then taught from 1883 to 1885. The near death of a sister during the delivery of a stillborn baby convinced Williams to enter the Woman's Medical College of the New York Infirmary for Women and Children. The same incident convinced her parents to support her. After she received her degree she remained at the college as an instructor in pathology and hygiene. She assisted ANNE S. DANIEL in the children's clinic and in the out-practice at the same time.

Williams became interested in the prevention and cure of diptheria in 1894, when she volunteered in the diagnostic laboratory of the New York City Department of Health. The purpose of this laboratory was to apply bacteriological techniques to the study of public health problems. Diphtheria, particularly in children, was a pressing problem. Working with the laboratory director, William Hallock Park, Williams searched for a diphtheria strain that would produce a toxin to replace the ineffective low-yield antitoxin that was currently used. The resulting toxin was known as "Park-Williams 8," a strong toxin producer. Williams believed that she alone was the discoverer, since she had discovered it when Park was on vacation. This discovery was crucial in the eradication of diphtheria in much of the world.

Williams became a full-time assistant bacteriologist for the laboratory in 1895, progressing to assistant director in 1905, a position she held until her retirement in 1934. Her laboratory was known for the number of women in it as well as for its smooth organization. Between 1894 and 1896, Williams studied the bacteriology of streptococcal and bacterial infections. She went to the Pasteur Institute in Paris to continue her search for a scarlet fever toxin in 1896, where she studied

with Alexander Marmorek. Through a series of studies on streptococci, she determined that several toxins were involved in streptococcal infections. She wrote a definitive monograph on the subject in 1932. During this same European trip, she worked with Emile Duclaux and Alexander Marmorek to improve upon the diagnosis of rabies and the preparation of a vaccine. She returned with the first culture of the rabies vaccine virus, and produced enough vaccine from this culture to vaccinate fifteen people. After her initial work, the United States became involved in large-scale production of this vaccine. Still it was difficult to diagnose rabid animals early enough so that the vaccine was effective. Williams discovered that the brain cells of rabid animals had a peculiar structure, but she was preempted by an Italian physician, Adelchi Negri, who also discovered the cells and published first. These cells became known as "Negri bodies." Williams did publish a new method of preparing and staining brain tissue that could detect Negri bodies in only minutes.

Williams worked with others on many other public health problems, including influenza, venereal diseases, pneumonia, meningitis, smallpox, and poliomyelitis. She studied trachoma, a chronic inflammatory eye infection, and discovered that many diagnoses of trachoma among schoolchildren were actually other, less damaging eye diseases.

Williams was forced to retire in 1934 by Mayor Fiorello La Guardia, obsessed by maintaining age limitations. She lived in Woodcliff Lake, New Jersey, for ten years and then moved to Westwood, where she lived with her sister Amelia Wilson. She died of heart failure in 1954.

An active participant in professional organizations, Williams was a member of the American Medical Association, the Society of American Bacteriologists, the New York Pathological Society, the Society of Experimental Biology, the American Association of Immunologists, the American Social Hygiene Association, and the New York Academy of Medicine. She held numerous high elective offices in professional organizations.   JH/MBO

PRIMARY SOURCES

Williams, Anna. "Persistence of Varieties of the Bacillus Diptheriae and of Diphtheria-like Bacilli." *Journal of Medical Research* (June 1902): 83–108.

———. "Reports of Studies of the Etiology of Vaccinia and Variola." *New York University Bulletin of Medical Science* 2, no. 4 (1902): 145–159.

———. With William Hallock Park. *Pathogenic Micro-organisms, Including Bacteria and Protozoa: A Practical Manual for Students, Physicians and Health Officers.* New York: Lea Brothers and Co., 1905.

———. "The Etiology and Diagnosis of Hydrophobia." *Journal of Infectious Disease* 3, no. 3 (1906): 452–458.

———. *Streptococci in Relation to Man in Health and Disease.* Baltimore: Williams and Wilkins, 1932.

———. Papers, 1846–1950s (inclusive), 1884–1954 (bulk), Schlesinger Library, Radcliffe College. Includes manuscript and typescript drafts, correspondence, notes and some printed material used in compiling her unpublished autobiography, a journal (1884–1887), letters, short stories by Williams, photographs, and more.

SECONDARY SOURCES
Dr. Anna W. Williams." *Medical Woman's Journal* 43 (June 1936): 160.

STANDARD SOURCES
Bailey; Lovejoy; *NAW*(M) (article by Elizabeth D. Robinton); *Notable;* Shearer and Shearer 1996; Siegel and Finley; Vare and Ptacek.

WILLIAMS, CICELY DELPHINE (1893–?)

British public health physician. Educated at Oxford and London. Professional experience: Colonial Medical Service, Gold Coast (Ghana) (seven years); College of Medicine, Singapore, Malaya, lecturer in pediatrics (twelve years); Malaysian government, senior specialist in child health; Child Health Department, Institute of Social Medicine, Oxford University, head; World Health Organization, head of the maternal and child health section (1948–1951); University of London, senior lecturer in nutrition (1953–1955); Family Planning Association, advisor to the training program (1964–1967). Death date unknown.

During her service in Ghana, Williams became the first person to describe the disease kwashiorkor (severe malnutrition in infants and children caused by protein deficiency). This disease is common in Africa in newly weaned children, who, for the first years of their lives, receive sufficient protein from breast milk but whose diet thereafter consists almost entirely of carbohydrates. JH/MBO

PRIMARY SOURCES
Williams, Cicely D. *Kwashiorkor: A Nutritional Disease of Children Associated with a Maize Diet.* Lancet 2, no. 5855 (16 November 1935).

———. *Population Problems in Developing Countries.* London: International Planned Parenthood Federation, 1970.

———. With Derrick B. Jelliffe. *Mother and Child Health: Delivering the Services.* London and New York: Oxford University Press, 1972.

SECONDARY SOURCES
Dally, Ann. *Cicely: The Story of a Doctor.* London: Gollancz, 1968.

STANDARD SOURCES
Uglow 1989.

WILLIAMS, MARGUERITE (THOMAS) (1895–?)

U.S. geologist and geographer. Born 24 December 1895 in Washington, D.C. Educated Howard University (A.B., 1923); Columbia University (A.M., 1930); Clark University (1933–1934); Catholic University (Ph.D., 1942). Professional experience: Washington, D.C., elementary schools, teacher (1916–1923); Miner Normal School, teacher (1923–1929); Miner Teachers College, chairman division of geography (from 1929), assistant professor of geography (1943–1946), associate professor (from 1946). Memberships: American Academy; Association of Geographers, Fellow; Academy of Political and Social Sciences. Death date unknown.

After teaching for seven years in Washington, D.C., elementary schools before she earned her bachelor's degree from Howard University, Marguerite Williams spent time in New York City working on a master's degree, and attended Clark University for a year. She returned to Washington, D.C., and earned her doctorate in geology from Catholic University. Before going to Clark she taught at Miner Normal School and in 1929 became chair of the Division of Geography. She remained at Miner for the remainder of her career, advancing to associate professor. During the summers from 1919 to 1925, she taught at North Carolina Teachers College in Winston-Salem, and from 1943 to 1944 was a teacher at the Army Specialized Training Program at Howard. Her research was on physical and economic geography, erosion, and conservation. JH/MBO

PRIMARY SOURCES
Williams, Marguerite Thomas. *A History of Erosion in the Anacostia Drainage Basin.* Washington, D.C.: The Catholic University of America Press, 1942.

STANDARD SOURCES
AMS 8, S&B 9–10; Rossiter 1995.

WILLMOTT, ELLEN ANN (1858–1934)

British horticulturist. Born 19 August 1858 in Isleworth, Middlesex. Honors and memberships: Linnean Society, Fellow (1904). Died 27 September 1934 in Brentwood, Essex.

Ellen Ann Willmott established gardens at Warley Place in Essex, Aix-les-Bains, and on the Riviera. She was elected a Fellow of the Linnean Society in 1904. The plant *Ceratostigma willmottianum Stapf* is named after her. The herbarium Warleyense is at Kew. JH/MBO

PRIMARY SOURCES

Willmott, Ellen Ann. *Warley Garden in Spring and Summer 1909.* London: B. Quavitch, 1909. This book was commissioned by Alfred Parsons to illustrate the genus *Rosa* and the text was by J. G. Baker.

———. *The Genus Rosa.* London: John Murray, 1914.

SECONDARY SOURCES

Kew Bulletin (1934): 397–398. Obituary notice.

Nature 134 (1934): 726. Obituary notice.

Proceedings of the Linnean Society (1934–1935): 195–197. Obituary notice.

STANDARD SOURCES

Desmond.

WILSON, ALICE EVELYN (1881–1964)

Canadian invertebrate paleontologist and stratigrapher. Born 26 August 1881 in Cobourg, Ontario. Two brothers, Alfred and Norman. Never married. Educated University of Toronto (B.A., 1911); University of Chicago (Ph.D., 1929). Professional experience: Geological Survey of Canada, researcher (1909–1946); Carleton University, Ottawa, lecturer (1948–1958). University of Toronto's Museum of Mineralogy, assistant; Geological Survey of Canada, clerk to the invertebrate paleontology section, assistant paleontologist, assistant geologist (1936), associate geologist (1940). Honors and memberships: Royal Society of Canada, Fellow; Geological Society of America, Fellow; Carleton University, honorary doctorate; Member of the Order of the British Empire. Died 15 April 1964.

Alice Wilson, the first woman to be employed professionally by the Geological Survey of Canada, came from an intellectually gifted family. Her father, John Wilson, was professor of classics at Victoria University, and her two brothers were recognized in their respective fields, geology and mathematics. The family enjoyed outdoor activities, and as a child Alice and her brothers collected fossils and minerals. Alice's interest in paleontology sprung from these early experiences. Often in poor health, Alice nevertheless entered the University of Toronto to study languages. She did not complete her degree, because in her last year she suffered a breakdown that necessitated a long convalescence.

After recovering from her illness, Wilson accepted a job as an assistant in the University of Toronto's Museum of Mineralogy. The experience that she had acquired made her eligible for a temporary position as clerk to the invertebrate paleontology section of the Geological Survey of Canada. This position involved cataloguing, arranging, and labeling collections in the new Victoria Memorial Museum. Wilson's language training bore fruit, for she was asked to translate materials from German. Her success in this venture prompted Percy Raymond to allow her to take a leave of absence from the survey (1910) so that she could take courses and complete her degree. When she returned in 1911 she was granted a permanent appointment at the survey.

At Raymond's urging, Wilson pursued her interest in the Ordovician sediments and fossils of the Ottawa valley. Her results were successful and she continued the research throughout her life. Encouraged again by Raymond, in 1913 Wilson published a description of a new species of brachiopods. Unfortunately for Wilson, Raymond left for Harvard University, leaving unhelpful and unsympathetic colleagues at the survey. Wilson routinely applied for leave to continue her academic work but was just as routinely refused. Not only did she have to concern herself with hostile colleagues but, after a fire destroyed the central block of the Parliament building, the Victoria Memorial Museum was sequestered to serve as the location for the wartime Parliament. After spending some time in wartime work, she returned in 1920 as assistant paleontologist when the survey was back in the Victoria Museum. In 1926, with the support of the Federation of University Women, Wilson again applied for academic leave. The new director, Edward M. Kindle, was supportive, and he encouraged her to take a leave of absence to work on her doctorate. She went to the University of Chicago, where she studied under Stuart Weller and, after his death, Carey Croneis. Her dissertation topic was the geology and paleontology of the district surrounding Cornwall, Ontario. When the St. Lawrence Seaway was being constructed, she served as an expert consultant.

Wilson should have been promoted upon receiving her doctoral degree. Instead, her promotions were very slow in coming, in spite of her accomplishments. She was upgraded to assistant geologist (geologists were considered to be higher on the scale than paleontologists) in 1936, the same year that she was elected a Fellow of the Geological Society of America. In 1938, she was elected a Fellow of the Royal Society of Canada. Wilson's second promotion, to associate geologist, came in 1940. There is some question as to whether she actually became a full geologist or not. Her duties involved reporting on all Paleozoic invertebrates (except those from the Devonian Period) submitted for examination. Even after she retired in 1946, she maintained an office at the survey and continued to work on her projects. Also following her retirement, she served as lecturer in paleontology at the newly opened Carleton University in Ottawa. Teaching, public lecturing, and working with children were among her favored activities.

Wilson contributed to knowledge of the stratigraphy of Ontario and Quebec and to Ordovician invertebrates of Ontario and Paleozoic invertebrate fossils throughout Canada.

She produced a reference collection of national type specimens of fossils. She authored many regional reports and pioneered studies in the Ordovician faunas of the Arctic and Rocky Mountains. She engaged in so-called reconnaissance paleontology, surveying the fossils found in the most important rocks. She produced over fifty publications in her field. Her contributions to the then "masculine" science of geology were many, and were accomplished against great odds. When she was asked to explain the male-female equation in geology, she replied: "If you meet a stone wall you don't pit yourself against it, you go around it and find a weakness. And as with other problems, when you look at it in these terms, then you don't get so personally involved." (Meadowcroft, 219).

She amassed many honors, including an honorary doctor of laws degree from Carleton University. She also was the first woman to be elected a Fellow of the Royal Society of Canada. In 1935 she was made a Member of the Order of British Empire.   JH/MBO

PRIMARY SOURCES

Wilson, Alice. "A New Genus and a New Species of Gastropod from the Upper Ordovician of British Columbia." *Canadian Field Naturalist* 38 (1924): 150–151.

———. "The Geology of the Cornwall District, Ontario." Ph.D. diss. University of Chicago, 1929.

———. "Brachiopoda of the Ottawa Formation of the Ottawa–Saint Lawrence Lowland." *Bulletin of the Geological Survey of Canada* 8 (1946).

———. "Trilobita of the Ottawa Formation of the Ottawa–St. Lawrence Lowland." *Bulletin of the Geological Survey of Canada* (1947): 9.

———. *The Earth Beneath Our Feet.* Toronto: Macmillan, 1947.

———. "Gastropoda and Conularida of the Ottawa Formation of the Ottawa–Saint Lawrence Lowland." *Bulletin of the Geological Survey of Canada* 17 (1951).

———. "A Guide to the Geology of the Ottawa district [Ontario-Quebec]." *Canadian Field Naturalist* (1956): 70.

SECONDARY SOURCES

Jones, Debbie. "Canada's First Woman Geologist." *Earth Science* 28, no. 6 (1975): 292.

McKenzie, G. D. "Wilson, Alice Evelyn (1881–1964)." In *Biographies of Geologists: Materials for the Study of the History of Geology, Prepared in Geology 851, a Seminar in the History of Geology.* Fourth Supplement, ed. Auréle La Roque. Columbus: Ohio State University Dept. of Geology. 13 pages.

Russell, Loris S. "Alice Evelyn Wilson 1881–1964." *Canadian Field Naturalist* 79 (1965): 159–161.

Sinclair, G. W. "Memorial to Alice E. Wilson (1881–1964)." *Bulletin of the Geological Society of America* 77, no. 11 (1966): 215–218.

———. "Memorial to Alice Evelyn Wilson 1881–1964." *Minutes of the Proceedings of the Royal Society of Canada* 16 (1965): 127–128.

STANDARD SOURCES

Ainley (article by B. Meadowcroft); O'Neill; Rossiter 1982; Sarjeant.

WILSON, APHRA PHYLLIS (ca. 1896–1976)

British botanist. Educated Imperial College, London. Professional experience: Swanley Horticultural College, plant pathologist (from 1922); helped establish Lenton Research Station (1936). Died 1976.

Aphra Wilson was a plant pathologist who was educated at Imperial College, London, and who was a plant pathologist at the Swanley Horticultural College.   JH/MBO

PRIMARY SOURCES

Boylesve, René. *A Gentlewoman of France,* trans. Aphra Wilson. New York: Brentano's, [1916].

STANDARD SOURCES

Desmond.

WILSON, EDITH (1896–?)

U.S. chemist. Educated Northwestern University (A.B., 1919); Iowa State College (M.S., 1922); Johns Hopkins University (Ph.D., 1928). Professional experience: Experimental Station, Iowa State College, research chemist (1920–1922); Johns Hopkins, assistant (1928–1929); Edgewood Arsenal, research chemist (1929–1930); Universal Oil Products Co., Chicago (1934–1935); Bloodgood Cancer Research Fund, Hopkins Hospital (1938–1940); Francis P. Garvan Cancer Research Fund, Johns Hopkins School of Medicine, researcher (1940–1942); Franklin Institute, Biochemical Research Foundation (1942–). Death date unknown.

After Edith Wilson earned her doctorate from Johns Hopkins University, she had several short-term positions. Like many women of science in the mid-twentieth century, she had an excellent education, but did not find a permanent position for many years. Her research area was physico-organic chemistry.   JH/MBO

STANDARD SOURCES

AMS 7.

WILSON, FIAMMETTA WORTHINGTON (1864–1920)

British astronomer. Born 1864 in Lowestoft to Helen (Till) and F. S. Worthington. Married S. A. Wilson. Educated by governesses; attended schools in Switzerland and Germany; musical study in Italy. Professional experience: Guildhall School of Music, teacher, orchestra conductor. Died 1920.

Although Fiammetta Wilson's father was a physician, his real interest was natural science. After he retired from practice he spent his time in microscopical studies and encouraged Fiammetta to learn about her natural surroundings. She became a proficient linguist and spent four years in Lausanne and one year in a school in Germany. Although she was trained as a musician, she became interested in astronomy after attending a series of lectures by astrophysicist Alfred Fowler in 1910. She joined the British Astronomical Association and became an enthusiastic observer of meteors, the aurora borealis, the zodiacal light, and comets. In July 1920 she was appointed to the E. C. Pickering Fellowship, a one-year research position established at the Harvard College Observatory in 1916. However, she died the same month that the fellowship was announced and never knew of the honor.

Wilson was acting director, with A. Grace Cook, of the Meteor Section of the British Astronomical Society. Between 1910 and 1920 she observed more than ten thousand meteors, and she discovered Westphal's Comet at its return in 1913. She published several papers and was elected a Fellow of the Royal Astronomical Society in 1916.   JH/MBO

PRIMARY SOURCES

Wilson, Fiametta Worthington. "The Meteoric Shower of January." *Monthly Notices of the Royal Astronomical Society* 78 (January 1918): 198–199.

SECONDARY SOURCES

Cook, A. Grace. *Journal of the British Astronomical Association* 30 (1920): 330–331. Obituary notice.

Denning, W. F. *Monthly Notices of the Royal Astronomical Society* 81 (1921): 266–269. Obituary notice.

Kidwell, Peggy Aldrich. "Women Astronomers in Britain, 1780–1930." *Isis* 75 (September 1984): 534–546.

WILSON, HILDA E. (1899–1968)

Scottish biologist. Born 1899 in Fordyce, Banffshire. Educated Aberdeen University. Professional experience: Banff Academy (until retirement in ca. 1961). Died 1968.

Hilda Wilson was a biology teacher who collected mosses and lichens in Scotland.   JH/MBO

SECONDARY SOURCES

Transactions of the Botanical Society of Edinburgh (1974): 173–179.

STANDARD SOURCES

Desmond.

WILSON, IRENE MOSSOM (1904–)

British botanist. Born 10 May 1904 in Broach, India, to Mossom (Thomson) and Robert Wilson. Educated University of London (B.Sc., 1928; M.Sc., 1931; Ph.D., 1937; D.Sc., 1963). Professional experience: University of Wales, Aberystwyth (from 1935), reader in botany (from 1965).

Irene Mossom Wilson was primarily a mycologist who worked on the cytology and development of fungi. She also published on rust diseases.   JH/MBO

PRIMARY SOURCES

Wilson, Irene M. "Marine Fungi: A Review of the Present Position." *Proceedings of the Linnean Society of London* 171 (1960): 53–70.

———. With D.F. Walshaw and J. Walker. "The New Groundsel Rust in Britain and Its Relationship to Certain Australasian Rusts." *Transactions of the British Mycological Society* 48 (1965): 501–511.

STANDARD SOURCES

Debus.

WILSON, LOUISE (PALMER) (1903–)

U.S. zoologist. Born 26 June 1903 in Mineola, Kans. Educated Southwestern College, Winfield, Kans. (A.B., 1925); University of Pennsylvania (M.A., 1930; Ph.D., 1936). Professional experience: New Jersey State Normal College, Glassboro, N.J., instructor (1930–1931); Bureau of Fisheries, assistant biologist (1931–1933); Wellesley College, instructor in zoology (1934–1939), assistant professor (1939–1945), associate professor (1945–1954), professor (1954–1968). Retired 1968. Honors and memberships: Society of Zoologists, New York Academy of Sciences, American Association for the Advancement of Science, Society for Developmental Biology, Cancer Society, Physiological Society.

From Kansas where she was born, educated, and earned her bachelor's degree, Louise Wilson moved east, where she received two advanced degrees from the University of Pennsylvania. While she was working on her doctoral degree, she worked for the bureau of fisheries. Two years before she completed this degree she moved to Wellesley College as an instructor in zoology. She remained at this rank for five years (during which time she got the degree) and then continued up the academic ladder to professor.

Her research interests involved problems in general physiology. Her early research stressed factors in growth and the effect of protein constituents on the growth of *Drosophila melanogaster*. She later became specifically interested in the natural history of the starfish, marine surveys, and ionic effects on *Arbacia*. Neural control of appetite in lower vertebrates also interested her. She was a member of the Society of Zoologists, the New York Academy of Sciences, the American Association for the Advancement of Science, Society for Developmental Biology, the Cancer Society, and the Physiological Society. JH/MBO

STANDARD SOURCES
AMS 6–8, B9, P&B 10–11.

WILSON, LUCY (1888–1980)

U.S. physicist. Born 19 October 1888 in Bloomington, Ill. to Lucy Barron (White) and John James Speed Wilson, Jr. Educated Wellesley College (A.B., 1909); Johns Hopkins, fellow (1916–1917; Ph.D., 1917). Professional experience: Mount Holyoke College, assistant in physics (1909–1911), instructor (1911–1914); Wellesley College, instructor, physics and psychology (1917–1920), assistant professor of physics (1920–1924), associate professor (1924–1935), professor (1935–1954), acting dean of college (1938–1939), dean of students (1939–1954). Retired 1954. Honors and memberships: Physical Society, Optical Society, Metrology Society, member; University of Manchester, fellow (1924); MIT, fellow (1935); Sarah Frances Whiting Professor, Wellesley College (1945); Lucy Wilson Scholarship Fund established in her name, Wellesley College (1954). Died 22 September 1980 in Wellesley.

Lucy Wilson was known from research on theories of vision, optics in pure physics, and X-ray spectroscopy. Wilson was hired first as an assistant in physics and then as an instructor at Mount Holyoke after she earned her bachelor's degree from Wellesley. She left this position to work on her doctorate and after she received it accepted an appointment in physics and psychology at Wellesley. Because her work involved both perception and optics, the combination worked well for her. She rose through the ranks to professor in 1935, and held administrative positions from 1938.

Wilson was the first dean of students at Wellesley College, and was revered in that capacity; she also continued as a member of the physics department. She was named to a professorship established in the physics department in honor of the Wellesley physicist and astronomer Sarah Frances Whiting. On her retirement in 1954, a scholarship fund was established in her name by the senior class. JH/MBO

PRIMARY SOURCES
Wilson, Lucy. "The Structure of the Mercury Line, [Gamma] 2536." *Astrophysical Journal* 46, no. 5 (1917): 340–354.

STANDARD SOURCES
AMS 3–8, P 9; Bailey; Kass-Simon and Farnes; Rossiter 1982; *WW in America* 1950–1951.

WILSON, LUCY LANGDON (WILLIAMS) (1864–1937)

U.S. biologist, anthropologist, science writer. Married. One son, David. Educated State Normal School, Vt. (1878); State Normal School, Philadelphia (1881); University of Pennsylvania (Ph.D., 1897); Cornell University; University of Chicago; Harvard University; Woods Hole Marine Biological Laboratory. Professional experience: public school teacher and principal (1882–1934); Temple University, lecturer in education (1934–1936). Honors and memberships: Paris Exposition, gold medal (1900); Anthropological Association; the American Geographical Society; American Association for the Advancement of Science. Died 1937.

Lucy L. Wilson was known for her use of laboratory methods for teaching natural science to elementary school children. She attended two normal schools and then taught school and was a principal. She earned her doctorate from the University of Pennsylvania, and did postdoctoral studies at several universities. She studied teaching methods in Europe and South America and lectured at seminars and congresses. After she retired, she became a lecturer at Temple University.

Although she listed herself as a biologist in the first edition of *American Men of Science*, she referred to herself as an anthropologist and geographer in the second through fifth editions. Wilson wrote eight books describing her educational methods. She conducted research on anthropogeography and American archeology. JH/MBO

PRIMARY SOURCES
Wilson, Lucy Langdon Williams. *Nature Study in Elementary Schools: First Reader.* New York: Macmillan, 1899.
———. *Handbook of Domestic Science and Household Arts: for Use in Elementary Schools.* New York: Macmillan, [ca. 1900].
———. *The New Schools of New Russia.* New York: Vanguard Press, [1928].

STANDARD SOURCES
AMS 1–5; Bailey.

WILSON, MABEL FLOREY (1906–)

U.S. chemist. Born 17 March 1906 in Omaha, Neb. Educated Buena Vista College (B.S., 1927); Michigan State College (M.A.,

1930; Ph.D. in physical chemistry, 1937). Married 1929. Two children. Professional experience: high schools in Iowa, teacher (1928–1929); Michigan State College, laboratory assistant (1935–1936); Burgess Labs, spectral analyst (1937–1938); Diamond Alkali Co., spectroscopist (1938–1944), senior research chemist (1944–1952); Air Reduction Co., Inc., Research Laboratory, senior spectroscopist (1952–1956), head instrument analysis section (1956–1962); Allied Chemical Corporation, group leader, plastics research (from 1962).

Married with two children, Mabel Wilson chose to follow her career as a physical chemist in industry rather than in academia. Consequently, much of her work was in applied chemistry. Her first research was in emission spectroscopy in trace metals in organics and polymers. She later worked with infrared, ultraviolet, and X-ray diffraction evaluation of polymers and resins. She was a member of the Chemical Society, the Society for Applied Spectroscopy, and the Society for Tests and Materials.

JH/MBO

STANDARD SOURCES
AMS 8, P 9; P&B 10–14.

WILSON, MAY GEORGIANA (1891–?)

U.S. pediatrician. Born 1 July 1991. Educated Cornell (M.D., 1911). Professional experience: Cornell University Medical School, instructor in clinical pediatrics (1912–1926), associate (1927–1930), assistant professor (1931–1941), associate professor (from 1941). Death date unknown.

May Georgiana Wilson got her medical degree at Cornell and then continued to work at that institution. She worked with heart disease in children, especially the etiology, epidemiology, diagnosis, and prognosis of rheumatic fever. She was a member of the American Medical Association, the Society for Pediatric Research, the Rheumatism Association, the American Heart Association, the New York Academy of Medicine, and the New York Heart Association.

JH/MBO

STANDARD SOURCES
AMS 7–8, B 9, P&B 10–11.

WILSON, MONICA HUNTER (1908–1982)

South African anthropologist and ethnographer. Born 3 January 1908 in the village of Lovedale in eastern South Africa to Jessie (McGregor) and David Alexander Hunter. Married Godfrey Wilson (1935). Two children. Educated Lovedale Mission School; Collegiate School for Girls in Port Elizabeth; Girton College, Cambridge (B.A. with honors, 1930); Cambridge University (Ph.D., 1934).

Professional experience: field work among the Pondo in the Eastern Cape (now the Transkei); Rockefeller Fellow (1935–1938); research in Northern Rhodesia (1938–1940?); University College of Fort Hare in the Eastern Cape, lecturer and warden of women students (1940?-1947?); Rhodes University College, faculty (1947–1952); University of Capetown, professor (1952–1973). Honors and memberships: Frazer Lecture (1959); Scott Holland Lectures at Cambridge (1971); honorary doctorates from the universities of Rhodes, York, and Witwatersrand; honorary fellowships from the Royal Anthropological Association and the American Anthropological Association; Girton College, Cambridge, honorary fellow; Royal Society of Southern Africa, Fellow; Rivers Medal for Fieldwork (1952); Simon Biesheuvel Medal for Research (1969). Died 1982 at home on her family estate in the Eastern Cape of cancer.

Monica Hunter Wilson was born to South African missionary parents who were tolerant of racial diversity. Her first school, the Lovedale Mission School, was unusual in South Africa, for it admitted both black and white students. For her university training she went to Girton College, Cambridge, where she read history. At that time she realized that South African history was written from a white standpoint and was totally lacking in information about black life. After she took her honors bachelor's degree, she returned to the Eastern Cape and did field work among the Pondo. Hunter had an advantage because she had learned their language, Xhosa, as a child. Returning to Cambridge, she worked on her doctoral degree.

The year after she received this degree, she married another anthropologist, Godfrey Wilson. Both became Rockefeller Fellows and participated in the Foundation's project for studying the impact of Western culture on African societies. Before they left for East Africa to do field work, they were a part of the Malinowski seminar at the London School of Economics. It is interesting that in their almost five years of field work when they compared notes they found that it was not unusual for them to have very different notes on the same event. Monica Wilson interpreted these differences as gender biases.

When Godfrey got a position as the first director of the Rhodes-Livingstone Institute for Social Research, the couple moved to Northern Rhodesia. During this time they produced a number of important papers and wrote their monograph *The Analysis of Social Change*, in which they stressed the concept of scale in attempting to understand change in African societies.

When World War II erupted, the Wilsons and their two small children left Northern Rhodesia and returned to South Africa. However, Godfrey died in 1944, and Monica became a single mother without a job. She was dismayed at gender inequalities in salary when she finally did get a job at the University College of Fort Hare. Finding a better position at

Rhodes University College, she was still making less money than her male colleagues. Leaving her full professorship at Rhodes, she moved to the University of Capetown, where wage discrimination was not a problem. She became the first woman appointed to a full professorship. For a time, she also served as dean of the Faculty of Arts and as head of the department where she remained until retirement in 1973.

Monica Wilson was interested in change as a theme, and in her monograph *Reaction to Conquest,* she included sections on life in reserves, farms, and towns. She also produced an early study on African urban life. During the 1950s, Monica's international reputation increased as her writings on the Nyakyusa people came out, including works that she done with Godfrey. The Nyakyusa corpus established her as an expert in the field of the study of religious practice and ritual.

In the middle 1960s, Wilson edited a two-volume work, the *Oxford History of South Africa,* often recognized as the summit of liberal historical scholarship in South Africa. One of the most important characteristics of Wilson's work was its interdisciplinary character. She drew from many different disciplines to make her points. Wilson also had many distinguished students.

Wilson was always aware of racial and gender inequalities, and she did what she could to improve the situation. In 1973, she retired to her family estate and died of cancer there nine years later. ЈН/МВО

PRIMARY SOURCES

Wilson, Monica Hunter. "Results of Culture Contact on the Pondo and Xosa Farmily." *South African Journal of Science* 29 (1932).

————. With Godfrey Wilson. *The Analysis of Social Change.* Cambridge: Cambridge University Press, 1945.

————. "Nyakyusa Age-Villages." *Journal of the Royal Anthropological Institute* 79 (1949): 21–25.

————. "Nyakyusa Kinship." In *African Systems of Kinship and Marriage,* ed. A. R. Radcliffe-Brown and D. Forde, 111–139. London: Oxford University Press, 1950.

————. *Good Company: A Study of Nyakyusa Age-Villages.* London: Published for the International African Institute by the Oxford University Press, 1951.

————. *Communal Rituals of the Nyakyusa.* London: Oxford University Press, 1959.

————. *Divine Kings and the "Breath of Men."* Cambridge: University Press, 1959.

————. With Archie Mafeje. *Langa: A Study of Social Groups in an African Township.* Cape Town: Oxford University Press, 1963.

————. With Godrey Wilson. "Scale." In *Beyond the Frontier: Social Process and Cultural Change,* ed. Paul Bohannan and Fred Plog, 239–253. New York: Natural History Press, 1967.

————, ed. With Leonard Thompson. *The Oxford History of South Africa.* 2 vols. Oxford: Clarendon Press, 1969 and 1971. Wilson was also a contributor.

SECONDARY SOURCES

Brokensha, D. "Monica Wilson 1908–1982." *Africa* 53 (1983): 3.

Richards, A. "Monica Wilson: An Appreciation." In *Religion and Social Change in Southern Africa: Essays in Honour of Monica Wilson,* ed. M. G. Whisson and M. E. West, 1–13. Cape Town and London: David Philip and Rex Collins, 1975.

West, M. E. "Monica Hunter Wilson: A Memoir." *Transactions of the Royal Society of South Africa* 45 (1984): 2.

STANDARD SOURCES

Gacs (article by Martin E. West).

WINLOCK, ANNA (1857–1904)

U.S. astronomer. Born in Cambridge, Mass., to Isabella (Lane) and Joseph Winlock. Never married. Harvard College Observatory, staff member (1875–1904). Died 1904.

The elder daughter of Joseph Winlock, the third director of the Harvard College Observatory, Anna Winlock was interested in her father's work from an early age and demonstrated an ability in mathematics. When she was twelve years old (1869), she accompanied her father on a solar eclipse expedition to Kentucky. Soon after Anna graduated from high school, Joseph Winlock died (June 1875). With no higher education, Anna Winlock attempted to follow in her father's footsteps. She became the first female paid staff member of the observatory, remaining at this institution until her death.

Much of Winlock's work was simply tedious computation connected with meridian circle observations; however, she also made some independent observations. The Harvard Observatory had joined with a number of foreign observatories in a project for preparing a comprehensive star catalogue. For this project the sky was divided into sections or zones by circles parallel to the celestial equator. Winlock began to work on the Cambridge zone while still a schoolgirl and continued after joining the Harvard Observatory staff. Her immediate supervisor was William Rogers, who was immediately responsible for the project. Although assistants came and went during the tedious preparation of the catalogue, Winlock remained. Before it was completed Rogers regarded her as a colleague rather than an assistant. The Cambridge zone became a part of the catalogue of the *Astronomischer Gesellschaft.*

Winlock's work on this catalogue occupied most of her life. However, she also aided in other research at the observatory. This work included the supervision of the preparation of a table (published in volume 38 of the Observatory *An-*

nals) that contains the positions of variable stars in clusters and of their comparison stars. She calculated the path of the asteroid Eros, and computed its circular orbit. She also computed a circular orbit for the asteroid Ocllo and later assisted in determining its elliptical elements. Winlock's most important independent investigations involved her study of stars close to the North and South Poles. A catalogue of these stars was published in volume 17, parts 9 and 10, of the *Annals* and was at that time the most complete catalogue of the stars near the poles ever assembled.

A self-taught mathematical astronomer, Anna Winlock argued convincingly that astronomy would do well to use the untapped skills of women. With little formal education she became an indispensable, if little rewarded, member of the team at the Harvard Observatory. JH/MBO

PRIMARY SOURCES

Rogers, William, and Anna Winlock. "A Catalogue of 130 Polar Stars for the Epoch of 1875. Resulting from All the Available Observations Made between 1860 and 1885 and Reduced to the System of the Catalogue of Publication 14 of the *Astronomische Gesellschaft*." *Memoirs of the American Academy of Arts and Science* n.s. 2 (1846): 227–299.

SECONDARY SOURCES

Byrd, Mary E. "Anna Winlock." *Popular Astronomy* (1904): 254–258. Short biographical sketch of Winlock.

Pickering, Edward C. *Annals of the Harvard College Observatory* 53 (1904): 1. Brief obituary notice.

STANDARD SOURCES

Barr; Jones and Boyd; Mozans; Ogilvie 1986.

WINNER, DAME ALBERTINE (1907–1988)

British physician. Born 4 March 1907 in London to Annie and Isidore Winner. Educated Francis Holland School, Clarence Gate, London; University College, University of London (B.Sc. 1929; Bachelor of Medicine; University Gold Medal 1933; M.D., 1934). Professional experience: Elizabeth Garrett Anderson Hospital, honorary assistant physician (1937); Mother's Hospital, Clapton, honorary physician (1937); Royal Army Medical Corps, lieutenant-colonel (1940–1946); Ministry of Health, deputy chief medical officer (1947–1967); St. Christopher's Hospice, president and deputy medical director. Honors and memberships: Royal College of Surgeons (1932); Royal College of Physicians, licentiate (1932), Fellow (1959); Faculty of Community Medicine (1973); Order of the British Empire (1945); Dame Commander of the British Empire (1967); Queen's Honorary Physician (1965–1968); University College, London, fellow (1965); Royal College of Physicians (1967–1978). Died 13 May 1988 in London.

Although never a research physician, Albertine Winner, through her contributions to Britain's health service, became one of that country's most important physicians. She was born into a well-to-do Jewish family, attended University College, London, for all of her degrees, and had two honorary positions before she joined the Royal Army Medical Corps during World War II. Her military service presaged her later career, for it was in the military that she became an able administrator. From the military she moved into the Ministry of Health, during the time that the National Health Service was being established by Aneurin Bevan and the Labor Government. The basic idea was that everybody should have access to all necessary medical care. Winner was invited to lecture at the London School of Economics from 1951 to 1963, became a fellow Of University College in 1965, and Linacre Fellow of the Royal College of Physicians from 1967 to 1973.

One of her most important accomplishments was to help establish the hospice movement at the end of the 1960s. Whereas the health plan provided excellent care for those acutely ill, it was incapable of meeting the needs of the chronically ill or dying. The idea of hospices was strongly supported by Dame Cicely Saunders, who found an advocate in Winner. After she retired from the civil service she took a refresher clinical course so that she could work at the St. Christopher's Hospice, newly established in southeast London. She became deputy medical director, and her administrative skills were vital in the success of the hospice. She not only worked on the financial and military side of the hospice but was helpful to the medical team and had excellent relationships with the patients.

Dame Albertine Winner published many articles in *Lancet, Public Health*, and other journals. JH/MBO

PRIMARY SOURCES

Winner, Albertine. *The Specialised Health Visitor for the Handicapped Baby, Young Child, and School Child*. London: the Foundation, [1979].

STANDARD SOURCES

Annual Obituary 1988.

WINTHROP, HANNAH FAYERWEATHER TOLMAN (18th century)

U.S. astronomer.

Hannah Winthrop was an almanac writer. JH/MBO

PRIMARY SOURCES

Winthrop, Hannah. *Diaries, 1779–1789*. Mss. in Harvard Archives. Consists of a series of almanacs which are annotated and interrelated.

STANDARD SOURCES
Arnold.

WINTON, KATE GRACE (BARBER) (1882–?)

U.S. histologist. Born 9 October 1882 in Charleston, R.I. Educated Rhode Island State College (B.S., 1903); Yale University (Ph.D., 1906). Married Andrew Lincoln Winton (he died in 1946). Professional experience: Connecticut Experimental Station, microscopist (1906–1907); U.S. Department of Agriculture, microanalyst, Bureau of Chemistry (1907–1911). Death date unknown.

Kate Winton earned a doctoral degree from Yale University and then worked for the Connecticut Experimental Station and the U.S. Department of Agriculture. Her research interest was the histology of foods. JH/MBO

PRIMARY SOURCES
Barber, Kate G. With Andrew L. Winton. *The Structure and Composition of Foods.* 4 vols. New York: J. Wiley & Sons and London: Chapman & Hall, 1932–1939.
———. With Andrew L. Winton. *The Analysis of Foods.* New York: J. Wiley & Sons, London: Chapman & Hall, [1945].

STANDARD SOURCES
AMS 4–8, B 9.

WIPF, FRANCES LOUISE (1906–)

U.S. cytologist. Born 18 August 1906 in Iola, Wis. Educated Wisconsin State Teachers College (B.E., 1930); University of Wisconsin (Ph.M., 1933; Ph.D., 1939). Professional experience: Oshkosh State Teachers College, Wisconsin, assistant biologist (1930–1932); University of Wisconsin, research assistant veterinary science (1839–1943), genetics assistant (1943–1947), instructor (1947–1949), veterinary science, instructor (1949–1952), assistant professor (1955–1972).

Frances Wipf was a cytologist who worked on root nodules, fur farm animals, and cytogenetics. Assistant professor was the highest rank that she attained, even though she had a doctoral degree from the University of Wisconsin. She was a member of the American Association for the Advancement of Science, the Genetics Society, and the American Conference of Research Workers on Animal Diseases. JH/MBO

STANDARD SOURCES
AMS 7–9, P&B 10–14.

WITHERS, AUGUSTA INNES (BAKER) (1792–1869)

British botanical artist. Born 1792 probably in Lisson Grove, London. Professional experience: painter of flowers to Queen Adelaide (1830 or 1833); flower and fruit painter in ordinary to Queen Victoria (1864). Honors and memberships: Society of Lady Artists. Died 1869.

Augusta Withers was a botanical artist who exhibited her flower paintings at the Royal Academy from 1826 to 1846. She also exhibited in other galleries. She drew plants for the *Transactions of the Horitcultural Society of London, Curtis's Botanical Magazine, Floral Cabinet,* and the *Pomological Magazine.* She also illustrated J. Bateman's *Orchidaceae of Mexico* and R. Thompson's *Gardener's Assistant.* JH/MBO

PRIMARY SOURCES
Drawings are at the British Museum (Natural History); Royal Horticultural Society, and the Fitzwilliam Museum, Cambridge.

SECONDARY SOURCES
Blunt, W. *Art of Botanical Illustration* (1955): 216.
Gardener's Magazine (1831): 95; (1834): 452.

STANDARD SOURCES
Desmond.

WOILLARD-ROUCOUX, GENEVIÈVE MARIE-AURÉLIE (1948–1981)

Belgian palynologist. Born 16 April 1948. Married Pierre Roucoux. Educated Catholic University in Louvain (doctorate 1974). Died 7 July 1981.

Geneviève Woillard received her doctorate in botanical sciences. She studied under William Mullenders at the Catholic University in Louvain in 1974. She received this degree with "la plus grande distinction." She married Pierre Roucoux in 1974. Her first scientific paper was published when she was only eighteen years old and dealt with the subject of the use of antibiotics in fish tanks. From what began as a hobby, she moved into science. She showed much promise, but died of cancer when she was only thirty-three years old.

Woillard-Roucoux studied the Quaternary strata of Haute-sâone in France and Belgium. She produced twenty-eight publications. Her research demonstrated that the balmy climate of the last interglacial period came to an abrupt end. She demonstrated this by her research on the Grande Pile Peat Bog. She meticulously took samples one millimeter apart and was able to demonstrate a sudden displacement of the last interglacial period's hardwood forest by a pine-birch taiga.   CK/MBO

PRIMARY SOURCES

Woillard-Roucoux, Genevieve. "Recherches palynologiques sur le Pleistocene dans l'est de la Belgique et dans les Vosges Lorraines." *Acta Geographica Lovaniensia* 14 (1975).

———. "Vegetation et climat des derniers 140,000 ans dans le tourbiere de la Grande Pile (N.E. France)." In *Paleoecology of Africa and the Surrounding Islands.* Vol. 10, 1975–1977, ed. E. M. Bakker Van Zinderen, Sr. and J. A. Coetzee, 125–134. Rotterdam: A. A. Balkema, 1978.

———. "Grand Pile Peat Bog: a Continuous Pollen Record for the Last 140,000 Years." *Quaternary Research* 9 (1978): 1–21.

———. "Abrupt End of the Last Interglacial s.s. in Northeast France." *Nature* 181 no. 5732 (1979): 558–562.

———. With Willem G. Mook. "Carbon-14 Dates at Grand Pile: Correlation of Land and Sea Chronologies." *Science* 215, no. 4529 (1982): 159–161.

SECONDARY SOURCES

Kukla, George, and Alan Hecht. "In Memory of Geneviève Woillard-Roucoux." *Quaternary Research* 17, no. 2 (1982): 275.

Munaut, Andrè V. "Geneviève Woillard-Roucoux." *Newsletter for the International Commission for Palynology* 5, no. 2 (1982): 2.

STANDARD SOURCES

Debus; Sarjeant.

WOKER, GERTRUD JAN (1878–1968)

Swiss biochemist. Born 16 December 1878 in Bern to Elisabeth (Müller) and Philipp Woker. Two siblings. Never married. Educated Girls' Secondary School, Bern; secondary teacher's examination in mathematics and natural sciences; University of Bern (doctorate and gymnasium teacher's examination in chemistry, physics, and botany); University of Berlin, studied physical chemistry, toxicology, pharmacology, and biology; qualified to teach university (1907) and venia legendi (permission to lecture) in Bern. Professional experience: Bern, Girls' Secondary School, teacher; Free Gymnasium, Bern, teacher; Institute of Physical and Chemical Biology, faculty (1911), professor of biochemistry (1933). Died 13 September 1968 in Marin/Neuenburger See.

The Swiss journalist Emmy Moore, who caused a stir in the 1930s with her reports from the courtrooms, wrote a eulogy in 1968 for Gertrud Woker. Woker's books and other publications had influenced Moore as a young person in her choice of her career. She explained that the media had ig-

nored this great woman chemist, and wanted it known that the Swiss, like the Czechoslovakians, the Americans, the Poles, and the Russians, had their martyrs for spiritual freedom.

Clara Ragaz, the long-term president of the International Women's League for Peace and Freedom honored Woker in her greetings presented for the seventieth birthday of the chemistry professor. She praised Woker for putting her scientific knowledge to common use. She noted Woker's concern about modern war methods and the helplessness of the civilian population when confronted with various poisons. Since Gertrude Woker's research was not aimed at a special field or a career in the traditional chemical categories, her broadly based knowledge was first criticized for "unproven" hypotheses. She recognized that nature and natural sciences had been defamed through synthetic inventions. These events, she concluded, were masculine aberrations, and she called for a more ecologically friendly scientific thought.

In November 1924 the International Women's Commission against war, founded by Gertrude Woker and the Swedish chemist Naima Sahlbom, had several meetings in Berlin. The members decided to approach the representatives of the natural sciences of all countries to demand that they not allow their new ideas and inventions to be misused for war. They stressed that women scientists must take responsibility for future generations. It was to be made clear that once in the history of the world internationally organized women took up the fight against chemical and bacteriological warfare methods.

Woker's father, Philipp Woker, wrote a book on the financial dealings of the popes (*Das Finanzwesen der Päpste*) which landed on the Catholic Church's Index of forbidden books. He immigrated from Westphalia to Switzerland in 1874 in order to occupy the chair for church history in the newly founded old Catholic Faculty of the University of Bern. In Bern he soon asked for the hand of Johanna Müller, whose mother would be the real cultural center of the family. Although she was a musician and an artist, her real gift lay in politics. A very intelligent woman, she was determined to give all people their rights. In 1888 Woker's father was given the chair for general history in Bern.

When Gertrud, after graduating from the Girls' Secondary School, wanted to go to the gymnasium, her otherwise liberal father objected to her plans. Gertrud was sent to her uncle in Erfurt, the chief physician of the Catholic hospital, in order to learn cooking. However, she studied mathematics at night clandestinely with the brother of a fellow student. Woker became ill and her uncle, an excellent surgeon, diagnosed chlorosis and made her take iron. He finally sent the patient back to Switzerland where the first female doctor who practiced in Bern came to understand what the so-called chlorosis was: fatigue. This physician knew from her own experience that a young girl could overwork herself trying to fight for her studies.

After she obtained a doctorate and a gymnasium teacher's examination in chemistry, physics, and botany, her interest revolved around an interdisciplinary approach to science, especially in biochemistry. In August 1911 Woker was celebrated in the *Frankfurter Zeitung* as the first woman in Germany to whom was offered an extraordinary (adjunct) professorship. The Bern government promised her a position, but did not deliver. During World War I, the excuse was the financial situation of the state.

During World War I the cry of misery from the neighboring states resounded to the neutrals. One of the conclusions of the International Women's Protest Congress in the Hague was to send the resolutions of the women via personal delegations to the warring as well as the neutral governments. They wanted to counteract the idea that man controls the fate of the world and woman is only his handmaiden. The resolutions of the Hague Women's Congress, which were presented to the Swiss president through the good offices of Gertrud Woker, were later found in President Wilson's Fourteen Points.

In 1916 Woker was denied a professorship by a tie vote. At the women's conference for international understanding held in April 1918 in Bern, Woker, president of the initiative committee, gave the welcoming speech. She noted that it was unfortunate that other foreign governments misjudged the importance of the congress and refused passports to many women. In contrast, the Swiss government allowed the women use of the convention hall for the evening presentations.

Many ideas were presented at the conference. The women discussed the hereditary implications of poisonous gases and determined that effects of the poison gases would be inherited and could ultimately damage the race. While Paris was being shelled, the women discussed contemporary problems for an entire week. Themes such as abortion, forced motherhood, strikes against bearing children, and improper education principles were all discussed, as well as financial means for a pacifist education and ways of mediating understanding between people.

In 1925 Gertrud Woker was a guest of an institute in Morristown, Pa., which concerned itself with biological and biochemical metabolic diseases. Because of political persecution, she was forced to give up her scientific research after half a year.

In 1933, with the help of foreign pacifist colleagues, she was finally named a professor in Bern. Her scientific goal was to understand life events. Her personal fight during her entire life concerned the equal rights of women and peace and understanding between peoples through publications and enlighted oral communication.

In 1925 Woker's popular book *Der kommende Giftgaskrieg* (*The Coming of the Poison Gas War*, Leipzig, 1924) was banned. This book cannot be found today in any Berlin library. The National Socialist Student Association burned the book on a large pyre.

In 1953 Ralph E. Oesper suggested in the *Journal of Chemical Education* that in order to get a complete picture of Woker's important research, one need only to consult the indices of the most important biochemical journals. But because she generously allowed her doctoral students to be named as the sole or primary author of the published papers on which she advised, many works that are her intellectual property can be found in the literature under others' names.

In 1951 Woker summarized her decades-long biogenetic connections in a two-volume work *Die Chemie der natürlichen Alkaloide,* which was widely praised in pharmaceutical journals. She began to gain recognition as the first natural scientist to propose that efficacious medications can be constructed according to the building plans of plants.

In the late sixties, Woker suffered increasingly from a persecution complex which focused on a belief that she would be sent to Vietnam. She died in 1968. She left her small fortune to the pension funds of the International Women's League for Peace and Freedom.   GVL

PRIMARY SOURCES
Woker, Gertrud. *Die Katalyse.* 4 vols. Stuttgart: Verlag Ferdinand Enke, 1910–1931.
———. *Der kommende Giftgaskrieg.* Leipzig: Verlag Ernst Oldenburg, 1925.
———. "Aus meinem Leben/Kinderjahre." In *Führende Frauen Europas,* ed. Elga Kern. Munich: Verlag Ernst Reinhardt, 1928.
———. *Die Chemie der natürlichen Alkaloide-mit bes. Berücksichtigung ihrer Biogenese.* 2 vols. Stuttgart: Verlag Ferdinand Enke, 1953–1956.

SECONDARY SOURCES
Larsen, Majken. *Der Kampf der Frauen gegen die Hölle fon Gift und Feuer: Die IFFF, Gertrud Woker und die Giftgasdiskussion in der Schweiz der Zwischenkriegszeit.* Zurich: Lizentiatsarbeit Historical Seminar, 1995.
Leitner, Gerit v. "Frauenraum Naturwissenschaften? Clara Immerwahr und Gertrud Woker." In *Friedensentwürfe: Positionen von Querdenkern des 20. Jahrhunderts,* ed. Dieter Kinkelbur and Friedhelm Zubke, 47–69. Munster: Agenda, 1955.
———. *Sollen wir unsere Hände in Unschuld waschen? Die Chemikerin Gertrud Woker und die Geschichte der Frauenliga.* Bern: Efef, 1997.
Oesper, Ralph E. "Gertrud Woker." *Journal of Chemical Education* 30 (1953): 435 ff.

Perlin, Frida. *Der Kamp der Frauen gegen die Hölle von Gift und Feuer.* Stuttgart: IFFF/Gruppe Würtemberg-Druck Glaser & Sulz, 1927.

STANDARD SOURCES
Debus; *Lexikon der Frau;* Poggendorff, vol. 7a.

WOLF, KATHERINE (1907–)

Austrian/U.S. psychologist. Born 3 June 1907 in Vienna, Austria. Educated University of Vienna (Ph.D., 1930). Professional experience: University of Vienna, research associate (1930–1938); Jean J. Rousseau school, Geneva, instructor (1939–1941); New York, psychoanalytic research project, problems of infancy (1941–1949); Yale University Child Study Center, instructor of psychology (1949–1950), assistant professor (1950–1953), associate professor (from 1953).

Although she was born and educated in Austria, Katherine Wolf immigrated to the United States and, after several research positions, became an instructor of psychology at Yale University. She moved up the ranks to associate professor. She held concurrent positions as a consultant to the Bureau of Applied Social Research at Columbia from 1944 to 1946, and was the psychologist for the New York City schools in 1948. She later was visiting professor in the graduate school of City College from 1950 to 1952. Her research centered around personality research and child development.

JH/MBO

STANDARD SOURCES
AMS S&B 9, Rossiter 1982.

WOLLSTEIN, MARTHA (1868–1939)

U. S. pathologist and medical researcher. Born 21 November 1868 in New York City to Minna (Cohn) and Louis Wollstein. One brother. Educated Woman's Medical College of the New York Infirmary (M.D., 1889). Professional experience: Babies Hospital, New York City, intern (1890–1891), pathologist (1892–1902), pediatric pathologist (1903–1935); Rockefeller Institute, assistant pathologist (1903–1921). Honors and memberships: New York Academy of Science, head of pediatric section (1928); American Pediatric Society (first woman elected, 1930). Died 30 September 1930 at Mount Sinai Hospital in New York City.

Martha Wollstein proved herself to be a thorough and productive medical scientist, producing over eighty papers during her lifetime, but she is little known today. She was born in New York City to a Jewish German family; there are few records of her early life. At the age of eighteen she began her studies of medicine at the Woman's Medical College of the

New York Infirmary, where she studied with MARY PUTNAM JACOBI, who encouraged her to do research and with whom she published a paper on a myosarcoma of the uterus in 1902, her first and Putnam Jacobi's last publication. Upon graduation in 1890, she obtained a position as an intern at Babies Hospital in New York and remained there as pathologist and then pediatric pathologist for the following forty years. During the early years, she focused on studies of malaria, tuberculosis, and other contagious diseases such as typhoid fever. When Christian Herter privately financed a new laboratory of pathology, she was able to turn to experimental studies, locating a dysentery bacillus in the stools of thirty-seven infants suffering from infant diarrhea.

Simon Flexner, who had isolated the same dysentery bacillus in the Philippines, invited Wollstein to join his laboratory at the Rockefeller Institute as an assistant researcher in 1904. She continued to hold her position at Babies Hospital, but her link to the Rockefeller Institute allowed her to work with a number of important researchers, including Flexner himself. Her experiments with him to transmit polio to monkeys failed; her studies were extended later by Flexner and others. She also worked with Samuel Meltzer on a series of studies of pneumonia, trying to examine and classify different types of pneumonia caused by different organisms. Other studies that she made with Harold Amoss were on the preparation of antimeningitis sera, a study that included the development of criteria for standardization of sera.

Her work on mumps, published in the *Journal of the American Medical Association* in 1918, indicated that the disease was viral in nature, as suggested by her ability to transmit the disease using a filtrated preparation from mumps patients to cats and from cats to other cats. She did not make any special claims for her research, though, and others received credit in the 1930s for identifying the virus and transmitting it from humans to monkeys.

In her last year of laboratory work at the Rockefeller, in 1920, Wollstein began to examine and classify bacterophage discovered by Felix d'Herelle in 1907. Although she was the first scientist at the Rockefeller to call attention to the importance of phage, this work was also extended and completed by others, notably by Jacob Bronfenbrenner. In spite of her prolific and useful experimental work, Wollstein was never made a full member of the institute. In fact, during this period FLORENCE SABIN was the only woman to be appointed to a higher rank.

Returning full time to Babies Hospital, Wollstein turned back to research directly related to pediatric pathology, especially such problems as leukemia, influenzal meningitis, hemolytic jaundice, and various contagious diseases. Appreciated by her colleagues, she was named head of the pediatric section of the New York Academy of Medicine and became a member of the American Pediatric Society, the first woman member to be elected, in 1930.

Although she was said to be "difficult" to work with, a common complaint about strong-minded women, her publication record shows close collaboration with a wide range of colleagues, male and female. She was a quiet woman, however, considered shy, and had few friends. She retired in 1935 and moved to Grand Rapids, Michigan. When she fell ill, she returned to New York and died in Mount Sinai Hospital in 1939. Saul Benison has commented about the "paltry witness" at her funeral and in her obituary notices to her distinguished record of research in pediatric pathology.

JH/MBO

PRIMARY SOURCES

Wollstein, Martha. With Mary Putnam Jacobi. "A Case of Myosarcoma of the Uterus." *American Journal of Obstetrics* 45 (1902): 218.

———. "Parameningococcus and Its Antiserum." *Journal of Experimental Medicine* 20 (1 September 1914): 201–217.

———. "An Immunological Study of Bacillus Influenzae." *Journal of Experimental Medicine* 22 (1 October 1915): 445–456.

———. "An Experimental Study of Parotitis (Mumps)." *Journal of the American Medical Association* (24 August 1918).

———. With Ralph C. Spence. "A Study of Tuberculosis in Infants and Young Children." *American Journal of Diseases of Children* (January 1921).

———. "Studies on the Phenomenon of d'Herelle with Bacillus Dysenteriae." *Journal of Experimental Medicine* 34 (1 November 1921).

———. With Katherine Kreidel. "Familial Hemolytic Anemia of Childhood—Von Jaksch." *American Journal of Diseases of Children* (January 1930).

STANDARD SOURCES

AMS 3–6; Hurd-Mead 1933; *NAW* (article by Saul Benison).

WONG AH MAE (fl. early 20th century)

Chinese physician. Educated Toronto University (M.D. degree); practiced medicine in Nanking and Shanghai.

Wong Ah Mae spent fourteen years as assistant to Ellen C. Fullerton, director and chief surgeon of St. Elizabeth's Hospital, Shanghai. Wanting to become a doctor, Wong Ah Mae began medical coursework at age thirty-seven at Toronto University. After receiving her medical degree, she served at a hospital at Nanjing, then spent the remainder of her career as one of the leading women physicians of Shanghai.

JH/MBO

STANDARD SOURCES

Lovejoy.

WOOD, EMILY ELIZABETH (d. 1940)

British physician. Born to Elizabeth N. Nicolson and Arthur John Wood. Married Percy Flemming (1892). Four children, two sons, two daughters. Educated Girton College, Cambridge (Natural Science Tripos, Pt. I, cl. 1, 1882; Pt. II, cl. 2, 1884); University of London (M.B., 1891; M.D., 1892). Professional experience: Mount St. Leonard School, St. Andrews, science teacher (1884–1885); London School of Medicine for Women, demonstrator of anatomy; Royal Free Hospital, medical registrar; New Hospital for Women, pathologist and physician to children's department; Mission Hospital, Canning Town, pathologist and physician to children's department; Elizabeth Garrett Anderson Hospital, Euston Road, pathologist and physician. Died 1940.

Physician Emily Elizabeth Wood attended Girton College, Cambridge, where she earned a first-class pass on Part I of her Natural Science Tripos and a second-class pass on Part II. She then went to the University of London for her medical training, earning a bachelor's degree in 1891 and a doctor of medicine degree in the following year. In 1892 she also married Percy Flemming, an ophthalmic surgeon. The couple had four children. She held numerous positions as pathologist and physician in the children's department.   JH/MBO

STANDARD SOURCES

Girton.

WOOD, EMILY MARGARET (1865–1907)

British botanist. Born 23 August 1865 in Calcutta, India. Educated in England. Professional experience: Liverpool University, lectured on botany; drew plants. Died 28 October 1907 in Cheshire.

Although Emily Wood was born in India, when she was six years old she went to England. She lectured on botany at the University of Liverpool and made over eight hundred drawings of plants.   JH/MBO

PRIMARY SOURCES

Green, C. T. *Flora of the Liverpool District.* Liverpool: D. Marples & Co., 1902. Wood contributed to this work.

Atkinson, George Francis. *First Studies of Plant Life.* London: Ginn, [1905]. Wood revised this work.

SECONDARY SOURCES

Journal of Botany (1907): 454–455. Obituary notice.

Transactions of the Liverpool Botanical Society (1909): 108. Obituary notice.

Weekly Courier, 25 April 1908. Obituary notice.

STANDARD SOURCES
Desmond.

WOOD, ETHEL (1871–1946)
See Shakespear, Dame Ethel Mary.

WOOD, RUTH GOULDING (1874–?)
U.S. mathematician. Born 19 January 1875. Educated Smith College (B.L., 1898); Yale University (Ph.D., 1898); University of Göttingen (1908–1909). Professional experience: Mount Holyoke College, instructor in mathematics (1901–1902); Smith College, instructor (1902–1909), associate professor (1909–1914), professor (1914–1935), emerita professor (from 1935). Death date unknown.

Ruth Goulding Wood was an undergraduate at Smith College and then went to Yale University as a fellow. After one year, she accepted a position at Mount Holyoke College, but then returned to Yale where she completed her Ph.D. She returned to teach at Smith, where she moved up the academic ladder to full professor.

Wood was known for her work on non-Euclidean geometry. She spent a year at the University of Göttingen honing her skills in this area.   JH/MBO

STANDARD SOURCES
AMS 1–6; Bailey; Siegel and Finley.

WOODARD, HELEN (QUINCY) (1900–1993)
U.S. chemist. Born 8 August 1900 in Detroit, Mich. Educated Stetson (B.S., 1920); Columbia University (A.M., 1921; Ph.D., 1925). Professional experience: Memorial Center for Cancer and Allied Diseases, research chemist (Sloan-Kettering Cancer Center) (1926–1956), associate chemist (from 1956), associate (from 1960). Concurrent experience: Cornell University Medical College, assistant professor (1952–1964), associate professor (from 1964). Honors and memberships: American Association for the Advancement of Science; Chemical Society; Radiation Research Society; Health Physics Society. Died 1993.

Biochemist Helen Quincy Woodard was an authority on bone disease. After she received her doctorate from Columbia in 1925, she joined what became the Memorial Sloan-Kettering Cancer Center in Manhattan. She conducted important research in understanding and identifying cancers induced by environmental radiation.

In the 1940s, she published pioneering papers on radiation-induced osteogenic sarcomas in people who paint radium dials on watches. She worked as a consultant to the New York City Health Department for twenty years. She also was a consultant to the International Council on Radiation Units.

Woodard endowed the Woodard Fellowships at Columbia University, a fellowship at the New York University School of Environmental Medicine, and the John Laughlin Professorship at the Sloan-Kettering Center. She was an active member of the Nature Conservancy.   JH/MBO

SECONDARY SOURCES
New York Times, 11 June 1993. Obituary.

STANDARD SOURCES
AMS 4–8, P 8; P&B 10–14.

WOODBRIDGE, MARY EMILY (1876–?)
U.S. botanist. Born 16 February 1876 in Sarcoxie, Mo. Educated University of Illinois (A.B., 1908); University of Chicago (A.M., 1911). Professional experience: high school teacher (1912–1914); Texas State Department of Agriculture, seed analyst (1918–1926); New York Experimental Station, Geneva, research assistant (1926–1939). Retired 1940. Death date unknown.

Mary Emily Woodbridge studied botany first as an undergraduate at the University of Illinois and then continued to do a master's degree at the University of Chicago. Not finding a position immediately in botany, she began to teach high school science until she found a position as a seed analyst with the Texas state agricultural department. She remained in Texas until 1926, when she had the opportunity to serve as an assistant botanist in the New York Experimental Station in Geneva, New York, where she remained until her retirement in 1940.   JH/MBO

STANDARD SOURCES
AMS 6–8, B 9.

WOOD-LORZ, THELMA (RITTENHOUSE) (1900–)
U.S. zoologist. Born 30 March 1900 in Conshohocken, Pa. Married Albert Lorz. Educated Ursinus College (A.B., 1921); Brown University (A.M., 1932; Ph.D., 1938). Professional experience: high school teacher in New Jersey (1921–1924); Cold Spring Harbor, assistant in genetics (1924–1930); Brown University, assistant in biology (1930–1939).

Thelma Rittenhouse Wood-Lorz was born in Pennsylvania and received her bachelor's degree at a small college. After college she taught for four years in the public high schools of

New Jersey, after which she served as an assistant in genetics at Cold Spring Harbor, where much exciting work in the field was taking place. This work sparked her interest in science, and she returned to graduate work at Brown University in 1930, receiving a master's degree in 1932 and a doctorate six years later. During this period and for a year after, she served as an assistant in the biology department. During the summers from 1931 on she returned to Cold Spring Harbor as an associate to do research on the genetics and life history of members of the genus *Cladocera*. She also studied the one-celled microscopic organism, *Daphnia longispina*. Sometime during this period, she married Albert Lorz.   JH/MBO

PRIMARY SOURCES
Wood, Thelma R. With Arthur Mangun Banta. "Genetic Evidence That the Cladocera Male Is Diploid." *Science* 67 (1928): 18–19.
————. With Arthur Mangun Banta. "Inheritance in Parthenogenesis and in Sexual Reproduction in Cladocera." *Zeitschrift für induktive Abstammungs-und Vererbungslehre*, supplement 1 (1928): 391–396.
————. With Arthur Mangun Banta. "A Thermal Race of Cladocera Originating by Mutation." *Zeitschrift für induktive Abstammungs-und Vererbungslehre*, supplement 1 (1928): 397–398.
————. "Activation of the Dormant Form of Freshwater Animals, with special reference to Cladocera." Brown University, Ph.D. diss., 1938. Her advisor was Arthur Mangun Banta.
————. With A. M. Banta, L. A. Brown, and Lester Ingle. *Studies on the Physiology, Genetics, and Evolution of Some Cladocera*. Carnegie Institution of Washington, publication 513. Washington, D.C.: Carnegie Institution of Washington, 1939.

STANDARD SOURCES
AMS 6–8, B 9.

WOODS, ELIZABETH LINDLEY (1885–?)

U.S. educational psychologist. Born 3 March 1884 in Streater, Ill. Educated University of Oregon (A.B., 1905; A.M., 1910); Clark University (Ph.D., 1913). Professional experience: Rhode Island Normal School, instructor in psychology (1913–1914); Vassar College, instructor in psychology (1913–1916); California Public Schools, clinical psychologist (1916–1917); Wisconsin State Department of Public Instruction, director of special education (1917–1925); Los Angeles City Schools, Division of Psychology and Educational Research (1925–1946), guidance and counseling, supervisor (1946–1950). Retired 1950. Summer experience: University of Wisconsin, instructor in psychology (1922–1925); University of California, Los Angeles, instructor in psychology (1927, 1928,

1931, 1934, 1935); University of Southern California, instructor in psychology (1936). Death date unknown.

Born in Illinois, Elizabeth Lindley Woods went to the University of Oregon for her undergraduate and her master's degree. She became interested in educational psychology and intelligence testing, and went to Clark University in Massachussetts, then a center for psychology, to study. Upon receiving her degree, she taught as an instructor in psychology first at the Rhode Island Normal School and then at Vassar College until 1916, when she received an appointment at the California public schools as a clinical psychologist. After a year, she moved to Wisconsin to serve as the director of special education in the State Department of Public Instruction, where she remained for the next seven years. During this period she also taught summer school at the University of Wisconsin. By 1925, she moved again to California, taking a position in the division of psychology and educational research, where she had the opportunity to evaluate pupil growth through a variety of tests. Again, she taught in the California universities in the summer, first at University of California at Los Angeles and then at the University of Southern California.   JH/MBO

PRIMARY SOURCES
Woods, Elizabeth Lindley. With Theodore Barrett. *What About Jobs?* Rev. ed. New York: McClure, 1936.

STANDARD SOURCES
AMS 3–8, S&B 9–10.

WOODS, ETHEL GERTRUDE (SKEAT) (1865–1939)

British stratigrapher, invertebrate paleontologist, and geographer. Born 1865 at Cambridge to Bertha Jones Skeat and W. W. Skeat. Two siblings. Married Henry Woods (1910). Educated Bateman House School, Cambridge; Newnham College, Cambridge (1891–1894, Natural Science Tripos, Pt. I, cl. 1, 1894); Trinity College, Dublin (D.Sc.). Professional experience: Penarth County School, mistress (1898–1904); Queens School, Chester, teacher (1904–1910); Cambridge Training College for Women, lecturer (1911–1913); Postal Censorship Code Department, researcher (1915–1919). Died 26 January 1939 in Meldreth.

Ethel Skeat was the third daughter of a well-known Cambridge scholar of etymology and Anglo-Saxon studies. She attended the prestigious Bateman House School, and it may have been the influence of her teachers there that led her to geology. She attended Newnham College and placed in the first class of Natural Sciences Tripos in 1894. After her first-class honors, she was elected to a Bathurst Studentship, which she held for two years. At Newnham, she met MAR-GARET CROSFIELD, with whom she later collaborated.

With her Bathurst Studentship, Skeat was able to go to Munich to work under the well-known geologist and historian of geology K. A. von Zittel. She investigated the paleontology of Jurassic, Neocomian, and Gault boulders found in Denmark and published a paper on her research. She later worked in Paris, Geneva, and Lausanne. The first woman to be admitted to the University of Munich, she met Victor Madsen, with whom she collaborated on an important work on the Glacial Boulders of the Mesozoic in Denmark. Upon returning home, she worked with Crosfield on the Jurassic and Cretaceous boulders in the drift of Denmark, the Jurassic of east Greenland, and in the stratigraphy of Carmarthen (Wales). In her later years, she became interested in geography and published several books in that field, including *Principles of Geography: Physical and Human* and *The Baltic Region*.

Skeat was a member of the Geologists' Association since 1893 and was awarded the Murchison Fund in 1908, the first woman to receive that honor.

Marriage did not keep her from doing research, for she continued to produce papers and books after she married Henry Woods 17 June 1910. Her knowledge of German and the Scandinavian languages enabled her to help in the war effort. She moved to Meldreth and devoted her time to her garden. She became president of the Meldreth Women's Conservative and Unionist Association and was Secretary and Registrar of the Cambridge Training College for Women. She became ill in June 1938 and died at Meldreth on 26 January 1939.   JH/MBO

PRIMARY SOURCES
Skeat, Ethel Gertrude. With Margaret Chorley Crosfield. "On the Geology of the Neighbourhood of Carmarthen." *Quarterly Journal of the Geological Society* 56 (1900): 415–494.
———. *The Principles of Geography; Physical and Human.* Oxford: Clarendon Press, 1923.
Woods, Ethel Gertrude. With Margaret Chorley Crosfield. "The Silurian Rocks of the Central Part of the Clwydian Range." *Quarterly Journal of the Geological Association* 81 (1925): 170–192.
———. *The Baltic Region.* London: Methuen Press & Co., Ltd., 1932.

SECONDARY SOURCES
[Woods, Henry]. "Mrs Ethel Gertrude Woods." *Proceedings Geologists' Association* 51 (1940): 114.

STANDARD SOURCES
Newnham, vol. 1; *Newnham Roll;* Sarjeant.

WOODWARD, GLADYS ESTELLE (1900–)
U.S. chemist. Born 20 September 1900 in Hartford, Conn. Educated Mount Holyoke College (A.B., 1922); Northwestern University (M.S., 1924). Professional experience: Northwestern University Chemistry Department, departmental secretary (1925–1926); American Petroleum Institute, fellow (1926–1928); Franklin Institute, Biochemical Research Foundation, researcher (1928–1966). Retired 1966. Honors and memberships: Public Health Institute, Fellow (1922–1924); Chemical Society, member.

Gladys Estelle Woodward was born in Connecticut and went to Mount Holyoke for her undergraduate training. She went on to study at the Public Health Institute of Northwestern University for two years until she received her master of science degree.

For a year following her degree, Woodward remained at the chemistry department at Northwestern, working as a secretary. At the end of this time, she was awarded an American Petroleum Institute Fellowship for two years, which enabled her to obtain a position as research chemist at the Biochemical Research Foundation of the Franklin Institute, a post she held until she retired.

Her research interests were in organic mercurials, in organic sulfur compounds, especially those found in petroleum. She also studied hydrogen ion concentration of blood, glutathione, glyoxalase, and ascorbic acid.   JH/MBO

STANDARD SOURCE
AMS 6–8, P 9, P&B 10–11.

WOOLDRIDGE, ELIZABETH (TAYLOR) (1908–)
U.S. mathematician and educational psychologist. Born 6 September 1908 in Salem, Ky. Married 1937. One child. Educated Murray State College (A.B., 1931); Peabody College (M.A., 1941); University of Nebraska (Ph.D. in educational psychology, 1964). Professional experience: Kentucky, high school teacher (1928–1929; 1936–1942), elementary school teacher (1933–1935); Louisiana, high school teacher (1942–1945); Wayne State College, English teacher (1946–1947), mathematics teacher (1947–1957); University of Nebraska, statistician (1958–1959); Wayne State College, associate professor of mathematics (1959–1962); Florence State College, professor (from 1962).

Elizabeth Taylor Wooldridge was first a teacher for many years in both high schools and elementary schools in various subjects. She became a statistician for the University of Nebraska for a year, and then became an associate professor at Wayne State College and in 1962 became professor at Florence State College. Wooldridge was a visiting scientist National Science Foundation lecturer in 1966. She was a member of the Mathematical Association and researched statistics as well as the factorial study of changes in ability patterns of students in college algebra.   JH/MBO

STANDARD SOURCES
AMS P&B 11–14.

WOOLLEY, ANN (1623–?)

British physician; nutritionist. Born 1623 in London. Married (1) the headmaster of a school in Newport, Essex (1644); (2) Chalinor of Westminster. Educated in medicine and languages through working with influential people. Professional experience: schoolmistress; housekeeper for educated people; developed remedies for various ailments. Death date unknown.

Ann (or Hannah) Woolley of London was apparently from a family of modest means. Reputedly attractive and well educated, she credited her mother and sisters for teaching her the secrets of "physic and surgery." When she was only fourteen years old she was a schoolmistress, later becoming a companion to a wealthy woman, a governess, and a housekeeper for influential people. She used her time in these positions to study medicine and languages. She married the headmaster of a school in Newport, Essex, and after his death, remarried. Woolley wrote popular books and articles; the best-known one was on diet and medicine for women. Called *Pharmacopolinum muliebris sexus,* it caught the imagination of the public and was translated into German and probably into French. Originally published in 1674, it was republished in 1688 and 1697.

Woolley also wrote cookbooks and pamphlets on cosmetics. One of these cookbooks in its final pages gives recipes in medicine and surgery. Among the many "cures" one finds a remedy for breast cancer to be goose dung and celandine juice. For forgetfulness she recommends rue, mint, and oil of roses, mixed with burned hair and used as an inhalant.

JH/MBO

PRIMARY SOURCES
Woolley, Ann. *The Accomplish'd Lady's Delight in Preserving, Physick, Beautifying, and Cookery.* London: Printed for B. Harris, 1675.
———. *The Gentlewoman's Companion: A Guide to the Female Sex.* London: Printed for T. J. for Edward Thomas, 1682.

STANDARD SOURCES
Hurd-Mead 1938.

WOOLLEY, HELEN BRADFORD (THOMPSON) (1874–1947)

U.S. psychologist. Born 6 November 1874 in Chicago to Isabella Perkins (Faxon) Thompson and David Wallace. Married Paul G. Woolley, pathologist (1905; separated, 1924). Two daughters. Educated Englewood High School; University of Chicago (Ph.B., 1897; Ph.D., 1900, summa cum laude); postgraduate studies in Paris and Berlin. Professional experience: Mount Holyoke, professor of psychology and director, psychology laboratory (1901–1905); Bureau for the Investigation of Working Children, director (1911?–1921); Merrill Palmer School, Detroit, associate director (1922–1926); Columbia University Teachers College, professor of education and director of Institute of Child Welfare Research (1926–1930). Honors and memberships: American Psychologists Association, Vocational Guidance Association (president, 1921). Died 24 December 1947 at her daughter's home in Havertown, Pa., of an aortic aneurysm.

Helen Bradford Thompson was the daughter of a Chicago shoe manufacturer and received her early education in local schools. She then went to the University of Chicago. Her doctoral thesis, "Psychological Norms in Men and Women," was published in 1903. She studied in Paris and Berlin on a fellowship of the Association of Collegiate Alumnae. On her return to the United States, she became an instructor and director of the psychological laboratory at Mount Holyoke College. In 1905, she traveled to Yokohama, Japan, to marry Paul Gerhardt Woolley, pathologist and director of the Serum Laboratory in Manila, Philippine Islands. Helen Woolley worked as an experimental psychologist with the Philippine Education Bureau before moving to Bangkok, Siam, in 1906. The Woolleys returned to the United States in 1908 and finally settled in Cincinnati, where both were on faculty at the university—she as an instructor in philosophy and he as a professor of pathology, later dean of the medical college.

In 1911, Helen Woolley was appointed director of the new Bureau for the Investigation of Working Children. This project developed into the Cincinnati Vocation Bureau, directed by Woolley and part of the public school system. The psychological laboratory of the Vocational Bureau followed 750 children who left school to go to work, comparing them mentally and physically to children who stayed in school. The full report was published in 1926 as *An Experimental Study of Children at Work and in School between the Ages of Fourteen and Eighteen Years.* Working with social economist M. Edith Campbell and the superintendent of public instruction, Woolley drafted and helped engineer passage of the Bing Law of 1921, which became a model for other compulsory school attendance and child labor laws.

Woolley was active in several community and national organizations, including the Council of National Defense, the

National Vocational Guidance Association, Cincinnati Community Chest, and Ohio Woman Suffrage Association. In late 1921, the Woolley family (with daughters Eleanor and Charlotte) moved to Detroit, and Woolley was appointed staff psychologist for the Merrill-Palmer School. She soon established one of the first nursery schools in the country, which served as a laboratory for the study of child development and the education of teachers. She also taught child psychology and child guidance and supervised graduate research. Her personal research and publications concerned mental and physical development in children and the development of personality. To measure developmental changes in three-year-olds, Woolley, with graduate student Elizabeth Cleveland, developed four performance tests based on Montessori apparatus. These were the first of what became the Merrill-Palmer Scale of Mental Tests.

In 1924, Paul Woolley left his family and moved to California. Helen Woolley immersed herself in her work, lecturing, writing, and serving on various committees. She served as vice-president of the American Association of University Women (1923–1925) and was instrumental in their procurement of a Laura Spelman Rockefeller Memorial Fund grant for educational studies. In 1925, Woolley went to New York City as professor of education at Columbia University Teachers College and director of the Institute of Child Welfare Research. In the short time she was there, she saw the institute move to its own building, organized two nursery schools, revised the educational clinic to center research on phases of child development and parental education.

While she was alone in a large and impersonal university and city, Woolley's emotional and physical state deteriorated. She took a two-year leave from Columbia University and spent some time in Europe. She returned to teaching in 1928 but was unable to cope effectively with her previous duties. In 1929, she appointed LOIS HAYDEN MEEK to be associate director of the institute. In 1930, the university asked her to resign. Eventually, she went to live with her daughter Eleanor in Havertown, Pennsylvania, and died there in 1947 of an aortic aneurysm.

Helen Thompson Woolley was a talented and dedicated psychologist, deeply concerned with understanding child development in all its aspects. She was well organized and able to pool insights and methodologies from several disciplines into comprehensive studies and reports. Her last major publication was the chapter on "Eating, Sleeping and Elimination" in *A Handbook of Child Psychology* (1931), edited by Carl Murchison. JH/MBO

PRIMARY SOURCES
Woolley, Helen Bradford Thompson. *Psychological Norms in Men and Women.* Chicago: University of Chicago Press, 1903. Also published as *The Mental Traits of Sex: An Experimental Investigation of the Normal Mind in Men and Women.* Chicago: University of Chicago Press, 1903.
———. *Facts about the Working Children of Cincinnati, and their Bearing upon Educational Problems.* Chicago: n.p., 1913.
———. With Charlotte Rust Fischer. *Mental and Physical Measurements of Working Children.* Psychological monographs 18 no. 1, whole no. 77. Princeton, N.J., and Lancaster, Pa.: Psychological Review Co., 1914..
———. *An Experimental Study of Children at Work and in School Between the Ages of Fourteen and Eighteen Years.* New York: Macmillan, 1926.
———. With E. Leona Vincent and Rachel Stutsman. *Merrill-Palmer Personality Studies of Young Children 1925–1927.* Contains Woolley's classic case studies: David, a study of the experience of a nursery school in training a child adopted from an institution; Agnes, a dominant personality in the making; and Peter, the beginnings of the juvenile court problem.
———. "Eating, Sleeping and Elimination." In *A Handbook of Child Psychology,* ed. Carl Murchison. Worcester, Mass.: Clark University Press; London: Oxford University Press, 1931.

SECONDARY SOURCES
Educational Forum (May 1948). Obituary notice.

STANDARD SOURCES
American Women 1974; *AMS* 3–7; Bailey; *NAW* (article by M. W. Zapoleon and L. M. Stolz); Siegel and Finley; Stevens and Gardner; *WWW(A),* vol. 3, 1951–1960.

WOOLLEY, MILDRED THOMPSON (1902–1949)
U.S. bacteriologist. Born 7 November 1902 in Oakland, Calif. Educated University of California (A.M.); University of Michigan (D.P.H., 1940). Professional experience: West Virginia State Hygienic Laboratory, researcher (1940–1941); Arizona State Laboratory, director (1941–1949). Died in 1949.

Little is known about the life of Mildred Thompson Woolley, other than her birth in California and her subsequent education there. By the time she completed her doctorate in public health at the University of Michigan, she was forty years old. Her work in bacteriology led immediately to a position in West Virginia in the public health bacteriology laboratories, and subsequently to the directorship of the state laboratories in Tucson, Arizona. Her death eight years later brought her career to an abrupt end at the age of forty-seven. Her research interests included not only bacteriology but indigenous fungal infections in the Southwest, such as coccidiodomycosis. JH/MBO

STANDARD SOURCES
AMS 7.

WOOTTON, BARBARA ADAM (1897–1988)

British sociologist. Born 14 April 1897 in Cambridge, England, to Mrs. and James Adam. Married (1) John Wesley Wootton (1917) (d. 1917); (2) George Percival Wright (1935) (d. 1964). Educated Perse High School for Girls, Cambridge; Girton College, Cambridge (starred first-class degree in economics, 1919; M.A., 1920). Professional experience: Girton College, director of studies and lecturer in economics (1920–1922); Trades Union Congress and Labour Party Joint Research Department, research officer (1922–1926); Morley College for Working Men and Women, London, principal (1926–1927); University of London, director of studies for tutorial classes (1927–1944), professor of social studies (1948–1952); Bedford College, University of London, Nuffield Research Fellow (1952–1957); created life peer and took seat in House of Lords (1958); Deputy Speaker (from 1967). Died 11 July 1988 in Surrey, England.

Barbara Wootton spent much of her life developing her socialist beliefs. They apparently had their source in her childhood at Cambridge, where both of her liberal parents were lecturers. Her hatred of inequality gained momentum when she could not receive a Cambridge University degree for the starred first that she received in economics, and her first lectures at that university were advertised under a man's name. When she first left Cambridge, she took a position at Morley College in Lambeth, which then offered different rates of pay for men and women doing the same work. Her views were also influenced by war, when her husband of five weeks and her brother were killed in the trenches.

Wootton became a highly respected teacher at London University, where she was director of studies at its extramural department for seventeen years and for an additional twelve years, professor of economics, sociology, and social studies at Bedford College. Many of her published studies were well received. She served on four royal commissions and innumerable committees, was a governor of the BBC, and was a magistrate for forty years.

Ironically, given her views, she was one of only four women chosen in the first group of life peers created in 1958 and one of only two holding the title of Companion of Honour. Refusing to identify with any political party, she nevertheless acted like a burr under the saddle for both the Labour and Conservative groups. She believed that the Labour government equivocated on the matter of equality, believing that government must be responsible for income distribution and that capitalism embodied inequality.

One of her most important academic works was published in 1959 and resulted from five years of research. In this work she reversed commonly accepted ideas about the criminal personality, juvenile delinquency, inherited behavior trends, and problems of illegitimacy.

Barbara Wootton's life seemed to involve a mass of contradictions. She accepted a title that entitled her to become a member of the House of Lords, yet denounced that body's opposition to her own ideals. She was an academic, but one who stressed the importance of practical solutions to social problems. However, pervading her entire life was her philosophical socialism, and she worked constantly to put her theories into practice.   KM

PRIMARY SOURCES
Wootton, Barbara. *Plan or No Plan.* London: Gollancz, 1934.
———. *Lament for Economics.* New York: Farrar and Rinehart, 1938.
———. *The Social Foundations of Wage Policy.* New York: Norton, 1955.
———. *Social Science and Social Pathology.* New York: Macmillan, 1959.
———. *Crime and the Criminal Law.* London: Stevens, 1963.
———. *In a World I Never Made.* London: Allen and Unwin, 1967. Wootton's autobiography.

STANDARD SOURCES
Annual Obituary 1988.

WORMINGTON, HANNAH MARIE (1914–1994)

U.S. prehistoric archeologist. Born 5 September 1914 in Denver, Colo., to Adrienne (Roucoulle) and Charles Watkin Wormington. Married George D. Volk (1940). Educated University of Denver (A.B., 1935); Radcliffe College (Harvard University) (M.A., 1950, Ph.D., 1954). Professional experience: Denver Museum of Natural History, curator of archeology (1937–1968); University of Colorado, lecturer; University of Denver, lecturer, visiting professor, adjunct professor (1954–1980s). Honors and memberships: Society for American Archaeology, president (1967), Distinguished Service Award (1983); Colorado State University, honorary doctorate (1977); Colorado State Archaeology Distinguished Service Award (1977). Died 1994.

American archeologist Hannah Marie Wormington was born in Colorado to a French mother who encouraged her interest in the French language and culture. After graduating from the University of Denver where she had studied with E. B. Renaud, she went to France. There she studied with a number of French Paleolithic archeologists, including Henri Martin, with whom she excavated in the Dordogne, and met a well-known American archeologist Edgar Howard, who worked on Paleo-Indian sites. Her visit with the archeologist

DOROTHY GARROD in England provided her with a new role model.

Returning to Denver in 1936, she catalogued material from the important early Indian sites held by the Denver Museum of Natural History (then called the Colorado Museum). The following year she was appointed curator of archeology, a position she held for more than thirty-three years, with some time out for educational and sabbatical leaves. She married George D. Volk, a petroleum geologist and engineer, in 1940, while continuing her work at the museum. In those early years, she produced two remarkable books on prehistoric American Indians.

She soon took a leave from the museum to pursue a graduate degree at Harvard University (although at that time, even advanced degrees were awarded only under Radcliffe College). She was one of the first women to enter the Harvard anthropology department as a graduate student and she was also the first woman archeologist to complete her dissertation there. After taking the required course work, she returned to the museum while she worked on her thesis, completing her dissertation on the archeology of the Upper Colorado Plateau in 1954. Soon after, she extended her archeological work to Utah, becoming an authority on the Fremont culture. During this period, she also began to survey in Alberta, Canada, to follow the migration routes of early Asian hunters from Siberia, and extended this to work on Siberian sites. In early 1960s, she explored an early metal-using culture in Siberia and related it to the Old Copper Cultures in North America. Shortly before her death, she completed her major book on ancient hunters of North America. Wormington was unusually receptive and encouraging to amateur archeologists, and felt that their unpaid labor, when properly done, was invaluable.

Honored by a number of prizes, including an honorary doctorate from Colorado State University, she received the Distinguished Service Award from the Society of American Archaeologists (1983), whom she had served as the first woman president in 1967. She was conscious of the need to make the field of archeology more accessible to women, but at the same time, she felt that her own work had been enabled by the support from her husband and her male colleagues. She died in 1994.   JH/MBO

PRIMARY SOURCES

Wormington, Hannah Marie. *Ancient Man in North America.* Denver: Museum of Natural History, 1939.

———. *Ice Age Hunters of the Rockies.* Niwot, Colo: Denver Museum of Natural History and University Press of Colorado, [1939].

———. *Prehistoric Indians of the Southwest.* Denver: Museum of Natural History, 1949.

———. "Archaeology of the Upper Colorado Plateau Area in the Northern Periphery of the Southwestern United States." Ph.D. diss., Radcliffe College (Harvard University), 1953.

———. "A Survey of Early American Prehistory." *American Scientist* 50 (1962): 230–242.

———. *Ancient Hunters and Gatherers of North America.* New York: Academic Press, [1989].

SECONDARY SOURCES

Cordell, Linda S. "Women Archaeologists in the Southwest." In *Hidden Scholars: Women Anthropologists and the Native American Southwest,* ed. Nancy J. Parezo, 202–220. Albuquerque: University of New Mexico Press, 1933.

Fox, Jennifer. "The Women Who Opened Doors: Interviewing Southwestern Anthropologists." In *Hidden Scholars: Women Anthropologists and the Native American Southwest,* ed. Nancy J. Parezo, 294–310. See page 304.

Plains Anthropologist 39 (1994): 475–476. Obituary notice.

STANDARD SOURCES

AMS 8, S&B 9–12.

WORNER, RUBY K. (1900–)

U.S. chemist. Born 22 November 1900 in San Jose, Ill. Educated University of Chicago (B.S., 1921; M.S., 1922; Ph.D. in chemistry, 1925). Professional experience: Oklahoma College for Women, Chickasha, Okla., associate professor of chemistry (1925–1927); U.S. Department of Agriculture, bureau of home economics, assistant chemist (1927–1929); National Bureau of Standards (1929–1940); U.S. Department of Agriculture, division of agricultural research service, from associate textile technologist to head textile technologist (1940–1962); United Nations Food and Agricultural Organization for Cotton Research, project for cotton research and technical division, Ministry of Agriculture Giza, United Arab Republic, technical officer (1963–1965); Bibliography of the American Association of Textile Chemists and Colorists Year Book, editor (from 1966).

Ruby Worner received her three degrees from the University of Chicago and then began a short-lived academic career in a small women's college in Oklahoma. After two years she moved to federal service and continued to expand into the international venue, working as a U.S. representative to the United Nations. An expert in textile chemistry, she served the Department of Agriculture and the United Nations.

Science and international politics overlapped in Worner's work. In 1960–1961, she was a visiting Fulbright professor and consultant in Alexandria, Egypt. She was a member of the U.S. delegation's technical committee for developing an international standard for textiles in 1951 and again in 1958. Her international connections included attending the Middle East Standardization Conference in Cairo in 1961.

As an applied chemist, Worner's research was on the chemical and physical properties of textile materials, the chemistry of cellulose, textile processing, and test methods. She applied the results of this research on a national and international venue. In 1939 when Ruby Worner was an assistant at the National Bureau of Standards, she was an outspoken critic of the way that women were treated in the federal government. In her "Opportunities for Women Chemists in Washington, D.C.," she expressed her disillusionment with a system that assured that women federal workers would be kept in a subordinate position. However, as her own career gained momentum, she agreed that the situation had improved and that women, indeed, had an opportunity to advance in the federal government.   JH/MBO

PRIMARY SOURCES

Worner, Ruby. With Ruth O'Brien and Esther C. Peterson. *Bibliography on the Relation of Clothing to Health.* Department of Agriculture, Bureau of Home Economics, miscellaneous publication no. 62. Washington, D.C.: U.S. Government Printing Office, 1929.

———. "Opportunities for Women Chemists in Washington." *Journal of Chemical Education* 16 (1939): 584.

———. *Registered Trade Names Applicable to the Finishing of Cotton Textiles.* Washington, D.C.: Bureau of Agricultural Research Administration, U.S. Department of Agriculture, 1943.

STANDARD SOURCES

AMS 5–8, P 9, P&B 10–12; Rossiter 1982.

WORTHINGTON, EUPHEMIA R. (1881–?)

U.S. mathematician. Born 22 December 1881 in Pittsburgh, Pa. Educated Wellesley College (A.B., 1904); Yale University (Ph.D., 1908). Professional experience: Wellesley College, instructor of mathematics (1909–1918); Gallaudet Aircraft Corporation, engineer (1918–1922); University of California, Los Angeles, instructor of mathematics (1922–1924), assistant professor (1924–1949), emerita assistant professor (1949–1953). Honors and memberships: American Association for the Advancement of Science; Mathematical Society. Death date unknown.

After Euphemia R. Worthington earned her doctoral degree from Yale University, she went to Wellesley College as an instructor. She remained at this level for nine years and then took a position with the Gallaudet Aircraft Corporation as an engineer. She stayed at Gallaudet for four years and then

went to the University of California, Los Angeles, where she was first an instructor and then an assistant professor. She remained at the rank of assistant until she retired in 1949.

JH/MBO

STANDARD SOURCES

AMS 3–8, P 9, P&B 10–11; Rossiter 1982.

WRANGELL, MARGARETHE VON (1876–1932)

German agricultural chemist. Born 25 December 1876 in Moscow to Ida and Karl von Wrangell. Two siblings. Married Duke Wladimir Andronikow. Educated Higher Girls' School and Female Teachers' Seminary, Reval, Estonia; University of Tübingen and University of Leipzig (graduated Leipzig 1909); London, studied with William Ramsay; Paris, studied with Marie Curie; Habilitates Agriculture College, Hohenheim. "Phosphorsäureaufnahme und Bodenreaktion" (1920). Professional experience: Chemical Institute, Strassburg, assistant; Agricultural Experimental Station, Reval, Estonia, chief (1912–1918); Kaiser Wilhelm Institute of Fritz Haber, Berlin, scientific coworker (1919); Institute for Pflanzenernährung, founder (1920); Agricultural College, Hohenheim, first woman to occupy chair (1923); Pflanzenernährung, chief. Died 31 March 1932 in Stuttgart/Hohenheim.

Margarethe von Wrangell was the youngest child of a noble Baltic family. Her brother Nikolai was her teacher and a strict disciplinarian. He developed her interest in natural sciences. At age seventeen, when she and her aunt visited Nikolai in Karlsruhe where he studied chemistry, she was surprised to find the scarred faces of the members of the dueling fraternities.

When she returned to school in Reval, she made outstanding scores on the teacher's examination. She was not satisfied with obtaining the teaching diploma, thinking that if she did not achieve higher goals her life would be impoverished. Consequently, she took art instruction, dabbled in literature, learned the theory of chess, and did mathematical computations late into the night. Her room became a natural history laboratory and a painting studio. She explained that she used to think of herself as being very gifted, but later came to realize that her perceived brilliance came only from a complicated brain and an inclination to do metaphysics.

After Nicolai died of tuberculosis, Margarethe decided to follow in his footsteps and study chemistry, though most of her relatives considered it a mad idea. In 1904 she moved to Tübingen with her mother to begin her studies in inorganic chemistry. She explained in a letter to her family that there were fourteen hundred students, almost all of whom were mutilated members of the dueling fraternities and only three of whom were female. She was impressed by the chemist Wislicenus who "without bells and whistles" accomplished everything as planned in the experiments. She admired his lectures, in which there was never a word too many or too few.

For von Wrangell, chemistry was poetry. In her writings, she expressed the belief that purity and beauty characterize chemical formulae, that in the formulae one can hear the impatient and easily susceptible heart beat of oxygen. To her, chemistry was about the changeable; she spoke of the compounds of manganese as being chameleon-like, and described "hearing" the heavy lazy bloodstream of the nitrogen.

After she graduated in 1909, von Wrangell was recommended by her teacher Wislicenus to William Ramsey in England for thorium research. She complained that in England, she was considered by certain conceited professors as inferior. However, after Ramsey officially complimented her on her results, previously aloof professors became supportive.

Von Wrangell then worked with MARIE CURIE in Paris. Curie valued her thorium work and trusted her with one hundred liters of uranium to check the work of a professor on radioactive uranium. Von Wrangell's mother suspected early on that the symptoms of Curie's illness pointed to radiation poisoning. She wrote in 1912 to Margarethe that she would be relieved when Margarethe was removed from this dangerous situation.

From 1912 to 1918, von Wrangell led an agricultural experimental station in her home, Reval. She was responsible for the control of seeds and artificial fertilizers and animal food. Because of the horrors of the war, she ceased her work on radiation and instead turned with complete abandonment to agricultural chemistry. She observed the influence of Estonian phosphates on the ability of plants to bloom and to set better fruits. This was the starting point of her later important research on phosphate fertilizers. When she was dislocated during the war, she searched desperately for Estonian rock and soil samples.

In the meantime, she fled from the Baltic and worked as a scientific coworker in an experimental station of the agricultural college in Hohenheim. Obtaining a paid position was a real problem for a foreigner, especially a female one. Fritz Haber gave her a temporary position in his Kaiser-Wilhelm Institute for Physical Chemistry in Berlin, thus smoothing her way considerably. In 1920 she qualified to teach university and was asked to form an Institute for Pflanzenernährung in the Agricultural College in Hohenheim. In 1921 she wrote that she still would have to be careful in constructing her future. It was vital to her to be able to keep her scientific freedom, so she only wanted to make what she actually needed even though the industry would allow her to make much more. She quoted Schiller's description of science that for the one it is the high, heavenly goddess, whereas for the other it is a good cow that supplies him with butter.

In 1923 von Wrangell became the first regular female professor of the newly established institute. She complained that it was difficult as a woman to be in a highly visible position, for she constantly experienced enmity.

At age fifty-two she married her childhood friend Duke Wladimir Andronikow. She had to get special permission to marry him, for a woman in her position was supposed to be unmarried and furthermore marriage to a stateless subject endangered her state employment.

Von Wrangell's research concentrated on plant physiological questions, especially the usability of phosphates by cultivated plants and the systemic research of the behavior of nutrients in the natural soil. With a sure judgment concerning the fertility and the necessity for fertilizer of any soil, she found that the German soil did not need as many phosphates as was generally assumed. She knew that it was possible to choose something more adaptable to this soil to accommodate cultured plants, and that with the right fertilizer and working the soil correctly, you could mobilize the phosphate capital in the soil and determine the connection of the different fertilizers to each other. She insisted that plant nourishment was a question of equilibrium and was not, as commonly thought, a dynamic event. She concluded that plants in general fed on ground water's dissolved materials and demanded instead of the expected results, an exact analysis of the ground water. She published many experiments in the field of plant nutrition and soil chemistry, and worked with aerobes, a system that fertilizes without foreign phosphates.

Von Wrangell was interested in solving questions that concerned the present but not those of an economic nature. In 1930, she gave a speech at the opening of the Tübingen female student home. Money, she explained, should not dominate the choice of a career. Female students, when deciding on a career, should choose one that answered their deep need to aspire to a higher life. GVL

PRIMARY SOURCES

Wrangell, Margarethe von. "Gesetzmässigkeiten bei der Phosphorernährung der Pflanzen." *Landwirtschaftliches Jahrbuch* 57 (1922).

———. "Über Bodenphosphate und Phosphorsäurebedürftigkeit." *Landwirtschaftliches Jahrbuch* 63 (1926).

———. *Ernährung und Düngung der Pflanzen*. N.p., 1928.

———. "Die Zusammensetzung von Bodenlösungen und das Wachstum von Pflanzen in sehr verdünnten Lösungen." *Ergebnisse der Agrikulturchemie* 2 (1930).

———. "Das atmosphärische Jod und die Pflanze." *Die Umschau* 34 (1930): 40.

SECONDARY SOURCES

Andronikow, Wladimir Fürst. *Margarete v. Wrangell: Das leben einer Frau 1876–1932*. Munich: A. Langen/G. Müller Verlag,

1935. Stories about his wife, who died after only four years of marriage. Contains many of her letters as well as memories of her mother from her youth and her student years.

Feyl, Renate. "Margarete v. Wrangell." In *Der lautlose Aufbruch: Frauen in der Wissenschaft.* Darmstadt und Neuwied: Luchterhand, 1983.

Glaser, Edith, and Susanne Stiefel. *Zwischen Waschzuber und Wohltätigkeit. Tübinger Frauengeschichten im 19. und frühen 20. Jahrhundert 20f.* Tübingen: Universitätsstadt Tübingen, Frauenbeauftragte und Kulturant, 1991.

Luck, Conradine. *Frauen.* Reutlingen: Ensslin & Laiblin, 1937.

STANDARD SOURCES
Lexikon der Frau; Poggendorff, vol. 7a.

WRESCHNER, MARIE (1887–?)

German chemist. Educated University of Berlin Technical Institute, philosophical faculty (thesis, 1918). Professional experience: Kaiser Wilhelm Institute for Physical Chemistry and Electrochemistry, researcher (1928?). Death date unknown.

Little is known about Marie Wreschner except that she was one of two women (with VERA BIRSTEIN) in the Kaiser Wilhelm Institute for Physical Chemistry and Electrochemistry. During 1928 she was listed as a "miscellaneous coworker." There were twenty-one miscellaneous coworkers in 1928, nineteen of whom were men. Wreschner completed her thesis at the University of Berlin in 1918.

Wreschner investigated some behaviors of uranium X and thorium in solution. Their results supported the hypothesis that these substances formed colloids. MM

PRIMARY SOURCES
Wreschner, Marie. "Uber drehungsumkehrung und anomale rotations-dispersion." Leipzig: J. A. Barth, 1918. Inaugural dissertation.

———. With H. Freundlich. "Über die Aufnahme von Uran X_1 und Thorium durch Kohle." *Zeitschrift für physikalische Chemie* 106 (1923): 366–377.

Robinson, Robert. *Versuch einer elektronentheorie organisch-chemischer reaktionen* (two lectures on an "Outline of an electrochemical (electronic) theory of the course of organic reactions"). Marie Wreschner, trans. Stuttgart: F. Enke, 1932.

SECONDARY SOURCES
Handbuch der Kaiser Wilhelm-Gesellschaft zur Förderung der Wissenschaften. Berlin: R. Hobbing, 1928.

STANDARD SOURCES
Meyer and von Schweidler; Vogt.

WRIGHT, LADY CATHERINE (ca. 1732–1802)

British practitioner of natural philosophy, especially chemistry. Born ca. 1732 at Grey's Court, Rotherfield, Oxfordshire, to Catherine (Paul) and Sir William Stapleton. Four siblings. Married Sir James Wright, His Majesty's Resident Minister to the Republic of Venice. Mainly self-educated. Professional experience: experiments in natural philosophy. Died 6 January 1802 at Bath, Somerset.

Although Lady Catherine Wright never published her ideas, her surviving letters provide a vivid testimony of the seriousness with which some intelligent women pursued their studies, despite social obstacles. As a child, her brother's tutor—who became her father-in-law—had encouraged her academic interests. Later she enjoyed conversing with learned men and spent her spare time reading, benefiting particularly from her husband's purchase of an auctioned book collection, which included many older alchemical texts. With the help of a neighboring doctor, she subsequently became so conversant with contemporary chemical research that she criticized new books, formulated her own theories, and invented a therapeutic vapor bath. In 1784, she instigated a postal course of instruction from her close friend William Withering, the famous medical botanist, chemist, and mineralogist, which continued for at least three years. Although Withering urged her to study botany, then seen as appropriate for women, she far preferred chemistry, proposing experiments on local Devon minerals and the shellfish she investigated with Thomas Martyn, a conchologist and entomologist.

Wright and her valetudinarian husband lived in Teignmouth (Devon), and London. In London, she was friendly with the portrait painter Maria Cosway, who presided over a fashionable salon of Italian emigrés. Wright's introduction to this circle possibly stemmed from her husband's Venetian connections. It was probably with Cosway and Marchioness Townshend that she started attending the treatment sessions of John de Mainauduc, England's leading animal magnetizer (Mesmerist). Exasperated by Withering's conservative attitudes, she insisted on the efficacy of this controversial medical therapy, and cogently argued that it should not be rejected without thorough consideration.

In her correspondence, this learned aristocrat articulated the frustrations of a married woman prevented from reading and experimenting by her social obligations. PF/AS

PRIMARY SOURCES
Withering Letters, Royal Society of Medicine, London.

SECONDARY SOURCES
Fara, Patricia. "An Attractive Therapy: Animal Magnetism in Eighteenth-Century England." *History of Science* 33 (1995): 127–177.

Lloyd, Stephen. "The Accomplished Maria Cosway: Anglo-Italian Artist, Musician, Salon Hostess and Educationalist (1759–1838)." *Journal of Anglo-Italian Studies* 2 (1992): 108–139.

Burke's Peerage and Baronetage. London: Burke's Peerage, 1975.

C[okayne], G. E., ed. *Complete Baronetage.* 5 vols. Exeter: W. Pollard & Co., 1900–1906.

Horn, D. B., ed. *British Diplomatic Representatives 1689–1789.* London: Offices of the Society, 1932.

WRIGHT, FRANCES MAY (1902–)

U.S. mathematician. Born 22 July 1902 in Worcester, Mass. Educated Brown University (A.B., 1923; A.M., 1924). Professional experience: University of Oklahoma, instructor of mathematics (1924–1927); Elmira College, assistant professor (1927–1942); National Research Council, technical aide, office of scientific personnel (from 1942); Triple Cities College (later Harpur College), assistant professor (1950–1957); Harpur College, State University of New York, Binghamton (1957–post-1967). Honors and memberships: Brown University, Emery fellow (1923–1924); Mathematics Association, Mathematics Society, member.

Frances May Wright taught for three years at the University of Oklahoma and fifteen years at Elmira College before she went to work for the National Research Council. Following that, Wright taught at Triple Cities College in Binghamtom, New York, (later Harpur College) and ended her career as associate professor of mathematics at Harpur College, State University of New York, Binghamton.   JH/MBO

STANDARD SOURCES
AMS 5–8, P 9, P&B 10–11.

WRIGHT, FRANCES WOODWORTH (1897–1989)

U.S. astronomer. Born 30 April 1897 in Providence, R.I., to Nellie (Woodworth) and George William Wright. Educated Pembroke College (A.B., 1919); Brown University (A.M., 1920); Radcliffe College, postgraduate work (1927–1930; Ph.D., 1958). Professional experience: Elmira College, faculty member (1920–1927); Harvard University, research assistant (1928–1961), department of astronomy, executive secretary (1946–1963), lecturer on astronomy (from 1958); Smithsonian Astrophysical Observatory, Cambridge, Mass., astronomer (from 1961).

After Frances Woodworth Wright received her doctoral degree, she taught for seven years at a small college and then went to Harvard, where she spent many years in various positions. At one time she was the executive secretary for the department of astronomy; at another, she was a lecturer in astronomy. She then moved to the Smithsonian Institute's Astrophysical Observatory.

Wright's research interests and her publications are on variable stars, marine navigation, meteors, interplanetary dust, and the large Magellanic clouds. She held memberships in the American Association for the Advancement of Science, the Meteoritical Society (fellow), American Astronomical Society Instrument Navigation (member editorial board, 1950–1953), Phi Beta Kappa, and Sigma Xi.

JH/MBO

PRIMARY SOURCES
Wright, Frances Woodworth. With B. J. Bok. *Basic Marine Navigation.* Boston: Houghton Mifflin, [1944].

———. With Paul W. Hodge and Dorrit Hoffleit. "An Annotated Bibliography on Interplanetary Dust." *Smithsonian Contributions to Astrophysics* 5 (1961): 85–111.

———. *Celestial Navigation: A Quick, Easy, and Thorough Explanation.* Cambridge, Md.: Cornell Maritime Press, 1969.

———. *Coastwise Navigation.* Centreville, Md.: Cornell Maritime Press, c. 1980.

———. "Constant Vigilance." Taped and transcribed by Charles A. Whitney, 1986–1987.

SECONDARY SOURCES
"Frances Wright, 1897–1989." *Sky & Telescope* 78 (1989): 460.

STANDARD SOURCES
AMS P&B 11–14; Debus.

WRIGHT, HELENA ROSA (LOWENFELD) (1887–1982)

British physician and birth control advocate. Born 17 September 1887 at Brixton, London, to Alice (Evens) and Heinz Lowenfeld. One sister. Married Henry Wardel Snarey Wright. Four sons. Educated Cheltenham Ladies' College; London School of Medicine for Women (later, the Royal Free Hospital Medical School for Women); postgraduate gynecological training. Professional experience: Hampstead General Hospital; Hospital for Sick Children, Great Ormond Street; Bethnal Green Hospital, Royal Army Medical Corps; Shantung Christian University, lecturer in gynecology (1922–1927); Kensington free clinic, London; lecturer on family planning and sexual counselor at Family Planning Association clinics (to 1958); private practice. Honors and memberships: National Birth Control Council, a founder (1930); International Planned Parenthood Federation, member. Died age ninety-four, 21 March 1982 in Royal Free Hospital, London, following an operation for gallstones.

Helena Lowenfeld's father was a Polish immigrant to England who built and owned the popular Apollo Theatre and became very wealthy. Her parents separated and were divorced in 1902. After the divorce, her father spent most of his time in Paris.

Educated at the elite Cheltenham Ladies' College, Lowenfeld was expected to continue in the society debutante style but chose instead to become a doctor. She trained at the Royal Free Hospital Medical School for Women, joined the Royal Army medical corps, and received further training at Bethnal Green Hospital during World War I. There she met and married Henry Wright, known as Peter, a surgeon.

After the war, Helena Wright took additional training in gynecology and, with her husband and two sons, went to China as a medical missionary. Helena Wright taught gynecology at Shantung Christian University for five years before the family returned to England. In Berlin, she learned of new contraceptive devices and began to focus her career on family planning, birth control, and sexual counseling. She worked in one of the first free clinics in London, helped to found the National Birth Control Council (later the Family Planning Association), and worked with the International Planned Parenthood Federation for high standards of service and specialized training for doctors. She worked for the FPA clinics until 1958, then ran her own practice so that she could travel and lecture and teach foreign students to carry family planning information back to their home communities. At age eighty, she wrote her second best-seller, *Sex and Society,* and continued as teacher, broadcaster, and public figure until her death in 1982.

A controversial figure, she was willing to recommend abortion for unwanted pregnancies, arrange (illegal) private third-party adoptions for unwanted babies, and was interested in prisoner welfare. She also tried to persuade the governor of Holloway Prison to give contraceptive advice to women prisoners.

Wright was convinced that fidelity was not necessary for a happy marriage, and she spent weekends and holidays with men friends. She and her husband stayed together until his death in 1976.   JH/MBO

PRIMARY SOURCES

Wright, Helena. *The Sex Factor in Marriage: A Book for Those Who Are or Are about to Be Married.* London: N. Douglas, 1930.

———. *What Is Sex? An Outline for Young People.* London: Williams & Norgate Ltd., 1932.

———. *Birth Control, Advice on Family Spacing and Healthy Sex Life.* London, Toronto [etc.]: Cassell and Co. Ltd., 1935.

———. *Sex Fulfillment in Married Women.* London: Williams & Norgate, 1947.

———. *Contraceptive Technique: A Handbook for Medical Practitioners and Senior Students.* London: Churchill, 1951.

———. *Sex and Society.* London: Allen & Unwin, 1968.

SECONDARY SOURCES

Evans, Barbara. *Freedom to Choose: The Life and Work of Dr. Helena Wright, Pioneer of Contraception.* London: Bodley Head, 1984.

STANDARD SOURCES

DNB; Uglow 1989.

WRIGHT, KATHARINE (1892–?)

U.S. physician. Born 17 September 1892 at Carroll Springs Sanitarium, Forest Glen, Md. Four siblings. Married Lewis Wright (1916). Three children. Educated University of Wisconsin (B.S., 1916); George Washington Medical (graduated 1918); licensesd to practice medicine in Washington, D.C. (1918), Maryland (1919), Illinois (1940); American Board of Neurology and Psychiatry, diplomate. Professional experience: Carroll Springs Sanitarium, medical director (1920); Elgin State Hospital, staff (1940–1943); Illinois Neuropsychiatric Hospital, teaching fellow (1943–1946); Psychopathic Hospital of Cook County, staff (1943–1946); private practice in psychiatry (from 1945); psychiatric Clinic of Chicago, founder and worker (from 1947); Mary Thompson Hospital, psychiatric consultant (from 1947). Honors and memberships: Katharine Wright Psychiatric Clinic named for her; Woman of the Year (1959); Distinguished Citizen of the Press Club of Chicago, honorary member; Illinois Group Psychotherapy Society, cofounder; Pan American Medical Association (1965); University of Wisconsin Alumni Association, Distinguished Service Award (1966); Illinois State Medical Society, appointed to the Fifty-Year Club (1968); American Medical Women's Association, Elizabeth Blackwell Award (1969). Death date unknown.

Katharine Wright's father was a homeopathic physician and her mother one of the first two women to graduate from the University of Chicago. Her parents encouraged her interest in medicine; she pursued her father's interest in psychiatry. Her career was put on hold as she married a patent attorney and had three children, one boy and two girls. Education for Wright was a continuous project. When the family moved to Chicago she obtained an Illinois medical license and obtained a position on the staff of Elgin State Hospital, where she studied clinical psychiatry by direct contact with the patients. She remained in this position for three years and then obtained a teaching fellowship at Illinois Neuropsychiatric Hospital, where she spent three years working with junior and senior Northwestern University Medical School students. She also worked as a staff member at the Psychopathic Hospital of Cook County.

One of Wright's special interests was group therapy; collaborating with another doctor, she produced a paper on this subject. From 1945, she was involved in private psychiatric practice while continuing to work part time in various mental health facilities. The Mary Thompson Hospital where she worked was renamed the Katharine Wright Psychiatric Clinic.

Wright received numerous awards and honors. She was especially interested in the American Medical Women's Association of which she was president of the local branch (1947), the national (1958), and the international association (1958).   JH/MBO

PRIMARY SOURCES
"Wright, Katharine." In Hellstedt, *Autobiographies.*

WRIGHT, MABEL OSGOOD (1859–1934)

U.S. nature writer and bird conservationist. Born 28 January 1858 in New York City to Ellen Haswell Murdock and Rev. Samuel Osgood. Two sisters. Married James Osborne Wright 25 September 1884. Educated privately and at home. Professional experience: writer on birds and nature; New York Evening Post, contributor (1893); Bird Lore magazine, school and executive department (1899–1910); created bird sanctuary in Connecticut. Honors and memberships: American Ornithological Union, associate (1895), full member (1901); Connecticut Audubon Society, founding member (president, 1898). Died 16 July 1934 of hypertensive myocardial disease in Fairfield, Conn.

Mabel Osgood Wright, who wrote extensively on bird lore, was the daughter of a Unitarian pastor, later an Episcopal minister, in New York City. Athough her education was limited to a private school on Fifth Avenue, she soon developed a skill and facility for the written language. At the age of twenty-six, she married an English dealer in rare books. For some years she lived in England, and then returned to make her home in Fairfield, Connecticut. In her mid-thirties she began to write articles on nature, first in the *New York Evening Post* and then as pieces collected into books on nature and birds. In 1895, she published a field guide to two hundred native birds. Two years later she collaborated with a noted naturalist, Elliott Coues, to produce *Citizen Bird.*

The ornithologist Frank M. Chapman appreciated Wright's writing style and the intimacy it revealed with birds and flowers. He encouraged her to work in the executive and school departments of his magazine, *Bird Lore* for over eleven years. At this point she published another bird book called *Gray Lady and the Birds.* By 1910, she was a regular contributor until her death twenty-four years later. She was a founding member of the Connecticut Audubon Society, and served as its president for many years. Her interest in nature extended to protection of birds' environment, and she established a bird sanctuary near her home in Fairfield.

Wright also began to write romantic fiction under a pseudonym, "Barbara" (for example, *The Garden of a Commuter's Wife* and *The Stranger at the Gate*); in it she displayed much more sentimentality and conventionality than she expressed in her own life, attacking both career women and feminism. When Wright was sixty-seven, she wrote *My New York,* in which she primarily discussed in an autobiographical form her father's social world and its moral and religious beliefs but failed to mention her own important work in nature studies or bird conservation. However, she continued to write for the magazine *Bird Lore* almost until her death in 1934.   JH/MBO

PRIMARY SOURCES
Wright, Mabel Osgood. *The Friendship of Nature.* New York: Macmillan, 1895.
———. *Birdcraft: A Field Book of Two Hundred Song, Game and Water Birds.* New York: Macmillan, 1895.
———. With Elliott Coues. *Citizen Bird.* New York: Macmillan, 1897.
———. With Elliott Coues. *Gray Lady and the Birds.* New York: Macmillan, 1907.

STANDARD SOURCES
Bailey; *NAW* (article by Robert Welker); *NCAB.*

WRINCH, DOROTHY MAUD (1894–1976)

British mathematician. Born 1894 in Rosario, Argentina, to Ada Minnie (Souter) and Hugh Edward Hart Wrinch. Married (1) John William Nicholson; (2) Otto Charles Glaser (1941). One child, Pamela, by Nicholson. Educated Surbiton High School, Surbiton (suburb of London); Girton College, Cambridge (graduated 1916 as Wrangler in mathematics; M.A., 1918); Oxford University (D.Sc., 1929). Professional experience: University College, London, lecturer in mathematics (1918–1921); Girton College, Cambridge, research scholar (1921–1923); Oxford University, tutor in mathematics at the five women's colleges (1923–1927), lecturer (1927–1935); Johns Hopkins University, Rockefeller Foundation Fellow (1935–1940); Amherst, Smith, and Mount Holyoke Colleges, joint visiting professor (1941–1950); Smith College, visiting research professor (1950–1971). Died 1976.

Although Dorothy Wrinch was born in Argentina, her parents were British subjects, and they soon returned to Surbiton, a suburb of London, where she grew up. She married twice, the first time to John William Nicholson, a Fellow of the Royal Society, and director of studies in physics and mathematics at Balliol College, Oxford. Nicholson proved to be an alcoholic who required permanent institutionalization, and the marriage was dissolved by a Church of England decree in 1938. At the time of the marriage dissolution, Wrinch had been mathematics tutor for the five women's colleges and a member of the reorganized Natural Science

Faculty at Oxford. She was the first woman to receive a doctorate of sciences from Oxford. Wrinch's status changed from a don's wife to that of a single mother with a child. Her daughter Pamela was born in 1927. Her radically reduced income and lowered status stimulated her to leave Oxford. She applied for and received a five-year grant from the Rockefeller Foundation to study the application of mathematical techniques to biological problems. When World War II broke out, Wrinch was a visiting professor at Johns Hopkins. Jobs were scarce, and despite applying in both Canada and the United States, she remained without a permanent job. However, in 1940 she met biologist Otto Charles Glasser, who was vice-president of Amherst College and who set up a joint visiting professorship for Wrinch at four colleges. The couple married in 1941. This marriage was to be short as well, however, for Glaser died of nephritis in 1950. Upon his death, Wrinch moved to a house on the Smith College campus, and remained there as a visiting research professor until she retired in 1971. Her daughter, Pamela, earned a doctoral degree in international relations, from Yale, in 1954. Pamela died tragically in an accidental fire, and Wright died several months later, in 1976.

Surprisingly, given her superlative performance on the mathematical tripos, Wrinch's early publications were in philosophy. Influenced by her mentor, Bertrand Russell, between 1918 and 1932 she published sixteen papers on scientific methodology and philosophy of science. At first her interests in these areas were mainly relating methodology and philosophy of science to relativity theory. By the middle to late 1920s, she expanded her scientific methodological interests to include new theories in biology, physics, and other sciences. At about the same time she published around twenty papers in pure and applied mathematics. These papers, two of which she wrote with her father and two with her husband, considered topics such as real and complex variable analysis, Cantor's theory of sets, transfinite arithmetic, applications of potential theory in seismology, elasticity, vibrations, aerodynamics, electrostatics, and electrodynamics.

The most interesting aspects of Wrinch's work began in 1932 when she was invited to become a founding member of the Biotheoretical Gathering. As a goal, this group planned to apply ideas from the theoretical revolution in physics to biology, believing that mathematical techniques could solve this problem. The founders of this society included Joseph Henri Woodger, Joseph Needham, Conrad Hal Waddington, and John D. Bernal. Wrinch was a natural addition to this group, because of her training in philosophy and her long-time conviction that knowledge was interdisciplinary. Wrinch was interested in applying topology to experimental embryology. She recognized the possibility of funding from the Rockefeller Foundation for a Gathering-sponsored Research Institute. Although the Rockefeller Foundation failed to fund an entire institute, it funded small individual proposals. In 1935, Wrinch received a research grant enabling her to devote the bulk of her time to developing mathematical applications to biological problems. The movement gained momentum after Bernal and his doctoral student Dorothy Crowfoot (later DOROTHY HODGKIN) published the first X-ray photograph of a protein. Wrinch found this subject interesting and focused on geometrical approaches to protein structure. She developed a new theory of protein structure that combined ideas of mathematical symmetry with the notion of a relatively rare type of chemical bond, the cyclol bond. Wrinch hypothesized that the two-dimensional cyclol bond was the main link between the amino acids that made up the proteins. Wrinch believed that the spatial structure of proteins, considered the source of their functional versatility, was built of fabrics instead of chains, as the current theory assumed. The fabric model, where the bonds were two-dimensional rather than linear, seemed to fit the trigonal symmetry of insulin, best known from the crystallographic work of Bernal and Crowfoot. Many other examples seemed to fit the new model. When it was first proposed, her model greatly interested protein researchers. She made numerous international trips to search for new data for her theory. Wrinch's model was presented and discussed at many interdisciplinary meetings in the late 1930s; it was, however, attacked from two directions in 1939. The first claim that her model was supported by X-ray photographs implied that the crystallographers were unable to interpret their own findings. Bernal was particularly peeved, for he was considering proposing his own theory of protein structure and it appeared to him that Wrinch was attempting to preempt him. The confrontation between the two became bitter, as evidenced in a series of articles in *Nature*. British X-ray crystallographers discredited her model and refused to give her additional data to interpret mathematically. The rift with the British crystallographers was an important factor in convincing Wrinch to settle in the United States. However, in the United States she ran up against Linus Pauling, who succeeded in discrediting Wrinch with the Rockefeller Foundation and with the chemical community. The cyclol bond was discovered in nature and in the laboratory during the 1950s, and Wrinch became rehabilitated in part. Nevertheless, by this time the most interesting research in molecular biology had shifted to nucleic acids and away from proteins. Wrinch unflinchingly kept on with her research on proteins and rejected the double helix.

Wrinch was important as an early physical scientist who applied mathematical skills to biological problems. This type of approach eventually led to the rise of molecular biology in the 1930s. Although Wrinch's theory has been supplanted, her theory was very creative and in the 1930s was important enough to lead to her nomination for the Nobel Prize. Her ideas stimulated research in many different areas.   JH/MBO

PRIMARY SOURCES

Wrinch, Dorothy Maud. "The Structure of Insulin and the Cyclol Hypotheses." *Nature* 143 (1939): 673.

———. "The Structure of the Globular Proteins." *Nature* 143 (1939): 482.

———. With I. Langmuir. "Nature of the Cyclol Bond." *Nature* 143 (1939): 49.

———. *Fourier Transforms and Structure Factors.* Cambridge, Mass.: Society for X-ray and Electron Diffraction, 1946.

SECONDARY SOURCES

Abir Am, Pnina. "The Biotheoretical Gathering, Transdisciplinary Authority and the Incipient Letimation of Molecular Biology in the 1930s." *History of Science* 25 (1987): 1–70.

Senechal, M., ed. *Structure of Matter and Patterns of Science.* Cambridge, Mass.: Schenkman Press, 1980.

STANDARD SOURCES

AMS 7–8; Bailey; Debus; Grinstein 1993 (article by Pnina G. Abir-Am); Kass-Simon and Farnes; Ireland; Rossiter 1982; *Uneasy Careers* (article by Pnina Abir-Am).

WU CHIEN-SHIUNG (1912–1997)

Chinese/U.S. physicist. Born May 1912 in Liu Ho (Liuhe), a small town near Shanghai, China, to Wu Zong-Ye and Wu F. H. Fan. Two brothers. Married Luke Chia Liu Yuan (1942). One son, Vincent W. C. Yuan. Educated high school in Soochow; National Central Universitiy, Nanjing (B.S., 1936); University of California, Berkeley (Ph.D., 1940). Professional experience: University of California, Berkeley, resident fellow and lecturer (1940–1942); Smith College, assistant professor (1942–1943); Princeton University, instructor (1943–1944); Columbia University, scientific staff, Division of War Research ("Manhattan Project") (1944–1946), research associate (1946–1952), associate professor (1952–1957), professor of physics (1958–1972), Michael I. Pupin professor of physics (1972–1981); National Institutes of Health, member, Advisory Committee to the Director (1975–1982). Honorary Degrees and professorships: Princeton University, D.Sc. (1958); Smith College (1959); Goucher College (1960); Rutgers University (1961); Yale University (1967); Russell Sage College (1971); Harvard University (1974); Bard College (1974); Adelphi University (1974); Dickinson College (1975); Chinese University, Hong Kong, LL.D. (1969); Nanking University; Science and Technology University; Beijing University; Tsao Hwa University; Nan Kai University; and Padua University (Italy). Honors and memberships: National Academy of Sciences, member (elected 1958); Research Corporation Award (1958); American Association of University Women, Achievement Award (1960); National Academy of Sciences, Com-

stock Award (1964); Chi-Tsin Cultural Foundation, Taiwan, Chi-Tsin Achievement Award (1965); Industrial Research Magazine, Scientist of the Year Award (1974); American Physical Society, Tom Bonner Prize (1975); National Medal of Science (U.S.) (1975); Wolf Prize in Physics, Israel (1978); Royal Society of Edinburgh, honorary Fellow; American Academy of Arts and Sciences, Fellow; American Association for the Advancement of Science, Fellow; American Physical Society, Fellow. Died February 1997.

Born in China, Wu Chien-Shiung lived and was educated there through her bachelor's degree. Her father, an ardent believer in women's rights, insisted that she have the best possible education. The family home was full of books and magazines, and the family read together in the evenings. The local school offered only four elementary grades. However, the family supported her in attending a boarding school in Suzhou, the Suzhou Girls School, which offered a complete Western curriculum. Wu enrolled in the teachers' training program, which was both free and assured her of a job when she graduated. However, she soon realized that other students were learning more about science. She borrowed their books and taught herself mathematics, physics, and chemistry. She studied there from 1922 until 1930, when she graduated. Wu became a student activist at that time. After graduating from Suzhou with the highest grades in her class, she was selected to attend National Central University in Nanjing. Encouraged by her father, she studied mathematics and physics. In order to continue her studies in physics, Wu came to the University of California, Berkeley. At Berkeley, she studied with Nobel Prize–winner and inventor of the cyclotron, Ernest O. Lawrence, working with the interactions in noble gases for her doctoral degree. Although she was not a major participant, Wu participated in diagnosing problems with the first nuclear reactors and continuing chain reactions. The chain reaction worked for several hours and then mysteriously quit. She correctly diagnosed that xenon, one of the noble gases produced by fission, was the culprit. While she was at Berkeley, she met and married Luke Yuan Chia Liu (Luke Yuan), who had received his doctoral degree in physics from the California Institute of Technology. She and Yuan had a commuter marriage for most of their lives. The couple moved to the East Coast, where Wu first taught at Smith College and Yuan worked in Princeton, New Jersey. Wu liked teaching at Smith but missed the research, so when Lawrence recommended her to Princeton University, she accepted a position teaching advanced undergraduate physics. She became the first woman instructor at Princeton. In 1944 she began her career at Columbia University, first with the staff of the Division of War Research, where she helped to develop sensitive radiation detectors for the atomic bomb project. Wu and Yuan's son, Vincent Weichen, was born in 1947. Wu was one of the few Manhattan Project physicists asked to remain at Columbia after the war. She progressed through the academic ranks there, eventually attaining an endowed professorship. Wu and Yuan had a chance to return to China after the war, but after much soul searching they decided that they did not want to raise Vincent in a Communist country. They became United States citizens in 1954. Wu returned to China in 1973, finding her parents and brothers dead. Her older brother had been killed during the Cultural Revolution and her younger brother had been interrogated repeatedly and finally committed suicide.

Wu had worked on the fission products of uranium for her dissertation, but then turned to detailed measurements of the spectra from beta particle decay. Theoretical physics postulated that beta decay was caused by the weak interaction force and involved the emission of either an electron or its antiparticle, a positron, and a neutrino or an antineutrino. Enrico Fermi had proposed a theory in 1933 to determine how the nucleus reacts during beta decay, but other experimenters had failed to corroborate his predictions. He postulated that most of the electrons would burst out of the nucleus at high speeds whereas other experimenters had found great numbers of slow electrons. In order to test this theory experimentally, Wu developed methods for making precise measurements of the beta spectra of decaying nuclei. Accurate and precise, Wu recognized that the experimental results that contradicted Fermi were done through thick sections of radioactive materials. The electrons traveling through thick sections ricocheted off other atoms and lost energy. She found that when she used a thin sheet of uniform thickness, Fermi's results were corroborated. She worked on beta decay problems from 1946 to 1952. Although she had long been a Columbia researcher she did not become an actual Columbia faculty member until 1952.

Wu spent the years 1952 to 1956 exploring new research areas. Thus she was interested when Tsung Dao Lee of Columbia and Chen Ning Yang of the Institute for Advanced Study, Princeton, asked her help on a problem created by a newly discovered particle, the K-meson. Lee and Wang postulated that experimental results on the decay of the K-mesons indicated that parity and symmetry, considered basic laws of physics, were violated by the weak interaction. They needed experimental verification of this theory, however, and asked Wu's help in demonstrating this parity violation. She developed an experiment that confirmed Lee and Wang's theory of the violation of parity. Other laboratories confirmed Wu's results.

After this major success, Wu began a new series of experiments on beta decay. She was searching for confirmation or violation of conservation laws. After devising tedious, delicate experiments, Wu's results helped destroy what had previously been considered a law of nature. Lee and Yang won the 1957 Nobel Prize for physics for originating the idea, although Wu and many others thought she should have shared the honor. She did, however, win many other prestigious prizes.

Richard Feynman and Murray Gell-Mann of Caltech had hypothesized a new law of nature, the conservation of vector current in beta decay. However many experiments performed all over the world failed to confirm their theory. Wu, in 1963, devised an experiment that confirmed the laws.

Wu entered the field of biophysics late in her career. She became interested in studying changes in hemoglobin during oxygenation and deoxygenation and then in the study of the causes of sickle-cell anemia.

Wu worked very hard and demanded equal dedication from her collaborators and students. She had a sharp tongue and when she felt that workers were not giving their all to their projects, she could be quite acerbic. Physics always occupied the number one position in her life. She loved her husband and son (who later became a physicist), but there was never a question about her priorities.   JH/MBO

PRIMARY SOURCES

Wu Chien-Shiung. With I. Shaknov "The Angular Correlation of Scattered Annihilation Radiation." *Physical Review* 77 (1950): 136.

———. With E. Ambler, R. W. Hayward, D. D. Hoppes, and R. P. Hudson. "Experimental Test of Parity Conservation in Beta Decay." *Physical Review* 105 (1957): 1413.

———. With Y. K. Lee and L. W. Mo. "Experimental Test of the Conserved Vector Current Theory of the Beta Spectra of B^{12} and N^{13}." *Physical Review Letters* 10 (1963): 253.

———. "The Universal Fermi Interaction and the Conserved Vector Current in Beta Decay." *Review of Modern Physics* 36 (1964): 618.

———. *Beta Decay.* New York: Interscience Publishers, 1966.

———. With L. Wilets. "Muonic Atoms and Nuclear Structure." *Annual Reviews of Nuclear Science* 19 (1969): 527.

SECONDARY SOURCES

Lubkin, Gloria. "Chien-Shiung Wu, the First Lady of Physics Research." *Smithsonian* (1971): 52–56.

McGrayne, Sharon Bertsch. *Nobel Prize Women in Science: Their Lives, Struggles and Momentous Discoveries.* New York: Birch Lane Press, 1993.

STANDARD SOURCES

Grinstein 1993 (article by Ruth Howes); *Notable.*

WUNDT, NORA (1895–?)

German physician. Born 13 September 1895 to a British-born mother and a father who was a German infantry officer. Two brothers.

Educated girls' school; Munich, private preparatory courses for girls; University of Munich (M.D., 1923). Professional experience: Stuttgart, assistant in a hospital for infants (1924–1925); voluntary work (1925); children's hospital in Greifswald, physician (1926–1930); Feuerbach in Stuttgart, private practice as a children's specialist (1930–1970). Honors and memberships: German Women's Medical Association (from 1930). Death date unknown.

Born in Germany to an infantry officer father and British-born mother, German physician Nora Wundt lived through two world wars. When she was nineteen years old, she joined the Red Cross and served as an auxiliary nurse for several months. However, she decided that medicine interested her more than nursing, and with the approval of her parents she decided to go to medical school. As her early education had been inadequate, she had to take remedial courses in Munich and take the examination as an extern in a Bavarian boys' school. Only after she passed the examination was she able to enter the University of Munich. The university was closed in the winter of 1918 through 1919, at which time she worked as a nurse in a hospital for infants. She was awarded her medical degree in 1923 after passing the final examination in 1922.

She spent a year as an assistant in a hospital for infants in Stuttgart, and then did voluntary work in the clinic of a well-known pediatrician. After these experiences she decided to specialize in pediatrics.

After four years when she was a physician in the children's hospital in Greifswald, she established her own practice as a children's specialist in Feuerbach, a highly industrialized part of Stuttgart. She remained there for forty years. Wundt was active in the German Women's Medical Association (GWMA) and attended most of the national and international medical women's conventions held in Europe. From 1953 to 1967 Wundt was chairperson of the Baden Württemberg section of the GWMA.

During the early part of World War II, her office was severely damaged by air raids, but she continued to practice, for there was a great need for doctors. Even after the war, the situation was very difficult, but life gradually returned to normal, and her patients reappeared. Wundt retired from active practice in 1969 and moved to the outskirts of Stuttgart.

KM

PRIMARY SOURCES
"Wundt, Nora." In Hellstedt, *Autobiographies.*

WYCKOFF, DELAPHINE GRACE (ROSA) (1906–)

U.S. microbiologist. Born 11 September 1906 in Beloit, Wis., to Grace (Chamberlin) and Charles Darwin Rosa. Married John

Franklin Wyckoff (1942). Educated University of Wisconsin (Ph.B., 1927; Ph.M., 1928; Ph.D., 1938). Professional experience: North Dakota Agricultural College, Fargo, faculty (1928–1937), assistant professor, bacteriology (1936–1937); Wellesley College, faculty (from 1938), professor (from 1957). Honors and memberships: American Association for the Advancement of Science, American Society of Microbiology, Society of General Microbiology, National Association of Biology Teachers, Sigma Xi, Sigma Delta Epsilon, Alpha Gamma Delta, Phi Delta Gamma.

Delaphine Grace Wyckoff earned three degrees at the University of Wisconsin before she took a position in Fargo, North Dakota, at the agricultural college, where she spent four years. She did not become assistant professor until 1937 and remained at that rank for only one year before leaving for a position at Wellesley College. She became professor at Wellesley in 1957. While at Wellesley, she worked on the Biological Sciences Curriculum Study, a project designed to promote a revolution in biology teaching.

Wyckoff's major research was on yeast metabolism and antibacteriological agents, subjects on which she published. She was a member of numerous professional organizations, including the American Association for the Advancement of Science, American Society of Microbiology, Society of General Microbiology, National Association of Biology Teachers, Sigma Xi, Sigma Delta Epsilon (national president, 1961), Alpha Gamma Delta, and Phi Delta Gamma.

JH/MBO

PRIMARY SOURCES
Wyckoff, Delaphine Grace Rosa. *A Laboratory Guide in General Bacteriology.* Minneapolis, Minn.: Burgess, 1944.

STANDARD SOURCES
AMS 8, B 9, P&B 10–14.

WYCKOFF, DOROTHY (1900–)

U.S. geologist. Born 22 July 1900 in Topsfield, Mass. Educated Bryn Mawr College (A.B., 1921; Workman fellow, 1928–1929; American-Scandinavian Foundation fellow, 1929–1930; Ph.D., 1932); Royal University of Norway (1928–1930). Professional experience: Misses Kirk's School, teacher (1922–1924); Bryn Mawr College, demonstrator in geology (1925–1928; 1931–1932), instructor (1932–1934), assistant professor (1934–1943), from associate professor to emerita professor (from 1945); U.S. Geological Survey, military geology unit, researcher (1943–1945).

Most of Dorothy Wyckoff's academic training was at Bryn Mawr where she earned both of her degrees. She remained at this institution after receiving her doctorate as an instructor, advancing to assistant professor. During World War II, she took two years out of her academic career to work for the military unit of the U.S. Geological Survey. After the war she returned to Bryn Mawr and advanced from associate professor to emerita professor. Her research was on the petrology of metamorphic rocks.   JH/MBO

PRIMARY SOURCES

Wyckoff, Dorothy. *Geology of the Mt. Gausta Region in Telemark, Norway.* Bryn Mawr, Pa.: Bryn Mawr College, 1933. Reprinted from *Norsk geologisk tidsskrift* (Oslo) 13, no. 1 (1933). Ph.D. dissertation.

———. With Ann M. H. Ehrich and Emilio O. Forrer. *Early Pottery of the Jebeleh Region.* Philadelphia: American Philosophical Society, 1939.

Watson, E. H. *Guidebook Illustrating the Geology of the Philadelphia Area.* [Bryn Mawr, Pa.]: Bryn Mawr College, 1951. Figures drawn by Dorothy Wyckoff.

STANDARD SOURCES

AMS 6–8, P 9, P&B 10–11.

WYLIE, MARGARET (1889–?)

U.S. psychologist. Born 7 December 1889 in Red Rock, Iowa. Educated University of Michigan (A.B., 1918; A.M., 1924); Butzel fellow, 1924–1925; Ph.D., 1928); Columbia University (1926). Professional experience: New York public schools, teacher (1910–1916); U.S. Public Health Service, Detroit, psychologist (1918–1919); Wayne County Psychopathic Clinic, researcher (1919–1925); Cornell University, assistant professor of child development (1925–1927); Institute of Juvenile Research, Chicago, psychologist (1928–1929); University of Michigan, acting assistant professor of child development (1929–1930); Cornell University, professor (from 1930). Death date unknown.

Psychologist Margaret Wylie was born in the Midwest, but in 1918, even before she got her bachelor's degree, went to New York, where she taught in the public schools. She returned to the University of Michigan, where she earned her three degrees. After she received her master's degree, she began work in Detroit as a psychologist with the U.S. Public Health Service and the Wayne County Psychopathic Clinic. While finishing her doctoral research, she taught at Cornell and then worked at the Institute of Juvenile Research in Chicago, returning for a year to teach at the University of Michigan before she obtained as academic position at Cornell University.   JH/MBO

PRIMARY SOURCES

Wylie, Margaret. *An Experimental Study of Recognition and Recall in Abnormal Mental Cases.* Princeton, N.J.: Psychological Review Company, [1930].

STANDARD SOURCES

AMS 5–8, S&B 9–10; Rossiter 1982.

WYNNE, FRANCES ELIZABETH (1916–1985)

U.S. botanist. Born 25 July 1916 in Wilkinsburg, Pa. Educated Allegheny College (A.B., 1938); University of Michigan (M.S., 1939; Ph.D., 1942). Professional experience: New York Botanical Garden, assistant curator (from 1938).

Botanist Frances Wynne earned her two higher degrees from the University of Michigan. She then went to the New York Botanical Garden, where she worked as an assistant curator.   JH/MBO

PRIMARY SOURCES

Wynne, Frances. *A Revision of the North American Species of Drepanocladus.* Ph.D. diss., University of Michigan, 1942.

———. With William C. Steere. "The Bryophyte Flora of the East Coast of Hudson Bay" *Bryologist* 46 (1943): 73–87.

STANDARD SOURCES

AMS 7–8.

WYTTENBACH, JEANNE GALLIEN (d. 1830)

German healer. Educated University of Marburg (degree, 1773). Married. Died 1830.

Jeanne Wyttenbach received a medical degree from the University of Marburg. The actual nature of that degree is unknown. Among other books, she wrote one on Greek medical history and another entitled *Beauty, Love and Friendship.*   JH/MBO

PRIMARY SOURCES

Wyttenbach, Jeanne. *Ho Alexis: Metaphrastheis apo ten Galliken glossan* [*hypo Phrankia Phournarake*]. Paris: Phirminou Didodou, 1823.

———. *Symposiaques: ou Propos de table.* Paris: Renouard, 1823.

SECONDARY SOURCES

Demaras, Konstantinos. *Coray et Jeanne Wyttenbach; quelques documents inedits 1823–1829.* Athens, 1947.

Y

YOUNG, ANNE SEWELL (1871–1961)

U.S. astronomer. Born 1871 in Bloomington, Wis., to Mary (Sewell) and Rev. Albert Young. Never married. Educated Carleton College (B.L., 1892; M.S., 1897); University of Chicago (1892; M.S., 1897); University of Chicago (1898 and 1902); Columbia University (Ph.D., 1906). Professional experience: Whitman College, Walla Walla, Wash., instructor (1892–1893), professor of mathematics (1893–1895); Mount Holyoke College, John Payson Williston Observatory, director; head of astronomy department, instructor, and later professor (1899–1936). Died 1961 in Claremont, Calif.

Anne Young's uncle, Charles Augustus Young, was professor of astronomy at Princeton University, so she may have been familiar with the subject from an early age. After receiving degrees from Carleton College, she first attended the University of Chicago and then went to Columbia University, where she received a doctoral degree. She wrote her dissertation on the double cluster in the constellation Perseus; it was based on measurements of early photographs. While a graduate student, Young taught mathematics at Whitman College, in Walla Walla, Washington. She then began her long career at Mount Holyoke. She was appointed director of the John Payson Williston Observatory and head of the department of astronomy in 1899, at first with the rank of instructor and later as professor. She retired from Mount Holyoke in 1936.

Young was a member of the Royal Astronomical Society, the American Astronomical Society, the Astronomical Society of the Pacific, the American Association for the Advancement of Science, and the Phi Beta Kappa honorary society. After she retired, she went with her sister, Elizabeth, to live in a settlement, Pilgrim Place, in Claremont, California, for the elderly relatives of missionaries.

Anne Young's scientific work consisted mostly of observing variable stars. She exchanged information with Harvard College Observatory director Edward Pickering. Young supervised an active program of observations and kept a daily record of sunspots. She promoted public interest in astronomy by providing a series of open nights at the Holyoke observatory and by writing a monthly column on astronomy for the *Springfield Republican*. She published some eleven papers, as well as newspaper articles, reports of observations made at the observatory, and notes on popular astronomy.

JH/MBO

PRIMARY SOURCES

Young, Anne. *Rutherford Photographs of the Stellar Clusters h or x Persei*. Contributions from the Observatory of Columbia University 24 (1906). Ph.D. diss., Columbia University.

SECONDARY SOURCES

Hogg, Helen Sawyer. "Anne Sewell Young." *Quarterly Journal of the Royal Astronomical Society* 3 (1962): 355–357.

STANDARD SOURCES

AMS 2–8, P 9; Jones and Boyd; Ogilvie 1986.

YOUNG, GRACE EMILY (CHISHOLM) (1868–1944)

British mathematician. Born 15 March 1868 in Haslemere, Surrey, to Anna Louisa (Bell) and Henry William Chisholm. Two surviving siblings. Married William Henry Young. Six children. Educated Girton College, Cambridge (1889–1892, first-class honors); Oxford University (sat informally for final mathematics examinations 1892, placed first); Göttingen University (Ph.D. magna cum laude, 1895). Died 1944 of a heart attack in England.

Grace Chisholm, the first woman to receive a doctorate in any field from a German university, received her early education at home. Her father was a career civil servant who went through the ranks to become the chief of Britain's weights and measures. Her brother, Hugh Chisholm, had a distinguished career as editor of the famous eleventh edition of the *Encyclopaedia Britannica*. She married the Cambridge mathematician William Henry Young, with whom she produced books on elementary mathematics.

Although Grace had initially wanted to study medicine, her mother forbade it, so she settled for mathematics, which she studied at Girton College, Cambridge. Her mathematical abilities were recognized, and she became Girton's Sir Francis Goldschmid Scholar of mathematics and graduated with first-class honors. She went to Göttingen University in 1893, where she attended lectures and produced a dissertation, "The Algebraic Groups of Spherical Trigonometry," under the important mathematician Felix Klein.

Chisholm married her former Girton tutor, William Henry Young, and after the birth of the first of their six children moved to Göttingen where William Young pursued a career in mathematics. Although Grace Young did not have a paid position, she supported her husband in his research. During this time, she was able to pursue her other interest, anatomy, which she studied at the university while raising the children. Although the family lived modestly, finances were always a problem, and William Young often traveled to earn money by teaching. The family moved from Göttingen to Geneva in 1908. William Young constantly sought a lucrative position in England, but failed to obtain one. He did, however, obtain one in Calcutta, India, which required him only to be in residence for a few months each year. At the end of World War I, he obtained a professorship at the University of Wales in Aberystwyth, where he remained for several years. During the time her husband was seeking a position and taking temporary jobs, Young and the family remained in Switzerland. Their final separation occurred in 1940, when she was in England and he in Switzerland. The outbreak of the war precluded them from seeing each other again. William Young died in 1942.

Grace Young had supplemented much of William Henry Young's mathematical works. Her most important work was done between 1914 and 1916, when she published papers on derivates of real functions and contributed to what is known as the Denjoy-Saks-Young theorem.

Most of Grace Young's mathematical productivity occurred before 1929, when she began a historical novel that was never published. She found writing fiction and children's books and exploring music, languages, and medicine occupied her time.   MBO

PRIMARY SOURCES

Young, Grace Chisholm. With William Henry Young. *The First Book of Geometry*. London: Dent, 1905.

———. "On the Form of a Certain Jordan Curve." *Quarterly Journal of Pure and Applied Mathematics* 37 (1905): 87–91.

———. With William Henry Young. *The Theory of Sets of Points*. Cambridge: Cambridge University Press, 1906.

———. With William Henry Young. "An Additional Note on Derivates and the Theorem of the Mean." *Quarterly Journal of Pure and Applied Mathematics* 40 (1909): 144–145.

———. "A Note on Derivatives and Differential Coefficients." *Acta Mathematica* 37 (1914): 141–154.

———. With William Henry Young. "On the Reduction of Sets of Intervals." *Proceedings of the London Mathematical Society* 14 (1914): 111–130.

———. "On the Solution of a Pair of Simultaneous Diophantine Equations Connected with the Nuptial Number of Plato." *Proceedings of the London Mathematical Society* 23 (1925): 27–44.

SECONDARY SOURCES

Cartwright, M. L. "Grace Chisholm Young." *Journal of the London Mathematical Society* 19 (1944): 185–192.

Grattan-Guinness, Ivor. "A Mathematical Union: William Henry and Grace Chisholm Young." *Annals of Science* 29 (1972): 105–186.

STANDARD SOURCES

Grinstein and Campbell; *Notable* (article by Lewis Pyenson).

YOUNG, LEONA ESTHER (1895–?)

U.S. chemist. Born 1895 in Alameda, Calif. Educated University of California (B.S., 1915; M.S., 1916; Ph.D., 1928). Professional experience: Eldorado Oil Works, California, research chemist (1918–1920), consulting chemist (1920–1922); Dr. Albert Rowe, research chemist and X-ray technician (1922–1923); Anna Head School, head, department of science (1923–1927); Mills College, assistant professor (1927–1937), associate professor (1937–1940), professor and head of department (1940–1957). Retired 1957. Death date unknown.

Leona Esther Young received all of her education at the University of California and spent her entire career on the West Coast. She advanced through the academic ranks at Mills College, and finally reached the rank of professor and head of the department. Her major research interest was in physical chemistry. She worked on calomel and silver electrodes, optically active compounds, the stereochemistry of deuterium compounds, alphamethylbenzyl amine, and molecular rearrangement induced by ultrasonic waves.   JH/MBO

PRIMARY SOURCES

Young, Leona Esther. "A Study on the Preparation and Properties of Phthalic Acid." Master's thesis, University of California, Berkeley, 1916.

———. "The Calomel and Silver Chloride Electrodes in Acid and Neutral Solutions. The Activity Coefficient of Acqueous Hydrochloric Acid and the Single Potential of the Decimolal calomel Electrode." *Journal of the American Chemical Society* 50 (1928): 989.

———. With C. W. Porter. "Stereochemistry of Deuterium Compounds. I. Optical Rotation of Methylhelyldeutero-carbinol." *Journal of the American Chemical Society* 59 (February 1937): 328–329.

———. With C. W. Porter. "Stereochemistry of Deuterium Compounds. II. Alphamethylbenzylamine." *Journal of the American Chemical Society* 59 (1937?): 1437–1438.

———. With C. W. Porter. "A Molecular Rearrangement Induced by Ultrasonic Waves." *Journal of the American Chemical Society* 60 (1938): 1497–1500.

———. With C. W. Porter. *General Chemistry: A First Course.* New York: Prentice-Hall, Inc., 1940. Prentice-Hall chemistry series.

———. "Flow Sheet and Material Balance of a Quantitative Experiment." *Journal of Chemical Education* 18 (January 1941): 32–34.

STANDARD SOURCES
AMS 5–8, P 9, P&B 10–11.

YOUNG, MABEL MINERVA (1872–1963)

U.S. mathematician. Born 18 July 1872 in Worcester, Mass. One half-sister, Mrs. H. Bramwell Shaw. Educated Worcester Classical High School; Wellesley College (A.B., 1898); Columbia University (A.M., 1899); Johns Hopkins University (Ph.D., 1914). Professional experience: Northfield Seminary, teacher (1899–1902); Wellesley College, assistant professor, associate professor, professor (1904–1941), emerita professor (1941–1963). Died 4 March 1963.

Mabel Young became a fixture at Wellesley, known for her teas, her love of music and gardening, and her ability to inspire students. Although she had an excellent sense of humor, she was a shy person who avoided publicity whenever possible.

Young's ancestors were English and Scots-Irish and had settled in Massachusetts by 1627. Her father was on the School Board and in the State Legislature, and she attributes her interest in civic affairs to his influence. She credited her mother with inspiring her love of music; she studied the piano for years. She grew up in Worcester, Massachusetts, and attended the Classical High School there. It had an excellent reputation, and Mabel was well prepared when she entered Wellesley in 1894.

After she received her bachelor's degree she studied for a year at Columbia University and received her master's degree in 1899. After receiving this degree, she took a teaching job at Northfield Seminary, where she taught mainly English. She left Northfield to accept a job as assistant in mathematics at Wellesley. This position involved teaching one or two freshman sections. Since this was a light load, Young was able to take some graduate courses each year and by doing so achieved the rank of instructor. During her instructorship she got a leave of absence to study at Johns Hopkins University, where she earned her doctoral degree. She continued up the academic ladder until she became Lewis Atterbury Stimson Professor of Mathematics.

Young's major emphasis was on teaching. For many years, she worked only with freshman. The students concluded that she was not "easy" but was always fair. Later her name became associated with the geometry courses. Although she was much more of a theoretician than an applied mathematician, she often taught a statistics course. She was also known for her service to the College. As a member of the Academic Council, her reports were clear, though technical.

Her research was on the projective properties of surfaces and curves. Her doctoral thesis from Johns Hopkins was in geometry—on Dupin's cyclide as a self-dual surface. She also published on curves arising from a single infinity of triangles tangent to a parabola.

Young was a member of Phi Beta Kappa, Sigma Xi, the American Mathematics Society, Mathematical Association of America, and the American Statistical Associations. She was also a member of the History of Science Society and the American Association of University Professors.

Young spent her last days in Weld House, a nursing home in Wellesley.

PRIMARY SOURCES
Young, Mabel M. "Curves Arising from a Single Infinity of Triangles." *American Mathematical Monthly* 40, no. 4 (April 1933): 196– 202. Ph.D. diss., Johns Hopkins University, 1914.

———. "Dupin's Cyclide as a Self-Dual Surface." *American Journal of Mathematics* 38, no. 3 (July 1916): 269–286.

SECONDARY SOURCES
"Courses Taken at Wellesley College by Mabel Minerva Young." Wellesley College Archives, Wellesley, Mass.

"Mabel Young, 89, Headed Math Dept. at Wellesley College." *Boston Globe,* 5 March 1963. Wellesley College Archives, Wellesley, Mass.

"Mabel M. Young Dies, Former Math Professor." *Worcester (Massachusetts) Gazette,* 5 March 1963.

Merrill, Helen A. "Mabel Minerva Young." *The Wellesley Magazine* (June 1941): 415–416. Wellesley College Archives, Wellesley, Mass.

"Professor Young of Wellesley." *Record-American,* 5 March 1963. Wellesley College Archives, Wellesley, Mass.

Stark, Marion E. "In Memoriam Mable M. Young." Wellesley College Archives, June 1963.

Wellesley College Alumnae Association. "1942 Biographical Record." Wellesley College Archives, Wellesley, Mass.

"Wellesley Professor Dies." *The Standard-Times.* 5 March 1963. Wellesley College, Archives, Wellesley, Mass.

STANDARD SOURCES
AMS 5–8, P 9.

YOUNG, MARY SOPHIE (1872?–1919)

U.S. botanist. Born 20 September 1870 or 1872 in Glendale, Ohio, to Emma Adams (Sawer?) and Charles Huntington Young. Brothers. Educated Ohio public schools; Harcourt Place Seminary; Wellesley College (A.B., 1895); University of Chicago (graduate student fellow, 1908–1910; Ph.D., 1910). Professional experience: Louis Academy, Sullivan, Mo., teacher; Dundee (Ill.) High School, teacher; Kansas City, Kans., teacher; Grafton Hill, Fond-du-Lac, Wis., teacher; University of Texas, tutor in botany (1910), instructor (1911), herbarium curator (1912–1919). Died of cancer 5 March 1919.

Botanist Mary Sophie Young received her early education in Ohio and then attended Wellesley College, where she earned a bachelor's degree. She continued her education at the University of Chicago where she received a doctoral degree.

Young taught at the University of Texas. Her taxonomic skills were recognized, and she was made curator of the university herbarium. Young conducted pioneering work in the field of plant classification throughout the Central and West Texas area, making many arduous field trips and bringing back to the university's herbarium thousands of plants previously unrepresented in the collections. After completing major publications on plants of the Austin area and increasing the herbarium's holdings from 2,500 specimens to 16,000, she became ill and died of cancer while in her late forties. Her journal for the 1914 summer expedition to the Trans-Pecos area was published many years after her death.

JH/MBO

PRIMARY SOURCES
Young, Mary Sophie. *A Key to the Families and Genera of the Wild Plants of Austin Texas.* Austin, Tex.: The University, [1917].
———. *The Seed Plants, Ferns, and Fern Allies of the Austin Region.* Austin, Tex.: The University, [1920].
———. *Journal of Botanical Explorations in Trans-Pecos Texas, August–September 1914.* Ed. B. C. Tharp and Chester V. Kielman. Austin, Tex.: s.n., 1962?
Her papers are in the Barker Texas History Center, University of Texas at Austin.

SECONDARY SOURCES
Tharp, B.C., and Chester V. Kielman, eds. "Mary S. Young's Journal of Botanical Explorations in Trans-Pecos Texas." *Southwestern Historical Quarterly* 65 (January, April 1962).

YOUNG, ROGER ARLINER (1889–1964)

U.S. zoologist. Born 1889 in Clifton Forge, Va. Educated Burgettstown, Pa., public schools; Howard University (B.A., 1923); University of Chicago (M.A., 1926); University of Pennsylvania (Ph.D., 1940). Professional experience: Howard University, instructor, assistant professor (1923–1935); North Carolina College for Negroes and Shaw University, North Carolina, faculty (1940–1947); other colleges in Texas, Louisiana, Mississippi, faculty member (1950–1959; Marine Biological Laboratories, Woods Hole, researcher (summers 1927–1936). Died 9 November 1964.

Roger Arliner Young was the first African-American woman to rise to prominence in scientific research. She completed her undergraduate degree in zoology at Howard University under the renowned black zoologist Ernest Everett Just and helped him to establish an excellent zoology department, shouldering much of the teaching as assistant professor from 1923 to 1935. In 1924 she published her first paper in *Science*, on the excretory mechanisms that control salt concentrations in Paramecium. During this period, she worked toward a master's degree in zoology, taking summer classes at the University of Chicago. She earned excellent grades and received the master's in 1926, but experienced difficulties as she went on to work toward the doctorate under Frank Lillie, Just's mentor. Possibly because of a severe bout of depression, she failed the qualifying examination in January 1930. She assisted Just in his research on ultraviolet radiation of marine invertebrate eggs at the Marine Biological Laboratories during the summers of 1927–1930. Her assistance was recognized in his applications for grants, but she was not given coauthor status in the resulting papers. In the mid-1930s, Just began to take extended leaves from Howard to travel to Europe, where he worked at the Naples Marine Research Station and in Germany. With the loss of her mentor's support, Young began to flounder under the burdens of heavy teaching loads and having little money or encouragement for research. Just had experienced subtle exclusion and tacit racism during his career, but the same prejudices were heightened for a black woman scientist, especially after she ceased to have Just's support. Her research at Woods Hole continued through the summer of 1936.

Losing her teaching position at Howard in 1936, finishing out her contract until spring 1937, she went to the University of Pennsylvania to study for her doctorate. During this difficult period, she published a number of original papers, some of them with L. V. Heilbrunn, her dissertation advisor, extending the work she had begun with Just on the effects of radiation on sea urchin eggs (1938) and on the embryological development of the annelid (1939). Her work on calcium activation in Mactra, however, remained unpublished, although it was cited by Heilbrunn. In 1940, she received her doctorate and moved to the South to teach at a series of black colleges in North Carolina from 1940 to 1947 and in Texas, Louisiana, and Mississippi during the 1950s. She had no opportunities for further independent research, and by the early 1960s she was again plagued by bouts of the depression that had affected her all her life. She died 9 November 1964.   JH/MBO

PRIMARY SOURCES

Young, R. A. "On the Excretory Apparatus in Paramecium." *Science* n.s. 60 (1924): 224.

———. With L. V. Heilbrunn. "Indirect Effects of Radiation on Sea-Urchin Eggs." *Biological Bulletin* 69 (1935): 274–279.

———. "The Effects of Roentgen Irradiation on Cleavage and Early Development of the Annelid, *Chaetopterusperga-mentaceu s.*" *Biological Bulletin* 75 (1938): 378.

———. With D. P. Costello. "The Mechanism of Membrane Elevation in the Egg of *Nereis.*" *Biological Bulletin* 77 (1939): 311.

SECONDARY SOURCES

Hammonds, Evelynn. "Roger Arliner Young." In *Black Women in America: An Historical Encyclopedia,* ed. Darlene Hine, 1298–1299. New York: Carlson, 1993.

Manning, Kenneth R. *Black Apollo of Science: The Life of Ernest Everett Just.* New York: Oxford University Press, 1983. See pages 109–110, 147–148, 217–220, and 272–273.

———. "Roger Arliner Young, Scientist." *Sage: A Scholarly Journal on Black Women* (Fall 1989).

Z

ZACHRY, CAROLINE BEAUMONT (1894–1945)

U.S. psychologist. Born 20 April 1894 in New York City to Elise Clarkson (Thompson) and James Greer Zachry. Educated Columbia University (B.S., 1924; A.M., 1925; Ph.D., 1929); Oxford University; New York School of Social Work. Professional experience: Lincoln School, instructor; Columbia University Teachers College, associate professor (1922–1923); New Jersey State Teachers College, Upper Montclair, N.J. (1925–1934); Progressive Education Association, director Research Commission Secondary School Curriculum and Chairman, study of adolescents (1934–1939); Institute for the Study of Personality Development, director (1943); Ethical Culture Schools, New York City, Mental Hygiene Consultant (1935–1942); Board of Education, New York City, Bureau of Child Guidance (from 1942); Columbia University, lecturer. Honors and memberships: Psychological Association, member; National Committee on Mental Hygiene; Orthopsychiatric Association, Fellow; Progressive Education Association, director; New York Academy of Science. Died 1945.

Caroline Zachry earned her three degrees from Columbia University and spent the first part of her career at the State Teachers College in Upper Montclair, New Jersey. Her research interests were in mental hygiene and in the personality adjustment of school children. Her study of the emotions and conduct of adolescents, particularly junior high school students, led to a plan in New York to reorganize secondary education.   KM

STANDARD SOURCES
AMS 5–7; Stevens and Gardner; *Women of Psychology.*

ZAKLINSKAIA, ELENA DMITRIEVNA (1910–1989)

Russian palynologist and biostratigrapher. Born 2 April 1910 in Vladivostok. Educated at secondary school in Moscow; Moscow State University. Candidate of geological-mineralogical sciences,
1950; doctor of geological-mineralogical sciences. Professional experience: Geological Institute of the Soviet Academy of Sciences, associate professor. Honors and memberships: State Prize, 1950; Erdtman gold medal, 1980. Died 10 October 1989.

Elena Dmitrievna Zaklinskaia graduated from secondary school in Moscow and passed the examinations to the Moscow Conservatory. However an injury to her arm forced her to abandon a musical career. Instead Zaklinskaia became a student at the Medical Institute, but soon transferred to the geology department of the Moscow State University. As a student she took part in an expedition to Lake Baikal headed by A. E. Fersman, whom she credited as being her first tutor.

Zaklinskaia came to palynology, the branch of geology concerned with pollen and spores, from geology while working as a field geologist in the Urals, Sakhalin, Western Siberia, and Kazakhstan. In 1933, she used a method of analysis of pollen and spores to differentiate strata for a hydrogeology project.

In 1939 Zaklinskaia became associated with the Geological Institute of the Soviet Academy of Sciences. There she organized the Laboratory for Spore and Pollen Analysis, the first of its kind in the Soviet Union, and began laying the groundwork for palynology as a distinct science. She was particularly concerned to define the border between the Mesozoic and the Cenozoic for purposes of correlating continental and oceanic sediments.

Zaklinskaia was awarded a candidate's degree (similar to a doctorate) in 1950. Her thesis discussed the stratigraphic significance of holosperms in Cenozoic deposits of the Irtysh and Northern Aral regions. Her doctoral thesis, which she defended in 1964, was a fundamental generalization of scientific studies in the field of biostratigraphy and palynology of the Kazakhstan Cenophytic.

Zaklinskaia published over 120 works. One series of publications was devoted to methods of palynological studies to be applied in stratigraphy and paleofloristics. She also wrote about longterm changes of basic floras. Much of her material she collected herself. As well as expeditions to Kazakhstan and the Far East, she made a sea voyage on the *Vitiaz* and accumulated a substantial collection of pollen of tropical plants.

Zaklinskaia took an active part in international conferences and she was an organizer of the palynological section of the Moscow branch of the All-Union Botanical Society of the USSR and president of the Palynological Commission of the Scientific Council of the Soviet Academy of Sciences. In 1971, together with M. I. Neishtadt, she organized the International Palynological Commission. Zaklinskaia served on a number of commissions and was a member of the editorial board of *Review of Palaeobotany and Palynology* and a consultant for *Grana Palynologica*.

Zaklinskaia received a State Prize in 1950. In 1980 she was awarded the Erdtman gold medal instituted by India.   ACH

PRIMARY SOURCES

Zaklinskaia, Elena Dmitrievna. "Pyl'tsa pokrytosemiannykh i ee znachenie dlia obosnovaniia stratigrafii." *Trudy Geologicheskogo instituta* 74 (1963).
———. With Vladimir P. Grichuk. *Palinologiia chetvertichnogo perioda*. Moscow: "Nauka," 1985.

SECONDARY SOURCES

Brattseva, G. "Elena Dmitrievna Zaklinskaya, 1910–1989." *Review of Palaeobotany and Palynology* (1989): 1–2. Obituary notice.
Rovnina, L. V., et al. "Elena Dmitrievna Zaklinskaia, 1910–1989." *Izvestiia Akademii nauk SSSR. Seriia geologicheskaia* 12 (1990): 12: 132–133. Obituary notice.

ZAKRZEWSKA, MARIE ELIZABETH (1829–1902)

U.S. physician. Born 6 September 1829 in Berlin, Germany, to Frederika C. W. (Urban) and Martin Ludwig Zakrzewski. Five siblings. Educated Berlin girl's school; Charité Hospital School for Midwives, Berlin (graduated 1851); Western Reserve (Cleveland Medical College) (M.D., 1856). Professional experience: Charité Hospital (Berlin), chief midwife and instructor (1852–1853); New York, private practice (1856–1857); New York Infirmary for Women and Children (1857–1859); New England Female Medical College, professor of obstetrics and diseases of women and children (1859–1862); New England Hospital for Women and Children, founder and attending physician (1862–1887), advisory physician (1888–1899). Concurrent experience: Boston private practice (1865–1899). Died 12 May 1902 in Jamaica Plain, Mass., of heart disease.

Marie Zakrzewska's father was a Pole who had served in the Prussian army but was dismissed for his liberal views. The family lived in poor circumstances in Berlin, supported only by his pension, which pushed Zakrzewska's mother to look for a position as a midwife. Accompanying her mother to the hospital, she was attracted to medicine.

Zakrzewska studied with and then became assistant to Dr. Joseph Hermann Schmidt, head of the school for Midwives at the Charité Hospital in Berlin. Schmidt attempted to install her as chief midwife and professor at the school upon his retirement, but she was in her early twenties, and her youth caused a great deal of resentment. She decided to leave Germany, where there was a prejudice against women physicians, and study medicine in the United States. Moving to New York with two of her sisters, Zakrzewska met ELIZABETH BLACKWELL, who took her under her wing and obtained a place for her at Western Reserve (Cleveland Medical College), where Elizabeth's sister, EMILY BLACKWELL, had studied. Receiving her medical degree after two years of study, Zakrzewska returned to New York and opened a small private practice in the back parlor of the Blackwell sisters' home. Within a year, Elizabeth and Emily Blackwell joined with her to open a woman's hospital, the New York Infirmary for Women and Children, the first staffed entirely by women.

Zakrzewska spent two years as resident physician and general manager, and the hospital was a success. She then accepted an offer from Dr. Samuel Gregory to move to Boston. She welcomed the opportunity to teach obstetrics and diseases of women and children at Gregory's New England Female Medical College and to establish a new hospital for women. After three years, during which Zakrzewska built a reputation for obstetrical and gynecological teaching, she and Gregory quarreled about inadequate teaching offered within other areas of the school and about his inclusion of dubious physicians. Upon her resignation, Gregory disbanded the small hospital she had initiated. Zakrzewska—with the help of interested patrons and other women physicians, including her former student and colleague, LUCY ELLEN SEWALL—then took the opportunity to found a new institution, the New England Hospital for Women and Children (now incorporated into Beth Israel Medical Center). Many young women who went on to become important physicians, including MARY PUTNAM JACOBI, the Englishwoman SOPHIA JEX-BLAKE, African-American CAROLINE VIRGINIA ANDERSON, and surgeon SUSAN DIMOCK, either studied or interned at the hospital.

Although Zakrzewska expended intense energy to make a success of the hospital, she also threw her support to the abolitionist movement, as a friend of Wendell Phillips, Theodore Parker, and William Lloyd Garrison. Patrons of the hospital came from the ranks of socially committed women and men such as Samuel Sewall, Lucy Sewall's father. She supported the woman's rights movement throughout her life and, like her friend, the radical German-American journalist Karl Heinzen, considered herself a free thinker. As she aged, she began to suffer from arthritis and heart disease and turned much of the daily surgical work and supervision over to her colleagues. She retired three years before her death.

JH/MBO

PRIMARY SOURCES

Zakrzewska, Marie Elizabeth. *Address before the Moral Education Association of Massachusetts: Introductory Lecture Delivered Wednesday, November 2, before the New England Female Medical College at the Opening of the Term of 1859–60.* Boston: C.H. Simonds & Co., 1888.

———. *A Practical Illustration of Woman's Right to Labor; or, A Letter from Marie E. Zakrzewska.* Ed. Caroline H. Dall. Boston: Walker, Wise, and Co., 1860.

SECONDARY SOURCES

Drachman, Virginia G. *Hospital with a Heart: Women Doctors and the Paradox of Separatism at the New England Hospital, 1862–1969.* Ithaca: Cornell University Press, 1984.

New England Hospital for Women and Children. *Marie Elizabeth Zakrzewska, 1829–1902: A Memoir.* Boston: The New England Hospital for Women and Children, 1903.

Tuchman, Arlene M. "'Only in a Republic Can It Be Proved That Science Has No Sex': Marie Elizabeth Zakrzewska (1829–1902) and the Multiple Meanings of Science in the Nineteenth Century in the United States." *Journal of Women's History* 11 (1999): 121–142.

Walsh, Mary Roth. *Doctors Wanted, No Women Need Apply.* New Haven: Yale University Press, 1977.

Vietor, Agnes C., ed. *A Woman's Quest: The Life of Marie E. Zakrzewska, M.D.* New York: D. Appleton and Co., 1924. Includes autobiographical chapters.

Correspondence can be found in the papers of the May and Goddard families, the Blackwell family, Caroline Wells Healey Dall, and Frances Rollins Morse, Schlesinger Library, Radcliffe College. Archives of the New England Hospital for Women and Children are in the Boston University Library.

STANDARD SOURCES

Bonner; Morantz-Sanchez; *NAW* (article by John B. Blake); Uglow 1982.

ZALESSKAYA-CHIRKOVA, ELENA (1894–1972)

Soviet geologist and paleontologist. Born 1894 to working-class parents. Married M. D. Zalesskiy. Educated Moscow gymnasium and historical-philological department of the Highest Women's Courses (completed 1918); University of Moscow (1924–1930); candidate and doctoral degree. Professional experience: Middle School teacher (1918–1924); Geological Committe, junior scientific researcher, senior scientific researcher (1929–1941); "Coal City" researcher (1941–1944); All-Union Institute of Raw Minerals, Coal Department, researcher (1945–1946); Petroleum Institute of the Academy of Sciences of the USSR (from 1948). Died 1972.

Elena Chirkova's father was from a peasant family and her mother from the petty bourgeoisie. They considered education important for their daughter, and she attended the Moscow *gymnasium* and finished the Highest Women's Courses. After completing these courses in 1918, she passed the government examinations, and taught in the middle schools for six years. Desiring more education, she entered Moscow University in 1924 and took courses in geology. From 1929, she worked on the Geological Committee as a junior scientific researcher, then as a senior scientific researcher, studying the coal-bearing series of Donbas; Kuzbas in the Permian and Lower Carboniferous of the Urals.

Elena's husband, M. D. Zalesskiy, was an outstanding paleobotanist—really the founder of Russian paleobotanical science. Elena herself became an expert on Paleozoic floras and became a corresponding member of the Academy of Sciences of the USSR. From 1941 to 1944, she contributed to the war effort by moving to Egorshino, known as Coal City, on the eastern side of the Urals. Coal, of course, was of major strategic importance to the Soviet Union during that time.

After the war, Elena and her husband moved to Moscow and worked in the coal department of the All-Union Institute of Raw Minerals, where they studied the flora of the Podmoskovniy coal basin.

After her beloved husband died in 1946, Zalesskaya-Chirkova did not work anywhere for two years. When she did return to work she changed her research topic and dropped the Carboniferous series and studied the paleoflora of oil and gas deposits, where she studied the Paleozoic flora of the Volga-Ural oil-bearing region. She studied core samples from numerous wells. In these samples she found not only the famous Permian and Carboniferous plants but the lesser known Devonian ones, including the very ancient Psilophyta.

In 1948, she entered the Petroleum Institute of the Academy of Science of the USSR, which was later reorganized in the Institute of Geology and Exploration of Combustible Fuels. She remained at that institute until retirement.

Elena Zalesskaya-Chirkova's scientific work was important, especially her studies of the unknown material of the Paleozoic of the USSR. In addition to her own materials, she studied and stored the much larger collection of her husband, M. D. Zalesskiy. These collections contained the richest, most unique Lower Permian plants of the Pechora coal-bearing basin and the entire western Urals. The collections from Donbas, Kuzbas, and all of the Ural deposits are also very important.

Zalesskaya-Chirkova published thirty-six works, most of which were dedicated to the floras of the coal-bearing series of Pechora, Donetsk, and the Kuzbas basins. She published less on the flora of the Volga-Ural oil-bearing basin. Although she defended her thesis at both a candidate and doctoral level, she never taught in the institutes of higher education.

CK

PRIMARY SOURCES

Chirkova, Elena. With M. D. Zalessky. "Carte de l'extension du continent de l'Angaride d'apres les decouvertes de la flore permienne." *Problemy paleontologii (Moscow Universitet Paleontologiskaia laboratoriia)* 5 (1938): 311–324. In French. Map of the extension of the Paleozoic Angarida continent in Russia based on the distribution of the Permian flora.

———. "Contribution a la flore permienne des rivages de la mer de Kara, du golfe d'Enissei et de la portion occidentale de la presqu'ile de Taimyr en general (bassin de la riv. Piassina)." *Byulleten'Moskovskogo Obshchestva Ispytateley Prirody, Otdel Geologicheskiy* 49, no. 19 (1941): 75–101. Describes elements of the Permian flora of the Kara sea shores, the Yenisei gulf and the western part of the Taimyr peninsula in general.

Zalesskaya-Chirkova, Elena. With S. M. Doroshko. "O prisutstvii nizhnedevonskikh otlozhenii v Severo-Minusinskoi vpadine." *Akademii Nauk SSSR, Inst. Nefti* 5 (1955): 17–21. Reports occurrence of lower Devonian deposits in the northern Minusinsk basin in Asiatic USSR.

———. "Materialy po nizhnedevonskoi flore Minusinskoi kotloviny." *Akademii Nauk SSSR, Inst. Nefti* 7 (1956): 60–70. Describes remains of plants from lower Devonian formations of the Minusinsk basin, USSR.

———. With Andrei Vasilevich Khizhnyakov. "K stratigrafii nizhnedevoniskikh otlozhenii Podolskogo Pridnestrovya." *Doklady Akademii Nauk SSSR* 228, no. 3 (1958): 569–572.

STANDARD SOURCES

Nalivkin.

ZANIEWSKA-CHILPALSKA, EUGENIA (1889–1980)

Polish mineralogist, igneous petrologist, and pedologist. Born 1889. Professional experience: Warsaw Polytechnic, the Geological Survey of Poland, and the Soils Institute, Warsaw Agricultural Academy. Died 1980.

Zaniewska-Chilpalska studied pegmatites, phosporites, and soil mineralogy.

JH/MBO

PRIMARY SOURCES

Zaniewska-Chlipalska, Eugenia. "O skladzie chemicznym pewnych adularow: sur la composition chimique de quelques adulaires." *Archiwum Mineralogiczne* 13 (1937): 20–31.

SECONDARY SOURCES

"Eugenia Zaniewska-Chlipalska." *Rocznik Polskiego Towarzystwa Geologicznego* 51, nos. 3–4 (1981): 617–622.

Siewniek-Witruk, Alina. "Wiktor Zajaczkowski 1902–1974." *Roczniki Polskiego Towarzystwa Geologicznego* 45, nos. 3–6 (1975): 467–468.

STANDARD SOURCES

Sarjeant.

ZECKWER, ISOLDE THERESE (1892–?)

U.S. pathologist. Born 10 October 1892 in Philadelphia, Pa., to Marie T. (D'Invilliers) and Richard Zeckwer. Educated Bryn Mawr College (A.B., 1915); Woman's Medical College of Pennsylvania (M.D., 1919). Professional experience: Mayo Clinic, Rochester, Minn., fellow in pathological anatomy (1921–1922); Harvard Medical school department of pathology, staff researcher (1922–1926); Lying-In Hospital, Boston, pathologist (1922–1926); University College, London, researcher in physiology (1926–1927); University of Pennsylvania School of Medicine, department of pathology, faculty (1927–1958), professor of pathology (1954–1958), emerita professor (from 1958). Death date unknown.

Isolde Zeckwer was a diplomate of the American Board of Pathology. She belonged to many professional societies, including the Society for Experimental Pathology, the American Association of Pathologists and Bacteriologists, the American Physiology Society, and the American Association for Cancer Research. She published papers on functional and structural changes in endocrine organs under physiological and pathological conditions in animals and worked on experimental tumors in animals.

JH/MBO

STANDARD SOURCES

Debus.

ZENARI, SILVIA (1895–1956)

Italian biologist and geologist. Born 31 March 1895 in Udine to Elisa Pitter and Aristide Gabelli. Educated Vittorio Veneto; Padua, gymnasium and lyceum; University of Padua (graduated 1918). Professional experience: Istituto di Geologia, assistant; Istituto Botanico, assistant. Died 30 June 1956 in an automobile accident.

Although Silvia Zenari was born in Udine, Italy, her engineer father was transferred to Valcelina, where he worked on the construction of one of the first hydroelectric facilities. Silvia was in constant contact with nature and she enjoyed learning about the flora, fauna, and minerals of the mountains. She was admitted to the University of Padua, where she studied geology, specifically mineralogy. She worked on the petrography, stratigraphy, and tectonics of the Alps and might have continued along this road if she had not found it impossible to receive an assistantship through the Institute of Geology. Instead she went to the Botanical Institute, where she was the assistant to Professor Beguinot and then Professor Gola. In 1930, she began to teach secondary school. She first taught in Rovigo, then in the science high school at Padua, in Pordenone, and again in the science high school.

From 1918 to 1938, Zenari collaborated with Professor Dal Piaz on the compilation of a geological map of Trevenezie. She also studied the vegetation from the Corniche pre-Alps to the central ridge of the high Friulana Plain. She also explored a large portion of the dolomite sector, the crystalline rock sector, and metamorphic rock between Adige, Isarco, and Rienza.

Her various explorations allowed her to produce several papers on the flora of the Cellina Valley (1920, 1923, and 1925). She also published on the conifers in the Alps and on the flora of the Comelico and the eastern Alps. Although much of her work involved listing the plants of the areas, by putting them into a geographical and geological context she was able to contribute to the study of phytogeography.

Zenari's first publication was in 1919, and during the course of the next thirty-six years she published over sixty papers.

JH/MBO

PRIMARY SOURCES

Zenari, Silvia. "Sulla tettonica dei dintorno di Lozzo in Cadore." *Accademia Scientifica Veneto-Trentino-Istriana, Atti 3* 24 (1934): 3–7.

———. "Particolarità tettoniche al Ponte della Chiusa in valle del Boite (Cadore)." *Accademia Scientifica Veneto-Trentino-Istriana, Atti 3* 25 (1935): 151–156.

———. "Intorno alla tettonica della valle del Piave nel tratto fra Lozzo e Pieve di Cadore." *Bollettino della Società Geologica Italiana* 54 (1935): 172–174.

———. "La valle d–Oten ed il monte Antelao." *Bollettino della Società Geologica Italiana* 55 (1936): 155–168.

———. "Particolarità tettoniche nelle Alpi Bellunesi: Studio geotettonico del gruppo m. Schiara, m. Pelf, m. Serva." *Bollettino della Società Geologica Italiana* 57 (1938): 49–76.

SECONDARY SOURCES

Zangheri, P. "Silvia Zenari (1895–1956)." *Archivio botanico e biogeografico italiano* ser. 4, 32 (1956): 106–109.

STANDARD SOURCES
Sarjeant.

ZHUZE, ANASTASIYA PANTELEYEMONOVNA (1905–1981)

Russian geologist. Born 31 July 1905 in Kazan'. Father P. K. Zhuze. Six siblings. Married K. K. Markov. Educated Baku University (graduated 1928); USSR Academy of Sciences candidate's dissertation (1939); doctoral degree (1959). Professional experience: Scientific Research Institute of Geological Prospecting, Laboratory of Paleobotany, Leningrad, researcher (1932–1937); Institute of Geography, USSR Academy of Sciences, researcher (1937–1951); Institute of Oceanography, USSR, researcher (1951–1981). Died 12 September 1981.

Anastasiya Panteleyemonovna was born in Kazan' to a professor at Kazan' University who was a specialist on the history and literature of the East. The family was Arabic in origin and moved to the USSR during the last part of the nineteenth century. Anastasiya Panteleyemonovna grew up in Baku, where P. K. Zhuze had been invited to organize the university. She graduated from the department of natural science at Baku, where she studied biology. After graduation, she moved to Leningrad, where she worked at the Scientific Research Institute of Geological Prospecting in the Laboratory of Paleobotany. In 1932, she married K. K. Markov, who later became a well-known geographer.

Zhuze's career was divided into several distinct parts. In the 1930s, she and her teacher, V. S. Poretskiy, founded and developed Diatom Analysis. From 1932 to 1939, she studied diatomaceous algae from the Quaternary deposits of Leningrad Oblast and from the European portion of the Soviet Union. Her work on this subject provided the theme for her candidate's dissertation. From 1937, Zhuze moved to Moscow, first to the Institute of Geography and later under contract for the Moscow Geological Prospecting Institute and the Urals Geological Administration. In about 1945, she began a series of studies on fossil diatomaceous algae from the Cretaceous and Paleogene in the Urals and from the Volga area. These works were important because they formed the basis of the stratigraphic distinction of silicaceous rock using diatom content. In 1951, Zhuze underwent another rather distinct career change: she went to the Institute of Oceanography, USSR Academy of Sciences. There she worked on the stratigraphy of deposits and paleogeography of the far eastern seas and then other oceanic regions. She increasingly concentrated on the study of the ancient flora of the ocean, while remaining a specialist in algology.

Zhuze served as the nucleus of a group of Soviet micropaleontologists. She was chair of the section on marine paleontology of the Oceanographic Commission, USSR Academy of Sciences. An excellent organizer, Zhuze arranged conferences on problems of marine micropaleontology, headed the Commission on Algae, and was on the organization committee for both national and international conferences. CK/MBO

PRIMARY SOURCES

Zhuze, Anastasiya Panteleyemonovna. "K istorii diatomovoi flory ozera Khanka." *Akademia Nauk SSSR, Institut Geog. Trudy* 51 (1952): 226–252.

———. "Stratigraficheskie i paleogeograficheskie issledovaniya v severo sapadnoi chasti Tikhogo okeana." Moscow: *Akademiya Nauk SSSR, Institut Okeanologii, Trudy* 1962.

———. "Drevniye diatomei i diatomovyye porody Tikhookeanskogo basseyna." *Litologiya i Poleznyye Iskopayemyye* Lithology and Mineral Resources 1 (1968): 16–32.

———. "Stratigrafiya verkhnekaynozoyskikh otlozheniy po diatomeyam." In *Geologicheskaya istoriya Chernogo morya po rezul'tatam glubokovoknogo bureniya,* ed. Yu. P. Neprochnov, 52–65. Moscow: Izdanja Nauka, 1980.

SECONDARY SOURCES

"Anastasiya Panteleyemonovna Zhuze (31 July 1905–12 September 1981)." *Oceanology* 22, no. 2 (1982): 260–261.

Krasheninnikov, V. A. "Pamyati Anastasii Panteleymonovnyy Zhuze (1905–1981)." In *Morskaya Mikropaleontologiya,* ed. A. P. Zhuze and V. A. Krasheninnikov, 4–10. Moscow: Izdanja Nauka, 1982.

ZIEGARNIK, BLIUMA (VULFOWNA) (1900–1988)

Russian psychologist. Educated Berlin University under Kurt Lewin (Ph.D., 1927). Professional experience: Moscow State University, professor of psychology. Died 1988.

Ziegarnik's dissertation was the first to test Lewin's theory that attainment of a goal or successful locomotion toward a positive valence relieves tension. Ziegarnik assumed that the assignment of a simple task creates tension. Her test involved simple tasks (solving simple puzzles, laying blocks in a pattern, clay figure modeling) given to subjects who were interrupted during completion of some tasks but not during others. An hour later the interrupted tasks were better recalled than those completed, lending support to Lewin's theory. The phenomenon has become known as the Zeigarnik effect.

Ziegarnik was one of the few clinical psychologists in the Western sense practicing in Russia, where most psychology concentrates almost exclusively on behavior pathology. Her area of research focused on the psychoses, and she published papers on the history of abnormal psychology in the USSR. She is considered part of the Luria and Vygotsky school of Soviet psychology. JH/MBO

PRIMARY SOURCES

Ziegarnik, Bliuma. *The Pathology of Thinking.* Trans. from Russian. New York: Consultants Bureau, 1965.

———. *Experimental Abnormal Psychology.* Trans. from Russian. New York: Plenum Press, 1972.

SECONDARY SOURCES

Sheehy, Noel, J. Chapman, and Wendy A. Conroy, eds. *Biographical Dictionary of Psychology.* London: Routledge Reference, 1997.

STANDARD SOURCES

Encyclopedia of Psychology.

ZLATAROVIC, RELY (fl. 1920)

Meteorologist who worked in Austria. Professional experience: Physical Institute of the University of Innsbruck, Austria, researcher.

Rely Zlatarovic developed a different method for measuring the quantity of radioactive gases in air samples, which she used to determine the effects of meteorological factors on this quantity. Her experiments, performed at the Physical Institute of the University of Innsbruck (Austria), showed that precipitation decreased the quantity of radium emanation (radon) in air. MM

PRIMARY SOURCES

Zlatarovic, Rely. "Messungen des Ra-Emanationsgehaltes in der Luft von Innsbruck." *Akademie der Wissenschaften, Vienna, Sitzungsberichte* 2a, 129 (1920): 59–66.

STANDARD SOURCES

Meyer and von Schweidler.

LIST OF SCIENTISTS
BY OCCUPATION

A

activists
  political
    Barney, Nora Stanton (Blatch) De Forest, 83
    Fleming, Amalia Coutsouris, Lady, 451–53
  public health
    Breckinridge, Mary, 175–76
  social
    Bissell, Emily P., 132
    Dennett, Mary Ware, 347

administrators
  medical
    Ann Medica of York, 40–41
    Dempsey, Sister Mary Joseph, 345
    Heloise, 582–83
    Palmer, Sophia French, 976–77
  public health
    Kovrigina, Mariia Dmitrievna, 722–23
  university
    Pendleton, Ellen Fitz, 1002–3

agriculturalists
  Sessions, Kate Olivia, 1177–78
  Strong, Harriet Williams (Russell), 1248–49

agronomists
  Pinckney, Eliza (Lucas), 1024–25
  Ushakova, Elizaveta Ivanovna, 1314

agrostologists
  Chase, Mary Agnes Meara, 246–47

alchemists
  Anne, Electress of Denmark, 41
  Bertereau, Martine De, Baroness De Beausoleil, 119
  Cleopatra, 269
  Flammel, Perrenelle, 451
  Mary the Jewess, 850
  Mildmay, Grace Sherrington, 894
  Paphnutia the Virgin, 978
  Theosebeia, 1278

algologists
  Gatty, Margaret (Scott), 490–91

anatomists
  Arconville, Geneviève Charlotte D', 49
  Bassi, Laura Maria Caterina, 88–89
  Biheron, Marie Catherine, 126
  Bishop, Katharine Scott, 131–32

Boyer, Esther Lydia, 168
Crosby, Elizabeth Caroline, 305–6
Delauney, Marguerite De Staël, 342
De Witt, Lydia Maria Adams, 353–54
Friant, M., 473
Gage, Susanna Phelps, 480–81
Galvani, Lucia (Galeazzi), 481–82
Giliani, Alessandra, 502
Lewis, Margaret Adaline Reed, 785–86
Logan, Myra Adele, 800
Manzolini, Anna Morandi, 841
Moody, Mary Blair, 910
Peretti, Zaffira, 1006
Pettracini, Maria, 1013
Sabin, Florence Rena, 1140–42
Scott, Flora Murray, 1168
Trotter, Mildred, 1303–4
White, Frances Emily, 1372

anthropologists
  Aberle, Sophie Bledsoe, 4–5
  Beckwith, Martha Warren, 102–3
  Benedict, Ruth (Fulton), 113
  Blackwood, Beatrice Mary, 139
  Bourdel, Leone, 163–64
  Bouteiller, Marcelle, 164
  Bunzel, Ruth Leah, 208
  Cadilla De Martínez, María, 218–19
  Carroll, Christiane (Mendrez), 232
  Curtis, Natalie, 318–19
  De Laguna, Fredericka Annis Lopez De Leo, 339–41
  Deloria, Ella Cara, 343–44
  Diggs, Ellen Irene, 357
  Du Bois, Cora, 377–78
  Dutton, Bertha, 390–91
  Ellis, Florence Hawley, 419
  Friant, M., 473
  Gardner, Elinor Wight, 483–84
  Garfield, Viola Edmundson, 485–86
  Genet-Varcin, E, 494
  Goldfrank, Esther Schiff, 513–14
  Green, Vera Mae, 526–27
  Gunther, Erna, 538
  Hanks, Jane Richardson, 552–53
  Herskovits, Frances S.(Shapiro), 590–91
  Hunt, Eva Verbitsky, 629–30

Hurston, Zora Neale, 632–33
Kaberry, Phyllis Mary, 673–74
Kelly, Isabel Truesdell, 686–87
Keur, Dorothy Louise (Strouse), 692–93
King, Georgina, 695
Kroeber, Theodora Kracaw, 725–26
Landes, Ruth (Schlossberg), 740–41
Leacock, Eleanor Burke, 757–58
Leakey, Mary Douglas (Nicol), 758–59
Lebedeva, Nataliia Ivanovna, 760
Leighton, Dorothea (Cross), 769–70
Leschi, Jeanne, 776
Luomala, Katharine, 811–12
Mair, Lucy Philip, 832
Marriott, Alice Lee, 844–45
Mead, Margaret, 872–74
Nuttall, Zelia Maria Magdalena, 954
Parsons, Elsie Worthington (Clews), 982–83
Pink, Olive Muriel, 1025–26
Powdermaker, Hortense, 1047–48
Reichard, Gladys Amanda, 1087
Richards, Audrey Isabel, 1093–94
Robeson, Eslanda Cordoza (Goode), 1110–11
Rubin, Vera (Dourmashkin), 1133–34
Schwidetsky, Ilse, 1166–67
Seligman, Brenda Zara, 1174–75
Shepardson, Mary, 1184
Smith, Anne Millspaugh (Cooke), 1201–2
Smith, Marian Wesley, 1207–8
Steed, Gitel Poznanski, 1224–25
Stevenson, Matilda Coxe (Evans), 1232–33
Stone, Doris Zemurray, 1240–41
Thompson, Laura, 1284
Tisserand, M., 1294
Trotter, Mildred, 1303–4
Tunakan, Seniha (Hüsnü), 1307
Wallis, Ruth Sawtell, 1342–44
Wedgwood, Camilla Hildegarde, 1354–56
Weltfish, Gene, 1364–66
Wessel, Bessie (Bloom), 1366
White, Marian Emily, 1373
Wilson, Lucy Langdon (Williams), 1386
Wilson, Monica Hunter, 1387–88

arachnologists
  Peckham, Elizabeth (Gifford), 999

archeologists
Armitage, Ella Sophia A.(Bulley), 52
Caetani-Bovatelli, Donna Ersilia, 219–20
De Laguna, Fredericka Annis Lopez De Leo, 339–40
Dohan, Edith Haywood Hall, 364–65
Dutton, Bertha, 390–91
Ellis, Florence Hawley, 419
Garrod, Dorothy Anne Elizabeth, 488–89
Goldman, Hetty, 514–15
Hansen, Hazel D., 553
Harrison, Jane Ellen, 558
Hawes, Harriet (Boyd), 568–69
Hawkes, Jacquetta (Hopkins), 569
Kelly, Isabel Truesdell, 686–87
Kent, Kate Peck, 690–91
Kenyon, Kathleen Mary, 691–92
Kletnova, E.N., 704–5
Leakey, Mary Douglas (Nicol), 758–59
Lewis, Madeline Dorothy (Kneberg), 784–85
Lewis, Mary Butler, 786–87
Meritt, Lucy Taxis (Shoe), 885
Murray, Margaret Alice, 926
Nuttall, Zelia Maria Magdalena, 954
Popenoe, Dorothy K.(Hughes), 1040–41
Porada, Edith, 1041–42
Proskouriakoff, Tatiana, 1057–58
Rydh, Hanna, 1139
Schliemann, Sophia (Kastromenos), 1160–61
Schmid, Elisabeth, 1161
Stevenson, Sara (Yorke), 1233
Stokes, Margaret McNair, 1239
Stone, Doris Zemurray, 1240–41
Swindler, Mary Hamilton, 1256
Uvarova, Countess Praskov'ia Sergeevna, 1314–15
Van Deman, Esther Boise, 1319
White, Marian Emily, 1373
Wormington, Hannah Marie, 1400–1401

architects
Barney, Nora Stanton (Blatch) De Forest, 83
landscape
Colvin, Brenda, 282–83
Jekyll, Gertrude, 655–56
King, Louisa Boyd (Yeomans), 697–98

artists
Adamson, Joy (Gessner), 8–9
botanical
Delaney (or Delany), Mary (Granville), 341
Earle, Marie Theresa (Villiers), 394
Everard, Barbara Mary Steyning, 430
Fielding, Mary Maria (Simpson), 444–45
Godfery, Hilda Margaret, 510
Hassall, Bessie Florence (Cory), 564
Lansdell, Kathleen Annie, 745
Mason, Marianne Harriet, 851
May, Caroline Rebecca, 859–60
Mee, Margaret Ursula (Brown), 876
Nicholson, Barbara Evelyn, 942
North, Marianne, 951–52
Pallis, Marietta, 973
Rice, Elsie (Garrett), 1092
Smith, Matilda, 1208
Snelling, Lilian, 1209–10
Telfair, Annabella (Chamberlain), 1273

Trower, Charlotte Georgiana, 1305
Turner, Mary (Palgrave), 1308–9
Withers, Augusta Innes (Baker), 1390
Brooke, Winifred, 184
Brooks, Sarah Theresa, 186
Danti or Dante, Theodora, 325
Lee, Sarah Wallis Bowdich, 765
Rodde, Dorothea von (Schlözer), 1117
Schurman, Anna Marie van, 1165–66
See also illustrators

astronomers
Aglaonike, 13–14
Albertson, Mary, 18
Barney, Ida, 82
Blagg, Mary Adela, 139–40
Brown, Elizabeth, 189
Byrd, Mary Emma, 216
Cannon, Annie Jump, 227–28
Cook, A.Grace, 287–88
Cunitz, Maria, 309–10
Cunningham, Susan, 311
Cushman, Florence, 319
De Breaute, Eleonore-Nell-Suzanne, 335
Dumee, Jeanne, 382
Eimmart, Marie Claire, 409
Evershed, Mary Orr, 431–32
Farnsworth, Alice Hall, 434
Fatima, 436
Fleming, Williamina Paton Stevens, 453–54
Furness, Caroline Ellen, 478–79
Gill, Jocelyn Ruth, 502–3
Hansen, Julie Marie Vinter, 554
Harwood, Margaret, 562–63
Herschel, Caroline Lucretia, 587–89
Hevelius, Elisabetha Koopman, 593
Hoffleit, Ellen Dorrit, 607–8
Hogg, Helen Sawyer, 608–9
Huggins, Margaret Lindsay (Murray), 626–27
Iwanowska, Wilhelmina, 647
Janssen, Mme, 653–54
Kent, Elizabeth Isis Pogson, 690
King, Susan (Raymond), 698–99
Kirch, Christine, 700
Kirch, Margaretha, 700
Kirch, Maria Margaretha Winkelmann, 700–701
Lalande, Marie Jeanne Amélie Harlay Lefrancais de, 735–36
Leavitt, Henrietta Swan, 759
Leland, Evelyn, 770
Lepaute, Nicole-Reine Hortense (Etable de La Brière), 772–73
Lewis, Florence Parthenia, 782–83
Lewis, Isabel (Martin), 783–84
Makemson, Maude (Worcester), 832–33
Maunder, Annie Scott Dill Russell, 855–56
Maury, Antonia Caetana de Paiva, 856–57
Meyer, Margaret Theodora, 890
Mitchell, Maria, 901–5
Palmer, Margaretta, 976
Payne-Gaposchkin, Cecilia Helena, 994–96
Pettit, Hannah Steele, 1013
Pierry, Louise Elizabeth du, 1024
Prince, Helen Walter (Dodson), 1055
Roberts, Dorothea Klumpke, 1106

Scarpellini, Caterina, 1156
Swope, Henrietta (Hill), 1256–57
Thome, Frances, 1282
Tinsley, Beatrice Muriel (Hill), 1292–93
Vivian, Roxana Hayward, 1329
Vyssotsky, Emma T. R. (Williams), 1333
Wang Zhenyi (Chen-i), 1345
Ward, Mary (King), 1346
Wells, Agnes Ermina, 1362
Wells, Louisa D., 1363
Whiting, Sarah Frances, 1374
Whitney, Mary Watson, 1374–75
Wilson, Fiammetta Worthington, 1385
Winlock, Anna, 1388–89
Winthrop, Hannah Fayerweather Tolman, 1389
Wright, Frances Woodworth, 1405
Young, Anne Sewell, 1413

astrophysicists
Douglas, Alice Vibert, 372
Gjellestad, Guro Else, 505
Massevitch, Alla Genrikhovna, 851–52
Sitterly, Charlotte Emma (Moore), 1197

authors. *See* writers

B

bacteriochemists
Ermol'eva, Zinaida Vissarionovna, 425

bacteriologists
Bengston, Ida Albertina, 114–15
Bliss, Eleanor Albert, 146
Broadhurst, Jean, 181–82
Collins, Katharine Richards, 282
Coyle, Elizabeth Eleanor, 299
Engelbrecht, Mildred Amanda, 422
Evans, Alice Catherine, 428–30
Fleming, Amalia Coutsouris, Lady, 451
Genung, Elizabeth Faith, 494–95
Gilbert, Ruth, 500–501
Hamilton, Alice, 549–50
Hefferan, Mary, 578
Hill, Justina Hamilton, 601
Jermoljeva, Zinaida Vissarionovna, 657
Kirkbride, Mary Butler, 701
Klieneberger-Nobel, Emmy, 705–6
Koch, Marie Louise, 712–13
Lancefield, Rebecca Craighill, 739–40
Lange, Linda Bartels, 743
McKinney, Ruth Alden, 870–71
Moore, Ruth Ella, 912
Myers, Mabel Adelaide, 929
Petran, Elizabeth Irene, 1012
Pittman, Margaret Jane, 1030–31
Povitsky, Olga Raissa, 1047
Rabinovitch-Kempner, Lydia, 1067
Smart, Helen Edith (Fox), 1200
South, Lillian Herrald, 1218
Stewart, Sarah Elizabeth, 1236
Tunnicliff, Ruth, 1307–8
Verder, Ada Elizabeth, 1326
Williams, Anna Wessels, 1380–82
Woolley, Mildred Thompson, 1399

bibliographers
Henrey, Blanche Elizabeth Edith, 584
Hooker, Marjorie, 615
Vavrinova, Milada, 1324–25

bioacousticians
Fish, Marie Poland, 448
biochemists
Anderson, Evelyn M., 35–36
Banga, Ilona, 75–76
Breyer, Maria Gerdina (Brandwijk), 179
Brown, Rachel Fuller, 191
Buell, Mary Van Rensselaer, 203
Chaix, Paulette Audemard, 242
Chick, Dame Harriette, 250–51
Chmielewska, Irene, 253–54
Cohn, Essie White, 278–79
Cori, Gerty Theresa Radnitz, 292–94
Daniels, Amy L., 325
Davis, Alice (Rohde), 329
Davis, Marguerite, 332–33
Dyer, Helen Marie, 391–92
Eichelberger, Lillian, 408
Einstein, Elizabeth Roboz, 410–11
Elion, Gertrude Belle, 415–16
Emerson, Gladys Ludwina (Anderson),
    420–21
Farr, Wanda Kirkbride, 435–36
Flock, Eunice Verna, 455
Graham, Helen (Treadway), 522
Jordan-Lloyd, Dorothy, 669
Kenny, Elizabeth (Sister Kenny), 689
Knake, Else, 708
Kobel, Maria, 711
Krasnow, Frances, 725
Lu Gwei Djen, 809–10
MacLean, Ida (Smedley), 826–27
Man, Evelyn Brower, 835–36
Maver, Mary Eugenie, 858
Menten, Maud L., 882–83
Miller, Elizabeth Cavert, 896–97
Minot, Ann Stone, 898–99
Morgan, Agnes Fay, 913
Needham, Dorothy Mary (Moyle), 932–33
Okey, Ruth Eliza, 961
Onslow, Muriel (Wheldale), 962–63
Parsons, Helen Tracy, 984
Perlmann, Gertrude Erika, 1007–8
Petermann, Mary Locke, 1010–11
Peterson, Ruth Dixon, 1011–12
Pirie, Antoinette, 1027
Pitt-Rivers, Rosalind Venetia, 1028–30
Porter, Helen Kemp Archbold, 1042–43
Ratner, Sarah, 1076–78
Reder, Ruth Elizabeth, 1082
Russell, Jane Anne, 1137–38
Sandiford, Irene, 1149
Seibert, Florence Barbara, 1173–74
Smith, Olive Watkins, 1208–9
Spiegel-Adolf, Mona, 1219
Staudinger, Magda (Woit), 1223–24
Stephenson, Marjory, 1227–29
Venning, Eleanor (Hill), 1325–26
Wang Chi Che, 1345
Wharton, Martha Lucille, 1368
Willcock, Edith Gertrude (Gardiner), 1380
Woker, Gertrud Jan, 1391–93
biographers
Metchnikova, Olga (Belokopytova), 887–88
scientifc, 1052–53

biologists
Altmann, Margaret, 27
Behre, Ellinor H., 108
Boveri, Marcella Imelda O'Grady, 165–67
Bunting, Martha, 206
Bush, Katharine Jeannette, 214–15
Byrnes, Esther Fussell, 216–17
Carson, Rachel Louise, 233–34
Chauchard, B., 248
Conklin, Marie (Eckhardt), 285
De Vesian, Dorothy Ellis, 353
Dunning, Wilhelmina Frances, 388
Erdmann, Rhoda, 422–25
Feichtinger, Nora, 439
Fell, Honor Bridget, Dame, 439–40
Fish, Marie Poland, 448
Geppert, Maria Pia, 495
Gregory, Louise Hoyt, 530
Hamerstrom, Frances, 548–49
Hardesty, Mary, 555
Harvey, Ethel Nicholson Browne, 561–62
Hertwig, Paula, 591–92
Hewitt, Dorothy, 594
Homer, Annie, 613–14
Hummel, Katharine Pattee, 628–29
King, Helen Dean, 695–97
Lange, Mathilde Margarethe, 743
Lebour, Marie Victoire, 761–62
Lepeshinskaia, Ol'ga Borisovna, 773–74
Marshall, Sheina Macalister, 846–47
Mateyko, Gladys Mary, 853–54
McVeigh, Ilda, 872
Metchnikova, Olga (Belokopytova), 887–88
molecular, 719–20
    Roger, Muriel, 1119–20
Moore, Emmeline, 911
Murray, Margaret Ransone, 927–28
Newbigin, Marion Isabel, 937
Parkins, Phyllis Virginia, 980
Peebles, Florence, 999–1000
Pereiaslavtseva, Sof'ia Mikhailovna, 1004–5
Philip, Anna-Ursula, 1016
Pickford, Grace Evelyn, 1020–21
Pink, Olive Muriel, 1025–26
Pythias of Assos, 1062
Randoin, Lucie Gabrielle (Fandard),
    1073–74
Ray, Dixy Lee, 1079–80
Rees, Florence Gwendolen, 1083–84
Robinson, Daisy Maude (Orleman), 1111
Robscheit-Robbins, Frieda Saur, 1115
Shattuck, Lydia White, 1182–83
Soshkina, Elizabeth D., 1217
Tessier, Marguerite, 1276
Tunakan, Seniha (Hüsnü), 1307
Waelsch, Salome Gluecksohn, 1335–36
Walker, Norma (Ford), 1341
Wilson, Hilda E., 1385
Wilson, Lucy Langdon (Williams), 1386
Zenari, Silvia, 1421–22
biophysicists
Clark, Janet Howell, 261–62
Giraud, Marthe, 504
Herrick, Julia Frances, 586
Quimby, Edith Smaw (Hinckley), 1063–64

biostatisticians
Sheps, Mindel (Cherniack), 1184–85
biostratigraphers
Zaklinskaia, Elena Dmitrievna, 1418–19
botanists
Acton, Frances (Knight), 6
Albertson, Mary, 18
Alcock, Nora Lilian Leopard, 19
Ames, Mary E. Pulsifer, 31
Amherst, Sarah (Archer), Countess, 31
Anderton-Smith, Mrs. W., 37
Andrews, Eliza Frances, 39
Anna Sophia of Denmark, 41
Anna Sophia of Hesse, 41
Arber, Agnes (Robertson), 47–48
Arbuthnot, Isobel Agnes, 48–49
Arden, Lady Margaret Elizabeth (Spencer
    Wilson), 49
Armitage, Eleanora, 51–52
Armitt, Sophia, 53
Artemisia of Caria II, 54
Attersoll, Maria, 58
Atwood, Martha Maria, 59
Austin, Rebecca, 61
Baker, Sarah Martha, 71–72
Ball, Anne Elizabeth, 73
Bancroft, Nellie, 75
Barber, Mary Elizabeth (Bowker), 78
Barkly, Lady Anna Maria (Pratt), 79
Barlow, Emma Nora (Darwin), 80
Barnard, Lady Anne (Lindsay), 81
Bateson, Anna, 91
Beatley, Janice Carson, 98–99
Beaufort, Harriet Henrietta, 99–100
Becker, Lydia Ernestine, 101
Beck, Sarah Coker (Adams), 100–101
Beever, Mary, 104
Beever, Susan, 104–5
Bentham, Lady Mary Sophia (Fordyce), 117
Berridge, Emily Mary, 118–19
Bitting, Katherine Eliza (Golden), 132–33
Blackburne, Anna, 134–35
Blackwell, Elizabeth Marianne, 138
Bliss, Mary Campbell, 146
Bluket, Nina Aleksandrovna, 150
Bodley, Rachel Littler, 152–53
Boley, Gertrude Maud, 155
Bolton, Edith, 155
Bolus, Harriet Margaret Louisa (Kensit),
    155–56
Bonnay, Marchioness Du, 156–57
Borisova-Bekriasheva, Antoniia Georgievna,
    162
Bracher, Rose, 168
Brandegee, Mary Katharine Layne, 171
Braun, (Emma) Lucy, 173–74
Brenchley, Winifred Elsie, 177
Britten, Lilian Louisa, 180–81
Britton, Elizabeth Knight, 181
Bromley, Helen Jean (Brown), 182–83
Brooks, Sarah Theresa, 186
Browne, Lady Isabel Mary (Peyronnet),
    192–93
Brown, Mabel Mary, 190
Bruce, Eileen Adelaide, 194–95

botanists (*cont.*)

Cadbury, Dorothy Adlington, 218
Campbell, May Sherwood, 226
Catlow, Maria Agnes, 237
Chandler, Elizabeth, 243–44
Charsley, Fanny Anne, 246
Chase, Mary Agnes Meara, 246–47
Cheesman, Lucy Evelyn, 248–49
Chute, Hettie Morse, 256–57
Clarke, Cora Huidekoper, 264
Clarke, Lilian Jane, 265
Clarke, Louisa (Lane), 265
Clark, Jessie Jane, 262
Clark, Lois, 262–63
Clemens, Mary Knapp (Strong), 268
Cleve, Astrid, 272
Colden, Jane, 280
Cole, Emma J., 280–81
Conway, Elsie (phillips), 287
Cooke, Alice Sophia (Smart), 288
Cooley, Jacquelin Smith, 289
Cotter, Brigid M., 296
Coyle, Elizabeth Eleanor, 299
Crosfield, Margaret Chorley, 306
Cummings, Clara Eaton, 308
Cutler, Catherine, 321
Czaplicka, Marie Antoinette, 321
Dale, Elizabeth, 322–23
Davy, Lady Joanna Charlotte (Flemmich), 333–34
Day, Gwendolen Helen, 334–35
Decker, Jane Cynthia (Mclaughlin), 335–36
De Fraine, Ethel Louise, 336–37
Delap, Maude Jane, 342
Delf-Smith, Ellen Marion, 343
De Mole, Fanny Elizabeth, 345
Derick, Carrie M., 349–50
Detmers, Frederica, 350
De Valera, Mairin, 352–53
De Vesian, Dorothy Ellis, 353
Dobson, Mildred E., 362
Dodgson, Sarah Elizabeth, 364
Dorety, Angela, 370
Dormon, Caroline, 370–71
Doubleday, Neltje Blanchan (De Graff), 371–72
Downie, Dorothy G., 374
Drew, Kathleen Mary, 376–77
Duncan, Ursula Katherine, 385–86
Dunn, Mary Douglas, 387
Eastwood, Alice, 394–96
Eckerson, Sophia Hennion, 397
Edgeworth, Maria, 400
Esau, Katherine, 426–27
Esdorn, Ilse, 427–28
Ewing, Elizabeth Raymond (Burden), 432
Farenden, Emma, 433
Farquharson, Marian Sarah (Ridley), 435
Fedchenko, Ol'ga Aleksandrovna, 438–39
Finch, Louisa (Thynne), Countess of Aylesford, 446
Findlater, Doris, 446
Fish, Margery, 447–48
Fitton, Sarah Mary, 450
Flood, Margaret Greer, 455

Forbes, Helena Madelain Lamond, 458
Fraine, Ethel Louise De, 464
Frampton, Mary, 464
Francini, Eleonora Corti, 464–65
Fulford, Margaret Hannah, 477–78
Gage, Catherine, 480
Garlick, Constance, 486
Gatty, Margaret (Scott), 490–91
Geldart, Alice Mary, 494
Gepp, Ethel Sarel (Barton), 495
Gerry, Eloise B., 497–98
Gibbons, E.Joan, 498–99
Gibbs, Lilian Suzette, 500
Gifford, Isabella, 500
Gilkey, Helen Margaret, 502
Gillett, Margaret (Clark), 503
Gilmore, Jane Georgina, 503
Glascott, Louisa S., 506
Goodrich, Sarah Frances, 519
Grainger, Jennie, 522
Gray, Maria Emma (Smith), 523–24
Gregory, Eliza Standerwick (Barnes), 528
Gregory, Emily L., 528
Griffiths, Amelia Elizabeth, 531
Griffiths, Amelia Warren (Rogers), 531
Grundy, Clara, 534
Grundy, Ellen, 534
Grundy, Maria Ann, 534
Gunn, Mary Davidson, 537–38
Haccius, Barbara, 541–42
Halket, Ann Cronin, 544
Hall, Agnes C., 545
Halliday, Nellie, 547
Hall, Kate Marion, 546
Hallowell, Susan Maria, 548
Hardy, Thora Marggraff Plitt, 557
Harvey, Elizabeth, 561
Hawkins, Mary Esther (Sibthorp), 570
Hayward, Ida Margaret, 572
Hedges, Florence, 577
Helene, Duchess of Aosta, 581
Henderson, Nellie Frater, 583
Henrey, Blanche Elizabeth Edith, 584
Henshaw, Julia Wilmotte, 584
Hewer, Dorothy, 594
Higgins, Vera (Cockburn), 596
Hoare, Sarah, 605
Hodgson, Eliza Amy, 607
Hoggan, Isme Aldyth, 609
Hooker, Frances Harriet Henslow, 614–15
Hooker, Henrietta Edgecomb, 615
Hopkins, Esther (Burton), 616
Hussey, Anna Maria (Reed), 633
Hutchins, Ellen, 633–35
Hynes, Sarah, 637
Ibbetson, Agnes (Thomson), 641
Jacson, Maria Elizabeth, 651
James, Lucy Jones, 653
Janaki Ammal, Edavaleth Kakkat, 653
Jesson, Enid Mary, 657
Johnson, Minnie May, 661
Joyce, Margaret Elizabeth, 671
Kablick, Josephine (Ettel), 674
Kane, Lady Katherine Sophia (Baily), 675
Kanouse, Bessie Bernice, 675–76

Karpowicz, Ludmila, 678
Kaye-Smith, A.Dulcie, 680
Keeler, Harriet Louise, 680
Keeney, Dorothea Lilian, 681
Keller, Ida Augusta, 682–83
Kellerman, Stella Victoria (Dennis), 683–84
Kerling, Louise Catharina Petronella, 692
King, Anastasia Kathleen (Murphy), 695
Kirby, Elizabeth, 699–700
Knowles, Matilda Cullen, 709–10
Lampe, Lois, 737–38
Langdon, Ladema M., 742–43
Lankester, Phoebe (Pope), 744–45
Larter, Clara Ethelinda, 747
Laughlin, Emma Eliza, 751–52
Laurie, Charlotte Louisa, 752
Lawder, Margaret, 754
Lawton, Elva, 755–56
Leebody, Mary Elizabeth, 765
Lefroy, Helena (Trench), 766
Lemmon, Sarah Plummer, 771
Levyns, Margaret Rutherford Bryan (Michell), 782
Libert, Marie-Anne, 789
Lister, Gulielma, 795
Lomax, Elizabeth Anne (Smithson), 801
Loudon, Jane (Webb), 805–6
Lyell, Katharine Murray (Horner), 813
Lynn, Mary Johnstone, 814
MacCallum, Bella Dytes (MacIntosh), 818
Manton, Irene, 838–39
Martin, Ella May, 847–48
Massee, Ivy, 851
Mathias, Mildred Esther, 854–55
McCracken, Eileen May, 865
McCrea, Adelia, 866
McVeigh, Ilda, 872
Measham, Charlotte Elizabeth (Cowper), 874
Mee, Margaret Ursula (Brown), 876
Meredith, Louisa Anne (Twamley), 884
Mexia, Ynes, 889–90
Mitchell, Anna Helena, 900
Mockeridge, Florence Annie, 906
Molesworth, Caroline, 907–8
Morehouse, Kathleen M., 912–13
Murray, Amelia Matilda, 925
Murray, Lady Charlotte, 925–26
Napper, Diana Margaret, 930
Neal, Marie Catherine, 932
Nicholson, Barbara Evelyn, 942
Noel, Emilia Frances, 948–49
Nolte, Margarethe, 950
North, Marianne, 951–52
Nuttall, Gertrude (Clarke), 953–54
O'Malley, Lady Emma Winifred (Hardcastle), 962
O'Reilly, Helen, 964
Oszast, Janina Celina, 968–69
Page, Mary Maud, 971–72
Page, Winifred Mary, 972
Parke, Mary Winifred, 978–79
Patrick, Ruth, 988–89
Patterson, Flora Wambaugh, 990
Penston, Norah Lilian, 1004
Pertz, Dorothea Frances Matilda, 1009

Pfeiffer, Norma Etta, 1014
Pfiester, Lois Ann, 1015
Plues, Margaret, 1033
Porter, Lilian E.(Baker), 1043
Potts, Eliza, 1046–47
Prankerd, Theodora Lisle, 1049–50
Preston, Isabella, 1052
Raisin, Catherine Alice, 1068–69
Ramsay, Christina (Broun), Countess of
    Dalhousie, 1070–71
Rathbone, Mary May, 1075
Rayner, Mabel Mary Cheveley, 1081
Rea, Margaret Williamson, 1081
Reames, Eleanor Louise, 1081
Reed, Eva M., 1083
Reid, Eleanor Mary (Wynne Edwards),
    1087–88
Richards, Mary Alice Eleanor (Stokes),
    1097–98
Rich, Mary Florence, 1093
Riddle, Lumina Cotton, 1099
Rob, Catherine Muriel, 1104
Roberts, Edith Adelaide, 1106–7
Roberts, Mary, 1108
Robinson, Harriet May Skidmore, 1112–13
Rockley, Lady Alicia Margaret (Amherst),
    1116
Rogers, Julia Ellen, 1120–21
Roper, Ida Mary, 1124
Roupell, Arabella Elizabeth (Piggott), 1129
Rozanova, Mariia Aleksandrovna, 1132–33
Russell, Anna (Worsley), 1136
Sampson, Kathleen Samuel, 1147
Sanborn, Ethel, 1147
Sargant, Ethel, 1151–52
Saunders, Edith Rebecca, 1154–55
Schaffner, Mabel (Brockett), 1156
Scott, Flora Murray, 1168
Scott, Henderina Victoria (Klaassen), 1168–69
Sharsmith, Helen Katherine, 1182
Shattuck, Lydia White, 1182–83
Sherbourne, Margaret Dorothea (Willis), 1185
Shove, Rosamund Flora, 1189
Sinskaia, Evgeniia Nikolaevna, 1196–97
Smith, Annie Lorrain, 1202–3
Smith, Annie Morrill, 1203
Smith, Isabel Seymour, 1207
Smith, Winifred, 1209
Snow, Julia Warner, 1210
Snow, Mary (Pilkington), 1210–11
Sommer, Anna Louise, 1216
Spalding, Effie Southworth, 1218
Spence, Eliza Jane (Edmondson), 1218
Sprague, Mary Letitia (Green), 1221
Spratt, Ethel Rose, 1221
Stackhouse, Emily, 1221–22
Stelfox, Margarita Dawson (Mitchell), 1226
Stokey, Alma Gracey, 1239–40
Stoppel, Rose, 1242–43
Stovin, Margaret, 1244–45
Strong, Miriam Carpenter, 1249
Sykes, Mary Gladys, 1257–58
Taylor, Rose H., 1272
Thiselton-Dyer, Lady Harriet Ann (Hooker),
    1278–79

Thomas, Ethel Nancy Miles, 1280–81
Thompson, Rachel Ford, 1285
Thomson, Agnes C., 1286
Thomson, Jane Smithson, 1286
Thring, Lydia Eliza Dyer (Meredith), 1286–87
Tilden, Josephine Elizabeth, 1289–90
Tindall, Isabella Mary, 1291
Todd, Emily Sophia, 1294–95
Traill, Catharine Parr (Strickland), 1300–1301
Treat, Mary Lua Adelia (Davis), 1301–2
Trimmer, Sarah (Kirby), 1302
Tristram, Ruth Mary (Cardew), 1302
Trower, Charlotte Georgiana, 1305
Turner, Mary (Palgrave), 1308–9
Twining, Elizabeth Mary, 1309
Vachell, Eleanor, 1316
Van Beverwijk, Agathe L., 1317–18
Vesian, Dorothy E. de, 1328
Vickers, Anna, 1328
Wakefield, Elsie Maud, 1336–37
Walker, Harriet Ann, 1339–40
Warren, Elizabeth Andrew, 1347
Watkins, Della Elizabeth (Ingram), 1349–50
Watt, Helen Winifred Boyd (de Lisle), 1351
Watt, Menie, 1351
Weber, Anne Antoinette (Van Bosse), 1352–53
Webster, Mary McCallum, 1353–54
Wedgwood, Mary Louisa (Bell), 1356
Weightman, Mary, 1358
Weishaupt, Clara Gertrude, 1359
Welch, Winona Hazel, 1361
Westall, Mary, 1367
West, Ethel, 1367
White, Eliza Catherine (Quekett), 1371
Whitehead, Lilian Elizabeth, 1373
Whiting, Marian Muriel, 1373
Wilson, Aphra Phyllis, 1384
Wilson, Irene Mossom, 1385
Woodbridge, Mary Emily, 1395
Wood, Emily Margaret, 1394
Wynne, Frances Elizabeth, 1412
Young, Mary Sophie, 1416

broadcasters
Kirkham, Nellie, 701

bryologists
Atwood, Martha Maria, 59
Clark, Lois, 262–63
Dalby, Mary, 322
Lawton, Elva, 755–56

C

cartographers
Fischer, Irene Kaminka, 447

chemists
Adams, Mildred, 7–8
Barnard, Edith Ethel, 81
Batchelder, Esther Lord, 89–90
Baum, Marie, 92
Berger, Emily V., 118
Bevier, Isabel, 121–22
Bilger, Leonora (Neuffer), 126–27
Birstein, Vera, 129
Bodley, Rachel Littler, 152–53
Bogdanovskaia, Vera Evstaf'Evna, 153
Bolschanina, M.A., 155

Breed, Mary (Bidwell), 177
Brock, Sylvia (Deantonis), 182
Brunetti, R., 196
Caldwell, Mary Letitia, 220–21
Capen, Bessie, 228
Carr, Emma Perry, 230–32
Cauquil, Germaine Anne, 240
Cioranescu-Nenitzescu, Ecaterina, 258
Cleve, Astrid, 272
Cobb, Rosalie M.Karapetoff, 276
Cotelle, Sonia, 295–96
Cotter, Brigid M., 296
Cremer, Erika, 301–2
Croll, Hilda M., 304–5
Curie, Marie (Maria Sklodowska), 311–17
Dane, Elisabeth, 324
Davis, Rose May, 334
Dawson, Maria, 334
De Milt, Clara Marie, 345
Denis, Willey Glover, 347
Dobrowolska, H., 361
Dodds, Mary Letitia, 363–64
Dorabialska, Alicja Domenica, 368–69
Dorenfeldt, Margot, 371
Dover, Mary Violette, 372–73
Eves, Florence, 432
Fage, Winifred E., 433
Fenwick, Florence, 442
Fieser, Mary, 445
Fomina-Zhukovskaia, Evdokiia Aleksan-
    drovna, 457–58
Fossler, Mary Louise, 460
Foster, Margaret D., 460–61
Freidlina, Rakhil' Khatskelevna, 468–69
Freund, Ida, 472–73
Fulhame, Elizabeth, 478
Gerould, Elizabeth Wood, 497
Gibbons, Vernette Lois, 499
Gleditsch, Ellen, 508–9
Goldthwaite, Nellie Esther, 517–18
Gotz, Iren Julia (Dienes), 521–22
Green, Arda A., 525–26
Griggs, Mary Amerman, 531
Haber-Immerwahr, Clara, 540–41
Hahn, Dorothy Anna, 543
Hall, Dorothy, 545
Hall, Julia Brainerd, 545–46
Hathaway, Millicent Louise, 565
Heimann, Berta, 579
Herxheimer, Franziska, 592
Hill, Mary Elliott, 601
Hitchcock, Fanny Rysam Mulford, 603
Hitchens, Ada Florence R., 604
Hoke, Calm (Morrison), 610
Hoobler, Icie Gertrude Macy, 614
Horowitz, Stephanie, 618
Jeanes, Allene Rosalind, 654–55
Johnson, Mary, 660
Kelley, Louise, 684
Kelly, Margaret W., 687
Kraus Ragins, Ida, 725
Leach, Mary Frances, 757
Le Beau, Désirée, 759–60
Lee, Julia Southard, 763
Lepin, Lidiia Karlovna, 774

chemists (*cont.*)
Lermontova, Iuliia Vsevolodovna, 775–76
Leslie (Burr), May Sybil, 776–77
Lewis, Helen Geneva, 783
Libby, Leona Woods Marshall, 787–88
Lieber, Clara Flora, 789–90
Linton, Laura Alberta, 793–94
Lloyd, Rachel, 798
Loewe, Lotte Luise Friedericke, 799
Löser, Margaret Sibylla Von, 805
MacGillavry, Carolina Henriette, 821
Mack, Pauline Beery, 822–24
MacLeod, Annie Louise, 827
Medes, Grace, 874–75
Metzger, Hélène (Bruhl), 888–89
Meurdrac, Marie, 889
Michael, Helen Cecilia Desilver Abbott, 891–92
Minor, Jessie Elizabeth, 898
Nightingale, Dorothy Virginia, 944
Noddack, Ida Eva Tacke, 947–48
Northrup, Ann Hero, 953
Novoselova, Aleksandra Vasil'evna, 953
O'Brien, Ruth, 956
Obrutsheva, A., 956–57
Palmer, Alice W., 974
Parker, Ivy May, 979–80
Parsons, Eloise, 981–82
Parsons, Helen Tracy, 984
Pennington, Mary Engle, 1003–4
Perrette, Berthe, 1008
Petermann, Mary Locke, 1010–11
Phelps, Martha Austin, 1016
Pickett, Lucy Weston, 1020
Pierce, Marion (Armbruster), 1023–24
Prins, Ada, 1057
Prytz, Milda Dorothea, 1059
Quiggle, Dorothy, 1063
Ramart-Lucas, Pauline, 1069–70
Reimer, Marie, 1088
Richards, Ellen Henrietta Swallow, 1095–97
Risseghem, Hortense van, 1102
Roberts, Charlotte Fitch, 1105–6
Robeson, Eslanda Cordoza (Goode), 1110–11
Robinson, Gertrude Maud (Walsh), 1111–12
Ronzoni, Ethel (Bishop), 1124
Rose, Glenola Behling, 1125
Rose, Mary Davies Swartz, 1125–26
Schroeder, Edith von, 1165
Shattuck, Lydia White, 1182–83
Sherrill, Mary Lura, 1186–87
Smith, Alice Emily, 1201
Sommer, Anna Louise, 1216
Spencer, Adelin Elam, 1218–19
Stanley, Louise, 1222
Stearns, Genevieve, 1224
Stiebeling, Hazel Katherine, 1236–37
Stieglitz, Mary Rising, 1237–38
Strassmann-Heckter, Maria Caroline, 1246–47
Sullivan, Betty Julia, 1250
Swope, Helen Gladys, 1256–57
Szeparowicz, Maria, 1258
Taylor, Clara Millicent, 1269
Telkes, Maria, 1273–74
Terry, Ethel Mary, 1275
Towara, Hélène, 1299
Veil, Suzanne Zélie Pauline, 1325
Vold, Marjorie Jean Young, 1331–32
Volkova, Anna Fedorovna, 1332–33
Wall, Florence, 1342
Waring, Sister Mary Grace, 1347
Wassell, Helen Erma, 1349
Watts, Betty (Monaghan), 1351–52
Weeks, Mary Elvira, 1358
Wertenstein, Mathilde, 1366
Wheeler, Elizabeth Lockwood, 1370
White, Elizabeth Juanita (Greer), 1371
White, Florence Roy, 1371–72
Whiteley, Martha Annie, 1373
Willard, Mary Louisa, 1379
Wilson, Edith, 1384
Wilson, Mabel Florey, 1386–87
Woodard, Helen (Quincy), 1395
Woodward, Gladys Estelle, 1397
Worner, Ruby K., 1401–2
Wrangell, Margarethe von, 1402–4
Wreschner, Marie, 1404
Wright, Lady Catherine, 1404–5
Young, Leona Esther, 1414–15

climatologists
Kaczorowska, Zofia, 674–75

collectors
art
Cone, Claribel, 284–85
botanical
Brooke, Winifred, 184
Burkill, Ethel Maud (Morrison), 209
Burton, Helen Marie Rousseay (Kan-Nemeyer), 212
Callcott, Lady Maria Graham, 223
Henry, Caroline (Orridge), 584
Talbot, Dorothy Amaury, 1262
Telfair, Annabella (Chamberlain), 1273
Tinne, Alexandrina Petronella Francina, 1291–92
ethnological
Tinne, Alexandrina Petronella Francina, 1291–92
fossil
Hastings, Barbara, Marchioness of, 565
Mantell, Mary Ann (Woodhouse), 837–38
Philpot, Elizabeth, 1018
Philpot, Margaret, 1018
Philpot, Mary, 1018
medical books
Diana of Poitiers, 354
museum
Howe Akeley, Delia Julia Denning, 622–23
natural history, 908
plant, 936–37
Baker, Anne Elizabeth, 70
Barnard, Alicia Mildred, 80–81
Barnard, Lady Anne (Lindsay), 81
Calvert, Catherine Louisa Waring (Atkinson), 223

compilers
Bailey, Ethel Zoe, 68–69
De Graffenried, Mary Clare, 337

computer science specialists
Hopper, Grace (Brewster Murray), 616–17

conchologists
Bidder, Anna McClean, 125
Law, Annie, 753
Lyell, Mary Elizabeth (Horner), 813–14
Massy, Anne L., 852–53
Neal, Marie Catherine, 932

conservationists
Akeley, Mary Lee (Jobe), 17–18
Bomhard, Miriam Lucile, 156
Braun, (Emma) Lucy, 173–74
Carson, Rachel Louise, 233–34
Colvin, Brenda, 282–83
Comstock, Anna Botsford, 283–84
Dormon, Caroline, 370–71

cosmologists
Hildegard of Bingen, 596–98
Tinsley, Beatrice Muriel (Hill), 1292–93

criminologists
Bronner, Augusta Fox, 183
Glueck, Eleanor (Touroff), 509

critics, literary
Andreas-Salome, Louise Lelia, 38–39

crystallographers
Brezina, Maria Aristides, 179
Donnay, Gabrielle (Hamburger), 367–68
Franklin, Rosalind Elsie, 465–66
Hodgkin, Dorothy Mary Crowfoot, 606–7
Kolaczkowska, Maria, 716
Lonsdale, Kathleen (Yardley), 804–5
MacGillavry, Carolina Henriette, 821
Porter, Mary Winearls, 1043–44
Slavikova, Ludmila (Kaplanova), 1199
X-ray, 910–11

cytogeneticists
Janaki Ammal, Edavaleth Kakkat, 653
McCracken, Elizabeth (Unger), 865
Stevens, Nettie Maria, 1230–32

cytologists
Blackburn, Kathleen Bever, 133–34
Bochantseva, Zinaida Petrovna, 152
Bonnevie, Kristine, 157–58
Boring, Alice Middleton, 160–62
Carothers, Estrella Eleanor, 229
Clinch, Phyllis E.M., 273
Erdmann, Rhoda, 422–25
Foot, Katherine, 458
Guthrie, Mary Jane, 538–39
Gwynne-Vaughan, Dame Helen Charlotte Isabella (Fraser), 539
Hughes-Schrader, Sally, 628
Manton, Irene, 838–389
McKinney, Ruth Alden, 870–71
Sorokin, Helen Petrovna (Beratynskaiia), 1216–17
Strobell, Ella Church, 1248
Wipf, Frances Louise, 1390

D

deans, school
Aldrich-Blake, Louisa Brandreth, 19–20
Talbot, Marion, 1262–63

demographers
Hagood, Margaret Loyd Jarman, 542–43
Taeuber, Irene Barnes, 1260–61

dentists

Hirschfeld-Tiburtius, Henriette (Pagelsen), 602–3

Michael, Helen Cecilia Desilver Abbott, 891–92

Taylor, Lucy Beaman (Hobbs), 1271

dermatologists

Buerk, Minerva (Smith), 203–4

Drant, Patricia (Hart), 375

Gundersen, Herdis, 537

designers, garden

Jekyll, Gertrude, 655–56

dieticians

Stern, Frances, 1229–30

dramatists

Hroswitha of Gandersheim, 624

Ring, Barbara Taylor, 1100–1101

E

ecologists

Boley, Gertrude Maud, 155

Braun, (Emma) Lucy, 173–74

Clements, Edith Gertrude (Schwartz), 268

Howard, Louise Ernestine (Matthaei), Lady, 619–20

Karpowicz, Ludmila, 678

Mcavoy, Blanche, 860–61

Pallis, Marietta, 973

Patrick, Ruth, 988–89

economists

Campbell, Persia Crawford, 226–27

home, 844, 913, 956

Abel, Mary Hinman, 2–3

Atwater, Helen Woodard, 58–59

Beecher, Catharine Esther, 103–4

Bevier, Isabel, 121–22

Campbell, Helen Stuart, 224–25

Dye, Marie, 391

Gregory, Louisa Catherine (Allen), 529–30

Herrick, Christine (Terhune), 586

Hunt, Caroline Louisa, 629

Justin, Margaret M., 672

Richards, Ellen Henrietta Swallow, 1095–97

Roberts, Lydia Jane, 1107–8

Rose, Flora, 1125

Stanley, Louise, 1222

Talbot, Marion, 1262–63

Van Rensselaer, Martha, 1320–21

Royer, Clémence, 1129–32

Wickens, Aryness Joy, 1376

editors

Barnum, Charlotte Cynthia, 83–84

Bingham, Millicent (Todd), 127–28

Bledsoe, Lucybelle, 144–45

Heath, Daisy Winifred, 575

Lavoisier, Marie Anne Pierrette Paulze, 752–53

Litchfield Henrietta Emma (Darwin), 795–96

Newbigin, Marion Isabel, 937

Nolte, Margarethe, 950

Pearl, Maud Dewitt, 998

Renooz, Céline, 1089–90

Salmon, Eleanor Seely, 1146

educators

Abella, 4

Anderson, Caroline Virginia (Still) Wiley, 32–33

Andrews, Eliza Frances, 39

Arnstein, Margaret Gene, 53–54

Beecher, Catharine Esther, 103–4

Blunt, Katharine, 151

Bocchi (Bucca), Dorotea, 151

Boole, Mary (Everest), 158–59

Bowen, Susan, 167

Bradley, Amy Morris, 168–69

Bryan, Margaret, 198–99

Cady, Bertha Louise Chapman, 219

Carlson, Lucille, 228

Clarke, Lilian Jane, 265

Cole, Emma J., 280–81

Coyle, Elizabeth Eleanor, 298–99

Crocker, Lucretia, 303–4

Fielde, Adele Marion, 444

Frantz, Virginia Kneeland, 467

Galindo, Beatrix, 481

Gaw, Esther Allen, 491–92

Griggs, Mary Amerman, 531

Guarna, Rebecca, 535

Hayes, Ellen Amanda, 570–71

Henderson, Nellie Frater, 583

Kittrell, Flemmie Pansy, 701–2

Krupskaia, Nadezhda Konstantinovna, 728–29

Lampe, Lois, 737–38

Laughlin, Emma Eliza, 751–52

Laurie, Charlotte Louisa, 752

Lawrence, Penelope, 754–55

Linton, Laura Alberta, 793–94

Lyon, Mary, 814–15

Malleson, Elizabeth, 834

McAvoy, Blanche, 860

McBride, Katharine Elizabeth, 861

McKeag, Anna Jane, 870

Palmer, Sophia French, 976–77

Phelps, Almira Hart Lincoln, 1015–16

Putnam, Helen Cordelia, 1059–60

Reames, Eleanor Louise, 1081

Stewart, Isabel Maitland, 1235–36

Taft, Jessie, 1261

Taussky-Todd, Olga, 1267–68

Taylor, Janet, 1270–71

Willard, Emma (Hart), 1378–79

electrochemists

Sidgwick, Eleanor (Balfour), 1192–93

embryologists

Adams, Amy Elizabeth Kemper, 7

Bochantseva, Zinaida Petrovna, 152

comparative, 1031–32

Ferguson, Margaret Clay, 441–42

Gage, Susanna Phelps, 480–81

Harvey, Ethel Nicholson Browne, 561–62

Mangold, Hilde (Proescholdt), 836

Morgan, Lilian Vaughan Sampson, 914–15

Nickerson, Margaret (Lewis), 942

Oppenheimer, Jane Marion, 963–64

Phisalix, Marie (Picot), 1018–19

Pythias of Assos, 1062

Randolph, Harriet, 1074

Rudnick, Dorothea, 1135

endocrinologists

Adams, Amy Elizabeth Kemper, 7

Finkler, Rita V.(Sapiro), 446–47

Gualco, Sellina, 535

Juhn, Mary, 671

Lutwak-Mann, Cecelia, 812

Pickford, Grace Evelyn, 1020–21

Ponse, Kitty, 1038–39

Price, Dorothy, 1053

Russell, Jane Anne, 1137–38

Smith, Olive Watkins, 1208–9

Van Wagenen, Gertrude, 1321–22

Venning, Eleanor (Hill), 1325–26

engineers

Barney, Nora Stanton (Blatch) De Forest, 82–83

Clarke, Edith, 264–65

Dennis, Olive Wetzel, 347–48

Eaves, Elsie, 396

Fishenden, Margaret White, 448–49

Flugge-Lotz, Irmgard, 456–57

Gleason, Kate, 507

Hall, Julia Brainerd, 545–46

Hamburger, Erna, 548

Harmon, Élise F., 557–58

Haslett, Dame Caroline, 563–64

Hicks, Beatrice Alice, 595–96

Knott-Ter Meer, Ilse, 709

Lamme, Bertha, 736–37

Lines, Dorolyn (Boyd), 793

Macgill, Elsie Gregory, 820

Morse, Meroë Marston, 918

Paris, Marie-Louise, 978

Parker, Ivy May, 979–80

Quiggle, Dorothy, 1063

Rigas, Harriett B., 1100

Rockwell, Mabel MacFerran, 1116–17

Rogers, Marguerite Moillet, 1121

Ross, Mary G., 1127–28

Telkes, Maria, 1273–74

Terzaghi, Ruth Doggett, 1275–76

Tipper, Constance Fligg (Elam), 1293–94

Welch, Betty, 1361

entomologists

Ball, Mary, 74

Branch, Hazel Elisabeth, 170

Braun, Annette Frances, 172–73

Cady, Bertha Louise Chapman, 219

Cheesman, Lucy Evelyn, 248–49

Clarke, Cora Huidekoper, 264

Cockrell, Wilmatte (Porter), 278

Dobroscky, Irene Dorothy, 361

Doering, Kathleen Clara, 364

Drebeneva-Ukhova, Varvara Pavlovna, 376

Fernald, Maria Elizabeth (Smith), 443

Griswold, Grace Hall, 533

Hussey, Priscilla Butler, 633

Knull, Dorothy J., 711

Lieu, K.O.Victoria, 790

Longfield, Cynthia, 801–2

McCracken, Mary Isabel, 865–66

Morris, Margaretta Hare, 917

Murtfeldt, Mary, 928–29

Palmer, Miriam Augusta, 976

Patch, Edith Marion, 987–88

entomologists (*cont.*)
Payne, Nellie Maria de Cottrell, 993
Peckham, Elizabeth (Gifford), 999
Sandhouse, Grace Adelbert, 1148–49
Scotland, Minnie (Brink), 1167
Slosson, Annie Trumbull, 1199
Smith, Emily Adelia (Pidgen), 1205
Talbot, Mary, 1263
Taylor, Charlotte de Bernier Scarborough, 1268
Taylor, Monica, 1272
Treat, Mary Lua Adelia (Davis), 1301–2
Wiley, Grace Olive, 1378
environmentalists
Strong, Harriet Williams (Russell), 1248–49
epidemiologists
Lane-Claypon, Janet Elizabeth, 741–42
MacDonald, Eleanor Josephine, 819
ethnographers
Durham, Mary Edith, 388–89
Efimenko, Aleksandra Iakovlevna, 405–6
Kharuzina, Vera Nikolaevna, 693
Laird, Carobeth (Tucker), 733–34
Lebedeva, Nataliia Ivanova, 760
Lisitsian, Srbui Stepanova, 794
Smith, Erminnie Adele (Platt), 1205–6
Terent'eva, Liudmila Nikolaevna, 1274–75
Vasilevich, Glafira Makar'evna, 1323
Wilson, Monica Hunter, 1387–88
ethnohistorians
Wheeler-Voeglin, Erminie Brooke, 1370
ethnologists
Czaplicka, Marie Antoinette, 321
De Laguna, Fredericka Annis Lopez De Leo, 339–41
Fletcher, Alice Cunningham, 454–55
Hanks, Jane Richardson, 552–53
Marriott, Alice Lee, 844–45
Parsons, Elsie Worthington (Clews), 982–83
Stevenson, Matilda Coxe (Evans), 1232–33
Wallis, Ruth Sawtell, 1342–44
ethnomusicologists
Curtis, Natalie, 318–19
Densmore, Frances Theresa, 348–49
eugenicists
Bluhm, Agnes, 149–50
Elderton, Ethel, 413
explorers
Akeley, Mary Lee (Jobe), 17–18
Boyd, Louise Arner, 167–68
Coudreau, Octavie, 296
Fedchenko, Ol'ga Aleksandrovna, 438–39
Howe Akeley, Delia Julia Denning, 622–23
Kingsley, Mary Henrietta, 699
Tinne, Alexandrina Petronella Francina, 1291–92

F
folklorists
Beckwith, Martha Warren, 102–3
Cadilla De Martínez, María, 218–19
Hurston, Zora Neale, 632–33
Lisitsian, Srbui Stepanova, 794
Murray, Margaret Alice, 926

Parsons, Elsie Worthington (Clews), 982–83
Vasilevich, Glafira Makar'evna, 1323
foresters
Gerry, Eloise B., 497–98

G
gardeners
Delaney (or Delany), Mary (Granville), 341
Gregory, Lady Isabella Augusta (Persse), 529
Lawrenson, Alice Louisa, 755
gastroenterologists
Jordan, Sara Claudia (Murray), 668–69
geneticists
Auerbach, Charlotte, 59–60
Austin, Mary Lellah, 61
Barlow, Emma Nora (Darwin), 80
Bell, Julia, 109
Blanchard, Frieda Cobb, 141–42
Bonnevie, Kristine, 157–58
Boring, Alice Middleton, 160–62
Carothers, Estrella Eleanor, 229
Carroll, Christiane (Mendrez), 232
Ferguson, Margaret Clay, 441–42
Garnjobst, Laura Flora, 487
Gruhn, Ruth, 533–34
Hertwig, Paula, 591–92
Herwerden, Marianne Van, 592
McClintock, Barbara, 862–64
Morgan, Lilian Vaughan Sampson, 914–15
Philip, Anna-Ursula, 1016
Redfield, Helen, 1082–83
Richards, Mildred Hoge (Albro), 1098
Sager, Ruth, 1144–45
Saunders, Edith Rebecca, 1154–55
Schiemann, Elisabeth, 1159–60
Stein, Emmy, 1225
Tammes, Jantine, 1264–65
Tenenbaum, Estera, 1274
Timofe'eff-Ressovsky, Elena Aleksandrovna (Fiedler), 1290–91
Ubisch, Gerta Von, 1312–13
geobotanists
Dokhman, Genrietta Isaakovna, 365–66
geochemists
Gata, Elena (Stefanescu), 489
Giammarino, Pia, 498
Iusupova, Saradzhan Mikhailovna, 644–45
Shishkina, Olga Vasil'yevna, 1188
Stadnichenko, Tasia Maximovna, 1222
geographers
Baber, Zonia, 65–66
Bingham, Millicent (Todd), 127–28
Bishop, Isabella Lucy Bird, 131
Boyd, Louise Arner, 167–68
Carlson, Lucille, 228
Chalubinska, Aniela, 242–43
Clerke, Ellen Mary, 271–72
Czaplicka, Marie Antoinette, 321
Fischer, Irene Kaminka, 447
Fisher, Elizabeth Florette, 449
Garnett, Alice, 486–87
Heslop, Mary Kingdon, 592–93
Hol, Jacoba Brigitta Louisa, 610
Johnson, Hildegarde (Binder), 660
Kaczorowska, Zofia, 674–75

Mason, Carol Y., 850–51
Newbigin, Marion Isabel, 937
Pfeiffer, Ida (Reyer), 1013–14
Semple, Ellen Churchill, 1176–77
Strong, Helen Mabel, 1249
Taylor, Eva Germaine Rimington, 1269–70
Williams, Marguerite (Thomas), 1382
Woods, Ethel Gertrude (Skeat), 1396–97
geologists
Adametz, Lotte, 7
Alexander, Frances Elizabeth Somerville (Caldwell), 21–22
Amalitskiya, Anna P., 28
Applin, Esther (Richards), 46–47
Barber, Helen Karen, 77–78
Barlett, Helen Blair, 79–80
Bascom, Florence, 87–88
Bauer, Grace M., 92
Beanland, Sarah, 98
Belaeva, Elizaveta Ivanovna, 108–9
Belyea, Helen Reynolds, 110–11
Benett, Etheldred, 114
Billings, Katharine Stevens (Fowler–Lunn), 127
Birdsall, Lucy Ellen, 128–29
Boos, Margaret Bradley (Fuller), 159–60
Briere, Yvonne, 180
Browne, Ida Alison (Brown), 191–92
Buchbinder, Laura G.Ordan, 200–201
Carne, Elizabeth Catherine (Thomas), 228–29
Carroll, Dorothy, 232–33
Chaudet, Maria Casanova De, 248
Child, Lydia Maria (Francis), 251–52
Christen, Sydney Mary (Thompson), 254–55
Cleve, Astrid, 272
Coignou, Caroline Pauline Marie, 279
Cornelius-Furlani, Marta, 294
Currie, Ethel Dobbie, 317
Curtis, Doris Sarah (Malkin), 317–18
Davidson, Ada D., 328
Dobrolubova, Tatiana A., 360–61
Ebers, Edith (Knote), 396
Echols, Dorothy Jung, 397
Edson, Fanny Carter, 402–3
Eyton, Charlotte, 432
Fisher, Elizabeth Florette, 449
Foley, Mary Cecilia, 457
Forster, Mary, 459
Fowler-Billings, Katharine Stevens, 462–63
Gardiner, Margaret Isabella, 483
Gardner, Elinor Wight, 483–84
Garretson, Mary (Welleck), 488
Gata, Elena (Stefanescu), 489
Halicka, Antonina (Yaroszewicz), 544
Hawn Mirabile, Margaret H., 570
Heermann, Margareta, 577–78
Hodgson, Elizabeth, 607
Holley, Mary Austin, 610
Holm, Esther (Aberdeen), 612
Hughes, Mary Caroline (Weston), 627–28
Ivanova, Elena Alekseevna, 645–46
Johnston, Mary Sophia, 660–61
Jordan, Louise, 667–68
Kelly, Agnes, 685–86
Kielan-Jaworowska, Zofia, 693–94

King, Georgina, 695
Kingsley, Louise, 699
Kline, Virginia Harriett, 706
Klosterman, Mary Jo, 706–7
Knopf, Eleanora Frances (Bliss), 708–9
Korringa, Marjorie K., 718–19
Kozlova, Ol'ga Grigoriyevna, 724
Krutikhovskaia, Zinaida Aleksandrovna, 729
Lee, Sarah Wallis Bowdich, 765
Lehmann, Inge, 766
Lyell, Mary Elizabeth (Horner), 813–14
Lyubimova, Yelena Aleksandrovna, 815–16
Marinov, Evelina, 843–44
Mason, Carol Y., 850–51
McGlamery, Josie Winifred, 868
Mirchink, Maria E., 899
Missuna, Anna Boleslavovna, 899–900
Morozova, Valentina Galaktionovna, 915–16
Nelson, Katherine Greacen, 933–34
Nicosia, Maria Luisa, 942–43
Ogilvie-Gordon, Dame Maria Matilda, 959–60
Ogilvie, Ida Helen, 958–59
Owen, Luella Agnes, 969
Palmer, Dorothy Bryant (Kemper), 974
Palmer, Katherine Evangeline Hilton (Van Winkle), 975–76
Pavlova, Mariia Vasil'evna, 992–93
Pensa-Joja, Josipa, 1004
Pokrovskaia, Irina Mitrofanovna, 1036
Rasskazova, Yelena Stepanovna, 1074–75
Rauzer-Chernousova, Dagmara M., 1078–79
Reid, Eleanor Mary (Wynne Edwards), 1087–88
Reynolds, Doris Livesey, 1090–91
Rhodes, Mary Louise, 1092
Robinson, Pamela Lamplugh, 1114–15
Salmon, Eleanor Seely, 1146
Scarpellini, Caterina, 1156
Semikhatova, Sofia Viktorovna (Karpova), 1175–76
Sheldon, Jennie Arms, 1183
Shishkina, Olga Vasil'yevna, 1188
Shulga-Nesterenko, Maria I., 1191–92
Silliman, Hepsa Ely, 1194–95
Skoczylas-Ciszewska, Kamila, 1197–98
Slater, Ida Lilian, 1198
Slavikova, Ludmila (Kaplanova), 1199
Smith, Erminnie Adele (Platt), 1205–6
Smith, Isabel Fothergill, 1206–7
Sokol'skaya, Anna Nikolayevna, 1211–12
Sollas, Igerna Brünhilda Johnson, 1212
Solomko-Sotiriadis, Evgeniia, 1213
Soshkina, Elizabeth D., 1217
Stose, Anna Isabel (Jonas), 1243–44
Syniewska, Janina, 1258
Todd, Ruth, 1295–96
Todtmann, Emmy Mercedes, 1296
Trizna, Valentina Borisovna, 1302–3
Tsvetaeva, Maria, 1305–6
Tumanskaya, Olga G. (Shirokobruhova), 1306–7
Turnbull, Priscilla Freudenheim, 1308
Varsanof'eva, Vera Aleksandrovna, 1322–23
Vavrinova, Milada, 1324–25

Waelsch, Salome Gluecksohn, 1335–36
Walcott, Helene B. (Stevens), 1337–38
Watson, Janet Vida, 1350–51
Weeks, Alice Mary (Dowse), 1356–57
Weinzierl, Laura (Lane), 1358–59
Wienholz, Eva, 1377–78
Williams, Marguerite (Thomas), 1382
Wyckoff, Dorothy, 1411
Zalesskaya-Chirkova, Elena, 1420–21
Zenari, Silvia, 1421–22
Zhuze, Anastasiya Panteleyemonovna, 1422–23

geomorphologists
Boswell, Katherine Cumming, 163
Ebers, Edith (Knote), 396
Johnston, Mary Sophia, 660–61

geophysicists
Folmer, Hermine Jacoba, 457
Robertson, Florence, 1108
Róna, Elisabeth, 1122–23

glaciologists
Ogilvie, Ida Helen, 958–59
Walcott, Mary Morris (Vaux), 1338

gynecologists
Angst-Horridge, Anita, 40
Barringer, Emily (Dunning), 84–85
Bourgeoise, Louyse, 164
Chang, Moon Gyung, 245
Farrar, Lillian K.P., 436
Guldberg, Estrid, 536
Jones, Mary Amanda Dixon, 666
Kleegman, Sophia, 702–3
Langsdorff, Toni Von, 744
Larsson, Elisabeth, 746
Levine, Lena, 781–82
Meigler, Marie J., 877
Tetsuo, Tamayo, 1276

H
healers
Amalosunta, 28
Antonia, Maestra, 44–45
Berthagyta, Abbess, 119
Berthildis of Chelles, 119
Bertile of Chelles, 120
Bridget, Saint, of Ireland, 179
Clara (Clare) of Assisi, Saint, 259
Clothilde of Burgundy, 274
De Valois, Madame, 353
Elizabeth of Poland, Queen of Hungary, 417
Elizabeth of Portugal, Saint, 417
Elizabeth of Schonau, 417
Erdmuthe, Sophie, 425
Etheldrida, Queen, 428
Euphemia, Abbess of Wherwell, 428
Faustina, 436
Fouquet, Marie De Maupeou, Vicomtesse De Vaux, 461
Frances of Brittany, 464
Haoys (La Meresse), 555
Hebel, Medicienne, 576
Hedwig of Silesia, Saint, 577
Hersende.Abbess of Fontevrault, 590
Hroswitha of Gandersheim, 624
Mahout, Countess of Artois, 831

Marcella, 841
Margery, 843
Matilde, 855
Mechthild of Magdeburg, 874
Origenia, 965
Pernell, 1008
Roper, Margaret, 1124–25
Sara of Saint-Gilles, 1151
Thelka, Saint, 1278
Wyttenbach, Jeanne Gallien, 1412

hematologists
Payne, Rose Marise, 993–94

herbalists
Leyel, Hilda Winifred Ivy (Wauton), 787
Welser, Philippine, 1363

herpetologists
Cochran, Doris Mabel, 277–78
Dickerson, Mary Cynthia, 355–56

histologists
Nickerson, Margaret (Lewis), 942
Phisalix, Marie (Picot), 1018–19
Sabin, Florence Rena, 1140–42

histopathologists
Bishop, Katharine Scott, 131–32

historians
Abbott, Maude Elizabeth Seymour, 1–2
Allan, Mary Eleanor (Mea), 23
Amherst, Sarah (Archer), Countess, 31
Arber, Agnes (Robertson), 47–48
Atkinson, Louisa (Calvert), 58
Barlow, Emma Nora (Darwin), 80
Bate, Dorothea Minola Alice, 90
Bentinck, Margaret Cavendish (Harley), Duchess of Portland, 117–18
Blackburne, Anna, 134–35
Brazier, Mary Agnes Burniston, 174–75
Crane, Agnes, 300
Eckstorm, Fannie Pearson (Hardy), 398
Efimenko, Aleksandra Iakovlevna, 405
Garrod, Dorothy Anne Elizabeth, 488–89
Hammer, Marie Signe, 551
Hart, J.B., 560
Heloise, 582–83
Kirkham, Nellie, 701
McCracken, Eileen May, 865
Metzger, Hélène (Bruhl), 888–89
Myers, Mabel Adelaide, 929
Oppenheimer, Jane Marion, 963–64
Potter, Beatrix, 1044–45
Tannery, Marie Alexandrine (Prisset), 1265
Taylor, Eva Germaine Rimington, 1269–70
Tonnelat, Marie-Antoinette (Baudot), 1297–98
Winton, Kate (Barber), 1390

horticulturists
Bailey, Ethel Zoe, 68–69
Bateson, Anna, 91
Clark, Jessie Jane, 262
Colvin, Brenda, 282–83
Crosbie, May, 305
Cuffe, Lady Charlotte Wheeler (Williams), 307
Dodgson, Sarah Elizabeth, 364
Earle, Marie Theresa (Villiers), 394
Fiennes, Celia, 445

horticulturists (*cont.*)
Findlater, Doris, 446
Fish, Margery, 447–48
Hawkins, Kate, 570
Jekyll, Gertrude, 655–56
Johnson, Minnie May, 661
King, Louisa Boyd (Yeomans), 697–98
La Mance, Lora Sarah (Nichols), 736
Logan, Martha Daniell, 799
Nevill, Lady Dorothy Frances (Walpole), 936–37
O'Brien, Charlotte Grace, 956
Perceval, Anne Mary (Flower), 1004
Pinckney, Eliza (Lucas), 1024–25
Pringle, Elizabeth Waties (Allston), 1055–56
Robb, Mary Anne (Boulton), 1105
Rohde, Eleanour Sinclair, 1122
Sackville-West, Victoria Mary, 1143
Sessions, Kate Olivia, 1177–78
Vilmorin, Elisa (Bailly), 1329
Willmott, Ellen Ann, 1382–83
humanitarians
Fleming, Amalia Coutsouris, Lady, 451
hygienists
Tracy, Martha, 1299–1300

I
ichthyologists
Clark, Frances N., 260–61
Eigenmann, Rosa Smith, 408–9
Fish, Marie Poland, 448
Hubbs, Laura Cornelia (Clark), 624–25
Lamonte, Francesca Raimonde, 737
Moore, Emmeline, 911
illustrators
Allen, Eliza (Stevens), 25
Ames, Blanche (Ames), 28–30
Atkinson, Louisa (Calvert), 58
Baker, Anne Elizabeth, 70
Barkly, Lady Elizabeth Helen (Timins or Timmins), 79
Barnard, Alicia Mildred, 80–81
Barnard, Lady Anne (Henslow), 81
Blackwell, Elizabeth, 137–38
Burkill, Ethel Maud (Morrison), 209
Burtt Davy, Alice (Bolton), 212
Bury, Priscilla Susan (Falkner), 213–14
Callcott, Lady Maria Graham, 223
Calvert, Catherine Louisa Waring (Atkinson), 223
Cumming, Lady Gordon Eeliza Maria Campbell), 308
Daulton, Agnes Warner Mcclelland, 327–28
Hitchcock, Orra White, 604
Lavoisier, Marie Anne Pierrette Paulze, 752–53
Prestwich, Grace Anne (Milne) M'Call, 1052–53
Say, Lucy (Sistare), 1155–56
Thiselton-Dyer, Lady Harriet Ann (Hooker), 1278–79
See also artists
immunogeneticists
Bennett, Dorothea, 116

immunologists
Ashby, Winifred Mayer, 55
Bliss, Eleanor Albert, 146
Koshland, Marian (Elliott), 719–20
Loveless, Mary Hewitt, 807
Parsons, Elizabeth Ingersoll, 982
Payne, Rose Marise, 993–94
Robertson, Muriel, 1109–10
Seegal, Beatrice Carrier, 1172–73
Steinhardt, Edna, 1225
Taliaferro, Lucy (Graves), 1264
Tunnicliff, Ruth, 1307–8
indexers
Dougal, Margaret Douie, 372
Heath, Daisy Winifred, 575
inventors
Ames, Blanche (Ames), 28–30
Besant, Annie (Wood), 120
Coade, Eleanor, 274
Cunio, Isabella, 309
Duryea, Nina, 389
Knight, Margaret, 708
Le Beau, Désirée, 759–60
Manning, Ann B.(Harned), 836–37
Masters, Sybilla (Righton), 853
Mather, Sarah, 854
Morse, Meroë Marston, 918
Westover, Cynthia May, 1368
investigators, social
De Graffenried, Mary Clare, 337

J
journalists
Allan, Mary Eleanor (Mea), 23
Garretson, Mary (Welleck), 487–88
Kent, Elizabeth, 690

L
landscape architects. *See* architects, landscape
librarians
Colcord, Mabel, 280
Day, Mary Anna, 335
Laughlin, Emma Eliza, 751–52
lichenologists
Atwood, Martha Maria, 59
limnologists
Patrick, Ruth, 988–89
linguists
Deloria, Ella Cara, 343–44
Laird, Carobeth (Tucker), 733–34
Vasilevich, Glafira Makar'evna, 1323
logicians
Karp, Carol Ruth (Vander Velde), 677–78
Ladd-Franklin, Christine, 731–32
Péter, Rózsa, 1009–10

M
mammalogists
Kellogg, Louise, 684–85
Lawrence, Barbara, 754
management specialists
Gilbreth, Lillian Evelyn Moller, 501–2
mathematicians
Agnesi, Maria Gaetana, 14–16
Andrews, Grace, 39

Ardinghelli, Maria Angela, 49–50
Bacon, Clara (Latimer), 66
Bari, Nina Karlovna, 78–79
Black, Florence, 133
Bredikhina, Evgeniia Aleksandrovna, 176–77
Browne, Marjorie Lee, 193–94
Bryant, Sophie (Willock), 199–200
Burgess, May (Ayres), 209
Byron, Augusta Ada, Countess of Lovelace, 217
Carlson, Elizabeth, 228
Cartwright, Dame Mary Lucy, 235
Carus, Mary Hegeler, 235–36
Cinquini, Maria Dei Conti Cibrario, 258
Cobbe, Anne Phillipa, 276
Cooper, Elizabeth Morgan, 290
Copeland, Lennie Phoebe, 292
Cornaro (Cornero), Elena (Helena) Lucretia, 295
Cummings, Louise Duffield, 309
Danti or Dante, Theodora, 325
Di Novella, Maria, 355
Eccello of Lucania, 396
Echecratia the Philiasian, 397
Edgerton, Winifred Haring, 399–400
Ehrenfest-Afanassjewa, Tatyana Alexeyevna, 407–8
Eisele, Carolyn, 412–13
Fawcett, Phillipa Garrett, 436–37
Fenchel, Kate (Sperling), 440–41
Flugge-Lotz, Irmgard, 456–57
Geiringer Hilda, 493–94
Geppert, Maria Pia, 495
Germain, Sophie, 496–97
Griffin, Harriet Madeline, 531
Hardcastle, Frances, 555
Hayes, Ellen Amanda, 570–71
Hazlett, Olive Clio, 574
Heloise, 582–83
Hennel, Cora Barbara, 583–84
Hightower, Ruby Usher, 596
Hopper, Grace (Brewster Murray), 616–17
Hubbs, Laura Cornelia (Clark), 624–25
Hudson, Hilda Phoebe, 625–26
Hypatia of Alexandria, 637–39
Ianovskaia, Sof'ia Aleksandrovna, 640–41
Karp, Carol Ruth (Vander Velde), 677–78
Keldysh, Liudmila Vsevolodovna, 682
Kendall, Claribel, 687–88
Kochina, Pelageia Iakovlevna, 713–14
Kovaleskaia, Sofia Vasilyevna, 720–22
Lassar, Edna Ernestine (Kramer), 748–49
Lehr, Marguerite (Anna Marie), 769
Lewis, Florence Parthenia, 782–83
Litvinova, Elizaveta Fedorovna, 796–97
Litzinger, Marie, 797–98
Logsdon, Mayme (Irwin), 800
Macintyre, Sheila Scott, 821–22
Maddison, Ada Isabel, 829–30
Martin, Emilie Norton, 848
McDonald, Janet, 866
Medaglia, Diamante, 874
Melissa, 879
Merrill, Helen Abbot, 885–86
Meyer, Margaret Theodora, 890

Miller, Bessie Irving, 895–96
Moufang, Ruth, 922
Neumann, Hanna (Von Caemmerer), 936
Newson, Mary Frances Winston, 937–38
Noether, Amalie Emmy, 949–50
Occello of Lucania, 957
Paine, Mary Esther (Trueblood), 972–73
Palmie, Anna Helene, 977
Parthenay, Catherine de (Dame de Rohan), 985
Pastori, Maria, 987
Pendleton, Ellen Fitz, 1002–3
Péter, Rózsa, 1009–10
Piazolla-Beloch, Margherita, 1019
Piccard, Sophie, 1019–20
Rees, Mina Spiegel, 1084–85
Reinhardt, Anna Barbara, 1088–89
Robinson, Julia (Bowman), 1113–14
Roe, Josephine Robinson, 1119
Sanford, Vera, 1149
Sargent, Winifred, 1152–53
Scott, Charlotte Angas, 1167–68
Short, Jessie May, 1188–89
Simons, Lao Genevra, 1195
Sinclair, Mary Emily, 1195–96
Smith, Clara Eliza, 1204–5
Sperry, Pauline, 1219
Stern, Catherine (Brieger), 1229
Stott, Alicia (Boole), 1244
Taussky-Todd, Olga, 1267–68
Theano, 1276–77
Vivian, Roxana Hayward, 1329
Wang Zhenyi (Chen-i), 1345
Weiss, Marie Johanna, 1359–60
Weiss, Mary Catherine (Bishop), 1360–61
Wells, Agnes Ermina, 1362
Wheeler, Anna Johnson Pell, 1369–70
Wood, Ruth Goulding, 1395
Wooldridge, Elizabeth (Taylor), 1397–98
Worthington, Euphemia R., 1402
Wright, Frances May, 1405
Wrinch, Dorothy Maud, 1407–9
Young, Grace Emily (Chisholm), 1413–14
Young, Mabel Minerva, 1415–16
medical administrators. *See* administrators, medical
metallurgists
Bertereau, Martine De, Baroness De Beausoleil, 119
Hoke, Calm (Morrison), 610
meteorologists
Blinova, Ekaterina Nikitichna, 145
Burns, Eleanor Irene, 211
Whedon, Frances Lovisa, 1368–69
Zlatarovic, Rely, 1423
microbiologists
Alexander, Hattie Elizabeth, 22–23
Bitting, Katherine Eliza (Golden), 132–33
Branham, Sara Elizabeth, 171–72
Bunting-Smith, Mary (Ingraham), 206–8
Dick, Gladys Rowena Henry, 355
Downs, Cornelia Mitchell, 374–75
Eddy, Bernice Elaine, 398–99
Ermol'eva, Zinaida Vissarionovna, 425
Friend, Charlotte, 474

Garnjobst, Laura Flora, 487
Golinevich, Elena Mikhailovna, 518
Hazen, Elizabeth Lee, 573–74
Hesse, Fanny, 593
Hobby, Gladys Lounsbury, 605–6
Hohl, Leonora Anita, 609–10
Jermoljeva, Zinaida Vissarionovna, 657
Kendrick, Pearl (Luella), 688
Klieneberger-Nobel, Emmy, 705–6
Korshunova, Olga Stepanovna, 719
Lambin, Suzanne, 736
Lwoff, Marguerite (Bourdaleix), 812–13
Panajiotatou, Angeliki, 977–78
Robertson, Muriel, 1109–10
Ruys (Ruijs), Anna Charlotte, 1138
Smirnovazamkova, Aleksandra Iivanovna, 1201
Sutter, Vera Laverne, 1253–54
Taliaferro, Lucy (Graves), 1264
Tilden, Evelyn Butler, 1289
Wyckoff, Delaphine Grace (Rosa), 1411
micropaleontologists
Deflandre-Rigaud, Marthe, 336
Dylazanka, Maria, 393
Messina, Angelina Rose, 886
Plummer, Helen Jeanne (Skewes), 1033–34
Polenova, Yelena Nikolayevna, 1037–38
Stewart, Grace Anne, 1234–35
Syniewska, Janina, 1258
microscopists
Booth, Mary Ann Allard, 160
Bury, Priscilla Susan (Falkner), 213–14
Farquharson, Marian Sarah (Ridley), 435
Herrick, Sophia Mcilvaine (Bledsoe), 586–87
Latham, Vida Annette, 750
Veley, Lilian Jane (Nutcombe), 1325
Ward, Mary (King), 1346
midwives
Boivin, Marie Gillain, 154
Cellier, Elizabeth, 241–42
Cobbe, Margaret, 277
Cramer, Catherine Gertrude Du Tertre Schraders, 299–300
De La Marche, Marguerite Du Tertre, 341
Du Coudray, Angelique (Marguerite Le Boursier), 381
Eleanora, Duchess of Mantua, 414
Fuss, Margarita, 479
Horenburg, Anna Elizabeth Von, 617
Kaltenbeiner, Victorine, 675
Keil, Elizabeth Marbareta, 681
La Chapelle, Marie Louise Duges, 731
Laïs, 735
Metrodora, 888
Nihell, Elizabeth, 946
Olympias of Thebes, 962
Perette of Rouen, 1006
Pye, Edith Mary, 1061–62
Salpe, 1146–47
Schraders, Catharina Geertruida, 1165
Sharp, Jane, 1181
Shaw, Hester, 1183
Siegemund, Justine Dittrich, 1193–94
Van Blarcom, Carolyn (Conant), 1318–19

mineralogists
Anderson, Violet Louise, 37
Barlett, Helen Blair, 79–80
Brezina, Maria Aristides, 179
Briere, Yvonne, 180
Foster, Margaret D., 460–61
Giammarino, Pia, 498
Glass, Jewell Jeanette, 506–7
Hamilton, Peggy-Kay, 550–51
Heslop, Mary Kingdon, 592–93
Hooker, Marjorie, 615
Kolaczkowska, Maria, 716
Korn, Doris Elfriede, 717–18
Linton, Laura Alberta, 793–94
Mackowsky, Marie-Therese, 825–26
Macrobert, Rachel (Workman), Lady of Douneside and Cromar, 829
Missuna, Anna Boleslavovna, 899–900
Nemcová-Hlobilová, Jindriska, 934
Shubnikova, Ol'ga Mikhailovna, 1190–91
Slavikova, Ludmila (Kaplanova), 1199
Zaniewska-Chilpalska, Eugenia, 1421
ministers
Blackwell, Antoinette Louise, 135–36
missionaries
Dengel, Anna Maria, 346–47
Parmelee, Ruth A., 980–81
musicologists
Armitt, Mary Louisa, 52–53
mycologists
Alcock, Nora Lilian Leopard, 19
Arden, Lady Margaret Elizabeth (Spencer Wilson), 49
Blacker, Margaret Constance Helen, 135
Bracher, Rose, 168
Burlingham, Gertrude Simmons, 210–11
Charles, Vera Katherine, 245–46
Cookson, Isabel Clifton, 289
Duncan, Catherine (Gross), 384
Fell, Honor Bridget, Dame, 439–40
Gwynne-Vaughan, Dame Helen Charlotte Isabella (Fraser), 539
Hazen, Elizabeth Lee, 572–73
Lister, Gulielma, 795
Morse, Elizabeth Eaton, 917
Page, Winifred Mary, 972
Savulescu, Olga, 1155
Van Beverwijk, Agathe L., 1317–18
Wakefield, Elsie Maud, 1336–37

N
naturalists
Armitt, Annie Maria, 52
Bailey, Florence Augusta (Merriam), 69–70
Bishop, Isabella Lucy Bird, 131
Brightwen, Eliza (Elder), 181
Buckland, Mary Morland, 202
Buckley, Arabella, 202–3
Burges, Mary Anne, 208–9
Christen, Sydney Mary (Thompson), 254–55
Coudreau, Octavie, 296
Dietrich, Amalie, 356–57
Fiennes, Celia, 445
Howitt, Mary (Botham), 623–24
Lamarck, Cornelie, 736

naturalists (*cont.*)
Laskey, Amelia (Rudolph), 747–48
Longstaff, Mary Jane (Donald), 803
Maxwell, Martha Dartt, 858–59
Merian, Maria Sibylla, 884–85
Pfeiffer, Ida (Reyer), 1013–14
Ward, Mary (King), 1346

neonatologists
Dunham, Ethel Collins, 386–87

neoplatonists
Asclepigenia, 55

neuroanatomists
Dejerine-Klumpke, Augusta, 338–39
Hines, Marion, 601–2

neuroembryologists
Reddick, Mary Logan, 1081–82

neurogeneticists
Harding, Anita, 556

neurologists
Albrecht, Grete, 19
Dimsdale, Helen Easdale (Brown), 358–59
Vogt, Cécile (Mugnier), 1329–30

neuropharmacologists
Beauvallet, Marcelle Jeanne, 100
Tum-Suden, Caroline, 1306
Vogt, Marthe Louise, 1330–31

neurophysiologists
Brazier, Mary Agnes Burniston, 174–75
Kennard, Margaret Alice, 688
Lapicque, Marcelle (de Heredia), 745–46
Tum-Suden, Caroline, 1306

neuroscientists
Einstein, Elizabeth Roboz, 410–11
Levi-Montalcini, Rita, 779–81
Lubinska, Liliana, 810
Murray, Margaret Ransone, 927–28
Platt, Julia Barlow, 1031–32

novelists
Duryea, Nina, 389
Edgeworth, Maria, 400
Moriarity, Henrietta Maria, 915
Prestwich, Grace Anne (Milne) M'Call, 1052–53
Sackville-West, Victoria Mary, 1143
Stratton Porter, Gene, 1247–48

nurses
Arnstein, Margaret Gene, 53–54
Barton, Clara Harlowe, 86
Bickerdyke, Mary Ann (Ball), 124–25
Blake, Mary Safford, 140–41
Bradley, Amy Morris, 168–69
Breckinridge, Mary, 175–76
Crandall, Ella Phillips, 300
Davis, Frances (Elliott), 330
Dempsey, Sister Mary Joseph, 345
Dix, Dorothea Lynde, 360
Dock, Lavinia Lloyd, 362–63
Gardner, Mary Sewall, 485
Kenny, Elizabeth (Sister Kenny), 689
Lees, Florence Sarah, 766
Maass, Clara Louise, 817
Marillac, Louise de, 843
Nightingale, Florence, 944–46
Nutting, Mary Adelaide, 954–55
Paget, Dame Mary Rosalind, 972

Palmer, Sophia French, 976–77
Parsons, Emily Elizabeth, 983–84
Safford, Mary Jane, 1143–44
Sanger, Margaret Higgins, 1149–51
Thoms, Adah B. (Samuels), 1285–86
Tompkins, Sally Louisa, 1297
Van Blarcom, Carolyn (Conant), 1318–19
Wald, Lillian D., 1338–39

nutritionists
Abel, Mary Hinman, 2–3
Aberle, Sophie Bledsoe, 4–5
Atwater, Helen Woodard, 58–59
Blunt, Katharine, 151
Caldwell, Mary Letitia, 220–21
Daniels, Amy L., 325
Davis, Adelle, 328–29
Davis, Katharine Bement, 331–32
Dye, Marie, 391
Eleanora, Duchess of Troppau and Jagerndorf, 414
Elsom, Katharine (O'Shea), 420
Emerson, Gladys Ludwina (Anderson), 420–21
Francoise, Marie-Therese, 464
Goldsmith, Grace Arabell, 516–17
Hathaway, Millicent Louise, 565
Hunscher, Helen Alvina, 629
Justin, Margaret M., 672
Kittrell, Flemmie Pansy, 701–2
Krogh, Birthe Marie (Jorgensen), 726–28
Leverton, Ruth Mandeville, 778
MacLeod, Grace, 827–28
Mitchell, Helen Swift, 901
Morgan, Agnes Fay, 913
O'Brien, Ruth, 956
Orent-Kelles, Elsa, 964
Randoin, Lucie Gabrielle (Fandard), 1073–74
Reid, Mary Elizabeth, 1088
Roberts, Lydia Jane, 1107–8
Smith, Janice Minerva, 1207
Sommer, Anna Louise, 1216
Stern, Frances, 1229–30
Stiebeling, Hazel Katherine, 1236–37
Swanson, Pearl Pauline, 1255
Swift, Mary, 1255–56
Taylor, Clara Mae, 1268–69
Woolley, Ann, 1398

O

obstetricians
Bourgeoise, Louyse, 164
Chang, Moon Gyung, 245
Edwards, Lena Frances, 403
Farrar, Lillian K.P., 436
Langsdorff, Toni Von, 744
Larsson, Elisabeth, 746
Tetsuo, Tamayo, 1276

oceanographers
Fish, Marie Poland, 448
Gorshkova, Tat'yana Ivanovna, 521
Pattullo, June Grace, 990
Robinson, Margaret (King), 1114

oceanologists
Kozlova, Ol'ga Grigoriyevna, 724

oncologists
Dunning, Wilhelmina Frances, 388
Gey, Margaret Lewis, 499
Miller, Elizabeth Cavert, 896–97
Stewart, Sarah Elizabeth, 1236

opthalmologists
Barrows, Katherine Isabel (Hayes) Chapin, 85–86
Bokova-Sechenova, Mariia Aleksandrovna, 154–55

ornithologists
Armitt, Mary Louisa, 52–53
Bailey, Florence Augusta (Merriam), 69–70
Black, Hortensia, 133
Comyns-Lewer, Ethel, 284
Eckstorm, Fannie Pearson (Hardy), 398
Hamerstrom, Frances, 548–49
Laskey, Amelia (Rudolph), 747–48
Lewis, Graceanna, 783
Nice, Margaret Morse, 939–40
Pabst, Marie B., 971
Palmer, Elizabeth Day, 974–75
Paulucci, Marianna, Marchesa, 991
Scotland, Minnie (Brink), 1167
Sherman, Althea Rosina, 1185–86
Snethlage, Emilie, 1210
Tyler, Martha G., 1310–11
Tyndall, A.C., 1311
Watt, Helen Winifred Boyd (de Lisle), 1351
Wedderburn, Jemima, 1354

osteologists
Schmid, Elisabeth, 1161

P

paleobotanists
Benson, Margaret Jane, 116–17
Chandler, Marjorie Elizabeth Jane, 244
Cookson, Isabel Clifton, 289
Czeczottowa, Hanna (Peretiatkowicza), 321
Dale, Elizabeth, 322–23
Leclercq, Suzanne (Céline), 763
Neuburg Maria Feodorovna, 935–36
Pabst, Marie B., 971
Rasskazova, Yelena Stepanovna, 1074–75
Sanborn, Ethel, 1147
Scott, Henderina Victoria (Klaassen), 1168–69
Stopes, Marie Charlotte Carmichael, 1242

paleontologists
Alimen, Henriette, 23
Anning, Mary, 41–42
Bate, Dorothea Minola Alice, 90
Carroll, Christiane (Mendrez), 232
Cattoi, Noemí Violeta, 238–39
Cook, Margaret C., 288
Coryndon, Shirley (Cameron), 295
Crane, Agnes, 300
Crespin, Irene, 302–3
Csepreghyne-Meznerics, Ilona, 306–7
Dobrolubova, Tatiana A., 360–61
Dolgopol De Saez, Mathilde, 366
Doreck, Hertha (Walburger Doris Sieverts), 369–70
Duncan, Helen, 384–85
Edinger, Johanna Gabrielle Otellie, 400–401
Elles, Gertrude Lilian, 417–18

Fritz, Madeleine Alberta, 475
Gardner, Julia Anna, 484–85
Garretson, Mary (Welleck), 487–88
Goldring, Winifred, 515–16
Gorizdro-Kulczycka, Zinaida, 521
Gromova, Vera Isaacovna, 533
Harrison, Janet Mitchell Marr (Dingwall), 559
Hart, J.B., 560
Hill, Dorothy, 600–601
Hofmann, Elise, 608
Holmes, Mary Emilee, 612
Holm, Esther (Aberdeen), 612
Hough, Margaret Jean Ringier, 619
Howard Wylde, Hildegarde, 620–22
Ivanova, Elena Alekseevna, 645–46
Johnston, Mary Sophia, 660–61
Kablick, Josephine (Ettel), 674
Keen, Angeline Myra, 680–81
Kielan-Jaworowska, Zofia, 693–94
Leclercq, Suzanne (Céline), 763
Le Maître, Dorothée, 770–71
Lermontova, Ekaterina Vladimirovna, 774–75
Maury, Carlotta Joaquina, 857–58
McGlamery, Josie Winifred, 868
Missuna, Anna Boleslavovna, 899–900
Morozova, Valentina Galaktionovna, 915–16
Mottl, Maria, 921
O'Connell, Marjorie, 957
Pavlova, Mariia Vasil'evna, 992–93
Pozarska, Krystyna (Maliszewski), 1048–49
Rauzer-Chernousova, Dagmara M., 1078–79
Richter, Emma (Hüther), 1098
Semikhatova, Sofia Viktorovna (Karpova), 1175–76
Shakespear, Dame Ethel Mary Reader (Wood), 1180–81
Shulga-Nesterenko, Maria I., 1191–92
Signeux, Jeanne, 1194
Soshkina, Elizabeth D., 1217
Stefanescu, Sabba, 1225
Stewart, Grace Anne, 1234–35
Talbot, Mignon, 1263–64
Trizna, Valentina Borisovna, 1302–3
Tumanskaya, Olga G. (Shirokobruhova), 1306–7
Turnbull, Priscilla Freudenheim, 1308
Weinzierl, Laura (Lane), 1358–59
Wilson, Alice Evelyn, 1383–84
Woods, Ethel Gertrude (Skeat), 1396–97
Zalesskaya-Chirkova, Elena, 1420–21

palynologists
Blackburn, Kathleen Bever, 133–34
Cookson, Isabel Clifton, 289
Cranwell, Lucy May, 301
Deflandre-Rigaud, Marthe, 336
Hofmann, Elise, 608
Naumova, Sofiya Nickolaevna, 931
Oszast, Janina Celina, 968–69
Pokrovskaia, Irina Mitrofanovna, 1036
Woillard-Roucoux, Geneviève Marie-Aurélie, 1390–91
Zaklinskaia, Elena Dmitrievna, 1418–19

parapsychologists
Rhine, Louise Ella (Weckesser), 1091

parasitologists
Bishop, Ann, 129–31
Cram, Eloise Blaine, 299
Petran, Elizabeth Irene, 1012
Rees, Florence Gwendolen, 1083–84
Rothschild, Miriam, 1128–29

pathologists
Andersen, Dorothy Hansine, 31–32
Catani, Giuseppina, 236–37
Claypole, Edith Jane, 267
Cone, Claribel, 284–85
De Witt, Lydia Maria Adams, 353–54
Dick, Gladys Rowena Henry, 354–55
Dunn, Thelma Brumfield, 387–88
Dutton, Loraine Orr, 391
Frantz, Virginia Kneeland, 466
Goldfeder, Anna, 512–13
Gravatt, Annie Evelyn (Rathbun), 522–23
Hamilton, Alice, 549–50
Hardy, Harriet, 557
Jones, Eva Elizabeth, 664–65
L'esperance, Elise Depew Strang, 777–78
Menten, Maud L., 882–83
Oppenheimer, Ella Hutzler, 963
Pearce, Louise, 997–98
plant
Allen, Ruth Florence, 25–26
Beckwith, Angie Maria, 102
Brown, Nellie Adalesa, 190–91
Bryan, Mary Katherine, 199
Charles, Vera Katherine, 245
Elliott, Charlotte, 418
Hart, Helen, 560
Jensen, Estelle Louise, 656
McGuire, Ruth Colvin Starrett, 1064–65
Nance, Nellie Ward, 930
Newton, Margaret, 938–39
Quirk, Agnes, 1064–65
Rumbold, Caroline (Thomas), 1136
Savulescu, Olga, 1155
Smith, Elizabeth (Hight), 1205
Spalding, Effie Southworth, 1218
Potter, Edith Louise, 1045–46
Ramsey, Elizabeth Mapelsden, 1071
Richards, Clarice Audrey, 1094–95
Ross, Joan Margaret, 1127
Russell, Dorothy, 1136–37
Silberberg, Ruth Katzenstein, 1194
Slye, Maud, 1199–1200
Smirnovazamkova, Aleksandra Iivanovna, 1201
Weld, Julia Tiffany, 1361
Westcott, Cynthia, 1367–68
Wollstein, Martha, 1393–94
Zeckwer, Isolde Therese, 1421

pathophysiologists
Medvedeva, Nina Borisovna, 875–76

pediatricians
Alexander, Hattie Elizabeth, 22–23
Andersen, Dorothy Hansine, 31–32
Bakwin, Ruth (Morris), 72
Bang, Duck-Heung, 75
Dodd, Katharine, 363
Dombrovskaia, Juliia Fominichna, 367
Dunham, Ethel Collins, 386–87

Hurler, Gertrud (Zach), 631–32
Ilg, Frances Lillian, 642–43
Mackay, Helen Marion MacPherson, 824
Shabanova, Anna Nikolaevna, 1179–80
Thelander, Hulda Evelin, 1277
Wilson, May Georgiana, 1387

pedologists
Zaniewska-Chilpalska, Eugenia, 1421

petrologists
Heslop, Mary Kingdon, 592–93
Hooker, Marjorie, 615
Jeremine, Elisabeth (Tschernaieff), 656–57
Kardymowiczowa, Irena, 676
Knopf, Eleanora Frances (Bliss), 708–9
Korringa, Marjorie K., 718–19
MacRobert, Rachel (Workman), 829
Nemcová-Hlobilová, Jindriska, 934
Prádacová, Marcella, 1049
Raisin, Catherine Alice, 1068–69
Stose, Anna Isabel (Jonas), 1243–44
Zaniewska-Chilpalska, Eugenia, 1421

pharmacists
Marillac, Louise de, 843
Stephens, Joanna, 1226–27
Walker, Elizabeth, 1339

pharmacologists
Artemisia of Caria II, 54
Greig, Margaret Elizabeth, 530
Kelly, Margaret G., 687
Langecker, Hedwig, 743
Maling, Harriet Florence (Mylander), 833–34
Robb, Jane (Sands), 1104–5

philanthropists
Bruce, Catherine Wolfe, 194
Dummer, Ethel (Sturges), 382–83
Hearst, Phoebe (Apperson), 574–75
Necker, Susanne (Curchod), 932
Putnam, Mary Louise (Duncan), 1061
Schliemann, Sophia (Kastromenos), 1160–61

philosophers
Abrotelia, 5
Aesara, 11–12
Arber, Agnes (Robertson), 47–48
Arete of Cyrene, 50
Arignote of Samos, 50
Aspasia of miletus, 55–56
Astell, Mary, 56–57
Axiothea of Phlius, 62
Barbapiccola, Giuseppa Eleonora, 77
Bassi, Laura Maria Caterina, 88–89
Baynard, Anne, 97
Beronice, 118
Borromeo, Clelia Grillo, 163
Calkins, Mary Whiton, 221–23
Carter, Elizabeth, 234–35
Castra, Anna De, 236
Cleachma, 267–68
Clements, Margaret, 268–69
Cleobulina of Rhodes, 269
Clifford, Lady Anne, 273
Conway, Anne, 286–87
Cornaro (Cornero), Elena (Helena) Lucretia, 295
Coste Blanche, Marie De, 295
Damo, 323–24

philosophers (*cont.*)

De La Cruz, Juana Ines, 339

Diotima of Mantinea, 359

Du Chatelet, Gabrielle-Emilie Le Tonnelier De Breteuil (Marquise), 378

Eccello of Lucania, 396

Echecratia the Philiasian, 397

Galindo, Beatrix, 481

Herrad of Hohenburg, 585–86

Hildegard of Bingen, 596–98

Hypatia of Alexandria, 637–39

Leontium, 771–72

Myia or Mya, 929

Occello of Lucania, 957

Parthenay, Catherine de (Dame de Rohan), 985

Perictione, 1007

Pisan, Christine de, 1028

Rodde, Dorothea von (Schlözer), 1117

Royer, Clémence, 1129–32

Sablière, Marguerite (Hessein) de la, 1142–43

Theano, 1276–77

Wright, Lady Catherine, 1404–5

photographers

Akeley, Mary Lee (Jobe), 17–18

Atkins, Anna, 57

Booth, Mary Ann Allard, 160

Howe Akeley, Delia Julia Denning, 622–23

Parsons, Mary, Countess of Rosse, 984–85

Stratton Porter, Gene, 1247–48

phrenologists

Wells, Charlotte Fowler, 1362–63

phycologists

Pfiester, Lois Ann, 1015

Pocock, Mary Agard, 1035–36

physicians

Abbott, Maude Elizabeth Seymour, 1–2

Aberle, Sophie Bledsoe, 4–5

Abouchdid, Edna, 5

Acosta-Sison, Honoria, 6

Adelberger, 10

Adelle, 10

Adelmota, 10

Aelfleda, 11

Aemilia, 11

Agamede, 12

Agnes, Countess of Aix, 14

Agnes of Bohemia, 14

Agnes of Jerusalem, 14

Agnes of Silesia, 14

Agnodike, 16

Aitken, Janet Kerr, 16–17

Ali, Safieh, 23

Aluwihare, Florence Kaushalya (Ram), 27–28

Ameline, 28

Anderson, Caroline Virginia (Still) Wiley, 32–33

Anderson, Elizabeth Garrett, 34–35

Anderson, Louisa Garrett, 36–37

Andromache, 39

Angst-Horridge, Anita, 40

Anicia or Amyte, 40

Antoine, Lore, 43–44

Antoinette De Bellegarde, 44

Apgar, Virginia, 45–46

Apsley (Hutchinson), Lady Lucy, 47

Arkhangel'skaia, Aleksandra Gavriilovna, 50–51

Aspasia the Physician, 56

Atkins, Louisa Catherine Fanny, 57–58

Auken, Kirsten (Lomholt), 60–61

Ayrton, Matilda (Chaplin), 64

Bagshaw, Elizabeth Catherine, 67

Baker, Sara Josephine, 70–71

Balaam, Ellen, 72–73

Balfour, Margaret Ida, 73

Barringer, Emily (Dunning), 84–85

Bass, Mary Elizabeth, 88

Bates, Mary E., 90–91

Baumann, Frieda, 92–93

Baumgartner, Leona, 94–95

Beatrice, Medica of Candia, 99

Belota [Johanna Belota], 110

Bennett, Alice, 115

Bentham, Ethel, 117

Bertillon, Caroline Schutze, 120

Bhatia, Sharju Pandit, 122–23

Biscot, Jeanne, 129

Bishop, Katharine Scott, 131–32

Blackwell, Elizabeth, 136

Blackwell, Emily, 138–39

Blake, Mary Safford, 140–41

Blatchford, Ellen C., 143

Bluhm, Agnes, 149–50

Borsarelli, Fernanda, 163

Bradley, Frances Sage, 169–70

Brand, Martha, 170–71

Brenk, Irene, 177–78

Bres Madeleine (Gébelin), 178–79

Bridget, Saint, of Scandinavia, 179

Broomall, Anna Elizabeth, 186–87

Brown, Charlotte Amanda Blake, 187–88

Brown, Dame Edith Mary, 188–89

Bruckner, Frau Dr., 195

Brunetta, 196

Brunfels, Frau Otto, 196

Bryant, Louise Stevens, 199

Buckel, Chloe A., 201–2

Buerk, Minerva (Smith), 203–4

Burns, Louisa, 211

Bury, Elizabeth (Lawrence), 212–13

Buttelini, Marchesa, 215

Calderone, Mary S., 220

Calenda, Constanza or Laurea Constantia, 221

Cambriere, Clarisse, 224

Carvajales Y Camino, Laura M.De, 236

Catherine Ursula, Countess of Baden, 237

Cesniece-Freudenfelde, Zelma, 242

Chang, Vivian, 245

Chenoweth, Alice Drew, 249–50

Chesser, Elizabeth (Sloan), 250

Chinchon, Countess of, 252

Chinn, May Edward, 252–53

Chisholm, Catherine, 253

Chodak-Gregory, Hazel Haward (Cuthbert), 254

Cilento, Lady Phyllis, 257–58

Clarisse of Rotomago (or Clarice of Rouen), 259

Clark, Nancy Talbot, 263–64

Cleopatra, 269

Cleveland, Emeline Horton, 272–73

Clisby, Harriet Jemima Winifred, 273–74

Cole, Rebecca J., 281

Collins, Katharine Richards, 282

Comnena (Comnenos), Anna, 283

Converse, Jeanne, 286

Cunningham, Gladys Story, 310–11

Cushier, Elizabeth, 319

Cuthbert-Browne, Grace Johnston, 320–21

Dalai, Maria Jolanda (Tosoni), 322

Dalle Donne, Maria, 323

Daniel, Anne Sturges, 324–25

De Gorzano, Leonetta, 337

Dejerine-Klumpke, Augusta, 338–39

De Lange, Cornelia Catharina, 341–42

De Lebrix, Francoise, 342–43

Demud, 346

Derscheid-Delcourt, Marie, 350

Dodd, Katharine, 363

Dolley, Sarah Read Adamson, 366–67

Durocher, Marie (Josefina Mathilde), 389

Dutcher, Adelaide, 389–90

Edwards, Emma Ward, 403

Edwards-Pilliet, Blanche, 403–5

Eleanora, Duchess of Troppau and Jagerndorf, 414

Elephantis, 414

Elgood, Cornelia Bonte Sheldon (Amos), 414–15

Eliot, Martha May, 416

Elsom, Katharine (O'Shea), 420

Erxleben, Dorothea Christiana (Leporin), 425–26

Fabiola, 433

Fage, Winifred E., 433

Favilla, 436

Fearn, Anne walter, 437–38

Felicie, Jacobina, 439

Ferrand, Elizabeth M., 443

Figner, Vera, 446

Florendo, Soledad Arcega, 455–56

Fowler, Lydia Folger, 461–62

Gantt, Love Rosa, 482–83

Ghilietta, 498

Gilette of Narbonne, 502

Gilroy, Helen (Turnbull), 503

Glasgow, Maude, 506

Gleason, Rachel Brooks, 508

Goldsmith, Grace Arabell, 516–17

Gray, Etta, 523

Gullett, Lucy E., 536

Hainault, Countess of, 543

Haldorsen, Inger Alida, 543–44

Halket, Lady Anne, 544–45

Hall-Brown, Lucy, 547

Hall, Rosetta Sherwood, 546–47

Harding, Anita, 556

Heim-Vogtlin, Marie, 580

Hellman, Johanna, 581

Hellstedt, Leone Mcgregor, 581–82

Herford, Ethilda B.Meakin, 585

Hickey, Amanda Sanford, 595

Higgins, Vera (Cockburn), 596

Hitzenberger, Annaliese, 604–5
Hoby, Lady, 606
Horney, Karen Clementine (Danielsen), 617–18
Hughes, Ellen Kent, 627
Hugonnai-Wartha, Vilma, 628
Hunt, Harriot Kezia, 630–31
Hutton, Lady Isabel Emilie, 635
Inglis, Elsie (Maude), 643
Jacobi, Mary Corinna Putnam, 648–50
Jacobina Medica of Bologna, 650
Jacobs, Aletta Henrietta, 650–51
Jacobson, Clara, 651
Jacopa of Passau, 651
Jex-Blake, Sophia, 657–59
Jhirad, Jerusha, 659–60
Johanna (Johanne, Joanna), 660
Jones, Mary Amanda Dixon, 666
Jordan, Sara Claudia (Murray), 668–69
Kahn, Ida, 675
Karamihailova, Elizabeth/Elizaveta [Kara-Michailova], 676
Kashevarovarudneva, Varvara Aleksandrovna, 678–80
Katherine, La Surgiene (The Surgeon), 680
Kendrick, Pearl (Luella), 688
Kil, Chung-Hee, 694–95
Kleegman, Sophia, 702–3
Koprowska, Irena Grasberg, 717
Kovrigina, Mariia Dmitrievna, 722–23
Krogh, Birthe Marie (Jorgensen), 726–28
Laïs, 735
Laubenstein, Linda, 751
Lazarus, Hilda Mary, 756–57
Lebedeva, Vera Pavlovna, 760–61
Ledingham, Una Christina (Garvin), 763
Lee, Rebecca, 764
Lehmus, Emilie, 767–68
Leoparda, 772
Lind-Campbell, Hjördis, 791
Lindsten-Thomasson, Marianne, 792–93
Lin Qiaozhi (Lin Chiao-Chi), 790–91
Linton, Laura Alberta, 793–94
Lipinska, Mélanie, 794
Lisovskaia, Sofiya Nikolaievna, 794
Lloyd-Green, Lorna, 798
Logan, Myra Adele, 800
Longshore, Hannah E.(Myers), 802–3
Lovejoy, Esther Pohl, 806–7
Loveless, Mary hewitt, 807
Lozier, Clemence Sophia (Harned), 809
Lukanina, Adelaida N., 810–11
Mackay, Helen Marion MacPherson, 824
Macrina, 828–29
Marshall, Clara, 845–46
Martinez-Alvarez, Josefina, 849–50
Massey, Patricia, 852
Mathisen, Karoline, 855
McConney, Florence, 864–65
McGee, Anita (Newcomb), 867–68
McLaren, Agnes, 871
Memmler, Ruth Lundeen, 880–81
Mendenhall, Dorothy (Reed), 881–82
Mentuhetep, Queen, 883–84
Mercuriade, 884

Mergler, Marie, 884
Meyling-Hylkema, Elisabeth, 891
Mildmay, Grace Sherrington, 894
Minoka-Hill, Lillie Rosa, 897–98
Miyaji, Kunie, 905–6
Moffat, Agnes K., 906–7
Montessori, Maria, 909–10
Moody, Mary Blair, 910
Morgan, Elizabeth Frances, 914
Morton, Rosalie Slaughter, 918–20
Mosher, Clelia Duel, 920–21
Murrell, Christine Mary, 928
Nasymuth, Dorothea Clara (Maude), 930–31
Nemir, Rosa Lee, 934–35
Netrasiri, Khunying Cherd-Chalong, 935
Nicerata, Saint, 940
Nieh, Chung-en, 943
Nolde, Helene Aldegonde De, 348
Odlum, Doris, 957–58
Ogino, G., 961
Ohnesorge, Lena, 961
Owens-Adair, Bethenia, 970
Owens, Margaret, 969–70
Panajiotatou, Angeliki, 977–78
Parmelee, Ruth A., 980–81
Parrish, Rebecca, 981
Parry, Angenette, 981
Parsons, Eloise, 981–82
Pastori, Giuseppina, 986–87
Pearce, Louise, 997–98
Pechey-Phipson, Mary Edith, 998–99
Pelletier, Madeleine, 1000–1002
Pereira de Queiroz, Carlota, 1005–6
Peretti, Zaffira, 1006
Pettit, Mary Dewitt, 1013
Pettracini, Maria, 1013
Picotte, Susan (La Flesche), 1022–23
Pirami, Edmea, 1026–27
Pokrovskaia, Mariia Ivanovna, 1036–37
Pollack, Flora, 1038
Potter, Ellen Culver, 1046
Preston, Ann, 1051–52
Price, Dorothy (Stopford), 1054
Putnam, Helen Cordelia, 1059–60
Rabinoff, Sophie, 1066–67
Radegonde, 1067
Rafatdjah, Safieh, 1067–68
Ramirez, Rosita Rivera, 1070
Ramsey, Elizabeth Mapelsden, 1071
Rancken, Saima Tawast, 1072
Rathbone, Mary May, 1075
Ratnayake, May, 1076
Raymond-Schroeder, Aimee J., 1080
Refshauge, Joan, 1086–87
Remond, Sarah Parker, 1089
Rice-Wray, Edris, 1092–93
Ripley, Martha (Rogers), 1102
Ritter, Mary Elizabeth (Bennett), 1103
Robertson, Jeannie (Smillie), 1108–9
Robinson, Daisy Maude (Orleman), 1111
Ross, Joan Margaret, 1127
Rucker, Augusta, 1134
Russell, Dorothy, 1136–37
Ruys (Ruijs), Anna Charlotte, 1138
Sabuco Banera D'Alcaraz, Olivia, 1143

Safford, Mary Jane, 1143–44
Sandford-Morgan, Elma (Linton), 1148
Sara of Würzburg, 1151
Satur, Dorothy May, 1153–54
Sawin, Martha, 1155
Scharlieb, Dame Mary Ann Dacomb (Bird), 1157–58
Schmidt-Fischer, Hildegard, 1162–63
Schoenfeld, Reba Willits, 1163
Schoental, Regina, 1163–64
Scudder, Ida Sophia, 1169–70
Sewall, Lucy, 1178
Sibelius, Helena, 1192
Siebold, Charlotte Marianne Heidenreich von, 1193
Siebold, Josepha (Henning) von, 1193
Smith, Erma Anita, 1205
Solis Quiroga, Margarita Delgado de, 1212
Sotira, 1217–18
Stenhouse, Caroline, 1226
Stephens, Joanna, 1226–27
Stevenson, Sarah Ann (Hackett), 1233–34
Stimson, Barbara Bartlett, 1238
Stone, Constance, 1240
Stowe, Emily Howard (Jennings), 1245
Stuart, Miranda, 1250
Summerskill, Edith Clara, 1251–52
Sundquist, Alma, 1252
Suslova, Nadezhda Prokof'evna, 1252–53
Svartz, Nanna Charlotta, 1254
Swain, Clara A., 1255
Szwajger, Adina Blady, 1259
Takeuchi, Shigeyo (Ide), 1261–62
Taussig, Helen Brooke, 1265–66
Theano, 1276–77
Thelberg, Elizabeth (Burr), 1277–78
Theodosia, Saint, 1278
Thomas, Mary Frame (Myers), 1281–82
Thompson, Mary Harris, 1284–85
Tiburtius, Franziska, 1288–89
Tisserand, M., 1294
Tomaszewicz-Dobrska, Anna, 1297
Tracy, Martha, 1299–1300
Trotula, 1304–5
Tyng, Anita E., 1311
Veretennikova, Anna Ivanovna, 1326–27
Vilar, Lola, 1328–29
Vytilingam, Kamala Israel, 1333–34
Walker, Eliza, 1339
Walker, Mary Edward, 1340–41
Welsh, Lillian, 1364
Widdowson, Elsie May, 1376–77
Williams, Cicely Delphine, 1382
Winner, Dame Albertine, 1389
Wong Ah Mae, 1394
Wood, Emily Elizabeth, 1394
Woolley, Ann, 1398
Wright, Helena Rosa (Lowenfeld), 1405–6
Wright, Katharine, 1406–7
Wundt, Nora, 1410–11
Zakrzewska, Marie Elizabeth, 1419–20

physicists
Albrecht, Eleonore, 18
Anderson, Elda Emma, 33–34
Anslow, Gladys Amelia, 42–43

physicists (*cont.*)
Ardinghelli, Maria Angela, 49–50
Arsenjewa, A., 54
Artner, Mathilde, 55
Ayrton, Hertha Marks, 62–63
Bahr-bergius, Eva Vilhelmina Julia Von, 68
Barnothy, Madeleine (Forro), 83
Becker-Rose, Herta, 101–2
Beckman, A., 102
Belar, Maria, 110
Bender, Wilma, 112
Blanquies, Lucie, 142–43
Blau, Marietta, 143–44
Blodgett, Katharine Burr, 148–49
Bohm-wendt, Cacilia, 153–54
Boron, Elizabeth (Riddle) Graves, 162–63
Brant, Laura, 172
Brooks, Harriet T., 184–85
Brown, Fay Cluff, 189–90
Brunetti, R., 196
Burns, Eleanor Irene, 211
Bussecker, Erna, 215
Cale, F.M., 221
Carter, Edna, 234
Cauchois, Yvette, 239
Caughlan, Georgeanne (Robertson), 239–40
Chamie, Catherine, 243
Chasman, Renate Wiener, 247–48
Clark, Bertha, 260
Clay-Jolles, Tettje Clasina, 265–66
Cordier, Marguerite Jeanne, 292
Curie, Marie (Maria Sklodowska), 311–17
Dallas, A.E.M.M., 323
Davis, Grace Evangeline, 330
Dewey, Jane Mary (Clark), 353
Dobrowolska, H., 361
Downey, K.Melvina, 374
Dunlop, Janette Gilchrist, 387
Ehrenfest-Afanassjewa, Tatyana Alexeyevna, 407–8
Einstein-Maric, Mileva, 411–12
Fishenden, Margaret White, 448–49
Fonovits-Smereker, H., 458
Freeman, Joan Maie, 467–68
Friedmann, Friederike, 474
Gabler, Anna, 480
Galabert, Renee, 481
Gates, Fanny Cook, 489–90
Glagoleva-Arkad'Yeva, Aleksandra Andreyevna, 506
Goeppert Mayer, Maria Gertrud Kate, 510–12
Goldhaber, Sulamith, 514
Goldschmidt, Frieda, 516
Graves, Elizabeth (Riddle), 523
Hausser, Isolde (Ganswindt), 566–68, 566–68
Hayner, Lucy Julia, 571–72
Heimann, Berta, 579
Herxheimer, Franziska, 592
Johnson, Dorothy Durfee Montgomery, 660
Joliot-Curie, Irene, 662–63
Jones, Lorella Margaret, 665
Joslin, Lulu, 669
Karlik, Berta, 677
Keith, Marcia Anna, 682
Kochanowská, Adéla, 713

Kohn, Hedwig, 714–15
Laird, Elizabeth Rebecca, 734–35
Langford, Grace, 743–44
Laski, Gerda, 748
Levi, Hilde, 778–79
Libby, Leona Woods Marshall, 787–88
Lowater, Frances, 807–8
Maltby, Margaret Eliza, 835
Maracineanu, Stefania, 841
McDowell, Louise Sherwood, 866–67
Meitner, Lise, 877–79
Meyer-Bjerrum, Kirstine, 890–91
Monin-Molinier, Madeline, 908
Mooney-Slater, Rose Camille Ledieu, 910–11
Naylor, Bertha, 931
Neumann, Elsa, 936
Nickerson, Dorothy, 942
Noyes, Mary Chilton, 953
Paget, Rose Elizabeth, 972
Pettersson, Dagmar, 1012–13
Phillips, Melba Newell, 1017–18
PIazolla-Beloch, Margherita, 1019
Pirret, Ruth, 1027–28
Pockels, Agnes, 1034–35
Ramstedt, Eva Julia Augusta, 1071–72
Richter, Grete, 1098–99
Rogers, Marguerite Moillet, 1121
Ross, Marion Amelia Spence, 1127
Salbach, Hilde, 1145–46
Sale, Rhoda, 1146
Shields, Margaret Calderwood, 1187
Slater, Jesse Mabel Wilkins, 1198–99
Sponer-Franck, Hertha Dorothea Elisabeth, 1219–21
Stewart, Maude, 1236
Stone, Isabelle, 1241–42
Szmidt, Jadwiga, 1258–59
Tonnelat, Marie-Antoinette (Baudot), 1297–98
Warga, Mary Elizabeth, 1346–47
Way, Katharine, 1352
Weeks, Dorothy W., 1357–58
White, Margaret Pirie, 1372
Whiting, Sarah Frances, 1374
Wick, Frances Gertrude, 1375–76
Wiebusch, Agnes (Townsend), 1377
Wilson, Lucy, 1386
Wu Chien-Shiung, 1409–10

physiologists
Anderson, Evelyn M., 35–36
Baetjer, Anna Medora, 66–67
Barbarshova, Zoiaivanovna, 77
Barton, Lela Viola, 86–87
Beauvallet, Marcelle Jeanne, 100
Bidder, Marion Greenwood, 125–26
Brooks, Matilda (Moldenhauer), 185–86
Buchanan, Florence, 200
Bulbring, Edith, 205
Chick, Dame Harriette, 250–51
Clark, Janet Howell, 261–62
Claypole, Edith Jane, 267
Clinch, Phyllis E.M., 273
Coates, Sarah J., 274–75
Collett, Mary Elizabeth, 282
Conklin, Ruth Emelene, 285–86

Coombs, Helen Copeland, 289–90
Cooper, Sybil, 291
Cullis, Winifred, 307–8
Day, Dorothy, 334
Denis, Willey Glover, 347
Drinker, Katherine (Rotan), 377
Dubuisson-Brouha, Adele, 378
Eckerson, Sophia Hennion, 397–98
Edkins, Nora Tweedy, 401–2
Eggleton, Marion Grace (Palmer), 406–7
Fitzgerald, Mabel Purefoy, 450
Galvani, Lucia (Galeazzi), 481–82
Gocholashvili, Mariia Mikievna, 509
Goldsmith, Marie, 517
Greisheimer, Esther Maud, 530
Hanson, Emmeline Jean, 554–55
Hartt, Constance Endicott, 560–61
Haywood, Charlotte, 572
Hebb, Catherine Olding, 575–76
Herrick, Julia Frances, 586
Herwerden, Marianne Van, 592
Hinrichs, Marie Agnes, 602
Holton, Pamela Margaret (Watson-Williams), 613
Hyde, Ida Henrietta, 635–36
Irwin, Marian, 643–44
Jacobson, Clara, 651
Joteyko, Josephine, 670–71
Karpowicz, Ludmila, 678
Keller, Ida Augusta, 682–83
King, Jessie Luella, 697
KrasnoseL'skaia, Tat'iana Abramovna, 724–25
Kunde, Margaret Meta H., 729–30
Lane-Claypon, Janet Elizabeth, 741–42
Latimer, Caroline Wormeley, 750–51
Le Breton, Elaine, 762
Lewis, Margaret Adaline Reed, 785–86
Lutwak-Mann, Cecelia, 812
Macklin, Madge (Thurlow), 824–25
Mangold, Hilde (Proescholdt), 836
Marsh, Mary Elizabeth, 845
Mellanby, May (Tweedy), 879–80
Minot, Ann Stone, 898–99
Mitchell, Helen Swift, 901
Moore, Anne, 911
Moore, Lillian Mary, 912
Moore, Mary Mitchell, 912
Mosher, Clelia Duel, 920–21
Payne, Nellie Maria de Cottrell, 993
Petrova, Maria Kapitonovna, 1012
Phisalix, Marie (Picot), 1018–19
Pickford, Lilian Mary, 1021–22
Pool, Judith Graham, 1039–40
Porter, Helen Kemp Archbold, 1042–43
Prichard, Marjorie Mabel Lucy, 1054
research, 726–28
Robb, Jane (Sands), 1104–5
Rose, Mary Davies Swartz, 1125–26
Schofield, Brenda Muriel, 1164–65
Shtern, Lina Solomonovna, 1189–90
Smith, Audrey U., 1203–4
Smith, Erma Anita, 1205
Stoppel, Rose, 1242–43
Stose, Anna Isabel (Jonas), 1243–44
Tebb, Mary Christine, 1272–73

Thomas, Caroline (Bedell), 1279
Turner, Abby Howe, 1308
Van Wagenen, Gertrude, 1321–22
Vaughan, Dame Janet, 1323–24
Warren, Madeleine (Field), 1347
White, Frances Emily, 1372

phytocenologists
Dokhman, Genrietta Isaakovna, 365–66

phytogeographers
Czeczottowa, Hanna (Peretiatkowicza), 321

phytopathologists
Watkins, Della Elizabeth (Ingram), 1349–50

playwrights
Gregory, Lady Isabella Augusta (Persse), 529
Kirkham, Nellie, 701

poets
Kirkham, Nellie, 701
Sackville-West, Victoria Mary, 1143

political activists. *See* activists, political

primatologists
Fossey, Dian, 458

professors
Scharrer, Berta (Vogel), 1158–59

protozoologists
Austin, Mary Lellah, 61
Bishop, Ann, 129–31
Matikashvili, Nina, 855
Taylor, Monica, 1272

psychiatrists
Bender, Lauretta, 111–12
Bibring, Grete Lehner, 123–24
Bruch, Hilde, 195
Brunswick, Ruth Jane (Mack), 196–97
Dooley, Lucile, 368
Dunbar, Helen Flanders, 383–84
Fox, Ruth, 463–64
Gitelson, Frances H., 505
Hilgard, Josephine Rohrs, 599
Josselyn, Irene (Milliken), 669–70
Lampl-De Groot, Jeanne, 738
Leighton, Dorothea (Cross), 769–70
Levine, Lena, 781–82
Pasternak, Lydia, 985–86
Pavenstedt, Eleanor, 991–92
Payne, Sylvia May (Moore), 994
Ring, Barbara Taylor, 1100–1101
Sherman, Irene Case, 1186
Thompson, Clara Mabel, 1283
Vogt, Cécile (Mugnier), 1329–30

psychoanalysts
Andreas-Salome, Louise Lelia, 38–39
Benedek, Therese F., 112–13
Brunswick, Ruth Jane (Mack), 196–97
Burlingham, Dorothy (Tiffany), 209–10
Deutsch, Helene Rosenback, 351–52
Frenkel-Brunswik, Else, 469–70
Freud, Anna, 470–72
Friedlander, Kate, 473
Heimann, Paula, 579–80
Hilgard, Josephine Rohrs, 599
Horney, Karen Clementine (Danielsen), 617–18
Hug-Hellmuth, Hermine Von, 626
Klein, Melanie (Reizes), 703–4
McLean, Helen (Vincent), 871–72

Pavenstedt, Eleanor, 991–92
Payne, Sylvia May (Moore), 994
Riviere, Joan (Verrall), 1103–4
Rosenfeld, Eva, 1126–27
Schmideberg, Melitta (Klein), 1161–62
Strachey, Alix (Sargant-Florence), 1245–46

psychologists
Abel, Theodora Mead, 3–4
Abramson, Jadwiga, 5
Achilles, Edith Mulhall, 5–6
Adkins, Dorothy Christina, 10–11
Allen, Doris Twitchell, 24–25
Alper, Thelma Gorfinkle, 26–27
Ames, Louise Bates, 30–31
Anderson, Rose Gustava, 37
Andrus, Ruth, 39–40
Antipoff, Helene, 43
Arlitt, Ada Hart, 51
Arnold, Magda Blondiau, 53
Arthur, Mary Grace, 54–55
Babcock, Harriet, 65
Bagley, Florence (Winger), 67
Ball, Josephine, 73–74
Banham, Katherine May, 77
Baumgarten-Tramer, Franziska, 93–94
Baxter, Mildred Frances, 95
Bayley, Nancy, 96–97
Benedek, Therese F., 112–13
Bird, Grace Electa, 128
Blanchard, Phyllis, 142
Block, Jeanne (Humphrey), 146–48
Bourdel, Leone, 163–64
Bouthilet, Lorraine, 164–65
Bridgman, Olga Louise, 180
Bronner, Augusta Fox, 183
Brousseau, Kate, 187
Bryan, Alice Isabel (Bever), 197–98
Buhler, Charlotte Bertha (Malachowski), 204–5
Bull, Nina Wilcox, 205–6
Bunch, Cordia, 206
Burrell, Anna Porter, 212
Burr, Emily Thorp, 211
Calkins, Mary Whiton, 221–23
Castle, Cora (Sutton), 236
Cattell, Psyche, 238
Clark, Mamie Katherine (Phipps), 263
Cobb, Margaret Vara, 275–76
Colby, Martha Guernsey, 279
Cooper, Clara Chassell, 290
Cooper-Ellis, Katharine Murdoch, 292
Cowan, Edwina Abbott, 296–97
Cox, Rachel (Dunaway), 298
Cunningham, Bess Virginia, 310
Cushing, Hazel Morton, 319–20
Dembo, Tamara, 344–45
Dennett, Mary Ware, 347
Deutsch, Helene Rosenback, 351–52
Dinnerstein, Dorothy, 359
Downey, June Etta, 373–74
Drummond, Margaret, 378
Duffy, Elizabeth, 381–82
Edgell, Beatrice, 399
Eng, Helga, 421–22
Fernald, Grace Maxwell, 442

Ferrero, Gina (Lombroso), 443–44
Fisher, Sara Carolyn, 450
Foster, Josephine Curtis, 460
Frank, Margaret, 465
Frenkel-Brunswik, Else, 469–70
Fromm, Erika Oppenheimer, 475–76
Frostig, Marianne Bellak, 476–77
Gamble, Eleanor Acheson Mcculloch, 482
Gaw, Esther Allen, 491–92
Gaw, Frances Isabel, 492–93
Gifford, Isabella, 500
Gilbreth, Lillian Evelyn Moller, 501–2
Gleason, Josephine Mixer, 507
Goldsmith, Marie, 517
Goodenough, Florence Laura, 518–19
Gordon, Kate, 520
Gracheva, Yekaterina Konstantinovna, 522
Gray, Susan Walton, 524–25
Grzigorzewska, Marja, 535
Hanfmann, Eugenia, 551–52
Hardwick, Rose Standish, 556
Harrower, Molly R., 559–60
Heidbreder, Edna Frances, 578–79
Heinlein, Julia Elizabeth Heil, 580–81
Hetzer, Hildegard, 593
Hildreth, Gertrude Howell, 598–99
Hilgard, Josephine Rohrs, 599
Hinman, Alice Hamlin, 602
Hollingworth, Leta Anna Stetter, 610–12
Howard Beckman, Ruth Winifred, 620
Howes, Ethel Dench Puffer, 623
Hubbard, Ruth Marilla, 624
Hurlock, Elizabeth Bergner, 632
Ide, Gladys Genevra, 642
Isaacs, Susan Sutherland (Fairhurst), 644
Ives, Margaret, 646–47
Jahoda, Marie, 651–53
Jones, Mary Cover, 666–67
Katz, Rosa Heine, 680
Kent, Grace Helen, 690
Kluckhohn, Florence Rockwood, 707
Koch, Helen Lois, 712
Kohler, Elsa, 714
Kohts, Nadie (Ladychin), 715–16
Ladd-Franklin, Christine, 731–32
MacLaughlin, Florence Edith Carothers, 826
Mahler, Margaret Schönberger, 830–31
Mallory, Edith (Brandt), 834–35
Manson, Grace Evelyn, 837
Martin, Lillien Jane, 848
Mateer, Florence Edna, 853
Mayo, Clara Alexandra (Weiss), 860
McBride, Katharine Elizabeth, 861
McCarthy, Dorothea Agnes, 861–62
McGraw, Myrtle Byram, 868–69
McHale, Kathryn, 869–70
McKeag, Anna Jane, 870
Meek, Lois Hayden, 876–77
Merrill-James, Maud Amanda, 886
Miles, Catherine Cox, 894
Mitchell, Evelyn Groesbeeck, 900–901
Mitchell, Mildred Bessie, 905
Montessori, Maria, 909–10
Mueller, Kate Heuvner, 922–23
Murphy, Lois Barclay, 924–25

psychologists (*cont.*)
Murrey, Margaret Mary Alberta, 927
Norsworthy, Naomi, 950–51
O'Shea, Harriet Eastabrooks, 967
Pacaud, Suzanne, 971
Paulsen, Alice Elizabeth, 990–91
Peak, Helen, 996–97
Pressey, Luella (Cole), 1051
Pruette, Lorine Livingston, 1057, 1058–59
Rand, Marie Gertrude, 1072–73
Rhine, Louise Ella (Weckesser), 1091
Ridenour, Nina, 1099–1100
Rioch, Margaret J., 1101
Rockwell, Alice Jones, 1116
Roe, Anne, 1117–19
Rogers, Agnes Lowe, 1120
Schubert, Anna, 1165
Sears, Pauline Snedden, 1171–72
Seward, Georgene Hoffman, 1178–79
Sherif, Carolyn (Wood), 1185
Shinn, Milicent Washburn, 1187–88
Shirley, Mary Margaret, 1188
Smith, Margaret Kiever, 1207
Stanton, Hazel Martha, 1223
Stinchfield, Sara Mae, 1239
Strang, Ruth May, 1246
Sullivan, Elizabeth Teresa, 1250–51
Sullivan, Ellen Blythe, 1251
Sunne, Dagny, 1252
Szeminska, Alina, 1258
Taft, Jessie, 1261
Teagarden, Florence Mabel, 1272
Thompson, Helen, 1283–84
Thurstone, Thelma Gwinn, 1287–88
Tolman, Ruth (Sherman), 1296–97
Toops, Laura Chassell (Merrill), 1298
Town, Clara Harrison, 1299
Tyler, Leona Elizabeth, 1309–10
Vernon, Magdalen Dorothea, 1327–28
Washburn, Margaret Floy, 1348–49
Washburn, Ruth Wendell, 1349
Wellman, Beth Lucy, 1361–62
Wolf, Katherine, 1393
Woods, Elizabeth Lindley, 1396
Wooldridge, Elizabeth (Taylor), 1397–98
Woolley, Helen Bradford (Thompson), 1398–99
Wylie, Margaret, 1412
Zachry, Caroline Beaumont, 1418
Ziegarnik, Bliuma, 1423
psychotherapists
Herford, Ethilda B.Meakin, 585
public health activists. *See* activists, public health
public health administrators. *See* administrators, public health

R
radiochemists
Perey, Marguerite Catherine, 1006–7
Róna, Elisabeth, 1122–23
reporters, newspaper
Seaman, Elizabeth Cochrane, 1170–71
rhetoricians
Aspasia of miletus, 55–56

S
scholars
Beatrice of Savoy, Countess of Provence, 99
Beaufort, Countess Margaret, 100
Bertile of Chelles, 120
Bury, Elizabeth (Lawrence), 212–13
Erdmuthe, Sophie, 425
Mildmay, Grace Sherrington, 894
Pisan, Christine de, 1028
Rodde, Dorothea von (Schlözer), 1117
Schurman, Anna Marie van, 1165–66
seismologists
Lehmann, Inge, 766
Rozovna, Evdokia Aleksandrovna, 1133
sexologists
Auken, Kirsten (Lomholt), 60–61
social activists. *See* activists, social
social reformers
Addams, Jane, 9–10
social workers
Underhill, Ruth Murray, 1313–14
sociologists
Glueck, Eleanor (Touroff), 509
Hagood, Margaret Loyd Jarman, 542–43
Kellor, Frances A., 685
Kluckhohn, Florence Rockwood, 707
Komarovsky, Mirra, 716–17
Lee, Rose Hum, 764
Martineau, Harriet, 849
Terent'eva, Liudmila Nikolaevna, 1274–75
Thomas, Dorothy Swaine (Thomas), 1279–80
Wootton, Barbara Adam, 1400
speleologists
Mottl, Mária, 921
Owen, Luella Agnes, 969
spiritualists
Jones, Amanda Theodosia, 663–64
statisticians
Castle, Cora (Sutton), 236
Cox, Gertrude Mary, 297–98
David, Florence N., 328
Hagood, Margaret Loyd Jarman, 542–43
Short, Jessie May, 1188–89
Walker, Helen Mary, 1340
Wickens, Aryness Joy, 1376
stratigraphers
Alimen, Henriette, 23
Cornelius-Furlani, Marta, 294
Crosfield, Margaret Chorley, 306
Csepreghyne-Meznerics, Ilona, 306–7
Elles, Gertrude Lilian, 417–18
Ellisor, Alva Christine, 419–20
Gardner, Julia Anna, 484–85
Goodyear, Edith, 519–20
Gorizdro-Kulczycka, Zinaida, 521
Hendricks, Eileen M., 583
Hill, Dorothy, 600–601
Ivanova, Elena Alekseevna, 645–46
King, Georgina, 695
Kline, Virginia Harriett, 706
Knopf, Eleanora Frances (Bliss), 708–9
Neuburg Maria Feodorovna, 935–36
Ogilvie, Ida Helen, 958–59
Pensa-Joja, Josipa, 1004
Skoczylas-Ciszewska, Kamila, 1197–98

Stefanescu, Sabba, 1225
Stewart, Grace Anne, 1234–35
Tyska, Maria, 1311
Wilson, Alice Evelyn, 1383–84
Woods, Ethel Gertrude (Skeat), 1396–97
surgeons
Aldrich-Blake, Louisa Brandreth, 19–20
Barringer, Emily (Dunning), 84–85
Bourgeoise, Louyse, 164
Dalby, Mary, 322
Dimock, Susan, 357–58
Du Luys, Guillemette, 381
Gorinevskaya, Valentina Valentinovna, 520–21
Inglis, Elsie (Maude), 643
Katherine, La Surgiene (The Surgeon), 680
Morton, Rosalie Slaughter, 918–20
Scharlieb, Dame Mary Ann Dacomb (Bird), 1157–58
Stimson, Barbara Bartlett, 1238
Thompson, Mary Harris, 1284–85
Tyng, Anita E., 1311
Van Hoosen, Bertha, 1319–20

T
teachers. *See* educators
theologians
Losa, Isabella, 805
topographers
Schmidt, Johanna Gertrud Alice, 1162
toxicologists
Baetjer, Anna Medora, 66–67
translators
Barbapiccola, Giuseppa Eleonora, 77
Guyton De Morveau, Claudine Poullet Picardet, 539
scientific works, 885
travelers
Callcott, Lady Maria Graham, 223
Clappe, Louisa Amelia (Smith), 259
Durham, Mary Edith, 388–89
Fiennes, Celia, 445
Piozzi, Hester Lynch, 1026
Seaman, Elizabeth Cochrane, 1170–71
Sharp, Emily Katharine (Dooris), 1181

U
university administrators. *See* administrators, university
university deans. *See* deans, school

V
virologists
Gey, Margaret Lewis, 499
Lwoff, Marguerite (Bourdaleix), 812–13
vulcanologists
Korringa, Marjorie K., 718–19

W
writers
Adamson, Joy (Gessner), 8–9
Agassiz, Elizabeth Cary, 12–13
Allan, Mary Eleanor (Mea), 23
Ames, Blanche (Ames), 28–30
Andreas-Salome, Louise Lelia, 38–39
Andrews, Eliza Frances, 39

Astell, Mary, 56–57
Atkinson, Louisa (Calvert), 58
Ballard, Julia Perkins Pratt, 74–75
Barnes (Berners), Juliana, 81–82
Barrera, Oliva Sabuca De Nantes, 84
Beecher, Catharine Esther, 103–4
Behn, Aphra, 105–8
Bishop, Isabella Lucy Bird, 131
Boole, Mary (Everest), 158–59
Bryan, Argaret, 198–99
Callcott, Lady Maria Graham, 223
Carne, Elizabeth Catherine (Thomas), 228–29
Carson, Rachel Louise, 233–34
Carter, Elizabeth, 234–35
Cavendish, Margaret, Duchess of Newcastle, 240–41
Church, Elda Rodman (Macilvaine), 256
Clappe, Louisa Amelia (Smith), 259
Cobbe, Frances Power, 276–77
Cooper, Susan Fenimore, 290–91
Daulton, Agnes Warner Mcclelland, 327–28
Davis, Adelle, 328–29
De Staël Holstein, Anne Louise Germaine Necker, 350
Doubleday, Neltje Blanchan (De Graff), 371–72
Drake, Judith, 375
Du Chatelet, Gabrielle-Emilie Le Tonnelier De Breteuil (Marquise), 378–80
Dupre, Marie, 388
Durham, Mary Edith, 388–89
Duryea, Nina, 389
Farnsworth, Vesta J., 434
Farquharson, Marian Sarah (Ridley), 435
Godding, D.W., 509–10
Hall, Agnes C., 545
Hawkes, Jacquetta (Hopkins), 569
Hildegard of Bingen, 596–98
Howard Wylde, Hildegarde, 620–22
Howitt, Mary (Botham), 623–24
Hurston, Zora Neale, 632–33
Kent, Elizabeth, 690
Knowles, Ruth Sheldon, 710–11
Kroeber, Theodora Kracaw, 725–26
Laurie, Charlotte Louisa, 752
Lawrenson, Alice Louisa, 755
Lee, Sarah Wallis Bowdich, 765
Loudon, Jane (Webb), 805–6
Marcet, Jane Haldimand, 842–43
Michelet, Athénais (Mialaret), 892–94
Miller, Olive Thorne, 897
Montague, Lady Mary Wortley, 908–9

Necker, Susanne (Curchod), 932
Parloa, Maria, 980
Piozzi, Hester Lynch, 1026
Potter, Beatrix, 1044–45
Prestwich, Grace Anne (Milne) M'Call, 1052–53
Renooz, Céline, 1089–90
Roberts, Mary, 1108
Rogers, Julia Eilen, 1120–21
Rohde, Eleanour Sinclair, 1122
Royer, Clémence, 1129–32
Sharp, Emily Katharine (Dooris), 1181
Somerville, Mary (Fairfax) Greig, 1213–15
Stratton Porter, Gene, 1247–48
Swift, Mary, 1255–56
Szwajger, Adina Blady, 1259
Taylor, Janet, 1270–71
Todd, Mabel Loomis, 1295
Trimmer, Sarah (Kirby), 1302
Wakefield, Priscilla (Bell), 1337
Walworth, Ellen Hardin, 1344–45
Watt, Helen Winifred Boyd (de Lisle), 1351
Welsh, Jane Kilby, 1363–64
Wilson, Lucy Langdon (Williams), 1386
Wright, Mabel Osgood, 1407
See also novelists

Z

zoologists
Alexander, Annie Montague, 20–21
Battle, Helen Irene, 92
Beckwith, Cora, 102
Beers, Catherine Virginia, 104
Berger, Katharina Bertha Charlotte, 118
Beutler, Ruth, 120–21
Boring, Alice Middleton, 160–62
Bowen, Susan, 167
Boyd, Elizabeth Margaret, 167
Bykhovskaia, Anna Markovna, 215–16
Calvert, Emily Amelia (Adelia) (Smith), 224
Carpenter, Esther, 230
Clapp, Cornelia Maria, 258–59
Claypole, Agnes Mary, 266–67
Coryndon, Shirley (Cameron), 295
Crane, Jocelyn, 300–301
Davenport, Gertrude (Crotty), 328
Davis, Olive Griffith Stull, 333
Dickerson, Mary Cynthia, 355–56
Edge, Rosalie Barrow, 399
Fisher, Edna Marie, 449
Gaige, Helen (Thompson), 481
Gregory, Emily Ray, 528–29

Gromova, Vera Isaacovna, 533
Guthrie, Mary Jane, 538–39
Heppenstall, Caroline A., 585
Hertz, Mathilde, 592
Hibbard, Hope, 594–95
Hinrichs, Marie Agnes, 602
Hubbard, Marian Elizabeth, 624
Hughes-Schrader, Sally, 628
Hyman, Libbie Henrietta, 636–37
invertebrate, 742
    Bliss, Dorothy Elizabeth, 145–46
    Randolph, Harriet, 1074
    Rogick, Mary Dora, 1121–22
    Rucker, Augusta, 1134
Jones, Eva Elizabeth, 664–65
Kaan, Helen Warton, 673
Keil, Elsa Marie, 681–82
Lawrence, Barbara, 754
Lewis, Lilian (Burwell), 784
MacDougall, Mary Stuart, 819–20
Manton, Sidnie Milana, 839–40
marine
    Rathbun, Mary Jane, 1075
Mitchell, Evelyn Groesbeeck, 900–901
Mohr, Erna W., 907
Morgan, Ann Haven, 913–14
Moser, Fanny, 920
Nichols, Mary Louise, 940–41
Pierce, Madelene Evans, 1023
Plehn, Marianne, 1032–33
Ray, Dixy Lee, 1079–80
Richards, Mildred Hoge (Albro), 1098
Rothschild, Miriam, 1128–29
Schantz, Viola Shelly, 1156–57
Scharrer, Berta (Vogel), 1158–59
Sheldon, Jennie Arms, 1183
Stephens, Jane, 1226
Svihla, Ruth Dowell, 1254–55
Talbot, Mary, 1263
Tenenbaum, Estera, 1274
Thompson, Caroline Burling, 1282
Veley, Lilian Jane (Nutcombe), 1325
Wallace, Louise Baird, 1342
White, Edith Grace, 1370–71
Wilder, Inez (Whipple), 1378
Willcox, Mary Alice, 1380
Wilson, Louise (Palmer), 1385–86
Wood-Lorz, Thelma (Rittenhouse), 1395–96
Young, Roger Arliner, 1416–17
zoopsychologists
Ladygina-Kots, Nadezhda Nikolaevna, 732–33

LIST OF SCIENTISTS BY TIME PERIOD

Antiquity (before 450)

Abrotelia, 5
Aemilia, 11
Aesara of Lucania, 11–12
Aglaonike, 13–14
Agnodike, 16
Andromache, 39
Anicia or Amyte, 40
Arete of Cyrene, 50
Artemisia of Caria II, 54
Asclepigenia, 55
Aspasia of Miletus, 55
Aspasia the Physician, 56
Axiothea of Phlius, 62
Beronice, 118
Caerellia (Caerelia), 219
Clea, 267
Cleachma, 267–68
Cleopatra, 269
Damo, 323–24
Diotima of Mantinea, 359
Eccello of Lucania, 396
Echecratia the Philiasian, 397
Elephantis, 414
Fabiola, 433
Faustina, 436
Favilla, 436
Hypatia of Alexandria, 637–39
Laïs, 735
Lasthenia of Mantinea, 749–50
Leontium, 771–72
Leoparda, 772
Macrina, 828–29
Marcella, 841
Mary the Jewess, 850
Melissa, 879
Metrodora, 888
Myia or Mya, 929
Nicerata, Saint, 940
Occello of Lucania, 957
Olympias of Thebes, 962
Origenia, 965
Paphnutia the Virgin, 978
Paula, 990
Perictione, 1007
Pulcheria, Empress, 1059

Pythias of Assos, 1062
Salpe, 1146–47
Sotira, 1217–18
Theano, 1276–77
Thelka, Saint, 1278
Theosebeia, 1278

Middle Ages (451–1399)

Abella, 4
Adelberger of Lombardy, 10
Adelle of the Saracens, 10
Adelmota of Carrara, 10
Aelfleda, 11
Agamede, 12
Agnes, Countess of Aix, 14
Agnes of Bohemia, 14
Agnes of Jerusalem, 14
Agnes of Silesia, 14
Ameline, 28
Anna of Bohemia, 41
Antoinette De Bellegarde, 44
Antonia, Maestra, 44–45
Arignote of Samos, 50
Barrera, Oliva Sabuca de Nantes, 84
Beatrice, Medica of Candia, 99
Beatrice of Savoy, Countess of Provence, 99
Belota [Johanna Belota], 110
Berthagyta, Abbess, 119
Berthildis of Chelles, 119
Bertile of Chelles, 120
Bocchi (Bucca), Dorotea, 151
Bridget, Saint, of Ireland, 179
Bridget, Saint, of Scandinavia, 179
Cambrière, Clarisse, 224
Catherine of Siena, Saint, 237
Clara (Clare) of Assisi, Saint, 259
Clarisse of Rotomago (or Clarice of Rouen), 259
Cleobulina of Rhodes, 269
Clothilde of Burgundy, 274
Comnena (Comnenos), Anna, 283
Converse, Jeanne, 286
Cunio, Isabella, 309
De Gorzano, Leonetta, 337
Demud, 346
De Valois, Madame, 353
Di Novella, Maria, 355

Elizabeth of Poland, Queen of Hungary, 417
Elizabeth of Portugal, Saint, 417
Elizabeth of Schönau, 417
Etheldrida, Queen, 428
Euphemia, Abbess of Wherwell, 428
Felicie, Jacobina, 439
Flammel, Perrenelle, 451
Frances of Brittany, 464
Gilette of Narbonne, 502
Giliani, Alessandra, 502
Guarna, Rebecca, 535
Hainault, Countess of, 543
Haoys (La Meresse), 555
Hebel, Medicienne, 576
Hedwig of Silesia, Saint, 577
Héloise, 582–83
Herrad of Hohenburg, 585–89
Hersende. Abbess of Fontevrault, 590
Hildegard of Bingen, 596–98
Hroswitha of Gandersheim, 624
Jacobina Medica of Bologna, 650
Katherine, La Surgiene (The Surgeon), 680
Mahout, Countess of Artois, 831
Margery, 843
Matilde, 855
Mechthild of Magdeburg, 874
Mercuriade, 884
Perette of Rouen, 1006
Pernell, 1008
Péronelle, 1008
Pisan, Christine de, 1028
Radegonde, 1067
Sara of Saint-Gilles, 1151
Theodosia, Saint, 1278
Trotula, 1304–5

Early Renaissance (1400–1599)

Amalosunta, 28
Anna Sophia of Denmark, 41
Ann Medica of York, 40–41
Antonia, Maestra, 44–45
Barnes (Berners), Juliana, 81–82
Barrera, Oliva Sabuca de Nantes, 84
Beaufort, Countess Margaret, 100
Bourgeoise, Louyse, 164
Brahe, Sophia, 170
Brunetta, 196

Brunfels, Frau Otto, 196
Calenda, Constanza or Laurea Constantia, 221
Catherine, Medica of Cracow, 237
Catherine of Bologna, Saint, 237
Catherine of Genoa, Saint, 237
Clements, Margaret, 268–69
Cobbe, Margaret, 277
Coste Blanche, Marie de, 295
Danti or Dante, Theodora, 325
De Lebrix, FranÇoise, 342–43
Diana of Poitiers, 354
Du Luys, Guillemette, 381
Fouquet, Marie de Maupeou, Vicomtesse De Vaux, 461
Fuss, Margarita, 479
Galindo, Beatrix, 481
Hatshepsut, Queen, 566
Hoby, Lady, 606
Horenburg, Anna Elizabeth Von, 617
Jacopa of Passau, 651
Johanna (Johanne, Joanna), 660
Losa, Isabella, 805
Marillac, Louise de, 843
Mentuhetep, Queen, 883–84
Mildmay, Grace Sherrington, 894
Molza, Tarquinia, 908
Parthenay, Catherine de (Dame de Rohan), 985
Perette of Rouen, 1006
Roper, Margaret, 1124–25
Sabuco Banera D'Alcaraz, Olivia, 1143
Sara of Würzburg, 1151
Strozzi, Lorenza, 1249–50
Welser, Philippine, 1363

Seventeenth Century (1600–1699)
Amherst, Sarah (Archer), Countess., 31
Anna Sophia of Hesse, 41
Anne, Electress of Denmark, 41
Apsley (Hutchinson), Lady Lucy, 47
Astell, Mary, 56–57
Baynard, Anne, 97
Behn, Aphra, 105–8
Bertereau, Martine de, Baroness de Beausoleil, 119
Biscot, Jeanne, 129
Bourgeoise, Louyse, 164
Brahe, Sophia, 170
Bury, Elizabeth (Lawrence), 212–13
Castra, Anna de, 236
Catherine Ursula, Countess of Baden, 237
Cavendish, Margaret, Duchess of Newcastle, 240–41
Cellier, Elizabeth, 241–42
Chinchon, Countess of, 252
Christina, Queen of Sweden, 255–56
Clifford, Lady Anne, 273
Cockburn, Catharine (Trotter), 278
Conway, Anne, 286–87
Cornaro (Cornero), Elena (Helena) Lucretia, 295
Coste Blanche, Marie de, 295
Cramer, Catherine Gertrude Du Tertre Schraders, 299–300
Cunitz, Maria, 309–10

Dashkova, Princess Ekaterina Romanovna, 326–27
De La Cruz, Juana Inés, 339
De La Marche, Marguerite Du Tertre, 341
Drake, Judith, 375
Dumée, Jeanne, 382
Dupré, Marie, 388
Eimmart, Marie Claire, 409
Eleanora, Duchess of Mantua, 414
Eleanora, Duchess of Troppau and Jagerndorf, 414
Elizabeth of Bohemia, 416–17
Erdmuthe, Sophie, 425
Fiennes, Celia, 445
Fouquet, Marie de Maupeou, Vicomtesse De Vaux, 461
Fuss, Margarita, 479
Grignan, FranÇoise Marguerite de Sevigne, Comtesse de, 532
Gsell, Maria Dorothea Henrica (Graf), 535
Halket, Lady Anne, 544–45
Hevelius, Elisabetha Koopman, 593
Jones, Katharine, Viscountess Ranelagh, 665
Keil, Elizabeth Marbareta, 681
Kirch, Maria Margaretha Winkelmann, 700–701
La Sablière, Marguerite Hessein, Madame de, 747
La Vigne, Anne de, 752
Löser, Margaret Sibylla Von, 805
Marillac, Louise de, 843
Masters, Sybilla (Righton), 853
Merian, Maria Sibylla, 884–85
Meurdrac, Marie, 889
Mildmay, Grace Sherrington, 894
Parthenay, Catherine de (Dame de Rohan), 985
Ruysch, Rachel, 1139
Sablière, Marguerite (Hessein) de la, 1142–43
Schraders, Catharina Geertruida, 1165
Schurman, Anna Marie van, 1165–66
Serment, Louise-Anastasia, 1177
Sharp, Jane, 1181
Shaw, Hester, 1183
Siegemund, Justine Dittrich, 1193–94
Sophia Charlotte, Queen of Prussia, 1216
Sophia, Electress of Hanover, 1216
Walker, Elizabeth, 1339
Woolley, Ann, 1398

Eighteenth Century (1700–1799)
Agnesi, Maria Gaetana, 14–16
Amherst, Sarah (Archer), Countess., 31
Anning, Mary, 41–42
Arconville, Geneviève Charlotte D', 49
Ardinghelli, Maria Angela, 49–50
Astell, Mary, 56–57
Baker, Anne Elizabeth, 70
Banks, Sarah Sophia, 76–77
Barbapiccola, Giuseppa Eleonora, 77
Bassi, Laura Maria Caterina, 88–89
Benett, Etheldred, 114
Bentham, Lady Mary Sophia (Fordyce), 117
Bentinck, Margaret Cavendish (Harley), Duchess of Portland, 117–18

Biheron, Marie Catherine, 126
Blackburne, Anna, 134–35
Blackwell, Elizabeth, 136
Boivin, Marie Gillain, 154
Bonnay, Marchioness du, 156–57
Borromeo, Clelia Grillo, 163
Brand, Martha, 170–71
Brückner, Frau Dr., 195
Bryan, Margaret, 198–99
Burges, Mary Anne, 208–9
Bury, Elizabeth (Lawrence), 212–13
Bury, Priscilla Susan (Falkner), 213–14
Buttelini, Marchesa, 215
Callcott, Lady Maria Graham, 223
Carter, Elizabeth, 234–35
Charlotte Sophia, Queen, 246
Coade, Eleanor, 274
Cockburn, Catharine (Trotter), 278
Colden, Jane, 280
Cornaro (Cornero), Elena (Helena) Lucretia, 295
Cramer, Catherine Gertrude Du Tertre Schraders, 299–300
Dalle Donne, Maria, 323
Dashkova, Princess Ekaterina Romanovna, 326–27
Déjerine-Klumpke, Augusta, 338–39
De La Marche, Marguerite Du Tertre, 341
Delauney, Marguerite de Staël, 342
De Staël Holstein, Anne Louise Germaine Necker, 350
Du Châtelet, Gabrielle-Emilie Le Tonnelier de Breteuil (Marquise), 378–80
Du Coudray, Angelique (Marguerite Le Boursier), 381
Edgeworth, Maria, 400
Eimmart, Marie Claire, 409
Erxleben, Dorothea Christiana (Leporin), 425–26
Fiennes, Celia, 445
Finch, Louisa (Thynne), Countess of Aylesford, 446
Frampton, Mary, 464
Galvani, Lucia (Galeazzi), 481–82
Germain, Sophie, 496–97
Greene, Catherine (Littlefield), 527–28
Griffiths, Amelia Warren (Rogers), 531
Grignan, FranÇoise Marguerite de Sevigne, Comtesse de, 532
Gsell, Maria Dorothea Henrica (Graf), 535
Guyton de Morveau, Claudine Poullet Picardet, 539
Hall, Agnes C., 545
Herschel, Caroline Lucretia, 587–89
Hoare, Sarah, 605
Ibbetson, Agnes (Thomson), 641
Jacson, Maria Elizabeth, 651
Kaltenbeiner, Victorine, 675
Kirch, Christine, 700
Kirch, Margaretha, 700
Kirch, Maria Margaretha Winkelmann, 700–701
La Chapelle, Marie Louise Dugès, 731
Lalande, Marie Jeanne Amélie Harlay Lefrancais de, 735–36

Eighteenth Century (*cont.*)

Lavoisier, Marie Anne Pierrette Paulze, 752–53

Lepaute, Nicole-Reine Hortense (Etable de La Brière), 772–73

Libert, Marie-Anne, 789

Logan, Martha Daniell, 799

Macaulay, Catharine (Sawbridge), 817–18

Manzolini, Anna Morandi, 841

Marcet, Jane Haldimand, 842–43

Medaglia, Diamante, 874

Monson, Lady Anne Vane, 908

Montague, Lady Mary Wortley, 908–9

Murray, Lady Charlotte, 925–26

Necker, Susanne (Curchod), 932

Nihell, Elizabeth, 946

Nolde, Hélène Aldegonde de, 348

Pettracini, Maria, 1013

Philpot, Mary, 1018

Pierry, Louise Elizabeth du, 1024

Pinckney, Eliza (Lucas), 1024–25

Piozzi, Hester Lynch, 1026

Pope, Clara Maria (Leigh), 1040

Reinhardt, Anna Barbara, 1088–89

Rodde, Dorothea von (Schlözer), 1117

Schraders, Catharina Geertruida, 1165

Siebold, Josepha (Henning) von, 1193

Smith, Pleasance (Reeve), 1209

Somerville, Mary (Fairfax) Greig, 1213–15

Stephens, Joanna, 1226–27

Stovin, Margaret, 1244–45

Trimmer, Sarah (Kirby), 1302

Turner, Mary (Palgrave), 1308–9

Wakefield, Priscilla (Bell), 1337

Wang Zhenyi (Chen-i), 1345

Winthrop, Hannah Fayerweather Tolman, 1389

Wright, Lady Catherine, 1404–5

Nineteenth Century (1800–1899)

Abbott, Maude Elizabeth Seymour, 1–2

Abel, Mary Hinman, 2–3

Abel, Theodora Mead, 3–4

Abramson, Jadwiga, 5

Acton, Frances (Knight), 6

Adametz, Lotte, 7

Agassiz, Elizabeth Cary, 12–13

Akeley, Mary Lee (Jobe), 17–18

Alexander, Annie Montague, 20–21

Allen, Eliza (Stevens), 25

Amalitskiya, Anna P., 28

Ames, Mary E. Pulsifer, 31

Anderson, Caroline Virginia (Still) Wiley, 32–33

Anderson, Elizabeth Garrett, 34–35

Anderson, Louisa Garrett, 36–37

Anderton-Smith, Mrs. W., 37

Andreas-Salomé, Louise Lelia, 38–39

Andrews, Eliza Frances, 39

Andrews, Grace, 39

Anning, Mary, 41–42

Arconville, Geneviève Charlotte D', 49

Arden, Lady Margaret Elizabeth (Spencer Wilson), 49

Arkhangel'skaia, Aleksandra Gavriilovna, 50–51

Arlitt, Ada Hart, 51

Armitage, Eleanora, 51–52

Armitage, Ella Sophia A. (Bulley), 52

Armitt, Annie Maria, 52

Armitt, Mary Louisa, 52–53

Armitt, Sophia, 53

Atkins, Anna, 57

Atkins, Louisa Catherine Fanny, 58

Atkinson, Louisa (Calvert), 58

Attersoll, Maria, 58

Atwater, Helen Woodard, 58–59

Atwood, Martha Maria, 59

Austin, Rebecca, 61

Ayrton, Hertha Marks, 62–63

Ayrton, Matilda (Chaplin), 64

Babcock, Harriet, 65

Baber, Zonia, 65–66

Bachman, Maria Martin, 66

Bacon, Clara (Latimer), 66

Bagley, Florence (Winger), 67

Bailey, Florence Augusta (Merriam), 69–70

Baker, Sara Josephine, 70–71

Balfour, Margaret Ida, 73

Ball, Anne Elizabeth, 73

Ballard, Julia Perkins Pratt, 74–75

Ball, Mary, 74

Banks, Sarah Sophia, 76–77

Barber, Mary Elizabeth (Bowker), 78

Barkly, Lady Anna Maria (Pratt), 79

Barkly, Lady Elizabeth Helen (Timins or Timmins), 79

Barnard, Alicia Mildred, 80–81

Barnard, Lady Anne (Henslow), 81

Barnard, Lady Anne (Lindsay), 81

Barnum, Charlotte Cynthia, 83–84

Barrows, Katherine Isabel (Hayes), 85–86

Barton, Clara Harlowe, 86

Bascom, Florence, 87–88

Bass, Mary Elizabeth, 88

Bate, Dorothea Minola Alice, 90

Bates, Mary E., 90–91

Bateson, Anna, 91

Baum, Marie, 92

Bayern, Therese Von, 95–96

Beaufort, Harriet Henrietta, 99–100

Becker, Lydia Ernestine, 101

Beck, Sarah Coker (Adams), 100–101

Beecher, Catharine Esther, 103–4

Beever, Mary, 104

Beever, Susan, 104–5

Benett, Etheldred, 114

Bennett, Alice, 115

Benson, Margaret Jane, 116–17

Bentham, Lady Mary Sophia (Fordyce), 117

Berridge, Emily Mary, 118–19

Bertillon, Caroline Schutze, 120

Besant, Annie (Wood), 120

Bevier, Isabel, 121–22

Bickerdyke, Mary Ann (Ball), 124–25

Bidder, Marion Greenwood, 125–26

Bingham, Millicent (Todd), 127–28

Bishop, Isabella Lucy Bird, 131

Bissell, Emily P., 132

Bitting, Katherine Eliza (Golden), 132–33

Black, Hortensia, 133

Blackwell, Antoinette Louise (Brown), 135–36

Blackwell, Elizabeth, 136

Blackwell, Elizabeth Marianne, 138

Blackwell, Emily, 138–39

Blagg, Mary Adela, 139–40

Blake, Mary Safford, 140–41

Bliss, Mary Campbell, 146

Bluhm, Agnes, 149–50

Blunt, Katharine, 151

Bodley, Rachel Littler, 152–53

Bogdanovskaia, Vera Evstaf'evna, 153

Boivin, Marie Gillain, 154

Bokova–Sechenova, Mariia Aleksandrovna, 154–55

Boley, Gertrude Maud, 155

Bolus, Harriet Margaret Louisa (Kensit), 155–56

Bonnevie, Kristine, 157–58

Boole, Mary (Everest), 158–59

Booth, Mary Ann Allard, 160

Boveri, Marcella Imelda O'Grady, 165–67

Bowen, Susan, 167

Bradley, Amy Morris, 168–69

Bradley, Frances Sage, 169–70

Branch, Hazel Elisabeth, 170

Brandegee, Mary Katharine Layne, 171

Brand, Martha, 170–71

Brès Madeleine (Gébelin), 178–79

Brightwen, Eliza (Elder), 181

Britton, Elizabeth Knight, 181

Brooks, Sarah Theresa, 186

Broomall, Anna Elizabeth, 186

Brousseau, Kate, 186–87

Brown, Charlotte Amanda Blake, 187–88

Brown, Dame Edith Mary, 188–89

Brown, Elizabeth, 189

Bruce, Catherine Wolfe, 194

Buckel, Chloe A., 201–2

Buckland, Mary Morland, 202

Buckley, Arabella, 202–3

Bunting, Martha, 206

Bunzel, Ruth Leah, 208

Burges, Mary Anne, 208–9

Burkill, Ethel Maud (Morrison), 209

Burns, Louisa, 211

Burtt Davy, Alice (Bolton), 212

Bury, Priscilla Susan (Falkner), 213–14

Bush, Katharine Jeannette, 214–15

Byrd, Mary Emma, 216

Byrnes, Esther Fussell, 216–17

Byron, Augusta Ada, Countess of Lovelace, 217

Caetani-Bovatelli, Donna Ersilia, 219–20

Calkins, Mary Whiton, 221–23

Callcott, Lady Maria Graham, 223

Calvert, Catherine Louisa Waring (Atkinson), 223

Campbell, Helen Stuart, 224–25

Cannon, Annie Jump, 227–28

Capen, Bessie, 228

Carne, Elizabeth Catherine (Thomas), 228–29

Carter, Edna, 234

Carter, Elizabeth, 234–35

Carus, Mary Hegeler, 235–36

Carvajales y Camino, Laura M. de, 236

Catani, Giuseppina, 236–37
Catlow, Maria Agnes, 237
Chandler, Elizabeth, 243–44
Charlotte Sophia, Queen, 246
Charsley, Fanny Anne, 246
Chase, Mary Agnes Meara, 246–47
Chick, Dame Harriette, 250–51
Child, Lydia Maria (Francis), 251–52
Christen, Sydney Mary (Thompson), 254–55
Church, Elda Rodman (Macilvaine), 256
Clapp, Cornelia Maria, 258–59
Clappe, Louisa Amelia (Smith), 259
Clarke, Cora Huidekoper, 264
Clarke, Lilian Jane, 265
Clarke, Louisa (Lane), 265
Clark, Lois, 262–63
Clark, Nancy Talbot, 263–64
Claypole, Agnes Mary, 266–67
Claypole, Edith Jane, 267
Clemens, Mary Knapp (Strong), 268
Clerke, Agnes Mary, 269–71
Clerke, Ellen Mary, 271–72
Cleveland, Emeline Horton, 272–73
Clisby, Harriet Jemima Winifred, 273–74
Coade, Eleanor, 274
Coates, Sarah J., 274–75
Cobbe, Frances Power, 276–77
Cockrell, Wilmatte (Porter), 278
Coignou, Caroline Pauline Marie, 279
Cole, Emma J., 280–81
Cole, Rebecca J., 281
Collet, Clara Elizabeth, 281
Collins, Katharine Richards, 282
Comstock, Anna Botsford, 283–84
Comyns-Lewer, Ethel, 284
Cone, Claribel, 284–85
Cooper, Susan Fenimore, 290–91
Crandall, Ella Phillips, 299
Crane, Agnes, 300
Crocker, Lucretia, 303–4
Crosfield, Margaret Chorley, 306
Cuffe, Lady Charlotte Wheeler (Williams), 307
Cullis, Winifred, 307–8
Cumming, Lady Gordon (Eliza Maria Campbell), 308
Cummings, Clara Eaton, 308
Cummings, Louise Duffield, 309
Cunningham, Susan, 311
Curie, Marie (Maria Sklodowska), 311–17
Cushman, Florence, 319
Cutler, Catherine, 321
Dale, Elizabeth, 322–23
Dalle Donne, Maria, 323
Daniel, Anne Sturges, 324–25
Darwin, Emma (Wedgwood), 325–26
Daulton, Agnes Warner McClelland, 327–28
Davenport, Gertrude (Crotty), 328
Davidson, Ada D., 328
Davis, Grace Evangeline, 330
Davis, Katharine Bement, 331–32
Dawson, Maria, 334
Day, Mary Anna, 335
De Bréauté, Eléonore-Nell-Suzanne, 335
De Graffenried, Mary Clare, 337

Déjerine-Klumpke, Augusta, 338–39
De Lange, Cornelia Catharina, 341–42
Delap, Maude Jane, 342
De Mole, Fanny Elizabeth, 345
Dempsey, Sister Mary Joseph, 345
Densmore, Frances Theresa, 348–49
Derick, Carrie M., 349–50
De Staël Holstein, Anne Louise Germaine Necker, 350
Detmers, Frederica, 350
De Witt, Lydia Maria Adams, 353–54
Dickerson, Mary Cynthia, 355–56
Dietrich, Amalie, 356–57
Dimock, Susan, 357–58
Dix, Dorothea Lynde, 360
Dock, Lavinia Lloyd, 362–63
Dodgson, Sarah Elizabeth, 364
Dohan, Edith Haywood Hall, 364–65
Dolley, Sarah Read Adamson, 366–67
Doubleday, Neltje Blanchan (de Graff), 371–72
Dougal, Margaret Douie, 372
Downey, June Etta, 373–74
Draper, Mary Anna Palmer, 375–76
Dummer, Ethel (Sturges), 382–83
Durocher, Marie (Josefina Mathilde), 389
Duryea, Nina, 389
Earle, Marie Theresa (Villiers), 394
Eastwood, Alice, 394–96
Ebers, Edith (Knote), 396
Eckstorm, Fannie Pearson (Hardy), 398
Edgell, Beatrice, 399
Edgerton, Winifred Haring, 399–400
Edgeworth, Maria, 400
Edwards, Emma Ward, 403
Edwards-Pilliet, Blanche, 403–5
Efimenko, Aleksandra Iakovlevna, 405
Ehrenfest-Afanassjewa, Tatyana Alexeyevna, 407–8
Eigenmann, Rosa Smith, 408–9
Einstein-Maric, Mileva, 411–12
Elles, Gertrude Lilian, 417–18
Erdmann, Rhoda, 422–25
Everett, Alice, 428–30
Evershed, Mary Orr, 431–32
Ewing, Elizabeth Raymond (Burden), 432
Eyton, Charlotte, 432
Farenden, Emma, 433
Farnsworth, Vesta J., 434
Farquharson, Marian Sarah (Ridley), 435
Fawcett, Phillipa Garrett, 436–37
Fearn, Anne Walter, 437–38
Fedchenko, Ol'ga Aleksandrovna, 438–39
Ferguson, Margaret Clay, 441–42
Fernald, Maria Elizabeth (Smith), 443
Ferrand, Elizabeth M., 443
Ferrero, Gina (Lombroso), 443–44
Fielde, Adele Marion, 444
Fielding, Mary Maria (Simpson), 444–45
Figner, Vera, 446
Finch, Louisa (Thynne), Countess of Aylesford, 446
Fisher, Elizabeth Florette, 449
Fitton, Sarah Mary, 450
Fitzgerald, Mabel Purefoy, 450

Fleming, Williamina Paton Stevens, 453–54
Fletcher, Alice Cunningham, 454–55
Fomina-Zhukovskaia, Evdokiia Aleksandrovna, 457–58
Foot, Katherine, 458
Fossler, Mary Louise, 460
Fowler, Lydia Folger, 461–62
Fraine, Ethel Louise de, 464
Frampton, Mary, 464
Freund, Ida, 472–73
Fulhame, Elizabeth, 478
Furness, Caroline Ellen, 478–79
Gage, Catherine, 480
Gage, Susanna Phelps, 480–81
Gamble, Eleanor Acheson McCulloch, 482
Gantt, Love Rosa, 482–83
Gardiner, Margaret Isabella, 483
Gardner, Mary Sewall, 485
Gates, Fanny Cook, 489–90
Gatty, Margaret (Scott), 490–91
Geldart, Alice Mary, 494
Gepp, Ethel Sarel (Barton), 495
Germain, Sophie, 496–97
Gibbons, Vernette Lois, 499
Gibbs, Lilian Suzette, 500
Gifford, Isabella, 500
Glasgow, Maude, 506
Gleason, Kate, 507
Gleason, Rachel Brooks, 508
Godding, D. W., 509–10
Godfery, Hilda Margaret, 510
Goldhaber, Sulamith, 514
Goldsmith, Marie, 517
Goldthwaite, Nellie Esther, 517–18
Goodrich, Sarah Frances, 519
Gracheva, Yekaterina Konstantinovna, 522
Gray, Maria Emma (Smith), 523–24
Greene, Catherine (Littlefield), 527–28
Gregory, Eliza Standerwick (Barnes), 528
Gregory, Emily L., 528
Gregory, Lady Isabella Augusta (Persse), 529
Gregory, Louisa Catherine (Allen), 529–30
Griffiths, Amelia Elizabeth, 531
Griffiths, Amelia Warren (Rogers), 531
Griswold, Grace Hall, 533
Grundy, Clara, 534
Grundy, Ellen, 534
Grundy, Maria Ann, 534
Guyton de Morveau, Claudine Poullet Picardet, 539
Hahn, Dorothy Anna, 543
Hall, Agnes C., 545
Hall-Brown, Lucy, 547
Hall, Julia Brainerd, 545–46
Hall, Kate Marion, 546
Hallowell, Susan Maria, 548
Hall, Rosetta Sherwood, 546–47
Hamilton, Alice, 549–50
Hardcastle, Frances, 555
Hardwick, Rose Standish, 556
Harrison, Jane Ellen, 558
Hart, Esther Hasting, 560
Hart, J. B., 560
Harvey, Elizabeth, 561
Hastings, Barbara, Marchioness of, 565

Nineteenth Century (*cont.*)

Hawes, Harriet (Boyd), 568–69
Hawkins, Mary Esther (Sibthorp), 570
Hayes, Ellen Amanda, 570–71
Hearst, Phoebe (Apperson), 574–75
Hefferan, Mary, 578
Heim-Vögtlin, Marie, 580
Hélène, Duchess of Aosta, 581
Henshaw, Julia Wilmotte, 584
Herrick, Christine (Terhune), 586
Herrick, Sophia McIlvaine (Bledsoe), 586–87
Herschel, Caroline Lucretia, 587–89
Herwerden, Marianne Van, 592
Hesse, Fanny, 593
Hickey, Amanda Sanford, 595
Hinman, Alice Hamlin, 602
Hirschfeld-Tiburtius, Henriette (Pagelsen), 602–3
Hitchcock, Fanny Rysam Mulford, 603
Hitchcock, Orra White, 604
Hoare, Sarah, 605
Hodgson, Elizabeth, 607
Holley, Mary Austin, 610
Holmes, Mary Emilee, 612
Hooker, Frances Harriet Henslow, 614–15
Hooker, Henrietta Edgecomb, 615
Hopkins, Esther (Burton), 616
Howes, Ethel Dench Puffer, 623
Howitt, Mary (Botham), 623–24
Hubbard, Marian Elizabeth, 624
Huggins, Margaret Lindsay (Murray), 626–27
Hugonnai-Wartha, Vilma, 628
Hunt, Caroline Louisa, 629
Hunt, Harriot Kezia, 630–31
Hussey, Anna Maria (Reed), 633
Hutchins, Ellen, 633–35
Hyde, Ida Henrietta, 635–36
Hynes, Sarah, 637
Ibbetson, Agnes (Thomson), 641
Inglis, Elsie (Maude), 643
Jacobi, Mary Corinna Putnam, 648–50
Jacobs, Aletta Henrietta, 650–51
Jacson, Maria Elizabeth, 651
James, Lucy Jones, 653
Janssen, Mme., 653–54
Jekyll, Gertrude, 655–56
Jérémine, Elisabeth (Tschernaieff), 656–57
Jex-Blake, Sophia, 657–59
Johnston, Mary Sophia, 660–61
Jones, Amanda Theodosia, 663–64
Jones, Mary Amanda Dixon, 666
Joteyko, Joséphine, 670–71
Julian, Hester Forbes (Pengelly), 671–72
Kablick, Josephine (Ettel), 674
Kahn, Ida, 675
Kane, Lady Katherine Sophia (Baily), 675–76
Kashevarovarudneva, Varvara Aleksandrovna, 678–80
Keeler, Harriet Louise, 680
Keith, Marcia Anna, 682
Keller, Ida Augusta, 682–83
Kellerman, Stella Victoria (Dennis), 683–84
Kellor, Frances A., 685
Kelly, Agnes, 685–86
Kent, Elizabeth, 690

Kent, Grace Helen, 690
Kharuzina, Vera Nikolaevna, 693
King, Georgina, 695
King, Helen Dean, 695–97
King, Louisa Boyd (Yeomans), 697–98
King, Martha, 698
Kingsley, Mary Henrietta, 699
Kirby, Elizabeth, 699–700
Kirkbride, Mary Butler, 701
Kletnova, E.N., 704–5
Knight, Margaret, 708
Knowles, Matilda Cullen, 709–10
Korobeinikova, Iuliia Ivanovna, 718
Kovaleskaia, Sofia Vasilyevna, 720–22
Krogh, Birthe Marie (Jorgensen), 726–28
Krupskaia, Nadezhda Konstantinovna, 728–29
L'esperance, Elise Depew Strang, 777–78
La Chapelle, Marie Louise Dugès, 731
Ladd-Franklin, Christine, 731–32
Laird, Elizabeth Rebecca, 734–35
Lalande, Marie Jeanne Amélie Harlay Lefrancais de, 735–36
La Mance, Lora Sarah (Nichols), 736
Lamarck, Cornelié, 736
Lamme, Bertha, 736–37
Lamonte, Francesca Raimonde, 737
Lane-claypon, Janet Elizabeth, 741–42
Langdon, Fanny E., 742
Langford, Grace, 743–44
Lankester, Phoebe (Pope), 744–45
Latham, Vida Annette, 750
Latimer, Caroline Wormeley, 750–51
Laughlin, Emma Eliza, 751–52
Laurie, Charlotte Louisa, 752
Lavoisier, Marie Anne Pierrette Paulze, 752–53
Law, Annie, 753
Lawrence, Penelope, 754–55
Lawrenson, Alice Louisa, 755
Leach, Mary Frances, 757
Leavitt, Henrietta Swan, 759
Leebody, Mary Elizabeth, 765
Lee, Rebecca, 764
Lee, Sarah Wallis Bowdich, 765
Lees, Florence Sarah, 766
Lefroy, Helena (Trench), 766
Leland, Evelyn, 770
Lemmon, Sarah Plummer, 771
Lermontova, Iuliia Vsevolodovna, 775–76
Lewis, Graceanna, 783
Libert, Marie-Anne, 789
Linton, Laura Alberta, 793–94
Litchfield Henrietta Emma (Darwin), 795–96
Litvinova, Elizaveta Fedorovna, 796–97
Lloyd, Rachel, 798
Lomax, Elizabeth Anne (Smithson), 800
Longshore, Hannah E.(Myers), 802–3
Longstaff, Mary Jane (Donald), 803
Loudon, Jane (Webb), 805–6
Lovejoy, Esther Pohl, 806–7
Lowater, Frances, 807–8
Lozier, Clemence Sophia (Harned), 809
Lukanina, Adelaida N., 810–11
Lyell, Katharine Murray (Horner), 813
Lyell, Mary Elizabeth (Horner), 813

Lyon, Mary, 814–15
Maass, Clara Louise, 817
Maddison, Ada Isabel, 829–30
Malleson, Elizabeth, 834
Maltby, Margaret Eliza, 835
Manning, Ann B.(Harned), 836–37
Mantell, Mary Ann (Woodhouse), 837–38
Marcet, Jane Haldimand, 842–43
Marlatt, Abby Lillian, 844
Marshall, Clara, 845–46
Martineau, Harriet, 849
Martin, Emilie Norton, 848
Martin, Lillien Jane, 848
Mason, Marianne Harriet, 851
Mather, Sarah, 854
Maunder, Annie Scott Dill Russell, 855–56
Maury, Antonia Caetana de Paiva, 856–57
Maury, Carlotta Joaquina, 857–58
Maxwell, Martha Dartt, 858–59
May, Caroline Rebecca, 859–60
McDowell, Louise Sherwood, 866–67
McGee, Anita (Newcomb), 867–68
McKeag, Anna Jane, 870
McNab, Catherine Mary, 872
Measham, Charlotte Elizabeth (Cowper), 874
Meigler, Marie J., 877
Mendenhall, Dorothy (Reed), 881–82
Meredith, Louisa Anne (Twamley), 884
Mergler, Marie, 884
Merrifield, Mary Philadelphia (Watkins), 885
Merrill, Helen Abbot, 885–86
Metchnikova, Olga (Belokopytova), 887–88
Mexia, Ynes, 889–90
Meyer-Bjerrum, Kirstine, 890–91
Meyer, Margaret Theodora, 890
Michael, Helen Cecilia Desilver Abbott, 891–92
Michelet, Athénaïs (Mialaret), 892–94
Miller, Olive Thorne, 897
Mill, Harriet Hardy Taylor, 894–95
Minoka-Hill, Lillie Rosa, 897–98
Missuna, Anna Boleslavovna, 899–900
Mitchell, Anna Helena, 900
Mitchell, Maria, 901–5
Molesworth, Caroline, 907–8
Montessori, Maria, 909–10
Moody, Mary Blair, 910
Moore, Anne, 911
Moore, Emmeline, 911
Morgan, Elizabeth Frances, 914
Morgan, Lilian Vaughan Sampson, 914–15
Moriarity, Henrietta Maria, 915
Morris, Margaretta Hare, 917
Morse, Elizabeth Eaton, 917
Morton, Emily L., 918
Morton, Rosalie Slaughter, 918–20
Moser, Fanny, 920
Mosher, Clelia Duel, 920–21
Murray, Amelia Matilda, 925
Murray, Margaret Alice, 926
Murtfeldt, Mary, 928–29
Neumann, Elsa, 936
Nevill, Lady Dorothy Frances (Walpole), 936–37
Newbigin, Marion Isabel, 937

Newson, Mary Frances Winston, 937–38
Nichols, Mary Louise, 940–41
Nichols, Mary Sargeant Neal Gove, 941–42
Nickerson, Margaret (Lewis), 942
Nightingale, Florence, 944–46
Norsworthy, Naomi, 950–51
North, Marianne, 951–52
Northrup, Ann Hero, 953
Noyes, Mary Chilton, 953
Nuttall, Gertrude (Clarke), 953–54
Nuttall, Zelia Maria Magdalena, 954
Nutting, Mary Adelaide, 954–55
O'Brien, Charlotte Grace, 956
O'Malley, Lady Emma Winifred (Hardcastle), 962
Ogilvie-Gordon, Dame Maria Matilda, 959–60
Ogino, G., 961
Ormerod, Eleanor Anne, 965–67
Owen, Luella Agnes, 969
Owens-Adair, Bethenia, 970
Paget, Dame Mary Rosalind, 972
Paget, Rose Elizabeth, 972
Paine, Mary Esther (Trueblood), 972–73
Palmer, Alice W., 974
Palmer, Elizabeth Day, 974–75
Palmer, Sophia French, 976–77
Palmie, Anna Helene, 977
Panajiotatou, Angeliki, 977–78
Parloa, Maria, 980
Parsons, Elsie Worthington (Clews), 982–83
Parsons, Emily Elizabeth, 983–84
Parsons, Mary, Countess of Rosse, 984–85
Patterson, Flora Wambaugh, 990
Paulucci, Marianna, Marchesa, 991
Pavlova, Mariia Vasil'evna, 992–93
Pechey-Phipson, Mary Edith, 998–99
Peckham, Elizabeth (Gifford), 999
Peebles, Florence, 999–1000
Pelletier, Madeleine, 1000–1002
Pendleton, Ellen Fitz, 1002–3
Pennington, Mary Engle, 1003–4
Perceval, Anne Mary (Flower), 1004
Peretti, Zaffira, 1006
Pertz, Dorothea Frances Matilda, 1009
Petrova, Maria Kapitonovna, 1012
Pfeiffer, Ida (Reyer), 1013–14
Phelps, Almira Hart Lincoln, 1015–16
Philpot, Elizabeth, 1018
Philpot, Margaret, 1018
Philpot, Mary, 1018
Phisalix, Marie (Picot), 1018–19
Picotte, Susan (La Flesche), 1022–23
Piozzi, Hester Lynch, 1026
Pirie, Mary, 1027
Pirret, Ruth, 1027–28
Platt, Julia Barlow, 1031–32
Plehn, Marianne, 1032–33
Plues, Margaret, 1033
Pockels, Agnes, 1034–35
Pokrovskaia, Mariia Ivanovna, 1036–37
Potts, Eliza, 1046–47
Pratt, Anne, 1050–51
Preston, Ann, 1051–52
Prestwich, Grace Anne (Milne) M'Call, 1052–53

Pringle, Elizabeth Waties (Allston), 1055–56
Putnam, Helen Cordelia, 1059–60
Putnam, Mary Louise (Duncan), 1061
Rabinovitch-Kempner, Lydia, 1067
Raisin, Catherine Alice, 1068–69
Ramsay, Christina (Broun), Countess of Dalhousie, 1070–71
Randolph, Harriet, 1074
Rathbun, Mary Jane, 1075
Reid, Eleanor Mary (Wynne Edwards), 1087–88
Remond, Sarah Parker, 1089
Renooz, Céline, 1089–90
Reynolds, Doris Livesey, 1090–91
Richards, Ellen Henrietta Swallow, 1095–97
Rich, Mary Florence, 1093
Riddle, Lumina Cotton, 1099
Ripley, Martha (Rogers), 1102
Ritter, Mary Elizabeth (Bennett), 1103
Robb, Mary Anne (Boulton), 1105
Roberts, Charlotte Fitch, 1105–6
Roberts, Dorothea Klumpke, 1106
Roberts, Lydia Jane, 1107–8
Roberts, Mary, 1108
Robinson, Daisy Maude (Orleman), 1111
Rockley, Lady Alicia Margaret (Amherst), 1116
Roe, Josephine Robinson, 1119
Rose, Flora, 1125
Rose, Mary Davies Swartz, 1125–26
Roupell, Arabella Elizabeth (Piggott), 1129
Royer, Clémence, 1129–32
Rucker, Augusta, 1134
Russell, Anna (Worsley), 1136
Rydh, Hanna, 1139
Safford, Mary Jane, 1143–44
Sargant, Ethel, 1151–52
Saunders, Edith Rebecca, 1154–55
Sawin, Martha, 1155
Say, Lucy (Sistare), 1155–56
Scarpellini, Caterina, 1156
Schaffner, Mabel (Brockett), 1156
Scharlieb, Dame Mary Ann Dacomb (Bird), 1157–58
Schliemann, Sophia (Kastromenos), 1160–61
Schubert, Anna, 1165
Scott, Charlotte Angas, 1167–68
Scudder, Ida Sophia, 1169–70
Seaman, Elizabeth Cochrane, 1170–71
Semple, Ellen Churchill, 1176–77
Sessions, Kate Olivia, 1177–78
Sewall, Lucy, 1178
Shabanova, Anna Nikolaevna, 1179–80
Shakespear, Dame Ethel Mary Reader (Wood), 1180–81
Sharp, Emily Katharine (Dooris), 1181
Shattuck, Lydia White, 1182–83
Sheldon, Jennie Arms, 1183
Sherbourne, Margaret Dorothea (Willis), 1185
Sherman, Althea Rosina, 1185–86
Shinn, Milicent Washburn, 1187–88
Sidgwick, Eleanor (Balfour), 1192–93
Siebold, Charlotte Marianne Heidenreich von, 1193

Siebold, Josepha (Henning) von, 1193
Silliman, Hepsa Ely, 1194–95
Slater, Jesse Mabel Wilkins, 1198–99
Slosson, Annie Trumbull, 1199
Smith, Annie Lorrain, 1202–3
Smith, Annie Morrill, 1203
Smith, Erminnie Adele (Platt), 1205–6
Smith, Margaret Kiever, 1207
Smith, Matilda, 1208
Smith, Pleasance (Reeve), 1209
Smith, Winifred, 1209
Snow, Julia Warner, 1210
Soddy, Winifred Moller (Beilby), 1211
Sollas, Igerna Brünhilda Johnson, 1212
Solomko-Sotiriadis, Evgeniia, 1213
Somerville, Mary (Fairfax) Greig, 1213–15
Spalding, Effie Southworth, 1218
Spence, Eliza Jane (Edmondson), 1218
Spencer, Adelin Elam, 1218–19
Stackhouse, Emily, 1221–22
Stefanescu, Sabba, 1225
Stephenson, Marjory, 1227–28
Stern, Frances, 1229–30
Stevens, Nettie Maria, 1230–32
Stevenson, Matilda Coxe (Evans), 1232–33
Stevenson, Sarah Ann (Hackett), 1233–34
Stevenson, Sara (Yorke), 1233
Stewart, Maude, 1236
Stokes, Margaret McNair, 1239
Stone, Constance, 1240
Stone, Isabelle, 1241–42
Stott, Alicia (Boole), 1244
Stovin, Margaret, 1244–45
Stowe, Emily Howard (Jennings), 1245
Stratton Porter, Gene, 1247–48
Strobell, Ella Church, 1248
Strong, Harriet Williams (Russell), 1248–49
Stuart, Miranda, 1250
Suslova, Nadezhda Prokof'evna, 1252–53
Swain, Clara A., 1255
Swift, Mary, 1255–56
Talbot, Marion, 1262–63
Tammes, Jantine, 1264–65
Tannery, Marie Alexandrine (Prisset), 1265
Taylor, Charlotte de Bernier Scarborough, 1268
Taylor, Helen, 1270
Taylor, Janet, 1270–71
Taylor, Lucy Beaman (Hobbs), 1271
Taylor, Monica, 1272
Tebb, Mary Christine, 1272–73
Telfair, Annabella (Chamberlain), 1273
Thelberg, Elizabeth (Burr), 1277–78
Thiselton-Dyer, Lady Harriet Ann (Hooker), 1278–79
Thomas, Mary Frame (Myers), 1281–82
Thompson, Mary Harris, 1284–85
Thompson, Rachel Ford, 1285
Thoms, Adah B.(Samuels), 1285–86
Thomson, Agnes C., 1286
Thomson, Jane Smithson, 1286
Thring, Lydia Eliza Dyer (Meredith), 1286–87
Tiburtius, Franziska, 1288–89
Tilden, Josephine Elizabeth, 1289–90
Tindall, Isabella Mary, 1291

Eighteenth Century (*cont.*)

Tinne, Alexandrina Petronella Francina, 1291–92
Todd, Emily Sophia, 1294–95
Todd, Mabel Loomis, 1295
Tomaszewicz-Dobrska, Anna, 1297
Tompkins, Sally Louisa, 1297
Tracy, Martha, 1299–1300
Traill, Catharine Parr (Strickland), 1300–1301
Treat, Mary Lua Adelia (Davis), 1301–2
Trizna, Valentina Borisovna, 1302–3
Trower, Charlotte Georgiana, 1305
Tsvetaeva, Maria, 1305–6
Tunnicliff, Ruth, 1307–8
Turner, Abby Howe, 1308
Turner, Mary (Palgrave), 1308–9
Twining, Elizabeth Mary, 1309
Tyndall, A.C., 1311
Tyng, Anita E., 1311
Uvarova, Countess Praskov'ia Sergeevna, 1314–15
Van Deman, Esther Boise, 1319
Van Hoosen, Bertha, 1319–20
Van Rensselaer, Martha, 1320–21
Veley, Lilian Jane (Nutcombe), 1325
Veretennikova, Anna Ivanovna, 1326–27
Vickers, Anna, 1328
Vilmorin, Elisa (Bailly), 1329
Vivian, Roxana Hayward, 1329
Vogt, Cécile (Mugnier), 1329–30
Volkova, Anna Fedorovna, 1332–33
Wakefield, Priscilla (Bell), 1337
Walcott, Helene B. (Stevens), 1337–38
Walcott, Mary Morris (Vaux), 1338
Wald, Lillian D., 1338–39
Walker, Eliza, 1339
Walker, Harriet Ann, 1339–40
Walker, Mary Edward, 1340–41
Wallace, Louise Baird, 1342
Walworth, Ellen Hardin, 1344–45
Ward, Mary (King), 1346
Warren, Elizabeth Andrew, 1347
Washburn, Margaret Floy, 1348–49
Weber, Anne Antoinette (Van Bosse), 1352–53
Wedderburn, Jemima, 1354
Wedgwood, Mary Louisa (Bell), 1356
Wells, Charlotte Fowler, 1362–63
Wells, Louisa D., 1363
Welsh, Jane Kilby, 1363–64
Welsh, Lillian, 1364
West, Ethel, 1367
Westover, Cynthia May, 1368
White, Eliza Catherine (Quekett), 1371
White, Frances Emily, 1372
Whiteley, Martha Annie, 1373
Whiting, Sarah Frances, 1374
Whitney, Mary Watson, 1374–75
Wick, Frances Gertrude, 1375–76
Wilder, Inez (Whipple), 1378
Willard, Emma (Hart), 1378–79
Willcox, Mary Alice, 1380
Williams, Anna Wessels, 1380–82
Willmott, Ellen Ann, 1382–83
Wilson, Fiammetta Worthington, 1385
Wilson, Lucy Langdon (Williams), 1386

Winlock, Anna, 1388–89
Withers, Augusta Innes (Baker), 1390
Wollstein, Martha, 1393–94
Wood, Emily Elizabeth, 1394
Wood, Emily Margaret, 1394
Wood, Ruth Goulding, 1395
Woods, Ethel Gertrude (Skeat), 1396–97
Wright, Mabel Osgood, 1407
Wyttenbach, Jeanne Gallien, 1412
Young, Anne Sewell, 1413
Young, Grace Emily (Chisholm), 1413–14
Young, Mabel Minerva, 1415–16
Young, Mary Sophie, 1416
Zakrzewska, Marie Elizabeth, 1419–20

Twentieth Century (1900–1999)

Abbott, Maude Elizabeth Seymour, 1–2
Abel, Mary Hinman, 2–3
Abel, Theodora Mead, 3–4
Aberle, Sophie Bledsoe, 4–5
Abouchdid, Edna, 5
Achilles, Edith Mulhall, 5–6
Acosta-Sison, Honoria, 6
Adametz, Lotte, 7
Adams, Amy Elizabeth Kemper, 7
Adams, Mildred, 7–8
Adamson, Joy (Gessner), 8–9
Addams, Jane, 9–10
Adkins, Dorothy Christina, 10–11
Agassiz, Elizabeth Cary, 12–13
Aitken, Janet Kerr, 16–17
Akeley, Mary Lee (Jobe), 17–18
Albertson, Mary, 17–18
Albrecht, Eleonore, 18
Albrecht, Grete, 19
Alcock, Nora Lilian Leopard, 19
Aldrich-Blake, Louisa Brandreth, 19–20
Alexander, Annie Montague, 20–21
Alexander, Frances Elizabeth Somerville (Caldwell), 21–22
Alexander, Hattie Elizabeth, 22–23
Alimen, Henriette, 23
Ali, Safieh, 23
Allan, Mary Eleanor (Mea), 23
Allen, Doris Twitchell, 24–25
Allen, Ruth Florence, 25–26
Alper, Thelma Gorfinkle, 26–27
Altmann, Margaret, 27
Aluwihare, Florence Kaushalya (Ram), 27–28
Amalitskiya, Anna P., 28
Ames, Blanche (Ames), 28–30
Ames, Louise Bates, 30–31
Ames, Mary E. Pulsifer, 31
Andersen, Dorothy Hansine, 31–32
Anderson, Caroline Virginia (Still) Wiley, 32–33
Anderson, Elda Emma, 33–34
Anderson, Elizabeth Garrett, 34–35
Anderson, Evelyn M., 35–36
Anderson, Louisa Garrett, 36–37
Anderson, Rose Gustava, 37
Anderson, Violet Louise, 37
Andreas-Salomé, Louise Lelia, 38–39
Andrews, Eliza Frances, 39
Andrews, Grace, 39
Andrus, Ruth, 39–40

Angst-Horridge, Anita, 40
Anslow, Gladys Amelia, 42–43
Antipoff, Helene, 43
Antoine, Lore, 43–44
Apgar, Virginia, 45–46
Applin, Esther (Richards), 46–47
Arber, Agnes (Robertson), 47–48
Arbuthnot, Isobel Agnes, 48–49
Arkhangel'skaia, Aleksandra Gavriilovna, 50–51
Arlitt, Ada Hart, 51
Armitage, Eleanora, 51–52
Armitage, Ella Sophia A. (Bulley), 52
Armitt, Annie Maria, 52
Armitt, Mary Louisa, 52–53
Armitt, Sophia, 53
Arnold, Magda Blondiau, 53
Arnstein, Margaret Gene, 53–54
Arsenjewa, A., 54
Arthur, Mary Grace, 54–55
Artner, Mathilde, 55
Ashby, Winifred Mayer, 55
Atwater, Helen Woodard, 58–59
Auerbach, Charlotte, 59–60
Auken, Kirsten (Lomholt), 60–61
Austin, Mary Lellah, 61
Ayrton, Hertha Marks, 62–63
Babcock, Harriet, 65
Baber, Zonia, 65–66
Bacon, Clara (Latimer), 66
Baetjer, Anna Medora, 66–67
Bagley, Florence (Winger), 67
Bagshaw, Elizabeth Catherine, 67
Bahr-Bergius, Eva Vilhelmina Julia, 68
Bailey, Ethel Zoe, 68–69
Bailey, Florence Augusta (Merriam), 69–70
Baker, Sarah Martha, 71–72
Baker, Sara Josephine, 70–71
Bakwin, Ruth (Morris), 72
Balaam, Ellen, 72–73
Balfour, Margaret Ida, 73
Ball, Josephine, 73–74
Bancroft, Nellie, 75
Banga, Ilona, 75–76
Bang, Duck-Heung, 75
Banham, Katherine May, 77
Barbarshova, Zoia Ivanovna, 77
Barber, Helen Karen, 77–78
Bari, Nina Karlovna, 78–79
Barkly, Lady Anna Maria (Pratt), 79
Barlett, Helen Blair, 79–80
Barlow, Emma Nora (Darwin), 80
Barnard, Alicia Mildred, 80–81
Barnard, Edith Ethel, 81
Barney, Ida, 82
Barney, Nora Stanton (Blatch) de Forest, 83
Barnothy, Madeleine (Forro), 83
Barnum, Charlotte Cynthia, 83–84
Barringer, Emily (Dunning), 84–85
Barrows, Katherine Isabel (Hayes), 85–86
Barton, Clara Harlowe, 86
Barton, Lela Viola, 86–87
Bascom, Florence, 87–88
Bass, Mary Elizabeth, 88
Batchelder, Esther Lord, 89–90

Bate, Dorothea Minola Alice, 90
Bates, Mary E., 90–91
Bateson, Anna, 91
Bateson, Beatrice, 91
Battle, Helen Irene, 92
Bauer, Grace M., 92
Baumann, Frieda, 92–93
Baumgarten-Trameh, Franziska, 93–94
Baumgartner, Leona, 94–95
Baum, Marie, 92
Baxter, Mildred Frances, 95
Bayern, Therese Von, 95–96
Bayley, Nancy, 96–97
Beanland, Sarah, 98
Beatley, Janice Carson, 98–99
Beauvallet, Marcelle Jeanne, 100
Becker-Rose, Herta, 101–2
Beckman, A., 102
Beck, Sarah Coker (Adams), 100–101
Beckwith, Angie Maria, 102
Beckwith, Cora, 102
Beckwith, Martha Warren, 102–3
Beers, Catherine Virginia, 104
Behre, Ellinor H., 108
Belaeva, Elizaveta Ivanovna, 108–9
Belar, Maria, 110
Bell, Julia, 109
Belyea, Helen Reynolds, 110–11
Bender, Hedwig, 111
Bender, Lauretta, 111–12
Bender, Wilma, 112
Benedek, Therese F., 112–13
Benedict, Ruth (Fulton), 113
Bengston, Ida Albertina, 114–15
Bennett, Alice, 115
Bennett, Dorothea, 116
Benson, Margaret Jane, 116–17
Bentham, Ethel, 117
Berger, Emily V., 118
Berger, Katharina Bertha Charlotte, 118
Berridge, Emily Mary, 118–19
Bertillon, Caroline Schutze, 120
Besant, Annie (Wood), 120
Beutler, Ruth, 120–21
Bevier, Isabel, 121–22
Bhatia, Sharju Pandit, 122–23
Bibring, Grete Lehner, 123–24
Bickerdyke, Mary Ann (Ball), 124–25
Bidder, Anna McClean, 125
Bidder, Marion Greenwood, 125–26
Bilger, Leonora (Neuffer), 126–27
Billings, Katharine Stevens, 127
Bingham, Millicent (Todd), 127–28
Bird, Grace Electa, 128
Birdsall, Lucy Ellen, 128–29
Birstein, Vera, 129
Bishop, Ann, 129–30
Bishop, Isabella Lucy Bird, 131
Bishop, Katharine Scott, 131–32
Bissell, Emily P., 132
Bitting, Katherine Eliza (Golden), 132–33
Blackburn, Kathleen Bever, 133–34
Blacker, Margaret Constance Helen, 135
Black, Florence, 133
Blackwell, Antoinette Louise (Brown), 135–36

Blackwell, Elizabeth, 136
Blackwell, Elizabeth Marianne, 138
Blackwell, Emily, 138–39
Blackwood, Beatrice Mary, 139
Blagg, Mary Adela, 139–40
Blake, Mary Safford, 140–41
Blanchard, Frieda Cobb, 141–42
Blanchard, Phyllis, 142
Blanquies, Lucie, 142–43
Blatchford, Ellen C., 143
Blau, Marietta, 143–44
Bledsoe, Lucybelle, 144–45
Blinova, Ekaterina Nikitichna, 145
Bliss, Dorothy Elizabeth, 145–46
Bliss, Eleanor Albert, 146
Bliss, Mary Campbell, 146
Block, Jeanne (Humphrey), 146–48
Blodgett, Katharine Burr, 148–49
Bluhm, Agnes, 149–50
Bluket, Nina Aleksandrovna, 150
Blunt, Katharine, 151
Bochantseva, Zinaida Petrovna, 152
Böhm-Wendt, Cäcilia, 153–54
Bokova–Sechenova, Mariia Aleksandrovna, 154–55
Boley, Gertrude Maud, 155
Bolschanina, M. A., 155
Bolton, Edith, 155
Bolus, Harriet Margaret Louisa (Kensit), 155–56
Bomhard, Miriam Lucile, 156
Bonnevie, Kristine, 157–58
Boole, Mary (Everest), 158–59
Boos, Margaret Bradley (Fuller), 159–60
Booth, Mary Ann Allard, 160
Boring, Alice Middleton, 160–62
Borisova-Bekriasheva, Antoniia, 162
Boron, Elizabeth (Riddle) Graves, 162–63
Borsarelli, Fernanda, 163
Boswell, Katherine Cumming, 163
Bourdel, Léone, 163–64
Bouteiller, Marcelle, 164
Bouthilet, Lorraine, 164–65
Boveri, Marcella Imelda O'Grady, 165–67
Boyd, Elizabeth Margaret, 167
Boyd, Louise Arner, 167–68
Boyer, Esther Lydia, 168
Bracher, Rose, 168
Bradley, Amy Morris, 168–69
Bradley, Frances Sage, 169–70
Branch, Hazel Elisabeth, 170
Brandegee, Mary Katharine Layne, 171
Branham, Sara Elizabeth, 171–72
Brant, Laura, 172
Braun, Annette Frances, 172–73
Braun, (Emma) Lucy, 173–74
Brazier, Mary Agnes Burniston (Brown), 174–75
Breckinridge, Mary, 175–76
Bredikhina, Evgeniia Aleksandrovna, 176–77
Brenchley, Winifred Elsie, 177
Brenk, Irene, 177–78
Breyer, Maria Gerdina (Brandwijk), 179
Brezina, Maria Aristides, 179
Bridgman, Olga Louise, 180

Brière, Yvonne, 180
Brightwen, Eliza (Elder), 181
Britten, Lilian Louisa, 180–81
Britton, Elizabeth Knight, 181
Broadhurst, Jean, 181–82
Brock, Sylvia (Deantonis), 182
Bromley, Helen Jean (Brown), 182–83
Bronner, Augusta Fox, 183
Brooke, Winifred, 184
Brooks, Harriet T., 184–85
Brooks, Matilda (Moldenhauer), 185–86
Brooks, Sarah Theresa, 186
Broomall, Anna Elizabeth, 186
Brousseau, Kate, 186–87
Brown, Charlotte Amanda Blake, 187–88
Brown, Dame Edith Mary, 188–89
Browne, Ida Alison (Brown), 191–92
Browne, Lady Isabel Mary (Peyronnet), 192–93
Browne, Marjorie Lee, 193–94
Brown, Fay Cluff, 189–90
Brown, Mabel Mary, 190
Brown, Nellie Adalesa, 190–91
Brown, Rachel Fuller, 191
Bruce, Catherine Wolfe, 194
Bruce, Eileen Adelaide, 194–95
Brüch, Hilde, 195
Brunetti, R., 196
Brunswick, Ruth Jane (Mack), 196–97
Bryan, Alice Isabel (Bever), 197–98
Bryan, Mary Katherine, 199
Bryant, Louise Stevens, 199
Bryant, Sophie (Willock), 199–200
Buchanan, Florence, 200
Buchbinder, Laura G. Ordan, 200–201
Buckel, Chloe A., 201–2
Buckley, Arabella, 202–3
Buell, Mary Van Rensselaer, 203
Buerk, Minerva (Smith), 203–4
Bühler, Charlotte Bertha (Malachowski), 204–5
Bülbring, Edith, 205
Bull, Nina Wilcox, 205–6
Bunch, Cordia, 206
Bunting, Martha, 206
Bunting-Smith, Mary (Ingraham), 206–8
Bunzel, Ruth Leah, 208
Burgess, May (Ayres), 209
Burkill, Ethel Maud (Morrison), 209
Burlingham, Dorothy (Tiffany), 209–10
Burlingham, Gertrude Simmons, 210–11
Burns, Eleanor Irene, 211
Burns, Louisa, 211
Burrell, Anna Porter, 212
Burr, Emily Thorp, 211
Burton, Helen Marie Rousseay (Kan-Nemeyer), 212
Burtt Davy, Alice (Bolton), 212
Bush, Katharine Jeannette, 214–15
Busk, Lady Marian (Balfour), 215
Bussecker, Erna, 215
Bykhovskaia, Anna Markovna, 215–16
Byrd, Mary Emma, 216
Byrnes, Esther Fussell, 216–17
Cadbury, Dorothy Adlington, 218

Twentieth Century (*cont.*)

Cadilla de Martínez, María, 218–19
Cady, Bertha Louise Chapman, 219
Calderone, Mary S., 220
Caldwell, Mary Letitia, 220–21
Cale, F. M., 221
Calkins, Mary Whiton, 221–23
Calvert, Emily Amelia (Adelia) (Smith), 224
Campbell, Dame Janet Mary, 226
Campbell, Helen Stuart, 224–25
Campbell, May Sherwood, 226
Campbell, Persia Crawford, 226–27
Cannon, Annie Jump, 227–28
Carlson, Elizabeth, 228
Carlson, Lucille, 228
Carothers, Estrella Eleanor, 229
Carpenter, Esther, 230
Carr, Emma Perry, 230–32
Carroll, Christiane (Mendrez), 232
Carroll, Dorothy, 232–33
Carson, Rachel Louise, 233–34
Carter, Edna, 234
Cartwright, Dame Mary Lucy, 235
Carus, Mary Hegeler, 235–36
Castle, Cora (Sutton), 236
Cattell, Psyche, 238
Cattoi, Noemí Violeta, 238–39
Cauchois, Yvette, 239
Caughlan, Georgeanne (Robertson), 239–40
Cauquil, Germaine Anne, 240
Cesniece-Freudenfelde, Zelma, 242
Chaix, Paulette Audemard, 242
Chalubinska, Aniela, 242–43
Chamié, Catherine, 243
Chandler, Marjorie Elizabeth Jane, 244
Chang, Moon Gyung, 245
Chang, Vivian, 245
Charles, Vera Katherine, 245–46
Charsley, Fanny Anne, 246
Chase, Mary Agnes Meara, 246–47
Chasman, Renate Wiener, 247–48
Chauchard, B., 248
Chaudet, Maria Casanova de, 248
Cheesman, Lucy Evelyn, 248–49
Chenoweth, Alice Drew, 249–50
Chesser, Elizabeth (Sloan), 250
Chick, Dame Harriette, 250–51
Chinn, May Edward, 252
Chisholm, Catherine, 253
Chmielewska, Irene, 253–54
Chodak-Gregory, Hazel Haward (Cuthbert), 254
Christen, Sydney Mary (Thompson), 254–55
Chute, Hettie Morse, 256–57
Cilento, Lady Phyllis, 257–58
Cinquini, Maria Dei Conti Cibrario, 258
Cioranescu-Nenitzescu, Ecaterina, 258
Clapp, Cornelia Maria, 258–59
Clappe, Louisa Amelia (Smith), 259
Clark, Bertha, 260
Clarke, Lilian Jane, 265
Clark, Frances N., 260–61
Clark, Janet Howell, 261–62
Clark, Jessie Jane, 262
Clark, Lois, 262–63

Clark, Mamie Katherine (Phipps), 263
Clark, Nancy Talbot, 263–64
Clay-Jolles, Tettje Clasina, 265–66
Claypole, Agnes Mary, 266–67
Claypole, Edith Jane, 267
Clemens, Mary Knapp (Strong), 268
Clements, Edith Gertrude, 268
Clerke, Agnes Mary, 269–71
Clerke, Ellen Mary, 271–72
Cleve, Astrid, 272
Clinch, Phyllis E. M., 273
Clisby, Harriet Jemima Winifred, 273–74
Cobbe, Anne Phillipa, 276
Cobbe, Frances Power, 276–77
Cobb, Margaret Vara, 275–76
Cobb, Rosalie M. Karapetoff, 276
Cochran, Doris Mabel, 277–78
Cohn, Essie White, 278–79
Coignou, Caroline Pauline Marie, 279
Colby, Martha Guernsey, 279
Colcord, Mabel, 280
Cole, Emma J., 280–81
Cole, Rebecca J., 281
Collet, Clara Elizabeth, 281
Collett, Mary Elizabeth, 281
Collins, Katharine Richards, 282
Colvin, Brenda, 282–83
Comstock, Anna Botsford, 283–84
Comyns-Lewer, Ethel, 284
Cone, Claribel, 284–85
Conklin, Marie (Eckhardt), 285
Conklin, Ruth Emelene, 285–86
Conway, Elsie (Phillips), 287
Cook, A. Grace, 287–88
Cooke, Alice Sophia (Smart), 288
Cook, Margaret C., 288
Cookson, Isabel Clifton, 289
Cooley, Jacquelin Smith, 289
Coombs, Helen Copeland, 289–90
Cooper, Clara Chassell, 290
Cooper, Elizabeth Morgan, 290
Cooper-Ellis, Katharine Murdoch, 292
Cooper, Sybil, 291
Copeland, Lennie Phoebe, 292
Cordier, Marguerite Jeanne, 292
Cori, Gerty Theresa Radnitz, 292–94
Cornelius-Furlani, Marta, 294
Coryndon, Shirley (Cameron), 295
Cotelle, Sonia, 295–96
Cotter, Brigid M., 296
Coudreau, Octavie, 296
Cowan, Edwina Abbott, 296–97
Cox, Gertrude Mary, 297–98
Cox, Rachel (Dunaway), 298
Coyle, Elizabeth Eleanor, 298–99
Cram, Eloise Blaine, 299
Crandall, Ella Phillips, 299
Crane, Jocelyn, 300–301
Cranwell, Lucy May, 301
Cremer, Erika, 301–2
Crespin, Irene, 302–3
Croll, Hilda M., 304–5
Crosbie, May, 305
Crosby, Elizabeth Caroline, 305–6
Crosfield, Margaret Chorley, 306

Csepreghyné-Meznerics, Ilona, 306–7
Cuffe, Lady Charlotte Wheeler (Williams), 307
Cullis, Winifred, 307–8
Cummings, Clara Eaton, 308
Cummings, Louise Duffield, 309
Cunningham, Bess Virginia, 310
Cunningham, Gladys Story, 310–11
Cunningham, Susan, 311
Curie, Marie (Maria Sklodowska), 311–17
Currie, Ethel Dobbie, 317
Curtis, Doris Sarah (Malkin), 317–18
Curtis, Natalie, 318–19
Cushier, Elizabeth, 319
Cushing, Hazel Morton, 319–20
Cushman, Florence, 319
Cuthbert-Browne, Grace Johnston, 320–21
Czaplicka, Marie Antoinette, 321
Czeczottowa, Hanna (Peretiatkowicza), 321
Dalai, Maria Jolanda (Tosoni), 322
Dalby, Mary, 322
Dallas, A. E. M. M., 323
Dane, Elisabeth, 324
Daniel, Anne Sturges, 324–25
Daniels, Amy L., 325
Daulton, Agnes Warner McClelland, 327–28
Davenport, Gertrude (Crotty), 328
David, Florence N., 328
Davis, Adelle, 328–29
Davis, Alice (Rohde), 329
Davis, Frances (Elliott), 330
Davis, Grace Evangeline, 330
Davis, Katharine Bement, 331–32
Davis, Marguerite, 332–33
Davis, Olive Griffith Stull, 333
Davis, Rose May, 334
Davy, Lady Joanna Charlotte (Flemmich), 333–34
Dawson, Maria, 334
Day, Dorothy, 334
Day, Gwendolen Helen, 334–35
Day, Mary Anna, 335
Decker, Jane Cynthia (McLaughlin), 335–36
Deflandre-Rigaud, Marthe, 336
De Fraine, Ethel Louise, 336–37
De Graffenried, Mary Clare, 337
Deichmann, Elisabeth, 337–38
Déjerine-Klumpke, Augusta, 338–39
De Laguna, Fredericka Annis Lopez de Leo, 339–41
De Lange, Cornelia Catharina, 341–42
Delap, Maude Jane, 342
Delf-Smith, Ellen Marion, 343
Deloria, Ella Cara, 343–44
Dembo, Tamara, 344–45
De Milt, Clara Marie, 345
Dempsey, Sister Mary Joseph, 345
Dengel, Anna Maria, 346–47
Denis, Willey Glover, 347
Dennett, Mary Ware, 347
Dennis, Olive Wetzel, 347–48
Densmore, Frances Theresa, 348–49
Derick, Carrie M., 349–50
Derscheid-Delcourt, Marie, 350
Detmers, Frederica, 350

Deutsch, Helene Rosenback, 351–52
De Valera, Mairin, 352–53
De Vesian, Dorothy Ellis, 353
Dewey, Jane Mary (Clark), 353
De Witt, Lydia Maria Adams, 353–54
Dickerson, Mary Cynthia, 355–56
Dick, Gladys Rowena Henry, 354–55
Diggs, Ellen Irene, 357
Dimsdale, Helen Easdale (Brown), 358–59
Dinnerstein, Dorothy, 359
Dobrolubova, Tatiana A., 360–61
Dobroscky, Irene Dorothy, 361
Dobrowolska, H., 361
Dobson, Mildred E., 362
Dock, Lavinia Lloyd, 362–63
Dodd, Katharine, 363
Dodds, Mary Letitia, 363–64
Dodgson, Sarah Elizabeth, 364
Doering, Kathleen Clara, 364
Dohan, Edith Haywood Hall, 364–65
Dokhman, Genrietta Isaakovna, 365–66
Dolgopol de Saez, Mathilde, 366
Dolley, Sarah Read Adamson, 366–67
Dombrovskaia, Iuliia Fominichna, 367
Donnay, Gabrielle (Hamburger), 367–68
Dooley, Lucile, 368
Dorabialska, Alicja Domenica, 368–69
Doreck, Hertha (Walburger Doris Sieverts), 369–70
Dorenfeldt, Margot, 371
Dorety, Angela, 370
Dormon, Caroline, 370–71
Doubleday, Neltje Blanchan (de Graff), 371–72
Dougal, Margaret Douie, 372
Douglas, Alice Vibert, 372
Dover, Mary Violette, 372–73
Downey, June Etta, 373–74
Downey, K. Melvina, 374
Downie, Dorothy G., 374
Downs, Cornelia Mitchell, 374–75
Drant, Patricia (Hart), 375
Draper, Mary Anna Palmer, 375–76
Drebeneva-Ukhova, Varvara Pavlovna, 376
Drew, Kathleen Mary, 376–77
Drinker, Katherine (Rotan), 377
Drummond, Margaret, 378
Du Bois, Cora, 377–78
Dubuisson-Brouha, Adele, 378
Duffy, Elizabeth, 381–82
Dummer, Ethel (Sturges), 382–83
Dunbar, Helen Flanders, 383–84
Duncan, Catherine (Gross), 384
Duncan, Helen, 384–85
Duncan, Ursula Katherine, 385–86
Dunham, Ethel Collins, 386–87
Dunlop, Janette Gilchrist, 387
Dunning, Wilhelmina Frances, 388
Dunn, Mary Douglas, 387
Dunn, Thelma Brumfield, 387–88
Durham, Mary Edith, 388–89
Duryea, Nina, 389
Dutcher, Adelaide, 389–90
Dutton, Bertha, 390–91
Dutton, Loraine Orr, 391

Dye, Marie, 391
Dyer, Helen Marie, 391–92
Dylazanka, Maria, 393
Earle, Marie Theresa (Villiers), 394
Eastwood, Alice, 394–96
Eaves, Elsie, 396
Ebers, Edith (Knote), 396
Echols, Dorothy Jung, 397
Eckerson, Sophia Hennion, 397
Eckstorm, Fannie Pearson (Hardy), 398
Eddy, Bernice Elaine, 398–99
Edgell, Beatrice, 399
Edge, Rosalie Barrow, 399
Edgerton, Winifred Haring, 399–400
Edinger, Johanna Gabrielle Otellie (Tilly), 400–401
Edkins, Nora Tweedy, 401–2
Edson, Fanny Carter, 402–3
Edwards, Lena Frances, 403
Edwards-Pilliet, Blanche, 403–5
Efimenko, Aleksandra Iakovlevna, 405
Eggleton, Marion Grace (Palmer), 406–7
Ehrenfest-Afanassjewa, Tatyana Alexeyevna, 407–8
Eichelberger, Lillian, 408
Eigenmann, Rosa Smith, 408–9
Einstein, Elizabeth Roboz, 410–11
Einstein-Maric, Mileva, 411–12
Eisele, Carolyn, 412–13
Elderton, Ethel, 413
Elgood, Cornelia Bonté Sheldon (Amos), 414–15
Elion, Gertrude Belle, 415–16
Eliot, Martha May, 416
Elles, Gertrude Lilian, 417–18
Elliott, Charlotte, 418
Ellis, Florence Hawley, 419
Ellisor, Alva Christine, 419–20
Elsom, Katharine (O'Shea), 420
Emerson, Gladys Ludwina (Anderson), 420–21
Engelbrecht, Mildred Amanda, 422
Eng, Helga, 421–22
Erdmann, Rhoda, 422–25
Ermol'eva, Zinaida Vissarionovna, 425
Esau, Katherine, 426–27
Esdorn, Ilse, 427–28
Evans, Alice Catherine, 428–30
Evans, Alice Margaret, 430
Everard, Barbara Mary Steyning, 430
Evershed, Mary Orr, 431–32
Eves, Florence, 432
Ewing, Elizabeth Raymond (Burden), 432
Fage, Winifred E., 433
Farnsworth, Alice Hall, 434
Farnsworth, Vesta J., 434
Farquharson, Marian Sarah (Ridley), 435
Farrar, Lillian K. P., 436
Farr, Wanda Kirkbride, 435–36
Fawcett, Phillipa Garrett, 436–37
Fearn, Anne Walter, 437–38
Fedchenko, Ol'ga Aleksandrovna, 438–39
Feichtinger, Nora, 439
Fell, Honor Bridget, Dame, 439–40
Fenchel, Käte (Sperling), 440–41

Fenwick, Florence, 442
Ferguson, Margaret Clay, 441–42
Fernald, Grace Maxwell, 442
Ferrand, Elizabeth M., 443
Ferrero, Gina (Lombroso), 443–44
Fielde, Adele Marion, 444
Fieser, Mary, 445
Findlater, Doris, 446
Finkler, Rita V. (Sapiro), 446–47
Fischer, Irene Kaminka, 447
Fishenden, Margaret White, 448–49
Fisher, Edna Marie, 449
Fisher, Elizabeth Florette, 449
Fisher, Sara Carolyn, 450
Fish, Margery, 447–48
Fish, Marie Poland, 448
Fitzgerald, Mabel Purefoy, 450
Fleming, Amalia Coutsouris, Lady, 451
Fleming, Williamina Paton Stevens, 453–54
Fletcher, Alice Cunningham, 454–55
Flock, Eunice Verna, 455
Flood, Margaret Greer, 455
Florendo, Soledad Arcega, 455–56
Flügge-Lotz, Irmgard, 456–57
Foley, Mary Cecilia, 457
Folmer, Hermine Jacoba, 457
Fonovits-Smereker, H., 458
Foot, Katherine, 458
Forbes, Helena Madelain Lamond, 458
Forster, Mary, 459
Fossey, Dian, 458
Fossler, Mary Louise, 460
Foster, Josephine Curtis, 460
Foster, Margaret D., 460–61
Fowler-Billings, Katharine Stevens, 462–63
Fox, Ruth, 463–64
Fraine, Ethel Louise de, 464
Francini, Eleonora Corti, 464–65
FranÇoise, Marie-Thérèse, 464
Franklin, Rosalind Elsie, 465–66
Frank, Margaret, 465
Frantz, Virginia Kneeland, 466
Freeman, Joan Maie, 467–68
Freidlina, Rakhil' Khatskelevna, 468–69
Frenkel-Brunswik, Else, 469–70
Freud, Anna, 470–72
Freund, Ida, 472–73
Friant, M., 473
Friedlander, Kate, 473
Friedmann, Friederike, 474
Friend, Charlotte, 474
Fritz, Madeleine Alberta, 475
Fromm, Erika Oppenheimer, 475–76
Frostig, Marianne Bellak, 476–77
Fulford, Margaret Hannah, 477–78
Furness, Caroline Ellen, 478–79
Gabler, Anna, 480
Gage, Susanna Phelps, 480–81
Gaige, Helen (Thompson), 481
Gamble, Eleanor Acheson McCulloch, 482
Gantt, Love Rosa, 482–83
Gardiner, Margaret Isabella, 483
Gardner, Elinor Wight, 483–84
Gardner, Julia Anna, 484–85
Gardner, Mary Sewall, 485

Twentieth Century (*cont.*)

Garfield, Viola Edmundson, 485–86
Garlick, Constance, 486
Garnett, Alice, 486–87
Garnjobst, Laura Flora, 487
Garretson, Mary (Welleck), 487–88
Garrod, Dorothy Anne Elizabeth, 488–89
Gàta, Elena (Stefanescu), 489
Gates, Fanny Cook, 489–90
Gaw, Esther Allen, 491–92
Gaw, Frances Isabel, 492–93
Geiringer Hilda, 493–94
Geldart, Alice Mary, 494
Genet-Varcin, E., 494
Genung, Elizabeth Faith, 494–95
Geppert, Maria Pia, 495
Gepp, Ethel Sarel (Barton), 495
Gerould, Elizabeth Wood, 497
Gerry, Eloise B., 497–98
Gey, Margaret Lewis, 499
Giammarino, Pia, 498
Gibbons, E. Joan, 498–99
Gibbons, Vernette Lois, 499
Gibbs, Lilian Suzette, 500
Gilbert, Ruth, 501–2
Gilbreth, Lillian Evelyn Moller, 501–2
Gilkey, Helen Margaret, 502
Gillett, Margaret (Clark), 503
Gill, Jocelyn Ruth, 502–3
Gilmore, Jane Georgina, 503
Gilroy, Helen (Turnbull), 503
Giraud, Marthe, 504
Gitelson, Frances H., 505
Gjellestad, Guro Else, 505
Glagoleva-Arkad'yeva, Aleksandra
    Andreyevna, 506
Glascott, Louisa S., 506
Glasgow, Maude, 506
Glass, Jewell Jeanette, 506–7
Gleason, Josephine Mixer, 507
Gleason, Kate, 507
Gleason, Rachel Brooks, 508
Gleditsch, Ellen, 508–9
Glueck, Eleanor (Touroff), 509
Gocholashvili, Mariia Mikievna, 509
Godfery, Hilda Margaret, 510
Goeppert Mayer, Maria Gertrud Käte, 510–11
Goldfeder, Anna, 512–13
Goldfrank, Esther Schiff, 513–14
Goldhaber, Sulamith, 514
Goldman, Hetty, 514–15
Goldring, Winifred, 515–16
Goldschmidt, Frieda, 516
Goldsmith, Grace Arabell, 516–17
Goldsmith, Marie, 517
Goldthwaite, Nellie Esther, 517–18
Golinevich, Elena Mikhailovna, 518
Goodenough, Florence Laura, 518–19
Goodrich, Sarah Frances, 519
Goodyear, Edith, 519–20
Gordon, Kate, 520
Gorinevskaya, Valentina Valentinovna, 520–21
Gorizdro-Kulczycka, Zinaida, 521
Gorshkova, Tat'yana Ivanovna, 521
Götz, Irén Julih (Dienes), 521–22

Gracheva, Yekaterina Konstantinovna, 522
Graham, Helen (Treadway), 522
Grainger, Jennie, 522
Gravatt, Annie Evelyn (Rathbun), 522–23
Graves, Elizabeth (Riddle), 523
Gray, Etta, 523
Gray, Susan Walton, 524–25
Green, Arda A., 525–26
Green, Vera Mae, 526–27
Gregory, Eliza Standerwick (Barnes), 528
Gregory, Lady Isabella Augusta (Persse), 529
Gregory, Louisa Catherine (Allen), 529–30
Gregory, Louise Hoyt, 530
Greig, Margaret Elizabeth, 530
Greisheimer, Esther Maud, 530
Griffin, Harriet Madeline, 531
Griggs, Mary Amerman, 531
Grinnell, Hilda Wood, 532
Griswold, Grace Hall, 533
Gromova, Vera Isaacovna, 533
Gruhn, Ruth, 533–34
Grzigorzewska, Marja, 534
Gualco, Sellina, 535
Guldberg, Estrid, 536
Gullett, Lucy E., 536
Gundersen, Herdis, 537
Gunn, Mary Davidson, 537–38
Gunther, Erna, 538
Guthrie, Mary Jane, 538–39
Gwynne-Vaughan, Dame Helen Charlotte
    Isabella (Fraser), 539
Haber-Immerwahr, Clara, 540–41
Haccius, Barbara, 541–42
Hagood, Margaret Loyd Jarman, 542–43
Hahn, Dorothy Anna, 543
Haldorsen, Inger Alida, 543–44
Halicka, Antonina (Yaroszewicz), 544
Halket, Ann Cronin, 544
Hall-Brown, Lucy, 547
Hall, Dorothy, 545
Halliday, Nellie, 547
Hall, Julia Brainerd, 545–46
Hall, Kate Marion, 546
Hallowell, Susan Maria, 548
Hall, Rosetta Sherwood, 546–47
Hamburger, Erna, 548
Hamerstrom, Frances (Flint), 548–49
Hamilton, Alice, 549–50
Hamilton, Peggy-Kay, 550–51
Hammer, Marie Signe, 551
Hanfmann, Eugenia, 551–52
Hanks, Jane Richardson, 552–53
Hansen, Hazel D., 553
Hansen, Julie Marie Vinter, 554
Hanson, Emmeline Jean, 554–55
Hardcastle, Frances, 555
Hardesty, Mary, 555
Harding, Anita, 556
Hardwick, Rose Standish, 556
Hardy, Harriet, 557
Hardy, Thora Marggraff Plitt, 557
Harmon, Élise F., 557–58
Harrison, Jane Ellen, 558
Harrison, Janet Mitchell Marr, 559
Harrower, Molly R., 559–60

Hart, Esther Hasting, 560
Hart, Helen, 560
Hartt, Constance Endicott, 560–61
Harvey, Ethel Nicholson Browne, 561–62
Harwood, Margaret, 562–63
Haslett, Dame Caroline, 563–64
Hassall, Bessie Florence (Cory), 564
Hathaway, Millicent Louise, 565
Hausser, Isolde (Ganswindt), 566–68
Hawes, Harriet (Boyd), 568–69
Hawkes, Jacquetta (Hopkins), 569
Hawkins, Kate, 570
Hawn Mirabile, Margaret H., 570
Hayes, Ellen Amanda, 570–71
Hayner, Lucy Julia, 571–72
Hayward, Ida Margaret, 572
Haywood, Charlotte, 572
Hazen, Elizabeth Lee, 572–73
Hazlett, Olive Clio, 574
Hearst, Phoebe (Apperson), 574–75
Heath, Daisy Winifred, 575
Hebb, Catherine Olding, 575–76
Hedges, Florence, 577
Heermann, Margareta, 577–78
Hefferan, Mary, 578
Heidbreder, Edna Frances, 578–79
Heimann, Berta, 579
Heimann, Paula, 579–80
Heim-Vögtlin, Marie, 580
Heinlein, Julia Elizabeth Heil, 580–81
Hellman, Johanna, 581
Hellstedt, Leone McGregor, 581–82
Henderson, Nellie Frater, 583
Hendricks, Eileen M., 583
Hennel, Cora Barbara, 583–84
Henrey, Blanche Elizabeth Edith, 584
Henry, Caroline (Orridge), 584
Henshaw, Julia Wilmotte, 584
Heppenstall, Caroline A., 585
Herford, Ethilda B. Meakin, 585
Herrick, Julia Frances, 586
Herrick, Sophia McIlvaine (Bledsoe), 586–87
Herskovits, Frances S. (Shapiro), 590–91
Hertwig, Paula, 591–92
Hertz, Mathilde, 592
Herwerden, Marianne Van, 592
Herxheimer, Franziska, 592
Heslop, Mary Kingdon, 592–93
Hesse, Fanny, 593
Hetzer, Hildegard, 593
Hewer, Dorothy, 594
Hewitt, Dorothy, 594
Hibbard, Hope, 594–95
Hickey, Amanda Sanford, 595
Hicks, Beatrice Alice, 595–96
Higgins, Vera (Cockburn), 596
Hightower, Ruby Usher, 596
Hildreth, Gertrude Howell, 598–99
Hilgard, Josephine Rohrs, 599
Hill, Dorothy, 600–601
Hill, Justina Hamilton, 601
Hill, Mary Elliott, 601
Hines, Marion, 601–2
Hinman, Alice Hamlin, 602
Hinrichs, Marie Agnes, 602

Hirschfeld-Tiburtius, Henriette (Pagelsen), 602–3
Hitchens, Ada Florence R., 604
Hitzenberger, Annaliese, 604–5
Hobby, Gladys Lounsbury, 605–6
Hodgkin, Dorothy Mary Crowfoot, 606–7
Hodgson, Eliza Amy, 607
Hoffleit, Ellen Dorrit, 607–8
Hofmann, Elise, 608
Hoggan, Ismé Aldyth, 609
Hogg, Helen Sawyer, 608–9
Hohl, Leonora Anita, 609–10
Hoke, Calm (Morrison), 610
Hol, Jacoba Brigitta Louisa, 610
Hollingworth, Leta Anna Stetter, 610–12
Holm, Esther (Aberdeen), 612
Holton, Pamela Margaret (Watson-Williams), 613
Homer, Annie, 613–14
Hoobler, Icie Gertrude Macy, 614
Hooker, Henrietta Edgecomb, 615
Hooker, Marjorie, 615
Hopper, Grace (Brewster Murray), 616–17
Horney, Karen Clementine (Danielsen), 617–18
Horowitz, Stephanie, 618
Hough, Margaret Jean Ringier, 619
Howard Beckman, Ruth Winifred, 620
Howard, Louise Ernestine (Matthaei), Lady, 619–20
Howard Wylde, Hildegarde, 620–22
Howe Akeley, Delia Julia Denning, 622–23
Howes, Ethel Dench Puffer, 623
Hubbard, Marian Elizabeth, 624
Hubbard, Ruth Marilla, 624
Hubbs, Laura Cornelia (Clark), 624–25
Hudson, Hilda Phoebe, 625–26
Huggins, Margaret Lindsay (Murray), 626–27
Hug-Hellmuth, Hermine Von, 626
Hughes, Ellen Kent, 627
Hughes, Mary Caroline (Weston), 627–28
Hughes-Schrader, Sally, 628
Hugonnai-Wartha, Vilma, 628
Hummel, Katharine Pattee, 628–29
Hunscher, Helen Alvina, 629
Hunt, Caroline Louisa, 629
Hunt, Eva Verbitsky, 629–30
Hurler, Gertrud (Zach), 631–32
Hurlock, Elizabeth Bergner, 632
Hurston, Zora Neale, 632–33
Hussey, Priscilla Butler, 633
Hutton, Lady Isabel Emilie, 635
Hyde, Ida Henrietta, 635–36
Hyman, Libbie Henrietta, 636–37
Hynes, Sarah, 637
Ianovskaia, Sof'ia Aleksandrovna, 640–41
Ide, Gladys Genevra, 642
Ilg, Frances Lillian, 642–43
Inglis, Elsie (Maude), 643
Irwin, Marian, 643–44
Isaacs, Susan Sutherland (Fairhurst), 644
Iusupova, Saradzhan Mikhailovna, 644–45
Ivanova, Elena Alekseevna, 645–46
Ives, Margaret, 646–47
Iwanowska, Wilhelmina, 647

Jacobi, Mary Corinna Putnam, 648–50
Jacobs, Aletta Henrietta, 650–51
Jacobson, Clara, 651
Jahoda, Marie, 651–53
Janaki Ammal, Edavaleth Kakkat, 653
Janssen, Mme., 653–54
Jeanes, Allene Rosalind, 654–55
Jekyll, Gertrude, 655–56
Jensen, Estelle Louise, 656
Jérémine, Elisabeth (Tschernaieff), 656–57
Jermoljeva, Zinaida Vissarionovna, 657
Jesson, Enid Mary, 657
Jex-Blake, Sophia, 657–59
Jhirad, Jerusha, 659–60
Johnson, Dorothy Durfee Montgomery, 660
Johnson, Hildegarde (Binder), 660
Johnson, Mary, 660
Johnson, Minnie May, 661
Johnston, Mary Sophia, 660–61
Joliot-Curie, Irène, 662–63
Jones, Amanda Theodosia, 663–64
Jones, Eva Elizabeth, 664–65
Jones, Lorella Margaret, 665
Jones, Mary Amanda Dixon, 666
Jones, Mary Cover, 666–67
Jordan-Lloyd, Dorothy, 669
Jordan, Louise, 667–68
Jordan, Sara Claudia (Murray), 668–69
Joslin, Lulu, 669
Josselyn, Irene (Milliken), 669–70
Joteyko, Joséphine, 670–71
Joyce, Margaret Elizabeth, 671
Juhn, Mary, 671
Julian, Hester Forbes (Pengelly), 671–72
Justin, Margaret M., 672
Kaan, Helen Warton, 673
Kaberry, Phyllis Mary, 673–74
Kaczorowska, Zofia, 674–75
Kanouse, Bessie Bernice, 675–76
Karamihailova, Elizabeth/Elizaveta [Kara-Michailova], 676
Kardymowiczowa, Irena, 676
Karlik, Berta, 677
Karp, Carol Ruth (Vander Velde), 677–78
Karpowicz, Ludmila, 678
Karrer, Annie May Hurd, 678
Katz, Rosa Heine, 680
Kaye-Smith, A.Dulcie, 680
Keeler, Harriet Louise, 680
Keen, Angeline Myra, 680–81
Keeney, Dorothea Lilian, 681
Keil, Elsa Marie, 681–82
Keith, Marcia Anna, 682
Keldysh, LIudmila Vsevolodovna, 682
Keller, Ida Augusta, 682–83
Kellerman, Stella Victoria (Dennis), 683–84
Kelley, Louise, 684
Kellogg, Louise, 684–85
Kellor, Frances A., 685
Kelly, Agnes, 685–86
Kelly, Isabel Truesdell, 686–87
Kelly, Margaret G., 687
Kelly, Margaret W., 687
Kendall, Claribel, 687–88
Kendrick, Pearl (Luella), 688

Kennard, Margaret Alice, 688
Kennedy, Cornelia, 688
Kenny, Elizabeth (Sister Kenny), 690
Kent, Elizabeth Isis Pogson, 690
Kent, Grace Helen, 690
Kent, Kate Peck, 690–91
Kenyon, Kathleen Mary, 691–92
Kerling, Louise Catharina Petronella, 692
Keur, Dorothy Louise (Strouse), 692–93
Kharuzina, Vera Nikolaevna, 693
Kielan-Jaworowska, Zofia, 693–94
Kil, Chung-Hee, 694–95
King, Anastasia Kathleen (Murphy), 695
King, Georgina, 695
King, Helen Dean, 695–97
King, Jessie Luella, 697
King, Louisa Boyd (Yeomans), 697–98
Kingsley, Louise, 699
King, Susan (Raymond), 698–99
Kirkbride, Mary Butler, 701
Kirkham, Nellie, 701
Kittrell, Flemmie Pansy, 701–2
Kleegman, Sophia, 702–3
Klein, Marthe, 703
Klein, Melanie (Reizes), 703–4
Kletnova, E.N., 704–5
Klieneberger-Nobel, Emmy, 705–6
Kline, Virginia Harriett, 706
Klosterman, Mary Jo, 706–7
Kluckhohn, Florence Rockwood, 707
Knake, Else, 708
Knopf, Eleanora Frances (Bliss), 708–9
Knott-Ter Meer, Ilse, 709
Knowles, Matilda Cullen, 709–10
Knowles, Ruth Sheldon, 710–11
Knull, Dorothy J., 711
Kobel, Maria, 711
Kochanowská, Adéla, 713
Koch, Helen Lois, 712
Kochina, Pelageia Iakovlevna, 713–14
Koch, Marie Louise, 712–13
Kohler, Elsa, 714
Kohn, Hedwig, 714–15
Kohts, Nadie (LadyChin), 715–16
Kolaczkowska, Maria, 716
Komarovsky, Mirra, 716–17
Koprowska, Irena Grasberg, 717
Korn, Doris Elfriede, 717–18
Korobeinikova, Iuliia Ivanovna, 718
Korringa, Marjorie K., 718–19
Korshunova, Olga Stepanovna, 719
Koshland, Marian (Elliott), 719–20
Kovrigina, Mariia Dmitrievna, 722–23
Kozlova, Ol'ga Grigoriyevna, 724
Krasnosel'skaia, Tat'iana Abramovna, 724–25
Krasnow, Frances, 725
Kraus Ragins, Ida, 725
Kroeber, Theodora Kracaw, 725–26
Krogh, Birthe Marie (Jorgensen), 726–28
Krupskaia, Nadezhda Konstantinovna, 728–29
Krutikhovskaia, Zinaida Aleksandrovna, 729
Kunde, Margaret Meta H., 729–30
L'esperance, Elise Depew Strang, 777–78
Ladd-Franklin, Christine, 731–32
Ladygina-Kots, Nadezhda Nikolaevna, 732–33

Twentieth Century (*cont.*)

Laird, Carobeth (Tucker), 733–34
Laird, Elizabeth Rebecca, 734–35
Lambin, Suzanne, 736
Lamme, Bertha, 736–37
Lampe, Lois, 737–38
Lampl-de Groot, Jeanne, 738
Lancefield, Rebecca Craighill, 739–40
Landes, Ruth (Schlossberg), 740–41
Lane-claypon, Janet Elizabeth, 741–42
Langdon, Ladema M., 742–43
Langecker, Hedwig, 743
Lange, Linda Bartels, 743
Lange, Mathilde Margarethe, 743
Langford, Grace, 743–44
Langsdorff, Toni Von, 744
Lansdell, Kathleen Annie, 745
Lapicque, Marcelle (de Heredia), 745–46
Larsson, Elisabeth, 746
Larter, Clara Ethelinda, 747
Laskey, Amelia (Rudolph), 747–48
Laski, Gerda, 748
Lassar, Edna Ernestine (Kramer), 748–49
Latham, Vida Annette, 750
Latimer, Caroline Wormeley, 750–51
Laubenstein, Linda, 751
Laughlin, Emma Eliza, 751–52
Laurie, Charlotte Louisa, 752
Lawder, Margaret, 754
Lawrence, Barbara, 754
Lawrence, Penelope, 754–55
Lawton, Elva, 755–56
Lazarus, Hilda Mary, 756–57
Leach, Mary Frances, 757
Leacock, Eleanor Burke, 757–58
Leakey, Mary Douglas (Nicol), 758–59
Leavitt, Henrietta Swan, 759
Le Beau, Désirée, 759–60
Lebedeva, Nataliia Ivanova, 760
Lebedeva, Vera Pavlovna, 760–61
Lebour, Marie Victoire, 761–62
Le Breton, Elaine, 762
Leclercq, Suzanne (Céline), 763
Ledingham, Una Christina (Garvin), 763
Lee, Julia Southard, 763
Lee, Rose Hum, 764
Lees, Florence Sarah, 766
Lehmann, Inge, 766
Lehmus, Emilie, 767–68
Lehr, Marguerite (Anna Marie), 769
Leighton, Dorothea (Cross), 769–70
Leland, Evelyn, 770
Le Maître, Dorothée, 770–71
Lepeshinskaia, Ol'ga Borisovna, 773–74
Lepin, Lidiia Karlovna, 774
Lermontova, Ekaterina Vladimirovna, 774–75
Leschi, Jeanne, 776
Leslie (Burr), May Sybil, 776–77
Leverton, Ruth Mandeville, 778
Levi, Hilde, 778–79
Levi-Montalcini, Rita, 779–81
Levine, Lena, 781–82
Levyns, Margaret Rutherford Bryan (Michell), 782
Lewis, Florence Parthenia, 782–83

Lewis, Helen Geneva, 783
Lewis, Isabel (Martin), 783–84
Lewis, Lilian (Burwell), 784
Lewis, Madeline Dorothy (Kneberg), 784–85
Lewis, Margaret Adaline Reed, 785–86
Lewis, Mary Butler, 786–87
Leyel, Hilda Winifred Ivy (Wauton), 787
Libby, Leona Woods Marshall, 787–88
Lieber, Clara Flora, 789–90
Lieu, K.O.Victoria, 790
Lind-Campbell, Hjördis, 791
Lindsten-Thomasson, Marianne, 792–93
Lines, Dorolyn (Boyd), 793
Lin Qiaozhi (Lin Chiao-Chi), 790–91
Lipinska, Mélanie, 794
Lisitsian, Srbui Stepanova, 794
Lisovskaia, Sofiya Nikolaievna, 794
Lister, Gulielma, 795
Litchfield Henrietta Emma (Darwin), 795–96
Litzinger, Marie, 797–98
Lloyd-Green, Lorna, 798
Lloyd, Rachel, 798
Lochman-Balk, Christina, 798–99
Loewe, Lotte Luise Friedericke, 799
Logan, Myra Adele, 800
Logsdon, Mayme (Irwin), 800
Longfield, Cynthia, 801–2
Longstaff, Mary Jane (Donald), 803
Lonsdale, Kathleen (Yardley), 804–5
Lovejoy, Esther Pohl, 806–7
Loveless, Mary Hewitt, 807
Lowater, Frances, 807–8
Lowell, Frances Erma, 808
Lubinska, Liliana, 810
Lu Gwei Djen, 809–10
Luomala, Katharine, 811–12
Lutwak-Mann, Cecelia, 812
Lwoff, Marguerite (Bourdaleix), 812–13
Lynn, Mary Johnstone, 814
Lyubimova, Yelena Aleksandrovna, 815–16
Maccallum, Bella Dytes (Macintosh), 818
Macdonald, Eleanor Josephine, 819
Macdougall, Mary Stuart, 819–20
Macgillavry, Carolina Henriette, 821
Macgill, Elsie Gregory, 820
Macintyre, Sheila Scott, 821–22
Mackay, Helen Marion MacPherson, 824
Macklin, Madge (Thurlow), 824–25
Mackowsky, Marie-Therese, 825–26
Mack, Pauline Beery, 822–24
Maclaughlin, Florence Edith Carothers, 826
MacLean, Ida (Smedley), 826–27
MacLeod, Annie Louise, 827
MacLeod, Grace, 827–28
MacRobert, Rachel (Workman), Lady of Douneside and Cromar, 829
Maddison, Ada Isabel, 829–30
Mahler, Margaret Schönberger, 830–31
Mair, Lucy Philip, 832
Makemson, Maude (Worcester), 832–33
Maling, Harriet Florence (Mylander), 833–34
Malleson, Elizabeth, 834
Mallory, Edith (Brandt), 834–35
Maltby, Margaret Eliza, 835
Man, Evelyn Brower, 835–36

Mangold, Hilde (Proescholdt), 836
Manson, Grace Evelyn, 837
Manton, Irene, 838–39
Manton, Sidnie Milana, 839–40
Maracineanu, Stefania, 841
Margulova, Tereza Kristoforovna, 843
Marinov, Evelina, 843–44
Marlatt, Abby Lillian, 844
Marriott, Alice Lee, 844–45
Marshall, Clara, 845–46
Marshall, Sheina Macalister, 846–47
Marsh, Mary Elizabeth, 845
Martin, Ella May, 847–48
Martin, Emilie Norton, 848
Martinez-Alvarez, Josefina, 849–50
Martin, Lillien Jane, 848
Mason, Carol Y., 850–51
Massee, Ivy, 851
Massevitch, Alla Genrikhovna, 851–52
Massey, Patricia, 852
Massy, Anne L., 852–53
Mateer, Florence Edna, 853
Mateyko, Gladys Mary, 853–54
Mathias, Mildred Esther, 854–55
Mathisen, Karoline, 855
Matikashvili, Nina, 855
Maunder, Annie Scott Dill Russell, 855–56
Maury, Antonia Caetana de Paiva, 856–57
Maury, Carlotta Joaquina, 857–58
Maver, Mary Eugenie, 858
Mayo, Clara Alexandra (Weiss), 860
McAvoy, Blanche, 860
McBride, Katharine Elizabeth, 861
McCarthy, Dorothea Agnes, 861–62
McClintock, Barbara, 862–64
McConney, Florence, 864–65
McCracken, Eileen May, 865
McCracken, Elizabeth (Unger), 865
McCracken, Mary Isabel, 865–66
McCrea, Adelia, 866
McDonald, Janet, 866
McDowell, Louise Sherwood, 866–67
McGee, Anita (Newcomb), 867–68
McGlamery, Josie Winifred, 868
McGraw, Myrtle Byram, 868–69
McGuire, Ruth Colvin Starrett, 869
McHale, Kathryn, 869–70
McKeag, Anna Jane, 870
McKinney, Ruth Alden, 870–71
McLaren, Agnes, 871
McLean, Helen (Vincent), 871–72
McVeigh, Ilda, 872
Mead, Margaret, 872–74
Medes, Grace, 874–75
Medvedeva, Nina Borisovna, 875–76
Meek, Lois Hayden, 876–77
Mee, Margaret Ursula (Brown), 876
Meitner, Lise, 877–79
Mellanby, May (Tweedy), 879–80
Memmler, Ruth Lundeen, 880–81
Mendenhall, Dorothy (Reed), 881–82
Menten, Maud L., 882–83
Meritt, Lucy Taxis (Shoe), 885
Merrill, Helen Abbot, 885–86
Merrill-James, Maud Amanda, 886

Messina, Angelina Rose, 886–87

Metchnikova, Olga (Belokopytova), 887–88

Metzger, Hélène (Bruhl), 888–89

Mexia, Ynes, 889–90

Meyer-Bjerrum, Kirstine, 890–91

Meyer, Margaret Theodora, 890

Meyling-Hylkema, Elisabeth, 891

Michael, Helen Cecilia Desilver Abbott, 891–92

Miles, Catherine Cox, 894

Miller, Bessie Irving, 895–96

Miller, Elizabeth Cavert, 896–97

Minoka-Hill, Lillie Rosa, 897–98

Minor, Jessie Elizabeth, 898

Minot, Ann Stone, 898–99

Mirchink, Maria E., 899

Mitchell, Evelyn Groesbeeck, 900–901

Mitchell, Helen Swift, 901

Mitchell, Mildred Bessie, 905

Miyaji, Kunie, 905–6

Mockeridge, Florence Annie, 906

Moffat, Agnes K., 906–7

Mohr, Erna W., 907

Monin-Molinier, Madeline, 908

Montel, Eliane, 909

Montessori, Maria, 909–10

Mooney-Slater, Rose Camille Ledieu, 910–11

Moore, Anne, 911

Moore, Emmeline, 911

Moore, Lillian Mary, 912

Moore, Mary Mitchell, 912

Moore, Ruth Ella, 912

Morehouse, Kathleen M., 912–13

Morgan, Agnes Fay, 913

Morgan, Ann Haven, 913–14

Morgan, Lilian Vaughan Sampson, 914–15

Morozova, Valentina Galaktionovna, 915–16

Morse, Elizabeth Eaton, 917

Morse, Meroë Marston, 918

Morton, Rosalie Slaughter, 918–20

Moser, Fanny, 920

Mosher, Clelia Duel, 920–21

Mottl, Mária, 921

Moufang, Ruth, 922

Mueller, Kate Heuvner, 922–23

Muir-Wood, Helen Marguerite, 923

Murphy, Lois Barclay, 924–25

Murray, Margaret Alice, 926

Murray, Margaret Mary Alberta, 927

Murray, Margaret Ransone, 928

Murrell, Christine Mary, 928

Muszhat, Aniela, 929

Myers, Mabel Adelaide, 929

Nance, Nellie Ward, 930

Napper, Diana Margaret, 930

Nasymuth, Dorothea Clara (Maude), 930–31

Naumova, Sofiya Nickolaevna, 931

Naylor, Bertha, 931

Neal, Marie Catherine, 932

Needham, Dorothy Mary (Moyle), 932–33

Nelson, Katherine Greacen, 933–34

Nemcová-Hlobilová, Jindriska, 934

Nemir, Rosa Lee, 934–35

Netrasiri, Khunying Cherd-Chalong, 935

Neuburg Maria Feodorovna, 935–36

Neumann, Hanna (Von Caemmerer), 936

Newson, Mary Frances Winston, 937–38

Newton, Margaret, 938–39

Nice, Margaret Morse, 939–40

Nichols, Mary Louise, 940–41

Nicholson, Barbara Evelyn, 942

Nickerson, Dorothy, 942

Nickerson, Margaret (Lewis), 942

Nicosia, Maria Luisa, 942–43

Nieh, Chung-en, 943

Nightingale, Dorothy Virginia, 944

Noddack, Ida Eva Tacke, 947–48

Noel, Emilia Frances, 948–49

Noether, Amalie Emmy, 949–50

Norsworthy, Naomi, 950–51

Northrup, Ann Hero, 953

Novoselova, Aleksandra Vasil'evna, 953

Noyes, Mary Chilton, 953

Nuttall, Zelia Maria Magdalena, 954

Nutting, Mary Adelaide, 954–55

O'Brien, Ruth, 956

O'Connell, Marjorie, 957

O'Reilly, Helen, 964

O'Shea, Harriet Eastabrooks, 967

Obrutsheva, A., 956–57

Odlum, Doris, 957–58

Ogilvie-Gordon, Dame Maria Matilda, 959–60

Ogilvie, Ida Helen, 958–59

Ohnesorge, Lena, 961

Okey, Ruth Eliza, 961

Onslow, Muriel (Wheldale), 962

Oppenheimer, Ella Hutzler, 963

Orent-Kelles, Elsa, 964

Oszast, Janina Celina, 968–69

Owens, Margaret, 969–70

Pabst, Marie B., 971

Pacaud, Suzanne, 971

Page, Mary Maud, 971–72

Paget, Dame Mary Rosalind, 972

Page, Winifred Mary, 972

Paine, Mary Esther (Trueblood), 972–73

Pajchlowa, Maria Leokadia, 973

Pallis, Marietta, 973

Palmer, Dorothy Bryant (Kemper), 974

Palmer, Elizabeth Day, 974–75

Palmer, Katherine Evangeline Hilton (Van Winkle), 975–76

Palmer, Margaretta, 976

Palmer, Miriam Augusta, 976

Palmie, Anna Helene, 977

Panajiotatou, Angeliki, 977–78

Paris, Marie-Louise, 978

Parke, Mary Winifred, 978–79

Parker, Ivy May, 979–80

Parkins, Phyllis Virginia, 980

Parloa, Maria, 980

Parmelee, Ruth A., 980–81

Parrish, Rebecca, 981

Parry, Angenette, 981

Parsons, Elizabeth Ingersoll, 982

Parsons, Eloise, 981–82

Parsons, Elsie Worthington (Clews), 982–83

Parsons, Helen Tracy, 984

Pasternak, Lydia, 985–86

Pasteur, Marie (Laurent), 986

Pastori, Giuseppina, 986–87

Pastori, Maria, 987

Patch, Edith Marion, 987–88

Patrick, Ruth, 988–89

Patterson, Flora Wambaugh, 990

Pattullo, June Grace, 990

Paulsen, Alice Elizabeth, 990–91

Pavenstedt, Eleanor, 991–92

Payne-Gaposchkin, Cecilia Helena, 994–96

Payne, Nellie Maria de Cottrell, 993

Payne, Rose Marise, 993–94

Payne, Sylvia May (Moore), 994

Peak, Helen, 996–97

Pearce, Louise, 997–98

Pearl, Maud Dewitt, 998

Peckham, Elizabeth (Gifford), 999

Peebles, Florence, 999–1000

Pelletier, Madeleine, 1000–1002

Pendleton, Ellen Fitz, 1002–3

Pennington, Mary Engle, 1003–4

Pensa-Joja, Josipa, 1004

Penston, Norah Lilian, 1004

Pereiaslavtseva, Sof'ia Mikhailovna, 1004–5

Pereira de Queiroz, Carlota, 1005–6

Perey, Marguerite Catherine, 1006–7

Perlmann, Gertrude Erika, 1007–8

Perrette, Berthe, 1008

Pertz, Dorothea Frances Matilda, 1009

Petermann, Mary Locke, 1010–11

Péter, Rózsa, 1009–10

Peterson, Edith (Runne), 1011

Peterson, Ruth Dixon, 1011–12

Petran, Elizabeth Irene, 1012

Petrova, Maria Kapitonovna, 1012

Pettersson, Dagmar, 1012–13

Pettit, Hannah Steele, 1013

Pettit, Mary Dewitt, 1013

Pfeiffer, Norma Etta, 1014

Pfiester, Lois Ann, 1015

Phelps, Martha Austin, 1016

Philip, Anna-Ursula, 1016

Phillips, Melba Newell, 1017–18

Phisalix, Marie (Picot), 1018–19

Piazolla-Beloch, Margherita, 1019

Piccard, Sophie, 1019–20

Pickett, Lucy Weston, 1020

Pickford, Grace Evelyn, 1020–21

Pickford, Lilian Mary, 1021–22

Picotte, Susan (La Flesche), 1022–23

Pierce, Madelene Evans, 1023

Pierce, Marion (Armbruster), 1023–24

Pink, Olive Muriel, 1025–26

Pirami, Edmea, 1026–27

Pirie, Antoinette, 1027

Pirret, Ruth, 1027–28

Pittman, Margaret Jane, 1030–31

Pitt-Rivers, Rosalind Venetia, 1028–30

Platt, Julia Barlow, 1031–32

Plehn, Marianne, 1032–33

Plues, Margaret, 1033

Plummer, Helen Jeanne (Skewes), 1033–34

Pockels, Agnes, 1034–35

Pocock, Mary Agard, 1035–36

Pokrovskaia, Irina Mitrofanovna, 1036

Twentieth Century (*cont.*)

Polenova, Yelena Nikolayevna, 1037–38
Pollack, Flora, 1038
Ponse, Kitty, 1038–39
Pool, Judith Graham, 1039–40
Popenoe, Dorothy K.(Hughes), 1040–41
Porada, Edith, 1041–42
Porter, Helen Kemp Archbold, 1042–43
Porter, Lilian E.(Baker), 1043
Porter, Mary Winearls, 1043–44
Potter, Beatrix, 1044–45
Potter, Edith Louise, 1045–46
Potter, Ellen Culver, 1046
Povitsky, Olga Raissa, 1047
Powdermaker, Hortense, 1047–48
Pozarska, Krystyna (Maliszewski), 1048–49
Prádacová, Marcella, 1049
Prankerd, Theodora Lisle, 1049–50
Pressey, Luella (Cole), 1051
Preston, Isabella, 1052
Price, Dorothy, 1053
Price, Dorothy (Stopford), 1054
Prichard, Marjorie Mabel Lucy, 1054
Prince, Helen Walter (Dodson), 1055
Pringle, Mia Lilly (Kellmer), 1056–57
Prins, Ada, 1057
Proctor, Mary, 1057
Proskouriakoff, Tatiana, 1057–58
Pruette, Lorine Livingston, 1058–59
Prytz, Milda Dorothea, 1059
Putnam, Helen Cordelia, 1059–60
Pye, Edith Mary, 1061–62
Quiggle, Dorothy, 1063
Quimby, Edith Smaw (Hinckley), 1063–64
Quirk, Agnes, 1064–65
Rabinoff, Sophie, 1066–67
Rabinovitch-Kempner, Lydia, 1067
Rafatdjah, Safieh, 1067–68
Raisin, Catherine Alice, 1068–69
Ramart-Lucas, Pauline, 1069–70
Ramirez, Rosita Rivera, 1070
Ramsey, Elizabeth Mapelsden, 1070–71
Ramstedt, Eva Julia Augusta, 1071–72
Rancken, Saima Tawast, 1072
Rand, Marie Gertrude, 1072–73
Randoin, Lucie Gabrielle (Fandard), 1073–74
Randolph, Harriet, 1074
Rasskazova, Yelena Stepanovna, 1074–75
Rathbone, Mary May, 1075
Rathbun, Mary Jane, 1075
Ratnayake, May, 1076
Ratner, Sarah, 1076–78
Rauzer-Chernousova, Dagmara M., 1078–79
Ray, Dixy Lee, 1079–80
Raymond-Schroeder, Aimee J., 1080
Rayner, Mabel Mary Cheveley, 1081
Rea, Margaret Williamson, 1081
Reames, Eleanor Louise, 1081
Reddick, Mary Logan, 1081–82
Reder, Ruth Elizabeth, 1082
Redfield, Helen, 1082–83
Reed, Eva M., 1083
Rees, Florence Gwendolen, 1083–84
Rees, Mina Spiegel, 1084–85
Refshauge, Joan, 1086–87

Reichard, Gladys Amanda, 1086–87
Reid, Eleanor Mary (Wynne Edwards), 1087–88
Reid, Mary Elizabeth, 1088
Reimer, Marie, 1088
Reynolds, Doris Livesey, 1090–91
Rhine, Louise Ella (Weckesser), 1091
Rhodes, Mary Louise, 1092
Rice, Elsie (Garrett), 1092
Rice-Wray, Edris, 1092–93
Richards, Audrey Isabel, 1093–94
Richards, Clarice Audrey, 1094–95
Richards, Mary Alice Eleanor, 1097–98
Richards, Mildred Hoge (Albro), 1098
Rich, Mary Florence, 1093
Richter, Emma (Hüther), 1098
Richter, Grete, 1098–99
Riddle, Lumina Cotton, 1099
Ridenour, Nina, 1099–1100
Rigas, Harriett B., 1100
Ring, Barbara Taylor, 1100–1101
Rioch, Margaret J., 1101
Ripley, Martha (Rogers), 1102
Risseghem, Hortense Van, 1102
Ritter, Mary Elizabeth (Bennett), 1103
Riviere, Joan (Verrall), 1103–4
Robb, Jane (Sands), 1104–5
Rob, Catherine Muriel, 1104
Roberts, Charlotte Fitch, 1105–6
Roberts, Dorothea Klumpke, 1106
Roberts, Edith Adelaide, 1106–7
Roberts, Lydia Jane, 1107–8
Robertson, Florence, 1108
Robertson, Jeannie (Smillie), 1108–9
Robertson, Muriel, 1109–10
Robeson, Eslanda Cordoza (Goode), 1110–11
Robinson, Daisy Maude (Orleman), 1111
Robinson, Gertrude Maud (Walsh), 1111–12
Robinson, Harriet May Skidmore, 1112–13
Robinson, Julia (Bowman), 1113–14
Robinson, Margaret (King), 1114
Robinson, Pamela Lamplugh, 1114–15
Robscheit-Robbins, Frieda Saur, 1115
Rockley, Lady Alicia Margaret (Amherst), 1116
Rockwell, Alice Jones, 1116
Rockwell, Mabel MacFerran, 1116–17
Roe, Anne, 1117–19
Roe, Josephine Robinson, 1119
Roger, Muriel, 1119–20
Rogers, Agnes Lowe, 1120
Rogers, Julia Ellen, 1120–21
Rogers, Marguerite Moillet, 1121
Rogick, Mary Dora, 1121–22
Rohde, Eleanour Sinclair, 1122
Róna, Elisabeth, 1122–23
Ronzoni, Ethel (Bishop), 1124
Roper, Ida Mary, 1124
Rose, Glenola Behling, 1125
Rose, Mary Davies Swartz, 1125–26
Rosenfeld, Eva, 1126–27
Ross, Joan Margaret, 1127
Ross, Marion Amelia Spence, 1127
Ross, Mary G., 1127–28
Rothschild, Miriam, 1128–29

Rozanova, Mariia Aleksandrovna, 1132–33
Rozovna, Evdokia Aleksandrovna, 1133
Rubin, Vera (Dourmashkin), 1133–34
Rucker, Augusta, 1134
Rudnick, Dorothea, 1135
Rumbold, Caroline (Thomas), 1136
Russell, Dorothy, 1136–37
Russell, Jane Anne, 1137–38
Ruys (Ruijs), Anna Charlotte, 1138
Sabin, Florence Rena, 1140–42
Sackville-West, Victoria Mary, 1143
Sager, Ruth, 1144–45
Salbach, Hilde, 1145–46
Sale, Rhoda, 1146
Salmon, Eleanor Seely, 1146
Sampson, Kathleen Samuel, 1147
Sanborn, Ethel, 1147
Sandford-Morgan, Elma (Linton), 1148
Sandhouse, Grace Adelbert, 1148–49
Sandiford, Irene, 1149
Sanford, Vera, 1149
Sanger, Margaret Higgins, 1149–51
Sargent, Winifred, 1152–53
Satur, Dorothy May, 1153–54
Saunders, Edith Rebecca, 1154–55
Savulescu, Olga, 1155
Schantz, Viola Shelly, 1156–57
Scharrer, Berta (Vogel), 1158–59
Schiemann, Elisabeth, 1159–60
Schmideberg, Melitta (Klein), 1161–62
Schmid, Elisabeth, 1161
Schmidt-Fischer, Hildegard, 1162–63
Schmidt, Johanna Gertrud Alice, 1162
Schoenfeld, Reba Willits, 1163
Schoental, Regina, 1163–64
Schofield, Brenda Muriel, 1164–65
Schroeder, Edith von, 1165
Schwidetsky, Ilse, 1166–67
Scotland, Minnie (Brink), 1167
Scott, Charlotte Angas, 1167–68
Scott, Flora Murray, 1168
Scott, Henderina Victoria (Klaassen), 1168–69
Scudder, Ida Sophia, 1169–70
Seaman, Elizabeth Cochrane, 1170–71
Sears, Pauline Snedden, 1171–72
Seegal, Beatrice Carrier, 1172–73
Seibert, Florence Barbara, 1173–74
Seligman, Brenda Zara, 1174–75
Semikhatova, Sofia Viktorovna (Karpova), 1175–76
Semple, Ellen Churchill, 1176–77
Sessions, Kate Olivia, 1177–78
Seward, Georgene Hoffman, 1178–79
Shabanova, Anna Nikolaevna, 1179–80
Shakespear, Dame Ethel Mary Reader (Wood), 1180–81
Sharp, Emily Katharine (Dooris), 1181
Sharsmith, Helen Katherine, 1182
Shepardson, Mary, 1184
Sheps, Mindel (Cherniack), 1184–85
Sherif, Carolyn (Wood), 1185
Sherman, Althea Rosina, 1185–86
Sherman, Irene Case, 1186
Sherrill, Mary Lura, 1186–87
Shields, Margaret Calderwood, 1187

Shinn, Milicent Washburn, 1187–88
Shirley, Mary Margaret, 1188
Shishkina, Olga Vasil'yevna, 1188
Short, Jessie May, 1188–89
Shove, Rosamund Flora, 1189
Shtern, Lina Solomonovna, 1189–90
Shubnikova, Ol'ga Mikhailovna, 1190–91
Shulga-Nesterenko, Maria I., 1191–92
Sibelius, Helena, 1192
Sidgwick, Eleanor (Balfour), 1192–93
Signeux, Jeanne, 1194
Silberberg, Ruth Katzenstein, 1194
Simons, Lao Genevra, 1195
Sinclair, Mary Emily, 1195–96
Sinskaia, Evgeniia Nikolaevna, 1196–97
Sitterly, Charlotte Emma (Moore), 1197
Skoczylas-Ciszewska, Kamila, 1197–98
Slater, Ida Lilian, 1198
Slater, Jesse Mabel Wilkins, 1198–99
Slavikova, Ludmila (Kaplanova), 1199
Slye, Maud, 1199–1200
Smart, Helen Edith (Fox), 1200
Smirnovazamkova, Aleksandra Ivanovna, 1201
Smith, Alice Emily, 1201
Smith, Anne Millspaugh (Cooke), 1201–2
Smith, Annie Lorrain, 1202–3
Smith, Annie Morrill, 1203
Smith, Audrey U., 1203–4
Smith, Clara Eliza, 1204–5
Smith, Elizabeth (Hight), 1205
Smith, Emily Adelia (Pidgen), 1205
Smith, Erma Anita, 1205
Smith, Isabel Fothergill, 1206–7
Smith, Isabel Seymour, 1207
Smith, Janice Minerva, 1207
Smith, Margaret Kiever, 1207
Smith, Marian Wesley, 1207–8
Smith, Olive Watkins, 1208–9
Smith, Winifred, 1209
Snelling, Lilian, 1209–10
Snethlage, Emilie, 1210
Snow, Julia Warner, 1210
Snow, Mary (Pilkington), 1210–11
Soddy, Winifred Moller (Beilby), 1211
Sokol'skaya, Anna Nikolayevna, 1211–12
Solis Quiroga, Margarita Delgado de, 1212
Sollas, Igerna Brünhilda Johnson, 1212
Sommer, Anna Louise, 1216
Sorokin, Helen Petrovna (Beratynskaiia),
  1216–17
Soshkina, Elizabeth D., 1217
Souczek, Helene, 1218
South, Lillian Herrald, 1218
Sowton, Sarah C.M., 1218
Spalding, Effie Southworth, 1218
Spencer, Adelin Elam, 1218–19
Sperry, Pauline, 1219
Spiegel-Adolf, Mona, 1219
Sponer-Franck, Hertha Dorothea Elisabeth,
  1219–21
Sprague, Mary Letitia (Green), 1221
Spratt, Ethel Rose, 1221
Stadnichenko, Tasia Maximovna, 1222
Stanley, Louise, 1222
Stanton, Hazel Martha, 1223

Staudinger, Magda (Woit), 1223–24
Stearns, Genevieve, 1224
Steed, Gitel Poznanski, 1224–25
Stefanescu, Sabba, 1225
Stein, Emmy, 1225
Steinhardt, Edna, 1225
Stelfox, Margarita Dawson (Mitchell), 1226
Stenhouse, Caroline, 1226
Stephens, Jane, 1226
Stephenson, Marjory, 1227–29
Stern, Catherine (Brieger), 1229
Stern, Frances, 1229–30
Stevens, Nettie Maria, 1230–32
Stevenson, Matilda Coxe (Evans), 1232–33
Stevenson, Sara (Yorke), 1233
Stewart, Grace Anne, 1234–35
Stewart, Isabel Maitland, 1235–36
Stewart, Maude, 1236
Stewart, Sarah Elizabeth, 1236
Stiebeling, Hazel Katherine, 1236–37
Stieglitz, Mary Rising, 1237–38
Stimson, Barbara Bartlett, 1238
Stinchfield, Sara Mae, 1239
Stokey, Alma Gracey, 1239–40
Stone, Doris Zemurray, 1240–41
Stone, Isabelle, 1241–42
Stopes, Marie Charlotte Carmichael, 1242
Stoppel, Rose, 1242–43
Stose, Anna Isabel (Jonas), 1243–44
Stott, Alicia (Boole), 1244
Strachey, Alix (Sargant-Florence), 1245–46
Strang, Ruth May, 1246
Strassmann-Heckter, Maria Caroline, 1246–47
Stratton Porter, Gene, 1247–48
Strong, Helen Mabel, 1249
Strong, Miriam Carpenter, 1249
Sullivan, Betty Julia, 1250
Sullivan, Elizabeth Teresa, 1250–51
Sullivan, Ellen Blythe, 1251
Summerskill, Edith Clara, 1251–52
Sundquist, Alma, 1252
Sunne, Dagny, 1252
Sutter, Vera Laverne, 1253–54
Svartz, Nanna Charlotta, 1254
Svihla, Ruth Dowell, 1254–55
Swanson, Pearl Pauline, 1255
Swindler, Mary Hamilton, 1256
Swope, Helen Gladys, 1257
Swope, Henrietta (Hill), 1256–57
Sykes, Mary Gladys, 1257–58
Syniewska, Janina, 1258
Szeminska, Alina, 1258
Szeparowicz, Maria, 1258
Szmidt, Jadwiga, 1258–59
Szwajger, Adina Blady, 1259
Taeuber, Irene Barnes, 1260–61
Taft, Jessie, 1261
Takeuchi, Shigeyo (Ide), 1261–62
Talbot, Dorothy Amaury, 1262
Talbot, Marion, 1262–63
Talbot, Mary, 1263
Talbot, Mignon, 1263–64
Taliaferro, Lucy (Graves), 1264
Tammes, Jantine, 1264–65
Tannery, Marie Alexandrine (Prisset), 1265

Taussig, Helen Brooke, 1265–66
Taussky-Todd, Olga, 1267–68
Taylor, Clara Mae, 1268–69
Taylor, Clara Millicent, 1269
Taylor, Eva Germaine Rimington, 1269–70
Taylor, Monica, 1272
Taylor, Rose H., 1272
Teagarden, Florence Mabel, 1272
Tebb, Mary Christine, 1272–73
Telkes, Maria, 1273–74
Tenenbaum, Estera, 1274
Terent'eva, Liudmila Nikolaevna, 1274
Terry, Ethel Mary, 1275
Terzaghi, Ruth Doggett, 1275–76
Tessier, Marguerite, 1276
Tetsuo, Tamayo, 1276
Thelander, Hulda Evelin, 1277
Thelberg, Elizabeth (Burr), 1277–78
Thiselton-Dyer, Lady Harriet Ann (Hooker),
  1278–79
Thomas, Caroline (Bedell), 1279
Thomas, Dorothy Swaine (Thomas), 1279–80
Thomas, Ethel Nancy Miles, 1280–81
Thome, Frances, 1282
Thompson, Caroline Burling, 1282
Thompson, Clara Mabel, 1283
Thompson, Helen, 1283–84
Thompson, Laura, 1284
Thoms, Adah B.(Samuels), 1285–86
Thomson, Jane Smithson, 1286
Thurstone, Thelma Gwinn, 1287–88
Tiburtius, Franziska, 1288–89
Tilden, Evelyn Butler, 1289
Tilden, Josephine Elizabeth, 1289–90
Timofe'eff-Ressovsky, Elena Aleksandrovna
  (Fiedler), 1290–91
Tinsley, Beatrice Muriel (Hill), 1292–93
Tipper, Constance Fligg (Elam), 1293–94
Tisserand, M., 1294
Todd, Emily Sophia, 1294–95
Todd, Ruth, 1295–96
Todtmann, Emmy Mercedes, 1296
Tolman, Ruth (Sherman), 1296–97
Tomaszewicz-Dobrska, Anna, 1297
Tonnelat, Marie-Antoinette (Baudot),
  1297–98
Toops, Laura Chassell (Merrill), 1298
Towara, Hélène, 1299
Town, Clara Harrison, 1299
Tracy, Martha, 1299–1300
Tristram, Ruth Mary (Cardew), 1302
Trotter, Mildred, 1303–4
Tumanskaya, Olga G. (Shirokobruhova),
  1306–7
Tum-Suden, Caroline, 1306
Tunakan, Seniha (Hüsnü), 1307
Tunnicliff, Ruth, 1307–8
Turnbull, Priscilla Freudenheim, 1308
Turner, Abby Howe, 1308
Tyler, Leona Elizabeth, 1309–10
Tyler, Martha G., 1310–11
Tyska, Maria, 1311
Ubisch, Gerta Von, 1312–13
Underhill, Ruth Murray, 1313–14
Ushakova, Elizaveta Ivanovna, 1314

List of Scientists by Time Period

Twentieth Century (*cont.*)

Uvarova, Countess Praskov'ia Sergeevna, 1314–15
Vachell, Eleanor, 1316
Valentine, Lila Hardaway (Meade), 1316–17
Van Beverwijk, Agathe L., 1317–18
Van Blarcom, Carolyn (Conant), 1318–19
Van Deman, Esther Boise, 1319
Van Hoosen, Bertha, 1319–20
Van Rensselaer, Martha, 1320–21
Van Wagenen, Gertrude, 1321–22
Varsanof'eva, Vera Aleksandrovna, 1322–23
Vasilevich, Glafira Makar'evna, 1323
Vaughan, Dame Janet, 1323–24
Vavrinova, Milada, 1324–25
Veil, Suzanne Zélie Pauline, 1325
Veley, Lilian Jane (Nutcombe), 1325
Venning, Eleanor (Hill), 1325–26
Verder, Ada Elizabeth, 1326
Vernon, Magdalen Dorothea, 1327–28
Vesian, Dorothy E. de, 1328
Vickers, Anna, 1328
Vilar, Lola, 1328–29
Vivian, Roxana Hayward, 1329
Vogt, Cécile (Mugnier), 1329–30
Vogt, Marthe Louise, 1330–31
Vold, Marjorie Jean Young, 1331–32
Vyssotsky, Emma T. R. (Williams), 1333
Vytilingam, Kamala Israel, 1333–34
Waelsch, Salome Gluecksohn, 1335–36
Wakefield, Elsie Maud, 1336–37
Wald, Lillian D., 1338–39
Walker, Harriet Ann, 1339–40
Walker, Helen Mary, 1340
Walker, Mary Edward, 1340–41
Walker, Norma (Ford), 1341
Wallace, Louise Baird, 1342
Wall, Florence, 1342
Wallis, Ruth Sawtell, 1342–44
Walworth, Ellen Hardin, 1344–45
Wang Chi Che, 1345
Warga, Mary Elizabeth, 1346–47
Waring, Sister Mary Grace, 1347
Warren, Madeleine (Field), 1347
Washburn, Margaret Floy, 1348–49
Washburn, Ruth Wendell, 1349
Wassell, Helen Erma, 1349
Watkins, Della Elizabeth (Ingram), 1349–50
Watson, Janet Vida, 1350–51
Watt, Helen Winifred Boyd (de Lisle), 1351
Watt, Menie, 1351
Watts, Betty (Monaghan), 1351–52
Way, Katharine, 1352
Weber, Anne Antoinette (Van Bosse), 1352–53
Webster, Mary McCallum, 1353–54
Wedgwood, Camilla Hildegarde, 1354–56
Wedgwood, Mary Louisa (Bell), 1356

Weeks, Alice Mary (Dowse), 1356–57
Weeks, Dorothy W., 1357–58
Weeks, Mary Elvira, 1358
Weightman, Mary, 1358
Weinzierl, Laura (Lane), 1358–59
Weishaupt, Clara Gertrude, 1359
Weisskopf-Joelson, Edith Adele, 1361
Weiss, Marie Johanna, 1359–60
Weiss, Mary Catherine (Bishop), 1360–61
Welch, Betty, 1361
Welch, Winona Hazel, 1361
Weld, Julia Tiffany, 1361
Wellman, Beth Lucy, 1361–62
Wells, Agnes Ermina, 1362
Welsh, Lillian, 1364
Weltfish, Gene, 1364–66
Wertenstein, Mathilde, 1366
Wessel, Bessie (Bloom), 1366
Westall, Mary, 1367
Westcott, Cynthia, 1367–68
West, Ethel, 1367
Westover, Cynthia May, 1368
Wharton, Martha Lucille, 1368
Whedon, Frances Lovisa, 1368–69
Wheeler, Anna Johnson Pell, 1369–70
Wheeler, Elizabeth Lockwood, 1370
Wheeler-Voeglin, Erminie Brooke, 1370
White, Edith Grace, 1370–71
White, Elizabeth Juanita (Greer), 1371
White, Florence Roy, 1371–72
Whitehead, Lilian Elizabeth, 1373
White, Margaret Pirie, 1372
White, Marian Emily, 1373
Whiting, Marian Muriel, 1373
Whiting, Sarah Frances, 1374
Whitney, Mary Watson, 1374–75
Wickens, Aryness Joy, 1376
Wick, Frances Gertrude, 1375–76
Widdowson, Elsie May, 1376–77
Wiebusch, Agnes (Townsend), 1377
Wienholz, Eva, 1377–78
Wilder, Inez (Whipple), 1378
Wiley, Grace Olive, 1378
Willard, Mary Louisa, 1379
Willcock, Edith Gertrude (Gardiner), 1380
Willcox, Mary Alice, 1380
Williams, Anna Wessels, 1380–82
Williams, Cicely Delphine, 1382
Williams, Marguerite (Thomas), 1382
Willmott, Ellen Ann, 1382–83
Wilson, Alice Evelyn, 1383–84
Wilson, Aphra Phyllis, 1384
Wilson, Edith, 1384
Wilson, Fiammetta Worthington, 1385
Wilson, Hilda E., 1385
Wilson, Irene Mossom, 1385
Wilson, Louise (Palmer), 1385–86
Wilson, Lucy, 1386

Wilson, Lucy Langdon (Williams), 1386
Wilson, Mabel Florey, 1386–87
Wilson, May Georgiana, 1387
Wilson, Monica Hunter, 1387–88
Winner, Dame Albertine, 1389
Winton, Kate (Barber), 1390
Wipf, Frances Louise, 1390
Woillard-Roucoux, Geneviève Marie-Aurélie, 1390–91
Woker, Gertrud Jan, 1391–93
Wolf, Katherine, 1393
Wollstein, Martha, 1393–94
Wong Ah Mae, 1394
Woodard, Helen (Quincy), 1395
Woodbridge, Mary Emily, 1395
Wood, Emily Elizabeth, 1394
Wood-Lorz, Thelma (Rittenhouse), 1395–96
Wood, Ruth Goulding, 1395
Woods, Elizabeth Lindley, 1396
Woods, Ethel Gertrude (Skeat), 1396–97
Woodward, Gladys Estelle, 1397
Wooldridge, Elizabeth (Taylor), 1397–98
Woolley, Helen Bradford (Thompson), 1398–99
Woolley, Mildred Thompson, 1399
Wootton, Barbara Adam, 1400
Wormington, Hannah Marie, 1400–1401
Worner, Ruby K., 1401–2
Worthington, Euphemia R., 1402
Wrangell, Margarethe von, 1402–4
Wreschner, Marie, 1404
Wright, Frances May, 1405
Wright, Frances Woodworth, 1405
Wright, Helena Rosa (Lowenfeld), 1405–6
Wright, Katharine, 1406–7
Wrinch, Dorothy Maud, 1407–9
Wu Chien-Shiung, 1409–10
Wundt, Nora, 1410–11
Wyckoff, Delaphine Grace (Rosa), 1411
Wyckoff, Dorothy, 1411
Wylie, Margaret, 1412
Wynne, Frances Elizabeth, 1412
Young, Anne Sewell, 1413
Young, Grace Emily (Chisholm), 1413–14
Young, Leona Esther, 1414–15
Young, Mabel Minerva, 1415–16
Young, Mary Sophie, 1416
Young, Roger Arliner, 1416–17
Zachry, Caroline Beaumont, 1418
Zaklinskaia, Elena Dmitrievna, 1418–19
Zalesskaya-Chirkova, Elena, 1420–21
Zaniewska-Chilpalska, Eugenia, 1421
Zeckwer, Isolde Therese, 1421
Zenari, Silvia, 1421–22
Zhuze, Anastasiya Panteleyemonovna, 1422–23
Ziegarnik, Bliuma, 1423
Zlatarovic, Rely, 1423

LIST OF SCIENTISTS
BY COUNTRY

A

Argentina

Cattoi, Noemí Violeta, 238–39
Chaudet, Maria Casanova De, 248
Dolgopol De Saez, Mathilde, 366
Hunt, Eva Verbitsky, 629–30

Australia

Atkinson, Louisa (Calvert), 58
Balaam, Ellen, 72–73
Brooks, Sarah Theresa, 186
Browne, Ida Alison (Brown), 191–92
Calvert, Catherine Louisa Waring (Atkinson), 223
Campbell, Persia Crawford, 226–27
Carroll, Dorothy, 232–33
Cilento, Lady Phyllis, 257–58
Clisby, Harriet Jemima Winifred, 273–74
Cookson, Isabel Clifton, 289
Crespin, Irene, 302–3
Cuthbert-Browne, Grace Johnston, 320–21
Freeman, Joan Maie, 467–68
Gullett, Lucy E., 536
Hill, Dorothy, 600–601
Hughes, Ellen Kent, 627
Hynes, Sarah, 637
Kenny, Elizabeth (Sister Kenny), 689
King, Georgina, 695
Lloyd-Green, Lorna, 798
Meredith, ,Louisa Anne (Twamley), 884
Pink, Olive Muriel, 1025–26
Refshauge, Joan, 1086–87
Richter, Grete, 1098–99
Sandford-Morgan, Elma (Linton), 1148
Spiegel-Adolf, Mona, 1219
Stone, Constance, 1240

Austria

Adametz, Lotte, 7
Adamson, Joy (Gessner), 8–9
Albrecht, Eleonore, 18
Antoine, Lore, 43–44
Arnold, Magda Blondiau, 53
Artner, Mathilde, 55
Bibring, Grete Lehner, 123–24
Blau, Marietta, 143–44
Böhm-Wendt, Cäcilia, 153–54

Brezina, Maria Aristides, 179
Bussecker, Erna, 215
Cremer, Erika, 301–2
Dengel, Anna Maria, 346–47
Feichtinger, Nora, 439
Fischer, Irene Kaminka, 447
Freud, Anna, 470–72
Freund, Ida, 472–73
Friedlander, Kate, 473
Friedmann, Friederike, 474
Frostig, Marianne Bellak, 476–77
Gabler, Anna, 480
Geiringer Hilda, 493–94
Goldhaber, Sulamith, 514
Hetzer, Hildegard, 593
Hitzenberger, Annaliese, 604–5
Hofmann, Elise, 608
Horowitz, Stephanie, 618
Hug-Hellmuth, Hermine Von, 626
Jacopa of Passau, 651
Jahoda, Marie, 651–53
Juhn, Mary, 671
Karlik, Berta, 677
Klein, Melanie (Reizes), 703–4
Kohler, Elsa, 714
Laski, Gerda, 748
Mayo, Clara Alexandra (Weiss), 860
Meitner, Lise, 877–79
Pfeiffer, Ida (Reyer), 1013–14
Porada, Edith, 1041–42
Rosenfeld, Eva, 1126–27
Schmideberg, Melitta (Klein), 1161–62
Szeparowicz, Maria, 1258
Weisskopf-Joelson, Edith Adele, 1361
Welser, Philippine, 1363
Zlatarovic, Rely, 1423

B

Belgium

Derscheid-Delcourt, Marie, 350
Dubuisson-Brouha, Adele, 378
Hélène, Duchess of Aosta, 581
Leclercq, Suzanne (Céline), 763
Libert, Marie-Anne, 789
Renooz, Céline, 1089–90
Risseghem, Hortense Van, 1102

Bohemia

Agnes of Bohemia, 14
Elizabeth of Bohemia, 416–17
Kablick, Josephine (Ettel), 674
Langecker, Hedwig, 743

Brazil

Durocher, Marie (Josefina Mathilde), 389
Pereira De Queiroz, Carlota, 1005–6

Bulgaria

Karamihailova, Elizabeth/Elizaveta [Kara-Michailova], 676
Marinov, Evelina, 843–44

Byzantium

Comnena (Comnenos), Anna, 283
Pulcheria, Empress, 1059

C

Canada

Abbott, Maude Elizabeth Seymour, 1–2
Anderson, Violet Louise, 37
Bagshaw, Elizabeth Catherine, 67
Banham, Katherine May, 77
Barber, Helen Karen, 77–78
Battle, Helen Irene, 92
Belyea, Helen Reynolds, 110–11
Blatchford, Ellen C., 143
Brooks, Harriet T., 184–85
Cale, F.M., 221
Cummings, Louise Duffield, 309
Cunningham, Gladys Story, 310–11
Derick, Carrie M., 349–50
Donnay, Gabrielle (Hamburger), 367–68
Douglas, Alice Vibert, 372
Dover, Mary Violette, 372–73
Fritz, Madeleine Alberta, 475
Greig, Margaret Elizabeth, 530
Hebb, Catherine Olding, 575–76
Hellstedt, Leone Mcgregor, 581–82
Henshaw, Julia Wilmotte, 584
Hogg, Helen Sawyer, 608–9
Kennard, Margaret Alice, 688
Laird, Elizabeth Rebecca, 734–35
MacGill, Elsie Gregory, 820
McConney, Florence, 864–65
Menten, Maud L., 882–83

Moffat, Agnes K., 906–7
Newton, Margaret, 938–39
Nutting, Mary Adelaide, 954–55
Owens, Margaret, 969–70
Preston, Isabella, 1052
Rigas, Harriett B., 1100
Robertson, Jeannie (Smillie), 1108–9
Schoenfeld, Reba Willits, 1163
Sheps, Mindel (Cherniack), 1184–85
Smith, Margaret Kiever, 1207
Stewart, Grace Anne, 1234–35
Stowe, Emily Howard (Jennings), 1245
Traill, Catharine Parr (Strickland), 1300–1301
Tyndall, A.C., 1311
Venning, Eleanor (Hill), 1325–26
Walker, Norma (Ford), 1341
Wilson, Alice Evelyn, 1383–84

China
Lieu, K.O. Victoria, 790
Lin Qiaozhi (Lin Chiao-Chi), 790–91
Lu Gwei Djen, 809–10
Nieh, Chung-en, 943
Wang Chi Che, 1345
Wang Zhenyi, 1345

Cuba
Carvajales y Camino, Laura M. de, 236

Czechoslovakia
Adamson, Joy (Gessner), 8–9
Agnes of Silesia, 14
Anna of Bohemia, 41
Kochanowská, Adéla, 713
Langecker, Hedwig, 743
Nemcová-Hlobilová, Jindriska, 934
Perlmann, Gertrude Erika, 1007–8
Prádacová, Marcella, 1049
Siegemund, Justine Dittrich, 1193
Slavikova, Ludmila (Kaplanova), 1199
Vavrinova, Milada, 1324–25

D

Denmark
Anna Sophia of Denmark, 41
Anne, Electress of Denmark, 41
Auken, Kirsten (Lomholt), 60–61
Brahe, Sophia, 170
Breyer, Maria Gerdina (Brandwijk), 179
Deichmann, Elisabeth, 337–38
Hammer, Marie Signe, 551
Hansen, Julie Marie Vinter, 554
Krogh, Birthe Marie (Jorgensen), 726–28
Lehmann, Inge, 766
Levi, Hilde, 778–79
Meyer-Bjerrum, Kirstine, 890–91

E

Egypt
Andromache, 39
Hatshepsut, Queen, 566
Hypatia of Alexandria, 637–39
Mary the Jewess, 850
Mentuhetep, Queen, 883–84
Paphnutia the Virgin, 978
Theosebeia, 1278

England. *See* Great Britain

F

Finland
Rancken, Saima Tawast, 1072
Sibelius, Helena, 1192

France
Abramson, Jadwiga, 5
Aemilia, 11
Agnes, Countess of Aix, 14
Alimen, Henriette, 23
Ameline, 28
Antoinette De Bellegarde, 44
Arconville, Geneviève Charlotte D', 49
Beatrice of Savoy, Countess of Provence, 99
Beauvallet, Marcelle Jeanne, 100
Belota [Johanna Belota], 110
Bertereau, Martine de, Baroness de Beausoleil, 119
Berthildis of Chelles, 119
Bertile of Chelles, 120
Bertillon, Caroline Schutze, 120
Biheron, Marie Catherine, 126
Biscot, Jeanne, 129
Blanquies, Lucie, 142–43
Boivin, Marie Gillain, 154
Bonnay, Marchioness Du, 156–57
Bourdel, Léone, 163–64
Bourgeoise, Louyse, 164
Bouteiller, Marcelle, 164
Brès Madeleine (Gébelin), 178–79
Brière, Yvonne, 180
Cambrière, Clarisse, 224
Carroll, Christiane (Mendrez), 232
Cauchois, Yvette, 239
Cauquil, Germaine Anne, 240
Chaix, Paulette Audemard, 242
Chamié, Catherine, 243
Chauchard, B., 248
Clarisse of Rotomago (or Clarice of Rouen), 259
Clothilde of Burgundy, 274
Converse, Jeanne, 286
Cordier, Marguerite Jeanne, 292
Coste Blanche, Marie de, 295
Cotelle, Sonia, 295–96
Coudreau, Octavie, 296
Curie, Marie (Maria Sklodowska), 311–17
De Bréauté, Eléonore-Nell-Suzanne, 335
Deflandre-Rigaud, Marthe, 336
Déjerine-Klumpke, Augusta, 338–39
De La Marche, Marguerite Du Tertre, 341
Delauney, Marguerite de Staël, 342
De Staël Holstein, Anne Louise Germaine Necker, 350
De Valois, Madame, 353
Diana of Poitiers, 354
Du Châtelet, Gabrielle-Emilie Le Tonnelier de Breteuil (Marquise), 378–80
Du Coudray, Angelique (Marguerite Le Boursier), 381
Du Luys, Guillemette, 381
Dumée, Jeanne, 382
Dupré, Marie, 388
Durocher, Marie (Josefina Mathilde), 389
Edwards-Pilliet, Blanche, 403–5
Flammel, Perrenelle, 451

Fouquet, Marie De Maupeou, Vicomtesse De Vaux, 461
Frances of Brittany, 464
Françoise, Marie-Thérèse, 464
Friant, M., 473
Galabert, Renee, 481
Genet-Varcin, E., 494
Germain, Sophie, 496–97
Gilette of Narbonne, 502
Giraud, Marthe, 504
Goldsmith, Marie, 517
Grignan, Francoise Marguerite de Sevigne, Comtesse de, 532
Guyton De Morveau, Claudine Poullet Picardet, 539
Hainault, Countess of, 543
Haoys (La Meresse), 555
Héloïse, 582–83
Herrad of Hohenburg, 585–86
Hersende. Abbess of Fontevrault, 590
Janssen, Mme., 653–54
Joliot-Curie, Irène, 662–63
La Chapelle, Marie Louise Dugès, 731
Lalande, Marie Jeanne Amélie Harlay Lefrancais de, 735–36
Lambin, Suzanne, 736
Lapicque, Marcelle (de Heredia), 745–46
La Sablière, Marguerite Hessein, Madame de, 747
La Vigne, Anne de, 752
Lavoisier, Marie Anne Pierrette Paulze, 752–53
Le Breton, Elaine, 762
Le Maître, Dorothée, 770–71
Lepaute, Nicole-Reine Hortense (Etable de La Brière), 772–73
Leschi, Jeanne, 776
Lipinska, Mélanie, 794
Lwoff, Marguerite (Bourdaleix), 812–13
Mahout, Countess of Artois, 831
Marillac, Louise de, 843
Metchnikova, Olga (Belokopytova), 887–88
Metzger, Hélène (Bruhl), 888–89
Meurdrac, Marie, 889
Michelet, Athénaïs (Mialaret), 892–94
Monin-Molinier, Madeline, 908
Montel, Eliane, 909
Necker, Susanne (Curchod), 932
Paris, Marie-Louise, 978
Parthenay, Catherine de (Dame de Rohan), 985
Pasteur, Marie (Laurent), 986
Pelletier, Madeleine, 1000–1002
Perette of Rouen, 1006
Perey, Marguerite Catherine, 1006–7
Péronelle, 1008
Perrette, Berthe, 1008
Phisalix, Marie (Picot), 1018–19
Pierry, Louise Elizabeth du, 1024
Pisan, Christine de, 1028
Radegonde, 1067
Ramart-Lucas, Pauline, 1069–70
Randoin, Lucie Gabrielle (Fandard), 1073–74
Renooz, Céline, 1089–90
Royer, Clémence, 1129–32

France (*cont.*)
Sablière, Marguerite (Hessein) de la, 1142–43
Sara of Saint-Gilles, 1151
Serment, Louise-Anastasia, 1177
Signeux, Jeanne, 1194
Tannery, Marie Alexandrine (Prisset), 1265
Tessier, Marguerite, 1276
Tisserand, M., 1294
Tonnelat, Marie-Antoinette (Baudot),
    1297–98
Veil, Suzanne Zélie Pauline, 1325
Vilmorin, Elisa (Bailly), 1329
Vogt, Cécile (Mugnier), 1329–30

G

Germany
Albrecht, Eleonore, 18
Albrecht, Grete, 19
Altmann, Margaret, 27
Andreas-Salomé, Louise Lelia, 38–39
Anna Sophia of Hesse, 41
Artner, Mathilde, 55
Auerbach, Charlotte, 59–60
Baum, Marie, 92
Bayern, Therese Von, 95–96
Becker-Rose, Herta, 101–2
Beckman, A., 102
Bender, Wilma, 112
Berger, Katharina Bertha Charlotte, 118
Beutler, Ruth, 120–21
Birstein, Vera, 129
Bluhm, Agnes, 149–50
Böhm-Wendt, Cäcilia, 153–54
Brüch, Hilde, 195
Brückner, Frau Dr., 195
Brunetta, 196
Bühler, Charlotte Bertha (Malachowski),
    204–5
Bülbring, Edith, 205
Bussecker, Erna, 215
Catherine Ursula, Countess of Baden, 237
Chasman, Renate Wiener, 247–48
Cremer, Erika, 301–2
Cunitz, Maria, 309–10
Dane, Elisabeth, 324
Demud, 346
Dietrich, Amalie, 356–57
Donnay, Gabrielle (Hamburger), 367–68
Doreck, Hertha (Walburger Doris Sieverts),
    369–70
Dorenfeldt, Margot, 371
Ebers, Edith (Knote), 396
Edinger, Johanna Gabrielle Otellie (Tilly),
    400–401
Eimmart, Marie Claire, 409
Eleanora, Duchess of Troppau and Jagerndorf,
    414
Elizabeth of Schönau, 417
Erdmann, Rhoda, 422–25
Erdmuthe, Sophie, 425
Erxleben, Dorothea Christiana (Leporin),
    425–26
Esdorn, Ilse, 427–28
Fenchel, Käte (Sperling), 440–41
Flügge-Lotz, Irmgard, 456–57

Fonovits-Smereker, H., 458
Friedmann, Friederike, 474
Fromm, Erika Oppenheimer, 475–76
Fuss, Margarita, 479
Gabler, Anna, 480
Goeppert Mayer, Maria Gertrud Käte, 510–11
Goldschmidt, Frieda, 516
Gruhn, Ruth, 533–34
Gsell, Maria Dorothea Henrica (Graf), 535
Haber-Immerwahr, Clara, 540–41
Haccius, Barbara, 541–42
Hausser, Isolde (Ganswindt), 566–68
Hebel, Medicienne, 576
Hedwig of Silesia, Saint, 577
Heimann, Berta, 579
Heimann, Paula, 579–80
Hellman, Johanna, 581
Herrad of Hohenburg, 585–86
Herschel, Caroline Lucretia, 587–89
Hertwig, Paula, 591–92
Hertz, Mathilde, 592
Herxheimer, Franziska, 592
Hildegard of Bingen, 596–98
Hirschfeld-Tiburtius, Henriette (Pagelsen),
    602–3
Horenburg, Anna Elizabeth Von, 617
Horney, Karen Clementine (Danielsen),
    617–18
Hroswitha of Gandersheim, 624
Hurler, Gertrud (Zach), 631–32
Johnson, Hildegarde (Binder), 660
Katz, Rosa Heine, 680
Keil, Elizabeth Marbareta, 681
Keller, Ida Augusta, 682–83
Kirch, Christine, 700
Kirch, Margaretha, 700
Kirch, Maria Margaretha Winkelmann,
    700–701
Klieneberger-Nobel, Emmy, 705–6
Knake, Else, 708
Knott-ter Meer, Ilse, 709
Kobel, Maria, 711
Kohn, Hedwig, 714–15
Korn, Doris Elfriede, 717–18
Kunde, Margaret Meta H., 729–30
Langecker, Hedwig, 743
Langsdorff, Toni Von, 744
Laski, Gerda, 748
Lehmus, Emilie, 767–68
Levi, Hilde, 778–79
Loewe, Lotte Luise Friedericke, 799
Löser, Margaret Sibylla Von, 805
Lutwak-Mann, Cecelia, 812
Mackowsky, Marie-Therese, 825–26
Mangold, Hilde (Proescholdt), 836
Mechthild of Magdeburg, 874
Meigler, Marie J., 877
Merian, Maria Sibylla, 884–85
Mohr, Erna W., 907
Moser, Fanny, 920
Moufang, Ruth, 922
Neumann, Elsa, 936
Neumann, Hanna (Von Caemmerer), 936
Noddack, Ida Eva Tacke, 947–48
Noether, Amalie Emmy, 949–50

Nolde, Hélène Aldegonde de, 348
Nolte, Margarethe, 950
Ohnesorge, Lena, 961
Philip, Anna-Ursula, 1016
Plehn, Marianne, 1032–33
Pockels, Agnes, 1034–35
Rabinovitch-Kempner, Lydia, 1067
Radegonde, 1067
Richter, Emma (Hüther), 1098
Robscheit-Robbins, Frieda Saur, 1115
Rodde, Dorothea von (Schlözer), 1117
Salbach, Hilde, 1145–46
Sara of Würzburg, 1151
Scharrer, Berta (Vogel), 1158–59
Schiemann, Elisabeth, 1159–60
Schmid, Elisabeth, 1161
Schmidt-Fischer, Hildegard, 1162–63
Schmidt, Johanna Gertrud Alice, 1162
Schroeder von , Edith, 1165
Schurman, Anna Marie Van, 1165–66
Schwidetsky, Ilse, 1166–67
Siebold, Charlotte Marianne Heidenreich Von,
    1193
Siebold, Josepha (Henning) Von, 1193
Silberberg, Ruth Katzenstein, 1194
Snethlage, Emilie, 1210
Sponer-Franck, Hertha Dorothea Elisabeth,
    1219–21
Staudinger, Magda (Woit), 1223–24
Stein, Emmy, 1225
Stoppel, Rose, 1242–43
Strassmann-Heckter, Maria Caroline, 1246–47
Taussky-Todd, Olga, 1267–68
Tiburtius, Franziska, 1288–89
Todtmann, Emmy Mercedes, 1296
Ubisch, Gerta Von, 1312–13
Vogt, Marthe Louise, 1330–31
Waelsch, Salome Gluecksohn, 1335–36
Welser, Philippine, 1363
Wienholz, Eva, 1377–78

Great Britain
Acton, Frances (Knight), 6
Aelfleda, 11
Aitken, Janet Kerr, 16–17
Alcock, Nora Lilian Leopard, 19
Aldrich-Blake, Louisa Brandreth, 19–20
Alexander, Frances Elizabeth Somerville
    (Caldwell), 21–22
Allan, Mary Eleanor (Mea), 23
Allen, Eliza (Stevens), 25
Aluwihare, Florence Kaushalya (Ram), 27–28
Amherst, Sarah (Archer), Countess, 31
Anderson, Elizabeth Garrett, 34–35
Anderson, Louisa Garrett, 36–37
Anderton-Smith, Mrs.W., 37
Angst-Horridge, Anita, 40
Anning, Mary, 41–42
Ann Medica of York, 40–41
Apsley (Hutchinson), Lady Lucy, 47
Arber, Agnes (Robertson), 47–48
Arden, Lady Margaret Elizabeth (Spencer
    Wilson), 49
Armitage, Eleanora, 51–52
Armitage, Ella Sophia A.(Bulley), 52
Armitt, Annie Maria, 52

Armitt, Mary Louisa, 52–53
Armitt, Sophia, 53
Ashby, Winifred Mayer, 55
Astell, Mary, 56–57
Atkins, Anna, 57
Atkins, Louisa Catherine Fanny, 57–58
Attersoll, Maria, 58
Atwood, Martha Maria, 59
Ayrton, Hertha Marks, 62–63
Ayrton, Matilda (Chaplin), 64
Baker, Anne Elizabeth, 70
Baker, Sarah Martha, 71–72
Balfour, Margaret Ida, 73
Bancroft, Nellie, 75
Banham, Katherine May, 77
Banks, Sarah Sophia, 76–77
Barber, Mary Elizabeth (Bowker), 78
Barkly, Lady Anna Maria (Pratt), 79
Barkly, Lady Elizabeth Helen (Timins or Timmins), 79
Barlow, Emma Nora (Darwin), 80
Barnard, Alicia Mildred, 80–81
Barnard, Lady Anne (Henslow), 81
Barnard, Lady Anne (Lindsay), 81
Barnes (Berners), Juliana, 81–82
Bate, Dorothea Minola Alice, 90
Bateson, Anna, 91
Bateson, Beatrice, 91
Bauer, Grace M., 92
Beaufort, Countess Margaret, 100
Beaufort, Harriet Henrietta, 99–100
Becker, Lydia Ernestine, 101
Beck, Sarah Coker (Adams), 100–101
Beever, Mary, 104
Beever, Susan, 104–5
Behn, Aphra, 105–8
Bell, Julia, 109
Benett, Etheldred, 114
Bengston, Ida Albertina, 114–15
Benson, Margaret Jane, 116–17
Bentham, Ethel, 117
Bentham, Lady Mary Sophia (Fordyce), 117
Bentinck, Margaret Cavendish (Harley), Duchess of Portland, 117–18
Berridge, Emily Mary, 118–19
Berthagyta, Abbess, 119
Besant, Annie (Wood), 120
Bidder, Anna McClean, 125
Bidder, Marion Greenwood, 125–26
Bishop, Ann, 129–30
Bishop, Isabella Lucy Bird, 131
Blackburne, Anna, 134–35
Blackburn, Kathleen Bever, 133–34
Blacker, Margaret Constance Helen, 135
Blackwell, Elizabeth, 136
Blackwell, Elizabeth Marianne, 138
Blackwell, Emily, 138–39
Blackwood, Beatrice Mary, 139
Blagg, Mary Adela, 139–40
Boley, Gertrude Maud, 155
Bolton, Edith, 155
Boole, Mary (Everest), 158–59
Boswell, Katherine Cumming, 163
Brazier, Mary Agnes Burniston (Brown), 174–75

Brenchley, Winifred Elsie, 177
Brightwen, Eliza (Elder), 181
Brooke, Winifred, 184
Brown, Dame Edith Mary, 188–89
Browne, Lady Isabel Mary (Peyronnet), 192–93
Brown, Elizabeth, 189
Bruce, Eileen Adelaide, 194–95
Bryan, Margaret, 198–99
Bryant, Sophie (Willock), 199–200
Buchanan, Florence, 200
Buckland, Mary Morland, 202
Buckley, Arabella, 202–3
Bülbring, Edith, 205
Burges, Mary Anne, 208–9
Burkill, Ethel Maud (Morrison), 209
Burlingham, Dorothy (Tiffany), 209–10
Burtt Davy, Alice (Bolton), 212
Bury, Elizabeth (Lawrence), 212–13
Bury, Priscilla Susan (Falkner), 213–14
Busk, Lady Marian (Balfour), 215
Byron, Augusta Ada, Countess of Lovelace, 217
Cadbury, Dorothy Adlington, 218
Callcott, Lady Maria Graham, 223
Calvert, Catherine Louisa Waring (Atkinson), 223
Campbell, Dame Janet Mary, 226
Campbell, May Sherwood, 226
Carne, Elizabeth Catherine (Thomas), 228–29
Carter, Elizabeth, 234–35
Cartwright, Dame Mary Lucy, 235
Catlow, Maria Agnes, 237
Cavendish, Margaret, Duchess of Newcastle, 240–41
Cellier, Elizabeth, 241–42
Chandler, Elizabeth, 243–44
Chandler, Marjorie Elizabeth Jane, 244
Charlotte Sophia, Queen, 246
Charsley, Fanny Anne, 246
Cheesman, Lucy Evelyn, 248–49
Chesser, Elizabeth (Sloan), 250
Chick, Dame Harriette, 250–51
Chisholm, Catherine, 253
Chodak-Gregory, Hazel Haward (Cuthbert), 254
Clarke, Lilian Jane, 265
Clarke, Louisa (Lane), 265
Clark, Jessie Jane, 262
Clements, Margaret, 268–69
Clifford, Lady Anne, 273
Clisby, Harriet Jemima Winifred, 273–74
Coade, Eleanor, 274
Cobbe, Anne Phillipa, 276
Cobbe, Margaret, 277
Cockburn, Catharine (Trotter), 278
Coignou, Caroline Pauline Marie, 279
Collet, Clara Elizabeth, 281
Colvin, Brenda, 282–83
Comyns-Lewer, Ethel, 284
Conway, Anne, 286–87
Conway, Elsie (Phillips), 287
Cook, A.Grace, 287–88
Cooke, Alice Sophia (Smart), 288
Cooper, Sybil, 291

Coryndon, Shirley (Cameron), 295
Crane, Agnes, 300
Crosfield, Margaret Chorley, 306
Cuffe, Lady Charlotte Wheeler (Williams), 307
Cullis, Winifred, 307–8
Cumming, Lady Gordon (Eliza Maria Campbell), 308
Cutler, Catherine, 321
Dalby, Mary, 322
Dale, Elizabeth, 322–23
Dallas, A.E.M.M., 323
Darwin, Emma (Wedgwood), 325–26
David, Florence N., 328
Davy, Lady Joanna Charlotte (Flemmich), 333–34
Dawson, Maria, 334
Day, Gwendolen Helen, 334–35
De Fraine, Ethel Louise, 336–37
Delaney (or Delany), Mary (Granville), 341
Delf-Smith, Ellen Marion, 343
De Mole, Fanny Elizabeth, 345
De Vesian, Dorothy Ellis, 353
Dimsdale, Helen Easdale (Brown), 358–59
Dodgson, Sarah Elizabeth, 364
Dougal, Margaret Douie, 372
Downie, Dorothy G., 374
Drake, Judith, 375
Drew, Kathleen Mary, 376–77
Duncan, Ursula Katherine, 385–86
Durham, Mary Edith, 388–89
Earle, Marie Theresa (Villiers), 394
Edgell, Beatrice, 399
Edkins, Nora Tweedy, 401–2
Eggleton, Marion Grace (Palmer), 406–7
Elderton, Ethel, 413
Elgood, Cornelia Bonté Sheldon (Amos), 414–15
Elles, Gertrude Lilian, 417–18
Etheldrida, Queen, 428
Euphemia, Abbess of Wherwell, 428
Evans, Alice Margaret, 430
Everard, Barbara Mary Steyning, 430
Everett, Alice, 428–30
Evershed, Mary Orr, 431–32
Eves, Florence, 432
Ewing, Elizabeth Raymond (Burden), 432
Eyton, Charlotte, 432
Fage, Winifred E., 433
Farenden, Emma, 433
Farquharson, Marian Sarah (Ridley), 435
Fawcett, Phillipa Garrett, 436–37
Fell, Honor Bridget, Dame, 439–40
Fielding, Mary Maria (Simpson), 444–45
Fiennes, Celia, 445
Finch, Louisa (Thynne), Countess of Aylesford, 446
Fishenden, Margaret White, 448–49
Fish, Margery, 447–48
Fitzgerald, Mabel Purefoy, 450
Fleming, Amalia Coutsouris, Lady, 451
Foley, Mary Cecilia, 457
Forbes, Helena Madelain Lamond, 458
Forster, Mary, 459
Fraine, Ethel Louise De, 464

Great Britain *(cont.)*

Frampton, Mary, 464
Franklin, Rosalind Elsie, 465–66
Freund, Ida, 472–73
Friedlander, Kate, 473
Fulhame, Elizabeth, 478
Gardiner, Margaret Isabella, 483
Gardner, Elinor Wight, 483–84
Garlick, Constance, 486
Garnett, Alice, 486–87
Garrod, Dorothy Anne Elizabeth, 488–89
Gatty, Margaret (Scott), 490–91
Geldart, Alice Mary, 494
Gepp, Ethel Sarel (Barton), 495
Gibbons, E. Joan, 498–99
Gibbs, Lilian Suzette, 500
Gifford, Isabella, 500
Gillett, Margaret (Clark), 503
Godfery, Hilda Margaret, 510
Goodyear, Edith, 519–20
Grainger, Jennie, 522
Gray, Maria Emma (Smith), 523–24
Gregory, Eliza Standerwick (Barnes), 528
Griffiths, Amelia Elizabeth, 531
Griffiths, Amelia Warren (Rogers), 531
Grundy, Clara, 534
Grundy, Ellen, 534
Grundy, Maria Ann, 534
Gunn, Mary Davidson, 537–38
Gwynne-Vaughan, Dame Helen Charlotte
    Isabella (Fraser), 539
Halket, Ann Cronin, 544
Halket, Lady Anne, 544–45
Hall, Agnes C., 545
Hall, Kate Marion, 546
Hanson, Emmeline Jean, 554–55
Hardcastle, Frances, 555
Harding, Anita, 556
Harrison, Jane Ellen, 558
Harrison, Janet Mitchell Marr, 559
Hart, J.B., 560
Harvey, Elizabeth, 561
Haslett, Dame Caroline, 563–64
Hassall, Bessie Florence (Cory), 564
Hastings, Barbara, Marchioness of, 565
Hawkes, Jacquetta (Hopkins), 569
Hawkins, Kate, 570
Hawkins, Mary Esther (Sibthorp), 570
Hayward, Ida Margaret, 572
Hebb, Catherine Olding, 575–76
Heimann, Paula, 579–80
Hendricks, Eileen M., 583
Henrey, Blanche Elizabeth Edith, 584
Henry, Caroline (Orridge), 584
Henshaw, Julia Wilmotte, 584
Herford, Ethilda B.Meakin, 585
Heslop, Mary Kingdon, 592–93
Hewer, Dorothy, 594
Higgins, Vera (Cockburn), 596
Hitchens, Ada Florence R., 604
Hoare, Sarah, 605
Hoby, Lady, 606
Hodgkin, Dorothy Mary Crowfoot, 606–7
Hodgson, Elizabeth, 607
Hoggan, Ismé Aldyth, 609

Holton, Pamela Margaret (Watson-Williams),
    613
Homer, Annie, 613–14
Hooker, Frances Harriet Henslow, 614–15
Hopkins, Esther (Burton), 616
Howard, Louise Ernestine (Matthaei), Lady,
    619–20
Howitt, Mary (Botham), 623–24
Hudson, Hilda Phoebe, 625–26
Hughes, Mary Caroline (Weston), 627–28
Hussey, Anna Maria (Reed), 633
Hutton, Lady Isabel Emilie, 635
Huxley, Henrietta Heathorn, 635–36
Ibbetson, Agnes (Thomson), 641
Isaacs, Susan Sutherland (Fairhurst), 644
Jacson, Maria Elizabeth, 651
Jahoda, Marie, 651–53
James, Lucy Jones, 653
Jekyll, Gertrude, 655–56
Jesson, Enid Mary, 657
Jex-Blake, Sophia, 657–59
Johanna (Johanne, Joanna), 660
Johnson, Mary, 660
Johnston, Mary Sophia, 660–61
Jones, Katharine, Viscountess Ranelagh, 665
Jordan-Lloyd, Dorothy, 669
Juhn, Mary, 671
Julian, Hester Forbes (Pengelly), 671–72
Kaberry, Phyllis Mary, 673–74
Katherine, La Surgiene (The Surgeon), 680
Kaye-Smith, A.Dulcie, 680
Kelly, Agnes, 685–86
Kent, Elizabeth, 690
Kent, Elizabeth Isis Pogson, 690
Kenyon, Kathleen Mary, 691–92
Kingsley, Mary Henrietta, 699
Kirby, Elizabeth, 699–700
Kirkham, Nellie, 701
Klein, Melanie (Reizes), 703–4
Klieneberger-Nobel, Emmy, 705–6
Kohn, Hedwig, 714–15
Lane-Claypon, Janet Elizabeth, 741–42
Lankester, Phoebe (Pope), 744–45
Larter, Clara Ethelinda, 747
Latham, Vida Annette, 750
Laurie, Charlotte Louisa, 752
Lawrence, Penelope, 754–55
Lebour, Marie Victoire, 761–62
Ledingham, Una Christina (Garvin), 763
Lee, Sarah Wallis Bowdich, 765
Lees, Florence Sarah, 766
Leslie (Burr), May Sybil, 776–77
Leyel, Hilda Winifred Ivy (Wauton), 787
Lister, Gulielma, 795
Litchfield Henrietta Emma (Darwin), 795–96
Lomax, Elizabeth Anne (Smithson), 800
Longfield, Cynthia, 801–2
Longstaff, Mary Jane (Donald), 803
Lonsdale, Kathleen (Yardley), 804–5
Loudon, Jane (Webb), 805–6
Lowater, Frances, 807–8
Lu Gwei Djen, 809–10
Lutwak-Mann, Cecelia, 812
Lyell, Katharine Murray (Horner), 813
Lyell, Mary Elizabeth (Horner), 813

Macaulay, Catharine (Sawbridge), 817–18
MacCallum, Bella Dytes (Macintosh), 818
Mackay, Helen Marion MacPherson, 824
Maclean, Ida (Smedley), 826–27
Maddison, Ada Isabel, 829–30
Mair, Lucy Philip, 832
Malleson, Elizabeth, 834
Mantell, Mary Ann (Woodhouse), 837–38
Manton, Irene, 838–39
Manton, Sidnie Milana, 839–40
Marcet, Jane Haldimand, 842–43
Margery, 843
Martineau, Harriet, 849
Mason, Marianne Harriet, 851
Massee, Ivy, 851
Matilde, 855
Maunder, Annie Scott Dill Russell, 855–56
May, Caroline Rebecca, 859–60
McNab, Catherine Mary, 872
Measham, Charlotte Elizabeth (Cowper), 874
Mee, Margaret Ursula (Brown), 876
Mellanby, May (Tweedy), 879–80
Meredith, ,Louisa Anne (Twamley), 884
Meyer, Margaret Theodora, 890
Mildmay, Grace Sherrington, 894
Mill, Harriet Hardy Taylor, 894–95
Mitchell, Anna Helena, 900
Mockeridge, Florence Annie, 906
Molesworth, Caroline, 907–8
Monson, Lady Anne Vane, 908
Montague, Lady Mary Wortley, 908–9
Morehouse, Kathleen M., 912–13
Morgan, Elizabeth Frances, 914
Moriarity, Henrietta Maria, 915
Muir-Wood, Helen Marguerite, 923
Murray, Amelia Matilda, 925
Murray, Lady Charlotte, 925–26
Murray, Margaret Alice, 926
Murrell, Christine Mary, 928
Napper, Diana Margaret, 930
Nasymuth, Dorothea Clara (Maude), 930–31
Naylor, Bertha, 931
Needham, Dorothy Mary (Moyle), 932–33
Neumann, Hanna (Von Caemmerer), 936
Nevill, Lady Dorothy Frances (Walpole),
    936–37
Newbigin, Marion Isabel, 937
Nicholson, Barbara Evelyn, 942
Nightingale, Florence, 944–46
Nihell, Elizabeth, 946
Noel, Emilia Frances, 948–49
North, Marianne, 951–52
Nuttall, Gertrude (Clarke), 953–54
O'Malley, Lady Emma Winifred (Hardcastle),
    962
Odlum, Doris, 957–58
Onslow, Muriel (Wheldale), 962
Ormerod, Eleanor Anne, 965–67
Pacaud, Suzanne, 971
Page, Mary Maud, 971–72
Paget, Dame Mary Rosalind, 972
Paget, Rose Elizabeth, 972
Page, Winifred Mary, 972
Pallis, Marietta, 973
Parke, Mary Winifred, 978–79

Parsons, Mary, Countess of Rosse, 984–85
Payne-Gaposchkin, Cecilia Helena, 994–96
Payne, Sylvia May (Moore), 994
Pechey-Phipson, Mary Edith, 998–99
Penston, Norah Lilian, 1004
Perceval, Anne Mary (Flower), 1004
Pernell, 1008
Pertz, Dorothea Frances Matilda, 1009
Philip, Anna-Ursula, 1016
Philpot, Elizabeth, 1018
Philpot, Margaret, 1018
Philpot, Mary, 1018
Pickford, Grace Evelyn, 1020–21
Pickford, Lilian Mary, 1021–22
Piozzi, Hester Lynch, 1026
Pirie, Antoinette, 1027
Pitt-Rivers, Rosalind Venetia, 1028–30
Plues, Margaret, 1033
Pope, Clara Maria (Leigh), 1040
Popenoe, Dorothy K.(Hughes), 1040–41
Porter, Helen Kemp Archbold, 1042–43
Porter, Lilian E.(Baker), 1043
Porter, Mary Winearls, 1043–44
Potter, Beatrix, 1044–45
Potts, Eliza, 1046–47
Prankerd, Theodora Lisle, 1049–50
Pratt, Anne, 1050–51
Preston, Isabella, 1052
Prestwich, Grace Anne (Milne) M'Call, 1052–53
Prichard, Marjorie Mabel Lucy, 1054
Pringle, Mia Lilly (Kellmer), 1056–57
Pye, Edith Mary, 1061–62
Raisin, Catherine Alice, 1068–69
Rathbone, Mary May, 1075
Rayner, Mabel Mary Cheveley, 1081
Rees, Florence Gwendolen, 1083–84
Reid, Eleanor Mary (Wynne Edwards), 1087–88
Reynolds, Doris Livesey, 1090–91
Rice, Elsie (Garrett), 1092
Richards, Audrey Isabel, 1093–94
Richards, Mary Alice Eleanor (Stokes), 1097–98
Rich, Mary Florence, 1093
Riviere, Joan (Verrall), 1103–4
Robb, Mary Anne (Boulton), 1105
Rob, Catherine Muriel, 1104
Roberts, Mary, 1108
Robertson, Muriel, 1109–10
Robinson, Gertrude Maud (Walsh), 1111–12
Robinson, Harriet May Skidmore, 1112–13
Robinson, Pamela Lamplugh, 1114–15
Rockley, Lady Alicia Margaret (Amherst), 1116
Rohde, Eleanour Sinclair, 1122
Roper, Ida Mary, 1124
Roper, Margaret, 1124–25
Ross, Joan Margaret, 1127
Rothschild, Miriam, 1128–29
Roupell, Arabella Elizabeth (Piggott), 1129
Russell, Anna (Worsley), 1136
Russell, Dorothy, 1136–37
Sackville-West, Victoria Mary, 1143
Sale, Rhoda, 1146

Sampson, Kathleen Samuel, 1147
Sargant, Ethel, 1151–52
Sargent, Winifred, 1152–53
Saunders, Edith Rebecca, 1154–55
Scharlieb, Dame Mary Ann Dacomb, 1157–58
Schmideberg, Melitta (Klein), 1161–62
Schoental, Regina, 1163–64
Schofield, Brenda Muriel, 1164–65
Scott, Charlotte Angas, 1167–68
Scott, Henderina Victoria (Klaassen), 1168–69
Seligman, Brenda Zara, 1174–75
Shakespear, Dame Ethel Mary Reader (Wood), 1180–81
Sharp, Emily Katharine (Dooris), 1181
Sharp, Jane, 1181
Shaw, Hester, 1183
Sherbourne, Margaret Dorothea (Willis), 1185
Shove, Rosamund Flora, 1189
Sidgwick, Eleanor (Balfour), 1192–93
Slater, Ida Lilian, 1198
Slater, Jesse Mabel Wilkins, 1198–99
Smith, Alice Emily, 1201
Smith, Annie Lorrain, 1202–3
Smith, Audrey U., 1203–4
Smith, Matilda, 1208
Smith, Pleasance (Reeve), 1209
Smith, Winifred, 1209
Snelling, Lilian, 1209–10
Snow, Mary (Pilkington), 1210–11
Sollas, Igerna Brünhilda Johnson, 1212
Sophia Charlotte, Queen of Prussia, 1216
Sophia, Electress of Hanover, 1216
Sowton, Sarah C.M., 1218
Sprague, Mary Letitia (Green), 1221
Spratt, Ethel Rose, 1221
Stackhouse, Emily, 1221–22
Stephens, Joanna, 1226–27
Stephenson, Marjory, 1227–28
Stopes, Marie Charlotte Carmichael, 1242
Stovin, Margaret, 1244–45
Strachey, Alix (Sargant-Florence), 1245–46
Summerskill, Edith Clara, 1251–52
Sykes, Mary Gladys, 1257–58
Talbot, Dorothy Amaury, 1262
Taylor, Clara Millicent, 1269
Taylor, Eva Germaine Rimington, 1269–70
Taylor, Helen, 1270
Taylor, Janet, 1270–71
Taylor, Monica, 1272
Tebb, Mary Christine, 1272–73
Telfair, Annabella (Chamberlain), 1273
Thiselton-Dyer, Lady Harriet Ann (Hooker), 1278–79
Thomas, Ethel Nancy Miles, 1280–81
Thompson, Rachel Ford, 1285
Thomson, Agnes C., 1286
Thring, Lydia Eliza Dyer (Meredith), 1286–87
Tindall, Isabella Mary, 1291
Tinsley, Beatrice Muriel (Hill), 1292–93
Tipper, Constance Fligg (Elam), 1293–94
Todd, Emily Sophia, 1294–95
Traill, Catharine Parr (Strickland), 1300–1301
Trimmer, Sarah (Kirby), 1302
Tristram, Ruth Mary (Cardew), 1302
Trower, Charlotte Georgiana, 1305

Turner, Mary (Palgrave), 1308–9
Twining, Elizabeth Mary, 1309
Vachell, Eleanor, 1316
Vaughan, Dame Janet, 1323–24
Veley, Lilian Jane (Nutcombe), 1325
Vernon, Magdalen Dorothea, 1327–28
Vesian, Dorothy E. de, 1328
Vickers, Anna, 1328
Vogt, Marthe Louise, 1330–31
Wakefield, Elsie Maud, 1336–37
Wakefield, Priscilla (Bell), 1337
Walker, Eliza, 1339
Walker, Elizabeth, 1339
Warren, Elizabeth Andrew, 1347
Watson, Janet Vida, 1350–51
Watt, Helen Winifred Boyd (de Lisle), 1351
Watt, Menie, 1351
Webster, Mary McCallum, 1353–54
Wedderburn, Jemima, 1354
Wedgwood, Camilla Hildegarde, 1354–56
Wedgwood, Mary Louisa (Bell), 1356
Weightman, Mary, 1358
West, Ethel, 1367
White, Eliza Catherine (Quekett), 1371
Whitehead, Lilian Elizabeth, 1373
Whiteley, Martha Annie, 1373
Whiting, Marian Muriel, 1373
Widdowson, Elsie May, 1376–77
Willcock, Edith Gertrude (Gardiner), 1380
Williams, Cicely Delphine, 1382
Willmott, Ellen Ann, 1382–83
Wilson, Aphra Phyllis, 1384
Wilson, Fiammetta Worthington, 1385
Wilson, Irene Mossom, 1385
Young, Grace Emily (Chisholm), 1413–14
See also Scotland

Greece
Abrotelia, 5
Aesara of Lucania, 11–12
Agamede, 12
Aglaonike, 13–14
Agnodike, 16
Anicia or Amyte, 40
Arete of Cyrene, 50
Arignote of Samos, 50
Artemisia of Caria II, 54
Asclepigenia, 55
Aspasia of Miletus, 55–56
Aspasia the Physician, 56
Axiothea of Phlius, 62
Cleachma, 267–68
Cleobulina of Rhodes, 269
Cleopatra, 269
Damo, 323–24
Diotima of Mantinea, 359
Eccello of Lucania, 396
Echecratia the Philiasian, 397
Elephantis, 414
Fleming, Amalia Coutsouris, Lady, 451
Laïs, 735
Lasthenia of Mantinea, 749–50
Leontium, 771–72
Macrina, 828–29
Melissa, 879
Metrodora, 888

Greece (*cont.*)
Myia or Mya, 929
Nicerata, Saint, 940
Occello of Lucania, 957
Olympias of Thebes, 962
Origenia, 965
Pallis, Marietta, 973
Panajiotatou, Angeliki, 977–78
Perictione, 1007
Pythias of Assos, 1062
Salpe, 1146–47
Schliemann, Sophia (Kastromenos), 1160–61
Sotira, 1217–18
Theano, 1276–77

H

Holland
Beckman, A., 102
Clay-Jolles, Tettje Clasina, 265–66
Cramer, Catherine Gertrude Du Tertre Schraders, 299–300
De Lange, Cornelia Catharina, 341–42
Ehrenfest-Afanassjewa, Tatyana Alexeyevna, 407–8
Folmer, Hermine Jacoba, 457
Herwerden, Marianne Van, 592
Hesse, Fanny, 593
Hol, Jacoba Brigitta Louisa, 610
Jacobs, Aletta Henrietta, 650–51
Kerling, Louise Catharina Petronella, 692
Van Beverwijk, Agathe L., 1317–18
Weber, Anne Antoinette (Van Bosse), 1352–53

Hungary
Anna of Bohemia, 41
Banga, Ilona, 75–76
Barnothy, Madeleine (Forro), 83
Belar, Maria, 110
Benedek, Therese F., 112–13
Cori, Gerty Theresa Radnitz, 292–94
Csepreghyné-Meznerics, Ilona, 306–7
Einstein, Elizabeth Roboz, 410–11
Elizabeth of Poland, Queen of Hungary, 417
Götz, Irén Julih (Dienes), 521–22
Heermann, Margareta, 577–78
Hugonnai-Wartha, Vilma, 628
Le Beau, Désirée, 759–60
Mahler, Margaret Schönberger, 830–31
Mottl, Mária, 921
Péter, Rózsa, 1009–10
Róna, Elisabeth, 1122–23
Telkes, Maria, 1273–74

I

India
Aluwihare, Florence, 27–28
Bhatia, Sharju Pandit, 122–23
Janaki Ammal, Edavaleth Kakkat, 653
Jhirad, Jerusha, 659–60
Lazarus, Hilda Mary, 756–57
Satur, Dorothy May, 1153–54
Vytilingam, Kamala Israel, 1333–34

Iran
Rafatdjah, Safieh, 1067–68

Iraq
Thelka, Saint, 1278

Ireland
Arbuthnot, Isobel Agnes, 48–49
Ball, Anne Elizabeth, 73
Ball, Mary, 74
Bentham, Ethel, 117
Bridget, Saint, of Ireland, 179
Brooks, Sarah Theresa, 186
Christen, Sydney Mary (Thompson), 254–55
Clerke, Agnes Mary, 269–71
Clerke, Ellen Mary, 271–72
Clinch, Phyllis E.M., 273
Cobbe, Frances Power, 276–77
Cotter, Brigid M., 296
Crosbie, May, 305
Cuffe, Lady Charlotte Wheeler (Williams), 307
Delap, Maude Jane, 342
De Valera, Mairin, 352–53
Edgeworth, Maria, 400
Findlater, Doris, 446
Fitton, Sarah Mary, 450
Flood, Margaret Greer, 455
Gage, Catherine, 480
Gilmore, Jane Georgina, 503
Glascott, Louisa S., 506
Gregory, Lady Isabella Augusta (Persse), 529
Huggins, Margaret Lindsay (Murray), 626–27
Hutchins, Ellen, 633–35
Joyce, Margaret Elizabeth, 671
Kane, Lady Katherine Sophia (Baily), 675
King, Anastasia Kathleen (Murphy), 695
King, Martha, 698
Knowles, Matilda Cullen, 709–10
Lawder, Margaret, 754
Lawrenson, Alice Louisa, 755
Leebody, Mary Elizabeth, 765
Lefroy, Helena (Trench), 766
Longfield, Cynthia, 801–2
Lynn, Mary Johnstone, 814
Massy, Anne L., 852–53
Maunder, Annie Scott Dill Russell, 855–56
McCracken, Eileen May, 865
O'Brien, Charlotte Grace, 956
O'Reilly, Helen, 964
Parsons, Mary, Countess of Rosse, 984–85
Price, Dorothy (Stopford), 1054
Rea, Margaret Williamson, 1081
Sharp, Emily Katharine (Dooris), 1181
Stelfox, Margarita Dawson (Mitchell), 1226
Stephens, Jane, 1226
Stokes, Margaret Mcnair, 1239
Stott, Alicia (Boole), 1244
Thomson, Jane Smithson, 1286
Ward, Mary (King), 1346

Israel
Buchbinder, Laura G.Ordan, 200–201

Italy
Abella, 4
Adelberger of Lombardy, 10
Adelle of the Saracens, 10
Adelmota of Carrara, 10
Aemilia, 11
Aesara of Lucania, 11–12
Agnesi, Maria Gaetana, 14–16
Amalosunta, 28

Antonia, Maestra, 44–45
Ardinghelli, Maria Angela, 49–50
Barbapiccola, Giuseppa Eleonora, 77
Bassi, Laura Maria Caterina, 88–89
Beatrice, Medica of Candia, 99
Beronice, 118
Bocchi (Bucca), Dorotea, 151
Borromeo, Clelia Grillo, 163
Borsarelli, Fernanda, 163
Brunetti, R., 196
Buttelini, Marchesa, 215
Caerellia (Caerelia), 219
Caetani-Bovatelli, Donna Ersilia, 219–20
Calenda, Constanza or Laurea Constantia, 221
Catani, Giuseppina, 236–37
Catherine of Bologna, Saint, 237
Catherine of Genoa, Saint, 237
Catherine of Siena, Saint, 237
Ccioranescu-Nenitzescu, Ecaterina, 258
Cinquini, Maria Dei Conti Cibrario, 258
Clara (Clare) of Assisi, Saint, 259
Cornaro (Cornero), Elena (Helena) Lucretia, 295
Cornelius-Furlani, Marta, 294
Cunio, Isabella, 309
Dalai, Maria Jolanda (Tosoni), 322
Dalle Donne, Maria, 323
Danti or Dante, Theodora, 325
De Gorzano, Leonetta, 337
Di Novella, Maria, 355
Eccello of Lucania, 396
Echecratia the Philiasian, 397
Eleanora, Duchess of Mantua, 414
Elizabeth of Portugal, Saint, 417
Fabiola, 433
Faustina, 436
Favilla, 436
Felicie, Jacobina, 439
Ferrero, Gina (Lombroso), 443–44
Francini, Eleonora Corti, 464–65
Galvani, Lucia (Galeazzi), 481–82
Ghilietta, 498
Giammarino, Pia, 498
Giliani, Alessandra, 502
Gualco, Sellina, 535
Guarna, Rebecca, 535
Hélène, Duchess of Aosta, 581
Jacobina Medica of Bologna, 650
Jacopa of Passau, 651
Leoparda, 772
Levi-Montalcini, Rita, 779–81
Manzolini, Anna Morandi, 841
Marcella, 841
Medaglia, Diamante, 874
Mercuriade, 884
Molza, Tarquinia, 908
Montessori, Maria, 909–10
Nicosia, Maria Luisa, 942–43
Pastori, Giuseppina, 986–87
Pastori, Maria, 987
Paula, 990
Paulucci, Marianna, Marchesa, 991
Peretti, Zaffira, 1006
Pettracini, Maria, 1013

Piazolla-Beloch, Margherita, 1019
Pirami, Edmea, 1026–27
Pisan, Christine de, 1028
Scarpellini, Caterina, 1156
Strozzi, Lorenza, 1249–50
Theodosia, Saint, 1278
Trotula, 1304–5
Zenari, Silvia, 1421–22

J
Japan
Miyaji, Kunie, 905–6
Ogino, G., 961
Takeuchi, Shigeyo (Ide), 1261–62
Tetsuo, Tamayo, 1276

K
Korea
Bang, Duck-Heung, 75
Chang, Moon Gyung, 245
Kil, Chung-Hee, 694–95

L
Latvia
Staudinger, Magda (Woit), 1223–24
Lebanon
Abouchdid, Edna, 5
Lithuania
Halicka, Antonina (Yaroszewicz), 544
Iwanowska, Wilhelmina, 647
Kardymowiczowa, Irena, 676
Rabinovitch-Kempner, Lydia, 1067

M
Mexico
De La Cruz, Juana Inés, 339
Solis Quiroga, Margarita Delgado de, 1212

N
Netherlands
Lampl-De Groot, Jeanne, 738
Macgillavry, Carolina Henriette, 821
Meyling-Hylkema, Elisabeth, 891
Prins, Ada, 1057
Ruysch, Rachel, 1139
Ruys (Ruijs), Anna Charlotte, 1138
Schraders, Catharina Geertruida, 1165
Schurman, Anna Marie Van, 1165–66
Tammes, Jantine, 1264–65
Tinne, Alexandrina Petronella Francina, 1291–92
New Zealand
Beanland, Sarah, 98
Cranwell, Lucy May, 301
Hodgson, Eliza Amy, 607
MacCallum, Bella Dytes (Macintosh), 818
Stenhouse, Caroline, 1226
Norway
Bonnevie, Kristine, 157–58
Dorenfeldt, Margot, 371
Eng, Helga, 421–22
Gjellestad, Guro Else, 505
Gleditsch, Ellen, 508–9
Guldberg, Estrid, 536
Gundersen, Herdis, 537

Haldorsen, Inger Alida, 543–44
Mathisen, Karoline, 855
Prytz, Milda Dorothea, 1059
Sunne, Dagny, 1252

P
Palestine
Agnes of Jerusalem, 14
Peru
Chinchon, Countess of, 252
Philippines
Acosta-Sison, Honoria, 6
Florendo, Soledad Arcega, 455–56
Parrish, Rebecca, 981
Ramirez, Rosita Rivera, 1070
Poland
Abramson, Jadwiga, 5
Baumgarten-Tramer, Franziska, 93–94
Bertillon, Caroline Schutze, 120
Catherine, Medica of Cracow, 237
Chalubinska, Aniela, 242–43
Chmielewska, Irene, 253–54
Cotelle, Sonia, 295–96
Curie, Marie (Maria Sklodowska), 311–17
Czaplicka, Marie Antoinette, 321
Deutsch, Helene Rosenback, 351–52
Dobrowolska, H., 361
Dorabialska, Alicja Domenica, 368–69
Dylazanka, Maria, 393
Elizabeth of Poland, Queen of Hungary, 417
Fonovits-Smereker, H., 458
Frenkel-Brunswik, Else, 469–70
Geppert, Maria Pia, 495
Goldfeder, Anna, 512–13
Gruhn, Ruth, 533–34
Grzigorzewska, Marja, 534
Hevelius, Elisabetha Koopman, 593
Horowitz, Stephanie, 618
Joteyko, Joséphine, 670–71
Kaczorowska, Zofia, 674–75
Karpowicz, Ludmila, 678
Kielan-Jaworowska, Zofia, 693–94
Kolaczkowska, Maria, 716
Koprowska, Irena Grasberg, 717
Lipinska, Mélanie, 794
Lubinska, Liliana, 810
Missuna, Anna Boleslavovna, 899–900
Muszhat, Aniela, 929
Oszast, Janina Celina, 968–69
Pacaud, Suzanne, 971
Pajchlowa, Maria Leokadia, 973
Pozarska, Krystyna (Maliszewski), 1048–49
Schoental, Regina, 1163–64
Siegemund, Justine Dittrich, 1193
Skoczylas-Ciszewska, Kamila, 1197–98
Stern, Catherine (Brieger), 1229
Syniewska, Janina, 1258
Szeminska, Alina, 1258
Szmidt, Jadwiga, 1258–59
Szwajger, Adina Blady, 1259
Tenenbaum, Estera, 1274
Tomaszewicz-Dobrska, Anna, 1297
Tyska, Maria, 1311
Wertenstein, Mathilde, 1366
Zaniewska-Chilpalska, Eugenia, 1421

Portugal
Elizabeth of Portugal, Saint, 417
Prussia
Sophia Charlotte, Queen of Prussia, 1216
Puerto Rico
Martinez-Alvarez, Josefina, 849–50

R
Romania
Gàta, Elena (Stefanescu), 489
Maracineanu, Stefania, 841
Savulescu, Olga, 1155
Stefanescu, Sabba, 1225
Russia
Amalitskiya, Anna P., 28
Andreas-Salomé, Louise Lelia, 38–39
Antipoff, Helene, 43
Arkhangel'Skaia, Aleksandra Gavriilovna, 50–51
Arsenjewa, A., 54
Barbarshova, Zoia Ivanovna, 77
Bari, Nina Karlovna, 78–79
Blinova, Ekaterina Nikitichna, 145
Bluket, Nina Aleksandrovna, 150
Bochantseva, Zinaida Petrovna, 152
Bogdanovskaia, Vera Evstaf'evna, 153
Bokova–Sechenova, Mariia Aleksandrovna, 154–55
Bolschanina, M.A., 155
Borisova-Bekriasheva, Antoniia Georgievna, 162
Bredikhina, Evgeniia Aleksandrovna, 176–77
Bykhovskaia, Anna Markovna, 215–16
Chamié, Catherine, 243
Czeczottowa, Hanna (Peretiatkowicza), 321
Dashkova, Princess Ekaterina Romanovna, 326–27
Dembo, Tamara, 344–45
Dobrolubova, Tatiana A., 360–61
Dokhman, Genrietta Isaakovna, 365–66
Dombrovskaia, Iuliia Fominichna, 367
Drebeneva-Ukhova, Varvara Pavlovna, 376
Efimenko, Aleksandra Iakovlevna, 405
Ehrenfest-Afanassjewa, Tatyana Alexeyevna, 407–8
Ermol'eva, Zinaida Vissarionovna, 425
Esau, Katherine, 426–27
Fedchenko, Ol'ga Aleksandrovna, 438–39
Figner, Vera, 446
Finkler, Rita V.(Sapiro), 446–47
Fomina-Zhukovskaia, Evdokiia Aleksan-drovna, 457–58
Freidlina, Rakhil' Khatskelevna, 468–69
Glagoleva-Arkad'Yeva, Aleksandra Andreyevna, 506
Gocholashvili, Mariia Mikievna, 509
Golinevich, Elena Mikhailovna, 518
Gorinevskaya, Valentina Valentinovna, 520–21
Gorizdro-Kulczycka, Zinaida, 521
Gorshkova, Tat'yana Ivanovna, 521
Gracheva, Yekaterina Konstantinovna, 522
Gromova, Vera Isaacovna, 533
Gsell, Maria Dorothea Henrica (Graf), 535
Hanfmann, Eugenia, 551–52
Ianovskaia, Sof'ia Aleksandrovna, 640–41

Russia (*cont.*)

Iusupova, Saradzhan Mikhailovna, 644–45
Ivanova, Elena Alekseevna, 645–46
Jérémine, Elisabeth (Tschernaieff), 656–57
Jermoljeva, Zinaida Vissarionovna, 657
Kashevarovarudneva, Varvara Aleksandrovna, 678–80
Katz, Rosa Heine, 680
Keldysh, Liudmila Vsevolodovna, 682
Kharuzina, Vera Nikolaevna, 693
Kleegman, Sophia, 702–3
Kletnova, E.N., 704–5
Kochina, Pelageia Iakovlevna, 713–14
Kohts, Nadie (Ladychin), 715–16
Komarovsky, Mirra, 716–17
Korobeinikova, Iuliia Ivanovna, 718
Korshunova, Olga Stepanovna, 719
Kovaleskaia, Sofia Vasilyevna, 720–22
Kovrigina, Mariia Dmitrievna, 722–23
Krasnosel'skaia, Tat'iana Abramovna, 724–25
Kraus Ragins, Ida, 725
Krupskaia, Nadezhda Konstantinovna, 728–29
Ladygina-Kots, Nadezhda Nikolaevna, 732–33
Lebedeva, Nataliia Ivanova, 760
Lebedeva, Vera Pavlovna, 760–61
Lepeshinskaia, Ol'ga Borisovna, 773–74
Lepin, Lidiia Karlovna, 774
Lermontova, Ekaterina Vladimirovna, 774–75
Lermontova, Iuliia Vsevolodovna, 775–76
Lisovskaia, Sofiya Nikolaievna, 794
Litvinova, Elizaveta Fedorovna, 796–97
Lukanina, Adelaida N., 810–11
Massevitch, Alla Genrikhovna, 851–52
Matikashvili, Nina, 855
Medvedeva, Nina Borisovna, 875–76
Metchnikova, Olga (Belokopytova), 887–88
Missuna, Anna Boleslavovna, 899–900
Neuburg Maria Feodorovna, 935–36
Novoselova, Aleksandra Vasil'evna, 953
Obrutsheva, A., 956–57
Orent-Kelles, Elsa, 964
Pasternak, Lydia, 985–86
Pavlova, Mariia Vasil'evna, 992–93
Pereiaslavtseva, Sof'ia Mikhailovna, 1004–5
Petrova, Maria Kapitonovna, 1012
Piccard, Sophie, 1019–20
Pokrovskaia, Mariia Ivanovna, 1036–37
Povitsky, Olga Raissa, 1047
Proskouriakoff, Tatiana, 1057–58
Rabinoff, Sophie, 1066–67
Rasskazova, Yelena Stepanovna, 1074–75
Rauzer-Chernousova, Dagmara M., 1078–79
Rozanova, Mariia Aleksandrovna, 1132–33
Rozovna, Evdokia Aleksandrovna, 1133
Rubin, Vera (Dourmashkin), 1133–34
Semikhatova, Sofia Viktorovna (Karpova), 1175–76
Shabanova, Anna Nikolaevna, 1179–80
Shishkina, Olga Vasil'Yevna, 1188
Shtern, Lina Solomonovna, 1189–90
Shubnikova, Ol'ga Mikhailovna, 1190–91
Sinskaia, Evgeniia Nikolaevna, 1196–97

Sokol'skaya, Anna Nikolayevna, 1212
Solomko-Sotiriadis, Evgeniia, 1213
Sorokin, Helen Petrovna (Beratynskaiia), 1216–17
Suslova, Nadezhda Prokof'evna, 1252–53
Szmidt, Jadwiga, 1258–59
Terent'eva, Liudmila Nikolaevna, 1274
Timofe'eff-Ressovsky, Elena Aleksandrovna (Fiedler), 1290–91
Towara, Hélèlne, 1299
Trizna, Valentina Borisovna, 1302–3
Tsvetaeva, Maria, 1305–6
Uvarova, Countess Praskov'ia Sergeevna, 1314–15
See also United Soviet Socialists Republic (U.S.S.R.)

S

Scotland

Currie, Ethel Dobbie, 317
Cuthbert-Browne, Grace Johnston, 320–21
Dallas, A.E.M.M., 323
Dobson, Mildred E., 362
Downie, Dorothy G., 374
Drummond, Margaret, 378
Dunlop, Janette Gilchrist, 387
Dunn, Mary Douglas, 387
Ewing, Elizabeth Raymond (Burden), 432
Fleming, Williamina Paton Stevens, 453–54
Hitchens, Ada Florence R., 604
Hutton, Lady Isabel Emilie, 635
Inglis, Elsie (Maude), 643
Macintyre, Sheila Scott, 821–22
Marshall, Sheina Macalister, 846–47
McLaren, Agnes, 871
Newbigin, Marion Isabel, 937
Ogilvie-Gordon, Dame Maria Matilda, 959–60
Pirie, Mary, 1027
Pirret, Ruth, 1027–28
Prytz, Milda Dorothea, 1059
Ramsay, Christina (Broun), Countess of Dalhousie, 1070–71
Rogers, Agnes Lowe, 1120
Ross, Marion Amelia Spence, 1127
Scott, Flora Murray, 1168
Soddy, Winifred Moller (Beilby), 1211–12
Somerville, Mary (Fairfax) Greig, 1213–15
Walker, Eliza, 1339
White, Margaret Pirie (Dunbar), 1372
Wilson, Hilda E., 1385
See also Great Britain

Serbia

Einstein-Maric, Mileva, 411–12

Sir Lanka

Ratnayake, May, 1076

South Africa

Arbuthnot, Isobel Agnes, 48–49
Barber, Mary Elizabeth (Bowker), 78
Bolus, Harriet Margaret Louisa (Kensit), 155–56
Breyer, Maria Gerdina (Brandwijk), 179
Britten, Lilian Louisa, 180–81
Burton, Helen Marie Rousseay (Kan-Ne-meyer), 212

Forbes, Helena Madelain Lamond, 458
Gunn, Mary Davidson, 537–38
Harrower, Molly R., 559–60
Lansdell, Kathleen Annie, 745
Lawder, Margaret, 754
Levyns, Margaret Rutherford Bryan (Michell), 782
Massey, Patricia, 852
Pocock, Mary Agard, 1035–36
Rice, Elsie (Garrett), 1092

Soviet Union. *See* **United Soviet Socialists Republic (U.S.S.R.)**

Spain

Agnes, Countess of Aix, 14
Barrera, Oliva Sabuca De Nantes, 84
Castra, Anna de, 236
Chinchon, Countess of, 252
De La Cruz, Juana Inés, 339
De Lebrix, FranÇoise, 342–43
Fatima, 436
Galindo, Beatrix, 481
Losa, Isabella, 805
Sabuco Banera D'Alcaraz, Olivia, 1143
Vilar, Lola, 1328–29

Sweden

Bahr-Bergius, Eva Vilhelmina Julia Von, 68
Bridget, Saint, of Scandinavia, 179
Christina, Queen of Sweden, 255–56
Cleve, Astrid, 272
Hellman, Johanna, 581
Hellstedt, Leone Mcgregor, 581–82
Larsson, Elisabeth, 746
Lind-Campbell, Hjördis, 791
Lindsten-Thomasson, Marianne, 792–93
Mitchell, Anna Helena, 900
Pettersson, Dagmar, 1012–13
Ramstedt, Eva Julia Augusta, 1071–72
Rydh, Hanna, 1139
Sundquist, Alma, 1252
Svartz, Nanna Charlotta, 1254

Switzerland

Angst-Horridge, Anita, 40
Antipoff, Helene, 43
Baumgarten-Tramer, Franziska, 93–94
Brenk, Irene, 177–78
Brückner, Frau Dr., 195
Brunfels, Frau Otto, 196
Einstein-Maric, Mileva, 411–12
Hamburger, Erna, 548
Heim-Vögtlin, Marie, 580
Kaltenbeiner, Victorine, 675
Necker, Susanne (Curchod), 932
Piccard, Sophie, 1019–20
Ponse, Kitty, 1038–39
Reinhardt, Anna Barbara, 1088–89
Schubert, Anna, 1165

Syria

Chamié, Catherine, 243

T

Thailand

Netrasiri, Khunying Cherd-Chalong, 935

Turkey

Ali, Safieh, 23
Tunakan, Seniha (Hüsnü), 1307

U

Ukraine

Smirnovazamkova, Aleksandra Ivanovna, 1201

United Soviet Socialists Republic (U.S.S.R.)

Amalitskiya, Anna P., 28

Belaeva, Elizaveta Ivanovna, 108–9

Cesniece-Freudenfelde, Zelma, 242

Czeczottowa, Hanna (Peretiatkowicza), 321

Dobrolubova, Tatiana A., 360–61

Kozlova, Ol'ga Grigoriyevna, 724

Krutikhovskaia, Zinaida Aleksandrovna, 729

Lisitsian, Srbui Stepanova, 794

Lyubimova, Yelena Aleksandrovna, 815–16

Margulova, Tereza Kristoforovna, 843

Mirchink, Maria E., 899

Morozova, Valentina Galaktionovna, 915–16

Naumova, Sofiya Nickolaevna, 931

Pokrovskaia, Irina Mitrofanovna, 1036

Polenova, Yelena Nikolayevna, 1037–38

Rauzer-Chernousova, Dagmara M., 1078–79

Shulga-Nesterenko, Maria I., 1191–92

Soshkina, Elizabeth D., 1217

Stadnichenko, Tasia Maximovna, 1222

Tumanskaya, Olga G. (Shirokobruhova), 1306–7

Ushakova, Elizaveta Ivanovna, 1314

Varsanof'eva, Vera Aleksandrovna, 1322–23

Vasilevich, Glafira Makar'evna, 1323

Veretennikova, Anna Ivanovna, 1326–27

Volkova, Anna Fedorovna, 1332–33

Zaklinskaia, Elena Dmitrievna, 1418–19

Zalesskaya-Chirkova, Elena, 1420–21

Zhuze, Anastasiya Panteleyemonovna, 1422–23

Ziegarnik, Bliuma, 1423

See also Russia

United States of America

Abel, Mary Hinman, 2–3

Abel, Theodora Mead, 3–4

Aberle, Sophie Bledsoe, 4–5

Achilles, Edith Mulhall, 5–6

Adams, Amy Elizabeth Kemper, 7

Adams, Mildred, 7–8

Addams, Jane, 9–10

Agassiz, Elizabeth Cary, 12–13

Akeley, Mary Lee (Jobe), 17–18

Albertson, Mary, 18

Alexander, Annie Montague, 20–21

Alexander, Hattie Elizabeth, 22–23

Allen, Doris Twitchell, 24–25

Allen, Ruth Florence, 25–26

Alper, Thelma Gorfinkle, 26–27

Altmann, Margaret, 27

Ames, Blanche (Ames), 28–30

Ames, Louise Bates, 30–31

Ames, Mary E.Pulsifer, 31

Andersen, Dorothy Hansine, 31–32

Anderson, Caroline Virginia (Still) Wiley, 32–33

Anderson, Elda Emma, 33–34

Anderson, Evelyn M., 35–36

Anderson, Rose Gustava, 37

Andrews, Eliza Frances, 39

Andrews, Grace, 39

Andrus, Ruth, 39–40

Anslow, Gladys Amelia, 42–43

Apgar, Virginia, 45–46

Applin, Esther (Richards), 46–47

Arlitt, Ada Hart, 51

Arnold, Magda Blondiau, 53

Arnstein, Margaret Gene, 53–54

Arthur, Mary Grace, 54–55

Ashby, Winifred Mayer, 55

Atwater, Helen Woodard, 58–59

Austin, Mary Lellah, 61

Austin, Rebecca, 61

Babcock, Harriet, 65

Baber, Zonia, 65–66

Bachman, Maria Martin, 66

Bacon, Clara (Latimer), 66

Baetjer, Anna Medora, 66–67

Bagley, Florence (Winger), 67

Bailey, Ethel Zoe, 68–69

Bailey, Florence Augusta (Merriam), 69–70

Baker, Sara Josephine, 70–71

Bakwin, Ruth (Morris), 72

Ballard, Julia Perkins Pratt, 74–75

Ball, Josephine, 73–74

Barlett, Helen Blair, 79–80

Barnard, Edith Ethel, 81

Barney, Ida, 82

Barney, Nora Stanton (Blatch) De Forest, 83

Barnothy, Madeleine (Forro), 83

Barnum, Charlotte Cynthia, 83–84

Barringer, Emily (Dunning), 84–85

Barrows, Katherine Isabel (Hayes) Chapin, 85–86

Barton, Clara Arlowe, 86

Barton, Lela Viola, 86–87

Bascom, Florence, 87–88

Bass, Mary Elizabeth, 88

Batchelder, Esther Lord, 89–90

Bates, Mary E., 90–91

Baumann, Frieda, 92–93

Baumgartner, Leona, 94–95

Baxter, Mildred Frances, 95

Bayley, Nancy, 96–97

Baynard, Anne, 97

Beatley, Janice Carson, 98–99

Beckwith, Angie Maria, 102

Beckwith, Cora, 102

Beckwith, Martha Warren, 102–3

Beecher, Catharine Esther, 103–4

Beers, Catherine Virginia, 104

Behre, Ellinor H., 108

Bender, Lauretta, 111–12

Benedict, Ruth (Fulton), 113

Bennett, Alice, 115

Bennett, Dorothea, 116

Berger, Emily V., 118

Bevier, Isabel, 121–22

Bibring, Grete Lehner, 123–24

Bickerdyke, Mary Ann (Ball), 124–25

Bilger, Leonora (Neuffer), 126–27

Billings, Katharine Stevens (Fowler–Lunn), 127

Bingham, Millicent (Todd), 127–28

Bird, Grace Electa, 128

Birdsall, Lucy Ellen, 128–29

Bishop, Katharine Scott, 131–32

Bissell, Emily P., 132

Bitting, Katherine Eliza (Golden), 132–33

Black, Florence, 133

Black, Hortensia, 133

Blackwell, Antoinette Louise (Brown), 135–36

Blackwell, Elizabeth, 136

Blake, Mary Safford, 140–41

Blanchard, Frieda Cobb, 141–42

Blanchard, Phyllis, 142

Bledsoe, Lucybelle, 144–45

Bliss, Dorothy Elizabeth, 145–46

Bliss, Eleanor Albert, 146

Bliss, Mary Campbell, 146

Block, Jeanne (Humphrey), 146–48

Blodgett, Katharine Burr, 148–49

Blunt, Katharine, 151

Bodley, Rachel Littler, 152–53

Bomhard, Miriam Lucile, 156

Boos, Margaret Bradley (Fuller), 159–60

Booth, Mary Ann Allard, 160

Boring, Alice Middleton, 160–62

Boron, Elizabeth (Riddle) Graves, 162–63

Bouthilet, Lorraine, 164–65

Boveri, Marcella Imelda O'Grady, 165–67

Bowen, Susan, 167

Boyd, Elizabeth Margaret, 167

Boyd, Louise Arner, 167–68

Boyer, Esther Lydia, 168

Bracher, Rose, 168

Bradley, Amy Morris, 168–69

Bradley, Frances Sage, 169–70

Branch, Hazel Elisabeth, 170

Brandegee, Mary Katharine Layne, 171

Brand, Martha, 170–71

Branham, Sara Elizabeth, 171–72

Brant, Laura, 172

Braun, Annette Frances, 172–73

Braun, (Emma) Lucy, 173–74

Brazier, Mary Agnes Burniston (Brown), 174–75

Breckinridge, Mary, 175–76

Breed, Mary (Bidwell), 177

Bridgman, Olga Louise, 180

Britton, Elizabeth Knight, 181

Broadhurst, Jean, 181–82

Brock, Sylvia (Deantonis), 182

Bromley, Helen Jean (Brown), 182–83

Bronner, Augusta Fox, 183

Brooks, Matilda (Moldenhauer), 185–86

Broomall, Anna Elizabeth, 186

Brousseau, Kate, 186–87

Brown, Charlotte Amanda Blake, 187–88

Browne, Marjorie Lee, 193–94

Brown, Fay Cluff, 189–90

Brown, Mabel Mary, 190

Brown, Nellie Adalesa, 190–91

Brown, Rachel Fuller, 191

Bruce, Catherine Wolfe, 194

Brüch, Hilde, 195

Brunswick, Ruth Jane (Mack), 196–97

Bryan, Alice Isabel (Bever), 197–98

Bryan, Mary Katherine, 199

Bryant, Louise Stevens, 199

Buchbinder, Laura G.Ordan, 200–201

Buckel, Chloe A., 201–2

United States of America (*cont.*)

Buell, Mary Van Rensselaer, 203
Buerk, Minerva (Smith), 203–4
Bühler, Charlotte Bertha (Malachowski), 204–5
Bull, Nina Wilcox, 205–6
Bunch, Cordia, 206
Bunting, Martha, 206
Bunting-Smith, Mary (Ingraham), 206–8
Bunzel, Ruth Leah, 208
Burgess, May (Ayres), 209
Burlingham, Dorothy (Tiffany), 209–10
Burlingham, Gertrude Simmons, 210–11
Burns, Eleanor Irene, 211
Burns, Louisa, 211
Burrell, Anna Porter, 212
Burr, Emily Thorp, 211
Burtt Davy, Alice (Bolton), 212
Bush, Katharine Jeannette, 214–15
Byrd, Mary Emma, 216
Byrnes, Esther Fussell, 216–17
Cadilla De Martínez, María, 218–19
Cady, Bertha Louise Chapman, 219
Calderone, Mary S., 220
Caldwell, Mary Letitia, 220–21
Calkins, Mary Whiton, 221–23
Calvert, Emily Amelia (Adelia) (Smith), 224
Campbell, Helen Stuart, 224–25
Campbell, Persia Crawford, 226–27
Cannon, Annie Jump, 227–28
Capen, Bessie, 228
Carlson, Elizabeth, 228
Carlson, Lucille, 228
Carothers, Estrella Eleanor, 229
Carpenter, Esther, 230
Carr, Emma Perry, 230–32
Carroll, Dorothy, 232–33
Carson, Rachel Louise, 233–34
Carter, Edna, 234
Carus, Mary Hegeler, 235–36
Castle, Cora (Sutton), 236
Cattell, Psyche, 238
Caughlan, Georgeanne (Robertson), 239–40
Chang, Vivian, 245
Charles, Vera Katherine, 245–46
Chase, Mary Agnes Meara, 246–47
Chasman, Renate Wiener, 247–48
Chenoweth, Alice Drew, 249–50
Child, Lydia Maria (Francis), 251–52
Chinn, May Edward, 252–53
Church, Elda Rodman (Macilvaine), 256
Chute, Hettie Morse, 256–57
Clapp, Cornelia Maria, 258–59
Clappe, Louisa Amelia (Smith), 259
Clark, Bertha, 260
Clarke, Cora Huidekoper, 264
Clarke, Edith, 264–65
Clark, Frances N., 260–61
Clark, Janet Howell, 261–62
Clark, Lois, 262–63
Clark, Mamie Katherine (Phipps), 263
Clark, Nancy Talbot, 263–64
Claypole, Agnes Mary, 266–67
Claypole, Edith Jane, 267
Clemens, Mary Knapp (Strong), 268

Clements, Edith Gertrude (Schwartz), 268
Cleveland, Emeline Horton, 272–73
Clisby, Harriet Jemima Winifred, 273–74
Coates, Sarah J., 274–75
Cobb, Margaret Vara, 275–76
Cobb, Rosalie M.Karapetoff, 276
Cochran, Doris Mabel, 277–78
Cockrell, Wilmatte (Porter), 278
Cohn, Essie White, 278–79
Colby, Martha Guernsey, 279
Colcord, Mabel, 280
Colden, Jane, 280
Cole, Emma J., 280–81
Cole, Rebecca J., 281
Collett, Mary Elizabeth, 282
Collins, Katharine Richards, 282
Comstock, Anna Botsford, 283–84
Cone, Claribel, 284–85
Conklin, Marie (Eckhardt), 285
Conklin, Ruth Emelene, 285–86
Cook, Margaret C., 288
Cooley, Jacquelin Smith, 289
Coombs, Helen Copeland, 289–90
Cooper, Clara Chassell, 290
Cooper, Elizabeth Morgan, 290
Cooper-Ellis, Katharine Murdoch, 292
Cooper, Susan Fenimore, 290–91
Copeland, Lennie Phoebe, 292
Cori, Gerty Theresa Radnitz, 292–94
Cowan, Edwina Abbott, 296–97
Cox, Gertrude Mary, 297–98
Cox, Rachel (Dunaway), 298
Coyle, Elizabeth Eleanor, 298–99
Cram, Eloise Blaine, 299
Crandall, Ella Phillips, 299
Crane, Jocelyn, 300–301
Crocker, Lucretia, 303–4
Croll, Hilda M., 304–5
Crosby, Elizabeth Caroline, 305–6
Cummings, Clara Eaton, 308
Cummings, Louise Duffield, 309
Cunningham, Bess Virginia, 310
Cunningham, Susan, 311
Curtis, Doris Sarah (Malkin), 317–18
Curtis, Natalie, 318–19
Cushier, Elizabeth, 319
Cushing, Hazel Morton, 319–20
Cushman, Florence, 319
Daniel, Anne Sturges, 324–25
Daniels, Amy L., 325
Daulton, Agnes Warner McClelland, 327–28
Davenport, Gertrude (Crotty), 328
David, Florence N., 328
Davidson, Ada D., 328
Davis, Adelle, 328–29
Davis, Alice (Rohde), 329
Davis, Frances (Elliott), 330
Davis, Grace Evangeline, 330
Davis, Katharine Bement, 331–32
Davis, Marguerite, 332–33
Davis, Olive Griffith Stull, 333
Davis, Rose May, 334
Day, Dorothy, 334
Day, Mary Anna, 335
Decker, Jane Cynthia (McLaughlin), 335–36

De Graffenried, Mary Clare, 337
Deichmann, Elisabeth, 337–38
Déjerine-Klumpke, Augusta, 338–39
De Laguna, Fredericka Annis Lopez De Leo, 339–41
Deloria, Ella Cara, 343–44
Dembo, Tamara, 344–45
De Milt, Clara Marie, 345
Dempsey, Sister Mary Joseph, 345
Denis, Willey Glover, 347
Dennett, Mary Ware, 347
Dennis, Olive Wetzel, 347–48
Densmore, Frances Theresa, 348–49
Detmers, Frederica, 350
Deutsch, Helene Rosenback, 351–52
Dewey, Jane Mary (Clark), 353
De Witt, Lydia Maria Adams, 353–54
Dickerson, Mary Cynthia, 355–56
Dick, Gladys Rowena Henry, 354–55
Diggs, Ellen Irene, 357
Dimock, Susan, 357–58
Dinnerstein, Dorothy, 359
Dix, Dorothea Lynde, 360
Dobroscky, Irene Dorothy, 361
Dock, Lavinia Lloyd, 362–63
Dodd, Katharine, 363
Dodds, Mary Letitia, 363–64
Doering, Kathleen Clara, 364
Dohan, Edith Haywood Hall, 364–65
Dolley, Sarah Read Adamson, 366–67
Donnay, Gabrielle (Hamburger), 367–68
Dooley, Lucile, 368
Dorety, Angela, 370
Dormon, Caroline, 370–71
Doubleday, Neltje Blanchan (de Graff), 371–72
Dover, Mary Violette, 372–73
Downey, June Etta, 373–74
Downey, K.Melvina, 374
Downs, Cornelia Mitchell, 374–75
Drant, Patricia (Hart), 375
Draper, Mary Anna Palmer, 375–76
Drinker, Katherine (Rotan), 377
Du Bois, Cora, 377–78
Duffy, Elizabeth, 381–82
Dummer, Ethel (Sturges), 382–83
Dunbar, Helen Flanders, 383–84
Duncan, Catherine (Gross), 384
Duncan, Helen, 384–85
Dunham, Ethel Collins, 386–87
Dunning, Wilhelmina Frances, 388
Dunn, Thelma Brumfield, 387–88
Duryea, Nina, 389
Dutcher, Adelaide, 389–90
Dutton, Bertha, 390–91
Dutton, Loraine Orr, 391
Dye, Marie, 391
Dyer, Helen Marie, 391–92
Eastwood, Alice, 394–96
Eaves, Elsie, 396
Echols, Dorothy Jung, 397
Eckerson, Sophia Hennion, 397
Eckstorm, Fannie Pearson (Hardy), 398
Eddy, Bernice Elaine, 398–99
Edge, Rosalie Barrow, 399

Edgerton, Winifred Haring, 399–400
Edinger, Johanna Gabrielle Otellie (Tilly), 400–401
Edson, Fanny Carter, 402–3
Edwards, Emma Ward, 403
Edwards, Lena Frances, 403
Eichelberger, Lillian, 408
Eigenmann, Rosa Smith, 408–9
Einstein, Elizabeth Roboz, 410–11
Eisele, Carolyn, 412–13
Elion, Gertrude Belle, 415–16
Eliot, Martha May, 416
Elliott, Charlotte, 418
Ellis, Florence Hawley, 419
Ellisor, Alva Christine, 419–20
Elsom, Katharine (O'Shea), 420
Emerson, Gladys Ludwina (Anderson), 420–21
Engelbrecht, Mildred Amanda, 422
Esau, Katherine, 426–27
Evans, Alice Catherine, 428–30
Farnsworth, Alice Hall, 434
Farnsworth, Vesta J., 434
Farrar, Lillian K.P., 436
Farr, Wanda Kirkbride, 435–36
Fearn, Anne Walter, 437–38
Fenwick, Florence, 442
Ferguson, Margaret Clay, 441–42
Fernald, Grace Maxwell, 442
Fernald, Maria Elizabeth (Smith), 443
Ferrand, Elizabeth M., 443
Fielde, Adele Marion, 444
Fieser, Mary, 445
Finkler, Rita V.(Sapiro), 446–47
Fischer, Irene Kaminka, 447
Fisher, Edna Marie, 449
Fisher, Elizabeth Florette, 449
Fisher, Sara Carolyn, 450
Fish, Marie Poland, 448
Fleming, Williamina Paton Stevens, 453–54
Fletcher, Alice Cunningham, 454–55
Flock, Eunice Verna, 455
Foot, Katherine, 458
Fossey, Dian, 458
Fossler, Mary Louise, 460
Foster, Josephine Curtis, 460
Foster, Margaret D., 460–61
Fowler-Billings, Katharine Stevens, 462–63
Fowler, Lydia Folger, 461–62
Fox, Ruth, 463–64
Frank, Margaret, 465
Frantz, Virginia Kneeland, 466
Frenkel-Brunswik, Else, 469–70
Friend, Charlotte, 474
Fromm, Erika Oppenheimer, 475–76
Frostig, Marianne Bellak, 476–77
Fulford, Margaret Hannah, 477–78
Furness, Caroline Ellen, 478–79
Gage, Susanna Phelps, 480–81
Gaige, Helen (Thompson), 481
Gamble, Eleanor Acheson Mcculloch, 482
Gantt, Love Rosa, 482–83
Gardner, Julia Anna, 484–85
Gardner, Mary Sewall, 485
Garfield, Viola Edmundson, 485–86

Garnjobst, Laura Flora, 487
Garretson, Mary (Welleck), 487–88
Gates, Fanny Cook, 489–90
Gaw, Esther Allen, 491–92
Gaw, Frances Isabel, 492–93
Genung, Elizabeth Faith, 494–95
Gerould, Elizabeth Wood, 497
Gerry, Eloise B., 497–98
Gey, Margaret Lewis, 499
Gibbons, Vernette Lois, 499
Gilbert, Ruth, 500–501
Gilbreth, Lillian Evelyn Moller, 501–2
Gilkey, Helen Margaret, 502
Gill, Jocelyn Ruth, 502–3
Gilroy, Helen (Turnbull), 503
Gitelson, Frances H., 505
Glasgow, Maude, 506
Glass, Jewell Jeanette, 506–7
Gleason, Josephine Mixer, 507
Gleason, Kate, 507
Gleason, Rachel Brooks, 508
Glueck, Eleanor (Touroff), 509
Goeppert Mayer, Maria Gertrud Käte, 510–11
Goldfeder, Anna, 512–13
Goldfrank, Esther Schiff, 513–14
Goldhaber, Sulamith, 514
Goldman, Hetty, 514–15
Goldring, Winifred, 515–16
Goldsmith, Grace Arabell, 516–17
Goldthwaite, Nellie Esther, 517–18
Goodenough, Florence Laura, 518–19
Goodrich, Sarah Frances, 519
Gordon, Kate, 520
Graham, Helen (Treadway), 522
Gravatt, Annie Evelyn (Rathbun), 522–23
Graves, Elizabeth (Riddle), 523
Gray, Etta, 523
Gray, Susan Walton, 524–25
Green, Arda A., 525–26
Greene, Catherine (Littlefield), 527–28
Green, Vera Mae, 526–27
Gregory, Emily L., 528
Gregory, Emily Ray, 528–29
Gregory, Louisa Catherine (Allen), 529–30
Gregory, Louise Hoyt, 530
Greig, Margaret Elizabeth, 530
Greisheimer, Esther Maud, 530
Griffin, Harriet Madeline, 531
Griggs, Mary Amerman, 531
Grinnell, Hilda Wood, 532
Griswold, Grace Hall, 533
Gunther, Erna, 538
Guthrie, Mary Jane, 538–39
Hagood, Margaret Loyd Jarman, 542–43
Hahn, Dorothy Anna, 543
Hall-Brown, Lucy, 547
Hall, Dorothy, 545
Halliday, Nellie, 547
Hall, Julia Brainerd, 545–46
Hallowell, Susan Maria, 548
Hall, Rosetta Sherwood, 546–47
Hamerstrom, Frances (Flint), 548–49
Hamilton, Alice, 549–50
Hamilton, Peggy-Kay, 550–51
Hanfmann, Eugenia, 551–52

Hanks, Jane Richardson, 552–53
Hansen, Hazel D., 553
Hardesty, Mary, 555
Hardwick, Rose Standish, 556
Hardy, Harriet, 557
Hardy, Thora Marggraff Plitt, 557
Harmon, Élise F., 557–58
Harrower, Molly R., 559–60
Hart, Esther Hasting, 560
Hart, Helen, 560
Hartt, Constance Endicott, 560–61
Harvey, Ethel Nicholson Browne, 561–62
Harwood, Margaret, 562–63
Hathaway, Millicent Louise, 565
Hawes, Harriet (Boyd), 568–69
Hawn Mirabile, Margaret H., 570
Hayes, Ellen Amanda, 570–71
Hayner, Lucy Julia, 571–72
Haywood, Charlotte, 572
Hazen, Elizabeth Lee, 572–73
Hazlett, Olive Clio, 574
Hearst, Phoebe (Apperson), 574–75
Heath, Daisy Winifred, 575
Hedges, Florence, 577
Hefferan, Mary, 578
Heidbreder, Edna Frances, 578–79
Heinlein, Julia Elizabeth Heil, 580–81
Henderson, Nellie Frater, 583
Hennel, Cora Barbara, 583–84
Heppenstall, Caroline A., 585
Herrick, Christine (Terhune), 586
Herrick, Julia Frances, 586
Herrick, Sophia Mcilvaine (Bledsoe), 586–87
Herskovits, Frances S.(Shapiro), 590–91
Hewitt, Dorothy, 594
Hibbard, Hope, 594–95
Hickey, Amanda Sanford, 595
Hicks, Beatrice Alice, 595–96
Hightower, Ruby Usher, 596
Hildreth, Gertrude Howell, 598–99
Hilgard, Josephine Rohrs, 599
Hill, Justina Hamilton, 601
Hill, Mary Elliott, 601
Hines, Marion, 601–2
Hinman, Alice Hamlin, 602
Hinrichs, Marie Agnes, 602
Hitchcock, Fanny Rysam Mulford, 603
Hitchcock, Orra White, 604
Hobby, Gladys Lounsbury, 605–6
Hoffleit, Ellen Dorrit, 607–8
Hoggan, Ismé Aldyth, 609
Hohl, Leonora Anita, 609–10
Hoke, Calm (Morrison), 610
Holley, Mary Austin, 610
Hollingworth, Leta Anna Stetter, 610–12
Holmes, Mary Emilee, 612
Holm, Esther (Aberdeen), 612
Hoobler, Icie Gertrude Macy, 614
Hooker, Henrietta Edgecomb, 615
Hooker, Marjorie, 615
Hopper, Grace (Brewster Murray), 616–17
Hough, Margaret Jean Ringier, 619
Howard Beckman, Ruth Winifred, 620
Howard Wylde, Hildegarde, 620–22
Howe Akeley, Delia Julia Denning, 622–23

United States of America (*cont.*)

Howes, Ethel Dench Puffer, 623
Hubbard, Marian Elizabeth, 624
Hubbard, Ruth Marilla, 624
Hubbs, Laura Cornelia (Clark), 624–25
Hughes-Schrader, Sally, 628
Hummel, Katharine Pattee, 628–29
Hunscher, Helen Alvina, 629
Hunt, Caroline Louisa, 629
Hunt, Eva Verbitsky, 629–30
Hunt, Harriot Kezia, 630–31
Hurlock, Elizabeth Bergner, 632
Hurston, Zora Neale, 632–33
Hussey, Priscilla Butler, 633
Hyde, Ida Henrietta, 635–36
Hyman, Libbie Henrietta, 636–37
Ide, Gladys Genevra, 642
Ilg, Frances Lillian, 642–43
Irwin, Marian, 643–44
Ives, Margaret, 646–47
Jacobi, Mary Corinna Putnam, 648–50
Jacobson, Clara, 651
Jeanes, Allene Rosalind, 654–55
Jensen, Estelle Louise, 656
Johnson, Dorothy Durfee Montgomery, 660
Johnson, Hildegarde (Binder), 660
Johnson, Minnie May, 661
Jones, Amanda Theodosia, 663–64
Jones, Eva Elizabeth, 664–65
Jones, Lorella Margaret, 665
Jones, Mary Amanda Dixon, 666
Jones, Mary Cover, 666–67
Jordan, Louise, 667–68
Jordan, Sara Claudia (Murray), 668–69
Joslin, Lulu, 669
Josselyn, Irene (Milliken), 669–70
Justin, Margaret M., 672
Kaan, Helen Warton, 673
Kahn, Ida, 675
Kanouse, Bessie Bernice, 675–76
Karp, Carol Ruth (Vander Velde), 677–78
Karrer, Annie May Hurd, 678
Keeler, Harriet Louise, 680
Keen, Angeline Myra, 680–81
Keeney, Dorothea Lilian, 681
Keil, Elsa Marie, 681–82
Keith, Marcia Anna, 682
Kellerman, Stella Victoria (Dennis), 683–84
Kelley, Louise, 684
Kellogg, Louise, 684–85
Kellor, Frances A., 685
Kelly, Isabel Truesdell, 686–87
Kelly, Margaret G., 687
Kelly, Margaret W., 687
Kendall, Claribel, 687–88
Kendrick, Pearl (Luella), 688
Kennard, Margaret Alice, 688
Kent, Grace Helen, 690
Kent, Kate Peck, 690–91
Keur, Dorothy Louise (Strouse), 692–93
King, Helen Dean, 695–97
King, Jessie Luella, 697
King, Louisa Boyd (Yeomans), 697–98
Kingsley, Louise, 699
King, Susan (Raymond), 698–99

Kirkbride, Mary Butler, 701
Kittrell, Flemmie Pansy, 701–2
Kleegman, Sophia, 702–3
Kline, Virginia Harriett, 706
Klosterman, Mary Jo, 706–7
Kluckhohn, Florence Rockwood, 707
Knight, Margaret, 708
Knopf, Eleanora Frances (Bliss), 708–9
Knowles, Ruth Sheldon, 710–11
Knull, Dorothy J., 711
Koch, Helen Lois, 712
Koch, Marie Louise, 712–13
Komarovsky, Mirra, 716–17
Koprowska, Irena Grasberg, 717
Korringa, Marjorie K., 718–19
Koshland, Marian (Elliott), 719–20
Krasnow, Frances, 725
Kroeber, Theodora Kracaw, 725–26
Kunde, Margaret Meta H., 729–30
L'esperance, Elise Depew Strang, 777–78
Ladd-Franklin, Christine, 731–32
Laird, Carobeth (Tucker), 733–34
Laird, Elizabeth Rebecca, 734–35
La Mance, Lora Sarah (Nichols), 736
Lamarck, Cornelié, 736
Lamme, Bertha, 736–37
Lamonte, Francesca Raimonde, 737
Lampe, Lois, 737–38
Lancefield, Rebecca Craighill, 739–40
Landes, Ruth (Schlossberg), 740–41
Langdon, Fanny E., 742
Langdon, Ladema M., 742–43
Lange, Linda Bartels, 743
Lange, Mathilde Margarethe, 743
Langford, Grace, 743–44
Larsson, Elisabeth, 746
Laskey, Amelia (Rudolph), 747–48
Lassar, Edna Ernestine (Kramer), 748–49
Latham, Vida Annette, 750
Latimer, Caroline Wormeley, 750–51
Laubenstein, Linda, 751
Laughlin, Emma Eliza, 751–52
Law, Annie, 753
Lawrence, Barbara, 754
Lawton, Elva, 755–56
Leach, Mary Frances, 757
Leacock, Eleanor Burke, 757–58
Leakey, Mary Douglas (Nicol), 758–59
Leavitt, Henrietta Swan, 759
Le Beau, Désirée, 759–60
Lee, Julia Southard, 763
Lee, Rebecca, 764
Lee, Rose Hum, 764
Lehr, Marguerite (Anna Marie), 769
Leighton, Dorothea (Cross), 769–70
Leland, Evelyn, 770
Lemmon, Sarah Plummer, 771
Leverton, Ruth Mandeville, 778
Levi-Montalcini, Rita, 779–81
Levine, Lena, 781–82
Lewis, Florence Parthenia, 782–83
Lewis, Graceanna, 783
Lewis, Helen Geneva, 783
Lewis, Isabel (Martin), 783–84
Lewis, Lilian (Burwell), 784

Lewis, Madeline Dorothy (Kneberg), 784–85
Lewis, Margaret Adaline Reed, 785–86
Lewis, Mary Butler, 786–87
Libby, Leona Woods Marshall, 787–88
Lieber, Clara Flora, 789–90
Lines, Dorolyn (Boyd), 793
Linton, Laura Alberta, 793–94
Litzinger, Marie, 797–98
Lloyd, Rachel, 798
Lochman-Balk, Christina, 798–99
Logan, Martha Daniell, 799
Logan, Myra Adele, 800
Logsdon, Mayme (Irwin), 800
Longshore, Hannah E.(Myers), 802–3
Lovejoy, Esther Pohl, 806–7
Loveless, Mary Hewitt, 807
Lowater, Frances, 807–8
Lowell, Frances Erma, 808
Lozier, Clemence Sophia (Harned), 809
Luomala, Katharine, 811–12
Lyon, Mary, 814–15
Maass, Clara Louise, 817
Macdonald, Eleanor Josephine, 819
MacDougall, Mary Stuart, 819–20
Macklin, Madge (Thurlow), 824–25
Mack, Pauline Beery, 822–24
Maclaughlin, Florence Edith Carothers, 826
Macleod, Annie Louise, 827
Macleod, Grace, 827–28
Macrobert, Rachel (Workman), Lady of Douneside and Cromar, 829
Mahler, Margaret Schönberger, 830–31
Makemson, Maude (Worcester), 832–33
Maling, Harriet Florence (Mylander), 833–34
Mallory, Edith (Brandt), 834–35
Maltby, Margaret Eliza, 835
Man, Evelyn Brower, 835–36
Manning, Ann B. (Harned), 836–37
Manson, Grace Evelyn, 837
Marlatt, Abby Lillian, 844
Marriott, Alice Lee, 844–45
Marshall, Clara, 845–46
Marsh, Mary Elizabeth, 845
Martin, Ella May, 847–48
Martin, Emilie Norton, 848
Martin, Lillien Jane, 848
Mason, Carol Y., 850–51
Masters, Sybilla (Righton), 853
Mateer, Florence Edna, 853
Mateyko, Gladys Mary, 853–54
Mather, Sarah, 854
Mathias, Mildred Esther, 854–55
Maury, Antonia Caetana de Paiva, 856–57
Maury, Carlotta Joaquina, 857–58
Maver, Mary Eugenie, 858
Maxwell, Martha Dartt, 858–59
Mayo, Clara Alexandra (Weiss), 860
McAvoy, Blanche, 860
McBride, Katharine Elizabeth, 861
McCarthy, Dorothea Agnes, 861–62
McClintock, Barbara, 862–64
McCracken, Elizabeth (Unger), 865
McCracken, Mary Isabel, 865–66
McCrea, Adelia, 866
McDonald, Janet, 866

McDowell, Louise Sherwood, 866–67
McGee, Anita (Newcomb), 867–68
McGlamery, Josie Winifred, 868
McGraw, Myrtle Byram, 868–69
McGuire, Ruth Colvin Starrett, 869
McHale, Kathryn, 869–70
McKeag, Anna Jane, 870
McKinney, Ruth Alden, 870–71
McLean, Helen (Vincent), 871–72
McVeigh, Ilda, 872
Mead, Margaret, 872–74
Medes, Grace, 874–75
Meek, Lois Hayden, 876–77
Meigler, Marie J., 877
Memmler, Ruth Lundeen, 880–81
Mendenhall, Dorothy (Reed), 881–82
Mergler, Marie, 884
Meritt, Lucy Taxis (Shoe), 885
Merrifield, Mary Philadelphia (Watkins), 885
Merrill, Helen Abbot, 885–86
Merrill-James, Maud Amanda, 886
Messina, Angelina Rose, 886–87
Mexia, Ynes, 889–90
Michael, Helen Cecilia Desilver Abbott, 891–92
Miles, Catherine Cox, 894
Miller, Bessie Irving, 895–96
Miller, Elizabeth Cavert, 896–97
Miller, Olive Thorne, 897
Minoka-Hill, Lillie Rosa, 897–98
Minor, Jessie Elizabeth, 898
Minot, Ann Stone, 898–99
Mitchell, Evelyn Groesbeeck, 900–901
Mitchell, Helen Swift, 901
Mitchell, Maria, 901–5
Mitchell, Mildred Bessie, 905
Moody, Mary Blair, 910
Mooney-Slater, Rose Camille Lediеu, 910–11
Moore, Anne, 911
Moore, Emmeline, 911
Moore, Lillian Mary, 912
Moore, Ruth Ella, 912
Morgan, Agnes Fay, 913
Morgan, Ann Haven, 913–14
Morgan, Lilian Vaughan Sampson, 914–15
Morris, Margaretta Hare, 917
Morse, Elizabeth Eaton, 917
Morse, Meroë Marston, 918
Morton, Emily L., 918
Morton, Rosalie Slaughter, 918–20
Mosher, Clelia Duel, 920–21
Mueller, Kate Heuvner, 922–23
Murphy, Lois Barclay, 924–25
Murray, Margaret Ransone, 928
Murtfeldt, Mary, 928–29
Myers, Mabel Adelaide, 929
Nance, Nellie Ward, 930
Neal, Marie Catherine, 932
Nelson, Katherine Greacen, 933–34
Nemir, Rosa Lee, 934–35
Newson, Mary Frances Winston, 937–38
Nice, Margaret Morse, 939–40
Nichols, Mary Louise, 940–41
Nichols, Mary Sargeant Neal Gove, 941–42
Nickerson, Dorothy, 942

Nickerson, Margaret (Lewis), 942
Nightingale, Dorothy Virginia, 944
Norsworthy, Naomi, 950–51
Northrup, Ann Hero, 953
Noyes, Mary Chilton, 953
Nuttall, Zelia Maria Magdalena, 954
Nutting, Mary Adelaide, 954–55
O'Brien, Ruth, 956
O'Connell, Marjorie, 957
O'Shea, Harriet Eastabrooks, 967
Ogilvie, Ida Helen, 958–59
Okey, Ruth Eliza, 961
Oppenheimer, Ella Hutzler, 963
Oppenheimer, Jane Marion, 963–64
Orent-Kelles, Elsa, 964
Owen, Luella Agnes, 969
Owens-Adair, Bethenia, 970
Pabst, Marie B., 971
Paine, Mary Esther (Trueblood), 972–73
Palmer, Alice W., 974
Palmer, Dorothy Bryant (Kemper), 974
Palmer, Elizabeth Day, 974–75
Palmer, Katherine Evangeline Hilton (Van Winkle), 975–76
Palmer, Margaretta, 976
Palmer, Miriam Augusta, 976
Palmer, Sophia French, 976–77
Palmie, Anna Helene, 977
Parker, Ivy May, 979–80
Parkins, Phyllis Virginia, 980
Parloa, Maria, 980
Parmelee, Ruth A., 980–81
Parrish, Rebecca, 981
Parry, Angenette, 981
Parsons, Elizabeth Ingersoll, 982
Parsons, Eloise, 981–82
Parsons, Elsie Worthington (Clews), 982–83
Parsons, Emily Elizabeth, 983–84
Parsons, Helen Tracy, 984
Patch, Edith Marion, 987–88
Patrick, Ruth, 988–89
Patterson, Flora Wambaugh, 990
Pattullo, June Grace, 990
Paulsen, Alice Elizabeth, 990–91
Pavenstedt, Eleanor, 991–92
Payne-Gaposchkin, Cecilia Helena, 994–96
Payne, Nellie Maria de Cottrell, 993
Payne, Rose Marise, 993–94
Peak, Helen, 996–97
Pearce, Louise, 997–98
Pearl, Maud Dewitt, 998
Peckham, Elizabeth (Gifford), 999
Peebles, Florence, 999–1000
Pendleton, Ellen Fitz, 1002–3
Pennington, Mary Engle, 1003–4
Perlmann, Gertrude Erika, 1007–8
Petermann, Mary Locke, 1010–11
Peterson, Edith (Runne), 1011
Peterson, Ruth Dixon, 1011–12
Petran, Elizabeth Irene, 1012
Pettit, Hannah Steele, 1013
Pettit, Mary Dewitt, 1013
Pfeiffer, Norma Etta, 1014
Pfiester, Lois Ann, 1015
Phelps, Almira Hart Lincoln, 1015–16

Phelps, Martha Austin, 1016
Phillips, Melba Newell, 1017–18
Pickett, Lucy Weston, 1020
Pickford, Grace Evelyn, 1020–21
Picotte, Susan (La Flesche), 1022–23
Pierce, Madelene Evans, 1023
Pierce, Marion (Armbruster), 1023–24
Pinckney, Eliza (Lucas), 1024–25
Pittman, Margaret Jane, 1030–31
Platt, Julia Barlow, 1031–32
Plummer, Helen Jeanne (Skewes), 1033–34
Pollack, Flora, 1038
Pool, Judith Graham, 1039–40
Porada, Edith, 1041–42
Porter, Mary Winearls, 1043–44
Potter, Edith Louise, 1045–46
Potter, Ellen Culver, 1046
Povitsky, Olga Raissa, 1047
Powdermaker, Hortense, 1047–48
Pressey, Luella (Cole), 1051
Preston, Ann, 1051–52
Price, Dorothy, 1053
Prince, Helen Walter (Dodson), 1055
Pringle, Elizabeth Waties (Allston), 1055–56
Proctor, Mary, 1057
Proskouriakoff, Tatiana, 1057–58
Pruette, Lorine Livingston, 1058–59
Putnam, Helen Cordelia, 1059–60
Putnam, Mary Louise (Duncan), 1061
Quiggle, Dorothy, 1063
Quimby, Edith Smaw (Hinckley), 1063–64
Quirk, Agnes, 1064–65
Rabinoff, Sophie, 1066–67
Ramsey, Elizabeth Mapelsden, 1070–71
Rand, Marie Gertrude, 1072–73
Randolph, Harriet, 1074
Rathbun, Mary Jane, 1075
Ratner, Sarah, 1076–78
Ray, Dixy Lee, 1079–80
Raymond-Schroeder, Aimee J., 1080
Reames, Eleanor Louise, 1081
Reddick, Mary Logan, 1081–82
Reder, Ruth Elizabeth, 1082
Redfield, Helen, 1082–83
Reed, Eva M., 1083
Rees, Mina Spiegel, 1084
Reichard, Gladys Amanda, 1087
Reid, Mary Elizabeth, 1088
Reimer, Marie, 1088
Remond, Sarah Parker, 1089
Rhine, Louise Ella (Weckesser), 1091
Rhodes, Mary Louise, 1092
Rice-Wray, Edris, 1092–93
Richards, Clarice Audrey, 1094–95
Richards, Ellen Henrietta Swallow, 1095–97
Richards, Mildred Hoge (Albro), 1098
Riddle, Lumina Cotton, 1099
Ridenour, Nina, 1099–1100
Rigas, Harriett B., 1100
Ring, Barbara Taylor, 1100–1101
Rioch, Margaret J., 1101
Ripley, Martha (Rogers), 1102
Ritter, Mary Elizabeth (Bennett), 1103
Robb, Jane (Sands), 1104–5
Roberts, Charlotte Fitch, 1105–6

United States of America (*cont.*)
Roberts, Dorothea Klumpke, 1106
Roberts, Edith Adelaide, 1106–7
Roberts, Lydia Jane, 1107–8
Robertson, Florence, 1108
Robeson, Eslanda Cordoza (Goode), 1110–11
Robinson, Daisy Maude (Orleman), 1111
Robinson, Julia (Bowman), 1113–14
Robinson, Margaret (King), 1114
Robscheit-Robbins, Frieda Saur, 1115
Rockwell, Alice Jones, 1116
Rockwell, Mabel MacFerran, 1116–17
Roe, Anne, 1117–19
Roe, Josephine Robinson, 1119
Roger, Muriel, 1119–20
Rogers, Agnes Lowe, 1120
Rogers, Julia Ellen, 1120–21
Rogers, Marguerite Moillet, 1121
Rogick, Mary Dora, 1121–22
Róna, Elisabeth, 1122–23
Ronzoni, Ethel (Bishop), 1124
Rose, Flora, 1125
Rose, Glenola Behling, 1125
Rose, Mary Davies Swartz, 1125–26
Ross, Mary G., 1127–28
Rubin, Vera (Dourmashkin), 1133–34
Rucker, Augusta, 1134
Rudnick, Dorothea, 1135
Rumbold, Caroline (Thomas), 1136
Russell, Jane Anne, 1137–38
Sabin, Florence Rena, 1140–42
Safford, Mary Jane, 1143–44
Sager, Ruth, 1144–45
Salmon, Eleanor Seely, 1146
Sanborn, Ethel, 1147
Sandhouse, Grace Adelbert, 1148–49
Sandiford, Irene, 1149
Sanford, Vera, 1149
Sanger, Margaret Higgins, 1149–51
Sawin, Martha, 1155
Say, Lucy (Sistare), 1155–56
Schaffner, Mabel (Brockett), 1156
Schantz, Viola Shelly, 1156–57
Scotland, Minnie (Brink), 1167
Scott, Charlotte Angas, 1167–68
Scott, Flora Murray, 1168
Scudder, Ida Sophia, 1169–70
Seaman, Elizabeth Cochrane, 1170–71
Sears, Pauline Snedden, 1171–72
Seegal, Beatrice Carrier, 1172–73
Seibert, Florence Barbara, 1173–74
Semple, Ellen Churchill, 1176–77
Sessions, Kate Olivia, 1177–78
Sewall, Lucy, 1178
Seward, Georgene Hoffman, 1178–79
Sharp, Emily Katharine (Dooris), 1181
Sharsmith, Helen Katherine, 1182
Shattuck, Lydia White, 1182–83
Sheldon, Jennie Arms, 1183
Shepardson, Mary, 1184
Sheps, Mindel (Cherniack), 1184–85
Sherif, Carolyn (Wood), 1185
Sherman, Althea Rosina, 1185–86
Sherman, Irene Case, 1186
Sherrill, Mary Lura, 1186–87

Shields, Margaret Calderwood, 1187
Shinn, Milicent Washburn, 1187–88
Shirley, Mary Margaret, 1188
Short, Jessie May, 1188–89
Silliman, Hepsa Ely, 1194–95
Simons, Lao Genevra, 1195
Sinclair, Mary Emily, 1195–96
Sitterly, Charlotte Emma (Moore), 1197
Slosson, Annie Trumbull, 1199
Slye, Maud, 1199–1200
Smart, Helen Edith (Fox), 1200
Smith, Anne Millspaugh (Cooke), 1201–2
Smith, Annie Morrill, 1203
Smith, Clara Eliza, 1204–5
Smith, Elizabeth (Hight), 1205
Smith, Emily Adelia (Pidgen), 1205
Smith, Erma Anita, 1205
Smith, Erminnie Adele (Platt), 1205–6
Smith, Isabel Fothergill, 1206–7
Smith, Isabel Seymour, 1207
Smith, Janice Minerva, 1207
Smith, Margaret Kiever, 1207
Smith, Marian Wesley, 1207–8
Smith, Olive Watkins, 1208–9
Snow, Julia Warner, 1210
Sommer, Anna Louise, 1216
Sorokin, Helen Petrovna (Beratynskaiia),
    1216–17
South, Lillian Herrald, 1218
Spalding, Effie Southworth, 1218
Spence, Eliza Jane (Edmondson), 1218
Spencer, Adelin Elam, 1218–19
Sperry, Pauline, 1219
Spiegel-Adolf, Mona, 1219
Sponer-Franck, Hertha Dorothea Elisabeth,
    1219–21
Stadnichenko, Tasia Maximovna, 1222
Stanley, Louise, 1222
Stanton, Hazel Martha, 1223
Stearns, Genevieve, 1224
Steed, Gitel Poznanski, 1224–25
Steinhardt, Edna, 1225
Stern, Catherine (Brieger), 1229
Stern, Frances, 1229–30
Stevens, Nettie Maria, 1230–32
Stevenson, Matilda Coxe (Evans), 1232
Stevenson, Sarah Ann (Hackett), 1233–34
Stevenson, Sara (Yorke), 1233
Stewart, Isabel Maitland, 1235–36
Stewart, Maude, 1236
Stewart, Sarah Elizabeth, 1236
Stiebeling, Hazel Katherine, 1236–37
Stieglitz, Mary Rising, 1237–38
Stimson, Barbara Bartlett, 1238
Stinchfield, Sara Mae, 1239
Stokey, Alma Gracey, 1239–40
Stone, Doris Zemurray, 1240–41
Stone, Isabelle, 1241–42
Stose, Anna Isabel (Jonas), 1243–44
Strang, Ruth May, 1246
Stratton Porter, Gene, 1247–48
Strobell, Ella Church, 1248
Strong, Harriet Williams (Russell), 1248–49
Strong, Helen Mabel, 1249
Strong, Miriam Carpenter, 1249

Stuart, Miranda, 1250
Sullivan, Betty Julia, 1250
Sullivan, Elizabeth Teresa, 1250–51
Sullivan, Ellen Blythe, 1251
Sunne, Dagny, 1252
Sutter, Vera Laverne, 1253–54
Svihla, Ruth Dowell, 1254–55
Swain, Clara A., 1255
Swanson, Pearl Pauline, 1255
Swift, Mary, 1255–56
Swindler, Mary Hamilton, 1256
Swope, Helen Gladys, 1256
Swope, Henrietta (Hill), 1256–57
Taeuber, Irene Barnes, 1260–61
Taft, Jessie, 1261
Talbot, Marion, 1262–63
Talbot, Mary, 1263
Talbot, Mignon, 1263–64
Taliaferro, Lucy (Graves), 1264
Taussig, Helen Brooke, 1265–66
Taussky-Todd, Olga, 1267–68
Taylor, Charlotte de Bernier Scarborough,
    1268
Taylor, Clara Mae, 1268–69
Taylor, Lucy Beaman (Hobbs), 1271
Taylor, Rose H., 1272
Teagarden, Florence Mabel, 1272
Telkes, Maria, 1273–74
Terry, Ethel Mary, 1275
Terzaghi, Ruth Doggett, 1275–76
Thelander, Hulda Evelin, 1277
Thelberg, Elizabeth (Burr), 1277–78
Thomas, Caroline (Bedell), 1279
Thomas, Dorothy Swaine (Thomas), 1279–80
Thomas, Mary Frame (Myers), 1281–82
Thome, Frances, 1282
Thompson, Caroline Burling, 1282
Thompson, Clara Mabel, 1283
Thompson, Helen, 1283–84
Thompson, Laura, 1284
Thompson, Mary Harris, 1284–85
Thoms, Adah B.(Samuels), 1285–86
Thurstone, Thelma Gwinn, 1287–88
Tilden, Evelyn Butler, 1289
Tilden, Josephine Elizabeth, 1289–90
Todd, Mabel Loomis, 1295
Todd, Ruth, 1295–96
Tolman, Ruth (Sherman), 1296–97
Tompkins, Sally Louisa, 1297
Toops, Laura Chassell (Merrill), 1298
Town, Clara Harrison, 1299
Tracy, Martha, 1299–1300
Treat, Mary Lua Adelia (Davis), 1301–2
Trotter, Mildred, 1303–4
Tum-Suden, Caroline, 1306
Tunnicliff, Ruth, 1307–8
Turnbull, Priscilla Freudenheim, 1308
Turner, Abby Howe, 1308
Tyler, Leona Elizabeth, 1309–10
Tyler, Martha G., 1310–11
Tyng, Anita E., 1311
Underhill, Ruth Murray, 1313–14
Valentine, Lila Hardaway (Meade), 1316–17
Van Blarcom, Carolyn (Conant), 1318–19
Van Deman, Esther Boise, 1319

Van Hoosen, Bertha, 1319–20
Van Rensselaer, Martha, 1320–21
Van Wagenen, Gertrude, 1321–22
Verder, Ada Elizabeth, 1326
Vivian, Roxana Hayward, 1329
Vold, Marjorie Jean Young, 1331–32
Vyssotsky, Emma T. R. (Williams), 1333
Walcott, Helene B. (Stevens), 1337–38
Walcott, Mary Morris (Vaux), 1338
Wald, Lillian D., 1338–39
Walker, Harriet Ann, 1339–40
Walker, Helen Mary, 1340
Walker, Mary Edward, 1340–41
Wallace, Louise Baird, 1342
Wall, Florence, 1342
Wallis, Ruth Sawtell, 1342–44
Walworth, Ellen Hardin, 1344–45
Warga, Mary Elizabeth, 1346–47
Waring, Sister Mary Grace, 1347
Warren, Madeleine (Field), 1347
Washburn, Margaret Floy, 1348–49
Washburn, Ruth, 1349
Wassell, Helen Erma, 1349
Watkins, Della Elizabeth (Ingram), 1349–50
Watts, Betty (Monaghan), 1351–52
Way, Katharine, 1352
Weeks, Alice Mary (Dowse), 1356–57
Weeks, Dorothy W., 1357–58
Weeks, Mary Elvira, 1358

Weinzierl, Laura (Lane), 1358–59
Weishaupt, Clara Gertrude, 1359
Weisskopf-Joelson, Edith Adele, 1361
Weiss, Marie Johanna, 1359–60
Weiss, Mary Catherine (Bishop), 1360–61
Welch, Betty, 1361
Welch, Winona Hazel, 1361
Weld, Julia Tiffany, 1361
Wellman, Beth Lucy, 1361–62
Wells, Agnes Ermina, 1362
Wells, Charlotte Fowler, 1362–63
Wells, Louisa, 1363
Welsh, Jane Kilby, 1363–64
Welsh, Lillian, 1364
Weltfish, Gene, 1364–66
Wessel, Bessie (Bloom), 1366
Westall, Mary, 1367
Westcott, Cynthia, 1367–68
Westover, Cynthia May, 1368
Wharton, Martha Lucille, 1368
Whedon, Frances Lovisa, 1368–69
Wheeler, Anna Johnson Pell, 1369–70
Wheeler, Elizabeth Lockwood, 1370
Wheeler-Voeglin, Erminie Brooke, 1370
White, Edith Grace, 1370–71
White, Elizabeth Juanita (Greer), 1371
White, Florence Roy, 1371–72
White, Frances Emily, 1372
White, Marian Emily, 1373

Whiting, Sarah Frances, 1374
Whitney, Mary Watson, 1374–75
Wickens, Aryness Joy, 1376
Wick, Frances Gertrude, 1375–76
Wiebusch, Agnes (Townsend), 1377
Wilder, Inez (Whipple), 1378
Wiley, Grace Olive, 1378
Willard, Emma (Hart), 1378–79
Willard, Mary Louisa, 1379
Willcox, Mary Alice, 1380
Williams, Anna Wessels, 1380–82
Williams, Marguerite (Thomas), 1382
Wilson, Edith, 1384
Wilson, Louise (Palmer), 1385–86
Young, Anne Sewell, 1413
Young, Leona Esther, 1414–15
Young, Mabel Minerva, 1415–16
Young, Mary Sophie, 1416
Young, Roger Arliner, 1416–17
Zachry, Caroline Beaumont, 1418
Zakrzewska, Marie Elizabeth, 1419–20
Zeckwer, Isolde Therese, 1421

W

Wales. *See* **Great Britain**

Y

Yugoslavia
Pensa-Joja, Josipa, 1004\

SUBJECT INDEX

NOTE: Boldface indicates dictionary entries.

A

Abbott, Maude Elizabeth Seymour, 1–2, 907
Abella, 4
Abel, Mary Hinman, 2–3
Abel, Theodora Mead, 3–4
Aberle, Sophie Bledsoe, 4–5
Abouchdid, Edna, 5
Abrahamson, Jadwiga, 5
Abrotelia, 5
Acosta-Sison, Honoria, 6
Acton, Frances (Knight), 6
Adametz, Lotte, 7
Adams, Amy Elizabeth Kemper, 7
Adams, Mildred, 7–8
Adamson, Joy (Gessner), 8–9
Addams, Jane, 9–10, 685, 925, 1308
Adelberger of Lombardy, 10
Adelle of the Saracens, 10
Adelmota of Carrara, 10
Adkins, Dorothy Christina, 10–11
Aelfleda, 11
Aemilia, 11
Aesara of Lucania, 11–12
Agamede, 12
Agassiz, Elizabeth Cary, 12–13, 1182
Aglaonike, 13–14
Agnes, Countess of Aix, 14
Agnesi, Maria Gaetana, 14–16, 874, 986
Agnes of Bohemia, 14
Agnes of Jerusalem, 14
Agnes of Silesia, 14
Agnodike, 16
agriculture, 1177–78, 1248–49
agronomy, 1024–25, 1314
agrostology, 246–47
Aitken, Janet Kerr, 16–17
Albertson, Mary, 18
Albrecht, Eleonore, 19
Albrecht, Grete, 19
alchemy, 41, 119, 269, 451, 1278
Alcock, Nora Lilian Leopard, 19
Aldrich-Blake, Louisa Brandreth, 19–20

Alexander, Annie Montague, 20–21
Alexander, Frances Elizabeth Somerville (Caldwell), 21–22
Alexander, Hattie Elizabeth, 22–23
algology, 490–91
Alimen, Henriette, 23
Ali, Safieh, 23
Allan, Mary Eleanor (Mea), 23
Allen, Doris Twitchell, 24–25
Allen, Eliza (Stevens), 25
Allen, Ruth Florence, 25–26
Alper, Thelma Gorfinkle, 26–27, 834
Altmann, Margaret, 27
Amalitskiya, Anna P., 28
Amalosunta, 28
Ameline, 28
Ames, Blanche (Ames), 28–29
Ames, Louise Bates, 30–31
Ames, Mary E. Plusifer, 31
anatomy
  fourteenth-century, 503
  seventeenth-century, 1139
  eighteenth-century, 49, 88–89, 126, 342, 841, 1006, 1013, 1139
  nineteenth-century, 338–39, 353–54, 910, 1006, 1140–42, 1372
  early twentieth-century, 131–32, 168, 305–6, 338–39, 353–54, 480–81, 800, 1140–42, 1158–59, 1168, 1303–4
  mid twentieth-century, 168, 305–6, 473, 785–86, 800, 1140–42, 1158–59, 1168
  late twentieth-century, 305–6, 800, 1158–59
  comparative, 473, 480–81
  plant, 1168
  See also neuroanatomy
Andersen, Dorothy Hansine, 31–32
Anderson, Caroline Virginia (Still) Wiley, 32–33, 1419
Anderson, Elda Emma, 33–34
Anderson, Elizabeth Garrett, 34–35, 945, 1157
Anderson, Evelyn M., 35–36
Anderson, Louisa Garrett, 36–37
Anderson, Rose Gustava, 37
Anderson, Violet Lousie, 37
Anderton-Smith, Mrs. W., 38

Andréas-Salomé, Louise Lelia, 38–39, 1245
Andrews, Eliza Frances, 39
Andrews, Grace, 39
Andromache, 39
Andrus, Ruth, 39–40
anesthesiology, 45–46, 143
Angst-Horridge, Anita, 40
Anica or Amyte, 40
Anna of Bohemia, 41
Anna Sophia of Denmark, 41
Anna Sophia of Hesse, 41
Anne, Electress of Denmark, 41
Anning, Mary, 41–42, 1018
Ann Medica of York, 40–41
Anslow, Gladys Amelia, 42–43
anthropology
  early nineteenth-century, 443–44
  mid nineteenth-century, 113, 163–64, 208, 339–41, 357, 419, 483–84, 485–86, 513–14, 526–27, 538, 552–53, 590–91, 629–30
  late nineteenth-century, 95–96, 552–53, 695, 954, 982–83, 1232–33
  early twentieth-century, 4–5, 95–96, 102–3, 113, 139, 163–64, 208, 218–19, 318–19, 339–41, 343–44, 357, 377–78, 390–91, 419, 443–44, 473, 483–84, 485–86, 513–14, 538, 552–53, 590–91, 590–91, 632–33, 673–74, 686–87, 692–93, 695, 725–26, 740–41, 760, 769–70, 811–12, 832, 872–74, 954, 982–83, 1025–26, 1047–48, 1086–87, 1093–94, 1110–11, 1133–34, 1166–67, 1174–75, 1201–2, 1207–8, 1232–33, 1240–41, 1284, 1303–4, 1307, 1354–56, 1364–66, 1387–88
  mid twentieth-century, 4–5, 139, 343–44, 377–78, 390–91, 494, 552–53, 590–91, 673–74, 686–87, 692–93, 725–26, 740–41, 757–58, 758–59, 760, 769–70, 776, 811–12, 832, 844–45, 872–74, 1047–48, 1086–87, 1093–94, 1133–34, 1166–67, 1174–75, 1184, 1201–2, 1207–8, 1224–25, 1240–41, 1284, 1303–4, 1307, 1354–56, 1364–66, 1373, 1387–88

anthropology (*cont.*)

   late twentieth-century, 4–5, 232–33, 339–41, 377–78, 419, 526–27, 552–53, 590–91, 629–30, 673–74, 686–87, 692–93, 725–26, 740–41, 757–58, 758–59, 769–70, 811–12, 832, 872–74, 1133–34, 1166–67, 1184, 1201–2, 1224–25, 1240–41, 1284, 1364–66, 1387–88

   cultural, 377–78, 590–91, 632–33, 632–33, 740–41, 757–58, 1133–34

   linguistic, 740–41

   medical, 769–70

   physical, 494, 776, 1166–67, 1303–4, 1307, 1342–44

   prehistoric, study of, 473

   social, 139, 1354–56

Antipoff, Helene, 43

Antoine, Lore, 43–44

Antoinette de Bellegarde, 44

Antonia, Maestra, 44–45

Apagar, Virginia, 45–46

Applin, Esther (Richards), 46–47

Apsley (Hutchinson), Lady Lucy, 47

arachnology, 999

Arakhangel'skaia, Aleksandra Gavriilovna, 50–51

Arber, Agnes (Robertson), 47–48, 1009, 1152

Arbuthnot, Isobel Agnes, 48

archeology

   nineteenth-century study, 52, 219–20, 553, 558, 568–69, 704–5, 926, 954, 1160–61, 1233, 1239, 1256, 1314–15, 1319

   early twentieth-century study, 52, 339–41, 364–65, 390–91, 419, 488–89, 514–15, 553, 558, 568–69, 568–69, 686–87, 690–91, 691–92, 704–5, 784–85, 786–87, 885, 926, 954, 1040–41, 1057–58, 1139, 1160–61, 1233, 1240–41, 1256, 1314–15, 1319

   mid twentieth-century study, 339–41, 390–91, 419, 553, 569, 686–87, 690–91, 691–92, 758–59, 784–85, 786–87, 885, 926, 1041–42, 1057–58, 1161, 1240–41, 1373

   late twentieth-century study, 339–41, 419, 569, 686–87, 690–91, 691–92, 758–59, 786–87, 885, 1041–42, 1057–58, 1161, 1240–41

   prehistoric, 1400–1401

   textile, 690–91

architecture, 82–83, 282–83

Arconville, Geneviév Charlotte d', 49

Arden, Lady Margaret Elizabeth (Spencer Wilson), 49

Ardinghelli, Maria Angela, 49–50, 874

Arete of Cyrene, 50

Arignote of Samos, 50

Arlitt, Ada Hart, 51

Armitage, Eleanora, 51–52

Armitage, Ella Sophia A. (Bulley), 52

Armitt, Annie Maria, 52

Armitt, Mary Louisa, 52–53

Armitt, Sophia, 53

Arnold, Magda Blondiau, 53

Arnstein, Margaret Gene, 53–54

Arsenjewa, A., 54

Artemisia of Caria II, 54

Arthur, Mary Grace, 54–55

Artner, Mathilde, 55

Ashby, Winifred Mayer, 55

Aspasia of Miletus, 55–56

Aspasia the Physician, 56

Astell, Mary, 56–57, 908

astronomy

   ancient, 13–14

   tenth-century, 436

   sixteenth-century, 170

   seventeenth-century, 309–10, 382, 593, 700–701

   eighteenth-century, 409, 587–89, 735–36, 772–73, 1024, 1345, 1389

   nineteenth-century, 189, 194, 216, 227–28, 269–71, 271–72, 311, 431–32, 453–54, 478–79, 554, 587–89, 626–27, 626–27, 653–54, 690, 759, 770, 782–83, 855–56, 856–57, 890, 901–5, 901–5, 1106, 1156, 1329, 1346, 1363, 1374–75, 1388–89, 1413

   early twentieth-century, 82, 139–40, 227–28, 271–72, 287–88, 320, 335, 431–32, 434, 478–79, 503–4, 554, 562–63, 607–8, 608–9, 647, 698–99, 759, 770, 782–83, 783–84, 832–33, 855–56, 856–57, 890, 976, 994–96, 1013, 1055, 1057, 1106, 1256–57, 1282, 1329, 1333, 1362, 1363, 1385, 1405, 1413

   mid twentieth-century, 82, 554, 562–63, 607–8, 608–9, 647, 698–99, 783–84, 832–33, 851–52, 994–96, 1055, 1256–57, 1405

   late twentieth-century, 554, 562–63, 607–8, 608–9, 647, 832–33, 851–52, 994–96, 1055, 1256–57, 1292–93

   literary treatment of, 106–7

   and religion, 270

astrophysics, 372, 505–6, 1197

Atkins, Anna, 57

Atkins, Louisa Catherine Fanny, 57

Atkinson, Louisa (Calvert), 57–58

Attersoll, Maria, 58

Atwater, Helen Woodard, 58–59

Atwood, Martha Maria, 59

Auerbach, Charlotte, 59–60

Aukenk, Kirsten (Lomholt), 60

Austin, Mary Lellah, 61

Austin, Rebecca, 31, **61**

Axiothea of Phlius, 62

Ayrton, Hertha Marks, 62–63, 314

Ayrton, Matilda (Chaplin), 64

B

Babcock, Harriet, 65

Bachman, Maria Martin, 66

Bacon, Clara (Latimer), 66

bacteriochemistry, 425

bacteriology

   late nineteenth-century, 1–2, 549–50, 578, 701, 1307–8, 1380–82

   early twentieth-century, 1–2, 114–15, 146, 181–82, 282, 298–99, 421–22, 428–30, 494–95, 500–501, 549–50, 578, 601, 657, 701, 705–6, 712–13, 739–40, 743, 870–71, 912, 929, 1012, 1030–31, 1047, 1067, 1200, 1218, 1236, 1307–8, 1326, 1380–82, 1399

   mid twentieth-century, 114–15, 146, 298–99, 421–22, 428–30, 451–52, 549–50, 657, 701, 705–6, 712–13, 739–40, 743, 870–71, 912, 929, 1012, 1030–31, 1047, 1200, 1218, 1236, 1326, 1399

   late twentieth-century, 298–99, 705–6, 739–40, 912, 929, 1030–31, 1326

   medical, 712–13

Baetjer, Anna Medora, 66–67

Bagley, Florence (Winger), 67

Bagshaw, Elizabeth Catherine, 67

Bahr-Bergius, Eva Vilhelmina Julia Von, 68

Bailey, Etherl Zoe, 68–69

Bailey, Florence Augusta (Merriam), 69–70

Baker, Anne Elizabeth, 70

Baker, Sarah Martha, 71–72

Baker, Sara Josephine, 70–71

Bakwin, Ruth (Morris), 72

Balaam, Ellen, 72–73

Balfour, Margaret Ida, 73

Balk, Christina (Lochman). *See* **Lochman-Balk, Christina**

Ball, Anne Elizabeth, 73

Ballard, Julia Perkins Pratt, 74–75

Ball, Josephine, 73–74

Ball, Mary, 73–74

Bancroft, Nellie, 75

Banga, Ilona, 75–76

Bang, Duck-Bangheung, 75

Banham, Katherine May, 76

Banks, Sarah Sophia, 76–77

Barbapiccola, Giuseppa Eleonora, 77

Barbarshova, Zoiaivanovna, 77

Barber, Helen Karen, 77–78

Barber, Mary Elizabeth (Bowker), 78

Barber, Zonia, 65–66

Bari, Nina Karlovna, 78–79

Barkly, Lady Anna Maria (Pratt), 79

Barkly, Lady Elizabeth Helen (Timins or Timmins), 79

Barlett, Helen Blair, 79–80

Barlow, Emma Nora (Darwin), 80

Barnard, Alicia Mildred, 80–81

Barnard, Edith Ethel, 81

Barnard, Lady Anne (Henslow), 81

Barnard, Lady Anne (Lindsay), 81

Barnes (Berners), Juliana, 81–82

Barney, Ida, 82

Barney, Nora Stanton (Blatch) De Forest, 82–83

Barnothy, Madeleine (Forro), 83

Barnum, Charlotte Cynthia, 83–84

Barrera, Oliva Sabuca de Nantes, 84

Barringer, Emily (Dunning), 84–85

Barrows, Katherine Isabel (Hayes) Chapin, 85–86

Barry, James (pseudonym). *See* **Stuart, Miranda**

Barton, Clara Harlowe, 86
Barton, Lela Viola, 86–87
Bascom, Florence, 87–88, 694, 708, 958, 1206
Bassi, Laura Maria Caterina, 88–89
Bass, Mary Elizabeth, 88
Batchelder, Esther Lord, 89–90
Bate, Dorothea Minola Alice, 90
Bates, Mary E., 90–91
Bateson, Anna, 91
Bateson, Beatrice, 91
Battle, Helen Irene, 92
Bauer, Grace M., 92
Baumann, Frieda, 92–93
Baumgarten-Tramer, Franziska, 93–94
Baumgartner, Leona, 94–95
Baum, Marie, 92
Baxter, Mildred Frances, 95
Bayern, Therese Von, 95–96
Bayley, Nancy, 96–97
Baynard, Anne, 97
Beanland, Sarah, 98
Beatley, Janice Carson, 98–99
Beatrice of Savoy, Countess of Provence, 99
Beaufort, Countess Margaret, 100
Beaufort, Harriet Henrietta, 99–100
Beausoleil, Martine de Bertereau. *See* Bertereau, Martine de (Baroness de Beausoleil)
Beauvallet, Marcellene Jeanne, 100
Becker, Lydia Ernestine, 101
Becker-Rose, Herta, 101–2
Beckman, A., 102
Beck, Sarah Coker (Adams), 100–101
Beckwith, Angie Maria, 102
Beckwith, Cora, 102
Beckwith, Martha Warren, 102–3
Beecher, Catharine Esther, 103
Beers, Catherine Virginia, 104
Beever, Mary, 104
Beever, Susan, 104–5
Behn, Aphra, 105–8
Behre, Ellinor H., 108
Beilby, Winifred. *See* Soddy, Winifred Moller (Bielby)
Belaeva, Elizaveta Ivanovna, 108–9
Belar, Maria, 110
Bell, Julia, 109
Belota [Johanna Belota], 110
Belyea, Helen Reynolds, 110–11
Bender, Hedwig, 111
Bender, Lauretta, 111–12
Bender, Wilma, 112
Benedict, Ruth (Fulton), 112–13, 208, 344, 740, 811, 873, 924, 982, 1086, 1224, 1313
Benett, Etheldred, 114
Bengston, Ida Albertina, 114–15
Bennett, Alice, 115
Bennett, Dorothea, 116
Benson, Margaret Jane, 116–17
Bentham, Ethel, 117
Bentham, Lady Mary Sophia (Fordyce), 117
Bentinck, Margaret Cavendish (Harley), Duchess of Portland, 117–18
Berenice. *See* Beronice

Berger, Emily V., 118
Berger, Katharina Bertha Charlotte, 118
Berners, Juliana. *See* Barnes, Juliana
Beronice, 118
Berridge, Emily Mary, 118–19
Bertereau, Martine de, Baroness de Beausoleil, 119
Berthagyta, Abbess, 119
Berthildis of Chelles, 119
Bertile of Chelles, 120
Bertillon, Caroline Schutze, 120
Besant, Annie (Wood), 120
Beutler, Ruth, 120–21
Bevier, Isabel, 121–22
Bhatia, Sharju Pandit, 122–23
Bhöm-wendt, Cäcilia, 153–54
Bibring, Grete Lehner, 123–24, 830
Bickerdyke, Mary Ann (Ball), 124–25, 140, 1144
Bidder, Anna McClean, 125
Bidder, Marion Greenwood, 125–26
Biheron, Marie Catherine, 126
Bilger, Leonora (Neuffer), 126–27
Billings, Katharine Stevens (Fowler-Lunn), 127
Bingham, Millicent (Todd), 127–28
biochemistry
  late nineteenth-century, 1227–28
  early twentieth-century, 35–36, 75–76, 179, 191, 203, 242, 250–51, 253–54, 278–79, 292–94, 325, 329, 391–93, 408, 410–11, 420–21, 435–36, 455, 522, 613–14, 669, 708, 711, 725, 826–27, 835–36, 858, 881–82, 898–99, 913, 932–33, 961, 962, 984, 1007–8, 1010–11, 1011–12, 1027, 1028–30, 1042–43, 1076–78, 1082, 1137–38, 1149, 1173–74, 1208–9, 1219, 1223–24, 1227–28, 1325–26, 1345, 1368, 1380, 1391–93
  mid twentieth-century, 35–36, 75–76, 179, 191, 203, 250–51, 253–54, 278–79, 292–94, 292–94, 325, 391–93, 408, 410–11, 415–16, 420–21, 435–36, 455, 522, 708, 711, 725, 809–10, 826–27, 835–36, 858, 881–82, 896–97, 898–99, 913, 932–33, 961, 1007–8, 1010–11, 1011–12, 1027, 1028–30, 1042–43, 1076–78, 1137–38, 1173–74, 1208–9, 1219, 1223–24, 1227–28, 1325–26, 1345, 1368
  late twentieth-century, 35–36, 250–51, 391–93, 410–11, 415–16, 420–21, 708, 809–10, 835–36, 858, 898–99, 932–33, 961, 1007–8, 1011–12, 1028–30, 1137–38, 1173–74, 1208–9, 1219
  plant, 962
biology
  fourth-century, 1062
  eighteenth-century, 114
  mid nineteenth-century, 1182–83
  nineteenth-century, 108, 114, 165–67, 206–8, 216–17, 695–97, 887–88, 937, 999–1000, 1111, 1182–83, 1386
  early twentieth-century, 27, 108, 165–67, 206–8, 206–8, 216–17, 233–34, 248,

285, 388, 423–25, 439, 530, 547, 555, 561–62, 591–92, 594, 628–29, 695–97, 743, 761–62, 773–74, 846–47, 853–54, 872, 887–88, 911, 927, 937, 963–64, 980, 998, 999–1000, 1004–5, 1016, 1020–21, 1073–74, 1079–80, 1083–84, 1111, 1115, 1217, 1276, 1307, 1385, 1386, 1421–22
  mid twentieth-century, 27, 220–21, 233–34, 285, 388, 439, 530, 548–49, 561–62, 561–62, 591–92, 594, 695–97, 719–20, 743, 761–62, 773–74, 846–47, 853–54, 872, 911, 927, 963–64, 980, 999–1000, 1020–21, 1073–74, 1079–80, 1083–84, 1115, 1119–20, 1276, 1307, 1341
  late twentieth-century, 27, 439, 548–49, 594, 719–20, 761–62, 846–47, 872, 927, 963–64, 980, 1119–20, 1341
  aquatic, 206
  cell, 439–40, 561–62, 927
  chemistry of, 220
  developmental, 1335–36
  invertebrate, 1083–84
  marine, 214–15, 761–62, 846–47, 1004–5
  mathematics applied to, 495
  Michurinist, 215
  molecular, 719–20, 1119–20
  natural history, 1182–83
  plant, 206
  race, 149–50
  reproductive, 555
  See also biophysics; microbiology; photobiology; radiobiology
biophysics, 586, 1063–64
biophysiology, 261–62
biostatistics, 1184–85
biostratigraphy, 1418–19
Bird, Grace Electa, 128
Bird, Isabella. *See* Bishop, Isabella Lucy Bird
Birdsall, Lucy Ellen, 128
Birstein, Vera, 129, 1404
Biscot, Jeanne, 129
Bishop, Ann, 129–31
Bishop, Isabella Bucy Bird, 131
Bishop, Katharine Scott, 131–32
Bissell, Emily P., 132
Bitting, Katherine Eliza (Golden), 132–33
Blackburne, Anna, 134–35
Blackburn, Kathleen Bever, 133–34
Blacker, Margaret Constance Helen, 135
Black, Florence, 133
Black, Hortensia, 133
Blackwell, Antoinette Louise (Brown), 135–36, 783
Blackwell, Elizabeth, 136–37, 808, 1051, 1104, 1361, 1419
Blackwell, Elizabeth Marianne, 138
Blackwell, Emily, 138–39, 319, 808, 1051, 1277, 1285, 1361, 1419
Blackwood, Beatrice Mary, 139
Blagg, Mary Adela, 139–40
Blake, Mary Safford, 140–41
Blanchan, Neltje (pseudonym). *See* Doubleday, Neltje Blanchan (de Graff)
Blanchard, Frieda Cobb, 141–42

Blanchard, Phyllis, 142
Blanquies, Lucie, 142–43
Blatchford, Ellen C., 143
Blatch, Nora Stanton. *See* Barney, Nora
    Stanton (Blatch) De Forest
Blau, Marietta, 143–44
Bledsoe, Lucybelle, 144–45
Blinova, Ekaterina Nikitichna, 145
Bliss, Dorothy Elizabeth, 145
Bliss, Eleanor Albert, 146
Bliss, Mary Campbell, 146
Block, Jeanne (Humphrey), 146–48
Blodgett, Katharine Burr, 148–49
Bluhm, Agnes, 149–50
Bluket, Nina Aleksandrovna, 150
Blunt, Katharine, 151, 1104
Bocchi (Bucca), Dorotea, 151
Bochantseva, Zinaida Petrovna, 152
Bodley, Rachel Littler, 152–53, 845, 1311,
    1372
Bogdanovskaia, Vera Evstaf'evna, 153
Boivin, Marie Gillain, 154
Bokova-Sechenova, Mariia Aleksandrovna,
    154–55, 1248
Boley, Gertrude Maud, 155
Bolschanina, M.A., 155
Bolton, Edith, 155
Bolus, Harriet Margaret Louisa (Kensit),
    155–56
Bomhard, Miriam Lucile, 156
Bonnay, Marchioness du, 156–57
Bonnevie, Kristine, 157–58
Boole, Mary (Everest), 158–59, 383
Boos, Margaret Bradley (Fuller), 159–60
Booth, Mary Ann Allard, 160
Boring, Alice Middleton, 160–62, 914
Borisova-Bekriasheva, Antoniia
    Georgievna, 162
Boron, Elizabeth (Riddle) Graves, 162–63
Borromeo, Clelia Grillo, 163, 874
Borsarelli, Fernanda, 163
Boswell, Katherine Cumming, 163
botany
    fourth-century B.C.E., 54
    seventeenth-century, 41, 1108
    eighteenth-century, 81
    mid eighteenth-century, 134–35, 156–57, 280
    late eighteenth-century, 134–35, 246, 446,
        545, 570, 651, 925–26, 1040, 1244–45,
        1273, 1302, 1308–9, 1337
    early nineteenth-century, 6, 31, 49, 57, 58, 59,
        79, 81, 99–100, 104, 117, 223, 243–44,
        400, 446, 464, 523–24, 531, 545, 561,
        570, 605, 633, 641–42, 651, 674, 675,
        690, 744–45, 765, 789, 872, 900, 907–8,
        915, 925, 925–26, 1040, 1070–71, 1136,
        1185, 1209, 1221–22, 1300–1301,
        1308–9, 1347, 1390
    mid nineteenth-century, 38, 57, 59, 73, 79,
        104, 117, 152–53, 223, 237, 243–44,
        246, 346, 433, 450, 480, 500, 523–24,
        561, 570, 614–15, 616, 633–35, 653,
        674, 690, 698, 699–700, 744–45, 755,
        765, 766, 789, 800, 813, 851, 859–60,
        872, 900, 907–8, 925, 951–52, 962,

    1027, 1046–47, 1136, 1182–83, 1209,
        1221–22, 1286–87, 1309, 1390
    late nineteenth-century, 6, 18, 25, 31, 39,
        51–52, 57–58, 61, 78, 79, 81, 91, 95–96,
        100–101, 104–5, 118–19, 132–33,
        152–53, 186, 209, 212, 246, 246–47,
        264, 265, 272, 280–81, 306, 308, 321,
        335, 342, 349–50, 364, 371–72, 394–96,
        433, 435, 438–39, 480, 500, 506, 519,
        523–24, 528, 534, 546, 548, 584,
        614–15, 614–15, 616, 637, 653, 680,
        682–83, 683–84, 709–10, 744–45,
        751–52, 755, 766, 771, 800, 813, 851,
        859–60, 874, 889–90, 951–52, 953–54,
        962, 990, 991, 1009, 1033, 1046–47,
        1068–69, 1083, 1087–88, 1092, 1099,
        1116, 1120–21, 1151–52, 1154–55,
        1156, 1168–69, 1182–83, 1189, 1202–3,
        1207, 1208, 1209, 1210, 1218, 1221,
        1221–22, 1272, 1285, 1286, 1286–87,
        1289–90, 1291, 1291–92, 1294–95,
        1300–1301, 1301–2, 1305, 1309, 1328,
        1339–40, 1371, 1394
    early twentieth-century, 19, 28–29, 39, 47–48,
        51–52, 53, 71–72, 75, 80, 91, 95–96,
        104–5, 118–19, 132–33, 138, 146, 150,
        155, 155–56, 162, 168, 173–74, 177,
        180–81, 182–83, 184, 190, 192–93,
        194–95, 209, 212, 218, 226, 246–47,
        248–49, 256–57, 262, 262–63, 268, 287,
        289, 298–99, 308, 321, 334–35, 336–37,
        342, 343, 349–50, 352–53, 362, 364,
        370, 370–71, 371–72, 374, 376–77,
        385–86, 387, 394–96, 397–98, 426–27,
        427–28, 430, 432, 438–39, 455, 458–59,
        464, 464–65, 477–78, 486, 490–91, 494,
        495, 497–98, 500, 503, 504, 522, 528,
        537–38, 541–42, 544, 544–45, 546, 547,
        548, 557, 564, 572, 577, 581, 583, 584,
        594, 596, 605, 609, 633–35, 637, 653,
        657, 661, 671, 675–76, 678, 680, 681,
        682–83, 692, 709–10, 718, 737–38,
        742–43, 745, 747, 751–52, 754, 755–56,
        766, 771, 782, 795, 814, 818, 838–39,
        847–48, 851, 854–55, 866, 872, 874,
        889–90, 906, 912–13, 932, 942, 948–49,
        950, 953–54, 968–69, 971–72, 973,
        978–79, 988–89, 990, 991, 1004, 1009,
        1014, 1033, 1043, 1049–50, 1052,
        1068–69, 1075, 1081, 1083, 1087–88,
        1092, 1093, 1097–98, 1099, 1106–7,
        1112–13, 1116, 1120–21, 1125,
        1132–33, 1147, 1151–52, 1154–55,
        1156, 1168, 1182, 1189, 1196–97,
        1202–3, 1207, 1208, 1209, 1209–10,
        1210–11, 1216, 1218, 1221, 1226,
        1239–40, 1242–43, 1244–45, 1249,
        1257–58, 1262, 1278–79, 1280–81,
        1286, 1289–90, 1291, 1294–95, 1301–2,
        1305, 1316, 1317–18, 1336–37,
        1339–40, 1349–50, 1351, 1352–53,
        1356, 1358, 1359, 1361, 1367, 1373,
        1384, 1385, 1395, 1412, 1416
    mid twentieth-century, 28–29, 47–48, 75,
        98–99, 138, 155, 155–56, 162, 173–74,

    177, 182–83, 194–95, 212, 218, 226,
        246–47, 248–49, 256–57, 296, 298–99,
        335–36, 343, 352–53, 364, 385–86, 387,
        394–96, 426–27, 427–28, 430, 446,
        447–48, 458–59, 464–65, 477–78,
        498–99, 522, 534, 537–38, 541–42,
        541–42, 548, 557, 564, 572, 577, 583,
        584, 596, 605, 653, 661, 675–76, 680,
        695, 718, 737–38, 742–43, 745, 751–52,
        754, 755–56, 782, 795, 838–39, 847–48,
        854–55, 865, 866, 872, 876, 884,
        889–90, 906, 912–13, 930, 942, 948–49,
        950, 964, 968–69, 972, 973, 978–79,
        988–89, 1004, 1014, 1043, 1050–51,
        1052, 1081, 1087–88, 1092, 1097–98,
        1104, 1106–7, 1112–13, 1129, 1132–33,
        1147, 1168, 1182, 1196–97, 1209–10,
        1210–11, 1221, 1226, 1239–40,
        1242–43, 1249, 1286, 1317–18, 1328,
        1336–37, 1351, 1353–54, 1359, 1361,
        1373
    late twentieth-century, 23, 98–99, 218, 226,
        296, 298–99, 335–36, 352–53, 385–86,
        426–27, 446, 498–99, 541–42, 564, 584,
        607, 653, 737–38, 742–43, 754, 755–56,
        838–39, 847–48, 854–55, 865, 872, 884,
        930, 964, 968–69, 972, 1004, 1015,
        1050–51, 1104, 1221, 1226, 1328,
        1353–54, 1359, 1361
    cryptogamic, 633–35
    See also geobotany; paleobotany
Bourdel, Léone, 163–64
Bourgeoise, Louyse, 164
Bouteiller, Marcelle, 164
Bouthilet, Lorraine, 164–65
Boveri, Marcella Imelda O'Grady, 165–67,
    1135
Bowen, Susan, 167
Boyd, Elizabeth Margaret, 167
Boyd, Louise Arner, 167–68
Boyer, Esther Lydia, 168
Bracher, Rose, 168
Bradley, Amy Morris, 168–69
Bradley, Frances Sage, 169–70
Brahe, Sophia, 170
Branch, Hazel Elisabeth, 170
Brandegee, Mary Katharine Layne, 171
Brand, Martha, 170–71
Branham, Sara Elizabeth, 171–72
Brant, Laura, 172
Braun, Annette Frances, 172–73
Braun, (Emma) Lucy, 173–74
Brazier, Mary Agnes Burniston, 174–75
Breckinridge, Mary, 175–76
Bredikhina, Evgeniia Aleksandrovna,
    176–77
Breed, Mary (Bidwell), 177
Brenchley, Winifred Elsie, 177
Brenk, Irene, 177–78
Brés Madeleine (Gébelin), 178–79
Breyer, Maria Gerdina (Brandwijk), 179
Brezina, Maria Aristides, 179
Bridget, Saint, of Ireland, 179
Bridget, Saint, of Scandinavia, 179
Bridgman, Olga Louise, 180

Briére, Nicole-Reine Etable de la. *See* Lepaute, Nicole-Reine
Briére, Yvonne, 180
Brightwen, Eliza (Elder), 180
Britten, Lilian Louisa, 180–81
Britton, Elizabeth Knight, 181
Broadhurst, Jean, 181–82
Brock, Sylvia (Deantonis), 182
Bromley, Helen Jean (Brown), 182–83
Bronner, Augusta Fox, 183
Brooke, Winifred, 184
Brooks, Harriet T., 184–85
Brooks, Matilda (Moldenhauer), 185–86
Brooks, Sarah Theresa, 186
Broomall, Anna Elizabeth, 186–87
Brousseau, Kate, 187
Brown, Charlotte Amanda Blake, 187–88
Brown, Charlotte Blake, 1103
Brown, Dame Edith Mary, 188–89
Browne, Ida Alison (Brown), 191–92
Browne, Lady Isabel Mary (Peyronnet), 192–93
Brown, Elizabeth, 189
Browne, Marjorie Lee, 193–94
Brown, Fay Cluff, 189–90
Brown, Mabel Mary, 190
Brown, Nellie Adalesa, 190–91
Brown, Rachel Fuller, 191
Bruce, Catherine Wolfe, 194
Bruce, Eileen Adelaide, 194–95
Brüch, Hilde, 195
Brückner, Frau Dr., 195
Brunetta, 196
Brunetti, R., 196
Brunfels, Frau Otto, 196
Brunswick, Ruth Jane (Mack), 196–97
Bryan, Alice Isabel (Bever), 197–98
Bryan, Margaret, 198–99
Bryan, Mary Katherine, 199
Bryant, Louise Stevens, 199
Bryant, Sophie (Willock), 199–200
bryology, 59, 181, 262–63, 755–56
Bucca, Dorotea. *See* Bocchi, Dorotea
Buchanan, Florence, 200
Buchbinder, Laura G. Ordan, 200–201
Buckel, Chloe H., 201–2
Buckland, Mary Morland, 202
Buckley, Arabella, 202–3, 801
Buell, Mary Van Rensselaer, 203
Buerk, Minerva (Smith), 203–4
Bühler, Charlotte Bertha (Malachowski), 204–5, 1178
Bülbring, Edith, 205, 1331
Bull, Nina Wilcox, 205–6
Bunch, Cordia, 206
Bunting, Martha, 206
Bunting-Smith, Mary (Ingraham), 206–8
Bunzel, Ruth Leah, 208, 873
Burges, Mary Anne, 208–9
Burgess, May (Ayres), 209
Burkill, Ethel Maud (Morrison), 209
Burlingham, Dorothy (Tiffany), 209–10, 470–72
Burlingham, Gertrude Simmons, 210–11
Burns, Eleanor Irene, 211

Burns, Louisa, 211
Burrell, Anna Porter, 212
Burr, Emily Throp, 65, 211
Burton, Helen Marie Rousseay (Kannemeyer), 212
Burtt Davy, Alice (Bolton), 212
Bury, Elizabeth (Lawrence), 212–13
Bury, Priscilla Susan (Falkner), 213–14
Bush, Katharine Jeannette, 214–15
Busk, Lady Marian (Balfour), 215
Byrd, Mary Emma, 216
Byrnes, Esther Fussell, 216–17
Byron, Augusta Ada, Countess of Lovelace, 217

C
Cadbury, Dorothy Adlington, 218
Cadilla de Martínez, María, 218–19
Cady, Bertha Louise Chapman, 219
Caerellia (Caerelia), 219
Calderone, Mary S., 220
Caldwell, Mary Letitia, 220
Cale, F. M., 221
Calenda, Constanza or Laurea Constantia, 221
Calkins, Mary Whiton, 221–23
Callcott, Lady Maria Graham, 223
Calvert, Catherine Louisa Waring (Atkinson), 223
Calvert, Emily Amelia (Adelia) (Smith), 224
Cambrière, Clarisse, 224
Campbell, Helen Stuart, 224–25
Campbell, May Sherwood, 226
Campbell, Persia Crawford, 226–27
Cannon, Annie Jump, 227–28
Capen, Bessie, 228
Carlson, Elizabeth, 228
Carlson, Lucille, 228
Carne, Elizabeth Catherine (Thomas), 228–29
Carothers, Estrella Eleanor, 229
Carpenter, Esther, 230
Carr, Emma Perry, 230–32, 1020
Carroll, Christiane (Mendrez), 232–33
Carroll, Dorothy, 232–33
Carson, Rachel Louise, 233–34
Carter, Edna, 166, 234
Carter, Elizabeth, 234–35
cartography, 447
Cartwright, Dame Mary Lucy, 235
Carus, Mary Hegeler, 235–36
Carvajales y Camino, Laura M. de, 236
Castle, Cora (Sutton), 236
Castra, Anna de, 236
Catani, Giuseppina, 236–37
Catherine of Bologna, Saint, 237
Catherine of Genoa, Saint, 237
Catherine of Siena, Saint, 237
Catherine Ursula, Countess of Baden, 237
Catlow, Maria Agnes, 237
Cattell, Psyche, 238
Cattoi, Noemí Violeta, 238–39
Cauchois, Yvette, 239
Caughlan, Georgeanne (Robertson), 239–40

Cauquil, Germaine Anne, 240
Cavendish, Margaret, Duchess of Newcastle, 240–41
Cellier, Elizabeth, 241–42
Cesniece-Freudenfelde, Zelma, 242
Chaix, Paulette Audemard, 242
Chalubinska, Aniela, 242–43
Chamié, Catherine, 243, 909
Chandler, Elizabeth, 243–44
Chandler, Marjorie Elizabeth Jane, 244–45
Chang, Moon Gyung, 245
Chang, Vivian, 245
Charles, Vera Katherine, 245–46, 990
Charlotte Sophia, Queen, 246
Charsley, Fanny Anne, 246
Chase, Mary Agnes Meara, 246–47
Chasman, Renate Wiener, 247–48
Châtelet, Gabrielle-Emilie le Tonnelier de Breuteuil, Marquise du. *See* Du Châtelet, Gabrielle-Emilie
Chauchard, B., 248
Chaudet, Naria Casanova de, 248
Cheesman, Lucy Evelyn, 248–49, 801
chemistry
first century, 850
second century, 850
fourth-century, 978
sixteenth-century, 170, 894
seventeenth-century, 805, 889
eighteenth-century, 478, 752–53
mid nineteenth-century, 126–27, 152–53, 1095–97, 1182–83
late nineteenth-century, 92, 121–22, 152–53, 177, 228, 272, 311–17, 334, 432, 457–58, 472–73, 544–45, 545–46, 603, 757, 775–76, 793–94, 798, 891–92, 953, 974, 1003–4, 1016, 1069–70, 1088, 1105, 1125–26, 1182–83, 1201, 1218–19, 1332–33, 1373
early twentieth-century, 7–8, 81, 89–90, 92, 112, 121–22, 126–27, 129, 155, 220–21, 240, 276, 295–96, 304–5, 311–17, 324, 332–33, 345, 347, 361, 363–64, 368–69, 370, 372–73, 433, 441, 445, 455, 460, 460–61, 478, 497, 499, 508–9, 517–18, 521–22, 525–26, 531–32, 540–41, 543, 545, 545–46, 565, 565–66, 579, 592, 601, 604, 610, 614, 618, 619, 654–55, 659, 660–61, 684, 687, 725, 757, 759–60, 763, 774, 776–77, 783, 787–88, 789–90, 798, 799, 821, 822–24, 827, 874–75, 888–89, 891–92, 898, 944, 947–48, 953, 956, 956–57, 979–80, 981–82, 984, 1003–4, 1008, 1010–11, 1016, 1019–20, 1023–24, 1057, 1059, 1063, 1069–70, 1088, 1102, 1105, 1110–11, 1111–12, 1124, 1125, 1125–26, 1165, 1186–87, 1216, 1218–19, 1222, 1224, 1236–37, 1237–38, 1246–47, 1250, 1256–57, 1258, 1269, 1273–74, 1275, 1299, 1325, 1331–32, 1342, 1347, 1351–52, 1358, 1366, 1370, 1371, 1371–72, 1379, 1384, 1386–87, 1395, 1397, 1401–2, 1402–4, 1414–15

chemistry (cont.)
mid twentieth-century, 7–8, 89–90, 92, 182,
230–32, 276, 296, 301–2, 324, 332–33,
363–64, 368–69, 455, 508–9, 565,
565–66, 601, 604, 614, 614–15, 618,
654–55, 659, 660–61, 684, 687, 725,
759–60, 763, 774, 787–88, 789–90, 799,
821, 822–24, 827, 874–75, 888–89, 898,
944, 947–48, 953, 956, 979–80,
1010–11, 1019–20, 1023–24, 1059,
1063, 1069–70, 1102, 1110–11,
1111–12, 1124, 1186–87, 1222, 1224,
1236–37, 1250, 1256–57, 1273–74,
1331–32, 1342, 1351–52, 1370, 1371,
1371–72, 1379, 1386–87, 1395, 1401–2,
1414–15
late twentieth-century, 182, 296, 301–2,
332–33, 565–66, 654–55, 659, 687,
787–88, 822–24, 874–75, 944, 979–80,
1250, 1273–74
agricultural, 1402–4
analytical, 601, 1057
biological, 7–8, 220
education in, 472–73
food, 1236–37
indexing of, 372
inorganic, 953
nutrition, 984
organic, 153, 258, 345, 445, 468–69, 684,
1088, 1111–12
physical, 230–32, 230–32, 301–2, 774, 1057,
1258, 1273–74, 1371
physiological, 304–5, 455, 517–18, 565,
565–66, 565–66, 565–66, 614, 614–15,
981–82, 1010–11
soil, 1216
textile, 763
See also bacteriochemistry; biochemistry;
electrochemistry; geochemistry
Chenoweth, Alice Drew, 249–50
Chesser, Elizabeth (Sloan), 250
Chick, Dame Harriette, 250–51, 1109
Child, Lydia Maria (Francis), 251–52
Children, Anna. See Atkins, Anna
Chinchon, Countess of, 252
Chinn, May Edward, 252–53
Chisholm, Catherine, 253
Chisholm, Grace Emily. See Young, Grace
Emily Chisholm
Chmielewska, Irene, 253–54
Chodak-Gregory, Hazel Haward
(Cuthbert), 254
Christen, Sydney Mary (Thompson),
254–55
Christina, Queen of Sweden, 255–56
Church, Elda Rodman (Macilvaine), 256
Chute, Hettie Morse, 256–57
Cilento, Lady Phyllis, 257–58
Cinquini, Maria dei Conti Cibrario, 258
Cioranescu-Nenitzescu, Ecaterina, 258
civil engineering, 82–83, 396
Clapp, Cornelia Maria, 258–59, 913, 1032,
1182, 1308
Clappe, Louisa Amelia (Smith), 259
Clara (Clare) of Assisi, Saint, 259

Clarisse of Rotomago (or Clarice of
Rouen), 259
Clark, Bertha, 260
Clarke, Cora Huidekoper, 264
Clarke, Edith, 264–65
Clarke, Lilian Jane, 265
Clarke, Louisa (Lane), 265
Clark, Frances N., 260–61
Clark, Janet Howell, 261–62
Clark, Jessie Jane, 262
Clark, Lois, 262–63
Clark, Mamie Katherine (Phipps), 263
Clark, Nancy Talbot, 263–64
Clay-Jolles, Tettje Clasina, 265–66
clay mineralogy, 232–33, 550–51
Claypole, Agnes Mary, 266–67
Claypole, Edith Jane, 267
Clea, 267
Cleachma, 267–68
Clemens, Mary Knapp (Strong), 268
Clements, Edith Gertrude (Schwartz), 268
Clements, Margaret, 268–69
Cleobulina of Rhodes, 269
Cleopatra, 269, 1278
Clerke, Agnes Mary, 269–71
Clerke, Ellen Mary, 271–72
Cleve, Astrid, 272
Cleveland, Emeline Horton, 272–73, 845–46,
1372
Clifford, Lady Anne, 273
climatology, 674–75
Clinch, Phyllis E. M., 273
Clisby, Harriet Jemima Winifred, 273–74
Clothilde of Burgundy, 274
Coade, Eleanor, 274
Coates, Sarah J., 274–75
Cobbe, Anne Phillipa, 276
Cobbe, Frances Power, 276–77
Cobbe, Margaret, 277
Cobb, Margaret Vara, 275–76
Cobb, Rosalie M. Karapetoff, 276
Cochran, Doris Mabel, 277–78
Cockburn, Catharine (Trotter), 278
Cockrell, Wilmatte (Porter), 278
Cohn, Essie White, 278–79
Coignou, Caroline Pauline Marie, 279
Colby, Martha Guernsey, 279
Colcord, Mabel, 280
Colden, Jane, 280
Cole, Emma J., 280–81
Cole, Luella, 281
Cole, Rebecca J., 281
Collet, Clara Elizabeth, 281
Collett, Mary Elizabeth, 282
Collins, Katharine Richards, 282
Colvin, Brenda, 282–83
Comnena (Comnenos), Anna, 283
computer science, 616–17
Comstock, Anna Botsford, 283–84, 1320
Comyns-Lewer, Ethel, 284
conchology, 125, 753, 813, 852–53, 932
Cone, Claribel, 284–85
Conklin, Marie (Eckhardt), 285
Conklin, Ruth, 727
Conklin, Ruth Emelene, 285–86

conservation, 17–18, 156, 173–74, 233–34,
370–71
Converse, Jeanne, 286
Conway, Anne, 286–87
Conway, Elsie (Phillips), 287
Cook, A. Grace, 287–88
Cooke, Alice Sophia (Smart), 288
Cook, Margaret C., 288
Cookson, Isabel Clifton, 289
Cooley, Jacquelin Smith, 289
Coombs, Helen Copeland, 289–90
Cooper, Clara Chassell, 290
Cooper, Elizabeth Morgan, 290
Cooper-Ellis, Katharine Murdoch, 292
Cooper, Susan Fenimore, 290–91
Cooper, Sybil, 291
Copeland, Lennie Phoebe, 292
Cordier, Marguerite Jeanne, 292
Cori, Gerty Theresa Radnitz, 292–94, 1042
Cornaro (Cornero), Elena (Helena) Lucre-
tia, 294
Cornelius-Furlani, Marta, 294
Coryndon, Shirley (Cameron), 295
cosmology, 596–98, 1292–93
Coste Blanche, Marie de, 295
Cotelle, Sonia, 295–96
Cotter, Brigid M., 296
Coudreau, Octavie, 296
Cowan, Edwina Abbott, 296–97
Cox, Gertrude Mary, 297–98
Cox, Rachel (Dunaway), 298
Coyle, Elizabeth Eleanor, 298–99
Cram, Eloise Blaine, 298
Cramer, Catherine Gertrude du Tertre
Schraders, 299–300
Crandall, Ella Phillips, 300
Crane, Agnes, 300
Crane, Jocelyn, 300–301
Cranwell, Lucy May, 301
Cremer, Erika, 301–2
Crespin, Irene, 302–3
criminology
nineteenth-century, 331–32, 443–44
twentieth-century, 183, 331–32, 443–44, 509
Crocker, Lucretia, 303–4
Croll, Hilda M., 304–5
Crosbie, May, 305
Crosby, Elizabeth Caroline, 305–6
Crosfield, Margaret Chorley, 306, 1397
crystallography
nineteenth-century, 179
early twentieth-century, 606–7, 716, 804–5,
821, 910–11, 1043–44, 1199
mid twentieth-century, 367–68, 465–66,
606–7, 716, 804–5, 821, 910–11
late twentieth-century, 367–68, 606–7
Csepreghyné-Meznerics, Ilona, 306–7
Cuffe, Lady Charlotte Wheeler, 307
Cullis, Winifred, 307–8
Cumming, Lady Gordon (Eliza Maria
Campbell), 308
Cummings, Clara Eaton, 308
Cummings, Louise Duffield, 309
Cunio, Isabella, 309
Cunitz, Maria, 309–10

Cunningham, Bess Virginia, 310
Cunningham, Gladys Story, 310–11
Cunningham, Susan, 311
Curie, Marie (Maria Sklodowska), 3–4, 64, 142, 184, 243, 295, **311–17**, 369, 508, 776, 957, 1006, 1069, 1123, 1141, 1366, 1403
Currie, Ethel Dobbie, 317
Curtis, Doris Sarah (Malkin), 317–18, 397
Curtis, Natalie, 318–19
Cushier, Elizabeth, 138, 319
Cushing, Hazel Morton, 319–20
Cushman, Florence, 320
Cuthbert-Browne, Grace Johnston, 320–21
Cutler, Catherine, 321
cytogenetics, 1230–32
cytology
    nineteenth-century, 458, 1248
    early twentieth-century, 133–34, 152, 157–58, 160–62, 190, 229, 423–25, 458, 539–0, 628, 865, 870–71, 1216–17, 1248, 1390
    mid twentieth-century, 133–34, 152, 160–62, 628, 838–39, 865, 870–71, 1390
    late twentieth-century, 628, 838–39
Czaplicka, Marie Antoinette, 321
Czeczottowa, Hanna (Peretiatkowicza), 321

D

Dalai, Maria Jolanda (Tosoni), 322
Dalby, Mary, 322
Dale, Elizabeth, 322–23
Dallas, A. E. M. M., 323
Dalle Donne, Maria, 323
Damo, 323–24, 879
Dane, Elisabeth, 324
Daniel, Anne Sturges, 324–25, 1381
Daniels, Amy L., 325
Danti or Dante, Theodora, 325
Darwin, Emma (Wedgwood), 325–26
Dashkova, Princess Ekaterina Romanovna, 326–27
Daulton, Agnes Warner Mcclelland, 327–28
Davenport, Gertrude (Crotty), 328
David, Florence N., 328
Davidson, Ada D., 328
Davis, Adelle, 328–29
Davis, Alice (Rohde), 329
Davis, Frances (Elliott), 330
Davis, Grace Evangeline, 330–31
Davis, Katharine Bement, 331–32
Davis, Marguerite, 332–33
Davis, Olive Griffith Stull, 333
Davis, Rose May, 333
Davy, Lady Joanna Charlotte (Flemmich), 333–34
Dawson, Maria, 334
Day, Dorothy, 334
Day, Gwendolen Helen, 334–35
Day, Mary Anna, 335
De Almania, Jacqueline Felicia. *See* Felicie, Jacoba
De Bréauté, Eléonore-Nell-Suzanne, 335
De Chantal, Mme.. *See* Sévigné, Marie de Rabutin-Chantal, Marquise de
Decker, Jane Cynthia (Mclaughlin), 335–36

Deflandre-Rigaud, Marthe, 336
De Forest, Nora Stanton. *See* Barney, Nora Stanton (Blatch) De Forest
De Fraine, Ethel Louise, 336–37
De Gorzano, Leonetta, 337
De Graffenried, Mary Clare, 337
Deichmann, Elisabeth, 337–38
Déjerine-Klumpke, Augusta, 338–39, 880, 1329
De La Cruz, Juana Inés, 339
De Laguna, Fredericka Annis Lopez de Leo, 339–41
De La Marche, Marguerite du Tertre, 339–41
Delaney (or Delany), Mary (Granville), 339
De Lange, Cornelia Catharina, 341–42
Delap, Maude Jane, 342
Delauney, Marguerite de Staël, 342
De Lebrix, Françoise, 342–43
Delf-Smith, Ellen Marion, 343
Deloria, Ella Cara, 343–44
De Marillac, Louise, Mlle, Le Gras. *See* Marillac, Louise, Mlle, Le Gras de
Dembo, Tamara, 344–45, 1162
De Milt, Clara Marie, 345
demography, 541–42, 542–43, 1260–61
De Mole, Fanny Elizabeth, 346
Dempsey, Sister Mary Joseph, 346
Demud, 346
dendochronology, 419
Dengel, Anna Maria, 346–47, 871
Denis, Willey Glover, 347
Dennett, Mary Ware, 347
Dennis, Olive Wetzel, 347–48
De Nolde, Hélène Aldegonde de, 348
Densmore, Frances Theresa, 348–49
dentistry, 602–3, 1271
Derick, Carrie M., 349–50
dermatology, 44, 203–4, 375, 537
Derscheid-Delcourt, Marie, 350
De Staël Holstein, Anne Louise Germaine Necker, 350
Detmers, Frederica, 350
Deutsch, Helene, 830, 1245
Deutsch, Helene Rosenback, 351–52
De Valera, Mairin, 352–53
De Valois, Madame, 353
De Vesian, Dorothy Ellis, 353
Dewey, Jane Mary (Clark), 353
De Witt, Lydia Maria Adams, 353–54
Diana of Poitiers, 354
Dickerson, Mary Cynthia, 355–56
Dick, Gladys Rowena Henry, 354–55
Dietrich, Amalie, 356–57
Diggs, Ellen Irene, 357
Dimock, Susan, 357–58, 1419
Dimsdale, Helen Easdale (Brown), 358–59
Dinnerstein, Dorothy, 359
Di Novella, Maria, 359
Diotima of Mantinea, 359
Dix, Dorothea Lynde, 201, 360
Dobrolubova, Tatiana A., 360–61, 1217
Dobroscky, Irene Dorothy, 361
Dobrowolska, H., 361
Dobson, Mildred E., 362
Dock, Lavinia Lloyd, 362–63

Dodd, Katharine, 363
Dodds, Mary Letitia, 363–64
Dodgson, Sarah Elizabeth, 364
Dodson, Helen Walter. *See* Prince, Helen Walter (Dodson)
Doering, Kathleen Clara, 364
Dohan, Edith Haywood Hall, 364–65
Dokhman, Genrietta Isaakovna, 365–66
Dolgopol de Saez, Mathilde, 366
Dolley, Sarah Read Adamson, 366–67
Dombrovskaia, Juliia Fominichna, 367
Donnay, Gabrielle (Hamburger), 367–68
Dooley, Lucile, 368
Dorabialska, Alicja Domenica, 368–69
Doreck, Hertha (Walburger Doris Sieverts), 369–70
Dorenfeldt, Margot, 370
Dorety, Angela, 370
Dormon, Caroline, 370–71
Doubleday, Neltje Blanchan (de Graff), 371–72
Dougal, Margaret Douie, 372
Douglas, Alice Vibert, 372
Dover, Mary Violette, 372–73
Downey, June Etta, 373–74
Downey, Katherine Melvina, 374
Downie, Dorothy G., 374
Downs, Cornelia Mitchell, 374–75
Drant, Patricia (Hart), 375
Draper, Mary Anna Palmer, 375–76, 856
Drebeneva-Ukhova, Varvara Pavlovna, 376
Drew, Kathleen Mary, 376–77
Drinker, Katherine (Rotan), 377
Drummond, Margaret, 377
Du Bois, Cora, 377–78
Dubuisson-Brouha, Adele, 378
Du Châtelet, Gabrielle-Emilie Le Tonnelier de BreteuiL (Marquise), 378–80
Du Coudray, Angelique (Marguerite Le Boursier), 381
Duffy, Elizabeth, 381–82
Duges, Marie-Louise. *See* LaChapelle, Marie Louise
Du Luys, Guillemette, 382
Dumée, Jeanne, 382
Dummer, Ethel (Sturges), 382–83
Dunbar, Helen Flanders, 383–84
Duncan, Catherine (Gross), 384
Duncan, Helen, 384–85
Duncan, Ursula Katherine, 385–86
Dunham, Ethel Collins, 386–87
Dunlop, Janette Gilchrist, 387
Dunning, Wilhelmina Frances, 388
Dunn, Mary Douglas, 387
Dunn, Thelma Brumfield, 387–88
Dupré, Marie, 388
Durham, Mary Edith, 388–89
Durocher, Marie (Josefina Mathilde), 389
Duryea, Nina, 389
Dutcher, Adelaide, 389–90
Dutton, Bertha, 390–91
Dutton, Loraine Orr, 391
Dye, Marie, 391
Dyer, Helen Marie, 391–93
Dylazanka, Maria, 393

E

Earle, Marie Theresa (Villiers), 394
Eastwood, Alice, 394–96
Eaves, Elsie, 396
Ebers, Edith (Knote), 396
Eccello of Lucania, 396
Echecratia the Philiasian, 397
Echols, Dorothy Jung, 397
Eckerson, Sophia Hennion, 397–98
Eckstorm, Fannie Pearson (Hardy), 398
ecology
    nineteenth-century, 619–20, 980
    early twentieth-century, 155, 173–74, 268,
        619–20, 678, 860, 973, 980, 988–89
    mid twentieth-century, 173–74, 860, 973,
        988–89
    late twentieth-century, 860
economics
    nineteenth-century, 844
    twentieth-century, 844, 1376
    home
        nineteenth-century, 2–3, 58–59, 103,
            121–22, 224–25, 529–30, 586, 629,
            1095–97, 1107–8
        early twentieth-century, 2–3, 121–22,
            224–25, 391, 629, 672, 913–14, 956,
            1095–97, 1107–8, 1125, 1222, 1262–63
        mid twentieth-century, 672, 913–14, 956,
            1125, 1222
Eddy, Bernice Elaine, 398–99
Edgell, Beatrice, 399
Edge, Rosalie Barrow, 399
Edgerton, Winifred Haring, 399–400
Edgeworth, Maria, 99–100, 400, 754, 842
**Edinger, Johanna Gabrielle Otellie (Tilly),
    400–401**
Edkins, Nora Tweedy, 401–2, 927
Edson, Fanny Carter, 402–3
education
    eighteenth-century, 198
    early nineteenth-century, 103, 814–15,
        1015–16
    mid nineteenth-century, 158–59, 304,
        814–15, 1015–16, 1270–71
    late nineteenth-century, 39, 151, 158–59,
        168–69, 187–88, 570–71, 728–29,
        751–52, 754–55, 793–94, 834, 870,
        976–77, 1059–60
    early twentieth-century, 39, 151, 168–69, 219,
        220, 275–76, 298–99, 310, 460, 466,
        491–92, 570–71, 583, 701–2, 728–29,
        737–38, 751–52, 754–55, 834, 860, 861,
        870, 976–77, 1059–60, 1171–72,
        1267–68
    mid twentieth-century, 168–69, 220, 298–99,
        466, 491–92, 524–25, 701–2, 737–38,
        751–52, 860, 861, 1171–72, 1267–68
    late twentieth-century, 298–99, 524–25,
        701–2, 737–38, 860, 861, 1171–72,
        1267–68
    chemistry, 472–73
    health care, 53–54, 187–88
    medical, 467
    of mentally challenged, 476–77
    natural history, 303–4

natural philosophy, 198
for nurses, 53–54
in psychology, 51, 54, 275–76, 310, 1171–72
psychology of, 460, 524–25
secondary, 52
sex, 220
Edwards, Emma Ward, 403
Edwards, Lena Frances, 403
Edwards-Pilliet, Blanche, 403–5
Efimenko, Aleksandra Iakovlevna, 405–6
Eggleton, Marion Grace (Palmer), 406–7
**Ehrenfest-Afanassjewa, Tatyana Alexeyevna,
    407–8**
Eichelberger, Lillian, 408
Eigenmann, Rosa Smith, 408–9
Eimmart, Marie Claire, 409
Einstein, Elizabeth Roboz, 410–11
Einstein-Maric, Mileva, 411–12
Eisele, Carolyn, 412–13
Elam, Constance Fligg Tipper. *See* **Tipper,
    Constance Fligg**
Elderton, Ethel, 413
Eleanora, Duchess of Mantua, 414
**Eleanora, Duchess of Troppau and Jagern-
    dorf, 414**
electrical engineering, 264–65
electrochemistry, 1192–93
electroencephalography, 174–75
Elephantis, 414
**Elgood, Cornelia Bonté Sheldon (Amos),
    414–15**
Elion, Gertrude Belle, 415–16
Eliot, Martha May, 386, 416
Elizabeth of Bohemia, 416–17
**Elizabeth of Poland, Queen of Hungary,
    417**
Elizabeth of Portugal, Saint, 417
Elizabeth of Schönau, 417
Elles, Gertrude Lilian, 417–18, 1090, 1180
Elliott, Charlotte, 418–19
Ellis, Florence Hawley, 419, 693
Ellisor, Alva Christine, 419–20
Elsom, Katharine (O'shea), 420
embryology
    fourth-century, 1062
    nineteenth-century, 441–42, 480–81, 914–15,
        942, 1031–32, 1074
    early twentieth-century, 7, 152, 441–42,
        480–81, 561–62, 561–62, 914–15, 942,
        963–64, 1018–19, 1031–32, 1074,
        1081–82, 1135
    mid twentieth-century, 7, 152, 561–62,
        561–62, 914–15, 963–64, 1081–82,
        1135
    late twentieth-century, 963–64, 1135
    plant, 464–65
**Emerson, Gladys Ludwina (Anderson),
    420–21**
endocrinology
    early twentieth-century, 446–47, 535, 671,
        812, 1020–21, 1038–39, 1053, 1137–38,
        1208–9, 1321–22, 1325–26
    mid twentieth-century, 671, 1020–21,
        1038–39, 1053, 1137–38, 1208–9,
        1321–22, 1325–26

    late twentieth-century, 1137–38, 1208–9
    reproductive, 671
Engelbrecht, Mildred Amanda, 422
Eng, Helga, 421–22
engineering
    nineteenth-century, 456–57, 507, 545–46,
        548, 736–37
    early twentieth-century, 347–48, 448–49,
        545–46, 548, 557–58, 563–64, 595–96,
        709, 736–37, 793, 820, 978, 979–80,
        1063, 1116–17, 1127–28, 1273–74,
        1275–76, 1293–94
    mid twentieth-century, 264–65, 347–48,
        456–57, 548, 557–58, 563–64, 595–96,
        709, 793, 820, 918, 978, 979–80, 1063,
        1100, 1116–17, 1121, 1127–28,
        1273–74, 1293–94, 1361
    late twentieth-century, 396, 548, 557–58,
        595–96, 820, 979–80, 1100, 1121,
        1127–28, 1273–74, 1361
    aeronautical, 820, 1116–17, 1361
    aerospace, 1127–28
    chemical, 1063
    civil, 82–83, 396, 1275–76
    electrical, 264–65, 563–64, 563–64, 736–37,
        1100, 1116–17
    mechanical, 507
    research, 347–48
entomology
    eighteenth-century, 917
    early nineteenth-century, 74, 1268
    late nineteenth-century, 264, 278
    mid nineteenth-century, 74, 928–29, 1199,
        1268
    late nineteenth-century, 560, 918, 965–67,
        999, 1199, 1205, 1272, 1301–2
    early twentieth-century, 170, 172–73, 219,
        224, 248–49, 278, 280, 361, 364, 376,
        560, 633, 801–2, 865, 965–67, 976,
        987–88, 993, 999, 1148–49, 1167,
        1263, 1272, 1301–2, 1378
    mid twentieth-century, 170, 172–73,
        248–49, 364, 711, 790, 801–2,
        865, 976, 1148–49, 1167, 1263,
        1272
    late twentieth-century, 801–2
environment. *See* conservation
epidemiology, 741–42, 819
Erdmann, Rhoda, 423–25, 785
Erdmuthe, Sophie, 425
Ermol'eva, Zinaida Vissarionovna, 425
**Erxleben, Dorothea Christiana (Leporin),
    425–26**
Esau, Katherine, 426–27
Esdorn, Ilse, 427–28
Etheldrida, Queen, 428
ethnography
    nineteenth-century, 405–6, 693, 1232–33
    early twentieth-century, 388–89, 733–34,
        760, 1232–33, 1274, 1323, 1342–44,
        1387–88
    mid twentieth-century, 733–34, 760, 844–45,
        1274, 1342–44, 1387–88
    late twentieth-century, 733–34, 1387–88
ethnohistory, 1370

ethnology
  nineteenth-century, 454–55, 552–53, 982–83, 1205–6
  twentieth-century, 321, 339–41, 454–55, 552–53, 982–83
ethnomusicology, 318–19, 348–49
eugenics, 149–50, 413
Euphemia, Abbess of Wherwell, 428
Evans, Alice Catherine, 428–30
Evans, Alice Margaret, 430
Everard, Barbara Mary Steyning, 430
Everett, Alice, 430–31
Evershed, Mary Orr, 431–32
Eves, Florence, 432
Ewing, Elizabeth Raymond (Burden), 432
Eyton, Charlotte, 432

F
Fabiola, 433
Fage, Winifred E., 433
Farenden, Emma, 433
Farnsworth, Alice Hall, 434
Farnsworth, Vesta J., 434–35
Farquharson, Marian Sarah (Ridley), 435
Farrar, Lillian K. P., 436
Farr, Wanda Kirkbride, 435–36
Fátima, 436
Faustina, 436
Favilla, 436
Fawcett, Phillipa Garrett, 436–37, 1002
Fearn, Anne Walter, 437–38
Fedchenko, Ol'ga Aleksandrovna, 438–39
Feichtinger, Nora, 439
Felicie, Jacobina, 439
Fell, Honor Bridget, Dame, 439–40
Fenchel, Käte (Sperling), 440–41
Fenwick, Florence, 441
Ferguson, Margaret Clay, 441–42
Fernald, Grace Maxwell, 442
Fernald, Maria Elizabeth (Smith), 443
Ferrand, Elizabeth M., 443
Ferrand, Jacqueline. *See* **Lelong-Ferrand, Jacqueline**
Ferrero, Gina (Lombroso), 443–44
Fielde, Adele Marion, 444
Fielding, Mary Maria (Simpson), 444–45
Fiennes, Celia, 445
Fieser, Mary, 445
Figner, Vera, 446
Finch, Louisa (Thynne), Countess of Aylesford, 446
Findlater, Doris, 446
Finkler, Rita V. (Sapiro), 446–47
Fischer, Irene Kaminka, 447
Fishenden, Margaret White, 448–49
Fisher, Edna Marie, 449
Fisher, Elizabeth Florette, 449
Fisher, Sara Carolyn, 450
Fish, Margery, 447–48
Fish, Marie Poland, 448
Fitton, Sarah Mary, 450
Fitzgerald, Mabel Purefoy, 450–51
Flammel, Perrenelle, 451
Fleming, Amalia Coutsouris, Lady, 451–52
Fleming, Williamina Paton Stevens, 453–54

Fletcher, Alice Cunningham, 348–49, 454–55, 1023, 1206, 1232
Flock, Eunice Verna, 455
Flood, Margaret Greer, 455
Florendo, Soledad Arcega, 455–56
Flügge-Lotz, Irmgard, 456–57
Foley, Mary Cecilia, 457
Folmer, Hermine Jacoba, 457
Fomina-Zhukovskaia, Evdokiia Aleksandrovna, 457–58
Fonovits-Smereker, H., 458
Foot, Katherine, 458, 1248
Forbes, Helena Madelain Lamond, 458–59
Forster, Mary, 459
Fossey, Dian, 459–60
Fossler, Mary Louise, 460
Foster, Josephine Curtis, 460
Foster, Margaret D., 460–61
Fouquet, Marie de Maupeou, Vicomtesse de Vaux, 461
Fowler-BIllings, Katharine Stevens, 461–62
Fox, Ruth, 463–64
Fraine, Ethel Louise de, 464
Frampton, Mary, 464
Frances of Brittany, 464
Francini, Eleonora Corti, 464–65
Françoise, Marie-Thérèse, 465
Franklin, Rosalind Elsie, 465–66
Frank, Margaret, 465
Frantz, Virginia Kneeland, 467
Freeman, Joan Maie, 467–68
Freidlina, RakhiL' Khatskelevna, 468–69
Frenkel-Brunswik, Else, 469–70
Freud, Anna, 38, 209, 470–72, 830, 925, 994, 1104, 1126, 1162
Freund, Ida, 472–73
Friant, M., 473
Friedlander, Kate, 473
Friedmann, Friederike, 474
Friend, Charlotte, 474
Fritz, Madeleine Alberta, 475
Fromm, Erika Oppenheimer, 475–76
Frostig, Marianne Bellak, 476–77
Fulford, Margaret Hannah, 477–78
Fulhame, Elizabeth, 478
Furness, Caroline Ellen, 478–79
Fuss, Margarita, 479

G
Gabler, Anna, 480
Gage, Catherine, 480
Gage, Susanna Phelps, 480–81
Gaige, Helen (Thompson), 481
Galabert, Renée, 481
Galindo, Beatrix, 481
Galvani, Lucia (Galeazzi), 481–82
Gamble, Eleanor Acheson McCulloch, 482
Gantt, Love Rosa, 482–83
Gaposchkin, Cecilia Payne. *See* **Payne-Gaposchkin, Cecilia Helena**
gardening, 529
Gardiner, Edith Gertrude (Willcock). *See* **Willcock, Edith Gertrude**
Gardiner, Margaret Isabella, 483
Gardner, Elinor Wight, 483–84

Gardner, Julia Anna, 484–85
Gardner, Mary Sewall, 485
Garfield, Viola Edmundson, 485–86
gargoylism, 631–32
Garlick, Constance, 486
Garnett, Alice, 486–87
Garnjobst, Laura Flora, 487
Garretson, Mary (Welleck), 487–88
Garrett, Elizabeth. *See* **Anderson, Elizabeth Garrett**
Garrod, Dorothy Anne Elizabeth, 90, 488–89
gastric physiology, 613
gastroenterology, 668–69
Gàta, Elena (Stefanescu), 489
Gates, Fanny Cook, 489–90
Gatty, Margaret (Scott), 490–91
Gaw, Esther Allen, 491–92
Gaw, Frances Isabel, 491
Geiringer Hilda, 493–94
Geldart, Alice Mary, 494
genetics
  nineteenth-century, 109, 441–42, 914–15, 1154–55, 1264–65
  early twentieth-century, 80, 141–42, 157–58, 160–62, 229, 862–64, 914–15, 1016, 1082–83, 1098, 1154–55, 1159–60, 1225, 1264–65, 1274, 1290–91, 1312–13
  mid twentieth-century, 59–60, 61, 160–62, 160–62, 487, 533–34, 591–92, 862–64, 914–15, 1082–83, 1098, 1144–45, 1159–60, 1264–65, 1290–91
  late twentieth-century, 59–60, 232–33, 862–64, 1144–45
  gene manipulation, 149–50
  plant, 441–42, 1159–60
  See also neurogenetics
Genet-Varcin, E., 494
Genung, Elizabeth Faith, 494–95
geobotany, 365–66
geochemistry, 489, 498, 521, 644–45, 1188, 1222
geography
  nineteenth-century, 65–66, 95–96, 131, 271–72, 937, 1013–14, 1176–77
  early twentieth-century, 65–66, 95–96, 127–28, 167–68, 228, 242–43, 271–72, 321, 449, 592–93, 610, 660, 674–75, 937, 1176–77, 1249, 1269–70, 1382, 1396–97
  mid twentieth-century, 127–28, 167–68, 228, 242–43, 447, 486–87, 610, 660, 674–75, 1249, 1269–70, 1382
  late twentieth-century, 167–68, 242–43
geology
  early nineteenth-century, 251–52, 290–91, 604, 610, 765, 813
  mid nineteenth-century, 228–29, 765, 813, 1194–95, 1205–6
  late nineteenth-century, 28, 87–88, 92, 228–29, 254–55, 272, 279, 328, 432, 457, 459, 483, 607, 627–28, 685–86, 695, 899–900, 959–60, 969, 992–93, 1087–88, 1156, 1183, 1213, 1305–6, 1337–38

geology (*cont.*)

  early twentieth-century, 7, 21–22, 28, 46–47,
      79–80, 87–88, 92, 108–9, 127, 159–60,
      180, 191–92, 232–33, 248, 254–55, 279,
      317, 360–61, 397, 402–3, 449, 457,
      461–62, 483–84, 487–88, 544, 570, 575,
      577–78, 604, 612, 645–46, 662, 667–68,
      671–72, 685–86, 695, 699, 708–9, 766,
      850–51, 868, 899–900, 915–16, 933–34,
      958–59, 959–60, 969, 974, 975–76,
      992–93, 1074–75, 1078–79, 1087–88,
      1090–91, 1175–76, 1191–92, 1197–98,
      1199, 1206–7, 1211–12, 1217, 1243–44,
      1258, 1295–96, 1302–3, 1306–7,
      1322–23, 1356–57, 1358–59, 1377–78,
      1382, 1411, 1419–20, 1421–22

  mid twentieth-century, 21–22, 46–47, 77–78,
      79–80, 92, 98, 110–11, 128–29, 159–60,
      191–92, 232–33, 294, 317, 317–18,
      360–61, 397, 461–62, 483–84, 487–88,
      489, 544, 570, 575, 577–78, 607, 612,
      667–68, 693–94, 699, 706, 708–9,
      710–11, 729, 766, 815–16, 843–44,
      850–51, 868, 915–16, 933–34, 942–43,
      958–59, 973, 974, 975–76, 1004,
      1074–75, 1087–88, 1090–91, 1092,
      1114–15, 1146, 1175–76, 1188,
      1197–98, 1206–7, 1211–12, 1243–44,
      1295–96, 1302–3, 1306–7, 1308,
      1324–25, 1350–51, 1356–57, 1382,
      1411, 1419–20

  late twentieth-century, 77–78, 98, 110–11,
      128–29, 159–60, 200–201, 317–18, 396,
      397, 570, 612, 693–94, 706–7, 710–11,
      718–19, 724, 729, 766, 815–16, 843–44,
      868, 933–34, 942–43, 975–76, 1090–91,
      1092, 1146, 1188, 1206–7, 1211–12,
      1306–7, 1308

  economic, 695, 1199, 1324–25

  engineering, 843–44, 1324–25

  marine, 1188

  mining, 487–88, 487–88

  petroleum, 46–47, 159–60, 402–3, 570,
      933–34, 974, 1358–59

  quaternary, 958–59

  soil, 489

  structural, 294, 708–9, 718–19, 1004,
      1197–98, 1243–44

geomorphology, 163, 396, 662

geophysics, 457, 1122–23

Geppert, Maria Pia, 495

Gepp, Ethel Sarel (Barton), 495, 1074

Germain, Sophie, 496–97

Gerould, Elizabeth Wood, 497

Gerry, Eloise B., 497–98

Gessner, Joy-Fredericke Victoria. *See* Adamson, Joy (Gessner)

Gey, Margaret Lewis, 498

Ghilietta, 498

Giammarino, Pia, 498

Gibbons, E. Joan, 498–99

Gibbons, Vernette Lois, 499

Gibbs, Lilian Suzette, 500

Gifford, Isabella, 500

Gilbert, Ruth, 500–501

Gilbreth, Lillian Evelyn Moller, 501–3

Gilette of Narbonne, 503

Giliani, Alessandra, 503

GIlkey, Helen Margaret, 503

Gillett, Margaret (Clark), 504

Gill, Jocelyn Ruth, 503–4

Gilmore, Jane Georgina, 504

Gilroy, Helen (Turnbull), 504–5

Giraud, Marthe, 505

Gitelson, Frances H., 505

Gjellestad, Guro Else, 505–6

glaciology, 958–59, 1338

**Glagoleva-Arkad'yeva, Aleksandra
      Andreyevna**, 506

Glascott, Louisa S., 506

Glasgow, Maude, 506

Glass, Jewell Jeanette, 506–7

Gleason, Josephine Mixer, 507

Gleason, Kate, 507

Gleason, Rachel Brooks, 508

Gleditsch, Ellen, 370, 508–9, 1028, 1071, 1123

Glueck, Eleanor (Touroff), 509

Gocholashvili, Mariia Mikievna, 509

Godding, D. W., 509–10

Godfery, Hilda Margaret, 510

Goeppert Mayer, Maria Gertrud Käte, 510–12

Goldfeder, Anna, 512–13

Goldfrank, Esther Schiff, 513–14

Goldhaber, Sulamith, 514

Goldman, Hetty, 514–15

Goldring, Winifred, 515–16

Goldschmidt, Frieda, 516

Goldsmith, Grace Arabell, 516–17

Goldsmith, Marie, 517

Goldthwaite, Nellie Esther, 517–18

Golinevich, Elena Mikhailovna, 518

Goodenough, Florence Laura, 518–19, 1310

Goodrich, Sarah Frances, 519

Goodyear, Edith, 519–20

Gordon, Kate, 520

Gordon, Maria Matilda Ogilvie, 685. *See* Ogilvie-Gordon, Maria

Gorinevskaya, Valentina Valentinovna, 520–21

Gorizdro-Kulczycka, Zinaida, 521

Gorshkova, Tat'yana Ivanovna, 521

Götz, Irén Julia (Dienes), 521–22

Gracheva, Yekaterina Konstantinovna, 522

Graham, Helen (Treadway), 522

Graham, Maria Dundas (Lady Calcott). *See* Calcott, Maria Graham

Grainger, Jennie, 522

grasses, study of. *See* agrostology

Gravatt, Annie Evelyn (Rathbun), 522–23

Graves, Elizabeth (Riddle), 523

Gray, Etta, 523

Gray, Maria Emma (Smith), 523–24

Gray, Susan Walton, 524–25

Green, Arda A., 525–26

Greene, Catherine (Littlefield), 527–28

Green, Mary Letitia. *See* Sprague, Mary Letitia

Green, Vera Mae, 526–27

Greenwood, Marion. *See* Bidder, Marion Greenwood

Gregg, Mary (Kirby). *See* Kirby, Mary

Gregory, Eliza Standerwick (Barnes), 528

Gregory, Emily L., 528

Gregory, Emily Ray, 528–29

Gregory, Lady Isabella Augusta (Persse), 529

Gregory, Louisa Catherine (Allen), 529–30

Gregory, Louise Hoyt, 530

Greig, Margaret Elizabeth, 530

Greisheimer, Esther Maud, 530

Griffin, Harriet Madeline, 531

Griffiths, Amelia Elizabeth, 531

Griffiths, Amelia Warren (Rogers), 531

Griggs, Mary Amerman, 531–32

Grignan, Françoise Marguerite de Sevigne, Comtesse de, 532

Grinnell, Hilda Wood, 532, 858

Griswold, Grace Hall, 533

Gromova, Vera Isaacovna, 533

Groot, Jeanne Lampl-de, 830

Gruhn, Ruth, 533–34

Grundy, Clara, 534

Grundy, Ellen, 534

Grundy, Maria Ann, 534

Grzigorzewska, Marja, 535

Gsell, Maria Dorothea Henrica (Graf), 535

Gualco, Sellina, 535

Guarna, Rebecca, 535

Guldberg, Estrid, 536

Gullett, Lucy E., 536

Gundersen, Herdis, 537

Gunn, Mary Davidson, 537–38

Gunther, Erna, 538, 873

Guthrie, Mary Jane, 538–39

Guyton de Morveau, Claudine Poullet Picardet, 539

Gwynne-Vaughan, Dame Helen Charlotte Isabella (Fraser), 539

gynecology

  first-century, 56

  fourth-century, 11

  seventeenth-century, 164

  nineteenth-century, 186–87, 666, 877

  early twentieth-century, 6, 40, 84–85,
      224–25, 245, 436, 536, 702–3, 744, 746,
      781–82, 877, 1276

  mid twentieth-century, 40, 84–85, 245,
      702–3, 744, 746, 781–82, 1276

  late twentieth-century, 40, 702–3, 744, 746,
      781–82, 1276

H

Haber-Immerwahr, Clara, 540–41

Halket, Ann Cronin, 544

Halket, Lady Anne, 544–45

Hall, Agnes C., 545

Hall-Brown, Lucy, 547

Hall, Dorothy, 545

Hall, Edith Hayward. *See* Dohan, Edith Hayward Hall

Halliday, Nellie, 547

Hall, Julia Brainerd, 545–46

Hall, Kate Marion, 546
Hallowell, Susan Maria, 548
Hall, Rosetta Sherwood, 546–47, 694
Hamburger, Erna, 548
Hamerstrom, Frances (Flint), 548–49
Hamilton, Alice, 549–50, 898, 1307
Hamilton, Peggy-Kay, 550–51
Hammer, Marie Signe, 551
Hanfmann, Eugenia, 551–52
Hanks, Jane Richardson, 552–53
Hansen, Julie Marie Vinter, 554
Hanson, Emmeline Jean, 554–55
Haoys (la Meresse), 555
Hardcastle, Frances, 555
Hardesty, Mary, 555
Harding, Anita, 556
Hardwick, Rose Standish, 556
Hardy, Harriet, 557
Hardy, Thora Marggraff Plitt, 557
Harmon, Élise F., 557–58
Harrison, Janet Mitchell Marr (Dingwall),
    559
Harrower, Molly R., 559–60
Hart, Esther Hasting, 560
Hart, Helen, 560
Hart, J. B., 560
Hartt, Constance Endicott, 560–61
Harvey, Elizabeth, 561
Harvey, Ethel Nicholson Browne, 561–62
Harwood, Margaret, 562–63
Haslett, Dame Caroline, 563–64
Hassall, Bessie Florence (Cory), 564
Hastings, Barbara, Marchioness of, 565
Hathaway, Millicent Louise, 565
Hatshepsut, Queen, 566
Hausser, Isolde (Ganswindt), 566–68
Hawes, Harriet (Boyd), 365, 568–69
Hawkins, Kate, 570
Hawkins, Mary Esther (Sibthorp), 570
Hawn Mirabile, Margaret H., 570
Hay, Elizey. *See* Andrews, Eliza Frances
Hayes, Ellen Amanda, 570–71
Hayes, Katherine Isabel Chapin. *See* Bar-
    rows, Katherine Isabel (Hayes)
    Chapin
Hayner, Lucy Julia, 571–72
Hayward, Ida Margaret, 572
Haywood, Charlotte, 572
Hazen, Elizabeth Lee, 191, 572–73
Hazlett, Olive Clio, 574
healing
    second-century, 965
    third-century, 1278
    fourth-century, 841, 990
    fifth-century, 179, 274, 436
    sixth-century, 119, 274
    seventh-century, 119, 120, 428
    tenth-century, 624
    eleventh-century, 590
    twelfth-century, 417, 590
    thirteenth-century, 259, 353, 428, 555, 577,
        831, 855, 874
    fourteenth-century, 44–45, 417, 576, 831,
        843, 1008, 1151
    fifteenth-century, 44–45, 464

    sixteenth-century, 1124–25
    seventeenth-century, 425, 461
    eighteenth-century, 1412
    See also medicine
Hearst, Phoebe (Apperson), 574–75
Heath, Daisy Winifred, 575
Hebb, Catherine Olding, 575–76
Hebel, Medicienne, 576
Heckter, Maria. *See* Strassmann, Maria C.
    Heckter
Hedges, Florence, 577
Hedwig of Silesia, Saint, 577
Heermann, Margareta, 577–78
Hefferan, Mary, 578
Heidbreder, Edna Frances, 578–79
Heimann, Berta, 579
Heimann, Paula, 579–80
Heim-Vögtlin, Marie, 580
Heinlein, Julia Elizabeth Heil, 580–81
Hélène, Duchess of Aosta, 581
Hellman, Johanna, 581
Héloise, 582–83
hematology, 993–94
Henderson, Nellie Frater, 583
Hendricks, Eileen M., 583
Hennel, Cora Barbara, 583–84
Henrey, Blanche Elizabeth Edith, 584
Henry, Caroline (Orridge), 584
Henshaw, Julia Wilmotte, 584
Heppenstall, Caroline A., 585
herbalism, 1363
Herford, Ethilda B. Meakin, 585
herpetology, 277–78, 355–56
Herrad of Hohenburg, 585–89
Herrick, Christine (Terhune), 586
Herrick, Julia Frances, 586
Herrick, Sophia McIlvaine (Bledsoe),
    586–87
Herschel, Caroline Lucretia, 587–89, 735
Hersende, Abbess of Fontevrault, 590
Herskovits, Frances S. (Shapiro), 590–91
Hertwig, Paula, 591–92
Herwerden, Marianne van, 592
Herxheimer, Franziska, 592
Heslop, Mary Kingdon, 592–93
Hesse, Fanny, 593
Hetzer, Hildegard, 204, 593
Hevelius, Elisabetha Koopman, 593
Hewer, Dorothy, 594
Hibbard, Hope, 594–95
Hickey, Amanda Sanford, 595
Hicks, Beatrice Alice, 595–96
Higgins, Vera (Cockburn), 596
Hightower, Ruby Usher, 596
Hildegard of Bingen, 596–98
Hildreth, Gertrude Howell, 598–99
Hilgard, Josephine Rohrs, 599
Hill, Dorothy, 600–601
Hill, Justina Hamilton, 601
Hill, Mary Elliott, 601
Hines, Marion, 601–2
Hinman, Alice Hamlin, 602
Hinrichs, Marie Agnes, 602
Hirschfeld-Tiburtius, Henriette (Pagelsen),
    602–3, 767, 1285

histology, 942, 1018–19, 1390
histopathology, 131–32
history
    twelfth-century study, 582–83
    eighteenth-century study, 908
    nineteenth-century study, 1–2, 398, 405–6,
        560, 892–94, 1044–45
    twentieth-century study, 1–2, 47–48, 398,
        701, 809–10, 929
    medical, 1–2
    of mining, 701
    natural
        twelfth-century study, 582–83
        eighteenth-century study, 117–18, 134–35,
            134–35, 1337
        nineteenth-century study, 12–13, 12–13,
            31, 57–58, 66, 290–91, 300, 303–4,
            434–35, 560, 699
        twentieth-century study, 8–9, 8–9, 434–35,
            532, 551
    prehistory, 488–89
    prehistory, study of, 90
    of science, 174–75, 809–10
Hitchcock, Fanny Rysam Mulford, 603
Hitchcock, Orra White, 604
Hitchens, Ada Florence R., 604
Hitzenberger, Annaliese, 604–5
Hoare, Sarah, 605
Hobby, Gladys Lounsbury, 605–6
Hoby, Lady, 606
Hodgkin, Dorothy Mary Crowfoot, 606–7,
    1404
Hodgson, Eliza Amy, 607
Hodgson, Elizabeth, 607
Hoffleit, Ellen Dorrit, 607–8
Hofmann, Elise, 608
Hoggan, Ismé Aldyth, 609
Hogg, Helen Sawyer, 608–9
Hohl, Leonora Anita, 609–10
Hoke, Calm (Morrison), 610
Hol, Jacoba Brigitta Louisa, 610
Holley, Mary Austin, 610
Hollingworth, Leta Anna Stetter, 610–12,
    1178
Holmes, Mary Emilee, 612
Holm, Esther (Aberdeen), 612
Holton, Pamela Margaret (Watson-
    Williams), 613
Homer, Annie, 613–14
Hoobler, Icie Gertrude Macy, 614
Hooker, Frances Harriet Henslow, 614–15
Hooker, Henrietta Edgecomb, 615
Hooker, Marjorie, 615
Hopkins, Esther (Burton), 616
Hopper, Grace (Brewster Murray), 616–17
Horenburg, Anna Elizabeth von, 617
Horney, Karen Clementine (Danielsen),
    617–18, 1162, 1283
Horowitz, Stephanie, 618
horticulture
    seventeenth-century, 445
    eighteenth-century, 445, 799, 1024–25
    nineteenth-century, 91, 394, 655–56, 697–98,
        736, 936–37, 956, 1004, 1055–56, 1105,
        1177–78, 1329

horticulture (*cont.*)
  early twentieth-century, 68–69, 91, 262,
    282–83, 305, 307, 570, 697–98, 956,
    1055–56, 1122, 1143, 1177–78,
    1382–83
  mid twentieth-century, 68–69, 282–83, 307,
    446, 447–48, 570, 1122, 1177–78
  late twentieth-century, 446, 570
Hough, Margaret Jean Ringier, 619
Howard Beckman, Ruth Winifred, 620
Howard, Louise Ernestine (Matthaei),
    619–20
Howard Wylde, Hildegarde, 620–22
Howe Akeley, Delia Julia Denning, 622–23
Howes, Ethel Dench Puffer, 623
Howitt, Mary (Botham), 623–24
Hroswitha of Gandersheim, 624
Hubbard, Marian Elizabeth, 624
Hubbard, Ruth Marilla, 624
Hubbs, Laura Cornelia (Clark), 624–25
Hudson, Hilda Phoebe, 625–26
Huggins, Margaret Lindsay (Murray),
    626–27
Hug-Hellmuth, Hermine Von, 626
Hug-Hellmuth, Hermine von, 703
Hughes, Ellen Kent, 627
Hughes, Mary Caroline (Weston), 627–28
Hughes-Schrader, Sally, 628
Hugonnai-Wartha, Vilma, 628
Hummel, Katharine Pattee, 628–29
Hunscher, Helen Alvina, 629
Hunt, Caroline Louisa, 629
Hunt, Eva Verbitsky, 629–30
Hunt, Harriot Kezia, 630–31
Hurd-Mead, Kate Campbell. *See* Mead,
    Kate Campbell Hurd
Hurler, Gertrud (Zach), 631–32
Hurlock, Elizabeth Bergner, 632
Hurston, Zora Neale, 632–33
Hussey, Anna Maria (Reed), 633
Hussey, Priscilla Butler, 633
Hutchins, Ellen, 633–35
Hutchinson, Dorothy (Hewitt). *See* Hewitt,
    Dorothy
Hutton, Lady Isabel Emilie, 635
Huxley, Henrietta Heathorn, 635–36
Hyde, Ida Henrietta, 635–36, 1044
hygiene, 434–35, 630–31
Hyman, Libbie Henrietta, 636–37
Hynes, Sarah, 637
Hypatia of Alexandria, 637–39

I

ichthyology
  nineteenth-century, 408–9
  twentieth-century, 260–61, 408–9, 448,
    624–25, 737, 911
immunogenetics, 116
immunology
  nineteenth-century, 1307–8
  twentieth-century, 55, 146, 719–20, 807, 982,
    993–94, 1109–10, 1172–73, 1225, 1264,
    1307–8
Inglis, Elsie, 806
insects, study of. *See* entomology

inventions
  thirteenth-century, 309
  seventeenth-century, 853
  eighteenth-century, 274, 853
  nineteenth-century, 663–64, 708, 836–37,
    854, 1368
  twentieth-century, 28–29, 389, 663–64, 708,
    759–60, 918
invertebrates
  twentieth-century zoological study, 145
  and evolution, 202–3
  marine, 214–15
  paleontology of, 417–18, 484–85, 487–88,
    600–601

J

Jacobi, Mary Putnam, 783, 808, 1060, 1277,
    1419
Jacobs, Aletta, 1150
Jex-Blake, Sophia, 871, 994, 1178, 1419
Joliot-Curie, Irène, 909, 1029
Jones, Ernest, 994

K

Kaan, Helen Warton, 673
Kaberry, Phyllis Mary, 673–74, 1025
Kablick [Kablíková], Josephine (Ettel), 674
Kaczorowska, Zofia, 674–75
Kahn, Ida, 675
Kaltenbeiner, Victorine, 675
Kane, Lady Katherine Sophia (Baily), 675
Kanouse, Bessie Bernice, 675–76
Karamihailova, Elizabeth/Elizaveta
    [Kara-Michailova], 676
Kardymowiczowa, Irena, 676
Karlik, Berta, 677
Karp, Carol Ruth (Vander Velde), 677–78
Karpowicz, Ludmila, 678
Karrer, Annie May Hurd, 678–80
Kashevarova-Rudneva, Varvara Aleksan-
    drovna, 678
Katherine, La Surgiene (the surgeon), 680
Katz, Rosa Heine, 680
Kaye-Smith, A. Dulcie, 680
Keeler, Harriet Louise, 680
Keen, Angeline Myra, 680–81
Keeney, Dorothea Lilian, 681–82
Keil, Elizabeth Marbareta, 681
Keil, Elsa Marie, 681
Keith, Marcia Anna, 682
Keldysh, Liudmila Vsevolodovna, 682
Keller, Ida Augusta, 682–83
Kellerman, Stella Victoria (Dennis), 683–84
Kellogg, Louise, 684–85
Kellor, Frances A., 685
Kelly, Agnes, 685–86
Kelly, Isabel Truesdell, 686–87, 693
Kelly, Margaret G., 687
Kelly, Margaret W., 687
Kendall, Claribel, 687–88
Kendrick, Pearl (Luella), 688
Kennard, Margaret Alice, 688
Kennedy, Cornelia, 689
Kenny, Elizabeth (Sister Kenny), 689
Kent, Elizabeth, 690

Kent, Elizabeth Isis Pogson, 690
Kent, Grace Helen, 690
Kent, Kate Peck, 690–91
Kenyon, Kathleen Mary, 691–92
Kerling, Louise Catharina Petronella, 692
Keur, Dorothy Louise (Strouse), 692–93
Kharuzina, Vera Nikolaevna, 693
Kielan-Jaworowska, Zofia, 693–94
Kil, Chung-Hee, 694–95
King, Anastasia Kathleen (Murphy), 695
King, Georgina, 695
King, Helen Dean, 695–97
King, Jessie Luella, 697
King, Louisa Boyd (Yeomans), 697–98
King, Martha, 698
Kingsley, Louise, 699
Kingsley, Mary Henrietta, 699
King, Susan (Raymond), 698
Kirby, Elizabeth, 699–700
Kirch, Christine, 700
Kirch, Margaretha, 700
Kirch, Maria Margaretha, 700–701
Kirkbride, Mary Butler, 701
Kirkham, Nellie, 701
Kittrell, Flemmie Pansy, 701–2
Kleegman, Sophia, 702–3
Klein, Marthe, 703
Klein, Melanie (Reizes), 703–4, 994, 1104,
    1127, 1161, 1245
Kletnova, E. N., 704–5
Klieneberger-Nobel, Emmy, 705–6
Kline, Virginia Harriett, 706
Klosterman, Mary Jo, 706–7
Kluckhohn, Florence Rockwood, 707
Knake, Else, 708
Knight, Margaret, 708
Knopf, Eleanora Frances (Bliss), 708–9, 1243
Knott-Ter Meer, Ilse, 709
Knowles, Matilda Cullen, 709–10
Knowles, Ruth Sheldon, 710–11
Knull, Dorothy J., 711
Kobel, Maria, 711
Kochanowská, Adéla, 713
Koch, Helen Lois, 712
Kochina, Pelageia Iakovlevna, 713–14
Koch, Marie Louise, 712–13
Kohler, Elsa, 714
Kohn, Hedwig, 714–15
Kohts, Nadie (Ladychin), 715–16
Kolaczkowska, Maria, 716
Komarovsky, Mirra, 716–17
Koprowska, Irena Grasberg, 717
Korn, Doris Elfriede, 717–18
Korobeinikova, Iuliia Ivanovna, 718
Korringa, Marjorie K., 718–19
Korshunova, Olga Stepanovna, 719
Koshland, Marian (Elliott), 719–20
Kovalevskaia, Sofia Vasilyevna, 714, 720–22,
    775
Kovrigina, Mariia Dmitrievna, 722–23
Kozlova, Ol'ga Grigoriyevna, 724
Krasnosel'skaia, Tat'iana Abramovna,
    724–25
Krasnow, Frances, 725
Kraus Ragins, Ida, 725

Kroeber, Theodora Kracaw, 725–26
Krogh, Birthe Marie (Jorgensen), 726–28
Kruna (pseudonym). *See* Ballard, Julia Perkins Pratt
Krupskaia, Nadezhda Konstantinovna, 728–29
Krutikhovskaia, Zinaida Aleksandrovna, 729
Kunde, Margarethe Meta H., 729–30

L

L'Esperance, Elise Depew Strang, 777–78
La Chapelle, Marie Louise Dugès, 731
Ladd-Franklin, Christine, 731–32, 938
Ladygina-Kots, Nadezhda Nikolaevna, 732–33
Laird, Carobeth (Tucker), 733–34
Laird, Elizabeth Rebecca, 734–35
Laïs, 735
Lalande, Marie Jeanne Amélie Harlay LefranÇais de, 735–36
La Mance, Lora Sarah (Nichols), 736
Lamarck, Cornelié, 736
Lambin, Suzanne, 736
Lamme, Bertha, 736–37
Lamonte, Francesca Raimonde, 737
Lampe, Lois, 737–38
Lampl-De Groot, Jeanne, 738
Lancefield, Rebecca Craighill, 739–40
Landes, Ruth (Schlossberg), 740–41
landscape architecture, 282–83, 655–56
Lane-Claypon, Janet Elizabeth, 741–42
Langdon, Fanny E., 742
Langdon, Ladema M., 742–43
Langecker, Hedwig, 743
Lange, Linda Bartels, 743
Lange, Mathilde Margarethe, 743
Langford, Grace, 743–44
Langsdorff, Toni Von, 744
languages. *See* linguistics
Lankester, Phoebe (Pope), 744–45
Lansdell, Kathleen Annie, 745
Lapicque, Marcelle (de Heredia), 745–46, 809
Larsson, Elisabeth, 746
Larter, Clara Ethelinda, 747
La Sablière, Marguerite Hessein, Madame de, 747
Laskey, Amelia (Rudolph), 747
Laski, Gerda, 748
Lassar, Edna Ernestine (Kramer), 748–49
Lasthenia of Mantinea, 749–50
Latham, Vida Annette, 750
Latimer, Caroline Wormeley, 750–51
Laubenstein, Linda, 751
Laughlin, Emma Eliza, 751–52
Laurie, Charlotte Louisa, 752
La Vigne, Anne de, 752
Lavoisier, Marie Anne Pierrette Paulze, 752–53
Law, Annie, 753
Lawder, Margaret, 754
Lawrence, Barbara, 754
Lawrence, Penelope, 754–55
Lawrenson, Alice Louisa, 755

Lawton, Elva, 755–56
Lazarus, Hilda Mary, 756–57
Leach, Mary Frances, 757
Leacock, Eleanor Burke, 757–58
Leakey, Mary Douglas (Nicol), 758–59
Leavitt, Henrietta Swan, 759
Le Beau, Désirée, 759–60
Lebedeva, Nataliia Ivanova, 760
Lebedeva, Vera Pavlovna, 723, 760–61
Lebour, Marie Victoire, 761–62
Le Breton, Elaine, 762
Leclercq, Suzanne (Cèline), 763
Ledingham, Una Christina (Garvin), 763
Leebody, Mary Elizabeth, 765
Lee, Julia Southard, 763
Lee, Rebecca, 764
Lee, Rose Hum, 764
Lee, Sarah Wallis Bowdich, 765
Lees, Florence Sarah, 766
Lefroy, Helena (Trench), 766
Lehmann, Inge, 766
Lehmus, Emilie, 767–69, 1285
Lehr, Marguerite (Anna Marie), 769
Leighton, Dorothea (Cross), 769–70
Leland, Evelyn, 770
Le Maître, Dorothée, 770–71
Lemmon, Sarah Plummer, 771
Leontium, 771–72
Leoparda, 772
Lepaute, Nicole-Reine Hortense (Etable de La Brière), 772–73
Lepeshinskaia, Ol'ga Borisovna, 773–74
Lepin, Lidiia Karlovna, 774
Lermontova, Ekaterina Vladimirovna, 774–75
Lermontova, Iuliia Vsevolodovna, 775, 775–76
Leschi, Jeanne, 776
Leslie (Burr), May Sybil, 776–77
Leverton, Ruth Mandeville, 778
Levi, Hilde, 727, 778–79
Levi-Montalcini, Rita, 779–81, 836
Levine, Lena, 781–82
Levyns, Margaret Rutherford Bryan (Michell), 782
Lewis, Florence Parthenia, 782–83
Lewis, Graceanna, 783
Lewis, Helen Geneva, 783
Lewis, Isabel (Martin), 783–84
Lewis, Lilian (Burwell), 784
Lewis, Madeline Dorothy (Kneberg), 784–85
Lewis, Margaret Adaline Reed, 785–86
Lewis, Margaret Reed, 928
Lewis, Mary Butler, 786–87
Leyel, Hilda Winifred Ivy (Wauton), 787
Libby, Leona Woods Marshall, 787–89
Libert, Marie-Anne, 789
lichenology
    nineteenth-century, 59, 308
    twentieth-century, 308, 385–86
Lieber, Clara Flora, 789–90
Lieu, K.O.Victoria, 790
limnology, 988–89
Lind-Campbell, Hjördis, 791
Lindsten-Thomasson, Marianne, 792–93

Lines, Dorolyn (Boyd), 793
linguistics, 343–44, 1323
Linton, Laura Alberta, 793–94
Lipinska, Mélanie, 794
lipochondrodystrophy, 631–32
Lisitsian, Srbui Stepanova, 794
Lisovskaia, Sofiya Nikolaevna, 794
Lister, Gulielma, 795
Litchfield, Henrietta Emma (Darwin), 326, 795–96
Litvinova, Elizaveta Fedorovna, 796–97
Litzinger, Marie, 797–98
Lloyd-Green, Lorna, 798
Lloyd, Rachel, 798
Lochman-Balk, Christina, 798–99, 1295
Loewe, Lotte Luise Friedericke, 799
Logan, Martha Daniell, 799
Logan, Myra Adele, 800
logic, 677–78, 731–32, 1009–10
Logsdon, Mayme (Irwin), 800
Lomax, Elizabeth Anne (Smithson), 800
Longfield, Cynthia, 801–2
Longshore, Hannah E.(Myers), 802–3, 1051, 1281
Longstaff, Mary Jane (Donald), 803
Lonsdale, Kathleen (Yardley), 804–5, 1110
Losa, Isabella, 805
Löser, Margaret Sibylla Von, 805
Loudon, Jane (Webb), 805–6
Lovejoy, Esther Pohl, 806–7
Loveless, Mary Hewitt, 807
Lowater, Frances, 807–8
Lowell, Frances Erma, 808
Lozier, Clemence Sophia (Harned), 809, 837, 1363
Lubinska, Liliana, 810
Lu Gwei Djen, 809–10
Lukanina, Adelaida N., 810–11
Luomala, Katharine, 811–12
Lutwak-Mann, Cecelia, 812
Lwoff, Marguerite (Bourdaleix), 746, 812–13
Lyell, Katharine Murray (Horner), 813, 1009
Lyell, Mary Elizabeth (Horner), 813
Lynn, Mary Johnstone, 814
Lyon, Mary, 814–15
Lyubimova, Yelena Aleksandrovna, 815–16

M

Maass, Clara Louise, 817
Macaulay, Catharine (Sawbridge), 817–18
Maccallum, Bella Dytes (Macintosh), 818
Macdonald, Eleanor Josephine, 819
Macdougall, Mary Stuart, 819–20
Macgillavry, Carolina Henriette, 821
MacGill, Elsie Gregory, 820
Macintyre, Sheila Scott, 821–22
Mackay, Helen Marion MacPherson, 824
Macklin, Madge (Thurlow), 824–25
Mackowsky, Marie-Therese, 825–26
Mack, Pauline Beery, 822–24
Maclaughlin, Florence Edith Carothers, 826
Maclean, Ida (Smedley), 826–27
Macleod, Annie Louise, 827
Macleod, Grace, 827–28
Macrina, 828–29

Macrobert, Rachel (Workman), Lady of Douneside and Cromar, 829
Maddison, Ada Isabel, 829–30
Mahler, Margaret Schönberger, 830–31
Mahout, Countess of Artois, 831
Mair, Lucy Philip, 832
Makemson, Maude (Worcester), 832–33
malacology, 991
Maling, Harriet Florence (Mylander), 833–34
Malleson, Elizabeth, 834
Mallory, Edith (Brandt), 834–35
Maltby, Margaret Eliza, 835
mammalogy, 684–85, 754
Man, Evelyn Brower, 835–36
Mangold, Hilde (Proescholdt), 836
Manning, Ann B. (Harned), 836–37
Manson, Grace Evelyn, 837
Mantell, Mary Ann (Woodhouse), 837–38
Manton, Irene, 838–39, 979
Manton, Sidnie Milana, 839–40
Manzolini, Anna Morandi, 841
Maracineanu, Stefania, 841
Marcella, 841
Marcet, Jane Haldimand, 842–43
Margery, 843
Margulova, Tereza Kristoforovna, 843
Marillac, Louise de, 843
marine science, 337–38
Marinov, Evelina, 843–44
Marks, Phoebe Sarah. *See* Ayrton, Hertha Marks
Marlatt, Abby Lillian, 844, 984
Marriott, Alice Lee, 844–45
Marshall, Clara, 845–46, 1300
Marshall, Sheina Macalister, 846–47
Marsh, Mary Elizabeth, 845
Martineau, Harriet, 842, 849
Martin, Ella May, 847–48
Martin, Emilie Norton, 848
Martinez-Alvarez, Josefina, 849–50
Martin, Lillien Jane, 848
Mary the Jewess (Maria), 850, 1278
Mason, Carol Y., 850–51
Mason, Marianne Harriet, 851
Massee, Ivy, 851
Massevitch, Alla Genrikhovna, 851–52
Massey, Patricia, 852
Massy, Anne L., 852–53
Masters, Sybilla (Righton), 853
Mateer, Florence Edna, 853
Mateyko, Gladys Mary, 853–54
mathematics
  fourth-century B.C.E., 396
  fifth-century B.C.E., 396, 397, 957
  sixth-century B.C.E., 879, 1276–77
  fourth-century, 637–39, 957
  fifth-century, 637–39
  twelfth-century, 582–83
  fourteenth-century, 359
  sixteenth-century, 325, 985
  seventeenth-century, 294, 874, 985
  eighteenth-century, 14–16, 49–50, 1088–89, 1119, 1345
  early nineteenth-century, 217, 496–97

mid nineteenth-century, 158–59, 217
late nineteenth-century, 39, 66, 83–84, 158–59, 199–200, 235–36, 309, 399–400, 436–37, 456–57, 555, 570–71, 570–71, 720–22, 782–83, 796–97, 829–30, 885–86, 890, 937–38, 972–73, 977, 1002–3, 1167, 1244, 1329, 1413–14, 1415–16
early twentieth-century, 39, 66, 78–79, 83–84, 133, 193–94, 199–200, 209, 228, 235, 235–36, 258, 276, 290, 292, 309, 407–8, 412–13, 436–37, 440–41, 493–94, 531, 555, 570–71, 570–71, 574, 583–84, 596, 616–17, 624–25, 625–26, 625–26, 640–41, 687–88, 748–49, 769, 782–83, 797–98, 800, 821–22, 829–30, 866, 885–86, 890, 895–96, 922, 937–38, 949–50, 972–73, 987, 1002–3, 1019, 1019–20, 1084–85, 1113–14, 1119, 1149, 1152–53, 1167, 1188–89, 1195, 1195–96, 1204–5, 1219, 1229, 1244, 1267–68, 1329, 1359–60, 1362, 1369–70, 1395, 1397–98, 1402, 1405, 1407–9, 1415–16
mid twentieth-century, 66, 78–79, 133, 176–77, 193–94, 228, 235, 258, 276, 292, 412–13, 440–41, 456–57, 493–94, 495, 531, 574, 616–17, 624–25, 640–41, 677–78, 682, 687–88, 713–14, 748–49, 769, 797–98, 800, 821–22, 866, 922, 936, 937–38, 949–50, 987, 1019–20, 1084–85, 1113–14, 1149, 1152–53, 1195, 1195–96, 1219, 1229, 1267–68, 1359–60, 1360–61, 1397–98, 1402, 1405, 1407–9, 1415–16
late twentieth-century, 133, 176–77, 412–13, 440–41, 495, 616–17, 624–25, 677–78, 748–49, 866, 922, 936, 987, 1084–85, 1113–14, 1152–53, 1267–68
applied to biology, 495
teaching of, 158
Mather, Sarah, 854
Mathias, Mildred Esther, 854–55
Mathisen, Karoline, 855
Matikashvili, Nina, 855
Matilde, 855
Maunder, Annie Scott Dill Russell, 855–56
Maury, Antonia Caetana de Paiva, 856–57
Maury, Carlotta Joaquina, 857–58
Maver, Mary Eugenie, 858
Maxwell, Martha Dartt, 858–59
May, Caroline Rebecca, 859–60
Mayo, Clara Alexandra (Weiss), 860
McAvoy, Blanche, 860
McBride, Katharine Elizabeth, 861
McCarthy, Dorothea Agnes, 861–62
McClintock, Barbara, 838, 862–64, 1144
McConney, Florence, 864–65
McCracken, Eileen May, 865
McCracken, Elizabeth (Unger), 865
McCracken, Mary Isabel, 865–66, 866
McCrea, Adelia, 866
McDonald, Janet, 866
McDowell, Louise Sherwood, 866–67
McGee, Anita (Newcomb), 867–68

McGlamery, Josie Winifred, 868
McGraw, Myrtle Byram, 868–69
McGuire, Ruth Colvin Starrett, 869
McHale, Kathryn, 869–70
McKeag, Anna Jane, 870
McKinney, Ruth Alden, 870–71
McLaren, Agnes, 871
McLean, Helen (Vincent), 871–72
McNab, Catherine Mary, 872
McVeigh, Ilda, 872
Mead, Margaret, 113, 872–74, 925, 1133, 1224
Measham, Charlotte Elizabeth (Cowper), 872–74
Mechthild of Magdeburg, 872–74
Medaglia, Diamante, 872–74
Medes, Grace, 874–75
medicine
  B.C.E., 269, 414, 735, 883–84, 1217–18, 1276–77
  first-century, 56, 1067
  second-century, 436
  fourth-century, 11, 16, 40, 433, 772, 828–29, 940
  fifth-century, 1278
  sixth-century, 39
  seventh-century, 11
  eighth-century, 10
  eleventh-century, 14, 283, 590, 1304–5
  twelfth-century, 10, 12, 14, 283, 577, 582–83, 590
  thirteenth-century, 28, 41, 346, 498, 543, 577
  fourteenth-century, 4, 10, 28, 44, 99–100, 151, 179, 224, 259, 286, 337, 439, 503, 535, 576, 650, 884
  fifteenth-century, 196, 221, 237, 651, 660, 1151
  sixteenth-century, 606, 894, 1143
  seventeenth-century, 47, 212–13, 237, 252, 348, 414, 544–45, 606, 843, 1398
  eighteenth-century, 195, 908–9, 1006, 1013, 1193, 1226–27
  early nineteenth-century, 42–43, 170–71, 323, 630–31, 1006, 1155, 1193, 1249
  mid nineteenth-century, 34–35, 42–43, 123–24, 136–37, 138–39, 201–2, 263–64, 272–73, 273–74, 366–67, 446, 461, 508, 630–31, 802–3, 809, 884, 1051–52, 1089, 1143–44, 1155, 1193, 1281–82, 1340, 1419–20
  late nineteenth-century, 1–2, 19–20, 32–33, 34–35, 50–51, 57, 70–71, 90–91, 115, 120, 136–37, 138–39, 178–79, 186–87, 187–88, 188–89, 201–2, 236, 250, 272–73, 273–74, 319, 324–25, 330–31, 338–39, 366–67, 403, 403–5, 437–38, 443, 461, 508, 546, 546–47, 580, 595, 628, 648–50, 650–51, 657–59, 666, 675, 678–80, 726–28, 764, 767–68, 793–94, 802–3, 806–7, 809, 810–11, 845–46, 867–68, 871, 890–91, 897–98, 909–10, 914, 920–21, 930–31, 936, 961, 970, 977–78, 998–99, 1000–1002, 1022–23, 1036–37, 1059–60, 1080, 1089, 1102, 1103, 1111, 1134, 1143–44, 1157–58,

1169–70, 1178, 1179–80, 1233–34, 1240, 1245, 1252–53, 1255, 1277–78, 1281–82, 1284–85, 1288–89, 1297, 1299–1300, 1311, 1326–27, 1340, 1364, 1394, 1419–20

early twentieth-century, 1–2, 4–5, 6, 16–17, 19, 19–20, 22–23, 31–32, 33–34, 34–35, 40, 43–44, 45–46, 53–54, 60, 67, 68, 70–71, 72, 72–73, 75, 84–85, 88, 92–93, 94–95, 115, 117, 120, 122–23, 123–24, 131–32, 148–49, 169–70, 177–78, 184–85, 196, 199, 203–4, 220, 242, 249–50, 252–53, 254, 257–58, 282, 310–11, 319, 320–21, 324–25, 330–31, 338–39, 346–47, 350, 363, 366–67, 374, 389–90, 403–5, 414–15, 416, 437–38, 482–83, 504–5, 506, 516–17, 523, 536, 543–44, 546, 546–47, 580, 581, 581–82, 585, 596, 604–5, 617–18, 627, 628, 631–32, 635, 642–43, 650–51, 659–60, 668–69, 688, 694–95, 702–3, 726–28, 756–57, 761–62, 763, 767–68, 790–91, 792–93, 794, 798, 800, 806–7, 824, 845–46, 849–50, 855, 864–65, 867–68, 871, 880–81, 881–82, 890–91, 897–98, 905–6, 906–7, 909–10, 918–20, 920–21, 928, 930–31, 934–35, 936, 942, 943, 957–58, 961, 969–70, 977–78, 980–81, 981–82, 986–87, 997–98, 1000–1002, 1005–6, 1011, 1013, 1022–23, 1026–27, 1038, 1046, 1054, 1059–60, 1066–67, 1067–68, 1070–71, 1071–72, 1075, 1076, 1080, 1086–87, 1092–93, 1102, 1103, 1108–9, 1111, 1127, 1134, 1136–37, 1138, 1148, 1153–54, 1157–58, 1162–63, 1163–64, 1169–70, 1179–80, 1192, 1205, 1212, 1218, 1226, 1238, 1240, 1245, 1251–52, 1252–53, 1254, 1255, 1259, 1261–62, 1265–66, 1277, 1277–78, 1284–85, 1288–89, 1297, 1299–1300, 1328–29, 1333–34, 1339, 1346–47, 1389, 1394, 1405–6, 1406–7, 1409–10, 1410–11, 1419–20

mid twentieth-century, 4–5, 6, 16–17, 22–23, 31–32, 33–34, 40, 43–44, 45–46, 53–54, 60, 67, 72, 72–73, 75, 84–85, 88, 92–93, 94–95, 122–23, 148–49, 203–4, 220, 245, 252–53, 310–11, 320–21, 322, 363, 416, 455–56, 504–5, 516–17, 543–44, 581, 585, 596, 617–18, 631–32, 635, 642–43, 660, 668–69, 688, 694–95, 702–3, 717, 722–23, 726–28, 756–57, 761–62, 763, 790–91, 792–93, 794, 798, 800, 807, 849–50, 852, 880–81, 881–82, 890–91, 897–98, 905–6, 906–7, 934–35, 942, 943, 957–58, 969–70, 980–81, 997–98, 1005–6, 1011, 1013, 1026–27, 1054, 1066–67, 1070, 1070–71, 1071–72, 1086–87, 1092–93, 1108–9, 1136–37, 1138, 1148, 1153–54, 1162–63, 1163–64, 1192, 1205, 1212, 1238, 1249, 1251–52, 1259, 1261–62, 1277, 1294, 1333–34, 1346–47, 1382, 1389, 1405–6, 1406–7, 1409–10, 1410–11

late twentieth-century, 4–5, 40, 45–46, 53–54, 60, 67, 75, 94–95, 203–4, 245, 252–53, 320–21, 416, 516–17, 581, 642–43, 688, 694–95, 702–3, 717, 722–23, 751, 756–57, 790–91, 792–93, 800, 849–50, 906–7, 934–35, 942, 1005–6, 1011, 1070, 1070–71, 1086–87, 1092–93, 1136–37, 1153–54, 1162–63, 1261–62, 1277, 1389, 1409–10

book collection, 354

discrimination in field of, 44

education in, 467

herbal, 54

preventative, 65

thirteenth century, 680

See also in List of Scientists by Field (following this index); healing; history, medical; nursing; *specific branches of field of medicine*

Medvedeva, Nina Borisovna, 875–76

Meek, Lois Hayden, 876–77, 1399

Mee, Margaret Ursula (Brown), 876

Meigler, Marie J., 877

Meitner, Lise, 68, 715, **877–79,** 1123, 1159, 1312

Melissa, 879

Mellanby, May (Tweedy), 879–80

Memmler, Ruth Lundeen, 880–81

Mendenhall, Dorothy (Reed), 881–82

Menten, Maud L., 882–83

Mentuhetep, Queen, 883–84

Mercuriade, 884

Meredith, Louisa Anne (Twamley), 884

Mergler, Marie, 884

Merian, Maria Sibylla, 674, **884–85**

Meritt, Lucy Taxis (Shoe), 885

Merrifield, Mary Philadelphia (Watkins), 885

Merrill, Helen Abbot, 885–86

Merrill-James, Maud Amanda, 886

Messina, Angelina Rose, 886–87

metallurgy, 119, 610

Metchnikova, Olga (Belokopytova), 887–88

meteorology, 145, 211, 1368–69, 1423

Metrodora, 888

Metzger, Hélène (Bruhl), 888–89

Meurdrac, Marie, 889

Mexia, Ynes, 889–90

Meyer-Bjerrum, Kirstine, 890–91

Meyer, Margaret Theodora, 890

Meyling-Hylkema, Elisabeth, 891

Michael, Helen Cecilia Desilver Abbott, 891–92

Michelet, Athénaïs (Mialaret), 892–94

microbiology

nineteenth-century, 132–33, 977–78

early twentieth-century, 132–33, 171–72, 206–8, 206–8, 354–55, 374–75, 398–99, 425, 487, 518, 572–73, 573–74, 593, 605–6, 609–10, 657, 688, 705–6, 812–13, 977–78, 1109–10, 1138, 1201, 1264, 1289, 1411

mid twentieth-century, 171–72, 206–8, 354–55, 374–75, 398–99, 425, 474, 487, 518, 573–74, 605–6, 609–10, 657, 688, 705–6, 719, 736, 812–13, 1138, 1201, 1253–54, 1264, 1289, 1411

late twentieth-century, 206–8, 425, 572–73, 605–6, 688, 705–6, 719, 736, 1253–54, 1264

application to nursing, 181–82

micropaleontology, 336, 393, 608, 886–87, 1037–38, 1234–35, 1258

microscopy, 160, 435, 586–87, 750, 1346

micrpaleontology, 1033–34

midwifery

B.C.E., 735, 888, 962, 1146–47

fourteenth-century, 1006

fifteenth-century, 277

sixteenth-century, 617

seventeenth-century, 241–42, 339–41, 414, 681, 1165, 1181, 1183, 1193

eighteenth-century, 299–300, 381, 675, 731, 946, 1165

nineteenth-century, 154, 224–25, 323, 731, 1061–62

twentieth-century, 122–23, 479, 1061–62, 1318–19

Mildmay, Grace Sherrington, 894

Miles, Catherine Cox, 894

Miller, Bessie Irving, 895–96

Miller, Elizabeth Cavert, 896–97

Miller, Olive Thorne, 897

Mill, Harriet Hardy Taylor, 894–95

mineralogy

nineteenth-century, 179, 793–94, 899–900

early twentieth-century, 37, 180, 460–61, 498, 506–7, 592–93, 615, 716, 829, 899–900, 1190–91, 1199

mid twentieth-century, 37, 498, 506–7, 550–51, 615, 615–16, 716, 717–18, 825–26, 829, 934, 1190–91, 1421

late twentieth-century, 615–16, 717–18, 825–26

clay, 232–33

mining, 259

Minoka-Hill, Lillie Rosa, 897–98

Minor, Jessie Elizabeth, 898

Minot, Ann Stone, 898–99

Mirchink, Maria E., 899, 900

Missuna, Anna Boleslavovna, 899–900

Mitchell, Anna Helena, 900

Mitchell, Evelyn Groesbeeck, 900–901

Mitchell, Helen Swift, 901

Mitchell, Maria, 18, 783, **901–5,** 1096, 1374

Mitchell, Mildred Bessie, 905

Miyaji, Kunie, 905–6

Mockeridge, Florence Annie, 906

Moffat, Agnes K., 906–7

Mohr, Erna W., 907

Molesworth, Caroline, 907–8

Molza, Tarquinia, 908

Monin-Molinier, Madeline, 908

Monson, Lady Anne Vane, 908

Montague, Lady Mary Wortley, 908–9

Montel, Eliane, 909

Montessori, Maria, 909–10

Moody, Mary Blair, 910

Mooney-Slater, Rose Camille Ledieu, 910–11

Moore, Anne, 911
Moore, Emmeline, 911
Moore, Lillian Mary, 912
Moore, Ruth Ella, 912
Morehouse, Kathleen M., 912–13
Morgan, Agnes Fay, 913
Morgan, Ann Haven, 913–14
Morgan, Elizabeth Frances, 914
Morgan, Lilian Vaughan Sampson, 914–15
Moriarity, Henrietta Maria, 915
Morozova, Valentina Galaktionovna, 915–16
Morris, Margaretta Hare, 917, 1268
Morse, Elizabeth Eaton, 917
Morse, Meroë Marston, 918
Morton, Emily L., 918
Morton, Rosalie Slaughter, 918–20
Moser, Fanny, 920
Mosher, Clelia Duel, 920–21
Mottl, Mária, 921
Moufang, Ruth, 922
Mueller, Kate Heuvner, 922–23
Muir-Wood, Helen Marguerite, 923
Murphy, Lois Barclay, 924–25, 1178
Murray, Amelia Matilda, 925
Murray, Lady Charlotte, 925–26
Murray, Margaret Alice, 927, 1011
Murray, Margaret Ransone, 927–28
Murrell, Christine Mary, 928
Murtfeldt, Mary, 928–29
musicology, 52–53. *See also* ethnomusicology
Muszhat, Aniela, 929
mycology, 573–74
    nineteenth-century, 49, 917
    early twentieth-century, 168, 210–11, 245–46,
        289, 384, 439–40, 539, 795, 917, 1155,
        1317–18, 1336–37
    mid twentieth-century, 135, 289, 384,
        439–40, 572–73, 795, 972, 1155,
        1317–18, 1336–37
    late twentieth-century, 135, 439–40, 972
Myers, Mabel Adelaide, 929
Myia or Mya, 879, 929

N
Nance, Nellie Ward, 930
Napper, Diana Margaret, 930
Nasymuth, Dorothea Clara (Maude),
    930–31
natural history. *See* history, natural
naturalism
    seventeenth-century, 445, 884–85
    eighteenth-century, 76–77, 208–9, 445
    early nineteenth-century, 76–77, 202, 208–9,
        623–24, 736, 1013–14
    mid nineteenth-century, 131, 202, 356–57,
        858–59, 1346
    late nineteenth-century, 52, 69–70, 131, 180,
        202–3, 254–55, 283–84, 296, 356–57,
        623–24, 803, 858–59, 1346
    early twentieth-century, 52, 69–70, 180,
        254–55, 283–84, 296, 747–48, 803
    mid twentieth-century, 747–48
natural philosophy
    B.C.E., 323–24, 396, 397
    seventh-century, 295, 388

twelfth-century, 596–98
sixteenth-century, 268–69
seventeenth-century, 240–41, 273, 294, 339,
    416–17, 532
eighteenth-century, 163, 198–99, 234–35,
    378–80
nature science, 73–74
Naumova, Sofiya Nickolaevna, 931
Naylor, Bertha, 931
Neal, Marie Catherine, 932
Necker, Suzanne (Curchod), 350, 932
Needham, Dorothy Mary (Moyle), 809,
    932–33
Nelson, Katherine Greacen, 933–34
nematology, 275
Nemcová-Hlobilová, Jindriska, 934
Nemir, Rosa Lee, 934–35
neonatology, 386–87
Netrasiri, Khunying Cherd-Chalong, 935
Neuburg Maria Feodorovna, 935–36, 1074
Neumann, Elsa, 936
Neumann, Hanna (Von Caemmerer), 936
neuroanatomy, 338–39, 601–2
neuroembryology, 1081–82
neuroendocrinology, 35–36
neurogenetics, 556
neurology, 19, 341–42, 358–59, 688, 1329–30
neuropathology, 211
neuropharmacology, 100, 289–90, 1306,
    1330–31
neurophysiology, 174–75, 289–90, 745–46,
    1306
neuropsychiatry, 5
neuroscience
    nineteenth-century, 1031–32
    twentieth-century, 410–11, 779–81, 810,
        927–28, 1031–32, 1158–59, 1158–59
Nevill, Lady Dorothy Frances (Walpole),
    936–37
Newbigin, Marion Isabel, 937
Newson, Mary Frances Winston, 937–38
Newton, Margaret, 938–39
Nice, Margaret Morse, 939–40
Nicerata, Saint, 940
Nichols, Mary Louise, 940–41
Nichols, Mary Sargeant Neal Gove, 941–42
Nicholson, Barbara Evelyn, 942
Nickerson, Dorothy, 942
Nickerson, Margaret (Lewis), 942
Nicosia, Maria Luisa, 942–43
Nieh, Chung-en, 943
Nightingale, Dorothy Virginia, 944
Nightingale, Florence, 944–46
Nihell, Elizabeth, 946
Noddack, Ida Eva Tacke, 947–48
Noel, Emilia Frances, 948–49
Noether, Amalie Emmy, 949–50, 1267, 1369
Nolte, Margarethe, 950
Norsworthy, Naomi, 950–51
North, Marianne, 951–52
Northrup, Ann Hero, 953
Novoselova, Aleksandra Vasil'evna, 953
Noyes, Mary Chilton, 953
nursing
    seventeenth-century, 843

mid nineteenth-century, 86, 124–25, 201–2,
    360, 944–46, 1143–44
late nineteenth-century, 86, 124–25, 140–41,
    168–69, 201–2, 346, 360, 362–63, 766,
    817, 834, 944–46, 954–55, 972, 976–77,
    983–84, 1143–44, 1297
early twentieth-century, 168–69, 175–76, 300,
    330, 346, 362–63, 485, 689, 766, 817,
    834, 954–55, 972, 976–77, 1149–51,
    1235–36, 1285–86, 1318–19, 1338–39
mid twentieth-century, 168–69, 330, 689,
    1149–51, 1235–36
late twentieth-century, 1235–36
education for, 53–54
microbiology applied to, 181–82
public health, 300
nutrition
    seventeenth-century, 414, 1398
    nineteenth-century, 2–3, 58–59, 328–29,
        331–32, 726–28, 980
    early twentieth-century, 2–3, 2–3, 7–8, 7–8,
        58–59, 325, 328–29, 331–32, 391, 420,
        420–21, 465, 565, 565–66, 629, 701–2,
        726–28, 778, 827–28, 901, 913, 956,
        964, 980, 1073–74, 1088, 1107–8, 1207,
        1216, 1229–30, 1236–37, 1255, 1268–69
    mid twentieth-century, 4–5, 7–8, 7–8, 325,
        328–29, 420–21, 465, 565, 565–66, 629,
        701–2, 726–28, 778, 827–28, 901, 913,
        956, 964, 1073–74, 1088, 1107–8, 1207,
        1236–37, 1255, 1268–69
    late twentieth-century, 420–21, 465, 565–66,
        629, 701–2, 778, 901, 1207, 1255,
        1268–69
    effects on mothers and children, 614
Nuttall, Gertrude (Clarke), 953–54
Nuttall, Zelia Maria Magdalena, 954
Nutting, Mary Adelaide, 954–55, 1235, 1338

O
O'Brien, Charlotte Grace, 956
O'Brien, Ruth, 956
O'Connell, Marjorie, 957
O'Malley, Lady Emma Winifred (Hardcas-
    tle), 962
O'Reilly, Helen, 964
O'Shea, Harriet Eastabrooks, 967
Obrutsheva, A., 956–57
obstetrics
    first-century, 56
    seventeenth-century, 164
    nineteenth-century, 186–87
    twentieth-century, 6, 224–25, 245, 403, 436,
        744, 746, 1276
Occello of Lucania, 957
oceanography, 521, 724, 990, 1114
Odlum, Doris, 957–58
Ogilvie-Gordon, Dame Maria Matilda,
    959–60
Ogilvie, Ida Helen, 958–59
Ogino, G., 961
Ohnesorge, Lena, 961
Okey, Ruth Eliza, 961
Olympias of Thebes, 962
oncology, 388, 498, 896–97, 1236

Onslow, Muriel (Wheldale), 962
Onslow, Muriel Wheldale, 1112
ophthalmology, 154–55
Oppenheimer, Ella Hutzler, 963
Oppenheimer, Jane Marion, 963–64, 1021, 1135
opthamology, 85–86, 1027
Orent-Kelles, Elsa, 964
Origenia, 965
Ormerod, Eleanor Anne, 965–67
ornithology
　nineteenth-century, 52–53, 69–70, 133, 284, 398, 548–49, 783, 974–75, 991, 1185–86, 1310–11, 1354
　twentieth-century, 69–70, 284, 398, 747–48, 939–40, 971, 974–75, 991, 1167, 1185–86, 1210, 1351
osteology, 1161
osteopathy, 211
Oszast, Janina Celina, 968–69
otology, 206
ovariotomy, 140–41, 187–88, 272–73
Owen, Luella Agnes, 969
Owens-Adair, Bethenia, 970
Owens, Margaret, 969–70

P
Pabst, Marie B., 971
Pacaud, Suzanne, 971
Page, Mary Maud, 971–72
Paget, Dame Mary Rosalind, 972
Paget, Rose Elizabeth, 972
Page, Winifred Mary, 972
Paine, Mary Esther (Trueblood), 972–73
Pajchlowa, Maria Leokadia, 973
paleobotany
　nineteenth-century, 116–17, 322–23
　twentieth-century, 116–17, 244–45, 289, 322–23, 763, 935–36, 971, 1147, 1242
paleontology
　early nineteenth-century, 41–42, 674
　mid nineteenth-century, 674, 1098
　late nineteenth-century, 300, 417–18, 560, 612, 803, 856–57, 899–900, 992–93, 1098, 1168–69, 1180–81, 1225, 1263–64
　early twentieth-century, 7, 23, 90, 238–39, 302–3, 306–7, 360–61, 369–70, 384–85, 417–18, 475, 484–85, 487–88, 515–16, 521, 533, 559, 600–601, 608, 612, 620–22, 645–46, 662, 680–81, 763, 770–71, 774–75, 798–99, 803, 856–57, 868, 899–900, 915–16, 921, 923, 933–34, 957, 968–69, 992–93, 1048–49, 1074–75, 1078–79, 1175–76, 1180–81, 1191–92, 1217, 1225, 1234–35, 1263–64, 1302–3, 1306–7, 1358–59, 1419–20
　mid twentieth-century, 23, 238–39, 295, 302–3, 306–7, 360–61, 384–85, 400–401, 487–88, 515–16, 533, 559, 600–601, 612, 620–22, 645–46, 680–81, 693–94, 763, 770–71, 798–99, 868, 915–16, 921, 923, 933–34, 968–69, 1048–49, 1074–75, 1175–76, 1191–92,
1194, 1234–35, 1302–3, 1306–7, 1308, 1419–20
　late twentieth-century, 232, 295, 302–3, 306–7, 612, 620–22, 680–81, 693–94, 798–99, 856–57, 868, 933–34, 968–69, 1048–49, 1175–76, 1194, 1306–7, 1308
　avian, 620–22
　invertebrate, 417–18, 417–18, 484–85, 487–88, 600–601, 798–99, 803, 923, 933–34, 1049, 1180–81, 1225, 1234–35, 1263–64
　vertebrate, 90, 232, 238–39, 288, 295, 306–7, 366, 400–401, 521, 559, 619, 921, 1225, 1263–64
paleornithology, 620–22
Pallis, Marietta, 973
Palmer, Alice W., 974
Palmer, Dorothy Bryant (Kemper), 974
Palmer, Elizabeth Day, 974–75
Palmer, Katherine Evangeline Hilton (Van Winkle), 975–76
Palmer, Margaretta, 976
Palmer, Miriam Augusta, 976
Palmer, Sophia French, 976–77
Palmie, Anna Helene, 977
palynology, 133–34, 289, 301, 608, 931, 1036, 1390–91, 1418–19
Panajiotatou, Angeliki, 977–78
Paphnutia the Virgin, 978, 1278
parasitology, 129–31, 299, 1012, 1083–84, 1128–29
Paris, Marie-Louise, 978
Parke, Mary Winifred, 838, 978–79
Parker, Ivy May, 979–80
Parkins, Phyllis Virginia, 980
Parloa, Maria, 980
Parmelee, Ruth A., 980–81
Parrish, Rebecca, 981
Parry, Angenette, 981
Parsons, Elizabeth Ingersoll, 982
Parsons, Eloise, 981–82
Parsons, Elsie Worthington (Clews), 113, 208, 811, 982–83, 1086
Parsons, Emily Elizabeth, 983–84
Parsons, Helen Tracy, 984
Parsons, Mary, Countess of Rosse, 984–85
Parthenay, Catherine de (Dame de Rohan), 985
parthenogenesis, 423–25
Pasternak, Lydia, 985–86
Pasteur, Marie (Laurent), 986
Pastori, Giuseppina, 986–87, 987
Pastori, Maria, 987
Patch, Edith Marion, 987–88
pathology
　nineteenth-century, 236–37, 267, 284–85, 549–50, 560, 777–78, 1199–1200, 1218, 1393–94
　early twentieth-century, 25–26, 31–32, 102, 199, 245–46, 267, 354–55, 387, 387–88, 391, 418, 466, 512–13, 522–23, 549–50, 557, 560, 777–78, 869, 881–82, 930, 938–39, 963, 997–98, 1045–46, 1064–65, 1070–71, 1094–95, 1127, 1136, 1136–37, 1155, 1194, 1199–
1200, 1201, 1205, 1218, 1361, 1393–94, 1421
　mid twentieth-century, 31–32, 354–55, 387, 387–88, 418, 466, 512–13, 549–50, 557, 560, 777–78, 869, 881–82, 930, 938–39, 963, 997–98, 1045–46, 1064–65, 1070–71, 1094–95, 1136, 1136–37, 1155, 1194, 1201, 1361, 1421
　late twentieth-century, 512–13, 557, 963, 1070–71, 1136–37, 1194
　child, 367
　comparative, 664–65
　experimental, 512–13
　forest, 522–23, 1094–95
　plant, 25–26, 102, 190, 199, 245–46, 418, 560, 656, 869, 930, 938–39, 1064–65, 1136, 1155, 1205, 1218, 1367–68
　poultry, 333
　surgical, 467
pathophysiology, 875–76
Patrick, Ruth, 988–89
Patterson, Flora Wambaugh, 245, 990
Pattullo, June Grace, 990
Paula, 990
Paulsen, Alice Elizabeth, 990–91
Paulucci, Marianna, Marchesa, 991
Pavenstedt, Eleanor, 991–92
Pavlova, Mariia Vasil'evna, 992–93, 1191
Payne-Gaposchkin, Cecilia Helena, 994–96
Payne, Nellie Maria de Cottrell, 993
Payne, Rose Marise, 993–94
Payne, Sylvia May (Moore), 994, 1245
Peak, Helen, 996–97
Pearce, Louise, 997–98
Pearl, Maud Dewitt, 998
Pechey-Phipson, Mary Edith, 998–99
Peckham, Elizabeth (Gifford), 999
pediatrics, 31–32, 341–42, 363, 367, 386–87, 1386
pedology, 1421
Peebles, Florence, 999
Pelletier, Madeleine, 1000–1002
Pendleton, Ellen Fitz, 1002–3
Pennington, Mary Engle, 1003–4
Pensa-Joja, Josipa, 1004
Penston, Norah Lilian, 1004
Perceval, Anne Mary (Flower), 1004
Pereiaslavtseva, Sof'ia Mikhailovna, 1004–5
Pereira De Queiroz, Carlota, 1005–6
Perette of Rouen, 1006
Peretti, Zaffira, 1006, 1013
Perey, Marguerite Catherine, 1006–7
Perictione, 1007
Perimede. *See* Agamede
Perlmann, Gertrude Erika, 1007–8
Pernell, 1008
Péronelle, 1008
Perrette, Berthe, 1008
Pertz, Dorothea Frances Matilda, 1009
Petermann, Mary Locke, 1010–11
Péter, Rózsa, 1009–10
Peterson, Edith (Runne), 1011
Peterson, Ruth Dixon, 1011–12
Petran, Elizabeth Irene, 1012
petrography, 87–88

petrology
 nineteenth-century, 1068–69
 twentieth-century, 192, 615–16, 656–57, 676,
  708–9, 718–19, 829, 934, 1049,
  1068–69, 1243–44
 igneous, 592–93, 676, 718–19, 829, 934,
  1068–69, 1243–44, 1421
 metamorphic, 676, 934, 1243–44
 sedimentary, 1068–69
Petrova, Maria Kapitonovna, 1012
Pettersson, Dagmar, 1012–13
Pettit, Hannah Steele, 1013
Pettit, Mary Dewitt, 1013
Pettracini, Maria, 1006, **1013**
Pfeiffer, Ida (Reyer), 1013–14
Pfeiffer, Norma Etta, 1014
Pfiester, Lois Ann, 1015
pharmacology
 fourth-century B.C.E., 54
 twentieth-century, 530, 687, 743, 833–34,
  1104–5
 See also neuropharmacology
Phelps, Almira Hart Lincoln, 1015–16
Phelps, Martha Austin, 1016
Pherenice. *See* **Beronice**
philanthropy
 eighteenth-century, 932
 nineteenth-century, 194, 574–75, 1061,
  1160–61
 twentieth-century, 382–83, 574–75, 1160–61
Philip, Anna-Ursula, 1016
Phillips, Melba Newell, 1017–18
philosophy
 B.C.E., 50, 55–56, 62, 267–68, 359, 749–50,
  771–72, 879, 929, 957, 1276–77
 first-century, 118
 fourth-century, 11–12, 637–39, 771–72, 957,
  1007
 fifth-century, 11–12
 sixth-century, 269
 twelfth-century, 585–89
 fourteenth-century, 1028
 sixteenth-century, 481, 908, 985
 seventeenth-century, 56–57, 84, 97, 286–87,
  747, 985, 1142–43, 1177, 1216
 eighteenth-century, 77, 88–89, 752, 842–43,
  1117, 1142–43, 1216
 nineteenth-century, 221–23, 842–43, 1129–32
 twentieth-century, 5, 221–23, 1129–32
 natural, 56–57, 88–89, 97, 585–86, 596–98,
  747, 752, 1404–5
 of science, 47–48
 student, 1177, 1216
 See also List of Scientists by Field (*following this
  index*); natural philosophy
Philpot, Elizabeth, 1018, **1018**
Philpot, Margaret, 1018, **1018**
Philpot, Mary, 1018, **1018**
Phisalix, Marie (Picot), 1018–19
photobiology, 261–62
photography
 nineteenth-century, 57, 160, 984–85
 twentieth-century, 17–18, 160, 622–23,
  622–23
 and botany, 213

photomicrography, 37
phrenology, 1362–63
phycology, 1035–36
physics
 fourteenth-century, 110
 seventeenth-century, 129
 eighteenth-century, 49–50
 nineteenth-century, 62–63, 64, 149–50,
  153–54, 311–17, 389, 411–12, 682,
  734–35, 743–44, 807–8, 835, 953, 972,
  1027–28, 1034–35, 1236, 1241–42,
  1374, 1375–76
 early twentieth-century, 33–34, 55, 62–63, 83,
  101–2, 110, 112, 142–43, 143–44,
  149–50, 163, 172, 189–90, 211, 221,
  239, 243, 247–48, 260, 265–66, 292,
  311–17, 323, 353, 361, 387, 411–12,
  420, 425–26, 433, 448–49, 458, 474,
  480, 481, 489–90, 506, 510–12, 514,
  516, 523, 571–72, 579, 592, 662–63,
  676, 677, 682, 714–15, 734–35, 743–44,
  748, 778–79, 787–88, 807–8, 835, 841,
  866–67, 877–79, 908, 910–11, 931, 953,
  1008, 1012–13, 1017–18, 1019,
  1027–28, 1034–35, 1098–99, 1108,
  1127, 1145–46, 1187, 1198–99, 1236,
  1241–42, 1258–59, 1297–98, 1352,
  1357–58, 1372, 1374, 1375–76, 1377
 mid twentieth-century, 33–34, 83, 143,
  143–44, 162–63, 239, 239–40, 247–48,
  292, 411–12, 425–26, 467–68, 510–12,
  514, 523, 571–72, 662–63, 665, 676,
  677, 713, 714–15, 734–35, 778–79,
  787–88, 841, 866–67, 877–79, 910–11,
  1017–18, 1019, 1108, 1121, 1127,
  1219–21, 1297–98, 1352, 1357–58,
  1377
 late twentieth-century, 239, 239–40, 247–48,
  510–12, 571–72, 665, 713, 778–79,
  787–88, 1017–18, 1121, 1127, 1219–21,
  1297–98, 1352
 biomedical, 566–68
 health, 33–34, 33–34
 high-energy, 42–43
 technical, 566–68
 theoretical, 1297–98
 See also astrophysics; biophysics; geophysics
physiology
 eighteenth-century, 274–75
 nineteenth-century, 125–26, 267, 274–75,
  307–8, 517, 554–55, 560–61, 635–36,
  682–83, 726–28, 750–51, 920–21,
  1125–26, 1272–73, 1372
 early twentieth-century, 35–36, 66–67,
  86–87, 100, 200, 250–51, 261–62, 267,
  273, 282, 285–86, 289–90, 291, 307–8,
  334, 347, 377, 378, 397, 401–2, 406–7,
  450–51, 509, 517, 530, 554–55, 560–61,
  572, 575–76, 586, 592, 602, 613,
  635–36, 651, 678, 682–83, 688, 697,
  724–25, 726–28, 729–30, 741–42,
  750–51, 762, 785–86, 812, 824–25, 845,
  879–80, 898–99, 901, 911, 912, 920–21,
  993, 1018–19, 1021–22, 1042–43, 1054,
  1104–5, 1125–26, 1189–90, 1203–4,

 1205, 1242–43, 1272–73, 1279, 1308,
  1321–22, 1323–24, 1347, 1376–77
 mid twentieth-century, 35–36, 66–67, 100,
  250–51, 261–62, 273, 291, 334, 406–7,
  509, 554–55, 560–61, 575–76, 586, 602,
  613, 678, 688, 697, 724–25, 726–28,
  729–30, 741–42, 762, 824–25, 845,
  879–80, 898–99, 901, 1012, 1021–22,
  1039–40, 1042–43, 1054, 1104–5,
  1164–65, 1189–90, 1203–4, 1205,
  1242–43, 1279, 1308, 1321–22,
  1323–24, 1376–77
 late twentieth-century, 35–36, 66–67, 77,
  250–51, 554–55, 575–76, 586, 613,
  898–99, 901, 1021–22, 1039–40,
  1164–65, 1279, 1376–77
 cardiovascular, 307–8
 experimental, 670–71
 gastric, 613
 marine, 572
 nutrition, 845
 plant, 86–87, 273, 334, 397–98, 509, 560–61,
  678, 682–83, 724–25, 1242–43
 See also biophysiology; neurophysiology
phytocenology, 365–66
phytopathology, 1349–50
Piazolla-Beloch, Margherita, 1019
Piccard, Sophie, 1019–20
Pickett, Lucy Weston, 1020
Pickford, Grace Evelyn, 963, **1020–21**, 1135
Pickford, Lilian Mary, 1021–22, 1029
Picotte, Susan (La Flesche), 1022–23
Pierce, Madelene Evans, 1023
Pierce, Marion (Armbruster), 1023–24
Pierry, Louise Elizabeth du, 1024
Pinckney, Eliza (Lucas), 1024–25
Pink, Olive Muriel, 1025–26
Piozzi, Hester Lynch, 1026
Pirami, Edmea, 1026–27
Pirie, Antoinette, 1027
Pirie, Mary, 1027
Pirret, Ruth, 1027–28
Pisan, Christine de, 1028
Pittman, Margaret Jane, 1030–31
Pitt-Rivers, Rosalind Venetia, 1028–30, 1324
plants
 biology of, 206
 embryology of, 464–65
 morphology of, 146
 pathology of, 25–26, 190, 199, 245–46, 418,
  560
 physiology of, 86–87, 273, 334, 397–98, 509,
  560–61
 See also botany
Platt, Julia Barlow, 1031–32, 1044
Plehn, Marianne, 1032–33
Plues, Margaret, 1033
Plummer, Helen Jeanne (Skewes), 1033–34
Pockels, Agnes, 1034–35
Pocock, Mary Agard, 1035–36
Pokrovskaia, Irina Mitrofanovna, 1036
Pokrovskaia, Mariia Ivanovna, 1036–37,
  1180
Polenova, Yelena Nikolayevna, 1037–38
Pollack, Flora, 1038

Ponse, Kitty, 1038–39
Pool, Judith Graham, 1039–40
Pope, Clara Maria (Leigh), 1040
Popenoe, Dorothy K.(Hughes), 1040–41
Porada, Edith, 1041–42
Porter, Helen Kemp Archbold, 1042–43, 1376
Porter, Lilian E.(Baker), 1043
Porter, Mary Winearls, 1043–44
Potter, Beatrix, 1044–45
Potter, Edith Louise, 1045–46
Potter, Ellen Culver, 1046
Potts, Eliza, 1046–47
Povitsky, Olga Raissa, 1047
Powdermaker, Hortense, 1047–48
Pozarska, Krystyna (Maliszewski), 1048–49
Prádacová, Marcella, 1049
Prankerd, Theodora Lisle, 1049–50
Pratt, Anne, 1050–51
prehistory, study of, 90, 488–89, 553
Pressey, Luella (Cole), 1051
Preston, Ann, 803, 1051–52, 1372
Preston, Isabella, 1052
Prestwich, Grace Anne (Milne) M'Call, 1052–53
Price, Dorothy, 1053
Price, Dorothy (Stopford), 1054
Prichard, Marjorie Mabel Lucy, 1054
primatology, 459–60
Prince, Helen Walter (Dodson), 1055
Pringle, Elizabeth Waties (Allston), 1055–56
Pringle, Mia Lilly (Kellmer), 1056–57
Prins, Ada, 1057
Proctor, Mary, 1057
Proskouriakoff, Tatiana, 1057–58
protozoology, 61, 129–31, 855, 1272
Pruette, Lorine Livingston, 1058–59
Prytz, Milda Dorothea, 1059
psychiatry
    early twentieth-century, 111–12, 195, 196–97, 368, 383–84, 505, 599, 669–70, 738, 769–70, 1186, 1329–30
    mid twentieth-century, 195, 368, 383–84, 505, 599, 669–70, 738, 769–70, 1186, 1329–30
    late twentieth-century, 599, 738, 769–70
    child, 111–12
    social, 769–70
    See also neuropsychiatry
psychoanalysis
    nineteenth-century, 38–39, 112–13
    early twentieth-century, 38–39, 112–13, 196–97, 209–10, 351–52, 469–70, 470–72, 473, 579–80, 599, 617–18, 626, 703–4, 871–72, 1126–27, 1161–62, 1245–46
    mid twentieth-century, 3–4, 3–4, 195, 469–70, 579–80, 599, 617–18, 703–4, 871–72, 1161–62
    late twentieth-century, 3–4, 599, 1161–62
    of children, 470–72
    teaching of, 123–24
psychobiology, 27
psychology
    mid nineteenth-century, 112–13, 500

late nineteenth-century, 26–27, 221–23, 359, 373–74, 377, 443–44, 500, 551–52, 556, 602, 623, 731–32, 870, 909–10, 950–51, 1165, 1187–88, 1207, 1347, 1348–49
early twentieth-century, 3–4, 5, 10–11, 24–25, 26–27, 39–40, 43, 51, 54–55, 65, 67, 73–74, 76, 93–94, 95, 112–13, 128, 142, 163–64, 164–65, 180, 183, 187, 197–98, 204–5, 205–6, 211–12, 221–23, 236, 238, 263, 275–76, 279, 289–90, 292, 296–97, 298, 310, 319–20, 344–45, 347, 351–52, 373–74, 377, 381–82, 399, 443–44, 450, 455, 460, 465, 469–70, 475–76, 476–77, 482, 491–92, 501–3, 507, 517, 518–19, 520, 522, 535, 551–52, 556, 559–60, 578–79, 580–81, 593, 598–99, 602, 610–12, 620, 623, 624, 632, 644, 646–47, 651–53, 666–67, 680, 690, 712, 714, 715–16, 731–32, 732–33, 781–82, 808, 826, 830–31, 834–35, 837, 853, 861, 861–62, 868–69, 869–70, 876–77, 886, 894, 900–901, 905, 909–10, 922–23, 924–25, 950–51, 967, 985–86, 990–91, 991–92, 994, 996–97, 1051, 1058–59, 1072–73, 1091, 1099–1100, 1100–1101, 1103–4, 1116, 1117–19, 1120, 1178–79, 1188, 1207, 1218, 1223, 1239, 1246, 1250–51, 1252, 1258, 1261, 1272, 1283, 1287–88, 1296–97, 1298, 1299, 1309–10, 1327–28, 1348–49, 1393, 1398–99, 1412, 1418, 1423
mid twentieth-century, 3–4, 10–11, 24–25, 26–27, 30–31, 39–40, 51, 53, 54–55, 65, 73–74, 76, 95, 146–48, 163–64, 164–65, 180, 197–98, 204–5, 205–6, 238, 263, 296–97, 298, 319–20, 344–45, 359, 381–82, 455, 463–64, 465, 469–70, 475–76, 476–77, 491–92, 501–3, 520, 524–25, 551–52, 559–60, 578–79, 580–81, 598–99, 602, 620, 624, 632, 644, 646–47, 651–53, 666–67, 690, 707, 712, 732–33, 781–82, 808, 830–31, 834–35, 837, 853, 860, 861, 861–62, 868–69, 869–70, 876–77, 886, 894, 905, 922–23, 924–25, 967, 985–86, 990–91, 991–92, 994, 996–97, 1056–57, 1058–59, 1072–73, 1091, 1099–1100, 1100–1101, 1117–19, 1178–79, 1185, 1188, 1223, 1246, 1250–51, 1261, 1272, 1283, 1283–84, 1287–88, 1296–97, 1309–10, 1327–28, 1361, 1418
late twentieth-century, 3–4, 10–11, 24–25, 30–31, 146–48, 164–65, 205, 298, 344–45, 381–82, 476–77, 524–25, 551–52, 559–60, 578–79, 598–99, 602, 620, 646–47, 651–53, 666–67, 707, 712, 781–82, 834–35, 860, 861, 861–62, 905, 922–23, 924–25, 967, 971, 996–97, 1091, 1101, 1117–19, 1178–79, 1185, 1246, 1261, 1283–84, 1287–88, 1309–10, 1361
and African Americans, 263
behavioral, 443–44
chemistry of, 455

child, 30–31, 51, 93–94, 96–97, 180, 522, 580–81, 830–31, 924–25, 1056–57, 1116
clinical, 624
comparative, 517
compilation of eminent women in, 236
developmental, 30–31, 1361–62
educational, 10–11, 30–31, 275–76, 310, 460, 524–25, 593, 610–12, 642, 808, 1396, 1397–98
experimental, 475–76
humanistic, 204–5
industrial, 211
life-span developmental, 204–5
of prisoners, 331–32
self-psychology, 221–22
social, 860, 924–25
zoo, 732–33
psychotherapy, 585
Pulcheria, Empress, 1059
Putnam, Helen Cordelia, 1059–60
Putnam-Jacobi, Mary, 1372
Putnam, Mary Louise (Duncan), 1061
Pye, Edith Mary, 1061–62
Pythias of Assos, 1062

Q
Quiggle, Dorothy, 1063
Quimby, Edith Smaw (Hinckley), 1063–64
Quirk, Agnes, 1064–65

R
Rabinoff, Sophie, 1066–67
Rabinovitch-Kempner, Lydia, 1067
Radegonde, 1067
radiochemistry, 1006–7, 1122–23
radiology, 66–67
Rafatdjah, Safieh, 1067–68
Raisin, Catherine Alice, 1068–69, 1090
Ramart-Lucas, Pauline, 1069–70
Ramirez, Rosita Rivera, 1070
Ramsay, Christina (Broun), Countess of Dalhousie, 1070–71
Ramsey, Elizabeth Mapelsden, 1071
Ramstedt, Eva Julia Augusta, 1071–72
Rancken, Saima Tawast, 1072
Rand, Marie Gertrude, 1072–73
Randoin, Lucie Gabrielle (Fandard), 1073–74
Randolph, Harriet, 1032, 1074
Rasskazova, Yelena Stepanovna, 1074–75
Rathbone, Mary May, 1075
Rathbun, Mary Jane, 1075
Ratnayake, May, 1076
Ratner, Sarah, 1076–78
Rauzer-Chernousova, Dagmara M., 1078–79
Ray, Dixy Lee, 1079–80
Raymond-Schroeder, Aimee J., 1080
Rayner, Mabel Mary Cheveley, 1081
Rea, Margaret Williamson, 1081
Reames, Eleanor Louise, 1081
Reddick, Mary Logan, 1081–82
Reder, Ruth Elizabeth, 1082
Redfield, Helen, 1082–83

Reed, Eva M., 1083
Rees, Florence Gwendolen, 1083–84
Rees, Mina Spiegel, 1084
Refshauge, Joan, 1086–87
Reichard, Gladys Amanda, 690, 873, 1087, 1313
Reid, Eleanor Mary (Wynne Edwards), 1087–88
Reid, Mary Elizabeth, 1088, 1126
Reimer, Marie, 1088
Reinhardt, Anna Barbara, 1088–89
religion, and science, 198, 270
Remond, Sarah Parker, 1089
Renooz, Céline, 1089–90
Rensselaer, Martha Van, 1125
research engineering, 347–48
Reynolds, Doris Livesey, 1068, 1090–91
Rhine, Louise Ella (Weckesser), 1091
Rhodes, Mary Louise, 1092
Rice, Elsie (Garrett), 1092
Rice-Wray, Edris, 1092–93
Richards, Audrey Isabel, 673, 1093–94
Richards, Clarice Audrey, 1094–95
Richards, Ellen Henrietta Swallow, 121, 304, 763, 827, 844, 881, **1095–96**, 1095–97, 1262
Richards, Mary Alice Eleanor (Stokes), 1097–98
Richards, Mildred Hoge (Albro), 1098
Rich, Mary Florence, 1093
Richter, Emma (Hüther), 1098
Richter, Grete, 1098–99
Riddle, Lumina Cotton, 1099
Ridenour, Nina, 1099–1100
Rigas, Harriett B., 1100
Ring, Barbara Taylor, 1100–1101
Rioch, Margaret J., 1101
Ripley, Martha (Rogers), 1102
Risseghem, Hortense Van, 1102
Ritter, Mary Elizabeth (Bennett), 1103
Riviere, Joan (Verrall), 994, 1103–4
Robb, Jane (Sands), 1104–5
Robb, Mary Anne (Boulton), 1105
Rob, Catherine Muriel, 1104
Roberts, Charlotte Fitch, 1105–6
Roberts, Dorothea Klumpke, 1106
Roberts, Edith Adelaide, 1106–7
Roberts, Lydia Jane, 1107–8
Roberts, Mary, 1108
Robertson, Florence, 1108
Robertson, Jeannie (Smillie), 1108–9
Robertson, Muriel, 1109–10
Robeson, Eslanda Cordoza (Goode), 1110–11
Robinson, Daisy Maude (Orleman), 1111
Robinson, Gertrude Maud (Walsh), 1111–12
Robinson, Harriet May Skidmore, 1112–13
Robinson, Julia (Bowman), 1113–14
Robinson, Margaret (King), 1114
Robinson, Pamela Lamplugh, 1114–15
Robscheit-Robbins, Frieda Saur, 1115
Rockley, Lady Alicia Margaret (Amherst), 1116
Rockwell, Alice Jones, 1116
Rockwell, Mabel MacFerran, 1116–17

Rodde, Dorothea von (Schlözer), 1117
Roe, Anne, 1117–19
Roe, Josephine Robinson, 1119
Roger, Muriel, 1119–20
Rogers, Agnes Lowe, 1120
Rogers, Julia Ellen, 1120–21
Rogers, Marguerite Moillet, 1121
Rogick, Mary Dora, 1121–22
Rohde, Eleanour Sinclair, 1122
Róna, Elisabeth, 909, 1122–23
Ronzoni, Ethel (Bishop), 1124
Roper, Ida Mary, 1124
Roper, Margaret, 1124–25
Rose, Flora, 1125, 1320
Rose, Glenola Behling, 1125
Rose, Mary Davies Swartz, 828, 984, 1125–26
Rosenfeld, Eva, 1126–27
Ross, Joan Margaret, 1127
Ross, Marion Amelia Spence, 1127
Ross, Mary G., 1127–28
Rothschild, Miriam, 762, 1128–29
Roupell, Arabella Elizabeth (Piggott), 1129
Royer, Clémence, 1090, 1129–32
Rozanova, Mariia Aleksandrovna, 1132–33
Rozovna, Evdokia Aleksandrovna, 1133
Rubin, Vera (Dourmashkin), 1133–34
Rucker, Augusta, 1134
Rudnick, Dorothea, 1135
Rumbold, Caroline (Thomas), 1136
Russell, Anna (Worsley), 1136
Russell, Dorothy, 1136–37
Russell, Jane Anne, 1137–38
Ruysch, Rachel, 1139
Ruys (Ruijs), Anna Charlotte, 1138
Rydh, Hanna, 1139

S
Sabin, Florence, 31, 863, 882, 984, 1140–42, 1393
Sabin, Florence Rena, 1140–42
Sablière, Marguerite (Hessein) de la, 1142–43
Sabuco Banera D'Alcaraz, Olivia, 1143
Sackville-West, Victoria Mary, 1143
Safford, Mary Jane, 1143–44
Sager, Ruth, 1144–45
Salbach, Hilde, 1145–46
Sale, Rhoda, 1146
Salmon, Eleanor Seely, 1146
Salpe, 1146–47
Sampson, Kathleen Samuel, 1147
Sanborn, Ethel, 1147
Sandford-Morgan, Elma (Linton), 1148
Sandhouse, Grace Adelbert, 1148–49
Sandiford, Irene, 1149
Sanford, Vera, 1149
Sanger, Margaret, 702
Sanger, Margaret Higgins, 1149–51
sanitary science, 331–32, 331–32
Sara of Saint-Gilles, 1151
Sara of Würzburg, 1151
Sargant, Ethel, 48, 1151–52, 1162
Sargent, Winifred, 1152–53

Satur, Dorothy May, 1153–54
Saunders, Edith Rebecca, 1009, 1154–55
Savulescu, Olga, 1155
Sawin, Martha, 1155
Say, Lucy (Sistare), 1155–56
Scarpellini, Caterina, 1156
Schaffner, Mabel (Brockett), 1156
Schantz, Viola Shelly, 1156–57
Scharlieb, Dame Mary Ann Dacomb, 1157–58
Scharrer, Berta (Vogel), 1158–59
Schiemann, Elisabeth, 1159–60
Schliemann, Sophia (Kastromenos), 1160–61
Schmideberg, Melitta (Klein), 1161–62
Schmid, Elisabeth, 1161
Schmidt-Fischer, Hildegard, 1162–63
Schmidt, Johanna Gertrud Alice, 1162
Schoenfeld, Reba Willits, 1163
Schoental, Regina, 1163–64
Schofield, Brenda Muriel, 1164–65
Schraders, Catharina Geertruida, 1165
Schroeder von , Edith, 1165
Schubert, Anna, 1165
Schulze, Caroline. *See* Bertillon, Caroline Schulze
Schurman, Anna Marie Van, 1165–66
Schwidetsky, Ilse, 1166–67
science
    history of, 23, 80, 174–75
    natural, 1212
    nuclear, 843
    philosophy of, 47–48
    and religion, 198, 270
Scotland, Minnie (Brink), 1167
Scott, Charlotte Angas, 148, 829, 949, 1167–68
Scott, Flora Murray, 1168
Scott, Henderina Victoria (Klaassen), 1168–69
Scudder, Ida Sophia, 1169–70, 1334
Seaman, Elizabeth Cochrane, 1170–71
Sears, Pauline Snedden, 1171–72
Seegal, Beatrice Carrier, 1172–73
Seibert, Florence Barbara, 984, 1173–74
seismology, 766, 1133
Seligman, Brenda Zara, 1174–75
Semikhatova, Sofia Viktorovna (Karpova), 1175–76
Semple, Ellen Churchill, 1176–77
Serment, Louise-Anastasia, 1177
Sessions, Kate Olivia, 1177–78
Sewall, Lucy Ellen, 1178, 1419
Seward, Georgene Hoffman, 1178–79
sex education, 6, 220, 347
sexology, 60
Shabanova, Anna Nikolaevna, 1179–80
Shakespear, Dame Ethel Mary Reader (Wood), 1180–81
Sharp, Emily Katharine (Dooris), 1181
Sharp, Jane, 1181
Sharsmith, Helen Katherine, 1182
Shattuck, Lydia White, 1182–83
Shaw, Hester, 1183
Sheldon, Jennie Arms, 1183

Shepardson, Mary, 1184
Sheps, Mindel (Cherniack), 1184–85
Sherbourne, Margaret Dorothea (Willis), 1185
Sherif, Carolyn (Wood), 1185
Sherman, Althea Rosina, 1185–86
Sherman, Irene Case, 1186
Sherrill, Mary Lura, 1020, 1186–87
Shields, Margaret Calderwood, 1187
Shinn, Milicent Washburn, 1187–88
Shirley, Mary Margaret, 1188
Shishkina, Olga Vasil'Yevna, 1188
Short, Jessie May, 1188–89
Shove, Rosamund Flora, 1189
Shtern, Lina Solomonovna, 1189–90
Shubnikova, Ol'ga Mikhailovna, 1190–91
Shulga-Nesterenko, Maria I., 1191–92
Sibelius, Helena, 1192
Sidgwick, Eleanor (Balfour), 1192–93
Siebold, Charlotte Marianne Heidenreich Von, 1193, 1193
Siebold, Josepha (Henning) Von, 1193
Siegemund, Justine Dittrich, 1193
Signeux, Jeanne, 1194
Silberberg, Ruth Katzenstein, 1194
Silliman, Hepsa Ely, 1194–95
Simons, Lao Genevra, 1195
Sinclair, Mary Emily, 1195–96
Sinskaia, Evgeniia Nikolaevna, 1196–97
Sitterly, Charlotte Emma (Moore), 1197
Skoczylas-Ciszewska, Kamila, 1197–98
Slater, Ida Lilian, 1198
Slater, Jesse Mabel Wilkins, 1198–99
Slavikova, Ludmila (Kaplanova), 1199
Slosson, Annie Trumbull, 1199
Slye, Maud, 1199–1200
Smart, Helen Edith (Fox), 1200
Smirnovazamkova, Aleksandra Ivanovna, 1201
Smith, Alice Emily, 1201
Smith, Anne Millspaugh (Cooke), 1201–2
Smith, Annie Lorrain, 1202–3
Smith, Annie Morrill, 1203
Smith, Audrey U., 1203–4
Smith, Clara Eliza, 1204–5
Smith, Elizabeth (Hight), 1205
Smith, Emily Adelia (Pidgen), 1205
Smith, Erma Anita, 1205
Smith, Erminnie Adele (Platt), 1205–6
Smith, Isabel Fothergill, 1206–7
Smith, Isabel Seymour, 1207
Smith, Janice Minerva, 1207
Smith, Margaret Kiever, 1207
Smith, Marian Wesley, 1207–8
Smith, Matilda, 1208
Smith, Olive Watkins, 1208–9
Smith, Pleasance (Reeve), 1209
Smith, Winifred, 1209
Snelling, Lilian, 1209–10
Snethlage, Emilie, 1210
Snow, Julia Warner, 1210
Snow, Mary (Pilkington), 1210–11
social sciences, 9–10, 56–57, 278
sociology
    nineteenth-century, 281, 685, 849

early twentieth-century, 281, 509, 541–42, 542–43, 685, 716–17, 764, 1274, 1279–80, 1400
mid twentieth-century, 509, 541–42, 542–43, 685, 707, 716–17, 764, 1274, 1279–80, 1400
late twentieth-century, 542–43, 707, 716–17, 764, 1279–80
Soddy, Frederick, 604
Soddy, Winifred Moller (Beilby), 1211–12
Sokol'skaya, Anna Nikolayevna, 1212
Solis Quiroga, Margarita Delgado de, 1212
Sollas, Igerna Brünhilda Johnson, 1212
Solomko-Sotiriadis, Evgeniia, 1213
Somerville, Mary (Fairfax) Greig, 902, 1213–15
Sommer, Anna Louise, 1216
Sophia Charlotte, Queen of Prussia, 1216
Sophia, Electress of Hanover, 1216
Sorokin, Helen Petrovna (Beratynskaiia), 1216–17
Soshkina, Elizabeth D., 1217
Sotira, 1217–18
South, Lillian Herrald, 1218
Sowton, Sarah C.M., 1218
Spalding, Effie Southworth, 1218
spectroscopy, 42–43, 111, 239, 626–27
    nuclear, 247
    stellar, 453
    X-ray, 239
speleology, 921, 969
Spence, Eliza Jane (Edmondson), 1218
Spencer, Adelin Elam, 1218–19
Sperry, Pauline, 1219
Spiegel-Adolf, Mona, 1219
Sponer-Franck, Hertha Dorothea Elisabeth, 1219–21
Sprague, Mary Letitia (Green), 1221
Spratt, Ethel Rose, 1221
Stackhouse, Emily, 1221–22
Stadnichenko, Tasia Maximovna, 1222
Staël, Madame de, 932
Stanley, Louise, 1222
Stanton, Hazel Martha, 1223
statistics
    nineteenth-century study, 337
    twentieth-century study, 236, 297–98, 328, 541–42, 542–43, 1339–40, 1376
    See also biostatistics
Staudinger, Magda (Woit), 1223–24
Stearns, Genevieve, 1224
Steed, Gitel Poznanski, 1224–25
Stefanescu, Sabba, 1225
Stein, Emmy, 1225
Steinhardt, Edna, 1225
Stelfox, Margarita Dawson (Mitchell), 1226
Stenhouse, Caroline, 1226
stenography, 85
Stephens, Jane, 1226
Stephens, Joanna, 1226–27
Stephenson, Marjory, 1109, 1227–28
stereochemistry, 153
Stern, Catherine (Brieger), 1229
Stern, Frances, 1229–30
Stevens, Nettie Maria, 914, 1230–32

Stevenson, Matilda Coxe (Evans), 1232
Stevenson, Sarah Ann (Hackett), 1233–34
Stevenson, Sara (Yorke), 1233
Stewart, Grace Anne, 1234–35
Stewart, Isabel Maitland, 1235–36
Stewart, Maude, 1236
Stewart, Sarah Elizabeth, 1236
Stiebeling, Hazel Katherine, 1236–37
Stieglitz, Mary Rising, 1237–38
Stimson, Barbara Bartlett, 1238
Stinchfield, Sara Mae, 1239
Stokes, Margaret Mcnair, 1239
Stokey, Alma Gracey, 1239–40
stone, artificial, 274
Stone, Constance, 1240
Stone, Doris Zemurray, 1240–41
Stone, Isabelle, 1241–42
Stopes, Marie Charlotte Carmichael, 1242
Stoppel, Rose, 1242–43
Stose, Anna Isabel (Jonas), 708, 1243–44
Stott, Alicia (Boole), 1244
Stovin, Margaret, 1244–45
Stowe, Emily Howard (Jennings), 1245
Strachey, Alix (Sargant-Florence), 1245–46
Strang, Ruth May, 1246
Strassmann-Heckter, Maria Caroline, 1246–47
stratigraphy
    nineteenth-century, 306, 417–18, 695, 1225
    early twentieth-century, 21–22, 23, 46, 417–18, 419–20, 484–85, 519–20, 583, 600–601, 645–46, 695, 708–9, 935–36, 958–59, 1197–98, 1225, 1234–35, 1383–84, 1396–97
    mid twentieth-century, 23, 294, 419–20, 519–20, 583, 600–601, 645–46, 706, 708–9, 935–36, 958–59, 1004, 1197–98, 1234–35, 1311, 1383–84
    late twentieth-century, 583, 600–601, 1311
    See also biostratigraphy
Stratton Porter, Gene, 1247–48
Strobell, Ella Church, 1248
Strong, Harriet Williams (Russell), 1248–49
Strong, Helen Mabel, 1249
Strong, Miriam Carpenter, 1249
Strozzi, Lorenza, 1249–50
Stuart, Miranda, 1250
Sullivan, Betty Julia, 1250
Sullivan, Elizabeth Teresa, 1250–51
Sullivan, Ellen Blythe, 1251
Summerskill, Edith Clara, 1251–52
Sundquist, Alma, 1252
Sunne, Dagny, 1252
surgery
    fifth-century, 382
    seventh-century, 11
    thirteenth-century, 680
    seventeenth-century, 164
    nineteenth-century, 19–20, 50–51, 272–73, 357–58, 1311, 1319–20
    twentieth-century, 19–20, 72–73, 581, 643, 855, 1238
    orthopedic, 1238
    psychological aspects, 3–4
    veterinary, 855

Suslova, Nadezhda Prokof'evna, 1252–53
Sutter, Vera Laverne, 1253–54
Svartz, Nanna Charlotta, 1254
Svihla, Ruth Dowell, 1254–55
Swain, Clara A., 1255
Swanson, Pearl Pauline, 1255
Swift, Mary, 1255–56
Swindler, Mary Hamilton, 1256
Swope, Helen Gladys, 1256
Swope, Henrietta (Hill), 1256–57
Sykes, Mary Gladys, 1257–58
Syniewska, Janina, 1258
Szeminska, Alina, 1258
Szeparowicz, Maria, 1258
Szmidt, Jadwiga, 1258–59
Szwajger, Adina Blady, 1259

T

Taeuber, Irene Barnes, 1260–61
Taft, Jessie, 1261
Takeuchi, Shigeyo (Ide), 1261–62
Talbot, Dorothy Amaury, 1262
Talbot, Marion, 1262–63
Talbot, Mary, 1263
Talbot, Mignon, 1263–64
Taliaferro, Lucy (Graves), 1264
Tammes, Jantine, 1264–65
Tannery, Marie Alexandrine (Prisset), 1265
Taussig, Helen Brooke, 1265–66
Taussky-Todd, Olga, 1267–68
Taylor, Charlotte de Bernier Scarborough, 1268
Taylor, Clara Mae, 1268–69
Taylor, Clara Millicent, 1269
Taylor, Eva Germaine Rimington, 1269–70
Taylor, Harriet, 1270
Taylor, Helen, 1270
Taylor, Janet, 1270–71
Taylor, Lucy Beaman (Hobbs), 1271
Taylor, Monica, 1272
Taylor, Rose H., 1272
Teagarden, Florence Mabel, 1272
Tebb, Mary Christine, 1272–73
Telfair, Annabella (Chamberlain), 1273
Telkes, Maria, 1273–74
Tenenbaum, Estera, 1274
teratology, 45
Terent'eva, Liudmila Nikolaevna, 1274
Terry, Ethel Mary, 1275
Terzaghi, Ruth Doggett, 1275–76
Tessier, Marguerite, 1276
Tetsuo, Tamayo, 1276
Theano, 879, 1276–77
Thelander, Hulda Evelin, 1277
Thelberg, Elizabeth (Burr), 1277–78
Thelka, Saint, 1278
Theodosia, Saint, 1278
theology, 805
Theosebeia, 1278
Thiselton-Dyer, Lady Harriet Ann (Hooker), 1278–79
Thomas, Caroline (Bedell), 1279
Thomas, Dorothy Swaine (Thomas), 1279–80
Thomas, Ethel Nancy Miles, 1280–81

Thomas, Mary Frame (Myers), 1281–82, 1285
Thome, Frances, 1282
Thompson, Caroline Burling, 1282
Thompson, Clara Mabel, 1283
Thompson, Helen, 1283–84
Thompson, Laura, 1284
Thompson, Mary Harris, 1284–85
Thompson, Rachel Ford, 1285
Thoms, Adah B.(Samuels), 1285–86
Thomson, Agnes C., 1286
Thomson, Jane Smithson, 1286
Thring, Lydia Eliza Dyer (Meredith), 1286–87
Thurstone, Thelma Gwinn, 1287–88
Tiburtius, Franziska, 1288–89
Tilden, Evelyn Butler, 1289
Tilden, Josephine Elizabeth, 1289–90
Timofe'eff-Ressovsky, Elena Aleksandrovna (Fiedler), 1274, 1290–91
Tindall, Isabella Mary, 1291
Tinne, Alexandrina Petronella Francina, 1291–92
Tinsley, Beatrice Muriel (Hill), 1292–93
Tipper, Constance Fligg (Elam), 1293–94
Tisserand, M., 1294
Todd, Emily Sophia, 1294–95
Todd, Mabel Loomis, 1295
Todd, Ruth, 1295–96
Todtmann, Emmy Mercedes, 1296
Tolman, Ruth (Sherman), 1296–97
Tomaszewicz-Dobrska, Anna, 1297
Tompkins, Sally Louisa, 1297
Tonnelat, Marie-Antoinette (Baudot), 1297–98
Toops, Laura Chassell (Merrill), 1298
topography, 1161–62
Towara, Hélèlne, 1299
Town, Clara Harrison, 1299
toxicology, 66–67
Tracy, Dean Martha, 846
Tracy, Martha, 1060, 1299–1300
Traill, Catharine Parr (Strickland), 1300–1301
Treat, Mary Lua Adelia (Davis), 1301–2
Trimmer, Sarah (Kirby), 1302
Tristram, Ruth Mary (Cardew), 1302
Trizna, Valentina Borisovna, 1302–3
Trotter, Mildred, 1303–4
Trotula, 1304–5
Trower, Charlotte Georgiana, 1305
Tsvetaeva, Maria, 1305–6
Tumanskaya, Olga G. (Shirokobruhova), 1306–7
Tum-Suden, Caroline, 1306
Tunakan, Seniha (Hüsnü), 1307
Tunnicliff, Ruth, 1307–8
Turnbull, Priscilla Freudenheim, 1308
Turner, Abby Howe, 727, 1308
Turner, Mary (Palgrave), 1308–9
Twining, Elizabeth Mary, 1309
Tyler, Leona Elizabeth, 1309–10
Tyler, Martha G., 1310–11
Tyndall, A.C., 1311
Tyng, Anita E., 1311
Tyska, Maria, 1311

U

Ubisch, Gerta Von, 1312–13
Underhill, Ruth, 811, 873
Underhill, Ruth Murray, 1313–14
urology, 601
Ushakova, Elizaveta Ivanovna, 1314
Uvarova, Countess Praskov'ia Sergeevna, 1314–15

V

Vachell, Eleanor, 1316
Valentine, Lila Hardaway (Meade), 1316–17
Van Beverwijk, Agathe L., 1317–18
Van Blarcom, Carolyn (Conant), 1318–19
Van Deman, Esther Boise, 1318–19
Van Hoosen, Bertha, 1319–20
Van Rensselaer, Martha, 1320–21
Van Wagenen, Gertrude, 1321–22
Varsanof'eva, Vera Aleksandrovna, 1322–23
Vasilevich, Glafira Makar'evna, 1323
Vaughan, Dame Janet, 1029, 1323–24
Vavrinova, Milada, 1324–25
Veil, Suzanne Zélie Pauline, 1325
Veley, Lilian Jane (Nutcombe), 1325
Venning, Eleanor (Hill), 1325–26
Verder, Ada Elizabeth, 1326
Veretennikova, Anna Ivanovna, 1326–27
Vernon, Magdalen Dorothea, 1327–28
Vesian, Dorothy E. de, 1328
Vickers, Anna, 1328
Vilar, Lola, 1328–29
Vilmorin, Elisa (Bailly), 1329
virology, 498, 812–13
Vivian, Roxana Hayward, 1329
Vogt, Cécile (Mugnier), 1329–30, 1331
Vogt, Marthe Louise, 1330–31
Vold, Marjorie Jean Young, 1331–32
Volkova, Anna Fedorovna, 1332–33
vulcanology, 718–19
Vyssotsky, Emma T. R. (Williams), 1333
Vytilingam, Kamala Israel, 1333–34

W

Waelsch, Salome Gluecksohn, 1335–36
Wakefield, Elsie Maud, 1336–37
Wakefield, Priscilla (Bell), 1337
Walcott, Helene B. (Stevens), 1337–38
Walcott, Mary Morris (Vaux), 1337, 1338
Wald, Lillian D., 53, 1338–39
Walker, Eliza, 1339
Walker, Elizabeth, 1339
Walker, Harriet Ann, 1339–40
Walker, Helen Mary, 1340
Walker, Mary Edward, 1340–41
Walker, Norma (Ford), 1341
Wallace, Louise Baird, 1342
Wall, Florence, 1342
Wallis, Ruth Sawtell, 1342–44
Walworth, Ellen Hardin, 1344–45
Wang Chi Che, 1345
Ward, Mary (King), 1346
Warga, Mary Elizabeth, 1346–47
Waring, Sister Mary Grace, 1347
Warren, Elizabeth Andrew, 1347
Warren, Madeleine (Field), 1347

Washburn, Margaret Floy, 863, 1348–49
Wassell, Helen Erma, 1349
Watson, Janet Vida, 1350–51
Watt, Helen Winifred Boyd (de Lisle), 1351
Watt, Menie, 1351
Watts, Betty (Monaghan), 1351–52
Way, Katharine, 1352
Weber, Anne Antoinette (Van Bosse), 1352–53
Webster, Mary McCallum, 1338, 1353–54
Wedderburn, Jemima, 1354
Wedgwood, Camilla Hildegarde, 1354–56
Weeks, Alice Mary (Dowse), 1356–57
Weeks, Dorothy W., 1357–58
Weeks, Mary Elvira, 1358
Weightman, Mary, 1358
Weinzierl, Laura (Lane), 1358–59
Weishaupt, Clara Gertrude, 1359
Weisskopf-Joelson, Edith Adele, 1361
Weiss, Marie Johanna, 1359–60
Weiss, Mary Catherine (Bishop), 1360–61
Welch, Betty, 1361
Welch, Winona Hazel, 1361
Weld, Julia Tiffany, 1361
Wellman, Beth Lucy, 1361–62
Wells, Agnes Ermina, 1362
Wells, Charlotte Fowler, 1362–63
Wells, Louisa D., 1363
Welser, Philippine, 1363
Welsh, Jane Kilby, 1363–64
Welsh, Lillian, 1364
Weltfish, Gene, 740, 873, 1364–66
Wertenstein, Mathilde, 1366
Wessel, Bessie (Bloom), 1366
Westall, Mary, 1367
Westcott, Cynthia, 1367–68
West, Ethel, 1367
Westover, Cynthia May, 1368
Wharton, Martha Lucille, 1368
Whedon, Frances Lovisa, 1368–69
Wheeler, Anna Johnson Pell, 949, 1369–70
Wheeler, Elizabeth Lockwood, 1370
Wheeler-Voeglin, Erminie Brooke, 1370
White, Edith Grace, 1370–71
White, Elizabeth Juanita (Greer), 1371
White, Eliza Catherine (Quekett), 1371
White, Florence Roy, 1371–72
White, Frances Emily, 1372
Whitehead, Lilian Elizabeth, 1373
Whiteley, Martha Annie, 1042, 1373
White, Margaret Pirie, 1372
White, Marian Emily, 1373
Whiting, Marian Muriel, 1373
Whiting, Sarah Frances, 866, 1374
Whitney, Mary Watson, 1374–75
Wickens, Aryness Joy, 1376
Wick, Frances Gertrude, 866, 1375–76
Widdowson, Elsie May, 1376–77
Wiebusch, Agnes (Townsend), 1377
Wienholz, Eva, 1377–78
Wilder, Inez (Whipple), 1378
Wiley, Grace Olive, 1378
Willard, Emma (Hart), 1013, 1378–79

Willard, Mary Louisa, 1379
Willcock, Edith Gertrude (Gardiner), 1380
Willcox, Mary Alice, 1380
Williams, Anna Wessels, 84, 982, 1030, 1047, 1380–82
Williams, Cicely Delphine, 1382
Williams, Marguerite (Thomas), 1382
Willmott, Ellen Ann, 1382–83
Wilson, Alice Evelyn, 1383–84
Wilson, Aphra Phyllis, 1384
Wilson, Edith, 1384
Wilson, Fiammetta Worthington, 1385
Wilson, Hilda E., 1385
Wilson, Irene Mossom, 1385
Wilson, Louise (Palmer), 1385–86
Wilson, Lucy, 1386
Wilson, Lucy Langdon (Williams), 1386
Wilson, Mabel Florey, 1386–87
Wilson, May Georgiana, 1387
Wilson, Monica Hunter, 1387–88
Winger, Florence. *See* Bagley, Florence (Winger)
Winlock, Anna, 1388–89
Winner, Dame Albertine, 1389
Winton, Kate (Barber), 1390
Wipf, Frances Louise, 1390
Withers, Augusta Innes (Baker), 1390
Witterly, John Altrayd (pseudonym). *See* Carne, Elizabeth Catherine (Thomas)
Woillard-Roucoux, Geneviève Marie-Aurélie, 1390–91
Woker, Gertrud Jan, 1391–93
Wolf, Katherine, 1393
Wollstein, Martha, 1393–94
Wong Ah Mae, 1394
Woodard, Helen (Quincy), 1395
Woodbridge, Mary Emily, 1395
Wood, Emily Elizabeth, 1394
Wood, Emily Margaret, 1394
Wood-Lorz, Thelma (Rittenhouse), 1395–96
Wood, Ruth Goulding, 1395
Woods, Elizabeth Lindley, 1396
Woods, Ethel Gertrude (Skeat), 1396–97
Woodward, Gladys Estelle, 1397
Wooldridge, Elizabeth (Taylor), 1397–98
Woolley, Ann, 1398
Woolley, Helen Bradford (Thompson), 1398–99
Woolley, Mildred Thompson, 1399
Wootton, Barbara Adam, 1400
Wormington, Hannah Marie, 1400–1401
Worner, Ruby K., 1401–2
Worthington, Euphemia R., 1402
Wrangell, Margarethe von, 1402–4
Wreschner, Marie, 1404
Wright, Frances May, 1405
Wright, Frances Woodworth, 1405
Wright, Helena Rosa (Lowenfeld), 1405–6
Wright, Katharine, 1406–7
Wright, Lady Catherine, 1404–5

Wright, Mabel Osgood, 1407
Wrinch, Dorothy Maud, 43, 1407–9
Wu Chien-Shiung, 1409–10
Wundt, Nora, 1410–11
Wyckoff, Delaphine Grace (Rosa), 1411
Wyckoff, Dorothy, 1411
Wylie, Margaret, 1412
Wynne, Frances Elizabeth, 1412
Wyttenbach, Jeanne Gallien, 1412

Y

Young, Anne Sewell, 1413
Young, Grace Emily (Chisholm), 1413–14
Young, Leona Esther, 1414–15
Young, Mabel Minerva, 1415–16
Young, Mary Sophie, 1416
Young, Roger Arliner, 784, 1082, 1416–17

Z

Zachry, Caroline Beaumont, 1418
Zaklinskaia, Elena Dmitrievna, 1418–19
Zakrzewska, Marie Elizabeth, 137–38, 358, 764, 1060, 1178, 1285, **1419–20**
Zalesskaya-Chirkova, Elena, 1420–21
Zaniewska-Chilpalska, Eugenia, 1421
Zeckwer, Isolde Therese, 1421
Zenari, Silvia, 1421–22
Zhuze, Anastasiya Panteleyemonovna, 1422–23
Ziegarnik, Bliuma, 1423
Zlatarovic, Rely, 1423
zoology
    nineteenth-century, 20–21, 95–96, 167, 258–59, 266–67, 328, 355–56, 624, 742, 940–41, 1032–33, 1074, 1075, 1134, 1183, 1282, 1325, 1380
    early twentieth-century, 7, 20–21, 61, 92, 95–96, 102, 104, 120–21, 160–62, 167, 215, 224, 230, 266–67, 300–301, 333, 355–56, 399, 449, 481, 528–29, 533, 538–39, 592, 594–95, 602, 624, 628, 636–37, 664–65, 673, 681–82, 754, 784, 819–20, 839–40, 900–901, 907, 913–14, 920, 940–41, 1023, 1032–33, 1074, 1075, 1079–80, 1098, 1121–22, 1128–29, 1134, 1156–57, 1158–59, 1226, 1254–55, 1263, 1274, 1282, 1342, 1370–71, 1378, 1380, 1385–86, 1395–96, 1416–17
    mid twentieth-century, 7, 20–21, 61, 92, 118, 145, 160–62, 167, 230, 295, 300–301, 333, 533, 538–39, 585, 594–95, 602, 628, 636–37, 664–65, 681–82, 754, 784, 819–20, 839–40, 907, 913–14, 1023, 1079–80, 1098, 1121–22, 1128–29, 1156–57, 1158–59, 1254–55, 1263, 1370–71, 1385–86, 1416–17
    late twentieth-century, 167, 295, 585, 594–95, 602, 628, 754, 839–40, 1156–57, 1158–59
    invertebrate, 145, 742, 1121–22, 1134
    marine, 92, 1075
    See also protozoology